City Crime Rankings
2014

Other titles in the State Fact Finder series

Crime State Rankings (now part of **State Stats**)
Education State Rankings (now part of **State Stats**)
Health Care State Rankings (now part of **State Stats**)
State Rankings

State Stats online database

What is **State Stats**? Drawing together the statistics from the *State Rankings* series of books by CQ Press and Morgan Quitno Press, **State Stats** is a regularly updated database from CQ Press that delivers a dynamic and engaging user experience that is unmatched in other resources. Featuring data from more than 80 different government and nongovernment sources and backed by a rich collection of more than 2,000 current and historical data series on popular topics of research interest, **State Stats** uniquely allows users to discover, view, and export key information measures for the 50 states and the District of Columbia.

Check it out online at http://library.cqpress.com/statestats.

State Stats makes research easy by providing in one place annual measures dating back more than 15 years. Data series are displayed in a clear and consistent format with detailed source information. Numerous topics are covered in categories including Agriculture; Crime and Law Enforcement; Defense; Demographics; Economics; Education; Employment and Labor; Geography, Energy, and the Environment; Health and Medicine; Social Welfare; Taxes and Government Finance; Transportation.

The benefit of **State Stats** is in its ease of use and clean and concise presentation of data and trends. An intuitive interface lets users easily browse by state or by topic, and then compare across states or across time. Users can then share, save, and export data. **State Stats** also features CQ Press's CiteNow!® function for generating source citations in APA, MLA, Chicago, or Bluebook styles.

Users can:

* Analyze data patterns by comparing across states, data series, and time

* Create and export custom visuals including line charts, scatter plots, and maps

* Generate tables and download data for statistical research

* Toggle user display between interactive visual and tabular data view

* Engage a moveable timeline to discover trends

* Explore interactive maps featuring zoom and hover functions

State Stats is cross-searchable with other CQ Press online products including *CQ Researcher* and the *CQ Press U.S. Political Stats.* Ongoing updates to **State Stats** throughout the year ensure that users have the most current data available.

Working on an advanced data research project? The optional advanced State Stats Data Cart allows for bulk data export across single-click download of complete data series and multiple series.

City Crime Rankings 2014

Crime in Metropolitan America

Kathleen O'Leary Morgan
and
Scott Morgan
with
Rachel Boba Santos

Los Angeles | London | New Delhi
Singapore | Washington DC

Los Angeles | London | New Delhi
Singapore | Washington DC

For information:

SAGE Publications, Inc.
2455 Teller Road
Thousand Oaks, California 91320
E-mail: order@sagepub.com

SAGE Publications Ltd.
1 Oliver's Yard
55 City Road
London, EC1Y 1SP
United Kingdom

SAGE Publications India Pvt. Ltd.
B 1/I 1 Mohan Cooperative Industrial Area
Mathura Road, New Delhi 110 044
India

SAGE Publications Asia-Pacific Pte. Ltd.
3 Church Street
#10-04 Samsung Hub
Singapore 049483

Printed in the United States of America.

Certified Chain of Custody
Promoting Sustainable Forestry
www.sfiprogram.org
SFI-01268

SFI label applies to text stock

Developmental Editor: John Martino
Production Editor: Tracy Buyan
Proofreader: Cheryl Rivard
Cover Designer: Michael Dubowe
Marketing Manager: Carmel Schrire

ISBN 978-1-4522-8331-9 (paper)

13 14 15 16 17 10 9 8 7 6 5 4 3 2 1

Contents

Detailed Table of Contents

III. METROPOLITAN AND CITY POPULATIONS

APPENDIX

Introduction and Methodology

City Crime Rankings 2014 analyzes the latest (2012) FBI crime statistics for U.S. metropolitan areas and cities with populations of 75,000 or more. *City Crime Rankings* starts off by describing the data and methodology used in the rankings; it then provides a comparative analysis of cities and metropolitan areas, a distribution analysis of comparison scores and rates, and additional information and caveats regarding the analyzed data. The data and their limitations, the methodology, and the results of the comparative analysis of six types of reported crime are discussed. Also presented are charts illustrating the distribution of values for selected analyses along with the related statistics for the median, mean, standard deviation, minimum value, and maximum value. Lastly, the definitions of crimes based on the FBI's coding system are presented with supporting facts and caveats that provide context to the numbers presented in this volume.

The two main sections of the book, Metropolitan Area Crime Statistics and City Crime Statistics, report the statistics for 382 metropolitan areas and 442 cities with populations of 75,000 or more. Each section has forty tables, presented in both alphabetical and rank order, that compare the actual numbers of reported crimes, crime rates, and percent changes over periods of one year (2011–2012) and five years (2008–2012). Each table spans four pages with the first two pages displaying the metro areas and cities in alphabetical order and the third and fourth pages displaying them in rank order. In addition, City Crime Statistics presents the actual numbers, rates, and percent change in police officers employed per capita by law enforcement agencies in each city.

To be included in this edition, cities must have reported crime data to the FBI for 2012. Metropolitan areas must have met two criteria: first, their central city or cities must have submitted twelve months of data in 2012, and second, at least 75 percent of all law enforcement agencies located in a specific metro area must have reported crime statistics for 2012. (The cities and metro areas not meeting these requirements were excluded from this edition of *City Crime Rankings* and are listed in the Missing Cities and Metro Areas section.)

The Metropolitan and City Populations Appendix presents population data for the cities and metro areas included in *City Crime Rankings*. The section consists of a description for each metropolitan area, including a list of cities and counties, a county index for 2012, tables illustrating rates for each reported crime category for the past twenty years with an examination of national trends and perspective of crime in the United States, and a summary of the 2012 national, metropolitan, and city crime statistics.

Purpose of This Book

The purpose of *City Crime Rankings* is to serve as a resource for researchers, city and law enforcement officials, and the community. The book provides the means by which individuals can compare local communities to other similar communities through contrast with the national level of reported crime—more specifically, crime rates per 100,000 for individual types of reported crime, for violent and property crime categories, and for overall crime.

In editions prior to the 2009–2010 edition, the terms *safest* and *dangerous* were used to describe the cities and metropolitan areas with the lowest and highest rankings in the comparative analysis, respectively. Even though the rankings are still provided, these terms are no longer used because perceptions of safety and danger are just that—perceptions. The data analyzed here are *reported crime* and *population*, which together constitute only two factors considered when determining safety or risk of crime victimization. Thus, the analyses in this book are purely descriptive. At no time do we attempt to explain why reported crime rates are higher or lower from one community to the next. These explanations—currently sought by criminologists and other social science researchers—are beyond the scope of this book.

Consequently, to enhance the usefulness of *City Crime Rankings*, a new section was introduced in the 2009–2010 edition and is continued in subsequent editions. The "Distribution Analysis" section (see page xii) provides histograms of the comparison score and reported crime rate distributions as well as such measures of central tendency as median, mean, standard deviation, and minimum and maximum values for each distribution. Because the rank ordering of scores and crime rates does not illustrate the relative difference between metro areas' and cities' values, this analysis is provided so the reader can better understand how the values are distributed and where a particular metro area's or city's ranking falls in comparison to others.

These statistics are used in a variety of ways, by a range of audiences, including the following:

- Law enforcement agencies use them to help identify crime problems for further study.
- City governments compare their cities' crime levels to those of other jurisdictions to determine how their rates appear in comparison.
- The federal government uses this type of analysis to allocate grant funding.
- The media report these results to report and compare crime rates across cities and years.

In addition, it is important to examine the statistics of a city along with its metro area when using *City Crime Rankings*. Although a city's scores and rates are useful for understanding the crime levels within the boundaries of that city and for making comparisons to other law enforcement jurisdictions, criminals and opportunities for crime do not adhere to city boundaries, but rather spill over to adjacent (i.e., metro) areas. In fact, crime rates and comparison scores tend to be lower in metro areas than in individual cities because many of the more populous cities are geographically small and include central business, retail, and industrial areas where residential population is low. These nonresidential areas contain more victims and targets (e.g., commuters, merchandise, vehicles) than do residential areas, so their crime rates appear higher when population is used as the denominator in the calculation of the crime rate. Researchers who study low-population areas within cities often use other denominators to determine rates, such as number of vehicles parked in lots for auto theft, number of businesses for commercial burglary, or square footage of retail establishments for shoplifting and theft (Santos, 2012).

However, these variables are not easily obtained for all U.S. cities. By expanding the geographic unit from city to metro area to include business, retail, industrial, and residential areas, using population of the entire area as a basis for determining rate is more practical. Thus, combining a major city with its suburbs provides an overall view of how crime is present in interrelated communities. For example, the table below compares the city of Syracuse, NY, with its metro area, showing differences between the city and its metro area for each variable with the city having higher crime rates. Thus, city statistics and metro area statistics both serve useful purposes and should be considered together when examining a city situated within a metro area.

The Data and Their Limitations

The data featured in *City Crime Rankings* come from the FBI publication *Crime in the United States* (2013), which is available every fall (e.g., September 2013) and presents information for the previous year (e.g., 2012). This report is based on data collected through the Uniform Crime Reporting (UCR) Program, which began in 1930. The purpose of the UCR Program has been to develop reliable information about crime reported to law enforcement that can be used by law enforcement as well as by criminologists, sociologists, legislators, municipal planners, and the media for a variety of research and planning purposes. Although the program is voluntary, in 2012, 18,290 city, university and college, county, state, tribal, and federal law enforcement agencies provided information representing 99 percent of the population (FBI, 2013a).

Although law enforcement agencies collect common information on crimes reported to and discovered by them, each state has slightly different criminal laws, and each law enforcement agency has its own policies and procedures for recording activity. These differences make it very difficult to compare statistics across agencies. To classify criminal activity consistently, the UCR Program was created. The UCR Program provides national standards for the uniform classification of crimes and arrests (for further details, visit the FBI's website at http://www.fbi.gov/stats-services/crimestats). Notably, the UCR crime definitions are distinct and do not conform to federal or state laws.

There are well-documented criticisms of the UCR data that must be considered when using these data for any purpose. But while the nature of the data and their limitations should be understood, they should not preclude researchers, practitioners, and others from using the data to understand crime and guide policy decisions. The following is a brief discussion of the major issues and concerns surrounding UCR data.

While individual law enforcement agencies classify reported crimes based on the laws of their own states and jurisdictions, these agencies reclassify these crimes according to UCR definitions when reporting them and provide aggregate counts of (a) particular crimes (known as Part I crimes: murder, rape, robbery, aggravated assault, burglary, larceny-theft, motor vehicle theft, and arson) and (b) arrests for all crimes. Note that the FBI does not report the aggregate counts of Part II crimes—including simple assault, fraud, prostitution, and DUI—it reports only the arrests that occur. Thus, when statistics about reported violent and property crime are published in this or any other book or article, they are based on only the eight Part I crimes.

In addition, UCR reporting requires the use of a hierarchical coding system that means if two crimes happen during one incident, only one is counted. For example, if one person is the victim of both rape and robbery, only the rape will be counted, or if a car is stolen out of a locked garage, it is considered a burglary, not a burglary and an auto theft. The UCR Program has specific rules for coding that are not detailed here; however, the result is that the actual number of reported crimes might be underestimated in that the number of incidents is counted and not the number of unique crimes that occur.

	2012 Population	Comparison Score	Overall Crime Rate	Violent Crime Rate	Property Crime Rate
Syracuse, NY, City	145,934	102.20	5,035.2	940.2	4,095.0
Syracuse, NY, Metro	666,129	–28.51	2,823.7	304.1	2,519.6

The factor of actual versus reported crime is probably the most important one to consider when interpreting statistics based on UCR data. That is, the data provided to the FBI contain only those crimes reported or known to law enforcement as opposed to all crime that has actually occurred. We know from victimization surveys that not all crimes are reported to law enforcement (Bureau of Justice Statistics, 2012) and that different types of crimes are reported at different levels. The Bureau of Justice Statistics estimates from the National Crime Victimization Survey that violent crime is reported 40 percent to 50 percent of the time and that property crime is reported 30 percent to 40 percent of the time (Bureau of Justice Statistics, 2012). When UCR data are analyzed, we must recognize that the data do not represent the actual amount of crime. However, if the data are collected accurately and consistently, they can be used, with caution, to make comparisons across geographic areas and over time.

Additional criticisms of the UCR data include inaccuracy due to inputting errors and handling of missing data (Lynch & Jarvis, 2008; Maltz, 1999), pressure on some law enforcement agencies to "doctor" the numbers, and the use of aggregate numbers that mask other factors such as time of day, location, and circumstance of the crime (e.g., whether the crime is committed by a stranger or family member). Yet, the UCR data are the most comprehensive and consistently collected data on crime in the United States. In most cases, analysis of UCR data begins the conversation, and additional in-depth analysis of crime in local areas is required to really understand the nature and context of crime problems (Santos, 2012).

Methodology

As noted above, the crimes tracked by the UCR Program include the violent crimes of murder, rape, robbery, and aggravated assault and the property crimes of burglary, larceny-theft, motor vehicle theft, and arson. This combination of crimes are also sometimes known as *Crime Index* offenses; the index is simply the total of the eight main offense categories. The FBI discontinued use of this measure in 2004 because its officials and advisory board of criminologists concluded that the index was no longer a true indicator of crime. The primary concern was that the Crime Index was inflated by a high number of larceny-thefts, which account for nearly 60 percent of reported crime, thereby diminishing the focus on more serious but less frequently reported offenses, such as murder and rape. The consensus of the FBI and its advisory groups was that the Crime Index no longer served its purpose and that a more meaningful index should be developed.

While the FBI considers how it will replace the Crime Index, *City Crime Rankings* continues to provide total crime numbers, rates, and trends for U.S. cities and metropolitan areas as a service to readers. We offer a cautionary note, however, that in 2012, larceny-theft comprised 68.5 percent of property crime and 60.4 percent of all reported crimes.

Our analyses are conducted on two geographic units: the city and the metropolitan statistical area (MSA) as provided by the FBI. The cities included in these analyses are those with populations of 75,000 or more. According to the FBI in 2012,

Each MSA contains a principal city or urbanized area with a population of at least 50,000 inhabitants. MSAs include the principal city; the county in which the city is located; and other adjacent counties that have, as defined by the OMB, a high degree of economic and social integration with the principal city and county as measured through commuting. In the UCR Program, counties within an MSA are considered metropolitan. In addition, MSAs may cross state boundaries.

In 2012, approximately 85.0 percent of the nation's population lived in MSAs. Some presentations in this publication refer to Metropolitan Divisions, which are subdivisions of an MSA that consists of a core with "a population of at least 2.5 million persons. A Metropolitan Division consists of one or more main/secondary counties that represent an employment center or centers, plus adjacent counties associated with the main county or counties through commuting ties," (Federal Register 65 [249]). Also, some tables reference suburban areas, which are subdivisions of MSAs that exclude the principal cities but include all the remaining cities (those having fewer than 50,000 inhabitants) and the unincorporated areas of the MSAs. (FBI, 2013b)

The methodology used to produce the statistics presented in this book is fairly straightforward. In the first analysis, a score is calculated for each metropolitan area and city; this score is a summary of the percent differences of the reported crime rate from the national rate of six crime types (excluding larceny-theft and arson). Because this formula is unique to this book, it is described in detail below. The rest of the analyses are simple calculations of reported crime rates per 100,000 population and percent change for one year and five years. Lastly, all the analyses present a ranking that is a simple sort of the values computed for the analysis and numbered from highest to lowest. In case of a tie, the rankings are listed alphabetically. Parentheses indicate negative numbers and rates (except in the data distribution charts). Data reported as "NA" are not available or could not be calculated. The national totals and rates appearing at the top of each table are for the entire United States, including both metropolitan and nonmetropolitan areas. Specific totals for metropolitan areas and larger cities are provided in the Appendix.

Comparison Score Methodology

The methodology for determining the city and metro area comparison crime rate rankings involves a multistep process in which the reported crime per 100,000 population rate are compared to the national reported crime per 100,000 population rate and then indexed to create a summary score and ranking across six areas of reported violent and property crime. The methodology used for this edition of the book has been used for the past thirteen editions and is described here in detail.

Reported crime rates per 100,000 population in 2012 across six crime categories—murder, rape, robbery, aggravated assault, burglary, and motor vehicle theft—were examined in this analysis. Larceny-theft was removed from this analysis because of the aforementioned concerns noted by the FBI and others.

Example: City A, Population 150,000

	Murder	Rape	Robbery	Aggravated Assault	Burglary	Motor Vehicle Theft
City Rate	7.33	20.67	84.00	250.00	638.00	116.67
National Rate	4.8	27.5	119.1	252.3	699.6	238.8
Percent Difference	52.71	(24.84)	(29.47)	(0.91)	(8.81)	(51.14)
Percent Difference	52.71	(24.84)	(29.47)	(0.91)	(8.81)	(51.14)
Weighting Factor	.1667	.1667	.1667	.1667	.1667	.1667
Resulting Score	8.62	(4.31)	(5.08)	(0.32)	(1.63)	(8.69)

Cities with populations of 75,000 or more that reported data for the six categories of crime measured were included in the analysis. There is no population minimum for metropolitan areas. In all, 437 cities and 350 metro areas were included in the results.

The following are steps for the comparison score calculation and examples that illustrate the calculations:

1. For each of the six categories of reported crime, the crime rate per 100,000 residents of a city or metropolitan area is calculated from the reported crime and population data provided to the FBI by local law enforcement agencies for a particular type of crime. In the example below, the calculation for murder is 11 divided by 150,000 multiplied by 100,000, which results in a 7.33 per capita reported murder rate per 100,000 people for that year.

2. The percent difference between the metro area or city rate and the national rate for each of the six crimes is then computed. The use of percent difference for each crime separately eliminates weighting more frequent crimes more heavily (e.g., a city may have 1 murder and 1,500 burglaries). Negative numbers are displayed in parentheses here and throughout the analysis tables. The formula for this calculation is:

$$\frac{\text{Metro Area Rate or City Rate} - \text{National Rate}}{\text{National Rate}} \times 100$$

3. The number is then scaled to be one-sixth of the index to make it comparable to scores in the previous editions of this book. A number of years ago, each of the six crimes was weighted based on the results of a telephone survey that determined which crimes were of greatest concern to Americans. The polls indicated that most Americans believed crimes such as burglary are more likely to happen in their lives than more serious crimes such as murder. Thus, burglary received the highest weight, and murder received the lowest weight in the formula. In subsequent years, the polling was discontinued and, consequently, the weights were eliminated. However, equal weight is assigned to the crimes during this step in the analysis so that future scores would be more closely comparable to the scores with the weighted factors.

4. The final comparison score for each metro area and city is the sum of the individual scores for the six crimes. In this case, the sum is −11.41. The interpretation of these scores is that the higher a metro area or city score, the further above the national score; the lower the score, the further below the national score; and a score of zero is equal to the national score.

5. The scores are then sorted from highest to lowest to produce the rankings. Note that the rankings do not indicate the actual difference between the scores, only their order. The 20th Annual America's Cities and Metropolitan Areas with the Highest and Lowest Crimes Rates tables on pages xx–xxvii provide the results of the metro area and city scores. The Metropolitan and Cities Comparison Scores Distribution Analysis for 2012 on pages xiii–xvi provides the results of the distribution of these scores.

This methodology results in a score for each metro area and city that compares its rate to the national rates, providing a means to gauge crime trends in communities.

References

Bureau of Justice Statistics. (2012). *Percent of total crime reported to the police.* Retrieved November 8, 2012, from http://bjs.ojp.usdoj.gov

FBI. (2013a). *Crime in the United States.* Retrieved October 5, 2013, from http://www.fbi.gov/about-us/cjis/ucr/crime-in-the-u.s/2012/crime-in-the-u.s.-2012

FBI. (2013b). *Area Definitions.* Retrieved October 5, 2013, from http://www.fbi.gov/about-us/cjis/ucr/crime-in-the-u.s/2012/crime-in-the-u.s.-2012/resource-pages/area-definitions/areadefinitions

Lynch, J. P., & Jarvis, J. P. (2008). Missing data and imputation in the Uniform Crime Reports and the effects on national estimates. *Journal of Contemporary Criminal Justice, 24,* 69–85.

Maltz, M. (1999). *Bridging gaps in police crime data.* Washington, DC: Bureau of Justice Statistics.

Santos, R. B. (2012). *Crime analysis with crime mapping.* Thousand Oaks, CA: Sage.

Distribution Analysis

This section presents charts depicting the distributions of the comparison scores as well as the individual and collective reported crime rates shown in *City Crime Rankings* to provide a mechanism of comparison beyond the rankings included in each analysis. The histograms in this section illustrate the distribution of values for the comparison score analyses as well as for the overall, violent, and property crime rate analyses. Along with each histogram, measures of central tendency, such as median, mean, standard deviation, and minimum and maximum values, are reported to provide further description of each distribution.

In each histogram (formatted as area charts for easier viewing), the values of the scores or rates are shown along the bottom (*x*-axis) and the frequency of cases (i.e., metro areas or cities) are shown along the left (*y*-axis). The values along the bottom are ranges for which the frequency of cases is totaled. These ranges and frequencies are different for each distribution, in this case, each histogram.

The median indicates the middle value of the distribution, meaning that 50 percent of the metro areas or cities have scores or rates above that value, and 50 percent have scores or rates below it. The mean is the average value of the distribution, and the standard deviation, described generally, is the measure of spread of all the values from the mean. The minimum and maximum values are the lowest and highest values of the distribution, respectively.

These statistics are based on a normal curve, so one standard deviation above and below the mean contains 68 percent of the distribution, two standard deviations above and below the mean contain 95 percent of the distribution, and three standard deviations above and below the mean contain 99.7 percent of the distribution. The use of these statistics is purely descriptive, but it does help the reader assess the distribution as a whole as well as illustrate where an individual value sits in terms of all the other values. For example, if a score is two or three standard deviations above or below the mean, it may be considered an outlier because it falls with only 5 percent or .3 percent of the values, respectively.

For example, Figure 1 depicts the comparison scores for metro areas in 2012. The median is –9.1, the mean is –5.5, the standard deviation is 38.2, the minimum value is –74.8, and the maximum value is 194.2. These statistics are interpreted as follows:

- The lowest comparison score for metro areas is –74.8.
- The highest comparison score for metro areas is 194.2.
- The range of scores (maximum minus minimum) is 269.0.
- 50 percent of the metro areas have comparison scores lower than –9.1, and 50 percent have scores higher than –9.1.
- The average comparison score for metro areas is –5.5 and the standard deviation is 38.2.
- 68 percent of the metro areas have scores between –43.7 and 32.7.
- 95 percent of the metro areas have scores between –81.9 and 70.9.
- 99.7 percent of the metro areas have scores between –120.1 and 109.1. (The fact that the lower end of this range [–120.1] is less than the minimum value of the distribution [–74.8] indicates the distribution is skewed.)

Assessing the score of 103.94 for the metropolitan area of Hammond, LA, for example, reveals that it is in the higher 50 percent of all the scores (above the median of –9.1) and falls between the second and third standard deviation above the mean indicating the value is an extreme outlier and is higher than nearly 97.5 percent of the other metro areas.

The remainder of this section presents a total of six charts and sets of statistics for both metropolitan areas and cities in the categories listed here:

1. Comparison Score
2. Overall Reported Crime
3. Reported Violent Crime
4. Reported Property Crime

A word of caution: These distribution analysis charts and statistics are provided to help the reader understand the nature of the values within each analysis, but the analyses are still based on data that must be interpreted within the constraints noted earlier. These charts are only descriptions of the data and do not provide predictions or explanations of why these values are different.

Figure 1 Metropolitan Areas Comparison Score Distribution Analysis for 2012

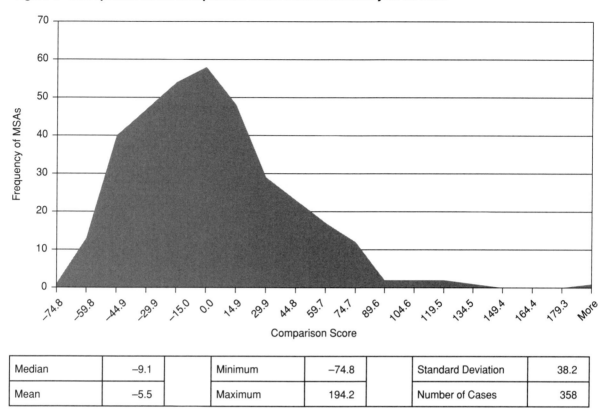

| Median | −9.1 | Minimum | −74.8 | Standard Deviation | 38.2 |
| Mean | −5.5 | Maximum | 194.2 | Number of Cases | 358 |

Figure 2 Cities Comparison Score Distribution Analysis for 2012

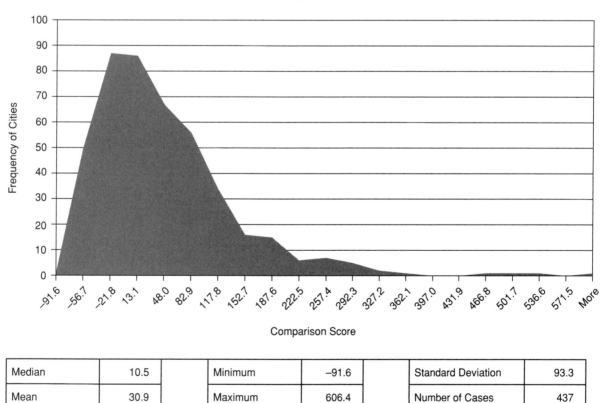

| Median | 10.5 | Minimum | −91.6 | Standard Deviation | 93.3 |
| Mean | 30.9 | Maximum | 606.4 | Number of Cases | 437 |

Figure 3   Metropolitan Areas Overall Reported Crime Rate Distribution Analysis for 2012

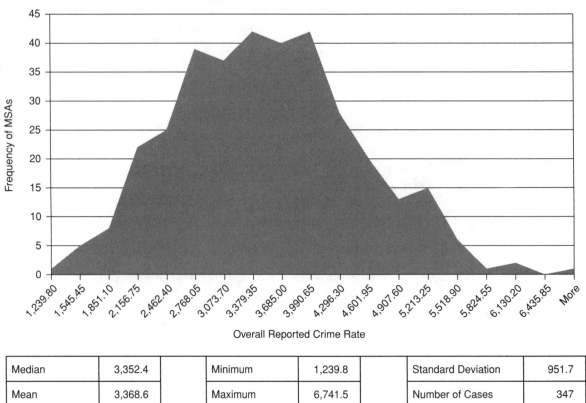

Median	3,352.4		Minimum	1,239.8		Standard Deviation	951.7
Mean	3,368.6		Maximum	6,741.5		Number of Cases	347

Figure 4   Cities Overall Reported Crime Rate Distribution Analysis for 2012

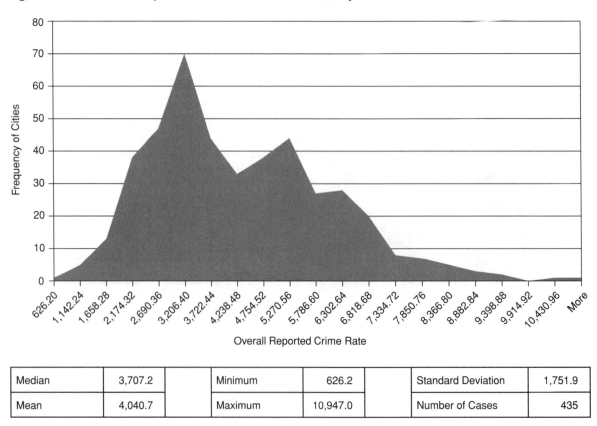

Median	3,707.2		Minimum	626.2		Standard Deviation	1,751.9
Mean	4,040.7		Maximum	10,947.0		Number of Cases	435

Figure 5 Metropolitan Areas Reported Violent Crime Rate Distribution Analysis for 2012

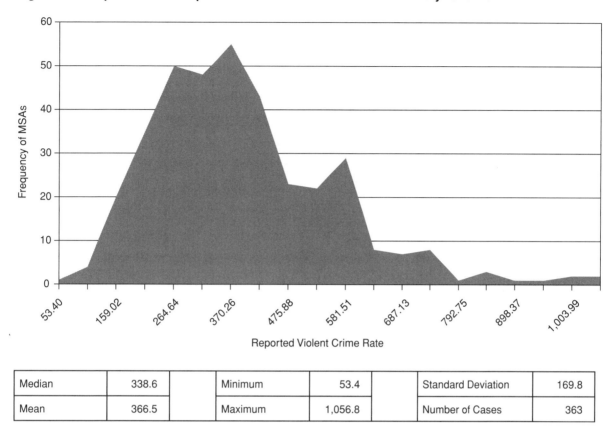

Median	338.6		Minimum	53.4		Standard Deviation	169.8
Mean	366.5		Maximum	1,056.8		Number of Cases	363

Figure 6 Cities Reported Violent Crime Rate Distribution Analysis for 2012

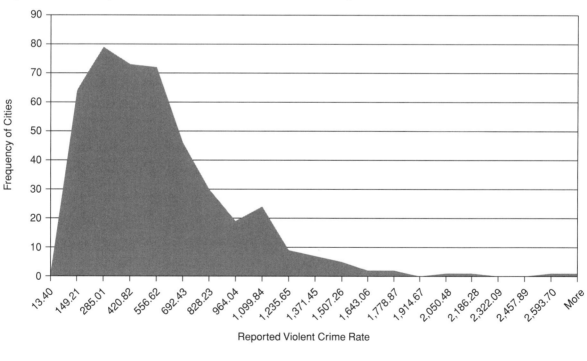

Median	423.2		Minimum	13.4		Standard Deviation	380.0
Mean	504.7		Maximum	2,729.5		Number of Cases	437

Figure 7   Metropolitan Areas Reported Property Crime Rate Distribution Analysis for 2012

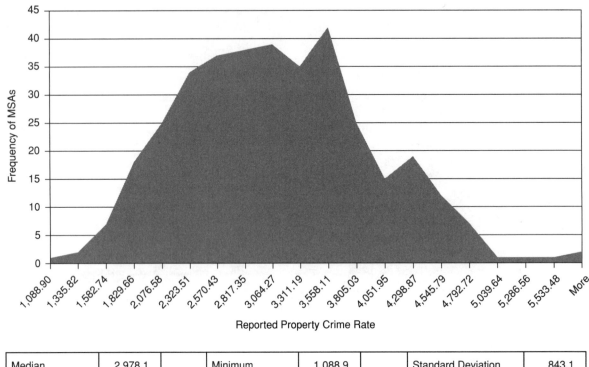

Median	2,978.1		Minimum	1,088.9		Standard Deviation	843.1
Mean	2,983.5		Maximum	5,780.4		Number of Cases	361

Figure 8   Cities Reported Property Crime Rate Distribution Analysis for 2012

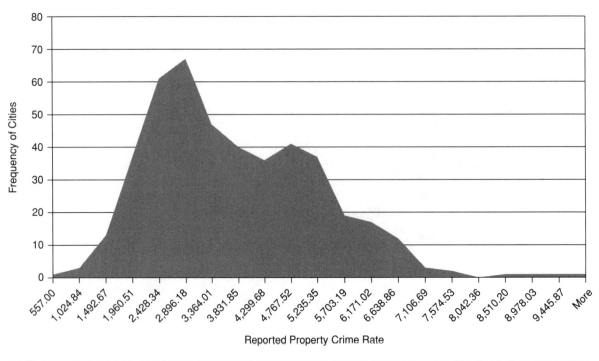

Median	3,203.1		Minimum	557.0		Standard Deviation	1,340.3
Mean	3,441.5		Maximum	6,594.0		Number of Cases	430

Missing Cities and Metropolitan Areas

To be included in the comparative analysis, cities and metro areas must report data for six crime categories: murder, rape, robbery, aggravated assault, burglary, and motor vehicle theft. All metro areas and all cities with populations of 75,000 or more that reported crime data to the FBI were included. A number of cities and metropolitan areas did not report complete crime information for 2012. This information is delineated as follows.

Missing Cities

The data collection method used by the city of Chicago, IL, and the state of Minnesota for the offense of forcible rape did not meet the Federal Bureau of Investigation's Uniform Crime Reporting (UCR) guidelines in 2012 (Minneapolis, MN; and St. Paul, MN, are exceptions). Given that the rape numbers were not available, the following cities are not included in the comparative analysis: Chicago, IL; Bloomington, MN; Brooklyn Park, MN; Duluth, MN; and Rochester, MN.

The FBI did not report crime data for fourteen other cities with populations larger than 75,000. Crime statistics for these cities were unavailable for a number of reasons, ranging from general reporting difficulties and computer issues to changes in reporting systems. Below is a list of cities with populations greater than 75,000 (according to the U.S. Census Bureau) but for which no information was available in the FBI's 2012 Uniform Crime Report. These cities are: Augusta-Richmond County, GA; Bend, OR; Chattanooga, TN; Columbia, SC; Columbus, OH; Concord, NC; Deltona, FL; Evanston, IN; Honolulu, HI; Kalamazoo, MI; Lewisville, TX; Palm Coast, FL; San Angelo, TX; and Suffolk, VA.

Missing Metropolitan Areas

For crime figures to be reported for a metropolitan area, 12 months of complete data must be submitted for 75 percent of agencies and for the principal city or cities within that area. A number of metropolitan areas are not included in the comparative analysis because of missing data for specific offenses. Forcible rape statistics were not available for the Chicago metropolitan area as well as all metropolitan areas in Minnesota.

Another group of metropolitan areas were not included in the comparative analysis because the FBI did not report data for them in its 2012 Crime in the United States report. These metropolitan areas are: Battle Creek, MI; Bend-Redmond, OR; Burlington-South Burlington, VT; Carbondale-Marion, IL; Charleston, WV; Charlotte-Concord-Gastonia, NC-SC; Chattanooga, TN-GA; Cleveland-Elyria, OH; Columbia, SC; Columbus, OH; Eau Claire, WI; Elkhart-Goshen, IN; Evansville, IN-KY; Grand Rapids-Wyoming, MI; Grants Pass, OR; Gulfport-Biloxi-Pascagoula, MS; Honolulu, HI; Hot Springs, AR; Huntington-Ashland, WV-KY-OH; Ithaca, NY; Jacksonville, NC; Jackson, MI; Lake Charles, LA; Muskegon, MI; Myrtle Beach-Conway-North Myrtle Beach, SC-NC; Niles-Benton Harbor, MI; San Angelo, TX; St. Cloud, MN; Weirton-Steubenville, WV-OH; and Wenatchee, WA.

An Overview of 2012 Crime

Crimes are reported by police agencies to the FBI as part of the Uniform Crime Reporting (UCR) Program. Almost 18,300 city, county, college and university, state, tribal, and federal law enforcement agencies participated in the program in 2012. Law enforcement agencies active in the program represented more than 99 percent of the total U.S. population in 2012.

Larcenies and thefts accounted for 60.4 percent of crimes, burglaries accounted for 20.6 percent, aggravated assaults for 7.5 percent, motor vehicle thefts for 7.1 percent, robberies for 3.5 percent, forcible rapes for 0.8 percent, and murders for 0.15 percent. The 2012 total crime rate of 3,246.1 crimes per 100,000 people is 1.4 percent lower than in 2011.

Violent Crime

Violent crimes include offenses of murder, forcible rape, robbery, and aggravated assault. A total of 1,214,462 such crimes were committed in 2012. Of these, 62.6 percent were aggravated assaults, 29.2 percent were robberies, 6.9 percent were forcible rapes, and 1.2 percent were murders. The 2012 national violent crime rate was 386.9 violent crimes per 100,000 population, statistically the same as in 2011.

Five- and ten-year trends show the 2012 violent crime rate was 15.6 percent lower than it was in 2008 and 18.7 percent lower than in 2003. Actual numbers of violent crimes dropped 12.9 percent from 2008 levels and 12.2 percent lower than in 2003.

Among those violent crimes for which weapons information was available, firearms were involved in 69.3 percent of murders, 41.0 percent of robberies, and 21.8 percent of aggravated assaults.

Murder

Murder and nonnegligent manslaughter, as defined by the FBI, involve the willful (nonnegligent) killing of one human being by another. There were 14,827 murders in 2012. Although the national murder rate was 4.7 per 100,000 population in both 2011 and 2012, the FBI reports a 0.4 percent increase based on unrounded rates. Five-year trends show the 2012 murder rate was 12.8 percent lower than in 2008. A ten-year comparison of murder rates shows a drop of 16.9 percent from levels recorded in 2003.

Of those murders for which complete weapons data were available, 69.3 percent involved firearms. FBI data showed that 22.5 percent of murders were committed in conjunction with felonies or suspected felonies such as robberies, drug deals, and rapes. Among murders for which the relationship between the victim and offender was known, strangers committed 22.2 percent of those murders in 2012. Approximately 78 percent of murder victims were male, 46.3 percent were white, and 51.1 percent were black.

Camden, NJ, had the highest murder rate in 2012 of any reporting city with more than 75,000 in population. The city's murder rate of 86.3 murders per 100,000 population was well above the national rate of 4.7 murders per 100,000 population.

Forcible Rape

The FBI defines forcible rape as the carnal knowledge of a female forcibly and against her will. While the definition includes assaults or attempts to commit rape by force or threat of force, it does not include statutory rape (without force) or other sex offenses. There is quite a bit of controversy surrounding this definition. Most states and the District of Columbia collect data for both male and female rapes; however, the UCR data reflect the narrower female-only definition. Sexual attacks on males are counted as aggravated assaults or sex offenses, depending on the circumstances and extent of injuries.

An estimated 52.9 of every 100,000 females in the United States were reported rape victims in 2012. Although the FBI's definition of rape is limited to female victims, the 2012 national rape rate of 26.9 per 100,000 applies to the entire U.S. population, both males and females. This national rape rate dropped 0.5 percent from levels recorded in 2011 and decreased 9.9 percent from 2008 levels.

A total of 84,376 rapes were reported to the FBI by law enforcement agencies in 2012. Of that total, 93.3 percent constituted rapes by force. The remainder included attempts or assaults to commit forcible rape.

Robbery

Robbery is the taking or attempt to take anything by force or threat of force. The 354,520 robberies that occurred in 2012 represented a decrease of 0.1 percent from levels recorded in 2011. The national rate of 112.9 robberies per 100,000 population is lower as well, having decreased 0.8 percent from 2011.

The average dollar loss per robbery was $1,167. Banks lost an average of $3,810 per robbery. Forty-three and a half percent of robberies occurred on streets or highways, 20.8 percent took place in commercial establishments, 16.9 percent were at residences, and 1.9 percent were at banks. The remaining robbery locations were termed "miscellaneous."

Firearms of various types were used in 41.0 percent of robberies in 2012. Strong-arm tactics were used in 42.5 percent of robberies, knives or cutting instruments were used in 7.8 percent, and other dangerous weapons were involved in the remaining 8.8 percent.

Aggravated Assault

Aggravated assault is the unlawful attack by one person upon another for the purpose of inflicting severe bodily injury. This type of assault usually involves the use of a dangerous weapon. The FBI aggravated assault data includes attempts.

The 760,739 aggravated assaults that occurred in 2012 represent a 1.1 percent increase from 2011 levels. The nation's 2012 rate of 242.3 aggravated assaults per 100,000 population is a 0.4 percent increase from 2011. Aggravated assault rates fell 12.7 percent from 2008 levels and 18.0 percent from 2003 levels.

Assailants chose a variety of weapons with which to carry out their attacks in 2012. Slightly less than 27 percent were committed with "personal weapons" (e.g., hands or feet), 21.8 percent with firearms, 18.8 percent with knives, and 32.6 percent of assaults with "other" weapons.

Property Crime

Property crime includes the crimes of burglary, larceny-theft, motor vehicle theft, and arson. These offenses involve the taking of money or property, but there is no force or threat of force against the victims. While arson is considered a property crime, data for arson offenses are not included in this book. The vast majority of crimes committed in the United States are property crimes; in 2012 they accounted for approximately 88.1 percent of all crimes reported.

A total of 8,975,438 property crimes occurred in the United States in 2012. The national property crime rate measured 2,859.2 property crimes per 100,000 population. Property crime decreased from 2011 to 2012 in both number and rate: the number of property crimes fell 0.9 percent from 2011, while the rate decreased 1.6 percent. Five-year trends show that property crime rates decreased 11.1 percent from 2008. A ten-year comparison shows a decline of 20.4 percent from 2003.

Property crimes accounted for an estimated $15.5 billion in losses in 2012. Larceny-thefts accounted for 68.5 percent of all property crimes, burglaries for 23.4 percent, and motor vehicle thefts for 8.0 percent.

Burglary

Burglary is defined as the unlawful entry of a structure to commit a felony or theft. The use of force to gain entry is not required for an offense to be classified as burglary. The FBI tracks data for three types of burglaries: forcible entry, unlawful entry where no force is used, and attempted forcible entry. Burglary accounted for 23.4 percent of the estimated number of property crimes committed in 2012.

A total of 2,103,787 burglaries were reported in 2012, a decrease of 3.7 percent from 2011. The year's burglary rate of 670.2 burglaries per 100,000 population is 4.4 percent lower than in 2011. Five- and ten-year trends show that burglary rates have decreased 8.6 percent since 2008 and 9.6 percent since 2003.

Burglaries of residential properties accounted for 74.5 percent of all burglary offenses. Burglary offenses cost victims an estimated $4.7 billion in lost property. The average dollar loss per burglary offense was $2,230.

Larceny-Theft

Larceny-theft is the unlawful taking of property from another person. It includes crimes such as shoplifting, pick-pocketing, purse-snatching, thefts from motor vehicles, thefts of motor vehicle parts and accessories, and bicycle thefts. No use of force, violence, or fraud is involved in these offenses. This category does not include embezzlement, "con" games, forgery, or worthless check writing.

A total of 6,150,598 thefts occurred in 2012, essentially unchanged from 2011. This number represents 68.5 percent of property crimes reported for the year. The national rate of 1,959.3 larcenies and thefts per 100,000 population represents a 0.7 percent decrease from 2011 levels. Five- and ten-year trends show that larceny-theft rates have decreased 9.5 percent since 2008 and are down 18.9 percent from 2003.

The average value of property stolen in 2012 was $987. Total losses from larceny-thefts measured more than $6.0 billion.

Motor Vehicle Theft

The motor vehicle theft category includes the stealing of automobiles, trucks, buses, motorcycles, motor scooters, snowmobiles, etc. The definition does not include the taking of a motor vehicle for temporary use by those persons having lawful access to the vehicle.

A total of 721,053 motor vehicle thefts were committed in 2012. This represents a 0.6 percent increase from 2011. The national rate of 229.7 vehicles stolen per 100,000 population represents a decrease of 0.1 percent from the prior year.

The total estimated value of these thefts was $4.3 billion, or an average of $6,019 per stolen vehicle. Automobiles were the most frequently stolen vehicle type, accounting for 73.9 percent of all those stolen.

Police Officers

Nationwide, a total of 670,439 sworn police officers were on the job in 2012, with an additional 285,883 civilian employees assisting. This equates to 2.4 full-time officers per 1,000 population.

Only police officers on each city's primary police force are reported in this volume. Many cities have a number of overlapping law enforcement agencies. For example, New York City has its Transit Police, Port Authority Police, and officials in other special law enforcement agencies. Those officers are not covered in City Crime Rankings.

Miscellaneous Notes Regarding City and Metro Crime Data

- 2012 crime statistics are not comparable to previous years' data for all cities in New York; Chandler, AZ; Thornton, CO; and Allentown, PA. Accordingly, one- and five-year crime rate trends are not available for these cities.

- 2012 crime statistics are not comparable to 2011 data for 105 Metropolitan Statistical Areas (MSAs) and to 2008 data for 124 MSAs. Some of these are because of changes in reporting practices but most are because the federal government redefines its MSAs every ten years following a decennial census. This was done in 2012 based on the 2010 census. As a result, new MSAs were created and significant changes were made in some existing MSAs. Where the changes created a one-year population change of 5 percent or greater, the editors determined that the data were not comparable. As a result, one- and five-year trends are not available for these metro areas.

- The population estimates reported in *City Crime Rankings 2014* are provided by the FBI. These estimates sometimes differ from those reported by the U.S. Census Bureau.

- Forcible rape data reported to the Uniform Crime Reporting (UCR) Program by Minnesota (with the exception of Minneapolis and St. Paul) and the city of Chicago, IL, were not in accordance with national UCR guidelines. Therefore, these numbers are not available for Chicago as well as most cities and metro areas in Minnesota.

- Larceny-theft data were not reported for either the cities or the metro areas of Toledo, OH, and Tucson, AZ, because they did not meet UCR guidelines. Thus, this information, as well as property crime statistics, is not available for these cities or metro areas.

- The Hamilton Township, NJ, data are for the township located in Mercer County.

- Honolulu, HI, has a combined city-county government. Therefore, the population and crime data provided in this book include areas outside the principal city of Honolulu.

- Charlotte, NC, crime and population data include Mecklenburg County.

- Indianapolis, IN, crime and population data include Marion County.

- Louisville, KY, data include offenses reported by the Louisville and Jefferson County Police Departments.

- Las Vegas, NV, has a metropolitan police department and its crime and population numbers include areas outside of the principal city of Las Vegas.

- Savannah, GA, crime and population data include Chatham County.

- Toms River Township, NJ, was formerly known as Dover Township.

- The population shown for the city of Mobile, AL, includes 55,819 inhabitants from the jurisdiction of the Mobile County Sheriff's Department.

- *City Crime Rankings 2014* also provides rankings for Metropolitan Divisions (MDs). These are subdivisions of eleven large Metropolitan Statistical Areas.

2013 Metropolitan Crime Rate Rankings*

RANK	METROPOLITAN AREA	SCORE	RANK	METROPOLITAN AREA	SCORE	RANK	METROPOLITAN AREA	SCORE
125	Abilene, TX	(23.05)	96	Cheyenne, WY	(32.15)	255	Gary, IN M.D.	13.34
203	Akron, OH	(3.41)	NA	Chicago (greater), IL-IN-WI**	NA	17	Gettysburg, PA	(57.32)
71	Albany-Schenectady-Troy, NY	(38.95)	NA	Chicago-Joilet-Naperville, IL M.D.**	NA	46	Glens Falls, NY	(46.45)
304	Albany, GA	38.74	228	Chico, CA	3.49	313	Goldsboro, NC	43.27
35	Albany, OR	(49.98)	170	Cincinnati, OH-KY-IN	(10.73)	NA	Grand Forks, ND-MN**	NA
NA	Albuquerque, NM**	NA	218	Clarksville, TN-KY	1.63	104	Grand Island, NE	(28.40)
NA	Alexandria, LA**	NA	217	Cleveland, TN	1.53	206	Grand Junction, CO	(2.31)
84	Allentown, PA-NJ	(35.84)	132	Coeur d'Alene, ID	(21.29)	62	Great Falls, MT	(41.17)
93	Altoona, PA	(32.85)	135	College Station-Bryan, TX	(20.24)	78	Greeley, CO	(37.35)
286	Amarillo, TX	25.88	NA	Colorado Springs, CO**	NA	44	Green Bay, WI	(46.69)
55	Ames, IA	(44.74)	138	Columbia, MO	(20.03)	224	Greensboro-High Point, NC	2.68
67	Anaheim-Santa Ana-Irvine, CA M.D.	(40.16)	294	Columbus, GA-AL	31.86	297	Greenville-Anderson, SC	33.83
337	Anchorage, AK	68.88	87	Columbus, IN	(34.35)	239	Greenville, NC	5.29
130	Ann Arbor, MI	(21.39)	NA	Corpus Christi, TX**	NA	85	Hagerstown-Martinsburg, MD-WV	(35.31)
289	Anniston-Oxford, AL	28.12	14	Corvallis, OR	(60.24)	346	Hammond, LA	103.94
5	Appleton, WI	(68.85)	143	Crestview-Fort Walton Beach, FL	(18.59)	212	Hanford-Corcoran, CA	(0.11)
140	Asheville, NC	(19.37)	130	Cumberland, MD-WV	(21.39)	110	Harrisburg-Carlisle, PA	(26.11)
184	Athens-Clarke County, GA	(7.63)	219	Dallas (greater), TX	1.65	10	Harrisonburg, VA	(63.50)
276	Atlanta, GA	21.45	222	Dallas-Plano-Irving, TX M.D.	2.25	122	Hartford, CT	(23.21)
NA	Atlantic City, NJ**	NA	89	Dalton, GA	(33.95)	60	Hattiesburg, MS	(42.00)
114	Auburn, AL	(25.65)	319	Danville, IL	46.59	149	Hickory, NC	(16.79)
285	Augusta, GA-SC	25.79	82	Daphne-Fairhope-Foley, AL	(36.42)	290	Hilton Head Island, SC	28.26
113	Austin-Round Rock, TX	(25.83)	129	Davenport, IA-IL	(21.91)	221	Hinesville, GA	2.22
341	Bakersfield, CA	73.75	213	Dayton, OH	(0.04)	100	Homosassa Springs, FL	(31.13)
308	Baltimore, MD	40.74	88	Decatur, AL	(34.14)	119	Houma, LA	(24.36)
57	Bangor, ME	(44.58)	227	Decatur, IL	3.40	NA	Houston, TX**	NA
134	Barnstable Town, MA	(20.65)	161	Deltona-Daytona Beach, FL	(12.72)	262	Huntsville, AL	15.36
NA	Baton Rouge, LA**	NA	216	Denver-Aurora, CO	1.40	20	Idaho Falls, ID	(55.15)
128	Bay City, MI	(22.08)	NA	Des Moines-West Des Moines, IA**	NA	310	Indianapolis, IN	41.55
282	Beaumont-Port Arthur, TX	25.19	330	Detroit (greater), MI	59.13	64	Iowa City, IA	(40.86)
295	Beckley, WV	32.43	350	Detroit-Dearborn-Livonia, MI M.D.	194.24	270	Jacksonville, FL	18.89
123	Bellingham, WA	(23.14)	259	Dothan, AL	14.37	324	Jackson, MS	51.03
144	Billings, MT	(18.43)	200	Dover, DE	(3.83)	338	Jackson, TN	70.46
76	Binghamton, NY	(37.67)	NA	Dubuque, IA**	NA	81	Janesville, WI	(36.70)
315	Birmingham-Hoover, AL	44.98	NA	Duluth, MN-WI**	NA	66	Jefferson City, MO	(40.18)
166	Bismarck, ND	(11.83)	248	Durham-Chapel Hill, NC	11.22	94	Johnson City, TN	(32.69)
33	Blacksburg, VA	(50.47)	6	Dutchess-Putnam, NY M.D.	(64.49)	68	Johnstown, PA	(39.99)
90	Bloomington, IL	(33.91)	127	East Stroudsburg, PA	(22.35)	238	Jonesboro, AR	5.24
116	Bloomington, IN	(25.09)	205	El Centro, CA	(2.89)	236	Joplin, MO	5.01
47	Bloomsburg-Berwick, PA	(46.16)	124	El Paso, TX	(23.11)	173	Kahului-Wailuku-Lahaina, HI	(10.10)
39	Boise City, ID	(48.15)	22	Elgin, IL M.D.	(52.82)	220	Kalamazoo-Portage, MI	1.71
102	Boston (greater), MA-NH	(29.07)	4	Elizabethtown-Fort Knox, KY	(69.61)	211	Kankakee, IL	(0.51)
195	Boston, MA M.D.	(4.31)	42	Elmira, NY	(47.17)	299	Kansas City, MO-KS	35.23
23	Boulder, CO	(52.79)	121	Erie, PA	(23.66)	80	Kennewick-Richland, WA	(37.03)
73	Bowling Green, KY	(38.57)	154	Eugene, OR	(15.60)	NA	Killeen-Temple, TX**	NA
168	Bremerton-Silverdale, WA	(11.15)	328	Fairbanks, AK	57.05	148	Kingsport, TN-VA	(16.88)
180	Bridgeport-Stamford, CT	(8.67)	NA	Fargo, ND-MN**	NA	8	Kingston, NY	(63.91)
107	Brownsville-Harlingen, TX	(27.74)	316	Farmington, NM	45.33	243	Knoxville, TN	7.04
260	Brunswick, GA	14.53	160	Fayetteville-Springdale, AR-MO	(12.89)	150	Kokomo, IN	(16.67)
210	Buffalo-Niagara Falls, NY	(1.10)	327	Fayetteville, NC	56.43	NA	La Crosse, WI-MN**	NA
190	Burlington, NC	(6.73)	106	Flagstaff, AZ	(28.15)	99	Lafayette, IN	(31.27)
31	California-Lexington Park, MD	(50.82)	349	Flint, MI	121.19	NA	Lafayette, LA**	NA
49	Cambridge-Newton, MA M.D.	(46.11)	167	Florence-Muscle Shoals, AL	(11.21)	19	Lake Co.-Kenosha Co., IL-WI M.D.	(55.31)
187	Camden, NJ M.D.	(7.29)	303	Florence, SC	37.60	141	Lake Havasu City-Kingman, AZ	(19.04)
197	Canton, OH	(4.19)	27	Fond du Lac, WI	(51.86)	194	Lakeland, FL	(4.32)
178	Cape Coral-Fort Myers, FL	(8.79)	37	Fort Collins, CO	(48.82)	38	Lancaster, PA	(48.62)
192	Cape Girardeau, MO-IL	(6.49)	267	Fort Lauderdale, FL M.D.	17.55	172	Lansing-East Lansing, MI	(10.19)
15	Carson City, NV	(58.60)	183	Fort Smith, AR-OK	(7.71)	189	Laredo, TX	(6.74)
70	Casper, WY	(39.09)	157	Fort Wayne, IN	(14.36)	196	Las Cruces, NM	(4.28)
NA	Cedar Rapids, IA**	NA	215	Fort Worth-Arlington, TX M.D.	0.80	325	Las Vegas-Henderson, NV	54.19
25	Chambersburg-Waynesboro, PA	(52.01)	335	Fresno, CA	67.21	165	Lawrence, KS	(12.00)
244	Champaign-Urbana, IL	7.50	293	Gadsden, AL	31.32	332	Lawton, OK	61.52
249	Charleston-North Charleston, SC	11.67	266	Gainesville, FL	16.88	24	Lebanon, PA	(52.56)
43	Charlottesville, VA	(46.71)	86	Gainesville, GA	(34.87)	74	Lewiston-Auburn, ME	(37.88)

Note: All listings are for Metropolitan Statistical Areas (M.S.A.s) except for those ending with "M.D." Listings with "M.D." are Metropolitan Divisions which are smaller parts of eleven large M.S.A.s. See explanatory note at beginning of metropolitan area section.

RANK	METROPOLITAN AREA	SCORE
48	Lewiston, ID-WA	(46.15)
225	Lexington-Fayette, KY	2.88
311	Lima, OH	42.59
177	Lincoln, NE	(8.88)
342	Little Rock, AR	74.33
1	Logan, UT-ID	(74.76)
254	Longview, TX	12.47
257	Longview, WA	14.32
271	Los Angeles County, CA M.D.	19.13
237	Los Angeles (greater), CA	5.22
252	Louisville, KY-IN	12.30
320	Lubbock, TX	47.14
26	Lynchburg, VA	(51.89)
314	Macon, GA	44.97
278	Madera, CA	22.85
61	Madison, WI	(41.65)
65	Manchester-Nashua, NH	(40.37)
45	Manhattan, KS	(46.58)
NA	Mankato-North Mankato, MN**	NA
193	Mansfield, OH	(5.56)
158	McAllen-Edinburg-Mission, TX	(14.27)
117	Medford, OR	(24.80)
347	Memphis, TN-MS-AR	112.85
334	Merced, CA	63.00
292	Miami (greater), FL	31.28
322	Miami-Dade County, FL M.D.	50.95
92	Michigan City-La Porte, IN	(33.45)
58	Midland, MI	(44.56)
95	Midland, TX	(32.27)
296	Milwaukee, WI	33.36
NA	Minneapolis-St. Paul, MN-WI**	NA
79	Missoula, MT	(37.12)
318	Mobile, AL	45.59
339	Modesto, CA	71.61
247	Monroe, LA	10.62
175	Monroe, MI	(9.28)
12	Montgomery County, PA M.D.	(61.01)
326	Montgomery, AL	54.91
63	Morgantown, WV	(41.09)
153	Morristown, TN	(15.70)
146	Mount Vernon-Anacortes, WA	(17.99)
91	Muncie, IN	(33.68)
108	Napa, CA	(27.47)
32	Naples-Marco Island, FL	(50.80)
269	Nashville-Davidson, TN	18.71
9	Nassau-Suffolk, NY M.D.	(63.54)
182	New Bern, NC	(7.72)
203	New Haven-Milford, CT	(3.41)
336	New Orleans, LA	68.73
NA	New York (greater), NY-NJ-PA**	NA
NA	New York-Jersey City, NY-NJ M.D.**	NA
208	Newark, NJ-PA M.D.	(1.66)
223	North Port-Sarasota-Bradenton, FL	2.31
145	Norwich-New London, CT	(18.35)
344	Oakland-Hayward, CA M.D.	84.63
240	Ocala, FL	5.31
101	Ocean City, NJ	(30.29)
306	Odessa, TX	40.09
29	Ogden-Clearfield, UT	(51.58)
333	Oklahoma City, OK	61.74
155	Olympia, WA	(15.44)
275	Omaha-Council Bluffs, NE-IA	20.87
277	Orlando, FL	22.84
11	Oshkosh-Neenah, WI	(62.67)

RANK	METROPOLITAN AREA	SCORE
36	Owensboro, KY	(49.81)
59	Oxnard-Thousand Oaks, CA	(43.97)
251	Palm Bay-Melbourne, FL	11.84
264	Panama City, FL	15.55
115	Parkersburg-Vienna, WV	(25.37)
281	Pensacola, FL	25.05
181	Peoria, IL	(7.79)
NA	Philadelphia (greater) PA-NJ-MD-DE**	NA
NA	Philadelphia, PA M.D.**	NA
NA	Phoenix-Mesa-Scottsdale, AZ**	NA
345	Pine Bluff, AR	93.80
NA	Pittsburgh, PA**	NA
137	Pittsfield, MA	(20.15)
56	Pocatello, ID	(44.72)
133	Port St. Lucie, FL	(21.24)
163	Portland-Vancouver, OR-WA	(12.11)
30	Portland, ME	(51.17)
111	Prescott, AZ	(26.10)
156	Providence-Warwick, RI-MA	(14.98)
2	Provo-Orem, UT	(72.57)
284	Pueblo, CO	25.46
28	Punta Gorda, FL	(51.76)
109	Racine, WI	(26.80)
83	Raleigh, NC	(36.14)
279	Rapid City, SD	23.88
169	Reading, PA	(10.93)
331	Redding, CA	61.19
179	Reno, NV	(8.70)
136	Richmond, VA	(20.22)
261	Riverside-San Bernardino, CA	14.85
98	Roanoke, VA	(31.48)
NA	Rochester, MN**	NA
120	Rochester, NY	(24.06)
312	Rockford, IL	43.14
34	Rockingham County, NH M.D.	(50.45)
300	Rocky Mount, NC	35.49
207	Rome, GA	(2.14)
265	Sacramento, CA	16.73
343	Saginaw, MI	81.44
142	Salem, OR	(19.03)
305	Salinas, CA	39.49
209	Salisbury, MD-DE	(1.41)
235	Salt Lake City, UT	4.74
273	San Antonio, TX	19.78
201	San Diego, CA	(3.68)
NA	San Francisco (greater), CA**	NA
287	San Francisco-Redwood, CA M.D.	26.10
229	San Jose, CA	3.51
105	San Luis Obispo, CA	(28.34)
NA	San Rafael, CA M.D.**	NA
230	Santa Cruz-Watsonville, CA	3.56
263	Santa Fe, NM	15.45
147	Santa Maria-Santa Barbara, CA	(17.02)
97	Santa Rosa, CA	(31.84)
234	Savannah, GA	3.93
75	Scranton--Wilkes-Barre, PA	(37.76)
NA	Seattle (greater), WA**	NA
242	Seattle-Bellevue-Everett, WA M.D.	6.57
51	Sebastian-Vero Beach, FL	(45.61)
151	Sebring, FL	(16.40)
50	Sheboygan, WI	(46.10)
126	Sherman-Denison, TX	(22.52)
NA	Shreveport-Bossier City, LA**	NA
188	Sierra Vista-Douglas, AZ	(6.80)

RANK	METROPOLITAN AREA	SCORE
21	Silver Spring-Frederick, MD M.D.	(54.40)
77	Sioux City, IA-NE-SD	(37.65)
159	Sioux Falls, SD	(14.06)
258	South Bend-Mishawaka, IN-MI	14.34
226	Spartanburg, SC	3.21
298	Spokane, WA	34.11
317	Springfield, IL	45.50
245	Springfield, MA	7.63
280	Springfield, MO	24.74
233	Springfield, OH	3.76
3	State College, PA	(70.75)
16	Staunton-Waynesboro, VA	(58.19)
348	Stockton-Lodi, CA	113.37
40	St. George, UT	(47.63)
176	St. Joseph, MO-KS	(9.00)
256	St. Louis, MO-IL	14.14
340	Sumter, SC	72.66
103	Syracuse, NY	(28.51)
NA	Tacoma, WA M.D.**	NA
307	Tallahassee, FL	40.73
174	Tampa-St Petersburg, FL	(9.38)
164	Terre Haute, IN	(12.04)
301	Texarkana, TX-AR	36.09
7	The Villages, FL	(63.96)
329	Toledo, OH	57.19
268	Topeka, KS	17.57
246	Trenton, NJ	9.26
291	Tucson, AZ	30.02
309	Tulsa, OK	41.40
232	Tuscaloosa, AL	3.73
202	Tyler, TX	(3.54)
54	Utica-Rome, NY	(45.53)
184	Valdosta, GA	(7.63)
321	Vallejo-Fairfield, CA	48.75
274	Victoria, TX	20.29
272	Vineland-Bridgeton, NJ	19.50
162	Virginia Beach-Norfolk, VA-NC	(12.45)
302	Visalia-Porterville, CA	36.34
231	Waco, TX	3.59
112	Walla Walla, WA	(26.01)
186	Warner Robins, GA	(7.53)
72	Warren-Troy, MI M.D.	(38.66)
139	Washington (greater) DC-VA-MD-WV	(19.81)
171	Washington, DC-VA-MD-WV M.D.	(10.35)
191	Waterloo-Cedar Falls, IA	(6.55)
18	Watertown-Fort Drum, NY	(56.59)
13	Wausau, WI	(60.33)
252	West Palm Beach, FL M.D.	12.30
53	Wheeling, WV-OH	(45.54)
241	Wichita Falls, TX	5.45
283	Wichita, KS	25.37
41	Williamsport, PA	(47.56)
288	Wilmington, DE-MD-NJ M.D.	27.53
214	Wilmington, NC	0.49
52	Winchester, VA-WV	(45.56)
199	Winston-Salem, NC	(3.87)
118	Worcester, MA-CT	(24.69)
323	Yakima, WA	51.01
69	York-Hanover, PA	(39.25)
198	Youngstown-Warren, OH-PA	(4.10)
250	Yuba City, CA	11.73
152	Yuma, AZ	(16.11)

Source: CQ Press using reported data from the F.B.I. "Crime in the United States 2012"

*Includes murder, rape, robbery, aggravated assault, burglary, and motor vehicle theft. A negative score (in parentheses) indicates a composite crime number below the national rate, a positive number is above the national rate. **Not available.

2013 Metropolitan Crime Rate Rankings* (continued)

RANK	METROPOLITAN AREA	SCORE	RANK	METROPOLITAN AREA	SCORE	RANK	METROPOLITAN AREA	SCORE
1	Logan, UT-ID	(74.76)	65	Manchester-Nashua, NH	(40.37)	129	Davenport, IA-IL	(21.91)
2	Provo-Orem, UT	(72.57)	66	Jefferson City, MO	(40.18)	130	Ann Arbor, MI	(21.39)
3	State College, PA	(70.75)	67	Anaheim-Santa Ana-Irvine, CA M.D.	(40.16)	130	Cumberland, MD-WV	(21.39)
4	Elizabethtown-Fort Knox, KY	(69.61)	68	Johnstown, PA	(39.99)	132	Coeur d'Alene, ID	(21.29)
5	Appleton, WI	(68.85)	69	York-Hanover, PA	(39.25)	133	Port St. Lucie, FL	(21.24)
6	Dutchess-Putnam, NY M.D.	(64.49)	70	Casper, WY	(39.09)	134	Barnstable Town, MA	(20.65)
7	The Villages, FL	(63.96)	71	Albany-Schenectady-Troy, NY	(38.95)	135	College Station-Bryan, TX	(20.24)
8	Kingston, NY	(63.91)	72	Warren-Troy, MI M.D.	(38.66)	136	Richmond, VA	(20.22)
9	Nassau-Suffolk, NY M.D.	(63.54)	73	Bowling Green, KY	(38.57)	137	Pittsfield, MA	(20.15)
10	Harrisonburg, VA	(63.50)	74	Lewiston-Auburn, ME	(37.88)	138	Columbia, MO	(20.03)
11	Oshkosh-Neenah, WI	(62.67)	75	Scranton--Wilkes-Barre, PA	(37.76)	139	Washington (greater) DC-VA-MD-WV	(19.81)
12	Montgomery County, PA M.D.	(61.01)	76	Binghamton, NY	(37.67)	140	Asheville, NC	(19.37)
13	Wausau, WI	(60.33)	77	Sioux City, IA-NE-SD	(37.65)	141	Lake Havasu City-Kingman, AZ	(19.04)
14	Corvallis, OR	(60.24)	78	Greeley, CO	(37.35)	142	Salem, OR	(19.03)
15	Carson City, NV	(58.60)	79	Missoula, MT	(37.12)	143	Crestview-Fort Walton Beach, FL	(18.59)
16	Staunton-Waynesboro, VA	(58.19)	80	Kennewick-Richland, WA	(37.03)	144	Billings, MT	(18.43)
17	Gettysburg, PA	(57.32)	81	Janesville, WI	(36.70)	145	Norwich-New London, CT	(18.35)
18	Watertown-Fort Drum, NY	(56.59)	82	Daphne-Fairhope-Foley, AL	(36.42)	146	Mount Vernon-Anacortes, WA	(17.99)
19	Lake Co.-Kenosha Co., IL-WI M.D.	(55.31)	83	Raleigh, NC	(36.14)	147	Santa Maria-Santa Barbara, CA	(17.02)
20	Idaho Falls, ID	(55.15)	84	Allentown, PA-NJ	(35.84)	148	Kingsport, TN-VA	(16.88)
21	Silver Spring-Frederick, MD M.D.	(54.40)	85	Hagerstown-Martinsburg, MD-WV	(35.31)	149	Hickory, NC	(16.79)
22	Elgin, IL M.D.	(52.82)	86	Gainesville, GA	(34.87)	150	Kokomo, IN	(16.67)
23	Boulder, CO	(52.79)	87	Columbus, IN	(34.35)	151	Sebring, FL	(16.40)
24	Lebanon, PA	(52.56)	88	Decatur, AL	(34.14)	152	Yuma, AZ	(16.11)
25	Chambersburg-Waynesboro, PA	(52.01)	89	Dalton, GA	(33.95)	153	Morristown, TN	(15.70)
26	Lynchburg, VA	(51.89)	90	Bloomington, IL	(33.91)	154	Eugene, OR	(15.60)
27	Fond du Lac, WI	(51.86)	91	Muncie, IN	(33.68)	155	Olympia, WA	(15.44)
28	Punta Gorda, FL	(51.76)	92	Michigan City-La Porte, IN	(33.45)	156	Providence-Warwick, RI-MA	(14.98)
29	Ogden-Clearfield, UT	(51.58)	93	Altoona, PA	(32.85)	157	Fort Wayne, IN	(14.36)
30	Portland, ME	(51.17)	94	Johnson City, TN	(32.69)	158	McAllen-Edinburg-Mission, TX	(14.27)
31	California-Lexington Park, MD	(50.82)	95	Midland, TX	(32.27)	159	Sioux Falls, SD	(14.06)
32	Naples-Marco Island, FL	(50.80)	96	Cheyenne, WY	(32.15)	160	Fayetteville-Springdale, AR-MO	(12.89)
33	Blacksburg, VA	(50.47)	97	Santa Rosa, CA	(31.84)	161	Deltona-Daytona Beach, FL	(12.72)
34	Rockingham County, NH M.D.	(50.45)	98	Roanoke, VA	(31.48)	162	Virginia Beach-Norfolk, VA-NC	(12.45)
35	Albany, OR	(49.98)	99	Lafayette, IN	(31.27)	163	Portland-Vancouver, OR-WA	(12.11)
36	Owensboro, KY	(49.81)	100	Homosassa Springs, FL	(31.13)	164	Terre Haute, IN	(12.04)
37	Fort Collins, CO	(48.82)	101	Ocean City, NJ	(30.29)	165	Lawrence, KS	(12.00)
38	Lancaster, PA	(48.62)	102	Boston (greater), MA-NH	(29.07)	166	Bismarck, ND	(11.83)
39	Boise City, ID	(48.15)	103	Syracuse, NY	(28.51)	167	Florence-Muscle Shoals, AL	(11.21)
40	St. George, UT	(47.63)	104	Grand Island, NE	(28.40)	168	Bremerton-Silverdale, WA	(11.15)
41	Williamsport, PA	(47.56)	105	San Luis Obispo, CA	(28.34)	169	Reading, PA	(10.93)
42	Elmira, NY	(47.17)	106	Flagstaff, AZ	(28.15)	170	Cincinnati, OH-KY-IN	(10.73)
43	Charlottesville, VA	(46.71)	107	Brownsville-Harlingen, TX	(27.74)	171	Washington, DC-VA-MD-WV M.D.	(10.35)
44	Green Bay, WI	(46.69)	108	Napa, CA	(27.47)	172	Lansing-East Lansing, MI	(10.19)
45	Manhattan, KS	(46.58)	109	Racine, WI	(26.80)	173	Kahului-Wailuku-Lahaina, HI	(10.10)
46	Glens Falls, NY	(46.45)	110	Harrisburg-Carlisle, PA	(26.11)	174	Tampa-St Petersburg, FL	(9.38)
47	Bloomsburg-Berwick, PA	(46.16)	111	Prescott, AZ	(26.10)	175	Monroe, MI	(9.28)
48	Lewiston, ID-WA	(46.15)	112	Walla Walla, WA	(26.01)	176	St. Joseph, MO-KS	(9.00)
49	Cambridge-Newton, MA M.D.	(46.11)	113	Austin-Round Rock, TX	(25.83)	177	Lincoln, NE	(8.88)
50	Sheboygan, WI	(46.10)	114	Auburn, AL	(25.65)	178	Cape Coral-Fort Myers, FL	(8.79)
51	Sebastian-Vero Beach, FL	(45.61)	115	Parkersburg-Vienna, WV	(25.37)	179	Reno, NV	(8.70)
52	Winchester, VA-WV	(45.56)	116	Bloomington, IN	(25.09)	180	Bridgeport-Stamford, CT	(8.67)
53	Wheeling, WV-OH	(45.54)	117	Medford, OR	(24.80)	181	Peoria, IL	(7.79)
54	Utica-Rome, NY	(45.53)	118	Worcester, MA-CT	(24.69)	182	New Bern, NC	(7.72)
55	Ames, IA	(44.74)	119	Houma, LA	(24.36)	183	Fort Smith, AR-OK	(7.71)
56	Pocatello, ID	(44.72)	120	Rochester, NY	(24.06)	184	Athens-Clarke County, GA	(7.63)
57	Bangor, ME	(44.58)	121	Erie, PA	(23.66)	184	Valdosta, GA	(7.63)
58	Midland, MI	(44.56)	122	Hartford, CT	(23.21)	186	Warner Robins, GA	(7.53)
59	Oxnard-Thousand Oaks, CA	(43.97)	123	Bellingham, WA	(23.14)	187	Camden, NJ M.D.	(7.29)
60	Hattiesburg, MS	(42.00)	124	El Paso, TX	(23.11)	188	Sierra Vista-Douglas, AZ	(6.80)
61	Madison, WI	(41.65)	125	Abilene, TX	(23.05)	189	Laredo, TX	(6.74)
62	Great Falls, MT	(41.17)	126	Sherman-Denison, TX	(22.52)	190	Burlington, NC	(6.73)
63	Morgantown, WV	(41.09)	127	East Stroudsburg, PA	(22.35)	191	Waterloo-Cedar Falls, IA	(6.55)
64	Iowa City, IA	(40.86)	128	Bay City, MI	(22.08)	192	Cape Girardeau, MO-IL	(6.49)

Note: All listings are for Metropolitan Statistical Areas (M.S.A.s) except for those ending with "M.D." Listings with "M.D." are Metropolitan Divisions which are smaller parts of eleven large M.S.A.s. See explanatory note at beginning of metropolitan area section.

RANK	METROPOLITAN AREA	SCORE	RANK	METROPOLITAN AREA	SCORE	RANK	METROPOLITAN AREA	SCORE
193	Mansfield, OH	(5.56)	257	Longview, WA	14.32	321	Vallejo-Fairfield, CA	48.75
194	Lakeland, FL	(4.32)	258	South Bend-Mishawaka, IN-MI	14.34	322	Miami-Dade County, FL M.D.	50.95
195	Boston, MA M.D.	(4.31)	259	Dothan, AL	14.37	323	Yakima, WA	51.01
196	Las Cruces, NM	(4.28)	260	Brunswick, GA	14.53	324	Jackson, MS	51.03
197	Canton, OH	(4.19)	261	Riverside-San Bernardino, CA	14.85	325	Las Vegas-Henderson, NV	54.19
198	Youngstown-Warren, OH-PA	(4.10)	262	Huntsville, AL	15.36	326	Montgomery, AL	54.91
199	Winston-Salem, NC	(3.87)	263	Santa Fe, NM	15.45	327	Fayetteville, NC	56.43
200	Dover, DE	(3.83)	264	Panama City, FL	15.55	328	Fairbanks, AK	57.05
201	San Diego, CA	(3.68)	265	Sacramento, CA	16.73	329	Toledo, OH	57.19
202	Tyler, TX	(3.54)	266	Gainesville, FL	16.88	330	Detroit (greater), MI	59.13
203	Akron, OH	(3.41)	267	Fort Lauderdale, FL M.D.	17.55	331	Redding, CA	61.19
203	New Haven-Milford, CT	(3.41)	268	Topeka, KS	17.57	332	Lawton, OK	61.52
205	El Centro, CA	(2.89)	269	Nashville-Davidson, TN	18.71	333	Oklahoma City, OK	61.74
206	Grand Junction, CO	(2.31)	270	Jacksonville, FL	18.89	334	Merced, CA	63.00
207	Rome, GA	(2.14)	271	Los Angeles County, CA M.D.	19.13	335	Fresno, CA	67.21
208	Newark, NJ-PA M.D.	(1.66)	272	Vineland-Bridgeton, NJ	19.50	336	New Orleans, LA	68.73
209	Salisbury, MD-DE	(1.41)	273	San Antonio, TX	19.78	337	Anchorage, AK	68.88
210	Buffalo-Niagara Falls, NY	(1.10)	274	Victoria, TX	20.29	338	Jackson, TN	70.46
211	Kankakee, IL	(0.51)	275	Omaha-Council Bluffs, NE-IA	20.87	339	Modesto, CA	71.61
212	Hanford-Corcoran, CA	(0.11)	276	Atlanta, GA	21.45	340	Sumter, SC	72.66
213	Dayton, OH	(0.04)	277	Orlando, FL	22.84	341	Bakersfield, CA	73.75
214	Wilmington, NC	0.49	278	Madera, CA	22.85	342	Little Rock, AR	74.33
215	Fort Worth-Arlington, TX M.D.	0.80	279	Rapid City, SD	23.88	343	Saginaw, MI	81.44
216	Denver-Aurora, CO	1.40	280	Springfield, MO	24.74	344	Oakland-Hayward, CA M.D.	84.63
217	Cleveland, TN	1.53	281	Pensacola, FL	25.05	345	Pine Bluff, AR	93.80
218	Clarksville, TN-KY	1.63	282	Beaumont-Port Arthur, TX	25.19	346	Hammond, LA	103.94
219	Dallas (greater), TX	1.65	283	Wichita, KS	25.37	347	Memphis, TN-MS-AR	112.85
220	Kalamazoo-Portage, MI	1.71	284	Pueblo, CO	25.46	348	Stockton-Lodi, CA	113.37
221	Hinesville, GA	2.22	285	Augusta, GA-SC	25.79	349	Flint, MI	121.19
222	Dallas-Plano-Irving, TX M.D.	2.25	286	Amarillo, TX	25.88	350	Detroit-Dearborn-Livonia, MI M.D.	194.24
223	North Port-Sarasota-Bradenton, FL	2.31	287	San Francisco-Redwood, CA M.D.	26.10	NA	Albuquerque, NM**	NA
224	Greensboro-High Point, NC	2.68	288	Wilmington, DE-MD-NJ M.D.	27.53	NA	Alexandria, LA**	NA
225	Lexington-Fayette, KY	2.88	289	Anniston-Oxford, AL	28.12	NA	Atlantic City, NJ**	NA
226	Spartanburg, SC	3.21	290	Hilton Head Island, SC	28.26	NA	Baton Rouge, LA**	NA
227	Decatur, IL	3.40	291	Tucson, AZ	30.02	NA	Cedar Rapids, IA**	NA
228	Chico, CA	3.49	292	Miami (greater), FL	31.28	NA	Chicago (greater), IL-IN-WI**	NA
229	San Jose, CA	3.51	293	Gadsden, AL	31.32	NA	Chicago-Joilet-Naperville, IL M.D.**	NA
230	Santa Cruz-Watsonville, CA	3.56	294	Columbus, GA-AL	31.86	NA	Colorado Springs, CO**	NA
231	Waco, TX	3.59	295	Beckley, WV	32.43	NA	Corpus Christi, TX**	NA
232	Tuscaloosa, AL	3.73	296	Milwaukee, WI	33.36	NA	Des Moines-West Des Moines, IA**	NA
233	Springfield, OH	3.76	297	Greenville-Anderson, SC	33.83	NA	Dubuque, IA**	NA
234	Savannah, GA	3.93	298	Spokane, WA	34.11	NA	Duluth, MN-WI**	NA
235	Salt Lake City, UT	4.74	299	Kansas City, MO-KS	35.23	NA	Fargo, ND-MN**	NA
236	Joplin, MO	5.01	300	Rocky Mount, NC	35.49	NA	Grand Forks, ND-MN**	NA
237	Los Angeles (greater), CA	5.22	301	Texarkana, TX-AR	36.09	NA	Houston, TX**	NA
238	Jonesboro, AR	5.24	302	Visalia-Porterville, CA	36.34	NA	Killeen-Temple, TX**	NA
239	Greenville, NC	5.29	303	Florence, SC	37.60	NA	La Crosse, WI-MN**	NA
240	Ocala, FL	5.31	304	Albany, GA	38.74	NA	Lafayette, LA**	NA
241	Wichita Falls, TX	5.45	305	Salinas, CA	39.49	NA	Mankato-North Mankato, MN**	NA
242	Seattle-Bellevue-Everett, WA M.D.	6.57	306	Odessa, TX	40.09	NA	Minneapolis-St. Paul, MN-WI**	NA
243	Knoxville, TN	7.04	307	Tallahassee, FL	40.73	NA	New York (greater), NY-NJ-PA**	NA
244	Champaign-Urbana, IL	7.50	308	Baltimore, MD	40.74	NA	New York-Jersey City, NY-NJ M.D.**	NA
245	Springfield, MA	7.63	309	Tulsa, OK	41.40	NA	Philadelphia (greater) PA-NJ-MD-DE**	NA
246	Trenton, NJ	9.26	310	Indianapolis, IN	41.55	NA	Philadelphia, PA M.D.**	NA
247	Monroe, LA	10.62	311	Lima, OH	42.59	NA	Phoenix-Mesa-Scottsdale, AZ**	NA
248	Durham-Chapel Hill, NC	11.22	312	Rockford, IL	43.14	NA	Pittsburgh, PA**	NA
249	Charleston-North Charleston, SC	11.67	313	Goldsboro, NC	43.27	NA	Rochester, MN**	NA
250	Yuba City, CA	11.73	314	Macon, GA	44.97	NA	San Francisco (greater), CA**	NA
251	Palm Bay-Melbourne, FL	11.84	315	Birmingham-Hoover, AL	44.98	NA	San Rafael, CA M.D.**	NA
252	Louisville, KY-IN	12.30	316	Farmington, NM	45.33	NA	Seattle (greater), WA**	NA
252	West Palm Beach, FL M.D.	12.30	317	Springfield, IL	45.50	NA	Shreveport-Bossier City, LA**	NA
254	Longview, TX	12.47	318	Mobile, AL	45.59	NA	Tacoma, WA M.D.**	NA
255	Gary, IN M.D.	13.34	319	Danville, IL	46.59			
256	St. Louis, MO-IL	14.14	320	Lubbock, TX	47.14			

Source: CQ Press using reported data from the F.B.I. "Crime in the United States 2012"

*Includes murder, rape, robbery, aggravated assault, burglary, and motor vehicle theft. A negative score (in parentheses) indicates a composite crime number below the national rate, a positive number is above the national rate. **Not available.

2013 City Crime Rate Rankings*

RANK	CITY	SCORE	RANK	CITY	SCORE	RANK	CITY	SCORE
182	Abilene, TX	(6.56)	20	Chino Hills, CA	(73.06)	271	Gainesville, FL	38.54
392	Akron, OH	141.71	142	Chino, CA	(20.15)	113	Garden Grove, CA	(33.86)
126	Alameda, CA	(27.86)	143	Chula Vista, CA	(20.12)	165	Garland, TX	(13.12)
360	Albany, GA	95.70	250	Cicero, IL	25.86	431	Gary, IN	307.84
293	Albany, NY	48.40	407	Cincinnati, OH	174.82	33	Gilbert, AZ	(64.38)
352	Albuquerque, NM	86.43	222	Citrus Heights, CA	11.03	289	Glendale, AZ	47.15
51	Alexandria, VA	(56.67)	8	Clarkstown, NY	(82.49)	28	Glendale, CA	(67.62)
73	Alhambra, CA	(48.92)	236	Clarksville, TN	19.84	162	Grand Prairie, TX	(13.97)
342	Allentown, PA	79.50	264	Clearwater, FL	32.36	296	Grand Rapids, MI	50.10
14	Allen, TX	(78.14)	432	Cleveland, OH	315.94	41	Greece, NY	(60.52)
303	Amarillo, TX	54.08	77	Clifton, NJ	(46.53)	164	Greeley, CO	(13.36)
6	Amherst, NY	(82.85)	128	Clinton Twnshp, MI	(27.30)	172	Green Bay, WI	(11.32)
210	Anaheim, CA	5.93	200	Clovis, CA	2.78	275	Greensboro, NC	40.03
333	Anchorage, AK	72.82	169	College Station, TX	(12.40)	269	Greenville, NC	36.41
94	Ann Arbor, MI	(40.50)	10	Colonie, NY	(80.97)	287	Gresham, OR	45.82
403	Antioch, CA	163.08	300	Colorado Springs, CO	52.26	80	Hamilton Twnshp, NJ	(46.26)
11	Arlington Heights, IL	(79.53)	189	Columbia, MO	(2.04)	336	Hammond, IN	74.89
241	Arlington, TX	22.34	310	Columbus, GA	56.42	147	Hampton, VA	(19.54)
58	Arvada, CO	(54.54)	413	Compton, CA	187.98	406	Hartford, CT	174.45
283	Asheville, NC	43.02	184	Concord, CA	(5.26)	343	Hawthorne, CA	80.90
226	Athens-Clarke, GA	14.00	56	Coral Springs, FL	(55.20)	326	Hayward, CA	68.69
420	Atlanta, GA	237.00	95	Corona, CA	(40.28)	280	Hemet, CA	42.02
263	Aurora, CO	32.25	266	Corpus Christi, TX	34.69	101	Henderson, NV	(38.16)
92	Aurora, IL	(41.45)	168	Costa Mesa, CA	(12.51)	246	Hesperia, CA	24.66
208	Austin, TX	5.85	96	Cranston, RI	(39.84)	155	Hialeah, FL	(17.80)
209	Avondale, AZ	5.87	375	Dallas, TX	110.56	242	High Point, NC	22.69
359	Bakersfield, CA	95.57	74	Daly City, CA	(47.46)	104	Hillsboro, OR	(37.92)
177	Baldwin Park, CA	(8.76)	63	Danbury, CT	(51.59)	270	Hollywood, FL	38.24
426	Baltimore, MD	268.30	260	Davenport, IA	30.87	62	Hoover, AL	(52.01)
409	Baton Rouge, LA	180.17	194	Davie, FL	0.52	388	Houston, TX	127.79
386	Beaumont, TX	124.71	416	Dayton, OH	192.87	69	Huntington Beach, CA	(49.48)
42	Beaverton, OR	(59.93)	166	Dearborn, MI	(12.99)	355	Huntsville, AL	88.43
76	Bellevue, WA	(46.85)	255	Decatur, IL	26.99	295	Independence, MO	50.01
267	Bellflower, CA	34.86	225	Deerfield Beach, FL	13.66	404	Indianapolis, IN	166.47
130	Bellingham, WA	(26.73)	180	Denton, TX	(7.84)	297	Indio, CA	50.60
290	Berkeley, CA	47.19	335	Denver, CO	74.13	354	Inglewood, CA	87.59
138	Bethlehem, PA	(21.93)	278	Des Moines, IA	41.66	12	Irvine, CA	(79.28)
204	Billings, MT	4.93	435	Detroit, MI	489.70	109	Irving, TX	(36.04)
428	Birmingham, AL	279.51	276	Downey, CA	40.28	302	Jacksonville, FL	53.01
170	Bloomington, IL	(12.01)	NA	Duluth, MN**	NA	427	Jackson, MS	272.88
154	Bloomington, IN	(18.13)	332	Durham, NC	72.53	272	Jersey City, NJ	39.31
NA	Bloomington, MN**	NA	204	Edinburg, TX	4.93	4	Johns Creek, GA	(88.01)
64	Boca Raton, FL	(51.05)	31	Edison Twnshp, NJ	(65.82)	176	Joliet, IL	(10.49)
88	Boise, ID	(41.82)	38	Edmond, OK	(61.70)	214	Jurupa Valley, CA	7.75
322	Boston, MA	66.17	186	El Cajon, CA	(3.90)	377	Kansas City, KS	112.54
93	Boulder, CO	(40.60)	204	El Monte, CA	4.93	418	Kansas City, MO	216.08
16	Brick Twnshp, NJ	(76.42)	148	El Paso, TX	(19.41)	140	Kennewick, WA	(21.29)
429	Bridgeport, CT	281.06	135	Elgin, IL	(24.84)	134	Kenosha, WI	(24.88)
349	Brockton, MA	84.27	389	Elizabeth, NJ	129.49	309	Kent, WA	55.94
75	Broken Arrow, OK	(47.29)	84	Elk Grove, CA	(42.99)	318	Killeen, TX	63.08
NA	Brooklyn Park, MN**	NA	274	Erie, PA	40.01	390	Knoxville, TN	135.90
111	Brownsville, TX	(35.15)	232	Escondido, CA	16.58	265	Lafayette, LA	34.00
157	Bryan, TX	(15.59)	188	Eugene, OR	(2.59)	22	Lake Forest, CA	(70.24)
133	Buena Park, CA	(25.11)	286	Evansville, IN	45.22	279	Lakeland, FL	41.99
415	Buffalo, NY	191.23	323	Everett, WA	66.56	23	Lakewood Twnshp, NJ	(69.48)
114	Burbank, CA	(33.78)	258	Fairfield, CA	30.25	150	Lakewood, CA	(18.97)
120	Cambridge, MA	(29.99)	341	Fall River, MA	79.18	249	Lakewood, CO	25.68
437	Camden, NJ	606.38	174	Fargo, ND	(10.72)	244	Lancaster, CA	23.40
55	Cape Coral, FL	(55.33)	44	Farmington Hills, MI	(59.48)	371	Lansing, MI	107.11
107	Carlsbad, CA	(37.72)	231	Fayetteville, AR	15.89	181	Laredo, TX	(6.80)
2	Carmel, IN	(89.67)	356	Fayetteville, NC	93.24	219	Largo, FL	10.49
83	Carrollton, TX	(44.62)	311	Federal Way, WA	56.97	239	Las Cruces, NM	21.20
284	Carson, CA	43.55	1	Fishers, IN	(91.55)	329	Las Vegas, NV	70.93
13	Cary, NC	(78.70)	436	Flint, MI	519.76	190	Lawrence, KS	(1.31)
159	Cedar Rapids, IA	(15.47)	212	Fontana, CA	7.65	365	Lawrence, MA	100.19
67	Centennial, CO	(50.44)	87	Fort Collins, CO	(42.07)	370	Lawton, OK	106.22
301	Champaign, IL	52.46	381	Fort Lauderdale, FL	116.86	29	League City, TX	(66.43)
106	Chandler, AZ	(37.84)	331	Fort Smith, AR	71.29	30	Lee's Summit, MO	(66.29)
163	Charleston, SC	(13.51)	237	Fort Wayne, IN	19.94	233	Lexington, KY	17.69
281	Charlotte, NC	42.60	299	Fort Worth, TX	51.42	191	Lincoln, NE	(1.25)
78	Cheektowaga, NY	(46.41)	79	Fremont, CA	(46.36)	419	Little Rock, AR	235.78
141	Chesapeake, VA	(20.31)	350	Fresno, CA	84.87	108	Livermore, CA	(37.25)
NA	Chicago, IL**	NA	15	Frisco, TX	(77.36)	89	Livonia, MI	(41.75)
211	Chico, CA	7.16	129	Fullerton, CA	(27.17)	315	Long Beach, CA	58.24

RANK	CITY	SCORE
49	Longmont, CO	(57.37)
308	Longview, TX	55.72
261	Los Angeles, CA	30.94
305	Louisville, KY	55.13
213	Lowell, MA	7.67
318	Lubbock, TX	63.08
158	Lynchburg, VA	(15.55)
292	Lynn, MA	48.31
399	Macon, GA	154.73
175	Madison, WI	(10.54)
240	Manchester, NH	21.98
34	McAllen, TX	(64.18)
70	McKinney, TX	(49.43)
228	Medford, OR	14.86
321	Melbourne, FL	65.73
424	Memphis, TN	246.70
103	Menifee, CA	(37.93)
378	Merced, CA	113.67
21	Meridian, ID	(72.69)
187	Mesa, AZ	(3.53)
199	Mesquite, TX	2.53
379	Miami Beach, FL	114.83
387	Miami Gardens, FL	125.76
402	Miami, FL	160.24
119	Midland, TX	(30.02)
414	Milwaukee, WI	189.94
400	Minneapolis, MN	158.91
171	Miramar, FL	(11.62)
9	Mission Viejo, CA	(81.71)
86	Mission, TX	(42.30)
291	Mobile, AL	47.94
380	Modesto, CA	115.77
372	Montgomery, AL	107.48
220	Moreno Valley, CA	10.71
37	Mountain View, CA	(62.08)
238	Murfreesboro, TN	21.10
27	Murrieta, CA	(68.36)
139	Nampa, ID	(21.73)
132	Napa, CA	(25.14)
16	Naperville, IL	(76.42)
100	Nashua, NH	(38.26)
373	Nashville, TN	107.61
344	New Bedford, MA	81.15
412	New Haven, CT	186.70
425	New Orleans, LA	252.61
39	New Rochelle, NY	(60.98)
196	New York, NY	1.39
430	Newark, NJ	287.93
47	Newport Beach, CA	(58.28)
235	Newport News, VA	18.28
7	Newton, MA	(82.57)
316	Norfolk, VA	62.75
115	Norman, OK	(33.09)
368	North Charleston, SC	105.21
304	North Las Vegas, NV	55.06
262	Norwalk, CA	31.35
105	Norwalk, CT	(37.87)
434	Oakland, CA	435.74
193	Oceanside, CA	0.18
327	Odessa, TX	68.71
18	O'Fallon, MO	(75.44)
198	Ogden, UT	1.86
401	Oklahoma City, OK	159.35
54	Olathe, KS	(55.93)
346	Omaha, NE	82.35
217	Ontario, CA	10.38
60	Orange, CA	(53.16)
24	Orem, UT	(69.23)
383	Orlando, FL	122.52
68	Overland Park, KS	(50.26)
146	Oxnard, CA	(19.64)
173	Palm Bay, FL	(11.08)
202	Palmdale, CA	4.12
3	Parma, OH	(89.20)

RANK	CITY	SCORE
149	Pasadena, CA	(19.15)
224	Pasadena, TX	12.43
394	Paterson, NJ	148.39
40	Pearland, TX	(60.80)
59	Pembroke Pines, FL	(53.25)
124	Peoria, AZ	(28.33)
320	Peoria, IL	64.41
408	Philadelphia, PA	176.53
338	Phoenix, AZ	77.02
324	Pittsburgh, PA	67.09
50	Plano, TX	(57.07)
179	Plantation, FL	(8.35)
361	Pomona, CA	95.77
363	Pompano Beach, FL	99.05
91	Port St. Lucie, FL	(41.61)
282	Portland, OR	42.93
313	Portsmouth, VA	57.74
358	Providence, RI	93.69
43	Provo, UT	(59.56)
337	Pueblo, CO	76.67
136	Quincy, MA	(23.16)
273	Racine, WI	39.47
203	Raleigh, NC	4.31
5	Ramapo, NY	(83.76)
131	Rancho Cucamon., CA	(26.34)
405	Reading, PA	169.02
351	Redding, CA	85.84
116	Redwood City, CA	(32.95)
218	Reno, NV	10.41
248	Renton, WA	25.17
312	Rialto, CA	57.28
110	Richardson, TX	(35.52)
423	Richmond, CA	244.75
369	Richmond, VA	105.89
102	Rio Rancho, NM	(38.12)
254	Riverside, CA	26.53
288	Roanoke, VA	46.32
NA	Rochester, MN**	NA
393	Rochester, NY	141.95
391	Rockford, IL	139.75
90	Roseville, CA	(41.66)
45	Roswell, GA	(58.58)
48	Round Rock, TX	(57.77)
348	Sacramento, CA	84.25
221	Salem, OR	11.00
367	Salinas, CA	103.06
362	Salt Lake City, UT	96.81
298	San Antonio, TX	51.14
417	San Bernardino, CA	208.56
216	San Diego, CA	8.81
345	San Francisco, CA	81.73
285	San Jose, CA	44.89
317	San Leandro, CA	62.88
117	San Marcos, CA	(31.55)
65	San Mateo, CA	(50.69)
112	Sandy Springs, GA	(34.76)
97	Sandy, UT	(39.68)
201	Santa Ana, CA	3.15
185	Santa Barbara, CA	(5.21)
99	Santa Clara, CA	(39.14)
66	Santa Clarita, CA	(50.51)
230	Santa Maria, CA	15.77
183	Santa Monica, CA	(5.51)
151	Santa Rosa, CA	(18.86)
253	Savannah, GA	26.29
72	Scottsdale, AZ	(49.15)
160	Scranton, PA	(15.24)
294	Seattle, WA	49.35
328	Shreveport, LA	70.37
36	Simi Valley, CA	(63.81)
178	Sioux City, IA	(8.54)
223	Sioux Falls, SD	11.59
125	Somerville, MA	(28.02)
382	South Bend, IN	121.67

RANK	CITY	SCORE
347	South Gate, CA	82.72
152	Sparks, NV	(18.65)
197	Spokane Valley, WA	1.76
384	Spokane, WA	123.09
364	Springfield, IL	100.09
376	Springfield, MA	110.69
395	Springfield, MO	149.76
118	Stamford, CT	(30.64)
61	Sterling Heights, MI	(52.49)
421	Stockton, CA	243.91
81	St. George, UT	(45.52)
247	St. Joseph, MO	24.93
433	St. Louis, MO	342.34
353	St. Paul, MN	87.04
339	St. Petersburg, FL	77.28
19	Sugar Land, TX	(73.07)
71	Sunnyvale, CA	(49.32)
137	Sunrise, FL	(22.82)
52	Surprise, AZ	(56.63)
366	Syracuse, NY	102.20
385	Tacoma, WA	124.15
357	Tallahassee, FL	93.52
229	Tampa, FL	15.12
57	Temecula, CA	(55.14)
252	Tempe, AZ	26.01
145	Thornton, CO	(19.86)
26	Thousand Oaks, CA	(68.63)
410	Toledo, OH	184.38
32	Toms River Twnshp, NJ	(64.62)
330	Topeka, KS	71.01
82	Torrance, CA	(45.04)
127	Tracy, CA	(27.84)
422	Trenton, NJ	244.27
35	Troy, MI	(63.90)
340	Tucson, AZ	78.51
397	Tulsa, OK	151.91
268	Tuscaloosa, AL	35.29
46	Tustin, CA	(58.39)
227	Tyler, TX	14.29
156	Upland, CA	(17.68)
215	Upper Darby Twnshp, PA	8.24
123	Vacaville, CA	(28.97)
411	Vallejo, CA	186.01
257	Vancouver, WA	30.10
153	Ventura, CA	(18.20)
325	Victorville, CA	68.25
85	Virginia Beach, VA	(42.55)
245	Visalia, CA	23.98
192	Vista, CA	(0.92)
256	Waco, TX	27.17
277	Warren, MI	40.99
53	Warwick, RI	(56.03)
396	Washington, DC	150.90
195	Waterbury, CT	1.32
207	Waukegan, IL	5.50
167	West Covina, CA	(12.86)
98	West Jordan, UT	(39.40)
374	West Palm Beach, FL	108.80
259	West Valley, UT	30.51
251	Westland, MI	25.89
144	Westminster, CA	(20.05)
121	Westminster, CO	(29.50)
122	Whittier, CA	(29.17)
243	Wichita Falls, TX	22.80
334	Wichita, KS	73.92
314	Wilmington, NC	57.89
307	Winston-Salem, NC	55.45
25	Woodbridge Twnshp, NJ	(69.04)
306	Worcester, MA	55.34
398	Yakima, WA	153.14
161	Yonkers, NY	(14.10)
234	Yuma, AZ	18.02

Source: CQ Press using reported data from the F.B.I. "Crime in the United States 2012"

*Includes murder, rape, robbery, aggravated assault, burglary, and motor vehicle theft. A negative score (in parentheses) indicates a composite crime number below the national rate, a positive number is above the national rate. **Not available.

2013 City Crime Rate Rankings* (continued)

RANK	CITY	SCORE	RANK	CITY	SCORE	RANK	CITY	SCORE
1	Fishers, IN	(91.55)	75	Broken Arrow, OK	(47.29)	149	Pasadena, CA	(19.15)
2	Carmel, IN	(89.67)	76	Bellevue, WA	(46.85)	150	Lakewood, CA	(18.97)
3	Parma, OH	(89.20)	77	Clifton, NJ	(46.53)	151	Santa Rosa, CA	(18.86)
4	Johns Creek, GA	(88.01)	78	Cheektowaga, NY	(46.41)	152	Sparks, NV	(18.65)
5	Ramapo, NY	(83.76)	79	Fremont, CA	(46.36)	153	Ventura, CA	(18.20)
6	Amherst, NY	(82.85)	80	Hamilton Twnshp, NJ	(46.26)	154	Bloomington, IN	(18.13)
7	Newton, MA	(82.57)	81	St. George, UT	(45.52)	155	Hialeah, FL	(17.80)
8	Clarkstown, NY	(82.49)	82	Torrance, CA	(45.04)	156	Upland, CA	(17.68)
9	Mission Viejo, CA	(81.71)	83	Carrollton, TX	(44.62)	157	Bryan, TX	(15.59)
10	Colonie, NY	(80.97)	84	Elk Grove, CA	(42.99)	158	Lynchburg, VA	(15.55)
11	Arlington Heights, IL	(79.53)	85	Virginia Beach, VA	(42.55)	159	Cedar Rapids, IA	(15.47)
12	Irvine, CA	(79.28)	86	Mission, TX	(42.30)	160	Scranton, PA	(15.24)
13	Cary, NC	(78.70)	87	Fort Collins, CO	(42.07)	161	Yonkers, NY	(14.10)
14	Allen, TX	(78.14)	88	Boise, ID	(41.82)	162	Grand Prairie, TX	(13.97)
15	Frisco, TX	(77.36)	89	Livonia, MI	(41.75)	163	Charleston, SC	(13.51)
16	Brick Twnshp, NJ	(76.42)	90	Roseville, CA	(41.66)	164	Greeley, CO	(13.36)
16	Naperville, IL	(76.42)	91	Port St. Lucie, FL	(41.61)	165	Garland, TX	(13.12)
18	O'Fallon, MO	(75.44)	92	Aurora, IL	(41.45)	166	Dearborn, MI	(12.99)
19	Sugar Land, TX	(73.07)	93	Boulder, CO	(40.60)	167	West Covina, CA	(12.86)
20	Chino Hills, CA	(73.06)	94	Ann Arbor, MI	(40.50)	168	Costa Mesa, CA	(12.51)
21	Meridian, ID	(72.69)	95	Corona, CA	(40.28)	169	College Station, TX	(12.40)
22	Lake Forest, CA	(70.24)	96	Cranston, RI	(39.84)	170	Bloomington, IL	(12.01)
23	Lakewood Twnshp, NJ	(69.48)	97	Sandy, UT	(39.68)	171	Miramar, FL	(11.62)
24	Orem, UT	(69.23)	98	West Jordan, UT	(39.40)	172	Green Bay, WI	(11.32)
25	Woodbridge Twnshp, NJ	(69.04)	99	Santa Clara, CA	(39.14)	173	Palm Bay, FL	(11.08)
26	Thousand Oaks, CA	(68.63)	100	Nashua, NH	(38.26)	174	Fargo, ND	(10.72)
27	Murrieta, CA	(68.36)	101	Henderson, NV	(38.16)	175	Madison, WI	(10.54)
28	Glendale, CA	(67.62)	102	Rio Rancho, NM	(38.12)	176	Joliet, IL	(10.49)
29	League City, TX	(66.43)	103	Menifee, CA	(37.93)	177	Baldwin Park, CA	(8.76)
30	Lee's Summit, MO	(66.29)	104	Hillsboro, OR	(37.92)	178	Sioux City, IA	(8.54)
31	Edison Twnshp, NJ	(65.82)	105	Norwalk, CT	(37.87)	179	Plantation, FL	(8.35)
32	Toms River Twnshp, NJ	(64.62)	106	Chandler, AZ	(37.84)	180	Denton, TX	(7.84)
33	Gilbert, AZ	(64.38)	107	Carlsbad, CA	(37.72)	181	Laredo, TX	(6.80)
34	McAllen, TX	(64.18)	108	Livermore, CA	(37.25)	182	Abilene, TX	(6.56)
35	Troy, MI	(63.90)	109	Irving, TX	(36.04)	183	Santa Monica, CA	(5.51)
36	Simi Valley, CA	(63.81)	110	Richardson, TX	(35.52)	184	Concord, CA	(5.26)
37	Mountain View, CA	(62.08)	111	Brownsville, TX	(35.15)	185	Santa Barbara, CA	(5.21)
38	Edmond, OK	(61.70)	112	Sandy Springs, GA	(34.76)	186	El Cajon, CA	(3.90)
39	New Rochelle, NY	(60.98)	113	Garden Grove, CA	(33.86)	187	Mesa, AZ	(3.53)
40	Pearland, TX	(60.80)	114	Burbank, CA	(33.78)	188	Eugene, OR	(2.59)
41	Greece, NY	(60.52)	115	Norman, OK	(33.09)	189	Columbia, MO	(2.04)
42	Beaverton, OR	(59.93)	116	Redwood City, CA	(32.95)	190	Lawrence, KS	(1.31)
43	Provo, UT	(59.56)	117	San Marcos, CA	(31.55)	191	Lincoln, NE	(1.25)
44	Farmington Hills, MI	(59.48)	118	Stamford, CT	(30.64)	192	Vista, CA	(0.92)
45	Roswell, GA	(58.58)	119	Midland, TX	(30.02)	193	Oceanside, CA	0.18
46	Tustin, CA	(58.39)	120	Cambridge, MA	(29.99)	194	Davie, FL	0.52
47	Newport Beach, CA	(58.28)	121	Westminster, CO	(29.50)	195	Waterbury, CT	1.32
48	Round Rock, TX	(57.77)	122	Whittier, CA	(29.17)	196	New York, NY	1.39
49	Longmont, CO	(57.37)	123	Vacaville, CA	(28.97)	197	Spokane Valley, WA	1.76
50	Plano, TX	(57.07)	124	Peoria, AZ	(28.33)	198	Ogden, UT	1.86
51	Alexandria, VA	(56.67)	125	Somerville, MA	(28.02)	199	Mesquite, TX	2.53
52	Surprise, AZ	(56.63)	126	Alameda, CA	(27.86)	200	Clovis, CA	2.78
53	Warwick, RI	(56.03)	127	Tracy, CA	(27.84)	201	Santa Ana, CA	3.15
54	Olathe, KS	(55.93)	128	Clinton Twnshp, MI	(27.30)	202	Palmdale, CA	4.12
55	Cape Coral, FL	(55.33)	129	Fullerton, CA	(27.17)	203	Raleigh, NC	4.31
56	Coral Springs, FL	(55.20)	130	Bellingham, WA	(26.73)	204	Billings, MT	4.93
57	Temecula, CA	(55.14)	131	Rancho Cucamon., CA	(26.34)	204	Edinburg, TX	4.93
58	Arvada, CO	(54.54)	132	Napa, CA	(25.14)	204	El Monte, CA	4.93
59	Pembroke Pines, FL	(53.25)	133	Buena Park, CA	(25.11)	207	Waukegan, IL	5.50
60	Orange, CA	(53.16)	134	Kenosha, WI	(24.88)	208	Austin, TX	5.85
61	Sterling Heights, MI	(52.49)	135	Elgin, IL	(24.84)	209	Avondale, AZ	5.87
62	Hoover, AL	(52.01)	136	Quincy, MA	(23.16)	210	Anaheim, CA	5.93
63	Danbury, CT	(51.59)	137	Sunrise, FL	(22.82)	211	Chico, CA	7.16
64	Boca Raton, FL	(51.05)	138	Bethlehem, PA	(21.93)	212	Fontana, CA	7.65
65	San Mateo, CA	(50.69)	139	Nampa, ID	(21.73)	213	Lowell, MA	7.67
66	Santa Clarita, CA	(50.51)	140	Kennewick, WA	(21.29)	214	Jurupa Valley, CA	7.75
67	Centennial, CO	(50.44)	141	Chesapeake, VA	(20.31)	215	Upper Darby Twnshp, PA	8.24
68	Overland Park, KS	(50.26)	142	Chino, CA	(20.15)	216	San Diego, CA	8.81
69	Huntington Beach, CA	(49.48)	143	Chula Vista, CA	(20.12)	217	Ontario, CA	10.38
70	McKinney, TX	(49.43)	144	Westminster, CA	(20.05)	218	Reno, NV	10.41
71	Sunnyvale, CA	(49.32)	145	Thornton, CO	(19.86)	219	Largo, FL	10.49
72	Scottsdale, AZ	(49.15)	146	Oxnard, CA	(19.64)	220	Moreno Valley, CA	10.71
73	Alhambra, CA	(48.92)	147	Hampton, VA	(19.54)	221	Salem, OR	11.00
74	Daly City, CA	(47.46)	148	El Paso, TX	(19.41)	222	Citrus Heights, CA	11.03

RANK	CITY	SCORE	RANK	CITY	SCORE	RANK	CITY	SCORE
223	Sioux Falls, SD	11.59	297	Indio, CA	50.60	371	Lansing, MI	107.11
224	Pasadena, TX	12.43	298	San Antonio, TX	51.14	372	Montgomery, AL	107.48
225	Deerfield Beach, FL	13.66	299	Fort Worth, TX	51.42	373	Nashville, TN	107.61
226	Athens-Clarke, GA	14.00	300	Colorado Springs, CO	52.26	374	West Palm Beach, FL	108.80
227	Tyler, TX	14.29	301	Champaign, IL	52.46	375	Dallas, TX	110.56
228	Medford, OR	14.86	302	Jacksonville, FL	53.01	376	Springfield, MA	110.69
229	Tampa, FL	15.12	303	Amarillo, TX	54.08	377	Kansas City, KS	112.54
230	Santa Maria, CA	15.77	304	North Las Vegas, NV	55.06	378	Merced, CA	113.67
231	Fayetteville, AR	15.89	305	Louisville, KY	55.13	379	Miami Beach, FL	114.83
232	Escondido, CA	16.58	306	Worcester, MA	55.34	380	Modesto, CA	115.77
233	Lexington, KY	17.69	307	Winston-Salem, NC	55.45	381	Fort Lauderdale, FL	116.86
234	Yuma, AZ	18.02	308	Longview, TX	55.72	382	South Bend, IN	121.67
235	Newport News, VA	18.28	309	Kent, WA	55.94	383	Orlando, FL	122.52
236	Clarksville, TN	19.84	310	Columbus, GA	56.42	384	Spokane, WA	123.09
237	Fort Wayne, IN	19.94	311	Federal Way, WA	56.97	385	Tacoma, WA	124.15
238	Murfreesboro, TN	21.10	312	Rialto, CA	57.28	386	Beaumont, TX	124.71
239	Las Cruces, NM	21.20	313	Portsmouth, VA	57.74	387	Miami Gardens, FL	125.76
240	Manchester, NH	21.98	314	Wilmington, NC	57.89	388	Houston, TX	127.79
241	Arlington, TX	22.34	315	Long Beach, CA	58.24	389	Elizabeth, NJ	129.49
242	High Point, NC	22.69	316	Norfolk, VA	62.75	390	Knoxville, TN	135.90
243	Wichita Falls, TX	22.80	317	San Leandro, CA	62.88	391	Rockford, IL	139.75
244	Lancaster, CA	23.40	318	Killeen, TX	63.08	392	Akron, OH	141.71
245	Visalia, CA	23.98	318	Lubbock, TX	63.08	393	Rochester, NY	141.95
246	Hesperia, CA	24.66	320	Peoria, IL	64.41	394	Paterson, NJ	148.39
247	St. Joseph, MO	24.93	321	Melbourne, FL	65.73	395	Springfield, MO	149.76
248	Renton, WA	25.17	322	Boston, MA	66.17	396	Washington, DC	150.90
249	Lakewood, CO	25.68	323	Everett, WA	66.56	397	Tulsa, OK	151.91
250	Cicero, IL	25.86	324	Pittsburgh, PA	67.09	398	Yakima, WA	153.14
251	Westland, MI	25.89	325	Victorville, CA	68.25	399	Macon, GA	154.73
252	Tempe, AZ	26.01	326	Hayward, CA	68.69	400	Minneapolis, MN	158.91
253	Savannah, GA	26.29	327	Odessa, TX	68.71	401	Oklahoma City, OK	159.35
254	Riverside, CA	26.53	328	Shreveport, LA	70.37	402	Miami, FL	160.24
255	Decatur, IL	26.99	329	Las Vegas, NV	70.93	403	Antioch, CA	163.08
256	Waco, TX	27.17	330	Topeka, KS	71.01	404	Indianapolis, IN	166.47
257	Vancouver, WA	30.10	331	Fort Smith, AR	71.29	405	Reading, PA	169.02
258	Fairfield, CA	30.25	332	Durham, NC	72.53	406	Hartford, CT	174.45
259	West Valley, UT	30.51	333	Anchorage, AK	72.82	407	Cincinnati, OH	174.82
260	Davenport, IA	30.87	334	Wichita, KS	73.92	408	Philadelphia, PA	176.53
261	Los Angeles, CA	30.94	335	Denver, CO	74.13	409	Baton Rouge, LA	180.17
262	Norwalk, CA	31.35	336	Hammond, IN	74.89	410	Toledo, OH	184.38
263	Aurora, CO	32.25	337	Pueblo, CO	76.67	411	Vallejo, CA	186.01
264	Clearwater, FL	32.36	338	Phoenix, AZ	77.02	412	New Haven, CT	186.70
265	Lafayette, LA	34.00	339	St. Petersburg, FL	77.28	413	Compton, CA	187.98
266	Corpus Christi, TX	34.69	340	Tucson, AZ	78.51	414	Milwaukee, WI	189.94
267	Bellflower, CA	34.86	341	Fall River, MA	79.18	415	Buffalo, NY	191.23
268	Tuscaloosa, AL	35.29	342	Allentown, PA	79.50	416	Dayton, OH	192.87
269	Greenville, NC	36.41	343	Hawthorne, CA	80.90	417	San Bernardino, CA	208.56
270	Hollywood, FL	38.24	344	New Bedford, MA	81.15	418	Kansas City, MO	216.08
271	Gainesville, FL	38.54	345	San Francisco, CA	81.73	419	Little Rock, AR	235.78
272	Jersey City, NJ	39.31	346	Omaha, NE	82.35	420	Atlanta, GA	237.00
273	Racine, WI	39.47	347	South Gate, CA	82.72	421	Stockton, CA	243.91
274	Erie, PA	40.01	348	Sacramento, CA	84.25	422	Trenton, NJ	244.27
275	Greensboro, NC	40.03	349	Brockton, MA	84.27	423	Richmond, CA	244.75
276	Downey, CA	40.28	350	Fresno, CA	84.87	424	Memphis, TN	246.70
277	Warren, MI	40.99	351	Redding, CA	85.84	425	New Orleans, LA	252.61
278	Des Moines, IA	41.66	352	Albuquerque, NM	86.43	426	Baltimore, MD	268.30
279	Lakeland, FL	41.99	353	St. Paul, MN	87.04	427	Jackson, MS	272.88
280	Hemet, CA	42.02	354	Inglewood, CA	87.59	428	Birmingham, AL	279.51
281	Charlotte, NC	42.60	355	Huntsville, AL	88.43	429	Bridgeport, CT	281.06
282	Portland, OR	42.93	356	Fayetteville, NC	93.24	430	Newark, NJ	287.93
283	Asheville, NC	43.02	357	Tallahassee, FL	93.52	431	Gary, IN	307.84
284	Carson, CA	43.55	358	Providence, RI	93.69	432	Cleveland, OH	315.94
285	San Jose, CA	44.89	359	Bakersfield, CA	95.57	433	St. Louis, MO	342.34
286	Evansville, IN	45.22	360	Albany, GA	95.70	434	Oakland, CA	435.74
287	Gresham, OR	45.82	361	Pomona, CA	95.77	435	Detroit, MI	489.70
288	Roanoke, VA	46.32	362	Salt Lake City, UT	96.81	436	Flint, MI	519.76
289	Glendale, AZ	47.15	363	Pompano Beach, FL	99.05	437	Camden, NJ	606.38
290	Berkeley, CA	47.19	364	Springfield, IL	100.09	NA	Bloomington, MN**	NA
291	Mobile, AL	47.94	365	Lawrence, MA	100.19	NA	Brooklyn Park, MN**	NA
292	Lynn, MA	48.31	366	Syracuse, NY	102.20	NA	Chicago, IL**	NA
293	Albany, NY	48.40	367	Salinas, CA	103.06	NA	Duluth, MN**	NA
294	Seattle, WA	49.35	368	North Charleston, SC	105.21	NA	Rochester, MN**	NA
295	Independence, MO	50.01	369	Richmond, VA	105.89			
296	Grand Rapids, MI	50.10	370	Lawton, OK	106.22			

Source: CQ Press using reported data from the F.B.I. "Crime in the United States 2012"

*Includes murder, rape, robbery, aggravated assault, burglary, and motor vehicle theft. A negative score (in parentheses) indicates a composite crime number below the national rate, a positive number is above the national rate. **Not available.

About the Editors

Kathleen O'Leary Morgan holds a master's degree in public administration and has served in a number of media and legislative liaison positions within the U.S. Department of Transportation, where she also served as deputy director of congressional affairs.

Scott Morgan is an attorney who served as chief counsel to Robert Dole's 1988 presidential campaign.

Rachel Boba Santos is an associate professor at Florida Atlantic University in the School of Criminology and Criminal Justice. She works with police departments and conducts research on police accountability, the effectiveness of crime reduction efforts by police, and crime analysis.

I. Metropolitan Area Crime Statistics

Please note the following for Tables 1 through 40 and 85 through 87:

- All listings are for Metropolitan Statistical Areas (M.S.A.'s) except for those ending with "M.D."
- Listings with "M.D." are Metropolitan Divisions, which are smaller parts of eleven large M.S.A.'s. These eleven M.S.A.'s divided into M.D.'s are identified using "(greater)" following the metropolitan area name.
- For example, the "Dallas (greater)" M.S.A. includes the two M.D.'s of Dallas-Plano-Irving and Fort Worth-Arlington. The data for the M.D.'s are included in the data for the overall M.S.A. as well.
- The name of a M.S.A. or M.D. is subject to change based on the changing proportional size of the large cities included within it. Percent changes are calculated in this book if the M.S.A. or M.D. has not substantially changed, despite the changes in name. Furthermore, the Office of Management and Budget (OMB) redefined a number of M.S.A.'s in 2013; if the redefined M.S.A. had a population change of 5 percent or greater from the previous definition, its data are treated as not comparable and are not included in the tables showing change over time.
- Some M.S.A. and M.D. names are abbreviated to preserve space within the tables.

1. Crimes in 2012
National Total = 10,189,900 Crimes*

RANK	METROPOLITAN AREA	CRIMES	RANK	METROPOLITAN AREA	CRIMES	RANK	METROPOLITAN AREA	CRIMES
230	Abilene, TX	5,635	313	Cheyenne, WY	2,943	78	Gary, IN M.D.	24,700
81	Akron, OH	23,514	NA	Chicago (greater), IL-IN-WI**	NA	344	Gettysburg, PA	1,323
79	Albany-Schenectady-Troy, NY	23,924	NA	Chicago-Joilet-Naperville, IL M.D.**	NA	330	Glens Falls, NY	2,378
173	Albany, GA	8,344	216	Chico, CA	6,343	233	Goldsboro, NC	5,463
289	Albany, OR	3,878	27	Cincinnati, OH-KY-IN	76,525	NA	Grand Forks, ND-MN**	NA
NA	Albuquerque, NM**	NA	178	Clarksville, TN-KY	8,141	308	Grand Island, NE	3,074
NA	Alexandria, LA**	NA	274	Cleveland, TN	4,209	254	Grand Junction, CO	4,777
92	Allentown, PA-NJ	20,047	250	Coeur d'Alene, ID	4,939	304	Great Falls, MT	3,305
326	Altoona, PA	2,434	193	College Station-Bryan, TX	7,238	210	Greeley, CO	6,502
145	Amarillo, TX	11,082	NA	Colorado Springs, CO**	NA	207	Green Bay, WI	6,574
336	Ames, IA	2,163	219	Columbia, MO	6,167	69	Greensboro-High Point, NC	28,921
28	Anaheim-Santa Ana-Irvine, CA M.D.	74,610	108	Columbus, GA-AL	15,872	55	Greenville-Anderson, SC	37,880
118	Anchorage, AK	13,887	315	Columbus, IN	2,902	204	Greenville, NC	6,734
163	Ann Arbor, MI	9,513	NA	Corpus Christi, TX**	NA	209	Hagerstown-Martinsburg, MD-WV	6,518
223	Anniston-Oxford, AL	6,017	342	Corvallis, OR	1,937	175	Hammond, LA	8,312
290	Appleton, WI	3,870	186	Crestview-Fort Walton Beach, FL	7,569	275	Hanford-Corcoran, CA	4,207
127	Asheville, NC	13,119	301	Cumberland, MD-WV	3,325	122	Harrisburg-Carlisle, PA	13,494
192	Athens-Clarke County, GA	7,276	4	Dallas (greater), TX	235,181	340	Harrisonburg, VA	1,968
5	Atlanta, GA	206,078	7	Dallas-Plano-Irving, TX M.D.	150,857	70	Hartford, CT	28,022
NA	Atlantic City, NJ**	NA	268	Dalton, GA	4,365	280	Hattiesburg, MS	4,077
266	Auburn, AL	4,395	294	Danville, IL	3,511	128	Hickory, NC	13,025
77	Augusta, GA-SC	24,842	235	Daphne-Fairhope-Foley, AL	5,434	200	Hilton Head Island, SC	6,822
32	Austin-Round Rock, TX	67,412	141	Davenport, IA-IL	11,301	320	Hinesville, GA	2,732
53	Bakersfield, CA	39,737	68	Dayton, OH	29,630	298	Homosassa Springs, FL	3,419
15	Baltimore, MD	99,349	252	Decatur, AL	4,924	188	Houma, LA	7,466
255	Bangor, ME	4,762	299	Decatur, IL	3,390	NA	Houston, TX**	NA
203	Barnstable Town, MA	6,736	86	Deltona-Daytona Beach, FL	21,647	106	Huntsville, AL	16,520
NA	Baton Rouge, LA**	NA	23	Denver-Aurora, CO	81,282	318	Idaho Falls, ID	2,782
329	Bay City, MI	2,411	NA	Des Moines-West Des Moines, IA**	NA	21	Indianapolis, IN	81,843
111	Beaumont-Port Arthur, TX	15,527	9	Detroit (greater), MI	141,725	296	Iowa City, IA	3,470
244	Beckley, WV	5,025	18	Detroit-Dearborn-Livonia, MI M.D.	89,334	38	Jacksonville, FL	54,766
201	Bellingham, WA	6,806	238	Dothan, AL	5,156	88	Jackson, MS	21,336
218	Billings, MT	6,216	196	Dover, DE	7,073	227	Jackson, TN	5,850
187	Binghamton, NY	7,483	NA	Dubuque, IA**	NA	239	Janesville, WI	5,155
45	Birmingham-Hoover, AL	49,596	NA	Duluth, MN-WI**	NA	283	Jefferson City, MO	4,046
303	Bismarck, ND	3,321	93	Durham-Chapel Hill, NC	20,035	206	Johnson City, TN	6,631
273	Blacksburg, VA	4,211	199	Dutchess-Putnam, NY M.D.	6,849	316	Johnstown, PA	2,892
260	Bloomington, IL	4,654	240	East Stroudsburg, PA	5,152	258	Jonesboro, AR	4,712
231	Bloomington, IN	5,534	198	El Centro, CA	6,990	176	Joplin, MO	8,179
341	Bloomsburg-Berwick, PA	1,940	82	El Paso, TX	22,680	212	Kahului-Wailuku-Lahaina, HI	6,414
120	Boise City, ID	13,796	140	Elgin, IL M.D.	11,468	152	Kalamazoo-Portage, MI	10,417
14	Boston (greater), MA-NH	108,277	334	Elizabethtown-Fort Knox, KY	2,275	293	Kankakee, IL	3,542
43	Boston, MA M.D.	51,398	326	Elmira, NY	2,434	24	Kansas City, MO-KS	80,593
183	Boulder, CO	7,718	179	Erie, PA	8,038	197	Kennewick-Richland, WA	7,024
270	Bowling Green, KY	4,234	115	Eugene, OR	14,380	NA	Killeen-Temple, TX**	NA
168	Bremerton-Silverdale, WA	8,823	343	Fairbanks, AK	1,732	150	Kingsport, TN-VA	10,498
98	Bridgeport-Stamford, CT	18,992	NA	Fargo, ND-MN**	NA	285	Kingston, NY	3,950
102	Brownsville-Harlingen, TX	17,834	284	Farmington, NM	4,024	62	Knoxville, TN	33,259
236	Brunswick, GA	5,240	119	Fayetteville-Springdale, AR-MO	13,870	323	Kokomo, IN	2,584
54	Buffalo-Niagara Falls, NY	38,409	84	Fayetteville, NC	22,145	NA	La Crosse, WI-MN**	NA
225	Burlington, NC	5,892	257	Flagstaff, AZ	4,724	220	Lafayette, IN	6,099
309	California-Lexington Park, MD	3,035	96	Flint, MI	19,209	NA	Lafayette, LA**	NA
49	Cambridge-Newton, MA M.D.	47,148	246	Florence-Muscle Shoals, AL	4,967	100	Lake Co.-Kenosha Co., IL-WI M.D.	18,478
57	Camden, NJ M.D.	36,603	146	Florence, SC	11,012	189	Lake Havasu City-Kingman, AZ	7,440
126	Canton, OH	13,154	339	Fond du Lac, WI	2,009	89	Lakeland, FL	21,258
105	Cape Coral-Fort Myers, FL	17,255	174	Fort Collins, CO	8,315	142	Lancaster, PA	11,172
277	Cape Girardeau, MO-IL	4,145	26	Fort Lauderdale, FL M.D.	76,652	134	Lansing-East Lansing, MI	12,004
346	Carson City, NV	1,239	162	Fort Smith, AR-OK	9,636	130	Laredo, TX	12,207
324	Casper, WY	2,498	124	Fort Wayne, IN	13,194	194	Las Cruces, NM	7,234
NA	Cedar Rapids, IA**	NA	20	Fort Worth-Arlington, TX M.D.	84,324	30	Las Vegas-Henderson, NV	73,094
321	Chambersburg-Waynesboro, PA	2,720	48	Fresno, CA	47,236	247	Lawrence, KS	4,964
190	Champaign-Urbana, IL	7,366	243	Gadsden, AL	5,072	205	Lawton, OK	6,634
74	Charleston-North Charleston, SC	25,415	151	Gainesville, FL	10,419	317	Lebanon, PA	2,857
256	Charlottesville, VA	4,761	261	Gainesville, GA	4,646	297	Lewiston-Auburn, ME	3,428

Note: All listings are for Metropolitan Statistical Areas (M.S.A.s) except for those ending with "M.D." Listings with "M.D." are Metropolitan Divisions which are smaller parts of eleven large M.S.A.s. See explanatory note at beginning of metropolitan area section.

RANK	METROPOLITAN AREA	CRIMES	RANK	METROPOLITAN AREA	CRIMES	RANK	METROPOLITAN AREA	CRIMES
335	Lewiston, ID-WA	2,247	305	Owensboro, KY	3,285	80	Silver Spring-Frederick, MD M.D.	23,869
90	Lexington-Fayette, KY	21,114	104	Oxnard-Thousand Oaks, CA	17,585	251	Sioux City, IA-NE-SD	4,930
265	Lima, OH	4,401	94	Palm Bay-Melbourne, FL	19,622	208	Sioux Falls, SD	6,529
132	Lincoln, NE	12,030	171	Panama City, FL	8,597	143	South Bend-Mishawaka, IN-MI	11,146
52	Little Rock, AR	41,440	311	Parkersburg-Vienna, WV	3,014	135	Spartanburg, SC	11,998
338	Logan, UT-ID	2,103	95	Pensacola, FL	19,432	66	Spokane, WA	31,512
164	Longview, TX	8,983	136	Peoria, IL	11,941	155	Springfield, IL	10,223
278	Longview, WA	4,089	NA	Philadelphia (greater) PA-NJ-MD-DE**	NA	85	Springfield, MA	22,083
2	Los Angeles County, CA M.D.	276,822	NA	Philadelphia, PA M.D.**	NA	83	Springfield, MO	22,509
1	Los Angeles (greater), CA	351,432	NA	Phoenix-Mesa-Scottsdale, AZ**	NA	222	Springfield, OH	6,046
46	Louisville, KY-IN	48,700	249	Pine Bluff, AR	4,943	331	State College, PA	2,350
110	Lubbock, TX	15,745	NA	Pittsburgh, PA**	NA	333	Staunton-Waynesboro, VA	2,317
245	Lynchburg, VA	4,991	295	Pittsfield, MA	3,507	59	Stockton-Lodi, CA	35,513
133	Macon, GA	12,027	331	Pocatello, ID	2,350	310	St. George, UT	3,017
248	Madera, CA	4,951	139	Port St. Lucie, FL	11,697	226	St. Joseph, MO-KS	5,875
107	Madison, WI	16,192	25	Portland-Vancouver, OR-WA	78,217	17	St. Louis, MO-IL	93,605
154	Manchester-Nashua, NH	10,270	123	Portland, ME	13,399	232	Sumter, SC	5,472
337	Manhattan, KS	2,105	241	Prescott, AZ	5,142	99	Syracuse, NY	18,810
NA	Mankato-North Mankato, MN**	NA	51	Providence-Warwick, RI-MA	45,477	NA	Tacoma, WA M.D.**	NA
221	Mansfield, OH	6,074	149	Provo-Orem, UT	10,577	112	Tallahassee, FL	15,349
63	McAllen-Edinburg-Mission, TX	33,102	165	Pueblo, CO	8,945	16	Tampa-St Petersburg, FL	93,687
172	Medford, OR	8,449	288	Punta Gorda, FL	3,906	202	Terre Haute, IN	6,748
31	Memphis, TN-MS-AR	72,879	229	Racine, WI	5,774	191	Texarkana, TX-AR	7,331
137	Merced, CA	11,924	64	Raleigh, NC	31,934	345	The Villages, FL	1,250
3	Miami (greater), FL	258,344	253	Rapid City, SD	4,900	NA	Toledo, OH**	NA
10	Miami-Dade County, FL M.D.	130,865	148	Reading, PA	10,681	157	Topeka, KS	10,029
286	Michigan City-La Porte, IN	3,948	185	Redding, CA	7,578	158	Trenton, NJ	9,845
347	Midland, MI	1,043	125	Reno, NV	13,191	NA	Tucson, AZ**	NA
276	Midland, TX	4,169	60	Richmond, VA	34,592	56	Tulsa, OK	36,632
36	Milwaukee, WI	61,392	8	Riverside-San Bernardino, CA	147,296	170	Tuscaloosa, AL	8,631
NA	Minneapolis-St. Paul, MN-WI**	NA	169	Roanoke, VA	8,821	182	Tyler, TX	7,741
287	Missoula, MT	3,937	NA	Rochester, MN**	NA	180	Utica-Rome, NY	7,793
91	Mobile, AL	20,094	65	Rochester, NY	31,835	262	Valdosta, GA	4,624
76	Modesto, CA	24,936	114	Rockford, IL	14,617	113	Vallejo-Fairfield, CA	15,077
167	Monroe, LA	8,918	161	Rockingham County, NH M.D.	9,731	291	Victoria, TX	3,707
263	Monroe, MI	4,501	213	Rocky Mount, NC	6,392	184	Vineland-Bridgeton, NJ	7,622
58	Montgomery County, PA M.D.	36,068	271	Rome, GA	4,230	37	Virginia Beach-Norfolk, VA-NC	57,966
101	Montgomery, AL	18,249	29	Sacramento, CA	73,948	103	Visalia-Porterville, CA	17,652
314	Morgantown, WV	2,934	217	Saginaw, MI	6,289	156	Waco, TX	10,188
269	Morristown, TN	4,353	121	Salem, OR	13,713	328	Walla Walla, WA	2,413
236	Mount Vernon-Anacortes, WA	5,240	131	Salinas, CA	12,164	181	Warner Robins, GA	7,762
279	Muncie, IN	4,084	116	Salisbury, MD-DE	14,347	41	Warren-Troy, MI M.D.	52,391
300	Napa, CA	3,348	42	Salt Lake City, UT	52,295	6	Washington (greater) DC-VA-MD-WV	152,340
214	Naples-Marco Island, FL	6,360	12	San Antonio, TX	113,144	11	Washington, DC-VA-MD-WV M.D.	128,471
35	Nashville-Davidson, TN	61,481	22	San Diego, CA	81,463	264	Waterloo-Cedar Falls, IA	4,452
47	Nassau-Suffolk, NY M.D.	48,144	NA	San Francisco (greater), CA**	NA	312	Watertown-Fort Drum, NY	2,994
242	New Bern, NC	5,114	34	San Francisco-Redwood, CA M.D.	62,109	325	Wausau, WI	2,452
71	New Haven-Milford, CT	27,606	40	San Jose, CA	54,174	44	West Palm Beach, FL M.D.	50,827
50	New Orleans, LA	45,566	195	San Luis Obispo, CA	7,158	302	Wheeling, WV-OH	3,322
NA	New York (greater), NY-NJ-PA**	NA	NA	San Rafael, CA M.D.**	NA	211	Wichita Falls, TX	6,438
NA	New York-Jersey City, NY-NJ M.D.**	NA	160	Santa Cruz-Watsonville, CA	9,750	67	Wichita, KS	29,995
39	Newark, NJ-PA M.D.	54,426	224	Santa Fe, NM	5,973	319	Williamsport, PA	2,741
75	North Port-Sarasota-Bradenton, FL	25,084	138	Santa Maria-Santa Barbara, CA	11,807	73	Wilmington, DE-MD-NJ M.D.	27,341
282	Norwich-New London, CT	4,055	153	Santa Rosa, CA	10,306	147	Wilmington, NC	11,007
NA	Oakland-Hayward, CA M.D.**	NA	129	Savannah, GA	12,433	306	Winchester, VA-WV	3,282
166	Ocala, FL	8,927	117	Scranton--Wilkes-Barre, PA	14,231	72	Winston-Salem, NC	27,517
259	Ocean City, NJ	4,665	NA	Seattle (greater), WA**	NA	87	Worcester, MA-CT	21,595
215	Odessa, TX	6,345	13	Seattle-Bellevue-Everett, WA M.D.	110,588	144	Yakima, WA	11,102
109	Ogden-Clearfield, UT	15,763	272	Sebastian-Vero Beach, FL	4,221	159	York-Hanover, PA	9,754
33	Oklahoma City, OK	63,214	307	Sebring, FL	3,112	97	Youngstown-Warren, OH-PA	19,204
177	Olympia, WA	8,142	322	Sheboygan, WI	2,647	234	Yuba City, CA	5,448
61	Omaha-Council Bluffs, NE-IA	33,336	281	Sherman-Denison, TX	4,071	228	Yuma, AZ	5,844
19	Orlando, FL	88,724	NA	Shreveport-Bossier City, LA**	NA			
291	Oshkosh-Neenah, WI	3,707	267	Sierra Vista-Douglas, AZ	4,387			

Source: CQ Press using reported data from the F.B.I. "Crime in the United States 2012"

*Includes murder, rape, robbery, aggravated assault, burglary, larceny-theft, and motor vehicle theft.

**Not available.

1. Crimes in 2012 (continued)
National Total = 10,189,900 Crimes*

RANK	METROPOLITAN AREA	CRIMES	RANK	METROPOLITAN AREA	CRIMES	RANK	METROPOLITAN AREA	CRIMES
1	Los Angeles (greater), CA	351,432	65	Rochester, NY	31,835	129	Savannah, GA	12,433
2	Los Angeles County, CA M.D.	276,822	66	Spokane, WA	31,512	130	Laredo, TX	12,207
3	Miami (greater), FL	258,344	67	Wichita, KS	29,995	131	Salinas, CA	12,164
4	Dallas (greater), TX	235,181	68	Dayton, OH	29,630	132	Lincoln, NE	12,030
5	Atlanta, GA	206,078	69	Greensboro-High Point, NC	28,921	133	Macon, GA	12,027
6	Washington (greater) DC-VA-MD-WV	152,340	70	Hartford, CT	28,022	134	Lansing-East Lansing, MI	12,004
7	Dallas-Plano-Irving, TX M.D.	150,857	71	New Haven-Milford, CT	27,606	135	Spartanburg, SC	11,998
8	Riverside-San Bernardino, CA	147,296	72	Winston-Salem, NC	27,517	136	Peoria, IL	11,941
9	Detroit (greater), MI	141,725	73	Wilmington, DE-MD-NJ M.D.	27,341	137	Merced, CA	11,924
10	Miami-Dade County, FL M.D.	130,865	74	Charleston-North Charleston, SC	25,415	138	Santa Maria-Santa Barbara, CA	11,807
11	Washington, DC-VA-MD-WV M.D.	128,471	75	North Port-Sarasota-Bradenton, FL	25,084	139	Port St. Lucie, FL	11,697
12	San Antonio, TX	113,144	76	Modesto, CA	24,936	140	Elgin, IL M.D.	11,468
13	Seattle-Bellevue-Everett, WA M.D.	110,588	77	Augusta, GA-SC	24,842	141	Davenport, IA-IL	11,301
14	Boston (greater), MA-NH	108,277	78	Gary, IN M.D.	24,700	142	Lancaster, PA	11,172
15	Baltimore, MD	99,349	79	Albany-Schenectady-Troy, NY	23,924	143	South Bend-Mishawaka, IN-MI	11,146
16	Tampa-St Petersburg, FL	93,687	80	Silver Spring-Frederick, MD M.D.	23,869	144	Yakima, WA	11,102
17	St. Louis, MO-IL	93,605	81	Akron, OH	23,514	145	Amarillo, TX	11,082
18	Detroit-Dearborn-Livonia, MI M.D.	89,334	82	El Paso, TX	22,680	146	Florence, SC	11,012
19	Orlando, FL	88,724	83	Springfield, MO	22,509	147	Wilmington, NC	11,007
20	Fort Worth-Arlington, TX M.D.	84,324	84	Fayetteville, NC	22,145	148	Reading, PA	10,681
21	Indianapolis, IN	81,843	85	Springfield, MA	22,083	149	Provo-Orem, UT	10,577
22	San Diego, CA	81,463	86	Deltona-Daytona Beach, FL	21,647	150	Kingsport, TN-VA	10,498
23	Denver-Aurora, CO	81,282	87	Worcester, MA-CT	21,595	151	Gainesville, FL	10,419
24	Kansas City, MO-KS	80,593	88	Jackson, MS	21,336	152	Kalamazoo-Portage, MI	10,417
25	Portland-Vancouver, OR-WA	78,217	89	Lakeland, FL	21,258	153	Santa Rosa, CA	10,306
26	Fort Lauderdale, FL M.D.	76,652	90	Lexington-Fayette, KY	21,114	154	Manchester-Nashua, NH	10,270
27	Cincinnati, OH-KY-IN	76,525	91	Mobile, AL	20,094	155	Springfield, IL	10,223
28	Anaheim-Santa Ana-Irvine, CA M.D.	74,610	92	Allentown, PA-NJ	20,047	156	Waco, TX	10,188
29	Sacramento, CA	73,948	93	Durham-Chapel Hill, NC	20,035	157	Topeka, KS	10,029
30	Las Vegas-Henderson, NV	73,094	94	Palm Bay-Melbourne, FL	19,622	158	Trenton, NJ	9,845
31	Memphis, TN-MS-AR	72,879	95	Pensacola, FL	19,432	159	York-Hanover, PA	9,754
32	Austin-Round Rock, TX	67,412	96	Flint, MI	19,209	160	Santa Cruz-Watsonville, CA	9,750
33	Oklahoma City, OK	63,214	97	Youngstown-Warren, OH-PA	19,204	161	Rockingham County, NH M.D.	9,731
34	San Francisco-Redwood, CA M.D.	62,109	98	Bridgeport-Stamford, CT	18,992	162	Fort Smith, AR-OK	9,636
35	Nashville-Davidson, TN	61,481	99	Syracuse, NY	18,810	163	Ann Arbor, MI	9,513
36	Milwaukee, WI	61,392	100	Lake Co.-Kenosha Co., IL-WI M.D.	18,478	164	Longview, TX	8,983
37	Virginia Beach-Norfolk, VA-NC	57,966	101	Montgomery, AL	18,249	165	Pueblo, CO	8,945
38	Jacksonville, FL	54,766	102	Brownsville-Harlingen, TX	17,834	166	Ocala, FL	8,927
39	Newark, NJ-PA M.D.	54,426	103	Visalia-Porterville, CA	17,652	167	Monroe, LA	8,918
40	San Jose, CA	54,174	104	Oxnard-Thousand Oaks, CA	17,585	168	Bremerton-Silverdale, WA	8,823
41	Warren-Troy, MI M.D.	52,391	105	Cape Coral-Fort Myers, FL	17,255	169	Roanoke, VA	8,821
42	Salt Lake City, UT	52,295	106	Huntsville, AL	16,520	170	Tuscaloosa, AL	8,631
43	Boston, MA M.D.	51,398	107	Madison, WI	16,192	171	Panama City, FL	8,597
44	West Palm Beach, FL M.D.	50,827	108	Columbus, GA-AL	15,872	172	Medford, OR	8,449
45	Birmingham-Hoover, AL	49,596	109	Ogden-Clearfield, UT	15,763	173	Albany, GA	8,344
46	Louisville, KY-IN	48,700	110	Lubbock, TX	15,745	174	Fort Collins, CO	8,315
47	Nassau-Suffolk, NY M.D.	48,144	111	Beaumont-Port Arthur, TX	15,527	175	Hammond, LA	8,312
48	Fresno, CA	47,236	112	Tallahassee, FL	15,349	176	Joplin, MO	8,179
49	Cambridge-Newton, MA M.D.	47,148	113	Vallejo-Fairfield, CA	15,077	177	Olympia, WA	8,142
50	New Orleans, LA	45,566	114	Rockford, IL	14,617	178	Clarksville, TN-KY	8,141
51	Providence-Warwick, RI-MA	45,477	115	Eugene, OR	14,380	179	Erie, PA	8,038
52	Little Rock, AR	41,440	116	Salisbury, MD-DE	14,347	180	Utica-Rome, NY	7,793
53	Bakersfield, CA	39,737	117	Scranton--Wilkes-Barre, PA	14,231	181	Warner Robins, GA	7,762
54	Buffalo-Niagara Falls, NY	38,409	118	Anchorage, AK	13,887	182	Tyler, TX	7,741
55	Greenville-Anderson, SC	37,880	119	Fayetteville-Springdale, AR-MO	13,870	183	Boulder, CO	7,718
56	Tulsa, OK	36,632	120	Boise City, ID	13,796	184	Vineland-Bridgeton, NJ	7,622
57	Camden, NJ M.D.	36,603	121	Salem, OR	13,713	185	Redding, CA	7,578
58	Montgomery County, PA M.D.	36,068	122	Harrisburg-Carlisle, PA	13,494	186	Crestview-Fort Walton Beach, FL	7,569
59	Stockton-Lodi, CA	35,513	123	Portland, ME	13,399	187	Binghamton, NY	7,483
60	Richmond, VA	34,592	124	Fort Wayne, IN	13,194	188	Houma, LA	7,466
61	Omaha-Council Bluffs, NE-IA	33,336	125	Reno, NV	13,191	189	Lake Havasu City-Kingman, AZ	7,440
62	Knoxville, TN	33,259	126	Canton, OH	13,154	190	Champaign-Urbana, IL	7,366
63	McAllen-Edinburg-Mission, TX	33,102	127	Asheville, NC	13,119	191	Texarkana, TX-AR	7,331
64	Raleigh, NC	31,934	128	Hickory, NC	13,025	192	Athens-Clarke County, GA	7,276

Note: All listings are for Metropolitan Statistical Areas (M.S.A.s) except for those ending with "M.D." Listings with "M.D." are Metropolitan Divisions which are smaller parts of eleven large M.S.A.s. See explanatory note at beginning of metropolitan area section.

RANK	METROPOLITAN AREA	CRIMES	RANK	METROPOLITAN AREA	CRIMES	RANK	METROPOLITAN AREA	CRIMES
193	College Station-Bryan, TX	7,238	257	Flagstaff, AZ	4,724	321	Chambersburg-Waynesboro, PA	2,720
194	Las Cruces, NM	7,234	258	Jonesboro, AR	4,712	322	Sheboygan, WI	2,647
195	San Luis Obispo, CA	7,158	259	Ocean City, NJ	4,665	323	Kokomo, IN	2,584
196	Dover, DE	7,073	260	Bloomington, IL	4,654	324	Casper, WY	2,498
197	Kennewick-Richland, WA	7,024	261	Gainesville, GA	4,646	325	Wausau, WI	2,452
198	El Centro, CA	6,990	262	Valdosta, GA	4,624	326	Altoona, PA	2,434
199	Dutchess-Putnam, NY M.D.	6,849	263	Monroe, MI	4,501	326	Elmira, NY	2,434
200	Hilton Head Island, SC	6,822	264	Waterloo-Cedar Falls, IA	4,452	328	Walla Walla, WA	2,413
201	Bellingham, WA	6,806	265	Lima, OH	4,401	329	Bay City, MI	2,411
202	Terre Haute, IN	6,748	266	Auburn, AL	4,395	330	Glens Falls, NY	2,378
203	Barnstable Town, MA	6,736	267	Sierra Vista-Douglas, AZ	4,387	331	Pocatello, ID	2,350
204	Greenville, NC	6,734	268	Dalton, GA	4,365	331	State College, PA	2,350
205	Lawton, OK	6,634	269	Morristown, TN	4,353	333	Staunton-Waynesboro, VA	2,317
206	Johnson City, TN	6,631	270	Bowling Green, KY	4,234	334	Elizabethtown-Fort Knox, KY	2,275
207	Green Bay, WI	6,574	271	Rome, GA	4,230	335	Lewiston, ID-WA	2,247
208	Sioux Falls, SD	6,529	272	Sebastian-Vero Beach, FL	4,221	336	Ames, IA	2,163
209	Hagerstown-Martinsburg, MD-WV	6,518	273	Blacksburg, VA	4,211	337	Manhattan, KS	2,105
210	Greeley, CO	6,502	274	Cleveland, TN	4,209	338	Logan, UT-ID	2,103
211	Wichita Falls, TX	6,438	275	Hanford-Corcoran, CA	4,207	339	Fond du Lac, WI	2,009
212	Kahului-Wailuku-Lahaina, HI	6,414	276	Midland, TX	4,169	340	Harrisonburg, VA	1,968
213	Rocky Mount, NC	6,392	277	Cape Girardeau, MO-IL	4,145	341	Bloomsburg-Berwick, PA	1,940
214	Naples-Marco Island, FL	6,360	278	Longview, WA	4,089	342	Corvallis, OR	1,937
215	Odessa, TX	6,345	279	Muncie, IN	4,084	343	Fairbanks, AK	1,732
216	Chico, CA	6,343	280	Hattiesburg, MS	4,077	344	Gettysburg, PA	1,323
217	Saginaw, MI	6,289	281	Sherman-Denison, TX	4,071	345	The Villages, FL	1,250
218	Billings, MT	6,216	282	Norwich-New London, CT	4,055	346	Carson City, NV	1,239
219	Columbia, MO	6,167	283	Jefferson City, MO	4,046	347	Midland, MI	1,043
220	Lafayette, IN	6,099	284	Farmington, NM	4,024	NA	Albuquerque, NM**	NA
221	Mansfield, OH	6,074	285	Kingston, NY	3,950	NA	Alexandria, LA**	NA
222	Springfield, OH	6,046	286	Michigan City-La Porte, IN	3,948	NA	Atlantic City, NJ**	NA
223	Anniston-Oxford, AL	6,017	287	Missoula, MT	3,937	NA	Baton Rouge, LA**	NA
224	Santa Fe, NM	5,973	288	Punta Gorda, FL	3,906	NA	Cedar Rapids, IA**	NA
225	Burlington, NC	5,892	289	Albany, OR	3,878	NA	Chicago (greater), IL-IN-WI**	NA
226	St. Joseph, MO-KS	5,875	290	Appleton, WI	3,870	NA	Chicago-Joilet-Naperville, IL M.D.**	NA
227	Jackson, TN	5,850	291	Oshkosh-Neenah, WI	3,707	NA	Colorado Springs, CO**	NA
228	Yuma, AZ	5,844	291	Victoria, TX	3,707	NA	Corpus Christi, TX**	NA
229	Racine, WI	5,774	293	Kankakee, IL	3,542	NA	Des Moines-West Des Moines, IA**	NA
230	Abilene, TX	5,635	294	Danville, IL	3,511	NA	Dubuque, IA**	NA
231	Bloomington, IN	5,534	295	Pittsfield, MA	3,507	NA	Duluth, MN-WI**	NA
232	Sumter, SC	5,472	296	Iowa City, IA	3,470	NA	Fargo, ND-MN**	NA
233	Goldsboro, NC	5,463	297	Lewiston-Auburn, ME	3,428	NA	Grand Forks, ND-MN**	NA
234	Yuba City, CA	5,448	298	Homosassa Springs, FL	3,419	NA	Houston, TX**	NA
235	Daphne-Fairhope-Foley, AL	5,434	299	Decatur, IL	3,390	NA	Killeen-Temple, TX**	NA
236	Brunswick, GA	5,240	300	Napa, CA	3,348	NA	La Crosse, WI-MN**	NA
236	Mount Vernon-Anacortes, WA	5,240	301	Cumberland, MD-WV	3,325	NA	Lafayette, LA**	NA
238	Dothan, AL	5,156	302	Wheeling, WV-OH	3,322	NA	Mankato-North Mankato, MN**	NA
239	Janesville, WI	5,155	303	Bismarck, ND	3,321	NA	Minneapolis-St. Paul, MN-WI**	NA
240	East Stroudsburg, PA	5,152	304	Great Falls, MT	3,305	NA	New York (greater), NY-NJ-PA**	NA
241	Prescott, AZ	5,142	305	Owensboro, KY	3,285	NA	New York-Jersey City, NY-NJ M.D.**	NA
242	New Bern, NC	5,114	306	Winchester, VA-WV	3,282	NA	Oakland-Hayward, CA M.D.**	NA
243	Gadsden, AL	5,072	307	Sebring, FL	3,112	NA	Philadelphia (greater) PA-NJ-MD-DE**	NA
244	Beckley, WV	5,025	308	Grand Island, NE	3,074	NA	Philadelphia, PA M.D.**	NA
245	Lynchburg, VA	4,991	309	California-Lexington Park, MD	3,035	NA	Phoenix-Mesa-Scottsdale, AZ**	NA
246	Florence-Muscle Shoals, AL	4,967	310	St. George, UT	3,017	NA	Pittsburgh, PA**	NA
247	Lawrence, KS	4,964	311	Parkersburg-Vienna, WV	3,014	NA	Rochester, MN**	NA
248	Madera, CA	4,951	312	Watertown-Fort Drum, NY	2,994	NA	San Francisco (greater), CA**	NA
249	Pine Bluff, AR	4,943	313	Cheyenne, WY	2,943	NA	San Rafael, CA M.D.**	NA
250	Coeur d'Alene, ID	4,939	314	Morgantown, WV	2,934	NA	Seattle (greater), WA**	NA
251	Sioux City, IA-NE-SD	4,930	315	Columbus, IN	2,902	NA	Shreveport-Bossier City, LA**	NA
252	Decatur, AL	4,924	316	Johnstown, PA	2,892	NA	Tacoma, WA M.D.**	NA
253	Rapid City, SD	4,900	317	Lebanon, PA	2,857	NA	Toledo, OH**	NA
254	Grand Junction, CO	4,777	318	Idaho Falls, ID	2,782	NA	Tucson, AZ**	NA
255	Bangor, ME	4,762	319	Williamsport, PA	2,741			
256	Charlottesville, VA	4,761	320	Hinesville, GA	2,732			

Source: CQ Press using reported data from the F.B.I. "Crime in the United States 2012"

*Includes murder, rape, robbery, aggravated assault, burglary, larceny-theft, and motor vehicle theft.

**Not available.

2. Crime Rate in 2012
National Rate = 3,246.1 Crimes per 100,000 Population*

RANK	METROPOLITAN AREA	RATE	RANK	METROPOLITAN AREA	RATE	RANK	METROPOLITAN AREA	RATE
176	Abilene, TX	3,336.2	202	Cheyenne, WY	3,130.0	153	Gary, IN M.D.	3,474.5
174	Akron, OH	3,352.4	NA	Chicago (greater), IL-IN-WI**	NA	345	Gettysburg, PA	1,302.2
251	Albany-Schenectady-Troy, NY	2,730.4	NA	Chicago-Joilet-Naperville, IL M.D.**	NA	335	Glens Falls, NY	1,833.6
9	Albany, GA	5,235.6	233	Chico, CA	2,853.3	54	Goldsboro, NC	4,373.1
182	Albany, OR	3,259.8	135	Cincinnati, OH-KY-IN	3,603.4	NA	Grand Forks, ND-MN**	NA
NA	Albuquerque, NM**	NA	212	Clarksville, TN-KY	3,058.3	126	Grand Island, NE	3,694.9
NA	Alexandria, LA**	NA	139	Cleveland, TN	3,573.0	192	Grand Junction, CO	3,203.5
288	Allentown, PA-NJ	2,425.2	152	Coeur d'Alene, ID	3,476.0	85	Great Falls, MT	4,010.7
332	Altoona, PA	1,912.0	210	College Station-Bryan, TX	3,078.8	286	Greeley, CO	2,479.6
60	Amarillo, TX	4,266.7	NA	Colorado Springs, CO**	NA	316	Green Bay, WI	2,118.9
291	Ames, IA	2,403.0	121	Columbia, MO	3,716.4	92	Greensboro-High Point, NC	3,917.8
289	Anaheim-Santa Ana-Irvine, CA M.D.	2,419.2	10	Columbus, GA-AL	5,216.0	45	Greenville-Anderson, SC	4,489.0
49	Anchorage, AK	4,429.3	122	Columbus, IN	3,715.1	98	Greenville, NC	3,896.3
250	Ann Arbor, MI	2,731.9	NA	Corpus Christi, TX**	NA	277	Hagerstown-Martinsburg, MD-WV	2,552.2
13	Anniston-Oxford, AL	5,087.5	303	Corvallis, OR	2,238.3	1	Hammond, LA	6,741.5
339	Appleton, WI	1,697.5	203	Crestview-Fort Walton Beach, FL	3,120.7	255	Hanford-Corcoran, CA	2,710.8
215	Asheville, NC	3,028.0	190	Cumberland, MD-WV	3,209.3	287	Harrisburg-Carlisle, PA	2,436.6
119	Athens-Clarke County, GA	3,724.0	148	Dallas (greater), TX	3,520.6	342	Harrisonburg, VA	1,538.0
110	Atlanta, GA	3,792.0	161	Dallas-Plano-Irving, TX M.D.	3,424.3	249	Hartford, CT	2,736.9
NA	Atlantic City, NJ**	NA	217	Dalton, GA	3,025.7	241	Hattiesburg, MS	2,797.4
213	Auburn, AL	3,051.2	58	Danville, IL	4,305.5	145	Hickory, NC	3,537.7
57	Augusta, GA-SC	4,316.0	228	Daphne-Fairhope-Foley, AL	2,898.6	141	Hilton Head Island, SC	3,559.0
120	Austin-Round Rock, TX	3,723.9	222	Davenport, IA-IL	2,957.7	173	Hinesville, GA	3,354.3
37	Bakersfield, CA	4,622.7	128	Dayton, OH	3,688.8	290	Homosassa Springs, FL	2,408.7
134	Baltimore, MD	3,605.5	194	Decatur, AL	3,183.2	142	Houma, LA	3,558.3
208	Bangor, ME	3,094.2	211	Decatur, IL	3,060.0	NA	Houston, TX**	NA
207	Barnstable Town, MA	3,094.3	133	Deltona-Daytona Beach, FL	3,606.2	102	Huntsville, AL	3,867.1
NA	Baton Rouge, LA**	NA	209	Denver-Aurora, CO	3,084.1	324	Idaho Falls, ID	2,048.5
302	Bay City, MI	2,249.3	NA	Des Moines-West Des Moines, IA**	NA	59	Indianapolis, IN	4,272.0
111	Beaumont-Port Arthur, TX	3,777.3	178	Detroit (greater), MI	3,304.4	304	Iowa City, IA	2,231.6
84	Beckley, WV	4,025.5	23	Detroit-Dearborn-Livonia, MI M.D.	4,953.6	87	Jacksonville, FL	3,972.0
177	Bellingham, WA	3,309.4	149	Dothan, AL	3,503.9	123	Jackson, MS	3,713.7
106	Billings, MT	3,835.1	64	Dover, DE	4,244.4	46	Jackson, TN	4,464.3
220	Binghamton, NY	2,976.3	NA	Dubuque, IA**	NA	189	Janesville, WI	3,211.7
55	Birmingham-Hoover, AL	4,362.8	NA	Duluth, MN-WI**	NA	260	Jefferson City, MO	2,683.7
245	Bismarck, ND	2,775.1	101	Durham-Chapel Hill, NC	3,867.3	180	Johnson City, TN	3,291.3
296	Blacksburg, VA	2,341.7	338	Dutchess-Putnam, NY M.D.	1,711.9	325	Johnstown, PA	2,008.9
285	Bloomington, IL	2,485.8	216	East Stroudsburg, PA	3,027.8	107	Jonesboro, AR	3,821.8
162	Bloomington, IN	3,420.2	94	El Centro, CA	3,911.6	38	Joplin, MO	4,616.1
300	Bloomsburg-Berwick, PA	2,258.2	254	El Paso, TX	2,711.1	82	Kahului-Wailuku-Lahaina, HI	4,040.1
311	Boise City, ID	2,183.2	334	Elgin, IL M.D.	1,834.0	195	Kalamazoo-Portage, MI	3,171.7
297	Boston (greater), MA-NH	2,339.1	344	Elizabethtown-Fort Knox, KY	1,499.5	204	Kankakee, IL	3,113.8
261	Boston, MA M.D.	2,675.7	252	Elmira, NY	2,725.0	88	Kansas City, MO-KS	3,963.8
279	Boulder, CO	2,542.8	232	Erie, PA	2,856.0	266	Kennewick-Richland, WA	2,633.5
268	Bowling Green, KY	2,630.1	81	Eugene, OR	4,040.2	NA	Killeen-Temple, TX**	NA
159	Bremerton-Silverdale, WA	3,431.4	18	Fairbanks, AK	5,005.4	172	Kingsport, TN-VA	3,358.1
322	Bridgeport-Stamford, CT	2,085.4	NA	Fargo, ND-MN**	NA	312	Kingston, NY	2,153.4
65	Brownsville-Harlingen, TX	4,242.9	201	Farmington, NM	3,133.9	95	Knoxville, TN	3,910.8
40	Brunswick, GA	4,591.4	225	Fayetteville-Springdale, AR-MO	2,916.4	206	Kokomo, IN	3,111.1
169	Buffalo-Niagara Falls, NY	3,368.8	3	Fayetteville, NC	5,860.6	NA	La Crosse, WI-MN**	NA
109	Burlington, NC	3,806.0	154	Flagstaff, AZ	3,474.0	219	Lafayette, IN	2,986.1
242	California-Lexington Park, MD	2,796.6	42	Flint, MI	4,547.8	NA	Lafayette, LA**	NA
323	Cambridge-Newton, MA M.D.	2,061.3	171	Florence-Muscle Shoals, AL	3,358.7	317	Lake Co.-Kenosha Co., IL-WI M.D.	2,113.5
226	Camden, NJ M.D.	2,909.4	7	Florence, SC	5,291.1	131	Lake Havasu City-Kingman, AZ	3,637.1
183	Canton, OH	3,257.2	326	Fond du Lac, WI	1,963.1	158	Lakeland, FL	3,440.8
257	Cape Coral-Fort Myers, FL	2,696.3	259	Fort Collins, CO	2,684.4	313	Lancaster, PA	2,130.2
61	Cape Girardeau, MO-IL	4,264.6	63	Fort Lauderdale, FL M.D.	4,247.9	274	Lansing-East Lansing, MI	2,578.9
308	Carson City, NV	2,206.0	166	Fort Smith, AR-OK	3,401.0	35	Laredo, TX	4,688.9
186	Casper, WY	3,224.3	200	Fort Wayne, IN	3,135.7	168	Las Cruces, NM	3,381.3
NA	Cedar Rapids, IA**	NA	124	Fort Worth-Arlington, TX M.D.	3,707.4	129	Las Vegas-Henderson, NV	3,662.5
337	Chambersburg-Waynesboro, PA	1,800.6	22	Fresno, CA	4,963.6	50	Lawrence, KS	4,401.3
196	Champaign-Urbana, IL	3,168.9	28	Gadsden, AL	4,843.3	19	Lawton, OK	4,995.3
127	Charleston-North Charleston, SC	3,690.8	103	Gainesville, FL	3,858.9	315	Lebanon, PA	2,123.7
314	Charlottesville, VA	2,129.3	283	Gainesville, GA	2,511.3	193	Lewiston-Auburn, ME	3,189.5

Note: All listings are for Metropolitan Statistical Areas (M.S.A.s) except for those ending with "M.D." Listings with "M.D." are Metropolitan Divisions which are smaller parts of eleven large M.S.A.s. See explanatory note at beginning of metropolitan area section.

RANK	METROPOLITAN AREA	RATE	RANK	METROPOLITAN AREA	RATE	RANK	METROPOLITAN AREA	RATE
132	Lewiston, ID-WA	3,626.6	234	Owensboro, KY	2,841.1	330	Silver Spring-Frederick, MD M.D.	1,927.4
51	Lexington-Fayette, KY	4,394.5	320	Oxnard-Thousand Oaks, CA	2,094.7	227	Sioux City, IA-NE-SD	2,903.3
74	Lima, OH	4,148.5	140	Palm Bay-Melbourne, FL	3,561.3	244	Sioux Falls, SD	2,777.7
97	Lincoln, NE	3,897.7	41	Panama City, FL	4,567.1	151	South Bend-Mishawaka, IN-MI	3,487.9
4	Little Rock, AR	5,815.4	185	Parkersburg-Vienna, WV	3,244.9	113	Spartanburg, SC	3,766.5
341	Logan, UT-ID	1,627.9	66	Pensacola, FL	4,229.9	2	Spokane, WA	5,885.7
79	Longview, TX	4,084.8	198	Peoria, IL	3,144.5	29	Springfield, IL	4,830.3
90	Longview, WA	3,951.4	NA	Philadelphia (greater) PA-NJ-MD-DE**	NA	147	Springfield, MA	3,521.2
246	Los Angeles County, CA M.D.	2,773.5	NA	Philadelphia, PA M.D.**	NA	12	Springfield, MO	5,104.4
258	Los Angeles (greater), CA	2,689.9	NA	Phoenix-Mesa-Scottsdale, AZ**	NA	53	Springfield, OH	4,391.3
96	Louisville, KY-IN	3,900.3	21	Pine Bluff, AR	4,977.9	343	State College, PA	1,516.4
8	Lubbock, TX	5,242.7	NA	Pittsburgh, PA**	NA	328	Staunton-Waynesboro, VA	1,931.9
327	Lynchburg, VA	1,942.3	263	Pittsfield, MA	2,664.5	15	Stockton-Lodi, CA	5,054.0
11	Macon, GA	5,109.1	243	Pocatello, ID	2,789.0	319	St. George, UT	2,101.2
191	Madera, CA	3,207.7	256	Port St. Lucie, FL	2,697.0	39	St. Joseph, MO-KS	4,595.6
267	Madison, WI	2,633.1	160	Portland-Vancouver, OR-WA	3,430.8	175	St. Louis, MO-IL	3,345.4
278	Manchester-Nashua, NH	2,551.8	272	Portland, ME	2,595.7	17	Sumter, SC	5,044.1
307	Manhattan, KS	2,206.4	294	Prescott, AZ	2,400.6	238	Syracuse, NY	2,823.7
NA	Mankato-North Mankato, MN**	NA	235	Providence-Warwick, RI-MA	2,835.1	NA	Tacoma, WA M.D.**	NA
24	Mansfield, OH	4,918.1	329	Provo-Orem, UT	1,929.6	76	Tallahassee, FL	4,095.2
78	McAllen-Edinburg-Mission, TX	4,087.9	5	Pueblo, CO	5,495.6	181	Tampa-St Petersburg, FL	3,272.1
75	Medford, OR	4,096.0	293	Punta Gorda, FL	2,400.7	99	Terre Haute, IN	3,896.0
6	Memphis, TN-MS-AR	5,424.1	223	Racine, WI	2,947.6	27	Texarkana, TX-AR	4,850.1
43	Merced, CA	4,545.8	253	Raleigh, NC	2,717.7	346	The Villages, FL	1,261.5
44	Miami (greater), FL	4,494.9	144	Rapid City, SD	3,544.7	NA	Toledo, OH**	NA
16	Miami-Dade County, FL M.D.	5,053.4	273	Reading, PA	2,583.4	62	Topeka, KS	4,252.4
146	Michigan City-La Porte, IN	3,533.7	68	Redding, CA	4,223.5	262	Trenton, NJ	2,669.0
347	Midland, MI	1,239.8	214	Reno, NV	3,030.8	NA	Tucson, AZ**	NA
236	Midland, TX	2,828.1	239	Richmond, VA	2,806.7	105	Tulsa, OK	3,844.7
91	Milwaukee, WI	3,919.8	167	Riverside-San Bernardino, CA	3,390.0	125	Tuscaloosa, AL	3,705.6
NA	Minneapolis-St. Paul, MN-WI**	NA	237	Roanoke, VA	2,824.9	138	Tyler, TX	3,574.3
143	Missoula, MT	3,549.9	NA	Rochester, MN**	NA	271	Utica-Rome, NY	2,597.2
26	Mobile, AL	4,850.9	224	Rochester, NY	2,929.9	188	Valdosta, GA	3,215.0
33	Modesto, CA	4,764.9	71	Rockford, IL	4,194.0	137	Vallejo-Fairfield, CA	3,586.9
20	Monroe, LA	4,990.4	298	Rockingham County, NH M.D.	2,312.1	104	Victoria, TX	3,853.1
221	Monroe, MI	2,967.7	73	Rocky Mount, NC	4,159.7	30	Vineland-Bridgeton, NJ	4,828.1
333	Montgomery County, PA M.D.	1,905.9	56	Rome, GA	4,360.3	165	Virginia Beach-Norfolk, VA-NC	3,402.7
32	Montgomery, AL	4,800.8	170	Sacramento, CA	3,366.8	100	Visalia-Porterville, CA	3,893.1
306	Morgantown, WV	2,218.5	197	Saginaw, MI	3,156.6	93	Waco, TX	3,913.2
114	Morristown, TN	3,763.1	157	Salem, OR	3,448.4	117	Walla Walla, WA	3,755.0
52	Mount Vernon-Anacortes, WA	4,393.5	231	Salinas, CA	2,856.6	72	Warner Robins, GA	4,185.7
155	Muncie, IN	3,460.2	115	Salisbury, MD-DE	3,762.9	318	Warren-Troy, MI M.D.	2,107.8
292	Napa, CA	2,402.3	36	Salt Lake City, UT	4,655.5	269	Washington (greater) DC-VA-MD-WV	2,614.8
331	Naples-Marco Island, FL	1,912.1	14	San Antonio, TX	5,078.8	240	Washington, DC-VA-MD-WV M.D.	2,800.3
136	Nashville-Davidson, TN	3,589.7	275	San Diego, CA	2,570.5	265	Waterloo-Cedar Falls, IA	2,635.2
340	Nassau-Suffolk, NY M.D.	1,684.1	NA	San Francisco (greater), CA**	NA	281	Watertown-Fort Drum, NY	2,525.6
89	New Bern, NC	3,956.1	86	San Francisco-Redwood, CA M.D.	3,995.9	336	Wausau, WI	1,819.8
164	New Haven-Milford, CT	3,409.1	230	San Jose, CA	2,877.4	116	West Palm Beach, FL M.D.	3,755.5
118	New Orleans, LA	3,734.8	270	San Luis Obispo, CA	2,607.8	301	Wheeling, WV-OH	2,256.9
NA	New York (greater), NY-NJ-PA**	NA	NA	San Rafael, CA M.D.**	NA	69	Wichita Falls, TX	4,221.3
NA	New York-Jersey City, NY-NJ M.D.**	NA	130	Santa Cruz-Watsonville, CA	3,655.2	34	Wichita, KS	4,711.6
310	Newark, NJ-PA M.D.	2,185.9	77	Santa Fe, NM	4,094.4	295	Williamsport, PA	2,344.0
150	North Port-Sarasota-Bradenton, FL	3,488.5	248	Santa Maria-Santa Barbara, CA	2,740.5	108	Wilmington, DE-MD-NJ M.D.	3,814.2
247	Norwich-New London, CT	2,770.0	321	Santa Rosa, CA	2,092.0	70	Wilmington, NC	4,198.6
NA	Oakland-Hayward, CA M.D.**	NA	156	Savannah, GA	3,459.6	284	Winchester, VA-WV	2,500.8
264	Ocala, FL	2,648.4	282	Scranton--Wilkes-Barre, PA	2,522.6	67	Winston-Salem, NC	4,226.1
31	Ocean City, NJ	4,805.4	NA	Seattle (greater), WA**	NA	280	Worcester, MA-CT	2,537.1
47	Odessa, TX	4,461.7	80	Seattle-Bellevue-Everett, WA M.D.	4,068.0	48	Yakima, WA	4,448.5
276	Ogden-Clearfield, UT	2,565.6	218	Sebastian-Vero Beach, FL	2,998.1	305	York-Hanover, PA	2,229.6
25	Oklahoma City, OK	4,915.9	205	Sebring, FL	3,112.8	163	Youngstown-Warren, OH-PA	3,411.6
199	Olympia, WA	3,142.3	299	Sheboygan, WI	2,292.9	187	Yuba City, CA	3,222.7
112	Omaha-Council Bluffs, NE-IA	3,775.9	179	Sherman-Denison, TX	3,303.4	229	Yuma, AZ	2,877.9
83	Orlando, FL	4,031.1	NA	Shreveport-Bossier City, LA**	NA			
309	Oshkosh-Neenah, WI	2,204.8	184	Sierra Vista-Douglas, AZ	3,255.8			

Source: CQ Press using reported data from the F.B.I. "Crime in the United States 2012"

*Includes murder, rape, robbery, aggravated assault, burglary, larceny-theft, and motor vehicle theft.

**Not available.

2. Crime Rate in 2012 (continued)
National Rate = 3,246.1 Crimes per 100,000 Population*

RANK	METROPOLITAN AREA	RATE	RANK	METROPOLITAN AREA	RATE	RANK	METROPOLITAN AREA	RATE
1	Hammond, LA	6,741.5	65	Brownsville-Harlingen, TX	4,242.9	129	Las Vegas-Henderson, NV	3,662.5
2	Spokane, WA	5,885.7	66	Pensacola, FL	4,229.9	130	Santa Cruz-Watsonville, CA	3,655.2
3	Fayetteville, NC	5,860.6	67	Winston-Salem, NC	4,226.1	131	Lake Havasu City-Kingman, AZ	3,637.1
4	Little Rock, AR	5,815.4	68	Redding, CA	4,223.5	132	Lewiston, ID-WA	3,626.6
5	Pueblo, CO	5,495.6	69	Wichita Falls, TX	4,221.3	133	Deltona-Daytona Beach, FL	3,606.2
6	Memphis, TN-MS-AR	5,424.1	70	Wilmington, NC	4,198.6	134	Baltimore, MD	3,605.5
7	Florence, SC	5,291.1	71	Rockford, IL	4,194.0	135	Cincinnati, OH-KY-IN	3,603.4
8	Lubbock, TX	5,242.7	72	Warner Robins, GA	4,185.7	136	Nashville-Davidson, TN	3,589.7
9	Albany, GA	5,235.6	73	Rocky Mount, NC	4,159.7	137	Vallejo-Fairfield, CA	3,586.9
10	Columbus, GA-AL	5,216.0	74	Lima, OH	4,148.5	138	Tyler, TX	3,574.3
11	Macon, GA	5,109.1	75	Medford, OR	4,096.0	139	Cleveland, TN	3,573.0
12	Springfield, MO	5,104.4	76	Tallahassee, FL	4,095.2	140	Palm Bay-Melbourne, FL	3,561.3
13	Anniston-Oxford, AL	5,087.5	77	Santa Fe, NM	4,094.4	141	Hilton Head Island, SC	3,559.0
14	San Antonio, TX	5,078.8	78	McAllen-Edinburg-Mission, TX	4,087.9	142	Houma, LA	3,558.3
15	Stockton-Lodi, CA	5,054.0	79	Longview, TX	4,084.8	143	Missoula, MT	3,549.9
16	Miami-Dade County, FL M.D.	5,053.4	80	Seattle-Bellevue-Everett, WA M.D.	4,068.0	144	Rapid City, SD	3,544.7
17	Sumter, SC	5,044.1	81	Eugene, OR	4,040.2	145	Hickory, NC	3,537.7
18	Fairbanks, AK	5,005.4	82	Kahului-Wailuku-Lahaina, HI	4,040.1	146	Michigan City-La Porte, IN	3,533.7
19	Lawton, OK	4,995.3	83	Orlando, FL	4,031.1	147	Springfield, MA	3,521.2
20	Monroe, LA	4,990.4	84	Beckley, WV	4,025.5	148	Dallas (greater), TX	3,520.6
21	Pine Bluff, AR	4,977.9	85	Great Falls, MT	4,010.7	149	Dothan, AL	3,503.9
22	Fresno, CA	4,963.6	86	San Francisco-Redwood, CA M.D.	3,995.9	150	North Port-Sarasota-Bradenton, FL	3,488.5
23	Detroit-Dearborn-Livonia, MI M.D.	4,953.6	87	Jacksonville, FL	3,972.0	151	South Bend-Mishawaka, IN-MI	3,487.9
24	Mansfield, OH	4,918.1	88	Kansas City, MO-KS	3,963.8	152	Coeur d'Alene, ID	3,476.0
25	Oklahoma City, OK	4,915.9	89	New Bern, NC	3,956.1	153	Gary, IN M.D.	3,474.5
26	Mobile, AL	4,850.9	90	Longview, WA	3,951.4	154	Flagstaff, AZ	3,474.0
27	Texarkana, TX-AR	4,850.1	91	Milwaukee, WI	3,919.8	155	Muncie, IN	3,460.2
28	Gadsden, AL	4,843.3	92	Greensboro-High Point, NC	3,917.8	156	Savannah, GA	3,459.6
29	Springfield, IL	4,830.3	93	Waco, TX	3,913.2	157	Salem, OR	3,448.4
30	Vineland-Bridgeton, NJ	4,828.1	94	El Centro, CA	3,911.6	158	Lakeland, FL	3,440.8
31	Ocean City, NJ	4,805.4	95	Knoxville, TN	3,910.8	159	Bremerton-Silverdale, WA	3,431.4
32	Montgomery, AL	4,800.8	96	Louisville, KY-IN	3,900.3	160	Portland-Vancouver, OR-WA	3,430.8
33	Modesto, CA	4,764.9	97	Lincoln, NE	3,897.7	161	Dallas-Plano-Irving, TX M.D.	3,424.3
34	Wichita, KS	4,711.6	98	Greenville, NC	3,896.3	162	Bloomington, IN	3,420.2
35	Laredo, TX	4,688.9	99	Terre Haute, IN	3,896.0	163	Youngstown-Warren, OH-PA	3,411.6
36	Salt Lake City, UT	4,655.5	100	Visalia-Porterville, CA	3,893.1	164	New Haven-Milford, CT	3,409.1
37	Bakersfield, CA	4,622.7	101	Durham-Chapel Hill, NC	3,867.3	165	Virginia Beach-Norfolk, VA-NC	3,402.7
38	Joplin, MO	4,616.1	102	Huntsville, AL	3,867.1	166	Fort Smith, AR-OK	3,401.0
39	St. Joseph, MO-KS	4,595.6	103	Gainesville, FL	3,858.9	167	Riverside-San Bernardino, CA	3,390.0
40	Brunswick, GA	4,591.4	104	Victoria, TX	3,853.1	168	Las Cruces, NM	3,381.3
41	Panama City, FL	4,567.1	105	Tulsa, OK	3,844.7	169	Buffalo-Niagara Falls, NY	3,368.8
42	Flint, MI	4,547.8	106	Billings, MT	3,835.1	170	Sacramento, CA	3,366.8
43	Merced, CA	4,545.8	107	Jonesboro, AR	3,821.8	171	Florence-Muscle Shoals, AL	3,358.7
44	Miami (greater), FL	4,494.9	108	Wilmington, DE-MD-NJ M.D.	3,814.2	172	Kingsport, TN-VA	3,358.1
45	Greenville-Anderson, SC	4,489.0	109	Burlington, NC	3,806.0	173	Hinesville, GA	3,354.3
46	Jackson, TN	4,464.9	110	Atlanta, GA	3,792.0	174	Akron, OH	3,352.4
47	Odessa, TX	4,461.7	111	Beaumont-Port Arthur, TX	3,777.3	175	St. Louis, MO-IL	3,345.4
48	Yakima, WA	4,448.5	112	Omaha-Council Bluffs, NE-IA	3,775.9	176	Abilene, TX	3,336.2
49	Anchorage, AK	4,429.3	113	Spartanburg, SC	3,766.5	177	Bellingham, WA	3,309.4
50	Lawrence, KS	4,401.3	114	Morristown, TN	3,763.1	178	Detroit (greater), MI	3,304.4
51	Lexington-Fayette, KY	4,394.5	115	Salisbury, MD-DE	3,762.9	179	Sherman-Denison, TX	3,303.4
52	Mount Vernon-Anacortes, WA	4,393.5	116	West Palm Beach, FL M.D.	3,755.5	180	Johnson City, TN	3,291.3
53	Springfield, OH	4,391.3	117	Walla Walla, WA	3,755.0	181	Tampa-St Petersburg, FL	3,272.1
54	Goldsboro, NC	4,373.1	118	New Orleans, LA	3,734.8	182	Albany, OR	3,259.8
55	Birmingham-Hoover, AL	4,362.8	119	Athens-Clarke County, GA	3,724.0	183	Canton, OH	3,257.2
56	Rome, GA	4,360.3	120	Austin-Round Rock, TX	3,723.9	184	Sierra Vista-Douglas, AZ	3,255.8
57	Augusta, GA-SC	4,316.0	121	Columbia, MO	3,716.4	185	Parkersburg-Vienna, WV	3,244.9
58	Danville, IL	4,305.5	122	Columbus, IN	3,715.1	186	Casper, WY	3,224.3
59	Indianapolis, IN	4,272.0	123	Jackson, MS	3,713.7	187	Yuba City, CA	3,222.7
60	Amarillo, TX	4,266.7	124	Fort Worth-Arlington, TX M.D.	3,707.4	188	Valdosta, GA	3,215.0
61	Cape Girardeau, MO-IL	4,264.6	125	Tuscaloosa, AL	3,705.6	189	Janesville, WI	3,211.7
62	Topeka, KS	4,252.4	126	Grand Island, NE	3,694.9	190	Cumberland, MD-WV	3,209.3
63	Fort Lauderdale, FL M.D.	4,247.9	127	Charleston-North Charleston, SC	3,690.8	191	Madera, CA	3,207.7
64	Dover, DE	4,244.4	128	Dayton, OH	3,688.8	192	Grand Junction, CO	3,203.5

Note: All listings are for Metropolitan Statistical Areas (M.S.A.s) except for those ending with "M.D." Listings with "M.D." are Metropolitan Divisions which are smaller parts of eleven large M.S.A.s. See explanatory note at beginning of metropolitan area section.

RANK	METROPOLITAN AREA	RATE	RANK	METROPOLITAN AREA	RATE	RANK	METROPOLITAN AREA	RATE
193	Lewiston-Auburn, ME	3,189.5	257	Cape Coral-Fort Myers, FL	2,696.3	321	Santa Rosa, CA	2,092.0
194	Decatur, AL	3,183.2	258	Los Angeles (greater), CA	2,689.9	322	Bridgeport-Stamford, CT	2,085.4
195	Kalamazoo-Portage, MI	3,171.7	259	Fort Collins, CO	2,684.4	323	Cambridge-Newton, MA M.D.	2,061.3
196	Champaign-Urbana, IL	3,168.9	260	Jefferson City, MO	2,683.7	324	Idaho Falls, ID	2,048.5
197	Saginaw, MI	3,156.6	261	Boston, MA M.D.	2,675.7	325	Johnstown, PA	2,008.9
198	Peoria, IL	3,144.5	262	Trenton, NJ	2,669.0	326	Fond du Lac, WI	1,963.1
199	Olympia, WA	3,142.3	263	Pittsfield, MA	2,664.5	327	Lynchburg, VA	1,942.3
200	Fort Wayne, IN	3,135.7	264	Ocala, FL	2,648.4	328	Staunton-Waynesboro, VA	1,931.9
201	Farmington, NM	3,133.9	265	Waterloo-Cedar Falls, IA	2,635.2	329	Provo-Orem, UT	1,929.6
202	Cheyenne, WY	3,130.0	266	Kennewick-Richland, WA	2,633.5	330	Silver Spring-Frederick, MD M.D.	1,927.4
203	Crestview-Fort Walton Beach, FL	3,120.7	267	Madison, WI	2,633.1	331	Naples-Marco Island, FL	1,912.1
204	Kankakee, IL	3,113.8	268	Bowling Green, KY	2,630.1	332	Altoona, PA	1,912.0
205	Sebring, FL	3,112.8	269	Washington (greater) DC-VA-MD-WV	2,614.8	333	Montgomery County, PA M.D.	1,905.9
206	Kokomo, IN	3,111.1	270	San Luis Obispo, CA	2,607.8	334	Elgin, IL M.D.	1,834.0
207	Barnstable Town, MA	3,094.3	271	Utica-Rome, NY	2,597.2	335	Glens Falls, NY	1,833.6
208	Bangor, ME	3,094.2	272	Portland, ME	2,595.7	336	Wausau, WI	1,819.8
209	Denver-Aurora, CO	3,084.1	273	Reading, PA	2,583.4	337	Chambersburg-Waynesboro, PA	1,800.6
210	College Station-Bryan, TX	3,078.8	274	Lansing-East Lansing, MI	2,578.9	338	Dutchess-Putnam, NY M.D.	1,711.9
211	Decatur, IL	3,060.0	275	San Diego, CA	2,570.5	339	Appleton, WI	1,697.5
212	Clarksville, TN-KY	3,058.3	276	Ogden-Clearfield, UT	2,565.6	340	Nassau-Suffolk, NY M.D.	1,684.1
213	Auburn, AL	3,051.2	277	Hagerstown-Martinsburg, MD-WV	2,552.2	341	Logan, UT-ID	1,627.9
214	Reno, NV	3,030.8	278	Manchester-Nashua, NH	2,551.8	342	Harrisonburg, VA	1,538.0
215	Asheville, NC	3,028.0	279	Boulder, CO	2,542.8	343	State College, PA	1,516.4
216	East Stroudsburg, PA	3,027.8	280	Worcester, MA-CT	2,537.1	344	Elizabethtown-Fort Knox, KY	1,499.5
217	Dalton, GA	3,025.7	281	Watertown-Fort Drum, NY	2,525.6	345	Gettysburg, PA	1,302.2
218	Sebastian-Vero Beach, FL	2,998.1	282	Scranton--Wilkes-Barre, PA	2,522.6	346	The Villages, FL	1,261.5
219	Lafayette, IN	2,986.1	283	Gainesville, GA	2,511.3	347	Midland, MI	1,239.8
220	Binghamton, NY	2,976.3	284	Winchester, VA-WV	2,500.8	NA	Albuquerque, NM**	NA
221	Monroe, MI	2,967.7	285	Bloomington, IL	2,485.8	NA	Alexandria, LA**	NA
222	Davenport, IA-IL	2,957.7	286	Greeley, CO	2,479.6	NA	Atlantic City, NJ**	NA
223	Racine, WI	2,947.6	287	Harrisburg-Carlisle, PA	2,436.6	NA	Baton Rouge, LA**	NA
224	Rochester, NY	2,929.9	288	Allentown, PA-NJ	2,425.2	NA	Cedar Rapids, IA**	NA
225	Fayetteville-Springdale, AR-MO	2,916.4	289	Anaheim-Santa Ana-Irvine, CA M.D.	2,419.2	NA	Chicago (greater), IL-IN-WI**	NA
226	Camden, NJ M.D.	2,909.4	290	Homosassa Springs, FL	2,408.7	NA	Chicago-Joliet-Naperville, IL M.D.**	NA
227	Sioux City, IA-NE-SD	2,903.3	291	Ames, IA	2,403.0	NA	Colorado Springs, CO**	NA
228	Daphne-Fairhope-Foley, AL	2,898.6	292	Napa, CA	2,402.3	NA	Corpus Christi, TX**	NA
229	Yuma, AZ	2,877.9	293	Punta Gorda, FL	2,400.7	NA	Des Moines-West Des Moines, IA**	NA
230	San Jose, CA	2,877.4	294	Prescott, AZ	2,400.6	NA	Dubuque, IA**	NA
231	Salinas, CA	2,856.6	295	Williamsport, PA	2,344.0	NA	Duluth, MN-WI**	NA
232	Erie, PA	2,856.0	296	Blacksburg, VA	2,341.7	NA	Fargo, ND-MN**	NA
233	Chico, CA	2,853.3	297	Boston (greater), MA-NH	2,339.1	NA	Grand Forks, ND-MN**	NA
234	Owensboro, KY	2,841.1	298	Rockingham County, NH M.D.	2,312.1	NA	Houston, TX**	NA
235	Providence-Warwick, RI-MA	2,835.1	299	Sheboygan, WI	2,292.9	NA	Killeen-Temple, TX**	NA
236	Midland, TX	2,828.1	300	Bloomsburg-Berwick, PA	2,258.2	NA	La Crosse, WI-MN**	NA
237	Roanoke, VA	2,824.9	301	Wheeling, WV-OH	2,256.9	NA	Lafayette, LA**	NA
238	Syracuse, NY	2,823.7	302	Bay City, MI	2,249.3	NA	Mankato-North Mankato, MN**	NA
239	Richmond, VA	2,806.7	303	Corvallis, OR	2,238.3	NA	Minneapolis-St. Paul, MN-WI**	NA
240	Washington, DC-VA-MD-WV M.D.	2,800.3	304	Iowa City, IA	2,231.6	NA	New York (greater), NY-NJ-PA**	NA
241	Hattiesburg, MS	2,797.4	305	York-Hanover, PA	2,229.6	NA	New York-Jersey City, NY-NJ M.D.**	NA
242	California-Lexington Park, MD	2,796.6	306	Morgantown, WV	2,218.5	NA	Oakland-Hayward, CA M.D.**	NA
243	Pocatello, ID	2,789.0	307	Manhattan, KS	2,206.4	NA	Philadelphia (greater) PA-NJ-MD-DE**	NA
244	Sioux Falls, SD	2,777.7	308	Carson City, NV	2,206.0	NA	Philadelphia, PA M.D.**	NA
245	Bismarck, ND	2,775.1	309	Oshkosh-Neenah, WI	2,204.8	NA	Phoenix-Mesa-Scottsdale, AZ**	NA
246	Los Angeles County, CA M.D.	2,773.5	310	Newark, NJ-PA M.D.	2,185.9	NA	Pittsburgh, PA**	NA
247	Norwich-New London, CT	2,770.0	311	Boise City, ID	2,183.2	NA	Rochester, MN**	NA
248	Santa Maria-Santa Barbara, CA	2,740.5	312	Kingston, NY	2,153.4	NA	San Francisco (greater), CA**	NA
249	Hartford, CT	2,736.9	313	Lancaster, PA	2,130.2	NA	San Rafael, CA M.D.**	NA
250	Ann Arbor, MI	2,731.9	314	Charlottesville, VA	2,129.3	NA	Seattle (greater), WA**	NA
251	Albany-Schenectady-Troy, NY	2,730.4	315	Lebanon, PA	2,123.7	NA	Shreveport-Bossier City, LA**	NA
252	Elmira, NY	2,725.0	316	Green Bay, WI	2,118.9	NA	Tacoma, WA M.D.**	NA
253	Raleigh, NC	2,717.7	317	Lake Co.-Kenosha Co., IL-WI M.D.	2,113.5	NA	Toledo, OH**	NA
254	El Paso, TX	2,711.1	318	Warren-Troy, MI M.D.	2,107.8	NA	Tucson, AZ**	NA
255	Hanford-Corcoran, CA	2,710.8	319	St. George, UT	2,101.2			
256	Port St. Lucie, FL	2,697.0	320	Oxnard-Thousand Oaks, CA	2,094.7			

Source: CQ Press using reported data from the F.B.I. "Crime in the United States 2012"

*Includes murder, rape, robbery, aggravated assault, burglary, larceny-theft, and motor vehicle theft.

**Not available.

3. Percent Change in Crime Rate: 2011 to 2012
National Percent Change = 1.4% Decrease*

RANK	METROPOLITAN AREA	% CHANGE	RANK	METROPOLITAN AREA	% CHANGE	RANK	METROPOLITAN AREA	% CHANGE
102	Abilene, TX	0.3	65	Cheyenne, WY	3.9	216	Gary, IN M.D.	(8.4)
205	Akron, OH	(7.3)	NA	Chicago (greater), IL-IN-WI**	NA	NA	Gettysburg, PA**	NA
NA	Albany-Schenectady-Troy, NY**	NA	NA	Chicago-Joilet-Naperville, IL M.D.**	NA	NA	Glens Falls, NY**	NA
39	Albany, GA	7.0	43	Chico, CA	6.7	177	Goldsboro, NC	(5.3)
NA	Albany, OR**	NA	NA	Cincinnati, OH-KY-IN**	NA	NA	Grand Forks, ND-MN**	NA
NA	Albuquerque, NM**	NA	200	Clarksville, TN-KY	(6.7)	NA	Grand Island, NE**	NA
NA	Alexandria, LA**	NA	136	Cleveland, TN	(2.6)	48	Grand Junction, CO	6.0
NA	Allentown, PA-NJ**	NA	NA	Coeur d'Alene, ID**	NA	60	Great Falls, MT	4.4
249	Altoona, PA	(14.6)	238	College Station-Bryan, TX	(13.4)	68	Greeley, CO	3.6
195	Amarillo, TX	(6.4)	NA	Colorado Springs, CO**	NA	21	Green Bay, WI	10.3
252	Ames, IA	(16.8)	80	Columbia, MO	2.3	NA	Greensboro-High Point, NC**	NA
30	Anaheim-Santa Ana-Irvine, CA M.D.	8.1	215	Columbus, GA-AL	(8.3)	NA	Greenville-Anderson, SC**	NA
NA	Anchorage, AK**	NA	245	Columbus, IN	(14.1)	NA	Greenville, NC**	NA
57	Ann Arbor, MI	4.6	NA	Corpus Christi, TX**	NA	NA	Hagerstown-Martinsburg, MD-WV**	NA
45	Anniston-Oxford, AL	6.4	252	Corvallis, OR	(16.8)	NA	Hammond, LA**	NA
209	Appleton, WI	(7.5)	175	Crestview-Fort Walton Beach, FL	(5.2)	52	Hanford-Corcoran, CA	5.5
23	Asheville, NC	10.1	112	Cumberland, MD-WV	(0.7)	137	Harrisburg-Carlisle, PA	(2.7)
223	Athens-Clarke County, GA	(9.2)	219	Dallas (greater), TX	(8.7)	35	Harrisonburg, VA	7.5
163	Atlanta, GA	(4.1)	214	Dallas-Plano-Irving, TX M.D.	(8.2)	105	Hartford, CT	0.0
NA	Atlantic City, NJ**	NA	180	Dalton, GA	(5.4)	NA	Hattiesburg, MS**	NA
231	Auburn, AL	(11.9)	201	Danville, IL	(7.0)	172	Hickory, NC	(4.9)
216	Augusta, GA-SC	(8.4)	NA	Daphne-Fairhope-Foley, AL**	NA	NA	Hilton Head Island, SC**	NA
109	Austin-Round Rock, TX	(0.3)	233	Davenport, IA-IL	(12.0)	190	Hinesville, GA	(6.1)
14	Bakersfield, CA	13.8	115	Dayton, OH	(1.1)	NA	Homosassa Springs, FL**	NA
134	Baltimore, MD	(2.3)	11	Decatur, AL	14.6	130	Houma, LA	(2.0)
37	Bangor, ME	7.3	242	Decatur, IL	(13.7)	NA	Houston, TX**	NA
169	Barnstable Town, MA	(4.5)	NA	Deltona-Daytona Beach, FL**	NA	147	Huntsville, AL	(3.6)
NA	Baton Rouge, LA**	NA	NA	Denver-Aurora, CO**	NA	221	Idaho Falls, ID	(9.1)
98	Bay City, MI	0.6	NA	Des Moines-West Des Moines, IA**	NA	NA	Indianapolis, IN**	NA
248	Beaumont-Port Arthur, TX	(14.5)	166	Detroit (greater), MI	(4.3)	33	Iowa City, IA	7.7
NA	Beckley, WV**	NA	163	Detroit-Dearborn-Livonia, MI M.D.	(4.1)	184	Jacksonville, FL	(5.6)
115	Bellingham, WA	(1.1)	75	Dothan, AL	2.8	NA	Jackson, MS**	NA
73	Billings, MT	3.0	112	Dover, DE	(0.7)	NA	Jackson, TN**	NA
NA	Binghamton, NY**	NA	NA	Dubuque, IA**	NA	127	Janesville, WI	(1.9)
182	Birmingham-Hoover, AL	(5.5)	NA	Duluth, MN-WI**	NA	154	Jefferson City, MO	(3.8)
64	Bismarck, ND	4.2	219	Durham-Chapel Hill, NC	(8.7)	124	Johnson City, TN	(1.7)
231	Blacksburg, VA	(11.9)	NA	Dutchess-Putnam, NY M.D.**	NA	240	Johnstown, PA	(13.6)
111	Bloomington, IL	(0.4)	NA	East Stroudsburg, PA**	NA	228	Jonesboro, AR	(11.4)
NA	Bloomington, IN**	NA	29	El Centro, CA	8.3	9	Joplin, MO	15.6
NA	Bloomsburg-Berwick, PA**	NA	140	El Paso, TX	(2.9)	NA	Kahului-Wailuku-Lahaina, HI**	NA
137	Boise City, ID	(2.7)	NA	Elgin, IL M.D.**	NA	NA	Kalamazoo-Portage, MI**	NA
NA	Boston (greater), MA-NH**	NA	NA	Elizabethtown-Fort Knox, KY**	NA	174	Kankakee, IL	(5.0)
NA	Boston, MA M.D.**	NA	NA	Elmira, NY**	NA	NA	Kansas City, MO-KS**	NA
45	Boulder, CO	6.4	139	Erie, PA	(2.8)	221	Kennewick-Richland, WA	(9.1)
201	Bowling Green, KY	(7.0)	53	Eugene, OR	5.3	NA	Killeen-Temple, TX**	NA
50	Bremerton-Silverdale, WA	5.6	32	Fairbanks, AK	7.9	209	Kingsport, TN-VA	(7.5)
191	Bridgeport-Stamford, CT	(6.2)	NA	Fargo, ND-MN**	NA	NA	Kingston, NY**	NA
148	Brownsville-Harlingen, TX	(3.7)	10	Farmington, NM	15.1	NA	Knoxville, TN**	NA
226	Brunswick, GA	(10.6)	NA	Fayetteville-Springdale, AR-MO**	NA	NA	Kokomo, IN**	NA
NA	Buffalo-Niagara Falls, NY**	NA	118	Fayetteville, NC	(1.4)	NA	La Crosse, WI-MN**	NA
236	Burlington, NC	(12.4)	213	Flagstaff, AZ	(8.0)	71	Lafayette, IN	3.4
NA	California-Lexington Park, MD**	NA	154	Flint, MI	(3.8)	NA	Lafayette, LA**	NA
NA	Cambridge-Newton, MA M.D.**	NA	4	Florence-Muscle Shoals, AL	23.6	143	Lake Co.-Kenosha Co., IL-WI M.D.	(3.2)
148	Camden, NJ M.D.	(3.7)	191	Florence, SC	(6.2)	35	Lake Havasu City-Kingman, AZ	7.5
161	Canton, OH	(4.0)	20	Fond du Lac, WI	10.8	205	Lakeland, FL	(7.3)
246	Cape Coral-Fort Myers, FL	(14.2)	122	Fort Collins, CO	(1.6)	148	Lancaster, PA	(3.7)
77	Cape Girardeau, MO-IL	2.7	184	Fort Lauderdale, FL M.D.	(5.6)	198	Lansing-East Lansing, MI	(6.6)
240	Carson City, NV	(13.6)	NA	Fort Smith, AR-OK**	NA	114	Laredo, TX	(0.9)
198	Casper, WY	(6.6)	57	Fort Wayne, IN	4.6	184	Las Cruces, NM	(5.6)
NA	Cedar Rapids, IA**	NA	224	Fort Worth-Arlington, TX M.D.	(9.8)	28	Las Vegas-Henderson, NV	8.5
NA	Chambersburg-Waynesboro, PA**	NA	89	Fresno, CA	1.7	98	Lawrence, KS	0.6
72	Champaign-Urbana, IL	3.3	115	Gadsden, AL	(1.1)	NA	Lawton, OK**	NA
NA	Charleston-North Charleston, SC**	NA	166	Gainesville, FL	(4.3)	40	Lebanon, PA	6.9
124	Charlottesville, VA	(1.7)	169	Gainesville, GA	(4.5)	78	Lewiston-Auburn, ME	2.6

Note: All listings are for Metropolitan Statistical Areas (M.S.A.s) except for those ending with "M.D." Listings with "M.D." are Metropolitan Divisions which are smaller parts of eleven large M.S.A.s. See explanatory note at beginning of metropolitan area section.

RANK	METROPOLITAN AREA	% CHANGE	RANK	METROPOLITAN AREA	% CHANGE	RANK	METROPOLITAN AREA	% CHANGE
NA	Lewiston, ID-WA**	NA	83	Owensboro, KY	2.1	180	Silver Spring-Frederick, MD M.D.	(5.4)
NA	Lexington-Fayette, KY**	NA	24	Oxnard-Thousand Oaks, CA	9.9	NA	Sioux City, IA-NE-SD**	NA
122	Lima, OH	(1.6)	216	Palm Bay-Melbourne, FL	(8.4)	41	Sioux Falls, SD	6.8
109	Lincoln, NE	(0.3)	NA	Panama City, FL**	NA	244	South Bend-Mishawaka, IN-MI	(13.9)
127	Little Rock, AR	(1.9)	NA	Parkersburg-Vienna, WV**	NA	NA	Spartanburg, SC**	NA
1	Logan, UT-ID	46.8	74	Pensacola, FL	2.9	NA	Spokane, WA**	NA
27	Longview, TX	8.9	118	Peoria, IL	(1.4)	144	Springfield, IL	(3.4)
25	Longview, WA	9.6	NA	Philadelphia (greater) PA-NJ-MD-DE**	NA	NA	Springfield, MA**	NA
101	Los Angeles County, CA M.D.	0.5	NA	Philadelphia, PA M.D.**	NA	88	Springfield, MO	1.8
86	Los Angeles (greater), CA	2.0	NA	Phoenix-Mesa-Scottsdale, AZ**	NA	118	Springfield, OH	(1.4)
201	Louisville, KY-IN	(7.0)	243	Pine Bluff, AR	(13.8)	227	State College, PA	(11.3)
134	Lubbock, TX	(2.3)	NA	Pittsburgh, PA**	NA	NA	Staunton-Waynesboro, VA**	NA
230	Lynchburg, VA	(11.6)	184	Pittsfield, MA	(5.6)	98	Stockton-Lodi, CA	0.6
239	Macon, GA	(13.5)	NA	Pocatello, ID**	NA	NA	St. George, UT**	NA
47	Madera, CA	6.3	247	Port St. Lucie, FL	(14.4)	15	St. Joseph, MO-KS	13.4
NA	Madison, WI**	NA	92	Portland-Vancouver, OR-WA	1.0	212	St. Louis, MO-IL	(7.7)
127	Manchester-Nashua, NH	(1.9)	165	Portland, ME	(4.2)	3	Sumter, SC	24.2
NA	Manhattan, KS**	NA	171	Prescott, AZ	(4.7)	NA	Syracuse, NY**	NA
NA	Mankato-North Mankato, MN**	NA	NA	Providence-Warwick, RI-MA**	NA	NA	Tacoma, WA M.D.**	NA
33	Mansfield, OH	7.7	250	Provo-Orem, UT	(15.3)	189	Tallahassee, FL	(5.9)
154	McAllen-Edinburg-Mission, TX	(3.8)	18	Pueblo, CO	11.2	209	Tampa-St Petersburg, FL	(7.5)
16	Medford, OR	12.4	234	Punta Gorda, FL	(12.2)	148	Terre Haute, IN	(3.7)
131	Memphis, TN-MS-AR	(2.1)	177	Racine, WI	(5.3)	NA	Texarkana, TX-AR**	NA
17	Merced, CA	11.6	166	Raleigh, NC	(4.3)	NA	The Villages, FL**	NA
191	Miami (greater), FL	(6.2)	NA	Rapid City, SD**	NA	NA	Toledo, OH**	NA
208	Miami-Dade County, FL M.D.	(7.4)	65	Reading, PA	3.9	205	Topeka, KS	(7.3)
197	Michigan City-La Porte, IN	(6.5)	5	Redding, CA	21.1	83	Trenton, NJ	2.1
NA	Midland, MI**	NA	38	Reno, NV	7.2	NA	Tucson, AZ**	NA
NA	Midland, TX**	NA	75	Richmond, VA	2.8	175	Tulsa, OK	(5.2)
54	Milwaukee, WI	5.2	41	Riverside-San Bernardino, CA	6.8	NA	Tuscaloosa, AL**	NA
NA	Minneapolis-St. Paul, MN-WI**	NA	105	Roanoke, VA	0.0	124	Tyler, TX	(1.7)
2	Missoula, MT	24.8	NA	Rochester, MN**	NA	NA	Utica-Rome, NY**	NA
225	Mobile, AL	(10.4)	NA	Rochester, NY**	NA	204	Valdosta, GA	(7.2)
13	Modesto, CA	14.4	22	Rockford, IL	10.2	31	Vallejo-Fairfield, CA	8.0
144	Monroe, LA	(3.4)	105	Rockingham County, NH M.D.	0.0	NA	Victoria, TX**	NA
44	Monroe, MI	6.6	182	Rocky Mount, NC	(5.5)	NA	Vineland-Bridgeton, NJ**	NA
NA	Montgomery County, PA M.D.**	NA	91	Rome, GA	1.1	195	Virginia Beach-Norfolk, VA-NC	(6.4)
26	Montgomery, AL	9.5	67	Sacramento, CA	3.7	94	Visalia-Porterville, CA	0.8
NA	Morgantown, WV**	NA	148	Saginaw, MI	(3.7)	NA	Waco, TX**	NA
NA	Morristown, TN**	NA	11	Salem, OR	14.6	NA	Walla Walla, WA**	NA
188	Mount Vernon-Anacortes, WA	(5.8)	90	Salinas, CA	1.3	NA	Warner Robins, GA**	NA
69	Muncie, IN	3.5	NA	Salisbury, MD-DE**	NA	158	Warren-Troy, MI M.D.	(3.9)
86	Napa, CA	2.0	56	Salt Lake City, UT	5.1	158	Washington (greater) DC-VA-MD-WV	(3.9)
235	Naples-Marco Island, FL	(12.3)	102	San Antonio, TX	0.3	148	Washington, DC-VA-MD-WV M.D.	(3.7)
NA	Nashville-Davidson, TN**	NA	49	San Diego, CA	5.8	19	Waterloo-Cedar Falls, IA	11.0
NA	Nassau-Suffolk, NY M.D.**	NA	NA	San Francisco (greater), CA**	NA	NA	Watertown-Fort Drum, NY**	NA
NA	New Bern, NC**	NA	8	San Francisco-Redwood, CA M.D.	19.6	194	Wausau, WI	(6.3)
108	New Haven-Milford, CT	(0.1)	7	San Jose, CA	19.8	161	West Palm Beach, FL M.D.	(4.0)
154	New Orleans, LA	(3.8)	69	San Luis Obispo, CA	3.5	NA	Wheeling, WV-OH**	NA
NA	New York (greater), NY-NJ-PA**	NA	NA	San Rafael, CA M.D.**	NA	57	Wichita Falls, TX	4.6
NA	New York-Jersey City, NY-NJ M.D.**	NA	131	Santa Cruz-Watsonville, CA	(2.1)	62	Wichita, KS	4.3
NA	Newark, NJ-PA M.D.**	NA	96	Santa Fe, NM	0.7	121	Williamsport, PA	(1.5)
251	North Port-Sarasota-Bradenton, FL	(15.9)	NA	Santa Maria-Santa Barbara, CA**	NA	80	Wilmington, DE-MD-NJ M.D.	2.3
50	Norwich-New London, CT	5.6	80	Santa Rosa, CA	2.3	NA	Wilmington, NC**	NA
NA	Oakland-Hayward, CA M.D.**	NA	237	Savannah, GA	(12.8)	83	Winchester, VA-WV	2.1
229	Ocala, FL	(11.5)	96	Scranton--Wilkes-Barre, PA	0.7	NA	Winston-Salem, NC**	NA
144	Ocean City, NJ	(3.4)	NA	Seattle (greater), WA**	NA	NA	Worcester, MA-CT**	NA
6	Odessa, TX	20.4	102	Seattle-Bellevue-Everett, WA M.D.	0.3	131	Yakima, WA	(2.1)
NA	Ogden-Clearfield, UT**	NA	172	Sebastian-Vero Beach, FL	(4.9)	141	York-Hanover, PA	(3.1)
79	Oklahoma City, OK	2.4	NA	Sebring, FL**	NA	NA	Youngstown-Warren, OH-PA**	NA
60	Olympia, WA	4.4	62	Sheboygan, WI	4.3	94	Yuba City, CA	0.8
92	Omaha-Council Bluffs, NE-IA	1.0	158	Sherman-Denison, TX	(3.9)	141	Yuma, AZ	(3.1)
177	Orlando, FL	(5.3)	NA	Shreveport-Bossier City, LA**	NA			
54	Oshkosh-Neenah, WI	5.2	NA	Sierra Vista-Douglas, AZ**	NA			

Source: CQ Press using reported data from the F.B.I. "Crime in the United States 2012"

*Includes murder, rape, robbery, aggravated assault, burglary, larceny-theft, and motor vehicle theft.

**Not available.

3. Percent Change in Crime Rate: 2011 to 2012 (continued)
National Percent Change = 1.4% Decrease*

RANK	METROPOLITAN AREA	% CHANGE	RANK	METROPOLITAN AREA	% CHANGE	RANK	METROPOLITAN AREA	% CHANGE
1	Logan, UT-ID	46.8	65	Cheyenne, WY	3.9	127	Manchester-Nashua, NH	(1.9)
2	Missoula, MT	24.8	65	Reading, PA	3.9	130	Houma, LA	(2.0)
3	Sumter, SC	24.2	67	Sacramento, CA	3.7	131	Memphis, TN-MS-AR	(2.1)
4	Florence-Muscle Shoals, AL	23.6	68	Greeley, CO	3.6	131	Santa Cruz-Watsonville, CA	(2.1)
5	Redding, CA	21.1	69	Muncie, IN	3.5	131	Yakima, WA	(2.1)
6	Odessa, TX	20.4	69	San Luis Obispo, CA	3.5	134	Baltimore, MD	(2.3)
7	San Jose, CA	19.8	71	Lafayette, IN	3.4	134	Lubbock, TX	(2.3)
8	San Francisco-Redwood, CA M.D.	19.6	72	Champaign-Urbana, IL	3.3	136	Cleveland, TN	(2.6)
9	Joplin, MO	15.6	73	Billings, MT	3.0	137	Boise City, ID	(2.7)
10	Farmington, NM	15.1	74	Pensacola, FL	2.9	137	Harrisburg-Carlisle, PA	(2.7)
11	Decatur, AL	14.6	75	Dothan, AL	2.8	139	Erie, PA	(2.8)
11	Salem, OR	14.6	75	Richmond, VA	2.8	140	El Paso, TX	(2.9)
13	Modesto, CA	14.4	77	Cape Girardeau, MO-IL	2.7	141	York-Hanover, PA	(3.1)
14	Bakersfield, CA	13.8	78	Lewiston-Auburn, ME	2.6	141	Yuma, AZ	(3.1)
15	St. Joseph, MO-KS	13.4	79	Oklahoma City, OK	2.4	143	Lake Co.-Kenosha Co., IL-WI M.D.	(3.2)
16	Medford, OR	12.4	80	Columbia, MO	2.3	144	Monroe, LA	(3.4)
17	Merced, CA	11.6	80	Santa Rosa, CA	2.3	144	Ocean City, NJ	(3.4)
18	Pueblo, CO	11.2	80	Wilmington, DE-MD-NJ M.D.	2.3	144	Springfield, IL	(3.4)
19	Waterloo-Cedar Falls, IA	11.0	83	Owensboro, KY	2.1	147	Huntsville, AL	(3.6)
20	Fond du Lac, WI	10.8	83	Trenton, NJ	2.1	148	Brownsville-Harlingen, TX	(3.7)
21	Green Bay, WI	10.3	83	Winchester, VA-WV	2.1	148	Camden, NJ M.D.	(3.7)
22	Rockford, IL	10.2	86	Los Angeles (greater), CA	2.0	148	Lancaster, PA	(3.7)
23	Asheville, NC	10.1	86	Napa, CA	2.0	148	Saginaw, MI	(3.7)
24	Oxnard-Thousand Oaks, CA	9.9	88	Springfield, MO	1.8	148	Terre Haute, IN	(3.7)
25	Longview, WA	9.6	89	Fresno, CA	1.7	148	Washington, DC-VA-MD-WV M.D.	(3.7)
26	Montgomery, AL	9.5	90	Salinas, CA	1.3	154	Flint, MI	(3.8)
27	Longview, TX	8.9	91	Rome, GA	1.1	154	Jefferson City, MO	(3.8)
28	Las Vegas-Henderson, NV	8.5	92	Omaha-Council Bluffs, NE-IA	1.0	154	McAllen-Edinburg-Mission, TX	(3.8)
29	El Centro, CA	8.3	92	Portland-Vancouver, OR-WA	1.0	154	New Orleans, LA	(3.8)
30	Anaheim-Santa Ana-Irvine, CA M.D.	8.1	94	Visalia-Porterville, CA	0.8	158	Sherman-Denison, TX	(3.9)
31	Vallejo-Fairfield, CA	8.0	94	Yuba City, CA	0.8	158	Warren-Troy, MI M.D.	(3.9)
32	Fairbanks, AK	7.9	96	Santa Fe, NM	0.7	158	Washington (greater) DC-VA-MD-WV	(3.9)
33	Iowa City, IA	7.7	96	Scranton--Wilkes-Barre, PA	0.7	161	Canton, OH	(4.0)
33	Mansfield, OH	7.7	98	Bay City, MI	0.6	161	West Palm Beach, FL M.D.	(4.0)
35	Harrisonburg, VA	7.5	98	Lawrence, KS	0.6	163	Atlanta, GA	(4.1)
35	Lake Havasu City-Kingman, AZ	7.5	98	Stockton-Lodi, CA	0.6	163	Detroit-Dearborn-Livonia, MI M.D.	(4.1)
37	Bangor, ME	7.3	101	Los Angeles County, CA M.D.	0.5	165	Portland, ME	(4.2)
38	Reno, NV	7.2	102	Abilene, TX	0.3	166	Detroit (greater), MI	(4.3)
39	Albany, GA	7.0	102	San Antonio, TX	0.3	166	Gainesville, FL	(4.3)
40	Lebanon, PA	6.9	102	Seattle-Bellevue-Everett, WA M.D.	0.3	166	Raleigh, NC	(4.3)
41	Riverside-San Bernardino, CA	6.8	105	Hartford, CT	0.0	169	Barnstable Town, MA	(4.5)
41	Sioux Falls, SD	6.8	105	Roanoke, VA	0.0	169	Gainesville, GA	(4.5)
43	Chico, CA	6.7	105	Rockingham County, NH M.D.	0.0	171	Prescott, AZ	(4.7)
44	Monroe, MI	6.6	108	New Haven-Milford, CT	(0.1)	172	Hickory, NC	(4.9)
45	Anniston-Oxford, AL	6.4	109	Austin-Round Rock, TX	(0.3)	172	Sebastian-Vero Beach, FL	(4.9)
45	Boulder, CO	6.4	109	Lincoln, NE	(0.3)	174	Kankakee, IL	(5.0)
47	Madera, CA	6.3	111	Bloomington, IL	(0.4)	175	Crestview-Fort Walton Beach, FL	(5.2)
48	Grand Junction, CO	6.0	112	Cumberland, MD-WV	(0.7)	175	Tulsa, OK	(5.2)
49	San Diego, CA	5.8	112	Dover, DE	(0.7)	177	Goldsboro, NC	(5.3)
50	Bremerton-Silverdale, WA	5.6	114	Laredo, TX	(0.9)	177	Orlando, FL	(5.3)
50	Norwich-New London, CT	5.6	115	Bellingham, WA	(1.1)	177	Racine, WI	(5.3)
52	Hanford-Corcoran, CA	5.5	115	Dayton, OH	(1.1)	180	Dalton, GA	(5.4)
53	Eugene, OR	5.3	115	Gadsden, AL	(1.1)	180	Silver Spring-Frederick, MD M.D.	(5.4)
54	Milwaukee, WI	5.2	118	Fayetteville, NC	(1.4)	182	Birmingham-Hoover, AL	(5.5)
54	Oshkosh-Neenah, WI	5.2	118	Peoria, IL	(1.4)	182	Rocky Mount, NC	(5.5)
56	Salt Lake City, UT	5.1	118	Springfield, OH	(1.4)	184	Fort Lauderdale, FL M.D.	(5.6)
57	Ann Arbor, MI	4.6	121	Williamsport, PA	(1.5)	184	Jacksonville, FL	(5.6)
57	Fort Wayne, IN	4.6	122	Fort Collins, CO	(1.6)	184	Las Cruces, NM	(5.6)
57	Wichita Falls, TX	4.6	122	Lima, OH	(1.6)	184	Pittsfield, MA	(5.6)
60	Great Falls, MT	4.4	124	Charlottesville, VA	(1.7)	188	Mount Vernon-Anacortes, WA	(5.8)
60	Olympia, WA	4.4	124	Johnson City, TN	(1.7)	189	Tallahassee, FL	(5.9)
62	Sheboygan, WI	4.3	124	Tyler, TX	(1.7)	190	Hinesville, GA	(6.1)
62	Wichita, KS	4.3	127	Janesville, WI	(1.9)	191	Bridgeport-Stamford, CT	(6.2)
64	Bismarck, ND	4.2	127	Little Rock, AR	(1.9)	191	Florence, SC	(6.2)

Note: All listings are for Metropolitan Statistical Areas (M.S.A.s) except for those ending with "M.D." Listings with "M.D." are Metropolitan Divisions which are smaller parts of eleven large M.S.A.s. See explanatory note at beginning of metropolitan area section.

RANK	METROPOLITAN AREA	% CHANGE	RANK	METROPOLITAN AREA	% CHANGE	RANK	METROPOLITAN AREA	% CHANGE
191	Miami (greater), FL	(6.2)	NA	Alexandria, LA**	NA	NA	Lexington-Fayette, KY**	NA
194	Wausau, WI	(6.3)	NA	Allentown, PA-NJ**	NA	NA	Madison, WI**	NA
195	Amarillo, TX	(6.4)	NA	Anchorage, AK**	NA	NA	Manhattan, KS**	NA
195	Virginia Beach-Norfolk, VA-NC	(6.4)	NA	Atlantic City, NJ**	NA	NA	Mankato-North Mankato, MN**	NA
197	Michigan City-La Porte, IN	(6.5)	NA	Baton Rouge, LA**	NA	NA	Midland, MI**	NA
198	Casper, WY	(6.6)	NA	Beckley, WV**	NA	NA	Midland, TX**	NA
198	Lansing-East Lansing, MI	(6.6)	NA	Binghamton, NY**	NA	NA	Minneapolis-St. Paul, MN-WI**	NA
200	Clarksville, TN-KY	(6.7)	NA	Bloomington, IN**	NA	NA	Montgomery County, PA M.D.**	NA
201	Bowling Green, KY	(7.0)	NA	Bloomsburg-Berwick, PA**	NA	NA	Morgantown, WV**	NA
201	Danville, IL	(7.0)	NA	Boston (greater), MA-NH**	NA	NA	Morristown, TN**	NA
201	Louisville, KY-IN	(7.0)	NA	Boston, MA M.D.**	NA	NA	Nashville-Davidson, TN**	NA
204	Valdosta, GA	(7.2)	NA	Buffalo-Niagara Falls, NY**	NA	NA	Nassau-Suffolk, NY M.D.**	NA
205	Akron, OH	(7.3)	NA	California-Lexington Park, MD**	NA	NA	New Bern, NC**	NA
205	Lakeland, FL	(7.3)	NA	Cambridge-Newton, MA M.D.**	NA	NA	New York (greater), NY-NJ-PA**	NA
205	Topeka, KS	(7.3)	NA	Cedar Rapids, IA**	NA	NA	New York-Jersey City, NY-NJ M.D.**	NA
208	Miami-Dade County, FL M.D.	(7.4)	NA	Chambersburg-Waynesboro, PA**	NA	NA	Newark, NJ-PA M.D.**	NA
209	Appleton, WI	(7.5)	NA	Charleston-North Charleston, SC**	NA	NA	Oakland-Hayward, CA M.D.**	NA
209	Kingsport, TN-VA	(7.5)	NA	Chicago (greater), IL-IN-WI**	NA	NA	Ogden-Clearfield, UT**	NA
209	Tampa-St Petersburg, FL	(7.5)	NA	Chicago-Joilet-Naperville, IL M.D.**	NA	NA	Panama City, FL**	NA
212	St. Louis, MO-IL	(7.7)	NA	Cincinnati, OH-KY-IN**	NA	NA	Parkersburg-Vienna, WV**	NA
213	Flagstaff, AZ	(8.0)	NA	Coeur d'Alene, ID**	NA	NA	Philadelphia (greater) PA-NJ-MD-DE**	NA
214	Dallas-Plano-Irving, TX M.D.	(8.2)	NA	Colorado Springs, CO**	NA	NA	Philadelphia, PA M.D.**	NA
215	Columbus, GA-AL	(8.3)	NA	Corpus Christi, TX**	NA	NA	Phoenix-Mesa-Scottsdale, AZ**	NA
216	Augusta, GA-SC	(8.4)	NA	Daphne-Fairhope-Foley, AL**	NA	NA	Pittsburgh, PA**	NA
216	Gary, IN M.D.	(8.4)	NA	Deltona-Daytona Beach, FL**	NA	NA	Pocatello, ID**	NA
216	Palm Bay-Melbourne, FL	(8.4)	NA	Denver-Aurora, CO**	NA	NA	Providence-Warwick, RI-MA**	NA
219	Dallas (greater), TX	(8.7)	NA	Des Moines-West Des Moines, IA**	NA	NA	Rapid City, SD**	NA
219	Durham-Chapel Hill, NC	(8.7)	NA	Dubuque, IA**	NA	NA	Rochester, MN**	NA
221	Idaho Falls, ID	(9.1)	NA	Duluth, MN-WI**	NA	NA	Rochester, NY**	NA
221	Kennewick-Richland, WA	(9.1)	NA	Dutchess-Putnam, NY M.D.**	NA	NA	Salisbury, MD-DE**	NA
223	Athens-Clarke County, GA	(9.2)	NA	East Stroudsburg, PA**	NA	NA	San Francisco (greater), CA**	NA
224	Fort Worth-Arlington, TX M.D.	(9.8)	NA	Elgin, IL M.D.**	NA	NA	San Rafael, CA M.D.**	NA
225	Mobile, AL	(10.4)	NA	Elizabethtown-Fort Knox, KY**	NA	NA	Santa Maria-Santa Barbara, CA**	NA
226	Brunswick, GA	(10.6)	NA	Elmira, NY**	NA	NA	Seattle (greater), WA**	NA
227	State College, PA	(11.3)	NA	Fargo, ND-MN**	NA	NA	Sebring, FL**	NA
228	Jonesboro, AR	(11.4)	NA	Fayetteville-Springdale, AR-MO**	NA	NA	Shreveport-Bossier City, LA**	NA
229	Ocala, FL	(11.5)	NA	Fort Smith, AR-OK**	NA	NA	Sierra Vista-Douglas, AZ**	NA
230	Lynchburg, VA	(11.6)	NA	Gettysburg, PA**	NA	NA	Sioux City, IA-NE-SD**	NA
231	Auburn, AL	(11.9)	NA	Glens Falls, NY**	NA	NA	Spartanburg, SC**	NA
231	Blacksburg, VA	(11.9)	NA	Grand Forks, ND-MN**	NA	NA	Spokane, WA**	NA
233	Davenport, IA-IL	(12.0)	NA	Grand Island, NE**	NA	NA	Springfield, MA**	NA
234	Punta Gorda, FL	(12.2)	NA	Greensboro-High Point, NC**	NA	NA	Staunton-Waynesboro, VA**	NA
235	Naples-Marco Island, FL	(12.3)	NA	Greenville-Anderson, SC**	NA	NA	St. George, UT**	NA
236	Burlington, NC	(12.4)	NA	Greenville, NC**	NA	NA	Syracuse, NY**	NA
237	Savannah, GA	(12.8)	NA	Hagerstown-Martinsburg, MD-WV**	NA	NA	Tacoma, WA M.D.**	NA
238	College Station-Bryan, TX	(13.4)	NA	Hammond, LA**	NA	NA	Texarkana, TX-AR**	NA
239	Macon, GA	(13.5)	NA	Hattiesburg, MS**	NA	NA	The Villages, FL**	NA
240	Carson City, NV	(13.6)	NA	Hilton Head Island, SC**	NA	NA	Toledo, OH**	NA
240	Johnstown, PA	(13.6)	NA	Homosassa Springs, FL**	NA	NA	Tucson, AZ**	NA
242	Decatur, IL	(13.7)	NA	Houston, TX**	NA	NA	Tuscaloosa, AL**	NA
243	Pine Bluff, AR	(13.8)	NA	Indianapolis, IN**	NA	NA	Utica-Rome, NY**	NA
244	South Bend-Mishawaka, IN-MI	(13.9)	NA	Jackson, MS**	NA	NA	Victoria, TX**	NA
245	Columbus, IN	(14.1)	NA	Jackson, TN**	NA	NA	Vineland-Bridgeton, NJ**	NA
246	Cape Coral-Fort Myers, FL	(14.2)	NA	Kahului-Wailuku-Lahaina, HI**	NA	NA	Waco, TX**	NA
247	Port St. Lucie, FL	(14.4)	NA	Kalamazoo-Portage, MI**	NA	NA	Walla Walla, WA**	NA
248	Beaumont-Port Arthur, TX	(14.5)	NA	Kansas City, MO-KS**	NA	NA	Warner Robins, GA**	NA
249	Altoona, PA	(14.6)	NA	Killeen-Temple, TX**	NA	NA	Watertown-Fort Drum, NY**	NA
250	Provo-Orem, UT	(15.3)	NA	Kingston, NY**	NA	NA	Wheeling, WV-OH**	NA
251	North Port-Sarasota-Bradenton, FL	(15.9)	NA	Knoxville, TN**	NA	NA	Wilmington, NC**	NA
252	Ames, IA	(16.8)	NA	Kokomo, IN**	NA	NA	Winston-Salem, NC**	NA
252	Corvallis, OR	(16.8)	NA	La Crosse, WI-MN**	NA	NA	Worcester, MA-CT**	NA
NA	Albany-Schenectady-Troy, NY**	NA	NA	Lafayette, LA**	NA	NA	Youngstown-Warren, OH-PA**	NA
NA	Albany, OR**	NA	NA	Lawton, OK**	NA			
NA	Albuquerque, NM**	NA	NA	Lewiston, ID-WA**	NA			

Source: CQ Press using reported data from the F.B.I. "Crime in the United States 2012"

*Includes murder, rape, robbery, aggravated assault, burglary, larceny-theft, and motor vehicle theft.

**Not available.

4. Percent Change in Crime Rate: 2008 to 2012
National Percent Change = 11.6% Decrease*

RANK	METROPOLITAN AREA	% CHANGE	RANK	METROPOLITAN AREA	% CHANGE	RANK	METROPOLITAN AREA	% CHANGE
97	Abilene, TX	(9.0)	163	Cheyenne, WY	(17.3)	NA	Gary, IN M.D.**	NA
93	Akron, OH	(8.4)	NA	Chicago (greater), IL-IN-WI**	NA	NA	Gettysburg, PA**	NA
NA	Albany-Schenectady-Troy, NY**	NA	NA	Chicago-Joilet-Naperville, IL M.D.**	NA	NA	Glens Falls, NY**	NA
NA	Albany, GA**	NA	155	Chico, CA	(16.4)	165	Goldsboro, NC	(17.6)
NA	Albany, OR**	NA	NA	Cincinnati, OH-KY-IN**	NA	NA	Grand Forks, ND-MN**	NA
NA	Albuquerque, NM**	NA	172	Clarksville, TN-KY	(18.8)	NA	Grand Island, NE**	NA
NA	Alexandria, LA**	NA	108	Cleveland, TN	(11.2)	61	Grand Junction, CO	(3.8)
NA	Allentown, PA-NJ**	NA	NA	Coeur d'Alene, ID**	NA	47	Great Falls, MT	(1.0)
191	Altoona, PA	(21.0)	227	College Station-Bryan, TX	(31.4)	135	Greeley, CO	(13.5)
166	Amarillo, TX	(17.8)	NA	Colorado Springs, CO**	NA	159	Green Bay, WI	(16.8)
175	Ames, IA	(19.2)	31	Columbia, MO	3.3	212	Greensboro-High Point, NC	(24.2)
39	Anaheim-Santa Ana-Irvine, CA M.D.	1.7	185	Columbus, GA-AL	(20.1)	NA	Greenville-Anderson, SC**	NA
NA	Anchorage, AK**	NA	15	Columbus, IN	13.4	225	Greenville, NC	(30.7)
118	Ann Arbor, MI	(11.8)	NA	Corpus Christi, TX**	NA	NA	Hagerstown-Martinsburg, MD-WV**	NA
NA	Anniston-Oxford, AL**	NA	107	Corvallis, OR	(10.7)	NA	Hammond, LA**	NA
232	Appleton, WI	(35.7)	NA	Crestview-Fort Walton Beach, FL**	NA	62	Hanford-Corcoran, CA	(3.9)
62	Asheville, NC	(3.9)	43	Cumberland, MD-WV	1.2	66	Harrisburg-Carlisle, PA	(4.2)
219	Athens-Clarke County, GA	(27.7)	201	Dallas (greater), TX	(22.1)	97	Harrisonburg, VA	(9.0)
152	Atlanta, GA	(15.7)	208	Dallas-Plano-Irving, TX M.D.	(23.7)	135	Hartford, CT	(13.5)
NA	Atlantic City, NJ**	NA	85	Dalton, GA	(6.8)	NA	Hattiesburg, MS**	NA
233	Auburn, AL	(42.4)	NA	Danville, IL**	NA	77	Hickory, NC	(6.0)
NA	Augusta, GA-SC**	NA	NA	Daphne-Fairhope-Foley, AL**	NA	NA	Hilton Head Island, SC**	NA
123	Austin-Round Rock, TX	(12.4)	NA	Davenport, IA-IL**	NA	203	Hinesville, GA	(22.7)
37	Bakersfield, CA	1.8	70	Dayton, OH	(4.7)	NA	Homosassa Springs, FL**	NA
159	Baltimore, MD	(16.8)	194	Decatur, AL	(21.5)	51	Houma, LA	(1.9)
86	Bangor, ME	(7.0)	NA	Decatur, IL**	NA	NA	Houston, TX**	NA
99	Barnstable Town, MA	(9.3)	170	Deltona-Daytona Beach, FL	(18.7)	123	Huntsville, AL	(12.4)
NA	Baton Rouge, LA**	NA	NA	Denver-Aurora, CO**	NA	194	Idaho Falls, ID	(21.5)
206	Bay City, MI	(23.5)	NA	Des Moines-West Des Moines, IA**	NA	95	Indianapolis, IN	(8.6)
142	Beaumont-Port Arthur, TX	(14.3)	NA	Detroit (greater), MI**	NA	78	Iowa City, IA	(6.4)
NA	Beckley, WV**	NA	NA	Detroit-Dearborn-Livonia, MI M.D.**	NA	222	Jacksonville, FL	(29.1)
148	Bellingham, WA	(14.8)	137	Dothan, AL	(13.8)	NA	Jackson, MS**	NA
29	Billings, MT	4.5	33	Dover, DE	2.8	NA	Jackson, TN**	NA
NA	Binghamton, NY**	NA	NA	Dubuque, IA**	NA	119	Janesville, WI	(12.0)
168	Birmingham-Hoover, AL	(18.2)	NA	Duluth, MN-WI**	NA	NA	Jefferson City, MO**	NA
11	Bismarck, ND	16.5	174	Durham-Chapel Hill, NC	(18.9)	36	Johnson City, TN	1.9
189	Blacksburg, VA	(20.7)	NA	Dutchess-Putnam, NY M.D.**	NA	82	Johnstown, PA	(6.7)
NA	Bloomington, IL**	NA	NA	East Stroudsburg, PA**	NA	130	Jonesboro, AR	(13.2)
7	Bloomington, IN	21.1	68	El Centro, CA	(4.5)	65	Joplin, MO	(4.1)
NA	Bloomsburg-Berwick, PA**	NA	207	El Paso, TX	(23.6)	NA	Kahului-Wailuku-Lahaina, HI**	NA
127	Boise City, ID	(12.6)	NA	Elgin, IL M.D.**	NA	208	Kalamazoo-Portage, MI	(23.7)
NA	Boston (greater), MA-NH**	NA	NA	Elizabethtown-Fort Knox, KY**	NA	NA	Kankakee, IL**	NA
NA	Boston, MA M.D.**	NA	NA	Elmira, NY**	NA	NA	Kansas City, MO-KS**	NA
NA	Boulder, CO**	NA	32	Erie, PA	2.9	96	Kennewick-Richland, WA	(8.9)
215	Bowling Green, KY	(25.1)	189	Eugene, OR	(20.7)	NA	Killeen-Temple, TX**	NA
22	Bremerton-Silverdale, WA	8.6	NA	Fairbanks, AK**	NA	115	Kingsport, TN-VA	(11.6)
134	Bridgeport-Stamford, CT	(13.4)	NA	Fargo, ND-MN**	NA	NA	Kingston, NY**	NA
180	Brownsville-Harlingen, TX	(19.7)	NA	Farmington, NM**	NA	NA	Knoxville, TN**	NA
NA	Brunswick, GA**	NA	27	Fayetteville-Springdale, AR-MO	5.3	NA	Kokomo, IN**	NA
NA	Buffalo-Niagara Falls, NY**	NA	130	Fayetteville, NC	(13.2)	NA	La Crosse, WI-MN**	NA
151	Burlington, NC	(15.6)	164	Flagstaff, AZ	(17.5)	54	Lafayette, IN	(2.5)
NA	California-Lexington Park, MD**	NA	34	Flint, MI	2.4	NA	Lafayette, LA**	NA
NA	Cambridge-Newton, MA M.D.**	NA	161	Florence-Muscle Shoals, AL	(17.0)	NA	Lake Co.-Kenosha Co., IL-WI M.D.**	NA
82	Camden, NJ M.D.	(6.7)	162	Florence, SC	(17.2)	62	Lake Havasu City-Kingman, AZ	(3.9)
NA	Canton, OH**	NA	75	Fond du Lac, WI	(5.8)	214	Lakeland, FL	(24.8)
230	Cape Coral-Fort Myers, FL	(32.2)	121	Fort Collins, CO	(12.1)	87	Lancaster, PA	(7.1)
16	Cape Girardeau, MO-IL	12.8	101	Fort Lauderdale, FL M.D.	(9.6)	169	Lansing-East Lansing, MI	(18.6)
183	Carson City, NV	(19.9)	NA	Fort Smith, AR-OK**	NA	226	Laredo, TX	(30.9)
186	Casper, WY	(20.4)	74	Fort Wayne, IN	(5.6)	82	Las Cruces, NM	(6.7)
NA	Cedar Rapids, IA**	NA	177	Fort Worth-Arlington, TX M.D.	(19.3)	172	Las Vegas-Henderson, NV	(18.8)
NA	Chambersburg-Waynesboro, PA**	NA	23	Fresno, CA	8.5	129	Lawrence, KS	(12.8)
NA	Champaign-Urbana, IL**	NA	8	Gadsden, AL	19.5	NA	Lawton, OK**	NA
199	Charleston-North Charleston, SC	(21.9)	205	Gainesville, FL	(23.4)	25	Lebanon, PA	6.2
204	Charlottesville, VA	(23.0)	NA	Gainesville, GA**	NA	3	Lewiston-Auburn, ME	29.6

Note: All listings are for Metropolitan Statistical Areas (M.S.A.s) except for those ending with "M.D." Listings with "M.D." are Metropolitan Divisions which are smaller parts of eleven large M.S.A.s. See explanatory note at beginning of metropolitan area section.

RANK	METROPOLITAN AREA	% CHANGE
6	Lewiston, ID-WA	22.6
NA	Lexington-Fayette, KY**	NA
182	Lima, OH	(19.8)
80	Lincoln, NE	(6.6)
67	Little Rock, AR	(4.4)
71	Logan, UT-ID	(5.0)
193	Longview, TX	(21.4)
52	Longview, WA	(2.2)
142	Los Angeles County, CA M.D.	(14.3)
112	Los Angeles (greater), CA	(11.4)
55	Louisville, KY-IN	(2.7)
112	Lubbock, TX	(11.4)
186	Lynchburg, VA	(20.4)
137	Macon, GA	(13.8)
9	Madera, CA	19.4
NA	Madison, WI**	NA
NA	Manchester-Nashua, NH**	NA
NA	Manhattan, KS**	NA
NA	Mankato-North Mankato, MN**	NA
12	Mansfield, OH	14.6
167	McAllen-Edinburg-Mission, TX	(17.9)
1	Medford, OR	42.1
200	Memphis, TN-MS-AR	(22.0)
24	Merced, CA	7.1
170	Miami (greater), FL	(18.7)
196	Miami-Dade County, FL M.D.	(21.6)
157	Michigan City-La Porte, IN	(16.7)
NA	Midland, MI**	NA
NA	Midland, TX**	NA
106	Milwaukee, WI	(10.4)
NA	Minneapolis-St. Paul, MN-WI**	NA
18	Missoula, MT	11.3
101	Mobile, AL	(9.6)
72	Modesto, CA	(5.3)
110	Monroe, LA	(11.3)
21	Monroe, MI	8.9
NA	Montgomery County, PA M.D.**	NA
72	Montgomery, AL	(5.3)
NA	Morgantown, WV**	NA
NA	Morristown, TN**	NA
87	Mount Vernon-Anacortes, WA	(7.1)
35	Muncie, IN	2.1
197	Napa, CA	(21.8)
157	Naples-Marco Island, FL	(16.7)
NA	Nashville-Davidson, TN**	NA
NA	Nassau-Suffolk, NY M.D.**	NA
NA	New Bern, NC**	NA
NA	New Haven-Milford, CT**	NA
175	New Orleans, LA	(19.2)
NA	New York (greater), NY-NJ-PA**	NA
NA	New York-Jersey City, NY-NJ M.D.**	NA
NA	Newark, NJ-PA M.D.**	NA
NA	North Port-Sarasota-Bradenton, FL**	NA
50	Norwich-New London, CT	(1.6)
NA	Oakland-Hayward, CA M.D.**	NA
153	Ocala, FL	(16.1)
87	Ocean City, NJ	(7.1)
57	Odessa, TX	(2.9)
NA	Ogden-Clearfield, UT**	NA
45	Oklahoma City, OK	0.8
141	Olympia, WA	(14.2)
58	Omaha-Council Bluffs, NE-IA	(3.2)
210	Orlando, FL	(23.8)
154	Oshkosh-Neenah, WI	(16.2)
NA	Owensboro, KY**	NA
91	Oxnard-Thousand Oaks, CA	(8.1)
144	Palm Bay-Melbourne, FL	(14.4)
NA	Panama City, FL**	NA
NA	Parkersburg-Vienna, WV**	NA
20	Pensacola, FL	9.6
NA	Peoria, IL**	NA
NA	Philadelphia (greater) PA-NJ-MD-DE**	NA
NA	Philadelphia, PA M.D.**	NA
NA	Phoenix-Mesa-Scottsdale, AZ**	NA
218	Pine Bluff, AR	(26.3)
NA	Pittsburgh, PA**	NA
48	Pittsfield, MA	(1.1)
NA	Pocatello, ID**	NA
216	Port St. Lucie, FL	(25.3)
59	Portland-Vancouver, OR-WA	(3.5)
42	Portland, ME	1.4
99	Prescott, AZ	(9.3)
105	Providence-Warwick, RI-MA	(10.1)
188	Provo-Orem, UT	(20.5)
NA	Pueblo, CO**	NA
231	Punta Gorda, FL	(34.0)
150	Racine, WI	(14.9)
NA	Raleigh, NC**	NA
NA	Rapid City, SD**	NA
104	Reading, PA	(10.0)
5	Redding, CA	23.3
221	Reno, NV	(28.4)
115	Richmond, VA	(11.6)
60	Riverside-San Bernardino, CA	(3.7)
117	Roanoke, VA	(11.7)
NA	Rochester, MN**	NA
NA	Rochester, NY**	NA
NA	Rockford, IL**	NA
10	Rockingham County, NH M.D.	16.6
NA	Rocky Mount, NC**	NA
NA	Rome, GA**	NA
128	Sacramento, CA	(12.7)
224	Saginaw, MI	(30.6)
80	Salem, OR	(6.6)
137	Salinas, CA	(13.8)
NA	Salisbury, MD-DE**	NA
92	Salt Lake City, UT	(8.2)
197	San Antonio, TX	(21.8)
192	San Diego, CA	(21.2)
NA	San Francisco (greater), CA**	NA
39	San Francisco-Redwood, CA M.D.	1.7
28	San Jose, CA	5.1
49	San Luis Obispo, CA	(1.3)
NA	San Rafael, CA M.D.**	NA
46	Santa Cruz-Watsonville, CA	0.1
13	Santa Fe, NM	13.8
NA	Santa Maria-Santa Barbara, CA**	NA
103	Santa Rosa, CA	(9.8)
222	Savannah, GA	(29.1)
52	Scranton--Wilkes-Barre, PA	(2.2)
NA	Seattle (greater), WA**	NA
NA	Seattle-Bellevue-Everett, WA M.D.**	NA
155	Sebastian-Vero Beach, FL	(16.4)
NA	Sebring, FL**	NA
183	Sheboygan, WI	(19.9)
30	Sherman-Denison, TX	3.5
NA	Shreveport-Bossier City, LA**	NA
NA	Sierra Vista-Douglas, AZ**	NA
229	Silver Spring-Frederick, MD M.D.	(31.7)
NA	Sioux City, IA-NE-SD**	NA
4	Sioux Falls, SD	25.0
220	South Bend-Mishawaka, IN-MI	(27.8)
NA	Spartanburg, SC**	NA
2	Spokane, WA	39.2
NA	Springfield, IL**	NA
NA	Springfield, MA**	NA
NA	Springfield, MO**	NA
78	Springfield, OH	(6.4)
179	State College, PA	(19.6)
NA	Staunton-Waynesboro, VA**	NA
132	Stockton-Lodi, CA	(13.3)
137	St. George, UT	(13.8)
14	St. Joseph, MO-KS	13.6
148	St. Louis, MO-IL	(14.8)
16	Sumter, SC	12.8
NA	Syracuse, NY**	NA
NA	Tacoma, WA M.D.**	NA
147	Tallahassee, FL	(14.7)
228	Tampa-St Petersburg, FL	(31.5)
NA	Terre Haute, IN**	NA
NA	Texarkana, TX-AR**	NA
NA	The Villages, FL**	NA
NA	Toledo, OH**	NA
110	Topeka, KS	(11.3)
37	Trenton, NJ	1.8
NA	Tucson, AZ**	NA
114	Tulsa, OK	(11.5)
NA	Tuscaloosa, AL**	NA
94	Tyler, TX	(8.5)
NA	Utica-Rome, NY**	NA
177	Valdosta, GA	(19.3)
146	Vallejo-Fairfield, CA	(14.6)
NA	Victoria, TX**	NA
19	Vineland-Bridgeton, NJ	10.0
123	Virginia Beach-Norfolk, VA-NC	(12.4)
132	Visalia-Porterville, CA	(13.3)
NA	Waco, TX**	NA
NA	Walla Walla, WA**	NA
NA	Warner Robins, GA**	NA
NA	Warren-Troy, MI M.D.**	NA
211	Washington (greater) DC-VA-MD-WV	(24.0)
202	Washington, DC-VA-MD-WV M.D.	(22.5)
144	Waterloo-Cedar Falls, IA	(14.4)
NA	Watertown-Fort Drum, NY**	NA
126	Wausau, WI	(12.5)
212	West Palm Beach, FL M.D.	(24.2)
39	Wheeling, WV-OH	1.7
217	Wichita Falls, TX	(26.2)
68	Wichita, KS	(4.5)
26	Williamsport, PA	5.7
108	Wilmington, DE-MD-NJ M.D.	(11.2)
NA	Wilmington, NC**	NA
119	Winchester, VA-WV	(12.0)
NA	Winston-Salem, NC**	NA
43	Worcester, MA-CT	1.2
180	Yakima, WA	(19.7)
122	York-Hanover, PA	(12.3)
76	Youngstown-Warren, OH-PA	(5.9)
56	Yuba City, CA	(2.8)
90	Yuma, AZ	(8.0)

Source: CQ Press using reported data from the F.B.I. "Crime in the United States 2012"

*Includes murder, rape, robbery, aggravated assault, burglary, larceny-theft, and motor vehicle theft.

**Not available.

4. Percent Change in Crime Rate: 2008 to 2012 (continued)
National Percent Change = 11.6% Decrease*

RANK	METROPOLITAN AREA	% CHANGE	RANK	METROPOLITAN AREA	% CHANGE	RANK	METROPOLITAN AREA	% CHANGE
1	Medford, OR	42.1	65	Joplin, MO	(4.1)	129	Lawrence, KS	(12.8)
2	Spokane, WA	39.2	66	Harrisburg-Carlisle, PA	(4.2)	130	Fayetteville, NC	(13.2)
3	Lewiston-Auburn, ME	29.6	67	Little Rock, AR	(4.4)	130	Jonesboro, AR	(13.2)
4	Sioux Falls, SD	25.0	68	El Centro, CA	(4.5)	132	Stockton-Lodi, CA	(13.3)
5	Redding, CA	23.3	68	Wichita, KS	(4.5)	132	Visalia-Porterville, CA	(13.3)
6	Lewiston, ID-WA	22.6	70	Dayton, OH	(4.7)	134	Bridgeport-Stamford, CT	(13.4)
7	Bloomington, IN	21.1	71	Logan, UT-ID	(5.0)	135	Greeley, CO	(13.5)
8	Gadsden, AL	19.5	72	Modesto, CA	(5.3)	135	Hartford, CT	(13.5)
9	Madera, CA	19.4	72	Montgomery, AL	(5.3)	137	Dothan, AL	(13.8)
10	Rockingham County, NH M.D.	16.6	74	Fort Wayne, IN	(5.6)	137	Macon, GA	(13.8)
11	Bismarck, ND	16.5	75	Fond du Lac, WI	(5.8)	137	Salinas, CA	(13.8)
12	Mansfield, OH	14.6	76	Youngstown-Warren, OH-PA	(5.9)	137	St. George, UT	(13.8)
13	Santa Fe, NM	13.8	77	Hickory, NC	(6.0)	141	Olympia, WA	(14.2)
14	St. Joseph, MO-KS	13.6	78	Iowa City, IA	(6.4)	142	Beaumont-Port Arthur, TX	(14.3)
15	Columbus, IN	13.4	78	Springfield, OH	(6.4)	142	Los Angeles County, CA M.D.	(14.3)
16	Cape Girardeau, MO-IL	12.8	80	Lincoln, NE	(6.6)	144	Palm Bay-Melbourne, FL	(14.4)
16	Sumter, SC	12.8	80	Salem, OR	(6.6)	144	Waterloo-Cedar Falls, IA	(14.4)
18	Missoula, MT	11.3	82	Camden, NJ M.D.	(6.7)	146	Vallejo-Fairfield, CA	(14.6)
19	Vineland-Bridgeton, NJ	10.0	82	Johnstown, PA	(6.7)	147	Tallahassee, FL	(14.7)
20	Pensacola, FL	9.6	82	Las Cruces, NM	(6.7)	148	Bellingham, WA	(14.8)
21	Monroe, MI	8.9	85	Dalton, GA	(6.8)	148	St. Louis, MO-IL	(14.8)
22	Bremerton-Silverdale, WA	8.6	86	Bangor, ME	(7.0)	150	Racine, WI	(14.9)
23	Fresno, CA	8.5	87	Lancaster, PA	(7.1)	151	Burlington, NC	(15.6)
24	Merced, CA	7.1	87	Mount Vernon-Anacortes, WA	(7.1)	152	Atlanta, GA	(15.7)
25	Lebanon, PA	6.2	87	Ocean City, NJ	(7.1)	153	Ocala, FL	(16.1)
26	Williamsport, PA	5.7	90	Yuma, AZ	(8.0)	154	Oshkosh-Neenah, WI	(16.2)
27	Fayetteville-Springdale, AR-MO	5.3	91	Oxnard-Thousand Oaks, CA	(8.1)	155	Chico, CA	(16.4)
28	San Jose, CA	5.1	92	Salt Lake City, UT	(8.2)	155	Sebastian-Vero Beach, FL	(16.4)
29	Billings, MT	4.5	93	Akron, OH	(8.4)	157	Michigan City-La Porte, IN	(16.7)
30	Sherman-Denison, TX	3.5	94	Tyler, TX	(8.5)	157	Naples-Marco Island, FL	(16.7)
31	Columbia, MO	3.3	95	Indianapolis, IN	(8.6)	159	Baltimore, MD	(16.8)
32	Erie, PA	2.9	96	Kennewick-Richland, WA	(8.9)	159	Green Bay, WI	(16.8)
33	Dover, DE	2.8	97	Abilene, TX	(9.0)	161	Florence-Muscle Shoals, AL	(17.0)
34	Flint, MI	2.4	97	Harrisonburg, VA	(9.0)	162	Florence, SC	(17.2)
35	Muncie, IN	2.1	99	Barnstable Town, MA	(9.3)	163	Cheyenne, WY	(17.3)
36	Johnson City, TN	1.9	99	Prescott, AZ	(9.3)	164	Flagstaff, AZ	(17.5)
37	Bakersfield, CA	1.8	101	Fort Lauderdale, FL M.D.	(9.6)	165	Goldsboro, NC	(17.6)
37	Trenton, NJ	1.8	101	Mobile, AL	(9.6)	166	Amarillo, TX	(17.8)
39	Anaheim-Santa Ana-Irvine, CA M.D.	1.7	103	Santa Rosa, CA	(9.8)	167	McAllen-Edinburg-Mission, TX	(17.9)
39	San Francisco-Redwood, CA M.D.	1.7	104	Reading, PA	(10.0)	168	Birmingham-Hoover, AL	(18.2)
39	Wheeling, WV-OH	1.7	105	Providence-Warwick, RI-MA	(10.1)	169	Lansing-East Lansing, MI	(18.6)
42	Portland, ME	1.4	106	Milwaukee, WI	(10.4)	170	Deltona-Daytona Beach, FL	(18.7)
43	Cumberland, MD-WV	1.2	107	Corvallis, OR	(10.7)	170	Miami (greater), FL	(18.7)
43	Worcester, MA-CT	1.2	108	Cleveland, TN	(11.2)	172	Clarksville, TN-KY	(18.8)
45	Oklahoma City, OK	0.8	108	Wilmington, DE-MD-NJ M.D.	(11.2)	172	Las Vegas-Henderson, NV	(18.8)
46	Santa Cruz-Watsonville, CA	0.1	110	Monroe, LA	(11.3)	174	Durham-Chapel Hill, NC	(18.9)
47	Great Falls, MT	(1.0)	110	Topeka, KS	(11.3)	175	Ames, IA	(19.2)
48	Pittsfield, MA	(1.1)	112	Los Angeles (greater), CA	(11.4)	175	New Orleans, LA	(19.2)
49	San Luis Obispo, CA	(1.3)	112	Lubbock, TX	(11.4)	177	Fort Worth-Arlington, TX M.D.	(19.3)
50	Norwich-New London, CT	(1.6)	114	Tulsa, OK	(11.5)	177	Valdosta, GA	(19.3)
51	Houma, LA	(1.9)	115	Kingsport, TN-VA	(11.6)	179	State College, PA	(19.6)
52	Longview, WA	(2.2)	115	Richmond, VA	(11.6)	180	Brownsville-Harlingen, TX	(19.7)
52	Scranton--Wilkes-Barre, PA	(2.2)	117	Roanoke, VA	(11.7)	180	Yakima, WA	(19.7)
54	Lafayette, IN	(2.5)	118	Ann Arbor, MI	(11.8)	182	Lima, OH	(19.8)
55	Louisville, KY-IN	(2.7)	119	Janesville, WI	(12.0)	183	Carson City, NV	(19.9)
56	Yuba City, CA	(2.8)	119	Winchester, VA-WV	(12.0)	183	Sheboygan, WI	(19.9)
57	Odessa, TX	(2.9)	121	Fort Collins, CO	(12.1)	185	Columbus, GA-AL	(20.1)
58	Omaha-Council Bluffs, NE-IA	(3.2)	122	York-Hanover, PA	(12.3)	186	Casper, WY	(20.4)
59	Portland-Vancouver, OR-WA	(3.5)	123	Austin-Round Rock, TX	(12.4)	186	Lynchburg, VA	(20.4)
60	Riverside-San Bernardino, CA	(3.7)	123	Huntsville, AL	(12.4)	188	Provo-Orem, UT	(20.5)
61	Grand Junction, CO	(3.8)	123	Virginia Beach-Norfolk, VA-NC	(12.4)	189	Blacksburg, VA	(20.7)
62	Asheville, NC	(3.9)	126	Wausau, WI	(12.5)	189	Eugene, OR	(20.7)
62	Hanford-Corcoran, CA	(3.9)	127	Boise City, ID	(12.6)	191	Altoona, PA	(21.0)
62	Lake Havasu City-Kingman, AZ	(3.9)	128	Sacramento, CA	(12.7)	192	San Diego, CA	(21.2)

Note: All listings are for Metropolitan Statistical Areas (M.S.A.s) except for those ending with "M.D." Listings with "M.D." are Metropolitan Divisions which are smaller parts of eleven large M.S.A.s. See explanatory note at beginning of metropolitan area section.

RANK	METROPOLITAN AREA	% CHANGE	RANK	METROPOLITAN AREA	% CHANGE	RANK	METROPOLITAN AREA	% CHANGE
193	Longview, TX	(21.4)	NA	Cedar Rapids, IA**	NA	NA	Montgomery County, PA M.D.**	NA
194	Decatur, AL	(21.5)	NA	Chambersburg-Waynesboro, PA**	NA	NA	Morgantown, WV**	NA
194	Idaho Falls, ID	(21.5)	NA	Champaign-Urbana, IL**	NA	NA	Morristown, TN**	NA
196	Miami-Dade County, FL M.D.	(21.6)	NA	Chicago (greater), IL-IN-WI**	NA	NA	Nashville-Davidson, TN**	NA
197	Napa, CA	(21.8)	NA	Chicago-Joilet-Naperville, IL M.D.**	NA	NA	Nassau-Suffolk, NY M.D.**	NA
197	San Antonio, TX	(21.8)	NA	Cincinnati, OH-KY-IN**	NA	NA	New Bern, NC**	NA
199	Charleston-North Charleston, SC	(21.9)	NA	Coeur d'Alene, ID**	NA	NA	New Haven-Milford, CT**	NA
200	Memphis, TN-MS-AR	(22.0)	NA	Colorado Springs, CO**	NA	NA	New York (greater), NY-NJ-PA**	NA
201	Dallas (greater), TX	(22.1)	NA	Corpus Christi, TX**	NA	NA	New York-Jersey City, NY-NJ M.D.**	NA
202	Washington, DC-VA-MD-WV M.D.	(22.5)	NA	Crestview-Fort Walton Beach, FL**	NA	NA	Newark, NJ-PA M.D.**	NA
203	Hinesville, GA	(22.7)	NA	Danville, IL**	NA	NA	North Port-Sarasota-Bradenton, FL**	NA
204	Charlottesville, VA	(23.0)	NA	Daphne-Fairhope-Foley, AL**	NA	NA	Oakland-Hayward, CA M.D.**	NA
205	Gainesville, FL	(23.4)	NA	Davenport, IA-IL**	NA	NA	Ogden-Clearfield, UT**	NA
206	Bay City, MI	(23.5)	NA	Decatur, IL**	NA	NA	Owensboro, KY**	NA
207	El Paso, TX	(23.6)	NA	Denver-Aurora, CO**	NA	NA	Panama City, FL**	NA
208	Dallas-Plano-Irving, TX M.D.	(23.7)	NA	Des Moines-West Des Moines, IA**	NA	NA	Parkersburg-Vienna, WV**	NA
208	Kalamazoo-Portage, MI	(23.7)	NA	Detroit (greater), MI**	NA	NA	Peoria, IL**	NA
210	Orlando, FL	(23.8)	NA	Detroit-Dearborn-Livonia, MI M.D.**	NA	NA	Philadelphia (greater) PA-NJ-MD-DE**	NA
211	Washington (greater) DC-VA-MD-WV	(24.0)	NA	Dubuque, IA**	NA	NA	Philadelphia, PA M.D.**	NA
212	Greensboro-High Point, NC	(24.2)	NA	Duluth, MN-WI**	NA	NA	Phoenix-Mesa-Scottsdale, AZ**	NA
212	West Palm Beach, FL M.D.	(24.2)	NA	Dutchess-Putnam, NY M.D.**	NA	NA	Pittsburgh, PA**	NA
214	Lakeland, FL	(24.8)	NA	East Stroudsburg, PA**	NA	NA	Pocatello, ID**	NA
215	Bowling Green, KY	(25.1)	NA	Elgin, IL M.D.**	NA	NA	Pueblo, CO**	NA
216	Port St. Lucie, FL	(25.3)	NA	Elizabethtown-Fort Knox, KY**	NA	NA	Raleigh, NC**	NA
217	Wichita Falls, TX	(26.2)	NA	Elmira, NY**	NA	NA	Rapid City, SD**	NA
218	Pine Bluff, AR	(26.3)	NA	Fairbanks, AK**	NA	NA	Rochester, MN**	NA
219	Athens-Clarke County, GA	(27.7)	NA	Fargo, ND-MN**	NA	NA	Rochester, NY**	NA
220	South Bend-Mishawaka, IN-MI	(27.8)	NA	Farmington, NM**	NA	NA	Rockford, IL**	NA
221	Reno, NV	(28.4)	NA	Fort Smith, AR-OK**	NA	NA	Rocky Mount, NC**	NA
222	Jacksonville, FL	(29.1)	NA	Gainesville, GA**	NA	NA	Rome, GA**	NA
222	Savannah, GA	(29.1)	NA	Gary, IN M.D.**	NA	NA	Salisbury, MD-DE**	NA
224	Saginaw, MI	(30.6)	NA	Gettysburg, PA**	NA	NA	San Francisco (greater), CA**	NA
225	Greenville, NC	(30.7)	NA	Glens Falls, NY**	NA	NA	San Rafael, CA M.D.**	NA
226	Laredo, TX	(30.9)	NA	Grand Forks, ND-MN**	NA	NA	Santa Maria-Santa Barbara, CA**	NA
227	College Station-Bryan, TX	(31.4)	NA	Grand Island, NE**	NA	NA	Seattle (greater), WA**	NA
228	Tampa-St Petersburg, FL	(31.5)	NA	Greenville-Anderson, SC**	NA	NA	Seattle-Bellevue-Everett, WA M.D.**	NA
229	Silver Spring-Frederick, MD M.D.	(31.7)	NA	Hagerstown-Martinsburg, MD-WV**	NA	NA	Sebring, FL**	NA
230	Cape Coral-Fort Myers, FL	(32.2)	NA	Hammond, LA**	NA	NA	Shreveport-Bossier City, LA**	NA
231	Punta Gorda, FL	(34.0)	NA	Hattiesburg, MS**	NA	NA	Sierra Vista-Douglas, AZ**	NA
232	Appleton, WI	(35.7)	NA	Hilton Head Island, SC**	NA	NA	Sioux City, IA-NE-SD**	NA
233	Auburn, AL	(42.4)	NA	Homosassa Springs, FL**	NA	NA	Spartanburg, SC**	NA
NA	Albany-Schenectady-Troy, NY**	NA	NA	Houston, TX**	NA	NA	Springfield, IL**	NA
NA	Albany, GA**	NA	NA	Jackson, MS**	NA	NA	Springfield, MA**	NA
NA	Albany, OR**	NA	NA	Jackson, TN**	NA	NA	Springfield, MO**	NA
NA	Albuquerque, NM**	NA	NA	Jefferson City, MO**	NA	NA	Staunton-Waynesboro, VA**	NA
NA	Alexandria, LA**	NA	NA	Kahului-Wailuku-Lahaina, HI**	NA	NA	Syracuse, NY**	NA
NA	Allentown, PA-NJ**	NA	NA	Kankakee, IL**	NA	NA	Tacoma, WA M.D.**	NA
NA	Anchorage, AK**	NA	NA	Kansas City, MO-KS**	NA	NA	Terre Haute, IN**	NA
NA	Anniston-Oxford, AL**	NA	NA	Killeen-Temple, TX**	NA	NA	Texarkana, TX-AR**	NA
NA	Atlantic City, NJ**	NA	NA	Kingston, NY**	NA	NA	The Villages, FL**	NA
NA	Augusta, GA-SC**	NA	NA	Knoxville, TN**	NA	NA	Toledo, OH**	NA
NA	Baton Rouge, LA**	NA	NA	Kokomo, IN**	NA	NA	Tucson, AZ**	NA
NA	Beckley, WV**	NA	NA	La Crosse, WI-MN**	NA	NA	Tuscaloosa, AL**	NA
NA	Binghamton, NY**	NA	NA	Lafayette, LA**	NA	NA	Utica-Rome, NY**	NA
NA	Bloomington, IL**	NA	NA	Lake Co.-Kenosha Co., IL-WI M.D.**	NA	NA	Victoria, TX**	NA
NA	Bloomsburg-Berwick, PA**	NA	NA	Lawton, OK**	NA	NA	Waco, TX**	NA
NA	Boston (greater), MA-NH**	NA	NA	Lexington-Fayette, KY**	NA	NA	Walla Walla, WA**	NA
NA	Boston, MA M.D.**	NA	NA	Madison, WI**	NA	NA	Warner Robins, GA**	NA
NA	Boulder, CO**	NA	NA	Manchester-Nashua, NH**	NA	NA	Warren-Troy, MI M.D.**	NA
NA	Brunswick, GA**	NA	NA	Manhattan, KS**	NA	NA	Watertown-Fort Drum, NY**	NA
NA	Buffalo-Niagara Falls, NY**	NA	NA	Mankato-North Mankato, MN**	NA	NA	Wilmington, NC**	NA
NA	California-Lexington Park, MD**	NA	NA	Midland, MI**	NA	NA	Winston-Salem, NC**	NA
NA	Cambridge-Newton, MA M.D.**	NA	NA	Midland, TX**	NA			
NA	Canton, OH**	NA	NA	Minneapolis-St. Paul, MN-WI**	NA			

Source: CQ Press using reported data from the F.B.I. "Crime in the United States 2012"

*Includes murder, rape, robbery, aggravated assault, burglary, larceny-theft, and motor vehicle theft.

**Not available.

5. Violent Crimes in 2012
National Total = 1,214,462 Violent Crimes*

RANK	METROPOLITAN AREA	CRIMES	RANK	METROPOLITAN AREA	CRIMES	RANK	METROPOLITAN AREA	CRIMES
246	Abilene, TX	555	326	Cheyenne, WY	227	101	Gary, IN M.D.	2,274
104	Akron, OH	2,227	NA	Chicago (greater), IL-IN-WI**	NA	359	Gettysburg, PA	112
98	Albany-Schenectady-Troy, NY	2,338	NA	Chicago-Joilet-Naperville, IL M.D.**	NA	334	Glens Falls, NY	200
168	Albany, GA	1,068	221	Chico, CA	684	248	Goldsboro, NC	533
353	Albany, OR	139	47	Cincinnati, OH-KY-IN	6,042	NA	Grand Forks, ND-MN**	NA
49	Albuquerque, NM	5,806	157	Clarksville, TN-KY	1,175	340	Grand Island, NE	183
NA	Alexandria, LA**	NA	226	Cleveland, TN	642	262	Grand Junction, CO	468
122	Allentown, PA-NJ	1,743	278	Coeur d'Alene, ID	417	339	Great Falls, MT	190
304	Altoona, PA	321	185	College Station-Bryan, TX	934	204	Greeley, CO	768
144	Amarillo, TX	1,366	93	Colorado Springs, CO	2,530	212	Green Bay, WI	717
356	Ames, IA	132	233	Columbia, MO	623	87	Greensboro-High Point, NC	2,726
41	Anaheim-Santa Ana-Irvine, CA M.D.	6,789	147	Columbus, GA-AL	1,331	60	Greenville-Anderson, SC	4,814
92	Anchorage, AK	2,543	355	Columbus, IN	135	216	Greenville, NC	704
172	Ann Arbor, MI	1,026	95	Corpus Christi, TX	2,458	230	Hagerstown-Martinsburg, MD-WV	628
222	Anniston-Oxford, AL	678	362	Corvallis, OR	96	154	Hammond, LA	1,185
300	Appleton, WI	351	163	Crestview-Fort Walton Beach, FL	1,116	206	Hanford-Corcoran, CA	767
177	Asheville, NC	976	301	Cumberland, MD-WV	346	126	Harrisburg-Carlisle, PA	1,659
231	Athens-Clarke County, GA	626	7	Dallas (greater), TX	23,028	344	Harrisonburg, VA	169
8	Atlanta, GA	22,207	18	Dallas-Plano-Irving, TX M.D.	14,378	81	Hartford, CT	2,926
NA	Atlantic City, NJ**	NA	295	Dalton, GA	375	342	Hattiesburg, MS	172
296	Auburn, AL	372	270	Danville, IL	454	201	Hickory, NC	821
118	Augusta, GA-SC	1,802	271	Daphne-Fairhope-Foley, AL	446	174	Hilton Head Island, SC	996
53	Austin-Round Rock, TX	5,299	139	Davenport, IA-IL	1,422	317	Hinesville, GA	275
59	Bakersfield, CA	4,976	97	Dayton, OH	2,343	263	Homosassa Springs, FL	465
13	Baltimore, MD	17,117	282	Decatur, AL	406	236	Houma, LA	611
353	Bangor, ME	139	273	Decatur, IL	427	3	Houston, TX	34,535
189	Barnstable Town, MA	901	96	Deltona-Daytona Beach, FL	2,424	103	Huntsville, AL	2,228
NA	Baton Rouge, LA**	NA	32	Denver-Aurora, CO	8,895	328	Idaho Falls, ID	223
304	Bay City, MI	321	124	Des Moines-West Des Moines, IA	1,685	26	Indianapolis, IN	11,485
107	Beaumont-Port Arthur, TX	2,175	5	Detroit (greater), MI	24,637	280	Iowa City, IA	412
255	Beckley, WV	492	10	Detroit-Dearborn-Livonia, MI M.D.	18,932	39	Jacksonville, FL	7,079
257	Bellingham, WA	488	244	Dothan, AL	567	105	Jackson, MS	2,224
266	Billings, MT	461	189	Dover, DE	901	150	Jackson, TN	1,256
228	Binghamton, NY	632	347	Dubuque, IA	153	291	Janesville, WI	384
43	Birmingham-Hoover, AL	6,424	NA	Duluth, MN-WI**	NA	261	Jefferson City, MO	469
275	Bismarck, ND	424	106	Durham-Chapel Hill, NC	2,214	229	Johnson City, TN	631
314	Blacksburg, VA	297	208	Dutchess-Putnam, NY M.D.	730	308	Johnstown, PA	320
239	Bloomington, IL	602	225	East Stroudsburg, PA	666	283	Jonesboro, AR	403
288	Bloomington, IN	392	252	El Centro, CA	519	227	Joplin, MO	634
352	Bloomsburg-Berwick, PA	140	75	El Paso, TX	3,319	281	Kahului-Wailuku-Lahaina, HI	411
146	Boise City, ID	1,335	160	Elgin, IL M.D.	1,146	155	Kalamazoo-Portage, MI	1,178
15	Boston (greater), MA-NH	16,444	358	Elizabethtown-Fort Knox, KY	115	290	Kankakee, IL	387
30	Boston, MA M.D.	9,532	329	Elmira, NY	222	28	Kansas City, MO-KS	9,926
236	Boulder, CO	611	219	Erie, PA	693	232	Kennewick-Richland, WA	624
324	Bowling Green, KY	231	197	Eugene, OR	842	136	Killeen-Temple, TX	1,501
218	Bremerton-Silverdale, WA	696	340	Fairbanks, AK	183	153	Kingsport, TN-VA	1,188
86	Bridgeport-Stamford, CT	2,736	NA	Fargo, ND-MN**	NA	316	Kingston, NY	279
166	Brownsville-Harlingen, TX	1,080	195	Farmington, NM	849	70	Knoxville, TN	3,584
251	Brunswick, GA	527	120	Fayetteville-Springdale, AR-MO	1,781	330	Kokomo, IN	221
58	Buffalo-Niagara Falls, NY	5,045	113	Fayetteville, NC	1,893	NA	La Crosse, WI-MN**	NA
223	Burlington, NC	674	268	Flagstaff, AZ	456	242	Lafayette, IN	577
318	California-Lexington Park, MD	257	66	Flint, MI	3,833	NA	Lafayette, LA**	NA
44	Cambridge-Newton, MA M.D.	6,298	253	Florence-Muscle Shoals, AL	513	141	Lake Co.-Kenosha Co., IL-WI M.D.	1,404
64	Camden, NJ M.D.	4,264	161	Florence, SC	1,132	297	Lake Havasu City-Kingman, AZ	367
152	Canton, OH	1,197	327	Fond du Lac, WI	225	108	Lakeland, FL	2,170
102	Cape Coral-Fort Myers, FL	2,234	215	Fort Collins, CO	710	191	Lancaster, PA	878
275	Cape Girardeau, MO-IL	424	33	Fort Lauderdale, FL M.D.	8,720	127	Lansing-East Lansing, MI	1,656
356	Carson City, NV	132	159	Fort Smith, AR-OK	1,161	162	Laredo, TX	1,127
348	Casper, WY	152	167	Fort Wayne, IN	1,078	211	Las Cruces, NM	723
264	Cedar Rapids, IA	464	35	Fort Worth-Arlington, TX M.D.	8,650	20	Las Vegas-Henderson, NV	13,901
332	Chambersburg-Waynesboro, PA	212	56	Fresno, CA	5,137	279	Lawrence, KS	416
151	Champaign-Urbana, IL	1,211	243	Gadsden, AL	568	179	Lawton, OK	959
82	Charleston-North Charleston, SC	2,907	133	Gainesville, FL	1,567	315	Lebanon, PA	287
292	Charlottesville, VA	381	303	Gainesville, GA	323	346	Lewiston-Auburn, ME	157

Note: All listings are for Metropolitan Statistical Areas (M.S.A.s) except for those ending with "M.D." Listings with "M.D." are Metropolitan Divisions which are smaller parts of eleven large M.S.A.s. See explanatory note at beginning of metropolitan area section.

RANK	METROPOLITAN AREA	CRIMES	RANK	METROPOLITAN AREA	CRIMES	RANK	METROPOLITAN AREA	CRIMES
359	Lewiston, ID-WA	112	351	Owensboro, KY	146	94	Silver Spring-Frederick, MD M.D.	2,497
137	Lexington-Fayette, KY	1,432	125	Oxnard-Thousand Oaks, CA	1,664	298	Sioux City, IA-NE-SD	361
245	Lima, OH	558	80	Palm Bay-Melbourne, FL	2,963	214	Sioux Falls, SD	713
165	Lincoln, NE	1,092	183	Panama City, FL	939	173	South Bend-Mishawaka, IN-MI	999
62	Little Rock, AR	4,739	309	Parkersburg-Vienna, WV	313	140	Spartanburg, SC	1,407
363	Logan, UT-ID	69	88	Pensacola, FL	2,687	115	Spokane, WA	1,859
180	Longview, TX	951	134	Peoria, IL	1,562	138	Springfield, IL	1,430
313	Longview, WA	304	NA	Philadelphia (greater) PA-NJ-MD-DE**	NA	77	Springfield, MA	3,134
2	Los Angeles County, CA M.D.	44,556	NA	Philadelphia, PA M.D.**	NA	111	Springfield, MO	2,123
1	Los Angeles (greater), CA	51,345	11	Phoenix-Mesa-Scottsdale, AZ	17,534	283	Springfield, OH	403
52	Louisville, KY-IN	5,310	210	Pine Bluff, AR	725	349	State College, PA	151
110	Lubbock, TX	2,163	NA	Pittsburgh, PA**	NA	335	Staunton-Waynesboro, VA	198
286	Lynchburg, VA	400	267	Pittsfield, MA	458	45	Stockton-Lodi, CA	6,249
184	Macon, GA	938	336	Pocatello, ID	195	321	St. George, UT	244
185	Madera, CA	934	135	Port St. Lucie, FL	1,527	285	St. Joseph, MO-KS	402
149	Madison, WI	1,273	46	Portland-Vancouver, OR-WA	6,076	21	St. Louis, MO-IL	12,971
174	Manchester-Nashua, NH	996	220	Portland, ME	686	200	Sumter, SC	827
325	Manhattan, KS	229	217	Prescott, AZ	700	112	Syracuse, NY	2,026
NA	Mankato-North Mankato, MN**	NA	51	Providence-Warwick, RI-MA	5,449	72	Tacoma, WA M.D.	3,510
322	Mansfield, OH	242	289	Provo-Orem, UT	388	99	Tallahassee, FL	2,299
90	McAllen-Edinburg-Mission, TX	2,585	198	Pueblo, CO	831	25	Tampa-St Petersburg, FL	11,718
224	Medford, OR	673	287	Punta Gorda, FL	399	302	Terre Haute, IN	328
19	Memphis, TN-MS-AR	14,199	260	Racine, WI	484	171	Texarkana, TX-AR	1,039
117	Merced, CA	1,833	83	Raleigh, NC	2,902	343	The Villages, FL	171
4	Miami (greater), FL	32,487	249	Rapid City, SD	529	67	Toledo, OH	3,735
12	Miami-Dade County, FL M.D.	17,173	143	Reading, PA	1,376	176	Topeka, KS	982
338	Michigan City-La Porte, IN	193	148	Redding, CA	1,298	128	Trenton, NJ	1,645
361	Midland, MI	102	123	Reno, NV	1,721	61	Tucson, AZ	4,771
264	Midland, TX	464	79	Richmond, VA	3,000	54	Tulsa, OK	5,171
31	Milwaukee, WI	9,015	17	Riverside-San Bernardino, CA	16,021	187	Tuscaloosa, AL	932
NA	Minneapolis-St. Paul, MN-WI**	NA	203	Roanoke, VA	794	196	Tyler, TX	847
304	Missoula, MT	321	NA	Rochester, MN**	NA	207	Utica-Rome, NY	739
100	Mobile, AL	2,287	78	Rochester, NY	3,090	258	Valdosta, GA	487
84	Modesto, CA	2,875	91	Rockford, IL	2,578	116	Vallejo-Fairfield, CA	1,850
202	Monroe, LA	814	235	Rockingham County, NH M.D.	614	254	Victoria, TX	500
277	Monroe, MI	421	181	Rocky Mount, NC	944	193	Vineland-Bridgeton, NJ	866
85	Montgomery County, PA M.D.	2,800	299	Rome, GA	353	57	Virginia Beach-Norfolk, VA-NC	5,124
145	Montgomery, AL	1,341	29	Sacramento, CA	9,688	109	Visalia-Porterville, CA	2,164
292	Morgantown, WV	381	130	Saginaw, MI	1,627	169	Waco, TX	1,057
269	Morristown, TN	455	182	Salem, OR	942	350	Walla Walla, WA	147
323	Mount Vernon-Anacortes, WA	232	114	Salinas, CA	1,866	209	Warner Robins, GA	727
311	Muncie, IN	308	121	Salisbury, MD-DE	1,758	50	Warren-Troy, MI M.D.	5,705
259	Napa, CA	485	68	Salt Lake City, UT	3,679	9	Washington (greater) DC-VA-MD-WV	19,381
199	Naples-Marco Island, FL	829	34	San Antonio, TX	8,703	14	Washington, DC-VA-MD-WV M.D.	16,884
27	Nashville-Davidson, TN	11,405	24	San Diego, CA	11,839	234	Waterloo-Cedar Falls, IA	616
63	Nassau-Suffolk, NY M.D.	4,578	6	San Francisco (greater), CA	24,411	330	Watertown-Fort Drum, NY	221
294	New Bern, NC	376	38	San Francisco-Redwood, CA M.D.	7,638	345	Wausau, WI	168
74	New Haven-Milford, CT	3,352	55	San Jose, CA	5,159	42	West Palm Beach, FL M.D.	6,594
48	New Orleans, LA	5,894	188	San Luis Obispo, CA	906	274	Wheeling, WV-OH	426
NA	New York (greater), NY-NJ-PA**	NA	256	San Rafael, CA M.D.	490	241	Wichita Falls, TX	584
NA	New York-Jersey City, NY-NJ M.D.**	NA	170	Santa Cruz-Watsonville, CA	1,041	73	Wichita, KS	3,368
37	Newark, NJ-PA M.D.	7,860	250	Santa Fe, NM	528	333	Williamsport, PA	211
76	North Port-Sarasota-Bradenton, FL	3,241	129	Santa Maria-Santa Barbara, CA	1,643	65	Wilmington, DE-MD-NJ M.D.	3,905
240	Norwich-New London, CT	594	119	Santa Rosa, CA	1,792	178	Wilmington, NC	966
16	Oakland-Hayward, CA M.D.	16,283	156	Savannah, GA	1,177	320	Winchester, VA-WV	247
131	Ocala, FL	1,616	142	Scranton--Wilkes-Barre, PA	1,390	89	Winston-Salem, NC	2,621
319	Ocean City, NJ	254	23	Seattle (greater), WA	11,904	71	Worcester, MA-CT	3,576
158	Odessa, TX	1,168	36	Seattle-Bellevue-Everett, WA M.D.	8,394	192	Yakima, WA	872
194	Ogden-Clearfield, UT	861	272	Sebastian-Vero Beach, FL	438	164	York-Hanover, PA	1,095
40	Oklahoma City, OK	7,054	312	Sebring, FL	306	132	Youngstown-Warren, OH-PA	1,605
247	Olympia, WA	552	336	Sheboygan, WI	195	238	Yuba City, CA	603
69	Omaha-Council Bluffs, NE-IA	3,594	310	Sherman-Denison, TX	311	213	Yuma, AZ	716
22	Orlando, FL	12,019	NA	Shreveport-Bossier City, LA**	NA			
304	Oshkosh-Neenah, WI	321	204	Sierra Vista-Douglas, AZ	768			

Source: Reported data from the F.B.I. "Crime in the United States 2012"
*Violent crimes are offenses of murder, forcible rape, robbery, and aggravated assault.
**Not available.

5. Violent Crimes in 2012 (continued)
National Total = 1,214,462 Violent Crimes*

RANK	METROPOLITAN AREA	CRIMES	RANK	METROPOLITAN AREA	CRIMES	RANK	METROPOLITAN AREA	CRIMES
1	Los Angeles (greater), CA	51,345	65	Wilmington, DE-MD-NJ M.D.	3,905	129	Santa Maria-Santa Barbara, CA	1,643
2	Los Angeles County, CA M.D.	44,556	66	Flint, MI	3,833	130	Saginaw, MI	1,627
3	Houston, TX	34,535	67	Toledo, OH	3,735	131	Ocala, FL	1,616
4	Miami (greater), FL	32,487	68	Salt Lake City, UT	3,679	132	Youngstown-Warren, OH-PA	1,605
5	Detroit (greater), MI	24,637	69	Omaha-Council Bluffs, NE-IA	3,594	133	Gainesville, FL	1,567
6	San Francisco (greater), CA	24,411	70	Knoxville, TN	3,584	134	Peoria, IL	1,562
7	Dallas (greater), TX	23,028	71	Worcester, MA-CT	3,576	135	Port St. Lucie, FL	1,527
8	Atlanta, GA	22,207	72	Tacoma, WA M.D.	3,510	136	Killeen-Temple, TX	1,501
9	Washington (greater) DC-VA-MD-WV	19,381	73	Wichita, KS	3,368	137	Lexington-Fayette, KY	1,432
10	Detroit-Dearborn-Livonia, MI M.D.	18,932	74	New Haven-Milford, CT	3,352	138	Springfield, IL	1,430
11	Phoenix-Mesa-Scottsdale, AZ	17,534	75	El Paso, TX	3,319	139	Davenport, IA-IL	1,422
12	Miami-Dade County, FL M.D.	17,173	76	North Port-Sarasota-Bradenton, FL	3,241	140	Spartanburg, SC	1,407
13	Baltimore, MD	17,117	77	Springfield, MA	3,134	141	Lake Co.-Kenosha Co., IL-WI M.D.	1,404
14	Washington, DC-VA-MD-WV M.D.	16,884	78	Rochester, NY	3,090	142	Scranton--Wilkes-Barre, PA	1,390
15	Boston (greater), MA-NH	16,444	79	Richmond, VA	3,000	143	Reading, PA	1,376
16	Oakland-Hayward, CA M.D.	16,283	80	Palm Bay-Melbourne, FL	2,963	144	Amarillo, TX	1,366
17	Riverside-San Bernardino, CA	16,021	81	Hartford, CT	2,926	145	Montgomery, AL	1,341
18	Dallas-Plano-Irving, TX M.D.	14,378	82	Charleston-North Charleston, SC	2,907	146	Boise City, ID	1,335
19	Memphis, TN-MS-AR	14,199	83	Raleigh, NC	2,902	147	Columbus, GA-AL	1,331
20	Las Vegas-Henderson, NV	13,901	84	Modesto, CA	2,875	148	Redding, CA	1,298
21	St. Louis, MO-IL	12,971	85	Montgomery County, PA M.D.	2,800	149	Madison, WI	1,273
22	Orlando, FL	12,019	86	Bridgeport-Stamford, CT	2,736	150	Jackson, TN	1,256
23	Seattle (greater), WA	11,904	87	Greensboro-High Point, NC	2,726	151	Champaign-Urbana, IL	1,211
24	San Diego, CA	11,839	88	Pensacola, FL	2,687	152	Canton, OH	1,197
25	Tampa-St Petersburg, FL	11,718	89	Winston-Salem, NC	2,621	153	Kingsport, TN-VA	1,188
26	Indianapolis, IN	11,485	90	McAllen-Edinburg-Mission, TX	2,585	154	Hammond, LA	1,185
27	Nashville-Davidson, TN	11,405	91	Rockford, IL	2,578	155	Kalamazoo-Portage, MI	1,178
28	Kansas City, MO-KS	9,926	92	Anchorage, AK	2,543	156	Savannah, GA	1,177
29	Sacramento, CA	9,688	93	Colorado Springs, CO	2,530	157	Clarksville, TN-KY	1,175
30	Boston, MA M.D.	9,532	94	Silver Spring-Frederick, MD M.D.	2,497	158	Odessa, TX	1,168
31	Milwaukee, WI	9,015	95	Corpus Christi, TX	2,458	159	Fort Smith, AR-OK	1,161
32	Denver-Aurora, CO	8,895	96	Deltona-Daytona Beach, FL	2,424	160	Elgin, IL M.D.	1,146
33	Fort Lauderdale, FL M.D.	8,720	97	Dayton, OH	2,343	161	Florence, SC	1,132
34	San Antonio, TX	8,703	98	Albany-Schenectady-Troy, NY	2,338	162	Laredo, TX	1,127
35	Fort Worth-Arlington, TX M.D.	8,650	99	Tallahassee, FL	2,299	163	Crestview-Fort Walton Beach, FL	1,116
36	Seattle-Bellevue-Everett, WA M.D.	8,394	100	Mobile, AL	2,287	164	York-Hanover, PA	1,095
37	Newark, NJ-PA M.D.	7,860	101	Gary, IN M.D.	2,274	165	Lincoln, NE	1,092
38	San Francisco-Redwood, CA M.D.	7,638	102	Cape Coral-Fort Myers, FL	2,234	166	Brownsville-Harlingen, TX	1,080
39	Jacksonville, FL	7,079	103	Huntsville, AL	2,228	167	Fort Wayne, IN	1,078
40	Oklahoma City, OK	7,054	104	Akron, OH	2,227	168	Albany, GA	1,068
41	Anaheim-Santa Ana-Irvine, CA M.D.	6,789	105	Jackson, MS	2,224	169	Waco, TX	1,057
42	West Palm Beach, FL M.D.	6,594	106	Durham-Chapel Hill, NC	2,214	170	Santa Cruz-Watsonville, CA	1,041
43	Birmingham-Hoover, AL	6,424	107	Beaumont-Port Arthur, TX	2,175	171	Texarkana, TX-AR	1,039
44	Cambridge-Newton, MA M.D.	6,298	108	Lakeland, FL	2,170	172	Ann Arbor, MI	1,026
45	Stockton-Lodi, CA	6,249	109	Visalia-Porterville, CA	2,164	173	South Bend-Mishawaka, IN-MI	999
46	Portland-Vancouver, OR-WA	6,076	110	Lubbock, TX	2,163	174	Hilton Head Island, SC	996
47	Cincinnati, OH-KY-IN	6,042	111	Springfield, MO	2,123	174	Manchester-Nashua, NH	996
48	New Orleans, LA	5,894	112	Syracuse, NY	2,026	176	Topeka, KS	982
49	Albuquerque, NM	5,806	113	Fayetteville, NC	1,893	177	Asheville, NC	976
50	Warren-Troy, MI M.D.	5,705	114	Salinas, CA	1,866	178	Wilmington, NC	966
51	Providence-Warwick, RI-MA	5,449	115	Spokane, WA	1,859	179	Lawton, OK	959
52	Louisville, KY-IN	5,310	116	Vallejo-Fairfield, CA	1,850	180	Longview, TX	951
53	Austin-Round Rock, TX	5,299	117	Merced, CA	1,833	181	Rocky Mount, NC	944
54	Tulsa, OK	5,171	118	Augusta, GA-SC	1,802	182	Salem, OR	942
55	San Jose, CA	5,159	119	Santa Rosa, CA	1,792	183	Panama City, FL	939
56	Fresno, CA	5,137	120	Fayetteville-Springdale, AR-MO	1,781	184	Macon, GA	938
57	Virginia Beach-Norfolk, VA-NC	5,124	121	Salisbury, MD-DE	1,758	185	College Station-Bryan, TX	934
58	Buffalo-Niagara Falls, NY	5,045	122	Allentown, PA-NJ	1,743	185	Madera, CA	934
59	Bakersfield, CA	4,976	123	Reno, NV	1,721	187	Tuscaloosa, AL	932
60	Greenville-Anderson, SC	4,814	124	Des Moines-West Des Moines, IA	1,685	188	San Luis Obispo, CA	906
61	Tucson, AZ	4,771	125	Oxnard-Thousand Oaks, CA	1,664	189	Barnstable Town, MA	901
62	Little Rock, AR	4,739	126	Harrisburg-Carlisle, PA	1,659	189	Dover, DE	901
63	Nassau-Suffolk, NY M.D.	4,578	127	Lansing-East Lansing, MI	1,656	191	Lancaster, PA	878
64	Camden, NJ M.D.	4,264	128	Trenton, NJ	1,645	192	Yakima, WA	872

Note: All listings are for Metropolitan Statistical Areas (M.S.A.s) except for those ending with "M.D." Listings with "M.D." are Metropolitan Divisions which are smaller parts of eleven large M.S.A.s. See explanatory note at beginning of metropolitan area section.

RANK	METROPOLITAN AREA	CRIMES	RANK	METROPOLITAN AREA	CRIMES	RANK	METROPOLITAN AREA	CRIMES
193	Vineland-Bridgeton, NJ	866	257	Bellingham, WA	488	321	St. George, UT	244
194	Ogden-Clearfield, UT	861	258	Valdosta, GA	487	322	Mansfield, OH	242
195	Farmington, NM	849	259	Napa, CA	485	323	Mount Vernon-Anacortes, WA	232
196	Tyler, TX	847	260	Racine, WI	484	324	Bowling Green, KY	231
197	Eugene, OR	842	261	Jefferson City, MO	469	325	Manhattan, KS	229
198	Pueblo, CO	831	262	Grand Junction, CO	468	326	Cheyenne, WY	227
199	Naples-Marco Island, FL	829	263	Homosassa Springs, FL	465	327	Fond du Lac, WI	225
200	Sumter, SC	827	264	Cedar Rapids, IA	464	328	Idaho Falls, ID	223
201	Hickory, NC	821	264	Midland, TX	464	329	Elmira, NY	222
202	Monroe, LA	814	266	Billings, MT	461	330	Kokomo, IN	221
203	Roanoke, VA	794	267	Pittsfield, MA	458	330	Watertown-Fort Drum, NY	221
204	Greeley, CO	768	268	Flagstaff, AZ	456	332	Chambersburg-Waynesboro, PA	212
204	Sierra Vista-Douglas, AZ	768	269	Morristown, TN	455	333	Williamsport, PA	211
206	Hanford-Corcoran, CA	767	270	Danville, IL	454	334	Glens Falls, NY	200
207	Utica-Rome, NY	739	271	Daphne-Fairhope-Foley, AL	446	335	Staunton-Waynesboro, VA	198
208	Dutchess-Putnam, NY M.D.	730	272	Sebastian-Vero Beach, FL	438	336	Pocatello, ID	195
209	Warner Robins, GA	727	273	Decatur, IL	427	336	Sheboygan, WI	195
210	Pine Bluff, AR	725	274	Wheeling, WV-OH	426	338	Michigan City-La Porte, IN	193
211	Las Cruces, NM	723	275	Bismarck, ND	424	339	Great Falls, MT	190
212	Green Bay, WI	717	275	Cape Girardeau, MO-IL	424	340	Fairbanks, AK	183
213	Yuma, AZ	716	277	Monroe, MI	421	340	Grand Island, NE	183
214	Sioux Falls, SD	713	278	Coeur d'Alene, ID	417	342	Hattiesburg, MS	172
215	Fort Collins, CO	710	279	Lawrence, KS	416	343	The Villages, FL	171
216	Greenville, NC	704	280	Iowa City, IA	412	344	Harrisonburg, VA	169
217	Prescott, AZ	700	281	Kahului-Wailuku-Lahaina, HI	411	345	Wausau, WI	168
218	Bremerton-Silverdale, WA	696	282	Decatur, AL	406	346	Lewiston-Auburn, ME	157
219	Erie, PA	693	283	Jonesboro, AR	403	347	Dubuque, IA	153
220	Portland, ME	686	283	Springfield, OH	403	348	Casper, WY	152
221	Chico, CA	684	285	St. Joseph, MO-KS	402	349	State College, PA	151
222	Anniston-Oxford, AL	678	286	Lynchburg, VA	400	350	Walla Walla, WA	147
223	Burlington, NC	674	287	Punta Gorda, FL	399	351	Owensboro, KY	146
224	Medford, OR	673	288	Bloomington, IN	392	352	Bloomsburg-Berwick, PA	140
225	East Stroudsburg, PA	666	289	Provo-Orem, UT	388	353	Albany, OR	139
226	Cleveland, TN	642	290	Kankakee, IL	387	353	Bangor, ME	139
227	Joplin, MO	634	291	Janesville, WI	384	355	Columbus, IN	135
228	Binghamton, NY	632	292	Charlottesville, VA	381	356	Ames, IA	132
229	Johnson City, TN	631	292	Morgantown, WV	381	356	Carson City, NV	132
230	Hagerstown-Martinsburg, MD-WV	628	294	New Bern, NC	376	358	Elizabethtown-Fort Knox, KY	115
231	Athens-Clarke County, GA	626	295	Dalton, GA	375	359	Gettysburg, PA	112
232	Kennewick-Richland, WA	624	296	Auburn, AL	372	359	Lewiston, ID-WA	112
233	Columbia, MO	623	297	Lake Havasu City-Kingman, AZ	367	361	Midland, MI	102
234	Waterloo-Cedar Falls, IA	616	298	Sioux City, IA-NE-SD	361	362	Corvallis, OR	96
235	Rockingham County, NH M.D.	614	299	Rome, GA	353	363	Logan, UT-ID	69
236	Boulder, CO	611	300	Appleton, WI	351	NA	Alexandria, LA**	NA
236	Houma, LA	611	301	Cumberland, MD-WV	346	NA	Atlantic City, NJ**	NA
238	Yuba City, CA	603	302	Terre Haute, IN	328	NA	Baton Rouge, LA**	NA
239	Bloomington, IL	602	303	Gainesville, GA	323	NA	Chicago (greater), IL-IN-WI**	NA
240	Norwich-New London, CT	594	304	Altoona, PA	321	NA	Chicago-Joilet-Naperville, IL M.D.**	NA
241	Wichita Falls, TX	584	304	Bay City, MI	321	NA	Duluth, MN-WI**	NA
242	Lafayette, IN	577	304	Missoula, MT	321	NA	Fargo, ND-MN**	NA
243	Gadsden, AL	568	304	Oshkosh-Neenah, WI	321	NA	Grand Forks, ND-MN**	NA
244	Dothan, AL	567	308	Johnstown, PA	320	NA	La Crosse, WI-MN**	NA
245	Lima, OH	558	309	Parkersburg-Vienna, WV	313	NA	Lafayette, LA**	NA
246	Abilene, TX	555	310	Sherman-Denison, TX	311	NA	Mankato-North Mankato, MN**	NA
247	Olympia, WA	552	311	Muncie, IN	308	NA	Minneapolis-St. Paul, MN-WI**	NA
248	Goldsboro, NC	533	312	Sebring, FL	306	NA	New York (greater), NY-NJ-PA**	NA
249	Rapid City, SD	529	313	Longview, WA	304	NA	New York-Jersey City, NY-NJ M.D.**	NA
250	Santa Fe, NM	528	314	Blacksburg, VA	297	NA	Philadelphia (greater) PA-NJ-MD-DE**	NA
251	Brunswick, GA	527	315	Lebanon, PA	287	NA	Philadelphia, PA M.D.**	NA
252	El Centro, CA	519	316	Kingston, NY	279	NA	Pittsburgh, PA**	NA
253	Florence-Muscle Shoals, AL	513	317	Hinesville, GA	275	NA	Rochester, MN**	NA
254	Victoria, TX	500	318	California-Lexington Park, MD	257	NA	Shreveport-Bossier City, LA**	NA
255	Beckley, WV	492	319	Ocean City, NJ	254			
256	San Rafael, CA M.D.	490	320	Winchester, VA-WV	247			

Source: Reported data from the F.B.I. "Crime in the United States 2012"

*Violent crimes are offenses of murder, forcible rape, robbery, and aggravated assault.

**Not available.

6. Violent Crime Rate in 2012
National Rate = 386.9 Violent Crimes per 100,000 Population*

RANK	METROPOLITAN AREA	RATE	RANK	METROPOLITAN AREA	RATE	RANK	METROPOLITAN AREA	RATE
193	Abilene, TX	328.6	279	Cheyenne, WY	241.4	203	Gary, IN M.D.	319.9
205	Akron, OH	317.5	NA	Chicago (greater), IL-IN-WI**	NA	358	Gettysburg, PA	110.2
250	Albany-Schenectady-Troy, NY	266.8	NA	Chicago-Joilet-Naperville, IL M.D.**	NA	340	Glens Falls, NY	154.2
20	Albany, GA	670.1	216	Chico, CA	307.7	106	Goldsboro, NC	426.7
356	Albany, OR	116.8	242	Cincinnati, OH-KY-IN	284.5	NA	Grand Forks, ND-MN**	NA
25	Albuquerque, NM	645.1	95	Clarksville, TN-KY	441.4	299	Grand Island, NE	220.0
NA	Alexandria, LA**	NA	52	Cleveland, TN	545.0	209	Grand Junction, CO	313.8
305	Allentown, PA-NJ	210.9	228	Coeur d'Alene, ID	293.5	291	Great Falls, MT	230.6
264	Altoona, PA	252.2	127	College Station-Bryan, TX	397.3	229	Greeley, CO	292.9
64	Amarillo, TX	525.9	146	Colorado Springs, CO	377.9	290	Green Bay, WI	231.1
344	Ames, IA	146.6	147	Columbia, MO	375.4	151	Greensboro-High Point, NC	369.3
298	Anaheim-Santa Ana-Irvine, CA M.D.	220.1	99	Columbus, GA-AL	437.4	39	Greenville-Anderson, SC	570.5
9	Anchorage, AK	811.1	325	Columbus, IN	172.8	118	Greenville, NC	407.3
226	Ann Arbor, MI	294.6	44	Corpus Christi, TX	561.4	275	Hagerstown-Martinsburg, MD-WV	245.9
38	Anniston-Oxford, AL	573.3	357	Corvallis, OR	110.9	3	Hammond, LA	961.1
341	Appleton, WI	154.0	88	Crestview-Fort Walton Beach, FL	460.1	75	Hanford-Corcoran, CA	494.2
295	Asheville, NC	225.3	189	Cumberland, MD-WV	334.0	222	Harrisburg-Carlisle, PA	299.6
202	Athens-Clarke County, GA	320.4	178	Dallas (greater), TX	344.7	351	Harrisonburg, VA	132.1
117	Atlanta, GA	408.6	199	Dallas-Plano-Irving, TX M.D.	326.4	240	Hartford, CT	285.8
NA	Atlantic City, NJ**	NA	257	Dalton, GA	259.9	355	Hattiesburg, MS	118.0
259	Auburn, AL	258.3	45	Danville, IL	556.7	296	Hickory, NC	223.0
211	Augusta, GA-SC	313.1	282	Daphne-Fairhope-Foley, AL	237.9	68	Hilton Head Island, SC	519.6
230	Austin-Round Rock, TX	292.7	150	Davenport, IA-IL	372.2	184	Hinesville, GA	337.6
35	Bakersfield, CA	578.9	232	Dayton, OH	291.7	194	Homosassa Springs, FL	327.6
27	Baltimore, MD	621.2	254	Decatur, AL	262.5	233	Houma, LA	291.2
360	Bangor, ME	90.3	139	Decatur, IL	385.4	43	Houston, TX	561.5
112	Barnstable Town, MA	413.9	123	Deltona-Daytona Beach, FL	403.8	65	Huntsville, AL	521.5
NA	Baton Rouge, LA**	NA	185	Denver-Aurora, CO	337.5	334	Idaho Falls, ID	164.2
223	Bay City, MI	299.5	238	Des Moines-West Des Moines, IA	289.3	32	Indianapolis, IN	599.5
60	Beaumont-Port Arthur, TX	529.1	37	Detroit (greater), MI	574.4	253	Iowa City, IA	265.0
130	Beckley, WV	394.1	2	Detroit-Dearborn-Livonia, MI M.D.	1,049.8	69	Jacksonville, FL	513.4
283	Bellingham, WA	237.3	140	Dothan, AL	385.3	138	Jackson, MS	387.1
243	Billings, MT	284.4	57	Dover, DE	540.7	4	Jackson, TN	958.6
265	Binghamton, NY	251.4	336	Dubuque, IA	161.0	281	Janesville, WI	239.2
42	Birmingham-Hoover, AL	565.1	NA	Duluth, MN-WI**	NA	213	Jefferson City, MO	311.1
166	Bismarck, ND	354.3	105	Durham-Chapel Hill, NC	427.4	210	Johnson City, TN	313.2
332	Blacksburg, VA	165.2	319	Dutchess-Putnam, NY M.D.	182.5	297	Johnstown, PA	222.3
201	Bloomington, IL	321.5	134	East Stroudsburg, PA	391.4	197	Jonesboro, AR	326.9
278	Bloomington, IN	242.3	235	El Centro, CA	290.4	162	Joplin, MO	357.8
335	Bloomsburg-Berwick, PA	163.0	128	El Paso, TX	396.7	258	Kahului-Wailuku-Lahaina, HI	258.9
304	Boise City, ID	211.3	318	Elgin, IL M.D.	183.3	161	Kalamazoo-Portage, MI	358.7
165	Boston (greater), MA-NH	355.2	361	Elizabethtown-Fort Knox, KY	75.8	179	Kankakee, IL	340.2
74	Boston, MA M.D.	496.2	268	Elmira, NY	248.5	77	Kansas City, MO-KS	488.2
308	Boulder, CO	201.3	274	Erie, PA	246.2	288	Kennewick-Richland, WA	234.0
347	Bowling Green, KY	143.5	286	Eugene, OR	236.6	160	Killeen-Temple, TX	359.3
249	Bremerton-Silverdale, WA	270.7	62	Fairbanks, AK	528.9	145	Kingsport, TN-VA	380.0
221	Bridgeport-Stamford, CT	300.4	NA	Fargo, ND-MN**	NA	342	Kingston, NY	152.1
260	Brownsville-Harlingen, TX	256.9	24	Farmington, NM	661.2	109	Knoxville, TN	421.4
86	Brunswick, GA	461.8	148	Fayetteville-Springdale, AR-MO	374.5	252	Kokomo, IN	266.1
93	Buffalo-Niagara Falls, NY	442.5	71	Fayetteville, NC	501.0	NA	La Crosse, WI-MN**	NA
101	Burlington, NC	435.4	188	Flagstaff, AZ	335.3	245	Lafayette, IN	282.5
285	California-Lexington Park, MD	236.8	5	Flint, MI	907.5	NA	Lafayette, LA**	NA
247	Cambridge-Newton, MA M.D.	275.3	177	Florence-Muscle Shoals, AL	346.9	337	Lake Co.-Kenosha Co., IL-WI M.D.	160.6
181	Camden, NJ M.D.	338.9	54	Florence, SC	543.9	322	Lake Havasu City-Kingman, AZ	179.4
225	Canton, OH	296.4	300	Fond du Lac, WI	219.9	171	Lakeland, FL	351.2
173	Cape Coral-Fort Myers, FL	349.1	293	Fort Collins, CO	229.2	331	Lancaster, PA	167.4
100	Cape Girardeau, MO-IL	436.2	79	Fort Lauderdale, FL M.D.	483.2	164	Lansing-East Lansing, MI	355.8
287	Carson City, NV	235.0	115	Fort Smith, AR-OK	409.8	102	Laredo, TX	432.9
310	Casper, WY	196.2	261	Fort Wayne, IN	256.2	183	Las Cruces, NM	337.9
323	Cedar Rapids, IA	177.4	144	Fort Worth-Arlington, TX M.D.	380.3	17	Las Vegas-Henderson, NV	696.5
348	Chambersburg-Waynesboro, PA	140.3	58	Fresno, CA	539.8	152	Lawrence, KS	368.8
66	Champaign-Urbana, IL	521.0	56	Gadsden, AL	542.4	14	Lawton, OK	722.1
108	Charleston-North Charleston, SC	422.2	34	Gainesville, FL	580.4	301	Lebanon, PA	213.3
328	Charlottesville, VA	170.4	324	Gainesville, GA	174.6	345	Lewiston-Auburn, ME	146.1

Note: All listings are for Metropolitan Statistical Areas (M.S.A.s) except for those ending with "M.D." Listings with "M.D." are Metropolitan Divisions which are smaller parts of eleven large M.S.A.s. See explanatory note at beginning of metropolitan area section.

RANK	METROPOLITAN AREA	RATE	RANK	METROPOLITAN AREA	RATE	RANK	METROPOLITAN AREA	RATE
320	Lewiston, ID-WA	180.8	352	Owensboro, KY	126.3	307	Silver Spring-Frederick, MD M.D.	201.6
224	Lexington-Fayette, KY	298.0	309	Oxnard-Thousand Oaks, CA	198.2	303	Sioux City, IA-NE-SD	212.6
63	Lima, OH	526.0	59	Palm Bay-Melbourne, FL	537.8	219	Sioux Falls, SD	303.3
167	Lincoln, NE	353.8	73	Panama City, FL	498.8	212	South Bend-Mishawaka, IN-MI	312.6
22	Little Rock, AR	665.0	186	Parkersburg-Vienna, WV	337.0	94	Spartanburg, SC	441.7
363	Logan, UT-ID	53.4	33	Pensacola, FL	584.9	176	Spokane, WA	347.2
103	Longview, TX	432.4	114	Peoria, IL	411.3	19	Springfield, IL	675.7
227	Longview, WA	293.8	NA	Philadelphia (greater) PA-NJ-MD-DE**	NA	72	Springfield, MA	499.7
91	Los Angeles County, CA M.D.	446.4	NA	Philadelphia, PA M.D.**	NA	81	Springfield, MO	481.4
132	Los Angeles (greater), CA	393.0	120	Phoenix-Mesa-Scottsdale, AZ	406.8	230	Springfield, OH	292.7
107	Louisville, KY-IN	425.3	12	Pine Bluff, AR	730.1	359	State College, PA	97.4
15	Lubbock, TX	720.2	NA	Pittsburgh, PA**	NA	333	Staunton-Waynesboro, VA	165.1
339	Lynchburg, VA	155.7	174	Pittsfield, MA	348.0	6	Stockton-Lodi, CA	889.3
126	Macon, GA	398.5	289	Pocatello, ID	231.4	329	St. George, UT	169.9
31	Madera, CA	605.1	170	Port St. Lucie, FL	352.1	208	St. Joseph, MO-KS	314.5
306	Madison, WI	207.0	251	Portland-Vancouver, OR-WA	266.5	85	St. Louis, MO-IL	463.6
269	Manchester-Nashua, NH	247.5	350	Portland, ME	132.9	10	Sumter, SC	762.3
280	Manhattan, KS	240.0	198	Prescott, AZ	326.8	218	Syracuse, NY	304.1
NA	Mankato-North Mankato, MN**	NA	180	Providence-Warwick, RI-MA	339.7	104	Tacoma, WA M.D.	430.2
311	Mansfield, OH	195.9	362	Provo-Orem, UT	70.8	30	Tallahassee, FL	613.4
204	McAllen-Edinburg-Mission, TX	319.2	70	Pueblo, CO	510.5	116	Tampa-St Petersburg, FL	409.3
200	Medford, OR	326.3	276	Punta Gorda, FL	245.2	315	Terre Haute, IN	189.4
1	Memphis, TN-MS-AR	1,056.8	270	Racine, WI	247.1	18	Texarkana, TX-AR	687.4
16	Merced, CA	698.8	271	Raleigh, NC	247.0	327	The Villages, FL	172.6
41	Miami (greater), FL	565.2	142	Rapid City, SD	382.7	29	Toledo, OH	613.5
23	Miami-Dade County, FL M.D.	663.1	190	Reading, PA	332.8	111	Topeka, KS	416.4
326	Michigan City-La Porte, IN	172.7	13	Redding, CA	723.4	92	Trenton, NJ	446.0
354	Midland, MI	121.2	129	Reno, NV	395.4	84	Tucson, AZ	476.9
207	Midland, TX	314.8	277	Richmond, VA	243.4	55	Tulsa, OK	542.7
36	Milwaukee, WI	575.6	153	Riverside-San Bernardino, CA	368.7	125	Tuscaloosa, AL	400.1
NA	Minneapolis-St. Paul, MN-WI**	NA	262	Roanoke, VA	254.3	135	Tyler, TX	391.1
236	Missoula, MT	289.4	NA	Rochester, MN**	NA	273	Utica-Rome, NY	246.3
46	Mobile, AL	552.1	243	Rochester, NY	284.4	182	Valdosta, GA	338.6
48	Modesto, CA	549.4	11	Rockford, IL	739.7	97	Vallejo-Fairfield, CA	440.1
89	Monroe, LA	455.5	346	Rockingham County, NH M.D.	145.9	67	Victoria, TX	519.7
246	Monroe, MI	277.6	28	Rocky Mount, NC	614.3	49	Vineland-Bridgeton, NJ	548.6
343	Montgomery County, PA M.D.	148.0	157	Rome, GA	363.9	220	Virginia Beach-Norfolk, VA-NC	300.8
168	Montgomery, AL	352.8	96	Sacramento, CA	441.1	83	Visalia-Porterville, CA	477.3
239	Morgantown, WV	288.1	8	Saginaw, MI	816.6	121	Waco, TX	406.0
131	Morristown, TN	393.3	284	Salem, OR	236.9	294	Walla Walla, WA	228.8
312	Mount Vernon-Anacortes, WA	194.5	98	Salinas, CA	438.2	133	Warner Robins, GA	392.0
256	Muncie, IN	261.0	87	Salisbury, MD-DE	461.1	292	Warren-Troy, MI M.D.	229.5
174	Napa, CA	348.0	195	Salt Lake City, UT	327.5	191	Washington (greater) DC-VA-MD-WV	332.7
267	Naples-Marco Island, FL	249.2	136	San Antonio, TX	390.7	155	Washington, DC-VA-MD-WV M.D.	368.0
21	Nashville-Davidson, TN	665.9	149	San Diego, CA	373.6	156	Waterloo-Cedar Falls, IA	364.6
338	Nassau-Suffolk, NY M.D.	160.1	47	San Francisco (greater), CA	550.8	317	Watertown-Fort Drum, NY	186.4
234	New Bern, NC	290.9	76	San Francisco-Redwood, CA M.D.	491.4	353	Wausau, WI	124.7
112	New Haven-Milford, CT	413.9	248	San Jose, CA	274.0	78	West Palm Beach, FL M.D.	487.2
80	New Orleans, LA	483.1	192	San Luis Obispo, CA	330.1	236	Wheeling, WV-OH	289.4
NA	New York (greater), NY-NJ-PA**	NA	314	San Rafael, CA M.D.	190.4	141	Wichita Falls, TX	382.9
NA	New York-Jersey City, NY-NJ M.D.**	NA	137	Santa Cruz-Watsonville, CA	390.3	61	Wichita, KS	529.0
206	Newark, NJ-PA M.D.	315.7	159	Santa Fe, NM	361.9	321	Williamsport, PA	180.4
90	North Port-Sarasota-Bradenton, FL	450.7	143	Santa Maria-Santa Barbara, CA	381.4	53	Wilmington, DE-MD-NJ M.D.	544.8
122	Norwich-New London, CT	405.8	158	Santa Rosa, CA	363.8	154	Wilmington, NC	368.5
26	Oakland-Hayward, CA M.D.	621.5	195	Savannah, GA	327.5	316	Winchester, VA-WV	188.2
82	Ocala, FL	479.4	272	Scranton--Wilkes-Barre, PA	246.4	124	Winston-Salem, NC	402.5
255	Ocean City, NJ	261.6	187	Seattle (greater), WA	336.8	110	Worcester, MA-CT	420.1
7	Odessa, TX	821.3	215	Seattle-Bellevue-Everett, WA M.D.	308.8	172	Yakima, WA	349.4
349	Ogden-Clearfield, UT	140.1	213	Sebastian-Vero Beach, FL	311.1	266	York-Hanover, PA	250.3
49	Oklahoma City, OK	548.6	217	Sebring, FL	306.1	241	Youngstown-Warren, OH-PA	285.1
302	Olympia, WA	213.0	330	Sheboygan, WI	168.9	163	Yuba City, CA	356.7
119	Omaha-Council Bluffs, NE-IA	407.1	263	Sherman-Denison, TX	252.4	169	Yuma, AZ	352.6
51	Orlando, FL	546.1	NA	Shreveport-Bossier City, LA**	NA			
313	Oshkosh-Neenah, WI	190.9	40	Sierra Vista-Douglas, AZ	570.0			

Source: Reported data from the F.B.I. "Crime in the United States 2012"

*Violent crimes are offenses of murder, forcible rape, robbery, and aggravated assault.

**Not available.

6. Violent Crime Rate in 2012 (continued)
National Rate = 386.9 Violent Crimes per 100,000 Population*

RANK	METROPOLITAN AREA	RATE	RANK	METROPOLITAN AREA	RATE	RANK	METROPOLITAN AREA	RATE
1	Memphis, TN-MS-AR	1,056.8	65	Huntsville, AL	521.5	129	Reno, NV	395.4
2	Detroit-Dearborn-Livonia, MI M.D.	1,049.8	66	Champaign-Urbana, IL	521.0	130	Beckley, WV	394.1
3	Hammond, LA	961.1	67	Victoria, TX	519.7	131	Morristown, TN	393.3
4	Jackson, TN	958.6	68	Hilton Head Island, SC	519.6	132	Los Angeles (greater), CA	393.0
5	Flint, MI	907.5	69	Jacksonville, FL	513.4	133	Warner Robins, GA	392.0
6	Stockton-Lodi, CA	889.3	70	Pueblo, CO	510.5	134	East Stroudsburg, PA	391.4
7	Odessa, TX	821.3	71	Fayetteville, NC	501.0	135	Tyler, TX	391.1
8	Saginaw, MI	816.6	72	Springfield, MA	499.7	136	San Antonio, TX	390.7
9	Anchorage, AK	811.1	73	Panama City, FL	498.8	137	Santa Cruz-Watsonville, CA	390.3
10	Sumter, SC	762.3	74	Boston, MA M.D.	496.2	138	Jackson, MS	387.1
11	Rockford, IL	739.7	75	Hanford-Corcoran, CA	494.2	139	Decatur, IL	385.4
12	Pine Bluff, AR	730.1	76	San Francisco-Redwood, CA M.D.	491.4	140	Dothan, AL	385.3
13	Redding, CA	723.4	77	Kansas City, MO-KS	488.2	141	Wichita Falls, TX	382.9
14	Lawton, OK	722.1	78	West Palm Beach, FL M.D.	487.2	142	Rapid City, SD	382.7
15	Lubbock, TX	720.2	79	Fort Lauderdale, FL M.D.	483.2	143	Santa Maria-Santa Barbara, CA	381.4
16	Merced, CA	698.8	80	New Orleans, LA	483.1	144	Fort Worth-Arlington, TX M.D.	380.3
17	Las Vegas-Henderson, NV	696.5	81	Springfield, MO	481.4	145	Kingsport, TN-VA	380.0
18	Texarkana, TX-AR	687.4	82	Ocala, FL	479.4	146	Colorado Springs, CO	377.9
19	Springfield, IL	675.7	83	Visalia-Porterville, CA	477.3	147	Columbia, MO	375.4
20	Albany, GA	670.1	84	Tucson, AZ	476.9	148	Fayetteville-Springdale, AR-MO	374.5
21	Nashville-Davidson, TN	665.9	85	St. Louis, MO-IL	463.6	149	San Diego, CA	373.6
22	Little Rock, AR	665.0	86	Brunswick, GA	461.8	150	Davenport, IA-IL	372.2
23	Miami-Dade County, FL M.D.	663.1	87	Salisbury, MD-DE	461.1	151	Greensboro-High Point, NC	369.3
24	Farmington, NM	661.2	88	Crestview-Fort Walton Beach, FL	460.1	152	Lawrence, KS	368.8
25	Albuquerque, NM	645.1	89	Monroe, LA	455.5	153	Riverside-San Bernardino, CA	368.7
26	Oakland-Hayward, CA M.D.	621.5	90	North Port-Sarasota-Bradenton, FL	450.7	154	Wilmington, NC	368.5
27	Baltimore, MD	621.2	91	Los Angeles County, CA M.D.	446.4	155	Washington, DC-VA-MD-WV M.D.	368.0
28	Rocky Mount, NC	614.3	92	Trenton, NJ	446.0	156	Waterloo-Cedar Falls, IA	364.6
29	Toledo, OH	613.5	93	Buffalo-Niagara Falls, NY	442.5	157	Rome, GA	363.9
30	Tallahassee, FL	613.4	94	Spartanburg, SC	441.7	158	Santa Rosa, CA	363.8
31	Madera, CA	605.1	95	Clarksville, TN-KY	441.4	159	Santa Fe, NM	361.9
32	Indianapolis, IN	599.5	96	Sacramento, CA	441.1	160	Killeen-Temple, TX	359.3
33	Pensacola, FL	584.9	97	Vallejo-Fairfield, CA	440.1	161	Kalamazoo-Portage, MI	358.7
34	Gainesville, FL	580.4	98	Salinas, CA	438.2	162	Joplin, MO	357.8
35	Bakersfield, CA	578.9	99	Columbus, GA-AL	437.4	163	Yuba City, CA	356.7
36	Milwaukee, WI	575.6	100	Cape Girardeau, MO-IL	436.2	164	Lansing-East Lansing, MI	355.8
37	Detroit (greater), MI	574.4	101	Burlington, NC	435.4	165	Boston (greater), MA-NH	355.2
38	Anniston-Oxford, AL	573.3	102	Laredo, TX	432.9	166	Bismarck, ND	354.3
39	Greenville-Anderson, SC	570.5	103	Longview, TX	432.4	167	Lincoln, NE	353.8
40	Sierra Vista-Douglas, AZ	570.0	104	Tacoma, WA M.D.	430.2	168	Montgomery, AL	352.8
41	Miami (greater), FL	565.2	105	Durham-Chapel Hill, NC	427.4	169	Yuma, AZ	352.6
42	Birmingham-Hoover, AL	565.1	106	Goldsboro, NC	426.7	170	Port St. Lucie, FL	352.1
43	Houston, TX	561.5	107	Louisville, KY-IN	425.3	171	Lakeland, FL	351.2
44	Corpus Christi, TX	561.4	108	Charleston-North Charleston, SC	422.2	172	Yakima, WA	349.4
45	Danville, IL	556.7	109	Knoxville, TN	421.4	173	Cape Coral-Fort Myers, FL	349.1
46	Mobile, AL	552.1	110	Worcester, MA-CT	420.1	174	Napa, CA	348.0
47	San Francisco (greater), CA	550.8	111	Topeka, KS	416.4	174	Pittsfield, MA	348.0
48	Modesto, CA	549.4	112	Barnstable Town, MA	413.9	176	Spokane, WA	347.2
49	Oklahoma City, OK	548.6	112	New Haven-Milford, CT	413.9	177	Florence-Muscle Shoals, AL	346.9
49	Vineland-Bridgeton, NJ	548.6	114	Peoria, IL	411.3	178	Dallas (greater), TX	344.7
51	Orlando, FL	546.1	115	Fort Smith, AR-OK	409.8	179	Kankakee, IL	340.2
52	Cleveland, TN	545.0	116	Tampa-St Petersburg, FL	409.3	180	Providence-Warwick, RI-MA	339.7
53	Wilmington, DE-MD-NJ M.D.	544.8	117	Atlanta, GA	408.6	181	Camden, NJ M.D.	338.9
54	Florence, SC	543.9	118	Greenville, NC	407.3	182	Valdosta, GA	338.6
55	Tulsa, OK	542.7	119	Omaha-Council Bluffs, NE-IA	407.1	183	Las Cruces, NM	337.9
56	Gadsden, AL	542.4	120	Phoenix-Mesa-Scottsdale, AZ	406.8	184	Hinesville, GA	337.6
57	Dover, DE	540.7	121	Waco, TX	406.0	185	Denver-Aurora, CO	337.5
58	Fresno, CA	539.8	122	Norwich-New London, CT	405.8	186	Parkersburg-Vienna, WV	337.0
59	Palm Bay-Melbourne, FL	537.8	123	Deltona-Daytona Beach, FL	403.8	187	Seattle (greater), WA	336.8
60	Beaumont-Port Arthur, TX	529.1	124	Winston-Salem, NC	402.5	188	Flagstaff, AZ	335.3
61	Wichita, KS	529.0	125	Tuscaloosa, AL	400.1	189	Cumberland, MD-WV	334.0
62	Fairbanks, AK	528.9	126	Macon, GA	398.5	190	Reading, PA	332.8
63	Lima, OH	526.0	127	College Station-Bryan, TX	397.3	191	Washington (greater) DC-VA-MD-WV	332.7
64	Amarillo, TX	525.9	128	El Paso, TX	396.7	192	San Luis Obispo, CA	330.1

Note: All listings are for Metropolitan Statistical Areas (M.S.A.s) except for those ending with "M.D." Listings with "M.D." are Metropolitan Divisions which are smaller parts of eleven large M.S.A.s. See explanatory note at beginning of metropolitan area section.

RANK	METROPOLITAN AREA	RATE	RANK	METROPOLITAN AREA	RATE	RANK	METROPOLITAN AREA	RATE
193	Abilene, TX	328.6	257	Dalton, GA	259.9	321	Williamsport, PA	180.4
194	Homosassa Springs, FL	327.6	258	Kahului-Wailuku-Lahaina, HI	258.9	322	Lake Havasu City-Kingman, AZ	179.4
195	Salt Lake City, UT	327.5	259	Auburn, AL	258.3	323	Cedar Rapids, IA	177.4
195	Savannah, GA	327.5	260	Brownsville-Harlingen, TX	256.9	324	Gainesville, GA	174.6
197	Jonesboro, AR	326.9	261	Fort Wayne, IN	256.2	325	Columbus, IN	172.8
198	Prescott, AZ	326.8	262	Roanoke, VA	254.3	326	Michigan City-La Porte, IN	172.7
199	Dallas-Plano-Irving, TX M.D.	326.4	263	Sherman-Denison, TX	252.4	327	The Villages, FL	172.6
200	Medford, OR	326.3	264	Altoona, PA	252.2	328	Charlottesville, VA	170.4
201	Bloomington, IL	321.5	265	Binghamton, NY	251.4	329	St. George, UT	169.9
202	Athens-Clarke County, GA	320.4	266	York-Hanover, PA	250.3	330	Sheboygan, WI	168.9
203	Gary, IN M.D.	319.9	267	Naples-Marco Island, FL	249.2	331	Lancaster, PA	167.4
204	McAllen-Edinburg-Mission, TX	319.2	268	Elmira, NY	248.5	332	Blacksburg, VA	165.2
205	Akron, OH	317.5	269	Manchester-Nashua, NH	247.5	333	Staunton-Waynesboro, VA	165.1
206	Newark, NJ-PA M.D.	315.7	270	Racine, WI	247.1	334	Idaho Falls, ID	164.2
207	Midland, TX	314.8	271	Raleigh, NC	247.0	335	Bloomsburg-Berwick, PA	163.0
208	St. Joseph, MO-KS	314.5	272	Scranton--Wilkes-Barre, PA	246.4	336	Dubuque, IA	161.0
209	Grand Junction, CO	313.8	273	Utica-Rome, NY	246.3	337	Lake Co.-Kenosha Co., IL-WI M.D.	160.6
210	Johnson City, TN	313.2	274	Erie, PA	246.2	338	Nassau-Suffolk, NY M.D.	160.1
211	Augusta, GA-SC	313.1	275	Hagerstown-Martinsburg, MD-WV	245.9	339	Lynchburg, VA	155.7
212	South Bend-Mishawaka, IN-MI	312.6	276	Punta Gorda, FL	245.2	340	Glens Falls, NY	154.2
213	Jefferson City, MO	311.1	277	Richmond, VA	243.4	341	Appleton, WI	154.0
213	Sebastian-Vero Beach, FL	311.1	278	Bloomington, IN	242.3	342	Kingston, NY	152.1
215	Seattle-Bellevue-Everett, WA M.D.	308.8	279	Cheyenne, WY	241.4	343	Montgomery County, PA M.D.	148.0
216	Chico, CA	307.7	280	Manhattan, KS	240.0	344	Ames, IA	146.6
217	Sebring, FL	306.1	281	Janesville, WI	239.2	345	Lewiston-Auburn, ME	146.1
218	Syracuse, NY	304.1	282	Daphne-Fairhope-Foley, AL	237.9	346	Rockingham County, NH M.D.	145.9
219	Sioux Falls, SD	303.3	283	Bellingham, WA	237.3	347	Bowling Green, KY	143.5
220	Virginia Beach-Norfolk, VA-NC	300.8	284	Salem, OR	236.9	348	Chambersburg-Waynesboro, PA	140.3
221	Bridgeport-Stamford, CT	300.4	285	California-Lexington Park, MD	236.8	349	Ogden-Clearfield, UT	140.1
222	Harrisburg-Carlisle, PA	299.6	286	Eugene, OR	236.6	350	Portland, ME	132.9
223	Bay City, MI	299.5	287	Carson City, NV	235.0	351	Harrisonburg, VA	132.1
224	Lexington-Fayette, KY	298.0	288	Kennewick-Richland, WA	234.0	352	Owensboro, KY	126.3
225	Canton, OH	296.4	289	Pocatello, ID	231.4	353	Wausau, WI	124.7
226	Ann Arbor, MI	294.6	290	Green Bay, WI	231.1	354	Midland, MI	121.2
227	Longview, WA	293.8	291	Great Falls, MT	230.6	355	Hattiesburg, MS	118.0
228	Coeur d'Alene, ID	293.5	292	Warren-Troy, MI M.D.	229.5	356	Albany, OR	116.8
229	Greeley, CO	292.9	293	Fort Collins, CO	229.2	357	Corvallis, OR	110.9
230	Austin-Round Rock, TX	292.7	294	Walla Walla, WA	228.8	358	Gettysburg, PA	110.2
230	Springfield, OH	292.7	295	Asheville, NC	225.3	359	State College, PA	97.4
232	Dayton, OH	291.7	296	Hickory, NC	223.0	360	Bangor, ME	90.3
233	Houma, LA	291.2	297	Johnstown, PA	222.3	361	Elizabethtown-Fort Knox, KY	75.8
234	New Bern, NC	290.9	298	Anaheim-Santa Ana-Irvine, CA M.D.	220.1	362	Provo-Orem, UT	70.8
235	El Centro, CA	290.4	299	Grand Island, NE	220.0	363	Logan, UT-ID	53.4
236	Missoula, MT	289.4	300	Fond du Lac, WI	219.9	NA	Alexandria, LA**	NA
236	Wheeling, WV-OH	289.4	301	Lebanon, PA	213.3	NA	Atlantic City, NJ**	NA
238	Des Moines-West Des Moines, IA	289.3	302	Olympia, WA	213.0	NA	Baton Rouge, LA**	NA
239	Morgantown, WV	288.1	303	Sioux City, IA-NE-SD	212.6	NA	Chicago (greater), IL-IN-WI**	NA
240	Hartford, CT	285.8	304	Boise City, ID	211.3	NA	Chicago-Joilet-Naperville, IL M.D.**	NA
241	Youngstown-Warren, OH-PA	285.1	305	Allentown, PA-NJ	210.9	NA	Duluth, MN-WI**	NA
242	Cincinnati, OH-KY-IN	284.5	306	Madison, WI	207.0	NA	Fargo, ND-MN**	NA
243	Billings, MT	284.4	307	Silver Spring-Frederick, MD M.D.	201.6	NA	Grand Forks, ND-MN**	NA
243	Rochester, NY	284.4	308	Boulder, CO	201.3	NA	La Crosse, WI-MN**	NA
245	Lafayette, IN	282.5	309	Oxnard-Thousand Oaks, CA	198.2	NA	Lafayette, LA**	NA
246	Monroe, MI	277.6	310	Casper, WY	196.2	NA	Mankato-North Mankato, MN**	NA
247	Cambridge-Newton, MA M.D.	275.3	311	Mansfield, OH	195.9	NA	Minneapolis-St. Paul, MN-WI**	NA
248	San Jose, CA	274.0	312	Mount Vernon-Anacortes, WA	194.5	NA	New York (greater), NY-NJ-PA**	NA
249	Bremerton-Silverdale, WA	270.7	313	Oshkosh-Neenah, WI	190.9	NA	New York-Jersey City, NY-NJ M.D.**	NA
250	Albany-Schenectady-Troy, NY	266.8	314	San Rafael, CA M.D.	190.4	NA	Philadelphia (greater) PA-NJ-MD-DE**	NA
251	Portland-Vancouver, OR-WA	266.5	315	Terre Haute, IN	189.4	NA	Philadelphia, PA M.D.**	NA
252	Kokomo, IN	266.1	316	Winchester, VA-WV	188.2	NA	Pittsburgh, PA**	NA
253	Iowa City, IA	265.0	317	Watertown-Fort Drum, NY	186.4	NA	Rochester, MN**	NA
254	Decatur, AL	262.5	318	Elgin, IL M.D.	183.3	NA	Shreveport-Bossier City, LA**	NA
255	Ocean City, NJ	261.6	319	Dutchess-Putnam, NY M.D.	182.5			
256	Muncie, IN	261.0	320	Lewiston, ID-WA	180.8			

Source: Reported data from the F.B.I. "Crime in the United States 2012"

*Violent crimes are offenses of murder, forcible rape, robbery, and aggravated assault.

**Not available.

7. Percent Change in Violent Crime Rate: 2011 to 2012
National Percent Change = 0.0% Change*

RANK	METROPOLITAN AREA	% CHANGE	RANK	METROPOLITAN AREA	% CHANGE	RANK	METROPOLITAN AREA	% CHANGE
45	Abilene, TX	10.5	152	Cheyenne, WY	(1.2)	124	Gary, IN M.D.	1.6
162	Akron, OH	(2.0)	NA	Chicago (greater), IL-IN-WI**	NA	NA	Gettysburg, PA**	NA
NA	Albany-Schenectady-Troy, NY**	NA	NA	Chicago-Joilet-Naperville, IL M.D.**	NA	NA	Glens Falls, NY**	NA
10	Albany, GA	27.0	17	Chico, CA	18.9	184	Goldsboro, NC	(3.8)
NA	Albany, OR**	NA	NA	Cincinnati, OH-KY-IN**	NA	NA	Grand Forks, ND-MN**	NA
169	Albuquerque, NM	(2.6)	131	Clarksville, TN-KY	1.3	NA	Grand Island, NE**	NA
NA	Alexandria, LA**	NA	243	Cleveland, TN	(13.1)	93	Grand Junction, CO	4.1
NA	Allentown, PA-NJ**	NA	NA	Coeur d'Alene, ID**	NA	209	Great Falls, MT	(7.2)
155	Altoona, PA	(1.4)	42	College Station-Bryan, TX	10.7	141	Greeley, CO	(0.1)
122	Amarillo, TX	1.8	130	Colorado Springs, CO	1.4	2	Green Bay, WI	59.4
265	Ames, IA	(47.2)	231	Columbia, MO	(10.7)	NA	Greensboro-High Point, NC**	NA
107	Anaheim-Santa Ana-Irvine, CA M.D.	3.0	73	Columbus, GA-AL	6.9	NA	Greenville-Anderson, SC**	NA
NA	Anchorage, AK**	NA	81	Columbus, IN	5.9	NA	Greenville, NC**	NA
195	Ann Arbor, MI	(4.8)	88	Corpus Christi, TX	4.6	NA	Hagerstown-Martinsburg, MD-WV**	NA
30	Anniston-Oxford, AL	12.5	152	Corvallis, OR	(1.2)	NA	Hammond, LA**	NA
54	Appleton, WI	8.8	61	Crestview-Fort Walton Beach, FL	7.8	5	Hanford-Corcoran, CA	41.1
105	Asheville, NC	3.3	110	Cumberland, MD-WV	2.8	166	Harrisburg-Carlisle, PA	(2.3)
249	Athens-Clarke County, GA	(14.9)	184	Dallas (greater), TX	(3.8)	36	Harrisonburg, VA	11.6
120	Atlanta, GA	1.9	174	Dallas-Plano-Irving, TX M.D.	(3.1)	169	Hartford, CT	(2.6)
NA	Atlantic City, NJ**	NA	21	Dalton, GA	16.3	NA	Hattiesburg, MS**	NA
13	Auburn, AL	23.0	201	Danville, IL	(5.4)	136	Hickory, NC	0.3
245	Augusta, GA-SC	(13.2)	NA	Daphne-Fairhope-Foley, AL**	NA	NA	Hilton Head Island, SC**	NA
117	Austin-Round Rock, TX	2.0	230	Davenport, IA-IL	(10.6)	147	Hinesville, GA	(0.9)
44	Bakersfield, CA	10.6	134	Dayton, OH	0.6	NA	Homosassa Springs, FL**	NA
187	Baltimore, MD	(3.9)	262	Decatur, IL	(24.5)	213	Houma, LA	(7.4)
28	Bangor, ME	13.0	18	Decatur, AL	18.6	120	Houston, TX	1.9
223	Barnstable Town, MA	(8.7)	NA	Deltona-Daytona Beach, FL**	NA	94	Huntsville, AL	3.9
NA	Baton Rouge, LA**	NA	NA	Denver-Aurora, CO**	NA	250	Idaho Falls, ID	(15.1)
52	Bay City, MI	9.3	91	Des Moines-West Des Moines, IA	4.2	NA	Indianapolis, IN**	NA
174	Beaumont-Port Arthur, TX	(3.1)	139	Detroit (greater), MI	0.1	45	Iowa City, IA	10.5
NA	Beckley, WV**	NA	142	Detroit-Dearborn-Livonia, MI M.D.	(0.2)	160	Jacksonville, FL	(1.9)
47	Bellingham, WA	10.4	191	Dothan, AL	(4.4)	NA	Jackson, MS**	NA
55	Billings, MT	8.5	243	Dover, DE	(13.1)	NA	Jackson, TN**	NA
NA	Binghamton, NY**	NA	98	Dubuque, IA	3.8	162	Janesville, WI	(2.0)
61	Birmingham-Hoover, AL	7.8	NA	Duluth, MN-WI**	NA	151	Jefferson City, MO	(1.1)
1	Bismarck, ND	60.0	174	Durham-Chapel Hill, NC	(3.1)	180	Johnson City, TN	(3.4)
38	Blacksburg, VA	11.2	NA	Dutchess-Putnam, NY M.D.**	NA	252	Johnstown, PA	(15.4)
137	Bloomington, IL	0.2	NA	East Stroudsburg, PA**	NA	247	Jonesboro, AR	(14.6)
NA	Bloomington, IN**	NA	69	El Centro, CA	7.3	26	Joplin, MO	14.2
NA	Bloomsburg-Berwick, PA**	NA	167	El Paso, TX	(2.5)	NA	Kahului-Wailuku-Lahaina, HI**	NA
132	Boise City, ID	1.1	NA	Elgin, IL M.D.**	NA	NA	Kalamazoo-Portage, MI**	NA
NA	Boston (greater), MA-NH**	NA	NA	Elizabethtown-Fort Knox, KY**	NA	239	Kankakee, IL	(12.0)
NA	Boston, MA M.D.**	NA	NA	Elmira, NY**	NA	NA	Kansas City, MO-KS**	NA
246	Boulder, CO	(13.5)	139	Erie, PA	0.1	216	Kennewick-Richland, WA	(8.2)
241	Bowling Green, KY	(12.1)	254	Eugene, OR	(16.0)	66	Killeen-Temple, TX	7.6
248	Bremerton-Silverdale, WA	(14.8)	202	Fairbanks, AK	(5.7)	88	Kingsport, TN-VA	4.6
113	Bridgeport-Stamford, CT	2.3	NA	Fargo, ND-MN**	NA	NA	Kingston, NY**	NA
242	Brownsville-Harlingen, TX	(12.4)	83	Farmington, NM	5.8	NA	Knoxville, TN**	NA
222	Brunswick, GA	(8.6)	NA	Fayetteville-Springdale, AR-MO**	NA	NA	Kokomo, IN**	NA
NA	Buffalo-Niagara Falls, NY**	NA	100	Fayetteville, NC	3.6	NA	La Crosse, WI-MN**	NA
103	Burlington, NC	3.5	259	Flagstaff, AZ	(19.1)	91	Lafayette, IN	4.2
NA	California-Lexington Park, MD**	NA	60	Flint, MI	7.9	NA	Lafayette, LA**	NA
NA	Cambridge-Newton, MA M.D.**	NA	3	Florence-Muscle Shoals, AL	52.2	126	Lake Co.-Kenosha Co., IL-WI M.D.	1.5
182	Camden, NJ M.D.	(3.6)	256	Florence, SC	(17.4)	234	Lake Havasu City-Kingman, AZ	(11.0)
147	Canton, OH	(0.9)	14	Fond du Lac, WI	22.0	253	Lakeland, FL	(15.7)
149	Cape Coral-Fort Myers, FL	(1.0)	71	Fort Collins, CO	7.0	214	Lancaster, PA	(7.8)
204	Cape Girardeau, MO-IL	(5.9)	164	Fort Lauderdale, FL M.D.	(2.1)	188	Lansing-East Lansing, MI	(4.0)
237	Carson City, NV	(11.5)	NA	Fort Smith, AR-OK**	NA	229	Laredo, TX	(10.5)
260	Casper, WY	(20.6)	25	Fort Wayne, IN	14.6	215	Las Cruces, NM	(8.1)
183	Cedar Rapids, IA	(3.7)	199	Fort Worth-Arlington, TX M.D.	(5.3)	65	Las Vegas-Henderson, NV	7.7
NA	Chambersburg-Waynesboro, PA**	NA	158	Fresno, CA	(1.7)	85	Lawrence, KS	5.5
217	Champaign-Urbana, IL	(8.3)	41	Gadsden, AL	10.9	NA	Lawton, OK**	NA
NA	Charleston-North Charleston, SC**	NA	172	Gainesville, FL	(3.0)	16	Lebanon, PA	19.1
106	Charlottesville, VA	3.1	33	Gainesville, GA	11.9	198	Lewiston-Auburn, ME	(5.2)

Note: All listings are for Metropolitan Statistical Areas (M.S.A.s) except for those ending with "M.D." Listings with "M.D." are Metropolitan Divisions which are smaller parts of eleven large M.S.A.s. See explanatory note at beginning of metropolitan area section.

RANK	METROPOLITAN AREA	% CHANGE	RANK	METROPOLITAN AREA	% CHANGE	RANK	METROPOLITAN AREA	% CHANGE
NA	Lewiston, ID-WA**	NA	234	Owensboro, KY	(11.0)	67	Silver Spring-Frederick, MD M.D.	7.5
NA	Lexington-Fayette, KY**	NA	178	Oxnard-Thousand Oaks, CA	(3.2)	NA	Sioux City, IA-NE-SD**	NA
39	Lima, OH	11.1	226	Palm Bay-Melbourne, FL	(9.2)	6	Sioux Falls, SD	41.0
53	Lincoln, NE	9.1	NA	Panama City, FL**	NA	232	South Bend-Mishawaka, IN-MI	(10.8)
233	Little Rock, AR	(10.9)	NA	Parkersburg-Vienna, WV**	NA	NA	Spartanburg, SC**	NA
33	Logan, UT-ID	11.9	40	Pensacola, FL	11.0	NA	Spokane, WA**	NA
32	Longview, TX	12.3	75	Peoria, IL	6.6	196	Springfield, IL	(5.0)
172	Longview, WA	(3.0)	NA	Philadelphia (greater) PA-NJ-MD-DE**	NA	NA	Springfield, MA**	NA
184	Los Angeles County, CA M.D.	(3.8)	NA	Philadelphia, PA M.D.**	NA	28	Springfield, MO	13.0
174	Los Angeles (greater), CA	(3.1)	NA	Phoenix-Mesa-Scottsdale, AZ**	NA	155	Springfield, OH	(1.4)
126	Louisville, KY-IN	1.5	197	Pine Bluff, AR	(5.1)	239	State College, PA	(12.0)
75	Lubbock, TX	6.6	NA	Pittsburgh, PA**	NA	NA	Staunton-Waynesboro, VA**	NA
228	Lynchburg, VA	(9.5)	251	Pittsfield, MA	(15.2)	57	Stockton-Lodi, CA	8.3
110	Macon, GA	2.8	NA	Pocatello, ID**	NA	NA	St. George, UT**	NA
22	Madera, CA	15.6	114	Port St. Lucie, FL	2.2	26	St. Joseph, MO-KS	14.2
NA	Madison, WI**	NA	112	Portland-Vancouver, OR-WA	2.6	206	St. Louis, MO-IL	(6.4)
171	Manchester-Nashua, NH	(2.8)	123	Portland, ME	1.7	4	Sumter, SC	50.7
NA	Manhattan, KS**	NA	223	Prescott, AZ	(8.7)	NA	Syracuse, NY**	NA
NA	Mankato-North Mankato, MN**	NA	NA	Providence-Warwick, RI-MA**	NA	108	Tacoma, WA M.D.	2.9
67	Mansfield, OH	7.5	193	Provo-Orem, UT	(4.5)	209	Tallahassee, FL	(7.2)
58	McAllen-Edinburg-Mission, TX	8.1	188	Pueblo, CO	(4.0)	205	Tampa-St Petersburg, FL	(6.0)
31	Medford, OR	12.4	135	Punta Gorda, FL	0.4	100	Terre Haute, IN	3.6
61	Memphis, TN-MS-AR	7.8	75	Racine, WI	6.6	NA	Texarkana, TX-AR**	NA
9	Merced, CA	28.4	126	Raleigh, NC	1.5	NA	The Villages, FL**	NA
199	Miami (greater), FL	(5.3)	NA	Rapid City, SD**	NA	NA	Toledo, OH**	NA
219	Miami-Dade County, FL M.D.	(8.4)	59	Reading, PA	8.0	42	Topeka, KS	10.7
108	Michigan City-La Porte, IN	2.9	144	Redding, CA	(0.4)	114	Trenton, NJ	2.2
NA	Midland, MI**	NA	133	Reno, NV	1.0	48	Tucson, AZ	10.0
NA	Midland, TX**	NA	99	Richmond, VA	3.7	164	Tulsa, OK	(2.1)
8	Milwaukee, WI	28.5	94	Riverside-San Bernardino, CA	3.9	NA	Tuscaloosa, AL**	NA
NA	Minneapolis-St. Paul, MN-WI**	NA	207	Roanoke, VA	(6.5)	81	Tyler, TX	5.9
22	Missoula, MT	15.6	NA	Rochester, MN**	NA	NA	Utica-Rome, NY**	NA
226	Mobile, AL	(9.2)	NA	Rochester, NY**	NA	154	Valdosta, GA	(1.3)
24	Modesto, CA	15.1	87	Rockford, IL	4.7	116	Vallejo-Fairfield, CA	2.1
264	Monroe, LA	(28.8)	167	Rockingham County, NH M.D.	(2.5)	NA	Victoria, TX**	NA
35	Monroe, MI	11.8	12	Rocky Mount, NC	23.1	NA	Vineland-Bridgeton, NJ**	NA
NA	Montgomery County, PA M.D.**	NA	263	Rome, GA	(26.9)	211	Virginia Beach-Norfolk, VA-NC	(7.3)
19	Montgomery, AL	18.4	86	Sacramento, CA	5.0	48	Visalia-Porterville, CA	10.0
NA	Morgantown, WV**	NA	94	Saginaw, MI	3.9	NA	Waco, TX**	NA
NA	Morristown, TN**	NA	84	Salem, OR	5.7	NA	Walla Walla, WA**	NA
194	Mount Vernon-Anacortes, WA	(4.6)	202	Salinas, CA	(5.7)	NA	Warner Robins, GA**	NA
266	Muncie, IN	(48.7)	NA	Salisbury, MD-DE**	NA	103	Warren-Troy, MI M.D.	3.5
78	Napa, CA	6.3	61	Salt Lake City, UT	7.8	145	Washington (greater) DC-VA-MD-WV	(0.6)
261	Naples-Marco Island, FL	(21.0)	160	San Antonio, TX	(1.9)	159	Washington, DC-VA-MD-WV M.D.	(1.8)
NA	Nashville-Davidson, TN**	NA	78	San Diego, CA	6.3	48	Waterloo-Cedar Falls, IA	10.0
NA	Nassau-Suffolk, NY M.D.**	NA	56	San Francisco (greater), CA	8.4	NA	Watertown-Fort Drum, NY**	NA
NA	New Bern, NC**	NA	20	San Francisco-Redwood, CA M.D.	16.5	254	Wausau, WI	(16.0)
37	New Haven-Milford, CT	11.5	71	San Jose, CA	7.0	149	West Palm Beach, FL M.D.	(1.0)
157	New Orleans, LA	(1.5)	7	San Luis Obispo, CA	32.4	NA	Wheeling, WV-OH**	NA
NA	New York (greater), NY-NJ-PA**	NA	NA	San Rafael, CA M.D.**	NA	70	Wichita Falls, TX	7.2
NA	New York-Jersey City, NY-NJ M.D.**	NA	236	Santa Cruz-Watsonville, CA	(11.4)	219	Wichita, KS	(8.4)
NA	Newark, NJ-PA M.D.**	NA	191	Santa Fe, NM	(4.4)	126	Williamsport, PA	1.5
225	North Port-Sarasota-Bradenton, FL	(8.8)	NA	Santa Maria-Santa Barbara, CA**	NA	137	Wilmington, DE-MD-NJ M.D.	0.2
117	Norwich-New London, CT	2.0	88	Santa Rosa, CA	4.6	NA	Wilmington, NC**	NA
51	Oakland-Hayward, CA M.D.	9.4	188	Savannah, GA	(4.0)	146	Winchester, VA-WV	(0.7)
181	Ocala, FL	(3.5)	221	Scranton--Wilkes-Barre, PA	(8.5)	NA	Winston-Salem, NC**	NA
256	Ocean City, NJ	(17.4)	117	Seattle (greater), WA	2.0	NA	Worcester, MA-CT**	NA
15	Odessa, TX	20.9	124	Seattle-Bellevue-Everett, WA M.D.	1.6	73	Yakima, WA	6.9
NA	Ogden-Clearfield, UT**	NA	179	Sebastian-Vero Beach, FL	(3.3)	258	York-Hanover, PA	(17.5)
94	Oklahoma City, OK	3.9	NA	Sebring, FL**	NA	NA	Youngstown-Warren, OH-PA**	NA
208	Olympia, WA	(7.0)	11	Sheboygan, WI	24.0	238	Yuba City, CA	(11.9)
80	Omaha-Council Bluffs, NE-IA	6.1	211	Sherman-Denison, TX	(7.3)	100	Yuma, AZ	3.6
217	Orlando, FL	(8.3)	NA	Shreveport-Bossier City, LA**	NA			
143	Oshkosh-Neenah, WI	(0.3)	NA	Sierra Vista-Douglas, AZ**	NA			

Source: CQ Press using reported data from the F.B.I. "Crime in the United States 2012"

*Violent crimes are offenses of murder, forcible rape, robbery, and aggravated assault.

**Not available.

7. Percent Change in Violent Crime Rate: 2011 to 2012 (continued)
National Percent Change = 0.0% Change*

RANK	METROPOLITAN AREA	% CHANGE	RANK	METROPOLITAN AREA	% CHANGE	RANK	METROPOLITAN AREA	% CHANGE
1	Bismarck, ND	60.0	65	Las Vegas-Henderson, NV	7.7	126	Williamsport, PA	1.5
2	Green Bay, WI	59.4	66	Killeen-Temple, TX	7.6	130	Colorado Springs, CO	1.4
3	Florence-Muscle Shoals, AL	52.2	67	Mansfield, OH	7.5	131	Clarksville, TN-KY	1.3
4	Sumter, SC	50.7	67	Silver Spring-Frederick, MD M.D.	7.5	132	Boise City, ID	1.1
5	Hanford-Corcoran, CA	41.1	69	El Centro, CA	7.3	133	Reno, NV	1.0
6	Sioux Falls, SD	41.0	70	Wichita Falls, TX	7.2	134	Dayton, OH	0.6
7	San Luis Obispo, CA	32.4	71	Fort Collins, CO	7.0	135	Punta Gorda, FL	0.4
8	Milwaukee, WI	28.5	71	San Jose, CA	7.0	136	Hickory, NC	0.3
9	Merced, CA	28.4	73	Columbus, GA-AL	6.9	137	Bloomington, IL	0.2
10	Albany, GA	27.0	73	Yakima, WA	6.9	137	Wilmington, DE-MD-NJ M.D.	0.2
11	Sheboygan, WI	24.0	75	Lubbock, TX	6.6	139	Detroit (greater), MI	0.1
12	Rocky Mount, NC	23.1	75	Peoria, IL	6.6	139	Erie, PA	0.1
13	Auburn, AL	23.0	75	Racine, WI	6.6	141	Greeley, CO	(0.1)
14	Fond du Lac, WI	22.0	78	Napa, CA	6.3	142	Detroit-Dearborn-Livonia, MI M.D.	(0.2)
15	Odessa, TX	20.9	78	San Diego, CA	6.3	143	Oshkosh-Neenah, WI	(0.3)
16	Lebanon, PA	19.1	80	Omaha-Council Bluffs, NE-IA	6.1	144	Redding, CA	(0.4)
17	Chico, CA	18.9	81	Columbus, IN	5.9	145	Washington (greater) DC-VA-MD-WV	(0.6)
18	Decatur, AL	18.6	81	Tyler, TX	5.9	146	Winchester, VA-WV	(0.7)
19	Montgomery, AL	18.4	83	Farmington, NM	5.8	147	Canton, OH	(0.9)
20	San Francisco-Redwood, CA M.D.	16.5	84	Salem, OR	5.7	147	Hinesville, GA	(0.9)
21	Dalton, GA	16.3	85	Lawrence, KS	5.5	149	Cape Coral-Fort Myers, FL	(1.0)
22	Madera, CA	15.6	86	Sacramento, CA	5.0	149	West Palm Beach, FL M.D.	(1.0)
22	Missoula, MT	15.6	87	Rockford, IL	4.7	151	Jefferson City, MO	(1.1)
24	Modesto, CA	15.1	88	Corpus Christi, TX	4.6	152	Cheyenne, WY	(1.2)
25	Fort Wayne, IN	14.6	88	Kingsport, TN-VA	4.6	152	Corvallis, OR	(1.2)
26	Joplin, MO	14.2	88	Santa Rosa, CA	4.6	154	Valdosta, GA	(1.3)
26	St. Joseph, MO-KS	14.2	91	Des Moines-West Des Moines, IA	4.2	155	Altoona, PA	(1.4)
28	Bangor, ME	13.0	91	Lafayette, IN	4.2	155	Springfield, OH	(1.4)
28	Springfield, MO	13.0	93	Grand Junction, CO	4.1	157	New Orleans, LA	(1.5)
30	Anniston-Oxford, AL	12.5	94	Huntsville, AL	3.9	158	Fresno, CA	(1.7)
31	Medford, OR	12.4	94	Oklahoma City, OK	3.9	159	Washington, DC-VA-MD-WV M.D.	(1.8)
32	Longview, TX	12.3	94	Riverside-San Bernardino, CA	3.9	160	Jacksonville, FL	(1.9)
33	Gainesville, GA	11.9	94	Saginaw, MI	3.9	160	San Antonio, TX	(1.9)
33	Logan, UT-ID	11.9	98	Dubuque, IA	3.8	162	Akron, OH	(2.0)
35	Monroe, MI	11.8	99	Richmond, VA	3.7	162	Janesville, WI	(2.0)
36	Harrisonburg, VA	11.6	100	Fayetteville, NC	3.6	164	Fort Lauderdale, FL M.D.	(2.1)
37	New Haven-Milford, CT	11.5	100	Terre Haute, IN	3.6	164	Tulsa, OK	(2.1)
38	Blacksburg, VA	11.2	100	Yuma, AZ	3.6	166	Harrisburg-Carlisle, PA	(2.3)
39	Lima, OH	11.1	103	Burlington, NC	3.5	167	El Paso, TX	(2.5)
40	Pensacola, FL	11.0	103	Warren-Troy, MI M.D.	3.5	167	Rockingham County, NH M.D.	(2.5)
41	Gadsden, AL	10.9	105	Asheville, NC	3.3	169	Albuquerque, NM	(2.6)
42	College Station-Bryan, TX	10.7	106	Charlottesville, VA	3.1	169	Hartford, CT	(2.6)
42	Topeka, KS	10.7	107	Anaheim-Santa Ana-Irvine, CA M.D.	3.0	171	Manchester-Nashua, NH	(2.8)
44	Bakersfield, CA	10.6	108	Michigan City-La Porte, IN	2.9	172	Gainesville, FL	(3.0)
45	Abilene, TX	10.5	108	Tacoma, WA M.D.	2.9	172	Longview, WA	(3.0)
45	Iowa City, IA	10.5	110	Cumberland, MD-WV	2.8	174	Beaumont-Port Arthur, TX	(3.1)
47	Bellingham, WA	10.4	110	Macon, GA	2.8	174	Dallas-Plano-Irving, TX M.D.	(3.1)
48	Tucson, AZ	10.0	112	Portland-Vancouver, OR-WA	2.6	174	Durham-Chapel Hill, NC	(3.1)
48	Visalia-Porterville, CA	10.0	113	Bridgeport-Stamford, CT	2.3	174	Los Angeles (greater), CA	(3.1)
48	Waterloo-Cedar Falls, IA	10.0	114	Port St. Lucie, FL	2.2	178	Oxnard-Thousand Oaks, CA	(3.2)
51	Oakland-Hayward, CA M.D.	9.4	114	Trenton, NJ	2.2	179	Sebastian-Vero Beach, FL	(3.3)
52	Bay City, MI	9.3	116	Vallejo-Fairfield, CA	2.1	180	Johnson City, TN	(3.4)
53	Lincoln, NE	9.1	117	Austin-Round Rock, TX	2.0	181	Ocala, FL	(3.5)
54	Appleton, WI	8.8	117	Norwich-New London, CT	2.0	182	Camden, NJ M.D.	(3.6)
55	Billings, MT	8.5	117	Seattle (greater), WA	2.0	183	Cedar Rapids, IA	(3.7)
56	San Francisco (greater), CA	8.4	120	Atlanta, GA	1.9	184	Dallas (greater), TX	(3.8)
57	Stockton-Lodi, CA	8.3	120	Houston, TX	1.9	184	Goldsboro, NC	(3.8)
58	McAllen-Edinburg-Mission, TX	8.1	122	Amarillo, TX	1.8	184	Los Angeles County, CA M.D.	(3.8)
59	Reading, PA	8.0	123	Portland, ME	1.7	187	Baltimore, MD	(3.9)
60	Flint, MI	7.9	124	Gary, IN M.D.	1.6	188	Lansing-East Lansing, MI	(4.0)
61	Birmingham-Hoover, AL	7.8	124	Seattle-Bellevue-Everett, WA M.D.	1.6	188	Pueblo, CO	(4.0)
61	Crestview-Fort Walton Beach, FL	7.8	126	Lake Co.-Kenosha Co., IL-WI M.D.	1.5	188	Savannah, GA	(4.0)
61	Memphis, TN-MS-AR	7.8	126	Louisville, KY-IN	1.5	191	Dothan, AL	(4.4)
61	Salt Lake City, UT	7.8	126	Raleigh, NC	1.5	191	Santa Fe, NM	(4.4)

Note: All listings are for Metropolitan Statistical Areas (M.S.A.s) except for those ending with "M.D." Listings with "M.D." are Metropolitan Divisions which are smaller parts of eleven large M.S.A.s. See explanatory note at beginning of metropolitan area section.

RANK	METROPOLITAN AREA	% CHANGE	RANK	METROPOLITAN AREA	% CHANGE	RANK	METROPOLITAN AREA	% CHANGE
193	Provo-Orem, UT	(4.5)	256	Ocean City, NJ	(17.4)	NA	Kokomo, IN**	NA
194	Mount Vernon-Anacortes, WA	(4.6)	258	York-Hanover, PA	(17.5)	NA	La Crosse, WI-MN**	NA
195	Ann Arbor, MI	(4.8)	259	Flagstaff, AZ	(19.1)	NA	Lafayette, LA**	NA
196	Springfield, IL	(5.0)	260	Casper, WY	(20.6)	NA	Lawton, OK**	NA
197	Pine Bluff, AR	(5.1)	261	Naples-Marco Island, FL	(21.0)	NA	Lewiston, ID-WA**	NA
198	Lewiston-Auburn, ME	(5.2)	262	Decatur, IL	(24.5)	NA	Lexington-Fayette, KY**	NA
199	Fort Worth-Arlington, TX M.D.	(5.3)	263	Rome, GA	(26.9)	NA	Madison, WI**	NA
199	Miami (greater), FL	(5.3)	264	Monroe, LA	(28.8)	NA	Manhattan, KS**	NA
201	Danville, IL	(5.4)	265	Ames, IA	(47.2)	NA	Mankato-North Mankato, MN**	NA
202	Fairbanks, AK	(5.7)	266	Muncie, IN	(48.7)	NA	Midland, MI**	NA
202	Salinas, CA	(5.7)	NA	Albany-Schenectady-Troy, NY**	NA	NA	Midland, TX**	NA
204	Cape Girardeau, MO-IL	(5.9)	NA	Albany, OR**	NA	NA	Minneapolis-St. Paul, MN-WI**	NA
205	Tampa-St Petersburg, FL	(6.0)	NA	Alexandria, LA**	NA	NA	Montgomery County, PA M.D.**	NA
206	St. Louis, MO-IL	(6.4)	NA	Allentown, PA-NJ**	NA	NA	Morgantown, WV**	NA
207	Roanoke, VA	(6.5)	NA	Anchorage, AK**	NA	NA	Morristown, TN**	NA
208	Olympia, WA	(7.0)	NA	Atlantic City, NJ**	NA	NA	Nashville-Davidson, TN**	NA
209	Great Falls, MT	(7.2)	NA	Baton Rouge, LA**	NA	NA	Nassau-Suffolk, NY M.D.**	NA
209	Tallahassee, FL	(7.2)	NA	Beckley, WV**	NA	NA	New Bern, NC**	NA
211	Sherman-Denison, TX	(7.3)	NA	Binghamton, NY**	NA	NA	New York (greater), NY-NJ-PA**	NA
211	Virginia Beach-Norfolk, VA-NC	(7.3)	NA	Bloomington, IN**	NA	NA	New York-Jersey City, NY-NJ M.D.**	NA
213	Houma, LA	(7.4)	NA	Bloomsburg-Berwick, PA**	NA	NA	Newark, NJ-PA M.D.**	NA
214	Lancaster, PA	(7.8)	NA	Boston (greater), MA-NH**	NA	NA	Ogden-Clearfield, UT**	NA
215	Las Cruces, NM	(8.1)	NA	Boston, MA M.D.**	NA	NA	Panama City, FL**	NA
216	Kennewick-Richland, WA	(8.2)	NA	Buffalo-Niagara Falls, NY**	NA	NA	Parkersburg-Vienna, WV**	NA
217	Champaign-Urbana, IL	(8.3)	NA	California-Lexington Park, MD**	NA	NA	Philadelphia (greater) PA-NJ-MD-DE**	NA
217	Orlando, FL	(8.3)	NA	Cambridge-Newton, MA M.D.**	NA	NA	Philadelphia, PA M.D.**	NA
219	Miami-Dade County, FL M.D.	(8.4)	NA	Chambersburg-Waynesboro, PA**	NA	NA	Phoenix-Mesa-Scottsdale, AZ**	NA
219	Wichita, KS	(8.4)	NA	Charleston-North Charleston, SC**	NA	NA	Pittsburgh, PA**	NA
221	Scranton--Wilkes-Barre, PA	(8.5)	NA	Chicago (greater), IL-IN-WI**	NA	NA	Pocatello, ID**	NA
222	Brunswick, GA	(8.6)	NA	Chicago-Joilet-Naperville, IL M.D.**	NA	NA	Providence-Warwick, RI-MA**	NA
223	Barnstable Town, MA	(8.7)	NA	Cincinnati, OH-KY-IN**	NA	NA	Rapid City, SD**	NA
223	Prescott, AZ	(8.7)	NA	Coeur d'Alene, ID**	NA	NA	Rochester, MN**	NA
225	North Port-Sarasota-Bradenton, FL	(8.8)	NA	Daphne-Fairhope-Foley, AL**	NA	NA	Rochester, NY**	NA
226	Mobile, AL	(9.2)	NA	Deltona-Daytona Beach, FL**	NA	NA	Salisbury, MD-DE**	NA
226	Palm Bay-Melbourne, FL	(9.2)	NA	Denver-Aurora, CO**	NA	NA	San Rafael, CA M.D.**	NA
228	Lynchburg, VA	(9.5)	NA	Duluth, MN-WI**	NA	NA	Santa Maria-Santa Barbara, CA**	NA
229	Laredo, TX	(10.5)	NA	Dutchess-Putnam, NY M.D.**	NA	NA	Sebring, FL**	NA
230	Davenport, IA-IL	(10.6)	NA	East Stroudsburg, PA**	NA	NA	Shreveport-Bossier City, LA**	NA
231	Columbia, MO	(10.7)	NA	Elgin, IL M.D.**	NA	NA	Sierra Vista-Douglas, AZ**	NA
232	South Bend-Mishawaka, IN-MI	(10.8)	NA	Elizabethtown-Fort Knox, KY**	NA	NA	Sioux City, IA-NE-SD**	NA
233	Little Rock, AR	(10.9)	NA	Elmira, NY**	NA	NA	Spartanburg, SC**	NA
234	Lake Havasu City-Kingman, AZ	(11.0)	NA	Fargo, ND-MN**	NA	NA	Spokane, WA**	NA
234	Owensboro, KY	(11.0)	NA	Fayetteville-Springdale, AR-MO**	NA	NA	Springfield, MA**	NA
236	Santa Cruz-Watsonville, CA	(11.4)	NA	Fort Smith, AR-OK**	NA	NA	Staunton-Waynesboro, VA**	NA
237	Carson City, NV	(11.5)	NA	Gettysburg, PA**	NA	NA	St. George, UT**	NA
238	Yuba City, CA	(11.9)	NA	Glens Falls, NY**	NA	NA	Syracuse, NY**	NA
239	Kankakee, IL	(12.0)	NA	Grand Forks, ND-MN**	NA	NA	Texarkana, TX-AR**	NA
239	State College, PA	(12.0)	NA	Grand Island, NE**	NA	NA	The Villages, FL**	NA
241	Bowling Green, KY	(12.1)	NA	Greensboro-High Point, NC**	NA	NA	Toledo, OH**	NA
242	Brownsville-Harlingen, TX	(12.4)	NA	Greenville-Anderson, SC**	NA	NA	Tuscaloosa, AL**	NA
243	Cleveland, TN	(13.1)	NA	Greenville, NC**	NA	NA	Utica-Rome, NY**	NA
243	Dover, DE	(13.1)	NA	Hagerstown-Martinsburg, MD-WV**	NA	NA	Victoria, TX**	NA
245	Augusta, GA-SC	(13.2)	NA	Hammond, LA**	NA	NA	Vineland-Bridgeton, NJ**	NA
246	Boulder, CO	(13.5)	NA	Hattiesburg, MS**	NA	NA	Waco, TX**	NA
247	Jonesboro, AR	(14.6)	NA	Hilton Head Island, SC**	NA	NA	Walla Walla, WA**	NA
248	Bremerton-Silverdale, WA	(14.8)	NA	Homosassa Springs, FL**	NA	NA	Warner Robins, GA**	NA
249	Athens-Clarke County, GA	(14.9)	NA	Indianapolis, IN**	NA	NA	Watertown-Fort Drum, NY**	NA
250	Idaho Falls, ID	(15.1)	NA	Jackson, MS**	NA	NA	Wheeling, WV-OH**	NA
251	Pittsfield, MA	(15.2)	NA	Jackson, TN**	NA	NA	Wilmington, NC**	NA
252	Johnstown, PA	(15.4)	NA	Kahului-Wailuku-Lahaina, HI**	NA	NA	Winston-Salem, NC**	NA
253	Lakeland, FL	(15.7)	NA	Kalamazoo-Portage, MI**	NA	NA	Worcester, MA-CT**	NA
254	Eugene, OR	(16.0)	NA	Kansas City, MO-KS**	NA	NA	Youngstown-Warren, OH-PA**	NA
254	Wausau, WI	(16.0)	NA	Kingston, NY**	NA			
256	Florence, SC	(17.4)	NA	Knoxville, TN**	NA			

Source: CQ Press using reported data from the F.B.I. "Crime in the United States 2012"

*Violent crimes are offenses of murder, forcible rape, robbery, and aggravated assault.

**Not available.

8. Percent Change in Violent Crime Rate: 2008 to 2012
National Percent Change = 15.6% Decrease*

RANK	METROPOLITAN AREA	% CHANGE	RANK	METROPOLITAN AREA	% CHANGE	RANK	METROPOLITAN AREA	% CHANGE
205	Abilene, TX	(26.9)	26	Cheyenne, WY	14.7	NA	Gary, IN M.D.**	NA
93	Akron, OH	(8.6)	NA	Chicago (greater), IL-IN-WI**	NA	NA	Gettysburg, PA**	NA
NA	Albany-Schenectady-Troy, NY**	NA	NA	Chicago-Joilet-Naperville, IL M.D.**	NA	NA	Glens Falls, NY**	NA
NA	Albany, GA**	NA	156	Chico, CA	(19.2)	116	Goldsboro, NC	(12.3)
NA	Albany, OR**	NA	NA	Cincinnati, OH-KY-IN**	NA	NA	Grand Forks, ND-MN**	NA
156	Albuquerque, NM	(19.2)	147	Clarksville, TN-KY	(18.0)	NA	Grand Island, NE**	NA
NA	Alexandria, LA**	NA	184	Cleveland, TN	(22.6)	79	Grand Junction, CO	(6.9)
NA	Allentown, PA-NJ**	NA	NA	Coeur d'Alene, ID**	NA	98	Great Falls, MT	(9.8)
134	Altoona, PA	(15.0)	161	College Station-Bryan, TX	(19.7)	73	Greeley, CO	(5.7)
144	Amarillo, TX	(17.6)	161	Colorado Springs, CO	(19.7)	24	Green Bay, WI	15.8
241	Ames, IA	(48.8)	29	Columbia, MO	13.8	215	Greensboro-High Point, NC	(28.8)
127	Anaheim-Santa Ana-Irvine, CA M.D.	(13.6)	171	Columbus, GA-AL	(20.8)	NA	Greenville-Anderson, SC**	NA
NA	Anchorage, AK**	NA	1	Columbus, IN	82.7	219	Greenville, NC	(31.1)
174	Ann Arbor, MI	(21.8)	109	Corpus Christi, TX	(11.2)	NA	Hagerstown-Martinsburg, MD-WV**	NA
NA	Anniston-Oxford, AL**	NA	143	Corvallis, OR	(17.5)	NA	Hammond, LA**	NA
8	Appleton, WI	33.3	NA	Crestview-Fort Walton Beach, FL**	NA	12	Hanford-Corcoran, CA	21.3
170	Asheville, NC	(20.7)	202	Cumberland, MD-WV	(26.6)	78	Harrisburg-Carlisle, PA	(6.6)
174	Athens-Clarke County, GA	(21.8)	192	Dallas (greater), TX	(24.7)	94	Harrisonburg, VA	(9.1)
149	Atlanta, GA	(18.4)	209	Dallas-Plano-Irving, TX M.D.	(28.0)	65	Hartford, CT	(3.9)
NA	Atlantic City, NJ**	NA	182	Dalton, GA	(22.5)	NA	Hattiesburg, MS**	NA
237	Auburn, AL	(44.4)	NA	Danville, IL**	NA	163	Hickory, NC	(20.0)
NA	Augusta, GA-SC**	NA	NA	Daphne-Fairhope-Foley, AL**	NA	NA	Hilton Head Island, SC**	NA
135	Austin-Round Rock, TX	(15.3)	NA	Davenport, IA-IL**	NA	187	Hinesville, GA	(23.6)
49	Bakersfield, CA	0.5	153	Dayton, OH	(18.7)	NA	Homosassa Springs, FL**	NA
149	Baltimore, MD	(18.4)	49	Decatur, AL	0.5	230	Houma, LA	(35.8)
18	Bangor, ME	18.8	NA	Decatur, IL**	NA	149	Houston, TX	(18.4)
68	Barnstable Town, MA	(4.8)	225	Deltona-Daytona Beach, FL	(31.8)	9	Huntsville, AL	23.8
NA	Baton Rouge, LA**	NA	NA	Denver-Aurora, CO**	NA	236	Idaho Falls, ID	(42.0)
79	Bay City, MI	(6.9)	121	Des Moines-West Des Moines, IA	(13.1)	77	Indianapolis, IN	(6.1)
59	Beaumont-Port Arthur, TX	(2.3)	NA	Detroit (greater), MI**	NA	91	Iowa City, IA	(8.2)
NA	Beckley, WV**	NA	NA	Detroit-Dearborn-Livonia, MI M.D.**	NA	231	Jacksonville, FL	(37.5)
41	Bellingham, WA	5.1	66	Dothan, AL	(4.2)	NA	Jackson, MS**	NA
20	Billings, MT	18.3	156	Dover, DE	(19.2)	NA	Jackson, TN**	NA
NA	Binghamton, NY**	NA	244	Dubuque, IA	(64.1)	64	Janesville, WI	(3.3)
70	Birmingham-Hoover, AL	(4.9)	NA	Duluth, MN-WI**	NA	NA	Jefferson City, MO**	NA
2	Bismarck, ND	67.0	140	Durham-Chapel Hill, NC	(16.8)	129	Johnson City, TN	(14.4)
207	Blacksburg, VA	(27.4)	NA	Dutchess-Putnam, NY M.D.**	NA	33	Johnstown, PA	12.4
NA	Bloomington, IL**	NA	NA	East Stroudsburg, PA**	NA	138	Jonesboro, AR	(16.0)
21	Bloomington, IN	18.0	53	El Centro, CA	0.3	92	Joplin, MO	(8.3)
NA	Bloomsburg-Berwick, PA**	NA	96	El Paso, TX	(9.2)	NA	Kahului-Wailuku-Lahaina, HI**	NA
109	Boise City, ID	(11.2)	NA	Elgin, IL M.D.**	NA	155	Kalamazoo-Portage, MI	(19.0)
NA	Boston (greater), MA-NH**	NA	NA	Elizabethtown-Fort Knox, KY**	NA	NA	Kankakee, IL**	NA
NA	Boston, MA M.D.**	NA	NA	Elmira, NY**	NA	NA	Kansas City, MO-KS**	NA
NA	Boulder, CO**	NA	159	Erie, PA	(19.4)	87	Kennewick-Richland, WA	(8.0)
243	Bowling Green, KY	(53.6)	208	Eugene, OR	(27.7)	108	Killeen-Temple, TX	(11.0)
235	Bremerton-Silverdale, WA	(41.7)	NA	Fairbanks, AK**	NA	39	Kingsport, TN-VA	5.8
89	Bridgeport-Stamford, CT	(8.1)	NA	Fargo, ND-MN**	NA	NA	Kingston, NY**	NA
233	Brownsville-Harlingen, TX	(39.2)	NA	Farmington, NM**	NA	NA	Knoxville, TN**	NA
NA	Brunswick, GA**	NA	14	Fayetteville-Springdale, AR-MO	20.0	NA	Kokomo, IN**	NA
NA	Buffalo-Niagara Falls, NY**	NA	221	Fayetteville, NC	(31.4)	NA	La Crosse, WI-MN**	NA
85	Burlington, NC	(7.8)	103	Flagstaff, AZ	(10.0)	16	Lafayette, IN	19.3
NA	California-Lexington Park, MD**	NA	11	Flint, MI	21.9	NA	Lafayette, LA**	NA
81	Camden, NJ M.D.	(7.0)	120	Florence-Muscle Shoals, AL	(13.0)	NA	Lake Co.-Kenosha Co., IL-WI M.D.**	NA
NA	Canton, OH**	NA	240	Florence, SC	(45.7)	169	Lake Havasu City-Kingman, AZ	(20.6)
196	Cape Coral-Fort Myers, FL	(25.5)	46	Fond du Lac, WI	2.5	213	Lakeland, FL	(28.6)
17	Cape Girardeau, MO-IL	19.0	135	Fort Collins, CO	(15.3)	117	Lancaster, PA	(12.4)
239	Carson City, NV	(44.7)	166	Fort Lauderdale, FL M.D.	(20.3)	149	Lansing-East Lansing, MI	(18.4)
198	Casper, WY	(25.9)	NA	Fort Smith, AR-OK**	NA	210	Laredo, TX	(28.1)
129	Cedar Rapids, IA	(14.4)	27	Fort Wayne, IN	14.6	177	Las Cruces, NM	(21.9)
NA	Chambersburg-Waynesboro, PA**	NA	148	Fort Worth-Arlington, TX M.D.	(18.3)	141	Las Vegas-Henderson, NV	(17.1)
NA	Champaign-Urbana, IL**	NA	28	Fresno, CA	14.3	81	Lawrence, KS	(7.0)
234	Charleston-North Charleston, SC	(41.4)	5	Gadsden, AL	39.9	NA	Lawton, OK**	NA
163	Charlottesville, VA	(20.0)	206	Gainesville, FL	(27.3)	105	Lebanon, PA	(10.5)
			NA	Gainesville, GA**	NA	61	Lewiston-Auburn, ME	(2.5)

Note: All listings are for Metropolitan Statistical Areas (M.S.A.s) except for those ending with "M.D." Listings with "M.D." are Metropolitan Divisions which are smaller parts of eleven large M.S.A.s. See explanatory note at beginning of metropolitan area section.

RANK	METROPOLITAN AREA	% CHANGE	RANK	METROPOLITAN AREA	% CHANGE	RANK	METROPOLITAN AREA	% CHANGE
10	Lewiston, ID-WA	22.3	NA	Owensboro, KY**	NA	178	Silver Spring-Frederick, MD M.D.	(22.0)
NA	Lexington-Fayette, KY**	NA	197	Oxnard-Thousand Oaks, CA	(25.8)	NA	Sioux City, IA-NE-SD**	NA
68	Lima, OH	(4.8)	173	Palm Bay-Melbourne, FL	(21.7)	15	Sioux Falls, SD	19.7
168	Lincoln, NE	(20.5)	NA	Panama City, FL**	NA	178	South Bend-Mishawaka, IN-MI	(22.0)
84	Little Rock, AR	(7.4)	NA	Parkersburg-Vienna, WV**	NA	NA	Spartanburg, SC**	NA
202	Logan, UT-ID	(26.6)	114	Pensacola, FL	(11.8)	139	Spokane, WA	(16.4)
226	Longview, TX	(31.9)	NA	Peoria, IL**	NA	NA	Springfield, IL**	NA
51	Longview, WA	0.4	NA	Philadelphia (greater) PA-NJ-MD-DE**	NA	NA	Springfield, MA**	NA
200	Los Angeles County, CA M.D.	(26.3)	NA	Philadelphia, PA M.D.**	NA	NA	Springfield, MO**	NA
194	Los Angeles (greater), CA	(25.0)	NA	Phoenix-Mesa-Scottsdale, AZ**	NA	18	Springfield, OH	18.8
55	Louisville, KY-IN	0.1	186	Pine Bluff, AR	(23.1)	38	State College, PA	5.9
129	Lubbock, TX	(14.4)	NA	Pittsburgh, PA**	NA	NA	Staunton-Waynesboro, VA**	NA
220	Lynchburg, VA	(31.3)	121	Pittsfield, MA	(13.1)	57	Stockton-Lodi, CA	(1.5)
202	Macon, GA	(26.6)	NA	Pocatello, ID**	NA	104	St. George, UT	(10.2)
13	Madera, CA	21.1	211	Port St. Lucie, FL	(28.2)	106	St. Joseph, MO-KS	(10.8)
NA	Madison, WI**	NA	94	Portland-Vancouver, OR-WA	(9.1)	114	St. Louis, MO-IL	(11.8)
NA	Manchester-Nashua, NH**	NA	56	Portland, ME	(1.3)	45	Sumter, SC	3.0
NA	Manhattan, KS**	NA	72	Prescott, AZ	(5.6)	NA	Syracuse, NY**	NA
NA	Mankato-North Mankato, MN**	NA	89	Providence-Warwick, RI-MA	(8.1)	NA	Tacoma, WA M.D.**	NA
54	Mansfield, OH	0.2	182	Provo-Orem, UT	(22.5)	221	Tallahassee, FL	(31.4)
112	McAllen-Edinburg-Mission, TX	(11.4)	NA	Pueblo, CO**	NA	232	Tampa-St Petersburg, FL	(38.1)
4	Medford, OR	42.7	217	Punta Gorda, FL	(29.5)	NA	Terre Haute, IN**	NA
118	Memphis, TN-MS-AR	(12.5)	192	Racine, WI	(24.7)	NA	Texarkana, TX-AR**	NA
30	Merced, CA	12.9	NA	Raleigh, NC**	NA	NA	The Villages, FL**	NA
199	Miami (greater), FL	(26.2)	NA	Rapid City, SD**	NA	NA	Toledo, OH**	NA
212	Miami-Dade County, FL M.D.	(28.5)	48	Reading, PA	0.7	36	Topeka, KS	10.8
113	Michigan City-La Porte, IN	(11.5)	34	Redding, CA	11.3	37	Trenton, NJ	10.3
NA	Midland, MI**	NA	201	Reno, NV	(26.5)	87	Tucson, AZ	(8.0)
NA	Midland, TX**	NA	218	Richmond, VA	(30.6)	172	Tulsa, OK	(20.9)
40	Milwaukee, WI	5.7	145	Riverside-San Bernardino, CA	(17.9)	NA	Tuscaloosa, AL**	NA
NA	Minneapolis-St. Paul, MN-WI**	NA	194	Roanoke, VA	(25.0)	166	Tyler, TX	(20.3)
41	Missoula, MT	5.1	NA	Rochester, MN**	NA	NA	Utica-Rome, NY**	NA
25	Mobile, AL	15.6	NA	Rochester, NY**	NA	154	Valdosta, GA	(18.8)
51	Modesto, CA	0.4	NA	Rockford, IL**	NA	188	Vallejo-Fairfield, CA	(23.7)
85	Monroe, LA	(7.8)	31	Rockingham County, NH M.D.	12.7	NA	Victoria, TX**	NA
32	Monroe, MI	12.5	NA	Rocky Mount, NC**	NA	133	Vineland-Bridgeton, NJ	(14.7)
NA	Montgomery County, PA M.D.**	NA	NA	Rome, GA**	NA	216	Virginia Beach-Norfolk, VA-NC	(29.3)
44	Montgomery, AL	4.0	137	Sacramento, CA	(15.5)	98	Visalia-Porterville, CA	(9.8)
NA	Morgantown, WV**	NA	223	Saginaw, MI	(31.5)	NA	Waco, TX**	NA
NA	Morristown, TN**	NA	63	Salem, OR	(3.1)	NA	Walla Walla, WA**	NA
71	Mount Vernon-Anacortes, WA	(5.4)	98	Salinas, CA	(9.8)	NA	Warner Robins, GA**	NA
185	Muncie, IN	(22.9)	NA	Salisbury, MD-DE**	NA	NA	Warren-Troy, MI M.D.**	NA
237	Napa, CA	(44.4)	76	Salt Lake City, UT	(6.0)	190	Washington (greater) DC-VA-MD-WV	(24.0)
226	Naples-Marco Island, FL	(31.9)	223	San Antonio, TX	(31.5)	191	Washington, DC-VA-MD-WV M.D.	(24.6)
NA	Nashville-Davidson, TN**	NA	126	San Diego, CA	(13.5)	178	Waterloo-Cedar Falls, IA	(22.0)
NA	Nassau-Suffolk, NY M.D.**	NA	125	San Francisco (greater), CA	(13.4)	NA	Watertown-Fort Drum, NY**	NA
NA	New Bern, NC**	NA	98	San Francisco-Redwood, CA M.D.	(9.8)	242	Wausau, WI	(53.0)
NA	New Haven-Milford, CT**	NA	123	San Jose, CA	(13.3)	214	West Palm Beach, FL M.D.	(28.7)
181	New Orleans, LA	(22.4)	34	San Luis Obispo, CA	11.3	7	Wheeling, WV-OH	33.7
NA	New York (greater), NY-NJ-PA**	NA	NA	San Rafael, CA M.D.**	NA	107	Wichita Falls, TX	(10.9)
NA	New York-Jersey City, NY-NJ M.D.**	NA	174	Santa Cruz-Watsonville, CA	(21.8)	123	Wichita, KS	(13.3)
NA	Newark, NJ-PA M.D.**	NA	96	Santa Fe, NM	(9.2)	23	Williamsport, PA	16.6
NA	North Port-Sarasota-Bradenton, FL**	NA	NA	Santa Maria-Santa Barbara, CA**	NA	165	Wilmington, DE-MD-NJ M.D.	(20.1)
22	Norwich-New London, CT	17.0	141	Santa Rosa, CA	(17.1)	NA	Wilmington, NC**	NA
109	Oakland-Hayward, CA M.D.	(11.2)	229	Savannah, GA	(34.2)	83	Winchester, VA-WV	(7.2)
189	Ocala, FL	(23.8)	75	Scranton--Wilkes-Barre, PA	(5.9)	NA	Winston-Salem, NC**	NA
160	Ocean City, NJ	(19.6)	NA	Seattle (greater), WA**	NA	47	Worcester, MA-CT	1.6
6	Odessa, TX	38.4	NA	Seattle-Bellevue-Everett, WA M.D.**	NA	41	Yakima, WA	5.1
NA	Ogden-Clearfield, UT**	NA	119	Sebastian-Vero Beach, FL	(12.9)	58	York-Hanover, PA	(1.8)
73	Oklahoma City, OK	(5.7)	NA	Sebring, FL**	NA	128	Youngstown-Warren, OH-PA	(13.8)
145	Olympia, WA	(17.9)	3	Sheboygan, WI	64.1	129	Yuba City, CA	(14.4)
60	Omaha-Council Bluffs, NE-IA	(2.4)	98	Sherman-Denison, TX	(9.8)	67	Yuma, AZ	(4.6)
228	Orlando, FL	(33.5)	NA	Shreveport-Bossier City, LA**	NA			
62	Oshkosh-Neenah, WI	(2.7)	NA	Sierra Vista-Douglas, AZ**	NA			

Source: CQ Press using reported data from the F.B.I. "Crime in the United States 2012"

*Violent crimes are offenses of murder, forcible rape, robbery, and aggravated assault.

**Not available.

8. Percent Change in Violent Crime Rate: 2008 to 2012 (continued)
National Percent Change = 15.6% Decrease*

RANK	METROPOLITAN AREA	% CHANGE	RANK	METROPOLITAN AREA	% CHANGE	RANK	METROPOLITAN AREA	% CHANGE
1	Columbus, IN	82.7	65	Hartford, CT	(3.9)	129	Cedar Rapids, IA	(14.4)
2	Bismarck, ND	67.0	66	Dothan, AL	(4.2)	129	Johnson City, TN	(14.4)
3	Sheboygan, WI	64.1	67	Yuma, AZ	(4.6)	129	Lubbock, TX	(14.4)
4	Medford, OR	42.7	68	Barnstable Town, MA	(4.8)	129	Yuba City, CA	(14.4)
5	Gadsden, AL	39.9	68	Lima, OH	(4.8)	133	Vineland-Bridgeton, NJ	(14.7)
6	Odessa, TX	38.4	70	Birmingham-Hoover, AL	(4.9)	134	Altoona, PA	(15.0)
7	Wheeling, WV-OH	33.7	71	Mount Vernon-Anacortes, WA	(5.4)	135	Austin-Round Rock, TX	(15.3)
8	Appleton, WI	33.3	72	Prescott, AZ	(5.6)	135	Fort Collins, CO	(15.3)
9	Huntsville, AL	23.8	73	Greeley, CO	(5.7)	137	Sacramento, CA	(15.5)
10	Lewiston, ID-WA	22.3	73	Oklahoma City, OK	(5.7)	138	Jonesboro, AR	(16.0)
11	Flint, MI	21.9	75	Scranton--Wilkes-Barre, PA	(5.9)	139	Spokane, WA	(16.4)
12	Hanford-Corcoran, CA	21.3	76	Salt Lake City, UT	(6.0)	140	Durham-Chapel Hill, NC	(16.8)
13	Madera, CA	21.1	77	Indianapolis, IN	(6.1)	141	Las Vegas-Henderson, NV	(17.1)
14	Fayetteville-Springdale, AR-MO	20.0	78	Harrisburg-Carlisle, PA	(6.6)	141	Santa Rosa, CA	(17.1)
15	Sioux Falls, SD	19.7	79	Bay City, MI	(6.9)	143	Corvallis, OR	(17.5)
16	Lafayette, IN	19.3	79	Grand Junction, CO	(6.9)	144	Amarillo, TX	(17.6)
17	Cape Girardeau, MO-IL	19.0	81	Camden, NJ M.D.	(7.0)	145	Olympia, WA	(17.9)
18	Bangor, ME	18.8	81	Lawrence, KS	(7.0)	145	Riverside-San Bernardino, CA	(17.9)
18	Springfield, OH	18.8	83	Winchester, VA-WV	(7.2)	147	Clarksville, TN-KY	(18.0)
20	Billings, MT	18.3	84	Little Rock, AR	(7.4)	148	Fort Worth-Arlington, TX M.D.	(18.3)
21	Bloomington, IN	18.0	85	Burlington, NC	(7.8)	149	Atlanta, GA	(18.4)
22	Norwich-New London, CT	17.0	85	Monroe, LA	(7.8)	149	Baltimore, MD	(18.4)
23	Williamsport, PA	16.6	87	Kennewick-Richland, WA	(8.0)	149	Houston, TX	(18.4)
24	Green Bay, WI	15.8	87	Tucson, AZ	(8.0)	149	Lansing-East Lansing, MI	(18.4)
25	Mobile, AL	15.6	89	Bridgeport-Stamford, CT	(8.1)	153	Dayton, OH	(18.7)
26	Cheyenne, WY	14.7	89	Providence-Warwick, RI-MA	(8.1)	154	Valdosta, GA	(18.8)
27	Fort Wayne, IN	14.6	91	Iowa City, IA	(8.2)	155	Kalamazoo-Portage, MI	(19.0)
28	Fresno, CA	14.3	92	Joplin, MO	(8.3)	156	Albuquerque, NM	(19.2)
29	Columbia, MO	13.8	93	Akron, OH	(8.6)	156	Chico, CA	(19.2)
30	Merced, CA	12.9	94	Harrisonburg, VA	(9.1)	156	Dover, DE	(19.2)
31	Rockingham County, NH M.D.	12.7	94	Portland-Vancouver, OR-WA	(9.1)	159	Erie, PA	(19.4)
32	Monroe, MI	12.5	96	El Paso, TX	(9.2)	160	Ocean City, NJ	(19.6)
33	Johnstown, PA	12.4	96	Santa Fe, NM	(9.2)	161	College Station-Bryan, TX	(19.7)
34	Redding, CA	11.3	98	Great Falls, MT	(9.8)	161	Colorado Springs, CO	(19.7)
34	San Luis Obispo, CA	11.3	98	Salinas, CA	(9.8)	163	Charlottesville, VA	(20.0)
36	Topeka, KS	10.8	98	San Francisco-Redwood, CA M.D.	(9.8)	163	Hickory, NC	(20.0)
37	Trenton, NJ	10.3	98	Sherman-Denison, TX	(9.8)	165	Wilmington, DE-MD-NJ M.D.	(20.1)
38	State College, PA	5.9	98	Visalia-Porterville, CA	(9.8)	166	Fort Lauderdale, FL M.D.	(20.3)
39	Kingsport, TN-VA	5.8	103	Flagstaff, AZ	(10.0)	166	Tyler, TX	(20.3)
40	Milwaukee, WI	5.7	104	St. George, UT	(10.2)	168	Lincoln, NE	(20.5)
41	Bellingham, WA	5.1	105	Lebanon, PA	(10.5)	169	Lake Havasu City-Kingman, AZ	(20.6)
41	Missoula, MT	5.1	106	St. Joseph, MO-KS	(10.8)	170	Asheville, NC	(20.7)
41	Yakima, WA	5.1	107	Wichita Falls, TX	(10.9)	171	Columbus, GA-AL	(20.8)
44	Montgomery, AL	4.0	108	Killeen-Temple, TX	(11.0)	172	Tulsa, OK	(20.9)
45	Sumter, SC	3.0	109	Boise City, ID	(11.2)	173	Palm Bay-Melbourne, FL	(21.7)
46	Fond du Lac, WI	2.5	109	Corpus Christi, TX	(11.2)	174	Ann Arbor, MI	(21.8)
47	Worcester, MA-CT	1.6	109	Oakland-Hayward, CA M.D.	(11.2)	174	Athens-Clarke County, GA	(21.8)
48	Reading, PA	0.7	112	McAllen-Edinburg-Mission, TX	(11.4)	174	Santa Cruz-Watsonville, CA	(21.8)
49	Bakersfield, CA	0.5	113	Michigan City-La Porte, IN	(11.5)	177	Las Cruces, NM	(21.9)
49	Decatur, AL	0.5	114	Pensacola, FL	(11.8)	178	Silver Spring-Frederick, MD M.D.	(22.0)
51	Longview, WA	0.4	114	St. Louis, MO-IL	(11.8)	178	South Bend-Mishawaka, IN-MI	(22.0)
51	Modesto, CA	0.4	116	Goldsboro, NC	(12.3)	178	Waterloo-Cedar Falls, IA	(22.0)
53	El Centro, CA	0.3	117	Lancaster, PA	(12.4)	181	New Orleans, LA	(22.4)
54	Mansfield, OH	0.2	118	Memphis, TN-MS-AR	(12.5)	182	Dalton, GA	(22.5)
55	Louisville, KY-IN	0.1	119	Sebastian-Vero Beach, FL	(12.9)	182	Provo-Orem, UT	(22.5)
56	Portland, ME	(1.3)	120	Florence-Muscle Shoals, AL	(13.0)	184	Cleveland, TN	(22.6)
57	Stockton-Lodi, CA	(1.5)	121	Des Moines-West Des Moines, IA	(13.1)	185	Muncie, IN	(22.9)
58	York-Hanover, PA	(1.8)	121	Pittsfield, MA	(13.1)	186	Pine Bluff, AR	(23.1)
59	Beaumont-Port Arthur, TX	(2.3)	123	San Jose, CA	(13.3)	187	Hinesville, GA	(23.6)
60	Omaha-Council Bluffs, NE-IA	(2.4)	123	Wichita, KS	(13.3)	188	Vallejo-Fairfield, CA	(23.7)
61	Lewiston-Auburn, ME	(2.5)	125	San Francisco (greater), CA	(13.4)	189	Ocala, FL	(23.8)
62	Oshkosh-Neenah, WI	(2.7)	126	San Diego, CA	(13.5)	190	Washington (greater) DC-VA-MD-WV	(24.0)
63	Salem, OR	(3.1)	127	Anaheim-Santa Ana-Irvine, CA M.D.	(13.6)	191	Washington, DC-VA-MD-WV M.D.	(24.6)
64	Janesville, WI	(3.3)	128	Youngstown-Warren, OH-PA	(13.8)	192	Dallas (greater), TX	(24.7)

Note: All listings are for Metropolitan Statistical Areas (M.S.A.s) except for those ending with "M.D." Listings with "M.D." are Metropolitan Divisions which are smaller parts of eleven large M.S.A.s. See explanatory note at beginning of metropolitan area section.

RANK	METROPOLITAN AREA	% CHANGE	RANK	METROPOLITAN AREA	% CHANGE	RANK	METROPOLITAN AREA	% CHANGE
192	Racine, WI	(24.7)	NA	Bloomington, IL**	NA	NA	Midland, MI**	NA
194	Los Angeles (greater), CA	(25.0)	NA	Bloomsburg-Berwick, PA**	NA	NA	Midland, TX**	NA
194	Roanoke, VA	(25.0)	NA	Boston (greater), MA-NH**	NA	NA	Minneapolis-St. Paul, MN-WI**	NA
196	Cape Coral-Fort Myers, FL	(25.5)	NA	Boston, MA M.D.**	NA	NA	Montgomery County, PA M.D.**	NA
197	Oxnard-Thousand Oaks, CA	(25.8)	NA	Boulder, CO**	NA	NA	Morgantown, WV**	NA
198	Casper, WY	(25.9)	NA	Brunswick, GA**	NA	NA	Morristown, TN**	NA
199	Miami (greater), FL	(26.2)	NA	Buffalo-Niagara Falls, NY**	NA	NA	Nashville-Davidson, TN**	NA
200	Los Angeles County, CA M.D.	(26.3)	NA	California-Lexington Park, MD**	NA	NA	Nassau-Suffolk, NY M.D.**	NA
201	Reno, NV	(26.5)	NA	Cambridge-Newton, MA M.D.**	NA	NA	New Bern, NC**	NA
202	Cumberland, MD-WV	(26.6)	NA	Canton, OH**	NA	NA	New Haven-Milford, CT**	NA
202	Logan, UT-ID	(26.6)	NA	Chambersburg-Waynesboro, PA**	NA	NA	New York (greater), NY-NJ-PA**	NA
202	Macon, GA	(26.6)	NA	Champaign-Urbana, IL**	NA	NA	New York-Jersey City, NY-NJ M.D.**	NA
205	Abilene, TX	(26.9)	NA	Chicago (greater), IL-IN-WI**	NA	NA	Newark, NJ-PA M.D.**	NA
206	Gainesville, FL	(27.3)	NA	Chicago-Joilet-Naperville, IL M.D.**	NA	NA	North Port-Sarasota-Bradenton, FL**	NA
207	Blacksburg, VA	(27.4)	NA	Cincinnati, OH-KY-IN**	NA	NA	Ogden-Clearfield, UT**	NA
208	Eugene, OR	(27.7)	NA	Coeur d'Alene, ID**	NA	NA	Owensboro, KY**	NA
209	Dallas-Plano-Irving, TX M.D.	(28.0)	NA	Crestview-Fort Walton Beach, FL**	NA	NA	Panama City, FL**	NA
210	Laredo, TX	(28.1)	NA	Danville, IL**	NA	NA	Parkersburg-Vienna, WV**	NA
211	Port St. Lucie, FL	(28.2)	NA	Daphne-Fairhope-Foley, AL**	NA	NA	Peoria, IL**	NA
212	Miami-Dade County, FL M.D.	(28.5)	NA	Davenport, IA-IL**	NA	NA	Philadelphia (greater) PA-NJ-MD-DE**	NA
213	Lakeland, FL	(28.6)	NA	Decatur, IL**	NA	NA	Philadelphia, PA M.D.**	NA
214	West Palm Beach, FL M.D.	(28.7)	NA	Denver-Aurora, CO**	NA	NA	Phoenix-Mesa-Scottsdale, AZ**	NA
215	Greensboro-High Point, NC	(28.8)	NA	Detroit (greater), MI**	NA	NA	Pittsburgh, PA**	NA
216	Virginia Beach-Norfolk, VA-NC	(29.3)	NA	Detroit-Dearborn-Livonia, MI M.D.**	NA	NA	Pocatello, ID**	NA
217	Punta Gorda, FL	(29.5)	NA	Duluth, MN-WI**	NA	NA	Pueblo, CO**	NA
218	Richmond, VA	(30.6)	NA	Dutchess-Putnam, NY M.D.**	NA	NA	Raleigh, NC**	NA
219	Greenville, NC	(31.1)	NA	East Stroudsburg, PA**	NA	NA	Rapid City, SD**	NA
220	Lynchburg, VA	(31.3)	NA	Elgin, IL M.D.**	NA	NA	Rochester, MN**	NA
221	Fayetteville, NC	(31.4)	NA	Elizabethtown-Fort Knox, KY**	NA	NA	Rochester, NY**	NA
221	Tallahassee, FL	(31.4)	NA	Elmira, NY**	NA	NA	Rockford, IL**	NA
223	Saginaw, MI	(31.5)	NA	Fairbanks, AK**	NA	NA	Rocky Mount, NC**	NA
223	San Antonio, TX	(31.5)	NA	Fargo, ND-MN**	NA	NA	Rome, GA**	NA
225	Deltona-Daytona Beach, FL	(31.8)	NA	Farmington, NM**	NA	NA	Salisbury, MD-DE**	NA
226	Longview, TX	(31.9)	NA	Fort Smith, AR-OK**	NA	NA	San Rafael, CA M.D.**	NA
226	Naples-Marco Island, FL	(31.9)	NA	Gainesville, GA**	NA	NA	Santa Maria-Santa Barbara, CA**	NA
228	Orlando, FL	(33.5)	NA	Gary, IN M.D.**	NA	NA	Seattle (greater), WA**	NA
229	Savannah, GA	(34.2)	NA	Gettysburg, PA**	NA	NA	Seattle-Bellevue-Everett, WA M.D.**	NA
230	Houma, LA	(35.8)	NA	Glens Falls, NY**	NA	NA	Sebring, FL**	NA
231	Jacksonville, FL	(37.5)	NA	Grand Forks, ND-MN**	NA	NA	Shreveport-Bossier City, LA**	NA
232	Tampa-St Petersburg, FL	(38.1)	NA	Grand Island, NE**	NA	NA	Sierra Vista-Douglas, AZ**	NA
233	Brownsville-Harlingen, TX	(39.2)	NA	Greenville-Anderson, SC**	NA	NA	Sioux City, IA-NE-SD**	NA
234	Charleston-North Charleston, SC	(41.4)	NA	Hagerstown-Martinsburg, MD-WV**	NA	NA	Spartanburg, SC**	NA
235	Bremerton-Silverdale, WA	(41.7)	NA	Hammond, LA**	NA	NA	Springfield, IL**	NA
236	Idaho Falls, ID	(42.0)	NA	Hattiesburg, MS**	NA	NA	Springfield, MA**	NA
237	Auburn, AL	(44.4)	NA	Hilton Head Island, SC**	NA	NA	Springfield, MO**	NA
237	Napa, CA	(44.4)	NA	Homosassa Springs, FL**	NA	NA	Staunton-Waynesboro, VA**	NA
239	Carson City, NV	(44.7)	NA	Jackson, MS**	NA	NA	Syracuse, NY**	NA
240	Florence, SC	(45.7)	NA	Jackson, TN**	NA	NA	Tacoma, WA M.D.**	NA
241	Ames, IA	(48.8)	NA	Jefferson City, MO**	NA	NA	Terre Haute, IN**	NA
242	Wausau, WI	(53.0)	NA	Kahului-Wailuku-Lahaina, HI**	NA	NA	Texarkana, TX-AR**	NA
243	Bowling Green, KY	(53.6)	NA	Kankakee, IL**	NA	NA	The Villages, FL**	NA
244	Dubuque, IA	(64.1)	NA	Kansas City, MO-KS**	NA	NA	Toledo, OH**	NA
NA	Albany-Schenectady-Troy, NY**	NA	NA	Kingston, NY**	NA	NA	Tuscaloosa, AL**	NA
NA	Albany, GA**	NA	NA	Knoxville, TN**	NA	NA	Utica-Rome, NY**	NA
NA	Albany, OR**	NA	NA	Kokomo, IN**	NA	NA	Victoria, TX**	NA
NA	Alexandria, LA**	NA	NA	La Crosse, WI-MN**	NA	NA	Waco, TX**	NA
NA	Allentown, PA-NJ**	NA	NA	Lafayette, LA**	NA	NA	Walla Walla, WA**	NA
NA	Anchorage, AK**	NA	NA	Lake Co.-Kenosha Co., IL-WI M.D.**	NA	NA	Warner Robins, GA**	NA
NA	Anniston-Oxford, AL**	NA	NA	Lawton, OK**	NA	NA	Warren-Troy, MI M.D.**	NA
NA	Atlantic City, NJ**	NA	NA	Lexington-Fayette, KY**	NA	NA	Watertown-Fort Drum, NY**	NA
NA	Augusta, GA-SC**	NA	NA	Madison, WI**	NA	NA	Wilmington, NC**	NA
NA	Baton Rouge, LA**	NA	NA	Manchester-Nashua, NH**	NA	NA	Winston-Salem, NC**	NA
NA	Beckley, WV**	NA	NA	Manhattan, KS**	NA			
NA	Binghamton, NY**	NA	NA	Mankato-North Mankato, MN**	NA			

Source: CQ Press using reported data from the F.B.I. "Crime in the United States 2012"

*Violent crimes are offenses of murder, forcible rape, robbery, and aggravated assault.

**Not available.

9. Murders in 2012
National Total = 14,827 Murders*

RANK	METROPOLITAN AREA	MURDERS	RANK	METROPOLITAN AREA	MURDERS	RANK	METROPOLITAN AREA	MURDERS
300	Abilene, TX	3	321	Cheyenne, WY	2	62	Gary, IN M.D.	66
108	Akron, OH	27	2	Chicago (greater), IL-IN-WI	679	250	Gettysburg, PA	5
120	Albany-Schenectady-Troy, NY	23	5	Chicago-Joilet-Naperville, IL M.D.	598	216	Glens Falls, NY	7
196	Albany, GA	9	178	Chico, CA	11	132	Goldsboro, NC	20
363	Albany, OR	0	57	Cincinnati, OH-KY-IN	75	341	Grand Forks, ND-MN	1
71	Albuquerque, NM	53	145	Clarksville, TN-KY	17	363	Grand Island, NE	0
196	Alexandria, LA	9	250	Cleveland, TN	5	250	Grand Junction, CO	5
93	Allentown, PA-NJ	34	341	Coeur d'Alene, ID	1	341	Great Falls, MT	1
230	Altoona, PA	6	230	College Station-Bryan, TX	6	230	Greeley, CO	6
178	Amarillo, TX	11	132	Colorado Springs, CO	20	216	Green Bay, WI	7
363	Ames, IA	0	300	Columbia, MO	3	81	Greensboro-High Point, NC	44
73	Anaheim-Santa Ana-Irvine, CA M.D.	51	138	Columbus, GA-AL	19	67	Greenville-Anderson, SC	54
149	Anchorage, AK	15	341	Columbus, IN	1	178	Greenville, NC	11
250	Ann Arbor, MI	5	120	Corpus Christi, TX	23	216	Hagerstown-Martinsburg, MD-WV	7
230	Anniston-Oxford, AL	6	341	Corvallis, OR	1	271	Hanford-Corcoran, CA	4
341	Appleton, WI	1	300	Crestview-Fort Walton Beach, FL	3	140	Harrisburg-Carlisle, PA	18
132	Asheville, NC	20	271	Cumberland, MD-WV	4	341	Harrisonburg, VA	1
230	Athens-Clarke County, GA	6	15	Dallas (greater), TX	277	91	Hartford, CT	37
13	Atlanta, GA	333	24	Dallas-Plano-Irving, TX M.D.	194	250	Hattiesburg, MS	5
101	Atlantic City, NJ	30	271	Dalton, GA	4	132	Hickory, NC	20
201	Auburn, AL	8	271	Danville, IL	4	127	Hilton Head Island, SC	21
77	Augusta, GA-SC	47	201	Daphne-Fairhope-Foley, AL	8	271	Hinesville, GA	4
86	Austin-Round Rock, TX	39	189	Davenport, IA-IL	10	250	Homosassa Springs, FL	5
63	Bakersfield, CA	65	100	Dayton, OH	31	196	Houma, LA	9
16	Baltimore, MD	262	321	Decatur, AL	2	12	Houston, TX	349
201	Bangor, ME	8	230	Decatur, IL	6	123	Huntsville, AL	22
341	Barnstable Town, MA	1	132	Deltona-Daytona Beach, FL	20	363	Idaho Falls, ID	0
42	Baton Rouge, LA	96	39	Denver-Aurora, CO	103	30	Indianapolis, IN	114
341	Bay City, MI	1	201	Des Moines-West Des Moines, IA	8	321	Iowa City, IA	2
115	Beaumont-Port Arthur, TX	24	8	Detroit (greater), MI	469	33	Jacksonville, FL	110
156	Beckley, WV	14	9	Detroit-Dearborn-Livonia, MI M.D.	430	54	Jackson, MS	77
271	Bellingham, WA	4	178	Dothan, AL	11	161	Jackson, TN	13
300	Billings, MT	3	271	Dover, DE	4	300	Janesville, WI	3
216	Binghamton, NY	7	321	Dubuque, IA	2	300	Jefferson City, MO	3
36	Birmingham-Hoover, AL	107	271	Duluth, MN-WI	4	250	Johnson City, TN	5
271	Bismarck, ND	4	108	Durham-Chapel Hill, NC	27	230	Johnstown, PA	6
321	Blacksburg, VA	2	250	Dutchess-Putnam, NY M.D.	5	230	Jonesboro, AR	6
341	Bloomington, IL	1	271	East Stroudsburg, PA	4	230	Joplin, MO	6
271	Bloomington, IN	4	300	El Centro, CA	3	250	Kahului-Wailuku-Lahaina, HI	5
321	Bloomsburg-Berwick, PA	2	106	El Paso, TX	28	170	Kalamazoo-Portage, MI	12
216	Boise City, ID	7	216	Elgin, IL M.D.	7	201	Kankakee, IL	8
43	Boston (greater), MA-NH	95	341	Elizabethtown-Fort Knox, KY	1	27	Kansas City, MO-KS	156
60	Boston, MA M.D.	71	271	Elmira, NY	4	321	Kennewick-Richland, WA	2
363	Boulder, CO	0	178	Erie, PA	11	132	Killeen-Temple, TX	20
271	Bowling Green, KY	4	216	Eugene, OR	7	196	Kingsport, TN-VA	9
250	Bremerton-Silverdale, WA	5	300	Fairbanks, AK	3	341	Kingston, NY	1
96	Bridgeport-Stamford, CT	33	321	Fargo, ND-MN	2	93	Knoxville, TN	34
161	Brownsville-Harlingen, TX	13	230	Farmington, NM	6	271	Kokomo, IN	4
201	Brunswick, GA	8	178	Fayetteville-Springdale, AR-MO	11	271	La Crosse, WI-MN	4
67	Buffalo-Niagara Falls, NY	54	101	Fayetteville, NC	30	341	Lafayette, IN	1
271	Burlington, NC	4	271	Flagstaff, AZ	4	93	Lafayette, LA	34
363	California-Lexington Park, MD	0	61	Flint, MI	69	201	Lake Co.-Kenosha Co., IL-WI M.D.	8
149	Cambridge-Newton, MA M.D.	15	250	Florence-Muscle Shoals, AL	5	170	Lake Havasu City-Kingman, AZ	12
50	Camden, NJ M.D.	80	146	Florence, SC	16	86	Lakeland, FL	39
161	Canton, OH	13	363	Fond du Lac, WI	0	149	Lancaster, PA	15
79	Cape Coral-Fort Myers, FL	45	300	Fort Collins, CO	3	146	Lansing-East Lansing, MI	16
250	Cape Girardeau, MO-IL	5	50	Fort Lauderdale, FL M.D.	80	201	Laredo, TX	8
363	Carson City, NV	0	201	Fort Smith, AR-OK	8	216	Las Cruces, NM	7
300	Casper, WY	3	115	Fort Wayne, IN	24	43	Las Vegas-Henderson, NV	95
271	Cedar Rapids, IA	4	49	Fort Worth-Arlington, TX M.D.	83	363	Lawrence, KS	0
250	Chambersburg-Waynesboro, PA	5	55	Fresno, CA	76	161	Lawton, OK	13
271	Champaign-Urbana, IL	4	321	Gadsden, AL	2	300	Lebanon, PA	3
76	Charleston-North Charleston, SC	48	189	Gainesville, FL	10	363	Lewiston-Auburn, ME	0
230	Charlottesville, VA	6	216	Gainesville, GA	7			

Note: All listings are for Metropolitan Statistical Areas (M.S.A.s) except for those ending with "M.D." Listings with "M.D." are Metropolitan Divisions which are smaller parts of eleven large M.S.A.s. See explanatory note at beginning of metropolitan area section.

RANK	METROPOLITAN AREA	MURDERS	RANK	METROPOLITAN AREA	MURDERS	RANK	METROPOLITAN AREA	MURDERS
363	Lewiston, ID-WA	0	363	Owensboro, KY	0	149	Silver Spring-Frederick, MD M.D.	15
140	Lexington-Fayette, KY	18	127	Oxnard-Thousand Oaks, CA	21	271	Sioux City, IA-NE-SD	4
201	Lima, OH	8	101	Palm Bay-Melbourne, FL	30	321	Sioux Falls, SD	2
271	Lincoln, NE	4	189	Panama City, FL	10	115	South Bend-Mishawaka, IN-MI	24
63	Little Rock, AR	65	341	Parkersburg-Vienna, WV	1	170	Spartanburg, SC	12
363	Logan, UT-ID	0	123	Pensacola, FL	22	127	Spokane, WA	21
201	Longview, TX	8	140	Peoria, IL	18	156	Springfield, IL	14
271	Longview, WA	4	7	Philadelphia (greater) PA-NJ-MD-DE	517	161	Springfield, MA	13
4	Los Angeles County, CA M.D.	600	11	Philadelphia, PA M.D.	361	123	Springfield, MO	22
3	Los Angeles (greater), CA	651	18	Phoenix-Mesa-Scottsdale, AZ	228	250	Springfield, OH	5
53	Louisville, KY-IN	78	156	Pine Bluff, AR	14	341	State College, PA	1
170	Lubbock, TX	12	41	Pittsburgh, PA	100	321	Staunton-Waynesboro, VA	2
230	Lynchburg, VA	6	363	Pittsfield, MA	0	45	Stockton-Lodi, CA	89
110	Macon, GA	26	300	Pocatello, ID	3	300	St. George, UT	3
321	Madera, CA	2	178	Port St. Lucie, FL	11	321	St. Joseph, MO-KS	2
149	Madison, WI	15	67	Portland-Vancouver, OR-WA	54	22	St. Louis, MO-IL	203
341	Manchester-Nashua, NH	1	216	Portland, ME	7	170	Sumter, SC	12
341	Manhattan, KS	1	170	Prescott, AZ	12	149	Syracuse, NY	15
363	Mankato-North Mankato, MN	0	89	Providence-Warwick, RI-MA	38	98	Tacoma, WA M.D.	32
300	Mansfield, OH	3	271	Provo-Orem, UT	4	123	Tallahassee, FL	22
101	McAllen-Edinburg-Mission, TX	30	201	Pueblo, CO	8	32	Tampa-St Petersburg, FL	111
271	Medford, OR	4	341	Punta Gorda, FL	1	201	Terre Haute, IN	8
28	Memphis, TN-MS-AR	155	230	Racine, WI	6	201	Texarkana, TX-AR	8
120	Merced, CA	23	127	Raleigh, NC	21	363	The Villages, FL	0
10	Miami (greater), FL	364	271	Rapid City, SD	4	83	Toledo, OH	43
19	Miami-Dade County, FL M.D.	210	138	Reading, PA	19	140	Topeka, KS	18
300	Michigan City-La Porte, IN	3	216	Redding, CA	7	110	Trenton, NJ	26
321	Midland, MI	2	170	Reno, NV	12	65	Tucson, AZ	57
250	Midland, TX	5	47	Richmond, VA	84	67	Tulsa, OK	54
35	Milwaukee, WI	108	25	Riverside-San Bernardino, CA	178	161	Tuscaloosa, AL	13
55	Minneapolis-St. Paul, MN-WI	76	178	Roanoke, VA	11	230	Tyler, TX	6
363	Missoula, MT	0	300	Rochester, MN	3	271	Utica-Rome, NY	4
78	Mobile, AL	46	81	Rochester, NY	44	250	Valdosta, GA	5
89	Modesto, CA	38	170	Rockford, IL	12	106	Vallejo-Fairfield, CA	28
178	Monroe, LA	11	196	Rockingham County, NH M.D.	9	230	Victoria, TX	6
250	Monroe, MI	5	156	Rocky Mount, NC	14	216	Vineland-Bridgeton, NJ	7
110	Montgomery County, PA M.D.	26	250	Rome, GA	5	29	Virginia Beach-Norfolk, VA-NC	116
71	Montgomery, AL	53	47	Sacramento, CA	84	91	Visalia-Porterville, CA	37
300	Morgantown, WV	3	101	Saginaw, MI	30	189	Waco, TX	10
300	Morristown, TN	3	161	Salem, OR	13	341	Walla Walla, WA	1
321	Mount Vernon-Anacortes, WA	2	79	Salinas, CA	45	201	Warner Robins, GA	8
341	Muncie, IN	1	149	Salisbury, MD-DE	15	86	Warren-Troy, MI M.D.	39
321	Napa, CA	2	113	Salt Lake City, UT	25	19	Washington (greater) DC-VA-MD-WV	210
230	Naples-Marco Island, FL	6	30	San Antonio, TX	114	23	Washington, DC-VA-MD-WV M.D.	195
46	Nashville-Davidson, TN	87	36	San Diego, CA	107	230	Waterloo-Cedar Falls, IA	6
73	Nassau-Suffolk, NY M.D.	51	14	San Francisco (greater), CA	288	341	Watertown-Fort Drum, NY	1
300	New Bern, NC	3	52	San Francisco-Redwood, CA M.D.	79	321	Wausau, WI	2
96	New Haven-Milford, CT	33	66	San Jose, CA	56	58	West Palm Beach, FL M.D.	74
17	New Orleans, LA	251	230	San Luis Obispo, CA	6	363	Wheeling, WV-OH	0
1	New York (greater), NY-NJ-PA	749	363	San Rafael, CA M.D.	0	216	Wichita Falls, TX	7
6	New York-Jersey City, NY-NJ M.D.	531	189	Santa Cruz-Watsonville, CA	10	115	Wichita, KS	24
26	Newark, NJ-PA M.D.	162	230	Santa Fe, NM	6	321	Williamsport, PA	2
83	North Port-Sarasota-Bradenton, FL	43	230	Santa Maria-Santa Barbara, CA	6	75	Wilmington, DE-MD-NJ M.D.	50
250	Norwich-New London, CT	5	271	Santa Rosa, CA	4	189	Wilmington, NC	10
21	Oakland-Hayward, CA M.D.	209	113	Savannah, GA	25	321	Winchester, VA-WV	2
127	Ocala, FL	21	161	Scranton--Wilkes-Barre, PA	13	161	Winston-Salem, NC	13
321	Ocean City, NJ	2	38	Seattle (greater), WA	104	156	Worcester, MA-CT	14
250	Odessa, TX	5	59	Seattle-Bellevue-Everett, WA M.D.	72	140	Yakima, WA	18
271	Ogden-Clearfield, UT	4	341	Sebastian-Vero Beach, FL	1	146	York-Hanover, PA	16
39	Oklahoma City, OK	103	300	Sebring, FL	3	98	Youngstown-Warren, OH-PA	32
189	Olympia, WA	10	250	Sheboygan, WI	5	178	Yuba City, CA	11
83	Omaha-Council Bluffs, NE-IA	43	300	Sherman-Denison, TX	3	216	Yuma, AZ	7
34	Orlando, FL	109	115	Shreveport-Bossier City, LA	24			
363	Oshkosh-Neenah, WI	0	271	Sierra Vista-Douglas, AZ	4			

Source: Reported data from the F.B.I. "Crime in the United States 2012"
*Includes nonnegligent manslaughter.

9. Murders in 2012 (continued)
National Total = 14,827 Murders*

RANK	METROPOLITAN AREA	MURDERS	RANK	METROPOLITAN AREA	MURDERS	RANK	METROPOLITAN AREA	MURDERS
1	New York (greater), NY-NJ-PA	749	65	Tucson, AZ	57	127	Oxnard-Thousand Oaks, CA	21
2	Chicago (greater), IL-IN-WI	679	66	San Jose, CA	56	127	Raleigh, NC	21
3	Los Angeles (greater), CA	651	67	Buffalo-Niagara Falls, NY	54	127	Spokane, WA	21
4	Los Angeles County, CA M.D.	600	67	Greenville-Anderson, SC	54	132	Asheville, NC	20
5	Chicago-Joilet-Naperville, IL M.D.	598	67	Portland-Vancouver, OR-WA	54	132	Colorado Springs, CO	20
6	New York-Jersey City, NY-NJ M.D.	531	67	Tulsa, OK	54	132	Deltona-Daytona Beach, FL	20
7	Philadelphia (greater) PA-NJ-MD-DE	517	71	Albuquerque, NM	53	132	Goldsboro, NC	20
8	Detroit (greater), MI	469	71	Montgomery, AL	53	132	Hickory, NC	20
9	Detroit-Dearborn-Livonia, MI M.D.	430	73	Anaheim-Santa Ana-Irvine, CA M.D.	51	132	Killeen-Temple, TX	20
10	Miami (greater), FL	364	73	Nassau-Suffolk, NY M.D.	51	138	Columbus, GA-AL	19
11	Philadelphia, PA M.D.	361	75	Wilmington, DE-MD-NJ M.D.	50	138	Reading, PA	19
12	Houston, TX	349	76	Charleston-North Charleston, SC	48	140	Harrisburg-Carlisle, PA	18
13	Atlanta, GA	333	77	Augusta, GA-SC	47	140	Lexington-Fayette, KY	18
14	San Francisco (greater), CA	288	78	Mobile, AL	46	140	Peoria, IL	18
15	Dallas (greater), TX	277	79	Cape Coral-Fort Myers, FL	45	140	Topeka, KS	18
16	Baltimore, MD	262	79	Salinas, CA	45	140	Yakima, WA	18
17	New Orleans, LA	251	81	Greensboro-High Point, NC	44	145	Clarksville, TN-KY	17
18	Phoenix-Mesa-Scottsdale, AZ	228	81	Rochester, NY	44	146	Florence, SC	16
19	Miami-Dade County, FL M.D.	210	83	North Port-Sarasota-Bradenton, FL	43	146	Lansing-East Lansing, MI	16
19	Washington (greater) DC-VA-MD-WV	210	83	Omaha-Council Bluffs, NE-IA	43	146	York-Hanover, PA	16
21	Oakland-Hayward, CA M.D.	209	83	Toledo, OH	43	149	Anchorage, AK	15
22	St. Louis, MO-IL	203	86	Austin-Round Rock, TX	39	149	Cambridge-Newton, MA M.D.	15
23	Washington, DC-VA-MD-WV M.D.	195	86	Lakeland, FL	39	149	Lancaster, PA	15
24	Dallas-Plano-Irving, TX M.D.	194	86	Warren-Troy, MI M.D.	39	149	Madison, WI	15
25	Riverside-San Bernardino, CA	178	89	Modesto, CA	38	149	Salisbury, MD-DE	15
26	Newark, NJ-PA M.D.	162	89	Providence-Warwick, RI-MA	38	149	Silver Spring-Frederick, MD M.D.	15
27	Kansas City, MO-KS	156	91	Hartford, CT	37	149	Syracuse, NY	15
28	Memphis, TN-MS-AR	155	91	Visalia-Porterville, CA	37	156	Beckley, WV	14
29	Virginia Beach-Norfolk, VA-NC	116	93	Allentown, PA-NJ	34	156	Pine Bluff, AR	14
30	Indianapolis, IN	114	93	Knoxville, TN	34	156	Rocky Mount, NC	14
30	San Antonio, TX	114	93	Lafayette, LA	34	156	Springfield, IL	14
32	Tampa-St Petersburg, FL	111	96	Bridgeport-Stamford, CT	33	156	Worcester, MA-CT	14
33	Jacksonville, FL	110	96	New Haven-Milford, CT	33	161	Brownsville-Harlingen, TX	13
34	Orlando, FL	109	98	Tacoma, WA M.D.	32	161	Canton, OH	13
35	Milwaukee, WI	108	98	Youngstown-Warren, OH-PA	32	161	Jackson, TN	13
36	Birmingham-Hoover, AL	107	100	Dayton, OH	31	161	Lawton, OK	13
36	San Diego, CA	107	101	Atlantic City, NJ	30	161	Salem, OR	13
38	Seattle (greater), WA	104	101	Fayetteville, NC	30	161	Scranton--Wilkes-Barre, PA	13
39	Denver-Aurora, CO	103	101	McAllen-Edinburg-Mission, TX	30	161	Springfield, MA	13
39	Oklahoma City, OK	103	101	Palm Bay-Melbourne, FL	30	161	Tuscaloosa, AL	13
41	Pittsburgh, PA	100	101	Saginaw, MI	30	161	Winston-Salem, NC	13
42	Baton Rouge, LA	96	106	El Paso, TX	28	170	Kalamazoo-Portage, MI	12
43	Boston (greater), MA-NH	95	106	Vallejo-Fairfield, CA	28	170	Lake Havasu City-Kingman, AZ	12
43	Las Vegas-Henderson, NV	95	108	Akron, OH	27	170	Lubbock, TX	12
45	Stockton-Lodi, CA	89	108	Durham-Chapel Hill, NC	27	170	Prescott, AZ	12
46	Nashville-Davidson, TN	87	110	Macon, GA	26	170	Reno, NV	12
47	Richmond, VA	84	110	Montgomery County, PA M.D.	26	170	Rockford, IL	12
47	Sacramento, CA	84	110	Trenton, NJ	26	170	Spartanburg, SC	12
49	Fort Worth-Arlington, TX M.D.	83	113	Salt Lake City, UT	25	170	Sumter, SC	12
50	Camden, NJ M.D.	80	113	Savannah, GA	25	178	Amarillo, TX	11
50	Fort Lauderdale, FL M.D.	80	115	Beaumont-Port Arthur, TX	24	178	Chico, CA	11
52	San Francisco-Redwood, CA M.D.	79	115	Fort Wayne, IN	24	178	Dothan, AL	11
53	Louisville, KY-IN	78	115	Shreveport-Bossier City, LA	24	178	Erie, PA	11
54	Jackson, MS	77	115	South Bend-Mishawaka, IN-MI	24	178	Fayetteville-Springdale, AR-MO	11
55	Fresno, CA	76	115	Wichita, KS	24	178	Greenville, NC	11
55	Minneapolis-St. Paul, MN-WI	76	120	Albany-Schenectady-Troy, NY	23	178	Hammond, LA	11
57	Cincinnati, OH-KY-IN	75	120	Corpus Christi, TX	23	178	Monroe, LA	11
58	West Palm Beach, FL M.D.	74	120	Merced, CA	23	178	Port St. Lucie, FL	11
59	Seattle-Bellevue-Everett, WA M.D.	72	123	Huntsville, AL	22	178	Roanoke, VA	11
60	Boston, MA M.D.	71	123	Pensacola, FL	22	178	Yuba City, CA	11
61	Flint, MI	69	123	Springfield, MO	22	189	Davenport, IA-IL	10
62	Gary, IN M.D.	66	123	Tallahassee, FL	22	189	Gainesville, FL	10
63	Bakersfield, CA	65	127	Hilton Head Island, SC	21	189	Olympia, WA	10
63	Little Rock, AR	65	127	Ocala, FL	21	189	Panama City, FL	10

Note: All listings are for Metropolitan Statistical Areas (M.S.A.s) except for those ending with "M.D." Listings with "M.D." are Metropolitan Divisions which are smaller parts of eleven large M.S.A.s. See explanatory note at beginning of metropolitan area section.

RANK	METROPOLITAN AREA	MURDERS	RANK	METROPOLITAN AREA	MURDERS	RANK	METROPOLITAN AREA	MURDERS
189	Santa Cruz-Watsonville, CA	10	250	Gettysburg, PA	5	321	Blacksburg, VA	2
189	Waco, TX	10	250	Grand Junction, CO	5	321	Bloomsburg-Berwick, PA	2
189	Wilmington, NC	10	250	Hattiesburg, MS	5	321	Cheyenne, WY	2
196	Albany, GA	9	250	Homosassa Springs, FL	5	321	Decatur, AL	2
196	Alexandria, LA	9	250	Johnson City, TN	5	321	Dubuque, IA	2
196	Houma, LA	9	250	Kahului-Wailuku-Lahaina, HI	5	321	Fargo, ND-MN	2
196	Kingsport, TN-VA	9	250	Midland, TX	5	321	Gadsden, AL	2
196	Rockingham County, NH M.D.	9	250	Monroe, MI	5	321	Iowa City, IA	2
201	Auburn, AL	8	250	Norwich-New London, CT	5	321	Kennewick-Richland, WA	2
201	Bangor, ME	8	250	Odessa, TX	5	321	Madera, CA	2
201	Brunswick, GA	8	250	Rome, GA	5	321	Midland, MI	2
201	Daphne-Fairhope-Foley, AL	8	250	Sheboygan, WI	5	321	Mount Vernon-Anacortes, WA	2
201	Des Moines-West Des Moines, IA	8	250	Springfield, OH	5	321	Napa, CA	2
201	Fort Smith, AR-OK	8	250	Valdosta, GA	5	321	Ocean City, NJ	2
201	Kankakee, IL	8	271	Bellingham, WA	4	321	Sioux Falls, SD	2
201	Lake Co.-Kenosha Co., IL-WI M.D.	8	271	Bismarck, ND	4	321	Staunton-Waynesboro, VA	2
201	Laredo, TX	8	271	Bloomington, IN	4	321	St. Joseph, MO-KS	2
201	Lima, OH	8	271	Bowling Green, KY	4	321	Wausau, WI	2
201	Longview, TX	8	271	Burlington, NC	4	321	Williamsport, PA	2
201	Pueblo, CO	8	271	Cedar Rapids, IA	4	321	Winchester, VA-WV	2
201	Terre Haute, IN	8	271	Champaign-Urbana, IL	4	341	Appleton, WI	1
201	Texarkana, TX-AR	8	271	Cumberland, MD-WV	4	341	Barnstable Town, MA	1
201	Warner Robins, GA	8	271	Dalton, GA	4	341	Bay City, MI	1
216	Binghamton, NY	7	271	Danville, IL	4	341	Bloomington, IL	1
216	Boise City, ID	7	271	Dover, DE	4	341	Coeur d'Alene, ID	1
216	Elgin, IL M.D.	7	271	Duluth, MN-WI	4	341	Columbus, IN	1
216	Eugene, OR	7	271	East Stroudsburg, PA	4	341	Corvallis, OR	1
216	Gainesville, GA	7	271	Elmira, NY	4	341	Elizabethtown-Fort Knox, KY	1
216	Glens Falls, NY	7	271	Flagstaff, AZ	4	341	Grand Forks, ND-MN	1
216	Green Bay, WI	7	271	Hanford-Corcoran, CA	4	341	Great Falls, MT	1
216	Hagerstown-Martinsburg, MD-WV	7	271	Hinesville, GA	4	341	Harrisonburg, VA	1
216	Las Cruces, NM	7	271	Kokomo, IN	4	341	Kingston, NY	1
216	Portland, ME	7	271	La Crosse, WI-MN	4	341	Lafayette, IN	1
216	Redding, CA	7	271	Lincoln, NE	4	341	Manchester-Nashua, NH	1
216	Vineland-Bridgeton, NJ	7	271	Longview, WA	4	341	Manhattan, KS	1
216	Wichita Falls, TX	7	271	Medford, OR	4	341	Muncie, IN	1
216	Yuma, AZ	7	271	Ogden-Clearfield, UT	4	341	Parkersburg-Vienna, WV	1
230	Altoona, PA	6	271	Provo-Orem, UT	4	341	Punta Gorda, FL	1
230	Anniston-Oxford, AL	6	271	Rapid City, SD	4	341	Sebastian-Vero Beach, FL	1
230	Athens-Clarke County, GA	6	271	Santa Rosa, CA	4	341	State College, PA	1
230	Charlottesville, VA	6	271	Sierra Vista-Douglas, AZ	4	341	Walla Walla, WA	1
230	College Station-Bryan, TX	6	271	Sioux City, IA-NE-SD	4	341	Watertown-Fort Drum, NY	1
230	Decatur, IL	6	271	Utica-Rome, NY	4	363	Albany, OR	0
230	Farmington, NM	6	300	Abilene, TX	3	363	Ames, IA	0
230	Greeley, CO	6	300	Billings, MT	3	363	Boulder, CO	0
230	Johnstown, PA	6	300	Casper, WY	3	363	California-Lexington Park, MD	0
230	Jonesboro, AR	6	300	Columbia, MO	3	363	Carson City, NV	0
230	Joplin, MO	6	300	Crestview-Fort Walton Beach, FL	3	363	Fond du Lac, WI	0
230	Lynchburg, VA	6	300	El Centro, CA	3	363	Grand Island, NE	0
230	Naples-Marco Island, FL	6	300	Fairbanks, AK	3	363	Idaho Falls, ID	0
230	Racine, WI	6	300	Fort Collins, CO	3	363	Lawrence, KS	0
230	San Luis Obispo, CA	6	300	Janesville, WI	3	363	Lewiston-Auburn, ME	0
230	Santa Fe, NM	6	300	Jefferson City, MO	3	363	Lewiston, ID-WA	0
230	Santa Maria-Santa Barbara, CA	6	300	Lebanon, PA	3	363	Logan, UT-ID	0
230	Tyler, TX	6	300	Mansfield, OH	3	363	Mankato-North Mankato, MN	0
230	Victoria, TX	6	300	Michigan City-La Porte, IN	3	363	Missoula, MT	0
230	Waterloo-Cedar Falls, IA	6	300	Morgantown, WV	3	363	Oshkosh-Neenah, WI	0
250	Ann Arbor, MI	5	300	Morristown, TN	3	363	Owensboro, KY	0
250	Bremerton-Silverdale, WA	5	300	New Bern, NC	3	363	Pittsfield, MA	0
250	Cape Girardeau, MO-IL	5	300	Pocatello, ID	3	363	San Rafael, CA M.D.	0
250	Chambersburg-Waynesboro, PA	5	300	Rochester, MN	3	363	The Villages, FL	0
250	Cleveland, TN	5	300	Sebring, FL	3	363	Wheeling, WV-OH	0
250	Dutchess-Putnam, NY M.D.	5	300	Sherman-Denison, TX	3			
250	Florence-Muscle Shoals, AL	5	300	St. George, UT	3			

Source: Reported data from the F.B.I. "Crime in the United States 2012"
*Includes nonnegligent manslaughter.

10. Murder Rate in 2012
National Rate = 4.7 Murders per 100,000 Population*

RANK	METROPOLITAN AREA	RATE	RANK	METROPOLITAN AREA	RATE	RANK	METROPOLITAN AREA	RATE
296	Abilene, TX	1.8	280	Cheyenne, WY	2.1	25	Gary, IN M.D.	9.3
174	Akron, OH	3.8	52	Chicago (greater), IL-IN-WI	7.1	121	Gettysburg, PA	4.9
245	Albany-Schenectady-Troy, NY	2.6	32	Chicago-Joilet-Naperville, IL M.D.	8.2	100	Glens Falls, NY	5.4
95	Albany, GA	5.6	121	Chico, CA	4.9	5	Goldsboro, NC	16.0
363	Albany, OR	0.0	198	Cincinnati, OH-KY-IN	3.5	337	Grand Forks, ND-MN	1.0
85	Albuquerque, NM	5.9	69	Clarksville, TN-KY	6.4	363	Grand Island, NE	0.0
88	Alexandria, LA	5.8	150	Cleveland, TN	4.2	203	Grand Junction, CO	3.4
154	Allentown, PA-NJ	4.1	348	Coeur d'Alene, ID	0.7	328	Great Falls, MT	1.2
133	Altoona, PA	4.7	245	College Station-Bryan, TX	2.6	266	Greeley, CO	2.3
150	Amarillo, TX	4.2	227	Colorado Springs, CO	3.0	266	Green Bay, WI	2.3
363	Ames, IA	0.0	296	Columbia, MO	1.8	81	Greensboro-High Point, NC	6.0
301	Anaheim-Santa Ana-Irvine, CA M.D.	1.7	75	Columbus, GA-AL	6.2	69	Greenville-Anderson, SC	6.4
128	Anchorage, AK	4.8	322	Columbus, IN	1.3	69	Greenville, NC	6.4
314	Ann Arbor, MI	1.4	105	Corpus Christi, TX	5.3	242	Hagerstown-Martinsburg, MD-WV	2.7
112	Anniston-Oxford, AL	5.1	328	Corvallis, OR	1.2	245	Hanford-Corcoran, CA	2.6
361	Appleton, WI	0.4	328	Crestview-Fort Walton Beach, FL	1.2	213	Harrisburg-Carlisle, PA	3.3
137	Asheville, NC	4.6	162	Cumberland, MD-WV	3.9	344	Harrisonburg, VA	0.8
222	Athens-Clarke County, GA	3.1	154	Dallas (greater), TX	4.1	190	Hartford, CT	3.6
80	Atlanta, GA	6.1	142	Dallas-Plano-Irving, TX M.D.	4.4	203	Hattiesburg, MS	3.4
18	Atlantic City, NJ	10.9	237	Dalton, GA	2.8	100	Hickory, NC	5.4
95	Auburn, AL	5.6	121	Danville, IL	4.9	16	Hilton Head Island, SC	11.0
32	Augusta, GA-SC	8.2	145	Daphne-Fairhope-Foley, AL	4.3	121	Hinesville, GA	4.9
275	Austin-Round Rock, TX	2.2	245	Davenport, IA-IL	2.6	198	Homosassa Springs, FL	3.5
43	Bakersfield, CA	7.6	162	Dayton, OH	3.9	145	Houma, LA	4.3
23	Baltimore, MD	9.5	322	Decatur, AL	1.3	90	Houston, TX	5.7
109	Bangor, ME	5.2	100	Decatur, IL	5.4	112	Huntsville, AL	5.1
357	Barnstable Town, MA	0.5	213	Deltona-Daytona Beach, FL	3.3	363	Idaho Falls, ID	0.0
11	Baton Rouge, LA	11.8	162	Denver-Aurora, CO	3.9	81	Indianapolis, IN	6.0
340	Bay City, MI	0.9	314	Des Moines-West Des Moines, IA	1.4	322	Iowa City, IA	1.3
88	Beaumont-Port Arthur, TX	5.8	18	Detroit (greater), MI	10.9	36	Jacksonville, FL	8.0
13	Beckley, WV	11.2	1	Detroit-Dearborn-Livonia, MI M.D.	23.8	9	Jackson, MS	13.4
290	Bellingham, WA	1.9	45	Dothan, AL	7.5	21	Jackson, TN	9.9
290	Billings, MT	1.9	257	Dover, DE	2.4	290	Janesville, WI	1.9
237	Binghamton, NY	2.8	280	Dubuque, IA	2.1	287	Jefferson City, MO	2.0
24	Birmingham-Hoover, AL	9.4	314	Duluth, MN-WI	1.4	252	Johnson City, TN	2.5
213	Bismarck, ND	3.3	109	Durham-Chapel Hill, NC	5.2	150	Johnstown, PA	4.2
333	Blacksburg, VA	1.1	328	Dutchess-Putnam, NY M.D.	1.2	121	Jonesboro, AR	4.9
357	Bloomington, IL	0.5	257	East Stroudsburg, PA	2.4	203	Joplin, MO	3.4
252	Bloomington, IN	2.5	301	El Centro, CA	1.7	222	Kahului-Wailuku-Lahaina, HI	3.1
266	Bloomsburg-Berwick, PA	2.3	213	El Paso, TX	3.3	183	Kalamazoo-Portage, MI	3.7
333	Boise City, ID	1.1	333	Elgin, IL M.D.	1.1	54	Kankakee, IL	7.0
280	Boston (greater), MA-NH	2.1	348	Elizabethtown-Fort Knox, KY	0.7	41	Kansas City, MO-KS	7.7
183	Boston, MA M.D.	3.7	141	Elmira, NY	4.5	348	Kennewick-Richland, WA	0.7
363	Boulder, CO	0.0	162	Erie, PA	3.9	128	Killeen-Temple, TX	4.8
252	Bowling Green, KY	2.5	287	Eugene, OR	2.0	232	Kingsport, TN-VA	2.9
290	Bremerton-Silverdale, WA	1.9	30	Fairbanks, AK	8.7	357	Kingston, NY	0.5
190	Bridgeport-Stamford, CT	3.6	340	Fargo, ND-MN	0.9	159	Knoxville, TN	4.0
222	Brownsville-Harlingen, TX	3.1	133	Farmington, NM	4.7	128	Kokomo, IN	4.8
54	Brunswick, GA	7.0	266	Fayetteville-Springdale, AR-MO	2.3	227	La Crosse, WI-MN	3.0
133	Buffalo-Niagara Falls, NY	4.7	40	Fayetteville, NC	7.9	357	Lafayette, IN	0.5
245	Burlington, NC	2.6	232	Flagstaff, AZ	2.9	50	Lafayette, LA	7.2
363	California-Lexington Park, MD	0.0	4	Flint, MI	16.3	340	Lake Co.-Kenosha Co., IL-WI M.D.	0.9
348	Cambridge-Newton, MA M.D.	0.7	203	Florence-Muscle Shoals, AL	3.4	85	Lake Havasu City-Kingman, AZ	5.9
69	Camden, NJ M.D.	6.4	41	Florence, SC	7.7	73	Lakeland, FL	6.3
221	Canton, OH	3.2	363	Fond du Lac, WI	0.0	232	Lancaster, PA	2.9
54	Cape Coral-Fort Myers, FL	7.0	337	Fort Collins, CO	1.0	203	Lansing-East Lansing, MI	3.4
112	Cape Girardeau, MO-IL	5.1	142	Fort Lauderdale, FL M.D.	4.4	222	Laredo, TX	3.1
363	Carson City, NV	0.0	237	Fort Smith, AR-OK	2.8	213	Las Cruces, NM	3.3
162	Casper, WY	3.9	90	Fort Wayne, IN	5.7	128	Las Vegas-Henderson, NV	4.8
311	Cedar Rapids, IA	1.5	190	Fort Worth-Arlington, TX M.D.	3.6	363	Lawrence, KS	0.0
213	Chambersburg-Waynesboro, PA	3.3	36	Fresno, CA	8.0	22	Lawton, OK	9.8
301	Champaign-Urbana, IL	1.7	290	Gadsden, AL	1.9	275	Lebanon, PA	2.2
54	Charleston-North Charleston, SC	7.0	183	Gainesville, FL	3.7	363	Lewiston-Auburn, ME	0.0
242	Charlottesville, VA	2.7	174	Gainesville, GA	3.8			

Note: All listings are for Metropolitan Statistical Areas (M.S.A.s) except for those ending with "M.D." Listings with "M.D." are Metropolitan Divisions which are smaller parts of eleven large M.S.A.s. See explanatory note at beginning of metropolitan area section.

RANK	METROPOLITAN AREA	RATE	RANK	METROPOLITAN AREA	RATE	RANK	METROPOLITAN AREA	RATE
363	Lewiston, ID-WA	0.0	363	Owensboro, KY	0.0	328	Silver Spring-Frederick, MD M.D.	1.2
183	Lexington-Fayette, KY	3.7	252	Oxnard-Thousand Oaks, CA	2.5	257	Sioux City, IA-NE-SD	2.4
45	Lima, OH	7.5	100	Palm Bay-Melbourne, FL	5.4	340	Sioux Falls, SD	0.9
322	Lincoln, NE	1.3	105	Panama City, FL	5.3	45	South Bend-Mishawaka, IN-MI	7.5
26	Little Rock, AR	9.1	333	Parkersburg-Vienna, WV	1.1	174	Spartanburg, SC	3.8
363	Logan, UT-ID	0.0	128	Pensacola, FL	4.8	162	Spokane, WA	3.9
190	Longview, TX	3.6	133	Peoria, IL	4.7	65	Springfield, IL	6.6
162	Longview, WA	3.9	31	Philadelphia (greater) PA-NJ-MD-DE	8.6	280	Springfield, MA	2.1
81	Los Angeles County, CA M.D.	6.0	3	Philadelphia, PA M.D.	16.8	118	Springfield, MO	5.0
118	Los Angeles (greater), CA	5.0	105	Phoenix-Mesa-Scottsdale, AZ	5.3	190	Springfield, OH	3.6
75	Louisville, KY-IN	6.2	7	Pine Bluff, AR	14.1	355	State College, PA	0.6
159	Lubbock, TX	4.0	150	Pittsburgh, PA	4.2	301	Staunton-Waynesboro, VA	1.7
266	Lynchburg, VA	2.3	363	Pittsfield, MA	0.0	10	Stockton-Lodi, CA	12.7
16	Macon, GA	11.0	190	Pocatello, ID	3.6	280	St. George, UT	2.1
322	Madera, CA	1.3	252	Port St. Lucie, FL	2.5	307	St. Joseph, MO-KS	1.6
257	Madison, WI	2.4	257	Portland-Vancouver, OR-WA	2.4	48	St. Louis, MO-IL	7.3
362	Manchester-Nashua, NH	0.2	314	Portland, ME	1.4	14	Sumter, SC	11.1
337	Manhattan, KS	1.0	95	Prescott, AZ	5.6	266	Syracuse, NY	2.3
363	Mankato-North Mankato, MN	0.0	257	Providence-Warwick, RI-MA	2.4	162	Tacoma, WA M.D.	3.9
257	Mansfield, OH	2.4	348	Provo-Orem, UT	0.7	85	Tallahassee, FL	5.9
183	McAllen-Edinburg-Mission, TX	3.7	121	Pueblo, CO	4.9	162	Tampa-St Petersburg, FL	3.9
290	Medford, OR	1.9	355	Punta Gorda, FL	0.6	137	Terre Haute, IN	4.6
12	Memphis, TN-MS-AR	11.5	222	Racine, WI	3.1	105	Texarkana, TX-AR	5.3
29	Merced, CA	8.8	296	Raleigh, NC	1.8	363	The Villages, FL	0.0
73	Miami (greater), FL	6.3	232	Rapid City, SD	2.9	52	Toledo, OH	7.1
35	Miami-Dade County, FL M.D.	8.1	137	Reading, PA	4.6	43	Topeka, KS	7.6
242	Michigan City-La Porte, IN	2.7	162	Redding, CA	3.9	54	Trenton, NJ	7.0
257	Midland, MI	2.4	237	Reno, NV	2.8	90	Tucson, AZ	5.7
203	Midland, TX	3.4	62	Richmond, VA	6.8	90	Tulsa, OK	5.7
61	Milwaukee, WI	6.9	154	Riverside-San Bernardino, CA	4.1	95	Tuscaloosa, AL	5.6
275	Minneapolis-St. Paul, MN-WI	2.2	198	Roanoke, VA	3.5	237	Tyler, TX	2.8
363	Missoula, MT	0.0	314	Rochester, MN	1.4	322	Utica-Rome, NY	1.3
14	Mobile, AL	11.1	159	Rochester, NY	4.0	198	Valdosta, GA	3.5
48	Modesto, CA	7.3	203	Rockford, IL	3.4	64	Vallejo-Fairfield, CA	6.7
75	Monroe, LA	6.2	280	Rockingham County, NH M.D.	2.1	75	Victoria, TX	6.2
213	Monroe, MI	3.3	26	Rocky Mount, NC	9.1	142	Vineland-Bridgeton, NJ	4.4
314	Montgomery County, PA M.D.	1.4	109	Rome, GA	5.2	62	Virginia Beach-Norfolk, VA-NC	6.8
8	Montgomery, AL	13.9	174	Sacramento, CA	3.8	32	Visalia-Porterville, CA	8.2
266	Morgantown, WV	2.3	6	Saginaw, MI	15.1	174	Waco, TX	3.8
245	Morristown, TN	2.6	213	Salem, OR	3.3	307	Walla Walla, WA	1.6
301	Mount Vernon-Anacortes, WA	1.7	162	Salisbury, MD-DE	3.9	145	Warner Robins, GA	4.3
344	Muncie, IN	0.8	275	Salt Lake City, UT	2.2	307	Warren-Troy, MI M.D.	1.6
314	Napa, CA	1.4	112	San Antonio, TX	5.1	190	Washington (greater) DC-VA-MD-WV	3.6
296	Naples-Marco Island, FL	1.8	203	San Diego, CA	3.4	145	Washington, DC-VA-MD-WV M.D.	4.3
112	Nashville-Davidson, TN	5.1	66	San Francisco (greater), CA	6.5	190	Waterloo-Cedar Falls, IA	3.6
296	Nassau-Suffolk, NY M.D.	1.8	112	San Francisco-Redwood, CA M.D.	5.1	344	Watertown-Fort Drum, NY	0.8
266	New Bern, NC	2.3	227	San Jose, CA	3.0	311	Wausau, WI	1.5
154	New Haven-Milford, CT	4.1	275	San Luis Obispo, CA	2.2	99	West Palm Beach, FL M.D.	5.5
2	New Orleans, LA	20.6	363	San Rafael, CA M.D.	0.0	363	Wheeling, WV-OH	0.0
174	New York (greater), NY-NJ-PA	3.8	183	Santa Cruz-Watsonville, CA	3.7	137	Wichita Falls, TX	4.6
174	New York-Jersey City, NY-NJ M.D.	3.8	154	Santa Fe, NM	4.1	174	Wichita, KS	3.8
66	Newark, NJ-PA M.D.	6.5	314	Santa Maria-Santa Barbara, CA	1.4	301	Williamsport, PA	1.7
81	North Port-Sarasota-Bradenton, FL	6.0	344	Santa Rosa, CA	0.8	54	Wilmington, DE-MD-NJ M.D.	7.0
203	Norwich-New London, CT	3.4	54	Savannah, GA	7.0	174	Wilmington, NC	3.8
36	Oakland-Hayward, CA M.D.	8.0	266	Scranton--Wilkes-Barre, PA	2.3	311	Winchester, VA-WV	1.5
75	Ocala, FL	6.2	232	Seattle (greater), WA	2.9	287	Winston-Salem, NC	2.0
280	Ocean City, NJ	2.1	245	Seattle-Bellevue-Everett, WA M.D.	2.6	307	Worcester, MA-CT	1.6
198	Odessa, TX	3.5	348	Sebastian-Vero Beach, FL	0.7	50	Yakima, WA	7.2
348	Ogden-Clearfield, UT	0.7	227	Sebring, FL	3.0	183	York-Hanover, PA	3.7
36	Oklahoma City, OK	8.0	145	Sheboygan, WI	4.3	90	Youngstown-Warren, OH-PA	5.7
162	Olympia, WA	3.9	257	Sherman-Denison, TX	2.4	66	Yuba City, CA	6.5
121	Omaha-Council Bluffs, NE-IA	4.9	100	Shreveport-Bossier City, LA	5.4	203	Yuma, AZ	3.4
118	Orlando, FL	5.0	227	Sierra Vista-Douglas, AZ	3.0			
363	Oshkosh-Neenah, WI	0.0						

Source: Reported data from the F.B.I. "Crime in the United States 2012"
*Includes nonnegligent manslaughter.

10. Murder Rate in 2012 (continued)
National Rate = 4.7 Murders per 100,000 Population*

RANK	METROPOLITAN AREA	RATE	RANK	METROPOLITAN AREA	RATE	RANK	METROPOLITAN AREA	RATE
1	Detroit-Dearborn-Livonia, MI M.D.	23.8	65	Springfield, IL	6.6	128	Killeen-Temple, TX	4.8
2	New Orleans, LA	20.6	66	Newark, NJ-PA M.D.	6.5	128	Kokomo, IN	4.8
3	Philadelphia, PA M.D.	16.8	66	San Francisco (greater), CA	6.5	128	Las Vegas-Henderson, NV	4.8
4	Flint, MI	16.3	66	Yuba City, CA	6.5	128	Pensacola, FL	4.8
5	Goldsboro, NC	16.0	69	Camden, NJ M.D.	6.4	133	Altoona, PA	4.7
6	Saginaw, MI	15.1	69	Clarksville, TN-KY	6.4	133	Buffalo-Niagara Falls, NY	4.7
7	Pine Bluff, AR	14.1	69	Greenville-Anderson, SC	6.4	133	Farmington, NM	4.7
8	Montgomery, AL	13.9	69	Greenville, NC	6.4	133	Peoria, IL	4.7
9	Jackson, MS	13.4	73	Lakeland, FL	6.3	137	Asheville, NC	4.6
10	Stockton-Lodi, CA	12.7	73	Miami (greater), FL	6.3	137	Reading, PA	4.6
11	Baton Rouge, LA	11.8	75	Columbus, GA-AL	6.2	137	Terre Haute, IN	4.6
12	Memphis, TN-MS-AR	11.5	75	Louisville, KY-IN	6.2	137	Wichita Falls, TX	4.6
13	Beckley, WV	11.2	75	Monroe, LA	6.2	141	Elmira, NY	4.5
14	Mobile, AL	11.1	75	Ocala, FL	6.2	142	Dallas-Plano-Irving, TX M.D.	4.4
14	Sumter, SC	11.1	75	Victoria, TX	6.2	142	Fort Lauderdale, FL M.D.	4.4
16	Hilton Head Island, SC	11.0	80	Atlanta, GA	6.1	142	Vineland-Bridgeton, NJ	4.4
16	Macon, GA	11.0	81	Greensboro-High Point, NC	6.0	145	Daphne-Fairhope-Foley, AL	4.3
18	Atlantic City, NJ	10.9	81	Indianapolis, IN	6.0	145	Houma, LA	4.3
18	Detroit (greater), MI	10.9	81	Los Angeles County, CA M.D.	6.0	145	Sheboygan, WI	4.3
20	Salinas, CA	10.6	81	North Port-Sarasota-Bradenton, FL	6.0	145	Warner Robins, GA	4.3
21	Jackson, TN	9.9	85	Albuquerque, NM	5.9	145	Washington, DC-VA-MD-WV M.D.	4.3
22	Lawton, OK	9.8	85	Lake Havasu City-Kingman, AZ	5.9	150	Amarillo, TX	4.2
23	Baltimore, MD	9.5	85	Tallahassee, FL	5.9	150	Cleveland, TN	4.2
24	Birmingham-Hoover, AL	9.4	88	Alexandria, LA	5.8	150	Johnstown, PA	4.2
25	Gary, IN M.D.	9.3	88	Beaumont-Port Arthur, TX	5.8	150	Pittsburgh, PA	4.2
26	Little Rock, AR	9.1	90	Fort Wayne, IN	5.7	154	Allentown, PA-NJ	4.1
26	Rocky Mount, NC	9.1	90	Houston, TX	5.7	154	Dallas (greater), TX	4.1
28	Hammond, LA	8.9	90	Tucson, AZ	5.7	154	New Haven-Milford, CT	4.1
29	Merced, CA	8.8	90	Tulsa, OK	5.7	154	Riverside-San Bernardino, CA	4.1
30	Fairbanks, AK	8.7	90	Youngstown-Warren, OH-PA	5.7	154	Santa Fe, NM	4.1
31	Philadelphia (greater) PA-NJ-MD-DE	8.6	95	Albany, GA	5.6	159	Knoxville, TN	4.0
32	Augusta, GA-SC	8.2	95	Auburn, AL	5.6	159	Lubbock, TX	4.0
32	Chicago-Joilet-Naperville, IL M.D.	8.2	95	Prescott, AZ	5.6	159	Rochester, NY	4.0
32	Visalia-Porterville, CA	8.2	95	Tuscaloosa, AL	5.6	162	Casper, WY	3.9
35	Miami-Dade County, FL M.D.	8.1	99	West Palm Beach, FL M.D.	5.5	162	Cumberland, MD-WV	3.9
36	Fresno, CA	8.0	100	Decatur, IL	5.4	162	Dayton, OH	3.9
36	Jacksonville, FL	8.0	100	Glens Falls, NY	5.4	162	Denver-Aurora, CO	3.9
36	Oakland-Hayward, CA M.D.	8.0	100	Hickory, NC	5.4	162	Erie, PA	3.9
36	Oklahoma City, OK	8.0	100	Palm Bay-Melbourne, FL	5.4	162	Longview, WA	3.9
40	Fayetteville, NC	7.9	100	Shreveport-Bossier City, LA	5.4	162	Olympia, WA	3.9
41	Florence, SC	7.7	105	Corpus Christi, TX	5.3	162	Redding, CA	3.9
41	Kansas City, MO-KS	7.7	105	Panama City, FL	5.3	162	Salisbury, MD-DE	3.9
43	Bakersfield, CA	7.6	105	Phoenix-Mesa-Scottsdale, AZ	5.3	162	Spokane, WA	3.9
43	Topeka, KS	7.6	105	Texarkana, TX-AR	5.3	162	Tacoma, WA M.D.	3.9
45	Dothan, AL	7.5	109	Bangor, ME	5.2	162	Tampa-St Petersburg, FL	3.9
45	Lima, OH	7.5	109	Durham-Chapel Hill, NC	5.2	174	Akron, OH	3.8
45	South Bend-Mishawaka, IN-MI	7.5	109	Rome, GA	5.2	174	Gainesville, GA	3.8
48	Modesto, CA	7.3	112	Anniston-Oxford, AL	5.1	174	New York (greater), NY-NJ-PA	3.8
48	St. Louis, MO-IL	7.3	112	Cape Girardeau, MO-IL	5.1	174	New York-Jersey City, NY-NJ M.D.	3.8
50	Lafayette, LA	7.2	112	Huntsville, AL	5.1	174	Sacramento, CA	3.8
50	Yakima, WA	7.2	112	Nashville-Davidson, TN	5.1	174	Spartanburg, SC	3.8
52	Chicago (greater), IL-IN-WI	7.1	112	San Antonio, TX	5.1	174	Waco, TX	3.8
52	Toledo, OH	7.1	112	San Francisco-Redwood, CA M.D.	5.1	174	Wichita, KS	3.8
54	Brunswick, GA	7.0	118	Los Angeles (greater), CA	5.0	174	Wilmington, NC	3.8
54	Cape Coral-Fort Myers, FL	7.0	118	Orlando, FL	5.0	183	Boston, MA M.D.	3.7
54	Charleston-North Charleston, SC	7.0	118	Springfield, MO	5.0	183	Gainesville, FL	3.7
54	Kankakee, IL	7.0	121	Chico, CA	4.9	183	Kalamazoo-Portage, MI	3.7
54	Savannah, GA	7.0	121	Danville, IL	4.9	183	Lexington-Fayette, KY	3.7
54	Trenton, NJ	7.0	121	Gettysburg, PA	4.9	183	McAllen-Edinburg-Mission, TX	3.7
54	Wilmington, DE-MD-NJ M.D.	7.0	121	Hinesville, GA	4.9	183	Santa Cruz-Watsonville, CA	3.7
61	Milwaukee, WI	6.9	121	Jonesboro, AR	4.9	183	York-Hanover, PA	3.7
62	Richmond, VA	6.8	121	Omaha-Council Bluffs, NE-IA	4.9	190	Bridgeport-Stamford, CT	3.6
62	Virginia Beach-Norfolk, VA-NC	6.8	121	Pueblo, CO	4.9	190	Fort Worth-Arlington, TX M.D.	3.6
64	Vallejo-Fairfield, CA	6.7	128	Anchorage, AK	4.8	190	Hartford, CT	3.6

Note: All listings are for Metropolitan Statistical Areas (M.S.A.s) except for those ending with "M.D." Listings with "M.D." are Metropolitan Divisions which are smaller parts of eleven large M.S.A.s. See explanatory note at beginning of metropolitan area section.

RANK	METROPOLITAN AREA	RATE	RANK	METROPOLITAN AREA	RATE	RANK	METROPOLITAN AREA	RATE
190	Longview, TX	3.6	257	Dover, DE	2.4	314	Santa Maria-Santa Barbara, CA	1.4
190	Pocatello, ID	3.6	257	East Stroudsburg, PA	2.4	322	Columbus, IN	1.3
190	Springfield, OH	3.6	257	Madison, WI	2.4	322	Decatur, AL	1.3
190	Washington (greater) DC-VA-MD-WV	3.6	257	Mansfield, OH	2.4	322	Iowa City, IA	1.3
190	Waterloo-Cedar Falls, IA	3.6	257	Midland, MI	2.4	322	Lincoln, NE	1.3
198	Cincinnati, OH-KY-IN	3.5	257	Portland-Vancouver, OR-WA	2.4	322	Madera, CA	1.3
198	Homosassa Springs, FL	3.5	257	Providence-Warwick, RI-MA	2.4	322	Utica-Rome, NY	1.3
198	Odessa, TX	3.5	257	Sherman-Denison, TX	2.4	328	Corvallis, OR	1.2
198	Roanoke, VA	3.5	257	Sioux City, IA-NE-SD	2.4	328	Crestview-Fort Walton Beach, FL	1.2
198	Valdosta, GA	3.5	266	Bloomsburg-Berwick, PA	2.3	328	Dutchess-Putnam, NY M.D.	1.2
203	Florence-Muscle Shoals, AL	3.4	266	Fayetteville-Springdale, AR-MO	2.3	328	Great Falls, MT	1.2
203	Grand Junction, CO	3.4	266	Greeley, CO	2.3	328	Silver Spring-Frederick, MD M.D.	1.2
203	Hattiesburg, MS	3.4	266	Green Bay, WI	2.3	333	Blacksburg, VA	1.1
203	Joplin, MO	3.4	266	Lynchburg, VA	2.3	333	Boise City, ID	1.1
203	Lansing-East Lansing, MI	3.4	266	Morgantown, WV	2.3	333	Elgin, IL M.D.	1.1
203	Midland, TX	3.4	266	New Bern, NC	2.3	333	Parkersburg-Vienna, WV	1.1
203	Norwich-New London, CT	3.4	266	Scranton--Wilkes-Barre, PA	2.3	337	Fort Collins, CO	1.0
203	Rockford, IL	3.4	266	Syracuse, NY	2.3	337	Grand Forks, ND-MN	1.0
203	San Diego, CA	3.4	275	Austin-Round Rock, TX	2.2	337	Manhattan, KS	1.0
203	Yuma, AZ	3.4	275	Lebanon, PA	2.2	340	Bay City, MI	0.9
213	Bismarck, ND	3.3	275	Minneapolis-St. Paul, MN-WI	2.2	340	Fargo, ND-MN	0.9
213	Chambersburg-Waynesboro, PA	3.3	275	Salt Lake City, UT	2.2	340	Lake Co.-Kenosha Co., IL-WI M.D.	0.9
213	Deltona-Daytona Beach, FL	3.3	275	San Luis Obispo, CA	2.2	340	Sioux Falls, SD	0.9
213	El Paso, TX	3.3	280	Boston (greater), MA-NH	2.1	344	Harrisonburg, VA	0.8
213	Harrisburg-Carlisle, PA	3.3	280	Cheyenne, WY	2.1	344	Muncie, IN	0.8
213	Las Cruces, NM	3.3	280	Dubuque, IA	2.1	344	Santa Rosa, CA	0.8
213	Monroe, MI	3.3	280	Ocean City, NJ	2.1	344	Watertown-Fort Drum, NY	0.8
213	Salem, OR	3.3	280	Rockingham County, NH M.D.	2.1	348	Cambridge-Newton, MA M.D.	0.7
221	Canton, OH	3.2	280	Springfield, MA	2.1	348	Coeur d'Alene, ID	0.7
222	Athens-Clarke County, GA	3.1	280	St. George, UT	2.1	348	Elizabethtown-Fort Knox, KY	0.7
222	Brownsville-Harlingen, TX	3.1	287	Eugene, OR	2.0	348	Kennewick-Richland, WA	0.7
222	Kahului-Wailuku-Lahaina, HI	3.1	287	Jefferson City, MO	2.0	348	Ogden-Clearfield, UT	0.7
222	Laredo, TX	3.1	287	Winston-Salem, NC	2.0	348	Provo-Orem, UT	0.7
222	Racine, WI	3.1	290	Bellingham, WA	1.9	348	Sebastian-Vero Beach, FL	0.7
227	Colorado Springs, CO	3.0	290	Billings, MT	1.9	355	Punta Gorda, FL	0.6
227	La Crosse, WI-MN	3.0	290	Bremerton-Silverdale, WA	1.9	355	State College, PA	0.6
227	San Jose, CA	3.0	290	Gadsden, AL	1.9	357	Barnstable Town, MA	0.5
227	Sebring, FL	3.0	290	Janesville, WI	1.9	357	Bloomington, IL	0.5
227	Sierra Vista-Douglas, AZ	3.0	290	Medford, OR	1.9	357	Kingston, NY	0.5
232	Flagstaff, AZ	2.9	296	Abilene, TX	1.8	357	Lafayette, IN	0.5
232	Kingsport, TN-VA	2.9	296	Columbia, MO	1.8	361	Appleton, WI	0.4
232	Lancaster, PA	2.9	296	Naples-Marco Island, FL	1.8	362	Manchester-Nashua, NH	0.2
232	Rapid City, SD	2.9	296	Nassau-Suffolk, NY M.D.	1.8	363	Albany, OR	0.0
232	Seattle (greater), WA	2.9	296	Raleigh, NC	1.8	363	Ames, IA	0.0
237	Binghamton, NY	2.8	301	Anaheim-Santa Ana-Irvine, CA M.D.	1.7	363	Boulder, CO	0.0
237	Dalton, GA	2.8	301	Champaign-Urbana, IL	1.7	363	California-Lexington Park, MD	0.0
237	Fort Smith, AR-OK	2.8	301	El Centro, CA	1.7	363	Carson City, NV	0.0
237	Reno, NV	2.8	301	Mount Vernon-Anacortes, WA	1.7	363	Fond du Lac, WI	0.0
237	Tyler, TX	2.8	301	Staunton-Waynesboro, VA	1.7	363	Grand Island, NE	0.0
242	Charlottesville, VA	2.7	301	Williamsport, PA	1.7	363	Idaho Falls, ID	0.0
242	Hagerstown-Martinsburg, MD-WV	2.7	307	St. Joseph, MO-KS	1.6	363	Lawrence, KS	0.0
242	Michigan City-La Porte, IN	2.7	307	Walla Walla, WA	1.6	363	Lewiston-Auburn, ME	0.0
245	Albany-Schenectady-Troy, NY	2.6	307	Warren-Troy, MI M.D.	1.6	363	Lewiston, ID-WA	0.0
245	Burlington, NC	2.6	307	Worcester, MA-CT	1.6	363	Logan, UT-ID	0.0
245	College Station-Bryan, TX	2.6	311	Cedar Rapids, IA	1.5	363	Mankato-North Mankato, MN	0.0
245	Davenport, IA-IL	2.6	311	Wausau, WI	1.5	363	Missoula, MT	0.0
245	Hanford-Corcoran, CA	2.6	311	Winchester, VA-WV	1.5	363	Oshkosh-Neenah, WI	0.0
245	Morristown, TN	2.6	314	Ann Arbor, MI	1.4	363	Owensboro, KY	0.0
245	Seattle-Bellevue-Everett, WA M.D.	2.6	314	Des Moines-West Des Moines, IA	1.4	363	Pittsfield, MA	0.0
252	Bloomington, IN	2.5	314	Duluth, MN-WI	1.4	363	San Rafael, CA M.D.	0.0
252	Bowling Green, KY	2.5	314	Montgomery County, PA M.D.	1.4	363	The Villages, FL	0.0
252	Johnson City, TN	2.5	314	Napa, CA	1.4	363	Wheeling, WV-OH	0.0
252	Oxnard-Thousand Oaks, CA	2.5	314	Portland, ME	1.4			
252	Port St. Lucie, FL	2.5	314	Rochester, MN	1.4			

Source: Reported data from the F.B.I. "Crime in the United States 2012"
*Includes nonnegligent manslaughter.

11. Percent Change in Murder Rate: 2011 to 2012
National Percent Change = 0.4% Increase*

RANK	METROPOLITAN AREA	% CHANGE	RANK	METROPOLITAN AREA	% CHANGE	RANK	METROPOLITAN AREA	% CHANGE
230	Abilene, TX	(40.0)	155	Cheyenne, WY	(4.5)	118	Gary, IN M.D.	4.5
192	Akron, OH	(19.1)	103	Chicago (greater), IL-IN-WI	10.9	NA	Gettysburg, PA**	NA
NA	Albany-Schenectady-Troy, NY**	NA	NA	Chicago-Joilet-Naperville, IL M.D.**	NA	NA	Glens Falls, NY**	NA
234	Albany, GA	(44.0)	61	Chico, CA	36.1	21	Goldsboro, NC	97.5
NA	Albany, OR**	NA	NA	Cincinnati, OH-KY-IN**	NA	NA	Grand Forks, ND-MN***	NA
91	Albuquerque, NM	18.0	34	Clarksville, TN-KY	60.0	NA	Grand Island, NE**	NA
25	Alexandria, LA	81.3	214	Cleveland, TN	(30.0)	27	Grand Junction, CO	70.0
NA	Allentown, PA-NJ**	NA	NA	Coeur d'Alene, ID**	NA	238	Great Falls, MT	(50.0)
8	Altoona, PA	193.8	77	College Station-Bryan, TX	23.8	131	Greeley, CO	0.0
169	Amarillo, TX	(10.6)	224	Colorado Springs, CO	(36.2)	6	Green Bay, WI	228.6
131	Ames, IA	0.0	196	Columbia, MO	(21.7)	NA	Greensboro-High Point, NC**	NA
213	Anaheim-Santa Ana-Irvine, CA M.D.	(29.2)	200	Columbus, GA-AL	(22.5)	NA	Greenville-Anderson, SC**	NA
NA	Anchorage, AK**	NA	131	Columbus, IN	0.0	NA	Greenville, NC**	NA
229	Ann Arbor, MI	(39.1)	71	Corpus Christi, TX	29.3	NA	Hagerstown-Martinsburg, MD-WV**	NA
249	Anniston-Oxford, AL	(56.8)	259	Corvallis, OR	(65.7)	NA	Hammond, LA**	NA
246	Appleton, WI	(55.6)	236	Crestview-Fort Walton Beach, FL	(45.5)	238	Hanford-Corcoran, CA	(50.0)
30	Asheville, NC	64.3	218	Cumberland, MD-WV	(32.8)	165	Harrisburg-Carlisle, PA	(8.3)
131	Athens-Clarke County, GA	0.0	167	Dallas (greater), TX	(8.9)	238	Harrisonburg, VA	(50.0)
128	Atlanta, GA	1.7	154	Dallas-Plano-Irving, TX M.D.	(4.3)	122	Hartford, CT	2.9
60	Atlantic City, NJ	36.3	17	Dalton, GA	100.0	NA	Hattiesburg, MS**	NA
9	Auburn, AL	166.7	66	Danville, IL	32.4	166	Hickory, NC	(8.5)
162	Augusta, GA-SC	(7.9)	NA	Daphne-Fairhope-Foley, AL**	NA	NA	Hilton Head Island, SC**	NA
204	Austin-Round Rock, TX	(24.1)	77	Davenport, IA-IL	23.8	152	Hinesville, GA	(3.9)
53	Bakersfield, CA	40.7	223	Dayton, OH	(36.1)	NA	Homosassa Springs, FL**	NA
130	Baltimore, MD	1.1	216	Decatur, AL	(31.6)	47	Houma, LA	48.3
94	Bangor, ME	15.6	230	Decatur, IL	(40.0)	112	Houston, TX	5.6
258	Barnstable Town, MA	(64.3)	NA	Deltona-Daytona Beach, FL**	NA	99	Huntsville, AL	13.3
149	Baton Rouge, LA	(0.8)	NA	Denver-Aurora, CO**	NA	264	Idaho Falls, ID	(100.0)
261	Bay City, MI	(67.9)	173	Des Moines-West Des Moines, IA	(12.5)	NA	Indianapolis, IN**	NA
172	Beaumont-Port Arthur, TX	(12.1)	100	Detroit (greater), MI	12.4	222	Iowa City, IA	(35.0)
NA	Beckley, WV**	NA	92	Detroit-Dearborn-Livonia, MI M.D.	17.2	76	Jacksonville, FL	25.0
75	Bellingham, WA	26.7	14	Dothan, AL	120.6	NA	Jackson, MS**	NA
131	Billings, MT	0.0	235	Dover, DE	(44.2)	NA	Jackson, TN**	NA
NA	Binghamton, NY**	NA	22	Dubuque, IA	90.9	202	Janesville, WI	(24.0)
112	Birmingham-Hoover, AL	5.6	74	Duluth, MN-WI	27.3	250	Jefferson City, MO	(57.4)
82	Bismarck, ND	22.2	208	Durham-Chapel Hill, NC	(27.8)	186	Johnson City, TN	(16.7)
228	Blacksburg, VA	(38.9)	NA	Dutchess-Putnam, NY M.D.**	NA	40	Johnstown, PA	50.0
251	Bloomington, IL	(58.3)	NA	East Stroudsburg, PA**	NA	46	Jonesboro, AR	48.5
NA	Bloomington, IN**	NA	131	El Centro, CA	0.0	17	Joplin, MO	100.0
NA	Bloomsburg-Berwick, PA**	NA	40	El Paso, TX	50.0	NA	Kahului-Wailuku-Lahaina, HI**	NA
180	Boise City, ID	(15.4)	NA	Elgin, IL M.D.**	NA	NA	Kalamazoo-Portage, MI**	NA
NA	Boston (greater), MA-NH**	NA	NA	Elizabethtown-Fort Knox, KY**	NA	17	Kankakee, IL	100.0
NA	Boston, MA M.D.**	NA	NA	Elmira, NY**	NA	NA	Kansas City, MO-KS**	NA
264	Boulder, CO	(100.0)	56	Erie, PA	39.3	256	Kennewick-Richland, WA	(63.2)
119	Bowling Green, KY	4.2	10	Eugene, OR	150.0	102	Killeen-Temple, TX	11.6
35	Bremerton-Silverdale, WA	58.3	40	Fairbanks, AK	50.0	131	Kingsport, TN-VA	0.0
131	Bridgeport-Stamford, CT	0.0	26	Fargo, ND-MN	80.0	NA	Kingston, NY**	NA
32	Brownsville-Harlingen, TX	63.2	79	Farmington, NM	23.7	NA	Knoxville, TN**	NA
96	Brunswick, GA	14.8	NA	Fayetteville-Springdale, AR-MO**	NA	NA	Kokomo, IN**	NA
NA	Buffalo-Niagara Falls, NY**	NA	171	Fayetteville, NC	(11.2)	NA	La Crosse, WI-MN***	NA
70	Burlington, NC	30.0	195	Flagstaff, AZ	(21.6)	260	Lafayette, IN	(66.7)
NA	California-Lexington Park, MD**	NA	109	Flint, MI	8.7	NA	Lafayette, LA**	NA
NA	Cambridge-Newton, MA M.D.**	NA	27	Florence-Muscle Shoals, AL	70.0	73	Lake Co.-Kenosha Co., IL-WI M.D.	28.6
80	Camden, NJ M.D.	23.1	95	Florence, SC	14.9	131	Lake Havasu City-Kingman, AZ	0.0
176	Canton, OH	(13.5)	264	Fond du Lac, WI	(100.0)	36	Lakeland, FL	53.7
96	Cape Coral-Fort Myers, FL	14.8	201	Fort Collins, CO	(23.1)	13	Lancaster, PA	123.1
3	Cape Girardeau, MO-IL	410.0	64	Fort Lauderdale, FL M.D.	33.3	174	Lansing-East Lansing, MI	(12.8)
264	Carson City, NV	(100.0)	NA	Fort Smith, AR-OK**	NA	209	Laredo, TX	(27.9)
40	Casper, WY	50.0	164	Fort Wayne, IN	(8.1)	131	Las Cruces, NM	0.0
24	Cedar Rapids, IA	87.5	185	Fort Worth-Arlington, TX M.D.	(16.3)	125	Las Vegas-Henderson, NV	2.1
NA	Chambersburg-Waynesboro, PA**	NA	49	Fresno, CA	45.5	131	Lawrence, KS	0.0
220	Champaign-Urbana, IL	(34.6)	253	Gadsden, AL	(60.4)	NA	Lawton, OK**	NA
NA	Charleston-North Charleston, SC**	NA	206	Gainesville, FL	(24.5)	7	Lebanon, PA	214.3
159	Charlottesville, VA	(6.9)	53	Gainesville, GA	40.7	264	Lewiston-Auburn, ME	(100.0)

Note: All listings are for Metropolitan Statistical Areas (M.S.A.s) except for those ending with "M.D." Listings with "M.D." are Metropolitan Divisions which are smaller parts of eleven large M.S.A.s. See explanatory note at beginning of metropolitan area section.

RANK	METROPOLITAN AREA	% CHANGE	RANK	METROPOLITAN AREA	% CHANGE	RANK	METROPOLITAN AREA	% CHANGE
NA	Lewiston, ID-WA**	NA	264	Owensboro, KY	(100.0)	194	Silver Spring-Frederick, MD M.D.	(20.0)
NA	Lexington-Fayette, KY**	NA	57	Oxnard-Thousand Oaks, CA	38.9	NA	Sioux City, IA-NE-SD**	NA
5	Lima, OH	294.7	17	Palm Bay-Melbourne, FL	100.0	252	Sioux Falls, SD	(59.1)
131	Lincoln, NE	0.0	NA	Panama City, FL**	NA	40	South Bend-Mishawaka, IN-MI	50.0
161	Little Rock, AR	(7.1)	NA	Parkersburg-Vienna, WV**	NA	NA	Spartanburg, SC**	NA
131	Logan, UT-ID	0.0	88	Pensacola, FL	20.0	NA	Spokane, WA**	NA
210	Longview, TX	(28.0)	191	Peoria, IL	(19.0)	37	Springfield, IL	53.5
124	Longview, WA	2.6	NA	Philadelphia (greater) PA-NJ-MD-DE**	NA	NA	Springfield, MA**	NA
114	Los Angeles County, CA M.D.	5.3	NA	Philadelphia, PA M.D.**	NA	12	Springfield, MO	138.1
126	Los Angeles (greater), CA	2.0	NA	Phoenix-Mesa-Scottsdale, AZ**	NA	31	Springfield, OH	63.6
52	Louisville, KY-IN	40.9	156	Pine Bluff, AR	(4.7)	NA	State College, PA***	NA
114	Lubbock, TX	5.3	105	Pittsburgh, PA	10.5	NA	Staunton-Waynesboro, VA**	NA
131	Lynchburg, VA	0.0	264	Pittsfield, MA	(100.0)	129	Stockton-Lodi, CA	1.6
50	Macon, GA	44.7	NA	Pocatello, ID**	NA	NA	St. George, UT**	NA
254	Madera, CA	(60.6)	243	Port St. Lucie, FL	(51.0)	237	St. Joseph, MO-KS	(48.4)
NA	Madison, WI**	NA	98	Portland-Vancouver, OR-WA	14.3	152	St. Louis, MO-IL	(3.9)
263	Manchester-Nashua, NH	(90.0)	55	Portland, ME	40.0	211	Sumter, SC	(28.8)
NA	Manhattan, KS**	NA	212	Prescott, AZ	(29.1)	NA	Syracuse, NY**	NA
264	Mankato-North Mankato, MN	(100.0)	NA	Providence-Warwick, RI-MA**	NA	85	Tacoma, WA M.D.	21.9
131	Mansfield, OH	0.0	197	Provo-Orem, UT	(22.2)	81	Tallahassee, FL	22.9
183	McAllen-Edinburg-Mission, TX	(15.9)	227	Pueblo, CO	(38.8)	187	Tampa-St Petersburg, FL	(17.0)
255	Medford, OR	(61.2)	238	Punta Gorda, FL	(50.0)	67	Terre Haute, IN	31.4
110	Memphis, TN-MS-AR	8.5	178	Racine, WI	(13.9)	NA	Texarkana, TX-AR**	NA
33	Merced, CA	63.0	215	Raleigh, NC	(30.8)	NA	The Villages, FL**	NA
120	Miami (greater), FL	3.3	NA	Rapid City, SD**	NA	NA	Toledo, OH**	NA
158	Miami-Dade County, FL M.D.	(5.8)	131	Reading, PA	0.0	89	Topeka, KS	18.8
207	Michigan City-La Porte, IN	(25.0)	90	Redding, CA	18.2	122	Trenton, NJ	2.9
NA	Midland, MI**	NA	238	Reno, NV	(50.0)	202	Tucson, AZ	(24.0)
NA	Midland, TX**	NA	87	Richmond, VA	21.4	184	Tulsa, OK	(16.2)
93	Milwaukee, WI	16.9	156	Riverside-San Bernardino, CA	(4.7)	NA	Tuscaloosa, AL**	NA
82	Minneapolis-St. Paul, MN-WI	22.2	108	Roanoke, VA	9.4	205	Tyler, TX	(24.3)
264	Missoula, MT	(100.0)	NA	Rochester, MN**	NA	NA	Utica-Rome, NY**	NA
150	Mobile, AL	(1.8)	NA	Rochester, NY**	NA	226	Valdosta, GA	(38.6)
101	Modesto, CA	12.3	248	Rockford, IL	(55.8)	159	Vallejo-Fairfield, CA	(6.9)
86	Monroe, LA	21.6	1	Rockingham County, NH M.D.	950.0	NA	Victoria, TX**	NA
29	Monroe, MI	65.0	197	Rocky Mount, NC	(22.2)	NA	Vineland-Bridgeton, NJ**	NA
NA	Montgomery County, PA M.D.**	NA	126	Rome, GA	2.0	121	Virginia Beach-Norfolk, VA-NC	3.0
63	Montgomery, AL	33.7	177	Sacramento, CA	(13.6)	162	Visalia-Porterville, CA	(7.9)
NA	Morgantown, WV**	NA	15	Saginaw, MI	115.7	NA	Waco, TX**	NA
NA	Morristown, TN**	NA	106	Salem, OR	10.0	NA	Walla Walla, WA**	NA
217	Mount Vernon-Anacortes, WA	(32.0)	68	Salinas, CA	30.9	NA	Warner Robins, GA**	NA
245	Muncie, IN	(52.9)	NA	Salisbury, MD-DE**	NA	182	Warren-Troy, MI M.D.	(15.8)
225	Napa, CA	(36.4)	117	Salt Lake City, UT	4.8	189	Washington (greater) DC-VA-MD-WV	(18.2)
233	Naples-Marco Island, FL	(41.9)	131	San Antonio, TX	0.0	190	Washington, DC-VA-MD-WV M.D.	(18.9)
NA	Nashville-Davidson, TN**	NA	69	San Diego, CA	30.8	40	Waterloo-Cedar Falls, IA	50.0
NA	Nassau-Suffolk, NY M.D.**	NA	111	San Francisco (greater), CA	8.3	NA	Watertown-Fort Drum, NY**	NA
NA	New Bern, NC**	NA	62	San Francisco-Redwood, CA M.D.	34.2	NA	Wausau, WI***	NA
219	New Haven-Milford, CT	(33.9)	168	San Jose, CA	(9.1)	106	West Palm Beach, FL M.D.	10.0
175	New Orleans, LA	(13.1)	82	San Luis Obispo, CA	22.2	NA	Wheeling, WV-OH**	NA
NA	New York (greater), NY-NJ-PA**	NA	NA	San Rafael, CA M.D.**	NA	2	Wichita Falls, TX	666.7
NA	New York-Jersey City, NY-NJ M.D.**	NA	151	Santa Cruz-Watsonville, CA	(2.6)	199	Wichita, KS	(22.4)
NA	Newark, NJ-PA M.D.**	NA	39	Santa Fe, NM	51.9	23	Williamsport, PA	88.9
64	North Port-Sarasota-Bradenton, FL	33.3	NA	Santa Maria-Santa Barbara, CA**	NA	51	Wilmington, DE-MD-NJ M.D.	42.9
131	Norwich-New London, CT	0.0	257	Santa Rosa, CA	(63.6)	NA	Wilmington, NC**	NA
114	Oakland-Hayward, CA M.D.	5.3	188	Savannah, GA	(17.6)	221	Winchester, VA-WV	(34.8)
48	Ocala, FL	47.6	179	Scranton--Wilkes-Barre, PA	(14.8)	NA	Winston-Salem, NC**	NA
16	Ocean City, NJ	110.0	59	Seattle (greater), WA	38.1	NA	Worcester, MA-CT**	NA
247	Odessa, TX	(55.7)	38	Seattle-Bellevue-Everett, WA M.D.	52.9	104	Yakima, WA	10.8
NA	Ogden-Clearfield, UT**	NA	262	Sebastian-Vero Beach, FL	(80.6)	193	York-Hanover, PA	(19.6)
72	Oklahoma City, OK	29.0	NA	Sebring, FL**	NA	NA	Youngstown-Warren, OH-PA**	NA
11	Olympia, WA	143.8	4	Sheboygan, WI	377.8	58	Yuba City, CA	38.3
181	Omaha-Council Bluffs, NE-IA	(15.5)	232	Sherman-Denison, TX	(41.5)	244	Yuma, AZ	(52.1)
170	Orlando, FL	(10.7)	NA	Shreveport-Bossier City, LA**	NA			
264	Oshkosh-Neenah, WI	(100.0)	NA	Sierra Vista-Douglas, AZ**	NA			

Source: CQ Press using reported data from the F.B.I. "Crime in the United States 2012"

*Includes nonnegligent manslaughter. **Not available. ***These metro areas had murder rates of 0 in 2011 but had at least one murder in 2012. Calculating percent increase from zero results in an infinite number. This is shown as "NA."

11. Percent Change in Murder Rate: 2011 to 2012 (continued)
National Percent Change = 0.4% Increase*

RANK	METROPOLITAN AREA	% CHANGE	RANK	METROPOLITAN AREA	% CHANGE	RANK	METROPOLITAN AREA	% CHANGE
1	Rockingham County, NH M.D.	950.0	64	North Port-Sarasota-Bradenton, FL	33.3	129	Stockton-Lodi, CA	1.6
2	Wichita Falls, TX	666.7	66	Danville, IL	32.4	130	Baltimore, MD	1.1
3	Cape Girardeau, MO-IL	410.0	67	Terre Haute, IN	31.4	131	Ames, IA	0.0
4	Sheboygan, WI	377.8	68	Salinas, CA	30.9	131	Athens-Clarke County, GA	0.0
5	Lima, OH	294.7	69	San Diego, CA	30.8	131	Billings, MT	0.0
6	Green Bay, WI	228.6	70	Burlington, NC	30.0	131	Bridgeport-Stamford, CT	0.0
7	Lebanon, PA	214.3	71	Corpus Christi, TX	29.3	131	Columbus, IN	0.0
8	Altoona, PA	193.8	72	Oklahoma City, OK	29.0	131	El Centro, CA	0.0
9	Auburn, AL	166.7	73	Lake Co.-Kenosha Co., IL-WI M.D.	28.6	131	Greeley, CO	0.0
10	Eugene, OR	150.0	74	Duluth, MN-WI	27.3	131	Kingsport, TN-VA	0.0
11	Olympia, WA	143.8	75	Bellingham, WA	26.7	131	Lake Havasu City-Kingman, AZ	0.0
12	Springfield, MO	138.1	76	Jacksonville, FL	25.0	131	Las Cruces, NM	0.0
13	Lancaster, PA	123.1	77	College Station-Bryan, TX	23.8	131	Lawrence, KS	0.0
14	Dothan, AL	120.6	77	Davenport, IA-IL	23.8	131	Lincoln, NE	0.0
15	Saginaw, MI	115.7	79	Farmington, NM	23.7	131	Logan, UT-ID	0.0
16	Ocean City, NJ	110.0	80	Camden, NJ M.D.	23.1	131	Lynchburg, VA	0.0
17	Dalton, GA	100.0	81	Tallahassee, FL	22.9	131	Mansfield, OH	0.0
17	Joplin, MO	100.0	82	Bismarck, ND	22.2	131	Norwich-New London, CT	0.0
17	Kankakee, IL	100.0	82	Minneapolis-St. Paul, MN-WI	22.2	131	Reading, PA	0.0
17	Palm Bay-Melbourne, FL	100.0	82	San Luis Obispo, CA	22.2	131	San Antonio, TX	0.0
21	Goldsboro, NC	97.5	85	Tacoma, WA M.D.	21.9	149	Baton Rouge, LA	(0.8)
22	Dubuque, IA	90.9	86	Monroe, LA	21.6	150	Mobile, AL	(1.8)
23	Williamsport, PA	88.9	87	Richmond, VA	21.4	151	Santa Cruz-Watsonville, CA	(2.6)
24	Cedar Rapids, IA	87.5	88	Pensacola, FL	20.0	152	Hinesville, GA	(3.9)
25	Alexandria, LA	81.3	89	Topeka, KS	18.8	152	St. Louis, MO-IL	(3.9)
26	Fargo, ND-MN	80.0	90	Redding, CA	18.2	154	Dallas-Plano-Irving, TX M.D.	(4.3)
27	Florence-Muscle Shoals, AL	70.0	91	Albuquerque, NM	18.0	155	Cheyenne, WY	(4.5)
27	Grand Junction, CO	70.0	92	Detroit-Dearborn-Livonia, MI M.D.	17.2	156	Pine Bluff, AR	(4.7)
29	Monroe, MI	65.0	93	Milwaukee, WI	16.9	156	Riverside-San Bernardino, CA	(4.7)
30	Asheville, NC	64.3	94	Bangor, ME	15.6	158	Miami-Dade County, FL M.D.	(5.8)
31	Springfield, OH	63.6	95	Florence, SC	14.9	159	Charlottesville, VA	(6.9)
32	Brownsville-Harlingen, TX	63.2	96	Brunswick, GA	14.8	159	Vallejo-Fairfield, CA	(6.9)
33	Merced, CA	63.0	96	Cape Coral-Fort Myers, FL	14.8	161	Little Rock, AR	(7.1)
34	Clarksville, TN-KY	60.0	98	Portland-Vancouver, OR-WA	14.3	162	Augusta, GA-SC	(7.9)
35	Bremerton-Silverdale, WA	58.3	99	Huntsville, AL	13.3	162	Visalia-Porterville, CA	(7.9)
36	Lakeland, FL	53.7	100	Detroit (greater), MI	12.4	164	Fort Wayne, IN	(8.1)
37	Springfield, IL	53.5	101	Modesto, CA	12.3	165	Harrisburg-Carlisle, PA	(8.3)
38	Seattle-Bellevue-Everett, WA M.D.	52.9	102	Killeen-Temple, TX	11.6	166	Hickory, NC	(8.5)
39	Santa Fe, NM	51.9	103	Chicago (greater), IL-IN-WI	10.9	167	Dallas (greater), TX	(8.9)
40	Casper, WY	50.0	104	Yakima, WA	10.8	168	San Jose, CA	(9.1)
40	El Paso, TX	50.0	105	Pittsburgh, PA	10.5	169	Amarillo, TX	(10.6)
40	Fairbanks, AK	50.0	106	Salem, OR	10.0	170	Orlando, FL	(10.7)
40	Johnstown, PA	50.0	106	West Palm Beach, FL M.D.	10.0	171	Fayetteville, NC	(11.2)
40	South Bend-Mishawaka, IN-MI	50.0	108	Roanoke, VA	9.4	172	Beaumont-Port Arthur, TX	(12.1)
40	Waterloo-Cedar Falls, IA	50.0	109	Flint, MI	8.7	173	Des Moines-West Des Moines, IA	(12.5)
46	Jonesboro, AR	48.5	110	Memphis, TN-MS-AR	8.5	174	Lansing-East Lansing, MI	(12.8)
47	Houma, LA	48.3	111	San Francisco (greater), CA	8.3	175	New Orleans, LA	(13.1)
48	Ocala, FL	47.6	112	Birmingham-Hoover, AL	5.6	176	Canton, OH	(13.5)
49	Fresno, CA	45.5	112	Houston, TX	5.6	177	Sacramento, CA	(13.6)
50	Macon, GA	44.7	114	Los Angeles County, CA M.D.	5.3	178	Racine, WI	(13.9)
51	Wilmington, DE-MD-NJ M.D.	42.9	114	Lubbock, TX	5.3	179	Scranton--Wilkes-Barre, PA	(14.8)
52	Louisville, KY-IN	40.9	114	Oakland-Hayward, CA M.D.	5.3	180	Boise City, ID	(15.4)
53	Bakersfield, CA	40.7	117	Salt Lake City, UT	4.8	181	Omaha-Council Bluffs, NE-IA	(15.5)
53	Gainesville, GA	40.7	118	Gary, IN M.D.	4.5	182	Warren-Troy, MI M.D.	(15.8)
55	Portland, ME	40.0	119	Bowling Green, KY	4.2	183	McAllen-Edinburg-Mission, TX	(15.9)
56	Erie, PA	39.3	120	Miami (greater), FL	3.3	184	Tulsa, OK	(16.2)
57	Oxnard-Thousand Oaks, CA	38.9	121	Virginia Beach-Norfolk, VA-NC	3.0	185	Fort Worth-Arlington, TX M.D.	(16.3)
58	Yuba City, CA	38.3	122	Hartford, CT	2.9	186	Johnson City, TN	(16.7)
59	Seattle (greater), WA	38.1	122	Trenton, NJ	2.9	187	Tampa-St Petersburg, FL	(17.0)
60	Atlantic City, NJ	36.3	124	Longview, WA	2.6	188	Savannah, GA	(17.6)
61	Chico, CA	36.1	125	Las Vegas-Henderson, NV	2.1	189	Washington (greater) DC-VA-MD-WV	(18.2)
62	San Francisco-Redwood, CA M.D.	34.2	126	Los Angeles (greater), CA	2.0	190	Washington, DC-VA-MD-WV M.D.	(18.9)
63	Montgomery, AL	33.7	126	Rome, GA	2.0	191	Peoria, IL	(19.0)
64	Fort Lauderdale, FL M.D.	33.3	128	Atlanta, GA	1.7	192	Akron, OH	(19.1)

Note: All listings are for Metropolitan Statistical Areas (M.S.A.s) except for those ending with "M.D." Listings with "M.D." are Metropolitan Divisions which are smaller parts of eleven large M.S.A.s. See explanatory note at beginning of metropolitan area section.

RANK	METROPOLITAN AREA	% CHANGE
193	York-Hanover, PA	(19.6)
194	Silver Spring-Frederick, MD M.D.	(20.0)
195	Flagstaff, AZ	(21.6)
196	Columbia, MO	(21.7)
197	Provo-Orem, UT	(22.2)
197	Rocky Mount, NC	(22.2)
199	Wichita, KS	(22.4)
200	Columbus, GA-AL	(22.5)
201	Fort Collins, CO	(23.1)
202	Janesville, WI	(24.0)
202	Tucson, AZ	(24.0)
204	Austin-Round Rock, TX	(24.1)
205	Tyler, TX	(24.3)
206	Gainesville, FL	(24.5)
207	Michigan City-La Porte, IN	(25.0)
208	Durham-Chapel Hill, NC	(27.8)
209	Laredo, TX	(27.9)
210	Longview, TX	(28.0)
211	Sumter, SC	(28.8)
212	Prescott, AZ	(29.1)
213	Anaheim-Santa Ana-Irvine, CA M.D.	(29.2)
214	Cleveland, TN	(30.0)
215	Raleigh, NC	(30.8)
216	Decatur, AL	(31.6)
217	Mount Vernon-Anacortes, WA	(32.0)
218	Cumberland, MD-WV	(32.8)
219	New Haven-Milford, CT	(33.9)
220	Champaign-Urbana, IL	(34.6)
221	Winchester, VA-WV	(34.8)
222	Iowa City, IA	(35.0)
223	Dayton, OH	(36.1)
224	Colorado Springs, CO	(36.2)
225	Napa, CA	(36.4)
226	Valdosta, GA	(38.6)
227	Pueblo, CO	(38.8)
228	Blacksburg, VA	(38.9)
229	Ann Arbor, MI	(39.1)
230	Abilene, TX	(40.0)
230	Decatur, IL	(40.0)
232	Sherman-Denison, TX	(41.5)
233	Naples-Marco Island, FL	(41.9)
234	Albany, GA	(44.0)
235	Dover, DE	(44.2)
236	Crestview-Fort Walton Beach, FL	(45.5)
237	St. Joseph, MO-KS	(48.4)
238	Great Falls, MT	(50.0)
238	Hanford-Corcoran, CA	(50.0)
238	Harrisonburg, VA	(50.0)
238	Punta Gorda, FL	(50.0)
238	Reno, NV	(50.0)
243	Port St. Lucie, FL	(51.0)
244	Yuma, AZ	(52.1)
245	Muncie, IN	(52.9)
246	Appleton, WI	(55.6)
247	Odessa, TX	(55.7)
248	Rockford, IL	(55.8)
249	Anniston-Oxford, AL	(56.8)
250	Jefferson City, MO	(57.4)
251	Bloomington, IL	(58.3)
252	Sioux Falls, SD	(59.1)
253	Gadsden, AL	(60.4)
254	Madera, CA	(60.6)
255	Medford, OR	(61.2)
256	Kennewick-Richland, WA	(63.2)
257	Santa Rosa, CA	(63.6)
258	Barnstable Town, MA	(64.3)
259	Corvallis, OR	(65.7)
260	Lafayette, IN	(66.7)
261	Bay City, MI	(67.9)
262	Sebastian-Vero Beach, FL	(80.6)
263	Manchester-Nashua, NH	(90.0)
264	Boulder, CO	(100.0)
264	Carson City, NV	(100.0)
264	Fond du Lac, WI	(100.0)
264	Idaho Falls, ID	(100.0)
264	Lewiston-Auburn, ME	(100.0)
264	Mankato-North Mankato, MN	(100.0)
264	Missoula, MT	(100.0)
264	Oshkosh-Neenah, WI	(100.0)
264	Owensboro, KY	(100.0)
264	Pittsfield, MA	(100.0)
NA	Albany-Schenectady-Troy, NY**	NA
NA	Albany, OR**	NA
NA	Allentown, PA-NJ**	NA
NA	Anchorage, AK**	NA
NA	Beckley, WV**	NA
NA	Binghamton, NY**	NA
NA	Bloomington, IN**	NA
NA	Bloomsburg-Berwick, PA**	NA
NA	Boston (greater), MA-NH**	NA
NA	Boston, MA M.D.**	NA
NA	Buffalo-Niagara Falls, NY**	NA
NA	California-Lexington Park, MD**	NA
NA	Cambridge-Newton, MA M.D.**	NA
NA	Chambersburg-Waynesboro, PA**	NA
NA	Charleston-North Charleston, SC**	NA
NA	Chicago-Joilet-Naperville, IL M.D.**	NA
NA	Cincinnati, OH-KY-IN**	NA
NA	Coeur d'Alene, ID**	NA
NA	Daphne-Fairhope-Foley, AL**	NA
NA	Deltona-Daytona Beach, FL**	NA
NA	Denver-Aurora, CO**	NA
NA	Dutchess-Putnam, NY M.D.**	NA
NA	East Stroudsburg, PA**	NA
NA	Elgin, IL M.D.**	NA
NA	Elizabethtown-Fort Knox, KY**	NA
NA	Elmira, NY**	NA
NA	Fayetteville-Springdale, AR-MO**	NA
NA	Fort Smith, AR-OK**	NA
NA	Gettysburg, PA**	NA
NA	Glens Falls, NY**	NA
NA	Grand Forks, ND-MN***	NA
NA	Grand Island, NE**	NA
NA	Greensboro-High Point, NC**	NA
NA	Greenville-Anderson, SC**	NA
NA	Greenville, NC**	NA
NA	Hagerstown-Martinsburg, MD-WV**	NA
NA	Hammond, LA**	NA
NA	Hattiesburg, MS**	NA
NA	Hilton Head Island, SC**	NA
NA	Homosassa Springs, FL**	NA
NA	Indianapolis, IN**	NA
NA	Jackson, MS**	NA
NA	Jackson, TN**	NA
NA	Kahului-Wailuku-Lahaina, HI**	NA
NA	Kalamazoo-Portage, MI**	NA
NA	Kansas City, MO-KS**	NA
NA	Kingston, NY**	NA
NA	Knoxville, TN**	NA
NA	Kokomo, IN**	NA
NA	La Crosse, WI-MN***	NA
NA	Lafayette, LA**	NA
NA	Lawton, OK**	NA
NA	Lewiston, ID-WA**	NA
NA	Lexington-Fayette, KY**	NA
NA	Madison, WI**	NA
NA	Manhattan, KS**	NA
NA	Midland, MI**	NA
NA	Midland, TX**	NA
NA	Montgomery County, PA M.D.**	NA
NA	Morgantown, WV**	NA
NA	Morristown, TN**	NA
NA	Nashville-Davidson, TN**	NA
NA	Nassau-Suffolk, NY M.D.**	NA
NA	New Bern, NC**	NA
NA	New York (greater), NY-NJ-PA**	NA
NA	New York-Jersey City, NY-NJ M.D.**	NA
NA	Newark, NJ-PA M.D.**	NA
NA	Ogden-Clearfield, UT**	NA
NA	Panama City, FL**	NA
NA	Parkersburg-Vienna, WV**	NA
NA	Philadelphia (greater) PA-NJ-MD-DE**	NA
NA	Philadelphia, PA M.D.**	NA
NA	Phoenix-Mesa-Scottsdale, AZ**	NA
NA	Pocatello, ID**	NA
NA	Providence-Warwick, RI-MA**	NA
NA	Rapid City, SD**	NA
NA	Rochester, MN**	NA
NA	Rochester, NY**	NA
NA	Salisbury, MD-DE**	NA
NA	San Rafael, CA M.D.**	NA
NA	Santa Maria-Santa Barbara, CA**	NA
NA	Sebring, FL**	NA
NA	Shreveport-Bossier City, LA**	NA
NA	Sierra Vista-Douglas, AZ**	NA
NA	Sioux City, IA-NE-SD**	NA
NA	Spartanburg, SC**	NA
NA	Spokane, WA**	NA
NA	Springfield, MA**	NA
NA	State College, PA***	NA
NA	Staunton-Waynesboro, VA**	NA
NA	St. George, UT**	NA
NA	Syracuse, NY**	NA
NA	Texarkana, TX-AR**	NA
NA	The Villages, FL**	NA
NA	Toledo, OH**	NA
NA	Tuscaloosa, AL**	NA
NA	Utica-Rome, NY**	NA
NA	Victoria, TX**	NA
NA	Vineland-Bridgeton, NJ**	NA
NA	Waco, TX**	NA
NA	Walla Walla, WA**	NA
NA	Warner Robins, GA**	NA
NA	Watertown-Fort Drum, NY**	NA
NA	Wausau, WI***	NA
NA	Wheeling, WV-OH**	NA
NA	Wilmington, NC**	NA
NA	Winston-Salem, NC**	NA
NA	Worcester, MA-CT**	NA
NA	Youngstown-Warren, OH-PA**	NA

Source: CQ Press using reported data from the F.B.I. "Crime in the United States 2012"

*Includes nonnegligent manslaughter. **Not available. ***These metro areas had murder rates of 0 in 2011 but had at least one murder in 2012. Calculating percent increase from zero results in an infinite number. This is shown as "NA."

12. Percent Change in Murder Rate: 2008 to 2012
National Percent Change = 12.8% Decrease*

RANK	METROPOLITAN AREA	% CHANGE	RANK	METROPOLITAN AREA	% CHANGE	RANK	METROPOLITAN AREA	% CHANGE
227	Abilene, TX	(59.1)	194	Cheyenne, WY	(38.2)	NA	Gary, IN M.D.**	NA
68	Akron, OH	11.8	NA	Chicago (greater), IL-IN-WI**	NA	NA	Gettysburg, PA**	NA
NA	Albany-Schenectady-Troy, NY**	NA	NA	Chicago-Joliet-Naperville, IL M.D.**	NA	NA	Glens Falls, NY**	NA
NA	Albany, GA**	NA	32	Chico, CA	53.1	29	Goldsboro, NC	64.9
NA	Albany, OR**	NA	NA	Cincinnati, OH-KY-IN**	NA	85	Grand Forks, ND-MN	0.0
155	Albuquerque, NM	(22.4)	12	Clarksville, TN-KY	146.2	NA	Grand Island, NE**	NA
NA	Alexandria, LA**	NA	31	Cleveland, TN	55.6	177	Grand Junction, CO	(30.6)
NA	Allentown, PA-NJ**	NA	NA	Coeur d'Alene, ID**	NA	211	Great Falls, MT	(50.0)
35	Altoona, PA	46.9	207	College Station-Bryan, TX	(46.9)	97	Greeley, CO	(4.2)
181	Amarillo, TX	(31.1)	196	Colorado Springs, CO	(40.0)	5	Green Bay, WI	228.6
242	Ames, IA	(100.0)	226	Columbia, MO	(58.1)	103	Greensboro-High Point, NC	(6.3)
172	Anaheim-Santa Ana-Irvine, CA M.D.	(29.2)	211	Columbus, GA-AL	(50.0)	NA	Greenville-Anderson, SC**	NA
NA	Anchorage, AK**	NA	215	Columbus, IN	(51.9)	39	Greenville, NC	39.1
NA	Anniston-Oxford, AL**	NA	82	Corpus Christi, TX	3.9	NA	Hagerstown-Martinsburg, MD-WV**	NA
223	Ann Arbor, MI	(54.8)	85	Corvallis, OR	0.0	NA	Hammond, LA**	NA
224	Appleton, WI	(55.6)	NA	Crestview-Fort Walton Beach, FL**	NA	204	Hanford-Corcoran, CA	(43.5)
14	Asheville, NC	109.1	156	Cumberland, MD-WV	(23.5)	113	Harrisburg-Carlisle, PA	(8.3)
56	Athens-Clarke County, GA	19.2	160	Dallas (greater), TX	(25.5)	218	Harrisonburg, VA	(52.9)
136	Atlanta, GA	(17.6)	168	Dallas-Plano-Irving, TX M.D.	(27.9)	128	Hartford, CT	(14.3)
37	Atlantic City, NJ	41.6	1	Dalton, GA	300.0	NA	Hattiesburg, MS**	NA
50	Auburn, AL	24.4	NA	Danville, IL**	NA	183	Hickory, NC	(32.5)
77	Augusta, GA-SC	6.5	NA	Daphne-Fairhope-Foley, AL**	NA	NA	Hilton Head Island, SC**	NA
71	Austin-Round Rock, TX	10.0	NA	Davenport, IA-IL**	NA	173	Hinesville, GA	(30.0)
76	Bakersfield, CA	7.0	158	Dayton, OH	(25.0)	NA	Homosassa Springs, FL**	NA
131	Baltimore, MD	(15.9)	231	Decatur, AL	(67.5)	149	Houma, LA	(20.4)
1	Bangor, ME	300.0	NA	Decatur, IL**	NA	165	Houston, TX	(26.9)
205	Barnstable Town, MA	(44.4)	71	Deltona-Daytona Beach, FL	10.0	79	Huntsville, AL	6.2
124	Baton Rouge, LA	(11.9)	NA	Denver-Aurora, CO**	NA	242	Idaho Falls, ID	(100.0)
232	Bay City, MI	(67.9)	214	Des Moines-West Des Moines, IA	(51.7)	143	Indianapolis, IN	(18.9)
54	Beaumont-Port Arthur, TX	20.8	NA	Detroit (greater), MI**	NA	237	Iowa City, IA	(75.9)
NA	Beckley, WV**	NA	NA	Detroit-Dearborn-Livonia, MI M.D.**	NA	135	Jacksonville, FL	(17.5)
20	Bellingham, WA	90.0	9	Dothan, AL	167.9	NA	Jackson, MS**	NA
100	Billings, MT	(5.0)	218	Dover, DE	(52.9)	NA	Jackson, TN**	NA
NA	Binghamton, NY**	NA	NA	Dubuque, IA***	NA	157	Janesville, WI	(24.0)
115	Birmingham-Hoover, AL	(8.7)	106	Duluth, MN-WI	(6.7)	NA	Jefferson City, MO**	NA
26	Bismarck, ND	73.7	185	Durham-Chapel Hill, NC	(33.3)	28	Johnson City, TN	66.7
236	Blacksburg, VA	(71.1)	NA	Dutchess-Putnam, NY M.D.**	NA	85	Johnstown, PA	0.0
NA	Bloomington, IL**	NA	NA	East Stroudsburg, PA**	NA	139	Jonesboro, AR	(18.3)
64	Bloomington, IN	13.6	230	El Centro, CA	(65.3)	132	Joplin, MO	(17.1)
NA	Bloomsburg-Berwick, PA**	NA	47	El Paso, TX	26.9	NA	Kahului-Wailuku-Lahaina, HI**	NA
40	Boise City, ID	37.5	NA	Elgin, IL M.D.**	NA	18	Kalamazoo-Portage, MI	94.7
NA	Boston (greater), MA-NH**	NA	NA	Elizabethtown-Fort Knox, KY**	NA	NA	Kankakee, IL**	NA
NA	Boston, MA M.D.**	NA	NA	Elmira, NY**	NA	NA	Kansas City, MO-KS**	NA
NA	Boulder, CO**	NA	51	Erie, PA	21.9	153	Kennewick-Richland, WA	(22.2)
NA	Bowling Green, KY***	NA	126	Eugene, OR	(13.0)	69	Killeen-Temple, TX	11.6
118	Bremerton-Silverdale, WA	(9.5)	NA	Fairbanks, AK**	NA	206	Kingsport, TN-VA	(45.3)
109	Bridgeport-Stamford, CT	(7.7)	NA	Fargo, ND-MN***	NA	NA	Kingston, NY**	NA
102	Brownsville-Harlingen, TX	(6.1)	167	Farmington, NM	(27.7)	NA	Knoxville, TN**	NA
NA	Brunswick, GA**	NA	45	Fayetteville-Springdale, AR-MO	27.8	NA	Kokomo, IN**	NA
NA	Buffalo-Niagara Falls, NY**	NA	179	Fayetteville, NC	(30.7)	4	La Crosse, WI-MN	275.0
95	Burlington, NC	(3.7)	48	Flagstaff, AZ	26.1	238	Lafayette, IN	(76.2)
NA	California-Lexington Park, MD**	NA	22	Flint, MI	89.5	NA	Lafayette, LA**	NA
NA	Cambridge-Newton, MA M.D.**	NA	144	Florence-Muscle Shoals, AL	(19.0)	NA	Lake Co.-Kenosha Co., IL-WI M.D.**	NA
84	Camden, NJ M.D.	1.6	173	Florence, SC	(30.0)	34	Lake Havasu City-Kingman, AZ	47.5
NA	Canton, OH**	NA	242	Fond du Lac, WI	(100.0)	132	Lakeland, FL	(17.1)
111	Cape Coral-Fort Myers, FL	(7.9)	198	Fort Collins, CO	(41.2)	15	Lancaster, PA	107.1
58	Cape Girardeau, MO-IL	18.6	113	Fort Lauderdale, FL M.D.	(8.3)	60	Lansing-East Lansing, MI	17.2
85	Carson City, NV	0.0	NA	Fort Smith, AR-OK**	NA	184	Laredo, TX	(32.6)
8	Casper, WY	178.6	105	Fort Wayne, IN	(6.6)	163	Las Cruces, NM	(26.7)
158	Cedar Rapids, IA	(25.0)	138	Fort Worth-Arlington, TX M.D.	(18.2)	189	Las Vegas-Henderson, NV	(34.2)
NA	Chambersburg-Waynesboro, PA**	NA	70	Fresno, CA	11.1	242	Lawrence, KS	(100.0)
NA	Champaign-Urbana, IL**	NA	228	Gadsden, AL	(60.4)	NA	Lawton, OK**	NA
106	Charleston-North Charleston, SC	(6.7)	30	Gainesville, FL	60.9	242	Lebanon, PA	37.5
199	Charlottesville, VA	(41.3)	NA	Gainesville, GA**	NA	242	Lewiston-Auburn, ME	(100.0)

Note: All listings are for Metropolitan Statistical Areas (M.S.A.s) except for those ending with "M.D." Listings with "M.D." are Metropolitan Divisions which are smaller parts of eleven large M.S.A.s. See explanatory note at beginning of metropolitan area section.

RANK	METROPOLITAN AREA	% CHANGE	RANK	METROPOLITAN AREA	% CHANGE	RANK	METROPOLITAN AREA	% CHANGE
242	Lewiston, ID-WA	(100.0)	NA	Owensboro, KY**	NA	202	Silver Spring-Frederick, MD M.D.	(42.9)
NA	Lexington-Fayette, KY**	NA	192	Oxnard-Thousand Oaks, CA	(35.9)	NA	Sioux City, IA-NE-SD**	NA
3	Lima, OH	294.7	43	Palm Bay-Melbourne, FL	31.7	234	Sioux Falls, SD	(70.0)
191	Lincoln, NE	(35.0)	NA	Panama City, FL**	NA	44	South Bend-Mishawaka, IN-MI	31.6
97	Little Rock, AR	(4.2)	NA	Parkersburg-Vienna, WV**	NA	NA	Spartanburg, SC**	NA
242	Logan, UT-ID	(100.0)	117	Pensacola, FL	(9.4)	99	Spokane, WA	(4.9)
213	Longview, TX	(50.7)	NA	Peoria, IL**	NA	NA	Springfield, IL**	NA
17	Longview, WA	95.0	NA	Philadelphia (greater) PA-NJ-MD-DE**	NA	NA	Springfield, MA**	NA
164	Los Angeles County, CA M.D.	(26.8)	NA	Philadelphia, PA M.D.**	NA	19	Springfield, MO	92.3
162	Los Angeles (greater), CA	(26.5)	NA	Phoenix-Mesa-Scottsdale, AZ**	NA	210	Springfield, OH	(49.3)
94	Louisville, KY-IN	(3.1)	182	Pine Bluff, AR	(32.2)	NA	State College, PA***	NA
53	Lubbock, TX	21.2	146	Pittsburgh, PA	(19.2)	NA	Staunton-Waynesboro, VA**	NA
175	Lynchburg, VA	(30.3)	242	Pittsfield, MA	(100.0)	11	Stockton-Lodi, CA	149.0
71	Macon, GA	10.0	NA	Pocatello, ID**	NA	33	St. George, UT	50.0
241	Madera, CA	(80.6)	152	Port St. Lucie, FL	(21.9)	185	St. Joseph, MO-KS	(33.3)
NA	Madison, WI**	NA	55	Portland-Vancouver, OR-WA	20.0	125	St. Louis, MO-IL	(12.0)
NA	Manchester-Nashua, NH**	NA	185	Portland, ME	(33.3)	122	Sumter, SC	(11.2)
NA	Manhattan, KS**	NA	6	Prescott, AZ	211.1	NA	Syracuse, NY**	NA
85	Mankato-North Mankato, MN	0.0	109	Providence-Warwick, RI-MA	(7.7)	NA	Tacoma, WA M.D.**	NA
85	Mansfield, OH	0.0	61	Provo-Orem, UT	16.7	42	Tallahassee, FL	37.2
208	McAllen-Edinburg-Mission, TX	(47.1)	NA	Pueblo, CO**	NA	176	Tampa-St Petersburg, FL	(30.4)
20	Medford, OR	90.0	234	Punta Gorda, FL	(70.0)	NA	Terre Haute, IN**	NA
115	Memphis, TN-MS-AR	(8.7)	195	Racine, WI	(39.2)	NA	Texarkana, TX-AR**	NA
81	Merced, CA	4.8	229	Raleigh, NC	(61.7)	NA	The Villages, FL**	NA
132	Miami (greater), FL	(17.1)	NA	Rapid City, SD**	NA	NA	Toledo, OH**	NA
129	Miami-Dade County, FL M.D.	(15.6)	59	Reading, PA	17.9	27	Topeka, KS	72.7
199	Michigan City-La Porte, IN	(41.3)	24	Redding, CA	77.3	80	Trenton, NJ	6.1
NA	Midland, MI**	NA	153	Reno, NV	(22.2)	196	Tucson, AZ	(40.0)
NA	Midland, TX**	NA	74	Richmond, VA	9.7	171	Tulsa, OK	(28.8)
38	Milwaukee, WI	40.8	137	Riverside-San Bernardino, CA	(18.0)	NA	Tuscaloosa, AL**	NA
141	Minneapolis-St. Paul, MN-WI	(18.5)	201	Roanoke, VA	(42.6)	225	Tyler, TX	(56.3)
242	Missoula, MT	(100.0)	NA	Rochester, MN**	NA	NA	Utica-Rome, NY**	NA
177	Mobile, AL	(30.6)	NA	Rochester, NY**	NA	67	Valdosta, GA	12.9
52	Modesto, CA	21.7	NA	Rockford, IL**	NA	64	Vallejo-Fairfield, CA	13.6
92	Monroe, LA	(1.6)	7	Rockingham County, NH M.D.	200.0	NA	Victoria, TX**	NA
10	Monroe, MI	153.8	NA	Rocky Mount, NC**	NA	221	Vineland-Bridgeton, NJ	(54.2)
NA	Montgomery County, PA M.D.**	NA	NA	Rome, GA**	NA	78	Virginia Beach-Norfolk, VA-NC	6.3
23	Montgomery, AL	82.9	170	Sacramento, CA	(28.3)	142	Visalia-Porterville, CA	(18.8)
NA	Morgantown, WV**	NA	49	Saginaw, MI	25.8	NA	Waco, TX**	NA
NA	Morristown, TN**	NA	147	Salem, OR	(19.5)	NA	Walla Walla, WA**	NA
240	Mount Vernon-Anacortes, WA	(77.6)	57	Salinas, CA	19.1	NA	Warner Robins, GA**	NA
119	Muncie, IN	(11.1)	NA	Salisbury, MD-DE**	NA	NA	Warren-Troy, MI M.D.**	NA
25	Napa, CA	75.0	62	Salt Lake City, UT	15.8	216	Washington (greater) DC-VA-MD-WV	(52.0)
169	Naples-Marco Island, FL	(28.0)	188	San Antonio, TX	(33.8)	217	Washington, DC-VA-MD-WV M.D.	(52.2)
NA	Nashville-Davidson, TN**	NA	66	San Diego, CA	13.3	16	Waterloo-Cedar Falls, IA	100.0
NA	Nassau-Suffolk, NY M.D.**	NA	148	San Francisco (greater), CA	(19.8)	NA	Watertown-Fort Drum, NY**	NA
112	New Orleans, LA	(8.0)	161	San Francisco-Redwood, CA M.D.	(26.1)	190	Wausau, WI	(34.8)
NA	New York (greater), NY-NJ-PA**	NA	83	San Jose, CA	3.4	166	West Palm Beach, FL M.D.	(27.6)
NA	New York-Jersey City, NY-NJ M.D.**	NA	36	San Luis Obispo, CA	46.7	242	Wheeling, WV-OH	(100.0)
NA	Newark, NJ-PA M.D.**	NA	NA	San Rafael, CA M.D.**	NA	93	Wichita Falls, TX	(2.1)
NA	North Port-Sarasota-Bradenton, FL**	NA	63	Santa Cruz-Watsonville, CA	15.6	180	Wichita, KS	(30.9)
144	Norwich-New London, CT	(19.0)	222	Santa Fe, NM	(54.4)	85	Williamsport, PA	0.0
119	Oakland-Hayward, CA M.D.	(11.1)	NA	Santa Maria-Santa Barbara, CA**	NA	123	Wilmington, DE-MD-NJ M.D.	(11.4)
108	Ocala, FL	(7.5)	233	Santa Rosa, CA	(69.2)	NA	Wilmington, NC**	NA
NA	Ocean City, NJ***	NA	127	Savannah, GA	(13.6)	103	Winchester, VA-WV	(6.3)
220	Odessa, TX	(53.9)	209	Scranton--Wilkes-Barre, PA	(47.7)	NA	Winston-Salem, NC**	NA
NA	Ogden-Clearfield, UT**	NA	NA	Seattle (greater), WA**	NA	130	Worcester, MA-CT	(15.8)
46	Oklahoma City, OK	27.0	NA	Seattle-Bellevue-Everett, WA M.D.**	NA	119	Yakima, WA	(11.1)
13	Olympia, WA	143.8	239	Sebastian-Vero Beach, FL	(76.7)	151	York-Hanover, PA	(21.3)
139	Omaha-Council Bluffs, NE-IA	(18.3)	NA	Sebring, FL**	NA	150	Youngstown-Warren, OH-PA	(20.8)
193	Orlando, FL	(36.7)	NA	Sheboygan, WI***	NA	75	Yuba City, CA	8.3
242	Oshkosh-Neenah, WI	(100.0)	96	Sherman-Denison, TX	(4.0)	101	Yuma, AZ	(5.6)
			203	Shreveport-Bossier City, LA	(43.2)			
			NA	Sierra Vista-Douglas, AZ**	NA			

Source: CQ Press using reported data from the F.B.I. "Crime in the United States 2012"

*Includes nonnegligent manslaughter. **Not available. ***These metro areas had murder rates of 0 in 2008 but had at least one murder in 2012. Calculating percent increase from zero results in an infinite number. This is shown as "NA."

12. Percent Change in Murder Rate: 2008 to 2012 (continued)
National Percent Change = 12.8% Decrease*

RANK	METROPOLITAN AREA	% CHANGE	RANK	METROPOLITAN AREA	% CHANGE	RANK	METROPOLITAN AREA	% CHANGE
1	Bangor, ME	300.0	64	Vallejo-Fairfield, CA	13.6	129	Miami-Dade County, FL M.D.	(15.6)
1	Dalton, GA	300.0	66	San Diego, CA	13.3	130	Worcester, MA-CT	(15.8)
3	Lima, OH	294.7	67	Valdosta, GA	12.9	131	Baltimore, MD	(15.9)
4	La Crosse, WI-MN	275.0	68	Akron, OH	11.8	132	Joplin, MO	(17.1)
5	Green Bay, WI	228.6	69	Killeen-Temple, TX	11.6	132	Lakeland, FL	(17.1)
6	Prescott, AZ	211.1	70	Fresno, CA	11.1	132	Miami (greater), FL	(17.1)
7	Rockingham County, NH M.D.	200.0	71	Austin-Round Rock, TX	10.0	135	Jacksonville, FL	(17.5)
8	Casper, WY	178.6	71	Deltona-Daytona Beach, FL	10.0	136	Atlanta, GA	(17.6)
9	Dothan, AL	167.9	71	Macon, GA	10.0	137	Riverside-San Bernardino, CA	(18.0)
10	Monroe, MI	153.8	74	Richmond, VA	9.7	138	Fort Worth-Arlington, TX M.D.	(18.2)
11	Stockton-Lodi, CA	149.0	75	Yuba City, CA	8.3	139	Jonesboro, AR	(18.3)
12	Clarksville, TN-KY	146.2	76	Bakersfield, CA	7.0	139	Omaha-Council Bluffs, NE-IA	(18.3)
13	Olympia, WA	143.8	77	Augusta, GA-SC	6.5	141	Minneapolis-St. Paul, MN-WI	(18.5)
14	Asheville, NC	109.1	78	Virginia Beach-Norfolk, VA-NC	6.3	142	Visalia-Porterville, CA	(18.8)
15	Lancaster, PA	107.1	79	Huntsville, AL	6.2	143	Indianapolis, IN	(18.9)
16	Waterloo-Cedar Falls, IA	100.0	80	Trenton, NJ	6.1	144	Florence-Muscle Shoals, AL	(19.0)
17	Longview, WA	95.0	81	Merced, CA	4.8	144	Norwich-New London, CT	(19.0)
18	Kalamazoo-Portage, MI	94.7	82	Corpus Christi, TX	3.9	146	Pittsburgh, PA	(19.2)
19	Springfield, MO	92.3	83	San Jose, CA	3.4	147	Salem, OR	(19.5)
20	Bellingham, WA	90.0	84	Camden, NJ M.D.	1.6	148	San Francisco (greater), CA	(19.8)
20	Medford, OR	90.0	85	Carson City, NV	0.0	149	Houma, LA	(20.4)
22	Flint, MI	89.5	85	Corvallis, OR	0.0	150	Youngstown-Warren, OH-PA	(20.8)
23	Montgomery, AL	82.9	85	Grand Forks, ND-MN	0.0	151	York-Hanover, PA	(21.3)
24	Redding, CA	77.3	85	Johnstown, PA	0.0	152	Port St. Lucie, FL	(21.9)
25	Napa, CA	75.0	85	Mankato-North Mankato, MN	0.0	153	Kennewick-Richland, WA	(22.2)
26	Bismarck, ND	73.7	85	Mansfield, OH	0.0	153	Reno, NV	(22.2)
27	Topeka, KS	72.7	85	Williamsport, PA	0.0	155	Albuquerque, NM	(22.4)
28	Johnson City, TN	66.7	92	Monroe, LA	(1.6)	156	Cumberland, MD-WV	(23.5)
29	Goldsboro, NC	64.9	93	Wichita Falls, TX	(2.1)	157	Janesville, WI	(24.0)
30	Gainesville, FL	60.9	94	Louisville, KY-IN	(3.1)	158	Cedar Rapids, IA	(25.0)
31	Cleveland, TN	55.6	95	Burlington, NC	(3.7)	158	Dayton, OH	(25.0)
32	Chico, CA	53.1	96	Sherman-Denison, TX	(4.0)	160	Dallas (greater), TX	(25.5)
33	St. George, UT	50.0	97	Greeley, CO	(4.2)	161	San Francisco-Redwood, CA M.D.	(26.1)
34	Lake Havasu City-Kingman, AZ	47.5	97	Little Rock, AR	(4.2)	162	Los Angeles (greater), CA	(26.5)
35	Altoona, PA	46.9	99	Spokane, WA	(4.9)	163	Las Cruces, NM	(26.7)
36	San Luis Obispo, CA	46.7	100	Billings, MT	(5.0)	164	Los Angeles County, CA M.D.	(26.8)
37	Atlantic City, NJ	41.6	101	Yuma, AZ	(5.6)	165	Houston, TX	(26.9)
38	Milwaukee, WI	40.8	102	Brownsville-Harlingen, TX	(6.1)	166	West Palm Beach, FL M.D.	(27.6)
39	Greenville, NC	39.1	103	Greensboro-High Point, NC	(6.3)	167	Farmington, NM	(27.7)
40	Boise City, ID	37.5	103	Winchester, VA-WV	(6.3)	168	Dallas-Plano-Irving, TX M.D.	(27.9)
40	Lebanon, PA	37.5	105	Fort Wayne, IN	(6.6)	169	Naples-Marco Island, FL	(28.0)
42	Tallahassee, FL	37.2	106	Charleston-North Charleston, SC	(6.7)	170	Sacramento, CA	(28.3)
43	Palm Bay-Melbourne, FL	31.7	106	Duluth, MN-WI	(6.7)	171	Tulsa, OK	(28.8)
44	South Bend-Mishawaka, IN-MI	31.6	108	Ocala, FL	(7.5)	172	Anaheim-Santa Ana-Irvine, CA M.D.	(29.2)
45	Fayetteville-Springdale, AR-MO	27.8	109	Bridgeport-Stamford, CT	(7.7)	173	Florence, SC	(30.0)
46	Oklahoma City, OK	27.0	109	Providence-Warwick, RI-MA	(7.7)	173	Hinesville, GA	(30.0)
47	El Paso, TX	26.9	111	Cape Coral-Fort Myers, FL	(7.9)	175	Lynchburg, VA	(30.3)
48	Flagstaff, AZ	26.1	112	New Orleans, LA	(8.0)	176	Tampa-St Petersburg, FL	(30.4)
49	Saginaw, MI	25.8	113	Fort Lauderdale, FL M.D.	(8.3)	177	Grand Junction, CO	(30.6)
50	Auburn, AL	24.4	113	Harrisburg-Carlisle, PA	(8.3)	177	Mobile, AL	(30.6)
51	Erie, PA	21.9	115	Birmingham-Hoover, AL	(8.7)	179	Fayetteville, NC	(30.7)
52	Modesto, CA	21.7	115	Memphis, TN-MS-AR	(8.7)	180	Wichita, KS	(30.9)
53	Lubbock, TX	21.2	117	Pensacola, FL	(9.4)	181	Amarillo, TX	(31.1)
54	Beaumont-Port Arthur, TX	20.8	118	Bremerton-Silverdale, WA	(9.5)	182	Pine Bluff, AR	(32.2)
55	Portland-Vancouver, OR-WA	20.0	119	Muncie, IN	(11.1)	183	Hickory, NC	(32.5)
56	Athens-Clarke County, GA	19.2	119	Oakland-Hayward, CA M.D.	(11.1)	184	Laredo, TX	(32.6)
57	Salinas, CA	19.1	119	Yakima, WA	(11.1)	185	Durham-Chapel Hill, NC	(33.3)
58	Cape Girardeau, MO-IL	18.6	122	Sumter, SC	(11.2)	185	Portland, ME	(33.3)
59	Reading, PA	17.9	123	Wilmington, DE-MD-NJ M.D.	(11.4)	185	St. Joseph, MO-KS	(33.3)
60	Lansing-East Lansing, MI	17.2	124	Baton Rouge, LA	(11.9)	188	San Antonio, TX	(33.8)
61	Provo-Orem, UT	16.7	125	St. Louis, MO-IL	(12.0)	189	Las Vegas-Henderson, NV	(34.2)
62	Salt Lake City, UT	15.8	126	Eugene, OR	(13.0)	190	Wausau, WI	(34.8)
63	Santa Cruz-Watsonville, CA	15.6	127	Savannah, GA	(13.6)	191	Lincoln, NE	(35.0)
64	Bloomington, IN	13.6	128	Hartford, CT	(14.3)	192	Oxnard-Thousand Oaks, CA	(35.9)

Note: All listings are for Metropolitan Statistical Areas (M.S.A.s) except for those ending with "M.D." Listings with "M.D." are Metropolitan Divisions which are smaller parts of eleven large M.S.A.s. See explanatory note at beginning of metropolitan area section.

RANK	METROPOLITAN AREA	% CHANGE	RANK	METROPOLITAN AREA	% CHANGE	RANK	METROPOLITAN AREA	% CHANGE
193	Orlando, FL	(36.7)	NA	Allentown, PA-NJ**	NA	NA	Manchester-Nashua, NH**	NA
194	Cheyenne, WY	(38.2)	NA	Anchorage, AK**	NA	NA	Manhattan, KS**	NA
195	Racine, WI	(39.2)	NA	Anniston-Oxford, AL**	NA	NA	Midland, MI**	NA
196	Colorado Springs, CO	(40.0)	NA	Beckley, WV**	NA	NA	Midland, TX**	NA
196	Tucson, AZ	(40.0)	NA	Binghamton, NY**	NA	NA	Montgomery County, PA M.D.**	NA
198	Fort Collins, CO	(41.2)	NA	Bloomington, IL**	NA	NA	Morgantown, WV**	NA
199	Charlottesville, VA	(41.3)	NA	Bloomsburg-Berwick, PA**	NA	NA	Morristown, TN**	NA
199	Michigan City-La Porte, IN	(41.3)	NA	Boston (greater), MA-NH**	NA	NA	Nashville-Davidson, TN**	NA
201	Roanoke, VA	(42.6)	NA	Boston, MA M.D.**	NA	NA	Nassau-Suffolk, NY M.D.**	NA
202	Silver Spring-Frederick, MD M.D.	(42.9)	NA	Boulder, CO**	NA	NA	New Bern, NC**	NA
203	Shreveport-Bossier City, LA	(43.2)	NA	Bowling Green, KY***	NA	NA	New Haven-Milford, CT**	NA
204	Hanford-Corcoran, CA	(43.5)	NA	Brunswick, GA**	NA	NA	New York (greater), NY-NJ-PA**	NA
205	Barnstable Town, MA	(44.4)	NA	Buffalo-Niagara Falls, NY**	NA	NA	New York-Jersey City, NY-NJ M.D.**	NA
206	Kingsport, TN-VA	(45.3)	NA	California-Lexington Park, MD**	NA	NA	Newark, NJ-PA M.D.**	NA
207	College Station-Bryan, TX	(46.9)	NA	Cambridge-Newton, MA M.D.**	NA	NA	North Port-Sarasota-Bradenton, FL**	NA
208	McAllen-Edinburg-Mission, TX	(47.1)	NA	Canton, OH**	NA	NA	Ocean City, NJ***	NA
209	Scranton--Wilkes-Barre, PA	(47.7)	NA	Chambersburg-Waynesboro, PA**	NA	NA	Ogden-Clearfield, UT**	NA
210	Springfield, OH	(49.3)	NA	Champaign-Urbana, IL**	NA	NA	Owensboro, KY**	NA
211	Columbus, GA-AL	(50.0)	NA	Chicago (greater), IL-IN-WI**	NA	NA	Panama City, FL**	NA
211	Great Falls, MT	(50.0)	NA	Chicago-Joilet-Naperville, IL M.D.**	NA	NA	Parkersburg-Vienna, WV**	NA
213	Longview, TX	(50.7)	NA	Cincinnati, OH-KY-IN**	NA	NA	Peoria, IL**	NA
214	Des Moines-West Des Moines, IA	(51.7)	NA	Coeur d'Alene, ID**	NA	NA	Philadelphia (greater) PA-NJ-MD-DE**	NA
215	Columbus, IN	(51.9)	NA	Crestview-Fort Walton Beach, FL**	NA	NA	Philadelphia, PA M.D.**	NA
216	Washington (greater) DC-VA-MD-WV	(52.0)	NA	Danville, IL**	NA	NA	Phoenix-Mesa-Scottsdale, AZ**	NA
217	Washington, DC-VA-MD-WV M.D.	(52.2)	NA	Daphne-Fairhope-Foley, AL**	NA	NA	Pocatello, ID**	NA
218	Dover, DE	(52.9)	NA	Davenport, IA-IL**	NA	NA	Pueblo, CO**	NA
218	Harrisonburg, VA	(52.9)	NA	Decatur, IL**	NA	NA	Rapid City, SD**	NA
220	Odessa, TX	(53.9)	NA	Denver-Aurora, CO**	NA	NA	Rochester, MN**	NA
221	Vineland-Bridgeton, NJ	(54.2)	NA	Detroit (greater), MI**	NA	NA	Rochester, NY**	NA
222	Santa Fe, NM	(54.4)	NA	Detroit-Dearborn-Livonia, MI M.D.**	NA	NA	Rockford, IL**	NA
223	Ann Arbor, MI	(54.8)	NA	Dubuque, IA***	NA	NA	Rocky Mount, NC**	NA
224	Appleton, WI	(55.6)	NA	Dutchess-Putnam, NY M.D.**	NA	NA	Rome, GA**	NA
225	Tyler, TX	(56.3)	NA	East Stroudsburg, PA**	NA	NA	Salisbury, MD-DE**	NA
226	Columbia, MO	(58.1)	NA	Elgin, IL M.D.**	NA	NA	San Rafael, CA M.D.**	NA
227	Abilene, TX	(59.1)	NA	Elizabethtown-Fort Knox, KY**	NA	NA	Santa Maria-Santa Barbara, CA**	NA
228	Gadsden, AL	(60.4)	NA	Elmira, NY**	NA	NA	Seattle (greater), WA**	NA
229	Raleigh, NC	(61.7)	NA	Fairbanks, AK**	NA	NA	Seattle-Bellevue-Everett, WA M.D.**	NA
230	El Centro, CA	(65.3)	NA	Fargo, ND-MN***	NA	NA	Sebring, FL**	NA
231	Decatur, AL	(67.5)	NA	Fort Smith, AR-OK**	NA	NA	Sheboygan, WI***	NA
232	Bay City, MI	(67.9)	NA	Gainesville, GA**	NA	NA	Sierra Vista-Douglas, AZ**	NA
233	Santa Rosa, CA	(69.2)	NA	Gary, IN M.D.**	NA	NA	Sioux City, IA-NE-SD**	NA
234	Punta Gorda, FL	(70.0)	NA	Gettysburg, PA**	NA	NA	Spartanburg, SC**	NA
234	Sioux Falls, SD	(70.0)	NA	Glens Falls, NY**	NA	NA	Springfield, IL**	NA
236	Blacksburg, VA	(71.1)	NA	Grand Island, NE**	NA	NA	Springfield, MA**	NA
237	Iowa City, IA	(75.9)	NA	Greenville-Anderson, SC**	NA	NA	State College, PA***	NA
238	Lafayette, IN	(76.2)	NA	Hagerstown-Martinsburg, MD-WV**	NA	NA	Staunton-Waynesboro, VA**	NA
239	Sebastian-Vero Beach, FL	(76.7)	NA	Hammond, LA**	NA	NA	Syracuse, NY**	NA
240	Mount Vernon-Anacortes, WA	(77.6)	NA	Hattiesburg, MS**	NA	NA	Tacoma, WA M.D.**	NA
241	Madera, CA	(80.6)	NA	Hilton Head Island, SC**	NA	NA	Terre Haute, IN**	NA
242	Ames, IA	(100.0)	NA	Homosassa Springs, FL**	NA	NA	Texarkana, TX-AR**	NA
242	Fond du Lac, WI	(100.0)	NA	Jackson, MS**	NA	NA	The Villages, FL**	NA
242	Idaho Falls, ID	(100.0)	NA	Jackson, TN**	NA	NA	Toledo, OH**	NA
242	Lawrence, KS	(100.0)	NA	Jefferson City, MO**	NA	NA	Tuscaloosa, AL**	NA
242	Lewiston-Auburn, ME	(100.0)	NA	Kahului-Wailuku-Lahaina, HI**	NA	NA	Utica-Rome, NY**	NA
242	Lewiston, ID-WA	(100.0)	NA	Kankakee, IL**	NA	NA	Victoria, TX**	NA
242	Logan, UT-ID	(100.0)	NA	Kansas City, MO-KS**	NA	NA	Waco, TX**	NA
242	Missoula, MT	(100.0)	NA	Kingston, NY**	NA	NA	Walla Walla, WA**	NA
242	Oshkosh-Neenah, WI	(100.0)	NA	Knoxville, TN**	NA	NA	Warner Robins, GA**	NA
242	Pittsfield, MA	(100.0)	NA	Kokomo, IN**	NA	NA	Warren-Troy, MI M.D.**	NA
242	Wheeling, WV-OH	(100.0)	NA	Lafayette, LA**	NA	NA	Watertown-Fort Drum, NY**	NA
NA	Albany-Schenectady-Troy, NY**	NA	NA	Lake Co.-Kenosha Co., IL-WI M.D.**	NA	NA	Wilmington, NC**	NA
NA	Albany, GA**	NA	NA	Lawton, OK**	NA	NA	Winston-Salem, NC**	NA
NA	Albany, OR**	NA	NA	Lexington-Fayette, KY**	NA			
NA	Alexandria, LA**	NA	NA	Madison, WI**	NA			

Source: CQ Press using reported data from the F.B.I. "Crime in the United States 2012"
*Includes nonnegligent manslaughter. **Not available. ***These metro areas had murder rates of 0 in 2008 but had at least one murder in 2012. Calculating percent increase from zero results in an infinite number. This is shown as "NA."

13. Rapes in 2012
National Total = 84,376 Rapes*

RANK	METROPOLITAN AREA	RAPES	RANK	METROPOLITAN AREA	RAPES	RANK	METROPOLITAN AREA	RAPES
259	Abilene, TX	45	302	Cheyenne, WY	33	121	Gary, IN M.D.	150
71	Akron, OH	278	NA	Chicago (greater), IL-IN-WI**	NA	363	Gettysburg, PA	14
113	Albany-Schenectady-Troy, NY	159	NA	Chicago-Joilet-Naperville, IL M.D.**	NA	319	Glens Falls, NY	29
294	Albany, GA	36	197	Chico, CA	75	370	Goldsboro, NC	9
336	Albany, OR	25	31	Cincinnati, OH-KY-IN	683	NA	Grand Forks, ND-MN**	NA
55	Albuquerque, NM	371	190	Clarksville, TN-KY	85	259	Grand Island, NE	45
253	Alexandria, LA	46	294	Cleveland, TN	36	162	Grand Junction, CO	107
116	Allentown, PA-NJ	156	239	Coeur d'Alene, ID	53	362	Great Falls, MT	16
266	Altoona, PA	44	195	College Station-Bryan, TX	77	215	Greeley, CO	64
150	Amarillo, TX	118	48	Colorado Springs, CO	447	212	Green Bay, WI	68
253	Ames, IA	46	253	Columbia, MO	46	131	Greensboro-High Point, NC	137
53	Anaheim-Santa Ana-Irvine, CA M.D.	398	226	Columbus, GA-AL	59	64	Greenville-Anderson, SC	305
63	Anchorage, AK	307	358	Columbus, IN	18	292	Greenville, NC	37
123	Ann Arbor, MI	148	78	Corpus Christi, TX	240	283	Hagerstown-Martinsburg, MD-WV	40
292	Anniston-Oxford, AL	37	355	Corvallis, OR	19	215	Hammond, LA	64
283	Appleton, WI	40	187	Crestview-Fort Walton Beach, FL	86	234	Hanford-Corcoran, CA	55
168	Asheville, NC	99	319	Cumberland, MD-WV	29	102	Harrisburg-Carlisle, PA	176
210	Athens-Clarke County, GA	69	4	Dallas (greater), TX	1,893	327	Harrisonburg, VA	27
13	Atlanta, GA	1,093	12	Dallas-Plano-Irving, TX M.D.	1,120	115	Hartford, CT	157
199	Atlantic City, NJ	74	327	Dalton, GA	27	336	Hattiesburg, MS	25
332	Auburn, AL	26	217	Danville, IL	63	229	Hickory, NC	57
110	Augusta, GA-SC	164	312	Daphne-Fairhope-Foley, AL	30	221	Hilton Head Island, SC	60
47	Austin-Round Rock, TX	453	151	Davenport, IA-IL	117	289	Hinesville, GA	38
104	Bakersfield, CA	174	65	Dayton, OH	302	327	Homosassa Springs, FL	27
33	Baltimore, MD	671	354	Decatur, AL	20	323	Houma, LA	28
355	Bangor, ME	19	288	Decatur, IL	39	7	Houston, TX	1,498
218	Barnstable Town, MA	62	164	Deltona-Daytona Beach, FL	104	160	Huntsville, AL	109
131	Baton Rouge, LA	137	11	Denver-Aurora, CO	1,150	253	Idaho Falls, ID	46
212	Bay City, MI	68	101	Des Moines-West Des Moines, IA	178	37	Indianapolis, IN	602
131	Beaumont-Port Arthur, TX	137	8	Detroit (greater), MI	1,468	235	Iowa City, IA	54
253	Beckley, WV	46	21	Detroit-Dearborn-Livonia, MI M.D.	799	49	Jacksonville, FL	426
166	Bellingham, WA	101	235	Dothan, AL	54	94	Jackson, MS	194
275	Billings, MT	43	248	Dover, DE	47	259	Jackson, TN	45
226	Binghamton, NY	59	342	Dubuque, IA	24	266	Janesville, WI	44
56	Birmingham-Hoover, AL	363	NA	Duluth, MN-WI**	NA	342	Jefferson City, MO	24
221	Bismarck, ND	60	159	Durham-Chapel Hill, NC	110	342	Johnson City, TN	24
229	Blacksburg, VA	57	289	Dutchess-Putnam, NY M.D.	38	312	Johnstown, PA	30
194	Bloomington, IL	78	243	East Stroudsburg, PA	50	248	Jonesboro, AR	47
232	Bloomington, IN	56	352	El Centro, CA	21	202	Joplin, MO	73
308	Bloomsburg-Berwick, PA	31	82	El Paso, TX	220	266	Kahului-Wailuku-Lahaina, HI	44
95	Boise City, ID	193	96	Elgin, IL M.D.	190	90	Kalamazoo-Portage, MI	200
14	Boston (greater), MA-NH	1,039	336	Elizabethtown-Fort Knox, KY	25	246	Kankakee, IL	49
42	Boston, MA M.D.	509	372	Elmira, NY	2	30	Kansas City, MO-KS	687
202	Boulder, CO	73	179	Erie, PA	93	193	Kennewick-Richland, WA	81
259	Bowling Green, KY	45	144	Eugene, OR	126	107	Killeen-Temple, TX	166
163	Bremerton-Silverdale, WA	105	319	Fairbanks, AK	29	169	Kingsport, TN-VA	98
44	Bridgeport-Stamford, CT	482	NA	Fargo, ND-MN**	NA	308	Kingston, NY	31
169	Brownsville-Harlingen, TX	98	139	Farmington, NM	132	73	Knoxville, TN	271
350	Brunswick, GA	22	76	Fayetteville-Springdale, AR-MO	254	355	Kokomo, IN	19
74	Buffalo-Niagara Falls, NY	258	177	Fayetteville, NC	95	NA	La Crosse, WI-MN**	NA
298	Burlington, NC	35	248	Flagstaff, AZ	47	207	Lafayette, IN	70
367	California-Lexington Park, MD	12	77	Flint, MI	243	184	Lafayette, LA	88
52	Cambridge-Newton, MA M.D.	399	266	Florence-Muscle Shoals, AL	44	83	Lake Co.-Kenosha Co., IL-WI M.D.	217
79	Camden, NJ M.D.	231	239	Florence, SC	53	308	Lake Havasu City-Kingman, AZ	31
147	Canton, OH	122	279	Fond du Lac, WI	41	144	Lakeland, FL	126
160	Cape Coral-Fort Myers, FL	109	187	Fort Collins, CO	86	156	Lancaster, PA	113
358	Cape Girardeau, MO-IL	18	51	Fort Lauderdale, FL M.D.	404	85	Lansing-East Lansing, MI	215
373	Carson City, NV	0	154	Fort Smith, AR-OK	115	187	Laredo, TX	86
371	Casper, WY	7	157	Fort Wayne, IN	112	173	Las Cruces, NM	97
207	Cedar Rapids, IA	70	22	Fort Worth-Arlington, TX M.D.	773	25	Las Vegas-Henderson, NV	739
300	Chambersburg-Waynesboro, PA	34	106	Fresno, CA	172	228	Lawrence, KS	58
125	Champaign-Urbana, IL	144	248	Gadsden, AL	47	277	Lawton, OK	42
92	Charleston-North Charleston, SC	198	130	Gainesville, FL	138	342	Lebanon, PA	24
232	Charlottesville, VA	56	294	Gainesville, GA	36	266	Lewiston-Auburn, ME	44

Note: All listings are for Metropolitan Statistical Areas (M.S.A.s) except for those ending with "M.D." Listings with "M.D." are Metropolitan Divisions which are smaller parts of eleven large M.S.A.s. See explanatory note at beginning of metropolitan area section.

RANK	METROPOLITAN AREA	RAPES	RANK	METROPOLITAN AREA	RAPES	RANK	METROPOLITAN AREA	RAPES
366	Lewiston, ID-WA	13	303	Owensboro, KY	32	116	Silver Spring-Frederick, MD M.D.	156
111	Lexington-Fayette, KY	161	167	Oxnard-Thousand Oaks, CA	100	279	Sioux City, IA-NE-SD	41
202	Lima, OH	73	91	Palm Bay-Melbourne, FL	199	114	Sioux Falls, SD	158
93	Lincoln, NE	196	199	Panama City, FL	74	151	South Bend-Mishawaka, IN-MI	117
62	Little Rock, AR	324	312	Parkersburg-Vienna, WV	30	169	Spartanburg, SC	98
347	Logan, UT-ID	23	97	Pensacola, FL	187	122	Spokane, WA	149
176	Longview, TX	96	173	Peoria, IL	97	158	Springfield, IL	111
202	Longview, WA	73	6	Philadelphia (greater) PA-NJ-MD-DE	1,667	81	Springfield, MA	222
3	Los Angeles County, CA M.D.	1,976	17	Philadelphia, PA M.D.	972	97	Springfield, MO	187
1	Los Angeles (greater), CA	2,374	10	Phoenix-Mesa-Scottsdale, AZ	1,188	259	Springfield, OH	45
72	Louisville, KY-IN	275	259	Pine Bluff, AR	45	303	State College, PA	32
125	Lubbock, TX	144	57	Pittsburgh, PA	359	332	Staunton-Waynesboro, VA	26
218	Lynchburg, VA	62	212	Pittsfield, MA	68	119	Stockton-Lodi, CA	152
221	Macon, GA	60	363	Pocatello, ID	14	275	St. George, UT	43
298	Madera, CA	35	129	Port St. Lucie, FL	140	336	St. Joseph, MO-KS	25
104	Madison, WI	174	27	Portland-Vancouver, OR-WA	724	23	St. Louis, MO-IL	759
127	Manchester-Nashua, NH	143	131	Portland, ME	137	323	Sumter, SC	28
312	Manhattan, KS	30	259	Prescott, AZ	45	118	Syracuse, NY	154
NA	Mankato-North Mankato, MN**	NA	46	Providence-Warwick, RI-MA	466	68	Tacoma, WA M.D.	286
266	Mansfield, OH	44	192	Provo-Orem, UT	83	109	Tallahassee, FL	165
89	McAllen-Edinburg-Mission, TX	202	352	Pueblo, CO	21	28	Tampa-St Petersburg, FL	701
199	Medford, OR	74	342	Punta Gorda, FL	24	266	Terre Haute, IN	44
36	Memphis, TN-MS-AR	604	283	Racine, WI	40	242	Texarkana, TX-AR	51
235	Merced, CA	54	88	Raleigh, NC	205	360	The Villages, FL	17
9	Miami (greater), FL	1,356	128	Rapid City, SD	142	80	Toledo, OH	225
39	Miami-Dade County, FL M.D.	570	179	Reading, PA	93	243	Topeka, KS	50
347	Michigan City-La Porte, IN	23	173	Redding, CA	97	243	Trenton, NJ	50
248	Midland, MI	47	190	Reno, NV	85	59	Tucson, AZ	342
347	Midland, TX	23	112	Richmond, VA	160	45	Tulsa, OK	470
61	Milwaukee, WI	326	24	Riverside-San Bernardino, CA	744	220	Tuscaloosa, AL	61
NA	Minneapolis-St. Paul, MN-WI**	NA	197	Roanoke, VA	75	181	Tyler, TX	91
279	Missoula, MT	41	NA	Rochester, MN**	NA	235	Utica-Rome, NY	54
185	Mobile, AL	87	75	Rochester, NY	256	221	Valdosta, GA	60
141	Modesto, CA	129	87	Rockford, IL	208	154	Vallejo-Fairfield, CA	115
303	Monroe, LA	32	140	Rockingham County, NH M.D.	131	246	Victoria, TX	49
207	Monroe, MI	70	308	Rocky Mount, NC	31	303	Vineland-Bridgeton, NJ	32
66	Montgomery County, PA M.D.	289	332	Rome, GA	26	58	Virginia Beach-Norfolk, VA-NC	350
185	Montgomery, AL	87	41	Sacramento, CA	530	151	Visalia-Porterville, CA	117
312	Morgantown, WV	30	148	Saginaw, MI	120	148	Waco, TX	120
319	Morristown, TN	29	183	Salem, OR	89	350	Walla Walla, WA	22
289	Mount Vernon-Anacortes, WA	38	178	Salinas, CA	94	294	Warner Robins, GA	36
369	Muncie, IN	11	142	Salisbury, MD-DE	127	34	Warren-Troy, MI M.D.	669
312	Napa, CA	30	43	Salt Lake City, UT	502	16	Washington (greater) DC-VA-MD-WV	983
279	Naples-Marco Island, FL	41	20	San Antonio, TX	811	19	Washington, DC-VA-MD-WV M.D.	827
40	Nashville-Davidson, TN	566	29	San Diego, CA	692	181	Waterloo-Cedar Falls, IA	91
146	Nassau-Suffolk, NY M.D.	124	18	San Francisco (greater), CA	892	363	Watertown-Fort Drum, NY	14
327	New Bern, NC	27	84	San Francisco-Redwood, CA M.D.	216	323	Wausau, WI	28
137	New Haven-Milford, CT	134	50	San Jose, CA	417	54	West Palm Beach, FL M.D.	382
69	New Orleans, LA	285	210	San Luis Obispo, CA	69	300	Wheeling, WV-OH	34
2	New York (greater), NY-NJ-PA	2,132	312	San Rafael, CA M.D.	30	253	Wichita Falls, TX	46
5	New York-Jersey City, NY-NJ M.D.	1,689	196	Santa Cruz-Watsonville, CA	76	67	Wichita, KS	288
70	Newark, NJ-PA M.D.	281	336	Santa Fe, NM	25	327	Williamsport, PA	27
86	North Port-Sarasota-Bradenton, FL	212	124	Santa Maria-Santa Barbara, CA	146	103	Wilmington, DE-MD-NJ M.D.	175
266	Norwich-New London, CT	44	119	Santa Rosa, CA	152	229	Wilmington, NC	57
35	Oakland-Hayward, CA M.D.	646	221	Savannah, GA	60	283	Winchester, VA-WV	40
107	Ocala, FL	166	142	Scranton--Wilkes-Barre, PA	127	137	Winston-Salem, NC	134
367	Ocean City, NJ	12	15	Seattle (greater), WA	1,015	100	Worcester, MA-CT	186
266	Odessa, TX	44	26	Seattle-Bellevue-Everett, WA M.D.	729	202	Yakima, WA	73
97	Ogden-Clearfield, UT	187	360	Sebastian-Vero Beach, FL	17	165	York-Hanover, PA	103
38	Oklahoma City, OK	596	332	Sebring, FL	26	135	Youngstown-Warren, OH-PA	135
169	Olympia, WA	98	336	Sheboygan, WI	25	239	Yuba City, CA	53
60	Omaha-Council Bluffs, NE-IA	335	303	Sherman-Denison, TX	32	277	Yuma, AZ	42
32	Orlando, FL	676	135	Shreveport-Bossier City, LA	135			
323	Oshkosh-Neenah, WI	28	283	Sierra Vista-Douglas, AZ	40			

Source: Reported data from the F.B.I. "Crime in the United States 2012"

*Forcible rape is the carnal knowledge of a female forcibly and against her will. Assaults or attempts to commit rape by force or threat of force are included. However, statutory rape without force and other sex offenses are excluded. **Not available

13. Rapes in 2012 (continued)
National Total = 84,376 Rapes*

RANK	METROPOLITAN AREA	RAPES	RANK	METROPOLITAN AREA	RAPES	RANK	METROPOLITAN AREA	RAPES
1	Los Angeles (greater), CA	2,374	65	Dayton, OH	302	129	Port St. Lucie, FL	140
2	New York (greater), NY-NJ-PA	2,132	66	Montgomery County, PA M.D.	289	130	Gainesville, FL	138
3	Los Angeles County, CA M.D.	1,976	67	Wichita, KS	288	131	Baton Rouge, LA	137
4	Dallas (greater), TX	1,893	68	Tacoma, WA M.D.	286	131	Beaumont-Port Arthur, TX	137
5	New York-Jersey City, NY-NJ M.D.	1,689	69	New Orleans, LA	285	131	Greensboro-High Point, NC	137
6	Philadelphia (greater) PA-NJ-MD-DE	1,667	70	Newark, NJ-PA M.D.	281	131	Portland, ME	137
7	Houston, TX	1,498	71	Akron, OH	278	135	Shreveport-Bossier City, LA	135
8	Detroit (greater), MI	1,468	72	Louisville, KY-IN	275	135	Youngstown-Warren, OH-PA	135
9	Miami (greater), FL	1,356	73	Knoxville, TN	271	137	New Haven-Milford, CT	134
10	Phoenix-Mesa-Scottsdale, AZ	1,188	74	Buffalo-Niagara Falls, NY	258	137	Winston-Salem, NC	134
11	Denver-Aurora, CO	1,150	75	Rochester, NY	256	139	Farmington, NM	132
12	Dallas-Plano-Irving, TX M.D.	1,120	76	Fayetteville-Springdale, AR-MO	254	140	Rockingham County, NH M.D.	131
13	Atlanta, GA	1,093	77	Flint, MI	243	141	Modesto, CA	129
14	Boston (greater), MA-NH	1,039	78	Corpus Christi, TX	240	142	Salisbury, MD-DE	127
15	Seattle (greater), WA	1,015	79	Camden, NJ M.D.	231	142	Scranton--Wilkes-Barre, PA	127
16	Washington (greater) DC-VA-MD-WV	983	80	Toledo, OH	225	144	Eugene, OR	126
17	Philadelphia, PA M.D.	972	81	Springfield, MA	222	144	Lakeland, FL	126
18	San Francisco (greater), CA	892	82	El Paso, TX	220	146	Nassau-Suffolk, NY M.D.	124
19	Washington, DC-VA-MD-WV M.D.	827	83	Lake Co.-Kenosha Co., IL-WI M.D.	217	147	Canton, OH	122
20	San Antonio, TX	811	84	San Francisco-Redwood, CA M.D.	216	148	Saginaw, MI	120
21	Detroit-Dearborn-Livonia, MI M.D.	799	85	Lansing-East Lansing, MI	215	148	Waco, TX	120
22	Fort Worth-Arlington, TX M.D.	773	86	North Port-Sarasota-Bradenton, FL	212	150	Amarillo, TX	118
23	St. Louis, MO-IL	759	87	Rockford, IL	208	151	Davenport, IA-IL	117
24	Riverside-San Bernardino, CA	744	88	Raleigh, NC	205	151	South Bend-Mishawaka, IN-MI	117
25	Las Vegas-Henderson, NV	739	89	McAllen-Edinburg-Mission, TX	202	151	Visalia-Porterville, CA	117
26	Seattle-Bellevue-Everett, WA M.D.	729	90	Kalamazoo-Portage, MI	200	154	Fort Smith, AR-OK	115
27	Portland-Vancouver, OR-WA	724	91	Palm Bay-Melbourne, FL	199	154	Vallejo-Fairfield, CA	115
28	Tampa-St Petersburg, FL	701	92	Charleston-North Charleston, SC	198	156	Lancaster, PA	113
29	San Diego, CA	692	93	Lincoln, NE	196	157	Fort Wayne, IN	112
30	Kansas City, MO-KS	687	94	Jackson, MS	194	158	Springfield, IL	111
31	Cincinnati, OH-KY-IN	683	95	Boise City, ID	193	159	Durham-Chapel Hill, NC	110
32	Orlando, FL	676	96	Elgin, IL M.D.	190	160	Cape Coral-Fort Myers, FL	109
33	Baltimore, MD	671	97	Ogden-Clearfield, UT	187	160	Huntsville, AL	109
34	Warren-Troy, MI M.D.	669	97	Pensacola, FL	187	162	Grand Junction, CO	107
35	Oakland-Hayward, CA M.D.	646	97	Springfield, MO	187	163	Bremerton-Silverdale, WA	105
36	Memphis, TN-MS-AR	604	100	Worcester, MA-CT	186	164	Deltona-Daytona Beach, FL	104
37	Indianapolis, IN	602	101	Des Moines-West Des Moines, IA	178	165	York-Hanover, PA	103
38	Oklahoma City, OK	596	102	Harrisburg-Carlisle, PA	176	166	Bellingham, WA	101
39	Miami-Dade County, FL M.D.	570	103	Wilmington, DE-MD-NJ M.D.	175	167	Oxnard-Thousand Oaks, CA	100
40	Nashville-Davidson, TN	566	104	Bakersfield, CA	174	168	Asheville, NC	99
41	Sacramento, CA	530	104	Madison, WI	174	169	Brownsville-Harlingen, TX	98
42	Boston, MA M.D.	509	106	Fresno, CA	172	169	Kingsport, TN-VA	98
43	Salt Lake City, UT	502	107	Killeen-Temple, TX	166	169	Olympia, WA	98
44	Bridgeport-Stamford, CT	482	107	Ocala, FL	166	169	Spartanburg, SC	98
45	Tulsa, OK	470	109	Tallahassee, FL	165	173	Las Cruces, NM	97
46	Providence-Warwick, RI-MA	466	110	Augusta, GA-SC	164	173	Peoria, IL	97
47	Austin-Round Rock, TX	453	111	Lexington-Fayette, KY	161	173	Redding, CA	97
48	Colorado Springs, CO	447	112	Richmond, VA	160	176	Longview, TX	96
49	Jacksonville, FL	426	113	Albany-Schenectady-Troy, NY	159	177	Fayetteville, NC	95
50	San Jose, CA	417	114	Sioux Falls, SD	158	178	Salinas, CA	94
51	Fort Lauderdale, FL M.D.	404	115	Hartford, CT	157	179	Erie, PA	93
52	Cambridge-Newton, MA M.D.	399	116	Allentown, PA-NJ	156	179	Reading, PA	93
53	Anaheim-Santa Ana-Irvine, CA M.D.	398	116	Silver Spring-Frederick, MD M.D.	156	181	Tyler, TX	91
54	West Palm Beach, FL M.D.	382	118	Syracuse, NY	154	181	Waterloo-Cedar Falls, IA	91
55	Albuquerque, NM	371	119	Santa Rosa, CA	152	183	Salem, OR	89
56	Birmingham-Hoover, AL	363	119	Stockton-Lodi, CA	152	184	Lafayette, LA	88
57	Pittsburgh, PA	359	121	Gary, IN M.D.	150	185	Mobile, AL	87
58	Virginia Beach-Norfolk, VA-NC	350	122	Spokane, WA	149	185	Montgomery, AL	87
59	Tucson, AZ	342	123	Ann Arbor, MI	148	187	Crestview-Fort Walton Beach, FL	86
60	Omaha-Council Bluffs, NE-IA	335	124	Santa Maria-Santa Barbara, CA	146	187	Fort Collins, CO	86
61	Milwaukee, WI	326	125	Champaign-Urbana, IL	144	187	Laredo, TX	86
62	Little Rock, AR	324	125	Lubbock, TX	144	190	Clarksville, TN-KY	85
63	Anchorage, AK	307	127	Manchester-Nashua, NH	143	190	Reno, NV	85
64	Greenville-Anderson, SC	305	128	Rapid City, SD	142	192	Provo-Orem, UT	83

Note: All listings are for Metropolitan Statistical Areas (M.S.A.s) except for those ending with "M.D." Listings with "M.D." are Metropolitan Divisions which are smaller parts of eleven large M.S.A.s. See explanatory note at beginning of metropolitan area section.

RANK	METROPOLITAN AREA	RAPES
193	Kennewick-Richland, WA	81
194	Bloomington, IL	78
195	College Station-Bryan, TX	77
196	Santa Cruz-Watsonville, CA	76
197	Chico, CA	75
197	Roanoke, VA	75
199	Atlantic City, NJ	74
199	Medford, OR	74
199	Panama City, FL	74
202	Boulder, CO	73
202	Joplin, MO	73
202	Lima, OH	73
202	Longview, WA	73
202	Yakima, WA	73
207	Cedar Rapids, IA	70
207	Lafayette, IN	70
207	Monroe, MI	70
210	Athens-Clarke County, GA	69
210	San Luis Obispo, CA	69
212	Bay City, MI	68
212	Green Bay, WI	68
212	Pittsfield, MA	68
215	Greeley, CO	64
215	Hammond, LA	64
217	Danville, IL	63
218	Barnstable Town, MA	62
218	Lynchburg, VA	62
220	Tuscaloosa, AL	61
221	Bismarck, ND	60
221	Hilton Head Island, SC	60
221	Macon, GA	60
221	Savannah, GA	60
221	Valdosta, GA	60
226	Binghamton, NY	59
226	Columbus, GA-AL	59
228	Lawrence, KS	58
229	Blacksburg, VA	57
229	Hickory, NC	57
229	Wilmington, NC	57
232	Bloomington, IN	56
232	Charlottesville, VA	56
234	Hanford-Corcoran, CA	55
235	Dothan, AL	54
235	Iowa City, IA	54
235	Merced, CA	54
235	Utica-Rome, NY	54
239	Coeur d'Alene, ID	53
239	Florence, SC	53
239	Yuba City, CA	53
242	Texarkana, TX-AR	51
243	East Stroudsburg, PA	50
243	Topeka, KS	50
243	Trenton, NJ	50
246	Kankakee, IL	49
246	Victoria, TX	49
248	Dover, DE	47
248	Flagstaff, AZ	47
248	Gadsden, AL	47
248	Jonesboro, AR	47
248	Midland, MI	47
253	Alexandria, LA	46
253	Ames, IA	46
253	Beckley, WV	46
253	Columbia, MO	46

RANK	METROPOLITAN AREA	RAPES
253	Idaho Falls, ID	46
253	Wichita Falls, TX	46
259	Abilene, TX	45
259	Bowling Green, KY	45
259	Grand Island, NE	45
259	Jackson, TN	45
259	Pine Bluff, AR	45
259	Prescott, AZ	45
259	Springfield, OH	45
266	Altoona, PA	44
266	Florence-Muscle Shoals, AL	44
266	Janesville, WI	44
266	Kahului-Wailuku-Lahaina, HI	44
266	Lewiston-Auburn, ME	44
266	Mansfield, OH	44
266	Norwich-New London, CT	44
266	Odessa, TX	44
266	Terre Haute, IN	44
275	Billings, MT	43
275	St. George, UT	43
277	Lawton, OK	42
277	Yuma, AZ	42
279	Fond du Lac, WI	41
279	Missoula, MT	41
279	Naples-Marco Island, FL	41
279	Sioux City, IA-NE-SD	41
283	Appleton, WI	40
283	Hagerstown-Martinsburg, MD-WV	40
283	Racine, WI	40
283	Sierra Vista-Douglas, AZ	40
283	Winchester, VA-WV	40
288	Decatur, IL	39
289	Dutchess-Putnam, NY M.D.	38
289	Hinesville, GA	38
289	Mount Vernon-Anacortes, WA	38
292	Anniston-Oxford, AL	37
292	Greenville, NC	37
294	Albany, GA	36
294	Cleveland, TN	36
294	Gainesville, GA	36
294	Warner Robins, GA	36
298	Burlington, NC	35
298	Madera, CA	35
300	Chambersburg-Waynesboro, PA	34
300	Wheeling, WV-OH	34
302	Cheyenne, WY	33
303	Monroe, LA	32
303	Owensboro, KY	32
303	Sherman-Denison, TX	32
303	State College, PA	32
303	Vineland-Bridgeton, NJ	32
308	Bloomsburg-Berwick, PA	31
308	Kingston, NY	31
308	Lake Havasu City-Kingman, AZ	31
308	Rocky Mount, NC	31
312	Daphne-Fairhope-Foley, AL	30
312	Johnstown, PA	30
312	Manhattan, KS	30
312	Morgantown, WV	30
312	Napa, CA	30
312	Parkersburg-Vienna, WV	30
312	San Rafael, CA M.D.	30
319	Cumberland, MD-WV	29
319	Fairbanks, AK	29

RANK	METROPOLITAN AREA	RAPES
319	Glens Falls, NY	29
319	Morristown, TN	29
323	Houma, LA	28
323	Oshkosh-Neenah, WI	28
323	Sumter, SC	28
323	Wausau, WI	28
327	Dalton, GA	27
327	Harrisonburg, VA	27
327	Homosassa Springs, FL	27
327	New Bern, NC	27
327	Williamsport, PA	27
332	Auburn, AL	26
332	Rome, GA	26
332	Sebring, FL	26
332	Staunton-Waynesboro, VA	26
336	Albany, OR	25
336	Elizabethtown-Fort Knox, KY	25
336	Hattiesburg, MS	25
336	Santa Fe, NM	25
336	Sheboygan, WI	25
336	St. Joseph, MO-KS	25
342	Dubuque, IA	24
342	Jefferson City, MO	24
342	Johnson City, TN	24
342	Lebanon, PA	24
342	Punta Gorda, FL	24
347	Logan, UT-ID	23
347	Michigan City-La Porte, IN	23
347	Midland, TX	23
350	Brunswick, GA	22
350	Walla Walla, WA	22
352	El Centro, CA	21
352	Pueblo, CO	21
354	Decatur, AL	20
355	Bangor, ME	19
355	Corvallis, OR	19
355	Kokomo, IN	19
358	Cape Girardeau, MO-IL	18
358	Columbus, IN	18
360	Sebastian-Vero Beach, FL	17
360	The Villages, FL	17
362	Great Falls, MT	16
363	Gettysburg, PA	14
363	Pocatello, ID	14
363	Watertown-Fort Drum, NY	14
366	Lewiston, ID-WA	13
367	California-Lexington Park, MD	12
367	Ocean City, NJ	12
369	Muncie, IN	11
370	Goldsboro, NC	9
371	Casper, WY	7
372	Elmira, NY	2
373	Carson City, NV	0
NA	Chicago (greater), IL-IN-WI**	NA
NA	Chicago-Joliet-Naperville, IL M.D.**	NA
NA	Duluth, MN-WI**	NA
NA	Fargo, ND-MN**	NA
NA	Grand Forks, ND-MN**	NA
NA	La Crosse, WI-MN**	NA
NA	Mankato-North Mankato, MN**	NA
NA	Minneapolis-St. Paul, MN-WI**	NA
NA	Rochester, MN**	NA

Source: Reported data from the F.B.I. "Crime in the United States 2012"

*Forcible rape is the carnal knowledge of a female forcibly and against her will. Assaults or attempts to commit rape by force or threat of force are included. However, statutory rape without force and other sex offenses are excluded. **Not available

14. Rape Rate in 2012
National Rate = 26.9 Rapes per 100,000 Population*

RANK	METROPOLITAN AREA	RATE	RANK	METROPOLITAN AREA	RATE	RANK	METROPOLITAN AREA	RATE
190	Abilene, TX	26.6	95	Cheyenne, WY	35.1	270	Gary, IN M.D.	21.1
69	Akron, OH	39.6	NA	Chicago (greater), IL-IN-WI**	NA	346	Gettysburg, PA	13.8
309	Albany-Schenectady-Troy, NY	18.1	NA	Chicago-Joliet-Naperville, IL M.D.**	NA	249	Glens Falls, NY	22.4
243	Albany, GA	22.6	111	Chico, CA	33.7	370	Goldsboro, NC	7.2
272	Albany, OR	21.0	123	Cincinnati, OH-KY-IN	32.2	NA	Grand Forks, ND-MN**	NA
61	Albuquerque, NM	41.2	124	Clarksville, TN-KY	31.9	20	Grand Island, NE	54.1
159	Alexandria, LA	29.6	144	Cleveland, TN	30.6	6	Grand Junction, CO	71.8
302	Allentown, PA-NJ	18.9	75	Coeur d'Alene, ID	37.3	297	Great Falls, MT	19.4
98	Altoona, PA	34.6	119	College Station-Bryan, TX	32.8	218	Greeley, CO	24.4
43	Amarillo, TX	45.4	10	Colorado Springs, CO	66.8	258	Green Bay, WI	21.9
29	Ames, IA	51.1	177	Columbia, MO	27.7	304	Greensboro-High Point, NC	18.6
350	Anaheim-Santa Ana-Irvine, CA M.D.	12.9	297	Columbus, GA-AL	19.4	83	Greenville-Anderson, SC	36.1
3	Anchorage, AK	97.9	237	Columbus, IN	23.0	267	Greenville, NC	21.4
56	Ann Arbor, MI	42.5	19	Corpus Christi, TX	54.8	336	Hagerstown-Martinsburg, MD-WV	15.7
135	Anniston-Oxford, AL	31.3	255	Corvallis, OR	22.0	26	Hammond, LA	51.9
317	Appleton, WI	17.5	88	Crestview-Fort Walton Beach, FL	35.5	90	Hanford-Corcoran, CA	35.4
240	Asheville, NC	22.8	173	Cumberland, MD-WV	28.0	128	Harrisburg-Carlisle, PA	31.8
93	Athens-Clarke County, GA	35.3	169	Dallas (greater), TX	28.3	270	Harrisonburg, VA	21.1
291	Atlanta, GA	20.1	205	Dallas-Plano-Irving, TX M.D.	25.4	339	Hartford, CT	15.3
186	Atlantic City, NJ	26.8	303	Dalton, GA	18.7	321	Hattiesburg, MS	17.2
309	Auburn, AL	18.1	5	Danville, IL	77.3	338	Hickory, NC	15.5
166	Augusta, GA-SC	28.5	334	Daphne-Fairhope-Foley, AL	16.0	135	Hilton Head Island, SC	31.3
211	Austin-Round Rock, TX	25.0	144	Davenport, IA-IL	30.6	37	Hinesville, GA	46.7
289	Bakersfield, CA	20.2	74	Dayton, OH	37.6	301	Homosassa Springs, FL	19.0
218	Baltimore, MD	24.4	350	Decatur, AL	12.9	348	Houma, LA	13.3
355	Bangor, ME	12.3	94	Decatur, IL	35.2	218	Houston, TX	24.4
166	Barnstable Town, MA	28.5	320	Deltona-Daytona Beach, FL	17.3	201	Huntsville, AL	25.5
326	Baton Rouge, LA	16.9	54	Denver-Aurora, CO	43.6	107	Idaho Falls, ID	33.9
12	Bay City, MI	63.4	144	Des Moines-West Des Moines, IA	30.6	132	Indianapolis, IN	31.4
114	Beaumont-Port Arthur, TX	33.3	103	Detroit (greater), MI	34.2	97	Iowa City, IA	34.7
79	Beckley, WV	36.9	51	Detroit-Dearborn-Livonia, MI M.D.	44.3	139	Jacksonville, FL	30.9
35	Bellingham, WA	49.1	80	Dothan, AL	36.7	109	Jackson, MS	33.8
192	Billings, MT	26.5	171	Dover, DE	28.2	101	Jackson, TN	34.3
230	Binghamton, NY	23.5	207	Dubuque, IA	25.3	182	Janesville, WI	27.4
124	Birmingham-Hoover, AL	31.9	NA	Duluth, MN-WI**	NA	335	Jefferson City, MO	15.9
32	Bismarck, ND	50.1	268	Durham-Chapel Hill, NC	21.2	359	Johnson City, TN	11.9
130	Blacksburg, VA	31.7	367	Dutchess-Putnam, NY M.D.	9.5	277	Johnstown, PA	20.8
59	Bloomington, IL	41.7	161	East Stroudsburg, PA	29.4	71	Jonesboro, AR	38.1
98	Bloomington, IN	34.6	361	El Centro, CA	11.8	61	Joplin, MO	41.2
83	Bloomsburg-Berwick, PA	36.1	195	El Paso, TX	26.3	177	Kahului-Wailuku-Lahaina, HI	27.7
147	Boise City, ID	30.5	149	Elgin, IL M.D.	30.4	14	Kalamazoo-Portage, MI	60.9
249	Boston (greater), MA-NH	22.4	332	Elizabethtown-Fort Knox, KY	16.5	55	Kankakee, IL	43.1
192	Boston, MA M.D.	26.5	372	Elmira, NY	2.2	109	Kansas City, MO-KS	33.8
222	Boulder, CO	24.1	116	Erie, PA	33.0	149	Kennewick-Richland, WA	30.4
173	Bowling Green, KY	28.0	90	Eugene, OR	35.4	68	Killeen-Temple, TX	39.7
64	Bremerton-Silverdale, WA	40.8	4	Fairbanks, AK	83.8	135	Kingsport, TN-VA	31.3
24	Bridgeport-Stamford, CT	52.9	NA	Fargo, ND-MN**	NA	326	Kingston, NY	16.9
233	Brownsville-Harlingen, TX	23.3	1	Farmington, NM	102.8	124	Knoxville, TN	31.9
300	Brunswick, GA	19.3	23	Fayetteville-Springdale, AR-MO	53.4	238	Kokomo, IN	22.9
243	Buffalo-Niagara Falls, NY	22.6	208	Fayetteville, NC	25.1	NA	La Crosse, WI-MN**	NA
243	Burlington, NC	22.6	98	Flagstaff, AZ	34.6	101	Lafayette, IN	34.3
365	California-Lexington Park, MD	11.1	157	Florence-Muscle Shoals, AL	29.8	304	Lafayette, LA	18.6
318	Cambridge-Newton, MA M.D.	17.4	201	Florence, SC	25.5	214	Lake Co.-Kenosha Co., IL-WI M.D.	24.8
307	Camden, NJ M.D.	18.4	67	Fond du Lac, WI	40.1	341	Lake Havasu City-Kingman, AZ	15.2
152	Canton, OH	30.2	175	Fort Collins, CO	27.8	286	Lakeland, FL	20.4
325	Cape Coral-Fort Myers, FL	17.0	249	Fort Lauderdale, FL M.D.	22.4	265	Lancaster, PA	21.5
306	Cape Girardeau, MO-IL	18.5	66	Fort Smith, AR-OK	40.6	39	Lansing-East Lansing, MI	46.2
373	Carson City, NV	0.0	190	Fort Wayne, IN	26.6	116	Laredo, TX	33.0
369	Casper, WY	9.0	106	Fort Worth-Arlington, TX M.D.	34.0	44	Las Cruces, NM	45.3
186	Cedar Rapids, IA	26.8	309	Fresno, CA	18.1	76	Las Vegas-Henderson, NV	37.0
246	Chambersburg-Waynesboro, PA	22.5	49	Gadsden, AL	44.9	28	Lawrence, KS	51.4
13	Champaign-Urbana, IL	62.0	29	Gainesville, FL	51.1	131	Lawton, OK	31.6
164	Charleston-North Charleston, SC	28.8	295	Gainesville, GA	19.5	315	Lebanon, PA	17.8
211	Charlottesville, VA	25.0				63	Lewiston-Auburn, ME	40.9

Note: All listings are for Metropolitan Statistical Areas (M.S.A.s) except for those ending with "M.D." Listings with "M.D." are Metropolitan Divisions which are smaller parts of eleven large M.S.A.s. See explanatory note at beginning of metropolitan area section.

RANK	METROPOLITAN AREA	RATE	RANK	METROPOLITAN AREA	RATE	RANK	METROPOLITAN AREA	RATE
272	Lewiston, ID-WA	21.0	177	Owensboro, KY	27.7	353	Silver Spring-Frederick, MD M.D.	12.6
113	Lexington-Fayette, KY	33.5	359	Oxnard-Thousand Oaks, CA	11.9	222	Sioux City, IA-NE-SD	24.1
8	Lima, OH	68.8	83	Palm Bay-Melbourne, FL	36.1	9	Sioux Falls, SD	67.2
11	Lincoln, NE	63.5	70	Panama City, FL	39.3	81	South Bend-Mishawaka, IN-MI	36.6
42	Little Rock, AR	45.5	121	Parkersburg-Vienna, WV	32.3	142	Spartanburg, SC	30.8
315	Logan, UT-ID	17.8	65	Pensacola, FL	40.7	175	Spokane, WA	27.8
53	Longview, TX	43.7	201	Peoria, IL	25.5	25	Springfield, IL	52.4
7	Longview, WA	70.5	177	Philadelphia (greater) PA-NJ-MD-DE	27.7	90	Springfield, MA	35.4
293	Los Angeles County, CA M.D.	19.8	44	Philadelphia, PA M.D.	45.3	57	Springfield, MO	42.4
308	Los Angeles (greater), CA	18.2	181	Phoenix-Mesa-Scottsdale, AZ	27.6	120	Springfield, OH	32.7
255	Louisville, KY-IN	22.0	44	Pine Bluff, AR	45.3	281	State College, PA	20.6
36	Lubbock, TX	47.9	341	Pittsburgh, PA	15.2	261	Staunton-Waynesboro, VA	21.7
222	Lynchburg, VA	24.1	27	Pittsfield, MA	51.7	264	Stockton-Lodi, CA	21.6
201	Macon, GA	25.5	331	Pocatello, ID	16.6	156	St. George, UT	29.9
241	Madera, CA	22.7	121	Port St. Lucie, FL	32.3	294	St. Joseph, MO-KS	19.6
169	Madison, WI	28.3	128	Portland-Vancouver, OR-WA	31.8	184	St. Louis, MO-IL	27.1
88	Manchester-Nashua, NH	35.5	192	Portland, ME	26.5	199	Sumter, SC	25.8
132	Manhattan, KS	31.4	272	Prescott, AZ	21.0	234	Syracuse, NY	23.1
NA	Mankato-North Mankato, MN**	NA	163	Providence-Warwick, RI-MA	29.1	95	Tacoma, WA M.D.	35.1
87	Mansfield, OH	35.6	343	Provo-Orem, UT	15.1	52	Tallahassee, FL	44.0
213	McAllen-Edinburg-Mission, TX	24.9	350	Pueblo, CO	12.9	217	Tampa-St Petersburg, FL	24.5
86	Medford, OR	35.9	344	Punta Gorda, FL	14.8	205	Terre Haute, IN	25.4
48	Memphis, TN-MS-AR	45.0	286	Racine, WI	20.4	111	Texarkana, TX-AR	33.7
281	Merced, CA	20.6	318	Raleigh, NC	17.4	321	The Villages, FL	17.2
228	Miami (greater), FL	23.6	2	Rapid City, SD	102.7	76	Toledo, OH	37.0
255	Miami-Dade County, FL M.D.	22.0	246	Reading, PA	22.5	268	Topeka, KS	21.2
281	Michigan City-La Porte, IN	20.6	20	Redding, CA	54.1	347	Trenton, NJ	13.6
18	Midland, MI	55.9	295	Reno, NV	19.5	103	Tucson, AZ	34.2
337	Midland, TX	15.6	349	Richmond, VA	13.0	33	Tulsa, OK	49.3
277	Milwaukee, WI	20.8	323	Riverside-San Bernardino, CA	17.1	196	Tuscaloosa, AL	26.2
NA	Minneapolis-St. Paul, MN-WI**	NA	226	Roanoke, VA	24.0	58	Tyler, TX	42.0
76	Missoula, MT	37.0	NA	Rochester, MN**	NA	312	Utica-Rome, NY	18.0
272	Mobile, AL	21.0	228	Rochester, NY	23.6	59	Valdosta, GA	41.7
216	Modesto, CA	24.6	16	Rockford, IL	59.7	182	Vallejo-Fairfield, CA	27.4
314	Monroe, LA	17.9	138	Rockingham County, NH M.D.	31.1	31	Victoria, TX	50.9
39	Monroe, MI	46.2	289	Rocky Mount, NC	20.2	288	Vineland-Bridgeton, NJ	20.3
339	Montgomery County, PA M.D.	15.3	186	Rome, GA	26.8	285	Virginia Beach-Norfolk, VA-NC	20.5
238	Montgomery, AL	22.9	222	Sacramento, CA	24.1	199	Visalia-Porterville, CA	25.8
241	Morgantown, WV	22.7	15	Saginaw, MI	60.2	41	Waco, TX	46.1
208	Morristown, TN	25.1	249	Salem, OR	22.4	103	Walla Walla, WA	34.2
124	Mount Vernon-Anacortes, WA	31.9	253	Salinas, CA	22.1	297	Warner Robins, GA	19.4
368	Muncie, IN	9.3	114	Salisbury, MD-DE	33.3	185	Warren-Troy, MI M.D.	26.9
265	Napa, CA	21.5	50	Salt Lake City, UT	44.7	326	Washington (greater) DC-VA-MD-WV	16.9
355	Naples-Marco Island, FL	12.3	82	San Antonio, TX	36.4	312	Washington, DC-VA-MD-WV M.D.	18.0
116	Nashville-Davidson, TN	33.0	260	San Diego, CA	21.8	22	Waterloo-Cedar Falls, IA	53.9
371	Nassau-Suffolk, NY M.D.	4.3	291	San Francisco (greater), CA	20.1	361	Watertown-Fort Drum, NY	11.8
276	New Bern, NC	20.9	345	San Francisco-Redwood, CA M.D.	13.9	277	Wausau, WI	20.8
332	New Haven-Milford, CT	16.5	253	San Jose, CA	22.1	171	West Palm Beach, FL M.D.	28.2
232	New Orleans, LA	23.4	208	San Luis Obispo, CA	25.1	234	Wheeling, WV-OH	23.1
366	New York (greater), NY-NJ-PA	10.8	363	San Rafael, CA M.D.	11.7	152	Wichita Falls, TX	30.2
358	New York-Jersey City, NY-NJ M.D.	12.0	166	Santa Cruz-Watsonville, CA	28.5	47	Wichita, KS	45.2
364	Newark, NJ-PA M.D.	11.3	323	Santa Fe, NM	17.1	234	Williamsport, PA	23.1
160	North Port-Sarasota-Bradenton, FL	29.5	107	Santa Maria-Santa Barbara, CA	33.9	218	Wilmington, DE-MD-NJ M.D.	24.4
155	Norwich-New London, CT	30.1	139	Santa Rosa, CA	30.9	261	Wilmington, NC	21.7
215	Oakland-Hayward, CA M.D.	24.7	329	Savannah, GA	16.7	147	Winchester, VA-WV	30.5
34	Ocala, FL	49.2	246	Scranton--Wilkes-Barre, PA	22.5	281	Winston-Salem, NC	20.6
354	Ocean City, NJ	12.4	165	Seattle (greater), WA	28.7	258	Worcester, MA-CT	21.9
139	Odessa, TX	30.9	186	Seattle-Bellevue-Everett, WA M.D.	26.8	162	Yakima, WA	29.3
149	Ogden-Clearfield, UT	30.4	357	Sebastian-Vero Beach, FL	12.1	230	York-Hanover, PA	23.5
38	Oklahoma City, OK	46.3	197	Sebring, FL	26.0	226	Youngstown-Warren, OH-PA	24.0
73	Olympia, WA	37.8	261	Sheboygan, WI	21.7	132	Yuba City, CA	31.4
72	Omaha-Council Bluffs, NE-IA	37.9	197	Sherman-Denison, TX	26.0	280	Yuma, AZ	20.7
143	Orlando, FL	30.7	152	Shreveport-Bossier City, LA	30.2			
329	Oshkosh-Neenah, WI	16.7	158	Sierra Vista-Douglas, AZ	29.7			

Source: Reported data from the F.B.I. "Crime in the United States 2012"

*Forcible rape is the carnal knowledge of a female forcibly and against her will. Assaults or attempts to commit rape by force or threat of force are included. However, statutory rape without force and other sex offenses are excluded. **Not available

14. Rape Rate in 2012 (continued)
National Rate = 26.9 Rapes per 100,000 Population*

RANK	METROPOLITAN AREA	RATE	RANK	METROPOLITAN AREA	RATE	RANK	METROPOLITAN AREA	RATE
1	Farmington, NM	102.8	65	Pensacola, FL	40.7	128	Portland-Vancouver, OR-WA	31.8
2	Rapid City, SD	102.7	66	Fort Smith, AR-OK	40.6	130	Blacksburg, VA	31.7
3	Anchorage, AK	97.9	67	Fond du Lac, WI	40.1	131	Lawton, OK	31.6
4	Fairbanks, AK	83.8	68	Killeen-Temple, TX	39.7	132	Indianapolis, IN	31.4
5	Danville, IL	77.3	69	Akron, OH	39.6	132	Manhattan, KS	31.4
6	Grand Junction, CO	71.8	70	Panama City, FL	39.3	132	Yuba City, CA	31.4
7	Longview, WA	70.5	71	Jonesboro, AR	38.1	135	Anniston-Oxford, AL	31.3
8	Lima, OH	68.8	72	Omaha-Council Bluffs, NE-IA	37.9	135	Hilton Head Island, SC	31.3
9	Sioux Falls, SD	67.2	73	Olympia, WA	37.8	135	Kingsport, TN-VA	31.3
10	Colorado Springs, CO	66.8	74	Dayton, OH	37.6	138	Rockingham County, NH M.D.	31.1
11	Lincoln, NE	63.5	75	Coeur d'Alene, ID	37.3	139	Jacksonville, FL	30.9
12	Bay City, MI	63.4	76	Las Vegas-Henderson, NV	37.0	139	Odessa, TX	30.9
13	Champaign-Urbana, IL	62.0	76	Missoula, MT	37.0	139	Santa Rosa, CA	30.9
14	Kalamazoo-Portage, MI	60.9	76	Toledo, OH	37.0	142	Spartanburg, SC	30.8
15	Saginaw, MI	60.2	79	Beckley, WV	36.9	143	Orlando, FL	30.7
16	Rockford, IL	59.7	80	Dothan, AL	36.7	144	Cleveland, TN	30.6
17	Flint, MI	57.5	81	South Bend-Mishawaka, IN-MI	36.6	144	Davenport, IA-IL	30.6
18	Midland, MI	55.9	82	San Antonio, TX	36.4	144	Des Moines-West Des Moines, IA	30.6
19	Corpus Christi, TX	54.8	83	Bloomsburg-Berwick, PA	36.1	147	Boise City, ID	30.5
20	Grand Island, NE	54.1	83	Greenville-Anderson, SC	36.1	147	Winchester, VA-WV	30.5
20	Redding, CA	54.1	83	Palm Bay-Melbourne, FL	36.1	149	Elgin, IL M.D.	30.4
22	Waterloo-Cedar Falls, IA	53.9	86	Medford, OR	35.9	149	Kennewick-Richland, WA	30.4
23	Fayetteville-Springdale, AR-MO	53.4	87	Mansfield, OH	35.6	149	Ogden-Clearfield, UT	30.4
24	Bridgeport-Stamford, CT	52.9	88	Crestview-Fort Walton Beach, FL	35.5	152	Canton, OH	30.2
25	Springfield, IL	52.4	88	Manchester-Nashua, NH	35.5	152	Shreveport-Bossier City, LA	30.2
26	Hammond, LA	51.9	90	Eugene, OR	35.4	152	Wichita Falls, TX	30.2
27	Pittsfield, MA	51.7	90	Hanford-Corcoran, CA	35.4	155	Norwich-New London, CT	30.1
28	Lawrence, KS	51.4	90	Springfield, MA	35.4	156	St. George, UT	29.9
29	Ames, IA	51.1	93	Athens-Clarke County, GA	35.3	157	Florence-Muscle Shoals, AL	29.8
29	Gainesville, FL	51.1	94	Decatur, IL	35.2	158	Sierra Vista-Douglas, AZ	29.7
31	Victoria, TX	50.9	95	Cheyenne, WY	35.1	159	Alexandria, LA	29.6
32	Bismarck, ND	50.1	95	Tacoma, WA M.D.	35.1	160	North Port-Sarasota-Bradenton, FL	29.5
33	Tulsa, OK	49.3	97	Iowa City, IA	34.7	161	East Stroudsburg, PA	29.4
34	Ocala, FL	49.2	98	Altoona, PA	34.6	162	Yakima, WA	29.3
35	Bellingham, WA	49.1	98	Bloomington, IN	34.6	163	Providence-Warwick, RI-MA	29.1
36	Lubbock, TX	47.9	98	Flagstaff, AZ	34.6	164	Charleston-North Charleston, SC	28.8
37	Hinesville, GA	46.7	101	Jackson, TN	34.3	165	Seattle (greater), WA	28.7
38	Oklahoma City, OK	46.3	101	Lafayette, IN	34.3	166	Augusta, GA-SC	28.5
39	Lansing-East Lansing, MI	46.2	103	Detroit (greater), MI	34.2	166	Barnstable Town, MA	28.5
39	Monroe, MI	46.2	103	Tucson, AZ	34.2	166	Santa Cruz-Watsonville, CA	28.5
41	Waco, TX	46.1	103	Walla Walla, WA	34.2	169	Dallas (greater), TX	28.3
42	Little Rock, AR	45.5	106	Fort Worth-Arlington, TX M.D.	34.0	169	Madison, WI	28.3
43	Amarillo, TX	45.4	107	Idaho Falls, ID	33.9	171	Dover, DE	28.2
44	Las Cruces, NM	45.3	107	Santa Maria-Santa Barbara, CA	33.9	171	West Palm Beach, FL M.D.	28.2
44	Philadelphia, PA M.D.	45.3	109	Jackson, MS	33.8	173	Bowling Green, KY	28.0
44	Pine Bluff, AR	45.3	109	Kansas City, MO-KS	33.8	173	Cumberland, MD-WV	28.0
47	Wichita, KS	45.2	111	Chico, CA	33.7	175	Fort Collins, CO	27.8
48	Memphis, TN-MS-AR	45.0	111	Texarkana, TX-AR	33.7	175	Spokane, WA	27.8
49	Gadsden, AL	44.9	113	Lexington-Fayette, KY	33.5	177	Columbia, MO	27.7
50	Salt Lake City, UT	44.7	114	Beaumont-Port Arthur, TX	33.3	177	Kahului-Wailuku-Lahaina, HI	27.7
51	Detroit-Dearborn-Livonia, MI M.D.	44.3	114	Salisbury, MD-DE	33.3	177	Owensboro, KY	27.7
52	Tallahassee, FL	44.0	116	Erie, PA	33.0	177	Philadelphia (greater) PA-NJ-MD-DE	27.7
53	Longview, TX	43.7	116	Laredo, TX	33.0	181	Phoenix-Mesa-Scottsdale, AZ	27.6
54	Denver-Aurora, CO	43.6	116	Nashville-Davidson, TN	33.0	182	Janesville, WI	27.4
55	Kankakee, IL	43.1	119	College Station-Bryan, TX	32.8	182	Vallejo-Fairfield, CA	27.4
56	Ann Arbor, MI	42.5	120	Springfield, OH	32.7	184	St. Louis, MO-IL	27.1
57	Springfield, MO	42.4	121	Parkersburg-Vienna, WV	32.3	185	Warren-Troy, MI M.D.	26.9
58	Tyler, TX	42.0	121	Port St. Lucie, FL	32.3	186	Atlantic City, NJ	26.8
59	Bloomington, IL	41.7	123	Cincinnati, OH-KY-IN	32.2	186	Cedar Rapids, IA	26.8
59	Valdosta, GA	41.7	124	Birmingham-Hoover, AL	31.9	186	Rome, GA	26.8
61	Albuquerque, NM	41.2	124	Clarksville, TN-KY	31.9	186	Seattle-Bellevue-Everett, WA M.D.	26.8
61	Joplin, MO	41.2	124	Knoxville, TN	31.9	190	Abilene, TX	26.6
63	Lewiston-Auburn, ME	40.9	124	Mount Vernon-Anacortes, WA	31.9	190	Fort Wayne, IN	26.6
64	Bremerton-Silverdale, WA	40.8	128	Harrisburg-Carlisle, PA	31.8	192	Billings, MT	26.5

Note: All listings are for Metropolitan Statistical Areas (M.S.A.s) except for those ending with "M.D." Listings with "M.D." are Metropolitan Divisions which are smaller parts of eleven large M.S.A.s. See explanatory note at beginning of metropolitan area section.

RANK	METROPOLITAN AREA	RATE	RANK	METROPOLITAN AREA	RATE	RANK	METROPOLITAN AREA	RATE
192	Boston, MA M.D.	26.5	255	Miami-Dade County, FL M.D.	22.0	321	Hattiesburg, MS	17.2
192	Portland, ME	26.5	258	Green Bay, WI	21.9	321	The Villages, FL	17.2
195	El Paso, TX	26.3	258	Worcester, MA-CT	21.9	323	Riverside-San Bernardino, CA	17.1
196	Tuscaloosa, AL	26.2	260	San Diego, CA	21.8	323	Santa Fe, NM	17.1
197	Sebring, FL	26.0	261	Sheboygan, WI	21.7	325	Cape Coral-Fort Myers, FL	17.0
197	Sherman-Denison, TX	26.0	261	Staunton-Waynesboro, VA	21.7	326	Baton Rouge, LA	16.9
199	Sumter, SC	25.8	261	Wilmington, NC	21.7	326	Kingston, NY	16.9
199	Visalia-Porterville, CA	25.8	264	Stockton-Lodi, CA	21.6	326	Washington (greater) DC-VA-MD-WV	16.9
201	Florence, SC	25.5	265	Lancaster, PA	21.5	329	Oshkosh-Neenah, WI	16.7
201	Huntsville, AL	25.5	265	Napa, CA	21.5	329	Savannah, GA	16.7
201	Macon, GA	25.5	267	Greenville, NC	21.4	331	Pocatello, ID	16.6
201	Peoria, IL	25.5	268	Durham-Chapel Hill, NC	21.2	332	Elizabethtown-Fort Knox, KY	16.5
205	Dallas-Plano-Irving, TX M.D.	25.4	268	Topeka, KS	21.2	332	New Haven-Milford, CT	16.5
205	Terre Haute, IN	25.4	270	Gary, IN M.D.	21.1	334	Daphne-Fairhope-Foley, AL	16.0
207	Dubuque, IA	25.3	270	Harrisonburg, VA	21.1	335	Jefferson City, MO	15.9
208	Fayetteville, NC	25.1	272	Albany, OR	21.0	336	Hagerstown-Martinsburg, MD-WV	15.7
208	Morristown, TN	25.1	272	Lewiston, ID-WA	21.0	337	Midland, TX	15.6
208	San Luis Obispo, CA	25.1	272	Mobile, AL	21.0	338	Hickory, NC	15.5
211	Austin-Round Rock, TX	25.0	272	Prescott, AZ	21.0	339	Hartford, CT	15.3
211	Charlottesville, VA	25.0	276	New Bern, NC	20.9	339	Montgomery County, PA M.D.	15.3
213	McAllen-Edinburg-Mission, TX	24.9	277	Johnstown, PA	20.8	341	Lake Havasu City-Kingman, AZ	15.2
214	Lake Co.-Kenosha Co., IL-WI M.D.	24.8	277	Milwaukee, WI	20.8	341	Pittsburgh, PA	15.2
215	Oakland-Hayward, CA M.D.	24.7	277	Wausau, WI	20.8	343	Provo-Orem, UT	15.1
216	Modesto, CA	24.6	280	Yuma, AZ	20.7	344	Punta Gorda, FL	14.8
217	Tampa-St Petersburg, FL	24.5	281	Merced, CA	20.6	345	San Francisco-Redwood, CA M.D.	13.9
218	Baltimore, MD	24.4	281	Michigan City-La Porte, IN	20.6	346	Gettysburg, PA	13.8
218	Greeley, CO	24.4	281	State College, PA	20.6	347	Trenton, NJ	13.6
218	Houston, TX	24.4	281	Winston-Salem, NC	20.6	348	Houma, LA	13.3
218	Wilmington, DE-MD-NJ M.D.	24.4	285	Virginia Beach-Norfolk, VA-NC	20.5	349	Richmond, VA	13.0
222	Boulder, CO	24.1	286	Lakeland, FL	20.4	350	Anaheim-Santa Ana-Irvine, CA M.D.	12.9
222	Lynchburg, VA	24.1	286	Racine, WI	20.4	350	Decatur, AL	12.9
222	Sacramento, CA	24.1	288	Vineland-Bridgeton, NJ	20.3	350	Pueblo, CO	12.9
222	Sioux City, IA-NE-SD	24.1	289	Bakersfield, CA	20.2	353	Silver Spring-Frederick, MD M.D.	12.6
226	Roanoke, VA	24.0	289	Rocky Mount, NC	20.2	354	Ocean City, NJ	12.4
226	Youngstown-Warren, OH-PA	24.0	291	Atlanta, GA	20.1	355	Bangor, ME	12.3
228	Miami (greater), FL	23.6	291	San Francisco (greater), CA	20.1	355	Naples-Marco Island, FL	12.3
228	Rochester, NY	23.6	293	Los Angeles County, CA M.D.	19.8	357	Sebastian-Vero Beach, FL	12.1
230	Binghamton, NY	23.5	294	St. Joseph, MO-KS	19.6	358	New York-Jersey City, NY-NJ M.D.	12.0
230	York-Hanover, PA	23.5	295	Gainesville, GA	19.5	359	Johnson City, TN	11.9
232	New Orleans, LA	23.4	295	Reno, NV	19.5	359	Oxnard-Thousand Oaks, CA	11.9
233	Brownsville-Harlingen, TX	23.3	297	Columbus, GA-AL	19.4	361	El Centro, CA	11.8
234	Syracuse, NY	23.1	297	Great Falls, MT	19.4	361	Watertown-Fort Drum, NY	11.8
234	Wheeling, WV-OH	23.1	297	Warner Robins, GA	19.4	363	San Rafael, CA M.D.	11.7
234	Williamsport, PA	23.1	300	Brunswick, GA	19.3	364	Newark, NJ-PA M.D.	11.3
237	Columbus, IN	23.0	301	Homosassa Springs, FL	19.0	365	California-Lexington Park, MD	11.1
238	Kokomo, IN	22.9	302	Allentown, PA-NJ	18.9	366	New York (greater), NY-NJ-PA	10.8
238	Montgomery, AL	22.9	303	Dalton, GA	18.7	367	Dutchess-Putnam, NY M.D.	9.5
240	Asheville, NC	22.8	304	Greensboro-High Point, NC	18.6	368	Muncie, IN	9.3
241	Madera, CA	22.7	304	Lafayette, LA	18.6	369	Casper, WY	9.0
241	Morgantown, WV	22.7	306	Cape Girardeau, MO-IL	18.5	370	Goldsboro, NC	7.2
243	Albany, GA	22.6	307	Camden, NJ M.D.	18.4	371	Nassau-Suffolk, NY M.D.	4.3
243	Buffalo-Niagara Falls, NY	22.6	308	Los Angeles (greater), CA	18.2	372	Elmira, NY	2.2
243	Burlington, NC	22.6	309	Albany-Schenectady-Troy, NY	18.1	373	Carson City, NV	0.0
246	Chambersburg-Waynesboro, PA	22.5	309	Auburn, AL	18.1	NA	Chicago (greater), IL-IN-WI**	NA
246	Reading, PA	22.5	309	Fresno, CA	18.1	NA	Chicago-Joilet-Naperville, IL M.D.**	NA
246	Scranton--Wilkes-Barre, PA	22.5	312	Utica-Rome, NY	18.0	NA	Duluth, MN-WI**	NA
249	Boston (greater), MA-NH	22.4	312	Washington, DC-VA-MD-WV M.D.	18.0	NA	Fargo, ND-MN**	NA
249	Fort Lauderdale, FL M.D.	22.4	314	Monroe, LA	17.9	NA	Grand Forks, ND-MN**	NA
249	Glens Falls, NY	22.4	315	Lebanon, PA	17.8	NA	La Crosse, WI-MN**	NA
249	Salem, OR	22.4	315	Logan, UT-ID	17.8	NA	Mankato-North Mankato, MN**	NA
253	Salinas, CA	22.1	317	Appleton, WI	17.5	NA	Minneapolis-St. Paul, MN-WI**	NA
253	San Jose, CA	22.1	318	Cambridge-Newton, MA M.D.	17.4	NA	Rochester, MN**	NA
255	Corvallis, OR	22.0	318	Raleigh, NC	17.4			
255	Louisville, KY-IN	22.0	320	Deltona-Daytona Beach, FL	17.3			

Source: Reported data from the F.B.I. "Crime in the United States 2012"

*Forcible rape is the carnal knowledge of a female forcibly and against her will. Assaults or attempts to commit rape by force or threat of force are included. However, statutory rape without force and other sex offenses are excluded. **Not available

15. Percent Change in Rape Rate: 2011 to 2012
National Percent Change = 0.5% Decrease*

RANK	METROPOLITAN AREA	% CHANGE	RANK	METROPOLITAN AREA	% CHANGE	RANK	METROPOLITAN AREA	% CHANGE
32	Abilene, TX	24.9	225	Cheyenne, WY	(16.8)	228	Gary, IN M.D.	(17.6)
100	Akron, OH	6.7	NA	Chicago (greater), IL-IN-WI**	NA	NA	Gettysburg, PA**	NA
NA	Albany-Schenectady-Troy, NY**	NA	NA	Chicago-Joilet-Naperville, IL M.D.**	NA	NA	Glens Falls, NY**	NA
252	Albany, GA	(29.4)	135	Chico, CA	0.0	12	Goldsboro, NC	50.0
NA	Albany, OR**	NA	NA	Cincinnati, OH-KY-IN**	NA	NA	Grand Forks, ND-MN**	NA
114	Albuquerque, NM	4.0	232	Clarksville, TN-KY	(19.2)	NA	Grand Island, NE**	NA
212	Alexandria, LA	(13.2)	89	Cleveland, TN	8.5	52	Grand Junction, CO	16.6
NA	Allentown, PA-NJ**	NA	NA	Coeur d'Alene, ID**	NA	138	Great Falls, MT	(0.5)
238	Altoona, PA	(21.2)	103	College Station-Bryan, TX	6.5	172	Greeley, CO	(6.2)
116	Amarillo, TX	3.4	74	Colorado Springs, CO	11.1	190	Green Bay, WI	(9.1)
10	Ames, IA	53.5	98	Columbia, MO	6.9	NA	Greensboro-High Point, NC**	NA
163	Anaheim-Santa Ana-Irvine, CA M.D.	(4.4)	222	Columbus, GA-AL	(16.0)	NA	Greenville-Anderson, SC**	NA
NA	Anchorage, AK**	NA	23	Columbus, IN	36.9	NA	Greenville, NC**	NA
215	Ann Arbor, MI	(13.4)	185	Corpus Christi, TX	(8.2)	NA	Hagerstown-Martinsburg, MD-WV**	NA
213	Anniston-Oxford, AL	(13.3)	105	Corvallis, OR	5.8	NA	Hammond, LA**	NA
204	Appleton, WI	(12.1)	88	Crestview-Fort Walton Beach, FL	8.6	4	Hanford-Corcoran, CA	82.5
25	Asheville, NC	34.1	224	Cumberland, MD-WV	(16.7)	152	Harrisburg-Carlisle, PA	(3.0)
9	Athens-Clarke County, GA	56.2	106	Dallas (greater), TX	5.2	239	Harrisonburg, VA	(21.3)
150	Atlanta, GA	(2.4)	91	Dallas-Plano-Irving, TX M.D.	8.1	242	Hartford, CT	(22.3)
34	Atlantic City, NJ	22.9	194	Dalton, GA	(10.1)	NA	Hattiesburg, MS**	NA
234	Auburn, AL	(20.3)	231	Danville, IL	(18.9)	56	Hickory, NC	14.8
241	Augusta, GA-SC	(21.7)	NA	Daphne-Fairhope-Foley, AL**	NA	NA	Hilton Head Island, SC**	NA
81	Austin-Round Rock, TX	9.6	258	Davenport, IA-IL	(33.3)	1	Hinesville, GA	130.0
178	Bakersfield, CA	(6.9)	87	Dayton, OH	8.7	NA	Homosassa Springs, FL**	NA
148	Baltimore, MD	(2.0)	264	Decatur, AL	(46.0)	265	Houma, LA	(46.4)
193	Bangor, ME	(9.6)	45	Decatur, IL	18.5	189	Houston, TX	(9.0)
259	Barnstable Town, MA	(37.5)	NA	Deltona-Daytona Beach, FL**	NA	164	Huntsville, AL	(4.5)
185	Baton Rouge, LA	(8.2)	NA	Denver-Aurora, CO**	NA	47	Idaho Falls, ID	17.7
184	Bay City, MI	(7.7)	140	Des Moines-West Des Moines, IA	(1.0)	NA	Indianapolis, IN**	NA
155	Beaumont-Port Arthur, TX	(3.5)	104	Detroit (greater), MI	5.9	86	Iowa City, IA	8.8
NA	Beckley, WV**	NA	113	Detroit-Dearborn-Livonia, MI M.D.	4.2	161	Jacksonville, FL	(4.0)
100	Bellingham, WA	6.7	37	Dothan, AL	21.9	NA	Jackson, MS**	NA
130	Billings, MT	0.8	263	Dover, DE	(45.6)	NA	Jackson, TN**	NA
NA	Binghamton, NY**	NA	60	Dubuque, IA	13.5	62	Janesville, WI	13.2
213	Birmingham-Hoover, AL	(13.3)	NA	Duluth, MN-WI**	NA	85	Jefferson City, MO	8.9
24	Bismarck, ND	35.0	181	Durham-Chapel Hill, NC	(7.4)	31	Johnson City, TN	25.3
167	Blacksburg, VA	(5.1)	NA	Dutchess-Putnam, NY M.D.**	NA	260	Johnstown, PA	(41.2)
246	Bloomington, IL	(24.6)	NA	East Stroudsburg, PA**	NA	239	Jonesboro, AR	(21.3)
NA	Bloomington, IN**	NA	257	El Centro, CA	(33.0)	80	Joplin, MO	9.9
NA	Bloomsburg-Berwick, PA**	NA	197	El Paso, TX	(10.8)	NA	Kahului-Wailuku-Lahaina, HI**	NA
39	Boise City, ID	21.0	NA	Elgin, IL M.D.**	NA	NA	Kalamazoo-Portage, MI**	NA
NA	Boston (greater), MA-NH**	NA	NA	Elizabethtown-Fort Knox, KY**	NA	225	Kankakee, IL	(16.8)
NA	Boston, MA M.D.**	NA	NA	Elmira, NY**	NA	NA	Kansas City, MO-KS**	NA
196	Boulder, CO	(10.7)	251	Erie, PA	(27.9)	211	Kennewick-Richland, WA	(13.1)
176	Bowling Green, KY	(6.7)	102	Eugene, OR	6.6	43	Killeen-Temple, TX	19.2
220	Bremerton-Silverdale, WA	(14.6)	6	Fairbanks, AK	69.0	165	Kingsport, TN-VA	(4.9)
2	Bridgeport-Stamford, CT	109.1	NA	Fargo, ND-MN**	NA	NA	Kingston, NY**	NA
107	Brownsville-Harlingen, TX	5.0	26	Farmington, NM	30.0	NA	Knoxville, TN**	NA
250	Brunswick, GA	(26.9)	NA	Fayetteville-Springdale, AR-MO**	NA	NA	Kokomo, IN**	NA
NA	Buffalo-Niagara Falls, NY**	NA	42	Fayetteville, NC	19.5	NA	La Crosse, WI-MN**	NA
33	Burlington, NC	23.5	254	Flagstaff, AZ	(31.6)	66	Lafayette, IN	12.1
NA	California-Lexington Park, MD**	NA	111	Flint, MI	4.5	NA	Lafayette, LA**	NA
NA	Cambridge-Newton, MA M.D.**	NA	3	Florence-Muscle Shoals, AL	100.0	55	Lake Co.-Kenosha Co., IL-WI M.D.	15.3
170	Camden, NJ M.D.	(5.6)	203	Florence, SC	(11.8)	253	Lake Havasu City-Kingman, AZ	(31.5)
158	Canton, OH	(3.8)	179	Fond du Lac, WI	(7.0)	210	Lakeland, FL	(12.8)
139	Cape Coral-Fort Myers, FL	(0.6)	202	Fort Collins, CO	(11.7)	151	Lancaster, PA	(2.7)
267	Cape Girardeau, MO-IL	(48.9)	223	Fort Lauderdale, FL M.D.	(16.1)	144	Lansing-East Lansing, MI	(1.3)
135	Carson City, NV	0.0	NA	Fort Smith, AR-OK**	NA	134	Laredo, TX	0.3
269	Casper, WY	(57.1)	180	Fort Wayne, IN	(7.3)	8	Las Cruces, NM	57.3
78	Cedar Rapids, IA	10.3	129	Fort Worth-Arlington, TX M.D.	0.9	168	Las Vegas-Henderson, NV	(5.4)
NA	Chambersburg-Waynesboro, PA**	NA	63	Fresno, CA	12.4	18	Lawrence, KS	46.9
70	Champaign-Urbana, IL	11.7	64	Gadsden, AL	12.3	NA	Lawton, OK**	NA
NA	Charleston-North Charleston, SC**	NA	77	Gainesville, FL	10.4	185	Lebanon, PA	(8.2)
181	Charlottesville, VA	(7.4)	93	Gainesville, GA	7.7	44	Lewiston-Auburn, ME	18.9

Note: All listings are for Metropolitan Statistical Areas (M.S.A.s) except for those ending with "M.D." Listings with "M.D." are Metropolitan Divisions which are smaller parts of eleven large M.S.A.s. See explanatory note at beginning of metropolitan area section.

RANK	METROPOLITAN AREA	% CHANGE	RANK	METROPOLITAN AREA	% CHANGE	RANK	METROPOLITAN AREA	% CHANGE
NA	Lewiston, ID-WA**	NA	261	Owensboro, KY	(42.9)	107	Silver Spring-Frederick, MD M.D.	5.0
NA	Lexington-Fayette, KY**	NA	146	Oxnard-Thousand Oaks, CA	(1.7)	NA	Sioux City, IA-NE-SD**	NA
84	Lima, OH	9.2	58	Palm Bay-Melbourne, FL	14.2	36	Sioux Falls, SD	22.2
73	Lincoln, NE	11.2	NA	Panama City, FL**	NA	94	South Bend-Mishawaka, IN-MI	7.6
147	Little Rock, AR	(1.9)	NA	Parkersburg-Vienna, WV**	NA	NA	Spartanburg, SC**	NA
5	Logan, UT-ID	74.5	173	Pensacola, FL	(6.4)	NA	Spokane, WA**	NA
29	Longview, TX	25.9	244	Peoria, IL	(23.7)	237	Springfield, IL	(21.1)
217	Longview, WA	(13.7)	NA	Philadelphia (greater) PA-NJ-MD-DE**	NA	NA	Springfield, MA**	NA
119	Los Angeles County, CA M.D.	3.1	NA	Philadelphia, PA M.D.**	NA	21	Springfield, MO	39.9
122	Los Angeles (greater), CA	2.2	NA	Phoenix-Mesa-Scottsdale, AZ**	NA	30	Springfield, OH	25.8
230	Louisville, KY-IN	(18.5)	174	Pine Bluff, AR	(6.6)	256	State College, PA	(32.2)
14	Lubbock, TX	48.3	221	Pittsburgh, PA	(15.6)	NA	Staunton-Waynesboro, VA**	NA
38	Lynchburg, VA	21.1	125	Pittsfield, MA	1.8	98	Stockton-Lodi, CA	6.9
48	Macon, GA	17.5	NA	Pocatello, ID**	NA	NA	St. George, UT**	NA
27	Madera, CA	28.2	19	Port St. Lucie, FL	46.2	217	St. Joseph, MO-KS	(13.7)
NA	Madison, WI**	NA	156	Portland-Vancouver, OR-WA	(3.6)	95	St. Louis, MO-IL	7.5
68	Manchester-Nashua, NH	12.0	130	Portland, ME	0.8	65	Sumter, SC	12.2
NA	Manhattan, KS**	NA	28	Prescott, AZ	28.0	NA	Syracuse, NY**	NA
NA	Mankato-North Mankato, MN**	NA	NA	Providence-Warwick, RI-MA**	NA	158	Tacoma, WA M.D.	(3.8)
183	Mansfield, OH	(7.5)	235	Provo-Orem, UT	(20.5)	112	Tallahassee, FL	4.3
206	McAllen-Edinburg-Mission, TX	(12.3)	268	Pueblo, CO	(49.0)	133	Tampa-St Petersburg, FL	0.4
115	Medford, OR	3.8	243	Punta Gorda, FL	(22.5)	96	Terre Haute, IN	7.2
118	Memphis, TN-MS-AR	3.2	15	Racine, WI	47.8	NA	Texarkana, TX-AR**	NA
208	Merced, CA	(12.7)	197	Raleigh, NC	(10.8)	NA	The Villages, FL**	NA
185	Miami (greater), FL	(8.2)	NA	Rapid City, SD**	NA	NA	Toledo, OH**	NA
208	Miami-Dade County, FL M.D.	(12.7)	11	Reading, PA	52.0	245	Topeka, KS	(24.3)
201	Michigan City-La Porte, IN	(11.2)	143	Redding, CA	(1.1)	170	Trenton, NJ	(5.6)
NA	Midland, MI**	NA	165	Reno, NV	(4.9)	41	Tucson, AZ	19.6
NA	Midland, TX**	NA	205	Richmond, VA	(12.2)	49	Tulsa, OK	17.1
79	Milwaukee, WI	10.1	154	Riverside-San Bernardino, CA	(3.4)	NA	Tuscaloosa, AL**	NA
NA	Minneapolis-St. Paul, MN-WI**	NA	121	Roanoke, VA	2.6	194	Tyler, TX	(10.1)
96	Missoula, MT	7.2	NA	Rochester, MN**	NA	NA	Utica-Rome, NY**	NA
135	Mobile, AL	0.0	NA	Rochester, NY**	NA	17	Valdosta, GA	47.3
83	Modesto, CA	9.3	35	Rockford, IL	22.3	127	Vallejo-Fairfield, CA	1.5
229	Monroe, LA	(18.3)	53	Rockingham County, NH M.D.	16.5	NA	Victoria, TX**	NA
119	Monroe, MI	3.1	13	Rocky Mount, NC	48.5	NA	Vineland-Bridgeton, NJ**	NA
NA	Montgomery County, PA M.D.**	NA	174	Rome, GA	(6.6)	169	Virginia Beach-Norfolk, VA-NC	(5.5)
61	Montgomery, AL	13.4	153	Sacramento, CA	(3.2)	51	Visalia-Porterville, CA	16.7
NA	Morgantown, WV**	NA	20	Saginaw, MI	40.0	NA	Waco, TX**	NA
NA	Morristown, TN**	NA	125	Salem, OR	1.8	NA	Walla Walla, WA**	NA
233	Mount Vernon-Anacortes, WA	(19.4)	144	Salinas, CA	(1.3)	NA	Warner Robins, GA**	NA
270	Muncie, IN	(82.0)	NA	Salisbury, MD-DE**	NA	89	Warren-Troy, MI M.D.	8.5
207	Napa, CA	(12.6)	68	Salt Lake City, UT	12.0	107	Washington (greater) DC-VA-MD-WV	5.0
199	Naples-Marco Island, FL	(10.9)	46	San Antonio, TX	17.8	110	Washington, DC-VA-MD-WV M.D.	4.7
NA	Nashville-Davidson, TN**	NA	117	San Diego, CA	3.3	76	Waterloo-Cedar Falls, IA	10.9
NA	Nassau-Suffolk, NY M.D.**	NA	140	San Francisco (greater), CA	(1.0)	NA	Watertown-Fort Drum, NY**	NA
NA	New Bern, NC**	NA	236	San Francisco-Redwood, CA M.D.	(21.0)	261	Wausau, WI	(42.9)
54	New Haven-Milford, CT	16.2	71	San Jose, CA	11.6	75	West Palm Beach, FL M.D.	11.0
200	New Orleans, LA	(11.0)	247	San Luis Obispo, CA	(24.9)	NA	Wheeling, WV-OH**	NA
NA	New York (greater), NY-NJ-PA**	NA	NA	San Rafael, CA M.D.**	NA	128	Wichita Falls, TX	1.3
NA	New York-Jersey City, NY-NJ M.D.**	NA	132	Santa Cruz-Watsonville, CA	0.7	191	Wichita, KS	(9.2)
NA	Newark, NJ-PA M.D.**	NA	227	Santa Fe, NM	(17.0)	66	Williamsport, PA	12.1
91	North Port-Sarasota-Bradenton, FL	8.1	NA	Santa Maria-Santa Barbara, CA**	NA	156	Wilmington, DE-MD-NJ M.D.	(3.6)
249	Norwich-New London, CT	(26.4)	81	Santa Rosa, CA	9.6	NA	Wilmington, NC**	NA
72	Oakland-Hayward, CA M.D.	11.3	216	Savannah, GA	(13.5)	140	Winchester, VA-WV	(1.0)
123	Ocala, FL	2.1	40	Scranton--Wilkes-Barre, PA	20.3	NA	Winston-Salem, NC**	NA
177	Ocean City, NJ	(6.8)	161	Seattle (greater), WA	(4.0)	NA	Worcester, MA-CT**	NA
59	Odessa, TX	14.0	160	Seattle-Bellevue-Everett, WA M.D.	(3.9)	255	Yakima, WA	(31.7)
NA	Ogden-Clearfield, UT**	NA	266	Sebastian-Vero Beach, FL	(47.2)	248	York-Hanover, PA	(26.3)
57	Oklahoma City, OK	14.6	NA	Sebring, FL**	NA	NA	Youngstown-Warren, OH-PA**	NA
22	Olympia, WA	38.5	16	Sheboygan, WI	47.6	124	Yuba City, CA	1.9
192	Omaha-Council Bluffs, NE-IA	(9.5)	7	Sherman-Denison, TX	68.8	219	Yuma, AZ	(14.5)
149	Orlando, FL	(2.2)	NA	Shreveport-Bossier City, LA**	NA			
50	Oshkosh-Neenah, WI	16.8	NA	Sierra Vista-Douglas, AZ**	NA			

Source: CQ Press using reported data from the F.B.I. "Crime in the United States 2012"

*Forcible rape is the carnal knowledge of a female forcibly and against her will. Assaults or attempts to commit rape by force or threat of force are included. However, statutory rape without force and other sex offenses are excluded. **Not available

15. Percent Change in Rape Rate: 2011 to 2012 (continued)
National Percent Change = 0.5% Decrease*

RANK	METROPOLITAN AREA	% CHANGE	RANK	METROPOLITAN AREA	% CHANGE	RANK	METROPOLITAN AREA	% CHANGE
1	Hinesville, GA	130.0	65	Sumter, SC	12.2	129	Fort Worth-Arlington, TX M.D.	0.9
2	Bridgeport-Stamford, CT	109.1	66	Lafayette, IN	12.1	130	Billings, MT	0.8
3	Florence-Muscle Shoals, AL	100.0	66	Williamsport, PA	12.1	130	Portland, ME	0.8
4	Hanford-Corcoran, CA	82.5	68	Manchester-Nashua, NH	12.0	132	Santa Cruz-Watsonville, CA	0.7
5	Logan, UT-ID	74.5	68	Salt Lake City, UT	12.0	133	Tampa-St Petersburg, FL	0.4
6	Fairbanks, AK	69.0	70	Champaign-Urbana, IL	11.7	134	Laredo, TX	0.3
7	Sherman-Denison, TX	68.8	71	San Jose, CA	11.6	135	Carson City, NV	0.0
8	Las Cruces, NM	57.3	72	Oakland-Hayward, CA M.D.	11.3	135	Chico, CA	0.0
9	Athens-Clarke County, GA	56.2	73	Lincoln, NE	11.2	135	Mobile, AL	0.0
10	Ames, IA	53.5	74	Colorado Springs, CO	11.1	138	Great Falls, MT	(0.5)
11	Reading, PA	52.0	75	West Palm Beach, FL M.D.	11.0	139	Cape Coral-Fort Myers, FL	(0.6)
12	Goldsboro, NC	50.0	76	Waterloo-Cedar Falls, IA	10.9	140	Des Moines-West Des Moines, IA	(1.0)
13	Rocky Mount, NC	48.5	77	Gainesville, FL	10.4	140	San Francisco (greater), CA	(1.0)
14	Lubbock, TX	48.3	78	Cedar Rapids, IA	10.3	140	Winchester, VA-WV	(1.0)
15	Racine, WI	47.8	79	Milwaukee, WI	10.1	143	Redding, CA	(1.1)
16	Sheboygan, WI	47.6	80	Joplin, MO	9.9	144	Lansing-East Lansing, MI	(1.3)
17	Valdosta, GA	47.3	81	Austin-Round Rock, TX	9.6	144	Salinas, CA	(1.3)
18	Lawrence, KS	46.9	81	Santa Rosa, CA	9.6	146	Oxnard-Thousand Oaks, CA	(1.7)
19	Port St. Lucie, FL	46.2	83	Modesto, CA	9.3	147	Little Rock, AR	(1.9)
20	Saginaw, MI	40.0	84	Lima, OH	9.2	148	Baltimore, MD	(2.0)
21	Springfield, MO	39.9	85	Jefferson City, MO	8.9	149	Orlando, FL	(2.2)
22	Olympia, WA	38.5	86	Iowa City, IA	8.8	150	Atlanta, GA	(2.4)
23	Columbus, IN	36.9	87	Dayton, OH	8.7	151	Lancaster, PA	(2.7)
24	Bismarck, ND	35.0	88	Crestview-Fort Walton Beach, FL	8.6	152	Harrisburg-Carlisle, PA	(3.0)
25	Asheville, NC	34.1	89	Cleveland, TN	8.5	153	Sacramento, CA	(3.2)
26	Farmington, NM	30.0	89	Warren-Troy, MI M.D.	8.5	154	Riverside-San Bernardino, CA	(3.4)
27	Madera, CA	28.2	91	Dallas-Plano-Irving, TX M.D.	8.1	155	Beaumont-Port Arthur, TX	(3.5)
28	Prescott, AZ	28.0	91	North Port-Sarasota-Bradenton, FL	8.1	156	Portland-Vancouver, OR-WA	(3.6)
29	Longview, TX	25.9	93	Gainesville, GA	7.7	156	Wilmington, DE-MD-NJ M.D.	(3.6)
30	Springfield, OH	25.8	94	South Bend-Mishawaka, IN-MI	7.6	158	Canton, OH	(3.8)
31	Johnson City, TN	25.3	95	St. Louis, MO-IL	7.5	158	Tacoma, WA M.D.	(3.8)
32	Abilene, TX	24.9	96	Missoula, MT	7.2	160	Seattle-Bellevue-Everett, WA M.D.	(3.9)
33	Burlington, NC	23.5	96	Terre Haute, IN	7.2	161	Jacksonville, FL	(4.0)
34	Atlantic City, NJ	22.9	98	Columbia, MO	6.9	161	Seattle (greater), WA	(4.0)
35	Rockford, IL	22.3	98	Stockton-Lodi, CA	6.9	163	Anaheim-Santa Ana-Irvine, CA M.D.	(4.4)
36	Sioux Falls, SD	22.2	100	Akron, OH	6.7	164	Huntsville, AL	(4.5)
37	Dothan, AL	21.9	100	Bellingham, WA	6.7	165	Kingsport, TN-VA	(4.9)
38	Lynchburg, VA	21.1	102	Eugene, OR	6.6	165	Reno, NV	(4.9)
39	Boise City, ID	21.0	103	College Station-Bryan, TX	6.5	167	Blacksburg, VA	(5.1)
40	Scranton--Wilkes-Barre, PA	20.3	104	Detroit (greater), MI	5.9	168	Las Vegas-Henderson, NV	(5.4)
41	Tucson, AZ	19.6	105	Corvallis, OR	5.8	169	Virginia Beach-Norfolk, VA-NC	(5.5)
42	Fayetteville, NC	19.5	106	Dallas (greater), TX	5.2	170	Camden, NJ M.D.	(5.6)
43	Killeen-Temple, TX	19.2	107	Brownsville-Harlingen, TX	5.0	170	Trenton, NJ	(5.6)
44	Lewiston-Auburn, ME	18.9	107	Silver Spring-Frederick, MD M.D.	5.0	172	Greeley, CO	(6.2)
45	Decatur, IL	18.5	107	Washington (greater) DC-VA-MD-WV	5.0	173	Pensacola, FL	(6.4)
46	San Antonio, TX	17.8	110	Washington, DC-VA-MD-WV M.D.	4.7	174	Pine Bluff, AR	(6.6)
47	Idaho Falls, ID	17.7	111	Flint, MI	4.5	174	Rome, GA	(6.6)
48	Macon, GA	17.5	112	Tallahassee, FL	4.3	176	Bowling Green, KY	(6.7)
49	Tulsa, OK	17.1	113	Detroit-Dearborn-Livonia, MI M.D.	4.2	177	Ocean City, NJ	(6.8)
50	Oshkosh-Neenah, WI	16.8	114	Albuquerque, NM	4.0	178	Bakersfield, CA	(6.9)
51	Visalia-Porterville, CA	16.7	115	Medford, OR	3.8	179	Fond du Lac, WI	(7.0)
52	Grand Junction, CO	16.6	116	Amarillo, TX	3.4	180	Fort Wayne, IN	(7.3)
53	Rockingham County, NH M.D.	16.5	117	San Diego, CA	3.3	181	Charlottesville, VA	(7.4)
54	New Haven-Milford, CT	16.2	118	Memphis, TN-MS-AR	3.2	181	Durham-Chapel Hill, NC	(7.4)
55	Lake Co.-Kenosha Co., IL-WI M.D.	15.3	119	Los Angeles County, CA M.D.	3.1	183	Mansfield, OH	(7.5)
56	Hickory, NC	14.8	119	Monroe, MI	3.1	184	Bay City, MI	(7.7)
57	Oklahoma City, OK	14.6	121	Roanoke, VA	2.6	185	Baton Rouge, LA	(8.2)
58	Palm Bay-Melbourne, FL	14.2	122	Los Angeles (greater), CA	2.2	185	Corpus Christi, TX	(8.2)
59	Odessa, TX	14.0	123	Ocala, FL	2.1	185	Lebanon, PA	(8.2)
60	Dubuque, IA	13.5	124	Yuba City, CA	1.9	185	Miami (greater), FL	(8.2)
61	Montgomery, AL	13.4	125	Pittsfield, MA	1.8	189	Houston, TX	(9.0)
62	Janesville, WI	13.2	125	Salem, OR	1.8	190	Green Bay, WI	(9.1)
63	Fresno, CA	12.4	127	Vallejo-Fairfield, CA	1.5	191	Wichita, KS	(9.2)
64	Gadsden, AL	12.3	128	Wichita Falls, TX	1.3	192	Omaha-Council Bluffs, NE-IA	(9.5)

Note: All listings are for Metropolitan Statistical Areas (M.S.A.s) except for those ending with "M.D." Listings with "M.D." are Metropolitan Divisions which are smaller parts of eleven large M.S.A.s. See explanatory note at beginning of metropolitan area section.

RANK	METROPOLITAN AREA	% CHANGE	RANK	METROPOLITAN AREA	% CHANGE	RANK	METROPOLITAN AREA	% CHANGE
193	Bangor, ME	(9.6)	257	El Centro, CA	(33.0)	NA	Knoxville, TN**	NA
194	Dalton, GA	(10.1)	258	Davenport, IA-IL	(33.3)	NA	Kokomo, IN**	NA
194	Tyler, TX	(10.1)	259	Barnstable Town, MA	(37.5)	NA	La Crosse, WI-MN**	NA
196	Boulder, CO	(10.7)	260	Johnstown, PA	(41.2)	NA	Lafayette, LA**	NA
197	El Paso, TX	(10.8)	261	Owensboro, KY	(42.9)	NA	Lawton, OK**	NA
197	Raleigh, NC	(10.8)	261	Wausau, WI	(42.9)	NA	Lewiston, ID-WA**	NA
199	Naples-Marco Island, FL	(10.9)	263	Dover, DE	(45.6)	NA	Lexington-Fayette, KY**	NA
200	New Orleans, LA	(11.0)	264	Decatur, AL	(46.0)	NA	Madison, WI**	NA
201	Michigan City-La Porte, IN	(11.2)	265	Houma, LA	(46.4)	NA	Manhattan, KS**	NA
202	Fort Collins, CO	(11.7)	266	Sebastian-Vero Beach, FL	(47.2)	NA	Mankato-North Mankato, MN**	NA
203	Florence, SC	(11.8)	267	Cape Girardeau, MO-IL	(48.9)	NA	Midland, MI**	NA
204	Appleton, WI	(12.1)	268	Pueblo, CO	(49.0)	NA	Midland, TX**	NA
205	Richmond, VA	(12.2)	269	Casper, WY	(57.1)	NA	Minneapolis-St. Paul, MN-WI**	NA
206	McAllen-Edinburg-Mission, TX	(12.3)	270	Muncie, IN	(82.0)	NA	Montgomery County, PA M.D.**	NA
207	Napa, CA	(12.6)	NA	Albany-Schenectady-Troy, NY**	NA	NA	Morgantown, WV**	NA
208	Merced, CA	(12.7)	NA	Albany, OR**	NA	NA	Morristown, TN**	NA
208	Miami-Dade County, FL M.D.	(12.7)	NA	Allentown, PA-NJ**	NA	NA	Nashville-Davidson, TN**	NA
210	Lakeland, FL	(12.8)	NA	Anchorage, AK**	NA	NA	Nassau-Suffolk, NY M.D.**	NA
211	Kennewick-Richland, WA	(13.1)	NA	Beckley, WV**	NA	NA	New Bern, NC**	NA
212	Alexandria, LA	(13.2)	NA	Binghamton, NY**	NA	NA	New York (greater), NY-NJ-PA**	NA
213	Anniston-Oxford, AL	(13.3)	NA	Bloomington, IN**	NA	NA	New York-Jersey City, NY-NJ M.D.**	NA
213	Birmingham-Hoover, AL	(13.3)	NA	Bloomsburg-Berwick, PA**	NA	NA	Newark, NJ-PA M.D.**	NA
215	Ann Arbor, MI	(13.4)	NA	Boston (greater), MA-NH**	NA	NA	Ogden-Clearfield, UT**	NA
216	Savannah, GA	(13.5)	NA	Boston, MA M.D.**	NA	NA	Panama City, FL**	NA
217	Longview, WA	(13.7)	NA	Buffalo-Niagara Falls, NY**	NA	NA	Parkersburg-Vienna, WV**	NA
217	St. Joseph, MO-KS	(13.7)	NA	California-Lexington Park, MD**	NA	NA	Philadelphia (greater) PA-NJ-MD-DE**	NA
219	Yuma, AZ	(14.5)	NA	Cambridge-Newton, MA M.D.**	NA	NA	Philadelphia, PA M.D.**	NA
220	Bremerton-Silverdale, WA	(14.6)	NA	Chambersburg-Waynesboro, PA**	NA	NA	Phoenix-Mesa-Scottsdale, AZ**	NA
221	Pittsburgh, PA	(15.6)	NA	Charleston-North Charleston, SC**	NA	NA	Pocatello, ID**	NA
222	Columbus, GA-AL	(16.0)	NA	Chicago (greater), IL-IN-WI**	NA	NA	Providence-Warwick, RI-MA**	NA
223	Fort Lauderdale, FL M.D.	(16.1)	NA	Chicago-Joilet-Naperville, IL M.D.**	NA	NA	Rapid City, SD**	NA
224	Cumberland, MD-WV	(16.7)	NA	Cincinnati, OH-KY-IN**	NA	NA	Rochester, MN**	NA
225	Cheyenne, WY	(16.8)	NA	Coeur d'Alene, ID**	NA	NA	Rochester, NY**	NA
225	Kankakee, IL	(16.8)	NA	Daphne-Fairhope-Foley, AL**	NA	NA	Salisbury, MD-DE**	NA
227	Santa Fe, NM	(17.0)	NA	Deltona-Daytona Beach, FL**	NA	NA	San Rafael, CA M.D.**	NA
228	Gary, IN M.D.	(17.6)	NA	Denver-Aurora, CO**	NA	NA	Santa Maria-Santa Barbara, CA**	NA
229	Monroe, LA	(18.3)	NA	Duluth, MN-WI**	NA	NA	Sebring, FL**	NA
230	Louisville, KY-IN	(18.5)	NA	Dutchess-Putnam, NY M.D.**	NA	NA	Shreveport-Bossier City, LA**	NA
231	Danville, IL	(18.9)	NA	East Stroudsburg, PA**	NA	NA	Sierra Vista-Douglas, AZ**	NA
232	Clarksville, TN-KY	(19.2)	NA	Elgin, IL M.D.**	NA	NA	Sioux City, IA-NE-SD**	NA
233	Mount Vernon-Anacortes, WA	(19.4)	NA	Elizabethtown-Fort Knox, KY**	NA	NA	Spartanburg, SC**	NA
234	Auburn, AL	(20.3)	NA	Elmira, NY**	NA	NA	Spokane, WA**	NA
235	Provo-Orem, UT	(20.5)	NA	Fargo, ND-MN**	NA	NA	Springfield, MA**	NA
236	San Francisco-Redwood, CA M.D.	(21.0)	NA	Fayetteville-Springdale, AR-MO**	NA	NA	Staunton-Waynesboro, VA**	NA
237	Springfield, IL	(21.1)	NA	Fort Smith, AR-OK**	NA	NA	St. George, UT**	NA
238	Altoona, PA	(21.2)	NA	Gettysburg, PA**	NA	NA	Syracuse, NY**	NA
239	Harrisonburg, VA	(21.3)	NA	Glens Falls, NY**	NA	NA	Texarkana, TX-AR**	NA
239	Jonesboro, AR	(21.3)	NA	Grand Forks, ND-MN**	NA	NA	The Villages, FL**	NA
241	Augusta, GA-SC	(21.7)	NA	Grand Island, NE**	NA	NA	Toledo, OH**	NA
242	Hartford, CT	(22.3)	NA	Greensboro-High Point, NC**	NA	NA	Tuscaloosa, AL**	NA
243	Punta Gorda, FL	(22.5)	NA	Greenville-Anderson, SC**	NA	NA	Utica-Rome, NY**	NA
244	Peoria, IL	(23.7)	NA	Greenville, NC**	NA	NA	Victoria, TX**	NA
245	Topeka, KS	(24.3)	NA	Hagerstown-Martinsburg, MD-WV**	NA	NA	Vineland-Bridgeton, NJ**	NA
246	Bloomington, IL	(24.6)	NA	Hammond, LA**	NA	NA	Waco, TX**	NA
247	San Luis Obispo, CA	(24.9)	NA	Hattiesburg, MS**	NA	NA	Walla Walla, WA**	NA
248	York-Hanover, PA	(26.3)	NA	Hilton Head Island, SC**	NA	NA	Warner Robins, GA**	NA
249	Norwich-New London, CT	(26.4)	NA	Homosassa Springs, FL**	NA	NA	Watertown-Fort Drum, NY**	NA
250	Brunswick, GA	(26.9)	NA	Indianapolis, IN**	NA	NA	Wheeling, WV-OH**	NA
251	Erie, PA	(27.9)	NA	Jackson, MS**	NA	NA	Wilmington, NC**	NA
252	Albany, GA	(29.4)	NA	Jackson, TN**	NA	NA	Winston-Salem, NC**	NA
253	Lake Havasu City-Kingman, AZ	(31.5)	NA	Kahului-Wailuku-Lahaina, HI**	NA	NA	Worcester, MA-CT**	NA
254	Flagstaff, AZ	(31.6)	NA	Kalamazoo-Portage, MI**	NA	NA	Youngstown-Warren, OH-PA**	NA
255	Yakima, WA	(31.7)	NA	Kansas City, MO-KS**	NA			
256	State College, PA	(32.2)	NA	Kingston, NY**	NA			

Source: CQ Press using reported data from the F.B.I. "Crime in the United States 2012"

*Forcible rape is the carnal knowledge of a female forcibly and against her will. Assaults or attempts to commit rape by force or threat of force are included. However, statutory rape without force and other sex offenses are excluded. **Not available

16. Percent Change in Rape Rate: 2008 to 2012
National Percent Change = 9.9% Decrease*

RANK	METROPOLITAN AREA	% CHANGE	RANK	METROPOLITAN AREA	% CHANGE	RANK	METROPOLITAN AREA	% CHANGE
246	Abilene, TX	(55.4)	65	Cheyenne, WY	6.4	NA	Gary, IN M.D.**	NA
94	Akron, OH	(1.7)	NA	Chicago (greater), IL-IN-WI**	NA	NA	Gettysburg, PA**	NA
NA	Albany-Schenectady-Troy, NY**	NA	NA	Chicago-Joilet-Naperville, IL M.D.**	NA	NA	Glens Falls, NY**	NA
NA	Albany, GA**	NA	171	Chico, CA	(19.6)	22	Goldsboro, NC	35.8
NA	Albany, OR**	NA	NA	Cincinnati, OH-KY-IN**	NA	NA	Grand Forks, ND-MN**	NA
222	Albuquerque, NM	(33.0)	147	Clarksville, TN-KY	(13.6)	NA	Grand Island, NE**	NA
NA	Alexandria, LA**	NA	107	Cleveland, TN	(5.0)	34	Grand Junction, CO	22.9
NA	Allentown, PA-NJ**	NA	NA	Coeur d'Alene, ID**	NA	15	Great Falls, MT	44.8
16	Altoona, PA	44.2	232	College Station-Bryan, TX	(40.3)	165	Greeley, CO	(17.8)
163	Amarillo, TX	(17.3)	90	Colorado Springs, CO	(0.4)	224	Green Bay, WI	(37.4)
45	Ames, IA	15.1	6	Columbia, MO	68.9	221	Greensboro-High Point, NC	(32.9)
131	Anaheim-Santa Ana-Irvine, CA M.D.	(9.8)	230	Columbus, GA-AL	(39.2)	NA	Greenville-Anderson, SC**	NA
NA	Anchorage, AK**	NA	3	Columbus, IN	243.3	24	Greenville, NC	33.8
43	Ann Arbor, MI	16.4	111	Corpus Christi, TX	(6.2)	NA	Hagerstown-Martinsburg, MD-WV**	NA
NA	Anniston-Oxford, AL**	NA	131	Corvallis, OR	(9.8)	NA	Hammond, LA**	NA
110	Appleton, WI	(5.9)	NA	Crestview-Fort Walton Beach, FL**	NA	5	Hanford-Corcoran, CA	97.8
94	Asheville, NC	(1.7)	54	Cumberland, MD-WV	10.2	75	Harrisburg-Carlisle, PA	3.6
71	Athens-Clarke County, GA	4.4	122	Dallas (greater), TX	(8.7)	40	Harrisonburg, VA	19.2
84	Atlanta, GA	1.5	127	Dallas-Plano-Irving, TX M.D.	(9.3)	203	Hartford, CT	(26.4)
57	Atlantic City, NJ	8.5	99	Dalton, GA	(2.6)	NA	Hattiesburg, MS**	NA
250	Auburn, AL	(63.0)	NA	Danville, IL**	NA	154	Hickory, NC	(14.4)
231	Augusta, GA-SC	(40.1)	NA	Daphne-Fairhope-Foley, AL**	NA	NA	Hilton Head Island, SC**	NA
144	Austin-Round Rock, TX	(13.2)	NA	Davenport, IA-IL**	NA	7	Hinesville, GA	66.8
215	Bakersfield, CA	(30.3)	112	Dayton, OH	(6.5)	NA	Homosassa Springs, FL**	NA
35	Baltimore, MD	21.4	244	Decatur, AL	(51.7)	242	Houma, LA	(48.0)
30	Bangor, ME	30.9	NA	Decatur, IL**	NA	180	Houston, TX	(20.8)
178	Barnstable Town, MA	(20.4)	239	Deltona-Daytona Beach, FL	(46.4)	190	Huntsville, AL	(23.4)
167	Baton Rouge, LA	(18.8)	NA	Denver-Aurora, CO**	NA	169	Idaho Falls, ID	(19.3)
88	Bay City, MI	0.6	219	Des Moines-West Des Moines, IA	(31.8)	135	Indianapolis, IN	(10.0)
199	Beaumont-Port Arthur, TX	(25.7)	NA	Detroit (greater), MI**	NA	98	Iowa City, IA	(2.3)
NA	Beckley, WV**	NA	NA	Detroit-Dearborn-Livonia, MI M.D.**	NA	62	Jacksonville, FL	6.9
20	Bellingham, WA	37.9	105	Dothan, AL	(4.2)	NA	Jackson, MS**	NA
200	Billings, MT	(25.8)	245	Dover, DE	(55.3)	NA	Jackson, TN**	NA
NA	Binghamton, NY**	NA	130	Dubuque, IA	(9.6)	184	Janesville, WI	(21.5)
196	Birmingham-Hoover, AL	(24.0)	NA	Duluth, MN-WI**	NA	NA	Jefferson City, MO**	NA
49	Bismarck, ND	13.9	113	Durham-Chapel Hill, NC	(7.4)	241	Johnson City, TN	(47.3)
148	Blacksburg, VA	(13.9)	NA	Dutchess-Putnam, NY M.D.**	NA	17	Johnstown, PA	42.5
NA	Bloomington, IL**	NA	NA	East Stroudsburg, PA**	NA	174	Jonesboro, AR	(20.1)
23	Bloomington, IN	35.7	141	El Centro, CA	(11.9)	108	Joplin, MO	(5.1)
NA	Bloomsburg-Berwick, PA**	NA	117	El Paso, TX	(8.0)	NA	Kahului-Wailuku-Lahaina, HI**	NA
180	Boise City, ID	(20.8)	NA	Elgin, IL M.D.**	NA	75	Kalamazoo-Portage, MI	3.6
NA	Boston (greater), MA-NH**	NA	NA	Elizabethtown-Fort Knox, KY**	NA	NA	Kankakee, IL**	NA
NA	Boston, MA M.D.**	NA	NA	Elmira, NY**	NA	NA	Kansas City, MO-KS**	NA
NA	Boulder, CO**	NA	207	Erie, PA	(27.0)	198	Kennewick-Richland, WA	(24.9)
228	Bowling Green, KY	(37.9)	52	Eugene, OR	11.3	87	Killeen-Temple, TX	0.8
243	Bremerton-Silverdale, WA	(50.3)	NA	Fairbanks, AK**	NA	169	Kingsport, TN-VA	(19.3)
2	Bridgeport-Stamford, CT	243.5	NA	Fargo, ND-MN**	NA	NA	Kingston, NY**	NA
217	Brownsville-Harlingen, TX	(31.1)	161	Farmington, NM	(15.6)	NA	Knoxville, TN**	NA
NA	Brunswick, GA**	NA	100	Fayetteville-Springdale, AR-MO	(2.7)	NA	Kokomo, IN**	NA
NA	Buffalo-Niagara Falls, NY**	NA	179	Fayetteville, NC	(20.6)	NA	La Crosse, WI-MN**	NA
85	Burlington, NC	0.9	238	Flagstaff, AZ	(44.6)	8	Lafayette, IN	61.8
NA	California-Lexington Park, MD**	NA	75	Flint, MI	3.6	NA	Lafayette, LA**	NA
NA	Cambridge-Newton, MA M.D.**	NA	139	Florence-Muscle Shoals, AL	(11.0)	NA	Lake Co.-Kenosha Co., IL-WI M.D.**	NA
186	Camden, NJ M.D.	(21.7)	237	Florence, SC	(43.2)	233	Lake Havasu City-Kingman, AZ	(40.6)
NA	Canton, OH**	NA	69	Fond du Lac, WI	4.7	210	Lakeland, FL	(28.4)
223	Cape Coral-Fort Myers, FL	(34.6)	226	Fort Collins, CO	(37.5)	135	Lancaster, PA	(10.0)
208	Cape Girardeau, MO-IL	(28.0)	192	Fort Lauderdale, FL M.D.	(23.8)	126	Lansing-East Lansing, MI	(9.2)
89	Carson City, NV	0.0	NA	Fort Smith, AR-OK**	NA	104	Laredo, TX	(4.1)
252	Casper, WY	(81.7)	143	Fort Wayne, IN	(13.1)	28	Las Cruces, NM	32.1
19	Cedar Rapids, IA	39.6	119	Fort Worth-Arlington, TX M.D.	(8.4)	183	Las Vegas-Henderson, NV	(21.4)
NA	Chambersburg-Waynesboro, PA**	NA	105	Fresno, CA	(4.2)	37	Lawrence, KS	21.2
NA	Champaign-Urbana, IL**	NA	102	Gadsden, AL	(3.2)	NA	Lawton, OK**	NA
212	Charleston-North Charleston, SC	(28.9)	96	Gainesville, FL	(1.9)	55	Lebanon, PA	9.2
164	Charlottesville, VA	(17.5)	NA	Gainesville, GA**	NA	35	Lewiston-Auburn, ME	21.4

Note: All listings are for Metropolitan Statistical Areas (M.S.A.s) except for those ending with "M.D." Listings with "M.D." are Metropolitan Divisions which are smaller parts of eleven large M.S.A.s. See explanatory note at beginning of metropolitan area section.

RANK	METROPOLITAN AREA	% CHANGE	RANK	METROPOLITAN AREA	% CHANGE	RANK	METROPOLITAN AREA	% CHANGE
68	Lewiston, ID-WA	5.5	NA	Owensboro, KY**	NA	113	Silver Spring-Frederick, MD M.D.	(7.4)
NA	Lexington-Fayette, KY**	NA	188	Oxnard-Thousand Oaks, CA	(23.2)	NA	Sioux City, IA-NE-SD**	NA
150	Lima, OH	(14.1)	58	Palm Bay-Melbourne, FL	8.4	64	Sioux Falls, SD	6.7
11	Lincoln, NE	57.6	NA	Panama City, FL**	NA	157	South Bend-Mishawaka, IN-MI	(14.9)
160	Little Rock, AR	(15.4)	NA	Parkersburg-Vienna, WV**	NA	NA	Spartanburg, SC**	NA
229	Logan, UT-ID	(38.2)	75	Pensacola, FL	3.6	109	Spokane, WA	(5.8)
116	Longview, TX	(7.8)	NA	Peoria, IL**	NA	NA	Springfield, IL**	NA
193	Longview, WA	(23.9)	NA	Philadelphia (greater) PA-NJ-MD-DE**	NA	NA	Springfield, MA**	NA
135	Los Angeles County, CA M.D.	(10.0)	NA	Philadelphia, PA M.D.**	NA	21	Springfield, MO	35.9
133	Los Angeles (greater), CA	(9.9)	NA	Phoenix-Mesa-Scottsdale, AZ**	NA	38	Springfield, OH	20.7
159	Louisville, KY-IN	(15.1)	240	Pine Bluff, AR	(47.0)	14	State College, PA	50.4
39	Lubbock, TX	19.5	201	Pittsburgh, PA	(25.9)	NA	Staunton-Waynesboro, VA**	NA
202	Lynchburg, VA	(26.3)	142	Pittsfield, MA	(12.8)	148	Stockton-Lodi, CA	(13.9)
140	Macon, GA	(11.1)	NA	Pocatello, ID**	NA	27	St. George, UT	32.9
120	Madera, CA	(8.5)	48	Port St. Lucie, FL	14.1	47	St. Joseph, MO-KS	14.6
NA	Madison, WI**	NA	150	Portland-Vancouver, OR-WA	(14.1)	26	St. Louis, MO-IL	33.5
NA	Manchester-Nashua, NH**	NA	172	Portland, ME	(19.9)	42	Sumter, SC	17.3
NA	Manhattan, KS**	NA	56	Prescott, AZ	8.8	NA	Syracuse, NY**	NA
NA	Mankato-North Mankato, MN**	NA	80	Providence-Warwick, RI-MA	2.5	NA	Tacoma, WA M.D.**	NA
123	Mansfield, OH	(9.0)	233	Provo-Orem, UT	(40.6)	157	Tallahassee, FL	(14.9)
79	McAllen-Edinburg-Mission, TX	3.3	NA	Pueblo, CO**	NA	213	Tampa-St Petersburg, FL	(29.4)
97	Medford, OR	(2.2)	13	Punta Gorda, FL	51.0	NA	Terre Haute, IN**	NA
51	Memphis, TN-MS-AR	11.4	9	Racine, WI	59.4	NA	Texarkana, TX-AR**	NA
206	Merced, CA	(26.7)	152	Raleigh, NC	(14.3)	NA	The Villages, FL**	NA
173	Miami (greater), FL	(20.0)	NA	Rapid City, SD**	NA	NA	Toledo, OH**	NA
193	Miami-Dade County, FL M.D.	(23.9)	18	Reading, PA	40.6	155	Topeka, KS	(14.5)
168	Michigan City-La Porte, IN	(19.2)	204	Redding, CA	(26.5)	127	Trenton, NJ	(9.3)
NA	Midland, MI**	NA	236	Reno, NV	(43.0)	82	Tucson, AZ	2.4
NA	Midland, TX**	NA	235	Richmond, VA	(41.4)	44	Tulsa, OK	15.7
80	Milwaukee, WI	2.5	209	Riverside-San Bernardino, CA	(28.2)	NA	Tuscaloosa, AL**	NA
NA	Minneapolis-St. Paul, MN-WI**	NA	162	Roanoke, VA	(17.2)	69	Tyler, TX	4.7
31	Missoula, MT	28.0	NA	Rochester, MN**	NA	NA	Utica-Rome, NY**	NA
29	Mobile, AL	31.3	NA	Rochester, NY**	NA	32	Valdosta, GA	27.1
133	Modesto, CA	(9.9)	NA	Rockford, IL**	NA	123	Vallejo-Fairfield, CA	(9.0)
61	Monroe, LA	7.2	41	Rockingham County, NH M.D.	18.3	NA	Victoria, TX**	NA
166	Monroe, MI	(18.7)	NA	Rocky Mount, NC**	NA	33	Vineland-Bridgeton, NJ	26.9
NA	Montgomery County, PA M.D.**	NA	NA	Rome, GA**	NA	211	Virginia Beach-Norfolk, VA-NC	(28.6)
156	Montgomery, AL	(14.6)	146	Sacramento, CA	(13.3)	67	Visalia-Porterville, CA	5.7
NA	Morgantown, WV**	NA	53	Saginaw, MI	10.3	NA	Waco, TX**	NA
NA	Morristown, TN**	NA	144	Salem, OR	(13.2)	NA	Walla Walla, WA**	NA
197	Mount Vernon-Anacortes, WA	(24.6)	129	Salinas, CA	(9.4)	NA	Warner Robins, GA**	NA
251	Muncie, IN	(72.6)	NA	Salisbury, MD-DE**	NA	NA	Warren-Troy, MI M.D.**	NA
205	Napa, CA	(26.6)	50	Salt Lake City, UT	12.6	118	Washington (greater) DC-VA-MD-WV	(8.2)
214	Naples-Marco Island, FL	(29.7)	46	San Antonio, TX	14.8	121	Washington, DC-VA-MD-WV M.D.	(8.6)
NA	Nashville-Davidson, TN**	NA	188	San Diego, CA	(23.2)	25	Waterloo-Cedar Falls, IA	33.7
NA	Nassau-Suffolk, NY M.D.**	NA	193	San Francisco (greater), CA	(23.9)	NA	Watertown-Fort Drum, NY**	NA
NA	New Bern, NC**	NA	216	San Francisco-Redwood, CA M.D.	(30.5)	187	Wausau, WI	(22.4)
NA	New Haven-Milford, CT**	NA	60	San Jose, CA	7.3	123	West Palm Beach, FL M.D.	(9.0)
85	New Orleans, LA	0.9	227	San Luis Obispo, CA	(37.7)	220	Wheeling, WV-OH	(31.9)
NA	New York (greater), NY-NJ-PA**	NA	NA	San Rafael, CA M.D.**	NA	177	Wichita Falls, TX	(20.3)
NA	New York-Jersey City, NY-NJ M.D.**	NA	115	Santa Cruz-Watsonville, CA	(7.5)	184	Wichita, KS	(21.5)
NA	Newark, NJ-PA M.D.**	NA	247	Santa Fe, NM	(56.7)	10	Williamsport, PA	58.2
NA	North Port-Sarasota-Bradenton, FL**	NA	NA	Santa Maria-Santa Barbara, CA**	NA	135	Wilmington, DE-MD-NJ M.D.	(10.0)
191	Norwich-New London, CT	(23.6)	91	Santa Rosa, CA	(1.3)	NA	Wilmington, NC**	NA
174	Oakland-Hayward, CA M.D.	(20.1)	103	Savannah, GA	(4.0)	224	Winchester, VA-WV	(37.4)
93	Ocala, FL	(1.6)	66	Scranton--Wilkes-Barre, PA	6.1	NA	Winston-Salem, NC**	NA
249	Ocean City, NJ	(61.8)	NA	Seattle (greater), WA**	NA	74	Worcester, MA-CT	4.3
1	Odessa, TX	896.8	NA	Seattle-Bellevue-Everett, WA M.D.**	NA	218	Yakima, WA	(31.2)
NA	Ogden-Clearfield, UT**	NA	248	Sebastian-Vero Beach, FL	(58.8)	71	York-Hanover, PA	4.4
62	Oklahoma City, OK	6.9	NA	Sebring, FL**	NA	152	Youngstown-Warren, OH-PA	(14.3)
71	Olympia, WA	4.4	12	Sheboygan, WI	55.0	91	Yuba City, CA	(1.3)
83	Omaha-Council Bluffs, NE-IA	2.2	4	Sherman-Denison, TX	108.0	58	Yuma, AZ	8.4
182	Orlando, FL	(20.9)	174	Shreveport-Bossier City, LA	(20.1)			
101	Oshkosh-Neenah, WI	(2.9)	NA	Sierra Vista-Douglas, AZ**	NA			

Source: CQ Press using reported data from the F.B.I. "Crime in the United States 2012"

*Forcible rape is the carnal knowledge of a female forcibly and against her will. Assaults or attempts to commit rape by force or threat of force are included. However, statutory rape without force and other sex offenses are excluded. **Not available

16. Percent Change in Rape Rate: 2008 to 2012 (continued)
National Percent Change = 9.9% Decrease*

RANK	METROPOLITAN AREA	% CHANGE	RANK	METROPOLITAN AREA	% CHANGE	RANK	METROPOLITAN AREA	% CHANGE
1	Odessa, TX	896.8	65	Cheyenne, WY	6.4	129	Salinas, CA	(9.4)
2	Bridgeport-Stamford, CT	243.5	66	Scranton--Wilkes-Barre, PA	6.1	130	Dubuque, IA	(9.6)
3	Columbus, IN	243.3	67	Visalia-Porterville, CA	5.7	131	Anaheim-Santa Ana-Irvine, CA M.D.	(9.8)
4	Sherman-Denison, TX	108.0	68	Lewiston, ID-WA	5.5	131	Corvallis, OR	(9.8)
5	Hanford-Corcoran, CA	97.8	69	Fond du Lac, WI	4.7	133	Los Angeles (greater), CA	(9.9)
6	Columbia, MO	68.9	69	Tyler, TX	4.7	133	Modesto, CA	(9.9)
7	Hinesville, GA	66.8	71	Athens-Clarke County, GA	4.4	135	Indianapolis, IN	(10.0)
8	Lafayette, IN	61.8	71	Olympia, WA	4.4	135	Lancaster, PA	(10.0)
9	Racine, WI	59.4	71	York-Hanover, PA	4.4	135	Los Angeles County, CA M.D.	(10.0)
10	Williamsport, PA	58.2	74	Worcester, MA-CT	4.3	135	Wilmington, DE-MD-NJ M.D.	(10.0)
11	Lincoln, NE	57.6	75	Flint, MI	3.6	139	Florence-Muscle Shoals, AL	(11.0)
12	Sheboygan, WI	55.0	75	Harrisburg-Carlisle, PA	3.6	140	Macon, GA	(11.1)
13	Punta Gorda, FL	51.0	75	Kalamazoo-Portage, MI	3.6	141	El Centro, CA	(11.9)
14	State College, PA	50.4	75	Pensacola, FL	3.6	142	Pittsfield, MA	(12.8)
15	Great Falls, MT	44.8	79	McAllen-Edinburg-Mission, TX	3.3	143	Fort Wayne, IN	(13.1)
16	Altoona, PA	44.2	80	Milwaukee, WI	2.5	144	Austin-Round Rock, TX	(13.2)
17	Johnstown, PA	42.5	80	Providence-Warwick, RI-MA	2.5	144	Salem, OR	(13.2)
18	Reading, PA	40.6	82	Tucson, AZ	2.4	146	Sacramento, CA	(13.3)
19	Cedar Rapids, IA	39.6	83	Omaha-Council Bluffs, NE-IA	2.2	147	Clarksville, TN-KY	(13.6)
20	Bellingham, WA	37.9	84	Atlanta, GA	1.5	148	Blacksburg, VA	(13.9)
21	Springfield, MO	35.9	85	Burlington, NC	0.9	148	Stockton-Lodi, CA	(13.9)
22	Goldsboro, NC	35.8	85	New Orleans, LA	0.9	150	Lima, OH	(14.1)
23	Bloomington, IN	35.7	87	Killeen-Temple, TX	0.8	150	Portland-Vancouver, OR-WA	(14.1)
24	Greenville, NC	33.8	88	Bay City, MI	0.6	152	Raleigh, NC	(14.3)
25	Waterloo-Cedar Falls, IA	33.7	89	Carson City, NV	0.0	152	Youngstown-Warren, OH-PA	(14.3)
26	St. Louis, MO-IL	33.5	90	Colorado Springs, CO	(0.4)	154	Hickory, NC	(14.4)
27	St. George, UT	32.9	91	Santa Rosa, CA	(1.3)	155	Topeka, KS	(14.5)
28	Las Cruces, NM	32.1	91	Yuba City, CA	(1.3)	156	Montgomery, AL	(14.6)
29	Mobile, AL	31.3	93	Ocala, FL	(1.6)	157	South Bend-Mishawaka, IN-MI	(14.9)
30	Bangor, ME	30.9	94	Akron, OH	(1.7)	157	Tallahassee, FL	(14.9)
31	Missoula, MT	28.0	94	Asheville, NC	(1.7)	159	Louisville, KY-IN	(15.1)
32	Valdosta, GA	27.1	96	Gainesville, FL	(1.9)	160	Little Rock, AR	(15.4)
33	Vineland-Bridgeton, NJ	26.9	97	Medford, OR	(2.2)	161	Farmington, NM	(15.6)
34	Grand Junction, CO	22.9	98	Iowa City, IA	(2.3)	162	Roanoke, VA	(17.2)
35	Baltimore, MD	21.4	99	Dalton, GA	(2.6)	163	Amarillo, TX	(17.3)
35	Lewiston-Auburn, ME	21.4	100	Fayetteville-Springdale, AR-MO	(2.7)	164	Charlottesville, VA	(17.5)
37	Lawrence, KS	21.2	101	Oshkosh-Neenah, WI	(2.9)	165	Greeley, CO	(17.8)
38	Springfield, OH	20.7	102	Gadsden, AL	(3.2)	166	Monroe, MI	(18.7)
39	Lubbock, TX	19.5	103	Savannah, GA	(4.0)	167	Baton Rouge, LA	(18.8)
40	Harrisonburg, VA	19.2	104	Laredo, TX	(4.1)	168	Michigan City-La Porte, IN	(19.2)
41	Rockingham County, NH M.D.	18.3	105	Dothan, AL	(4.2)	169	Idaho Falls, ID	(19.3)
42	Sumter, SC	17.3	105	Fresno, CA	(4.2)	169	Kingsport, TN-VA	(19.3)
43	Ann Arbor, MI	16.4	107	Cleveland, TN	(5.0)	171	Chico, CA	(19.6)
44	Tulsa, OK	15.7	108	Joplin, MO	(5.1)	172	Portland, ME	(19.9)
45	Ames, IA	15.1	109	Spokane, WA	(5.8)	173	Miami (greater), FL	(20.0)
46	San Antonio, TX	14.8	110	Appleton, WI	(5.9)	174	Jonesboro, AR	(20.1)
47	St. Joseph, MO-KS	14.6	111	Corpus Christi, TX	(6.2)	174	Oakland-Hayward, CA M.D.	(20.1)
48	Port St. Lucie, FL	14.1	112	Dayton, OH	(6.5)	174	Shreveport-Bossier City, LA	(20.1)
49	Bismarck, ND	13.9	113	Durham-Chapel Hill, NC	(7.4)	177	Wichita Falls, TX	(20.3)
50	Salt Lake City, UT	12.6	113	Silver Spring-Frederick, MD M.D.	(7.4)	178	Barnstable Town, MA	(20.4)
51	Memphis, TN-MS-AR	11.4	115	Santa Cruz-Watsonville, CA	(7.5)	179	Fayetteville, NC	(20.6)
52	Eugene, OR	11.3	116	Longview, TX	(7.8)	180	Boise City, ID	(20.8)
53	Saginaw, MI	10.3	117	El Paso, TX	(8.0)	180	Houston, TX	(20.8)
54	Cumberland, MD-WV	10.2	118	Washington (greater) DC-VA-MD-WV	(8.2)	182	Orlando, FL	(20.9)
55	Lebanon, PA	9.2	119	Fort Worth-Arlington, TX M.D.	(8.4)	183	Las Vegas-Henderson, NV	(21.4)
56	Prescott, AZ	8.8	120	Madera, CA	(8.5)	184	Janesville, WI	(21.5)
57	Atlantic City, NJ	8.5	121	Washington, DC-VA-MD-WV M.D.	(8.6)	184	Wichita, KS	(21.5)
58	Palm Bay-Melbourne, FL	8.4	122	Dallas (greater), TX	(8.7)	186	Camden, NJ M.D.	(21.7)
58	Yuma, AZ	8.4	123	Mansfield, OH	(9.0)	187	Wausau, WI	(22.4)
60	San Jose, CA	7.3	123	Vallejo-Fairfield, CA	(9.0)	188	Oxnard-Thousand Oaks, CA	(23.2)
61	Monroe, LA	7.2	123	West Palm Beach, FL M.D.	(9.0)	188	San Diego, CA	(23.2)
62	Jacksonville, FL	6.9	126	Lansing-East Lansing, MI	(9.2)	190	Huntsville, AL	(23.4)
62	Oklahoma City, OK	6.9	127	Dallas-Plano-Irving, TX M.D.	(9.3)	191	Norwich-New London, CT	(23.6)
64	Sioux Falls, SD	6.7	127	Trenton, NJ	(9.3)	192	Fort Lauderdale, FL M.D.	(23.8)

Note: All listings are for Metropolitan Statistical Areas (M.S.A.s) except for those ending with "M.D." Listings with "M.D." are Metropolitan Divisions which are smaller parts of eleven large M.S.A.s. See explanatory note at beginning of metropolitan area section.

RANK	METROPOLITAN AREA	% CHANGE	RANK	METROPOLITAN AREA	% CHANGE	RANK	METROPOLITAN AREA	% CHANGE
193	Longview, WA	(23.9)	NA	Allentown, PA-NJ**	NA	NA	Madison, WI**	NA
193	Miami-Dade County, FL M.D.	(23.9)	NA	Anchorage, AK**	NA	NA	Manchester-Nashua, NH**	NA
193	San Francisco (greater), CA	(23.9)	NA	Anniston-Oxford, AL**	NA	NA	Manhattan, KS**	NA
196	Birmingham-Hoover, AL	(24.0)	NA	Beckley, WV**	NA	NA	Mankato-North Mankato, MN**	NA
197	Mount Vernon-Anacortes, WA	(24.6)	NA	Binghamton, NY**	NA	NA	Midland, MI**	NA
198	Kennewick-Richland, WA	(24.9)	NA	Bloomington, IL**	NA	NA	Midland, TX**	NA
199	Beaumont-Port Arthur, TX	(25.7)	NA	Bloomsburg-Berwick, PA**	NA	NA	Minneapolis-St. Paul, MN-WI**	NA
200	Billings, MT	(25.8)	NA	Boston (greater), MA-NH**	NA	NA	Montgomery County, PA M.D.**	NA
201	Pittsburgh, PA	(25.9)	NA	Boston, MA M.D.**	NA	NA	Morgantown, WV**	NA
202	Lynchburg, VA	(26.3)	NA	Boulder, CO**	NA	NA	Morristown, TN**	NA
203	Hartford, CT	(26.4)	NA	Brunswick, GA**	NA	NA	Nashville-Davidson, TN**	NA
204	Redding, CA	(26.5)	NA	Buffalo-Niagara Falls, NY**	NA	NA	Nassau-Suffolk, NY M.D.**	NA
205	Napa, CA	(26.6)	NA	California-Lexington Park, MD**	NA	NA	New Bern, NC**	NA
206	Merced, CA	(26.7)	NA	Cambridge-Newton, MA M.D.**	NA	NA	New Haven-Milford, CT**	NA
207	Erie, PA	(27.0)	NA	Canton, OH**	NA	NA	New York (greater), NY-NJ-PA**	NA
208	Cape Girardeau, MO-IL	(28.0)	NA	Chambersburg-Waynesboro, PA**	NA	NA	New York-Jersey City, NY-NJ M.D.**	NA
209	Riverside-San Bernardino, CA	(28.2)	NA	Champaign-Urbana, IL**	NA	NA	Newark, NJ-PA M.D.**	NA
210	Lakeland, FL	(28.4)	NA	Chicago (greater), IL-IN-WI**	NA	NA	North Port-Sarasota-Bradenton, FL**	NA
211	Virginia Beach-Norfolk, VA-NC	(28.6)	NA	Chicago-Joilet-Naperville, IL M.D.**	NA	NA	Ogden-Clearfield, UT**	NA
212	Charleston-North Charleston, SC	(28.9)	NA	Cincinnati, OH-KY-IN**	NA	NA	Owensboro, KY**	NA
213	Tampa-St Petersburg, FL	(29.4)	NA	Coeur d'Alene, ID**	NA	NA	Panama City, FL**	NA
214	Naples-Marco Island, FL	(29.7)	NA	Crestview-Fort Walton Beach, FL**	NA	NA	Parkersburg-Vienna, WV**	NA
215	Bakersfield, CA	(30.3)	NA	Danville, IL**	NA	NA	Peoria, IL**	NA
216	San Francisco-Redwood, CA M.D.	(30.5)	NA	Daphne-Fairhope-Foley, AL**	NA	NA	Philadelphia (greater) PA-NJ-MD-DE**	NA
217	Brownsville-Harlingen, TX	(31.1)	NA	Davenport, IA-IL**	NA	NA	Philadelphia, PA M.D.**	NA
218	Yakima, WA	(31.2)	NA	Decatur, IL**	NA	NA	Phoenix-Mesa-Scottsdale, AZ**	NA
219	Des Moines-West Des Moines, IA	(31.8)	NA	Denver-Aurora, CO**	NA	NA	Pocatello, ID**	NA
220	Wheeling, WV-OH	(31.9)	NA	Detroit (greater), MI**	NA	NA	Pueblo, CO**	NA
221	Greensboro-High Point, NC	(32.9)	NA	Detroit-Dearborn-Livonia, MI M.D.**	NA	NA	Rapid City, SD**	NA
222	Albuquerque, NM	(33.0)	NA	Duluth, MN-WI**	NA	NA	Rochester, MN**	NA
223	Cape Coral-Fort Myers, FL	(34.6)	NA	Dutchess-Putnam, NY M.D.**	NA	NA	Rochester, NY**	NA
224	Green Bay, WI	(37.4)	NA	East Stroudsburg, PA**	NA	NA	Rockford, IL**	NA
224	Winchester, VA-WV	(37.4)	NA	Elgin, IL M.D.**	NA	NA	Rocky Mount, NC**	NA
226	Fort Collins, CO	(37.5)	NA	Elizabethtown-Fort Knox, KY**	NA	NA	Rome, GA**	NA
227	San Luis Obispo, CA	(37.7)	NA	Elmira, NY**	NA	NA	Salisbury, MD-DE**	NA
228	Bowling Green, KY	(37.9)	NA	Fairbanks, AK**	NA	NA	San Rafael, CA M.D.**	NA
229	Logan, UT-ID	(38.2)	NA	Fargo, ND-MN**	NA	NA	Santa Maria-Santa Barbara, CA**	NA
230	Columbus, GA-AL	(39.2)	NA	Fort Smith, AR-OK**	NA	NA	Seattle (greater), WA**	NA
231	Augusta, GA-SC	(40.1)	NA	Gainesville, GA**	NA	NA	Seattle-Bellevue-Everett, WA M.D.**	NA
232	College Station-Bryan, TX	(40.3)	NA	Gary, IN M.D.**	NA	NA	Sebring, FL**	NA
233	Lake Havasu City-Kingman, AZ	(40.6)	NA	Gettysburg, PA**	NA	NA	Sierra Vista-Douglas, AZ**	NA
233	Provo-Orem, UT	(40.6)	NA	Glens Falls, NY**	NA	NA	Sioux City, IA-NE-SD**	NA
235	Richmond, VA	(41.4)	NA	Grand Forks, ND-MN**	NA	NA	Spartanburg, SC**	NA
236	Reno, NV	(43.0)	NA	Grand Island, NE**	NA	NA	Springfield, IL**	NA
237	Florence, SC	(43.2)	NA	Greenville-Anderson, SC**	NA	NA	Springfield, MA**	NA
238	Flagstaff, AZ	(44.6)	NA	Hagerstown-Martinsburg, MD-WV**	NA	NA	Staunton-Waynesboro, VA**	NA
239	Deltona-Daytona Beach, FL	(46.4)	NA	Hammond, LA**	NA	NA	Syracuse, NY**	NA
240	Pine Bluff, AR	(47.0)	NA	Hattiesburg, MS**	NA	NA	Tacoma, WA M.D.**	NA
241	Johnson City, TN	(47.3)	NA	Hilton Head Island, SC**	NA	NA	Terre Haute, IN**	NA
242	Houma, LA	(48.0)	NA	Homosassa Springs, FL**	NA	NA	Texarkana, TX-AR**	NA
243	Bremerton-Silverdale, WA	(50.3)	NA	Jackson, MS**	NA	NA	The Villages, FL**	NA
244	Decatur, AL	(51.7)	NA	Jackson, TN**	NA	NA	Toledo, OH**	NA
245	Dover, DE	(55.3)	NA	Jefferson City, MO**	NA	NA	Tuscaloosa, AL**	NA
246	Abilene, TX	(55.4)	NA	Kahului-Wailuku-Lahaina, HI**	NA	NA	Utica-Rome, NY**	NA
247	Santa Fe, NM	(56.7)	NA	Kankakee, IL**	NA	NA	Victoria, TX**	NA
248	Sebastian-Vero Beach, FL	(58.8)	NA	Kansas City, MO-KS**	NA	NA	Waco, TX**	NA
249	Ocean City, NJ	(61.8)	NA	Kingston, NY**	NA	NA	Walla Walla, WA**	NA
250	Auburn, AL	(63.0)	NA	Knoxville, TN**	NA	NA	Warner Robins, GA**	NA
251	Muncie, IN	(72.6)	NA	Kokomo, IN**	NA	NA	Warren-Troy, MI M.D.**	NA
252	Casper, WY	(81.7)	NA	La Crosse, WI-MN**	NA	NA	Watertown-Fort Drum, NY**	NA
NA	Albany-Schenectady-Troy, NY**	NA	NA	Lafayette, LA**	NA	NA	Wilmington, NC**	NA
NA	Albany, GA**	NA	NA	Lake Co.-Kenosha Co., IL-WI M.D.**	NA	NA	Winston-Salem, NC**	NA
NA	Albany, OR**	NA	NA	Lawton, OK**	NA			
NA	Alexandria, LA**	NA	NA	Lexington-Fayette, KY**	NA			

Source: CQ Press using reported data from the F.B.I. "Crime in the United States 2012"

*Forcible rape is the carnal knowledge of a female forcibly and against her will. Assaults or attempts to commit rape by force or threat of force are included. However, statutory rape without force and other sex offenses are excluded. **Not available

17. Robberies in 2012
National Total = 354,520 Robberies*

RANK	METROPOLITAN AREA	ROBBERY	RANK	METROPOLITAN AREA	ROBBERY	RANK	METROPOLITAN AREA	ROBBERY
224	Abilene, TX	136	353	Cheyenne, WY	27	98	Gary, IN M.D.	706
95	Akron, OH	732	5	Chicago (greater), IL-IN-WI	17,518	381	Gettysburg, PA	6
103	Albany-Schenectady-Troy, NY	698	6	Chicago-Joilet-Naperville, IL M.D.	16,207	372	Glens Falls, NY	16
165	Albany, GA	258	207	Chico, CA	167	242	Goldsboro, NC	110
339	Albany, OR	42	39	Cincinnati, OH-KY-IN	2,798	353	Grand Forks, ND-MN	27
71	Albuquerque, NM	1,229	200	Clarksville, TN-KY	174	370	Grand Island, NE	21
199	Alexandria, LA	175	315	Cleveland, TN	55	334	Grand Junction, CO	44
100	Allentown, PA-NJ	704	367	Coeur d'Alene, ID	22	358	Great Falls, MT	26
342	Altoona, PA	38	236	College Station-Bryan, TX	116	261	Greeley, CO	94
161	Amarillo, TX	280	118	Colorado Springs, CO	567	252	Green Bay, WI	100
379	Ames, IA	8	196	Columbia, MO	180	88	Greensboro-High Point, NC	856
46	Anaheim-Santa Ana-Irvine, CA M.D.	2,132	128	Columbus, GA-AL	506	101	Greenville-Anderson, SC	703
130	Anchorage, AK	496	360	Columbus, IN	25	182	Greenville, NC	209
191	Ann Arbor, MI	187	140	Corpus Christi, TX	412	206	Hagerstown-Martinsburg, MD-WV	170
228	Anniston-Oxford, AL	131	371	Corvallis, OR	18	193	Hammond, LA	183
345	Appleton, WI	37	230	Crestview-Fort Walton Beach, FL	126	246	Hanford-Corcoran, CA	106
173	Asheville, NC	236	324	Cumberland, MD-WV	48	113	Harrisburg-Carlisle, PA	608
197	Athens-Clarke County, GA	179	14	Dallas (greater), TX	8,007	352	Harrisonburg, VA	29
13	Atlanta, GA	8,382	21	Dallas-Plano-Irving, TX M.D.	5,765	75	Hartford, CT	1,194
132	Atlantic City, NJ	477	334	Dalton, GA	44	278	Hattiesburg, MS	80
281	Auburn, AL	77	268	Danville, IL	88	186	Hickory, NC	200
97	Augusta, GA-SC	715	283	Daphne-Fairhope-Foley, AL	76	205	Hilton Head Island, SC	171
74	Austin-Round Rock, TX	1,195	168	Davenport, IA-IL	245	334	Hinesville, GA	44
69	Bakersfield, CA	1,313	79	Dayton, OH	1,016	302	Homosassa Springs, FL	61
19	Baltimore, MD	5,901	262	Decatur, AL	93	228	Houma, LA	131
302	Bangor, ME	61	241	Decatur, IL	111	7	Houston, TX	13,524
279	Barnstable Town, MA	78	135	Deltona-Daytona Beach, FL	462	123	Huntsville, AL	548
63	Baton Rouge, LA	1,460	44	Denver-Aurora, CO	2,224	374	Idaho Falls, ID	15
340	Bay City, MI	41	160	Des Moines-West Des Moines, IA	284	30	Indianapolis, IN	3,755
111	Beaumont-Port Arthur, TX	613	17	Detroit (greater), MI	7,013	329	Iowa City, IA	47
231	Beckley, WV	123	20	Detroit-Dearborn-Livonia, MI M.D.	5,887	59	Jacksonville, FL	1,610
299	Bellingham, WA	65	234	Dothan, AL	119	84	Jackson, MS	926
292	Billings, MT	69	213	Dover, DE	161	188	Jackson, TN	199
219	Binghamton, NY	142	364	Dubuque, IA	23	257	Janesville, WI	96
54	Birmingham-Hoover, AL	1,769	227	Duluth, MN-WI	133	306	Jefferson City, MO	59
353	Bismarck, ND	27	96	Durham-Chapel Hill, NC	725	294	Johnson City, TN	68
347	Blacksburg, VA	36	202	Dutchess-Putnam, NY M.D.	173	324	Johnstown, PA	48
258	Bloomington, IL	95	258	East Stroudsburg, PA	95	268	Jonesboro, AR	88
315	Bloomington, IN	55	232	El Centro, CA	120	272	Joplin, MO	86
377	Bloomsburg-Berwick, PA	12	127	El Paso, TX	508	238	Kahului-Wailuku-Lahaina, HI	115
235	Boise City, ID	117	179	Elgin, IL M.D.	221	169	Kalamazoo-Portage, MI	242
25	Boston (greater), MA-NH	4,312	334	Elizabethtown-Fort Knox, KY	44	271	Kankakee, IL	87
38	Boston, MA M.D.	2,869	332	Elmira, NY	46	42	Kansas City, MO-KS	2,421
250	Boulder, CO	102	177	Erie, PA	223	253	Kennewick-Richland, WA	99
275	Bowling Green, KY	83	164	Eugene, OR	261	145	Killeen-Temple, TX	376
242	Bremerton-Silverdale, WA	110	341	Fairbanks, AK	39	245	Kingsport, TN-VA	109
82	Bridgeport-Stamford, CT	946	306	Fargo, ND-MN	59	342	Kingston, NY	38
172	Brownsville-Harlingen, TX	237	313	Farmington, NM	56	92	Knoxville, TN	759
223	Brunswick, GA	137	247	Fayetteville-Springdale, AR-MO	104	301	Kokomo, IN	63
52	Buffalo-Niagara Falls, NY	1,811	94	Fayetteville, NC	753	338	La Crosse, WI-MN	43
221	Burlington, NC	138	313	Flagstaff, AZ	56	265	Lafayette, IN	89
322	California-Lexington Park, MD	51	81	Flint, MI	980	136	Lafayette, LA	436
66	Cambridge-Newton, MA M.D.	1,354	264	Florence-Muscle Shoals, AL	90	144	Lake Co.-Kenosha Co., IL-WI M.D.	384
60	Camden, NJ M.D.	1,596	183	Florence, SC	205	309	Lake Havasu City-Kingman, AZ	57
114	Canton, OH	589	376	Fond du Lac, WI	13	137	Lakeland, FL	421
122	Cape Coral-Fort Myers, FL	553	285	Fort Collins, CO	75	148	Lancaster, PA	331
288	Cape Girardeau, MO-IL	73	32	Fort Lauderdale, FL M.D.	3,425	159	Lansing-East Lansing, MI	294
375	Carson City, NV	14	242	Fort Smith, AR-OK	110	191	Laredo, TX	187
377	Casper, WY	12	134	Fort Wayne, IN	472	268	Las Cruces, NM	88
250	Cedar Rapids, IA	102	43	Fort Worth-Arlington, TX M.D.	2,242	24	Las Vegas-Henderson, NV	4,422
329	Chambersburg-Waynesboro, PA	47	64	Fresno, CA	1,421	309	Lawrence, KS	57
175	Champaign-Urbana, IL	228	226	Gadsden, AL	134	200	Lawton, OK	174
109	Charleston-North Charleston, SC	618	166	Gainesville, FL	254	296	Lebanon, PA	66
288	Charlottesville, VA	73	258	Gainesville, GA	95	296	Lewiston-Auburn, ME	66

Note: All listings are for Metropolitan Statistical Areas (M.S.A.s) except for those ending with "M.D." Listings with "M.D." are Metropolitan Divisions which are smaller parts of eleven large M.S.A.s. See explanatory note at beginning of metropolitan area section.

RANK	METROPOLITAN AREA	ROBBERY
372	Lewiston, ID-WA	16
102	Lexington-Fayette, KY	702
232	Lima, OH	120
185	Lincoln, NE	201
72	Little Rock, AR	1,202
382	Logan, UT-ID	4
197	Longview, TX	179
296	Longview, WA	66
4	Los Angeles County, CA M.D.	18,923
3	Los Angeles (greater), CA	21,055
57	Louisville, KY-IN	1,711
150	Lubbock, TX	329
302	Lynchburg, VA	61
153	Macon, GA	313
220	Madera, CA	139
158	Madison, WI	297
162	Manchester-Nashua, NH	276
358	Manhattan, KS	26
349	Mankato-North Mankato, MN	33
236	Mansfield, OH	116
133	McAllen-Edinburg-Mission, TX	474
276	Medford, OR	82
29	Memphis, TN-MS-AR	3,839
148	Merced, CA	331
10	Miami (greater), FL	11,322
18	Miami-Dade County, FL M.D.	6,006
287	Michigan City-La Porte, IN	74
380	Midland, MI	7
318	Midland, TX	54
31	Milwaukee, WI	3,446
35	Minneapolis-St. Paul, MN-WI	3,084
342	Missoula, MT	38
106	Mobile, AL	661
91	Modesto, CA	788
194	Monroe, LA	182
255	Monroe, MI	98
87	Montgomery County, PA M.D.	875
121	Montgomery, AL	554
324	Morgantown, WV	48
273	Morristown, TN	85
332	Mount Vernon-Anacortes, WA	46
247	Muncie, IN	104
290	Napa, CA	71
216	Naples-Marco Island, FL	151
45	Nashville-Davidson, TN	2,184
51	Nassau-Suffolk, NY M.D.	1,837
292	New Bern, NC	69
67	New Haven-Milford, CT	1,349
56	New Orleans, LA	1,722
1	New York (greater), NY-NJ-PA	31,798
2	New York-Jersey City, NY-NJ M.D.	25,636
26	Newark, NJ-PA M.D.	4,152
104	North Port-Sarasota-Bradenton, FL	676
253	Norwich-New London, CT	99
15	Oakland-Hayward, CA M.D.	7,822
211	Ocala, FL	162
319	Ocean City, NJ	53
210	Odessa, TX	163
217	Ogden-Clearfield, UT	147
62	Oklahoma City, OK	1,479
265	Olympia, WA	89
83	Omaha-Council Bluffs, NE-IA	939
41	Orlando, FL	2,673
363	Oshkosh-Neenah, WI	24

RANK	METROPOLITAN AREA	ROBBERY
324	Owensboro, KY	48
110	Oxnard-Thousand Oaks, CA	617
129	Palm Bay-Melbourne, FL	505
202	Panama City, FL	173
348	Parkersburg-Vienna, WV	34
124	Pensacola, FL	529
141	Peoria, IL	403
8	Philadelphia (greater) PA-NJ-MD-DE	12,651
11	Philadelphia, PA M.D.	8,851
22	Phoenix-Mesa-Scottsdale, AZ	5,488
218	Pine Bluff, AR	143
47	Pittsburgh, PA	2,125
305	Pittsfield, MA	60
360	Pocatello, ID	25
154	Port St. Lucie, FL	311
53	Portland-Vancouver, OR-WA	1,780
189	Portland, ME	197
329	Prescott, AZ	47
65	Providence-Warwick, RI-MA	1,407
294	Provo-Orem, UT	68
184	Pueblo, CO	203
345	Punta Gorda, FL	37
176	Racine, WI	226
86	Raleigh, NC	893
315	Rapid City, SD	55
131	Reading, PA	482
209	Redding, CA	165
138	Reno, NV	416
76	Richmond, VA	1,165
23	Riverside-San Bernardino, CA	5,272
208	Roanoke, VA	166
306	Rochester, MN	59
78	Rochester, NY	1,060
115	Rockford, IL	583
265	Rockingham County, NH M.D.	89
211	Rocky Mount, NC	162
309	Rome, GA	57
37	Sacramento, CA	2,919
169	Saginaw, MI	242
186	Salem, OR	200
98	Salinas, CA	706
147	Salisbury, MD-DE	356
90	Salt Lake City, UT	823
48	San Antonio, TX	2,118
33	San Diego, CA	3,200
9	San Francisco (greater), CA	12,040
27	San Francisco-Redwood, CA M.D.	4,062
58	San Jose, CA	1,672
279	San Luis Obispo, CA	78
214	San Rafael, CA M.D.	156
180	Santa Cruz-Watsonville, CA	220
221	Santa Fe, NM	138
154	Santa Maria-Santa Barbara, CA	311
174	Santa Rosa, CA	232
120	Savannah, GA	555
143	Scranton--Wilkes-Barre, PA	395
28	Seattle (greater), WA	3,913
36	Seattle-Bellevue-Everett, WA M.D.	2,998
300	Sebastian-Vero Beach, FL	64
281	Sebring, FL	77
364	Sheboygan, WI	23
324	Sherman-Denison, TX	48
124	Shreveport-Bossier City, LA	529
319	Sierra Vista-Douglas, AZ	53

RANK	METROPOLITAN AREA	ROBBERY
80	Silver Spring-Frederick, MD M.D.	1,009
322	Sioux City, IA-NE-SD	51
291	Sioux Falls, SD	70
142	South Bend-Mishawaka, IN-MI	398
163	Spartanburg, SC	270
105	Spokane, WA	662
156	Springfield, IL	304
89	Springfield, MA	824
145	Springfield, MO	376
194	Springfield, OH	182
353	State College, PA	27
367	Staunton-Waynesboro, VA	22
49	Stockton-Lodi, CA	1,992
350	St. George, UT	30
262	St. Joseph, MO-KS	93
34	St. Louis, MO-IL	3,121
247	Sumter, SC	104
117	Syracuse, NY	576
85	Tacoma, WA M.D.	915
112	Tallahassee, FL	612
40	Tampa-St Petersburg, FL	2,711
256	Terre Haute, IN	97
225	Texarkana, TX-AR	135
364	The Villages, FL	23
70	Toledo, OH	1,239
167	Topeka, KS	246
93	Trenton, NJ	758
61	Tucson, AZ	1,481
73	Tulsa, OK	1,200
171	Tuscaloosa, AL	238
238	Tyler, TX	115
204	Utica-Rome, NY	172
240	Valdosta, GA	113
107	Vallejo-Fairfield, CA	660
321	Victoria, TX	52
152	Vineland-Bridgeton, NJ	315
55	Virginia Beach-Norfolk, VA-NC	1,742
139	Visalia-Porterville, CA	415
177	Waco, TX	223
367	Walla Walla, WA	22
190	Warner Robins, GA	194
77	Warren-Troy, MI M.D.	1,126
12	Washington (greater) DC-VA-MD-WV	8,773
16	Washington, DC-VA-MD-WV M.D.	7,764
283	Waterloo-Cedar Falls, IA	76
353	Watertown-Fort Drum, NY	27
360	Wausau, WI	25
50	West Palm Beach, FL M.D.	1,891
309	Wheeling, WV-OH	57
214	Wichita Falls, TX	156
126	Wichita, KS	526
277	Williamsport, PA	81
68	Wilmington, DE-MD-NJ M.D.	1,329
151	Wilmington, NC	316
350	Winchester, VA-WV	30
115	Winston-Salem, NC	583
108	Worcester, MA-CT	658
181	Yakima, WA	211
157	York-Hanover, PA	303
119	Youngstown-Warren, OH-PA	557
274	Yuba City, CA	84
285	Yuma, AZ	75

Source: Reported data from the F.B.I. "Crime in the United States 2012"
*Robbery is the taking of anything of value by force or threat of force. Attempts are included.

17. Robberies in 2012 (continued)
National Total = 354,520 Robberies*

RANK	METROPOLITAN AREA	ROBBERY	RANK	METROPOLITAN AREA	ROBBERY	RANK	METROPOLITAN AREA	ROBBERY
1	New York (greater), NY-NJ-PA	31,798	65	Providence-Warwick, RI-MA	1,407	129	Palm Bay-Melbourne, FL	505
2	New York-Jersey City, NY-NJ M.D.	25,636	66	Cambridge-Newton, MA M.D.	1,354	130	Anchorage, AK	496
3	Los Angeles (greater), CA	21,055	67	New Haven-Milford, CT	1,349	131	Reading, PA	482
4	Los Angeles County, CA M.D.	18,923	68	Wilmington, DE-MD-NJ M.D.	1,329	132	Atlantic City, NJ	477
5	Chicago (greater), IL-IN-WI	17,518	69	Bakersfield, CA	1,313	133	McAllen-Edinburg-Mission, TX	474
6	Chicago-Joilet-Naperville, IL M.D.	16,207	70	Toledo, OH	1,239	134	Fort Wayne, IN	472
7	Houston, TX	13,524	71	Albuquerque, NM	1,229	135	Deltona-Daytona Beach, FL	462
8	Philadelphia (greater) PA-NJ-MD-DE	12,651	72	Little Rock, AR	1,202	136	Lafayette, LA	436
9	San Francisco (greater), CA	12,040	73	Tulsa, OK	1,200	137	Lakeland, FL	421
10	Miami (greater), FL	11,322	74	Austin-Round Rock, TX	1,195	138	Reno, NV	416
11	Philadelphia, PA M.D.	8,851	75	Hartford, CT	1,194	139	Visalia-Porterville, CA	415
12	Washington (greater) DC-VA-MD-WV	8,773	76	Richmond, VA	1,165	140	Corpus Christi, TX	412
13	Atlanta, GA	8,382	77	Warren-Troy, MI M.D.	1,126	141	Peoria, IL	403
14	Dallas (greater), TX	8,007	78	Rochester, NY	1,060	142	South Bend-Mishawaka, IN-MI	398
15	Oakland-Hayward, CA M.D.	7,822	79	Dayton, OH	1,016	143	Scranton--Wilkes-Barre, PA	395
16	Washington, DC-VA-MD-WV M.D.	7,764	80	Silver Spring-Frederick, MD M.D.	1,009	144	Lake Co.-Kenosha Co., IL-WI M.D.	384
17	Detroit (greater), MI	7,013	81	Flint, MI	980	145	Killeen-Temple, TX	376
18	Miami-Dade County, FL M.D.	6,006	82	Bridgeport-Stamford, CT	946	145	Springfield, MO	376
19	Baltimore, MD	5,901	83	Omaha-Council Bluffs, NE-IA	939	147	Salisbury, MD-DE	356
20	Detroit-Dearborn-Livonia, MI M.D.	5,887	84	Jackson, MS	926	148	Lancaster, PA	331
21	Dallas-Plano-Irving, TX M.D.	5,765	85	Tacoma, WA M.D.	915	148	Merced, CA	331
22	Phoenix-Mesa-Scottsdale, AZ	5,488	86	Raleigh, NC	893	150	Lubbock, TX	329
23	Riverside-San Bernardino, CA	5,272	87	Montgomery County, PA M.D.	875	151	Wilmington, NC	316
24	Las Vegas-Henderson, NV	4,422	88	Greensboro-High Point, NC	856	152	Vineland-Bridgeton, NJ	315
25	Boston (greater), MA-NH	4,312	89	Springfield, MA	824	153	Macon, GA	313
26	Newark, NJ-PA M.D.	4,152	90	Salt Lake City, UT	823	154	Port St. Lucie, FL	311
27	San Francisco-Redwood, CA M.D.	4,062	91	Modesto, CA	788	154	Santa Maria-Santa Barbara, CA	311
28	Seattle (greater), WA	3,913	92	Knoxville, TN	759	156	Springfield, IL	304
29	Memphis, TN-MS-AR	3,839	93	Trenton, NJ	758	157	York-Hanover, PA	303
30	Indianapolis, IN	3,755	94	Fayetteville, NC	753	158	Madison, WI	297
31	Milwaukee, WI	3,446	95	Akron, OH	732	159	Lansing-East Lansing, MI	294
32	Fort Lauderdale, FL M.D.	3,425	96	Durham-Chapel Hill, NC	725	160	Des Moines-West Des Moines, IA	284
33	San Diego, CA	3,200	97	Augusta, GA-SC	715	161	Amarillo, TX	280
34	St. Louis, MO-IL	3,121	98	Gary, IN M.D.	706	162	Manchester-Nashua, NH	276
35	Minneapolis-St. Paul, MN-WI	3,084	98	Salinas, CA	706	163	Spartanburg, SC	270
36	Seattle-Bellevue-Everett, WA M.D.	2,998	100	Allentown, PA-NJ	704	164	Eugene, OR	261
37	Sacramento, CA	2,919	101	Greenville-Anderson, SC	703	165	Albany, GA	258
38	Boston, MA M.D.	2,869	102	Lexington-Fayette, KY	702	166	Gainesville, FL	254
39	Cincinnati, OH-KY-IN	2,798	103	Albany-Schenectady-Troy, NY	698	167	Topeka, KS	246
40	Tampa-St Petersburg, FL	2,711	104	North Port-Sarasota-Bradenton, FL	676	168	Davenport, IA-IL	245
41	Orlando, FL	2,673	105	Spokane, WA	662	169	Kalamazoo-Portage, MI	242
42	Kansas City, MO-KS	2,421	106	Mobile, AL	661	169	Saginaw, MI	242
43	Fort Worth-Arlington, TX M.D.	2,242	107	Vallejo-Fairfield, CA	660	171	Tuscaloosa, AL	238
44	Denver-Aurora, CO	2,224	108	Worcester, MA-CT	658	172	Brownsville-Harlingen, TX	237
45	Nashville-Davidson, TN	2,184	109	Charleston-North Charleston, SC	618	173	Asheville, NC	236
46	Anaheim-Santa Ana-Irvine, CA M.D.	2,132	110	Oxnard-Thousand Oaks, CA	617	174	Santa Rosa, CA	232
47	Pittsburgh, PA	2,125	111	Beaumont-Port Arthur, TX	613	175	Champaign-Urbana, IL	228
48	San Antonio, TX	2,118	112	Tallahassee, FL	612	176	Racine, WI	226
49	Stockton-Lodi, CA	1,992	113	Harrisburg-Carlisle, PA	608	177	Erie, PA	223
50	West Palm Beach, FL M.D.	1,891	114	Canton, OH	589	177	Waco, TX	223
51	Nassau-Suffolk, NY M.D.	1,837	115	Rockford, IL	583	179	Elgin, IL M.D.	221
52	Buffalo-Niagara Falls, NY	1,811	115	Winston-Salem, NC	583	180	Santa Cruz-Watsonville, CA	220
53	Portland-Vancouver, OR-WA	1,780	117	Syracuse, NY	576	181	Yakima, WA	211
54	Birmingham-Hoover, AL	1,769	118	Colorado Springs, CO	567	182	Greenville, NC	209
55	Virginia Beach-Norfolk, VA-NC	1,742	119	Youngstown-Warren, OH-PA	557	183	Florence, SC	205
56	New Orleans, LA	1,722	120	Savannah, GA	555	184	Pueblo, CO	203
57	Louisville, KY-IN	1,711	121	Montgomery, AL	554	185	Lincoln, NE	201
58	San Jose, CA	1,672	122	Cape Coral-Fort Myers, FL	553	186	Hickory, NC	200
59	Jacksonville, FL	1,610	123	Huntsville, AL	548	186	Salem, OR	200
60	Camden, NJ M.D.	1,596	124	Pensacola, FL	529	188	Jackson, TN	199
61	Tucson, AZ	1,481	124	Shreveport-Bossier City, LA	529	189	Portland, ME	197
62	Oklahoma City, OK	1,479	126	Wichita, KS	526	190	Warner Robins, GA	194
63	Baton Rouge, LA	1,460	127	El Paso, TX	508	191	Ann Arbor, MI	187
64	Fresno, CA	1,421	128	Columbus, GA-AL	506	191	Laredo, TX	187

Note: All listings are for Metropolitan Statistical Areas (M.S.A.s) except for those ending with "M.D." Listings with "M.D." are Metropolitan Divisions which are smaller parts of eleven large M.S.A.s. See explanatory note at beginning of metropolitan area section.

RANK	METROPOLITAN AREA	ROBBERY	RANK	METROPOLITAN AREA	ROBBERY	RANK	METROPOLITAN AREA	ROBBERY
193	Hammond, LA	183	257	Janesville, WI	96	321	Victoria, TX	52
194	Monroe, LA	182	258	Bloomington, IL	95	322	California-Lexington Park, MD	51
194	Springfield, OH	182	258	East Stroudsburg, PA	95	322	Sioux City, IA-NE-SD	51
196	Columbia, MO	180	258	Gainesville, GA	95	324	Cumberland, MD-WV	48
197	Athens-Clarke County, GA	179	261	Greeley, CO	94	324	Johnstown, PA	48
197	Longview, TX	179	262	Decatur, AL	93	324	Morgantown, WV	48
199	Alexandria, LA	175	262	St. Joseph, MO-KS	93	324	Owensboro, KY	48
200	Clarksville, TN-KY	174	264	Florence-Muscle Shoals, AL	90	324	Sherman-Denison, TX	48
200	Lawton, OK	174	265	Lafayette, IN	89	329	Chambersburg-Waynesboro, PA	47
202	Dutchess-Putnam, NY M.D.	173	265	Olympia, WA	89	329	Iowa City, IA	47
202	Panama City, FL	173	265	Rockingham County, NH M.D.	89	329	Prescott, AZ	47
204	Utica-Rome, NY	172	268	Danville, IL	88	332	Elmira, NY	46
205	Hilton Head Island, SC	171	268	Jonesboro, AR	88	332	Mount Vernon-Anacortes, WA	46
206	Hagerstown-Martinsburg, MD-WV	170	268	Las Cruces, NM	88	334	Dalton, GA	44
207	Chico, CA	167	271	Kankakee, IL	87	334	Elizabethtown-Fort Knox, KY	44
208	Roanoke, VA	166	272	Joplin, MO	86	334	Grand Junction, CO	44
209	Redding, CA	165	273	Morristown, TN	85	334	Hinesville, GA	44
210	Odessa, TX	163	274	Yuba City, CA	84	338	La Crosse, WI-MN	43
211	Ocala, FL	162	275	Bowling Green, KY	83	339	Albany, OR	42
211	Rocky Mount, NC	162	276	Medford, OR	82	340	Bay City, MI	41
213	Dover, DE	161	277	Williamsport, PA	81	341	Fairbanks, AK	39
214	San Rafael, CA M.D.	156	278	Hattiesburg, MS	80	342	Altoona, PA	38
214	Wichita Falls, TX	156	279	Barnstable Town, MA	78	342	Kingston, NY	38
216	Naples-Marco Island, FL	151	279	San Luis Obispo, CA	78	342	Missoula, MT	38
217	Ogden-Clearfield, UT	147	281	Auburn, AL	77	345	Appleton, WI	37
218	Pine Bluff, AR	143	281	Sebring, FL	77	345	Punta Gorda, FL	37
219	Binghamton, NY	142	283	Daphne-Fairhope-Foley, AL	76	347	Blacksburg, VA	36
220	Madera, CA	139	283	Waterloo-Cedar Falls, IA	76	348	Parkersburg-Vienna, WV	34
221	Burlington, NC	138	285	Fort Collins, CO	75	349	Mankato-North Mankato, MN	33
221	Santa Fe, NM	138	285	Yuma, AZ	75	350	St. George, UT	30
223	Brunswick, GA	137	287	Michigan City-La Porte, IN	74	350	Winchester, VA-WV	30
224	Abilene, TX	136	288	Cape Girardeau, MO-IL	73	352	Harrisonburg, VA	29
225	Texarkana, TX-AR	135	288	Charlottesville, VA	73	353	Bismarck, ND	27
226	Gadsden, AL	134	290	Napa, CA	71	353	Cheyenne, WY	27
227	Duluth, MN-WI	133	291	Sioux Falls, SD	70	353	Grand Forks, ND-MN	27
228	Anniston-Oxford, AL	131	292	Billings, MT	69	353	State College, PA	27
228	Houma, LA	131	292	New Bern, NC	69	353	Watertown-Fort Drum, NY	27
230	Crestview-Fort Walton Beach, FL	126	294	Johnson City, TN	68	358	Great Falls, MT	26
231	Beckley, WV	123	294	Provo-Orem, UT	68	358	Manhattan, KS	26
232	El Centro, CA	120	296	Lebanon, PA	66	360	Columbus, IN	25
232	Lima, OH	120	296	Lewiston-Auburn, ME	66	360	Pocatello, ID	25
234	Dothan, AL	119	296	Longview, WA	66	360	Wausau, WI	25
235	Boise City, ID	117	299	Bellingham, WA	65	363	Oshkosh-Neenah, WI	24
236	College Station-Bryan, TX	116	300	Sebastian-Vero Beach, FL	64	364	Dubuque, IA	23
236	Mansfield, OH	116	301	Kokomo, IN	63	364	Sheboygan, WI	23
238	Kahului-Wailuku-Lahaina, HI	115	302	Bangor, ME	61	364	The Villages, FL	23
238	Tyler, TX	115	302	Homosassa Springs, FL	61	367	Coeur d'Alene, ID	22
240	Valdosta, GA	113	302	Lynchburg, VA	61	367	Staunton-Waynesboro, VA	22
241	Decatur, IL	111	305	Pittsfield, MA	60	367	Walla Walla, WA	22
242	Bremerton-Silverdale, WA	110	306	Fargo, ND-MN	59	370	Grand Island, NE	21
242	Fort Smith, AR-OK	110	306	Jefferson City, MO	59	371	Corvallis, OR	18
242	Goldsboro, NC	110	306	Rochester, MN	59	372	Glens Falls, NY	16
245	Kingsport, TN-VA	109	309	Lake Havasu City-Kingman, AZ	57	372	Lewiston, ID-WA	16
246	Hanford-Corcoran, CA	106	309	Lawrence, KS	57	374	Idaho Falls, ID	15
247	Fayetteville-Springdale, AR-MO	104	309	Rome, GA	57	375	Carson City, NV	14
247	Muncie, IN	104	309	Wheeling, WV-OH	57	376	Fond du Lac, WI	13
247	Sumter, SC	104	313	Farmington, NM	56	377	Bloomsburg-Berwick, PA	12
250	Boulder, CO	102	313	Flagstaff, AZ	56	377	Casper, WY	12
250	Cedar Rapids, IA	102	315	Bloomington, IN	55	379	Ames, IA	8
252	Green Bay, WI	100	315	Cleveland, TN	55	380	Midland, MI	7
253	Kennewick-Richland, WA	99	315	Rapid City, SD	55	381	Gettysburg, PA	6
253	Norwich-New London, CT	99	318	Midland, TX	54	382	Logan, UT-ID	4
255	Monroe, MI	98	319	Ocean City, NJ	53			
256	Terre Haute, IN	97	319	Sierra Vista-Douglas, AZ	53			

Source: Reported data from the F.B.I. "Crime in the United States 2012"

*Robbery is the taking of anything of value by force or threat of force. Attempts are included.

18. Robbery Rate in 2012
National Rate = 112.9 Robberies per 100,000 Population*

RANK	METROPOLITAN AREA	RATE	RANK	METROPOLITAN AREA	RATE	RANK	METROPOLITAN AREA	RATE
186	Abilene, TX	80.5	338	Cheyenne, WY	28.7	131	Gary, IN M.D.	99.3
122	Akron, OH	104.4	25	Chicago (greater), IL-IN-WI	184.2	381	Gettysburg, PA	5.9
187	Albany-Schenectady-Troy, NY	79.7	10	Chicago-Joilet-Naperville, IL M.D.	222.0	377	Glens Falls, NY	12.3
38	Albany, GA	161.9	197	Chico, CA	75.1	168	Goldsboro, NC	88.1
312	Albany, OR	35.3	71	Cincinnati, OH-KY-IN	131.8	344	Grand Forks, ND-MN	27.1
67	Albuquerque, NM	136.5	222	Clarksville, TN-KY	65.4	346	Grand Island, NE	25.2
106	Alexandria, LA	112.6	274	Cleveland, TN	46.7	336	Grand Junction, CO	29.5
175	Allentown, PA-NJ	85.2	371	Coeur d'Alene, ID	15.5	327	Great Falls, MT	31.6
333	Altoona, PA	29.8	265	College Station-Bryan, TX	49.3	310	Greeley, CO	35.8
117	Amarillo, TX	107.8	177	Colorado Springs, CO	84.7	324	Green Bay, WI	32.2
379	Ames, IA	8.9	115	Columbia, MO	108.5	99	Greensboro-High Point, NC	116.0
213	Anaheim-Santa Ana-Irvine, CA M.D.	69.1	34	Columbus, GA-AL	166.3	180	Greenville-Anderson, SC	83.3
44	Anchorage, AK	158.2	325	Columbus, IN	32.0	90	Greenville, NC	120.9
251	Ann Arbor, MI	53.7	145	Corpus Christi, TX	94.1	219	Hagerstown-Martinsburg, MD-WV	66.6
110	Anniston-Oxford, AL	110.8	362	Corvallis, OR	20.8	56	Hammond, LA	148.4
370	Appleton, WI	16.2	256	Crestview-Fort Walton Beach, FL	52.0	215	Hanford-Corcoran, CA	68.3
247	Asheville, NC	54.5	275	Cumberland, MD-WV	46.3	113	Harrisburg-Carlisle, PA	109.8
155	Athens-Clarke County, GA	91.6	93	Dallas (greater), TX	119.9	355	Harrisonburg, VA	22.7
48	Atlanta, GA	154.2	74	Dallas-Plano-Irving, TX M.D.	130.9	97	Hartford, CT	116.6
28	Atlantic City, NJ	173.0	330	Dalton, GA	30.5	245	Hattiesburg, MS	54.9
252	Auburn, AL	53.5	116	Danville, IL	107.9	248	Hickory, NC	54.3
85	Augusta, GA-SC	124.2	292	Daphne-Fairhope-Foley, AL	40.5	164	Hilton Head Island, SC	89.2
221	Austin-Round Rock, TX	66.0	226	Davenport, IA-IL	64.1	250	Hinesville, GA	54.0
49	Bakersfield, CA	152.7	80	Dayton, OH	126.5	286	Homosassa Springs, FL	43.0
14	Baltimore, MD	214.2	235	Decatur, AL	60.1	230	Houma, LA	62.4
295	Bangor, ME	39.6	130	Decatur, IL	100.2	13	Houston, TX	219.9
310	Barnstable Town, MA	35.8	192	Deltona-Daytona Beach, FL	77.0	75	Huntsville, AL	128.3
27	Baton Rouge, LA	179.6	179	Denver-Aurora, CO	84.4	378	Idaho Falls, ID	11.0
303	Bay City, MI	38.3	267	Des Moines-West Des Moines, IA	48.8	21	Indianapolis, IN	196.0
55	Beaumont-Port Arthur, TX	149.1	36	Detroit (greater), MI	163.5	331	Iowa City, IA	30.2
134	Beckley, WV	98.5	2	Detroit-Dearborn-Livonia, MI M.D.	326.4	96	Jacksonville, FL	116.8
327	Bellingham, WA	31.6	185	Dothan, AL	80.9	39	Jackson, MS	161.2
288	Billings, MT	42.6	138	Dover, DE	96.6	50	Jackson, TN	151.9
241	Binghamton, NY	56.5	348	Dubuque, IA	24.2	236	Janesville, WI	59.8
46	Birmingham-Hoover, AL	155.6	271	Duluth, MN-WI	47.3	297	Jefferson City, MO	39.1
357	Bismarck, ND	22.6	64	Durham-Chapel Hill, NC	139.9	319	Johnson City, TN	33.8
364	Blacksburg, VA	20.0	285	Dutchess-Putnam, NY M.D.	43.2	322	Johnstown, PA	33.3
261	Bloomington, IL	50.7	244	East Stroudsburg, PA	55.8	209	Jonesboro, AR	71.4
318	Bloomington, IN	34.0	218	El Centro, CA	67.2	268	Joplin, MO	48.5
374	Bloomsburg-Berwick, PA	14.0	233	El Paso, TX	60.7	205	Kahului-Wailuku-Lahaina, HI	72.4
367	Boise City, ID	18.5	312	Elgin, IL M.D.	35.3	199	Kalamazoo-Portage, MI	73.7
150	Boston (greater), MA-NH	93.2	337	Elizabethtown-Fort Knox, KY	29.0	194	Kankakee, IL	76.5
53	Boston, MA M.D.	149.4	258	Elmira, NY	51.5	94	Kansas City, MO-KS	119.1
321	Boulder, CO	33.6	188	Erie, PA	79.2	305	Kennewick-Richland, WA	37.1
257	Bowling Green, KY	51.6	202	Eugene, OR	73.3	159	Killeen-Temple, TX	90.0
287	Bremerton-Silverdale, WA	42.8	105	Fairbanks, AK	112.7	314	Kingsport, TN-VA	34.9
124	Bridgeport-Stamford, CT	103.9	342	Fargo, ND-MN	27.3	363	Kingston, NY	20.7
242	Brownsville-Harlingen, TX	56.4	283	Farmington, NM	43.6	164	Knoxville, TN	89.2
92	Brunswick, GA	120.0	358	Fayetteville-Springdale, AR-MO	21.9	196	Kokomo, IN	75.8
43	Buffalo-Niagara Falls, NY	158.8	19	Fayetteville, NC	199.3	326	La Crosse, WI-MN	31.9
166	Burlington, NC	89.1	290	Flagstaff, AZ	41.2	283	Lafayette, IN	43.6
273	California-Lexington Park, MD	47.0	8	Flint, MI	232.0	151	Lafayette, LA	92.0
237	Cambridge-Newton, MA M.D.	59.2	232	Florence-Muscle Shoals, AL	60.9	282	Lake Co.-Kenosha Co., IL-WI M.D.	43.9
79	Camden, NJ M.D.	126.9	134	Florence, SC	98.5	341	Lake Havasu City-Kingman, AZ	27.9
59	Canton, OH	145.8	375	Fond du Lac, WI	12.7	216	Lakeland, FL	68.1
172	Cape Coral-Fort Myers, FL	86.4	348	Fort Collins, CO	24.2	229	Lancaster, PA	63.1
197	Cape Girardeau, MO-IL	75.1	22	Fort Lauderdale, FL M.D.	189.8	228	Lansing-East Lansing, MI	63.2
347	Carson City, NV	24.9	300	Fort Smith, AR-OK	38.8	207	Laredo, TX	71.8
371	Casper, WY	15.5	107	Fort Wayne, IN	112.2	291	Las Cruces, NM	41.1
298	Cedar Rapids, IA	39.0	133	Fort Worth-Arlington, TX M.D.	98.6	11	Las Vegas-Henderson, NV	221.6
329	Chambersburg-Waynesboro, PA	31.1	54	Fresno, CA	149.3	262	Lawrence, KS	50.5
136	Champaign-Urbana, IL	98.1	76	Gadsden, AL	128.0	73	Lawton, OK	131.0
161	Charleston-North Charleston, SC	89.7	145	Gainesville, FL	94.1	266	Lebanon, PA	49.1
323	Charlottesville, VA	32.6	259	Gainesville, GA	51.3	231	Lewiston-Auburn, ME	61.4

Note: All listings are for Metropolitan Statistical Areas (M.S.A.s) except for those ending with "M.D." Listings with "M.D." are Metropolitan Divisions which are smaller parts of eleven large M.S.A.s. See explanatory note at beginning of metropolitan area section.

RANK	METROPOLITAN AREA	RATE	RANK	METROPOLITAN AREA	RATE	RANK	METROPOLITAN AREA	RATE
345	Lewiston, ID-WA	25.8	289	Owensboro, KY	41.5	183	Silver Spring-Frederick, MD M.D.	81.5
58	Lexington-Fayette, KY	146.1	200	Oxnard-Thousand Oaks, CA	73.5	332	Sioux City, IA-NE-SD	30.0
104	Lima, OH	113.1	154	Palm Bay-Melbourne, FL	91.7	333	Sioux Falls, SD	29.8
223	Lincoln, NE	65.1	153	Panama City, FL	91.9	84	South Bend-Mishawaka, IN-MI	124.5
30	Little Rock, AR	168.7	307	Parkersburg-Vienna, WV	36.6	176	Spartanburg, SC	84.8
382	Logan, UT-ID	3.1	101	Pensacola, FL	115.1	86	Spokane, WA	123.6
184	Longview, TX	81.4	119	Peoria, IL	106.1	62	Springfield, IL	143.6
227	Longview, WA	63.8	15	Philadelphia (greater) PA-NJ-MD-DE	210.4	72	Springfield, MA	131.4
23	Los Angeles County, CA M.D.	189.6	1	Philadelphia, PA M.D.	412.6	174	Springfield, MO	85.3
39	Los Angeles (greater), CA	161.2	78	Phoenix-Mesa-Scottsdale, AZ	127.3	70	Springfield, OH	132.2
66	Louisville, KY-IN	137.0	61	Pine Bluff, AR	144.0	369	State College, PA	17.4
114	Lubbock, TX	109.5	160	Pittsburgh, PA	89.9	368	Staunton-Waynesboro, VA	18.3
351	Lynchburg, VA	23.7	277	Pittsfield, MA	45.6	5	Stockton-Lodi, CA	283.5
68	Macon, GA	133.0	335	Pocatello, ID	29.7	361	St. George, UT	20.9
158	Madera, CA	90.1	208	Port St. Lucie, FL	71.7	204	St. Joseph, MO-KS	72.7
269	Madison, WI	48.3	190	Portland-Vancouver, OR-WA	78.1	109	St. Louis, MO-IL	111.5
214	Manchester-Nashua, NH	68.6	304	Portland, ME	38.2	139	Sumter, SC	95.9
342	Manhattan, KS	27.3	358	Prescott, AZ	21.9	171	Syracuse, NY	86.5
320	Mankato-North Mankato, MN	33.7	170	Providence-Warwick, RI-MA	87.7	107	Tacoma, WA M.D.	112.2
148	Mansfield, OH	93.9	376	Provo-Orem, UT	12.4	37	Tallahassee, FL	163.3
239	McAllen-Edinburg-Mission, TX	58.5	83	Pueblo, CO	124.7	142	Tampa-St Petersburg, FL	94.7
293	Medford, OR	39.8	355	Punta Gorda, FL	22.7	243	Terre Haute, IN	56.0
4	Memphis, TN-MS-AR	285.7	100	Racine, WI	115.4	163	Texarkana, TX-AR	89.3
81	Merced, CA	126.2	195	Raleigh, NC	76.0	352	The Villages, FL	23.2
20	Miami (greater), FL	197.0	293	Rapid City, SD	39.8	17	Toledo, OH	203.5
9	Miami-Dade County, FL M.D.	231.9	97	Reading, PA	116.6	123	Topeka, KS	104.3
220	Michigan City-La Porte, IN	66.2	151	Redding, CA	92.0	16	Trenton, NJ	205.5
380	Midland, MI	8.3	140	Reno, NV	95.6	57	Tucson, AZ	148.0
307	Midland, TX	36.6	144	Richmond, VA	94.5	82	Tulsa, OK	125.9
12	Milwaukee, WI	220.0	89	Riverside-San Bernardino, CA	121.3	127	Tuscaloosa, AL	102.2
157	Minneapolis-St. Paul, MN-WI	90.5	254	Roanoke, VA	53.2	255	Tyler, TX	53.1
315	Missoula, MT	34.3	340	Rochester, MN	28.1	240	Utica-Rome, NY	57.3
42	Mobile, AL	159.6	137	Rochester, NY	97.6	189	Valdosta, GA	78.6
51	Modesto, CA	150.6	31	Rockford, IL	167.3	45	Vallejo-Fairfield, CA	157.0
128	Monroe, LA	101.8	360	Rockingham County, NH M.D.	21.1	249	Victoria, TX	54.1
224	Monroe, MI	64.6	120	Rocky Mount, NC	105.4	18	Vineland-Bridgeton, NJ	199.5
276	Montgomery County, PA M.D.	46.2	238	Rome, GA	58.8	125	Virginia Beach-Norfolk, VA-NC	102.3
60	Montgomery, AL	145.7	69	Sacramento, CA	132.9	156	Visalia-Porterville, CA	91.5
309	Morgantown, WV	36.3	87	Saginaw, MI	121.5	173	Waco, TX	85.7
200	Morristown, TN	73.5	263	Salem, OR	50.3	317	Walla Walla, WA	34.2
302	Mount Vernon-Anacortes, WA	38.6	35	Salinas, CA	165.8	121	Warner Robins, GA	104.6
168	Muncie, IN	88.1	149	Salisbury, MD-DE	93.4	280	Warren-Troy, MI M.D.	45.3
260	Napa, CA	50.9	202	Salt Lake City, UT	73.3	51	Washington (greater) DC-VA-MD-WV	150.6
279	Naples-Marco Island, FL	45.4	141	San Antonio, TX	95.1	29	Washington, DC-VA-MD-WV M.D.	169.2
77	Nashville-Davidson, TN	127.5	129	San Diego, CA	101.0	281	Waterloo-Cedar Falls, IA	45.0
225	Nassau-Suffolk, NY M.D.	64.3	6	San Francisco (greater), CA	271.7	354	Watertown-Fort Drum, NY	22.8
253	New Bern, NC	53.4	7	San Francisco-Redwood, CA M.D.	261.3	366	Wausau, WI	18.6
33	New Haven-Milford, CT	166.6	167	San Jose, CA	88.8	65	West Palm Beach, FL M.D.	139.7
63	New Orleans, LA	141.1	339	San Luis Obispo, CA	28.4	301	Wheeling, WV-OH	38.7
41	New York (greater), NY-NJ-PA	160.7	234	San Rafael, CA M.D.	60.6	125	Wichita Falls, TX	102.3
26	New York-Jersey City, NY-NJ M.D.	182.6	182	Santa Cruz-Watsonville, CA	82.5	181	Wichita, KS	82.6
32	Newark, NJ-PA M.D.	166.8	143	Santa Fe, NM	94.6	211	Williamsport, PA	69.3
147	North Port-Sarasota-Bradenton, FL	94.0	206	Santa Maria-Santa Barbara, CA	72.2	24	Wilmington, DE-MD-NJ M.D.	185.4
217	Norwich-New London, CT	67.6	272	Santa Rosa, CA	47.1	91	Wilmington, NC	120.5
3	Oakland-Hayward, CA M.D.	298.5	47	Savannah, GA	154.4	353	Winchester, VA-WV	22.9
270	Ocala, FL	48.1	210	Scranton--Wilkes-Barre, PA	70.0	162	Winston-Salem, NC	89.5
246	Ocean City, NJ	54.6	111	Seattle (greater), WA	110.7	191	Worcester, MA-CT	77.3
103	Odessa, TX	114.6	112	Seattle-Bellevue-Everett, WA M.D.	110.3	178	Yakima, WA	84.5
350	Ogden-Clearfield, UT	23.9	278	Sebastian-Vero Beach, FL	45.5	211	York-Hanover, PA	69.3
102	Oklahoma City, OK	115.0	192	Sebring, FL	77.0	132	Youngstown-Warren, OH-PA	99.0
315	Olympia, WA	34.3	365	Sheboygan, WI	19.9	264	Yuba City, CA	49.7
118	Omaha-Council Bluffs, NE-IA	106.4	299	Sherman-Denison, TX	38.9	306	Yuma, AZ	36.9
88	Orlando, FL	121.4	95	Shreveport-Bossier City, LA	118.2			
373	Oshkosh-Neenah, WI	14.3	296	Sierra Vista-Douglas, AZ	39.3			

Source: Reported data from the F.B.I. "Crime in the United States 2012"

*Robbery is the taking of anything of value by force or threat of force. Attempts are included.

18. Robbery Rate in 2012 (continued)
National Rate = 112.9 Robberies per 100,000 Population*

RANK	METROPOLITAN AREA	RATE	RANK	METROPOLITAN AREA	RATE	RANK	METROPOLITAN AREA	RATE
1	Philadelphia, PA M.D.	412.6	65	West Palm Beach, FL M.D.	139.7	129	San Diego, CA	101.0
2	Detroit-Dearborn-Livonia, MI M.D.	326.4	66	Louisville, KY-IN	137.0	130	Decatur, IL	100.2
3	Oakland-Hayward, CA M.D.	298.5	67	Albuquerque, NM	136.5	131	Gary, IN M.D.	99.3
4	Memphis, TN-MS-AR	285.7	68	Macon, GA	133.0	132	Youngstown-Warren, OH-PA	99.0
5	Stockton-Lodi, CA	283.5	69	Sacramento, CA	132.9	133	Fort Worth-Arlington, TX M.D.	98.6
6	San Francisco (greater), CA	271.7	70	Springfield, OH	132.2	134	Beckley, WV	98.5
7	San Francisco-Redwood, CA M.D.	261.3	71	Cincinnati, OH-KY-IN	131.8	134	Florence, SC	98.5
8	Flint, MI	232.0	72	Springfield, MA	131.4	136	Champaign-Urbana, IL	98.1
9	Miami-Dade County, FL M.D.	231.9	73	Lawton, OK	131.0	137	Rochester, NY	97.6
10	Chicago-Joilet-Naperville, IL M.D.	222.0	74	Dallas-Plano-Irving, TX M.D.	130.9	138	Dover, DE	96.6
11	Las Vegas-Henderson, NV	221.6	75	Huntsville, AL	128.3	139	Sumter, SC	95.9
12	Milwaukee, WI	220.0	76	Gadsden, AL	128.0	140	Reno, NV	95.6
13	Houston, TX	219.9	77	Nashville-Davidson, TN	127.5	141	San Antonio, TX	95.1
14	Baltimore, MD	214.2	78	Phoenix-Mesa-Scottsdale, AZ	127.3	142	Tampa-St Petersburg, FL	94.7
15	Philadelphia (greater) PA-NJ-MD-DE	210.4	79	Camden, NJ M.D.	126.9	143	Santa Fe, NM	94.6
16	Trenton, NJ	205.5	80	Dayton, OH	126.5	144	Richmond, VA	94.5
17	Toledo, OH	203.5	81	Merced, CA	126.2	145	Corpus Christi, TX	94.1
18	Vineland-Bridgeton, NJ	199.5	82	Tulsa, OK	125.9	145	Gainesville, FL	94.1
19	Fayetteville, NC	199.3	83	Pueblo, CO	124.7	147	North Port-Sarasota-Bradenton, FL	94.0
20	Miami (greater), FL	197.0	84	South Bend-Mishawaka, IN-MI	124.5	148	Mansfield, OH	93.9
21	Indianapolis, IN	196.0	85	Augusta, GA-SC	124.2	149	Salisbury, MD-DE	93.4
22	Fort Lauderdale, FL M.D.	189.8	86	Spokane, WA	123.6	150	Boston (greater), MA-NH	93.2
23	Los Angeles County, CA M.D.	189.6	87	Saginaw, MI	121.5	151	Lafayette, LA	92.0
24	Wilmington, DE-MD-NJ M.D.	185.4	88	Orlando, FL	121.4	151	Redding, CA	92.0
25	Chicago (greater), IL-IN-WI	184.2	89	Riverside-San Bernardino, CA	121.3	153	Panama City, FL	91.9
26	New York-Jersey City, NY-NJ M.D.	182.6	90	Greenville, NC	120.9	154	Palm Bay-Melbourne, FL	91.7
27	Baton Rouge, LA	179.6	91	Wilmington, NC	120.5	155	Athens-Clarke County, GA	91.6
28	Atlantic City, NJ	173.0	92	Brunswick, GA	120.0	156	Visalia-Porterville, CA	91.5
29	Washington, DC-VA-MD-WV M.D.	169.2	93	Dallas (greater), TX	119.9	157	Minneapolis-St. Paul, MN-WI	90.5
30	Little Rock, AR	168.7	94	Kansas City, MO-KS	119.1	158	Madera, CA	90.1
31	Rockford, IL	167.3	95	Shreveport-Bossier City, LA	118.2	159	Killeen-Temple, TX	90.0
32	Newark, NJ-PA M.D.	166.8	96	Jacksonville, FL	116.8	160	Pittsburgh, PA	89.9
33	New Haven-Milford, CT	166.6	97	Hartford, CT	116.6	161	Charleston-North Charleston, SC	89.7
34	Columbus, GA-AL	166.3	97	Reading, PA	116.6	162	Winston-Salem, NC	89.5
35	Salinas, CA	165.8	99	Greensboro-High Point, NC	116.0	163	Texarkana, TX-AR	89.3
36	Detroit (greater), MI	163.5	100	Racine, WI	115.4	164	Hilton Head Island, SC	89.2
37	Tallahassee, FL	163.3	101	Pensacola, FL	115.1	164	Knoxville, TN	89.2
38	Albany, GA	161.9	102	Oklahoma City, OK	115.0	166	Burlington, NC	89.1
39	Jackson, MS	161.2	103	Odessa, TX	114.6	167	San Jose, CA	88.8
39	Los Angeles (greater), CA	161.2	104	Lima, OH	113.1	168	Goldsboro, NC	88.1
41	New York (greater), NY-NJ-PA	160.7	105	Fairbanks, AK	112.7	168	Muncie, IN	88.1
42	Mobile, AL	159.6	106	Alexandria, LA	112.6	170	Providence-Warwick, RI-MA	87.7
43	Buffalo-Niagara Falls, NY	158.8	107	Fort Wayne, IN	112.2	171	Syracuse, NY	86.5
44	Anchorage, AK	158.2	107	Tacoma, WA M.D.	112.2	172	Cape Coral-Fort Myers, FL	86.4
45	Vallejo-Fairfield, CA	157.0	109	St. Louis, MO-IL	111.5	173	Waco, TX	85.7
46	Birmingham-Hoover, AL	155.6	110	Anniston-Oxford, AL	110.8	174	Springfield, MO	85.3
47	Savannah, GA	154.4	111	Seattle (greater), WA	110.7	175	Allentown, PA-NJ	85.2
48	Atlanta, GA	154.2	112	Seattle-Bellevue-Everett, WA M.D.	110.3	176	Spartanburg, SC	84.8
49	Bakersfield, CA	152.7	113	Harrisburg-Carlisle, PA	109.8	177	Colorado Springs, CO	84.7
50	Jackson, TN	151.9	114	Lubbock, TX	109.5	178	Yakima, WA	84.5
51	Modesto, CA	150.6	115	Columbia, MO	108.5	179	Denver-Aurora, CO	84.4
51	Washington (greater) DC-VA-MD-WV	150.6	116	Danville, IL	107.9	180	Greenville-Anderson, SC	83.3
53	Boston, MA M.D.	149.4	117	Amarillo, TX	107.8	181	Wichita, KS	82.6
54	Fresno, CA	149.3	118	Omaha-Council Bluffs, NE-IA	106.4	182	Santa Cruz-Watsonville, CA	82.5
55	Beaumont-Port Arthur, TX	149.1	119	Peoria, IL	106.1	183	Silver Spring-Frederick, MD M.D.	81.5
56	Hammond, LA	148.4	120	Rocky Mount, NC	105.4	184	Longview, TX	81.4
57	Tucson, AZ	148.0	121	Warner Robins, GA	104.6	185	Dothan, AL	80.9
58	Lexington-Fayette, KY	146.1	122	Akron, OH	104.4	186	Abilene, TX	80.5
59	Canton, OH	145.8	123	Topeka, KS	104.3	187	Albany-Schenectady-Troy, NY	79.7
60	Montgomery, AL	145.7	124	Bridgeport-Stamford, CT	103.9	188	Erie, PA	79.2
61	Pine Bluff, AR	144.0	125	Virginia Beach-Norfolk, VA-NC	102.3	189	Valdosta, GA	78.6
62	Springfield, IL	143.6	125	Wichita Falls, TX	102.3	190	Portland-Vancouver, OR-WA	78.1
63	New Orleans, LA	141.1	127	Tuscaloosa, AL	102.2	191	Worcester, MA-CT	77.3
64	Durham-Chapel Hill, NC	139.9	128	Monroe, LA	101.8	192	Deltona-Daytona Beach, FL	77.0

Note: All listings are for Metropolitan Statistical Areas (M.S.A.s) except for those ending with "M.D." Listings with "M.D." are Metropolitan Divisions which are smaller parts of eleven large M.S.A.s. See explanatory note at beginning of metropolitan area section.

RANK	METROPOLITAN AREA	RATE	RANK	METROPOLITAN AREA	RATE	RANK	METROPOLITAN AREA	RATE
192	Sebring, FL	77.0	257	Bowling Green, KY	51.6	321	Boulder, CO	33.6
194	Kankakee, IL	76.5	258	Elmira, NY	51.5	322	Johnstown, PA	33.3
195	Raleigh, NC	76.0	259	Gainesville, GA	51.3	323	Charlottesville, VA	32.6
196	Kokomo, IN	75.8	260	Napa, CA	50.9	324	Green Bay, WI	32.2
197	Cape Girardeau, MO-IL	75.1	261	Bloomington, IL	50.7	325	Columbus, IN	32.0
197	Chico, CA	75.1	262	Lawrence, KS	50.5	326	La Crosse, WI-MN	31.9
199	Kalamazoo-Portage, MI	73.7	263	Salem, OR	50.3	327	Bellingham, WA	31.6
200	Morristown, TN	73.5	264	Yuba City, CA	49.7	327	Great Falls, MT	31.6
200	Oxnard-Thousand Oaks, CA	73.5	265	College Station-Bryan, TX	49.3	329	Chambersburg-Waynesboro, PA	31.1
202	Eugene, OR	73.3	266	Lebanon, PA	49.1	330	Dalton, GA	30.5
202	Salt Lake City, UT	73.3	267	Des Moines-West Des Moines, IA	48.8	331	Iowa City, IA	30.2
204	St. Joseph, MO-KS	72.7	268	Joplin, MO	48.5	332	Sioux City, IA-NE-SD	30.0
205	Kahului-Wailuku-Lahaina, HI	72.4	269	Madison, WI	48.3	333	Altoona, PA	29.8
206	Santa Maria-Santa Barbara, CA	72.2	270	Ocala, FL	48.1	333	Sioux Falls, SD	29.8
207	Laredo, TX	71.8	271	Duluth, MN-WI	47.3	335	Pocatello, ID	29.7
208	Port St. Lucie, FL	71.7	272	Santa Rosa, CA	47.1	336	Grand Junction, CO	29.5
209	Jonesboro, AR	71.4	273	California-Lexington Park, MD	47.0	337	Elizabethtown-Fort Knox, KY	29.0
210	Scranton--Wilkes-Barre, PA	70.0	274	Cleveland, TN	46.7	338	Cheyenne, WY	28.7
211	Williamsport, PA	69.3	275	Cumberland, MD-WV	46.3	339	San Luis Obispo, CA	28.4
211	York-Hanover, PA	69.3	276	Montgomery County, PA M.D.	46.2	340	Rochester, MN	28.1
213	Anaheim-Santa Ana-Irvine, CA M.D.	69.1	277	Pittsfield, MA	45.6	341	Lake Havasu City-Kingman, AZ	27.9
214	Manchester-Nashua, NH	68.6	278	Sebastian-Vero Beach, FL	45.5	342	Fargo, ND-MN	27.3
215	Hanford-Corcoran, CA	68.3	279	Naples-Marco Island, FL	45.4	342	Manhattan, KS	27.3
216	Lakeland, FL	68.1	280	Warren-Troy, MI M.D.	45.3	344	Grand Forks, ND-MN	27.1
217	Norwich-New London, CT	67.6	281	Waterloo-Cedar Falls, IA	45.0	345	Lewiston, ID-WA	25.8
218	El Centro, CA	67.2	282	Lake Co.-Kenosha Co., IL-WI M.D.	43.9	346	Grand Island, NE	25.2
219	Hagerstown-Martinsburg, MD-WV	66.6	283	Farmington, NM	43.6	347	Carson City, NV	24.9
220	Michigan City-La Porte, IN	66.2	283	Lafayette, IN	43.6	348	Dubuque, IA	24.2
221	Austin-Round Rock, TX	66.0	285	Dutchess-Putnam, NY M.D.	43.2	348	Fort Collins, CO	24.2
222	Clarksville, TN-KY	65.4	286	Homosassa Springs, FL	43.0	350	Ogden-Clearfield, UT	23.9
223	Lincoln, NE	65.1	287	Bremerton-Silverdale, WA	42.8	351	Lynchburg, VA	23.7
224	Monroe, MI	64.6	288	Billings, MT	42.6	352	The Villages, FL	23.2
225	Nassau-Suffolk, NY M.D.	64.3	289	Owensboro, KY	41.5	353	Winchester, VA-WV	22.9
226	Davenport, IA-IL	64.1	290	Flagstaff, AZ	41.2	354	Watertown-Fort Drum, NY	22.8
227	Longview, WA	63.8	291	Las Cruces, NM	41.1	355	Harrisonburg, VA	22.7
228	Lansing-East Lansing, MI	63.2	292	Daphne-Fairhope-Foley, AL	40.5	355	Punta Gorda, FL	22.7
229	Lancaster, PA	63.1	293	Medford, OR	39.8	357	Bismarck, ND	22.6
230	Houma, LA	62.4	293	Rapid City, SD	39.8	358	Fayetteville-Springdale, AR-MO	21.9
231	Lewiston-Auburn, ME	61.4	295	Bangor, ME	39.6	358	Prescott, AZ	21.9
232	Florence-Muscle Shoals, AL	60.9	296	Sierra Vista-Douglas, AZ	39.3	360	Rockingham County, NH M.D.	21.1
233	El Paso, TX	60.7	297	Jefferson City, MO	39.1	361	St. George, UT	20.9
234	San Rafael, CA M.D.	60.6	298	Cedar Rapids, IA	39.0	362	Corvallis, OR	20.8
235	Decatur, AL	60.1	299	Sherman-Denison, TX	38.9	363	Kingston, NY	20.7
236	Janesville, WI	59.8	300	Fort Smith, AR-OK	38.8	364	Blacksburg, VA	20.0
237	Cambridge-Newton, MA M.D.	59.2	301	Wheeling, WV-OH	38.7	365	Sheboygan, WI	19.9
238	Rome, GA	58.8	302	Mount Vernon-Anacortes, WA	38.6	366	Wausau, WI	18.6
239	McAllen-Edinburg-Mission, TX	58.5	303	Bay City, MI	38.3	367	Boise City, ID	18.5
240	Utica-Rome, NY	57.3	304	Portland, ME	38.2	368	Staunton-Waynesboro, VA	18.3
241	Binghamton, NY	56.5	305	Kennewick-Richland, WA	37.1	369	State College, PA	17.4
242	Brownsville-Harlingen, TX	56.4	306	Yuma, AZ	36.9	370	Appleton, WI	16.2
243	Terre Haute, IN	56.0	307	Midland, TX	36.6	371	Casper, WY	15.5
244	East Stroudsburg, PA	55.8	307	Parkersburg-Vienna, WV	36.6	371	Coeur d'Alene, ID	15.5
245	Hattiesburg, MS	54.9	309	Morgantown, WV	36.3	373	Oshkosh-Neenah, WI	14.3
246	Ocean City, NJ	54.6	310	Barnstable Town, MA	35.8	374	Bloomsburg-Berwick, PA	14.0
247	Asheville, NC	54.5	310	Greeley, CO	35.8	375	Fond du Lac, WI	12.7
248	Hickory, NC	54.3	312	Albany, OR	35.3	376	Provo-Orem, UT	12.4
249	Victoria, TX	54.1	312	Elgin, IL M.D.	35.3	377	Glens Falls, NY	12.3
250	Hinesville, GA	54.0	314	Kingsport, TN-VA	34.9	378	Idaho Falls, ID	11.0
251	Ann Arbor, MI	53.7	315	Missoula, MT	34.3	379	Ames, IA	8.9
252	Auburn, AL	53.5	315	Olympia, WA	34.3	380	Midland, MI	8.3
253	New Bern, NC	53.4	317	Walla Walla, WA	34.2	381	Gettysburg, PA	5.9
254	Roanoke, VA	53.2	318	Bloomington, IN	34.0	382	Logan, UT-ID	3.1
255	Tyler, TX	53.1	319	Johnson City, TN	33.8			
256	Crestview-Fort Walton Beach, FL	52.0	320	Mankato-North Mankato, MN	33.7			

Source: Reported data from the F.B.I. "Crime in the United States 2012"

*Robbery is the taking of anything of value by force or threat of force. Attempts are included.

19. Percent Change in Robbery Rate: 2011 to 2012
National Percent Change = 0.8% Decrease*

RANK	METROPOLITAN AREA	% CHANGE	RANK	METROPOLITAN AREA	% CHANGE	RANK	METROPOLITAN AREA	% CHANGE
68	Abilene, TX	11.3	211	Cheyenne, WY	(11.4)	223	Gary, IN M.D.	(14.0)
241	Akron, OH	(18.4)	162	Chicago (greater), IL-IN-WI	(3.4)	NA	Gettysburg, PA**	NA
NA	Albany-Schenectady-Troy, NY**	NA	NA	Chicago-Joilet-Naperville, IL M.D.**	NA	NA	Glens Falls, NY**	NA
23	Albany, GA	27.8	89	Chico, CA	5.8	226	Goldsboro, NC	(14.5)
NA	Albany, OR**	NA	NA	Cincinnati, OH-KY-IN**	NA	1	Grand Forks, ND-MN	125.8
97	Albuquerque, NM	4.8	195	Clarksville, TN-KY	(9.2)	NA	Grand Island, NE**	NA
168	Alexandria, LA	(3.9)	155	Cleveland, TN	(2.5)	230	Grand Junction, CO	(15.2)
NA	Allentown, PA-NJ**	NA	NA	Coeur d'Alene, ID**	NA	251	Great Falls, MT	(21.4)
248	Altoona, PA	(20.7)	178	College Station-Bryan, TX	(5.7)	194	Greeley, CO	(8.9)
56	Amarillo, TX	14.1	44	Colorado Springs, CO	16.3	2	Green Bay, WI	76.9
274	Ames, IA	(38.2)	108	Columbia, MO	3.3	NA	Greensboro-High Point, NC**	NA
181	Anaheim-Santa Ana-Irvine, CA M.D.	(6.2)	85	Columbus, GA-AL	6.7	NA	Greenville-Anderson, SC**	NA
NA	Anchorage, AK**	NA	109	Columbus, IN	2.9	NA	Greenville, NC**	NA
221	Ann Arbor, MI	(13.5)	107	Corpus Christi, TX	3.4	NA	Hagerstown-Martinsburg, MD-WV**	NA
41	Anniston-Oxford, AL	16.9	62	Corvallis, OR	12.4	NA	Hammond, LA**	NA
69	Appleton, WI	11.0	233	Crestview-Fort Walton Beach, FL	(15.7)	77	Hanford-Corcoran, CA	8.9
221	Asheville, NC	(13.5)	267	Cumberland, MD-WV	(31.2)	100	Harrisburg-Carlisle, PA	4.2
33	Athens-Clarke County, GA	21.5	163	Dallas (greater), TX	(3.5)	17	Harrisonburg, VA	36.7
125	Atlanta, GA	1.0	163	Dallas-Plano-Irving, TX M.D.	(3.5)	93	Hartford, CT	5.1
249	Atlantic City, NJ	(21.0)	74	Dalton, GA	9.7	NA	Hattiesburg, MS**	NA
245	Auburn, AL	(19.8)	92	Danville, IL	5.2	88	Hickory, NC	6.3
179	Augusta, GA-SC	(5.8)	NA	Daphne-Fairhope-Foley, AL**	NA	NA	Hilton Head Island, SC**	NA
215	Austin-Round Rock, TX	(12.2)	44	Davenport, IA-IL	16.3	264	Hinesville, GA	(28.9)
27	Bakersfield, CA	26.1	136	Dayton, OH	(0.6)	NA	Homosassa Springs, FL**	NA
151	Baltimore, MD	(1.8)	18	Decatur, AL	36.6	208	Houma, LA	(10.9)
22	Bangor, ME	29.8	235	Decatur, IL	(16.3)	49	Houston, TX	15.8
262	Barnstable Town, MA	(26.6)	NA	Deltona-Daytona Beach, FL**	NA	83	Huntsville, AL	8.1
60	Baton Rouge, LA	12.7	NA	Denver-Aurora, CO**	NA	34	Idaho Falls, ID	20.9
193	Bay City, MI	(8.4)	72	Des Moines-West Des Moines, IA	9.9	NA	Indianapolis, IN**	NA
176	Beaumont-Port Arthur, TX	(5.6)	132	Detroit (greater), MI	(0.1)	3	Iowa City, IA	71.6
NA	Beckley, WV**	NA	129	Detroit-Dearborn-Livonia, MI M.D.	0.3	229	Jacksonville, FL	(14.8)
216	Bellingham, WA	(12.7)	170	Dothan, AL	(4.5)	NA	Jackson, MS**	NA
5	Billings, MT	65.8	239	Dover, DE	(17.9)	NA	Jackson, TN**	NA
NA	Binghamton, NY**	NA	266	Dubuque, IA	(31.1)	129	Janesville, WI	0.3
106	Birmingham-Hoover, AL	3.5	96	Duluth, MN-WI	4.9	234	Jefferson City, MO	(16.1)
7	Bismarck, ND	55.9	219	Durham-Chapel Hill, NC	(13.3)	253	Johnson City, TN	(22.1)
16	Blacksburg, VA	37.0	NA	Dutchess-Putnam, NY M.D.**	NA	276	Johnstown, PA	(45.5)
140	Bloomington, IL	(1.0)	NA	East Stroudsburg, PA**	NA	192	Jonesboro, AR	(8.3)
NA	Bloomington, IN**	NA	21	El Centro, CA	30.5	51	Joplin, MO	15.5
NA	Bloomsburg-Berwick, PA**	NA	142	El Paso, TX	(1.1)	NA	Kahului-Wailuku-Lahaina, HI**	NA
25	Boise City, ID	26.7	NA	Elgin, IL M.D.**	NA	NA	Kalamazoo-Portage, MI**	NA
NA	Boston (greater), MA-NH**	NA	NA	Elizabethtown-Fort Knox, KY**	NA	275	Kankakee, IL	(38.3)
NA	Boston, MA M.D.**	NA	NA	Elmira, NY**	NA	NA	Kansas City, MO-KS**	NA
48	Boulder, CO	15.9	43	Erie, PA	16.6	73	Kennewick-Richland, WA	9.8
153	Bowling Green, KY	(2.3)	113	Eugene, OR	2.5	31	Killeen-Temple, TX	23.8
187	Bremerton-Silverdale, WA	(6.8)	84	Fairbanks, AK	7.2	243	Kingsport, TN-VA	(18.6)
225	Bridgeport-Stamford, CT	(14.4)	197	Fargo, ND-MN	(9.6)	NA	Kingston, NY**	NA
128	Brownsville-Harlingen, TX	0.4	82	Farmington, NM	8.2	NA	Knoxville, TN**	NA
196	Brunswick, GA	(9.5)	NA	Fayetteville-Springdale, AR-MO**	NA	NA	Kokomo, IN**	NA
NA	Buffalo-Niagara Falls, NY**	NA	75	Fayetteville, NC	9.4	8	La Crosse, WI-MN	47.7
125	Burlington, NC	1.0	148	Flagstaff, AZ	(1.4)	14	Lafayette, IN	38.0
NA	California-Lexington Park, MD**	NA	87	Flint, MI	6.6	NA	Lafayette, LA**	NA
NA	Cambridge-Newton, MA M.D.**	NA	12	Florence-Muscle Shoals, AL	38.4	181	Lake Co.-Kenosha Co., IL-WI M.D.	(6.2)
176	Camden, NJ M.D.	(5.6)	185	Florence, SC	(6.5)	138	Lake Havasu City-Kingman, AZ	(0.7)
117	Canton, OH	1.9	131	Fond du Lac, WI	0.0	250	Lakeland, FL	(21.3)
200	Cape Coral-Fort Myers, FL	(10.0)	37	Fort Collins, CO	19.2	163	Lancaster, PA	(3.5)
270	Cape Girardeau, MO-IL	(32.2)	158	Fort Lauderdale, FL M.D.	(3.2)	227	Lansing-East Lansing, MI	(14.6)
218	Carson City, NV	(13.2)	NA	Fort Smith, AR-OK**	NA	237	Laredo, TX	(17.4)
277	Casper, WY	(48.7)	15	Fort Wayne, IN	37.7	160	Las Cruces, NM	(3.3)
47	Cedar Rapids, IA	16.1	160	Fort Worth-Arlington, TX M.D.	(3.3)	49	Las Vegas-Henderson, NV	15.8
NA	Chambersburg-Waynesboro, PA**	NA	117	Fresno, CA	1.9	11	Lawrence, KS	40.7
101	Champaign-Urbana, IL	4.1	6	Gadsden, AL	58.0	NA	Lawton, OK**	NA
NA	Charleston-North Charleston, SC**	NA	208	Gainesville, FL	(10.9)	227	Lebanon, PA	(14.6)
257	Charlottesville, VA	(22.7)	58	Gainesville, GA	14.0	71	Lewiston-Auburn, ME	10.2

Note: All listings are for Metropolitan Statistical Areas (M.S.A.s) except for those ending with "M.D." Listings with "M.D." are Metropolitan Divisions which are smaller parts of eleven large M.S.A.s. See explanatory note at beginning of metropolitan area section.

RANK	METROPOLITAN AREA	% CHANGE	RANK	METROPOLITAN AREA	% CHANGE	RANK	METROPOLITAN AREA	% CHANGE
NA	Lewiston, ID-WA**	NA	55	Owensboro, KY	14.3	147	Silver Spring-Frederick, MD M.D.	(1.3)
NA	Lexington-Fayette, KY**	NA	135	Oxnard-Thousand Oaks, CA	(0.5)	NA	Sioux City, IA-NE-SD**	NA
110	Lima, OH	2.8	200	Palm Bay-Melbourne, FL	(10.0)	204	Sioux Falls, SD	(10.5)
64	Lincoln, NE	12.0	NA	Panama City, FL**	NA	252	South Bend-Mishawaka, IN-MI	(21.6)
181	Little Rock, AR	(6.2)	199	Pensacola, FL	(9.9)	NA	Spartanburg, SC**	NA
247	Logan, UT-ID	(20.5)	79	Peoria, IL	8.8	NA	Spokane, WA**	NA
20	Longview, TX	31.1	NA	Philadelphia (greater) PA-NJ-MD-DE**	NA	115	Springfield, IL	2.3
70	Longview, WA	10.6	NA	Philadelphia, PA M.D.**	NA	NA	Springfield, MA**	NA
172	Los Angeles County, CA M.D.	(5.3)	NA	Phoenix-Mesa-Scottsdale, AZ**	NA	59	Springfield, MO	13.3
174	Los Angeles (greater), CA	(5.5)	207	Pine Bluff, AR	(10.8)	231	Springfield, OH	(15.3)
204	Louisville, KY-IN	(10.5)	145	Pittsburgh, PA	(1.2)	220	State College, PA	(13.4)
142	Lubbock, TX	(1.1)	102	Pittsfield, MA	3.9	NA	Staunton-Waynesboro, VA**	NA
269	Lynchburg, VA	(31.9)	NA	Pocatello, ID**	NA	56	Stockton-Lodi, CA	14.1
111	Macon, GA	2.6	256	Port St. Lucie, FL	(22.6)	NA	St. George, UT**	NA
142	Madera, CA	(1.1)	105	Portland-Vancouver, OR-WA	3.6	64	St. Joseph, MO-KS	12.0
NA	Madison, WI**	NA	90	Portland, ME	5.5	236	St. Louis, MO-IL	(16.8)
93	Manchester-Nashua, NH	5.1	9	Prescott, AZ	46.0	202	Sumter, SC	(10.1)
NA	Manhattan, KS**	NA	NA	Providence-Warwick, RI-MA**	NA	NA	Syracuse, NY**	NA
26	Mankato-North Mankato, MN	26.2	54	Provo-Orem, UT	14.8	149	Tacoma, WA M.D.	(1.5)
99	Mansfield, OH	4.4	60	Pueblo, CO	12.7	156	Tallahassee, FL	(2.6)
145	McAllen-Edinburg-Mission, TX	(1.2)	265	Punta Gorda, FL	(30.6)	198	Tampa-St Petersburg, FL	(9.7)
63	Medford, OR	12.1	127	Racine, WI	0.7	214	Terre Haute, IN	(11.8)
77	Memphis, TN-MS-AR	8.9	180	Raleigh, NC	(6.1)	NA	Texarkana, TX-AR**	NA
37	Merced, CA	19.2	NA	Rapid City, SD**	NA	NA	The Villages, FL**	NA
163	Miami (greater), FL	(3.5)	85	Reading, PA	6.7	NA	Toledo, OH**	NA
171	Miami-Dade County, FL M.D.	(4.7)	29	Redding, CA	25.0	121	Topeka, KS	1.5
36	Michigan City-La Porte, IN	19.7	224	Reno, NV	(14.2)	75	Trenton, NJ	9.4
NA	Midland, MI**	NA	134	Richmond, VA	(0.4)	98	Tucson, AZ	4.7
NA	Midland, TX**	NA	93	Riverside-San Bernardino, CA	5.1	163	Tulsa, OK	(3.5)
103	Milwaukee, WI	3.8	257	Roanoke, VA	(22.7)	NA	Tuscaloosa, AL**	NA
133	Minneapolis-St. Paul, MN-WI	(0.2)	NA	Rochester, MN**	NA	66	Tyler, TX	11.6
10	Missoula, MT	45.3	NA	Rochester, NY**	NA	NA	Utica-Rome, NY**	NA
261	Mobile, AL	(25.9)	188	Rockford, IL	(7.0)	203	Valdosta, GA	(10.4)
66	Modesto, CA	11.6	191	Rockingham County, NH M.D.	(7.9)	173	Vallejo-Fairfield, CA	(5.4)
34	Monroe, LA	20.9	240	Rocky Mount, NC	(18.2)	NA	Victoria, TX**	NA
13	Monroe, MI	38.3	260	Rome, GA	(25.5)	NA	Vineland-Bridgeton, NJ**	NA
NA	Montgomery County, PA M.D.**	NA	121	Sacramento, CA	1.5	254	Virginia Beach-Norfolk, VA-NC	(22.3)
24	Montgomery, AL	26.9	80	Saginaw, MI	8.5	28	Visalia-Porterville, CA	26.0
NA	Morgantown, WV**	NA	46	Salem, OR	16.2	NA	Waco, TX**	NA
NA	Morristown, TN**	NA	32	Salinas, CA	21.7	NA	Walla Walla, WA**	NA
263	Mount Vernon-Anacortes, WA	(28.4)	NA	Salisbury, MD-DE**	NA	NA	Warner Robins, GA**	NA
208	Muncie, IN	(10.9)	113	Salt Lake City, UT	2.5	124	Warren-Troy, MI M.D.	1.1
119	Napa, CA	1.8	121	San Antonio, TX	1.5	174	Washington (greater) DC-VA-MD-WV	(5.5)
267	Naples-Marco Island, FL	(31.2)	104	San Diego, CA	3.7	181	Washington, DC-VA-MD-WV M.D.	(6.2)
NA	Nashville-Davidson, TN**	NA	53	San Francisco (greater), CA	14.9	41	Waterloo-Cedar Falls, IA	16.9
NA	Nassau-Suffolk, NY M.D.**	NA	30	San Francisco-Redwood, CA M.D.	24.7	NA	Watertown-Fort Drum, NY**	NA
NA	New Bern, NC**	NA	115	San Jose, CA	2.3	206	Wausau, WI	(10.6)
81	New Haven-Milford, CT	8.3	169	San Luis Obispo, CA	(4.4)	136	West Palm Beach, FL M.D.	(0.6)
186	New Orleans, LA	(6.6)	NA	San Rafael, CA M.D.**	NA	NA	Wheeling, WV-OH**	NA
NA	New York (greater), NY-NJ-PA**	NA	217	Santa Cruz-Watsonville, CA	(13.1)	91	Wichita Falls, TX	5.4
NA	New York-Jersey City, NY-NJ M.D.**	NA	19	Santa Fe, NM	33.8	152	Wichita, KS	(2.1)
NA	Newark, NJ-PA M.D.**	NA	NA	Santa Maria-Santa Barbara, CA**	NA	52	Williamsport, PA	15.3
244	North Port-Sarasota-Bradenton, FL	(19.5)	149	Santa Rosa, CA	(1.5)	158	Wilmington, DE-MD-NJ M.D.	(3.2)
189	Norwich-New London, CT	(7.4)	139	Savannah, GA	(0.8)	NA	Wilmington, NC**	NA
40	Oakland-Hayward, CA M.D.	17.1	140	Scranton--Wilkes-Barre, PA	(1.0)	273	Winchester, VA-WV	(36.7)
232	Ocala, FL	(15.5)	120	Seattle (greater), WA	1.6	NA	Winston-Salem, NC**	NA
272	Ocean City, NJ	(36.6)	111	Seattle-Bellevue-Everett, WA M.D.	2.6	NA	Worcester, MA-CT**	NA
4	Odessa, TX	69.0	255	Sebastian-Vero Beach, FL	(22.4)	212	Yakima, WA	(11.5)
NA	Ogden-Clearfield, UT**	NA	NA	Sebring, FL**	NA	271	York-Hanover, PA	(35.1)
157	Oklahoma City, OK	(3.0)	259	Sheboygan, WI	(23.2)	NA	Youngstown-Warren, OH-PA**	NA
153	Olympia, WA	(2.3)	246	Sherman-Denison, TX	(20.0)	238	Yuba City, CA	(17.7)
39	Omaha-Council Bluffs, NE-IA	17.7	NA	Shreveport-Bossier City, LA**	NA	242	Yuma, AZ	(18.5)
212	Orlando, FL	(11.5)	NA	Sierra Vista-Douglas, AZ**	NA			
190	Oshkosh-Neenah, WI	(7.7)						

Source: CQ Press using reported data from the F.B.I. "Crime in the United States 2012"

*Robbery is the taking of anything of value by force or threat of force. Attempts are included.

**Not available.

19. Percent Change in Robbery Rate: 2011 to 2012 (continued)
National Percent Change = 0.8% Decrease*

RANK	METROPOLITAN AREA	% CHANGE	RANK	METROPOLITAN AREA	% CHANGE	RANK	METROPOLITAN AREA	% CHANGE
1	Grand Forks, ND-MN	125.8	64	St. Joseph, MO-KS	12.0	129	Detroit-Dearborn-Livonia, MI M.D.	0.3
2	Green Bay, WI	76.9	66	Modesto, CA	11.6	129	Janesville, WI	0.3
3	Iowa City, IA	71.6	66	Tyler, TX	11.6	131	Fond du Lac, WI	0.0
4	Odessa, TX	69.0	68	Abilene, TX	11.3	132	Detroit (greater), MI	(0.1)
5	Billings, MT	65.8	69	Appleton, WI	11.0	133	Minneapolis-St. Paul, MN-WI	(0.2)
6	Gadsden, AL	58.0	70	Longview, WA	10.6	134	Richmond, VA	(0.4)
7	Bismarck, ND	55.9	71	Lewiston-Auburn, ME	10.2	135	Oxnard-Thousand Oaks, CA	(0.5)
8	La Crosse, WI-MN	47.7	72	Des Moines-West Des Moines, IA	9.9	136	Dayton, OH	(0.6)
9	Prescott, AZ	46.0	73	Kennewick-Richland, WA	9.8	136	West Palm Beach, FL M.D.	(0.6)
10	Missoula, MT	45.3	74	Dalton, GA	9.7	138	Lake Havasu City-Kingman, AZ	(0.7)
11	Lawrence, KS	40.7	75	Fayetteville, NC	9.4	139	Savannah, GA	(0.8)
12	Florence-Muscle Shoals, AL	38.4	75	Trenton, NJ	9.4	140	Bloomington, IL	(1.0)
13	Monroe, MI	38.3	77	Hanford-Corcoran, CA	8.9	140	Scranton--Wilkes-Barre, PA	(1.0)
14	Lafayette, IN	38.0	77	Memphis, TN-MS-AR	8.9	142	El Paso, TX	(1.1)
15	Fort Wayne, IN	37.7	79	Peoria, IL	8.8	142	Lubbock, TX	(1.1)
16	Blacksburg, VA	37.0	80	Saginaw, MI	8.5	142	Madera, CA	(1.1)
17	Harrisonburg, VA	36.7	81	New Haven-Milford, CT	8.3	145	McAllen-Edinburg-Mission, TX	(1.2)
18	Decatur, AL	36.6	82	Farmington, NM	8.2	145	Pittsburgh, PA	(1.2)
19	Santa Fe, NM	33.8	83	Huntsville, AL	8.1	147	Silver Spring-Frederick, MD M.D.	(1.3)
20	Longview, TX	31.1	84	Fairbanks, AK	7.2	148	Flagstaff, AZ	(1.4)
21	El Centro, CA	30.5	85	Columbus, GA-AL	6.7	149	Santa Rosa, CA	(1.5)
22	Bangor, ME	29.8	85	Reading, PA	6.7	149	Tacoma, WA M.D.	(1.5)
23	Albany, GA	27.8	87	Flint, MI	6.6	151	Baltimore, MD	(1.8)
24	Montgomery, AL	26.9	88	Hickory, NC	6.3	152	Wichita, KS	(2.1)
25	Boise City, ID	26.7	89	Chico, CA	5.8	153	Bowling Green, KY	(2.3)
26	Mankato-North Mankato, MN	26.2	90	Portland, ME	5.5	153	Olympia, WA	(2.3)
27	Bakersfield, CA	26.1	91	Wichita Falls, TX	5.4	155	Cleveland, TN	(2.5)
28	Visalia-Porterville, CA	26.0	92	Danville, IL	5.2	156	Tallahassee, FL	(2.6)
29	Redding, CA	25.0	93	Hartford, CT	5.1	157	Oklahoma City, OK	(3.0)
30	San Francisco-Redwood, CA M.D.	24.7	93	Manchester-Nashua, NH	5.1	158	Fort Lauderdale, FL M.D.	(3.2)
31	Killeen-Temple, TX	23.8	93	Riverside-San Bernardino, CA	5.1	158	Wilmington, DE-MD-NJ M.D.	(3.2)
32	Salinas, CA	21.7	96	Duluth, MN-WI	4.9	160	Fort Worth-Arlington, TX M.D.	(3.3)
33	Athens-Clarke County, GA	21.5	97	Albuquerque, NM	4.8	160	Las Cruces, NM	(3.3)
34	Idaho Falls, ID	20.9	98	Tucson, AZ	4.7	162	Chicago (greater), IL-IN-WI	(3.4)
34	Monroe, LA	20.9	99	Mansfield, OH	4.4	163	Dallas (greater), TX	(3.5)
36	Michigan City-La Porte, IN	19.7	100	Harrisburg-Carlisle, PA	4.2	163	Dallas-Plano-Irving, TX M.D.	(3.5)
37	Fort Collins, CO	19.2	101	Champaign-Urbana, IL	4.1	163	Lancaster, PA	(3.5)
37	Merced, CA	19.2	102	Pittsfield, MA	3.9	163	Miami (greater), FL	(3.5)
39	Omaha-Council Bluffs, NE-IA	17.7	103	Milwaukee, WI	3.8	163	Tulsa, OK	(3.5)
40	Oakland-Hayward, CA M.D.	17.1	104	San Diego, CA	3.7	168	Alexandria, LA	(3.9)
41	Anniston-Oxford, AL	16.9	105	Portland-Vancouver, OR-WA	3.6	169	San Luis Obispo, CA	(4.4)
41	Waterloo-Cedar Falls, IA	16.9	106	Birmingham-Hoover, AL	3.5	170	Dothan, AL	(4.5)
43	Erie, PA	16.6	107	Corpus Christi, TX	3.4	171	Miami-Dade County, FL M.D.	(4.7)
44	Colorado Springs, CO	16.3	108	Columbia, MO	3.3	172	Los Angeles County, CA M.D.	(5.3)
44	Davenport, IA-IL	16.3	109	Columbus, IN	2.9	173	Vallejo-Fairfield, CA	(5.4)
46	Salem, OR	16.2	110	Lima, OH	2.8	174	Los Angeles (greater), CA	(5.5)
47	Cedar Rapids, IA	16.1	111	Macon, GA	2.6	174	Washington (greater) DC-VA-MD-WV	(5.5)
48	Boulder, CO	15.9	111	Seattle-Bellevue-Everett, WA M.D.	2.6	176	Beaumont-Port Arthur, TX	(5.6)
49	Houston, TX	15.8	113	Eugene, OR	2.5	176	Camden, NJ M.D.	(5.6)
49	Las Vegas-Henderson, NV	15.8	113	Salt Lake City, UT	2.5	178	College Station-Bryan, TX	(5.7)
51	Joplin, MO	15.5	115	San Jose, CA	2.3	179	Augusta, GA-SC	(5.8)
52	Williamsport, PA	15.3	115	Springfield, IL	2.3	180	Raleigh, NC	(6.1)
53	San Francisco (greater), CA	14.9	117	Canton, OH	1.9	181	Anaheim-Santa Ana-Irvine, CA M.D.	(6.2)
54	Provo-Orem, UT	14.8	117	Fresno, CA	1.9	181	Lake Co.-Kenosha Co., IL-WI M.D.	(6.2)
55	Owensboro, KY	14.3	119	Napa, CA	1.8	181	Little Rock, AR	(6.2)
56	Amarillo, TX	14.1	120	Seattle (greater), WA	1.6	181	Washington, DC-VA-MD-WV M.D.	(6.2)
56	Stockton-Lodi, CA	14.1	121	Sacramento, CA	1.5	185	Florence, SC	(6.5)
58	Gainesville, GA	14.0	121	San Antonio, TX	1.5	186	New Orleans, LA	(6.6)
59	Springfield, MO	13.3	121	Topeka, KS	1.5	187	Bremerton-Silverdale, WA	(6.8)
60	Baton Rouge, LA	12.7	124	Warren-Troy, MI M.D.	1.1	188	Rockford, IL	(7.0)
60	Pueblo, CO	12.7	125	Atlanta, GA	1.0	189	Norwich-New London, CT	(7.4)
62	Corvallis, OR	12.4	125	Burlington, NC	1.0	190	Oshkosh-Neenah, WI	(7.7)
63	Medford, OR	12.1	127	Racine, WI	0.7	191	Rockingham County, NH M.D.	(7.9)
64	Lincoln, NE	12.0	128	Brownsville-Harlingen, TX	0.4	192	Jonesboro, AR	(8.3)

Note: All listings are for Metropolitan Statistical Areas (M.S.A.s) except for those ending with "M.D." Listings with "M.D." are Metropolitan Divisions which are smaller parts of eleven large M.S.A.s. See explanatory note at beginning of metropolitan area section.

RANK	METROPOLITAN AREA	% CHANGE	RANK	METROPOLITAN AREA	% CHANGE	RANK	METROPOLITAN AREA	% CHANGE
193	Bay City, MI	(8.4)	257	Charlottesville, VA	(22.7)	NA	Kalamazoo-Portage, MI**	NA
194	Greeley, CO	(8.9)	257	Roanoke, VA	(22.7)	NA	Kansas City, MO-KS**	NA
195	Clarksville, TN-KY	(9.2)	259	Sheboygan, WI	(23.2)	NA	Kingston, NY**	NA
196	Brunswick, GA	(9.5)	260	Rome, GA	(25.5)	NA	Knoxville, TN**	NA
197	Fargo, ND-MN	(9.6)	261	Mobile, AL	(25.9)	NA	Kokomo, IN**	NA
198	Tampa-St Petersburg, FL	(9.7)	262	Barnstable Town, MA	(26.6)	NA	Lafayette, LA**	NA
199	Pensacola, FL	(9.9)	263	Mount Vernon-Anacortes, WA	(28.4)	NA	Lawton, OK**	NA
200	Cape Coral-Fort Myers, FL	(10.0)	264	Hinesville, GA	(28.9)	NA	Lewiston, ID-WA**	NA
200	Palm Bay-Melbourne, FL	(10.0)	265	Punta Gorda, FL	(30.6)	NA	Lexington-Fayette, KY**	NA
202	Sumter, SC	(10.1)	266	Dubuque, IA	(31.1)	NA	Madison, WI**	NA
203	Valdosta, GA	(10.4)	267	Cumberland, MD-WV	(31.2)	NA	Manhattan, KS**	NA
204	Louisville, KY-IN	(10.5)	267	Naples-Marco Island, FL	(31.2)	NA	Midland, MI**	NA
204	Sioux Falls, SD	(10.5)	269	Lynchburg, VA	(31.9)	NA	Midland, TX**	NA
206	Wausau, WI	(10.6)	270	Cape Girardeau, MO-IL	(32.2)	NA	Montgomery County, PA M.D.**	NA
207	Pine Bluff, AR	(10.8)	271	York-Hanover, PA	(35.1)	NA	Morgantown, WV**	NA
208	Gainesville, FL	(10.9)	272	Ocean City, NJ	(36.6)	NA	Morristown, TN**	NA
208	Houma, LA	(10.9)	273	Winchester, VA-WV	(36.7)	NA	Nashville-Davidson, TN**	NA
208	Muncie, IN	(10.9)	274	Ames, IA	(38.2)	NA	Nassau-Suffolk, NY M.D.**	NA
211	Cheyenne, WY	(11.4)	275	Kankakee, IL	(38.3)	NA	New Bern, NC**	NA
212	Orlando, FL	(11.5)	276	Johnstown, PA	(45.5)	NA	New York (greater), NY-NJ-PA**	NA
212	Yakima, WA	(11.5)	277	Casper, WY	(48.7)	NA	New York-Jersey City, NY-NJ M.D.**	NA
214	Terre Haute, IN	(11.8)	NA	Albany-Schenectady-Troy, NY**	NA	NA	Newark, NJ-PA M.D.**	NA
215	Austin-Round Rock, TX	(12.2)	NA	Albany, OR**	NA	NA	Ogden-Clearfield, UT**	NA
216	Bellingham, WA	(12.7)	NA	Allentown, PA-NJ**	NA	NA	Panama City, FL**	NA
217	Santa Cruz-Watsonville, CA	(13.1)	NA	Anchorage, AK**	NA	NA	Parkersburg-Vienna, WV**	NA
218	Carson City, NV	(13.2)	NA	Beckley, WV**	NA	NA	Philadelphia (greater) PA-NJ-MD-DE**	NA
219	Durham-Chapel Hill, NC	(13.3)	NA	Binghamton, NY**	NA	NA	Philadelphia, PA M.D.**	NA
220	State College, PA	(13.4)	NA	Bloomington, IN**	NA	NA	Phoenix-Mesa-Scottsdale, AZ**	NA
221	Ann Arbor, MI	(13.5)	NA	Bloomsburg-Berwick, PA**	NA	NA	Pocatello, ID**	NA
221	Asheville, NC	(13.5)	NA	Boston (greater), MA-NH**	NA	NA	Providence-Warwick, RI-MA**	NA
223	Gary, IN M.D.	(14.0)	NA	Boston, MA M.D.**	NA	NA	Rapid City, SD**	NA
224	Reno, NV	(14.2)	NA	Buffalo-Niagara Falls, NY**	NA	NA	Rochester, MN**	NA
225	Bridgeport-Stamford, CT	(14.4)	NA	California-Lexington Park, MD**	NA	NA	Rochester, NY**	NA
226	Goldsboro, NC	(14.5)	NA	Cambridge-Newton, MA M.D.**	NA	NA	Salisbury, MD-DE**	NA
227	Lansing-East Lansing, MI	(14.6)	NA	Chambersburg-Waynesboro, PA**	NA	NA	San Rafael, CA M.D.**	NA
227	Lebanon, PA	(14.6)	NA	Charleston-North Charleston, SC**	NA	NA	Santa Maria-Santa Barbara, CA**	NA
229	Jacksonville, FL	(14.8)	NA	Chicago-Joilet-Naperville, IL M.D.**	NA	NA	Sebring, FL**	NA
230	Grand Junction, CO	(15.2)	NA	Cincinnati, OH-KY-IN**	NA	NA	Shreveport-Bossier City, LA**	NA
231	Springfield, OH	(15.3)	NA	Coeur d'Alene, ID**	NA	NA	Sierra Vista-Douglas, AZ**	NA
232	Ocala, FL	(15.5)	NA	Daphne-Fairhope-Foley, AL**	NA	NA	Sioux City, IA-NE-SD**	NA
233	Crestview-Fort Walton Beach, FL	(15.7)	NA	Deltona-Daytona Beach, FL**	NA	NA	Spartanburg, SC**	NA
234	Jefferson City, MO	(16.1)	NA	Denver-Aurora, CO**	NA	NA	Spokane, WA**	NA
235	Decatur, IL	(16.3)	NA	Dutchess-Putnam, NY M.D.**	NA	NA	Springfield, MA**	NA
236	St. Louis, MO-IL	(16.8)	NA	East Stroudsburg, PA**	NA	NA	Staunton-Waynesboro, VA**	NA
237	Laredo, TX	(17.4)	NA	Elgin, IL M.D.**	NA	NA	St. George, UT**	NA
238	Yuba City, CA	(17.7)	NA	Elizabethtown-Fort Knox, KY**	NA	NA	Syracuse, NY**	NA
239	Dover, DE	(17.9)	NA	Elmira, NY**	NA	NA	Texarkana, TX-AR**	NA
240	Rocky Mount, NC	(18.2)	NA	Fayetteville-Springdale, AR-MO**	NA	NA	The Villages, FL**	NA
241	Akron, OH	(18.4)	NA	Fort Smith, AR-OK**	NA	NA	Toledo, OH**	NA
242	Yuma, AZ	(18.5)	NA	Gettysburg, PA**	NA	NA	Tuscaloosa, AL**	NA
243	Kingsport, TN-VA	(18.6)	NA	Glens Falls, NY**	NA	NA	Utica-Rome, NY**	NA
244	North Port-Sarasota-Bradenton, FL	(19.5)	NA	Grand Island, NE**	NA	NA	Victoria, TX**	NA
245	Auburn, AL	(19.8)	NA	Greensboro-High Point, NC**	NA	NA	Vineland-Bridgeton, NJ**	NA
246	Sherman-Denison, TX	(20.0)	NA	Greenville-Anderson, SC**	NA	NA	Waco, TX**	NA
247	Logan, UT-ID	(20.5)	NA	Greenville, NC**	NA	NA	Walla Walla, WA**	NA
248	Altoona, PA	(20.7)	NA	Hagerstown-Martinsburg, MD-WV**	NA	NA	Warner Robins, GA**	NA
249	Atlantic City, NJ	(21.0)	NA	Hammond, LA**	NA	NA	Watertown-Fort Drum, NY**	NA
250	Lakeland, FL	(21.3)	NA	Hattiesburg, MS**	NA	NA	Wheeling, WV-OH**	NA
251	Great Falls, MT	(21.4)	NA	Hilton Head Island, SC**	NA	NA	Wilmington, NC**	NA
252	South Bend-Mishawaka, IN-MI	(21.6)	NA	Homosassa Springs, FL**	NA	NA	Winston-Salem, NC**	NA
253	Johnson City, TN	(22.1)	NA	Indianapolis, IN**	NA	NA	Worcester, MA-CT**	NA
254	Virginia Beach-Norfolk, VA-NC	(22.3)	NA	Jackson, MS**	NA	NA	Youngstown-Warren, OH-PA**	NA
255	Sebastian-Vero Beach, FL	(22.4)	NA	Jackson, TN**	NA			
256	Port St. Lucie, FL	(22.6)	NA	Kahului-Wailuku-Lahaina, HI**	NA			

Source: CQ Press using reported data from the F.B.I. "Crime in the United States 2012"

*Robbery is the taking of anything of value by force or threat of force. Attempts are included.

**Not available.

20. Percent Change in Robbery Rate: 2008 to 2012
National Percent Change = 22.6% Decrease*

RANK	METROPOLITAN AREA	% CHANGE	RANK	METROPOLITAN AREA	% CHANGE	RANK	METROPOLITAN AREA	% CHANGE
193	Abilene, TX	(31.8)	109	Cheyenne, WY	(15.8)	NA	Gary, IN M.D.**	NA
157	Akron, OH	(26.0)	NA	Chicago (greater), IL-IN-WI**	NA	NA	Gettysburg, PA**	NA
NA	Albany-Schenectady-Troy, NY**	NA	NA	Chicago-Joilet-Naperville, IL M.D.**	NA	NA	Glens Falls, NY**	NA
NA	Albany, GA**	NA	52	Chico, CA	(2.3)	210	Goldsboro, NC	(36.9)
NA	Albany, OR**	NA	NA	Cincinnati, OH-KY-IN**	NA	7	Grand Forks, ND-MN	65.2
167	Albuquerque, NM	(27.5)	234	Clarksville, TN-KY	(42.8)	NA	Grand Island, NE**	NA
NA	Alexandria, LA**	NA	55	Cleveland, TN	(3.1)	79	Grand Junction, CO	(9.0)
NA	Allentown, PA-NJ**	NA	NA	Coeur d'Alene, ID**	NA	114	Great Falls, MT	(16.2)
257	Altoona, PA	(59.1)	225	College Station-Bryan, TX	(40.7)	67	Greeley, CO	(5.8)
125	Amarillo, TX	(20.0)	62	Colorado Springs, CO	(4.5)	95	Green Bay, WI	(12.7)
143	Ames, IA	(23.9)	29	Columbia, MO	17.2	240	Greensboro-High Point, NC	(45.1)
192	Anaheim-Santa Ana-Irvine, CA M.D.	(31.7)	201	Columbus, GA-AL	(33.5)	NA	Greenville-Anderson, SC**	NA
NA	Anchorage, AK**	NA	4	Columbus, IN	72.0	190	Greenville, NC	(31.5)
209	Ann Arbor, MI	(36.4)	166	Corpus Christi, TX	(27.4)	NA	Hagerstown-Martinsburg, MD-WV**	NA
NA	Anniston-Oxford, AL**	NA	105	Corvallis, OR	(14.8)	NA	Hammond, LA**	NA
12	Appleton, WI	48.6	NA	Crestview-Fort Walton Beach, FL**	NA	69	Hanford-Corcoran, CA	(6.4)
218	Asheville, NC	(37.9)	33	Cumberland, MD-WV	11.3	124	Harrisburg-Carlisle, PA	(19.9)
188	Athens-Clarke County, GA	(30.9)	204	Dallas (greater), TX	(35.4)	60	Harrisonburg, VA	(4.2)
178	Atlanta, GA	(29.4)	210	Dallas-Plano-Irving, TX M.D.	(36.9)	61	Hartford, CT	(4.3)
84	Atlantic City, NJ	(10.8)	141	Dalton, GA	(23.8)	NA	Hattiesburg, MS**	NA
258	Auburn, AL	(61.2)	NA	Danville, IL**	NA	157	Hickory, NC	(26.0)
203	Augusta, GA-SC	(35.0)	NA	Daphne-Fairhope-Foley, AL**	NA	NA	Hilton Head Island, SC**	NA
179	Austin-Round Rock, TX	(29.7)	NA	Davenport, IA-IL**	NA	244	Hinesville, GA	(46.4)
64	Bakersfield, CA	(4.7)	130	Dayton, OH	(20.8)	NA	Homosassa Springs, FL**	NA
126	Baltimore, MD	(20.2)	198	Decatur, AL	(32.7)	163	Houma, LA	(26.8)
10	Bangor, ME	54.7	NA	Decatur, IL**	NA	101	Houston, TX	(13.9)
109	Barnstable Town, MA	(15.8)	246	Deltona-Daytona Beach, FL	(47.0)	50	Huntsville, AL	(2.2)
49	Baton Rouge, LA	(1.4)	NA	Denver-Aurora, CO**	NA	83	Idaho Falls, ID	(10.6)
164	Bay City, MI	(27.3)	172	Des Moines-West Des Moines, IA	(28.6)	133	Indianapolis, IN	(21.6)
71	Beaumont-Port Arthur, TX	(6.6)	NA	Detroit (greater), MI**	NA	225	Iowa City, IA	(40.7)
NA	Beckley, WV**	NA	NA	Detroit-Dearborn-Livonia, MI M.D.**	NA	254	Jacksonville, FL	(53.5)
171	Bellingham, WA	(28.5)	248	Dothan, AL	(47.5)	NA	Jackson, MS**	NA
28	Billings, MT	17.4	138	Dover, DE	(22.7)	NA	Jackson, TN**	NA
NA	Binghamton, NY**	NA	82	Dubuque, IA	(10.0)	111	Janesville, WI	(15.9)
205	Birmingham-Hoover, AL	(36.0)	146	Duluth, MN-WI	(24.8)	NA	Jefferson City, MO**	NA
6	Bismarck, ND	68.7	223	Durham-Chapel Hill, NC	(39.6)	88	Johnson City, TN	(11.1)
146	Blacksburg, VA	(24.8)	NA	Dutchess-Putnam, NY M.D.**	NA	118	Johnstown, PA	(17.4)
NA	Bloomington, IL**	NA	NA	East Stroudsburg, PA**	NA	100	Jonesboro, AR	(13.6)
65	Bloomington, IN	(4.8)	99	El Centro, CA	(13.4)	26	Joplin, MO	18.0
NA	Bloomsburg-Berwick, PA**	NA	97	El Paso, TX	(12.9)	NA	Kahului-Wailuku-Lahaina, HI**	NA
95	Boise City, ID	(12.7)	NA	Elgin, IL M.D.**	NA	180	Kalamazoo-Portage, MI	(29.9)
NA	Boston (greater), MA-NH**	NA	NA	Elizabethtown-Fort Knox, KY**	NA	NA	Kankakee, IL**	NA
NA	Boston, MA M.D.**	NA	NA	Elmira, NY**	NA	NA	Kansas City, MO-KS**	NA
NA	Boulder, CO**	NA	222	Erie, PA	(38.7)	120	Kennewick-Richland, WA	(18.6)
206	Bowling Green, KY	(36.1)	111	Eugene, OR	(15.9)	92	Killeen-Temple, TX	(11.9)
81	Bremerton-Silverdale, WA	(9.3)	NA	Fairbanks, AK**	NA	91	Kingsport, TN-VA	(11.6)
141	Bridgeport-Stamford, CT	(23.8)	14	Fargo, ND-MN	47.6	NA	Kingston, NY**	NA
187	Brownsville-Harlingen, TX	(30.8)	34	Farmington, NM	9.5	NA	Knoxville, TN**	NA
NA	Brunswick, GA**	NA	47	Fayetteville-Springdale, AR-MO	0.9	NA	Kokomo, IN**	NA
NA	Buffalo-Niagara Falls, NY**	NA	134	Fayetteville, NC	(22.1)	36	La Crosse, WI-MN	7.4
135	Burlington, NC	(22.2)	162	Flagstaff, AZ	(26.7)	22	Lafayette, IN	24.2
NA	California-Lexington Park, MD**	NA	38	Flint, MI	6.9	NA	Lafayette, LA**	NA
NA	Cambridge-Newton, MA M.D.**	NA	189	Florence-Muscle Shoals, AL	(31.2)	NA	Lake Co.-Kenosha Co., IL-WI M.D.**	NA
90	Camden, NJ M.D.	(11.5)	230	Florence, SC	(41.8)	103	Lake Havasu City-Kingman, AZ	(14.4)
NA	Canton, OH**	NA	20	Fond du Lac, WI	25.7	237	Lakeland, FL	(44.2)
197	Cape Coral-Fort Myers, FL	(32.6)	43	Fort Collins, CO	3.9	86	Lancaster, PA	(10.9)
40	Cape Girardeau, MO-IL	6.5	119	Fort Lauderdale, FL M.D.	(17.7)	145	Lansing-East Lansing, MI	(24.6)
236	Carson City, NV	(43.7)	NA	Fort Smith, AR-OK**	NA	245	Laredo, TX	(46.8)
242	Casper, WY	(46.0)	76	Fort Wayne, IN	(8.0)	93	Las Cruces, NM	(12.0)
180	Cedar Rapids, IA	(29.9)	183	Fort Worth-Arlington, TX M.D.	(30.1)	170	Las Vegas-Henderson, NV	(28.0)
NA	Chambersburg-Waynesboro, PA**	NA	41	Fresno, CA	5.6	159	Lawrence, KS	(26.2)
NA	Champaign-Urbana, IL**	NA	108	Gadsden, AL	(15.7)	NA	Lawton, OK**	NA
256	Charleston-North Charleston, SC	(57.0)	199	Gainesville, FL	(32.8)	37	Lebanon, PA	7.2
250	Charlottesville, VA	(48.9)	NA	Gainesville, GA**	NA	17	Lewiston-Auburn, ME	36.4

Note: All listings are for Metropolitan Statistical Areas (M.S.A.s) except for those ending with "M.D." Listings with "M.D." are Metropolitan Divisions which are smaller parts of eleven large M.S.A.s. See explanatory note at beginning of metropolitan area section.

RANK	METROPOLITAN AREA	% CHANGE	RANK	METROPOLITAN AREA	% CHANGE	RANK	METROPOLITAN AREA	% CHANGE
16	Lewiston, ID-WA	41.0	NA	Owensboro, KY**	NA	176	Silver Spring-Frederick, MD M.D.	(29.2)
NA	Lexington-Fayette, KY**	NA	195	Oxnard-Thousand Oaks, CA	(32.2)	NA	Sioux City, IA-NE-SD**	NA
213	Lima, OH	(37.3)	156	Palm Bay-Melbourne, FL	(25.7)	13	Sioux Falls, SD	48.3
89	Lincoln, NE	(11.3)	NA	Panama City, FL**	NA	139	South Bend-Mishawaka, IN-MI	(23.5)
102	Little Rock, AR	(14.1)	NA	Parkersburg-Vienna, WV**	NA	NA	Spartanburg, SC**	NA
3	Logan, UT-ID	93.8	164	Pensacola, FL	(27.3)	46	Spokane, WA	2.1
229	Longview, TX	(41.5)	NA	Peoria, IL**	NA	NA	Springfield, IL**	NA
42	Longview, WA	4.4	NA	Philadelphia (greater) PA-NJ-MD-DE**	NA	NA	Springfield, MA**	NA
182	Los Angeles County, CA M.D.	(30.0)	NA	Philadelphia, PA M.D.**	NA	32	Springfield, MO	11.5
185	Los Angeles (greater), CA	(30.3)	NA	Phoenix-Mesa-Scottsdale, AZ**	NA	19	Springfield, OH	26.7
127	Louisville, KY-IN	(20.4)	238	Pine Bluff, AR	(44.6)	50	State College, PA	(2.2)
66	Lubbock, TX	(5.4)	153	Pittsburgh, PA	(25.5)	NA	Staunton-Waynesboro, VA**	NA
255	Lynchburg, VA	(54.7)	2	Pittsfield, MA	119.2	62	Stockton-Lodi, CA	(4.5)
202	Macon, GA	(34.0)	NA	Pocatello, ID**	NA	73	St. George, UT	(7.1)
167	Madera, CA	(27.5)	235	Port St. Lucie, FL	(43.1)	57	St. Joseph, MO-KS	(3.7)
NA	Madison, WI**	NA	98	Portland-Vancouver, OR-WA	(13.1)	153	St. Louis, MO-IL	(25.5)
NA	Manchester-Nashua, NH**	NA	54	Portland, ME	(2.8)	231	Sumter, SC	(42.5)
NA	Manhattan, KS**	NA	44	Prescott, AZ	3.8	NA	Syracuse, NY**	NA
1	Mankato-North Mankato, MN	121.7	84	Providence-Warwick, RI-MA	(10.8)	NA	Tacoma, WA M.D.**	NA
23	Mansfield, OH	22.6	68	Provo-Orem, UT	(6.1)	169	Tallahassee, FL	(27.8)
206	McAllen-Edinburg-Mission, TX	(36.1)	NA	Pueblo, CO**	NA	243	Tampa-St Petersburg, FL	(46.3)
25	Medford, OR	18.1	253	Punta Gorda, FL	(52.0)	NA	Terre Haute, IN**	NA
183	Memphis, TN-MS-AR	(30.1)	193	Racine, WI	(31.8)	NA	Texarkana, TX-AR**	NA
27	Merced, CA	17.6	232	Raleigh, NC	(42.6)	NA	The Villages, FL**	NA
174	Miami (greater), FL	(28.9)	NA	Rapid City, SD**	NA	NA	Toledo, OH**	NA
191	Miami-Dade County, FL M.D.	(31.6)	107	Reading, PA	(15.6)	113	Topeka, KS	(16.0)
144	Michigan City-La Porte, IN	(24.3)	8	Redding, CA	59.7	45	Trenton, NJ	3.0
NA	Midland, MI**	NA	215	Reno, NV	(37.8)	116	Tucson, AZ	(16.8)
NA	Midland, TX**	NA	220	Richmond, VA	(38.4)	72	Tulsa, OK	(6.7)
70	Milwaukee, WI	(6.5)	123	Riverside-San Bernardino, CA	(19.7)	NA	Tuscaloosa, AL**	NA
137	Minneapolis-St. Paul, MN-WI	(22.6)	218	Roanoke, VA	(37.9)	195	Tyler, TX	(32.2)
11	Missoula, MT	53.1	NA	Rochester, MN**	NA	NA	Utica-Rome, NY**	NA
241	Mobile, AL	(45.5)	NA	Rochester, NY**	NA	210	Valdosta, GA	(36.9)
58	Modesto, CA	(3.9)	NA	Rockford, IL**	NA	176	Vallejo-Fairfield, CA	(29.2)
78	Monroe, LA	(8.9)	31	Rockingham County, NH M.D.	13.4	NA	Victoria, TX**	NA
9	Monroe, MI	59.5	NA	Rocky Mount, NC**	NA	87	Vineland-Bridgeton, NJ	(11.0)
NA	Montgomery County, PA M.D.**	NA	NA	Rome, GA**	NA	247	Virginia Beach-Norfolk, VA-NC	(47.1)
53	Montgomery, AL	(2.7)	151	Sacramento, CA	(25.3)	115	Visalia-Porterville, CA	(16.7)
NA	Morgantown, WV**	NA	220	Saginaw, MI	(38.4)	NA	Waco, TX**	NA
NA	Morristown, TN**	NA	77	Salem, OR	(8.4)	NA	Walla Walla, WA**	NA
117	Mount Vernon-Anacortes, WA	(17.0)	30	Salinas, CA	14.7	NA	Warner Robins, GA**	NA
24	Muncie, IN	19.2	NA	Salisbury, MD-DE**	NA	NA	Warren-Troy, MI M.D.**	NA
56	Napa, CA	(3.4)	127	Salt Lake City, UT	(20.4)	161	Washington (greater) DC-VA-MD-WV	(26.4)
215	Naples-Marco Island, FL	(37.8)	214	San Antonio, TX	(37.6)	160	Washington, DC-VA-MD-WV M.D.	(26.3)
NA	Nashville-Davidson, TN**	NA	149	San Diego, CA	(25.1)	224	Waterloo-Cedar Falls, IA	(40.2)
NA	Nassau-Suffolk, NY M.D.**	NA	94	San Francisco (greater), CA	(12.1)	NA	Watertown-Fort Drum, NY**	NA
NA	New Bern, NC**	NA	80	San Francisco-Redwood, CA M.D.	(9.1)	173	Wausau, WI	(28.7)
NA	New Haven-Milford, CT**	NA	74	San Jose, CA	(7.3)	215	West Palm Beach, FL M.D.	(37.8)
140	New Orleans, LA	(23.7)	200	San Luis Obispo, CA	(33.3)	131	Wheeling, WV-OH	(21.2)
NA	New York (greater), NY-NJ-PA**	NA	NA	San Rafael, CA M.D.**	NA	175	Wichita Falls, TX	(29.1)
NA	New York-Jersey City, NY-NJ M.D.**	NA	151	Santa Cruz-Watsonville, CA	(25.3)	59	Wichita, KS	(4.0)
NA	Newark, NJ-PA M.D.**	NA	15	Santa Fe, NM	43.6	18	Williamsport, PA	34.3
NA	North Port-Sarasota-Bradenton, FL**	NA	NA	Santa Maria-Santa Barbara, CA**	NA	122	Wilmington, DE-MD-NJ M.D.	(19.3)
39	Norwich-New London, CT	6.8	127	Santa Rosa, CA	(20.4)	NA	Wilmington, NC**	NA
75	Oakland-Hayward, CA M.D.	(7.9)	233	Savannah, GA	(42.7)	249	Winchester, VA-WV	(47.7)
251	Ocala, FL	(49.2)	21	Scranton--Wilkes-Barre, PA	25.0	NA	Winston-Salem, NC**	NA
186	Ocean City, NJ	(30.6)	NA	Seattle (greater), WA**	NA	34	Worcester, MA-CT	9.5
5	Odessa, TX	70.3	NA	Seattle-Bellevue-Everett, WA M.D.**	NA	121	Yakima, WA	(18.8)
NA	Ogden-Clearfield, UT**	NA	227	Sebastian-Vero Beach, FL	(40.8)	228	York-Hanover, PA	(41.0)
148	Oklahoma City, OK	(25.0)	NA	Sebring, FL**	NA	106	Youngstown-Warren, OH-PA	(15.3)
155	Olympia, WA	(25.6)	132	Sheboygan, WI	(21.3)	208	Yuba City, CA	(36.3)
104	Omaha-Council Bluffs, NE-IA	(14.7)	48	Sherman-Denison, TX	(1.0)	136	Yuma, AZ	(22.5)
252	Orlando, FL	(49.3)	149	Shreveport-Bossier City, LA	(25.1)			
238	Oshkosh-Neenah, WI	(44.6)	NA	Sierra Vista-Douglas, AZ**	NA			

Source: CQ Press using reported data from the F.B.I. "Crime in the United States 2012"

*Robbery is the taking of anything of value by force or threat of force. Attempts are included.

**Not available.

20. Percent Change in Robbery Rate: 2008 to 2012 (continued)
National Percent Change = 22.6% Decrease*

RANK	METROPOLITAN AREA	% CHANGE	RANK	METROPOLITAN AREA	% CHANGE	RANK	METROPOLITAN AREA	% CHANGE
1	Mankato-North Mankato, MN	121.7	65	Bloomington, IN	(4.8)	127	Santa Rosa, CA	(20.4)
2	Pittsfield, MA	119.2	66	Lubbock, TX	(5.4)	130	Dayton, OH	(20.8)
3	Logan, UT-ID	93.8	67	Greeley, CO	(5.8)	131	Wheeling, WV-OH	(21.2)
4	Columbus, IN	72.0	68	Provo-Orem, UT	(6.1)	132	Sheboygan, WI	(21.3)
5	Odessa, TX	70.3	69	Hanford-Corcoran, CA	(6.4)	133	Indianapolis, IN	(21.6)
6	Bismarck, ND	68.7	70	Milwaukee, WI	(6.5)	134	Fayetteville, NC	(22.1)
7	Grand Forks, ND-MN	65.2	71	Beaumont-Port Arthur, TX	(6.6)	135	Burlington, NC	(22.2)
8	Redding, CA	59.7	72	Tulsa, OK	(6.7)	136	Yuma, AZ	(22.5)
9	Monroe, MI	59.5	73	St. George, UT	(7.1)	137	Minneapolis-St. Paul, MN-WI	(22.6)
10	Bangor, ME	54.7	74	San Jose, CA	(7.3)	138	Dover, DE	(22.7)
11	Missoula, MT	53.1	75	Oakland-Hayward, CA M.D.	(7.9)	139	South Bend-Mishawaka, IN-MI	(23.5)
12	Appleton, WI	48.6	76	Fort Wayne, IN	(8.0)	140	New Orleans, LA	(23.7)
13	Sioux Falls, SD	48.3	77	Salem, OR	(8.4)	141	Bridgeport-Stamford, CT	(23.8)
14	Fargo, ND-MN	47.6	78	Monroe, LA	(8.9)	141	Dalton, GA	(23.8)
15	Santa Fe, NM	43.6	79	Grand Junction, CO	(9.0)	143	Ames, IA	(23.9)
16	Lewiston, ID-WA	41.0	80	San Francisco-Redwood, CA M.D.	(9.1)	144	Michigan City-La Porte, IN	(24.3)
17	Lewiston-Auburn, ME	36.4	81	Bremerton-Silverdale, WA	(9.3)	145	Lansing-East Lansing, MI	(24.6)
18	Williamsport, PA	34.3	82	Dubuque, IA	(10.0)	146	Blacksburg, VA	(24.8)
19	Springfield, OH	26.7	83	Idaho Falls, ID	(10.6)	146	Duluth, MN-WI	(24.8)
20	Fond du Lac, WI	25.7	84	Atlantic City, NJ	(10.8)	148	Oklahoma City, OK	(25.0)
21	Scranton--Wilkes-Barre, PA	25.0	84	Providence-Warwick, RI-MA	(10.8)	149	San Diego, CA	(25.1)
22	Lafayette, IN	24.2	86	Lancaster, PA	(10.9)	149	Shreveport-Bossier City, LA	(25.1)
23	Mansfield, OH	22.6	87	Vineland-Bridgeton, NJ	(11.0)	151	Sacramento, CA	(25.3)
24	Muncie, IN	19.2	88	Johnson City, TN	(11.1)	151	Santa Cruz-Watsonville, CA	(25.3)
25	Medford, OR	18.1	89	Lincoln, NE	(11.3)	153	Pittsburgh, PA	(25.5)
26	Joplin, MO	18.0	90	Camden, NJ M.D.	(11.5)	153	St. Louis, MO-IL	(25.5)
27	Merced, CA	17.6	91	Kingsport, TN-VA	(11.6)	155	Olympia, WA	(25.6)
28	Billings, MT	17.4	92	Killeen-Temple, TX	(11.9)	156	Palm Bay-Melbourne, FL	(25.7)
29	Columbia, MO	17.2	93	Las Cruces, NM	(12.0)	157	Akron, OH	(26.0)
30	Salinas, CA	14.7	94	San Francisco (greater), CA	(12.1)	157	Hickory, NC	(26.0)
31	Rockingham County, NH M.D.	13.4	95	Boise City, ID	(12.7)	159	Lawrence, KS	(26.2)
32	Springfield, MO	11.5	95	Green Bay, WI	(12.7)	160	Washington, DC-VA-MD-WV M.D.	(26.3)
33	Cumberland, MD-WV	11.3	97	El Paso, TX	(12.9)	161	Washington (greater) DC-VA-MD-WV	(26.4)
34	Farmington, NM	9.5	98	Portland-Vancouver, OR-WA	(13.1)	162	Flagstaff, AZ	(26.7)
34	Worcester, MA-CT	9.5	99	El Centro, CA	(13.4)	163	Houma, LA	(26.8)
36	La Crosse, WI-MN	7.4	100	Jonesboro, AR	(13.6)	164	Bay City, MI	(27.3)
37	Lebanon, PA	7.2	101	Houston, TX	(13.9)	164	Pensacola, FL	(27.3)
38	Flint, MI	6.9	102	Little Rock, AR	(14.1)	166	Corpus Christi, TX	(27.4)
39	Norwich-New London, CT	6.8	103	Lake Havasu City-Kingman, AZ	(14.4)	167	Albuquerque, NM	(27.5)
40	Cape Girardeau, MO-IL	6.5	104	Omaha-Council Bluffs, NE-IA	(14.7)	167	Madera, CA	(27.5)
41	Fresno, CA	5.6	105	Corvallis, OR	(14.8)	169	Tallahassee, FL	(27.8)
42	Longview, WA	4.4	106	Youngstown-Warren, OH-PA	(15.3)	170	Las Vegas-Henderson, NV	(28.0)
43	Fort Collins, CO	3.9	107	Reading, PA	(15.6)	171	Bellingham, WA	(28.5)
44	Prescott, AZ	3.8	108	Gadsden, AL	(15.7)	172	Des Moines-West Des Moines, IA	(28.6)
45	Trenton, NJ	3.0	109	Barnstable Town, MA	(15.8)	173	Wausau, WI	(28.7)
46	Spokane, WA	2.1	109	Cheyenne, WY	(15.8)	174	Miami (greater), FL	(28.9)
47	Fayetteville-Springdale, AR-MO	0.9	111	Eugene, OR	(15.9)	175	Wichita Falls, TX	(29.1)
48	Sherman-Denison, TX	(1.0)	111	Janesville, WI	(15.9)	176	Silver Spring-Frederick, MD M.D.	(29.2)
49	Baton Rouge, LA	(1.4)	113	Topeka, KS	(16.0)	176	Vallejo-Fairfield, CA	(29.2)
50	Huntsville, AL	(2.2)	114	Great Falls, MT	(16.2)	178	Atlanta, GA	(29.4)
50	State College, PA	(2.2)	115	Visalia-Porterville, CA	(16.7)	179	Austin-Round Rock, TX	(29.7)
52	Chico, CA	(2.3)	116	Tucson, AZ	(16.8)	180	Cedar Rapids, IA	(29.9)
53	Montgomery, AL	(2.7)	117	Mount Vernon-Anacortes, WA	(17.0)	180	Kalamazoo-Portage, MI	(29.9)
54	Portland, ME	(2.8)	118	Johnstown, PA	(17.4)	182	Los Angeles County, CA M.D.	(30.0)
55	Cleveland, TN	(3.1)	119	Fort Lauderdale, FL M.D.	(17.7)	183	Fort Worth-Arlington, TX M.D.	(30.1)
56	Napa, CA	(3.4)	120	Kennewick-Richland, WA	(18.6)	183	Memphis, TN-MS-AR	(30.1)
57	St. Joseph, MO-KS	(3.7)	121	Yakima, WA	(18.8)	185	Los Angeles (greater), CA	(30.3)
58	Modesto, CA	(3.9)	122	Wilmington, DE-MD-NJ M.D.	(19.3)	186	Ocean City, NJ	(30.6)
59	Wichita, KS	(4.0)	123	Riverside-San Bernardino, CA	(19.7)	187	Brownsville-Harlingen, TX	(30.8)
60	Harrisonburg, VA	(4.2)	124	Harrisburg-Carlisle, PA	(19.9)	188	Athens-Clarke County, GA	(30.9)
61	Hartford, CT	(4.3)	125	Amarillo, TX	(20.0)	189	Florence-Muscle Shoals, AL	(31.2)
62	Colorado Springs, CO	(4.5)	126	Baltimore, MD	(20.2)	190	Greenville, NC	(31.5)
62	Stockton-Lodi, CA	(4.5)	127	Louisville, KY-IN	(20.4)	191	Miami-Dade County, FL M.D.	(31.6)
64	Bakersfield, CA	(4.7)	127	Salt Lake City, UT	(20.4)	192	Anaheim-Santa Ana-Irvine, CA M.D.	(31.7)

Note: All listings are for Metropolitan Statistical Areas (M.S.A.s) except for those ending with "M.D." Listings with "M.D." are Metropolitan Divisions which are smaller parts of eleven large M.S.A.s. See explanatory note at beginning of metropolitan area section.

RANK	METROPOLITAN AREA	% CHANGE	RANK	METROPOLITAN AREA	% CHANGE	RANK	METROPOLITAN AREA	% CHANGE
193	Abilene, TX	(31.8)	257	Altoona, PA	(59.1)	NA	Lawton, OK**	NA
193	Racine, WI	(31.8)	258	Auburn, AL	(61.2)	NA	Lexington-Fayette, KY**	NA
195	Oxnard-Thousand Oaks, CA	(32.2)	NA	Albany-Schenectady-Troy, NY**	NA	NA	Madison, WI**	NA
195	Tyler, TX	(32.2)	NA	Albany, GA**	NA	NA	Manchester-Nashua, NH**	NA
197	Cape Coral-Fort Myers, FL	(32.6)	NA	Albany, OR**	NA	NA	Manhattan, KS**	NA
198	Decatur, AL	(32.7)	NA	Alexandria, LA**	NA	NA	Midland, MI**	NA
199	Gainesville, FL	(32.8)	NA	Allentown, PA-NJ**	NA	NA	Midland, TX**	NA
200	San Luis Obispo, CA	(33.3)	NA	Anchorage, AK**	NA	NA	Montgomery County, PA M.D.**	NA
201	Columbus, GA-AL	(33.5)	NA	Anniston-Oxford, AL**	NA	NA	Morgantown, WV**	NA
202	Macon, GA	(34.0)	NA	Beckley, WV**	NA	NA	Morristown, TN**	NA
203	Augusta, GA-SC	(35.0)	NA	Binghamton, NY**	NA	NA	Nashville-Davidson, TN**	NA
204	Dallas (greater), TX	(35.4)	NA	Bloomington, IL**	NA	NA	Nassau-Suffolk, NY M.D.**	NA
205	Birmingham-Hoover, AL	(36.0)	NA	Bloomsburg-Berwick, PA**	NA	NA	New Bern, NC**	NA
206	Bowling Green, KY	(36.1)	NA	Boston (greater), MA-NH**	NA	NA	New Haven-Milford, CT**	NA
206	McAllen-Edinburg-Mission, TX	(36.1)	NA	Boston, MA M.D.**	NA	NA	New York (greater), NY-NJ-PA**	NA
208	Yuba City, CA	(36.3)	NA	Boulder, CO**	NA	NA	New York-Jersey City, NY-NJ M.D.**	NA
209	Ann Arbor, MI	(36.4)	NA	Brunswick, GA**	NA	NA	Newark, NJ-PA M.D.**	NA
210	Dallas-Plano-Irving, TX M.D.	(36.9)	NA	Buffalo-Niagara Falls, NY**	NA	NA	North Port-Sarasota-Bradenton, FL**	NA
210	Goldsboro, NC	(36.9)	NA	California-Lexington Park, MD**	NA	NA	Ogden-Clearfield, UT**	NA
210	Valdosta, GA	(36.9)	NA	Cambridge-Newton, MA M.D.**	NA	NA	Owensboro, KY**	NA
213	Lima, OH	(37.3)	NA	Canton, OH**	NA	NA	Panama City, FL**	NA
214	San Antonio, TX	(37.6)	NA	Chambersburg-Waynesboro, PA**	NA	NA	Parkersburg-Vienna, WV**	NA
215	Naples-Marco Island, FL	(37.8)	NA	Champaign-Urbana, IL**	NA	NA	Peoria, IL**	NA
215	Reno, NV	(37.8)	NA	Chicago (greater), IL-IN-WI**	NA	NA	Philadelphia (greater) PA-NJ-MD-DE**	NA
215	West Palm Beach, FL M.D.	(37.8)	NA	Chicago-Joilet-Naperville, IL M.D.**	NA	NA	Philadelphia, PA M.D.**	NA
218	Asheville, NC	(37.9)	NA	Cincinnati, OH-KY-IN**	NA	NA	Phoenix-Mesa-Scottsdale, AZ**	NA
218	Roanoke, VA	(37.9)	NA	Coeur d'Alene, ID**	NA	NA	Pocatello, ID**	NA
220	Richmond, VA	(38.4)	NA	Crestview-Fort Walton Beach, FL**	NA	NA	Pueblo, CO**	NA
220	Saginaw, MI	(38.4)	NA	Danville, IL**	NA	NA	Rapid City, SD**	NA
222	Erie, PA	(38.7)	NA	Daphne-Fairhope-Foley, AL**	NA	NA	Rochester, MN**	NA
223	Durham-Chapel Hill, NC	(39.6)	NA	Davenport, IA-IL**	NA	NA	Rochester, NY**	NA
224	Waterloo-Cedar Falls, IA	(40.2)	NA	Decatur, IL**	NA	NA	Rockford, IL**	NA
225	College Station-Bryan, TX	(40.7)	NA	Denver-Aurora, CO**	NA	NA	Rocky Mount, NC**	NA
225	Iowa City, IA	(40.7)	NA	Detroit (greater), MI**	NA	NA	Rome, GA**	NA
227	Sebastian-Vero Beach, FL	(40.8)	NA	Detroit-Dearborn-Livonia, MI M.D.**	NA	NA	Salisbury, MD-DE**	NA
228	York-Hanover, PA	(41.0)	NA	Dutchess-Putnam, NY M.D.**	NA	NA	San Rafael, CA M.D.**	NA
229	Longview, TX	(41.5)	NA	East Stroudsburg, PA**	NA	NA	Santa Maria-Santa Barbara, CA**	NA
230	Florence, SC	(41.8)	NA	Elgin, IL M.D.**	NA	NA	Seattle (greater), WA**	NA
231	Sumter, SC	(42.5)	NA	Elizabethtown-Fort Knox, KY**	NA	NA	Seattle-Bellevue-Everett, WA M.D.**	NA
232	Raleigh, NC	(42.6)	NA	Elmira, NY**	NA	NA	Sebring, FL**	NA
233	Savannah, GA	(42.7)	NA	Fairbanks, AK**	NA	NA	Sierra Vista-Douglas, AZ**	NA
234	Clarksville, TN-KY	(42.8)	NA	Fort Smith, AR-OK**	NA	NA	Sioux City, IA-NE-SD**	NA
235	Port St. Lucie, FL	(43.1)	NA	Gainesville, GA**	NA	NA	Spartanburg, SC**	NA
236	Carson City, NV	(43.7)	NA	Gary, IN M.D.**	NA	NA	Springfield, IL**	NA
237	Lakeland, FL	(44.2)	NA	Gettysburg, PA**	NA	NA	Springfield, MA**	NA
238	Oshkosh-Neenah, WI	(44.6)	NA	Glens Falls, NY**	NA	NA	Staunton-Waynesboro, VA**	NA
238	Pine Bluff, AR	(44.6)	NA	Grand Island, NE**	NA	NA	Syracuse, NY**	NA
240	Greensboro-High Point, NC	(45.1)	NA	Greenville-Anderson, SC**	NA	NA	Tacoma, WA M.D.**	NA
241	Mobile, AL	(45.5)	NA	Hagerstown-Martinsburg, MD-WV**	NA	NA	Terre Haute, IN**	NA
242	Casper, WY	(46.0)	NA	Hammond, LA**	NA	NA	Texarkana, TX-AR**	NA
243	Tampa-St Petersburg, FL	(46.3)	NA	Hattiesburg, MS**	NA	NA	The Villages, FL**	NA
244	Hinesville, GA	(46.4)	NA	Hilton Head Island, SC**	NA	NA	Toledo, OH**	NA
245	Laredo, TX	(46.8)	NA	Homosassa Springs, FL**	NA	NA	Tuscaloosa, AL**	NA
246	Deltona-Daytona Beach, FL	(47.0)	NA	Jackson, MS**	NA	NA	Utica-Rome, NY**	NA
247	Virginia Beach-Norfolk, VA-NC	(47.1)	NA	Jackson, TN**	NA	NA	Victoria, TX**	NA
248	Dothan, AL	(47.5)	NA	Jefferson City, MO**	NA	NA	Waco, TX**	NA
249	Winchester, VA-WV	(47.7)	NA	Kahului-Wailuku-Lahaina, HI**	NA	NA	Walla Walla, WA**	NA
250	Charlottesville, VA	(48.9)	NA	Kankakee, IL**	NA	NA	Warner Robins, GA**	NA
251	Ocala, FL	(49.2)	NA	Kansas City, MO-KS**	NA	NA	Warren-Troy, MI M.D.**	NA
252	Orlando, FL	(49.3)	NA	Kingston, NY**	NA	NA	Watertown-Fort Drum, NY**	NA
253	Punta Gorda, FL	(52.0)	NA	Knoxville, TN**	NA	NA	Wilmington, NC**	NA
254	Jacksonville, FL	(53.5)	NA	Kokomo, IN**	NA	NA	Winston-Salem, NC**	NA
255	Lynchburg, VA	(54.7)	NA	Lafayette, LA**	NA			
256	Charleston-North Charleston, SC	(57.0)	NA	Lake Co.-Kenosha Co., IL-WI M.D.**	NA			

Source: CQ Press using reported data from the F.B.I. "Crime in the United States 2012"
*Robbery is the taking of anything of value by force or threat of force. Attempts are included.
**Not available.

21. Aggravated Assaults in 2012
National Total = 760,739 Aggravated Assaults*

RANK	METROPOLITAN AREA	ASSAULTS	RANK	METROPOLITAN AREA	ASSAULTS	RANK	METROPOLITAN AREA	ASSAULTS
256	Abilene, TX	371	330	Cheyenne, WY	165	111	Gary, IN M.D.	1,352
121	Akron, OH	1,190	4	Chicago (greater), IL-IN-WI	19,272	360	Gettysburg, PA	87
106	Albany-Schenectady-Troy, NY	1,458	6	Chicago-Joilet-Naperville, IL M.D.	16,397	336	Glens Falls, NY	148
161	Albany, GA	765	235	Chico, CA	431	242	Goldsboro, NC	394
364	Albany, OR	72	71	Cincinnati, OH-KY-IN	2,486	334	Grand Forks, ND-MN	155
46	Albuquerque, NM	4,153	147	Clarksville, TN-KY	899	348	Grand Island, NE	117
NA	Alexandria, LA**	NA	201	Cleveland, TN	546	276	Grand Junction, CO	312
153	Allentown, PA-NJ	849	266	Coeur d'Alene, ID	341	338	Great Falls, MT	147
308	Altoona, PA	233	168	College Station-Bryan, TX	735	191	Greeley, CO	604
140	Amarillo, TX	957	104	Colorado Springs, CO	1,496	204	Green Bay, WI	542
363	Ames, IA	78	242	Columbia, MO	394	93	Greensboro-High Point, NC	1,689
44	Anaheim-Santa Ana-Irvine, CA M.D.	4,208	165	Columbus, GA-AL	747	49	Greenville-Anderson, SC	3,752
92	Anchorage, AK	1,725	358	Columbus, IN	91	228	Greenville, NC	447
177	Ann Arbor, MI	686	88	Corpus Christi, TX	1,783	240	Hagerstown-Martinsburg, MD-WV	411
217	Anniston-Oxford, AL	504	367	Corvallis, OR	58	144	Hammond, LA	927
290	Appleton, WI	273	146	Crestview-Fort Walton Beach, FL	901	192	Hanford-Corcoran, CA	602
189	Asheville, NC	621	295	Cumberland, MD-WV	265	151	Harrisburg-Carlisle, PA	857
254	Athens-Clarke County, GA	372	8	Dallas (greater), TX	12,851	350	Harrisonburg, VA	112
9	Atlanta, GA	12,399	27	Dallas-Plano-Irving, TX M.D.	7,299	100	Hartford, CT	1,538
NA	Atlantic City, NJ**	NA	282	Dalton, GA	300	366	Hattiesburg, MS	62
299	Auburn, AL	261	284	Danville, IL	299	203	Hickory, NC	544
149	Augusta, GA-SC	876	271	Daphne-Fairhope-Foley, AL	332	166	Hilton Head Island, SC	744
51	Austin-Round Rock, TX	3,612	126	Davenport, IA-IL	1,050	319	Hinesville, GA	189
56	Bakersfield, CA	3,424	138	Dayton, OH	994	254	Homosassa Springs, FL	372
15	Baltimore, MD	10,283	285	Decatur, AL	291	231	Houma, LA	443
368	Bangor, ME	51	291	Decatur, IL	271	5	Houston, TX	19,164
162	Barnstable Town, MA	760	86	Deltona-Daytona Beach, FL	1,838	99	Huntsville, AL	1,549
NA	Baton Rouge, LA**	NA	35	Denver-Aurora, CO	5,418	332	Idaho Falls, ID	162
312	Bay City, MI	211	119	Des Moines-West Des Moines, IA	1,215	28	Indianapolis, IN	7,014
110	Beaumont-Port Arthur, TX	1,401	7	Detroit (greater), MI	15,687	277	Iowa City, IA	309
277	Beckley, WV	309	10	Detroit-Dearborn-Livonia, MI M.D.	11,816	37	Jacksonville, FL	4,933
275	Bellingham, WA	318	247	Dothan, AL	383	130	Jackson, MS	1,027
264	Billings, MT	346	176	Dover, DE	689	137	Jackson, TN	999
237	Binghamton, NY	424	352	Dubuque, IA	104	306	Janesville, WI	241
45	Birmingham-Hoover, AL	4,185	228	Duluth, MN-WI	447	247	Jefferson City, MO	383
270	Bismarck, ND	333	111	Durham-Chapel Hill, NC	1,352	208	Johnson City, TN	534
314	Blacksburg, VA	202	213	Dutchess-Putnam, NY M.D.	514	307	Johnstown, PA	236
236	Bloomington, IL	428	212	East Stroudsburg, PA	517	298	Jonesboro, AR	262
288	Bloomington, IN	277	251	El Centro, CA	375	224	Joplin, MO	469
356	Bloomsburg-Berwick, PA	95	67	El Paso, TX	2,563	302	Kahului-Wailuku-Lahaina, HI	247
134	Boise City, ID	1,018	172	Elgin, IL M.D.	728	173	Kalamazoo-Portage, MI	724
12	Boston (greater), MA-NH	10,998	371	Elizabethtown-Fort Knox, KY	45	304	Kankakee, IL	243
32	Boston, MA M.D.	6,083	328	Elmira, NY	170	30	Kansas City, MO-KS	6,662
234	Boulder, CO	436	257	Erie, PA	366	233	Kennewick-Richland, WA	442
355	Bowling Green, KY	99	227	Eugene, OR	448	142	Killeen-Temple, TX	939
221	Bremerton-Silverdale, WA	476	350	Fairbanks, AK	112	139	Kingsport, TN-VA	972
115	Bridgeport-Stamford, CT	1,275	241	Fargo, ND-MN	401	313	Kingston, NY	209
170	Brownsville-Harlingen, TX	732	184	Farmington, NM	655	70	Knoxville, TN	2,520
258	Brunswick, GA	360	108	Fayetteville-Springdale, AR-MO	1,412	342	Kokomo, IN	135
62	Buffalo-Niagara Falls, NY	2,922	135	Fayetteville, NC	1,015	341	La Crosse, WI-MN	141
218	Burlington, NC	497	263	Flagstaff, AZ	349	239	Lafayette, IN	417
316	California-Lexington Park, MD	194	68	Flint, MI	2,541	NA	Lafayette, LA**	NA
42	Cambridge-Newton, MA M.D.	4,530	253	Florence-Muscle Shoals, AL	374	158	Lake Co.-Kenosha Co., IL-WI M.D.	795
72	Camden, NJ M.D.	2,357	150	Florence, SC	858	294	Lake Havasu City-Kingman, AZ	267
222	Canton, OH	473	326	Fond du Lac, WI	171	98	Lakeland, FL	1,584
102	Cape Coral-Fort Myers, FL	1,527	201	Fort Collins, CO	546	238	Lancaster, PA	419
273	Cape Girardeau, MO-IL	328	40	Fort Lauderdale, FL M.D.	4,811	124	Lansing-East Lansing, MI	1,131
347	Carson City, NV	118	143	Fort Smith, AR-OK	928	154	Laredo, TX	846
344	Casper, WY	130	223	Fort Wayne, IN	470	209	Las Cruces, NM	531
286	Cedar Rapids, IA	288	34	Fort Worth-Arlington, TX M.D.	5,552	20	Las Vegas-Henderson, NV	8,645
345	Chambersburg-Waynesboro, PA	126	54	Fresno, CA	3,468	281	Lawrence, KS	301
156	Champaign-Urbana, IL	835	245	Gadsden, AL	385	171	Lawton, OK	730
81	Charleston-North Charleston, SC	2,043	123	Gainesville, FL	1,165	316	Lebanon, PA	194
303	Charlottesville, VA	246	321	Gainesville, GA	185	369	Lewiston-Auburn, ME	47

Note: All listings are for Metropolitan Statistical Areas (M.S.A.s) except for those ending with "M.D." Listings with "M.D." are Metropolitan Divisions which are smaller parts of eleven large M.S.A.s. See explanatory note at beginning of metropolitan area section.

RANK	METROPOLITAN AREA	ASSAULTS	RANK	METROPOLITAN AREA	ASSAULTS	RANK	METROPOLITAN AREA	ASSAULTS
361	Lewiston, ID-WA	83	365	Owensboro, KY	66	113	Silver Spring-Frederick, MD M.D.	1,317
200	Lexington-Fayette, KY	551	145	Oxnard-Thousand Oaks, CA	926	295	Sioux City, IA-NE-SD	265
260	Lima, OH	357	78	Palm Bay-Melbourne, FL	2,229	220	Sioux Falls, SD	483
175	Lincoln, NE	691	179	Panama City, FL	682	225	South Bend-Mishawaka, IN-MI	460
60	Little Rock, AR	3,148	300	Parkersburg-Vienna, WV	248	130	Spartanburg, SC	1,027
372	Logan, UT-ID	42	82	Pensacola, FL	1,949	130	Spokane, WA	1,027
182	Longview, TX	668	128	Peoria, IL	1,044	136	Springfield, IL	1,001
333	Longview, WA	161	NA	Philadelphia (greater) PA-NJ-MD-DE**	NA	80	Springfield, MA	2,075
2	Los Angeles County, CA M.D.	23,057	NA	Philadelphia, PA M.D.**	NA	100	Springfield, MO	1,538
1	Los Angeles (greater), CA	27,265	13	Phoenix-Mesa-Scottsdale, AZ	10,630	326	Springfield, OH	171
59	Louisville, KY-IN	3,246	210	Pine Bluff, AR	523	358	State College, PA	91
94	Lubbock, TX	1,678	NA	Pittsburgh, PA**	NA	336	Staunton-Waynesboro, VA	148
291	Lynchburg, VA	271	272	Pittsfield, MA	330	47	Stockton-Lodi, CA	4,016
206	Macon, GA	539	335	Pocatello, ID	153	329	St. George, UT	168
163	Madera, CA	758	125	Port St. Lucie, FL	1,065	287	St. Joseph, MO-KS	282
159	Madison, WI	787	53	Portland-Vancouver, OR-WA	3,518	19	St. Louis, MO-IL	8,888
198	Manchester-Nashua, NH	576	265	Portland, ME	345	178	Sumter, SC	683
325	Manhattan, KS	172	194	Prescott, AZ	596	114	Syracuse, NY	1,281
346	Mankato-North Mankato, MN	119	52	Providence-Warwick, RI-MA	3,538	76	Tacoma, WA M.D.	2,277
362	Mansfield, OH	79	308	Provo-Orem, UT	233	103	Tallahassee, FL	1,500
85	McAllen-Edinburg-Mission, TX	1,879	193	Pueblo, CO	599	23	Tampa-St Petersburg, FL	8,195
214	Medford, OR	513	268	Punta Gorda, FL	337	322	Terre Haute, IN	179
17	Memphis, TN-MS-AR	9,601	311	Racine, WI	212	155	Texarkana, TX-AR	845
107	Merced, CA	1,425	88	Raleigh, NC	1,783	343	The Villages, FL	131
3	Miami (greater), FL	19,445	273	Rapid City, SD	328	79	Toledo, OH	2,228
14	Miami-Dade County, FL M.D.	10,387	160	Reading, PA	782	182	Topeka, KS	668
357	Michigan City-La Porte, IN	93	129	Redding, CA	1,029	157	Trenton, NJ	811
370	Midland, MI	46	120	Reno, NV	1,208	64	Tucson, AZ	2,891
249	Midland, TX	382	97	Richmond, VA	1,591	55	Tulsa, OK	3,447
36	Milwaukee, WI	5,135	16	Riverside-San Bernardino, CA	9,827	190	Tuscaloosa, AL	620
39	Minneapolis-St. Paul, MN-WI	4,820	204	Roanoke, VA	542	187	Tyler, TX	635
305	Missoula, MT	242	330	Rochester, MN	165	216	Utica-Rome, NY	509
105	Mobile, AL	1,493	91	Rochester, NY	1,730	277	Valdosta, GA	309
83	Modesto, CA	1,920	90	Rockford, IL	1,775	127	Vallejo-Fairfield, CA	1,047
196	Monroe, LA	589	245	Rockingham County, NH M.D.	385	244	Victoria, TX	393
300	Monroe, MI	248	167	Rocky Mount, NC	737	215	Vineland-Bridgeton, NJ	512
95	Montgomery County, PA M.D.	1,610	295	Rome, GA	265	63	Virginia Beach-Norfolk, VA-NC	2,916
185	Montgomery, AL	647	31	Sacramento, CA	6,155	96	Visalia-Porterville, CA	1,595
282	Morgantown, WV	300	118	Saginaw, MI	1,235	174	Waco, TX	704
267	Morristown, TN	338	186	Salem, OR	640	353	Walla Walla, WA	102
339	Mount Vernon-Anacortes, WA	146	133	Salinas, CA	1,021	219	Warner Robins, GA	489
318	Muncie, IN	192	117	Salisbury, MD-DE	1,260	48	Warren-Troy, MI M.D.	3,871
249	Napa, CA	382	74	Salt Lake City, UT	2,329	18	Washington (greater) DC-VA-MD-WV	9,415
188	Naples-Marco Island, FL	631	33	San Antonio, TX	5,660	24	Washington, DC-VA-MD-WV M.D.	8,098
21	Nashville-Davidson, TN	8,568	25	San Diego, CA	7,840	231	Waterloo-Cedar Falls, IA	443
66	Nassau-Suffolk, NY M.D.	2,566	11	San Francisco (greater), CA	11,191	322	Watertown-Fort Drum, NY	179
288	New Bern, NC	277	57	San Francisco-Redwood, CA M.D.	3,281	349	Wausau, WI	113
87	New Haven-Milford, CT	1,836	61	San Jose, CA	3,014	43	West Palm Beach, FL M.D.	4,247
50	New Orleans, LA	3,636	164	San Luis Obispo, CA	753	269	Wheeling, WV-OH	335
NA	New York (greater), NY-NJ-PA**	NA	280	San Rafael, CA M.D.	304	251	Wichita Falls, TX	375
NA	New York-Jersey City, NY-NJ M.D.**	NA	168	Santa Cruz-Watsonville, CA	735	69	Wichita, KS	2,530
58	Newark, NJ-PA M.D.	3,265	259	Santa Fe, NM	359	354	Williamsport, PA	101
75	North Port-Sarasota-Bradenton, FL	2,310	122	Santa Maria-Santa Barbara, CA	1,180	73	Wilmington, DE-MD-NJ M.D.	2,351
230	Norwich-New London, CT	446	109	Santa Rosa, CA	1,404	197	Wilmington, NC	583
26	Oakland-Hayward, CA M.D.	7,606	207	Savannah, GA	537	324	Winchester, VA-WV	175
116	Ocala, FL	1,267	152	Scranton--Wilkes-Barre, PA	855	84	Winston-Salem, NC	1,891
320	Ocean City, NJ	187	29	Seattle (greater), WA	6,872	65	Worcester, MA-CT	2,718
141	Odessa, TX	956	41	Seattle-Bellevue-Everett, WA M.D.	4,595	199	Yakima, WA	570
210	Ogden-Clearfield, UT	523	261	Sebastian-Vero Beach, FL	356	180	York-Hanover, PA	673
38	Oklahoma City, OK	4,876	315	Sebring, FL	200	148	Youngstown-Warren, OH-PA	881
262	Olympia, WA	355	340	Sheboygan, WI	142	226	Yuba City, CA	455
76	Omaha-Council Bluffs, NE-IA	2,277	310	Sherman-Denison, TX	228	195	Yuma, AZ	592
22	Orlando, FL	8,561	NA	Shreveport-Bossier City, LA**	NA			
293	Oshkosh-Neenah, WI	269	181	Sierra Vista-Douglas, AZ	671			

Source: Reported data from the F.B.I. "Crime in the United States 2012"

*Aggravated assault is an attack for the purpose of inflicting severe bodily injury.

**Not available.

21. Aggravated Assaults in 2012 (continued)
National Total = 760,739 Aggravated Assaults*

RANK	METROPOLITAN AREA	ASSAULTS	RANK	METROPOLITAN AREA	ASSAULTS	RANK	METROPOLITAN AREA	ASSAULTS
1	Los Angeles (greater), CA	27,265	65	Worcester, MA-CT	2,718	129	Redding, CA	1,029
2	Los Angeles County, CA M.D.	23,057	66	Nassau-Suffolk, NY M.D.	2,566	130	Jackson, MS	1,027
3	Miami (greater), FL	19,445	67	El Paso, TX	2,563	130	Spartanburg, SC	1,027
4	Chicago (greater), IL-IN-WI	19,272	68	Flint, MI	2,541	130	Spokane, WA	1,027
5	Houston, TX	19,164	69	Wichita, KS	2,530	133	Salinas, CA	1,021
6	Chicago-Joilet-Naperville, IL M.D.	16,397	70	Knoxville, TN	2,520	134	Boise City, ID	1,018
7	Detroit (greater), MI	15,687	71	Cincinnati, OH-KY-IN	2,486	135	Fayetteville, NC	1,015
8	Dallas (greater), TX	12,851	72	Camden, NJ M.D.	2,357	136	Springfield, IL	1,001
9	Atlanta, GA	12,399	73	Wilmington, DE-MD-NJ M.D.	2,351	137	Jackson, TN	999
10	Detroit-Dearborn-Livonia, MI M.D.	11,816	74	Salt Lake City, UT	2,329	138	Dayton, OH	994
11	San Francisco (greater), CA	11,191	75	North Port-Sarasota-Bradenton, FL	2,310	139	Kingsport, TN-VA	972
12	Boston (greater), MA-NH	10,998	76	Omaha-Council Bluffs, NE-IA	2,277	140	Amarillo, TX	957
13	Phoenix-Mesa-Scottsdale, AZ	10,630	76	Tacoma, WA M.D.	2,277	141	Odessa, TX	956
14	Miami-Dade County, FL M.D.	10,387	78	Palm Bay-Melbourne, FL	2,229	142	Killeen-Temple, TX	939
15	Baltimore, MD	10,283	79	Toledo, OH	2,228	143	Fort Smith, AR-OK	928
16	Riverside-San Bernardino, CA	9,827	80	Springfield, MA	2,075	144	Hammond, LA	927
17	Memphis, TN-MS-AR	9,601	81	Charleston-North Charleston, SC	2,043	145	Oxnard-Thousand Oaks, CA	926
18	Washington (greater) DC-VA-MD-WV	9,415	82	Pensacola, FL	1,949	146	Crestview-Fort Walton Beach, FL	901
19	St. Louis, MO-IL	8,888	83	Modesto, CA	1,920	147	Clarksville, TN-KY	899
20	Las Vegas-Henderson, NV	8,645	84	Winston-Salem, NC	1,891	148	Youngstown-Warren, OH-PA	881
21	Nashville-Davidson, TN	8,568	85	McAllen-Edinburg-Mission, TX	1,879	149	Augusta, GA-SC	876
22	Orlando, FL	8,561	86	Deltona-Daytona Beach, FL	1,838	150	Florence, SC	858
23	Tampa-St Petersburg, FL	8,195	87	New Haven-Milford, CT	1,836	151	Harrisburg-Carlisle, PA	857
24	Washington, DC-VA-MD-WV M.D.	8,098	88	Corpus Christi, TX	1,783	152	Scranton--Wilkes-Barre, PA	855
25	San Diego, CA	7,840	88	Raleigh, NC	1,783	153	Allentown, PA-NJ	849
26	Oakland-Hayward, CA M.D.	7,606	90	Rockford, IL	1,775	154	Laredo, TX	846
27	Dallas-Plano-Irving, TX M.D.	7,299	91	Rochester, NY	1,730	155	Texarkana, TX-AR	845
28	Indianapolis, IN	7,014	92	Anchorage, AK	1,725	156	Champaign-Urbana, IL	835
29	Seattle (greater), WA	6,872	93	Greensboro-High Point, NC	1,689	157	Trenton, NJ	811
30	Kansas City, MO-KS	6,662	94	Lubbock, TX	1,678	158	Lake Co.-Kenosha Co., IL-WI M.D.	795
31	Sacramento, CA	6,155	95	Montgomery County, PA M.D.	1,610	159	Madison, WI	787
32	Boston, MA M.D.	6,083	96	Visalia-Porterville, CA	1,595	160	Reading, PA	782
33	San Antonio, TX	5,660	97	Richmond, VA	1,591	161	Albany, GA	765
34	Fort Worth-Arlington, TX M.D.	5,552	98	Lakeland, FL	1,584	162	Barnstable Town, MA	760
35	Denver-Aurora, CO	5,418	99	Huntsville, AL	1,549	163	Madera, CA	758
36	Milwaukee, WI	5,135	100	Hartford, CT	1,538	164	San Luis Obispo, CA	753
37	Jacksonville, FL	4,933	100	Springfield, MO	1,538	165	Columbus, GA-AL	747
38	Oklahoma City, OK	4,876	102	Cape Coral-Fort Myers, FL	1,527	166	Hilton Head Island, SC	744
39	Minneapolis-St. Paul, MN-WI	4,820	103	Tallahassee, FL	1,500	167	Rocky Mount, NC	737
40	Fort Lauderdale, FL M.D.	4,811	104	Colorado Springs, CO	1,496	168	College Station-Bryan, TX	735
41	Seattle-Bellevue-Everett, WA M.D.	4,595	105	Mobile, AL	1,493	168	Santa Cruz-Watsonville, CA	735
42	Cambridge-Newton, MA M.D.	4,530	106	Albany-Schenectady-Troy, NY	1,458	170	Brownsville-Harlingen, TX	732
43	West Palm Beach, FL M.D.	4,247	107	Merced, CA	1,425	171	Lawton, OK	730
44	Anaheim-Santa Ana-Irvine, CA M.D.	4,208	108	Fayetteville-Springdale, AR-MO	1,412	172	Elgin, IL M.D.	728
45	Birmingham-Hoover, AL	4,185	109	Santa Rosa, CA	1,404	173	Kalamazoo-Portage, MI	724
46	Albuquerque, NM	4,153	110	Beaumont-Port Arthur, TX	1,401	174	Waco, TX	704
47	Stockton-Lodi, CA	4,016	111	Durham-Chapel Hill, NC	1,352	175	Lincoln, NE	691
48	Warren-Troy, MI M.D.	3,871	111	Gary, IN M.D.	1,352	176	Dover, DE	689
49	Greenville-Anderson, SC	3,752	113	Silver Spring-Frederick, MD M.D.	1,317	177	Ann Arbor, MI	686
50	New Orleans, LA	3,636	114	Syracuse, NY	1,281	178	Sumter, SC	683
51	Austin-Round Rock, TX	3,612	115	Bridgeport-Stamford, CT	1,275	179	Panama City, FL	682
52	Providence-Warwick, RI-MA	3,538	116	Ocala, FL	1,267	180	York-Hanover, PA	673
53	Portland-Vancouver, OR-WA	3,518	117	Salisbury, MD-DE	1,260	181	Sierra Vista-Douglas, AZ	671
54	Fresno, CA	3,468	118	Saginaw, MI	1,235	182	Longview, TX	668
55	Tulsa, OK	3,447	119	Des Moines-West Des Moines, IA	1,215	182	Topeka, KS	668
56	Bakersfield, CA	3,424	120	Reno, NV	1,208	184	Farmington, NM	655
57	San Francisco-Redwood, CA M.D.	3,281	121	Akron, OH	1,190	185	Montgomery, AL	647
58	Newark, NJ-PA M.D.	3,265	122	Santa Maria-Santa Barbara, CA	1,180	186	Salem, OR	640
59	Louisville, KY-IN	3,246	123	Gainesville, FL	1,165	187	Tyler, TX	635
60	Little Rock, AR	3,148	124	Lansing-East Lansing, MI	1,131	188	Naples-Marco Island, FL	631
61	San Jose, CA	3,014	125	Port St. Lucie, FL	1,065	189	Asheville, NC	621
62	Buffalo-Niagara Falls, NY	2,922	126	Davenport, IA-IL	1,050	190	Tuscaloosa, AL	620
63	Virginia Beach-Norfolk, VA-NC	2,916	127	Vallejo-Fairfield, CA	1,047	191	Greeley, CO	604
64	Tucson, AZ	2,891	128	Peoria, IL	1,044	192	Hanford-Corcoran, CA	602

Note: All listings are for Metropolitan Statistical Areas (M.S.A.s) except for those ending with "M.D." Listings with "M.D." are Metropolitan Divisions which are smaller parts of eleven large M.S.A.s. See explanatory note at beginning of metropolitan area section.

RANK	METROPOLITAN AREA	ASSAULTS	RANK	METROPOLITAN AREA	ASSAULTS	RANK	METROPOLITAN AREA	ASSAULTS
193	Pueblo, CO	599	257	Erie, PA	366	321	Gainesville, GA	185
194	Prescott, AZ	596	258	Brunswick, GA	360	322	Terre Haute, IN	179
195	Yuma, AZ	592	259	Santa Fe, NM	359	322	Watertown-Fort Drum, NY	179
196	Monroe, LA	589	260	Lima, OH	357	324	Winchester, VA-WV	175
197	Wilmington, NC	583	261	Sebastian-Vero Beach, FL	356	325	Manhattan, KS	172
198	Manchester-Nashua, NH	576	262	Olympia, WA	355	326	Fond du Lac, WI	171
199	Yakima, WA	570	263	Flagstaff, AZ	349	326	Springfield, OH	171
200	Lexington-Fayette, KY	551	264	Billings, MT	346	328	Elmira, NY	170
201	Cleveland, TN	546	265	Portland, ME	345	329	St. George, UT	168
201	Fort Collins, CO	546	266	Coeur d'Alene, ID	341	330	Cheyenne, WY	165
203	Hickory, NC	544	267	Morristown, TN	338	330	Rochester, MN	165
204	Green Bay, WI	542	268	Punta Gorda, FL	337	332	Idaho Falls, ID	162
204	Roanoke, VA	542	269	Wheeling, WV-OH	335	333	Longview, WA	161
206	Macon, GA	539	270	Bismarck, ND	333	334	Grand Forks, ND-MN	155
207	Savannah, GA	537	271	Daphne-Fairhope-Foley, AL	332	335	Pocatello, ID	153
208	Johnson City, TN	534	272	Pittsfield, MA	330	336	Glens Falls, NY	148
209	Las Cruces, NM	531	273	Cape Girardeau, MO-IL	328	336	Staunton-Waynesboro, VA	148
210	Ogden-Clearfield, UT	523	273	Rapid City, SD	328	338	Great Falls, MT	147
210	Pine Bluff, AR	523	275	Bellingham, WA	318	339	Mount Vernon-Anacortes, WA	146
212	East Stroudsburg, PA	517	276	Grand Junction, CO	312	340	Sheboygan, WI	142
213	Dutchess-Putnam, NY M.D.	514	277	Beckley, WV	309	341	La Crosse, WI-MN	141
214	Medford, OR	513	277	Iowa City, IA	309	342	Kokomo, IN	135
215	Vineland-Bridgeton, NJ	512	277	Valdosta, GA	309	343	The Villages, FL	131
216	Utica-Rome, NY	509	280	San Rafael, CA M.D.	304	344	Casper, WY	130
217	Anniston-Oxford, AL	504	281	Lawrence, KS	301	345	Chambersburg-Waynesboro, PA	126
218	Burlington, NC	497	282	Dalton, GA	300	346	Mankato-North Mankato, MN	119
219	Warner Robins, GA	489	282	Morgantown, WV	300	347	Carson City, NV	118
220	Sioux Falls, SD	483	284	Danville, IL	299	348	Grand Island, NE	117
221	Bremerton-Silverdale, WA	476	285	Decatur, AL	291	349	Wausau, WI	113
222	Canton, OH	473	286	Cedar Rapids, IA	288	350	Fairbanks, AK	112
223	Fort Wayne, IN	470	287	St. Joseph, MO-KS	282	350	Harrisonburg, VA	112
224	Joplin, MO	469	288	Bloomington, IN	277	352	Dubuque, IA	104
225	South Bend-Mishawaka, IN-MI	460	288	New Bern, NC	277	353	Walla Walla, WA	102
226	Yuba City, CA	455	290	Appleton, WI	273	354	Williamsport, PA	101
227	Eugene, OR	448	291	Decatur, IL	271	355	Bowling Green, KY	99
228	Duluth, MN-WI	447	291	Lynchburg, VA	271	356	Bloomsburg-Berwick, PA	95
228	Greenville, NC	447	293	Oshkosh-Neenah, WI	269	357	Michigan City-La Porte, IN	93
230	Norwich-New London, CT	446	294	Lake Havasu City-Kingman, AZ	267	358	Columbus, IN	91
231	Houma, LA	443	295	Cumberland, MD-WV	265	358	State College, PA	91
231	Waterloo-Cedar Falls, IA	443	295	Rome, GA	265	360	Gettysburg, PA	87
233	Kennewick-Richland, WA	442	295	Sioux City, IA-NE-SD	265	361	Lewiston, ID-WA	83
234	Boulder, CO	436	298	Jonesboro, AR	262	362	Mansfield, OH	79
235	Chico, CA	431	299	Auburn, AL	261	363	Ames, IA	78
236	Bloomington, IL	428	300	Monroe, MI	248	364	Albany, OR	72
237	Binghamton, NY	424	300	Parkersburg-Vienna, WV	248	365	Owensboro, KY	66
238	Lancaster, PA	419	302	Kahului-Wailuku-Lahaina, HI	247	366	Hattiesburg, MS	62
239	Lafayette, IN	417	303	Charlottesville, VA	246	367	Corvallis, OR	58
240	Hagerstown-Martinsburg, MD-WV	411	304	Kankakee, IL	243	368	Bangor, ME	51
241	Fargo, ND-MN	401	305	Missoula, MT	242	369	Lewiston-Auburn, ME	47
242	Columbia, MO	394	306	Janesville, WI	241	370	Midland, MI	46
242	Goldsboro, NC	394	307	Johnstown, PA	236	371	Elizabethtown-Fort Knox, KY	45
244	Victoria, TX	393	308	Altoona, PA	233	372	Logan, UT-ID	42
245	Gadsden, AL	385	308	Provo-Orem, UT	233	NA	Alexandria, LA**	NA
245	Rockingham County, NH M.D.	385	310	Sherman-Denison, TX	228	NA	Atlantic City, NJ**	NA
247	Dothan, AL	383	311	Racine, WI	212	NA	Baton Rouge, LA**	NA
247	Jefferson City, MO	383	312	Bay City, MI	211	NA	Lafayette, LA**	NA
249	Midland, TX	382	313	Kingston, NY	209	NA	New York (greater), NY-NJ-PA**	NA
249	Napa, CA	382	314	Blacksburg, VA	202	NA	New York-Jersey City, NY-NJ M.D.**	NA
251	El Centro, CA	375	315	Sebring, FL	200	NA	Philadelphia (greater) PA-NJ-MD-DE**	NA
251	Wichita Falls, TX	375	316	California-Lexington Park, MD	194	NA	Philadelphia, PA M.D.**	NA
253	Florence-Muscle Shoals, AL	374	316	Lebanon, PA	194	NA	Pittsburgh, PA**	NA
254	Athens-Clarke County, GA	372	318	Muncie, IN	192	NA	Shreveport-Bossier City, LA**	NA
254	Homosassa Springs, FL	372	319	Hinesville, GA	189			
256	Abilene, TX	371	320	Ocean City, NJ	187			

Source: Reported data from the F.B.I. "Crime in the United States 2012"

*Aggravated assault is an attack for the purpose of inflicting severe bodily injury.

**Not available.

22. Aggravated Assault Rate in 2012
National Rate = 242.3 Aggravated Assaults per 100,000 Population*

RANK	METROPOLITAN AREA	RATE	RANK	METROPOLITAN AREA	RATE	RANK	METROPOLITAN AREA	RATE
194	Abilene, TX	219.6	247	Cheyenne, WY	175.5	229	Gary, IN M.D.	190.2
254	Akron, OH	169.7	214	Chicago (greater), IL-IN-WI	202.6	351	Gettysburg, PA	85.6
260	Albany-Schenectady-Troy, NY	166.4	186	Chicago-Joilet-Naperville, IL M.D.	224.6	329	Glens Falls, NY	114.1
22	Albany, GA	480.0	222	Chico, CA	193.9	89	Goldsboro, NC	315.4
363	Albany, OR	60.5	323	Cincinnati, OH-KY-IN	117.1	281	Grand Forks, ND-MN	155.3
26	Albuquerque, NM	461.4	70	Clarksville, TN-KY	337.7	300	Grand Island, NE	140.6
NA	Alexandria, LA**	NA	25	Cleveland, TN	463.5	205	Grand Junction, CO	209.2
343	Allentown, PA-NJ	102.7	166	Coeur d'Alene, ID	240.0	243	Great Falls, MT	178.4
237	Altoona, PA	183.0	92	College Station-Bryan, TX	312.6	175	Greeley, CO	230.3
49	Amarillo, TX	368.5	188	Colorado Springs, CO	223.5	248	Green Bay, WI	174.7
349	Ames, IA	86.7	170	Columbia, MO	237.4	177	Greensboro-High Point, NC	228.8
303	Anaheim-Santa Ana-Irvine, CA M.D.	136.4	162	Columbus, GA-AL	245.5	27	Greenville-Anderson, SC	444.6
13	Anchorage, AK	550.2	326	Columbus, IN	116.5	141	Greenville, NC	258.6
219	Ann Arbor, MI	197.0	36	Corpus Christi, TX	407.2	269	Hagerstown-Martinsburg, MD-WV	160.9
31	Anniston-Oxford, AL	426.1	359	Corvallis, OR	67.0	2	Hammond, LA	751.8
320	Appleton, WI	119.7	48	Crestview-Fort Walton Beach, FL	371.5	44	Hanford-Corcoran, CA	387.9
297	Asheville, NC	143.3	146	Cumberland, MD-WV	255.8	282	Harrisburg-Carlisle, PA	154.7
227	Athens-Clarke County, GA	190.4	224	Dallas (greater), TX	192.4	348	Harrisonburg, VA	87.5
180	Atlanta, GA	228.2	261	Dallas-Plano-Irving, TX M.D.	165.7	290	Hartford, CT	150.2
NA	Atlantic City, NJ**	NA	208	Dalton, GA	208.0	368	Hattiesburg, MS	42.5
239	Auburn, AL	181.2	54	Danville, IL	366.7	293	Hickory, NC	147.8
286	Augusta, GA-SC	152.2	244	Daphne-Fairhope-Foley, AL	177.1	43	Hilton Head Island, SC	388.1
216	Austin-Round Rock, TX	199.5	120	Davenport, IA-IL	274.8	172	Hinesville, GA	232.1
40	Bakersfield, CA	398.3	315	Dayton, OH	123.7	136	Homosassa Springs, FL	262.1
47	Baltimore, MD	373.2	232	Decatur, AL	188.1	201	Houma, LA	211.1
370	Bangor, ME	33.1	163	Decatur, IL	244.6	93	Houston, TX	311.6
66	Barnstable Town, MA	349.1	96	Deltona-Daytona Beach, FL	306.2	59	Huntsville, AL	362.6
NA	Baton Rouge, LA**	NA	211	Denver-Aurora, CO	205.6	321	Idaho Falls, ID	119.3
220	Bay City, MI	196.9	207	Des Moines-West Des Moines, IA	208.6	55	Indianapolis, IN	366.1
68	Beaumont-Port Arthur, TX	340.8	57	Detroit (greater), MI	365.8	217	Iowa City, IA	198.7
156	Beckley, WV	247.5	5	Detroit-Dearborn-Livonia, MI M.D.	655.2	64	Jacksonville, FL	357.8
283	Bellingham, WA	154.6	138	Dothan, AL	260.3	241	Jackson, MS	178.8
199	Billings, MT	213.5	33	Dover, DE	413.5	1	Jackson, TN	762.5
257	Binghamton, NY	168.6	337	Dubuque, IA	109.5	290	Janesville, WI	150.2
50	Birmingham-Hoover, AL	368.1	274	Duluth, MN-WI	158.8	148	Jefferson City, MO	254.0
115	Bismarck, ND	278.3	137	Durham-Chapel Hill, NC	261.0	132	Johnson City, TN	265.1
331	Blacksburg, VA	112.3	311	Dutchess-Putnam, NY M.D.	128.5	263	Johnstown, PA	163.9
178	Bloomington, IL	228.6	98	East Stroudsburg, PA	303.8	200	Jonesboro, AR	212.5
251	Bloomington, IN	171.2	204	El Centro, CA	209.9	133	Joplin, MO	264.7
333	Bloomsburg-Berwick, PA	110.6	95	El Paso, TX	306.4	279	Kahului-Wailuku-Lahaina, HI	155.6
268	Boise City, ID	161.1	327	Elgin, IL M.D.	116.4	192	Kalamazoo-Portage, MI	220.4
169	Boston (greater), MA-NH	237.6	372	Elizabethtown-Fort Knox, KY	29.7	198	Kankakee, IL	213.6
88	Boston, MA M.D.	316.7	228	Elmira, NY	190.3	78	Kansas City, MO-KS	327.7
296	Boulder, CO	143.6	309	Erie, PA	130.0	261	Kennewick-Richland, WA	165.7
362	Bowling Green, KY	61.5	313	Eugene, OR	125.9	185	Killeen-Temple, TX	224.8
235	Bremerton-Silverdale, WA	185.1	82	Fairbanks, AK	323.7	94	Kingsport, TN-VA	310.9
301	Bridgeport-Stamford, CT	140.0	234	Fargo, ND-MN	185.6	330	Kingston, NY	113.9
249	Brownsville-Harlingen, TX	174.2	17	Farmington, NM	510.1	103	Knoxville, TN	296.3
89	Brunswick, GA	315.4	101	Fayetteville-Springdale, AR-MO	296.9	266	Kokomo, IN	162.5
145	Buffalo-Niagara Falls, NY	256.3	127	Fayetteville, NC	268.6	341	La Crosse, WI-MN	104.5
85	Burlington, NC	321.0	143	Flagstaff, AZ	256.7	213	Lafayette, IN	204.2
241	California-Lexington Park, MD	178.8	8	Flint, MI	601.6	NA	Lafayette, LA**	NA
218	Cambridge-Newton, MA M.D.	198.1	149	Florence-Muscle Shoals, AL	252.9	346	Lake Co.-Kenosha Co., IL-WI M.D.	90.9
233	Camden, NJ M.D.	187.3	34	Florence, SC	412.3	308	Lake Havasu City-Kingman, AZ	130.5
323	Canton, OH	117.1	259	Fond du Lac, WI	167.1	144	Lakeland, FL	256.4
168	Cape Coral-Fort Myers, FL	238.6	246	Fort Collins, CO	176.3	357	Lancaster, PA	79.9
71	Cape Girardeau, MO-IL	337.5	130	Fort Lauderdale, FL M.D.	266.6	165	Lansing-East Lansing, MI	243.0
203	Carson City, NV	210.1	79	Fort Smith, AR-OK	327.5	80	Laredo, TX	325.0
258	Casper, WY	167.8	332	Fort Wayne, IN	111.7	155	Las Cruces, NM	248.2
335	Cedar Rapids, IA	110.1	164	Fort Worth-Arlington, TX M.D.	244.1	29	Las Vegas-Henderson, NV	433.2
355	Chambersburg-Waynesboro, PA	83.4	58	Fresno, CA	364.4	129	Lawrence, KS	266.9
63	Champaign-Urbana, IL	359.2	52	Gadsden, AL	367.6	14	Lawton, OK	549.7
102	Charleston-North Charleston, SC	296.7	30	Gainesville, FL	431.5	294	Lebanon, PA	144.2
336	Charlottesville, VA	110.0	344	Gainesville, GA	100.0	367	Lewiston-Auburn, ME	43.7

Note: All listings are for Metropolitan Statistical Areas (M.S.A.s) except for those ending with "M.D." Listings with "M.D." are Metropolitan Divisions which are smaller parts of eleven large M.S.A.s. See explanatory note at beginning of metropolitan area section.

RANK	METROPOLITAN AREA	RATE	RANK	METROPOLITAN AREA	RATE	RANK	METROPOLITAN AREA	RATE
304	Lewiston, ID-WA	134.0	365	Owensboro, KY	57.1	339	Silver Spring-Frederick, MD M.D.	106.3
328	Lexington-Fayette, KY	114.7	334	Oxnard-Thousand Oaks, CA	110.3	277	Sioux City, IA-NE-SD	156.1
72	Lima, OH	336.5	37	Palm Bay-Melbourne, FL	404.5	212	Sioux Falls, SD	205.5
187	Lincoln, NE	223.9	60	Panama City, FL	362.3	295	South Bend-Mishawaka, IN-MI	143.9
28	Little Rock, AR	441.8	128	Parkersburg-Vienna, WV	267.0	83	Spartanburg, SC	322.4
371	Logan, UT-ID	32.5	32	Pensacola, FL	424.2	226	Spokane, WA	191.8
98	Longview, TX	303.8	119	Peoria, IL	274.9	24	Springfield, IL	473.0
279	Longview, WA	155.6	NA	Philadelphia (greater) PA-NJ-MD-DE**	NA	73	Springfield, MA	330.9
174	Los Angeles County, CA M.D.	231.0	NA	Philadelphia, PA M.D.**	NA	67	Springfield, MO	348.8
206	Los Angeles (greater), CA	208.7	158	Phoenix-Mesa-Scottsdale, AZ	246.6	314	Springfield, OH	124.2
139	Louisville, KY-IN	260.0	16	Pine Bluff, AR	526.7	364	State College, PA	58.7
12	Lubbock, TX	558.7	NA	Pittsburgh, PA**	NA	316	Staunton-Waynesboro, VA	123.4
340	Lynchburg, VA	105.5	152	Pittsfield, MA	250.7	10	Stockton-Lodi, CA	571.5
176	Macon, GA	229.0	238	Pocatello, ID	181.6	325	St. George, UT	117.0
21	Madera, CA	491.1	161	Port St. Lucie, FL	245.6	190	St. Joseph, MO-KS	220.6
312	Madison, WI	128.0	284	Portland-Vancouver, OR-WA	154.3	87	St. Louis, MO-IL	317.7
298	Manchester-Nashua, NH	143.1	360	Portland, ME	66.8	6	Sumter, SC	629.6
240	Manhattan, KS	180.3	116	Prescott, AZ	278.2	225	Syracuse, NY	192.3
319	Mankato-North Mankato, MN	121.6	190	Providence-Warwick, RI-MA	220.6	114	Tacoma, WA M.D.	279.1
361	Mansfield, OH	64.0	368	Provo-Orem, UT	42.5	39	Tallahassee, FL	400.2
173	McAllen-Edinburg-Mission, TX	232.0	51	Pueblo, CO	368.0	110	Tampa-St Petersburg, FL	286.2
154	Medford, OR	248.7	210	Punta Gorda, FL	207.1	342	Terre Haute, IN	103.3
3	Memphis, TN-MS-AR	714.6	338	Racine, WI	108.2	11	Texarkana, TX-AR	559.0
15	Merced, CA	543.3	287	Raleigh, NC	151.7	306	The Villages, FL	132.2
69	Miami (greater), FL	338.3	171	Rapid City, SD	237.3	56	Toledo, OH	365.9
38	Miami-Dade County, FL M.D.	401.1	231	Reading, PA	189.1	112	Topeka, KS	283.2
356	Michigan City-La Porte, IN	83.2	9	Redding, CA	573.5	193	Trenton, NJ	219.9
366	Midland, MI	54.7	117	Reno, NV	277.6	109	Tucson, AZ	289.0
140	Midland, TX	259.1	310	Richmond, VA	129.1	61	Tulsa, OK	361.8
77	Milwaukee, WI	327.9	184	Riverside-San Bernardino, CA	226.2	131	Tuscaloosa, AL	266.2
299	Minneapolis-St. Paul, MN-WI	141.4	250	Roanoke, VA	173.6	104	Tyler, TX	293.2
195	Missoula, MT	218.2	358	Rochester, MN	78.6	255	Utica-Rome, NY	169.6
62	Mobile, AL	360.4	273	Rochester, NY	159.2	196	Valdosta, GA	214.8
53	Modesto, CA	366.9	18	Rockford, IL	509.3	153	Vallejo-Fairfield, CA	249.1
75	Monroe, LA	329.6	345	Rockingham County, NH M.D.	91.5	35	Victoria, TX	408.5
264	Monroe, MI	163.5	23	Rocky Mount, NC	479.6	81	Vineland-Bridgeton, NJ	324.3
352	Montgomery County, PA M.D.	85.1	124	Rome, GA	273.2	251	Virginia Beach-Norfolk, VA-NC	171.2
253	Montgomery, AL	170.2	113	Sacramento, CA	280.2	65	Visalia-Porterville, CA	351.8
182	Morgantown, WV	226.8	7	Saginaw, MI	619.9	125	Waco, TX	270.4
105	Morristown, TN	292.2	269	Salem, OR	160.9	275	Walla Walla, WA	158.7
318	Mount Vernon-Anacortes, WA	122.4	167	Salinas, CA	239.8	134	Warner Robins, GA	263.7
265	Muncie, IN	162.7	74	Salisbury, MD-DE	330.5	278	Warren-Troy, MI M.D.	155.7
122	Napa, CA	274.1	209	Salt Lake City, UT	207.3	267	Washington (greater) DC-VA-MD-WV	161.6
230	Naples-Marco Island, FL	189.7	147	San Antonio, TX	254.1	245	Washington, DC-VA-MD-WV M.D.	176.5
19	Nashville-Davidson, TN	500.3	157	San Diego, CA	247.4	135	Waterloo-Cedar Falls, IA	262.2
347	Nassau-Suffolk, NY M.D.	89.8	151	San Francisco (greater), CA	252.5	289	Watertown-Fort Drum, NY	151.0
197	New Bern, NC	214.3	201	San Francisco-Redwood, CA M.D.	211.1	354	Wausau, WI	83.9
183	New Haven-Milford, CT	226.7	271	San Jose, CA	160.1	91	West Palm Beach, FL M.D.	313.8
100	New Orleans, LA	298.0	121	San Luis Obispo, CA	274.3	181	Wheeling, WV-OH	227.6
NA	New York (greater), NY-NJ-PA**	NA	322	San Rafael, CA M.D.	118.1	160	Wichita Falls, TX	245.9
NA	New York-Jersey City, NY-NJ M.D.**	NA	118	Santa Cruz-Watsonville, CA	275.5	41	Wichita, KS	397.4
307	Newark, NJ-PA M.D.	131.1	159	Santa Fe, NM	246.1	350	Williamsport, PA	86.4
84	North Port-Sarasota-Bradenton, FL	321.3	123	Santa Maria-Santa Barbara, CA	273.9	76	Wilmington, DE-MD-NJ M.D.	328.0
97	Norwich-New London, CT	304.7	111	Santa Rosa, CA	285.0	189	Wilmington, NC	222.4
108	Oakland-Hayward, CA M.D.	290.3	292	Savannah, GA	149.4	305	Winchester, VA-WV	133.3
46	Ocala, FL	375.9	288	Scranton--Wilkes-Barre, PA	151.6	107	Winston-Salem, NC	290.4
223	Ocean City, NJ	192.6	221	Seattle (greater), WA	194.4	86	Worcester, MA-CT	319.3
4	Odessa, TX	672.2	256	Seattle-Bellevue-Everett, WA M.D.	169.0	179	Yakima, WA	228.4
352	Ogden-Clearfield, UT	85.1	149	Sebastian-Vero Beach, FL	252.9	285	York-Hanover, PA	153.8
45	Oklahoma City, OK	379.2	215	Sebring, FL	200.0	276	Youngstown-Warren, OH-PA	156.5
302	Olympia, WA	137.0	317	Sheboygan, WI	123.0	126	Yuba City, CA	269.2
142	Omaha-Council Bluffs, NE-IA	257.9	236	Sherman-Denison, TX	185.0	106	Yuma, AZ	291.5
42	Orlando, FL	389.0	NA	Shreveport-Bossier City, LA**	NA			
272	Oshkosh-Neenah, WI	160.0	20	Sierra Vista-Douglas, AZ	498.0			

Source: Reported data from the F.B.I. "Crime in the United States 2012"

*Aggravated assault is an attack for the purpose of inflicting severe bodily injury.

**Not available.

22. Aggravated Assault Rate in 2012 (continued)
National Rate = 242.3 Aggravated Assaults per 100,000 Population*

RANK	METROPOLITAN AREA	RATE	RANK	METROPOLITAN AREA	RATE	RANK	METROPOLITAN AREA	RATE
1	Jackson, TN	762.5	65	Visalia-Porterville, CA	351.8	129	Lawrence, KS	266.9
2	Hammond, LA	751.8	66	Barnstable Town, MA	349.1	130	Fort Lauderdale, FL M.D.	266.6
3	Memphis, TN-MS-AR	714.6	67	Springfield, MO	348.8	131	Tuscaloosa, AL	266.2
4	Odessa, TX	672.2	68	Beaumont-Port Arthur, TX	340.8	132	Johnson City, TN	265.1
5	Detroit-Dearborn-Livonia, MI M.D.	655.2	69	Miami (greater), FL	338.3	133	Joplin, MO	264.7
6	Sumter, SC	629.6	70	Clarksville, TN-KY	337.7	134	Warner Robins, GA	263.7
7	Saginaw, MI	619.9	71	Cape Girardeau, MO-IL	337.5	135	Waterloo-Cedar Falls, IA	262.2
8	Flint, MI	601.6	72	Lima, OH	336.5	136	Homosassa Springs, FL	262.1
9	Redding, CA	573.5	73	Springfield, MA	330.9	137	Durham-Chapel Hill, NC	261.0
10	Stockton-Lodi, CA	571.5	74	Salisbury, MD-DE	330.5	138	Dothan, AL	260.3
11	Texarkana, TX-AR	559.0	75	Monroe, LA	329.6	139	Louisville, KY-IN	260.0
12	Lubbock, TX	558.7	76	Wilmington, DE-MD-NJ M.D.	328.0	140	Midland, TX	259.1
13	Anchorage, AK	550.2	77	Milwaukee, WI	327.9	141	Greenville, NC	258.6
14	Lawton, OK	549.7	78	Kansas City, MO-KS	327.7	142	Omaha-Council Bluffs, NE-IA	257.9
15	Merced, CA	543.3	79	Fort Smith, AR-OK	327.5	143	Flagstaff, AZ	256.7
16	Pine Bluff, AR	526.7	80	Laredo, TX	325.0	144	Lakeland, FL	256.4
17	Farmington, NM	510.1	81	Vineland-Bridgeton, NJ	324.3	145	Buffalo-Niagara Falls, NY	256.3
18	Rockford, IL	509.3	82	Fairbanks, AK	323.7	146	Cumberland, MD-WV	255.8
19	Nashville-Davidson, TN	500.3	83	Spartanburg, SC	322.4	147	San Antonio, TX	254.1
20	Sierra Vista-Douglas, AZ	498.0	84	North Port-Sarasota-Bradenton, FL	321.3	148	Jefferson City, MO	254.0
21	Madera, CA	491.1	85	Burlington, NC	321.0	149	Florence-Muscle Shoals, AL	252.9
22	Albany, GA	480.0	86	Worcester, MA-CT	319.3	149	Sebastian-Vero Beach, FL	252.9
23	Rocky Mount, NC	479.6	87	St. Louis, MO-IL	317.7	151	San Francisco (greater), CA	252.5
24	Springfield, IL	473.0	88	Boston, MA M.D.	316.7	152	Pittsfield, MA	250.7
25	Cleveland, TN	463.5	89	Brunswick, GA	315.4	153	Vallejo-Fairfield, CA	249.1
26	Albuquerque, NM	461.4	89	Goldsboro, NC	315.4	154	Medford, OR	248.7
27	Greenville-Anderson, SC	444.6	91	West Palm Beach, FL M.D.	313.8	155	Las Cruces, NM	248.2
28	Little Rock, AR	441.8	92	College Station-Bryan, TX	312.6	156	Beckley, WV	247.5
29	Las Vegas-Henderson, NV	433.2	93	Houston, TX	311.6	157	San Diego, CA	247.4
30	Gainesville, FL	431.5	94	Kingsport, TN-VA	310.9	158	Phoenix-Mesa-Scottsdale, AZ	246.6
31	Anniston-Oxford, AL	426.1	95	El Paso, TX	306.4	159	Santa Fe, NM	246.1
32	Pensacola, FL	424.2	96	Deltona-Daytona Beach, FL	306.2	160	Wichita Falls, TX	245.9
33	Dover, DE	413.5	97	Norwich-New London, CT	304.7	161	Port St. Lucie, FL	245.6
34	Florence, SC	412.3	98	East Stroudsburg, PA	303.8	162	Columbus, GA-AL	245.5
35	Victoria, TX	408.5	98	Longview, TX	303.8	163	Decatur, IL	244.6
36	Corpus Christi, TX	407.2	100	New Orleans, LA	298.0	164	Fort Worth-Arlington, TX M.D.	244.1
37	Palm Bay-Melbourne, FL	404.5	101	Fayetteville-Springdale, AR-MO	296.9	165	Lansing-East Lansing, MI	243.0
38	Miami-Dade County, FL M.D.	401.1	102	Charleston-North Charleston, SC	296.7	166	Coeur d'Alene, ID	240.0
39	Tallahassee, FL	400.2	103	Knoxville, TN	296.3	167	Salinas, CA	239.8
40	Bakersfield, CA	398.3	104	Tyler, TX	293.2	168	Cape Coral-Fort Myers, FL	238.6
41	Wichita, KS	397.4	105	Morristown, TN	292.2	169	Boston (greater), MA-NH	237.6
42	Orlando, FL	389.0	106	Yuma, AZ	291.5	170	Columbia, MO	237.4
43	Hilton Head Island, SC	388.1	107	Winston-Salem, NC	290.4	171	Rapid City, SD	237.3
44	Hanford-Corcoran, CA	387.9	108	Oakland-Hayward, CA M.D.	290.3	172	Hinesville, GA	232.1
45	Oklahoma City, OK	379.2	109	Tucson, AZ	289.0	173	McAllen-Edinburg-Mission, TX	232.0
46	Ocala, FL	375.9	110	Tampa-St Petersburg, FL	286.2	174	Los Angeles County, CA M.D.	231.0
47	Baltimore, MD	373.2	111	Santa Rosa, CA	285.0	175	Greeley, CO	230.3
48	Crestview-Fort Walton Beach, FL	371.5	112	Topeka, KS	283.2	176	Macon, GA	229.0
49	Amarillo, TX	368.5	113	Sacramento, CA	280.2	177	Greensboro-High Point, NC	228.8
50	Birmingham-Hoover, AL	368.1	114	Tacoma, WA M.D.	279.1	178	Bloomington, IL	228.6
51	Pueblo, CO	368.0	115	Bismarck, ND	278.3	179	Yakima, WA	228.4
52	Gadsden, AL	367.6	116	Prescott, AZ	278.2	180	Atlanta, GA	228.2
53	Modesto, CA	366.9	117	Reno, NV	277.6	181	Wheeling, WV-OH	227.6
54	Danville, IL	366.7	118	Santa Cruz-Watsonville, CA	275.5	182	Morgantown, WV	226.8
55	Indianapolis, IN	366.1	119	Peoria, IL	274.9	183	New Haven-Milford, CT	226.7
56	Toledo, OH	365.9	120	Davenport, IA-IL	274.8	184	Riverside-San Bernardino, CA	226.2
57	Detroit (greater), MI	365.8	121	San Luis Obispo, CA	274.3	185	Killeen-Temple, TX	224.8
58	Fresno, CA	364.4	122	Napa, CA	274.1	186	Chicago-Joilet-Naperville, IL M.D.	224.6
59	Huntsville, AL	362.6	123	Santa Maria-Santa Barbara, CA	273.9	187	Lincoln, NE	223.9
60	Panama City, FL	362.3	124	Rome, GA	273.2	188	Colorado Springs, CO	223.5
61	Tulsa, OK	361.8	125	Waco, TX	270.4	189	Wilmington, NC	222.4
62	Mobile, AL	360.4	126	Yuba City, CA	269.2	190	Providence-Warwick, RI-MA	220.6
63	Champaign-Urbana, IL	359.2	127	Fayetteville, NC	268.6	190	St. Joseph, MO-KS	220.6
64	Jacksonville, FL	357.8	128	Parkersburg-Vienna, WV	267.0	192	Kalamazoo-Portage, MI	220.4

Note: All listings are for Metropolitan Statistical Areas (M.S.A.s) except for those ending with "M.D." Listings with "M.D." are Metropolitan Divisions which are smaller parts of eleven large M.S.A.s. See explanatory note at beginning of metropolitan area section.

RANK	METROPOLITAN AREA	RATE	RANK	METROPOLITAN AREA	RATE	RANK	METROPOLITAN AREA	RATE
193	Trenton, NJ	219.9	257	Binghamton, NY	168.6	321	Idaho Falls, ID	119.3
194	Abilene, TX	219.6	258	Casper, WY	167.8	322	San Rafael, CA M.D.	118.1
195	Missoula, MT	218.2	259	Fond du Lac, WI	167.1	323	Canton, OH	117.1
196	Valdosta, GA	214.8	260	Albany-Schenectady-Troy, NY	166.4	323	Cincinnati, OH-KY-IN	117.1
197	New Bern, NC	214.3	261	Dallas-Plano-Irving, TX M.D.	165.7	325	St. George, UT	117.0
198	Kankakee, IL	213.6	261	Kennewick-Richland, WA	165.7	326	Columbus, IN	116.5
199	Billings, MT	213.5	263	Johnstown, PA	163.9	327	Elgin, IL M.D.	116.4
200	Jonesboro, AR	212.5	264	Monroe, MI	163.5	328	Lexington-Fayette, KY	114.7
201	Houma, LA	211.1	265	Muncie, IN	162.7	329	Glens Falls, NY	114.1
201	San Francisco-Redwood, CA M.D.	211.1	266	Kokomo, IN	162.5	330	Kingston, NY	113.9
203	Carson City, NV	210.1	267	Washington (greater) DC-VA-MD-WV	161.6	331	Blacksburg, VA	112.3
204	El Centro, CA	209.9	268	Boise City, ID	161.1	332	Fort Wayne, IN	111.7
205	Grand Junction, CO	209.2	269	Hagerstown-Martinsburg, MD-WV	160.9	333	Bloomsburg-Berwick, PA	110.6
206	Los Angeles (greater), CA	208.7	269	Salem, OR	160.9	334	Oxnard-Thousand Oaks, CA	110.3
207	Des Moines-West Des Moines, IA	208.6	271	San Jose, CA	160.1	335	Cedar Rapids, IA	110.1
208	Dalton, GA	208.0	272	Oshkosh-Neenah, WI	160.0	336	Charlottesville, VA	110.0
209	Salt Lake City, UT	207.3	273	Rochester, NY	159.2	337	Dubuque, IA	109.5
210	Punta Gorda, FL	207.1	274	Duluth, MN-WI	158.8	338	Racine, WI	108.2
211	Denver-Aurora, CO	205.6	275	Walla Walla, WA	158.7	339	Silver Spring-Frederick, MD M.D.	106.3
212	Sioux Falls, SD	205.5	276	Youngstown-Warren, OH-PA	156.5	340	Lynchburg, VA	105.5
213	Lafayette, IN	204.2	277	Sioux City, IA-NE-SD	156.1	341	La Crosse, WI-MN	104.5
214	Chicago (greater), IL-IN-WI	202.6	278	Warren-Troy, MI M.D.	155.7	342	Terre Haute, IN	103.3
215	Sebring, FL	200.0	279	Kahului-Wailuku-Lahaina, HI	155.6	343	Allentown, PA-NJ	102.7
216	Austin-Round Rock, TX	199.5	279	Longview, WA	155.6	344	Gainesville, GA	100.0
217	Iowa City, IA	198.7	281	Grand Forks, ND-MN	155.3	345	Rockingham County, NH M.D.	91.5
218	Cambridge-Newton, MA M.D.	198.1	282	Harrisburg-Carlisle, PA	154.7	346	Lake Co.-Kenosha Co., IL-WI M.D.	90.9
219	Ann Arbor, MI	197.0	283	Bellingham, WA	154.6	347	Nassau-Suffolk, NY M.D.	89.8
220	Bay City, MI	196.9	284	Portland-Vancouver, OR-WA	154.3	348	Harrisonburg, VA	87.5
221	Seattle (greater), WA	194.4	285	York-Hanover, PA	153.8	349	Ames, IA	86.7
222	Chico, CA	193.9	286	Augusta, GA-SC	152.2	350	Williamsport, PA	86.4
223	Ocean City, NJ	192.6	287	Raleigh, NC	151.7	351	Gettysburg, PA	85.6
224	Dallas (greater), TX	192.4	288	Scranton--Wilkes-Barre, PA	151.6	352	Montgomery County, PA M.D.	85.1
225	Syracuse, NY	192.3	289	Watertown-Fort Drum, NY	151.0	352	Ogden-Clearfield, UT	85.1
226	Spokane, WA	191.8	290	Hartford, CT	150.2	354	Wausau, WI	83.9
227	Athens-Clarke County, GA	190.4	290	Janesville, WI	150.2	355	Chambersburg-Waynesboro, PA	83.4
228	Elmira, NY	190.3	292	Savannah, GA	149.4	356	Michigan City-La Porte, IN	83.2
229	Gary, IN M.D.	190.2	293	Hickory, NC	147.8	357	Lancaster, PA	79.9
230	Naples-Marco Island, FL	189.7	294	Lebanon, PA	144.2	358	Rochester, MN	78.6
231	Reading, PA	189.1	295	South Bend-Mishawaka, IN-MI	143.9	359	Corvallis, OR	67.0
232	Decatur, AL	188.1	296	Boulder, CO	143.6	360	Portland, ME	66.8
233	Camden, NJ M.D.	187.3	297	Asheville, NC	143.3	361	Mansfield, OH	64.0
234	Fargo, ND-MN	185.6	298	Manchester-Nashua, NH	143.1	362	Bowling Green, KY	61.5
235	Bremerton-Silverdale, WA	185.1	299	Minneapolis-St. Paul, MN-WI	141.4	363	Albany, OR	60.5
236	Sherman-Denison, TX	185.0	300	Grand Island, NE	140.6	364	State College, PA	58.7
237	Altoona, PA	183.0	301	Bridgeport-Stamford, CT	140.0	365	Owensboro, KY	57.1
238	Pocatello, ID	181.6	302	Olympia, WA	137.0	366	Midland, MI	54.7
239	Auburn, AL	181.2	303	Anaheim-Santa Ana-Irvine, CA M.D.	136.4	367	Lewiston-Auburn, ME	43.7
240	Manhattan, KS	180.3	304	Lewiston, ID-WA	134.0	368	Hattiesburg, MS	42.5
241	California-Lexington Park, MD	178.8	305	Winchester, VA-WV	133.3	368	Provo-Orem, UT	42.5
241	Jackson, MS	178.8	306	The Villages, FL	132.2	370	Bangor, ME	33.1
243	Great Falls, MT	178.4	307	Newark, NJ-PA M.D.	131.1	371	Logan, UT-ID	32.5
244	Daphne-Fairhope-Foley, AL	177.1	308	Lake Havasu City-Kingman, AZ	130.5	372	Elizabethtown-Fort Knox, KY	29.7
245	Washington, DC-VA-MD-WV M.D.	176.5	309	Erie, PA	130.0	NA	Alexandria, LA**	NA
246	Fort Collins, CO	176.3	310	Richmond, VA	129.1	NA	Atlantic City, NJ**	NA
247	Cheyenne, WY	175.5	311	Dutchess-Putnam, NY M.D.	128.5	NA	Baton Rouge, LA**	NA
248	Green Bay, WI	174.7	312	Madison, WI	128.0	NA	Lafayette, LA**	NA
249	Brownsville-Harlingen, TX	174.2	313	Eugene, OR	125.9	NA	New York (greater), NY-NJ-PA**	NA
250	Roanoke, VA	173.6	314	Springfield, OH	124.2	NA	New York-Jersey City, NY-NJ M.D.**	NA
251	Bloomington, IN	171.2	315	Dayton, OH	123.7	NA	Philadelphia (greater) PA-NJ-MD-DE**	NA
251	Virginia Beach-Norfolk, VA-NC	171.2	316	Staunton-Waynesboro, VA	123.4	NA	Philadelphia, PA M.D.**	NA
253	Montgomery, AL	170.2	317	Sheboygan, WI	123.0	NA	Pittsburgh, PA**	NA
254	Akron, OH	169.7	318	Mount Vernon-Anacortes, WA	122.4	NA	Shreveport-Bossier City, LA**	NA
255	Utica-Rome, NY	169.6	319	Mankato-North Mankato, MN	121.6			
256	Seattle-Bellevue-Everett, WA M.D.	169.0	320	Appleton, WI	119.7			

Source: Reported data from the F.B.I. "Crime in the United States 2012"

*Aggravated assault is an attack for the purpose of inflicting severe bodily injury.

**Not available.

23. Percent Change in Aggravated Assault Rate: 2011 to 2012
National Percent Change = 0.4% Increase*

RANK	METROPOLITAN AREA	% CHANGE	RANK	METROPOLITAN AREA	% CHANGE	RANK	METROPOLITAN AREA	% CHANGE
68	Abilene, TX	9.3	111	Cheyenne, WY	4.7	37	Gary, IN M.D.	15.2
63	Akron, OH	9.8	160	Chicago (greater), IL-IN-WI	(1.3)	NA	Gettysburg, PA**	NA
NA	Albany-Schenectady-Troy, NY**	NA	NA	Chicago-Joilet-Naperville, IL M.D.**	NA	NA	Glens Falls, NY**	NA
15	Albany, GA	33.7	18	Chico, CA	28.8	191	Goldsboro, NC	(3.8)
NA	Albany, OR**	NA	NA	Cincinnati, OH-KY-IN**	NA	56	Grand Forks, ND-MN	10.8
205	Albuquerque, NM	(5.3)	106	Clarksville, TN-KY	5.4	NA	Grand Island, NE**	NA
NA	Alexandria, LA**	NA	247	Cleveland, TN	(15.0)	122	Grand Junction, CO	3.1
NA	Allentown, PA-NJ**	NA	NA	Coeur d'Alene, ID**	NA	195	Great Falls, MT	(4.3)
97	Altoona, PA	6.0	39	College Station-Bryan, TX	14.2	135	Greeley, CO	2.1
160	Amarillo, TX	(1.3)	199	Colorado Springs, CO	(5.0)	2	Green Bay, WI	71.1
273	Ames, IA	(62.3)	255	Columbia, MO	(17.3)	NA	Greensboro-High Point, NC**	NA
62	Anaheim-Santa Ana-Irvine, CA M.D.	9.9	57	Columbus, GA-AL	10.6	NA	Greenville-Anderson, SC**	NA
NA	Anchorage, AK**	NA	134	Columbus, IN	2.2	NA	Greenville, NC**	NA
146	Ann Arbor, MI	0.6	93	Corpus Christi, TX	6.7	NA	Hagerstown-Martinsburg, MD-WV**	NA
34	Anniston-Oxford, AL	16.2	187	Corvallis, OR	(3.5)	NA	Hammond, LA**	NA
47	Appleton, WI	12.6	49	Crestview-Fort Walton Beach, FL	12.5	10	Hanford-Corcoran, CA	47.5
98	Asheville, NC	5.9	31	Cumberland, MD-WV	17.2	213	Harrisburg-Carlisle, PA	(6.2)
270	Athens-Clarke County, GA	(30.8)	199	Dallas (greater), TX	(5.0)	27	Harrisonburg, VA	19.2
125	Atlanta, GA	2.9	194	Dallas-Plano-Irving, TX M.D.	(4.2)	211	Hartford, CT	(5.7)
NA	Atlantic City, NJ**	NA	24	Dalton, GA	19.9	NA	Hattiesburg, MS**	NA
7	Auburn, AL	52.9	205	Danville, IL	(5.3)	175	Hickory, NC	(2.6)
254	Augusta, GA-SC	(17.2)	NA	Daphne-Fairhope-Foley, AL**	NA	NA	Hilton Head Island, SC**	NA
89	Austin-Round Rock, TX	7.0	237	Davenport, IA-IL	(12.2)	180	Hinesville, GA	(3.0)
95	Bakersfield, CA	6.1	143	Dayton, OH	1.2	NA	Homosassa Springs, FL**	NA
202	Baltimore, MD	(5.2)	21	Decatur, AL	24.2	177	Houma, LA	(2.8)
95	Bangor, ME	6.1	269	Decatur, IL	(30.5)	202	Houston, TX	(5.2)
172	Barnstable Town, MA	(2.4)	NA	Deltona-Daytona Beach, FL**	NA	123	Huntsville, AL	3.0
NA	Baton Rouge, LA**	NA	NA	Denver-Aurora, CO**	NA	264	Idaho Falls, ID	(20.9)
22	Bay City, MI	22.6	118	Des Moines-West Des Moines, IA	3.9	NA	Indianapolis, IN**	NA
165	Beaumont-Port Arthur, TX	(1.8)	153	Detroit (greater), MI	(0.6)	105	Iowa City, IA	5.5
NA	Beckley, WV**	NA	160	Detroit-Dearborn-Livonia, MI M.D.	(1.3)	128	Jacksonville, FL	2.8
30	Bellingham, WA	17.8	225	Dothan, AL	(8.7)	NA	Jackson, MS**	NA
132	Billings, MT	2.5	218	Dover, DE	(7.7)	NA	Jackson, TN**	NA
NA	Binghamton, NY**	NA	45	Dubuque, IA	13.2	198	Janesville, WI	(4.8)
50	Birmingham-Hoover, AL	12.2	13	Duluth, MN-WI	36.9	135	Jefferson City, MO	2.1
3	Bismarck, ND	66.4	112	Durham-Chapel Hill, NC	4.6	158	Johnson City, TN	(1.2)
43	Blacksburg, VA	13.7	NA	Dutchess-Putnam, NY M.D.**	NA	150	Johnstown, PA	0.1
88	Bloomington, IL	7.1	NA	East Stroudsburg, PA**	NA	251	Jonesboro, AR	(16.1)
NA	Bloomington, IN**	NA	109	El Centro, CA	5.0	41	Joplin, MO	14.0
NA	Bloomsburg-Berwick, PA**	NA	168	El Paso, TX	(2.3)	NA	Kahului-Wailuku-Lahaina, HI**	NA
193	Boise City, ID	(4.1)	NA	Elgin, IL M.D.**	NA	NA	Kalamazoo-Portage, MI**	NA
NA	Boston (greater), MA-NH**	NA	NA	Elizabethtown-Fort Knox, KY**	NA	123	Kankakee, IL	3.0
NA	Boston, MA M.D.**	NA	NA	Elmira, NY**	NA	NA	Kansas City, MO-KS**	NA
256	Boulder, CO	(18.0)	148	Erie, PA	0.5	229	Kennewick-Richland, WA	(10.0)
265	Bowling Green, KY	(21.3)	267	Eugene, OR	(28.5)	146	Killeen-Temple, TX	0.6
252	Bremerton-Silverdale, WA	(16.9)	259	Fairbanks, AK	(19.1)	70	Kingsport, TN-VA	9.2
168	Bridgeport-Stamford, CT	(2.3)	103	Fargo, ND-MN	5.6	NA	Kingston, NY**	NA
257	Brownsville-Harlingen, TX	(18.3)	140	Farmington, NM	1.6	NA	Knoxville, TN**	NA
217	Brunswick, GA	(7.2)	NA	Fayetteville-Springdale, AR-MO**	NA	NA	Kokomo, IN**	NA
NA	Buffalo-Niagara Falls, NY**	NA	157	Fayetteville, NC	(1.1)	250	La Crosse, WI-MN	(15.9)
128	Burlington, NC	2.8	260	Flagstaff, AZ	(19.4)	163	Lafayette, IN	(1.6)
NA	California-Lexington Park, MD**	NA	73	Flint, MI	8.7	NA	Lafayette, LA**	NA
NA	Cambridge-Newton, MA M.D.**	NA	8	Florence-Muscle Shoals, AL	51.3	139	Lake Co.-Kenosha Co., IL-WI M.D.	1.8
176	Camden, NJ M.D.	(2.7)	263	Florence, SC	(20.3)	230	Lake Havasu City-Kingman, AZ	(10.2)
183	Canton, OH	(3.3)	14	Fond du Lac, WI	36.4	248	Lakeland, FL	(15.3)
135	Cape Coral-Fort Myers, FL	2.1	66	Fort Collins, CO	9.4	245	Lancaster, PA	(13.8)
91	Cape Girardeau, MO-IL	6.9	152	Fort Lauderdale, FL M.D.	(0.4)	158	Lansing-East Lansing, MI	(1.2)
224	Carson City, NV	(8.5)	NA	Fort Smith, AR-OK**	NA	228	Laredo, TX	(9.6)
241	Casper, WY	(13.2)	115	Fort Wayne, IN	4.3	248	Las Cruces, NM	(15.3)
238	Cedar Rapids, IA	(12.4)	215	Fort Worth-Arlington, TX M.D.	(6.6)	108	Las Vegas-Henderson, NV	5.2
NA	Chambersburg-Waynesboro, PA**	NA	197	Fresno, CA	(4.4)	195	Lawrence, KS	(4.3)
243	Champaign-Urbana, IL	(13.6)	143	Gadsden, AL	1.2	NA	Lawton, OK**	NA
NA	Charleston-North Charleston, SC**	NA	168	Gainesville, FL	(2.3)	11	Lebanon, PA	42.1
29	Charlottesville, VA	18.0	53	Gainesville, GA	11.0	266	Lewiston-Auburn, ME	(27.6)

Note: All listings are for Metropolitan Statistical Areas (M.S.A.s) except for those ending with "M.D." Listings with "M.D." are Metropolitan Divisions which are smaller parts of eleven large M.S.A.s. See explanatory note at beginning of metropolitan area section.

RANK	METROPOLITAN AREA	% CHANGE	RANK	METROPOLITAN AREA	% CHANGE	RANK	METROPOLITAN AREA	% CHANGE
NA	Lewiston, ID-WA**	NA	141	Owensboro, KY	1.4	34	Silver Spring-Frederick, MD M.D.	16.2
NA	Lexington-Fayette, KY**	NA	210	Oxnard-Thousand Oaks, CA	(5.6)	NA	Sioux City, IA-NE-SD**	NA
47	Lima, OH	12.6	235	Palm Bay-Melbourne, FL	(11.3)	4	Sioux Falls, SD	64.8
84	Lincoln, NE	7.6	NA	Panama City, FL**	NA	211	South Bend-Mishawaka, IN-MI	(5.7)
242	Little Rock, AR	(13.4)	NA	Parkersburg-Vienna, WV**	NA	NA	Spartanburg, SC**	NA
190	Logan, UT-ID	(3.6)	23	Pensacola, FL	20.6	NA	Spokane, WA**	NA
87	Longview, TX	7.2	59	Peoria, IL	10.4	209	Springfield, IL	(5.5)
173	Longview, WA	(2.5)	NA	Philadelphia (greater) PA-NJ-MD-DE**	NA	NA	Springfield, MA**	NA
183	Los Angeles County, CA M.D.	(3.3)	NA	Philadelphia, PA M.D.**	NA	64	Springfield, MO	9.6
163	Los Angeles (greater), CA	(1.6)	NA	Phoenix-Mesa-Scottsdale, AZ**	NA	61	Springfield, OH	10.2
54	Louisville, KY-IN	10.9	183	Pine Bluff, AR	(3.3)	173	State College, PA	(2.5)
101	Lubbock, TX	5.7	NA	Pittsburgh, PA**	NA	NA	Staunton-Waynesboro, VA**	NA
222	Lynchburg, VA	(8.3)	262	Pittsfield, MA	(19.9)	99	Stockton-Lodi, CA	5.8
149	Macon, GA	0.2	NA	Pocatello, ID**	NA	NA	St. George, UT**	NA
26	Madera, CA	19.4	68	Port St. Lucie, FL	9.3	25	St. Joseph, MO-KS	19.5
NA	Madison, WI**	NA	120	Portland-Vancouver, OR-WA	3.3	183	St. Louis, MO-IL	(3.3)
220	Manchester-Nashua, NH	(8.0)	156	Portland, ME	(0.7)	1	Sumter, SC	74.6
NA	Manhattan, KS**	NA	239	Prescott, AZ	(12.7)	NA	Syracuse, NY**	NA
5	Mankato-North Mankato, MN	64.5	NA	Providence-Warwick, RI-MA**	NA	103	Tacoma, WA M.D.	5.6
20	Mansfield, OH	24.5	167	Provo-Orem, UT	(2.1)	233	Tallahassee, FL	(10.4)
40	McAllen-Edinburg-Mission, TX	14.1	202	Pueblo, CO	(5.2)	199	Tampa-St Petersburg, FL	(5.0)
36	Medford, OR	15.6	76	Punta Gorda, FL	8.3	51	Terre Haute, IN	11.9
84	Memphis, TN-MS-AR	7.6	76	Racine, WI	8.3	NA	Texarkana, TX-AR**	NA
16	Merced, CA	32.6	79	Raleigh, NC	8.1	NA	The Villages, FL**	NA
213	Miami (greater), FL	(6.2)	NA	Rapid City, SD**	NA	NA	Toledo, OH**	NA
230	Miami-Dade County, FL M.D.	(10.2)	107	Reading, PA	5.3	28	Topeka, KS	18.6
178	Michigan City-La Porte, IN	(2.9)	187	Redding, CA	(3.5)	182	Trenton, NJ	(3.2)
NA	Midland, MI**	NA	70	Reno, NV	9.2	46	Tucson, AZ	12.9
NA	Midland, TX**	NA	81	Richmond, VA	8.0	187	Tulsa, OK	(3.5)
6	Milwaukee, WI	55.0	117	Riverside-San Bernardino, CA	4.0	NA	Tuscaloosa, AL**	NA
145	Minneapolis-St. Paul, MN-WI	0.8	165	Roanoke, VA	(1.8)	79	Tyler, TX	8.1
41	Missoula, MT	14.0	NA	Rochester, MN**	NA	NA	Utica-Rome, NY**	NA
151	Mobile, AL	0.0	NA	Rochester, NY**	NA	178	Valdosta, GA	(2.9)
32	Modesto, CA	17.1	76	Rockford, IL	8.3	81	Vallejo-Fairfield, CA	8.0
271	Monroe, LA	(37.6)	222	Rockingham County, NH M.D.	(8.3)	NA	Victoria, TX**	NA
101	Monroe, MI	5.7	12	Rocky Mount, NC	39.1	NA	Vineland-Bridgeton, NJ**	NA
NA	Montgomery County, PA M.D.**	NA	268	Rome, GA	(29.1)	116	Virginia Beach-Norfolk, VA-NC	4.1
52	Montgomery, AL	11.6	83	Sacramento, CA	7.8	94	Visalia-Porterville, CA	6.5
NA	Morgantown, WV**	NA	153	Saginaw, MI	(0.6)	NA	Waco, TX**	NA
NA	Morristown, TN**	NA	120	Salem, OR	3.3	NA	Walla Walla, WA**	NA
44	Mount Vernon-Anacortes, WA	13.5	261	Salinas, CA	(19.5)	NA	Warner Robins, GA**	NA
272	Muncie, IN	(54.4)	NA	Salisbury, MD-DE**	NA	119	Warren-Troy, MI M.D.	3.5
66	Napa, CA	9.4	72	Salt Lake City, UT	8.9	113	Washington (greater) DC-VA-MD-WV	4.5
258	Naples-Marco Island, FL	(18.4)	205	San Antonio, TX	(5.3)	131	Washington, DC-VA-MD-WV M.D.	2.6
NA	Nashville-Davidson, TN**	NA	86	San Diego, CA	7.4	75	Waterloo-Cedar Falls, IA	8.4
NA	Nassau-Suffolk, NY M.D.**	NA	125	San Francisco (greater), CA	2.9	NA	Watertown-Fort Drum, NY**	NA
NA	New Bern, NC**	NA	58	San Francisco-Redwood, CA M.D.	10.5	221	Wausau, WI	(8.1)
38	New Haven-Milford, CT	15.0	65	San Jose, CA	9.5	168	West Palm Beach, FL M.D.	(2.3)
125	New Orleans, LA	2.9	9	San Luis Obispo, CA	48.8	NA	Wheeling, WV-OH**	NA
NA	New York (greater), NY-NJ-PA**	NA	NA	San Rafael, CA M.D.**	NA	89	Wichita Falls, TX	7.0
NA	New York-Jersey City, NY-NJ M.D.**	NA	236	Santa Cruz-Watsonville, CA	(12.1)	226	Wichita, KS	(9.3)
NA	Newark, NJ-PA M.D.**	NA	243	Santa Fe, NM	(13.6)	230	Williamsport, PA	(10.2)
216	North Port-Sarasota-Bradenton, FL	(7.1)	NA	Santa Maria-Santa Barbara, CA**	NA	138	Wilmington, DE-MD-NJ M.D.	1.9
73	Norwich-New London, CT	8.7	99	Santa Rosa, CA	5.8	NA	Wilmington, NC**	NA
133	Oakland-Hayward, CA M.D.	2.4	208	Savannah, GA	(5.4)	54	Winchester, VA-WV	10.9
180	Ocala, FL	(3.0)	246	Scranton--Wilkes-Barre, PA	(14.4)	NA	Winston-Salem, NC**	NA
234	Ocean City, NJ	(10.9)	130	Seattle (greater), WA	2.7	NA	Worcester, MA-CT**	NA
33	Odessa, TX	16.6	141	Seattle-Bellevue-Everett, WA M.D.	1.4	19	Yakima, WA	25.7
NA	Ogden-Clearfield, UT**	NA	91	Sebastian-Vero Beach, FL	6.9	192	York-Hanover, PA	(4.0)
114	Oklahoma City, OK	4.4	NA	Sebring, FL**	NA	NA	Youngstown-Warren, OH-PA**	NA
253	Olympia, WA	(17.0)	17	Sheboygan, WI	29.7	240	Yuba City, CA	(12.9)
109	Omaha-Council Bluffs, NE-IA	5.0	227	Sherman-Denison, TX	(9.4)	59	Yuma, AZ	10.4
218	Orlando, FL	(7.7)	NA	Shreveport-Bossier City, LA**	NA			
153	Oshkosh-Neenah, WI	(0.6)	NA	Sierra Vista-Douglas, AZ**	NA			

Source: CQ Press using reported data from the F.B.I. "Crime in the United States 2012"

*Aggravated assault is an attack for the purpose of inflicting severe bodily injury.

**Not available.

23. Percent Change in Aggravated Assault Rate: 2011 to 2012 (continued)
National Percent Change = 0.4% Increase*

RANK	METROPOLITAN AREA	% CHANGE	RANK	METROPOLITAN AREA	% CHANGE	RANK	METROPOLITAN AREA	% CHANGE
1	Sumter, SC	74.6	65	San Jose, CA	9.5	128	Jacksonville, FL	2.8
2	Green Bay, WI	71.1	66	Fort Collins, CO	9.4	130	Seattle (greater), WA	2.7
3	Bismarck, ND	66.4	66	Napa, CA	9.4	131	Washington, DC-VA-MD-WV M.D.	2.6
4	Sioux Falls, SD	64.8	68	Abilene, TX	9.3	132	Billings, MT	2.5
5	Mankato-North Mankato, MN	64.5	68	Port St. Lucie, FL	9.3	133	Oakland-Hayward, CA M.D.	2.4
6	Milwaukee, WI	55.0	70	Kingsport, TN-VA	9.2	134	Columbus, IN	2.2
7	Auburn, AL	52.9	70	Reno, NV	9.2	135	Cape Coral-Fort Myers, FL	2.1
8	Florence-Muscle Shoals, AL	51.3	72	Salt Lake City, UT	8.9	135	Greeley, CO	2.1
9	San Luis Obispo, CA	48.8	73	Flint, MI	8.7	135	Jefferson City, MO	2.1
10	Hanford-Corcoran, CA	47.5	73	Norwich-New London, CT	8.7	138	Wilmington, DE-MD-NJ M.D.	1.9
11	Lebanon, PA	42.1	75	Waterloo-Cedar Falls, IA	8.4	139	Lake Co.-Kenosha Co., IL-WI M.D.	1.8
12	Rocky Mount, NC	39.1	76	Punta Gorda, FL	8.3	140	Farmington, NM	1.6
13	Duluth, MN-WI	36.9	76	Racine, WI	8.3	141	Owensboro, KY	1.4
14	Fond du Lac, WI	36.4	76	Rockford, IL	8.3	141	Seattle-Bellevue-Everett, WA M.D.	1.4
15	Albany, GA	33.7	79	Raleigh, NC	8.1	143	Dayton, OH	1.2
16	Merced, CA	32.6	79	Tyler, TX	8.1	143	Gadsden, AL	1.2
17	Sheboygan, WI	29.7	81	Richmond, VA	8.0	145	Minneapolis-St. Paul, MN-WI	0.8
18	Chico, CA	28.8	81	Vallejo-Fairfield, CA	8.0	146	Ann Arbor, MI	0.6
19	Yakima, WA	25.7	83	Sacramento, CA	7.8	146	Killeen-Temple, TX	0.6
20	Mansfield, OH	24.5	84	Lincoln, NE	7.6	148	Erie, PA	0.5
21	Decatur, AL	24.2	84	Memphis, TN-MS-AR	7.6	149	Macon, GA	0.2
22	Bay City, MI	22.6	86	San Diego, CA	7.4	150	Johnstown, PA	0.1
23	Pensacola, FL	20.6	87	Longview, TX	7.2	151	Mobile, AL	0.0
24	Dalton, GA	19.9	88	Bloomington, IL	7.1	152	Fort Lauderdale, FL M.D.	(0.4)
25	St. Joseph, MO-KS	19.5	89	Austin-Round Rock, TX	7.0	153	Detroit (greater), MI	(0.6)
26	Madera, CA	19.4	89	Wichita Falls, TX	7.0	153	Oshkosh-Neenah, WI	(0.6)
27	Harrisonburg, VA	19.2	91	Cape Girardeau, MO-IL	6.9	153	Saginaw, MI	(0.6)
28	Topeka, KS	18.6	91	Sebastian-Vero Beach, FL	6.9	156	Portland, ME	(0.7)
29	Charlottesville, VA	18.0	93	Corpus Christi, TX	6.7	157	Fayetteville, NC	(1.1)
30	Bellingham, WA	17.8	94	Visalia-Porterville, CA	6.5	158	Johnson City, TN	(1.2)
31	Cumberland, MD-WV	17.2	95	Bakersfield, CA	6.1	158	Lansing-East Lansing, MI	(1.2)
32	Modesto, CA	17.1	95	Bangor, ME	6.1	160	Amarillo, TX	(1.3)
33	Odessa, TX	16.6	97	Altoona, PA	6.0	160	Chicago (greater), IL-IN-WI	(1.3)
34	Anniston-Oxford, AL	16.2	98	Asheville, NC	5.9	160	Detroit-Dearborn-Livonia, MI M.D.	(1.3)
34	Silver Spring-Frederick, MD M.D.	16.2	99	Santa Rosa, CA	5.8	163	Lafayette, IN	(1.6)
36	Medford, OR	15.6	99	Stockton-Lodi, CA	5.8	163	Los Angeles (greater), CA	(1.6)
37	Gary, IN M.D.	15.2	101	Lubbock, TX	5.7	165	Beaumont-Port Arthur, TX	(1.8)
38	New Haven-Milford, CT	15.0	101	Monroe, MI	5.7	165	Roanoke, VA	(1.8)
39	College Station-Bryan, TX	14.2	103	Fargo, ND-MN	5.6	167	Provo-Orem, UT	(2.1)
40	McAllen-Edinburg-Mission, TX	14.1	103	Tacoma, WA M.D.	5.6	168	Bridgeport-Stamford, CT	(2.3)
41	Joplin, MO	14.0	105	Iowa City, IA	5.5	168	El Paso, TX	(2.3)
41	Missoula, MT	14.0	106	Clarksville, TN-KY	5.4	168	Gainesville, FL	(2.3)
43	Blacksburg, VA	13.7	107	Reading, PA	5.3	168	West Palm Beach, FL M.D.	(2.3)
44	Mount Vernon-Anacortes, WA	13.5	108	Las Vegas-Henderson, NV	5.2	172	Barnstable Town, MA	(2.4)
45	Dubuque, IA	13.2	109	El Centro, CA	5.0	173	Longview, WA	(2.5)
46	Tucson, AZ	12.9	109	Omaha-Council Bluffs, NE-IA	5.0	173	State College, PA	(2.5)
47	Appleton, WI	12.6	111	Cheyenne, WY	4.7	175	Hickory, NC	(2.6)
47	Lima, OH	12.6	112	Durham-Chapel Hill, NC	4.6	176	Camden, NJ M.D.	(2.7)
49	Crestview-Fort Walton Beach, FL	12.5	113	Washington (greater) DC-VA-MD-WV	4.5	177	Houma, LA	(2.8)
50	Birmingham-Hoover, AL	12.2	114	Oklahoma City, OK	4.4	178	Michigan City-La Porte, IN	(2.9)
51	Terre Haute, IN	11.9	115	Fort Wayne, IN	4.3	178	Valdosta, GA	(2.9)
52	Montgomery, AL	11.6	116	Virginia Beach-Norfolk, VA-NC	4.1	180	Hinesville, GA	(3.0)
53	Gainesville, GA	11.0	117	Riverside-San Bernardino, CA	4.0	180	Ocala, FL	(3.0)
54	Louisville, KY-IN	10.9	118	Des Moines-West Des Moines, IA	3.9	182	Trenton, NJ	(3.2)
54	Winchester, VA-WV	10.9	119	Warren-Troy, MI M.D.	3.5	183	Canton, OH	(3.3)
56	Grand Forks, ND-MN	10.8	120	Portland-Vancouver, OR-WA	3.3	183	Los Angeles County, CA M.D.	(3.3)
57	Columbus, GA-AL	10.6	120	Salem, OR	3.3	183	Pine Bluff, AR	(3.3)
58	San Francisco-Redwood, CA M.D.	10.5	122	Grand Junction, CO	3.1	183	St. Louis, MO-IL	(3.3)
59	Peoria, IL	10.4	123	Huntsville, AL	3.0	187	Corvallis, OR	(3.5)
59	Yuma, AZ	10.4	123	Kankakee, IL	3.0	187	Redding, CA	(3.5)
61	Springfield, OH	10.2	125	Atlanta, GA	2.9	187	Tulsa, OK	(3.5)
62	Anaheim-Santa Ana-Irvine, CA M.D.	9.9	125	New Orleans, LA	2.9	190	Logan, UT-ID	(3.6)
63	Akron, OH	9.8	125	San Francisco (greater), CA	2.9	191	Goldsboro, NC	(3.8)
64	Springfield, MO	9.6	128	Burlington, NC	2.8	192	York-Hanover, PA	(4.0)

Note: All listings are for Metropolitan Statistical Areas (M.S.A.s) except for those ending with "M.D." Listings with "M.D." are Metropolitan Divisions which are smaller parts of eleven large M.S.A.s. See explanatory note at beginning of metropolitan area section.

RANK	METROPOLITAN AREA	% CHANGE	RANK	METROPOLITAN AREA	% CHANGE	RANK	METROPOLITAN AREA	% CHANGE
193	Boise City, ID	(4.1)	257	Brownsville-Harlingen, TX	(18.3)	NA	Kansas City, MO-KS**	NA
194	Dallas-Plano-Irving, TX M.D.	(4.2)	258	Naples-Marco Island, FL	(18.4)	NA	Kingston, NY**	NA
195	Great Falls, MT	(4.3)	259	Fairbanks, AK	(19.1)	NA	Knoxville, TN**	NA
195	Lawrence, KS	(4.3)	260	Flagstaff, AZ	(19.4)	NA	Kokomo, IN**	NA
197	Fresno, CA	(4.4)	261	Salinas, CA	(19.5)	NA	Lafayette, LA**	NA
198	Janesville, WI	(4.8)	262	Pittsfield, MA	(19.9)	NA	Lawton, OK**	NA
199	Colorado Springs, CO	(5.0)	263	Florence, SC	(20.3)	NA	Lewiston, ID-WA**	NA
199	Dallas (greater), TX	(5.0)	264	Idaho Falls, ID	(20.9)	NA	Lexington-Fayette, KY**	NA
199	Tampa-St Petersburg, FL	(5.0)	265	Bowling Green, KY	(21.3)	NA	Madison, WI**	NA
202	Baltimore, MD	(5.2)	266	Lewiston-Auburn, ME	(27.6)	NA	Manhattan, KS**	NA
202	Houston, TX	(5.2)	267	Eugene, OR	(28.5)	NA	Midland, MI**	NA
202	Pueblo, CO	(5.2)	268	Rome, GA	(29.1)	NA	Midland, TX**	NA
205	Albuquerque, NM	(5.3)	269	Decatur, IL	(30.5)	NA	Montgomery County, PA M.D.**	NA
205	Danville, IL	(5.3)	270	Athens-Clarke County, GA	(30.8)	NA	Morgantown, WV**	NA
205	San Antonio, TX	(5.3)	271	Monroe, LA	(37.6)	NA	Morristown, TN**	NA
208	Savannah, GA	(5.4)	272	Muncie, IN	(54.4)	NA	Nashville-Davidson, TN**	NA
209	Springfield, IL	(5.5)	273	Ames, IA	(62.3)	NA	Nassau-Suffolk, NY M.D.**	NA
210	Oxnard-Thousand Oaks, CA	(5.6)	NA	Albany-Schenectady-Troy, NY**	NA	NA	New Bern, NC**	NA
211	Hartford, CT	(5.7)	NA	Albany, OR**	NA	NA	New York (greater), NY-NJ-PA**	NA
211	South Bend-Mishawaka, IN-MI	(5.7)	NA	Alexandria, LA**	NA	NA	New York-Jersey City, NY-NJ M.D.**	NA
213	Harrisburg-Carlisle, PA	(6.2)	NA	Allentown, PA-NJ**	NA	NA	Newark, NJ-PA M.D.**	NA
213	Miami (greater), FL	(6.2)	NA	Anchorage, AK**	NA	NA	Ogden-Clearfield, UT**	NA
215	Fort Worth-Arlington, TX M.D.	(6.6)	NA	Atlantic City, NJ**	NA	NA	Panama City, FL**	NA
216	North Port-Sarasota-Bradenton, FL	(7.1)	NA	Baton Rouge, LA**	NA	NA	Parkersburg-Vienna, WV**	NA
217	Brunswick, GA	(7.2)	NA	Beckley, WV**	NA	NA	Philadelphia (greater) PA-NJ-MD-DE**	NA
218	Dover, DE	(7.7)	NA	Binghamton, NY**	NA	NA	Philadelphia, PA M.D.**	NA
218	Orlando, FL	(7.7)	NA	Bloomington, IN**	NA	NA	Phoenix-Mesa-Scottsdale, AZ**	NA
220	Manchester-Nashua, NH	(8.0)	NA	Bloomsburg-Berwick, PA**	NA	NA	Pittsburgh, PA**	NA
221	Wausau, WI	(8.1)	NA	Boston (greater), MA-NH**	NA	NA	Pocatello, ID**	NA
222	Lynchburg, VA	(8.3)	NA	Boston, MA M.D.**	NA	NA	Providence-Warwick, RI-MA**	NA
222	Rockingham County, NH M.D.	(8.3)	NA	Buffalo-Niagara Falls, NY**	NA	NA	Rapid City, SD**	NA
224	Carson City, NV	(8.5)	NA	California-Lexington Park, MD**	NA	NA	Rochester, MN**	NA
225	Dothan, AL	(8.7)	NA	Cambridge-Newton, MA M.D.**	NA	NA	Rochester, NY**	NA
226	Wichita, KS	(9.3)	NA	Chambersburg-Waynesboro, PA**	NA	NA	Salisbury, MD-DE**	NA
227	Sherman-Denison, TX	(9.4)	NA	Charleston-North Charleston, SC**	NA	NA	San Rafael, CA M.D.**	NA
228	Laredo, TX	(9.6)	NA	Chicago-Joilet-Naperville, IL M.D.**	NA	NA	Santa Maria-Santa Barbara, CA**	NA
229	Kennewick-Richland, WA	(10.0)	NA	Cincinnati, OH-KY-IN**	NA	NA	Sebring, FL**	NA
230	Lake Havasu City-Kingman, AZ	(10.2)	NA	Coeur d'Alene, ID**	NA	NA	Shreveport-Bossier City, LA**	NA
230	Miami-Dade County, FL M.D.	(10.2)	NA	Daphne-Fairhope-Foley, AL**	NA	NA	Sierra Vista-Douglas, AZ**	NA
230	Williamsport, PA	(10.2)	NA	Deltona-Daytona Beach, FL**	NA	NA	Sioux City, IA-NE-SD**	NA
233	Tallahassee, FL	(10.4)	NA	Denver-Aurora, CO**	NA	NA	Spartanburg, SC**	NA
234	Ocean City, NJ	(10.9)	NA	Dutchess-Putnam, NY M.D.**	NA	NA	Spokane, WA**	NA
235	Palm Bay-Melbourne, FL	(11.3)	NA	East Stroudsburg, PA**	NA	NA	Springfield, MA**	NA
236	Santa Cruz-Watsonville, CA	(12.1)	NA	Elgin, IL M.D.**	NA	NA	Staunton-Waynesboro, VA**	NA
237	Davenport, IA-IL	(12.2)	NA	Elizabethtown-Fort Knox, KY**	NA	NA	St. George, UT**	NA
238	Cedar Rapids, IA	(12.4)	NA	Elmira, NY**	NA	NA	Syracuse, NY**	NA
239	Prescott, AZ	(12.7)	NA	Fayetteville-Springdale, AR-MO**	NA	NA	Texarkana, TX-AR**	NA
240	Yuba City, CA	(12.9)	NA	Fort Smith, AR-OK**	NA	NA	The Villages, FL**	NA
241	Casper, WY	(13.2)	NA	Gettysburg, PA**	NA	NA	Toledo, OH**	NA
242	Little Rock, AR	(13.4)	NA	Glens Falls, NY**	NA	NA	Tuscaloosa, AL**	NA
243	Champaign-Urbana, IL	(13.6)	NA	Grand Island, NE**	NA	NA	Utica-Rome, NY**	NA
243	Santa Fe, NM	(13.6)	NA	Greensboro-High Point, NC**	NA	NA	Victoria, TX**	NA
245	Lancaster, PA	(13.8)	NA	Greenville-Anderson, SC**	NA	NA	Vineland-Bridgeton, NJ**	NA
246	Scranton--Wilkes-Barre, PA	(14.4)	NA	Greenville, NC**	NA	NA	Waco, TX**	NA
247	Cleveland, TN	(15.0)	NA	Hagerstown-Martinsburg, MD-WV**	NA	NA	Walla Walla, WA**	NA
248	Lakeland, FL	(15.3)	NA	Hammond, LA**	NA	NA	Warner Robins, GA**	NA
248	Las Cruces, NM	(15.3)	NA	Hattiesburg, MS**	NA	NA	Watertown-Fort Drum, NY**	NA
250	La Crosse, WI-MN	(15.9)	NA	Hilton Head Island, SC**	NA	NA	Wheeling, WV-OH**	NA
251	Jonesboro, AR	(16.1)	NA	Homosassa Springs, FL**	NA	NA	Wilmington, NC**	NA
252	Bremerton-Silverdale, WA	(16.9)	NA	Indianapolis, IN**	NA	NA	Winston-Salem, NC**	NA
253	Olympia, WA	(17.0)	NA	Jackson, MS**	NA	NA	Worcester, MA-CT**	NA
254	Augusta, GA-SC	(17.2)	NA	Jackson, TN**	NA	NA	Youngstown-Warren, OH-PA**	NA
255	Columbia, MO	(17.3)	NA	Kahului-Wailuku-Lahaina, HI**	NA			
256	Boulder, CO	(18.0)	NA	Kalamazoo-Portage, MI**	NA			

Source: CQ Press using reported data from the F.B.I. "Crime in the United States 2012"

*Aggravated assault is an attack for the purpose of inflicting severe bodily injury.

**Not available.

24. Percent Change in Aggravated Assault Rate: 2008 to 2012
National Percent Change = 12.7% Decrease*

RANK	METROPOLITAN AREA	% CHANGE	RANK	METROPOLITAN AREA	% CHANGE	RANK	METROPOLITAN AREA	% CHANGE
159	Abilene, TX	(17.9)	28	Cheyenne, WY	25.4	NA	Gary, IN M.D.**	NA
62	Akron, OH	4.5	NA	Chicago (greater), IL-IN-WI**	NA	NA	Gettysburg, PA**	NA
NA	Albany-Schenectady-Troy, NY**	NA	NA	Chicago-Joliet-Naperville, IL M.D.**	NA	NA	Glens Falls, NY**	NA
NA	Albany, GA**	NA	206	Chico, CA	(25.0)	99	Goldsboro, NC	(4.9)
NA	Albany, OR**	NA	NA	Cincinnati, OH-KY-IN**	NA	76	Grand Forks, ND-MN	(0.1)
141	Albuquerque, NM	(14.8)	125	Clarksville, TN-KY	(12.1)	NA	Grand Island, NE**	NA
NA	Alexandria, LA**	NA	209	Cleveland, TN	(25.3)	133	Grand Junction, CO	(13.3)
NA	Allentown, PA-NJ**	NA	NA	Coeur d'Alene, ID**	NA	124	Great Falls, MT	(11.7)
102	Altoona, PA	(7.0)	123	College Station-Bryan, TX	(11.2)	96	Greeley, CO	(4.2)
151	Amarillo, TX	(16.7)	218	Colorado Springs, CO	(27.8)	14	Green Bay, WI	37.6
248	Ames, IA	(61.4)	53	Columbia, MO	9.5	149	Greensboro-High Point, NC	(16.4)
77	Anaheim-Santa Ana-Irvine, CA M.D.	(0.2)	98	Columbus, GA-AL	(4.7)	NA	Greenville-Anderson, SC**	NA
NA	Anchorage, AK**	NA	5	Columbus, IN	74.9	232	Greenville, NC	(34.4)
187	Ann Arbor, MI	(22.0)	104	Corpus Christi, TX	(7.2)	NA	Hagerstown-Martinsburg, MD-WV**	NA
NA	Anniston-Oxford, AL**	NA	175	Corvallis, OR	(20.5)	NA	Hammond, LA**	NA
11	Appleton, WI	40.8	NA	Crestview-Fort Walton Beach, FL**	NA	29	Hanford-Corcoran, CA	24.4
147	Asheville, NC	(16.1)	229	Cumberland, MD-WV	(33.2)	64	Harrisburg-Carlisle, PA	3.6
177	Athens-Clarke County, GA	(20.8)	163	Dallas (greater), TX	(18.2)	140	Harrisonburg, VA	(14.5)
121	Atlanta, GA	(10.6)	184	Dallas-Plano-Irving, TX M.D.	(21.8)	79	Hartford, CT	(0.4)
NA	Atlantic City, NJ**	NA	205	Dalton, GA	(24.4)	NA	Hattiesburg, MS**	NA
231	Auburn, AL	(33.7)	NA	Danville, IL**	NA	156	Hickory, NC	(17.6)
NA	Augusta, GA-SC**	NA	NA	Daphne-Fairhope-Foley, AL**	NA	NA	Hilton Head Island, SC**	NA
116	Austin-Round Rock, TX	(9.6)	NA	Davenport, IA-IL**	NA	202	Hinesville, GA	(24.2)
61	Bakersfield, CA	5.0	169	Dayton, OH	(19.7)	NA	Homosassa Springs, FL**	NA
168	Baltimore, MD	(19.1)	16	Decatur, AL	33.1	238	Houma, LA	(37.5)
150	Bangor, ME	(16.6)	NA	Decatur, IL**	NA	179	Houston, TX	(21.0)
83	Barnstable Town, MA	(1.8)	211	Deltona-Daytona Beach, FL	(25.7)	9	Huntsville, AL	43.8
NA	Baton Rouge, LA**	NA	NA	Denver-Aurora, CO**	NA	245	Idaho Falls, ID	(47.5)
90	Bay City, MI	(3.1)	95	Des Moines-West Des Moines, IA	(3.8)	59	Indianapolis, IN	5.8
67	Beaumont-Port Arthur, TX	2.5	NA	Detroit (greater), MI**	NA	73	Iowa City, IA	0.9
NA	Beckley, WV**	NA	NA	Detroit-Dearborn-Livonia, MI M.D.**	NA	227	Jacksonville, FL	(32.7)
58	Bellingham, WA	6.6	27	Dothan, AL	25.6	NA	Jackson, MS**	NA
21	Billings, MT	28.2	131	Dover, DE	(13.1)	NA	Jackson, TN**	NA
NA	Binghamton, NY**	NA	250	Dubuque, IA	(72.2)	56	Janesville, WI	8.1
30	Birmingham-Hoover, AL	23.2	38	Duluth, MN-WI	17.7	NA	Jefferson City, MO**	NA
4	Bismarck, ND	82.0	63	Durham-Chapel Hill, NC	3.7	129	Johnson City, TN	(12.7)
223	Blacksburg, VA	(29.9)	NA	Dutchess-Putnam, NY M.D.**	NA	36	Johnstown, PA	18.1
NA	Bloomington, IL**	NA	NA	East Stroudsburg, PA**	NA	144	Jonesboro, AR	(16.0)
33	Bloomington, IN	20.6	55	El Centro, CA	8.4	126	Joplin, MO	(12.2)
NA	Bloomsburg-Berwick, PA**	NA	113	El Paso, TX	(8.9)	NA	Kahului-Wailuku-Lahaina, HI**	NA
114	Boise City, ID	(9.2)	NA	Elgin, IL M.D.**	NA	175	Kalamazoo-Portage, MI	(20.5)
NA	Boston (greater), MA-NH**	NA	NA	Elizabethtown-Fort Knox, KY**	NA	NA	Kankakee, IL**	NA
NA	Boston, MA M.D.**	NA	NA	Elmira, NY**	NA	NA	Kansas City, MO-KS**	NA
NA	Boulder, CO**	NA	70	Erie, PA	1.5	82	Kennewick-Richland, WA	(0.9)
249	Bowling Green, KY	(66.5)	240	Eugene, OR	(38.9)	130	Killeen-Temple, TX	(12.8)
242	Bremerton-Silverdale, WA	(44.4)	NA	Fairbanks, AK**	NA	46	Kingsport, TN-VA	12.8
164	Bridgeport-Stamford, CT	(18.3)	12	Fargo, ND-MN	40.3	NA	Kingston, NY**	NA
241	Brownsville-Harlingen, TX	(42.8)	NA	Farmington, NM**	NA	NA	Knoxville, TN**	NA
NA	Brunswick, GA**	NA	25	Fayetteville-Springdale, AR-MO	27.0	NA	Kokomo, IN**	NA
NA	Buffalo-Niagara Falls, NY**	NA	239	Fayetteville, NC	(37.7)	232	La Crosse, WI-MN	(34.4)
92	Burlington, NC	(3.5)	68	Flagstaff, AZ	2.1	43	Lafayette, IN	14.4
NA	California-Lexington Park, MD**	NA	18	Flint, MI	29.8	NA	Lafayette, LA**	NA
NA	Cambridge-Newton, MA M.D.**	NA	104	Florence-Muscle Shoals, AL	(7.2)	NA	Lake Co.-Kenosha Co., IL-WI M.D.**	NA
85	Camden, NJ M.D.	(2.0)	244	Florence, SC	(47.0)	172	Lake Havasu City-Kingman, AZ	(20.2)
NA	Canton, OH**	NA	71	Fond du Lac, WI	1.2	193	Lakeland, FL	(23.1)
191	Cape Coral-Fort Myers, FL	(22.3)	127	Fort Collins, CO	(12.3)	144	Lancaster, PA	(16.0)
26	Cape Girardeau, MO-IL	26.8	187	Fort Lauderdale, FL M.D.	(22.0)	165	Lansing-East Lansing, MI	(18.5)
243	Carson City, NV	(44.9)	NA	Fort Smith, AR-OK**	NA	201	Laredo, TX	(24.1)
116	Casper, WY	(9.6)	7	Fort Wayne, IN	71.8	220	Las Cruces, NM	(28.5)
142	Cedar Rapids, IA	(15.6)	136	Fort Worth-Arlington, TX M.D.	(13.7)	115	Las Vegas-Henderson, NV	(9.4)
NA	Chambersburg-Waynesboro, PA**	NA	35	Fresno, CA	19.6	100	Lawrence, KS	(5.4)
NA	Champaign-Urbana, IL**	NA	2	Gadsden, AL	99.0	NA	Lawton, OK**	NA
236	Charleston-North Charleston, SC	(36.1)	221	Gainesville, FL	(28.6)	155	Lebanon, PA	(17.5)
93	Charlottesville, VA	(3.6)	NA	Gainesville, GA**	NA	237	Lewiston-Auburn, ME	(36.9)

Note: All listings are for Metropolitan Statistical Areas (M.S.A.s) except for those ending with "M.D." Listings with "M.D." are Metropolitan Divisions which are smaller parts of eleven large M.S.A.s. See explanatory note at beginning of metropolitan area section.

RANK	METROPOLITAN AREA	% CHANGE	RANK	METROPOLITAN AREA	% CHANGE	RANK	METROPOLITAN AREA	% CHANGE
22	Lewiston, ID-WA	28.1	NA	Owensboro, KY**	NA	152	Silver Spring-Frederick, MD M.D.	(16.8)
NA	Lexington-Fayette, KY**	NA	178	Oxnard-Thousand Oaks, CA	(20.9)	NA	Sioux City, IA-NE-SD**	NA
40	Lima, OH	16.0	193	Palm Bay-Melbourne, FL	(23.1)	31	Sioux Falls, SD	23.0
226	Lincoln, NE	(32.0)	NA	Panama City, FL**	NA	199	South Bend-Mishawaka, IN-MI	(23.9)
94	Little Rock, AR	(3.7)	106	Pensacola, FL	(7.9)	NA	Spartanburg, SC**	NA
173	Logan, UT-ID	(20.3)	NA	Peoria, IL**	NA	214	Spokane, WA	(26.4)
225	Longview, TX	(31.1)	NA	Philadelphia (greater) PA-NJ-MD-DE**	NA	NA	Springfield, IL**	NA
45	Longview, WA	13.7	NA	Philadelphia, PA M.D.**	NA	NA	Springfield, MA**	NA
202	Los Angeles County, CA M.D.	(24.2)	NA	Phoenix-Mesa-Scottsdale, AZ**	NA	NA	Springfield, MO**	NA
181	Los Angeles (greater), CA	(21.4)	116	Pine Bluff, AR	(9.6)	42	Springfield, OH	15.1
36	Louisville, KY-IN	18.1	NA	Pittsburgh, PA**	NA	88	State College, PA	(2.8)
161	Lubbock, TX	(18.1)	180	Pittsfield, MA	(21.3)	NA	Staunton-Waynesboro, VA**	NA
198	Lynchburg, VA	(23.7)	NA	Pocatello, ID**	NA	81	Stockton-Lodi, CA	(0.7)
204	Macon, GA	(24.3)	212	Port St. Lucie, FL	(26.2)	161	St. George, UT	(18.1)
10	Madera, CA	42.8	101	Portland-Vancouver, OR-WA	(6.1)	139	St. Joseph, MO-KS	(14.3)
NA	Madison, WI**	NA	48	Portland, ME	11.1	111	St. Louis, MO-IL	(8.6)
NA	Manchester-Nashua, NH**	NA	110	Prescott, AZ	(8.5)	39	Sumter, SC	16.9
NA	Manhattan, KS**	NA	107	Providence-Warwick, RI-MA	(8.2)	NA	Syracuse, NY**	NA
15	Mankato-North Mankato, MN	34.7	167	Provo-Orem, UT	(18.7)	NA	Tacoma, WA M.D.**	NA
153	Mansfield, OH	(17.3)	NA	Pueblo, CO**	NA	234	Tallahassee, FL	(34.7)
86	McAllen-Edinburg-Mission, TX	(2.3)	219	Punta Gorda, FL	(28.3)	235	Tampa-St Petersburg, FL	(35.5)
8	Medford, OR	58.2	196	Racine, WI	(23.3)	NA	Terre Haute, IN**	NA
96	Memphis, TN-MS-AR	(4.2)	NA	Raleigh, NC**	NA	NA	Texarkana, TX-AR**	NA
44	Merced, CA	14.3	NA	Rapid City, SD**	NA	NA	The Villages, FL**	NA
207	Miami (greater), FL	(25.1)	51	Reading, PA	9.7	NA	Toledo, OH**	NA
215	Miami-Dade County, FL M.D.	(27.0)	49	Redding, CA	11.0	23	Topeka, KS	27.3
57	Michigan City-La Porte, IN	7.4	170	Reno, NV	(19.9)	34	Trenton, NJ	20.2
NA	Midland, MI**	NA	197	Richmond, VA	(23.5)	89	Tucson, AZ	(2.9)
NA	Midland, TX**	NA	144	Riverside-San Bernardino, CA	(16.0)	217	Tulsa, OK	(27.7)
41	Milwaukee, WI	15.4	174	Roanoke, VA	(20.4)	NA	Tuscaloosa, AL**	NA
154	Minneapolis-St. Paul, MN-WI	(17.4)	NA	Rochester, MN**	NA	170	Tyler, TX	(19.9)
83	Missoula, MT	(1.8)	NA	Rochester, NY**	NA	NA	Utica-Rome, NY**	NA
1	Mobile, AL	135.9	NA	Rockford, IL**	NA	148	Valdosta, GA	(16.3)
66	Modesto, CA	2.7	54	Rockingham County, NH M.D.	9.1	185	Vallejo-Fairfield, CA	(21.9)
107	Monroe, LA	(8.2)	NA	Rocky Mount, NC**	NA	NA	Victoria, TX**	NA
50	Monroe, MI	10.4	NA	Rome, GA**	NA	156	Vineland-Bridgeton, NJ	(17.6)
NA	Montgomery County, PA M.D.**	NA	119	Sacramento, CA	(9.9)	131	Virginia Beach-Norfolk, VA-NC	(13.1)
51	Montgomery, AL	9.7	229	Saginaw, MI	(33.2)	111	Visalia-Porterville, CA	(8.6)
NA	Morgantown, WV**	NA	74	Salem, OR	0.7	NA	Waco, TX**	NA
NA	Morristown, TN**	NA	190	Salinas, CA	(22.1)	NA	Walla Walla, WA**	NA
47	Mount Vernon-Anacortes, WA	12.2	NA	Salisbury, MD-DE**	NA	NA	Warner Robins, GA**	NA
222	Muncie, IN	(29.2)	91	Salt Lake City, UT	(3.4)	NA	Warren-Troy, MI M.D.**	NA
246	Napa, CA	(49.5)	228	San Antonio, TX	(32.9)	187	Washington (greater) DC-VA-MD-WV	(22.0)
224	Naples-Marco Island, FL	(30.6)	102	San Diego, CA	(7.0)	193	Washington, DC-VA-MD-WV M.D.	(23.1)
NA	Nashville-Davidson, TN**	NA	135	San Francisco (greater), CA	(13.6)	207	Waterloo-Cedar Falls, IA	(25.1)
NA	Nassau-Suffolk, NY M.D.**	NA	107	San Francisco-Redwood, CA M.D.	(8.2)	NA	Watertown-Fort Drum, NY**	NA
NA	New Bern, NC**	NA	165	San Jose, CA	(18.5)	247	Wausau, WI	(60.1)
NA	New Haven-Milford, CT**	NA	19	San Luis Obispo, CA	29.3	209	West Palm Beach, FL M.D.	(25.3)
199	New Orleans, LA	(23.9)	NA	San Rafael, CA M.D.**	NA	6	Wheeling, WV-OH	73.2
NA	New York (greater), NY-NJ-PA**	NA	191	Santa Cruz-Watsonville, CA	(22.3)	71	Wichita Falls, TX	1.2
NA	New York-Jersey City, NY-NJ M.D.**	NA	134	Santa Fe, NM	(13.4)	138	Wichita, KS	(13.8)
NA	Newark, NJ-PA M.D.**	NA	NA	Santa Maria-Santa Barbara, CA**	NA	80	Williamsport, PA	(0.5)
NA	North Port-Sarasota-Bradenton, FL**	NA	156	Santa Rosa, CA	(17.6)	181	Wilmington, DE-MD-NJ M.D.	(21.4)
24	Norwich-New London, CT	27.1	213	Savannah, GA	(26.3)	NA	Wilmington, NC**	NA
136	Oakland-Hayward, CA M.D.	(13.7)	143	Scranton--Wilkes-Barre, PA	(15.9)	32	Winchester, VA-WV	22.6
181	Ocala, FL	(21.4)	NA	Seattle (greater), WA**	NA	NA	Winston-Salem, NC**	NA
120	Ocean City, NJ	(10.0)	NA	Seattle-Bellevue-Everett, WA M.D.**	NA	77	Worcester, MA-CT	(0.2)
17	Odessa, TX	30.4	69	Sebastian-Vero Beach, FL	2.0	20	Yakima, WA	28.5
NA	Ogden-Clearfield, UT**	NA	NA	Sebring, FL**	NA	13	York-Hanover, PA	39.3
75	Oklahoma City, OK	0.2	3	Sheboygan, WI	93.1	127	Youngstown-Warren, OH-PA	(12.3)
185	Olympia, WA	(21.9)	160	Sherman-Denison, TX	(18.0)	121	Yuba City, CA	(10.6)
65	Omaha-Council Bluffs, NE-IA	3.4	NA	Shreveport-Bossier City, LA**	NA	87	Yuma, AZ	(2.6)
216	Orlando, FL	(27.2)	NA	Sierra Vista-Douglas, AZ**	NA			
59	Oshkosh-Neenah, WI	5.8						

Source: CQ Press using reported data from the F.B.I. "Crime in the United States 2012"

*Aggravated assault is an attack for the purpose of inflicting severe bodily injury.

**Not available.

24. Percent Change in Aggravated Assault Rate: 2008 to 2012 (continued)
National Percent Change = 12.7% Decrease*

RANK	METROPOLITAN AREA	% CHANGE	RANK	METROPOLITAN AREA	% CHANGE	RANK	METROPOLITAN AREA	% CHANGE
1	Mobile, AL	135.9	65	Omaha-Council Bluffs, NE-IA	3.4	129	Johnson City, TN	(12.7)
2	Gadsden, AL	99.0	66	Modesto, CA	2.7	130	Killeen-Temple, TX	(12.8)
3	Sheboygan, WI	93.1	67	Beaumont-Port Arthur, TX	2.5	131	Dover, DE	(13.1)
4	Bismarck, ND	82.0	68	Flagstaff, AZ	2.1	131	Virginia Beach-Norfolk, VA-NC	(13.1)
5	Columbus, IN	74.9	69	Sebastian-Vero Beach, FL	2.0	133	Grand Junction, CO	(13.3)
6	Wheeling, WV-OH	73.2	70	Erie, PA	1.5	134	Santa Fe, NM	(13.4)
7	Fort Wayne, IN	71.8	71	Fond du Lac, WI	1.2	135	San Francisco (greater), CA	(13.6)
8	Medford, OR	58.2	71	Wichita Falls, TX	1.2	136	Fort Worth-Arlington, TX M.D.	(13.7)
9	Huntsville, AL	43.8	73	Iowa City, IA	0.9	136	Oakland-Hayward, CA M.D.	(13.7)
10	Madera, CA	42.8	74	Salem, OR	0.7	138	Wichita, KS	(13.8)
11	Appleton, WI	40.8	75	Oklahoma City, OK	0.2	139	St. Joseph, MO-KS	(14.3)
12	Fargo, ND-MN	40.3	76	Grand Forks, ND-MN	(0.1)	140	Harrisonburg, VA	(14.5)
13	York-Hanover, PA	39.3	77	Anaheim-Santa Ana-Irvine, CA M.D.	(0.2)	141	Albuquerque, NM	(14.8)
14	Green Bay, WI	37.6	77	Worcester, MA-CT	(0.2)	142	Cedar Rapids, IA	(15.6)
15	Mankato-North Mankato, MN	34.7	79	Hartford, CT	(0.4)	143	Scranton--Wilkes-Barre, PA	(15.9)
16	Decatur, AL	33.1	80	Williamsport, PA	(0.5)	144	Jonesboro, AR	(16.0)
17	Odessa, TX	30.4	81	Stockton-Lodi, CA	(0.7)	144	Lancaster, PA	(16.0)
18	Flint, MI	29.8	82	Kennewick-Richland, WA	(0.9)	144	Riverside-San Bernardino, CA	(16.0)
19	San Luis Obispo, CA	29.3	83	Barnstable Town, MA	(1.8)	147	Asheville, NC	(16.1)
20	Yakima, WA	28.5	83	Missoula, MT	(1.8)	148	Valdosta, GA	(16.3)
21	Billings, MT	28.2	85	Camden, NJ M.D.	(2.0)	149	Greensboro-High Point, NC	(16.4)
22	Lewiston, ID-WA	28.1	86	McAllen-Edinburg-Mission, TX	(2.3)	150	Bangor, ME	(16.6)
23	Topeka, KS	27.3	87	Yuma, AZ	(2.6)	151	Amarillo, TX	(16.7)
24	Norwich-New London, CT	27.1	88	State College, PA	(2.8)	152	Silver Spring-Frederick, MD M.D.	(16.8)
25	Fayetteville-Springdale, AR-MO	27.0	89	Tucson, AZ	(2.9)	153	Mansfield, OH	(17.3)
26	Cape Girardeau, MO-IL	26.8	90	Bay City, MI	(3.1)	154	Minneapolis-St. Paul, MN-WI	(17.4)
27	Dothan, AL	25.6	91	Salt Lake City, UT	(3.4)	155	Lebanon, PA	(17.5)
28	Cheyenne, WY	25.4	92	Burlington, NC	(3.5)	156	Hickory, NC	(17.6)
29	Hanford-Corcoran, CA	24.4	93	Charlottesville, VA	(3.6)	156	Santa Rosa, CA	(17.6)
30	Birmingham-Hoover, AL	23.2	94	Little Rock, AR	(3.7)	156	Vineland-Bridgeton, NJ	(17.6)
31	Sioux Falls, SD	23.0	95	Des Moines-West Des Moines, IA	(3.8)	159	Abilene, TX	(17.9)
32	Winchester, VA-WV	22.6	96	Greeley, CO	(4.2)	160	Sherman-Denison, TX	(18.0)
33	Bloomington, IN	20.6	96	Memphis, TN-MS-AR	(4.2)	161	Lubbock, TX	(18.1)
34	Trenton, NJ	20.2	98	Columbus, GA-AL	(4.7)	161	St. George, UT	(18.1)
35	Fresno, CA	19.6	99	Goldsboro, NC	(4.9)	163	Dallas (greater), TX	(18.2)
36	Johnstown, PA	18.1	100	Lawrence, KS	(5.4)	164	Bridgeport-Stamford, CT	(18.3)
36	Louisville, KY-IN	18.1	101	Portland-Vancouver, OR-WA	(6.1)	165	Lansing-East Lansing, MI	(18.5)
38	Duluth, MN-WI	17.7	102	Altoona, PA	(7.0)	165	San Jose, CA	(18.5)
39	Sumter, SC	16.9	102	San Diego, CA	(7.0)	167	Provo-Orem, UT	(18.7)
40	Lima, OH	16.0	104	Corpus Christi, TX	(7.2)	168	Baltimore, MD	(19.1)
41	Milwaukee, WI	15.4	104	Florence-Muscle Shoals, AL	(7.2)	169	Dayton, OH	(19.7)
42	Springfield, OH	15.1	106	Pensacola, FL	(7.9)	170	Reno, NV	(19.9)
43	Lafayette, IN	14.4	107	Monroe, LA	(8.2)	170	Tyler, TX	(19.9)
44	Merced, CA	14.3	107	Providence-Warwick, RI-MA	(8.2)	172	Lake Havasu City-Kingman, AZ	(20.2)
45	Longview, WA	13.7	107	San Francisco-Redwood, CA M.D.	(8.2)	173	Logan, UT-ID	(20.3)
46	Kingsport, TN-VA	12.8	110	Prescott, AZ	(8.5)	174	Roanoke, VA	(20.4)
47	Mount Vernon-Anacortes, WA	12.2	111	St. Louis, MO-IL	(8.6)	175	Corvallis, OR	(20.5)
48	Portland, ME	11.1	111	Visalia-Porterville, CA	(8.6)	175	Kalamazoo-Portage, MI	(20.5)
49	Redding, CA	11.0	113	El Paso, TX	(8.9)	177	Athens-Clarke County, GA	(20.8)
50	Monroe, MI	10.4	114	Boise City, ID	(9.2)	178	Oxnard-Thousand Oaks, CA	(20.9)
51	Montgomery, AL	9.7	115	Las Vegas-Henderson, NV	(9.4)	179	Houston, TX	(21.0)
51	Reading, PA	9.7	116	Austin-Round Rock, TX	(9.6)	180	Pittsfield, MA	(21.3)
53	Columbia, MO	9.5	116	Casper, WY	(9.6)	181	Los Angeles (greater), CA	(21.4)
54	Rockingham County, NH M.D.	9.1	116	Pine Bluff, AR	(9.6)	181	Ocala, FL	(21.4)
55	El Centro, CA	8.4	119	Sacramento, CA	(9.9)	181	Wilmington, DE-MD-NJ M.D.	(21.4)
56	Janesville, WI	8.1	120	Ocean City, NJ	(10.0)	184	Dallas-Plano-Irving, TX M.D.	(21.8)
57	Michigan City-La Porte, IN	7.4	121	Atlanta, GA	(10.6)	185	Olympia, WA	(21.9)
58	Bellingham, WA	6.6	121	Yuba City, CA	(10.6)	185	Vallejo-Fairfield, CA	(21.9)
59	Indianapolis, IN	5.8	123	College Station-Bryan, TX	(11.2)	187	Ann Arbor, MI	(22.0)
59	Oshkosh-Neenah, WI	5.8	124	Great Falls, MT	(11.7)	187	Fort Lauderdale, FL M.D.	(22.0)
61	Bakersfield, CA	5.0	125	Clarksville, TN-KY	(12.1)	187	Washington (greater) DC-VA-MD-WV	(22.0)
62	Akron, OH	4.5	126	Joplin, MO	(12.2)	190	Salinas, CA	(22.1)
63	Durham-Chapel Hill, NC	3.7	127	Fort Collins, CO	(12.3)	191	Cape Coral-Fort Myers, FL	(22.3)
64	Harrisburg-Carlisle, PA	3.6	127	Youngstown-Warren, OH-PA	(12.3)	191	Santa Cruz-Watsonville, CA	(22.3)

Note: All listings are for Metropolitan Statistical Areas (M.S.A.s) except for those ending with "M.D." Listings with "M.D." are Metropolitan Divisions which are smaller parts of eleven large M.S.A.s. See explanatory note at beginning of metropolitan area section.

RANK	METROPOLITAN AREA	% CHANGE	RANK	METROPOLITAN AREA	% CHANGE	RANK	METROPOLITAN AREA	% CHANGE
193	Lakeland, FL	(23.1)	NA	Anniston-Oxford, AL**	NA	NA	Manhattan, KS**	NA
193	Palm Bay-Melbourne, FL	(23.1)	NA	Atlantic City, NJ**	NA	NA	Midland, MI**	NA
193	Washington, DC-VA-MD-WV M.D.	(23.1)	NA	Augusta, GA-SC**	NA	NA	Midland, TX**	NA
196	Racine, WI	(23.3)	NA	Baton Rouge, LA**	NA	NA	Montgomery County, PA M.D.**	NA
197	Richmond, VA	(23.5)	NA	Beckley, WV**	NA	NA	Morgantown, WV**	NA
198	Lynchburg, VA	(23.7)	NA	Binghamton, NY**	NA	NA	Morristown, TN**	NA
199	New Orleans, LA	(23.9)	NA	Bloomington, IL**	NA	NA	Nashville-Davidson, TN**	NA
199	South Bend-Mishawaka, IN-MI	(23.9)	NA	Bloomsburg-Berwick, PA**	NA	NA	Nassau-Suffolk, NY M.D.**	NA
201	Laredo, TX	(24.1)	NA	Boston (greater), MA-NH**	NA	NA	New Bern, NC**	NA
202	Hinesville, GA	(24.2)	NA	Boston, MA M.D.**	NA	NA	New Haven-Milford, CT**	NA
202	Los Angeles County, CA M.D.	(24.2)	NA	Boulder, CO**	NA	NA	New York (greater), NY-NJ-PA**	NA
204	Macon, GA	(24.3)	NA	Brunswick, GA**	NA	NA	New York-Jersey City, NY-NJ M.D.**	NA
205	Dalton, GA	(24.4)	NA	Buffalo-Niagara Falls, NY**	NA	NA	Newark, NJ-PA M.D.**	NA
206	Chico, CA	(25.0)	NA	California-Lexington Park, MD**	NA	NA	North Port-Sarasota-Bradenton, FL**	NA
207	Miami (greater), FL	(25.1)	NA	Cambridge-Newton, MA M.D.**	NA	NA	Ogden-Clearfield, UT**	NA
207	Waterloo-Cedar Falls, IA	(25.1)	NA	Canton, OH**	NA	NA	Owensboro, KY**	NA
209	Cleveland, TN	(25.3)	NA	Chambersburg-Waynesboro, PA**	NA	NA	Panama City, FL**	NA
209	West Palm Beach, FL M.D.	(25.3)	NA	Champaign-Urbana, IL**	NA	NA	Parkersburg-Vienna, WV**	NA
211	Deltona-Daytona Beach, FL	(25.7)	NA	Chicago (greater), IL-IN-WI**	NA	NA	Peoria, IL**	NA
212	Port St. Lucie, FL	(26.2)	NA	Chicago-Joilet-Naperville, IL M.D.**	NA	NA	Philadelphia (greater) PA-NJ-MD-DE**	NA
213	Savannah, GA	(26.3)	NA	Cincinnati, OH-KY-IN**	NA	NA	Philadelphia, PA M.D.**	NA
214	Spokane, WA	(26.4)	NA	Coeur d'Alene, ID**	NA	NA	Phoenix-Mesa-Scottsdale, AZ**	NA
215	Miami-Dade County, FL M.D.	(27.0)	NA	Crestview-Fort Walton Beach, FL**	NA	NA	Pittsburgh, PA**	NA
216	Orlando, FL	(27.2)	NA	Danville, IL**	NA	NA	Pocatello, ID**	NA
217	Tulsa, OK	(27.7)	NA	Daphne-Fairhope-Foley, AL**	NA	NA	Pueblo, CO**	NA
218	Colorado Springs, CO	(27.8)	NA	Davenport, IA-IL**	NA	NA	Raleigh, NC**	NA
219	Punta Gorda, FL	(28.3)	NA	Decatur, IL**	NA	NA	Rapid City, SD**	NA
220	Las Cruces, NM	(28.5)	NA	Denver-Aurora, CO**	NA	NA	Rochester, MN**	NA
221	Gainesville, FL	(28.6)	NA	Detroit (greater), MI**	NA	NA	Rochester, NY**	NA
222	Muncie, IN	(29.2)	NA	Detroit-Dearborn-Livonia, MI M.D.**	NA	NA	Rockford, IL**	NA
223	Blacksburg, VA	(29.9)	NA	Dutchess-Putnam, NY M.D.**	NA	NA	Rocky Mount, NC**	NA
224	Naples-Marco Island, FL	(30.6)	NA	East Stroudsburg, PA**	NA	NA	Rome, GA**	NA
225	Longview, TX	(31.1)	NA	Elgin, IL M.D.**	NA	NA	Salisbury, MD-DE**	NA
226	Lincoln, NE	(32.0)	NA	Elizabethtown-Fort Knox, KY**	NA	NA	San Rafael, CA M.D.**	NA
227	Jacksonville, FL	(32.7)	NA	Elmira, NY**	NA	NA	Santa Maria-Santa Barbara, CA**	NA
228	San Antonio, TX	(32.9)	NA	Fairbanks, AK**	NA	NA	Seattle (greater), WA**	NA
229	Cumberland, MD-WV	(33.2)	NA	Farmington, NM**	NA	NA	Seattle-Bellevue-Everett, WA M.D.**	NA
229	Saginaw, MI	(33.2)	NA	Fort Smith, AR-OK**	NA	NA	Sebring, FL**	NA
231	Auburn, AL	(33.7)	NA	Gainesville, GA**	NA	NA	Shreveport-Bossier City, LA**	NA
232	Greenville, NC	(34.4)	NA	Gary, IN M.D.**	NA	NA	Sierra Vista-Douglas, AZ**	NA
232	La Crosse, WI-MN	(34.4)	NA	Gettysburg, PA**	NA	NA	Sioux City, IA-NE-SD**	NA
234	Tallahassee, FL	(34.7)	NA	Glens Falls, NY**	NA	NA	Spartanburg, SC**	NA
235	Tampa-St Petersburg, FL	(35.5)	NA	Grand Island, NE**	NA	NA	Springfield, IL**	NA
236	Charleston-North Charleston, SC	(36.1)	NA	Greenville-Anderson, SC**	NA	NA	Springfield, MA**	NA
237	Lewiston-Auburn, ME	(36.9)	NA	Hagerstown-Martinsburg, MD-WV**	NA	NA	Springfield, MO**	NA
238	Houma, LA	(37.5)	NA	Hammond, LA**	NA	NA	Staunton-Waynesboro, VA**	NA
239	Fayetteville, NC	(37.7)	NA	Hattiesburg, MS**	NA	NA	Syracuse, NY**	NA
240	Eugene, OR	(38.9)	NA	Hilton Head Island, SC**	NA	NA	Tacoma, WA M.D.**	NA
241	Brownsville-Harlingen, TX	(42.8)	NA	Homosassa Springs, FL**	NA	NA	Terre Haute, IN**	NA
242	Bremerton-Silverdale, WA	(44.4)	NA	Jackson, MS**	NA	NA	Texarkana, TX-AR**	NA
243	Carson City, NV	(44.9)	NA	Jackson, TN**	NA	NA	The Villages, FL**	NA
244	Florence, SC	(47.0)	NA	Jefferson City, MO**	NA	NA	Toledo, OH**	NA
245	Idaho Falls, ID	(47.5)	NA	Kahului-Wailuku-Lahaina, HI**	NA	NA	Tuscaloosa, AL**	NA
246	Napa, CA	(49.5)	NA	Kankakee, IL**	NA	NA	Utica-Rome, NY**	NA
247	Wausau, WI	(60.1)	NA	Kansas City, MO-KS**	NA	NA	Victoria, TX**	NA
248	Ames, IA	(61.4)	NA	Kingston, NY**	NA	NA	Waco, TX**	NA
249	Bowling Green, KY	(66.5)	NA	Knoxville, TN**	NA	NA	Walla Walla, WA**	NA
250	Dubuque, IA	(72.2)	NA	Kokomo, IN**	NA	NA	Warner Robins, GA**	NA
NA	Albany-Schenectady-Troy, NY**	NA	NA	Lafayette, LA**	NA	NA	Warren-Troy, MI M.D.**	NA
NA	Albany, GA**	NA	NA	Lake Co.-Kenosha Co., IL-WI M.D.**	NA	NA	Watertown-Fort Drum, NY**	NA
NA	Albany, OR**	NA	NA	Lawton, OK**	NA	NA	Wilmington, NC**	NA
NA	Alexandria, LA**	NA	NA	Lexington-Fayette, KY**	NA	NA	Winston-Salem, NC**	NA
NA	Allentown, PA-NJ**	NA	NA	Madison, WI**	NA			
NA	Anchorage, AK**	NA	NA	Manchester-Nashua, NH**	NA			

Source: CQ Press using reported data from the F.B.I. "Crime in the United States 2012"

*Aggravated assault is an attack for the purpose of inflicting severe bodily injury.

**Not available.

25. Property Crimes in 2012
National Total = 8,975,438 Property Crimes*

RANK	METROPOLITAN AREA	CRIMES	RANK	METROPOLITAN AREA	CRIMES	RANK	METROPOLITAN AREA	CRIMES
238	Abilene, TX	5,080	326	Cheyenne, WY	2,716	83	Gary, IN M.D.	22,426
88	Akron, OH	21,287	3	Chicago (greater), IL-IN-WI	254,619	358	Gettysburg, PA	1,211
86	Albany-Schenectady-Troy, NY	21,586	8	Chicago-Joilet-Naperville, IL M.D.	204,797	343	Glens Falls, NY	2,178
186	Albany, GA	7,276	224	Chico, CA	5,659	241	Goldsboro, NC	4,930
288	Albany, OR	3,739	29	Cincinnati, OH-KY-IN	70,483	340	Grand Forks, ND-MN	2,232
NA	Albuquerque, NM**	NA	192	Clarksville, TN-KY	6,966	318	Grand Island, NE	2,891
NA	Alexandria, LA**	NA	296	Cleveland, TN	3,567	266	Grand Junction, CO	4,309
97	Allentown, PA-NJ	18,304	256	Coeur d'Alene, ID	4,522	308	Great Falls, MT	3,115
348	Altoona, PA	2,113	204	College Station-Bryan, TX	6,304	222	Greeley, CO	5,734
155	Amarillo, TX	9,716	NA	Colorado Springs, CO**	NA	215	Green Bay, WI	5,857
351	Ames, IA	2,031	226	Columbia, MO	5,544	76	Greensboro-High Point, NC	26,195
34	Anaheim-Santa Ana-Irvine, CA M.D.	67,821	115	Columbus, GA-AL	14,541	63	Greenville-Anderson, SC	33,066
135	Anchorage, AK	11,344	324	Columbus, IN	2,767	211	Greenville, NC	6,030
169	Ann Arbor, MI	8,487	NA	Corpus Christi, TX**	NA	214	Hagerstown-Martinsburg, MD-WV	5,890
232	Anniston-Oxford, AL	5,339	353	Corvallis, OR	1,841	187	Hammond, LA	7,127
297	Appleton, WI	3,519	200	Crestview-Fort Walton Beach, FL	6,453	300	Hanford-Corcoran, CA	3,440
128	Asheville, NC	12,143	313	Cumberland, MD-WV	2,979	133	Harrisburg-Carlisle, PA	11,835
197	Athens-Clarke County, GA	6,650	7	Dallas (greater), TX	212,153	355	Harrisonburg, VA	1,799
9	Atlanta, GA	183,871	11	Dallas-Plano-Irving, TX M.D.	136,479	77	Hartford, CT	25,096
171	Atlantic City, NJ	8,404	276	Dalton, GA	3,990	278	Hattiesburg, MS	3,905
273	Auburn, AL	4,023	310	Danville, IL	3,057	127	Hickory, NC	12,204
81	Augusta, GA-SC	23,040	240	Daphne-Fairhope-Foley, AL	4,988	219	Hilton Head Island, SC	5,826
36	Austin-Round Rock, TX	62,113	154	Davenport, IA-IL	9,879	334	Hinesville, GA	2,457
60	Bakersfield, CA	34,761	74	Dayton, OH	27,287	315	Homosassa Springs, FL	2,954
20	Baltimore, MD	82,232	257	Decatur, AL	4,518	194	Houma, LA	6,855
249	Bangor, ME	4,623	314	Decatur, IL	2,963	NA	Houston, TX**	NA
217	Barnstable Town, MA	5,835	93	Deltona-Daytona Beach, FL	19,223	116	Huntsville, AL	14,292
NA	Baton Rouge, LA**	NA	25	Denver-Aurora, CO	72,387	330	Idaho Falls, ID	2,559
349	Bay City, MI	2,090	NA	Des Moines-West Des Moines, IA**	NA	31	Indianapolis, IN	70,358
119	Beaumont-Port Arthur, TX	13,352	14	Detroit (greater), MI	117,088	309	Iowa City, IA	3,058
255	Beckley, WV	4,533	30	Detroit-Dearborn-Livonia, MI M.D.	70,402	46	Jacksonville, FL	47,687
203	Bellingham, WA	6,318	252	Dothan, AL	4,589	94	Jackson, MS	19,112
221	Billings, MT	5,755	208	Dover, DE	6,172	250	Jackson, TN	4,594
195	Binghamton, NY	6,851	NA	Dubuque, IA**	NA	243	Janesville, WI	4,771
53	Birmingham-Hoover, AL	43,172	164	Duluth, MN-WI	8,836	295	Jefferson City, MO	3,577
316	Bismarck, ND	2,897	99	Durham-Chapel Hill, NC	17,821	213	Johnson City, TN	6,000
277	Blacksburg, VA	3,914	210	Dutchess-Putnam, NY M.D.	6,119	328	Johnstown, PA	2,572
272	Bloomington, IL	4,052	259	East Stroudsburg, PA	4,486	266	Jonesboro, AR	4,309
236	Bloomington, IN	5,142	199	El Centro, CA	6,471	183	Joplin, MO	7,545
354	Bloomsburg-Berwick, PA	1,800	92	El Paso, TX	19,361	212	Kahului-Wailuku-Lahaina, HI	6,003
126	Boise City, ID	12,461	143	Elgin, IL M.D.	10,322	159	Kalamazoo-Portage, MI	9,239
19	Boston (greater), MA-NH	91,833	344	Elizabethtown-Fort Knox, KY	2,160	306	Kankakee, IL	3,155
55	Boston, MA M.D.	41,866	341	Elmira, NY	2,212	28	Kansas City, MO-KS	70,667
188	Boulder, CO	7,107	184	Erie, PA	7,345	202	Kennewick-Richland, WA	6,400
275	Bowling Green, KY	4,003	118	Eugene, OR	13,538	NA	Killeen-Temple, TX**	NA
173	Bremerton-Silverdale, WA	8,127	357	Fairbanks, AK	1,549	156	Kingsport, TN-VA	9,310
108	Bridgeport-Stamford, CT	16,256	245	Fargo, ND-MN	4,729	292	Kingston, NY	3,671
105	Brownsville-Harlingen, TX	16,754	305	Farmington, NM	3,175	69	Knoxville, TN	29,675
246	Brunswick, GA	4,713	130	Fayetteville-Springdale, AR-MO	12,089	336	Kokomo, IN	2,363
61	Buffalo-Niagara Falls, NY	33,364	90	Fayetteville, NC	20,252	303	La Crosse, WI-MN	3,266
234	Burlington, NC	5,218	268	Flagstaff, AZ	4,268	228	Lafayette, IN	5,522
321	California-Lexington Park, MD	2,778	111	Flint, MI	15,376	NA	Lafayette, LA**	NA
56	Cambridge-Newton, MA M.D.	40,850	260	Florence-Muscle Shoals, AL	4,454	102	Lake Co.-Kenosha Co., IL-WI M.D.	17,074
64	Camden, NJ M.D.	32,339	153	Florence, SC	9,880	189	Lake Havasu City-Kingman, AZ	7,073
132	Canton, OH	11,957	356	Fond du Lac, WI	1,784	95	Lakeland, FL	19,088
112	Cape Coral-Fort Myers, FL	15,021	181	Fort Collins, CO	7,605	145	Lancaster, PA	10,294
289	Cape Girardeau, MO-IL	3,721	33	Fort Lauderdale, FL M.D.	67,932	142	Lansing-East Lansing, MI	10,348
359	Carson City, NV	1,107	170	Fort Smith, AR-OK	8,475	138	Laredo, TX	11,080
337	Casper, WY	2,346	129	Fort Wayne, IN	12,116	198	Las Cruces, NM	6,511
NA	Cedar Rapids, IA**	NA	24	Fort Worth-Arlington, TX M.D.	75,674	37	Las Vegas-Henderson, NV	59,193
333	Chambersburg-Waynesboro, PA	2,508	54	Fresno, CA	42,099	254	Lawrence, KS	4,548
209	Champaign-Urbana, IL	6,155	258	Gadsden, AL	4,504	223	Lawton, OK	5,675
82	Charleston-North Charleston, SC	22,508	163	Gainesville, FL	8,852	329	Lebanon, PA	2,570
263	Charlottesville, VA	4,380	265	Gainesville, GA	4,323	302	Lewiston-Auburn, ME	3,271

Note: All listings are for Metropolitan Statistical Areas (M.S.A.s) except for those ending with "M.D." Listings with "M.D." are Metropolitan Divisions which are smaller parts of eleven large M.S.A.s. See explanatory note at beginning of metropolitan area section.

RANK	METROPOLITAN AREA	CRIMES	RANK	METROPOLITAN AREA	CRIMES	RANK	METROPOLITAN AREA	CRIMES
346	Lewiston, ID-WA	2,135	307	Owensboro, KY	3,139	87	Silver Spring-Frederick, MD M.D.	21,372
91	Lexington-Fayette, KY	19,682	109	Oxnard-Thousand Oaks, CA	15,921	253	Sioux City, IA-NE-SD	4,569
281	Lima, OH	3,843	107	Palm Bay-Melbourne, FL	16,659	220	Sioux Falls, SD	5,816
139	Lincoln, NE	10,938	180	Panama City, FL	7,658	150	South Bend-Mishawaka, IN-MI	10,147
59	Little Rock, AR	36,701	327	Parkersburg-Vienna, WV	2,701	140	Spartanburg, SC	10,591
350	Logan, UT-ID	2,034	106	Pensacola, FL	16,745	70	Spokane, WA	29,653
176	Longview, TX	8,032	141	Peoria, IL	10,379	165	Springfield, IL	8,793
283	Longview, WA	3,785	10	Philadelphia (greater) PA-NJ-MD-DE	160,273	96	Springfield, MA	18,949
5	Los Angeles County, CA M.D.	232,266	27	Philadelphia, PA M.D.	71,230	89	Springfield, MO	20,386
2	Los Angeles (greater), CA	300,087	NA	Phoenix-Mesa-Scottsdale, AZ**	NA	225	Springfield, OH	5,643
52	Louisville, KY-IN	43,390	269	Pine Bluff, AR	4,218	342	State College, PA	2,199
117	Lubbock, TX	13,582	49	Pittsburgh, PA	44,920	347	Staunton-Waynesboro, VA	2,119
251	Lynchburg, VA	4,591	311	Pittsfield, MA	3,049	71	Stockton-Lodi, CA	29,264
137	Macon, GA	11,089	345	Pocatello, ID	2,155	322	St. George, UT	2,773
274	Madera, CA	4,017	148	Port St. Lucie, FL	10,170	229	St. Joseph, MO-KS	5,473
113	Madison, WI	14,919	26	Portland-Vancouver, OR-WA	72,141	22	St. Louis, MO-IL	80,634
158	Manchester-Nashua, NH	9,274	124	Portland, ME	12,713	248	Sumter, SC	4,645
352	Manhattan, KS	1,876	261	Prescott, AZ	4,442	104	Syracuse, NY	16,784
325	Mankato-North Mankato, MN	2,733	57	Providence-Warwick, RI-MA	40,028	NA	Tacoma, WA M.D.**	NA
218	Mansfield, OH	5,832	147	Provo-Orem, UT	10,189	121	Tallahassee, FL	13,050
67	McAllen-Edinburg-Mission, TX	30,517	174	Pueblo, CO	8,114	21	Tampa-St Petersburg, FL	81,969
178	Medford, OR	7,776	298	Punta Gorda, FL	3,507	201	Terre Haute, IN	6,420
38	Memphis, TN-MS-AR	58,680	233	Racine, WI	5,290	205	Texarkana, TX-AR	6,292
151	Merced, CA	10,091	72	Raleigh, NC	29,032	360	The Villages, FL	1,079
6	Miami (greater), FL	225,857	264	Rapid City, SD	4,371	NA	Toledo, OH**	NA
15	Miami-Dade County, FL M.D.	113,692	157	Reading, PA	9,305	162	Topeka, KS	9,047
287	Michigan City-La Porte, IN	3,755	206	Redding, CA	6,280	172	Trenton, NJ	8,200
361	Midland, MI	941	134	Reno, NV	11,470	NA	Tucson, AZ**	NA
290	Midland, TX	3,705	65	Richmond, VA	31,592	66	Tulsa, OK	31,461
42	Milwaukee, WI	52,377	13	Riverside-San Bernardino, CA	131,275	179	Tuscaloosa, AL	7,699
NA	Minneapolis-St. Paul, MN-WI**	NA	177	Roanoke, VA	8,027	193	Tyler, TX	6,894
294	Missoula, MT	3,616	291	Rochester, MN	3,697	190	Utica-Rome, NY	7,054
100	Mobile, AL	17,807	73	Rochester, NY	28,745	270	Valdosta, GA	4,137
84	Modesto, CA	22,061	131	Rockford, IL	12,039	120	Vallejo-Fairfield, CA	13,227
175	Monroe, LA	8,104	161	Rockingham County, NH M.D.	9,117	304	Victoria, TX	3,207
271	Monroe, MI	4,080	230	Rocky Mount, NC	5,448	196	Vineland-Bridgeton, NJ	6,756
62	Montgomery County, PA M.D.	33,268	280	Rome, GA	3,877	41	Virginia Beach-Norfolk, VA-NC	52,842
103	Montgomery, AL	16,908	35	Sacramento, CA	64,260	110	Visalia-Porterville, CA	15,488
331	Morgantown, WV	2,553	247	Saginaw, MI	4,662	160	Waco, TX	9,131
279	Morristown, TN	3,898	123	Salem, OR	12,771	339	Walla Walla, WA	2,266
239	Mount Vernon-Anacortes, WA	5,008	144	Salinas, CA	10,298	191	Warner Robins, GA	7,035
285	Muncie, IN	3,776	125	Salisbury, MD-DE	12,589	47	Warren-Troy, MI M.D.	46,686
319	Napa, CA	2,863	45	Salt Lake City, UT	48,616	12	Washington (greater) DC-VA-MD-WV	132,959
227	Naples-Marco Island, FL	5,531	17	San Antonio, TX	104,441	16	Washington, DC-VA-MD-WV M.D.	111,587
43	Nashville-Davidson, TN	50,076	32	San Diego, CA	69,624	282	Waterloo-Cedar Falls, IA	3,836
51	Nassau-Suffolk, NY M.D.	43,566	NA	San Francisco (greater), CA**	NA	322	Watertown-Fort Drum, NY	2,773
244	New Bern, NC	4,738	40	San Francisco-Redwood, CA M.D.	54,471	338	Wausau, WI	2,284
79	New Haven-Milford, CT	24,254	44	San Jose, CA	49,015	50	West Palm Beach, FL M.D.	44,233
58	New Orleans, LA	39,672	207	San Luis Obispo, CA	6,252	317	Wheeling, WV-OH	2,896
1	New York (greater), NY-NJ-PA	337,353	NA	San Rafael, CA M.D.**	NA	216	Wichita Falls, TX	5,854
4	New York-Jersey City, NY-NJ M.D.	241,102	166	Santa Cruz-Watsonville, CA	8,709	75	Wichita, KS	26,627
48	Newark, NJ-PA M.D.	46,566	231	Santa Fe, NM	5,445	332	Williamsport, PA	2,530
85	North Port-Sarasota-Bradenton, FL	21,843	149	Santa Maria-Santa Barbara, CA	10,164	80	Wilmington, DE-MD-NJ M.D.	23,436
299	Norwich-New London, CT	3,461	168	Santa Rosa, CA	8,514	152	Wilmington, NC	10,041
NA	Oakland-Hayward, CA M.D.**	NA	136	Savannah, GA	11,256	312	Winchester, VA-WV	3,035
185	Ocala, FL	7,311	122	Scranton--Wilkes-Barre, PA	12,841	78	Winston-Salem, NC	24,896
262	Ocean City, NJ	4,411	NA	Seattle (greater), WA**	NA	98	Worcester, MA-CT	18,019
235	Odessa, TX	5,177	18	Seattle-Bellevue-Everett, WA M.D.	102,194	146	Yakima, WA	10,230
114	Ogden-Clearfield, UT	14,902	284	Sebastian-Vero Beach, FL	3,783	167	York-Hanover, PA	8,659
39	Oklahoma City, OK	56,160	320	Sebring, FL	2,806	101	Youngstown-Warren, OH-PA	17,599
182	Olympia, WA	7,590	335	Sheboygan, WI	2,452	242	Yuba City, CA	4,845
68	Omaha-Council Bluffs, NE-IA	29,742	286	Sherman-Denison, TX	3,760	237	Yuma, AZ	5,128
23	Orlando, FL	76,705	NA	Shreveport-Bossier City, LA**	NA			
301	Oshkosh-Neenah, WI	3,386	293	Sierra Vista-Douglas, AZ	3,619			

Source: Reported data from the F.B.I. "Crime in the United States 2012"

*Property crimes are offenses of burglary, larceny-theft, and motor vehicle theft. Attempts are included.

**Not available.

25. Property Crimes in 2012 (continued)
National Total = 8,975,438 Property Crimes*

RANK	METROPOLITAN AREA	CRIMES	RANK	METROPOLITAN AREA	CRIMES	RANK	METROPOLITAN AREA	CRIMES
1	New York (greater), NY-NJ-PA	337,353	65	Richmond, VA	31,592	129	Fort Wayne, IN	12,116
2	Los Angeles (greater), CA	300,087	66	Tulsa, OK	31,461	130	Fayetteville-Springdale, AR-MO	12,089
3	Chicago (greater), IL-IN-WI	254,619	67	McAllen-Edinburg-Mission, TX	30,517	131	Rockford, IL	12,039
4	New York-Jersey City, NY-NJ M.D.	241,102	68	Omaha-Council Bluffs, NE-IA	29,742	132	Canton, OH	11,957
5	Los Angeles County, CA M.D.	232,266	69	Knoxville, TN	29,675	133	Harrisburg-Carlisle, PA	11,835
6	Miami (greater), FL	225,857	70	Spokane, WA	29,653	134	Reno, NV	11,470
7	Dallas (greater), TX	212,153	71	Stockton-Lodi, CA	29,264	135	Anchorage, AK	11,344
8	Chicago-Joilet-Naperville, IL M.D.	204,797	72	Raleigh, NC	29,032	136	Savannah, GA	11,256
9	Atlanta, GA	183,871	73	Rochester, NY	28,745	137	Macon, GA	11,089
10	Philadelphia (greater) PA-NJ-MD-DE	160,273	74	Dayton, OH	27,287	138	Laredo, TX	11,080
11	Dallas-Plano-Irving, TX M.D.	136,479	75	Wichita, KS	26,627	139	Lincoln, NE	10,938
12	Washington (greater) DC-VA-MD-WV	132,959	76	Greensboro-High Point, NC	26,195	140	Spartanburg, SC	10,591
13	Riverside-San Bernardino, CA	131,275	77	Hartford, CT	25,096	141	Peoria, IL	10,379
14	Detroit (greater), MI	117,088	78	Winston-Salem, NC	24,896	142	Lansing-East Lansing, MI	10,348
15	Miami-Dade County, FL M.D.	113,692	79	New Haven-Milford, CT	24,254	143	Elgin, IL M.D.	10,322
16	Washington, DC-VA-MD-WV M.D.	111,587	80	Wilmington, DE-MD-NJ M.D.	23,436	144	Salinas, CA	10,298
17	San Antonio, TX	104,441	81	Augusta, GA-SC	23,040	145	Lancaster, PA	10,294
18	Seattle-Bellevue-Everett, WA M.D.	102,194	82	Charleston-North Charleston, SC	22,508	146	Yakima, WA	10,230
19	Boston (greater), MA-NH	91,833	83	Gary, IN M.D.	22,426	147	Provo-Orem, UT	10,18¹
20	Baltimore, MD	82,232	84	Modesto, CA	22,061	148	Port St. Lucie, FL	10,170
21	Tampa-St Petersburg, FL	81,969	85	North Port-Sarasota-Bradenton, FL	21,843	149	Santa Maria-Santa Barbara, CA	10,164
22	St. Louis, MO-IL	80,634	86	Albany-Schenectady-Troy, NY	21,586	150	South Bend-Mishawaka, IN-MI	10,147
23	Orlando, FL	76,705	87	Silver Spring-Frederick, MD M.D.	21,372	151	Merced, CA	10,091
24	Fort Worth-Arlington, TX M.D.	75,674	88	Akron, OH	21,287	152	Wilmington, NC	10,041
25	Denver-Aurora, CO	72,387	89	Springfield, MO	20,386	153	Florence, SC	9,880
26	Portland-Vancouver, OR-WA	72,141	90	Fayetteville, NC	20,252	154	Davenport, IA-IL	9,879
27	Philadelphia, PA M.D.	71,230	91	Lexington-Fayette, KY	19,682	155	Amarillo, TX	9,716
28	Kansas City, MO-KS	70,667	92	El Paso, TX	19,361	156	Kingsport, TN-VA	9,310
29	Cincinnati, OH-KY-IN	70,483	93	Deltona-Daytona Beach, FL	19,223	157	Reading, PA	9,305
30	Detroit-Dearborn-Livonia, MI M.D.	70,402	94	Jackson, MS	19,112	158	Manchester-Nashua, NH	9,274
31	Indianapolis, IN	70,358	95	Lakeland, FL	19,088	159	Kalamazoo-Portage, MI	9,239
32	San Diego, CA	69,624	96	Springfield, MA	18,949	160	Waco, TX	9,131
33	Fort Lauderdale, FL M.D.	67,932	97	Allentown, PA-NJ	18,304	161	Rockingham County, NH M.D.	9,117
34	Anaheim-Santa Ana-Irvine, CA M.D.	67,821	98	Worcester, MA-CT	18,019	162	Topeka, KS	9,047
35	Sacramento, CA	64,260	99	Durham-Chapel Hill, NC	17,821	163	Gainesville, FL	8,852
36	Austin-Round Rock, TX	62,113	100	Mobile, AL	17,807	164	Duluth, MN-WI	8,836
37	Las Vegas-Henderson, NV	59,193	101	Youngstown-Warren, OH-PA	17,599	165	Springfield, IL	8,793
38	Memphis, TN-MS-AR	58,680	102	Lake Co.-Kenosha Co., IL-WI M.D.	17,074	166	Santa Cruz-Watsonville, CA	8,709
39	Oklahoma City, OK	56,160	103	Montgomery, AL	16,908	167	York-Hanover, PA	8,659
40	San Francisco-Redwood, CA M.D.	54,471	104	Syracuse, NY	16,784	168	Santa Rosa, CA	8,5¹
41	Virginia Beach-Norfolk, VA-NC	52,842	105	Brownsville-Harlingen, TX	16,754	169	Ann Arbor, MI	8,4...
42	Milwaukee, WI	52,377	106	Pensacola, FL	16,745	170	Fort Smith, AR-OK	8,475
43	Nashville-Davidson, TN	50,076	107	Palm Bay-Melbourne, FL	16,659	171	Atlantic City, NJ	8,404
44	San Jose, CA	49,015	108	Bridgeport-Stamford, CT	16,256	172	Trenton, NJ	8,200
45	Salt Lake City, UT	48,616	109	Oxnard-Thousand Oaks, CA	15,921	173	Bremerton-Silverdale, WA	8,127
46	Jacksonville, FL	47,687	110	Visalia-Porterville, CA	15,488	174	Pueblo, CO	8,114
47	Warren-Troy, MI M.D.	46,686	111	Flint, MI	15,376	175	Monroe, LA	8,104
48	Newark, NJ-PA M.D.	46,566	112	Cape Coral-Fort Myers, FL	15,021	176	Longview, TX	8,032
49	Pittsburgh, PA	44,920	113	Madison, WI	14,919	177	Roanoke, VA	8,027
50	West Palm Beach, FL M.D.	44,233	114	Ogden-Clearfield, UT	14,902	178	Medford, OR	7,776
51	Nassau-Suffolk, NY M.D.	43,566	115	Columbus, GA-AL	14,541	179	Tuscaloosa, AL	7,699
52	Louisville, KY-IN	43,390	116	Huntsville, AL	14,292	180	Panama City, FL	7,658
53	Birmingham-Hoover, AL	43,172	117	Lubbock, TX	13,582	181	Fort Collins, CO	7,605
54	Fresno, CA	42,099	118	Eugene, OR	13,538	182	Olympia, WA	7,590
55	Boston, MA M.D.	41,866	119	Beaumont-Port Arthur, TX	13,352	183	Joplin, MO	7,545
56	Cambridge-Newton, MA M.D.	40,850	120	Vallejo-Fairfield, CA	13,227	184	Erie, PA	7,345
57	Providence-Warwick, RI-MA	40,028	121	Tallahassee, FL	13,050	185	Ocala, FL	7,311
58	New Orleans, LA	39,672	122	Scranton--Wilkes-Barre, PA	12,841	186	Albany, GA	7,276
59	Little Rock, AR	36,701	123	Salem, OR	12,771	187	Hammond, LA	7,127
60	Bakersfield, CA	34,761	124	Portland, ME	12,713	188	Boulder, CO	7,107
61	Buffalo-Niagara Falls, NY	33,364	125	Salisbury, MD-DE	12,589	189	Lake Havasu City-Kingman, AZ	7,073
62	Montgomery County, PA M.D.	33,268	126	Boise City, ID	12,461	190	Utica-Rome, NY	7,054
63	Greenville-Anderson, SC	33,066	127	Hickory, NC	12,204	191	Warner Robins, GA	7,035
64	Camden, NJ M.D.	32,339	128	Asheville, NC	12,143	192	Clarksville, TN-KY	6,966

Note: All listings are for Metropolitan Statistical Areas (M.S.A.s) except for those ending with "M.D." Listings with "M.D." are Metropolitan Divisions which are smaller parts of eleven large M.S.A.s. See explanatory note at beginning of metropolitan area section.

RANK	METROPOLITAN AREA	CRIMES
193	Tyler, TX	6,894
194	Houma, LA	6,855
195	Binghamton, NY	6,851
196	Vineland-Bridgeton, NJ	6,756
197	Athens-Clarke County, GA	6,650
198	Las Cruces, NM	6,511
199	El Centro, CA	6,471
200	Crestview-Fort Walton Beach, FL	6,453
201	Terre Haute, IN	6,420
202	Kennewick-Richland, WA	6,400
203	Bellingham, WA	6,318
204	College Station-Bryan, TX	6,304
205	Texarkana, TX-AR	6,292
206	Redding, CA	6,280
207	San Luis Obispo, CA	6,252
208	Dover, DE	6,172
209	Champaign-Urbana, IL	6,155
210	Dutchess-Putnam, NY M.D.	6,119
211	Greenville, NC	6,030
212	Kahului-Wailuku-Lahaina, HI	6,003
213	Johnson City, TN	6,000
214	Hagerstown-Martinsburg, MD-WV	5,890
215	Green Bay, WI	5,857
216	Wichita Falls, TX	5,854
217	Barnstable Town, MA	5,835
218	Mansfield, OH	5,832
219	Hilton Head Island, SC	5,826
220	Sioux Falls, SD	5,816
221	Billings, MT	5,755
222	Greeley, CO	5,734
223	Lawton, OK	5,675
224	Chico, CA	5,659
225	Springfield, OH	5,643
226	Columbia, MO	5,544
227	Naples-Marco Island, FL	5,531
228	Lafayette, IN	5,522
229	St. Joseph, MO-KS	5,473
230	Rocky Mount, NC	5,448
231	Santa Fe, NM	5,445
232	Anniston-Oxford, AL	5,339
233	Racine, WI	5,290
234	Burlington, NC	5,218
235	Odessa, TX	5,177
236	Bloomington, IN	5,142
237	Yuma, AZ	5,128
238	Abilene, TX	5,080
239	Mount Vernon-Anacortes, WA	5,008
240	Daphne-Fairhope-Foley, AL	4,988
241	Goldsboro, NC	4,930
242	Yuba City, CA	4,845
243	Janesville, WI	4,771
244	New Bern, NC	4,738
245	Fargo, ND-MN	4,729
246	Brunswick, GA	4,713
247	Saginaw, MI	4,662
248	Sumter, SC	4,645
249	Bangor, ME	4,623
250	Jackson, TN	4,594
251	Lynchburg, VA	4,591
252	Dothan, AL	4,589
253	Sioux City, IA-NE-SD	4,569
254	Lawrence, KS	4,548
255	Beckley, WV	4,533
256	Coeur d'Alene, ID	4,522
257	Decatur, AL	4,518
258	Gadsden, AL	4,504
259	East Stroudsburg, PA	4,486
260	Florence-Muscle Shoals, AL	4,454
261	Prescott, AZ	4,442
262	Ocean City, NJ	4,411
263	Charlottesville, VA	4,380
264	Rapid City, SD	4,371
265	Gainesville, GA	4,323
266	Grand Junction, CO	4,309
266	Jonesboro, AR	4,309
268	Flagstaff, AZ	4,268
269	Pine Bluff, AR	4,218
270	Valdosta, GA	4,137
271	Monroe, MI	4,080
272	Bloomington, IL	4,052
273	Auburn, AL	4,023
274	Madera, CA	4,017
275	Bowling Green, KY	4,003
276	Dalton, GA	3,990
277	Blacksburg, VA	3,914
278	Hattiesburg, MS	3,905
279	Morristown, TN	3,898
280	Rome, GA	3,877
281	Lima, OH	3,843
282	Waterloo-Cedar Falls, IA	3,836
283	Longview, WA	3,785
284	Sebastian-Vero Beach, FL	3,783
285	Muncie, IN	3,776
286	Sherman-Denison, TX	3,760
287	Michigan City-La Porte, IN	3,755
288	Albany, OR	3,739
289	Cape Girardeau, MO-IL	3,721
290	Midland, TX	3,705
291	Rochester, MN	3,697
292	Kingston, NY	3,671
293	Sierra Vista-Douglas, AZ	3,619
294	Missoula, MT	3,616
295	Jefferson City, MO	3,577
296	Cleveland, TN	3,567
297	Appleton, WI	3,519
298	Punta Gorda, FL	3,507
299	Norwich-New London, CT	3,461
300	Hanford-Corcoran, CA	3,440
301	Oshkosh-Neenah, WI	3,386
302	Lewiston-Auburn, ME	3,271
303	La Crosse, WI-MN	3,266
304	Victoria, TX	3,207
305	Farmington, NM	3,175
306	Kankakee, IL	3,155
307	Owensboro, KY	3,139
308	Great Falls, MT	3,115
309	Iowa City, IA	3,058
310	Danville, IL	3,057
311	Pittsfield, MA	3,049
312	Winchester, VA-WV	3,035
313	Cumberland, MD-WV	2,979
314	Decatur, IL	2,963
315	Homosassa Springs, FL	2,954
316	Bismarck, ND	2,897
317	Wheeling, WV-OH	2,896
318	Grand Island, NE	2,891
319	Napa, CA	2,863
320	Sebring, FL	2,806
321	California-Lexington Park, MD	2,778
322	St. George, UT	2,773
322	Watertown-Fort Drum, NY	2,773
324	Columbus, IN	2,767
325	Mankato-North Mankato, MN	2,733
326	Cheyenne, WY	2,716
327	Parkersburg-Vienna, WV	2,701
328	Johnstown, PA	2,572
329	Lebanon, PA	2,570
330	Idaho Falls, ID	2,559
331	Morgantown, WV	2,553
332	Williamsport, PA	2,530
333	Chambersburg-Waynesboro, PA	2,508
334	Hinesville, GA	2,457
335	Sheboygan, WI	2,452
336	Kokomo, IN	2,363
337	Casper, WY	2,346
338	Wausau, WI	2,284
339	Walla Walla, WA	2,266
340	Grand Forks, ND-MN	2,232
341	Elmira, NY	2,212
342	State College, PA	2,199
343	Glens Falls, NY	2,178
344	Elizabethtown-Fort Knox, KY	2,160
345	Pocatello, ID	2,155
346	Lewiston, ID-WA	2,135
347	Staunton-Waynesboro, VA	2,119
348	Altoona, PA	2,113
349	Bay City, MI	2,090
350	Logan, UT-ID	2,034
351	Ames, IA	2,031
352	Manhattan, KS	1,876
353	Corvallis, OR	1,841
354	Bloomsburg-Berwick, PA	1,800
355	Harrisonburg, VA	1,799
356	Fond du Lac, WI	1,784
357	Fairbanks, AK	1,549
358	Gettysburg, PA	1,211
359	Carson City, NV	1,107
360	The Villages, FL	1,079
361	Midland, MI	941
NA	Albuquerque, NM**	NA
NA	Alexandria, LA**	NA
NA	Baton Rouge, LA**	NA
NA	Cedar Rapids, IA**	NA
NA	Colorado Springs, CO**	NA
NA	Corpus Christi, TX**	NA
NA	Des Moines-West Des Moines, IA**	NA
NA	Dubuque, IA**	NA
NA	Houston, TX**	NA
NA	Killeen-Temple, TX**	NA
NA	Lafayette, LA**	NA
NA	Minneapolis-St. Paul, MN-WI**	NA
NA	Oakland-Hayward, CA M.D.**	NA
NA	Phoenix-Mesa-Scottsdale, AZ**	NA
NA	San Francisco (greater), CA**	NA
NA	San Rafael, CA M.D.**	NA
NA	Seattle (greater), WA**	NA
NA	Shreveport-Bossier City, LA**	NA
NA	Tacoma, WA M.D.**	NA
NA	Toledo, OH**	NA
NA	Tucson, AZ**	NA

Source: Reported data from the F.B.I. "Crime in the United States 2012"
*Property crimes are offenses of burglary, larceny-theft, and motor vehicle theft. Attempts are included.
**Not available.

26. Property Crime Rate in 2012
National Rate = 2,859.2 Property Crimes per 100,000 Population*

RANK	METROPOLITAN AREA	RATE	RANK	METROPOLITAN AREA	RATE	RANK	METROPOLITAN AREA	RATE
175	Abilene, TX	3,007.6	192	Cheyenne, WY	2,888.6	149	Gary, IN M.D.	3,154.6
167	Akron, OH	3,034.9	222	Chicago (greater), IL-IN-WI	2,677.0	359	Gettysburg, PA	1,192.0
252	Albany-Schenectady-Troy, NY	2,463.6	202	Chicago-Joilet-Naperville, IL M.D.	2,805.1	347	Glens Falls, NY	1,679.4
12	Albany, GA	4,565.5	241	Chico, CA	2,545.6	49	Goldsboro, NC	3,946.4
151	Albany, OR	3,143.0	124	Cincinnati, OH-KY-IN	3,318.9	287	Grand Forks, ND-MN	2,236.8
NA	Albuquerque, NM**	NA	231	Clarksville, TN-KY	2,616.9	101	Grand Island, NE	3,474.9
NA	Alexandria, LA**	NA	169	Cleveland, TN	3,028.0	191	Grand Junction, CO	2,889.7
291	Allentown, PA-NJ	2,214.3	142	Coeur d'Alene, ID	3,182.5	63	Great Falls, MT	3,780.1
350	Altoona, PA	1,659.8	219	College Station-Bryan, TX	2,681.5	295	Greeley, CO	2,186.7
69	Amarillo, TX	3,740.8	NA	Colorado Springs, CO**	NA	329	Green Bay, WI	1,887.8
285	Ames, IA	2,256.4	118	Columbia, MO	3,341.0	85	Greensboro-High Point, NC	3,548.5
292	Anaheim-Santa Ana-Irvine, CA M.D.	2,199.1	6	Columbus, GA-AL	4,778.6	51	Greenville-Anderson, SC	3,918.5
83	Anchorage, AK	3,618.2	88	Columbus, IN	3,542.3	96	Greenville, NC	3,489.0
256	Ann Arbor, MI	2,437.3	NA	Corpus Christi, TX**	NA	278	Hagerstown-Martinsburg, MD-WV	2,306.3
16	Anniston-Oxford, AL	4,514.2	304	Corvallis, OR	2,127.4	1	Hammond, LA	5,780.4
353	Appleton, WI	1,543.5	226	Crestview-Fort Walton Beach, FL	2,660.6	290	Hanford-Corcoran, CA	2,216.6
203	Asheville, NC	2,802.7	196	Cumberland, MD-WV	2,875.3	303	Harrisburg-Carlisle, PA	2,137.0
109	Athens-Clarke County, GA	3,403.6	144	Dallas (greater), TX	3,175.9	358	Harrisonburg, VA	1,405.9
111	Atlanta, GA	3,383.4	158	Dallas-Plano-Irving, TX M.D.	3,097.9	255	Hartford, CT	2,451.1
162	Atlantic City, NJ	3,048.4	207	Dalton, GA	2,765.8	221	Hattiesburg, MS	2,679.4
205	Auburn, AL	2,792.9	68	Danville, IL	3,748.8	125	Hickory, NC	3,314.7
46	Augusta, GA-SC	4,002.9	225	Daphne-Fairhope-Foley, AL	2,660.7	165	Hilton Head Island, SC	3,039.4
107	Austin-Round Rock, TX	3,431.2	235	Davenport, IA-IL	2,585.5	173	Hinesville, GA	3,016.7
44	Bakersfield, CA	4,043.8	110	Dayton, OH	3,397.1	308	Homosassa Springs, FL	2,081.1
179	Baltimore, MD	2,984.3	189	Decatur, AL	2,920.7	133	Houma, LA	3,267.1
176	Bangor, ME	3,003.9	223	Decatur, IL	2,674.6	NA	Houston, TX**	NA
220	Barnstable Town, MA	2,680.4	139	Deltona-Daytona Beach, FL	3,202.4	116	Huntsville, AL	3,345.6
NA	Baton Rouge, LA**	NA	208	Denver-Aurora, CO	2,746.6	330	Idaho Falls, ID	1,884.3
323	Bay City, MI	1,949.8	NA	Des Moines-West Des Moines, IA**	NA	73	Indianapolis, IN	3,672.5
137	Beaumont-Port Arthur, TX	3,248.2	210	Detroit (greater), MI	2,730.0	318	Iowa City, IA	1,966.6
80	Beckley, WV	3,631.4	52	Detroit-Dearborn-Livonia, MI M.D.	3,903.8	102	Jacksonville, FL	3,458.6
160	Bellingham, WA	3,072.1	156	Dothan, AL	3,118.6	121	Jackson, MS	3,326.6
84	Billings, MT	3,550.7	72	Dover, DE	3,703.7	91	Jackson, TN	3,506.3
211	Binghamton, NY	2,724.9	NA	Dubuque, IA**	NA	182	Janesville, WI	2,972.5
60	Birmingham-Hoover, AL	3,797.7	152	Duluth, MN-WI	3,139.6	264	Jefferson City, MO	2,372.6
261	Bismarck, ND	2,420.8	106	Durham-Chapel Hill, NC	3,439.9	180	Johnson City, TN	2,978.1
297	Blacksburg, VA	2,176.5	354	Dutchess-Putnam, NY M.D.	1,529.4	334	Johnstown, PA	1,786.6
300	Bloomington, IL	2,164.3	229	East Stroudsburg, PA	2,636.4	94	Jonesboro, AR	3,494.9
143	Bloomington, IN	3,177.9	82	El Centro, CA	3,621.2	30	Joplin, MO	4,258.3
307	Bloomsburg-Berwick, PA	2,095.2	276	El Paso, TX	2,314.4	62	Kahului-Wailuku-Lahaina, HI	3,781.2
315	Boise City, ID	1,971.9	351	Elgin, IL M.D.	1,650.7	200	Kalamazoo-Portage, MI	2,813.0
313	Boston (greater), MA-NH	1,983.9	356	Elizabethtown-Fort Knox, KY	1,423.7	206	Kankakee, IL	2,773.6
296	Boston, MA M.D.	2,179.5	248	Elmira, NY	2,476.5	99	Kansas City, MO-KS	3,475.6
270	Boulder, CO	2,341.5	232	Erie, PA	2,609.8	263	Kennewick-Richland, WA	2,399.5
247	Bowling Green, KY	2,486.6	59	Eugene, OR	3,803.6	NA	Killeen-Temple, TX**	NA
148	Bremerton-Silverdale, WA	3,160.7	17	Fairbanks, AK	4,476.5	180	Kingsport, TN-VA	2,978.1
337	Bridgeport-Stamford, CT	1,785.0	294	Fargo, ND-MN	2,188.8	312	Kingston, NY	2,001.3
48	Brownsville-Harlingen, TX	3,986.0	250	Farmington, NM	2,472.7	95	Knoxville, TN	3,489.4
39	Brunswick, GA	4,129.6	242	Fayetteville-Springdale, AR-MO	2,541.9	199	Kokomo, IN	2,845.0
186	Buffalo-Niagara Falls, NY	2,926.3	3	Fayetteville, NC	5,359.6	260	La Crosse, WI-MN	2,421.0
112	Burlington, NC	3,370.6	153	Flagstaff, AZ	3,138.7	213	Lafayette, IN	2,703.6
239	California-Lexington Park, MD	2,559.8	79	Flint, MI	3,640.3	NA	Lafayette, LA**	NA
336	Cambridge-Newton, MA M.D.	1,786.0	174	Florence-Muscle Shoals, AL	3,011.8	322	Lake Co.-Kenosha Co., IL-WI M.D.	1,952.9
237	Camden, NJ M.D.	2,570.5	7	Florence, SC	4,747.2	103	Lake Havasu City-Kingman, AZ	3,457.7
184	Canton, OH	2,960.8	341	Fond du Lac, WI	1,743.2	159	Lakeland, FL	3,089.6
268	Cape Coral-Fort Myers, FL	2,347.2	254	Fort Collins, CO	2,455.2	320	Lancaster, PA	1,962.8
57	Cape Girardeau, MO-IL	3,828.4	66	Fort Lauderdale, FL M.D.	3,764.7	288	Lansing-East Lansing, MI	2,223.1
316	Carson City, NV	1,971.0	178	Fort Smith, AR-OK	2,991.2	31	Laredo, TX	4,256.0
168	Casper, WY	3,028.1	194	Fort Wayne, IN	2,879.5	163	Las Cruces, NM	3,043.4
NA	Cedar Rapids, IA**	NA	120	Fort Worth-Arlington, TX M.D.	3,327.1	183	Las Vegas-Henderson, NV	2,966.0
349	Chambersburg-Waynesboro, PA	1,660.3	19	Fresno, CA	4,423.8	45	Lawrence, KS	4,032.5
227	Champaign-Urbana, IL	2,647.9	24	Gadsden, AL	4,300.9	29	Lawton, OK	4,273.2
131	Charleston-North Charleston, SC	3,268.6	129	Gainesville, FL	3,278.5	326	Lebanon, PA	1,910.4
321	Charlottesville, VA	1,958.9	273	Gainesville, GA	2,336.7	163	Lewiston-Auburn, ME	3,043.4

Note: All listings are for Metropolitan Statistical Areas (M.S.A.s) except for those ending with "M.D." Listings with "M.D." are Metropolitan Divisions which are smaller parts of eleven large M.S.A.s. See explanatory note at beginning of metropolitan area section.

RANK	METROPOLITAN AREA	RATE	RANK	METROPOLITAN AREA	RATE	RANK	METROPOLITAN AREA	RATE
105	Lewiston, ID-WA	3,445.8	212	Owensboro, KY	2,714.8	343	Silver Spring-Frederick, MD M.D.	1,725.8
42	Lexington-Fayette, KY	4,096.5	328	Oxnard-Thousand Oaks, CA	1,896.5	215	Sioux City, IA-NE-SD	2,690.7
81	Lima, OH	3,622.5	170	Palm Bay-Melbourne, FL	3,023.5	249	Sioux Falls, SD	2,474.4
87	Lincoln, NE	3,543.9	43	Panama City, FL	4,068.3	145	South Bend-Mishawaka, IN-MI	3,175.3
4	Little Rock, AR	5,150.4	190	Parkersburg-Vienna, WV	2,907.9	122	Spartanburg, SC	3,324.8
352	Logan, UT-ID	1,574.5	77	Pensacola, FL	3,645.0	2	Spokane, WA	5,538.5
76	Longview, TX	3,652.4	209	Peoria, IL	2,733.2	38	Springfield, IL	4,154.6
75	Longview, WA	3,657.6	224	Philadelphia (greater) PA-NJ-MD-DE	2,665.7	171	Springfield, MA	3,021.5
274	Los Angeles County, CA M.D.	2,327.1	123	Philadelphia, PA M.D.	3,320.8	11	Springfield, MO	4,623.0
280	Los Angeles (greater), CA	2,296.9	NA	Phoenix-Mesa-Scottsdale, AZ**	NA	41	Springfield, OH	4,098.6
100	Louisville, KY-IN	3,475.0	32	Pine Bluff, AR	4,247.8	357	State College, PA	1,419.0
15	Lubbock, TX	4,522.5	327	Pittsburgh, PA	1,900.5	338	Staunton-Waynesboro, VA	1,766.8
334	Lynchburg, VA	1,786.6	275	Pittsfield, MA	2,316.5	36	Stockton-Lodi, CA	4,164.7
9	Macon, GA	4,710.6	240	Pocatello, ID	2,557.6	324	St. George, UT	1,931.3
234	Madera, CA	2,602.6	269	Port St. Lucie, FL	2,344.9	27	St. Joseph, MO-KS	4,281.1
258	Madison, WI	2,426.1	146	Portland-Vancouver, OR-WA	3,164.3	193	St. Louis, MO-IL	2,881.8
279	Manchester-Nashua, NH	2,304.3	253	Portland, ME	2,462.8	26	Sumter, SC	4,281.8
319	Manhattan, KS	1,966.4	309	Prescott, AZ	2,073.8	244	Syracuse, NY	2,519.6
204	Mankato-North Mankato, MN	2,793.7	246	Providence-Warwick, RI-MA	2,495.4	NA	Tacoma, WA M.D.**	NA
8	Mansfield, OH	4,722.2	333	Provo-Orem, UT	1,858.8	98	Tallahassee, FL	3,481.8
65	McAllen-Edinburg-Mission, TX	3,768.7	5	Pueblo, CO	4,985.1	198	Tampa-St Petersburg, FL	2,862.8
64	Medford, OR	3,769.7	302	Punta Gorda, FL	2,155.5	71	Terre Haute, IN	3,706.6
21	Memphis, TN-MS-AR	4,367.3	214	Racine, WI	2,700.5	37	Texarkana, TX-AR	4,162.7
53	Merced, CA	3,847.0	251	Raleigh, NC	2,470.7	361	The Villages, FL	1,088.9
50	Miami (greater), FL	3,929.7	147	Rapid City, SD	3,162.0	NA	Toledo, OH**	NA
20	Miami-Dade County, FL M.D.	4,390.3	286	Reading, PA	2,250.6	55	Topeka, KS	3,836.0
115	Michigan City-La Porte, IN	3,361.0	93	Redding, CA	3,500.1	289	Trenton, NJ	2,223.0
360	Midland, MI	1,118.6	230	Reno, NV	2,635.4	NA	Tucson, AZ**	NA
245	Midland, TX	2,513.3	238	Richmond, VA	2,563.3	127	Tulsa, OK	3,302.0
117	Milwaukee, WI	3,344.2	172	Riverside-San Bernardino, CA	3,021.3	126	Tuscaloosa, AL	3,305.5
NA	Minneapolis-St. Paul, MN-WI**	NA	236	Roanoke, VA	2,570.6	141	Tyler, TX	3,183.2
135	Missoula, MT	3,260.5	339	Rochester, MN	1,761.9	267	Utica-Rome, NY	2,350.9
25	Mobile, AL	4,298.8	228	Rochester, NY	2,645.5	195	Valdosta, GA	2,876.4
33	Modesto, CA	4,215.5	104	Rockford, IL	3,454.3	150	Vallejo-Fairfield, CA	3,146.8
14	Monroe, LA	4,534.9	299	Rockingham County, NH M.D.	2,166.2	119	Victoria, TX	3,333.4
216	Monroe, MI	2,690.1	86	Rocky Mount, NC	3,545.4	28	Vineland-Bridgeton, NJ	4,279.5
340	Montgomery County, PA M.D.	1,757.9	47	Rome, GA	3,996.4	157	Virginia Beach-Norfolk, VA-NC	3,101.9
18	Montgomery, AL	4,448.0	187	Sacramento, CA	2,925.7	108	Visalia-Porterville, CA	3,415.8
325	Morgantown, WV	1,930.4	271	Saginaw, MI	2,340.0	90	Waco, TX	3,507.2
113	Morristown, TN	3,369.8	138	Salem, OR	3,211.5	89	Walla Walla, WA	3,526.2
34	Mount Vernon-Anacortes, WA	4,199.0	262	Salinas, CA	2,418.4	61	Warner Robins, GA	3,793.7
140	Muncie, IN	3,199.2	128	Salisbury, MD-DE	3,301.8	331	Warren-Troy, MI M.D.	1,878.3
310	Napa, CA	2,054.3	23	Salt Lake City, UT	4,328.0	281	Washington (greater) DC-VA-MD-WV	2,282.1
348	Naples-Marco Island, FL	1,662.9	10	San Antonio, TX	4,688.1	257	Washington, DC-VA-MD-WV M.D.	2,432.3
188	Nashville-Davidson, TN	2,923.8	293	San Diego, CA	2,196.9	284	Waterloo-Cedar Falls, IA	2,270.6
355	Nassau-Suffolk, NY M.D.	1,524.0	NA	San Francisco (greater), CA**	NA	272	Watertown-Fort Drum, NY	2,339.2
74	New Bern, NC	3,665.2	92	San Francisco-Redwood, CA M.D.	3,504.5	346	Wausau, WI	1,695.1
177	New Haven-Milford, CT	2,995.2	233	San Jose, CA	2,603.4	132	West Palm Beach, FL M.D.	3,268.3
136	New Orleans, LA	3,251.7	282	San Luis Obispo, CA	2,277.7	317	Wheeling, WV-OH	1,967.5
345	New York (greater), NY-NJ-PA	1,704.5	NA	San Rafael, CA M.D.**	NA	54	Wichita Falls, TX	3,838.4
344	New York-Jersey City, NY-NJ M.D.	1,716.9	134	Santa Cruz-Watsonville, CA	3,264.9	35	Wichita, KS	4,182.6
332	Newark, NJ-PA M.D.	1,870.2	70	Santa Fe, NM	3,732.5	301	Williamsport, PA	2,163.6
166	North Port-Sarasota-Bradenton, FL	3,037.8	266	Santa Maria-Santa Barbara, CA	2,359.1	130	Wilmington, DE-MD-NJ M.D.	3,269.4
265	Norwich-New London, CT	2,364.2	342	Santa Rosa, CA	1,728.2	56	Wilmington, NC	3,830.1
NA	Oakland-Hayward, CA M.D.**	NA	154	Savannah, GA	3,132.1	277	Winchester, VA-WV	2,312.6
298	Ocala, FL	2,169.0	283	Scranton--Wilkes-Barre, PA	2,276.2	58	Winston-Salem, NC	3,823.6
13	Ocean City, NJ	4,543.8	NA	Seattle (greater), WA**	NA	306	Worcester, MA-CT	2,117.0
78	Odessa, TX	3,640.4	67	Seattle-Bellevue-Everett, WA M.D.	3,759.2	40	Yakima, WA	4,099.1
259	Ogden-Clearfield, UT	2,425.5	217	Sebastian-Vero Beach, FL	2,687.0	314	York-Hanover, PA	1,979.3
21	Oklahoma City, OK	4,367.3	201	Sebring, FL	2,806.7	155	Youngstown-Warren, OH-PA	3,126.5
185	Olympia, WA	2,929.3	305	Sheboygan, WI	2,124.0	197	Yuba City, CA	2,866.0
114	Omaha-Council Bluffs, NE-IA	3,368.8	161	Sherman-Denison, TX	3,051.0	243	Yuma, AZ	2,525.3
97	Orlando, FL	3,485.0	NA	Shreveport-Bossier City, LA**	NA			
311	Oshkosh-Neenah, WI	2,013.9	218	Sierra Vista-Douglas, AZ	2,685.8			

Source: Reported data from the F.B.I. "Crime in the United States 2012"

*Property crimes are offenses of burglary, larceny-theft, and motor vehicle theft. Attempts are included.

**Not available.

26. Property Crime Rate in 2012 (continued)
National Rate = 2,859.2 Property Crimes per 100,000 Population*

RANK	METROPOLITAN AREA	RATE	RANK	METROPOLITAN AREA	RATE	RANK	METROPOLITAN AREA	RATE
1	Hammond, LA	5,780.4	65	McAllen-Edinburg-Mission, TX	3,768.7	129	Gainesville, FL	3,278.5
2	Spokane, WA	5,538.5	66	Fort Lauderdale, FL M.D.	3,764.7	130	Wilmington, DE-MD-NJ M.D.	3,269.4
3	Fayetteville, NC	5,359.6	67	Seattle-Bellevue-Everett, WA M.D.	3,759.2	131	Charleston-North Charleston, SC	3,268.6
4	Little Rock, AR	5,150.4	68	Danville, IL	3,748.8	132	West Palm Beach, FL M.D.	3,268.3
5	Pueblo, CO	4,985.1	69	Amarillo, TX	3,740.8	133	Houma, LA	3,267.1
6	Columbus, GA-AL	4,778.6	70	Santa Fe, NM	3,732.5	134	Santa Cruz-Watsonville, CA	3,264.9
7	Florence, SC	4,747.2	71	Terre Haute, IN	3,706.6	135	Missoula, MT	3,260.5
8	Mansfield, OH	4,722.2	72	Dover, DE	3,703.7	136	New Orleans, LA	3,251.7
9	Macon, GA	4,710.6	73	Indianapolis, IN	3,672.5	137	Beaumont-Port Arthur, TX	3,248.2
10	San Antonio, TX	4,688.1	74	New Bern, NC	3,665.2	138	Salem, OR	3,211.5
11	Springfield, MO	4,623.0	75	Longview, WA	3,657.6	139	Deltona-Daytona Beach, FL	3,202.4
12	Albany, GA	4,565.5	76	Longview, TX	3,652.4	140	Muncie, IN	3,199.2
13	Ocean City, NJ	4,543.8	77	Pensacola, FL	3,645.0	141	Tyler, TX	3,183.2
14	Monroe, LA	4,534.9	78	Odessa, TX	3,640.4	142	Coeur d'Alene, ID	3,182.5
15	Lubbock, TX	4,522.5	79	Flint, MI	3,640.3	143	Bloomington, IN	3,177.9
16	Anniston-Oxford, AL	4,514.2	80	Beckley, WV	3,631.4	144	Dallas (greater), TX	3,175.9
17	Fairbanks, AK	4,476.5	81	Lima, OH	3,622.5	145	South Bend-Mishawaka, IN-MI	3,175.3
18	Montgomery, AL	4,448.0	82	El Centro, CA	3,621.2	146	Portland-Vancouver, OR-WA	3,164.3
19	Fresno, CA	4,423.8	83	Anchorage, AK	3,618.2	147	Rapid City, SD	3,162.0
20	Miami-Dade County, FL M.D.	4,390.3	84	Billings, MT	3,550.7	148	Bremerton-Silverdale, WA	3,160.7
21	Memphis, TN-MS-AR	4,367.3	85	Greensboro-High Point, NC	3,548.5	149	Gary, IN M.D.	3,154.6
21	Oklahoma City, OK	4,367.3	86	Rocky Mount, NC	3,545.4	150	Vallejo-Fairfield, CA	3,146.8
23	Salt Lake City, UT	4,328.0	87	Lincoln, NE	3,543.9	151	Albany, OR	3,143.0
24	Gadsden, AL	4,300.9	88	Columbus, IN	3,542.3	152	Duluth, MN-WI	3,139.6
25	Mobile, AL	4,298.8	89	Walla Walla, WA	3,526.2	153	Flagstaff, AZ	3,138.7
26	Sumter, SC	4,281.8	90	Waco, TX	3,507.2	154	Savannah, GA	3,132.1
27	St. Joseph, MO-KS	4,281.1	91	Jackson, TN	3,506.3	155	Youngstown-Warren, OH-PA	3,126.5
28	Vineland-Bridgeton, NJ	4,279.5	92	San Francisco-Redwood, CA M.D.	3,504.5	156	Dothan, AL	3,118.6
29	Lawton, OK	4,273.2	93	Redding, CA	3,500.1	157	Virginia Beach-Norfolk, VA-NC	3,101.9
30	Joplin, MO	4,258.3	94	Jonesboro, AR	3,494.9	158	Dallas-Plano-Irving, TX M.D.	3,097.9
31	Laredo, TX	4,256.0	95	Knoxville, TN	3,489.4	159	Lakeland, FL	3,089.6
32	Pine Bluff, AR	4,247.8	96	Greenville, NC	3,489.0	160	Bellingham, WA	3,072.1
33	Modesto, CA	4,215.5	97	Orlando, FL	3,485.0	161	Sherman-Denison, TX	3,051.0
34	Mount Vernon-Anacortes, WA	4,199.0	98	Tallahassee, FL	3,481.8	162	Atlantic City, NJ	3,048.4
35	Wichita, KS	4,182.6	99	Kansas City, MO-KS	3,475.6	163	Las Cruces, NM	3,043.4
36	Stockton-Lodi, CA	4,164.7	100	Louisville, KY-IN	3,475.0	163	Lewiston-Auburn, ME	3,043.4
37	Texarkana, TX-AR	4,162.7	101	Grand Island, NE	3,474.9	165	Hilton Head Island, SC	3,039.4
38	Springfield, IL	4,154.6	102	Jacksonville, FL	3,458.6	166	North Port-Sarasota-Bradenton, FL	3,037.8
39	Brunswick, GA	4,129.6	103	Lake Havasu City-Kingman, AZ	3,457.7	167	Akron, OH	3,034.9
40	Yakima, WA	4,099.1	104	Rockford, IL	3,454.3	168	Casper, WY	3,028.1
41	Springfield, OH	4,098.6	105	Lewiston, ID-WA	3,445.8	169	Cleveland, TN	3,028.0
42	Lexington-Fayette, KY	4,096.5	106	Durham-Chapel Hill, NC	3,439.9	170	Palm Bay-Melbourne, FL	3,023.5
43	Panama City, FL	4,068.3	107	Austin-Round Rock, TX	3,431.2	171	Springfield, MA	3,021.5
44	Bakersfield, CA	4,043.8	108	Visalia-Porterville, CA	3,415.8	172	Riverside-San Bernardino, CA	3,021.3
45	Lawrence, KS	4,032.5	109	Athens-Clarke County, GA	3,403.6	173	Hinesville, GA	3,016.7
46	Augusta, GA-SC	4,002.9	110	Dayton, OH	3,397.1	174	Florence-Muscle Shoals, AL	3,011.8
47	Rome, GA	3,996.4	111	Atlanta, GA	3,383.4	175	Abilene, TX	3,007.6
48	Brownsville-Harlingen, TX	3,986.0	112	Burlington, NC	3,370.6	176	Bangor, ME	3,003.9
49	Goldsboro, NC	3,946.4	113	Morristown, TN	3,369.8	177	New Haven-Milford, CT	2,995.2
50	Miami (greater), FL	3,929.7	114	Omaha-Council Bluffs, NE-IA	3,368.8	178	Fort Smith, AR-OK	2,991.2
51	Greenville-Anderson, SC	3,918.5	115	Michigan City-La Porte, IN	3,361.0	179	Baltimore, MD	2,984.3
52	Detroit-Dearborn-Livonia, MI M.D.	3,903.8	116	Huntsville, AL	3,345.6	180	Johnson City, TN	2,978.1
53	Merced, CA	3,847.0	117	Milwaukee, WI	3,344.2	180	Kingsport, TN-VA	2,978.1
54	Wichita Falls, TX	3,838.4	118	Columbia, MO	3,341.0	182	Janesville, WI	2,972.5
55	Topeka, KS	3,836.0	119	Victoria, TX	3,333.4	183	Las Vegas-Henderson, NV	2,966.0
56	Wilmington, NC	3,830.1	120	Fort Worth-Arlington, TX M.D.	3,327.1	184	Canton, OH	2,960.8
57	Cape Girardeau, MO-IL	3,828.4	121	Jackson, MS	3,326.6	185	Olympia, WA	2,929.3
58	Winston-Salem, NC	3,823.6	122	Spartanburg, SC	3,324.8	186	Buffalo-Niagara Falls, NY	2,926.3
59	Eugene, OR	3,803.6	123	Philadelphia, PA M.D.	3,320.8	187	Sacramento, CA	2,925.7
60	Birmingham-Hoover, AL	3,797.7	124	Cincinnati, OH-KY-IN	3,318.9	188	Nashville-Davidson, TN	2,923.8
61	Warner Robins, GA	3,793.7	125	Hickory, NC	3,314.7	189	Decatur, AL	2,920.7
62	Kahului-Wailuku-Lahaina, HI	3,781.2	126	Tuscaloosa, AL	3,305.5	190	Parkersburg-Vienna, WV	2,907.9
63	Great Falls, MT	3,780.1	127	Tulsa, OK	3,302.0	191	Grand Junction, CO	2,889.7
64	Medford, OR	3,769.7	128	Salisbury, MD-DE	3,301.8	192	Cheyenne, WY	2,888.6

Note: All listings are for Metropolitan Statistical Areas (M.S.A.s) except for those ending with "M.D." Listings with "M.D." are Metropolitan Divisions which are smaller parts of eleven large M.S.A.s. See explanatory note at beginning of metropolitan area section.

RANK	METROPOLITAN AREA	RATE	RANK	METROPOLITAN AREA	RATE	RANK	METROPOLITAN AREA	RATE
193	St. Louis, MO-IL	2,881.8	257	Washington, DC-VA-MD-WV M.D.	2,432.3	321	Charlottesville, VA	1,958.9
194	Fort Wayne, IN	2,879.5	258	Madison, WI	2,426.1	322	Lake Co.-Kenosha Co., IL-WI M.D.	1,952.9
195	Valdosta, GA	2,876.4	259	Ogden-Clearfield, UT	2,425.5	323	Bay City, MI	1,949.8
196	Cumberland, MD-WV	2,875.3	260	La Crosse, WI-MN	2,421.0	324	St. George, UT	1,931.3
197	Yuba City, CA	2,866.0	261	Bismarck, ND	2,420.8	325	Morgantown, WV	1,930.4
198	Tampa-St Petersburg, FL	2,862.8	262	Salinas, CA	2,418.4	326	Lebanon, PA	1,910.4
199	Kokomo, IN	2,845.0	263	Kennewick-Richland, WA	2,399.5	327	Pittsburgh, PA	1,900.5
200	Kalamazoo-Portage, MI	2,813.0	264	Jefferson City, MO	2,372.6	328	Oxnard-Thousand Oaks, CA	1,896.5
201	Sebring, FL	2,806.7	265	Norwich-New London, CT	2,364.2	329	Green Bay, WI	1,887.8
202	Chicago-Joilet-Naperville, IL M.D.	2,805.1	266	Santa Maria-Santa Barbara, CA	2,359.1	330	Idaho Falls, ID	1,884.3
203	Asheville, NC	2,802.7	267	Utica-Rome, NY	2,350.9	331	Warren-Troy, MI M.D.	1,878.3
204	Mankato-North Mankato, MN	2,793.7	268	Cape Coral-Fort Myers, FL	2,347.2	332	Newark, NJ-PA M.D.	1,870.2
205	Auburn, AL	2,792.9	269	Port St. Lucie, FL	2,344.9	333	Provo-Orem, UT	1,858.8
206	Kankakee, IL	2,773.6	270	Boulder, CO	2,341.5	334	Johnstown, PA	1,786.6
207	Dalton, GA	2,765.8	271	Saginaw, MI	2,340.0	334	Lynchburg, VA	1,786.6
208	Denver-Aurora, CO	2,746.6	272	Watertown-Fort Drum, NY	2,339.2	336	Cambridge-Newton, MA M.D.	1,786.0
209	Peoria, IL	2,733.2	273	Gainesville, GA	2,336.7	337	Bridgeport-Stamford, CT	1,785.0
210	Detroit (greater), MI	2,730.0	274	Los Angeles County, CA M.D.	2,327.1	338	Staunton-Waynesboro, VA	1,766.8
211	Binghamton, NY	2,724.9	275	Pittsfield, MA	2,316.5	339	Rochester, MN	1,761.9
212	Owensboro, KY	2,714.8	276	El Paso, TX	2,314.4	340	Montgomery County, PA M.D.	1,757.9
213	Lafayette, IN	2,703.6	277	Winchester, VA-WV	2,312.6	341	Fond du Lac, WI	1,743.2
214	Racine, WI	2,700.5	278	Hagerstown-Martinsburg, MD-WV	2,306.3	342	Santa Rosa, CA	1,728.2
215	Sioux City, IA-NE-SD	2,690.7	279	Manchester-Nashua, NH	2,304.3	343	Silver Spring-Frederick, MD M.D.	1,725.8
216	Monroe, MI	2,690.1	280	Los Angeles (greater), CA	2,296.9	344	New York-Jersey City, NY-NJ M.D.	1,716.9
217	Sebastian-Vero Beach, FL	2,687.0	281	Washington (greater) DC-VA-MD-WV	2,282.1	345	New York (greater), NY-NJ-PA	1,704.5
218	Sierra Vista-Douglas, AZ	2,685.8	282	San Luis Obispo, CA	2,277.7	346	Wausau, WI	1,695.1
219	College Station-Bryan, TX	2,681.5	283	Scranton--Wilkes-Barre, PA	2,276.2	347	Glens Falls, NY	1,679.4
220	Barnstable Town, MA	2,680.4	284	Waterloo-Cedar Falls, IA	2,270.6	348	Naples-Marco Island, FL	1,662.9
221	Hattiesburg, MS	2,679.4	285	Ames, IA	2,256.4	349	Chambersburg-Waynesboro, PA	1,660.3
222	Chicago (greater), IL-IN-WI	2,677.0	286	Reading, PA	2,250.6	350	Altoona, PA	1,659.8
223	Decatur, IL	2,674.6	287	Grand Forks, ND-MN	2,236.8	351	Elgin, IL M.D.	1,650.7
224	Philadelphia (greater) PA-NJ-MD-DE	2,665.7	288	Lansing-East Lansing, MI	2,223.1	352	Logan, UT-ID	1,574.5
225	Daphne-Fairhope-Foley, AL	2,660.7	289	Trenton, NJ	2,223.0	353	Appleton, WI	1,543.5
226	Crestview-Fort Walton Beach, FL	2,660.6	290	Hanford-Corcoran, CA	2,216.6	354	Dutchess-Putnam, NY M.D.	1,529.4
227	Champaign-Urbana, IL	2,647.9	291	Allentown, PA-NJ	2,214.3	355	Nassau-Suffolk, NY M.D.	1,524.0
228	Rochester, NY	2,645.5	292	Anaheim-Santa Ana-Irvine, CA M.D.	2,199.1	356	Elizabethtown-Fort Knox, KY	1,423.7
229	East Stroudsburg, PA	2,636.4	293	San Diego, CA	2,196.9	357	State College, PA	1,419.0
230	Reno, NV	2,635.4	294	Fargo, ND-MN	2,188.8	358	Harrisonburg, VA	1,405.9
231	Clarksville, TN-KY	2,616.9	295	Greeley, CO	2,186.7	359	Gettysburg, PA	1,192.0
232	Erie, PA	2,609.8	296	Boston, MA M.D.	2,179.5	360	Midland, MI	1,118.6
233	San Jose, CA	2,603.4	297	Blacksburg, VA	2,176.5	361	The Villages, FL	1,088.9
234	Madera, CA	2,602.6	298	Ocala, FL	2,169.0	NA	Albuquerque, NM**	NA
235	Davenport, IA-IL	2,585.5	299	Rockingham County, NH M.D.	2,166.2	NA	Alexandria, LA**	NA
236	Roanoke, VA	2,570.6	300	Bloomington, IL	2,164.3	NA	Baton Rouge, LA**	NA
237	Camden, NJ M.D.	2,570.5	301	Williamsport, PA	2,163.6	NA	Cedar Rapids, IA**	NA
238	Richmond, VA	2,563.3	302	Punta Gorda, FL	2,155.5	NA	Colorado Springs, CO**	NA
239	California-Lexington Park, MD	2,559.8	303	Harrisburg-Carlisle, PA	2,137.0	NA	Corpus Christi, TX**	NA
240	Pocatello, ID	2,557.6	304	Corvallis, OR	2,127.4	NA	Des Moines-West Des Moines, IA**	NA
241	Chico, CA	2,545.6	305	Sheboygan, WI	2,124.0	NA	Dubuque, IA**	NA
242	Fayetteville-Springdale, AR-MO	2,541.9	306	Worcester, MA-CT	2,117.0	NA	Houston, TX**	NA
243	Yuma, AZ	2,525.3	307	Bloomsburg-Berwick, PA	2,095.2	NA	Killeen-Temple, TX**	NA
244	Syracuse, NY	2,519.6	308	Homosassa Springs, FL	2,081.1	NA	Lafayette, LA**	NA
245	Midland, TX	2,513.3	309	Prescott, AZ	2,073.8	NA	Minneapolis-St. Paul, MN-WI**	NA
246	Providence-Warwick, RI-MA	2,495.4	310	Napa, CA	2,054.3	NA	Oakland-Hayward, CA M.D.**	NA
247	Bowling Green, KY	2,486.6	311	Oshkosh-Neenah, WI	2,013.9	NA	Phoenix-Mesa-Scottsdale, AZ**	NA
248	Elmira, NY	2,476.5	312	Kingston, NY	2,001.3	NA	San Francisco (greater), CA**	NA
249	Sioux Falls, SD	2,474.4	313	Boston (greater), MA-NH	1,983.9	NA	San Rafael, CA M.D.**	NA
250	Farmington, NM	2,472.7	314	York-Hanover, PA	1,979.3	NA	Seattle (greater), WA**	NA
251	Raleigh, NC	2,470.7	315	Boise City, ID	1,971.9	NA	Shreveport-Bossier City, LA**	NA
252	Albany-Schenectady-Troy, NY	2,463.6	316	Carson City, NV	1,971.0	NA	Tacoma, WA M.D.**	NA
253	Portland, ME	2,462.8	317	Wheeling, WV-OH	1,967.5	NA	Toledo, OH**	NA
254	Fort Collins, CO	2,455.2	318	Iowa City, IA	1,966.6	NA	Tucson, AZ**	NA
255	Hartford, CT	2,451.1	319	Manhattan, KS	1,966.4			
256	Ann Arbor, MI	2,437.3	320	Lancaster, PA	1,962.8			

Source: Reported data from the F.B.I. "Crime in the United States 2012"

*Property crimes are offenses of burglary, larceny-theft, and motor vehicle theft. Attempts are included.

**Not available.

27. Percent Change in Property Crime Rate: 2011 to 2012
National Percent Change = 1.6% Decrease*

RANK	METROPOLITAN AREA	% CHANGE	RANK	METROPOLITAN AREA	% CHANGE	RANK	METROPOLITAN AREA	% CHANGE
113	Abilene, TX	(0.7)	62	Cheyenne, WY	4.4	228	Gary, IN M.D.	(9.4)
212	Akron, OH	(7.8)	158	Chicago (greater), IL-IN-WI	(4.1)	NA	Gettysburg, PA**	NA
NA	Albany-Schenectady-Troy, NY**	NA	NA	Chicago-Joilet-Naperville, IL M.D.**	NA	NA	Glens Falls, NY**	NA
60	Albany, GA	4.6	55	Chico, CA	5.4	183	Goldsboro, NC	(5.5)
NA	Albany, OR**	NA	NA	Cincinnati, OH-KY-IN**	NA	133	Grand Forks, ND-MN	(2.1)
NA	Albuquerque, NM**	NA	213	Clarksville, TN-KY	(7.9)	NA	Grand Island, NE**	NA
NA	Alexandria, LA**	NA	110	Cleveland, TN	(0.5)	45	Grand Junction, CO	6.2
NA	Allentown, PA-NJ**	NA	NA	Coeur d'Alene, ID**	NA	57	Great Falls, MT	5.2
258	Altoona, PA	(16.3)	256	College Station-Bryan, TX	(16.1)	65	Greeley, CO	4.1
209	Amarillo, TX	(7.5)	NA	Colorado Springs, CO**	NA	43	Green Bay, WI	6.3
245	Ames, IA	(13.6)	66	Columbia, MO	4.0	NA	Greensboro-High Point, NC**	NA
30	Anaheim-Santa Ana-Irvine, CA M.D.	8.6	230	Columbus, GA-AL	(9.5)	NA	Greenville-Anderson, SC**	NA
NA	Anchorage, AK**	NA	252	Columbus, IN	(14.9)	NA	Greenville, NC**	NA
49	Ann Arbor, MI	5.8	NA	Corpus Christi, TX**	NA	NA	Hagerstown-Martinsburg, MD-WV**	NA
50	Anniston-Oxford, AL	5.7	261	Corvallis, OR	(17.5)	NA	Hammond, LA**	NA
222	Appleton, WI	(8.9)	205	Crestview-Fort Walton Beach, FL	(7.1)	107	Hanford-Corcoran, CA	(0.1)
23	Asheville, NC	10.6	119	Cumberland, MD-WV	(1.0)	140	Harrisburg-Carlisle, PA	(2.7)
220	Athens-Clarke County, GA	(8.7)	226	Dallas (greater), TX	(9.2)	40	Harrisonburg, VA	7.1
172	Atlanta, GA	(4.7)	220	Dallas-Plano-Irving, TX M.D.	(8.7)	100	Hartford, CT	0.3
232	Atlantic City, NJ	(10.6)	203	Dalton, GA	(7.0)	NA	Hattiesburg, MS**	NA
249	Auburn, AL	(14.2)	206	Danville, IL	(7.2)	180	Hickory, NC	(5.2)
216	Augusta, GA-SC	(8.0)	NA	Daphne-Fairhope-Foley, AL**	NA	NA	Hilton Head Island, SC**	NA
110	Austin-Round Rock, TX	(0.5)	240	Davenport, IA-IL	(12.2)	198	Hinesville, GA	(6.7)
13	Bakersfield, CA	14.2	121	Dayton, OH	(1.2)	NA	Homosassa Springs, FL**	NA
130	Baltimore, MD	(1.9)	13	Decatur, AL	14.2	124	Houma, LA	(1.5)
40	Bangor, ME	7.1	239	Decatur, IL	(11.9)	NA	Houston, TX**	NA
154	Barnstable Town, MA	(3.8)	NA	Deltona-Daytona Beach, FL**	NA	170	Huntsville, AL	(4.6)
NA	Baton Rouge, LA**	NA	NA	Denver-Aurora, CO**	NA	219	Idaho Falls, ID	(8.6)
112	Bay City, MI	(0.6)	NA	Des Moines-West Des Moines, IA**	NA	NA	Indianapolis, IN**	NA
256	Beaumont-Port Arthur, TX	(16.1)	180	Detroit (greater), MI	(5.2)	38	Iowa City, IA	7.3
NA	Beckley, WV**	NA	179	Detroit-Dearborn-Livonia, MI M.D.	(5.1)	191	Jacksonville, FL	(6.1)
130	Bellingham, WA	(1.9)	69	Dothan, AL	3.7	NA	Jackson, MS**	NA
81	Billings, MT	2.6	91	Dover, DE	1.4	NA	Jackson, TN**	NA
NA	Binghamton, NY**	NA	NA	Dubuque, IA**	NA	130	Janesville, WI	(1.9)
206	Birmingham-Hoover, AL	(7.2)	158	Duluth, MN-WI	(4.1)	158	Jefferson City, MO	(4.1)
115	Bismarck, ND	(0.8)	228	Durham-Chapel Hill, NC	(9.4)	124	Johnson City, TN	(1.5)
242	Blacksburg, VA	(13.2)	NA	Dutchess-Putnam, NY M.D.**	NA	243	Johnstown, PA	(13.3)
109	Bloomington, IL	(0.4)	NA	East Stroudsburg, PA**	NA	236	Jonesboro, AR	(11.1)
NA	Bloomington, IN**	NA	34	El Centro, CA	8.4	10	Joplin, MO	15.7
NA	Bloomsburg-Berwick, PA**	NA	142	El Paso, TX	(2.9)	NA	Kahului-Wailuku-Lahaina, HI**	NA
143	Boise City, ID	(3.1)	NA	Elgin, IL M.D.**	NA	NA	Kalamazoo-Portage, MI**	NA
NA	Boston (greater), MA-NH**	NA	NA	Elizabethtown-Fort Knox, KY**	NA	158	Kankakee, IL	(4.1)
NA	Boston, MA M.D.**	NA	NA	Elmira, NY**	NA	NA	Kansas City, MO-KS**	NA
32	Boulder, CO	8.5	143	Erie, PA	(3.1)	226	Kennewick-Richland, WA	(9.2)
198	Bowling Green, KY	(6.7)	42	Eugene, OR	7.0	NA	Killeen-Temple, TX**	NA
36	Bremerton-Silverdale, WA	7.8	24	Fairbanks, AK	9.8	222	Kingsport, TN-VA	(8.9)
209	Bridgeport-Stamford, CT	(7.5)	54	Fargo, ND-MN	5.6	NA	Kingston, NY**	NA
143	Brownsville-Harlingen, TX	(3.1)	9	Farmington, NM	17.9	NA	Knoxville, TN**	NA
234	Brunswick, GA	(10.8)	NA	Fayetteville-Springdale, AR-MO**	NA	NA	Kokomo, IN**	NA
NA	Buffalo-Niagara Falls, NY**	NA	128	Fayetteville, NC	(1.8)	61	La Crosse, WI-MN	4.5
248	Burlington, NC	(14.1)	198	Flagstaff, AZ	(6.7)	73	Lafayette, IN	3.3
NA	California-Lexington Park, MD**	NA	195	Flint, MI	(6.3)	NA	Lafayette, LA**	NA
NA	Cambridge-Newton, MA M.D.**	NA	5	Florence-Muscle Shoals, AL	21.0	149	Lake Co.-Kenosha Co., IL-WI M.D.	(3.6)
153	Camden, NJ M.D.	(3.7)	172	Florence, SC	(4.7)	30	Lake Havasu City-Kingman, AZ	8.6
165	Canton, OH	(4.3)	25	Fond du Lac, WI	9.5	193	Lakeland, FL	(6.2)
255	Cape Coral-Fort Myers, FL	(15.9)	135	Fort Collins, CO	(2.4)	148	Lancaster, PA	(3.4)
67	Cape Girardeau, MO-IL	3.8	190	Fort Lauderdale, FL M.D.	(6.0)	203	Lansing-East Lansing, MI	(7.0)
247	Carson City, NV	(13.8)	NA	Fort Smith, AR-OK**	NA	102	Laredo, TX	0.2
183	Casper, WY	(5.5)	67	Fort Wayne, IN	3.8	182	Las Cruces, NM	(5.3)
NA	Cedar Rapids, IA**	NA	231	Fort Worth-Arlington, TX M.D.	(10.3)	29	Las Vegas-Henderson, NV	8.7
NA	Chambersburg-Waynesboro, PA**	NA	84	Fresno, CA	2.2	102	Lawrence, KS	0.2
48	Champaign-Urbana, IL	6.0	135	Gadsden, AL	(2.4)	NA	Lawton, OK**	NA
NA	Charleston-North Charleston, SC**	NA	170	Gainesville, FL	(4.6)	50	Lebanon, PA	5.7
133	Charlottesville, VA	(2.1)	186	Gainesville, GA	(5.6)	74	Lewiston-Auburn, ME	3.0

Note: All listings are for Metropolitan Statistical Areas (M.S.A.s) except for those ending with "M.D." Listings with "M.D." are Metropolitan Divisions which are smaller parts of eleven large M.S.A.s. See explanatory note at beginning of metropolitan area section.

RANK	METROPOLITAN AREA	% CHANGE	RANK	METROPOLITAN AREA	% CHANGE	RANK	METROPOLITAN AREA	% CHANGE
NA	Lewiston, ID-WA**	NA	77	Owensboro, KY	2.8	198	Silver Spring-Frederick, MD M.D.	(6.7)
NA	Lexington-Fayette, KY**	NA	19	Oxnard-Thousand Oaks, CA	11.5	NA	Sioux City, IA-NE-SD**	NA
146	Lima, OH	(3.2)	218	Palm Bay-Melbourne, FL	(8.3)	69	Sioux Falls, SD	3.7
120	Lincoln, NE	(1.1)	NA	Panama City, FL**	NA	249	South Bend-Mishawaka, IN-MI	(14.2)
113	Little Rock, AR	(0.7)	NA	Parkersburg-Vienna, WV**	NA	NA	Spartanburg, SC**	NA
1	Logan, UT-ID	48.3	90	Pensacola, FL	1.6	NA	Spokane, WA**	NA
32	Longview, TX	8.5	138	Peoria, IL	(2.5)	146	Springfield, IL	(3.2)
22	Longview, WA	10.8	NA	Philadelphia (greater) PA-NJ-MD-DE**	NA	NA	Springfield, MA**	NA
92	Los Angeles County, CA M.D.	1.3	NA	Philadelphia, PA M.D.**	NA	96	Springfield, MO	0.8
76	Los Angeles (greater), CA	2.9	NA	Phoenix-Mesa-Scottsdale, AZ**	NA	123	Springfield, OH	(1.4)
216	Louisville, KY-IN	(8.0)	253	Pine Bluff, AR	(15.2)	237	State College, PA	(11.3)
149	Lubbock, TX	(3.6)	121	Pittsburgh, PA	(1.2)	NA	Staunton-Waynesboro, VA**	NA
238	Lynchburg, VA	(11.8)	155	Pittsfield, MA	(3.9)	116	Stockton-Lodi, CA	(0.9)
251	Macon, GA	(14.6)	NA	Pocatello, ID**	NA	NA	St. George, UT**	NA
62	Madera, CA	4.4	259	Port St. Lucie, FL	(16.4)	15	St. Joseph, MO-KS	13.4
NA	Madison, WI**	NA	95	Portland-Vancouver, OR-WA	0.9	213	St. Louis, MO-IL	(7.9)
128	Manchester-Nashua, NH	(1.8)	168	Portland, ME	(4.5)	6	Sumter, SC	20.4
NA	Manhattan, KS**	NA	158	Prescott, AZ	(4.1)	NA	Syracuse, NY**	NA
149	Mankato-North Mankato, MN	(3.6)	NA	Providence-Warwick, RI-MA**	NA	NA	Tacoma, WA M.D.**	NA
37	Mansfield, OH	7.7	254	Provo-Orem, UT	(15.7)	186	Tallahassee, FL	(5.6)
172	McAllen-Edinburg-Mission, TX	(4.7)	16	Pueblo, CO	13.1	211	Tampa-St Petersburg, FL	(7.7)
18	Medford, OR	12.3	244	Punta Gorda, FL	(13.4)	158	Terre Haute, IN	(4.1)
165	Memphis, TN-MS-AR	(4.3)	193	Racine, WI	(6.2)	NA	Texarkana, TX-AR**	NA
26	Merced, CA	9.0	176	Raleigh, NC	(4.8)	NA	The Villages, FL**	NA
195	Miami (greater), FL	(6.3)	NA	Rapid City, SD**	NA	NA	Toledo, OH**	NA
208	Miami-Dade County, FL M.D.	(7.3)	72	Reading, PA	3.4	222	Topeka, KS	(8.9)
202	Michigan City-La Porte, IN	(6.9)	2	Redding, CA	26.7	86	Trenton, NJ	2.1
NA	Midland, MI**	NA	35	Reno, NV	8.2	NA	Tucson, AZ**	NA
NA	Midland, TX**	NA	78	Richmond, VA	2.7	188	Tulsa, OK	(5.7)
87	Milwaukee, WI	2.0	39	Riverside-San Bernardino, CA	7.2	NA	Tuscaloosa, AL**	NA
NA	Minneapolis-St. Paul, MN-WI**	NA	97	Roanoke, VA	0.7	139	Tyler, TX	(2.6)
3	Missoula, MT	25.7	NA	Rochester, MN**	NA	NA	Utica-Rome, NY**	NA
232	Mobile, AL	(10.6)	NA	Rochester, NY**	NA	213	Valdosta, GA	(7.9)
12	Modesto, CA	14.4	20	Rockford, IL	11.4	27	Vallejo-Fairfield, CA	8.9
102	Monroe, LA	0.2	102	Rockingham County, NH M.D.	0.2	NA	Victoria, TX**	NA
46	Monroe, MI	6.1	225	Rocky Mount, NC	(9.1)	NA	Vineland-Bridgeton, NJ**	NA
NA	Montgomery County, PA M.D.**	NA	59	Rome, GA	4.7	195	Virginia Beach-Norfolk, VA-NC	(6.3)
27	Montgomery, AL	8.9	71	Sacramento, CA	3.5	108	Visalia-Porterville, CA	(0.3)
NA	Morgantown, WV**	NA	191	Saginaw, MI	(6.1)	NA	Waco, TX**	NA
NA	Morristown, TN**	NA	11	Salem, OR	15.3	NA	Walla Walla, WA**	NA
189	Mount Vernon-Anacortes, WA	(5.8)	78	Salinas, CA	2.7	NA	Warner Robins, GA**	NA
17	Muncie, IN	12.9	NA	Salisbury, MD-DE**	NA	172	Warren-Troy, MI M.D.	(4.7)
92	Napa, CA	1.3	58	Salt Lake City, UT	4.9	167	Washington (greater) DC-VA-MD-WV	(4.4)
234	Naples-Marco Island, FL	(10.8)	98	San Antonio, TX	0.4	156	Washington, DC-VA-MD-WV M.D.	(4.0)
NA	Nashville-Davidson, TN**	NA	50	San Diego, CA	5.7	21	Waterloo-Cedar Falls, IA	11.1
NA	Nassau-Suffolk, NY M.D.**	NA	NA	San Francisco (greater), CA**	NA	NA	Watertown-Fort Drum, NY**	NA
NA	New Bern, NC**	NA	8	San Francisco-Redwood, CA M.D.	20.0	183	Wausau, WI	(5.5)
126	New Haven-Milford, CT	(1.6)	4	San Jose, CA	21.3	168	West Palm Beach, FL M.D.	(4.5)
164	New Orleans, LA	(4.2)	100	San Luis Obispo, CA	0.3	NA	Wheeling, WV-OH**	NA
NA	New York (greater), NY-NJ-PA**	NA	NA	San Rafael, CA M.D.**	NA	62	Wichita Falls, TX	4.4
NA	New York-Jersey City, NY-NJ M.D.**	NA	116	Santa Cruz-Watsonville, CA	(0.9)	46	Wichita, KS	6.1
NA	Newark, NJ-PA M.D.**	NA	94	Santa Fe, NM	1.2	127	Williamsport, PA	(1.7)
260	North Port-Sarasota-Bradenton, FL	(16.8)	NA	Santa Maria-Santa Barbara, CA**	NA	78	Wilmington, DE-MD-NJ M.D.	2.7
43	Norwich-New London, CT	6.3	88	Santa Rosa, CA	1.9	NA	Wilmington, NC**	NA
NA	Oakland-Hayward, CA M.D.**	NA	245	Savannah, GA	(13.6)	83	Winchester, VA-WV	2.3
241	Ocala, FL	(13.1)	89	Scranton--Wilkes-Barre, PA	1.8	NA	Winston-Salem, NC**	NA
135	Ocean City, NJ	(2.4)	NA	Seattle (greater), WA**	NA	NA	Worcester, MA-CT**	NA
7	Odessa, TX	20.3	102	Seattle-Bellevue-Everett, WA M.D.	0.2	141	Yakima, WA	(2.8)
NA	Ogden-Clearfield, UT**	NA	178	Sebastian-Vero Beach, FL	(5.0)	116	York-Hanover, PA	(0.9)
84	Oklahoma City, OK	2.2	NA	Sebring, FL**	NA	NA	Youngstown-Warren, OH-PA**	NA
55	Olympia, WA	5.4	74	Sheboygan, WI	3.0	81	Yuba City, CA	2.6
98	Omaha-Council Bluffs, NE-IA	0.4	149	Sherman-Denison, TX	(3.6)	156	Yuma, AZ	(4.0)
177	Orlando, FL	(4.9)	NA	Shreveport-Bossier City, LA**	NA			
50	Oshkosh-Neenah, WI	5.7	NA	Sierra Vista-Douglas, AZ**	NA			

Source: CQ Press using reported data from the F.B.I. "Crime in the United States 2012"

*Property crimes are offenses of burglary, larceny-theft, and motor vehicle theft. Attempts are included.

**Not available.

27. Percent Change in Property Crime Rate: 2011 to 2012 (continued)
National Percent Change = 1.6% Decrease*

RANK	METROPOLITAN AREA	% CHANGE	RANK	METROPOLITAN AREA	% CHANGE	RANK	METROPOLITAN AREA	% CHANGE
1	Logan, UT-ID	48.3	65	Greeley, CO	4.1	128	Manchester-Nashua, NH	(1.8)
2	Redding, CA	26.7	66	Columbia, MO	4.0	130	Baltimore, MD	(1.9)
3	Missoula, MT	25.7	67	Cape Girardeau, MO-IL	3.8	130	Bellingham, WA	(1.9)
4	San Jose, CA	21.3	67	Fort Wayne, IN	3.8	130	Janesville, WI	(1.9)
5	Florence-Muscle Shoals, AL	21.0	69	Dothan, AL	3.7	133	Charlottesville, VA	(2.1)
6	Sumter, SC	20.4	69	Sioux Falls, SD	3.7	133	Grand Forks, ND-MN	(2.1)
7	Odessa, TX	20.3	71	Sacramento, CA	3.5	135	Fort Collins, CO	(2.4)
8	San Francisco-Redwood, CA M.D.	20.0	72	Reading, PA	3.4	135	Gadsden, AL	(2.4)
9	Farmington, NM	17.9	73	Lafayette, IN	3.3	135	Ocean City, NJ	(2.4)
10	Joplin, MO	15.7	74	Lewiston-Auburn, ME	3.0	138	Peoria, IL	(2.5)
11	Salem, OR	15.3	74	Sheboygan, WI	3.0	139	Tyler, TX	(2.6)
12	Modesto, CA	14.4	76	Los Angeles (greater), CA	2.9	140	Harrisburg-Carlisle, PA	(2.7)
13	Bakersfield, CA	14.2	77	Owensboro, KY	2.8	141	Yakima, WA	(2.8)
13	Decatur, AL	14.2	78	Richmond, VA	2.7	142	El Paso, TX	(2.9)
15	St. Joseph, MO-KS	13.4	78	Salinas, CA	2.7	143	Boise City, ID	(3.1)
16	Pueblo, CO	13.1	78	Wilmington, DE-MD-NJ M.D.	2.7	143	Brownsville-Harlingen, TX	(3.1)
17	Muncie, IN	12.9	81	Billings, MT	2.6	143	Erie, PA	(3.1)
18	Medford, OR	12.3	81	Yuba City, CA	2.6	146	Lima, OH	(3.2)
19	Oxnard-Thousand Oaks, CA	11.5	83	Winchester, VA-WV	2.3	146	Springfield, IL	(3.2)
20	Rockford, IL	11.4	84	Fresno, CA	2.2	148	Lancaster, PA	(3.4)
21	Waterloo-Cedar Falls, IA	11.1	84	Oklahoma City, OK	2.2	149	Lake Co.-Kenosha Co., IL-WI M.D.	(3.6)
22	Longview, WA	10.8	86	Trenton, NJ	2.1	149	Lubbock, TX	(3.6)
23	Asheville, NC	10.6	87	Milwaukee, WI	2.0	149	Mankato-North Mankato, MN	(3.6)
24	Fairbanks, AK	9.8	88	Santa Rosa, CA	1.9	149	Sherman-Denison, TX	(3.6)
25	Fond du Lac, WI	9.5	89	Scranton--Wilkes-Barre, PA	1.8	153	Camden, NJ M.D.	(3.7)
26	Merced, CA	9.0	90	Pensacola, FL	1.6	154	Barnstable Town, MA	(3.8)
27	Montgomery, AL	8.9	91	Dover, DE	1.4	155	Pittsfield, MA	(3.9)
27	Vallejo-Fairfield, CA	8.9	92	Los Angeles County, CA M.D.	1.3	156	Washington, DC-VA-MD-WV M.D.	(4.0)
29	Las Vegas-Henderson, NV	8.7	92	Napa, CA	1.3	156	Yuma, AZ	(4.0)
30	Anaheim-Santa Ana-Irvine, CA M.D.	8.6	94	Santa Fe, NM	1.2	158	Chicago (greater), IL-IN-WI	(4.1)
30	Lake Havasu City-Kingman, AZ	8.6	95	Portland-Vancouver, OR-WA	0.9	158	Duluth, MN-WI	(4.1)
32	Boulder, CO	8.5	96	Springfield, MO	0.8	158	Jefferson City, MO	(4.1)
32	Longview, TX	8.5	97	Roanoke, VA	0.7	158	Kankakee, IL	(4.1)
34	El Centro, CA	8.4	98	Omaha-Council Bluffs, NE-IA	0.4	158	Prescott, AZ	(4.1)
35	Reno, NV	8.2	98	San Antonio, TX	0.4	158	Terre Haute, IN	(4.1)
36	Bremerton-Silverdale, WA	7.8	100	Hartford, CT	0.3	164	New Orleans, LA	(4.2)
37	Mansfield, OH	7.7	100	San Luis Obispo, CA	0.3	165	Canton, OH	(4.3)
38	Iowa City, IA	7.3	102	Laredo, TX	0.2	165	Memphis, TN-MS-AR	(4.3)
39	Riverside-San Bernardino, CA	7.2	102	Lawrence, KS	0.2	167	Washington (greater) DC-VA-MD-WV	(4.4)
40	Bangor, ME	7.1	102	Monroe, LA	0.2	168	Portland, ME	(4.5)
40	Harrisonburg, VA	7.1	102	Rockingham County, NH M.D.	0.2	168	West Palm Beach, FL M.D.	(4.5)
42	Eugene, OR	7.0	102	Seattle-Bellevue-Everett, WA M.D.	0.2	170	Gainesville, FL	(4.6)
43	Green Bay, WI	6.3	107	Hanford-Corcoran, CA	(0.1)	170	Huntsville, AL	(4.6)
43	Norwich-New London, CT	6.3	108	Visalia-Porterville, CA	(0.3)	172	Atlanta, GA	(4.7)
45	Grand Junction, CO	6.2	109	Bloomington, IL	(0.4)	172	Florence, SC	(4.7)
46	Monroe, MI	6.1	110	Austin-Round Rock, TX	(0.5)	172	McAllen-Edinburg-Mission, TX	(4.7)
46	Wichita, KS	6.1	110	Cleveland, TN	(0.5)	172	Warren-Troy, MI M.D.	(4.7)
48	Champaign-Urbana, IL	6.0	112	Bay City, MI	(0.6)	176	Raleigh, NC	(4.8)
49	Ann Arbor, MI	5.8	113	Abilene, TX	(0.7)	177	Orlando, FL	(4.9)
50	Anniston-Oxford, AL	5.7	113	Little Rock, AR	(0.7)	178	Sebastian-Vero Beach, FL	(5.0)
50	Lebanon, PA	5.7	115	Bismarck, ND	(0.8)	179	Detroit-Dearborn-Livonia, MI M.D.	(5.1)
50	Oshkosh-Neenah, WI	5.7	116	Santa Cruz-Watsonville, CA	(0.9)	180	Detroit (greater), MI	(5.2)
50	San Diego, CA	5.7	116	Stockton-Lodi, CA	(0.9)	180	Hickory, NC	(5.2)
54	Fargo, ND-MN	5.6	116	York-Hanover, PA	(0.9)	182	Las Cruces, NM	(5.3)
55	Chico, CA	5.4	119	Cumberland, MD-WV	(1.0)	183	Casper, WY	(5.5)
55	Olympia, WA	5.4	120	Lincoln, NE	(1.1)	183	Goldsboro, NC	(5.5)
57	Great Falls, MT	5.2	121	Dayton, OH	(1.2)	183	Wausau, WI	(5.5)
58	Salt Lake City, UT	4.9	121	Pittsburgh, PA	(1.2)	186	Gainesville, GA	(5.6)
59	Rome, GA	4.7	123	Springfield, OH	(1.4)	186	Tallahassee, FL	(5.6)
60	Albany, GA	4.6	124	Houma, LA	(1.5)	188	Tulsa, OK	(5.7)
61	La Crosse, WI-MN	4.5	124	Johnson City, TN	(1.5)	189	Mount Vernon-Anacortes, WA	(5.8)
62	Cheyenne, WY	4.4	126	New Haven-Milford, CT	(1.6)	190	Fort Lauderdale, FL M.D.	(6.0)
62	Madera, CA	4.4	127	Williamsport, PA	(1.7)	191	Jacksonville, FL	(6.1)
62	Wichita Falls, TX	4.4	128	Fayetteville, NC	(1.8)	191	Saginaw, MI	(6.1)

Note: All listings are for Metropolitan Statistical Areas (M.S.A.s) except for those ending with "M.D." Listings with "M.D." are Metropolitan Divisions which are smaller parts of eleven large M.S.A.s. See explanatory note at beginning of metropolitan area section.

RANK	METROPOLITAN AREA	% CHANGE	RANK	METROPOLITAN AREA	% CHANGE	RANK	METROPOLITAN AREA	% CHANGE
193	Lakeland, FL	(6.2)	256	College Station-Bryan, TX	(16.1)	NA	Lawton, OK**	NA
193	Racine, WI	(6.2)	258	Altoona, PA	(16.3)	NA	Lewiston, ID-WA**	NA
195	Flint, MI	(6.3)	259	Port St. Lucie, FL	(16.4)	NA	Lexington-Fayette, KY**	NA
195	Miami (greater), FL	(6.3)	260	North Port-Sarasota-Bradenton, FL	(16.8)	NA	Madison, WI**	NA
195	Virginia Beach-Norfolk, VA-NC	(6.3)	261	Corvallis, OR	(17.5)	NA	Manhattan, KS**	NA
198	Bowling Green, KY	(6.7)	NA	Albany-Schenectady-Troy, NY**	NA	NA	Midland, MI**	NA
198	Flagstaff, AZ	(6.7)	NA	Albany, OR**	NA	NA	Midland, TX**	NA
198	Hinesville, GA	(6.7)	NA	Albuquerque, NM**	NA	NA	Minneapolis-St. Paul, MN-WI**	NA
198	Silver Spring-Frederick, MD M.D.	(6.7)	NA	Alexandria, LA**	NA	NA	Montgomery County, PA M.D.**	NA
202	Michigan City-La Porte, IN	(6.9)	NA	Allentown, PA-NJ**	NA	NA	Morgantown, WV**	NA
203	Dalton, GA	(7.0)	NA	Anchorage, AK**	NA	NA	Morristown, TN**	NA
203	Lansing-East Lansing, MI	(7.0)	NA	Baton Rouge, LA**	NA	NA	Nashville-Davidson, TN**	NA
205	Crestview-Fort Walton Beach, FL	(7.1)	NA	Beckley, WV**	NA	NA	Nassau-Suffolk, NY M.D.**	NA
206	Birmingham-Hoover, AL	(7.2)	NA	Binghamton, NY**	NA	NA	New Bern, NC**	NA
206	Danville, IL	(7.2)	NA	Bloomington, IN**	NA	NA	New York (greater), NY-NJ-PA**	NA
208	Miami-Dade County, FL M.D.	(7.3)	NA	Bloomsburg-Berwick, PA**	NA	NA	New York-Jersey City, NY-NJ M.D.**	NA
209	Amarillo, TX	(7.5)	NA	Boston (greater), MA-NH**	NA	NA	Newark, NJ-PA M.D.**	NA
209	Bridgeport-Stamford, CT	(7.5)	NA	Boston, MA M.D.**	NA	NA	Oakland-Hayward, CA M.D.**	NA
211	Tampa-St Petersburg, FL	(7.7)	NA	Buffalo-Niagara Falls, NY**	NA	NA	Ogden-Clearfield, UT**	NA
212	Akron, OH	(7.8)	NA	California-Lexington Park, MD**	NA	NA	Panama City, FL**	NA
213	Clarksville, TN-KY	(7.9)	NA	Cambridge-Newton, MA M.D.**	NA	NA	Parkersburg-Vienna, WV**	NA
213	St. Louis, MO-IL	(7.9)	NA	Cedar Rapids, IA**	NA	NA	Philadelphia (greater) PA-NJ-MD-DE**	NA
213	Valdosta, GA	(7.9)	NA	Chambersburg-Waynesboro, PA**	NA	NA	Philadelphia, PA M.D.**	NA
216	Augusta, GA-SC	(8.0)	NA	Charleston-North Charleston, SC**	NA	NA	Phoenix-Mesa-Scottsdale, AZ**	NA
216	Louisville, KY-IN	(8.0)	NA	Chicago-Joilet-Naperville, IL M.D.**	NA	NA	Pocatello, ID**	NA
218	Palm Bay-Melbourne, FL	(8.3)	NA	Cincinnati, OH-KY-IN**	NA	NA	Providence-Warwick, RI-MA**	NA
219	Idaho Falls, ID	(8.6)	NA	Coeur d'Alene, ID**	NA	NA	Rapid City, SD**	NA
220	Athens-Clarke County, GA	(8.7)	NA	Colorado Springs, CO**	NA	NA	Rochester, MN**	NA
220	Dallas-Plano-Irving, TX M.D.	(8.7)	NA	Corpus Christi, TX**	NA	NA	Rochester, NY**	NA
222	Appleton, WI	(8.9)	NA	Daphne-Fairhope-Foley, AL**	NA	NA	Salisbury, MD-DE**	NA
222	Kingsport, TN-VA	(8.9)	NA	Deltona-Daytona Beach, FL**	NA	NA	San Francisco (greater), CA**	NA
222	Topeka, KS	(8.9)	NA	Denver-Aurora, CO**	NA	NA	San Rafael, CA M.D.**	NA
225	Rocky Mount, NC	(9.1)	NA	Des Moines-West Des Moines, IA**	NA	NA	Santa Maria-Santa Barbara, CA**	NA
226	Dallas (greater), TX	(9.2)	NA	Dubuque, IA**	NA	NA	Seattle (greater), WA**	NA
226	Kennewick-Richland, WA	(9.2)	NA	Dutchess-Putnam, NY M.D.**	NA	NA	Sebring, FL**	NA
228	Durham-Chapel Hill, NC	(9.4)	NA	East Stroudsburg, PA**	NA	NA	Shreveport-Bossier City, LA**	NA
228	Gary, IN M.D.	(9.4)	NA	Elgin, IL M.D.**	NA	NA	Sierra Vista-Douglas, AZ**	NA
230	Columbus, GA-AL	(9.5)	NA	Elizabethtown-Fort Knox, KY**	NA	NA	Sioux City, IA-NE-SD**	NA
231	Fort Worth-Arlington, TX M.D.	(10.3)	NA	Elmira, NY**	NA	NA	Spartanburg, SC**	NA
232	Atlantic City, NJ	(10.6)	NA	Fayetteville-Springdale, AR-MO**	NA	NA	Spokane, WA**	NA
232	Mobile, AL	(10.6)	NA	Fort Smith, AR-OK**	NA	NA	Springfield, MA**	NA
234	Brunswick, GA	(10.8)	NA	Gettysburg, PA**	NA	NA	Staunton-Waynesboro, VA**	NA
234	Naples-Marco Island, FL	(10.8)	NA	Glens Falls, NY**	NA	NA	St. George, UT**	NA
236	Jonesboro, AR	(11.1)	NA	Grand Island, NE**	NA	NA	Syracuse, NY**	NA
237	State College, PA	(11.3)	NA	Greensboro-High Point, NC**	NA	NA	Tacoma, WA M.D.**	NA
238	Lynchburg, VA	(11.8)	NA	Greenville-Anderson, SC**	NA	NA	Texarkana, TX-AR**	NA
239	Decatur, IL	(11.9)	NA	Greenville, NC**	NA	NA	The Villages, FL**	NA
240	Davenport, IA-IL	(12.2)	NA	Hagerstown-Martinsburg, MD-WV**	NA	NA	Toledo, OH**	NA
241	Ocala, FL	(13.1)	NA	Hammond, LA**	NA	NA	Tucson, AZ**	NA
242	Blacksburg, VA	(13.2)	NA	Hattiesburg, MS**	NA	NA	Tuscaloosa, AL**	NA
243	Johnstown, PA	(13.3)	NA	Hilton Head Island, SC**	NA	NA	Utica-Rome, NY**	NA
244	Punta Gorda, FL	(13.4)	NA	Homosassa Springs, FL**	NA	NA	Victoria, TX**	NA
245	Ames, IA	(13.6)	NA	Houston, TX**	NA	NA	Vineland-Bridgeton, NJ**	NA
245	Savannah, GA	(13.6)	NA	Indianapolis, IN**	NA	NA	Waco, TX**	NA
247	Carson City, NV	(13.8)	NA	Jackson, MS**	NA	NA	Walla Walla, WA**	NA
248	Burlington, NC	(14.1)	NA	Jackson, TN**	NA	NA	Warner Robins, GA**	NA
249	Auburn, AL	(14.2)	NA	Kahului-Wailuku-Lahaina, HI**	NA	NA	Watertown-Fort Drum, NY**	NA
249	South Bend-Mishawaka, IN-MI	(14.2)	NA	Kalamazoo-Portage, MI**	NA	NA	Wheeling, WV-OH**	NA
251	Macon, GA	(14.6)	NA	Kansas City, MO-KS**	NA	NA	Wilmington, NC**	NA
252	Columbus, IN	(14.9)	NA	Killeen-Temple, TX**	NA	NA	Winston-Salem, NC**	NA
253	Pine Bluff, AR	(15.2)	NA	Kingston, NY**	NA	NA	Worcester, MA-CT**	NA
254	Provo-Orem, UT	(15.7)	NA	Knoxville, TN**	NA	NA	Youngstown-Warren, OH-PA**	NA
255	Cape Coral-Fort Myers, FL	(15.9)	NA	Kokomo, IN**	NA			
256	Beaumont-Port Arthur, TX	(16.1)	NA	Lafayette, LA**	NA			

Source: CQ Press using reported data from the F.B.I. "Crime in the United States 2012"

*Property crimes are offenses of burglary, larceny-theft, and motor vehicle theft. Attempts are included.

**Not available.

28. Percent Change in Property Crime Rate: 2008 to 2012
National Percent Change = 11.1% Decrease*

RANK	METROPOLITAN AREA	% CHANGE	RANK	METROPOLITAN AREA	% CHANGE	RANK	METROPOLITAN AREA	% CHANGE
83	Abilene, TX	(6.5)	188	Cheyenne, WY	(19.2)	NA	Gary, IN M.D.**	NA
98	Akron, OH	(8.4)	NA	Chicago (greater), IL-IN-WI**	NA	NA	Gettysburg, PA**	NA
NA	Albany-Schenectady-Troy, NY**	NA	NA	Chicago-Joilet-Naperville, IL M.D.**	NA	NA	Glens Falls, NY**	NA
NA	Albany, GA**	NA	165	Chico, CA	(16.1)	177	Goldsboro, NC	(18.1)
NA	Albany, OR**	NA	NA	Cincinnati, OH-KY-IN**	NA	137	Grand Forks, ND-MN	(12.9)
NA	Albuquerque, NM**	NA	184	Clarksville, TN-KY	(18.9)	NA	Grand Island, NE**	NA
NA	Alexandria, LA**	NA	103	Cleveland, TN	(8.8)	65	Grand Junction, CO	(3.5)
NA	Allentown, PA-NJ**	NA	NA	Coeur d'Alene, ID**	NA	49	Great Falls, MT	(0.4)
205	Altoona, PA	(21.9)	238	College Station-Bryan, TX	(32.9)	153	Greeley, CO	(14.4)
176	Amarillo, TX	(17.9)	NA	Colorado Springs, CO**	NA	192	Green Bay, WI	(19.6)
162	Ames, IA	(16.0)	41	Columbia, MO	2.3	218	Greensboro-High Point, NC	(23.7)
34	Anaheim-Santa Ana-Irvine, CA M.D.	3.6	196	Columbus, GA-AL	(20.1)	NA	Greenville-Anderson, SC**	NA
NA	Anchorage, AK**	NA	21	Columbus, IN	11.3	235	Greenville, NC	(30.6)
118	Ann Arbor, MI	(10.4)	NA	Corpus Christi, TX**	NA	NA	Hagerstown-Martinsburg, MD-WV**	NA
NA	Anniston-Oxford, AL**	NA	116	Corvallis, OR	(10.3)	NA	Hammond, LA**	NA
241	Appleton, WI	(38.9)	NA	Crestview-Fort Walton Beach, FL**	NA	96	Hanford-Corcoran, CA	(8.1)
55	Asheville, NC	(2.3)	28	Cumberland, MD-WV	5.8	67	Harrisburg-Carlisle, PA	(3.8)
229	Athens-Clarke County, GA	(28.2)	205	Dallas (greater), TX	(21.9)	105	Harrisonburg, VA	(9.0)
158	Atlanta, GA	(15.3)	215	Dallas-Plano-Irving, TX M.D.	(23.2)	154	Hartford, CT	(14.5)
NA	Atlantic City, NJ**	NA	76	Dalton, GA	(5.0)	NA	Hattiesburg, MS**	NA
242	Auburn, AL	(42.2)	NA	Danville, IL**	NA	74	Hickory, NC	(4.9)
172	Augusta, GA-SC	(17.2)	NA	Daphne-Fairhope-Foley, AL**	NA	NA	Hilton Head Island, SC**	NA
130	Austin-Round Rock, TX	(12.1)	NA	Davenport, IA-IL**	NA	211	Hinesville, GA	(22.6)
42	Bakersfield, CA	1.9	62	Dayton, OH	(3.3)	NA	Homosassa Springs, FL**	NA
167	Baltimore, MD	(16.5)	213	Decatur, AL	(23.0)	39	Houma, LA	2.9
93	Bangor, ME	(7.6)	NA	Decatur, IL**	NA	NA	Houston, TX**	NA
113	Barnstable Town, MA	(10.0)	169	Deltona-Daytona Beach, FL	(16.7)	166	Huntsville, AL	(16.2)
NA	Baton Rouge, LA**	NA	NA	Denver-Aurora, CO**	NA	185	Idaho Falls, ID	(19.0)
224	Bay City, MI	(25.5)	NA	Des Moines-West Des Moines, IA**	NA	104	Indianapolis, IN	(8.9)
161	Beaumont-Port Arthur, TX	(15.9)	NA	Detroit (greater), MI**	NA	81	Iowa City, IA	(6.2)
NA	Beckley, WV**	NA	NA	Detroit-Dearborn-Livonia, MI M.D.**	NA	228	Jacksonville, FL	(27.7)
162	Bellingham, WA	(16.0)	156	Dothan, AL	(14.8)	NA	Jackson, MS**	NA
34	Billings, MT	3.6	26	Dover, DE	7.0	NA	Jackson, TN**	NA
NA	Binghamton, NY**	NA	NA	Dubuque, IA**	NA	134	Janesville, WI	(12.6)
193	Birmingham-Hoover, AL	(19.8)	109	Duluth, MN-WI	(9.5)	NA	Jefferson City, MO**	NA
20	Bismarck, ND	11.6	186	Durham-Chapel Hill, NC	(19.1)	33	Johnson City, TN	4.0
196	Blacksburg, VA	(20.1)	NA	Dutchess-Putnam, NY M.D.**	NA	101	Johnstown, PA	(8.6)
NA	Bloomington, IL**	NA	NA	East Stroudsburg, PA**	NA	137	Jonesboro, AR	(12.9)
7	Bloomington, IN	21.4	73	El Centro, CA	(4.8)	66	Joplin, MO	(3.7)
NA	Bloomsburg-Berwick, PA**	NA	225	El Paso, TX	(25.6)	NA	Kahului-Wailuku-Lahaina, HI**	NA
135	Boise City, ID	(12.7)	NA	Elgin, IL M.D.**	NA	221	Kalamazoo-Portage, MI	(24.2)
NA	Boston (greater), MA-NH**	NA	NA	Elizabethtown-Fort Knox, KY**	NA	NA	Kankakee, IL**	NA
NA	Boston, MA M.D.**	NA	NA	Elmira, NY**	NA	NA	Kansas City, MO-KS**	NA
NA	Boulder, CO**	NA	29	Erie, PA	5.7	105	Kennewick-Richland, WA	(9.0)
209	Bowling Green, KY	(22.4)	198	Eugene, OR	(20.2)	NA	Killeen-Temple, TX**	NA
10	Bremerton-Silverdale, WA	17.2	NA	Fairbanks, AK**	NA	144	Kingsport, TN-VA	(13.4)
152	Bridgeport-Stamford, CT	(14.3)	NA	Fargo, ND-MN**	NA	NA	Kingston, NY**	NA
177	Brownsville-Harlingen, TX	(18.1)	40	Farmington, NM	2.6	NA	Knoxville, TN**	NA
NA	Brunswick, GA**	NA	38	Fayetteville-Springdale, AR-MO	3.4	NA	Kokomo, IN**	NA
NA	Buffalo-Niagara Falls, NY**	NA	121	Fayetteville, NC	(11.0)	92	La Crosse, WI-MN	(7.5)
168	Burlington, NC	(16.6)	179	Flagstaff, AZ	(18.2)	70	Lafayette, IN	(4.3)
NA	California-Lexington Park, MD**	NA	51	Flint, MI	(1.5)	NA	Lafayette, LA**	NA
NA	Cambridge-Newton, MA M.D.**	NA	174	Florence-Muscle Shoals, AL	(17.4)	NA	Lake Co.-Kenosha Co., IL-WI M.D.**	NA
86	Camden, NJ M.D.	(6.7)	126	Florence, SC	(11.8)	57	Lake Havasu City-Kingman, AZ	(2.9)
NA	Canton, OH**	NA	86	Fond du Lac, WI	(6.7)	222	Lakeland, FL	(24.3)
239	Cape Coral-Fort Myers, FL	(33.1)	126	Fort Collins, CO	(11.8)	84	Lancaster, PA	(6.6)
18	Cape Girardeau, MO-IL	12.1	95	Fort Lauderdale, FL M.D.	(8.0)	182	Lansing-East Lansing, MI	(18.6)
159	Carson City, NV	(15.4)	NA	Fort Smith, AR-OK**	NA	236	Laredo, TX	(31.2)
194	Casper, WY	(20.0)	90	Fort Wayne, IN	(7.0)	72	Las Cruces, NM	(4.6)
NA	Cedar Rapids, IA**	NA	191	Fort Worth-Arlington, TX M.D.	(19.4)	186	Las Vegas-Henderson, NV	(19.1)
NA	Chambersburg-Waynesboro, PA**	NA	24	Fresno, CA	7.8	143	Lawrence, KS	(13.3)
NA	Champaign-Urbana, IL**	NA	9	Gadsden, AL	17.3	NA	Lawton, OK**	NA
180	Charleston-North Charleston, SC	(18.4)	212	Gainesville, FL	(22.7)	22	Lebanon, PA	8.5
215	Charlottesville, VA	(23.2)	NA	Gainesville, GA**	NA	3	Lewiston-Auburn, ME	31.7

Note: All listings are for Metropolitan Statistical Areas (M.S.A.s) except for those ending with "M.D." Listings with "M.D." are Metropolitan Divisions which are smaller parts of eleven large M.S.A.s. See explanatory note at beginning of metropolitan area section.

RANK	METROPOLITAN AREA	% CHANGE	RANK	METROPOLITAN AREA	% CHANGE	RANK	METROPOLITAN AREA	% CHANGE
6	Lewiston, ID-WA	22.6	NA	Owensboro, KY**	NA	237	Silver Spring-Frederick, MD M.D.	(32.7)
NA	Lexington-Fayette, KY**	NA	78	Oxnard-Thousand Oaks, CA	(5.8)	NA	Sioux City, IA-NE-SD**	NA
204	Lima, OH	(21.6)	137	Palm Bay-Melbourne, FL	(12.9)	5	Sioux Falls, SD	25.7
74	Lincoln, NE	(4.9)	NA	Panama City, FL**	NA	230	South Bend-Mishawaka, IN-MI	(28.4)
68	Little Rock, AR	(4.0)	NA	Parkersburg-Vienna, WV**	NA	NA	Spartanburg, SC**	NA
69	Logan, UT-ID	(4.1)	17	Pensacola, FL	14.1	1	Spokane, WA	45.3
194	Longview, TX	(20.0)	NA	Peoria, IL**	NA	NA	Springfield, IL**	NA
56	Longview, WA	(2.4)	NA	Philadelphia (greater) PA-NJ-MD-DE**	NA	NA	Springfield, MA**	NA
124	Los Angeles County, CA M.D.	(11.5)	NA	Philadelphia, PA M.D.**	NA	44	Springfield, MO	1.6
101	Los Angeles (greater), CA	(8.6)	NA	Phoenix-Mesa-Scottsdale, AZ**	NA	94	Springfield, OH	(7.8)
59	Louisville, KY-IN	(3.0)	226	Pine Bluff, AR	(26.8)	201	State College, PA	(20.9)
121	Lubbock, TX	(11.0)	128	Pittsburgh, PA	(11.9)	NA	Staunton-Waynesboro, VA**	NA
188	Lynchburg, VA	(19.2)	47	Pittsfield, MA	1.0	159	Stockton-Lodi, CA	(15.4)
133	Macon, GA	(12.5)	NA	Pocatello, ID**	NA	150	St. George, UT	(14.1)
8	Madera, CA	19.0	223	Port St. Lucie, FL	(24.9)	13	St. Joseph, MO-KS	15.9
NA	Madison, WI**	NA	59	Portland-Vancouver, OR-WA	(3.0)	157	St. Louis, MO-IL	(15.2)
NA	Manchester-Nashua, NH**	NA	44	Portland, ME	1.6	15	Sumter, SC	14.7
NA	Manhattan, KS**	NA	112	Prescott, AZ	(9.9)	NA	Syracuse, NY**	NA
64	Mankato-North Mankato, MN	(3.4)	118	Providence-Warwick, RI-MA	(10.4)	NA	Tacoma, WA M.D.**	NA
14	Mansfield, OH	15.3	199	Provo-Orem, UT	(20.4)	120	Tallahassee, FL	(10.9)
180	McAllen-Edinburg-Mission, TX	(18.4)	NA	Pueblo, CO**	NA	234	Tampa-St Petersburg, FL	(30.4)
2	Medford, OR	42.0	240	Punta Gorda, FL	(34.4)	NA	Terre Haute, IN**	NA
219	Memphis, TN-MS-AR	(24.0)	147	Racine, WI	(13.8)	NA	Texarkana, TX-AR**	NA
27	Merced, CA	6.1	114	Raleigh, NC	(10.1)	NA	The Villages, FL**	NA
175	Miami (greater), FL	(17.5)	NA	Rapid City, SD**	NA	NA	Toledo, OH**	NA
200	Miami-Dade County, FL M.D.	(20.5)	123	Reading, PA	(11.4)	142	Topeka, KS	(13.2)
171	Michigan City-La Porte, IN	(16.9)	4	Redding, CA	26.1	48	Trenton, NJ	0.3
NA	Midland, MI**	NA	232	Reno, NV	(28.7)	NA	Tucson, AZ**	NA
NA	Midland, TX**	NA	108	Richmond, VA	(9.2)	111	Tulsa, OK	(9.7)
135	Milwaukee, WI	(12.7)	52	Riverside-San Bernardino, CA	(1.6)	NA	Tuscaloosa, AL**	NA
NA	Minneapolis-St. Paul, MN-WI**	NA	114	Roanoke, VA	(10.1)	88	Tyler, TX	(6.8)
19	Missoula, MT	11.9	NA	Rochester, MN**	NA	NA	Utica-Rome, NY**	NA
129	Mobile, AL	(12.0)	NA	Rochester, NY**	NA	190	Valdosta, GA	(19.3)
79	Modesto, CA	(6.0)	NA	Rockford, IL**	NA	141	Vallejo-Fairfield, CA	(13.1)
125	Monroe, LA	(11.7)	11	Rockingham County, NH M.D.	16.9	NA	Victoria, TX**	NA
22	Monroe, MI	8.5	NA	Rocky Mount, NC**	NA	16	Vineland-Bridgeton, NJ	14.3
NA	Montgomery County, PA M.D.**	NA	NA	Rome, GA**	NA	116	Virginia Beach-Norfolk, VA-NC	(10.3)
79	Montgomery, AL	(6.0)	131	Sacramento, CA	(12.2)	146	Visalia-Porterville, CA	(13.7)
NA	Morgantown, WV**	NA	233	Saginaw, MI	(30.3)	NA	Waco, TX**	NA
NA	Morristown, TN**	NA	88	Salem, OR	(6.8)	NA	Walla Walla, WA**	NA
91	Mount Vernon-Anacortes, WA	(7.2)	154	Salinas, CA	(14.5)	NA	Warner Robins, GA**	NA
30	Muncie, IN	4.9	NA	Salisbury, MD-DE**	NA	NA	Warren-Troy, MI M.D.**	NA
162	Napa, CA	(16.0)	98	Salt Lake City, UT	(8.4)	219	Washington (greater) DC-VA-MD-WV	(24.0)
147	Naples-Marco Island, FL	(13.8)	201	San Antonio, TX	(20.9)	208	Washington, DC-VA-MD-WV M.D.	(22.1)
NA	Nashville-Davidson, TN**	NA	209	San Diego, CA	(22.4)	140	Waterloo-Cedar Falls, IA	(13.0)
NA	Nassau-Suffolk, NY M.D.**	NA	NA	San Francisco (greater), CA**	NA	NA	Watertown-Fort Drum, NY**	NA
NA	New Bern, NC**	NA	37	San Francisco-Redwood, CA M.D.	3.5	84	Wausau, WI	(6.6)
NA	New Haven-Milford, CT**	NA	25	San Jose, CA	7.5	217	West Palm Beach, FL M.D.	(23.5)
183	New Orleans, LA	(18.7)	57	San Luis Obispo, CA	(2.9)	53	Wheeling, WV-OH	(1.7)
NA	New York (greater), NY-NJ-PA**	NA	NA	San Rafael, CA M.D.**	NA	227	Wichita Falls, TX	(27.4)
NA	New York-Jersey City, NY-NJ M.D.**	NA	34	Santa Cruz-Watsonville, CA	3.6	61	Wichita, KS	(3.2)
NA	Newark, NJ-PA M.D.**	NA	12	Santa Fe, NM	16.6	30	Williamsport, PA	4.9
NA	North Port-Sarasota-Bradenton, FL**	NA	NA	Santa Maria-Santa Barbara, CA**	NA	109	Wilmington, DE-MD-NJ M.D.	(9.5)
70	Norwich-New London, CT	(4.3)	96	Santa Rosa, CA	(8.1)	NA	Wilmington, NC**	NA
NA	Oakland-Hayward, CA M.D.**	NA	231	Savannah, GA	(28.5)	132	Winchester, VA-WV	(12.4)
151	Ocala, FL	(14.2)	53	Scranton--Wilkes-Barre, PA	(1.7)	NA	Winston-Salem, NC**	NA
81	Ocean City, NJ	(6.2)	NA	Seattle (greater), WA**	NA	46	Worcester, MA-CT	1.1
107	Odessa, TX	(9.1)	NA	Seattle-Bellevue-Everett, WA M.D.**	NA	203	Yakima, WA	(21.3)
NA	Ogden-Clearfield, UT**	NA	170	Sebastian-Vero Beach, FL	(16.8)	145	York-Hanover, PA	(13.5)
43	Oklahoma City, OK	1.7	NA	Sebring, FL**	NA	77	Youngstown-Warren, OH-PA	(5.1)
149	Olympia, WA	(14.0)	213	Sheboygan, WI	(23.0)	50	Yuba City, CA	(1.1)
62	Omaha-Council Bluffs, NE-IA	(3.3)	32	Sherman-Denison, TX	4.8	98	Yuma, AZ	(8.4)
207	Orlando, FL	(22.0)	NA	Shreveport-Bossier City, LA**	NA			
173	Oshkosh-Neenah, WI	(17.3)	NA	Sierra Vista-Douglas, AZ**	NA			

Source: CQ Press using reported data from the F.B.I. "Crime in the United States 2012"

*Property crimes are offenses of burglary, larceny-theft, and motor vehicle theft. Attempts are included.

**Not available.

28. Percent Change in Property Crime Rate: 2008 to 2012 (continued)
National Percent Change = 11.1% Decrease*

RANK	METROPOLITAN AREA	% CHANGE	RANK	METROPOLITAN AREA	% CHANGE	RANK	METROPOLITAN AREA	% CHANGE
1	Spokane, WA	45.3	65	Grand Junction, CO	(3.5)	129	Mobile, AL	(12.0)
2	Medford, OR	42.0	66	Joplin, MO	(3.7)	130	Austin-Round Rock, TX	(12.1)
3	Lewiston-Auburn, ME	31.7	67	Harrisburg-Carlisle, PA	(3.8)	131	Sacramento, CA	(12.2)
4	Redding, CA	26.1	68	Little Rock, AR	(4.0)	132	Winchester, VA-WV	(12.4)
5	Sioux Falls, SD	25.7	69	Logan, UT-ID	(4.1)	133	Macon, GA	(12.5)
6	Lewiston, ID-WA	22.6	70	Lafayette, IN	(4.3)	134	Janesville, WI	(12.6)
7	Bloomington, IN	21.4	70	Norwich-New London, CT	(4.3)	135	Boise City, ID	(12.7)
8	Madera, CA	19.0	72	Las Cruces, NM	(4.6)	135	Milwaukee, WI	(12.7)
9	Gadsden, AL	17.3	73	El Centro, CA	(4.8)	137	Grand Forks, ND-MN	(12.9)
10	Bremerton-Silverdale, WA	17.2	74	Hickory, NC	(4.9)	137	Jonesboro, AR	(12.9)
11	Rockingham County, NH M.D.	16.9	74	Lincoln, NE	(4.9)	137	Palm Bay-Melbourne, FL	(12.9)
12	Santa Fe, NM	16.6	76	Dalton, GA	(5.0)	140	Waterloo-Cedar Falls, IA	(13.0)
13	St. Joseph, MO-KS	15.9	77	Youngstown-Warren, OH-PA	(5.1)	141	Vallejo-Fairfield, CA	(13.1)
14	Mansfield, OH	15.3	78	Oxnard-Thousand Oaks, CA	(5.8)	142	Topeka, KS	(13.2)
15	Sumter, SC	14.7	79	Modesto, CA	(6.0)	143	Lawrence, KS	(13.3)
16	Vineland-Bridgeton, NJ	14.3	79	Montgomery, AL	(6.0)	144	Kingsport, TN-VA	(13.4)
17	Pensacola, FL	14.1	81	Iowa City, IA	(6.2)	145	York-Hanover, PA	(13.5)
18	Cape Girardeau, MO-IL	12.1	81	Ocean City, NJ	(6.2)	146	Visalia-Porterville, CA	(13.7)
19	Missoula, MT	11.9	83	Abilene, TX	(6.5)	147	Naples-Marco Island, FL	(13.8)
20	Bismarck, ND	11.6	84	Lancaster, PA	(6.6)	147	Racine, WI	(13.8)
21	Columbus, IN	11.3	84	Wausau, WI	(6.6)	149	Olympia, WA	(14.0)
22	Lebanon, PA	8.5	86	Camden, NJ M.D.	(6.7)	150	St. George, UT	(14.1)
22	Monroe, MI	8.5	86	Fond du Lac, WI	(6.7)	151	Ocala, FL	(14.2)
24	Fresno, CA	7.8	88	Salem, OR	(6.8)	152	Bridgeport-Stamford, CT	(14.3)
25	San Jose, CA	7.5	88	Tyler, TX	(6.8)	153	Greeley, CO	(14.4)
26	Dover, DE	7.0	90	Fort Wayne, IN	(7.0)	154	Hartford, CT	(14.5)
27	Merced, CA	6.1	91	Mount Vernon-Anacortes, WA	(7.2)	154	Salinas, CA	(14.5)
28	Cumberland, MD-WV	5.8	92	La Crosse, WI-MN	(7.5)	156	Dothan, AL	(14.8)
29	Erie, PA	5.7	93	Bangor, ME	(7.6)	157	St. Louis, MO-IL	(15.2)
30	Muncie, IN	4.9	94	Springfield, OH	(7.8)	158	Atlanta, GA	(15.3)
30	Williamsport, PA	4.9	95	Fort Lauderdale, FL M.D.	(8.0)	159	Carson City, NV	(15.4)
32	Sherman-Denison, TX	4.8	96	Hanford-Corcoran, CA	(8.1)	159	Stockton-Lodi, CA	(15.4)
33	Johnson City, TN	4.0	96	Santa Rosa, CA	(8.1)	161	Beaumont-Port Arthur, TX	(15.9)
34	Anaheim-Santa Ana-Irvine, CA M.D.	3.6	98	Akron, OH	(8.4)	162	Ames, IA	(16.0)
34	Billings, MT	3.6	98	Salt Lake City, UT	(8.4)	162	Bellingham, WA	(16.0)
34	Santa Cruz-Watsonville, CA	3.6	98	Yuma, AZ	(8.4)	162	Napa, CA	(16.0)
37	San Francisco-Redwood, CA M.D.	3.5	101	Johnstown, PA	(8.6)	165	Chico, CA	(16.1)
38	Fayetteville-Springdale, AR-MO	3.4	101	Los Angeles (greater), CA	(8.6)	166	Huntsville, AL	(16.2)
39	Houma, LA	2.9	103	Cleveland, TN	(8.8)	167	Baltimore, MD	(16.5)
40	Farmington, NM	2.6	104	Indianapolis, IN	(8.9)	168	Burlington, NC	(16.6)
41	Columbia, MO	2.3	105	Harrisonburg, VA	(9.0)	169	Deltona-Daytona Beach, FL	(16.7)
42	Bakersfield, CA	1.9	105	Kennewick-Richland, WA	(9.0)	170	Sebastian-Vero Beach, FL	(16.8)
43	Oklahoma City, OK	1.7	107	Odessa, TX	(9.1)	171	Michigan City-La Porte, IN	(16.9)
44	Portland, ME	1.6	108	Richmond, VA	(9.2)	172	Augusta, GA-SC	(17.2)
44	Springfield, MO	1.6	109	Duluth, MN-WI	(9.5)	173	Oshkosh-Neenah, WI	(17.3)
46	Worcester, MA-CT	1.1	109	Wilmington, DE-MD-NJ M.D.	(9.5)	174	Florence-Muscle Shoals, AL	(17.4)
47	Pittsfield, MA	1.0	111	Tulsa, OK	(9.7)	175	Miami (greater), FL	(17.5)
48	Trenton, NJ	0.3	112	Prescott, AZ	(9.9)	176	Amarillo, TX	(17.9)
49	Great Falls, MT	(0.4)	113	Barnstable Town, MA	(10.0)	177	Brownsville-Harlingen, TX	(18.1)
50	Yuba City, CA	(1.1)	114	Raleigh, NC	(10.1)	177	Goldsboro, NC	(18.1)
51	Flint, MI	(1.5)	114	Roanoke, VA	(10.1)	179	Flagstaff, AZ	(18.2)
52	Riverside-San Bernardino, CA	(1.6)	116	Corvallis, OR	(10.3)	180	Charleston-North Charleston, SC	(18.4)
53	Scranton--Wilkes-Barre, PA	(1.7)	116	Virginia Beach-Norfolk, VA-NC	(10.3)	180	McAllen-Edinburg-Mission, TX	(18.4)
53	Wheeling, WV-OH	(1.7)	118	Ann Arbor, MI	(10.4)	182	Lansing-East Lansing, MI	(18.6)
55	Asheville, NC	(2.3)	118	Providence-Warwick, RI-MA	(10.4)	183	New Orleans, LA	(18.7)
56	Longview, WA	(2.4)	120	Tallahassee, FL	(10.9)	184	Clarksville, TN-KY	(18.9)
57	Lake Havasu City-Kingman, AZ	(2.9)	121	Fayetteville, NC	(11.0)	185	Idaho Falls, ID	(19.0)
57	San Luis Obispo, CA	(2.9)	121	Lubbock, TX	(11.0)	186	Durham-Chapel Hill, NC	(19.1)
59	Louisville, KY-IN	(3.0)	123	Reading, PA	(11.4)	186	Las Vegas-Henderson, NV	(19.1)
59	Portland-Vancouver, OR-WA	(3.0)	124	Los Angeles County, CA M.D.	(11.5)	188	Cheyenne, WY	(19.2)
61	Wichita, KS	(3.2)	125	Monroe, LA	(11.7)	188	Lynchburg, VA	(19.2)
62	Dayton, OH	(3.3)	126	Florence, SC	(11.8)	190	Valdosta, GA	(19.3)
62	Omaha-Council Bluffs, NE-IA	(3.3)	126	Fort Collins, CO	(11.8)	191	Fort Worth-Arlington, TX M.D.	(19.4)
64	Mankato-North Mankato, MN	(3.4)	128	Pittsburgh, PA	(11.9)	192	Green Bay, WI	(19.6)

Note: All listings are for Metropolitan Statistical Areas (M.S.A.s) except for those ending with "M.D." Listings with "M.D." are Metropolitan Divisions which are smaller parts of eleven large M.S.A.s. See explanatory note at beginning of metropolitan area section.

RANK	METROPOLITAN AREA	% CHANGE	RANK	METROPOLITAN AREA	% CHANGE	RANK	METROPOLITAN AREA	% CHANGE
193	Birmingham-Hoover, AL	(19.8)	NA	Boston (greater), MA-NH**	NA	NA	Midland, MI**	NA
194	Casper, WY	(20.0)	NA	Boston, MA M.D.**	NA	NA	Midland, TX**	NA
194	Longview, TX	(20.0)	NA	Boulder, CO**	NA	NA	Minneapolis-St. Paul, MN-WI**	NA
196	Blacksburg, VA	(20.1)	NA	Brunswick, GA**	NA	NA	Montgomery County, PA M.D.**	NA
196	Columbus, GA-AL	(20.1)	NA	Buffalo-Niagara Falls, NY**	NA	NA	Morgantown, WV**	NA
198	Eugene, OR	(20.2)	NA	California-Lexington Park, MD**	NA	NA	Morristown, TN**	NA
199	Provo-Orem, UT	(20.4)	NA	Cambridge-Newton, MA M.D.**	NA	NA	Nashville-Davidson, TN**	NA
200	Miami-Dade County, FL M.D.	(20.5)	NA	Canton, OH**	NA	NA	Nassau-Suffolk, NY M.D.**	NA
201	San Antonio, TX	(20.9)	NA	Cedar Rapids, IA**	NA	NA	New Bern, NC**	NA
201	State College, PA	(20.9)	NA	Chambersburg-Waynesboro, PA**	NA	NA	New Haven-Milford, CT**	NA
203	Yakima, WA	(21.3)	NA	Champaign-Urbana, IL**	NA	NA	New York (greater), NY-NJ-PA**	NA
204	Lima, OH	(21.6)	NA	Chicago (greater), IL-IN-WI**	NA	NA	New York-Jersey City, NY-NJ M.D.**	NA
205	Altoona, PA	(21.9)	NA	Chicago-Joilet-Naperville, IL M.D.**	NA	NA	Newark, NJ-PA M.D.**	NA
205	Dallas (greater), TX	(21.9)	NA	Cincinnati, OH-KY-IN**	NA	NA	North Port-Sarasota-Bradenton, FL**	NA
207	Orlando, FL	(22.0)	NA	Coeur d'Alene, ID**	NA	NA	Oakland-Hayward, CA M.D.**	NA
208	Washington, DC-VA-MD-WV M.D.	(22.1)	NA	Colorado Springs, CO**	NA	NA	Ogden-Clearfield, UT**	NA
209	Bowling Green, KY	(22.4)	NA	Corpus Christi, TX**	NA	NA	Owensboro, KY**	NA
209	San Diego, CA	(22.4)	NA	Crestview-Fort Walton Beach, FL**	NA	NA	Panama City, FL**	NA
211	Hinesville, GA	(22.6)	NA	Danville, IL**	NA	NA	Parkersburg-Vienna, WV**	NA
212	Gainesville, FL	(22.7)	NA	Daphne-Fairhope-Foley, AL**	NA	NA	Peoria, IL**	NA
213	Decatur, AL	(23.0)	NA	Davenport, IA-IL**	NA	NA	Philadelphia (greater) PA-NJ-MD-DE**	NA
213	Sheboygan, WI	(23.0)	NA	Decatur, IL**	NA	NA	Philadelphia, PA M.D.**	NA
215	Charlottesville, VA	(23.2)	NA	Denver-Aurora, CO**	NA	NA	Phoenix-Mesa-Scottsdale, AZ**	NA
215	Dallas-Plano-Irving, TX M.D.	(23.2)	NA	Des Moines-West Des Moines, IA**	NA	NA	Pocatello, ID**	NA
217	West Palm Beach, FL M.D.	(23.5)	NA	Detroit (greater), MI**	NA	NA	Pueblo, CO**	NA
218	Greensboro-High Point, NC	(23.7)	NA	Detroit-Dearborn-Livonia, MI M.D.**	NA	NA	Rapid City, SD**	NA
219	Memphis, TN-MS-AR	(24.0)	NA	Dubuque, IA**	NA	NA	Rochester, MN**	NA
219	Washington (greater) DC-VA-MD-WV	(24.0)	NA	Dutchess-Putnam, NY M.D.**	NA	NA	Rochester, NY**	NA
221	Kalamazoo-Portage, MI	(24.2)	NA	East Stroudsburg, PA**	NA	NA	Rockford, IL**	NA
222	Lakeland, FL	(24.3)	NA	Elgin, IL M.D.**	NA	NA	Rocky Mount, NC**	NA
223	Port St. Lucie, FL	(24.9)	NA	Elizabethtown-Fort Knox, KY**	NA	NA	Rome, GA**	NA
224	Bay City, MI	(25.5)	NA	Elmira, NY**	NA	NA	Salisbury, MD-DE**	NA
225	El Paso, TX	(25.6)	NA	Fairbanks, AK**	NA	NA	San Francisco (greater), CA**	NA
226	Pine Bluff, AR	(26.8)	NA	Fargo, ND-MN**	NA	NA	San Rafael, CA M.D.**	NA
227	Wichita Falls, TX	(27.4)	NA	Fort Smith, AR-OK**	NA	NA	Santa Maria-Santa Barbara, CA**	NA
228	Jacksonville, FL	(27.7)	NA	Gainesville, GA**	NA	NA	Seattle (greater), WA**	NA
229	Athens-Clarke County, GA	(28.2)	NA	Gary, IN M.D.**	NA	NA	Seattle-Bellevue-Everett, WA M.D.**	NA
230	South Bend-Mishawaka, IN-MI	(28.4)	NA	Gettysburg, PA**	NA	NA	Sebring, FL**	NA
231	Savannah, GA	(28.5)	NA	Glens Falls, NY**	NA	NA	Shreveport-Bossier City, LA**	NA
232	Reno, NV	(28.7)	NA	Grand Island, NE**	NA	NA	Sierra Vista-Douglas, AZ**	NA
233	Saginaw, MI	(30.3)	NA	Greenville-Anderson, SC**	NA	NA	Sioux City, IA-NE-SD**	NA
234	Tampa-St Petersburg, FL	(30.4)	NA	Hagerstown-Martinsburg, MD-WV**	NA	NA	Spartanburg, SC**	NA
235	Greenville, NC	(30.6)	NA	Hammond, LA**	NA	NA	Springfield, IL**	NA
236	Laredo, TX	(31.2)	NA	Hattiesburg, MS**	NA	NA	Springfield, MA**	NA
237	Silver Spring-Frederick, MD M.D.	(32.7)	NA	Hilton Head Island, SC**	NA	NA	Staunton-Waynesboro, VA**	NA
238	College Station-Bryan, TX	(32.9)	NA	Homosassa Springs, FL**	NA	NA	Syracuse, NY**	NA
239	Cape Coral-Fort Myers, FL	(33.1)	NA	Houston, TX**	NA	NA	Tacoma, WA M.D.**	NA
240	Punta Gorda, FL	(34.4)	NA	Jackson, MS**	NA	NA	Terre Haute, IN**	NA
241	Appleton, WI	(38.9)	NA	Jackson, TN**	NA	NA	Texarkana, TX-AR**	NA
242	Auburn, AL	(42.2)	NA	Jefferson City, MO**	NA	NA	The Villages, FL**	NA
NA	Albany-Schenectady-Troy, NY**	NA	NA	Kahului-Wailuku-Lahaina, HI**	NA	NA	Toledo, OH**	NA
NA	Albany, GA**	NA	NA	Kankakee, IL**	NA	NA	Tucson, AZ**	NA
NA	Albany, OR**	NA	NA	Kansas City, MO-KS**	NA	NA	Tuscaloosa, AL**	NA
NA	Albuquerque, NM**	NA	NA	Killeen-Temple, TX**	NA	NA	Utica-Rome, NY**	NA
NA	Alexandria, LA**	NA	NA	Kingston, NY**	NA	NA	Victoria, TX**	NA
NA	Allentown, PA-NJ**	NA	NA	Knoxville, TN**	NA	NA	Waco, TX**	NA
NA	Anchorage, AK**	NA	NA	Kokomo, IN**	NA	NA	Walla Walla, WA**	NA
NA	Anniston-Oxford, AL**	NA	NA	Lafayette, LA**	NA	NA	Warner Robins, GA**	NA
NA	Atlantic City, NJ**	NA	NA	Lake Co.-Kenosha Co., IL-WI M.D.**	NA	NA	Warren-Troy, MI M.D.**	NA
NA	Baton Rouge, LA**	NA	NA	Lawton, OK**	NA	NA	Watertown-Fort Drum, NY**	NA
NA	Beckley, WV**	NA	NA	Lexington-Fayette, KY**	NA	NA	Wilmington, NC**	NA
NA	Binghamton, NY**	NA	NA	Madison, WI**	NA	NA	Winston-Salem, NC**	NA
NA	Bloomington, IL**	NA	NA	Manchester-Nashua, NH**	NA			
NA	Bloomsburg-Berwick, PA**	NA	NA	Manhattan, KS**	NA			

Source: CQ Press using reported data from the F.B.I. "Crime in the United States 2012"

*Property crimes are offenses of burglary, larceny-theft, and motor vehicle theft. Attempts are included.

**Not available.

29. Burglaries in 2012
National Total = 2,103,787 Burglaries*

RANK	METROPOLITAN AREA	BURGLARY	RANK	METROPOLITAN AREA	BURGLARY	RANK	METROPOLITAN AREA	BURGLARY
247	Abilene, TX	1,245	346	Cheyenne, WY	425	95	Gary, IN M.D.	5,033
87	Akron, OH	5,708	4	Chicago (greater), IL-IN-WI	50,771	366	Gettysburg, PA	263
106	Albany-Schenectady-Troy, NY	4,205	8	Chicago-Joilet-Naperville, IL M.D.	40,385	349	Glens Falls, NY	403
167	Albany, GA	2,090	181	Chico, CA	1,919	211	Goldsboro, NC	1,601
313	Albany, OR	707	31	Cincinnati, OH-KY-IN	16,869	352	Grand Forks, ND-MN	394
NA	Albuquerque, NM**	NA	186	Clarksville, TN-KY	1,848	330	Grand Island, NE	517
183	Alexandria, LA	1,879	299	Cleveland, TN	788	326	Grand Junction, CO	576
119	Allentown, PA-NJ	3,525	254	Coeur d'Alene, ID	1,165	353	Great Falls, MT	391
354	Altoona, PA	387	226	College Station-Bryan, TX	1,474	266	Greeley, CO	1,026
157	Amarillo, TX	2,346	NA	Colorado Springs, CO**	NA	245	Green Bay, WI	1,265
344	Ames, IA	448	267	Columbia, MO	1,023	71	Greensboro-High Point, NC	7,404
41	Anaheim-Santa Ana-Irvine, CA M.D.	11,819	117	Columbus, GA-AL	3,685	64	Greenville-Anderson, SC	8,158
248	Anchorage, AK	1,236	356	Columbus, IN	384	193	Greenville, NC	1,785
158	Ann Arbor, MI	2,334	NA	Corpus Christi, TX**	NA	224	Hagerstown-Martinsburg, MD-WV	1,488
200	Anniston-Oxford, AL	1,710	363	Corvallis, OR	322	145	Hammond, LA	2,666
331	Appleton, WI	516	243	Crestview-Fort Walton Beach, FL	1,295	294	Hanford-Corcoran, CA	813
124	Asheville, NC	3,229	314	Cumberland, MD-WV	702	159	Harrisburg-Carlisle, PA	2,333
215	Athens-Clarke County, GA	1,568	3	Dallas (greater), TX	52,335	358	Harrisonburg, VA	356
7	Atlanta, GA	47,384	12	Dallas-Plano-Irving, TX M.D.	34,242	98	Hartford, CT	4,764
191	Atlantic City, NJ	1,791	273	Dalton, GA	970	269	Hattiesburg, MS	1,019
276	Auburn, AL	954	275	Danville, IL	955	116	Hickory, NC	3,716
84	Augusta, GA-SC	5,844	274	Daphne-Fairhope-Foley, AL	967	221	Hilton Head Island, SC	1,497
42	Austin-Round Rock, TX	11,173	179	Davenport, IA-IL	1,976	304	Hinesville, GA	758
44	Bakersfield, CA	10,931	72	Dayton, OH	7,255	303	Homosassa Springs, FL	763
28	Baltimore, MD	17,483	239	Decatur, AL	1,326	227	Houma, LA	1,464
284	Bangor, ME	912	260	Decatur, IL	1,090	NA	Houston, TX**	NA
163	Barnstable Town, MA	2,224	99	Deltona-Daytona Beach, FL	4,546	118	Huntsville, AL	3,615
65	Baton Rouge, LA	8,142	38	Denver-Aurora, CO	13,163	343	Idaho Falls, ID	456
345	Bay City, MI	441	NA	Des Moines-West Des Moines, IA**	NA	22	Indianapolis, IN	18,955
111	Beaumont-Port Arthur, TX	4,037	14	Detroit (greater), MI	29,873	325	Iowa City, IA	635
235	Beckley, WV	1,367	20	Detroit-Dearborn-Livonia, MI M.D.	20,047	49	Jacksonville, FL	10,259
238	Bellingham, WA	1,332	231	Dothan, AL	1,396	81	Jackson, MS	6,267
272	Billings, MT	999	249	Dover, DE	1,226	225	Jackson, TN	1,481
230	Binghamton, NY	1,400	NA	Dubuque, IA**	NA	287	Janesville, WI	884
39	Birmingham-Hoover, AL	12,756	206	Duluth, MN-WI	1,640	301	Jefferson City, MO	773
332	Bismarck, ND	515	88	Durham-Chapel Hill, NC	5,673	222	Johnson City, TN	1,494
309	Blacksburg, VA	734	258	Dutchess-Putnam, NY M.D.	1,104	322	Johnstown, PA	657
291	Bloomington, IL	849	250	East Stroudsburg, PA	1,202	213	Jonesboro, AR	1,574
268	Bloomington, IN	1,022	168	El Centro, CA	2,087	220	Joplin, MO	1,506
357	Bloomsburg-Berwick, PA	375	156	El Paso, TX	2,380	263	Kahului-Wailuku-Lahaina, HI	1,067
148	Boise City, ID	2,629	177	Elgin, IL M.D.	1,978	172	Kalamazoo-Portage, MI	2,059
23	Boston (greater), MA-NH	18,439	341	Elizabethtown-Fort Knox, KY	471	315	Kankakee, IL	701
59	Boston, MA M.D.	8,705	350	Elmira, NY	398	32	Kansas City, MO-KS	15,310
253	Boulder, CO	1,169	190	Erie, PA	1,808	233	Kennewick-Richland, WA	1,379
286	Bowling Green, KY	909	149	Eugene, OR	2,621	NA	Killeen-Temple, TX**	NA
170	Bremerton-Silverdale, WA	2,080	369	Fairbanks, AK	148	180	Kingsport, TN-VA	1,926
126	Bridgeport-Stamford, CT	3,205	296	Fargo, ND-MN	799	310	Kingston, NY	731
129	Brownsville-Harlingen, TX	3,092	318	Farmington, NM	677	69	Knoxville, TN	7,676
237	Brunswick, GA	1,348	143	Fayetteville-Springdale, AR-MO	2,675	316	Kokomo, IN	682
70	Buffalo-Niagara Falls, NY	7,461	76	Fayetteville, NC	6,905	317	La Crosse, WI-MN	678
228	Burlington, NC	1,438	327	Flagstaff, AZ	555	252	Lafayette, IN	1,170
305	California-Lexington Park, MD	753	82	Flint, MI	6,118	113	Lafayette, LA	3,858
62	Cambridge-Newton, MA M.D.	8,340	246	Florence-Muscle Shoals, AL	1,260	122	Lake Co.-Kenosha Co., IL-WI M.D.	3,375
68	Camden, NJ M.D.	7,693	147	Florence, SC	2,641	192	Lake Havasu City-Kingman, AZ	1,790
115	Canton, OH	3,729	367	Fond du Lac, WI	251	85	Lakeland, FL	5,796
108	Cape Coral-Fort Myers, FL	4,171	259	Fort Collins, CO	1,100	199	Lancaster, PA	1,720
295	Cape Girardeau, MO-IL	812	29	Fort Lauderdale, FL M.D.	17,469	146	Lansing-East Lansing, MI	2,662
364	Carson City, NV	298	162	Fort Smith, AR-OK	2,240	188	Laredo, TX	1,825
339	Casper, WY	474	150	Fort Wayne, IN	2,538	200	Las Cruces, NM	1,710
NA	Cedar Rapids, IA**	NA	25	Fort Worth-Arlington, TX M.D.	18,093	26	Las Vegas-Henderson, NV	17,539
335	Chambersburg-Waynesboro, PA	497	46	Fresno, CA	10,552	308	Lawrence, KS	740
203	Champaign-Urbana, IL	1,708	241	Gadsden, AL	1,310	200	Lawton, OK	1,710
103	Charleston-North Charleston, SC	4,373	175	Gainesville, FL	2,011	355	Lebanon, PA	386
293	Charlottesville, VA	823	281	Gainesville, GA	923	302	Lewiston-Auburn, ME	768

Note: All listings are for Metropolitan Statistical Areas (M.S.A.s) except for those ending with "M.D." Listings with "M.D." are Metropolitan Divisions which are smaller parts of eleven large M.S.A.s. See explanatory note at beginning of metropolitan area section.

RANK	METROPOLITAN AREA	BURGLARY	RANK	METROPOLITAN AREA	BURGLARY	RANK	METROPOLITAN AREA	BURGLARY
347	Lewiston, ID-WA	419	324	Owensboro, KY	639	123	Silver Spring-Frederick, MD M.D.	3,360
105	Lexington-Fayette, KY	4,326	128	Oxnard-Thousand Oaks, CA	3,113	288	Sioux City, IA-NE-SD	857
265	Lima, OH	1,042	112	Palm Bay-Melbourne, FL	3,945	256	Sioux Falls, SD	1,130
194	Lincoln, NE	1,780	204	Panama City, FL	1,683	131	South Bend-Mishawaka, IN-MI	3,038
51	Little Rock, AR	9,833	323	Parkersburg-Vienna, WV	656	140	Spartanburg, SC	2,695
351	Logan, UT-ID	397	100	Pensacola, FL	4,496	77	Spokane, WA	6,634
178	Longview, TX	1,977	138	Peoria, IL	2,721	165	Springfield, IL	2,153
289	Longview, WA	853	13	Philadelphia (greater) PA-NJ-MD-DE	33,848	93	Springfield, MA	5,254
5	Los Angeles County, CA M.D.	49,107	36	Philadelphia, PA M.D.	14,542	114	Springfield, MO	3,735
1	Los Angeles (greater), CA	60,926	11	Phoenix-Mesa-Scottsdale, AZ	35,341	196	Springfield, OH	1,750
47	Louisville, KY-IN	10,482	218	Pine Bluff, AR	1,544	359	State College, PA	355
121	Lubbock, TX	3,452	54	Pittsburgh, PA	9,420	365	Staunton-Waynesboro, VA	281
277	Lynchburg, VA	951	280	Pittsfield, MA	935	66	Stockton-Lodi, CA	8,019
133	Macon, GA	2,894	362	Pocatello, ID	328	334	St. George, UT	502
205	Madera, CA	1,654	137	Port St. Lucie, FL	2,722	251	St. Joseph, MO-KS	1,201
136	Madison, WI	2,742	40	Portland-Vancouver, OR-WA	12,057	30	St. Louis, MO-IL	16,980
198	Manchester-Nashua, NH	1,732	151	Portland, ME	2,499	209	Sumter, SC	1,604
361	Manhattan, KS	338	278	Prescott, AZ	948	110	Syracuse, NY	4,046
338	Mankato-North Mankato, MN	489	53	Providence-Warwick, RI-MA	9,606	NA	Tacoma, WA M.D.**	NA
189	Mansfield, OH	1,824	240	Provo-Orem, UT	1,315	109	Tallahassee, FL	4,079
78	McAllen-Edinburg-Mission, TX	6,465	168	Pueblo, CO	2,087	21	Tampa-St Petersburg, FL	19,377
270	Medford, OR	1,014	285	Punta Gorda, FL	910	209	Terre Haute, IN	1,604
27	Memphis, TN-MS-AR	17,511	229	Racine, WI	1,430	208	Texarkana, TX-AR	1,622
141	Merced, CA	2,686	73	Raleigh, NC	7,240	359	The Villages, FL	355
6	Miami (greater), FL	48,856	305	Rapid City, SD	753	61	Toledo, OH	8,460
18	Miami-Dade County, FL M.D.	21,109	153	Reading, PA	2,456	185	Topeka, KS	1,868
292	Michigan City-La Porte, IN	843	195	Redding, CA	1,754	154	Trenton, NJ	2,447
368	Midland, MI	209	142	Reno, NV	2,684	63	Tucson, AZ	8,323
312	Midland, TX	714	80	Richmond, VA	6,301	57	Tulsa, OK	8,972
50	Milwaukee, WI	10,040	10	Riverside-San Bernardino, CA	37,893	171	Tuscaloosa, AL	2,078
NA	Minneapolis-St. Paul, MN-WI**	NA	212	Roanoke, VA	1,575	182	Tyler, TX	1,894
342	Missoula, MT	461	300	Rochester, MN	777	223	Utica-Rome, NY	1,490
101	Mobile, AL	4,458	79	Rochester, NY	6,304	255	Valdosta, GA	1,132
90	Modesto, CA	5,551	125	Rockford, IL	3,217	104	Vallejo-Fairfield, CA	4,342
161	Monroe, LA	2,283	232	Rockingham County, NH M.D.	1,394	296	Victoria, TX	799
262	Monroe, MI	1,088	184	Rocky Mount, NC	1,873	174	Vineland-Bridgeton, NJ	2,033
89	Montgomery County, PA M.D.	5,620	279	Rome, GA	941	56	Virginia Beach-Norfolk, VA-NC	9,084
97	Montgomery, AL	4,903	33	Sacramento, CA	15,279	102	Visalia-Porterville, CA	4,375
329	Morgantown, WV	519	197	Saginaw, MI	1,746	160	Waco, TX	2,321
296	Morristown, TN	799	164	Salem, OR	2,185	336	Walla Walla, WA	496
244	Mount Vernon-Anacortes, WA	1,275	132	Salinas, CA	2,912	217	Warner Robins, GA	1,548
282	Muncie, IN	914	127	Salisbury, MD-DE	3,184	52	Warren-Troy, MI M.D.	9,826
321	Napa, CA	658	75	Salt Lake City, UT	7,049	24	Washington (greater) DC-VA-MD-WV	18,193
236	Naples-Marco Island, FL	1,356	19	San Antonio, TX	20,597	35	Washington, DC-VA-MD-WV M.D.	14,833
43	Nashville-Davidson, TN	10,975	37	San Diego, CA	14,076	257	Waterloo-Cedar Falls, IA	1,115
74	Nassau-Suffolk, NY M.D.	7,106	NA	San Francisco (greater), CA**	NA	340	Watertown-Fort Drum, NY	472
173	New Bern, NC	2,054	60	San Francisco-Redwood, CA M.D.	8,674	337	Wausau, WI	492
107	New Haven-Milford, CT	4,188	55	San Jose, CA	9,297	48	West Palm Beach, FL M.D.	10,278
58	New Orleans, LA	8,827	215	San Luis Obispo, CA	1,568	307	Wheeling, WV-OH	752
2	New York (greater), NY-NJ-PA	57,780	NA	San Rafael, CA M.D.**	NA	219	Wichita Falls, TX	1,527
9	New York-Jersey City, NY-NJ M.D.	38,827	207	Santa Cruz-Watsonville, CA	1,633	94	Wichita, KS	5,240
45	Newark, NJ-PA M.D.	10,743	139	Santa Fe, NM	2,715	332	Williamsport, PA	515
92	North Port-Sarasota-Bradenton, FL	5,461	155	Santa Maria-Santa Barbara, CA	2,430	83	Wilmington, DE-MD-NJ M.D.	5,993
320	Norwich-New London, CT	670	187	Santa Rosa, CA	1,826	144	Wilmington, NC	2,674
16	Oakland-Hayward, CA M.D.	21,801	134	Savannah, GA	2,773	328	Winchester, VA-WV	548
176	Ocala, FL	1,989	135	Scranton--Wilkes-Barre, PA	2,748	67	Winston-Salem, NC	7,949
264	Ocean City, NJ	1,054	NA	Seattle (greater), WA**	NA	96	Worcester, MA-CT	4,951
260	Odessa, TX	1,090	15	Seattle-Bellevue-Everett, WA M.D.	22,872	130	Yakima, WA	3,039
152	Ogden-Clearfield, UT	2,457	290	Sebastian-Vero Beach, FL	851	242	York-Hanover, PA	1,309
34	Oklahoma City, OK	14,924	282	Sebring, FL	914	86	Youngstown-Warren, OH-PA	5,733
166	Olympia, WA	2,137	348	Sheboygan, WI	408	234	Yuba City, CA	1,370
91	Omaha-Council Bluffs, NE-IA	5,496	271	Sherman-Denison, TX	1,013	214	Yuma, AZ	1,569
17	Orlando, FL	21,316	120	Shreveport-Bossier City, LA	3,494			
319	Oshkosh-Neenah, WI	675	311	Sierra Vista-Douglas, AZ	723			

Source: Reported data from the F.B.I. "Crime in the United States 2012"

*Burglary is the unlawful entry of a structure to commit a felony or theft. Attempts are included.

**Not available.

29. Burglaries in 2012 (continued)
National Total = 2,103,787 Burglaries*

RANK	METROPOLITAN AREA	BURGLARY	RANK	METROPOLITAN AREA	BURGLARY	RANK	METROPOLITAN AREA	BURGLARY
1	Los Angeles (greater), CA	60,926	65	Baton Rouge, LA	8,142	129	Brownsville-Harlingen, TX	3,092
2	New York (greater), NY-NJ-PA	57,780	66	Stockton-Lodi, CA	8,019	130	Yakima, WA	3,039
3	Dallas (greater), TX	52,335	67	Winston-Salem, NC	7,949	131	South Bend-Mishawaka, IN-MI	3,038
4	Chicago (greater), IL-IN-WI	50,771	68	Camden, NJ M.D.	7,693	132	Salinas, CA	2,912
5	Los Angeles County, CA M.D.	49,107	69	Knoxville, TN	7,676	133	Macon, GA	2,894
6	Miami (greater), FL	48,856	70	Buffalo-Niagara Falls, NY	7,461	134	Savannah, GA	2,773
7	Atlanta, GA	47,384	71	Greensboro-High Point, NC	7,404	135	Scranton--Wilkes-Barre, PA	2,748
8	Chicago-Joilet-Naperville, IL M.D.	40,385	72	Dayton, OH	7,255	136	Madison, WI	2,742
9	New York-Jersey City, NY-NJ M.D.	38,827	73	Raleigh, NC	7,240	137	Port St. Lucie, FL	2,722
10	Riverside-San Bernardino, CA	37,893	74	Nassau-Suffolk, NY M.D.	7,106	138	Peoria, IL	2,721
11	Phoenix-Mesa-Scottsdale, AZ	35,341	75	Salt Lake City, UT	7,049	139	Santa Fe, NM	2,715
12	Dallas-Plano-Irving, TX M.D.	34,242	76	Fayetteville, NC	6,905	140	Spartanburg, SC	2,695
13	Philadelphia (greater) PA-NJ-MD-DE	33,848	77	Spokane, WA	6,634	141	Merced, CA	2,686
14	Detroit (greater), MI	29,873	78	McAllen-Edinburg-Mission, TX	6,465	142	Reno, NV	2,684
15	Seattle-Bellevue-Everett, WA M.D.	22,872	79	Rochester, NY	6,304	143	Fayetteville-Springdale, AR-MO	2,675
16	Oakland-Hayward, CA M.D.	21,801	80	Richmond, VA	6,301	144	Wilmington, NC	2,674
17	Orlando, FL	21,316	81	Jackson, MS	6,267	145	Hammond, LA	2,666
18	Miami-Dade County, FL M.D.	21,109	82	Flint, MI	6,118	146	Lansing-East Lansing, MI	2,662
19	San Antonio, TX	20,597	83	Wilmington, DE-MD-NJ M.D.	5,993	147	Florence, SC	2,641
20	Detroit-Dearborn-Livonia, MI M.D.	20,047	84	Augusta, GA-SC	5,844	148	Boise City, ID	2,629
21	Tampa-St Petersburg, FL	19,377	85	Lakeland, FL	5,796	149	Eugene, OR	2,621
22	Indianapolis, IN	18,955	86	Youngstown-Warren, OH-PA	5,733	150	Fort Wayne, IN	2,538
23	Boston (greater), MA-NH	18,439	87	Akron, OH	5,708	151	Portland, ME	2,499
24	Washington (greater) DC-VA-MD-WV	18,193	88	Durham-Chapel Hill, NC	5,673	152	Ogden-Clearfield, UT	2,457
25	Fort Worth-Arlington, TX M.D.	18,093	89	Montgomery County, PA M.D.	5,620	153	Reading, PA	2,456
26	Las Vegas-Henderson, NV	17,539	90	Modesto, CA	5,551	154	Trenton, NJ	2,447
27	Memphis, TN-MS-AR	17,511	91	Omaha-Council Bluffs, NE-IA	5,496	155	Santa Maria-Santa Barbara, CA	2,430
28	Baltimore, MD	17,483	92	North Port-Sarasota-Bradenton, FL	5,461	156	El Paso, TX	2,380
29	Fort Lauderdale, FL M.D.	17,469	93	Springfield, MA	5,254	157	Amarillo, TX	2,346
30	St. Louis, MO-IL	16,980	94	Wichita, KS	5,240	158	Ann Arbor, MI	2,334
31	Cincinnati, OH-KY-IN	16,869	95	Gary, IN M.D.	5,033	159	Harrisburg-Carlisle, PA	2,333
32	Kansas City, MO-KS	15,310	96	Worcester, MA-CT	4,951	160	Waco, TX	2,321
33	Sacramento, CA	15,279	97	Montgomery, AL	4,903	161	Monroe, LA	2,283
34	Oklahoma City, OK	14,924	98	Hartford, CT	4,764	162	Fort Smith, AR-OK	2,240
35	Washington, DC-VA-MD-WV M.D.	14,833	99	Deltona-Daytona Beach, FL	4,546	163	Barnstable Town, MA	2,224
36	Philadelphia, PA M.D.	14,542	100	Pensacola, FL	4,496	164	Salem, OR	2,185
37	San Diego, CA	14,076	101	Mobile, AL	4,458	165	Springfield, IL	2,153
38	Denver-Aurora, CO	13,163	102	Visalia-Porterville, CA	4,375	166	Olympia, WA	2,137
39	Birmingham-Hoover, AL	12,756	103	Charleston-North Charleston, SC	4,373	167	Albany, GA	2,090
40	Portland-Vancouver, OR-WA	12,057	104	Vallejo-Fairfield, CA	4,342	168	El Centro, CA	2,087
41	Anaheim-Santa Ana-Irvine, CA M.D.	11,819	105	Lexington-Fayette, KY	4,326	168	Pueblo, CO	2,087
42	Austin-Round Rock, TX	11,173	106	Albany-Schenectady-Troy, NY	4,205	170	Bremerton-Silverdale, WA	2,080
43	Nashville-Davidson, TN	10,975	107	New Haven-Milford, CT	4,188	171	Tuscaloosa, AL	2,078
44	Bakersfield, CA	10,931	108	Cape Coral-Fort Myers, FL	4,171	172	Kalamazoo-Portage, MI	2,059
45	Newark, NJ-PA M.D.	10,743	109	Tallahassee, FL	4,079	173	New Bern, NC	2,054
46	Fresno, CA	10,552	110	Syracuse, NY	4,046	174	Vineland-Bridgeton, NJ	2,033
47	Louisville, KY-IN	10,482	111	Beaumont-Port Arthur, TX	4,037	175	Gainesville, FL	2,011
48	West Palm Beach, FL M.D.	10,278	112	Palm Bay-Melbourne, FL	3,945	176	Ocala, FL	1,989
49	Jacksonville, FL	10,259	113	Lafayette, LA	3,858	177	Elgin, IL M.D.	1,978
50	Milwaukee, WI	10,040	114	Springfield, MO	3,735	178	Longview, TX	1,977
51	Little Rock, AR	9,833	115	Canton, OH	3,729	179	Davenport, IA-IL	1,976
52	Warren-Troy, MI M.D.	9,826	116	Hickory, NC	3,716	180	Kingsport, TN-VA	1,926
53	Providence-Warwick, RI-MA	9,606	117	Columbus, GA-AL	3,685	181	Chico, CA	1,919
54	Pittsburgh, PA	9,420	118	Huntsville, AL	3,615	182	Tyler, TX	1,894
55	San Jose, CA	9,297	119	Allentown, PA-NJ	3,525	183	Alexandria, LA	1,879
56	Virginia Beach-Norfolk, VA-NC	9,084	120	Shreveport-Bossier City, LA	3,494	184	Rocky Mount, NC	1,873
57	Tulsa, OK	8,972	121	Lubbock, TX	3,452	185	Topeka, KS	1,868
58	New Orleans, LA	8,827	122	Lake Co.-Kenosha Co., IL-WI M.D.	3,375	186	Clarksville, TN-KY	1,848
59	Boston, MA M.D.	8,705	123	Silver Spring-Frederick, MD M.D.	3,360	187	Santa Rosa, CA	1,826
60	San Francisco-Redwood, CA M.D.	8,674	124	Asheville, NC	3,229	188	Laredo, TX	1,825
61	Toledo, OH	8,460	125	Rockford, IL	3,217	189	Mansfield, OH	1,824
62	Cambridge-Newton, MA M.D.	8,340	126	Bridgeport-Stamford, CT	3,205	190	Erie, PA	1,808
63	Tucson, AZ	8,323	127	Salisbury, MD-DE	3,184	191	Atlantic City, NJ	1,791
64	Greenville-Anderson, SC	8,158	128	Oxnard-Thousand Oaks, CA	3,113	192	Lake Havasu City-Kingman, AZ	1,790

Note: All listings are for Metropolitan Statistical Areas (M.S.A.s) except for those ending with "M.D." Listings with "M.D." are Metropolitan Divisions which are smaller parts of eleven large M.S.A.s. See explanatory note at beginning of metropolitan area section.

RANK	METROPOLITAN AREA	BURGLARY	RANK	METROPOLITAN AREA	BURGLARY	RANK	METROPOLITAN AREA	BURGLARY
193	Greenville, NC	1,785	257	Waterloo-Cedar Falls, IA	1,115	321	Napa, CA	658
194	Lincoln, NE	1,780	258	Dutchess-Putnam, NY M.D.	1,104	322	Johnstown, PA	657
195	Redding, CA	1,754	259	Fort Collins, CO	1,100	323	Parkersburg-Vienna, WV	656
196	Springfield, OH	1,750	260	Decatur, IL	1,090	324	Owensboro, KY	639
197	Saginaw, MI	1,746	260	Odessa, TX	1,090	325	Iowa City, IA	635
198	Manchester-Nashua, NH	1,732	262	Monroe, MI	1,088	326	Grand Junction, CO	576
199	Lancaster, PA	1,720	263	Kahului-Wailuku-Lahaina, HI	1,067	327	Flagstaff, AZ	555
200	Anniston-Oxford, AL	1,710	264	Ocean City, NJ	1,054	328	Winchester, VA-WV	548
200	Las Cruces, NM	1,710	265	Lima, OH	1,042	329	Morgantown, WV	519
200	Lawton, OK	1,710	266	Greeley, CO	1,026	330	Grand Island, NE	517
203	Champaign-Urbana, IL	1,708	267	Columbia, MO	1,023	331	Appleton, WI	516
204	Panama City, FL	1,683	268	Bloomington, IN	1,022	332	Bismarck, ND	515
205	Madera, CA	1,654	269	Hattiesburg, MS	1,019	332	Williamsport, PA	515
206	Duluth, MN-WI	1,640	270	Medford, OR	1,014	334	St. George, UT	502
207	Santa Cruz-Watsonville, CA	1,633	271	Sherman-Denison, TX	1,013	335	Chambersburg-Waynesboro, PA	497
208	Texarkana, TX-AR	1,622	272	Billings, MT	999	336	Walla Walla, WA	496
209	Sumter, SC	1,604	273	Dalton, GA	970	337	Wausau, WI	492
209	Terre Haute, IN	1,604	274	Daphne-Fairhope-Foley, AL	967	338	Mankato-North Mankato, MN	489
211	Goldsboro, NC	1,601	275	Danville, IL	955	339	Casper, WY	474
212	Roanoke, VA	1,575	276	Auburn, AL	954	340	Watertown-Fort Drum, NY	472
213	Jonesboro, AR	1,574	277	Lynchburg, VA	951	341	Elizabethtown-Fort Knox, KY	471
214	Yuma, AZ	1,569	278	Prescott, AZ	948	342	Missoula, MT	461
215	Athens-Clarke County, GA	1,568	279	Rome, GA	941	343	Idaho Falls, ID	456
215	San Luis Obispo, CA	1,568	280	Pittsfield, MA	935	344	Ames, IA	448
217	Warner Robins, GA	1,548	281	Gainesville, GA	923	345	Bay City, MI	441
218	Pine Bluff, AR	1,544	282	Muncie, IN	914	346	Cheyenne, WY	425
219	Wichita Falls, TX	1,527	282	Sebring, FL	914	347	Lewiston, ID-WA	419
220	Joplin, MO	1,506	284	Bangor, ME	912	348	Sheboygan, WI	408
221	Hilton Head Island, SC	1,497	285	Punta Gorda, FL	910	349	Glens Falls, NY	403
222	Johnson City, TN	1,494	286	Bowling Green, KY	909	350	Elmira, NY	398
223	Utica-Rome, NY	1,490	287	Janesville, WI	884	351	Logan, UT-ID	397
224	Hagerstown-Martinsburg, MD-WV	1,488	288	Sioux City, IA-NE-SD	857	352	Grand Forks, ND-MN	394
225	Jackson, TN	1,481	289	Longview, WA	853	353	Great Falls, MT	391
226	College Station-Bryan, TX	1,474	290	Sebastian-Vero Beach, FL	851	354	Altoona, PA	387
227	Houma, LA	1,464	291	Bloomington, IL	849	355	Lebanon, PA	386
228	Burlington, NC	1,438	292	Michigan City-La Porte, IN	843	356	Columbus, IN	384
229	Racine, WI	1,430	293	Charlottesville, VA	823	357	Bloomsburg-Berwick, PA	375
230	Binghamton, NY	1,400	294	Hanford-Corcoran, CA	813	358	Harrisonburg, VA	356
231	Dothan, AL	1,396	295	Cape Girardeau, MO-IL	812	359	State College, PA	355
232	Rockingham County, NH M.D.	1,394	296	Fargo, ND-MN	799	359	The Villages, FL	355
233	Kennewick-Richland, WA	1,379	296	Morristown, TN	799	361	Manhattan, KS	338
234	Yuba City, CA	1,370	296	Victoria, TX	799	362	Pocatello, ID	328
235	Beckley, WV	1,367	299	Cleveland, TN	788	363	Corvallis, OR	322
236	Naples-Marco Island, FL	1,356	300	Rochester, MN	777	364	Carson City, NV	298
237	Brunswick, GA	1,348	301	Jefferson City, MO	773	365	Staunton-Waynesboro, VA	281
238	Bellingham, WA	1,332	302	Lewiston-Auburn, ME	768	366	Gettysburg, PA	263
239	Decatur, AL	1,326	303	Homosassa Springs, FL	763	367	Fond du Lac, WI	251
240	Provo-Orem, UT	1,315	304	Hinesville, GA	758	368	Midland, MI	209
241	Gadsden, AL	1,310	305	California-Lexington Park, MD	753	369	Fairbanks, AK	148
242	York-Hanover, PA	1,309	305	Rapid City, SD	753	NA	Albuquerque, NM**	NA
243	Crestview-Fort Walton Beach, FL	1,295	307	Wheeling, WV-OH	752	NA	Cedar Rapids, IA**	NA
244	Mount Vernon-Anacortes, WA	1,275	308	Lawrence, KS	740	NA	Colorado Springs, CO**	NA
245	Green Bay, WI	1,265	309	Blacksburg, VA	734	NA	Corpus Christi, TX**	NA
246	Florence-Muscle Shoals, AL	1,260	310	Kingston, NY	731	NA	Des Moines-West Des Moines, IA**	NA
247	Abilene, TX	1,245	311	Sierra Vista-Douglas, AZ	723	NA	Dubuque, IA**	NA
248	Anchorage, AK	1,236	312	Midland, TX	714	NA	Houston, TX**	NA
249	Dover, DE	1,226	313	Albany, OR	707	NA	Killeen-Temple, TX**	NA
250	East Stroudsburg, PA	1,202	314	Cumberland, MD-WV	702	NA	Minneapolis-St. Paul, MN-WI**	NA
251	St. Joseph, MO-KS	1,201	315	Kankakee, IL	701	NA	San Francisco (greater), CA**	NA
252	Lafayette, IN	1,170	316	Kokomo, IN	682	NA	San Rafael, CA M.D.**	NA
253	Boulder, CO	1,169	317	La Crosse, WI-MN	678	NA	Seattle (greater), WA**	NA
254	Coeur d'Alene, ID	1,165	318	Farmington, NM	677	NA	Tacoma, WA M.D.**	NA
255	Valdosta, GA	1,132	319	Oshkosh-Neenah, WI	675			
256	Sioux Falls, SD	1,130	320	Norwich-New London, CT	670			

Source: Reported data from the F.B.I. "Crime in the United States 2012"

*Burglary is the unlawful entry of a structure to commit a felony or theft. Attempts are included.

**Not available.

30. Burglary Rate in 2012
National Rate = 670.2 Burglaries per 100,000 Population*

RANK	METROPOLITAN AREA	RATE	RANK	METROPOLITAN AREA	RATE	RANK	METROPOLITAN AREA	RATE
157	Abilene, TX	737.1	289	Cheyenne, WY	452.0	169	Gary, IN M.D.	708.0
128	Akron, OH	813.8	251	Chicago (greater), IL-IN-WI	533.8	362	Gettysburg, PA	258.9
280	Albany-Schenectady-Troy, NY	479.9	243	Chicago-Joilet-Naperville, IL M.D.	553.1	349	Glens Falls, NY	310.7
12	Albany, GA	1,311.4	101	Chico, CA	863.2	18	Goldsboro, NC	1,281.6
NA	Albuquerque, NM**	NA	135	Cincinnati, OH-KY-IN	794.3	318	Grand Forks, ND-MN	394.9
31	Alexandria, LA	1,209.0	177	Clarksville, TN-KY	694.2	208	Grand Island, NE	621.4
300	Allentown, PA-NJ	426.4	188	Cleveland, TN	668.9	323	Grand Junction, CO	386.3
352	Altoona, PA	304.0	125	Coeur d'Alene, ID	819.9	281	Great Falls, MT	474.5
87	Amarillo, TX	903.2	205	College Station-Bryan, TX	627.0	321	Greeley, CO	391.3
270	Ames, IA	497.7	NA	Colorado Springs, CO**	NA	309	Green Bay, WI	407.7
326	Anaheim-Santa Ana-Irvine, CA M.D.	383.2	211	Columbia, MO	616.5	61	Greensboro-High Point, NC	1,003.0
319	Anchorage, AK	394.2	30	Columbus, GA-AL	1,211.0	73	Greenville-Anderson, SC	966.8
187	Ann Arbor, MI	670.3	274	Columbus, IN	491.6	53	Greenville, NC	1,032.8
9	Anniston-Oxford, AL	1,445.8	NA	Corpus Christi, TX**	NA	229	Hagerstown-Martinsburg, MD-WV	582.6
369	Appleton, WI	226.3	327	Corvallis, OR	372.1	256	Hanford-Corcoran, CA	523.9
153	Asheville, NC	745.3	250	Crestview-Fort Walton Beach, FL	533.9	301	Harrisburg-Carlisle, PA	421.3
131	Athens-Clarke County, GA	802.5	182	Cumberland, MD-WV	677.6	358	Harrisonburg, VA	278.2
100	Atlanta, GA	871.9	139	Dallas (greater), TX	783.5	284	Hartford, CT	465.3
195	Atlantic City, NJ	649.6	142	Dallas-Plano-Irving, TX M.D.	777.2	173	Hattiesburg, MS	699.2
190	Auburn, AL	662.3	185	Dalton, GA	672.4	60	Hickory, NC	1,009.3
59	Augusta, GA-SC	1,015.3	33	Danville, IL	1,171.1	140	Hilton Head Island, SC	781.0
209	Austin-Round Rock, TX	617.2	260	Daphne-Fairhope-Foley, AL	515.8	80	Hinesville, GA	930.7
21	Bakersfield, CA	1,271.6	257	Davenport, IA-IL	517.2	248	Homosassa Springs, FL	537.5
201	Baltimore, MD	634.5	87	Dayton, OH	903.2	174	Houma, LA	697.8
226	Bangor, ME	592.6	102	Decatur, AL	857.2	NA	Houston, TX**	NA
55	Barnstable Town, MA	1,021.6	65	Decatur, IL	983.9	107	Huntsville, AL	846.2
62	Baton Rouge, LA	1,001.4	150	Deltona-Daytona Beach, FL	757.3	342	Idaho Falls, ID	335.8
305	Bay City, MI	411.4	268	Denver-Aurora, CO	499.5	64	Indianapolis, IN	989.4
67	Beaumont-Port Arthur, TX	982.1	NA	Des Moines-West Des Moines, IA**	NA	306	Iowa City, IA	408.4
42	Beckley, WV	1,095.1	175	Detroit (greater), MI	696.5	155	Jacksonville, FL	744.0
196	Bellingham, WA	647.7	40	Detroit-Dearborn-Livonia, MI M.D.	1,111.6	44	Jackson, MS	1,090.8
212	Billings, MT	616.4	76	Dothan, AL	948.7	38	Jackson, TN	1,130.3
242	Binghamton, NY	556.8	159	Dover, DE	735.7	245	Janesville, WI	550.8
39	Birmingham-Hoover, AL	1,122.1	NA	Dubuque, IA**	NA	261	Jefferson City, MO	512.7
297	Bismarck, ND	430.3	228	Duluth, MN-WI	582.7	156	Johnson City, TN	741.6
307	Blacksburg, VA	408.2	43	Durham-Chapel Hill, NC	1,095.0	286	Johnstown, PA	456.4
287	Bloomington, IL	453.5	360	Dutchess-Putnam, NY M.D.	275.9	20	Jonesboro, AR	1,276.6
202	Bloomington, IN	631.6	170	East Stroudsburg, PA	706.4	104	Joplin, MO	850.0
295	Bloomsburg-Berwick, PA	436.5	34	El Centro, CA	1,167.9	186	Kahului-Wailuku-Lahaina, HI	672.1
303	Boise City, ID	416.0	357	El Paso, TX	284.5	206	Kalamazoo-Portage, MI	626.9
315	Boston (greater), MA-NH	398.3	347	Elgin, IL M.D.	316.3	213	Kankakee, IL	616.3
288	Boston, MA M.D.	453.2	350	Elizabethtown-Fort Knox, KY	310.4	152	Kansas City, MO-KS	753.0
325	Boulder, CO	385.1	291	Elmira, NY	445.6	259	Kennewick-Richland, WA	517.0
236	Bowling Green, KY	564.7	197	Erie, PA	642.4	NA	Killeen-Temple, TX**	NA
130	Bremerton-Silverdale, WA	808.9	158	Eugene, OR	736.4	214	Kingsport, TN-VA	616.1
340	Bridgeport-Stamford, CT	351.9	299	Fairbanks, AK	427.7	313	Kingston, NY	398.5
160	Brownsville-Harlingen, TX	735.6	332	Fargo, ND-MN	369.8	89	Knoxville, TN	902.6
32	Brunswick, GA	1,181.1	255	Farmington, NM	527.2	123	Kokomo, IN	821.1
193	Buffalo-Niagara Falls, NY	654.4	239	Fayetteville-Springdale, AR-MO	562.5	266	La Crosse, WI-MN	502.6
81	Burlington, NC	928.9	3	Fayetteville, NC	1,827.4	233	Lafayette, IN	572.8
178	California-Lexington Park, MD	693.9	307	Flagstaff, AZ	408.2	127	Lafayette, LA	814.4
335	Cambridge-Newton, MA M.D.	364.6	8	Flint, MI	1,448.4	324	Lake Co.-Kenosha Co., IL-WI M.D.	386.0
218	Camden, NJ M.D.	611.5	103	Florence-Muscle Shoals, AL	852.0	97	Lake Havasu City-Kingman, AZ	875.1
84	Canton, OH	923.4	23	Florence, SC	1,269.0	79	Lakeland, FL	938.2
194	Cape Coral-Fort Myers, FL	651.8	365	Fond du Lac, WI	245.3	345	Lancaster, PA	328.0
113	Cape Girardeau, MO-IL	835.4	337	Fort Collins, CO	355.1	234	Lansing-East Lansing, MI	571.9
253	Carson City, NV	530.6	72	Fort Lauderdale, FL M.D.	968.1	172	Laredo, TX	701.0
217	Casper, WY	611.8	137	Fort Smith, AR-OK	790.6	132	Las Cruces, NM	799.3
NA	Cedar Rapids, IA**	NA	222	Fort Wayne, IN	603.2	95	Las Vegas-Henderson, NV	878.9
344	Chambersburg-Waynesboro, PA	329.0	134	Fort Worth-Arlington, TX M.D.	795.5	192	Lawrence, KS	656.1
161	Champaign-Urbana, IL	734.8	41	Fresno, CA	1,108.8	16	Lawton, OK	1,287.6
200	Charleston-North Charleston, SC	635.1	24	Gadsden, AL	1,250.9	356	Lebanon, PA	286.9
333	Charlottesville, VA	368.1	154	Gainesville, FL	744.8	167	Lewiston-Auburn, ME	714.6
			269	Gainesville, GA	498.9			

Note: All listings are for Metropolitan Statistical Areas (M.S.A.s) except for those ending with "M.D." Listings with "M.D." are Metropolitan Divisions which are smaller parts of eleven large M.S.A.s. See explanatory note at beginning of metropolitan area section.

RANK	METROPOLITAN AREA	RATE	RANK	METROPOLITAN AREA	RATE	RANK	METROPOLITAN AREA	RATE
184	Lewiston, ID-WA	676.3	244	Owensboro, KY	552.6	361	Silver Spring-Frederick, MD M.D.	271.3
90	Lexington-Fayette, KY	900.4	328	Oxnard-Thousand Oaks, CA	370.8	264	Sioux City, IA-NE-SD	504.7
66	Lima, OH	982.2	166	Palm Bay-Melbourne, FL	716.0	279	Sioux Falls, SD	480.8
232	Lincoln, NE	576.7	92	Panama City, FL	894.1	75	South Bend-Mishawaka, IN-MI	950.7
11	Little Rock, AR	1,379.9	171	Parkersburg-Vienna, WV	706.3	108	Spartanburg, SC	846.0
351	Logan, UT-ID	307.3	68	Pensacola, FL	978.7	25	Spokane, WA	1,239.1
91	Longview, TX	899.0	165	Peoria, IL	716.6	58	Springfield, IL	1,017.3
120	Longview, WA	824.3	238	Philadelphia (greater) PA-NJ-MD-DE	563.0	111	Springfield, MA	837.8
273	Los Angeles County, CA M.D.	492.0	181	Philadelphia, PA M.D.	678.0	106	Springfield, MO	847.0
283	Los Angeles (greater), CA	466.3	124	Phoenix-Mesa-Scottsdale, AZ	820.0	22	Springfield, OH	1,271.0
110	Louisville, KY-IN	839.5	5	Pine Bluff, AR	1,554.9	368	State College, PA	229.1
36	Lubbock, TX	1,149.4	313	Pittsburgh, PA	398.5	367	Staunton-Waynesboro, VA	234.3
331	Lynchburg, VA	370.1	168	Pittsfield, MA	710.4	37	Stockton-Lodi, CA	1,141.2
26	Macon, GA	1,229.4	322	Pocatello, ID	389.3	341	St. George, UT	349.6
49	Madera, CA	1,071.6	203	Port St. Lucie, FL	627.6	78	St. Joseph, MO-KS	939.5
290	Madison, WI	445.9	254	Portland-Vancouver, OR-WA	528.8	220	St. Louis, MO-IL	606.9
297	Manchester-Nashua, NH	430.3	278	Portland, ME	484.1	6	Sumter, SC	1,478.6
338	Manhattan, KS	354.3	293	Prescott, AZ	442.6	219	Syracuse, NY	607.4
267	Mankato-North Mankato, MN	499.9	223	Providence-Warwick, RI-MA	598.8	NA	Tacoma, WA M.D.**	NA
7	Mansfield, OH	1,476.9	366	Provo-Orem, UT	239.9	45	Tallahassee, FL	1,088.3
133	McAllen-Edinburg-Mission, TX	798.4	17	Pueblo, CO	1,282.2	183	Tampa-St Petersburg, FL	676.7
274	Medford, OR	491.6	240	Punta Gorda, FL	559.3	82	Terre Haute, IN	926.1
13	Memphis, TN-MS-AR	1,303.3	162	Racine, WI	730.0	48	Texarkana, TX-AR	1,073.1
54	Merced, CA	1,024.0	214	Raleigh, NC	616.1	336	The Villages, FL	358.3
104	Miami (greater), FL	850.0	247	Rapid City, SD	544.7	10	Toledo, OH	1,389.5
126	Miami-Dade County, FL M.D.	815.1	225	Reading, PA	594.0	136	Topeka, KS	792.0
151	Michigan City-La Porte, IN	754.5	69	Redding, CA	977.6	189	Trenton, NJ	663.4
364	Midland, MI	248.4	210	Reno, NV	616.7	117	Tucson, AZ	832.0
277	Midland, TX	484.3	262	Richmond, VA	511.3	77	Tulsa, OK	941.7
198	Milwaukee, WI	641.0	99	Riverside-San Bernardino, CA	872.1	93	Tuscaloosa, AL	892.2
NA	Minneapolis-St. Paul, MN-WI**	NA	265	Roanoke, VA	504.4	98	Tyler, TX	874.5
304	Missoula, MT	415.7	330	Rochester, MN	370.3	271	Utica-Rome, NY	496.6
47	Mobile, AL	1,076.2	231	Rochester, NY	580.2	138	Valdosta, GA	787.1
51	Modesto, CA	1,060.7	85	Rockford, IL	923.0	52	Vallejo-Fairfield, CA	1,033.0
19	Monroe, LA	1,277.6	343	Rockingham County, NH M.D.	331.2	118	Victoria, TX	830.5
164	Monroe, MI	717.3	28	Rocky Mount, NC	1,218.9	15	Vineland-Bridgeton, NJ	1,287.8
354	Montgomery County, PA M.D.	297.0	70	Rome, GA	970.0	252	Virginia Beach-Norfolk, VA-NC	533.2
14	Montgomery, AL	1,289.8	176	Sacramento, CA	695.6	74	Visalia-Porterville, CA	964.9
320	Morgantown, WV	392.4	96	Saginaw, MI	876.4	94	Waco, TX	891.5
179	Morristown, TN	690.7	246	Salem, OR	549.5	145	Walla Walla, WA	771.8
50	Mount Vernon-Anacortes, WA	1,069.0	180	Salinas, CA	683.9	115	Warner Robins, GA	834.8
143	Muncie, IN	774.4	114	Salisbury, MD-DE	835.1	317	Warren-Troy, MI M.D.	395.3
282	Napa, CA	472.1	204	Salt Lake City, UT	627.5	348	Washington (greater) DC-VA-MD-WV	312.3
309	Naples-Marco Island, FL	407.7	83	San Antonio, TX	924.5	346	Washington, DC-VA-MD-WV M.D.	323.3
199	Nashville-Davidson, TN	640.8	292	San Diego, CA	444.2	191	Waterloo-Cedar Falls, IA	660.0
363	Nassau-Suffolk, NY M.D.	248.6	NA	San Francisco (greater), CA**	NA	316	Watertown-Fort Drum, NY	398.2
4	New Bern, NC	1,588.9	241	San Francisco-Redwood, CA M.D.	558.1	334	Wausau, WI	365.1
257	New Haven-Milford, CT	517.2	272	San Jose, CA	493.8	149	West Palm Beach, FL M.D.	759.4
163	New Orleans, LA	723.5	235	San Luis Obispo, CA	571.2	263	Wheeling, WV-OH	510.9
355	New York (greater), NY-NJ-PA	291.9	NA	San Rafael, CA M.D.**	NA	63	Wichita Falls, TX	1,001.2
359	New York-Jersey City, NY-NJ M.D.	276.5	216	Santa Cruz-Watsonville, CA	612.2	121	Wichita, KS	823.1
296	Newark, NJ-PA M.D.	431.5	2	Santa Fe, NM	1,861.1	294	Williamsport, PA	440.4
148	North Port-Sarasota-Bradenton, FL	759.5	237	Santa Maria-Santa Barbara, CA	564.0	112	Wilmington, DE-MD-NJ M.D.	836.1
285	Norwich-New London, CT	457.7	329	Santa Rosa, CA	370.7	56	Wilmington, NC	1,020.0
116	Oakland-Hayward, CA M.D.	832.1	146	Savannah, GA	771.6	302	Winchester, VA-WV	417.6
227	Ocala, FL	590.1	276	Scranton--Wilkes-Barre, PA	487.1	27	Winston-Salem, NC	1,220.8
46	Ocean City, NJ	1,085.7	NA	Seattle (greater), WA**	NA	230	Worcester, MA-CT	581.7
147	Odessa, TX	766.5	109	Seattle-Bellevue-Everett, WA M.D.	841.3	29	Yakima, WA	1,217.7
312	Ogden-Clearfield, UT	399.9	221	Sebastian-Vero Beach, FL	604.5	353	York-Hanover, PA	299.2
35	Oklahoma City, OK	1,160.6	86	Sebring, FL	914.2	57	Youngstown-Warren, OH-PA	1,018.5
119	Olympia, WA	824.8	339	Sheboygan, WI	353.4	129	Yuba City, CA	810.4
207	Omaha-Council Bluffs, NE-IA	622.5	122	Sherman-Denison, TX	822.0	144	Yuma, AZ	772.7
71	Orlando, FL	968.5	141	Shreveport-Bossier City, LA	780.8			
311	Oshkosh-Neenah, WI	401.5	249	Sierra Vista-Douglas, AZ	536.6			

Source: Reported data from the F.B.I. "Crime in the United States 2012"

*Burglary is the unlawful entry of a structure to commit a felony or theft. Attempts are included.

**Not available.

30. Burglary Rate in 2012 (continued)
National Rate = 670.2 Burglaries per 100,000 Population*

RANK	METROPOLITAN AREA	RATE	RANK	METROPOLITAN AREA	RATE	RANK	METROPOLITAN AREA	RATE
1	Hammond, LA	2,162.3	65	Decatur, IL	983.9	129	Yuba City, CA	810.4
2	Santa Fe, NM	1,861.1	66	Lima, OH	982.2	130	Bremerton-Silverdale, WA	808.9
3	Fayetteville, NC	1,827.4	67	Beaumont-Port Arthur, TX	982.1	131	Athens-Clarke County, GA	802.5
4	New Bern, NC	1,588.9	68	Pensacola, FL	978.7	132	Las Cruces, NM	799.3
5	Pine Bluff, AR	1,554.9	69	Redding, CA	977.6	133	McAllen-Edinburg-Mission, TX	798.4
6	Sumter, SC	1,478.6	70	Rome, GA	970.0	134	Fort Worth-Arlington, TX M.D.	795.5
7	Mansfield, OH	1,476.9	71	Orlando, FL	968.5	135	Cincinnati, OH-KY-IN	794.3
8	Flint, MI	1,448.4	72	Fort Lauderdale, FL M.D.	968.1	136	Topeka, KS	792.0
9	Anniston-Oxford, AL	1,445.8	73	Greenville-Anderson, SC	966.8	137	Fort Smith, AR-OK	790.6
10	Toledo, OH	1,389.5	74	Visalia-Porterville, CA	964.9	138	Valdosta, GA	787.1
11	Little Rock, AR	1,379.9	75	South Bend-Mishawaka, IN-MI	950.7	139	Dallas (greater), TX	783.5
12	Albany, GA	1,311.4	76	Dothan, AL	948.7	140	Hilton Head Island, SC	781.0
13	Memphis, TN-MS-AR	1,303.3	77	Tulsa, OK	941.7	141	Shreveport-Bossier City, LA	780.8
14	Montgomery, AL	1,289.8	78	St. Joseph, MO-KS	939.5	142	Dallas-Plano-Irving, TX M.D.	777.2
15	Vineland-Bridgeton, NJ	1,287.8	79	Lakeland, FL	938.2	143	Muncie, IN	774.4
16	Lawton, OK	1,287.6	80	Hinesville, GA	930.7	144	Yuma, AZ	772.7
17	Pueblo, CO	1,282.2	81	Burlington, NC	928.9	145	Walla Walla, WA	771.8
18	Goldsboro, NC	1,281.6	82	Terre Haute, IN	926.1	146	Savannah, GA	771.6
19	Monroe, LA	1,277.6	83	San Antonio, TX	924.5	147	Odessa, TX	766.5
20	Jonesboro, AR	1,276.6	84	Canton, OH	923.4	148	North Port-Sarasota-Bradenton, FL	759.5
21	Bakersfield, CA	1,271.6	85	Rockford, IL	923.0	149	West Palm Beach, FL M.D.	759.4
22	Springfield, OH	1,271.0	86	Sebring, FL	914.2	150	Deltona-Daytona Beach, FL	757.3
23	Florence, SC	1,269.0	87	Amarillo, TX	903.2	151	Michigan City-La Porte, IN	754.5
24	Gadsden, AL	1,250.9	87	Dayton, OH	903.2	152	Kansas City, MO-KS	753.0
25	Spokane, WA	1,239.1	89	Knoxville, TN	902.6	153	Asheville, NC	745.3
26	Macon, GA	1,229.4	90	Lexington-Fayette, KY	900.4	154	Gainesville, FL	744.8
27	Winston-Salem, NC	1,220.8	91	Longview, TX	899.0	155	Jacksonville, FL	744.0
28	Rocky Mount, NC	1,218.9	92	Panama City, FL	894.1	156	Johnson City, TN	741.6
29	Yakima, WA	1,217.7	93	Tuscaloosa, AL	892.2	157	Abilene, TX	737.1
30	Columbus, GA-AL	1,211.0	94	Waco, TX	891.5	158	Eugene, OR	736.4
31	Alexandria, LA	1,209.0	95	Las Vegas-Henderson, NV	878.8	159	Dover, DE	735.7
32	Brunswick, GA	1,181.1	96	Saginaw, MI	876.4	160	Brownsville-Harlingen, TX	735.6
33	Danville, IL	1,171.1	97	Lake Havasu City-Kingman, AZ	875.1	161	Champaign-Urbana, IL	734.8
34	El Centro, CA	1,167.9	98	Tyler, TX	874.5	162	Racine, WI	730.0
35	Oklahoma City, OK	1,160.6	99	Riverside-San Bernardino, CA	872.1	163	New Orleans, LA	723.5
36	Lubbock, TX	1,149.4	100	Atlanta, GA	871.9	164	Monroe, MI	717.3
37	Stockton-Lodi, CA	1,141.2	101	Chico, CA	863.2	165	Peoria, IL	716.6
38	Jackson, TN	1,130.3	102	Decatur, AL	857.2	166	Palm Bay-Melbourne, FL	716.0
39	Birmingham-Hoover, AL	1,122.1	103	Florence-Muscle Shoals, AL	852.0	167	Lewiston-Auburn, ME	714.6
40	Detroit-Dearborn-Livonia, MI M.D.	1,111.6	104	Joplin, MO	850.0	168	Pittsfield, MA	710.4
41	Fresno, CA	1,108.8	104	Miami (greater), FL	850.0	169	Gary, IN M.D.	708.0
42	Beckley, WV	1,095.1	106	Springfield, MO	847.0	170	East Stroudsburg, PA	706.4
43	Durham-Chapel Hill, NC	1,095.0	107	Huntsville, AL	846.2	171	Parkersburg-Vienna, WV	706.3
44	Jackson, MS	1,090.8	108	Spartanburg, SC	846.0	172	Laredo, TX	701.0
45	Tallahassee, FL	1,088.3	109	Seattle-Bellevue-Everett, WA M.D.	841.3	173	Hattiesburg, MS	699.2
46	Ocean City, NJ	1,085.7	110	Louisville, KY-IN	839.5	174	Houma, LA	697.8
47	Mobile, AL	1,076.2	111	Springfield, MA	837.8	175	Detroit (greater), MI	696.5
48	Texarkana, TX-AR	1,073.1	112	Wilmington, DE-MD-NJ M.D.	836.1	176	Sacramento, CA	695.6
49	Madera, CA	1,071.6	113	Cape Girardeau, MO-IL	835.4	177	Clarksville, TN-KY	694.2
50	Mount Vernon-Anacortes, WA	1,069.0	114	Salisbury, MD-DE	835.1	178	California-Lexington Park, MD	693.9
51	Modesto, CA	1,060.7	115	Warner Robins, GA	834.8	179	Morristown, TN	690.7
52	Vallejo-Fairfield, CA	1,033.0	116	Oakland-Hayward, CA M.D.	832.1	180	Salinas, CA	683.9
53	Greenville, NC	1,032.8	117	Tucson, AZ	832.0	181	Philadelphia, PA M.D.	678.0
54	Merced, CA	1,024.0	118	Victoria, TX	830.5	182	Cumberland, MD-WV	677.6
55	Barnstable Town, MA	1,021.6	119	Olympia, WA	824.8	183	Tampa-St Petersburg, FL	676.7
56	Wilmington, NC	1,020.0	120	Longview, WA	824.3	184	Lewiston, ID-WA	676.3
57	Youngstown-Warren, OH-PA	1,018.5	121	Wichita, KS	823.1	185	Dalton, GA	672.4
58	Springfield, IL	1,017.3	122	Sherman-Denison, TX	822.0	186	Kahului-Wailuku-Lahaina, HI	672.1
59	Augusta, GA-SC	1,015.3	123	Kokomo, IN	821.1	187	Ann Arbor, MI	670.3
60	Hickory, NC	1,009.3	124	Phoenix-Mesa-Scottsdale, AZ	820.0	188	Cleveland, TN	668.9
61	Greensboro-High Point, NC	1,003.0	125	Coeur d'Alene, ID	819.9	189	Trenton, NJ	663.4
62	Baton Rouge, LA	1,001.4	126	Miami-Dade County, FL M.D.	815.1	190	Auburn, AL	662.3
63	Wichita Falls, TX	1,001.2	127	Lafayette, LA	814.4	191	Waterloo-Cedar Falls, IA	660.0
64	Indianapolis, IN	989.4	128	Akron, OH	813.8	192	Lawrence, KS	656.1

Note: All listings are for Metropolitan Statistical Areas (M.S.A.s) except for those ending with "M.D." Listings with "M.D." are Metropolitan Divisions which are smaller parts of eleven large M.S.A.s. See explanatory note at beginning of metropolitan area section.

RANK	METROPOLITAN AREA	RATE	RANK	METROPOLITAN AREA	RATE	RANK	METROPOLITAN AREA	RATE
193	Buffalo-Niagara Falls, NY	654.4	257	Davenport, IA-IL	517.2	321	Greeley, CO	391.3
194	Cape Coral-Fort Myers, FL	651.8	257	New Haven-Milford, CT	517.2	322	Pocatello, ID	389.3
195	Atlantic City, NJ	649.6	259	Kennewick-Richland, WA	517.0	323	Grand Junction, CO	386.3
196	Bellingham, WA	647.7	260	Daphne-Fairhope-Foley, AL	515.8	324	Lake Co.-Kenosha Co., IL-WI M.D.	386.0
197	Erie, PA	642.4	261	Jefferson City, MO	512.7	325	Boulder, CO	385.1
198	Milwaukee, WI	641.0	262	Richmond, VA	511.3	326	Anaheim-Santa Ana-Irvine, CA M.D.	383.2
199	Nashville-Davidson, TN	640.8	263	Wheeling, WV-OH	510.9	327	Corvallis, OR	372.1
200	Charleston-North Charleston, SC	635.1	264	Sioux City, IA-NE-SD	504.7	328	Oxnard-Thousand Oaks, CA	370.8
201	Baltimore, MD	634.5	265	Roanoke, VA	504.4	329	Santa Rosa, CA	370.7
202	Bloomington, IN	631.6	266	La Crosse, WI-MN	502.6	330	Rochester, MN	370.3
203	Port St. Lucie, FL	627.6	267	Mankato-North Mankato, MN	499.9	331	Lynchburg, VA	370.1
204	Salt Lake City, UT	627.5	268	Denver-Aurora, CO	499.5	332	Fargo, ND-MN	369.8
205	College Station-Bryan, TX	627.0	269	Gainesville, GA	498.9	333	Charlottesville, VA	368.1
206	Kalamazoo-Portage, MI	626.9	270	Ames, IA	497.7	334	Wausau, WI	365.1
207	Omaha-Council Bluffs, NE-IA	622.5	271	Utica-Rome, NY	496.6	335	Cambridge-Newton, MA M.D.	364.6
208	Grand Island, NE	621.4	272	San Jose, CA	493.8	336	The Villages, FL	358.3
209	Austin-Round Rock, TX	617.2	273	Los Angeles County, CA M.D.	492.0	337	Fort Collins, CO	355.1
210	Reno, NV	616.7	274	Columbus, IN	491.6	338	Manhattan, KS	354.3
211	Columbia, MO	616.5	274	Medford, OR	491.6	339	Sheboygan, WI	353.4
212	Billings, MT	616.4	276	Scranton--Wilkes-Barre, PA	487.1	340	Bridgeport-Stamford, CT	351.9
213	Kankakee, IL	616.3	277	Midland, TX	484.3	341	St. George, UT	349.6
214	Kingsport, TN-VA	616.1	278	Portland, ME	484.1	342	Idaho Falls, ID	335.8
214	Raleigh, NC	616.1	279	Sioux Falls, SD	480.8	343	Rockingham County, NH M.D.	331.2
216	Santa Cruz-Watsonville, CA	612.2	280	Albany-Schenectady-Troy, NY	479.9	344	Chambersburg-Waynesboro, PA	329.0
217	Casper, WY	611.8	281	Great Falls, MT	474.5	345	Lancaster, PA	328.0
218	Camden, NJ M.D.	611.5	282	Napa, CA	472.1	346	Washington, DC-VA-MD-WV M.D.	323.3
219	Syracuse, NY	607.4	283	Los Angeles (greater), CA	466.3	347	Elgin, IL M.D.	316.3
220	St. Louis, MO-IL	606.9	284	Hartford, CT	465.3	348	Washington (greater) DC-VA-MD-WV	312.3
221	Sebastian-Vero Beach, FL	604.5	285	Norwich-New London, CT	457.7	349	Glens Falls, NY	310.7
222	Fort Wayne, IN	603.2	286	Johnstown, PA	456.4	350	Elizabethtown-Fort Knox, KY	310.4
223	Providence-Warwick, RI-MA	598.8	287	Bloomington, IL	453.5	351	Logan, UT-ID	307.3
224	Albany, OR	594.3	288	Boston, MA M.D.	453.2	352	Altoona, PA	304.0
225	Reading, PA	594.0	289	Cheyenne, WY	452.0	353	York-Hanover, PA	299.2
226	Bangor, ME	592.6	290	Madison, WI	445.9	354	Montgomery County, PA M.D.	297.0
227	Ocala, FL	590.1	291	Elmira, NY	445.6	355	New York (greater), NY-NJ-PA	291.9
228	Duluth, MN-WI	582.7	292	San Diego, CA	444.2	356	Lebanon, PA	286.9
229	Hagerstown-Martinsburg, MD-WV	582.6	293	Prescott, AZ	442.6	357	El Paso, TX	284.5
230	Worcester, MA-CT	581.7	294	Williamsport, PA	440.4	358	Harrisonburg, VA	278.2
231	Rochester, NY	580.2	295	Bloomsburg-Berwick, PA	436.5	359	New York-Jersey City, NY-NJ M.D.	276.5
232	Lincoln, NE	576.7	296	Newark, NJ-PA M.D.	431.5	360	Dutchess-Putnam, NY M.D.	275.9
233	Lafayette, IN	572.8	297	Bismarck, ND	430.3	361	Silver Spring-Frederick, MD M.D.	271.3
234	Lansing-East Lansing, MI	571.9	297	Manchester-Nashua, NH	430.3	362	Gettysburg, PA	258.9
235	San Luis Obispo, CA	571.2	299	Fairbanks, AK	427.7	363	Nassau-Suffolk, NY M.D.	248.6
236	Bowling Green, KY	564.7	300	Allentown, PA-NJ	426.4	364	Midland, MI	248.4
237	Santa Maria-Santa Barbara, CA	564.0	301	Harrisburg-Carlisle, PA	421.3	365	Fond du Lac, WI	245.3
238	Philadelphia (greater) PA-NJ-MD-DE	563.0	302	Winchester, VA-WV	417.6	366	Provo-Orem, UT	239.9
239	Fayetteville-Springdale, AR-MO	562.5	303	Boise City, ID	416.0	367	Staunton-Waynesboro, VA	234.3
240	Punta Gorda, FL	559.3	304	Missoula, MT	415.7	368	State College, PA	229.1
241	San Francisco-Redwood, CA M.D.	558.1	305	Bay City, MI	411.4	369	Appleton, WI	226.3
242	Binghamton, NY	556.8	306	Iowa City, IA	408.4	NA	Albuquerque, NM**	NA
243	Chicago-Joilet-Naperville, IL M.D.	553.1	307	Blacksburg, VA	408.2	NA	Cedar Rapids, IA**	NA
244	Owensboro, KY	552.6	307	Flagstaff, AZ	408.2	NA	Colorado Springs, CO**	NA
245	Janesville, WI	550.8	309	Green Bay, WI	407.7	NA	Corpus Christi, TX**	NA
246	Salem, OR	549.5	309	Naples-Marco Island, FL	407.7	NA	Des Moines-West Des Moines, IA**	NA
247	Rapid City, SD	544.7	311	Oshkosh-Neenah, WI	401.5	NA	Dubuque, IA**	NA
248	Homosassa Springs, FL	537.5	312	Ogden-Clearfield, UT	399.9	NA	Houston, TX**	NA
249	Sierra Vista-Douglas, AZ	536.6	313	Kingston, NY	398.5	NA	Killeen-Temple, TX**	NA
250	Crestview-Fort Walton Beach, FL	533.9	313	Pittsburgh, PA	398.5	NA	Minneapolis-St. Paul, MN-WI**	NA
251	Chicago (greater), IL-IN-WI	533.8	315	Boston (greater), MA-NH	398.3	NA	San Francisco (greater), CA**	NA
252	Virginia Beach-Norfolk, VA-NC	533.2	316	Watertown-Fort Drum, NY	398.2	NA	San Rafael, CA M.D.**	NA
253	Carson City, NV	530.6	317	Warren-Troy, MI M.D.	395.3	NA	Seattle (greater), WA**	NA
254	Portland-Vancouver, OR-WA	528.8	318	Grand Forks, ND-MN	394.9	NA	Tacoma, WA M.D.**	NA
255	Farmington, NM	527.2	319	Anchorage, AK	394.2			
256	Hanford-Corcoran, CA	523.9	320	Morgantown, WV	392.4			

Source: Reported data from the F.B.I. "Crime in the United States 2012"

*Burglary is the unlawful entry of a structure to commit a felony or theft. Attempts are included.

**Not available.

31. Percent Change in Burglary Rate: 2011 to 2012
National Percent Change = 4.4% Decrease*

RANK	METROPOLITAN AREA	% CHANGE	RANK	METROPOLITAN AREA	% CHANGE	RANK	METROPOLITAN AREA	% CHANGE
155	Abilene, TX	(7.0)	69	Cheyenne, WY	6.1	246	Gary, IN M.D.	(18.7)
228	Akron, OH	(15.4)	176	Chicago (greater), IL-IN-WI	(9.9)	NA	Gettysburg, PA**	NA
NA	Albany-Schenectady-Troy, NY**	NA	NA	Chicago-Joilet-Naperville, IL M.D.**	NA	NA	Glens Falls, NY**	NA
66	Albany, GA	6.3	11	Chico, CA	22.9	132	Goldsboro, NC	(3.6)
NA	Albany, OR**	NA	NA	Cincinnati, OH-KY-IN**	NA	223	Grand Forks, ND-MN	(14.9)
NA	Albuquerque, NM**	NA	254	Clarksville, TN-KY	(20.3)	252	Grand Junction, CO	(20.1)
61	Alexandria, LA	7.2	124	Cleveland, TN	(2.2)	NA	Grand Island, NE**	NA
NA	Allentown, PA-NJ**	NA	NA	Coeur d'Alene, ID**	NA	30	Great Falls, MT	13.2
264	Altoona, PA	(26.5)	204	College Station-Bryan, TX	(12.7)	185	Greeley, CO	(10.6)
103	Amarillo, TX	0.4	NA	Colorado Springs, CO**	NA	12	Green Bay, WI	21.6
176	Ames, IA	(9.9)	92	Columbia, MO	2.3	NA	Greensboro-High Point, NC**	NA
48	Anaheim-Santa Ana-Irvine, CA M.D.	8.9	230	Columbus, GA-AL	(15.7)	NA	Greenville-Anderson, SC**	NA
NA	Anchorage, AK**	NA	173	Columbus, IN	(9.4)	NA	Greenville, NC**	NA
16	Ann Arbor, MI	18.0	NA	Corpus Christi, TX**	NA	NA	Hagerstown-Martinsburg, MD-WV**	NA
109	Anniston-Oxford, AL	(0.3)	247	Corvallis, OR	(18.9)	NA	Hammond, LA**	NA
163	Appleton, WI	(8.1)	121	Crestview-Fort Walton Beach, FL	(1.9)	142	Hanford-Corcoran, CA	(5.6)
123	Asheville, NC	(2.0)	166	Cumberland, MD-WV	(8.6)	147	Harrisburg-Carlisle, PA	(6.1)
240	Athens-Clarke County, GA	(17.3)	227	Dallas (greater), TX	(15.1)	3	Harrisonburg, VA	32.5
182	Atlanta, GA	(10.5)	210	Dallas-Plano-Irving, TX M.D.	(13.5)	134	Hartford, CT	(4.9)
235	Atlantic City, NJ	(16.5)	110	Dalton, GA	(0.5)	NA	Hattiesburg, MS**	NA
193	Auburn, AL	(11.4)	238	Danville, IL	(16.8)	182	Hickory, NC	(10.5)
213	Augusta, GA-SC	(13.9)	NA	Daphne-Fairhope-Foley, AL**	NA	NA	Hilton Head Island, SC**	NA
106	Austin-Round Rock, TX	0.0	232	Davenport, IA-IL	(16.1)	193	Hinesville, GA	(11.4)
26	Bakersfield, CA	14.2	137	Dayton, OH	(5.2)	NA	Homosassa Springs, FL**	NA
125	Baltimore, MD	(2.7)	174	Decatur, AL	(9.5)	219	Houma, LA	(14.5)
116	Bangor, ME	(1.0)	236	Decatur, IL	(16.7)	NA	Houston, TX**	NA
129	Barnstable Town, MA	(3.3)	NA	Deltona-Daytona Beach, FL**	NA	243	Huntsville, AL	(18.3)
159	Baton Rouge, LA	(7.5)	NA	Denver-Aurora, CO**	NA	259	Idaho Falls, ID	(22.4)
241	Bay City, MI	(17.7)	NA	Des Moines-West Des Moines, IA**	NA	NA	Indianapolis, IN**	NA
217	Beaumont-Port Arthur, TX	(14.4)	198	Detroit (greater), MI	(12.0)	40	Iowa City, IA	10.3
NA	Beckley, WV**	NA	201	Detroit-Dearborn-Livonia, MI M.D.	(12.3)	192	Jacksonville, FL	(11.2)
166	Bellingham, WA	(8.6)	6	Dothan, AL	28.8	NA	Jackson, MS**	NA
22	Billings, MT	15.5	79	Dover, DE	4.2	NA	Jackson, TN**	NA
NA	Binghamton, NY**	NA	NA	Dubuque, IA**	NA	243	Janesville, WI	(18.3)
208	Birmingham-Hoover, AL	(13.2)	188	Duluth, MN-WI	(10.9)	114	Jefferson City, MO	(0.9)
45	Bismarck, ND	9.2	225	Durham-Chapel Hill, NC	(15.0)	121	Johnson City, TN	(1.9)
146	Blacksburg, VA	(6.0)	NA	Dutchess-Putnam, NY M.D.**	NA	216	Johnstown, PA	(14.2)
217	Bloomington, IL	(14.4)	NA	East Stroudsburg, PA**	NA	189	Jonesboro, AR	(11.0)
NA	Bloomington, IN**	NA	80	El Centro, CA	3.8	38	Joplin, MO	10.7
NA	Bloomsburg-Berwick, PA**	NA	157	El Paso, TX	(7.1)	NA	Kahului-Wailuku-Lahaina, HI**	NA
58	Boise City, ID	7.4	NA	Elgin, IL M.D.**	NA	NA	Kalamazoo-Portage, MI**	NA
NA	Boston (greater), MA-NH**	NA	NA	Elizabethtown-Fort Knox, KY**	NA	155	Kankakee, IL	(7.0)
NA	Boston, MA M.D.**	NA	NA	Elmira, NY**	NA	NA	Kansas City, MO-KS**	NA
93	Boulder, CO	1.8	174	Erie, PA	(9.5)	151	Kennewick-Richland, WA	(6.5)
43	Bowling Green, KY	9.5	73	Eugene, OR	5.0	NA	Killeen-Temple, TX**	NA
95	Bremerton-Silverdale, WA	1.7	91	Fairbanks, AK	2.4	233	Kingsport, TN-VA	(16.3)
198	Bridgeport-Stamford, CT	(12.0)	33	Fargo, ND-MN	12.4	NA	Kingston, NY**	NA
133	Brownsville-Harlingen, TX	(4.3)	7	Farmington, NM	27.7	NA	Knoxville, TN**	NA
138	Brunswick, GA	(5.4)	NA	Fayetteville-Springdale, AR-MO**	NA	NA	Kokomo, IN**	NA
NA	Buffalo-Niagara Falls, NY**	NA	153	Fayetteville, NC	(6.9)	37	La Crosse, WI-MN	11.0
215	Burlington, NC	(14.1)	70	Flagstaff, AZ	5.4	96	Lafayette, IN	1.4
NA	California-Lexington Park, MD**	NA	160	Flint, MI	(7.8)	NA	Lafayette, LA**	NA
NA	Cambridge-Newton, MA M.D.**	NA	4	Florence-Muscle Shoals, AL	32.0	84	Lake Co.-Kenosha Co., IL-WI M.D.	3.5
127	Camden, NJ M.D.	(2.8)	112	Florence, SC	(0.7)	56	Lake Havasu City-Kingman, AZ	7.5
117	Canton, OH	(1.2)	72	Fond du Lac, WI	5.2	141	Lakeland, FL	(5.5)
262	Cape Coral-Fort Myers, FL	(23.2)	105	Fort Collins, CO	0.1	171	Lancaster, PA	(9.1)
31	Cape Girardeau, MO-IL	12.6	169	Fort Lauderdale, FL M.D.	(8.8)	248	Lansing-East Lansing, MI	(19.1)
150	Carson City, NV	(6.4)	NA	Fort Smith, AR-OK**	NA	147	Laredo, TX	(6.1)
25	Casper, WY	15.2	64	Fort Wayne, IN	6.5	172	Las Cruces, NM	(9.2)
NA	Cedar Rapids, IA**	NA	242	Fort Worth-Arlington, TX M.D.	(18.1)	52	Las Vegas-Henderson, NV	8.2
NA	Chambersburg-Waynesboro, PA**	NA	73	Fresno, CA	5.0	28	Lawrence, KS	14.0
35	Champaign-Urbana, IL	12.1	82	Gadsden, AL	3.7	NA	Lawton, OK**	NA
NA	Charleston-North Charleston, SC**	NA	144	Gainesville, FL	(5.8)	212	Lebanon, PA	(13.8)
2	Charlottesville, VA	49.3	249	Gainesville, GA	(19.2)	164	Lewiston-Auburn, ME	(8.3)

Note: All listings are for Metropolitan Statistical Areas (M.S.A.s) except for those ending with "M.D." Listings with "M.D." are Metropolitan Divisions which are smaller parts of eleven large M.S.A.s. See explanatory note at beginning of metropolitan area section.

RANK	METROPOLITAN AREA	% CHANGE	RANK	METROPOLITAN AREA	% CHANGE	RANK	METROPOLITAN AREA	% CHANGE
NA	Lewiston, ID-WA**	NA	185	Owensboro, KY	(10.6)	228	Silver Spring-Frederick, MD M.D.	(15.4)
NA	Lexington-Fayette, KY**	NA	20	Oxnard-Thousand Oaks, CA	16.4	NA	Sioux City, IA-NE-SD**	NA
193	Lima, OH	(11.4)	220	Palm Bay-Melbourne, FL	(14.6)	96	Sioux Falls, SD	1.4
23	Lincoln, NE	15.4	NA	Panama City, FL**	NA	236	South Bend-Mishawaka, IN-MI	(16.7)
147	Little Rock, AR	(6.1)	NA	Parkersburg-Vienna, WV**	NA	NA	Spartanburg, SC**	NA
1	Logan, UT-ID	80.1	33	Pensacola, FL	12.4	NA	Spokane, WA**	NA
44	Longview, TX	9.3	165	Peoria, IL	(8.4)	170	Springfield, IL	(9.0)
8	Longview, WA	25.5	NA	Philadelphia (greater) PA-NJ-MD-DE**	NA	NA	Springfield, MA**	NA
114	Los Angeles County, CA M.D.	(0.9)	NA	Philadelphia, PA M.D.**	NA	89	Springfield, MO	3.1
101	Los Angeles (greater), CA	0.8	NA	Phoenix-Mesa-Scottsdale, AZ**	NA	144	Springfield, OH	(5.8)
214	Louisville, KY-IN	(14.0)	257	Pine Bluff, AR	(21.8)	260	State College, PA	(23.1)
221	Lubbock, TX	(14.8)	152	Pittsburgh, PA	(6.8)	NA	Staunton-Waynesboro, VA**	NA
206	Lynchburg, VA	(12.8)	189	Pittsfield, MA	(11.0)	108	Stockton-Lodi, CA	(0.2)
230	Macon, GA	(15.7)	NA	Pocatello, ID**	NA	NA	St. George, UT**	NA
102	Madera, CA	0.5	251	Port St. Lucie, FL	(19.7)	71	St. Joseph, MO-KS	5.3
NA	Madison, WI**	NA	54	Portland-Vancouver, OR-WA	7.8	245	St. Louis, MO-IL	(18.5)
168	Manchester-Nashua, NH	(8.7)	221	Portland, ME	(14.8)	5	Sumter, SC	31.9
NA	Manhattan, KS**	NA	225	Prescott, AZ	(15.0)	NA	Syracuse, NY**	NA
250	Mankato-North Mankato, MN	(19.3)	NA	Providence-Warwick, RI-MA**	NA	NA	Tacoma, WA M.D.**	NA
10	Mansfield, OH	23.3	256	Provo-Orem, UT	(21.2)	204	Tallahassee, FL	(12.7)
106	McAllen-Edinburg-Mission, TX	0.0	53	Pueblo, CO	7.9	208	Tampa-St Petersburg, FL	(13.2)
18	Medford, OR	17.4	255	Punta Gorda, FL	(20.7)	120	Terre Haute, IN	(1.7)
160	Memphis, TN-MS-AR	(7.8)	162	Racine, WI	(8.0)	NA	Texarkana, TX-AR**	NA
93	Merced, CA	1.8	153	Raleigh, NC	(6.9)	NA	The Villages, FL**	NA
197	Miami (greater), FL	(11.8)	NA	Rapid City, SD**	NA	NA	Toledo, OH**	NA
223	Miami-Dade County, FL M.D.	(14.9)	64	Reading, PA	6.5	260	Topeka, KS	(23.1)
68	Michigan City-La Porte, IN	6.2	9	Redding, CA	23.8	66	Trenton, NJ	6.3
NA	Midland, MI**	NA	125	Reno, NV	(2.7)	119	Tucson, AZ	(1.6)
NA	Midland, TX**	NA	99	Richmond, VA	1.2	211	Tulsa, OK	(13.6)
63	Milwaukee, WI	6.6	58	Riverside-San Bernardino, CA	7.4	NA	Tuscaloosa, AL**	NA
NA	Minneapolis-St. Paul, MN-WI**	NA	85	Roanoke, VA	3.4	19	Tyler, TX	16.8
17	Missoula, MT	17.8	NA	Rochester, MN**	NA	NA	Utica-Rome, NY**	NA
265	Mobile, AL	(27.4)	NA	Rochester, NY**	NA	233	Valdosta, GA	(16.3)
87	Modesto, CA	3.3	21	Rockford, IL	15.8	46	Vallejo-Fairfield, CA	9.1
207	Monroe, LA	(12.9)	180	Rockingham County, NH M.D.	(10.4)	NA	Victoria, TX**	NA
128	Monroe, MI	(3.1)	135	Rocky Mount, NC	(5.0)	NA	Vineland-Bridgeton, NJ**	NA
NA	Montgomery County, PA M.D.**	NA	48	Rome, GA	8.9	201	Virginia Beach-Norfolk, VA-NC	(12.3)
26	Montgomery, AL	14.2	90	Sacramento, CA	2.7	51	Visalia-Porterville, CA	8.3
NA	Morgantown, WV**	NA	198	Saginaw, MI	(12.0)	NA	Waco, TX**	NA
NA	Morristown, TN**	NA	40	Salem, OR	10.3	NA	Walla Walla, WA**	NA
85	Mount Vernon-Anacortes, WA	3.4	50	Salinas, CA	8.4	NA	Warner Robins, GA**	NA
15	Muncie, IN	18.2	NA	Salisbury, MD-DE**	NA	180	Warren-Troy, MI M.D.	(10.4)
87	Napa, CA	3.3	77	Salt Lake City, UT	4.5	201	Washington (greater) DC-VA-MD-WV	(12.3)
182	Naples-Marco Island, FL	(10.5)	104	San Antonio, TX	0.3	196	Washington, DC-VA-MD-WV M.D.	(11.5)
NA	Nashville-Davidson, TN**	NA	78	San Diego, CA	4.4	36	Waterloo-Cedar Falls, IA	12.0
NA	Nassau-Suffolk, NY M.D.**	NA	NA	San Francisco (greater), CA**	NA	NA	Watertown-Fort Drum, NY**	NA
NA	New Bern, NC**	NA	29	San Francisco-Redwood, CA M.D.	13.4	110	Wausau, WI	(0.5)
158	New Haven-Milford, CT	(7.4)	13	San Jose, CA	21.2	179	West Palm Beach, FL M.D.	(10.3)
187	New Orleans, LA	(10.8)	39	San Luis Obispo, CA	10.4	NA	Wheeling, WV-OH**	NA
NA	New York (greater), NY-NJ-PA**	NA	NA	San Rafael, CA M.D.**	NA	75	Wichita Falls, TX	4.8
NA	New York-Jersey City, NY-NJ M.D.**	NA	239	Santa Cruz-Watsonville, CA	(17.0)	113	Wichita, KS	(0.8)
NA	Newark, NJ-PA M.D.**	NA	138	Santa Fe, NM	(5.4)	131	Williamsport, PA	(3.4)
253	North Port-Sarasota-Bradenton, FL	(20.2)	NA	Santa Maria-Santa Barbara, CA**	NA	56	Wilmington, DE-MD-NJ M.D.	7.5
82	Norwich-New London, CT	3.7	46	Santa Rosa, CA	9.1	NA	Wilmington, NC**	NA
55	Oakland-Hayward, CA M.D.	7.6	189	Savannah, GA	(11.0)	138	Winchester, VA-WV	(5.4)
258	Ocala, FL	(22.0)	61	Scranton--Wilkes-Barre, PA	7.2	NA	Winston-Salem, NC**	NA
118	Ocean City, NJ	(1.4)	NA	Seattle (greater), WA**	NA	NA	Worcester, MA-CT**	NA
14	Odessa, TX	19.2	80	Seattle-Bellevue-Everett, WA M.D.	3.8	178	Yakima, WA	(10.2)
NA	Ogden-Clearfield, UT**	NA	263	Sebastian-Vero Beach, FL	(23.6)	143	York-Hanover, PA	(5.7)
98	Oklahoma City, OK	1.3	NA	Sebring, FL**	NA	NA	Youngstown-Warren, OH-PA**	NA
40	Olympia, WA	10.3	31	Sheboygan, WI	12.6	24	Yuba City, CA	15.3
129	Omaha-Council Bluffs, NE-IA	(3.3)	100	Sherman-Denison, TX	1.1	75	Yuma, AZ	4.8
136	Orlando, FL	(5.1)	NA	Shreveport-Bossier City, LA**	NA			
58	Oshkosh-Neenah, WI	7.4	NA	Sierra Vista-Douglas, AZ**	NA			

Source: CQ Press using reported data from the F.B.I. "Crime in the United States 2012"

*Burglary is the unlawful entry of a structure to commit a felony or theft. Attempts are included.

**Not available.

31. Percent Change in Burglary Rate: 2011 to 2012 (continued)
National Percent Change = 4.4% Decrease*

RANK	METROPOLITAN AREA	% CHANGE	RANK	METROPOLITAN AREA	% CHANGE	RANK	METROPOLITAN AREA	% CHANGE
1	Logan, UT-ID	80.1	64	Reading, PA	6.5	129	Barnstable Town, MA	(3.3)
2	Charlottesville, VA	49.3	66	Albany, GA	6.3	129	Omaha-Council Bluffs, NE-IA	(3.3)
3	Harrisonburg, VA	32.5	66	Trenton, NJ	6.3	131	Williamsport, PA	(3.4)
4	Florence-Muscle Shoals, AL	32.0	68	Michigan City-La Porte, IN	6.2	132	Goldsboro, NC	(3.6)
5	Sumter, SC	31.9	69	Cheyenne, WY	6.1	133	Brownsville-Harlingen, TX	(4.3)
6	Dothan, AL	28.8	70	Flagstaff, AZ	5.4	134	Hartford, CT	(4.9)
7	Farmington, NM	27.7	71	St. Joseph, MO-KS	5.3	135	Rocky Mount, NC	(5.0)
8	Longview, WA	25.5	72	Fond du Lac, WI	5.2	136	Orlando, FL	(5.1)
9	Redding, CA	23.8	73	Eugene, OR	5.0	137	Dayton, OH	(5.2)
10	Mansfield, OH	23.3	73	Fresno, CA	5.0	138	Brunswick, GA	(5.4)
11	Chico, CA	22.9	75	Wichita Falls, TX	4.8	138	Santa Fe, NM	(5.4)
12	Green Bay, WI	21.6	75	Yuma, AZ	4.8	138	Winchester, VA-WV	(5.4)
13	San Jose, CA	21.2	77	Salt Lake City, UT	4.5	141	Lakeland, FL	(5.5)
14	Odessa, TX	19.2	78	San Diego, CA	4.4	142	Hanford-Corcoran, CA	(5.6)
15	Muncie, IN	18.2	79	Dover, DE	4.2	143	York-Hanover, PA	(5.7)
16	Ann Arbor, MI	18.0	80	El Centro, CA	3.8	144	Gainesville, FL	(5.8)
17	Missoula, MT	17.8	80	Seattle-Bellevue-Everett, WA M.D.	3.8	144	Springfield, OH	(5.8)
18	Medford, OR	17.4	82	Gadsden, AL	3.7	146	Blacksburg, VA	(6.0)
19	Tyler, TX	16.8	82	Norwich-New London, CT	3.7	147	Harrisburg-Carlisle, PA	(6.1)
20	Oxnard-Thousand Oaks, CA	16.4	84	Lake Co.-Kenosha Co., IL-WI M.D.	3.5	147	Laredo, TX	(6.1)
21	Rockford, IL	15.8	85	Mount Vernon-Anacortes, WA	3.4	147	Little Rock, AR	(6.1)
22	Billings, MT	15.5	85	Roanoke, VA	3.4	150	Carson City, NV	(6.4)
23	Lincoln, NE	15.4	87	Modesto, CA	3.3	151	Kennewick-Richland, WA	(6.5)
24	Yuba City, CA	15.3	87	Napa, CA	3.3	152	Pittsburgh, PA	(6.8)
25	Casper, WY	15.2	89	Springfield, MO	3.1	153	Fayetteville, NC	(6.9)
26	Bakersfield, CA	14.2	90	Sacramento, CA	2.7	153	Raleigh, NC	(6.9)
26	Montgomery, AL	14.2	91	Fairbanks, AK	2.4	155	Abilene, TX	(7.0)
28	Lawrence, KS	14.0	92	Columbia, MO	2.3	155	Kankakee, IL	(7.0)
29	San Francisco-Redwood, CA M.D.	13.4	93	Boulder, CO	1.8	157	El Paso, TX	(7.1)
30	Great Falls, MT	13.2	93	Merced, CA	1.8	158	New Haven-Milford, CT	(7.4)
31	Cape Girardeau, MO-IL	12.6	95	Bremerton-Silverdale, WA	1.7	159	Baton Rouge, LA	(7.5)
31	Sheboygan, WI	12.6	96	Lafayette, IN	1.4	160	Flint, MI	(7.8)
33	Fargo, ND-MN	12.4	96	Sioux Falls, SD	1.4	160	Memphis, TN-MS-AR	(7.8)
33	Pensacola, FL	12.4	98	Oklahoma City, OK	1.3	162	Racine, WI	(8.0)
35	Champaign-Urbana, IL	12.1	99	Richmond, VA	1.2	163	Appleton, WI	(8.1)
36	Waterloo-Cedar Falls, IA	12.0	100	Sherman-Denison, TX	1.1	164	Lewiston-Auburn, ME	(8.3)
37	La Crosse, WI-MN	11.0	101	Los Angeles (greater), CA	0.8	165	Peoria, IL	(8.4)
38	Joplin, MO	10.7	102	Madera, CA	0.5	166	Bellingham, WA	(8.6)
39	San Luis Obispo, CA	10.4	103	Amarillo, TX	0.4	166	Cumberland, MD-WV	(8.6)
40	Iowa City, IA	10.3	104	San Antonio, TX	0.3	168	Manchester-Nashua, NH	(8.7)
40	Olympia, WA	10.3	105	Fort Collins, CO	0.1	169	Fort Lauderdale, FL M.D.	(8.8)
40	Salem, OR	10.3	106	Austin-Round Rock, TX	0.0	170	Springfield, IL	(9.0)
43	Bowling Green, KY	9.5	106	McAllen-Edinburg-Mission, TX	0.0	171	Lancaster, PA	(9.1)
44	Longview, TX	9.3	108	Stockton-Lodi, CA	(0.2)	172	Las Cruces, NM	(9.2)
45	Bismarck, ND	9.2	109	Anniston-Oxford, AL	(0.3)	173	Columbus, IN	(9.4)
46	Santa Rosa, CA	9.1	110	Dalton, GA	(0.5)	174	Decatur, AL	(9.5)
46	Vallejo-Fairfield, CA	9.1	110	Wausau, WI	(0.5)	174	Erie, PA	(9.5)
48	Anaheim-Santa Ana-Irvine, CA M.D.	8.9	112	Florence, SC	(0.7)	176	Ames, IA	(9.9)
48	Rome, GA	8.9	113	Wichita, KS	(0.8)	176	Chicago (greater), IL-IN-WI	(9.9)
50	Salinas, CA	8.4	114	Jefferson City, MO	(0.9)	178	Yakima, WA	(10.2)
51	Visalia-Porterville, CA	8.3	114	Los Angeles County, CA M.D.	(0.9)	179	West Palm Beach, FL M.D.	(10.3)
52	Las Vegas-Henderson, NV	8.2	116	Bangor, ME	(1.0)	180	Rockingham County, NH M.D.	(10.4)
53	Pueblo, CO	7.9	117	Canton, OH	(1.2)	180	Warren-Troy, MI M.D.	(10.4)
54	Portland-Vancouver, OR-WA	7.8	118	Ocean City, NJ	(1.4)	182	Atlanta, GA	(10.5)
55	Oakland-Hayward, CA M.D.	7.6	119	Tucson, AZ	(1.6)	182	Hickory, NC	(10.5)
56	Lake Havasu City-Kingman, AZ	7.5	120	Terre Haute, IN	(1.7)	182	Naples-Marco Island, FL	(10.5)
56	Wilmington, DE-MD-NJ M.D.	7.5	121	Crestview-Fort Walton Beach, FL	(1.9)	185	Greeley, CO	(10.6)
58	Boise City, ID	7.4	121	Johnson City, TN	(1.9)	185	Owensboro, KY	(10.6)
58	Oshkosh-Neenah, WI	7.4	123	Asheville, NC	(2.0)	187	New Orleans, LA	(10.8)
58	Riverside-San Bernardino, CA	7.4	124	Cleveland, TN	(2.2)	188	Duluth, MN-WI	(10.9)
61	Alexandria, LA	7.2	125	Baltimore, MD	(2.7)	189	Jonesboro, AR	(11.0)
61	Scranton--Wilkes-Barre, PA	7.2	125	Reno, NV	(2.7)	189	Pittsfield, MA	(11.0)
63	Milwaukee, WI	6.6	127	Camden, NJ M.D.	(2.8)	189	Savannah, GA	(11.0)
64	Fort Wayne, IN	6.5	128	Monroe, MI	(3.1)	192	Jacksonville, FL	(11.2)

Note: All listings are for Metropolitan Statistical Areas (M.S.A.s) except for those ending with "M.D." Listings with "M.D." are Metropolitan Divisions which are smaller parts of eleven large M.S.A.s. See explanatory note at beginning of metropolitan area section.

RANK	METROPOLITAN AREA	% CHANGE	RANK	METROPOLITAN AREA	% CHANGE	RANK	METROPOLITAN AREA	% CHANGE
193	Auburn, AL	(11.4)	257	Pine Bluff, AR	(21.8)	NA	Kokomo, IN**	NA
193	Hinesville, GA	(11.4)	258	Ocala, FL	(22.0)	NA	Lafayette, LA**	NA
193	Lima, OH	(11.4)	259	Idaho Falls, ID	(22.4)	NA	Lawton, OK**	NA
196	Washington, DC-VA-MD-WV M.D.	(11.5)	260	State College, PA	(23.1)	NA	Lewiston, ID-WA**	NA
197	Miami (greater), FL	(11.8)	260	Topeka, KS	(23.1)	NA	Lexington-Fayette, KY**	NA
198	Bridgeport-Stamford, CT	(12.0)	262	Cape Coral-Fort Myers, FL	(23.2)	NA	Madison, WI**	NA
198	Detroit (greater), MI	(12.0)	263	Sebastian-Vero Beach, FL	(23.6)	NA	Manhattan, KS**	NA
198	Saginaw, MI	(12.0)	264	Altoona, PA	(26.5)	NA	Midland, MI**	NA
201	Detroit-Dearborn-Livonia, MI M.D.	(12.3)	265	Mobile, AL	(27.4)	NA	Midland, TX**	NA
201	Virginia Beach-Norfolk, VA-NC	(12.3)	NA	Albany-Schenectady-Troy, NY**	NA	NA	Minneapolis-St. Paul, MN-WI**	NA
201	Washington (greater) DC-VA-MD-WV	(12.3)	NA	Albany, OR**	NA	NA	Montgomery County, PA M.D.**	NA
204	College Station-Bryan, TX	(12.7)	NA	Albuquerque, NM**	NA	NA	Morgantown, WV**	NA
204	Tallahassee, FL	(12.7)	NA	Allentown, PA-NJ**	NA	NA	Morristown, TN**	NA
206	Lynchburg, VA	(12.8)	NA	Anchorage, AK**	NA	NA	Nashville-Davidson, TN**	NA
207	Monroe, LA	(12.9)	NA	Beckley, WV**	NA	NA	Nassau-Suffolk, NY M.D.**	NA
208	Birmingham-Hoover, AL	(13.2)	NA	Binghamton, NY**	NA	NA	New Bern, NC**	NA
208	Tampa-St Petersburg, FL	(13.2)	NA	Bloomington, IN**	NA	NA	New York (greater), NY-NJ-PA**	NA
210	Dallas-Plano-Irving, TX M.D.	(13.5)	NA	Bloomsburg-Berwick, PA**	NA	NA	New York-Jersey City, NY-NJ M.D.**	NA
211	Tulsa, OK	(13.6)	NA	Boston (greater), MA-NH**	NA	NA	Newark, NJ-PA M.D.**	NA
212	Lebanon, PA	(13.8)	NA	Boston, MA M.D.**	NA	NA	Ogden-Clearfield, UT**	NA
213	Augusta, GA-SC	(13.9)	NA	Buffalo-Niagara Falls, NY**	NA	NA	Panama City, FL**	NA
214	Louisville, KY-IN	(14.0)	NA	California-Lexington Park, MD**	NA	NA	Parkersburg-Vienna, WV**	NA
215	Burlington, NC	(14.1)	NA	Cambridge-Newton, MA M.D.**	NA	NA	Philadelphia (greater) PA-NJ-MD-DE**	NA
216	Johnstown, PA	(14.2)	NA	Cedar Rapids, IA**	NA	NA	Philadelphia, PA M.D.**	NA
217	Beaumont-Port Arthur, TX	(14.4)	NA	Chambersburg-Waynesboro, PA**	NA	NA	Phoenix-Mesa-Scottsdale, AZ**	NA
217	Bloomington, IL	(14.4)	NA	Charleston-North Charleston, SC**	NA	NA	Pocatello, ID**	NA
219	Houma, LA	(14.5)	NA	Chicago-Joilet-Naperville, IL M.D.**	NA	NA	Providence-Warwick, RI-MA**	NA
220	Palm Bay-Melbourne, FL	(14.6)	NA	Cincinnati, OH-KY-IN**	NA	NA	Rapid City, SD**	NA
221	Lubbock, TX	(14.8)	NA	Coeur d'Alene, ID**	NA	NA	Rochester, MN**	NA
221	Portland, ME	(14.8)	NA	Colorado Springs, CO**	NA	NA	Rochester, NY**	NA
223	Grand Forks, ND-MN	(14.9)	NA	Corpus Christi, TX**	NA	NA	Salisbury, MD-DE**	NA
223	Miami-Dade County, FL M.D.	(14.9)	NA	Daphne-Fairhope-Foley, AL**	NA	NA	San Francisco (greater), CA**	NA
225	Durham-Chapel Hill, NC	(15.0)	NA	Deltona-Daytona Beach, FL**	NA	NA	San Rafael, CA M.D.**	NA
225	Prescott, AZ	(15.0)	NA	Denver-Aurora, CO**	NA	NA	Santa Maria-Santa Barbara, CA**	NA
227	Dallas (greater), TX	(15.1)	NA	Des Moines-West Des Moines, IA**	NA	NA	Seattle (greater), WA**	NA
228	Akron, OH	(15.4)	NA	Dubuque, IA**	NA	NA	Sebring, FL**	NA
228	Silver Spring-Frederick, MD M.D.	(15.4)	NA	Dutchess-Putnam, NY M.D.**	NA	NA	Shreveport-Bossier City, LA**	NA
230	Columbus, GA-AL	(15.7)	NA	East Stroudsburg, PA**	NA	NA	Sierra Vista-Douglas, AZ**	NA
230	Macon, GA	(15.7)	NA	Elgin, IL M.D.**	NA	NA	Sioux City, IA-NE-SD**	NA
232	Davenport, IA-IL	(16.1)	NA	Elizabethtown-Fort Knox, KY**	NA	NA	Spartanburg, SC**	NA
233	Kingsport, TN-VA	(16.3)	NA	Elmira, NY**	NA	NA	Spokane, WA**	NA
233	Valdosta, GA	(16.3)	NA	Fayetteville-Springdale, AR-MO**	NA	NA	Springfield, MA**	NA
235	Atlantic City, NJ	(16.5)	NA	Fort Smith, AR-OK**	NA	NA	Staunton-Waynesboro, VA**	NA
236	Decatur, IL	(16.7)	NA	Gettysburg, PA**	NA	NA	St. George, UT**	NA
236	South Bend-Mishawaka, IN-MI	(16.7)	NA	Glens Falls, NY**	NA	NA	Syracuse, NY**	NA
238	Danville, IL	(16.8)	NA	Grand Island, NE**	NA	NA	Tacoma, WA M.D.**	NA
239	Santa Cruz-Watsonville, CA	(17.0)	NA	Greensboro-High Point, NC**	NA	NA	Texarkana, TX-AR**	NA
240	Athens-Clarke County, GA	(17.3)	NA	Greenville-Anderson, SC**	NA	NA	The Villages, FL**	NA
241	Bay City, MI	(17.7)	NA	Greenville, NC**	NA	NA	Toledo, OH**	NA
242	Fort Worth-Arlington, TX M.D.	(18.1)	NA	Hagerstown-Martinsburg, MD-WV**	NA	NA	Tuscaloosa, AL**	NA
243	Huntsville, AL	(18.3)	NA	Hammond, LA**	NA	NA	Utica-Rome, NY**	NA
243	Janesville, WI	(18.3)	NA	Hattiesburg, MS**	NA	NA	Victoria, TX**	NA
245	St. Louis, MO-IL	(18.5)	NA	Hilton Head Island, SC**	NA	NA	Vineland-Bridgeton, NJ**	NA
246	Gary, IN M.D.	(18.7)	NA	Homosassa Springs, FL**	NA	NA	Waco, TX**	NA
247	Corvallis, OR	(18.9)	NA	Houston, TX**	NA	NA	Walla Walla, WA**	NA
248	Lansing-East Lansing, MI	(19.1)	NA	Indianapolis, IN**	NA	NA	Warner Robins, GA**	NA
249	Gainesville, GA	(19.2)	NA	Jackson, MS**	NA	NA	Watertown-Fort Drum, NY**	NA
250	Mankato-North Mankato, MN	(19.3)	NA	Jackson, TN**	NA	NA	Wheeling, WV-OH**	NA
251	Port St. Lucie, FL	(19.7)	NA	Kahului-Wailuku-Lahaina, HI**	NA	NA	Wilmington, NC**	NA
252	Grand Junction, CO	(20.1)	NA	Kalamazoo-Portage, MI**	NA	NA	Winston-Salem, NC**	NA
253	North Port-Sarasota-Bradenton, FL	(20.2)	NA	Kansas City, MO-KS**	NA	NA	Worcester, MA-CT**	NA
254	Clarksville, TN-KY	(20.3)	NA	Killeen-Temple, TX**	NA	NA	Youngstown-Warren, OH-PA**	NA
255	Punta Gorda, FL	(20.7)	NA	Kingston, NY**	NA			
256	Provo-Orem, UT	(21.2)	NA	Knoxville, TN**	NA			

Source: CQ Press using reported data from the F.B.I. "Crime in the United States 2012"

*Burglary is the unlawful entry of a structure to commit a felony or theft. Attempts are included.

**Not available.

32. Percent Change in Burglary Rate: 2008 to 2012
National Percent Change = 8.6% Decrease*

RANK	METROPOLITAN AREA	% CHANGE	RANK	METROPOLITAN AREA	% CHANGE	RANK	METROPOLITAN AREA	% CHANGE
174	Abilene, TX	(17.2)	101	Cheyenne, WY	(3.5)	NA	Gary, IN M.D.**	NA
119	Akron, OH	(7.8)	NA	Chicago (greater), IL-IN-WI**	NA	NA	Gettysburg, PA**	NA
NA	Albany-Schenectady-Troy, NY**	NA	NA	Chicago-Joilet-Naperville, IL M.D.**	NA	NA	Glens Falls, NY**	NA
NA	Albany, GA**	NA	78	Chico, CA	1.9	159	Goldsboro, NC	(13.8)
NA	Albany, OR**	NA	NA	Cincinnati, OH-KY-IN**	NA	106	Grand Forks, ND-MN	(4.4)
NA	Albuquerque, NM**	NA	221	Clarksville, TN-KY	(28.3)	NA	Grand Island, NE**	NA
NA	Alexandria, LA**	NA	149	Cleveland, TN	(12.7)	238	Grand Junction, CO	(34.4)
NA	Allentown, PA-NJ**	NA	NA	Coeur d'Alene, ID**	NA	25	Great Falls, MT	18.5
244	Altoona, PA	(41.3)	242	College Station-Bryan, TX	(37.4)	234	Greeley, CO	(33.0)
166	Amarillo, TX	(16.0)	NA	Colorado Springs, CO**	NA	94	Green Bay, WI	(1.1)
161	Ames, IA	(14.7)	146	Columbia, MO	(12.0)	226	Greensboro-High Point, NC	(30.4)
86	Anaheim-Santa Ana-Irvine, CA M.D.	(0.8)	156	Columbus, GA-AL	(13.4)	NA	Greenville-Anderson, SC**	NA
NA	Anchorage, AK**	NA	1	Columbus, IN	68.6	240	Greenville, NC	(36.4)
75	Ann Arbor, MI	2.1	NA	Corpus Christi, TX**	NA	NA	Hagerstown-Martinsburg, MD-WV**	NA
NA	Anniston-Oxford, AL**	NA	118	Corvallis, OR	(7.4)	NA	Hammond, LA**	NA
205	Appleton, WI	(25.0)	NA	Crestview-Fort Walton Beach, FL**	NA	129	Hanford-Corcoran, CA	(9.6)
127	Asheville, NC	(9.3)	68	Cumberland, MD-WV	3.5	79	Harrisburg-Carlisle, PA	1.6
237	Athens-Clarke County, GA	(33.7)	190	Dallas (greater), TX	(21.5)	151	Harrisonburg, VA	(12.9)
184	Atlanta, GA	(19.1)	201	Dallas-Plano-Irving, TX M.D.	(23.7)	97	Hartford, CT	(2.4)
NA	Atlantic City, NJ**	NA	41	Dalton, GA	12.2	NA	Hattiesburg, MS**	NA
246	Auburn, AL	(59.1)	NA	Danville, IL**	NA	74	Hickory, NC	2.2
158	Augusta, GA-SC	(13.7)	NA	Daphne-Fairhope-Foley, AL**	NA	NA	Hilton Head Island, SC**	NA
193	Austin-Round Rock, TX	(21.7)	NA	Davenport, IA-IL**	NA	220	Hinesville, GA	(27.8)
46	Bakersfield, CA	10.5	70	Dayton, OH	2.8	NA	Homosassa Springs, FL**	NA
145	Baltimore, MD	(11.5)	168	Decatur, AL	(16.3)	12	Houma, LA	33.3
54	Bangor, ME	7.7	NA	Decatur, IL**	NA	NA	Houston, TX**	NA
63	Barnstable Town, MA	4.8	210	Deltona-Daytona Beach, FL	(25.5)	142	Huntsville, AL	(11.1)
122	Baton Rouge, LA	(8.9)	NA	Denver-Aurora, CO**	NA	225	Idaho Falls, ID	(29.9)
228	Bay City, MI	(30.5)	NA	Des Moines-West Des Moines, IA**	NA	98	Indianapolis, IN	(2.6)
182	Beaumont-Port Arthur, TX	(18.8)	NA	Detroit (greater), MI**	NA	175	Iowa City, IA	(17.4)
NA	Beckley, WV**	NA	NA	Detroit-Dearborn-Livonia, MI M.D.**	NA	243	Jacksonville, FL	(37.6)
149	Bellingham, WA	(12.7)	67	Dothan, AL	3.8	NA	Jackson, MS**	NA
24	Billings, MT	19.0	85	Dover, DE	(0.3)	NA	Jackson, TN**	NA
NA	Binghamton, NY**	NA	NA	Dubuque, IA**	NA	137	Janesville, WI	(10.6)
136	Birmingham-Hoover, AL	(10.5)	63	Duluth, MN-WI	4.8	NA	Jefferson City, MO**	NA
7	Bismarck, ND	41.1	146	Durham-Chapel Hill, NC	(12.0)	40	Johnson City, TN	12.3
229	Blacksburg, VA	(30.6)	NA	Dutchess-Putnam, NY M.D.**	NA	28	Johnstown, PA	17.6
NA	Bloomington, IL**	NA	NA	East Stroudsburg, PA**	NA	181	Jonesboro, AR	(18.5)
75	Bloomington, IN	2.1	96	El Centro, CA	(1.9)	81	Joplin, MO	1.4
NA	Bloomsburg-Berwick, PA**	NA	198	El Paso, TX	(22.8)	NA	Kahului-Wailuku-Lahaina, HI**	NA
161	Boise City, ID	(14.7)	NA	Elgin, IL M.D.**	NA	232	Kalamazoo-Portage, MI	(31.8)
NA	Boston (greater), MA-NH**	NA	NA	Elizabethtown-Fort Knox, KY**	NA	NA	Kankakee, IL**	NA
NA	Boston, MA M.D.**	NA	NA	Elmira, NY**	NA	NA	Kansas City, MO-KS**	NA
NA	Boulder, CO**	NA	70	Erie, PA	2.8	163	Kennewick-Richland, WA	(14.8)
152	Bowling Green, KY	(13.0)	169	Eugene, OR	(16.4)	NA	Killeen-Temple, TX**	NA
33	Bremerton-Silverdale, WA	14.6	NA	Fairbanks, AK**	NA	206	Kingsport, TN-VA	(25.1)
94	Bridgeport-Stamford, CT	(1.1)	NA	Fargo, ND-MN**	NA	NA	Kingston, NY**	NA
222	Brownsville-Harlingen, TX	(29.0)	245	Farmington, NM	(44.0)	NA	Knoxville, TN**	NA
NA	Brunswick, GA**	NA	114	Fayetteville-Springdale, AR-MO	(6.7)	NA	Kokomo, IN**	NA
NA	Buffalo-Niagara Falls, NY**	NA	72	Fayetteville, NC	2.3	19	La Crosse, WI-MN	23.3
198	Burlington, NC	(22.8)	215	Flagstaff, AZ	(26.9)	108	Lafayette, IN	(5.0)
NA	California-Lexington Park, MD**	NA	43	Flint, MI	11.3	NA	Lafayette, LA**	NA
NA	Cambridge-Newton, MA M.D.**	NA	142	Florence-Muscle Shoals, AL	(11.1)	NA	Lake Co.-Kenosha Co., IL-WI M.D.**	NA
57	Camden, NJ M.D.	6.2	101	Florence, SC	(3.5)	120	Lake Havasu City-Kingman, AZ	(8.0)
NA	Canton, OH**	NA	66	Fond du Lac, WI	4.1	180	Lakeland, FL	(18.4)
240	Cape Coral-Fort Myers, FL	(36.4)	216	Fort Collins, CO	(27.3)	152	Lancaster, PA	(13.0)
13	Cape Girardeau, MO-IL	31.8	51	Fort Lauderdale, FL M.D.	8.3	169	Lansing-East Lansing, MI	(16.4)
91	Carson City, NV	(1.0)	NA	Fort Smith, AR-OK**	NA	209	Laredo, TX	(25.3)
135	Casper, WY	(10.4)	164	Fort Wayne, IN	(14.9)	35	Las Cruces, NM	13.9
NA	Cedar Rapids, IA**	NA	172	Fort Worth-Arlington, TX M.D.	(16.8)	157	Las Vegas-Henderson, NV	(13.5)
NA	Chambersburg-Waynesboro, PA**	NA	15	Fresno, CA	30.9	191	Lawrence, KS	(21.6)
NA	Champaign-Urbana, IL**	NA	2	Gadsden, AL	58.7	NA	Lawton, OK**	NA
206	Charleston-North Charleston, SC	(25.1)	236	Gainesville, FL	(33.2)	114	Lebanon, PA	(6.7)
59	Charlottesville, VA	5.6	NA	Gainesville, GA**	NA	4	Lewiston-Auburn, ME	55.0

Note: All listings are for Metropolitan Statistical Areas (M.S.A.s) except for those ending with "M.D." Listings with "M.D." are Metropolitan Divisions which are smaller parts of eleven large M.S.A.s. See explanatory note at beginning of metropolitan area section.

RANK	METROPOLITAN AREA	% CHANGE	RANK	METROPOLITAN AREA	% CHANGE	RANK	METROPOLITAN AREA	% CHANGE
23	Lewiston, ID-WA	20.9	NA	Owensboro, KY**	NA	223	Silver Spring-Frederick, MD M.D.	(29.5)
NA	Lexington-Fayette, KY**	NA	129	Oxnard-Thousand Oaks, CA	(9.6)	NA	Sioux City, IA-NE-SD**	NA
203	Lima, OH	(24.1)	196	Palm Bay-Melbourne, FL	(22.1)	10	Sioux Falls, SD	37.6
86	Lincoln, NE	(0.8)	NA	Panama City, FL**	NA	187	South Bend-Mishawaka, IN-MI	(20.7)
110	Little Rock, AR	(6.0)	NA	Parkersburg-Vienna, WV**	NA	NA	Spartanburg, SC**	NA
104	Logan, UT-ID	(3.8)	17	Pensacola, FL	26.4	3	Spokane, WA	56.5
176	Longview, TX	(17.6)	NA	Peoria, IL**	NA	NA	Springfield, IL**	NA
35	Longview, WA	13.9	NA	Philadelphia (greater) PA-NJ-MD-DE**	NA	NA	Springfield, MA**	NA
139	Los Angeles County, CA M.D.	(10.9)	NA	Philadelphia, PA M.D.**	NA	44	Springfield, MO	10.8
125	Los Angeles (greater), CA	(9.2)	NA	Phoenix-Mesa-Scottsdale, AZ**	NA	6	Springfield, OH	46.3
91	Louisville, KY-IN	(1.0)	203	Pine Bluff, AR	(24.1)	233	State College, PA	(32.6)
160	Lubbock, TX	(13.9)	129	Pittsburgh, PA	(9.6)	NA	Staunton-Waynesboro, VA**	NA
60	Lynchburg, VA	5.5	132	Pittsfield, MA	(9.8)	79	Stockton-Lodi, CA	1.6
117	Macon, GA	(7.3)	NA	Pocatello, ID**	NA	216	St. George, UT	(27.3)
5	Madera, CA	53.0	212	Port St. Lucie, FL	(25.9)	45	St. Joseph, MO-KS	10.6
NA	Madison, WI**	NA	56	Portland-Vancouver, OR-WA	6.6	144	St. Louis, MO-IL	(11.3)
NA	Manchester-Nashua, NH**	NA	69	Portland, ME	3.3	21	Sumter, SC	23.0
NA	Manhattan, KS**	NA	197	Prescott, AZ	(22.3)	NA	Syracuse, NY**	NA
31	Mankato-North Mankato, MN	17.0	86	Providence-Warwick, RI-MA	(0.8)	NA	Tacoma, WA M.D.**	NA
14	Mansfield, OH	31.2	231	Provo-Orem, UT	(31.4)	178	Tallahassee, FL	(18.3)
191	McAllen-Edinburg-Mission, TX	(21.6)	NA	Pueblo, CO**	NA	239	Tampa-St Petersburg, FL	(35.0)
8	Medford, OR	38.8	235	Punta Gorda, FL	(33.1)	NA	Terre Haute, IN**	NA
189	Memphis, TN-MS-AR	(21.1)	154	Racine, WI	(13.1)	NA	Texarkana, TX-AR**	NA
38	Merced, CA	12.4	141	Raleigh, NC	(11.0)	NA	The Villages, FL**	NA
171	Miami (greater), FL	(16.5)	NA	Rapid City, SD**	NA	NA	Toledo, OH**	NA
211	Miami-Dade County, FL M.D.	(25.7)	38	Reading, PA	12.4	188	Topeka, KS	(20.8)
112	Michigan City-La Porte, IN	(6.5)	20	Redding, CA	23.2	9	Trenton, NJ	38.5
NA	Midland, MI**	NA	219	Reno, NV	(27.4)	86	Tucson, AZ	(0.8)
NA	Midland, TX**	NA	134	Richmond, VA	(10.1)	139	Tulsa, OK	(10.9)
61	Milwaukee, WI	5.4	50	Riverside-San Bernardino, CA	8.5	NA	Tuscaloosa, AL**	NA
NA	Minneapolis-St. Paul, MN-WI**	NA	101	Roanoke, VA	(3.5)	37	Tyler, TX	12.6
18	Missoula, MT	23.4	NA	Rochester, MN**	NA	NA	Utica-Rome, NY**	NA
165	Mobile, AL	(15.2)	NA	Rochester, NY**	NA	112	Valdosta, GA	(6.5)
99	Modesto, CA	(2.9)	NA	Rockford, IL**	NA	52	Vallejo-Fairfield, CA	7.8
132	Monroe, LA	(9.8)	27	Rockingham County, NH M.D.	17.9	NA	Victoria, TX**	NA
29	Monroe, MI	17.4	NA	Rocky Mount, NC**	NA	11	Vineland-Bridgeton, NJ	34.4
NA	Montgomery County, PA M.D.**	NA	NA	Rome, GA**	NA	123	Virginia Beach-Norfolk, VA-NC	(9.0)
83	Montgomery, AL	0.2	127	Sacramento, CA	(9.3)	65	Visalia-Porterville, CA	4.7
NA	Morgantown, WV**	NA	230	Saginaw, MI	(30.7)	NA	Waco, TX**	NA
NA	Morristown, TN**	NA	125	Salem, OR	(9.2)	NA	Walla Walla, WA**	NA
26	Mount Vernon-Anacortes, WA	18.2	124	Salinas, CA	(9.1)	NA	Warner Robins, GA**	NA
16	Muncie, IN	30.1	NA	Salisbury, MD-DE**	NA	NA	Warren-Troy, MI M.D.**	NA
178	Napa, CA	(18.3)	146	Salt Lake City, UT	(12.0)	213	Washington (greater) DC-VA-MD-WV	(26.0)
105	Naples-Marco Island, FL	(3.9)	198	San Antonio, TX	(22.8)	208	Washington, DC-VA-MD-WV M.D.	(25.2)
NA	Nashville-Davidson, TN**	NA	194	San Diego, CA	(21.8)	86	Waterloo-Cedar Falls, IA	(0.8)
NA	Nassau-Suffolk, NY M.D.**	NA	NA	San Francisco (greater), CA**	NA	NA	Watertown-Fort Drum, NY**	NA
NA	New Bern, NC**	NA	75	San Francisco-Redwood, CA M.D.	2.1	109	Wausau, WI	(5.2)
NA	New Haven-Milford, CT**	NA	22	San Jose, CA	21.6	216	West Palm Beach, FL M.D.	(27.3)
226	New Orleans, LA	(30.4)	91	San Luis Obispo, CA	(1.0)	32	Wheeling, WV-OH	14.7
NA	New York (greater), NY-NJ-PA**	NA	NA	San Rafael, CA M.D.**	NA	182	Wichita Falls, TX	(18.8)
NA	New York-Jersey City, NY-NJ M.D.**	NA	100	Santa Cruz-Watsonville, CA	(3.4)	121	Wichita, KS	(8.5)
NA	Newark, NJ-PA M.D.**	NA	42	Santa Fe, NM	11.4	106	Williamsport, PA	(4.4)
NA	North Port-Sarasota-Bradenton, FL**	NA	NA	Santa Maria-Santa Barbara, CA**	NA	58	Wilmington, DE-MD-NJ M.D.	5.8
116	Norwich-New London, CT	(7.0)	172	Santa Rosa, CA	(16.8)	NA	Wilmington, NC**	NA
52	Oakland-Hayward, CA M.D.	7.8	223	Savannah, GA	(29.5)	202	Winchester, VA-WV	(23.9)
177	Ocala, FL	(17.7)	48	Scranton--Wilkes-Barre, PA	9.8	NA	Winston-Salem, NC**	NA
55	Ocean City, NJ	7.5	NA	Seattle (greater), WA**	NA	62	Worcester, MA-CT	5.3
167	Odessa, TX	(16.1)	NA	Seattle-Bellevue-Everett, WA M.D.**	NA	111	Yakima, WA	(6.3)
NA	Ogden-Clearfield, UT**	NA	214	Sebastian-Vero Beach, FL	(26.3)	195	York-Hanover, PA	(22.0)
83	Oklahoma City, OK	0.2	NA	Sebring, FL**	NA	47	Youngstown-Warren, OH-PA	10.0
30	Olympia, WA	17.1	155	Sheboygan, WI	(13.2)	72	Yuba City, CA	2.3
82	Omaha-Council Bluffs, NE-IA	0.3	49	Sherman-Denison, TX	9.5	34	Yuma, AZ	14.3
186	Orlando, FL	(20.1)	138	Shreveport-Bossier City, LA	(10.7)			
185	Oshkosh-Neenah, WI	(19.9)	NA	Sierra Vista-Douglas, AZ**	NA			

Source: CQ Press using reported data from the F.B.I. "Crime in the United States 2012"

*Burglary is the unlawful entry of a structure to commit a felony or theft. Attempts are included.

**Not available.

32. Percent Change in Burglary Rate: 2008 to 2012 (continued)
National Percent Change = 8.6% Decrease*

RANK	METROPOLITAN AREA	% CHANGE	RANK	METROPOLITAN AREA	% CHANGE	RANK	METROPOLITAN AREA	% CHANGE
1	Columbus, IN	68.6	65	Visalia-Porterville, CA	4.7	129	Hanford-Corcoran, CA	(9.6)
2	Gadsden, AL	58.7	66	Fond du Lac, WI	4.1	129	Oxnard-Thousand Oaks, CA	(9.6)
3	Spokane, WA	56.5	67	Dothan, AL	3.8	129	Pittsburgh, PA	(9.6)
4	Lewiston-Auburn, ME	55.0	68	Cumberland, MD-WV	3.5	132	Monroe, LA	(9.8)
5	Madera, CA	53.0	69	Portland, ME	3.3	132	Pittsfield, MA	(9.8)
6	Springfield, OH	46.3	70	Dayton, OH	2.8	134	Richmond, VA	(10.1)
7	Bismarck, ND	41.1	70	Erie, PA	2.8	135	Casper, WY	(10.4)
8	Medford, OR	38.8	72	Fayetteville, NC	2.3	136	Birmingham-Hoover, AL	(10.5)
9	Trenton, NJ	38.5	72	Yuba City, CA	2.3	137	Janesville, WI	(10.6)
10	Sioux Falls, SD	37.6	74	Hickory, NC	2.2	138	Shreveport-Bossier City, LA	(10.7)
11	Vineland Bridgeton, NJ	34.4	75	Ann Arbor, MI	2.1	139	Los Angeles County, CA M.D.	(10.9)
12	Houma, LA	33.3	75	Bloomington, IN	2.1	139	Tulsa, OK	(10.9)
13	Cape Girardeau, MO-IL	31.8	75	San Francisco-Redwood, CA M.D.	2.1	141	Raleigh, NC	(11.0)
14	Mansfield, OH	31.2	78	Chico, CA	1.9	142	Florence-Muscle Shoals, AL	(11.1)
15	Fresno, CA	30.9	79	Harrisburg-Carlisle, PA	1.6	142	Huntsville, AL	(11.1)
16	Muncie, IN	30.1	79	Stockton-Lodi, CA	1.6	144	St. Louis, MO-IL	(11.3)
17	Pensacola, FL	26.4	81	Joplin, MO	1.4	145	Baltimore, MD	(11.5)
18	Missoula, MT	23.4	82	Omaha-Council Bluffs, NE-IA	0.3	146	Columbia, MO	(12.0)
19	La Crosse, WI-MN	23.3	83	Montgomery, AL	0.2	146	Durham-Chapel Hill, NC	(12.0)
20	Redding, CA	23.2	83	Oklahoma City, OK	0.2	146	Salt Lake City, UT	(12.0)
21	Sumter, SC	23.0	85	Dover, DE	(0.3)	149	Bellingham, WA	(12.7)
22	San Jose, CA	21.6	86	Anaheim-Santa Ana-Irvine, CA M.D.	(0.8)	149	Cleveland, TN	(12.7)
23	Lewiston, ID-WA	20.9	86	Lincoln, NE	(0.8)	151	Harrisonburg, VA	(12.9)
24	Billings, MT	19.0	86	Providence-Warwick, RI-MA	(0.8)	152	Bowling Green, KY	(13.0)
25	Great Falls, MT	18.5	86	Tucson, AZ	(0.8)	152	Lancaster, PA	(13.0)
26	Mount Vernon-Anacortes, WA	18.2	86	Waterloo-Cedar Falls, IA	(0.8)	154	Racine, WI	(13.1)
27	Rockingham County, NH M.D.	17.9	91	Carson City, NV	(1.0)	155	Sheboygan, WI	(13.2)
28	Johnstown, PA	17.6	91	Louisville, KY-IN	(1.0)	156	Columbus, GA-AL	(13.4)
29	Monroe, MI	17.4	91	San Luis Obispo, CA	(1.0)	157	Las Vegas-Henderson, NV	(13.5)
30	Olympia, WA	17.1	94	Bridgeport-Stamford, CT	(1.1)	158	Augusta, GA-SC	(13.7)
31	Mankato-North Mankato, MN	17.0	94	Green Bay, WI	(1.1)	159	Goldsboro, NC	(13.8)
32	Wheeling, WV-OH	14.7	96	El Centro, CA	(1.9)	160	Lubbock, TX	(13.9)
33	Bremerton-Silverdale, WA	14.6	97	Hartford, CT	(2.4)	161	Ames, IA	(14.7)
34	Yuma, AZ	14.3	98	Indianapolis, IN	(2.6)	161	Boise City, ID	(14.7)
35	Las Cruces, NM	13.9	99	Modesto, CA	(2.9)	163	Kennewick-Richland, WA	(14.8)
35	Longview, WA	13.9	100	Santa Cruz-Watsonville, CA	(3.4)	164	Fort Wayne, IN	(14.9)
37	Tyler, TX	12.6	101	Cheyenne, WY	(3.5)	165	Mobile, AL	(15.2)
38	Merced, CA	12.4	101	Florence, SC	(3.5)	166	Amarillo, TX	(16.0)
38	Reading, PA	12.4	101	Roanoke, VA	(3.5)	167	Odessa, TX	(16.1)
40	Johnson City, TN	12.3	104	Logan, UT-ID	(3.8)	168	Decatur, AL	(16.3)
41	Dalton, GA	12.2	105	Naples-Marco Island, FL	(3.9)	169	Eugene, OR	(16.4)
42	Santa Fe, NM	11.4	106	Grand Forks, ND-MN	(4.4)	169	Lansing-East Lansing, MI	(16.4)
43	Flint, MI	11.3	106	Williamsport, PA	(4.4)	171	Miami (greater), FL	(16.5)
44	Springfield, MO	10.8	108	Lafayette, IN	(5.0)	172	Fort Worth-Arlington, TX M.D.	(16.8)
45	St. Joseph, MO-KS	10.6	109	Wausau, WI	(5.2)	172	Santa Rosa, CA	(16.8)
46	Bakersfield, CA	10.5	110	Little Rock, AR	(6.0)	174	Abilene, TX	(17.2)
47	Youngstown-Warren, OH-PA	10.0	111	Yakima, WA	(6.3)	175	Iowa City, IA	(17.4)
48	Scranton--Wilkes-Barre, PA	9.8	112	Michigan City-La Porte, IN	(6.5)	176	Longview, TX	(17.6)
49	Sherman-Denison, TX	9.5	112	Valdosta, GA	(6.5)	177	Ocala, FL	(17.7)
50	Riverside-San Bernardino, CA	8.5	114	Fayetteville-Springdale, AR-MO	(6.7)	178	Napa, CA	(18.3)
51	Fort Lauderdale, FL M.D.	8.3	114	Lebanon, PA	(6.7)	178	Tallahassee, FL	(18.3)
52	Oakland-Hayward, CA M.D.	7.8	116	Norwich-New London, CT	(7.0)	180	Lakeland, FL	(18.4)
52	Vallejo-Fairfield, CA	7.8	117	Macon, GA	(7.3)	181	Jonesboro, AR	(18.5)
54	Bangor, ME	7.7	118	Corvallis, OR	(7.4)	182	Beaumont-Port Arthur, TX	(18.8)
55	Ocean City, NJ	7.5	119	Akron, OH	(7.8)	182	Wichita Falls, TX	(18.8)
56	Portland-Vancouver, OR-WA	6.6	120	Lake Havasu City-Kingman, AZ	(8.0)	184	Atlanta, GA	(19.1)
57	Camden, NJ M.D.	6.2	121	Wichita, KS	(8.5)	185	Oshkosh-Neenah, WI	(19.9)
58	Wilmington, DE-MD-NJ M.D.	5.8	122	Baton Rouge, LA	(8.9)	186	Orlando, FL	(20.1)
59	Charlottesville, VA	5.6	123	Virginia Beach-Norfolk, VA-NC	(9.0)	187	South Bend-Mishawaka, IN-MI	(20.7)
60	Lynchburg, VA	5.5	124	Salinas, CA	(9.1)	188	Topeka, KS	(20.8)
61	Milwaukee, WI	5.4	125	Los Angeles (greater), CA	(9.2)	189	Memphis, TN-MS-AR	(21.1)
62	Worcester, MA-CT	5.3	125	Salem, OR	(9.2)	190	Dallas (greater), TX	(21.5)
63	Barnstable Town, MA	4.8	127	Asheville, NC	(9.3)	191	Lawrence, KS	(21.6)
63	Duluth, MN-WI	4.8	127	Sacramento, CA	(9.3)	191	McAllen-Edinburg-Mission, TX	(21.6)

Note: All listings are for Metropolitan Statistical Areas (M.S.A.s) except for those ending with "M.D." Listings with "M.D." are Metropolitan Divisions which are smaller parts of eleven large M.S.A.s. See explanatory note at beginning of metropolitan area section.

RANK	METROPOLITAN AREA	% CHANGE	RANK	METROPOLITAN AREA	% CHANGE	RANK	METROPOLITAN AREA	% CHANGE
193	Austin-Round Rock, TX	(21.7)	NA	Binghamton, NY**	NA	NA	Madison, WI**	NA
194	San Diego, CA	(21.8)	NA	Bloomington, IL**	NA	NA	Manchester-Nashua, NH**	NA
195	York-Hanover, PA	(22.0)	NA	Bloomsburg-Berwick, PA**	NA	NA	Manhattan, KS**	NA
196	Palm Bay-Melbourne, FL	(22.1)	NA	Boston (greater), MA-NH**	NA	NA	Midland, MI**	NA
197	Prescott, AZ	(22.3)	NA	Boston, MA M.D.**	NA	NA	Midland, TX**	NA
198	Burlington, NC	(22.8)	NA	Boulder, CO**	NA	NA	Minneapolis-St. Paul, MN-WI**	NA
198	El Paso, TX	(22.8)	NA	Brunswick, GA**	NA	NA	Montgomery County, PA M.D.**	NA
198	San Antonio, TX	(22.8)	NA	Buffalo-Niagara Falls, NY**	NA	NA	Morgantown, WV**	NA
201	Dallas-Plano-Irving, TX M.D.	(23.7)	NA	California-Lexington Park, MD**	NA	NA	Morristown, TN**	NA
202	Winchester, VA-WV	(23.9)	NA	Cambridge-Newton, MA M.D.**	NA	NA	Nashville-Davidson, TN**	NA
203	Lima, OH	(24.1)	NA	Canton, OH**	NA	NA	Nassau-Suffolk, NY M.D.**	NA
203	Pine Bluff, AR	(24.1)	NA	Cedar Rapids, IA**	NA	NA	New Bern, NC**	NA
205	Appleton, WI	(25.0)	NA	Chambersburg-Waynesboro, PA**	NA	NA	New Haven-Milford, CT**	NA
206	Charleston-North Charleston, SC	(25.1)	NA	Champaign-Urbana, IL**	NA	NA	New York (greater), NY-NJ-PA**	NA
206	Kingsport, TN-VA	(25.1)	NA	Chicago (greater), IL-IN-WI**	NA	NA	New York-Jersey City, NY-NJ M.D.**	NA
208	Washington, DC-VA-MD-WV M.D.	(25.2)	NA	Chicago-Joilet-Naperville, IL M.D.**	NA	NA	Newark, NJ-PA M.D.**	NA
209	Laredo, TX	(25.3)	NA	Cincinnati, OH-KY-IN**	NA	NA	North Port-Sarasota-Bradenton, FL**	NA
210	Deltona-Daytona Beach, FL	(25.5)	NA	Coeur d'Alene, ID**	NA	NA	Ogden-Clearfield, UT**	NA
211	Miami-Dade County, FL M.D.	(25.7)	NA	Colorado Springs, CO**	NA	NA	Owensboro, KY**	NA
212	Port St. Lucie, FL	(25.9)	NA	Corpus Christi, TX**	NA	NA	Panama City, FL**	NA
213	Washington (greater) DC-VA-MD-WV	(26.0)	NA	Crestview-Fort Walton Beach, FL**	NA	NA	Parkersburg-Vienna, WV**	NA
214	Sebastian-Vero Beach, FL	(26.3)	NA	Danville, IL**	NA	NA	Peoria, IL**	NA
215	Flagstaff, AZ	(26.9)	NA	Daphne-Fairhope-Foley, AL**	NA	NA	Philadelphia (greater) PA-NJ-MD-DE**	NA
216	Fort Collins, CO	(27.3)	NA	Davenport, IA-IL**	NA	NA	Philadelphia, PA M.D.**	NA
216	St. George, UT	(27.3)	NA	Decatur, IL**	NA	NA	Phoenix-Mesa-Scottsdale, AZ**	NA
216	West Palm Beach, FL M.D.	(27.3)	NA	Denver-Aurora, CO**	NA	NA	Pocatello, ID**	NA
219	Reno, NV	(27.4)	NA	Des Moines-West Des Moines, IA**	NA	NA	Pueblo, CO**	NA
220	Hinesville, GA	(27.8)	NA	Detroit (greater), MI**	NA	NA	Rapid City, SD**	NA
221	Clarksville, TN-KY	(28.3)	NA	Detroit-Dearborn-Livonia, MI M.D.**	NA	NA	Rochester, MN**	NA
222	Brownsville-Harlingen, TX	(29.0)	NA	Dubuque, IA**	NA	NA	Rochester, NY**	NA
223	Savannah, GA	(29.5)	NA	Dutchess-Putnam, NY M.D.**	NA	NA	Rockford, IL**	NA
223	Silver Spring-Frederick, MD M.D.	(29.5)	NA	East Stroudsburg, PA**	NA	NA	Rocky Mount, NC**	NA
225	Idaho Falls, ID	(29.9)	NA	Elgin, IL M.D.**	NA	NA	Rome, GA**	NA
226	Greensboro-High Point, NC	(30.4)	NA	Elizabethtown-Fort Knox, KY**	NA	NA	Salisbury, MD-DE**	NA
226	New Orleans, LA	(30.4)	NA	Elmira, NY**	NA	NA	San Francisco (greater), CA**	NA
228	Bay City, MI	(30.5)	NA	Fairbanks, AK**	NA	NA	San Rafael, CA M.D.**	NA
229	Blacksburg, VA	(30.6)	NA	Fargo, ND-MN**	NA	NA	Santa Maria-Santa Barbara, CA**	NA
230	Saginaw, MI	(30.7)	NA	Fort Smith, AR-OK**	NA	NA	Seattle (greater), WA**	NA
231	Provo-Orem, UT	(31.4)	NA	Gainesville, GA**	NA	NA	Seattle-Bellevue-Everett, WA M.D.**	NA
232	Kalamazoo-Portage, MI	(31.8)	NA	Gary, IN M.D.**	NA	NA	Sebring, FL**	NA
233	State College, PA	(32.6)	NA	Gettysburg, PA**	NA	NA	Sierra Vista-Douglas, AZ**	NA
234	Greeley, CO	(33.0)	NA	Glens Falls, NY**	NA	NA	Sioux City, IA-NE-SD**	NA
235	Punta Gorda, FL	(33.1)	NA	Grand Island, NE**	NA	NA	Spartanburg, SC**	NA
236	Gainesville, FL	(33.2)	NA	Greenville-Anderson, SC**	NA	NA	Springfield, IL**	NA
237	Athens-Clarke County, GA	(33.7)	NA	Hagerstown-Martinsburg, MD-WV**	NA	NA	Springfield, MA**	NA
238	Grand Junction, CO	(34.4)	NA	Hammond, LA**	NA	NA	Staunton-Waynesboro, VA**	NA
239	Tampa-St Petersburg, FL	(35.0)	NA	Hattiesburg, MS**	NA	NA	Syracuse, NY**	NA
240	Cape Coral-Fort Myers, FL	(36.4)	NA	Hilton Head Island, SC**	NA	NA	Tacoma, WA M.D.**	NA
240	Greenville, NC	(36.4)	NA	Homosassa Springs, FL**	NA	NA	Terre Haute, IN**	NA
242	College Station-Bryan, TX	(37.4)	NA	Houston, TX**	NA	NA	Texarkana, TX-AR**	NA
243	Jacksonville, FL	(37.6)	NA	Jackson, MS**	NA	NA	The Villages, FL**	NA
244	Altoona, PA	(41.3)	NA	Jackson, TN**	NA	NA	Toledo, OH**	NA
245	Farmington, NM	(44.0)	NA	Jefferson City, MO**	NA	NA	Tuscaloosa, AL**	NA
246	Auburn, AL	(59.1)	NA	Kahului-Wailuku-Lahaina, HI**	NA	NA	Utica-Rome, NY**	NA
NA	Albany-Schenectady-Troy, NY**	NA	NA	Kankakee, IL**	NA	NA	Victoria, TX**	NA
NA	Albany, GA**	NA	NA	Kansas City, MO-KS**	NA	NA	Waco, TX**	NA
NA	Albany, OR**	NA	NA	Killeen-Temple, TX**	NA	NA	Walla Walla, WA**	NA
NA	Albuquerque, NM**	NA	NA	Kingston, NY**	NA	NA	Warner Robins, GA**	NA
NA	Alexandria, LA**	NA	NA	Knoxville, TN**	NA	NA	Warren-Troy, MI M.D.**	NA
NA	Allentown, PA-NJ**	NA	NA	Kokomo, IN**	NA	NA	Watertown-Fort Drum, NY**	NA
NA	Anchorage, AK**	NA	NA	Lafayette, LA**	NA	NA	Wilmington, NC**	NA
NA	Anniston-Oxford, AL**	NA	NA	Lake Co.-Kenosha Co., IL-WI M.D.**	NA	NA	Winston-Salem, NC**	NA
NA	Atlantic City, NJ**	NA	NA	Lawton, OK**	NA			
NA	Beckley, WV**	NA	NA	Lexington-Fayette, KY**	NA			

Source: CQ Press using reported data from the F.B.I. "Crime in the United States 2012"

*Burglary is the unlawful entry of a structure to commit a felony or theft. Attempts are included.

**Not available.

33. Larceny-Thefts in 2012
National Total = 6,150,598 Larceny-Thefts*

RANK	METROPOLITAN AREA	THEFTS	RANK	METROPOLITAN AREA	THEFTS	RANK	METROPOLITAN AREA	THEFTS
246	Abilene, TX	3,631	329	Cheyenne, WY	2,147	93	Gary, IN M.D.	15,243
96	Akron, OH	14,492	4	Chicago (greater), IL-IN-WI	179,630	373	Gettysburg, PA	898
86	Albany-Schenectady-Troy, NY	16,721	6	Chicago-Joilet-Naperville, IL M.D.	143,093	354	Glens Falls, NY	1,719
204	Albany, GA	4,849	267	Chico, CA	3,147	271	Goldsboro, NC	3,062
289	Albany, OR	2,821	30	Cincinnati, OH-KY-IN	50,790	355	Grand Forks, ND-MN	1,715
NA	Albuquerque, NM**	NA	207	Clarksville, TN-KY	4,787	323	Grand Island, NE	2,268
213	Alexandria, LA	4,636	307	Cleveland, TN	2,580	255	Grand Junction, CO	3,470
99	Allentown, PA-NJ	13,906	269	Coeur d'Alene, ID	3,084	309	Great Falls, MT	2,567
358	Altoona, PA	1,647	212	College Station-Bryan, TX	4,641	219	Greeley, CO	4,400
167	Amarillo, TX	6,685	95	Colorado Springs, CO	14,950	221	Green Bay, WI	4,392
365	Ames, IA	1,534	223	Columbia, MO	4,321	83	Greensboro-High Point, NC	17,563
33	Anaheim-Santa Ana-Irvine, CA M.D.	48,899	126	Columbus, GA-AL	9,753	70	Greenville-Anderson, SC	22,368
133	Anchorage, AK	9,235	328	Columbus, IN	2,148	230	Greenville, NC	4,054
184	Ann Arbor, MI	5,713	98	Corpus Christi, TX	13,925	231	Hagerstown-Martinsburg, MD-WV	4,050
253	Anniston-Oxford, AL	3,482	368	Corvallis, OR	1,460	229	Hammond, LA	4,243
280	Appleton, WI	2,920	203	Crestview-Fort Walton Beach, FL	4,869	324	Hanford-Corcoran, CA	2,222
146	Asheville, NC	8,093	325	Cumberland, MD-WV	2,189	134	Harrisburg-Carlisle, PA	9,108
210	Athens-Clarke County, GA	4,734	8	Dallas (greater), TX	142,186	370	Harrisonburg, VA	1,367
10	Atlanta, GA	116,101	14	Dallas-Plano-Irving, TX M.D.	89,570	80	Hartford, CT	18,154
176	Atlantic City, NJ	6,312	287	Dalton, GA	2,841	295	Hattiesburg, MS	2,748
278	Auburn, AL	2,941	337	Danville, IL	1,978	148	Hickory, NC	7,921
94	Augusta, GA-SC	15,212	239	Daphne-Fairhope-Foley, AL	3,829	231	Hilton Head Island, SC	4,050
34	Austin-Round Rock, TX	47,929	153	Davenport, IA-IL	7,446	361	Hinesville, GA	1,600
82	Bakersfield, CA	17,584	79	Dayton, OH	18,571	333	Homosassa Springs, FL	2,055
25	Baltimore, MD	57,582	274	Decatur, AL	2,976	200	Houma, LA	5,071
250	Bangor, ME	3,573	347	Decatur, IL	1,776	9	Houston, TX	141,416
257	Barnstable Town, MA	3,455	100	Deltona-Daytona Beach, FL	13,553	127	Huntsville, AL	9,702
67	Baton Rouge, LA	22,952	29	Denver-Aurora, CO	51,402	336	Idaho Falls, ID	1,997
364	Bay City, MI	1,560	109	Des Moines-West Des Moines, IA	12,093	37	Indianapolis, IN	45,572
140	Beaumont-Port Arthur, TX	8,516	21	Detroit (greater), MI	67,897	320	Iowa City, IA	2,321
274	Beckley, WV	2,976	48	Detroit-Dearborn-Livonia, MI M.D.	35,071	47	Jacksonville, FL	35,335
208	Bellingham, WA	4,751	277	Dothan, AL	2,958	118	Jackson, MS	11,313
227	Billings, MT	4,262	209	Dover, DE	4,735	282	Jackson, TN	2,912
195	Binghamton, NY	5,310	371	Dubuque, IA	1,322	240	Janesville, WI	3,738
58	Birmingham-Hoover, AL	27,958	165	Duluth, MN-WI	6,787	302	Jefferson City, MO	2,661
326	Bismarck, ND	2,180	119	Durham-Chapel Hill, NC	11,162	228	Johnson City, TN	4,245
272	Blacksburg, VA	3,052	206	Dutchess-Putnam, NY M.D.	4,833	345	Johnstown, PA	1,822
268	Bloomington, IL	3,100	265	East Stroudsburg, PA	3,185	306	Jonesboro, AR	2,610
238	Bloomington, IN	3,850	244	El Centro, CA	3,636	190	Joplin, MO	5,528
369	Bloomsburg-Berwick, PA	1,392	90	El Paso, TX	15,623	218	Kahului-Wailuku-Lahaina, HI	4,419
129	Boise City, ID	9,405	147	Elgin, IL M.D.	8,054	166	Kalamazoo-Portage, MI	6,762
23	Boston (greater), MA-NH	67,269	360	Elizabethtown-Fort Knox, KY	1,613	319	Kankakee, IL	2,350
54	Boston, MA M.D.	30,235	348	Elmira, NY	1,768	35	Kansas City, MO-KS	47,477
188	Boulder, CO	5,609	194	Erie, PA	5,326	214	Kennewick-Richland, WA	4,583
283	Bowling Green, KY	2,887	123	Eugene, OR	10,055	149	Killeen-Temple, TX	7,763
193	Bremerton-Silverdale, WA	5,421	372	Fairbanks, AK	1,283	163	Kingsport, TN-VA	6,885
114	Bridgeport-Stamford, CT	11,536	241	Fargo, ND-MN	3,694	285	Kingston, NY	2,863
102	Brownsville-Harlingen, TX	13,186	321	Farmington, NM	2,315	76	Knoxville, TN	19,995
264	Brunswick, GA	3,224	137	Fayetteville-Springdale, AR-MO	8,875	362	Kokomo, IN	1,574
65	Buffalo-Niagara Falls, NY	24,194	106	Fayetteville, NC	12,330	312	La Crosse, WI-MN	2,506
252	Burlington, NC	3,530	248	Flagstaff, AZ	3,596	233	Lafayette, IN	4,043
339	California-Lexington Park, MD	1,938	142	Flint, MI	8,319	115	Lafayette, LA	11,483
56	Cambridge-Newton, MA M.D.	29,612	274	Florence-Muscle Shoals, AL	2,976	101	Lake Co.-Kenosha Co., IL-WI M.D.	13,240
69	Camden, NJ M.D.	22,602	168	Florence, SC	6,664	205	Lake Havasu City-Kingman, AZ	4,839
152	Canton, OH	7,493	366	Fond du Lac, WI	1,479	103	Lakeland, FL	12,467
124	Cape Coral-Fort Myers, FL	9,927	177	Fort Collins, CO	6,254	145	Lancaster, PA	8,227
290	Cape Girardeau, MO-IL	2,790	36	Fort Lauderdale, FL M.D.	46,079	159	Lansing-East Lansing, MI	7,118
374	Carson City, NV	731	183	Fort Smith, AR-OK	5,872	138	Laredo, TX	8,845
352	Casper, WY	1,739	136	Fort Wayne, IN	9,016	217	Las Cruces, NM	4,420
216	Cedar Rapids, IA	4,512	27	Fort Worth-Arlington, TX M.D.	52,616	51	Las Vegas-Henderson, NV	33,435
341	Chambersburg-Waynesboro, PA	1,931	63	Fresno, CA	24,603	249	Lawrence, KS	3,590
225	Champaign-Urbana, IL	4,268	284	Gadsden, AL	2,884	245	Lawton, OK	3,635
87	Charleston-North Charleston, SC	16,280	171	Gainesville, FL	6,468	332	Lebanon, PA	2,104
259	Charlottesville, VA	3,351	270	Gainesville, GA	3,076	316	Lewiston-Auburn, ME	2,400

Note: All listings are for Metropolitan Statistical Areas (M.S.A.s) except for those ending with "M.D." Listings with "M.D." are Metropolitan Divisions which are smaller parts of eleven large M.S.A.s. See explanatory note at beginning of metropolitan area section.

RANK	METROPOLITAN AREA	THEFTS	RANK	METROPOLITAN AREA	THEFTS	RANK	METROPOLITAN AREA	THEFTS
359	Lewiston, ID-WA	1,622	318	Owensboro, KY	2,353	85	Silver Spring-Frederick, MD M.D.	16,741
97	Lexington-Fayette, KY	14,219	117	Oxnard-Thousand Oaks, CA	11,404	258	Sioux City, IA-NE-SD	3,450
301	Lima, OH	2,668	111	Palm Bay-Melbourne, FL	11,867	222	Sioux Falls, SD	4,342
139	Lincoln, NE	8,825	185	Panama City, FL	5,672	169	South Bend-Mishawaka, IN-MI	6,530
64	Little Rock, AR	24,485	342	Parkersburg-Vienna, WV	1,925	157	Spartanburg, SC	7,241
363	Logan, UT-ID	1,568	116	Pensacola, FL	11,469	75	Spokane, WA	20,009
189	Longview, TX	5,529	156	Peoria, IL	7,273	175	Springfield, IL	6,331
297	Longview, WA	2,701	11	Philadelphia (greater) PA-NJ-MD-DE	114,494	105	Springfield, MA	12,376
7	Los Angeles County, CA M.D.	142,604	32	Philadelphia, PA M.D.	49,637	92	Springfield, MO	15,248
2	Los Angeles (greater), CA	191,503	13	Phoenix-Mesa-Scottsdale, AZ	98,449	242	Springfield, OH	3,683
55	Louisville, KY-IN	29,863	315	Pine Bluff, AR	2,406	346	State College, PA	1,800
131	Lubbock, TX	9,298	50	Pittsburgh, PA	33,694	351	Staunton-Waynesboro, VA	1,750
256	Lynchburg, VA	3,461	335	Pittsfield, MA	2,002	84	Stockton-Lodi, CA	16,847
155	Macon, GA	7,410	350	Pocatello, ID	1,761	331	St. George, UT	2,141
355	Madera, CA	1,715	161	Port St. Lucie, FL	7,042	237	St. Joseph, MO-KS	3,851
113	Madison, WI	11,729	28	Portland-Vancouver, OR-WA	52,421	26	St. Louis, MO-IL	56,689
158	Manchester-Nashua, NH	7,195	125	Portland, ME	9,846	298	Sumter, SC	2,696
367	Manhattan, KS	1,470	263	Prescott, AZ	3,268	110	Syracuse, NY	12,011
327	Mankato-North Mankato, MN	2,154	61	Providence-Warwick, RI-MA	27,000	72	Tacoma, WA M.D.	20,852
236	Mansfield, OH	3,857	141	Provo-Orem, UT	8,506	144	Tallahassee, FL	8,256
68	McAllen-Edinburg-Mission, TX	22,631	192	Pueblo, CO	5,478	24	Tampa-St Petersburg, FL	58,203
173	Medford, OR	6,449	313	Punta Gorda, FL	2,475	220	Terre Haute, IN	4,398
42	Memphis, TN-MS-AR	37,380	243	Racine, WI	3,673	224	Texarkana, TX-AR	4,293
181	Merced, CA	6,047	74	Raleigh, NC	20,217	376	The Villages, FL	670
5	Miami (greater), FL	160,505	260	Rapid City, SD	3,347	NA	Toledo, OH**	NA
17	Miami-Dade County, FL M.D.	83,124	180	Reading, PA	6,062	174	Topeka, KS	6,434
294	Michigan City-La Porte, IN	2,759	247	Redding, CA	3,623	201	Trenton, NJ	5,039
375	Midland, MI	719	151	Reno, NV	7,542	NA	Tucson, AZ**	NA
292	Midland, TX	2,773	66	Richmond, VA	23,242	77	Tulsa, OK	19,371
44	Milwaukee, WI	36,932	19	Riverside-San Bernardino, CA	72,682	197	Tuscaloosa, AL	5,234
20	Minneapolis-St. Paul, MN-WI	71,629	179	Roanoke, VA	6,069	211	Tyler, TX	4,679
273	Missoula, MT	3,009	292	Rochester, MN	2,773	196	Utica-Rome, NY	5,306
107	Mobile, AL	12,315	71	Rochester, NY	21,341	286	Valdosta, GA	2,843
104	Modesto, CA	12,425	143	Rockford, IL	8,274	172	Vallejo-Fairfield, CA	6,451
186	Monroe, LA	5,622	154	Rockingham County, NH M.D.	7,422	322	Victoria, TX	2,275
296	Monroe, MI	2,746	261	Rocky Mount, NC	3,324	215	Vineland-Bridgeton, NJ	4,559
62	Montgomery County, PA M.D.	26,478	291	Rome, GA	2,786	39	Virginia Beach-Norfolk, VA-NC	41,271
122	Montgomery, AL	10,635	40	Sacramento, CA	39,256	132	Visalia-Porterville, CA	9,265
342	Morgantown, WV	1,925	300	Saginaw, MI	2,690	170	Waco, TX	6,518
281	Morristown, TN	2,917	130	Salem, OR	9,313	357	Walla Walla, WA	1,664
254	Mount Vernon-Anacortes, WA	3,478	187	Salinas, CA	5,612	198	Warner Robins, GA	5,209
303	Muncie, IN	2,630	135	Salisbury, MD-DE	9,046	52	Warren-Troy, MI M.D.	32,826
344	Napa, CA	1,895	43	Salt Lake City, UT	37,145	12	Washington (greater) DC-VA-MD-WV	102,052
235	Naples-Marco Island, FL	3,932	18	San Antonio, TX	76,280	16	Washington, DC-VA-MD-WV M.D.	85,311
45	Nashville-Davidson, TN	36,505	38	San Diego, CA	43,412	308	Waterloo-Cedar Falls, IA	2,577
49	Nassau-Suffolk, NY M.D.	34,276	NA	San Francisco (greater), CA**	NA	330	Watertown-Fort Drum, NY	2,144
310	New Bern, NC	2,523	41	San Francisco-Redwood, CA M.D.	38,850	353	Wausau, WI	1,720
81	New Haven-Milford, CT	17,972	57	San Jose, CA	28,617	53	West Palm Beach, FL M.D.	31,302
60	New Orleans, LA	27,168	226	San Luis Obispo, CA	4,266	334	Wheeling, WV-OH	2,021
1	New York (greater), NY-NJ-PA	254,913	NA	San Rafael, CA M.D.**	NA	233	Wichita Falls, TX	4,043
3	New York-Jersey City, NY-NJ M.D.	188,193	178	Santa Cruz-Watsonville, CA	6,104	78	Wichita, KS	19,291
59	Newark, NJ-PA M.D.	27,611	314	Santa Fe, NM	2,466	340	Williamsport, PA	1,935
91	North Port-Sarasota-Bradenton, FL	15,600	162	Santa Maria-Santa Barbara, CA	6,933	89	Wilmington, DE-MD-NJ M.D.	15,777
305	Norwich-New London, CT	2,617	182	Santa Rosa, CA	5,982	164	Wilmington, NC	6,821
NA	Oakland-Hayward, CA M.D.**	NA	150	Savannah, GA	7,666	317	Winchester, VA-WV	2,355
199	Ocala, FL	5,080	128	Scranton--Wilkes-Barre, PA	9,528	88	Winston-Salem, NC	15,806
262	Ocean City, NJ	3,273	15	Seattle (greater), WA	88,216	108	Worcester, MA-CT	12,103
251	Odessa, TX	3,571	22	Seattle-Bellevue-Everett, WA M.D.	67,364	191	Yakima, WA	5,511
112	Ogden-Clearfield, UT	11,787	288	Sebastian-Vero Beach, FL	2,830	160	York-Hanover, PA	7,058
46	Oklahoma City, OK	35,430	348	Sebring, FL	1,768	121	Youngstown-Warren, OH-PA	11,082
202	Olympia, WA	5,013	338	Sheboygan, WI	1,964	279	Yuba City, CA	2,934
73	Omaha-Council Bluffs, NE-IA	20,464	311	Sherman-Denison, TX	2,510	266	Yuma, AZ	3,159
31	Orlando, FL	50,130	120	Shreveport-Bossier City, LA	11,106			
304	Oshkosh-Neenah, WI	2,621	298	Sierra Vista-Douglas, AZ	2,696			

Source: Reported data from the F.B.I. "Crime in the United States 2012"
*Larceny-theft is the unlawful taking of property. Attempts are included.
**Not available.

33. Larceny-Thefts in 2012 (continued)
National Total = 6,150,598 Larceny-Thefts*

RANK	METROPOLITAN AREA	THEFTS	RANK	METROPOLITAN AREA	THEFTS	RANK	METROPOLITAN AREA	THEFTS
1	New York (greater), NY-NJ-PA	254,913	65	Buffalo-Niagara Falls, NY	24,194	129	Boise City, ID	9,405
2	Los Angeles (greater), CA	191,503	66	Richmond, VA	23,242	130	Salem, OR	9,313
3	New York-Jersey City, NY-NJ M.D.	188,193	67	Baton Rouge, LA	22,952	131	Lubbock, TX	9,298
4	Chicago (greater), IL-IN-WI	179,630	68	McAllen-Edinburg-Mission, TX	22,631	132	Visalia-Porterville, CA	9,265
5	Miami (greater), FL	160,505	69	Camden, NJ M.D.	22,602	133	Anchorage, AK	9,235
6	Chicago-Joilet-Naperville, IL M.D.	143,093	70	Greenville-Anderson, SC	22,368	134	Harrisburg-Carlisle, PA	9,108
7	Los Angeles County, CA M.D.	142,604	71	Rochester, NY	21,341	135	Salisbury, MD-DE	9,046
8	Dallas (greater), TX	142,186	72	Tacoma, WA M.D.	20,852	136	Fort Wayne, IN	9,016
9	Houston, TX	141,416	73	Omaha-Council Bluffs, NE-IA	20,464	137	Fayetteville-Springdale, AR-MO	8,875
10	Atlanta, GA	116,101	74	Raleigh, NC	20,217	138	Laredo, TX	8,845
11	Philadelphia (greater) PA-NJ-MD-DE	114,494	75	Spokane, WA	20,009	139	Lincoln, NE	8,825
12	Washington (greater) DC-VA-MD-WV	102,052	76	Knoxville, TN	19,995	140	Beaumont-Port Arthur, TX	8,516
13	Phoenix-Mesa-Scottsdale, AZ	98,449	77	Tulsa, OK	19,371	141	Provo-Orem, UT	8,506
14	Dallas-Plano-Irving, TX M.D.	89,570	78	Wichita, KS	19,291	142	Flint, MI	8,319
15	Seattle (greater), WA	88,216	79	Dayton, OH	18,571	143	Rockford, IL	8,274
16	Washington, DC-VA-MD-WV M.D.	85,311	80	Hartford, CT	18,154	144	Tallahassee, FL	8,256
17	Miami-Dade County, FL M.D.	83,124	81	New Haven-Milford, CT	17,972	145	Lancaster, PA	8,227
18	San Antonio, TX	76,280	82	Bakersfield, CA	17,584	146	Asheville, NC	8,093
19	Riverside-San Bernardino, CA	72,682	83	Greensboro-High Point, NC	17,563	147	Elgin, IL M.D.	8,054
20	Minneapolis-St. Paul, MN-WI	71,629	84	Stockton-Lodi, CA	16,847	148	Hickory, NC	7,921
21	Detroit (greater), MI	67,897	85	Silver Spring-Frederick, MD M.D.	16,741	149	Killeen-Temple, TX	7,763
22	Seattle-Bellevue-Everett, WA M.D.	67,364	86	Albany-Schenectady-Troy, NY	16,721	150	Savannah, GA	7,666
23	Boston (greater), MA-NH	67,269	87	Charleston-North Charleston, SC	16,280	151	Reno, NV	7,542
24	Tampa-St Petersburg, FL	58,203	88	Winston-Salem, NC	15,806	152	Canton, OH	7,493
25	Baltimore, MD	57,582	89	Wilmington, DE-MD-NJ M.D.	15,777	153	Davenport, IA-IL	7,446
26	St. Louis, MO-IL	56,689	90	El Paso, TX	15,623	154	Rockingham County, NH M.D.	7,422
27	Fort Worth-Arlington, TX M.D.	52,616	91	North Port-Sarasota-Bradenton, FL	15,600	155	Macon, GA	7,410
28	Portland-Vancouver, OR-WA	52,421	92	Springfield, MO	15,248	156	Peoria, IL	7,273
29	Denver-Aurora, CO	51,402	93	Gary, IN M.D.	15,243	157	Spartanburg, SC	7,241
30	Cincinnati, OH-KY-IN	50,790	94	Augusta, GA-SC	15,212	158	Manchester-Nashua, NH	7,195
31	Orlando, FL	50,130	95	Colorado Springs, CO	14,950	159	Lansing-East Lansing, MI	7,118
32	Philadelphia, PA M.D.	49,637	96	Akron, OH	14,492	160	York-Hanover, PA	7,058
33	Anaheim-Santa Ana-Irvine, CA M.D.	48,899	97	Lexington-Fayette, KY	14,219	161	Port St. Lucie, FL	7,042
34	Austin-Round Rock, TX	47,929	98	Corpus Christi, TX	13,925	162	Santa Maria-Santa Barbara, CA	6,933
35	Kansas City, MO-KS	47,477	99	Allentown, PA-NJ	13,906	163	Kingsport, TN-VA	6,885
36	Fort Lauderdale, FL M.D.	46,079	100	Deltona-Daytona Beach, FL	13,553	164	Wilmington, NC	6,821
37	Indianapolis, IN	45,572	101	Lake Co.-Kenosha Co., IL-WI M.D.	13,240	165	Duluth, MN-WI	6,787
38	San Diego, CA	43,412	102	Brownsville-Harlingen, TX	13,186	166	Kalamazoo-Portage, MI	6,762
39	Virginia Beach-Norfolk, VA-NC	41,271	103	Lakeland, FL	12,467	167	Amarillo, TX	6,685
40	Sacramento, CA	39,256	104	Modesto, CA	12,425	168	Florence, SC	6,664
41	San Francisco-Redwood, CA M.D.	38,850	105	Springfield, MA	12,376	169	South Bend-Mishawaka, IN-MI	6,530
42	Memphis, TN-MS-AR	37,380	106	Fayetteville, NC	12,330	170	Waco, TX	6,518
43	Salt Lake City, UT	37,145	107	Mobile, AL	12,315	171	Gainesville, FL	6,468
44	Milwaukee, WI	36,932	108	Worcester, MA-CT	12,103	172	Vallejo-Fairfield, CA	6,451
45	Nashville-Davidson, TN	36,505	109	Des Moines-West Des Moines, IA	12,093	173	Medford, OR	6,449
46	Oklahoma City, OK	35,430	110	Syracuse, NY	12,011	174	Topeka, KS	6,434
47	Jacksonville, FL	35,335	111	Palm Bay-Melbourne, FL	11,867	175	Springfield, IL	6,331
48	Detroit-Dearborn-Livonia, MI M.D.	35,071	112	Ogden-Clearfield, UT	11,787	176	Atlantic City, NJ	6,312
49	Nassau-Suffolk, NY M.D.	34,276	113	Madison, WI	11,729	177	Fort Collins, CO	6,254
50	Pittsburgh, PA	33,694	114	Bridgeport-Stamford, CT	11,536	178	Santa Cruz-Watsonville, CA	6,104
51	Las Vegas-Henderson, NV	33,435	115	Lafayette, LA	11,483	179	Roanoke, VA	6,069
52	Warren-Troy, MI M.D.	32,826	116	Pensacola, FL	11,469	180	Reading, PA	6,062
53	West Palm Beach, FL M.D.	31,302	117	Oxnard-Thousand Oaks, CA	11,404	181	Merced, CA	6,047
54	Boston, MA M.D.	30,235	118	Jackson, MS	11,313	182	Santa Rosa, CA	5,982
55	Louisville, KY-IN	29,863	119	Durham-Chapel Hill, NC	11,162	183	Fort Smith, AR-OK	5,872
56	Cambridge-Newton, MA M.D.	29,612	120	Shreveport-Bossier City, LA	11,106	184	Ann Arbor, MI	5,713
57	San Jose, CA	28,617	121	Youngstown-Warren, OH-PA	11,082	185	Panama City, FL	5,672
58	Birmingham-Hoover, AL	27,958	122	Montgomery, AL	10,635	186	Monroe, LA	5,622
59	Newark, NJ-PA M.D.	27,611	123	Eugene, OR	10,055	187	Salinas, CA	5,612
60	New Orleans, LA	27,168	124	Cape Coral-Fort Myers, FL	9,927	188	Boulder, CO	5,609
61	Providence-Warwick, RI-MA	27,000	125	Portland, ME	9,846	189	Longview, TX	5,529
62	Montgomery County, PA M.D.	26,478	126	Columbus, GA-AL	9,753	190	Joplin, MO	5,528
63	Fresno, CA	24,603	127	Huntsville, AL	9,702	191	Yakima, WA	5,511
64	Little Rock, AR	24,485	128	Scranton--Wilkes-Barre, PA	9,528	192	Pueblo, CO	5,478

Note: All listings are for Metropolitan Statistical Areas (M.S.A.s) except for those ending with "M.D." Listings with "M.D." are Metropolitan Divisions which are smaller parts of eleven large M.S.A.s. See explanatory note at beginning of metropolitan area section.

RANK	METROPOLITAN AREA	THEFTS	RANK	METROPOLITAN AREA	THEFTS	RANK	METROPOLITAN AREA	THEFTS
193	Bremerton-Silverdale, WA	5,421	257	Barnstable Town, MA	3,455	321	Farmington, NM	2,315
194	Erie, PA	5,326	258	Sioux City, IA-NE-SD	3,450	322	Victoria, TX	2,275
195	Binghamton, NY	5,310	259	Charlottesville, VA	3,351	323	Grand Island, NE	2,268
196	Utica-Rome, NY	5,306	260	Rapid City, SD	3,347	324	Hanford-Corcoran, CA	2,222
197	Tuscaloosa, AL	5,234	261	Rocky Mount, NC	3,324	325	Cumberland, MD-WV	2,189
198	Warner Robins, GA	5,209	262	Ocean City, NJ	3,273	326	Bismarck, ND	2,180
199	Ocala, FL	5,080	263	Prescott, AZ	3,268	327	Mankato-North Mankato, MN	2,154
200	Houma, LA	5,071	264	Brunswick, GA	3,224	328	Columbus, IN	2,148
201	Trenton, NJ	5,039	265	East Stroudsburg, PA	3,185	329	Cheyenne, WY	2,147
202	Olympia, WA	5,013	266	Yuma, AZ	3,159	330	Watertown-Fort Drum, NY	2,144
203	Crestview-Fort Walton Beach, FL	4,869	267	Chico, CA	3,147	331	St. George, UT	2,141
204	Albany, GA	4,849	268	Bloomington, IL	3,100	332	Lebanon, PA	2,104
205	Lake Havasu City-Kingman, AZ	4,839	269	Coeur d'Alene, ID	3,084	333	Homosassa Springs, FL	2,055
206	Dutchess-Putnam, NY M.D.	4,833	270	Gainesville, GA	3,076	334	Wheeling, WV-OH	2,021
207	Clarksville, TN-KY	4,787	271	Goldsboro, NC	3,062	335	Pittsfield, MA	2,002
208	Bellingham, WA	4,751	272	Blacksburg, VA	3,052	336	Idaho Falls, ID	1,997
209	Dover, DE	4,735	273	Missoula, MT	3,009	337	Danville, IL	1,978
210	Athens-Clarke County, GA	4,734	274	Beckley, WV	2,976	338	Sheboygan, WI	1,964
211	Tyler, TX	4,679	274	Decatur, AL	2,976	339	California-Lexington Park, MD	1,938
212	College Station-Bryan, TX	4,641	274	Florence-Muscle Shoals, AL	2,976	340	Williamsport, PA	1,935
213	Alexandria, LA	4,636	277	Dothan, AL	2,958	341	Chambersburg-Waynesboro, PA	1,931
214	Kennewick-Richland, WA	4,583	278	Auburn, AL	2,941	342	Morgantown, WV	1,925
215	Vineland-Bridgeton, NJ	4,559	279	Yuba City, CA	2,934	342	Parkersburg-Vienna, WV	1,925
216	Cedar Rapids, IA	4,512	280	Appleton, WI	2,920	344	Napa, CA	1,895
217	Las Cruces, NM	4,420	281	Morristown, TN	2,917	345	Johnstown, PA	1,822
218	Kahului-Wailuku-Lahaina, HI	4,419	282	Jackson, TN	2,912	346	State College, PA	1,800
219	Greeley, CO	4,400	283	Bowling Green, KY	2,887	347	Decatur, IL	1,776
220	Terre Haute, IN	4,398	284	Gadsden, AL	2,884	348	Elmira, NY	1,768
221	Green Bay, WI	4,392	285	Kingston, NY	2,863	348	Sebring, FL	1,768
222	Sioux Falls, SD	4,342	286	Valdosta, GA	2,843	350	Pocatello, ID	1,761
223	Columbia, MO	4,321	287	Dalton, GA	2,841	351	Staunton-Waynesboro, VA	1,750
224	Texarkana, TX-AR	4,293	288	Sebastian-Vero Beach, FL	2,830	352	Casper, WY	1,739
225	Champaign-Urbana, IL	4,268	289	Albany, OR	2,821	353	Wausau, WI	1,720
226	San Luis Obispo, CA	4,266	290	Cape Girardeau, MO-IL	2,790	354	Glens Falls, NY	1,719
227	Billings, MT	4,262	291	Rome, GA	2,786	355	Grand Forks, ND-MN	1,715
228	Johnson City, TN	4,245	292	Midland, TX	2,773	355	Madera, CA	1,715
229	Hammond, LA	4,243	292	Rochester, MN	2,773	357	Walla Walla, WA	1,664
230	Greenville, NC	4,054	294	Michigan City-La Porte, IN	2,759	358	Altoona, PA	1,647
231	Hagerstown-Martinsburg, MD-WV	4,050	295	Hattiesburg, MS	2,748	359	Lewiston, ID-WA	1,622
231	Hilton Head Island, SC	4,050	296	Monroe, MI	2,746	360	Elizabethtown-Fort Knox, KY	1,613
233	Lafayette, IN	4,043	297	Longview, WA	2,701	361	Hinesville, GA	1,600
233	Wichita Falls, TX	4,043	298	Sierra Vista-Douglas, AZ	2,696	362	Kokomo, IN	1,574
235	Naples-Marco Island, FL	3,932	298	Sumter, SC	2,696	363	Logan, UT-ID	1,568
236	Mansfield, OH	3,857	300	Saginaw, MI	2,690	364	Bay City, MI	1,560
237	St. Joseph, MO-KS	3,851	301	Lima, OH	2,668	365	Ames, IA	1,534
238	Bloomington, IN	3,850	302	Jefferson City, MO	2,661	366	Fond du Lac, WI	1,479
239	Daphne-Fairhope-Foley, AL	3,829	303	Muncie, IN	2,630	367	Manhattan, KS	1,470
240	Janesville, WI	3,738	304	Oshkosh-Neenah, WI	2,621	368	Corvallis, OR	1,460
241	Fargo, ND-MN	3,694	305	Norwich-New London, CT	2,617	369	Bloomsburg-Berwick, PA	1,392
242	Springfield, OH	3,683	306	Jonesboro, AR	2,610	370	Harrisonburg, VA	1,367
243	Racine, WI	3,673	307	Cleveland, TN	2,580	371	Dubuque, IA	1,322
244	El Centro, CA	3,636	308	Waterloo-Cedar Falls, IA	2,577	372	Fairbanks, AK	1,283
245	Lawton, OK	3,635	309	Great Falls, MT	2,567	373	Gettysburg, PA	898
246	Abilene, TX	3,631	310	New Bern, NC	2,523	374	Carson City, NV	731
247	Redding, CA	3,623	311	Sherman-Denison, TX	2,510	375	Midland, MI	719
248	Flagstaff, AZ	3,596	312	La Crosse, WI-MN	2,506	376	The Villages, FL	670
249	Lawrence, KS	3,590	313	Punta Gorda, FL	2,475	NA	Albuquerque, NM**	NA
250	Bangor, ME	3,573	314	Santa Fe, NM	2,466	NA	Oakland-Hayward, CA M.D.**	NA
251	Odessa, TX	3,571	315	Pine Bluff, AR	2,406	NA	San Francisco (greater), CA**	NA
252	Burlington, NC	3,530	316	Lewiston-Auburn, ME	2,400	NA	San Rafael, CA M.D.**	NA
253	Anniston-Oxford, AL	3,482	317	Winchester, VA-WV	2,355	NA	Toledo, OH**	NA
254	Mount Vernon-Anacortes, WA	3,478	318	Owensboro, KY	2,353	NA	Tucson, AZ**	NA
255	Grand Junction, CO	3,470	319	Kankakee, IL	2,350			
256	Lynchburg, VA	3,461	320	Iowa City, IA	2,321			

Source: Reported data from the F.B.I. "Crime in the United States 2012"

*Larceny-theft is the unlawful taking of property. Attempts are included.

**Not available.

34. Larceny-Theft Rate in 2012
National Rate = 1,959.3 Larceny-Thefts per 100,000 Population*

RANK	METROPOLITAN AREA	RATE	RANK	METROPOLITAN AREA	RATE	RANK	METROPOLITAN AREA	RATE
161	Abilene, TX	2,149.7	134	Cheyenne, WY	2,283.4	162	Gary, IN M.D.	2,144.2
182	Akron, OH	2,066.1	234	Chicago (greater), IL-IN-WI	1,888.6	374	Gettysburg, PA	883.9
228	Albany-Schenectady-Troy, NY	1,908.4	218	Chicago-Joilet-Naperville, IL M.D.	1,959.9	350	Glens Falls, NY	1,325.4
25	Albany, GA	3,042.6	337	Chico, CA	1,415.6	89	Goldsboro, NC	2,451.1
110	Albany, OR	2,371.4	102	Cincinnati, OH-KY-IN	2,391.6	273	Grand Forks, ND-MN	1,718.7
NA	Albuquerque, NM**	NA	255	Clarksville, TN-KY	1,798.3	56	Grand Island, NE	2,726.1
30	Alexandria, LA	2,982.9	153	Cleveland, TN	2,190.2	120	Grand Junction, CO	2,327.0
283	Allentown, PA-NJ	1,682.3	154	Coeur d'Alene, ID	2,170.5	23	Great Falls, MT	3,115.1
356	Altoona, PA	1,293.7	210	College Station-Bryan, TX	1,974.1	284	Greeley, CO	1,678.0
71	Amarillo, TX	2,573.8	142	Colorado Springs, CO	2,233.2	337	Green Bay, WI	1,415.6
276	Ames, IA	1,704.2	67	Columbia, MO	2,604.0	105	Greensboro-High Point, NC	2,379.1
299	Anaheim-Santa Ana-Irvine, CA M.D.	1,585.5	13	Columbus, GA-AL	3,205.2	60	Greenville-Anderson, SC	2,650.8
33	Anchorage, AK	2,945.5	53	Columbus, IN	2,749.8	116	Greenville, NC	2,345.7
291	Ann Arbor, MI	1,640.7	16	Corpus Christi, TX	3,180.4	298	Hagerstown-Martinsburg, MD-WV	1,585.8
34	Anniston-Oxford, AL	2,944.1	281	Corvallis, OR	1,687.1	4	Hammond, LA	3,441.3
359	Appleton, WI	1,280.8	205	Crestview-Fort Walton Beach, FL	2,007.5	333	Hanford-Corcoran, CA	1,431.8
240	Asheville, NC	1,867.9	170	Cumberland, MD-WV	2,112.8	290	Harrisburg-Carlisle, PA	1,644.6
93	Athens-Clarke County, GA	2,423.0	167	Dallas (greater), TX	2,128.5	372	Harrisonburg, VA	1,068.3
164	Atlanta, GA	2,136.4	194	Dallas-Plano-Irving, TX M.D.	2,033.1	263	Hartford, CT	1,773.1
131	Atlantic City, NJ	2,289.5	213	Dalton, GA	1,969.3	236	Hattiesburg, MS	1,885.5
190	Auburn, AL	2,041.7	91	Danville, IL	2,425.6	160	Hickory, NC	2,151.4
63	Augusta, GA-SC	2,642.9	189	Daphne-Fairhope-Foley, AL	2,042.5	170	Hilton Head Island, SC	2,112.8
61	Austin-Round Rock, TX	2,647.7	221	Davenport, IA-IL	1,948.8	216	Hinesville, GA	1,964.5
186	Bakersfield, CA	2,045.6	126	Dayton, OH	2,312.0	331	Homosassa Springs, FL	1,447.8
177	Baltimore, MD	2,089.7	225	Decatur, AL	1,923.9	97	Houma, LA	2,416.9
121	Bangor, ME	2,321.6	296	Decatur, IL	1,603.1	129	Houston, TX	2,299.3
297	Barnstable Town, MA	1,587.1	139	Deltona-Daytona Beach, FL	2,257.9	138	Huntsville, AL	2,271.1
44	Baton Rouge, LA	2,823.0	220	Denver-Aurora, CO	1,950.4	324	Idaho Falls, ID	1,470.4
329	Bay City, MI	1,455.4	178	Des Moines-West Des Moines, IA	2,076.0	106	Indianapolis, IN	2,378.8
181	Beaumont-Port Arthur, TX	2,071.8	300	Detroit (greater), MI	1,583.1	321	Iowa City, IA	1,492.7
103	Beckley, WV	2,384.1	222	Detroit-Dearborn-Livonia, MI M.D.	1,944.7	72	Jacksonville, FL	2,562.7
127	Bellingham, WA	2,310.1	203	Dothan, AL	2,010.2	214	Jackson, MS	1,969.1
64	Billings, MT	2,629.5	40	Dover, DE	2,841.4	146	Jackson, TN	2,222.5
172	Binghamton, NY	2,112.0	340	Dubuque, IA	1,391.4	119	Janesville, WI	2,328.9
88	Birmingham-Hoover, AL	2,459.3	98	Duluth, MN-WI	2,411.5	266	Jefferson City, MO	1,765.0
250	Bismarck, ND	1,821.6	158	Durham-Chapel Hill, NC	2,154.6	174	Johnson City, TN	2,107.0
278	Blacksburg, VA	1,697.2	366	Dutchess-Putnam, NY M.D.	1,208.0	363	Johnstown, PA	1,265.6
288	Bloomington, IL	1,655.8	239	East Stroudsburg, PA	1,871.8	169	Jonesboro, AR	2,116.9
104	Bloomington, IN	2,379.4	193	El Centro, CA	2,034.7	22	Joplin, MO	3,120.0
293	Bloomsburg-Berwick, PA	1,620.3	241	El Paso, TX	1,867.5	49	Kahului-Wailuku-Lahaina, HI	2,783.4
323	Boise City, ID	1,488.3	357	Elgin, IL M.D.	1,288.0	185	Kalamazoo-Portage, MI	2,058.8
330	Boston (greater), MA-NH	1,453.2	373	Elizabethtown-Fort Knox, KY	1,063.2	184	Kankakee, IL	2,065.9
301	Boston, MA M.D.	1,574.0	208	Elmira, NY	1,979.4	118	Kansas City, MO-KS	2,335.0
247	Boulder, CO	1,848.0	233	Erie, PA	1,892.4	274	Kennewick-Richland, WA	1,718.3
258	Bowling Green, KY	1,793.4	42	Eugene, OR	2,825.0	244	Killeen-Temple, TX	1,858.2
173	Bremerton-Silverdale, WA	2,108.3	2	Fairbanks, AK	3,707.8	150	Kingsport, TN-VA	2,202.4
362	Bridgeport-Stamford, CT	1,266.7	275	Fargo, ND-MN	1,709.7	304	Kingston, NY	1,560.8
19	Brownsville-Harlingen, TX	3,137.1	254	Farmington, NM	1,802.9	115	Knoxville, TN	2,351.2
43	Brunswick, GA	2,824.9	242	Fayetteville-Springdale, AR-MO	1,866.1	232	Kokomo, IN	1,895.0
168	Buffalo-Niagara Falls, NY	2,122.0	11	Fayetteville, NC	3,263.1	245	La Crosse, WI-MN	1,857.6
135	Burlington, NC	2,280.2	62	Flagstaff, AZ	2,644.5	207	Lafayette, IN	1,979.5
262	California-Lexington Park, MD	1,785.8	212	Flint, MI	1,969.5	92	Lafayette, LA	2,423.8
355	Cambridge-Newton, MA M.D.	1,294.6	202	Florence-Muscle Shoals, AL	2,012.4	318	Lake Co.-Kenosha Co., IL-WI M.D.	1,514.4
256	Camden, NJ M.D.	1,796.5	14	Florence, SC	3,202.0	111	Lake Havasu City-Kingman, AZ	2,365.6
246	Canton, OH	1,855.4	332	Fond du Lac, WI	1,445.2	201	Lakeland, FL	2,017.9
309	Cape Coral-Fort Myers, FL	1,551.2	200	Fort Collins, CO	2,019.0	302	Lancaster, PA	1,568.7
38	Cape Girardeau, MO-IL	2,870.5	74	Fort Lauderdale, FL M.D.	2,553.6	312	Lansing-East Lansing, MI	1,529.2
354	Carson City, NV	1,301.5	179	Fort Smith, AR-OK	2,072.5	7	Laredo, TX	3,397.5
141	Casper, WY	2,244.6	163	Fort Wayne, IN	2,142.8	183	Las Cruces, NM	2,066.0
271	Cedar Rapids, IA	1,724.9	124	Fort Worth-Arlington, TX M.D.	2,313.4	285	Las Vegas-Henderson, NV	1,675.3
360	Chambersburg-Waynesboro, PA	1,278.3	70	Fresno, CA	2,585.3	15	Lawrence, KS	3,183.1
249	Champaign-Urbana, IL	1,836.1	52	Gadsden, AL	2,754.0	54	Lawton, OK	2,737.1
113	Charleston-North Charleston, SC	2,364.2	100	Gainesville, FL	2,395.5	303	Lebanon, PA	1,564.0
320	Charlottesville, VA	1,498.7	287	Gainesville, GA	1,662.7	143	Lewiston-Auburn, ME	2,233.0

Note: All listings are for Metropolitan Statistical Areas (M.S.A.s) except for those ending with "M.D." Listings with "M.D." are Metropolitan Divisions which are smaller parts of eleven large M.S.A.s. See explanatory note at beginning of metropolitan area section.

RANK	METROPOLITAN AREA	RATE
65	Lewiston, ID-WA	2,617.9
32	Lexington-Fayette, KY	2,959.5
77	Lima, OH	2,514.9
39	Lincoln, NE	2,859.3
5	Little Rock, AR	3,436.0
365	Logan, UT-ID	1,213.8
78	Longview, TX	2,514.2
66	Longview, WA	2,610.1
334	Los Angeles County, CA M.D.	1,428.8
326	Los Angeles (greater), CA	1,465.8
101	Louisville, KY-IN	2,391.7
24	Lubbock, TX	3,096.0
348	Lynchburg, VA	1,346.8
17	Macon, GA	3,147.8
370	Madera, CA	1,111.2
229	Madison, WI	1,907.4
259	Manchester-Nashua, NH	1,787.7
310	Manhattan, KS	1,540.8
151	Mankato-North Mankato, MN	2,201.8
21	Mansfield, OH	3,123.0
47	McAllen-Edinburg-Mission, TX	2,794.8
20	Medford, OR	3,126.4
50	Memphis, TN-MS-AR	2,782.1
128	Merced, CA	2,305.3
48	Miami (greater), FL	2,792.6
12	Miami-Dade County, FL M.D.	3,209.9
87	Michigan City-La Porte, IN	2,469.5
375	Midland, MI	854.7
237	Midland, TX	1,881.1
114	Milwaukee, WI	2,358.0
175	Minneapolis-St. Paul, MN-WI	2,101.5
57	Missoula, MT	2,713.2
31	Mobile, AL	2,973.0
107	Modesto, CA	2,374.2
18	Monroe, LA	3,146.0
251	Monroe, MI	1,810.5
339	Montgomery County, PA M.D.	1,399.1
46	Montgomery, AL	2,797.7
328	Morgantown, WV	1,455.5
76	Morristown, TN	2,521.7
35	Mount Vernon-Anacortes, WA	2,916.1
144	Muncie, IN	2,228.3
344	Napa, CA	1,359.7
368	Naples-Marco Island, FL	1,182.2
166	Nashville-Davidson, TN	2,131.5
367	Nassau-Suffolk, NY M.D.	1,199.0
219	New Bern, NC	1,951.7
147	New Haven-Milford, CT	2,219.4
145	New Orleans, LA	2,226.8
357	New York (greater), NY-NJ-PA	1,288.0
349	New York-Jersey City, NY-NJ M.D.	1,340.1
371	Newark, NJ-PA M.D.	1,108.9
155	North Port-Sarasota-Bradenton, FL	2,169.6
259	Norwich-New London, CT	1,787.7
NA	Oakland-Hayward, CA M.D.**	NA
319	Ocala, FL	1,507.1
8	Ocean City, NJ	3,371.6
79	Odessa, TX	2,511.1
226	Ogden-Clearfield, UT	1,918.5
51	Oklahoma City, OK	2,755.3
224	Olympia, WA	1,934.7
122	Omaha-Council Bluffs, NE-IA	2,317.9
136	Orlando, FL	2,277.6
305	Oshkosh-Neenah, WI	1,558.9

RANK	METROPOLITAN AREA	RATE
192	Owensboro, KY	2,035.0
345	Oxnard-Thousand Oaks, CA	1,358.5
159	Palm Bay-Melbourne, FL	2,153.8
27	Panama City, FL	3,013.3
179	Parkersburg-Vienna, WV	2,072.5
82	Pensacola, FL	2,496.5
227	Peoria, IL	1,915.3
231	Philadelphia (greater) PA-NJ-MD-DE	1,904.3
123	Philadelphia, PA M.D.	2,314.1
133	Phoenix-Mesa-Scottsdale, AZ	2,284.3
93	Pine Bluff, AR	2,423.0
335	Pittsburgh, PA	1,425.6
316	Pittsfield, MA	1,521.1
176	Pocatello, ID	2,090.0
292	Port St. Lucie, FL	1,623.7
129	Portland-Vancouver, OR-WA	2,299.3
229	Portland, ME	1,907.4
313	Prescott, AZ	1,525.7
282	Providence-Warwick, RI-MA	1,683.2
308	Provo-Orem, UT	1,551.8
9	Pueblo, CO	3,365.6
315	Punta Gorda, FL	1,521.2
238	Racine, WI	1,875.1
272	Raleigh, NC	1,720.5
96	Rapid City, SD	2,421.2
325	Reading, PA	1,466.2
199	Redding, CA	2,019.3
270	Reno, NV	1,732.9
235	Richmond, VA	1,885.8
286	Riverside-San Bernardino, CA	1,672.8
223	Roanoke, VA	1,943.5
351	Rochester, MN	1,321.6
217	Rochester, NY	1,964.1
108	Rockford, IL	2,374.0
267	Rockingham County, NH M.D.	1,763.5
156	Rocky Mount, NC	2,163.2
37	Rome, GA	2,871.8
261	Sacramento, CA	1,787.3
347	Saginaw, MI	1,350.2
117	Salem, OR	2,341.9
353	Salinas, CA	1,318.0
109	Salisbury, MD-DE	2,372.5
10	Salt Lake City, UT	3,306.8
6	San Antonio, TX	3,424.0
342	San Diego, CA	1,369.8
NA	San Francisco (greater), CA**	NA
81	San Francisco-Redwood, CA M.D.	2,499.5
317	San Jose, CA	1,520.0
307	San Luis Obispo, CA	1,554.1
NA	San Rafael, CA M.D.**	NA
132	Santa Cruz-Watsonville, CA	2,288.3
279	Santa Fe, NM	1,690.4
295	Santa Maria-Santa Barbara, CA	1,609.2
364	Santa Rosa, CA	1,214.3
165	Savannah, GA	2,133.2
280	Scranton--Wilkes-Barre, PA	1,689.0
83	Seattle (greater), WA	2,496.0
86	Seattle-Bellevue-Everett, WA M.D.	2,478.0
204	Sebastian-Vero Beach, FL	2,010.1
264	Sebring, FL	1,768.4
277	Sheboygan, WI	1,701.3
191	Sherman-Denison, TX	2,036.7
85	Shreveport-Bossier City, LA	2,481.7
206	Sierra Vista-Douglas, AZ	2,000.8

RANK	METROPOLITAN AREA	RATE
346	Silver Spring-Frederick, MD M.D.	1,351.8
197	Sioux City, IA-NE-SD	2,031.7
248	Sioux Falls, SD	1,847.3
187	South Bend-Mishawaka, IN-MI	2,043.4
137	Spartanburg, SC	2,273.1
1	Spokane, WA	3,737.3
29	Springfield, IL	2,991.3
211	Springfield, MA	1,973.4
3	Springfield, MO	3,457.8
58	Springfield, OH	2,675.0
369	State College, PA	1,161.5
327	Staunton-Waynesboro, VA	1,459.1
99	Stockton-Lodi, CA	2,397.6
322	St. George, UT	1,491.2
28	St. Joseph, MO-KS	3,012.4
198	St. Louis, MO-IL	2,026.0
84	Sumter, SC	2,485.2
253	Syracuse, NY	1,803.1
73	Tacoma, WA M.D.	2,555.9
149	Tallahassee, FL	2,202.8
196	Tampa-St Petersburg, FL	2,032.7
75	Terre Haute, IN	2,539.2
41	Texarkana, TX-AR	2,840.2
376	The Villages, FL	676.2
NA	Toledo, OH**	NA
55	Topeka, KS	2,728.1
343	Trenton, NJ	1,366.1
NA	Tucson, AZ**	NA
194	Tulsa, OK	2,033.1
140	Tuscaloosa, AL	2,247.2
157	Tyler, TX	2,160.4
265	Utica-Rome, NY	1,768.3
209	Valdosta, GA	1,976.7
311	Vallejo-Fairfield, CA	1,534.7
112	Victoria, TX	2,364.7
36	Vineland-Bridgeton, NJ	2,887.8
95	Virginia Beach-Norfolk, VA-NC	2,422.7
187	Visalia-Porterville, CA	2,043.4
80	Waco, TX	2,503.6
69	Walla Walla, WA	2,589.4
45	Warner Robins, GA	2,809.0
352	Warren-Troy, MI M.D.	1,320.7
268	Washington (greater) DC-VA-MD-WV	1,751.6
243	Washington, DC-VA-MD-WV M.D.	1,859.6
314	Waterloo-Cedar Falls, IA	1,525.4
252	Watertown-Fort Drum, NY	1,808.6
361	Wausau, WI	1,276.5
125	West Palm Beach, FL M.D.	2,312.8
341	Wheeling, WV-OH	1,373.0
59	Wichita Falls, TX	2,651.0
26	Wichita, KS	3,030.2
289	Williamsport, PA	1,654.8
152	Wilmington, DE-MD-NJ M.D.	2,201.0
68	Wilmington, NC	2,601.8
257	Winchester, VA-WV	1,794.5
90	Winston-Salem, NC	2,427.5
336	Worcester, MA-CT	1,421.9
148	Yakima, WA	2,208.3
294	York-Hanover, PA	1,613.3
215	Youngstown-Warren, OH-PA	1,968.7
269	Yuba City, CA	1,735.6
306	Yuma, AZ	1,555.7

Source: Reported data from the F.B.I. "Crime in the United States 2012"

*Larceny-theft is the unlawful taking of property. Attempts are included.

**Not available.

34. Larceny-Theft Rate in 2012 (continued)
National Rate = 1,959.3 Larceny-Thefts per 100,000 Population*

RANK	METROPOLITAN AREA	RATE	RANK	METROPOLITAN AREA	RATE	RANK	METROPOLITAN AREA	RATE
1	Spokane, WA	3,737.3	65	Lewiston, ID-WA	2,617.9	129	Houston, TX	2,299.3
2	Fairbanks, AK	3,707.8	66	Longview, WA	2,610.1	129	Portland-Vancouver, OR-WA	2,299.3
3	Springfield, MO	3,457.8	67	Columbia, MO	2,604.0	131	Atlantic City, NJ	2,289.5
4	Hammond, LA	3,441.3	68	Wilmington, NC	2,601.8	132	Santa Cruz-Watsonville, CA	2,288.3
5	Little Rock, AR	3,436.0	69	Walla Walla, WA	2,589.4	133	Phoenix-Mesa-Scottsdale, AZ	2,284.3
6	San Antonio, TX	3,424.0	70	Fresno, CA	2,585.3	134	Cheyenne, WY	2,283.4
7	Laredo, TX	3,397.5	71	Amarillo, TX	2,573.8	135	Burlington, NC	2,280.2
8	Ocean City, NJ	3,371.6	72	Jacksonville, FL	2,562.7	136	Orlando, FL	2,277.6
9	Pueblo, CO	3,365.6	73	Tacoma, WA M.D.	2,555.9	137	Spartanburg, SC	2,273.1
10	Salt Lake City, UT	3,306.8	74	Fort Lauderdale, FL M.D.	2,553.6	138	Huntsville, AL	2,271.1
11	Fayetteville, NC	3,263.1	75	Terre Haute, IN	2,539.2	139	Deltona-Daytona Beach, FL	2,257.9
12	Miami-Dade County, FL M.D.	3,209.9	76	Morristown, TN	2,521.7	140	Tuscaloosa, AL	2,247.2
13	Columbus, GA-AL	3,205.2	77	Lima, OH	2,514.9	141	Casper, WY	2,244.6
14	Florence, SC	3,202.0	78	Longview, TX	2,514.2	142	Colorado Springs, CO	2,233.2
15	Lawrence, KS	3,183.1	79	Odessa, TX	2,511.1	143	Lewiston-Auburn, ME	2,233.0
16	Corpus Christi, TX	3,180.4	80	Waco, TX	2,503.6	144	Muncie, IN	2,228.3
17	Macon, GA	3,147.8	81	San Francisco-Redwood, CA M.D.	2,499.5	145	New Orleans, LA	2,226.8
18	Monroe, LA	3,146.0	82	Pensacola, FL	2,496.5	146	Jackson, TN	2,222.5
19	Brownsville-Harlingen, TX	3,137.1	83	Seattle (greater), WA	2,496.0	147	New Haven-Milford, CT	2,219.4
20	Medford, OR	3,126.4	84	Sumter, SC	2,485.2	148	Yakima, WA	2,208.3
21	Mansfield, OH	3,123.0	85	Shreveport-Bossier City, LA	2,481.7	149	Tallahassee, FL	2,202.8
22	Joplin, MO	3,120.0	86	Seattle-Bellevue-Everett, WA M.D.	2,478.0	150	Kingsport, TN-VA	2,202.4
23	Great Falls, MT	3,115.1	87	Michigan City-La Porte, IN	2,469.5	151	Mankato-North Mankato, MN	2,201.8
24	Lubbock, TX	3,096.0	88	Birmingham-Hoover, AL	2,459.3	152	Wilmington, DE-MD-NJ M.D.	2,201.0
25	Albany, GA	3,042.6	89	Goldsboro, NC	2,451.1	153	Cleveland, TN	2,190.2
26	Wichita, KS	3,030.2	90	Winston-Salem, NC	2,427.5	154	Coeur d'Alene, ID	2,170.5
27	Panama City, FL	3,013.3	91	Danville, IL	2,425.6	155	North Port-Sarasota-Bradenton, FL	2,169.6
28	St. Joseph, MO-KS	3,012.4	92	Lafayette, LA	2,423.8	156	Rocky Mount, NC	2,163.2
29	Springfield, IL	2,991.3	93	Athens-Clarke County, GA	2,423.0	157	Tyler, TX	2,160.4
30	Alexandria, LA	2,982.9	93	Pine Bluff, AR	2,423.0	158	Durham-Chapel Hill, NC	2,154.6
31	Mobile, AL	2,973.0	95	Virginia Beach-Norfolk, VA-NC	2,422.7	159	Palm Bay-Melbourne, FL	2,153.8
32	Lexington-Fayette, KY	2,959.5	96	Rapid City, SD	2,421.2	160	Hickory, NC	2,151.4
33	Anchorage, AK	2,945.5	97	Houma, LA	2,416.9	161	Abilene, TX	2,149.7
34	Anniston-Oxford, AL	2,944.1	98	Duluth, MN-WI	2,411.5	162	Gary, IN M.D.	2,144.2
35	Mount Vernon-Anacortes, WA	2,916.1	99	Stockton-Lodi, CA	2,397.6	163	Fort Wayne, IN	2,142.8
36	Vineland-Bridgeton, NJ	2,887.8	100	Gainesville, FL	2,395.5	164	Atlanta, GA	2,136.4
37	Rome, GA	2,871.8	101	Louisville, KY-IN	2,391.7	165	Savannah, GA	2,133.2
38	Cape Girardeau, MO-IL	2,870.5	102	Cincinnati, OH-KY-IN	2,391.6	166	Nashville-Davidson, TN	2,131.5
39	Lincoln, NE	2,859.3	103	Beckley, WV	2,384.1	167	Dallas (greater), TX	2,128.5
40	Dover, DE	2,841.4	104	Bloomington, IN	2,379.4	168	Buffalo-Niagara Falls, NY	2,122.0
41	Texarkana, TX-AR	2,840.2	105	Greensboro-High Point, NC	2,379.1	169	Jonesboro, AR	2,116.9
42	Eugene, OR	2,825.0	106	Indianapolis, IN	2,378.8	170	Cumberland, MD-WV	2,112.8
43	Brunswick, GA	2,824.9	107	Modesto, CA	2,374.2	170	Hilton Head Island, SC	2,112.8
44	Baton Rouge, LA	2,823.0	108	Rockford, IL	2,374.0	172	Binghamton, NY	2,112.0
45	Warner Robins, GA	2,809.0	109	Salisbury, MD-DE	2,372.5	173	Bremerton-Silverdale, WA	2,108.3
46	Montgomery, AL	2,797.7	110	Albany, OR	2,371.4	174	Johnson City, TN	2,107.0
47	McAllen-Edinburg-Mission, TX	2,794.8	111	Lake Havasu City-Kingman, AZ	2,365.6	175	Minneapolis-St. Paul, MN-WI	2,101.5
48	Miami (greater), FL	2,792.6	112	Victoria, TX	2,364.7	176	Pocatello, ID	2,090.0
49	Kahului-Wailuku-Lahaina, HI	2,783.4	113	Charleston-North Charleston, SC	2,364.2	177	Baltimore, MD	2,089.7
50	Memphis, TN-MS-AR	2,782.1	114	Milwaukee, WI	2,358.0	178	Des Moines-West Des Moines, IA	2,076.0
51	Oklahoma City, OK	2,755.3	115	Knoxville, TN	2,351.2	179	Fort Smith, AR-OK	2,072.5
52	Gadsden, AL	2,754.0	116	Greenville, NC	2,345.7	179	Parkersburg-Vienna, WV	2,072.5
53	Columbus, IN	2,749.8	117	Salem, OR	2,341.9	181	Beaumont-Port Arthur, TX	2,071.8
54	Lawton, OK	2,737.1	118	Kansas City, MO-KS	2,335.0	182	Akron, OH	2,066.1
55	Topeka, KS	2,728.1	119	Janesville, WI	2,328.9	183	Las Cruces, NM	2,066.0
56	Grand Island, NE	2,726.1	120	Grand Junction, CO	2,327.0	184	Kankakee, IL	2,065.9
57	Missoula, MT	2,713.2	121	Bangor, ME	2,321.6	185	Kalamazoo-Portage, MI	2,058.8
58	Springfield, OH	2,675.0	122	Omaha-Council Bluffs, NE-IA	2,317.9	186	Bakersfield, CA	2,045.6
59	Wichita Falls, TX	2,651.0	123	Philadelphia, PA M.D.	2,314.1	187	South Bend-Mishawaka, IN-MI	2,043.4
60	Greenville-Anderson, SC	2,650.8	124	Fort Worth-Arlington, TX M.D.	2,313.4	187	Visalia-Porterville, CA	2,043.4
61	Austin-Round Rock, TX	2,647.7	125	West Palm Beach, FL M.D.	2,312.8	189	Daphne-Fairhope-Foley, AL	2,042.5
62	Flagstaff, AZ	2,644.5	126	Dayton, OH	2,312.0	190	Auburn, AL	2,041.7
63	Augusta, GA-SC	2,642.9	127	Bellingham, WA	2,310.1	191	Sherman-Denison, TX	2,036.7
64	Billings, MT	2,629.5	128	Merced, CA	2,305.3	192	Owensboro, KY	2,035.0

Note: All listings are for Metropolitan Statistical Areas (M.S.A.s) except for those ending with "M.D." Listings with "M.D." are Metropolitan Divisions which are smaller parts of eleven large M.S.A.s. See explanatory note at beginning of metropolitan area section.

RANK	METROPOLITAN AREA	RATE	RANK	METROPOLITAN AREA	RATE	RANK	METROPOLITAN AREA	RATE
193	El Centro, CA	2,034.7	257	Winchester, VA-WV	1,794.5	321	Iowa City, IA	1,492.7
194	Dallas-Plano-Irving, TX M.D.	2,033.1	258	Bowling Green, KY	1,793.4	322	St. George, UT	1,491.2
194	Tulsa, OK	2,033.1	259	Manchester-Nashua, NH	1,787.7	323	Boise City, ID	1,488.3
196	Tampa-St Petersburg, FL	2,032.7	259	Norwich-New London, CT	1,787.7	324	Idaho Falls, ID	1,470.4
197	Sioux City, IA-NE-SD	2,031.7	261	Sacramento, CA	1,787.3	325	Reading, PA	1,466.2
198	St. Louis, MO-IL	2,026.0	262	California-Lexington Park, MD	1,785.8	326	Los Angeles (greater), CA	1,465.8
199	Redding, CA	2,019.3	263	Hartford, CT	1,773.1	327	Staunton-Waynesboro, VA	1,459.1
200	Fort Collins, CO	2,019.0	264	Sebring, FL	1,768.4	328	Morgantown, WV	1,455.5
201	Lakeland, FL	2,017.9	265	Utica-Rome, NY	1,768.3	329	Bay City, MI	1,455.4
202	Florence-Muscle Shoals, AL	2,012.4	266	Jefferson City, MO	1,765.0	330	Boston (greater), MA-NH	1,453.2
203	Dothan, AL	2,010.2	267	Rockingham County, NH M.D.	1,763.5	331	Homosassa Springs, FL	1,447.8
204	Sebastian-Vero Beach, FL	2,010.1	268	Washington (greater) DC-VA-MD-WV	1,751.6	332	Fond du Lac, WI	1,445.2
205	Crestview-Fort Walton Beach, FL	2,007.5	269	Yuba City, CA	1,735.6	333	Hanford-Corcoran, CA	1,431.8
206	Sierra Vista-Douglas, AZ	2,000.8	270	Reno, NV	1,732.9	334	Los Angeles County, CA M.D.	1,428.8
207	Lafayette, IN	1,979.5	271	Cedar Rapids, IA	1,724.9	335	Pittsburgh, PA	1,425.6
208	Elmira, NY	1,979.4	272	Raleigh, NC	1,720.5	336	Worcester, MA-CT	1,421.9
209	Valdosta, GA	1,976.7	273	Grand Forks, ND-MN	1,718.7	337	Chico, CA	1,415.6
210	College Station-Bryan, TX	1,974.1	274	Kennewick-Richland, WA	1,718.3	337	Green Bay, WI	1,415.6
211	Springfield, MA	1,973.4	275	Fargo, ND-MN	1,709.7	339	Montgomery County, PA M.D.	1,399.1
212	Flint, MI	1,969.5	276	Ames, IA	1,704.2	340	Dubuque, IA	1,391.4
213	Dalton, GA	1,969.3	277	Sheboygan, WI	1,701.3	341	Wheeling, WV-OH	1,373.0
214	Jackson, MS	1,969.1	278	Blacksburg, VA	1,697.2	342	San Diego, CA	1,369.8
215	Youngstown-Warren, OH-PA	1,968.7	279	Santa Fe, NM	1,690.4	343	Trenton, NJ	1,366.1
216	Hinesville, GA	1,964.5	280	Scranton--Wilkes-Barre, PA	1,689.0	344	Napa, CA	1,359.7
217	Rochester, NY	1,964.1	281	Corvallis, OR	1,687.1	345	Oxnard-Thousand Oaks, CA	1,358.5
218	Chicago-Joilet-Naperville, IL M.D.	1,959.9	282	Providence-Warwick, RI-MA	1,683.2	346	Silver Spring-Frederick, MD M.D.	1,351.8
219	New Bern, NC	1,951.7	283	Allentown, PA-NJ	1,682.3	347	Saginaw, MI	1,350.2
220	Denver-Aurora, CO	1,950.4	284	Greeley, CO	1,678.0	348	Lynchburg, VA	1,346.8
221	Davenport, IA-IL	1,948.8	285	Las Vegas-Henderson, NV	1,675.3	349	New York-Jersey City, NY-NJ M.D.	1,340.1
222	Detroit-Dearborn-Livonia, MI M.D.	1,944.7	286	Riverside-San Bernardino, CA	1,672.8	350	Glens Falls, NY	1,325.4
223	Roanoke, VA	1,943.5	287	Gainesville, GA	1,662.7	351	Rochester, MN	1,321.6
224	Olympia, WA	1,934.7	288	Bloomington, IL	1,655.8	352	Warren-Troy, MI M.D.	1,320.7
225	Decatur, AL	1,923.9	289	Williamsport, PA	1,654.8	353	Salinas, CA	1,318.0
226	Ogden-Clearfield, UT	1,918.5	290	Harrisburg-Carlisle, PA	1,644.6	354	Carson City, NV	1,301.5
227	Peoria, IL	1,915.3	291	Ann Arbor, MI	1,640.7	355	Cambridge-Newton, MA M.D.	1,294.6
228	Albany-Schenectady-Troy, NY	1,908.4	292	Port St. Lucie, FL	1,623.7	356	Altoona, PA	1,293.7
229	Madison, WI	1,907.4	293	Bloomsburg-Berwick, PA	1,620.3	357	Elgin, IL M.D.	1,288.0
229	Portland, ME	1,907.4	294	York-Hanover, PA	1,613.3	357	New York (greater), NY-NJ-PA	1,288.0
231	Philadelphia (greater) PA-NJ-MD-DE	1,904.3	295	Santa Maria-Santa Barbara, CA	1,609.2	359	Appleton, WI	1,280.8
232	Kokomo, IN	1,895.0	296	Decatur, IL	1,603.1	360	Chambersburg-Waynesboro, PA	1,278.3
233	Erie, PA	1,892.4	297	Barnstable Town, MA	1,587.1	361	Wausau, WI	1,276.5
234	Chicago (greater), IL-IN-WI	1,888.6	298	Hagerstown-Martinsburg, MD-WV	1,585.8	362	Bridgeport-Stamford, CT	1,266.7
235	Richmond, VA	1,885.8	299	Anaheim-Santa Ana-Irvine, CA M.D.	1,585.5	363	Johnstown, PA	1,265.6
236	Hattiesburg, MS	1,885.5	300	Detroit (greater), MI	1,583.1	364	Santa Rosa, CA	1,214.3
237	Midland, TX	1,881.1	301	Boston, MA M.D.	1,574.0	365	Logan, UT-ID	1,213.8
238	Racine, WI	1,875.1	302	Lancaster, PA	1,568.7	366	Dutchess-Putnam, NY M.D.	1,208.0
239	East Stroudsburg, PA	1,871.8	303	Lebanon, PA	1,564.0	367	Nassau-Suffolk, NY M.D.	1,199.0
240	Asheville, NC	1,867.9	304	Kingston, NY	1,560.8	368	Naples-Marco Island, FL	1,182.2
241	El Paso, TX	1,867.5	305	Oshkosh-Neenah, WI	1,558.9	369	State College, PA	1,161.5
242	Fayetteville-Springdale, AR-MO	1,866.1	306	Yuma, AZ	1,555.7	370	Madera, CA	1,111.2
243	Washington, DC-VA-MD-WV M.D.	1,859.6	307	San Luis Obispo, CA	1,554.1	371	Newark, NJ-PA M.D.	1,108.9
244	Killeen-Temple, TX	1,858.2	308	Provo-Orem, UT	1,551.8	372	Harrisonburg, VA	1,068.3
245	La Crosse, WI-MN	1,857.6	309	Cape Coral-Fort Myers, FL	1,551.2	373	Elizabethtown-Fort Knox, KY	1,063.2
246	Canton, OH	1,855.4	310	Manhattan, KS	1,540.8	374	Gettysburg, PA	883.9
247	Boulder, CO	1,848.0	311	Vallejo-Fairfield, CA	1,534.7	375	Midland, MI	854.7
248	Sioux Falls, SD	1,847.3	312	Lansing-East Lansing, MI	1,529.2	376	The Villages, FL	676.2
249	Champaign-Urbana, IL	1,836.1	313	Prescott, AZ	1,525.7	NA	Albuquerque, NM**	NA
250	Bismarck, ND	1,821.6	314	Waterloo-Cedar Falls, IA	1,525.4	NA	Oakland-Hayward, CA M.D.**	NA
251	Monroe, MI	1,810.5	315	Punta Gorda, FL	1,521.2	NA	San Francisco (greater), CA**	NA
252	Watertown-Fort Drum, NY	1,808.6	316	Pittsfield, MA	1,521.1	NA	San Rafael, CA M.D.**	NA
253	Syracuse, NY	1,803.1	317	San Jose, CA	1,520.0	NA	Toledo, OH**	NA
254	Farmington, NM	1,802.9	318	Lake Co.-Kenosha Co., IL-WI M.D.	1,514.4	NA	Tucson, AZ**	NA
255	Clarksville, TN-KY	1,798.3	319	Ocala, FL	1,507.1			
256	Camden, NJ M.D.	1,796.5	320	Charlottesville, VA	1,498.7			

Source: Reported data from the F.B.I. "Crime in the United States 2012"
*Larceny-theft is the unlawful taking of property. Attempts are included.
**Not available.

35. Percent Change in Larceny-Theft Rate: 2011 to 2012
National Percent Change = 0.7% Decrease*

RANK	METROPOLITAN AREA	% CHANGE	RANK	METROPOLITAN AREA	% CHANGE	RANK	METROPOLITAN AREA	% CHANGE
93	Abilene, TX	1.6	87	Cheyenne, WY	2.1	204	Gary, IN M.D.	(5.2)
189	Akron, OH	(3.9)	141	Chicago (greater), IL-IN-WI	(1.3)	NA	Gettysburg, PA**	NA
NA	Albany-Schenectady-Troy, NY**	NA	NA	Chicago-Joilet-Naperville, IL M.D.**	NA	NA	Glens Falls, NY**	NA
63	Albany, GA	4.1	142	Chico, CA	(1.4)	217	Goldsboro, NC	(6.3)
NA	Albany, OR**	NA	NA	Cincinnati, OH-KY-IN**	NA	93	Grand Forks, ND-MN	1.6
NA	Albuquerque, NM**	NA	142	Clarksville, TN-KY	(1.4)	NA	Grand Island, NE**	NA
115	Alexandria, LA	0.2	115	Cleveland, TN	0.2	22	Grand Junction, CO	11.4
NA	Allentown, PA-NJ**	NA	NA	Coeur d'Alene, ID**	NA	74	Great Falls, MT	2.7
259	Altoona, PA	(14.2)	271	College Station-Bryan, TX	(17.3)	36	Greeley, CO	9.1
246	Amarillo, TX	(10.6)	42	Colorado Springs, CO	7.7	73	Green Bay, WI	2.8
256	Ames, IA	(13.6)	58	Columbia, MO	4.4	NA	Greensboro-High Point, NC**	NA
45	Anaheim-Santa Ana-Irvine, CA M.D.	7.1	213	Columbus, GA-AL	(5.9)	NA	Greenville-Anderson, SC**	NA
NA	Anchorage, AK**	NA	269	Columbus, IN	(15.9)	NA	Greenville, NC**	NA
87	Ann Arbor, MI	2.1	179	Corpus Christi, TX	(3.3)	NA	Hagerstown-Martinsburg, MD-WV**	NA
27	Anniston-Oxford, AL	10.7	270	Corvallis, OR	(16.9)	NA	Hammond, LA**	NA
233	Appleton, WI	(8.5)	241	Crestview-Fort Walton Beach, FL	(8.9)	101	Hanford-Corcoran, CA	1.3
7	Asheville, NC	17.2	115	Cumberland, MD-WV	0.2	125	Harrisburg-Carlisle, PA	(0.4)
212	Athens-Clarke County, GA	(5.8)	220	Dallas (greater), TX	(6.7)	83	Harrisonburg, VA	2.2
169	Atlanta, GA	(3.0)	217	Dallas-Plano-Irving, TX M.D.	(6.3)	105	Hartford, CT	1.1
239	Atlantic City, NJ	(8.8)	224	Dalton, GA	(6.9)	NA	Hattiesburg, MS**	NA
266	Auburn, AL	(15.4)	179	Danville, IL	(3.3)	174	Hickory, NC	(3.2)
210	Augusta, GA-SC	(5.5)	NA	Daphne-Fairhope-Foley, AL**	NA	NA	Hilton Head Island, SC**	NA
133	Austin-Round Rock, TX	(1.0)	249	Davenport, IA-IL	(11.2)	162	Hinesville, GA	(2.4)
28	Bakersfield, CA	10.5	115	Dayton, OH	0.2	NA	Homosassa Springs, FL**	NA
137	Baltimore, MD	(1.2)	2	Decatur, AL	34.1	74	Houma, LA	2.7
32	Bangor, ME	9.8	229	Decatur, IL	(7.9)	149	Houston, TX	(1.6)
179	Barnstable Town, MA	(3.3)	NA	Deltona-Daytona Beach, FL**	NA	83	Huntsville, AL	2.2
133	Baton Rouge, LA	(1.0)	NA	Denver-Aurora, CO**	NA	182	Idaho Falls, ID	(3.4)
61	Bay City, MI	4.2	221	Des Moines-West Des Moines, IA	(6.8)	NA	Indianapolis, IN**	NA
272	Beaumont-Port Arthur, TX	(17.8)	174	Detroit (greater), MI	(3.2)	46	Iowa City, IA	6.7
NA	Beckley, WV**	NA	187	Detroit-Dearborn-Livonia, MI M.D.	(3.6)	189	Jacksonville, FL	(3.9)
120	Bellingham, WA	0.0	197	Dothan, AL	(4.5)	NA	Jackson, MS**	NA
152	Billings, MT	(1.7)	113	Dover, DE	0.4	NA	Jackson, TN**	NA
NA	Binghamton, NY**	NA	174	Dubuque, IA	(3.2)	76	Janesville, WI	2.6
164	Birmingham-Hoover, AL	(2.6)	169	Duluth, MN-WI	(3.0)	210	Jefferson City, MO	(5.5)
192	Bismarck, ND	(4.0)	226	Durham-Chapel Hill, NC	(7.4)	152	Johnson City, TN	(1.7)
262	Blacksburg, VA	(14.6)	NA	Dutchess-Putnam, NY M.D.**	NA	257	Johnstown, PA	(13.8)
59	Bloomington, IL	4.3	NA	East Stroudsburg, PA**	NA	247	Jonesboro, AR	(11.0)
NA	Bloomington, IN**	NA	13	El Centro, CA	13.8	6	Joplin, MO	18.2
NA	Bloomsburg-Berwick, PA**	NA	122	El Paso, TX	(0.1)	NA	Kahului-Wailuku-Lahaina, HI**	NA
207	Boise City, ID	(5.3)	NA	Elgin, IL M.D.**	NA	NA	Kalamazoo-Portage, MI**	NA
NA	Boston (greater), MA-NH**	NA	NA	Elizabethtown-Fort Knox, KY**	NA	185	Kankakee, IL	(3.5)
NA	Boston, MA M.D.**	NA	NA	Elmira, NY**	NA	NA	Kansas City, MO-KS**	NA
25	Boulder, CO	10.8	133	Erie, PA	(1.0)	244	Kennewick-Richland, WA	(9.2)
251	Bowling Green, KY	(11.5)	37	Eugene, OR	8.9	56	Killeen-Temple, TX	4.5
29	Bremerton-Silverdale, WA	10.4	40	Fairbanks, AK	8.5	229	Kingsport, TN-VA	(7.9)
201	Bridgeport-Stamford, CT	(4.8)	67	Fargo, ND-MN	3.9	NA	Kingston, NY**	NA
169	Brownsville-Harlingen, TX	(3.0)	11	Farmington, NM	15.2	NA	Knoxville, TN**	NA
255	Brunswick, GA	(12.6)	NA	Fayetteville-Springdale, AR-MO**	NA	NA	Kokomo, IN**	NA
NA	Buffalo-Niagara Falls, NY**	NA	95	Fayetteville, NC	1.5	66	La Crosse, WI-MN	4.0
265	Burlington, NC	(15.3)	233	Flagstaff, AZ	(8.5)	70	Lafayette, IN	3.5
NA	California-Lexington Park, MD**	NA	137	Flint, MI	(1.2)	NA	Lafayette, LA**	NA
NA	Cambridge-Newton, MA M.D.**	NA	10	Florence-Muscle Shoals, AL	16.0	200	Lake Co.-Kenosha Co., IL-WI M.D.	(4.7)
196	Camden, NJ M.D.	(4.3)	219	Florence, SC	(6.5)	43	Lake Havasu City-Kingman, AZ	7.5
233	Canton, OH	(8.5)	20	Fond du Lac, WI	11.5	221	Lakeland, FL	(6.8)
261	Cape Coral-Fort Myers, FL	(14.5)	163	Fort Collins, CO	(2.5)	157	Lancaster, PA	(2.1)
101	Cape Girardeau, MO-IL	1.3	203	Fort Lauderdale, FL M.D.	(5.0)	168	Lansing-East Lansing, MI	(2.9)
273	Carson City, NV	(18.5)	NA	Fort Smith, AR-OK**	NA	72	Laredo, TX	2.9
252	Casper, WY	(11.8)	76	Fort Wayne, IN	2.6	174	Las Cruces, NM	(3.2)
142	Cedar Rapids, IA	(1.4)	227	Fort Worth-Arlington, TX M.D.	(7.5)	16	Las Vegas-Henderson, NV	12.0
NA	Chambersburg-Waynesboro, PA**	NA	81	Fresno, CA	2.4	161	Lawrence, KS	(2.3)
63	Champaign-Urbana, IL	4.1	185	Gadsden, AL	(3.5)	NA	Lawton, OK**	NA
NA	Charleston-North Charleston, SC**	NA	182	Gainesville, FL	(3.4)	30	Lebanon, PA	10.2
243	Charlottesville, VA	(9.1)	155	Gainesville, GA	(1.9)	53	Lewiston-Auburn, ME	5.5

Note: All listings are for Metropolitan Statistical Areas (M.S.A.s) except for those ending with "M.D." Listings with "M.D." are Metropolitan Divisions which are smaller parts of eleven large M.S.A.s. See explanatory note at beginning of metropolitan area section.

RANK	METROPOLITAN AREA	% CHANGE	RANK	METROPOLITAN AREA	% CHANGE	RANK	METROPOLITAN AREA	% CHANGE
NA	Lewiston, ID-WA**	NA	48	Owensboro, KY	6.3	194	Silver Spring-Frederick, MD M.D.	(4.1)
NA	Lexington-Fayette, KY**	NA	41	Oxnard-Thousand Oaks, CA	7.8	NA	Sioux City, IA-NE-SD**	NA
89	Lima, OH	2.0	225	Palm Bay-Melbourne, FL	(7.3)	67	Sioux Falls, SD	3.9
182	Lincoln, NE	(3.4)	NA	Panama City, FL**	NA	258	South Bend-Mishawaka, IN-MI	(13.9)
95	Little Rock, AR	1.5	NA	Parkersburg-Vienna, WV**	NA	NA	Spartanburg, SC**	NA
1	Logan, UT-ID	41.9	142	Pensacola, FL	(1.4)	NA	Spokane, WA**	NA
31	Longview, TX	10.1	107	Peoria, IL	0.7	142	Springfield, IL	(1.4)
25	Longview, WA	10.8	NA	Philadelphia (greater) PA-NJ-MD-DE**	NA	NA	Springfield, MA**	NA
76	Los Angeles County, CA M.D.	2.6	NA	Philadelphia, PA M.D.**	NA	125	Springfield, MO	(0.4)
69	Los Angeles (greater), CA	3.7	NA	Phoenix-Mesa-Scottsdale, AZ**	NA	95	Springfield, OH	1.5
216	Louisville, KY-IN	(6.2)	228	Pine Bluff, AR	(7.6)	231	State College, PA	(8.1)
110	Lubbock, TX	0.5	110	Pittsburgh, PA	0.5	NA	Staunton-Waynesboro, VA**	NA
247	Lynchburg, VA	(11.0)	110	Pittsfield, MA	0.5	237	Stockton-Lodi, CA	(8.6)
259	Macon, GA	(14.2)	NA	Pocatello, ID**	NA	NA	St. George, UT**	NA
51	Madera, CA	5.8	266	Port St. Lucie, FL	(15.4)	12	St. Joseph, MO-KS	13.9
NA	Madison, WI**	NA	159	Portland-Vancouver, OR-WA	(2.2)	208	St. Louis, MO-IL	(5.4)
125	Manchester-Nashua, NH	(0.4)	132	Portland, ME	(0.9)	15	Sumter, SC	13.2
NA	Manhattan, KS**	NA	137	Prescott, AZ	(1.2)	NA	Syracuse, NY**	NA
106	Mankato-North Mankato, MN	1.0	NA	Providence-Warwick, RI-MA**	NA	47	Tacoma, WA M.D.	6.5
83	Mansfield, OH	2.2	262	Provo-Orem, UT	(14.6)	192	Tallahassee, FL	(4.0)
204	McAllen-Edinburg-Mission, TX	(5.2)	9	Pueblo, CO	16.3	213	Tampa-St Petersburg, FL	(5.9)
24	Medford, OR	11.0	250	Punta Gorda, FL	(11.3)	197	Terre Haute, IN	(4.5)
137	Memphis, TN-MS-AR	(1.2)	208	Racine, WI	(5.4)	NA	Texarkana, TX-AR**	NA
39	Merced, CA	8.6	188	Raleigh, NC	(3.7)	NA	The Villages, FL**	NA
189	Miami (greater), FL	(3.9)	NA	Rapid City, SD**	NA	NA	Toledo, OH**	NA
194	Miami-Dade County, FL M.D.	(4.1)	115	Reading, PA	0.2	204	Topeka, KS	(5.2)
232	Michigan City-La Porte, IN	(8.2)	4	Redding, CA	20.9	123	Trenton, NJ	(0.2)
NA	Midland, MI**	NA	38	Reno, NV	8.7	NA	Tucson, AZ**	NA
NA	Midland, TX**	NA	71	Richmond, VA	3.1	149	Tulsa, OK	(1.6)
107	Milwaukee, WI	0.7	61	Riverside-San Bernardino, CA	4.2	NA	Tuscaloosa, AL**	NA
152	Minneapolis-St. Paul, MN-WI	(1.7)	109	Roanoke, VA	0.6	233	Tyler, TX	(8.5)
3	Missoula, MT	27.5	NA	Rochester, MN**	NA	NA	Utica-Rome, NY**	NA
142	Mobile, AL	(1.4)	NA	Rochester, NY**	NA	174	Valdosta, GA	(3.2)
8	Modesto, CA	16.4	18	Rockford, IL	11.8	91	Vallejo-Fairfield, CA	1.9
44	Monroe, LA	7.2	76	Rockingham County, NH M.D.	2.6	NA	Victoria, TX**	NA
34	Monroe, MI	9.4	253	Rocky Mount, NC	(12.0)	NA	Vineland-Bridgeton, NJ**	NA
NA	Montgomery County, PA M.D.**	NA	56	Rome, GA	4.5	199	Virginia Beach-Norfolk, VA-NC	(4.6)
54	Montgomery, AL	5.0	81	Sacramento, CA	2.4	172	Visalia-Porterville, CA	(3.1)
NA	Morgantown, WV**	NA	155	Saginaw, MI	(1.9)	NA	Waco, TX**	NA
NA	Morristown, TN**	NA	18	Salem, OR	11.8	NA	Walla Walla, WA**	NA
241	Mount Vernon-Anacortes, WA	(8.9)	129	Salinas, CA	(0.7)	NA	Warner Robins, GA**	NA
16	Muncie, IN	12.0	NA	Salisbury, MD-DE**	NA	164	Warren-Troy, MI M.D.	(2.6)
159	Napa, CA	(2.2)	51	Salt Lake City, UT	5.8	133	Washington (greater) DC-VA-MD-WV	(1.0)
253	Naples-Marco Island, FL	(12.0)	120	San Antonio, TX	0.0	128	Washington, DC-VA-MD-WV M.D.	(0.5)
NA	Nashville-Davidson, TN**	NA	49	San Diego, CA	6.1	20	Waterloo-Cedar Falls, IA	11.5
NA	Nassau-Suffolk, NY M.D.**	NA	NA	San Francisco (greater), CA**	NA	NA	Watertown-Fort Drum, NY**	NA
103	New Haven-Milford, CT	1.2	5	San Francisco-Redwood, CA M.D.	19.5	221	Wausau, WI	(6.8)
124	New Orleans, LA	(0.3)	23	San Jose, CA	11.1	157	West Palm Beach, FL M.D.	(2.1)
NA	New York (greater), NY-NJ-PA**	NA	167	San Luis Obispo, CA	(2.8)	NA	Wheeling, WV-OH**	NA
NA	New York-Jersey City, NY-NJ M.D.**	NA	NA	San Rafael, CA M.D.**	NA	63	Wichita Falls, TX	4.1
NA	Newark, NJ-PA M.D.**	NA	91	Santa Cruz-Watsonville, CA	1.9	33	Wichita, KS	9.7
268	North Port-Sarasota-Bradenton, FL	(15.7)	34	Santa Fe, NM	9.4	131	Williamsport, PA	(0.8)
50	Norwich-New London, CT	6.0	NA	Santa Maria-Santa Barbara, CA**	NA	129	Wilmington, DE-MD-NJ M.D.	(0.7)
NA	Oakland-Hayward, CA M.D.**	NA	149	Santa Rosa, CA	(1.6)	NA	Wilmington, NC**	NA
239	Ocala, FL	(8.8)	264	Savannah, GA	(15.0)	55	Winchester, VA-WV	4.9
172	Ocean City, NJ	(3.1)	95	Scranton--Wilkes-Barre, PA	1.5	NA	Winston-Salem, NC**	NA
14	Odessa, TX	13.6	114	Seattle (greater), WA	0.3	NA	Worcester, MA-CT**	NA
NA	Ogden-Clearfield, UT**	NA	148	Seattle-Bellevue-Everett, WA M.D.	(1.5)	215	Yakima, WA	(6.0)
83	Oklahoma City, OK	2.2	76	Sebastian-Vero Beach, FL	2.6	99	York-Hanover, PA	1.4
89	Olympia, WA	2.0	NA	Sebring, FL**	NA	NA	Youngstown-Warren, OH-PA**	NA
103	Omaha-Council Bluffs, NE-IA	1.2	99	Sheboygan, WI	1.4	164	Yuba City, CA	(2.6)
201	Orlando, FL	(4.8)	237	Sherman-Denison, TX	(8.6)	244	Yuma, AZ	(9.2)
59	Oshkosh-Neenah, WI	4.3	NA	Shreveport-Bossier City, LA**	NA			
			NA	Sierra Vista-Douglas, AZ**	NA			

Source: CQ Press using reported data from the F.B.I. "Crime in the United States 2012"

*Larceny-theft is the unlawful taking of property. Attempts are included.

**Not available.

35. Percent Change in Larceny-Theft Rate: 2011 to 2012 (continued)
National Percent Change = 0.7% Decrease*

RANK	METROPOLITAN AREA	% CHANGE	RANK	METROPOLITAN AREA	% CHANGE	RANK	METROPOLITAN AREA	% CHANGE
1	Logan, UT-ID	41.9	63	Wichita Falls, TX	4.1	129	Salinas, CA	(0.7)
2	Decatur, AL	34.1	66	La Crosse, WI-MN	4.0	129	Wilmington, DE-MD-NJ M.D.	(0.7)
3	Missoula, MT	27.5	67	Fargo, ND-MN	3.9	131	Williamsport, PA	(0.8)
4	Redding, CA	20.9	67	Sioux Falls, SD	3.9	132	Portland, ME	(0.9)
5	San Francisco-Redwood, CA M.D.	19.5	69	Los Angeles (greater), CA	3.7	133	Austin-Round Rock, TX	(1.0)
6	Joplin, MO	18.2	70	Lafayette, IN	3.5	133	Baton Rouge, LA	(1.0)
7	Asheville, NC	17.2	71	Richmond, VA	3.1	133	Erie, PA	(1.0)
8	Modesto, CA	16.4	72	Laredo, TX	2.9	133	Washington (greater) DC-VA-MD-WV	(1.0)
9	Pueblo, CO	16.3	73	Green Bay, WI	2.8	137	Baltimore, MD	(1.2)
10	Florence-Muscle Shoals, AL	16.0	74	Great Falls, MT	2.7	137	Flint, MI	(1.2)
11	Farmington, NM	15.2	74	Houma, LA	2.7	137	Memphis, TN-MS-AR	(1.2)
12	St. Joseph, MO-KS	13.9	76	Fort Wayne, IN	2.6	137	Prescott, AZ	(1.2)
13	El Centro, CA	13.8	76	Janesville, WI	2.6	141	Chicago (greater), IL-IN-WI	(1.3)
14	Odessa, TX	13.6	76	Los Angeles County, CA M.D.	2.6	142	Cedar Rapids, IA	(1.4)
15	Sumter, SC	13.2	76	Rockingham County, NH M.D.	2.6	142	Chico, CA	(1.4)
16	Las Vegas-Henderson, NV	12.0	76	Sebastian-Vero Beach, FL	2.6	142	Clarksville, TN-KY	(1.4)
16	Muncie, IN	12.0	81	Fresno, CA	2.4	142	Mobile, AL	(1.4)
18	Rockford, IL	11.8	81	Sacramento, CA	2.4	142	Pensacola, FL	(1.4)
18	Salem, OR	11.8	83	Harrisonburg, VA	2.2	142	Springfield, IL	(1.4)
20	Fond du Lac, WI	11.5	83	Huntsville, AL	2.2	148	Seattle-Bellevue-Everett, WA M.D.	(1.5)
20	Waterloo-Cedar Falls, IA	11.5	83	Mansfield, OH	2.2	149	Houston, TX	(1.6)
22	Grand Junction, CO	11.4	83	Oklahoma City, OK	2.2	149	Santa Rosa, CA	(1.6)
23	San Jose, CA	11.1	87	Ann Arbor, MI	2.1	149	Tulsa, OK	(1.6)
24	Medford, OR	11.0	87	Cheyenne, WY	2.1	152	Billings, MT	(1.7)
25	Boulder, CO	10.8	89	Lima, OH	2.0	152	Johnson City, TN	(1.7)
25	Longview, WA	10.8	89	Olympia, WA	2.0	152	Minneapolis-St. Paul, MN-WI	(1.7)
27	Anniston-Oxford, AL	10.7	91	Santa Cruz-Watsonville, CA	1.9	155	Gainesville, GA	(1.9)
28	Bakersfield, CA	10.5	91	Vallejo-Fairfield, CA	1.9	155	Saginaw, MI	(1.9)
29	Bremerton-Silverdale, WA	10.4	93	Abilene, TX	1.6	157	Lancaster, PA	(2.1)
30	Lebanon, PA	10.2	93	Grand Forks, ND-MN	1.6	157	West Palm Beach, FL M.D.	(2.1)
31	Longview, TX	10.1	95	Fayetteville, NC	1.5	159	Napa, CA	(2.2)
32	Bangor, ME	9.8	95	Little Rock, AR	1.5	159	Portland-Vancouver, OR-WA	(2.2)
33	Wichita, KS	9.7	95	Scranton--Wilkes-Barre, PA	1.5	161	Lawrence, KS	(2.3)
34	Monroe, MI	9.4	95	Springfield, OH	1.5	162	Hinesville, GA	(2.4)
34	Santa Fe, NM	9.4	99	Sheboygan, WI	1.4	163	Fort Collins, CO	(2.5)
36	Greeley, CO	9.1	99	York-Hanover, PA	1.4	164	Birmingham-Hoover, AL	(2.6)
37	Eugene, OR	8.9	101	Cape Girardeau, MO-IL	1.3	164	Warren-Troy, MI M.D.	(2.6)
38	Reno, NV	8.7	101	Hanford-Corcoran, CA	1.3	164	Yuba City, CA	(2.6)
39	Merced, CA	8.6	103	New Haven-Milford, CT	1.2	167	San Luis Obispo, CA	(2.8)
40	Fairbanks, AK	8.5	103	Omaha-Council Bluffs, NE-IA	1.2	168	Lansing-East Lansing, MI	(2.9)
41	Oxnard-Thousand Oaks, CA	7.8	105	Hartford, CT	1.1	169	Atlanta, GA	(3.0)
42	Colorado Springs, CO	7.7	106	Mankato-North Mankato, MN	1.0	169	Brownsville-Harlingen, TX	(3.0)
43	Lake Havasu City-Kingman, AZ	7.5	107	Milwaukee, WI	0.7	169	Duluth, MN-WI	(3.0)
44	Monroe, LA	7.2	107	Peoria, IL	0.7	172	Ocean City, NJ	(3.1)
45	Anaheim-Santa Ana-Irvine, CA M.D.	7.1	109	Roanoke, VA	0.6	172	Visalia-Porterville, CA	(3.1)
46	Iowa City, IA	6.7	110	Lubbock, TX	0.5	174	Detroit (greater), MI	(3.2)
47	Tacoma, WA M.D.	6.5	110	Pittsburgh, PA	0.5	174	Dubuque, IA	(3.2)
48	Owensboro, KY	6.3	110	Pittsfield, MA	0.5	174	Hickory, NC	(3.2)
49	San Diego, CA	6.1	113	Dover, DE	0.4	174	Las Cruces, NM	(3.2)
50	Norwich-New London, CT	6.0	114	Seattle (greater), WA	0.3	174	Valdosta, GA	(3.2)
51	Madera, CA	5.8	115	Alexandria, LA	0.2	179	Barnstable Town, MA	(3.3)
51	Salt Lake City, UT	5.8	115	Cleveland, TN	0.2	179	Corpus Christi, TX	(3.3)
53	Lewiston-Auburn, ME	5.5	115	Cumberland, MD-WV	0.2	179	Danville, IL	(3.3)
54	Montgomery, AL	5.0	115	Dayton, OH	0.2	182	Gainesville, FL	(3.4)
55	Winchester, VA-WV	4.9	115	Reading, PA	0.2	182	Idaho Falls, ID	(3.4)
56	Killeen-Temple, TX	4.5	120	Bellingham, WA	0.0	182	Lincoln, NE	(3.4)
56	Rome, GA	4.5	120	San Antonio, TX	0.0	185	Gadsden, AL	(3.5)
58	Columbia, MO	4.4	122	El Paso, TX	(0.1)	185	Kankakee, IL	(3.5)
59	Bloomington, IL	4.3	123	Trenton, NJ	(0.2)	187	Detroit-Dearborn-Livonia, MI M.D.	(3.6)
59	Oshkosh-Neenah, WI	4.3	124	New Orleans, LA	(0.3)	188	Raleigh, NC	(3.7)
61	Bay City, MI	4.2	125	Harrisburg-Carlisle, PA	(0.4)	189	Akron, OH	(3.9)
61	Riverside-San Bernardino, CA	4.2	125	Manchester-Nashua, NH	(0.4)	189	Jacksonville, FL	(3.9)
63	Albany, GA	4.1	125	Springfield, MO	(0.4)	189	Miami (greater), FL	(3.9)
63	Champaign-Urbana, IL	4.1	128	Washington, DC-VA-MD-WV M.D.	(0.5)	192	Bismarck, ND	(4.0)

Note: All listings are for Metropolitan Statistical Areas (M.S.A.s) except for those ending with "M.D." Listings with "M.D." are Metropolitan Divisions which are smaller parts of eleven large M.S.A.s. See explanatory note at beginning of metropolitan area section.

RANK	METROPOLITAN AREA	% CHANGE	RANK	METROPOLITAN AREA	% CHANGE	RANK	METROPOLITAN AREA	% CHANGE
192	Tallahassee, FL	(4.0)	257	Johnstown, PA	(13.8)	NA	Knoxville, TN**	NA
194	Miami-Dade County, FL M.D.	(4.1)	258	South Bend-Mishawaka, IN-MI	(13.9)	NA	Kokomo, IN**	NA
194	Silver Spring-Frederick, MD M.D.	(4.1)	259	Altoona, PA	(14.2)	NA	Lafayette, LA**	NA
196	Camden, NJ M.D.	(4.3)	259	Macon, GA	(14.2)	NA	Lawton, OK**	NA
197	Dothan, AL	(4.5)	261	Cape Coral-Fort Myers, FL	(14.5)	NA	Lewiston, ID-WA**	NA
197	Terre Haute, IN	(4.5)	262	Blacksburg, VA	(14.6)	NA	Lexington-Fayette, KY**	NA
199	Virginia Beach-Norfolk, VA-NC	(4.6)	262	Provo-Orem, UT	(14.6)	NA	Madison, WI**	NA
200	Lake Co.-Kenosha Co., IL-WI M.D.	(4.7)	264	Savannah, GA	(15.0)	NA	Manhattan, KS**	NA
201	Bridgeport-Stamford, CT	(4.8)	265	Burlington, NC	(15.3)	NA	Midland, MI**	NA
201	Orlando, FL	(4.8)	266	Auburn, AL	(15.4)	NA	Midland, TX**	NA
203	Fort Lauderdale, FL M.D.	(5.0)	266	Port St. Lucie, FL	(15.4)	NA	Montgomery County, PA M.D.**	NA
204	Gary, IN M.D.	(5.2)	268	North Port-Sarasota-Bradenton, FL	(15.7)	NA	Morgantown, WV**	NA
204	McAllen-Edinburg-Mission, TX	(5.2)	269	Columbus, IN	(15.9)	NA	Morristown, TN**	NA
204	Topeka, KS	(5.2)	270	Corvallis, OR	(16.9)	NA	Nashville-Davidson, TN**	NA
207	Boise City, ID	(5.3)	271	College Station-Bryan, TX	(17.3)	NA	Nassau-Suffolk, NY M.D.**	NA
208	Racine, WI	(5.4)	272	Beaumont-Port Arthur, TX	(17.8)	NA	New Bern, NC**	NA
208	St. Louis, MO-IL	(5.4)	273	Carson City, NV	(18.5)	NA	New York (greater), NY-NJ-PA**	NA
210	Augusta, GA-SC	(5.5)	NA	Albany-Schenectady-Troy, NY**	NA	NA	New York-Jersey City, NY-NJ M.D.**	NA
210	Jefferson City, MO	(5.5)	NA	Albany, OR**	NA	NA	Newark, NJ-PA M.D.**	NA
212	Athens-Clarke County, GA	(5.8)	NA	Albuquerque, NM**	NA	NA	Oakland-Hayward, CA M.D.**	NA
213	Columbus, GA-AL	(5.9)	NA	Allentown, PA-NJ**	NA	NA	Ogden-Clearfield, UT**	NA
213	Tampa-St Petersburg, FL	(5.9)	NA	Anchorage, AK**	NA	NA	Panama City, FL**	NA
215	Yakima, WA	(6.0)	NA	Beckley, WV**	NA	NA	Parkersburg-Vienna, WV**	NA
216	Louisville, KY-IN	(6.2)	NA	Binghamton, NY**	NA	NA	Philadelphia (greater) PA-NJ-MD-DE**	NA
217	Dallas-Plano-Irving, TX M.D.	(6.3)	NA	Bloomington, IN**	NA	NA	Philadelphia, PA M.D.**	NA
217	Goldsboro, NC	(6.3)	NA	Bloomsburg-Berwick, PA**	NA	NA	Phoenix-Mesa-Scottsdale, AZ**	NA
219	Florence, SC	(6.5)	NA	Boston (greater), MA-NH**	NA	NA	Pocatello, ID**	NA
220	Dallas (greater), TX	(6.7)	NA	Boston, MA M.D.**	NA	NA	Providence-Warwick, RI-MA**	NA
221	Des Moines-West Des Moines, IA	(6.8)	NA	Buffalo-Niagara Falls, NY**	NA	NA	Rapid City, SD**	NA
221	Lakeland, FL	(6.8)	NA	California-Lexington Park, MD**	NA	NA	Rochester, MN**	NA
221	Wausau, WI	(6.8)	NA	Cambridge-Newton, MA M.D.**	NA	NA	Rochester, NY**	NA
224	Dalton, GA	(6.9)	NA	Chambersburg-Waynesboro, PA**	NA	NA	Salisbury, MD-DE**	NA
225	Palm Bay-Melbourne, FL	(7.3)	NA	Charleston-North Charleston, SC**	NA	NA	San Francisco (greater), CA**	NA
226	Durham-Chapel Hill, NC	(7.4)	NA	Chicago-Joilet-Naperville, IL M.D.**	NA	NA	San Rafael, CA M.D.**	NA
227	Fort Worth-Arlington, TX M.D.	(7.5)	NA	Cincinnati, OH-KY-IN**	NA	NA	Santa Maria-Santa Barbara, CA**	NA
228	Pine Bluff, AR	(7.6)	NA	Coeur d'Alene, ID**	NA	NA	Sebring, FL**	NA
229	Decatur, IL	(7.9)	NA	Daphne-Fairhope-Foley, AL**	NA	NA	Shreveport-Bossier City, LA**	NA
229	Kingsport, TN-VA	(7.9)	NA	Deltona-Daytona Beach, FL**	NA	NA	Sierra Vista-Douglas, AZ**	NA
231	State College, PA	(8.1)	NA	Denver-Aurora, CO**	NA	NA	Sioux City, IA-NE-SD**	NA
232	Michigan City-La Porte, IN	(8.2)	NA	Dutchess-Putnam, NY M.D.**	NA	NA	Spartanburg, SC**	NA
233	Appleton, WI	(8.5)	NA	East Stroudsburg, PA**	NA	NA	Spokane, WA**	NA
233	Canton, OH	(8.5)	NA	Elgin, IL M.D.**	NA	NA	Springfield, MA**	NA
233	Flagstaff, AZ	(8.5)	NA	Elizabethtown-Fort Knox, KY**	NA	NA	Staunton-Waynesboro, VA**	NA
233	Tyler, TX	(8.5)	NA	Elmira, NY**	NA	NA	St. George, UT**	NA
237	Sherman-Denison, TX	(8.6)	NA	Fayetteville-Springdale, AR-MO**	NA	NA	Syracuse, NY**	NA
237	Stockton-Lodi, CA	(8.6)	NA	Fort Smith, AR-OK**	NA	NA	Texarkana, TX-AR**	NA
239	Atlantic City, NJ	(8.8)	NA	Gettysburg, PA**	NA	NA	The Villages, FL**	NA
239	Ocala, FL	(8.8)	NA	Glens Falls, NY**	NA	NA	Toledo, OH**	NA
241	Crestview-Fort Walton Beach, FL	(8.9)	NA	Grand Island, NE**	NA	NA	Tucson, AZ**	NA
241	Mount Vernon-Anacortes, WA	(8.9)	NA	Greensboro-High Point, NC**	NA	NA	Tuscaloosa, AL**	NA
243	Charlottesville, VA	(9.1)	NA	Greenville-Anderson, SC**	NA	NA	Utica-Rome, NY**	NA
244	Kennewick-Richland, WA	(9.2)	NA	Greenville, NC**	NA	NA	Victoria, TX**	NA
244	Yuma, AZ	(9.2)	NA	Hagerstown-Martinsburg, MD-WV**	NA	NA	Vineland-Bridgeton, NJ**	NA
246	Amarillo, TX	(10.6)	NA	Hammond, LA**	NA	NA	Waco, TX**	NA
247	Jonesboro, AR	(11.0)	NA	Hattiesburg, MS**	NA	NA	Walla Walla, WA**	NA
247	Lynchburg, VA	(11.0)	NA	Hilton Head Island, SC**	NA	NA	Warner Robins, GA**	NA
249	Davenport, IA-IL	(11.2)	NA	Homosassa Springs, FL**	NA	NA	Watertown-Fort Drum, NY**	NA
250	Punta Gorda, FL	(11.3)	NA	Indianapolis, IN**	NA	NA	Wheeling, WV-OH**	NA
251	Bowling Green, KY	(11.5)	NA	Jackson, MS**	NA	NA	Wilmington, NC**	NA
252	Casper, WY	(11.8)	NA	Jackson, TN**	NA	NA	Winston-Salem, NC**	NA
253	Naples-Marco Island, FL	(12.0)	NA	Kahului-Wailuku-Lahaina, HI**	NA	NA	Worcester, MA-CT**	NA
253	Rocky Mount, NC	(12.0)	NA	Kalamazoo-Portage, MI**	NA	NA	Youngstown-Warren, OH-PA**	NA
255	Brunswick, GA	(12.6)	NA	Kansas City, MO-KS**	NA			
256	Ames, IA	(13.6)	NA	Kingston, NY**	NA			

Source: CQ Press using reported data from the F.B.I. "Crime in the United States 2012"

*Larceny-theft is the unlawful taking of property. Attempts are included.

**Not available.

36. Percent Change in Larceny-Theft Rate: 2008 to 2012
National Percent Change = 9.5% Decrease*

RANK	METROPOLITAN AREA	% CHANGE	RANK	METROPOLITAN AREA	% CHANGE	RANK	METROPOLITAN AREA	% CHANGE
48	Abilene, TX	(0.6)	224	Cheyenne, WY	(22.4)	NA	Gary, IN M.D.**	NA
94	Akron, OH	(6.6)	NA	Chicago (greater), IL-IN-WI**	NA	NA	Gettysburg, PA**	NA
NA	Albany-Schenectady-Troy, NY**	NA	NA	Chicago-Joilet-Naperville, IL M.D.**	NA	NA	Glens Falls, NY**	NA
NA	Albany, GA**	NA	226	Chico, CA	(22.6)	190	Goldsboro, NC	(16.9)
NA	Albany, OR**	NA	NA	Cincinnati, OH-KY-IN**	NA	167	Grand Forks, ND-MN	(14.3)
NA	Albuquerque, NM**	NA	153	Clarksville, TN-KY	(12.7)	NA	Grand Island, NE**	NA
NA	Alexandria, LA**	NA	103	Cleveland, TN	(7.5)	26	Grand Junction, CO	6.5
NA	Allentown, PA-NJ**	NA	NA	Coeur d'Alene, ID**	NA	61	Great Falls, MT	(2.9)
173	Altoona, PA	(14.7)	247	College Station-Bryan, TX	(29.7)	96	Greeley, CO	(6.7)
198	Amarillo, TX	(18.3)	36	Colorado Springs, CO	3.1	227	Green Bay, WI	(22.7)
165	Ames, IA	(14.1)	25	Columbia, MO	6.8	195	Greensboro-High Point, NC	(18.1)
27	Anaheim-Santa Ana-Irvine, CA M.D.	6.3	195	Columbus, GA-AL	(18.1)	NA	Greenville-Anderson, SC**	NA
NA	Anchorage, AK**	NA	43	Columbus, IN	1.1	239	Greenville, NC	(25.3)
155	Ann Arbor, MI	(13.0)	221	Corpus Christi, TX	(21.4)	NA	Hagerstown-Martinsburg, MD-WV**	NA
NA	Anniston-Oxford, AL**	NA	107	Corvallis, OR	(8.3)	NA	Hammond, LA**	NA
254	Appleton, WI	(40.4)	NA	Crestview-Fort Walton Beach, FL**	NA	74	Hanford-Corcoran, CA	(4.8)
37	Asheville, NC	2.9	27	Cumberland, MD-WV	6.3	69	Harrisburg-Carlisle, PA	(3.7)
237	Athens-Clarke County, GA	(25.1)	207	Dallas (greater), TX	(19.5)	84	Harrisonburg, VA	(5.4)
137	Atlanta, GA	(11.6)	212	Dallas-Plano-Irving, TX M.D.	(19.9)	171	Hartford, CT	(14.4)
140	Atlantic City, NJ	(11.8)	112	Dalton, GA	(8.7)	NA	Hattiesburg, MS**	NA
252	Auburn, AL	(33.3)	NA	Danville, IL**	NA	82	Hickory, NC	(5.3)
189	Augusta, GA-SC	(16.8)	NA	Daphne-Fairhope-Foley, AL**	NA	NA	Hilton Head Island, SC**	NA
113	Austin-Round Rock, TX	(8.8)	NA	Davenport, IA-IL**	NA	210	Hinesville, GA	(19.8)
86	Bakersfield, CA	(5.6)	53	Dayton, OH	(1.8)	NA	Homosassa Springs, FL**	NA
166	Baltimore, MD	(14.2)	243	Decatur, AL	(27.3)	49	Houma, LA	(0.9)
128	Bangor, ME	(10.5)	NA	Decatur, IL**	NA	73	Houston, TX	(4.7)
187	Barnstable Town, MA	(16.6)	135	Deltona-Daytona Beach, FL	(11.1)	176	Huntsville, AL	(15.1)
30	Baton Rouge, LA	5.4	NA	Denver-Aurora, CO**	NA	173	Idaho Falls, ID	(14.7)
229	Bay City, MI	(23.2)	99	Des Moines-West Des Moines, IA	(7.1)	104	Indianapolis, IN	(7.6)
158	Beaumont-Port Arthur, TX	(13.5)	NA	Detroit (greater), MI**	NA	51	Iowa City, IA	(1.0)
NA	Beckley, WV**	NA	NA	Detroit-Dearborn-Livonia, MI M.D.**	NA	213	Jacksonville, FL	(20.2)
179	Bellingham, WA	(15.3)	218	Dothan, AL	(21.0)	NA	Jackson, MS**	NA
57	Billings, MT	(2.2)	13	Dover, DE	13.8	NA	Jackson, TN**	NA
NA	Binghamton, NY**	NA	185	Dubuque, IA	(15.9)	133	Janesville, WI	(11.0)
216	Birmingham-Hoover, AL	(20.5)	147	Duluth, MN-WI	(12.2)	NA	Jefferson City, MO**	NA
31	Bismarck, ND	5.2	219	Durham-Chapel Hill, NC	(21.1)	39	Johnson City, TN	2.2
182	Blacksburg, VA	(15.7)	NA	Dutchess-Putnam, NY M.D.**	NA	177	Johnstown, PA	(15.2)
NA	Bloomington, IL**	NA	NA	East Stroudsburg, PA**	NA	107	Jonesboro, AR	(8.3)
4	Bloomington, IN	28.7	33	El Centro, CA	4.3	77	Joplin, MO	(5.1)
NA	Bloomsburg-Berwick, PA**	NA	208	El Paso, TX	(19.6)	NA	Kahului-Wailuku-Lahaina, HI**	NA
126	Boise City, ID	(10.3)	NA	Elgin, IL M.D.**	NA	215	Kalamazoo-Portage, MI	(20.4)
NA	Boston (greater), MA-NH**	NA	NA	Elizabethtown-Fort Knox, KY**	NA	NA	Kankakee, IL**	NA
NA	Boston, MA M.D.**	NA	NA	Elmira, NY**	NA	NA	Kansas City, MO-KS**	NA
NA	Boulder, CO**	NA	20	Erie, PA	8.3	91	Kennewick-Richland, WA	(6.4)
240	Bowling Green, KY	(26.0)	159	Eugene, OR	(13.7)	147	Killeen-Temple, TX	(12.2)
14	Bremerton-Silverdale, WA	13.4	NA	Fairbanks, AK**	NA	107	Kingsport, TN-VA	(8.3)
175	Bridgeport-Stamford, CT	(14.9)	123	Fargo, ND-MN	(10.1)	NA	Kingston, NY**	NA
159	Brownsville-Harlingen, TX	(13.7)	2	Farmington, NM	43.7	NA	Knoxville, TN**	NA
NA	Brunswick, GA**	NA	23	Fayetteville-Springdale, AR-MO	7.6	NA	Kokomo, IN**	NA
NA	Buffalo-Niagara Falls, NY**	NA	177	Fayetteville, NC	(15.2)	139	La Crosse, WI-MN	(11.7)
164	Burlington, NC	(14.0)	187	Flagstaff, AZ	(16.6)	70	Lafayette, IN	(3.8)
NA	California-Lexington Park, MD**	NA	54	Flint, MI	(1.9)	NA	Lafayette, LA**	NA
NA	Cambridge-Newton, MA M.D.**	NA	220	Florence-Muscle Shoals, AL	(21.2)	NA	Lake Co.-Kenosha Co., IL-WI M.D.**	NA
105	Camden, NJ M.D.	(8.1)	145	Florence, SC	(12.1)	44	Lake Havasu City-Kingman, AZ	0.8
NA	Canton, OH**	NA	100	Fond du Lac, WI	(7.4)	230	Lakeland, FL	(23.8)
250	Cape Coral-Fort Myers, FL	(30.6)	90	Fort Collins, CO	(6.3)	63	Lancaster, PA	(3.2)
29	Cape Girardeau, MO-IL	5.9	124	Fort Lauderdale, FL M.D.	(10.2)	208	Lansing-East Lansing, MI	(19.6)
204	Carson City, NV	(19.1)	NA	Fort Smith, AR-OK**	NA	234	Laredo, TX	(24.6)
225	Casper, WY	(22.5)	55	Fort Wayne, IN	(2.0)	113	Las Cruces, NM	(8.8)
203	Cedar Rapids, IA	(19.0)	204	Fort Worth-Arlington, TX M.D.	(19.1)	145	Las Vegas-Henderson, NV	(12.1)
NA	Chambersburg-Waynesboro, PA**	NA	46	Fresno, CA	(0.3)	142	Lawrence, KS	(12.0)
NA	Champaign-Urbana, IL**	NA	35	Gadsden, AL	3.5	NA	Lawton, OK**	NA
157	Charleston-North Charleston, SC	(13.4)	186	Gainesville, FL	(16.3)	15	Lebanon, PA	13.2
242	Charlottesville, VA	(26.6)	NA	Gainesville, GA**	NA	5	Lewiston-Auburn, ME	27.3

Note: All listings are for Metropolitan Statistical Areas (M.S.A.s) except for those ending with "M.D." Listings with "M.D." are Metropolitan Divisions which are smaller parts of eleven large M.S.A.s. See explanatory note at beginning of metropolitan area section.

RANK	METROPOLITAN AREA	% CHANGE	RANK	METROPOLITAN AREA	% CHANGE	RANK	METROPOLITAN AREA	% CHANGE
8	Lewiston, ID-WA	21.7	NA	Owensboro, KY**	NA	251	Silver Spring-Frederick, MD M.D.	(30.9)
NA	Lexington-Fayette, KY**	NA	81	Oxnard-Thousand Oaks, CA	(5.2)	NA	Sioux City, IA-NE-SD**	NA
199	Lima, OH	(18.4)	98	Palm Bay-Melbourne, FL	(7.0)	6	Sioux Falls, SD	24.1
84	Lincoln, NE	(5.4)	NA	Panama City, FL**	NA	248	South Bend-Mishawaka, IN-MI	(30.4)
59	Little Rock, AR	(2.5)	NA	Parkersburg-Vienna, WV**	NA	NA	Spartanburg, SC**	NA
77	Logan, UT-ID	(5.1)	16	Pensacola, FL	13.1	1	Spokane, WA	47.3
199	Longview, TX	(18.4)	NA	Peoria, IL**	NA	NA	Springfield, IL**	NA
63	Longview, WA	(3.2)	NA	Philadelphia (greater) PA-NJ-MD-DE**	NA	NA	Springfield, MA**	NA
77	Los Angeles County, CA M.D.	(5.1)	NA	Philadelphia, PA M.D.**	NA	46	Springfield, MO	(0.3)
58	Los Angeles (greater), CA	(2.4)	NA	Phoenix-Mesa-Scottsdale, AZ**	NA	201	Springfield, OH	(18.5)
55	Louisville, KY-IN	(2.0)	236	Pine Bluff, AR	(24.9)	192	State College, PA	(17.4)
136	Lubbock, TX	(11.3)	119	Pittsburgh, PA	(9.4)	NA	Staunton-Waynesboro, VA**	NA
222	Lynchburg, VA	(21.9)	22	Pittsfield, MA	8.2	231	Stockton-Lodi, CA	(23.9)
128	Macon, GA	(10.5)	NA	Pocatello, ID**	NA	117	St. George, UT	(9.2)
62	Madera, CA	(3.0)	231	Port St. Lucie, FL	(23.9)	11	St. Joseph, MO-KS	14.6
NA	Madison, WI**	NA	71	Portland-Vancouver, OR-WA	(4.4)	156	St. Louis, MO-IL	(13.3)
NA	Manchester-Nashua, NH**	NA	38	Portland, ME	2.4	12	Sumter, SC	14.5
NA	Manhattan, KS**	NA	72	Prescott, AZ	(4.5)	NA	Syracuse, NY**	NA
87	Mankato-North Mankato, MN	(6.1)	142	Providence-Warwick, RI-MA	(12.0)	NA	Tacoma, WA M.D.**	NA
19	Mansfield, OH	9.3	193	Provo-Orem, UT	(17.5)	97	Tallahassee, FL	(6.8)
154	McAllen-Edinburg-Mission, TX	(12.8)	NA	Pueblo, CO**	NA	240	Tampa-St Petersburg, FL	(26.0)
3	Medford, OR	43.2	253	Punta Gorda, FL	(33.9)	NA	Terre Haute, IN**	NA
223	Memphis, TN-MS-AR	(22.1)	147	Racine, WI	(12.2)	NA	Texarkana, TX-AR**	NA
42	Merced, CA	1.4	105	Raleigh, NC	(8.1)	NA	The Villages, FL**	NA
161	Miami (greater), FL	(13.9)	NA	Rapid City, SD**	NA	NA	Toledo, OH**	NA
167	Miami-Dade County, FL M.D.	(14.3)	172	Reading, PA	(14.6)	131	Topeka, KS	(10.7)
194	Michigan City-La Porte, IN	(17.8)	10	Redding, CA	16.4	115	Trenton, NJ	(9.0)
NA	Midland, MI**	NA	248	Reno, NV	(30.4)	NA	Tucson, AZ**	NA
NA	Midland, TX**	NA	92	Richmond, VA	(6.5)	122	Tulsa, OK	(9.9)
161	Milwaukee, WI	(13.9)	76	Riverside-San Bernardino, CA	(4.9)	NA	Tuscaloosa, AL**	NA
167	Minneapolis-St. Paul, MN-WI	(14.3)	132	Roanoke, VA	(10.8)	133	Tyler, TX	(11.0)
17	Missoula, MT	11.7	NA	Rochester, MN**	NA	NA	Utica-Rome, NY**	NA
92	Mobile, AL	(6.5)	NA	Rochester, NY**	NA	217	Valdosta, GA	(20.8)
121	Modesto, CA	(9.6)	NA	Rockford, IL**	NA	233	Vallejo-Fairfield, CA	(24.3)
130	Monroe, LA	(10.6)	9	Rockingham County, NH M.D.	18.8	NA	Victoria, TX**	NA
32	Monroe, MI	4.5	NA	Rocky Mount, NC**	NA	18	Vineland-Bridgeton, NJ	10.0
NA	Montgomery County, PA M.D.**	NA	NA	Rome, GA**	NA	110	Virginia Beach-Norfolk, VA-NC	(8.4)
124	Montgomery, AL	(10.2)	152	Sacramento, CA	(12.6)	167	Visalia-Porterville, CA	(14.3)
NA	Morgantown, WV**	NA	245	Saginaw, MI	(28.5)	NA	Waco, TX**	NA
NA	Morristown, TN**	NA	100	Salem, OR	(7.4)	NA	Walla Walla, WA**	NA
151	Mount Vernon-Anacortes, WA	(12.5)	197	Salinas, CA	(18.2)	NA	Warner Robins, GA**	NA
60	Muncie, IN	(2.6)	NA	Salisbury, MD-DE**	NA	NA	Warren-Troy, MI M.D.**	NA
191	Napa, CA	(17.0)	94	Salt Lake City, UT	(6.6)	202	Washington (greater) DC-VA-MD-WV	(18.7)
183	Naples-Marco Island, FL	(15.8)	210	San Antonio, TX	(19.8)	183	Washington, DC-VA-MD-WV M.D.	(15.8)
NA	Nashville-Davidson, TN**	NA	161	San Diego, CA	(13.9)	179	Waterloo-Cedar Falls, IA	(15.3)
NA	Nassau-Suffolk, NY M.D.**	NA	NA	San Francisco (greater), CA**	NA	NA	Watertown-Fort Drum, NY**	NA
NA	New Bern, NC**	NA	24	San Francisco-Redwood, CA M.D.	7.1	87	Wausau, WI	(6.1)
NA	New Haven-Milford, CT**	NA	82	San Jose, CA	(5.3)	206	West Palm Beach, FL M.D.	(19.2)
111	New Orleans, LA	(8.5)	77	San Luis Obispo, CA	(5.1)	66	Wheeling, WV-OH	(3.5)
NA	New York (greater), NY-NJ-PA**	NA	NA	San Rafael, CA M.D.**	NA	244	Wichita Falls, TX	(27.7)
NA	New York-Jersey City, NY-NJ M.D.**	NA	40	Santa Cruz-Watsonville, CA	2.1	49	Wichita, KS	(0.9)
NA	Newark, NJ-PA M.D.**	NA	7	Santa Fe, NM	22.9	20	Williamsport, PA	8.3
NA	North Port-Sarasota-Bradenton, FL**	NA	NA	Santa Maria-Santa Barbara, CA**	NA	140	Wilmington, DE-MD-NJ M.D.	(11.8)
66	Norwich-New London, CT	(3.5)	66	Santa Rosa, CA	(3.5)	NA	Wilmington, NC**	NA
NA	Oakland-Hayward, CA M.D.**	NA	235	Savannah, GA	(24.8)	89	Winchester, VA-WV	(6.2)
116	Ocala, FL	(9.1)	65	Scranton--Wilkes-Barre, PA	(3.3)	NA	Winston-Salem, NC**	NA
120	Ocean City, NJ	(9.5)	NA	Seattle (greater), WA**	NA	34	Worcester, MA-CT	3.8
127	Odessa, TX	(10.4)	NA	Seattle-Bellevue-Everett, WA M.D.**	NA	246	Yakima, WA	(29.6)
NA	Ogden-Clearfield, UT**	NA	150	Sebastian-Vero Beach, FL	(12.4)	118	York-Hanover, PA	(9.3)
41	Oklahoma City, OK	1.8	NA	Sebring, FL**	NA	100	Youngstown-Warren, OH-PA	(7.4)
228	Olympia, WA	(22.8)	237	Sheboygan, WI	(25.1)	52	Yuba City, CA	(1.1)
74	Omaha-Council Bluffs, NE-IA	(4.8)	45	Sherman-Denison, TX	0.2	137	Yuma, AZ	(11.6)
213	Orlando, FL	(20.2)	142	Shreveport-Bossier City, LA	(12.0)			
181	Oshkosh-Neenah, WI	(15.5)	NA	Sierra Vista-Douglas, AZ**	NA			

Source: CQ Press using reported data from the F.B.I. "Crime in the United States 2012"

*Larceny-theft is the unlawful taking of property. Attempts are included.

**Not available.

36. Percent Change in Larceny-Theft Rate: 2008 to 2012 (continued)
National Percent Change = 9.5% Decrease*

RANK	METROPOLITAN AREA	% CHANGE	RANK	METROPOLITAN AREA	% CHANGE	RANK	METROPOLITAN AREA	% CHANGE
1	Spokane, WA	47.3	65	Scranton--Wilkes-Barre, PA	(3.3)	128	Macon, GA	(10.5)
2	Farmington, NM	43.7	66	Norwich-New London, CT	(3.5)	130	Monroe, LA	(10.6)
3	Medford, OR	43.2	66	Santa Rosa, CA	(3.5)	131	Topeka, KS	(10.7)
4	Bloomington, IN	28.7	66	Wheeling, WV-OH	(3.5)	132	Roanoke, VA	(10.8)
5	Lewiston-Auburn, ME	27.3	69	Harrisburg-Carlisle, PA	(3.7)	133	Janesville, WI	(11.0)
6	Sioux Falls, SD	24.1	70	Lafayette, IN	(3.8)	133	Tyler, TX	(11.0)
7	Santa Fe, NM	22.9	71	Portland-Vancouver, OR-WA	(4.4)	135	Deltona-Daytona Beach, FL	(11.1)
8	Lewiston, ID-WA	21.7	72	Prescott, AZ	(4.5)	136	Lubbock, TX	(11.3)
9	Rockingham County, NH M.D.	18.8	73	Houston, TX	(4.7)	137	Atlanta, GA	(11.6)
10	Redding, CA	16.4	74	Hanford-Corcoran, CA	(4.8)	137	Yuma, AZ	(11.6)
11	St. Joseph, MO-KS	14.6	74	Omaha-Council Bluffs, NE-IA	(4.8)	139	La Crosse, WI-MN	(11.7)
12	Sumter, SC	14.5	76	Riverside-San Bernardino, CA	(4.9)	140	Atlantic City, NJ	(11.8)
13	Dover, DE	13.8	77	Joplin, MO	(5.1)	140	Wilmington, DE-MD-NJ M.D.	(11.8)
14	Bremerton-Silverdale, WA	13.4	77	Logan, UT-ID	(5.1)	142	Lawrence, KS	(12.0)
15	Lebanon, PA	13.2	77	Los Angeles County, CA M.D.	(5.1)	142	Providence-Warwick, RI-MA	(12.0)
16	Pensacola, FL	13.1	77	San Luis Obispo, CA	(5.1)	142	Shreveport-Bossier City, LA	(12.0)
17	Missoula, MT	11.7	81	Oxnard-Thousand Oaks, CA	(5.2)	145	Florence, SC	(12.1)
18	Vineland-Bridgeton, NJ	10.0	82	Hickory, NC	(5.3)	145	Las Vegas-Henderson, NV	(12.1)
19	Mansfield, OH	9.3	82	San Jose, CA	(5.3)	147	Duluth, MN-WI	(12.2)
20	Erie, PA	8.3	84	Harrisonburg, VA	(5.4)	147	Killeen-Temple, TX	(12.2)
20	Williamsport, PA	8.3	84	Lincoln, NE	(5.4)	147	Racine, WI	(12.2)
22	Pittsfield, MA	8.2	86	Bakersfield, CA	(5.6)	150	Sebastian-Vero Beach, FL	(12.4)
23	Fayetteville-Springdale, AR-MO	7.6	87	Mankato-North Mankato, MN	(6.1)	151	Mount Vernon-Anacortes, WA	(12.5)
24	San Francisco-Redwood, CA M.D.	7.1	87	Wausau, WI	(6.1)	152	Sacramento, CA	(12.6)
25	Columbia, MO	6.8	89	Winchester, VA-WV	(6.2)	153	Clarksville, TN-KY	(12.7)
26	Grand Junction, CO	6.5	90	Fort Collins, CO	(6.3)	154	McAllen-Edinburg-Mission, TX	(12.8)
27	Anaheim-Santa Ana-Irvine, CA M.D.	6.3	91	Kennewick-Richland, WA	(6.4)	155	Ann Arbor, MI	(13.0)
27	Cumberland, MD-WV	6.3	92	Mobile, AL	(6.5)	156	St. Louis, MO-IL	(13.3)
29	Cape Girardeau, MO-IL	5.9	92	Richmond, VA	(6.5)	157	Charleston-North Charleston, SC	(13.4)
30	Baton Rouge, LA	5.4	94	Akron, OH	(6.6)	158	Beaumont-Port Arthur, TX	(13.5)
31	Bismarck, ND	5.2	94	Salt Lake City, UT	(6.6)	159	Brownsville-Harlingen, TX	(13.7)
32	Monroe, MI	4.5	96	Greeley, CO	(6.7)	159	Eugene, OR	(13.7)
33	El Centro, CA	4.3	97	Tallahassee, FL	(6.8)	161	Miami (greater), FL	(13.9)
34	Worcester, MA-CT	3.8	98	Palm Bay-Melbourne, FL	(7.0)	161	Milwaukee, WI	(13.9)
35	Gadsden, AL	3.5	99	Des Moines-West Des Moines, IA	(7.1)	161	San Diego, CA	(13.9)
36	Colorado Springs, CO	3.1	100	Fond du Lac, WI	(7.4)	164	Burlington, NC	(14.0)
37	Asheville, NC	2.9	100	Salem, OR	(7.4)	165	Ames, IA	(14.1)
38	Portland, ME	2.4	100	Youngstown-Warren, OH-PA	(7.4)	166	Baltimore, MD	(14.2)
39	Johnson City, TN	2.2	103	Cleveland, TN	(7.5)	167	Grand Forks, ND-MN	(14.3)
40	Santa Cruz-Watsonville, CA	2.1	104	Indianapolis, IN	(7.6)	167	Miami-Dade County, FL M.D.	(14.3)
41	Oklahoma City, OK	1.8	105	Camden, NJ M.D.	(8.1)	167	Minneapolis-St. Paul, MN-WI	(14.3)
42	Merced, CA	1.4	105	Raleigh, NC	(8.1)	167	Visalia-Porterville, CA	(14.3)
43	Columbus, IN	1.1	107	Corvallis, OR	(8.3)	171	Hartford, CT	(14.4)
44	Lake Havasu City-Kingman, AZ	0.8	107	Jonesboro, AR	(8.3)	172	Reading, PA	(14.6)
45	Sherman-Denison, TX	0.2	107	Kingsport, TN-VA	(8.3)	173	Altoona, PA	(14.7)
46	Fresno, CA	(0.3)	110	Virginia Beach-Norfolk, VA-NC	(8.4)	173	Idaho Falls, ID	(14.7)
46	Springfield, MO	(0.3)	111	New Orleans, LA	(8.5)	175	Bridgeport-Stamford, CT	(14.9)
48	Abilene, TX	(0.6)	112	Dalton, GA	(8.7)	176	Huntsville, AL	(15.1)
49	Houma, LA	(0.9)	113	Austin-Round Rock, TX	(8.8)	177	Fayetteville, NC	(15.2)
49	Wichita, KS	(0.9)	113	Las Cruces, NM	(8.8)	177	Johnstown, PA	(15.2)
51	Iowa City, IA	(1.0)	115	Trenton, NJ	(9.0)	179	Bellingham, WA	(15.3)
52	Yuba City, CA	(1.1)	116	Ocala, FL	(9.1)	179	Waterloo-Cedar Falls, IA	(15.3)
53	Dayton, OH	(1.8)	117	St. George, UT	(9.2)	181	Oshkosh-Neenah, WI	(15.5)
54	Flint, MI	(1.9)	118	York-Hanover, PA	(9.3)	182	Blacksburg, VA	(15.7)
55	Fort Wayne, IN	(2.0)	119	Pittsburgh, PA	(9.4)	183	Naples-Marco Island, FL	(15.8)
55	Louisville, KY-IN	(2.0)	120	Ocean City, NJ	(9.5)	183	Washington, DC-VA-MD-WV M.D.	(15.8)
57	Billings, MT	(2.2)	121	Modesto, CA	(9.6)	185	Dubuque, IA	(15.9)
58	Los Angeles (greater), CA	(2.4)	122	Tulsa, OK	(9.9)	186	Gainesville, FL	(16.3)
59	Little Rock, AR	(2.5)	123	Fargo, ND-MN	(10.1)	187	Barnstable Town, MA	(16.6)
60	Muncie, IN	(2.6)	124	Fort Lauderdale, FL M.D.	(10.2)	187	Flagstaff, AZ	(16.6)
61	Great Falls, MT	(2.9)	124	Montgomery, AL	(10.2)	189	Augusta, GA-SC	(16.8)
62	Madera, CA	(3.0)	126	Boise City, ID	(10.3)	190	Goldsboro, NC	(16.9)
63	Lancaster, PA	(3.2)	127	Odessa, TX	(10.4)	191	Napa, CA	(17.0)
63	Longview, WA	(3.2)	128	Bangor, ME	(10.5)	192	State College, PA	(17.4)

Note: All listings are for Metropolitan Statistical Areas (M.S.A.s) except for those ending with "M.D." Listings with "M.D." are Metropolitan Divisions which are smaller parts of eleven large M.S.A.s. See explanatory note at beginning of metropolitan area section.

RANK	METROPOLITAN AREA	% CHANGE	RANK	METROPOLITAN AREA	% CHANGE	RANK	METROPOLITAN AREA	% CHANGE
193	Provo-Orem, UT	(17.5)	NA	Albany, OR**	NA	NA	Manchester-Nashua, NH**	NA
194	Michigan City-La Porte, IN	(17.8)	NA	Albuquerque, NM**	NA	NA	Manhattan, KS**	NA
195	Columbus, GA-AL	(18.1)	NA	Alexandria, LA**	NA	NA	Midland, MI**	NA
195	Greensboro-High Point, NC	(18.1)	NA	Allentown, PA-NJ**	NA	NA	Midland, TX**	NA
197	Salinas, CA	(18.2)	NA	Anchorage, AK**	NA	NA	Montgomery County, PA M.D.**	NA
198	Amarillo, TX	(18.3)	NA	Anniston-Oxford, AL**	NA	NA	Morgantown, WV**	NA
199	Lima, OH	(18.4)	NA	Beckley, WV**	NA	NA	Morristown, TN**	NA
199	Longview, TX	(18.4)	NA	Binghamton, NY**	NA	NA	Nashville-Davidson, TN**	NA
201	Springfield, OH	(18.5)	NA	Bloomington, IL**	NA	NA	Nassau-Suffolk, NY M.D.**	NA
202	Washington (greater) DC-VA-MD-WV	(18.7)	NA	Bloomsburg-Berwick, PA**	NA	NA	New Bern, NC**	NA
203	Cedar Rapids, IA	(19.0)	NA	Boston (greater), MA-NH**	NA	NA	New Haven-Milford, CT**	NA
204	Carson City, NV	(19.1)	NA	Boston, MA M.D.**	NA	NA	New York (greater), NY-NJ-PA**	NA
204	Fort Worth-Arlington, TX M.D.	(19.1)	NA	Boulder, CO**	NA	NA	New York-Jersey City, NY-NJ M.D.**	NA
206	West Palm Beach, FL M.D.	(19.2)	NA	Brunswick, GA**	NA	NA	Newark, NJ-PA M.D.**	NA
207	Dallas (greater), TX	(19.5)	NA	Buffalo-Niagara Falls, NY**	NA	NA	North Port-Sarasota-Bradenton, FL**	NA
208	El Paso, TX	(19.6)	NA	California-Lexington Park, MD**	NA	NA	Oakland-Hayward, CA M.D.**	NA
208	Lansing-East Lansing, MI	(19.6)	NA	Cambridge-Newton, MA M.D.**	NA	NA	Ogden-Clearfield, UT**	NA
210	Hinesville, GA	(19.8)	NA	Canton, OH**	NA	NA	Owensboro, KY**	NA
210	San Antonio, TX	(19.8)	NA	Chambersburg-Waynesboro, PA**	NA	NA	Panama City, FL**	NA
212	Dallas-Plano-Irving, TX M.D.	(19.9)	NA	Champaign-Urbana, IL**	NA	NA	Parkersburg-Vienna, WV**	NA
213	Jacksonville, FL	(20.2)	NA	Chicago (greater), IL-IN-WI**	NA	NA	Peoria, IL**	NA
213	Orlando, FL	(20.2)	NA	Chicago-Joilet-Naperville, IL M.D.**	NA	NA	Philadelphia (greater) PA-NJ-MD-DE**	NA
215	Kalamazoo-Portage, MI	(20.4)	NA	Cincinnati, OH-KY-IN**	NA	NA	Philadelphia, PA M.D.**	NA
216	Birmingham-Hoover, AL	(20.5)	NA	Coeur d'Alene, ID**	NA	NA	Phoenix-Mesa-Scottsdale, AZ**	NA
217	Valdosta, GA	(20.8)	NA	Crestview-Fort Walton Beach, FL**	NA	NA	Pocatello, ID**	NA
218	Dothan, AL	(21.0)	NA	Danville, IL**	NA	NA	Pueblo, CO**	NA
219	Durham-Chapel Hill, NC	(21.1)	NA	Daphne-Fairhope-Foley, AL**	NA	NA	Rapid City, SD**	NA
220	Florence-Muscle Shoals, AL	(21.2)	NA	Davenport, IA-IL**	NA	NA	Rochester, MN**	NA
221	Corpus Christi, TX	(21.4)	NA	Decatur, IL**	NA	NA	Rochester, NY**	NA
222	Lynchburg, VA	(21.9)	NA	Denver-Aurora, CO**	NA	NA	Rockford, IL**	NA
223	Memphis, TN-MS-AR	(22.1)	NA	Detroit (greater), MI**	NA	NA	Rocky Mount, NC**	NA
224	Cheyenne, WY	(22.4)	NA	Detroit-Dearborn-Livonia, MI M.D.**	NA	NA	Rome, GA**	NA
225	Casper, WY	(22.5)	NA	Dutchess-Putnam, NY M.D.**	NA	NA	Salisbury, MD-DE**	NA
226	Chico, CA	(22.6)	NA	East Stroudsburg, PA**	NA	NA	San Francisco (greater), CA**	NA
227	Green Bay, WI	(22.7)	NA	Elgin, IL M.D.**	NA	NA	San Rafael, CA M.D.**	NA
228	Olympia, WA	(22.8)	NA	Elizabethtown-Fort Knox, KY**	NA	NA	Santa Maria-Santa Barbara, CA**	NA
229	Bay City, MI	(23.2)	NA	Elmira, NY**	NA	NA	Seattle (greater), WA**	NA
230	Lakeland, FL	(23.8)	NA	Fairbanks, AK**	NA	NA	Seattle-Bellevue-Everett, WA M.D.**	NA
231	Port St. Lucie, FL	(23.9)	NA	Fort Smith, AR-OK**	NA	NA	Sebring, FL**	NA
231	Stockton-Lodi, CA	(23.9)	NA	Gainesville, GA**	NA	NA	Sierra Vista-Douglas, AZ**	NA
233	Vallejo-Fairfield, CA	(24.3)	NA	Gary, IN M.D.**	NA	NA	Sioux City, IA-NE-SD**	NA
234	Laredo, TX	(24.6)	NA	Gettysburg, PA**	NA	NA	Spartanburg, SC**	NA
235	Savannah, GA	(24.8)	NA	Glens Falls, NY**	NA	NA	Springfield, IL**	NA
236	Pine Bluff, AR	(24.9)	NA	Grand Island, NE**	NA	NA	Springfield, MA**	NA
237	Athens-Clarke County, GA	(25.1)	NA	Greenville-Anderson, SC**	NA	NA	Staunton-Waynesboro, VA**	NA
237	Sheboygan, WI	(25.1)	NA	Hagerstown-Martinsburg, MD-WV**	NA	NA	Syracuse, NY**	NA
239	Greenville, NC	(25.3)	NA	Hammond, LA**	NA	NA	Tacoma, WA M.D.**	NA
240	Bowling Green, KY	(26.0)	NA	Hattiesburg, MS**	NA	NA	Terre Haute, IN**	NA
240	Tampa-St Petersburg, FL	(26.0)	NA	Hilton Head Island, SC**	NA	NA	Texarkana, TX-AR**	NA
242	Charlottesville, VA	(26.6)	NA	Homosassa Springs, FL**	NA	NA	The Villages, FL**	NA
243	Decatur, AL	(27.3)	NA	Jackson, MS**	NA	NA	Toledo, OH**	NA
244	Wichita Falls, TX	(27.7)	NA	Jackson, TN**	NA	NA	Tucson, AZ**	NA
245	Saginaw, MI	(28.5)	NA	Jefferson City, MO**	NA	NA	Tuscaloosa, AL**	NA
246	Yakima, WA	(29.6)	NA	Kahului-Wailuku-Lahaina, HI**	NA	NA	Utica-Rome, NY**	NA
247	College Station-Bryan, TX	(29.7)	NA	Kankakee, IL**	NA	NA	Victoria, TX**	NA
248	Reno, NV	(30.4)	NA	Kansas City, MO-KS**	NA	NA	Waco, TX**	NA
248	South Bend-Mishawaka, IN-MI	(30.4)	NA	Kingston, NY**	NA	NA	Walla Walla, WA**	NA
250	Cape Coral-Fort Myers, FL	(30.6)	NA	Knoxville, TN**	NA	NA	Warner Robins, GA**	NA
251	Silver Spring-Frederick, MD M.D.	(30.9)	NA	Kokomo, IN**	NA	NA	Warren-Troy, MI M.D.**	NA
252	Auburn, AL	(33.3)	NA	Lafayette, LA**	NA	NA	Watertown-Fort Drum, NY**	NA
253	Punta Gorda, FL	(33.9)	NA	Lake Co.-Kenosha Co., IL-WI M.D.**	NA	NA	Wilmington, NC**	NA
254	Appleton, WI	(40.4)	NA	Lawton, OK**	NA	NA	Winston-Salem, NC**	NA
NA	Albany-Schenectady-Troy, NY**	NA	NA	Lexington-Fayette, KY**	NA			
NA	Albany, GA**	NA	NA	Madison, WI**	NA			

Source: CQ Press using reported data from the F.B.I. "Crime in the United States 2012"
*Larceny-theft is the unlawful taking of property. Attempts are included.
**Not available.

37. Motor Vehicle Thefts in 2012
National Total = 721,053 Motor Vehicle Thefts*

RANK	METROPOLITAN AREA	THEFTS	RANK	METROPOLITAN AREA	THEFTS	RANK	METROPOLITAN AREA	THEFTS
270	Abilene, TX	204	304	Cheyenne, WY	144	75	Gary, IN M.D.	2,150
113	Akron, OH	1,087	5	Chicago (greater), IL-IN-WI	24,218	372	Gettysburg, PA	50
147	Albany-Schenectady-Troy, NY	660	7	Chicago-Joilet-Naperville, IL M.D.	21,319	369	Glens Falls, NY	56
208	Albany, GA	337	152	Chico, CA	593	237	Goldsboro, NC	267
264	Albany, OR	211	65	Cincinnati, OH-KY-IN	2,824	322	Grand Forks, ND-MN	123
57	Albuquerque, NM	3,446	211	Clarksville, TN-KY	331	332	Grand Island, NE	106
NA	Alexandria, LA**	NA	276	Cleveland, TN	199	239	Grand Junction, CO	263
124	Allentown, PA-NJ	873	233	Coeur d'Alene, ID	273	293	Great Falls, MT	157
358	Altoona, PA	79	281	College Station-Bryan, TX	189	222	Greeley, CO	308
146	Amarillo, TX	685	79	Colorado Springs, CO	2,078	273	Green Bay, WI	200
373	Ames, IA	49	273	Columbia, MO	200	106	Greensboro-High Point, NC	1,228
33	Anaheim-Santa Ana-Irvine, CA M.D.	7,103	111	Columbus, GA-AL	1,103	68	Greenville-Anderson, SC	2,540
124	Anchorage, AK	873	252	Columbus, IN	235	279	Greenville, NC	191
177	Ann Arbor, MI	440	153	Corpus Christi, TX	588	202	Hagerstown-Martinsburg, MD-WV	352
300	Anniston-Oxford, AL	147	368	Corvallis, OR	59	259	Hammond, LA	218
352	Appleton, WI	83	229	Crestview-Fort Walton Beach, FL	289	188	Hanford-Corcoran, CA	405
130	Asheville, NC	821	348	Cumberland, MD-WV	88	190	Harrisburg-Carlisle, PA	394
203	Athens-Clarke County, GA	348	12	Dallas (greater), TX	17,632	361	Harrisonburg, VA	76
9	Atlanta, GA	20,386	18	Dallas-Plano-Irving, TX M.D.	12,667	74	Hartford, CT	2,178
224	Atlantic City, NJ	301	286	Dalton, GA	179	309	Hattiesburg, MS	138
317	Auburn, AL	128	320	Danville, IL	124	158	Hickory, NC	567
83	Augusta, GA-SC	1,984	278	Daphne-Fairhope-Foley, AL	192	231	Hilton Head Island, SC	279
61	Austin-Round Rock, TX	3,011	174	Davenport, IA-IL	457	340	Hinesville, GA	99
39	Bakersfield, CA	6,246	95	Dayton, OH	1,461	311	Homosassa Springs, FL	136
32	Baltimore, MD	7,167	263	Decatur, AL	216	216	Houma, LA	320
309	Bangor, ME	138	342	Decatur, IL	97	6	Houston, TX	23,272
295	Barnstable Town, MA	156	110	Deltona-Daytona Beach, FL	1,124	118	Huntsville, AL	975
NA	Baton Rouge, LA**	NA	29	Denver-Aurora, CO	7,822	332	Idaho Falls, ID	106
347	Bay City, MI	89	114	Des Moines-West Des Moines, IA	1,086	41	Indianapolis, IN	5,831
133	Beaumont-Port Arthur, TX	799	11	Detroit (greater), MI	19,318	338	Iowa City, IA	102
280	Beckley, WV	190	15	Detroit-Dearborn-Livonia, MI M.D.	15,284	78	Jacksonville, FL	2,093
252	Bellingham, WA	235	252	Dothan, AL	235	93	Jackson, MS	1,532
171	Billings, MT	494	264	Dover, DE	211	272	Jackson, TN	201
307	Binghamton, NY	141	361	Dubuque, IA	76	299	Janesville, WI	149
70	Birmingham-Hoover, AL	2,458	186	Duluth, MN-WI	409	306	Jefferson City, MO	143
271	Bismarck, ND	202	117	Durham-Chapel Hill, NC	986	241	Johnson City, TN	261
317	Blacksburg, VA	128	284	Dutchess-Putnam, NY M.D.	182	344	Johnstown, PA	93
336	Bloomington, IL	103	340	East Stroudsburg, PA	99	319	Jonesboro, AR	125
235	Bloomington, IN	270	139	El Centro, CA	748	169	Joplin, MO	511
376	Bloomsburg-Berwick, PA	33	100	El Paso, TX	1,358	167	Kahului-Wailuku-Lahaina, HI	517
180	Boise City, ID	427	228	Elgin, IL M.D.	290	182	Kalamazoo-Portage, MI	418
40	Boston (greater), MA-NH	6,125	361	Elizabethtown-Fort Knox, KY	76	335	Kankakee, IL	104
63	Boston, MA M.D.	2,926	374	Elmira, NY	46	28	Kansas City, MO-KS	7,880
213	Boulder, CO	329	264	Erie, PA	211	179	Kennewick-Richland, WA	438
268	Bowling Green, KY	207	126	Eugene, OR	862	199	Killeen-Temple, TX	365
151	Bremerton-Silverdale, WA	626	327	Fairbanks, AK	118	170	Kingsport, TN-VA	499
94	Bridgeport-Stamford, CT	1,515	251	Fargo, ND-MN	236	360	Kingston, NY	77
172	Brownsville-Harlingen, TX	476	283	Farmington, NM	183	82	Knoxville, TN	2,004
307	Brunswick, GA	141	165	Fayetteville-Springdale, AR-MO	539	331	Kokomo, IN	107
88	Buffalo-Niagara Falls, NY	1,709	116	Fayetteville, NC	1,017	353	La Crosse, WI-MN	82
246	Burlington, NC	250	328	Flagstaff, AZ	117	220	Lafayette, IN	309
350	California-Lexington Park, MD	87	121	Flint, MI	939	NA	Lafayette, LA**	NA
64	Cambridge-Newton, MA M.D.	2,898	259	Florence-Muscle Shoals, AL	218	173	Lake Co.-Kenosha Co., IL-WI M.D.	459
81	Camden, NJ M.D.	2,044	156	Florence, SC	575	176	Lake Havasu City-Kingman, AZ	444
141	Canton, OH	735	370	Fond du Lac, WI	54	129	Lakeland, FL	825
122	Cape Coral-Fort Myers, FL	923	244	Fort Collins, CO	251	204	Lancaster, PA	347
326	Cape Girardeau, MO-IL	119	49	Fort Lauderdale, FL M.D.	4,384	157	Lansing-East Lansing, MI	568
359	Carson City, NV	78	200	Fort Smith, AR-OK	363	185	Laredo, TX	410
312	Casper, WY	133	160	Fort Wayne, IN	562	194	Las Cruces, NM	381
209	Cedar Rapids, IA	333	45	Fort Worth-Arlington, TX M.D.	4,965	26	Las Vegas-Henderson, NV	8,219
354	Chambersburg-Waynesboro, PA	80	37	Fresno, CA	6,944	259	Lawrence, KS	218
286	Champaign-Urbana, IL	179	218	Gadsden, AL	310	212	Lawton, OK	330
84	Charleston-North Charleston, SC	1,855	196	Gainesville, FL	373	354	Lebanon, PA	80
269	Charlottesville, VA	206	214	Gainesville, GA	324	336	Lewiston-Auburn, ME	103

Note: All listings are for Metropolitan Statistical Areas (M.S.A.s) except for those ending with "M.D." Listings with "M.D." are Metropolitan Divisions which are smaller parts of eleven large M.S.A.s. See explanatory note at beginning of metropolitan area section.

RANK	METROPOLITAN AREA	THEFTS	RANK	METROPOLITAN AREA	THEFTS	RANK	METROPOLITAN AREA	THEFTS
343	Lewiston, ID-WA	94	300	Owensboro, KY	147	104	Silver Spring-Frederick, MD M.D.	1,271
109	Lexington-Fayette, KY	1,137	97	Oxnard-Thousand Oaks, CA	1,404	240	Sioux City, IA-NE-SD	262
312	Lima, OH	133	127	Palm Bay-Melbourne, FL	847	207	Sioux Falls, SD	344
209	Lincoln, NE	333	223	Panama City, FL	303	155	South Bend-Mishawaka, IN-MI	579
72	Little Rock, AR	2,383	325	Parkersburg-Vienna, WV	120	149	Spartanburg, SC	655
365	Logan, UT-ID	69	138	Pensacola, FL	780	62	Spokane, WA	3,010
166	Longview, TX	526	192	Peoria, IL	385	220	Springfield, IL	309
256	Longview, WA	231	21	Philadelphia (greater) PA-NJ-MD-DE	11,931	102	Springfield, MA	1,319
2	Los Angeles County, CA M.D.	40,555	34	Philadelphia, PA M.D.	7,051	98	Springfield, MO	1,403
1	Los Angeles (greater), CA	47,658	NA	Phoenix-Mesa-Scottsdale, AZ**	NA	267	Springfield, OH	210
60	Louisville, KY-IN	3,045	236	Pine Bluff, AR	268	375	State College, PA	44
128	Lubbock, TX	832	86	Pittsburgh, PA	1,806	348	Staunton-Waynesboro, VA	88
286	Lynchburg, VA	179	329	Pittsfield, MA	112	47	Stockton-Lodi, CA	4,398
135	Macon, GA	785	367	Pocatello, ID	66	316	St. George, UT	130
150	Madera, CA	648	187	Port St. Lucie, FL	406	181	St. Joseph, MO-KS	421
175	Madison, WI	448	30	Portland-Vancouver, OR-WA	7,663	35	St. Louis, MO-IL	6,965
204	Manchester-Nashua, NH	347	197	Portland, ME	368	206	Sumter, SC	345
366	Manhattan, KS	68	257	Prescott, AZ	226	142	Syracuse, NY	727
345	Mankato-North Mankato, MN	90	58	Providence-Warwick, RI-MA	3,422	51	Tacoma, WA M.D.	4,065
297	Mansfield, OH	151	197	Provo-Orem, UT	368	143	Tallahassee, FL	715
96	McAllen-Edinburg-Mission, TX	1,421	161	Pueblo, CO	549	48	Tampa-St Petersburg, FL	4,389
217	Medford, OR	313	324	Punta Gorda, FL	122	182	Terre Haute, IN	418
53	Memphis, TN-MS-AR	3,789	282	Racine, WI	187	195	Texarkana, TX-AR	377
100	Merced, CA	1,358	92	Raleigh, NC	1,575	370	The Villages, FL	54
13	Miami (greater), FL	16,496	234	Rapid City, SD	271	91	Toledo, OH	1,622
25	Miami-Dade County, FL M.D.	9,459	134	Reading, PA	787	140	Topeka, KS	745
296	Michigan City-La Porte, IN	153	123	Redding, CA	903	144	Trenton, NJ	714
377	Midland, MI	13	105	Reno, NV	1,244	56	Tucson, AZ	3,613
259	Midland, TX	218	80	Richmond, VA	2,049	59	Tulsa, OK	3,118
43	Milwaukee, WI	5,405	8	Riverside-San Bernardino, CA	20,700	191	Tuscaloosa, AL	387
38	Minneapolis-St. Paul, MN-WI	6,601	193	Roanoke, VA	383	215	Tyler, TX	321
303	Missoula, MT	146	300	Rochester, MN	147	242	Utica-Rome, NY	258
115	Mobile, AL	1,034	112	Rochester, NY	1,100	291	Valdosta, GA	162
50	Modesto, CA	4,085	162	Rockford, IL	548	71	Vallejo-Fairfield, CA	2,434
276	Monroe, LA	199	224	Rockingham County, NH M.D.	301	312	Victoria, TX	133
247	Monroe, MI	246	244	Rocky Mount, NC	251	290	Vineland-Bridgeton, NJ	164
107	Montgomery County, PA M.D.	1,170	298	Rome, GA	150	69	Virginia Beach-Norfolk, VA-NC	2,487
99	Montgomery, AL	1,370	24	Sacramento, CA	9,725	85	Visalia-Porterville, CA	1,848
330	Morgantown, WV	109	257	Saginaw, MI	226	226	Waco, TX	292
284	Morristown, TN	182	103	Salem, OR	1,273	332	Walla Walla, WA	106
243	Mount Vernon-Anacortes, WA	255	87	Salinas, CA	1,774	232	Warner Robins, GA	278
255	Muncie, IN	232	201	Salisbury, MD-DE	359	52	Warren-Troy, MI M.D.	4,034
218	Napa, CA	310	46	Salt Lake City, UT	4,422	17	Washington (greater) DC-VA-MD-WV	12,714
248	Naples-Marco Island, FL	243	31	San Antonio, TX	7,564	22	Washington, DC-VA-MD-WV M.D.	11,443
67	Nashville-Davidson, TN	2,596	19	San Diego, CA	12,136	304	Waterloo-Cedar Falls, IA	144
73	Nassau-Suffolk, NY M.D.	2,184	3	San Francisco (greater), CA	27,833	293	Watertown-Fort Drum, NY	157
292	New Bern, NC	161	36	San Francisco-Redwood, CA M.D.	6,947	364	Wausau, WI	72
77	New Haven-Milford, CT	2,094	23	San Jose, CA	11,101	66	West Palm Beach, FL M.D.	2,653
55	New Orleans, LA	3,677	182	San Luis Obispo, CA	418	322	Wheeling, WV-OH	123
4	New York (greater), NY-NJ-PA	24,660	154	San Rafael, CA M.D.	584	230	Wichita Falls, TX	284
16	New York-Jersey City, NY-NJ M.D.	14,082	119	Santa Cruz-Watsonville, CA	972	76	Wichita, KS	2,096
27	Newark, NJ-PA M.D.	8,212	238	Santa Fe, NM	264	354	Williamsport, PA	80
137	North Port-Sarasota-Bradenton, FL	782	132	Santa Maria-Santa Barbara, CA	801	90	Wilmington, DE-MD-NJ M.D.	1,666
289	Norwich-New London, CT	174	145	Santa Rosa, CA	706	163	Wilmington, NC	546
10	Oakland-Hayward, CA M.D.	20,302	131	Savannah, GA	817	315	Winchester, VA-WV	132
249	Ocala, FL	242	159	Scranton--Wilkes-Barre, PA	565	108	Winston-Salem, NC	1,141
351	Ocean City, NJ	84	14	Seattle (greater), WA	16,023	120	Worcester, MA-CT	965
168	Odessa, TX	516	20	Seattle-Bellevue-Everett, WA M.D.	11,958	89	Yakima, WA	1,680
148	Ogden-Clearfield, UT	658	338	Sebastian-Vero Beach, FL	102	226	York-Hanover, PA	292
42	Oklahoma City, OK	5,806	320	Sebring, FL	124	136	Youngstown-Warren, OH-PA	784
177	Olympia, WA	440	354	Sheboygan, WI	80	164	Yuba City, CA	541
54	Omaha-Council Bluffs, NE-IA	3,782	250	Sherman-Denison, TX	237	189	Yuma, AZ	400
44	Orlando, FL	5,259	NA	Shreveport-Bossier City, LA**	NA			
345	Oshkosh-Neenah, WI	90	273	Sierra Vista-Douglas, AZ	200			

Source: Reported data from the F.B.I. "Crime in the United States 2012"
*Motor vehicle theft includes the theft or attempted theft of a self-propelled vehicle. Excludes motorboats, construction equipment, airplanes, and farming equipment. **Not available.

37. Motor Vehicle Thefts in 2012 (continued)
National Total = 721,053 Motor Vehicle Thefts*

RANK	METROPOLITAN AREA	THEFTS	RANK	METROPOLITAN AREA	THEFTS	RANK	METROPOLITAN AREA	THEFTS
1	Los Angeles (greater), CA	47,658	65	Cincinnati, OH-KY-IN	2,824	129	Lakeland, FL	825
2	Los Angeles County, CA M.D.	40,555	66	West Palm Beach, FL M.D.	2,653	130	Asheville, NC	821
3	San Francisco (greater), CA	27,833	67	Nashville-Davidson, TN	2,596	131	Savannah, GA	817
4	New York (greater), NY-NJ-PA	24,660	68	Greenville-Anderson, SC	2,540	132	Santa Maria-Santa Barbara, CA	801
5	Chicago (greater), IL-IN-WI	24,218	69	Virginia Beach-Norfolk, VA-NC	2,487	133	Beaumont-Port Arthur, TX	799
6	Houston, TX	23,272	70	Birmingham-Hoover, AL	2,458	134	Reading, PA	787
7	Chicago-Joilet-Naperville, IL M.D.	21,319	71	Vallejo-Fairfield, CA	2,434	135	Macon, GA	785
8	Riverside-San Bernardino, CA	20,700	72	Little Rock, AR	2,383	136	Youngstown-Warren, OH-PA	784
9	Atlanta, GA	20,386	73	Nassau-Suffolk, NY M.D.	2,184	137	North Port-Sarasota-Bradenton, FL	782
10	Oakland-Hayward, CA M.D.	20,302	74	Hartford, CT	2,178	138	Pensacola, FL	780
11	Detroit (greater), MI	19,318	75	Gary, IN M.D.	2,150	139	El Centro, CA	748
12	Dallas (greater), TX	17,632	76	Wichita, KS	2,096	140	Topeka, KS	745
13	Miami (greater), FL	16,496	77	New Haven-Milford, CT	2,094	141	Canton, OH	735
14	Seattle (greater), WA	16,023	78	Jacksonville, FL	2,093	142	Syracuse, NY	727
15	Detroit-Dearborn-Livonia, MI M.D.	15,284	79	Colorado Springs, CO	2,078	143	Tallahassee, FL	715
16	New York-Jersey City, NY-NJ M.D.	14,082	80	Richmond, VA	2,049	144	Trenton, NJ	714
17	Washington (greater) DC-VA-MD-WV	12,714	81	Camden, NJ M.D.	2,044	145	Santa Rosa, CA	706
18	Dallas-Plano-Irving, TX M.D.	12,667	82	Knoxville, TN	2,004	146	Amarillo, TX	685
19	San Diego, CA	12,136	83	Augusta, GA-SC	1,984	147	Albany-Schenectady-Troy, NY	660
20	Seattle-Bellevue-Everett, WA M.D.	11,958	84	Charleston-North Charleston, SC	1,855	148	Ogden-Clearfield, UT	658
21	Philadelphia (greater) PA-NJ-MD-DE	11,931	85	Visalia-Porterville, CA	1,848	149	Spartanburg, SC	655
22	Washington, DC-VA-MD-WV M.D.	11,443	86	Pittsburgh, PA	1,806	150	Madera, CA	648
23	San Jose, CA	11,101	87	Salinas, CA	1,774	151	Bremerton-Silverdale, WA	626
24	Sacramento, CA	9,725	88	Buffalo-Niagara Falls, NY	1,709	152	Chico, CA	593
25	Miami-Dade County, FL M.D.	9,459	89	Yakima, WA	1,680	153	Corpus Christi, TX	588
26	Las Vegas-Henderson, NV	8,219	90	Wilmington, DE-MD-NJ M.D.	1,666	154	San Rafael, CA M.D.	584
27	Newark, NJ-PA M.D.	8,212	91	Toledo, OH	1,622	155	South Bend-Mishawaka, IN-MI	579
28	Kansas City, MO-KS	7,880	92	Raleigh, NC	1,575	156	Florence, SC	575
29	Denver-Aurora, CO	7,822	93	Jackson, MS	1,532	157	Lansing-East Lansing, MI	568
30	Portland-Vancouver, OR-WA	7,663	94	Bridgeport-Stamford, CT	1,515	158	Hickory, NC	567
31	San Antonio, TX	7,564	95	Dayton, OH	1,461	159	Scranton--Wilkes-Barre, PA	565
32	Baltimore, MD	7,167	96	McAllen-Edinburg-Mission, TX	1,421	160	Fort Wayne, IN	562
33	Anaheim-Santa Ana-Irvine, CA M.D.	7,103	97	Oxnard-Thousand Oaks, CA	1,404	161	Pueblo, CO	549
34	Philadelphia, PA M.D.	7,051	98	Springfield, MO	1,403	162	Rockford, IL	548
35	St. Louis, MO-IL	6,965	99	Montgomery, AL	1,370	163	Wilmington, NC	546
36	San Francisco-Redwood, CA M.D.	6,947	100	El Paso, TX	1,358	164	Yuba City, CA	541
37	Fresno, CA	6,944	100	Merced, CA	1,358	165	Fayetteville-Springdale, AR-MO	539
38	Minneapolis-St. Paul, MN-WI	6,601	102	Springfield, MA	1,319	166	Longview, TX	526
39	Bakersfield, CA	6,246	103	Salem, OR	1,273	167	Kahului-Wailuku-Lahaina, HI	517
40	Boston (greater), MA-NH	6,125	104	Silver Spring-Frederick, MD M.D.	1,271	168	Odessa, TX	516
41	Indianapolis, IN	5,831	105	Reno, NV	1,244	169	Joplin, MO	511
42	Oklahoma City, OK	5,806	106	Greensboro-High Point, NC	1,228	170	Kingsport, TN-VA	499
43	Milwaukee, WI	5,405	107	Montgomery County, PA M.D.	1,170	171	Billings, MT	494
44	Orlando, FL	5,259	108	Winston-Salem, NC	1,141	172	Brownsville-Harlingen, TX	476
45	Fort Worth-Arlington, TX M.D.	4,965	109	Lexington-Fayette, KY	1,137	173	Lake Co.-Kenosha Co., IL-WI M.D.	459
46	Salt Lake City, UT	4,422	110	Deltona-Daytona Beach, FL	1,124	174	Davenport, IA-IL	457
47	Stockton-Lodi, CA	4,398	111	Columbus, GA-AL	1,103	175	Madison, WI	448
48	Tampa-St Petersburg, FL	4,389	112	Rochester, NY	1,100	176	Lake Havasu City-Kingman, AZ	444
49	Fort Lauderdale, FL M.D.	4,384	113	Akron, OH	1,087	177	Ann Arbor, MI	440
50	Modesto, CA	4,085	114	Des Moines-West Des Moines, IA	1,086	177	Olympia, WA	440
51	Tacoma, WA M.D.	4,065	115	Mobile, AL	1,034	179	Kennewick-Richland, WA	438
52	Warren-Troy, MI M.D.	4,034	116	Fayetteville, NC	1,017	180	Boise City, ID	427
53	Memphis, TN-MS-AR	3,789	117	Durham-Chapel Hill, NC	986	181	St. Joseph, MO-KS	421
54	Omaha-Council Bluffs, NE-IA	3,782	118	Huntsville, AL	975	182	Kalamazoo-Portage, MI	418
55	New Orleans, LA	3,677	119	Santa Cruz-Watsonville, CA	972	182	San Luis Obispo, CA	418
56	Tucson, AZ	3,613	120	Worcester, MA-CT	965	182	Terre Haute, IN	418
57	Albuquerque, NM	3,446	121	Flint, MI	939	185	Laredo, TX	410
58	Providence-Warwick, RI-MA	3,422	122	Cape Coral-Fort Myers, FL	923	186	Duluth, MN-WI	409
59	Tulsa, OK	3,118	123	Redding, CA	903	187	Port St. Lucie, FL	406
60	Louisville, KY-IN	3,045	124	Allentown, PA-NJ	873	188	Hanford-Corcoran, CA	405
61	Austin-Round Rock, TX	3,011	124	Anchorage, AK	873	189	Yuma, AZ	400
62	Spokane, WA	3,010	126	Eugene, OR	862	190	Harrisburg-Carlisle, PA	394
63	Boston, MA M.D.	2,926	127	Palm Bay-Melbourne, FL	847	191	Tuscaloosa, AL	387
64	Cambridge-Newton, MA M.D.	2,898	128	Lubbock, TX	832	192	Peoria, IL	385

Note: All listings are for Metropolitan Statistical Areas (M.S.A.s) except for those ending with "M.D." Listings with "M.D." are Metropolitan Divisions which are smaller parts of eleven large M.S.A.s. See explanatory note at beginning of metropolitan area section.

RANK	METROPOLITAN AREA	THEFTS	RANK	METROPOLITAN AREA	THEFTS	RANK	METROPOLITAN AREA	THEFTS
193	Roanoke, VA	383	257	Prescott, AZ	226	320	Sebring, FL	124
194	Las Cruces, NM	381	257	Saginaw, MI	226	322	Grand Forks, ND-MN	123
195	Texarkana, TX-AR	377	259	Florence-Muscle Shoals, AL	218	322	Wheeling, WV-OH	123
196	Gainesville, FL	373	259	Hammond, LA	218	324	Punta Gorda, FL	122
197	Portland, ME	368	259	Lawrence, KS	218	325	Parkersburg-Vienna, WV	120
197	Provo-Orem, UT	368	259	Midland, TX	218	326	Cape Girardeau, MO-IL	119
199	Killeen-Temple, TX	365	263	Decatur, AL	216	327	Fairbanks, AK	118
200	Fort Smith, AR-OK	363	264	Albany, OR	211	328	Flagstaff, AZ	117
201	Salisbury, MD-DE	359	264	Dover, DE	211	329	Pittsfield, MA	112
202	Hagerstown-Martinsburg, MD-WV	352	264	Erie, PA	211	330	Morgantown, WV	109
203	Athens-Clarke County, GA	348	267	Springfield, OH	210	331	Kokomo, IN	107
204	Lancaster, PA	347	268	Bowling Green, KY	207	332	Grand Island, NE	106
204	Manchester-Nashua, NH	347	269	Charlottesville, VA	206	332	Idaho Falls, ID	106
206	Sumter, SC	345	270	Abilene, TX	204	332	Walla Walla, WA	106
207	Sioux Falls, SD	344	271	Bismarck, ND	202	335	Kankakee, IL	104
208	Albany, GA	337	272	Jackson, TN	201	336	Bloomington, IL	103
209	Cedar Rapids, IA	333	273	Columbia, MO	200	336	Lewiston-Auburn, ME	103
209	Lincoln, NE	333	273	Green Bay, WI	200	338	Iowa City, IA	102
211	Clarksville, TN-KY	331	273	Sierra Vista-Douglas, AZ	200	338	Sebastian-Vero Beach, FL	102
212	Lawton, OK	330	276	Cleveland, TN	199	340	East Stroudsburg, PA	99
213	Boulder, CO	329	276	Monroe, LA	199	340	Hinesville, GA	99
214	Gainesville, GA	324	278	Daphne-Fairhope-Foley, AL	192	342	Decatur, IL	97
215	Tyler, TX	321	279	Greenville, NC	191	343	Lewiston, ID-WA	94
216	Houma, LA	320	280	Beckley, WV	190	344	Johnstown, PA	93
217	Medford, OR	313	281	College Station-Bryan, TX	189	345	Mankato-North Mankato, MN	90
218	Gadsden, AL	310	282	Racine, WI	187	345	Oshkosh-Neenah, WI	90
218	Napa, CA	310	283	Farmington, NM	183	347	Bay City, MI	89
220	Lafayette, IN	309	284	Dutchess-Putnam, NY M.D.	182	348	Cumberland, MD-WV	88
220	Springfield, IL	309	284	Morristown, TN	182	348	Staunton-Waynesboro, VA	88
222	Greeley, CO	308	286	Champaign-Urbana, IL	179	350	California-Lexington Park, MD	87
223	Panama City, FL	303	286	Dalton, GA	179	351	Ocean City, NJ	84
224	Atlantic City, NJ	301	286	Lynchburg, VA	179	352	Appleton, WI	83
224	Rockingham County, NH M.D.	301	289	Norwich-New London, CT	174	353	La Crosse, WI-MN	82
226	Waco, TX	292	290	Vineland-Bridgeton, NJ	164	354	Chambersburg-Waynesboro, PA	80
226	York-Hanover, PA	292	291	Valdosta, GA	162	354	Lebanon, PA	80
228	Elgin, IL M.D.	290	292	New Bern, NC	161	354	Sheboygan, WI	80
229	Crestview-Fort Walton Beach, FL	289	293	Great Falls, MT	157	354	Williamsport, PA	80
230	Wichita Falls, TX	284	293	Watertown-Fort Drum, NY	157	358	Altoona, PA	79
231	Hilton Head Island, SC	279	295	Barnstable Town, MA	156	359	Carson City, NV	78
232	Warner Robins, GA	278	296	Michigan City-La Porte, IN	153	360	Kingston, NY	77
233	Coeur d'Alene, ID	273	297	Mansfield, OH	151	361	Dubuque, IA	76
234	Rapid City, SD	271	298	Rome, GA	150	361	Elizabethtown-Fort Knox, KY	76
235	Bloomington, IN	270	299	Janesville, WI	149	361	Harrisonburg, VA	76
236	Pine Bluff, AR	268	300	Anniston-Oxford, AL	147	364	Wausau, WI	72
237	Goldsboro, NC	267	300	Owensboro, KY	147	365	Logan, UT-ID	69
238	Santa Fe, NM	264	300	Rochester, MN	147	366	Manhattan, KS	68
239	Grand Junction, CO	263	303	Missoula, MT	146	367	Pocatello, ID	66
240	Sioux City, IA-NE-SD	262	304	Cheyenne, WY	144	368	Corvallis, OR	59
241	Johnson City, TN	261	304	Waterloo-Cedar Falls, IA	144	369	Glens Falls, NY	56
242	Utica-Rome, NY	258	306	Jefferson City, MO	143	370	Fond du Lac, WI	54
243	Mount Vernon-Anacortes, WA	255	307	Binghamton, NY	141	370	The Villages, FL	54
244	Fort Collins, CO	251	307	Brunswick, GA	141	372	Gettysburg, PA	50
244	Rocky Mount, NC	251	309	Bangor, ME	138	373	Ames, IA	49
246	Burlington, NC	250	309	Hattiesburg, MS	138	374	Elmira, NY	46
247	Monroe, MI	246	311	Homosassa Springs, FL	136	375	State College, PA	44
248	Naples-Marco Island, FL	243	312	Casper, WY	133	376	Bloomsburg-Berwick, PA	33
249	Ocala, FL	242	312	Lima, OH	133	377	Midland, MI	13
250	Sherman-Denison, TX	237	312	Victoria, TX	133	NA	Alexandria, LA**	NA
251	Fargo, ND-MN	236	315	Winchester, VA-WV	132	NA	Baton Rouge, LA**	NA
252	Bellingham, WA	235	316	St. George, UT	130	NA	Lafayette, LA**	NA
252	Columbus, IN	235	317	Auburn, AL	128	NA	Phoenix-Mesa-Scottsdale, AZ**	NA
252	Dothan, AL	235	317	Blacksburg, VA	128	NA	Shreveport-Bossier City, LA**	NA
255	Muncie, IN	232	319	Jonesboro, AR	125			
256	Longview, WA	231	320	Danville, IL	124			

Source: Reported data from the F.B.I. "Crime in the United States 2012"
*Motor vehicle theft includes the theft or attempted theft of a self-propelled vehicle. Excludes motorboats, construction equipment, airplanes, and farming equipment. **Not available.

38. Motor Vehicle Theft Rate in 2012
National Rate = 229.7 Motor Vehicle Thefts per 100,000 Population*

RANK	METROPOLITAN AREA	RATE	RANK	METROPOLITAN AREA	RATE	RANK	METROPOLITAN AREA	RATE
257	Abilene, TX	120.8	190	Cheyenne, WY	153.1	64	Gary, IN M.D.	302.4
183	Akron, OH	155.0	90	Chicago (greater), IL-IN-WI	254.6	369	Gettysburg, PA	49.2
325	Albany-Schenectady-Troy, NY	75.3	70	Chicago-Joliet-Naperville, IL M.D.	292.0	372	Glens Falls, NY	43.2
121	Albany, GA	211.5	82	Chico, CA	266.7	118	Goldsboro, NC	213.7
151	Albany, OR	177.4	227	Cincinnati, OH-KY-IN	133.0	251	Grand Forks, ND-MN	123.3
31	Albuquerque, NM	382.9	246	Clarksville, TN-KY	124.3	236	Grand Island, NE	127.4
NA	Alexandria, LA**	NA	160	Cleveland, TN	168.9	153	Grand Junction, CO	176.4
279	Allentown, PA-NJ	105.6	135	Coeur d'Alene, ID	192.1	137	Great Falls, MT	190.5
351	Altoona, PA	62.1	317	College Station-Bryan, TX	80.4	262	Greeley, CO	117.5
86	Amarillo, TX	263.7	61	Colorado Springs, CO	310.4	350	Green Bay, WI	64.5
360	Ames, IA	54.4	258	Columbia, MO	120.5	165	Greensboro-High Point, NC	166.3
106	Anaheim-Santa Ana-Irvine, CA M.D.	230.3	39	Columbus, GA-AL	362.5	66	Greenville-Anderson, SC	301.0
76	Anchorage, AK	278.4	67	Columbus, IN	300.8	271	Greenville, NC	110.5
242	Ann Arbor, MI	126.4	223	Corpus Christi, TX	134.3	221	Hagerstown-Martinsburg, MD-WV	137.8
246	Anniston-Oxford, AL	124.3	343	Corvallis, OR	68.2	152	Hammond, LA	176.8
375	Appleton, WI	36.4	260	Crestview-Fort Walton Beach, FL	119.2	87	Hanford-Corcoran, CA	261.0
140	Asheville, NC	189.5	312	Cumberland, MD-WV	84.9	338	Harrisburg-Carlisle, PA	71.1
149	Athens-Clarke County, GA	178.1	85	Dallas (greater), TX	264.0	355	Harrisonburg, VA	59.4
34	Atlanta, GA	375.1	72	Dallas-Plano-Irving, TX M.D.	287.5	120	Hartford, CT	212.7
272	Atlantic City, NJ	109.2	248	Dalton, GA	124.1	294	Hattiesburg, MS	94.7
303	Auburn, AL	88.9	196	Danville, IL	152.1	186	Hickory, NC	154.0
43	Augusta, GA-SC	344.7	283	Daphne-Fairhope-Foley, AL	102.4	211	Hilton Head Island, SC	145.6
165	Austin-Round Rock, TX	166.3	259	Davenport, IA-IL	119.6	256	Hinesville, GA	121.6
5	Bakersfield, CA	726.6	146	Dayton, OH	181.9	290	Homosassa Springs, FL	95.8
88	Baltimore, MD	260.1	216	Decatur, AL	139.6	191	Houma, LA	152.5
302	Bangor, ME	89.7	304	Decatur, IL	87.6	33	Houston, TX	378.4
333	Barnstable Town, MA	71.7	141	Deltona-Daytona Beach, FL	187.3	107	Huntsville, AL	228.2
NA	Baton Rouge, LA**	NA	68	Denver-Aurora, CO	296.8	321	Idaho Falls, ID	78.1
314	Bay City, MI	83.0	142	Des Moines-West Des Moines, IA	186.4	63	Indianapolis, IN	304.4
130	Beaumont-Port Arthur, TX	194.4	18	Detroit (greater), MI	450.4	348	Iowa City, IA	65.6
195	Beckley, WV	152.2	1	Detroit-Dearborn-Livonia, MI M.D.	847.5	197	Jacksonville, FL	151.8
263	Bellingham, WA	114.3	178	Dothan, AL	159.7	82	Jackson, MS	266.7
62	Billings, MT	304.8	241	Dover, DE	126.6	188	Jackson, TN	153.4
357	Binghamton, NY	56.1	319	Dubuque, IA	80.0	297	Janesville, WI	92.8
116	Birmingham-Hoover, AL	216.2	212	Duluth, MN-WI	145.3	293	Jefferson City, MO	94.9
161	Bismarck, ND	168.8	139	Durham-Chapel Hill, NC	190.3	231	Johnson City, TN	129.5
337	Blacksburg, VA	71.2	371	Dutchess-Putnam, NY M.D.	45.5	349	Johnstown, PA	64.6
358	Bloomington, IL	55.0	356	East Stroudsburg, PA	58.2	284	Jonesboro, AR	101.4
163	Bloomington, IN	166.9	24	El Centro, CA	418.6	71	Joplin, MO	288.4
374	Bloomsburg-Berwick, PA	38.4	173	El Paso, TX	162.3	55	Kahului-Wailuku-Lahaina, HI	325.6
344	Boise City, ID	67.6	370	Elgin, IL M.D.	46.4	237	Kalamazoo-Portage, MI	127.3
229	Boston (greater), MA-NH	132.3	368	Elizabethtown-Fort Knox, KY	50.1	300	Kankakee, IL	91.4
193	Boston, MA M.D.	152.3	367	Elmira, NY	51.5	30	Kansas City, MO-KS	387.6
276	Boulder, CO	108.4	326	Erie, PA	75.0	170	Kennewick-Richland, WA	164.2
234	Bowling Green, KY	128.6	99	Eugene, OR	242.2	305	Killeen-Temple, TX	87.4
97	Bremerton-Silverdale, WA	243.5	44	Fairbanks, AK	341.0	179	Kingsport, TN-VA	159.6
164	Bridgeport-Stamford, CT	166.4	272	Fargo, ND-MN	109.2	373	Kingston, NY	42.0
267	Brownsville-Harlingen, TX	113.2	215	Farmington, NM	142.5	104	Knoxville, TN	235.6
250	Brunswick, GA	123.5	266	Fayetteville-Springdale, AR-MO	113.3	233	Kokomo, IN	128.8
202	Buffalo-Niagara Falls, NY	149.9	81	Fayetteville, NC	269.1	353	La Crosse, WI-MN	60.8
176	Burlington, NC	161.5	308	Flagstaff, AZ	86.0	201	Lafayette, IN	151.3
318	California-Lexington Park, MD	80.2	112	Flint, MI	222.3	NA	Lafayette, LA**	NA
240	Cambridge-Newton, MA M.D.	126.7	207	Florence-Muscle Shoals, AL	147.4	366	Lake Co.-Kenosha Co., IL-WI M.D.	52.5
172	Camden, NJ M.D.	162.5	78	Florence, SC	276.3	115	Lake Havasu City-Kingman, AZ	217.1
145	Canton, OH	182.0	365	Fond du Lac, WI	52.8	226	Lakeland, FL	133.5
213	Cape Coral-Fort Myers, FL	144.2	316	Fort Collins, CO	81.0	347	Lancaster, PA	66.2
253	Cape Girardeau, MO-IL	122.4	98	Fort Lauderdale, FL M.D.	243.0	255	Lansing-East Lansing, MI	122.0
218	Carson City, NV	138.9	235	Fort Smith, AR-OK	128.1	180	Laredo, TX	157.5
157	Casper, WY	171.7	225	Fort Wayne, IN	133.6	149	Las Cruces, NM	178.1
237	Cedar Rapids, IA	127.3	113	Fort Worth-Arlington, TX M.D.	218.3	26	Las Vegas-Henderson, NV	411.8
364	Chambersburg-Waynesboro, PA	53.0	4	Fresno, CA	729.7	133	Lawrence, KS	193.3
322	Champaign-Urbana, IL	77.0	69	Gadsden, AL	296.0	95	Lawton, OK	248.5
80	Charleston-North Charleston, SC	269.4	220	Gainesville, FL	138.1	354	Lebanon, PA	59.5
298	Charlottesville, VA	92.1	156	Gainesville, GA	175.1	290	Lewiston-Auburn, ME	95.8

Note: All listings are for Metropolitan Statistical Areas (M.S.A.s) except for those ending with "M.D." Listings with "M.D." are Metropolitan Divisions which are smaller parts of eleven large M.S.A.s. See explanatory note at beginning of metropolitan area section.

RANK	METROPOLITAN AREA	RATE
198	Lewiston, ID-WA	151.7
103	Lexington-Fayette, KY	236.6
243	Lima, OH	125.4
277	Lincoln, NE	107.9
48	Little Rock, AR	334.4
362	Logan, UT-ID	53.4
101	Longview, TX	239.2
110	Longview, WA	223.2
28	Los Angeles County, CA M.D.	406.3
36	Los Angeles (greater), CA	364.8
96	Louisville, KY-IN	243.9
77	Lubbock, TX	277.0
340	Lynchburg, VA	69.7
49	Macon, GA	333.5
23	Madera, CA	419.8
330	Madison, WI	72.9
307	Manchester-Nashua, NH	86.2
335	Manhattan, KS	71.3
299	Mankato-North Mankato, MN	92.0
254	Mansfield, OH	122.3
154	McAllen-Edinburg-Mission, TX	175.5
198	Medford, OR	151.7
75	Memphis, TN-MS-AR	282.0
12	Merced, CA	517.7
73	Miami (greater), FL	287.0
35	Miami-Dade County, FL M.D.	365.3
222	Michigan City-La Porte, IN	136.9
377	Midland, MI	15.5
206	Midland, TX	147.9
42	Milwaukee, WI	345.1
131	Minneapolis-St. Paul, MN-WI	193.7
230	Missoula, MT	131.6
91	Mobile, AL	249.6
2	Modesto, CA	780.6
270	Monroe, LA	111.4
175	Monroe, MI	162.2
352	Montgomery County, PA M.D.	61.8
41	Montgomery, AL	360.4
315	Morgantown, WV	82.4
181	Morristown, TN	157.3
117	Mount Vernon-Anacortes, WA	213.8
127	Muncie, IN	196.6
111	Napa, CA	222.4
329	Naples-Marco Island, FL	73.1
200	Nashville-Davidson, TN	151.6
323	Nassau-Suffolk, NY M.D.	76.4
245	New Bern, NC	124.5
89	New Haven-Milford, CT	258.6
65	New Orleans, LA	301.4
244	New York (greater), NY-NJ-PA	124.6
288	New York-Jersey City, NY-NJ M.D.	100.3
50	Newark, NJ-PA M.D.	329.8
275	North Port-Sarasota-Bradenton, FL	108.8
261	Norwich-New London, CT	118.9
3	Oakland-Hayward, CA M.D.	774.9
332	Ocala, FL	71.8
306	Ocean City, NJ	86.5
38	Odessa, TX	362.8
278	Ogden-Clearfield, UT	107.1
17	Oklahoma City, OK	451.5
158	Olympia, WA	169.8
22	Omaha-Council Bluffs, NE-IA	428.4
102	Orlando, FL	238.9
361	Oshkosh-Neenah, WI	53.5

RANK	METROPOLITAN AREA	RATE
239	Owensboro, KY	127.1
162	Oxnard-Thousand Oaks, CA	167.2
187	Palm Bay-Melbourne, FL	153.7
177	Panama City, FL	161.0
232	Parkersburg-Vienna, WV	129.2
158	Pensacola, FL	169.8
284	Peoria, IL	101.4
125	Philadelphia (greater) PA-NJ-MD-DE	198.4
53	Philadelphia, PA M.D.	328.7
NA	Phoenix-Mesa-Scottsdale, AZ**	NA
79	Pine Bluff, AR	269.9
323	Pittsburgh, PA	76.4
311	Pittsfield, MA	85.1
320	Pocatello, ID	78.3
296	Port St. Lucie, FL	93.6
47	Portland-Vancouver, OR-WA	336.1
335	Portland, ME	71.3
280	Prescott, AZ	105.5
119	Providence-Warwick, RI-MA	213.3
345	Provo-Orem, UT	67.1
46	Pueblo, CO	337.3
326	Punta Gorda, FL	75.0
292	Racine, WI	95.5
224	Raleigh, NC	134.0
128	Rapid City, SD	196.0
138	Reading, PA	190.4
13	Redding, CA	503.3
74	Reno, NV	285.8
165	Richmond, VA	166.3
15	Riverside-San Bernardino, CA	476.4
252	Roanoke, VA	122.7
339	Rochester, MN	70.1
286	Rochester, NY	101.2
182	Rockford, IL	157.2
334	Rockingham County, NH M.D.	71.5
171	Rocky Mount, NC	163.3
184	Rome, GA	154.6
20	Sacramento, CA	442.8
264	Saginaw, MI	113.4
56	Salem, OR	320.1
25	Salinas, CA	416.6
295	Salisbury, MD-DE	94.2
29	Salt Lake City, UT	393.7
45	San Antonio, TX	339.5
31	San Diego, CA	382.9
7	San Francisco (greater), CA	628.0
19	San Francisco-Redwood, CA M.D.	446.9
9	San Jose, CA	589.6
193	San Luis Obispo, CA	152.3
109	San Rafael, CA M.D.	226.9
37	Santa Cruz-Watsonville, CA	364.4
148	Santa Fe, NM	181.0
144	Santa Maria-Santa Barbara, CA	185.9
214	Santa Rosa, CA	143.3
108	Savannah, GA	227.3
289	Scranton--Wilkes-Barre, PA	100.2
16	Seattle (greater), WA	453.4
21	Seattle-Bellevue-Everett, WA M.D.	439.9
331	Sebastian-Vero Beach, FL	72.4
249	Sebring, FL	124.0
341	Sheboygan, WI	69.3
134	Sherman-Denison, TX	192.3
NA	Shreveport-Bossier City, LA**	NA
204	Sierra Vista-Douglas, AZ	148.4

RANK	METROPOLITAN AREA	RATE
282	Silver Spring-Frederick, MD M.D.	102.6
185	Sioux City, IA-NE-SD	154.3
208	Sioux Falls, SD	146.4
147	South Bend-Mishawaka, IN-MI	181.2
124	Spartanburg, SC	205.6
11	Spokane, WA	562.2
209	Springfield, IL	146.0
122	Springfield, MA	210.3
58	Springfield, MO	318.2
191	Springfield, OH	152.5
376	State College, PA	28.4
328	Staunton-Waynesboro, VA	73.4
8	Stockton-Lodi, CA	625.9
301	St. George, UT	90.5
51	St. Joseph, MO-KS	329.3
94	St. Louis, MO-IL	248.9
59	Sumter, SC	318.0
274	Syracuse, NY	109.1
14	Tacoma, WA M.D.	498.3
136	Tallahassee, FL	190.8
189	Tampa-St Petersburg, FL	153.3
100	Terre Haute, IN	241.3
92	Texarkana, TX-AR	249.4
359	The Villages, FL	54.5
84	Toledo, OH	266.4
60	Topeka, KS	315.9
132	Trenton, NJ	193.6
40	Tucson, AZ	361.2
54	Tulsa, OK	327.3
168	Tuscaloosa, AL	166.2
205	Tyler, TX	148.2
308	Utica-Rome, NY	86.0
268	Valdosta, GA	112.6
10	Vallejo-Fairfield, CA	579.1
219	Victoria, TX	138.2
281	Vineland-Bridgeton, NJ	103.9
209	Virginia Beach-Norfolk, VA-NC	146.0
27	Visalia-Porterville, CA	407.6
269	Waco, TX	112.2
169	Walla Walla, WA	164.9
202	Warner Robins, GA	149.9
173	Warren-Troy, MI M.D.	162.3
114	Washington (greater) DC-VA-MD-WV	218.2
92	Washington, DC-VA-MD-WV M.D.	249.4
310	Waterloo-Cedar Falls, IA	85.2
228	Watertown-Fort Drum, NY	132.4
362	Wausau, WI	53.4
128	West Palm Beach, FL M.D.	196.0
313	Wheeling, WV-OH	83.6
143	Wichita Falls, TX	186.2
52	Wichita, KS	329.2
342	Williamsport, PA	68.4
105	Wilmington, DE-MD-NJ M.D.	232.4
123	Wilmington, NC	208.3
287	Winchester, VA-WV	100.6
155	Winston-Salem, NC	175.2
264	Worcester, MA-CT	113.4
6	Yakima, WA	673.2
346	York-Hanover, PA	66.7
217	Youngstown-Warren, OH-PA	139.3
57	Yuba City, CA	320.0
126	Yuma, AZ	197.0

Source: Reported data from the F.B.I. "Crime in the United States 2012"

*Motor vehicle theft includes the theft or attempted theft of a self-propelled vehicle. Excludes motorboats, construction equipment, airplanes, and farming equipment. **Not available.

38. Motor Vehicle Theft Rate in 2012 (continued)
National Rate = 229.7 Motor Vehicle Thefts per 100,000 Population*

RANK	METROPOLITAN AREA	RATE	RANK	METROPOLITAN AREA	RATE	RANK	METROPOLITAN AREA	RATE
1	Detroit-Dearborn-Livonia, MI M.D.	847.5	65	New Orleans, LA	301.4	128	West Palm Beach, FL M.D.	196.0
2	Modesto, CA	780.6	66	Greenville-Anderson, SC	301.0	130	Beaumont-Port Arthur, TX	194.4
3	Oakland-Hayward, CA M.D.	774.9	67	Columbus, IN	300.8	131	Minneapolis-St. Paul, MN-WI	193.7
4	Fresno, CA	729.7	68	Denver-Aurora, CO	296.8	132	Trenton, NJ	193.6
5	Bakersfield, CA	726.6	69	Gadsden, AL	296.0	133	Lawrence, KS	193.3
6	Yakima, WA	673.2	70	Chicago-Joilet-Naperville, IL M.D.	292.0	134	Sherman-Denison, TX	192.3
7	San Francisco (greater), CA	628.0	71	Joplin, MO	288.4	135	Coeur d'Alene, ID	192.1
8	Stockton-Lodi, CA	625.9	72	Dallas-Plano-Irving, TX M.D.	287.5	136	Tallahassee, FL	190.8
9	San Jose, CA	589.6	73	Miami (greater), FL	287.0	137	Great Falls, MT	190.5
10	Vallejo-Fairfield, CA	579.1	74	Reno, NV	285.8	138	Reading, PA	190.4
11	Spokane, WA	562.2	75	Memphis, TN-MS-AR	282.0	139	Durham-Chapel Hill, NC	190.3
12	Merced, CA	517.7	76	Anchorage, AK	278.4	140	Asheville, NC	189.5
13	Redding, CA	503.3	77	Lubbock, TX	277.0	141	Deltona-Daytona Beach, FL	187.3
14	Tacoma, WA M.D.	498.3	78	Florence, SC	276.3	142	Des Moines-West Des Moines, IA	186.4
15	Riverside-San Bernardino, CA	476.4	79	Pine Bluff, AR	269.9	143	Wichita Falls, TX	186.2
16	Seattle (greater), WA	453.4	80	Charleston-North Charleston, SC	269.4	144	Santa Maria-Santa Barbara, CA	185.9
17	Oklahoma City, OK	451.5	81	Fayetteville, NC	269.1	145	Canton, OH	182.0
18	Detroit (greater), MI	450.4	82	Chico, CA	266.7	146	Dayton, OH	181.9
19	San Francisco-Redwood, CA M.D.	446.9	82	Jackson, MS	266.7	147	South Bend-Mishawaka, IN-MI	181.2
20	Sacramento, CA	442.8	84	Toledo, OH	266.4	148	Santa Fe, NM	181.0
21	Seattle-Bellevue-Everett, WA M.D.	439.9	85	Dallas (greater), TX	264.0	149	Athens-Clarke County, GA	178.1
22	Omaha-Council Bluffs, NE-IA	428.4	86	Amarillo, TX	263.7	149	Las Cruces, NM	178.1
23	Madera, CA	419.8	87	Hanford-Corcoran, CA	261.0	151	Albany, OR	177.4
24	El Centro, CA	418.6	88	Baltimore, MD	260.1	152	Hammond, LA	176.8
25	Salinas, CA	416.6	89	New Haven-Milford, CT	258.6	153	Grand Junction, CO	176.4
26	Las Vegas-Henderson, NV	411.8	90	Chicago (greater), IL-IN-WI	254.6	154	McAllen-Edinburg-Mission, TX	175.5
27	Visalia-Porterville, CA	407.6	91	Mobile, AL	249.6	155	Winston-Salem, NC	175.2
28	Los Angeles County, CA M.D.	406.3	92	Texarkana, TX-AR	249.4	156	Gainesville, GA	175.1
29	Salt Lake City, UT	393.7	92	Washington, DC-VA-MD-WV M.D.	249.4	157	Casper, WY	171.7
30	Kansas City, MO-KS	387.6	94	St. Louis, MO-IL	248.9	158	Olympia, WA	169.8
31	Albuquerque, NM	382.9	95	Lawton, OK	248.5	158	Pensacola, FL	169.8
31	San Diego, CA	382.9	96	Louisville, KY-IN	243.9	160	Cleveland, TN	168.9
33	Houston, TX	378.4	97	Bremerton-Silverdale, WA	243.5	161	Bismarck, ND	168.8
34	Atlanta, GA	375.1	98	Fort Lauderdale, FL M.D.	243.0	162	Oxnard-Thousand Oaks, CA	167.2
35	Miami-Dade County, FL M.D.	365.3	99	Eugene, OR	242.2	163	Bloomington, IN	166.9
36	Los Angeles (greater), CA	364.8	100	Terre Haute, IN	241.3	164	Bridgeport-Stamford, CT	166.4
37	Santa Cruz-Watsonville, CA	364.4	101	Longview, TX	239.2	165	Austin-Round Rock, TX	166.3
38	Odessa, TX	362.8	102	Orlando, FL	238.9	165	Greensboro-High Point, NC	166.3
39	Columbus, GA-AL	362.5	103	Lexington-Fayette, KY	236.6	165	Richmond, VA	166.3
40	Tucson, AZ	361.2	104	Knoxville, TN	235.6	168	Tuscaloosa, AL	166.2
41	Montgomery, AL	360.4	105	Wilmington, DE-MD-NJ M.D.	232.4	169	Walla Walla, WA	164.9
42	Milwaukee, WI	345.1	106	Anaheim-Santa Ana-Irvine, CA M.D.	230.3	170	Kennewick-Richland, WA	164.2
43	Augusta, GA-SC	344.7	107	Huntsville, AL	228.2	171	Rocky Mount, NC	163.3
44	Fairbanks, AK	341.0	108	Savannah, GA	227.3	172	Camden, NJ M.D.	162.5
45	San Antonio, TX	339.5	109	San Rafael, CA M.D.	226.9	173	El Paso, TX	162.3
46	Pueblo, CO	337.3	110	Longview, WA	223.2	173	Warren-Troy, MI M.D.	162.3
47	Portland-Vancouver, OR-WA	336.1	111	Napa, CA	222.4	175	Monroe, MI	162.2
48	Little Rock, AR	334.4	112	Flint, MI	222.3	176	Burlington, NC	161.5
49	Macon, GA	333.5	113	Fort Worth-Arlington, TX M.D.	218.3	177	Panama City, FL	161.0
50	Newark, NJ-PA M.D.	329.8	114	Washington (greater) DC-VA-MD-WV	218.2	178	Dothan, AL	159.7
51	St. Joseph, MO-KS	329.3	115	Lake Havasu City-Kingman, AZ	217.1	179	Kingsport, TN-VA	159.6
52	Wichita, KS	329.2	116	Birmingham-Hoover, AL	216.2	180	Laredo, TX	157.5
53	Philadelphia, PA M.D.	328.7	117	Mount Vernon-Anacortes, WA	213.8	181	Morristown, TN	157.3
54	Tulsa, OK	327.3	118	Goldsboro, NC	213.7	182	Rockford, IL	157.2
55	Kahului-Wailuku-Lahaina, HI	325.6	119	Providence-Warwick, RI-MA	213.3	183	Akron, OH	155.0
56	Salem, OR	320.1	120	Hartford, CT	212.7	184	Rome, GA	154.6
57	Yuba City, CA	320.0	121	Albany, GA	211.5	185	Sioux City, IA-NE-SD	154.3
58	Springfield, MO	318.2	122	Springfield, MA	210.3	186	Hickory, NC	154.0
59	Sumter, SC	318.0	123	Wilmington, NC	208.3	187	Palm Bay-Melbourne, FL	153.7
60	Topeka, KS	315.9	124	Spartanburg, SC	205.6	188	Jackson, TN	153.4
61	Colorado Springs, CO	310.4	125	Philadelphia (greater) PA-NJ-MD-DE	198.4	189	Tampa-St Petersburg, FL	153.3
62	Billings, MT	304.8	126	Yuma, AZ	197.0	190	Cheyenne, WY	153.1
63	Indianapolis, IN	304.4	127	Muncie, IN	196.6	191	Houma, LA	152.5
64	Gary, IN M.D.	302.4	128	Rapid City, SD	196.0	191	Springfield, OH	152.5

Note: All listings are for Metropolitan Statistical Areas (M.S.A.s) except for those ending with "M.D." Listings with "M.D." are Metropolitan Divisions which are smaller parts of eleven large M.S.A.s. See explanatory note at beginning of metropolitan area section.

RANK	METROPOLITAN AREA	RATE	RANK	METROPOLITAN AREA	RATE	RANK	METROPOLITAN AREA	RATE
193	Boston, MA M.D.	152.3	257	Abilene, TX	120.8	321	Idaho Falls, ID	78.1
193	San Luis Obispo, CA	152.3	258	Columbia, MO	120.5	322	Champaign-Urbana, IL	77.0
195	Beckley, WV	152.2	259	Davenport, IA-IL	119.6	323	Nassau-Suffolk, NY M.D.	76.4
196	Danville, IL	152.1	260	Crestview-Fort Walton Beach, FL	119.2	323	Pittsburgh, PA	76.4
197	Jacksonville, FL	151.8	261	Norwich-New London, CT	118.9	325	Albany-Schenectady-Troy, NY	75.3
198	Lewiston, ID-WA	151.7	262	Greeley, CO	117.5	326	Erie, PA	75.0
198	Medford, OR	151.7	263	Bellingham, WA	114.3	326	Punta Gorda, FL	75.0
200	Nashville-Davidson, TN	151.6	264	Saginaw, MI	113.4	328	Staunton-Waynesboro, VA	73.4
201	Lafayette, IN	151.3	264	Worcester, MA-CT	113.4	329	Naples-Marco Island, FL	73.1
202	Buffalo-Niagara Falls, NY	149.9	266	Fayetteville-Springdale, AR-MO	113.3	330	Madison, WI	72.9
202	Warner Robins, GA	149.9	267	Brownsville-Harlingen, TX	113.2	331	Sebastian-Vero Beach, FL	72.4
204	Sierra Vista-Douglas, AZ	148.4	268	Valdosta, GA	112.6	332	Ocala, FL	71.8
205	Tyler, TX	148.2	269	Waco, TX	112.2	333	Barnstable Town, MA	71.7
206	Midland, TX	147.9	270	Monroe, LA	111.4	334	Rockingham County, NH M.D.	71.5
207	Florence-Muscle Shoals, AL	147.4	271	Greenville, NC	110.5	335	Manhattan, KS	71.3
208	Sioux Falls, SD	146.4	272	Atlantic City, NJ	109.2	335	Portland, ME	71.3
209	Springfield, IL	146.0	272	Fargo, ND-MN	109.2	337	Blacksburg, VA	71.2
209	Virginia Beach-Norfolk, VA-NC	146.0	274	Syracuse, NY	109.1	338	Harrisburg-Carlisle, PA	71.1
211	Hilton Head Island, SC	145.6	275	North Port-Sarasota-Bradenton, FL	108.8	339	Rochester, MN	70.1
212	Duluth, MN-WI	145.3	276	Boulder, CO	108.4	340	Lynchburg, VA	69.7
213	Cape Coral-Fort Myers, FL	144.2	277	Lincoln, NE	107.9	341	Sheboygan, WI	69.3
214	Santa Rosa, CA	143.3	278	Ogden-Clearfield, UT	107.1	342	Williamsport, PA	68.4
215	Farmington, NM	142.5	279	Allentown, PA-NJ	105.6	343	Corvallis, OR	68.2
216	Decatur, AL	139.6	280	Prescott, AZ	105.5	344	Boise City, ID	67.6
217	Youngstown-Warren, OH-PA	139.3	281	Vineland-Bridgeton, NJ	103.9	345	Provo-Orem, UT	67.1
218	Carson City, NV	138.9	282	Silver Spring-Frederick, MD M.D.	102.6	346	York-Hanover, PA	66.7
219	Victoria, TX	138.2	283	Daphne-Fairhope-Foley, AL	102.4	347	Lancaster, PA	66.2
220	Gainesville, FL	138.1	284	Jonesboro, AR	101.4	348	Iowa City, IA	65.6
221	Hagerstown-Martinsburg, MD-WV	137.8	284	Peoria, IL	101.4	349	Johnstown, PA	64.6
222	Michigan City-La Porte, IN	136.9	286	Rochester, NY	101.2	350	Green Bay, WI	64.5
223	Corpus Christi, TX	134.3	287	Winchester, VA-WV	100.6	351	Altoona, PA	62.1
224	Raleigh, NC	134.0	288	New York-Jersey City, NY-NJ M.D.	100.3	352	Montgomery County, PA M.D.	61.8
225	Fort Wayne, IN	133.6	289	Scranton--Wilkes-Barre, PA	100.2	353	La Crosse, WI-MN	60.8
226	Lakeland, FL	133.5	290	Homosassa Springs, FL	95.8	354	Lebanon, PA	59.5
227	Cincinnati, OH-KY-IN	133.0	290	Lewiston-Auburn, ME	95.8	355	Harrisonburg, VA	59.4
228	Watertown-Fort Drum, NY	132.4	292	Racine, WI	95.5	356	East Stroudsburg, PA	58.2
229	Boston (greater), MA-NH	132.3	293	Jefferson City, MO	94.9	357	Binghamton, NY	56.1
230	Missoula, MT	131.6	294	Hattiesburg, MS	94.7	358	Bloomington, IL	55.0
231	Johnson City, TN	129.5	295	Salisbury, MD-DE	94.2	359	The Villages, FL	54.5
232	Parkersburg-Vienna, WV	129.2	296	Port St. Lucie, FL	93.6	360	Ames, IA	54.4
233	Kokomo, IN	128.8	297	Janesville, WI	92.8	361	Oshkosh-Neenah, WI	53.5
234	Bowling Green, KY	128.6	298	Charlottesville, VA	92.1	362	Logan, UT-ID	53.4
235	Fort Smith, AR-OK	128.1	299	Mankato-North Mankato, MN	92.0	362	Wausau, WI	53.4
236	Grand Island, NE	127.4	300	Kankakee, IL	91.4	364	Chambersburg-Waynesboro, PA	53.0
237	Cedar Rapids, IA	127.3	301	St. George, UT	90.5	365	Fond du Lac, WI	52.8
237	Kalamazoo-Portage, MI	127.3	302	Bangor, ME	89.7	366	Lake Co.-Kenosha Co., IL-WI M.D.	52.5
239	Owensboro, KY	127.1	303	Auburn, AL	88.9	367	Elmira, NY	51.5
240	Cambridge-Newton, MA M.D.	126.7	304	Decatur, IL	87.6	368	Elizabethtown-Fort Knox, KY	50.1
241	Dover, DE	126.6	305	Killeen-Temple, TX	87.4	369	Gettysburg, PA	49.2
242	Ann Arbor, MI	126.4	306	Ocean City, NJ	86.5	370	Elgin, IL M.D.	46.4
243	Lima, OH	125.4	307	Manchester-Nashua, NH	86.2	371	Dutchess-Putnam, NY M.D.	45.5
244	New York (greater), NY-NJ-PA	124.6	308	Flagstaff, AZ	86.0	372	Glens Falls, NY	43.2
245	New Bern, NC	124.5	308	Utica-Rome, NY	86.0	373	Kingston, NY	42.0
246	Anniston-Oxford, AL	124.3	310	Waterloo-Cedar Falls, IA	85.2	374	Bloomsburg-Berwick, PA	38.4
246	Clarksville, TN-KY	124.3	311	Pittsfield, MA	85.1	375	Appleton, WI	36.4
248	Dalton, GA	124.1	312	Cumberland, MD-WV	84.9	376	State College, PA	28.4
249	Sebring, FL	124.0	313	Wheeling, WV-OH	83.6	377	Midland, MI	15.5
250	Brunswick, GA	123.5	314	Bay City, MI	83.0	NA	Alexandria, LA**	NA
251	Grand Forks, ND-MN	123.3	315	Morgantown, WV	82.4	NA	Baton Rouge, LA**	NA
252	Roanoke, VA	122.7	316	Fort Collins, CO	81.0	NA	Lafayette, LA**	NA
253	Cape Girardeau, MO-IL	122.4	317	College Station-Bryan, TX	80.4	NA	Phoenix-Mesa-Scottsdale, AZ**	NA
254	Mansfield, OH	122.3	318	California-Lexington Park, MD	80.2	NA	Shreveport-Bossier City, LA**	NA
255	Lansing-East Lansing, MI	122.0	319	Dubuque, IA	80.0			
256	Hinesville, GA	121.6	320	Pocatello, ID	78.3			

Source: Reported data from the F.B.I. "Crime in the United States 2012"

*Motor vehicle theft includes the theft or attempted theft of a self-propelled vehicle. Excludes motorboats, construction equipment, airplanes, and farming equipment. **Not available.

39. Percent Change in Motor Vehicle Theft Rate: 2011 to 2012
National Percent Change = 0.1% Decrease*

RANK	METROPOLITAN AREA	% CHANGE	RANK	METROPOLITAN AREA	% CHANGE	RANK	METROPOLITAN AREA	% CHANGE
135	Abilene, TX	(0.6)	11	Cheyenne, WY	45.9	218	Gary, IN M.D.	(13.1)
222	Akron, OH	(13.6)	206	Chicago (greater), IL-IN-WI	(10.9)	NA	Gettysburg, PA**	NA
NA	Albany-Schenectady-Troy, NY**	NA	NA	Chicago-Joilet-Naperville, IL M.D.**	NA	NA	Glens Falls, NY**	NA
123	Albany, GA	1.5	161	Chico, CA	(3.5)	187	Goldsboro, NC	(7.2)
NA	Albany, OR**	NA	NA	Cincinnati, OH-KY-IN**	NA	163	Grand Forks, ND-MN	(3.8)
155	Albuquerque, NM	(2.9)	239	Clarksville, TN-KY	(16.2)	NA	Grand Island, NE**	NA
NA	Alexandria, LA**	NA	149	Cleveland, TN	(2.3)	46	Grand Junction, CO	18.6
NA	Allentown, PA-NJ**	NA	NA	Coeur d'Alene, ID**	NA	18	Great Falls, MT	35.9
138	Altoona, PA	(1.0)	211	College Station-Bryan, TX	(11.1)	175	Greeley, CO	(5.5)
131	Amarillo, TX	0.0	10	Colorado Springs, CO	46.5	125	Green Bay, WI	1.3
275	Ames, IA	(38.0)	103	Columbia, MO	4.0	NA	Greensboro-High Point, NC**	NA
40	Anaheim-Santa Ana-Irvine, CA M.D.	20.1	247	Columbus, GA-AL	(17.4)	NA	Greenville-Anderson, SC**	NA
NA	Anchorage, AK**	NA	224	Columbus, IN	(14.0)	NA	Greenville, NC**	NA
138	Ann Arbor, MI	(1.0)	141	Corpus Christi, TX	(1.5)	NA	Hagerstown-Martinsburg, MD-WV**	NA
262	Anniston-Oxford, AL	(23.3)	258	Corvallis, OR	(22.4)	NA	Hammond, LA**	NA
260	Appleton, WI	(22.9)	129	Crestview-Fort Walton Beach, FL	0.7	106	Hanford-Corcoran, CA	3.9
84	Asheville, NC	6.6	7	Cumberland, MD-WV	52.4	269	Harrisburg-Carlisle, PA	(26.3)
158	Athens-Clarke County, GA	(3.2)	204	Dallas (greater), TX	(10.6)	97	Harrisonburg, VA	4.6
134	Atlanta, GA	(0.5)	214	Dallas-Plano-Irving, TX M.D.	(11.6)	85	Hartford, CT	6.0
201	Atlantic City, NJ	(9.4)	273	Dalton, GA	(32.5)	NA	Hattiesburg, MS**	NA
178	Auburn, AL	(5.8)	38	Danville, IL	22.1	103	Hickory, NC	4.0
195	Augusta, GA-SC	(8.6)	NA	Daphne-Fairhope-Foley, AL**	NA	NA	Hilton Head Island, SC**	NA
89	Austin-Round Rock, TX	5.5	206	Davenport, IA-IL	(10.9)	270	Hinesville, GA	(28.3)
29	Bakersfield, CA	26.3	121	Dayton, OH	1.9	NA	Homosassa Springs, FL**	NA
173	Baltimore, MD	(5.2)	254	Decatur, AL	(20.4)	109	Houma, LA	3.3
140	Bangor, ME	(1.4)	265	Decatur, IL	(24.5)	62	Houston, TX	11.5
249	Barnstable Town, MA	(18.4)	NA	Deltona-Daytona Beach, FL**	NA	198	Huntsville, AL	(8.9)
NA	Baton Rouge, LA**	NA	NA	Denver-Aurora, CO**	NA	268	Idaho Falls, ID	(25.9)
31	Bay City, MI	25.9	167	Des Moines-West Des Moines, IA	(4.3)	NA	Indianapolis, IN**	NA
180	Beaumont-Port Arthur, TX	(5.9)	132	Detroit (greater), MI	(0.2)	107	Iowa City, IA	3.8
NA	Beckley, WV**	NA	114	Detroit-Dearborn-Livonia, MI M.D.	2.4	234	Jacksonville, FL	(15.1)
109	Bellingham, WA	3.3	160	Dothan, AL	(3.4)	NA	Jackson, MS**	NA
42	Billings, MT	19.7	78	Dover, DE	7.6	NA	Jackson, TN**	NA
NA	Binghamton, NY**	NA	28	Dubuque, IA	27.6	64	Janesville, WI	10.7
256	Birmingham-Hoover, AL	(21.2)	76	Duluth, MN-WI	8.0	87	Jefferson City, MO	5.7
58	Bismarck, ND	12.5	89	Durham-Chapel Hill, NC	5.5	116	Johnson City, TN	2.2
246	Blacksburg, VA	(17.3)	NA	Dutchess-Putnam, NY M.D.**	NA	82	Johnstown, PA	7.0
161	Bloomington, IL	(3.5)	NA	East Stroudsburg, PA**	NA	222	Jonesboro, AR	(13.6)
NA	Bloomington, IN**	NA	146	El Centro, CA	(2.0)	91	Joplin, MO	5.4
NA	Bloomsburg-Berwick, PA**	NA	258	El Paso, TX	(22.4)	NA	Kahului-Wailuku-Lahaina, HI**	NA
202	Boise City, ID	(9.6)	NA	Elgin, IL M.D.**	NA	NA	Kalamazoo-Portage, MI**	NA
NA	Boston (greater), MA-NH**	NA	NA	Elizabethtown-Fort Knox, KY**	NA	119	Kankakee, IL	2.0
NA	Boston, MA M.D.**	NA	NA	Elmira, NY**	NA	NA	Kansas City, MO-KS**	NA
144	Boulder, CO	(1.8)	111	Erie, PA	3.0	238	Kennewick-Richland, WA	(16.0)
93	Bowling Green, KY	5.2	188	Eugene, OR	(7.3)	203	Killeen-Temple, TX	(10.5)
80	Bremerton-Silverdale, WA	7.5	13	Fairbanks, AK	40.7	59	Kingsport, TN-VA	12.2
243	Bridgeport-Stamford, CT	(16.7)	67	Fargo, ND-MN	10.1	NA	Kingston, NY**	NA
100	Brownsville-Harlingen, TX	4.3	43	Farmington, NM	19.3	NA	Knoxville, TN**	NA
245	Brunswick, GA	(16.8)	NA	Fayetteville-Springdale, AR-MO**	NA	NA	Kokomo, IN**	NA
NA	Buffalo-Niagara Falls, NY**	NA	167	Fayetteville, NC	(4.3)	263	La Crosse, WI-MN	(23.7)
68	Burlington, NC	9.9	127	Flagstaff, AZ	1.1	73	Lafayette, IN	8.5
NA	California-Lexington Park, MD**	NA	271	Flint, MI	(31.1)	NA	Lafayette, LA**	NA
NA	Cambridge-Newton, MA M.D.**	NA	19	Florence-Muscle Shoals, AL	33.6	236	Lake Co.-Kenosha Co., IL-WI M.D.	(15.5)
137	Camden, NJ M.D.	(0.9)	136	Florence, SC	(0.8)	27	Lake Havasu City-Kingman, AZ	29.2
16	Canton, OH	37.2	237	Fond du Lac, WI	(15.8)	152	Lakeland, FL	(2.6)
54	Cape Coral-Fort Myers, FL	13.5	195	Fort Collins, CO	(8.6)	157	Lancaster, PA	(3.1)
73	Cape Girardeau, MO-IL	8.5	170	Fort Lauderdale, FL M.D.	(4.4)	57	Lansing-East Lansing, MI	13.0
59	Carson City, NV	12.2	NA	Fort Smith, AR-OK**	NA	255	Laredo, TX	(20.8)
20	Casper, WY	33.2	65	Fort Wayne, IN	10.2	206	Las Cruces, NM	(10.9)
48	Cedar Rapids, IA	18.3	189	Fort Worth-Arlington, TX M.D.	(7.4)	145	Las Vegas-Henderson, NV	(1.9)
NA	Chambersburg-Waynesboro, PA**	NA	154	Fresno, CA	(2.8)	129	Lawrence, KS	0.7
153	Champaign-Urbana, IL	(2.7)	228	Gadsden, AL	(14.2)	NA	Lawton, OK**	NA
NA	Charleston-North Charleston, SC**	NA	242	Gainesville, FL	(16.5)	77	Lebanon, PA	7.8
220	Charlottesville, VA	(13.4)	75	Gainesville, GA	8.4	4	Lewiston-Auburn, ME	63.8

Note: All listings are for Metropolitan Statistical Areas (M.S.A.s) except for those ending with "M.D." Listings with "M.D." are Metropolitan Divisions which are smaller parts of eleven large M.S.A.s. See explanatory note at beginning of metropolitan area section.

RANK	METROPOLITAN AREA	% CHANGE	RANK	METROPOLITAN AREA	% CHANGE	RANK	METROPOLITAN AREA	% CHANGE
NA	Lewiston, ID-WA**	NA	47	Owensboro, KY	18.5	225	Silver Spring-Frederick, MD M.D.	(14.1)
NA	Lexington-Fayette, KY**	NA	15	Oxnard-Thousand Oaks, CA	37.4	NA	Sioux City, IA-NE-SD**	NA
266	Lima, OH	(24.6)	55	Palm Bay-Melbourne, FL	13.2	71	Sioux Falls, SD	8.8
230	Lincoln, NE	(14.4)	NA	Panama City, FL**	NA	155	South Bend-Mishawaka, IN-MI	(2.9)
123	Little Rock, AR	1.5	NA	Parkersburg-Vienna, WV**	NA	NA	Spartanburg, SC**	NA
8	Logan, UT-ID	51.7	184	Pensacola, FL	(6.7)	NA	Spokane, WA**	NA
191	Longview, TX	(7.6)	225	Peoria, IL	(14.1)	91	Springfield, IL	5.4
260	Longview, WA	(22.9)	NA	Philadelphia (greater) PA-NJ-MD-DE**	NA	NA	Springfield, MA**	NA
133	Los Angeles County, CA M.D.	(0.3)	NA	Philadelphia, PA M.D.**	NA	71	Springfield, MO	8.8
116	Los Angeles (greater), CA	2.2	NA	Phoenix-Mesa-Scottsdale, AZ**	NA	212	Springfield, OH	(11.3)
150	Louisville, KY-IN	(2.4)	272	Pine Bluff, AR	(32.3)	264	State College, PA	(24.3)
97	Lubbock, TX	4.6	150	Pittsburgh, PA	(2.4)	NA	Staunton-Waynesboro, VA**	NA
256	Lynchburg, VA	(21.2)	228	Pittsfield, MA	(14.2)	12	Stockton-Lodi, CA	43.8
233	Macon, GA	(14.9)	NA	Pocatello, ID**	NA	NA	St. George, UT**	NA
61	Madera, CA	11.6	215	Port St. Lucie, FL	(11.8)	17	St. Joseph, MO-KS	37.1
NA	Madison, WI**	NA	55	Portland-Vancouver, OR-WA	13.2	116	St. Louis, MO-IL	2.2
81	Manchester-Nashua, NH	7.3	251	Portland, ME	(18.9)	21	Sumter, SC	32.9
NA	Manhattan, KS**	NA	70	Prescott, AZ	9.1	NA	Syracuse, NY**	NA
175	Mankato-North Mankato, MN	(5.5)	NA	Providence-Warwick, RI-MA**	NA	158	Tacoma, WA M.D.	(3.2)
181	Mansfield, OH	(6.0)	252	Provo-Orem, UT	(19.1)	25	Tallahassee, FL	30.4
241	McAllen-Edinburg-Mission, TX	(16.3)	111	Pueblo, CO	3.0	171	Tampa-St Petersburg, FL	(4.8)
33	Medford, OR	25.6	78	Punta Gorda, FL	7.6	197	Terre Haute, IN	(8.7)
235	Memphis, TN-MS-AR	(15.3)	194	Racine, WI	(8.1)	NA	Texarkana, TX-AR**	NA
26	Merced, CA	29.8	199	Raleigh, NC	(9.2)	NA	The Villages, FL**	NA
209	Miami (greater), FL	(11.0)	NA	Rapid City, SD**	NA	NA	Toledo, OH**	NA
232	Miami-Dade County, FL M.D.	(14.8)	39	Reading, PA	21.4	97	Topeka, KS	4.6
274	Michigan City-La Porte, IN	(34.5)	2	Redding, CA	66.5	96	Trenton, NJ	4.7
NA	Midland, MI**	NA	14	Reno, NV	37.5	182	Tucson, AZ	(6.2)
NA	Midland, TX**	NA	108	Richmond, VA	3.4	174	Tulsa, OK	(5.4)
114	Milwaukee, WI	2.4	45	Riverside-San Bernardino, CA	18.7	NA	Tuscaloosa, AL**	NA
103	Minneapolis-St. Paul, MN-WI	4.0	192	Roanoke, VA	(7.9)	178	Tyler, TX	(5.8)
51	Missoula, MT	15.1	NA	Rochester, MN**	NA	NA	Utica-Rome, NY**	NA
252	Mobile, AL	(19.1)	NA	Rochester, NY**	NA	250	Valdosta, GA	(18.8)
30	Modesto, CA	26.1	220	Rockford, IL	(13.4)	23	Vallejo-Fairfield, CA	32.4
213	Monroe, LA	(11.4)	167	Rockingham County, NH M.D.	(4.3)	NA	Victoria, TX**	NA
52	Monroe, MI	14.6	128	Rocky Mount, NC	0.8	NA	Vineland-Bridgeton, NJ**	NA
NA	Montgomery County, PA M.D.**	NA	216	Rome, GA	(12.3)	204	Virginia Beach-Norfolk, VA-NC	(10.6)
34	Montgomery, AL	24.0	69	Sacramento, CA	9.8	171	Visalia-Porterville, CA	(4.8)
NA	Morgantown, WV**	NA	165	Saginaw, MI	(3.9)	NA	Waco, TX**	NA
NA	Morristown, TN**	NA	3	Salem, OR	65.4	NA	Walla Walla, WA**	NA
163	Mount Vernon-Anacortes, WA	(3.8)	95	Salinas, CA	4.8	NA	Warner Robins, GA**	NA
100	Muncie, IN	4.3	NA	Salisbury, MD-DE**	NA	186	Warren-Troy, MI M.D.	(6.9)
36	Napa, CA	23.3	143	Salt Lake City, UT	(1.7)	239	Washington (greater) DC-VA-MD-WV	(16.2)
63	Naples-Marco Island, FL	10.8	85	San Antonio, TX	6.0	243	Washington, DC-VA-MD-WV M.D.	(16.7)
NA	Nashville-Davidson, TN**	NA	88	San Diego, CA	5.6	141	Waterloo-Cedar Falls, IA	(1.5)
NA	Nassau-Suffolk, NY M.D.**	NA	40	San Francisco (greater), CA	20.1	NA	Watertown-Fort Drum, NY**	NA
NA	New Bern, NC**	NA	22	San Francisco-Redwood, CA M.D.	32.8	183	Wausau, WI	(6.6)
209	New Haven-Milford, CT	(11.0)	5	San Jose, CA	59.3	189	West Palm Beach, FL M.D.	(7.4)
218	New Orleans, LA	(13.1)	148	San Luis Obispo, CA	(2.2)	NA	Wheeling, WV-OH**	NA
NA	New York (greater), NY-NJ-PA**	NA	NA	San Rafael, CA M.D.**	NA	82	Wichita Falls, TX	7.0
NA	New York-Jersey City, NY-NJ M.D.**	NA	49	Santa Cruz-Watsonville, CA	17.7	177	Wichita, KS	(5.6)
NA	Newark, NJ-PA M.D.**	NA	121	Santa Fe, NM	1.9	217	Williamsport, PA	(12.4)
231	North Port-Sarasota-Bradenton, FL	(14.5)	NA	Santa Maria-Santa Barbara, CA**	NA	35	Wilmington, DE-MD-NJ M.D.	23.8
37	Norwich-New London, CT	22.7	50	Santa Rosa, CA	16.5	NA	Wilmington, NC**	NA
44	Oakland-Hayward, CA M.D.	18.8	199	Savannah, GA	(9.2)	185	Winchester, VA-WV	(6.8)
248	Ocala, FL	(17.5)	225	Scranton--Wilkes-Barre, PA	(14.1)	NA	Winston-Salem, NC**	NA
53	Ocean City, NJ	14.1	125	Seattle (greater), WA	1.3	NA	Worcester, MA-CT**	NA
1	Odessa, TX	110.0	113	Seattle-Bellevue-Everett, WA M.D.	2.9	24	Yakima, WA	31.5
NA	Ogden-Clearfield, UT**	NA	192	Sebastian-Vero Beach, FL	(7.9)	267	York-Hanover, PA	(25.6)
94	Oklahoma City, OK	5.0	NA	Sebring, FL**	NA	NA	Youngstown-Warren, OH-PA**	NA
32	Olympia, WA	25.8	146	Sheboygan, WI	(2.0)	102	Yuba City, CA	4.1
119	Omaha-Council Bluffs, NE-IA	2.0	6	Sherman-Denison, TX	56.1	65	Yuma, AZ	10.2
166	Orlando, FL	(4.2)	NA	Shreveport-Bossier City, LA**	NA			
9	Oshkosh-Neenah, WI	49.4	NA	Sierra Vista-Douglas, AZ**	NA			

Source: CQ Press using reported data from the F.B.I. "Crime in the United States 2012"

*Motor vehicle theft includes the theft or attempted theft of a self-propelled vehicle. Excludes motorboats, construction equipment, airplanes, and farming equipment. **Not available.

39. Percent Change in Motor Vehicle Theft Rate: 2011 to 2012 (continued)
National Percent Change = 0.1% Decrease*

RANK	METROPOLITAN AREA	% CHANGE	RANK	METROPOLITAN AREA	% CHANGE	RANK	METROPOLITAN AREA	% CHANGE
1	Odessa, TX	110.0	65	Fort Wayne, IN	10.2	129	Crestview-Fort Walton Beach, FL	0.7
2	Redding, CA	66.5	65	Yuma, AZ	10.2	129	Lawrence, KS	0.7
3	Salem, OR	65.4	67	Fargo, ND-MN	10.1	131	Amarillo, TX	0.0
4	Lewiston-Auburn, ME	63.8	68	Burlington, NC	9.9	132	Detroit (greater), MI	(0.2)
5	San Jose, CA	59.3	69	Sacramento, CA	9.8	133	Los Angeles County, CA M.D.	(0.3)
6	Sherman-Denison, TX	56.1	70	Prescott, AZ	9.1	134	Atlanta, GA	(0.5)
7	Cumberland, MD-WV	52.4	71	Sioux Falls, SD	8.8	135	Abilene, TX	(0.6)
8	Logan, UT-ID	51.7	71	Springfield, MO	8.8	136	Florence, SC	(0.8)
9	Oshkosh-Neenah, WI	49.4	73	Cape Girardeau, MO-IL	8.5	137	Camden, NJ M.D.	(0.9)
10	Colorado Springs, CO	46.5	73	Lafayette, IN	8.5	138	Altoona, PA	(1.0)
11	Cheyenne, WY	45.9	75	Gainesville, GA	8.4	138	Ann Arbor, MI	(1.0)
12	Stockton-Lodi, CA	43.8	76	Duluth, MN-WI	8.0	140	Bangor, ME	(1.4)
13	Fairbanks, AK	40.7	77	Lebanon, PA	7.8	141	Corpus Christi, TX	(1.5)
14	Reno, NV	37.5	78	Dover, DE	7.6	141	Waterloo-Cedar Falls, IA	(1.5)
15	Oxnard-Thousand Oaks, CA	37.4	78	Punta Gorda, FL	7.6	143	Salt Lake City, UT	(1.7)
16	Canton, OH	37.2	80	Bremerton-Silverdale, WA	7.5	144	Boulder, CO	(1.8)
17	St. Joseph, MO-KS	37.1	81	Manchester-Nashua, NH	7.3	145	Las Vegas-Henderson, NV	(1.9)
18	Great Falls, MT	35.9	82	Johnstown, PA	7.0	146	El Centro, CA	(2.0)
19	Florence-Muscle Shoals, AL	33.6	82	Wichita Falls, TX	7.0	146	Sheboygan, WI	(2.0)
20	Casper, WY	33.2	84	Asheville, NC	6.6	148	San Luis Obispo, CA	(2.2)
21	Sumter, SC	32.9	85	Hartford, CT	6.0	149	Cleveland, TN	(2.3)
22	San Francisco-Redwood, CA M.D.	32.8	85	San Antonio, TX	6.0	150	Louisville, KY-IN	(2.4)
23	Vallejo-Fairfield, CA	32.4	87	Jefferson City, MO	5.7	150	Pittsburgh, PA	(2.4)
24	Yakima, WA	31.5	88	San Diego, CA	5.6	152	Lakeland, FL	(2.6)
25	Tallahassee, FL	30.4	89	Austin-Round Rock, TX	5.5	153	Champaign-Urbana, IL	(2.7)
26	Merced, CA	29.8	89	Durham-Chapel Hill, NC	5.5	154	Fresno, CA	(2.8)
27	Lake Havasu City-Kingman, AZ	29.2	91	Joplin, MO	5.4	155	Albuquerque, NM	(2.9)
28	Dubuque, IA	27.6	91	Springfield, IL	5.4	155	South Bend-Mishawaka, IN-MI	(2.9)
29	Bakersfield, CA	26.3	93	Bowling Green, KY	5.2	157	Lancaster, PA	(3.1)
30	Modesto, CA	26.1	94	Oklahoma City, OK	5.0	158	Athens-Clarke County, GA	(3.2)
31	Bay City, MI	25.9	95	Salinas, CA	4.8	158	Tacoma, WA M.D.	(3.2)
32	Olympia, WA	25.8	96	Trenton, NJ	4.7	160	Dothan, AL	(3.4)
33	Medford, OR	25.6	97	Harrisonburg, VA	4.6	161	Bloomington, IL	(3.5)
34	Montgomery, AL	24.0	97	Lubbock, TX	4.6	161	Chico, CA	(3.5)
35	Wilmington, DE-MD-NJ M.D.	23.8	97	Topeka, KS	4.6	163	Grand Forks, ND-MN	(3.8)
36	Napa, CA	23.3	100	Brownsville-Harlingen, TX	4.3	163	Mount Vernon-Anacortes, WA	(3.8)
37	Norwich-New London, CT	22.7	100	Muncie, IN	4.3	165	Saginaw, MI	(3.9)
38	Danville, IL	22.1	102	Yuba City, CA	4.1	166	Orlando, FL	(4.2)
39	Reading, PA	21.4	103	Columbia, MO	4.0	167	Des Moines-West Des Moines, IA	(4.3)
40	Anaheim-Santa Ana-Irvine, CA M.D.	20.1	103	Hickory, NC	4.0	167	Fayetteville, NC	(4.3)
40	San Francisco (greater), CA	20.1	103	Minneapolis-St. Paul, MN-WI	4.0	167	Rockingham County, NH M.D.	(4.3)
42	Billings, MT	19.7	106	Hanford-Corcoran, CA	3.9	170	Fort Lauderdale, FL M.D.	(4.4)
43	Farmington, NM	19.3	107	Iowa City, IA	3.8	171	Tampa-St Petersburg, FL	(4.8)
44	Oakland-Hayward, CA M.D.	18.8	108	Richmond, VA	3.4	171	Visalia-Porterville, CA	(4.8)
45	Riverside-San Bernardino, CA	18.7	109	Bellingham, WA	3.3	173	Baltimore, MD	(5.2)
46	Grand Junction, CO	18.6	109	Houma, LA	3.3	174	Tulsa, OK	(5.4)
47	Owensboro, KY	18.5	111	Erie, PA	3.0	175	Greeley, CO	(5.5)
48	Cedar Rapids, IA	18.3	111	Pueblo, CO	3.0	175	Mankato-North Mankato, MN	(5.5)
49	Santa Cruz-Watsonville, CA	17.7	113	Seattle-Bellevue-Everett, WA M.D.	2.9	177	Wichita, KS	(5.6)
50	Santa Rosa, CA	16.5	114	Detroit-Dearborn-Livonia, MI M.D.	2.4	178	Auburn, AL	(5.8)
51	Missoula, MT	15.1	114	Milwaukee, WI	2.4	178	Tyler, TX	(5.8)
52	Monroe, MI	14.6	116	Johnson City, TN	2.2	180	Beaumont-Port Arthur, TX	(5.9)
53	Ocean City, NJ	14.1	116	Los Angeles (greater), CA	2.2	181	Mansfield, OH	(6.0)
54	Cape Coral-Fort Myers, FL	13.5	116	St. Louis, MO-IL	2.2	182	Tucson, AZ	(6.2)
55	Palm Bay-Melbourne, FL	13.2	119	Kankakee, IL	2.0	183	Wausau, WI	(6.6)
55	Portland-Vancouver, OR-WA	13.2	119	Omaha-Council Bluffs, NE-IA	2.0	184	Pensacola, FL	(6.7)
57	Lansing-East Lansing, MI	13.0	121	Dayton, OH	1.9	185	Winchester, VA-WV	(6.8)
58	Bismarck, ND	12.5	121	Santa Fe, NM	1.9	186	Warren-Troy, MI M.D.	(6.9)
59	Carson City, NV	12.2	123	Albany, GA	1.5	187	Goldsboro, NC	(7.2)
59	Kingsport, TN-VA	12.2	123	Little Rock, AR	1.5	188	Eugene, OR	(7.3)
61	Madera, CA	11.6	125	Green Bay, WI	1.3	189	Fort Worth-Arlington, TX M.D.	(7.4)
62	Houston, TX	11.5	125	Seattle (greater), WA	1.3	189	West Palm Beach, FL M.D.	(7.4)
63	Naples-Marco Island, FL	10.8	127	Flagstaff, AZ	1.1	191	Longview, TX	(7.6)
64	Janesville, WI	10.7	128	Rocky Mount, NC	0.8	192	Roanoke, VA	(7.9)

Note: All listings are for Metropolitan Statistical Areas (M.S.A.s) except for those ending with "M.D." Listings with "M.D." are Metropolitan Divisions which are smaller parts of eleven large M.S.A.s. See explanatory note at beginning of metropolitan area section.

RANK	METROPOLITAN AREA	% CHANGE	RANK	METROPOLITAN AREA	% CHANGE	RANK	METROPOLITAN AREA	% CHANGE
192	Sebastian-Vero Beach, FL	(7.9)	256	Lynchburg, VA	(21.2)	NA	Kalamazoo-Portage, MI**	NA
194	Racine, WI	(8.1)	258	Corvallis, OR	(22.4)	NA	Kansas City, MO-KS**	NA
195	Augusta, GA-SC	(8.6)	258	El Paso, TX	(22.4)	NA	Kingston, NY**	NA
195	Fort Collins, CO	(8.6)	260	Appleton, WI	(22.9)	NA	Knoxville, TN**	NA
197	Terre Haute, IN	(8.7)	260	Longview, WA	(22.9)	NA	Kokomo, IN**	NA
198	Huntsville, AL	(8.9)	262	Anniston-Oxford, AL	(23.3)	NA	Lafayette, LA**	NA
199	Raleigh, NC	(9.2)	263	La Crosse, WI-MN	(23.7)	NA	Lawton, OK**	NA
199	Savannah, GA	(9.2)	264	State College, PA	(24.3)	NA	Lewiston, ID-WA**	NA
201	Atlantic City, NJ	(9.4)	265	Decatur, IL	(24.5)	NA	Lexington-Fayette, KY**	NA
202	Boise City, ID	(9.6)	266	Lima, OH	(24.6)	NA	Madison, WI**	NA
203	Killeen-Temple, TX	(10.5)	267	York-Hanover, PA	(25.6)	NA	Manhattan, KS**	NA
204	Dallas (greater), TX	(10.6)	268	Idaho Falls, ID	(25.9)	NA	Midland, MI**	NA
204	Virginia Beach-Norfolk, VA-NC	(10.6)	269	Harrisburg-Carlisle, PA	(26.3)	NA	Midland, TX**	NA
206	Chicago (greater), IL-IN-WI	(10.9)	270	Hinesville, GA	(28.3)	NA	Montgomery County, PA M.D.**	NA
206	Davenport, IA-IL	(10.9)	271	Flint, MI	(31.1)	NA	Morgantown, WV**	NA
206	Las Cruces, NM	(10.9)	272	Pine Bluff, AR	(32.3)	NA	Morristown, TN**	NA
209	Miami (greater), FL	(11.0)	273	Dalton, GA	(32.5)	NA	Nashville-Davidson, TN**	NA
209	New Haven-Milford, CT	(11.0)	274	Michigan City-La Porte, IN	(34.5)	NA	Nassau-Suffolk, NY M.D.**	NA
211	College Station-Bryan, TX	(11.1)	275	Ames, IA	(38.0)	NA	New Bern, NC**	NA
212	Springfield, OH	(11.3)	NA	Albany-Schenectady-Troy, NY**	NA	NA	New York (greater), NY-NJ-PA**	NA
213	Monroe, LA	(11.4)	NA	Albany, OR**	NA	NA	New York-Jersey City, NY-NJ M.D.**	NA
214	Dallas-Plano-Irving, TX M.D.	(11.6)	NA	Alexandria, LA**	NA	NA	Newark, NJ-PA M.D.**	NA
215	Port St. Lucie, FL	(11.8)	NA	Allentown, PA-NJ**	NA	NA	Ogden-Clearfield, UT**	NA
216	Rome, GA	(12.3)	NA	Anchorage, AK**	NA	NA	Panama City, FL**	NA
217	Williamsport, PA	(12.4)	NA	Baton Rouge, LA**	NA	NA	Parkersburg-Vienna, WV**	NA
218	Gary, IN M.D.	(13.1)	NA	Beckley, WV**	NA	NA	Philadelphia (greater) PA-NJ-MD-DE**	NA
218	New Orleans, LA	(13.1)	NA	Binghamton, NY**	NA	NA	Philadelphia, PA M.D.**	NA
220	Charlottesville, VA	(13.4)	NA	Bloomington, IN**	NA	NA	Phoenix-Mesa-Scottsdale, AZ**	NA
220	Rockford, IL	(13.4)	NA	Bloomsburg-Berwick, PA**	NA	NA	Pocatello, ID**	NA
222	Akron, OH	(13.6)	NA	Boston (greater), MA-NH**	NA	NA	Providence-Warwick, RI-MA**	NA
222	Jonesboro, AR	(13.6)	NA	Boston, MA M.D.**	NA	NA	Rapid City, SD**	NA
224	Columbus, IN	(14.0)	NA	Buffalo-Niagara Falls, NY**	NA	NA	Rochester, MN**	NA
225	Peoria, IL	(14.1)	NA	California-Lexington Park, MD**	NA	NA	Rochester, NY**	NA
225	Scranton--Wilkes-Barre, PA	(14.1)	NA	Cambridge-Newton, MA M.D.**	NA	NA	Salisbury, MD-DE**	NA
225	Silver Spring-Frederick, MD M.D.	(14.1)	NA	Chambersburg-Waynesboro, PA**	NA	NA	San Rafael, CA M.D.**	NA
228	Gadsden, AL	(14.2)	NA	Charleston-North Charleston, SC**	NA	NA	Santa Maria-Santa Barbara, CA**	NA
228	Pittsfield, MA	(14.2)	NA	Chicago-Joilet-Naperville, IL M.D.**	NA	NA	Sebring, FL**	NA
230	Lincoln, NE	(14.4)	NA	Cincinnati, OH-KY-IN**	NA	NA	Shreveport-Bossier City, LA**	NA
231	North Port-Sarasota-Bradenton, FL	(14.5)	NA	Coeur d'Alene, ID**	NA	NA	Sierra Vista-Douglas, AZ**	NA
232	Miami-Dade County, FL M.D.	(14.8)	NA	Daphne-Fairhope-Foley, AL**	NA	NA	Sioux City, IA-NE-SD**	NA
233	Macon, GA	(14.9)	NA	Deltona-Daytona Beach, FL**	NA	NA	Spartanburg, SC**	NA
234	Jacksonville, FL	(15.1)	NA	Denver-Aurora, CO**	NA	NA	Spokane, WA**	NA
235	Memphis, TN-MS-AR	(15.3)	NA	Dutchess-Putnam, NY M.D.**	NA	NA	Springfield, MA**	NA
236	Lake Co.-Kenosha Co., IL-WI M.D.	(15.5)	NA	East Stroudsburg, PA**	NA	NA	Staunton-Waynesboro, VA**	NA
237	Fond du Lac, WI	(15.8)	NA	Elgin, IL M.D.**	NA	NA	St. George, UT**	NA
238	Kennewick-Richland, WA	(16.0)	NA	Elizabethtown-Fort Knox, KY**	NA	NA	Syracuse, NY**	NA
239	Clarksville, TN-KY	(16.2)	NA	Elmira, NY**	NA	NA	Texarkana, TX-AR**	NA
239	Washington (greater) DC-VA-MD-WV	(16.2)	NA	Fayetteville-Springdale, AR-MO**	NA	NA	The Villages, FL**	NA
241	McAllen-Edinburg-Mission, TX	(16.3)	NA	Fort Smith, AR-OK**	NA	NA	Toledo, OH**	NA
242	Gainesville, FL	(16.5)	NA	Gettysburg, PA**	NA	NA	Tuscaloosa, AL**	NA
243	Bridgeport-Stamford, CT	(16.7)	NA	Glens Falls, NY**	NA	NA	Utica-Rome, NY**	NA
243	Washington, DC-VA-MD-WV M.D.	(16.7)	NA	Grand Island, NE**	NA	NA	Victoria, TX**	NA
245	Brunswick, GA	(16.8)	NA	Greensboro-High Point, NC**	NA	NA	Vineland-Bridgeton, NJ**	NA
246	Blacksburg, VA	(17.3)	NA	Greenville-Anderson, SC**	NA	NA	Waco, TX**	NA
247	Columbus, GA-AL	(17.4)	NA	Greenville, NC**	NA	NA	Walla Walla, WA**	NA
248	Ocala, FL	(17.5)	NA	Hagerstown-Martinsburg, MD-WV**	NA	NA	Warner Robins, GA**	NA
249	Barnstable Town, MA	(18.4)	NA	Hammond, LA**	NA	NA	Watertown-Fort Drum, NY**	NA
250	Valdosta, GA	(18.8)	NA	Hattiesburg, MS**	NA	NA	Wheeling, WV-OH**	NA
251	Portland, ME	(18.9)	NA	Hilton Head Island, SC**	NA	NA	Wilmington, NC**	NA
252	Mobile, AL	(19.1)	NA	Homosassa Springs, FL**	NA	NA	Winston-Salem, NC**	NA
252	Provo-Orem, UT	(19.1)	NA	Indianapolis, IN**	NA	NA	Worcester, MA-CT**	NA
254	Decatur, AL	(20.4)	NA	Jackson, MS**	NA	NA	Youngstown-Warren, OH-PA**	NA
255	Laredo, TX	(20.8)	NA	Jackson, TN**	NA			
256	Birmingham-Hoover, AL	(21.2)	NA	Kahului-Wailuku-Lahaina, HI**	NA			

Source: CQ Press using reported data from the F.B.I. "Crime in the United States 2012"
*Motor vehicle theft includes the theft or attempted theft of a self-propelled vehicle. Excludes motorboats, construction equipment, airplanes, and farming equipment. **Not available.

40. Percent Change in Motor Vehicle Theft Rate: 2008 to 2012
National Percent Change = 27.2% Decrease*

RANK	METROPOLITAN AREA	% CHANGE	RANK	METROPOLITAN AREA	% CHANGE	RANK	METROPOLITAN AREA	% CHANGE
127	Abilene, TX	(27.1)	53	Cheyenne, WY	(6.5)	NA	Gary, IN M.D.**	NA
137	Akron, OH	(28.4)	NA	Chicago (greater), IL-IN-WI**	NA	NA	Gettysburg, PA**	NA
NA	Albany-Schenectady-Troy, NY**	NA	NA	Chicago-Joilet-Naperville, IL M.D.**	NA	NA	Glens Falls, NY**	NA
NA	Albany, GA**	NA	122	Chico, CA	(25.6)	219	Goldsboro, NC	(44.2)
NA	Albany, OR**	NA	NA	Cincinnati, OH-KY-IN**	NA	88	Grand Forks, ND-MN	(17.4)
220	Albuquerque, NM	(44.3)	178	Clarksville, TN-KY	(37.2)	NA	Grand Island, NE**	NA
NA	Alexandria, LA**	NA	61	Cleveland, TN	(9.1)	100	Grand Junction, CO	(20.1)
NA	Allentown, PA-NJ**	NA	NA	Coeur d'Alene, ID**	NA	37	Great Falls, MT	1.6
144	Altoona, PA	(30.1)	251	College Station-Bryan, TX	(56.6)	154	Greeley, CO	(32.0)
98	Amarillo, TX	(20.0)	9	Colorado Springs, CO	38.8	176	Green Bay, WI	(36.9)
248	Ames, IA	(53.9)	50	Columbia, MO	(5.3)	223	Greensboro-High Point, NC	(45.4)
52	Anaheim-Santa Ana-Irvine, CA M.D.	(6.2)	225	Columbus, GA-AL	(45.6)	NA	Greenville-Anderson, SC**	NA
NA	Anchorage, AK**	NA	4	Columbus, IN	75.1	252	Greenville, NC	(57.9)
132	Ann Arbor, MI	(28.0)	166	Corpus Christi, TX	(35.2)	NA	Hagerstown-Martinsburg, MD-WV**	NA
NA	Anniston-Oxford, AL**	NA	232	Corvallis, OR	(47.8)	NA	Hammond, LA**	NA
240	Appleton, WI	(49.7)	NA	Crestview-Fort Walton Beach, FL**	NA	105	Hanford-Corcoran, CA	(20.9)
92	Asheville, NC	(18.0)	25	Cumberland, MD-WV	13.0	134	Harrisburg-Carlisle, PA	(28.3)
194	Athens-Clarke County, GA	(39.7)	178	Dallas (greater), TX	(37.2)	185	Harrisonburg, VA	(37.8)
117	Atlanta, GA	(24.9)	192	Dallas-Plano-Irving, TX M.D.	(39.4)	156	Hartford, CT	(33.2)
162	Atlantic City, NJ	(34.6)	96	Dalton, GA	(19.4)	NA	Hattiesburg, MS**	NA
214	Auburn, AL	(43.5)	NA	Danville, IL**	NA	153	Hickory, NC	(31.9)
138	Augusta, GA-SC	(28.6)	NA	Daphne-Fairhope-Foley, AL**	NA	NA	Hilton Head Island, SC**	NA
107	Austin-Round Rock, TX	(21.2)	NA	Davenport, IA-IL**	NA	118	Hinesville, GA	(25.1)
27	Bakersfield, CA	11.7	163	Dayton, OH	(34.9)	NA	Homosassa Springs, FL**	NA
186	Baltimore, MD	(38.0)	24	Decatur, AL	13.2	134	Houma, LA	(28.3)
77	Bangor, ME	(14.0)	NA	Decatur, IL**	NA	79	Houston, TX	(14.7)
141	Barnstable Town, MA	(29.5)	163	Deltona-Daytona Beach, FL	(34.9)	182	Huntsville, AL	(37.7)
NA	Baton Rouge, LA**	NA	NA	Denver-Aurora, CO**	NA	174	Idaho Falls, ID	(36.8)
172	Bay City, MI	(36.5)	41	Des Moines-West Des Moines, IA	(0.6)	149	Indianapolis, IN	(31.3)
119	Beaumont-Port Arthur, TX	(25.3)	NA	Detroit (greater), MI**	NA	144	Iowa City, IA	(30.1)
NA	Beckley, WV**	NA	NA	Detroit-Dearborn-Livonia, MI M.D.**	NA	253	Jacksonville, FL	(59.6)
196	Bellingham, WA	(39.9)	109	Dothan, AL	(21.3)	NA	Jackson, MS**	NA
10	Billings, MT	37.7	217	Dover, DE	(44.1)	NA	Jackson, TN**	NA
NA	Binghamton, NY**	NA	111	Dubuque, IA	(22.6)	224	Janesville, WI	(45.5)
221	Birmingham-Hoover, AL	(44.7)	74	Duluth, MN-WI	(13.0)	NA	Jefferson City, MO**	NA
14	Bismarck, ND	26.2	151	Durham-Chapel Hill, NC	(31.5)	58	Johnson City, TN	(8.9)
205	Blacksburg, VA	(42.1)	NA	Dutchess-Putnam, NY M.D.**	NA	79	Johnstown, PA	(14.7)
NA	Bloomington, IL**	NA	NA	East Stroudsburg, PA**	NA	125	Jonesboro, AR	(26.9)
28	Bloomington, IN	10.8	177	El Centro, CA	(37.0)	44	Joplin, MO	(3.1)
NA	Bloomsburg-Berwick, PA**	NA	255	El Paso, TX	(61.2)	NA	Kahului-Wailuku-Lahaina, HI**	NA
197	Boise City, ID	(40.3)	NA	Elgin, IL M.D.**	NA	188	Kalamazoo-Portage, MI	(38.2)
NA	Boston (greater), MA-NH**	NA	NA	Elizabethtown-Fort Knox, KY**	NA	NA	Kankakee, IL**	NA
NA	Boston, MA M.D.**	NA	NA	Elmira, NY**	NA	NA	Kansas City, MO-KS**	NA
NA	Boulder, CO**	NA	111	Erie, PA	(22.6)	83	Kennewick-Richland, WA	(16.0)
44	Bowling Green, KY	(3.1)	254	Eugene, OR	(60.6)	181	Killeen-Temple, TX	(37.3)
2	Bremerton-Silverdale, WA	84.7	NA	Fairbanks, AK**	NA	121	Kingsport, TN-VA	(25.5)
144	Bridgeport-Stamford, CT	(30.1)	157	Fargo, ND-MN	(33.3)	NA	Kingston, NY**	NA
201	Brownsville-Harlingen, TX	(41.6)	158	Farmington, NM	(33.5)	NA	Knoxville, TN**	NA
NA	Brunswick, GA**	NA	54	Fayetteville-Springdale, AR-MO	(6.7)	NA	Kokomo, IN**	NA
NA	Buffalo-Niagara Falls, NY**	NA	148	Fayetteville, NC	(30.8)	206	La Crosse, WI-MN	(42.2)
70	Burlington, NC	(12.4)	101	Flagstaff, AZ	(20.2)	56	Lafayette, IN	(8.4)
NA	California-Lexington Park, MD**	NA	209	Flint, MI	(42.5)	NA	Lafayette, LA**	NA
NA	Cambridge-Newton, MA M.D.**	NA	32	Florence-Muscle Shoals, AL	9.0	NA	Lake Co.-Kenosha Co., IL-WI M.D.**	NA
127	Camden, NJ M.D.	(27.1)	169	Florence, SC	(35.5)	89	Lake Havasu City-Kingman, AZ	(17.5)
NA	Canton, OH**	NA	130	Fond du Lac, WI	(27.2)	246	Lakeland, FL	(53.0)
201	Cape Coral-Fort Myers, FL	(41.6)	204	Fort Collins, CO	(41.9)	178	Lancaster, PA	(37.2)
3	Cape Girardeau, MO-IL	78.9	149	Fort Lauderdale, FL M.D.	(31.3)	84	Lansing-East Lansing, MI	(16.6)
116	Carson City, NV	(24.6)	NA	Fort Smith, AR-OK**	NA	256	Laredo, TX	(78.7)
86	Casper, WY	(17.3)	159	Fort Wayne, IN	(34.1)	104	Las Cruces, NM	(20.5)
131	Cedar Rapids, IA	(27.5)	143	Fort Worth-Arlington, TX M.D.	(29.9)	222	Las Vegas-Henderson, NV	(44.8)
NA	Chambersburg-Waynesboro, PA**	NA	29	Fresno, CA	9.9	42	Lawrence, KS	(0.8)
NA	Champaign-Urbana, IL**	NA	11	Gadsden, AL	37.3	NA	Lawton, OK**	NA
173	Charleston-North Charleston, SC	(36.7)	231	Gainesville, FL	(47.6)	90	Lebanon, PA	(17.6)
206	Charlottesville, VA	(42.2)	NA	Gainesville, GA**	NA	40	Lewiston-Auburn, ME	0.2

Note: All listings are for Metropolitan Statistical Areas (M.S.A.s) except for those ending with "M.D." Listings with "M.D." are Metropolitan Divisions which are smaller parts of eleven large M.S.A.s. See explanatory note at beginning of metropolitan area section.

RANK	METROPOLITAN AREA	% CHANGE	RANK	METROPOLITAN AREA	% CHANGE	RANK	METROPOLITAN AREA	% CHANGE
6	Lewiston, ID-WA	52.3	NA	Owensboro, KY**	NA	249	Silver Spring-Frederick, MD M.D.	(54.2)
NA	Lexington-Fayette, KY**	NA	43	Oxnard-Thousand Oaks, CA	(1.8)	NA	Sioux City, IA-NE-SD**	NA
232	Lima, OH	(47.8)	163	Palm Bay-Melbourne, FL	(34.9)	26	Sioux Falls, SD	12.8
72	Lincoln, NE	(12.6)	NA	Panama City, FL**	NA	189	South Bend-Mishawaka, IN-MI	(38.7)
62	Little Rock, AR	(9.4)	NA	Parkersburg-Vienna, WV**	NA	NA	Spartanburg, SC**	NA
16	Logan, UT-ID	25.9	97	Pensacola, FL	(19.8)	22	Spokane, WA	16.3
189	Longview, TX	(38.7)	NA	Peoria, IL**	NA	NA	Springfield, IL**	NA
152	Longview, WA	(31.7)	NA	Philadelphia (greater) PA-NJ-MD-DE**	NA	NA	Springfield, MA**	NA
140	Los Angeles County, CA M.D.	(29.1)	NA	Philadelphia, PA M.D.**	NA	38	Springfield, MO	1.0
124	Los Angeles (greater), CA	(26.6)	NA	Phoenix-Mesa-Scottsdale, AZ**	NA	237	Springfield, OH	(48.9)
86	Louisville, KY-IN	(17.3)	238	Pine Bluff, AR	(49.1)	200	State College, PA	(40.8)
31	Lubbock, TX	9.1	230	Pittsburgh, PA	(47.2)	NA	Staunton-Waynesboro, VA**	NA
236	Lynchburg, VA	(48.8)	82	Pittsfield, MA	(15.6)	47	Stockton-Lodi, CA	(3.9)
187	Macon, GA	(38.1)	NA	Pocatello, ID**	NA	133	St. George, UT	(28.1)
17	Madera, CA	23.1	155	Port St. Lucie, FL	(32.9)	5	St. Joseph, MO-KS	52.9
NA	Madison, WI**	NA	55	Portland-Vancouver, OR-WA	(7.4)	161	St. Louis, MO-IL	(34.3)
NA	Manchester-Nashua, NH**	NA	113	Portland, ME	(23.3)	67	Sumter, SC	(11.5)
NA	Manhattan, KS**	NA	105	Prescott, AZ	(20.9)	NA	Syracuse, NY**	NA
115	Mankato-North Mankato, MN	(23.8)	102	Providence-Warwick, RI-MA	(20.4)	NA	Tacoma, WA M.D.**	NA
33	Mansfield, OH	8.7	166	Provo-Orem, UT	(35.2)	64	Tallahassee, FL	(10.2)
250	McAllen-Edinburg-Mission, TX	(55.3)	NA	Pueblo, CO**	NA	245	Tampa-St Petersburg, FL	(52.9)
13	Medford, OR	29.0	240	Punta Gorda, FL	(49.7)	NA	Terre Haute, IN**	NA
227	Memphis, TN-MS-AR	(46.4)	194	Racine, WI	(39.7)	NA	Texarkana, TX-AR**	NA
20	Merced, CA	17.4	127	Raleigh, NC	(27.1)	NA	The Villages, FL**	NA
209	Miami (greater), FL	(42.5)	NA	Rapid City, SD**	NA	NA	Toledo, OH**	NA
226	Miami-Dade County, FL M.D.	(46.1)	166	Reading, PA	(35.2)	75	Topeka, KS	(13.4)
203	Michigan City-La Porte, IN	(41.8)	1	Redding, CA	103.8	91	Trenton, NJ	(17.9)
NA	Midland, MI**	NA	95	Reno, NV	(19.2)	243	Tucson, AZ	(51.8)
NA	Midland, TX**	NA	147	Richmond, VA	(30.5)	49	Tulsa, OK	(4.7)
134	Milwaukee, WI	(28.3)	51	Riverside-San Bernardino, CA	(5.9)	NA	Tuscaloosa, AL**	NA
102	Minneapolis-St. Paul, MN-WI	(20.4)	110	Roanoke, VA	(22.3)	142	Tyler, TX	(29.8)
69	Missoula, MT	(11.9)	NA	Rochester, MN**	NA	NA	Utica-Rome, NY**	NA
213	Mobile, AL	(43.1)	NA	Rochester, NY**	NA	242	Valdosta, GA	(50.7)
36	Modesto, CA	2.2	NA	Rockford, IL**	NA	58	Vallejo-Fairfield, CA	(8.9)
216	Monroe, LA	(43.8)	93	Rockingham County, NH M.D.	(18.7)	NA	Victoria, TX**	NA
18	Monroe, MI	20.7	NA	Rocky Mount, NC**	NA	171	Vineland-Bridgeton, NJ	(36.1)
NA	Montgomery County, PA M.D.**	NA	NA	Rome, GA**	NA	170	Virginia Beach-Norfolk, VA-NC	(36.0)
30	Montgomery, AL	9.4	81	Sacramento, CA	(15.1)	182	Visalia-Porterville, CA	(37.7)
NA	Morgantown, WV**	NA	217	Saginaw, MI	(44.1)	NA	Waco, TX**	NA
NA	Morristown, TN**	NA	35	Salem, OR	3.1	NA	Walla Walla, WA**	NA
123	Mount Vernon-Anacortes, WA	(26.1)	65	Salinas, CA	(10.7)	NA	Warner Robins, GA**	NA
19	Muncie, IN	17.7	NA	Salisbury, MD-DE**	NA	NA	Warren-Troy, MI M.D.**	NA
46	Napa, CA	(3.7)	85	Salt Lake City, UT	(16.7)	235	Washington (greater) DC-VA-MD-WV	(48.7)
126	Naples-Marco Island, FL	(27.0)	119	San Antonio, TX	(25.3)	234	Washington, DC-VA-MD-WV M.D.	(48.3)
NA	Nashville-Davidson, TN**	NA	211	San Diego, CA	(42.9)	199	Waterloo-Cedar Falls, IA	(40.7)
NA	Nassau-Suffolk, NY M.D.**	NA	78	San Francisco (greater), CA	(14.4)	NA	Watertown-Fort Drum, NY**	NA
NA	New Bern, NC**	NA	67	San Francisco-Redwood, CA M.D.	(11.5)	114	Wausau, WI	(23.5)
NA	New Haven-Milford, CT**	NA	8	San Jose, CA	43.3	227	West Palm Beach, FL M.D.	(46.4)
211	New Orleans, LA	(42.9)	23	San Luis Obispo, CA	16.1	182	Wheeling, WV-OH	(37.7)
NA	New York (greater), NY-NJ-PA**	NA	NA	San Rafael, CA M.D.**	NA	243	Wichita Falls, TX	(51.8)
NA	New York-Jersey City, NY-NJ M.D.**	NA	12	Santa Cruz-Watsonville, CA	30.9	63	Wichita, KS	(9.7)
NA	Newark, NJ-PA M.D.**	NA	21	Santa Fe, NM	17.1	57	Williamsport, PA	(8.6)
NA	North Port-Sarasota-Bradenton, FL**	NA	NA	Santa Maria-Santa Barbara, CA**	NA	138	Wilmington, DE-MD-NJ M.D.	(28.6)
48	Norwich-New London, CT	(4.5)	93	Santa Rosa, CA	(18.7)	NA	Wilmington, NC**	NA
75	Oakland-Hayward, CA M.D.	(13.4)	239	Savannah, GA	(49.3)	215	Winchester, VA-WV	(43.6)
246	Ocala, FL	(53.0)	107	Scranton--Wilkes-Barre, PA	(21.2)	NA	Winston-Salem, NC**	NA
98	Ocean City, NJ	(20.0)	NA	Seattle (greater), WA**	NA	159	Worcester, MA-CT	(34.1)
15	Odessa, TX	26.1	NA	Seattle-Bellevue-Everett, WA M.D.**	NA	73	Yakima, WA	(12.7)
NA	Ogden-Clearfield, UT**	NA	174	Sebastian-Vero Beach, FL	(36.8)	229	York-Hanover, PA	(47.0)
34	Oklahoma City, OK	4.9	NA	Sebring, FL**	NA	208	Youngstown-Warren, OH-PA	(42.4)
70	Olympia, WA	(12.4)	65	Sheboygan, WI	(10.7)	60	Yuba City, CA	(9.0)
39	Omaha-Council Bluffs, NE-IA	0.6	7	Sherman-Denison, TX	50.5	191	Yuma, AZ	(38.9)
198	Orlando, FL	(40.6)	NA	Shreveport-Bossier City, LA**	NA			
193	Oshkosh-Neenah, WI	(39.5)	NA	Sierra Vista-Douglas, AZ**	NA			

Source: CQ Press using reported data from the F.B.I. "Crime in the United States 2012"

*Motor vehicle theft includes the theft or attempted theft of a self-propelled vehicle. Excludes motorboats, construction equipment, airplanes, and farming equipment. **Not available.

40. Percent Change in Motor Vehicle Theft Rate: 2008 to 2012 (continued)
National Percent Change = 27.2% Decrease*

RANK	METROPOLITAN AREA	% CHANGE	RANK	METROPOLITAN AREA	% CHANGE	RANK	METROPOLITAN AREA	% CHANGE
1	Redding, CA	103.8	65	Salinas, CA	(10.7)	127	Raleigh, NC	(27.1)
2	Bremerton-Silverdale, WA	84.7	65	Sheboygan, WI	(10.7)	130	Fond du Lac, WI	(27.2)
3	Cape Girardeau, MO-IL	78.9	67	San Francisco-Redwood, CA M.D.	(11.5)	131	Cedar Rapids, IA	(27.5)
4	Columbus, IN	75.1	67	Sumter, SC	(11.5)	132	Ann Arbor, MI	(28.0)
5	St. Joseph, MO-KS	52.9	69	Missoula, MT	(11.9)	133	St. George, UT	(28.1)
6	Lewiston, ID-WA	52.3	70	Burlington, NC	(12.4)	134	Harrisburg-Carlisle, PA	(28.3)
7	Sherman-Denison, TX	50.5	70	Olympia, WA	(12.4)	134	Houma, LA	(28.3)
8	San Jose, CA	43.3	72	Lincoln, NE	(12.6)	134	Milwaukee, WI	(28.3)
9	Colorado Springs, CO	38.8	73	Yakima, WA	(12.7)	137	Akron, OH	(28.4)
10	Billings, MT	37.7	74	Duluth, MN-WI	(13.0)	138	Augusta, GA-SC	(28.6)
11	Gadsden, AL	37.3	75	Oakland-Hayward, CA M.D.	(13.4)	138	Wilmington, DE-MD-NJ M.D.	(28.6)
12	Santa Cruz-Watsonville, CA	30.9	75	Topeka, KS	(13.4)	140	Los Angeles County, CA M.D.	(29.1)
13	Medford, OR	29.0	77	Bangor, ME	(14.0)	141	Barnstable Town, MA	(29.5)
14	Bismarck, ND	26.2	78	San Francisco (greater), CA	(14.4)	142	Tyler, TX	(29.8)
15	Odessa, TX	26.1	79	Houston, TX	(14.7)	143	Fort Worth-Arlington, TX M.D.	(29.9)
16	Logan, UT-ID	25.9	79	Johnstown, PA	(14.7)	144	Altoona, PA	(30.1)
17	Madera, CA	23.1	81	Sacramento, CA	(15.1)	144	Bridgeport-Stamford, CT	(30.1)
18	Monroe, MI	20.7	82	Pittsfield, MA	(15.6)	144	Iowa City, IA	(30.1)
19	Muncie, IN	17.7	83	Kennewick-Richland, WA	(16.0)	147	Richmond, VA	(30.5)
20	Merced, CA	17.4	84	Lansing-East Lansing, MI	(16.6)	148	Fayetteville, NC	(30.8)
21	Santa Fe, NM	17.1	85	Salt Lake City, UT	(16.7)	149	Fort Lauderdale, FL M.D.	(31.3)
22	Spokane, WA	16.3	86	Casper, WY	(17.3)	149	Indianapolis, IN	(31.3)
23	San Luis Obispo, CA	16.1	86	Louisville, KY-IN	(17.3)	151	Durham-Chapel Hill, NC	(31.5)
24	Decatur, AL	13.2	88	Grand Forks, ND-MN	(17.4)	152	Longview, WA	(31.7)
25	Cumberland, MD-WV	13.0	89	Lake Havasu City-Kingman, AZ	(17.5)	153	Hickory, NC	(31.9)
26	Sioux Falls, SD	12.8	90	Lebanon, PA	(17.6)	154	Greeley, CO	(32.0)
27	Bakersfield, CA	11.7	91	Trenton, NJ	(17.9)	155	Port St. Lucie, FL	(32.9)
28	Bloomington, IN	10.8	92	Asheville, NC	(18.0)	156	Hartford, CT	(33.2)
29	Fresno, CA	9.9	93	Rockingham County, NH M.D.	(18.7)	157	Fargo, ND-MN	(33.3)
30	Montgomery, AL	9.4	93	Santa Rosa, CA	(18.7)	158	Farmington, NM	(33.5)
31	Lubbock, TX	9.1	95	Reno, NV	(19.2)	159	Fort Wayne, IN	(34.1)
32	Florence-Muscle Shoals, AL	9.0	96	Dalton, GA	(19.4)	159	Worcester, MA-CT	(34.1)
33	Mansfield, OH	8.7	97	Pensacola, FL	(19.8)	161	St. Louis, MO-IL	(34.3)
34	Oklahoma City, OK	4.9	98	Amarillo, TX	(20.0)	162	Atlantic City, NJ	(34.6)
35	Salem, OR	3.1	98	Ocean City, NJ	(20.0)	163	Dayton, OH	(34.9)
36	Modesto, CA	2.2	100	Grand Junction, CO	(20.1)	163	Deltona-Daytona Beach, FL	(34.9)
37	Great Falls, MT	1.6	101	Flagstaff, AZ	(20.2)	163	Palm Bay-Melbourne, FL	(34.9)
38	Springfield, MO	1.0	102	Minneapolis-St. Paul, MN-WI	(20.4)	166	Corpus Christi, TX	(35.2)
39	Omaha-Council Bluffs, NE-IA	0.6	102	Providence-Warwick, RI-MA	(20.4)	166	Provo-Orem, UT	(35.2)
40	Lewiston-Auburn, ME	0.2	104	Las Cruces, NM	(20.5)	166	Reading, PA	(35.2)
41	Des Moines-West Des Moines, IA	(0.6)	105	Hanford-Corcoran, CA	(20.9)	169	Florence, SC	(35.5)
42	Lawrence, KS	(0.8)	105	Prescott, AZ	(20.9)	170	Virginia Beach-Norfolk, VA-NC	(36.0)
43	Oxnard-Thousand Oaks, CA	(1.8)	107	Austin-Round Rock, TX	(21.2)	171	Vineland-Bridgeton, NJ	(36.1)
44	Bowling Green, KY	(3.1)	107	Scranton--Wilkes-Barre, PA	(21.2)	172	Bay City, MI	(36.5)
44	Joplin, MO	(3.1)	109	Dothan, AL	(21.3)	173	Charleston-North Charleston, SC	(36.7)
46	Napa, CA	(3.7)	110	Roanoke, VA	(22.3)	174	Idaho Falls, ID	(36.8)
47	Stockton-Lodi, CA	(3.9)	111	Dubuque, IA	(22.6)	174	Sebastian-Vero Beach, FL	(36.8)
48	Norwich-New London, CT	(4.5)	111	Erie, PA	(22.6)	176	Green Bay, WI	(36.9)
49	Tulsa, OK	(4.7)	113	Portland, ME	(23.3)	177	El Centro, CA	(37.0)
50	Columbia, MO	(5.3)	114	Wausau, WI	(23.5)	178	Clarksville, TN-KY	(37.2)
51	Riverside-San Bernardino, CA	(5.9)	115	Mankato-North Mankato, MN	(23.8)	178	Dallas (greater), TX	(37.2)
52	Anaheim-Santa Ana-Irvine, CA M.D.	(6.2)	116	Carson City, NV	(24.6)	178	Lancaster, PA	(37.2)
53	Cheyenne, WY	(6.5)	117	Atlanta, GA	(24.9)	181	Killeen-Temple, TX	(37.3)
54	Fayetteville-Springdale, AR-MO	(6.7)	118	Hinesville, GA	(25.1)	182	Huntsville, AL	(37.7)
55	Portland-Vancouver, OR-WA	(7.4)	119	Beaumont-Port Arthur, TX	(25.3)	182	Visalia-Porterville, CA	(37.7)
56	Lafayette, IN	(8.4)	119	San Antonio, TX	(25.3)	182	Wheeling, WV-OH	(37.7)
57	Williamsport, PA	(8.6)	121	Kingsport, TN-VA	(25.5)	185	Harrisonburg, VA	(37.8)
58	Johnson City, TN	(8.9)	122	Chico, CA	(25.6)	186	Baltimore, MD	(38.0)
58	Vallejo-Fairfield, CA	(8.9)	123	Mount Vernon-Anacortes, WA	(26.1)	187	Macon, GA	(38.1)
60	Yuba City, CA	(9.0)	124	Los Angeles (greater), CA	(26.6)	188	Kalamazoo-Portage, MI	(38.2)
61	Cleveland, TN	(9.1)	125	Jonesboro, AR	(26.9)	189	Longview, TX	(38.7)
62	Little Rock, AR	(9.4)	126	Naples-Marco Island, FL	(27.0)	189	South Bend-Mishawaka, IN-MI	(38.7)
63	Wichita, KS	(9.7)	127	Abilene, TX	(27.1)	191	Yuma, AZ	(38.9)
64	Tallahassee, FL	(10.2)	127	Camden, NJ M.D.	(27.1)	192	Dallas-Plano-Irving, TX M.D.	(39.4)

Note: All listings are for Metropolitan Statistical Areas (M.S.A.s) except for those ending with "M.D." Listings with "M.D." are Metropolitan Divisions which are smaller parts of eleven large M.S.A.s. See explanatory note at beginning of metropolitan area section.

RANK	METROPOLITAN AREA	% CHANGE	RANK	METROPOLITAN AREA	% CHANGE	RANK	METROPOLITAN AREA	% CHANGE
193	Oshkosh-Neenah, WI	(39.5)	NA	Albany-Schenectady-Troy, NY**	NA	NA	Lexington-Fayette, KY**	NA
194	Athens-Clarke County, GA	(39.7)	NA	Albany, GA**	NA	NA	Madison, WI**	NA
194	Racine, WI	(39.7)	NA	Albany, OR**	NA	NA	Manchester-Nashua, NH**	NA
196	Bellingham, WA	(39.9)	NA	Alexandria, LA**	NA	NA	Manhattan, KS**	NA
197	Boise City, ID	(40.3)	NA	Allentown, PA-NJ**	NA	NA	Midland, MI**	NA
198	Orlando, FL	(40.6)	NA	Anchorage, AK**	NA	NA	Midland, TX**	NA
199	Waterloo-Cedar Falls, IA	(40.7)	NA	Anniston-Oxford, AL**	NA	NA	Montgomery County, PA M.D.**	NA
200	State College, PA	(40.8)	NA	Baton Rouge, LA**	NA	NA	Morgantown, WV**	NA
201	Brownsville-Harlingen, TX	(41.6)	NA	Beckley, WV**	NA	NA	Morristown, TN**	NA
201	Cape Coral-Fort Myers, FL	(41.6)	NA	Binghamton, NY**	NA	NA	Nashville-Davidson, TN**	NA
203	Michigan City-La Porte, IN	(41.8)	NA	Bloomington, IL**	NA	NA	Nassau-Suffolk, NY M.D.**	NA
204	Fort Collins, CO	(41.9)	NA	Bloomsburg-Berwick, PA**	NA	NA	New Bern, NC**	NA
205	Blacksburg, VA	(42.1)	NA	Boston (greater), MA-NH**	NA	NA	New Haven-Milford, CT**	NA
206	Charlottesville, VA	(42.2)	NA	Boston, MA M.D.**	NA	NA	New York (greater), NY-NJ-PA**	NA
206	La Crosse, WI-MN	(42.2)	NA	Boulder, CO**	NA	NA	New York-Jersey City, NY-NJ M.D.**	NA
208	Youngstown-Warren, OH-PA	(42.4)	NA	Brunswick, GA**	NA	NA	Newark, NJ-PA M.D.**	NA
209	Flint, MI	(42.5)	NA	Buffalo-Niagara Falls, NY**	NA	NA	North Port-Sarasota-Bradenton, FL**	NA
209	Miami (greater), FL	(42.5)	NA	California-Lexington Park, MD**	NA	NA	Ogden-Clearfield, UT**	NA
211	New Orleans, LA	(42.9)	NA	Cambridge-Newton, MA M.D.**	NA	NA	Owensboro, KY**	NA
211	San Diego, CA	(42.9)	NA	Canton, OH**	NA	NA	Panama City, FL**	NA
213	Mobile, AL	(43.1)	NA	Chambersburg-Waynesboro, PA**	NA	NA	Parkersburg-Vienna, WV**	NA
214	Auburn, AL	(43.5)	NA	Champaign-Urbana, IL**	NA	NA	Peoria, IL**	NA
215	Winchester, VA-WV	(43.6)	NA	Chicago (greater), IL-IN-WI**	NA	NA	Philadelphia (greater) PA-NJ-MD-DE**	NA
216	Monroe, LA	(43.8)	NA	Chicago-Joilet-Naperville, IL M.D.**	NA	NA	Philadelphia, PA M.D.**	NA
217	Dover, DE	(44.1)	NA	Cincinnati, OH-KY-IN**	NA	NA	Phoenix-Mesa-Scottsdale, AZ**	NA
217	Saginaw, MI	(44.1)	NA	Coeur d'Alene, ID**	NA	NA	Pocatello, ID**	NA
219	Goldsboro, NC	(44.2)	NA	Crestview-Fort Walton Beach, FL**	NA	NA	Pueblo, CO**	NA
220	Albuquerque, NM	(44.3)	NA	Danville, IL**	NA	NA	Rapid City, SD**	NA
221	Birmingham-Hoover, AL	(44.7)	NA	Daphne-Fairhope-Foley, AL**	NA	NA	Rochester, MN**	NA
222	Las Vegas-Henderson, NV	(44.8)	NA	Davenport, IA-IL**	NA	NA	Rochester, NY**	NA
223	Greensboro-High Point, NC	(45.4)	NA	Decatur, IL**	NA	NA	Rockford, IL**	NA
224	Janesville, WI	(45.5)	NA	Denver-Aurora, CO**	NA	NA	Rocky Mount, NC**	NA
225	Columbus, GA-AL	(45.6)	NA	Detroit (greater), MI**	NA	NA	Rome, GA**	NA
226	Miami-Dade County, FL M.D.	(46.1)	NA	Detroit-Dearborn-Livonia, MI M.D.**	NA	NA	Salisbury, MD-DE**	NA
227	Memphis, TN-MS-AR	(46.4)	NA	Dutchess-Putnam, NY M.D.**	NA	NA	San Rafael, CA M.D.**	NA
227	West Palm Beach, FL M.D.	(46.4)	NA	East Stroudsburg, PA**	NA	NA	Santa Maria-Santa Barbara, CA**	NA
229	York-Hanover, PA	(47.0)	NA	Elgin, IL M.D.**	NA	NA	Seattle (greater), WA**	NA
230	Pittsburgh, PA	(47.2)	NA	Elizabethtown-Fort Knox, KY**	NA	NA	Seattle-Bellevue-Everett, WA M.D.**	NA
231	Gainesville, FL	(47.6)	NA	Elmira, NY**	NA	NA	Sebring, FL**	NA
232	Corvallis, OR	(47.8)	NA	Fairbanks, AK**	NA	NA	Shreveport-Bossier City, LA**	NA
232	Lima, OH	(47.8)	NA	Fort Smith, AR-OK**	NA	NA	Sierra Vista-Douglas, AZ**	NA
234	Washington, DC-VA-MD-WV M.D.	(48.3)	NA	Gainesville, GA**	NA	NA	Sioux City, IA-NE-SD**	NA
235	Washington (greater) DC-VA-MD-WV	(48.7)	NA	Gary, IN M.D.**	NA	NA	Spartanburg, SC**	NA
236	Lynchburg, VA	(48.8)	NA	Gettysburg, PA**	NA	NA	Springfield, IL**	NA
237	Springfield, OH	(48.9)	NA	Glens Falls, NY**	NA	NA	Springfield, MA**	NA
238	Pine Bluff, AR	(49.1)	NA	Grand Island, NE**	NA	NA	Staunton-Waynesboro, VA**	NA
239	Savannah, GA	(49.3)	NA	Greenville-Anderson, SC**	NA	NA	Syracuse, NY**	NA
240	Appleton, WI	(49.7)	NA	Hagerstown-Martinsburg, MD-WV**	NA	NA	Tacoma, WA M.D.**	NA
240	Punta Gorda, FL	(49.7)	NA	Hammond, LA**	NA	NA	Terre Haute, IN**	NA
242	Valdosta, GA	(50.7)	NA	Hattiesburg, MS**	NA	NA	Texarkana, TX-AR**	NA
243	Tucson, AZ	(51.8)	NA	Hilton Head Island, SC**	NA	NA	The Villages, FL**	NA
243	Wichita Falls, TX	(51.8)	NA	Homosassa Springs, FL**	NA	NA	Toledo, OH**	NA
245	Tampa-St Petersburg, FL	(52.9)	NA	Jackson, MS**	NA	NA	Tuscaloosa, AL**	NA
246	Lakeland, FL	(53.0)	NA	Jackson, TN**	NA	NA	Utica-Rome, NY**	NA
246	Ocala, FL	(53.0)	NA	Jefferson City, MO**	NA	NA	Victoria, TX**	NA
248	Ames, IA	(53.9)	NA	Kahului-Wailuku-Lahaina, HI**	NA	NA	Waco, TX**	NA
249	Silver Spring-Frederick, MD M.D.	(54.2)	NA	Kankakee, IL**	NA	NA	Walla Walla, WA**	NA
250	McAllen-Edinburg-Mission, TX	(55.3)	NA	Kansas City, MO-KS**	NA	NA	Warner Robins, GA**	NA
251	College Station-Bryan, TX	(56.6)	NA	Kingston, NY**	NA	NA	Warren-Troy, MI M.D.**	NA
252	Greenville, NC	(57.9)	NA	Knoxville, TN**	NA	NA	Watertown-Fort Drum, NY**	NA
253	Jacksonville, FL	(59.6)	NA	Kokomo, IN**	NA	NA	Wilmington, NC**	NA
254	Eugene, OR	(60.6)	NA	Lafayette, LA**	NA	NA	Winston-Salem, NC**	NA
255	El Paso, TX	(61.2)	NA	Lake Co.-Kenosha Co., IL-WI M.D.**	NA			
256	Laredo, TX	(78.7)	NA	Lawton, OK**	NA			

Source: CQ Press using reported data from the F.B.I. "Crime in the United States 2012"

*Motor vehicle theft includes the theft or attempted theft of a self-propelled vehicle. Excludes motorboats, construction equipment, airplanes, and farming equipment. **Not available.

II. City Crime Statistics
(for cities larger than 75,000 population)

Please note the following for Tables 41 through 84 and 88 through 90:

• All listings are for cities of 75,000 or more in population that reported data to the F.B.I. for 2012. The reported populations for crime reporting purposes may vary from Census populations.

41. Crimes in 2012
National Total = 10,189,900 Crimes*

RANK	CITY	CRIMES	RANK	CITY	CRIMES	RANK	CITY	CRIMES
207	Abilene, TX	4,865	428	Chino Hills, CA	1,020	159	Gainesville, FL	6,052
86	Akron, OH	11,793	357	Chino, CA	2,407	228	Garden Grove, CA	4,456
390	Alameda, CA	2,052	174	Chula Vista, CA	5,662	102	Garland, TX	9,215
167	Albany, GA	5,814	349	Cicero, IL	2,600	189	Gary, IN	5,203
191	Albany, NY	5,142	42	Cincinnati, OH	21,060	275	Gilbert, AZ	3,591
25	Albuquerque, NM	33,869	290	Citrus Heights, CA	3,446	57	Glendale, AZ	16,079
300	Alexandria, VA	3,233	417	Clarkstown, NY	1,587	297	Glendale, CA	3,276
388	Alhambra, CA	2,068	220	Clarksville, TN	4,616	169	Grand Prairie, TX	5,745
188	Allentown, PA	5,256	202	Clearwater, FL	4,991	117	Grand Rapids, MI	8,083
420	Allen, TX	1,487	31	Cleveland, OH	29,758	342	Greece, NY	2,685
98	Amarillo, TX	10,178	408	Clifton, NJ	1,763	267	Greeley, CO	3,669
363	Amherst, NY	2,349	353	Clinton Twnshp, MI	2,521	284	Green Bay, WI	3,492
91	Anaheim, CA	11,349	240	Clovis, CA	4,244	70	Greensboro, NC	13,619
76	Anchorage, AK	13,022	323	College Station, TX	2,889	239	Greenville, NC	4,300
320	Ann Arbor, MI	2,953	381	Colonie, NY	2,163	183	Gresham, OR	5,345
166	Antioch, CA	5,825	45	Colorado Springs, CO	19,867	380	Hamilton Twnshp, NJ	2,166
429	Arlington Heights, IL	1,019	215	Columbia, MO	4,697	247	Hammond, IN	4,113
51	Arlington, TX	17,018	82	Columbus, GA	12,260	204	Hampton, VA	4,971
335	Arvada, CO	2,763	272	Compton, CA	3,617	135	Hartford, CT	6,974
185	Asheville, NC	5,333	221	Concord, CA	4,584	325	Hawthorne, CA	2,818
196	Athens-Clarke, GA	5,056	313	Coral Springs, FL	3,049	180	Hayward, CA	5,405
23	Atlanta, GA	34,581	236	Corona, CA	4,353	255	Hemet, CA	3,892
89	Aurora, CO	11,492	55	Corpus Christi, TX	16,118	170	Henderson, NV	5,740
246	Aurora, IL	4,128	238	Costa Mesa, CA	4,333	322	Hesperia, CA	2,904
12	Austin, TX	46,877	391	Cranston, RI	2,038	119	Hialeah, FL	8,004
254	Avondale, AZ	3,915	7	Dallas, TX	62,680	203	High Point, NC	4,973
46	Bakersfield, CA	19,683	394	Daly City, CA	2,019	365	Hillsboro, OR	2,334
403	Baldwin Park, CA	1,846	412	Danbury, CT	1,671	115	Hollywood, FL	8,356
17	Baltimore, MD	37,938	216	Davenport, IA	4,692	372	Hoover, AL	2,266
63	Baton Rouge, LA	14,566	257	Davie, FL	3,842	2	Houston, TX	129,288
134	Beaumont, TX	7,066	100	Dayton, OH	9,769	168	Huntington Beach, CA	5,783
414	Beaverton, OR	1,612	273	Dearborn, MI	3,604	94	Huntsville, AL	10,957
269	Bellevue, WA	3,664	330	Decatur, IL	2,800	121	Independence, MO	7,689
384	Bellflower, CA	2,106	325	Deerfield Beach, FL	2,818	9	Indianapolis, IN	56,840
243	Bellingham, WA	4,195	271	Denton, TX	3,631	299	Indio, CA	3,241
153	Berkeley, CA	6,183	34	Denver, CO	27,214	289	Inglewood, CA	3,453
378	Bethlehem, PA	2,186	92	Des Moines, IA	11,304	294	Irvine, CA	3,414
190	Billings, MT	5,182	10	Detroit, MI	55,967	138	Irving, TX	6,814
50	Birmingham, AL	18,025	253	Downey, CA	3,918	15	Jacksonville, FL	39,863
379	Bloomington, IL	2,169	NA	Duluth, MN**	NA	74	Jackson, MS	13,236
285	Bloomington, IN	3,487	85	Durham, NC	11,989	126	Jersey City, NJ	7,326
NA	Bloomington, MN**	NA	193	Edinburg, TX	5,089	434	Johns Creek, GA	569
341	Boca Raton, FL	2,721	415	Edison Twnshp, NJ	1,603	237	Joliet, IL	4,341
164	Boise, ID	5,909	407	Edmond, OK	1,765	286	Jurupa Valley, CA	3,486
38	Boston, MA	23,615	333	El Cajon, CA	2,779	113	Kansas City, KS	8,415
304	Boulder, CO	3,186	345	El Monte, CA	2,625	30	Kansas City, MO	31,504
422	Brick Twnshp, NJ	1,326	47	El Paso, TX	19,270	348	Kennewick, WA	2,601
136	Bridgeport, CT	6,913	374	Elgin, IL	2,239	298	Kenosha, WI	3,273
245	Brockton, MA	4,159	182	Elizabeth, NJ	5,358	160	Kent, WA	6,011
364	Broken Arrow, OK	2,342	259	Elk Grove, CA	3,804	165	Killeen, TX	5,837
NA	Brooklyn Park, MN**	NA	252	Erie, PA	3,968	69	Knoxville, TN	13,943
105	Brownsville, TX	8,810	223	Escondido, CA	4,515	123	Lafayette, LA	7,594
332	Bryan, TX	2,785	111	Eugene, OR	8,434	427	Lake Forest, CA	1,195
370	Buena Park, CA	2,272	142	Evansville, IN	6,643	172	Lakeland, FL	5,681
52	Buffalo, NY	16,836	137	Everett, WA	6,897	426	Lakewood Twnshp, NJ	1,213
339	Burbank, CA	2,736	261	Fairfield, CA	3,771	367	Lakewood, CA	2,289
280	Cambridge, MA	3,522	270	Fall River, MA	3,660	124	Lakewood, CO	7,381
161	Camden, NJ	6,000	301	Fargo, ND	3,229	234	Lancaster, CA	4,357
262	Cape Coral, FL	3,750	421	Farmington Hills, MI	1,338	208	Lansing, MI	4,852
359	Carlsbad, CA	2,374	292	Fayetteville, AR	3,431	87	Laredo, TX	11,721
432	Carmel, IN	819	66	Fayetteville, NC	14,349	282	Largo, FL	3,511
274	Carrollton, TX	3,594	181	Federal Way, WA	5,402	213	Las Cruces, NM	4,813
301	Carson, CA	3,229	431	Fishers, IN	835	8	Las Vegas, NV	58,025
393	Cary, NC	2,024	112	Flint, MI	8,419	232	Lawrence, KS	4,367
195	Cedar Rapids, IA	5,079	184	Fontana, CA	5,344	336	Lawrence, MA	2,750
416	Centennial, CO	1,596	224	Fort Collins, CO	4,510	156	Lawton, OK	6,128
291	Champaign, IL	3,441	88	Fort Lauderdale, FL	11,503	404	League City, TX	1,813
130	Chandler, AZ	7,199	178	Fort Smith, AR	5,458	375	Lee's Summit, MO	2,236
267	Charleston, SC	3,669	96	Fort Wayne, IN	10,446	65	Lexington, KY	14,465
18	Charlotte, NC	37,825	20	Fort Worth, TX	37,038	93	Lincoln, NE	11,221
317	Cheektowaga, NY	2,996	222	Fremont, CA	4,565	49	Little Rock, AR	18,383
131	Chesapeake, VA	7,131	32	Fresno, CA	28,485	384	Livermore, CA	2,106
NA	Chicago, IL**	NA	345	Frisco, TX	2,625	371	Livonia, MI	2,270
350	Chico, CA	2,573	231	Fullerton, CA	4,389	52	Long Beach, CA	16,836

RANK	CITY	CRIMES	RANK	CITY	CRIMES	RANK	CITY	CRIMES
361	Longmont, CO	2,357	258	Pasadena, CA	3,812	311	South Gate, CA	3,098
218	Longview, TX	4,675	150	Pasadena, TX	6,232	331	Sparks, NV	2,793
3	Los Angeles, CA	106,025	152	Paterson, NJ	6,192	201	Spokane Valley, WA	5,001
28	Louisville, KY	32,595	400	Pearland, TX	1,876	43	Spokane, WA	19,891
265	Lowell, MA	3,710	226	Pembroke Pines, FL	4,476	117	Springfield, IL	8,083
67	Lubbock, TX	14,235	205	Peoria, AZ	4,969	109	Springfield, MA	8,630
360	Lynchburg, VA	2,360	162	Peoria, IL	5,941	56	Springfield, MO	16,100
296	Lynn, MA	3,343	5	Philadelphia, PA	74,850	368	Stamford, CT	2,283
128	Macon, GA	7,282	6	Phoenix, AZ	70,235	327	Sterling Heights, MI	2,810
108	Madison, WI	8,650	75	Pittsburgh, PA	13,038	44	Stockton, CA	19,888
227	Manchester, NH	4,472	139	Plano, TX	6,811	411	St. George, UT	1,716
175	McAllen, TX	5,631	264	Plantation, FL	3,721	199	St. Joseph, MO	5,031
315	McKinney, TX	3,015	157	Pomona, CA	6,076	33	St. Louis, MO	27,656
210	Medford, OR	4,843	143	Pompano Beach, FL	6,622	68	St. Paul, MN	13,994
249	Melbourne, FL	4,032	293	Port St. Lucie, FL	3,426	62	St. Petersburg, FL	14,690
11	Memphis, TN	53,010	27	Portland, OR	33,547	413	Sugar Land, TX	1,650
392	Menifee, CA	2,029	187	Portsmouth, VA	5,282	340	Sunnyvale, CA	2,725
206	Merced, CA	4,921	104	Providence, RI	9,110	288	Sunrise, FL	3,459
423	Meridian, ID	1,322	347	Provo, UT	2,614	344	Surprise, AZ	2,650
58	Mesa, AZ	15,944	120	Pueblo, CO	7,827	125	Syracuse, NY	7,348
140	Mesquite, TX	6,727	399	Quincy, MA	1,955	64	Tacoma, WA	14,481
99	Miami Beach, FL	9,969	278	Racine, WI	3,555	97	Tallahassee, FL	10,199
171	Miami Gardens, FL	5,715	60	Raleigh, NC	15,559	84	Tampa, FL	12,109
35	Miami, FL	27,127	433	Ramapo, NY	796	352	Temecula, CA	2,537
295	Midland, TX	3,406	217	Rancho Cucamon., CA	4,683	107	Tempe, AZ	8,702
16	Milwaukee, WI	37,987	230	Reading, PA	4,440	276	Thornton, CO	3,589
40	Minneapolis, MN	23,231	194	Redding, CA	5,085	396	Thousand Oaks, CA	1,995
281	Miramar, FL	3,521	395	Redwood City, CA	2,008	NA	Toledo, OH**	NA
425	Mission Viejo, CA	1,270	110	Reno, NV	8,615	318	Toms River Twnshp, NJ	2,974
356	Mission, TX	2,474	209	Renton, WA	4,845	122	Topeka, KS	7,613
72	Mobile, AL	13,417	248	Rialto, CA	4,080	324	Torrance, CA	2,880
78	Modesto, CA	12,866	305	Richardson, TX	3,175	366	Tracy, CA	2,303
77	Montgomery, AL	12,885	154	Richmond, CA	6,180	251	Trenton, NJ	3,997
132	Moreno Valley, CA	7,077	95	Richmond, VA	10,451	410	Troy, MI	1,724
419	Mountain View, CA	1,574	384	Rio Rancho, NM	2,106	NA	Tucson, AZ**	NA
214	Murfreesboro, TN	4,707	83	Riverside, CA	12,207	36	Tulsa, OK	24,756
405	Murrieta, CA	1,785	186	Roanoke, VA	5,313	211	Tuscaloosa, AL	4,827
358	Nampa, ID	2,383	NA	Rochester, MN**	NA	406	Tustin, CA	1,767
401	Napa, CA	1,859	73	Rochester, NY	13,352	197	Tyler, TX	5,042
381	Naperville, IL	2,163	101	Rockford, IL	9,691	355	Upland, CA	2,476
351	Nashua, NH	2,565	277	Roseville, CA	3,581	354	Upper Darby Twnshp, PA	2,492
26	Nashville, TN	33,602	402	Roswell, GA	1,853	369	Vacaville, CA	2,277
241	New Bedford, MA	4,210	334	Round Rock, TX	2,777	141	Vallejo, CA	6,722
114	New Haven, CT	8,386	39	Sacramento, CA	23,487	133	Vancouver, WA	7,070
54	New Orleans, LA	16,647	127	Salem, OR	7,295	243	Ventura, CA	4,195
418	New Rochelle, NY	1,577	163	Salinas, CA	5,933	192	Victorville, CA	5,141
1	New York, NY	195,753	59	Salt Lake City, UT	15,657	81	Virginia Beach, VA	12,475
71	Newark, NJ	13,419	4	San Antonio, TX	89,611	158	Visalia, CA	6,075
373	Newport Beach, CA	2,252	80	San Bernardino, CA	12,532	362	Vista, CA	2,350
147	Newport News, VA	6,476	19	San Diego, CA	37,229	146	Waco, TX	6,479
430	Newton, MA	970	13	San Francisco, CA	44,675	225	Warren, MI	4,502
79	Norfolk, VA	12,723	29	San Jose, CA	32,010	376	Warwick, RI	2,219
303	Norman, OK	3,223	250	San Leandro, CA	4,022	21	Washington, DC	36,712
145	North Charleston, SC	6,494	409	San Marcos, CA	1,729	198	Waterbury, CT	5,041
129	North Las Vegas, NV	7,229	383	San Mateo, CA	2,137	310	Waukegan, IL	3,108
314	Norwalk, CA	3,042	321	Sandy Springs, GA	2,937	283	West Covina, CA	3,505
398	Norwalk, CT	1,985	327	Sandy, UT	2,810	306	West Jordan, UT	3,165
24	Oakland, CA	34,305	106	Santa Ana, CA	8,723	151	West Palm Beach, FL	6,225
200	Oceanside, CA	5,017	287	Santa Barbara, CA	3,478	155	West Valley, UT	6,168
212	Odessa, TX	4,820	279	Santa Clara, CA	3,527	338	Westland, MI	2,748
424	O'Fallon, MO	1,320	312	Santa Clarita, CA	3,084	307	Westminster, CA	3,159
235	Ogden, UT	4,354	308	Santa Maria, CA	3,120	309	Westminster, CO	3,114
14	Oklahoma City, OK	40,864	260	Santa Monica, CA	3,793	337	Whittier, CA	2,749
343	Olathe, KS	2,671	229	Santa Rosa, CA	4,454	177	Wichita Falls, TX	5,496
41	Omaha, NE	21,663	103	Savannah, GA	9,203	37	Wichita, KS	23,939
176	Ontario, CA	5,590	148	Scottsdale, AZ	6,376	144	Wilmington, NC	6,528
319	Orange, CA	2,968	329	Scranton, PA	2,805	61	Winston-Salem, NC	15,257
377	Orem, UT	2,209	22	Seattle, WA	35,677	387	Woodbridge Twnshp, NJ	2,089
48	Orlando, FL	18,812	90	Shreveport, LA	11,412	116	Worcester, MA	8,190
233	Overland Park, KS	4,364	389	Simi Valley, CA	2,057	149	Yakima, WA	6,340
219	Oxnard, CA	4,674	263	Sioux City, IA	3,744	266	Yonkers, NY	3,698
316	Palm Bay, FL	3,010	173	Sioux Falls, SD	5,672	256	Yuma, AZ	3,861
242	Palmdale, CA	4,205	397	Somerville, MA	1,993			
435	Parma, OH	507	179	South Bend, IN	5,449			

Source: CQ Press using reported data from the F.B.I. "Crime in the United States 2012"

*Includes murder, rape, robbery, aggravated assault, burglary, larceny-theft, and motor vehicle theft.

**Not available.

41. Crimes in 2012 (continued)
National Total = 10,189,900 Crimes*

RANK	CITY	CRIMES	RANK	CITY	CRIMES	RANK	CITY	CRIMES
1	New York, NY	195,753	75	Pittsburgh, PA	13,038	149	Yakima, WA	6,340
2	Houston, TX	129,288	76	Anchorage, AK	13,022	150	Pasadena, TX	6,232
3	Los Angeles, CA	106,025	77	Montgomery, AL	12,885	151	West Palm Beach, FL	6,225
4	San Antonio, TX	89,611	78	Modesto, CA	12,866	152	Paterson, NJ	6,192
5	Philadelphia, PA	74,850	79	Norfolk, VA	12,723	153	Berkeley, CA	6,183
6	Phoenix, AZ	70,235	80	San Bernardino, CA	12,532	154	Richmond, CA	6,180
7	Dallas, TX	62,680	81	Virginia Beach, VA	12,475	155	West Valley, UT	6,168
8	Las Vegas, NV	58,025	82	Columbus, GA	12,260	156	Lawton, OK	6,128
9	Indianapolis, IN	56,840	83	Riverside, CA	12,207	157	Pomona, CA	6,076
10	Detroit, MI	55,967	84	Tampa, FL	12,109	158	Visalia, CA	6,075
11	Memphis, TN	53,010	85	Durham, NC	11,989	159	Gainesville, FL	6,052
12	Austin, TX	46,877	86	Akron, OH	11,793	160	Kent, WA	6,011
13	San Francisco, CA	44,675	87	Laredo, TX	11,721	161	Camden, NJ	6,000
14	Oklahoma City, OK	40,864	88	Fort Lauderdale, FL	11,503	162	Peoria, IL	5,941
15	Jacksonville, FL	39,863	89	Aurora, CO	11,492	163	Salinas, CA	5,933
16	Milwaukee, WI	37,987	90	Shreveport, LA	11,412	164	Boise, ID	5,909
17	Baltimore, MD	37,938	91	Anaheim, CA	11,349	165	Killeen, TX	5,837
18	Charlotte, NC	37,825	92	Des Moines, IA	11,304	166	Antioch, CA	5,825
19	San Diego, CA	37,229	93	Lincoln, NE	11,221	167	Albany, GA	5,814
20	Fort Worth, TX	37,038	94	Huntsville, AL	10,957	168	Huntington Beach, CA	5,783
21	Washington, DC	36,712	95	Richmond, VA	10,451	169	Grand Prairie, TX	5,745
22	Seattle, WA	35,677	96	Fort Wayne, IN	10,446	170	Henderson, NV	5,740
23	Atlanta, GA	34,581	97	Tallahassee, FL	10,199	171	Miami Gardens, FL	5,715
24	Oakland, CA	34,305	98	Amarillo, TX	10,178	172	Lakeland, FL	5,681
25	Albuquerque, NM	33,869	99	Miami Beach, FL	9,969	173	Sioux Falls, SD	5,672
26	Nashville, TN	33,602	100	Dayton, OH	9,769	174	Chula Vista, CA	5,662
27	Portland, OR	33,547	101	Rockford, IL	9,691	175	McAllen, TX	5,631
28	Louisville, KY	32,595	102	Garland, TX	9,215	176	Ontario, CA	5,590
29	San Jose, CA	32,010	103	Savannah, GA	9,203	177	Wichita Falls, TX	5,496
30	Kansas City, MO	31,504	104	Providence, RI	9,110	178	Fort Smith, AR	5,458
31	Cleveland, OH	29,758	105	Brownsville, TX	8,810	179	South Bend, IN	5,449
32	Fresno, CA	28,485	106	Santa Ana, CA	8,723	180	Hayward, CA	5,405
33	St. Louis, MO	27,656	107	Tempe, AZ	8,702	181	Federal Way, WA	5,402
34	Denver, CO	27,214	108	Madison, WI	8,650	182	Elizabeth, NJ	5,358
35	Miami, FL	27,127	109	Springfield, MA	8,630	183	Gresham, OR	5,345
36	Tulsa, OK	24,756	110	Reno, NV	8,615	184	Fontana, CA	5,344
37	Wichita, KS	23,939	111	Eugene, OR	8,434	185	Asheville, NC	5,333
38	Boston, MA	23,615	112	Flint, MI	8,419	186	Roanoke, VA	5,313
39	Sacramento, CA	23,487	113	Kansas City, KS	8,415	187	Portsmouth, VA	5,282
40	Minneapolis, MN	23,231	114	New Haven, CT	8,386	188	Allentown, PA	5,256
41	Omaha, NE	21,663	115	Hollywood, FL	8,356	189	Gary, IN	5,203
42	Cincinnati, OH	21,060	116	Worcester, MA	8,190	190	Billings, MT	5,182
43	Spokane, WA	19,891	117	Grand Rapids, MI	8,083	191	Albany, NY	5,142
44	Stockton, CA	19,888	117	Springfield, IL	8,083	192	Victorville, CA	5,141
45	Colorado Springs, CO	19,867	119	Hialeah, FL	8,004	193	Edinburg, TX	5,089
46	Bakersfield, CA	19,683	120	Pueblo, CO	7,827	194	Redding, CA	5,085
47	El Paso, TX	19,270	121	Independence, MO	7,689	195	Cedar Rapids, IA	5,079
48	Orlando, FL	18,812	122	Topeka, KS	7,613	196	Athens-Clarke, GA	5,056
49	Little Rock, AR	18,383	123	Lafayette, LA	7,594	197	Tyler, TX	5,042
50	Birmingham, AL	18,025	124	Lakewood, CO	7,381	198	Waterbury, CT	5,041
51	Arlington, TX	17,018	125	Syracuse, NY	7,348	199	St. Joseph, MO	5,031
52	Buffalo, NY	16,836	126	Jersey City, NJ	7,326	200	Oceanside, CA	5,017
52	Long Beach, CA	16,836	127	Salem, OR	7,295	201	Spokane Valley, WA	5,001
54	New Orleans, LA	16,647	128	Macon, GA	7,282	202	Clearwater, FL	4,991
55	Corpus Christi, TX	16,118	129	North Las Vegas, NV	7,229	203	High Point, NC	4,973
56	Springfield, MO	16,100	130	Chandler, AZ	7,199	204	Hampton, VA	4,971
57	Glendale, AZ	16,079	131	Chesapeake, VA	7,131	205	Peoria, AZ	4,969
58	Mesa, AZ	15,944	132	Moreno Valley, CA	7,077	206	Merced, CA	4,921
59	Salt Lake City, UT	15,657	133	Vancouver, WA	7,070	207	Abilene, TX	4,865
60	Raleigh, NC	15,559	134	Beaumont, TX	7,066	208	Lansing, MI	4,852
61	Winston-Salem, NC	15,257	135	Hartford, CT	6,974	209	Renton, WA	4,845
62	St. Petersburg, FL	14,690	136	Bridgeport, CT	6,913	210	Medford, OR	4,843
63	Baton Rouge, LA	14,566	137	Everett, WA	6,897	211	Tuscaloosa, AL	4,827
64	Tacoma, WA	14,481	138	Irving, TX	6,814	212	Odessa, TX	4,820
65	Lexington, KY	14,465	139	Plano, TX	6,811	213	Las Cruces, NM	4,813
66	Fayetteville, NC	14,349	140	Mesquite, TX	6,727	214	Murfreesboro, TN	4,707
67	Lubbock, TX	14,235	141	Vallejo, CA	6,722	215	Columbia, MO	4,697
68	St. Paul, MN	13,994	142	Evansville, IN	6,643	216	Davenport, IA	4,692
69	Knoxville, TN	13,943	143	Pompano Beach, FL	6,622	217	Rancho Cucamon., CA	4,683
70	Greensboro, NC	13,619	144	Wilmington, NC	6,528	218	Longview, TX	4,675
71	Newark, NJ	13,419	145	North Charleston, SC	6,494	219	Oxnard, CA	4,674
72	Mobile, AL	13,417	146	Waco, TX	6,479	220	Clarksville, TN	4,616
73	Rochester, NY	13,352	147	Newport News, VA	6,476	221	Concord, CA	4,584
74	Jackson, MS	13,236	148	Scottsdale, AZ	6,376	222	Fremont, CA	4,565

RANK	CITY	CRIMES	RANK	CITY	CRIMES	RANK	CITY	CRIMES
223	Escondido, CA	4,515	297	Glendale, CA	3,276	371	Livonia, MI	2,270
224	Fort Collins, CO	4,510	298	Kenosha, WI	3,273	372	Hoover, AL	2,266
225	Warren, MI	4,502	299	Indio, CA	3,241	373	Newport Beach, CA	2,252
226	Pembroke Pines, FL	4,476	300	Alexandria, VA	3,233	374	Elgin, IL	2,239
227	Manchester, NH	4,472	301	Carson, CA	3,229	375	Lee's Summit, MO	2,236
228	Garden Grove, CA	4,456	301	Fargo, ND	3,229	376	Warwick, RI	2,219
229	Santa Rosa, CA	4,454	303	Norman, OK	3,223	377	Orem, UT	2,209
230	Reading, PA	4,440	304	Boulder, CO	3,186	378	Bethlehem, PA	2,186
231	Fullerton, CA	4,389	305	Richardson, TX	3,175	379	Bloomington, IL	2,169
232	Lawrence, KS	4,367	306	West Jordan, UT	3,165	380	Hamilton Twnshp, NJ	2,166
233	Overland Park, KS	4,364	307	Westminster, CA	3,159	381	Colonie, NY	2,163
234	Lancaster, CA	4,357	308	Santa Maria, CA	3,120	381	Naperville, IL	2,163
235	Ogden, UT	4,354	309	Westminster, CO	3,114	383	San Mateo, CA	2,137
236	Corona, CA	4,353	310	Waukegan, IL	3,108	384	Bellflower, CA	2,106
237	Joliet, IL	4,341	311	South Gate, CA	3,098	384	Livermore, CA	2,106
238	Costa Mesa, CA	4,333	312	Santa Clarita, CA	3,084	384	Rio Rancho, NM	2,106
239	Greenville, NC	4,300	313	Coral Springs, FL	3,049	387	Woodbridge Twnshp, NJ	2,089
240	Clovis, CA	4,244	314	Norwalk, CA	3,042	388	Alhambra, CA	2,068
241	New Bedford, MA	4,210	315	McKinney, TX	3,015	389	Simi Valley, CA	2,057
242	Palmdale, CA	4,205	316	Palm Bay, FL	3,010	390	Alameda, CA	2,052
243	Bellingham, WA	4,195	317	Cheektowaga, NY	2,996	391	Cranston, RI	2,038
243	Ventura, CA	4,195	318	Toms River Twnshp, NJ	2,974	392	Menifee, CA	2,029
245	Brockton, MA	4,159	319	Orange, CA	2,968	393	Cary, NC	2,024
246	Aurora, IL	4,128	320	Ann Arbor, MI	2,953	394	Daly City, CA	2,019
247	Hammond, IN	4,113	321	Sandy Springs, GA	2,937	395	Redwood City, CA	2,008
248	Rialto, CA	4,080	322	Hesperia, CA	2,904	396	Thousand Oaks, CA	1,995
249	Melbourne, FL	4,032	323	College Station, TX	2,889	397	Somerville, MA	1,993
250	San Leandro, CA	4,022	324	Torrance, CA	2,880	398	Norwalk, CT	1,985
251	Trenton, NJ	3,997	325	Deerfield Beach, FL	2,818	399	Quincy, MA	1,955
252	Erie, PA	3,968	325	Hawthorne, CA	2,818	400	Pearland, TX	1,876
253	Downey, CA	3,918	327	Sandy, UT	2,810	401	Napa, CA	1,859
254	Avondale, AZ	3,915	327	Sterling Heights, MI	2,810	402	Roswell, GA	1,853
255	Hemet, CA	3,892	329	Scranton, PA	2,805	403	Baldwin Park, CA	1,846
256	Yuma, AZ	3,861	330	Decatur, IL	2,800	404	League City, TX	1,813
257	Davie, FL	3,842	331	Sparks, NV	2,793	405	Murrieta, CA	1,785
258	Pasadena, CA	3,812	332	Bryan, TX	2,785	406	Tustin, CA	1,767
259	Elk Grove, CA	3,804	333	El Cajon, CA	2,779	407	Edmond, OK	1,765
260	Santa Monica, CA	3,793	334	Round Rock, TX	2,777	408	Clifton, NJ	1,763
261	Fairfield, CA	3,771	335	Arvada, CO	2,763	409	San Marcos, CA	1,729
262	Cape Coral, FL	3,750	336	Lawrence, MA	2,750	410	Troy, MI	1,724
263	Sioux City, IA	3,744	337	Whittier, CA	2,749	411	St. George, UT	1,716
264	Plantation, FL	3,721	338	Westland, MI	2,748	412	Danbury, CT	1,671
265	Lowell, MA	3,710	339	Burbank, CA	2,736	413	Sugar Land, TX	1,650
266	Yonkers, NY	3,698	340	Sunnyvale, CA	2,725	414	Beaverton, OR	1,612
267	Charleston, SC	3,669	341	Boca Raton, FL	2,721	415	Edison Twnshp, NJ	1,603
267	Greeley, CO	3,669	342	Greece, NY	2,685	416	Centennial, CO	1,596
269	Bellevue, WA	3,664	343	Olathe, KS	2,671	417	Clarkstown, NY	1,587
270	Fall River, MA	3,660	344	Surprise, AZ	2,650	418	New Rochelle, NY	1,577
271	Denton, TX	3,631	345	El Monte, CA	2,625	419	Mountain View, CA	1,574
272	Compton, CA	3,617	345	Frisco, TX	2,625	420	Allen, TX	1,487
273	Dearborn, MI	3,604	347	Provo, UT	2,614	421	Farmington Hills, MI	1,338
274	Carrollton, TX	3,594	348	Kennewick, WA	2,601	422	Brick Twnshp, NJ	1,326
275	Gilbert, AZ	3,591	349	Cicero, IL	2,600	423	Meridian, ID	1,322
276	Thornton, CO	3,589	350	Chico, CA	2,573	424	O'Fallon, MO	1,320
277	Roseville, CA	3,581	351	Nashua, NH	2,565	425	Mission Viejo, CA	1,270
278	Racine, WI	3,555	352	Temecula, CA	2,537	426	Lakewood Twnshp, NJ	1,213
279	Santa Clara, CA	3,527	353	Clinton Twnshp, MI	2,521	427	Lake Forest, CA	1,195
280	Cambridge, MA	3,522	354	Upper Darby Twnshp, PA	2,492	428	Chino Hills, CA	1,020
281	Miramar, FL	3,521	355	Upland, CA	2,476	429	Arlington Heights, IL	1,019
282	Largo, FL	3,511	356	Mission, TX	2,474	430	Newton, MA	970
283	West Covina, CA	3,505	357	Chino, CA	2,407	431	Fishers, IN	835
284	Green Bay, WI	3,492	358	Nampa, ID	2,383	432	Carmel, IN	819
285	Bloomington, IN	3,487	359	Carlsbad, CA	2,374	433	Ramapo, NY	796
286	Jurupa Valley, CA	3,486	360	Lynchburg, VA	2,360	434	Johns Creek, GA	569
287	Santa Barbara, CA	3,478	361	Longmont, CO	2,357	435	Parma, OH	507
288	Sunrise, FL	3,459	362	Vista, CA	2,350	NA	Bloomington, MN**	NA
289	Inglewood, CA	3,453	363	Amherst, NY	2,349	NA	Brooklyn Park, MN**	NA
290	Citrus Heights, CA	3,446	364	Broken Arrow, OK	2,342	NA	Chicago, IL**	NA
291	Champaign, IL	3,441	365	Hillsboro, OR	2,334	NA	Duluth, MN**	NA
292	Fayetteville, AR	3,431	366	Tracy, CA	2,303	NA	Rochester, MN**	NA
293	Port St. Lucie, FL	3,426	367	Lakewood, CA	2,289	NA	Toledo, OH**	NA
294	Irvine, CA	3,414	368	Stamford, CT	2,283	NA	Tucson, AZ**	NA
295	Midland, TX	3,406	369	Vacaville, CA	2,277			
296	Lynn, MA	3,343	370	Buena Park, CA	2,272			

Source: CQ Press using reported data from the F.B.I. "Crime in the United States 2012"

*Includes murder, rape, robbery, aggravated assault, burglary, larceny-theft, and motor vehicle theft.

**Not available.

42. Crime Rate in 2012
National Rate = 3,246.1 Crimes per 100,000 Population*

RANK	CITY	RATE	RANK	CITY	RATE	RANK	CITY	RATE
196	Abilene, TX	4,058.0	427	Chino Hills, CA	1,331.0	145	Gainesville, FL	4,764.0
67	Akron, OH	5,944.4	282	Chino, CA	3,016.6	343	Garden Grove, CA	2,545.1
327	Alameda, CA	2,719.1	371	Chula Vista, CA	2,266.3	207	Garland, TX	3,921.5
19	Albany, GA	7,405.2	272	Cicero, IL	3,084.2	39	Gary, IN	6,465.6
105	Albany, NY	5,236.9	22	Cincinnati, OH	7,110.0	413	Gilbert, AZ	1,676.0
59	Albuquerque, NM	6,117.0	197	Citrus Heights, CA	4,048.8	24	Glendale, AZ	6,900.9
374	Alexandria, VA	2,216.0	402	Clarkstown, NY	1,979.1	412	Glendale, CA	1,680.8
352	Alhambra, CA	2,448.2	247	Clarksville, TN	3,360.6	265	Grand Prairie, TX	3,160.4
170	Allentown, PA	4,404.4	161	Clearwater, FL	4,568.2	179	Grand Rapids, MI	4,255.3
414	Allen, TX	1,674.9	17	Cleveland, OH	7,557.0	318	Greece, NY	2,775.1
110	Amarillo, TX	5,177.6	388	Clifton, NJ	2,081.9	214	Greeley, CO	3,810.9
399	Amherst, NY	1,997.6	338	Clinton Twnshp, MI	2,598.9	253	Green Bay, WI	3,291.9
251	Anaheim, CA	3,294.1	174	Clovis, CA	4,338.2	130	Greensboro, NC	4,932.0
173	Anchorage, AK	4,353.1	285	College Station, TX	2,991.7	128	Greenville, NC	4,950.0
341	Ann Arbor, MI	2,567.6	317	Colonie, NY	2,778.3	129	Gresham, OR	4,939.8
90	Antioch, CA	5,547.1	159	Colorado Springs, CO	4,595.8	357	Hamilton Twnshp, NJ	2,430.7
426	Arlington Heights, IL	1,350.3	182	Columbia, MO	4,245.1	118	Hammond, IN	5,077.2
166	Arlington, TX	4,486.7	52	Columbus, GA	6,249.4	228	Hampton, VA	3,604.7
347	Arvada, CO	2,534.2	220	Compton, CA	3,688.7	89	Hartford, CT	5,570.2
51	Asheville, NC	6,252.4	224	Concord, CA	3,661.2	254	Hawthorne, CA	3,288.5
177	Athens-Clarke, GA	4,304.6	354	Coral Springs, FL	2,438.8	223	Hayward, CA	3,666.3
12	Atlanta, GA	7,912.5	319	Corona, CA	2,766.6	142	Hemet, CA	4,792.3
245	Aurora, CO	3,410.6	112	Corpus Christi, TX	5,156.7	378	Henderson, NV	2,178.6
392	Aurora, IL	2,066.4	212	Costa Mesa, CA	3,846.9	267	Hesperia, CA	3,143.4
84	Austin, TX	5,628.2	345	Cranston, RI	2,537.5	243	Hialeah, FL	3,433.6
127	Avondale, AZ	4,995.9	120	Dallas, TX	5,048.5	152	High Point, NC	4,656.3
91	Bakersfield, CA	5,533.7	403	Daly City, CA	1,954.3	349	Hillsboro, OR	2,479.8
359	Baldwin Park, CA	2,408.5	394	Danbury, CT	2,040.5	76	Hollywood, FL	5,750.3
62	Baltimore, MD	6,065.5	155	Davenport, IA	4,636.7	322	Hoover, AL	2,752.3
49	Baton Rouge, LA	6,292.0	198	Davie, FL	4,046.3	68	Houston, TX	5,938.1
72	Beaumont, TX	5,872.5	26	Dayton, OH	6,872.8	286	Huntington Beach, CA	2,970.6
409	Beaverton, OR	1,746.9	218	Dearborn, MI	3,707.2	65	Huntsville, AL	5,964.9
300	Bellevue, WA	2,907.4	222	Decatur, IL	3,677.9	34	Independence, MO	6,547.6
330	Bellflower, CA	2,704.0	227	Deerfield Beach, FL	3,639.4	30	Indianapolis, IN	6,777.6
119	Bellingham, WA	5,074.7	277	Denton, TX	3,052.7	192	Indio, CA	4,128.6
99	Berkeley, CA	5,378.3	176	Denver, CO	4,329.7	271	Inglewood, CA	3,097.2
301	Bethlehem, PA	2,899.7	95	Des Moines, IA	5,450.3	420	Irvine, CA	1,569.5
135	Billings, MT	4,871.6	11	Detroit, MI	7,915.0	279	Irving, TX	3,041.9
7	Birmingham, AL	8,451.9	241	Downey, CA	3,448.1	147	Jacksonville, FL	4,741.9
310	Bloomington, IL	2,813.0	NA	Duluth, MN**	NA	18	Jackson, MS	7,523.1
178	Bloomington, IN	4,271.4	117	Durham, NC	5,089.5	299	Jersey City, NJ	2,912.3
NA	Bloomington, MN**	NA	47	Edinburg, TX	6,335.0	434	Johns Creek, GA	710.9
266	Boca Raton, FL	3,145.9	419	Edison Twnshp, NJ	1,587.0	296	Joliet, IL	2,923.8
314	Boise, ID	2,792.9	383	Edmond, OK	2,114.5	231	Jurupa Valley, CA	3,572.6
216	Boston, MA	3,744.6	326	El Cajon, CA	2,728.1	77	Kansas City, KS	5,716.7
262	Boulder, CO	3,177.8	370	El Monte, CA	2,275.6	28	Kansas City, MO	6,788.6
408	Brick Twnshp, NJ	1,749.1	306	El Paso, TX	2,852.5	246	Kennewick, WA	3,379.2
148	Bridgeport, CT	4,734.0	393	Elgin, IL	2,051.2	257	Kenosha, WI	3,273.2
172	Brockton, MA	4,370.7	183	Elizabeth, NJ	4,242.9	132	Kent, WA	4,922.9
366	Broken Arrow, OK	2,326.0	356	Elk Grove, CA	2,433.1	169	Killeen, TX	4,423.1
NA	Brooklyn Park, MN**	NA	209	Erie, PA	3,891.3	15	Knoxville, TN	7,650.3
136	Brownsville, TX	4,864.7	276	Escondido, CA	3,063.4	57	Lafayette, LA	6,181.4
233	Bryan, TX	3,548.7	101	Eugene, OR	5,336.5	424	Lake Forest, CA	1,509.5
321	Buena Park, CA	2,753.8	85	Evansville, IN	5,620.4	80	Lakeland, FL	5,684.8
43	Buffalo, NY	6,415.3	33	Everett, WA	6,548.7	429	Lakewood Twnshp, NJ	1,294.0
337	Burbank, CA	2,604.3	237	Fairfield, CA	3,520.7	311	Lakewood, CO	2,812.7
252	Cambridge, MA	3,292.2	193	Fall River, MA	4,077.9	121	Lakewood, CO	5,041.5
14	Camden, NJ	7,725.5	294	Fargo, ND	2,940.5	324	Lancaster, CA	2,737.6
365	Cape Coral, FL	2,349.3	416	Farmington Hills, MI	1,665.9	186	Lansing, MI	4,230.6
375	Carlsbad, CA	2,200.6	163	Fayetteville, AR	4,551.2	144	Laredo, TX	4,773.2
432	Carmel, IN	1,001.0	23	Fayetteville, NC	6,966.7	168	Largo, FL	4,456.5
302	Carrollton, TX	2,887.3	71	Federal Way, WA	5,873.1	138	Las Cruces, NM	4,821.5
239	Carson, CA	3,463.4	431	Fishers, IN	1,052.0	206	Las Vegas, NV	3,922.2
425	Cary, NC	1,435.3	8	Flint, MI	8,283.8	133	Lawrence, KS	4,896.8
205	Cedar Rapids, IA	3,955.6	332	Fontana, CA	2,660.4	235	Lawrence, MA	3,541.0
422	Centennial, CO	1,534.3	280	Fort Collins, CO	3,031.1	55	Lawton, OK	6,203.6
185	Champaign, IL	4,231.0	31	Fort Lauderdale, FL	6,733.7	385	League City, TX	2,105.0
287	Chandler, AZ	2,966.0	53	Fort Smith, AR	6,238.9	355	Lee's Summit, MO	2,434.7
288	Charleston, SC	2,962.3	194	Fort Wayne, IN	4,070.5	143	Lexington, KY	4,784.5
151	Charlotte, NC	4,678.4	141	Fort Worth, TX	4,809.5	181	Lincoln, NE	4,247.6
215	Cheektowaga, NY	3,783.9	387	Fremont, CA	2,085.2	3	Little Rock, AR	9,376.5
269	Chesapeake, VA	3,134.1	83	Fresno, CA	5,629.3	344	Livermore, CA	2,543.5
NA	Chicago, IL**	NA	381	Frisco, TX	2,130.6	362	Livonia, MI	2,363.9
291	Chico, CA	2,954.4	263	Fullerton, CA	3,170.0	229	Long Beach, CA	3,582.9

RANK	CITY	RATE
333	Longmont, CO	2,650.5
81	Longview, TX	5,663.0
323	Los Angeles, CA	2,750.2
134	Louisville, KY	4,892.7
244	Lowell, MA	3,418.1
63	Lubbock, TX	6,000.2
278	Lynchburg, VA	3,051.2
226	Lynn, MA	3,639.8
13	Macon, GA	7,843.9
225	Madison, WI	3,642.0
195	Manchester, NH	4,064.0
191	McAllen, TX	4,148.2
377	McKinney, TX	2,183.1
44	Medford, OR	6,369.3
106	Melbourne, FL	5,227.3
10	Memphis, TN	8,063.1
346	Menifee, CA	2,534.8
61	Merced, CA	6,077.1
411	Meridian, ID	1,710.9
236	Mesa, AZ	3,532.2
154	Mesquite, TX	4,645.4
1	Miami Beach, FL	10,947.0
114	Miami Gardens, FL	5,140.5
35	Miami, FL	6,547.2
293	Midland, TX	2,945.4
46	Milwaukee, WI	6,337.6
66	Minneapolis, MN	5,953.0
313	Miramar, FL	2,794.5
428	Mission Viejo, CA	1,328.5
275	Mission, TX	3,071.1
102	Mobile, AL	5,334.5
50	Modesto, CA	6,287.4
58	Montgomery, AL	6,164.5
234	Moreno Valley, CA	3,544.3
391	Mountain View, CA	2,072.9
188	Murfreesboro, TN	4,193.4
415	Murrieta, CA	1,670.7
304	Nampa, ID	2,860.2
361	Napa, CA	2,365.5
423	Naperville, IL	1,514.3
292	Nashua, NH	2,952.7
98	Nashville, TN	5,411.9
171	New Bedford, MA	4,384.0
40	New Haven, CT	6,454.0
160	New Orleans, LA	4,587.5
396	New Rochelle, NY	2,021.1
363	New York, NY	2,361.5
140	Newark, NJ	4,811.3
340	Newport Beach, CA	2,580.0
232	Newport News, VA	3,566.3
430	Newton, MA	1,118.7
108	Norfolk, VA	5,186.6
309	Norman, OK	2,828.0
41	North Charleston, SC	6,450.5
258	North Las Vegas, NV	3,258.0
308	Norwalk, CA	2,835.2
368	Norwalk, CT	2,289.7
6	Oakland, CA	8,587.3
295	Oceanside, CA	2,931.5
153	Odessa, TX	4,650.9
417	O'Fallon, MO	1,636.3
116	Ogden, UT	5,117.4
27	Oklahoma City, OK	6,860.9
389	Olathe, KS	2,077.6
109	Omaha, NE	5,182.9
249	Ontario, CA	3,328.7
382	Orange, CA	2,124.7
360	Orem, UT	2,402.3
16	Orlando, FL	7,631.2
350	Overland Park, KS	2,464.4
367	Oxnard, CA	2,316.2
303	Palm Bay, FL	2,876.7
329	Palmdale, CA	2,707.8
435	Parma, OH	626.2

RANK	CITY	RATE
325	Pasadena, CA	2,734.9
200	Pasadena, TX	4,032.0
187	Paterson, NJ	4,208.0
401	Pearland, TX	1,981.0
312	Pembroke Pines, FL	2,802.0
268	Peoria, AZ	3,138.0
113	Peoria, IL	5,153.2
137	Philadelphia, PA	4,863.7
149	Phoenix, AZ	4,728.0
189	Pittsburgh, PA	4,177.3
348	Plano, TX	2,487.4
184	Plantation, FL	4,242.6
202	Pomona, CA	4,010.3
42	Pompano Beach, FL	6,428.9
395	Port St. Lucie, FL	2,034.2
86	Portland, OR	5,609.5
94	Portsmouth, VA	5,460.1
115	Providence, RI	5,121.4
373	Provo, UT	2,236.5
20	Pueblo, CO	7,176.5
386	Quincy, MA	2,085.6
164	Racine, WI	4,496.9
219	Raleigh, NC	3,699.3
433	Ramapo, NY	931.6
320	Rancho Cucamon., CA	2,766.5
126	Reading, PA	5,013.7
87	Redding, CA	5,589.5
342	Redwood City, CA	2,559.1
217	Reno, NV	3,737.8
111	Renton, WA	5,169.5
201	Rialto, CA	4,015.9
274	Richardson, TX	3,074.6
74	Richmond, CA	5,810.6
125	Richmond, VA	5,029.4
364	Rio Rancho, NM	2,354.1
208	Riverside, CA	3,893.4
97	Roanoke, VA	5,433.6
NA	Rochester, MN**	NA
48	Rochester, NY	6,298.3
45	Rockford, IL	6,363.4
298	Roseville, CA	2,913.8
398	Roswell, GA	2,011.0
335	Round Rock, TX	2,614.1
131	Sacramento, CA	4,928.5
156	Salem, OR	4,636.1
213	Salinas, CA	3,842.3
9	Salt Lake City, UT	8,135.0
38	San Antonio, TX	6,493.0
73	San Bernardino, CA	5,829.2
316	San Diego, CA	2,781.4
96	San Francisco, CA	5,445.8
255	San Jose, CA	3,278.2
157	San Leandro, CA	4,630.0
397	San Marcos, CA	2,014.9
380	San Mateo, CA	2,152.0
284	Sandy Springs, GA	3,000.3
270	Sandy, UT	3,108.2
334	Santa Ana, CA	2,623.6
210	Santa Barbara, CA	3,870.0
290	Santa Clara, CA	2,954.9
410	Santa Clarita, CA	1,720.5
273	Santa Maria, CA	3,082.8
190	Santa Monica, CA	4,158.3
336	Santa Rosa, CA	2,606.8
203	Savannah, GA	3,979.1
305	Scottsdale, AZ	2,853.7
221	Scranton, PA	3,685.1
79	Seattle, WA	5,691.3
82	Shreveport, LA	5,644.9
418	Simi Valley, CA	1,623.7
165	Sioux City, IA	4,495.2
230	Sioux Falls, SD	3,581.8
339	Somerville, MA	2,581.6
100	South Bend, IN	5,373.9

RANK	CITY	RATE
260	South Gate, CA	3,228.2
281	Sparks, NV	3,023.2
93	Spokane Valley, WA	5,485.7
4	Spokane, WA	9,375.3
25	Springfield, IL	6,900.8
88	Springfield, MA	5,585.1
2	Springfield, MO	10,002.4
407	Stamford, CT	1,838.1
379	Sterling Heights, MI	2,162.0
32	Stockton, CA	6,649.2
372	St. George, UT	2,264.4
36	St. Joseph, MO	6,505.9
5	St. Louis, MO	8,678.7
139	St. Paul, MN	4,813.9
69	St. Petersburg, FL	5,915.3
400	Sugar Land, TX	1,989.8
405	Sunnyvale, CA	1,897.6
204	Sunrise, FL	3,968.2
376	Surprise, AZ	2,193.8
124	Syracuse, NY	5,035.2
21	Tacoma, WA	7,146.0
92	Tallahassee, FL	5,499.3
240	Tampa, FL	3,452.2
351	Temecula, CA	2,453.2
104	Tempe, AZ	5,240.2
297	Thornton, CO	2,915.2
421	Thousand Oaks, CA	1,544.5
NA	Toledo, OH**	NA
261	Toms River Twnshp, NJ	3,228.0
70	Topeka, KS	5,908.7
404	Torrance, CA	1,947.9
328	Tracy, CA	2,707.9
150	Trenton, NJ	4,684.9
384	Troy, MI	2,113.6
NA	Tucson, AZ**	NA
54	Tulsa, OK	6,206.0
103	Tuscaloosa, AL	5,248.3
369	Tustin, CA	2,282.9
122	Tyler, TX	5,040.0
256	Upland, CA	3,278.1
283	Upper Darby Twnshp, PA	3,003.2
358	Vacaville, CA	2,423.6
78	Vallejo, CA	5,700.9
180	Vancouver, WA	4,249.4
211	Ventura, CA	3,866.0
175	Victorville, CA	4,331.6
315	Virginia Beach, VA	2,787.2
146	Visalia, CA	4,760.8
353	Vista, CA	2,445.7
123	Waco, TX	5,038.3
248	Warren, MI	3,351.2
331	Warwick, RI	2,696.8
75	Washington, DC	5,805.9
162	Waterbury, CT	4,562.6
238	Waukegan, IL	3,473.8
259	West Covina, CA	3,249.6
289	West Jordan, UT	2,955.1
60	West Palm Beach, FL	6,077.8
158	West Valley, UT	4,612.5
250	Westland, MI	3,299.0
242	Westminster, CA	3,437.1
307	Westminster, CO	2,844.8
264	Whittier, CA	3,169.2
107	Wichita Falls, TX	5,210.1
56	Wichita, KS	6,195.2
64	Wilmington, NC	5,968.7
37	Winston-Salem, NC	6,501.0
390	Woodbridge Twnshp, NJ	2,076.3
167	Worcester, MA	4,469.4
29	Yakima, WA	6,786.6
406	Yonkers, NY	1,863.3
199	Yuma, AZ	4,040.1

Source: CQ Press using reported data from the F.B.I. "Crime in the United States 2012"

*Includes murder, rape, robbery, aggravated assault, burglary, larceny-theft, and motor vehicle theft.

**Not available.

42. Crime Rate in 2012 (continued)
National Rate = 3,246.1 Crimes per 100,000 Population*

RANK	CITY	RATE	RANK	CITY	RATE	RANK	CITY	RATE
1	Miami Beach, FL	10,947.0	75	Washington, DC	5,805.9	149	Phoenix, AZ	4,728.0
2	Springfield, MO	10,002.4	76	Hollywood, FL	5,750.3	150	Trenton, NJ	4,684.9
3	Little Rock, AR	9,376.5	77	Kansas City, KS	5,716.7	151	Charlotte, NC	4,678.4
4	Spokane, WA	9,375.3	78	Vallejo, CA	5,700.9	152	High Point, NC	4,656.3
5	St. Louis, MO	8,678.7	79	Seattle, WA	5,691.3	153	Odessa, TX	4,650.9
6	Oakland, CA	8,587.3	80	Lakeland, FL	5,684.8	154	Mesquite, TX	4,645.4
7	Birmingham, AL	8,451.9	81	Longview, TX	5,663.0	155	Davenport, IA	4,636.7
8	Flint, MI	8,283.8	82	Shreveport, LA	5,644.9	156	Salem, OR	4,636.1
9	Salt Lake City, UT	8,135.0	83	Fresno, CA	5,629.3	157	San Leandro, CA	4,630.0
10	Memphis, TN	8,063.1	84	Austin, TX	5,628.2	158	West Valley, UT	4,612.5
11	Detroit, MI	7,915.0	85	Evansville, IN	5,620.4	159	Colorado Springs, CO	4,595.8
12	Atlanta, GA	7,912.5	86	Portland, OR	5,609.5	160	New Orleans, LA	4,587.5
13	Macon, GA	7,843.9	87	Redding, CA	5,589.5	161	Clearwater, FL	4,568.2
14	Camden, NJ	7,725.5	88	Springfield, MA	5,585.1	162	Waterbury, CT	4,562.6
15	Knoxville, TN	7,650.3	89	Hartford, CT	5,570.2	163	Fayetteville, AR	4,551.2
16	Orlando, FL	7,631.2	90	Antioch, CA	5,547.1	164	Racine, WI	4,496.9
17	Cleveland, OH	7,557.0	91	Bakersfield, CA	5,533.7	165	Sioux City, IA	4,495.2
18	Jackson, MS	7,523.1	92	Tallahassee, FL	5,499.3	166	Arlington, TX	4,486.7
19	Albany, GA	7,405.2	93	Spokane Valley, WA	5,485.7	167	Worcester, MA	4,469.4
20	Pueblo, CO	7,176.5	94	Portsmouth, VA	5,460.1	168	Largo, FL	4,456.5
21	Tacoma, WA	7,146.0	95	Des Moines, IA	5,450.3	169	Killeen, TX	4,423.1
22	Cincinnati, OH	7,110.0	96	San Francisco, CA	5,445.8	170	Allentown, PA	4,404.4
23	Fayetteville, NC	6,966.7	97	Roanoke, VA	5,433.6	171	New Bedford, MA	4,384.0
24	Glendale, AZ	6,900.9	98	Nashville, TN	5,411.9	172	Brockton, MA	4,370.7
25	Springfield, IL	6,900.8	99	Berkeley, CA	5,378.3	173	Anchorage, AK	4,353.1
26	Dayton, OH	6,872.8	100	South Bend, IN	5,373.9	174	Clovis, CA	4,338.2
27	Oklahoma City, OK	6,860.9	101	Eugene, OR	5,336.5	175	Victorville, CA	4,331.6
28	Kansas City, MO	6,788.6	102	Mobile, AL	5,334.5	176	Denver, CO	4,329.7
29	Yakima, WA	6,786.6	103	Tuscaloosa, AL	5,248.3	177	Athens-Clarke, GA	4,304.6
30	Indianapolis, IN	6,777.6	104	Tempe, AZ	5,240.2	178	Bloomington, IN	4,271.4
31	Fort Lauderdale, FL	6,733.7	105	Albany, NY	5,236.9	179	Grand Rapids, MI	4,255.3
32	Stockton, CA	6,649.2	106	Melbourne, FL	5,227.3	180	Vancouver, WA	4,249.4
33	Everett, WA	6,548.7	107	Wichita Falls, TX	5,210.1	181	Lincoln, NE	4,247.6
34	Independence, MO	6,547.6	108	Norfolk, VA	5,186.6	182	Columbia, MO	4,245.1
35	Miami, FL	6,547.2	109	Omaha, NE	5,182.9	183	Elizabeth, NJ	4,242.9
36	St. Joseph, MO	6,505.9	110	Amarillo, TX	5,177.6	184	Plantation, FL	4,242.6
37	Winston-Salem, NC	6,501.0	111	Renton, WA	5,169.5	185	Champaign, IL	4,231.0
38	San Antonio, TX	6,493.0	112	Corpus Christi, TX	5,156.7	186	Lansing, MI	4,230.6
39	Gary, IN	6,465.6	113	Peoria, IL	5,153.2	187	Paterson, NJ	4,208.0
40	New Haven, CT	6,454.0	114	Miami Gardens, FL	5,140.5	188	Murfreesboro, TN	4,193.4
41	North Charleston, SC	6,450.5	115	Providence, RI	5,121.4	189	Pittsburgh, PA	4,177.3
42	Pompano Beach, FL	6,428.9	116	Ogden, UT	5,117.4	190	Santa Monica, CA	4,158.3
43	Buffalo, NY	6,415.3	117	Durham, NC	5,089.5	191	McAllen, TX	4,148.2
44	Medford, OR	6,369.3	118	Hammond, IN	5,077.2	192	Indio, CA	4,128.6
45	Rockford, IL	6,363.4	119	Bellingham, WA	5,074.7	193	Fall River, MA	4,077.9
46	Milwaukee, WI	6,337.6	120	Dallas, TX	5,048.5	194	Fort Wayne, IN	4,070.5
47	Edinburg, TX	6,335.0	121	Lakewood, CO	5,041.5	195	Manchester, NH	4,064.0
48	Rochester, NY	6,298.3	122	Tyler, TX	5,040.0	196	Abilene, TX	4,058.0
49	Baton Rouge, LA	6,292.0	123	Waco, TX	5,038.3	197	Citrus Heights, CA	4,048.8
50	Modesto, CA	6,287.4	124	Syracuse, NY	5,035.2	198	Davie, FL	4,046.3
51	Asheville, NC	6,252.4	125	Richmond, VA	5,029.4	199	Yuma, AZ	4,040.1
52	Columbus, GA	6,249.4	126	Reading, PA	5,013.7	200	Pasadena, TX	4,032.0
53	Fort Smith, AR	6,238.9	127	Avondale, AZ	4,995.9	201	Rialto, CA	4,015.9
54	Tulsa, OK	6,206.0	128	Greenville, NC	4,950.0	202	Pomona, CA	4,010.3
55	Lawton, OK	6,203.6	129	Gresham, OR	4,939.8	203	Savannah, GA	3,979.1
56	Wichita, KS	6,195.2	130	Greensboro, NC	4,932.0	204	Sunrise, FL	3,968.2
57	Lafayette, LA	6,181.4	131	Sacramento, CA	4,928.5	205	Cedar Rapids, IA	3,955.6
58	Montgomery, AL	6,164.5	132	Kent, WA	4,922.9	206	Las Vegas, NV	3,922.2
59	Albuquerque, NM	6,117.0	133	Lawrence, KS	4,896.8	207	Garland, TX	3,921.5
60	West Palm Beach, FL	6,077.8	134	Louisville, KY	4,892.7	208	Riverside, CA	3,893.4
61	Merced, CA	6,077.1	135	Billings, MT	4,871.6	209	Erie, PA	3,891.3
62	Baltimore, MD	6,065.5	136	Brownsville, TX	4,864.7	210	Santa Barbara, CA	3,870.0
63	Lubbock, TX	6,000.2	137	Philadelphia, PA	4,863.7	211	Ventura, CA	3,866.0
64	Wilmington, NC	5,968.7	138	Las Cruces, NM	4,821.5	212	Costa Mesa, CA	3,846.9
65	Huntsville, AL	5,964.9	139	St. Paul, MN	4,813.9	213	Salinas, CA	3,842.3
66	Minneapolis, MN	5,953.0	140	Newark, NJ	4,811.3	214	Greeley, CO	3,810.9
67	Akron, OH	5,944.4	141	Fort Worth, TX	4,809.5	215	Cheektowaga, NY	3,783.9
68	Houston, TX	5,938.1	142	Hemet, CA	4,792.3	216	Boston, MA	3,744.6
69	St. Petersburg, FL	5,915.3	143	Lexington, KY	4,784.5	217	Reno, NV	3,737.8
70	Topeka, KS	5,908.7	144	Laredo, TX	4,773.2	218	Dearborn, MI	3,707.2
71	Federal Way, WA	5,873.1	145	Gainesville, FL	4,764.0	219	Raleigh, NC	3,699.3
72	Beaumont, TX	5,872.5	146	Visalia, CA	4,760.8	220	Compton, CA	3,688.7
73	San Bernardino, CA	5,829.2	147	Jacksonville, FL	4,741.9	221	Scranton, PA	3,685.1
74	Richmond, CA	5,810.6	148	Bridgeport, CT	4,734.0	222	Decatur, IL	3,677.9

RANK	CITY	RATE	RANK	CITY	RATE	RANK	CITY	RATE
223	Hayward, CA	3,666.3	297	Thornton, CO	2,915.2	371	Chula Vista, CA	2,266.3
224	Concord, CA	3,661.2	298	Roseville, CA	2,913.8	372	St. George, UT	2,264.4
225	Madison, WI	3,642.0	299	Jersey City, NJ	2,912.3	373	Provo, UT	2,236.5
226	Lynn, MA	3,639.8	300	Bellevue, WA	2,907.4	374	Alexandria, VA	2,216.0
227	Deerfield Beach, FL	3,639.4	301	Bethlehem, PA	2,899.7	375	Carlsbad, CA	2,200.6
228	Hampton, VA	3,604.7	302	Carrollton, TX	2,887.3	376	Surprise, AZ	2,193.8
229	Long Beach, CA	3,582.9	303	Palm Bay, FL	2,876.7	377	McKinney, TX	2,183.1
230	Sioux Falls, SD	3,581.8	304	Nampa, ID	2,860.2	378	Henderson, NV	2,178.6
231	Jurupa Valley, CA	3,572.6	305	Scottsdale, AZ	2,853.7	379	Sterling Heights, MI	2,162.0
232	Newport News, VA	3,566.3	306	El Paso, TX	2,852.5	380	San Mateo, CA	2,152.0
233	Bryan, TX	3,548.7	307	Westminster, CO	2,844.8	381	Frisco, TX	2,130.6
234	Moreno Valley, CA	3,544.3	308	Norwalk, CA	2,835.2	382	Orange, CA	2,124.7
235	Lawrence, MA	3,541.0	309	Norman, OK	2,828.0	383	Edmond, OK	2,114.5
236	Mesa, AZ	3,532.2	310	Bloomington, IL	2,813.0	384	Troy, MI	2,113.6
237	Fairfield, CA	3,520.7	311	Lakewood, CA	2,812.7	385	League City, TX	2,105.0
238	Waukegan, IL	3,473.9	312	Pembroke Pines, FL	2,802.0	386	Quincy, MA	2,085.6
239	Carson, CA	3,463.4	313	Miramar, FL	2,794.5	387	Fremont, CA	2,085.2
240	Tampa, FL	3,452.2	314	Boise, ID	2,792.9	388	Clifton, NJ	2,081.9
241	Downey, CA	3,448.1	315	Virginia Beach, VA	2,787.2	389	Olathe, KS	2,077.6
242	Westminster, CA	3,437.1	316	San Diego, CA	2,781.4	390	Woodbridge Twnshp, NJ	2,076.3
243	Hialeah, FL	3,433.6	317	Colonie, NY	2,778.3	391	Mountain View, CA	2,072.9
244	Lowell, MA	3,418.1	318	Greece, NY	2,775.1	392	Aurora, IL	2,066.4
245	Aurora, CO	3,410.6	319	Corona, CA	2,766.6	393	Elgin, IL	2,051.2
246	Kennewick, WA	3,379.2	320	Rancho Cucamon., CA	2,766.5	394	Danbury, CT	2,040.5
247	Clarksville, TN	3,360.6	321	Buena Park, CA	2,753.8	395	Port St. Lucie, FL	2,034.2
248	Warren, MI	3,351.2	322	Hoover, AL	2,752.3	396	New Rochelle, NY	2,021.1
249	Ontario, CA	3,328.7	323	Los Angeles, CA	2,750.2	397	San Marcos, CA	2,014.9
250	Westland, MI	3,299.0	324	Lancaster, CA	2,737.6	398	Roswell, GA	2,011.0
251	Anaheim, CA	3,294.1	325	Pasadena, CA	2,734.9	399	Amherst, NY	1,997.6
252	Cambridge, MA	3,292.2	326	El Cajon, CA	2,728.1	400	Sugar Land, TX	1,989.8
253	Green Bay, WI	3,291.9	327	Alameda, CA	2,719.1	401	Pearland, TX	1,981.0
254	Hawthorne, CA	3,288.5	328	Tracy, CA	2,707.9	402	Clarkstown, NY	1,979.1
255	San Jose, CA	3,278.2	329	Palmdale, CA	2,707.8	403	Daly City, CA	1,954.3
256	Upland, CA	3,278.1	330	Bellflower, CA	2,704.0	404	Torrance, CA	1,947.9
257	Kenosha, WI	3,273.2	331	Warwick, RI	2,696.8	405	Sunnyvale, CA	1,897.6
258	North Las Vegas, NV	3,258.0	332	Fontana, CA	2,660.4	406	Yonkers, NY	1,863.3
259	West Covina, CA	3,249.6	333	Longmont, CO	2,650.5	407	Stamford, CT	1,838.1
260	South Gate, CA	3,228.2	334	Santa Ana, CA	2,623.6	408	Brick Twnshp, NJ	1,749.1
261	Toms River Twnshp, NJ	3,228.0	335	Round Rock, TX	2,614.1	409	Beaverton, OR	1,746.9
262	Boulder, CO	3,177.8	336	Santa Rosa, CA	2,606.8	410	Santa Clarita, CA	1,720.5
263	Fullerton, CA	3,170.0	337	Burbank, CA	2,604.3	411	Meridian, ID	1,710.9
264	Whittier, CA	3,169.2	338	Clinton Twnshp, MI	2,598.9	412	Glendale, CA	1,680.8
265	Grand Prairie, TX	3,160.4	339	Somerville, MA	2,581.6	413	Gilbert, AZ	1,676.0
266	Boca Raton, FL	3,145.9	340	Newport Beach, CA	2,580.0	414	Allen, TX	1,674.9
267	Hesperia, CA	3,143.4	341	Ann Arbor, MI	2,567.6	415	Murrieta, CA	1,670.7
268	Peoria, AZ	3,138.0	342	Redwood City, CA	2,559.1	416	Farmington Hills, MI	1,665.9
269	Chesapeake, VA	3,134.1	343	Garden Grove, CA	2,545.1	417	O'Fallon, MO	1,636.3
270	Sandy, UT	3,108.2	344	Livermore, CA	2,543.5	418	Simi Valley, CA	1,623.7
271	Inglewood, CA	3,097.2	345	Cranston, RI	2,537.5	419	Edison Twnshp, NJ	1,587.0
272	Cicero, IL	3,084.2	346	Menifee, CA	2,534.8	420	Irvine, CA	1,569.5
273	Santa Maria, CA	3,082.8	347	Arvada, CO	2,534.2	421	Thousand Oaks, CA	1,544.5
274	Richardson, TX	3,074.6	348	Plano, TX	2,487.4	422	Centennial, CO	1,534.3
275	Mission, TX	3,071.1	349	Hillsboro, OR	2,479.8	423	Naperville, IL	1,514.3
276	Escondido, CA	3,063.4	350	Overland Park, KS	2,464.4	424	Lake Forest, CA	1,509.5
277	Denton, TX	3,052.7	351	Temecula, CA	2,453.2	425	Cary, NC	1,435.3
278	Lynchburg, VA	3,051.2	352	Alhambra, CA	2,448.2	426	Arlington Heights, IL	1,350.3
279	Irving, TX	3,041.9	353	Vista, CA	2,445.7	427	Chino Hills, CA	1,331.0
280	Fort Collins, CO	3,031.1	354	Coral Springs, FL	2,438.8	428	Mission Viejo, CA	1,328.5
281	Sparks, NV	3,023.2	355	Lee's Summit, MO	2,434.7	429	Lakewood Twnshp, NJ	1,294.0
282	Chino, CA	3,016.6	356	Elk Grove, CA	2,433.1	430	Newton, MA	1,118.7
283	Upper Darby Twnshp, PA	3,003.2	357	Hamilton Twnshp, NJ	2,430.7	431	Fishers, IN	1,052.0
284	Sandy Springs, GA	3,000.3	358	Vacaville, CA	2,423.6	432	Carmel, IN	1,001.0
285	College Station, TX	2,991.7	359	Baldwin Park, CA	2,408.5	433	Ramapo, NY	931.6
286	Huntington Beach, CA	2,970.6	360	Orem, UT	2,402.3	434	Johns Creek, GA	710.9
287	Chandler, AZ	2,966.0	361	Napa, CA	2,365.5	435	Parma, OH	626.2
288	Charleston, SC	2,962.3	362	Livonia, MI	2,363.9	NA	Bloomington, MN**	NA
289	West Jordan, UT	2,955.1	363	New York, NY	2,361.5	NA	Brooklyn Park, MN**	NA
290	Santa Clara, CA	2,954.9	364	Rio Rancho, NM	2,354.1	NA	Chicago, IL**	NA
291	Chico, CA	2,954.4	365	Cape Coral, FL	2,349.3	NA	Duluth, MN**	NA
292	Nashua, NH	2,952.7	366	Broken Arrow, OK	2,326.0	NA	Rochester, MN**	NA
293	Midland, TX	2,945.4	367	Oxnard, CA	2,316.2	NA	Toledo, OH**	NA
294	Fargo, ND	2,940.5	368	Norwalk, CT	2,289.7	NA	Tucson, AZ**	NA
295	Oceanside, CA	2,931.5	369	Tustin, CA	2,282.9			
296	Joliet, IL	2,923.8	370	El Monte, CA	2,275.6			

Source: CQ Press using reported data from the F.B.I. "Crime in the United States 2012"

*Includes murder, rape, robbery, aggravated assault, burglary, larceny-theft, and motor vehicle theft.

**Not available.

43. Percent Change in Crime Rate: 2011 to 2012
National Percent Change = 1.4% Decrease*

RANK	CITY	% CHANGE	RANK	CITY	% CHANGE	RANK	CITY	% CHANGE
171	Abilene, TX	0.8	255	Chino Hills, CA	(3.7)	263	Gainesville, FL	(4.2)
310	Akron, OH	(6.3)	132	Chino, CA	2.6	25	Garden Grove, CA	14.7
253	Alameda, CA	(3.5)	226	Chula Vista, CA	(1.5)	221	Garland, TX	(1.4)
75	Albany, GA	8.4	48	Cicero, IL	11.6	378	Gary, IN	(12.7)
NA	Albany, NY**	NA	354	Cincinnati, OH	(10.2)	372	Gilbert, AZ	(12.1)
107	Albuquerque, NM	4.9	314	Citrus Heights, CA	(6.9)	186	Glendale, AZ	0.1
337	Alexandria, VA	(8.6)	NA	Clarkstown, NY**	NA	372	Glendale, CA	(12.1)
174	Alhambra, CA	0.7	364	Clarksville, TN	(11.6)	409	Grand Prairie, TX	(25.0)
NA	Allentown, PA**	NA	159	Clearwater, FL	1.1	101	Grand Rapids, MI	5.6
350	Allen, TX	(9.8)	235	Cleveland, OH	(2.4)	NA	Greece, NY**	NA
288	Amarillo, TX	(5.0)	293	Clifton, NJ	(5.2)	154	Greeley, CO	1.3
NA	Amherst, NY**	NA	260	Clinton Twnshp, MI	(4.1)	6	Green Bay, WI	23.2
25	Anaheim, CA	14.7	154	Clovis, CA	1.3	NA	Greensboro, NC**	NA
66	Anchorage, AK	9.2	377	College Station, TX	(12.6)	NA	Greenville, NC**	NA
118	Ann Arbor, MI	4.0	NA	Colonie, NY**	NA	49	Gresham, OR	11.5
10	Antioch, CA	22.5	61	Colorado Springs, CO	9.8	79	Hamilton Twnshp, NJ	7.8
352	Arlington Heights, IL	(10.1)	278	Columbia, MO	(4.6)	299	Hammond, IN	(5.5)
374	Arlington, TX	(12.3)	354	Columbus, GA	(10.2)	359	Hampton, VA	(10.8)
154	Arvada, CO	1.3	334	Compton, CA	(8.4)	237	Hartford, CT	(2.5)
15	Asheville, NC	20.2	86	Concord, CA	6.8	141	Hawthorne, CA	2.1
279	Athens-Clarke, GA	(4.7)	336	Coral Springs, FL	(8.5)	9	Hayward, CA	22.6
318	Atlanta, GA	(7.1)	16	Corona, CA	20.0	200	Hemet, CA	(0.5)
199	Aurora, CO	(0.4)	282	Corpus Christi, TX	(4.8)	95	Henderson, NV	5.9
328	Aurora, IL	(8.0)	34	Costa Mesa, CA	13.7	46	Hesperia, CA	11.9
205	Austin, TX	(0.7)	292	Cranston, RI	(5.1)	311	Hialeah, FL	(6.4)
321	Avondale, AZ	(7.3)	368	Dallas, TX	(12.0)	381	High Point, NC	(13.0)
20	Bakersfield, CA	16.5	248	Daly City, CA	(3.1)	119	Hillsboro, OR	3.8
196	Baldwin Park, CA	(0.3)	302	Danbury, CT	(5.6)	242	Hollywood, FL	(2.9)
229	Baltimore, MD	(1.8)	398	Davenport, IA	(16.4)	182	Hoover, AL	0.2
255	Baton Rouge, LA	(3.7)	296	Davie, FL	(5.3)	226	Houston, TX	(1.5)
330	Beaumont, TX	(8.2)	176	Dayton, OH	0.6	28	Huntington Beach, CA	14.3
403	Beaverton, OR	(18.5)	366	Dearborn, MI	(11.7)	263	Huntsville, AL	(4.2)
229	Bellevue, WA	(1.8)	393	Decatur, IL	(15.3)	86	Independence, MO	6.8
216	Bellflower, CA	(1.0)	200	Deerfield Beach, FL	(0.5)	176	Indianapolis, IN	0.6
95	Bellingham, WA	5.9	237	Denton, TX	(2.5)	110	Indio, CA	4.5
55	Berkeley, CA	10.5	166	Denver, CO	0.9	153	Inglewood, CA	1.4
108	Bethlehem, PA	4.8	299	Des Moines, IA	(5.5)	210	Irvine, CA	(0.8)
136	Billings, MT	2.3	271	Detroit, MI	(4.4)	329	Irving, TX	(8.1)
389	Birmingham, AL	(14.2)	337	Downey, CA	(8.6)	263	Jacksonville, FL	(4.2)
129	Bloomington, IL	2.9	NA	Duluth, MN**	NA	343	Jackson, MS	(9.2)
116	Bloomington, IN	4.1	344	Durham, NC	(9.3)	284	Jersey City, NJ	(4.9)
NA	Bloomington, MN**	NA	159	Edinburg, TX	1.1	344	Johns Creek, GA	(9.3)
303	Boca Raton, FL	(5.7)	404	Edison Twnshp, NJ	(19.4)	217	Joliet, IL	(1.2)
200	Boise, ID	(0.5)	141	Edmond, OK	2.1	NA	Jurupa Valley, CA**	NA
304	Boston, MA	(5.8)	334	El Cajon, CA	(8.4)	288	Kansas City, KS	(5.0)
33	Boulder, CO	13.8	253	El Monte, CA	(3.5)	171	Kansas City, MO	0.8
313	Brick Twnshp, NJ	(6.8)	221	El Paso, TX	(1.4)	361	Kennewick, WA	(11.1)
246	Bridgeport, CT	(3.0)	299	Elgin, IL	(5.5)	226	Kenosha, WI	(1.5)
306	Brockton, MA	(6.0)	401	Elizabeth, NJ	(17.1)	400	Kent, WA	(17.0)
271	Broken Arrow, OK	(4.4)	205	Elk Grove, CA	(0.7)	260	Killeen, TX	(4.1)
NA	Brooklyn Park, MN**	NA	279	Erie, PA	(4.7)	293	Knoxville, TN	(5.2)
186	Brownsville, TX	0.1	14	Escondido, CA	20.4	136	Lafayette, LA	2.3
401	Bryan, TX	(17.1)	163	Eugene, OR	1.0	32	Lake Forest, CA	13.9
91	Buena Park, CA	6.4	49	Evansville, IN	11.5	221	Lakeland, FL	(1.4)
NA	Buffalo, NY**	NA	387	Everett, WA	(13.8)	120	Lakewood Twnshp, NJ	3.5
210	Burbank, CA	(0.8)	56	Fairfield, CA	10.4	79	Lakewood, CA	7.8
268	Cambridge, MA	(4.3)	390	Fall River, MA	(14.7)	81	Lakewood, CO	7.7
348	Camden, NJ	(9.4)	122	Fargo, ND	3.3	89	Lancaster, CA	6.7
381	Cape Coral, FL	(13.0)	242	Farmington Hills, MI	(2.9)	363	Lansing, MI	(11.4)
82	Carlsbad, CA	7.6	182	Fayetteville, AR	0.2	196	Laredo, TX	(0.3)
306	Carmel, IN	(6.0)	166	Fayetteville, NC	0.9	134	Largo, FL	2.5
200	Carrollton, TX	(0.5)	NA	Federal Way, WA**	NA	263	Las Cruces, NM	(4.2)
62	Carson, CA	9.5	29	Fishers, IN	14.2	62	Las Vegas, NV	9.5
357	Cary, NC	(10.7)	305	Flint, MI	(5.9)	109	Lawrence, KS	4.6
260	Cedar Rapids, IA	(4.1)	90	Fontana, CA	6.5	396	Lawrence, MA	(16.1)
121	Centennial, CO	3.4	298	Fort Collins, CO	(5.4)	275	Lawton, OK	(4.5)
29	Champaign, IL	14.2	258	Fort Lauderdale, FL	(3.9)	344	League City, TX	(9.3)
NA	Chandler, AZ**	NA	139	Fort Smith, AR	2.2	180	Lee's Summit, MO	0.4
384	Charleston, SC	(13.3)	98	Fort Wayne, IN	5.7	NA	Lexington, KY**	NA
180	Charlotte, NC	0.4	331	Fort Worth, TX	(8.3)	205	Lincoln, NE	(0.7)
NA	Cheektowaga, NY**	NA	115	Fremont, CA	4.2	205	Little Rock, AR	(0.7)
376	Chesapeake, VA	(12.5)	204	Fresno, CA	(0.6)	145	Livermore, CA	2.0
NA	Chicago, IL**	NA	221	Frisco, TX	(1.4)	176	Livonia, MI	0.6
66	Chico, CA	9.2	42	Fullerton, CA	12.4	84	Long Beach, CA	6.9

RANK	CITY	% CHANGE
95	Longmont, CO	5.9
56	Longview, TX	10.4
210	Los Angeles, CA	(0.8)
349	Louisville, KY	(9.7)
306	Lowell, MA	(6.0)
154	Lubbock, TX	1.3
391	Lynchburg, VA	(15.1)
250	Lynn, MA	(3.4)
384	Macon, GA	(13.3)
237	Madison, WI	(2.5)
321	Manchester, NH	(7.3)
352	McAllen, TX	(10.1)
279	McKinney, TX	(4.7)
37	Medford, OR	12.6
393	Melbourne, FL	(15.3)
194	Memphis, TN	(0.1)
18	Menifee, CA	19.5
1	Merced, CA	32.6
43	Meridian, ID	12.3
320	Mesa, AZ	(7.2)
271	Mesquite, TX	(4.4)
317	Miami Beach, FL	(7.0)
378	Miami Gardens, FL	(12.7)
275	Miami, FL	(4.5)
325	Midland, TX	(7.7)
105	Milwaukee, WI	5.0
182	Minneapolis, MN	0.2
318	Miramar, FL	(7.1)
249	Mission Viejo, CA	(3.2)
392	Mission, TX	(15.2)
368	Mobile, AL	(12.0)
4	Modesto, CA	24.2
52	Montgomery, AL	11.3
86	Moreno Valley, CA	6.8
126	Mountain View, CA	3.1
398	Murfreesboro, TN	(16.4)
65	Murrieta, CA	9.3
378	Nampa, ID	(12.7)
186	Napa, CA	0.1
246	Naperville, IL	(3.0)
66	Nashua, NH	9.2
342	Nashville, TN	(9.1)
293	New Bedford, MA	(5.2)
145	New Haven, CT	2.0
288	New Orleans, LA	(5.0)
NA	New Rochelle, NY**	NA
NA	New York, NY**	NA
166	Newark, NJ	0.9
284	Newport Beach, CA	(4.9)
296	Newport News, VA	(5.3)
408	Newton, MA	(24.0)
314	Norfolk, VA	(6.9)
386	Norman, OK	(13.6)
141	North Charleston, SC	2.1
NA	North Las Vegas, NV**	NA
27	Norwalk, CA	14.5
374	Norwalk, CT	(12.3)
6	Oakland, CA	23.2
53	Oceanside, CA	10.9
11	Odessa, TX	22.3
179	O'Fallon, MO	0.5
356	Ogden, UT	(10.4)
134	Oklahoma City, OK	2.5
78	Olathe, KS	8.3
152	Omaha, NE	1.5
124	Ontario, CA	3.2
112	Orange, CA	4.4
337	Orem, UT	(8.6)
312	Orlando, FL	(6.6)
194	Overland Park, KS	(0.1)
37	Oxnard, CA	12.6
351	Palm Bay, FL	(9.9)
126	Palmdale, CA	3.1
NA	Parma, OH**	NA

RANK	CITY	% CHANGE
323	Pasadena, CA	(7.6)
103	Pasadena, TX	5.2
210	Paterson, NJ	(0.8)
196	Pearland, TX	(0.3)
397	Pembroke Pines, FL	(16.3)
250	Peoria, AZ	(3.4)
284	Peoria, IL	(4.9)
271	Philadelphia, PA	(4.4)
275	Phoenix, AZ	(4.5)
130	Pittsburgh, PA	2.8
331	Plano, TX	(8.3)
383	Plantation, FL	(13.1)
37	Pomona, CA	12.6
163	Pompano Beach, FL	1.0
405	Port St. Lucie, FL	(19.8)
186	Portland, OR	0.1
341	Portsmouth, VA	(8.8)
NA	Providence, RI**	NA
395	Provo, UT	(15.6)
8	Pueblo, CO	23.1
359	Quincy, MA	(10.8)
344	Racine, WI	(9.3)
159	Raleigh, NC	1.1
NA	Ramapo, NY**	NA
60	Rancho Cucamon., CA	9.9
71	Reading, PA	9.1
5	Redding, CA	24.0
18	Redwood City, CA	19.5
53	Reno, NV	10.9
98	Renton, WA	5.7
20	Rialto, CA	16.5
110	Richardson, TX	4.5
66	Richmond, CA	9.2
124	Richmond, VA	3.2
23	Rio Rancho, NM	15.8
64	Riverside, CA	9.4
141	Roanoke, VA	2.1
NA	Rochester, MN**	NA
NA	Rochester, NY**	NA
98	Rockford, IL	5.7
323	Roseville, CA	(7.6)
186	Roswell, GA	0.1
116	Round Rock, TX	4.1
93	Sacramento, CA	6.1
47	Salem, OR	11.8
113	Salinas, CA	4.3
58	Salt Lake City, UT	10.3
186	San Antonio, TX	0.1
17	San Bernardino, CA	19.9
103	San Diego, CA	5.2
22	San Francisco, CA	16.0
3	San Jose, CA	24.6
51	San Leandro, CA	11.4
126	San Marcos, CA	3.1
83	San Mateo, CA	7.0
73	Sandy Springs, GA	8.6
158	Sandy, UT	1.2
66	Santa Ana, CA	9.2
37	Santa Barbara, CA	12.6
45	Santa Clara, CA	12.0
74	Santa Clarita, CA	8.5
219	Santa Maria, CA	(1.3)
36	Santa Monica, CA	13.0
166	Santa Rosa, CA	0.9
388	Savannah, GA	(13.9)
366	Scottsdale, AZ	(11.7)
159	Scranton, PA	1.1
210	Seattle, WA	(0.8)
145	Shreveport, LA	2.0
37	Simi Valley, CA	12.6
242	Sioux City, IA	(2.9)
75	Sioux Falls, SD	8.4
241	Somerville, MA	(2.8)
406	South Bend, IN	(20.1)

RANK	CITY	% CHANGE
362	South Gate, CA	(11.2)
174	Sparks, NV	0.7
250	Spokane Valley, WA	(3.4)
12	Spokane, WA	21.7
282	Springfield, IL	(4.8)
258	Springfield, MA	(3.9)
149	Springfield, MO	1.8
284	Stamford, CT	(4.9)
237	Sterling Heights, MI	(2.5)
193	Stockton, CA	0.0
NA	St. George, UT**	NA
24	St. Joseph, MO	15.6
368	St. Louis, MO	(12.0)
182	St. Paul, MN	0.2
268	St. Petersburg, FL	(4.3)
105	Sugar Land, TX	5.0
2	Sunnyvale, CA	26.9
368	Sunrise, FL	(12.0)
263	Surprise, AZ	(4.2)
NA	Syracuse, NY**	NA
93	Tacoma, WA	6.1
331	Tallahassee, FL	(8.3)
314	Tampa, FL	(6.9)
205	Temecula, CA	(0.7)
364	Tempe, AZ	(11.6)
NA	Thornton, CO**	NA
130	Thousand Oaks, CA	2.8
NA	Toledo, OH**	NA
340	Toms River Twnshp, NJ	(8.7)
327	Topeka, KS	(7.9)
242	Torrance, CA	(2.9)
232	Tracy, CA	(1.9)
101	Trenton, NJ	5.6
325	Troy, MI	(7.7)
NA	Tucson, AZ**	NA
288	Tulsa, OK	(5.0)
219	Tuscaloosa, AL	(1.3)
75	Tustin, CA	8.4
166	Tyler, TX	0.9
145	Upland, CA	2.0
309	Upper Darby Twnshp, PA	(6.1)
13	Vacaville, CA	21.1
72	Vallejo, CA	8.8
221	Vancouver, WA	(1.4)
29	Ventura, CA	14.2
59	Victorville, CA	10.0
268	Virginia Beach, VA	(4.3)
84	Visalia, CA	6.9
255	Vista, CA	(3.7)
357	Waco, TX	(10.7)
229	Warren, MI	(1.8)
234	Warwick, RI	(2.2)
150	Washington, DC	1.7
136	Waterbury, CT	2.3
NA	Waukegan, IL**	NA
217	West Covina, CA	(1.2)
210	West Jordan, UT	(0.8)
186	West Palm Beach, FL	0.1
139	West Valley, UT	2.2
151	Westland, MI	1.6
35	Westminster, CA	13.3
171	Westminster, CO	0.8
235	Whittier, CA	(2.4)
113	Wichita Falls, TX	4.3
91	Wichita, KS	6.4
163	Wilmington, NC	1.0
233	Winston-Salem, NC	(2.1)
407	Woodbridge Twnshp, NJ	(22.2)
122	Worcester, MA	3.3
44	Yakima, WA	12.1
NA	Yonkers, NY**	NA
132	Yuma, AZ	2.6

Source: CQ Press using reported data from the F.B.I. "Crime in the United States 2012"

*Includes murder, rape, robbery, aggravated assault, burglary, larceny-theft, and motor vehicle theft.

**Not available.

43. Percent Change in Crime Rate: 2011 to 2012 (continued)
National Percent Change = 1.4% Decrease*

RANK	CITY	% CHANGE	RANK	CITY	% CHANGE	RANK	CITY	% CHANGE
1	Merced, CA	32.6	75	Albany, GA	8.4	149	Springfield, MO	1.8
2	Sunnyvale, CA	26.9	75	Sioux Falls, SD	8.4	150	Washington, DC	1.7
3	San Jose, CA	24.6	75	Tustin, CA	8.4	151	Westland, MI	1.6
4	Modesto, CA	24.2	78	Olathe, KS	8.3	152	Omaha, NE	1.5
5	Redding, CA	24.0	79	Hamilton Twnshp, NJ	7.8	153	Inglewood, CA	1.4
6	Green Bay, WI	23.2	79	Lakewood, CA	7.8	154	Arvada, CO	1.3
6	Oakland, CA	23.2	81	Lakewood, CO	7.7	154	Clovis, CA	1.3
8	Pueblo, CO	23.1	82	Carlsbad, CA	7.6	154	Greeley, CO	1.3
9	Hayward, CA	22.6	83	San Mateo, CA	7.0	154	Lubbock, TX	1.3
10	Antioch, CA	22.5	84	Long Beach, CA	6.9	158	Sandy, UT	1.2
11	Odessa, TX	22.3	84	Visalia, CA	6.9	159	Clearwater, FL	1.1
12	Spokane, WA	21.7	86	Concord, CA	6.8	159	Edinburg, TX	1.1
13	Vacaville, CA	21.1	86	Independence, MO	6.8	159	Raleigh, NC	1.1
14	Escondido, CA	20.4	86	Moreno Valley, CA	6.8	159	Scranton, PA	1.1
15	Asheville, NC	20.2	89	Lancaster, CA	6.7	163	Eugene, OR	1.0
16	Corona, CA	20.0	90	Fontana, CA	6.5	163	Pompano Beach, FL	1.0
17	San Bernardino, CA	19.9	91	Buena Park, CA	6.4	163	Wilmington, NC	1.0
18	Menifee, CA	19.5	91	Wichita, KS	6.4	166	Denver, CO	0.9
18	Redwood City, CA	19.5	93	Sacramento, CA	6.1	166	Fayetteville, NC	0.9
20	Bakersfield, CA	16.5	93	Tacoma, WA	6.1	166	Newark, NJ	0.9
20	Rialto, CA	16.5	95	Bellingham, WA	5.9	166	Santa Rosa, CA	0.9
22	San Francisco, CA	16.0	95	Henderson, NV	5.9	166	Tyler, TX	0.9
23	Rio Rancho, NM	15.8	95	Longmont, CO	5.9	171	Abilene, TX	0.8
24	St. Joseph, MO	15.6	98	Fort Wayne, IN	5.7	171	Kansas City, MO	0.8
25	Anaheim, CA	14.7	98	Renton, WA	5.7	171	Westminster, CO	0.8
25	Garden Grove, CA	14.7	98	Rockford, IL	5.7	174	Alhambra, CA	0.7
27	Norwalk, CA	14.5	101	Grand Rapids, MI	5.6	174	Sparks, NV	0.7
28	Huntington Beach, CA	14.3	101	Trenton, NJ	5.6	176	Dayton, OH	0.6
29	Champaign, IL	14.2	103	Pasadena, TX	5.2	176	Indianapolis, IN	0.6
29	Fishers, IN	14.2	103	San Diego, CA	5.2	176	Livonia, MI	0.6
29	Ventura, CA	14.2	105	Milwaukee, WI	5.0	179	O'Fallon, MO	0.5
32	Lake Forest, CA	13.9	105	Sugar Land, TX	5.0	180	Charlotte, NC	0.4
33	Boulder, CO	13.8	107	Albuquerque, NM	4.9	180	Lee's Summit, MO	0.4
34	Costa Mesa, CA	13.7	108	Bethlehem, PA	4.8	182	Fayetteville, AR	0.2
35	Westminster, CA	13.3	109	Lawrence, KS	4.6	182	Hoover, AL	0.2
36	Santa Monica, CA	13.0	110	Indio, CA	4.5	182	Minneapolis, MN	0.2
37	Medford, OR	12.6	110	Richardson, TX	4.5	182	St. Paul, MN	0.2
37	Oxnard, CA	12.6	112	Orange, CA	4.4	186	Brownsville, TX	0.1
37	Pomona, CA	12.6	113	Salinas, CA	4.3	186	Glendale, AZ	0.1
37	Santa Barbara, CA	12.6	113	Wichita Falls, TX	4.3	186	Napa, CA	0.1
37	Simi Valley, CA	12.6	115	Fremont, CA	4.2	186	Portland, OR	0.1
42	Fullerton, CA	12.4	116	Bloomington, IN	4.1	186	Roswell, GA	0.1
43	Meridian, ID	12.3	116	Round Rock, TX	4.1	186	San Antonio, TX	0.1
44	Yakima, WA	12.1	118	Ann Arbor, MI	4.0	186	West Palm Beach, FL	0.1
45	Santa Clara, CA	12.0	119	Hillsboro, OR	3.8	193	Stockton, CA	0.0
46	Hesperia, CA	11.9	120	Lakewood Twnshp, NJ	3.5	194	Memphis, TN	(0.1)
47	Salem, OR	11.8	121	Centennial, CO	3.4	194	Overland Park, KS	(0.1)
48	Cicero, IL	11.6	122	Fargo, ND	3.3	196	Baldwin Park, CA	(0.3)
49	Evansville, IN	11.5	122	Worcester, MA	3.3	196	Laredo, TX	(0.3)
49	Gresham, OR	11.5	124	Ontario, CA	3.2	196	Pearland, TX	(0.3)
51	San Leandro, CA	11.4	124	Richmond, VA	3.2	199	Aurora, CO	(0.4)
52	Montgomery, AL	11.3	126	Mountain View, CA	3.1	200	Boise, ID	(0.5)
53	Oceanside, CA	10.9	126	Palmdale, CA	3.1	200	Carrollton, TX	(0.5)
53	Reno, NV	10.9	126	San Marcos, CA	3.1	200	Deerfield Beach, FL	(0.5)
55	Berkeley, CA	10.5	129	Bloomington, IL	2.9	200	Hemet, CA	(0.5)
56	Fairfield, CA	10.4	130	Pittsburgh, PA	2.8	204	Fresno, CA	(0.6)
56	Longview, TX	10.4	130	Thousand Oaks, CA	2.8	205	Austin, TX	(0.7)
58	Salt Lake City, UT	10.3	132	Chino, CA	2.6	205	Elk Grove, CA	(0.7)
59	Victorville, CA	10.0	132	Yuma, AZ	2.6	205	Lincoln, NE	(0.7)
60	Rancho Cucamon., CA	9.9	134	Largo, FL	2.5	205	Little Rock, AR	(0.7)
61	Colorado Springs, CO	9.8	134	Oklahoma City, OK	2.5	205	Temecula, CA	(0.7)
62	Carson, CA	9.5	136	Billings, MT	2.3	210	Burbank, CA	(0.8)
62	Las Vegas, NV	9.5	136	Lafayette, LA	2.3	210	Irvine, CA	(0.8)
64	Riverside, CA	9.4	136	Waterbury, CT	2.3	210	Los Angeles, CA	(0.8)
65	Murrieta, CA	9.3	139	Fort Smith, AR	2.2	210	Paterson, NJ	(0.8)
66	Anchorage, AK	9.2	139	West Valley, UT	2.2	210	Seattle, WA	(0.8)
66	Chico, CA	9.2	141	Edmond, OK	2.1	210	West Jordan, UT	(0.8)
66	Nashua, NH	9.2	141	Hawthorne, CA	2.1	216	Bellflower, CA	(1.0)
66	Richmond, CA	9.2	141	North Charleston, SC	2.1	217	Joliet, IL	(1.2)
66	Santa Ana, CA	9.2	141	Roanoke, VA	2.1	217	West Covina, CA	(1.2)
71	Reading, PA	9.1	145	Livermore, CA	2.0	219	Santa Maria, CA	(1.3)
72	Vallejo, CA	8.8	145	New Haven, CT	2.0	219	Tuscaloosa, AL	(1.3)
73	Sandy Springs, GA	8.6	145	Shreveport, LA	2.0	221	El Paso, TX	(1.4)
74	Santa Clarita, CA	8.5	145	Upland, CA	2.0	221	Frisco, TX	(1.4)

RANK	CITY	% CHANGE	RANK	CITY	% CHANGE	RANK	CITY	% CHANGE
221	Garland, TX	(1.4)	296	Newport News, VA	(5.3)	368	Sunrise, FL	(12.0)
221	Lakeland, FL	(1.4)	298	Fort Collins, CO	(5.4)	372	Gilbert, AZ	(12.1)
221	Vancouver, WA	(1.4)	299	Des Moines, IA	(5.5)	372	Glendale, CA	(12.1)
226	Chula Vista, CA	(1.5)	299	Elgin, IL	(5.5)	374	Arlington, TX	(12.3)
226	Houston, TX	(1.5)	299	Hammond, IN	(5.5)	374	Norwalk, CT	(12.3)
226	Kenosha, WI	(1.5)	302	Danbury, CT	(5.6)	376	Chesapeake, VA	(12.5)
229	Baltimore, MD	(1.8)	303	Boca Raton, FL	(5.7)	377	College Station, TX	(12.6)
229	Bellevue, WA	(1.8)	304	Boston, MA	(5.8)	378	Gary, IN	(12.7)
229	Warren, MI	(1.8)	305	Flint, MI	(5.9)	378	Miami Gardens, FL	(12.7)
232	Tracy, CA	(1.9)	306	Brockton, MA	(6.0)	378	Nampa, ID	(12.7)
233	Winston-Salem, NC	(2.1)	306	Carmel, IN	(6.0)	381	Cape Coral, FL	(13.0)
234	Warwick, RI	(2.2)	306	Lowell, MA	(6.0)	381	High Point, NC	(13.0)
235	Cleveland, OH	(2.4)	309	Upper Darby Twnshp, PA	(6.1)	383	Plantation, FL	(13.1)
235	Whittier, CA	(2.4)	310	Akron, OH	(6.3)	384	Charleston, SC	(13.3)
237	Denton, TX	(2.5)	311	Hialeah, FL	(6.4)	384	Macon, GA	(13.3)
237	Hartford, CT	(2.5)	312	Orlando, FL	(6.6)	386	Norman, OK	(13.6)
237	Madison, WI	(2.5)	313	Brick Twnshp, NJ	(6.8)	387	Everett, WA	(13.8)
237	Sterling Heights, MI	(2.5)	314	Citrus Heights, CA	(6.9)	388	Savannah, GA	(13.9)
241	Somerville, MA	(2.8)	314	Norfolk, VA	(6.9)	389	Birmingham, AL	(14.2)
242	Farmington Hills, MI	(2.9)	314	Tampa, FL	(6.9)	390	Fall River, MA	(14.7)
242	Hollywood, FL	(2.9)	317	Miami Beach, FL	(7.0)	391	Lynchburg, VA	(15.1)
242	Sioux City, IA	(2.9)	318	Atlanta, GA	(7.1)	392	Mission, TX	(15.2)
242	Torrance, CA	(2.9)	318	Miramar, FL	(7.1)	393	Decatur, IL	(15.3)
246	Bridgeport, CT	(3.0)	320	Mesa, AZ	(7.2)	393	Melbourne, FL	(15.3)
246	Naperville, IL	(3.0)	321	Avondale, AZ	(7.3)	395	Provo, UT	(15.6)
248	Daly City, CA	(3.1)	321	Manchester, NH	(7.3)	396	Lawrence, MA	(16.1)
249	Mission Viejo, CA	(3.2)	323	Pasadena, CA	(7.6)	397	Pembroke Pines, FL	(16.3)
250	Lynn, MA	(3.4)	323	Roseville, CA	(7.6)	398	Davenport, IA	(16.4)
250	Peoria, AZ	(3.4)	325	Midland, TX	(7.7)	398	Murfreesboro, TN	(16.4)
250	Spokane Valley, WA	(3.4)	325	Troy, MI	(7.7)	400	Kent, WA	(17.0)
253	Alameda, CA	(3.5)	327	Topeka, KS	(7.9)	401	Bryan, TX	(17.1)
253	El Monte, CA	(3.5)	328	Aurora, IL	(8.0)	401	Elizabeth, NJ	(17.1)
255	Baton Rouge, LA	(3.7)	329	Irving, TX	(8.1)	403	Beaverton, OR	(18.5)
255	Chino Hills, CA	(3.7)	330	Beaumont, TX	(8.2)	404	Edison Twnshp, NJ	(19.4)
255	Vista, CA	(3.7)	331	Fort Worth, TX	(8.3)	405	Port St. Lucie, FL	(19.8)
258	Fort Lauderdale, FL	(3.9)	331	Plano, TX	(8.3)	406	South Bend, IN	(20.1)
258	Springfield, MA	(3.9)	331	Tallahassee, FL	(8.3)	407	Woodbridge Twnshp, NJ	(22.2)
260	Cedar Rapids, IA	(4.1)	334	Compton, CA	(8.4)	408	Newton, MA	(24.0)
260	Clinton Twnshp, MI	(4.1)	334	El Cajon, CA	(8.4)	409	Grand Prairie, TX	(25.0)
260	Killeen, TX	(4.1)	336	Coral Springs, FL	(8.5)	NA	Albany, NY**	NA
263	Gainesville, FL	(4.2)	337	Alexandria, VA	(8.6)	NA	Allentown, PA**	NA
263	Huntsville, AL	(4.2)	337	Downey, CA	(8.6)	NA	Amherst, NY**	NA
263	Jacksonville, FL	(4.2)	337	Orem, UT	(8.6)	NA	Bloomington, MN**	NA
263	Las Cruces, NM	(4.2)	340	Toms River Twnshp, NJ	(8.7)	NA	Brooklyn Park, MN**	NA
263	Surprise, AZ	(4.2)	341	Portsmouth, VA	(8.8)	NA	Buffalo, NY**	NA
268	Cambridge, MA	(4.3)	342	Nashville, TN	(9.1)	NA	Chandler, AZ**	NA
268	St. Petersburg, FL	(4.3)	343	Jackson, MS	(9.2)	NA	Cheektowaga, NY**	NA
268	Virginia Beach, VA	(4.3)	344	Durham, NC	(9.3)	NA	Chicago, IL**	NA
271	Broken Arrow, OK	(4.4)	344	Johns Creek, GA	(9.3)	NA	Clarkstown, NY**	NA
271	Detroit, MI	(4.4)	344	League City, TX	(9.3)	NA	Colonie, NY**	NA
271	Mesquite, TX	(4.4)	344	Racine, WI	(9.3)	NA	Duluth, MN**	NA
271	Philadelphia, PA	(4.4)	348	Camden, NJ	(9.4)	NA	Federal Way, WA**	NA
275	Lawton, OK	(4.5)	349	Louisville, KY	(9.7)	NA	Greece, NY**	NA
275	Miami, FL	(4.5)	350	Allen, TX	(9.8)	NA	Greensboro, NC**	NA
275	Phoenix, AZ	(4.5)	351	Palm Bay, FL	(9.9)	NA	Greenville, NC**	NA
278	Columbia, MO	(4.6)	352	Arlington Heights, IL	(10.1)	NA	Jurupa Valley, CA**	NA
279	Athens-Clarke, GA	(4.7)	352	McAllen, TX	(10.1)	NA	Lexington, KY**	NA
279	Erie, PA	(4.7)	354	Cincinnati, OH	(10.2)	NA	New Rochelle, NY**	NA
279	McKinney, TX	(4.7)	354	Columbus, GA	(10.2)	NA	New York, NY**	NA
282	Corpus Christi, TX	(4.8)	356	Ogden, UT	(10.4)	NA	North Las Vegas, NV**	NA
282	Springfield, IL	(4.8)	357	Cary, NC	(10.7)	NA	Parma, OH**	NA
284	Jersey City, NJ	(4.9)	357	Waco, TX	(10.7)	NA	Providence, RI**	NA
284	Newport Beach, CA	(4.9)	359	Hampton, VA	(10.8)	NA	Ramapo, NY**	NA
284	Peoria, IL	(4.9)	359	Quincy, MA	(10.8)	NA	Rochester, MN**	NA
284	Stamford, CT	(4.9)	361	Kennewick, WA	(11.1)	NA	Rochester, NY**	NA
288	Amarillo, TX	(5.0)	362	South Gate, CA	(11.2)	NA	St. George, UT**	NA
288	Kansas City, KS	(5.0)	363	Lansing, MI	(11.4)	NA	Syracuse, NY**	NA
288	New Orleans, LA	(5.0)	364	Clarksville, TN	(11.6)	NA	Thornton, CO**	NA
288	Tulsa, OK	(5.0)	364	Tempe, AZ	(11.6)	NA	Toledo, OH**	NA
292	Cranston, RI	(5.1)	366	Dearborn, MI	(11.7)	NA	Tucson, AZ**	NA
293	Clifton, NJ	(5.2)	366	Scottsdale, AZ	(11.7)	NA	Waukegan, IL**	NA
293	Knoxville, TN	(5.2)	368	Dallas, TX	(12.0)	NA	Yonkers, NY**	NA
293	New Bedford, MA	(5.2)	368	Mobile, AL	(12.0)			
296	Davie, FL	(5.3)	368	St. Louis, MO	(12.0)			

Source: CQ Press using reported data from the F.B.I. "Crime in the United States 2012"

*Includes murder, rape, robbery, aggravated assault, burglary, larceny-theft, and motor vehicle theft.

**Not available.

44. Percent Change in Crime Rate: 2008 to 2012
National Percent Change = 11.6% Decrease*

RANK	CITY	% CHANGE	RANK	CITY	% CHANGE	RANK	CITY	% CHANGE
142	Abilene, TX	(8.3)	310	Chino Hills, CA	(21.1)	319	Gainesville, FL	(23.0)
89	Akron, OH	(2.6)	61	Chino, CA	1.4	114	Garden Grove, CA	(5.4)
148	Alameda, CA	(8.7)	372	Chula Vista, CA	(31.1)	218	Garland, TX	(14.2)
NA	Albany, GA**	NA	NA	Cicero, IL**	NA	9	Gary, IN	22.8
NA	Albany, NY**	NA	97	Cincinnati, OH	(3.3)	358	Gilbert, AZ	(28.6)
193	Albuquerque, NM	(12.1)	252	Citrus Heights, CA	(17.0)	13	Glendale, AZ	20.0
237	Alexandria, VA	(15.9)	NA	Clarkstown, NY**	NA	334	Glendale, CA	(25.6)
170	Alhambra, CA	(10.3)	355	Clarksville, TN	(27.7)	388	Grand Prairie, TX	(36.6)
NA	Allentown, PA**	NA	252	Clearwater, FL	(17.0)	346	Grand Rapids, MI	(26.6)
168	Allen, TX	(10.0)	45	Cleveland, OH	4.8	NA	Greece, NY**	NA
261	Amarillo, TX	(17.5)	324	Clifton, NJ	(23.8)	176	Greeley, CO	(11.0)
NA	Amherst, NY**	NA	179	Clinton Twnshp, MI	(11.3)	142	Green Bay, WI	(8.3)
21	Anaheim, CA	14.0	12	Clovis, CA	21.3	374	Greensboro, NC	(31.5)
50	Anchorage, AK	2.8	328	College Station, TX	(24.7)	377	Greenville, NC	(32.7)
208	Ann Arbor, MI	(13.4)	NA	Colonie, NY**	NA	22	Gresham, OR	13.7
2	Antioch, CA	50.0	100	Colorado Springs, CO	(3.7)	36	Hamilton Twnshp, NJ	6.8
NA	Arlington Heights, IL**	NA	77	Columbia, MO	(1.2)	231	Hammond, IN	(15.4)
329	Arlington, TX	(24.8)	345	Columbus, GA	(26.4)	120	Hampton, VA	(6.1)
134	Arvada, CO	(7.2)	373	Compton, CA	(31.2)	187	Hartford, CT	(11.9)
98	Asheville, NC	(3.4)	158	Concord, CA	(9.3)	106	Hawthorne, CA	(4.6)
364	Athens-Clarke, GA	(29.7)	116	Coral Springs, FL	(5.6)	105	Hayward, CA	(4.4)
155	Atlanta, GA	(9.1)	94	Corona, CA	(3.1)	155	Hemet, CA	(9.1)
194	Aurora, CO	(12.2)	335	Corpus Christi, TX	(25.7)	190	Henderson, NV	(12.0)
NA	Aurora, IL**	NA	24	Costa Mesa, CA	12.7	15	Hesperia, CA	18.2
203	Austin, TX	(13.0)	197	Cranston, RI	(12.5)	384	Hialeah, FL	(34.5)
257	Avondale, AZ	(17.3)	342	Dallas, TX	(26.1)	369	High Point, NC	(30.2)
76	Bakersfield, CA	(1.1)	234	Daly City, CA	(15.6)	207	Hillsboro, OR	(13.3)
134	Baldwin Park, CA	(7.2)	123	Danbury, CT	(6.2)	48	Hollywood, FL	3.1
113	Baltimore, MD	(5.3)	366	Davenport, IA	(29.8)	292	Hoover, AL	(19.8)
119	Baton Rouge, LA	(5.8)	104	Davie, FL	(4.2)	83	Houston, TX	(1.9)
211	Beaumont, TX	(13.6)	108	Dayton, OH	(4.8)	11	Huntington Beach, CA	21.7
360	Beaverton, OR	(29.1)	374	Dearborn, MI	(31.5)	206	Huntsville, AL	(13.2)
295	Bellevue, WA	(20.1)	NA	Decatur, IL**	NA	281	Independence, MO	(19.0)
342	Bellflower, CA	(26.1)	243	Deerfield Beach, FL	(16.6)	129	Indianapolis, IN	(7.0)
187	Bellingham, WA	(11.9)	73	Denton, TX	(0.5)	20	Indio, CA	14.8
351	Berkeley, CA	(27.3)	23	Denver, CO	13.2	211	Inglewood, CA	(13.6)
303	Bethlehem, PA	(20.5)	115	Des Moines, IA	(5.5)	81	Irvine, CA	(1.7)
26	Billings, MT	10.9	56	Detroit, MI	1.7	382	Irving, TX	(34.3)
256	Birmingham, AL	(17.2)	236	Downey, CA	(15.8)	363	Jacksonville, FL	(29.5)
NA	Bloomington, IL**	NA	NA	Duluth, MN**	NA	173	Jackson, MS	(10.5)
62	Bloomington, IN	1.3	267	Durham, NC	(18.0)	356	Jersey City, NJ	(27.8)
NA	Bloomington, MN**	NA	75	Edinburg, TX	(1.0)	NA	Johns Creek, GA**	NA
320	Boca Raton, FL	(23.1)	384	Edison Twnshp, NJ	(34.5)	NA	Joliet, IL**	NA
184	Boise, ID	(11.7)	162	Edmond, OK	(9.6)	NA	Jurupa Valley, CA**	NA
313	Boston, MA	(22.2)	387	El Cajon, CA	(35.2)	NA	Kansas City, KS**	NA
107	Boulder, CO	(4.7)	285	El Monte, CA	(19.2)	179	Kansas City, MO	(11.3)
303	Brick Twnshp, NJ	(20.5)	315	El Paso, TX	(22.5)	277	Kennewick, WA	(18.7)
260	Bridgeport, CT	(17.4)	NA	Elgin, IL**	NA	92	Kenosha, WI	(2.7)
NA	Brockton, MA**	NA	318	Elizabeth, NJ	(22.9)	289	Kent, WA	(19.4)
151	Broken Arrow, OK	(8.9)	298	Elk Grove, CA	(20.2)	155	Killeen, TX	(9.1)
NA	Brooklyn Park, MN**	NA	103	Erie, PA	(3.8)	71	Knoxville, TN	(0.4)
295	Brownsville, TX	(20.1)	187	Escondido, CA	(11.9)	199	Lafayette, LA	(12.6)
391	Bryan, TX	(39.0)	314	Eugene, OR	(22.3)	25	Lake Forest, CA	11.0
151	Buena Park, CA	(8.9)	28	Evansville, IN	10.3	150	Lakeland, FL	(8.8)
NA	Buffalo, NY**	NA	305	Everett, WA	(20.6)	NA	Lakewood Twnshp, NJ**	NA
228	Burbank, CA	(15.0)	285	Fairfield, CA	(19.2)	158	Lakewood, CA	(9.3)
120	Cambridge, MA	(6.1)	292	Fall River, MA	(19.8)	42	Lakewood, CO	5.5
190	Camden, NJ	(12.0)	216	Fargo, ND	(14.1)	364	Lancaster, CA	(29.7)
361	Cape Coral, FL	(29.2)	338	Farmington Hills, MI	(25.8)	178	Lansing, MI	(11.1)
248	Carlsbad, CA	(16.9)	31	Fayetteville, AR	9.0	376	Laredo, TX	(32.2)
380	Carmel, IN	(33.5)	308	Fayetteville, NC	(21.0)	225	Largo, FL	(14.6)
218	Carrollton, TX	(14.2)	54	Federal Way, WA	2.2	164	Las Cruces, NM	(9.7)
46	Carson, CA	4.3	316	Fishers, IN	(22.8)	298	Las Vegas, NV	(20.2)
346	Cary, NC	(26.6)	52	Flint, MI	2.3	190	Lawrence, KS	(12.0)
311	Cedar Rapids, IA	(21.5)	118	Fontana, CA	(5.7)	59	Lawrence, MA	1.5
167	Centennial, CO	(9.9)	298	Fort Collins, CO	(20.2)	34	Lawton, OK	8.1
NA	Champaign, IL**	NA	52	Fort Lauderdale, FL	2.3	248	League City, TX	(16.9)
NA	Chandler, AZ**	NA	79	Fort Smith, AR	(1.4)	216	Lee's Summit, MO	(14.1)
390	Charleston, SC	(38.0)	140	Fort Wayne, IN	(8.1)	NA	Lexington, KY**	NA
382	Charlotte, NC	(34.3)	233	Fort Worth, TX	(15.5)	126	Lincoln, NE	(6.7)
NA	Cheektowaga, NY**	NA	321	Fremont, CA	(23.4)	59	Little Rock, AR	1.5
184	Chesapeake, VA	(11.7)	35	Fresno, CA	7.8	89	Livermore, CA	(2.6)
NA	Chicago, IL**	NA	301	Frisco, TX	(20.3)	87	Livonia, MI	(2.3)
257	Chico, CA	(17.3)	137	Fullerton, CA	(7.6)	47	Long Beach, CA	3.6

RANK	CITY	% CHANGE	RANK	CITY	% CHANGE	RANK	CITY	% CHANGE
NA	Longmont, CO**	NA	263	Pasadena, CA	(17.7)	129	South Gate, CA	(7.0)
339	Longview, TX	(25.9)	39	Pasadena, TX	5.9	371	Sparks, NV	(31.0)
248	Los Angeles, CA	(16.9)	55	Paterson, NJ	1.8	6	Spokane Valley, WA	27.0
148	Louisville, KY	(8.7)	213	Pearland, TX	(13.8)	1	Spokane, WA	52.6
321	Lowell, MA	(23.4)	381	Pembroke Pines, FL	(34.1)	NA	Springfield, IL**	NA
142	Lubbock, TX	(8.3)	237	Peoria, AZ	(15.9)	145	Springfield, MA	(8.5)
359	Lynchburg, VA	(29.0)	NA	Peoria, IL**	NA	71	Springfield, MO	(0.4)
223	Lynn, MA	(14.4)	237	Philadelphia, PA	(15.9)	210	Stamford, CT	(13.5)
240	Macon, GA	(16.0)	291	Phoenix, AZ	(19.5)	166	Sterling Heights, MI	(9.8)
138	Madison, WI	(7.9)	281	Pittsburgh, PA	(19.0)	197	Stockton, CA	(12.5)
30	Manchester, NH	9.3	327	Plano, TX	(24.3)	335	St. George, UT	(25.7)
386	McAllen, TX	(34.6)	308	Plantation, FL	(21.0)	7	St. Joseph, MO	24.6
141	McKinney, TX	(8.2)	64	Pomona, CA	0.8	272	St. Louis, MO	(18.3)
3	Medford, OR	47.0	111	Pompano Beach, FL	(5.2)	95	St. Paul, MN	(3.2)
312	Melbourne, FL	(21.9)	330	Port St. Lucie, FL	(25.4)	321	St. Petersburg, FL	(23.4)
280	Memphis, TN	(18.9)	110	Portland, OR	(5.1)	202	Sugar Land, TX	(12.9)
NA	Menifee, CA**	NA	201	Portsmouth, VA	(12.7)	171	Sunnyvale, CA	(10.4)
16	Merced, CA	17.5	223	Providence, RI	(14.4)	267	Sunrise, FL	(18.0)
111	Meridian, ID	(5.2)	241	Provo, UT	(16.1)	248	Surprise, AZ	(16.9)
275	Mesa, AZ	(18.5)	NA	Pueblo, CO**	NA	NA	Syracuse, NY**	NA
127	Mesquite, TX	(6.9)	175	Quincy, MA	(10.7)	262	Tacoma, WA	(17.6)
74	Miami Beach, FL	(0.6)	257	Racine, WI	(17.3)	225	Tallahassee, FL	(14.6)
353	Miami Gardens, FL	(27.4)	129	Raleigh, NC	(7.0)	389	Tampa, FL	(37.0)
67	Miami, FL	0.4	NA	Ramapo, NY**	NA	125	Temecula, CA	(6.3)
306	Midland, TX	(20.8)	19	Rancho Cucamon., CA	16.1	244	Tempe, AZ	(16.7)
204	Milwaukee, WI	(13.1)	295	Reading, PA	(20.1)	NA	Thornton, CO**	NA
194	Minneapolis, MN	(12.2)	5	Redding, CA	33.6	68	Thousand Oaks, CA	0.0
348	Miramar, FL	(26.7)	306	Redwood City, CA	(20.8)	NA	Toledo, OH**	NA
100	Mission Viejo, CA	(3.7)	353	Reno, NV	(27.4)	18	Toms River Twnshp, NJ	16.3
362	Mission, TX	(29.3)	NA	Renton, WA**	NA	147	Topeka, KS	(8.6)
176	Mobile, AL	(11.0)	4	Rialto, CA	43.1	270	Torrance, CA	(18.2)
43	Modesto, CA	5.1	229	Richardson, TX	(15.2)	278	Tracy, CA	(18.8)
123	Montgomery, AL	(6.2)	88	Richmond, CA	(2.4)	37	Trenton, NJ	6.2
116	Moreno Valley, CA	(5.6)	48	Richmond, VA	3.1	199	Troy, MI	(12.6)
370	Mountain View, CA	(30.8)	254	Rio Rancho, NM	(17.1)	NA	Tucson, AZ**	NA
231	Murfreesboro, TN	(15.4)	169	Riverside, CA	(10.2)	218	Tulsa, OK	(14.2)
28	Murrieta, CA	10.3	222	Roanoke, VA	(14.3)	288	Tuscaloosa, AL	(19.3)
173	Nampa, ID	(10.5)	NA	Rochester, MN**	NA	85	Tustin, CA	(2.2)
272	Napa, CA	(18.3)	NA	Rochester, NY**	NA	99	Tyler, TX	(3.5)
NA	Naperville, IL**	NA	254	Rockford, IL	(17.1)	263	Upland, CA	(17.7)
NA	Nashua, NH**	NA	335	Roseville, CA	(25.7)	274	Upper Darby Twnshp, PA	(18.4)
294	Nashville, TN	(20.0)	379	Roswell, GA	(33.2)	136	Vacaville, CA	(7.4)
184	New Bedford, MA	(11.7)	109	Round Rock, TX	(5.0)	89	Vallejo, CA	(2.6)
NA	New Haven, CT**	NA	229	Sacramento, CA	(15.2)	65	Vancouver, WA	0.7
351	New Orleans, LA	(27.3)	138	Salem, OR	(7.9)	32	Ventura, CA	8.6
NA	New Rochelle, NY**	NA	204	Salinas, CA	(13.1)	57	Victorville, CA	1.6
NA	New York, NY**	NA	242	Salt Lake City, UT	(16.5)	181	Virginia Beach, VA	(11.4)
33	Newark, NJ	8.5	270	San Antonio, TX	(18.2)	158	Visalia, CA	(9.3)
196	Newport Beach, CA	(12.3)	57	San Bernardino, CA	1.6	349	Vista, CA	(26.9)
339	Newport News, VA	(25.9)	324	San Diego, CA	(23.8)	344	Waco, TX	(26.3)
326	Newton, MA	(24.2)	63	San Francisco, CA	1.0	NA	Warren, MI**	NA
213	Norfolk, VA	(13.8)	14	San Jose, CA	19.4	289	Warwick, RI	(19.4)
208	Norman, OK	(13.4)	276	San Leandro, CA	(18.6)	127	Washington, DC	(6.9)
341	North Charleston, SC	(26.0)	164	San Marcos, CA	(9.7)	284	Waterbury, CT	(19.1)
263	North Las Vegas, NV	(17.7)	331	San Mateo, CA	(25.5)	NA	Waukegan, IL**	NA
79	Norwalk, CA	(1.4)	331	Sandy Springs, GA	(25.5)	246	West Covina, CA	(16.8)
266	Norwalk, CT	(17.9)	316	Sandy, UT	(22.8)	145	West Jordan, UT	(8.5)
17	Oakland, CA	17.3	51	Santa Ana, CA	2.4	171	West Palm Beach, FL	(10.4)
69	Oceanside, CA	(0.2)	27	Santa Barbara, CA	10.5	281	West Valley, UT	(19.0)
85	Odessa, TX	(2.2)	66	Santa Clara, CA	0.5	218	Westland, MI	(14.2)
285	O'Fallon, MO	(19.2)	244	Santa Clarita, CA	(16.7)	37	Westminster, CA	6.2
129	Ogden, UT	(7.0)	246	Santa Maria, CA	(16.8)	302	Westminster, CO	(20.4)
69	Oklahoma City, OK	(0.2)	39	Santa Monica, CA	5.9	43	Whittier, CA	5.1
NA	Olathe, KS**	NA	151	Santa Rosa, CA	(8.9)	368	Wichita Falls, TX	(30.0)
41	Omaha, NE	5.7	378	Savannah, GA	(32.9)	93	Wichita, KS	(2.9)
161	Ontario, CA	(9.5)	269	Scottsdale, AZ	(18.1)	95	Wilmington, NC	(3.2)
183	Orange, CA	(11.6)	133	Scranton, PA	(7.1)	213	Winston-Salem, NC	(13.8)
225	Orem, UT	(14.6)	120	Seattle, WA	(6.1)	366	Woodbridge Twnshp, NJ	(29.8)
331	Orlando, FL	(25.5)	162	Shreveport, LA	(9.6)	83	Worcester, MA	(1.9)
100	Overland Park, KS	(3.7)	151	Simi Valley, CA	(8.9)	182	Yakima, WA	(11.5)
234	Oxnard, CA	(15.6)	10	Sioux City, IA	22.4	NA	Yonkers, NY**	NA
77	Palm Bay, FL	(1.2)	7	Sioux Falls, SD	24.6	82	Yuma, AZ	(1.8)
278	Palmdale, CA	(18.8)	350	Somerville, MA	(27.0)			
NA	Parma, OH**	NA	357	South Bend, IN	(28.5)			

Source: CQ Press using reported data from the F.B.I. "Crime in the United States 2012"

*Includes murder, rape, robbery, aggravated assault, burglary, larceny-theft, and motor vehicle theft.

**Not available.

44. Percent Change in Crime Rate: 2008 to 2012 (continued)
National Percent Change = 11.6% Decrease*

RANK	CITY	% CHANGE	RANK	CITY	% CHANGE	RANK	CITY	% CHANGE
1	Spokane, WA	52.6	75	Edinburg, TX	(1.0)	148	Louisville, KY	(8.7)
2	Antioch, CA	50.0	76	Bakersfield, CA	(1.1)	150	Lakeland, FL	(8.8)
3	Medford, OR	47.0	77	Columbia, MO	(1.2)	151	Broken Arrow, OK	(8.9)
4	Rialto, CA	43.1	77	Palm Bay, FL	(1.2)	151	Buena Park, CA	(8.9)
5	Redding, CA	33.6	79	Fort Smith, AR	(1.4)	151	Santa Rosa, CA	(8.9)
6	Spokane Valley, WA	27.0	79	Norwalk, CA	(1.4)	151	Simi Valley, CA	(8.9)
7	Sioux Falls, SD	24.6	81	Irvine, CA	(1.7)	155	Atlanta, GA	(9.1)
7	St. Joseph, MO	24.6	82	Yuma, AZ	(1.8)	155	Hemet, CA	(9.1)
9	Gary, IN	22.8	83	Houston, TX	(1.9)	155	Killeen, TX	(9.1)
10	Sioux City, IA	22.4	83	Worcester, MA	(1.9)	158	Concord, CA	(9.3)
11	Huntington Beach, CA	21.7	85	Odessa, TX	(2.2)	158	Lakewood, CA	(9.3)
12	Clovis, CA	21.3	85	Tustin, CA	(2.2)	158	Visalia, CA	(9.3)
13	Glendale, AZ	20.0	87	Livonia, MI	(2.3)	161	Ontario, CA	(9.5)
14	San Jose, CA	19.4	88	Richmond, CA	(2.4)	162	Edmond, OK	(9.6)
15	Hesperia, CA	18.2	89	Akron, OH	(2.6)	162	Shreveport, LA	(9.6)
16	Merced, CA	17.5	89	Livermore, CA	(2.6)	164	Las Cruces, NM	(9.7)
17	Oakland, CA	17.3	89	Vallejo, CA	(2.6)	164	San Marcos, CA	(9.7)
18	Toms River Twnshp, NJ	16.3	92	Kenosha, WI	(2.7)	166	Sterling Heights, MI	(9.8)
19	Rancho Cucamon., CA	16.1	93	Wichita, KS	(2.9)	167	Centennial, CO	(9.9)
20	Indio, CA	14.8	94	Corona, CA	(3.1)	168	Allen, TX	(10.0)
21	Anaheim, CA	14.0	95	St. Paul, MN	(3.2)	169	Riverside, CA	(10.2)
22	Gresham, OR	13.7	95	Wilmington, NC	(3.2)	170	Alhambra, CA	(10.3)
23	Denver, CO	13.2	97	Cincinnati, OH	(3.3)	171	Sunnyvale, CA	(10.4)
24	Costa Mesa, CA	12.7	98	Asheville, NC	(3.4)	171	West Palm Beach, FL	(10.4)
25	Lake Forest, CA	11.0	99	Tyler, TX	(3.5)	173	Jackson, MS	(10.5)
26	Billings, MT	10.9	100	Colorado Springs, CO	(3.7)	173	Nampa, ID	(10.5)
27	Santa Barbara, CA	10.5	100	Mission Viejo, CA	(3.7)	175	Quincy, MA	(10.7)
28	Evansville, IN	10.3	100	Overland Park, KS	(3.7)	176	Greeley, CO	(11.0)
28	Murrieta, CA	10.3	103	Erie, PA	(3.8)	176	Mobile, AL	(11.0)
30	Manchester, NH	9.3	104	Davie, FL	(4.2)	178	Lansing, MI	(11.1)
31	Fayetteville, AR	9.0	105	Hayward, CA	(4.4)	179	Clinton Twnshp, MI	(11.3)
32	Ventura, CA	8.6	106	Hawthorne, CA	(4.6)	179	Kansas City, MO	(11.3)
33	Newark, NJ	8.5	107	Boulder, CO	(4.7)	181	Virginia Beach, VA	(11.4)
34	Lawton, OK	8.1	108	Dayton, OH	(4.8)	182	Yakima, WA	(11.5)
35	Fresno, CA	7.8	109	Round Rock, TX	(5.0)	183	Orange, CA	(11.6)
36	Hamilton Twnshp, NJ	6.8	110	Portland, OR	(5.1)	184	Boise, ID	(11.7)
37	Trenton, NJ	6.2	111	Meridian, ID	(5.2)	184	Chesapeake, VA	(11.7)
37	Westminster, CA	6.2	111	Pompano Beach, FL	(5.2)	184	New Bedford, MA	(11.7)
39	Pasadena, TX	5.9	113	Baltimore, MD	(5.3)	187	Bellingham, WA	(11.9)
39	Santa Monica, CA	5.9	114	Garden Grove, CA	(5.4)	187	Escondido, CA	(11.9)
41	Omaha, NE	5.7	115	Des Moines, IA	(5.5)	187	Hartford, CT	(11.9)
42	Lakewood, CO	5.5	116	Coral Springs, FL	(5.6)	190	Camden, NJ	(12.0)
43	Modesto, CA	5.1	116	Moreno Valley, CA	(5.6)	190	Henderson, NV	(12.0)
43	Whittier, CA	5.1	118	Fontana, CA	(5.7)	190	Lawrence, KS	(12.0)
45	Cleveland, OH	4.8	119	Baton Rouge, LA	(5.8)	193	Albuquerque, NM	(12.1)
46	Carson, CA	4.3	120	Cambridge, MA	(6.1)	194	Aurora, CO	(12.2)
47	Long Beach, CA	3.6	120	Hampton, VA	(6.1)	194	Minneapolis, MN	(12.2)
48	Hollywood, FL	3.1	120	Seattle, WA	(6.1)	196	Newport Beach, CA	(12.3)
48	Richmond, VA	3.1	123	Danbury, CT	(6.2)	197	Cranston, RI	(12.5)
50	Anchorage, AK	2.8	123	Montgomery, AL	(6.2)	197	Stockton, CA	(12.5)
51	Santa Ana, CA	2.4	125	Temecula, CA	(6.3)	199	Lafayette, LA	(12.6)
52	Flint, MI	2.3	126	Lincoln, NE	(6.7)	199	Troy, MI	(12.6)
52	Fort Lauderdale, FL	2.3	127	Mesquite, TX	(6.9)	201	Portsmouth, VA	(12.7)
54	Federal Way, WA	2.2	127	Washington, DC	(6.9)	202	Sugar Land, TX	(12.9)
55	Paterson, NJ	1.8	129	Indianapolis, IN	(7.0)	203	Austin, TX	(13.0)
56	Detroit, MI	1.7	129	Ogden, UT	(7.0)	204	Milwaukee, WI	(13.1)
57	San Bernardino, CA	1.6	129	Raleigh, NC	(7.0)	204	Salinas, CA	(13.1)
57	Victorville, CA	1.6	129	South Gate, CA	(7.0)	206	Huntsville, AL	(13.2)
59	Lawrence, MA	1.5	133	Scranton, PA	(7.1)	207	Hillsboro, OR	(13.3)
59	Little Rock, AR	1.5	134	Arvada, CO	(7.2)	208	Ann Arbor, MI	(13.4)
61	Chino, CA	1.4	134	Baldwin Park, CA	(7.2)	208	Norman, OK	(13.4)
62	Bloomington, IN	1.3	136	Vacaville, CA	(7.4)	210	Stamford, CT	(13.5)
63	San Francisco, CA	1.0	137	Fullerton, CA	(7.6)	211	Beaumont, TX	(13.6)
64	Pomona, CA	0.8	138	Madison, WI	(7.9)	211	Inglewood, CA	(13.6)
65	Vancouver, WA	0.7	138	Salem, OR	(7.9)	213	Norfolk, VA	(13.8)
66	Santa Clara, CA	0.5	140	Fort Wayne, IN	(8.1)	213	Pearland, TX	(13.8)
67	Miami, FL	0.4	141	McKinney, TX	(8.2)	213	Winston-Salem, NC	(13.8)
68	Thousand Oaks, CA	0.0	142	Abilene, TX	(8.3)	216	Fargo, ND	(14.1)
69	Oceanside, CA	(0.2)	142	Green Bay, WI	(8.3)	216	Lee's Summit, MO	(14.1)
69	Oklahoma City, OK	(0.2)	142	Lubbock, TX	(8.3)	218	Carrollton, TX	(14.2)
71	Knoxville, TN	(0.4)	145	Springfield, MA	(8.5)	218	Garland, TX	(14.2)
71	Springfield, MO	(0.4)	145	West Jordan, UT	(8.5)	218	Tulsa, OK	(14.2)
73	Denton, TX	(0.5)	147	Topeka, KS	(8.6)	218	Westland, MI	(14.2)
74	Miami Beach, FL	(0.6)	148	Alameda, CA	(8.7)	222	Roanoke, VA	(14.3)

RANK	CITY	% CHANGE	RANK	CITY	% CHANGE	RANK	CITY	% CHANGE
223	Lynn, MA	(14.4)	295	Reading, PA	(20.1)	371	Sparks, NV	(31.0)
223	Providence, RI	(14.4)	298	Elk Grove, CA	(20.2)	372	Chula Vista, CA	(31.1)
225	Largo, FL	(14.6)	298	Fort Collins, CO	(20.2)	373	Compton, CA	(31.2)
225	Orem, UT	(14.6)	298	Las Vegas, NV	(20.2)	374	Dearborn, MI	(31.5)
225	Tallahassee, FL	(14.6)	301	Frisco, TX	(20.3)	374	Greensboro, NC	(31.5)
228	Burbank, CA	(15.0)	302	Westminster, CO	(20.4)	376	Laredo, TX	(32.2)
229	Richardson, TX	(15.2)	303	Bethlehem, PA	(20.5)	377	Greenville, NC	(32.7)
229	Sacramento, CA	(15.2)	303	Brick Twnshp, NJ	(20.5)	378	Savannah, GA	(32.9)
231	Hammond, IN	(15.4)	305	Everett, WA	(20.6)	379	Roswell, GA	(33.2)
231	Murfreesboro, TN	(15.4)	306	Midland, TX	(20.8)	380	Carmel, IN	(33.5)
233	Fort Worth, TX	(15.5)	306	Redwood City, CA	(20.8)	381	Pembroke Pines, FL	(34.1)
234	Daly City, CA	(15.6)	308	Fayetteville, NC	(21.0)	382	Charlotte, NC	(34.3)
234	Oxnard, CA	(15.6)	308	Plantation, FL	(21.0)	382	Irving, TX	(34.3)
236	Downey, CA	(15.8)	310	Chino Hills, CA	(21.1)	384	Edison Twnshp, NJ	(34.5)
237	Alexandria, VA	(15.9)	311	Cedar Rapids, IA	(21.5)	384	Hialeah, FL	(34.5)
237	Peoria, AZ	(15.9)	312	Melbourne, FL	(21.9)	386	McAllen, TX	(34.6)
237	Philadelphia, PA	(15.9)	313	Boston, MA	(22.2)	387	El Cajon, CA	(35.2)
240	Macon, GA	(16.0)	314	Eugene, OR	(22.3)	388	Grand Prairie, TX	(36.6)
241	Provo, UT	(16.1)	315	El Paso, TX	(22.5)	389	Tampa, FL	(37.0)
242	Salt Lake City, UT	(16.5)	316	Fishers, IN	(22.8)	390	Charleston, SC	(38.0)
243	Deerfield Beach, FL	(16.6)	316	Sandy, UT	(22.8)	391	Bryan, TX	(39.0)
244	Santa Clarita, CA	(16.7)	318	Elizabeth, NJ	(22.9)	NA	Albany, GA**	NA
244	Tempe, AZ	(16.7)	319	Gainesville, FL	(23.0)	NA	Albany, NY**	NA
246	Santa Maria, CA	(16.8)	320	Boca Raton, FL	(23.1)	NA	Allentown, PA**	NA
246	West Covina, CA	(16.8)	321	Fremont, CA	(23.4)	NA	Amherst, NY**	NA
248	Carlsbad, CA	(16.9)	321	Lowell, MA	(23.4)	NA	Arlington Heights, IL**	NA
248	League City, TX	(16.9)	321	St. Petersburg, FL	(23.4)	NA	Aurora, IL**	NA
248	Los Angeles, CA	(16.9)	324	Clifton, NJ	(23.8)	NA	Bloomington, IL**	NA
248	Surprise, AZ	(16.9)	324	San Diego, CA	(23.8)	NA	Bloomington, MN**	NA
252	Citrus Heights, CA	(17.0)	326	Newton, MA	(24.2)	NA	Brockton, MA**	NA
252	Clearwater, FL	(17.0)	327	Plano, TX	(24.3)	NA	Brooklyn Park, MN**	NA
254	Rio Rancho, NM	(17.1)	328	College Station, TX	(24.7)	NA	Buffalo, NY**	NA
254	Rockford, IL	(17.1)	329	Arlington, TX	(24.8)	NA	Champaign, IL**	NA
256	Birmingham, AL	(17.2)	330	Port St. Lucie, FL	(25.4)	NA	Chandler, AZ**	NA
257	Avondale, AZ	(17.3)	331	Orlando, FL	(25.5)	NA	Cheektowaga, NY**	NA
257	Chico, CA	(17.3)	331	San Mateo, CA	(25.5)	NA	Chicago, IL**	NA
257	Racine, WI	(17.3)	331	Sandy Springs, GA	(25.5)	NA	Cicero, IL**	NA
260	Bridgeport, CT	(17.4)	334	Glendale, CA	(25.6)	NA	Clarkstown, NY**	NA
261	Amarillo, TX	(17.5)	335	Corpus Christi, TX	(25.7)	NA	Colonie, NY**	NA
262	Tacoma, WA	(17.6)	335	Roseville, CA	(25.7)	NA	Decatur, IL**	NA
263	North Las Vegas, NV	(17.7)	335	St. George, UT	(25.7)	NA	Duluth, MN**	NA
263	Pasadena, CA	(17.7)	338	Farmington Hills, MI	(25.8)	NA	Elgin, IL**	NA
263	Upland, CA	(17.7)	339	Longview, TX	(25.9)	NA	Greece, NY**	NA
266	Norwalk, CT	(17.9)	339	Newport News, VA	(25.9)	NA	Johns Creek, GA**	NA
267	Durham, NC	(18.0)	341	North Charleston, SC	(26.0)	NA	Joliet, IL**	NA
267	Sunrise, FL	(18.0)	342	Bellflower, CA	(26.1)	NA	Jurupa Valley, CA**	NA
269	Scottsdale, AZ	(18.1)	342	Dallas, TX	(26.1)	NA	Kansas City, KS**	NA
270	San Antonio, TX	(18.2)	344	Waco, TX	(26.3)	NA	Lakewood Twnshp, NJ**	NA
270	Torrance, CA	(18.2)	345	Columbus, GA	(26.4)	NA	Lexington, KY**	NA
272	Napa, CA	(18.3)	346	Cary, NC	(26.6)	NA	Longmont, CO**	NA
272	St. Louis, MO	(18.3)	346	Grand Rapids, MI	(26.6)	NA	Menifee, CA**	NA
274	Upper Darby Twnshp, PA	(18.4)	348	Miramar, FL	(26.7)	NA	Naperville, IL**	NA
275	Mesa, AZ	(18.5)	349	Vista, CA	(26.9)	NA	Nashua, NH**	NA
276	San Leandro, CA	(18.6)	350	Somerville, MA	(27.0)	NA	New Haven, CT**	NA
277	Kennewick, WA	(18.7)	351	Berkeley, CA	(27.3)	NA	New Rochelle, NY**	NA
278	Palmdale, CA	(18.8)	351	New Orleans, LA	(27.3)	NA	New York, NY**	NA
278	Tracy, CA	(18.8)	353	Miami Gardens, FL	(27.4)	NA	Olathe, KS**	NA
280	Memphis, TN	(18.9)	353	Reno, NV	(27.4)	NA	Parma, OH**	NA
281	Independence, MO	(19.0)	355	Clarksville, TN	(27.7)	NA	Peoria, IL**	NA
281	Pittsburgh, PA	(19.0)	356	Jersey City, NJ	(27.8)	NA	Pueblo, CO**	NA
281	West Valley, UT	(19.0)	357	South Bend, IN	(28.5)	NA	Ramapo, NY**	NA
284	Waterbury, CT	(19.1)	358	Gilbert, AZ	(28.6)	NA	Renton, WA**	NA
285	El Monte, CA	(19.2)	359	Lynchburg, VA	(29.0)	NA	Rochester, MN**	NA
285	Fairfield, CA	(19.2)	360	Beaverton, OR	(29.1)	NA	Rochester, NY**	NA
285	O'Fallon, MO	(19.2)	361	Cape Coral, FL	(29.2)	NA	Springfield, IL**	NA
288	Tuscaloosa, AL	(19.3)	362	Mission, TX	(29.3)	NA	Syracuse, NY**	NA
289	Kent, WA	(19.4)	363	Jacksonville, FL	(29.5)	NA	Thornton, CO**	NA
289	Warwick, RI	(19.4)	364	Athens-Clarke, GA	(29.7)	NA	Toledo, OH**	NA
291	Phoenix, AZ	(19.5)	364	Lancaster, CA	(29.7)	NA	Tucson, AZ**	NA
292	Fall River, MA	(19.8)	366	Davenport, IA	(29.8)	NA	Warren, MI**	NA
292	Hoover, AL	(19.8)	366	Woodbridge Twnshp, NJ	(29.8)	NA	Waukegan, IL**	NA
294	Nashville, TN	(20.0)	368	Wichita Falls, TX	(30.0)	NA	Yonkers, NY**	NA
295	Bellevue, WA	(20.1)	369	High Point, NC	(30.2)			
295	Brownsville, TX	(20.1)	370	Mountain View, CA	(30.8)			

Source: CQ Press using reported data from the F.B.I. "Crime in the United States 2012"

*Includes murder, rape, robbery, aggravated assault, burglary, larceny-theft, and motor vehicle theft.

**Not available.

45. Violent Crimes in 2012
National Total = 1,214,462 Violent Crimes*

RANK	CITY	CRIMES	RANK	CITY	CRIMES	RANK	CITY	CRIMES
231	Abilene, TX	472	428	Chino Hills, CA	64	143	Gainesville, FL	851
76	Akron, OH	1,759	305	Chino, CA	291	244	Garden Grove, CA	439
376	Alameda, CA	160	197	Chula Vista, CA	581	209	Garland, TX	540
150	Albany, GA	813	268	Cicero, IL	379	165	Gary, IN	728
154	Albany, NY	802	46	Cincinnati, OH	2,887	353	Gilbert, AZ	205
30	Albuquerque, NM	4,151	287	Citrus Heights, CA	329	112	Glendale, AZ	1,145
328	Alexandria, VA	243	422	Clarkstown, NY	76	334	Glendale, CA	233
383	Alhambra, CA	149	141	Clarksville, TN	875	222	Grand Prairie, TX	499
178	Allentown, PA	653	167	Clearwater, FL	727	93	Grand Rapids, MI	1,465
431	Allen, TX	55	23	Cleveland, OH	5,449	395	Greece, NY	129
105	Amarillo, TX	1,278	364	Clifton, NJ	184	250	Greeley, CO	426
414	Amherst, NY	88	305	Clinton Twnshp, MI	291	216	Green Bay, WI	514
104	Anaheim, CA	1,279	347	Clovis, CA	219	89	Greensboro, NC	1,555
56	Anchorage, AK	2,479	223	College Station, TX	491	237	Greenville, NC	455
342	Ann Arbor, MI	227	432	Colonie, NY	46	224	Gresham, OR	487
120	Antioch, CA	1,068	66	Colorado Springs, CO	1,968	361	Hamilton Twnshp, NJ	188
434	Arlington Heights, IL	41	228	Columbia, MO	476	176	Hammond, IN	665
69	Arlington, TX	1,909	129	Columbus, GA	994	293	Hampton, VA	314
377	Arvada, CO	158	108	Compton, CA	1,218	82	Hartford, CT	1,655
252	Asheville, NC	423	255	Concord, CA	402	180	Hawthorne, CA	637
237	Athens-Clarke, GA	455	338	Coral Springs, FL	229	190	Hayward, CA	613
17	Atlanta, GA	6,027	350	Corona, CA	210	254	Hemet, CA	406
94	Aurora, CO	1,433	63	Corpus Christi, TX	2,057	242	Henderson, NV	445
201	Aurora, IL	563	323	Costa Mesa, CA	254	255	Hesperia, CA	402
39	Austin, TX	3,405	394	Cranston, RI	130	152	Hialeah, FL	810
334	Avondale, AZ	233	11	Dallas, TX	8,380	203	High Point, NC	556
68	Bakersfield, CA	1,929	348	Daly City, CA	216	366	Hillsboro, OR	180
320	Baldwin Park, CA	261	404	Danbury, CT	109	179	Hollywood, FL	643
10	Baltimore, MD	8,789	191	Davenport, IA	604	416	Hoover, AL	86
54	Baton Rouge, LA	2,507	273	Davie, FL	369	2	Houston, TX	21,610
107	Beaumont, TX	1,242	96	Dayton, OH	1,384	294	Huntington Beach, CA	313
389	Beaverton, OR	141	291	Dearborn, MI	322	79	Huntsville, AL	1,696
375	Bellevue, WA	161	282	Decatur, IL	352	210	Independence, MO	537
299	Bellflower, CA	304	277	Deerfield Beach, FL	360	8	Indianapolis, IN	9,942
346	Bellingham, WA	220	273	Denton, TX	369	241	Indio, CA	450
224	Berkeley, CA	487	34	Denver, CO	3,871	157	Inglewood, CA	780
331	Bethlehem, PA	238	117	Des Moines, IA	1,094	402	Irvine, CA	110
271	Billings, MT	370	5	Detroit, MI	15,011	220	Irving, TX	507
42	Birmingham, AL	3,237	267	Downey, CA	381	26	Jacksonville, FL	5,189
270	Bloomington, IL	372	NA	Duluth, MN**	NA	81	Jackson, MS	1,668
328	Bloomington, IN	243	78	Durham, NC	1,710	71	Jersey City, NJ	1,847
NA	Bloomington, MN**	NA	279	Edinburg, TX	357	433	Johns Creek, GA	43
373	Boca Raton, FL	164	397	Edison Twnshp, NJ	122	221	Joliet, IL	506
198	Boise, ID	567	417	Edmond, OK	85	295	Jurupa Valley, CA	312
24	Boston, MA	5,266	275	El Cajon, CA	365	140	Kansas City, KS	877
325	Boulder, CO	249	259	El Monte, CA	395	18	Kansas City, MO	5,862
418	Brick Twnshp, NJ	81	48	El Paso, TX	2,859	338	Kennewick, WA	229
75	Bridgeport, CT	1,760	322	Elgin, IL	257	314	Kenosha, WI	274
118	Brockton, MA	1,088	128	Elizabeth, NJ	1,007	207	Kent, WA	543
380	Broken Arrow, OK	155	217	Elk Grove, CA	512	143	Killeen, TX	851
NA	Brooklyn Park, MN**	NA	236	Erie, PA	458	74	Knoxville, TN	1,774
230	Brownsville, TX	473	184	Escondido, CA	628	158	Lafayette, LA	779
295	Bryan, TX	312	249	Eugene, OR	430	407	Lake Forest, CA	107
352	Buena Park, CA	206	202	Evansville, IN	560	232	Lakeland, FL	465
40	Buffalo, NY	3,382	226	Everett, WA	481	402	Lakewood Twnshp, NJ	110
328	Burbank, CA	243	239	Fairfield, CA	454	342	Lakewood, CA	227
248	Cambridge, MA	431	130	Fall River, MA	954	174	Lakewood, CO	676
65	Camden, NJ	1,993	262	Fargo, ND	394	142	Lancaster, CA	859
338	Cape Coral, FL	229	424	Farmington Hills, MI	74	119	Lansing, MI	1,078
319	Carlsbad, CA	265	266	Fayetteville, AR	388	124	Laredo, TX	1,036
437	Carmel, IN	11	110	Fayetteville, NC	1,186	262	Largo, FL	394
366	Carrollton, TX	180	301	Federal Way, WA	296	262	Las Cruces, NM	394
214	Carson, CA	520	436	Fishers, IN	14	6	Las Vegas, NV	11,598
400	Cary, NC	115	49	Flint, MI	2,774	271	Lawrence, KS	370
280	Cedar Rapids, IA	356	145	Fontana, CA	850	156	Lawrence, MA	785
378	Centennial, CO	157	265	Fort Collins, CO	391	134	Lawton, OK	920
163	Champaign, IL	741	92	Fort Lauderdale, FL	1,543	421	League City, TX	79
184	Chandler, AZ	628	173	Fort Smith, AR	687	404	Lee's Summit, MO	109
301	Charleston, SC	296	132	Fort Wayne, IN	931	121	Lexington, KY	1,066
25	Charlotte, NC	5,238	29	Fort Worth, TX	4,524	123	Lincoln, NE	1,050
368	Cheektowaga, NY	175	298	Fremont, CA	306	52	Little Rock, AR	2,579
146	Chesapeake, VA	839	50	Fresno, CA	2,748	300	Livermore, CA	301
NA	Chicago, IL**	NA	411	Frisco, TX	98	387	Livonia, MI	146
311	Chico, CA	282	240	Fullerton, CA	452	51	Long Beach, CA	2,705

RANK	CITY	CRIMES	RANK	CITY	CRIMES	RANK	CITY	CRIMES
361	Longmont, CO	188	246	Pasadena, CA	433	204	South Gate, CA	553
234	Longview, TX	463	187	Pasadena, TX	622	333	Sparks, NV	234
3	Los Angeles, CA	18,547	90	Paterson, NJ	1,552	358	Spokane Valley, WA	196
31	Louisville, KY	3,989	396	Pearland, TX	123	98	Spokane, WA	1,369
195	Lowell, MA	585	331	Pembroke Pines, FL	238	113	Springfield, IL	1,138
67	Lubbock, TX	1,962	301	Peoria, AZ	296	84	Springfield, MA	1,606
318	Lynchburg, VA	267	135	Peoria, IL	919	85	Springfield, MO	1,596
161	Lynn, MA	754	4	Philadelphia, PA	17,853	283	Stamford, CT	351
196	Macon, GA	583	9	Phoenix, AZ	9,458	336	Sterling Heights, MI	232
136	Madison, WI	897	57	Pittsburgh, PA	2,347	28	Stockton, CA	4,630
186	Manchester, NH	624	278	Plano, TX	358	380	St. George, UT	155
372	McAllen, TX	166	313	Plantation, FL	278	290	St. Joseph, MO	323
338	McKinney, TX	229	127	Pomona, CA	1,021	20	St. Louis, MO	5,661
251	Medford, OR	425	122	Pompano Beach, FL	1,060	60	St. Paul, MN	2,101
177	Melbourne, FL	658	259	Port St. Lucie, FL	395	58	St. Petersburg, FL	2,239
7	Memphis, TN	11,507	44	Portland, OR	3,093	404	Sugar Land, TX	109
415	Menifee, CA	87	235	Portsmouth, VA	461	371	Sunnyvale, CA	170
152	Merced, CA	810	114	Providence, RI	1,133	337	Sunrise, FL	230
413	Meridian, ID	92	383	Provo, UT	149	374	Surprise, AZ	162
72	Mesa, AZ	1,804	155	Pueblo, CO	797	97	Syracuse, NY	1,372
243	Mesquite, TX	442	257	Quincy, MA	401	83	Tacoma, WA	1,615
131	Miami Beach, FL	941	269	Racine, WI	374	87	Tallahassee, FL	1,582
132	Miami Gardens, FL	931	73	Raleigh, NC	1,780	59	Tampa, FL	2,162
27	Miami, FL	4,856	420	Ramapo, NY	80	412	Temecula, CA	97
258	Midland, TX	398	292	Rancho Cucamon., CA	321	137	Tempe, AZ	878
13	Milwaukee, WI	7,759	147	Reading, PA	828	286	Thornton, CO	332
33	Minneapolis, MN	3,872	170	Redding, CA	705	378	Thousand Oaks, CA	157
210	Miramar, FL	537	351	Redwood City, CA	208	41	Toledo, OH	3,352
426	Mission Viejo, CA	73	109	Reno, NV	1,192	418	Toms River Twnshp, NJ	81
408	Mission, TX	104	310	Renton, WA	283	159	Topeka, KS	772
102	Mobile, AL	1,314	218	Rialto, CA	509	360	Torrance, CA	190
86	Modesto, CA	1,590	370	Richardson, TX	171	388	Tracy, CA	145
148	Montgomery, AL	827	111	Richmond, CA	1,162	106	Trenton, NJ	1,251
169	Moreno Valley, CA	706	99	Richmond, VA	1,348	429	Troy, MI	60
380	Mountain View, CA	155	356	Rio Rancho, NM	202	35	Tucson, AZ	3,851
171	Murfreesboro, TN	701	95	Riverside, CA	1,389	32	Tulsa, OK	3,949
427	Murrieta, CA	70	208	Roanoke, VA	542	227	Tuscaloosa, AL	478
355	Nampa, ID	203	NA	Rochester, MN**	NA	401	Tustin, CA	114
348	Napa, CA	216	62	Rochester, NY	2,069	212	Tyler, TX	536
399	Naperville, IL	119	61	Rockford, IL	2,083	385	Upland, CA	148
354	Nashua, NH	204	304	Roseville, CA	293	215	Upper Darby Twnshp, PA	517
14	Nashville, TN	7,550	393	Roswell, GA	132	327	Vacaville, CA	246
125	New Bedford, MA	1,030	389	Round Rock, TX	141	137	Vallejo, CA	878
70	New Haven, CT	1,870	38	Sacramento, CA	3,520	194	Vancouver, WA	592
45	New Orleans, LA	2,958	200	Salem, OR	564	297	Ventura, CA	310
365	New Rochelle, NY	181	126	Salinas, CA	1,027	174	Victorville, CA	676
1	New York, NY	52,993	103	Salt Lake City, UT	1,300	160	Virginia Beach, VA	758
43	Newark, NJ	3,220	16	San Antonio, TX	6,943	206	Visalia, CA	544
410	Newport Beach, CA	101	64	San Bernardino, CA	2,022	232	Vista, CA	465
161	Newport News, VA	754	21	San Diego, CA	5,529	182	Waco, TX	635
422	Newton, MA	76	19	San Francisco, CA	5,777	168	Warren, MI	715
101	Norfolk, VA	1,332	37	San Jose, CA	3,547	409	Warwick, RI	102
369	Norman, OK	173	245	San Leandro, CA	437	15	Washington, DC	7,448
164	North Charleston, SC	737	342	San Marcos, CA	227	289	Waterbury, CT	328
80	North Las Vegas, NV	1,695	320	San Mateo, CA	261	253	Waukegan, IL	420
246	Norwalk, CA	433	363	Sandy Springs, GA	187	312	West Covina, CA	281
316	Norwalk, CT	272	386	Sandy, UT	147	357	West Jordan, UT	199
12	Oakland, CA	7,963	100	Santa Ana, CA	1,334	149	West Palm Beach, FL	821
165	Oceanside, CA	728	276	Santa Barbara, CA	363	193	West Valley, UT	599
116	Odessa, TX	1,103	345	Santa Clara, CA	221	285	Westland, MI	338
424	O'Fallon, MO	74	284	Santa Clarita, CA	342	308	Westminster, CA	284
281	Ogden, UT	353	172	Santa Maria, CA	690	308	Westminster, CO	284
22	Oklahoma City, OK	5,474	259	Santa Monica, CA	395	326	Whittier, CA	247
359	Olathe, KS	191	181	Santa Rosa, CA	636	229	Wichita Falls, TX	475
55	Omaha, NE	2,485	137	Savannah, GA	878	47	Wichita, KS	2,869
213	Ontario, CA	534	287	Scottsdale, AZ	329	189	Wilmington, NC	618
392	Orange, CA	135	324	Scranton, PA	252	88	Winston-Salem, NC	1,556
434	Orem, UT	41	36	Seattle, WA	3,746	397	Woodbridge Twnshp, NJ	122
53	Orlando, FL	2,508	91	Shreveport, LA	1,550	77	Worcester, MA	1,758
307	Overland Park, KS	285	389	Simi Valley, CA	141	199	Yakima, WA	566
192	Oxnard, CA	603	314	Sioux City, IA	274	114	Yonkers, NY	1,133
204	Palm Bay, FL	553	183	Sioux Falls, SD	631	219	Yuma, AZ	508
151	Palmdale, CA	812	317	Somerville, MA	269			
430	Parma, OH	56	187	South Bend, IN	622			

Source: Reported data from the F.B.I. "Crime in the United States 2012"

*Violent crimes are offenses of murder, forcible rape, robbery, and aggravated assault.

**Not available.

45. Violent Crimes in 2012 (continued)
National Total = 1,214,462 Violent Crimes*

RANK	CITY	CRIMES	RANK	CITY	CRIMES	RANK	CITY	CRIMES
1	New York, NY	52,993	75	Bridgeport, CT	1,760	149	West Palm Beach, FL	821
2	Houston, TX	21,610	76	Akron, OH	1,759	150	Albany, GA	813
3	Los Angeles, CA	18,547	77	Worcester, MA	1,758	151	Palmdale, CA	812
4	Philadelphia, PA	17,853	78	Durham, NC	1,710	152	Hialeah, FL	810
5	Detroit, MI	15,011	79	Huntsville, AL	1,696	152	Merced, CA	810
6	Las Vegas, NV	11,598	80	North Las Vegas, NV	1,695	154	Albany, NY	802
7	Memphis, TN	11,507	81	Jackson, MS	1,668	155	Pueblo, CO	797
8	Indianapolis, IN	9,942	82	Hartford, CT	1,655	156	Lawrence, MA	785
9	Phoenix, AZ	9,458	83	Tacoma, WA	1,615	157	Inglewood, CA	780
10	Baltimore, MD	8,789	84	Springfield, MA	1,606	158	Lafayette, LA	779
11	Dallas, TX	8,380	85	Springfield, MO	1,596	159	Topeka, KS	772
12	Oakland, CA	7,963	86	Modesto, CA	1,590	160	Virginia Beach, VA	758
13	Milwaukee, WI	7,759	87	Tallahassee, FL	1,582	161	Lynn, MA	754
14	Nashville, TN	7,550	88	Winston-Salem, NC	1,556	161	Newport News, VA	754
15	Washington, DC	7,448	89	Greensboro, NC	1,555	163	Champaign, IL	741
16	San Antonio, TX	6,943	90	Paterson, NJ	1,552	164	North Charleston, SC	737
17	Atlanta, GA	6,027	91	Shreveport, LA	1,550	165	Gary, IN	728
18	Kansas City, MO	5,862	92	Fort Lauderdale, FL	1,543	165	Oceanside, CA	728
19	San Francisco, CA	5,777	93	Grand Rapids, MI	1,465	167	Clearwater, FL	727
20	St. Louis, MO	5,661	94	Aurora, CO	1,433	168	Warren, MI	715
21	San Diego, CA	5,529	95	Riverside, CA	1,389	169	Moreno Valley, CA	706
22	Oklahoma City, OK	5,474	96	Dayton, OH	1,384	170	Redding, CA	705
23	Cleveland, OH	5,449	97	Syracuse, NY	1,372	171	Murfreesboro, TN	701
24	Boston, MA	5,266	98	Spokane, WA	1,369	172	Santa Maria, CA	690
25	Charlotte, NC	5,238	99	Richmond, VA	1,348	173	Fort Smith, AR	687
26	Jacksonville, FL	5,189	100	Santa Ana, CA	1,334	174	Lakewood, CO	676
27	Miami, FL	4,856	101	Norfolk, VA	1,332	174	Victorville, CA	676
28	Stockton, CA	4,630	102	Mobile, AL	1,314	176	Hammond, IN	665
29	Fort Worth, TX	4,524	103	Salt Lake City, UT	1,300	177	Melbourne, FL	658
30	Albuquerque, NM	4,151	104	Anaheim, CA	1,279	178	Allentown, PA	653
31	Louisville, KY	3,989	105	Amarillo, TX	1,278	179	Hollywood, FL	643
32	Tulsa, OK	3,949	106	Trenton, NJ	1,251	180	Hawthorne, CA	637
33	Minneapolis, MN	3,872	107	Beaumont, TX	1,242	181	Santa Rosa, CA	636
34	Denver, CO	3,871	108	Compton, CA	1,218	182	Waco, TX	635
35	Tucson, AZ	3,851	109	Reno, NV	1,192	183	Sioux Falls, SD	631
36	Seattle, WA	3,746	110	Fayetteville, NC	1,186	184	Chandler, AZ	628
37	San Jose, CA	3,547	111	Richmond, CA	1,162	184	Escondido, CA	628
38	Sacramento, CA	3,520	112	Glendale, AZ	1,145	186	Manchester, NH	624
39	Austin, TX	3,405	113	Springfield, IL	1,138	187	Pasadena, TX	622
40	Buffalo, NY	3,382	114	Providence, RI	1,133	187	South Bend, IN	622
41	Toledo, OH	3,352	114	Yonkers, NY	1,133	189	Wilmington, NC	618
42	Birmingham, AL	3,237	116	Odessa, TX	1,103	190	Hayward, CA	613
43	Newark, NJ	3,220	117	Des Moines, IA	1,094	191	Davenport, IA	604
44	Portland, OR	3,093	118	Brockton, MA	1,088	192	Oxnard, CA	603
45	New Orleans, LA	2,958	119	Lansing, MI	1,078	193	West Valley, UT	599
46	Cincinnati, OH	2,887	120	Antioch, CA	1,068	194	Vancouver, WA	592
47	Wichita, KS	2,869	121	Lexington, KY	1,066	195	Lowell, MA	585
48	El Paso, TX	2,859	122	Pompano Beach, FL	1,060	196	Macon, GA	583
49	Flint, MI	2,774	123	Lincoln, NE	1,050	197	Chula Vista, CA	581
50	Fresno, CA	2,748	124	Laredo, TX	1,036	198	Boise, ID	567
51	Long Beach, CA	2,705	125	New Bedford, MA	1,030	199	Yakima, WA	566
52	Little Rock, AR	2,579	126	Salinas, CA	1,027	200	Salem, OR	564
53	Orlando, FL	2,508	127	Pomona, CA	1,021	201	Aurora, IL	563
54	Baton Rouge, LA	2,507	128	Elizabeth, NJ	1,007	202	Evansville, IN	560
55	Omaha, NE	2,485	129	Columbus, GA	994	203	High Point, NC	556
56	Anchorage, AK	2,479	130	Fall River, MA	954	204	Palm Bay, FL	553
57	Pittsburgh, PA	2,347	131	Miami Beach, FL	941	204	South Gate, CA	553
58	St. Petersburg, FL	2,239	132	Fort Wayne, IN	931	206	Visalia, CA	544
59	Tampa, FL	2,162	132	Miami Gardens, FL	931	207	Kent, WA	543
60	St. Paul, MN	2,101	134	Lawton, OK	920	208	Roanoke, VA	542
61	Rockford, IL	2,083	135	Peoria, IL	919	209	Garland, TX	540
62	Rochester, NY	2,069	136	Madison, WI	897	210	Independence, MO	537
63	Corpus Christi, TX	2,057	137	Savannah, GA	878	210	Miramar, FL	537
64	San Bernardino, CA	2,022	137	Tempe, AZ	878	212	Tyler, TX	536
65	Camden, NJ	1,993	137	Vallejo, CA	878	213	Ontario, CA	534
66	Colorado Springs, CO	1,968	140	Kansas City, KS	877	214	Carson, CA	520
67	Lubbock, TX	1,962	141	Clarksville, TN	875	215	Upper Darby Twnshp, PA	517
68	Bakersfield, CA	1,929	142	Lancaster, CA	859	216	Green Bay, WI	514
69	Arlington, TX	1,909	143	Gainesville, FL	851	217	Elk Grove, CA	512
70	New Haven, CT	1,870	143	Killeen, TX	851	218	Rialto, CA	509
71	Jersey City, NJ	1,847	145	Fontana, CA	850	219	Yuma, AZ	508
72	Mesa, AZ	1,804	146	Chesapeake, VA	839	220	Irving, TX	507
73	Raleigh, NC	1,780	147	Reading, PA	828	221	Joliet, IL	506
74	Knoxville, TN	1,774	148	Montgomery, AL	827	222	Grand Prairie, TX	499

RANK	CITY	CRIMES	RANK	CITY	CRIMES	RANK	CITY	CRIMES
223	College Station, TX	491	297	Ventura, CA	310	371	Sunnyvale, CA	170
224	Berkeley, CA	487	298	Fremont, CA	306	372	McAllen, TX	166
224	Gresham, OR	487	299	Bellflower, CA	304	373	Boca Raton, FL	164
226	Everett, WA	481	300	Livermore, CA	301	374	Surprise, AZ	162
227	Tuscaloosa, AL	478	301	Charleston, SC	296	375	Bellevue, WA	161
228	Columbia, MO	476	301	Federal Way, WA	296	376	Alameda, CA	160
229	Wichita Falls, TX	475	301	Peoria, AZ	296	377	Arvada, CO	158
230	Brownsville, TX	473	304	Roseville, CA	293	378	Centennial, CO	157
231	Abilene, TX	472	305	Chino, CA	291	378	Thousand Oaks, CA	157
232	Lakeland, FL	465	305	Clinton Twnshp, MI	291	380	Broken Arrow, OK	155
232	Vista, CA	465	307	Overland Park, KS	285	380	Mountain View, CA	155
234	Longview, TX	463	308	Westminster, CA	284	380	St. George, UT	155
235	Portsmouth, VA	461	308	Westminster, CO	284	383	Alhambra, CA	149
236	Erie, PA	458	310	Renton, WA	283	383	Provo, UT	149
237	Athens-Clarke, GA	455	311	Chico, CA	282	385	Upland, CA	148
237	Greenville, NC	455	312	West Covina, CA	281	386	Sandy, UT	147
239	Fairfield, CA	454	313	Plantation, FL	278	387	Livonia, MI	146
240	Fullerton, CA	452	314	Kenosha, WI	274	388	Tracy, CA	145
241	Indio, CA	450	314	Sioux City, IA	274	389	Beaverton, OR	141
242	Henderson, NV	445	316	Norwalk, CT	272	389	Round Rock, TX	141
243	Mesquite, TX	442	317	Somerville, MA	269	389	Simi Valley, CA	141
244	Garden Grove, CA	439	318	Lynchburg, VA	267	392	Orange, CA	135
245	San Leandro, CA	437	319	Carlsbad, CA	265	393	Roswell, GA	132
246	Norwalk, CA	433	320	Baldwin Park, CA	261	394	Cranston, RI	130
246	Pasadena, CA	433	320	San Mateo, CA	261	395	Greece, NY	129
248	Cambridge, MA	431	322	Elgin, IL	257	396	Pearland, TX	123
249	Eugene, OR	430	323	Costa Mesa, CA	254	397	Edison Twnshp, NJ	122
250	Greeley, CO	426	324	Scranton, PA	252	397	Woodbridge Twnshp, NJ	122
251	Medford, OR	425	325	Boulder, CO	249	399	Naperville, IL	119
252	Asheville, NC	423	326	Whittier, CA	247	400	Cary, NC	115
253	Waukegan, IL	420	327	Vacaville, CA	246	401	Tustin, CA	114
254	Hemet, CA	406	328	Alexandria, VA	243	402	Irvine, CA	110
255	Concord, CA	402	328	Bloomington, IN	243	402	Lakewood Twnshp, NJ	110
255	Hesperia, CA	402	328	Burbank, CA	243	404	Danbury, CT	109
257	Quincy, MA	401	331	Bethlehem, PA	238	404	Lee's Summit, MO	109
258	Midland, TX	398	331	Pembroke Pines, FL	238	404	Sugar Land, TX	109
259	El Monte, CA	395	333	Sparks, NV	234	407	Lake Forest, CA	107
259	Port St. Lucie, FL	395	334	Avondale, AZ	233	408	Mission, TX	104
259	Santa Monica, CA	395	334	Glendale, CA	233	409	Warwick, RI	102
262	Fargo, ND	394	336	Sterling Heights, MI	232	410	Newport Beach, CA	101
262	Largo, FL	394	337	Sunrise, FL	230	411	Frisco, TX	98
262	Las Cruces, NM	394	338	Cape Coral, FL	229	412	Temecula, CA	97
265	Fort Collins, CO	391	338	Coral Springs, FL	229	413	Meridian, ID	92
266	Fayetteville, AR	388	338	Kennewick, WA	229	414	Amherst, NY	88
267	Downey, CA	381	338	McKinney, TX	229	415	Menifee, CA	87
268	Cicero, IL	379	342	Ann Arbor, MI	227	416	Hoover, AL	86
269	Racine, WI	374	342	Lakewood, CA	227	417	Edmond, OK	85
270	Bloomington, IL	372	342	San Marcos, CA	227	418	Brick Twnshp, NJ	81
271	Billings, MT	370	345	Santa Clara, CA	221	418	Toms River Twnshp, NJ	81
271	Lawrence, KS	370	346	Bellingham, WA	220	420	Ramapo, NY	80
273	Davie, FL	369	347	Clovis, CA	219	421	League City, TX	79
273	Denton, TX	369	348	Daly City, CA	216	422	Clarkstown, NY	76
275	El Cajon, CA	365	348	Napa, CA	216	422	Newton, MA	76
276	Santa Barbara, CA	363	350	Corona, CA	210	424	Farmington Hills, MI	74
277	Deerfield Beach, FL	360	351	Redwood City, CA	208	424	O'Fallon, MO	74
278	Plano, TX	358	352	Buena Park, CA	206	426	Mission Viejo, CA	73
279	Edinburg, TX	357	353	Gilbert, AZ	205	427	Murrieta, CA	70
280	Cedar Rapids, IA	356	354	Nashua, NH	204	428	Chino Hills, CA	64
281	Ogden, UT	353	355	Nampa, ID	203	429	Troy, MI	60
282	Decatur, IL	352	356	Rio Rancho, NM	202	430	Parma, OH	56
283	Stamford, CT	351	357	West Jordan, UT	199	431	Allen, TX	55
284	Santa Clarita, CA	342	358	Spokane Valley, WA	196	432	Colonie, NY	46
285	Westland, MI	338	359	Olathe, KS	191	433	Johns Creek, GA	43
286	Thornton, CO	332	360	Torrance, CA	190	434	Arlington Heights, IL	41
287	Citrus Heights, CA	329	361	Hamilton Twnshp, NJ	188	434	Orem, UT	41
287	Scottsdale, AZ	329	361	Longmont, CO	188	436	Fishers, IN	14
289	Waterbury, CT	328	363	Sandy Springs, GA	187	437	Carmel, IN	11
290	St. Joseph, MO	323	364	Clifton, NJ	184	NA	Bloomington, MN**	NA
291	Dearborn, MI	322	365	New Rochelle, NY	181	NA	Brooklyn Park, MN**	NA
292	Rancho Cucamon., CA	321	366	Carrollton, TX	180	NA	Chicago, IL**	NA
293	Hampton, VA	314	366	Hillsboro, OR	180	NA	Duluth, MN**	NA
294	Huntington Beach, CA	313	368	Cheektowaga, NY	175	NA	Rochester, MN**	NA
295	Bryan, TX	312	369	Norman, OK	173			
295	Jurupa Valley, CA	312	370	Richardson, TX	171			

Source: Reported data from the F.B.I. "Crime in the United States 2012"

*Violent crimes are offenses of murder, forcible rape, robbery, and aggravated assault.

**Not available.

46. Violent Crime Rate in 2012
National Rate = 386.9 Violent Crimes per 100,000 Population*

RANK	CITY	RATE	RANK	CITY	RATE	RANK	CITY	RATE
240	Abilene, TX	393.7	421	Chino Hills, CA	83.5	107	Gainesville, FL	669.9
67	Akron, OH	886.6	250	Chino, CA	364.7	317	Garden Grove, CA	250.7
339	Alameda, CA	212.0	327	Chula Vista, CA	232.6	330	Garland, TX	229.8
37	Albany, GA	1,035.5	198	Cicero, IL	449.6	64	Gary, IN	904.7
76	Albany, NY	816.8	50	Cincinnati, OH	974.7	412	Gilbert, AZ	95.7
90	Albuquerque, NM	749.7	244	Citrus Heights, CA	386.5	180	Glendale, AZ	491.4
361	Alexandria, VA	166.6	413	Clarkstown, NY	94.8	400	Glendale, CA	119.5
357	Alhambra, CA	176.4	118	Clarksville, TN	637.0	300	Grand Prairie, TX	274.5
150	Allentown, PA	547.2	108	Clearwater, FL	665.4	86	Grand Rapids, MI	771.2
430	Allen, TX	61.9	12	Cleveland, OH	1,383.8	385	Greece, NY	133.3
112	Amarillo, TX	650.1	337	Clifton, NJ	217.3	204	Greeley, CO	442.5
426	Amherst, NY	74.8	287	Clinton Twnshp, MI	300.0	181	Green Bay, WI	484.5
248	Anaheim, CA	371.2	335	Clovis, CA	223.9	145	Greensboro, NC	563.1
72	Anchorage, AK	828.7	170	College Station, TX	508.5	162	Greenville, NC	523.8
345	Ann Arbor, MI	197.4	431	Colonie, NY	59.1	197	Gresham, OR	450.1
42	Antioch, CA	1,017.1	195	Colorado Springs, CO	455.3	341	Hamilton Twnshp, NJ	211.0
432	Arlington Heights, IL	54.3	208	Columbia, MO	430.2	74	Hammond, IN	820.9
172	Arlington, TX	503.3	171	Columbus, GA	506.7	331	Hampton, VA	227.7
377	Arvada, CO	144.9	20	Compton, CA	1,242.1	15	Hartford, CT	1,321.9
178	Asheville, NC	495.9	276	Concord, CA	321.1	92	Hawthorne, CA	743.4
243	Athens-Clarke, GA	387.4	355	Coral Springs, FL	183.2	222	Hayward, CA	415.8
13	Atlanta, GA	1,379.0	384	Corona, CA	133.5	177	Hemet, CA	499.9
214	Aurora, CO	425.3	111	Corpus Christi, TX	658.1	360	Henderson, NV	168.9
296	Aurora, IL	281.8	334	Costa Mesa, CA	225.5	206	Hesperia, CA	435.1
227	Austin, TX	408.8	365	Cranston, RI	161.9	262	Hialeah, FL	347.5
291	Avondale, AZ	297.3	105	Dallas, TX	675.0	165	High Point, NC	520.6
153	Bakersfield, CA	542.3	342	Daly City, CA	209.1	347	Hillsboro, OR	191.2
267	Baldwin Park, CA	340.5	386	Danbury, CT	133.1	204	Hollywood, FL	442.5
11	Baltimore, MD	1,405.2	133	Davenport, IA	596.9	409	Hoover, AL	104.5
31	Baton Rouge, LA	1,082.9	242	Davie, FL	388.6	45	Houston, TX	992.5
39	Beaumont, TX	1,032.2	51	Dayton, OH	973.7	367	Huntington Beach, CA	160.8
369	Beaverton, OR	152.8	269	Dearborn, MI	331.2	61	Huntsville, AL	923.3
393	Bellevue, WA	127.8	191	Decatur, IL	462.4	193	Independence, MO	457.3
241	Bellflower, CA	390.3	190	Deerfield Beach, FL	464.9	23	Indianapolis, IN	1,185.5
305	Bellingham, WA	266.1	283	Denton, TX	310.2	140	Indio, CA	573.2
216	Berkeley, CA	423.6	127	Denver, CO	615.9	102	Inglewood, CA	699.6
280	Bethlehem, PA	315.7	161	Des Moines, IA	527.5	434	Irvine, CA	50.6
261	Billings, MT	347.8	3	Detroit, MI	2,122.9	332	Irving, TX	226.3
8	Birmingham, AL	1,517.8	268	Downey, CA	335.3	125	Jacksonville, FL	617.3
183	Bloomington, IL	482.4	NA	Duluth, MN**	NA	55	Jackson, MS	948.1
289	Bloomington, IN	297.7	98	Durham, NC	725.9	95	Jersey City, NJ	734.2
NA	Bloomington, MN**	NA	202	Edinburg, TX	444.4	433	Johns Creek, GA	53.7
350	Boca Raton, FL	189.6	399	Edison Twnshp, NJ	120.8	266	Joliet, IL	340.8
304	Boise, ID	268.0	410	Edmond, OK	101.8	277	Jurupa Valley, CA	319.7
71	Boston, MA	835.0	256	El Cajon, CA	358.3	134	Kansas City, KS	595.8
319	Boulder, CO	248.4	265	El Monte, CA	342.4	19	Kansas City, MO	1,263.2
408	Brick Twnshp, NJ	106.8	217	El Paso, TX	423.2	290	Kennewick, WA	297.5
22	Bridgeport, CT	1,205.2	324	Elgin, IL	235.4	301	Kenosha, WI	274.0
29	Brockton, MA	1,143.4	79	Elizabeth, NJ	797.4	201	Kent, WA	444.7
368	Broken Arrow, OK	153.9	272	Elk Grove, CA	327.5	116	Killeen, TX	644.9
NA	Brooklyn Park, MN**	NA	199	Erie, PA	449.1	52	Knoxville, TN	973.4
312	Brownsville, TX	261.2	212	Escondido, CA	426.1	121	Lafayette, LA	634.1
236	Bryan, TX	397.6	302	Eugene, OR	272.1	382	Lake Forest, CA	135.2
318	Buena Park, CA	249.7	186	Evansville, IN	473.8	189	Lakeland, FL	465.3
18	Buffalo, NY	1,288.7	194	Everett, WA	456.7	404	Lakewood Twnshp, NJ	117.3
329	Burbank, CA	231.3	215	Fairfield, CA	423.9	297	Lakewood, CA	278.9
231	Cambridge, MA	402.9	34	Fall River, MA	1,062.9	192	Lakewood, CO	461.7
2	Camden, NJ	2,566.1	254	Fargo, ND	358.8	154	Lancaster, CA	539.7
379	Cape Coral, FL	143.5	416	Farmington Hills, MI	92.1	58	Lansing, MI	939.9
320	Carlsbad, CA	245.6	169	Fayetteville, AR	514.7	220	Laredo, TX	421.9
437	Carmel, IN	13.4	138	Fayetteville, NC	575.8	176	Largo, FL	500.1
378	Carrollton, TX	144.6	275	Federal Way, WA	321.8	239	Las Cruces, NM	394.7
148	Carson, CA	557.7	436	Fishers, IN	17.6	83	Las Vegas, NV	784.0
423	Cary, NC	81.6	1	Flint, MI	2,729.5	224	Lawrence, KS	414.9
298	Cedar Rapids, IA	277.3	217	Fontana, CA	423.2	43	Lawrence, MA	1,010.8
372	Centennial, CO	150.9	309	Fort Collins, CO	262.8	60	Lawton, OK	931.4
63	Champaign, IL	911.1	65	Fort Lauderdale, FL	903.3	417	League City, TX	91.7
315	Chandler, AZ	258.7	82	Fort Smith, AR	785.3	402	Lee's Summit, MO	118.7
322	Charleston, SC	239.0	253	Fort Wayne, IN	362.8	259	Lexington, KY	352.6
114	Charlotte, NC	647.9	136	Fort Worth, TX	587.5	237	Lincoln, NE	397.5
336	Cheektowaga, NY	221.0	381	Fremont, CA	139.8	16	Little Rock, AR	1,315.4
249	Chesapeake, VA	368.7	151	Fresno, CA	543.1	251	Livermore, CA	363.5
NA	Chicago, IL**	NA	424	Frisco, TX	79.5	370	Livonia, MI	152.0
274	Chico, CA	323.8	273	Fullerton, CA	326.5	139	Long Beach, CA	575.7

RANK	CITY	RATE
340	Longmont, CO	211.4
146	Longview, TX	560.8
184	Los Angeles, CA	481.1
131	Louisville, KY	598.8
155	Lowell, MA	539.0
73	Lubbock, TX	827.0
263	Lynchburg, VA	345.2
74	Lynn, MA	820.9
122	Macon, GA	628.0
246	Madison, WI	377.7
143	Manchester, NH	567.1
396	McAllen, TX	122.3
362	McKinney, TX	165.8
147	Medford, OR	558.9
68	Melbourne, FL	853.1
6	Memphis, TN	1,750.3
407	Menifee, CA	108.7
44	Merced, CA	1,000.3
401	Meridian, ID	119.1
234	Mesa, AZ	399.7
285	Mesquite, TX	305.2
38	Miami Beach, FL	1,033.3
70	Miami Gardens, FL	837.4
25	Miami, FL	1,172.0
264	Midland, TX	344.2
17	Milwaukee, WI	1,294.5
46	Minneapolis, MN	992.2
211	Miramar, FL	426.2
425	Mission Viejo, CA	76.4
391	Mission, TX	129.1
164	Mobile, AL	522.4
84	Modesto, CA	777.0
238	Montgomery, AL	395.7
258	Moreno Valley, CA	353.6
344	Mountain View, CA	204.1
123	Murfreesboro, TN	624.5
429	Murrieta, CA	65.5
321	Nampa, ID	243.7
299	Napa, CA	274.8
422	Naperville, IL	83.3
325	Nashua, NH	234.8
21	Nashville, TN	1,216.0
32	New Bedford, MA	1,072.6
10	New Haven, CT	1,439.2
77	New Orleans, LA	815.2
328	New Rochelle, NY	232.0
117	New York, NY	639.3
28	Newark, NJ	1,154.5
405	Newport Beach, CA	115.7
223	Newport News, VA	415.2
420	Newton, MA	87.6
152	Norfolk, VA	543.0
371	Norman, OK	151.8
96	North Charleston, SC	732.1
88	North Las Vegas, NV	763.9
230	Norwalk, CA	403.6
281	Norwalk, CT	313.8
4	Oakland, CA	1,993.3
213	Oceanside, CA	425.4
33	Odessa, TX	1,064.3
417	O'Fallon, MO	91.7
224	Ogden, UT	414.9
62	Oklahoma City, OK	919.1
374	Olathe, KS	148.6
135	Omaha, NE	594.5
278	Ontario, CA	318.0
411	Orange, CA	96.6
435	Orem, UT	44.6
41	Orlando, FL	1,017.4
366	Overland Park, KS	160.9
288	Oxnard, CA	298.8
160	Palm Bay, FL	528.5
163	Palmdale, CA	522.9
428	Parma, OH	69.2

RANK	CITY	RATE
282	Pasadena, CA	310.7
232	Pasadena, TX	402.4
35	Paterson, NJ	1,054.7
390	Pearland, TX	129.9
373	Pembroke Pines, FL	149.0
352	Peoria, AZ	186.9
80	Peoria, IL	797.1
27	Philadelphia, PA	1,160.1
120	Phoenix, AZ	636.7
89	Pittsburgh, PA	752.0
389	Plano, TX	130.7
279	Plantation, FL	317.0
106	Pomona, CA	673.9
40	Pompano Beach, FL	1,029.1
326	Port St. Lucie, FL	234.5
167	Portland, OR	517.2
185	Portsmouth, VA	476.5
119	Providence, RI	636.9
394	Provo, UT	127.5
97	Pueblo, CO	730.8
209	Quincy, MA	427.8
187	Racine, WI	473.1
217	Raleigh, NC	423.2
415	Ramapo, NY	93.6
350	Rancho Cucamon., CA	189.6
59	Reading, PA	935.0
85	Redding, CA	774.9
306	Redwood City, CA	265.1
167	Reno, NV	517.2
286	Renton, WA	302.0
175	Rialto, CA	501.0
363	Richardson, TX	165.6
30	Richmond, CA	1,092.5
113	Richmond, VA	648.7
333	Rio Rancho, NM	225.8
203	Riverside, CA	443.0
149	Roanoke, VA	554.3
NA	Rochester, MN**	NA
49	Rochester, NY	976.0
14	Rockford, IL	1,367.8
323	Roseville, CA	238.4
380	Roswell, GA	143.3
387	Round Rock, TX	132.7
94	Sacramento, CA	738.6
255	Salem, OR	358.4
109	Salinas, CA	665.1
104	Salt Lake City, UT	675.6
173	San Antonio, TX	503.1
56	San Bernardino, CA	940.5
226	San Diego, CA	413.1
101	San Francisco, CA	704.2
252	San Jose, CA	363.3
173	San Leandro, CA	503.1
307	San Marcos, CA	264.5
309	San Mateo, CA	262.8
348	Sandy Springs, GA	191.0
364	Sandy, UT	162.6
233	Santa Ana, CA	401.2
229	Santa Barbara, CA	403.9
354	Santa Clara, CA	185.2
349	Santa Clarita, CA	190.8
103	Santa Maria, CA	681.8
207	Santa Monica, CA	433.0
247	Santa Rosa, CA	372.2
245	Savannah, GA	379.6
376	Scottsdale, AZ	147.2
270	Scranton, PA	331.1
132	Seattle, WA	597.6
87	Shreveport, LA	766.7
406	Simi Valley, CA	111.3
271	Sioux City, IA	329.0
235	Sioux Falls, SD	398.5
260	Somerville, MA	348.4
128	South Bend, IN	613.4

RANK	CITY	RATE
137	South Gate, CA	576.2
316	Sparks, NV	253.3
338	Spokane Valley, WA	215.0
115	Spokane, WA	645.3
53	Springfield, IL	971.6
36	Springfield, MA	1,039.4
47	Springfield, MO	991.5
295	Stamford, CT	282.6
356	Sterling Heights, MI	178.5
7	Stockton, CA	1,548.0
343	St. George, UT	204.5
221	St. Joseph, MO	417.7
5	St. Louis, MO	1,776.5
100	St. Paul, MN	722.7
66	St. Petersburg, FL	901.6
388	Sugar Land, TX	131.4
403	Sunnyvale, CA	118.4
308	Sunrise, FL	263.9
383	Surprise, AZ	134.1
57	Syracuse, NY	940.2
81	Tacoma, WA	797.0
69	Tallahassee, FL	853.0
126	Tampa, FL	616.4
414	Temecula, CA	93.8
159	Tempe, AZ	528.7
303	Thornton, CO	269.7
397	Thousand Oaks, CA	121.5
26	Toledo, OH	1,171.9
419	Toms River Twnshp, NJ	87.9
130	Topeka, KS	599.2
392	Torrance, CA	128.5
358	Tracy, CA	170.5
9	Trenton, NJ	1,466.3
427	Troy, MI	73.6
99	Tucson, AZ	724.5
48	Tulsa, OK	990.0
166	Tuscaloosa, AL	519.7
375	Tustin, CA	147.3
156	Tyler, TX	535.8
346	Upland, CA	195.9
124	Upper Darby Twnshp, PA	623.1
311	Vacaville, CA	261.8
91	Vallejo, CA	744.6
257	Vancouver, WA	355.8
293	Ventura, CA	285.7
142	Victorville, CA	569.6
359	Virginia Beach, VA	169.4
210	Visalia, CA	426.3
182	Vista, CA	483.9
179	Waco, TX	493.8
157	Warren, MI	532.2
395	Warwick, RI	124.0
24	Washington, DC	1,177.9
292	Waterbury, CT	296.9
188	Waukegan, IL	469.4
313	West Covina, CA	260.5
353	West Jordan, UT	185.8
78	West Palm Beach, FL	801.6
200	West Valley, UT	447.9
228	Westland, MI	405.8
284	Westminster, CA	309.0
314	Westminster, CO	259.5
294	Whittier, CA	284.8
196	Wichita Falls, TX	450.3
93	Wichita, KS	742.5
144	Wilmington, NC	565.1
110	Winston-Salem, NC	663.0
398	Woodbridge Twnshp, NJ	121.3
54	Worcester, MA	959.4
129	Yakima, WA	605.9
141	Yonkers, NY	570.9
158	Yuma, AZ	531.6

Source: CQ Press using reported data from the F.B.I. "Crime in the United States 2012"

*Violent crimes are offenses of murder, forcible rape, robbery, and aggravated assault.

**Not available.

46. Violent Crime Rate in 2012 (continued)
National Rate = 386.9 Violent Crimes per 100,000 Population*

RANK	CITY	RATE	RANK	CITY	RATE	RANK	CITY	RATE
1	Flint, MI	2,729.5	74	Lynn, MA	820.9	149	Roanoke, VA	554.3
2	Camden, NJ	2,566.1	76	Albany, NY	816.8	150	Allentown, PA	547.2
3	Detroit, MI	2,122.9	77	New Orleans, LA	815.2	151	Fresno, CA	543.1
4	Oakland, CA	1,993.3	78	West Palm Beach, FL	801.6	152	Norfolk, VA	543.0
5	St. Louis, MO	1,776.5	79	Elizabeth, NJ	797.4	153	Bakersfield, CA	542.3
6	Memphis, TN	1,750.3	80	Peoria, IL	797.1	154	Lancaster, CA	539.7
7	Stockton, CA	1,548.0	81	Tacoma, WA	797.0	155	Lowell, MA	539.0
8	Birmingham, AL	1,517.8	82	Fort Smith, AR	785.3	156	Tyler, TX	535.8
9	Trenton, NJ	1,466.3	83	Las Vegas, NV	784.0	157	Warren, MI	532.2
10	New Haven, CT	1,439.2	84	Modesto, CA	777.0	158	Yuma, AZ	531.6
11	Baltimore, MD	1,405.2	85	Redding, CA	774.9	159	Tempe, AZ	528.7
12	Cleveland, OH	1,383.8	86	Grand Rapids, MI	771.2	160	Palm Bay, FL	528.5
13	Atlanta, GA	1,379.0	87	Shreveport, LA	766.7	161	Des Moines, IA	527.5
14	Rockford, IL	1,367.8	88	North Las Vegas, NV	763.9	162	Greenville, NC	523.8
15	Hartford, CT	1,321.9	89	Pittsburgh, PA	752.0	163	Palmdale, CA	522.9
16	Little Rock, AR	1,315.4	90	Albuquerque, NM	749.7	164	Mobile, AL	522.4
17	Milwaukee, WI	1,294.5	91	Vallejo, CA	744.6	165	High Point, NC	520.6
18	Buffalo, NY	1,288.7	92	Hawthorne, CA	743.4	166	Tuscaloosa, AL	519.7
19	Kansas City, MO	1,263.2	93	Wichita, KS	742.5	167	Portland, OR	517.2
20	Compton, CA	1,242.1	94	Sacramento, CA	738.6	167	Reno, NV	517.2
21	Nashville, TN	1,216.0	95	Jersey City, NJ	734.2	169	Fayetteville, AR	514.7
22	Bridgeport, CT	1,205.2	96	North Charleston, SC	732.1	170	College Station, TX	508.5
23	Indianapolis, IN	1,185.5	97	Pueblo, CO	730.8	171	Columbus, GA	506.7
24	Washington, DC	1,177.9	98	Durham, NC	725.9	172	Arlington, TX	503.3
25	Miami, FL	1,172.0	99	Tucson, AZ	724.5	173	San Antonio, TX	503.1
26	Toledo, OH	1,171.9	100	St. Paul, MN	722.7	173	San Leandro, CA	503.1
27	Philadelphia, PA	1,160.1	101	San Francisco, CA	704.2	175	Rialto, CA	501.0
28	Newark, NJ	1,154.5	102	Inglewood, CA	699.6	176	Largo, FL	500.1
29	Brockton, MA	1,143.4	103	Santa Maria, CA	681.8	177	Hemet, CA	499.9
30	Richmond, CA	1,092.5	104	Salt Lake City, UT	675.4	178	Asheville, NC	495.9
31	Baton Rouge, LA	1,082.9	105	Dallas, TX	675.0	179	Waco, TX	493.8
32	New Bedford, MA	1,072.6	106	Pomona, CA	673.9	180	Glendale, AZ	491.4
33	Odessa, TX	1,064.3	107	Gainesville, FL	669.9	181	Green Bay, WI	484.5
34	Fall River, MA	1,062.9	108	Clearwater, FL	665.4	182	Vista, CA	483.9
35	Paterson, NJ	1,054.7	109	Salinas, CA	665.1	183	Bloomington, IL	482.4
36	Springfield, MA	1,039.4	110	Winston-Salem, NC	663.0	184	Los Angeles, CA	481.1
37	Albany, GA	1,035.5	111	Corpus Christi, TX	658.1	185	Portsmouth, VA	476.5
38	Miami Beach, FL	1,033.3	112	Amarillo, TX	650.1	186	Evansville, IN	473.8
39	Beaumont, TX	1,032.2	113	Richmond, VA	648.7	187	Racine, WI	473.1
40	Pompano Beach, FL	1,029.1	114	Charlotte, NC	647.9	188	Waukegan, IL	469.4
41	Orlando, FL	1,017.4	115	Spokane, WA	645.3	189	Lakeland, FL	465.3
42	Antioch, CA	1,017.1	116	Killeen, TX	644.9	190	Deerfield Beach, FL	464.9
43	Lawrence, MA	1,010.8	117	New York, NY	639.3	191	Decatur, IL	462.4
44	Merced, CA	1,000.3	118	Clarksville, TN	637.0	192	Lakewood, CO	461.7
45	Houston, TX	992.5	119	Providence, RI	636.9	193	Independence, MO	457.3
46	Minneapolis, MN	992.2	120	Phoenix, AZ	636.7	194	Everett, WA	456.7
47	Springfield, MO	991.5	121	Lafayette, LA	634.1	195	Colorado Springs, CO	455.3
48	Tulsa, OK	990.0	122	Macon, GA	628.0	196	Wichita Falls, TX	450.3
49	Rochester, NY	976.0	123	Murfreesboro, TN	624.5	197	Gresham, OR	450.1
50	Cincinnati, OH	974.7	124	Upper Darby Twnshp, PA	623.1	198	Cicero, IL	449.6
51	Dayton, OH	973.7	125	Jacksonville, FL	617.3	199	Erie, PA	449.1
52	Knoxville, TN	973.4	126	Tampa, FL	616.4	200	West Valley, UT	447.9
53	Springfield, IL	971.6	127	Denver, CO	615.9	201	Kent, WA	444.7
54	Worcester, MA	959.4	128	South Bend, IN	613.4	202	Edinburg, TX	444.4
55	Jackson, MS	948.1	129	Yakima, WA	605.9	203	Riverside, CA	443.0
56	San Bernardino, CA	940.5	130	Topeka, KS	599.2	204	Greeley, CO	442.5
57	Syracuse, NY	940.2	131	Louisville, KY	598.8	204	Hollywood, FL	442.5
58	Lansing, MI	939.9	132	Seattle, WA	597.6	206	Hesperia, CA	435.1
59	Reading, PA	935.0	133	Davenport, IA	596.9	207	Santa Monica, CA	433.0
60	Lawton, OK	931.4	134	Kansas City, KS	595.8	208	Columbia, MO	430.2
61	Huntsville, AL	923.3	135	Omaha, NE	594.5	209	Quincy, MA	427.8
62	Oklahoma City, OK	919.1	136	Fort Worth, TX	587.5	210	Visalia, CA	426.3
63	Champaign, IL	911.1	137	South Gate, CA	576.2	211	Miramar, FL	426.2
64	Gary, IN	904.7	138	Fayetteville, NC	575.8	212	Escondido, CA	426.1
65	Fort Lauderdale, FL	903.3	139	Long Beach, CA	575.7	213	Oceanside, CA	425.4
66	St. Petersburg, FL	901.6	140	Indio, CA	573.2	214	Aurora, CO	425.3
67	Akron, OH	886.6	141	Yonkers, NY	570.9	215	Fairfield, CA	423.9
68	Melbourne, FL	853.1	142	Victorville, CA	569.6	216	Berkeley, CA	423.6
69	Tallahassee, FL	853.0	143	Manchester, NH	567.1	217	El Paso, TX	423.2
70	Miami Gardens, FL	837.4	144	Wilmington, NC	565.1	217	Fontana, CA	423.2
71	Boston, MA	835.0	145	Greensboro, NC	563.1	217	Raleigh, NC	423.2
72	Anchorage, AK	828.7	146	Longview, TX	560.8	220	Laredo, TX	421.9
73	Lubbock, TX	827.0	147	Medford, OR	558.9	221	St. Joseph, MO	417.7
74	Hammond, IN	820.9	148	Carson, CA	557.7	222	Hayward, CA	415.8

RANK	CITY	RATE	RANK	CITY	RATE	RANK	CITY	RATE
223	Newport News, VA	415.2	297	Lakewood, CA	278.9	371	Norman, OK	151.8
224	Lawrence, KS	414.9	298	Cedar Rapids, IA	277.3	372	Centennial, CO	150.9
224	Ogden, UT	414.9	299	Napa, CA	274.8	373	Pembroke Pines, FL	149.0
226	San Diego, CA	413.1	300	Grand Prairie, TX	274.5	374	Olathe, KS	148.6
227	Austin, TX	408.8	301	Kenosha, WI	274.0	375	Tustin, CA	147.3
228	Westland, MI	405.8	302	Eugene, OR	272.1	376	Scottsdale, AZ	147.2
229	Santa Barbara, CA	403.9	303	Thornton, CO	269.7	377	Arvada, CO	144.9
230	Norwalk, CA	403.6	304	Boise, ID	268.0	378	Carrollton, TX	144.6
231	Cambridge, MA	402.9	305	Bellingham, WA	266.1	379	Cape Coral, FL	143.5
232	Pasadena, TX	402.4	306	Redwood City, CA	265.1	380	Roswell, GA	143.3
233	Santa Ana, CA	401.2	307	San Marcos, CA	264.5	381	Fremont, CA	139.8
234	Mesa, AZ	399.7	308	Sunrise, FL	263.9	382	Lake Forest, CA	135.2
235	Sioux Falls, SD	398.5	309	Fort Collins, CO	262.8	383	Surprise, AZ	134.1
236	Bryan, TX	397.6	309	San Mateo, CA	262.8	384	Corona, CA	133.5
237	Lincoln, NE	397.5	311	Vacaville, CA	261.8	385	Greece, NY	133.3
238	Montgomery, AL	395.7	312	Brownsville, TX	261.2	386	Danbury, CT	133.1
239	Las Cruces, NM	394.7	313	West Covina, CA	260.5	387	Round Rock, TX	132.7
240	Abilene, TX	393.7	314	Westminster, CO	259.5	388	Sugar Land, TX	131.4
241	Bellflower, CA	390.3	315	Chandler, AZ	258.7	389	Plano, TX	130.7
242	Davie, FL	388.6	316	Sparks, NV	253.3	390	Pearland, TX	129.9
243	Athens-Clarke, GA	387.4	317	Garden Grove, CA	250.7	391	Mission, TX	129.1
244	Citrus Heights, CA	386.5	318	Buena Park, CA	249.7	392	Torrance, CA	128.5
245	Savannah, GA	379.6	319	Boulder, CO	248.4	393	Bellevue, WA	127.8
246	Madison, WI	377.7	320	Carlsbad, CA	245.6	394	Provo, UT	127.5
247	Santa Rosa, CA	372.2	321	Nampa, ID	243.7	395	Warwick, RI	124.0
248	Anaheim, CA	371.2	322	Charleston, SC	239.0	396	McAllen, TX	122.3
249	Chesapeake, VA	368.7	323	Roseville, CA	238.4	397	Thousand Oaks, CA	121.5
250	Chino, CA	364.7	324	Elgin, IL	235.4	398	Woodbridge Twnshp, NJ	121.3
251	Livermore, CA	363.5	325	Nashua, NH	234.8	399	Edison Twnshp, NJ	120.8
252	San Jose, CA	363.3	326	Port St. Lucie, FL	234.5	400	Glendale, CA	119.5
253	Fort Wayne, IN	362.8	327	Chula Vista, CA	232.6	401	Meridian, ID	119.1
254	Fargo, ND	358.8	328	New Rochelle, NY	232.0	402	Lee's Summit, MO	118.7
255	Salem, OR	358.4	329	Burbank, CA	231.3	403	Sunnyvale, CA	118.4
256	El Cajon, CA	358.3	330	Garland, TX	229.8	404	Lakewood Twnshp, NJ	117.3
257	Vancouver, WA	355.8	331	Hampton, VA	227.7	405	Newport Beach, CA	115.7
258	Moreno Valley, CA	353.6	332	Irving, TX	226.3	406	Simi Valley, CA	111.3
259	Lexington, KY	352.6	333	Rio Rancho, NM	225.8	407	Menifee, CA	108.7
260	Somerville, MA	348.4	334	Costa Mesa, CA	225.5	408	Brick Twnshp, NJ	106.8
261	Billings, MT	347.8	335	Clovis, CA	223.9	409	Hoover, AL	104.5
262	Hialeah, FL	347.5	336	Cheektowaga, NY	221.0	410	Edmond, OK	101.8
263	Lynchburg, VA	345.2	337	Clifton, NJ	217.3	411	Orange, CA	96.6
264	Midland, TX	344.2	338	Spokane Valley, WA	215.0	412	Gilbert, AZ	95.7
265	El Monte, CA	342.4	339	Alameda, CA	212.0	413	Clarkstown, NY	94.8
266	Joliet, IL	340.8	340	Longmont, CO	211.4	414	Temecula, CA	93.8
267	Baldwin Park, CA	340.5	341	Hamilton Twnshp, NJ	211.0	415	Ramapo, NY	93.6
268	Downey, CA	335.3	342	Daly City, CA	209.1	416	Farmington Hills, MI	92.1
269	Dearborn, MI	331.2	343	St. George, UT	204.5	417	League City, TX	91.7
270	Scranton, PA	331.1	344	Mountain View, CA	204.1	417	O'Fallon, MO	91.7
271	Sioux City, IA	329.0	345	Ann Arbor, MI	197.4	419	Toms River Twnshp, NJ	87.9
272	Elk Grove, CA	327.5	346	Upland, CA	195.9	420	Newton, MA	87.6
273	Fullerton, CA	326.5	347	Hillsboro, OR	191.2	421	Chino Hills, CA	83.5
274	Chico, CA	323.8	348	Sandy Springs, GA	191.0	422	Naperville, IL	83.3
275	Federal Way, WA	321.8	349	Santa Clarita, CA	190.8	423	Cary, NC	81.6
276	Concord, CA	321.1	350	Boca Raton, FL	189.6	424	Frisco, TX	79.5
277	Jurupa Valley, CA	319.7	350	Rancho Cucamon., CA	189.6	425	Mission Viejo, CA	76.4
278	Ontario, CA	318.0	352	Peoria, AZ	186.9	426	Amherst, NY	74.8
279	Plantation, FL	317.0	353	West Jordan, UT	185.8	427	Troy, MI	73.6
280	Bethlehem, PA	315.7	354	Santa Clara, CA	185.2	428	Parma, OH	69.2
281	Norwalk, CT	313.8	355	Coral Springs, FL	183.2	429	Murrieta, CA	65.5
282	Pasadena, CA	310.7	356	Sterling Heights, MI	178.5	430	Allen, TX	61.9
283	Denton, TX	310.2	357	Alhambra, CA	176.4	431	Colonie, NY	59.1
284	Westminster, CA	309.0	358	Tracy, CA	170.5	432	Arlington Heights, IL	54.3
285	Mesquite, TX	305.2	359	Virginia Beach, VA	169.4	433	Johns Creek, GA	53.7
286	Renton, WA	302.0	360	Henderson, NV	168.9	434	Irvine, CA	50.6
287	Clinton Twnshp, MI	300.0	361	Alexandria, VA	166.6	435	Orem, UT	44.6
288	Oxnard, CA	298.8	362	McKinney, TX	165.8	436	Fishers, IN	17.6
289	Bloomington, IN	297.7	363	Richardson, TX	165.6	437	Carmel, IN	13.4
290	Kennewick, WA	297.5	364	Sandy, UT	162.6	NA	Bloomington, MN**	NA
291	Avondale, AZ	297.3	365	Cranston, RI	161.9	NA	Brooklyn Park, MN**	NA
292	Waterbury, CT	296.9	366	Overland Park, KS	160.9	NA	Chicago, IL**	NA
293	Ventura, CA	285.7	367	Huntington Beach, CA	160.8	NA	Duluth, MN**	NA
294	Whittier, CA	284.8	368	Broken Arrow, OK	153.9	NA	Rochester, MN**	NA
295	Stamford, CT	282.6	369	Beaverton, OR	152.8			
296	Aurora, IL	281.8	370	Livonia, MI	152.0			

Source: CQ Press using reported data from the F.B.I. "Crime in the United States 2012"

*Violent crimes are offenses of murder, forcible rape, robbery, and aggravated assault.

**Not available.

47. Percent Change in Violent Crime Rate: 2011 to 2012
National Percent Change = 0.0% Change*

RANK	CITY	% CHANGE	RANK	CITY	% CHANGE	RANK	CITY	% CHANGE
100	Abilene, TX	9.9	313	Chino Hills, CA	(7.1)	317	Gainesville, FL	(7.4)
221	Akron, OH	(0.7)	50	Chino, CA	16.5	269	Garden Grove, CA	(3.5)
395	Alameda, CA	(23.5)	364	Chula Vista, CA	(14.3)	209	Garland, TX	0.4
15	Albany, GA	26.9	97	Cicero, IL	10.0	66	Gary, IN	14.3
NA	Albany, NY**	NA	292	Cincinnati, OH	(5.6)	69	Gilbert, AZ	13.7
234	Albuquerque, NM	(1.6)	243	Citrus Heights, CA	(2.5)	194	Glendale, AZ	1.4
304	Alexandria, VA	(6.4)	NA	Clarkstown, NY**	NA	345	Glendale, CA	(10.2)
242	Alhambra, CA	(2.4)	260	Clarksville, TN	(3.2)	377	Grand Prairie, TX	(16.8)
NA	Allentown, PA**	NA	340	Clearwater, FL	(9.3)	157	Grand Rapids, MI	3.9
399	Allen, TX	(26.0)	196	Cleveland, OH	1.3	NA	Greece, NY**	NA
163	Amarillo, TX	3.5	366	Clifton, NJ	(14.7)	276	Greeley, CO	(4.3)
NA	Amherst, NY**	NA	275	Clinton Twnshp, MI	(4.2)	10	Green Bay, WI	35.8
231	Anaheim, CA	(1.4)	176	Clovis, CA	2.7	NA	Greensboro, NC**	NA
169	Anchorage, AK	3.0	2	College Station, TX	69.2	NA	Greenville, NC**	NA
362	Ann Arbor, MI	(13.9)	NA	Colonie, NY**	NA	59	Gresham, OR	15.5
13	Antioch, CA	28.8	164	Colorado Springs, CO	3.4	197	Hamilton Twnshp, NJ	1.2
368	Arlington Heights, IL	(14.8)	387	Columbia, MO	(19.5)	27	Hammond, IN	21.9
213	Arlington, TX	0.2	154	Columbus, GA	4.5	342	Hampton, VA	(9.5)
257	Arvada, CO	(3.1)	71	Compton, CA	13.6	201	Hartford, CT	0.8
295	Asheville, NC	(5.7)	322	Concord, CA	(7.8)	186	Hawthorne, CA	1.8
110	Athens-Clarke, GA	8.8	285	Coral Springs, FL	(4.7)	150	Hayward, CA	4.8
270	Atlanta, GA	(3.8)	171	Corona, CA	2.9	92	Hemet, CA	10.2
252	Aurora, CO	(2.9)	168	Corpus Christi, TX	3.2	394	Henderson, NV	(23.1)
358	Aurora, IL	(12.0)	111	Costa Mesa, CA	8.6	16	Hesperia, CA	26.8
287	Austin, TX	(5.0)	20	Cranston, RI	25.0	325	Hialeah, FL	(8.0)
307	Avondale, AZ	(6.6)	224	Dallas, TX	(0.9)	330	High Point, NC	(8.3)
183	Bakersfield, CA	2.2	53	Daly City, CA	16.3	30	Hillsboro, OR	21.2
121	Baldwin Park, CA	7.3	409	Danbury, CT	(34.2)	276	Hollywood, FL	(4.3)
224	Baltimore, MD	(0.9)	330	Davenport, IA	(8.3)	6	Hoover, AL	45.3
191	Baton Rouge, LA	1.6	193	Davie, FL	1.5	186	Houston, TX	1.8
47	Beaumont, TX	16.6	186	Dayton, OH	1.8	396	Huntington Beach, CA	(23.9)
375	Beaverton, OR	(16.5)	342	Dearborn, MI	(9.5)	94	Huntsville, AL	10.1
73	Bellevue, WA	13.5	401	Decatur, IL	(26.6)	120	Independence, MO	7.4
137	Bellflower, CA	5.8	267	Deerfield Beach, FL	(3.4)	118	Indianapolis, IN	7.7
100	Bellingham, WA	9.9	59	Denton, TX	15.5	179	Indio, CA	2.6
214	Berkeley, CA	0.1	194	Denver, CO	1.4	272	Inglewood, CA	(3.9)
112	Bethlehem, PA	8.5	200	Des Moines, IA	0.9	340	Irvine, CA	(9.3)
45	Billings, MT	16.8	221	Detroit, MI	(0.7)	248	Irving, TX	(2.8)
182	Birmingham, AL	2.3	248	Downey, CA	(2.8)	220	Jacksonville, FL	(0.6)
176	Bloomington, IL	2.7	NA	Duluth, MN**	NA	185	Jackson, MS	1.9
231	Bloomington, IN	(1.4)	236	Durham, NC	(1.7)	276	Jersey City, NJ	(4.3)
NA	Bloomington, MN**	NA	22	Edinburg, TX	24.1	34	Johns Creek, GA	19.3
336	Boca Raton, FL	(8.9)	366	Edison Twnshp, NJ	(14.7)	243	Joliet, IL	(2.5)
105	Boise, ID	9.3	8	Edmond, OK	44.4	NA	Jurupa Valley, CA**	NA
229	Boston, MA	(1.2)	407	El Cajon, CA	(31.8)	321	Kansas City, KS	(7.7)
346	Boulder, CO	(10.5)	307	El Monte, CA	(6.6)	147	Kansas City, MO	5.3
388	Brick Twnshp, NJ	(19.6)	237	El Paso, TX	(1.9)	229	Kennewick, WA	(1.2)
32	Bridgeport, CT	20.4	351	Elgin, IL	(11.0)	240	Kenosha, WI	(2.1)
312	Brockton, MA	(7.0)	397	Elizabeth, NJ	(24.0)	406	Kent, WA	(27.7)
126	Broken Arrow, OK	6.8	254	Elk Grove, CA	(3.0)	167	Killeen, TX	3.3
NA	Brooklyn Park, MN**	NA	132	Erie, PA	6.4	157	Knoxville, TN	3.9
307	Brownsville, TX	(6.6)	19	Escondido, CA	25.3	333	Lafayette, LA	(8.4)
403	Bryan, TX	(27.2)	307	Eugene, OR	(6.6)	35	Lake Forest, CA	18.7
354	Buena Park, CA	(11.5)	68	Evansville, IN	13.9	371	Lakeland, FL	(16.1)
NA	Buffalo, NY**	NA	134	Everett, WA	6.2	35	Lakewood Twnshp, NJ	18.7
17	Burbank, CA	26.6	133	Fairfield, CA	6.3	141	Lakewood, CA	5.6
351	Cambridge, MA	(11.0)	361	Fall River, MA	(12.7)	107	Lakewood, CO	9.2
318	Camden, NJ	(7.5)	211	Fargo, ND	0.3	205	Lancaster, CA	0.5
280	Cape Coral, FL	(4.5)	405	Farmington Hills, MI	(27.4)	329	Lansing, MI	(8.2)
21	Carlsbad, CA	24.6	14	Fayetteville, AR	27.6	338	Laredo, TX	(9.2)
411	Carmel, IN	(37.4)	84	Fayetteville, NC	11.4	143	Largo, FL	5.5
365	Carrollton, TX	(14.6)	NA	Federal Way, WA**	NA	328	Las Cruces, NM	(8.1)
47	Carson, CA	16.6	24	Fishers, IN	23.1	140	Las Vegas, NV	5.7
164	Cary, NC	3.4	45	Flint, MI	16.8	107	Lawrence, KS	9.2
234	Cedar Rapids, IA	(1.6)	47	Fontana, CA	16.6	189	Lawrence, MA	1.7
286	Centennial, CO	(4.9)	330	Fort Collins, CO	(8.3)	97	Lawton, OK	10.0
197	Champaign, IL	1.2	260	Fort Lauderdale, FL	(3.2)	377	League City, TX	(16.8)
NA	Chandler, AZ**	NA	73	Fort Smith, AR	13.5	189	Lee's Summit, MO	1.7
402	Charleston, SC	(27.0)	40	Fort Wayne, IN	17.8	NA	Lexington, KY**	NA
126	Charlotte, NC	6.8	247	Fort Worth, TX	(2.7)	121	Lincoln, NE	7.3
NA	Cheektowaga, NY**	NA	391	Fremont, CA	(21.2)	356	Little Rock, AR	(11.7)
313	Chesapeake, VA	(7.1)	311	Fresno, CA	(6.7)	83	Livermore, CA	11.5
NA	Chicago, IL**	NA	392	Frisco, TX	(22.1)	359	Livonia, MI	(12.3)
63	Chico, CA	15.2	5	Fullerton, CA	45.9	296	Long Beach, CA	(5.8)

RANK	CITY	% CHANGE
392	Longmont, CO	(22.1)
81	Longview, TX	11.8
323	Los Angeles, CA	(7.9)
243	Louisville, KY	(2.5)
404	Lowell, MA	(27.3)
118	Lubbock, TX	7.7
287	Lynchburg, VA	(5.0)
315	Lynn, MA	(7.2)
176	Macon, GA	2.7
112	Madison, WI	8.5
204	Manchester, NH	0.7
408	McAllen, TX	(34.1)
323	McKinney, TX	(7.9)
105	Medford, OR	9.3
359	Melbourne, FL	(12.3)
89	Memphis, TN	10.5
3	Menifee, CA	60.8
4	Merced, CA	58.9
374	Meridian, ID	(16.3)
260	Mesa, AZ	(3.2)
102	Mesquite, TX	9.7
161	Miami Beach, FL	3.7
336	Miami Gardens, FL	(8.9)
240	Miami, FL	(2.1)
44	Midland, TX	17.0
12	Milwaukee, WI	29.6
174	Minneapolis, MN	2.8
179	Miramar, FL	2.6
335	Mission Viejo, CA	(8.7)
191	Mission, TX	1.6
382	Mobile, AL	(18.7)
79	Modesto, CA	11.9
57	Montgomery, AL	15.7
291	Moreno Valley, CA	(5.5)
215	Mountain View, CA	0.0
150	Murfreesboro, TN	4.8
410	Murrieta, CA	(34.7)
354	Nampa, ID	(11.5)
280	Napa, CA	(4.5)
137	Naperville, IL	5.8
273	Nashua, NH	(4.1)
171	Nashville, TN	2.9
299	New Bedford, MA	(6.1)
124	New Haven, CT	7.1
171	New Orleans, LA	2.9
NA	New Rochelle, NY**	NA
NA	New York, NY**	NA
227	Newark, NJ	(1.0)
363	Newport Beach, CA	(14.0)
344	Newport News, VA	(10.1)
301	Newton, MA	(6.2)
302	Norfolk, VA	(6.3)
350	Norman, OK	(10.9)
88	North Charleston, SC	10.6
NA	North Las Vegas, NV**	NA
54	Norwalk, CA	16.2
380	Norwalk, CT	(17.4)
39	Oakland, CA	18.5
56	Oceanside, CA	16.0
7	Odessa, TX	45.2
174	O'Fallon, MO	2.8
347	Ogden, UT	(10.6)
143	Oklahoma City, OK	5.5
376	Olathe, KS	(16.7)
134	Omaha, NE	6.2
125	Ontario, CA	7.0
369	Orange, CA	(15.1)
349	Orem, UT	(10.8)
290	Orlando, FL	(5.2)
248	Overland Park, KS	(2.8)
267	Oxnard, CA	(3.4)
325	Palm Bay, FL	(8.0)
169	Palmdale, CA	3.0
NA	Parma, OH**	NA

RANK	CITY	% CHANGE
224	Pasadena, CA	(0.9)
115	Pasadena, TX	8.2
160	Paterson, NJ	3.8
260	Pearland, TX	(3.2)
398	Pembroke Pines, FL	(24.6)
254	Peoria, AZ	(3.0)
77	Peoria, IL	13.0
248	Philadelphia, PA	(2.8)
62	Phoenix, AZ	15.4
302	Pittsburgh, PA	(6.3)
385	Plano, TX	(19.2)
305	Plantation, FL	(6.5)
103	Pomona, CA	9.6
71	Pompano Beach, FL	13.6
145	Port St. Lucie, FL	5.4
205	Portland, OR	0.5
372	Portsmouth, VA	(16.2)
NA	Providence, RI**	NA
237	Provo, UT	(1.9)
283	Pueblo, CO	(4.6)
201	Quincy, MA	0.8
58	Racine, WI	15.6
209	Raleigh, NC	0.4
NA	Ramapo, NY**	NA
115	Rancho Cucamon., CA	8.2
109	Reading, PA	9.0
205	Redding, CA	0.5
52	Redwood City, CA	16.4
136	Reno, NV	6.0
280	Renton, WA	(4.5)
152	Rialto, CA	4.7
254	Richardson, TX	(3.0)
87	Richmond, CA	10.7
299	Richmond, VA	(6.1)
86	Rio Rancho, NM	11.0
156	Riverside, CA	4.0
319	Roanoke, VA	(7.6)
NA	Rochester, MN**	NA
NA	Rochester, NY**	NA
219	Rockford, IL	(0.4)
59	Roseville, CA	15.5
1	Roswell, GA	78.2
42	Round Rock, TX	17.6
157	Sacramento, CA	3.9
117	Salem, OR	7.9
338	Salinas, CA	(9.2)
137	Salt Lake City, UT	5.8
257	San Antonio, TX	(3.1)
121	San Bernardino, CA	7.3
129	San Diego, CA	6.6
126	San Francisco, CA	6.8
114	San Jose, CA	8.4
40	San Leandro, CA	17.8
270	San Marcos, CA	(3.8)
148	San Mateo, CA	5.1
35	Sandy Springs, GA	18.7
33	Sandy, UT	19.8
211	Santa Ana, CA	0.3
75	Santa Barbara, CA	13.3
23	Santa Clara, CA	23.3
11	Santa Clarita, CA	29.9
273	Santa Maria, CA	(4.1)
131	Santa Monica, CA	6.5
316	Santa Rosa, CA	(7.3)
264	Savannah, GA	(3.3)
383	Scottsdale, AZ	(18.9)
81	Scranton, PA	11.8
201	Seattle, WA	0.8
217	Shreveport, LA	(0.1)
31	Simi Valley, CA	20.6
386	Sioux City, IA	(19.3)
9	Sioux Falls, SD	41.1
296	Somerville, MA	(5.8)
372	South Bend, IN	(16.2)

RANK	CITY	% CHANGE
289	South Gate, CA	(5.1)
384	Sparks, NV	(19.1)
78	Spokane Valley, WA	12.0
149	Spokane, WA	5.0
353	Springfield, IL	(11.4)
197	Springfield, MA	1.2
29	Springfield, MO	21.5
348	Stamford, CT	(10.7)
67	Sterling Heights, MI	14.0
97	Stockton, CA	10.0
NA	St. George, UT**	NA
64	St. Joseph, MO	14.5
276	St. Louis, MO	(4.3)
91	St. Paul, MN	10.3
356	St. Petersburg, FL	(11.7)
94	Sugar Land, TX	10.1
79	Sunnyvale, CA	11.9
370	Sunrise, FL	(16.0)
26	Surprise, AZ	22.0
NA	Syracuse, NY**	NA
129	Tacoma, WA	6.6
292	Tallahassee, FL	(5.6)
298	Tampa, FL	(5.9)
215	Temecula, CA	0.0
92	Tempe, AZ	10.2
NA	Thornton, CO**	NA
69	Thousand Oaks, CA	13.7
43	Toledo, OH	17.4
390	Toms River Twnshp, NJ	(20.3)
94	Topeka, KS	10.1
183	Torrance, CA	2.2
162	Tracy, CA	3.6
164	Trenton, NJ	3.4
379	Troy, MI	(17.3)
85	Tucson, AZ	11.1
227	Tulsa, OK	(1.0)
104	Tuscaloosa, AL	9.4
55	Tustin, CA	16.1
145	Tyler, TX	5.4
389	Upland, CA	(20.1)
25	Upper Darby Twnshp, PA	22.3
18	Vacaville, CA	25.6
264	Vallejo, CA	(3.3)
319	Vancouver, WA	(7.6)
292	Ventura, CA	(5.6)
246	Victorville, CA	(2.6)
264	Virginia Beach, VA	(3.3)
90	Visalia, CA	10.4
35	Vista, CA	18.7
381	Waco, TX	(17.9)
223	Warren, MI	(0.8)
27	Warwick, RI	21.9
155	Washington, DC	4.2
334	Waterbury, CT	(8.6)
NA	Waukegan, IL**	NA
217	West Covina, CA	(0.1)
305	West Jordan, UT	(6.5)
141	West Palm Beach, FL	5.6
205	West Valley, UT	0.5
239	Westland, MI	(2.0)
76	Westminster, CA	13.1
65	Westminster, CO	14.4
400	Whittier, CA	(26.4)
152	Wichita Falls, TX	4.7
257	Wichita, KS	(3.1)
325	Wilmington, NC	(8.0)
233	Winston-Salem, NC	(1.5)
283	Woodbridge Twnshp, NJ	(4.6)
252	Worcester, MA	(2.9)
50	Yakima, WA	16.5
NA	Yonkers, NY**	NA
181	Yuma, AZ	2.4

Source: CQ Press using reported data from the F.B.I. "Crime in the United States 2012"

*Violent crimes are offenses of murder, forcible rape, robbery, and aggravated assault.

**Not available.

47. Percent Change in Violent Crime Rate: 2011 to 2012 (continued)
National Percent Change = 0.0% Change*

RANK CITY	% CHANGE	RANK CITY	% CHANGE	RANK CITY	% CHANGE
1 Roswell, GA	78.2	75 Santa Barbara, CA	13.3	149 Spokane, WA	5.0
2 College Station, TX	69.2	76 Westminster, CA	13.1	150 Hayward, CA	4.8
3 Menifee, CA	60.8	77 Peoria, IL	13.0	150 Murfreesboro, TN	4.8
4 Merced, CA	58.9	78 Spokane Valley, WA	12.0	152 Rialto, CA	4.7
5 Fullerton, CA	45.9	79 Modesto, CA	11.9	152 Wichita Falls, TX	4.7
6 Hoover, AL	45.3	79 Sunnyvale, CA	11.9	154 Columbus, GA	4.5
7 Odessa, TX	45.2	81 Longview, TX	11.8	155 Washington, DC	4.2
8 Edmond, OK	44.4	81 Scranton, PA	11.8	156 Riverside, CA	4.0
9 Sioux Falls, SD	41.1	83 Livermore, CA	11.5	157 Grand Rapids, MI	3.9
10 Green Bay, WI	35.8	84 Fayetteville, NC	11.4	157 Knoxville, TN	3.9
11 Santa Clarita, CA	29.9	85 Tucson, AZ	11.1	157 Sacramento, CA	3.9
12 Milwaukee, WI	29.6	86 Rio Rancho, NM	11.0	160 Paterson, NJ	3.8
13 Antioch, CA	28.8	87 Richmond, CA	10.7	161 Miami Beach, FL	3.7
14 Fayetteville, AR	27.6	88 North Charleston, SC	10.6	162 Tracy, CA	3.6
15 Albany, GA	26.9	89 Memphis, TN	10.5	163 Amarillo, TX	3.5
16 Hesperia, CA	26.8	90 Visalia, CA	10.4	164 Cary, NC	3.4
17 Burbank, CA	26.6	91 St. Paul, MN	10.3	164 Colorado Springs, CO	3.4
18 Vacaville, CA	25.6	92 Hemet, CA	10.2	164 Trenton, NJ	3.4
19 Escondido, CA	25.3	92 Tempe, AZ	10.2	167 Killeen, TX	3.3
20 Cranston, RI	25.0	94 Huntsville, AL	10.1	168 Corpus Christi, TX	3.2
21 Carlsbad, CA	24.6	94 Sugar Land, TX	10.1	169 Anchorage, AK	3.0
22 Edinburg, TX	24.1	94 Topeka, KS	10.1	169 Palmdale, CA	3.0
23 Santa Clara, CA	23.3	97 Cicero, IL	10.0	171 Corona, CA	2.9
24 Fishers, IN	23.1	97 Lawton, OK	10.0	171 Nashville, TN	2.9
25 Upper Darby Twnshp, PA	22.3	97 Stockton, CA	10.0	171 New Orleans, LA	2.9
26 Surprise, AZ	22.0	100 Abilene, TX	9.9	174 Minneapolis, MN	2.8
27 Hammond, IN	21.9	100 Bellingham, WA	9.9	174 O'Fallon, MO	2.8
27 Warwick, RI	21.9	102 Mesquite, TX	9.7	176 Bloomington, IL	2.7
29 Springfield, MO	21.5	103 Pomona, CA	9.6	176 Clovis, CA	2.7
30 Hillsboro, OR	21.2	104 Tuscaloosa, AL	9.4	176 Macon, GA	2.7
31 Simi Valley, CA	20.6	105 Boise, ID	9.3	179 Indio, CA	2.6
32 Bridgeport, CT	20.4	105 Medford, OR	9.3	179 Miramar, FL	2.6
33 Sandy, UT	19.8	107 Lakewood, CO	9.2	181 Yuma, AZ	2.4
34 Johns Creek, GA	19.3	107 Lawrence, KS	9.2	182 Birmingham, AL	2.3
35 Lake Forest, CA	18.7	109 Reading, PA	9.0	183 Bakersfield, CA	2.2
35 Lakewood Twnshp, NJ	18.7	110 Athens-Clarke, GA	8.8	183 Torrance, CA	2.2
35 Sandy Springs, GA	18.7	111 Costa Mesa, CA	8.6	185 Jackson, MS	1.9
35 Vista, CA	18.7	112 Bethlehem, PA	8.5	186 Dayton, OH	1.8
39 Oakland, CA	18.5	112 Madison, WI	8.5	186 Hawthorne, CA	1.8
40 Fort Wayne, IN	17.8	114 San Jose, CA	8.4	186 Houston, TX	1.8
40 San Leandro, CA	17.8	115 Pasadena, TX	8.2	189 Lawrence, MA	1.7
42 Round Rock, TX	17.6	115 Rancho Cucamon., CA	8.2	189 Lee's Summit, MO	1.7
43 Toledo, OH	17.4	117 Salem, OR	7.9	191 Baton Rouge, LA	1.6
44 Midland, TX	17.0	118 Indianapolis, IN	7.7	191 Mission, TX	1.6
45 Billings, MT	16.8	118 Lubbock, TX	7.7	193 Davie, FL	1.5
45 Flint, MI	16.8	120 Independence, MO	7.4	194 Denver, CO	1.4
47 Beaumont, TX	16.6	121 Baldwin Park, CA	7.3	194 Glendale, AZ	1.4
47 Carson, CA	16.6	121 Lincoln, NE	7.3	196 Cleveland, OH	1.3
47 Fontana, CA	16.6	121 San Bernardino, CA	7.3	197 Champaign, IL	1.2
50 Chino, CA	16.5	124 New Haven, CT	7.1	197 Hamilton Twnshp, NJ	1.2
50 Yakima, WA	16.5	125 Ontario, CA	7.0	197 Springfield, MA	1.2
52 Redwood City, CA	16.4	126 Broken Arrow, OK	6.8	200 Des Moines, IA	0.9
53 Daly City, CA	16.3	126 Charlotte, NC	6.8	201 Hartford, CT	0.8
54 Norwalk, CA	16.2	126 San Francisco, CA	6.8	201 Quincy, MA	0.8
55 Tustin, CA	16.1	129 San Diego, CA	6.6	201 Seattle, WA	0.8
56 Oceanside, CA	16.0	129 Tacoma, WA	6.6	204 Manchester, NH	0.7
57 Montgomery, AL	15.7	131 Santa Monica, CA	6.5	205 Lancaster, CA	0.5
58 Racine, WI	15.6	132 Erie, PA	6.4	205 Portland, OR	0.5
59 Denton, TX	15.5	133 Fairfield, CA	6.3	205 Redding, CA	0.5
59 Gresham, OR	15.5	134 Everett, WA	6.2	205 West Valley, UT	0.5
59 Roseville, CA	15.5	134 Omaha, NE	6.2	209 Garland, TX	0.4
62 Phoenix, AZ	15.4	136 Reno, NV	6.0	209 Raleigh, NC	0.4
63 Chico, CA	15.2	137 Bellflower, CA	5.8	211 Fargo, ND	0.3
64 St. Joseph, MO	14.5	137 Naperville, IL	5.8	211 Santa Ana, CA	0.3
65 Westminster, CO	14.4	137 Salt Lake City, UT	5.8	213 Arlington, TX	0.2
66 Gary, IN	14.3	140 Las Vegas, NV	5.7	214 Berkeley, CA	0.1
67 Sterling Heights, MI	14.0	141 Lakewood, CA	5.6	215 Mountain View, CA	0.0
68 Evansville, IN	13.9	141 West Palm Beach, FL	5.6	215 Temecula, CA	0.0
69 Gilbert, AZ	13.7	143 Largo, FL	5.5	217 Shreveport, LA	(0.1)
69 Thousand Oaks, CA	13.7	143 Oklahoma City, OK	5.5	217 West Covina, CA	(0.1)
71 Compton, CA	13.6	145 Port St. Lucie, FL	5.4	219 Rockford, IL	(0.4)
71 Pompano Beach, FL	13.6	145 Tyler, TX	5.4	220 Jacksonville, FL	(0.6)
73 Bellevue, WA	13.5	147 Kansas City, MO	5.3	221 Akron, OH	(0.7)
73 Fort Smith, AR	13.5	148 San Mateo, CA	5.1	221 Detroit, MI	(0.7)

RANK	CITY	% CHANGE
223	Warren, MI	(0.8)
224	Baltimore, MD	(0.9)
224	Dallas, TX	(0.9)
224	Pasadena, CA	(0.9)
227	Newark, NJ	(1.0)
227	Tulsa, OK	(1.0)
229	Boston, MA	(1.2)
229	Kennewick, WA	(1.2)
231	Anaheim, CA	(1.4)
231	Bloomington, IN	(1.4)
233	Winston-Salem, NC	(1.5)
234	Albuquerque, NM	(1.6)
234	Cedar Rapids, IA	(1.6)
236	Durham, NC	(1.7)
237	El Paso, TX	(1.9)
237	Provo, UT	(1.9)
239	Westland, MI	(2.0)
240	Kenosha, WI	(2.1)
240	Miami, FL	(2.1)
242	Alhambra, CA	(2.4)
243	Citrus Heights, CA	(2.5)
243	Joliet, IL	(2.5)
243	Louisville, KY	(2.5)
246	Victorville, CA	(2.6)
247	Fort Worth, TX	(2.7)
248	Downey, CA	(2.8)
248	Irving, TX	(2.8)
248	Overland Park, KS	(2.8)
248	Philadelphia, PA	(2.8)
252	Aurora, CO	(2.9)
252	Worcester, MA	(2.9)
254	Elk Grove, CA	(3.0)
254	Peoria, AZ	(3.0)
254	Richardson, TX	(3.0)
257	Arvada, CO	(3.1)
257	San Antonio, TX	(3.1)
257	Wichita, KS	(3.1)
260	Clarksville, TN	(3.2)
260	Fort Lauderdale, FL	(3.2)
260	Mesa, AZ	(3.2)
260	Pearland, TX	(3.2)
264	Savannah, GA	(3.3)
264	Vallejo, CA	(3.3)
264	Virginia Beach, VA	(3.3)
267	Deerfield Beach, FL	(3.4)
267	Oxnard, CA	(3.4)
269	Garden Grove, CA	(3.5)
270	Atlanta, GA	(3.8)
270	San Marcos, CA	(3.8)
272	Inglewood, CA	(3.9)
273	Nashua, NH	(4.1)
273	Santa Maria, CA	(4.1)
275	Clinton Twnshp, MI	(4.2)
276	Greeley, CO	(4.3)
276	Hollywood, FL	(4.3)
276	Jersey City, NJ	(4.3)
276	St. Louis, MO	(4.3)
280	Cape Coral, FL	(4.5)
280	Napa, CA	(4.5)
280	Renton, WA	(4.5)
283	Pueblo, CO	(4.6)
283	Woodbridge Twnshp, NJ	(4.6)
285	Coral Springs, FL	(4.7)
286	Centennial, CO	(4.9)
287	Austin, TX	(5.0)
287	Lynchburg, VA	(5.0)
289	South Gate, CA	(5.1)
290	Orlando, FL	(5.2)
291	Moreno Valley, CA	(5.5)
292	Cincinnati, OH	(5.6)
292	Tallahassee, FL	(5.6)
292	Ventura, CA	(5.6)
295	Asheville, NC	(5.7)
296	Long Beach, CA	(5.8)

RANK	CITY	% CHANGE
296	Somerville, MA	(5.8)
298	Tampa, FL	(5.9)
299	New Bedford, MA	(6.1)
299	Richmond, VA	(6.1)
301	Newton, MA	(6.2)
302	Norfolk, VA	(6.3)
302	Pittsburgh, PA	(6.3)
304	Alexandria, VA	(6.4)
305	Plantation, FL	(6.5)
305	West Jordan, UT	(6.5)
307	Avondale, AZ	(6.6)
307	Brownsville, TX	(6.6)
307	El Monte, CA	(6.6)
307	Eugene, OR	(6.6)
311	Fresno, CA	(6.7)
312	Brockton, MA	(7.0)
313	Chesapeake, VA	(7.1)
313	Chino Hills, CA	(7.1)
315	Lynn, MA	(7.2)
316	Santa Rosa, CA	(7.3)
317	Gainesville, FL	(7.4)
318	Camden, NJ	(7.5)
319	Roanoke, VA	(7.6)
319	Vancouver, WA	(7.6)
321	Kansas City, KS	(7.7)
322	Concord, CA	(7.8)
323	Los Angeles, CA	(7.9)
323	McKinney, TX	(7.9)
325	Hialeah, FL	(8.0)
325	Palm Bay, FL	(8.0)
325	Wilmington, NC	(8.0)
328	Las Cruces, NM	(8.1)
329	Lansing, MI	(8.2)
330	Davenport, IA	(8.3)
330	Fort Collins, CO	(8.3)
330	High Point, NC	(8.3)
333	Lafayette, LA	(8.4)
334	Waterbury, CT	(8.6)
335	Mission Viejo, CA	(8.7)
336	Boca Raton, FL	(8.9)
336	Miami Gardens, FL	(8.9)
338	Laredo, TX	(9.2)
338	Salinas, CA	(9.2)
340	Clearwater, FL	(9.3)
340	Irvine, CA	(9.3)
342	Dearborn, MI	(9.5)
342	Hampton, VA	(9.5)
344	Newport News, VA	(10.1)
345	Glendale, CA	(10.2)
346	Boulder, CO	(10.5)
347	Ogden, UT	(10.6)
348	Stamford, CT	(10.7)
349	Orem, UT	(10.8)
350	Norman, OK	(10.9)
351	Cambridge, MA	(11.0)
351	Elgin, IL	(11.0)
353	Springfield, IL	(11.4)
354	Buena Park, CA	(11.5)
354	Nampa, ID	(11.5)
356	Little Rock, AR	(11.7)
356	St. Petersburg, FL	(11.7)
358	Aurora, IL	(12.0)
359	Livonia, MI	(12.3)
359	Melbourne, FL	(12.3)
361	Fall River, MA	(12.7)
362	Ann Arbor, MI	(13.9)
363	Newport Beach, CA	(14.0)
364	Chula Vista, CA	(14.3)
365	Carrollton, TX	(14.6)
366	Clifton, NJ	(14.7)
366	Edison Twnshp, NJ	(14.7)
368	Arlington Heights, IL	(14.8)
369	Orange, CA	(15.1)
370	Sunrise, FL	(16.0)

RANK	CITY	% CHANGE
371	Lakeland, FL	(16.1)
372	Portsmouth, VA	(16.2)
372	South Bend, IN	(16.2)
374	Meridian, ID	(16.3)
375	Beaverton, OR	(16.5)
376	Olathe, KS	(16.7)
377	Grand Prairie, TX	(16.8)
377	League City, TX	(16.8)
379	Troy, MI	(17.3)
380	Norwalk, CT	(17.4)
381	Waco, TX	(17.9)
382	Mobile, AL	(18.7)
383	Scottsdale, AZ	(18.9)
384	Sparks, NV	(19.1)
385	Plano, TX	(19.2)
386	Sioux City, IA	(19.3)
387	Columbia, MO	(19.5)
388	Brick Twnshp, NJ	(19.6)
389	Upland, CA	(20.1)
390	Toms River Twnshp, NJ	(20.3)
391	Fremont, CA	(21.2)
392	Frisco, TX	(22.1)
392	Longmont, CO	(22.1)
394	Henderson, NV	(23.1)
395	Alameda, CA	(23.5)
396	Huntington Beach, CA	(23.9)
397	Elizabeth, NJ	(24.0)
398	Pembroke Pines, FL	(24.6)
399	Allen, TX	(26.0)
400	Whittier, CA	(26.4)
401	Decatur, IL	(26.6)
402	Charleston, SC	(27.0)
403	Bryan, TX	(27.2)
404	Lowell, MA	(27.3)
405	Farmington Hills, MI	(27.4)
406	Kent, WA	(27.7)
407	El Cajon, CA	(31.8)
408	McAllen, TX	(34.1)
409	Danbury, CT	(34.2)
410	Murrieta, CA	(34.7)
411	Carmel, IN	(37.4)
NA	Albany, NY**	NA
NA	Allentown, PA**	NA
NA	Amherst, NY**	NA
NA	Bloomington, MN**	NA
NA	Brooklyn Park, MN**	NA
NA	Buffalo, NY**	NA
NA	Chandler, AZ**	NA
NA	Cheektowaga, NY**	NA
NA	Chicago, IL**	NA
NA	Clarkstown, NY**	NA
NA	Colonie, NY**	NA
NA	Duluth, MN**	NA
NA	Federal Way, WA**	NA
NA	Greece, NY**	NA
NA	Greensboro, NC**	NA
NA	Greenville, NC**	NA
NA	Jurupa Valley, CA**	NA
NA	Lexington, KY**	NA
NA	New Rochelle, NY**	NA
NA	New York, NY**	NA
NA	North Las Vegas, NV**	NA
NA	Parma, OH**	NA
NA	Providence, RI**	NA
NA	Ramapo, NY**	NA
NA	Rochester, MN**	NA
NA	Rochester, NY**	NA
NA	St. George, UT**	NA
NA	Syracuse, NY**	NA
NA	Thornton, CO**	NA
NA	Waukegan, IL**	NA
NA	Yonkers, NY**	NA

Source: CQ Press using reported data from the F.B.I. "Crime in the United States 2012"

*Violent crimes are offenses of murder, forcible rape, robbery, and aggravated assault.

**Not available.

48. Percent Change in Violent Crime Rate: 2008 to 2012
National Percent Change = 15.6% Decrease*

RANK	CITY	% CHANGE	RANK	CITY	% CHANGE	RANK	CITY	% CHANGE
306	Abilene, TX	(29.4)	115	Chino Hills, CA	(6.2)	292	Gainesville, FL	(27.4)
97	Akron, OH	(3.3)	3	Chino, CA	55.1	326	Garden Grove, CA	(31.8)
304	Alameda, CA	(29.3)	355	Chula Vista, CA	(37.5)	343	Garland, TX	(34.9)
NA	Albany, GA**	NA	NA	Cicero, IL**	NA	93	Gary, IN	(2.7)
NA	Albany, NY**	NA	256	Cincinnati, OH	(22.9)	158	Gilbert, AZ	(11.4)
194	Albuquerque, NM	(16.2)	248	Citrus Heights, CA	(22.2)	108	Glendale, AZ	(5.2)
294	Alexandria, VA	(27.6)	NA	Clarkstown, NY**	NA	333	Glendale, CA	(32.9)
379	Alhambra, CA	(44.8)	221	Clarksville, TN	(18.9)	215	Grand Prairie, TX	(18.1)
NA	Allentown, PA**	NA	307	Clearwater, FL	(29.5)	273	Grand Rapids, MI	(24.8)
243	Allen, TX	(21.9)	95	Cleveland, OH	(3.1)	NA	Greece, NY**	NA
204	Amarillo, TX	(17.2)	181	Clifton, NJ	(14.6)	240	Greeley, CO	(21.5)
NA	Amherst, NY**	NA	161	Clinton Twnshp, MI	(11.9)	94	Green Bay, WI	(3.0)
111	Anaheim, CA	(5.6)	8	Clovis, CA	42.0	342	Greensboro, NC	(34.8)
163	Anchorage, AK	(12.3)	1	College Station, TX	70.0	346	Greenville, NC	(35.4)
258	Ann Arbor, MI	(23.0)	NA	Colonie, NY**	NA	125	Gresham, OR	(8.2)
27	Antioch, CA	17.1	173	Colorado Springs, CO	(13.8)	46	Hamilton Twnshp, NJ	8.3
NA	Arlington Heights, IL**	NA	37	Columbia, MO	10.9	117	Hammond, IN	(6.4)
195	Arlington, TX	(16.4)	281	Columbus, GA	(25.9)	309	Hampton, VA	(29.6)
299	Arvada, CO	(28.0)	330	Compton, CA	(32.5)	41	Hartford, CT	9.6
323	Asheville, NC	(31.2)	132	Concord, CA	(8.8)	191	Hawthorne, CA	(15.8)
209	Athens-Clarke, GA	(17.5)	281	Coral Springs, FL	(25.9)	330	Hayward, CA	(32.5)
81	Atlanta, GA	(0.7)	295	Corona, CA	(27.7)	192	Hemet, CA	(16.0)
201	Aurora, CO	(17.1)	186	Corpus Christi, TX	(15.3)	217	Henderson, NV	(18.2)
NA	Aurora, IL**	NA	312	Costa Mesa, CA	(29.8)	9	Hesperia, CA	36.6
241	Austin, TX	(21.7)	106	Cranston, RI	(4.8)	352	Hialeah, FL	(37.1)
378	Avondale, AZ	(44.5)	270	Dallas, TX	(24.6)	280	High Point, NC	(25.8)
182	Bakersfield, CA	(14.9)	279	Daly City, CA	(25.7)	34	Hillsboro, OR	11.4
80	Baldwin Park, CA	(0.5)	91	Danbury, CT	(2.6)	245	Hollywood, FL	(22.0)
160	Baltimore, MD	(11.5)	277	Davenport, IA	(25.5)	336	Hoover, AL	(33.4)
131	Baton Rouge, LA	(8.6)	154	Davie, FL	(11.0)	146	Houston, TX	(10.3)
36	Beaumont, TX	11.0	145	Dayton, OH	(10.2)	228	Huntington Beach, CA	(19.9)
309	Beaverton, OR	(29.6)	271	Dearborn, MI	(24.7)	13	Huntsville, AL	30.6
120	Bellevue, WA	(6.9)	NA	Decatur, IL**	NA	363	Independence, MO	(38.7)
375	Bellflower, CA	(43.4)	339	Deerfield Beach, FL	(34.6)	86	Indianapolis, IN	(1.6)
28	Bellingham, WA	15.8	59	Denton, TX	4.5	12	Indio, CA	31.5
338	Berkeley, CA	(34.3)	45	Denver, CO	8.6	223	Inglewood, CA	(19.5)
64	Bethlehem, PA	1.8	245	Des Moines, IA	(22.0)	213	Irvine, CA	(17.9)
11	Billings, MT	31.9	39	Detroit, MI	10.3	353	Irving, TX	(37.2)
50	Birmingham, AL	6.7	225	Downey, CA	(19.6)	359	Jacksonville, FL	(38.0)
NA	Bloomington, IL**	NA	NA	Duluth, MN**	NA	73	Jackson, MS	0.3
225	Bloomington, IN	(19.6)	156	Durham, NC	(11.3)	248	Jersey City, NJ	(22.2)
NA	Bloomington, MN**	NA	32	Edinburg, TX	11.9	NA	Johns Creek, GA**	NA
264	Boca Raton, FL	(23.6)	384	Edison Twnshp, NJ	(48.6)	NA	Joliet, IL**	NA
82	Boise, ID	(0.9)	70	Edmond, OK	1.2	NA	Jurupa Valley, CA**	NA
268	Boston, MA	(24.4)	354	El Cajon, CA	(37.4)	NA	Kansas City, KS**	NA
29	Boulder, CO	15.4	383	El Monte, CA	(47.3)	134	Kansas City, MO	(9.0)
233	Brick Twnshp, NJ	(20.4)	128	El Paso, TX	(8.3)	232	Kennewick, WA	(20.3)
73	Bridgeport, CT	0.3	NA	Elgin, IL**	NA	254	Kenosha, WI	(22.5)
NA	Brockton, MA**	NA	158	Elizabeth, NJ	(11.4)	317	Kent, WA	(30.4)
275	Broken Arrow, OK	(25.4)	321	Elk Grove, CA	(30.8)	188	Killeen, TX	(15.5)
NA	Brooklyn Park, MN**	NA	297	Erie, PA	(27.8)	142	Knoxville, TN	(9.8)
291	Brownsville, TX	(27.1)	62	Escondido, CA	2.6	376	Lafayette, LA	(43.5)
386	Bryan, TX	(49.5)	209	Eugene, OR	(17.5)	109	Lake Forest, CA	(5.3)
267	Buena Park, CA	(24.3)	22	Evansville, IN	18.6	218	Lakeland, FL	(18.3)
NA	Buffalo, NY**	NA	256	Everett, WA	(22.9)	NA	Lakewood Twnshp, NJ**	NA
63	Burbank, CA	2.0	220	Fairfield, CA	(18.5)	370	Lakewood, CA	(40.7)
85	Cambridge, MA	(1.3)	156	Fall River, MA	(11.3)	150	Lakewood, CO	(10.7)
40	Camden, NJ	10.0	16	Fargo, ND	22.1	335	Lancaster, CA	(33.3)
346	Cape Coral, FL	(35.4)	387	Farmington Hills, MI	(49.7)	133	Lansing, MI	(8.9)
54	Carlsbad, CA	5.7	31	Fayetteville, AR	14.0	320	Laredo, TX	(30.7)
393	Carmel, IN	(61.6)	367	Fayetteville, NC	(39.1)	339	Largo, FL	(34.6)
359	Carrollton, TX	(38.0)	188	Federal Way, WA	(15.5)	286	Las Cruces, NM	(26.1)
124	Carson, CA	(8.0)	391	Fishers, IN	(52.2)	233	Las Vegas, NV	(20.4)
104	Cary, NC	(4.4)	10	Flint, MI	34.8	128	Lawrence, KS	(8.3)
237	Cedar Rapids, IA	(21.4)	123	Fontana, CA	(7.7)	4	Lawrence, MA	54.7
21	Centennial, CO	19.2	345	Fort Collins, CO	(35.0)	182	Lawton, OK	(14.9)
NA	Champaign, IL**	NA	67	Fort Lauderdale, FL	1.5	324	League City, TX	(31.6)
NA	Chandler, AZ**	NA	71	Fort Smith, AR	1.0	122	Lee's Summit, MO	(7.3)
394	Charleston, SC	(66.6)	33	Fort Wayne, IN	11.7	NA	Lexington, KY**	NA
318	Charlotte, NC	(30.5)	147	Fort Worth, TX	(10.4)	245	Lincoln, NE	(22.0)
NA	Cheektowaga, NY**	NA	390	Fremont, CA	(51.1)	57	Little Rock, AR	5.0
192	Chesapeake, VA	(16.0)	121	Fresno, CA	(7.1)	2	Livermore, CA	62.1
NA	Chicago, IL**	NA	275	Frisco, TX	(25.4)	51	Livonia, MI	6.3
147	Chico, CA	(10.4)	54	Fullerton, CA	5.7	182	Long Beach, CA	(14.9)

RANK	CITY	% CHANGE
NA	Longmont, CO**	NA
382	Longview, TX	(46.2)
314	Los Angeles, CA	(30.2)
164	Louisville, KY	(12.4)
385	Lowell, MA	(49.1)
172	Lubbock, TX	(13.4)
302	Lynchburg, VA	(28.6)
140	Lynn, MA	(9.4)
337	Macon, GA	(34.2)
89	Madison, WI	(2.0)
20	Manchester, NH	19.4
392	McAllen, TX	(57.1)
236	McKinney, TX	(21.3)
6	Medford, OR	44.7
329	Melbourne, FL	(32.0)
136	Memphis, TN	(9.1)
NA	Menifee, CA**	NA
14	Merced, CA	28.5
263	Meridian, ID	(23.4)
231	Mesa, AZ	(20.2)
212	Mesquite, TX	(17.7)
165	Miami Beach, FL	(12.7)
199	Miami Gardens, FL	(17.0)
162	Miami, FL	(12.2)
174	Midland, TX	(13.9)
52	Milwaukee, WI	6.2
242	Minneapolis, MN	(21.8)
165	Miramar, FL	(12.7)
301	Mission Viejo, CA	(28.4)
274	Mission, TX	(25.3)
43	Mobile, AL	8.9
35	Modesto, CA	11.1
130	Montgomery, AL	(8.4)
348	Moreno Valley, CA	(36.1)
388	Mountain View, CA	(50.3)
82	Murfreesboro, TN	(0.9)
248	Murrieta, CA	(22.2)
287	Nampa, ID	(26.2)
213	Napa, CA	(17.9)
NA	Naperville, IL**	NA
NA	Nashua, NH**	NA
167	Nashville, TN	(12.9)
211	New Bedford, MA	(17.6)
NA	New Haven, CT**	NA
230	New Orleans, LA	(20.0)
NA	New Rochelle, NY**	NA
NA	New York, NY**	NA
18	Newark, NJ	21.4
365	Newport Beach, CA	(38.8)
368	Newport News, VA	(40.1)
357	Newton, MA	(37.7)
339	Norfolk, VA	(34.6)
87	Norman, OK	(1.8)
389	North Charleston, SC	(50.6)
47	North Las Vegas, NV	7.7
225	Norwalk, CA	(19.6)
350	Norwalk, CT	(36.9)
69	Oakland, CA	1.3
152	Oceanside, CA	(10.8)
5	Odessa, TX	54.0
41	O'Fallon, MO	9.6
147	Ogden, UT	(10.4)
113	Oklahoma City, OK	(6.0)
NA	Olathe, KS**	NA
87	Omaha, NE	(1.8)
358	Ontario, CA	(37.8)
371	Orange, CA	(40.8)
349	Orem, UT	(36.3)
366	Orlando, FL	(38.9)
138	Overland Park, KS	(9.3)
326	Oxnard, CA	(31.8)
77	Palm Bay, FL	(0.2)
175	Palmdale, CA	(14.0)
NA	Parma, OH**	NA

RANK	CITY	% CHANGE
295	Pasadena, CA	(27.7)
125	Pasadena, TX	(8.2)
56	Paterson, NJ	5.4
75	Pearland, TX	0.1
381	Pembroke Pines, FL	(45.6)
144	Peoria, AZ	(10.1)
NA	Peoria, IL**	NA
223	Philadelphia, PA	(19.5)
98	Phoenix, AZ	(3.5)
319	Pittsburgh, PA	(30.6)
373	Plano, TX	(42.3)
281	Plantation, FL	(25.9)
152	Pomona, CA	(10.8)
171	Pompano Beach, FL	(13.3)
96	Port St. Lucie, FL	(3.2)
199	Portland, OR	(17.0)
330	Portsmouth, VA	(32.5)
116	Providence, RI	(6.3)
208	Provo, UT	(17.4)
NA	Pueblo, CO**	NA
26	Quincy, MA	17.2
300	Racine, WI	(28.2)
289	Raleigh, NC	(26.7)
NA	Ramapo, NY**	NA
187	Rancho Cucamon., CA	(15.4)
167	Reading, PA	(12.9)
37	Redding, CA	10.9
248	Redwood City, CA	(22.2)
287	Reno, NV	(26.2)
NA	Renton, WA**	NA
150	Rialto, CA	(10.7)
362	Richardson, TX	(38.1)
66	Richmond, CA	1.6
219	Richmond, VA	(18.4)
255	Rio Rancho, NM	(22.8)
322	Riverside, CA	(31.0)
324	Roanoke, VA	(31.6)
NA	Rochester, MN**	NA
NA	Rochester, NY**	NA
91	Rockford, IL	(2.6)
207	Roseville, CA	(17.3)
293	Roswell, GA	(27.5)
52	Round Rock, TX	6.2
284	Sacramento, CA	(26.0)
100	Salem, OR	(3.6)
136	Salinas, CA	(9.1)
176	Salt Lake City, UT	(14.1)
313	San Antonio, TX	(29.9)
134	San Bernardino, CA	(9.0)
170	San Diego, CA	(13.1)
196	San Francisco, CA	(16.7)
112	San Jose, CA	(5.7)
266	San Leandro, CA	(24.0)
68	San Marcos, CA	1.4
334	San Mateo, CA	(33.1)
303	Sandy Springs, GA	(28.9)
77	Sandy, UT	(0.2)
235	Santa Ana, CA	(21.0)
309	Santa Barbara, CA	(29.6)
155	Santa Clara, CA	(11.2)
237	Santa Clarita, CA	(21.4)
107	Santa Maria, CA	(4.9)
304	Santa Monica, CA	(29.3)
261	Santa Rosa, CA	(23.2)
355	Savannah, GA	(37.5)
198	Scottsdale, AZ	(16.9)
72	Scranton, PA	0.5
60	Seattle, WA	3.7
222	Shreveport, LA	(19.4)
284	Simi Valley, CA	(26.0)
201	Sioux City, IA	(17.1)
23	Sioux Falls, SD	18.4
185	Somerville, MA	(15.2)
253	South Bend, IN	(22.4)

RANK	CITY	% CHANGE
117	South Gate, CA	(6.4)
380	Sparks, NV	(45.1)
328	Spokane Valley, WA	(31.9)
102	Spokane, WA	(3.8)
NA	Springfield, IL**	NA
204	Springfield, MA	(17.2)
7	Springfield, MO	44.0
176	Stamford, CT	(14.1)
76	Sterling Heights, MI	0.0
57	Stockton, CA	5.0
110	St. George, UT	(5.5)
141	St. Joseph, MO	(9.6)
179	St. Louis, MO	(14.3)
138	St. Paul, MN	(9.3)
343	St. Petersburg, FL	(34.9)
248	Sugar Land, TX	(22.2)
190	Sunnyvale, CA	(15.7)
376	Sunrise, FL	(43.5)
24	Surprise, AZ	17.9
NA	Syracuse, NY**	NA
237	Tacoma, WA	(21.4)
269	Tallahassee, FL	(24.5)
314	Tampa, FL	(30.2)
363	Temecula, CA	(38.7)
43	Tempe, AZ	8.9
NA	Thornton, CO**	NA
64	Thousand Oaks, CA	1.8
61	Toledo, OH	2.7
265	Toms River Twnshp, NJ	(23.8)
19	Topeka, KS	20.6
369	Torrance, CA	(40.5)
49	Tracy, CA	7.2
17	Trenton, NJ	21.8
351	Troy, MI	(37.0)
143	Tucson, AZ	(9.9)
258	Tulsa, OK	(23.0)
79	Tuscaloosa, AL	(0.3)
101	Tustin, CA	(3.7)
228	Tyler, TX	(19.9)
374	Upland, CA	(43.3)
98	Upper Darby Twnshp, PA	(3.5)
201	Vacaville, CA	(17.1)
243	Vallejo, CA	(21.9)
102	Vancouver, WA	(3.8)
277	Ventura, CA	(25.5)
105	Victorville, CA	(4.7)
307	Virginia Beach, VA	(29.5)
260	Visalia, CA	(23.1)
178	Vista, CA	(14.2)
372	Waco, TX	(41.0)
47	Warren, MI	7.7
15	Warwick, RI	26.0
179	Washington, DC	(14.3)
204	Waterbury, CT	(17.2)
NA	Waukegan, IL**	NA
316	West Covina, CA	(30.3)
125	West Jordan, UT	(8.2)
196	West Palm Beach, FL	(16.7)
119	West Valley, UT	(6.6)
271	Westland, MI	(24.7)
30	Westminster, CA	15.2
90	Westminster, CO	(2.4)
262	Whittier, CA	(23.3)
215	Wichita Falls, TX	(18.1)
167	Wichita, KS	(12.9)
289	Wilmington, NC	(26.7)
297	Winston-Salem, NC	(27.8)
359	Woodbridge Twnshp, NJ	(38.0)
84	Worcester, MA	(1.1)
25	Yakima, WA	17.3
NA	Yonkers, NY**	NA
114	Yuma, AZ	(6.1)

Source: CQ Press using reported data from the F.B.I. "Crime in the United States 2012"

*Violent crimes are offenses of murder, forcible rape, robbery, and aggravated assault.

**Not available.

48. Percent Change in Violent Crime Rate: 2008 to 2012 (continued)
National Percent Change = 15.6% Decrease*

RANK	CITY	% CHANGE	RANK	CITY	% CHANGE	RANK	CITY	% CHANGE
1	College Station, TX	70.0	75	Pearland, TX	0.1	147	Ogden, UT	(10.4)
2	Livermore, CA	62.1	76	Sterling Heights, MI	0.0	150	Lakewood, CO	(10.7)
3	Chino, CA	55.1	77	Palm Bay, FL	(0.2)	150	Rialto, CA	(10.7)
4	Lawrence, MA	54.7	77	Sandy, UT	(0.2)	152	Oceanside, CA	(10.8)
5	Odessa, TX	54.0	79	Tuscaloosa, AL	(0.3)	152	Pomona, CA	(10.8)
6	Medford, OR	44.7	80	Baldwin Park, CA	(0.5)	154	Davie, FL	(11.0)
7	Springfield, MO	44.0	81	Atlanta, GA	(0.7)	155	Santa Clara, CA	(11.2)
8	Clovis, CA	42.0	82	Boise, ID	(0.9)	156	Durham, NC	(11.3)
9	Hesperia, CA	36.6	82	Murfreesboro, TN	(0.9)	156	Fall River, MA	(11.3)
10	Flint, MI	34.8	84	Worcester, MA	(1.1)	158	Elizabeth, NJ	(11.4)
11	Billings, MT	31.9	85	Cambridge, MA	(1.3)	158	Gilbert, AZ	(11.4)
12	Indio, CA	31.5	86	Indianapolis, IN	(1.6)	160	Baltimore, MD	(11.5)
13	Huntsville, AL	30.6	87	Norman, OK	(1.8)	161	Clinton Twnshp, MI	(11.9)
14	Merced, CA	28.5	87	Omaha, NE	(1.8)	162	Miami, FL	(12.2)
15	Warwick, RI	26.0	89	Madison, WI	(2.0)	163	Anchorage, AK	(12.3)
16	Fargo, ND	22.1	90	Westminster, CO	(2.4)	164	Louisville, KY	(12.4)
17	Trenton, NJ	21.8	91	Danbury, CT	(2.6)	165	Miami Beach, FL	(12.7)
18	Newark, NJ	21.4	91	Rockford, IL	(2.6)	165	Miramar, FL	(12.7)
19	Topeka, KS	20.6	93	Gary, IN	(2.7)	167	Nashville, TN	(12.9)
20	Manchester, NH	19.4	94	Green Bay, WI	(3.0)	167	Reading, PA	(12.9)
21	Centennial, CO	19.2	95	Cleveland, OH	(3.1)	167	Wichita, KS	(12.9)
22	Evansville, IN	18.6	96	Port St. Lucie, FL	(3.2)	170	San Diego, CA	(13.1)
23	Sioux Falls, SD	18.4	97	Akron, OH	(3.3)	171	Pompano Beach, FL	(13.3)
24	Surprise, AZ	17.9	98	Phoenix, AZ	(3.5)	172	Lubbock, TX	(13.4)
25	Yakima, WA	17.3	98	Upper Darby Twnshp, PA	(3.5)	173	Colorado Springs, CO	(13.8)
26	Quincy, MA	17.2	100	Salem, OR	(3.6)	174	Midland, TX	(13.9)
27	Antioch, CA	17.1	101	Tustin, CA	(3.7)	175	Palmdale, CA	(14.0)
28	Bellingham, WA	15.8	102	Spokane, WA	(3.8)	176	Salt Lake City, UT	(14.1)
29	Boulder, CO	15.4	102	Vancouver, WA	(3.8)	176	Stamford, CT	(14.1)
30	Westminster, CA	15.2	104	Cary, NC	(4.4)	178	Vista, CA	(14.2)
31	Fayetteville, AR	14.0	105	Victorville, CA	(4.7)	179	St. Louis, MO	(14.3)
32	Edinburg, TX	11.9	106	Cranston, RI	(4.8)	179	Washington, DC	(14.3)
33	Fort Wayne, IN	11.7	107	Santa Maria, CA	(4.9)	181	Clifton, NJ	(14.6)
34	Hillsboro, OR	11.4	108	Glendale, AZ	(5.2)	182	Bakersfield, CA	(14.9)
35	Modesto, CA	11.1	109	Lake Forest, CA	(5.3)	182	Lawton, OK	(14.9)
36	Beaumont, TX	11.0	110	St. George, UT	(5.5)	182	Long Beach, CA	(14.9)
37	Columbia, MO	10.9	111	Anaheim, CA	(5.6)	185	Somerville, MA	(15.2)
37	Redding, CA	10.9	112	San Jose, CA	(5.7)	186	Corpus Christi, TX	(15.3)
39	Detroit, MI	10.3	113	Oklahoma City, OK	(6.0)	187	Rancho Cucamon., CA	(15.4)
40	Camden, NJ	10.0	114	Yuma, AZ	(6.1)	188	Federal Way, WA	(15.5)
41	Hartford, CT	9.6	115	Chino Hills, CA	(6.2)	188	Killeen, TX	(15.5)
41	O'Fallon, MO	9.6	116	Providence, RI	(6.3)	190	Sunnyvale, CA	(15.7)
43	Mobile, AL	8.9	117	Hammond, IN	(6.4)	191	Hawthorne, CA	(15.8)
43	Tempe, AZ	8.9	117	South Gate, CA	(6.4)	192	Chesapeake, VA	(16.0)
45	Denver, CO	8.6	119	West Valley, UT	(6.6)	192	Hemet, CA	(16.0)
46	Hamilton Twnshp, NJ	8.3	120	Bellevue, WA	(6.9)	194	Albuquerque, NM	(16.2)
47	North Las Vegas, NV	7.7	121	Fresno, CA	(7.1)	195	Arlington, TX	(16.4)
47	Warren, MI	7.7	122	Lee's Summit, MO	(7.3)	196	San Francisco, CA	(16.7)
49	Tracy, CA	7.2	123	Fontana, CA	(7.7)	196	West Palm Beach, FL	(16.7)
50	Birmingham, AL	6.7	124	Carson, CA	(8.0)	198	Scottsdale, AZ	(16.9)
51	Livonia, MI	6.3	125	Gresham, OR	(8.2)	199	Miami Gardens, FL	(17.0)
52	Milwaukee, WI	6.2	125	Pasadena, TX	(8.2)	199	Portland, OR	(17.0)
52	Round Rock, TX	6.2	125	West Jordan, UT	(8.2)	201	Aurora, CO	(17.1)
54	Carlsbad, CA	5.7	128	El Paso, TX	(8.3)	201	Sioux City, IA	(17.1)
54	Fullerton, CA	5.7	128	Lawrence, KS	(8.3)	201	Vacaville, CA	(17.1)
56	Paterson, NJ	5.4	130	Montgomery, AL	(8.4)	204	Amarillo, TX	(17.2)
57	Little Rock, AR	5.0	131	Baton Rouge, LA	(8.6)	204	Springfield, MA	(17.2)
57	Stockton, CA	5.0	132	Concord, CA	(8.8)	204	Waterbury, CT	(17.2)
59	Denton, TX	4.5	133	Lansing, MI	(8.9)	207	Roseville, CA	(17.3)
60	Seattle, WA	3.7	134	Kansas City, MO	(9.0)	208	Provo, UT	(17.4)
61	Toledo, OH	2.7	134	San Bernardino, CA	(9.0)	209	Athens-Clarke, GA	(17.5)
62	Escondido, CA	2.6	136	Memphis, TN	(9.1)	209	Eugene, OR	(17.5)
63	Burbank, CA	2.0	136	Salinas, CA	(9.1)	211	New Bedford, MA	(17.6)
64	Bethlehem, PA	1.8	138	Overland Park, KS	(9.3)	212	Mesquite, TX	(17.7)
64	Thousand Oaks, CA	1.8	138	St. Paul, MN	(9.3)	213	Irvine, CA	(17.9)
66	Richmond, CA	1.6	140	Lynn, MA	(9.4)	213	Napa, CA	(17.9)
67	Fort Lauderdale, FL	1.5	141	St. Joseph, MO	(9.6)	215	Grand Prairie, TX	(18.1)
68	San Marcos, CA	1.4	142	Knoxville, TN	(9.8)	215	Wichita Falls, TX	(18.1)
69	Oakland, CA	1.3	143	Tucson, AZ	(9.9)	217	Henderson, NV	(18.2)
70	Edmond, OK	1.2	144	Peoria, AZ	(10.1)	218	Lakeland, FL	(18.3)
71	Fort Smith, AR	1.0	145	Dayton, OH	(10.2)	219	Richmond, VA	(18.4)
72	Scranton, PA	0.5	146	Houston, TX	(10.3)	220	Fairfield, CA	(18.5)
73	Bridgeport, CT	0.3	147	Chico, CA	(10.4)	221	Clarksville, TN	(18.9)
73	Jackson, MS	0.3	147	Fort Worth, TX	(10.4)	222	Shreveport, LA	(19.4)

RANK	CITY	% CHANGE	RANK	CITY	% CHANGE	RANK	CITY	% CHANGE
223	Inglewood, CA	(19.5)	297	Erie, PA	(27.8)	371	Orange, CA	(40.8)
223	Philadelphia, PA	(19.5)	297	Winston-Salem, NC	(27.8)	372	Waco, TX	(41.0)
225	Bloomington, IN	(19.6)	299	Arvada, CO	(28.0)	373	Plano, TX	(42.3)
225	Downey, CA	(19.6)	300	Racine, WI	(28.2)	374	Upland, CA	(43.3)
225	Norwalk, CA	(19.6)	301	Mission Viejo, CA	(28.4)	375	Bellflower, CA	(43.4)
228	Huntington Beach, CA	(19.9)	302	Lynchburg, VA	(28.6)	376	Lafayette, LA	(43.5)
228	Tyler, TX	(19.9)	303	Sandy Springs, GA	(28.9)	376	Sunrise, FL	(43.5)
230	New Orleans, LA	(20.0)	304	Alameda, CA	(29.3)	378	Avondale, AZ	(44.5)
231	Mesa, AZ	(20.2)	304	Santa Monica, CA	(29.3)	379	Alhambra, CA	(44.8)
232	Kennewick, WA	(20.3)	306	Abilene, TX	(29.4)	380	Sparks, NV	(45.1)
233	Brick Twnshp, NJ	(20.4)	307	Clearwater, FL	(29.5)	381	Pembroke Pines, FL	(45.6)
233	Las Vegas, NV	(20.4)	307	Virginia Beach, VA	(29.5)	382	Longview, TX	(46.2)
235	Santa Ana, CA	(21.0)	309	Beaverton, OR	(29.6)	383	El Monte, CA	(47.3)
236	McKinney, TX	(21.3)	309	Hampton, VA	(29.6)	384	Edison Twnshp, NJ	(48.6)
237	Cedar Rapids, IA	(21.4)	309	Santa Barbara, CA	(29.6)	385	Lowell, MA	(49.1)
237	Santa Clarita, CA	(21.4)	312	Costa Mesa, CA	(29.8)	386	Bryan, TX	(49.5)
237	Tacoma, WA	(21.4)	313	San Antonio, TX	(29.9)	387	Farmington Hills, MI	(49.7)
240	Greeley, CO	(21.5)	314	Los Angeles, CA	(30.2)	388	Mountain View, CA	(50.3)
241	Austin, TX	(21.7)	314	Tampa, FL	(30.2)	389	North Charleston, SC	(50.6)
242	Minneapolis, MN	(21.8)	316	West Covina, CA	(30.3)	390	Fremont, CA	(51.1)
243	Allen, TX	(21.9)	317	Kent, WA	(30.4)	391	Fishers, IN	(52.2)
243	Vallejo, CA	(21.9)	318	Charlotte, NC	(30.5)	392	McAllen, TX	(57.1)
245	Des Moines, IA	(22.0)	319	Pittsburgh, PA	(30.6)	393	Carmel, IN	(61.6)
245	Hollywood, FL	(22.0)	320	Laredo, TX	(30.7)	394	Charleston, SC	(66.6)
245	Lincoln, NE	(22.0)	321	Elk Grove, CA	(30.8)	NA	Albany, GA**	NA
248	Citrus Heights, CA	(22.2)	322	Riverside, CA	(31.0)	NA	Albany, NY**	NA
248	Jersey City, NJ	(22.2)	323	Asheville, NC	(31.2)	NA	Allentown, PA**	NA
248	Murrieta, CA	(22.2)	324	League City, TX	(31.6)	NA	Amherst, NY**	NA
248	Redwood City, CA	(22.2)	324	Roanoke, VA	(31.6)	NA	Arlington Heights, IL**	NA
248	Sugar Land, TX	(22.2)	326	Garden Grove, CA	(31.8)	NA	Aurora, IL**	NA
253	South Bend, IN	(22.4)	326	Oxnard, CA	(31.8)	NA	Bloomington, IL**	NA
254	Kenosha, WI	(22.5)	328	Spokane Valley, WA	(31.9)	NA	Bloomington, MN**	NA
255	Rio Rancho, NM	(22.8)	329	Melbourne, FL	(32.0)	NA	Brockton, MA**	NA
256	Cincinnati, OH	(22.9)	330	Compton, CA	(32.5)	NA	Brooklyn Park, MN**	NA
256	Everett, WA	(22.9)	330	Hayward, CA	(32.5)	NA	Buffalo, NY**	NA
258	Ann Arbor, MI	(23.0)	330	Portsmouth, VA	(32.5)	NA	Champaign, IL**	NA
258	Tulsa, OK	(23.0)	333	Glendale, CA	(32.9)	NA	Chandler, AZ**	NA
260	Visalia, CA	(23.1)	334	San Mateo, CA	(33.1)	NA	Cheektowaga, NY**	NA
261	Santa Rosa, CA	(23.2)	335	Lancaster, CA	(33.3)	NA	Chicago, IL**	NA
262	Whittier, CA	(23.3)	336	Hoover, AL	(33.4)	NA	Cicero, IL**	NA
263	Meridian, ID	(23.4)	337	Macon, GA	(34.2)	NA	Clarkstown, NY**	NA
264	Boca Raton, FL	(23.6)	338	Berkeley, CA	(34.3)	NA	Colonie, NY**	NA
265	Toms River Twnshp, NJ	(23.8)	339	Deerfield Beach, FL	(34.6)	NA	Decatur, IL**	NA
266	San Leandro, CA	(24.0)	339	Largo, FL	(34.6)	NA	Duluth, MN**	NA
267	Buena Park, CA	(24.3)	339	Norfolk, VA	(34.6)	NA	Elgin, IL**	NA
268	Boston, MA	(24.4)	342	Greensboro, NC	(34.8)	NA	Greece, NY**	NA
269	Tallahassee, FL	(24.5)	343	Garland, TX	(34.9)	NA	Johns Creek, GA**	NA
270	Dallas, TX	(24.6)	343	St. Petersburg, FL	(34.9)	NA	Joliet, IL**	NA
271	Dearborn, MI	(24.7)	345	Fort Collins, CO	(35.0)	NA	Jurupa Valley, CA**	NA
271	Westland, MI	(24.7)	346	Cape Coral, FL	(35.4)	NA	Kansas City, KS**	NA
273	Grand Rapids, MI	(24.8)	346	Greenville, NC	(35.4)	NA	Lakewood Twnshp, NJ**	NA
274	Mission, TX	(25.3)	348	Moreno Valley, CA	(36.1)	NA	Lexington, KY**	NA
275	Broken Arrow, OK	(25.4)	349	Orem, UT	(36.3)	NA	Longmont, CO**	NA
275	Frisco, TX	(25.4)	350	Norwalk, CT	(36.9)	NA	Menifee, CA**	NA
277	Davenport, IA	(25.5)	351	Troy, MI	(37.0)	NA	Naperville, IL**	NA
277	Ventura, CA	(25.5)	352	Hialeah, FL	(37.1)	NA	Nashua, NH**	NA
279	Daly City, CA	(25.7)	353	Irving, TX	(37.2)	NA	New Haven, CT**	NA
280	High Point, NC	(25.8)	354	El Cajon, CA	(37.4)	NA	New Rochelle, NY**	NA
281	Columbus, GA	(25.9)	355	Chula Vista, CA	(37.5)	NA	New York, NY**	NA
281	Coral Springs, FL	(25.9)	355	Savannah, GA	(37.5)	NA	Olathe, KS**	NA
281	Plantation, FL	(25.9)	357	Newton, MA	(37.7)	NA	Parma, OH**	NA
284	Sacramento, CA	(26.0)	358	Ontario, CA	(37.8)	NA	Peoria, IL**	NA
284	Simi Valley, CA	(26.0)	359	Carrollton, TX	(38.0)	NA	Pueblo, CO**	NA
286	Las Cruces, NM	(26.1)	359	Jacksonville, FL	(38.0)	NA	Ramapo, NY**	NA
287	Nampa, ID	(26.2)	359	Woodbridge Twnshp, NJ	(38.0)	NA	Renton, WA**	NA
287	Reno, NV	(26.2)	362	Richardson, TX	(38.1)	NA	Rochester, MN**	NA
289	Raleigh, NC	(26.7)	363	Independence, MO	(38.7)	NA	Rochester, NY**	NA
289	Wilmington, NC	(26.7)	363	Temecula, CA	(38.7)	NA	Springfield, IL**	NA
291	Brownsville, TX	(27.1)	365	Newport Beach, CA	(38.8)	NA	Syracuse, NY**	NA
292	Gainesville, FL	(27.4)	366	Orlando, FL	(38.9)	NA	Thornton, CO**	NA
293	Roswell, GA	(27.5)	367	Fayetteville, NC	(39.1)	NA	Waukegan, IL**	NA
294	Alexandria, VA	(27.6)	368	Newport News, VA	(40.1)	NA	Yonkers, NY**	NA
295	Corona, CA	(27.7)	369	Torrance, CA	(40.5)			
295	Pasadena, CA	(27.7)	370	Lakewood, CA	(40.7)			

Source: CQ Press using reported data from the F.B.I. "Crime in the United States 2012"

*Violent crimes are offenses of murder, forcible rape, robbery, and aggravated assault.

**Not available.

49. Murders in 2012
National Total = 14,827 Murders*

RANK	CITY	MURDERS	RANK	CITY	MURDERS	RANK	CITY	MURDERS
237	Abilene, TX	3	376	Chino Hills, CA	0	176	Gainesville, FL	6
65	Akron, OH	24	323	Chino, CA	1	323	Garden Grove, CA	1
323	Alameda, CA	1	155	Chula Vista, CA	8	167	Garland, TX	7
213	Albany, GA	4	190	Cicero, IL	5	55	Gary, IN	37
213	Albany, NY	4	41	Cincinnati, OH	46	190	Gilbert, AZ	5
49	Albuquerque, NM	41	269	Citrus Heights, CA	2	125	Glendale, AZ	12
376	Alexandria, VA	0	376	Clarkstown, NY	0	376	Glendale, CA	0
376	Alhambra, CA	0	142	Clarksville, TN	10	323	Grand Prairie, TX	1
105	Allentown, PA	15	237	Clearwater, FL	3	100	Grand Rapids, MI	16
376	Allen, TX	0	22	Cleveland, OH	84	376	Greece, NY	0
142	Amarillo, TX	10	376	Clifton, NJ	0	323	Greeley, CO	1
376	Amherst, NY	0	376	Clinton Twnshp, MI	0	323	Green Bay, WI	1
105	Anaheim, CA	15	237	Clovis, CA	3	78	Greensboro, NC	21
105	Anchorage, AK	15	237	College Station, TX	3	167	Greenville, NC	7
323	Ann Arbor, MI	1	376	Colonie, NY	0	213	Gresham, OR	4
142	Antioch, CA	10	88	Colorado Springs, CO	18	376	Hamilton Twnshp, NJ	0
323	Arlington Heights, IL	1	237	Columbia, MO	3	176	Hammond, IN	6
92	Arlington, TX	17	92	Columbus, GA	17	148	Hampton, VA	9
376	Arvada, CO	0	78	Compton, CA	21	69	Hartford, CT	23
176	Asheville, NC	6	376	Concord, CA	0	167	Hawthorne, CA	7
190	Athens-Clarke, GA	5	323	Coral Springs, FL	1	176	Hayward, CA	6
23	Atlanta, GA	83	323	Corona, CA	1	323	Hemet, CA	1
63	Aurora, CO	29	100	Corpus Christi, TX	16	213	Henderson, NV	4
376	Aurora, IL	0	213	Costa Mesa, CA	4	176	Hesperia, CA	6
62	Austin, TX	31	269	Cranston, RI	2	213	Hialeah, FL	4
167	Avondale, AZ	7	9	Dallas, TX	154	190	High Point, NC	5
57	Bakersfield, CA	34	376	Daly City, CA	0	269	Hillsboro, OR	2
269	Baldwin Park, CA	2	323	Danbury, CT	1	190	Hollywood, FL	5
6	Baltimore, MD	218	213	Davenport, IA	4	269	Hoover, AL	2
30	Baton Rouge, LA	66	190	Davie, FL	5	7	Houston, TX	217
119	Beaumont, TX	13	65	Dayton, OH	24	237	Huntington Beach, CA	3
376	Beaverton, OR	0	323	Dearborn, MI	1	112	Huntsville, AL	14
269	Bellevue, WA	2	176	Decatur, IL	6	190	Independence, MO	5
176	Bellflower, CA	6	213	Deerfield Beach, FL	4	15	Indianapolis, IN	97
376	Bellingham, WA	0	323	Denton, TX	1	269	Indio, CA	2
190	Berkeley, CA	5	52	Denver, CO	39	112	Inglewood, CA	14
269	Bethlehem, PA	2	167	Des Moines, IA	7	269	Irvine, CA	2
237	Billings, MT	3	3	Detroit, MI	386	237	Irving, TX	3
28	Birmingham, AL	67	176	Downey, CA	6	17	Jacksonville, FL	93
323	Bloomington, IL	1	269	Duluth, MN	2	31	Jackson, MS	63
237	Bloomington, IN	3	78	Durham, NC	21	132	Jersey City, NJ	11
376	Bloomington, MN	0	323	Edinburg, TX	1	376	Johns Creek, GA	0
376	Boca Raton, FL	0	376	Edison Twnshp, NJ	0	132	Joliet, IL	11
323	Boise, ID	1	269	Edmond, OK	2	323	Jurupa Valley, CA	1
35	Boston, MA	57	269	El Cajon, CA	2	105	Kansas City, KS	15
376	Boulder, CO	0	213	El Monte, CA	4	14	Kansas City, MO	105
376	Brick Twnshp, NJ	0	69	El Paso, TX	23	323	Kennewick, WA	1
75	Bridgeport, CT	22	269	Elgin, IL	2	323	Kenosha, WI	1
176	Brockton, MA	6	112	Elizabeth, NJ	14	269	Kent, WA	2
323	Broken Arrow, OK	1	323	Elk Grove, CA	1	125	Killeen, TX	12
213	Brooklyn Park, MN	4	155	Erie, PA	8	88	Knoxville, TN	18
237	Brownsville, TX	3	190	Escondido, CA	5	132	Lafayette, LA	11
323	Bryan, TX	1	376	Eugene, OR	0	376	Lake Forest, CA	0
323	Buena Park, CA	1	155	Evansville, IN	8	142	Lakeland, FL	10
38	Buffalo, NY	48	323	Everett, WA	1	269	Lakewood Twnshp, NJ	2
269	Burbank, CA	2	155	Fairfield, CA	8	323	Lakewood, CA	1
323	Cambridge, MA	1	269	Fall River, MA	2	269	Lakewood, CO	2
28	Camden, NJ	67	269	Fargo, ND	2	155	Lancaster, CA	8
213	Cape Coral, FL	4	323	Farmington Hills, MI	1	119	Lansing, MI	13
269	Carlsbad, CA	2	323	Fayetteville, AR	1	155	Laredo, TX	8
376	Carmel, IN	0	75	Fayetteville, NC	22	323	Largo, FL	1
269	Carrollton, TX	2	237	Federal Way, WA	3	190	Las Cruces, NM	5
167	Carson, CA	7	376	Fishers, IN	0	24	Las Vegas, NV	76
376	Cary, NC	0	31	Flint, MI	63	376	Lawrence, KS	0
237	Cedar Rapids, IA	3	190	Fontana, CA	5	269	Lawrence, MA	2
323	Centennial, CO	1	269	Fort Collins, CO	2	119	Lawton, OK	13
237	Champaign, IL	3	100	Fort Lauderdale, FL	16	376	League City, TX	0
213	Chandler, AZ	4	190	Fort Smith, AR	5	376	Lee's Summit, MO	0
125	Charleston, SC	12	75	Fort Wayne, IN	22	125	Lexington, KY	12
36	Charlotte, NC	52	44	Fort Worth, TX	44	237	Lincoln, NE	3
376	Cheektowaga, NY	0	269	Fremont, CA	2	42	Little Rock, AR	45
125	Chesapeake, VA	12	37	Fresno, CA	51	376	Livermore, CA	0
1	Chicago, IL	500	376	Frisco, TX	0	237	Livonia, MI	3
323	Chico, CA	1	376	Fullerton, CA	0	60	Long Beach, CA	32

RANK	CITY	MURDERS	RANK	CITY	MURDERS	RANK	CITY	MURDERS
376	Longmont, CO	0	190	Pasadena, CA	5	148	South Gate, CA	9
167	Longview, TX	7	155	Pasadena, TX	8	323	Sparks, NV	1
5	Los Angeles, CA	299	78	Paterson, NJ	21	323	Spokane Valley, WA	1
33	Louisville, KY	62	323	Pearland, TX	1	119	Spokane, WA	13
376	Lowell, MA	0	269	Pembroke Pines, FL	2	142	Springfield, IL	10
132	Lubbock, TX	11	148	Peoria, AZ	9	132	Springfield, MA	11
237	Lynchburg, VA	3	142	Peoria, IL	10	100	Springfield, MO	16
269	Lynn, MA	2	4	Philadelphia, PA	331	190	Stamford, CT	5
78	Macon, GA	21	12	Phoenix, AZ	123	213	Sterling Heights, MI	4
237	Madison, WI	3	49	Pittsburgh, PA	41	25	Stockton, CA	71
323	Manchester, NH	1	323	Plano, TX	1	376	St. George, UT	0
323	McAllen, TX	1	213	Plantation, FL	4	323	St. Joseph, MO	1
376	McKinney, TX	0	92	Pomona, CA	17	13	St. Louis, MO	113
269	Medford, OR	2	190	Pompano Beach, FL	5	119	St. Paul, MN	13
176	Melbourne, FL	6	213	Port St. Lucie, FL	4	105	St. Petersburg, FL	15
10	Memphis, TN	133	85	Portland, OR	20	376	Sugar Land, TX	0
323	Menifee, CA	1	132	Portsmouth, VA	11	237	Sunnyvale, CA	3
148	Merced, CA	9	92	Providence, RI	17	323	Sunrise, FL	1
376	Meridian, ID	0	376	Provo, UT	0	237	Surprise, AZ	3
112	Mesa, AZ	14	155	Pueblo, CO	8	112	Syracuse, NY	14
269	Mesquite, TX	2	376	Quincy, MA	0	125	Tacoma, WA	12
190	Miami Beach, FL	5	213	Racine, WI	4	125	Tallahassee, FL	12
64	Miami Gardens, FL	25	92	Raleigh, NC	17	69	Tampa, FL	23
26	Miami, FL	69	376	Ramapo, NY	0	376	Temecula, CA	0
213	Midland, TX	4	213	Rancho Cucamon., CA	4	132	Tempe, AZ	11
18	Milwaukee, WI	91	105	Reading, PA	15	323	Thornton, CO	1
52	Minneapolis, MN	39	237	Redding, CA	3	376	Thousand Oaks, CA	0
269	Miramar, FL	2	376	Redwood City, CA	0	52	Toledo, OH	39
376	Mission Viejo, CA	0	167	Reno, NV	7	323	Toms River Twnshp, NJ	1
237	Mission, TX	3	269	Renton, WA	2	105	Topeka, KS	15
60	Mobile, AL	32	213	Rialto, CA	4	213	Torrance, CA	4
85	Modesto, CA	20	269	Richardson, TX	2	213	Tracy, CA	4
44	Montgomery, AL	44	88	Richmond, CA	18	65	Trenton, NJ	24
190	Moreno Valley, CA	5	47	Richmond, VA	42	269	Troy, MI	2
376	Mountain View, CA	0	269	Rio Rancho, NM	2	46	Tucson, AZ	43
237	Murfreesboro, TN	3	100	Riverside, CA	16	47	Tulsa, OK	42
323	Murrieta, CA	1	148	Roanoke, VA	9	213	Tuscaloosa, AL	4
269	Nampa, ID	2	269	Rochester, MN	2	376	Tustin, CA	0
269	Napa, CA	2	56	Rochester, NY	36	237	Tyler, TX	3
237	Naperville, IL	3	148	Rockford, IL	9	376	Upland, CA	0
376	Nashua, NH	0	269	Roseville, CA	2	237	Upper Darby Twnshp, PA	3
33	Nashville, TN	62	323	Roswell, GA	1	237	Vacaville, CA	3
269	New Bedford, MA	2	376	Round Rock, TX	0	112	Vallejo, CA	14
92	New Haven, CT	17	57	Sacramento, CA	34	190	Vancouver, WA	5
8	New Orleans, LA	193	167	Salem, OR	7	323	Ventura, CA	1
376	New Rochelle, NY	0	78	Salinas, CA	21	176	Victorville, CA	6
2	New York, NY	419	155	Salt Lake City, UT	8	78	Virginia Beach, VA	21
16	Newark, NJ	96	19	San Antonio, TX	89	190	Visalia, CA	5
323	Newport Beach, CA	1	39	San Bernardino, CA	47	323	Vista, CA	1
85	Newport News, VA	20	39	San Diego, CA	47	176	Waco, TX	6
376	Newton, MA	0	26	San Francisco, CA	69	376	Warren, MI	0
57	Norfolk, VA	34	42	San Jose, CA	45	323	Warwick, RI	1
323	Norman, OK	1	269	San Leandro, CA	2	20	Washington, DC	88
119	North Charleston, SC	13	269	San Marcos, CA	2	190	Waterbury, CT	5
112	North Las Vegas, NV	14	376	San Mateo, CA	0	269	Waukegan, IL	2
132	Norwalk, CA	11	237	Sandy Springs, GA	3	269	West Covina, CA	2
237	Norwalk, CT	3	269	Sandy, UT	2	269	West Jordan, UT	2
11	Oakland, CA	127	132	Santa Ana, CA	11	92	West Palm Beach, FL	17
155	Oceanside, CA	8	376	Santa Barbara, CA	0	323	West Valley, UT	1
190	Odessa, TX	5	376	Santa Clara, CA	0	323	Westland, MI	1
269	O'Fallon, MO	2	323	Santa Clarita, CA	1	269	Westminster, CA	2
269	Ogden, UT	2	376	Santa Maria, CA	0	269	Westminster, CO	2
21	Oklahoma City, OK	85	269	Santa Monica, CA	2	376	Whittier, CA	0
376	Olathe, KS	0	269	Santa Rosa, CA	2	190	Wichita Falls, TX	5
49	Omaha, NE	41	69	Savannah, GA	23	69	Wichita, KS	23
237	Ontario, CA	3	237	Scottsdale, AZ	3	155	Wilmington, NC	8
213	Orange, CA	4	376	Scranton, PA	0	176	Winston-Salem, NC	6
269	Orem, UT	2	69	Seattle, WA	23	376	Woodbridge Twnshp, NJ	0
65	Orlando, FL	24	92	Shreveport, LA	17	155	Worcester, MA	8
269	Overland Park, KS	2	237	Simi Valley, CA	3	132	Yakima, WA	11
148	Oxnard, CA	9	269	Sioux City, IA	2	213	Yonkers, NY	4
237	Palm Bay, FL	3	269	Sioux Falls, SD	2	190	Yuma, AZ	5
176	Palmdale, CA	6	376	Somerville, MA	0			
376	Parma, OH	0	88	South Bend, IN	18			

Source: Reported data from the F.B.I. "Crime in the United States 2012"

*Includes nonnegligent manslaughter.

49. Murders in 2012 (continued)
National Total = 14,827 Murders*

RANK	CITY	MURDERS	RANK	CITY	MURDERS	RANK	CITY	MURDERS
1	Chicago, IL	500	75	Bridgeport, CT	22	148	Merced, CA	9
2	New York, NY	419	75	Fayetteville, NC	22	148	Oxnard, CA	9
3	Detroit, MI	386	75	Fort Wayne, IN	22	148	Peoria, AZ	9
4	Philadelphia, PA	331	78	Compton, CA	21	148	Roanoke, VA	9
5	Los Angeles, CA	299	78	Durham, NC	21	148	Rockford, IL	9
6	Baltimore, MD	218	78	Greensboro, NC	21	148	South Gate, CA	9
7	Houston, TX	217	78	Macon, GA	21	155	Chula Vista, CA	8
8	New Orleans, LA	193	78	Paterson, NJ	21	155	Erie, PA	8
9	Dallas, TX	154	78	Salinas, CA	21	155	Evansville, IN	8
10	Memphis, TN	133	78	Virginia Beach, VA	21	155	Fairfield, CA	8
11	Oakland, CA	127	85	Modesto, CA	20	155	Lancaster, CA	8
12	Phoenix, AZ	123	85	Newport News, VA	20	155	Laredo, TX	8
13	St. Louis, MO	113	85	Portland, OR	20	155	Oceanside, CA	8
14	Kansas City, MO	105	88	Colorado Springs, CO	18	155	Pasadena, TX	8
15	Indianapolis, IN	97	88	Knoxville, TN	18	155	Pueblo, CO	8
16	Newark, NJ	96	88	Richmond, CA	18	155	Salt Lake City, UT	8
17	Jacksonville, FL	93	88	South Bend, IN	18	155	Wilmington, NC	8
18	Milwaukee, WI	91	92	Arlington, TX	17	155	Worcester, MA	8
19	San Antonio, TX	89	92	Columbus, GA	17	167	Avondale, AZ	7
20	Washington, DC	88	92	New Haven, CT	17	167	Carson, CA	7
21	Oklahoma City, OK	85	92	Pomona, CA	17	167	Des Moines, IA	7
22	Cleveland, OH	84	92	Providence, RI	17	167	Garland, TX	7
23	Atlanta, GA	83	92	Raleigh, NC	17	167	Greenville, NC	7
24	Las Vegas, NV	76	92	Shreveport, LA	17	167	Hawthorne, CA	7
25	Stockton, CA	71	92	West Palm Beach, FL	17	167	Longview, TX	7
26	Miami, FL	69	100	Corpus Christi, TX	16	167	Reno, NV	7
26	San Francisco, CA	69	100	Fort Lauderdale, FL	16	167	Salem, OR	7
28	Birmingham, AL	67	100	Grand Rapids, MI	16	176	Asheville, NC	6
28	Camden, NJ	67	100	Riverside, CA	16	176	Bellflower, CA	6
30	Baton Rouge, LA	66	100	Springfield, MO	16	176	Brockton, MA	6
31	Flint, MI	63	105	Allentown, PA	15	176	Decatur, IL	6
31	Jackson, MS	63	105	Anaheim, CA	15	176	Downey, CA	6
33	Louisville, KY	62	105	Anchorage, AK	15	176	Gainesville, FL	6
33	Nashville, TN	62	105	Kansas City, KS	15	176	Hammond, IN	6
35	Boston, MA	57	105	Reading, PA	15	176	Hayward, CA	6
36	Charlotte, NC	52	105	St. Petersburg, FL	15	176	Hesperia, CA	6
37	Fresno, CA	51	105	Topeka, KS	15	176	Melbourne, FL	6
38	Buffalo, NY	48	112	Elizabeth, NJ	14	176	Palmdale, CA	6
39	San Bernardino, CA	47	112	Huntsville, AL	14	176	Victorville, CA	6
39	San Diego, CA	47	112	Inglewood, CA	14	176	Waco, TX	6
41	Cincinnati, OH	46	112	Mesa, AZ	14	176	Winston-Salem, NC	6
42	Little Rock, AR	45	112	North Las Vegas, NV	14	190	Athens-Clarke, GA	5
42	San Jose, CA	45	112	Syracuse, NY	14	190	Berkeley, CA	5
44	Fort Worth, TX	44	112	Vallejo, CA	14	190	Cicero, IL	5
44	Montgomery, AL	44	119	Beaumont, TX	13	190	Davie, FL	5
46	Tucson, AZ	43	119	Lansing, MI	13	190	Escondido, CA	5
47	Richmond, VA	42	119	Lawton, OK	13	190	Fontana, CA	5
47	Tulsa, OK	42	119	North Charleston, SC	13	190	Fort Smith, AR	5
49	Albuquerque, NM	41	119	Spokane, WA	13	190	Gilbert, AZ	5
49	Omaha, NE	41	119	St. Paul, MN	13	190	High Point, NC	5
49	Pittsburgh, PA	41	125	Charleston, SC	12	190	Hollywood, FL	5
52	Denver, CO	39	125	Chesapeake, VA	12	190	Independence, MO	5
52	Minneapolis, MN	39	125	Glendale, AZ	12	190	Las Cruces, NM	5
52	Toledo, OH	39	125	Killeen, TX	12	190	Miami Beach, FL	5
55	Gary, IN	37	125	Lexington, KY	12	190	Moreno Valley, CA	5
56	Rochester, NY	36	125	Tacoma, WA	12	190	Odessa, TX	5
57	Bakersfield, CA	34	125	Tallahassee, FL	12	190	Pasadena, CA	5
57	Norfolk, VA	34	132	Jersey City, NJ	11	190	Pompano Beach, FL	5
57	Sacramento, CA	34	132	Joliet, IL	11	190	Stamford, CT	5
60	Long Beach, CA	32	132	Lafayette, LA	11	190	Vancouver, WA	5
60	Mobile, AL	32	132	Lubbock, TX	11	190	Visalia, CA	5
62	Austin, TX	31	132	Norwalk, CA	11	190	Waterbury, CT	5
63	Aurora, CO	29	132	Portsmouth, VA	11	190	Wichita Falls, TX	5
64	Miami Gardens, FL	25	132	Santa Ana, CA	11	190	Yuma, AZ	5
65	Akron, OH	24	132	Springfield, MA	11	213	Albany, GA	4
65	Dayton, OH	24	132	Tempe, AZ	11	213	Albany, NY	4
65	Orlando, FL	24	132	Yakima, WA	11	213	Brooklyn Park, MN	4
65	Trenton, NJ	24	142	Amarillo, TX	10	213	Cape Coral, FL	4
69	El Paso, TX	23	142	Antioch, CA	10	213	Chandler, AZ	4
69	Hartford, CT	23	142	Clarksville, TN	10	213	Costa Mesa, CA	4
69	Savannah, GA	23	142	Lakeland, FL	10	213	Davenport, IA	4
69	Seattle, WA	23	142	Peoria, IL	10	213	Deerfield Beach, FL	4
69	Tampa, FL	23	142	Springfield, IL	10	213	El Monte, CA	4
69	Wichita, KS	23	148	Hampton, VA	9	213	Gresham, OR	4

RANK	CITY	MURDERS	RANK	CITY	MURDERS	RANK	CITY	MURDERS
213	Henderson, NV	4	269	Nampa, ID	2	323	Ventura, CA	1
213	Hialeah, FL	4	269	Napa, CA	2	323	Vista, CA	1
213	Midland, TX	4	269	New Bedford, MA	2	323	Warwick, RI	1
213	Orange, CA	4	269	O'Fallon, MO	2	323	West Valley, UT	1
213	Plantation, FL	4	269	Ogden, UT	2	323	Westland, MI	1
213	Port St. Lucie, FL	4	269	Orem, UT	2	376	Alexandria, VA	0
213	Racine, WI	4	269	Overland Park, KS	2	376	Alhambra, CA	0
213	Rancho Cucamon., CA	4	269	Pembroke Pines, FL	2	376	Allen, TX	0
213	Rialto, CA	4	269	Renton, WA	2	376	Amherst, NY	0
213	Sterling Heights, MI	4	269	Richardson, TX	2	376	Arvada, CO	0
213	Torrance, CA	4	269	Rio Rancho, NM	2	376	Aurora, IL	0
213	Tracy, CA	4	269	Rochester, MN	2	376	Beaverton, OR	0
213	Tuscaloosa, AL	4	269	Roseville, CA	2	376	Bellingham, WA	0
213	Yonkers, NY	4	269	San Leandro, CA	2	376	Bloomington, MN	0
237	Abilene, TX	3	269	San Marcos, CA	2	376	Boca Raton, FL	0
237	Billings, MT	3	269	Sandy, UT	2	376	Boulder, CO	0
237	Bloomington, IN	3	269	Santa Monica, CA	2	376	Brick Twnshp, NJ	0
237	Brownsville, TX	3	269	Santa Rosa, CA	2	376	Carmel, IN	0
237	Cedar Rapids, IA	3	269	Sioux City, IA	2	376	Cary, NC	0
237	Champaign, IL	3	269	Sioux Falls, SD	2	376	Cheektowaga, NY	0
237	Clearwater, FL	3	269	Troy, MI	2	376	Chino Hills, CA	0
237	Clovis, CA	3	269	Waukegan, IL	2	376	Clarkstown, NY	0
237	College Station, TX	3	269	West Covina, CA	2	376	Clifton, NJ	0
237	Columbia, MO	3	269	West Jordan, UT	2	376	Clinton Twnshp, MI	0
237	Federal Way, WA	3	269	Westminster, CA	2	376	Colonie, NY	0
237	Huntington Beach, CA	3	269	Westminster, CO	2	376	Concord, CA	0
237	Irving, TX	3	323	Alameda, CA	1	376	Daly City, CA	0
237	Lincoln, NE	3	323	Ann Arbor, MI	1	376	Edison Twnshp, NJ	0
237	Livonia, MI	3	323	Arlington Heights, IL	1	376	Eugene, OR	0
237	Lynchburg, VA	3	323	Bloomington, IL	1	376	Fishers, IN	0
237	Madison, WI	3	323	Boise, ID	1	376	Frisco, TX	0
237	Mission, TX	3	323	Broken Arrow, OK	1	376	Fullerton, CA	0
237	Murfreesboro, TN	3	323	Bryan, TX	1	376	Glendale, CA	0
237	Naperville, IL	3	323	Buena Park, CA	1	376	Greece, NY	0
237	Norwalk, CT	3	323	Cambridge, MA	1	376	Hamilton Twnshp, NJ	0
237	Ontario, CA	3	323	Centennial, CO	1	376	Johns Creek, GA	0
237	Palm Bay, FL	3	323	Chico, CA	1	376	Lake Forest, CA	0
237	Redding, CA	3	323	Chino, CA	1	376	Lawrence, KS	0
237	Sandy Springs, GA	3	323	Coral Springs, FL	1	376	League City, TX	0
237	Scottsdale, AZ	3	323	Corona, CA	1	376	Lee's Summit, MO	0
237	Simi Valley, CA	3	323	Danbury, CT	1	376	Livermore, CA	0
237	Sunnyvale, CA	3	323	Dearborn, MI	1	376	Longmont, CO	0
237	Surprise, AZ	3	323	Denton, TX	1	376	Lowell, MA	0
237	Tyler, TX	3	323	Edinburg, TX	1	376	McKinney, TX	0
237	Upper Darby Twnshp, PA	3	323	Elk Grove, CA	1	376	Meridian, ID	0
237	Vacaville, CA	3	323	Everett, WA	1	376	Mission Viejo, CA	0
269	Baldwin Park, CA	2	323	Farmington Hills, MI	1	376	Mountain View, CA	0
269	Bellevue, WA	2	323	Fayetteville, AR	1	376	Nashua, NH	0
269	Bethlehem, PA	2	323	Garden Grove, CA	1	376	New Rochelle, NY	0
269	Burbank, CA	2	323	Grand Prairie, TX	1	376	Newton, MA	0
269	Carlsbad, CA	2	323	Greeley, CO	1	376	Olathe, KS	0
269	Carrollton, TX	2	323	Green Bay, WI	1	376	Parma, OH	0
269	Citrus Heights, CA	2	323	Hemet, CA	1	376	Provo, UT	0
269	Cranston, RI	2	323	Jurupa Valley, CA	1	376	Quincy, MA	0
269	Duluth, MN	2	323	Kennewick, WA	1	376	Ramapo, NY	0
269	Edmond, OK	2	323	Kenosha, WI	1	376	Redwood City, CA	0
269	El Cajon, CA	2	323	Lakewood, CA	1	376	Round Rock, TX	0
269	Elgin, IL	2	323	Largo, FL	1	376	San Mateo, CA	0
269	Fall River, MA	2	323	Manchester, NH	1	376	Santa Barbara, CA	0
269	Fargo, ND	2	323	McAllen, TX	1	376	Santa Clara, CA	0
269	Fort Collins, CO	2	323	Menifee, CA	1	376	Santa Maria, CA	0
269	Fremont, CA	2	323	Murrieta, CA	1	376	Scranton, PA	0
269	Hillsboro, OR	2	323	Newport Beach, CA	1	376	Somerville, MA	0
269	Hoover, AL	2	323	Norman, OK	1	376	St. George, UT	0
269	Indio, CA	2	323	Pearland, TX	1	376	Sugar Land, TX	0
269	Irvine, CA	2	323	Plano, TX	1	376	Temecula, CA	0
269	Kent, WA	2	323	Roswell, GA	1	376	Thousand Oaks, CA	0
269	Lakewood Twnshp, NJ	2	323	Santa Clarita, CA	1	376	Tustin, CA	0
269	Lakewood, CO	2	323	Sparks, NV	1	376	Upland, CA	0
269	Lawrence, MA	2	323	Spokane Valley, WA	1	376	Warren, MI	0
269	Lynn, MA	2	323	St. Joseph, MO	1	376	Whittier, CA	0
269	Medford, OR	2	323	Sunrise, FL	1	376	Woodbridge Twnshp, NJ	0
269	Mesquite, TX	2	323	Thornton, CO	1			
269	Miramar, FL	2	323	Toms River Twnshp, NJ	1			

Source: Reported data from the F.B.I. "Crime in the United States 2012"

*Includes nonnegligent manslaughter.

50. Murder Rate in 2012
National Rate = 4.7 Murders per 100,000 Population*

RANK	CITY	RATE	RANK	CITY	RATE	RANK	CITY	RATE
250	Abilene, TX	2.5	376	Chino Hills, CA	0.0	170	Gainesville, FL	4.7
54	Akron, OH	12.1	312	Chino, CA	1.3	369	Garden Grove, CA	0.6
312	Alameda, CA	1.3	226	Chula Vista, CA	3.2	234	Garland, TX	3.0
157	Albany, GA	5.1	142	Cicero, IL	5.9	5	Gary, IN	46.0
194	Albany, NY	4.1	37	Cincinnati, OH	15.5	268	Gilbert, AZ	2.3
118	Albuquerque, NM	7.4	268	Citrus Heights, CA	2.3	152	Glendale, AZ	5.2
376	Alexandria, VA	0.0	376	Clarkstown, NY	0.0	376	Glendale, CA	0.0
376	Alhambra, CA	0.0	121	Clarksville, TN	7.3	369	Grand Prairie, TX	0.6
51	Allentown, PA	12.6	241	Clearwater, FL	2.7	102	Grand Rapids, MI	8.4
376	Allen, TX	0.0	22	Cleveland, OH	21.3	376	Greece, NY	0.0
157	Amarillo, TX	5.1	376	Clifton, NJ	0.0	347	Greeley, CO	1.0
376	Amherst, NY	0.0	376	Clinton Twnshp, MI	0.0	354	Green Bay, WI	0.9
184	Anaheim, CA	4.4	228	Clovis, CA	3.1	114	Greensboro, NC	7.6
165	Anchorage, AK	5.0	228	College Station, TX	3.1	107	Greenville, NC	8.1
354	Ann Arbor, MI	0.9	376	Colonie, NY	0.0	204	Gresham, OR	3.7
86	Antioch, CA	9.5	192	Colorado Springs, CO	4.2	376	Hamilton Twnshp, NJ	0.0
312	Arlington Heights, IL	1.3	241	Columbia, MO	2.7	118	Hammond, IN	7.4
180	Arlington, TX	4.5	96	Columbus, GA	8.7	131	Hampton, VA	6.5
376	Arvada, CO	0.0	21	Compton, CA	21.4	28	Hartford, CT	18.4
126	Asheville, NC	7.0	376	Concord, CA	0.0	106	Hawthorne, CA	8.2
188	Athens-Clarke, GA	4.3	364	Coral Springs, FL	0.8	194	Hayward, CA	4.1
26	Atlanta, GA	19.0	369	Corona, CA	0.6	327	Hemet, CA	1.2
98	Aurora, CO	8.6	157	Corpus Christi, TX	5.1	308	Henderson, NV	1.5
376	Aurora, IL	0.0	210	Costa Mesa, CA	3.6	131	Hesperia, CA	6.5
204	Austin, TX	3.7	250	Cranston, RI	2.5	300	Hialeah, FL	1.7
94	Avondale, AZ	8.9	53	Dallas, TX	12.4	170	High Point, NC	4.7
83	Bakersfield, CA	9.6	376	Daly City, CA	0.0	282	Hillsboro, OR	2.1
246	Baldwin Park, CA	2.6	327	Danbury, CT	1.2	217	Hollywood, FL	3.4
8	Baltimore, MD	34.9	196	Davenport, IA	4.0	260	Hoover, AL	2.4
12	Baton Rouge, LA	28.5	149	Davie, FL	5.3	72	Houston, TX	10.0
66	Beaumont, TX	10.8	32	Dayton, OH	16.9	308	Huntington Beach, CA	1.5
376	Beaverton, OR	0.0	347	Dearborn, MI	1.0	114	Huntsville, AL	7.6
302	Bellevue, WA	1.6	109	Decatur, IL	7.9	188	Independence, MO	4.3
113	Bellflower, CA	7.7	152	Deerfield Beach, FL	5.2	57	Indianapolis, IN	11.6
376	Bellingham, WA	0.0	364	Denton, TX	0.8	250	Indio, CA	2.5
188	Berkeley, CA	4.3	138	Denver, CO	6.2	51	Inglewood, CA	12.6
241	Bethlehem, PA	2.7	217	Des Moines, IA	3.4	354	Irvine, CA	0.9
240	Billings, MT	2.8	3	Detroit, MI	54.6	312	Irving, TX	1.3
11	Birmingham, AL	31.4	149	Downey, CA	5.3	62	Jacksonville, FL	11.1
312	Bloomington, IL	1.3	268	Duluth, MN	2.3	6	Jackson, MS	35.8
204	Bloomington, IN	3.7	94	Durham, NC	8.9	184	Jersey City, NJ	4.4
376	Bloomington, MN	0.0	327	Edinburg, TX	1.2	376	Johns Creek, GA	0.0
376	Boca Raton, FL	0.0	376	Edison Twnshp, NJ	0.0	118	Joliet, IL	7.4
374	Boise, ID	0.5	260	Edmond, OK	2.4	347	Jurupa Valley, CA	1.0
92	Boston, MA	9.0	288	El Cajon, CA	2.0	70	Kansas City, KS	10.2
376	Boulder, CO	0.0	213	El Monte, CA	3.5	16	Kansas City, MO	22.6
376	Brick Twnshp, NJ	0.0	217	El Paso, TX	3.4	312	Kennewick, WA	1.3
39	Bridgeport, CT	15.1	295	Elgin, IL	1.8	347	Kenosha, WI	1.0
136	Brockton, MA	6.3	62	Elizabeth, NJ	11.1	302	Kent, WA	1.6
347	Broken Arrow, OK	1.0	369	Elk Grove, CA	0.6	91	Killeen, TX	9.1
152	Brooklyn Park, MN	5.2	110	Erie, PA	7.8	76	Knoxville, TN	9.9
300	Brownsville, TX	1.7	217	Escondido, CA	3.4	92	Lafayette, LA	9.0
312	Bryan, TX	1.3	376	Eugene, OR	0.0	376	Lake Forest, CA	0.0
327	Buena Park, CA	1.2	127	Evansville, IN	6.8	72	Lakeland, FL	10.0
29	Buffalo, NY	18.3	354	Everett, WA	0.9	282	Lakewood Twnshp, NJ	2.1
290	Burbank, CA	1.9	116	Fairfield, CA	7.5	327	Lakewood, CA	1.2
354	Cambridge, MA	0.9	274	Fall River, MA	2.2	310	Lakewood, CO	1.4
1	Camden, NJ	86.3	295	Fargo, ND	1.8	165	Lancaster, CA	5.0
250	Cape Coral, FL	2.5	327	Farmington Hills, MI	1.2	60	Lansing, MI	11.3
290	Carlsbad, CA	1.9	312	Fayetteville, AR	1.3	221	Laredo, TX	3.3
376	Carmel, IN	0.0	67	Fayetteville, NC	10.7	312	Largo, FL	1.3
302	Carrollton, TX	1.6	221	Federal Way, WA	3.3	165	Las Cruces, NM	5.0
116	Carson, CA	7.5	376	Fishers, IN	0.0	157	Las Vegas, NV	5.1
376	Cary, NC	0.0	2	Flint, MI	62.0	376	Lawrence, KS	0.0
268	Cedar Rapids, IA	2.3	250	Fontana, CA	2.5	246	Lawrence, MA	2.6
347	Centennial, CO	1.0	312	Fort Collins, CO	1.3	46	Lawton, OK	13.2
204	Champaign, IL	3.7	87	Fort Lauderdale, FL	9.4	376	League City, TX	0.0
302	Chandler, AZ	1.6	145	Fort Smith, AR	5.7	376	Lee's Summit, MO	0.0
81	Charleston, SC	9.7	98	Fort Wayne, IN	8.6	196	Lexington, KY	4.0
134	Charlotte, NC	6.4	145	Fort Worth, TX	5.7	337	Lincoln, NE	1.1
376	Cheektowaga, NY	0.0	354	Fremont, CA	0.9	15	Little Rock, AR	23.0
149	Chesapeake, VA	5.3	71	Fresno, CA	10.1	376	Livermore, CA	0.0
27	Chicago, IL	18.5	376	Frisco, TX	0.0	228	Livonia, MI	3.1
337	Chico, CA	1.1	376	Fullerton, CA	0.0	127	Long Beach, CA	6.8

RANK	CITY	RATE	RANK	CITY	RATE	RANK	CITY	RATE
376	Longmont, CO	0.0	210	Pasadena, CA	3.6	87	South Gate, CA	9.4
100	Longview, TX	8.5	152	Pasadena, TX	5.2	337	Sparks, NV	1.1
110	Los Angeles, CA	7.8	40	Paterson, NJ	14.3	337	Spokane Valley, WA	1.1
89	Louisville, KY	9.3	337	Pearland, TX	1.1	139	Spokane, WA	6.1
376	Lowell, MA	0.0	312	Pembroke Pines, FL	1.3	100	Springfield, IL	8.5
177	Lubbock, TX	4.6	145	Peoria, AZ	5.7	124	Springfield, MA	7.1
200	Lynchburg, VA	3.9	96	Peoria, IL	8.7	76	Springfield, MO	9.9
274	Lynn, MA	2.2	20	Philadelphia, PA	21.5	196	Stamford, CT	4.0
16	Macon, GA	22.6	105	Phoenix, AZ	8.3	228	Sterling Heights, MI	3.1
312	Madison, WI	1.3	47	Pittsburgh, PA	13.1	14	Stockton, CA	23.7
354	Manchester, NH	0.9	375	Plano, TX	0.4	376	St. George, UT	0.0
367	McAllen, TX	0.7	177	Plantation, FL	4.6	312	St. Joseph, MO	1.3
376	McKinney, TX	0.0	61	Pomona, CA	11.2	7	St. Louis, MO	35.5
246	Medford, OR	2.6	168	Pompano Beach, FL	4.9	180	St. Paul, MN	4.5
110	Melbourne, FL	7.8	260	Port St. Lucie, FL	2.4	140	St. Petersburg, FL	6.0
24	Memphis, TN	20.2	221	Portland, OR	3.3	376	Sugar Land, TX	0.0
327	Menifee, CA	1.2	59	Portsmouth, VA	11.4	282	Sunnyvale, CA	2.1
62	Merced, CA	11.1	83	Providence, RI	9.6	337	Sunrise, FL	1.1
376	Meridian, ID	0.0	376	Provo, UT	0.0	250	Surprise, AZ	2.5
228	Mesa, AZ	3.1	121	Pueblo, CO	7.3	83	Syracuse, NY	9.6
310	Mesquite, TX	1.4	376	Quincy, MA	0.0	142	Tacoma, WA	5.9
148	Miami Beach, FL	5.5	157	Racine, WI	5.1	131	Tallahassee, FL	6.5
18	Miami Gardens, FL	22.5	196	Raleigh, NC	4.0	129	Tampa, FL	6.6
35	Miami, FL	16.7	376	Ramapo, NY	0.0	376	Temecula, CA	0.0
213	Midland, TX	3.5	260	Rancho Cucamon., CA	2.4	129	Tempe, AZ	6.6
38	Milwaukee, WI	15.2	32	Reading, PA	16.9	364	Thornton, CO	0.8
72	Minneapolis, MN	10.0	221	Redding, CA	3.3	376	Thousand Oaks, CA	0.0
302	Miramar, FL	1.6	376	Redwood City, CA	0.0	44	Toledo, OH	13.6
376	Mission Viejo, CA	0.0	234	Reno, NV	3.0	337	Toms River Twnshp, NJ	1.1
204	Mission, TX	3.7	282	Renton, WA	2.1	57	Topeka, KS	11.6
50	Mobile, AL	12.7	200	Rialto, CA	3.9	241	Torrance, CA	2.7
79	Modesto, CA	9.8	290	Richardson, TX	1.9	170	Tracy, CA	4.7
23	Montgomery, AL	21.1	32	Richmond, CA	16.9	13	Trenton, NJ	28.1
250	Moreno Valley, CA	2.5	24	Richmond, VA	20.2	250	Troy, MI	2.5
376	Mountain View, CA	0.0	274	Rio Rancho, NM	2.2	107	Tucson, AZ	8.1
241	Murfreesboro, TN	2.7	157	Riverside, CA	5.1	68	Tulsa, OK	10.5
354	Murrieta, CA	0.9	90	Roanoke, VA	9.2	188	Tuscaloosa, AL	4.3
260	Nampa, ID	2.4	295	Rochester, MN	1.8	376	Tustin, CA	0.0
250	Napa, CA	2.5	31	Rochester, NY	17.0	234	Tyler, TX	3.0
282	Naperville, IL	2.1	142	Rockford, IL	5.9	376	Upland, CA	0.0
376	Nashua, NH	0.0	302	Roseville, CA	1.6	210	Upper Darby Twnshp, PA	3.6
72	Nashville, TN	10.0	337	Roswell, GA	1.1	226	Vacaville, CA	3.2
282	New Bedford, MA	2.1	376	Round Rock, TX	0.0	55	Vallejo, CA	11.9
47	New Haven, CT	13.1	124	Sacramento, CA	7.1	234	Vancouver, WA	3.0
4	New Orleans, LA	53.2	184	Salem, OR	4.4	354	Ventura, CA	0.9
376	New Rochelle, NY	0.0	44	Salinas, CA	13.6	157	Victorville, CA	5.1
157	New York, NY	5.1	192	Salt Lake City, UT	4.2	170	Virginia Beach, VA	4.7
9	Newark, NJ	34.4	134	San Antonio, TX	6.4	200	Visalia, CA	3.9
337	Newport Beach, CA	1.1	19	San Bernardino, CA	21.9	347	Vista, CA	1.0
65	Newport News, VA	11.0	213	San Diego, CA	3.5	170	Waco, TX	4.7
376	Newton, MA	0.0	102	San Francisco, CA	8.4	376	Warren, MI	0.0
42	Norfolk, VA	13.9	177	San Jose, CA	4.6	327	Warwick, RI	1.2
354	Norman, OK	0.9	268	San Leandro, CA	2.3	42	Washington, DC	13.9
49	North Charleston, SC	12.9	268	San Marcos, CA	2.3	180	Waterbury, CT	4.5
136	North Las Vegas, NV	6.3	376	San Mateo, CA	0.0	274	Waukegan, IL	2.2
69	Norwalk, CA	10.3	228	Sandy Springs, GA	3.1	290	West Covina, CA	1.9
213	Norwalk, CT	3.5	274	Sandy, UT	2.2	290	West Jordan, UT	1.9
10	Oakland, CA	31.8	221	Santa Ana, CA	3.3	36	West Palm Beach, FL	16.6
170	Oceanside, CA	4.7	376	Santa Barbara, CA	0.0	367	West Valley, UT	0.7
169	Odessa, TX	4.8	376	Santa Clara, CA	0.0	327	Westland, MI	1.2
250	O'Fallon, MO	2.5	369	Santa Clarita, CA	0.6	274	Westminster, CA	2.2
260	Ogden, UT	2.4	376	Santa Maria, CA	0.0	295	Westminster, CO	1.8
40	Oklahoma City, OK	14.3	274	Santa Monica, CA	2.2	376	Whittier, CA	0.0
376	Olathe, KS	0.0	327	Santa Rosa, CA	1.2	170	Wichita Falls, TX	4.7
79	Omaha, NE	9.8	76	Savannah, GA	9.9	140	Wichita, KS	6.0
295	Ontario, CA	1.8	312	Scottsdale, AZ	1.3	121	Wilmington, NC	7.3
238	Orange, CA	2.9	376	Scranton, PA	0.0	246	Winston-Salem, NC	2.6
274	Orem, UT	2.2	204	Seattle, WA	3.7	376	Woodbridge Twnshp, NJ	0.0
81	Orlando, FL	9.7	102	Shreveport, LA	8.4	184	Worcester, MA	4.4
337	Overland Park, KS	1.1	260	Simi Valley, CA	2.4	56	Yakima, WA	11.8
180	Oxnard, CA	4.5	260	Sioux City, IA	2.4	288	Yonkers, NY	2.0
238	Palm Bay, FL	2.9	312	Sioux Falls, SD	1.3	152	Yuma, AZ	5.2
200	Palmdale, CA	3.9	376	Somerville, MA	0.0			
376	Parma, OH	0.0	30	South Bend, IN	17.8			

Source: CQ Press using reported data from the F.B.I. "Crime in the United States 2012"

*Includes nonnegligent manslaughter.

50. Murder Rate in 2012 (continued)
National Rate = 4.7 Murders per 100,000 Population*

RANK	CITY	RATE	RANK	CITY	RATE	RANK	CITY	RATE
1	Camden, NJ	86.3	72	Nashville, TN	10.0	149	Chesapeake, VA	5.3
2	Flint, MI	62.0	76	Knoxville, TN	9.9	149	Davie, FL	5.3
3	Detroit, MI	54.6	76	Savannah, GA	9.9	149	Downey, CA	5.3
4	New Orleans, LA	53.2	76	Springfield, MO	9.9	152	Brooklyn Park, MN	5.2
5	Gary, IN	46.0	79	Modesto, CA	9.8	152	Deerfield Beach, FL	5.2
6	Jackson, MS	35.8	79	Omaha, NE	9.8	152	Glendale, AZ	5.2
7	St. Louis, MO	35.5	81	Charleston, SC	9.7	152	Pasadena, TX	5.2
8	Baltimore, MD	34.9	81	Orlando, FL	9.7	152	Yuma, AZ	5.2
9	Newark, NJ	34.4	83	Bakersfield, CA	9.6	157	Albany, GA	5.1
10	Oakland, CA	31.8	83	Providence, RI	9.6	157	Amarillo, TX	5.1
11	Birmingham, AL	31.4	83	Syracuse, NY	9.6	157	Corpus Christi, TX	5.1
12	Baton Rouge, LA	28.5	86	Antioch, CA	9.5	157	Las Vegas, NV	5.1
13	Trenton, NJ	28.1	87	Fort Lauderdale, FL	9.4	157	New York, NY	5.1
14	Stockton, CA	23.7	87	South Gate, CA	9.4	157	Racine, WI	5.1
15	Little Rock, AR	23.0	89	Louisville, KY	9.3	157	Riverside, CA	5.1
16	Kansas City, MO	22.6	90	Roanoke, VA	9.2	157	Victorville, CA	5.1
16	Macon, GA	22.6	91	Killeen, TX	9.1	165	Anchorage, AK	5.0
18	Miami Gardens, FL	22.5	92	Boston, MA	9.0	165	Lancaster, CA	5.0
19	San Bernardino, CA	21.9	92	Lafayette, LA	9.0	165	Las Cruces, NM	5.0
20	Philadelphia, PA	21.5	94	Avondale, AZ	8.9	168	Pompano Beach, FL	4.9
21	Compton, CA	21.4	94	Durham, NC	8.9	169	Odessa, TX	4.8
22	Cleveland, OH	21.3	96	Columbus, GA	8.7	170	Gainesville, FL	4.7
23	Montgomery, AL	21.1	96	Peoria, IL	8.7	170	High Point, NC	4.7
24	Memphis, TN	20.2	98	Aurora, CO	8.6	170	Oceanside, CA	4.7
24	Richmond, VA	20.2	98	Fort Wayne, IN	8.6	170	Tracy, CA	4.7
26	Atlanta, GA	19.0	100	Longview, TX	8.5	170	Virginia Beach, VA	4.7
27	Chicago, IL	18.5	100	Springfield, IL	8.5	170	Waco, TX	4.7
28	Hartford, CT	18.4	102	Grand Rapids, MI	8.4	170	Wichita Falls, TX	4.7
29	Buffalo, NY	18.3	102	San Francisco, CA	8.4	177	Lubbock, TX	4.6
30	South Bend, IN	17.8	102	Shreveport, LA	8.4	177	Plantation, FL	4.6
31	Rochester, NY	17.0	105	Phoenix, AZ	8.3	177	San Jose, CA	4.6
32	Dayton, OH	16.9	106	Hawthorne, CA	8.2	180	Arlington, TX	4.5
32	Reading, PA	16.9	107	Greenville, NC	8.1	180	Oxnard, CA	4.5
32	Richmond, CA	16.9	107	Tucson, AZ	8.1	180	St. Paul, MN	4.5
35	Miami, FL	16.7	109	Decatur, IL	7.9	180	Waterbury, CT	4.5
36	West Palm Beach, FL	16.6	110	Erie, PA	7.8	184	Anaheim, CA	4.4
37	Cincinnati, OH	15.5	110	Los Angeles, CA	7.8	184	Jersey City, NJ	4.4
38	Milwaukee, WI	15.2	110	Melbourne, FL	7.8	184	Salem, OR	4.4
39	Bridgeport, CT	15.1	113	Bellflower, CA	7.7	184	Worcester, MA	4.4
40	Oklahoma City, OK	14.3	114	Greensboro, NC	7.6	188	Athens-Clarke, GA	4.3
40	Paterson, NJ	14.3	114	Huntsville, AL	7.6	188	Berkeley, CA	4.3
42	Norfolk, VA	13.9	116	Carson, CA	7.5	188	Independence, MO	4.3
42	Washington, DC	13.9	116	Fairfield, CA	7.5	188	Tuscaloosa, AL	4.3
44	Salinas, CA	13.6	118	Albuquerque, NM	7.4	192	Colorado Springs, CO	4.2
44	Toledo, OH	13.6	118	Hammond, IN	7.4	192	Salt Lake City, UT	4.2
46	Lawton, OK	13.2	118	Joliet, IL	7.4	194	Albany, NY	4.1
47	New Haven, CT	13.1	121	Clarksville, TN	7.3	194	Hayward, CA	4.1
47	Pittsburgh, PA	13.1	121	Pueblo, CO	7.3	196	Davenport, IA	4.0
49	North Charleston, SC	12.9	121	Wilmington, NC	7.3	196	Lexington, KY	4.0
50	Mobile, AL	12.7	124	Sacramento, CA	7.1	196	Raleigh, NC	4.0
51	Allentown, PA	12.6	124	Springfield, MA	7.1	196	Stamford, CT	4.0
51	Inglewood, CA	12.6	126	Asheville, NC	7.0	200	Lynchburg, VA	3.9
53	Dallas, TX	12.4	127	Evansville, IN	6.8	200	Palmdale, CA	3.9
54	Akron, OH	12.1	127	Long Beach, CA	6.8	200	Rialto, CA	3.9
55	Vallejo, CA	11.9	129	Tampa, FL	6.6	200	Visalia, CA	3.9
56	Yakima, WA	11.8	129	Tempe, AZ	6.6	204	Austin, TX	3.7
57	Indianapolis, IN	11.6	131	Hampton, VA	6.5	204	Bloomington, IN	3.7
57	Topeka, KS	11.6	131	Hesperia, CA	6.5	204	Champaign, IL	3.7
59	Portsmouth, VA	11.4	131	Tallahassee, FL	6.5	204	Gresham, OR	3.7
60	Lansing, MI	11.3	134	Charlotte, NC	6.4	204	Mission, TX	3.7
61	Pomona, CA	11.2	134	San Antonio, TX	6.4	204	Seattle, WA	3.7
62	Elizabeth, NJ	11.1	136	Brockton, MA	6.3	210	Costa Mesa, CA	3.6
62	Jacksonville, FL	11.1	136	North Las Vegas, NV	6.3	210	Pasadena, CA	3.6
62	Merced, CA	11.1	138	Denver, CO	6.2	210	Upper Darby Twnshp, PA	3.6
65	Newport News, VA	11.0	139	Spokane, WA	6.1	213	El Monte, CA	3.5
66	Beaumont, TX	10.8	140	St. Petersburg, FL	6.0	213	Midland, TX	3.5
67	Fayetteville, NC	10.7	140	Wichita, KS	6.0	213	Norwalk, CT	3.5
68	Tulsa, OK	10.5	142	Cicero, IL	5.9	213	San Diego, CA	3.5
69	Norwalk, CA	10.3	142	Rockford, IL	5.9	217	Des Moines, IA	3.4
70	Kansas City, KS	10.2	142	Tacoma, WA	5.9	217	El Paso, TX	3.4
71	Fresno, CA	10.1	145	Fort Smith, AR	5.7	217	Escondido, CA	3.4
72	Houston, TX	10.0	145	Fort Worth, TX	5.7	217	Hollywood, FL	3.4
72	Lakeland, FL	10.0	145	Peoria, AZ	5.7	221	Federal Way, WA	3.3
72	Minneapolis, MN	10.0	148	Miami Beach, FL	5.5	221	Laredo, TX	3.3

RANK	CITY	RATE	RANK	CITY	RATE	RANK	CITY	RATE
221	Portland, OR	3.3	295	Ontario, CA	1.8	369	Garden Grove, CA	0.6
221	Redding, CA	3.3	295	Rochester, MN	1.8	369	Grand Prairie, TX	0.6
221	Santa Ana, CA	3.3	295	Westminster, CO	1.8	369	Santa Clarita, CA	0.6
226	Chula Vista, CA	3.2	300	Brownsville, TX	1.7	374	Boise, ID	0.5
226	Vacaville, CA	3.2	300	Hialeah, FL	1.7	375	Plano, TX	0.4
228	Clovis, CA	3.1	302	Bellevue, WA	1.6	376	Alexandria, VA	0.0
228	College Station, TX	3.1	302	Carrollton, TX	1.6	376	Alhambra, CA	0.0
228	Livonia, MI	3.1	302	Chandler, AZ	1.6	376	Allen, TX	0.0
228	Mesa, AZ	3.1	302	Kent, WA	1.6	376	Amherst, NY	0.0
228	Sandy Springs, GA	3.1	302	Miramar, FL	1.6	376	Arvada, CO	0.0
228	Sterling Heights, MI	3.1	302	Roseville, CA	1.6	376	Aurora, IL	0.0
234	Garland, TX	3.0	308	Henderson, NV	1.5	376	Beaverton, OR	0.0
234	Reno, NV	3.0	308	Huntington Beach, CA	1.5	376	Bellingham, WA	0.0
234	Tyler, TX	3.0	310	Lakewood, CO	1.4	376	Bloomington, MN	0.0
234	Vancouver, WA	3.0	310	Mesquite, TX	1.4	376	Boca Raton, FL	0.0
238	Orange, CA	2.9	312	Alameda, CA	1.3	376	Boulder, CO	0.0
238	Palm Bay, FL	2.9	312	Arlington Heights, IL	1.3	376	Brick Twnshp, NJ	0.0
240	Billings, MT	2.8	312	Bloomington, IL	1.3	376	Carmel, IN	0.0
241	Bethlehem, PA	2.7	312	Bryan, TX	1.3	376	Cary, NC	0.0
241	Clearwater, FL	2.7	312	Chino, CA	1.3	376	Cheektowaga, NY	0.0
241	Columbia, MO	2.7	312	Fayetteville, AR	1.3	376	Chino Hills, CA	0.0
241	Murfreesboro, TN	2.7	312	Fort Collins, CO	1.3	376	Clarkstown, NY	0.0
241	Torrance, CA	2.7	312	Irving, TX	1.3	376	Clifton, NJ	0.0
246	Baldwin Park, CA	2.6	312	Kennewick, WA	1.3	376	Clinton Twnshp, MI	0.0
246	Lawrence, MA	2.6	312	Largo, FL	1.3	376	Colonie, NY	0.0
246	Medford, OR	2.6	312	Madison, WI	1.3	376	Concord, CA	0.0
246	Winston-Salem, NC	2.6	312	Pembroke Pines, FL	1.3	376	Daly City, CA	0.0
250	Abilene, TX	2.5	312	Scottsdale, AZ	1.3	376	Edison Twnshp, NJ	0.0
250	Cape Coral, FL	2.5	312	Sioux Falls, SD	1.3	376	Eugene, OR	0.0
250	Cranston, RI	2.5	312	St. Joseph, MO	1.3	376	Fishers, IN	0.0
250	Fontana, CA	2.5	327	Buena Park, CA	1.2	376	Frisco, TX	0.0
250	Indio, CA	2.5	327	Danbury, CT	1.2	376	Fullerton, CA	0.0
250	Moreno Valley, CA	2.5	327	Edinburg, TX	1.2	376	Glendale, CA	0.0
250	Napa, CA	2.5	327	Farmington Hills, MI	1.2	376	Greece, NY	0.0
250	O'Fallon, MO	2.5	327	Hemet, CA	1.2	376	Hamilton Twnshp, NJ	0.0
250	Surprise, AZ	2.5	327	Lakewood, CA	1.2	376	Johns Creek, GA	0.0
250	Troy, MI	2.5	327	Menifee, CA	1.2	376	Lake Forest, CA	0.0
260	Edmond, OK	2.4	327	Santa Rosa, CA	1.2	376	Lawrence, KS	0.0
260	Hoover, AL	2.4	327	Warwick, RI	1.2	376	League City, TX	0.0
260	Nampa, ID	2.4	327	Westland, MI	1.2	376	Lee's Summit, MO	0.0
260	Ogden, UT	2.4	337	Chico, CA	1.1	376	Livermore, CA	0.0
260	Port St. Lucie, FL	2.4	337	Lincoln, NE	1.1	376	Longmont, CO	0.0
260	Rancho Cucamon., CA	2.4	337	Newport Beach, CA	1.1	376	Lowell, MA	0.0
260	Simi Valley, CA	2.4	337	Overland Park, KS	1.1	376	McKinney, TX	0.0
260	Sioux City, IA	2.4	337	Pearland, TX	1.1	376	Meridian, ID	0.0
268	Cedar Rapids, IA	2.3	337	Roswell, GA	1.1	376	Mission Viejo, CA	0.0
268	Citrus Heights, CA	2.3	337	Sparks, NV	1.1	376	Mountain View, CA	0.0
268	Duluth, MN	2.3	337	Spokane Valley, WA	1.1	376	Nashua, NH	0.0
268	Gilbert, AZ	2.3	337	Sunrise, FL	1.1	376	New Rochelle, NY	0.0
268	San Leandro, CA	2.3	337	Toms River Twnshp, NJ	1.1	376	Newton, MA	0.0
268	San Marcos, CA	2.3	347	Broken Arrow, OK	1.0	376	Olathe, KS	0.0
274	Fall River, MA	2.2	347	Centennial, CO	1.0	376	Parma, OH	0.0
274	Lynn, MA	2.2	347	Dearborn, MI	1.0	376	Provo, UT	0.0
274	Orem, UT	2.2	347	Greeley, CO	1.0	376	Quincy, MA	0.0
274	Rio Rancho, NM	2.2	347	Jurupa Valley, CA	1.0	376	Ramapo, NY	0.0
274	Sandy, UT	2.2	347	Kenosha, WI	1.0	376	Redwood City, CA	0.0
274	Santa Monica, CA	2.2	347	Vista, CA	1.0	376	Round Rock, TX	0.0
274	Waukegan, IL	2.2	354	Ann Arbor, MI	0.9	376	San Mateo, CA	0.0
274	Westminster, CA	2.2	354	Cambridge, MA	0.9	376	Santa Barbara, CA	0.0
282	Hillsboro, OR	2.1	354	Everett, WA	0.9	376	Santa Clara, CA	0.0
282	Lakewood Twnshp, NJ	2.1	354	Fremont, CA	0.9	376	Santa Maria, CA	0.0
282	Naperville, IL	2.1	354	Green Bay, WI	0.9	376	Scranton, PA	0.0
282	New Bedford, MA	2.1	354	Irvine, CA	0.9	376	Somerville, MA	0.0
282	Renton, WA	2.1	354	Manchester, NH	0.9	376	St. George, UT	0.0
282	Sunnyvale, CA	2.1	354	Murrieta, CA	0.9	376	Sugar Land, TX	0.0
288	El Cajon, CA	2.0	354	Norman, OK	0.9	376	Temecula, CA	0.0
288	Yonkers, NY	2.0	354	Ventura, CA	0.9	376	Thousand Oaks, CA	0.0
290	Burbank, CA	1.9	364	Coral Springs, FL	0.8	376	Tustin, CA	0.0
290	Carlsbad, CA	1.9	364	Denton, TX	0.8	376	Upland, CA	0.0
290	Richardson, TX	1.9	364	Thornton, CO	0.8	376	Warren, MI	0.0
290	West Covina, CA	1.9	367	McAllen, TX	0.7	376	Whittier, CA	0.0
290	West Jordan, UT	1.9	367	West Valley, UT	0.7	376	Woodbridge Twnshp, NJ	0.0
295	Elgin, IL	1.8	369	Corona, CA	0.6			
295	Fargo, ND	1.8	369	Elk Grove, CA	0.6			

Source: CQ Press using reported data from the F.B.I. "Crime in the United States 2012"

*Includes nonnegligent manslaughter.

51. Percent Change in Murder Rate: 2011 to 2012
National Percent Change = 0.4% Increase*

RANK	CITY	% CHANGE	RANK	CITY	% CHANGE	RANK	CITY	% CHANGE
300	Abilene, TX	(40.5)	163	Chino Hills, CA	0.0	223	Gainesville, FL	(2.1)
243	Akron, OH	(11.0)	307	Chino, CA	(48.0)	308	Garden Grove, CA	(50.0)
163	Alameda, CA	0.0	91	Chula Vista, CA	33.3	88	Garland, TX	36.4
341	Albany, GA	(69.3)	2	Cicero, IL	391.7	106	Gary, IN	23.7
NA	Albany, NY**	NA	268	Cincinnati, OH	(24.4)	22	Gilbert, AZ	155.6
126	Albuquerque, NM	17.5	45	Citrus Heights, CA	91.7	305	Glendale, AZ	(45.8)
357	Alexandria, VA	(100.0)	NA	Clarkstown, NY**	NA	163	Glendale, CA	0.0
357	Alhambra, CA	(100.0)	113	Clarksville, TN	21.7	356	Grand Prairie, TX	(88.0)
NA	Allentown, PA**	NA	342	Clearwater, FL	(70.7)	63	Grand Rapids, MI	58.5
163	Allen, TX	0.0	132	Cleveland, OH	14.5	NA	Greece, NY**	NA
163	Amarillo, TX	0.0	357	Clifton, NJ	(100.0)	239	Greeley, CO	(9.1)
NA	Amherst, NY**	NA	357	Clinton Twnshp, MI	(100.0)	324	Green Bay, WI	(52.6)
163	Anaheim, CA	0.0	268	Clovis, CA	(24.4)	NA	Greensboro, NC**	NA
103	Anchorage, AK	25.0	14	College Station, TX	210.0	NA	Greenville, NC**	NA
NA	Ann Arbor, MI***	NA	NA	Colonie, NY**	NA	6	Gresham, OR	311.1
42	Antioch, CA	97.9	281	Colorado Springs, CO	(31.1)	163	Hamilton Twnshp, NJ	0.0
320	Arlington Heights, IL	(51.9)	68	Columbia, MO	50.0	285	Hammond, IN	(33.3)
266	Arlington, TX	(23.7)	140	Columbus, GA	11.5	163	Hampton, VA	0.0
357	Arvada, CO	(100.0)	109	Compton, CA	23.0	248	Hartford, CT	(14.8)
124	Asheville, NC	18.6	357	Concord, CA	(100.0)	82	Hawthorne, CA	39.0
250	Athens-Clarke, GA	(15.7)	163	Coral Springs, FL	0.0	247	Hayward, CA	(14.6)
235	Atlanta, GA	(8.2)	327	Corona, CA	(53.8)	353	Hemet, CA	(81.0)
13	Aurora, CO	218.5	96	Corpus Christi, TX	30.8	50	Henderson, NV	87.5
357	Aurora, IL	(100.0)	163	Costa Mesa, CA	0.0	17	Hesperia, CA	195.5
151	Austin, TX	5.7	29	Cranston, RI	108.3	228	Hialeah, FL	(5.6)
133	Avondale, AZ	14.1	134	Dallas, TX	13.8	54	High Point, NC	67.9
49	Bakersfield, CA	88.2	357	Daly City, CA	(100.0)	46	Hillsboro, OR	90.9
30	Baldwin Park, CA	100.0	163	Danbury, CT	0.0	114	Hollywood, FL	21.4
140	Baltimore, MD	11.5	259	Davenport, IA	(20.0)	NA	Hoover, AL***	NA
156	Baton Rouge, LA	3.3	3	Davie, FL	381.8	145	Houston, TX	8.7
163	Beaumont, TX	0.0	273	Dayton, OH	(27.5)	277	Huntington Beach, CA	(28.6)
163	Beaverton, OR	0.0	338	Dearborn, MI	(67.7)	152	Huntsville, AL	5.6
30	Bellevue, WA	100.0	299	Decatur, IL	(39.7)	23	Independence, MO	152.9
71	Bellflower, CA	48.1	7	Deerfield Beach, FL	300.0	161	Indianapolis, IN	0.9
357	Bellingham, WA	(100.0)	326	Denton, TX	(52.9)	294	Indio, CA	(35.9)
4	Berkeley, CA	377.8	143	Denver, CO	10.7	146	Inglewood, CA	7.7
283	Bethlehem, PA	(32.5)	244	Des Moines, IA	(12.8)	163	Irvine, CA	0.0
73	Billings, MT	47.4	136	Detroit, MI	13.3	335	Irving, TX	(63.9)
104	Birmingham, AL	24.1	18	Downey, CA	194.4	98	Jacksonville, FL	30.6
163	Bloomington, IL	0.0	NA	Duluth, MN***	NA	123	Jackson, MS	19.7
270	Bloomington, IN	(24.5)	267	Durham, NC	(23.9)	297	Jersey City, NJ	(38.9)
163	Bloomington, MN	0.0	232	Edinburg, TX	(7.7)	163	Johns Creek, GA	0.0
163	Boca Raton, FL	0.0	357	Edison Twnshp, NJ	(100.0)	87	Joliet, IL	37.0
163	Boise, ID	0.0	30	Edmond, OK	100.0	NA	Jurupa Valley, CA**	NA
242	Boston, MA	(10.9)	163	El Cajon, CA	0.0	301	Kansas City, KS	(44.6)
357	Boulder, CO	(100.0)	8	El Monte, CA	288.9	226	Kansas City, MO	(3.4)
163	Brick Twnshp, NJ	0.0	80	El Paso, TX	41.7	320	Kennewick, WA	(51.9)
144	Bridgeport, CT	9.4	333	Elgin, IL	(60.9)	NA	Kenosha, WI***	NA
290	Brockton, MA	(33.7)	253	Elizabeth, NJ	(18.4)	74	Kent, WA	45.5
NA	Broken Arrow, OK***	NA	339	Elk Grove, CA	(68.4)	262	Killeen, TX	(20.9)
259	Brooklyn Park, MN	(20.0)	92	Erie, PA	32.2	153	Knoxville, TN	5.3
19	Brownsville, TX	183.3	57	Escondido, CA	61.9	51	Lafayette, LA	83.7
308	Bryan, TX	(50.0)	163	Eugene, OR	0.0	357	Lake Forest, CA	(100.0)
337	Buena Park, CA	(67.6)	21	Evansville, IN	172.0	56	Lakeland, FL	63.9
NA	Buffalo, NY**	NA	354	Everett, WA	(81.3)	163	Lakewood Twnshp, NJ	0.0
48	Burbank, CA	90.0	62	Fairfield, CA	59.6	322	Lakewood, CA	(52.0)
352	Cambridge, MA	(80.9)	163	Fall River, MA	0.0	344	Lakewood, CO	(74.5)
78	Camden, NJ	42.4	30	Fargo, ND	100.0	30	Lancaster, CA	100.0
94	Cape Coral, FL	31.6	322	Farmington Hills, MI	(52.0)	58	Lansing, MI	61.4
308	Carlsbad, CA	(50.0)	163	Fayetteville, AR	0.0	276	Laredo, TX	(28.3)
357	Carmel, IN	(100.0)	245	Fayetteville, NC	(13.0)	163	Largo, FL	0.0
295	Carrollton, TX	(36.0)	NA	Federal Way, WA**	NA	55	Las Cruces, NM	66.7
83	Carson, CA	38.9	163	Fishers, IN	0.0	238	Las Vegas, NV	(8.9)
357	Cary, NC	(100.0)	111	Flint, MI	22.0	163	Lawrence, KS	0.0
77	Cedar Rapids, IA	43.8	163	Fontana, CA	0.0	350	Lawrence, MA	(80.0)
NA	Centennial, CO***	NA	292	Fort Collins, CO	(35.0)	60	Lawton, OK	61.0
16	Champaign, IL	208.3	98	Fort Lauderdale, FL	30.6	357	League City, TX	(100.0)
NA	Chandler, AZ**	NA	222	Fort Smith, AR	(1.7)	163	Lee's Summit, MO	0.0
150	Charleston, SC	6.6	237	Fort Wayne, IN	(8.5)	NA	Lexington, KY**	NA
241	Charlotte, NC	(9.9)	240	Fort Worth, TX	(9.5)	271	Lincoln, NE	(26.7)
NA	Cheektowaga, NY**	NA	163	Fremont, CA	0.0	116	Little Rock, AR	21.1
163	Chesapeake, VA	0.0	76	Fresno, CA	44.3	357	Livermore, CA	(100.0)
127	Chicago, IL	16.4	357	Frisco, TX	(100.0)	14	Livonia, MI	210.0
351	Chico, CA	(80.7)	357	Fullerton, CA	(100.0)	102	Long Beach, CA	28.3

RANK	CITY	% CHANGE
357	Longmont, CO	(100.0)
53	Longview, TX	73.5
160	Los Angeles, CA	1.3
101	Louisville, KY	29.2
357	Lowell, MA	(100.0)
89	Lubbock, TX	35.3
163	Lynchburg, VA	0.0
285	Lynn, MA	(33.3)
58	Macon, GA	61.4
334	Madison, WI	(61.8)
308	Manchester, NH	(50.0)
346	McAllen, TX	(76.7)
357	McKinney, TX	(100.0)
336	Medford, OR	(67.1)
30	Melbourne, FL	100.0
137	Memphis, TN	12.8
327	Menifee, CA	(53.8)
142	Merced, CA	11.0
357	Meridian, ID	(100.0)
265	Mesa, AZ	(22.5)
163	Mesquite, TX	0.0
110	Miami Beach, FL	22.2
157	Miami Gardens, FL	1.8
219	Miami, FL	(0.6)
163	Midland, TX	0.0
148	Milwaukee, WI	7.0
119	Minneapolis, MN	20.5
308	Miramar, FL	(50.0)
163	Mission Viejo, CA	0.0
72	Mission, TX	48.0
149	Mobile, AL	6.7
79	Modesto, CA	42.0
81	Montgomery, AL	40.7
280	Moreno Valley, CA	(30.6)
163	Mountain View, CA	0.0
163	Murfreesboro, TN	0.0
324	Murrieta, CA	(52.6)
NA	Nampa, ID***	NA
44	Napa, CA	92.3
68	Naperville, IL	50.0
357	Nashua, NH	(100.0)
111	Nashville, TN	22.0
308	New Bedford, MA	(50.0)
308	New Haven, CT	(50.0)
231	New Orleans, LA	(7.6)
NA	New Rochelle, NY**	NA
NA	New York, NY**	NA
157	Newark, NJ	1.8
NA	Newport Beach, CA***	NA
90	Newport News, VA	34.1
163	Newton, MA	0.0
125	Norfolk, VA	17.8
308	Norman, OK	(50.0)
23	North Charleston, SC	152.9
NA	North Las Vegas, NV**	NA
27	Norwalk, CA	119.1
163	Norwalk, CT	0.0
117	Oakland, CA	20.9
131	Oceanside, CA	14.6
255	Odessa, TX	(18.6)
NA	O'Fallon, MO***	NA
163	Ogden, UT	0.0
75	Oklahoma City, OK	44.4
357	Olathe, KS	(100.0)
229	Omaha, NE	(5.8)
308	Ontario, CA	(50.0)
93	Orange, CA	31.8
NA	Orem, UT***	NA
257	Orlando, FL	(19.2)
163	Overland Park, KS	0.0
138	Oxnard, CA	12.5
67	Palm Bay, FL	52.6
284	Palmdale, CA	(32.8)
NA	Parma, OH**	NA

RANK	CITY	% CHANGE
275	Pasadena, CA	(28.0)
64	Pasadena, TX	57.6
107	Paterson, NJ	23.3
306	Pearland, TX	(47.6)
308	Pembroke Pines, FL	(50.0)
5	Peoria, AZ	338.5
296	Peoria, IL	(37.4)
159	Philadelphia, PA	1.4
154	Phoenix, AZ	5.1
236	Pittsburgh, PA	(8.4)
349	Plano, TX	(78.9)
10	Plantation, FL	283.3
66	Pomona, CA	53.4
163	Pompano Beach, FL	0.0
285	Port St. Lucie, FL	(33.3)
224	Portland, OR	(2.9)
234	Portsmouth, VA	(8.1)
NA	Providence, RI**	NA
357	Provo, UT	(100.0)
291	Pueblo, CO	(34.2)
357	Quincy, MA	(100.0)
256	Racine, WI	(19.0)
227	Raleigh, NC	(4.8)
NA	Ramapo, NY**	NA
285	Rancho Cucamon., CA	(33.3)
130	Reading, PA	15.0
163	Redding, CA	0.0
163	Redwood City, CA	0.0
319	Reno, NV	(51.6)
46	Renton, WA	90.9
292	Rialto, CA	(35.0)
NA	Richardson, TX***	NA
282	Richmond, CA	(31.9)
128	Richmond, VA	16.1
NA	Rio Rancho, NM***	NA
114	Riverside, CA	21.4
135	Roanoke, VA	13.6
30	Rochester, MN	100.0
NA	Rochester, NY**	NA
330	Rockford, IL	(56.9)
30	Roseville, CA	100.0
NA	Roswell, GA***	NA
357	Round Rock, TX	(100.0)
230	Sacramento, CA	(6.6)
25	Salem, OR	131.6
86	Salinas, CA	37.4
95	Salt Lake City, UT	31.2
225	San Antonio, TX	(3.0)
65	San Bernardino, CA	55.3
118	San Diego, CA	20.7
85	San Francisco, CA	37.7
139	San Jose, CA	12.2
343	San Leandro, CA	(71.6)
NA	San Marcos, CA***	NA
357	San Mateo, CA	(100.0)
20	Sandy Springs, GA	181.8
30	Sandy, UT	100.0
252	Santa Ana, CA	(17.5)
163	Santa Barbara, CA	0.0
357	Santa Clara, CA	(100.0)
348	Santa Clarita, CA	(78.6)
357	Santa Maria, CA	(100.0)
30	Santa Monica, CA	100.0
331	Santa Rosa, CA	(58.6)
246	Savannah, GA	(13.9)
274	Scottsdale, AZ	(27.8)
357	Scranton, PA	(100.0)
129	Seattle, WA	15.6
221	Shreveport, LA	(1.2)
NA	Simi Valley, CA***	NA
30	Sioux City, IA	100.0
332	Sioux Falls, SD	(59.4)
163	Somerville, MA	0.0
30	South Bend, IN	100.0

RANK	CITY	% CHANGE
70	South Gate, CA	49.2
355	Sparks, NV	(85.7)
NA	Spokane Valley, WA***	NA
11	Spokane, WA	221.1
108	Springfield, IL	23.2
303	Springfield, MA	(45.4)
12	Springfield, MO	219.4
253	Stamford, CT	(18.4)
9	Sterling Heights, MI	287.5
121	Stockton, CA	20.3
NA	St. George, UT**	NA
345	St. Joseph, MO	(75.0)
162	St. Louis, MO	0.6
61	St. Paul, MN	60.7
279	St. Petersburg, FL	(29.4)
357	Sugar Land, TX	(100.0)
163	Sunnyvale, CA	0.0
340	Sunrise, FL	(68.6)
NA	Surprise, AZ***	NA
NA	Syracuse, NY**	NA
147	Tacoma, WA	7.3
120	Tallahassee, FL	20.4
258	Tampa, FL	(19.5)
163	Temecula, CA	0.0
26	Tempe, AZ	120.0
NA	Thornton, CO**	NA
357	Thousand Oaks, CA	(100.0)
96	Toledo, OH	30.8
163	Toms River Twnshp, NJ	0.0
220	Topeka, KS	(0.9)
43	Torrance, CA	92.9
NA	Tracy, CA***	NA
155	Trenton, NJ	4.1
NA	Troy, MI***	NA
251	Tucson, AZ	(16.5)
249	Tulsa, OK	(15.3)
100	Tuscaloosa, AL	30.3
357	Tustin, CA	(100.0)
163	Tyler, TX	0.0
357	Upland, CA	(100.0)
163	Upper Darby Twnshp, PA	0.0
163	Vacaville, CA	0.0
264	Vallejo, CA	(22.2)
304	Vancouver, WA	(45.5)
163	Ventura, CA	0.0
163	Victorville, CA	0.0
84	Virginia Beach, VA	38.2
298	Visalia, CA	(39.1)
NA	Vista, CA***	NA
302	Waco, TX	(45.3)
357	Warren, MI	(100.0)
NA	Warwick, RI***	NA
261	Washington, DC	(20.6)
277	Waterbury, CT	(28.6)
NA	Waukegan, IL**	NA
28	West Covina, CA	111.1
NA	West Jordan, UT***	NA
121	West Palm Beach, FL	20.3
346	West Valley, UT	(76.7)
163	Westland, MI	0.0
285	Westminster, CA	(33.3)
318	Westminster, CO	(51.4)
357	Whittier, CA	(100.0)
1	Wichita Falls, TX	422.2
232	Wichita, KS	(7.7)
263	Wilmington, NC	(21.5)
329	Winston-Salem, NC	(56.7)
357	Woodbridge Twnshp, NJ	(100.0)
271	Worcester, MA	(26.7)
52	Yakima, WA	81.5
NA	Yonkers, NY**	NA
105	Yuma, AZ	23.8

Source: CQ Press using reported data from the F.B.I. "Crime in the United States 2012"

*Includes nonnegligent manslaughter. **Not available. ***These cities had murder rates of 0 in 2011 but had at least one murder in 2012. Calculating percent increase from zero results in an infinite number. These are shown as "NA."

51. Percent Change in Murder Rate: 2011 to 2012 (continued)
National Percent Change = 0.4% Increase*

RANK	CITY	% CHANGE	RANK	CITY	% CHANGE	RANK	CITY	% CHANGE
1	Wichita Falls, TX	422.2	75	Oklahoma City, OK	44.4	149	Mobile, AL	6.7
2	Cicero, IL	391.7	76	Fresno, CA	44.3	150	Charleston, SC	6.6
3	Davie, FL	381.8	77	Cedar Rapids, IA	43.8	151	Austin, TX	5.7
4	Berkeley, CA	377.8	78	Camden, NJ	42.4	152	Huntsville, AL	5.6
5	Peoria, AZ	338.5	79	Modesto, CA	42.0	153	Knoxville, TN	5.3
6	Gresham, OR	311.1	80	El Paso, TX	41.7	154	Phoenix, AZ	5.1
7	Deerfield Beach, FL	300.0	81	Montgomery, AL	40.7	155	Trenton, NJ	4.1
8	El Monte, CA	288.9	82	Hawthorne, CA	39.0	156	Baton Rouge, LA	3.3
9	Sterling Heights, MI	287.5	83	Carson, CA	38.9	157	Miami Gardens, FL	1.8
10	Plantation, FL	283.3	84	Virginia Beach, VA	38.2	157	Newark, NJ	1.8
11	Spokane, WA	221.1	85	San Francisco, CA	37.7	159	Philadelphia, PA	1.4
12	Springfield, MO	219.4	86	Salinas, CA	37.4	160	Los Angeles, CA	1.3
13	Aurora, CO	218.5	87	Joliet, IL	37.0	161	Indianapolis, IN	0.9
14	College Station, TX	210.0	88	Garland, TX	36.4	162	St. Louis, MO	0.6
14	Livonia, MI	210.0	89	Lubbock, TX	35.3	163	Alameda, CA	0.0
16	Champaign, IL	208.3	90	Newport News, VA	34.1	163	Allen, TX	0.0
17	Hesperia, CA	195.5	91	Chula Vista, CA	33.3	163	Amarillo, TX	0.0
18	Downey, CA	194.4	92	Erie, PA	32.2	163	Anaheim, CA	0.0
19	Brownsville, TX	183.3	93	Orange, CA	31.8	163	Beaumont, TX	0.0
20	Sandy Springs, GA	181.8	94	Cape Coral, FL	31.6	163	Beaverton, OR	0.0
21	Evansville, IN	172.0	95	Salt Lake City, UT	31.2	163	Bloomington, IL	0.0
22	Gilbert, AZ	155.6	96	Corpus Christi, TX	30.8	163	Bloomington, MN	0.0
23	Independence, MO	152.9	96	Toledo, OH	30.8	163	Boca Raton, FL	0.0
23	North Charleston, SC	152.9	98	Fort Lauderdale, FL	30.6	163	Boise, ID	0.0
25	Salem, OR	131.6	98	Jacksonville, FL	30.6	163	Brick Twnshp, NJ	0.0
26	Tempe, AZ	120.0	100	Tuscaloosa, AL	30.3	163	Chesapeake, VA	0.0
27	Norwalk, CA	119.1	101	Louisville, KY	29.2	163	Chino Hills, CA	0.0
28	West Covina, CA	111.1	102	Long Beach, CA	28.3	163	Coral Springs, FL	0.0
29	Cranston, RI	108.3	103	Anchorage, AK	25.0	163	Costa Mesa, CA	0.0
30	Baldwin Park, CA	100.0	104	Birmingham, AL	24.1	163	Danbury, CT	0.0
30	Bellevue, WA	100.0	105	Yuma, AZ	23.8	163	El Cajon, CA	0.0
30	Edmond, OK	100.0	106	Gary, IN	23.7	163	Eugene, OR	0.0
30	Fargo, ND	100.0	107	Paterson, NJ	23.3	163	Fall River, MA	0.0
30	Lancaster, CA	100.0	108	Springfield, IL	23.2	163	Fayetteville, AR	0.0
30	Melbourne, FL	100.0	109	Compton, CA	23.0	163	Fishers, IN	0.0
30	Rochester, MN	100.0	110	Miami Beach, FL	22.2	163	Fontana, CA	0.0
30	Roseville, CA	100.0	111	Flint, MI	22.0	163	Fremont, CA	0.0
30	Sandy, UT	100.0	111	Nashville, TN	22.0	163	Glendale, CA	0.0
30	Santa Monica, CA	100.0	113	Clarksville, TN	21.7	163	Hamilton Twnshp, NJ	0.0
30	Sioux City, IA	100.0	114	Hollywood, FL	21.4	163	Hampton, VA	0.0
30	South Bend, IN	100.0	114	Riverside, CA	21.4	163	Irvine, CA	0.0
42	Antioch, CA	97.9	116	Little Rock, AR	21.1	163	Johns Creek, GA	0.0
43	Torrance, CA	92.9	117	Oakland, CA	20.9	163	Lakewood Twnshp, NJ	0.0
44	Napa, CA	92.3	118	San Diego, CA	20.7	163	Largo, FL	0.0
45	Citrus Heights, CA	91.7	119	Minneapolis, MN	20.5	163	Lawrence, KS	0.0
46	Hillsboro, OR	90.9	120	Tallahassee, FL	20.4	163	Lee's Summit, MO	0.0
46	Renton, WA	90.9	121	Stockton, CA	20.3	163	Lynchburg, VA	0.0
48	Burbank, CA	90.0	121	West Palm Beach, FL	20.3	163	Mesquite, TX	0.0
49	Bakersfield, CA	88.2	123	Jackson, MS	19.7	163	Midland, TX	0.0
50	Henderson, NV	87.5	124	Asheville, NC	18.6	163	Mission Viejo, CA	0.0
51	Lafayette, LA	83.7	125	Norfolk, VA	17.8	163	Mountain View, CA	0.0
52	Yakima, WA	81.5	126	Albuquerque, NM	17.5	163	Murfreesboro, TN	0.0
53	Longview, TX	73.5	127	Chicago, IL	16.4	163	Newton, MA	0.0
54	High Point, NC	67.9	128	Richmond, VA	16.1	163	Norwalk, CT	0.0
55	Las Cruces, NM	66.7	129	Seattle, WA	15.6	163	Ogden, UT	0.0
56	Lakeland, FL	63.9	130	Reading, PA	15.0	163	Overland Park, KS	0.0
57	Escondido, CA	61.9	131	Oceanside, CA	14.6	163	Pompano Beach, FL	0.0
58	Lansing, MI	61.4	132	Cleveland, OH	14.5	163	Redding, CA	0.0
58	Macon, GA	61.4	133	Avondale, AZ	14.1	163	Redwood City, CA	0.0
60	Lawton, OK	61.0	134	Dallas, TX	13.8	163	Santa Barbara, CA	0.0
61	St. Paul, MN	60.7	135	Roanoke, VA	13.6	163	Somerville, MA	0.0
62	Fairfield, CA	59.6	136	Detroit, MI	13.3	163	Sunnyvale, CA	0.0
63	Grand Rapids, MI	58.5	137	Memphis, TN	12.8	163	Temecula, CA	0.0
64	Pasadena, TX	57.6	138	Oxnard, CA	12.5	163	Toms River Twnshp, NJ	0.0
65	San Bernardino, CA	55.3	139	San Jose, CA	12.2	163	Tyler, TX	0.0
66	Pomona, CA	53.4	140	Baltimore, MD	11.5	163	Upper Darby Twnshp, PA	0.0
67	Palm Bay, FL	52.6	140	Columbus, GA	11.5	163	Vacaville, CA	0.0
68	Columbia, MO	50.0	142	Merced, CA	11.0	163	Ventura, CA	0.0
68	Naperville, IL	50.0	143	Denver, CO	10.7	163	Victorville, CA	0.0
70	South Gate, CA	49.2	144	Bridgeport, CT	9.4	163	Westland, MI	0.0
71	Bellflower, CA	48.1	145	Houston, TX	8.7	219	Miami, FL	(0.6)
72	Mission, TX	48.0	146	Inglewood, CA	7.7	220	Topeka, KS	(0.9)
73	Billings, MT	47.4	147	Tacoma, WA	7.3	221	Shreveport, LA	(1.2)
74	Kent, WA	45.5	148	Milwaukee, WI	7.0	222	Fort Smith, AR	(1.7)

RANK	CITY	% CHANGE	RANK	CITY	% CHANGE	RANK	CITY	% CHANGE
223	Gainesville, FL	(2.1)	297	Jersey City, NJ	(38.9)	357	Fullerton, CA	(100.0)
224	Portland, OR	(2.9)	298	Visalia, CA	(39.1)	357	Lake Forest, CA	(100.0)
225	San Antonio, TX	(3.0)	299	Decatur, IL	(39.7)	357	League City, TX	(100.0)
226	Kansas City, MO	(3.4)	300	Abilene, TX	(40.5)	357	Livermore, CA	(100.0)
227	Raleigh, NC	(4.8)	301	Kansas City, KS	(44.6)	357	Longmont, CO	(100.0)
228	Hialeah, FL	(5.6)	302	Waco, TX	(45.3)	357	Lowell, MA	(100.0)
229	Omaha, NE	(5.8)	303	Springfield, MA	(45.4)	357	McKinney, TX	(100.0)
230	Sacramento, CA	(6.6)	304	Vancouver, WA	(45.5)	357	Meridian, ID	(100.0)
231	New Orleans, LA	(7.6)	305	Glendale, AZ	(45.8)	357	Nashua, NH	(100.0)
232	Edinburg, TX	(7.7)	306	Pearland, TX	(47.6)	357	Olathe, KS	(100.0)
232	Wichita, KS	(7.7)	307	Chino, CA	(48.0)	357	Provo, UT	(100.0)
234	Portsmouth, VA	(8.1)	308	Bryan, TX	(50.0)	357	Quincy, MA	(100.0)
235	Atlanta, GA	(8.2)	308	Carlsbad, CA	(50.0)	357	Round Rock, TX	(100.0)
236	Pittsburgh, PA	(8.4)	308	Garden Grove, CA	(50.0)	357	San Mateo, CA	(100.0)
237	Fort Wayne, IN	(8.5)	308	Manchester, NH	(50.0)	357	Santa Clara, CA	(100.0)
238	Las Vegas, NV	(8.9)	308	Miramar, FL	(50.0)	357	Santa Maria, CA	(100.0)
239	Greeley, CO	(9.1)	308	New Bedford, MA	(50.0)	357	Scranton, PA	(100.0)
240	Fort Worth, TX	(9.5)	308	New Haven, CT	(50.0)	357	Sugar Land, TX	(100.0)
241	Charlotte, NC	(9.9)	308	Norman, OK	(50.0)	357	Thousand Oaks, CA	(100.0)
242	Boston, MA	(10.9)	308	Ontario, CA	(50.0)	357	Tustin, CA	(100.0)
243	Akron, OH	(11.0)	308	Pembroke Pines, FL	(50.0)	357	Upland, CA	(100.0)
244	Des Moines, IA	(12.8)	318	Westminster, CO	(51.4)	357	Warren, MI	(100.0)
245	Fayetteville, NC	(13.0)	319	Reno, NV	(51.6)	357	Whittier, CA	(100.0)
246	Savannah, GA	(13.9)	320	Arlington Heights, IL	(51.9)	357	Woodbridge Twnshp, NJ	(100.0)
247	Hayward, CA	(14.6)	320	Kennewick, WA	(51.9)	NA	Albany, NY**	NA
248	Hartford, CT	(14.8)	322	Farmington Hills, MI	(52.0)	NA	Allentown, PA**	NA
249	Tulsa, OK	(15.3)	322	Lakewood, CA	(52.0)	NA	Amherst, NY**	NA
250	Athens-Clarke, GA	(15.7)	324	Green Bay, WI	(52.6)	NA	Ann Arbor, MI***	NA
251	Tucson, AZ	(16.5)	324	Murrieta, CA	(52.6)	NA	Broken Arrow, OK***	NA
252	Santa Ana, CA	(17.5)	326	Denton, TX	(52.9)	NA	Buffalo, NY**	NA
253	Elizabeth, NJ	(18.4)	327	Corona, CA	(53.8)	NA	Centennial, CO***	NA
253	Stamford, CT	(18.4)	327	Menifee, CA	(53.8)	NA	Chandler, AZ**	NA
255	Odessa, TX	(18.6)	329	Winston-Salem, NC	(56.7)	NA	Cheektowaga, NY**	NA
256	Racine, WI	(19.0)	330	Rockford, IL	(56.9)	NA	Clarkstown, NY**	NA
257	Orlando, FL	(19.2)	331	Santa Rosa, CA	(58.6)	NA	Colonie, NY**	NA
258	Tampa, FL	(19.5)	332	Sioux Falls, SD	(59.4)	NA	Duluth, MN***	NA
259	Brooklyn Park, MN	(20.0)	333	Elgin, IL	(60.9)	NA	Federal Way, WA**	NA
259	Davenport, IA	(20.0)	334	Madison, WI	(61.8)	NA	Greece, NY**	NA
261	Washington, DC	(20.6)	335	Irving, TX	(63.9)	NA	Greensboro, NC**	NA
262	Killeen, TX	(20.9)	336	Medford, OR	(67.1)	NA	Greenville, NC**	NA
263	Wilmington, NC	(21.5)	337	Buena Park, CA	(67.6)	NA	Hoover, AL***	NA
264	Vallejo, CA	(22.2)	338	Dearborn, MI	(67.7)	NA	Jurupa Valley, CA**	NA
265	Mesa, AZ	(22.5)	339	Elk Grove, CA	(68.4)	NA	Kenosha, WI***	NA
266	Arlington, TX	(23.7)	340	Sunrise, FL	(68.6)	NA	Lexington, KY**	NA
267	Durham, NC	(23.9)	341	Albany, GA	(69.3)	NA	Nampa, ID***	NA
268	Cincinnati, OH	(24.4)	342	Clearwater, FL	(70.7)	NA	New Rochelle, NY**	NA
268	Clovis, CA	(24.4)	343	San Leandro, CA	(71.6)	NA	New York, NY**	NA
270	Bloomington, IN	(24.5)	344	Lakewood, CO	(74.5)	NA	Newport Beach, CA***	NA
271	Lincoln, NE	(26.7)	345	St. Joseph, MO	(75.0)	NA	North Las Vegas, NV**	NA
271	Worcester, MA	(26.7)	346	McAllen, TX	(76.7)	NA	O'Fallon, MO***	NA
273	Dayton, OH	(27.5)	346	West Valley, UT	(76.7)	NA	Orem, UT***	NA
274	Scottsdale, AZ	(27.8)	348	Santa Clarita, CA	(78.6)	NA	Parma, OH**	NA
275	Pasadena, CA	(28.0)	349	Plano, TX	(78.9)	NA	Providence, RI**	NA
276	Laredo, TX	(28.3)	350	Lawrence, MA	(80.0)	NA	Ramapo, NY**	NA
277	Huntington Beach, CA	(28.6)	351	Chico, CA	(80.7)	NA	Richardson, TX***	NA
277	Waterbury, CT	(28.6)	352	Cambridge, MA	(80.9)	NA	Rio Rancho, NM***	NA
279	St. Petersburg, FL	(29.4)	353	Hemet, CA	(81.0)	NA	Rochester, NY**	NA
280	Moreno Valley, CA	(30.6)	354	Everett, WA	(81.3)	NA	Roswell, GA***	NA
281	Colorado Springs, CO	(31.1)	355	Sparks, NV	(85.7)	NA	San Marcos, CA***	NA
282	Richmond, CA	(31.9)	356	Grand Prairie, TX	(88.0)	NA	Simi Valley, CA***	NA
283	Bethlehem, PA	(32.5)	357	Alexandria, VA	(100.0)	NA	Spokane Valley, WA***	NA
284	Palmdale, CA	(32.8)	357	Alhambra, CA	(100.0)	NA	St. George, UT**	NA
285	Hammond, IN	(33.3)	357	Arvada, CO	(100.0)	NA	Surprise, AZ***	NA
285	Lynn, MA	(33.3)	357	Aurora, IL	(100.0)	NA	Syracuse, NY**	NA
285	Port St. Lucie, FL	(33.3)	357	Bellingham, WA	(100.0)	NA	Thornton, CO**	NA
285	Rancho Cucamon., CA	(33.3)	357	Boulder, CO	(100.0)	NA	Tracy, CA***	NA
285	Westminster, CA	(33.3)	357	Carmel, IN	(100.0)	NA	Troy, MI***	NA
290	Brockton, MA	(33.7)	357	Cary, NC	(100.0)	NA	Vista, CA***	NA
291	Pueblo, CO	(34.2)	357	Clifton, NJ	(100.0)	NA	Warwick, RI***	NA
292	Fort Collins, CO	(35.0)	357	Clinton Twnshp, MI	(100.0)	NA	Waukegan, IL**	NA
292	Rialto, CA	(35.0)	357	Concord, CA	(100.0)	NA	West Jordan, UT***	NA
294	Indio, CA	(35.9)	357	Daly City, CA	(100.0)	NA	Yonkers, NY**	NA
295	Carrollton, TX	(36.0)	357	Edison Twnshp, NJ	(100.0)			
296	Peoria, IL	(37.4)	357	Frisco, TX	(100.0)			

Source: CQ Press using reported data from the F.B.I. "Crime in the United States 2012"

*Includes nonnegligent manslaughter. **Not available. ***These cities had murder rates of 0 in 2011 but had at least one murder in 2012. Calculating percent increase from zero results in an infinite number. These are shown as "NA."

52. Percent Change in Murder Rate: 2008 to 2012
National Percent Change = 12.8% Decrease*

RANK	CITY	% CHANGE	RANK	CITY	% CHANGE	RANK	CITY	% CHANGE
303	Abilene, TX	(58.3)	335	Chino Hills, CA	(100.0)	31	Gainesville, FL	80.8
48	Akron, OH	47.6	263	Chino, CA	(45.8)	316	Garden Grove, CA	(66.7)
293	Alameda, CA	(55.2)	82	Chula Vista, CA	18.5	241	Garland, TX	(34.8)
NA	Albany, GA**	NA	NA	Cicero, IL**	NA	161	Gary, IN	(10.2)
NA	Albany, NY**	NA	224	Cincinnati, OH	(29.2)	NA	Gilbert, AZ***	NA
106	Albuquerque, NM	2.8	24	Citrus Heights, CA	91.7	191	Glendale, AZ	(21.2)
335	Alexandria, VA	(100.0)	NA	Clarkstown, NY**	NA	335	Glendale, CA	(100.0)
335	Alhambra, CA	(100.0)	46	Clarksville, TN	49.0	333	Grand Prairie, TX	(86.0)
NA	Allentown, PA**	NA	324	Clearwater, FL	(74.3)	99	Grand Rapids, MI	7.7
335	Allen, TX	(100.0)	157	Cleveland, OH	(9.4)	NA	Greece, NY**	NA
212	Amarillo, TX	(26.1)	335	Clifton, NJ	(100.0)	331	Greeley, CO	(77.3)
NA	Amherst, NY**	NA	335	Clinton Twnshp, MI	(100.0)	290	Green Bay, WI	(55.0)
63	Anaheim, CA	33.3	47	Clovis, CA	47.6	188	Greensboro, NC	(20.8)
57	Anchorage, AK	38.9	7	College Station, TX	158.3	104	Greenville, NC	5.2
NA	Ann Arbor, MI***	NA	NA	Colonie, NY**	NA	246	Gresham, OR	(37.3)
79	Antioch, CA	20.3	234	Colorado Springs, CO	(33.3)	335	Hamilton Twnshp, NJ	(100.0)
NA	Arlington Heights, IL**	NA	261	Columbia, MO	(44.9)	297	Hammond, IN	(56.5)
215	Arlington, TX	(26.2)	264	Columbus, GA	(46.0)	83	Hampton, VA	18.2
335	Arvada, CO	(100.0)	222	Compton, CA	(27.7)	214	Hartford, CT	(26.1)
6	Asheville, NC	159.3	335	Concord, CA	(100.0)	35	Hawthorne, CA	74.5
9	Athens-Clarke, GA	138.9	326	Coral Springs, FL	(75.0)	177	Hayward, CA	(18.0)
134	Atlanta, GA	(3.6)	329	Corona, CA	(76.9)	300	Hemet, CA	(57.1)
44	Aurora, CO	50.9	199	Corpus Christi, TX	(22.7)	207	Henderson, NV	(25.0)
335	Aurora, IL	(100.0)	2	Costa Mesa, CA	300.0	26	Hesperia, CA	91.2
81	Austin, TX	19.4	22	Cranston, RI	92.3	294	Hialeah, FL	(55.3)
245	Avondale, AZ	(36.9)	147	Dallas, TX	(6.8)	298	High Point, NC	(56.5)
70	Bakersfield, CA	24.7	335	Daly City, CA	(100.0)	NA	Hillsboro, OR***	NA
325	Baldwin Park, CA	(74.8)	152	Danbury, CT	(7.7)	310	Hollywood, FL	(63.0)
143	Baltimore, MD	(5.4)	240	Davenport, IA	(34.4)	169	Hoover, AL	(14.3)
133	Baton Rouge, LA	(3.4)	8	Davie, FL	140.9	204	Houston, TX	(23.7)
39	Beaumont, TX	68.8	225	Dayton, OH	(29.6)	145	Huntington Beach, CA	(6.3)
111	Beaverton, OR	0.0	NA	Dearborn, MI***	NA	220	Huntsville, AL	(26.9)
NA	Bellevue, WA***	NA	NA	Decatur, IL**	NA	266	Independence, MO	(47.6)
181	Bellflower, CA	(18.9)	NA	Deerfield Beach, FL***	NA	176	Indianapolis, IN	(17.7)
335	Bellingham, WA	(100.0)	NA	Denton, TX***	NA	91	Indio, CA	13.6
262	Berkeley, CA	(45.6)	151	Denver, CO	(7.5)	97	Inglewood, CA	9.6
NA	Bethlehem, PA***	NA	259	Des Moines, IA	(44.3)	32	Irvine, CA	80.0
49	Billings, MT	47.4	41	Detroit, MI	61.5	309	Irving, TX	(62.9)
164	Birmingham, AL	(12.5)	27	Downey, CA	89.3	196	Jacksonville, FL	(22.4)
NA	Bloomington, IL**	NA	135	Duluth, MN	(4.2)	129	Jackson, MS	(0.8)
158	Bloomington, IN	(9.8)	174	Durham, NC	(17.6)	301	Jersey City, NJ	(57.3)
335	Bloomington, MN	(100.0)	323	Edinburg, TX	(71.4)	NA	Johns Creek, GA**	NA
335	Boca Raton, FL	(100.0)	335	Edison Twnshp, NJ	(100.0)	13	Joliet, IL	124.2
111	Boise, ID	0.0	NA	Edmond, OK***	NA	NA	Jurupa Valley, CA**	NA
165	Boston, MA	(12.6)	30	El Cajon, CA	81.8	NA	Kansas City, KS**	NA
111	Boulder, CO	0.0	311	El Monte, CA	(64.3)	162	Kansas City, MO	(11.4)
111	Brick Twnshp, NJ	0.0	77	El Paso, TX	21.4	180	Kennewick, WA	(18.8)
108	Bridgeport, CT	2.7	141	Elgin, IL	(5.3)	319	Kenosha, WI	(67.7)
NA	Brockton, MA**	NA	101	Elizabeth, NJ	6.7	234	Kent, WA	(33.3)
328	Broken Arrow, OK	(76.7)	NA	Elk Grove, CA***	NA	102	Killeen, TX	5.8
3	Brooklyn Park, MN	271.4	89	Erie, PA	16.4	242	Knoxville, TN	(34.9)
212	Brownsville, TX	(26.1)	86	Escondido, CA	17.2	109	Lafayette, LA	2.3
327	Bryan, TX	(76.4)	335	Eugene, OR	(100.0)	335	Lake Forest, CA	(100.0)
276	Buena Park, CA	(52.0)	42	Evansville, IN	58.1	150	Lakeland, FL	(7.4)
NA	Buffalo, NY**	NA	159	Everett, WA	(10.0)	270	Lakewood Twnshp, NJ	(50.0)
111	Burbank, CA	0.0	43	Fairfield, CA	56.3	276	Lakewood, CA	(52.0)
290	Cambridge, MA	(55.0)	234	Fall River, MA	(33.3)	16	Lakewood, CO	100.0
75	Camden, NJ	21.7	NA	Fargo, ND***	NA	216	Lancaster, CA	(26.5)
256	Cape Coral, FL	(41.9)	NA	Farmington Hills, MI***	NA	85	Lansing, MI	17.7
140	Carlsbad, CA	(5.0)	148	Fayetteville, AR	(7.1)	217	Laredo, TX	(26.7)
111	Carmel, IN	0.0	185	Fayetteville, NC	(20.1)	320	Largo, FL	(68.3)
270	Carrollton, TX	(50.0)	315	Federal Way, WA	(64.9)	90	Las Cruces, NM	16.3
166	Carson, CA	(12.8)	111	Fishers, IN	0.0	257	Las Vegas, NV	(42.7)
335	Cary, NC	(100.0)	14	Flint, MI	119.9	335	Lawrence, KS	(100.0)
135	Cedar Rapids, IA	(4.2)	306	Fontana, CA	(60.3)	289	Lawrence, MA	(54.4)
111	Centennial, CO	0.0	167	Fort Collins, CO	(13.3)	16	Lawton, OK	100.0
NA	Champaign, IL**	NA	192	Fort Lauderdale, FL	(21.7)	335	League City, TX	(100.0)
NA	Chandler, AZ**	NA	11	Fort Smith, AR	137.5	335	Lee's Summit, MO	(100.0)
197	Charleston, SC	(22.4)	168	Fort Wayne, IN	(14.0)	NA	Lexington, KY**	NA
255	Charlotte, NC	(41.3)	178	Fort Worth, TX	(18.6)	230	Lincoln, NE	(31.3)
NA	Cheektowaga, NY**	NA	159	Fremont, CA	(10.0)	98	Little Rock, AR	8.0
131	Chesapeake, VA	(1.9)	80	Fresno, CA	20.2	335	Livermore, CA	(100.0)
106	Chicago, IL	2.8	335	Frisco, TX	(100.0)	NA	Livonia, MI***	NA
287	Chico, CA	(54.2)	335	Fullerton, CA	(100.0)	189	Long Beach, CA	(20.9)

RANK	CITY	% CHANGE	RANK	CITY	% CHANGE	RANK	CITY	% CHANGE
NA	Longmont, CO**	NA	36	Pasadena, CA	71.4	12	South Gate, CA	129.3
218	Longview, TX	(26.7)	228	Pasadena, TX	(30.7)	NA	Sparks, NV***	NA
194	Los Angeles, CA	(22.0)	73	Paterson, NJ	22.2	154	Spokane Valley, WA	(8.3)
175	Louisville, KY	(17.7)	154	Pearland, TX	(8.3)	144	Spokane, WA	(6.2)
335	Lowell, MA	(100.0)	249	Pembroke Pines, FL	(38.1)	NA	Springfield, IL**	NA
68	Lubbock, TX	27.8	100	Peoria, AZ	7.5	203	Springfield, MA	(23.7)
227	Lynchburg, VA	(30.4)	NA	Peoria, IL**	NA	37	Springfield, MO	70.7
318	Lynn, MA	(67.2)	146	Philadelphia, PA	(6.5)	139	Stamford, CT	(4.8)
96	Macon, GA	10.2	190	Phoenix, AZ	(21.0)	20	Sterling Heights, MI	93.8
322	Madison, WI	(69.8)	258	Pittsburgh, PA	(43.5)	5	Stockton, CA	189.0
270	Manchester, NH	(50.0)	332	Plano, TX	(84.6)	335	St. George, UT	(100.0)
334	McAllen, TX	(89.9)	135	Plantation, FL	(4.2)	316	St. Joseph, MO	(66.7)
335	McKinney, TX	(100.0)	170	Pomona, CA	(14.5)	206	St. Louis, MO	(24.3)
NA	Medford, OR***	NA	260	Pompano Beach, FL	(44.3)	229	St. Paul, MN	(30.8)
207	Melbourne, FL	(25.0)	69	Port St. Lucie, FL	26.3	219	St. Petersburg, FL	(26.8)
130	Memphis, TN	(1.5)	226	Portland, OR	(29.8)	111	Sugar Land, TX	0.0
NA	Menifee, CA**	NA	198	Portsmouth, VA	(22.4)	55	Sunnyvale, CA	40.0
187	Merced, CA	(20.7)	60	Providence, RI	37.1	111	Sunrise, FL	0.0
335	Meridian, ID	(100.0)	111	Provo, UT	0.0	NA	Surprise, AZ***	NA
163	Mesa, AZ	(11.4)	NA	Pueblo, CO**	NA	NA	Syracuse, NY**	NA
252	Mesquite, TX	(39.1)	335	Quincy, MA	(100.0)	195	Tacoma, WA	(22.4)
202	Miami Beach, FL	(23.6)	302	Racine, WI	(58.2)	59	Tallahassee, FL	38.3
88	Miami Gardens, FL	16.6	286	Raleigh, NC	(54.0)	173	Tampa, FL	(17.5)
92	Miami, FL	13.6	NA	Ramapo, NY**	NA	335	Temecula, CA	(100.0)
153	Midland, TX	(7.9)	15	Rancho Cucamon., CA	118.2	19	Tempe, AZ	94.1
67	Milwaukee, WI	28.8	62	Reading, PA	36.3	NA	Thornton, CO**	NA
110	Minneapolis, MN	2.0	111	Redding, CA	0.0	335	Thousand Oaks, CA	(100.0)
312	Miramar, FL	(64.4)	335	Redwood City, CA	(100.0)	10	Toledo, OH	138.6
111	Mission Viejo, CA	0.0	299	Reno, NV	(56.5)	267	Toms River Twnshp, NJ	(47.6)
269	Mission, TX	(49.3)	NA	Renton, WA**	NA	54	Topeka, KS	41.5
205	Mobile, AL	(24.0)	314	Rialto, CA	(64.9)	21	Torrance, CA	92.9
93	Modesto, CA	12.6	282	Richardson, TX	(52.5)	NA	Tracy, CA***	NA
28	Montgomery, AL	86.7	244	Richmond, CA	(36.5)	76	Trenton, NJ	21.6
275	Moreno Valley, CA	(51.0)	65	Richmond, VA	30.3	111	Troy, MI	0.0
335	Mountain View, CA	(100.0)	38	Rio Rancho, NM	69.2	238	Tucson, AZ	(34.1)
288	Murfreesboro, TN	(54.2)	182	Riverside, CA	(19.0)	184	Tulsa, OK	(19.8)
111	Murrieta, CA	0.0	201	Roanoke, VA	(23.3)	313	Tuscaloosa, AL	(64.8)
NA	Nampa, ID***	NA	290	Rochester, MN	(55.0)	335	Tustin, CA	(100.0)
22	Napa, CA	92.3	NA	Rochester, NY**	NA	254	Tyler, TX	(41.2)
45	Naperville, IL	50.0	285	Rockford, IL	(53.5)	335	Upland, CA	(100.0)
NA	Nashua, NH**	NA	NA	Roseville, CA***	NA	305	Upper Darby Twnshp, PA	(59.6)
186	Nashville, TN	(20.6)	111	Roswell, GA	0.0	4	Vacaville, CA	190.9
280	New Bedford, MA	(52.3)	111	Round Rock, TX	0.0	103	Vallejo, CA	5.3
NA	New Haven, CT**	NA	233	Sacramento, CA	(32.4)	NA	Vancouver, WA***	NA
172	New Orleans, LA	(16.4)	209	Salem, OR	(25.4)	283	Ventura, CA	(52.6)
NA	New Rochelle, NY**	NA	193	Salinas, CA	(21.8)	52	Victorville, CA	45.7
NA	New York, NY**	NA	243	Salt Lake City, UT	(36.4)	50	Virginia Beach, VA	46.9
53	Newark, NJ	43.9	210	San Antonio, TX	(25.6)	281	Visalia, CA	(52.4)
NA	Newport Beach, CA***	NA	61	San Bernardino, CA	36.9	156	Vista, CA	(9.1)
73	Newport News, VA	22.2	179	San Diego, CA	(18.6)	265	Waco, TX	(47.2)
111	Newton, MA	0.0	231	San Francisco, CA	(31.7)	335	Warren, MI	(100.0)
87	Norfolk, VA	16.8	56	San Jose, CA	39.4	NA	Warwick, RI***	NA
283	Norman, OK	(52.6)	34	San Leandro, CA	76.9	295	Washington, DC	(55.7)
171	North Charleston, SC	(14.6)	24	San Marcos, CA	91.7	138	Waterbury, CT	(4.3)
64	North Las Vegas, NV	31.3	335	San Mateo, CA	(100.0)	NA	Waukegan, IL**	NA
33	Norwalk, CA	77.6	NA	Sandy Springs, GA***	NA	232	West Covina, CA	(32.1)
51	Norwalk, CT	45.8	NA	Sandy, UT***	NA	NA	West Jordan, UT***	NA
95	Oakland, CA	11.2	308	Santa Ana, CA	(62.5)	149	West Palm Beach, FL	(7.3)
40	Oceanside, CA	62.1	335	Santa Barbara, CA	(100.0)	296	West Valley, UT	(56.3)
234	Odessa, TX	(33.3)	335	Santa Clara, CA	(100.0)	276	Westland, MI	(52.0)
239	O'Fallon, MO	(34.2)	270	Santa Clarita, CA	(50.0)	16	Westminster, CA	100.0
270	Ogden, UT	(50.0)	335	Santa Maria, CA	(100.0)	141	Westminster, CO	(5.3)
58	Oklahoma City, OK	38.8	279	Santa Monica, CA	(52.2)	335	Whittier, CA	(100.0)
NA	Olathe, KS**	NA	329	Santa Rosa, CA	(76.9)	78	Wichita Falls, TX	20.5
132	Omaha, NE	(3.0)	183	Savannah, GA	(19.5)	223	Wichita, KS	(27.7)
248	Ontario, CA	(37.9)	249	Scottsdale, AZ	(38.1)	251	Wilmington, NC	(38.7)
1	Orange, CA	314.3	335	Scranton, PA	(100.0)	321	Winston-Salem, NC	(69.0)
105	Orem, UT	4.8	200	Seattle, WA	(22.9)	335	Woodbridge Twnshp, NJ	(100.0)
268	Orlando, FL	(48.1)	247	Shreveport, LA	(37.8)	66	Worcester, MA	29.4
29	Overland Park, KS	83.3	221	Simi Valley, CA	(27.3)	71	Yakima, WA	22.9
253	Oxnard, CA	(40.0)	307	Sioux City, IA	(60.7)	NA	Yonkers, NY**	NA
211	Palm Bay, FL	(25.6)	304	Sioux Falls, SD	(59.4)	83	Yuma, AZ	18.2
94	Palmdale, CA	11.4	335	Somerville, MA	(100.0)			
NA	Parma, OH**	NA	72	South Bend, IN	22.8			

Source: CQ Press using reported data from the F.B.I. "Crime in the United States 2012"

*Includes nonnegligent manslaughter. **Not available. ***These cities had murder rates of 0 in 2008 but had at least one murder in 2012. Calculating percent increase from zero results in an infinite number. These are shown as "NA."

52. Percent Change in Murder Rate: 2008 to 2012 (continued)
National Percent Change = 12.8% Decrease*

RANK	CITY	% CHANGE	RANK	CITY	% CHANGE	RANK	CITY	% CHANGE
1	Orange, CA	314.3	75	Camden, NJ	21.7	149	West Palm Beach, FL	(7.3)
2	Costa Mesa, CA	300.0	76	Trenton, NJ	21.6	150	Lakeland, FL	(7.4)
3	Brooklyn Park, MN	271.4	77	El Paso, TX	21.4	151	Denver, CO	(7.5)
4	Vacaville, CA	190.9	78	Wichita Falls, TX	20.5	152	Danbury, CT	(7.7)
5	Stockton, CA	189.0	79	Antioch, CA	20.3	153	Midland, TX	(7.9)
6	Asheville, NC	159.3	80	Fresno, CA	20.2	154	Pearland, TX	(8.3)
7	College Station, TX	158.3	81	Austin, TX	19.4	154	Spokane Valley, WA	(8.3)
8	Davie, FL	140.9	82	Chula Vista, CA	18.5	156	Vista, CA	(9.1)
9	Athens-Clarke, GA	138.9	83	Hampton, VA	18.2	157	Cleveland, OH	(9.4)
10	Toledo, OH	138.6	83	Yuma, AZ	18.2	158	Bloomington, IN	(9.8)
11	Fort Smith, AR	137.5	85	Lansing, MI	17.7	159	Everett, WA	(10.0)
12	South Gate, CA	129.3	86	Escondido, CA	17.2	159	Fremont, CA	(10.0)
13	Joliet, IL	124.2	87	Norfolk, VA	16.8	161	Gary, IN	(10.2)
14	Flint, MI	119.9	88	Miami Gardens, FL	16.6	162	Kansas City, MO	(11.4)
15	Rancho Cucamon., CA	118.2	89	Erie, PA	16.4	163	Mesa, AZ	(11.4)
16	Lakewood, CO	100.0	90	Las Cruces, NM	16.3	164	Birmingham, AL	(12.5)
16	Lawton, OK	100.0	91	Indio, CA	13.6	165	Boston, MA	(12.6)
16	Westminster, CA	100.0	92	Miami, FL	13.6	166	Carson, CA	(12.8)
19	Tempe, AZ	94.1	93	Modesto, CA	12.6	167	Fort Collins, CO	(13.3)
20	Sterling Heights, MI	93.8	94	Palmdale, CA	11.4	168	Fort Wayne, IN	(14.0)
21	Torrance, CA	92.9	95	Oakland, CA	11.2	169	Hoover, AL	(14.3)
22	Cranston, RI	92.3	96	Macon, GA	10.2	170	Pomona, CA	(14.5)
22	Napa, CA	92.3	97	Inglewood, CA	9.6	171	North Charleston, SC	(14.6)
24	Citrus Heights, CA	91.7	98	Little Rock, AR	8.0	172	New Orleans, LA	(16.4)
24	San Marcos, CA	91.7	99	Grand Rapids, MI	7.7	173	Tampa, FL	(17.5)
26	Hesperia, CA	91.2	100	Peoria, AZ	7.5	174	Durham, NC	(17.6)
27	Downey, CA	89.3	101	Elizabeth, NJ	6.7	175	Louisville, KY	(17.7)
28	Montgomery, AL	86.7	102	Killeen, TX	5.8	176	Indianapolis, IN	(17.7)
29	Overland Park, KS	83.3	103	Vallejo, CA	5.3	177	Hayward, CA	(18.0)
30	El Cajon, CA	81.8	104	Greenville, NC	5.2	178	Fort Worth, TX	(18.6)
31	Gainesville, FL	80.8	105	Orem, UT	4.8	179	San Diego, CA	(18.6)
32	Irvine, CA	80.0	106	Albuquerque, NM	2.8	180	Kennewick, WA	(18.8)
33	Norwalk, CA	77.6	106	Chicago, IL	2.8	181	Bellflower, CA	(18.9)
34	San Leandro, CA	76.9	108	Bridgeport, CT	2.7	182	Riverside, CA	(19.0)
35	Hawthorne, CA	74.5	109	Lafayette, LA	2.3	183	Savannah, GA	(19.5)
36	Pasadena, CA	71.4	110	Minneapolis, MN	2.0	184	Tulsa, OK	(19.8)
37	Springfield, MO	70.7	111	Beaverton, OR	0.0	185	Fayetteville, NC	(20.1)
38	Rio Rancho, NM	69.2	111	Boise, ID	0.0	186	Nashville, TN	(20.6)
39	Beaumont, TX	68.8	111	Boulder, CO	0.0	187	Merced, CA	(20.7)
40	Oceanside, CA	62.1	111	Brick Twnshp, NJ	0.0	188	Greensboro, NC	(20.8)
41	Detroit, MI	61.5	111	Burbank, CA	0.0	189	Long Beach, CA	(20.9)
42	Evansville, IN	58.1	111	Carmel, IN	0.0	190	Phoenix, AZ	(21.0)
43	Fairfield, CA	56.3	111	Centennial, CO	0.0	191	Glendale, AZ	(21.2)
44	Aurora, CO	50.9	111	Fishers, IN	0.0	192	Fort Lauderdale, FL	(21.7)
45	Naperville, IL	50.0	111	Mission Viejo, CA	0.0	193	Salinas, CA	(21.8)
46	Clarksville, TN	49.0	111	Murrieta, CA	0.0	194	Los Angeles, CA	(22.0)
47	Clovis, CA	47.6	111	Newton, MA	0.0	195	Tacoma, WA	(22.4)
48	Akron, OH	47.6	111	Provo, UT	0.0	196	Jacksonville, FL	(22.4)
49	Billings, MT	47.4	111	Redding, CA	0.0	197	Charleston, SC	(22.4)
50	Virginia Beach, VA	46.9	111	Roswell, GA	0.0	198	Portsmouth, VA	(22.4)
51	Norwalk, CT	45.8	111	Round Rock, TX	0.0	199	Corpus Christi, TX	(22.7)
52	Victorville, CA	45.7	111	Sugar Land, TX	0.0	200	Seattle, WA	(22.9)
53	Newark, NJ	43.9	111	Sunrise, FL	0.0	201	Roanoke, VA	(23.3)
54	Topeka, KS	41.5	111	Troy, MI	0.0	202	Miami Beach, FL	(23.6)
55	Sunnyvale, CA	40.0	129	Jackson, MS	(0.8)	203	Springfield, MA	(23.7)
56	San Jose, CA	39.4	130	Memphis, TN	(1.5)	204	Houston, TX	(23.7)
57	Anchorage, AK	38.9	131	Chesapeake, VA	(1.9)	205	Mobile, AL	(24.0)
58	Oklahoma City, OK	38.8	132	Omaha, NE	(3.0)	206	St. Louis, MO	(24.3)
59	Tallahassee, FL	38.3	133	Baton Rouge, LA	(3.4)	207	Henderson, NV	(25.0)
60	Providence, RI	37.1	134	Atlanta, GA	(3.6)	207	Melbourne, FL	(25.0)
61	San Bernardino, CA	36.9	135	Cedar Rapids, IA	(4.2)	209	Salem, OR	(25.4)
62	Reading, PA	36.3	135	Duluth, MN	(4.2)	210	San Antonio, TX	(25.6)
63	Anaheim, CA	33.3	135	Plantation, FL	(4.2)	211	Palm Bay, FL	(25.6)
64	North Las Vegas, NV	31.3	138	Waterbury, CT	(4.3)	212	Amarillo, TX	(26.1)
65	Richmond, VA	30.3	139	Stamford, CT	(4.8)	212	Brownsville, TX	(26.1)
66	Worcester, MA	29.4	140	Carlsbad, CA	(5.0)	214	Hartford, CT	(26.1)
67	Milwaukee, WI	28.8	141	Elgin, IL	(5.3)	215	Arlington, TX	(26.2)
68	Lubbock, TX	27.8	141	Westminster, CO	(5.3)	216	Lancaster, CA	(26.5)
69	Port St. Lucie, FL	26.3	143	Baltimore, MD	(5.4)	217	Laredo, TX	(26.7)
70	Bakersfield, CA	24.7	144	Spokane, WA	(6.2)	218	Longview, TX	(26.7)
71	Yakima, WA	22.9	145	Huntington Beach, CA	(6.3)	219	St. Petersburg, FL	(26.8)
72	South Bend, IN	22.8	146	Philadelphia, PA	(6.5)	220	Huntsville, AL	(26.9)
73	Newport News, VA	22.2	147	Dallas, TX	(6.8)	221	Simi Valley, CA	(27.3)
73	Paterson, NJ	22.2	148	Fayetteville, AR	(7.1)	222	Compton, CA	(27.7)

RANK	CITY	% CHANGE	RANK	CITY	% CHANGE	RANK	CITY	% CHANGE
223	Wichita, KS	(27.7)	297	Hammond, IN	(56.5)	335	Somerville, MA	(100.0)
224	Cincinnati, OH	(29.2)	298	High Point, NC	(56.5)	335	St. George, UT	(100.0)
225	Dayton, OH	(29.6)	299	Reno, NV	(56.5)	335	Temecula, CA	(100.0)
226	Portland, OR	(29.8)	300	Hemet, CA	(57.1)	335	Thousand Oaks, CA	(100.0)
227	Lynchburg, VA	(30.4)	301	Jersey City, NJ	(57.3)	335	Tustin, CA	(100.0)
228	Pasadena, TX	(30.7)	302	Racine, WI	(58.2)	335	Upland, CA	(100.0)
229	St. Paul, MN	(30.8)	303	Abilene, TX	(58.3)	335	Warren, MI	(100.0)
230	Lincoln, NE	(31.3)	304	Sioux Falls, SD	(59.4)	335	Whittier, CA	(100.0)
231	San Francisco, CA	(31.7)	305	Upper Darby Twnshp, PA	(59.6)	335	Woodbridge Twnshp, NJ	(100.0)
232	West Covina, CA	(32.1)	306	Fontana, CA	(60.3)	NA	Albany, GA**	NA
233	Sacramento, CA	(32.4)	307	Sioux City, IA	(60.7)	NA	Albany, NY**	NA
234	Colorado Springs, CO	(33.3)	308	Santa Ana, CA	(62.5)	NA	Allentown, PA**	NA
234	Fall River, MA	(33.3)	309	Irving, TX	(62.9)	NA	Amherst, NY**	NA
234	Kent, WA	(33.3)	310	Hollywood, FL	(63.0)	NA	Ann Arbor, MI***	NA
234	Odessa, TX	(33.3)	311	El Monte, CA	(64.3)	NA	Arlington Heights, IL**	NA
238	Tucson, AZ	(34.1)	312	Miramar, FL	(64.4)	NA	Bellevue, WA***	NA
239	O'Fallon, MO	(34.2)	313	Tuscaloosa, AL	(64.8)	NA	Bethlehem, PA***	NA
240	Davenport, IA	(34.4)	314	Rialto, CA	(64.9)	NA	Bloomington, IL**	NA
241	Garland, TX	(34.8)	315	Federal Way, WA	(64.9)	NA	Brockton, MA**	NA
242	Knoxville, TN	(34.9)	316	Garden Grove, CA	(66.7)	NA	Buffalo, NY**	NA
243	Salt Lake City, UT	(36.4)	316	St. Joseph, MO	(66.7)	NA	Champaign, IL**	NA
244	Richmond, CA	(36.5)	318	Lynn, MA	(67.2)	NA	Chandler, AZ**	NA
245	Avondale, AZ	(36.9)	319	Kenosha, WI	(67.7)	NA	Cheektowaga, NY**	NA
246	Gresham, OR	(37.3)	320	Largo, FL	(68.3)	NA	Cicero, IL**	NA
247	Shreveport, LA	(37.8)	321	Winston-Salem, NC	(69.0)	NA	Clarkstown, NY**	NA
248	Ontario, CA	(37.9)	322	Madison, WI	(69.8)	NA	Colonie, NY**	NA
249	Pembroke Pines, FL	(38.1)	323	Edinburg, TX	(71.4)	NA	Dearborn, MI***	NA
249	Scottsdale, AZ	(38.1)	324	Clearwater, FL	(74.3)	NA	Decatur, IL**	NA
251	Wilmington, NC	(38.7)	325	Baldwin Park, CA	(74.8)	NA	Deerfield Beach, FL***	NA
252	Mesquite, TX	(39.1)	326	Coral Springs, FL	(75.0)	NA	Denton, TX***	NA
253	Oxnard, CA	(40.0)	327	Bryan, TX	(76.4)	NA	Edmond, OK***	NA
254	Tyler, TX	(41.2)	328	Broken Arrow, OK	(76.7)	NA	Elk Grove, CA***	NA
255	Charlotte, NC	(41.3)	329	Corona, CA	(76.9)	NA	Fargo, ND***	NA
256	Cape Coral, FL	(41.9)	329	Santa Rosa, CA	(76.9)	NA	Farmington Hills, MI***	NA
257	Las Vegas, NV	(42.7)	331	Greeley, CO	(77.3)	NA	Gilbert, AZ***	NA
258	Pittsburgh, PA	(43.5)	332	Plano, TX	(84.6)	NA	Greece, NY**	NA
259	Des Moines, IA	(44.3)	333	Grand Prairie, TX	(86.0)	NA	Hillsboro, OR***	NA
260	Pompano Beach, FL	(44.3)	334	McAllen, TX	(89.9)	NA	Johns Creek, GA**	NA
261	Columbia, MO	(44.9)	335	Alexandria, VA	(100.0)	NA	Jurupa Valley, CA**	NA
262	Berkeley, CA	(45.6)	335	Alhambra, CA	(100.0)	NA	Kansas City, KS**	NA
263	Chino, CA	(45.8)	335	Allen, TX	(100.0)	NA	Lexington, KY**	NA
264	Columbus, GA	(46.0)	335	Arvada, CO	(100.0)	NA	Livonia, MI***	NA
265	Waco, TX	(47.2)	335	Aurora, IL	(100.0)	NA	Longmont, CO**	NA
266	Independence, MO	(47.6)	335	Bellingham, WA	(100.0)	NA	Medford, OR***	NA
267	Toms River Twnshp, NJ	(47.6)	335	Bloomington, MN	(100.0)	NA	Menifee, CA**	NA
268	Orlando, FL	(48.1)	335	Boca Raton, FL	(100.0)	NA	Nampa, ID***	NA
269	Mission, TX	(49.3)	335	Cary, NC	(100.0)	NA	Nashua, NH**	NA
270	Carrollton, TX	(50.0)	335	Chino Hills, CA	(100.0)	NA	New Haven, CT**	NA
270	Lakewood Twnshp, NJ	(50.0)	335	Clifton, NJ	(100.0)	NA	New Rochelle, NY**	NA
270	Manchester, NH	(50.0)	335	Clinton Twnshp, MI	(100.0)	NA	New York, NY**	NA
270	Ogden, UT	(50.0)	335	Concord, CA	(100.0)	NA	Newport Beach, CA***	NA
270	Santa Clarita, CA	(50.0)	335	Daly City, CA	(100.0)	NA	Olathe, KS**	NA
275	Moreno Valley, CA	(51.0)	335	Edison Twnshp, NJ	(100.0)	NA	Parma, OH**	NA
276	Buena Park, CA	(52.0)	335	Eugene, OR	(100.0)	NA	Peoria, IL**	NA
276	Lakewood, CA	(52.0)	335	Frisco, TX	(100.0)	NA	Pueblo, CO**	NA
276	Westland, MI	(52.0)	335	Fullerton, CA	(100.0)	NA	Ramapo, NY**	NA
279	Santa Monica, CA	(52.2)	335	Glendale, CA	(100.0)	NA	Renton, WA**	NA
280	New Bedford, MA	(52.3)	335	Hamilton Twnshp, NJ	(100.0)	NA	Rochester, NY**	NA
281	Visalia, CA	(52.4)	335	Lake Forest, CA	(100.0)	NA	Roseville, CA***	NA
282	Richardson, TX	(52.5)	335	Lawrence, KS	(100.0)	NA	Sandy Springs, GA***	NA
283	Norman, OK	(52.6)	335	League City, TX	(100.0)	NA	Sandy, UT***	NA
283	Ventura, CA	(52.6)	335	Lee's Summit, MO	(100.0)	NA	Sparks, NV***	NA
285	Rockford, IL	(53.5)	335	Livermore, CA	(100.0)	NA	Springfield, IL**	NA
286	Raleigh, NC	(54.0)	335	Lowell, MA	(100.0)	NA	Surprise, AZ***	NA
287	Chico, CA	(54.2)	335	McKinney, TX	(100.0)	NA	Syracuse, NY**	NA
288	Murfreesboro, TN	(54.2)	335	Meridian, ID	(100.0)	NA	Thornton, CO**	NA
289	Lawrence, MA	(54.4)	335	Mountain View, CA	(100.0)	NA	Tracy, CA***	NA
290	Cambridge, MA	(55.0)	335	Quincy, MA	(100.0)	NA	Vancouver, WA***	NA
290	Green Bay, WI	(55.0)	335	Redwood City, CA	(100.0)	NA	Warwick, RI***	NA
290	Rochester, MN	(55.0)	335	San Mateo, CA	(100.0)	NA	Waukegan, IL**	NA
293	Alameda, CA	(55.2)	335	Santa Barbara, CA	(100.0)	NA	West Jordan, UT***	NA
294	Hialeah, FL	(55.3)	335	Santa Clara, CA	(100.0)	NA	Yonkers, NY**	NA
295	Washington, DC	(55.7)	335	Santa Maria, CA	(100.0)			
296	West Valley, UT	(56.3)	335	Scranton, PA	(100.0)			

Source: CQ Press using reported data from the F.B.I. "Crime in the United States 2012"

*Includes nonnegligent manslaughter. **Not available. ***These cities had murder rates of 0 in 2008 but had at least one murder in 2012. Calculating percent increase from zero results in an infinite number. These are shown as "NA."

53. Rapes in 2012
National Total = 84,376 Rapes*

RANK	CITY	RAPES	RANK	CITY	RAPES	RANK	CITY	RAPES
208	Abilene, TX	38	432	Chino Hills, CA	2	98	Gainesville, FL	74
48	Akron, OH	167	388	Chino, CA	9	338	Garden Grove, CA	16
388	Alameda, CA	9	234	Chula Vista, CA	33	162	Garland, TX	47
267	Albany, GA	27	327	Cicero, IL	18	131	Gary, IN	56
181	Albany, NY	43	38	Cincinnati, OH	188	318	Gilbert, AZ	19
26	Albuquerque, NM	278	359	Citrus Heights, CA	13	141	Glendale, AZ	54
388	Alexandria, VA	9	421	Clarkstown, NY	4	412	Glendale, CA	6
432	Alhambra, CA	2	166	Clarksville, TN	46	154	Grand Prairie, TX	50
141	Allentown, PA	54	125	Clearwater, FL	59	166	Grand Rapids, MI	46
372	Allen, TX	11	17	Cleveland, OH	363	327	Greece, NY	18
69	Amarillo, TX	110	359	Clifton, NJ	13	196	Greeley, CO	40
405	Amherst, NY	7	208	Clinton Twnshp, MI	38	174	Green Bay, WI	44
88	Anaheim, CA	82	230	Clovis, CA	34	106	Greensboro, NC	70
24	Anchorage, AK	303	230	College Station, TX	34	295	Greenville, NC	23
229	Ann Arbor, MI	35	437	Colonie, NY	0	234	Gresham, OR	33
261	Antioch, CA	29	18	Colorado Springs, CO	358	383	Hamilton Twnshp, NJ	10
405	Arlington Heights, IL	7	191	Columbia, MO	41	327	Hammond, IN	18
55	Arlington, TX	135	247	Columbus, GA	31	338	Hampton, VA	16
305	Arvada, CO	22	234	Compton, CA	33	267	Hartford, CT	27
234	Asheville, NC	33	318	Concord, CA	19	275	Hawthorne, CA	26
156	Athens-Clarke, GA	48	383	Coral Springs, FL	10	166	Hayward, CA	46
65	Atlanta, GA	113	332	Corona, CA	17	309	Hemet, CA	21
44	Aurora, CO	179	40	Corpus Christi, TX	184	122	Henderson, NV	61
114	Aurora, IL	65	243	Costa Mesa, CA	32	332	Hesperia, CA	17
36	Austin, TX	209	338	Cranston, RI	16	196	Hialeah, FL	40
421	Avondale, AZ	4	8	Dallas, TX	486	318	High Point, NC	19
130	Bakersfield, CA	57	388	Daly City, CA	9	230	Hillsboro, OR	34
415	Baldwin Park, CA	5	295	Danbury, CT	23	208	Hollywood, FL	38
21	Baltimore, MD	315	196	Davenport, IA	40	359	Hoover, AL	13
116	Baton Rouge, LA	64	295	Davie, FL	23	4	Houston, TX	665
92	Beaumont, TX	76	67	Dayton, OH	112	247	Huntington Beach, CA	31
309	Beaverton, OR	21	287	Dearborn, MI	24	102	Huntsville, AL	72
275	Bellevue, WA	26	275	Decatur, IL	26	181	Independence, MO	43
372	Bellflower, CA	11	332	Deerfield Beach, FL	17	10	Indianapolis, IN	436
261	Bellingham, WA	29	85	Denton, TX	86	305	Indio, CA	22
204	Berkeley, CA	39	16	Denver, CO	376	267	Inglewood, CA	27
318	Bethlehem, PA	19	75	Des Moines, IA	100	396	Irvine, CA	8
208	Billings, MT	38	9	Detroit, MI	441	267	Irving, TX	27
49	Birmingham, AL	152	315	Downey, CA	20	19	Jacksonville, FL	341
188	Bloomington, IL	42	NA	Duluth, MN**	NA	55	Jackson, MS	135
327	Bloomington, IN	18	119	Durham, NC	63	171	Jersey City, NJ	45
NA	Bloomington, MN**	NA	261	Edinburg, TX	29	426	Johns Creek, GA	3
369	Boca Raton, FL	12	388	Edison Twnshp, NJ	9	257	Joliet, IL	30
95	Boise, ID	75	369	Edmond, OK	12	369	Jurupa Valley, CA	12
28	Boston, MA	249	287	El Cajon, CA	24	86	Kansas City, KS	85
243	Boulder, CO	32	353	El Monte, CA	14	29	Kansas City, MO	246
412	Brick Twnshp, NJ	6	40	El Paso, TX	184	234	Kennewick, WA	33
15	Bridgeport, CT	388	111	Elgin, IL	67	223	Kenosha, WI	36
156	Brockton, MA	48	217	Elizabeth, NJ	37	110	Kent, WA	68
234	Broken Arrow, OK	33	315	Elk Grove, CA	20	88	Killeen, TX	82
NA	Brooklyn Park, MN**	NA	116	Erie, PA	64	60	Knoxville, TN	119
208	Brownsville, TX	38	208	Escondido, CA	38	372	Lafayette, LA	11
247	Bryan, TX	31	102	Eugene, OR	72	396	Lake Forest, CA	8
359	Buena Park, CA	13	131	Evansville, IN	56	234	Lakeland, FL	33
52	Buffalo, NY	138	166	Everett, WA	46	435	Lakewood Twnshp, NJ	1
287	Burbank, CA	24	257	Fairfield, CA	30	359	Lakewood, CA	13
315	Cambridge, MA	20	148	Fall River, MA	52	76	Lakewood, CO	94
98	Camden, NJ	74	108	Fargo, ND	69	141	Lancaster, CA	54
338	Cape Coral, FL	16	347	Farmington Hills, MI	15	80	Lansing, MI	92
275	Carlsbad, CA	26	127	Fayetteville, AR	58	90	Laredo, TX	81
432	Carmel, IN	2	106	Fayetteville, NC	70	181	Largo, FL	43
405	Carrollton, TX	7	181	Federal Way, WA	43	131	Las Cruces, NM	56
353	Carson, CA	14	435	Fishers, IN	1	5	Las Vegas, NV	596
372	Cary, NC	11	70	Flint, MI	108	148	Lawrence, KS	52
181	Cedar Rapids, IA	43	247	Fontana, CA	31	279	Lawrence, MA	25
196	Centennial, CO	40	174	Fort Collins, CO	44	208	Lawton, OK	38
153	Champaign, IL	51	156	Fort Lauderdale, FL	48	338	League City, TX	16
116	Chandler, AZ	64	108	Fort Smith, AR	69	359	Lee's Summit, MO	13
318	Charleston, SC	19	78	Fort Wayne, IN	93	74	Lexington, KY	102
35	Charlotte, NC	223	13	Fort Worth, TX	391	43	Lincoln, NE	182
318	Cheektowaga, NY	19	353	Fremont, CA	14	53	Little Rock, AR	137
223	Chesapeake, VA	36	141	Fresno, CA	54	347	Livermore, CA	15
NA	Chicago, IL**	NA	396	Frisco, TX	8	318	Livonia, MI	19
166	Chico, CA	46	247	Fullerton, CA	31	62	Long Beach, CA	115

RANK	CITY	RAPES	RANK	CITY	RAPES	RANK	CITY	RAPES
372	Longmont, CO	11	309	Pasadena, CA	21	347	South Gate, CA	15
265	Longview, TX	28	148	Pasadena, TX	52	243	Sparks, NV	32
2	Los Angeles, CA	936	305	Paterson, NJ	22	247	Spokane Valley, WA	31
42	Louisville, KY	183	327	Pearland, TX	18	90	Spokane, WA	81
217	Lowell, MA	37	353	Pembroke Pines, FL	14	92	Springfield, IL	76
72	Lubbock, TX	104	287	Peoria, AZ	24	204	Springfield, MA	39
230	Lynchburg, VA	34	279	Peoria, IL	25	50	Springfield, MO	141
156	Lynn, MA	48	3	Philadelphia, PA	880	279	Stamford, CT	25
191	Macon, GA	41	6	Phoenix, AZ	556	338	Sterling Heights, MI	16
64	Madison, WI	114	162	Pittsburgh, PA	47	83	Stockton, CA	90
102	Manchester, NH	72	135	Plano, TX	55	267	St. George, UT	27
426	McAllen, TX	3	372	Plantation, FL	11	305	St. Joseph, MO	22
141	McKinney, TX	54	119	Pomona, CA	63	37	St. Louis, MO	199
204	Medford, OR	39	217	Pompano Beach, FL	37	47	St. Paul, MN	168
156	Melbourne, FL	48	162	Port St. Lucie, FL	47	76	St. Petersburg, FL	94
11	Memphis, TN	420	32	Portland, OR	231	421	Sugar Land, TX	4
421	Menifee, CA	4	191	Portsmouth, VA	41	353	Sunnyvale, CA	14
279	Merced, CA	25	87	Providence, RI	84	318	Sunrise, FL	19
359	Meridian, ID	13	223	Provo, UT	36	396	Surprise, AZ	8
45	Mesa, AZ	172	309	Pueblo, CO	21	95	Syracuse, NY	75
353	Mesquite, TX	14	247	Quincy, MA	31	78	Tacoma, WA	93
188	Miami Beach, FL	42	247	Racine, WI	31	62	Tallahassee, FL	115
338	Miami Gardens, FL	16	65	Raleigh, NC	113	181	Tampa, FL	43
114	Miami, FL	65	415	Ramapo, NY	5	383	Temecula, CA	10
309	Midland, TX	21	338	Rancho Cucamon., CA	16	174	Tempe, AZ	44
33	Milwaukee, WI	230	174	Reading, PA	44	127	Thornton, CO	58
12	Minneapolis, MN	403	113	Redding, CA	66	295	Thousand Oaks, CA	23
247	Miramar, FL	31	359	Redwood City, CA	13	45	Toledo, OH	172
426	Mission Viejo, CA	3	234	Reno, NV	33	426	Toms River Twnshp, NJ	3
412	Mission, TX	6	267	Renton, WA	27	204	Topeka, KS	39
171	Mobile, AL	45	332	Rialto, CA	17	332	Torrance, CA	17
125	Modesto, CA	59	267	Richardson, TX	27	396	Tracy, CA	8
191	Montgomery, AL	41	223	Richmond, CA	36	295	Trenton, NJ	23
279	Moreno Valley, CA	25	208	Richmond, VA	38	388	Troy, MI	9
415	Mountain View, CA	5	295	Rio Rancho, NM	23	31	Tucson, AZ	234
135	Murfreesboro, TN	55	92	Riverside, CA	76	20	Tulsa, OK	316
396	Murrieta, CA	8	196	Roanoke, VA	40	217	Tuscaloosa, AL	37
174	Nampa, ID	44	NA	Rochester, MN**	NA	372	Tustin, CA	11
332	Napa, CA	17	67	Rochester, NY	112	171	Tyler, TX	45
405	Naperville, IL	7	58	Rockford, IL	124	396	Upland, CA	8
217	Nashua, NH	37	347	Roseville, CA	15	338	Upper Darby Twnshp, PA	16
22	Nashville, TN	311	405	Roswell, GA	7	287	Vacaville, CA	24
141	New Bedford, MA	54	243	Round Rock, TX	32	174	Vallejo, CA	44
135	New Haven, CT	55	57	Sacramento, CA	125	102	Vancouver, WA	72
54	New Orleans, LA	136	196	Salem, OR	40	287	Ventura, CA	24
426	New Rochelle, NY	3	191	Salinas, CA	41	196	Victorville, CA	40
1	New York, NY	1,162	59	Salt Lake City, UT	122	127	Virginia Beach, VA	58
135	Newark, NJ	55	7	San Antonio, TX	549	174	Visalia, CA	44
372	Newport Beach, CA	11	131	San Bernardino, CA	56	279	Vista, CA	25
154	Newport News, VA	50	23	San Diego, CA	304	119	Waco, TX	63
415	Newton, MA	5	70	San Francisco, CA	108	82	Warren, MI	91
95	Norfolk, VA	75	25	San Jose, CA	280	347	Warwick, RI	15
148	Norman, OK	52	347	San Leandro, CA	15	30	Washington, DC	236
122	North Charleston, SC	61	372	San Marcos, CA	11	405	Waterbury, CT	7
101	North Las Vegas, NV	73	359	San Mateo, CA	13	162	Waukegan, IL	47
359	Norwalk, CA	13	415	Sandy Springs, GA	5	372	West Covina, CA	11
388	Norwalk, CT	9	287	Sandy, UT	24	287	West Jordan, UT	24
27	Oakland, CA	271	135	Santa Ana, CA	55	247	West Palm Beach, FL	31
156	Oceanside, CA	48	147	Santa Barbara, CA	53	83	West Valley, UT	90
181	Odessa, TX	43	383	Santa Clara, CA	10	122	Westland, MI	61
415	O'Fallon, MO	5	257	Santa Clarita, CA	30	388	Westminster, CA	9
279	Ogden, UT	25	309	Santa Maria, CA	21	261	Westminster, CO	29
14	Oklahoma City, OK	389	295	Santa Monica, CA	23	383	Whittier, CA	10
208	Olathe, KS	38	111	Santa Rosa, CA	67	223	Wichita Falls, TX	36
39	Omaha, NE	187	279	Savannah, GA	25	34	Wichita, KS	228
223	Ontario, CA	36	188	Scottsdale, AZ	42	295	Wilmington, NC	23
396	Orange, CA	8	295	Scranton, PA	23	98	Winston-Salem, NC	74
372	Orem, UT	11	60	Seattle, WA	119	426	Woodbridge Twnshp, NJ	3
73	Orlando, FL	103	80	Shreveport, LA	92	234	Worcester, MA	33
196	Overland Park, KS	40	405	Simi Valley, CA	7	148	Yakima, WA	52
396	Oxnard, CA	8	257	Sioux City, IA	30	265	Yonkers, NY	28
318	Palm Bay, FL	19	51	Sioux Falls, SD	139	267	Yuma, AZ	27
217	Palmdale, CA	37	295	Somerville, MA	23			
421	Parma, OH	4	135	South Bend, IN	55			

Source: Reported data from the F.B.I. "Crime in the United States 2012"

*Forcible rape is the carnal knowledge of a female forcibly and against her will. Assaults or attempts to commit rape by force or threat of force are included. However, statutory rape without force and other sex offenses are excluded. **Not available

53. Rapes in 2012 (continued)
National Total = 84,376 Rapes*

RANK CITY	RAPES	RANK CITY	RAPES	RANK CITY	RAPES
1 New York, NY	1,162	75 Des Moines, IA	100	148 Lawrence, KS	52
2 Los Angeles, CA	936	76 Lakewood, CO	94	148 Norman, OK	52
3 Philadelphia, PA	880	76 St. Petersburg, FL	94	148 Pasadena, TX	52
4 Houston, TX	665	78 Fort Wayne, IN	93	148 Yakima, WA	52
5 Las Vegas, NV	596	78 Tacoma, WA	93	153 Champaign, IL	51
6 Phoenix, AZ	556	80 Lansing, MI	92	154 Grand Prairie, TX	50
7 San Antonio, TX	549	80 Shreveport, LA	92	154 Newport News, VA	50
8 Dallas, TX	486	82 Warren, MI	91	156 Athens-Clarke, GA	48
9 Detroit, MI	441	83 Stockton, CA	90	156 Brockton, MA	48
10 Indianapolis, IN	436	83 West Valley, UT	90	156 Fort Lauderdale, FL	48
11 Memphis, TN	420	85 Denton, TX	86	156 Lynn, MA	48
12 Minneapolis, MN	403	86 Kansas City, KS	85	156 Melbourne, FL	48
13 Fort Worth, TX	391	87 Providence, RI	84	156 Oceanside, CA	48
14 Oklahoma City, OK	389	88 Anaheim, CA	82	162 Garland, TX	47
15 Bridgeport, CT	388	88 Killeen, TX	82	162 Pittsburgh, PA	47
16 Denver, CO	376	90 Laredo, TX	81	162 Port St. Lucie, FL	47
17 Cleveland, OH	363	90 Spokane, WA	81	162 Waukegan, IL	47
18 Colorado Springs, CO	358	92 Beaumont, TX	76	166 Chico, CA	46
19 Jacksonville, FL	341	92 Riverside, CA	76	166 Clarksville, TN	46
20 Tulsa, OK	316	92 Springfield, IL	76	166 Everett, WA	46
21 Baltimore, MD	315	95 Boise, ID	75	166 Grand Rapids, MI	46
22 Nashville, TN	311	95 Norfolk, VA	75	166 Hayward, CA	46
23 San Diego, CA	304	95 Syracuse, NY	75	171 Jersey City, NJ	45
24 Anchorage, AK	303	98 Camden, NJ	74	171 Mobile, AL	45
25 San Jose, CA	280	98 Gainesville, FL	74	171 Tyler, TX	45
26 Albuquerque, NM	278	98 Winston-Salem, NC	74	174 Fort Collins, CO	44
27 Oakland, CA	271	101 North Las Vegas, NV	73	174 Green Bay, WI	44
28 Boston, MA	249	102 Eugene, OR	72	174 Nampa, ID	44
29 Kansas City, MO	246	102 Huntsville, AL	72	174 Reading, PA	44
30 Washington, DC	236	102 Manchester, NH	72	174 Tempe, AZ	44
31 Tucson, AZ	234	102 Vancouver, WA	72	174 Vallejo, CA	44
32 Portland, OR	231	106 Fayetteville, NC	70	174 Visalia, CA	44
33 Milwaukee, WI	230	106 Greensboro, NC	70	181 Albany, NY	43
34 Wichita, KS	228	108 Fargo, ND	69	181 Cedar Rapids, IA	43
35 Charlotte, NC	223	108 Fort Smith, AR	69	181 Federal Way, WA	43
36 Austin, TX	209	110 Kent, WA	68	181 Independence, MO	43
37 St. Louis, MO	199	111 Elgin, IL	67	181 Largo, FL	43
38 Cincinnati, OH	188	111 Santa Rosa, CA	67	181 Odessa, TX	43
39 Omaha, NE	187	113 Redding, CA	66	181 Tampa, FL	43
40 Corpus Christi, TX	184	114 Aurora, IL	65	188 Bloomington, IL	42
40 El Paso, TX	184	114 Miami, FL	65	188 Miami Beach, FL	42
42 Louisville, KY	183	116 Baton Rouge, LA	64	188 Scottsdale, AZ	42
43 Lincoln, NE	182	116 Chandler, AZ	64	191 Columbia, MO	41
44 Aurora, CO	179	116 Erie, PA	64	191 Macon, GA	41
45 Mesa, AZ	172	119 Durham, NC	63	191 Montgomery, AL	41
45 Toledo, OH	172	119 Pomona, CA	63	191 Portsmouth, VA	41
47 St. Paul, MN	168	119 Waco, TX	63	191 Salinas, CA	41
48 Akron, OH	167	122 Henderson, NV	61	196 Centennial, CO	40
49 Birmingham, AL	152	122 North Charleston, SC	61	196 Davenport, IA	40
50 Springfield, MO	141	122 Westland, MI	61	196 Greeley, CO	40
51 Sioux Falls, SD	139	125 Clearwater, FL	59	196 Hialeah, FL	40
52 Buffalo, NY	138	125 Modesto, CA	59	196 Overland Park, KS	40
53 Little Rock, AR	137	127 Fayetteville, AR	58	196 Roanoke, VA	40
54 New Orleans, LA	136	127 Thornton, CO	58	196 Salem, OR	40
55 Arlington, TX	135	127 Virginia Beach, VA	58	196 Victorville, CA	40
55 Jackson, MS	135	130 Bakersfield, CA	57	204 Berkeley, CA	39
57 Sacramento, CA	125	131 Evansville, IN	56	204 Medford, OR	39
58 Rockford, IL	124	131 Gary, IN	56	204 Springfield, MA	39
59 Salt Lake City, UT	122	131 Las Cruces, NM	56	204 Topeka, KS	39
60 Knoxville, TN	119	131 San Bernardino, CA	56	208 Abilene, TX	38
60 Seattle, WA	119	135 Murfreesboro, TN	55	208 Billings, MT	38
62 Long Beach, CA	115	135 New Haven, CT	55	208 Brownsville, TX	38
62 Tallahassee, FL	115	135 Newark, NJ	55	208 Clinton Twnshp, MI	38
64 Madison, WI	114	135 Plano, TX	55	208 Escondido, CA	38
65 Atlanta, GA	113	135 Santa Ana, CA	55	208 Hollywood, FL	38
65 Raleigh, NC	113	135 South Bend, IN	55	208 Lawton, OK	38
67 Dayton, OH	112	141 Allentown, PA	54	208 Olathe, KS	38
67 Rochester, NY	112	141 Fresno, CA	54	208 Richmond, VA	38
69 Amarillo, TX	110	141 Glendale, AZ	54	217 Elizabeth, NJ	37
70 Flint, MI	108	141 Lancaster, CA	54	217 Lowell, MA	37
70 San Francisco, CA	108	141 McKinney, TX	54	217 Nashua, NH	37
72 Lubbock, TX	104	141 New Bedford, MA	54	217 Palmdale, CA	37
73 Orlando, FL	103	147 Santa Barbara, CA	53	217 Pompano Beach, FL	37
74 Lexington, KY	102	148 Fall River, MA	52	217 Tuscaloosa, AL	37

RANK	CITY	RAPES	RANK	CITY	RAPES	RANK	CITY	RAPES
223	Chesapeake, VA	36	295	Greenville, NC	23	369	Jurupa Valley, CA	12
223	Kenosha, WI	36	295	Rio Rancho, NM	23	372	Allen, TX	11
223	Ontario, CA	36	295	Santa Monica, CA	23	372	Bellflower, CA	11
223	Provo, UT	36	295	Scranton, PA	23	372	Cary, NC	11
223	Richmond, CA	36	295	Somerville, MA	23	372	Lafayette, LA	11
223	Wichita Falls, TX	36	295	Thousand Oaks, CA	23	372	Longmont, CO	11
229	Ann Arbor, MI	35	295	Trenton, NJ	23	372	Newport Beach, CA	11
230	Clovis, CA	34	295	Wilmington, NC	23	372	Orem, UT	11
230	College Station, TX	34	305	Arvada, CO	22	372	Plantation, FL	11
230	Hillsboro, OR	34	305	Indio, CA	22	372	San Marcos, CA	11
230	Lynchburg, VA	34	305	Paterson, NJ	22	372	Tustin, CA	11
234	Asheville, NC	33	305	St. Joseph, MO	22	372	West Covina, CA	11
234	Broken Arrow, OK	33	309	Beaverton, OR	21	383	Coral Springs, FL	10
234	Chula Vista, CA	33	309	Hemet, CA	21	383	Hamilton Twnshp, NJ	10
234	Compton, CA	33	309	Midland, TX	21	383	Santa Clara, CA	10
234	Gresham, OR	33	309	Pasadena, CA	21	383	Temecula, CA	10
234	Kennewick, WA	33	309	Pueblo, CO	21	383	Whittier, CA	10
234	Lakeland, FL	33	309	Santa Maria, CA	21	388	Alameda, CA	9
234	Reno, NV	33	315	Cambridge, MA	20	388	Alexandria, VA	9
234	Worcester, MA	33	315	Downey, CA	20	388	Chino, CA	9
243	Boulder, CO	32	315	Elk Grove, CA	20	388	Daly City, CA	9
243	Costa Mesa, CA	32	318	Bethlehem, PA	19	388	Edison Twnshp, NJ	9
243	Round Rock, TX	32	318	Charleston, SC	19	388	Norwalk, CT	9
243	Sparks, NV	32	318	Cheektowaga, NY	19	388	Troy, MI	9
247	Bryan, TX	31	318	Concord, CA	19	388	Westminster, CA	9
247	Columbus, GA	31	318	Gilbert, AZ	19	396	Frisco, TX	8
247	Fontana, CA	31	318	High Point, NC	19	396	Irvine, CA	8
247	Fullerton, CA	31	318	Livonia, MI	19	396	Lake Forest, CA	8
247	Huntington Beach, CA	31	318	Palm Bay, FL	19	396	Murrieta, CA	8
247	Miramar, FL	31	318	Sunrise, FL	19	396	Orange, CA	8
247	Quincy, MA	31	327	Bloomington, IN	18	396	Oxnard, CA	8
247	Racine, WI	31	327	Cicero, IL	18	396	Surprise, AZ	8
247	Spokane Valley, WA	31	327	Greece, NY	18	396	Tracy, CA	8
247	West Palm Beach, FL	31	327	Hammond, IN	18	396	Upland, CA	8
257	Fairfield, CA	30	327	Pearland, TX	18	405	Amherst, NY	7
257	Joliet, IL	30	332	Corona, CA	17	405	Arlington Heights, IL	7
257	Santa Clarita, CA	30	332	Deerfield Beach, FL	17	405	Carrollton, TX	7
257	Sioux City, IA	30	332	Hesperia, CA	17	405	Naperville, IL	7
261	Antioch, CA	29	332	Napa, CA	17	405	Roswell, GA	7
261	Bellingham, WA	29	332	Rialto, CA	17	405	Simi Valley, CA	7
261	Edinburg, TX	29	332	Torrance, CA	17	405	Waterbury, CT	7
261	Westminster, CO	29	338	Cape Coral, FL	16	412	Brick Twnshp, NJ	6
265	Longview, TX	28	338	Cranston, RI	16	412	Glendale, CA	6
265	Yonkers, NY	28	338	Garden Grove, CA	16	412	Mission, TX	6
267	Albany, GA	27	338	Hampton, VA	16	415	Baldwin Park, CA	5
267	Hartford, CT	27	338	League City, TX	16	415	Mountain View, CA	5
267	Inglewood, CA	27	338	Miami Gardens, FL	16	415	Newton, MA	5
267	Irving, TX	27	338	Rancho Cucamon., CA	16	415	O'Fallon, MO	5
267	Renton, WA	27	338	Sterling Heights, MI	16	415	Ramapo, NY	5
267	Richardson, TX	27	338	Upper Darby Twnshp, PA	16	415	Sandy Springs, GA	5
267	St. George, UT	27	347	Farmington Hills, MI	15	421	Avondale, AZ	4
267	Yuma, AZ	27	347	Livermore, CA	15	421	Clarkstown, NY	4
275	Bellevue, WA	26	347	Roseville, CA	15	421	Menifee, CA	4
275	Carlsbad, CA	26	347	San Leandro, CA	15	421	Parma, OH	4
275	Decatur, IL	26	347	South Gate, CA	15	421	Sugar Land, TX	4
275	Hawthorne, CA	26	347	Warwick, RI	15	426	Johns Creek, GA	3
279	Lawrence, MA	25	353	Carson, CA	14	426	McAllen, TX	3
279	Merced, CA	25	353	El Monte, CA	14	426	Mission Viejo, CA	3
279	Moreno Valley, CA	25	353	Fremont, CA	14	426	New Rochelle, NY	3
279	Ogden, UT	25	353	Mesquite, TX	14	426	Toms River Twnshp, NJ	3
279	Peoria, IL	25	353	Pembroke Pines, FL	14	426	Woodbridge Twnshp, NJ	3
279	Savannah, GA	25	353	Sunnyvale, CA	14	432	Alhambra, CA	2
279	Stamford, CT	25	359	Buena Park, CA	13	432	Carmel, IN	2
279	Vista, CA	25	359	Citrus Heights, CA	13	432	Chino Hills, CA	2
287	Burbank, CA	24	359	Clifton, NJ	13	435	Fishers, IN	1
287	Dearborn, MI	24	359	Hoover, AL	13	435	Lakewood Twnshp, NJ	1
287	El Cajon, CA	24	359	Lakewood, CA	13	437	Colonie, NY	0
287	Peoria, AZ	24	359	Lee's Summit, MO	13	NA	Bloomington, MN**	NA
287	Sandy, UT	24	359	Meridian, ID	13	NA	Brooklyn Park, MN**	NA
287	Vacaville, CA	24	359	Norwalk, CA	13	NA	Chicago, IL**	NA
287	Ventura, CA	24	359	Redwood City, CA	13	NA	Duluth, MN**	NA
287	West Jordan, UT	24	359	San Mateo, CA	13	NA	Rochester, MN**	NA
295	Danbury, CT	23	369	Boca Raton, FL	12			
295	Davie, FL	23	369	Edmond, OK	12			

Source: Reported data from the F.B.I. "Crime in the United States 2012"

*Forcible rape is the carnal knowledge of a female forcibly and against her will. Assaults or attempts to commit rape by force or threat of force are included. However, statutory rape without force and other sex offenses are excluded. **Not available

54. Rape Rate in 2012
National Rate = 26.9 Rapes per 100,000 Population*

RANK	CITY	RATE	RANK	CITY	RATE	RANK	CITY	RATE
184	Abilene, TX	31.7	431	Chino Hills, CA	2.6	52	Gainesville, FL	58.3
9	Akron, OH	84.2	371	Chino, CA	11.3	389	Garden Grove, CA	9.1
367	Alameda, CA	11.9	348	Chula Vista, CA	13.2	287	Garland, TX	20.0
160	Albany, GA	34.4	277	Cicero, IL	21.4	23	Gary, IN	69.6
103	Albany, NY	43.8	34	Cincinnati, OH	63.5	391	Gilbert, AZ	8.9
81	Albuquerque, NM	50.2	331	Citrus Heights, CA	15.3	261	Glendale, AZ	23.2
408	Alexandria, VA	6.2	418	Clarkstown, NY	5.0	428	Glendale, CA	3.1
432	Alhambra, CA	2.4	174	Clarksville, TN	33.5	219	Grand Prairie, TX	27.5
97	Allentown, PA	45.3	66	Clearwater, FL	54.0	252	Grand Rapids, MI	24.2
357	Allen, TX	12.4	6	Cleveland, OH	92.2	299	Greece, NY	18.6
60	Amarillo, TX	56.0	329	Clifton, NJ	15.4	113	Greeley, CO	41.5
410	Amherst, NY	6.0	125	Clinton Twnshp, MI	39.2	113	Green Bay, WI	41.5
258	Anaheim, CA	23.8	157	Clovis, CA	34.8	242	Greensboro, NC	25.4
4	Anchorage, AK	101.3	155	College Station, TX	35.2	227	Greenville, NC	26.5
192	Ann Arbor, MI	30.4	437	Colonie, NY	0.0	190	Gresham, OR	30.5
216	Antioch, CA	27.6	10	Colorado Springs, CO	82.8	372	Hamilton Twnshp, NJ	11.2
388	Arlington Heights, IL	9.3	143	Columbia, MO	37.1	269	Hammond, IN	22.2
152	Arlington, TX	35.6	323	Columbus, GA	15.8	368	Hampton, VA	11.6
283	Arvada, CO	20.2	170	Compton, CA	33.7	275	Hartford, CT	21.6
131	Asheville, NC	38.7	333	Concord, CA	15.2	193	Hawthorne, CA	30.3
116	Athens-Clarke, GA	40.9	396	Coral Springs, FL	8.0	186	Hayward, CA	31.2
237	Atlanta, GA	25.9	374	Corona, CA	10.8	237	Hemet, CA	25.9
67	Aurora, CO	53.1	51	Corpus Christi, TX	58.9	261	Henderson, NV	23.2
181	Aurora, IL	32.5	207	Costa Mesa, CA	28.4	301	Hesperia, CA	18.4
247	Austin, TX	25.1	288	Cranston, RI	19.9	314	Hialeah, FL	17.2
416	Avondale, AZ	5.1	129	Dallas, TX	39.1	310	High Point, NC	17.8
320	Bakersfield, CA	16.0	394	Daly City, CA	8.7	146	Hillsboro, OR	36.1
404	Baldwin Park, CA	6.5	210	Danbury, CT	28.1	232	Hollywood, FL	26.2
79	Baltimore, MD	50.4	122	Davenport, IA	39.5	323	Hoover, AL	15.8
216	Baton Rouge, LA	27.6	252	Davie, FL	24.2	190	Houston, TX	30.5
36	Beaumont, TX	63.2	15	Dayton, OH	78.8	322	Huntington Beach, CA	15.9
263	Beaverton, OR	22.8	248	Dearborn, MI	24.7	125	Huntsville, AL	39.2
282	Bellevue, WA	20.6	161	Decatur, IL	34.2	144	Independence, MO	36.6
344	Bellflower, CA	14.1	271	Deerfield Beach, FL	22.0	75	Indianapolis, IN	52.0
156	Bellingham, WA	35.1	20	Denton, TX	72.3	212	Indio, CA	28.0
166	Berkeley, CA	33.9	48	Denver, CO	59.8	252	Inglewood, CA	24.2
244	Bethlehem, PA	25.2	86	Des Moines, IA	48.2	425	Irvine, CA	3.7
151	Billings, MT	35.7	40	Detroit, MI	62.4	363	Irving, TX	12.1
21	Birmingham, AL	71.3	312	Downey, CA	17.6	118	Jacksonville, FL	40.6
64	Bloomington, IL	54.5	NA	Duluth, MN**	NA	17	Jackson, MS	76.7
271	Bloomington, IN	22.0	225	Durham, NC	26.7	308	Jersey City, NJ	17.9
NA	Bloomington, MN**	NA	146	Edinburg, TX	36.1	425	Johns Creek, GA	3.7
347	Boca Raton, FL	13.9	391	Edison Twnshp, NJ	8.9	283	Joliet, IL	20.2
154	Boise, ID	35.4	339	Edmond, OK	14.4	359	Jurupa Valley, CA	12.3
122	Boston, MA	39.5	260	El Cajon, CA	23.6	56	Kansas City, KS	57.7
183	Boulder, CO	31.9	363	El Monte, CA	12.1	68	Kansas City, MO	53.0
397	Brick Twnshp, NJ	7.9	222	El Paso, TX	27.2	107	Kennewick, WA	42.9
1	Bridgeport, CT	265.7	45	Elgin, IL	61.4	148	Kenosha, WI	36.0
79	Brockton, MA	50.4	203	Elizabeth, NJ	29.3	61	Kent, WA	55.7
180	Broken Arrow, OK	32.8	352	Elk Grove, CA	12.8	43	Killeen, TX	62.1
NA	Brooklyn Park, MN**	NA	37	Erie, PA	62.8	29	Knoxville, TN	65.3
279	Brownsville, TX	21.0	239	Escondido, CA	25.8	390	Lafayette, LA	9.0
122	Bryan, TX	39.5	94	Eugene, OR	45.6	380	Lake Forest, CA	10.1
323	Buena Park, CA	15.8	88	Evansville, IN	47.4	177	Lakeland, FL	33.0
72	Buffalo, NY	52.6	105	Everett, WA	43.7	436	Lakewood Twnshp, NJ	1.1
263	Burbank, CA	22.8	212	Fairfield, CA	28.0	320	Lakewood, CA	16.0
297	Cambridge, MA	18.7	54	Fall River, MA	57.9	32	Lakewood, CO	64.2
5	Camden, NJ	95.3	37	Fargo, ND	62.8	166	Lancaster, CA	33.9
381	Cape Coral, FL	10.0	297	Farmington Hills, MI	18.7	12	Lansing, MI	80.2
256	Carlsbad, CA	24.1	16	Fayetteville, AR	76.9	177	Laredo, TX	33.0
432	Carmel, IN	2.4	164	Fayetteville, NC	34.0	63	Largo, FL	54.6
414	Carrollton, TX	5.6	91	Federal Way, WA	46.8	59	Las Cruces, NM	56.1
337	Carson, CA	15.0	435	Fishers, IN	1.3	119	Las Vegas, NV	40.3
398	Cary, NC	7.8	2	Flint, MI	106.3	52	Lawrence, KS	58.3
174	Cedar Rapids, IA	33.5	329	Fontana, CA	15.4	182	Lawrence, MA	32.2
133	Centennial, CO	38.5	200	Fort Collins, CO	29.6	133	Lawton, OK	38.5
39	Champaign, IL	62.7	210	Fort Lauderdale, FL	28.1	299	League City, TX	18.6
231	Chandler, AZ	26.4	14	Fort Smith, AR	78.9	342	Lee's Summit, MO	14.2
331	Charleston, SC	15.3	145	Fort Wayne, IN	36.2	170	Lexington, KY	33.7
216	Charlotte, NC	27.6	78	Fort Worth, TX	50.8	24	Lincoln, NE	68.9
257	Cheektowaga, NY	24.0	406	Fremont, CA	6.4	22	Little Rock, AR	69.9
323	Chesapeake, VA	15.8	376	Fresno, CA	10.7	306	Livermore, CA	18.1
NA	Chicago, IL**	NA	404	Frisco, TX	6.5	289	Livonia, MI	19.8
69	Chico, CA	52.8	267	Fullerton, CA	22.4	250	Long Beach, CA	24.5

RANK	CITY	RATE	RANK	CITY	RATE	RANK	CITY	RATE
357	Longmont, CO	12.4	335	Pasadena, CA	15.1	328	South Gate, CA	15.6
166	Longview, TX	33.9	173	Pasadena, TX	33.6	158	Sparks, NV	34.6
251	Los Angeles, CA	24.3	337	Paterson, NJ	15.0	164	Spokane Valley, WA	34.0
219	Louisville, KY	27.5	294	Pearland, TX	19.0	136	Spokane, WA	38.2
162	Lowell, MA	34.1	393	Pembroke Pines, FL	8.8	31	Springfield, IL	64.9
103	Lubbock, TX	43.8	333	Peoria, AZ	15.2	244	Springfield, MA	25.2
101	Lynchburg, VA	44.0	274	Peoria, IL	21.7	8	Springfield, MO	87.6
74	Lynn, MA	52.3	57	Philadelphia, PA	57.2	285	Stamford, CT	20.1
100	Macon, GA	44.2	140	Phoenix, AZ	37.4	359	Sterling Heights, MI	12.3
87	Madison, WI	48.0	335	Pittsburgh, PA	15.1	197	Stockton, CA	30.1
28	Manchester, NH	65.4	285	Plano, TX	20.1	152	St. George, UT	35.6
434	McAllen, TX	2.2	355	Plantation, FL	12.5	207	St. Joseph, MO	28.4
129	McKinney, TX	39.1	112	Pomona, CA	41.6	40	St. Louis, MO	62.4
77	Medford, OR	51.3	150	Pompano Beach, FL	35.9	55	St. Paul, MN	57.8
42	Melbourne, FL	62.2	215	Port St. Lucie, FL	27.9	138	St. Petersburg, FL	37.9
33	Memphis, TN	63.9	132	Portland, OR	38.6	422	Sugar Land, TX	4.8
418	Menifee, CA	5.0	109	Portsmouth, VA	42.4	383	Sunnyvale, CA	9.7
187	Merced, CA	30.9	89	Providence, RI	47.2	273	Sunrise, FL	21.8
315	Meridian, ID	16.8	188	Provo, UT	30.8	402	Surprise, AZ	6.6
137	Mesa, AZ	38.1	292	Pueblo, CO	19.3	76	Syracuse, NY	51.4
383	Mesquite, TX	9.7	176	Quincy, MA	33.1	93	Tacoma, WA	45.9
92	Miami Beach, FL	46.1	125	Racine, WI	39.2	44	Tallahassee, FL	62.0
339	Miami Gardens, FL	14.4	224	Raleigh, NC	26.9	359	Tampa, FL	12.3
327	Miami, FL	15.7	411	Ramapo, NY	5.9	383	Temecula, CA	9.7
303	Midland, TX	18.2	386	Rancho Cucamon., CA	9.5	227	Tempe, AZ	26.5
135	Milwaukee, WI	38.4	83	Reading, PA	49.7	90	Thornton, CO	47.1
3	Minneapolis, MN	103.3	19	Redding, CA	72.5	310	Thousand Oaks, CA	17.8
249	Miramar, FL	24.6	318	Redwood City, CA	16.6	47	Toledo, OH	60.1
428	Mission Viejo, CA	3.1	341	Reno, NV	14.3	427	Toms River Twnshp, NJ	3.3
401	Mission, TX	7.4	204	Renton, WA	28.8	193	Topeka, KS	30.3
308	Mobile, AL	17.9	316	Rialto, CA	16.7	369	Torrance, CA	11.5
204	Modesto, CA	28.8	234	Richardson, TX	26.1	387	Tracy, CA	9.4
291	Montgomery, AL	19.6	169	Richmond, CA	33.8	223	Trenton, NJ	27.0
355	Moreno Valley, CA	12.5	302	Richmond, VA	18.3	373	Troy, MI	11.0
402	Mountain View, CA	6.6	240	Rio Rancho, NM	25.7	101	Tucson, AZ	44.0
84	Murfreesboro, TN	49.0	252	Riverside, CA	24.2	13	Tulsa, OK	79.2
400	Murrieta, CA	7.5	116	Roanoke, VA	40.9	120	Tuscaloosa, AL	40.2
69	Nampa, ID	52.8	NA	Rochester, MN**	NA	342	Tustin, CA	14.2
275	Napa, CA	21.6	69	Rochester, NY	52.8	98	Tyler, TX	45.0
420	Naperville, IL	4.9	11	Rockford, IL	81.4	377	Upland, CA	10.6
108	Nashua, NH	42.6	362	Roseville, CA	12.2	292	Upper Darby Twnshp, PA	19.3
82	Nashville, TN	50.1	399	Roswell, GA	7.6	241	Vacaville, CA	25.5
58	New Bedford, MA	56.2	197	Round Rock, TX	30.1	141	Vallejo, CA	37.3
110	New Haven, CT	42.3	232	Sacramento, CA	26.2	106	Vancouver, WA	43.3
139	New Orleans, LA	37.5	242	Salem, OR	25.4	270	Ventura, CA	22.1
424	New Rochelle, NY	3.8	35	Salt Lake City, UT	63.4	170	Victorville, CA	33.7
346	New York, NY	14.0	121	San Antonio, TX	39.8	351	Virginia Beach, VA	13.0
290	Newark, NJ	19.7	235	San Bernardino, CA	26.0	159	Visalia, CA	34.5
354	Newport Beach, CA	12.6	265	San Diego, CA	22.7	235	Vista, CA	26.0
219	Newport News, VA	27.5	348	San Francisco, CA	13.2	84	Waco, TX	49.0
412	Newton, MA	5.8	206	San Jose, CA	28.7	26	Warren, MI	67.7
189	Norfolk, VA	30.6	313	San Leandro, CA	17.3	303	Warwick, RI	18.2
94	Norman, OK	45.6	352	San Marcos, CA	12.8	141	Washington, DC	37.3
46	North Charleston, SC	60.6	350	San Mateo, CA	13.1	407	Waterbury, CT	6.3
179	North Las Vegas, NV	32.9	416	Sandy Springs, GA	5.1	73	Waukegan, IL	52.5
363	Norwalk, CA	12.1	227	Sandy, UT	26.5	379	West Covina, CA	10.2
378	Norwalk, CT	10.4	319	Santa Ana, CA	16.5	267	West Jordan, UT	22.4
25	Oakland, CA	67.8	49	Santa Barbara, CA	59.0	193	West Palm Beach, FL	30.3
212	Oceanside, CA	28.0	395	Santa Clara, CA	8.4	27	West Valley, UT	67.3
113	Odessa, TX	41.5	316	Santa Clarita, CA	16.7	18	Westland, MI	73.2
408	O'Fallon, MO	6.2	281	Santa Maria, CA	20.7	382	Westminster, CA	9.8
202	Ogden, UT	29.4	244	Santa Monica, CA	25.2	227	Westminster, CO	26.5
29	Oklahoma City, OK	65.3	125	Santa Rosa, CA	39.2	369	Whittier, CA	11.5
200	Olathe, KS	29.6	374	Savannah, GA	10.8	162	Wichita Falls, TX	34.1
99	Omaha, NE	44.7	296	Scottsdale, AZ	18.8	49	Wichita, KS	59.0
277	Ontario, CA	21.4	196	Scranton, PA	30.2	279	Wilmington, NC	21.0
413	Orange, CA	5.7	294	Seattle, WA	19.0	185	Winston-Salem, NC	31.5
366	Orem, UT	12.0	96	Shreveport, LA	45.5	430	Woodbridge Twnshp, NJ	3.0
111	Orlando, FL	41.8	415	Simi Valley, CA	5.5	307	Worcester, MA	18.0
266	Overland Park, KS	22.6	148	Sioux City, IA	36.0	61	Yakima, WA	55.7
423	Oxnard, CA	4.0	7	Sioux Falls, SD	87.8	344	Yonkers, NY	14.1
303	Palm Bay, FL	18.2	199	Somerville, MA	29.8	209	Yuma, AZ	28.3
258	Palmdale, CA	23.8	65	South Bend, IN	54.2			
420	Parma, OH	4.9						

Source: CQ Press using reported data from the F.B.I. "Crime in the United States 2012"

*Forcible rape is the carnal knowledge of a female forcibly and against her will. Assaults or attempts to commit rape by force or threat of force are included. However, statutory rape without force and other sex offenses are excluded. **Not available

54. Rape Rate in 2012 (continued)
National Rate = 26.9 Rapes per 100,000 Population*

RANK	CITY	RATE	RANK	CITY	RATE	RANK	CITY	RATE
1	Bridgeport, CT	265.7	75	Indianapolis, IN	52.0	148	Sioux City, IA	36.0
2	Flint, MI	106.3	76	Syracuse, NY	51.4	150	Pompano Beach, FL	35.9
3	Minneapolis, MN	103.3	77	Medford, OR	51.3	151	Billings, MT	35.7
4	Anchorage, AK	101.3	78	Fort Worth, TX	50.8	152	Arlington, TX	35.6
5	Camden, NJ	95.3	79	Baltimore, MD	50.4	152	St. George, UT	35.6
6	Cleveland, OH	92.2	79	Brockton, MA	50.4	154	Boise, ID	35.4
7	Sioux Falls, SD	87.8	81	Albuquerque, NM	50.2	155	College Station, TX	35.2
8	Springfield, MO	87.6	82	Nashville, TN	50.1	156	Bellingham, WA	35.1
9	Akron, OH	84.2	83	Reading, PA	49.7	157	Clovis, CA	34.8
10	Colorado Springs, CO	82.8	84	Murfreesboro, TN	49.0	158	Sparks, NV	34.6
11	Rockford, IL	81.4	84	Waco, TX	49.0	159	Visalia, CA	34.5
12	Lansing, MI	80.2	86	Des Moines, IA	48.2	160	Albany, GA	34.4
13	Tulsa, OK	79.2	87	Madison, WI	48.0	161	Decatur, IL	34.2
14	Fort Smith, AR	78.9	88	Evansville, IN	47.4	162	Lowell, MA	34.1
15	Dayton, OH	78.8	89	Providence, RI	47.2	162	Wichita Falls, TX	34.1
16	Fayetteville, AR	76.9	90	Thornton, CO	47.1	164	Fayetteville, NC	34.0
17	Jackson, MS	76.7	91	Federal Way, WA	46.8	164	Spokane Valley, WA	34.0
18	Westland, MI	73.2	92	Miami Beach, FL	46.1	166	Berkeley, CA	33.9
19	Redding, CA	72.5	93	Tacoma, WA	45.9	166	Lancaster, CA	33.9
20	Denton, TX	72.3	94	Eugene, OR	45.6	166	Longview, TX	33.9
21	Birmingham, AL	71.3	94	Norman, OK	45.6	169	Richmond, CA	33.8
22	Little Rock, AR	69.9	96	Shreveport, LA	45.5	170	Compton, CA	33.7
23	Gary, IN	69.6	97	Allentown, PA	45.3	170	Lexington, KY	33.7
24	Lincoln, NE	68.9	98	Tyler, TX	45.0	170	Victorville, CA	33.7
25	Oakland, CA	67.8	99	Omaha, NE	44.7	173	Pasadena, TX	33.6
26	Warren, MI	67.7	100	Macon, GA	44.2	174	Cedar Rapids, IA	33.5
27	West Valley, UT	67.3	101	Lynchburg, VA	44.0	174	Clarksville, TN	33.5
28	Manchester, NH	65.4	101	Tucson, AZ	44.0	176	Quincy, MA	33.1
29	Knoxville, TN	65.3	103	Albany, NY	43.8	177	Lakeland, FL	33.0
29	Oklahoma City, OK	65.3	103	Lubbock, TX	43.8	177	Laredo, TX	33.0
31	Springfield, IL	64.9	105	Everett, WA	43.7	179	North Las Vegas, NV	32.9
32	Lakewood, CO	64.2	106	Vancouver, WA	43.3	180	Broken Arrow, OK	32.8
33	Memphis, TN	63.9	107	Kennewick, WA	42.9	181	Aurora, IL	32.5
34	Cincinnati, OH	63.5	108	Nashua, NH	42.6	182	Lawrence, MA	32.2
35	Salt Lake City, UT	63.4	109	Portsmouth, VA	42.4	183	Boulder, CO	31.9
36	Beaumont, TX	63.2	110	New Haven, CT	42.3	184	Abilene, TX	31.7
37	Erie, PA	62.8	111	Orlando, FL	41.8	185	Winston-Salem, NC	31.5
37	Fargo, ND	62.8	112	Pomona, CA	41.6	186	Hayward, CA	31.2
39	Champaign, IL	62.7	113	Greeley, CO	41.5	187	Merced, CA	30.9
40	Detroit, MI	62.4	113	Green Bay, WI	41.5	188	Provo, UT	30.8
40	St. Louis, MO	62.4	113	Odessa, TX	41.5	189	Norfolk, VA	30.6
42	Melbourne, FL	62.2	116	Athens-Clarke, GA	40.9	190	Gresham, OR	30.5
43	Killeen, TX	62.1	116	Roanoke, VA	40.9	190	Houston, TX	30.5
44	Tallahassee, FL	62.0	118	Jacksonville, FL	40.6	192	Ann Arbor, MI	30.4
45	Elgin, IL	61.4	119	Las Vegas, NV	40.3	193	Hawthorne, CA	30.3
46	North Charleston, SC	60.6	120	Tuscaloosa, AL	40.2	193	Topeka, KS	30.3
47	Toledo, OH	60.1	121	San Antonio, TX	39.8	193	West Palm Beach, FL	30.3
48	Denver, CO	59.8	122	Boston, MA	39.5	196	Scranton, PA	30.2
49	Santa Barbara, CA	59.0	122	Bryan, TX	39.5	197	Round Rock, TX	30.1
49	Wichita, KS	59.0	122	Davenport, IA	39.5	197	Stockton, CA	30.1
51	Corpus Christi, TX	58.9	125	Clinton Twnshp, MI	39.2	199	Somerville, MA	29.8
52	Gainesville, FL	58.3	125	Huntsville, AL	39.2	200	Fort Collins, CO	29.6
52	Lawrence, KS	58.3	125	Racine, WI	39.2	200	Olathe, KS	29.6
54	Fall River, MA	57.9	125	Santa Rosa, CA	39.2	202	Ogden, UT	29.4
55	St. Paul, MN	57.8	129	Dallas, TX	39.1	203	Elizabeth, NJ	29.3
56	Kansas City, KS	57.7	129	McKinney, TX	39.1	204	Modesto, CA	28.8
57	Philadelphia, PA	57.2	131	Asheville, NC	38.7	204	Renton, WA	28.8
58	New Bedford, MA	56.2	132	Portland, OR	38.6	206	San Jose, CA	28.7
59	Las Cruces, NM	56.1	133	Centennial, CO	38.5	207	Costa Mesa, CA	28.4
60	Amarillo, TX	56.0	133	Lawton, OK	38.5	207	St. Joseph, MO	28.4
61	Kent, WA	55.7	135	Milwaukee, WI	38.4	209	Yuma, AZ	28.3
61	Yakima, WA	55.7	136	Spokane, WA	38.2	210	Danbury, CT	28.1
63	Largo, FL	54.6	137	Mesa, AZ	38.1	210	Fort Lauderdale, FL	28.1
64	Bloomington, IL	54.5	138	St. Petersburg, FL	37.9	212	Fairfield, CA	28.0
65	South Bend, IN	54.2	139	New Orleans, LA	37.5	212	Indio, CA	28.0
66	Clearwater, FL	54.0	140	Phoenix, AZ	37.4	212	Oceanside, CA	28.0
67	Aurora, CO	53.1	141	Vallejo, CA	37.3	215	Port St. Lucie, FL	27.9
68	Kansas City, MO	53.0	141	Washington, DC	37.3	216	Antioch, CA	27.6
69	Chico, CA	52.8	143	Columbia, MO	37.1	216	Baton Rouge, LA	27.6
69	Nampa, ID	52.8	144	Independence, MO	36.6	216	Charlotte, NC	27.6
69	Rochester, NY	52.8	145	Fort Wayne, IN	36.2	219	Grand Prairie, TX	27.5
72	Buffalo, NY	52.6	146	Edinburg, TX	36.1	219	Louisville, KY	27.5
73	Waukegan, IL	52.5	146	Hillsboro, OR	36.1	219	Newport News, VA	27.5
74	Lynn, MA	52.3	148	Kenosha, WI	36.0	222	El Paso, TX	27.2

RANK	CITY	RATE	RANK	CITY	RATE	RANK	CITY	RATE
223	Trenton, NJ	27.0	297	Cambridge, MA	18.7	371	Chino, CA	11.3
224	Raleigh, NC	26.9	297	Farmington Hills, MI	18.7	372	Hamilton Twnshp, NJ	11.2
225	Durham, NC	26.7	299	Greece, NY	18.6	373	Troy, MI	11.0
226	Salinas, CA	26.6	299	League City, TX	18.6	374	Corona, CA	10.8
227	Greenville, NC	26.5	301	Hesperia, CA	18.4	374	Savannah, GA	10.8
227	Sandy, UT	26.5	302	Richmond, VA	18.3	376	Fresno, CA	10.7
227	Tempe, AZ	26.5	303	Midland, TX	18.2	377	Upland, CA	10.6
227	Westminster, CO	26.5	303	Palm Bay, FL	18.2	378	Norwalk, CT	10.4
231	Chandler, AZ	26.4	303	Warwick, RI	18.2	379	West Covina, CA	10.2
232	Hollywood, FL	26.2	306	Livermore, CA	18.1	380	Lake Forest, CA	10.1
232	Sacramento, CA	26.2	307	Worcester, MA	18.0	381	Cape Coral, FL	10.0
234	Richardson, TX	26.1	308	Jersey City, NJ	17.9	382	Westminster, CA	9.8
235	San Bernardino, CA	26.0	308	Mobile, AL	17.9	383	Mesquite, TX	9.7
235	Vista, CA	26.0	310	High Point, NC	17.8	383	Sunnyvale, CA	9.7
237	Atlanta, GA	25.9	310	Thousand Oaks, CA	17.8	383	Temecula, CA	9.7
237	Hemet, CA	25.9	312	Downey, CA	17.6	386	Rancho Cucamon., CA	9.5
239	Escondido, CA	25.8	313	San Leandro, CA	17.3	387	Tracy, CA	9.4
240	Rio Rancho, NM	25.7	314	Hialeah, FL	17.2	388	Arlington Heights, IL	9.3
241	Vacaville, CA	25.5	315	Meridian, ID	16.8	389	Garden Grove, CA	9.1
242	Greensboro, NC	25.4	316	Rialto, CA	16.7	390	Lafayette, LA	9.0
242	Salem, OR	25.4	316	Santa Clarita, CA	16.7	391	Edison Twnshp, NJ	8.9
244	Bethlehem, PA	25.2	318	Redwood City, CA	16.6	391	Gilbert, AZ	8.9
244	Santa Monica, CA	25.2	319	Santa Ana, CA	16.5	393	Pembroke Pines, FL	8.8
244	Springfield, MA	25.2	320	Bakersfield, CA	16.0	394	Daly City, CA	8.7
247	Austin, TX	25.1	320	Lakewood, CA	16.0	395	Santa Clara, CA	8.4
248	Dearborn, MI	24.7	322	Huntington Beach, CA	15.9	396	Coral Springs, FL	8.0
249	Miramar, FL	24.6	323	Buena Park, CA	15.8	397	Brick Twnshp, NJ	7.9
250	Long Beach, CA	24.5	323	Chesapeake, VA	15.8	398	Cary, NC	7.8
251	Los Angeles, CA	24.3	323	Columbus, GA	15.8	399	Roswell, GA	7.6
252	Davie, FL	24.2	323	Hoover, AL	15.8	400	Murrieta, CA	7.5
252	Grand Rapids, MI	24.2	327	Miami, FL	15.7	401	Mission, TX	7.4
252	Inglewood, CA	24.2	328	South Gate, CA	15.6	402	Mountain View, CA	6.6
252	Riverside, CA	24.2	329	Clifton, NJ	15.4	402	Surprise, AZ	6.6
256	Carlsbad, CA	24.1	329	Fontana, CA	15.4	404	Baldwin Park, CA	6.5
257	Cheektowaga, NY	24.0	331	Charleston, SC	15.3	404	Frisco, TX	6.5
258	Anaheim, CA	23.8	331	Citrus Heights, CA	15.3	406	Fremont, CA	6.4
258	Palmdale, CA	23.8	333	Concord, CA	15.2	407	Waterbury, CT	6.3
260	El Cajon, CA	23.6	333	Peoria, AZ	15.2	408	Alexandria, VA	6.2
261	Glendale, AZ	23.2	335	Pasadena, CA	15.1	408	O'Fallon, MO	6.2
261	Henderson, NV	23.2	335	Pittsburgh, PA	15.1	410	Amherst, NY	6.0
263	Beaverton, OR	22.8	337	Carson, CA	15.0	411	Ramapo, NY	5.9
263	Burbank, CA	22.8	337	Paterson, NJ	15.0	412	Newton, MA	5.8
265	San Diego, CA	22.7	339	Edmond, OK	14.4	413	Orange, CA	5.7
266	Overland Park, KS	22.6	339	Miami Gardens, FL	14.4	414	Carrollton, TX	5.6
267	Fullerton, CA	22.4	341	Reno, NV	14.3	415	Simi Valley, CA	5.5
267	West Jordan, UT	22.4	342	Lee's Summit, MO	14.2	416	Avondale, AZ	5.1
269	Hammond, IN	22.2	342	Tustin, CA	14.2	416	Sandy Springs, GA	5.1
270	Ventura, CA	22.1	344	Bellflower, CA	14.1	418	Clarkstown, NY	5.0
271	Bloomington, IN	22.0	344	Yonkers, NY	14.1	418	Menifee, CA	5.0
271	Deerfield Beach, FL	22.0	346	New York, NY	14.0	420	Naperville, IL	4.9
273	Sunrise, FL	21.8	347	Boca Raton, FL	13.9	420	Parma, OH	4.9
274	Peoria, IL	21.7	348	Chula Vista, CA	13.2	422	Sugar Land, TX	4.8
275	Hartford, CT	21.6	348	San Francisco, CA	13.2	423	Oxnard, CA	4.0
275	Napa, CA	21.6	350	San Mateo, CA	13.1	424	New Rochelle, NY	3.8
277	Cicero, IL	21.4	351	Virginia Beach, VA	13.0	425	Irvine, CA	3.7
277	Ontario, CA	21.4	352	Elk Grove, CA	12.8	425	Johns Creek, GA	3.7
279	Brownsville, TX	21.0	352	San Marcos, CA	12.8	427	Toms River Twnshp, NJ	3.3
279	Wilmington, NC	21.0	354	Newport Beach, CA	12.6	428	Glendale, CA	3.1
281	Santa Maria, CA	20.7	355	Moreno Valley, CA	12.5	428	Mission Viejo, CA	3.1
282	Bellevue, WA	20.6	355	Plantation, FL	12.5	430	Woodbridge Twnshp, NJ	3.0
283	Arvada, CO	20.2	357	Allen, TX	12.4	431	Chino Hills, CA	2.6
283	Joliet, IL	20.2	357	Longmont, CO	12.4	432	Alhambra, CA	2.4
285	Plano, TX	20.1	359	Jurupa Valley, CA	12.3	432	Carmel, IN	2.4
285	Stamford, CT	20.1	359	Sterling Heights, MI	12.3	434	McAllen, TX	2.2
287	Garland, TX	20.0	359	Tampa, FL	12.3	435	Fishers, IN	1.3
288	Cranston, RI	19.9	362	Roseville, CA	12.2	436	Lakewood Twnshp, NJ	1.1
289	Livonia, MI	19.8	363	El Monte, CA	12.1	437	Colonie, NY	0.0
290	Newark, NJ	19.7	363	Irving, TX	12.1	NA	Bloomington, MN**	NA
291	Montgomery, AL	19.6	363	Norwalk, CA	12.1	NA	Brooklyn Park, MN**	NA
292	Pueblo, CO	19.3	366	Orem, UT	12.0	NA	Chicago, IL**	NA
292	Upper Darby Twnshp, PA	19.3	367	Alameda, CA	11.9	NA	Duluth, MN**	NA
294	Pearland, TX	19.0	368	Hampton, VA	11.6	NA	Rochester, MN**	NA
294	Seattle, WA	19.0	369	Torrance, CA	11.5			
296	Scottsdale, AZ	18.8	369	Whittier, CA	11.5			

Source: CQ Press using reported data from the F.B.I. "Crime in the United States 2012"

*Forcible rape is the carnal knowledge of a female forcibly and against her will. Assaults or attempts to commit rape by force or threat of force are included. However, statutory rape without force and other sex offenses are excluded. **Not available

55. Percent Change in Rape Rate: 2011 to 2012
National Percent Change = 0.5% Decrease*

RANK	CITY	% CHANGE	RANK	CITY	% CHANGE	RANK	CITY	% CHANGE
124	Abilene, TX	14.9	399	Chino Hills, CA	(50.9)	259	Gainesville, FL	(10.4)
186	Akron, OH	1.7	199	Chino, CA	(0.9)	290	Garden Grove, CA	(17.3)
385	Alameda, CA	(40.8)	227	Chula Vista, CA	(4.3)	283	Garland, TX	(15.6)
343	Albany, GA	(27.1)	333	Cicero, IL	(24.9)	109	Gary, IN	19.6
NA	Albany, NY**	NA	180	Cincinnati, OH	3.1	256	Gilbert, AZ	(10.1)
162	Albuquerque, NM	5.0	274	Citrus Heights, CA	(14.0)	105	Glendale, AZ	21.5
376	Alexandria, VA	(37.4)	NA	Clarkstown, NY**	NA	401	Glendale, CA	(56.9)
407	Alhambra, CA	(71.1)	338	Clarksville, TN	(26.4)	351	Grand Prairie, TX	(28.6)
NA	Allentown, PA**	NA	44	Clearwater, FL	47.5	389	Grand Rapids, MI	(43.9)
264	Allen, TX	(11.4)	175	Cleveland, OH	3.5	NA	Greece, NY**	NA
163	Amarillo, TX	4.9	78	Clifton, NJ	30.5	178	Greeley, CO	3.2
NA	Amherst, NY**	NA	26	Clinton Twnshp, MI	64.7	307	Green Bay, WI	(19.7)
323	Anaheim, CA	(23.0)	81	Clovis, CA	29.4	NA	Greensboro, NC**	NA
154	Anchorage, AK	6.3	144	College Station, TX	9.0	NA	Greenville, NC**	NA
224	Ann Arbor, MI	(3.8)	NA	Colonie, NY**	NA	159	Gresham, OR	5.2
65	Antioch, CA	36.0	140	Colorado Springs, CO	10.0	199	Hamilton Twnshp, NJ	(0.9)
55	Arlington Heights, IL	40.9	143	Columbia, MO	9.1	403	Hammond, IN	(59.9)
212	Arlington, TX	(2.2)	329	Columbus, GA	(24.0)	280	Hampton, VA	(15.3)
268	Arvada, CO	(12.6)	342	Compton, CA	(26.9)	399	Hartford, CT	(50.9)
43	Asheville, NC	48.3	204	Concord, CA	(1.3)	176	Hawthorne, CA	3.4
32	Athens-Clarke, GA	59.8	6	Coral Springs, FL	142.4	177	Hayward, CA	3.3
336	Atlanta, GA	(25.6)	24	Corona, CA	66.2	64	Hemet, CA	37.8
226	Aurora, CO	(4.0)	233	Corpus Christi, TX	(5.5)	171	Henderson, NV	4.0
136	Aurora, IL	11.3	159	Costa Mesa, CA	5.2	363	Hesperia, CA	(32.8)
224	Austin, TX	(3.8)	263	Cranston, RI	(11.2)	87	Hialeah, FL	26.5
371	Avondale, AZ	(34.6)	131	Dallas, TX	11.7	333	High Point, NC	(24.9)
49	Bakersfield, CA	44.1	375	Daly City, CA	(36.5)	47	Hillsboro, OR	45.6
390	Baldwin Park, CA	(44.9)	365	Danbury, CT	(33.1)	310	Hollywood, FL	(20.4)
240	Baltimore, MD	(7.4)	335	Davenport, IA	(25.3)	17	Hoover, AL	85.9
88	Baton Rouge, LA	25.5	72	Davie, FL	33.0	280	Houston, TX	(15.3)
119	Beaumont, TX	17.5	127	Dayton, OH	13.9	257	Huntington Beach, CA	(10.2)
204	Beaverton, OR	(1.3)	138	Dearborn, MI	10.3	61	Huntsville, AL	39.0
135	Bellevue, WA	11.4	16	Decatur, IL	86.9	230	Independence, MO	(4.7)
316	Bellflower, CA	(22.1)	344	Deerfield Beach, FL	(27.2)	196	Indianapolis, IN	(0.4)
293	Bellingham, WA	(17.6)	34	Denton, TX	57.9	258	Indio, CA	(10.3)
12	Berkeley, CA	103.0	245	Denver, CO	(7.9)	300	Inglewood, CA	(18.5)
133	Bethlehem, PA	11.5	228	Des Moines, IA	(4.4)	345	Irvine, CA	(27.5)
170	Billings, MT	4.1	169	Detroit, MI	4.2	149	Irving, TX	7.1
286	Birmingham, AL	(16.4)	271	Downey, CA	(13.3)	214	Jacksonville, FL	(3.1)
381	Bloomington, IL	(39.3)	NA	Duluth, MN**	NA	156	Jackson, MS	6.1
204	Bloomington, IN	(1.3)	222	Durham, NC	(3.6)	249	Jersey City, NJ	(9.1)
NA	Bloomington, MN**	NA	188	Edinburg, TX	1.4	232	Johns Creek, GA	(5.1)
396	Boca Raton, FL	(48.3)	203	Edison Twnshp, NJ	(1.1)	197	Joliet, IL	(0.5)
131	Boise, ID	11.7	23	Edmond, OK	69.4	NA	Jurupa Valley, CA**	NA
252	Boston, MA	(9.4)	277	El Cajon, CA	(15.1)	262	Kansas City, KS	(11.0)
253	Boulder, CO	(9.6)	402	El Monte, CA	(57.8)	241	Kansas City, MO	(7.7)
277	Brick Twnshp, NJ	(15.1)	288	El Paso, TX	(16.8)	111	Kennewick, WA	19.2
2	Bridgeport, CT	230.9	276	Elgin, IL	(14.6)	349	Kenosha, WI	(28.3)
315	Brockton, MA	(22.0)	218	Elizabeth, NJ	(3.3)	270	Kent, WA	(12.8)
41	Broken Arrow, OK	49.1	138	Elk Grove, CA	10.3	117	Killeen, TX	17.6
NA	Brooklyn Park, MN**	NA	287	Erie, PA	(16.7)	90	Knoxville, TN	25.3
188	Brownsville, TX	1.4	67	Escondido, CA	34.4	341	Lafayette, LA	(26.8)
58	Bryan, TX	39.6	241	Eugene, OR	(7.7)	1	Lake Forest, CA	676.9
30	Buena Park, CA	61.2	192	Evansville, IN	0.0	253	Lakeland, FL	(9.6)
NA	Buffalo, NY**	NA	237	Everett, WA	(6.6)	409	Lakewood Twnshp, NJ	(82.8)
57	Burbank, CA	39.9	52	Fairfield, CA	42.1	49	Lakewood, CA	44.1
293	Cambridge, MA	(17.6)	197	Fall River, MA	(0.5)	156	Lakewood, CO	6.1
130	Camden, NJ	12.1	31	Fargo, ND	60.6	84	Lancaster, CA	27.9
137	Cape Coral, FL	11.1	66	Farmington Hills, MI	35.5	185	Lansing, MI	1.8
7	Carlsbad, CA	134.0	107	Fayetteville, AR	21.3	165	Laredo, TX	4.8
408	Carmel, IN	(76.2)	97	Fayetteville, NC	23.2	68	Largo, FL	34.2
22	Carrollton, TX	69.7	NA	Federal Way, WA**	NA	3	Las Cruces, NM	226.2
149	Carson, CA	7.1	NA	Fishers, IN***	NA	253	Las Vegas, NV	(9.6)
297	Cary, NC	(17.9)	83	Flint, MI	28.1	35	Lawrence, KS	55.9
174	Cedar Rapids, IA	3.7	313	Fontana, CA	(21.8)	11	Lawrence, MA	106.4
46	Centennial, CO	45.8	318	Fort Collins, CO	(22.5)	366	Lawton, OK	(33.8)
248	Champaign, IL	(9.0)	395	Fort Lauderdale, FL	(48.2)	331	League City, TX	(24.4)
NA	Chandler, AZ**	NA	145	Fort Smith, AR	8.8	346	Lee's Summit, MO	(27.6)
378	Charleston, SC	(38.1)	211	Fort Wayne, IN	(1.9)	NA	Lexington, KY**	NA
192	Charlotte, NC	0.0	140	Fort Worth, TX	10.0	147	Lincoln, NE	8.2
NA	Cheektowaga, NY**	NA	404	Fremont, CA	(60.5)	282	Little Rock, AR	(15.4)
322	Chesapeake, VA	(22.9)	163	Fresno, CA	4.9	158	Livermore, CA	5.8
NA	Chicago, IL**	NA	79	Frisco, TX	30.0	191	Livonia, MI	1.0
91	Chico, CA	24.5	100	Fullerton, CA	22.4	181	Long Beach, CA	2.5

RANK	CITY	% CHANGE	RANK	CITY	% CHANGE	RANK	CITY	% CHANGE
382	Longmont, CO	(39.5)	304	Pasadena, CA	(19.3)	42	South Gate, CA	48.6
59	Longview, TX	39.5	291	Pasadena, TX	(17.4)	358	Sparks, NV	(31.5)
129	Los Angeles, CA	12.5	387	Paterson, NJ	(43.6)	54	Spokane Valley, WA	41.1
306	Louisville, KY	(19.4)	115	Pearland, TX	18.0	221	Spokane, WA	(3.5)
187	Lowell, MA	1.5	398	Pembroke Pines, FL	(50.8)	339	Springfield, IL	(26.5)
45	Lubbock, TX	46.5	359	Peoria, AZ	(32.1)	89	Springfield, MA	25.4
39	Lynchburg, VA	52.8	330	Peoria, IL	(24.1)	85	Springfield, MO	27.5
27	Lynn, MA	63.9	161	Philadelphia, PA	5.1	320	Stamford, CT	(22.7)
95	Macon, GA	23.8	210	Phoenix, AZ	(1.8)	48	Sterling Heights, MI	44.7
40	Madison, WI	51.9	357	Pittsburgh, PA	(30.4)	204	Stockton, CA	(1.3)
171	Manchester, NH	4.0	71	Plano, TX	33.1	NA	St. George, UT**	NA
410	McAllen, TX	(89.2)	348	Plantation, FL	(28.2)	171	St. Joseph, MO	4.0
33	McKinney, TX	58.9	121	Pomona, CA	16.2	154	St. Louis, MO	6.3
184	Medford, OR	2.2	264	Pompano Beach, FL	(11.4)	208	St. Paul, MN	(1.5)
15	Melbourne, FL	92.0	36	Port St. Lucie, FL	55.0	168	St. Petersburg, FL	4.4
165	Memphis, TN	4.8	266	Portland, OR	(11.7)	319	Sugar Land, TX	(22.6)
14	Menifee, CA	92.3	261	Portsmouth, VA	(10.9)	370	Sunnyvale, CA	(34.5)
96	Merced, CA	23.6	NA	Providence, RI**	NA	10	Sunrise, FL	107.6
363	Meridian, ID	(32.8)	76	Provo, UT	31.1	372	Surprise, AZ	(34.7)
80	Mesa, AZ	29.6	394	Pueblo, CO	(47.7)	NA	Syracuse, NY**	NA
20	Mesquite, TX	73.2	199	Quincy, MA	(0.9)	337	Tacoma, WA	(26.0)
182	Miami Beach, FL	2.4	9	Racine, WI	121.5	152	Tallahassee, FL	6.5
295	Miami Gardens, FL	(17.7)	273	Raleigh, NC	(13.5)	346	Tampa, FL	(27.6)
366	Miami, FL	(33.8)	NA	Ramapo, NY**	NA	56	Temecula, CA	40.6
209	Midland, TX	(1.6)	102	Rancho Cucamon., CA	21.8	218	Tempe, AZ	(3.3)
114	Milwaukee, WI	18.2	13	Reading, PA	99.6	NA	Thornton, CO**	NA
178	Minneapolis, MN	3.2	167	Redding, CA	4.6	8	Thousand Oaks, CA	128.2
327	Miramar, FL	(23.8)	397	Redwood City, CA	(50.4)	60	Toledo, OH	39.4
214	Mission Viejo, CA	(3.1)	108	Reno, NV	20.2	192	Toms River Twnshp, NJ	0.0
213	Mission, TX	(2.6)	304	Renton, WA	(19.3)	340	Topeka, KS	(26.6)
235	Mobile, AL	(6.3)	238	Rialto, CA	(6.7)	199	Torrance, CA	(0.9)
267	Modesto, CA	(12.5)	4	Richardson, TX	193.3	368	Tracy, CA	(34.3)
152	Montgomery, AL	6.5	249	Richmond, CA	(9.1)	244	Trenton, NJ	(7.8)
327	Moreno Valley, CA	(23.8)	275	Richmond, VA	(14.1)	393	Troy, MI	(47.6)
352	Mountain View, CA	(29.0)	29	Rio Rancho, NM	62.7	128	Tucson, AZ	13.7
18	Murfreesboro, TN	79.5	77	Riverside, CA	30.8	116	Tulsa, OK	17.9
382	Murrieta, CA	(39.5)	103	Roanoke, VA	21.7	235	Tuscaloosa, AL	(6.3)
117	Nampa, ID	17.6	NA	Rochester, MN**	NA	37	Tustin, CA	54.3
355	Napa, CA	(29.9)	NA	Rochester, NY**	NA	216	Tyler, TX	(3.2)
19	Naperville, IL	75.0	133	Rockford, IL	11.5	387	Upland, CA	(43.6)
38	Nashua, NH	53.8	380	Roseville, CA	(39.0)	308	Upper Darby Twnshp, PA	(19.9)
295	Nashville, TN	(17.7)	379	Roswell, GA	(38.2)	111	Vacaville, CA	19.2
247	New Bedford, MA	(8.9)	99	Round Rock, TX	22.9	292	Vallejo, CA	(17.5)
192	New Haven, CT	0.0	241	Sacramento, CA	(7.7)	356	Vancouver, WA	(30.3)
309	New Orleans, LA	(20.2)	94	Salem, OR	23.9	113	Ventura, CA	18.8
NA	New Rochelle, NY**	NA	110	Salinas, CA	19.3	151	Victorville, CA	6.6
NA	New York, NY**	NA	190	Salt Lake City, UT	1.3	223	Virginia Beach, VA	(3.7)
234	Newark, NJ	(5.7)	142	San Antonio, TX	9.6	146	Visalia, CA	8.5
362	Newport Beach, CA	(32.3)	350	San Bernardino, CA	(28.4)	321	Vista, CA	(22.8)
216	Newport News, VA	(3.2)	183	San Diego, CA	2.3	260	Waco, TX	(10.7)
5	Newton, MA	152.2	298	San Francisco, CA	(18.0)	92	Warren, MI	24.2
239	Norfolk, VA	(7.3)	104	San Jose, CA	21.6	377	Warwick, RI	(37.5)
326	Norman, OK	(23.7)	312	San Leandro, CA	(21.7)	68	Washington, DC	34.2
21	North Charleston, SC	70.7	386	San Marcos, CA	(42.9)	317	Waterbury, CT	(22.2)
NA	North Las Vegas, NV**	NA	373	San Mateo, CA	(35.5)	NA	Waukegan, IL**	NA
82	Norwalk, CA	28.7	301	Sandy Springs, GA	(19.0)	391	West Covina, CA	(45.2)
384	Norwalk, CT	(40.6)	62	Sandy, UT	38.7	324	West Jordan, UT	(23.5)
73	Oakland, CA	32.7	269	Santa Ana, CA	(12.7)	374	West Palm Beach, FL	(36.1)
299	Oceanside, CA	(18.4)	51	Santa Barbara, CA	42.5	123	West Valley, UT	15.4
126	Odessa, TX	14.3	354	Santa Clara, CA	(29.4)	98	Westland, MI	23.0
28	O'Fallon, MO	63.2	25	Santa Clarita, CA	65.3	301	Westminster, CA	(19.0)
93	Ogden, UT	24.1	122	Santa Maria, CA	15.6	284	Westminster, CO	(15.9)
63	Oklahoma City, OK	38.1	229	Santa Monica, CA	(4.5)	53	Whittier, CA	42.0
314	Olathe, KS	(21.9)	125	Santa Rosa, CA	14.6	106	Wichita Falls, TX	21.4
285	Omaha, NE	(16.1)	359	Savannah, GA	(32.1)	230	Wichita, KS	(4.7)
75	Ontario, CA	31.3	101	Scottsdale, AZ	22.1	353	Wilmington, NC	(29.3)
74	Orange, CA	32.6	359	Scranton, PA	(32.1)	311	Winston-Salem, NC	(21.3)
392	Orem, UT	(45.9)	120	Seattle, WA	17.3	405	Woodbridge Twnshp, NJ	(62.5)
279	Orlando, FL	(15.2)	331	Shreveport, LA	(24.4)	249	Worcester, MA	(9.1)
368	Overland Park, KS	(34.3)	325	Simi Valley, CA	(23.6)	148	Yakima, WA	7.3
406	Oxnard, CA	(69.2)	289	Sioux City, IA	(16.9)	NA	Yonkers, NY**	NA
271	Palm Bay, FL	(13.3)	86	Sioux Falls, SD	26.7	303	Yuma, AZ	(19.1)
218	Palmdale, CA	(3.3)	70	Somerville, MA	33.6			
NA	Parma, OH**	NA	246	South Bend, IN	(8.1)			

Source: CQ Press using reported data from the F.B.I. "Crime in the United States 2012"

*Forcible rape is the carnal knowledge of a female forcibly and against her will. **Not available. ***Fishers, IN had a rape rate of 0 in 2011 but had 1 rape in 2012. Calculating percent increase from zero results in an infinite number. This is shown as "NA."

55. Percent Change in Rape Rate: 2011 to 2012 (continued)
National Percent Change = 0.5% Decrease*

RANK	CITY	% CHANGE	RANK	CITY	% CHANGE	RANK	CITY	% CHANGE
1	Lake Forest, CA	676.9	75	Ontario, CA	31.3	149	Carson, CA	7.1
2	Bridgeport, CT	230.9	76	Provo, UT	31.1	149	Irving, TX	7.1
3	Las Cruces, NM	226.2	77	Riverside, CA	30.8	151	Victorville, CA	6.6
4	Richardson, TX	193.3	78	Clifton, NJ	30.5	152	Montgomery, AL	6.5
5	Newton, MA	152.2	79	Frisco, TX	30.0	152	Tallahassee, FL	6.5
6	Coral Springs, FL	142.4	80	Mesa, AZ	29.6	154	Anchorage, AK	6.3
7	Carlsbad, CA	134.0	81	Clovis, CA	29.4	154	St. Louis, MO	6.3
8	Thousand Oaks, CA	128.2	82	Norwalk, CA	28.7	156	Jackson, MS	6.1
9	Racine, WI	121.5	83	Flint, MI	28.1	156	Lakewood, CO	6.1
10	Sunrise, FL	107.6	84	Lancaster, CA	27.9	158	Livermore, CA	5.8
11	Lawrence, MA	106.4	85	Springfield, MO	27.5	159	Costa Mesa, CA	5.2
12	Berkeley, CA	103.0	86	Sioux Falls, SD	26.7	159	Gresham, OR	5.2
13	Reading, PA	99.6	87	Hialeah, FL	26.5	161	Philadelphia, PA	5.1
14	Menifee, CA	92.3	88	Baton Rouge, LA	25.5	162	Albuquerque, NM	5.0
15	Melbourne, FL	92.0	89	Springfield, MA	25.4	163	Amarillo, TX	4.9
16	Decatur, IL	86.9	90	Knoxville, TN	25.3	163	Fresno, CA	4.9
17	Hoover, AL	85.9	91	Chico, CA	24.5	165	Laredo, TX	4.8
18	Murfreesboro, TN	79.5	92	Warren, MI	24.2	165	Memphis, TN	4.8
19	Naperville, IL	75.0	93	Ogden, UT	24.1	167	Redding, CA	4.6
20	Mesquite, TX	73.2	94	Salem, OR	23.9	168	St. Petersburg, FL	4.4
21	North Charleston, SC	70.7	95	Macon, GA	23.8	169	Detroit, MI	4.2
22	Carrollton, TX	69.7	96	Merced, CA	23.6	170	Billings, MT	4.1
23	Edmond, OK	69.4	97	Fayetteville, NC	23.2	171	Henderson, NV	4.0
24	Corona, CA	66.2	98	Westland, MI	23.0	171	Manchester, NH	4.0
25	Santa Clarita, CA	65.3	99	Round Rock, TX	22.9	171	St. Joseph, MO	4.0
26	Clinton Twnshp, MI	64.7	100	Fullerton, CA	22.4	174	Cedar Rapids, IA	3.7
27	Lynn, MA	63.9	101	Scottsdale, AZ	22.1	175	Cleveland, OH	3.5
28	O'Fallon, MO	63.2	102	Rancho Cucamon., CA	21.8	176	Hawthorne, CA	3.4
29	Rio Rancho, NM	62.7	103	Roanoke, VA	21.7	177	Hayward, CA	3.3
30	Buena Park, CA	61.2	104	San Jose, CA	21.6	178	Greeley, CO	3.2
31	Fargo, ND	60.6	105	Glendale, AZ	21.5	178	Minneapolis, MN	3.2
32	Athens-Clarke, GA	59.8	106	Wichita Falls, TX	21.4	180	Cincinnati, OH	3.1
33	McKinney, TX	58.9	107	Fayetteville, AR	21.3	181	Long Beach, CA	2.5
34	Denton, TX	57.9	108	Reno, NV	20.2	182	Miami Beach, FL	2.4
35	Lawrence, KS	55.9	109	Gary, IN	19.6	183	San Diego, CA	2.3
36	Port St. Lucie, FL	55.0	110	Salinas, CA	19.3	184	Medford, OR	2.2
37	Tustin, CA	54.3	111	Kennewick, WA	19.2	185	Lansing, MI	1.8
38	Nashua, NH	53.8	111	Vacaville, CA	19.2	186	Akron, OH	1.7
39	Lynchburg, VA	52.8	113	Ventura, CA	18.8	187	Lowell, MA	1.5
40	Madison, WI	51.9	114	Milwaukee, WI	18.2	188	Brownsville, TX	1.4
41	Broken Arrow, OK	49.1	115	Pearland, TX	18.0	188	Edinburg, TX	1.4
42	South Gate, CA	48.6	116	Tulsa, OK	17.9	190	Salt Lake City, UT	1.3
43	Asheville, NC	48.3	117	Killeen, TX	17.6	191	Livonia, MI	1.0
44	Clearwater, FL	47.5	117	Nampa, ID	17.6	192	Charlotte, NC	0.0
45	Lubbock, TX	46.5	119	Beaumont, TX	17.5	192	Evansville, IN	0.0
46	Centennial, CO	45.8	120	Seattle, WA	17.3	192	New Haven, CT	0.0
47	Hillsboro, OR	45.6	121	Pomona, CA	16.2	192	Toms River Twnshp, NJ	0.0
48	Sterling Heights, MI	44.7	122	Santa Maria, CA	15.6	196	Indianapolis, IN	(0.4)
49	Bakersfield, CA	44.1	123	West Valley, UT	15.4	197	Fall River, MA	(0.5)
49	Lakewood, CA	44.1	124	Abilene, TX	14.9	197	Joliet, IL	(0.5)
51	Santa Barbara, CA	42.5	125	Santa Rosa, CA	14.6	199	Chino, CA	(0.9)
52	Fairfield, CA	42.1	126	Odessa, TX	14.3	199	Hamilton Twnshp, NJ	(0.9)
53	Whittier, CA	42.0	127	Dayton, OH	13.9	199	Quincy, MA	(0.9)
54	Spokane Valley, WA	41.1	128	Tucson, AZ	13.7	199	Torrance, CA	(0.9)
55	Arlington Heights, IL	40.9	129	Los Angeles, CA	12.5	203	Edison Twnshp, NJ	(1.1)
56	Temecula, CA	40.6	130	Camden, NJ	12.1	204	Beaverton, OR	(1.3)
57	Burbank, CA	39.9	131	Boise, ID	11.7	204	Bloomington, IN	(1.3)
58	Bryan, TX	39.6	131	Dallas, TX	11.7	204	Concord, CA	(1.3)
59	Longview, TX	39.5	133	Bethlehem, PA	11.5	204	Stockton, CA	(1.3)
60	Toledo, OH	39.4	133	Rockford, IL	11.5	208	St. Paul, MN	(1.5)
61	Huntsville, AL	39.0	135	Bellevue, WA	11.4	209	Midland, TX	(1.6)
62	Sandy, UT	38.7	136	Aurora, IL	11.3	210	Phoenix, AZ	(1.8)
63	Oklahoma City, OK	38.1	137	Cape Coral, FL	11.1	211	Fort Wayne, IN	(1.9)
64	Hemet, CA	37.8	138	Dearborn, MI	10.3	212	Arlington, TX	(2.2)
65	Antioch, CA	36.0	138	Elk Grove, CA	10.3	213	Mission, TX	(2.6)
66	Farmington Hills, MI	35.5	140	Colorado Springs, CO	10.0	214	Jacksonville, FL	(3.1)
67	Escondido, CA	34.4	140	Fort Worth, TX	10.0	214	Mission Viejo, CA	(3.1)
68	Largo, FL	34.2	142	San Antonio, TX	9.6	216	Newport News, VA	(3.2)
68	Washington, DC	34.2	143	Columbia, MO	9.1	216	Tyler, TX	(3.2)
70	Somerville, MA	33.6	144	College Station, TX	9.0	218	Elizabeth, NJ	(3.3)
71	Plano, TX	33.1	145	Fort Smith, AR	8.8	218	Palmdale, CA	(3.3)
72	Davie, FL	33.0	146	Visalia, CA	8.5	218	Tempe, AZ	(3.3)
73	Oakland, CA	32.7	147	Lincoln, NE	8.2	221	Spokane, WA	(3.5)
74	Orange, CA	32.6	148	Yakima, WA	7.3	222	Durham, NC	(3.6)

RANK	CITY	% CHANGE	RANK	CITY	% CHANGE	RANK	CITY	% CHANGE
223	Virginia Beach, VA	(3.7)	297	Cary, NC	(17.9)	371	Avondale, AZ	(34.6)
224	Ann Arbor, MI	(3.8)	298	San Francisco, CA	(18.0)	372	Surprise, AZ	(34.7)
224	Austin, TX	(3.8)	299	Oceanside, CA	(18.4)	373	San Mateo, CA	(35.5)
226	Aurora, CO	(4.0)	300	Inglewood, CA	(18.5)	374	West Palm Beach, FL	(36.1)
227	Chula Vista, CA	(4.3)	301	Sandy Springs, GA	(19.0)	375	Daly City, CA	(36.5)
228	Des Moines, IA	(4.4)	301	Westminster, CA	(19.0)	376	Alexandria, VA	(37.4)
229	Santa Monica, CA	(4.5)	303	Yuma, AZ	(19.1)	377	Warwick, RI	(37.5)
230	Independence, MO	(4.7)	304	Pasadena, CA	(19.3)	378	Charleston, SC	(38.1)
230	Wichita, KS	(4.7)	304	Renton, WA	(19.3)	379	Roswell, GA	(38.2)
232	Johns Creek, GA	(5.1)	306	Louisville, KY	(19.4)	380	Roseville, CA	(39.0)
233	Corpus Christi, TX	(5.5)	307	Green Bay, WI	(19.7)	381	Bloomington, IL	(39.3)
234	Newark, NJ	(5.7)	308	Upper Darby Twnshp, PA	(19.9)	382	Longmont, CO	(39.5)
235	Mobile, AL	(6.3)	309	New Orleans, LA	(20.2)	382	Murrieta, CA	(39.5)
235	Tuscaloosa, AL	(6.3)	310	Hollywood, FL	(20.4)	384	Norwalk, CT	(40.6)
237	Everett, WA	(6.6)	311	Winston-Salem, NC	(21.3)	385	Alameda, CA	(40.8)
238	Rialto, CA	(6.7)	312	San Leandro, CA	(21.7)	386	San Marcos, CA	(42.9)
239	Norfolk, VA	(7.3)	313	Fontana, CA	(21.8)	387	Paterson, NJ	(43.6)
240	Baltimore, MD	(7.4)	314	Olathe, KS	(21.9)	387	Upland, CA	(43.6)
241	Eugene, OR	(7.7)	315	Brockton, MA	(22.0)	389	Grand Rapids, MI	(43.9)
241	Kansas City, MO	(7.7)	316	Bellflower, CA	(22.1)	390	Baldwin Park, CA	(44.9)
241	Sacramento, CA	(7.7)	317	Waterbury, CT	(22.2)	391	West Covina, CA	(45.2)
244	Trenton, NJ	(7.8)	318	Fort Collins, CO	(22.5)	392	Orem, UT	(45.9)
245	Denver, CO	(7.9)	319	Sugar Land, TX	(22.6)	393	Troy, MI	(47.6)
246	South Bend, IN	(8.1)	320	Stamford, CT	(22.7)	394	Pueblo, CO	(47.7)
247	New Bedford, MA	(8.9)	321	Vista, CA	(22.8)	395	Fort Lauderdale, FL	(48.2)
248	Champaign, IL	(9.0)	322	Chesapeake, VA	(22.9)	396	Boca Raton, FL	(48.3)
249	Jersey City, NJ	(9.1)	323	Anaheim, CA	(23.0)	397	Redwood City, CA	(50.4)
249	Richmond, CA	(9.1)	324	West Jordan, UT	(23.5)	398	Pembroke Pines, FL	(50.8)
249	Worcester, MA	(9.1)	325	Simi Valley, CA	(23.6)	399	Chino Hills, CA	(50.9)
252	Boston, MA	(9.4)	326	Norman, OK	(23.7)	399	Hartford, CT	(50.9)
253	Boulder, CO	(9.6)	327	Miramar, FL	(23.8)	401	Glendale, CA	(56.9)
253	Lakeland, FL	(9.6)	327	Moreno Valley, CA	(23.8)	402	El Monte, CA	(57.8)
253	Las Vegas, NV	(9.6)	329	Columbus, GA	(24.0)	403	Hammond, IN	(59.9)
256	Gilbert, AZ	(10.1)	330	Peoria, IL	(24.1)	404	Fremont, CA	(60.5)
257	Huntington Beach, CA	(10.2)	331	League City, TX	(24.4)	405	Woodbridge Twnshp, NJ	(62.5)
258	Indio, CA	(10.3)	331	Shreveport, LA	(24.4)	406	Oxnard, CA	(69.2)
259	Gainesville, FL	(10.4)	333	Cicero, IL	(24.9)	407	Alhambra, CA	(71.1)
260	Waco, TX	(10.7)	333	High Point, NC	(24.9)	408	Carmel, IN	(76.2)
261	Portsmouth, VA	(10.9)	335	Davenport, IA	(25.3)	409	Lakewood Twnshp, NJ	(82.8)
262	Kansas City, KS	(11.0)	336	Atlanta, GA	(25.6)	410	McAllen, TX	(89.2)
263	Cranston, RI	(11.2)	337	Tacoma, WA	(26.0)	NA	Albany, NY**	NA
264	Allen, TX	(11.4)	338	Clarksville, TN	(26.4)	NA	Allentown, PA**	NA
264	Pompano Beach, FL	(11.4)	339	Springfield, IL	(26.5)	NA	Amherst, NY**	NA
266	Portland, OR	(11.7)	340	Topeka, KS	(26.6)	NA	Bloomington, MN**	NA
267	Modesto, CA	(12.5)	341	Lafayette, LA	(26.8)	NA	Brooklyn Park, MN**	NA
268	Arvada, CO	(12.6)	342	Compton, CA	(26.9)	NA	Buffalo, NY**	NA
269	Santa Ana, CA	(12.7)	343	Albany, GA	(27.1)	NA	Chandler, AZ**	NA
270	Kent, WA	(12.8)	344	Deerfield Beach, FL	(27.2)	NA	Cheektowaga, NY**	NA
271	Downey, CA	(13.3)	345	Irvine, CA	(27.5)	NA	Chicago, IL**	NA
271	Palm Bay, FL	(13.3)	346	Lee's Summit, MO	(27.6)	NA	Clarkstown, NY**	NA
273	Raleigh, NC	(13.5)	346	Tampa, FL	(27.6)	NA	Colonie, NY**	NA
274	Citrus Heights, CA	(14.0)	348	Plantation, FL	(28.2)	NA	Duluth, MN**	NA
275	Richmond, VA	(14.1)	349	Kenosha, WI	(28.3)	NA	Federal Way, WA**	NA
276	Elgin, IL	(14.6)	350	San Bernardino, CA	(28.4)	NA	Fishers, IN***	NA
277	Brick Twnshp, NJ	(15.1)	351	Grand Prairie, TX	(28.6)	NA	Greece, NY**	NA
277	El Cajon, CA	(15.1)	352	Mountain View, CA	(29.0)	NA	Greensboro, NC**	NA
279	Orlando, FL	(15.2)	353	Wilmington, NC	(29.3)	NA	Greenville, NC**	NA
280	Hampton, VA	(15.3)	354	Santa Clara, CA	(29.4)	NA	Jurupa Valley, CA**	NA
280	Houston, TX	(15.3)	355	Napa, CA	(29.9)	NA	Lexington, KY**	NA
282	Little Rock, AR	(15.4)	356	Vancouver, WA	(30.3)	NA	New Rochelle, NY**	NA
283	Garland, TX	(15.6)	357	Pittsburgh, PA	(30.4)	NA	New York, NY**	NA
284	Westminster, CO	(15.9)	358	Sparks, NV	(31.5)	NA	North Las Vegas, NV**	NA
285	Omaha, NE	(16.1)	359	Peoria, AZ	(32.1)	NA	Parma, OH**	NA
286	Birmingham, AL	(16.4)	359	Savannah, GA	(32.1)	NA	Providence, RI**	NA
287	Erie, PA	(16.7)	359	Scranton, PA	(32.1)	NA	Ramapo, NY**	NA
288	El Paso, TX	(16.8)	362	Newport Beach, CA	(32.3)	NA	Rochester, MN**	NA
289	Sioux City, IA	(16.9)	363	Hesperia, CA	(32.8)	NA	Rochester, NY**	NA
290	Garden Grove, CA	(17.3)	363	Meridian, ID	(32.8)	NA	St. George, UT**	NA
291	Pasadena, TX	(17.4)	365	Danbury, CT	(33.1)	NA	Syracuse, NY**	NA
292	Vallejo, CA	(17.5)	366	Lawton, OK	(33.8)	NA	Thornton, CO**	NA
293	Bellingham, WA	(17.6)	366	Miami, FL	(33.8)	NA	Waukegan, IL**	NA
293	Cambridge, MA	(17.6)	368	Overland Park, KS	(34.3)	NA	Yonkers, NY**	NA
295	Miami Gardens, FL	(17.7)	368	Tracy, CA	(34.3)			
295	Nashville, TN	(17.7)	370	Sunnyvale, CA	(34.5)			

Source: CQ Press using reported data from the F.B.I. "Crime in the United States 2012"

*Forcible rape is the carnal knowledge of a female forcibly and against her will. Assaults or attempts to commit rape by force or threat of force are included. However, statutory rape without force and other sex offenses are excluded. **Not available

56. Percent Change in Rape Rate: 2008 to 2012
National Percent Change = 9.9% Decrease*

RANK	CITY	% CHANGE	RANK	CITY	% CHANGE	RANK	CITY	% CHANGE
346	Abilene, TX	(58.1)	351	Chino Hills, CA	(60.6)	254	Gainesville, FL	(24.1)
113	Akron, OH	4.3	282	Chino, CA	(31.5)	258	Garden Grove, CA	(24.8)
391	Alameda, CA	(92.2)	325	Chula Vista, CA	(46.3)	324	Garland, TX	(45.9)
NA	Albany, GA**	NA	NA	Cicero, IL**	NA	56	Gary, IN	30.6
NA	Albany, NY**	NA	235	Cincinnati, OH	(21.5)	256	Gilbert, AZ	(24.6)
272	Albuquerque, NM	(28.4)	295	Citrus Heights, CA	(35.4)	171	Glendale, AZ	(9.7)
369	Alexandria, VA	(70.9)	NA	Clarkstown, NY**	NA	370	Glendale, CA	(71.0)
374	Alhambra, CA	(74.2)	279	Clarksville, TN	(31.1)	166	Grand Prairie, TX	(8.6)
NA	Allentown, PA**	NA	35	Clearwater, FL	49.2	316	Grand Rapids, MI	(42.2)
37	Allen, TX	47.6	153	Cleveland, OH	(5.5)	NA	Greece, NY**	NA
192	Amarillo, TX	(13.8)	50	Clifton, NJ	33.9	204	Greeley, CO	(17.2)
NA	Amherst, NY**	NA	73	Clinton Twnshp, MI	21.7	323	Green Bay, WI	(45.1)
146	Anaheim, CA	(4.4)	15	Clovis, CA	72.3	315	Greensboro, NC	(41.9)
105	Anchorage, AK	7.9	280	College Station, TX	(31.4)	26	Greenville, NC	58.7
97	Ann Arbor, MI	9.4	NA	Colonie, NY**	NA	344	Gresham, OR	(57.2)
145	Antioch, CA	(4.2)	158	Colorado Springs, CO	(6.4)	90	Hamilton Twnshp, NJ	12.0
NA	Arlington Heights, IL**	NA	10	Columbia, MO	97.3	336	Hammond, IN	(54.1)
148	Arlington, TX	(5.1)	349	Columbus, GA	(59.2)	350	Hampton, VA	(59.7)
223	Arvada, CO	(20.2)	290	Compton, CA	(33.7)	339	Hartford, CT	(55.9)
388	Asheville, NC	(88.6)	29	Concord, CA	53.5	42	Hawthorne, CA	42.3
191	Athens-Clarke, GA	(13.7)	3	Coral Springs, FL	400.0	243	Hayward, CA	(22.8)
96	Atlanta, GA	9.7	290	Corona, CA	(33.7)	386	Hemet, CA	(86.3)
175	Aurora, CO	(10.6)	183	Corpus Christi, TX	(12.1)	292	Henderson, NV	(33.9)
NA	Aurora, IL**	NA	226	Costa Mesa, CA	(20.7)	143	Hesperia, CA	(3.7)
277	Austin, TX	(30.7)	128	Cranston, RI	(0.5)	156	Hialeah, FL	(6.0)
340	Avondale, AZ	(56.4)	125	Dallas, TX	0.0	306	High Point, NC	(39.2)
99	Bakersfield, CA	8.8	361	Daly City, CA	(65.1)	150	Hillsboro, OR	(5.2)
319	Baldwin Park, CA	(43.5)	34	Danbury, CT	49.5	275	Hollywood, FL	(30.3)
5	Baltimore, MD	133.3	196	Davenport, IA	(14.9)	381	Hoover, AL	(82.0)
140	Baton Rouge, LA	(3.5)	215	Davie, FL	(19.1)	170	Houston, TX	(9.0)
161	Beaumont, TX	(8.0)	84	Dayton, OH	15.7	159	Huntington Beach, CA	(7.0)
184	Beaverton, OR	(12.3)	190	Dearborn, MI	(13.6)	268	Huntsville, AL	(27.1)
251	Bellevue, WA	(23.4)	NA	Decatur, IL**	NA	273	Independence, MO	(29.1)
394	Bellflower, CA	(95.5)	387	Deerfield Beach, FL	(88.3)	179	Indianapolis, IN	(11.6)
75	Bellingham, WA	20.2	67	Denton, TX	24.2	201	Indio, CA	(16.4)
48	Berkeley, CA	37.2	64	Denver, CO	25.6	164	Inglewood, CA	(8.3)
382	Bethlehem, PA	(82.9)	321	Des Moines, IA	(44.5)	342	Irvine, CA	(57.0)
161	Billings, MT	(8.0)	17	Detroit, MI	71.4	238	Irving, TX	(21.9)
249	Birmingham, AL	(23.3)	226	Downey, CA	(20.7)	66	Jacksonville, FL	24.9
NA	Bloomington, IL**	NA	NA	Duluth, MN**	NA	132	Jackson, MS	(1.4)
356	Bloomington, IN	(63.0)	228	Durham, NC	(21.0)	180	Jersey City, NJ	(11.8)
NA	Bloomington, MN**	NA	353	Edinburg, TX	(62.5)	NA	Johns Creek, GA**	NA
235	Boca Raton, FL	(21.5)	36	Edison Twnshp, NJ	48.3	NA	Joliet, IL**	NA
177	Boise, ID	(11.1)	253	Edmond, OK	(23.8)	NA	Jurupa Valley, CA**	NA
121	Boston, MA	0.8	304	El Cajon, CA	(37.9)	NA	Kansas City, KS**	NA
262	Boulder, CO	(25.5)	333	El Monte, CA	(53.5)	140	Kansas City, MO	(3.5)
28	Brick Twnshp, NJ	54.9	163	El Paso, TX	(8.1)	285	Kennewick, WA	(32.5)
2	Bridgeport, CT	525.2	NA	Elgin, IL**	NA	185	Kenosha, WI	(12.6)
NA	Brockton, MA**	NA	54	Elizabeth, NJ	30.8	320	Kent, WA	(43.7)
13	Broken Arrow, OK	88.5	213	Elk Grove, CA	(19.0)	98	Killeen, TX	9.1
NA	Brooklyn Park, MN**	NA	264	Erie, PA	(25.9)	193	Knoxville, TN	(14.0)
41	Brownsville, TX	42.9	87	Escondido, CA	13.7	385	Lafayette, LA	(86.0)
372	Bryan, TX	(71.2)	85	Eugene, OR	14.3	100	Lake Forest, CA	8.6
111	Buena Park, CA	4.6	199	Evansville, IN	(15.7)	196	Lakeland, FL	(14.9)
NA	Buffalo, NY**	NA	318	Everett, WA	(43.3)	395	Lakewood Twnshp, NJ	(99.2)
45	Burbank, CA	39.0	109	Fairfield, CA	4.9	135	Lakewood, CA	(3.0)
49	Cambridge, MA	35.5	215	Fall River, MA	(19.1)	112	Lakewood, CO	4.4
116	Camden, NJ	3.7	89	Fargo, ND	12.1	208	Lancaster, CA	(18.3)
328	Cape Coral, FL	(47.4)	187	Farmington Hills, MI	(13.4)	138	Lansing, MI	(3.4)
133	Carlsbad, CA	(2.0)	61	Fayetteville, AR	29.2	155	Laredo, TX	(5.7)
365	Carmel, IN	(68.4)	213	Fayetteville, NC	(19.0)	368	Largo, FL	(70.5)
348	Carrollton, TX	(58.5)	52	Federal Way, WA	32.2	44	Las Cruces, NM	39.6
265	Carson, CA	(26.5)	392	Fishers, IN	(92.4)	260	Las Vegas, NV	(25.2)
211	Cary, NC	(18.8)	80	Flint, MI	17.1	51	Lawrence, KS	32.8
65	Cedar Rapids, IA	25.0	311	Fontana, CA	(40.5)	378	Lawrence, MA	(78.4)
4	Centennial, CO	171.1	327	Fort Collins, CO	(46.4)	338	Lawton, OK	(54.9)
NA	Champaign, IL**	NA	274	Fort Lauderdale, FL	(29.6)	347	League City, TX	(58.4)
NA	Chandler, AZ**	NA	263	Fort Smith, AR	(25.6)	8	Lee's Summit, MO	100.0
373	Charleston, SC	(71.5)	150	Fort Wayne, IN	(5.2)	NA	Lexington, KY**	NA
244	Charlotte, NC	(22.9)	119	Fort Worth, TX	1.8	29	Lincoln, NE	53.5
NA	Cheektowaga, NY**	NA	362	Fremont, CA	(65.2)	127	Little Rock, AR	(0.4)
325	Chesapeake, VA	(46.3)	299	Fresno, CA	(36.3)	219	Livermore, CA	(19.2)
NA	Chicago, IL**	NA	342	Frisco, TX	(57.0)	43	Livonia, MI	40.4
39	Chico, CA	43.1	205	Fullerton, CA	(17.3)	147	Long Beach, CA	(4.7)

RANK	CITY	% CHANGE
NA	Longmont, CO**	NA
314	Longview, TX	(41.8)
131	Los Angeles, CA	(1.2)
231	Louisville, KY	(21.2)
174	Lowell, MA	(10.5)
77	Lubbock, TX	17.4
367	Lynchburg, VA	(68.7)
54	Lynn, MA	30.8
126	Macon, GA	(0.2)
6	Madison, WI	122.2
122	Manchester, NH	0.5
384	McAllen, TX	(84.1)
135	McKinney, TX	(3.0)
166	Medford, OR	(8.6)
27	Melbourne, FL	55.1
78	Memphis, TN	17.2
NA	Menifee, CA**	NA
215	Merced, CA	(19.1)
173	Meridian, ID	(10.2)
103	Mesa, AZ	8.2
59	Mesquite, TX	29.3
244	Miami Beach, FL	(22.9)
354	Miami Gardens, FL	(62.8)
25	Miami, FL	60.2
370	Midland, TX	(71.0)
92	Milwaukee, WI	11.3
106	Minneapolis, MN	6.1
317	Miramar, FL	(42.5)
137	Mission Viejo, CA	(3.1)
389	Mission, TX	(90.5)
20	Mobile, AL	65.7
169	Modesto, CA	(8.9)
208	Montgomery, AL	(18.3)
355	Moreno Valley, CA	(62.9)
390	Mountain View, CA	(91.5)
21	Murfreesboro, TN	62.3
293	Murrieta, CA	(34.2)
282	Nampa, ID	(31.5)
360	Napa, CA	(65.0)
NA	Naperville, IL**	NA
NA	Nashua, NH**	NA
124	Nashville, TN	0.2
186	New Bedford, MA	(12.9)
NA	New Haven, CT**	NA
21	New Orleans, LA	62.3
NA	New Rochelle, NY**	NA
NA	New York, NY**	NA
103	Newark, NJ	8.2
8	Newport Beach, CA	100.0
288	Newport News, VA	(32.8)
308	Newton, MA	(39.6)
201	Norfolk, VA	(16.4)
90	Norman, OK	12.0
210	North Charleston, SC	(18.5)
53	North Las Vegas, NV	31.6
113	Norwalk, CA	4.3
271	Norwalk, CT	(27.8)
220	Oakland, CA	(19.5)
240	Oceanside, CA	(22.2)
1	Odessa, TX	1,975.0
275	O'Fallon, MO	(30.3)
313	Ogden, UT	(41.7)
88	Oklahoma City, OK	13.4
NA	Olathe, KS**	NA
102	Omaha, NE	8.5
312	Ontario, CA	(41.4)
138	Orange, CA	(3.4)
329	Orem, UT	(48.5)
266	Orlando, FL	(26.7)
94	Overland Park, KS	10.8
358	Oxnard, CA	(64.6)
244	Palm Bay, FL	(22.9)
303	Palmdale, CA	(37.7)
NA	Parma, OH**	NA

RANK	CITY	% CHANGE
115	Pasadena, CA	4.1
206	Pasadena, TX	(17.6)
148	Paterson, NJ	(5.1)
256	Pearland, TX	(24.6)
194	Pembroke Pines, FL	(14.6)
335	Peoria, AZ	(53.9)
NA	Peoria, IL**	NA
225	Philadelphia, PA	(20.6)
69	Phoenix, AZ	23.4
363	Pittsburgh, PA	(65.6)
93	Plano, TX	11.0
337	Plantation, FL	(54.7)
16	Pomona, CA	71.9
302	Pompano Beach, FL	(37.0)
78	Port St. Lucie, FL	17.2
194	Portland, OR	(14.6)
267	Portsmouth, VA	(26.9)
14	Providence, RI	83.7
164	Provo, UT	(8.3)
NA	Pueblo, CO**	NA
7	Quincy, MA	109.5
18	Racine, WI	69.7
95	Raleigh, NC	10.2
NA	Ramapo, NY**	NA
130	Rancho Cucamon., CA	(1.0)
72	Reading, PA	21.8
251	Redding, CA	(23.4)
383	Redwood City, CA	(83.8)
352	Reno, NV	(62.4)
NA	Renton, WA**	NA
134	Rialto, CA	(2.3)
86	Richardson, TX	14.0
160	Richmond, CA	(7.1)
278	Richmond, VA	(30.9)
177	Rio Rancho, NM	(11.1)
289	Riverside, CA	(33.5)
237	Roanoke, VA	(21.6)
NA	Rochester, MN**	NA
NA	Rochester, NY**	NA
117	Rockford, IL	2.4
322	Roseville, CA	(45.0)
332	Roswell, GA	(52.2)
23	Round Rock, TX	61.8
269	Sacramento, CA	(27.2)
286	Salem, OR	(32.6)
123	Salinas, CA	0.4
31	Salt Lake City, UT	52.8
62	San Antonio, TX	26.8
222	San Bernardino, CA	(19.8)
249	San Diego, CA	(23.3)
301	San Francisco, CA	(36.5)
70	San Jose, CA	23.2
228	San Leandro, CA	(21.0)
56	San Marcos, CA	30.6
344	San Mateo, CA	(57.2)
375	Sandy Springs, GA	(75.1)
81	Sandy, UT	16.7
196	Santa Ana, CA	(14.9)
12	Santa Barbara, CA	94.7
334	Santa Clara, CA	(53.6)
33	Santa Clarita, CA	50.5
366	Santa Maria, CA	(68.5)
108	Santa Monica, CA	5.0
68	Santa Rosa, CA	24.1
305	Savannah, GA	(38.3)
24	Scottsdale, AZ	60.7
377	Scranton, PA	(77.5)
172	Seattle, WA	(10.0)
188	Shreveport, LA	(13.5)
330	Simi Valley, CA	(48.6)
238	Sioux City, IA	(21.9)
110	Sioux Falls, SD	4.8
379	Somerville, MA	(80.3)
247	South Bend, IN	(23.1)

RANK	CITY	% CHANGE
224	South Gate, CA	(20.4)
309	Sparks, NV	(39.7)
83	Spokane Valley, WA	16.4
207	Spokane, WA	(18.2)
NA	Springfield, IL**	NA
364	Springfield, MA	(67.4)
39	Springfield, MO	43.1
180	Stamford, CT	(11.8)
309	Sterling Heights, MI	(39.7)
231	Stockton, CA	(21.2)
120	St. George, UT	1.7
19	St. Joseph, MO	67.1
157	St. Louis, MO	(6.2)
100	St. Paul, MN	8.6
200	St. Petersburg, FL	(16.2)
234	Sugar Land, TX	(21.3)
261	Sunnyvale, CA	(25.4)
58	Sunrise, FL	29.8
203	Surprise, AZ	(16.5)
NA	Syracuse, NY**	NA
299	Tacoma, WA	(36.3)
231	Tallahassee, FL	(21.2)
331	Tampa, FL	(50.0)
298	Temecula, CA	(36.2)
47	Tempe, AZ	37.3
NA	Thornton, CO**	NA
46	Thousand Oaks, CA	38.0
38	Toledo, OH	44.5
359	Toms River Twnshp, NJ	(64.9)
107	Topeka, KS	5.9
241	Torrance, CA	(22.3)
11	Tracy, CA	95.8
142	Trenton, NJ	(3.6)
284	Troy, MI	(32.1)
152	Tucson, AZ	(5.4)
74	Tulsa, OK	20.4
59	Tuscaloosa, AL	29.3
380	Tustin, CA	(80.5)
144	Tyler, TX	(4.1)
393	Upland, CA	(93.3)
175	Upper Darby Twnshp, PA	(10.6)
211	Vacaville, CA	(18.8)
63	Vallejo, CA	26.4
286	Vancouver, WA	(32.6)
128	Ventura, CA	(0.5)
82	Victorville, CA	16.6
242	Virginia Beach, VA	(22.6)
168	Visalia, CA	(8.7)
297	Vista, CA	(36.1)
220	Waco, TX	(19.5)
32	Warren, MI	50.8
215	Warwick, RI	(19.1)
76	Washington, DC	18.8
357	Waterbury, CT	(64.4)
NA	Waukegan, IL**	NA
270	West Covina, CA	(27.7)
307	West Jordan, UT	(39.3)
294	West Palm Beach, FL	(35.3)
182	West Valley, UT	(12.0)
71	Westland, MI	22.0
228	Westminster, CA	(21.0)
296	Westminster, CO	(35.7)
188	Whittier, CA	(13.5)
259	Wichita Falls, TX	(24.9)
247	Wichita, KS	(23.1)
341	Wilmington, NC	(56.7)
280	Winston-Salem, NC	(31.4)
376	Woodbridge Twnshp, NJ	(75.4)
254	Worcester, MA	(24.1)
154	Yakima, WA	(5.6)
NA	Yonkers, NY**	NA
118	Yuma, AZ	2.2

Source: CQ Press using reported data from the F.B.I. "Crime in the United States 2012"

*Forcible rape is the carnal knowledge of a female forcibly and against her will. Assaults or attempts to commit rape by force or threat of force are included. However, statutory rape without force and other sex offenses are excluded. **Not available

56. Percent Change in Rape Rate: 2008 to 2012 (continued)
National Percent Change = 9.9% Decrease*

RANK	CITY	% CHANGE	RANK	CITY	% CHANGE	RANK	CITY	% CHANGE
1	Odessa, TX	1,975.0	75	Bellingham, WA	20.2	148	Paterson, NJ	(5.1)
2	Bridgeport, CT	525.2	76	Washington, DC	18.8	150	Fort Wayne, IN	(5.2)
3	Coral Springs, FL	400.0	77	Lubbock, TX	17.4	150	Hillsboro, OR	(5.2)
4	Centennial, CO	171.1	78	Memphis, TN	17.2	152	Tucson, AZ	(5.4)
5	Baltimore, MD	133.3	78	Port St. Lucie, FL	17.2	153	Cleveland, OH	(5.5)
6	Madison, WI	122.2	80	Flint, MI	17.1	154	Yakima, WA	(5.6)
7	Quincy, MA	109.5	81	Sandy, UT	16.7	155	Laredo, TX	(5.7)
8	Lee's Summit, MO	100.0	82	Victorville, CA	16.6	156	Hialeah, FL	(6.0)
8	Newport Beach, CA	100.0	83	Spokane Valley, WA	16.4	157	St. Louis, MO	(6.2)
10	Columbia, MO	97.3	84	Dayton, OH	15.7	158	Colorado Springs, CO	(6.4)
11	Tracy, CA	95.8	85	Eugene, OR	14.3	159	Huntington Beach, CA	(7.0)
12	Santa Barbara, CA	94.7	86	Richardson, TX	14.0	160	Richmond, CA	(7.1)
13	Broken Arrow, OK	88.5	87	Escondido, CA	13.7	161	Beaumont, TX	(8.0)
14	Providence, RI	83.7	88	Oklahoma City, OK	13.4	161	Billings, MT	(8.0)
15	Clovis, CA	72.3	89	Fargo, ND	12.1	163	El Paso, TX	(8.1)
16	Pomona, CA	71.9	90	Hamilton Twnshp, NJ	12.0	164	Inglewood, CA	(8.3)
17	Detroit, MI	71.4	90	Norman, OK	12.0	164	Provo, UT	(8.3)
18	Racine, WI	69.7	92	Milwaukee, WI	11.3	166	Grand Prairie, TX	(8.6)
19	St. Joseph, MO	67.1	93	Plano, TX	11.0	166	Medford, OR	(8.6)
20	Mobile, AL	65.7	94	Overland Park, KS	10.8	168	Visalia, CA	(8.7)
21	Murfreesboro, TN	62.3	95	Raleigh, NC	10.2	169	Modesto, CA	(8.9)
21	New Orleans, LA	62.3	96	Atlanta, GA	9.7	170	Houston, TX	(9.0)
23	Round Rock, TX	61.8	97	Ann Arbor, MI	9.4	171	Glendale, AZ	(9.7)
24	Scottsdale, AZ	60.7	98	Killeen, TX	9.1	172	Seattle, WA	(10.0)
25	Miami, FL	60.2	99	Bakersfield, CA	8.8	173	Meridian, ID	(10.2)
26	Greenville, NC	58.7	100	Lake Forest, CA	8.6	174	Lowell, MA	(10.5)
27	Melbourne, FL	55.1	100	St. Paul, MN	8.6	175	Aurora, CO	(10.6)
28	Brick Twnshp, NJ	54.9	102	Omaha, NE	8.5	175	Upper Darby Twnshp, PA	(10.6)
29	Concord, CA	53.5	103	Mesa, AZ	8.2	177	Boise, ID	(11.1)
29	Lincoln, NE	53.5	103	Newark, NJ	8.2	177	Rio Rancho, NM	(11.1)
31	Salt Lake City, UT	52.8	105	Anchorage, AK	7.9	179	Indianapolis, IN	(11.6)
32	Warren, MI	50.8	106	Minneapolis, MN	6.1	180	Jersey City, NJ	(11.8)
33	Santa Clarita, CA	50.5	107	Topeka, KS	5.9	180	Stamford, CT	(11.8)
34	Danbury, CT	49.5	108	Santa Monica, CA	5.0	182	West Valley, UT	(12.0)
35	Clearwater, FL	49.2	109	Fairfield, CA	4.9	183	Corpus Christi, TX	(12.1)
36	Edison Twnshp, NJ	48.3	110	Sioux Falls, SD	4.8	184	Beaverton, OR	(12.3)
37	Allen, TX	47.6	111	Buena Park, CA	4.6	185	Kenosha, WI	(12.6)
38	Toledo, OH	44.5	112	Lakewood, CO	4.4	186	New Bedford, MA	(12.9)
39	Chico, CA	43.1	113	Akron, OH	4.3	187	Farmington Hills, MI	(13.4)
39	Springfield, MO	43.1	113	Norwalk, CA	4.3	188	Shreveport, LA	(13.5)
41	Brownsville, TX	42.9	115	Pasadena, CA	4.1	188	Whittier, CA	(13.5)
42	Hawthorne, CA	42.3	116	Camden, NJ	3.7	190	Dearborn, MI	(13.6)
43	Livonia, MI	40.4	117	Rockford, IL	2.4	191	Athens-Clarke, GA	(13.7)
44	Las Cruces, NM	39.6	118	Yuma, AZ	2.2	192	Amarillo, TX	(13.8)
45	Burbank, CA	39.0	119	Fort Worth, TX	1.8	193	Knoxville, TN	(14.0)
46	Thousand Oaks, CA	38.0	120	St. George, UT	1.7	194	Pembroke Pines, FL	(14.6)
47	Tempe, AZ	37.3	121	Boston, MA	0.8	194	Portland, OR	(14.6)
48	Berkeley, CA	37.2	122	Manchester, NH	0.5	196	Davenport, IA	(14.9)
49	Cambridge, MA	35.5	123	Salinas, CA	0.4	196	Lakeland, FL	(14.9)
50	Clifton, NJ	33.9	124	Nashville, TN	0.2	196	Santa Ana, CA	(14.9)
51	Lawrence, KS	32.8	125	Dallas, TX	0.0	199	Evansville, IN	(15.7)
52	Federal Way, WA	32.2	126	Macon, GA	(0.2)	200	St. Petersburg, FL	(16.2)
53	North Las Vegas, NV	31.6	127	Little Rock, AR	(0.4)	201	Indio, CA	(16.4)
54	Elizabeth, NJ	30.8	128	Cranston, RI	(0.5)	201	Norfolk, VA	(16.4)
54	Lynn, MA	30.8	128	Ventura, CA	(0.5)	203	Surprise, AZ	(16.5)
56	Gary, IN	30.6	130	Rancho Cucamon., CA	(1.0)	204	Greeley, CO	(17.2)
56	San Marcos, CA	30.6	131	Los Angeles, CA	(1.2)	205	Fullerton, CA	(17.3)
58	Sunrise, FL	29.8	132	Jackson, MS	(1.4)	206	Pasadena, TX	(17.6)
59	Mesquite, TX	29.3	133	Carlsbad, CA	(2.0)	207	Spokane, WA	(18.2)
59	Tuscaloosa, AL	29.3	134	Rialto, CA	(2.3)	208	Lancaster, CA	(18.3)
61	Fayetteville, AR	29.2	135	Lakewood, CA	(3.0)	208	Montgomery, AL	(18.3)
62	San Antonio, TX	26.8	135	McKinney, TX	(3.0)	210	North Charleston, SC	(18.5)
63	Vallejo, CA	26.4	137	Mission Viejo, CA	(3.1)	211	Cary, NC	(18.8)
64	Denver, CO	25.6	138	Lansing, MI	(3.4)	211	Vacaville, CA	(18.8)
65	Cedar Rapids, IA	25.0	138	Orange, CA	(3.4)	213	Elk Grove, CA	(19.0)
66	Jacksonville, FL	24.9	140	Baton Rouge, LA	(3.5)	213	Fayetteville, NC	(19.0)
67	Denton, TX	24.2	140	Kansas City, MO	(3.5)	215	Davie, FL	(19.1)
68	Santa Rosa, CA	24.1	142	Trenton, NJ	(3.6)	215	Fall River, MA	(19.1)
69	Phoenix, AZ	23.4	143	Hesperia, CA	(3.7)	215	Merced, CA	(19.1)
70	San Jose, CA	23.2	144	Tyler, TX	(4.1)	215	Warwick, RI	(19.1)
71	Westland, MI	22.0	145	Antioch, CA	(4.2)	219	Livermore, CA	(19.2)
72	Reading, PA	21.8	146	Anaheim, CA	(4.4)	220	Oakland, CA	(19.5)
73	Clinton Twnshp, MI	21.7	147	Long Beach, CA	(4.7)	220	Waco, TX	(19.5)
74	Tulsa, OK	20.4	148	Arlington, TX	(5.1)	222	San Bernardino, CA	(19.8)

RANK	CITY	% CHANGE	RANK	CITY	% CHANGE	RANK	CITY	% CHANGE
223	Arvada, CO	(20.2)	297	Vista, CA	(36.1)	370	Midland, TX	(71.0)
224	South Gate, CA	(20.4)	298	Temecula, CA	(36.2)	372	Bryan, TX	(71.2)
225	Philadelphia, PA	(20.6)	299	Fresno, CA	(36.3)	373	Charleston, SC	(71.5)
226	Costa Mesa, CA	(20.7)	299	Tacoma, WA	(36.3)	374	Alhambra, CA	(74.2)
226	Downey, CA	(20.7)	301	San Francisco, CA	(36.5)	375	Sandy Springs, GA	(75.1)
228	Durham, NC	(21.0)	302	Pompano Beach, FL	(37.0)	376	Woodbridge Twnshp, NJ	(75.4)
228	San Leandro, CA	(21.0)	303	Palmdale, CA	(37.7)	377	Scranton, PA	(77.5)
228	Westminster, CA	(21.0)	304	El Cajon, CA	(37.9)	378	Lawrence, MA	(78.4)
231	Louisville, KY	(21.2)	305	Savannah, GA	(38.3)	379	Somerville, MA	(80.3)
231	Stockton, CA	(21.2)	306	High Point, NC	(39.2)	380	Tustin, CA	(80.5)
231	Tallahassee, FL	(21.2)	307	West Jordan, UT	(39.3)	381	Hoover, AL	(82.0)
234	Sugar Land, TX	(21.3)	308	Newton, MA	(39.6)	382	Bethlehem, PA	(82.9)
235	Boca Raton, FL	(21.5)	309	Sparks, NV	(39.7)	383	Redwood City, CA	(83.8)
235	Cincinnati, OH	(21.5)	309	Sterling Heights, MI	(39.7)	384	McAllen, TX	(84.1)
237	Roanoke, VA	(21.6)	311	Fontana, CA	(40.5)	385	Lafayette, LA	(86.0)
238	Irving, TX	(21.9)	312	Ontario, CA	(41.4)	386	Hemet, CA	(86.3)
238	Sioux City, IA	(21.9)	313	Ogden, UT	(41.7)	387	Deerfield Beach, FL	(88.3)
240	Oceanside, CA	(22.2)	314	Longview, TX	(41.8)	388	Asheville, NC	(88.6)
241	Torrance, CA	(22.3)	315	Greensboro, NC	(41.9)	389	Mission, TX	(90.5)
242	Virginia Beach, VA	(22.6)	316	Grand Rapids, MI	(42.2)	390	Mountain View, CA	(91.5)
243	Hayward, CA	(22.8)	317	Miramar, FL	(42.5)	391	Alameda, CA	(92.2)
244	Charlotte, NC	(22.9)	318	Everett, WA	(43.3)	392	Fishers, IN	(92.4)
244	Miami Beach, FL	(22.9)	319	Baldwin Park, CA	(43.5)	393	Upland, CA	(93.3)
244	Palm Bay, FL	(22.9)	320	Kent, WA	(43.7)	394	Bellflower, CA	(95.5)
247	South Bend, IN	(23.1)	321	Des Moines, IA	(44.5)	395	Lakewood Twnshp, NJ	(99.2)
247	Wichita, KS	(23.1)	322	Roseville, CA	(45.0)	NA	Albany, GA**	NA
249	Birmingham, AL	(23.3)	323	Green Bay, WI	(45.1)	NA	Albany, NY**	NA
249	San Diego, CA	(23.3)	324	Garland, TX	(45.9)	NA	Allentown, PA**	NA
251	Bellevue, WA	(23.4)	325	Chesapeake, VA	(46.3)	NA	Amherst, NY**	NA
251	Redding, CA	(23.4)	325	Chula Vista, CA	(46.3)	NA	Arlington Heights, IL**	NA
253	Edmond, OK	(23.8)	327	Fort Collins, CO	(46.4)	NA	Aurora, IL**	NA
254	Gainesville, FL	(24.1)	328	Cape Coral, FL	(47.4)	NA	Bloomington, IL**	NA
254	Worcester, MA	(24.1)	329	Orem, UT	(48.5)	NA	Bloomington, MN**	NA
256	Gilbert, AZ	(24.6)	330	Simi Valley, CA	(48.6)	NA	Brockton, MA**	NA
256	Pearland, TX	(24.6)	331	Tampa, FL	(50.0)	NA	Brooklyn Park, MN**	NA
258	Garden Grove, CA	(24.8)	332	Roswell, GA	(52.2)	NA	Buffalo, NY**	NA
259	Wichita Falls, TX	(24.9)	333	El Monte, CA	(53.5)	NA	Champaign, IL**	NA
260	Las Vegas, NV	(25.2)	334	Santa Clara, CA	(53.6)	NA	Chandler, AZ**	NA
261	Sunnyvale, CA	(25.4)	335	Peoria, AZ	(53.9)	NA	Cheektowaga, NY**	NA
262	Boulder, CO	(25.5)	336	Hammond, IN	(54.1)	NA	Chicago, IL**	NA
263	Fort Smith, AR	(25.6)	337	Plantation, FL	(54.7)	NA	Cicero, IL**	NA
264	Erie, PA	(25.9)	338	Lawton, OK	(54.9)	NA	Clarkstown, NY**	NA
265	Carson, CA	(26.5)	339	Hartford, CT	(55.9)	NA	Colonie, NY**	NA
266	Orlando, FL	(26.7)	340	Avondale, AZ	(56.4)	NA	Decatur, IL**	NA
267	Portsmouth, VA	(26.9)	341	Wilmington, NC	(56.7)	NA	Duluth, MN**	NA
268	Huntsville, AL	(27.1)	342	Frisco, TX	(57.0)	NA	Elgin, IL**	NA
269	Sacramento, CA	(27.2)	342	Irvine, CA	(57.0)	NA	Greece, NY**	NA
270	West Covina, CA	(27.7)	344	Gresham, OR	(57.2)	NA	Johns Creek, GA**	NA
271	Norwalk, CT	(27.8)	344	San Mateo, CA	(57.2)	NA	Joliet, IL**	NA
272	Albuquerque, NM	(28.4)	346	Abilene, TX	(58.1)	NA	Jurupa Valley, CA**	NA
273	Independence, MO	(29.1)	347	League City, TX	(58.4)	NA	Kansas City, KS**	NA
274	Fort Lauderdale, FL	(29.6)	348	Carrollton, TX	(58.5)	NA	Lexington, KY**	NA
275	Hollywood, FL	(30.3)	349	Columbus, GA	(59.2)	NA	Longmont, CO**	NA
275	O'Fallon, MO	(30.3)	350	Hampton, VA	(59.7)	NA	Menifee, CA**	NA
277	Austin, TX	(30.7)	351	Chino Hills, CA	(60.6)	NA	Naperville, IL**	NA
278	Richmond, VA	(30.9)	352	Reno, NV	(62.4)	NA	Nashua, NH**	NA
279	Clarksville, TN	(31.1)	353	Edinburg, TX	(62.5)	NA	New Haven, CT**	NA
280	College Station, TX	(31.4)	354	Miami Gardens, FL	(62.8)	NA	New Rochelle, NY**	NA
280	Winston-Salem, NC	(31.4)	355	Moreno Valley, CA	(62.9)	NA	New York, NY**	NA
282	Chino, CA	(31.5)	356	Bloomington, IN	(63.0)	NA	Olathe, KS**	NA
282	Nampa, ID	(31.5)	357	Waterbury, CT	(64.4)	NA	Parma, OH**	NA
284	Troy, MI	(32.1)	358	Oxnard, CA	(64.6)	NA	Peoria, IL**	NA
285	Kennewick, WA	(32.5)	359	Toms River Twnshp, NJ	(64.9)	NA	Pueblo, CO**	NA
286	Salem, OR	(32.6)	360	Napa, CA	(65.0)	NA	Ramapo, NY**	NA
286	Vancouver, WA	(32.6)	361	Daly City, CA	(65.1)	NA	Renton, WA**	NA
288	Newport News, VA	(32.8)	362	Fremont, CA	(65.2)	NA	Rochester, MN**	NA
289	Riverside, CA	(33.5)	363	Pittsburgh, PA	(65.6)	NA	Rochester, NY**	NA
290	Compton, CA	(33.7)	364	Springfield, MA	(67.4)	NA	Springfield, IL**	NA
290	Corona, CA	(33.7)	365	Carmel, IN	(68.4)	NA	Syracuse, NY**	NA
292	Henderson, NV	(33.9)	366	Santa Maria, CA	(68.5)	NA	Thornton, CO**	NA
293	Murrieta, CA	(34.2)	367	Lynchburg, VA	(68.7)	NA	Waukegan, IL**	NA
294	West Palm Beach, FL	(35.3)	368	Largo, FL	(70.5)	NA	Yonkers, NY**	NA
295	Citrus Heights, CA	(35.4)	369	Alexandria, VA	(70.9)			
296	Westminster, CO	(35.7)	370	Glendale, CA	(71.0)			

Source: CQ Press using reported data from the F.B.I. "Crime in the United States 2012"

*Forcible rape is the carnal knowledge of a female forcibly and against her will. **Not available. ***Fishers, IN had a rape rate in 2008 but had 1 rape in 2012. Calculating percent increase from zero results in an infinite number. This is shown as "NA."

57. Robberies in 2012
National Total = 354,520 Robberies*

RANK	CITY	ROBBERY	RANK	CITY	ROBBERY	RANK	CITY	ROBBERY
253	Abilene, TX	127	422	Chino Hills, CA	22	204	Gainesville, FL	171
74	Akron, OH	577	362	Chino, CA	52	241	Garden Grove, CA	135
308	Alameda, CA	80	164	Chula Vista, CA	227	162	Garland, TX	236
166	Albany, GA	224	191	Cicero, IL	183	145	Gary, IN	275
158	Albany, NY	249	25	Cincinnati, OH	1,725	345	Gilbert, AZ	59
44	Albuquerque, NM	1,092	277	Citrus Heights, CA	100	113	Glendale, AZ	413
238	Alexandria, VA	138	414	Clarkstown, NY	27	267	Glendale, CA	108
334	Alhambra, CA	66	278	Clarksville, TN	99	211	Grand Prairie, TX	160
122	Allentown, PA	374	174	Clearwater, FL	206	98	Grand Rapids, MI	462
434	Allen, TX	13	16	Cleveland, OH	3,252	370	Greece, NY	46
142	Amarillo, TX	278	308	Clifton, NJ	80	337	Greeley, CO	64
410	Amherst, NY	28	348	Clinton Twnshp, MI	58	298	Green Bay, WI	87
105	Anaheim, CA	440	350	Clovis, CA	57	78	Greensboro, NC	556
92	Anchorage, AK	488	390	College Station, TX	38	208	Greenville, NC	169
366	Ann Arbor, MI	50	405	Colonie, NY	29	173	Gresham, OR	207
124	Antioch, CA	372	86	Colorado Springs, CO	523	279	Hamilton Twnshp, NJ	98
440	Arlington Heights, IL	8	210	Columbia, MO	162	187	Hammond, IN	192
83	Arlington, TX	532	109	Columbus, GA	423	226	Hampton, VA	146
405	Arvada, CO	29	107	Compton, CA	428	66	Hartford, CT	640
233	Asheville, NC	141	214	Concord, CA	153	139	Hawthorne, CA	307
213	Athens-Clarke, GA	158	312	Coral Springs, FL	78	128	Hayward, CA	342
18	Atlanta, GA	2,276	275	Corona, CA	102	226	Hemet, CA	146
95	Aurora, CO	483	121	Corpus Christi, TX	375	200	Henderson, NV	172
257	Aurora, IL	125	301	Costa Mesa, CA	83	326	Hesperia, CA	69
50	Austin, TX	978	397	Cranston, RI	34	154	Hialeah, FL	260
322	Avondale, AZ	72	8	Dallas, TX	4,093	189	High Point, NC	185
62	Bakersfield, CA	697	316	Daly City, CA	76	362	Hillsboro, OR	52
320	Baldwin Park, CA	73	378	Danbury, CT	45	142	Hollywood, FL	278
11	Baltimore, MD	3,605	217	Davenport, IA	151	370	Hoover, AL	46
47	Baton Rouge, LA	1,033	319	Davie, FL	74	3	Houston, TX	9,385
114	Beaumont, TX	408	67	Dayton, OH	633	301	Huntington Beach, CA	83
392	Beaverton, OR	36	269	Dearborn, MI	107	101	Huntsville, AL	456
331	Bellevue, WA	67	270	Decatur, IL	106	253	Independence, MO	127
241	Bellflower, CA	135	220	Deerfield Beach, FL	149	14	Indianapolis, IN	3,442
359	Bellingham, WA	53	304	Denton, TX	82	214	Indio, CA	153
129	Berkeley, CA	335	41	Denver, CO	1,165	123	Inglewood, CA	373
259	Bethlehem, PA	121	157	Des Moines, IA	250	405	Irvine, CA	29
328	Billings, MT	68	6	Detroit, MI	4,843	241	Irving, TX	135
49	Birmingham, AL	983	188	Downey, CA	190	34	Jacksonville, FL	1,371
378	Bloomington, IL	45	295	Duluth, MN	90	60	Jackson, MS	799
381	Bloomington, IN	42	69	Durham, NC	615	52	Jersey City, NJ	880
345	Bloomington, MN	59	366	Edinburg, TX	50	431	Johns Creek, GA	16
341	Boca Raton, FL	62	345	Edison Twnshp, NJ	59	273	Joliet, IL	104
337	Boise, ID	64	426	Edmond, OK	20	289	Jurupa Valley, CA	93
21	Boston, MA	1,910	224	El Cajon, CA	147	144	Kansas City, KS	277
368	Boulder, CO	48	177	El Monte, CA	203	28	Kansas City, MO	1,647
431	Brick Twnshp, NJ	16	96	El Paso, TX	471	395	Kennewick, WA	35
70	Bridgeport, CT	606	316	Elgin, IL	76	272	Kenosha, WI	105
165	Brockton, MA	225	82	Elizabeth, NJ	535	186	Kent, WA	194
388	Broken Arrow, OK	39	284	Elk Grove, CA	95	162	Killeen, TX	236
292	Brooklyn Park, MN	91	200	Erie, PA	172	84	Knoxville, TN	528
257	Brownsville, TX	125	174	Escondido, CA	206	179	Lafayette, LA	202
326	Bryan, TX	69	185	Eugene, OR	196	426	Lake Forest, CA	20
314	Buena Park, CA	77	182	Evansville, IN	199	230	Lakeland, FL	144
33	Buffalo, NY	1,388	194	Everett, WA	182	370	Lakewood Twnshp, NJ	46
265	Burbank, CA	111	237	Fairfield, CA	139	275	Lakewood, CA	102
241	Cambridge, MA	135	152	Fall River, MA	262	222	Lakewood, CO	148
61	Camden, NJ	755	370	Fargo, ND	46	138	Lancaster, CA	313
383	Cape Coral, FL	41	437	Farmington Hills, MI	12	177	Lansing, MI	203
353	Carlsbad, CA	55	385	Fayetteville, AR	40	191	Laredo, TX	183
441	Carmel, IN	6	77	Fayetteville, NC	560	263	Largo, FL	114
318	Carrollton, TX	75	270	Federal Way, WA	106	324	Las Cruces, NM	70
232	Carson, CA	142	438	Fishers, IN	9	9	Las Vegas, NV	3,824
405	Cary, NC	29	63	Flint, MI	673	359	Lawrence, KS	53
281	Cedar Rapids, IA	97	141	Fontana, CA	291	168	Lawrence, MA	223
399	Centennial, CO	33	385	Fort Collins, CO	40	199	Lawton, OK	173
241	Champaign, IL	135	55	Fort Lauderdale, FL	835	410	League City, TX	28
220	Chandler, AZ	149	284	Fort Smith, AR	95	416	Lee's Summit, MO	24
273	Charleston, SC	104	104	Fort Wayne, IN	447	70	Lexington, KY	606
23	Charlotte, NC	1,798	35	Fort Worth, TX	1,280	184	Lincoln, NE	197
334	Cheektowaga, NY	66	249	Fremont, CA	132	58	Little Rock, AR	807
179	Chesapeake, VA	202	48	Fresno, CA	1,015	401	Livermore, CA	32
2	Chicago, IL	13,476	416	Frisco, TX	24	401	Livonia, MI	32
284	Chico, CA	95	240	Fullerton, CA	137	37	Long Beach, CA	1,239

RANK	CITY	ROBBERY
403	Longmont, CO	30
250	Longview, TX	131
4	Los Angeles, CA	8,983
32	Louisville, KY	1,394
198	Lowell, MA	174
134	Lubbock, TX	325
370	Lynchburg, VA	46
206	Lynn, MA	170
159	Macon, GA	242
160	Madison, WI	241
176	Manchester, NH	205
352	McAllen, TX	56
348	McKinney, TX	58
337	Medford, OR	64
248	Melbourne, FL	133
15	Memphis, TN	3,382
416	Menifee, CA	24
170	Merced, CA	215
439	Meridian, ID	9
97	Mesa, AZ	469
191	Mesquite, TX	183
115	Miami Beach, FL	407
125	Miami Gardens, FL	369
19	Miami, FL	2,096
362	Midland, TX	52
17	Milwaukee, WI	3,027
27	Minneapolis, MN	1,719
209	Miramar, FL	163
410	Mission Viejo, CA	28
370	Mission, TX	46
99	Mobile, AL	460
103	Modesto, CA	450
100	Montgomery, AL	459
131	Moreno Valley, CA	331
397	Mountain View, CA	34
246	Murfreesboro, TN	134
423	Murrieta, CA	21
426	Nampa, ID	20
388	Napa, CA	39
416	Naperville, IL	24
368	Nashua, NH	48
26	Nashville, TN	1,724
146	New Bedford, MA	272
54	New Haven, CT	844
45	New Orleans, LA	1,065
292	New Rochelle, NY	91
1	New York, NY	20,201
20	Newark, NJ	1,976
414	Newport Beach, CA	27
147	Newport News, VA	271
430	Newton, MA	17
90	Norfolk, VA	491
357	Norman, OK	54
171	North Charleston, SC	212
117	North Las Vegas, NV	389
204	Norwalk, CA	171
328	Norwalk, CT	68
7	Oakland, CA	4,338
197	Oceanside, CA	175
233	Odessa, TX	141
442	O'Fallon, MO	4
282	Ogden, UT	96
39	Oklahoma City, OK	1,209
416	Olathe, KS	24
57	Omaha, NE	815
150	Ontario, CA	266
357	Orange, CA	54
423	Orem, UT	21
72	Orlando, FL	603
381	Overland Park, KS	42
140	Oxnard, CA	304
312	Palm Bay, FL	78
166	Palmdale, CA	224
433	Parma, OH	14

RANK	CITY	ROBBERY
200	Pasadena, CA	172
224	Pasadena, TX	147
53	Paterson, NJ	854
410	Pearland, TX	28
301	Pembroke Pines, FL	83
314	Peoria, AZ	77
135	Peoria, IL	324
5	Philadelphia, PA	7,984
12	Phoenix, AZ	3,516
42	Pittsburgh, PA	1,134
266	Plano, TX	110
253	Plantation, FL	127
120	Pomona, CA	377
111	Pompano Beach, FL	419
353	Port St. Lucie, FL	55
51	Portland, OR	950
194	Portsmouth, VA	182
126	Providence, RI	362
429	Provo, UT	19
182	Pueblo, CO	199
299	Quincy, MA	84
172	Racine, WI	211
64	Raleigh, NC	665
434	Ramapo, NY	13
264	Rancho Cucamon., CA	112
118	Reading, PA	382
250	Redding, CA	131
296	Redwood City, CA	88
132	Reno, NV	327
261	Renton, WA	115
181	Rialto, CA	201
308	Richardson, TX	80
116	Richmond, CA	391
67	Richmond, VA	633
423	Rio Rancho, NM	21
87	Riverside, CA	517
233	Roanoke, VA	141
353	Rochester, MN	55
56	Rochester, NY	817
88	Rockford, IL	499
299	Roseville, CA	84
340	Roswell, GA	63
378	Round Rock, TX	45
38	Sacramento, CA	1,211
238	Salem, OR	138
92	Salinas, CA	488
136	Salt Lake City, UT	316
22	San Antonio, TX	1,864
59	San Bernardino, CA	803
30	San Diego, CA	1,517
13	San Francisco, CA	3,484
40	San Jose, CA	1,208
147	San Leandro, CA	271
350	San Marcos, CA	57
306	San Mateo, CA	81
279	Sandy Springs, GA	98
395	Sandy, UT	35
80	Santa Ana, CA	541
284	Santa Barbara, CA	95
343	Santa Clara, CA	61
282	Santa Clarita, CA	96
228	Santa Maria, CA	145
217	Santa Monica, CA	151
256	Santa Rosa, CA	126
90	Savannah, GA	491
261	Scottsdale, AZ	115
252	Scranton, PA	129
31	Seattle, WA	1,421
106	Shreveport, LA	433
392	Simi Valley, CA	36
370	Sioux City, IA	46
324	Sioux Falls, SD	70
304	Somerville, MA	82
136	South Bend, IN	316

RANK	CITY	ROBBERY
151	South Gate, CA	265
328	Sparks, NV	68
331	Spokane Valley, WA	67
81	Spokane, WA	537
154	Springfield, IL	260
79	Springfield, MA	542
127	Springfield, MO	353
228	Stamford, CT	145
403	Sterling Heights, MI	30
29	Stockton, CA	1,556
421	St. George, UT	23
292	St. Joseph, MO	91
24	St. Louis, MO	1,778
65	St. Paul, MN	658
73	St. Petersburg, FL	585
391	Sugar Land, TX	37
323	Sunnyvale, CA	71
288	Sunrise, FL	94
341	Surprise, AZ	62
102	Syracuse, NY	454
94	Tacoma, WA	486
85	Tallahassee, FL	525
76	Tampa, FL	573
359	Temecula, CA	53
156	Tempe, AZ	253
383	Thornton, CO	41
370	Thousand Oaks, CA	46
43	Toledo, OH	1,126
385	Toms River Twnshp, NJ	40
161	Topeka, KS	237
290	Torrance, CA	92
334	Tracy, CA	66
74	Trenton, NJ	577
434	Troy, MI	13
36	Tucson, AZ	1,260
46	Tulsa, OK	1,062
206	Tuscaloosa, AL	170
392	Tustin, CA	36
290	Tyler, TX	92
331	Upland, CA	67
149	Upper Darby Twnshp, PA	270
320	Vacaville, CA	73
119	Vallejo, CA	380
200	Vancouver, WA	172
236	Ventura, CA	140
169	Victorville, CA	222
133	Virginia Beach, VA	326
246	Visalia, CA	134
230	Vista, CA	144
194	Waco, TX	182
222	Warren, MI	148
405	Warwick, RI	29
10	Washington, DC	3,725
189	Waterbury, CT	185
211	Waukegan, IL	160
267	West Covina, CA	108
399	West Jordan, UT	33
130	West Palm Beach, FL	334
260	West Valley, UT	120
308	Westland, MI	80
296	Westminster, CA	88
365	Westminster, CO	51
306	Whittier, CA	81
219	Wichita Falls, TX	150
89	Wichita, KS	495
153	Wilmington, NC	261
107	Winston-Salem, NC	428
353	Woodbridge Twnshp, NJ	55
111	Worcester, MA	419
216	Yakima, WA	152
110	Yonkers, NY	422
343	Yuma, AZ	61

Source: Reported data from the F.B.I. "Crime in the United States 2012"

*Robbery is the taking of anything of value by force or threat of force. Attempts are included.

57. Robberies in 2012 (continued)
National Total = 354,520 Robberies*

RANK	CITY	ROBBERY	RANK	CITY	ROBBERY	RANK	CITY	ROBBERY
1	New York, NY	20,201	74	Trenton, NJ	577	149	Upper Darby Twnshp, PA	270
2	Chicago, IL	13,476	76	Tampa, FL	573	150	Ontario, CA	266
3	Houston, TX	9,385	77	Fayetteville, NC	560	151	South Gate, CA	265
4	Los Angeles, CA	8,983	78	Greensboro, NC	556	152	Fall River, MA	262
5	Philadelphia, PA	7,984	79	Springfield, MA	542	153	Wilmington, NC	261
6	Detroit, MI	4,843	80	Santa Ana, CA	541	154	Hialeah, FL	260
7	Oakland, CA	4,338	81	Spokane, WA	537	154	Springfield, IL	260
8	Dallas, TX	4,093	82	Elizabeth, NJ	535	156	Tempe, AZ	253
9	Las Vegas, NV	3,824	83	Arlington, TX	532	157	Des Moines, IA	250
10	Washington, DC	3,725	84	Knoxville, TN	528	158	Albany, NY	249
11	Baltimore, MD	3,605	85	Tallahassee, FL	525	159	Macon, GA	242
12	Phoenix, AZ	3,516	86	Colorado Springs, CO	523	160	Madison, WI	241
13	San Francisco, CA	3,484	87	Riverside, CA	517	161	Topeka, KS	237
14	Indianapolis, IN	3,442	88	Rockford, IL	499	162	Garland, TX	236
15	Memphis, TN	3,382	89	Wichita, KS	495	162	Killeen, TX	236
16	Cleveland, OH	3,252	90	Norfolk, VA	491	164	Chula Vista, CA	227
17	Milwaukee, WI	3,027	90	Savannah, GA	491	165	Brockton, MA	225
18	Atlanta, GA	2,276	92	Anchorage, AK	488	166	Albany, GA	224
19	Miami, FL	2,096	92	Salinas, CA	488	166	Palmdale, CA	224
20	Newark, NJ	1,976	94	Tacoma, WA	486	168	Lawrence, MA	223
21	Boston, MA	1,910	95	Aurora, CO	483	169	Victorville, CA	222
22	San Antonio, TX	1,864	96	El Paso, TX	471	170	Merced, CA	215
23	Charlotte, NC	1,798	97	Mesa, AZ	469	171	North Charleston, SC	212
24	St. Louis, MO	1,778	98	Grand Rapids, MI	462	172	Racine, WI	211
25	Cincinnati, OH	1,725	99	Mobile, AL	460	173	Gresham, OR	207
26	Nashville, TN	1,724	100	Montgomery, AL	459	174	Clearwater, FL	206
27	Minneapolis, MN	1,719	101	Huntsville, AL	456	174	Escondido, CA	206
28	Kansas City, MO	1,647	102	Syracuse, NY	454	176	Manchester, NH	205
29	Stockton, CA	1,556	103	Modesto, CA	450	177	El Monte, CA	203
30	San Diego, CA	1,517	104	Fort Wayne, IN	447	177	Lansing, MI	203
31	Seattle, WA	1,421	105	Anaheim, CA	440	179	Chesapeake, VA	202
32	Louisville, KY	1,394	106	Shreveport, LA	433	179	Lafayette, LA	202
33	Buffalo, NY	1,388	107	Compton, CA	428	181	Rialto, CA	201
34	Jacksonville, FL	1,371	107	Winston-Salem, NC	428	182	Evansville, IN	199
35	Fort Worth, TX	1,280	109	Columbus, GA	423	182	Pueblo, CO	199
36	Tucson, AZ	1,260	110	Yonkers, NY	422	184	Lincoln, NE	197
37	Long Beach, CA	1,239	111	Pompano Beach, FL	419	185	Eugene, OR	196
38	Sacramento, CA	1,211	111	Worcester, MA	419	186	Kent, WA	194
39	Oklahoma City, OK	1,209	113	Glendale, AZ	413	187	Hammond, IN	192
40	San Jose, CA	1,208	114	Beaumont, TX	408	188	Downey, CA	190
41	Denver, CO	1,165	115	Miami Beach, FL	407	189	High Point, NC	185
42	Pittsburgh, PA	1,134	116	Richmond, CA	391	189	Waterbury, CT	185
43	Toledo, OH	1,126	117	North Las Vegas, NV	389	191	Cicero, IL	183
44	Albuquerque, NM	1,092	118	Reading, PA	382	191	Laredo, TX	183
45	New Orleans, LA	1,065	119	Vallejo, CA	380	191	Mesquite, TX	183
46	Tulsa, OK	1,062	120	Pomona, CA	377	194	Everett, WA	182
47	Baton Rouge, LA	1,033	121	Corpus Christi, TX	375	194	Portsmouth, VA	182
48	Fresno, CA	1,015	122	Allentown, PA	374	194	Waco, TX	182
49	Birmingham, AL	983	123	Inglewood, CA	373	197	Oceanside, CA	175
50	Austin, TX	978	124	Antioch, CA	372	198	Lowell, MA	174
51	Portland, OR	950	125	Miami Gardens, FL	369	199	Lawton, OK	173
52	Jersey City, NJ	880	126	Providence, RI	362	200	Erie, PA	172
53	Paterson, NJ	854	127	Springfield, MO	353	200	Henderson, NV	172
54	New Haven, CT	844	128	Hayward, CA	342	200	Pasadena, CA	172
55	Fort Lauderdale, FL	835	129	Berkeley, CA	335	200	Vancouver, WA	172
56	Rochester, NY	817	130	West Palm Beach, FL	334	204	Gainesville, FL	171
57	Omaha, NE	815	131	Moreno Valley, CA	331	204	Norwalk, CA	171
58	Little Rock, AR	807	132	Reno, NV	327	206	Lynn, MA	170
59	San Bernardino, CA	803	133	Virginia Beach, VA	326	206	Tuscaloosa, AL	170
60	Jackson, MS	799	134	Lubbock, TX	325	208	Greenville, NC	169
61	Camden, NJ	755	135	Peoria, IL	324	209	Miramar, FL	163
62	Bakersfield, CA	697	136	Salt Lake City, UT	316	210	Columbia, MO	162
63	Flint, MI	673	136	South Bend, IN	316	211	Grand Prairie, TX	160
64	Raleigh, NC	665	138	Lancaster, CA	313	211	Waukegan, IL	160
65	St. Paul, MN	658	139	Hawthorne, CA	307	213	Athens-Clarke, GA	158
66	Hartford, CT	640	140	Oxnard, CA	304	214	Concord, CA	153
67	Dayton, OH	633	141	Fontana, CA	291	214	Indio, CA	153
67	Richmond, VA	633	142	Amarillo, TX	278	216	Yakima, WA	152
69	Durham, NC	615	142	Hollywood, FL	278	217	Davenport, IA	151
70	Bridgeport, CT	606	144	Kansas City, KS	277	217	Santa Monica, CA	151
70	Lexington, KY	606	145	Gary, IN	275	219	Wichita Falls, TX	150
72	Orlando, FL	603	146	New Bedford, MA	272	220	Chandler, AZ	149
73	St. Petersburg, FL	585	147	Newport News, VA	271	220	Deerfield Beach, FL	149
74	Akron, OH	577	147	San Leandro, CA	271	222	Lakewood, CO	148

RANK	CITY	ROBBERY	RANK	CITY	ROBBERY	RANK	CITY	ROBBERY
222	Warren, MI	148	296	Westminster, CA	88	370	Greece, NY	46
224	El Cajon, CA	147	298	Green Bay, WI	87	370	Hoover, AL	46
224	Pasadena, TX	147	299	Quincy, MA	84	370	Lakewood Twnshp, NJ	46
226	Hampton, VA	146	299	Roseville, CA	84	370	Lynchburg, VA	46
226	Hemet, CA	146	301	Costa Mesa, CA	83	370	Mission, TX	46
228	Santa Maria, CA	145	301	Huntington Beach, CA	83	370	Sioux City, IA	46
228	Stamford, CT	145	301	Pembroke Pines, FL	83	370	Thousand Oaks, CA	46
230	Lakeland, FL	144	304	Denton, TX	82	378	Bloomington, IL	45
230	Vista, CA	144	304	Somerville, MA	82	378	Danbury, CT	45
232	Carson, CA	142	306	San Mateo, CA	81	378	Round Rock, TX	45
233	Asheville, NC	141	306	Whittier, CA	81	381	Bloomington, IN	42
233	Odessa, TX	141	308	Alameda, CA	80	381	Overland Park, KS	42
233	Roanoke, VA	141	308	Clifton, NJ	80	383	Cape Coral, FL	41
236	Ventura, CA	140	308	Richardson, TX	80	383	Thornton, CO	41
237	Fairfield, CA	139	308	Westland, MI	80	385	Fayetteville, AR	40
238	Alexandria, VA	138	312	Coral Springs, FL	78	385	Fort Collins, CO	40
238	Salem, OR	138	312	Palm Bay, FL	78	385	Toms River Twnshp, NJ	40
240	Fullerton, CA	137	314	Buena Park, CA	77	388	Broken Arrow, OK	39
241	Bellflower, CA	135	314	Peoria, AZ	77	388	Napa, CA	39
241	Cambridge, MA	135	316	Daly City, CA	76	390	College Station, TX	38
241	Champaign, IL	135	316	Elgin, IL	76	391	Sugar Land, TX	37
241	Garden Grove, CA	135	318	Carrollton, TX	75	392	Beaverton, OR	36
241	Irving, TX	135	319	Davie, FL	74	392	Simi Valley, CA	36
246	Murfreesboro, TN	134	320	Baldwin Park, CA	73	392	Tustin, CA	36
246	Visalia, CA	134	320	Vacaville, CA	73	395	Kennewick, WA	35
248	Melbourne, FL	133	322	Avondale, AZ	72	395	Sandy, UT	35
249	Fremont, CA	132	323	Sunnyvale, CA	71	397	Cranston, RI	34
250	Longview, TX	131	324	Las Cruces, NM	70	397	Mountain View, CA	34
250	Redding, CA	131	324	Sioux Falls, SD	70	399	Centennial, CO	33
252	Scranton, PA	129	326	Bryan, TX	69	399	West Jordan, UT	33
253	Abilene, TX	127	326	Hesperia, CA	69	401	Livermore, CA	32
253	Independence, MO	127	328	Billings, MT	68	401	Livonia, MI	32
253	Plantation, FL	127	328	Norwalk, CT	68	403	Longmont, CO	30
256	Santa Rosa, CA	126	328	Sparks, NV	68	403	Sterling Heights, MI	30
257	Aurora, IL	125	331	Bellevue, WA	67	405	Arvada, CO	29
257	Brownsville, TX	125	331	Spokane Valley, WA	67	405	Cary, NC	29
259	Bethlehem, PA	121	331	Upland, CA	67	405	Colonie, NY	29
260	West Valley, UT	120	334	Alhambra, CA	66	405	Irvine, CA	29
261	Renton, WA	115	334	Cheektowaga, NY	66	405	Warwick, RI	29
261	Scottsdale, AZ	115	334	Tracy, CA	66	410	Amherst, NY	28
263	Largo, FL	114	337	Boise, ID	64	410	League City, TX	28
264	Rancho Cucamon., CA	112	337	Greeley, CO	64	410	Mission Viejo, CA	28
265	Burbank, CA	111	337	Medford, OR	64	410	Pearland, TX	28
266	Plano, TX	110	340	Roswell, GA	63	414	Clarkstown, NY	27
267	Glendale, CA	108	341	Boca Raton, FL	62	414	Newport Beach, CA	27
267	West Covina, CA	108	341	Surprise, AZ	62	416	Frisco, TX	24
269	Dearborn, MI	107	343	Santa Clara, CA	61	416	Lee's Summit, MO	24
270	Decatur, IL	106	343	Yuma, AZ	61	416	Menifee, CA	24
270	Federal Way, WA	106	345	Bloomington, MN	59	416	Naperville, IL	24
272	Kenosha, WI	105	345	Edison Twnshp, NJ	59	416	Olathe, KS	24
273	Charleston, SC	104	345	Gilbert, AZ	59	421	St. George, UT	23
273	Joliet, IL	104	348	Clinton Twnshp, MI	58	422	Chino Hills, CA	22
275	Corona, CA	102	348	McKinney, TX	58	423	Murrieta, CA	21
275	Lakewood, CA	102	350	Clovis, CA	57	423	Orem, UT	21
277	Citrus Heights, CA	100	350	San Marcos, CA	57	423	Rio Rancho, NM	21
278	Clarksville, TN	99	352	McAllen, TX	56	426	Edmond, OK	20
279	Hamilton Twnshp, NJ	98	353	Carlsbad, CA	55	426	Lake Forest, CA	20
279	Sandy Springs, GA	98	353	Port St. Lucie, FL	55	426	Nampa, ID	20
281	Cedar Rapids, IA	97	353	Rochester, MN	55	429	Provo, UT	19
282	Ogden, UT	96	353	Woodbridge Twnshp, NJ	55	430	Newton, MA	17
282	Santa Clarita, CA	96	357	Norman, OK	54	431	Brick Twnshp, NJ	16
284	Chico, CA	95	357	Orange, CA	54	431	Johns Creek, GA	16
284	Elk Grove, CA	95	359	Bellingham, WA	53	433	Parma, OH	14
284	Fort Smith, AR	95	359	Lawrence, KS	53	434	Allen, TX	13
284	Santa Barbara, CA	95	359	Temecula, CA	53	434	Ramapo, NY	13
288	Sunrise, FL	94	362	Chino, CA	52	434	Troy, MI	13
289	Jurupa Valley, CA	93	362	Hillsboro, OR	52	437	Farmington Hills, MI	12
290	Torrance, CA	92	362	Midland, TX	52	438	Fishers, IN	9
290	Tyler, TX	92	365	Westminster, CO	51	439	Meridian, ID	9
292	Brooklyn Park, MN	91	366	Ann Arbor, MI	50	440	Arlington Heights, IL	8
292	New Rochelle, NY	91	366	Edinburg, TX	50	441	Carmel, IN	6
292	St. Joseph, MO	91	368	Boulder, CO	48	442	O'Fallon, MO	4
295	Duluth, MN	90	368	Nashua, NH	48			
296	Redwood City, CA	88	370	Fargo, ND	46			

Source: Reported data from the F.B.I. "Crime in the United States 2012"

*Robbery is the taking of anything of value by force or threat of force. Attempts are included.

58. Robbery Rate in 2012
National Rate = 112.9 Robberies per 100,000 Population*

RANK	CITY	RATE	RANK	CITY	RATE	RANK	CITY	RATE
250	Abilene, TX	105.9	408	Chino Hills, CA	28.7	211	Gainesville, FL	134.6
68	Akron, OH	290.8	323	Chino, CA	65.2	296	Garden Grove, CA	77.1
249	Alameda, CA	106.0	277	Chula Vista, CA	90.9	262	Garland, TX	100.4
71	Albany, GA	285.3	110	Cicero, IL	217.1	49	Gary, IN	341.7
86	Albany, NY	253.6	10	Cincinnati, OH	582.4	410	Gilbert, AZ	27.5
124	Albuquerque, NM	197.2	232	Citrus Heights, CA	117.5	148	Glendale, AZ	177.3
271	Alexandria, VA	94.6	394	Clarkstown, NY	33.7	345	Glendale, CA	55.4
291	Alhambra, CA	78.1	308	Clarksville, TN	72.1	282	Grand Prairie, TX	88.0
59	Allentown, PA	313.4	133	Clearwater, FL	188.5	92	Grand Rapids, MI	243.2
436	Allen, TX	14.6	3	Cleveland, OH	825.8	367	Greece, NY	47.5
204	Amarillo, TX	141.4	272	Clifton, NJ	94.5	319	Greeley, CO	66.5
418	Amherst, NY	23.8	337	Clinton Twnshp, MI	59.8	288	Green Bay, WI	82.0
217	Anaheim, CA	127.7	342	Clovis, CA	58.3	119	Greensboro, NC	201.4
172	Anchorage, AK	163.1	385	College Station, TX	39.4	129	Greenville, NC	194.5
376	Ann Arbor, MI	43.5	391	Colonie, NY	37.2	131	Gresham, OR	191.3
46	Antioch, CA	354.3	226	Colorado Springs, CO	121.0	243	Hamilton Twnshp, NJ	110.0
440	Arlington Heights, IL	10.6	190	Columbia, MO	146.4	95	Hammond, IN	237.0
205	Arlington, TX	140.3	111	Columbus, GA	215.6	250	Hampton, VA	105.9
412	Arvada, CO	26.6	30	Compton, CA	436.5	19	Hartford, CT	511.2
167	Asheville, NC	165.3	225	Concord, CA	122.2	44	Hawthorne, CA	358.3
212	Athens-Clarke, GA	134.5	329	Coral Springs, FL	62.4	101	Hayward, CA	232.0
15	Atlanta, GA	520.8	324	Corona, CA	64.8	145	Hemet, CA	179.8
199	Aurora, CO	143.3	228	Corpus Christi, TX	120.0	322	Henderson, NV	65.3
328	Aurora, IL	62.6	302	Costa Mesa, CA	73.7	298	Hesperia, CA	74.7
233	Austin, TX	117.4	380	Cranston, RI	42.3	240	Hialeah, FL	111.5
276	Avondale, AZ	91.9	53	Dallas, TX	329.7	155	High Point, NC	173.2
126	Bakersfield, CA	196.0	304	Daly City, CA	73.6	347	Hillsboro, OR	55.2
269	Baldwin Park, CA	95.2	349	Danbury, CT	55.0	131	Hollywood, FL	191.3
12	Baltimore, MD	576.4	188	Davenport, IA	149.2	344	Hoover, AL	55.9
27	Baton Rouge, LA	446.2	292	Davie, FL	77.9	32	Houston, TX	431.0
50	Beaumont, TX	339.1	28	Dayton, OH	445.3	378	Huntington Beach, CA	42.6
386	Beaverton, OR	39.0	242	Dearborn, MI	110.1	89	Huntsville, AL	248.2
352	Bellevue, WA	53.2	207	Decatur, IL	139.2	246	Independence, MO	108.1
154	Bellflower, CA	173.3	130	Deerfield Beach, FL	192.4	37	Indianapolis, IN	410.4
325	Bellingham, WA	64.1	316	Denton, TX	68.9	128	Indio, CA	194.9
67	Berkeley, CA	291.4	138	Denver, CO	185.3	51	Inglewood, CA	334.6
176	Bethlehem, PA	160.5	227	Des Moines, IA	120.5	437	Irvine, CA	13.3
326	Billings, MT	63.9	5	Detroit, MI	684.9	334	Irving, TX	60.3
24	Birmingham, AL	460.9	162	Downey, CA	167.2	172	Jacksonville, FL	163.1
340	Bloomington, IL	58.4	257	Duluth, MN	103.7	25	Jackson, MS	454.1
356	Bloomington, IN	51.4	82	Durham, NC	261.1	48	Jersey City, NJ	349.8
312	Bloomington, MN	69.7	330	Edinburg, TX	62.2	425	Johns Creek, GA	20.0
309	Boca Raton, FL	71.7	340	Edison Twnshp, NJ	58.4	311	Joliet, IL	70.0
404	Boise, ID	30.3	416	Edmond, OK	24.0	268	Jurupa Valley, CA	95.3
64	Boston, MA	302.9	194	El Cajon, CA	144.3	134	Kansas City, KS	188.2
366	Boulder, CO	47.9	150	El Monte, CA	176.0	45	Kansas City, MO	354.9
423	Brick Twnshp, NJ	21.1	312	El Paso, TX	69.7	371	Kennewick, WA	45.5
35	Bridgeport, CT	415.0	314	Elgin, IL	69.6	254	Kenosha, WI	105.0
98	Brockton, MA	236.5	34	Elizabeth, NJ	423.7	179	Kent, WA	158.9
387	Broken Arrow, OK	38.7	333	Elk Grove, CA	60.8	146	Killeen, TX	178.8
230	Brooklyn Park, MN	117.7	159	Erie, PA	168.7	69	Knoxville, TN	289.7
315	Brownsville, TX	69.0	206	Escondido, CA	139.8	169	Lafayette, LA	164.4
283	Bryan, TX	87.9	221	Eugene, OR	124.0	415	Lake Forest, CA	25.3
274	Buena Park, CA	93.3	160	Evansville, IN	168.4	197	Lakeland, FL	144.1
14	Buffalo, NY	528.9	156	Everett, WA	172.8	364	Lakewood Twnshp, NJ	49.1
252	Burbank, CA	105.7	213	Fairfield, CA	129.8	220	Lakewood, CA	125.3
219	Cambridge, MA	126.2	66	Fall River, MA	291.9	261	Lakewood, CO	101.1
2	Camden, NJ	972.1	382	Fargo, ND	41.9	125	Lancaster, CA	196.7
414	Cape Coral, FL	25.7	435	Farmington Hills, MI	14.9	149	Lansing, MI	177.0
360	Carlsbad, CA	51.0	353	Fayetteville, AR	53.1	300	Laredo, TX	74.5
441	Carmel, IN	7.3	77	Fayetteville, NC	271.9	193	Largo, FL	144.7
334	Carrollton, TX	60.3	236	Federal Way, WA	115.2	310	Las Cruces, NM	70.1
185	Carson, CA	152.3	439	Fishers, IN	11.3	84	Las Vegas, NV	258.5
424	Cary, NC	20.6	7	Flint, MI	662.2	339	Lawrence, KS	59.4
297	Cedar Rapids, IA	75.5	191	Fontana, CA	144.9	70	Lawrence, MA	287.1
400	Centennial, CO	31.7	411	Fort Collins, CO	26.9	152	Lawton, OK	175.1
164	Champaign, IL	166.0	23	Fort Lauderdale, FL	488.8	399	League City, TX	32.5
332	Chandler, AZ	61.4	245	Fort Smith, AR	108.6	413	Lee's Summit, MO	26.1
286	Charleston, SC	84.0	153	Fort Wayne, IN	174.2	121	Lexington, KY	200.4
105	Charlotte, NC	222.4	163	Fort Worth, TX	166.2	299	Lincoln, NE	74.6
287	Cheektowaga, NY	83.4	334	Fremont, CA	60.3	36	Little Rock, AR	411.6
280	Chesapeake, VA	88.8	120	Fresno, CA	200.6	390	Livermore, CA	38.6
22	Chicago, IL	497.6	428	Frisco, TX	19.5	396	Livonia, MI	33.3
244	Chico, CA	109.1	265	Fullerton, CA	98.9	81	Long Beach, CA	263.7

RANK	CITY	RATE
394	Longmont, CO	33.7
181	Longview, TX	158.7
100	Los Angeles, CA	233.0
116	Louisville, KY	209.2
177	Lowell, MA	160.3
208	Lubbock, TX	137.0
338	Lynchburg, VA	59.5
139	Lynn, MA	185.1
83	Macon, GA	260.7
260	Madison, WI	101.5
137	Manchester, NH	186.3
383	McAllen, TX	41.3
381	McKinney, TX	42.0
285	Medford, OR	84.2
157	Melbourne, FL	172.4
18	Memphis, TN	514.4
405	Menifee, CA	30.0
80	Merced, CA	265.5
438	Meridian, ID	11.6
256	Mesa, AZ	103.9
218	Mesquite, TX	126.4
26	Miami Beach, FL	446.9
52	Miami Gardens, FL	331.9
20	Miami, FL	505.9
372	Midland, TX	45.0
21	Milwaukee, WI	505.0
29	Minneapolis, MN	440.5
214	Miramar, FL	129.4
407	Mission Viejo, CA	29.3
343	Mission, TX	57.1
142	Mobile, AL	182.9
107	Modesto, CA	219.9
108	Montgomery, AL	219.6
165	Moreno Valley, CA	165.8
373	Mountain View, CA	44.8
229	Murfreesboro, TN	119.4
426	Murrieta, CA	19.7
416	Nampa, ID	24.0
362	Napa, CA	49.6
431	Naperville, IL	16.8
346	Nashua, NH	55.3
75	Nashville, TN	277.7
72	New Bedford, MA	283.2
8	New Haven, CT	649.6
65	New Orleans, LA	293.5
235	New Rochelle, NY	116.6
91	New York, NY	243.7
4	Newark, NJ	708.5
401	Newport Beach, CA	30.9
188	Newport News, VA	149.2
427	Newton, MA	19.6
122	Norfolk, VA	200.2
368	Norman, OK	47.4
115	North Charleston, SC	210.6
151	North Las Vegas, NV	175.3
178	Norwalk, CA	159.4
290	Norwalk, CT	78.4
1	Oakland, CA	1,085.9
259	Oceanside, CA	102.3
209	Odessa, TX	136.1
442	O'Fallon, MO	5.0
238	Ogden, UT	112.8
118	Oklahoma City, OK	203.0
429	Olathe, KS	18.7
127	Omaha, NE	195.0
182	Ontario, CA	158.4
387	Orange, CA	38.7
422	Orem, UT	22.8
90	Orlando, FL	244.6
419	Overland Park, KS	23.7
186	Oxnard, CA	150.6
300	Palm Bay, FL	74.5
195	Palmdale, CA	144.2
430	Parma, OH	17.3

RANK	CITY	RATE
223	Pasadena, CA	123.4
270	Pasadena, TX	95.1
11	Paterson, NJ	580.4
406	Pearland, TX	29.6
354	Pembroke Pines, FL	52.0
365	Peoria, AZ	48.6
74	Peoria, IL	281.0
17	Philadelphia, PA	518.8
97	Phoenix, AZ	236.7
43	Pittsburgh, PA	363.3
384	Plano, TX	40.2
192	Plantation, FL	144.8
88	Pomona, CA	248.8
38	Pompano Beach, FL	406.8
398	Port St. Lucie, FL	32.7
179	Portland, OR	158.9
135	Portsmouth, VA	188.1
117	Providence, RI	203.5
432	Provo, UT	16.3
143	Pueblo, CO	182.5
279	Quincy, MA	89.6
78	Racine, WI	266.9
183	Raleigh, NC	158.1
434	Ramapo, NY	15.2
321	Rancho Cucamon., CA	66.2
31	Reading, PA	431.4
198	Redding, CA	144.0
239	Redwood City, CA	112.2
202	Reno, NV	141.9
224	Renton, WA	122.7
123	Rialto, CA	197.8
295	Richardson, TX	77.5
42	Richmond, CA	367.6
63	Richmond, VA	304.6
420	Rio Rancho, NM	23.5
168	Riverside, CA	164.9
195	Roanoke, VA	144.2
361	Rochester, MN	50.7
40	Rochester, NY	385.4
54	Rockford, IL	327.7
317	Roseville, CA	68.4
317	Roswell, GA	68.4
379	Round Rock, TX	42.4
85	Sacramento, CA	254.1
284	Salem, OR	87.7
58	Salinas, CA	316.0
170	Salt Lake City, UT	164.2
210	San Antonio, TX	135.1
41	San Bernardino, CA	373.5
237	San Diego, CA	113.3
33	San Francisco, CA	424.7
222	San Jose, CA	123.7
60	San Leandro, CA	312.0
320	San Marcos, CA	66.4
289	San Mateo, CA	81.6
263	Sandy Springs, GA	100.1
387	Sandy, UT	38.7
174	Santa Ana, CA	162.7
252	Santa Barbara, CA	105.7
359	Santa Clara, CA	51.1
351	Santa Clarita, CA	53.6
199	Santa Maria, CA	143.3
166	Santa Monica, CA	165.5
302	Santa Rosa, CA	73.7
114	Savannah, GA	212.3
355	Scottsdale, AZ	51.5
158	Scranton, PA	169.5
103	Seattle, WA	226.7
112	Shreveport, LA	214.2
409	Simi Valley, CA	28.4
347	Sioux City, IA	55.2
375	Sioux Falls, SD	44.2
248	Somerville, MA	106.2
61	South Bend, IN	311.6

RANK	CITY	RATE
76	South Gate, CA	276.1
304	Sparks, NV	73.6
306	Spokane Valley, WA	73.5
87	Spokane, WA	253.1
106	Springfield, IL	222.0
47	Springfield, MA	350.8
109	Springfield, MO	219.3
234	Stamford, CT	116.7
421	Sterling Heights, MI	23.1
16	Stockton, CA	520.2
403	St. George, UT	30.4
230	St. Joseph, MO	117.7
13	St. Louis, MO	557.9
104	St. Paul, MN	226.4
99	St. Petersburg, FL	235.6
374	Sugar Land, TX	44.6
363	Sunnyvale, CA	49.4
247	Sunrise, FL	107.8
357	Surprise, AZ	51.3
62	Syracuse, NY	311.1
93	Tacoma, WA	239.8
73	Tallahassee, FL	283.1
171	Tampa, FL	163.4
357	Temecula, CA	51.3
184	Tempe, AZ	152.4
396	Thornton, CO	33.3
392	Thousand Oaks, CA	35.6
39	Toledo, OH	393.7
377	Toms River Twnshp, NJ	43.4
141	Topeka, KS	183.9
330	Torrance, CA	62.2
294	Tracy, CA	77.6
6	Trenton, NJ	676.3
433	Troy, MI	15.9
95	Tucson, AZ	237.0
79	Tulsa, OK	266.2
140	Tuscaloosa, AL	184.8
370	Tustin, CA	46.5
275	Tyler, TX	92.0
281	Upland, CA	88.7
56	Upper Darby Twnshp, PA	325.4
293	Vacaville, CA	77.7
57	Vallejo, CA	322.3
258	Vancouver, WA	103.4
215	Ventura, CA	129.0
136	Victorville, CA	187.0
307	Virginia Beach, VA	72.8
254	Visalia, CA	105.0
187	Vista, CA	149.9
203	Waco, TX	141.5
241	Warren, MI	110.2
393	Warwick, RI	35.2
9	Washington, DC	589.1
161	Waterbury, CT	167.4
146	Waukegan, IL	178.8
263	West Covina, CA	100.1
402	West Jordan, UT	30.8
55	West Palm Beach, FL	326.1
278	West Valley, UT	89.7
266	Westland, MI	96.0
267	Westminster, CA	95.7
369	Westminster, CO	46.6
273	Whittier, CA	93.4
201	Wichita Falls, TX	142.2
216	Wichita, KS	128.1
94	Wilmington, NC	238.6
144	Winston-Salem, NC	182.4
350	Woodbridge Twnshp, NJ	54.7
102	Worcester, MA	228.7
174	Yakima, WA	162.7
113	Yonkers, NY	212.6
327	Yuma, AZ	63.8

Source: CQ Press using reported data from the F.B.I. "Crime in the United States 2012"

*Robbery is the taking of anything of value by force or threat of force. Attempts are included.

58. Robbery Rate in 2012 (continued)
National Rate = 112.9 Robberies per 100,000 Population*

RANK	CITY	RATE	RANK	CITY	RATE	RANK	CITY	RATE
1	Oakland, CA	1,085.9	75	Nashville, TN	277.7	149	Lansing, MI	177.0
2	Camden, NJ	972.1	76	South Gate, CA	276.1	150	El Monte, CA	176.0
3	Cleveland, OH	825.8	77	Fayetteville, NC	271.9	151	North Las Vegas, NV	175.3
4	Newark, NJ	708.5	78	Racine, WI	266.9	152	Lawton, OK	175.1
5	Detroit, MI	684.9	79	Tulsa, OK	266.2	153	Fort Wayne, IN	174.2
6	Trenton, NJ	676.3	80	Merced, CA	265.5	154	Bellflower, CA	173.3
7	Flint, MI	662.2	81	Long Beach, CA	263.7	155	High Point, NC	173.2
8	New Haven, CT	649.6	82	Durham, NC	261.1	156	Everett, WA	172.8
9	Washington, DC	589.1	83	Macon, GA	260.7	157	Melbourne, FL	172.4
10	Cincinnati, OH	582.4	84	Las Vegas, NV	258.5	158	Scranton, PA	169.5
11	Paterson, NJ	580.4	85	Sacramento, CA	254.1	159	Erie, PA	168.7
12	Baltimore, MD	576.4	86	Albany, NY	253.6	160	Evansville, IN	168.4
13	St. Louis, MO	557.9	87	Spokane, WA	253.1	161	Waterbury, CT	167.4
14	Buffalo, NY	528.9	88	Pomona, CA	248.8	162	Downey, CA	167.2
15	Atlanta, GA	520.8	89	Huntsville, AL	248.2	163	Fort Worth, TX	166.2
16	Stockton, CA	520.2	90	Orlando, FL	244.6	164	Champaign, IL	166.0
17	Philadelphia, PA	518.8	91	New York, NY	243.7	165	Moreno Valley, CA	165.8
18	Memphis, TN	514.4	92	Grand Rapids, MI	243.2	166	Santa Monica, CA	165.5
19	Hartford, CT	511.2	93	Tacoma, WA	239.8	167	Asheville, NC	165.3
20	Miami, FL	505.9	94	Wilmington, NC	238.6	168	Riverside, CA	164.9
21	Milwaukee, WI	505.0	95	Hammond, IN	237.0	169	Lafayette, LA	164.4
22	Chicago, IL	497.6	95	Tucson, AZ	237.0	170	Salt Lake City, UT	164.2
23	Fort Lauderdale, FL	488.8	97	Phoenix, AZ	236.7	171	Tampa, FL	163.4
24	Birmingham, AL	460.9	98	Brockton, MA	236.5	172	Anchorage, AK	163.1
25	Jackson, MS	454.1	99	St. Petersburg, FL	235.6	172	Jacksonville, FL	163.1
26	Miami Beach, FL	446.9	100	Los Angeles, CA	233.0	174	Santa Ana, CA	162.7
27	Baton Rouge, LA	446.2	101	Hayward, CA	232.0	174	Yakima, WA	162.7
28	Dayton, OH	445.3	102	Worcester, MA	228.7	176	Bethlehem, PA	160.5
29	Minneapolis, MN	440.5	103	Seattle, WA	226.7	177	Lowell, MA	160.3
30	Compton, CA	436.5	104	St. Paul, MN	226.4	178	Norwalk, CA	159.4
31	Reading, PA	431.4	105	Charlotte, NC	222.4	179	Kent, WA	158.9
32	Houston, TX	431.0	106	Springfield, IL	222.0	179	Portland, OR	158.9
33	San Francisco, CA	424.7	107	Modesto, CA	219.9	181	Longview, TX	158.7
34	Elizabeth, NJ	423.7	108	Montgomery, AL	219.6	182	Ontario, CA	158.4
35	Bridgeport, CT	415.0	109	Springfield, MO	219.3	183	Raleigh, NC	158.1
36	Little Rock, AR	411.6	110	Cicero, IL	217.1	184	Tempe, AZ	152.4
37	Indianapolis, IN	410.4	111	Columbus, GA	215.6	185	Carson, CA	152.3
38	Pompano Beach, FL	406.8	112	Shreveport, LA	214.2	186	Oxnard, CA	150.6
39	Toledo, OH	393.7	113	Yonkers, NY	212.6	187	Vista, CA	149.9
40	Rochester, NY	385.4	114	Savannah, GA	212.3	188	Davenport, IA	149.2
41	San Bernardino, CA	373.5	115	North Charleston, SC	210.6	188	Newport News, VA	149.2
42	Richmond, CA	367.6	116	Louisville, KY	209.2	190	Columbia, MO	146.4
43	Pittsburgh, PA	363.3	117	Providence, RI	203.5	191	Fontana, CA	144.9
44	Hawthorne, CA	358.3	118	Oklahoma City, OK	203.0	192	Plantation, FL	144.8
45	Kansas City, MO	354.9	119	Greensboro, NC	201.4	193	Largo, FL	144.7
46	Antioch, CA	354.3	120	Fresno, CA	200.6	194	El Cajon, CA	144.3
47	Springfield, MA	350.8	121	Lexington, KY	200.4	195	Palmdale, CA	144.2
48	Jersey City, NJ	349.8	122	Norfolk, VA	200.2	195	Roanoke, VA	144.2
49	Gary, IN	341.7	123	Rialto, CA	197.8	197	Lakeland, FL	144.1
50	Beaumont, TX	339.1	124	Albuquerque, NM	197.2	198	Redding, CA	144.0
51	Inglewood, CA	334.6	125	Lancaster, CA	196.7	199	Aurora, CO	143.3
52	Miami Gardens, FL	331.9	126	Bakersfield, CA	196.0	199	Santa Maria, CA	143.3
53	Dallas, TX	329.7	127	Omaha, NE	195.0	201	Wichita Falls, TX	142.2
54	Rockford, IL	327.7	128	Indio, CA	194.9	202	Reno, NV	141.9
55	West Palm Beach, FL	326.1	129	Greenville, NC	194.5	203	Waco, TX	141.5
56	Upper Darby Twnshp, PA	325.4	130	Deerfield Beach, FL	192.4	204	Amarillo, TX	141.4
57	Vallejo, CA	322.3	131	Gresham, OR	191.3	205	Arlington, TX	140.3
58	Salinas, CA	316.0	131	Hollywood, FL	191.3	206	Escondido, CA	139.8
59	Allentown, PA	313.4	133	Clearwater, FL	188.5	207	Decatur, IL	139.2
60	San Leandro, CA	312.0	134	Kansas City, KS	188.2	208	Lubbock, TX	137.0
61	South Bend, IN	311.6	135	Portsmouth, VA	188.1	209	Odessa, TX	136.1
62	Syracuse, NY	311.1	136	Victorville, CA	187.0	210	San Antonio, TX	135.1
63	Richmond, VA	304.6	137	Manchester, NH	186.3	211	Gainesville, FL	134.6
64	Boston, MA	302.9	138	Denver, CO	185.3	212	Athens-Clarke, GA	134.5
65	New Orleans, LA	293.5	139	Lynn, MA	185.1	213	Fairfield, CA	129.8
66	Fall River, MA	291.9	140	Tuscaloosa, AL	184.8	214	Miramar, FL	129.4
67	Berkeley, CA	291.4	141	Topeka, KS	183.9	215	Ventura, CA	129.0
68	Akron, OH	290.8	142	Mobile, AL	182.9	216	Wichita, KS	128.1
69	Knoxville, TN	289.7	143	Pueblo, CO	182.5	217	Anaheim, CA	127.7
70	Lawrence, MA	287.1	144	Winston-Salem, NC	182.4	218	Mesquite, TX	126.4
71	Albany, GA	285.3	145	Hemet, CA	179.8	219	Cambridge, MA	126.2
72	New Bedford, MA	283.2	146	Killeen, TX	178.8	220	Lakewood, CA	125.3
73	Tallahassee, FL	283.1	146	Waukegan, IL	178.8	221	Eugene, OR	124.0
74	Peoria, IL	281.0	148	Glendale, AZ	177.3	222	San Jose, CA	123.7

RANK	CITY	RATE	RANK	CITY	RATE	RANK	CITY	RATE
223	Pasadena, CA	123.4	297	Cedar Rapids, IA	75.5	371	Kennewick, WA	45.5
224	Renton, WA	122.7	298	Hesperia, CA	74.7	372	Midland, TX	45.0
225	Concord, CA	122.2	299	Lincoln, NE	74.6	373	Mountain View, CA	44.8
226	Colorado Springs, CO	121.0	300	Laredo, TX	74.5	374	Sugar Land, TX	44.6
227	Des Moines, IA	120.5	300	Palm Bay, FL	74.5	375	Sioux Falls, SD	44.2
228	Corpus Christi, TX	120.0	302	Costa Mesa, CA	73.7	376	Ann Arbor, MI	43.5
229	Murfreesboro, TN	119.4	302	Santa Rosa, CA	73.7	377	Toms River Twnshp, NJ	43.4
230	Brooklyn Park, MN	117.7	304	Daly City, CA	73.6	378	Huntington Beach, CA	42.6
230	St. Joseph, MO	117.7	304	Sparks, NV	73.6	379	Round Rock, TX	42.4
232	Citrus Heights, CA	117.5	306	Spokane Valley, WA	73.5	380	Cranston, RI	42.3
233	Austin, TX	117.4	307	Virginia Beach, VA	72.8	381	McKinney, TX	42.0
234	Stamford, CT	116.7	308	Clarksville, TN	72.1	382	Fargo, ND	41.9
235	New Rochelle, NY	116.6	309	Boca Raton, FL	71.7	383	McAllen, TX	41.3
236	Federal Way, WA	115.2	310	Las Cruces, NM	70.1	384	Plano, TX	40.2
237	San Diego, CA	113.3	311	Joliet, IL	70.0	385	College Station, TX	39.4
238	Ogden, UT	112.8	312	Bloomington, MN	69.7	386	Beaverton, OR	39.0
239	Redwood City, CA	112.2	312	El Paso, TX	69.7	387	Broken Arrow, OK	38.7
240	Hialeah, FL	111.5	314	Elgin, IL	69.6	387	Orange, CA	38.7
241	Warren, MI	110.2	315	Brownsville, TX	69.0	387	Sandy, UT	38.7
242	Dearborn, MI	110.1	316	Denton, TX	68.9	390	Livermore, CA	38.6
243	Hamilton Twnshp, NJ	110.0	317	Roseville, CA	68.4	391	Colonie, NY	37.2
244	Chico, CA	109.1	317	Roswell, GA	68.4	392	Thousand Oaks, CA	35.6
245	Fort Smith, AR	108.6	319	Greeley, CO	66.5	393	Warwick, RI	35.2
246	Independence, MO	108.1	320	San Marcos, CA	66.4	394	Clarkstown, NY	33.7
247	Sunrise, FL	107.8	321	Rancho Cucamon., CA	66.2	394	Longmont, CO	33.7
248	Somerville, MA	106.2	322	Henderson, NV	65.3	396	Livonia, MI	33.3
249	Alameda, CA	106.0	323	Chino, CA	65.2	396	Thornton, CO	33.3
250	Abilene, TX	105.9	324	Corona, CA	64.8	398	Port St. Lucie, FL	32.7
250	Hampton, VA	105.9	325	Bellingham, WA	64.1	399	League City, TX	32.5
252	Burbank, CA	105.7	326	Billings, MT	63.9	400	Centennial, CO	31.7
252	Santa Barbara, CA	105.7	327	Yuma, AZ	63.8	401	Newport Beach, CA	30.9
254	Kenosha, WI	105.0	328	Aurora, IL	62.6	402	West Jordan, UT	30.8
254	Visalia, CA	105.0	329	Coral Springs, FL	62.4	403	St. George, UT	30.4
256	Mesa, AZ	103.9	330	Edinburg, TX	62.2	404	Boise, ID	30.3
257	Duluth, MN	103.7	330	Torrance, CA	62.2	405	Menifee, CA	30.0
258	Vancouver, WA	103.4	332	Chandler, AZ	61.4	406	Pearland, TX	29.6
259	Oceanside, CA	102.3	333	Elk Grove, CA	60.8	407	Mission Viejo, CA	29.3
260	Madison, WI	101.5	334	Carrollton, TX	60.3	408	Chino Hills, CA	28.7
261	Lakewood, CO	101.1	334	Fremont, CA	60.3	409	Simi Valley, CA	28.4
262	Garland, TX	100.4	334	Irving, TX	60.3	410	Gilbert, AZ	27.5
263	Sandy Springs, GA	100.1	337	Clinton Twnshp, MI	59.8	411	Fort Collins, CO	26.9
263	West Covina, CA	100.1	338	Lynchburg, VA	59.5	412	Arvada, CO	26.6
265	Fullerton, CA	98.9	339	Lawrence, KS	59.4	413	Lee's Summit, MO	26.1
266	Westland, MI	96.0	340	Bloomington, IL	58.4	414	Cape Coral, FL	25.7
267	Westminster, CA	95.7	340	Edison Twnshp, NJ	58.4	415	Lake Forest, CA	25.3
268	Jurupa Valley, CA	95.3	342	Clovis, CA	58.3	416	Edmond, OK	24.0
269	Baldwin Park, CA	95.2	343	Mission, TX	57.1	416	Nampa, ID	24.0
270	Pasadena, TX	95.1	344	Hoover, AL	55.9	418	Amherst, NY	23.8
271	Alexandria, VA	94.6	345	Glendale, CA	55.4	419	Overland Park, KS	23.7
272	Clifton, NJ	94.5	346	Nashua, NH	55.3	420	Rio Rancho, NM	23.5
273	Whittier, CA	93.4	347	Hillsboro, OR	55.2	421	Sterling Heights, MI	23.1
274	Buena Park, CA	93.3	347	Sioux City, IA	55.2	422	Orem, UT	22.8
275	Tyler, TX	92.0	349	Danbury, CT	55.0	423	Brick Twnshp, NJ	21.1
276	Avondale, AZ	91.9	350	Woodbridge Twnshp, NJ	54.7	424	Cary, NC	20.6
277	Chula Vista, CA	90.9	351	Santa Clarita, CA	53.6	425	Johns Creek, GA	20.0
278	West Valley, UT	89.7	352	Bellevue, WA	53.2	426	Murrieta, CA	19.7
279	Quincy, MA	89.6	353	Fayetteville, AR	53.1	427	Newton, MA	19.6
280	Chesapeake, VA	88.8	354	Pembroke Pines, FL	52.0	428	Frisco, TX	19.5
281	Upland, CA	88.7	355	Scottsdale, AZ	51.5	429	Olathe, KS	18.7
282	Grand Prairie, TX	88.0	356	Bloomington, IN	51.4	430	Parma, OH	17.3
283	Bryan, TX	87.9	357	Surprise, AZ	51.3	431	Naperville, IL	16.8
284	Salem, OR	87.7	357	Temecula, CA	51.3	432	Provo, UT	16.3
285	Medford, OR	84.2	359	Santa Clara, CA	51.1	433	Troy, MI	15.9
286	Charleston, SC	84.0	360	Carlsbad, CA	51.0	434	Ramapo, NY	15.2
287	Cheektowaga, NY	83.4	361	Rochester, MN	50.7	435	Farmington Hills, MI	14.9
288	Green Bay, WI	82.0	362	Napa, CA	49.6	436	Allen, TX	14.6
289	San Mateo, CA	81.6	363	Sunnyvale, CA	49.4	437	Irvine, CA	13.3
290	Norwalk, CT	78.4	364	Lakewood Twnshp, NJ	49.1	438	Meridian, ID	11.6
291	Alhambra, CA	78.1	365	Peoria, AZ	48.6	439	Fishers, IN	11.3
292	Davie, FL	77.9	366	Boulder, CO	47.9	440	Arlington Heights, IL	10.6
293	Vacaville, CA	77.7	367	Greece, NY	47.5	441	Carmel, IN	7.3
294	Tracy, CA	77.6	368	Norman, OK	47.4	442	O'Fallon, MO	5.0
295	Richardson, TX	77.5	369	Westminster, CO	46.6			
296	Garden Grove, CA	77.1	370	Tustin, CA	46.5			

Source: CQ Press using reported data from the F.B.I. "Crime in the United States 2012"

*Robbery is the taking of anything of value by force or threat of force. Attempts are included.

59. Percent Change in Robbery Rate: 2011 to 2012
National Percent Change = 0.8% Decrease*

RANK	CITY	% CHANGE	RANK	CITY	% CHANGE	RANK	CITY	% CHANGE
149	Abilene, TX	5.5	28	Chino Hills, CA	36.0	290	Gainesville, FL	(7.8)
365	Akron, OH	(19.3)	319	Chino, CA	(11.3)	378	Garden Grove, CA	(22.0)
345	Alameda, CA	(15.8)	247	Chula Vista, CA	(3.7)	275	Garland, TX	(5.8)
49	Albany, GA	27.2	104	Cicero, IL	12.8	347	Gary, IN	(15.9)
NA	Albany, NY**	NA	233	Cincinnati, OH	(2.4)	161	Gilbert, AZ	3.8
129	Albuquerque, NM	9.1	378	Citrus Heights, CA	(22.0)	269	Glendale, AZ	(5.4)
161	Alexandria, VA	3.8	NA	Clarkstown, NY**	NA	207	Glendale, CA	(0.5)
85	Alhambra, CA	15.2	387	Clarksville, TN	(24.4)	376	Grand Prairie, TX	(21.6)
NA	Allentown, PA**	NA	99	Clearwater, FL	13.1	220	Grand Rapids, MI	(1.5)
392	Allen, TX	(26.3)	159	Cleveland, OH	3.9	NA	Greece, NY**	NA
75	Amarillo, TX	17.1	372	Clifton, NJ	(21.0)	353	Greeley, CO	(16.2)
NA	Amherst, NY**	NA	360	Clinton Twnshp, MI	(18.5)	9	Green Bay, WI	78.6
236	Anaheim, CA	(2.6)	172	Clovis, CA	2.6	NA	Greensboro, NC**	NA
157	Anchorage, AK	4.2	73	College Station, TX	18.0	NA	Greenville, NC**	NA
350	Ann Arbor, MI	(16.0)	NA	Colonie, NY**	NA	69	Gresham, OR	18.7
50	Antioch, CA	26.5	93	Colorado Springs, CO	14.2	62	Hamilton Twnshp, NJ	20.5
414	Arlington Heights, IL	(53.1)	254	Columbia, MO	(3.9)	154	Hammond, IN	4.6
240	Arlington, TX	(3.0)	198	Columbus, GA	0.4	265	Hampton, VA	(4.9)
343	Arvada, CO	(15.3)	109	Compton, CA	12.1	147	Hartford, CT	6.1
384	Asheville, NC	(22.9)	306	Concord, CA	(9.6)	190	Hawthorne, CA	1.2
66	Athens-Clarke, GA	19.3	341	Coral Springs, FL	(14.9)	276	Hayward, CA	(6.0)
269	Atlanta, GA	(5.4)	262	Corona, CA	(4.8)	83	Hemet, CA	15.4
276	Aurora, CO	(6.0)	192	Corpus Christi, TX	1.1	337	Henderson, NV	(13.9)
375	Aurora, IL	(21.4)	214	Costa Mesa, CA	(1.2)	397	Hesperia, CA	(28.2)
338	Austin, TX	(14.3)	99	Cranston, RI	13.1	198	Hialeah, FL	0.4
405	Avondale, AZ	(31.0)	210	Dallas, TX	(0.8)	299	High Point, NC	(8.5)
53	Bakersfield, CA	25.7	46	Daly City, CA	27.6	14	Hillsboro, OR	46.0
365	Baldwin Park, CA	(19.3)	413	Danbury, CT	(41.4)	185	Hollywood, FL	1.5
155	Baltimore, MD	4.5	36	Davenport, IA	32.3	37	Hoover, AL	30.9
80	Baton Rouge, LA	15.7	404	Davie, FL	(30.8)	91	Houston, TX	14.7
88	Beaumont, TX	15.1	214	Dayton, OH	(1.2)	386	Huntington Beach, CA	(24.2)
227	Beaverton, OR	(1.8)	159	Dearborn, MI	3.9	117	Huntsville, AL	10.9
96	Bellevue, WA	13.9	338	Decatur, IL	(14.3)	85	Independence, MO	15.2
79	Bellflower, CA	15.8	128	Deerfield Beach, FL	9.2	187	Indianapolis, IN	1.4
256	Bellingham, WA	(4.2)	15	Denton, TX	45.1	26	Indio, CA	36.3
233	Berkeley, CA	(2.4)	212	Denver, CO	(1.0)	135	Inglewood, CA	8.2
55	Bethlehem, PA	24.4	95	Des Moines, IA	14.1	400	Irvine, CA	(28.5)
8	Billings, MT	86.3	222	Detroit, MI	(1.6)	322	Irving, TX	(11.8)
239	Birmingham, AL	(2.8)	288	Downey, CA	(7.3)	335	Jacksonville, FL	(13.7)
382	Bloomington, IL	(22.6)	125	Duluth, MN	10.0	232	Jackson, MS	(2.1)
399	Bloomington, IN	(28.4)	334	Durham, NC	(13.6)	306	Jersey City, NJ	(9.6)
19	Bloomington, MN	42.0	304	Edinburg, TX	(9.3)	65	Johns Creek, GA	19.8
236	Boca Raton, FL	(2.6)	310	Edison Twnshp, NJ	(9.9)	68	Joliet, IL	19.0
144	Boise, ID	6.7	214	Edmond, OK	(1.2)	NA	Jurupa Valley, CA**	NA
213	Boston, MA	(1.1)	381	El Cajon, CA	(22.3)	267	Kansas City, KS	(5.1)
31	Boulder, CO	35.7	169	El Monte, CA	3.1	222	Kansas City, MO	(1.6)
371	Brick Twnshp, NJ	(20.7)	204	El Paso, TX	(0.4)	233	Kennewick, WA	(2.4)
225	Bridgeport, CT	(1.7)	291	Elgin, IL	(7.9)	148	Kenosha, WI	5.7
250	Brockton, MA	(3.8)	394	Elizabeth, NJ	(26.5)	401	Kent, WA	(29.0)
272	Broken Arrow, OK	(5.6)	254	Elk Grove, CA	(3.9)	29	Killeen, TX	35.8
329	Brooklyn Park, MN	(12.8)	90	Erie, PA	14.8	280	Knoxville, TN	(6.5)
99	Brownsville, TX	13.1	89	Escondido, CA	15.0	335	Lafayette, LA	(13.7)
326	Bryan, TX	(12.4)	120	Eugene, OR	10.6	312	Lake Forest, CA	(10.0)
202	Buena Park, CA	0.0	41	Evansville, IN	29.0	184	Lakeland, FL	1.6
NA	Buffalo, NY**	NA	51	Everett, WA	26.4	13	Lakewood Twnshp, NJ	47.4
10	Burbank, CA	62.6	282	Fairfield, CA	(6.6)	163	Lakewood, CA	3.6
325	Cambridge, MA	(12.2)	262	Fall River, MA	(4.8)	108	Lakewood, CO	12.2
324	Camden, NJ	(12.0)	258	Fargo, ND	(4.3)	93	Lancaster, CA	14.2
403	Cape Coral, FL	(30.7)	416	Farmington Hills, MI	(57.5)	394	Lansing, MI	(26.5)
12	Carlsbad, CA	55.5	164	Fayetteville, AR	3.5	355	Laredo, TX	(16.5)
1	Carmel, IN	192.0	112	Fayetteville, NC	11.6	104	Largo, FL	12.8
373	Carrollton, TX	(21.2)	NA	Federal Way, WA**	NA	183	Las Cruces, NM	1.7
34	Carson, CA	33.4	132	Fishers, IN	8.7	136	Las Vegas, NV	7.9
406	Cary, NC	(31.1)	111	Flint, MI	11.7	20	Lawrence, KS	41.4
113	Cedar Rapids, IA	11.5	66	Fontana, CA	19.3	306	Lawrence, MA	(9.6)
21	Centennial, CO	40.9	338	Fort Collins, CO	(14.3)	230	Lawton, OK	(2.0)
43	Champaign, IL	28.5	145	Fort Lauderdale, FL	6.4	390	League City, TX	(25.1)
NA	Chandler, AZ**	NA	272	Fort Smith, AR	(5.6)	370	Lee's Summit, MO	(20.2)
411	Charleston, SC	(37.0)	16	Fort Wayne, IN	43.3	NA	Lexington, KY**	NA
130	Charlotte, NC	8.9	209	Fort Worth, TX	(0.7)	127	Lincoln, NE	9.9
NA	Cheektowaga, NY**	NA	354	Fremont, CA	(16.3)	280	Little Rock, AR	(6.5)
361	Chesapeake, VA	(18.8)	222	Fresno, CA	(1.6)	363	Livermore, CA	(18.9)
247	Chicago, IL	(3.7)	195	Frisco, TX	1.0	368	Livonia, MI	(19.4)
165	Chico, CA	3.4	40	Fullerton, CA	30.0	282	Long Beach, CA	(6.6)

RANK	CITY	% CHANGE	RANK	CITY	% CHANGE	RANK	CITY	% CHANGE
315	Longmont, CO	(10.4)	250	Pasadena, CA	(3.8)	230	South Gate, CA	(2.0)
70	Longview, TX	18.5	142	Pasadena, TX	7.2	316	Sparks, NV	(10.7)
319	Los Angeles, CA	(11.3)	98	Paterson, NJ	13.4	81	Spokane Valley, WA	15.6
343	Louisville, KY	(15.3)	262	Pearland, TX	(4.8)	114	Spokane, WA	11.0
179	Lowell, MA	2.2	407	Pembroke Pines, FL	(31.5)	201	Springfield, IL	0.3
172	Lubbock, TX	2.6	29	Peoria, AZ	35.8	185	Springfield, MA	1.5
410	Lynchburg, VA	(36.8)	107	Peoria, IL	12.5	59	Springfield, MO	22.7
287	Lynn, MA	(7.1)	247	Philadelphia, PA	(3.7)	388	Stamford, CT	(24.5)
229	Macon, GA	(1.9)	156	Phoenix, AZ	4.4	242	Sterling Heights, MI	(3.3)
327	Madison, WI	(12.6)	204	Pittsburgh, PA	(0.4)	78	Stockton, CA	16.0
102	Manchester, NH	12.9	389	Plano, TX	(24.9)	NA	St. George, UT**	NA
385	McAllen, TX	(23.9)	242	Plantation, FL	(3.3)	120	St. Joseph, MO	10.6
45	McKinney, TX	27.7	118	Pomona, CA	10.7	347	St. Louis, MO	(15.9)
146	Medford, OR	6.2	63	Pompano Beach, FL	20.0	137	St. Paul, MN	7.8
347	Melbourne, FL	(15.9)	316	Port St. Lucie, FL	(10.7)	361	St. Petersburg, FL	(18.8)
130	Memphis, TN	8.9	177	Portland, OR	2.3	56	Sugar Land, TX	23.9
175	Menifee, CA	2.4	382	Portsmouth, VA	(22.6)	170	Sunnyvale, CA	2.9
18	Merced, CA	42.4	NA	Providence, RI**	NA	289	Sunrise, FL	(7.7)
2	Meridian, ID	190.0	397	Provo, UT	(28.2)	64	Surprise, AZ	19.9
285	Mesa, AZ	(6.9)	92	Pueblo, CO	14.4	NA	Syracuse, NY**	NA
180	Mesquite, TX	1.9	300	Quincy, MA	(8.6)	134	Tacoma, WA	8.4
139	Miami Beach, FL	7.5	97	Racine, WI	13.7	180	Tallahassee, FL	1.9
328	Miami Gardens, FL	(12.7)	265	Raleigh, NC	(4.9)	268	Tampa, FL	(5.3)
177	Miami, FL	2.3	NA	Ramapo, NY**	NA	250	Temecula, CA	(3.8)
323	Midland, TX	(11.9)	139	Rancho Cucamon., CA	7.5	149	Tempe, AZ	5.5
182	Milwaukee, WI	1.8	192	Reading, PA	1.1	NA	Thornton, CO**	NA
143	Minneapolis, MN	6.9	37	Redding, CA	30.9	33	Thousand Oaks, CA	34.3
356	Miramar, FL	(16.6)	25	Redwood City, CA	38.3	227	Toledo, OH	(1.8)
291	Mission Viejo, CA	(7.9)	345	Reno, NV	(15.8)	408	Toms River Twnshp, NJ	(34.8)
60	Mission, TX	21.5	219	Renton, WA	(1.4)	198	Topeka, KS	0.4
396	Mobile, AL	(27.7)	238	Rialto, CA	(2.7)	196	Torrance, CA	0.6
151	Modesto, CA	5.3	166	Richardson, TX	3.3	258	Tracy, CA	(4.3)
44	Montgomery, AL	28.3	48	Richmond, CA	27.3	114	Trenton, NJ	11.0
225	Moreno Valley, CA	(1.7)	285	Richmond, VA	(6.9)	294	Troy, MI	(8.1)
359	Mountain View, CA	(18.1)	23	Rio Rancho, NM	39.1	139	Tucson, AZ	7.5
202	Murfreesboro, TN	0.0	118	Riverside, CA	10.7	242	Tulsa, OK	(3.3)
412	Murrieta, CA	(39.4)	364	Roanoke, VA	(19.1)	333	Tuscaloosa, AL	(13.4)
3	Nampa, ID	120.2	352	Rochester, MN	(16.1)	302	Tustin, CA	(8.8)
358	Napa, CA	(17.9)	NA	Rochester, NY**	NA	84	Tyler, TX	15.3
208	Naperville, IL	(0.6)	318	Rockford, IL	(11.2)	357	Upland, CA	(17.3)
256	Nashua, NH	(4.2)	5	Roseville, CA	91.1	106	Upper Darby Twnshp, PA	12.6
310	Nashville, TN	(9.9)	5	Roswell, GA	91.1	17	Vacaville, CA	42.6
291	New Bedford, MA	(7.9)	114	Round Rock, TX	11.0	331	Vallejo, CA	(13.1)
122	New Haven, CT	10.3	168	Sacramento, CA	3.2	295	Vancouver, WA	(8.2)
250	New Orleans, LA	(3.8)	85	Salem, OR	15.2	170	Ventura, CA	2.9
NA	New Rochelle, NY**	NA	42	Salinas, CA	28.6	350	Victorville, CA	(16.0)
NA	New York, NY**	NA	295	Salt Lake City, UT	(8.2)	377	Virginia Beach, VA	(21.7)
204	Newark, NJ	(0.4)	172	San Antonio, TX	2.6	23	Visalia, CA	39.1
218	Newport Beach, CA	(1.3)	123	San Bernardino, CA	10.2	74	Vista, CA	17.6
402	Newport News, VA	(29.7)	175	San Diego, CA	2.4	393	Waco, TX	(26.4)
321	Newton, MA	(11.7)	109	San Francisco, CA	12.1	269	Warren, MI	(5.4)
374	Norfolk, VA	(21.3)	138	San Jose, CA	7.6	11	Warwick, RI	61.5
157	Norman, OK	4.2	57	San Leandro, CA	23.6	241	Washington, DC	(3.1)
102	North Charleston, SC	12.9	279	San Marcos, CA	(6.2)	192	Waterbury, CT	1.1
NA	North Las Vegas, NV**	NA	77	San Mateo, CA	16.2	NA	Waukegan, IL**	NA
58	Norwalk, CA	23.4	190	Sandy Springs, GA	1.2	332	West Covina, CA	(13.3)
391	Norwalk, CT	(25.3)	35	Sandy, UT	32.5	39	West Jordan, UT	30.5
46	Oakland, CA	27.6	306	Santa Ana, CA	(9.6)	22	West Palm Beach, FL	40.6
260	Oceanside, CA	(4.5)	72	Santa Barbara, CA	18.2	278	West Valley, UT	(6.1)
7	Odessa, TX	90.3	314	Santa Clara, CA	(10.2)	297	Westland, MI	(8.3)
415	O'Fallon, MO	(55.8)	52	Santa Clarita, CA	25.8	125	Westminster, CA	10.0
210	Ogden, UT	(0.8)	274	Santa Maria, CA	(5.7)	153	Westminster, CO	4.7
245	Oklahoma City, OK	(3.4)	76	Santa Monica, CA	16.5	365	Whittier, CA	(19.3)
71	Olathe, KS	18.4	282	Santa Rosa, CA	(6.6)	166	Wichita Falls, TX	3.3
81	Omaha, NE	15.6	220	Savannah, GA	(1.5)	196	Wichita, KS	0.6
53	Ontario, CA	25.7	303	Scottsdale, AZ	(9.2)	189	Wilmington, NC	1.3
408	Orange, CA	(34.8)	27	Scranton, PA	36.1	260	Winston-Salem, NC	(4.5)
4	Orem, UT	105.4	214	Seattle, WA	(1.2)	152	Woodbridge Twnshp, NJ	5.2
342	Orlando, FL	(15.2)	61	Shreveport, LA	21.4	187	Worcester, MA	1.4
132	Overland Park, KS	8.7	330	Simi Valley, CA	(12.9)	246	Yakima, WA	(3.6)
124	Oxnard, CA	10.1	32	Sioux City, IA	35.0	NA	Yonkers, NY**	NA
369	Palm Bay, FL	(19.6)	297	Sioux Falls, SD	(8.3)	301	Yuma, AZ	(8.7)
305	Palmdale, CA	(9.4)	313	Somerville, MA	(10.1)			
NA	Parma, OH**	NA	378	South Bend, IN	(22.0)			

Source: CQ Press using reported data from the F.B.I. "Crime in the United States 2012"

*Robbery is the taking of anything of value by force or threat of force. Attempts are included.

**Not available.

59. Percent Change in Robbery Rate: 2011 to 2012 (continued)
National Percent Change = 0.8% Decrease*

RANK	CITY	% CHANGE	RANK	CITY	% CHANGE	RANK	CITY	% CHANGE
1	Carmel, IN	192.0	75	Amarillo, TX	17.1	149	Abilene, TX	5.5
2	Meridian, ID	190.0	76	Santa Monica, CA	16.5	149	Tempe, AZ	5.5
3	Nampa, ID	120.2	77	San Mateo, CA	16.2	151	Modesto, CA	5.3
4	Orem, UT	105.4	78	Stockton, CA	16.0	152	Woodbridge Twnshp, NJ	5.2
5	Roseville, CA	91.1	79	Bellflower, CA	15.8	153	Westminster, CO	4.7
5	Roswell, GA	91.1	80	Baton Rouge, LA	15.7	154	Hammond, IN	4.6
7	Odessa, TX	90.3	81	Omaha, NE	15.6	155	Baltimore, MD	4.5
8	Billings, MT	86.3	81	Spokane Valley, WA	15.6	156	Phoenix, AZ	4.4
9	Green Bay, WI	78.6	83	Hemet, CA	15.4	157	Anchorage, AK	4.2
10	Burbank, CA	62.6	84	Tyler, TX	15.3	157	Norman, OK	4.2
11	Warwick, RI	61.5	85	Alhambra, CA	15.2	159	Cleveland, OH	3.9
12	Carlsbad, CA	55.5	85	Independence, MO	15.2	159	Dearborn, MI	3.9
13	Lakewood Twnshp, NJ	47.4	85	Salem, OR	15.2	161	Alexandria, VA	3.8
14	Hillsboro, OR	46.0	88	Beaumont, TX	15.1	161	Gilbert, AZ	3.8
15	Denton, TX	45.1	89	Escondido, CA	15.0	163	Lakewood, CA	3.6
16	Fort Wayne, IN	43.3	90	Erie, PA	14.8	164	Fayetteville, AR	3.5
17	Vacaville, CA	42.6	91	Houston, TX	14.7	165	Chico, CA	3.4
18	Merced, CA	42.4	92	Pueblo, CO	14.4	166	Richardson, TX	3.3
19	Bloomington, MN	42.0	93	Colorado Springs, CO	14.2	166	Wichita Falls, TX	3.3
20	Lawrence, KS	41.4	93	Lancaster, CA	14.2	168	Sacramento, CA	3.2
21	Centennial, CO	40.9	95	Des Moines, IA	14.1	169	El Monte, CA	3.1
22	West Palm Beach, FL	40.6	96	Bellevue, WA	13.9	170	Sunnyvale, CA	2.9
23	Rio Rancho, NM	39.1	97	Racine, WI	13.7	170	Ventura, CA	2.9
23	Visalia, CA	39.1	98	Paterson, NJ	13.4	172	Clovis, CA	2.6
25	Redwood City, CA	38.3	99	Brownsville, TX	13.1	172	Lubbock, TX	2.6
26	Indio, CA	36.3	99	Clearwater, FL	13.1	172	San Antonio, TX	2.6
27	Scranton, PA	36.1	99	Cranston, RI	13.1	175	Menifee, CA	2.4
28	Chino Hills, CA	36.0	102	Manchester, NH	12.9	175	San Diego, CA	2.4
29	Killeen, TX	35.8	102	North Charleston, SC	12.9	177	Miami, FL	2.3
29	Peoria, AZ	35.8	104	Cicero, IL	12.8	177	Portland, OR	2.3
31	Boulder, CO	35.7	104	Largo, FL	12.8	179	Lowell, MA	2.2
32	Sioux City, IA	35.0	106	Upper Darby Twnshp, PA	12.6	180	Mesquite, TX	1.9
33	Thousand Oaks, CA	34.3	107	Peoria, IL	12.5	180	Tallahassee, FL	1.9
34	Carson, CA	33.4	108	Lakewood, CO	12.2	182	Milwaukee, WI	1.8
35	Sandy, UT	32.5	109	Compton, CA	12.1	183	Las Cruces, NM	1.7
36	Davenport, IA	32.3	109	San Francisco, CA	12.1	184	Lakeland, FL	1.6
37	Hoover, AL	30.9	111	Flint, MI	11.7	185	Hollywood, FL	1.5
37	Redding, CA	30.9	112	Fayetteville, NC	11.6	185	Springfield, MA	1.5
39	West Jordan, UT	30.5	113	Cedar Rapids, IA	11.5	187	Indianapolis, IN	1.4
40	Fullerton, CA	30.0	114	Round Rock, TX	11.0	187	Worcester, MA	1.4
41	Evansville, IN	29.0	114	Spokane, WA	11.0	189	Wilmington, NC	1.3
42	Salinas, CA	28.6	114	Trenton, NJ	11.0	190	Hawthorne, CA	1.2
43	Champaign, IL	28.5	117	Huntsville, AL	10.9	190	Sandy Springs, GA	1.2
44	Montgomery, AL	28.3	118	Pomona, CA	10.7	192	Corpus Christi, TX	1.1
45	McKinney, TX	27.7	118	Riverside, CA	10.7	192	Reading, PA	1.1
46	Daly City, CA	27.6	120	Eugene, OR	10.6	192	Waterbury, CT	1.1
46	Oakland, CA	27.6	120	St. Joseph, MO	10.6	195	Frisco, TX	1.0
48	Richmond, CA	27.3	122	New Haven, CT	10.3	196	Torrance, CA	0.6
49	Albany, GA	27.2	123	San Bernardino, CA	10.2	196	Wichita, KS	0.6
50	Antioch, CA	26.5	124	Oxnard, CA	10.1	198	Columbus, GA	0.4
51	Everett, WA	26.4	125	Duluth, MN	10.0	198	Hialeah, FL	0.4
52	Santa Clarita, CA	25.8	125	Westminster, CA	10.0	198	Topeka, KS	0.4
53	Bakersfield, CA	25.7	127	Lincoln, NE	9.9	201	Springfield, IL	0.3
53	Ontario, CA	25.7	128	Deerfield Beach, FL	9.2	202	Buena Park, CA	0.0
55	Bethlehem, PA	24.4	129	Albuquerque, NM	9.1	202	Murfreesboro, TN	0.0
56	Sugar Land, TX	23.9	130	Charlotte, NC	8.9	204	El Paso, TX	(0.4)
57	San Leandro, CA	23.6	130	Memphis, TN	8.9	204	Newark, NJ	(0.4)
58	Norwalk, CA	23.4	132	Fishers, IN	8.7	204	Pittsburgh, PA	(0.4)
59	Springfield, MO	22.7	132	Overland Park, KS	8.7	207	Glendale, CA	(0.5)
60	Mission, TX	21.5	134	Tacoma, WA	8.4	208	Naperville, IL	(0.6)
61	Shreveport, LA	21.4	135	Inglewood, CA	8.2	209	Fort Worth, TX	(0.7)
62	Hamilton Twnshp, NJ	20.5	136	Las Vegas, NV	7.9	210	Dallas, TX	(0.8)
63	Pompano Beach, FL	20.0	137	St. Paul, MN	7.8	210	Ogden, UT	(0.8)
64	Surprise, AZ	19.9	138	San Jose, CA	7.6	212	Denver, CO	(1.0)
65	Johns Creek, GA	19.8	139	Miami Beach, FL	7.5	213	Boston, MA	(1.1)
66	Athens-Clarke, GA	19.3	139	Rancho Cucamon., CA	7.5	214	Costa Mesa, CA	(1.2)
66	Fontana, CA	19.3	139	Tucson, AZ	7.5	214	Dayton, OH	(1.2)
68	Joliet, IL	19.0	142	Pasadena, TX	7.2	214	Edmond, OK	(1.2)
69	Gresham, OR	18.7	143	Minneapolis, MN	6.9	214	Seattle, WA	(1.2)
70	Longview, TX	18.5	144	Boise, ID	6.7	218	Newport Beach, CA	(1.3)
71	Olathe, KS	18.4	145	Fort Lauderdale, FL	6.4	219	Renton, WA	(1.4)
72	Santa Barbara, CA	18.2	146	Medford, OR	6.2	220	Grand Rapids, MI	(1.5)
73	College Station, TX	18.0	147	Hartford, CT	6.1	220	Savannah, GA	(1.5)
74	Vista, CA	17.6	148	Kenosha, WI	5.7	222	Detroit, MI	(1.6)

RANK	CITY	% CHANGE	RANK	CITY	% CHANGE	RANK	CITY	% CHANGE
222	Fresno, CA	(1.6)	297	Sioux Falls, SD	(8.3)	371	Brick Twnshp, NJ	(20.7)
222	Kansas City, MO	(1.6)	297	Westland, MI	(8.3)	372	Clifton, NJ	(21.0)
225	Bridgeport, CT	(1.7)	299	High Point, NC	(8.5)	373	Carrollton, TX	(21.2)
225	Moreno Valley, CA	(1.7)	300	Quincy, MA	(8.6)	374	Norfolk, VA	(21.3)
227	Beaverton, OR	(1.8)	301	Yuma, AZ	(8.7)	375	Aurora, IL	(21.4)
227	Toledo, OH	(1.8)	302	Tustin, CA	(8.8)	376	Grand Prairie, TX	(21.6)
229	Macon, GA	(1.9)	303	Scottsdale, AZ	(9.2)	377	Virginia Beach, VA	(21.7)
230	Lawton, OK	(2.0)	304	Edinburg, TX	(9.3)	378	Citrus Heights, CA	(22.0)
230	South Gate, CA	(2.0)	305	Palmdale, CA	(9.4)	378	Garden Grove, CA	(22.0)
232	Jackson, MS	(2.1)	306	Concord, CA	(9.6)	378	South Bend, IN	(22.0)
233	Berkeley, CA	(2.4)	306	Jersey City, NJ	(9.6)	381	El Cajon, CA	(22.3)
233	Cincinnati, OH	(2.4)	306	Lawrence, MA	(9.6)	382	Bloomington, IL	(22.6)
233	Kennewick, WA	(2.4)	306	Santa Ana, CA	(9.6)	382	Portsmouth, VA	(22.6)
236	Anaheim, CA	(2.6)	310	Edison Twnshp, NJ	(9.9)	384	Asheville, NC	(22.9)
236	Boca Raton, FL	(2.6)	310	Nashville, TN	(9.9)	385	McAllen, TX	(23.9)
238	Rialto, CA	(2.7)	312	Lake Forest, CA	(10.0)	386	Huntington Beach, CA	(24.2)
239	Birmingham, AL	(2.8)	313	Somerville, MA	(10.1)	387	Clarksville, TN	(24.4)
240	Arlington, TX	(3.0)	314	Santa Clara, CA	(10.2)	388	Stamford, CT	(24.5)
241	Washington, DC	(3.1)	315	Longmont, CO	(10.4)	389	Plano, TX	(24.9)
242	Plantation, FL	(3.3)	316	Port St. Lucie, FL	(10.7)	390	League City, TX	(25.1)
242	Sterling Heights, MI	(3.3)	316	Sparks, NV	(10.7)	391	Norwalk, CT	(25.3)
242	Tulsa, OK	(3.3)	318	Rockford, IL	(11.2)	392	Allen, TX	(26.3)
245	Oklahoma City, OK	(3.4)	319	Chino, CA	(11.3)	393	Waco, TX	(26.4)
246	Yakima, WA	(3.6)	319	Los Angeles, CA	(11.3)	394	Elizabeth, NJ	(26.5)
247	Chicago, IL	(3.7)	321	Newton, MA	(11.7)	394	Lansing, MI	(26.5)
247	Chula Vista, CA	(3.7)	322	Irving, TX	(11.8)	396	Mobile, AL	(27.7)
247	Philadelphia, PA	(3.7)	323	Midland, TX	(11.9)	397	Hesperia, CA	(28.2)
250	Brockton, MA	(3.8)	324	Camden, NJ	(12.0)	397	Provo, UT	(28.2)
250	New Orleans, LA	(3.8)	325	Cambridge, MA	(12.2)	399	Bloomington, IN	(28.4)
250	Pasadena, CA	(3.8)	326	Bryan, TX	(12.4)	400	Irvine, CA	(28.5)
250	Temecula, CA	(3.8)	327	Madison, WI	(12.6)	401	Kent, WA	(29.0)
254	Columbia, MO	(3.9)	328	Miami Gardens, FL	(12.7)	402	Newport News, VA	(29.7)
254	Elk Grove, CA	(3.9)	329	Brooklyn Park, MN	(12.8)	403	Cape Coral, FL	(30.7)
256	Bellingham, WA	(4.2)	330	Simi Valley, CA	(12.9)	404	Davie, FL	(30.8)
256	Nashua, NH	(4.2)	331	Vallejo, CA	(13.1)	405	Avondale, AZ	(31.0)
258	Fargo, ND	(4.3)	332	West Covina, CA	(13.3)	406	Cary, NC	(31.1)
258	Tracy, CA	(4.3)	333	Tuscaloosa, AL	(13.4)	407	Pembroke Pines, FL	(31.5)
260	Oceanside, CA	(4.5)	334	Durham, NC	(13.6)	408	Orange, CA	(34.8)
260	Winston-Salem, NC	(4.5)	335	Jacksonville, FL	(13.7)	408	Toms River Twnshp, NJ	(34.8)
262	Corona, CA	(4.8)	335	Lafayette, LA	(13.7)	410	Lynchburg, VA	(36.8)
262	Fall River, MA	(4.8)	337	Henderson, NV	(13.9)	411	Charleston, SC	(37.0)
262	Pearland, TX	(4.8)	338	Austin, TX	(14.3)	412	Murrieta, CA	(39.4)
265	Hampton, VA	(4.9)	338	Decatur, IL	(14.3)	413	Danbury, CT	(41.4)
265	Raleigh, NC	(4.9)	338	Fort Collins, CO	(14.3)	414	Arlington Heights, IL	(53.1)
267	Kansas City, KS	(5.1)	341	Coral Springs, FL	(14.9)	415	O'Fallon, MO	(55.8)
268	Tampa, FL	(5.3)	342	Orlando, FL	(15.2)	416	Farmington Hills, MI	(57.5)
269	Atlanta, GA	(5.4)	343	Arvada, CO	(15.3)	NA	Albany, NY**	NA
269	Glendale, AZ	(5.4)	343	Louisville, KY	(15.3)	NA	Allentown, PA**	NA
269	Warren, MI	(5.4)	345	Alameda, CA	(15.8)	NA	Amherst, NY**	NA
272	Broken Arrow, OK	(5.6)	345	Reno, NV	(15.8)	NA	Buffalo, NY**	NA
272	Fort Smith, AR	(5.6)	347	Gary, IN	(15.9)	NA	Chandler, AZ**	NA
274	Santa Maria, CA	(5.7)	347	Melbourne, FL	(15.9)	NA	Cheektowaga, NY**	NA
275	Garland, TX	(5.8)	347	St. Louis, MO	(15.9)	NA	Clarkstown, NY**	NA
276	Aurora, CO	(6.0)	350	Ann Arbor, MI	(16.0)	NA	Colonie, NY**	NA
276	Hayward, CA	(6.0)	350	Victorville, CA	(16.0)	NA	Federal Way, WA**	NA
278	West Valley, UT	(6.1)	352	Rochester, MN	(16.1)	NA	Greece, NY**	NA
279	San Marcos, CA	(6.2)	353	Greeley, CO	(16.2)	NA	Greensboro, NC**	NA
280	Knoxville, TN	(6.5)	354	Fremont, CA	(16.3)	NA	Greenville, NC**	NA
280	Little Rock, AR	(6.5)	355	Laredo, TX	(16.5)	NA	Jurupa Valley, CA**	NA
282	Fairfield, CA	(6.6)	356	Miramar, FL	(16.6)	NA	Lexington, KY**	NA
282	Long Beach, CA	(6.6)	357	Upland, CA	(17.3)	NA	New Rochelle, NY**	NA
282	Santa Rosa, CA	(6.6)	358	Napa, CA	(17.9)	NA	New York, NY**	NA
285	Mesa, AZ	(6.9)	359	Mountain View, CA	(18.1)	NA	North Las Vegas, NV**	NA
285	Richmond, VA	(6.9)	360	Clinton Twnshp, MI	(18.5)	NA	Parma, OH**	NA
287	Lynn, MA	(7.1)	361	Chesapeake, VA	(18.8)	NA	Providence, RI**	NA
288	Downey, CA	(7.3)	361	St. Petersburg, FL	(18.8)	NA	Ramapo, NY**	NA
289	Sunrise, FL	(7.7)	363	Livermore, CA	(18.9)	NA	Rochester, NY**	NA
290	Gainesville, FL	(7.8)	364	Roanoke, VA	(19.1)	NA	St. George, UT**	NA
291	Elgin, IL	(7.9)	365	Akron, OH	(19.3)	NA	Syracuse, NY**	NA
291	Mission Viejo, CA	(7.9)	365	Baldwin Park, CA	(19.3)	NA	Thornton, CO**	NA
291	New Bedford, MA	(7.9)	365	Whittier, CA	(19.3)	NA	Waukegan, IL**	NA
294	Troy, MI	(8.1)	368	Livonia, MI	(19.4)	NA	Yonkers, NY**	NA
295	Salt Lake City, UT	(8.2)	369	Palm Bay, FL	(19.6)			
295	Vancouver, WA	(8.2)	370	Lee's Summit, MO	(20.2)			

Source: CQ Press using reported data from the F.B.I. "Crime in the United States 2012"

*Robbery is the taking of anything of value by force or threat of force. Attempts are included.

**Not available.

60. Percent Change in Robbery Rate: 2008 to 2012
National Percent Change = 22.6% Decrease*

RANK	CITY	% CHANGE	RANK	CITY	% CHANGE	RANK	CITY	% CHANGE
282	Abilene, TX	(31.6)	71	Chino Hills, CA	(1.7)	311	Gainesville, FL	(35.1)
220	Akron, OH	(24.9)	334	Chino, CA	(38.7)	382	Garden Grove, CA	(48.5)
276	Alameda, CA	(30.7)	321	Chula Vista, CA	(36.7)	291	Garland, TX	(32.3)
NA	Albany, GA**	NA	NA	Cicero, IL**	NA	19	Gary, IN	28.7
NA	Albany, NY**	NA	179	Cincinnati, OH	(19.9)	82	Gilbert, AZ	(3.8)
205	Albuquerque, NM	(22.9)	259	Citrus Heights, CA	(29.2)	203	Glendale, AZ	(22.6)
118	Alexandria, VA	(10.6)	NA	Clarkstown, NY**	NA	245	Glendale, CA	(27.7)
396	Alhambra, CA	(56.7)	399	Clarksville, TN	(58.1)	302	Grand Prairie, TX	(33.7)
NA	Allentown, PA**	NA	328	Clearwater, FL	(37.8)	335	Grand Rapids, MI	(38.8)
95	Allen, TX	(6.4)	92	Cleveland, OH	(5.9)	NA	Greece, NY**	NA
168	Amarillo, TX	(18.1)	126	Clifton, NJ	(12.0)	121	Greeley, CO	(11.5)
NA	Amherst, NY**	NA	174	Clinton Twnshp, MI	(18.9)	184	Green Bay, WI	(20.8)
227	Anaheim, CA	(25.6)	44	Clovis, CA	7.4	385	Greensboro, NC	(49.6)
150	Anchorage, AK	(16.0)	346	College Station, TX	(41.3)	326	Greenville, NC	(37.6)
214	Ann Arbor, MI	(24.1)	NA	Colonie, NY**	NA	24	Gresham, OR	23.7
116	Antioch, CA	(10.3)	124	Colorado Springs, CO	(11.6)	47	Hamilton Twnshp, NJ	6.8
NA	Arlington Heights, IL**	NA	45	Columbia, MO	7.2	194	Hammond, IN	(21.9)
213	Arlington, TX	(24.0)	323	Columbus, GA	(36.8)	238	Hampton, VA	(26.8)
391	Arvada, CO	(54.1)	276	Compton, CA	(30.7)	62	Hartford, CT	1.3
389	Asheville, NC	(51.1)	283	Concord, CA	(31.7)	180	Hawthorne, CA	(20.0)
220	Athens-Clarke, GA	(24.9)	183	Coral Springs, FL	(20.4)	321	Hayward, CA	(36.7)
152	Atlanta, GA	(16.1)	224	Corona, CA	(25.3)	88	Hemet, CA	(5.1)
169	Aurora, CO	(18.3)	264	Corpus Christi, TX	(29.8)	187	Henderson, NV	(21.1)
257	Aurora, IL	(29.1)	295	Costa Mesa, CA	(33.1)	225	Hesperia, CA	(25.4)
301	Austin, TX	(33.6)	332	Cranston, RI	(38.5)	349	Hialeah, FL	(42.6)
369	Avondale, AZ	(46.6)	310	Dallas, TX	(34.9)	351	High Point, NC	(42.8)
112	Bakersfield, CA	(9.7)	378	Daly City, CA	(48.2)	150	Hillsboro, OR	(16.0)
267	Baldwin Park, CA	(29.9)	46	Danbury, CT	7.0	281	Hollywood, FL	(31.5)
107	Baltimore, MD	(9.2)	228	Davenport, IA	(25.7)	316	Hoover, AL	(36.3)
72	Baton Rouge, LA	(1.9)	366	Davie, FL	(45.5)	105	Houston, TX	(9.0)
34	Beaumont, TX	11.8	144	Dayton, OH	(15.0)	272	Huntington Beach, CA	(30.3)
127	Beaverton, OR	(12.4)	329	Dearborn, MI	(37.9)	53	Huntsville, AL	4.1
110	Bellevue, WA	(9.5)	NA	Decatur, IL**	NA	238	Independence, MO	(26.8)
361	Bellflower, CA	(44.2)	58	Deerfield Beach, FL	2.0	162	Indianapolis, IN	(17.5)
138	Bellingham, WA	(14.4)	120	Denton, TX	(10.9)	10	Indio, CA	46.5
344	Berkeley, CA	(40.6)	31	Denver, CO	15.5	206	Inglewood, CA	(23.2)
42	Bethlehem, PA	8.8	228	Des Moines, IA	(25.7)	380	Irvine, CA	(48.4)
26	Billings, MT	22.2	61	Detroit, MI	1.5	384	Irving, TX	(49.2)
264	Birmingham, AL	(29.8)	250	Downey, CA	(28.2)	394	Jacksonville, FL	(55.3)
NA	Bloomington, IL**	NA	286	Duluth, MN	(31.8)	147	Jackson, MS	(15.8)
133	Bloomington, IN	(13.5)	307	Durham, NC	(34.6)	292	Jersey City, NJ	(32.5)
36	Bloomington, MN	10.6	313	Edinburg, TX	(35.3)	NA	Johns Creek, GA**	NA
166	Boca Raton, FL	(18.0)	243	Edison Twnshp, NJ	(27.4)	325	Joliet, IL	(37.3)
80	Boise, ID	(3.5)	132	Edmond, OK	(13.4)	NA	Jurupa Valley, CA**	NA
210	Boston, MA	(23.6)	308	El Cajon, CA	(34.8)	NA	Kansas City, KS**	NA
16	Boulder, CO	35.7	169	El Monte, CA	(18.3)	208	Kansas City, MO	(23.3)
130	Brick Twnshp, NJ	(13.2)	95	El Paso, TX	(6.4)	252	Kennewick, WA	(28.5)
206	Bridgeport, CT	(23.2)	128	Elgin, IL	(12.6)	187	Kenosha, WI	(21.1)
NA	Brockton, MA**	NA	261	Elizabeth, NJ	(29.4)	187	Kent, WA	(21.1)
67	Broken Arrow, OK	(1.0)	355	Elk Grove, CA	(43.1)	86	Killeen, TX	(4.1)
251	Brooklyn Park, MN	(28.3)	363	Erie, PA	(44.7)	180	Knoxville, TN	(20.0)
261	Brownsville, TX	(29.4)	74	Escondido, CA	(2.1)	337	Lafayette, LA	(39.1)
314	Bryan, TX	(36.0)	155	Eugene, OR	(16.4)	343	Lake Forest, CA	(40.2)
269	Buena Park, CA	(30.1)	7	Evansville, IN	57.1	294	Lakeland, FL	(32.9)
NA	Buffalo, NY**	NA	210	Everett, WA	(23.6)	401	Lakewood Twnshp, NJ	(62.6)
20	Burbank, CA	27.3	351	Fairfield, CA	(42.8)	395	Lakewood, CA	(56.1)
162	Cambridge, MA	(17.5)	37	Fall River, MA	10.4	241	Lakewood, CO	(27.2)
106	Camden, NJ	(9.1)	12	Fargo, ND	44.0	169	Lancaster, CA	(18.3)
392	Cape Coral, FL	(54.8)	389	Farmington Hills, MI	(51.1)	219	Lansing, MI	(24.7)
76	Carlsbad, CA	(2.3)	119	Fayetteville, AR	(10.8)	369	Laredo, TX	(46.6)
84	Carmel, IN	(3.9)	255	Fayetteville, NC	(28.6)	194	Largo, FL	(21.9)
356	Carrollton, TX	(43.5)	348	Federal Way, WA	(42.5)	161	Las Cruces, NM	(17.3)
303	Carson, CA	(34.0)	299	Fishers, IN	(33.5)	257	Las Vegas, NV	(29.1)
365	Cary, NC	(45.1)	41	Flint, MI	9.5	274	Lawrence, KS	(30.6)
263	Cedar Rapids, IA	(29.5)	77	Fontana, CA	(2.8)	2	Lawrence, MA	92.7
6	Centennial, CO	74.2	94	Fort Collins, CO	(6.3)	182	Lawton, OK	(20.3)
NA	Champaign, IL**	NA	51	Fort Lauderdale, FL	5.4	242	League City, TX	(27.3)
NA	Chandler, AZ**	NA	135	Fort Smith, AR	(13.9)	312	Lee's Summit, MO	(35.2)
404	Charleston, SC	(67.4)	104	Fort Wayne, IN	(8.7)	NA	Lexington, KY**	NA
356	Charlotte, NC	(43.5)	283	Fort Worth, TX	(31.7)	125	Lincoln, NE	(11.9)
NA	Cheektowaga, NY**	NA	373	Fremont, CA	(47.7)	91	Little Rock, AR	(5.5)
367	Chesapeake, VA	(46.0)	78	Fresno, CA	(3.0)	323	Livermore, CA	(36.8)
145	Chicago, IL	(15.5)	4	Frisco, TX	75.7	252	Livonia, MI	(28.5)
107	Chico, CA	(9.2)	109	Fullerton, CA	(9.4)	158	Long Beach, CA	(17.2)

RANK	CITY	% CHANGE
NA	Longmont, CO**	NA
360	Longview, TX	(44.0)
295	Los Angeles, CA	(33.1)
223	Louisville, KY	(25.2)
192	Lowell, MA	(21.5)
63	Lubbock, TX	1.0
398	Lynchburg, VA	(57.7)
103	Lynn, MA	(8.4)
308	Macon, GA	(34.8)
315	Madison, WI	(36.2)
25	Manchester, NH	22.4
400	McAllen, TX	(60.2)
21	McKinney, TX	26.5
8	Medford, OR	50.1
341	Melbourne, FL	(40.0)
247	Memphis, TN	(27.8)
NA	Menifee, CA**	NA
15	Merced, CA	36.4
331	Meridian, ID	(38.0)
244	Mesa, AZ	(27.6)
70	Mesquite, TX	(1.4)
102	Miami Beach, FL	(7.7)
306	Miami Gardens, FL	(34.5)
117	Miami, FL	(10.4)
387	Midland, TX	(49.7)
89	Milwaukee, WI	(5.2)
158	Minneapolis, MN	(17.2)
233	Miramar, FL	(26.4)
274	Mission Viejo, CA	(30.6)
236	Mission, TX	(26.5)
371	Mobile, AL	(47.5)
49	Modesto, CA	5.5
78	Montgomery, AL	(3.0)
339	Moreno Valley, CA	(39.7)
349	Mountain View, CA	(42.6)
216	Murfreesboro, TN	(24.4)
157	Murrieta, CA	(16.9)
64	Nampa, ID	(0.4)
177	Napa, CA	(19.7)
48	Naperville, IL	5.7
NA	Nashua, NH**	NA
267	Nashville, TN	(29.9)
135	New Bedford, MA	(13.9)
NA	New Haven, CT**	NA
212	New Orleans, LA	(23.9)
NA	New Rochelle, NY**	NA
NA	New York, NY**	NA
13	Newark, NJ	42.9
359	Newport Beach, CA	(43.9)
373	Newport News, VA	(47.7)
137	Newton, MA	(14.0)
393	Norfolk, VA	(55.2)
99	Norman, OK	(6.9)
403	North Charleston, SC	(65.7)
245	North Las Vegas, NV	(27.7)
186	Norwalk, CA	(21.0)
372	Norwalk, CT	(47.6)
18	Oakland, CA	31.2
115	Oceanside, CA	(10.2)
3	Odessa, TX	82.0
402	O'Fallon, MO	(64.3)
231	Ogden, UT	(26.0)
233	Oklahoma City, OK	(26.4)
NA	Olathe, KS**	NA
114	Omaha, NE	(10.1)
248	Ontario, CA	(27.9)
376	Orange, CA	(47.8)
1	Orem, UT	137.5
397	Orlando, FL	(57.4)
289	Overland Park, KS	(32.1)
329	Oxnard, CA	(37.9)
56	Palm Bay, FL	2.5
283	Palmdale, CA	(31.7)
NA	Parma, OH**	NA

RANK	CITY	% CHANGE
280	Pasadena, CA	(31.4)
143	Pasadena, TX	(14.7)
40	Paterson, NJ	9.6
30	Pearland, TX	17.5
387	Pembroke Pines, FL	(49.7)
260	Peoria, AZ	(29.3)
NA	Peoria, IL**	NA
199	Philadelphia, PA	(22.3)
198	Phoenix, AZ	(22.2)
240	Pittsburgh, PA	(27.0)
230	Plano, TX	(25.8)
201	Plantation, FL	(22.5)
165	Pomona, CA	(17.7)
72	Pompano Beach, FL	(1.9)
28	Port St. Lucie, FL	18.9
200	Portland, OR	(22.4)
364	Portsmouth, VA	(45.0)
269	Providence, RI	(30.1)
101	Provo, UT	(7.4)
NA	Pueblo, CO**	NA
174	Quincy, MA	(18.9)
222	Racine, WI	(25.1)
341	Raleigh, NC	(40.0)
NA	Ramapo, NY**	NA
187	Rancho Cucamon., CA	(21.1)
204	Reading, PA	(22.8)
5	Redding, CA	74.5
39	Redwood City, CA	9.8
318	Reno, NV	(36.5)
NA	Renton, WA**	NA
138	Rialto, CA	(14.4)
273	Richardson, TX	(30.4)
252	Richmond, CA	(28.5)
194	Richmond, VA	(21.9)
368	Rio Rancho, NM	(46.5)
288	Riverside, CA	(32.0)
327	Roanoke, VA	(37.7)
192	Rochester, MN	(21.5)
NA	Rochester, NY**	NA
121	Rockford, IL	(11.5)
38	Roseville, CA	10.3
337	Roswell, GA	(39.1)
11	Round Rock, TX	44.7
293	Sacramento, CA	(32.6)
66	Salem, OR	(0.8)
17	Salinas, CA	34.6
336	Salt Lake City, UT	(39.0)
298	San Antonio, TX	(33.4)
82	San Bernardino, CA	(3.8)
256	San Diego, CA	(28.7)
162	San Francisco, CA	(17.5)
54	San Jose, CA	4.0
289	San Leandro, CA	(32.1)
68	San Marcos, CA	(1.3)
320	San Mateo, CA	(36.6)
380	Sandy Springs, GA	(48.4)
52	Sandy, UT	4.3
305	Santa Ana, CA	(34.4)
201	Santa Barbara, CA	(22.5)
287	Santa Clara, CA	(31.9)
249	Santa Clarita, CA	(28.1)
23	Santa Maria, CA	24.3
299	Santa Monica, CA	(33.5)
209	Santa Rosa, CA	(23.4)
361	Savannah, GA	(44.2)
90	Scottsdale, AZ	(5.3)
22	Scranton, PA	26.2
149	Seattle, WA	(15.9)
113	Shreveport, LA	(9.9)
347	Simi Valley, CA	(41.4)
158	Sioux City, IA	(17.2)
9	Sioux Falls, SD	48.8
264	Somerville, MA	(29.8)
187	South Bend, IN	(21.1)

RANK	CITY	% CHANGE
197	South Gate, CA	(22.0)
383	Sparks, NV	(48.9)
87	Spokane Valley, WA	(4.7)
35	Spokane, WA	10.9
NA	Springfield, IL**	NA
95	Springfield, MA	(6.4)
29	Springfield, MO	17.7
176	Stamford, CT	(19.5)
340	Sterling Heights, MI	(39.8)
74	Stockton, CA	(2.1)
129	St. George, UT	(13.1)
57	St. Joseph, MO	2.2
218	St. Louis, MO	(24.6)
169	St. Paul, MN	(18.3)
373	St. Petersburg, FL	(47.7)
184	Sugar Land, TX	(20.8)
64	Sunnyvale, CA	(0.4)
379	Sunrise, FL	(48.3)
32	Surprise, AZ	15.3
NA	Syracuse, NY**	NA
214	Tacoma, WA	(24.1)
226	Tallahassee, FL	(25.5)
377	Tampa, FL	(47.9)
93	Temecula, CA	(6.2)
156	Tempe, AZ	(16.8)
NA	Thornton, CO**	NA
27	Thousand Oaks, CA	19.5
111	Toledo, OH	(9.6)
146	Toms River Twnshp, NJ	(15.6)
166	Topeka, KS	(18.0)
385	Torrance, CA	(49.6)
98	Tracy, CA	(6.7)
59	Trenton, NJ	1.7
141	Troy, MI	(14.5)
134	Tucson, AZ	(13.6)
100	Tulsa, OK	(7.0)
154	Tuscaloosa, AL	(16.3)
316	Tustin, CA	(36.3)
269	Tyler, TX	(30.1)
358	Upland, CA	(43.8)
68	Upper Darby Twnshp, PA	(1.3)
333	Vacaville, CA	(38.6)
142	Vallejo, CA	(14.6)
84	Vancouver, WA	(3.9)
138	Ventura, CA	(14.4)
147	Victorville, CA	(15.8)
345	Virginia Beach, VA	(41.1)
303	Visalia, CA	(34.0)
121	Vista, CA	(11.5)
278	Waco, TX	(30.8)
173	Warren, MI	(18.6)
14	Warwick, RI	41.4
152	Washington, DC	(16.1)
49	Waterbury, CT	5.5
NA	Waukegan, IL**	NA
318	West Covina, CA	(36.5)
33	West Jordan, UT	12.4
237	West Palm Beach, FL	(26.6)
297	West Valley, UT	(33.3)
232	Westland, MI	(26.2)
131	Westminster, CA	(13.3)
177	Westminster, CO	(19.7)
233	Whittier, CA	(26.4)
278	Wichita Falls, TX	(30.8)
81	Wichita, KS	(3.6)
217	Wilmington, NC	(24.5)
353	Winston-Salem, NC	(42.9)
353	Woodbridge Twnshp, NJ	(42.9)
43	Worcester, MA	8.6
60	Yakima, WA	1.6
NA	Yonkers, NY**	NA
55	Yuma, AZ	2.7

Source: CQ Press using reported data from the F.B.I. "Crime in the United States 2012"

*Robbery is the taking of anything of value by force or threat of force. Attempts are included.

**Not available.

60. Percent Change in Robbery Rate: 2008 to 2012 (continued)
National Percent Change = 22.6% Decrease*

RANK	CITY	% CHANGE	RANK	CITY	% CHANGE	RANK	CITY	% CHANGE
1	Orem, UT	137.5	74	Stockton, CA	(2.1)	149	Seattle, WA	(15.9)
2	Lawrence, MA	92.7	76	Carlsbad, CA	(2.3)	150	Anchorage, AK	(16.0)
3	Odessa, TX	82.0	77	Fontana, CA	(2.8)	150	Hillsboro, OR	(16.0)
4	Frisco, TX	75.7	78	Fresno, CA	(3.0)	152	Atlanta, GA	(16.1)
5	Redding, CA	74.5	78	Montgomery, AL	(3.0)	152	Washington, DC	(16.1)
6	Centennial, CO	74.2	80	Boise, ID	(3.5)	154	Tuscaloosa, AL	(16.3)
7	Evansville, IN	57.1	81	Wichita, KS	(3.6)	155	Eugene, OR	(16.4)
8	Medford, OR	50.1	82	Gilbert, AZ	(3.8)	156	Tempe, AZ	(16.8)
9	Sioux Falls, SD	48.8	82	San Bernardino, CA	(3.8)	157	Murrieta, CA	(16.9)
10	Indio, CA	46.5	84	Carmel, IN	(3.9)	158	Long Beach, CA	(17.2)
11	Round Rock, TX	44.7	84	Vancouver, WA	(3.9)	158	Minneapolis, MN	(17.2)
12	Fargo, ND	44.0	86	Killeen, TX	(4.1)	158	Sioux City, IA	(17.2)
13	Newark, NJ	42.9	87	Spokane Valley, WA	(4.7)	161	Las Cruces, NM	(17.3)
14	Warwick, RI	41.4	88	Hemet, CA	(5.1)	162	Cambridge, MA	(17.5)
15	Merced, CA	36.4	89	Milwaukee, WI	(5.2)	162	Indianapolis, IN	(17.5)
16	Boulder, CO	35.7	90	Scottsdale, AZ	(5.3)	162	San Francisco, CA	(17.5)
17	Salinas, CA	34.6	91	Little Rock, AR	(5.5)	165	Pomona, CA	(17.7)
18	Oakland, CA	31.2	92	Cleveland, OH	(5.9)	166	Boca Raton, FL	(18.0)
19	Gary, IN	28.7	93	Temecula, CA	(6.2)	166	Topeka, KS	(18.0)
20	Burbank, CA	27.3	94	Fort Collins, CO	(6.3)	168	Amarillo, TX	(18.1)
21	McKinney, TX	26.5	95	Allen, TX	(6.4)	169	Aurora, CO	(18.3)
22	Scranton, PA	26.2	95	El Paso, TX	(6.4)	169	El Monte, CA	(18.3)
23	Santa Maria, CA	24.3	95	Springfield, MA	(6.4)	169	Lancaster, CA	(18.3)
24	Gresham, OR	23.7	98	Tracy, CA	(6.7)	169	St. Paul, MN	(18.3)
25	Manchester, NH	22.4	99	Norman, OK	(6.9)	173	Warren, MI	(18.6)
26	Billings, MT	22.2	100	Tulsa, OK	(7.0)	174	Clinton Twnshp, MI	(18.9)
27	Thousand Oaks, CA	19.5	101	Provo, UT	(7.4)	174	Quincy, MA	(18.9)
28	Port St. Lucie, FL	18.9	102	Miami Beach, FL	(7.7)	176	Stamford, CT	(19.5)
29	Springfield, MO	17.7	103	Lynn, MA	(8.4)	177	Napa, CA	(19.7)
30	Pearland, TX	17.5	104	Fort Wayne, IN	(8.7)	177	Westminster, CO	(19.7)
31	Denver, CO	15.5	105	Houston, TX	(9.0)	179	Cincinnati, OH	(19.9)
32	Surprise, AZ	15.3	106	Camden, NJ	(9.1)	180	Hawthorne, CA	(20.0)
33	West Jordan, UT	12.4	107	Baltimore, MD	(9.2)	180	Knoxville, TN	(20.0)
34	Beaumont, TX	11.8	107	Chico, CA	(9.2)	182	Lawton, OK	(20.3)
35	Spokane, WA	10.9	109	Fullerton, CA	(9.4)	183	Coral Springs, FL	(20.4)
36	Bloomington, MN	10.6	110	Bellevue, WA	(9.5)	184	Green Bay, WI	(20.8)
37	Fall River, MA	10.4	111	Toledo, OH	(9.6)	184	Sugar Land, TX	(20.8)
38	Roseville, CA	10.3	112	Bakersfield, CA	(9.7)	186	Norwalk, CA	(21.0)
39	Redwood City, CA	9.8	113	Shreveport, LA	(9.9)	187	Henderson, NV	(21.1)
40	Paterson, NJ	9.6	114	Omaha, NE	(10.1)	187	Kenosha, WI	(21.1)
41	Flint, MI	9.5	115	Oceanside, CA	(10.2)	187	Kent, WA	(21.1)
42	Bethlehem, PA	8.8	116	Antioch, CA	(10.3)	187	Rancho Cucamon., CA	(21.1)
43	Worcester, MA	8.6	117	Miami, FL	(10.4)	187	South Bend, IN	(21.1)
44	Clovis, CA	7.4	118	Alexandria, VA	(10.6)	192	Lowell, MA	(21.5)
45	Columbia, MO	7.2	119	Fayetteville, AR	(10.8)	192	Rochester, MN	(21.5)
46	Danbury, CT	7.0	120	Denton, TX	(10.9)	194	Hammond, IN	(21.9)
47	Hamilton Twnshp, NJ	6.8	121	Greeley, CO	(11.5)	194	Largo, FL	(21.9)
48	Naperville, IL	5.7	121	Rockford, IL	(11.5)	194	Richmond, VA	(21.9)
49	Modesto, CA	5.5	121	Vista, CA	(11.5)	197	South Gate, CA	(22.0)
49	Waterbury, CT	5.5	124	Colorado Springs, CO	(11.6)	198	Phoenix, AZ	(22.2)
51	Fort Lauderdale, FL	5.4	125	Lincoln, NE	(11.9)	199	Philadelphia, PA	(22.3)
52	Sandy, UT	4.3	126	Clifton, NJ	(12.0)	200	Portland, OR	(22.4)
53	Huntsville, AL	4.1	127	Beaverton, OR	(12.4)	201	Plantation, FL	(22.5)
54	San Jose, CA	4.0	128	Elgin, IL	(12.6)	201	Santa Barbara, CA	(22.5)
55	Yuma, AZ	2.7	129	St. George, UT	(13.1)	203	Glendale, AZ	(22.6)
56	Palm Bay, FL	2.5	130	Brick Twnshp, NJ	(13.2)	204	Reading, PA	(22.8)
57	St. Joseph, MO	2.2	131	Westminster, CA	(13.3)	205	Albuquerque, NM	(22.9)
58	Deerfield Beach, FL	2.0	132	Edmond, OK	(13.4)	206	Bridgeport, CT	(23.2)
59	Trenton, NJ	1.7	133	Bloomington, IN	(13.5)	206	Inglewood, CA	(23.2)
60	Yakima, WA	1.6	134	Tucson, AZ	(13.6)	208	Kansas City, MO	(23.3)
61	Detroit, MI	1.5	135	Fort Smith, AR	(13.9)	209	Santa Rosa, CA	(23.4)
62	Hartford, CT	1.3	135	New Bedford, MA	(13.9)	210	Boston, MA	(23.6)
63	Lubbock, TX	1.0	137	Newton, MA	(14.0)	210	Everett, WA	(23.6)
64	Nampa, ID	(0.4)	138	Bellingham, WA	(14.4)	212	New Orleans, LA	(23.9)
64	Sunnyvale, CA	(0.4)	138	Rialto, CA	(14.4)	213	Arlington, TX	(24.0)
66	Salem, OR	(0.8)	138	Ventura, CA	(14.4)	214	Ann Arbor, MI	(24.1)
67	Broken Arrow, OK	(1.0)	141	Troy, MI	(14.5)	214	Tacoma, WA	(24.1)
68	San Marcos, CA	(1.3)	142	Vallejo, CA	(14.6)	216	Murfreesboro, TN	(24.4)
68	Upper Darby Twnshp, PA	(1.3)	143	Pasadena, TX	(14.7)	217	Wilmington, NC	(24.5)
70	Mesquite, TX	(1.4)	144	Dayton, OH	(15.0)	218	St. Louis, MO	(24.6)
71	Chino Hills, CA	(1.7)	145	Chicago, IL	(15.5)	219	Lansing, MI	(24.7)
72	Baton Rouge, LA	(1.9)	146	Toms River Twnshp, NJ	(15.6)	220	Akron, OH	(24.9)
72	Pompano Beach, FL	(1.9)	147	Jackson, MS	(15.8)	220	Athens-Clarke, GA	(24.9)
74	Escondido, CA	(2.1)	147	Victorville, CA	(15.8)	222	Racine, WI	(25.1)

RANK CITY	% CHANGE	RANK CITY	% CHANGE	RANK CITY	% CHANGE
223 Louisville, KY	(25.2)	297 West Valley, UT	(33.3)	371 Mobile, AL	(47.5)
224 Corona, CA	(25.3)	298 San Antonio, TX	(33.4)	372 Norwalk, CT	(47.6)
225 Hesperia, CA	(25.4)	299 Fishers, IN	(33.5)	373 Fremont, CA	(47.7)
226 Tallahassee, FL	(25.5)	299 Santa Monica, CA	(33.5)	373 Newport News, VA	(47.7)
227 Anaheim, CA	(25.6)	301 Austin, TX	(33.6)	373 St. Petersburg, FL	(47.7)
228 Davenport, IA	(25.7)	302 Grand Prairie, TX	(33.7)	376 Orange, CA	(47.8)
228 Des Moines, IA	(25.7)	303 Carson, CA	(34.0)	377 Tampa, FL	(47.9)
230 Plano, TX	(25.8)	303 Visalia, CA	(34.0)	378 Daly City, CA	(48.2)
231 Ogden, UT	(26.0)	305 Santa Ana, CA	(34.4)	379 Sunrise, FL	(48.3)
232 Westland, MI	(26.2)	306 Miami Gardens, FL	(34.5)	380 Irvine, CA	(48.4)
233 Miramar, FL	(26.4)	307 Durham, NC	(34.6)	380 Sandy Springs, GA	(48.4)
233 Oklahoma City, OK	(26.4)	308 El Cajon, CA	(34.8)	382 Garden Grove, CA	(48.5)
233 Whittier, CA	(26.4)	308 Macon, GA	(34.8)	383 Sparks, NV	(48.9)
236 Mission, TX	(26.5)	310 Dallas, TX	(34.9)	384 Irving, TX	(49.2)
237 West Palm Beach, FL	(26.6)	311 Gainesville, FL	(35.1)	385 Greensboro, NC	(49.6)
238 Hampton, VA	(26.8)	312 Lee's Summit, MO	(35.2)	385 Torrance, CA	(49.6)
238 Independence, MO	(26.8)	313 Edinburg, TX	(35.3)	387 Midland, TX	(49.7)
240 Pittsburgh, PA	(27.0)	314 Bryan, TX	(36.0)	387 Pembroke Pines, FL	(49.7)
241 Lakewood, CO	(27.2)	315 Madison, WI	(36.2)	389 Asheville, NC	(51.1)
242 League City, TX	(27.3)	316 Hoover, AL	(36.3)	389 Farmington Hills, MI	(51.1)
243 Edison Twnshp, NJ	(27.4)	316 Tustin, CA	(36.3)	391 Arvada, CO	(54.1)
244 Mesa, AZ	(27.6)	318 Reno, NV	(36.5)	392 Cape Coral, FL	(54.8)
245 Glendale, CA	(27.7)	318 West Covina, CA	(36.5)	393 Norfolk, VA	(55.2)
245 North Las Vegas, NV	(27.7)	320 San Mateo, CA	(36.6)	394 Jacksonville, FL	(55.3)
247 Memphis, TN	(27.8)	321 Chula Vista, CA	(36.7)	395 Lakewood, CA	(56.1)
248 Ontario, CA	(27.9)	321 Hayward, CA	(36.7)	396 Alhambra, CA	(56.7)
249 Santa Clarita, CA	(28.1)	323 Columbus, GA	(36.8)	397 Orlando, FL	(57.4)
250 Downey, CA	(28.2)	323 Livermore, CA	(36.8)	398 Lynchburg, VA	(57.7)
251 Brooklyn Park, MN	(28.3)	325 Joliet, IL	(37.3)	399 Clarksville, TN	(58.1)
252 Kennewick, WA	(28.5)	326 Greenville, NC	(37.6)	400 McAllen, TX	(60.2)
252 Livonia, MI	(28.5)	327 Roanoke, VA	(37.7)	401 Lakewood Twnshp, NJ	(62.6)
252 Richmond, CA	(28.5)	328 Clearwater, FL	(37.8)	402 O'Fallon, MO	(64.3)
255 Fayetteville, NC	(28.6)	329 Dearborn, MI	(37.9)	403 North Charleston, SC	(65.7)
256 San Diego, CA	(28.7)	329 Oxnard, CA	(37.9)	404 Charleston, SC	(67.4)
257 Aurora, IL	(29.1)	331 Meridian, ID	(38.0)	NA Albany, GA**	NA
257 Las Vegas, NV	(29.1)	332 Cranston, RI	(38.5)	NA Albany, NY**	NA
259 Citrus Heights, CA	(29.2)	333 Vacaville, CA	(38.6)	NA Allentown, PA**	NA
260 Peoria, AZ	(29.3)	334 Chino, CA	(38.7)	NA Amherst, NY**	NA
261 Brownsville, TX	(29.4)	335 Grand Rapids, MI	(38.8)	NA Arlington Heights, IL**	NA
261 Elizabeth, NJ	(29.4)	336 Salt Lake City, UT	(39.0)	NA Bloomington, IL**	NA
263 Cedar Rapids, IA	(29.5)	337 Lafayette, LA	(39.1)	NA Brockton, MA**	NA
264 Birmingham, AL	(29.8)	337 Roswell, GA	(39.1)	NA Buffalo, NY**	NA
264 Corpus Christi, TX	(29.8)	339 Moreno Valley, CA	(39.7)	NA Champaign, IL**	NA
264 Somerville, MA	(29.8)	340 Sterling Heights, MI	(39.8)	NA Chandler, AZ**	NA
267 Baldwin Park, CA	(29.9)	341 Melbourne, FL	(40.0)	NA Cheektowaga, NY**	NA
267 Nashville, TN	(29.9)	341 Raleigh, NC	(40.0)	NA Cicero, IL**	NA
269 Buena Park, CA	(30.1)	343 Lake Forest, CA	(40.2)	NA Clarkstown, NY**	NA
269 Providence, RI	(30.1)	344 Berkeley, CA	(40.6)	NA Colonie, NY**	NA
269 Tyler, TX	(30.1)	345 Virginia Beach, VA	(41.1)	NA Decatur, IL**	NA
272 Huntington Beach, CA	(30.3)	346 College Station, TX	(41.3)	NA Greece, NY**	NA
273 Richardson, TX	(30.4)	347 Simi Valley, CA	(41.4)	NA Johns Creek, GA**	NA
274 Lawrence, KS	(30.6)	348 Federal Way, WA	(42.5)	NA Jurupa Valley, CA**	NA
274 Mission Viejo, CA	(30.6)	349 Hialeah, FL	(42.6)	NA Kansas City, KS**	NA
276 Alameda, CA	(30.7)	349 Mountain View, CA	(42.6)	NA Lexington, KY**	NA
276 Compton, CA	(30.7)	351 Fairfield, CA	(42.8)	NA Longmont, CO**	NA
278 Waco, TX	(30.8)	351 High Point, NC	(42.8)	NA Menifee, CA**	NA
278 Wichita Falls, TX	(30.8)	353 Winston-Salem, NC	(42.9)	NA Nashua, NH**	NA
280 Pasadena, CA	(31.4)	353 Woodbridge Twnshp, NJ	(42.9)	NA New Haven, CT**	NA
281 Hollywood, FL	(31.5)	355 Elk Grove, CA	(43.1)	NA New Rochelle, NY**	NA
282 Abilene, TX	(31.6)	356 Carrollton, TX	(43.5)	NA New York, NY**	NA
283 Concord, CA	(31.7)	356 Charlotte, NC	(43.5)	NA Olathe, KS**	NA
283 Fort Worth, TX	(31.7)	358 Upland, CA	(43.8)	NA Parma, OH**	NA
283 Palmdale, CA	(31.7)	359 Newport Beach, CA	(43.9)	NA Peoria, IL**	NA
286 Duluth, MN	(31.8)	360 Longview, TX	(44.0)	NA Pueblo, CO**	NA
287 Santa Clara, CA	(31.9)	361 Bellflower, CA	(44.2)	NA Ramapo, NY**	NA
288 Riverside, CA	(32.0)	361 Savannah, GA	(44.2)	NA Renton, WA**	NA
289 Overland Park, KS	(32.1)	363 Erie, PA	(44.7)	NA Rochester, NY**	NA
289 San Leandro, CA	(32.1)	364 Portsmouth, VA	(45.0)	NA Springfield, IL**	NA
291 Garland, TX	(32.3)	365 Cary, NC	(45.1)	NA Syracuse, NY**	NA
292 Jersey City, NJ	(32.5)	366 Davie, FL	(45.5)	NA Thornton, CO**	NA
293 Sacramento, CA	(32.6)	367 Chesapeake, VA	(46.0)	NA Waukegan, IL**	NA
294 Lakeland, FL	(32.9)	368 Rio Rancho, NM	(46.5)	NA Yonkers, NY**	NA
295 Costa Mesa, CA	(33.1)	369 Avondale, AZ	(46.6)		
295 Los Angeles, CA	(33.1)	369 Laredo, TX	(46.6)		

Source: CQ Press using reported data from the F.B.I. "Crime in the United States 2012"

*Robbery is the taking of anything of value by force or threat of force. Attempts are included.

**Not available.

61. Aggravated Assaults in 2012
National Total = 760,739 Aggravated Assaults*

RANK	CITY	ASSAULTS	RANK	CITY	ASSAULTS	RANK	CITY	ASSAULTS
216	Abilene, TX	304	427	Chino Hills, CA	40	127	Gainesville, FL	600
82	Akron, OH	991	263	Chino, CA	229	224	Garden Grove, CA	287
397	Alameda, CA	70	212	Chula Vista, CA	313	250	Garland, TX	250
135	Albany, GA	558	305	Cicero, IL	173	194	Gary, IN	360
150	Albany, NY	506	88	Cincinnati, OH	928	347	Gilbert, AZ	122
28	Albuquerque, NM	2,740	271	Citrus Heights, CA	214	119	Glendale, AZ	666
366	Alexandria, VA	96	425	Clarkstown, NY	45	349	Glendale, CA	119
386	Alhambra, CA	81	111	Clarksville, TN	720	223	Grand Prairie, TX	288
278	Allentown, PA	210	161	Clearwater, FL	459	86	Grand Rapids, MI	941
435	Allen, TX	31	47	Cleveland, OH	1,750	406	Greece, NY	65
92	Amarillo, TX	880	373	Clifton, NJ	91	209	Greeley, CO	321
421	Amherst, NY	53	288	Clinton Twnshp, MI	195	184	Green Bay, WI	382
104	Anaheim, CA	742	346	Clovis, CA	125	91	Greensboro, NC	908
49	Anchorage, AK	1,673	172	College Station, TX	416	247	Greenville, NC	256
330	Ann Arbor, MI	141	439	Colonie, NY	17	252	Gresham, OR	243
120	Antioch, CA	657	75	Colorado Springs, CO	1,069	388	Hamilton Twnshp, NJ	80
436	Arlington Heights, IL	25	240	Columbia, MO	270	164	Hammond, IN	449
63	Arlington, TX	1,225	144	Columbus, GA	523	329	Hampton, VA	143
358	Arvada, CO	107	108	Compton, CA	736	84	Hartford, CT	965
252	Asheville, NC	243	261	Concord, CA	230	217	Hawthorne, CA	297
251	Athens-Clarke, GA	244	331	Coral Springs, FL	140	267	Hayward, CA	219
20	Atlanta, GA	3,555	374	Corona, CA	90	255	Hemet, CA	238
104	Aurora, CO	742	56	Corpus Christi, TX	1,482	280	Henderson, NV	208
188	Aurora, IL	373	339	Costa Mesa, CA	135	213	Hesperia, CA	310
34	Austin, TX	2,187	390	Cranston, RI	78	150	Hialeah, FL	506
322	Avondale, AZ	150	18	Dallas, TX	3,647	199	High Point, NC	347
67	Bakersfield, CA	1,141	342	Daly City, CA	131	371	Hillsboro, OR	92
301	Baldwin Park, CA	181	427	Danbury, CT	40	208	Hollywood, FL	322
12	Baltimore, MD	4,651	177	Davenport, IA	409	436	Hoover, AL	25
59	Baton Rouge, LA	1,344	241	Davie, FL	267	3	Houston, TX	11,343
102	Beaumont, TX	745	126	Dayton, OH	615	285	Huntington Beach, CA	196
382	Beaverton, OR	84	293	Dearborn, MI	190	65	Huntsville, AL	1,154
403	Bellevue, WA	66	271	Decatur, IL	214	191	Independence, MO	362
321	Bellflower, CA	152	293	Deerfield Beach, FL	190	9	Indianapolis, IN	5,967
336	Bellingham, WA	138	284	Denton, TX	200	239	Indio, CA	273
357	Berkeley, CA	108	33	Denver, CO	2,291	190	Inglewood, CA	366
366	Bethlehem, PA	96	107	Des Moines, IA	737	396	Irvine, CA	71
246	Billings, MT	261	4	Detroit, MI	9,341	204	Irving, TX	342
40	Birmingham, AL	2,035	310	Downey, CA	165	22	Jacksonville, FL	3,384
227	Bloomington, IL	284	274	Duluth, MN	213	116	Jackson, MS	671
302	Bloomington, IN	180	80	Durham, NC	1,011	90	Jersey City, NJ	911
409	Bloomington, MN	63	235	Edinburg, TX	277	438	Johns Creek, GA	24
374	Boca Raton, FL	90	419	Edison Twnshp, NJ	54	192	Joliet, IL	361
169	Boise, ID	427	422	Edmond, OK	51	281	Jurupa Valley, CA	206
25	Boston, MA	3,050	289	El Cajon, CA	192	153	Kansas City, KS	500
306	Boulder, CO	169	304	El Monte, CA	174	15	Kansas City, MO	3,864
416	Brick Twnshp, NJ	59	36	El Paso, TX	2,181	314	Kennewick, WA	160
103	Bridgeport, CT	744	355	Elgin, IL	112	341	Kenosha, WI	132
96	Brockton, MA	809	170	Elizabeth, NJ	421	232	Kent, WA	279
384	Broken Arrow, OK	82	179	Elk Grove, CA	396	146	Killeen, TX	521
347	Brooklyn Park, MN	122	271	Erie, PA	214	70	Knoxville, TN	1,109
214	Brownsville, TX	307	185	Escondido, CA	379	136	Lafayette, LA	555
276	Bryan, TX	211	312	Eugene, OR	162	389	Lake Forest, CA	79
354	Buena Park, CA	115	217	Evansville, IN	297	234	Lakeland, FL	278
45	Buffalo, NY	1,808	249	Everett, WA	252	414	Lakewood Twnshp, NJ	61
360	Burbank, CA	106	235	Fairfield, CA	277	356	Lakewood, CA	111
238	Cambridge, MA	275	123	Fall River, MA	638	168	Lakewood, CO	432
72	Camden, NJ	1,097	235	Fargo, ND	277	156	Lancaster, CA	484
308	Cape Coral, FL	168	424	Farmington Hills, MI	46	100	Lansing, MI	770
299	Carlsbad, CA	182	221	Fayetteville, AR	289	101	Laredo, TX	764
442	Carmel, IN	3	141	Fayetteville, NC	534	257	Largo, FL	236
366	Carrollton, TX	96	328	Federal Way, WA	144	245	Las Cruces, NM	263
195	Carson, CA	357	441	Fishers, IN	4	8	Las Vegas, NV	7,102
393	Cary, NC	75	43	Flint, MI	1,930	243	Lawrence, KS	265
274	Cedar Rapids, IA	213	144	Fontana, CA	523	140	Lawrence, MA	535
383	Centennial, CO	83	215	Fort Collins, CO	305	114	Lawton, OK	696
137	Champaign, IL	552	122	Fort Lauderdale, FL	644	433	League City, TX	35
176	Chandler, AZ	411	148	Fort Smith, AR	518	395	Lee's Summit, MO	72
313	Charleston, SC	161	189	Fort Wayne, IN	369	200	Lexington, KY	346
24	Charlotte, NC	3,165	27	Fort Worth, TX	2,809	118	Lincoln, NE	668
374	Cheektowaga, NY	90	316	Fremont, CA	158	51	Little Rock, AR	1,590
129	Chesapeake, VA	589	50	Fresno, CA	1,628	248	Livermore, CA	254
2	Chicago, IL	12,272	403	Frisco, TX	66	371	Livonia, MI	92
331	Chico, CA	140	227	Fullerton, CA	284	60	Long Beach, CA	1,319

RANK	CITY	ASSAULTS	RANK	CITY	ASSAULTS	RANK	CITY	ASSAULTS
325	Longmont, CO	147	258	Pasadena, CA	235	244	South Gate, CA	264
217	Longview, TX	297	173	Pasadena, TX	415	340	Sparks, NV	133
6	Los Angeles, CA	8,329	121	Paterson, NJ	655	365	Spokane Valley, WA	97
31	Louisville, KY	2,350	392	Pearland, TX	76	106	Spokane, WA	738
187	Lowell, MA	374	334	Pembroke Pines, FL	139	97	Springfield, IL	792
55	Lubbock, TX	1,522	296	Peoria, AZ	186	79	Springfield, MA	1,014
298	Lynchburg, VA	184	134	Peoria, IL	560	74	Springfield, MO	1,086
141	Lynn, MA	534	5	Philadelphia, PA	8,658	303	Stamford, CT	176
232	Macon, GA	279	11	Phoenix, AZ	5,263	299	Sterling Heights, MI	182
139	Madison, WI	539	68	Pittsburgh, PA	1,125	26	Stockton, CA	2,913
200	Manchester, NH	346	289	Plano, TX	192	362	St. George, UT	105
360	McAllen, TX	106	338	Plantation, FL	136	279	St. Joseph, MO	209
351	McKinney, TX	117	132	Pomona, CA	564	19	St. Louis, MO	3,571
211	Medford, OR	320	128	Pompano Beach, FL	599	62	St. Paul, MN	1,262
160	Melbourne, FL	471	221	Port St. Lucie, FL	289	53	St. Petersburg, FL	1,545
7	Memphis, TN	7,572	44	Portland, OR	1,892	400	Sugar Land, TX	68
417	Menifee, CA	58	266	Portsmouth, VA	227	384	Sunnyvale, CA	82
133	Merced, CA	561	117	Providence, RI	670	352	Sunrise, FL	116
397	Meridian, ID	70	370	Provo, UT	94	377	Surprise, AZ	89
66	Mesa, AZ	1,149	131	Pueblo, CO	569	94	Syracuse, NY	829
252	Mesquite, TX	243	226	Quincy, MA	286	78	Tacoma, WA	1,024
155	Miami Beach, FL	487	345	Racine, WI	128	87	Tallahassee, FL	930
146	Miami Gardens, FL	521	83	Raleigh, NC	985	54	Tampa, FL	1,523
29	Miami, FL	2,626	411	Ramapo, NY	62	434	Temecula, CA	34
209	Midland, TX	321	295	Rancho Cucamon., CA	189	130	Tempe, AZ	570
14	Milwaukee, WI	4,411	182	Reading, PA	387	260	Thornton, CO	232
48	Minneapolis, MN	1,711	152	Redding, CA	505	378	Thousand Oaks, CA	88
205	Miramar, FL	341	358	Redwood City, CA	107	41	Toledo, OH	2,015
426	Mission Viejo, CA	42	95	Reno, NV	825	431	Toms River Twnshp, NJ	37
423	Mission, TX	49	334	Renton, WA	139	157	Topeka, KS	481
99	Mobile, AL	777	224	Rialto, CA	287	391	Torrance, CA	77
76	Modesto, CA	1,061	411	Richardson, TX	62	401	Tracy, CA	67
230	Montgomery, AL	283	112	Richmond, CA	717	125	Trenton, NJ	627
202	Moreno Valley, CA	345	124	Richmond, VA	635	432	Troy, MI	36
352	Mountain View, CA	116	319	Rio Rancho, NM	156	32	Tucson, AZ	2,314
149	Murfreesboro, TN	509	98	Riverside, CA	780	30	Tulsa, OK	2,529
427	Murrieta, CA	40	197	Roanoke, VA	352	241	Tuscaloosa, AL	267
337	Nampa, ID	137	363	Rochester, MN	104	401	Tustin, CA	67
316	Napa, CA	158	71	Rochester, NY	1,104	179	Tyler, TX	396
381	Naperville, IL	85	57	Rockford, IL	1,451	394	Upland, CA	73
349	Nashua, NH	119	289	Roseville, CA	192	265	Upper Darby Twnshp, PA	228
10	Nashville, TN	5,453	414	Roswell, GA	61	326	Vacaville, CA	146
113	New Bedford, MA	702	407	Round Rock, TX	64	166	Vallejo, CA	440
85	New Haven, CT	954	37	Sacramento, CA	2,150	203	Vancouver, WA	343
52	New Orleans, LA	1,564	185	Salem, OR	379	327	Ventura, CA	145
379	New Rochelle, NY	87	158	Salinas, CA	477	178	Victorville, CA	408
1	New York, NY	31,211	93	Salt Lake City, UT	854	196	Virginia Beach, VA	353
73	Newark, NJ	1,093	13	San Antonio, TX	4,441	192	Visalia, CA	361
411	Newport Beach, CA	62	69	San Bernardino, CA	1,116	220	Vista, CA	295
175	Newport News, VA	413	17	San Diego, CA	3,661	183	Waco, TX	384
419	Newton, MA	54	39	San Francisco, CA	2,116	159	Warren, MI	476
109	Norfolk, VA	732	42	San Jose, CA	2,014	418	Warwick, RI	57
403	Norman, OK	66	324	San Leandro, CA	149	21	Washington, DC	3,399
163	North Charleston, SC	451	318	San Marcos, CA	157	342	Waterbury, CT	131
64	North Las Vegas, NV	1,219	309	San Mateo, CA	167	276	Waukegan, IL	211
255	Norwalk, CA	238	386	Sandy Springs, GA	81	314	West Covina, CA	160
289	Norwalk, CT	192	380	Sandy, UT	86	331	West Jordan, UT	140
23	Oakland, CA	3,227	110	Santa Ana, CA	727	167	West Palm Beach, FL	439
154	Oceanside, CA	497	269	Santa Barbara, CA	215	181	West Valley, UT	388
89	Odessa, TX	914	322	Santa Clara, CA	150	285	Westland, MI	196
409	O'Fallon, MO	63	269	Santa Clarita, CA	215	297	Westminster, CA	185
261	Ogden, UT	230	143	Santa Maria, CA	524	282	Westminster, CO	202
16	Oklahoma City, OK	3,791	267	Santa Monica, CA	219	319	Whittier, CA	156
344	Olathe, KS	129	165	Santa Rosa, CA	441	227	Wichita Falls, TX	284
58	Omaha, NE	1,442	206	Savannah, GA	339	38	Wichita, KS	2,123
263	Ontario, CA	229	306	Scottsdale, AZ	169	207	Wilmington, NC	326
399	Orange, CA	69	364	Scranton, PA	100	77	Winston-Salem, NC	1,048
440	Orem, UT	7	35	Seattle, WA	2,183	407	Woodbridge Twnshp, NJ	64
46	Orlando, FL	1,778	81	Shreveport, LA	1,008	61	Worcester, MA	1,298
283	Overland Park, KS	201	369	Simi Valley, CA	95	198	Yakima, WA	351
231	Oxnard, CA	282	285	Sioux City, IA	196	115	Yonkers, NY	679
162	Palm Bay, FL	453	171	Sioux Falls, SD	420	173	Yuma, AZ	415
138	Palmdale, CA	545	311	Somerville, MA	164			
430	Parma, OH	38	259	South Bend, IN	233			

Source: Reported data from the F.B.I. "Crime in the United States 2012"

*Aggravated assault is an attack for the purpose of inflicting severe bodily injury.

61. Aggravated Assaults in 2012 (continued)
National Total = 760,739 Aggravated Assaults*

RANK	CITY	ASSAULTS	RANK	CITY	ASSAULTS	RANK	CITY	ASSAULTS
1	New York, NY	31,211	75	Colorado Springs, CO	1,069	149	Murfreesboro, TN	509
2	Chicago, IL	12,272	76	Modesto, CA	1,061	150	Albany, NY	506
3	Houston, TX	11,343	77	Winston-Salem, NC	1,048	150	Hialeah, FL	506
4	Detroit, MI	9,341	78	Tacoma, WA	1,024	152	Redding, CA	505
5	Philadelphia, PA	8,658	79	Springfield, MA	1,014	153	Kansas City, KS	500
6	Los Angeles, CA	8,329	80	Durham, NC	1,011	154	Oceanside, CA	497
7	Memphis, TN	7,572	81	Shreveport, LA	1,008	155	Miami Beach, FL	487
8	Las Vegas, NV	7,102	82	Akron, OH	991	156	Lancaster, CA	484
9	Indianapolis, IN	5,967	83	Raleigh, NC	985	157	Topeka, KS	481
10	Nashville, TN	5,453	84	Hartford, CT	965	158	Salinas, CA	477
11	Phoenix, AZ	5,263	85	New Haven, CT	954	159	Warren, MI	476
12	Baltimore, MD	4,651	86	Grand Rapids, MI	941	160	Melbourne, FL	471
13	San Antonio, TX	4,441	87	Tallahassee, FL	930	161	Clearwater, FL	459
14	Milwaukee, WI	4,411	88	Cincinnati, OH	928	162	Palm Bay, FL	453
15	Kansas City, MO	3,864	89	Odessa, TX	914	163	North Charleston, SC	451
16	Oklahoma City, OK	3,791	90	Jersey City, NJ	911	164	Hammond, IN	449
17	San Diego, CA	3,661	91	Greensboro, NC	908	165	Santa Rosa, CA	441
18	Dallas, TX	3,647	92	Amarillo, TX	880	166	Vallejo, CA	440
19	St. Louis, MO	3,571	93	Salt Lake City, UT	854	167	West Palm Beach, FL	439
20	Atlanta, GA	3,555	94	Syracuse, NY	829	168	Lakewood, CO	432
21	Washington, DC	3,399	95	Reno, NV	825	169	Boise, ID	427
22	Jacksonville, FL	3,384	96	Brockton, MA	809	170	Elizabeth, NJ	421
23	Oakland, CA	3,227	97	Springfield, IL	792	171	Sioux Falls, SD	420
24	Charlotte, NC	3,165	98	Riverside, CA	780	172	College Station, TX	416
25	Boston, MA	3,050	99	Mobile, AL	777	173	Pasadena, TX	415
26	Stockton, CA	2,913	100	Lansing, MI	770	173	Yuma, AZ	415
27	Fort Worth, TX	2,809	101	Laredo, TX	764	175	Newport News, VA	413
28	Albuquerque, NM	2,740	102	Beaumont, TX	745	176	Chandler, AZ	411
29	Miami, FL	2,626	103	Bridgeport, CT	744	177	Davenport, IA	409
30	Tulsa, OK	2,529	104	Anaheim, CA	742	178	Victorville, CA	408
31	Louisville, KY	2,350	104	Aurora, CO	742	179	Elk Grove, CA	396
32	Tucson, AZ	2,314	106	Spokane, WA	738	179	Tyler, TX	396
33	Denver, CO	2,291	107	Des Moines, IA	737	181	West Valley, UT	388
34	Austin, TX	2,187	108	Compton, CA	736	182	Reading, PA	387
35	Seattle, WA	2,183	109	Norfolk, VA	732	183	Waco, TX	384
36	El Paso, TX	2,181	110	Santa Ana, CA	727	184	Green Bay, WI	382
37	Sacramento, CA	2,150	111	Clarksville, TN	720	185	Escondido, CA	379
38	Wichita, KS	2,123	112	Richmond, CA	717	185	Salem, OR	379
39	San Francisco, CA	2,116	113	New Bedford, MA	702	187	Lowell, MA	374
40	Birmingham, AL	2,035	114	Lawton, OK	696	188	Aurora, IL	373
41	Toledo, OH	2,015	115	Yonkers, NY	679	189	Fort Wayne, IN	369
42	San Jose, CA	2,014	116	Jackson, MS	671	190	Inglewood, CA	366
43	Flint, MI	1,930	117	Providence, RI	670	191	Independence, MO	362
44	Portland, OR	1,892	118	Lincoln, NE	668	192	Joliet, IL	361
45	Buffalo, NY	1,808	119	Glendale, AZ	666	192	Visalia, CA	361
46	Orlando, FL	1,778	120	Antioch, CA	657	194	Gary, IN	360
47	Cleveland, OH	1,750	121	Paterson, NJ	655	195	Carson, CA	357
48	Minneapolis, MN	1,711	122	Fort Lauderdale, FL	644	196	Virginia Beach, VA	353
49	Anchorage, AK	1,673	123	Fall River, MA	638	197	Roanoke, VA	352
50	Fresno, CA	1,628	124	Richmond, VA	635	198	Yakima, WA	351
51	Little Rock, AR	1,590	125	Trenton, NJ	627	199	High Point, NC	347
52	New Orleans, LA	1,564	126	Dayton, OH	615	200	Lexington, KY	346
53	St. Petersburg, FL	1,545	127	Gainesville, FL	600	200	Manchester, NH	346
54	Tampa, FL	1,523	128	Pompano Beach, FL	599	202	Moreno Valley, CA	345
55	Lubbock, TX	1,522	129	Chesapeake, VA	589	203	Vancouver, WA	343
56	Corpus Christi, TX	1,482	130	Tempe, AZ	570	204	Irving, TX	342
57	Rockford, IL	1,451	131	Pueblo, CO	569	205	Miramar, FL	341
58	Omaha, NE	1,442	132	Pomona, CA	564	206	Savannah, GA	339
59	Baton Rouge, LA	1,344	133	Merced, CA	561	207	Wilmington, NC	326
60	Long Beach, CA	1,319	134	Peoria, IL	560	208	Hollywood, FL	322
61	Worcester, MA	1,298	135	Albany, GA	558	209	Greeley, CO	321
62	St. Paul, MN	1,262	136	Lafayette, LA	555	209	Midland, TX	321
63	Arlington, TX	1,225	137	Champaign, IL	552	211	Medford, OR	320
64	North Las Vegas, NV	1,219	138	Palmdale, CA	545	212	Chula Vista, CA	313
65	Huntsville, AL	1,154	139	Madison, WI	539	213	Hesperia, CA	310
66	Mesa, AZ	1,149	140	Lawrence, MA	535	214	Brownsville, TX	307
67	Bakersfield, CA	1,141	141	Fayetteville, NC	534	215	Fort Collins, CO	305
68	Pittsburgh, PA	1,125	141	Lynn, MA	534	216	Abilene, TX	304
69	San Bernardino, CA	1,116	143	Santa Maria, CA	524	217	Evansville, IN	297
70	Knoxville, TN	1,109	144	Columbus, GA	523	217	Hawthorne, CA	297
71	Rochester, NY	1,104	144	Fontana, CA	523	217	Longview, TX	297
72	Camden, NJ	1,097	146	Killeen, TX	521	220	Vista, CA	295
73	Newark, NJ	1,093	146	Miami Gardens, FL	521	221	Fayetteville, AR	289
74	Springfield, MO	1,086	148	Fort Smith, AR	518	221	Port St. Lucie, FL	289

RANK	CITY	ASSAULTS	RANK	CITY	ASSAULTS	RANK	CITY	ASSAULTS
223	Grand Prairie, TX	288	297	Westminster, CA	185	371	Hillsboro, OR	92
224	Garden Grove, CA	287	298	Lynchburg, VA	184	371	Livonia, MI	92
224	Rialto, CA	287	299	Carlsbad, CA	182	373	Clifton, NJ	91
226	Quincy, MA	286	299	Sterling Heights, MI	182	374	Boca Raton, FL	90
227	Bloomington, IL	284	301	Baldwin Park, CA	181	374	Cheektowaga, NY	90
227	Fullerton, CA	284	302	Bloomington, IN	180	374	Corona, CA	90
227	Wichita Falls, TX	284	303	Stamford, CT	176	377	Surprise, AZ	89
230	Montgomery, AL	283	304	El Monte, CA	174	378	Thousand Oaks, CA	88
231	Oxnard, CA	282	305	Cicero, IL	173	379	New Rochelle, NY	87
232	Kent, WA	279	306	Boulder, CO	169	380	Sandy, UT	86
232	Macon, GA	279	306	Scottsdale, AZ	169	381	Naperville, IL	85
234	Lakeland, FL	278	308	Cape Coral, FL	168	382	Beaverton, OR	84
235	Edinburg, TX	277	309	San Mateo, CA	167	383	Centennial, CO	83
235	Fairfield, CA	277	310	Downey, CA	165	384	Broken Arrow, OK	82
235	Fargo, ND	277	311	Somerville, MA	164	384	Sunnyvale, CA	82
238	Cambridge, MA	275	312	Eugene, OR	162	386	Alhambra, CA	81
239	Indio, CA	273	313	Charleston, SC	161	386	Sandy Springs, GA	81
240	Columbia, MO	270	314	Kennewick, WA	160	388	Hamilton Twnshp, NJ	80
241	Davie, FL	267	314	West Covina, CA	160	389	Lake Forest, CA	79
241	Tuscaloosa, AL	267	316	Fremont, CA	158	390	Cranston, RI	78
243	Lawrence, KS	265	316	Napa, CA	158	391	Torrance, CA	77
244	South Gate, CA	264	318	San Marcos, CA	157	392	Pearland, TX	76
245	Las Cruces, NM	263	319	Rio Rancho, NM	156	393	Cary, NC	75
246	Billings, MT	261	319	Whittier, CA	156	394	Upland, CA	73
247	Greenville, NC	256	321	Bellflower, CA	152	395	Lee's Summit, MO	72
248	Livermore, CA	254	322	Avondale, AZ	150	396	Irvine, CA	71
249	Everett, WA	252	322	Santa Clara, CA	150	397	Alameda, CA	70
250	Garland, TX	250	324	San Leandro, CA	149	397	Meridian, ID	70
251	Athens-Clarke, GA	244	325	Longmont, CO	147	399	Orange, CA	69
252	Asheville, NC	243	326	Vacaville, CA	146	400	Sugar Land, TX	68
252	Gresham, OR	243	327	Ventura, CA	145	401	Tracy, CA	67
252	Mesquite, TX	243	328	Federal Way, WA	144	401	Tustin, CA	67
255	Hemet, CA	238	329	Hampton, VA	143	403	Bellevue, WA	66
255	Norwalk, CA	238	330	Ann Arbor, MI	141	403	Frisco, TX	66
257	Largo, FL	236	331	Chico, CA	140	403	Norman, OK	66
258	Pasadena, CA	235	331	Coral Springs, FL	140	406	Greece, NY	65
259	South Bend, IN	233	331	West Jordan, UT	140	407	Round Rock, TX	64
260	Thornton, CO	232	334	Pembroke Pines, FL	139	407	Woodbridge Twnshp, NJ	64
261	Concord, CA	230	334	Renton, WA	139	409	Bloomington, MN	63
261	Ogden, UT	230	336	Bellingham, WA	138	409	O'Fallon, MO	63
263	Chino, CA	229	337	Nampa, ID	137	411	Newport Beach, CA	62
263	Ontario, CA	229	338	Plantation, FL	136	411	Ramapo, NY	62
265	Upper Darby Twnshp, PA	228	339	Costa Mesa, CA	135	411	Richardson, TX	62
266	Portsmouth, VA	227	340	Sparks, NV	133	414	Lakewood Twnshp, NJ	61
267	Hayward, CA	219	341	Kenosha, WI	132	414	Roswell, GA	61
267	Santa Monica, CA	219	342	Daly City, CA	131	416	Brick Twnshp, NJ	59
269	Santa Barbara, CA	215	342	Waterbury, CT	131	417	Menifee, CA	58
269	Santa Clarita, CA	215	344	Olathe, KS	129	418	Warwick, RI	57
271	Citrus Heights, CA	214	345	Racine, WI	128	419	Edison Twnshp, NJ	54
271	Decatur, IL	214	346	Clovis, CA	125	419	Newton, MA	54
271	Erie, PA	214	347	Brooklyn Park, MN	122	421	Amherst, NY	53
274	Cedar Rapids, IA	213	347	Gilbert, AZ	122	422	Edmond, OK	51
274	Duluth, MN	213	349	Glendale, CA	119	423	Mission, TX	49
276	Bryan, TX	211	349	Nashua, NH	119	424	Farmington Hills, MI	46
276	Waukegan, IL	211	351	McKinney, TX	117	425	Clarkstown, NY	45
278	Allentown, PA	210	352	Mountain View, CA	116	426	Mission Viejo, CA	42
279	St. Joseph, MO	209	352	Sunrise, FL	116	427	Chino Hills, CA	40
280	Henderson, NV	208	354	Buena Park, CA	115	427	Danbury, CT	40
281	Jurupa Valley, CA	206	355	Elgin, IL	112	427	Murrieta, CA	40
282	Westminster, CO	202	356	Lakewood, CA	111	430	Parma, OH	38
283	Overland Park, KS	201	357	Berkeley, CA	108	431	Toms River Twnshp, NJ	37
284	Denton, TX	200	358	Arvada, CO	107	432	Troy, MI	36
285	Huntington Beach, CA	196	358	Redwood City, CA	107	433	League City, TX	35
285	Sioux City, IA	196	360	Burbank, CA	106	434	Temecula, CA	34
285	Westland, MI	196	360	McAllen, TX	106	435	Allen, TX	31
288	Clinton Twnshp, MI	195	362	St. George, UT	105	436	Arlington Heights, IL	25
289	El Cajon, CA	192	363	Rochester, MN	104	436	Hoover, AL	25
289	Norwalk, CT	192	364	Scranton, PA	100	438	Johns Creek, GA	24
289	Plano, TX	192	365	Spokane Valley, WA	97	439	Colonie, NY	17
289	Roseville, CA	192	366	Alexandria, VA	96	440	Orem, UT	7
293	Dearborn, MI	190	366	Bethlehem, PA	96	441	Fishers, IN	4
293	Deerfield Beach, FL	190	366	Carrollton, TX	96	442	Carmel, IN	3
295	Rancho Cucamon., CA	189	369	Simi Valley, CA	95			
296	Peoria, AZ	186	370	Provo, UT	94			

Source: Reported data from the F.B.I. "Crime in the United States 2012"

*Aggravated assault is an attack for the purpose of inflicting severe bodily injury.

62. Aggravated Assault Rate in 2012
National Rate = 242.3 Aggravated Assaults per 100,000 Population*

RANK	CITY	RATE	RANK	CITY	RATE	RANK	CITY	RATE
217	Abilene, TX	253.6	422	Chino Hills, CA	52.2	81	Gainesville, FL	472.3
73	Akron, OH	499.5	185	Chino, CA	287.0	296	Garden Grove, CA	163.9
368	Alameda, CA	92.8	335	Chula Vista, CA	125.3	348	Garland, TX	106.4
26	Albany, GA	710.7	262	Cicero, IL	205.2	89	Gary, IN	447.4
69	Albany, NY	515.3	162	Cincinnati, OH	313.3	416	Gilbert, AZ	56.9
76	Albuquerque, NM	494.9	221	Citrus Heights, CA	251.4	186	Glendale, AZ	285.8
402	Alexandria, VA	65.8	417	Clarkstown, NY	56.1	406	Glendale, CA	61.1
363	Alhambra, CA	95.9	62	Clarksville, TN	524.2	299	Grand Prairie, TX	158.4
279	Allentown, PA	176.0	107	Clearwater, FL	420.1	75	Grand Rapids, MI	495.4
433	Allen, TX	34.9	92	Cleveland, OH	444.4	400	Greece, NY	67.2
88	Amarillo, TX	447.7	347	Clifton, NJ	107.5	150	Greeley, CO	333.4
427	Amherst, NY	45.1	267	Clinton Twnshp, MI	201.0	129	Green Bay, WI	360.1
254	Anaheim, CA	215.4	331	Clovis, CA	127.8	152	Greensboro, NC	328.8
55	Anchorage, AK	559.3	103	College Station, TX	430.8	179	Greenville, NC	294.7
336	Ann Arbor, MI	122.6	439	Colonie, NY	21.8	245	Gresham, OR	224.6
44	Antioch, CA	625.7	224	Colorado Springs, CO	247.3	371	Hamilton Twnshp, NJ	89.8
434	Arlington Heights, IL	33.1	228	Columbia, MO	244.0	57	Hammond, IN	554.3
155	Arlington, TX	323.0	204	Columbus, GA	266.6	352	Hampton, VA	103.7
359	Arvada, CO	98.1	17	Compton, CA	750.6	150	Hartford, CT	770.7
187	Asheville, NC	284.9	276	Concord, CA	183.7	16	Hartford, CT	770.7
259	Athens-Clarke, GA	207.7	344	Coral Springs, FL	112.0	141	Hawthorne, CA	346.6
13	Atlanta, GA	813.4	414	Corona, CA	57.2	308	Hayward, CA	148.6
250	Aurora, CO	220.2	80	Corpus Christi, TX	474.1	181	Hemet, CA	293.1
274	Aurora, IL	186.7	337	Costa Mesa, CA	119.9	149	Hesperia, CA	335.6
207	Austin, TX	262.6	361	Cranston, RI	97.1	252	Hialeah, FL	217.1
271	Avondale, AZ	191.4	180	Dallas, TX	293.7	154	High Point, NC	324.9
159	Bakersfield, CA	320.8	333	Daly City, CA	126.8	360	Hillsboro, OR	97.7
235	Baldwin Park, CA	236.2	425	Danbury, CT	48.8	247	Hollywood, FL	221.6
18	Baltimore, MD	743.6	108	Davenport, IA	404.2	437	Hoover, AL	30.4
52	Baton Rouge, LA	580.6	190	Davie, FL	281.2	64	Houston, TX	521.0
46	Beaumont, TX	619.2	101	Dayton, OH	432.7	356	Huntington Beach, CA	100.7
369	Beaverton, OR	91.0	269	Dearborn, MI	195.4	43	Huntsville, AL	628.2
421	Bellevue, WA	52.4	191	Decatur, IL	281.1	166	Independence, MO	308.3
270	Bellflower, CA	195.2	225	Deerfield Beach, FL	245.4	24	Indianapolis, IN	711.5
292	Bellingham, WA	166.9	290	Denton, TX	168.1	139	Indio, CA	347.8
367	Berkeley, CA	93.9	126	Denver, CO	364.5	153	Inglewood, CA	328.3
332	Bethlehem, PA	127.3	133	Des Moines, IA	355.4	436	Irvine, CA	32.6
225	Billings, MT	245.4	3	Detroit, MI	1,321.0	306	Irving, TX	152.7
7	Birmingham, AL	954.2	312	Downey, CA	145.2	109	Jacksonville, FL	402.5
124	Bloomington, IL	368.3	227	Duluth, MN	245.3	116	Jackson, MS	381.4
249	Bloomington, IN	220.5	104	Durham, NC	429.2	127	Jersey City, NJ	362.1
391	Bloomington, MN	74.5	143	Edinburg, TX	344.8	438	Johns Creek, GA	30.0
351	Boca Raton, FL	104.1	419	Edison Twnshp, NJ	53.5	229	Joliet, IL	243.1
265	Boise, ID	201.8	406	Edmond, OK	61.1	256	Jurupa Valley, CA	211.1
78	Boston, MA	483.6	272	El Cajon, CA	188.5	148	Kansas City, KS	339.7
287	Boulder, CO	168.6	307	El Monte, CA	150.8	12	Kansas City, MO	832.6
387	Brick Twnshp, NJ	77.8	156	El Paso, TX	322.9	258	Kennewick, WA	207.9
70	Bridgeport, CT	509.5	353	Elgin, IL	102.6	327	Kenosha, WI	132.0
11	Brockton, MA	850.2	150	Elizabeth, NJ	333.4	242	Kent, WA	228.5
377	Broken Arrow, OK	81.4	218	Elk Grove, CA	253.3	111	Killeen, TX	394.8
300	Brooklyn Park, MN	157.7	257	Erie, PA	209.9	48	Knoxville, TN	608.5
284	Brownsville, TX	169.5	214	Escondido, CA	257.1	85	Lafayette, LA	451.8
202	Bryan, TX	268.9	354	Eugene, OR	102.5	358	Lake Forest, CA	99.8
318	Buena Park, CA	139.4	222	Evansville, IN	251.3	193	Lakeland, FL	278.2
31	Buffalo, NY	688.9	232	Everett, WA	239.3	403	Lakewood Twnshp, NJ	65.1
355	Burbank, CA	100.9	211	Fairfield, CA	258.6	321	Lakewood, CA	136.4
214	Cambridge, MA	257.1	25	Fall River, MA	710.8	178	Lakewood, CO	295.1
2	Camden, NJ	1,412.5	220	Fargo, ND	252.2	171	Lancaster, CA	304.1
350	Cape Coral, FL	105.2	413	Farmington Hills, MI	57.3	37	Lansing, MI	671.4
286	Carlsbad, CA	168.7	114	Fayetteville, AR	383.4	163	Laredo, TX	311.1
442	Carmel, IN	3.7	209	Fayetteville, NC	259.3	173	Largo, FL	299.6
388	Carrollton, TX	77.1	301	Federal Way, WA	156.6	206	Las Cruces, NM	263.5
115	Carson, CA	382.9	441	Fishers, IN	5.0	79	Las Vegas, NV	480.1
420	Cary, NC	53.2	1	Flint, MI	1,899.0	177	Lawrence, KS	297.2
293	Cedar Rapids, IA	165.9	208	Fontana, CA	260.4	31	Lawrence, MA	688.9
380	Centennial, CO	79.8	264	Fort Collins, CO	205.0	28	Lawton, OK	704.6
33	Champaign, IL	678.7	117	Fort Lauderdale, FL	377.0	430	League City, TX	40.6
285	Chandler, AZ	169.3	49	Fort Smith, AR	592.1	384	Lee's Summit, MO	78.4
330	Charleston, SC	130.0	314	Fort Wayne, IN	143.8	341	Lexington, KY	114.4
113	Charlotte, NC	391.5	125	Fort Worth, TX	364.8	219	Lincoln, NE	252.9
342	Cheektowaga, NY	113.7	395	Fremont, CA	72.2	14	Little Rock, AR	811.0
210	Chesapeake, VA	258.9	158	Fresno, CA	321.7	168	Livermore, CA	306.8
84	Chicago, IL	453.1	418	Frisco, TX	53.6	364	Livonia, MI	95.8
298	Chico, CA	160.8	263	Fullerton, CA	205.1	192	Long Beach, CA	280.7

RANK	CITY	RATE	RANK	CITY	RATE	RANK	CITY	RATE
294	Longmont, CO	165.3	287	Pasadena, CA	168.6	195	South Gate, CA	275.1
131	Longview, TX	359.8	203	Pasadena, TX	268.5	313	Sparks, NV	144.0
253	Los Angeles, CA	216.1	91	Paterson, NJ	445.1	348	Spokane Valley, WA	106.4
136	Louisville, KY	352.7	379	Pearland, TX	80.3	139	Spokane, WA	347.8
144	Lowell, MA	344.6	372	Pembroke Pines, FL	87.0	34	Springfield, IL	676.2
39	Lubbock, TX	641.5	340	Peoria, AZ	117.5	38	Springfield, MA	656.2
234	Lynchburg, VA	237.9	77	Peoria, IL	485.7	35	Springfield, MO	674.7
51	Lynn, MA	581.4	54	Philadelphia, PA	562.6	315	Stamford, CT	141.7
172	Macon, GA	300.5	134	Phoenix, AZ	354.3	316	Sterling Heights, MI	140.0
244	Madison, WI	226.9	128	Pittsburgh, PA	360.4	6	Stockton, CA	973.9
161	Manchester, NH	314.4	397	Plano, TX	70.1	319	St. George, UT	138.6
385	McAllen, TX	78.1	304	Plantation, FL	155.1	199	St. Joseph, MO	270.3
374	McKinney, TX	84.7	123	Pomona, CA	372.3	5	St. Louis, MO	1,120.6
106	Medford, OR	420.8	50	Pompano Beach, FL	581.5	99	St. Paul, MN	434.1
47	Melbourne, FL	610.6	282	Port St. Lucie, FL	171.6	45	St. Petersburg, FL	622.1
4	Memphis, TN	1,151.7	160	Portland, OR	316.4	376	Sugar Land, TX	82.0
394	Menifee, CA	72.5	239	Portsmouth, VA	234.7	415	Sunnyvale, CA	57.1
30	Merced, CA	692.8	118	Providence, RI	376.7	326	Sunrise, FL	133.1
370	Meridian, ID	90.6	378	Provo, UT	80.4	392	Surprise, AZ	73.7
216	Mesa, AZ	254.5	63	Pueblo, CO	521.7	53	Syracuse, NY	568.1
291	Mesquite, TX	167.8	170	Quincy, MA	305.1	71	Tacoma, WA	505.3
61	Miami Beach, FL	534.8	297	Racine, WI	161.9	72	Tallahassee, FL	501.5
82	Miami Gardens, FL	468.6	240	Raleigh, NC	234.2	97	Tampa, FL	434.2
42	Miami, FL	633.8	393	Ramapo, NY	72.6	435	Temecula, CA	32.9
194	Midland, TX	277.6	345	Rancho Cucamon., CA	111.7	146	Tempe, AZ	343.2
19	Milwaukee, WI	735.9	95	Reading, PA	437.0	273	Thornton, CO	188.4
94	Minneapolis, MN	438.4	56	Redding, CA	555.1	399	Thousand Oaks, CA	68.1
198	Miramar, FL	270.6	321	Redwood City, CA	136.4	29	Toledo, OH	704.5
429	Mission Viejo, CA	43.9	132	Reno, NV	357.9	431	Toms River Twnshp, NJ	40.2
408	Mission, TX	60.8	309	Renton, WA	148.3	121	Topeka, KS	373.3
164	Mobile, AL	308.9	189	Rialto, CA	282.5	423	Torrance, CA	52.1
67	Modesto, CA	518.5	410	Richardson, TX	60.0	383	Tracy, CA	78.8
324	Montgomery, AL	135.4	36	Richmond, CA	674.1	20	Trenton, NJ	734.9
281	Moreno Valley, CA	172.8	169	Richmond, VA	305.6	428	Troy, MI	44.1
305	Mountain View, CA	152.8	280	Rio Rancho, NM	174.4	96	Tucson, AZ	435.3
83	Murfreesboro, TN	453.5	223	Riverside, CA	248.8	41	Tulsa, OK	634.0
432	Murrieta, CA	37.4	130	Roanoke, VA	360.0	183	Tuscaloosa, AL	290.3
295	Nampa, ID	164.4	364	Rochester, MN	95.8	373	Tustin, CA	86.6
267	Napa, CA	201.0	65	Rochester, NY	520.8	110	Tyler, TX	395.8
411	Naperville, IL	59.5	8	Rockford, IL	952.8	362	Upland, CA	96.6
320	Nashua, NH	137.0	302	Roseville, CA	156.2	196	Upper Darby Twnshp, PA	274.8
10	Nashville, TN	878.3	401	Roswell, GA	66.2	303	Vacaville, CA	155.4
22	New Bedford, MA	731.0	409	Round Rock, TX	60.2	122	Vallejo, CA	373.2
21	New Haven, CT	734.2	86	Sacramento, CA	451.2	261	Vancouver, WA	206.2
102	New Orleans, LA	431.0	230	Salem, OR	240.9	325	Ventura, CA	133.6
346	New Rochelle, NY	111.5	164	Salinas, CA	308.9	145	Victorville, CA	343.8
119	New York, NY	376.5	93	Salt Lake City, UT	443.7	381	Virginia Beach, VA	78.9
112	Newark, NJ	391.9	157	San Antonio, TX	321.8	188	Visalia, CA	282.9
396	Newport Beach, CA	71.0	66	San Bernardino, CA	519.1	167	Vista, CA	307.0
243	Newport News, VA	227.4	197	San Diego, CA	273.5	174	Waco, TX	298.6
405	Newton, MA	62.3	213	San Francisco, CA	257.9	134	Warren, MI	354.3
175	Norfolk, VA	298.4	260	San Jose, CA	206.3	398	Warwick, RI	69.3
412	Norman, OK	57.9	283	San Leandro, CA	171.5	60	Washington, DC	537.5
87	North Charleston, SC	448.0	277	San Marcos, CA	183.0	339	Waterbury, CT	118.6
58	North Las Vegas, NV	549.4	289	San Mateo, CA	168.2	236	Waukegan, IL	235.8
246	Norwalk, CA	221.8	375	Sandy Springs, GA	82.7	309	West Covina, CA	148.3
248	Norwalk, CT	221.5	366	Sandy, UT	95.1	329	West Jordan, UT	130.7
15	Oakland, CA	807.8	251	Santa Ana, CA	218.7	105	West Palm Beach, FL	428.6
182	Oceanside, CA	290.4	233	Santa Barbara, CA	239.2	184	West Valley, UT	290.1
9	Odessa, TX	881.9	334	Santa Clara, CA	125.7	237	Westland, MI	235.3
385	O'Fallon, MO	78.1	337	Santa Clarita, CA	119.9	266	Westminster, CA	201.3
199	Ogden, UT	270.3	68	Santa Maria, CA	517.8	275	Westminster, CO	184.5
40	Oklahoma City, OK	636.5	231	Santa Monica, CA	240.1	278	Whittier, CA	179.8
357	Olathe, KS	100.3	212	Santa Rosa, CA	258.1	201	Wichita Falls, TX	269.2
142	Omaha, NE	345.0	311	Savannah, GA	146.6	58	Wichita, KS	549.4
321	Ontario, CA	136.4	389	Scottsdale, AZ	75.6	176	Wilmington, NC	298.1
424	Orange, CA	49.4	328	Scranton, PA	131.4	90	Winston-Salem, NC	446.6
440	Orem, UT	7.6	138	Seattle, WA	348.2	404	Woodbridge Twnshp, NJ	63.6
23	Orlando, FL	721.3	74	Shreveport, LA	498.6	27	Worcester, MA	708.3
343	Overland Park, KS	113.5	390	Simi Valley, CA	75.0	120	Yakima, WA	375.7
317	Oxnard, CA	139.7	237	Sioux City, IA	235.3	147	Yonkers, NY	342.1
100	Palm Bay, FL	432.9	205	Sioux Falls, SD	265.2	97	Yuma, AZ	434.2
137	Palmdale, CA	350.9	255	Somerville, MA	212.4			
426	Parma, OH	46.9	241	South Bend, IN	229.8			

Source: CQ Press using reported data from the F.B.I. "Crime in the United States 2012"

*Aggravated assault is an attack for the purpose of inflicting severe bodily injury.

62. Aggravated Assault Rate in 2012 (continued)
National Rate = 242.3 Aggravated Assaults per 100,000 Population*

RANK	CITY	RATE	RANK	CITY	RATE	RANK	CITY	RATE
1	Flint, MI	1,899.0	75	Grand Rapids, MI	495.4	149	Hesperia, CA	335.6
2	Camden, NJ	1,412.5	76	Albuquerque, NM	494.9	150	Elizabeth, NJ	333.4
3	Detroit, MI	1,321.0	77	Peoria, IL	485.7	150	Greeley, CO	333.4
4	Memphis, TN	1,151.7	78	Boston, MA	483.6	152	Greensboro, NC	328.8
5	St. Louis, MO	1,120.6	79	Las Vegas, NV	480.1	153	Inglewood, CA	328.3
6	Stockton, CA	973.9	80	Corpus Christi, TX	474.1	154	High Point, NC	324.9
7	Birmingham, AL	954.2	81	Gainesville, FL	472.3	155	Arlington, TX	323.0
8	Rockford, IL	952.8	82	Miami Gardens, FL	468.6	156	El Paso, TX	322.9
9	Odessa, TX	881.9	83	Murfreesboro, TN	453.5	157	San Antonio, TX	321.8
10	Nashville, TN	878.3	84	Chicago, IL	453.1	158	Fresno, CA	321.7
11	Brockton, MA	850.2	85	Lafayette, LA	451.8	159	Bakersfield, CA	320.8
12	Kansas City, MO	832.6	86	Sacramento, CA	451.2	160	Portland, OR	316.4
13	Atlanta, GA	813.4	87	North Charleston, SC	448.0	161	Manchester, NH	314.4
14	Little Rock, AR	811.0	88	Amarillo, TX	447.7	162	Cincinnati, OH	313.3
15	Oakland, CA	807.8	89	Gary, IN	447.4	163	Laredo, TX	311.1
16	Hartford, CT	770.7	90	Winston-Salem, NC	446.6	164	Mobile, AL	308.9
17	Compton, CA	750.6	91	Paterson, NJ	445.1	164	Salinas, CA	308.9
18	Baltimore, MD	743.6	92	Cleveland, OH	444.4	166	Independence, MO	308.3
19	Milwaukee, WI	735.9	93	Salt Lake City, UT	443.7	167	Vista, CA	307.0
20	Trenton, NJ	734.9	94	Minneapolis, MN	438.4	168	Livermore, CA	306.8
21	New Haven, CT	734.2	95	Reading, PA	437.0	169	Richmond, VA	305.6
22	New Bedford, MA	731.0	96	Tucson, AZ	435.3	170	Quincy, MA	305.1
23	Orlando, FL	721.3	97	Tampa, FL	434.2	171	Lancaster, CA	304.1
24	Indianapolis, IN	711.5	97	Yuma, AZ	434.2	172	Macon, GA	300.5
25	Fall River, MA	710.8	99	St. Paul, MN	434.1	173	Largo, FL	299.6
26	Albany, GA	710.7	100	Palm Bay, FL	432.9	174	Waco, TX	298.6
27	Worcester, MA	708.3	101	Dayton, OH	432.7	175	Norfolk, VA	298.4
28	Lawton, OK	704.6	102	New Orleans, LA	431.0	176	Wilmington, NC	298.1
29	Toledo, OH	704.5	103	College Station, TX	430.8	177	Lawrence, KS	297.2
30	Merced, CA	692.8	104	Durham, NC	429.2	178	Lakewood, CO	295.1
31	Buffalo, NY	688.9	105	West Palm Beach, FL	428.6	179	Greenville, NC	294.7
31	Lawrence, MA	688.9	106	Medford, OR	420.8	180	Dallas, TX	293.7
33	Champaign, IL	678.7	107	Clearwater, FL	420.1	181	Hemet, CA	293.1
34	Springfield, IL	676.2	108	Davenport, IA	404.2	182	Oceanside, CA	290.4
35	Springfield, MO	674.7	109	Jacksonville, FL	402.5	183	Tuscaloosa, AL	290.3
36	Richmond, CA	674.1	110	Tyler, TX	395.8	184	West Valley, UT	290.1
37	Lansing, MI	671.4	111	Killeen, TX	394.8	185	Chino, CA	287.0
38	Springfield, MA	656.2	112	Newark, NJ	391.9	186	Glendale, AZ	285.8
39	Lubbock, TX	641.5	113	Charlotte, NC	391.5	187	Asheville, NC	284.9
40	Oklahoma City, OK	636.5	114	Fayetteville, AR	383.4	188	Visalia, CA	282.9
41	Tulsa, OK	634.0	115	Carson, CA	382.9	189	Rialto, CA	282.5
42	Miami, FL	633.8	116	Jackson, MS	381.4	190	Davie, FL	281.2
43	Huntsville, AL	628.2	117	Fort Lauderdale, FL	377.0	191	Decatur, IL	281.1
44	Antioch, CA	625.7	118	Providence, RI	376.7	192	Long Beach, CA	280.7
45	St. Petersburg, FL	622.1	119	New York, NY	376.5	193	Lakeland, FL	278.2
46	Beaumont, TX	619.2	120	Yakima, WA	375.7	194	Midland, TX	277.6
47	Melbourne, FL	610.6	121	Topeka, KS	373.3	195	South Gate, CA	275.1
48	Knoxville, TN	608.5	122	Vallejo, CA	373.2	196	Upper Darby Twnshp, PA	274.8
49	Fort Smith, AR	592.1	123	Pomona, CA	372.3	197	San Diego, CA	273.5
50	Pompano Beach, FL	581.5	124	Bloomington, IL	368.3	198	Miramar, FL	270.6
51	Lynn, MA	581.4	125	Fort Worth, TX	364.8	199	Ogden, UT	270.3
52	Baton Rouge, LA	580.6	126	Denver, CO	364.5	199	St. Joseph, MO	270.3
53	Syracuse, NY	568.1	127	Jersey City, NJ	362.1	201	Wichita Falls, TX	269.2
54	Philadelphia, PA	562.6	128	Pittsburgh, PA	360.4	202	Bryan, TX	268.9
55	Anchorage, AK	559.3	129	Green Bay, WI	360.1	203	Pasadena, TX	268.5
56	Redding, CA	555.1	130	Roanoke, VA	360.0	204	Columbus, GA	266.6
57	Hammond, IN	554.3	131	Longview, TX	359.8	205	Sioux Falls, SD	265.2
58	North Las Vegas, NV	549.4	132	Reno, NV	357.9	206	Las Cruces, NM	263.5
58	Wichita, KS	549.4	133	Des Moines, IA	355.4	207	Austin, TX	262.6
60	Washington, DC	537.5	134	Phoenix, AZ	354.3	208	Fontana, CA	260.4
61	Miami Beach, FL	534.8	134	Warren, MI	354.3	209	Fayetteville, NC	259.3
62	Clarksville, TN	524.2	136	Louisville, KY	352.7	210	Chesapeake, VA	258.9
63	Pueblo, CO	521.7	137	Palmdale, CA	350.9	211	Fairfield, CA	258.6
64	Houston, TX	521.0	138	Seattle, WA	348.2	212	Santa Rosa, CA	258.1
65	Rochester, NY	520.8	139	Indio, CA	347.8	213	San Francisco, CA	257.9
66	San Bernardino, CA	519.1	139	Spokane, WA	347.8	214	Cambridge, MA	257.1
67	Modesto, CA	518.5	141	Hawthorne, CA	346.6	214	Escondido, CA	257.1
68	Santa Maria, CA	517.8	142	Omaha, NE	345.0	216	Mesa, AZ	254.5
69	Albany, NY	515.3	143	Edinburg, TX	344.8	217	Abilene, TX	253.6
70	Bridgeport, CT	509.5	144	Lowell, MA	344.6	218	Elk Grove, CA	253.3
71	Tacoma, WA	505.3	145	Victorville, CA	343.8	219	Lincoln, NE	252.9
72	Tallahassee, FL	501.5	146	Tempe, AZ	343.2	220	Fargo, ND	252.2
73	Akron, OH	499.5	147	Yonkers, NY	342.1	221	Citrus Heights, CA	251.4
74	Shreveport, LA	498.6	148	Kansas City, KS	339.7	222	Evansville, IN	251.3

RANK	CITY	RATE	RANK	CITY	RATE	RANK	CITY	RATE
223	Riverside, CA	248.8	297	Racine, WI	161.9	371	Hamilton Twnshp, NJ	89.8
224	Colorado Springs, CO	247.3	298	Chico, CA	160.8	372	Pembroke Pines, FL	87.0
225	Billings, MT	245.4	299	Grand Prairie, TX	158.4	373	Tustin, CA	86.6
225	Deerfield Beach, FL	245.4	300	Brooklyn Park, MN	157.7	374	McKinney, TX	84.7
227	Duluth, MN	245.3	301	Federal Way, WA	156.6	375	Sandy Springs, GA	82.7
228	Columbia, MO	244.0	302	Roseville, CA	156.2	376	Sugar Land, TX	82.0
229	Joliet, IL	243.1	303	Vacaville, CA	155.4	377	Broken Arrow, OK	81.4
230	Salem, OR	240.9	304	Plantation, FL	155.1	378	Provo, UT	80.4
231	Santa Monica, CA	240.1	305	Mountain View, CA	152.8	379	Pearland, TX	80.3
232	Everett, WA	239.3	306	Irving, TX	152.7	380	Centennial, CO	79.8
233	Santa Barbara, CA	239.2	307	El Monte, CA	150.8	381	Henderson, NV	78.9
234	Lynchburg, VA	237.9	308	Hayward, CA	148.6	381	Virginia Beach, VA	78.9
235	Baldwin Park, CA	236.2	309	Renton, WA	148.3	383	Tracy, CA	78.8
236	Waukegan, IL	235.8	309	West Covina, CA	148.3	384	Lee's Summit, MO	78.4
237	Sioux City, IA	235.3	311	Savannah, GA	146.6	385	McAllen, TX	78.1
237	Westland, MI	235.3	312	Downey, CA	145.2	385	O'Fallon, MO	78.1
239	Portsmouth, VA	234.7	313	Sparks, NV	144.0	387	Brick Twnshp, NJ	77.8
240	Raleigh, NC	234.2	314	Fort Wayne, IN	143.8	388	Carrollton, TX	77.1
241	South Bend, IN	229.8	315	Stamford, CT	141.7	389	Scottsdale, AZ	75.6
242	Kent, WA	228.5	316	Sterling Heights, MI	140.0	390	Simi Valley, CA	75.0
243	Newport News, VA	227.4	317	Oxnard, CA	139.7	391	Bloomington, MN	74.5
244	Madison, WI	226.9	318	Buena Park, CA	139.4	392	Surprise, AZ	73.7
245	Gresham, OR	224.6	319	St. George, UT	138.6	393	Ramapo, NY	72.6
246	Norwalk, CA	221.8	320	Nashua, NH	137.0	394	Menifee, CA	72.5
247	Hollywood, FL	221.6	321	Lakewood, CA	136.4	395	Fremont, CA	72.2
248	Norwalk, CT	221.5	321	Ontario, CA	136.4	396	Newport Beach, CA	71.0
249	Bloomington, IN	220.5	321	Redwood City, CA	136.4	397	Plano, TX	70.1
250	Aurora, CO	220.2	324	Montgomery, AL	135.4	398	Warwick, RI	69.3
251	Santa Ana, CA	218.7	325	Ventura, CA	133.6	399	Thousand Oaks, CA	68.1
252	Hialeah, FL	217.1	326	Sunrise, FL	133.1	400	Greece, NY	67.2
253	Los Angeles, CA	216.1	327	Kenosha, WI	132.0	401	Roswell, GA	66.2
254	Anaheim, CA	215.4	328	Scranton, PA	131.4	402	Alexandria, VA	65.8
255	Somerville, MA	212.4	329	West Jordan, UT	130.7	403	Lakewood Twnshp, NJ	65.1
256	Jurupa Valley, CA	211.1	330	Charleston, SC	130.0	404	Woodbridge Twnshp, NJ	63.6
257	Erie, PA	209.9	331	Clovis, CA	127.8	405	Newton, MA	62.3
258	Kennewick, WA	207.9	332	Bethlehem, PA	127.3	406	Edmond, OK	61.1
259	Athens-Clarke, GA	207.7	333	Daly City, CA	126.8	406	Glendale, CA	61.1
260	San Jose, CA	206.3	334	Santa Clara, CA	125.7	408	Mission, TX	60.8
261	Vancouver, WA	206.2	335	Chula Vista, CA	125.3	409	Round Rock, TX	60.2
262	Cicero, IL	205.2	336	Ann Arbor, MI	122.6	410	Richardson, TX	60.0
263	Fullerton, CA	205.1	337	Costa Mesa, CA	119.9	411	Naperville, IL	59.5
264	Fort Collins, CO	205.0	337	Santa Clarita, CA	119.9	412	Norman, OK	57.9
265	Boise, ID	201.8	339	Waterbury, CT	118.6	413	Farmington Hills, MI	57.3
266	Westminster, CA	201.3	340	Peoria, AZ	117.5	414	Corona, CA	57.2
267	Clinton Twnshp, MI	201.0	341	Lexington, KY	114.4	415	Sunnyvale, CA	57.1
267	Napa, CA	201.0	342	Cheektowaga, NY	113.7	416	Gilbert, AZ	56.9
269	Dearborn, MI	195.4	343	Overland Park, KS	113.5	417	Clarkstown, NY	56.1
270	Bellflower, CA	195.2	344	Coral Springs, FL	112.0	418	Frisco, TX	53.6
271	Avondale, AZ	191.4	345	Rancho Cucamon., CA	111.7	419	Edison Twnshp, NJ	53.5
272	El Cajon, CA	188.5	346	New Rochelle, NY	111.5	420	Cary, NC	53.2
273	Thornton, CO	188.4	347	Clifton, NJ	107.5	421	Bellevue, WA	52.4
274	Aurora, IL	186.7	348	Garland, TX	106.4	422	Chino Hills, CA	52.2
275	Westminster, CO	184.5	348	Spokane Valley, WA	106.4	423	Torrance, CA	52.1
276	Concord, CA	183.7	350	Cape Coral, FL	105.2	424	Orange, CA	49.4
277	San Marcos, CA	183.0	351	Boca Raton, FL	104.1	425	Danbury, CT	48.8
278	Whittier, CA	179.8	352	Hampton, VA	103.7	426	Parma, OH	46.9
279	Allentown, PA	176.0	353	Elgin, IL	102.6	427	Amherst, NY	45.1
280	Rio Rancho, NM	174.4	354	Eugene, OR	102.5	428	Troy, MI	44.1
281	Moreno Valley, CA	172.8	355	Burbank, CA	100.9	429	Mission Viejo, CA	43.9
282	Port St. Lucie, FL	171.6	356	Huntington Beach, CA	100.7	430	League City, TX	40.6
283	San Leandro, CA	171.5	357	Olathe, KS	100.3	431	Toms River Twnshp, NJ	40.2
284	Brownsville, TX	169.5	358	Lake Forest, CA	99.8	432	Murrieta, CA	37.4
285	Chandler, AZ	169.3	359	Arvada, CO	98.1	433	Allen, TX	34.9
286	Carlsbad, CA	168.7	360	Hillsboro, OR	97.7	434	Arlington Heights, IL	33.1
287	Boulder, CO	168.6	361	Cranston, RI	97.1	435	Temecula, CA	32.9
287	Pasadena, CA	168.6	362	Upland, CA	96.6	436	Irvine, CA	32.6
289	San Mateo, CA	168.2	363	Alhambra, CA	95.9	437	Hoover, AL	30.4
290	Denton, TX	168.1	364	Livonia, MI	95.8	438	Johns Creek, GA	30.0
291	Mesquite, TX	167.8	364	Rochester, MN	95.8	439	Colonie, NY	21.8
292	Bellingham, WA	166.9	366	Sandy, UT	95.1	440	Orem, UT	7.6
293	Cedar Rapids, IA	165.9	367	Berkeley, CA	93.9	441	Fishers, IN	5.0
294	Longmont, CO	165.3	368	Alameda, CA	92.8	442	Carmel, IN	3.7
295	Nampa, ID	164.4	369	Beaverton, OR	91.0			
296	Garden Grove, CA	163.9	370	Meridian, ID	90.6			

Source: CQ Press using reported data from the F.B.I. "Crime in the United States 2012"

*Aggravated assault is an attack for the purpose of inflicting severe bodily injury.

63. Percent Change in Aggravated Assault Rate: 2011 to 2012
National Percent Change = 0.4% Increase*

RANK	CITY	% CHANGE	RANK	CITY	% CHANGE	RANK	CITY	% CHANGE
93	Abilene, TX	12.3	373	Chino Hills, CA	(17.7)	299	Gainesville, FL	(7.0)
76	Akron, OH	14.5	38	Chino, CA	27.2	107	Garden Grove, CA	10.3
399	Alameda, CA	(28.6)	385	Chula Vista, CA	(22.1)	106	Garland, TX	10.5
24	Albany, GA	34.7	113	Cicero, IL	10.0	11	Gary, IN	54.3
NA	Albany, NY**	NA	337	Cincinnati, OH	(11.3)	50	Gilbert, AZ	21.6
287	Albuquerque, NM	(6.1)	103	Citrus Heights, CA	10.9	143	Glendale, AZ	6.5
355	Alexandria, VA	(13.8)	NA	Clarkstown, NY**	NA	345	Glendale, CA	(12.8)
301	Alhambra, CA	(7.3)	190	Clarksville, TN	2.5	317	Grand Prairie, TX	(9.1)
NA	Allentown, PA**	NA	380	Clearwater, FL	(19.4)	104	Grand Rapids, MI	10.8
405	Allen, TX	(30.2)	266	Cleveland, OH	(4.2)	NA	Greece, NY**	NA
226	Amarillo, TX	(0.3)	334	Clifton, NJ	(11.0)	251	Greeley, CO	(2.5)
NA	Amherst, NY**	NA	292	Clinton Twnshp, MI	(6.5)	19	Green Bay, WI	39.9
190	Anaheim, CA	2.5	241	Clovis, CA	(1.8)	NA	Greensboro, NC**	NA
201	Anchorage, AK	2.0	3	College Station, TX	84.3	NA	Greenville, NC**	NA
364	Ann Arbor, MI	(15.9)	NA	Colonie, NY**	NA	83	Gresham, OR	13.0
33	Antioch, CA	29.1	246	Colorado Springs, CO	(2.2)	361	Hamilton Twnshp, NJ	(15.2)
181	Arlington Heights, IL	3.8	401	Columbia, MO	(29.5)	14	Hammond, IN	45.8
190	Arlington, TX	2.5	107	Columbus, GA	10.3	354	Hampton, VA	(13.7)
178	Arvada, CO	4.1	71	Compton, CA	17.2	214	Hartford, CT	0.9
204	Asheville, NC	1.9	268	Concord, CA	(4.3)	205	Hawthorne, CA	1.6
249	Athens-Clarke, GA	(2.3)	251	Coral Springs, FL	(2.5)	35	Hayward, CA	29.0
239	Atlanta, GA	(1.6)	148	Corona, CA	6.3	132	Hemet, CA	7.5
257	Aurora, CO	(3.2)	169	Corpus Christi, TX	4.7	410	Henderson, NV	(34.7)
337	Aurora, IL	(11.3)	73	Costa Mesa, CA	17.0	8	Hesperia, CA	60.3
226	Austin, TX	(0.3)	18	Cranston, RI	41.8	353	Hialeah, FL	(13.6)
83	Avondale, AZ	13.0	254	Dallas, TX	(3.0)	304	High Point, NC	(7.7)
330	Bakersfield, CA	(10.6)	64	Daly City, CA	18.0	179	Hillsboro, OR	3.9
40	Baldwin Park, CA	26.9	393	Danbury, CT	(25.4)	299	Hollywood, FL	(7.0)
272	Baltimore, MD	(4.7)	363	Davenport, IA	(15.8)	13	Hoover, AL	46.9
306	Baton Rouge, LA	(7.9)	96	Davie, FL	12.1	285	Houston, TX	(5.9)
69	Beaumont, TX	17.8	170	Dayton, OH	4.6	394	Huntington Beach, CA	(25.6)
390	Beaverton, OR	(24.2)	370	Dearborn, MI	(16.7)	123	Huntsville, AL	8.4
94	Bellevue, WA	12.2	412	Decatur, IL	(35.5)	157	Independence, MO	5.7
229	Bellflower, CA	(0.5)	328	Deerfield Beach, FL	(10.3)	90	Indianapolis, IN	12.5
40	Bellingham, WA	26.9	257	Denton, TX	(3.2)	314	Indio, CA	(8.7)
344	Berkeley, CA	(12.3)	176	Denver, CO	4.3	349	Inglewood, CA	(13.1)
287	Bethlehem, PA	(6.1)	243	Des Moines, IA	(2.0)	171	Irvine, CA	4.5
129	Billings, MT	7.9	230	Detroit, MI	(0.9)	197	Irving, TX	2.2
152	Birmingham, AL	6.2	201	Downey, CA	2.0	158	Jacksonville, FL	5.5
51	Bloomington, IL	21.5	31	Duluth, MN	30.0	167	Jackson, MS	4.8
120	Bloomington, IN	8.7	125	Durham, NC	8.2	190	Jersey City, NJ	2.5
336	Bloomington, MN	(11.1)	22	Edinburg, TX	36.4	47	Johns Creek, GA	23.0
257	Boca Raton, FL	(3.2)	378	Edison Twnshp, NJ	(18.7)	310	Joliet, IL	(8.3)
116	Boise, ID	9.3	5	Edmond, OK	67.4	NA	Jurupa Valley, CA**	NA
226	Boston, MA	(0.3)	414	El Cajon, CA	(39.2)	296	Kansas City, KS	(6.7)
373	Boulder, CO	(17.7)	320	El Monte, CA	(9.4)	114	Kansas City, MO	9.8
381	Brick Twnshp, NJ	(19.7)	231	El Paso, TX	(1.0)	261	Kennewick, WA	(3.7)
165	Bridgeport, CT	5.0	314	Elgin, IL	(8.7)	212	Kenosha, WI	1.1
292	Brockton, MA	(6.5)	386	Elizabeth, NJ	(22.2)	403	Kent, WA	(29.9)
222	Broken Arrow, OK	0.4	254	Elk Grove, CA	(3.0)	305	Killeen, TX	(7.8)
64	Brooklyn Park, MN	18.0	124	Erie, PA	8.3	131	Knoxville, TN	7.6
358	Brownsville, TX	(14.2)	30	Escondido, CA	30.4	297	Lafayette, LA	(6.8)
411	Bryan, TX	(35.2)	383	Eugene, OR	(21.1)	48	Lake Forest, CA	21.9
382	Buena Park, CA	(20.6)	138	Evansville, IN	6.7	391	Lakeland, FL	(24.9)
NA	Buffalo, NY**	NA	231	Everett, WA	(1.0)	77	Lakewood Twnshp, NJ	14.4
218	Burbank, CA	0.5	114	Fairfield, CA	9.8	164	Lakewood, CA	5.2
314	Cambridge, MA	(8.7)	367	Fall River, MA	(16.5)	105	Lakewood, CO	10.6
301	Camden, NJ	(7.3)	306	Fargo, ND	(7.9)	320	Lancaster, CA	(9.4)
188	Cape Coral, FL	2.8	389	Farmington Hills, MI	(23.9)	261	Lansing, MI	(3.7)
92	Carlsbad, CA	12.4	26	Fayetteville, AR	33.4	310	Laredo, TX	(8.3)
415	Carmel, IN	(50.7)	100	Fayetteville, NC	11.1	236	Largo, FL	(1.4)
339	Carrollton, TX	(11.6)	NA	Federal Way, WA**	NA	387	Las Cruces, NM	(22.6)
101	Carson, CA	11.0	36	Fishers, IN	28.2	148	Las Vegas, NV	6.3
21	Cary, NC	37.5	66	Flint, MI	17.9	234	Lawrence, KS	(1.1)
308	Cedar Rapids, IA	(8.0)	63	Fontana, CA	18.7	148	Lawrence, MA	6.3
396	Centennial, CO	(27.3)	272	Fort Collins, CO	(4.7)	72	Lawton, OK	17.1
257	Champaign, IL	(3.2)	312	Fort Lauderdale, FL	(8.5)	166	League City, TX	4.9
NA	Chandler, AZ**	NA	60	Fort Smith, AR	18.8	48	Lee's Summit, MO	21.9
379	Charleston, SC	(19.0)	189	Fort Wayne, IN	2.7	NA	Lexington, KY**	NA
143	Charlotte, NC	6.5	274	Fort Worth, TX	(4.9)	143	Lincoln, NE	6.5
NA	Cheektowaga, NY**	NA	376	Fremont, CA	(18.1)	360	Little Rock, AR	(14.5)
231	Chesapeake, VA	(1.0)	334	Fresno, CA	(11.0)	59	Livermore, CA	19.1
235	Chicago, IL	(1.3)	400	Frisco, TX	(28.8)	357	Livonia, MI	(14.1)
42	Chico, CA	26.3	9	Fullerton, CA	60.2	289	Long Beach, CA	(6.2)

RANK	CITY	% CHANGE
384	Longmont, CO	(22.0)
148	Longview, TX	6.3
289	Los Angeles, CA	(6.2)
125	Louisville, KY	8.2
413	Lowell, MA	(37.2)
138	Lubbock, TX	6.7
218	Lynchburg, VA	0.5
330	Lynn, MA	(10.6)
207	Macon, GA	1.5
75	Madison, WI	15.3
284	Manchester, NH	(5.8)
398	McAllen, TX	(27.6)
407	McKinney, TX	(30.5)
87	Medford, OR	12.6
367	Melbourne, FL	(16.5)
97	Memphis, TN	11.6
1	Menifee, CA	118.4
4	Merced, CA	69.8
376	Meridian, ID	(18.1)
274	Mesa, AZ	(4.9)
78	Mesquite, TX	14.1
217	Miami Beach, FL	0.6
291	Miami Gardens, FL	(6.3)
268	Miami, FL	(4.3)
43	Midland, TX	25.5
7	Milwaukee, WI	61.2
236	Minneapolis, MN	(1.4)
55	Miramar, FL	20.4
325	Mission Viejo, CA	(9.9)
347	Mission, TX	(13.0)
356	Mobile, AL	(13.9)
74	Modesto, CA	16.4
238	Montgomery, AL	(1.5)
297	Moreno Valley, CA	(6.8)
119	Mountain View, CA	9.1
205	Murfreesboro, TN	1.6
404	Murrieta, CA	(30.1)
392	Nampa, ID	(25.1)
187	Napa, CA	2.9
183	Naperville, IL	3.3
342	Nashua, NH	(12.1)
117	Nashville, TN	9.2
276	New Bedford, MA	(5.0)
137	New Haven, CT	6.9
85	New Orleans, LA	12.8
NA	New Rochelle, NY**	NA
NA	New York, NY**	NA
246	Newark, NJ	(2.2)
365	Newport Beach, CA	(16.2)
141	Newport News, VA	6.6
322	Newton, MA	(9.6)
147	Norfolk, VA	6.4
312	Norman, OK	(8.5)
186	North Charleston, SC	3.0
NA	North Las Vegas, NV**	NA
120	Norwalk, CA	8.7
346	Norwalk, CT	(12.9)
135	Oakland, CA	7.1
28	Oceanside, CA	31.3
17	Odessa, TX	42.4
160	O'Fallon, MO	5.4
370	Ogden, UT	(16.7)
160	Oklahoma City, OK	5.4
366	Olathe, KS	(16.4)
160	Omaha, NE	5.4
324	Ontario, CA	(9.8)
183	Orange, CA	3.3
416	Orem, UT	(54.5)
224	Orlando, FL	(0.2)
167	Overland Park, KS	4.8
326	Oxnard, CA	(10.0)
282	Palm Bay, FL	(5.7)
110	Palmdale, CA	10.2
NA	Parma, OH**	NA

RANK	CITY	% CHANGE
174	Pasadena, CA	4.4
94	Pasadena, TX	12.2
270	Paterson, NJ	(4.4)
280	Pearland, TX	(5.3)
358	Pembroke Pines, FL	(14.2)
340	Peoria, AZ	(11.7)
70	Peoria, IL	17.5
253	Philadelphia, PA	(2.8)
39	Phoenix, AZ	27.0
327	Pittsburgh, PA	(10.2)
388	Plano, TX	(23.1)
317	Plantation, FL	(9.1)
133	Pomona, CA	7.4
99	Pompano Beach, FL	11.5
171	Port St. Lucie, FL	4.5
209	Portland, OR	1.3
340	Portsmouth, VA	(11.7)
NA	Providence, RI**	NA
223	Provo, UT	0.2
294	Pueblo, CO	(6.6)
171	Quincy, MA	4.5
130	Racine, WI	7.8
143	Raleigh, NC	6.5
NA	Ramapo, NY**	NA
117	Rancho Cucamon., CA	9.2
97	Reading, PA	11.6
282	Redding, CA	(5.7)
54	Redwood City, CA	20.5
60	Reno, NV	18.8
266	Renton, WA	(4.2)
90	Rialto, CA	12.5
408	Richardson, TX	(31.0)
154	Richmond, CA	6.0
286	Richmond, VA	(6.0)
197	Rio Rancho, NM	2.2
246	Riverside, CA	(2.2)
278	Roanoke, VA	(5.2)
212	Rochester, MN	1.1
NA	Rochester, NY**	NA
181	Rockford, IL	3.8
176	Roseville, CA	4.3
2	Roswell, GA	104.3
44	Round Rock, TX	25.4
163	Sacramento, CA	5.3
185	Salem, OR	3.1
409	Salinas, CA	(32.1)
86	Salt Lake City, UT	12.7
294	San Antonio, TX	(6.6)
141	San Bernardino, CA	6.6
122	San Diego, CA	8.6
224	San Francisco, CA	(0.2)
134	San Jose, CA	7.3
60	San Leandro, CA	18.8
216	San Marcos, CA	0.7
153	San Mateo, CA	6.1
12	Sandy Springs, GA	51.2
111	Sandy, UT	10.1
101	Santa Ana, CA	11.0
155	Santa Barbara, CA	5.9
10	Santa Clara, CA	57.5
29	Santa Clarita, CA	31.2
256	Santa Maria, CA	(3.1)
208	Santa Monica, CA	1.4
323	Santa Rosa, CA	(9.7)
244	Savannah, GA	(2.1)
402	Scottsdale, AZ	(29.7)
138	Scranton, PA	6.7
209	Seattle, WA	1.3
271	Shreveport, LA	(4.6)
15	Simi Valley, CA	42.9
395	Sioux City, IA	(27.0)
6	Sioux Falls, SD	63.9
303	Somerville, MA	(7.5)
349	South Bend, IN	(13.1)

RANK	CITY	% CHANGE
333	South Gate, CA	(10.9)
367	Sparks, NV	(16.5)
200	Spokane Valley, WA	2.1
215	Spokane, WA	0.8
351	Springfield, IL	(13.3)
211	Springfield, MA	1.2
58	Springfield, MO	19.4
125	Stamford, CT	8.2
81	Sterling Heights, MI	13.4
135	Stockton, CA	7.1
NA	St. George, UT**	NA
57	St. Joseph, MO	19.7
201	St. Louis, MO	2.0
82	St. Paul, MN	13.1
319	St. Petersburg, FL	(9.3)
125	Sugar Land, TX	8.2
20	Sunnyvale, CA	39.6
397	Sunrise, FL	(27.4)
33	Surprise, AZ	29.1
NA	Syracuse, NY**	NA
111	Tacoma, WA	10.1
332	Tallahassee, FL	(10.7)
276	Tampa, FL	(5.0)
244	Temecula, CA	(2.1)
87	Tempe, AZ	12.6
NA	Thornton, CO**	NA
278	Thousand Oaks, CA	(5.2)
32	Toledo, OH	29.6
195	Toms River Twnshp, NJ	2.3
52	Topeka, KS	21.2
197	Torrance, CA	2.2
79	Tracy, CA	14.0
249	Trenton, NJ	(2.3)
347	Troy, MI	(13.0)
80	Tucson, AZ	13.6
240	Tulsa, OK	(1.7)
25	Tuscaloosa, AL	34.6
27	Tustin, CA	32.4
174	Tyler, TX	4.4
372	Upland, CA	(17.2)
16	Upper Darby Twnshp, PA	42.7
56	Vacaville, CA	20.1
107	Vallejo, CA	10.3
218	Vancouver, WA	0.5
362	Ventura, CA	(15.4)
158	Victorville, CA	5.5
53	Virginia Beach, VA	21.0
179	Visalia, CA	3.9
46	Vista, CA	24.5
352	Waco, TX	(13.5)
242	Warren, MI	(1.9)
23	Warwick, RI	36.1
87	Washington, DC	12.6
375	Waterbury, CT	(18.0)
NA	Waukegan, IL**	NA
66	West Covina, CA	17.9
328	West Jordan, UT	(10.3)
308	West Palm Beach, FL	(8.0)
218	West Valley, UT	0.5
281	Westland, MI	(5.4)
66	Westminster, CA	17.9
45	Westminster, CO	25.3
406	Whittier, CA	(30.4)
195	Wichita Falls, TX	2.3
263	Wichita, KS	(3.8)
343	Wilmington, NC	(12.2)
194	Winston-Salem, NC	2.4
263	Woodbridge Twnshp, NJ	(3.8)
265	Worcester, MA	(3.9)
36	Yakima, WA	28.2
NA	Yonkers, NY**	NA
155	Yuma, AZ	5.9

Source: CQ Press using reported data from the F.B.I. "Crime in the United States 2012"

*Aggravated assault is an attack for the purpose of inflicting severe bodily injury.

**Not available.

63. Percent Change in Aggravated Assault Rate: 2011 to 2012 (continued)
National Percent Change = 0.4% Increase*

RANK	CITY	% CHANGE	RANK	CITY	% CHANGE	RANK	CITY	% CHANGE
1	Menifee, CA	118.4	75	Madison, WI	15.3	148	Las Vegas, NV	6.3
2	Roswell, GA	104.3	76	Akron, OH	14.5	148	Lawrence, MA	6.3
3	College Station, TX	84.3	77	Lakewood Twnshp, NJ	14.4	148	Longview, TX	6.3
4	Merced, CA	69.8	78	Mesquite, TX	14.1	152	Birmingham, AL	6.2
5	Edmond, OK	67.4	79	Tracy, CA	14.0	153	San Mateo, CA	6.1
6	Sioux Falls, SD	63.9	80	Tucson, AZ	13.6	154	Richmond, CA	6.0
7	Milwaukee, WI	61.2	81	Sterling Heights, MI	13.4	155	Santa Barbara, CA	5.9
8	Hesperia, CA	60.3	82	St. Paul, MN	13.1	155	Yuma, AZ	5.9
9	Fullerton, CA	60.2	83	Avondale, AZ	13.0	157	Independence, MO	5.7
10	Santa Clara, CA	57.5	83	Gresham, OR	13.0	158	Jacksonville, FL	5.5
11	Gary, IN	54.3	85	New Orleans, LA	12.8	158	Victorville, CA	5.5
12	Sandy Springs, GA	51.2	86	Salt Lake City, UT	12.7	160	O'Fallon, MO	5.4
13	Hoover, AL	46.9	87	Medford, OR	12.6	160	Oklahoma City, OK	5.4
14	Hammond, IN	45.8	87	Tempe, AZ	12.6	160	Omaha, NE	5.4
15	Simi Valley, CA	42.9	87	Washington, DC	12.6	163	Sacramento, CA	5.3
16	Upper Darby Twnshp, PA	42.7	90	Indianapolis, IN	12.5	164	Lakewood, CA	5.2
17	Odessa, TX	42.4	90	Rialto, CA	12.5	165	Bridgeport, CT	5.0
18	Cranston, RI	41.8	92	Carlsbad, CA	12.4	166	League City, TX	4.9
19	Green Bay, WI	39.9	93	Abilene, TX	12.3	167	Jackson, MS	4.8
20	Sunnyvale, CA	39.6	94	Bellevue, WA	12.2	167	Overland Park, KS	4.8
21	Cary, NC	37.5	94	Pasadena, TX	12.2	169	Corpus Christi, TX	4.7
22	Edinburg, TX	36.4	96	Davie, FL	12.1	170	Dayton, OH	4.6
23	Warwick, RI	36.1	97	Memphis, TN	11.6	171	Irvine, CA	4.5
24	Albany, GA	34.7	97	Reading, PA	11.6	171	Port St. Lucie, FL	4.5
25	Tuscaloosa, AL	34.6	99	Pompano Beach, FL	11.5	171	Quincy, MA	4.5
26	Fayetteville, AR	33.4	100	Fayetteville, NC	11.1	174	Pasadena, CA	4.4
27	Tustin, CA	32.4	101	Carson, CA	11.0	174	Tyler, TX	4.4
28	Oceanside, CA	31.3	101	Santa Ana, CA	11.0	176	Denver, CO	4.3
29	Santa Clarita, CA	31.2	103	Citrus Heights, CA	10.9	176	Roseville, CA	4.3
30	Escondido, CA	30.4	104	Grand Rapids, MI	10.8	178	Arvada, CO	4.1
31	Duluth, MN	30.0	105	Lakewood, CO	10.6	179	Hillsboro, OR	3.9
32	Toledo, OH	29.6	106	Garland, TX	10.5	179	Visalia, CA	3.9
33	Antioch, CA	29.1	107	Columbus, GA	10.3	181	Arlington Heights, IL	3.8
33	Surprise, AZ	29.1	107	Garden Grove, CA	10.3	181	Rockford, IL	3.8
35	Hayward, CA	29.0	107	Vallejo, CA	10.3	183	Naperville, IL	3.3
36	Fishers, IN	28.2	110	Palmdale, CA	10.2	183	Orange, CA	3.3
36	Yakima, WA	28.2	111	Sandy, UT	10.1	185	Salem, OR	3.1
38	Chino, CA	27.2	111	Tacoma, WA	10.1	186	North Charleston, SC	3.0
39	Phoenix, AZ	27.0	113	Cicero, IL	10.0	187	Napa, CA	2.9
40	Baldwin Park, CA	26.9	114	Fairfield, CA	9.8	188	Cape Coral, FL	2.8
40	Bellingham, WA	26.9	114	Kansas City, MO	9.8	189	Fort Wayne, IN	2.7
42	Chico, CA	26.3	116	Boise, ID	9.3	190	Anaheim, CA	2.5
43	Midland, TX	25.5	117	Nashville, TN	9.2	190	Arlington, TX	2.5
44	Round Rock, TX	25.4	117	Rancho Cucamon., CA	9.2	190	Clarksville, TN	2.5
45	Westminster, CO	25.3	119	Mountain View, CA	9.1	190	Jersey City, NJ	2.5
46	Vista, CA	24.5	120	Bloomington, IN	8.7	194	Winston-Salem, NC	2.4
47	Johns Creek, GA	23.0	120	Norwalk, CA	8.7	195	Toms River Twnshp, NJ	2.3
48	Lake Forest, CA	21.9	122	San Diego, CA	8.6	195	Wichita Falls, TX	2.3
48	Lee's Summit, MO	21.9	123	Huntsville, AL	8.4	197	Irving, TX	2.2
50	Gilbert, AZ	21.6	124	Erie, PA	8.3	197	Rio Rancho, NM	2.2
51	Bloomington, IL	21.5	125	Durham, NC	8.2	197	Torrance, CA	2.2
52	Topeka, KS	21.2	125	Louisville, KY	8.2	200	Spokane Valley, WA	2.1
53	Virginia Beach, VA	21.0	125	Stamford, CT	8.2	201	Anchorage, AK	2.0
54	Redwood City, CA	20.5	125	Sugar Land, TX	8.2	201	Downey, CA	2.0
55	Miramar, FL	20.4	129	Billings, MT	7.9	201	St. Louis, MO	2.0
56	Vacaville, CA	20.1	130	Racine, WI	7.8	204	Asheville, NC	1.9
57	St. Joseph, MO	19.7	131	Knoxville, TN	7.6	205	Hawthorne, CA	1.6
58	Springfield, MO	19.4	132	Hemet, CA	7.5	205	Murfreesboro, TN	1.6
59	Livermore, CA	19.1	133	Pomona, CA	7.4	207	Macon, GA	1.5
60	Fort Smith, AR	18.8	134	San Jose, CA	7.3	208	Santa Monica, CA	1.4
60	Reno, NV	18.8	135	Oakland, CA	7.1	209	Portland, OR	1.3
60	San Leandro, CA	18.8	135	Stockton, CA	7.1	209	Seattle, WA	1.3
63	Fontana, CA	18.7	137	New Haven, CT	6.9	211	Springfield, MA	1.2
64	Brooklyn Park, MN	18.0	138	Evansville, IN	6.7	212	Kenosha, WI	1.1
64	Daly City, CA	18.0	138	Lubbock, TX	6.7	212	Rochester, MN	1.1
66	Flint, MI	17.9	138	Scranton, PA	6.7	214	Hartford, CT	0.9
66	West Covina, CA	17.9	141	Newport News, VA	6.6	215	Spokane, WA	0.8
66	Westminster, CA	17.9	141	San Bernardino, CA	6.6	216	San Marcos, CA	0.7
69	Beaumont, TX	17.8	143	Charlotte, NC	6.5	217	Miami Beach, FL	0.6
70	Peoria, IL	17.5	143	Glendale, AZ	6.5	218	Burbank, CA	0.5
71	Compton, CA	17.2	143	Lincoln, NE	6.5	218	Lynchburg, VA	0.5
72	Lawton, OK	17.1	143	Raleigh, NC	6.5	218	Vancouver, WA	0.5
73	Costa Mesa, CA	17.0	147	Norfolk, VA	6.4	218	West Valley, UT	0.5
74	Modesto, CA	16.4	148	Corona, CA	6.3	222	Broken Arrow, OK	0.4

RANK	CITY	% CHANGE	RANK	CITY	% CHANGE	RANK	CITY	% CHANGE
223	Provo, UT	0.2	297	Lafayette, LA	(6.8)	370	Ogden, UT	(16.7)
224	Orlando, FL	(0.2)	297	Moreno Valley, CA	(6.8)	372	Upland, CA	(17.2)
224	San Francisco, CA	(0.2)	299	Gainesville, FL	(7.0)	373	Boulder, CO	(17.7)
226	Amarillo, TX	(0.3)	299	Hollywood, FL	(7.0)	373	Chino Hills, CA	(17.7)
226	Austin, TX	(0.3)	301	Alhambra, CA	(7.3)	375	Waterbury, CT	(18.0)
226	Boston, MA	(0.3)	301	Camden, NJ	(7.3)	376	Fremont, CA	(18.1)
229	Bellflower, CA	(0.5)	303	Somerville, MA	(7.5)	376	Meridian, ID	(18.1)
230	Detroit, MI	(0.9)	304	High Point, NC	(7.7)	378	Edison Twnshp, NJ	(18.7)
231	Chesapeake, VA	(1.0)	305	Killeen, TX	(7.8)	379	Charleston, SC	(19.0)
231	El Paso, TX	(1.0)	306	Baton Rouge, LA	(7.9)	380	Clearwater, FL	(19.4)
231	Everett, WA	(1.0)	306	Fargo, ND	(7.9)	381	Brick Twnshp, NJ	(19.7)
234	Lawrence, KS	(1.1)	308	Cedar Rapids, IA	(8.0)	382	Buena Park, CA	(20.6)
235	Chicago, IL	(1.3)	308	West Palm Beach, FL	(8.0)	383	Eugene, OR	(21.1)
236	Largo, FL	(1.4)	310	Joliet, IL	(8.3)	384	Longmont, CO	(22.0)
236	Minneapolis, MN	(1.4)	310	Laredo, TX	(8.3)	385	Chula Vista, CA	(22.1)
238	Montgomery, AL	(1.5)	312	Fort Lauderdale, FL	(8.5)	386	Elizabeth, NJ	(22.2)
239	Atlanta, GA	(1.6)	312	Norman, OK	(8.5)	387	Las Cruces, NM	(22.6)
240	Tulsa, OK	(1.7)	314	Cambridge, MA	(8.7)	388	Plano, TX	(23.1)
241	Clovis, CA	(1.8)	314	Elgin, IL	(8.7)	389	Farmington Hills, MI	(23.9)
242	Warren, MI	(1.9)	314	Indio, CA	(8.7)	390	Beaverton, OR	(24.2)
243	Des Moines, IA	(2.0)	317	Grand Prairie, TX	(9.1)	391	Lakeland, FL	(24.9)
244	Savannah, GA	(2.1)	317	Plantation, FL	(9.1)	392	Nampa, ID	(25.1)
244	Temecula, CA	(2.1)	319	St. Petersburg, FL	(9.3)	393	Danbury, CT	(25.4)
246	Colorado Springs, CO	(2.2)	320	El Monte, CA	(9.4)	394	Huntington Beach, CA	(25.6)
246	Newark, NJ	(2.2)	320	Lancaster, CA	(9.4)	395	Sioux City, IA	(27.0)
246	Riverside, CA	(2.2)	322	Newton, MA	(9.6)	396	Centennial, CO	(27.3)
249	Athens-Clarke, GA	(2.3)	323	Santa Rosa, CA	(9.7)	397	Sunrise, FL	(27.4)
249	Trenton, NJ	(2.3)	324	Ontario, CA	(9.8)	398	McAllen, TX	(27.6)
251	Coral Springs, FL	(2.5)	325	Mission Viejo, CA	(9.9)	399	Alameda, CA	(28.6)
251	Greeley, CO	(2.5)	326	Oxnard, CA	(10.0)	400	Frisco, TX	(28.8)
253	Philadelphia, PA	(2.8)	327	Pittsburgh, PA	(10.2)	401	Columbia, MO	(29.5)
254	Dallas, TX	(3.0)	328	Deerfield Beach, FL	(10.3)	402	Scottsdale, AZ	(29.7)
254	Elk Grove, CA	(3.0)	328	West Jordan, UT	(10.3)	403	Kent, WA	(29.9)
256	Santa Maria, CA	(3.1)	330	Bakersfield, CA	(10.6)	404	Murrieta, CA	(30.1)
257	Aurora, CO	(3.2)	330	Lynn, MA	(10.6)	405	Allen, TX	(30.2)
257	Boca Raton, FL	(3.2)	332	Tallahassee, FL	(10.7)	406	Whittier, CA	(30.4)
257	Champaign, IL	(3.2)	333	South Gate, CA	(10.9)	407	McKinney, TX	(30.5)
257	Denton, TX	(3.2)	334	Clifton, NJ	(11.0)	408	Richardson, TX	(31.0)
261	Kennewick, WA	(3.7)	334	Fresno, CA	(11.0)	409	Salinas, CA	(32.1)
261	Lansing, MI	(3.7)	336	Bloomington, MN	(11.1)	410	Henderson, NV	(34.7)
263	Wichita, KS	(3.8)	337	Aurora, IL	(11.3)	411	Bryan, TX	(35.2)
263	Woodbridge Twnshp, NJ	(3.8)	337	Cincinnati, OH	(11.3)	412	Decatur, IL	(35.5)
265	Worcester, MA	(3.9)	339	Carrollton, TX	(11.6)	413	Lowell, MA	(37.2)
266	Cleveland, OH	(4.2)	340	Peoria, AZ	(11.7)	414	El Cajon, CA	(39.2)
266	Renton, WA	(4.2)	340	Portsmouth, VA	(11.7)	415	Carmel, IN	(50.7)
268	Concord, CA	(4.3)	342	Nashua, NH	(12.1)	416	Orem, UT	(54.5)
268	Miami, FL	(4.3)	343	Wilmington, NC	(12.2)	NA	Albany, NY**	NA
270	Paterson, NJ	(4.4)	344	Berkeley, CA	(12.3)	NA	Allentown, PA**	NA
271	Shreveport, LA	(4.6)	345	Glendale, CA	(12.8)	NA	Amherst, NY**	NA
272	Baltimore, MD	(4.7)	346	Norwalk, CT	(12.9)	NA	Buffalo, NY**	NA
272	Fort Collins, CO	(4.7)	347	Mission, TX	(13.0)	NA	Chandler, AZ**	NA
274	Fort Worth, TX	(4.9)	347	Troy, MI	(13.0)	NA	Cheektowaga, NY**	NA
274	Mesa, AZ	(4.9)	349	Inglewood, CA	(13.1)	NA	Clarkstown, NY**	NA
276	New Bedford, MA	(5.0)	349	South Bend, IN	(13.1)	NA	Colonie, NY**	NA
276	Tampa, FL	(5.0)	351	Springfield, IL	(13.3)	NA	Federal Way, WA**	NA
278	Roanoke, VA	(5.2)	352	Waco, TX	(13.5)	NA	Greece, NY**	NA
278	Thousand Oaks, CA	(5.2)	353	Hialeah, FL	(13.6)	NA	Greensboro, NC**	NA
280	Pearland, TX	(5.3)	354	Hampton, VA	(13.7)	NA	Greenville, NC**	NA
281	Westland, MI	(5.4)	355	Alexandria, VA	(13.8)	NA	Jurupa Valley, CA**	NA
282	Palm Bay, FL	(5.7)	356	Mobile, AL	(13.9)	NA	Lexington, KY**	NA
282	Redding, CA	(5.7)	357	Livonia, MI	(14.1)	NA	New Rochelle, NY**	NA
284	Manchester, NH	(5.8)	358	Brownsville, TX	(14.2)	NA	New York, NY**	NA
285	Houston, TX	(5.9)	358	Pembroke Pines, FL	(14.2)	NA	North Las Vegas, NV**	NA
286	Richmond, VA	(6.0)	360	Little Rock, AR	(14.5)	NA	Parma, OH**	NA
287	Albuquerque, NM	(6.1)	361	Hamilton Twnshp, NJ	(15.2)	NA	Providence, RI**	NA
287	Bethlehem, PA	(6.1)	362	Ventura, CA	(15.4)	NA	Ramapo, NY**	NA
289	Long Beach, CA	(6.2)	363	Davenport, IA	(15.8)	NA	Rochester, NY**	NA
289	Los Angeles, CA	(6.2)	364	Ann Arbor, MI	(15.9)	NA	St. George, UT**	NA
291	Miami Gardens, FL	(6.3)	365	Newport Beach, CA	(16.2)	NA	Syracuse, NY**	NA
292	Brockton, MA	(6.5)	366	Olathe, KS	(16.4)	NA	Thornton, CO**	NA
292	Clinton Twnshp, MI	(6.5)	367	Fall River, MA	(16.5)	NA	Waukegan, IL**	NA
294	Pueblo, CO	(6.6)	367	Melbourne, FL	(16.5)	NA	Yonkers, NY**	NA
294	San Antonio, TX	(6.6)	367	Sparks, NV	(16.5)			
296	Kansas City, KS	(6.7)	370	Dearborn, MI	(16.7)			

Source: CQ Press using reported data from the F.B.I. "Crime in the United States 2012"

*Aggravated assault is an attack for the purpose of inflicting severe bodily injury.

**Not available.

64. Percent Change in Aggravated Assault Rate: 2008 to 2012
National Percent Change = 12.7% Decrease*

RANK	CITY	% CHANGE	RANK	CITY	% CHANGE	RANK	CITY	% CHANGE
258	Abilene, TX	(20.9)	111	Chino Hills, CA	0.8	287	Gainesville, FL	(25.8)
60	Akron, OH	13.3	2	Chino, CA	161.1	250	Garden Grove, CA	(19.7)
318	Alameda, CA	(29.4)	359	Chula Vista, CA	(37.8)	349	Garland, TX	(34.7)
NA	Albany, GA**	NA	NA	Cicero, IL**	NA	252	Gary, IN	(20.1)
NA	Albany, NY**	NA	306	Cincinnati, OH	(27.8)	214	Gilbert, AZ	(15.8)
183	Albuquerque, NM	(11.8)	235	Citrus Heights, CA	(17.8)	76	Glendale, AZ	11.3
349	Alexandria, VA	(34.7)	NA	Clarkstown, NY**	NA	333	Glendale, CA	(31.6)
284	Alhambra, CA	(25.4)	146	Clarksville, TN	(6.3)	142	Grand Prairie, TX	(5.6)
NA	Allentown, PA**	NA	317	Clearwater, FL	(29.3)	202	Grand Rapids, MI	(14.4)
353	Allen, TX	(35.5)	102	Cleveland, OH	3.3	NA	Greece, NY**	NA
229	Amarillo, TX	(17.2)	222	Clifton, NJ	(16.8)	274	Greeley, CO	(23.2)
NA	Amherst, NY**	NA	194	Clinton Twnshp, MI	(13.6)	62	Green Bay, WI	13.1
75	Anaheim, CA	11.4	8	Clovis, CA	57.8	251	Greensboro, NC	(20.0)
202	Anchorage, AK	(14.4)	3	College Station, TX	140.1	361	Greenville, NC	(37.9)
312	Ann Arbor, MI	(28.3)	NA	Colonie, NY**	NA	187	Gresham, OR	(13.1)
21	Antioch, CA	43.2	219	Colorado Springs, CO	(16.6)	77	Hamilton Twnshp, NJ	11.0
NA	Arlington Heights, IL**	NA	90	Columbia, MO	7.2	82	Hammond, IN	9.0
193	Arlington, TX	(13.5)	156	Columbus, GA	(7.6)	312	Hampton, VA	(28.3)
217	Arvada, CO	(16.2)	345	Compton, CA	(33.5)	41	Hartford, CT	22.8
207	Asheville, NC	(15.1)	52	Concord, CA	16.0	209	Hawthorne, CA	(15.4)
197	Athens-Clarke, GA	(13.9)	335	Coral Springs, FL	(31.7)	298	Hayward, CA	(27.0)
68	Atlanta, GA	12.2	301	Corona, CA	(27.6)	246	Hemet, CA	(19.4)
242	Aurora, CO	(19.1)	179	Corpus Christi, TX	(10.9)	168	Henderson, NV	(9.0)
363	Aurora, IL	(39.3)	331	Costa Mesa, CA	(31.3)	5	Hesperia, CA	71.4
201	Austin, TX	(14.2)	44	Cranston, RI	21.4	352	Hialeah, FL	(35.4)
375	Avondale, AZ	(43.3)	185	Dallas, TX	(12.5)	171	High Point, NC	(9.4)
245	Bakersfield, CA	(19.3)	73	Daly City, CA	11.8	18	Hillsboro, OR	44.1
35	Baldwin Park, CA	28.0	282	Danbury, CT	(25.2)	160	Hollywood, FL	(8.1)
224	Baltimore, MD	(17.0)	292	Davenport, IA	(26.3)	357	Hoover, AL	(36.8)
196	Baton Rouge, LA	(13.7)	88	Davie, FL	7.6	181	Houston, TX	(11.2)
68	Beaumont, TX	12.2	156	Dayton, OH	(7.6)	222	Huntington Beach, CA	(16.8)
359	Beaverton, OR	(37.8)	219	Dearborn, MI	(16.6)	10	Huntsville, AL	55.3
107	Bellevue, WA	1.9	NA	Decatur, IL**	NA	374	Independence, MO	(42.8)
381	Bellflower, CA	(45.0)	388	Deerfield Beach, FL	(51.3)	67	Indianapolis, IN	12.3
26	Bellingham, WA	35.6	97	Denton, TX	4.2	31	Indio, CA	30.2
269	Berkeley, CA	(22.8)	101	Denver, CO	3.5	226	Inglewood, CA	(17.1)
186	Bethlehem, PA	(12.9)	212	Des Moines, IA	(15.6)	43	Irvine, CA	21.6
20	Billings, MT	43.9	71	Detroit, MI	12.1	332	Irving, TX	(31.4)
14	Birmingham, AL	49.6	163	Downey, CA	(8.7)	330	Jacksonville, FL	(31.2)
NA	Bloomington, IL**	NA	93	Duluth, MN	5.9	29	Jackson, MS	30.4
218	Bloomington, IN	(16.5)	57	Durham, NC	14.7	162	Jersey City, NJ	(8.3)
114	Bloomington, MN	0.5	33	Edinburg, TX	28.8	NA	Johns Creek, GA**	NA
295	Boca Raton, FL	(26.6)	399	Edison Twnshp, NJ	(63.8)	122	Joliet, IL	(1.2)
108	Boise, ID	1.5	64	Edmond, OK	12.9	NA	Jurupa Valley, CA**	NA
294	Boston, MA	(26.5)	365	El Cajon, CA	(39.6)	NA	Kansas City, KS**	NA
39	Boulder, CO	23.1	398	El Monte, CA	(62.2)	126	Kansas City, MO	(1.5)
287	Brick Twnshp, NJ	(25.8)	166	El Paso, TX	(8.9)	216	Kennewick, WA	(16.1)
212	Bridgeport, CT	(15.6)	347	Elgin, IL	(34.0)	281	Kenosha, WI	(25.1)
NA	Brockton, MA**	NA	37	Elizabeth, NJ	24.6	337	Kent, WA	(32.1)
376	Broken Arrow, OK	(44.1)	306	Elk Grove, CA	(27.8)	269	Killeen, TX	(22.8)
293	Brooklyn Park, MN	(26.4)	153	Erie, PA	(6.8)	129	Knoxville, TN	(2.9)
325	Brownsville, TX	(30.4)	98	Escondido, CA	4.1	369	Lafayette, LA	(42.0)
394	Bryan, TX	(54.3)	298	Eugene, OR	(27.0)	77	Lake Forest, CA	11.0
266	Buena Park, CA	(22.0)	86	Evansville, IN	8.4	166	Lakeland, FL	(8.9)
NA	Buffalo, NY**	NA	224	Everett, WA	(17.0)	NA	Lakewood Twnshp, NJ**	NA
248	Burbank, CA	(19.5)	124	Fairfield, CA	(1.3)	235	Lakewood, CA	(17.8)
89	Cambridge, MA	7.3	230	Fall River, MA	(17.3)	149	Lakewood, CO	(6.7)
34	Camden, NJ	28.4	45	Fargo, ND	20.7	368	Lancaster, CA	(41.6)
290	Cape Coral, FL	(25.9)	395	Farmington Hills, MI	(56.3)	135	Lansing, MI	(4.7)
81	Carlsbad, CA	9.8	63	Fayetteville, AR	13.0	301	Laredo, TX	(27.6)
403	Carmel, IN	(83.7)	387	Fayetteville, NC	(49.1)	370	Largo, FL	(42.4)
321	Carrollton, TX	(29.8)	54	Federal Way, WA	15.4	351	Las Cruces, NM	(34.8)
80	Carson, CA	10.4	400	Fishers, IN	(64.8)	197	Las Vegas, NV	(13.9)
15	Cary, NC	48.2	16	Flint, MI	46.0	149	Lawrence, KS	(6.7)
276	Cedar Rapids, IA	(23.4)	145	Fontana, CA	(6.1)	19	Lawrence, MA	44.0
202	Centennial, CO	(14.4)	354	Fort Collins, CO	(35.7)	174	Lawton, OK	(10.0)
NA	Champaign, IL**	NA	113	Fort Lauderdale, FL	0.7	346	League City, TX	(33.9)
NA	Chandler, AZ**	NA	82	Fort Smith, AR	9.0	118	Lee's Summit, MO	0.3
401	Charleston, SC	(66.9)	6	Fort Wayne, IN	67.2	NA	Lexington, KY**	NA
255	Charlotte, NC	(20.4)	104	Fort Worth, TX	2.5	343	Lincoln, NE	(33.2)
NA	Cheektowaga, NY**	NA	391	Fremont, CA	(52.3)	74	Little Rock, AR	11.7
87	Chesapeake, VA	8.1	164	Fresno, CA	(8.8)	4	Livermore, CA	119.9
279	Chicago, IL	(24.7)	340	Frisco, TX	(32.5)	50	Livonia, MI	16.4
256	Chico, CA	(20.5)	48	Fullerton, CA	19.9	190	Long Beach, CA	(13.2)

RANK	CITY	% CHANGE	RANK	CITY	% CHANGE	RANK	CITY	% CHANGE
NA	Longmont, CO**	NA	305	Pasadena, CA	(27.7)	53	South Gate, CA	15.7
385	Longview, TX	(47.8)	133	Pasadena, TX	(3.7)	379	Sparks, NV	(44.6)
320	Los Angeles, CA	(29.5)	115	Paterson, NJ	0.4	386	Spokane Valley, WA	(48.9)
125	Louisville, KY	(1.4)	103	Pearland, TX	2.8	178	Spokane, WA	(10.7)
396	Lowell, MA	(57.5)	381	Pembroke Pines, FL	(45.0)	NA	Springfield, IL**	NA
233	Lubbock, TX	(17.6)	51	Peoria, AZ	16.3	230	Springfield, MA	(17.3)
246	Lynchburg, VA	(19.4)	NA	Peoria, IL**	NA	11	Springfield, MO	55.0
182	Lynn, MA	(11.6)	226	Philadelphia, PA	(17.1)	172	Stamford, CT	(9.6)
362	Macon, GA	(38.7)	66	Phoenix, AZ	12.5	49	Sterling Heights, MI	18.4
60	Madison, WI	13.3	328	Pittsburgh, PA	(30.6)	85	Stockton, CA	8.6
40	Manchester, NH	22.9	393	Plano, TX	(53.8)	172	St. George, UT	(9.6)
390	McAllen, TX	(51.4)	286	Plantation, FL	(25.6)	226	St. Joseph, MO	(17.1)
358	McKinney, TX	(37.3)	177	Pomona, CA	(10.6)	160	St. Louis, MO	(8.1)
9	Medford, OR	56.0	234	Pompano Beach, FL	(17.7)	141	St. Paul, MN	(5.5)
344	Melbourne, FL	(33.3)	170	Port St. Lucie, FL	(9.3)	318	St. Petersburg, FL	(29.4)
109	Memphis, TN	1.2	200	Portland, OR	(14.1)	271	Sugar Land, TX	(22.9)
NA	Menifee, CA**	NA	249	Portsmouth, VA	(19.6)	282	Sunnyvale, CA	(25.2)
30	Merced, CA	30.3	93	Providence, RI	5.9	379	Sunrise, FL	(44.6)
301	Meridian, ID	(27.6)	267	Provo, UT	(22.1)	47	Surprise, AZ	20.2
252	Mesa, AZ	(20.1)	NA	Pueblo, CO**	NA	NA	Syracuse, NY**	NA
309	Mesquite, TX	(28.0)	32	Quincy, MA	28.9	238	Tacoma, WA	(18.2)
210	Miami Beach, FL	(15.5)	364	Racine, WI	(39.5)	279	Tallahassee, FL	(24.7)
96	Miami Gardens, FL	5.6	219	Raleigh, NC	(16.6)	242	Tampa, FL	(19.1)
206	Miami, FL	(15.0)	NA	Ramapo, NY**	NA	397	Temecula, CA	(58.9)
58	Midland, TX	13.9	194	Rancho Cucamon., CA	(13.6)	41	Tempe, AZ	22.8
56	Milwaukee, WI	15.0	138	Reading, PA	(5.3)	NA	Thornton, CO**	NA
324	Minneapolis, MN	(30.3)	91	Redding, CA	7.1	169	Thousand Oaks, CA	(9.1)
106	Miramar, FL	2.1	348	Redwood City, CA	(34.2)	91	Toledo, OH	7.1
312	Mission Viejo, CA	(28.3)	230	Reno, NV	(17.3)	275	Toms River Twnshp, NJ	(23.3)
315	Mission, TX	(28.5)	NA	Renton, WA**	NA	7	Topeka, KS	58.3
1	Mobile, AL	198.2	146	Rialto, CA	(6.3)	333	Torrance, CA	(31.6)
55	Modesto, CA	15.1	392	Richardson, TX	(53.6)	79	Tracy, CA	10.8
256	Montgomery, AL	(20.5)	27	Richmond, CA	35.5	13	Trenton, NJ	50.5
306	Moreno Valley, CA	(27.8)	214	Richmond, VA	(15.8)	378	Troy, MI	(44.5)
388	Mountain View, CA	(51.3)	254	Rio Rancho, NM	(20.2)	154	Tucson, AZ	(7.5)
100	Murfreesboro, TN	4.0	323	Riverside, CA	(30.2)	329	Tulsa, OK	(31.1)
268	Murrieta, CA	(22.6)	322	Roanoke, VA	(30.0)	65	Tuscaloosa, AL	12.8
310	Nampa, ID	(28.2)	300	Rochester, MN	(27.5)	23	Tustin, CA	37.2
210	Napa, CA	(15.5)	NA	Rochester, NY**	NA	240	Tyler, TX	(18.5)
149	Naperville, IL	(6.7)	110	Rockford, IL	1.1	373	Upland, CA	(42.7)
NA	Nashua, NH**	NA	276	Roseville, CA	(23.4)	132	Upper Darby Twnshp, PA	(3.6)
146	Nashville, TN	(6.3)	128	Roswell, GA	(2.8)	121	Vacaville, CA	(1.0)
242	New Bedford, MA	(19.1)	265	Round Rock, TX	(21.9)	325	Vallejo, CA	(30.4)
NA	New Haven, CT**	NA	262	Sacramento, CA	(21.4)	98	Vancouver, WA	4.1
261	New Orleans, LA	(21.2)	115	Salem, OR	0.4	355	Ventura, CA	(36.0)
NA	New Rochelle, NY**	NA	336	Salinas, CA	(31.8)	118	Victorville, CA	0.3
NA	New York, NY**	NA	140	Salt Lake City, UT	(5.4)	238	Virginia Beach, VA	(18.2)
136	Newark, NJ	(5.1)	339	San Antonio, TX	(32.2)	241	Visalia, CA	(18.9)
377	Newport Beach, CA	(44.4)	187	San Bernardino, CA	(13.1)	187	Vista, CA	(13.1)
356	Newport News, VA	(36.3)	130	San Diego, CA	(3.3)	384	Waco, TX	(46.9)
370	Newton, MA	(42.4)	190	San Francisco, CA	(13.2)	58	Warren, MI	13.9
179	Norfolk, VA	(10.9)	199	San Jose, CA	(14.0)	25	Warwick, RI	35.9
137	Norman, OK	(5.2)	134	San Leandro, CA	(4.4)	184	Washington, DC	(11.9)
370	North Charleston, SC	(42.4)	118	San Marcos, CA	0.3	342	Waterbury, CT	(33.1)
36	North Las Vegas, NV	25.7	301	San Mateo, CA	(27.6)	NA	Waukegan, IL**	NA
264	Norwalk, CA	(21.6)	12	Sandy Springs, GA	52.6	285	West Covina, CA	(25.5)
341	Norwalk, CT	(33.0)	158	Sandy, UT	(7.8)	138	West Jordan, UT	(5.3)
262	Oakland, CA	(21.4)	144	Santa Ana, CA	(5.7)	142	West Palm Beach, FL	(5.6)
175	Oceanside, CA	(10.3)	367	Santa Barbara, CA	(40.9)	84	West Valley, UT	8.8
17	Odessa, TX	45.2	68	Santa Clara, CA	12.2	337	Westland, MI	(32.1)
24	O'Fallon, MO	36.8	273	Santa Clarita, CA	(23.1)	22	Westminster, CA	39.5
95	Ogden, UT	5.8	126	Santa Maria, CA	(1.5)	72	Westminster, CO	12.0
115	Oklahoma City, OK	0.4	310	Santa Monica, CA	(28.2)	258	Whittier, CA	(20.9)
NA	Olathe, KS**	NA	297	Santa Rosa, CA	(26.7)	164	Wichita Falls, TX	(8.8)
105	Omaha, NE	2.3	287	Savannah, GA	(25.8)	192	Wichita, KS	(13.4)
383	Ontario, CA	(45.9)	327	Scottsdale, AZ	(30.5)	278	Wilmington, NC	(24.4)
366	Orange, CA	(40.0)	176	Scranton, PA	(10.4)	237	Winston-Salem, NC	(18.0)
402	Orem, UT	(78.3)	38	Seattle, WA	24.0	295	Woodbridge Twnshp, NJ	(26.6)
316	Orlando, FL	(29.0)	272	Shreveport, LA	(23.0)	130	Worcester, MA	(3.3)
149	Overland Park, KS	(6.7)	205	Simi Valley, CA	(14.8)	28	Yakima, WA	30.5
260	Oxnard, CA	(21.1)	208	Sioux City, IA	(15.3)	NA	Yonkers, NY**	NA
111	Palm Bay, FL	0.8	45	Sioux Falls, SD	20.7	159	Yuma, AZ	(8.0)
122	Palmdale, CA	(1.2)	154	Somerville, MA	(7.5)			
NA	Parma, OH**	NA	291	South Bend, IN	(26.1)			

Source: CQ Press using reported data from the F.B.I. "Crime in the United States 2012"

*Aggravated assault is an attack for the purpose of inflicting severe bodily injury.

**Not available.

64. Percent Change in Aggravated Assault Rate: 2008 to 2012 (continued)
National Percent Change = 12.7% Decrease*

RANK	CITY	% CHANGE	RANK	CITY	% CHANGE	RANK	CITY	% CHANGE
1	Mobile, AL	198.2	75	Anaheim, CA	11.4	149	Lakewood, CO	(6.7)
2	Chino, CA	161.1	76	Glendale, AZ	11.3	149	Lawrence, KS	(6.7)
3	College Station, TX	140.1	77	Hamilton Twnshp, NJ	11.0	149	Naperville, IL	(6.7)
4	Livermore, CA	119.9	77	Lake Forest, CA	11.0	149	Overland Park, KS	(6.7)
5	Hesperia, CA	71.4	79	Tracy, CA	10.8	153	Erie, PA	(6.8)
6	Fort Wayne, IN	67.2	80	Carson, CA	10.4	154	Somerville, MA	(7.5)
7	Topeka, KS	58.3	81	Carlsbad, CA	9.8	154	Tucson, AZ	(7.5)
8	Clovis, CA	57.8	82	Fort Smith, AR	9.0	156	Columbus, GA	(7.6)
9	Medford, OR	56.0	82	Hammond, IN	9.0	156	Dayton, OH	(7.6)
10	Huntsville, AL	55.3	84	West Valley, UT	8.8	158	Sandy, UT	(7.8)
11	Springfield, MO	55.0	85	Stockton, CA	8.6	159	Yuma, AZ	(8.0)
12	Sandy Springs, GA	52.6	86	Evansville, IN	8.4	160	Hollywood, FL	(8.1)
13	Trenton, NJ	50.5	87	Chesapeake, VA	8.1	160	St. Louis, MO	(8.1)
14	Birmingham, AL	49.6	88	Davie, FL	7.6	162	Jersey City, NJ	(8.3)
15	Cary, NC	48.2	89	Cambridge, MA	7.3	163	Downey, CA	(8.7)
16	Flint, MI	46.0	90	Columbia, MO	7.2	164	Fresno, CA	(8.8)
17	Odessa, TX	45.2	91	Redding, CA	7.1	164	Wichita Falls, TX	(8.8)
18	Hillsboro, OR	44.1	91	Toledo, OH	7.1	166	El Paso, TX	(8.9)
19	Lawrence, MA	44.0	93	Duluth, MN	5.9	166	Lakeland, FL	(8.9)
20	Billings, MT	43.9	93	Providence, RI	5.9	168	Henderson, NV	(9.0)
21	Antioch, CA	43.2	95	Ogden, UT	5.8	169	Thousand Oaks, CA	(9.1)
22	Westminster, CA	39.5	96	Miami Gardens, FL	5.6	170	Port St. Lucie, FL	(9.3)
23	Tustin, CA	37.2	97	Denton, TX	4.2	171	High Point, NC	(9.4)
24	O'Fallon, MO	36.8	98	Escondido, CA	4.1	172	Stamford, CT	(9.6)
25	Warwick, RI	35.9	98	Vancouver, WA	4.1	172	St. George, UT	(9.6)
26	Bellingham, WA	35.6	100	Murfreesboro, TN	4.0	174	Lawton, OK	(10.0)
27	Richmond, CA	35.5	101	Denver, CO	3.5	175	Oceanside, CA	(10.3)
28	Yakima, WA	30.5	102	Cleveland, OH	3.3	176	Scranton, PA	(10.4)
29	Jackson, MS	30.4	103	Pearland, TX	2.8	177	Pomona, CA	(10.6)
30	Merced, CA	30.3	104	Fort Worth, TX	2.5	178	Spokane, WA	(10.7)
31	Indio, CA	30.2	105	Omaha, NE	2.3	179	Corpus Christi, TX	(10.9)
32	Quincy, MA	28.9	106	Miramar, FL	2.1	179	Norfolk, VA	(10.9)
33	Edinburg, TX	28.8	107	Bellevue, WA	1.9	181	Houston, TX	(11.2)
34	Camden, NJ	28.4	108	Boise, ID	1.5	182	Lynn, MA	(11.6)
35	Baldwin Park, CA	28.0	109	Memphis, TN	1.2	183	Albuquerque, NM	(11.8)
36	North Las Vegas, NV	25.7	110	Rockford, IL	1.1	184	Washington, DC	(11.9)
37	Elizabeth, NJ	24.6	111	Chino Hills, CA	0.8	185	Dallas, TX	(12.5)
38	Seattle, WA	24.0	111	Palm Bay, FL	0.8	186	Bethlehem, PA	(12.9)
39	Boulder, CO	23.1	113	Fort Lauderdale, FL	0.7	187	Gresham, OR	(13.1)
40	Manchester, NH	22.9	114	Bloomington, MN	0.5	187	San Bernardino, CA	(13.1)
41	Hartford, CT	22.8	115	Oklahoma City, OK	0.4	187	Vista, CA	(13.1)
41	Tempe, AZ	22.8	115	Paterson, NJ	0.4	190	Long Beach, CA	(13.2)
43	Irvine, CA	21.6	115	Salem, OR	0.4	190	San Francisco, CA	(13.2)
44	Cranston, RI	21.4	118	Lee's Summit, MO	0.3	192	Wichita, KS	(13.4)
45	Fargo, ND	20.7	118	San Marcos, CA	0.3	193	Arlington, TX	(13.5)
45	Sioux Falls, SD	20.7	118	Victorville, CA	0.3	194	Clinton Twnshp, MI	(13.6)
47	Surprise, AZ	20.2	121	Vacaville, CA	(1.0)	194	Rancho Cucamon., CA	(13.6)
48	Fullerton, CA	19.9	122	Joliet, IL	(1.2)	196	Baton Rouge, LA	(13.7)
49	Sterling Heights, MI	18.4	122	Palmdale, CA	(1.2)	197	Athens-Clarke, GA	(13.9)
50	Livonia, MI	16.4	124	Fairfield, CA	(1.3)	197	Las Vegas, NV	(13.9)
51	Peoria, AZ	16.3	125	Louisville, KY	(1.4)	199	San Jose, CA	(14.0)
52	Concord, CA	16.0	126	Kansas City, MO	(1.5)	200	Portland, OR	(14.1)
53	South Gate, CA	15.7	126	Santa Maria, CA	(1.5)	201	Austin, TX	(14.2)
54	Federal Way, WA	15.4	128	Roswell, GA	(2.8)	202	Anchorage, AK	(14.4)
55	Modesto, CA	15.1	129	Knoxville, TN	(2.9)	202	Centennial, CO	(14.4)
56	Milwaukee, WI	15.0	130	San Diego, CA	(3.3)	202	Grand Rapids, MI	(14.4)
57	Durham, NC	14.7	130	Worcester, MA	(3.3)	205	Simi Valley, CA	(14.8)
58	Midland, TX	13.9	132	Upper Darby Twnshp, PA	(3.6)	206	Miami, FL	(15.0)
58	Warren, MI	13.9	133	Pasadena, TX	(3.7)	207	Asheville, NC	(15.1)
60	Akron, OH	13.3	134	San Leandro, CA	(4.4)	208	Sioux City, IA	(15.3)
60	Madison, WI	13.3	135	Lansing, MI	(4.7)	209	Hawthorne, CA	(15.4)
62	Green Bay, WI	13.1	136	Newark, NJ	(5.1)	210	Miami Beach, FL	(15.5)
63	Fayetteville, AR	13.0	137	Norman, OK	(5.2)	210	Napa, CA	(15.5)
64	Edmond, OK	12.9	138	Reading, PA	(5.3)	212	Bridgeport, CT	(15.6)
65	Tuscaloosa, AL	12.8	138	West Jordan, UT	(5.3)	212	Des Moines, IA	(15.6)
66	Phoenix, AZ	12.5	140	Salt Lake City, UT	(5.4)	214	Gilbert, AZ	(15.8)
67	Indianapolis, IN	12.3	141	St. Paul, MN	(5.5)	214	Richmond, VA	(15.8)
68	Atlanta, GA	12.2	142	Grand Prairie, TX	(5.6)	216	Kennewick, WA	(16.1)
68	Beaumont, TX	12.2	142	West Palm Beach, FL	(5.6)	217	Arvada, CO	(16.2)
68	Santa Clara, CA	12.2	144	Santa Ana, CA	(5.7)	218	Bloomington, IN	(16.5)
71	Detroit, MI	12.1	145	Fontana, CA	(6.1)	219	Colorado Springs, CO	(16.6)
72	Westminster, CO	12.0	146	Clarksville, TN	(6.3)	219	Dearborn, MI	(16.6)
73	Daly City, CA	11.8	146	Nashville, TN	(6.3)	219	Raleigh, NC	(16.6)
74	Little Rock, AR	11.7	146	Rialto, CA	(6.3)	222	Clifton, NJ	(16.8)

RANK	CITY	% CHANGE	RANK	CITY	% CHANGE	RANK	CITY	% CHANGE
222	Huntington Beach, CA	(16.8)	297	Santa Rosa, CA	(26.7)	370	Newton, MA	(42.4)
224	Baltimore, MD	(17.0)	298	Eugene, OR	(27.0)	370	North Charleston, SC	(42.4)
224	Everett, WA	(17.0)	298	Hayward, CA	(27.0)	373	Upland, CA	(42.7)
226	Inglewood, CA	(17.1)	300	Rochester, MN	(27.5)	374	Independence, MO	(42.8)
226	Philadelphia, PA	(17.1)	301	Corona, CA	(27.6)	375	Avondale, AZ	(43.3)
226	St. Joseph, MO	(17.1)	301	Laredo, TX	(27.6)	376	Broken Arrow, OK	(44.1)
229	Amarillo, TX	(17.2)	301	Meridian, ID	(27.6)	377	Newport Beach, CA	(44.4)
230	Fall River, MA	(17.3)	301	San Mateo, CA	(27.6)	378	Troy, MI	(44.5)
230	Reno, NV	(17.3)	305	Pasadena, CA	(27.7)	379	Sparks, NV	(44.6)
230	Springfield, MA	(17.3)	306	Cincinnati, OH	(27.8)	379	Sunrise, FL	(44.6)
233	Lubbock, TX	(17.6)	306	Elk Grove, CA	(27.8)	381	Bellflower, CA	(45.0)
234	Pompano Beach, FL	(17.7)	306	Moreno Valley, CA	(27.8)	381	Pembroke Pines, FL	(45.0)
235	Citrus Heights, CA	(17.8)	309	Mesquite, TX	(28.0)	383	Ontario, CA	(45.9)
235	Lakewood, CA	(17.8)	310	Nampa, ID	(28.2)	384	Waco, TX	(46.9)
237	Winston-Salem, NC	(18.0)	310	Santa Monica, CA	(28.2)	385	Longview, TX	(47.8)
238	Tacoma, WA	(18.2)	312	Ann Arbor, MI	(28.3)	386	Spokane Valley, WA	(48.9)
238	Virginia Beach, VA	(18.2)	312	Hampton, VA	(28.3)	387	Fayetteville, NC	(49.1)
240	Tyler, TX	(18.5)	312	Mission Viejo, CA	(28.3)	388	Deerfield Beach, FL	(51.3)
241	Visalia, CA	(18.9)	315	Mission, TX	(28.5)	388	Mountain View, CA	(51.3)
242	Aurora, CO	(19.1)	316	Orlando, FL	(29.0)	390	McAllen, TX	(51.4)
242	New Bedford, MA	(19.1)	317	Clearwater, FL	(29.3)	391	Fremont, CA	(52.3)
242	Tampa, FL	(19.1)	318	Alameda, CA	(29.4)	392	Richardson, TX	(53.6)
245	Bakersfield, CA	(19.3)	318	St. Petersburg, FL	(29.4)	393	Plano, TX	(53.8)
246	Hemet, CA	(19.4)	320	Los Angeles, CA	(29.5)	394	Bryan, TX	(54.3)
246	Lynchburg, VA	(19.4)	321	Carrollton, TX	(29.8)	395	Farmington Hills, MI	(56.3)
248	Burbank, CA	(19.5)	322	Roanoke, VA	(30.0)	396	Lowell, MA	(57.5)
249	Portsmouth, VA	(19.6)	323	Riverside, CA	(30.2)	397	Temecula, CA	(58.9)
250	Garden Grove, CA	(19.7)	324	Minneapolis, MN	(30.3)	398	El Monte, CA	(62.2)
251	Greensboro, NC	(20.0)	325	Brownsville, TX	(30.4)	399	Edison Twnshp, NJ	(63.8)
252	Gary, IN	(20.1)	325	Vallejo, CA	(30.4)	400	Fishers, IN	(64.8)
252	Mesa, AZ	(20.1)	327	Scottsdale, AZ	(30.5)	401	Charleston, SC	(66.9)
254	Rio Rancho, NM	(20.2)	328	Pittsburgh, PA	(30.6)	402	Orem, UT	(78.3)
255	Charlotte, NC	(20.4)	329	Tulsa, OK	(31.1)	403	Carmel, IN	(83.7)
256	Chico, CA	(20.5)	330	Jacksonville, FL	(31.2)	NA	Albany, GA**	NA
256	Montgomery, AL	(20.5)	331	Costa Mesa, CA	(31.3)	NA	Albany, NY**	NA
258	Abilene, TX	(20.9)	332	Irving, TX	(31.4)	NA	Allentown, PA**	NA
258	Whittier, CA	(20.9)	333	Glendale, CA	(31.6)	NA	Amherst, NY**	NA
260	Oxnard, CA	(21.1)	333	Torrance, CA	(31.6)	NA	Arlington Heights, IL**	NA
261	New Orleans, LA	(21.2)	335	Coral Springs, FL	(31.7)	NA	Bloomington, IL**	NA
262	Oakland, CA	(21.4)	336	Salinas, CA	(31.8)	NA	Brockton, MA**	NA
262	Sacramento, CA	(21.4)	337	Kent, WA	(32.1)	NA	Buffalo, NY**	NA
264	Norwalk, CA	(21.6)	337	Westland, MI	(32.1)	NA	Champaign, IL**	NA
265	Round Rock, TX	(21.9)	339	San Antonio, TX	(32.2)	NA	Chandler, AZ**	NA
266	Buena Park, CA	(22.0)	340	Frisco, TX	(32.5)	NA	Cheektowaga, NY**	NA
267	Provo, UT	(22.1)	341	Norwalk, CT	(33.0)	NA	Cicero, IL**	NA
268	Murrieta, CA	(22.6)	342	Waterbury, CT	(33.1)	NA	Clarkstown, NY**	NA
269	Berkeley, CA	(22.8)	343	Lincoln, NE	(33.2)	NA	Colonie, NY**	NA
269	Killeen, TX	(22.8)	344	Melbourne, FL	(33.3)	NA	Decatur, IL**	NA
271	Sugar Land, TX	(22.9)	345	Compton, CA	(33.5)	NA	Greece, NY**	NA
272	Shreveport, LA	(23.0)	346	League City, TX	(33.9)	NA	Johns Creek, GA**	NA
273	Santa Clarita, CA	(23.1)	347	Elgin, IL	(34.0)	NA	Jurupa Valley, CA**	NA
274	Greeley, CO	(23.2)	348	Redwood City, CA	(34.2)	NA	Kansas City, KS**	NA
275	Toms River Twnshp, NJ	(23.3)	349	Alexandria, VA	(34.7)	NA	Lakewood Twnshp, NJ**	NA
276	Cedar Rapids, IA	(23.4)	349	Garland, TX	(34.7)	NA	Lexington, KY**	NA
276	Roseville, CA	(23.4)	351	Las Cruces, NM	(34.8)	NA	Longmont, CO**	NA
278	Wilmington, NC	(24.4)	352	Hialeah, FL	(35.4)	NA	Menifee, CA**	NA
279	Chicago, IL	(24.7)	353	Allen, TX	(35.5)	NA	Nashua, NH**	NA
279	Tallahassee, FL	(24.7)	354	Fort Collins, CO	(35.7)	NA	New Haven, CT**	NA
281	Kenosha, WI	(25.1)	355	Ventura, CA	(36.0)	NA	New Rochelle, NY**	NA
282	Danbury, CT	(25.2)	356	Newport News, VA	(36.3)	NA	New York, NY**	NA
282	Sunnyvale, CA	(25.2)	357	Hoover, AL	(36.8)	NA	Olathe, KS**	NA
284	Alhambra, CA	(25.4)	358	McKinney, TX	(37.3)	NA	Parma, OH**	NA
285	West Covina, CA	(25.5)	359	Beaverton, OR	(37.8)	NA	Peoria, IL**	NA
286	Plantation, FL	(25.6)	359	Chula Vista, CA	(37.8)	NA	Pueblo, CO**	NA
287	Brick Twnshp, NJ	(25.8)	361	Greenville, NC	(37.9)	NA	Ramapo, NY**	NA
287	Gainesville, FL	(25.8)	362	Macon, GA	(38.7)	NA	Renton, WA**	NA
287	Savannah, GA	(25.8)	363	Aurora, IL	(39.3)	NA	Rochester, NY**	NA
290	Cape Coral, FL	(25.9)	364	Racine, WI	(39.5)	NA	Springfield, IL**	NA
291	South Bend, IN	(26.1)	365	El Cajon, CA	(39.6)	NA	Syracuse, NY**	NA
292	Davenport, IA	(26.3)	366	Orange, CA	(40.0)	NA	Thornton, CO**	NA
293	Brooklyn Park, MN	(26.4)	367	Santa Barbara, CA	(40.9)	NA	Waukegan, IL**	NA
294	Boston, MA	(26.5)	368	Lancaster, CA	(41.6)	NA	Yonkers, NY**	NA
295	Boca Raton, FL	(26.6)	369	Lafayette, LA	(42.0)			
295	Woodbridge Twnshp, NJ	(26.6)	370	Largo, FL	(42.4)			

Source: CQ Press using reported data from the F.B.I. "Crime in the United States 2012"

*Aggravated assault is an attack for the purpose of inflicting severe bodily injury.

**Not available.

65. Property Crimes in 2012
National Total = 8,975,438 Property Crimes*

RANK	CITY	CRIMES	RANK	CITY	CRIMES	RANK	CITY	CRIMES
204	Abilene, TX	4,393	434	Chino Hills, CA	956	163	Gainesville, FL	5,201
91	Akron, OH	10,034	373	Chino, CA	2,116	225	Garden Grove, CA	4,017
393	Alameda, CA	1,892	166	Chula Vista, CA	5,081	100	Garland, TX	8,675
173	Albany, GA	5,001	359	Cicero, IL	2,221	199	Gary, IN	4,475
209	Albany, NY	4,340	44	Cincinnati, OH	18,173	261	Gilbert, AZ	3,386
23	Albuquerque, NM	29,718	283	Citrus Heights, CA	3,117	52	Glendale, AZ	14,934
295	Alexandria, VA	2,990	418	Clarkstown, NY	1,511	289	Glendale, CA	3,043
388	Alhambra, CA	1,919	241	Clarksville, TN	3,741	160	Grand Prairie, TX	5,246
194	Allentown, PA	4,603	211	Clearwater, FL	4,264	124	Grand Rapids, MI	6,618
423	Allen, TX	1,432	33	Cleveland, OH	24,309	330	Greece, NY	2,556
99	Amarillo, TX	8,900	413	Clifton, NJ	1,579	275	Greeley, CO	3,243
356	Amherst, NY	2,261	357	Clinton Twnshp, MI	2,230	297	Green Bay, WI	2,978
89	Anaheim, CA	10,070	224	Clovis, CA	4,025	70	Greensboro, NC	12,064
83	Anchorage, AK	10,543	350	College Station, TX	2,398	236	Greenville, NC	3,845
312	Ann Arbor, MI	2,726	371	Colonie, NY	2,117	177	Gresham, OR	4,858
186	Antioch, CA	4,757	45	Colorado Springs, CO	17,899	381	Hamilton Twnshp, NJ	1,978
433	Arlington Heights, IL	978	214	Columbia, MO	4,221	256	Hammond, IN	3,448
51	Arlington, TX	15,109	79	Columbus, GA	11,266	192	Hampton, VA	4,657
324	Arvada, CO	2,605	349	Compton, CA	2,399	158	Hartford, CT	5,319
175	Asheville, NC	4,910	216	Concord, CA	4,182	361	Hawthorne, CA	2,181
195	Athens-Clarke, GA	4,601	306	Coral Springs, FL	2,820	182	Hayward, CA	4,792
27	Atlanta, GA	28,554	217	Corona, CA	4,143	253	Hemet, CA	3,486
90	Aurora, CO	10,059	58	Corpus Christi, TX	14,061	159	Henderson, NV	5,295
247	Aurora, IL	3,565	221	Costa Mesa, CA	4,079	335	Hesperia, CA	2,502
11	Austin, TX	43,472	391	Cranston, RI	1,908	114	Hialeah, FL	7,194
243	Avondale, AZ	3,682	8	Dallas, TX	54,300	203	High Point, NC	4,417
46	Bakersfield, CA	17,754	398	Daly City, CA	1,803	367	Hillsboro, OR	2,154
412	Baldwin Park, CA	1,585	414	Danbury, CT	1,562	109	Hollywood, FL	7,713
25	Baltimore, MD	29,149	220	Davenport, IA	4,088	362	Hoover, AL	2,180
71	Baton Rouge, LA	12,059	254	Davie, FL	3,473	3	Houston, TX	107,678
141	Beaumont, TX	5,824	102	Dayton, OH	8,385	153	Huntington Beach, CA	5,470
421	Beaverton, OR	1,471	271	Dearborn, MI	3,282	96	Huntsville, AL	9,261
251	Bellevue, WA	3,503	344	Decatur, IL	2,448	115	Independence, MO	7,152
399	Bellflower, CA	1,802	342	Deerfield Beach, FL	2,458	9	Indianapolis, IN	46,898
230	Bellingham, WA	3,975	272	Denton, TX	3,262	307	Indio, CA	2,791
145	Berkeley, CA	5,696	34	Denver, CO	23,343	319	Inglewood, CA	2,673
385	Bethlehem, PA	1,948	86	Des Moines, IA	10,210	268	Irvine, CA	3,304
180	Billings, MT	4,812	13	Detroit, MI	40,956	132	Irving, TX	6,307
53	Birmingham, AL	14,788	248	Downey, CA	3,537	16	Jacksonville, FL	34,674
401	Bloomington, IL	1,797	234	Duluth, MN	3,861	75	Jackson, MS	11,568
274	Bloomington, IN	3,244	85	Durham, NC	10,279	152	Jersey City, NJ	5,479
278	Bloomington, MN	3,212	187	Edinburg, TX	4,732	439	Johns Creek, GA	526
329	Boca Raton, FL	2,557	420	Edison Twnshp, NJ	1,481	237	Joliet, IL	3,835
157	Boise, ID	5,342	408	Edmond, OK	1,680	281	Jurupa Valley, CA	3,174
43	Boston, MA	18,349	347	El Cajon, CA	2,414	111	Kansas City, KS	7,538
299	Boulder, CO	2,937	357	El Monte, CA	2,230	32	Kansas City, MO	25,642
428	Brick Twnshp, NJ	1,245	47	El Paso, TX	16,411	351	Kennewick, WA	2,372
164	Bridgeport, CT	5,153	380	Elgin, IL	1,982	294	Kenosha, WI	2,999
287	Brockton, MA	3,071	207	Elizabeth, NJ	4,351	154	Kent, WA	5,468
360	Broken Arrow, OK	2,187	269	Elk Grove, CA	3,292	174	Killeen, TX	4,986
322	Brooklyn Park, MN	2,629	250	Erie, PA	3,510	68	Knoxville, TN	12,169
103	Brownsville, TX	8,337	232	Escondido, CA	3,887	120	Lafayette, LA	6,815
340	Bryan, TX	2,473	105	Eugene, OR	8,004	432	Lake Forest, CA	1,088
376	Buena Park, CA	2,066	135	Evansville, IN	6,083	161	Lakeland, FL	5,216
62	Buffalo, NY	13,454	130	Everett, WA	6,416	431	Lakewood Twnshp, NJ	1,103
337	Burbank, CA	2,493	266	Fairfield, CA	3,317	377	Lakewood, CA	2,062
286	Cambridge, MA	3,091	315	Fall River, MA	2,706	122	Lakewood, CO	6,705
226	Camden, NJ	4,007	302	Fargo, ND	2,835	252	Lancaster, CA	3,498
249	Cape Coral, FL	3,521	426	Farmington Hills, MI	1,264	240	Lansing, MI	3,774
374	Carlsbad, CA	2,109	289	Fayetteville, AR	3,043	82	Laredo, TX	10,685
437	Carmel, IN	808	64	Fayetteville, NC	13,163	283	Largo, FL	3,117
258	Carrollton, TX	3,414	165	Federal Way, WA	5,106	201	Las Cruces, NM	4,419
314	Carson, CA	2,709	436	Fishers, IN	821	10	Las Vegas, NV	46,427
390	Cary, NC	1,909	146	Flint, MI	5,645	229	Lawrence, KS	3,997
188	Cedar Rapids, IA	4,723	198	Fontana, CA	4,494	384	Lawrence, MA	1,965
422	Centennial, CO	1,439	218	Fort Collins, CO	4,119	162	Lawton, OK	5,208
316	Champaign, IL	2,700	92	Fort Lauderdale, FL	9,960	403	League City, TX	1,734
125	Chandler, AZ	6,571	184	Fort Smith, AR	4,771	369	Lee's Summit, MO	2,127
264	Charleston, SC	3,373	95	Fort Wayne, IN	9,515	63	Lexington, KY	13,399
17	Charlotte, NC	32,587	18	Fort Worth, TX	32,514	88	Lincoln, NE	10,171
305	Cheektowaga, NY	2,821	212	Fremont, CA	4,259	49	Little Rock, AR	15,804
133	Chesapeake, VA	6,292	31	Fresno, CA	25,737	397	Livermore, CA	1,805
2	Chicago, IL	112,466	334	Frisco, TX	2,527	370	Livonia, MI	2,124
355	Chico, CA	2,291	231	Fullerton, CA	3,937	57	Long Beach, CA	14,131

RANK	CITY	CRIMES	RANK	CITY	CRIMES	RANK	CITY	CRIMES
364	Longmont, CO	2,169	262	Pasadena, CA	3,379	333	South Gate, CA	2,545
215	Longview, TX	4,212	147	Pasadena, TX	5,610	328	Sparks, NV	2,559
4	Los Angeles, CA	87,478	193	Paterson, NJ	4,640	181	Spokane Valley, WA	4,805
26	Louisville, KY	28,606	402	Pearland, TX	1,753	42	Spokane, WA	18,522
282	Lowell, MA	3,125	213	Pembroke Pines, FL	4,238	118	Springfield, IL	6,945
67	Lubbock, TX	12,273	191	Peoria, AZ	4,673	117	Springfield, MA	7,024
375	Lynchburg, VA	2,093	170	Peoria, IL	5,022	54	Springfield, MO	14,504
325	Lynn, MA	2,589	7	Philadelphia, PA	56,997	387	Stamford, CT	1,932
123	Macon, GA	6,699	6	Phoenix, AZ	60,777	326	Sterling Heights, MI	2,578
108	Madison, WI	7,753	81	Pittsburgh, PA	10,691	50	Stockton, CA	15,258
235	Manchester, NH	3,848	128	Plano, TX	6,453	415	St. George, UT	1,561
155	McAllen, TX	5,465	257	Plantation, FL	3,443	190	St. Joseph, MO	4,708
308	McKinney, TX	2,786	168	Pomona, CA	5,055	36	St. Louis, MO	21,995
202	Medford, OR	4,418	149	Pompano Beach, FL	5,562	73	St. Paul, MN	11,893
263	Melbourne, FL	3,374	291	Port St. Lucie, FL	3,031	66	St. Petersburg, FL	12,451
12	Memphis, TN	41,503	21	Portland, OR	30,454	417	Sugar Land, TX	1,541
386	Menifee, CA	1,942	179	Portsmouth, VA	4,821	331	Sunnyvale, CA	2,555
219	Merced, CA	4,111	106	Providence, RI	7,977	276	Sunrise, FL	3,229
429	Meridian, ID	1,230	341	Provo, UT	2,465	338	Surprise, AZ	2,488
56	Mesa, AZ	14,140	116	Pueblo, CO	7,030	137	Syracuse, NY	5,976
134	Mesquite, TX	6,285	416	Quincy, MA	1,554	65	Tacoma, WA	12,866
98	Miami Beach, FL	9,028	279	Racine, WI	3,181	101	Tallahassee, FL	8,617
183	Miami Gardens, FL	4,784	59	Raleigh, NC	13,779	93	Tampa, FL	9,947
35	Miami, FL	22,271	438	Ramapo, NY	716	345	Temecula, CA	2,440
292	Midland, TX	3,008	206	Rancho Cucamon., CA	4,362	107	Tempe, AZ	7,824
22	Milwaukee, WI	30,228	244	Reading, PA	3,612	273	Thornton, CO	3,257
40	Minneapolis, MN	19,359	205	Redding, CA	4,380	396	Thousand Oaks, CA	1,838
296	Miramar, FL	2,984	400	Redwood City, CA	1,800	NA	Toledo, OH**	NA
430	Mission Viejo, CA	1,197	112	Reno, NV	7,423	300	Toms River Twnshp, NJ	2,893
352	Mission, TX	2,370	196	Renton, WA	4,562	119	Topeka, KS	6,841
69	Mobile, AL	12,103	246	Rialto, CA	3,571	317	Torrance, CA	2,690
78	Modesto, CA	11,276	293	Richardson, TX	3,004	366	Tracy, CA	2,158
72	Montgomery, AL	12,058	172	Richmond, CA	5,018	310	Trenton, NJ	2,746
131	Moreno Valley, CA	6,371	97	Richmond, VA	9,103	409	Troy, MI	1,664
424	Mountain View, CA	1,419	392	Rio Rancho, NM	1,904	NA	Tucson, AZ**	NA
227	Murfreesboro, TN	4,006	80	Riverside, CA	10,818	38	Tulsa, OK	20,807
406	Murrieta, CA	1,715	184	Roanoke, VA	4,771	208	Tuscaloosa, AL	4,349
362	Nampa, ID	2,180	313	Rochester, MN	2,721	410	Tustin, CA	1,653
411	Napa, CA	1,643	77	Rochester, NY	11,283	197	Tyler, TX	4,506
378	Naperville, IL	2,044	110	Rockford, IL	7,608	354	Upland, CA	2,328
353	Nashua, NH	2,361	270	Roseville, CA	3,288	382	Upper Darby Twnshp, PA	1,975
30	Nashville, TN	26,052	405	Roswell, GA	1,721	379	Vacaville, CA	2,031
280	New Bedford, MA	3,180	321	Round Rock, TX	2,636	139	Vallejo, CA	5,844
126	New Haven, CT	6,516	39	Sacramento, CA	19,967	127	Vancouver, WA	6,478
61	New Orleans, LA	13,689	121	Salem, OR	6,731	233	Ventura, CA	3,885
425	New Rochelle, NY	1,396	176	Salinas, CA	4,906	200	Victorville, CA	4,465
1	New York, NY	142,760	55	Salt Lake City, UT	14,357	74	Virginia Beach, VA	11,717
87	Newark, NJ	10,199	5	San Antonio, TX	82,668	151	Visalia, CA	5,531
368	Newport Beach, CA	2,151	84	San Bernardino, CA	10,510	394	Vista, CA	1,885
144	Newport News, VA	5,722	20	San Diego, CA	31,700	139	Waco, TX	5,844
435	Newton, MA	894	14	San Francisco, CA	38,898	239	Warren, MI	3,787
76	Norfolk, VA	11,391	28	San Jose, CA	28,463	371	Warwick, RI	2,117
288	Norman, OK	3,050	245	San Leandro, CA	3,585	24	Washington, DC	29,264
143	North Charleston, SC	5,757	419	San Marcos, CA	1,502	189	Waterbury, CT	4,713
150	North Las Vegas, NV	5,534	395	San Mateo, CA	1,876	318	Waukegan, IL	2,688
323	Norwalk, CA	2,609	309	Sandy Springs, GA	2,750	277	West Covina, CA	3,224
407	Norwalk, CT	1,713	320	Sandy, UT	2,663	298	West Jordan, UT	2,966
29	Oakland, CA	26,342	113	Santa Ana, CA	7,389	156	West Palm Beach, FL	5,404
210	Oceanside, CA	4,289	285	Santa Barbara, CA	3,115	148	West Valley, UT	5,569
242	Odessa, TX	3,717	267	Santa Clara, CA	3,306	348	Westland, MI	2,410
427	O'Fallon, MO	1,246	311	Santa Clarita, CA	2,742	301	Westminster, CA	2,875
228	Ogden, UT	4,001	346	Santa Maria, CA	2,430	304	Westminster, CO	2,830
15	Oklahoma City, OK	35,390	259	Santa Monica, CA	3,398	335	Whittier, CA	2,502
339	Olathe, KS	2,480	238	Santa Rosa, CA	3,818	171	Wichita Falls, TX	5,021
41	Omaha, NE	19,178	104	Savannah, GA	8,325	37	Wichita, KS	21,070
167	Ontario, CA	5,056	136	Scottsdale, AZ	6,047	138	Wilmington, NC	5,910
303	Orange, CA	2,833	332	Scranton, PA	2,553	60	Winston-Salem, NC	13,701
365	Orem, UT	2,168	19	Seattle, WA	31,931	383	Woodbridge Twnshp, NJ	1,967
48	Orlando, FL	16,304	94	Shreveport, LA	9,862	129	Worcester, MA	6,432
221	Overland Park, KS	4,079	389	Simi Valley, CA	1,916	142	Yakima, WA	5,774
223	Oxnard, CA	4,071	255	Sioux City, IA	3,470	327	Yonkers, NY	2,565
343	Palm Bay, FL	2,457	169	Sioux Falls, SD	5,041	265	Yuma, AZ	3,353
260	Palmdale, CA	3,393	404	Somerville, MA	1,724			
440	Parma, OH	451	178	South Bend, IN	4,827			

Source: Reported data from the F.B.I. "Crime in the United States 2012"

*Property crimes are offenses of burglary, larceny-theft, and motor vehicle theft. Attempts are included.

**Not available.

65. Property Crimes in 2012 (continued)
National Total = 8,975,438 Property Crimes*

RANK	CITY	CRIMES	RANK	CITY	CRIMES	RANK	CITY	CRIMES
1	New York, NY	142,760	75	Jackson, MS	11,568	149	Pompano Beach, FL	5,562
2	Chicago, IL	112,466	76	Norfolk, VA	11,391	150	North Las Vegas, NV	5,534
3	Houston, TX	107,678	77	Rochester, NY	11,283	151	Visalia, CA	5,531
4	Los Angeles, CA	87,478	78	Modesto, CA	11,276	152	Jersey City, NJ	5,479
5	San Antonio, TX	82,668	79	Columbus, GA	11,266	153	Huntington Beach, CA	5,470
6	Phoenix, AZ	60,777	80	Riverside, CA	10,818	154	Kent, WA	5,468
7	Philadelphia, PA	56,997	81	Pittsburgh, PA	10,691	155	McAllen, TX	5,465
8	Dallas, TX	54,300	82	Laredo, TX	10,685	156	West Palm Beach, FL	5,404
9	Indianapolis, IN	46,898	83	Anchorage, AK	10,543	157	Boise, ID	5,342
10	Las Vegas, NV	46,427	84	San Bernardino, CA	10,510	158	Hartford, CT	5,319
11	Austin, TX	43,472	85	Durham, NC	10,279	159	Henderson, NV	5,295
12	Memphis, TN	41,503	86	Des Moines, IA	10,210	160	Grand Prairie, TX	5,246
13	Detroit, MI	40,956	87	Newark, NJ	10,199	161	Lakeland, FL	5,216
14	San Francisco, CA	38,898	88	Lincoln, NE	10,171	162	Lawton, OK	5,208
15	Oklahoma City, OK	35,390	89	Anaheim, CA	10,070	163	Gainesville, FL	5,201
16	Jacksonville, FL	34,674	90	Aurora, CO	10,059	164	Bridgeport, CT	5,153
17	Charlotte, NC	32,587	91	Akron, OH	10,034	165	Federal Way, WA	5,106
18	Fort Worth, TX	32,514	92	Fort Lauderdale, FL	9,960	166	Chula Vista, CA	5,081
19	Seattle, WA	31,931	93	Tampa, FL	9,947	167	Ontario, CA	5,056
20	San Diego, CA	31,700	94	Shreveport, LA	9,862	168	Pomona, CA	5,055
21	Portland, OR	30,454	95	Fort Wayne, IN	9,515	169	Sioux Falls, SD	5,041
22	Milwaukee, WI	30,228	96	Huntsville, AL	9,261	170	Peoria, IL	5,022
23	Albuquerque, NM	29,718	97	Richmond, VA	9,103	171	Wichita Falls, TX	5,021
24	Washington, DC	29,264	98	Miami Beach, FL	9,028	172	Richmond, CA	5,018
25	Baltimore, MD	29,149	99	Amarillo, TX	8,900	173	Albany, GA	5,001
26	Louisville, KY	28,606	100	Garland, TX	8,675	174	Killeen, TX	4,986
27	Atlanta, GA	28,554	101	Tallahassee, FL	8,617	175	Asheville, NC	4,910
28	San Jose, CA	28,463	102	Dayton, OH	8,385	176	Salinas, CA	4,906
29	Oakland, CA	26,342	103	Brownsville, TX	8,337	177	Gresham, OR	4,858
30	Nashville, TN	26,052	104	Savannah, GA	8,325	178	South Bend, IN	4,827
31	Fresno, CA	25,737	105	Eugene, OR	8,004	179	Portsmouth, VA	4,821
32	Kansas City, MO	25,642	106	Providence, RI	7,977	180	Billings, MT	4,812
33	Cleveland, OH	24,309	107	Tempe, AZ	7,824	181	Spokane Valley, WA	4,805
34	Denver, CO	23,343	108	Madison, WI	7,753	182	Hayward, CA	4,792
35	Miami, FL	22,271	109	Hollywood, FL	7,713	183	Miami Gardens, FL	4,784
36	St. Louis, MO	21,995	110	Rockford, IL	7,608	184	Fort Smith, AR	4,771
37	Wichita, KS	21,070	111	Kansas City, KS	7,538	184	Roanoke, VA	4,771
38	Tulsa, OK	20,807	112	Reno, NV	7,423	186	Antioch, CA	4,757
39	Sacramento, CA	19,967	113	Santa Ana, CA	7,389	187	Edinburg, TX	4,732
40	Minneapolis, MN	19,359	114	Hialeah, FL	7,194	188	Cedar Rapids, IA	4,723
41	Omaha, NE	19,178	115	Independence, MO	7,152	189	Waterbury, CT	4,713
42	Spokane, WA	18,522	116	Pueblo, CO	7,030	190	St. Joseph, MO	4,708
43	Boston, MA	18,349	117	Springfield, MA	7,024	191	Peoria, AZ	4,673
44	Cincinnati, OH	18,173	118	Springfield, IL	6,945	192	Hampton, VA	4,657
45	Colorado Springs, CO	17,899	119	Topeka, KS	6,841	193	Paterson, NJ	4,640
46	Bakersfield, CA	17,754	120	Lafayette, LA	6,815	194	Allentown, PA	4,603
47	El Paso, TX	16,411	121	Salem, OR	6,731	195	Athens-Clarke, GA	4,601
48	Orlando, FL	16,304	122	Lakewood, CO	6,705	196	Renton, WA	4,562
49	Little Rock, AR	15,804	123	Macon, GA	6,699	197	Tyler, TX	4,506
50	Stockton, CA	15,258	124	Grand Rapids, MI	6,618	198	Fontana, CA	4,494
51	Arlington, TX	15,109	125	Chandler, AZ	6,571	199	Gary, IN	4,475
52	Glendale, AZ	14,934	126	New Haven, CT	6,516	200	Victorville, CA	4,465
53	Birmingham, AL	14,788	127	Vancouver, WA	6,478	201	Las Cruces, NM	4,419
54	Springfield, MO	14,504	128	Plano, TX	6,453	202	Medford, OR	4,418
55	Salt Lake City, UT	14,357	129	Worcester, MA	6,432	203	High Point, NC	4,417
56	Mesa, AZ	14,140	130	Everett, WA	6,416	204	Abilene, TX	4,393
57	Long Beach, CA	14,131	131	Moreno Valley, CA	6,371	205	Redding, CA	4,380
58	Corpus Christi, TX	14,061	132	Irving, TX	6,307	206	Rancho Cucamon., CA	4,362
59	Raleigh, NC	13,779	133	Chesapeake, VA	6,292	207	Elizabeth, NJ	4,351
60	Winston-Salem, NC	13,701	134	Mesquite, TX	6,285	208	Tuscaloosa, AL	4,349
61	New Orleans, LA	13,689	135	Evansville, IN	6,083	209	Albany, NY	4,340
62	Buffalo, NY	13,454	136	Scottsdale, AZ	6,047	210	Oceanside, CA	4,289
63	Lexington, KY	13,399	137	Syracuse, NY	5,976	211	Clearwater, FL	4,264
64	Fayetteville, NC	13,163	138	Wilmington, NC	5,910	212	Fremont, CA	4,259
65	Tacoma, WA	12,866	139	Vallejo, CA	5,844	213	Pembroke Pines, FL	4,238
66	St. Petersburg, FL	12,451	139	Waco, TX	5,844	214	Columbia, MO	4,221
67	Lubbock, TX	12,273	141	Beaumont, TX	5,824	215	Longview, TX	4,212
68	Knoxville, TN	12,169	142	Yakima, WA	5,774	216	Concord, CA	4,182
69	Mobile, AL	12,103	143	North Charleston, SC	5,757	217	Corona, CA	4,143
70	Greensboro, NC	12,064	144	Newport News, VA	5,722	218	Fort Collins, CO	4,119
71	Baton Rouge, LA	12,059	145	Berkeley, CA	5,696	219	Merced, CA	4,111
72	Montgomery, AL	12,058	146	Flint, MI	5,645	220	Davenport, IA	4,088
73	St. Paul, MN	11,893	147	Pasadena, TX	5,610	221	Costa Mesa, CA	4,079
74	Virginia Beach, VA	11,717	148	West Valley, UT	5,569	221	Overland Park, KS	4,079

RANK	CITY	CRIMES	RANK	CITY	CRIMES	RANK	CITY	CRIMES
223	Oxnard, CA	4,071	297	Green Bay, WI	2,978	371	Colonie, NY	2,117
224	Clovis, CA	4,025	298	West Jordan, UT	2,966	371	Warwick, RI	2,117
225	Garden Grove, CA	4,017	299	Boulder, CO	2,937	373	Chino, CA	2,116
226	Camden, NJ	4,007	300	Toms River Twnshp, NJ	2,893	374	Carlsbad, CA	2,109
227	Murfreesboro, TN	4,006	301	Westminster, CA	2,875	375	Lynchburg, VA	2,093
228	Ogden, UT	4,001	302	Fargo, ND	2,835	376	Buena Park, CA	2,066
229	Lawrence, KS	3,997	303	Orange, CA	2,833	377	Lakewood, CA	2,062
230	Bellingham, WA	3,975	304	Westminster, CO	2,830	378	Naperville, IL	2,044
231	Fullerton, CA	3,937	305	Cheektowaga, NY	2,821	379	Vacaville, CA	2,031
232	Escondido, CA	3,887	306	Coral Springs, FL	2,820	380	Elgin, IL	1,982
233	Ventura, CA	3,885	307	Indio, CA	2,791	381	Hamilton Twnshp, NJ	1,978
234	Duluth, MN	3,861	308	McKinney, TX	2,786	382	Upper Darby Twnshp, PA	1,975
235	Manchester, NH	3,848	309	Sandy Springs, GA	2,750	383	Woodbridge Twnshp, NJ	1,967
236	Greenville, NC	3,845	310	Trenton, NJ	2,746	384	Lawrence, MA	1,965
237	Joliet, IL	3,835	311	Santa Clarita, CA	2,742	385	Bethlehem, PA	1,948
238	Santa Rosa, CA	3,818	312	Ann Arbor, MI	2,726	386	Menifee, CA	1,942
239	Warren, MI	3,787	313	Rochester, MN	2,721	387	Stamford, CT	1,932
240	Lansing, MI	3,774	314	Carson, CA	2,709	388	Alhambra, CA	1,919
241	Clarksville, TN	3,741	315	Fall River, MA	2,706	389	Simi Valley, CA	1,916
242	Odessa, TX	3,717	316	Champaign, IL	2,700	390	Cary, NC	1,909
243	Avondale, AZ	3,682	317	Torrance, CA	2,690	391	Cranston, RI	1,908
244	Reading, PA	3,612	318	Waukegan, IL	2,688	392	Rio Rancho, NM	1,904
245	San Leandro, CA	3,585	319	Inglewood, CA	2,673	393	Alameda, CA	1,892
246	Rialto, CA	3,571	320	Sandy, UT	2,663	394	Vista, CA	1,885
247	Aurora, IL	3,565	321	Round Rock, TX	2,636	395	San Mateo, CA	1,876
248	Downey, CA	3,537	322	Brooklyn Park, MN	2,629	396	Thousand Oaks, CA	1,838
249	Cape Coral, FL	3,521	323	Norwalk, CA	2,609	397	Livermore, CA	1,805
250	Erie, PA	3,510	324	Arvada, CO	2,605	398	Daly City, CA	1,803
251	Bellevue, WA	3,503	325	Lynn, MA	2,589	399	Bellflower, CA	1,802
252	Lancaster, CA	3,498	326	Sterling Heights, MI	2,578	400	Redwood City, CA	1,800
253	Hemet, CA	3,486	327	Yonkers, NY	2,565	401	Bloomington, IL	1,797
254	Davie, FL	3,473	328	Sparks, NV	2,559	402	Pearland, TX	1,753
255	Sioux City, IA	3,470	329	Boca Raton, FL	2,557	403	League City, TX	1,734
256	Hammond, IN	3,448	330	Greece, NY	2,556	404	Somerville, MA	1,724
257	Plantation, FL	3,443	331	Sunnyvale, CA	2,555	405	Roswell, GA	1,721
258	Carrollton, TX	3,414	332	Scranton, PA	2,553	406	Murrieta, CA	1,715
259	Santa Monica, CA	3,398	333	South Gate, CA	2,545	407	Norwalk, CT	1,713
260	Palmdale, CA	3,393	334	Frisco, TX	2,527	408	Edmond, OK	1,680
261	Gilbert, AZ	3,386	335	Hesperia, CA	2,502	409	Troy, MI	1,664
262	Pasadena, CA	3,379	335	Whittier, CA	2,502	410	Tustin, CA	1,653
263	Melbourne, FL	3,374	337	Burbank, CA	2,493	411	Napa, CA	1,643
264	Charleston, SC	3,373	338	Surprise, AZ	2,488	412	Baldwin Park, CA	1,585
265	Yuma, AZ	3,353	339	Olathe, KS	2,480	413	Clifton, NJ	1,579
266	Fairfield, CA	3,317	340	Bryan, TX	2,473	414	Danbury, CT	1,562
267	Santa Clara, CA	3,306	341	Provo, UT	2,465	415	St. George, UT	1,561
268	Irvine, CA	3,304	342	Deerfield Beach, FL	2,458	416	Quincy, MA	1,554
269	Elk Grove, CA	3,292	343	Palm Bay, FL	2,457	417	Sugar Land, TX	1,541
270	Roseville, CA	3,288	344	Decatur, IL	2,448	418	Clarkstown, NY	1,511
271	Dearborn, MI	3,282	345	Temecula, CA	2,440	419	San Marcos, CA	1,502
272	Denton, TX	3,262	346	Santa Maria, CA	2,430	420	Edison Twnshp, NJ	1,481
273	Thornton, CO	3,257	347	El Cajon, CA	2,414	421	Beaverton, OR	1,471
274	Bloomington, IN	3,244	348	Westland, MI	2,410	422	Centennial, CO	1,439
275	Greeley, CO	3,243	349	Compton, CA	2,399	423	Allen, TX	1,432
276	Sunrise, FL	3,229	350	College Station, TX	2,398	424	Mountain View, CA	1,419
277	West Covina, CA	3,224	351	Kennewick, WA	2,372	425	New Rochelle, NY	1,396
278	Bloomington, MN	3,212	352	Mission, TX	2,370	426	Farmington Hills, MI	1,264
279	Racine, WI	3,181	353	Nashua, NH	2,361	427	O'Fallon, MO	1,246
280	New Bedford, MA	3,180	354	Upland, CA	2,328	428	Brick Twnshp, NJ	1,245
281	Jurupa Valley, CA	3,174	355	Chico, CA	2,291	429	Meridian, ID	1,230
282	Lowell, MA	3,125	356	Amherst, NY	2,261	430	Mission Viejo, CA	1,197
283	Citrus Heights, CA	3,117	357	Clinton Twnshp, MI	2,230	431	Lakewood Twnshp, NJ	1,103
283	Largo, FL	3,117	357	El Monte, CA	2,230	432	Lake Forest, CA	1,088
285	Santa Barbara, CA	3,115	359	Cicero, IL	2,221	433	Arlington Heights, IL	978
286	Cambridge, MA	3,091	360	Broken Arrow, OK	2,187	434	Chino Hills, CA	956
287	Brockton, MA	3,071	361	Hawthorne, CA	2,181	435	Newton, MA	894
288	Norman, OK	3,050	362	Hoover, AL	2,180	436	Fishers, IN	821
289	Fayetteville, AR	3,043	362	Nampa, ID	2,180	437	Carmel, IN	808
289	Glendale, CA	3,043	364	Longmont, CO	2,169	438	Ramapo, NY	716
291	Port St. Lucie, FL	3,031	365	Orem, UT	2,168	439	Johns Creek, GA	526
292	Midland, TX	3,008	366	Tracy, CA	2,158	440	Parma, OH	451
293	Richardson, TX	3,004	367	Hillsboro, OR	2,154	NA	Toledo, OH**	NA
294	Kenosha, WI	2,999	368	Newport Beach, CA	2,151	NA	Tucson, AZ**	NA
295	Alexandria, VA	2,990	369	Lee's Summit, MO	2,127			
296	Miramar, FL	2,984	370	Livonia, MI	2,124			

Source: Reported data from the F.B.I. "Crime in the United States 2012"

*Property crimes are offenses of burglary, larceny-theft, and motor vehicle theft. Attempts are included.

**Not available.

66. Property Crime Rate in 2012
National Rate = 2,859.2 Property Crimes per 100,000 Population*

RANK	CITY	RATE	RANK	CITY	RATE	RANK	CITY	RATE
184	Abilene, TX	3,664.3	433	Chino Hills, CA	1,247.5	154	Gainesville, FL	4,094.1
74	Akron, OH	5,057.7	292	Chino, CA	2,651.9	347	Garden Grove, CA	2,294.4
314	Alameda, CA	2,507.1	377	Chula Vista, CA	2,033.8	182	Garland, TX	3,691.7
17	Albany, GA	6,369.7	297	Cicero, IL	2,634.6	40	Gary, IN	5,560.9
125	Albany, NY	4,420.1	22	Cincinnati, OH	6,135.3	416	Gilbert, AZ	1,580.3
51	Albuquerque, NM	5,367.3	185	Citrus Heights, CA	3,662.2	15	Glendale, AZ	6,409.5
375	Alexandria, VA	2,049.5	395	Clarkstown, NY	1,884.4	418	Glendale, CA	1,561.3
350	Alhambra, CA	2,271.8	280	Clarksville, TN	2,723.6	261	Grand Prairie, TX	2,885.9
170	Allentown, PA	3,857.2	168	Clearwater, FL	3,902.8	202	Grand Rapids, MI	3,484.0
412	Allen, TX	1,612.9	21	Cleveland, OH	6,173.2	295	Greece, NY	2,641.8
113	Amarillo, TX	4,527.5	398	Clifton, NJ	1,864.6	211	Greeley, CO	3,368.4
392	Amherst, NY	1,922.8	346	Clinton Twnshp, MI	2,298.9	271	Green Bay, WI	2,807.3
254	Anaheim, CA	2,922.9	152	Clovis, CA	4,114.4	129	Greensboro, NC	4,368.9
197	Anchorage, AK	3,524.4	319	College Station, TX	2,483.2	124	Greenville, NC	4,426.2
334	Ann Arbor, MI	2,370.3	282	Colonie, NY	2,719.2	117	Gresham, OR	4,489.8
112	Antioch, CA	4,530.1	148	Colorado Springs, CO	4,140.5	357	Hamilton Twnshp, NJ	2,219.7
430	Arlington Heights, IL	1,296.0	172	Columbia, MO	3,814.9	140	Hammond, IN	4,256.3
163	Arlington, TX	3,983.4	37	Columbus, GA	5,742.7	209	Hampton, VA	3,377.0
330	Arvada, CO	2,389.3	322	Compton, CA	2,446.5	141	Hartford, CT	4,248.3
36	Asheville, NC	5,756.5	213	Concord, CA	3,340.1	309	Hawthorne, CA	2,545.2
167	Athens-Clarke, GA	3,917.2	352	Coral Springs, FL	2,255.6	221	Hayward, CA	3,250.5
13	Atlanta, GA	6,533.5	298	Corona, CA	2,633.1	137	Hemet, CA	4,292.4
248	Aurora, CO	2,985.3	116	Corpus Christi, TX	4,498.6	383	Henderson, NV	2,009.7
405	Aurora, IL	1,784.6	189	Costa Mesa, CA	3,621.4	284	Hesperia, CA	2,708.3
59	Austin, TX	5,219.3	332	Cranston, RI	2,375.6	239	Hialeah, FL	3,086.1
102	Avondale, AZ	4,698.6	128	Dallas, TX	4,373.6	149	High Point, NC	4,135.7
80	Bakersfield, CA	4,991.3	408	Daly City, CA	1,745.2	349	Hillsboro, OR	2,288.6
371	Baldwin Park, CA	2,068.0	393	Danbury, CT	1,907.4	54	Hollywood, FL	5,307.9
103	Baltimore, MD	4,660.3	158	Davenport, IA	4,039.8	293	Hoover, AL	2,647.8
61	Baton Rouge, LA	5,209.1	186	Davie, FL	3,657.6	85	Houston, TX	4,945.5
91	Beaumont, TX	4,840.3	29	Dayton, OH	5,899.2	269	Huntington Beach, CA	2,809.8
414	Beaverton, OR	1,594.1	210	Dearborn, MI	3,376.0	76	Huntsville, AL	5,041.6
272	Bellevue, WA	2,779.7	225	Decatur, IL	3,215.5	24	Independence, MO	6,090.3
344	Bellflower, CA	2,313.6	229	Deerfield Beach, FL	3,174.4	39	Indianapolis, IN	5,592.1
94	Bellingham, WA	4,808.6	279	Denton, TX	2,742.5	195	Indio, CA	3,555.4
84	Berkeley, CA	4,954.7	178	Denver, CO	3,713.8	329	Inglewood, CA	2,397.6
304	Bethlehem, PA	2,584.0	86	Des Moines, IA	4,922.9	422	Irvine, CA	1,518.9
114	Billings, MT	4,523.8	34	Detroit, MI	5,792.1	268	Irving, TX	2,815.5
7	Birmingham, AL	6,934.1	237	Downey, CA	3,112.8	151	Jacksonville, FL	4,124.6
342	Bloomington, IL	2,330.5	121	Duluth, MN	4,446.6	12	Jackson, MS	6,575.0
164	Bloomington, IN	3,973.7	130	Durham, NC	4,363.6	363	Jersey City, NJ	2,178.1
173	Bloomington, MN	3,796.9	30	Edinburg, TX	5,890.6	439	Johns Creek, GA	657.2
249	Boca Raton, FL	2,956.3	424	Edison Twnshp, NJ	1,466.2	305	Joliet, IL	2,583.0
313	Boise, ID	2,524.9	382	Edmond, OK	2,012.6	220	Jurupa Valley, CA	3,252.8
256	Boston, MA	2,909.5	335	El Cajon, CA	2,369.8	66	Kansas City, KS	5,120.9
253	Boulder, CO	2,929.5	390	El Monte, CA	1,933.1	44	Kansas City, MO	5,525.4
411	Brick Twnshp, NJ	1,642.3	325	El Paso, TX	2,429.3	241	Kennewick, WA	3,081.7
196	Bridgeport, CT	3,528.7	402	Elgin, IL	1,815.8	246	Kenosha, WI	2,999.2
222	Brockton, MA	3,227.3	205	Elizabeth, NJ	3,445.5	120	Kent, WA	4,478.2
364	Broken Arrow, OK	2,172.1	369	Elk Grove, CA	2,105.6	174	Killeen, TX	3,778.3
208	Brooklyn Park, MN	3,399.0	206	Erie, PA	3,442.1	9	Knoxville, TN	6,676.9
107	Brownsville, TX	4,603.5	296	Escondido, CA	2,637.3	43	Lafayette, LA	5,547.3
231	Bryan, TX	3,151.2	73	Eugene, OR	5,064.4	428	Lake Forest, CA	1,374.3
317	Buena Park, CA	2,504.1	64	Evansville, IN	5,146.6	58	Lakeland, FL	5,219.4
65	Buffalo, NY	5,126.6	23	Everett, WA	6,092.0	434	Lakewood Twnshp, NJ	1,176.6
333	Burbank, CA	2,373.0	238	Fairfield, CA	3,096.8	311	Lakewood, CA	2,533.7
260	Cambridge, MA	2,889.3	242	Fall River, MA	3,014.9	109	Lakewood, CO	4,579.8
63	Camden, NJ	5,159.3	306	Fargo, ND	2,581.7	360	Lancaster, CA	2,197.9
359	Cape Coral, FL	2,205.8	417	Farmington Hills, MI	1,573.8	217	Lansing, MI	3,290.7
387	Carlsbad, CA	1,955.0	159	Fayetteville, AR	4,036.5	132	Laredo, TX	4,351.3
437	Carmel, IN	987.5	16	Fayetteville, NC	6,390.9	165	Largo, FL	3,956.4
278	Carrollton, TX	2,742.7	42	Federal Way, WA	5,551.3	123	Las Cruces, NM	4,426.8
258	Carson, CA	2,905.6	435	Fishers, IN	1,034.3	234	Las Vegas, NV	3,138.2
429	Cary, NC	1,353.7	41	Flint, MI	5,554.4	119	Lawrence, KS	4,481.9
183	Cedar Rapids, IA	3,678.3	353	Fontana, CA	2,237.2	312	Lawrence, MA	2,530.2
427	Centennial, CO	1,383.4	276	Fort Collins, CO	2,768.3	56	Lawton, OK	5,272.3
215	Champaign, IL	3,319.8	32	Fort Lauderdale, FL	5,830.5	381	League City, TX	2,013.3
285	Chandler, AZ	2,707.2	46	Fort Smith, AR	5,453.6	343	Lee's Summit, MO	2,316.0
281	Charleston, SC	2,723.3	179	Fort Wayne, IN	3,707.7	122	Lexington, KY	4,431.9
160	Charlotte, NC	4,030.5	142	Fort Worth, TX	4,222.0	171	Lincoln, NE	3,850.1
194	Cheektowaga, NY	3,562.9	389	Fremont, CA	1,945.4	4	Little Rock, AR	8,061.0
277	Chesapeake, VA	2,765.3	71	Fresno, CA	5,086.3	362	Livermore, CA	2,180.0
147	Chicago, IL	4,152.5	374	Frisco, TX	2,051.1	358	Livonia, MI	2,211.9
299	Chico, CA	2,630.6	264	Fullerton, CA	2,843.5	244	Long Beach, CA	3,007.3

RANK	CITY	RATE
323	Longmont, CO	2,439.1
67	Longview, TX	5,102.1
351	Los Angeles, CA	2,269.1
136	Louisville, KY	4,293.9
263	Lowell, MA	2,879.1
62	Lubbock, TX	5,173.2
287	Lynchburg, VA	2,706.0
267	Lynn, MA	2,818.8
6	Macon, GA	7,216.0
219	Madison, WI	3,264.3
201	Manchester, NH	3,496.9
161	McAllen, TX	4,025.9
380	McKinney, TX	2,017.3
33	Medford, OR	5,810.3
127	Melbourne, FL	4,374.3
19	Memphis, TN	6,312.9
326	Menifee, CA	2,426.1
72	Merced, CA	5,076.8
415	Meridian, ID	1,591.8
235	Mesa, AZ	3,132.5
133	Mesquite, TX	4,340.1
1	Miami Beach, FL	9,913.7
135	Miami Gardens, FL	4,303.0
50	Miami, FL	5,375.2
302	Midland, TX	2,601.2
75	Milwaukee, WI	5,043.1
82	Minneapolis, MN	4,960.8
337	Miramar, FL	2,368.3
432	Mission Viejo, CA	1,252.1
252	Mission, TX	2,942.0
93	Mobile, AL	4,812.0
45	Modesto, CA	5,510.4
35	Montgomery, AL	5,768.9
226	Moreno Valley, CA	3,190.7
396	Mountain View, CA	1,868.8
193	Murfreesboro, TN	3,568.9
413	Murrieta, CA	1,605.2
301	Nampa, ID	2,616.5
370	Napa, CA	2,090.6
425	Naperville, IL	1,431.0
283	Nashua, NH	2,717.9
143	Nashville, TN	4,195.9
216	New Bedford, MA	3,311.4
77	New Haven, CT	5,014.9
175	New Orleans, LA	3,772.4
404	New Rochelle, NY	1,789.2
409	New York, NY	1,722.2
187	Newark, NJ	3,656.8
321	Newport Beach, CA	2,464.3
232	Newport News, VA	3,151.0
436	Newton, MA	1,031.0
105	Norfolk, VA	4,643.6
288	Norman, OK	2,676.2
38	North Charleston, SC	5,718.4
318	North Las Vegas, NV	2,494.1
324	Norwalk, CA	2,431.6
385	Norwalk, CT	1,975.9
11	Oakland, CA	6,594.0
315	Oceanside, CA	2,506.1
191	Odessa, TX	3,586.6
420	O'Fallon, MO	1,544.6
101	Ogden, UT	4,702.5
27	Oklahoma City, OK	5,941.8
391	Olathe, KS	1,929.1
108	Omaha, NE	4,588.4
243	Ontario, CA	3,010.7
378	Orange, CA	2,028.0
339	Orem, UT	2,357.7
10	Orlando, FL	6,613.8
345	Overland Park, KS	2,303.4
379	Oxnard, CA	2,017.4
341	Palm Bay, FL	2,348.2
361	Palmdale, CA	2,184.9
440	Parma, OH	557.0

RANK	CITY	RATE
327	Pasadena, CA	2,424.3
188	Pasadena, TX	3,629.6
230	Paterson, NJ	3,153.3
400	Pearland, TX	1,851.1
290	Pembroke Pines, FL	2,653.0
250	Peoria, AZ	2,951.1
131	Peoria, IL	4,356.0
181	Philadelphia, PA	3,703.6
155	Phoenix, AZ	4,091.3
207	Pittsburgh, PA	3,425.4
340	Plano, TX	2,356.7
166	Plantation, FL	3,925.7
214	Pomona, CA	3,336.4
49	Pompano Beach, FL	5,399.8
403	Port St. Lucie, FL	1,799.7
70	Portland, OR	5,092.3
81	Portsmouth, VA	4,983.5
118	Providence, RI	4,484.4
368	Provo, UT	2,109.0
14	Pueblo, CO	6,445.7
410	Quincy, MA	1,657.8
162	Racine, WI	4,023.8
218	Raleigh, NC	3,276.1
438	Ramapo, NY	837.9
307	Rancho Cucamon., CA	2,576.9
157	Reading, PA	4,078.7
92	Redding, CA	4,814.6
348	Redwood City, CA	2,294.0
223	Reno, NV	3,220.6
90	Renton, WA	4,867.6
198	Rialto, CA	3,514.9
257	Richardson, TX	2,909.0
99	Richmond, CA	4,718.1
126	Richmond, VA	4,380.7
367	Rio Rancho, NM	2,128.3
204	Riverside, CA	3,450.4
88	Roanoke, VA	4,879.3
316	Rochester, MN	2,505.9
52	Rochester, NY	5,322.3
79	Rockford, IL	4,995.6
289	Roseville, CA	2,675.4
397	Roswell, GA	1,867.8
320	Round Rock, TX	2,481.4
144	Sacramento, CA	4,189.8
138	Salem, OR	4,277.6
228	Salinas, CA	3,177.2
5	Salt Lake City, UT	7,459.5
26	San Antonio, TX	5,989.9
87	San Bernardino, CA	4,888.7
336	San Diego, CA	2,368.4
97	San Francisco, CA	4,741.6
255	San Jose, CA	2,914.9
150	San Leandro, CA	4,126.9
407	San Marcos, CA	1,750.4
394	San Mateo, CA	1,889.2
270	Sandy Springs, GA	2,809.3
251	Sandy, UT	2,945.6
356	Santa Ana, CA	2,222.4
203	Santa Barbara, CA	3,466.1
274	Santa Clara, CA	2,769.8
421	Santa Clarita, CA	1,529.7
328	Santa Maria, CA	2,401.4
177	Santa Monica, CA	3,725.3
354	Santa Rosa, CA	2,234.6
190	Savannah, GA	3,599.5
286	Scottsdale, AZ	2,706.4
212	Scranton, PA	3,354.0
69	Seattle, WA	5,093.8
89	Shreveport, LA	4,878.2
423	Simi Valley, CA	1,512.4
145	Sioux City, IA	4,166.2
227	Sioux Falls, SD	3,183.4
355	Somerville, MA	2,233.2
95	South Bend, IN	4,760.4

RANK	CITY	RATE
291	South Gate, CA	2,652.0
273	Sparks, NV	2,769.9
57	Spokane Valley, WA	5,270.7
3	Spokane, WA	8,730.1
28	Springfield, IL	5,929.3
110	Springfield, MA	4,545.7
2	Springfield, MO	9,010.8
419	Stamford, CT	1,555.5
384	Sterling Heights, MI	1,983.5
68	Stockton, CA	5,101.2
372	St. George, UT	2,059.9
25	St. Joseph, MO	6,088.2
8	St. Louis, MO	6,902.2
156	St. Paul, MN	4,091.2
78	St. Petersburg, FL	5,013.7
399	Sugar Land, TX	1,858.3
406	Sunnyvale, CA	1,779.2
180	Sunrise, FL	3,704.3
373	Surprise, AZ	2,059.7
153	Syracuse, NY	4,095.0
18	Tacoma, WA	6,349.0
104	Tallahassee, FL	4,646.3
265	Tampa, FL	2,835.9
338	Temecula, CA	2,359.4
100	Tempe, AZ	4,711.5
294	Thornton, CO	2,645.5
426	Thousand Oaks, CA	1,422.9
NA	Toledo, OH**	NA
233	Toms River Twnshp, NJ	3,140.1
53	Topeka, KS	5,309.6
401	Torrance, CA	1,819.4
310	Tracy, CA	2,537.4
224	Trenton, NJ	3,218.6
376	Troy, MI	2,040.0
NA	Tucson, AZ**	NA
60	Tulsa, OK	5,216.0
98	Tuscaloosa, AL	4,728.6
366	Tustin, CA	2,135.7
115	Tyler, TX	4,504.2
240	Upland, CA	3,082.2
331	Upper Darby Twnshp, PA	2,380.1
365	Vacaville, CA	2,161.8
83	Vallejo, CA	4,956.2
169	Vancouver, WA	3,893.6
192	Ventura, CA	3,580.3
176	Victorville, CA	3,762.0
300	Virginia Beach, VA	2,617.8
134	Visalia, CA	4,334.5
386	Vista, CA	1,961.8
111	Waco, TX	4,544.5
266	Warren, MI	2,819.0
308	Warwick, RI	2,572.9
106	Washington, DC	4,628.0
139	Waterbury, CT	4,265.7
245	Waukegan, IL	3,004.4
247	West Covina, CA	2,989.0
275	West Jordan, UT	2,769.3
55	West Palm Beach, FL	5,276.2
146	West Valley, UT	4,164.5
259	Westland, MI	2,893.2
236	Westminster, CA	3,128.1
303	Westminster, CO	2,585.4
262	Whittier, CA	2,884.5
96	Wichita Falls, TX	4,759.8
47	Wichita, KS	5,452.8
48	Wilmington, NC	5,403.7
31	Winston-Salem, NC	5,838.0
387	Woodbridge Twnshp, NJ	1,955.0
199	Worcester, MA	3,510.0
20	Yakima, WA	6,180.8
431	Yonkers, NY	1,292.4
200	Yuma, AZ	3,508.5

Source: CQ Press using reported data from the F.B.I. "Crime in the United States 2012"

*Property crimes are offenses of burglary, larceny-theft, and motor vehicle theft. Attempts are included.

**Not available.

66. Property Crime Rate in 2012 (continued)
National Rate = 2,859.2 Property Crimes per 100,000 Population*

RANK	CITY	RATE	RANK	CITY	RATE	RANK	CITY	RATE
1	Miami Beach, FL	9,913.7	75	Milwaukee, WI	5,043.1	149	High Point, NC	4,135.7
2	Springfield, MO	9,010.8	76	Huntsville, AL	5,041.6	150	San Leandro, CA	4,126.9
3	Spokane, WA	8,730.1	77	New Haven, CT	5,014.9	151	Jacksonville, FL	4,124.6
4	Little Rock, AR	8,061.0	78	St. Petersburg, FL	5,013.7	152	Clovis, CA	4,114.4
5	Salt Lake City, UT	7,459.5	79	Rockford, IL	4,995.6	153	Syracuse, NY	4,095.0
6	Macon, GA	7,216.0	80	Bakersfield, CA	4,991.3	154	Gainesville, FL	4,094.1
7	Birmingham, AL	6,934.1	81	Portsmouth, VA	4,983.5	155	Phoenix, AZ	4,091.3
8	St. Louis, MO	6,902.2	82	Minneapolis, MN	4,960.8	156	St. Paul, MN	4,091.2
9	Knoxville, TN	6,676.9	83	Vallejo, CA	4,956.2	157	Reading, PA	4,078.7
10	Orlando, FL	6,613.8	84	Berkeley, CA	4,954.7	158	Davenport, IA	4,039.8
11	Oakland, CA	6,594.0	85	Houston, TX	4,945.5	159	Fayetteville, AR	4,036.5
12	Jackson, MS	6,575.0	86	Des Moines, IA	4,922.9	160	Charlotte, NC	4,030.5
13	Atlanta, GA	6,533.5	87	San Bernardino, CA	4,888.7	161	McAllen, TX	4,025.9
14	Pueblo, CO	6,445.7	88	Roanoke, VA	4,879.3	162	Racine, WI	4,023.8
15	Glendale, AZ	6,409.5	89	Shreveport, LA	4,878.2	163	Arlington, TX	3,983.4
16	Fayetteville, NC	6,390.9	90	Renton, WA	4,867.6	164	Bloomington, IN	3,973.7
17	Albany, GA	6,369.7	91	Beaumont, TX	4,840.3	165	Largo, FL	3,956.4
18	Tacoma, WA	6,349.0	92	Redding, CA	4,814.6	166	Plantation, FL	3,925.7
19	Memphis, TN	6,312.9	93	Mobile, AL	4,812.0	167	Athens-Clarke, GA	3,917.2
20	Yakima, WA	6,180.8	94	Bellingham, WA	4,808.6	168	Clearwater, FL	3,902.8
21	Cleveland, OH	6,173.2	95	South Bend, IN	4,760.4	169	Vancouver, WA	3,893.6
22	Cincinnati, OH	6,135.3	96	Wichita Falls, TX	4,759.8	170	Allentown, PA	3,857.2
23	Everett, WA	6,092.0	97	San Francisco, CA	4,741.6	171	Lincoln, NE	3,850.1
24	Independence, MO	6,090.3	98	Tuscaloosa, AL	4,728.6	172	Columbia, MO	3,814.9
25	St. Joseph, MO	6,088.2	99	Richmond, CA	4,718.1	173	Bloomington, MN	3,796.9
26	San Antonio, TX	5,989.9	100	Tempe, AZ	4,711.5	174	Killeen, TX	3,778.3
27	Oklahoma City, OK	5,941.8	101	Ogden, UT	4,702.5	175	New Orleans, LA	3,772.4
28	Springfield, IL	5,929.3	102	Avondale, AZ	4,698.6	176	Victorville, CA	3,762.0
29	Dayton, OH	5,899.2	103	Baltimore, MD	4,660.3	177	Santa Monica, CA	3,725.3
30	Edinburg, TX	5,890.6	104	Tallahassee, FL	4,646.3	178	Denver, CO	3,713.8
31	Winston-Salem, NC	5,838.0	105	Norfolk, VA	4,643.6	179	Fort Wayne, IN	3,707.7
32	Fort Lauderdale, FL	5,830.5	106	Washington, DC	4,628.0	180	Sunrise, FL	3,704.3
33	Medford, OR	5,810.3	107	Brownsville, TX	4,603.5	181	Philadelphia, PA	3,703.6
34	Detroit, MI	5,792.1	108	Omaha, NE	4,588.4	182	Garland, TX	3,691.7
35	Montgomery, AL	5,768.9	109	Lakewood, CO	4,579.8	183	Cedar Rapids, IA	3,678.3
36	Asheville, NC	5,756.5	110	Springfield, MA	4,545.7	184	Abilene, TX	3,664.3
37	Columbus, GA	5,742.7	111	Waco, TX	4,544.5	185	Citrus Heights, CA	3,662.2
38	North Charleston, SC	5,718.4	112	Antioch, CA	4,530.1	186	Davie, FL	3,657.6
39	Indianapolis, IN	5,592.1	113	Amarillo, TX	4,527.5	187	Newark, NJ	3,656.8
40	Gary, IN	5,560.9	114	Billings, MT	4,523.8	188	Pasadena, TX	3,629.6
41	Flint, MI	5,554.4	115	Tyler, TX	4,504.2	189	Costa Mesa, CA	3,621.4
42	Federal Way, WA	5,551.3	116	Corpus Christi, TX	4,498.6	190	Savannah, GA	3,599.5
43	Lafayette, LA	5,547.3	117	Gresham, OR	4,489.8	191	Odessa, TX	3,586.6
44	Kansas City, MO	5,525.4	118	Providence, RI	4,484.4	192	Ventura, CA	3,580.3
45	Modesto, CA	5,510.4	119	Lawrence, KS	4,481.9	193	Murfreesboro, TN	3,568.9
46	Fort Smith, AR	5,453.6	120	Kent, WA	4,478.2	194	Cheektowaga, NY	3,562.9
47	Wichita, KS	5,452.8	121	Duluth, MN	4,446.6	195	Indio, CA	3,555.4
48	Wilmington, NC	5,403.7	122	Lexington, KY	4,431.9	196	Bridgeport, CT	3,528.7
49	Pompano Beach, FL	5,399.8	123	Las Cruces, NM	4,426.8	197	Anchorage, AK	3,524.4
50	Miami, FL	5,375.2	124	Greenville, NC	4,426.2	198	Rialto, CA	3,514.9
51	Albuquerque, NM	5,367.3	125	Albany, NY	4,420.1	199	Worcester, MA	3,510.0
52	Rochester, NY	5,322.3	126	Richmond, VA	4,380.7	200	Yuma, AZ	3,508.5
53	Topeka, KS	5,309.6	127	Melbourne, FL	4,374.3	201	Manchester, NH	3,496.9
54	Hollywood, FL	5,307.9	128	Dallas, TX	4,373.6	202	Grand Rapids, MI	3,484.0
55	West Palm Beach, FL	5,276.2	129	Greensboro, NC	4,368.9	203	Santa Barbara, CA	3,466.1
56	Lawton, OK	5,272.3	130	Durham, NC	4,363.6	204	Riverside, CA	3,450.4
57	Spokane Valley, WA	5,270.7	131	Peoria, IL	4,356.0	205	Elizabeth, NJ	3,445.5
58	Lakeland, FL	5,219.4	132	Laredo, TX	4,351.3	206	Erie, PA	3,442.1
59	Austin, TX	5,219.3	133	Mesquite, TX	4,340.1	207	Pittsburgh, PA	3,425.4
60	Tulsa, OK	5,216.0	134	Visalia, CA	4,334.5	208	Brooklyn Park, MN	3,399.0
61	Baton Rouge, LA	5,209.1	135	Miami Gardens, FL	4,303.0	209	Hampton, VA	3,377.0
62	Lubbock, TX	5,173.2	136	Louisville, KY	4,293.9	210	Dearborn, MI	3,376.0
63	Camden, NJ	5,159.3	137	Hemet, CA	4,292.4	211	Greeley, CO	3,368.4
64	Evansville, IN	5,146.6	138	Salem, OR	4,277.6	212	Scranton, PA	3,354.0
65	Buffalo, NY	5,126.6	139	Waterbury, CT	4,265.7	213	Concord, CA	3,340.1
66	Kansas City, KS	5,120.9	140	Hammond, IN	4,256.3	214	Pomona, CA	3,336.4
67	Longview, TX	5,102.1	141	Hartford, CT	4,248.3	215	Champaign, IL	3,319.8
68	Stockton, CA	5,101.2	142	Fort Worth, TX	4,222.0	216	New Bedford, MA	3,311.4
69	Seattle, WA	5,093.8	143	Nashville, TN	4,195.9	217	Lansing, MI	3,290.7
70	Portland, OR	5,092.3	144	Sacramento, CA	4,189.8	218	Raleigh, NC	3,276.1
71	Fresno, CA	5,086.3	145	Sioux City, IA	4,166.2	219	Madison, WI	3,264.3
72	Merced, CA	5,076.8	146	West Valley, UT	4,164.5	220	Jurupa Valley, CA	3,252.8
73	Eugene, OR	5,064.4	147	Chicago, IL	4,152.5	221	Hayward, CA	3,250.5
74	Akron, OH	5,057.7	148	Colorado Springs, CO	4,140.5	222	Brockton, MA	3,227.3

RANK	CITY	RATE	RANK	CITY	RATE	RANK	CITY	RATE
223	Reno, NV	3,220.6	297	Cicero, IL	2,634.6	371	Baldwin Park, CA	2,068.0
224	Trenton, NJ	3,218.6	298	Corona, CA	2,633.1	372	St. George, UT	2,059.9
225	Decatur, IL	3,215.5	299	Chico, CA	2,630.6	373	Surprise, AZ	2,059.7
226	Moreno Valley, CA	3,190.7	300	Virginia Beach, VA	2,617.8	374	Frisco, TX	2,051.1
227	Sioux Falls, SD	3,183.4	301	Nampa, ID	2,616.5	375	Alexandria, VA	2,049.5
228	Salinas, CA	3,177.2	302	Midland, TX	2,601.2	376	Troy, MI	2,040.0
229	Deerfield Beach, FL	3,174.4	303	Westminster, CO	2,585.4	377	Chula Vista, CA	2,033.8
230	Paterson, NJ	3,153.3	304	Bethlehem, PA	2,584.0	378	Orange, CA	2,028.0
231	Bryan, TX	3,151.2	305	Joliet, IL	2,583.0	379	Oxnard, CA	2,017.4
232	Newport News, VA	3,151.0	306	Fargo, ND	2,581.7	380	McKinney, TX	2,017.3
233	Toms River Twnshp, NJ	3,140.1	307	Rancho Cucamon., CA	2,576.9	381	League City, TX	2,013.3
234	Las Vegas, NV	3,138.2	308	Warwick, RI	2,572.9	382	Edmond, OK	2,012.6
235	Mesa, AZ	3,132.5	309	Hawthorne, CA	2,545.2	383	Henderson, NV	2,009.7
236	Westminster, CA	3,128.1	310	Tracy, CA	2,537.4	384	Sterling Heights, MI	1,983.5
237	Downey, CA	3,112.8	311	Lakewood, CA	2,533.7	385	Norwalk, CT	1,975.9
238	Fairfield, CA	3,096.8	312	Lawrence, MA	2,530.2	386	Vista, CA	1,961.8
239	Hialeah, FL	3,086.1	313	Boise, ID	2,524.9	387	Carlsbad, CA	1,955.0
240	Upland, CA	3,082.2	314	Alameda, CA	2,507.1	387	Woodbridge Twnshp, NJ	1,955.0
241	Kennewick, WA	3,081.7	315	Oceanside, CA	2,506.1	389	Fremont, CA	1,945.4
242	Fall River, MA	3,014.9	316	Rochester, MN	2,505.9	390	El Monte, CA	1,933.1
243	Ontario, CA	3,010.7	317	Buena Park, CA	2,504.1	391	Olathe, KS	1,929.1
244	Long Beach, CA	3,007.3	318	North Las Vegas, NV	2,494.1	392	Amherst, NY	1,922.8
245	Waukegan, IL	3,004.4	319	College Station, TX	2,483.2	393	Danbury, CT	1,907.4
246	Kenosha, WI	2,999.2	320	Round Rock, TX	2,481.4	394	San Mateo, CA	1,889.2
247	West Covina, CA	2,989.0	321	Newport Beach, CA	2,464.3	395	Clarkstown, NY	1,884.4
248	Aurora, CO	2,985.3	322	Compton, CA	2,446.5	396	Mountain View, CA	1,868.8
249	Boca Raton, FL	2,956.3	323	Longmont, CO	2,439.1	397	Roswell, GA	1,867.8
250	Peoria, AZ	2,951.1	324	Norwalk, CA	2,431.6	398	Clifton, NJ	1,864.6
251	Sandy, UT	2,945.6	325	El Paso, TX	2,429.3	399	Sugar Land, TX	1,858.3
252	Mission, TX	2,942.0	326	Menifee, CA	2,426.1	400	Pearland, TX	1,851.1
253	Boulder, CO	2,929.5	327	Pasadena, CA	2,424.3	401	Torrance, CA	1,819.4
254	Anaheim, CA	2,922.9	328	Santa Maria, CA	2,401.0	402	Elgin, IL	1,815.8
255	San Jose, CA	2,914.9	329	Inglewood, CA	2,397.6	403	Port St. Lucie, FL	1,799.7
256	Boston, MA	2,909.5	330	Arvada, CO	2,389.3	404	New Rochelle, NY	1,789.2
257	Richardson, TX	2,909.0	331	Upper Darby Twnshp, PA	2,380.1	405	Aurora, IL	1,784.6
258	Carson, CA	2,905.6	332	Cranston, RI	2,375.6	406	Sunnyvale, CA	1,779.2
259	Westland, MI	2,893.2	333	Burbank, CA	2,373.0	407	San Marcos, CA	1,750.4
260	Cambridge, MA	2,889.3	334	Ann Arbor, MI	2,370.3	408	Daly City, CA	1,745.2
261	Grand Prairie, TX	2,885.9	335	El Cajon, CA	2,369.8	409	New York, NY	1,722.2
262	Whittier, CA	2,884.5	336	San Diego, CA	2,368.4	410	Quincy, MA	1,657.8
263	Lowell, MA	2,879.1	337	Miramar, FL	2,368.3	411	Brick Twnshp, NJ	1,642.3
264	Fullerton, CA	2,843.5	338	Temecula, CA	2,359.4	412	Allen, TX	1,612.9
265	Tampa, FL	2,835.9	339	Orem, UT	2,357.7	413	Murrieta, CA	1,605.2
266	Warren, MI	2,819.0	340	Plano, TX	2,356.7	414	Beaverton, OR	1,594.1
267	Lynn, MA	2,818.8	341	Palm Bay, FL	2,348.2	415	Meridian, ID	1,591.8
268	Irving, TX	2,815.5	342	Bloomington, IL	2,330.5	416	Gilbert, AZ	1,580.3
269	Huntington Beach, CA	2,809.8	343	Lee's Summit, MO	2,316.0	417	Farmington Hills, MI	1,573.8
270	Sandy Springs, GA	2,809.3	344	Bellflower, CA	2,313.6	418	Glendale, CA	1,561.3
271	Green Bay, WI	2,807.3	345	Overland Park, KS	2,303.4	419	Stamford, CT	1,555.5
272	Bellevue, WA	2,779.7	346	Clinton Twnshp, MI	2,298.9	420	O'Fallon, MO	1,544.6
273	Sparks, NV	2,769.9	347	Garden Grove, CA	2,294.4	421	Santa Clarita, CA	1,529.7
274	Santa Clara, CA	2,769.8	348	Redwood City, CA	2,294.0	422	Irvine, CA	1,518.9
275	West Jordan, UT	2,769.3	349	Hillsboro, OR	2,288.6	423	Simi Valley, CA	1,512.4
276	Fort Collins, CO	2,768.3	350	Alhambra, CA	2,271.8	424	Edison Twnshp, NJ	1,466.2
277	Chesapeake, VA	2,765.3	351	Los Angeles, CA	2,269.1	425	Naperville, IL	1,431.0
278	Carrollton, TX	2,742.7	352	Coral Springs, FL	2,255.6	426	Thousand Oaks, CA	1,422.9
279	Denton, TX	2,742.5	353	Fontana, CA	2,237.2	427	Centennial, CO	1,383.4
280	Clarksville, TN	2,723.6	354	Santa Rosa, CA	2,234.6	428	Lake Forest, CA	1,374.3
281	Charleston, SC	2,723.3	355	Somerville, MA	2,233.2	429	Cary, NC	1,353.7
282	Colonie, NY	2,719.2	356	Santa Ana, CA	2,222.4	430	Arlington Heights, IL	1,296.0
283	Nashua, NH	2,717.9	357	Hamilton Twnshp, NJ	2,219.7	431	Yonkers, NY	1,292.4
284	Hesperia, CA	2,708.3	358	Livonia, MI	2,211.9	432	Mission Viejo, CA	1,252.1
285	Chandler, AZ	2,707.2	359	Cape Coral, FL	2,205.8	433	Chino Hills, CA	1,247.5
286	Scottsdale, AZ	2,706.4	360	Lancaster, CA	2,197.9	434	Lakewood Twnshp, NJ	1,176.6
287	Lynchburg, VA	2,706.0	361	Palmdale, CA	2,184.9	435	Fishers, IN	1,034.3
288	Norman, OK	2,676.2	362	Livermore, CA	2,180.0	436	Newton, MA	1,031.0
289	Roseville, CA	2,675.4	363	Jersey City, NJ	2,178.1	437	Carmel, IN	987.5
290	Pembroke Pines, FL	2,653.0	364	Broken Arrow, OK	2,172.1	438	Ramapo, NY	837.9
291	South Gate, CA	2,652.0	365	Vacaville, CA	2,161.8	439	Johns Creek, GA	657.2
292	Chino, CA	2,651.9	366	Tustin, CA	2,135.7	440	Parma, OH	557.0
293	Hoover, AL	2,647.8	367	Rio Rancho, NM	2,128.3	NA	Toledo, OH**	NA
294	Thornton, CO	2,645.5	368	Provo, UT	2,109.0	NA	Tucson, AZ**	NA
295	Greece, NY	2,641.8	369	Elk Grove, CA	2,105.6			
296	Escondido, CA	2,637.3	370	Napa, CA	2,090.6			

Source: CQ Press using reported data from the F.B.I. "Crime in the United States 2012"

*Property crimes are offenses of burglary, larceny-theft, and motor vehicle theft. Attempts are included.

**Not available.

67. Percent Change in Property Crime Rate: 2011 to 2012
National Percent Change = 1.6% Decrease*

RANK	CITY	% CHANGE	RANK	CITY	% CHANGE	RANK	CITY	% CHANGE
192	Abilene, TX	(0.1)	255	Chino Hills, CA	(3.5)	258	Gainesville, FL	(3.6)
313	Akron, OH	(7.2)	158	Chino, CA	1.0	24	Garden Grove, CA	17.1
219	Alameda, CA	(1.4)	181	Chula Vista, CA	0.2	222	Garland, TX	(1.5)
100	Albany, GA	5.9	47	Cicero, IL	11.9	397	Gary, IN	(15.9)
NA	Albany, NY**	NA	353	Cincinnati, OH	(10.9)	375	Gilbert, AZ	(13.3)
100	Albuquerque, NM	5.9	317	Citrus Heights, CA	(7.4)	189	Glendale, AZ	0.0
330	Alexandria, VA	(8.7)	NA	Clarkstown, NY**	NA	370	Glendale, CA	(12.3)
158	Alhambra, CA	1.0	377	Clarksville, TN	(13.4)	414	Grand Prairie, TX	(25.7)
NA	Allentown, PA**	NA	129	Clearwater, FL	3.2	99	Grand Rapids, MI	6.0
337	Allen, TX	(9.1)	248	Cleveland, OH	(3.2)	NA	Greece, NY**	NA
300	Amarillo, TX	(6.1)	263	Clifton, NJ	(3.9)	144	Greeley, CO	2.1
NA	Amherst, NY**	NA	266	Clinton Twnshp, MI	(4.0)	12	Green Bay, WI	21.2
24	Anaheim, CA	17.1	155	Clovis, CA	1.2	NA	Greensboro, NC**	NA
60	Anchorage, AK	10.7	408	College Station, TX	(20.5)	NA	Greenville, NC**	NA
100	Ann Arbor, MI	5.9	NA	Colonie, NY**	NA	53	Gresham, OR	11.1
13	Antioch, CA	21.1	62	Colorado Springs, CO	10.6	79	Hamilton Twnshp, NJ	8.4
345	Arlington Heights, IL	(9.9)	239	Columbia, MO	(2.6)	342	Hammond, IN	(9.5)
383	Arlington, TX	(13.6)	358	Columbus, GA	(11.3)	353	Hampton, VA	(10.9)
149	Arvada, CO	1.6	402	Compton, CA	(16.7)	255	Hartford, CT	(3.5)
10	Asheville, NC	23.1	77	Concord, CA	8.5	141	Hawthorne, CA	2.2
296	Athens-Clarke, GA	(5.9)	333	Coral Springs, FL	(8.8)	7	Hayward, CA	25.4
321	Atlanta, GA	(7.8)	14	Corona, CA	21.0	226	Hemet, CA	(1.6)
189	Aurora, CO	0.0	296	Corpus Christi, TX	(5.9)	72	Henderson, NV	9.3
314	Aurora, IL	(7.3)	35	Costa Mesa, CA	14.0	69	Hesperia, CA	9.9
196	Austin, TX	(0.3)	305	Cranston, RI	(6.6)	301	Hialeah, FL	(6.2)
314	Avondale, AZ	(7.3)	380	Dallas, TX	(13.5)	383	High Point, NC	(13.6)
20	Bakersfield, CA	18.2	280	Daly City, CA	(5.0)	136	Hillsboro, OR	2.6
222	Baldwin Park, CA	(1.5)	241	Danbury, CT	(2.7)	243	Hollywood, FL	(2.8)
227	Baltimore, MD	(2.0)	404	Davenport, IA	(17.5)	212	Hoover, AL	(1.0)
277	Baton Rouge, LA	(4.8)	298	Davie, FL	(6.0)	229	Houston, TX	(2.1)
369	Beaumont, TX	(12.2)	173	Dayton, OH	0.4	22	Huntington Beach, CA	17.7
405	Beaverton, OR	(18.7)	365	Dearborn, MI	(11.9)	303	Huntsville, AL	(6.4)
236	Bellevue, WA	(2.4)	377	Decatur, IL	(13.4)	91	Independence, MO	6.7
229	Bellflower, CA	(2.1)	192	Deerfield Beach, FL	(0.1)	209	Indianapolis, IN	(0.8)
104	Bellingham, WA	5.7	268	Denton, TX	(4.2)	112	Indio, CA	4.8
50	Berkeley, CA	11.4	164	Denver, CO	0.8	132	Inglewood, CA	3.0
118	Bethlehem, PA	4.4	301	Des Moines, IA	(6.2)	204	Irvine, CA	(0.5)
154	Billings, MT	1.3	292	Detroit, MI	(5.7)	327	Irving, TX	(8.5)
403	Birmingham, AL	(17.1)	340	Downey, CA	(9.2)	274	Jacksonville, FL	(4.7)
134	Bloomington, IL	2.9	356	Duluth, MN	(11.1)	351	Jackson, MS	(10.6)
117	Bloomington, IN	4.5	350	Durham, NC	(10.5)	284	Jersey City, NJ	(5.1)
165	Bloomington, MN	0.7	196	Edinburg, TX	(0.3)	355	Johns Creek, GA	(11.0)
290	Boca Raton, FL	(5.5)	407	Edison Twnshp, NJ	(19.7)	214	Joliet, IL	(1.1)
222	Boise, ID	(1.5)	169	Edmond, OK	0.6	NA	Jurupa Valley, CA**	NA
310	Boston, MA	(7.0)	253	El Cajon, CA	(3.4)	274	Kansas City, KS	(4.7)
27	Boulder, CO	16.5	246	El Monte, CA	(2.9)	195	Kansas City, MO	(0.2)
294	Brick Twnshp, NJ	(5.8)	217	El Paso, TX	(1.3)	367	Kennewick, WA	(12.0)
337	Bridgeport, CT	(9.1)	274	Elgin, IL	(4.7)	219	Kenosha, WI	(1.4)
292	Brockton, MA	(5.7)	392	Elizabeth, NJ	(15.3)	395	Kent, WA	(15.7)
284	Broken Arrow, OK	(5.1)	196	Elk Grove, CA	(0.3)	287	Killeen, TX	(5.3)
330	Brooklyn Park, MN	(8.7)	298	Erie, PA	(6.0)	303	Knoxville, TN	(6.4)
172	Brownsville, TX	0.5	17	Escondido, CA	19.6	124	Lafayette, LA	3.7
394	Bryan, TX	(15.6)	151	Eugene, OR	1.5	38	Lake Forest, CA	13.4
76	Buena Park, CA	8.6	51	Evansville, IN	11.3	183	Lakeland, FL	0.1
NA	Buffalo, NY**	NA	391	Everett, WA	(15.0)	144	Lakewood Twnshp, NJ	2.1
246	Burbank, CA	(2.9)	54	Fairfield, CA	11.0	83	Lakewood, CA	8.1
248	Cambridge, MA	(3.2)	393	Fall River, MA	(15.4)	88	Lakewood, CO	7.6
347	Camden, NJ	(10.3)	124	Fargo, ND	3.7	80	Lancaster, CA	8.3
380	Cape Coral, FL	(13.5)	212	Farmington Hills, MI	(1.0)	370	Lansing, MI	(12.3)
103	Carlsbad, CA	5.8	238	Fayetteville, AR	(2.5)	165	Laredo, TX	0.7
289	Carmel, IN	(5.4)	183	Fayetteville, NC	0.1	141	Largo, FL	2.2
173	Carrollton, TX	0.4	NA	Federal Way, WA**	NA	263	Las Cruces, NM	(3.9)
82	Carson, CA	8.2	35	Fishers, IN	14.0	63	Las Vegas, NV	10.5
360	Cary, NC	(11.4)	388	Flint, MI	(14.1)	120	Lawrence, KS	4.2
269	Cedar Rapids, IA	(4.3)	112	Fontana, CA	4.8	410	Lawrence, MA	(21.6)
118	Centennial, CO	4.4	284	Fort Collins, CO	(5.1)	307	Lawton, OK	(6.7)
19	Champaign, IL	18.3	266	Fort Lauderdale, FL	(4.0)	335	League City, TX	(8.9)
NA	Chandler, AZ**	NA	165	Fort Smith, AR	0.7	173	Lee's Summit, MO	0.4
365	Charleston, SC	(11.9)	116	Fort Wayne, IN	4.6	NA	Lexington, KY**	NA
206	Charlotte, NC	(0.6)	336	Fort Worth, TX	(9.0)	222	Lincoln, NE	(1.5)
NA	Cheektowaga, NY**	NA	93	Fremont, CA	6.6	153	Little Rock, AR	1.4
374	Chesapeake, VA	(13.2)	183	Fresno, CA	0.1	169	Livermore, CA	0.6
280	Chicago, IL	(5.0)	200	Frisco, TX	(0.4)	149	Livonia, MI	1.6
77	Chico, CA	8.5	71	Fullerton, CA	9.5	70	Long Beach, CA	9.7

RANK	CITY	% CHANGE	RANK	CITY	% CHANGE	RANK	CITY	% CHANGE
72	Longmont, CO	9.3	326	Pasadena, CA	(8.4)	372	South Gate, CA	(12.4)
65	Longview, TX	10.2	111	Pasadena, TX	4.9	132	Sparks, NV	3.0
161	Los Angeles, CA	0.9	233	Paterson, NJ	(2.3)	263	Spokane Valley, WA	(3.9)
351	Louisville, KY	(10.6)	192	Pearland, TX	(0.1)	9	Spokane, WA	23.2
204	Lowell, MA	(0.5)	396	Pembroke Pines, FL	(15.8)	259	Springfield, IL	(3.7)
173	Lubbock, TX	0.4	253	Peoria, AZ	(3.4)	280	Springfield, MA	(5.0)
400	Lynchburg, VA	(16.2)	318	Peoria, IL	(7.6)	189	Springfield, MO	0.0
231	Lynn, MA	(2.2)	278	Philadelphia, PA	(4.9)	261	Stamford, CT	(3.8)
389	Macon, GA	(14.5)	310	Phoenix, AZ	(7.0)	261	Sterling Heights, MI	(3.8)
259	Madison, WI	(3.7)	318	Plano, TX	(7.6)	239	Stockton, CA	(2.6)
327	Manchester, NH	(8.5)	383	Plantation, FL	(13.6)	NA	St. George, UT**	NA
337	McAllen, TX	(9.1)	40	Pomona, CA	13.2	31	St. Joseph, MO	15.7
270	McKinney, TX	(4.4)	214	Pompano Beach, FL	(1.1)	386	St. Louis, MO	(13.8)
41	Medford, OR	12.9	411	Port St. Lucie, FL	(22.2)	219	St. Paul, MN	(1.4)
397	Melbourne, FL	(15.9)	183	Portland, OR	0.1	243	St. Petersburg, FL	(2.8)
241	Memphis, TN	(2.7)	322	Portsmouth, VA	(8.0)	114	Sugar Land, TX	4.7
21	Menifee, CA	18.1	NA	Providence, RI**	NA	3	Sunnyvale, CA	28.0
2	Merced, CA	28.4	401	Provo, UT	(16.3)	364	Sunrise, FL	(11.7)
33	Meridian, ID	15.2	4	Pueblo, CO	27.2	290	Surprise, AZ	(5.5)
320	Mesa, AZ	(7.7)	375	Quincy, MA	(13.3)	NA	Syracuse, NY**	NA
287	Mesquite, TX	(5.3)	363	Racine, WI	(11.6)	98	Tacoma, WA	6.1
322	Miami Beach, FL	(8.0)	155	Raleigh, NC	1.2	333	Tallahassee, FL	(8.8)
377	Miami Gardens, FL	(13.4)	NA	Ramapo, NY**	NA	312	Tampa, FL	(7.1)
280	Miami, FL	(5.0)	66	Rancho Cucamon., CA	10.1	207	Temecula, CA	(0.7)
346	Midland, TX	(10.2)	74	Reading, PA	9.2	380	Tempe, AZ	(13.5)
183	Milwaukee, WI	0.1	1	Redding, CA	28.9	NA	Thornton, CO**	NA
196	Minneapolis, MN	(0.3)	16	Redwood City, CA	19.9	148	Thousand Oaks, CA	2.0
330	Miramar, FL	(8.7)	48	Reno, NV	11.7	NA	Toledo, OH**	NA
243	Mission Viejo, CA	(2.8)	95	Renton, WA	6.5	325	Toms River Twnshp, NJ	(8.3)
397	Mission, TX	(15.9)	18	Rialto, CA	18.4	342	Topeka, KS	(9.5)
357	Mobile, AL	(11.2)	108	Richardson, TX	5.0	248	Torrance, CA	(3.2)
6	Modesto, CA	26.1	75	Richmond, CA	8.9	233	Tracy, CA	(2.3)
54	Montgomery, AL	11.0	114	Richmond, VA	4.7	91	Trenton, NJ	6.7
80	Moreno Valley, CA	8.3	28	Rio Rancho, NM	16.3	314	Troy, MI	(7.3)
126	Mountain View, CA	3.5	66	Riverside, CA	10.1	NA	Tucson, AZ**	NA
406	Murfreesboro, TN	(19.3)	128	Roanoke, VA	3.4	294	Tulsa, OK	(5.8)
43	Murrieta, CA	12.4	29	Rochester, MN	16.1	236	Tuscaloosa, AL	(2.4)
373	Nampa, ID	(12.8)	NA	Rochester, NY**	NA	84	Tustin, CA	7.9
165	Napa, CA	0.7	88	Rockford, IL	7.6	179	Tyler, TX	0.3
255	Naperville, IL	(3.5)	340	Roseville, CA	(9.2)	123	Upland, CA	3.9
63	Nashua, NH	10.5	248	Roswell, GA	(3.2)	361	Upper Darby Twnshp, PA	(11.5)
368	Nashville, TN	(12.1)	126	Round Rock, TX	3.5	15	Vacaville, CA	20.5
278	New Bedford, MA	(4.9)	95	Sacramento, CA	6.5	57	Vallejo, CA	10.9
169	New Haven, CT	0.6	44	Salem, OR	12.2	209	Vancouver, WA	(0.8)
305	New Orleans, LA	(6.6)	87	Salinas, CA	7.7	29	Ventura, CA	16.1
NA	New Rochelle, NY**	NA	59	Salt Lake City, UT	10.8	44	Victorville, CA	12.2
NA	New York, NY**	NA	173	San Antonio, TX	0.4	270	Virginia Beach, VA	(4.4)
151	Newark, NJ	1.5	11	San Bernardino, CA	22.7	93	Visalia, CA	6.6
272	Newport Beach, CA	(4.5)	108	San Diego, CA	5.0	322	Vista, CA	(8.0)
273	Newport News, VA	(4.6)	23	San Francisco, CA	17.5	344	Waco, TX	(9.8)
413	Newton, MA	(25.2)	5	San Jose, CA	27.0	227	Warren, MI	(2.0)
309	Norfolk, VA	(6.9)	60	San Leandro, CA	10.7	248	Warwick, RI	(3.2)
386	Norman, OK	(13.8)	120	San Marcos, CA	4.2	158	Washington, DC	1.0
157	North Charleston, SC	1.1	90	San Mateo, CA	7.3	129	Waterbury, CT	3.2
NA	North Las Vegas, NV**	NA	84	Sandy Springs, GA	7.9	NA	Waukegan, IL**	NA
34	Norwalk, CA	14.2	179	Sandy, UT	0.3	216	West Covina, CA	(1.2)
361	Norwalk, CT	(11.5)	54	Santa Ana, CA	11.0	200	West Jordan, UT	(0.4)
8	Oakland, CA	24.7	42	Santa Barbara, CA	12.5	207	West Palm Beach, FL	(0.7)
66	Oceanside, CA	10.1	51	Santa Clara, CA	11.3	138	West Valley, UT	2.4
26	Odessa, TX	16.8	97	Santa Clarita, CA	6.3	141	Westland, MI	2.2
173	O'Fallon, MO	0.4	200	Santa Maria, CA	(0.4)	38	Westminster, CA	13.4
349	Ogden, UT	(10.4)	37	Santa Monica, CA	13.8	200	Westminster, CO	(0.4)
144	Oklahoma City, OK	2.1	138	Santa Rosa, CA	2.4	161	Whittier, CA	0.9
57	Olathe, KS	10.9	390	Savannah, GA	(14.9)	120	Wichita Falls, TX	4.2
161	Omaha, NE	0.9	358	Scottsdale, AZ	(11.3)	86	Wichita, KS	7.8
135	Ontario, CA	2.8	181	Scranton, PA	0.2	144	Wilmington, NC	2.1
105	Orange, CA	5.5	211	Seattle, WA	(0.9)	231	Winston-Salem, NC	(2.2)
329	Orem, UT	(8.6)	138	Shreveport, LA	2.4	412	Woodbridge Twnshp, NJ	(23.0)
308	Orlando, FL	(6.8)	46	Simi Valley, CA	12.0	107	Worcester, MA	5.2
183	Overland Park, KS	0.1	217	Sioux City, IA	(1.3)	48	Yakima, WA	11.7
32	Oxnard, CA	15.4	106	Sioux Falls, SD	5.3	NA	Yonkers, NY**	NA
347	Palm Bay, FL	(10.3)	233	Somerville, MA	(2.3)	136	Yuma, AZ	2.6
129	Palmdale, CA	3.2	409	South Bend, IN	(20.6)			
NA	Parma, OH**	NA						

Source: CQ Press using reported data from the F.B.I. "Crime in the United States 2012"

*Property crimes are offenses of burglary, larceny-theft, and motor vehicle theft. Attempts are included.

**Not available.

67. Percent Change in Property Crime Rate: 2011 to 2012 (continued)
National Percent Change = 1.6% Decrease*

RANK	CITY	% CHANGE	RANK	CITY	% CHANGE	RANK	CITY	% CHANGE
1	Redding, CA	28.9	75	Richmond, CA	8.9	149	Arvada, CO	1.6
2	Merced, CA	28.4	76	Buena Park, CA	8.6	149	Livonia, MI	1.6
3	Sunnyvale, CA	28.0	77	Chico, CA	8.5	151	Eugene, OR	1.5
4	Pueblo, CO	27.2	77	Concord, CA	8.5	151	Newark, NJ	1.5
5	San Jose, CA	27.0	79	Hamilton Twnshp, NJ	8.4	153	Little Rock, AR	1.4
6	Modesto, CA	26.1	80	Lancaster, CA	8.3	154	Billings, MT	1.3
7	Hayward, CA	25.4	80	Moreno Valley, CA	8.3	155	Clovis, CA	1.2
8	Oakland, CA	24.7	82	Carson, CA	8.2	155	Raleigh, NC	1.2
9	Spokane, WA	23.2	83	Lakewood, CA	8.1	157	North Charleston, SC	1.1
10	Asheville, NC	23.1	84	Sandy Springs, GA	7.9	158	Alhambra, CA	1.0
11	San Bernardino, CA	22.7	84	Tustin, CA	7.9	158	Chino, CA	1.0
12	Green Bay, WI	21.2	86	Wichita, KS	7.8	158	Washington, DC	1.0
13	Antioch, CA	21.1	87	Salinas, CA	7.7	161	Los Angeles, CA	0.9
14	Corona, CA	21.0	88	Lakewood, CO	7.6	161	Omaha, NE	0.9
15	Vacaville, CA	20.5	88	Rockford, IL	7.6	161	Whittier, CA	0.9
16	Redwood City, CA	19.9	90	San Mateo, CA	7.3	164	Denver, CO	0.8
17	Escondido, CA	19.6	91	Independence, MO	6.7	165	Bloomington, MN	0.7
18	Rialto, CA	18.4	91	Trenton, NJ	6.7	165	Fort Smith, AR	0.7
19	Champaign, IL	18.3	93	Fremont, CA	6.6	165	Laredo, TX	0.7
20	Bakersfield, CA	18.2	93	Visalia, CA	6.6	165	Napa, CA	0.7
21	Menifee, CA	18.1	95	Renton, WA	6.5	169	Edmond, OK	0.6
22	Huntington Beach, CA	17.7	95	Sacramento, CA	6.5	169	Livermore, CA	0.6
23	San Francisco, CA	17.5	97	Santa Clarita, CA	6.3	169	New Haven, CT	0.6
24	Anaheim, CA	17.1	98	Tacoma, WA	6.1	172	Brownsville, TX	0.5
24	Garden Grove, CA	17.1	99	Grand Rapids, MI	6.0	173	Carrollton, TX	0.4
26	Odessa, TX	16.8	100	Albany, GA	5.9	173	Dayton, OH	0.4
27	Boulder, CO	16.5	100	Albuquerque, NM	5.9	173	Lee's Summit, MO	0.4
28	Rio Rancho, NM	16.3	100	Ann Arbor, MI	5.9	173	Lubbock, TX	0.4
29	Rochester, MN	16.1	103	Carlsbad, CA	5.8	173	O'Fallon, MO	0.4
29	Ventura, CA	16.1	104	Bellingham, WA	5.7	173	San Antonio, TX	0.4
31	St. Joseph, MO	15.7	105	Orange, CA	5.5	179	Sandy, UT	0.3
32	Oxnard, CA	15.4	106	Sioux Falls, SD	5.3	179	Tyler, TX	0.3
33	Meridian, ID	15.2	107	Worcester, MA	5.2	181	Chula Vista, CA	0.2
34	Norwalk, CA	14.2	108	Pittsburgh, PA	5.0	181	Scranton, PA	0.2
35	Costa Mesa, CA	14.0	108	Richardson, TX	5.0	183	Fayetteville, NC	0.1
35	Fishers, IN	14.0	108	San Diego, CA	5.0	183	Fresno, CA	0.1
37	Santa Monica, CA	13.8	111	Pasadena, TX	4.9	183	Lakeland, FL	0.1
38	Lake Forest, CA	13.4	112	Fontana, CA	4.8	183	Milwaukee, WI	0.1
38	Westminster, CA	13.4	112	Indio, CA	4.8	183	Overland Park, KS	0.1
40	Pomona, CA	13.2	114	Richmond, VA	4.7	183	Portland, OR	0.1
41	Medford, OR	12.9	114	Sugar Land, TX	4.7	189	Aurora, CO	0.0
42	Santa Barbara, CA	12.5	116	Fort Wayne, IN	4.6	189	Glendale, AZ	0.0
43	Murrieta, CA	12.4	117	Bloomington, IN	4.5	189	Springfield, MO	0.0
44	Salem, OR	12.2	118	Bethlehem, PA	4.4	192	Abilene, TX	(0.1)
44	Victorville, CA	12.2	118	Centennial, CO	4.4	192	Deerfield Beach, FL	(0.1)
46	Simi Valley, CA	12.0	120	Lawrence, KS	4.2	192	Pearland, TX	(0.1)
47	Cicero, IL	11.9	120	San Marcos, CA	4.2	195	Kansas City, MO	(0.2)
48	Reno, NV	11.7	120	Wichita Falls, TX	4.2	196	Austin, TX	(0.3)
48	Yakima, WA	11.7	123	Upland, CA	3.9	196	Edinburg, TX	(0.3)
50	Berkeley, CA	11.4	124	Fargo, ND	3.7	196	Elk Grove, CA	(0.3)
51	Evansville, IN	11.3	124	Lafayette, LA	3.7	196	Minneapolis, MN	(0.3)
51	Santa Clara, CA	11.3	126	Mountain View, CA	3.5	200	Frisco, TX	(0.4)
53	Gresham, OR	11.1	126	Round Rock, TX	3.5	200	Santa Maria, CA	(0.4)
54	Fairfield, CA	11.0	128	Roanoke, VA	3.4	200	West Jordan, UT	(0.4)
54	Montgomery, AL	11.0	129	Clearwater, FL	3.2	200	Westminster, CO	(0.4)
54	Santa Ana, CA	11.0	129	Palmdale, CA	3.2	204	Irvine, CA	(0.5)
57	Olathe, KS	10.9	129	Waterbury, CT	3.2	204	Lowell, MA	(0.5)
57	Vallejo, CA	10.9	132	Inglewood, CA	3.0	206	Charlotte, NC	(0.6)
59	Salt Lake City, UT	10.8	132	Sparks, NV	3.0	207	Temecula, CA	(0.7)
60	Anchorage, AK	10.7	134	Bloomington, IL	2.9	207	West Palm Beach, FL	(0.7)
60	San Leandro, CA	10.7	135	Ontario, CA	2.8	209	Indianapolis, IN	(0.8)
62	Colorado Springs, CO	10.6	136	Hillsboro, OR	2.6	209	Vancouver, WA	(0.8)
63	Las Vegas, NV	10.5	136	Yuma, AZ	2.6	211	Seattle, WA	(0.9)
63	Nashua, NH	10.5	138	Santa Rosa, CA	2.4	212	Farmington Hills, MI	(1.0)
65	Longview, TX	10.2	138	Shreveport, LA	2.4	212	Hoover, AL	(1.0)
66	Oceanside, CA	10.1	138	West Valley, UT	2.4	214	Joliet, IL	(1.1)
66	Rancho Cucamon., CA	10.1	141	Hawthorne, CA	2.2	214	Pompano Beach, FL	(1.1)
66	Riverside, CA	10.1	141	Largo, FL	2.2	216	West Covina, CA	(1.2)
69	Hesperia, CA	9.9	141	Westland, MI	2.2	217	El Paso, TX	(1.3)
70	Long Beach, CA	9.7	144	Greeley, CO	2.1	217	Sioux City, IA	(1.3)
71	Fullerton, CA	9.5	144	Lakewood Twnshp, NJ	2.1	219	Alameda, CA	(1.4)
72	Henderson, NV	9.3	144	Oklahoma City, OK	2.1	219	Kenosha, WI	(1.4)
72	Longmont, CO	9.3	144	Wilmington, NC	2.1	219	St. Paul, MN	(1.4)
74	Reading, PA	9.2	148	Thousand Oaks, CA	2.0	222	Baldwin Park, CA	(1.5)

RANK	CITY	% CHANGE	RANK	CITY	% CHANGE	RANK	CITY	% CHANGE
222	Boise, ID	(1.5)	296	Corpus Christi, TX	(5.9)	370	Lansing, MI	(12.3)
222	Garland, TX	(1.5)	298	Davie, FL	(6.0)	372	South Gate, CA	(12.4)
222	Lincoln, NE	(1.5)	298	Erie, PA	(6.0)	373	Nampa, ID	(12.8)
226	Hemet, CA	(1.6)	300	Amarillo, TX	(6.1)	374	Chesapeake, VA	(13.2)
227	Baltimore, MD	(2.0)	301	Des Moines, IA	(6.2)	375	Gilbert, AZ	(13.3)
227	Warren, MI	(2.0)	301	Hialeah, FL	(6.2)	375	Quincy, MA	(13.3)
229	Bellflower, CA	(2.1)	303	Huntsville, AL	(6.4)	377	Clarksville, TN	(13.4)
229	Houston, TX	(2.1)	303	Knoxville, TN	(6.4)	377	Decatur, IL	(13.4)
231	Lynn, MA	(2.2)	305	Cranston, RI	(6.6)	377	Miami Gardens, FL	(13.4)
231	Winston-Salem, NC	(2.2)	305	New Orleans, LA	(6.6)	380	Cape Coral, FL	(13.5)
233	Paterson, NJ	(2.3)	307	Lawton, OK	(6.7)	380	Dallas, TX	(13.5)
233	Somerville, MA	(2.3)	308	Orlando, FL	(6.8)	380	Tempe, AZ	(13.5)
233	Tracy, CA	(2.3)	309	Norfolk, VA	(6.9)	383	Arlington, TX	(13.6)
236	Bellevue, WA	(2.4)	310	Boston, MA	(7.0)	383	High Point, NC	(13.6)
236	Tuscaloosa, AL	(2.4)	310	Phoenix, AZ	(7.0)	383	Plantation, FL	(13.6)
238	Fayetteville, AR	(2.5)	312	Tampa, FL	(7.1)	386	Norman, OK	(13.8)
239	Columbia, MO	(2.6)	313	Akron, OH	(7.2)	386	St. Louis, MO	(13.8)
239	Stockton, CA	(2.6)	314	Aurora, IL	(7.3)	388	Flint, MI	(14.1)
241	Danbury, CT	(2.7)	314	Avondale, AZ	(7.3)	389	Macon, GA	(14.5)
241	Memphis, TN	(2.7)	314	Troy, MI	(7.3)	390	Savannah, GA	(14.9)
243	Hollywood, FL	(2.8)	317	Citrus Heights, CA	(7.4)	391	Everett, WA	(15.0)
243	Mission Viejo, CA	(2.8)	318	Peoria, IL	(7.6)	392	Elizabeth, NJ	(15.3)
243	St. Petersburg, FL	(2.8)	318	Plano, TX	(7.6)	393	Fall River, MA	(15.4)
246	Burbank, CA	(2.9)	320	Mesa, AZ	(7.7)	394	Bryan, TX	(15.6)
246	El Monte, CA	(2.9)	321	Atlanta, GA	(7.8)	395	Kent, WA	(15.7)
248	Cambridge, MA	(3.2)	322	Miami Beach, FL	(8.0)	396	Pembroke Pines, FL	(15.8)
248	Cleveland, OH	(3.2)	322	Portsmouth, VA	(8.0)	397	Gary, IN	(15.9)
248	Roswell, GA	(3.2)	322	Vista, CA	(8.0)	397	Melbourne, FL	(15.9)
248	Torrance, CA	(3.2)	325	Toms River Twnshp, NJ	(8.3)	397	Mission, TX	(15.9)
248	Warwick, RI	(3.2)	326	Pasadena, CA	(8.4)	400	Lynchburg, VA	(16.2)
253	El Cajon, CA	(3.4)	327	Irving, TX	(8.5)	401	Provo, UT	(16.3)
253	Peoria, AZ	(3.4)	327	Manchester, NH	(8.5)	402	Compton, CA	(16.7)
255	Chino Hills, CA	(3.5)	329	Orem, UT	(8.6)	403	Birmingham, AL	(17.1)
255	Hartford, CT	(3.5)	330	Alexandria, VA	(8.7)	404	Davenport, IA	(17.5)
255	Naperville, IL	(3.5)	330	Brooklyn Park, MN	(8.7)	405	Beaverton, OR	(18.7)
258	Gainesville, FL	(3.6)	330	Miramar, FL	(8.7)	406	Murfreesboro, TN	(19.3)
259	Madison, WI	(3.7)	333	Coral Springs, FL	(8.8)	407	Edison Twnshp, NJ	(19.7)
259	Springfield, IL	(3.7)	333	Tallahassee, FL	(8.8)	408	College Station, TX	(20.5)
261	Stamford, CT	(3.8)	335	League City, TX	(8.9)	409	South Bend, IN	(20.6)
261	Sterling Heights, MI	(3.8)	336	Fort Worth, TX	(9.0)	410	Lawrence, MA	(21.6)
263	Clifton, NJ	(3.9)	337	Allen, TX	(9.1)	411	Port St. Lucie, FL	(22.2)
263	Las Cruces, NM	(3.9)	337	Bridgeport, CT	(9.1)	412	Woodbridge Twnshp, NJ	(23.0)
263	Spokane Valley, WA	(3.9)	337	McAllen, TX	(9.1)	413	Newton, MA	(25.2)
266	Clinton Twnshp, MI	(4.0)	340	Downey, CA	(9.2)	414	Grand Prairie, TX	(25.7)
266	Fort Lauderdale, FL	(4.0)	340	Roseville, CA	(9.2)	NA	Albany, NY**	NA
268	Denton, TX	(4.2)	342	Hammond, IN	(9.5)	NA	Allentown, PA**	NA
269	Cedar Rapids, IA	(4.3)	342	Topeka, KS	(9.5)	NA	Amherst, NY**	NA
270	McKinney, TX	(4.4)	344	Waco, TX	(9.8)	NA	Buffalo, NY**	NA
270	Virginia Beach, VA	(4.4)	345	Arlington Heights, IL	(9.9)	NA	Chandler, AZ**	NA
272	Newport Beach, CA	(4.5)	346	Midland, TX	(10.2)	NA	Cheektowaga, NY**	NA
273	Newport News, VA	(4.6)	347	Camden, NJ	(10.3)	NA	Clarkstown, NY**	NA
274	Elgin, IL	(4.7)	347	Palm Bay, FL	(10.3)	NA	Colonie, NY**	NA
274	Jacksonville, FL	(4.7)	349	Ogden, UT	(10.4)	NA	Federal Way, WA**	NA
274	Kansas City, KS	(4.7)	350	Durham, NC	(10.5)	NA	Greece, NY**	NA
277	Baton Rouge, LA	(4.8)	351	Jackson, MS	(10.6)	NA	Greensboro, NC**	NA
278	New Bedford, MA	(4.9)	351	Louisville, KY	(10.6)	NA	Greenville, NC**	NA
278	Philadelphia, PA	(4.9)	353	Cincinnati, OH	(10.9)	NA	Jurupa Valley, CA**	NA
280	Chicago, IL	(5.0)	353	Hampton, VA	(10.9)	NA	Lexington, KY**	NA
280	Daly City, CA	(5.0)	355	Johns Creek, GA	(11.0)	NA	New Rochelle, NY**	NA
280	Miami, FL	(5.0)	356	Duluth, MN	(11.1)	NA	New York, NY**	NA
280	Springfield, MA	(5.0)	357	Mobile, AL	(11.2)	NA	North Las Vegas, NV**	NA
284	Broken Arrow, OK	(5.1)	358	Columbus, GA	(11.3)	NA	Parma, OH**	NA
284	Fort Collins, CO	(5.1)	358	Scottsdale, AZ	(11.3)	NA	Providence, RI**	NA
284	Jersey City, NJ	(5.1)	360	Cary, NC	(11.4)	NA	Ramapo, NY**	NA
287	Killeen, TX	(5.3)	361	Norwalk, CT	(11.5)	NA	Rochester, NY**	NA
287	Mesquite, TX	(5.3)	361	Upper Darby Twnshp, PA	(11.5)	NA	St. George, UT**	NA
289	Carmel, IN	(5.4)	363	Racine, WI	(11.6)	NA	Syracuse, NY**	NA
290	Boca Raton, FL	(5.5)	364	Sunrise, FL	(11.7)	NA	Thornton, CO**	NA
290	Surprise, AZ	(5.5)	365	Charleston, SC	(11.9)	NA	Toledo, OH**	NA
292	Brockton, MA	(5.7)	365	Dearborn, MI	(11.9)	NA	Tucson, AZ**	NA
292	Detroit, MI	(5.7)	367	Kennewick, WA	(12.0)	NA	Waukegan, IL**	NA
294	Brick Twnshp, NJ	(5.8)	368	Nashville, TN	(12.1)	NA	Yonkers, NY**	NA
294	Tulsa, OK	(5.8)	369	Beaumont, TX	(12.2)			
296	Athens-Clarke, GA	(5.9)	370	Glendale, CA	(12.3)			

Source: CQ Press using reported data from the F.B.I. "Crime in the United States 2012"

*Property crimes are offenses of burglary, larceny-theft, and motor vehicle theft. Attempts are included.

**Not available.

68. Percent Change in Property Crime Rate: 2008 to 2012
National Percent Change = 11.1% Decrease*

RANK	CITY	% CHANGE	RANK	CITY	% CHANGE	RANK	CITY	% CHANGE
122	Abilene, TX	(5.3)	319	Chino Hills, CA	(21.9)	325	Gainesville, FL	(22.2)
96	Akron, OH	(2.4)	101	Chino, CA	(3.2)	85	Garden Grove, CA	(1.2)
133	Alameda, CA	(6.4)	376	Chula Vista, CA	(30.2)	207	Garland, TX	(12.5)
NA	Albany, GA**	NA	NA	Cicero, IL**	NA	7	Gary, IN	28.3
NA	Albany, NY**	NA	69	Cincinnati, OH	0.7	370	Gilbert, AZ	(29.4)
191	Albuquerque, NM	(11.5)	254	Citrus Heights, CA	(16.4)	14	Glendale, AZ	22.4
234	Alexandria, VA	(14.8)	NA	Clarkstown, NY**	NA	342	Glendale, CA	(25.0)
126	Alhambra, CA	(5.7)	375	Clarksville, TN	(29.6)	399	Grand Prairie, TX	(38.0)
NA	Allentown, PA**	NA	229	Clearwater, FL	(14.4)	351	Grand Rapids, MI	(26.9)
167	Allen, TX	(9.5)	45	Cleveland, OH	6.7	NA	Greece, NY**	NA
267	Amarillo, TX	(17.6)	341	Clifton, NJ	(24.7)	165	Greeley, CO	(9.4)
NA	Amherst, NY**	NA	188	Clinton Twnshp, MI	(11.2)	163	Green Bay, WI	(9.2)
19	Anaheim, CA	17.1	15	Clovis, CA	20.3	382	Greensboro, NC	(31.0)
42	Anchorage, AK	7.2	387	College Station, TX	(32.5)	385	Greenville, NC	(32.4)
207	Ann Arbor, MI	(12.5)	NA	Colonie, NY**	NA	21	Gresham, OR	16.5
1	Antioch, CA	60.1	98	Colorado Springs, CO	(2.5)	45	Hamilton Twnshp, NJ	6.7
NA	Arlington Heights, IL**	NA	96	Columbia, MO	(2.4)	261	Hammond, IN	(17.0)
346	Arlington, TX	(25.7)	348	Columbus, GA	(26.4)	114	Hampton, VA	(3.9)
125	Arvada, CO	(5.6)	378	Compton, CA	(30.6)	259	Hartford, CT	(16.9)
74	Asheville, NC	0.1	165	Concord, CA	(9.4)	80	Hawthorne, CA	(0.8)
379	Athens-Clarke, GA	(30.7)	107	Coral Springs, FL	(3.5)	65	Hayward, CA	1.0
180	Atlanta, GA	(10.7)	88	Corona, CA	(1.4)	154	Hemet, CA	(8.2)
190	Aurora, CO	(11.4)	352	Corpus Christi, TX	(27.0)	191	Henderson, NV	(11.5)
359	Aurora, IL	(28.4)	19	Costa Mesa, CA	17.1	22	Hesperia, CA	15.7
202	Austin, TX	(12.2)	214	Cranston, RI	(13.0)	395	Hialeah, FL	(34.2)
232	Avondale, AZ	(14.7)	347	Dallas, TX	(26.3)	379	High Point, NC	(30.7)
69	Bakersfield, CA	0.7	228	Daly City, CA	(14.2)	234	Hillsboro, OR	(14.8)
155	Baldwin Park, CA	(8.3)	133	Danbury, CT	(6.4)	47	Hollywood, FL	6.0
102	Baltimore, MD	(3.3)	377	Davenport, IA	(30.4)	284	Hoover, AL	(19.1)
121	Baton Rouge, LA	(5.2)	107	Davie, FL	(3.5)	76	Houston, TX	0.0
265	Beaumont, TX	(17.5)	114	Dayton, OH	(3.9)	10	Huntington Beach, CA	25.5
365	Beaverton, OR	(29.1)	383	Dearborn, MI	(32.1)	271	Huntsville, AL	(18.2)
303	Bellevue, WA	(20.6)	NA	Decatur, IL**	NA	261	Independence, MO	(17.0)
323	Bellflower, CA	(22.1)	217	Deerfield Beach, FL	(13.1)	152	Indianapolis, IN	(8.1)
214	Bellingham, WA	(13.0)	81	Denton, TX	(1.0)	28	Indio, CA	12.5
350	Berkeley, CA	(26.7)	24	Denver, CO	14.0	195	Inglewood, CA	(11.7)
328	Bethlehem, PA	(22.6)	102	Des Moines, IA	(3.3)	81	Irvine, CA	(1.0)
32	Billings, MT	9.6	85	Detroit, MI	(1.2)	394	Irving, TX	(34.1)
311	Birmingham, AL	(21.1)	239	Downey, CA	(15.4)	358	Jacksonville, FL	(28.0)
NA	Bloomington, IL**	NA	183	Duluth, MN	(11.1)	200	Jackson, MS	(11.9)
56	Bloomington, IN	3.3	284	Durham, NC	(19.1)	373	Jersey City, NJ	(29.5)
116	Bloomington, MN	(4.3)	92	Edinburg, TX	(1.9)	NA	Johns Creek, GA**	NA
333	Boca Raton, FL	(23.1)	389	Edison Twnshp, NJ	(33.0)	99	Joliet, IL	(2.7)
212	Boise, ID	(12.7)	174	Edmond, OK	(10.1)	NA	Jurupa Valley, CA**	NA
315	Boston, MA	(21.6)	397	El Cajon, CA	(34.9)	NA	Kansas City, KS**	NA
129	Boulder, CO	(6.1)	182	El Monte, CA	(10.8)	196	Kansas City, MO	(11.8)
303	Brick Twnshp, NJ	(20.6)	340	El Paso, TX	(24.5)	280	Kennewick, WA	(18.6)
323	Bridgeport, CT	(22.1)	278	Elgin, IL	(18.5)	79	Kenosha, WI	(0.4)
NA	Brockton, MA**	NA	343	Elizabeth, NJ	(25.1)	271	Kent, WA	(18.2)
145	Broken Arrow, OK	(7.5)	271	Elk Grove, CA	(18.2)	149	Killeen, TX	(7.9)
294	Brooklyn Park, MN	(20.1)	71	Erie, PA	0.6	62	Knoxville, TN	1.1
291	Brownsville, TX	(19.7)	223	Escondido, CA	(13.9)	136	Lafayette, LA	(6.7)
398	Bryan, TX	(37.4)	327	Eugene, OR	(22.5)	26	Lake Forest, CA	12.9
140	Buena Park, CA	(7.0)	33	Evansville, IN	9.5	149	Lakeland, FL	(7.9)
NA	Buffalo, NY**	NA	301	Everett, WA	(20.4)	401	Lakewood Twnshp, NJ	(41.4)
254	Burbank, CA	(16.4)	288	Fairfield, CA	(19.3)	110	Lakewood, CA	(3.7)
136	Cambridge, MA	(6.7)	326	Fall River, MA	(22.4)	40	Lakewood, CO	7.4
293	Camden, NJ	(20.0)	265	Fargo, ND	(17.5)	362	Lancaster, CA	(28.7)
363	Cape Coral, FL	(28.8)	336	Farmington Hills, MI	(23.7)	193	Lansing, MI	(11.6)
283	Carlsbad, CA	(19.0)	35	Fayetteville, AR	8.3	385	Laredo, TX	(32.4)
388	Carmel, IN	(32.8)	281	Fayetteville, NC	(18.8)	183	Largo, FL	(11.1)
207	Carrollton, TX	(12.5)	54	Federal Way, WA	3.5	149	Las Cruces, NM	(7.9)
43	Carson, CA	7.1	322	Fishers, IN	(22.0)	294	Las Vegas, NV	(20.1)
355	Cary, NC	(27.6)	157	Flint, MI	(8.5)	203	Lawrence, KS	(12.3)
313	Cedar Rapids, IA	(21.5)	122	Fontana, CA	(5.3)	180	Lawrence, MA	(10.7)
203	Centennial, CO	(12.3)	276	Fort Collins, CO	(18.4)	25	Lawton, OK	13.5
NA	Champaign, IL**	NA	58	Fort Lauderdale, FL	2.4	246	League City, TX	(16.0)
NA	Chandler, AZ**	NA	91	Fort Smith, AR	(1.8)	229	Lee's Summit, MO	(14.4)
389	Charleston, SC	(33.0)	169	Fort Wayne, IN	(9.7)	NA	Lexington, KY**	NA
396	Charlotte, NC	(34.8)	251	Fort Worth, TX	(16.2)	118	Lincoln, NE	(4.8)
NA	Cheektowaga, NY**	NA	294	Fremont, CA	(20.1)	65	Little Rock, AR	1.0
183	Chesapeake, VA	(11.1)	31	Fresno, CA	9.7	159	Livermore, CA	(8.6)
176	Chicago, IL	(10.4)	294	Frisco, TX	(20.1)	100	Livonia, MI	(2.9)
270	Chico, CA	(18.1)	162	Fullerton, CA	(8.9)	37	Long Beach, CA	8.1

RANK	CITY	% CHANGE	RANK	CITY	% CHANGE	RANK	CITY	% CHANGE
NA	Longmont, CO**	NA	251	Pasadena, CA	(16.2)	141	South Gate, CA	(7.1)
329	Longview, TX	(22.7)	38	Pasadena, TX	7.8	370	Sparks, NV	(29.4)
218	Los Angeles, CA	(13.3)	71	Paterson, NJ	0.6	6	Spokane Valley, WA	31.7
152	Louisville, KY	(8.1)	231	Pearland, TX	(14.6)	2	Spokane, WA	59.6
239	Lowell, MA	(15.4)	391	Pembroke Pines, FL	(33.4)	NA	Springfield, IL**	NA
143	Lubbock, TX	(7.4)	253	Peoria, AZ	(16.3)	132	Springfield, MA	(6.3)
365	Lynchburg, VA	(29.1)	NA	Peoria, IL**	NA	110	Springfield, MO	(3.7)
243	Lynn, MA	(15.8)	232	Philadelphia, PA	(14.7)	219	Stamford, CT	(13.4)
223	Macon, GA	(13.9)	313	Phoenix, AZ	(21.5)	179	Sterling Heights, MI	(10.6)
159	Madison, WI	(8.6)	246	Pittsburgh, PA	(16.0)	257	Stockton, CA	(16.7)
38	Manchester, NH	7.8	332	Plano, TX	(23.0)	353	St. George, UT	(27.2)
392	McAllen, TX	(33.5)	303	Plantation, FL	(20.6)	8	St. Joseph, MO	28.0
139	McKinney, TX	(6.9)	54	Pomona, CA	3.5	286	St. Louis, MO	(19.2)
4	Medford, OR	47.2	106	Pompano Beach, FL	(3.4)	93	St. Paul, MN	(2.0)
289	Melbourne, FL	(19.5)	355	Port St. Lucie, FL	(27.6)	308	St. Petersburg, FL	(20.9)
312	Memphis, TN	(21.2)	110	Portland, OR	(3.7)	201	Sugar Land, TX	(12.1)
NA	Menifee, CA**	NA	175	Portsmouth, VA	(10.2)	172	Sunnyvale, CA	(10.0)
23	Merced, CA	15.6	239	Providence, RI	(15.4)	237	Sunrise, FL	(15.3)
107	Meridian, ID	(3.5)	246	Provo, UT	(16.0)	278	Surprise, AZ	(18.5)
275	Mesa, AZ	(18.3)	NA	Pueblo, CO**	NA	NA	Syracuse, NY**	NA
129	Mesquite, TX	(6.1)	243	Quincy, MA	(15.8)	264	Tacoma, WA	(17.1)
67	Miami Beach, FL	0.9	243	Racine, WI	(15.8)	206	Tallahassee, FL	(12.4)
367	Miami Gardens, FL	(29.2)	110	Raleigh, NC	(3.7)	400	Tampa, FL	(38.4)
53	Miami, FL	3.6	NA	Ramapo, NY**	NA	116	Temecula, CA	(4.3)
315	Midland, TX	(21.6)	16	Rancho Cucamon., CA	19.4	282	Tempe, AZ	(18.9)
259	Milwaukee, WI	(16.9)	315	Reading, PA	(21.6)	NA	Thornton, CO**	NA
172	Minneapolis, MN	(10.0)	5	Redding, CA	38.1	77	Thousand Oaks, CA	(0.2)
363	Miramar, FL	(28.8)	306	Redwood City, CA	(20.7)	NA	Toledo, OH**	NA
90	Mission Viejo, CA	(1.7)	354	Reno, NV	(27.5)	18	Toms River Twnshp, NJ	18.0
373	Mission, TX	(29.5)	NA	Renton, WA**	NA	183	Topeka, KS	(11.1)
213	Mobile, AL	(12.8)	3	Rialto, CA	56.6	246	Torrance, CA	(16.0)
50	Modesto, CA	4.3	219	Richardson, TX	(13.4)	294	Tracy, CA	(20.1)
127	Montgomery, AL	(6.0)	102	Richmond, CA	(3.3)	73	Trenton, NJ	0.3
78	Moreno Valley, CA	(0.3)	40	Richmond, VA	7.4	189	Troy, MI	(11.3)
357	Mountain View, CA	(27.7)	254	Rio Rancho, NM	(16.4)	NA	Tucson, AZ**	NA
267	Murfreesboro, TN	(17.6)	135	Riverside, CA	(6.6)	203	Tulsa, OK	(12.3)
29	Murrieta, CA	12.3	196	Roanoke, VA	(11.8)	310	Tuscaloosa, AL	(21.0)
161	Nampa, ID	(8.7)	193	Rochester, MN	(11.6)	94	Tustin, CA	(2.1)
276	Napa, CA	(18.4)	NA	Rochester, NY**	NA	83	Tyler, TX	(1.1)
236	Naperville, IL	(15.1)	300	Rockford, IL	(20.3)	237	Upland, CA	(15.3)
NA	Nashua, NH**	NA	348	Roseville, CA	(26.4)	315	Upper Darby Twnshp, PA	(21.6)
319	Nashville, TN	(21.9)	393	Roswell, GA	(33.6)	129	Vacaville, CA	(6.1)
169	New Bedford, MA	(9.7)	124	Round Rock, TX	(5.5)	62	Vallejo, CA	1.1
NA	New Haven, CT**	NA	214	Sacramento, CA	(13.0)	62	Vancouver, WA	1.1
361	New Orleans, LA	(28.6)	155	Salem, OR	(8.3)	27	Ventura, CA	12.7
NA	New Rochelle, NY**	NA	223	Salinas, CA	(13.9)	57	Victorville, CA	2.7
NA	New York, NY**	NA	257	Salt Lake City, UT	(16.7)	171	Virginia Beach, VA	(9.9)
49	Newark, NJ	4.9	261	San Antonio, TX	(17.0)	146	Visalia, CA	(7.6)
177	Newport Beach, CA	(10.5)	52	San Bernardino, CA	3.9	370	Vista, CA	(29.4)
335	Newport News, VA	(23.5)	345	San Diego, CA	(25.4)	338	Waco, TX	(24.3)
330	Newton, MA	(22.8)	50	San Francisco, CA	4.3	NA	Warren, MI**	NA
177	Norfolk, VA	(10.5)	12	San Jose, CA	23.6	306	Warwick, RI	(20.7)
226	Norman, OK	(14.0)	269	San Leandro, CA	(17.9)	118	Washington, DC	(4.8)
308	North Charleston, SC	(20.9)	183	San Marcos, CA	(11.1)	286	Waterbury, CT	(19.2)
334	North Las Vegas, NV	(23.2)	338	San Mateo, CA	(24.3)	NA	Waukegan, IL**	NA
58	Norwalk, CA	2.4	344	Sandy Springs, GA	(25.3)	239	West Covina, CA	(15.4)
222	Norwalk, CT	(13.8)	337	Sandy, UT	(23.8)	157	West Jordan, UT	(8.5)
13	Oakland, CA	23.2	36	Santa Ana, CA	8.2	164	West Palm Beach, FL	(9.3)
60	Oceanside, CA	1.8	17	Santa Barbara, CA	18.4	294	West Valley, UT	(20.1)
196	Odessa, TX	(11.8)	61	Santa Clara, CA	1.4	207	Westland, MI	(12.5)
302	O'Fallon, MO	(20.5)	250	Santa Clarita, CA	(16.1)	48	Westminster, CA	5.4
136	Ogden, UT	(6.7)	290	Santa Maria, CA	(19.6)	319	Westminster, CO	(21.9)
68	Oklahoma City, OK	0.8	29	Santa Monica, CA	12.3	34	Whittier, CA	9.1
NA	Olathe, KS**	NA	127	Santa Rosa, CA	(6.0)	381	Wichita Falls, TX	(30.9)
44	Omaha, NE	6.8	384	Savannah, GA	(32.3)	87	Wichita, KS	(1.3)
120	Ontario, CA	(5.0)	271	Scottsdale, AZ	(18.2)	74	Wilmington, NC	0.1
167	Orange, CA	(9.5)	147	Scranton, PA	(7.8)	196	Winston-Salem, NC	(11.8)
226	Orem, UT	(14.0)	142	Seattle, WA	(7.2)	367	Woodbridge Twnshp, NJ	(29.2)
331	Orlando, FL	(22.9)	147	Shreveport, LA	(7.8)	95	Worcester, MA	(2.2)
102	Overland Park, KS	(3.3)	143	Simi Valley, CA	(7.4)	221	Yakima, WA	(13.6)
207	Oxnard, CA	(12.5)	9	Sioux City, IA	27.2	NA	Yonkers, NY**	NA
88	Palm Bay, FL	(1.4)	11	Sioux Falls, SD	25.4	83	Yuma, AZ	(1.1)
292	Palmdale, CA	(19.9)	360	Somerville, MA	(28.5)			
NA	Parma, OH**	NA	367	South Bend, IN	(29.2)			

Source: CQ Press using reported data from the F.B.I. "Crime in the United States 2012"

*Property crimes are offenses of burglary, larceny-theft, and motor vehicle theft. Attempts are included.

**Not available.

68. Percent Change in Property Crime Rate: 2008 to 2012 (continued)
National Percent Change = 11.1% Decrease*

RANK	CITY	% CHANGE	RANK	CITY	% CHANGE	RANK	CITY	% CHANGE
1	Antioch, CA	60.1	74	Wilmington, NC	0.1	149	Killeen, TX	(7.9)
2	Spokane, WA	59.6	76	Houston, TX	0.0	149	Lakeland, FL	(7.9)
3	Rialto, CA	56.6	77	Thousand Oaks, CA	(0.2)	149	Las Cruces, NM	(7.9)
4	Medford, OR	47.2	78	Moreno Valley, CA	(0.3)	152	Indianapolis, IN	(8.1)
5	Redding, CA	38.1	79	Kenosha, WI	(0.4)	152	Louisville, KY	(8.1)
6	Spokane Valley, WA	31.7	80	Hawthorne, CA	(0.8)	154	Hemet, CA	(8.2)
7	Gary, IN	28.3	81	Denton, TX	(1.0)	155	Baldwin Park, CA	(8.3)
8	St. Joseph, MO	28.0	81	Irvine, CA	(1.0)	155	Salem, OR	(8.3)
9	Sioux City, IA	27.2	83	Tyler, TX	(1.1)	157	Flint, MI	(8.5)
10	Huntington Beach, CA	25.5	83	Yuma, AZ	(1.1)	157	West Jordan, UT	(8.5)
11	Sioux Falls, SD	25.4	85	Detroit, MI	(1.2)	159	Livermore, CA	(8.6)
12	San Jose, CA	23.6	85	Garden Grove, CA	(1.2)	159	Madison, WI	(8.6)
13	Oakland, CA	23.2	87	Wichita, KS	(1.3)	161	Nampa, ID	(8.7)
14	Glendale, AZ	22.4	88	Corona, CA	(1.4)	162	Fullerton, CA	(8.9)
15	Clovis, CA	20.3	88	Palm Bay, FL	(1.4)	163	Green Bay, WI	(9.2)
16	Rancho Cucamon., CA	19.4	90	Mission Viejo, CA	(1.7)	164	West Palm Beach, FL	(9.3)
17	Santa Barbara, CA	18.4	91	Fort Smith, AR	(1.8)	165	Concord, CA	(9.4)
18	Toms River Twnshp, NJ	18.0	92	Edinburg, TX	(1.9)	165	Greeley, CO	(9.4)
19	Anaheim, CA	17.1	93	St. Paul, MN	(2.0)	167	Allen, TX	(9.5)
19	Costa Mesa, CA	17.1	94	Tustin, CA	(2.1)	167	Orange, CA	(9.5)
21	Gresham, OR	16.5	95	Worcester, MA	(2.2)	169	Fort Wayne, IN	(9.7)
22	Hesperia, CA	15.7	96	Akron, OH	(2.4)	169	New Bedford, MA	(9.7)
23	Merced, CA	15.6	96	Columbia, MO	(2.4)	171	Virginia Beach, VA	(9.9)
24	Denver, CO	14.0	98	Colorado Springs, CO	(2.5)	172	Minneapolis, MN	(10.0)
25	Lawton, OK	13.5	99	Joliet, IL	(2.7)	172	Sunnyvale, CA	(10.0)
26	Lake Forest, CA	12.9	100	Livonia, MI	(2.9)	174	Edmond, OK	(10.1)
27	Ventura, CA	12.7	101	Chino, CA	(3.2)	175	Portsmouth, VA	(10.2)
28	Indio, CA	12.5	102	Baltimore, MD	(3.3)	176	Chicago, IL	(10.4)
29	Murrieta, CA	12.3	102	Des Moines, IA	(3.3)	177	Newport Beach, CA	(10.5)
29	Santa Monica, CA	12.3	102	Overland Park, KS	(3.3)	177	Norfolk, VA	(10.5)
31	Fresno, CA	9.7	102	Richmond, CA	(3.3)	179	Sterling Heights, MI	(10.6)
32	Billings, MT	9.6	106	Pompano Beach, FL	(3.4)	180	Atlanta, GA	(10.7)
33	Evansville, IN	9.5	107	Coral Springs, FL	(3.5)	180	Lawrence, MA	(10.7)
34	Whittier, CA	9.1	107	Davie, FL	(3.5)	182	El Monte, CA	(10.8)
35	Fayetteville, AR	8.3	107	Meridian, ID	(3.5)	183	Chesapeake, VA	(11.1)
36	Santa Ana, CA	8.2	110	Lakewood, CA	(3.7)	183	Duluth, MN	(11.1)
37	Long Beach, CA	8.1	110	Portland, OR	(3.7)	183	Largo, FL	(11.1)
38	Manchester, NH	7.8	110	Raleigh, NC	(3.7)	183	San Marcos, CA	(11.1)
38	Pasadena, TX	7.8	110	Springfield, MO	(3.7)	183	Topeka, KS	(11.1)
40	Lakewood, CO	7.4	114	Dayton, OH	(3.9)	188	Clinton Twnshp, MI	(11.2)
40	Richmond, VA	7.4	114	Hampton, VA	(3.9)	189	Troy, MI	(11.3)
42	Anchorage, AK	7.2	116	Bloomington, MN	(4.3)	190	Aurora, CO	(11.4)
43	Carson, CA	7.1	116	Temecula, CA	(4.3)	191	Albuquerque, NM	(11.5)
44	Omaha, NE	6.8	118	Lincoln, NE	(4.8)	191	Henderson, NV	(11.5)
45	Cleveland, OH	6.7	118	Washington, DC	(4.8)	193	Lansing, MI	(11.6)
45	Hamilton Twnshp, NJ	6.7	120	Ontario, CA	(5.0)	193	Rochester, MN	(11.6)
47	Hollywood, FL	6.0	121	Baton Rouge, LA	(5.2)	195	Inglewood, CA	(11.7)
48	Westminster, CA	5.4	122	Abilene, TX	(5.3)	196	Kansas City, MO	(11.8)
49	Newark, NJ	4.9	122	Fontana, CA	(5.3)	196	Odessa, TX	(11.8)
50	Modesto, CA	4.3	124	Round Rock, TX	(5.5)	196	Roanoke, VA	(11.8)
50	San Francisco, CA	4.3	125	Arvada, CO	(5.6)	196	Winston-Salem, NC	(11.8)
52	San Bernardino, CA	3.9	126	Alhambra, CA	(5.7)	200	Jackson, MS	(11.9)
53	Miami, FL	3.6	127	Montgomery, AL	(6.0)	201	Sugar Land, TX	(12.1)
54	Federal Way, WA	3.5	127	Santa Rosa, CA	(6.0)	202	Austin, TX	(12.2)
54	Pomona, CA	3.5	129	Boulder, CO	(6.1)	203	Centennial, CO	(12.3)
56	Bloomington, IN	3.3	129	Mesquite, TX	(6.1)	203	Lawrence, KS	(12.3)
57	Victorville, CA	2.7	129	Vacaville, CA	(6.1)	203	Tulsa, OK	(12.3)
58	Fort Lauderdale, FL	2.4	132	Springfield, MA	(6.3)	206	Tallahassee, FL	(12.4)
58	Norwalk, CA	2.4	133	Alameda, CA	(6.4)	207	Ann Arbor, MI	(12.5)
60	Oceanside, CA	1.8	133	Danbury, CT	(6.4)	207	Carrollton, TX	(12.5)
61	Santa Clara, CA	1.4	135	Riverside, CA	(6.6)	207	Garland, TX	(12.5)
62	Knoxville, TN	1.1	136	Cambridge, MA	(6.7)	207	Oxnard, CA	(12.5)
62	Vallejo, CA	1.1	136	Lafayette, LA	(6.7)	207	Westland, MI	(12.5)
62	Vancouver, WA	1.1	136	Ogden, UT	(6.7)	212	Boise, ID	(12.7)
65	Hayward, CA	1.0	139	McKinney, TX	(6.9)	213	Mobile, AL	(12.8)
65	Little Rock, AR	1.0	140	Buena Park, CA	(7.0)	214	Bellingham, WA	(13.0)
67	Miami Beach, FL	0.9	141	South Gate, CA	(7.1)	214	Cranston, RI	(13.0)
68	Oklahoma City, OK	0.8	142	Seattle, WA	(7.2)	214	Sacramento, CA	(13.0)
69	Bakersfield, CA	0.7	143	Lubbock, TX	(7.4)	217	Deerfield Beach, FL	(13.1)
69	Cincinnati, OH	0.7	143	Simi Valley, CA	(7.4)	218	Los Angeles, CA	(13.3)
71	Erie, PA	0.6	145	Broken Arrow, OK	(7.5)	219	Richardson, TX	(13.4)
71	Paterson, NJ	0.6	146	Visalia, CA	(7.6)	219	Stamford, CT	(13.4)
73	Trenton, NJ	0.3	147	Scranton, PA	(7.8)	221	Yakima, WA	(13.6)
74	Asheville, NC	0.1	147	Shreveport, LA	(7.8)	222	Norwalk, CT	(13.8)

RANK	CITY	% CHANGE	RANK	CITY	% CHANGE	RANK	CITY	% CHANGE
223	Escondido, CA	(13.9)	294	Las Vegas, NV	(20.1)	370	Sparks, NV	(29.4)
223	Macon, GA	(13.9)	294	Tracy, CA	(20.1)	370	Vista, CA	(29.4)
223	Salinas, CA	(13.9)	294	West Valley, UT	(20.1)	373	Jersey City, NJ	(29.5)
226	Norman, OK	(14.0)	300	Rockford, IL	(20.3)	373	Mission, TX	(29.5)
226	Orem, UT	(14.0)	301	Everett, WA	(20.4)	375	Clarksville, TN	(29.6)
228	Daly City, CA	(14.2)	302	O'Fallon, MO	(20.5)	376	Chula Vista, CA	(30.2)
229	Clearwater, FL	(14.4)	303	Bellevue, WA	(20.6)	377	Davenport, IA	(30.4)
229	Lee's Summit, MO	(14.4)	303	Brick Twnshp, NJ	(20.6)	378	Compton, CA	(30.6)
231	Pearland, TX	(14.6)	303	Plantation, FL	(20.6)	379	Athens-Clarke, GA	(30.7)
232	Avondale, AZ	(14.7)	306	Redwood City, CA	(20.7)	379	High Point, NC	(30.7)
232	Philadelphia, PA	(14.7)	306	Warwick, RI	(20.7)	381	Wichita Falls, TX	(30.9)
234	Alexandria, VA	(14.8)	308	North Charleston, SC	(20.9)	382	Greensboro, NC	(31.0)
234	Hillsboro, OR	(14.8)	308	St. Petersburg, FL	(20.9)	383	Dearborn, MI	(32.1)
236	Naperville, IL	(15.1)	310	Tuscaloosa, AL	(21.0)	384	Savannah, GA	(32.3)
237	Sunrise, FL	(15.3)	311	Birmingham, AL	(21.1)	385	Greenville, NC	(32.4)
237	Upland, CA	(15.3)	312	Memphis, TN	(21.2)	385	Laredo, TX	(32.4)
239	Downey, CA	(15.4)	313	Cedar Rapids, IA	(21.5)	387	College Station, TX	(32.5)
239	Lowell, MA	(15.4)	313	Phoenix, AZ	(21.5)	388	Carmel, IN	(32.8)
239	Providence, RI	(15.4)	315	Boston, MA	(21.6)	389	Charleston, SC	(33.0)
239	West Covina, CA	(15.4)	315	Midland, TX	(21.6)	389	Edison Twnshp, NJ	(33.0)
243	Lynn, MA	(15.8)	315	Reading, PA	(21.6)	391	Pembroke Pines, FL	(33.4)
243	Quincy, MA	(15.8)	315	Upper Darby Twnshp, PA	(21.6)	392	McAllen, TX	(33.5)
243	Racine, WI	(15.8)	319	Chino Hills, CA	(21.9)	393	Roswell, GA	(33.6)
246	League City, TX	(16.0)	319	Nashville, TN	(21.9)	394	Irving, TX	(34.1)
246	Pittsburgh, PA	(16.0)	319	Westminster, CO	(21.9)	395	Hialeah, FL	(34.2)
246	Provo, UT	(16.0)	322	Fishers, IN	(22.0)	396	Charlotte, NC	(34.8)
246	Torrance, CA	(16.0)	323	Bellflower, CA	(22.1)	397	El Cajon, CA	(34.9)
250	Santa Clarita, CA	(16.1)	323	Bridgeport, CT	(22.1)	398	Bryan, TX	(37.4)
251	Fort Worth, TX	(16.2)	325	Gainesville, FL	(22.2)	399	Grand Prairie, TX	(38.0)
251	Pasadena, CA	(16.2)	326	Fall River, MA	(22.4)	400	Tampa, FL	(38.4)
253	Peoria, AZ	(16.3)	327	Eugene, OR	(22.5)	401	Lakewood Twnshp, NJ	(41.4)
254	Burbank, CA	(16.4)	328	Bethlehem, PA	(22.6)	NA	Albany, GA**	NA
254	Citrus Heights, CA	(16.4)	329	Longview, TX	(22.7)	NA	Albany, NY**	NA
254	Rio Rancho, NM	(16.4)	330	Newton, MA	(22.8)	NA	Allentown, PA**	NA
257	Salt Lake City, UT	(16.7)	331	Orlando, FL	(22.9)	NA	Amherst, NY**	NA
257	Stockton, CA	(16.7)	332	Plano, TX	(23.0)	NA	Arlington Heights, IL**	NA
259	Hartford, CT	(16.9)	333	Boca Raton, FL	(23.1)	NA	Bloomington, IL**	NA
259	Milwaukee, WI	(16.9)	334	North Las Vegas, NV	(23.2)	NA	Brockton, MA**	NA
261	Hammond, IN	(17.0)	335	Newport News, VA	(23.5)	NA	Buffalo, NY**	NA
261	Independence, MO	(17.0)	336	Farmington Hills, MI	(23.7)	NA	Champaign, IL**	NA
261	San Antonio, TX	(17.0)	337	Sandy, UT	(23.8)	NA	Chandler, AZ**	NA
264	Tacoma, WA	(17.1)	338	San Mateo, CA	(24.3)	NA	Cheektowaga, NY**	NA
265	Beaumont, TX	(17.5)	338	Waco, TX	(24.3)	NA	Cicero, IL**	NA
265	Fargo, ND	(17.5)	340	El Paso, TX	(24.5)	NA	Clarkstown, NY**	NA
267	Amarillo, TX	(17.6)	341	Clifton, NJ	(24.7)	NA	Colonie, NY**	NA
267	Murfreesboro, TN	(17.6)	342	Glendale, CA	(25.0)	NA	Decatur, IL**	NA
269	San Leandro, CA	(17.9)	343	Elizabeth, NJ	(25.1)	NA	Greece, NY**	NA
270	Chico, CA	(18.1)	344	Sandy Springs, GA	(25.3)	NA	Johns Creek, GA**	NA
271	Elk Grove, CA	(18.2)	345	San Diego, CA	(25.4)	NA	Jurupa Valley, CA**	NA
271	Huntsville, AL	(18.2)	346	Arlington, TX	(25.7)	NA	Kansas City, KS**	NA
271	Kent, WA	(18.2)	347	Dallas, TX	(26.3)	NA	Lexington, KY**	NA
271	Scottsdale, AZ	(18.2)	348	Columbus, GA	(26.4)	NA	Longmont, CO**	NA
275	Mesa, AZ	(18.3)	348	Roseville, CA	(26.4)	NA	Menifee, CA**	NA
276	Fort Collins, CO	(18.4)	350	Berkeley, CA	(26.7)	NA	Nashua, NH**	NA
276	Napa, CA	(18.4)	351	Grand Rapids, MI	(26.9)	NA	New Haven, CT**	NA
278	Elgin, IL	(18.5)	352	Corpus Christi, TX	(27.0)	NA	New Rochelle, NY**	NA
278	Surprise, AZ	(18.5)	353	St. George, UT	(27.2)	NA	New York, NY**	NA
280	Kennewick, WA	(18.6)	354	Reno, NV	(27.5)	NA	Olathe, KS**	NA
281	Fayetteville, NC	(18.8)	355	Cary, NC	(27.6)	NA	Parma, OH**	NA
282	Tempe, AZ	(18.9)	355	Port St. Lucie, FL	(27.6)	NA	Peoria, IL**	NA
283	Carlsbad, CA	(19.0)	357	Mountain View, CA	(27.7)	NA	Pueblo, CO**	NA
284	Durham, NC	(19.1)	358	Jacksonville, FL	(28.0)	NA	Ramapo, NY**	NA
284	Hoover, AL	(19.1)	359	Aurora, IL	(28.4)	NA	Renton, WA**	NA
286	St. Louis, MO	(19.2)	360	Somerville, MA	(28.5)	NA	Rochester, NY**	NA
286	Waterbury, CT	(19.2)	361	New Orleans, LA	(28.6)	NA	Springfield, IL**	NA
288	Fairfield, CA	(19.3)	362	Lancaster, CA	(28.7)	NA	Syracuse, NY**	NA
289	Melbourne, FL	(19.5)	363	Cape Coral, FL	(28.8)	NA	Thornton, CO**	NA
290	Santa Maria, CA	(19.6)	363	Miramar, FL	(28.8)	NA	Toledo, OH**	NA
291	Brownsville, TX	(19.7)	365	Beaverton, OR	(29.1)	NA	Tucson, AZ**	NA
292	Palmdale, CA	(19.9)	365	Lynchburg, VA	(29.1)	NA	Warren, MI**	NA
293	Camden, NJ	(20.0)	367	Miami Gardens, FL	(29.2)	NA	Waukegan, IL**	NA
294	Brooklyn Park, MN	(20.1)	367	South Bend, IN	(29.2)	NA	Yonkers, NY**	NA
294	Fremont, CA	(20.1)	367	Woodbridge Twnshp, NJ	(29.2)			
294	Frisco, TX	(20.1)	370	Gilbert, AZ	(29.4)			

Source: CQ Press using reported data from the F.B.I. "Crime in the United States 2012"

*Property crimes are offenses of burglary, larceny-theft, and motor vehicle theft. Attempts are included.

**Not available.

69. Burglaries in 2012
National Total = 2,103,787 Burglaries*

RANK	CITY	BURGLARY	RANK	CITY	BURGLARY	RANK	CITY	BURGLARY
188	Abilene, TX	1,037	384	Chino Hills, CA	350	194	Gainesville, FL	1,009
58	Akron, OH	3,429	313	Chino, CA	562	255	Garden Grove, CA	761
404	Alameda, CA	296	215	Chula Vista, CA	926	93	Garland, TX	2,218
140	Albany, GA	1,408	267	Cicero, IL	711	120	Gary, IN	1,634
229	Albany, NY	887	32	Cincinnati, OH	5,483	261	Gilbert, AZ	726
24	Albuquerque, NM	6,677	291	Citrus Heights, CA	625	76	Glendale, AZ	2,847
410	Alexandria, VA	281	439	Clarkstown, NY	107	327	Glendale, CA	516
394	Alhambra, CA	325	200	Clarksville, TN	976	145	Grand Prairie, TX	1,298
157	Allentown, PA	1,248	218	Clearwater, FL	919	105	Grand Rapids, MI	1,917
426	Allen, TX	215	14	Cleveland, OH	9,740	359	Greece, NY	410
97	Amarillo, TX	2,087	380	Clifton, NJ	358	317	Greeley, CO	542
427	Amherst, NY	214	343	Clinton Twnshp, MI	477	282	Green Bay, WI	659
124	Anaheim, CA	1,605	203	Clovis, CA	955	61	Greensboro, NC	3,345
166	Anchorage, AK	1,158	305	College Station, TX	576	171	Greenville, NC	1,130
265	Ann Arbor, MI	714	427	Colonie, NY	214	230	Gresham, OR	886
116	Antioch, CA	1,741	55	Colorado Springs, CO	3,641	342	Hamilton Twnshp, NJ	489
435	Arlington Heights, IL	140	248	Columbia, MO	784	212	Hammond, IN	936
56	Arlington, TX	3,543	79	Columbus, GA	2,709	256	Hampton, VA	758
368	Arvada, CO	390	308	Compton, CA	574	182	Hartford, CT	1,050
257	Asheville, NC	742	242	Concord, CA	829	306	Hawthorne, CA	575
167	Athens-Clarke, GA	1,149	310	Coral Springs, FL	572	172	Hayward, CA	1,109
27	Atlanta, GA	6,192	232	Corona, CA	861	181	Hemet, CA	1,052
113	Aurora, CO	1,791	87	Corpus Christi, TX	2,452	140	Henderson, NV	1,408
208	Aurora, IL	944	279	Costa Mesa, CA	668	219	Hesperia, CA	917
19	Austin, TX	7,244	367	Cranston, RI	392	183	Hialeah, FL	1,048
274	Avondale, AZ	685	6	Dallas, TX	16,090	162	High Point, NC	1,188
37	Bakersfield, CA	4,994	364	Daly City, CA	395	395	Hillsboro, OR	323
392	Baldwin Park, CA	335	407	Danbury, CT	287	103	Hollywood, FL	1,958
16	Baltimore, MD	7,770	227	Davenport, IA	890	366	Hoover, AL	393
52	Baton Rouge, LA	3,826	280	Davie, FL	667	1	Houston, TX	26,630
109	Beaumont, TX	1,828	67	Dayton, OH	3,043	246	Huntington Beach, CA	797
430	Beaverton, OR	196	349	Dearborn, MI	462	95	Huntsville, AL	2,165
274	Bellevue, WA	685	217	Decatur, IL	921	155	Independence, MO	1,253
358	Bellflower, CA	417	301	Deerfield Beach, FL	594	8	Indianapolis, IN	14,774
296	Bellingham, WA	614	289	Denton, TX	632	241	Indio, CA	836
201	Berkeley, CA	971	35	Denver, CO	5,129	284	Inglewood, CA	646
370	Bethlehem, PA	377	85	Des Moines, IA	2,514	312	Irvine, CA	570
247	Billings, MT	793	10	Detroit, MI	13,488	151	Irving, TX	1,277
40	Birmingham, AL	4,704	278	Downey, CA	670	18	Jacksonville, FL	7,632
381	Bloomington, IL	357	285	Duluth, MN	642	47	Jackson, MS	4,124
293	Bloomington, IN	622	64	Durham, NC	3,284	138	Jersey City, NJ	1,426
421	Bloomington, MN	227	234	Edinburg, TX	857	440	Johns Creek, GA	104
341	Boca Raton, FL	491	388	Edison Twnshp, NJ	341	206	Joliet, IL	954
221	Boise, ID	913	401	Edmond, OK	303	260	Jurupa Valley, CA	731
62	Boston, MA	3,325	338	El Cajon, CA	493	114	Kansas City, KS	1,772
347	Boulder, CO	472	311	El Monte, CA	571	22	Kansas City, MO	6,964
415	Brick Twnshp, NJ	265	111	El Paso, TX	1,826	352	Kennewick, WA	450
142	Bridgeport, CT	1,377	381	Elgin, IL	357	269	Kenosha, WI	707
244	Brockton, MA	815	199	Elizabeth, NJ	987	158	Kent, WA	1,239
372	Broken Arrow, OK	374	277	Elk Grove, CA	674	134	Killeen, TX	1,498
338	Brooklyn Park, MN	493	175	Erie, PA	1,095	74	Knoxville, TN	2,882
169	Brownsville, TX	1,145	254	Escondido, CA	764	143	Lafayette, LA	1,330
335	Bryan, TX	496	133	Eugene, OR	1,515	421	Lake Forest, CA	227
387	Buena Park, CA	342	170	Evansville, IN	1,132	146	Lakeland, FL	1,296
49	Buffalo, NY	3,976	165	Everett, WA	1,165	414	Lakewood Twnshp, NJ	274
369	Burbank, CA	383	276	Fairfield, CA	676	374	Lakewood, CA	371
332	Cambridge, MA	502	251	Fall River, MA	774	219	Lakewood, CO	917
177	Camden, NJ	1,089	351	Fargo, ND	451	186	Lancaster, CA	1,043
233	Cape Coral, FL	860	420	Farmington Hills, MI	231	144	Lansing, MI	1,307
334	Carlsbad, CA	497	330	Fayetteville, AR	504	117	Laredo, TX	1,718
438	Carmel, IN	113	48	Fayetteville, NC	4,109	308	Largo, FL	574
252	Carrollton, TX	771	208	Federal Way, WA	944	198	Las Cruces, NM	991
299	Carson, CA	601	441	Fishers, IN	101	9	Las Vegas, NV	14,220
375	Cary, NC	370	69	Flint, MI	2,979	298	Lawrence, KS	604
202	Cedar Rapids, IA	966	174	Fontana, CA	1,099	319	Lawrence, MA	536
412	Centennial, CO	277	300	Fort Collins, CO	598	129	Lawton, OK	1,560
263	Champaign, IL	722	72	Fort Lauderdale, FL	2,951	403	League City, TX	299
168	Chandler, AZ	1,147	179	Fort Smith, AR	1,064	416	Lee's Summit, MO	263
372	Charleston, SC	374	101	Fort Wayne, IN	2,025	75	Lexington, KY	2,854
17	Charlotte, NC	7,761	15	Fort Worth, TX	8,442	123	Lincoln, NE	1,616
389	Cheektowaga, NY	338	164	Fremont, CA	1,176	46	Little Rock, AR	4,244
190	Chesapeake, VA	1,034	29	Fresno, CA	5,902	399	Livermore, CA	310
2	Chicago, IL	22,748	355	Frisco, TX	440	395	Livonia, MI	323
249	Chico, CA	778	257	Fullerton, CA	742	53	Long Beach, CA	3,799

RANK	CITY	BURGLARY	RANK	CITY	BURGLARY	RANK	CITY	BURGLARY
379	Longmont, CO	359	226	Pasadena, CA	891	359	South Gate, CA	410
207	Longview, TX	950	195	Pasadena, TX	999	297	Sparks, NV	609
5	Los Angeles, CA	16,388	122	Paterson, NJ	1,619	228	Spokane Valley, WA	889
20	Louisville, KY	7,008	412	Pearland, TX	277	51	Spokane, WA	3,827
236	Lowell, MA	849	239	Pembroke Pines, FL	846	119	Springfield, IL	1,670
66	Lubbock, TX	3,099	213	Peoria, AZ	929	89	Springfield, MA	2,317
377	Lynchburg, VA	365	139	Peoria, IL	1,420	94	Springfield, MO	2,215
272	Lynn, MA	698	12	Philadelphia, PA	12,004	405	Stamford, CT	290
109	Macon, GA	1,828	4	Phoenix, AZ	17,912	381	Sterling Heights, MI	357
125	Madison, WI	1,601	84	Pittsburgh, PA	2,537	44	Stockton, CA	4,416
236	Manchester, NH	849	175	Plano, TX	1,095	400	St. George, UT	307
331	McAllen, TX	503	270	Plantation, FL	702	197	St. Joseph, MO	993
340	McKinney, TX	492	222	Pomona, CA	901	38	St. Louis, MO	4,986
343	Medford, OR	477	150	Pompano Beach, FL	1,283	65	St. Paul, MN	3,150
283	Melbourne, FL	648	243	Port St. Lucie, FL	816	73	St. Petersburg, FL	2,933
11	Memphis, TN	12,575	43	Portland, OR	4,471	406	Sugar Land, TX	289
329	Menifee, CA	507	160	Portsmouth, VA	1,218	323	Sunnyvale, CA	524
203	Merced, CA	955	104	Providence, RI	1,929	245	Sunrise, FL	799
424	Meridian, ID	220	402	Provo, UT	301	324	Surprise, AZ	519
81	Mesa, AZ	2,681	107	Pueblo, CO	1,895	106	Syracuse, NY	1,896
128	Mesquite, TX	1,568	336	Quincy, MA	495	71	Tacoma, WA	2,965
183	Miami Beach, FL	1,048	173	Racine, WI	1,101	82	Tallahassee, FL	2,630
148	Miami Gardens, FL	1,290	68	Raleigh, NC	3,036	86	Tampa, FL	2,476
45	Miami, FL	4,255	436	Ramapo, NY	137	302	Temecula, CA	588
314	Midland, TX	559	135	Rancho Cucamon., CA	1,460	156	Tempe, AZ	1,250
21	Milwaukee, WI	6,977	137	Reading, PA	1,447	345	Thornton, CO	476
39	Minneapolis, MN	4,782	178	Redding, CA	1,088	411	Thousand Oaks, CA	278
231	Miramar, FL	862	322	Redwood City, CA	526	23	Toledo, OH	6,729
425	Mission Viejo, CA	216	121	Reno, NV	1,633	287	Toms River Twnshp, NJ	640
357	Mission, TX	423	225	Renton, WA	897	151	Topeka, KS	1,277
78	Mobile, AL	2,796	224	Rialto, CA	898	321	Torrance, CA	529
83	Modesto, CA	2,571	272	Richardson, TX	698	409	Tracy, CA	284
60	Montgomery, AL	3,409	132	Richmond, CA	1,537	147	Trenton, NJ	1,291
102	Moreno Valley, CA	2,018	100	Richmond, VA	2,030	432	Troy, MI	181
434	Mountain View, CA	178	378	Rio Rancho, NM	364	36	Tucson, AZ	5,021
216	Murfreesboro, TN	923	91	Riverside, CA	2,247	26	Tulsa, OK	6,235
361	Murrieta, CA	408	210	Roanoke, VA	940	163	Tuscaloosa, AL	1,182
328	Nampa, ID	510	336	Rochester, MN	495	419	Tustin, CA	240
385	Napa, CA	349	70	Rochester, NY	2,978	193	Tyler, TX	1,025
417	Naperville, IL	255	92	Rockford, IL	2,224	288	Upland, CA	633
371	Nashua, NH	375	324	Roseville, CA	519	423	Upper Darby Twnshp, PA	223
31	Nashville, TN	5,736	362	Roswell, GA	399	397	Vacaville, CA	319
213	New Bedford, MA	929	391	Round Rock, TX	336	80	Vallejo, CA	2,688
136	New Haven, CT	1,451	42	Sacramento, CA	4,474	185	Vancouver, WA	1,044
59	New Orleans, LA	3,423	186	Salem, OR	1,043	249	Ventura, CA	778
433	New Rochelle, NY	180	160	Salinas, CA	1,218	108	Victorville, CA	1,837
3	New York, NY	18,635	112	Salt Lake City, UT	1,824	126	Virginia Beach, VA	1,573
96	Newark, NJ	2,144	7	San Antonio, TX	15,668	159	Visalia, CA	1,227
354	Newport Beach, CA	445	77	San Bernardino, CA	2,809	356	Vista, CA	438
192	Newport News, VA	1,029	29	San Diego, CA	5,902	131	Waco, TX	1,550
431	Newton, MA	185	33	San Francisco, CA	5,317	195	Warren, MI	999
90	Norfolk, VA	2,261	34	San Jose, CA	5,206	393	Warwick, RI	334
290	Norman, OK	629	271	San Leandro, CA	699	57	Washington, DC	3,519
235	North Charleston, SC	854	376	San Marcos, CA	366	281	Waterbury, CT	662
130	North Las Vegas, NV	1,557	408	San Mateo, CA	285	291	Waukegan, IL	625
318	Norwalk, CA	539	268	Sandy Springs, GA	709	316	West Covina, CA	546
418	Norwalk, CT	250	350	Sandy, UT	453	346	West Jordan, UT	474
28	Oakland, CA	6,168	191	Santa Ana, CA	1,032	149	West Palm Beach, FL	1,289
240	Oceanside, CA	841	315	Santa Barbara, CA	558	210	West Valley, UT	940
253	Odessa, TX	770	304	Santa Clara, CA	584	306	Westland, MI	575
437	O'Fallon, MO	125	295	Santa Clarita, CA	616	348	Westminster, CA	466
259	Ogden, UT	734	266	Santa Maria, CA	712	364	Westminster, CO	395
13	Oklahoma City, OK	9,854	303	Santa Monica, CA	586	353	Whittier, CA	449
398	Olathe, KS	315	262	Santa Rosa, CA	725	153	Wichita Falls, TX	1,259
63	Omaha, NE	3,311	98	Savannah, GA	2,083	50	Wichita, KS	3,919
180	Ontario, CA	1,058	154	Scottsdale, AZ	1,255	118	Wilmington, NC	1,694
333	Orange, CA	500	286	Scranton, PA	641	41	Winston-Salem, NC	4,529
429	Orem, UT	203	25	Seattle, WA	6,523	389	Woodbridge Twnshp, NJ	338
54	Orlando, FL	3,778	88	Shreveport, LA	2,425	99	Worcester, MA	2,040
326	Overland Park, KS	517	363	Simi Valley, CA	398	126	Yakima, WA	1,573
238	Oxnard, CA	848	294	Sioux City, IA	621	320	Yonkers, NY	535
264	Palm Bay, FL	719	223	Sioux Falls, SD	899	203	Yuma, AZ	955
189	Palmdale, CA	1,035	386	Somerville, MA	348			
442	Parma, OH	47	115	South Bend, IN	1,744			

Source: Reported data from the F.B.I. "Crime in the United States 2012"

*Burglary is the unlawful entry of a structure to commit a felony or theft. Attempts are included.

69. Burglaries in 2012 (continued)
National Total = 2,103,787 Burglaries*

RANK	CITY	BURGLARY	RANK	CITY	BURGLARY	RANK	CITY	BURGLARY
1	Houston, TX	26,630	75	Lexington, KY	2,854	149	West Palm Beach, FL	1,289
2	Chicago, IL	22,748	76	Glendale, AZ	2,847	150	Pompano Beach, FL	1,283
3	New York, NY	18,635	77	San Bernardino, CA	2,809	151	Irving, TX	1,277
4	Phoenix, AZ	17,912	78	Mobile, AL	2,796	151	Topeka, KS	1,277
5	Los Angeles, CA	16,388	79	Columbus, GA	2,709	153	Wichita Falls, TX	1,259
6	Dallas, TX	16,090	80	Vallejo, CA	2,688	154	Scottsdale, AZ	1,255
7	San Antonio, TX	15,668	81	Mesa, AZ	2,681	155	Independence, MO	1,253
8	Indianapolis, IN	14,774	82	Tallahassee, FL	2,630	156	Tempe, AZ	1,250
9	Las Vegas, NV	14,220	83	Modesto, CA	2,571	157	Allentown, PA	1,248
10	Detroit, MI	13,488	84	Pittsburgh, PA	2,537	158	Kent, WA	1,239
11	Memphis, TN	12,575	85	Des Moines, IA	2,514	159	Visalia, CA	1,227
12	Philadelphia, PA	12,004	86	Tampa, FL	2,476	160	Portsmouth, VA	1,218
13	Oklahoma City, OK	9,854	87	Corpus Christi, TX	2,452	160	Salinas, CA	1,218
14	Cleveland, OH	9,740	88	Shreveport, LA	2,425	162	High Point, NC	1,188
15	Fort Worth, TX	8,442	89	Springfield, MA	2,317	163	Tuscaloosa, AL	1,182
16	Baltimore, MD	7,770	90	Norfolk, VA	2,261	164	Fremont, CA	1,176
17	Charlotte, NC	7,761	91	Riverside, CA	2,247	165	Everett, WA	1,165
18	Jacksonville, FL	7,632	92	Rockford, IL	2,224	166	Anchorage, AK	1,158
19	Austin, TX	7,244	93	Garland, TX	2,218	167	Athens-Clarke, GA	1,149
20	Louisville, KY	7,008	94	Springfield, MO	2,215	168	Chandler, AZ	1,147
21	Milwaukee, WI	6,977	95	Huntsville, AL	2,165	169	Brownsville, TX	1,145
22	Kansas City, MO	6,964	96	Newark, NJ	2,144	170	Evansville, IN	1,132
23	Toledo, OH	6,729	97	Amarillo, TX	2,087	171	Greenville, NC	1,130
24	Albuquerque, NM	6,677	98	Savannah, GA	2,083	172	Hayward, CA	1,109
25	Seattle, WA	6,523	99	Worcester, MA	2,040	173	Racine, WI	1,101
26	Tulsa, OK	6,235	100	Richmond, VA	2,030	174	Fontana, CA	1,099
27	Atlanta, GA	6,192	101	Fort Wayne, IN	2,025	175	Erie, PA	1,095
28	Oakland, CA	6,168	102	Moreno Valley, CA	2,018	175	Plano, TX	1,095
29	Fresno, CA	5,902	103	Hollywood, FL	1,958	177	Camden, NJ	1,089
29	San Diego, CA	5,902	104	Providence, RI	1,929	178	Redding, CA	1,088
31	Nashville, TN	5,736	105	Grand Rapids, MI	1,917	179	Fort Smith, AR	1,064
32	Cincinnati, OH	5,483	106	Syracuse, NY	1,896	180	Ontario, CA	1,058
33	San Francisco, CA	5,317	107	Pueblo, CO	1,895	181	Hemet, CA	1,052
34	San Jose, CA	5,206	108	Victorville, CA	1,837	182	Hartford, CT	1,050
35	Denver, CO	5,129	109	Beaumont, TX	1,828	183	Hialeah, FL	1,048
36	Tucson, AZ	5,021	109	Macon, GA	1,828	183	Miami Beach, FL	1,048
37	Bakersfield, CA	4,994	111	El Paso, TX	1,826	185	Vancouver, WA	1,044
38	St. Louis, MO	4,986	112	Salt Lake City, UT	1,824	186	Lancaster, CA	1,043
39	Minneapolis, MN	4,782	113	Aurora, CO	1,791	186	Salem, OR	1,043
40	Birmingham, AL	4,704	114	Kansas City, KS	1,772	188	Abilene, TX	1,037
41	Winston-Salem, NC	4,529	115	South Bend, IN	1,744	189	Palmdale, CA	1,035
42	Sacramento, CA	4,474	116	Antioch, CA	1,741	190	Chesapeake, VA	1,034
43	Portland, OR	4,471	117	Laredo, TX	1,718	191	Santa Ana, CA	1,032
44	Stockton, CA	4,416	118	Wilmington, NC	1,694	192	Newport News, VA	1,029
45	Miami, FL	4,255	119	Springfield, IL	1,670	193	Tyler, TX	1,025
46	Little Rock, AR	4,244	120	Gary, IN	1,634	194	Gainesville, FL	1,009
47	Jackson, MS	4,124	121	Reno, NV	1,633	195	Pasadena, TX	999
48	Fayetteville, NC	4,109	122	Paterson, NJ	1,619	195	Warren, MI	999
49	Buffalo, NY	3,976	123	Lincoln, NE	1,616	197	St. Joseph, MO	993
50	Wichita, KS	3,919	124	Anaheim, CA	1,605	198	Las Cruces, NM	991
51	Spokane, WA	3,827	125	Madison, WI	1,601	199	Elizabeth, NJ	987
52	Baton Rouge, LA	3,826	126	Virginia Beach, VA	1,573	200	Clarksville, TN	976
53	Long Beach, CA	3,799	126	Yakima, WA	1,573	201	Berkeley, CA	971
54	Orlando, FL	3,778	128	Mesquite, TX	1,568	202	Cedar Rapids, IA	966
55	Colorado Springs, CO	3,641	129	Lawton, OK	1,560	203	Clovis, CA	955
56	Arlington, TX	3,543	130	North Las Vegas, NV	1,557	203	Merced, CA	955
57	Washington, DC	3,519	131	Waco, TX	1,550	203	Yuma, AZ	955
58	Akron, OH	3,429	132	Richmond, CA	1,537	206	Joliet, IL	954
59	New Orleans, LA	3,423	133	Eugene, OR	1,515	207	Longview, TX	950
60	Montgomery, AL	3,409	134	Killeen, TX	1,498	208	Aurora, IL	944
61	Greensboro, NC	3,345	135	Rancho Cucamon., CA	1,460	208	Federal Way, WA	944
62	Boston, MA	3,325	136	New Haven, CT	1,451	210	Roanoke, VA	940
63	Omaha, NE	3,311	137	Reading, PA	1,447	210	West Valley, UT	940
64	Durham, NC	3,284	138	Jersey City, NJ	1,426	212	Hammond, IN	936
65	St. Paul, MN	3,150	139	Peoria, IL	1,420	213	New Bedford, MA	929
66	Lubbock, TX	3,099	140	Albany, GA	1,408	213	Peoria, AZ	929
67	Dayton, OH	3,043	140	Henderson, NV	1,408	215	Chula Vista, CA	926
68	Raleigh, NC	3,036	142	Bridgeport, CT	1,377	216	Murfreesboro, TN	923
69	Flint, MI	2,979	143	Lafayette, LA	1,330	217	Decatur, IL	921
70	Rochester, NY	2,978	144	Lansing, MI	1,307	218	Clearwater, FL	919
71	Tacoma, WA	2,965	145	Grand Prairie, TX	1,298	219	Hesperia, CA	917
72	Fort Lauderdale, FL	2,951	146	Lakeland, FL	1,296	219	Lakewood, CO	917
73	St. Petersburg, FL	2,933	147	Trenton, NJ	1,291	221	Boise, ID	913
74	Knoxville, TN	2,882	148	Miami Gardens, FL	1,290	222	Pomona, CA	901

RANK	CITY	BURGLARY	RANK	CITY	BURGLARY	RANK	CITY	BURGLARY
223	Sioux Falls, SD	899	297	Sparks, NV	609	371	Nashua, NH	375
224	Rialto, CA	898	298	Lawrence, KS	604	372	Broken Arrow, OK	374
225	Renton, WA	897	299	Carson, CA	601	372	Charleston, SC	374
226	Pasadena, CA	891	300	Fort Collins, CO	598	374	Lakewood, CA	371
227	Davenport, IA	890	301	Deerfield Beach, FL	594	375	Cary, NC	370
228	Spokane Valley, WA	889	302	Temecula, CA	588	376	San Marcos, CA	366
229	Albany, NY	887	303	Santa Monica, CA	586	377	Lynchburg, VA	365
230	Gresham, OR	886	304	Santa Clara, CA	584	378	Rio Rancho, NM	364
231	Miramar, FL	862	305	College Station, TX	576	379	Longmont, CO	359
232	Corona, CA	861	306	Hawthorne, CA	575	380	Clifton, NJ	358
233	Cape Coral, FL	860	306	Westland, MI	575	381	Bloomington, IL	357
234	Edinburg, TX	857	308	Compton, CA	574	381	Elgin, IL	357
235	North Charleston, SC	854	308	Largo, FL	574	381	Sterling Heights, MI	357
236	Lowell, MA	849	310	Coral Springs, FL	572	384	Chino Hills, CA	350
236	Manchester, NH	849	311	El Monte, CA	571	385	Napa, CA	349
238	Oxnard, CA	848	312	Irvine, CA	570	386	Somerville, MA	348
239	Pembroke Pines, FL	846	313	Chino, CA	562	387	Buena Park, CA	342
240	Oceanside, CA	841	314	Midland, TX	559	388	Edison Twnshp, NJ	341
241	Indio, CA	836	315	Santa Barbara, CA	558	389	Cheektowaga, NY	338
242	Concord, CA	829	316	West Covina, CA	546	389	Woodbridge Twnshp, NJ	338
243	Port St. Lucie, FL	816	317	Greeley, CO	542	391	Round Rock, TX	336
244	Brockton, MA	815	318	Norwalk, CA	539	392	Baldwin Park, CA	335
245	Sunrise, FL	799	319	Lawrence, MA	536	393	Warwick, RI	334
246	Huntington Beach, CA	797	320	Yonkers, NY	535	394	Alhambra, CA	325
247	Billings, MT	793	321	Torrance, CA	529	395	Hillsboro, OR	323
248	Columbia, MO	784	322	Redwood City, CA	526	395	Livonia, MI	323
249	Chico, CA	778	323	Sunnyvale, CA	524	397	Vacaville, CA	319
249	Ventura, CA	778	324	Roseville, CA	519	398	Olathe, KS	315
251	Fall River, MA	774	324	Surprise, AZ	519	399	Livermore, CA	310
252	Carrollton, TX	771	326	Overland Park, KS	517	400	St. George, UT	307
253	Odessa, TX	770	327	Glendale, CA	516	401	Edmond, OK	303
254	Escondido, CA	764	328	Nampa, ID	510	402	Provo, UT	301
255	Garden Grove, CA	761	329	Menifee, CA	507	403	League City, TX	299
256	Hampton, VA	758	330	Fayetteville, AR	504	404	Alameda, CA	296
257	Asheville, NC	742	331	McAllen, TX	503	405	Stamford, CT	290
257	Fullerton, CA	742	332	Cambridge, MA	502	406	Sugar Land, TX	289
259	Ogden, UT	734	333	Orange, CA	500	407	Danbury, CT	287
260	Jurupa Valley, CA	731	334	Carlsbad, CA	497	408	San Mateo, CA	285
261	Gilbert, AZ	726	335	Bryan, TX	496	409	Tracy, CA	284
262	Santa Rosa, CA	725	336	Quincy, MA	495	410	Alexandria, VA	281
263	Champaign, IL	722	336	Rochester, MN	495	411	Thousand Oaks, CA	278
264	Palm Bay, FL	719	338	Brooklyn Park, MN	493	412	Centennial, CO	277
265	Ann Arbor, MI	714	338	El Cajon, CA	493	412	Pearland, TX	277
266	Santa Maria, CA	712	340	McKinney, TX	492	414	Lakewood Twnshp, NJ	274
267	Cicero, IL	711	341	Boca Raton, FL	491	415	Brick Twnshp, NJ	265
268	Sandy Springs, GA	709	342	Hamilton Twnshp, NJ	489	416	Lee's Summit, MO	263
269	Kenosha, WI	707	343	Clinton Twnshp, MI	477	417	Naperville, IL	255
270	Plantation, FL	702	343	Medford, OR	477	418	Norwalk, CT	250
271	San Leandro, CA	699	345	Thornton, CO	476	419	Tustin, CA	240
272	Lynn, MA	698	346	West Jordan, UT	474	420	Farmington Hills, MI	231
272	Richardson, TX	698	347	Boulder, CO	472	421	Bloomington, MN	227
274	Avondale, AZ	685	348	Westminster, CA	466	421	Lake Forest, CA	227
274	Bellevue, WA	685	349	Dearborn, MI	462	423	Upper Darby Twnshp, PA	223
276	Fairfield, CA	676	350	Sandy, UT	453	424	Meridian, ID	220
277	Elk Grove, CA	674	351	Fargo, ND	451	425	Mission Viejo, CA	216
278	Downey, CA	670	352	Kennewick, WA	450	426	Allen, TX	215
279	Costa Mesa, CA	668	353	Whittier, CA	449	427	Amherst, NY	214
280	Davie, FL	667	354	Newport Beach, CA	445	427	Colonie, NY	214
281	Waterbury, CT	662	355	Frisco, TX	440	429	Orem, UT	203
282	Green Bay, WI	659	356	Vista, CA	438	430	Beaverton, OR	196
283	Melbourne, FL	648	357	Mission, TX	423	431	Newton, MA	185
284	Inglewood, CA	646	358	Bellflower, CA	417	432	Troy, MI	181
285	Duluth, MN	642	359	Greece, NY	410	433	New Rochelle, NY	180
286	Scranton, PA	641	359	South Gate, CA	410	434	Mountain View, CA	178
287	Toms River Twnshp, NJ	640	361	Murrieta, CA	408	435	Arlington Heights, IL	140
288	Upland, CA	633	362	Roswell, GA	399	436	Ramapo, NY	137
289	Denton, TX	632	363	Simi Valley, CA	398	437	O'Fallon, MO	125
290	Norman, OK	629	364	Daly City, CA	395	438	Carmel, IN	113
291	Citrus Heights, CA	625	364	Westminster, CO	395	439	Clarkstown, NY	107
291	Waukegan, IL	625	366	Hoover, AL	393	440	Johns Creek, GA	104
293	Bloomington, IN	622	367	Cranston, RI	392	441	Fishers, IN	101
294	Sioux City, IA	621	368	Arvada, CO	390	442	Parma, OH	47
295	Santa Clarita, CA	616	369	Burbank, CA	383			
296	Bellingham, WA	614	370	Bethlehem, PA	377			

Source: Reported data from the F.B.I. "Crime in the United States 2012"

*Burglary is the unlawful entry of a structure to commit a felony or theft. Attempts are included.

70. Burglary Rate in 2012
National Rate = 670.2 Burglaries per 100,000 Population*

RANK	CITY	RATE	RANK	CITY	RATE	RANK	CITY	RATE
161	Abilene, TX	865.0	327	Chino Hills, CA	456.7	183	Gainesville, FL	794.3
20	Akron, OH	1,728.4	219	Chino, CA	704.3	338	Garden Grove, CA	434.7
362	Alameda, CA	392.2	370	Chula Vista, CA	370.7	143	Garland, TX	943.9
17	Albany, GA	1,793.4	168	Cicero, IL	843.4	9	Gary, IN	2,030.5
152	Albany, NY	903.4	15	Cincinnati, OH	1,851.1	389	Gilbert, AZ	338.8
79	Albuquerque, NM	1,205.9	207	Citrus Heights, CA	734.3	74	Glendale, AZ	1,221.9
432	Alexandria, VA	192.6	439	Clarkstown, NY	133.4	416	Glendale, CA	264.7
365	Alhambra, CA	384.8	214	Clarksville, TN	710.6	213	Grand Prairie, TX	714.0
115	Allentown, PA	1,045.8	171	Clearwater, FL	841.2	123	Grand Rapids, MI	1,009.2
421	Allen, TX	242.2	2	Cleveland, OH	2,473.5	349	Greece, NY	423.8
113	Amarillo, TX	1,061.7	350	Clifton, NJ	422.7	279	Greeley, CO	563.0
434	Amherst, NY	182.0	309	Clinton Twnshp, MI	491.7	257	Green Bay, WI	621.2
323	Anaheim, CA	465.9	130	Clovis, CA	976.2	77	Greensboro, NC	1,211.4
363	Anchorage, AK	387.1	264	College Station, TX	596.5	59	Greenville, NC	1,300.8
259	Ann Arbor, MI	620.8	169	Colorado Springs, CO	842.3	177	Gresham, OR	818.8
24	Antioch, CA	1,658.0	215	Columbia, MO	708.6	284	Hamilton Twnshp, NJ	548.8
433	Arlington Heights, IL	185.5	54	Columbus, GA	1,380.9	92	Hammond, IN	1,155.4
147	Arlington, TX	934.1	270	Compton, CA	585.4	283	Hampton, VA	549.7
378	Arvada, CO	357.7	239	Concord, CA	662.1	174	Hartford, CT	838.6
159	Asheville, NC	869.9	326	Coral Springs, FL	457.5	234	Hawthorne, CA	671.0
128	Athens-Clarke, GA	978.2	285	Corona, CA	547.2	197	Hayward, CA	752.3
48	Atlanta, GA	1,416.8	187	Corpus Christi, TX	784.5	63	Hemet, CA	1,295.4
294	Aurora, CO	531.5	267	Costa Mesa, CA	593.1	292	Henderson, NV	534.4
318	Aurora, IL	472.6	312	Cranston, RI	488.1	126	Hesperia, CA	992.6
160	Austin, TX	869.7	62	Dallas, TX	1,296.0	333	Hialeah, FL	449.6
158	Avondale, AZ	874.1	366	Daly City, CA	382.3	100	High Point, NC	1,112.3
50	Bakersfield, CA	1,404.0	382	Danbury, CT	350.5	387	Hillsboro, OR	343.2
337	Baldwin Park, CA	437.1	157	Davenport, IA	879.5	56	Hollywood, FL	1,347.4
70	Baltimore, MD	1,242.3	222	Davie, FL	702.5	316	Hoover, AL	477.3
26	Baton Rouge, LA	1,652.7	8	Dayton, OH	2,140.9	73	Houston, TX	1,223.1
37	Beaumont, TX	1,519.2	317	Dearborn, MI	475.2	355	Huntington Beach, CA	409.4
431	Beaverton, OR	212.4	78	Decatur, IL	1,209.8	88	Huntsville, AL	1,178.6
287	Bellevue, WA	543.6	193	Deerfield Beach, FL	767.1	110	Independence, MO	1,067.0
291	Bellflower, CA	535.4	295	Denton, TX	531.4	18	Indianapolis, IN	1,761.6
205	Bellingham, WA	742.8	178	Denver, CO	816.0	112	Indio, CA	1,065.0
167	Berkeley, CA	844.6	76	Des Moines, IA	1,212.2	272	Inglewood, CA	579.4
307	Bethlehem, PA	500.1	14	Detroit, MI	1,907.5	418	Irvine, CA	262.0
202	Billings, MT	745.5	268	Downey, CA	589.6	273	Irving, TX	570.1
6	Birmingham, AL	2,205.7	206	Duluth, MN	739.4	151	Jacksonville, FL	907.9
324	Bloomington, IL	463.0	52	Durham, NC	1,394.1	4	Jackson, MS	2,344.0
194	Bloomington, IN	761.9	111	Edinburg, TX	1,066.8	277	Jersey City, NJ	566.9
414	Bloomington, MN	268.3	390	Edison Twnshp, NJ	337.8	440	Johns Creek, GA	129.9
275	Boca Raton, FL	567.7	374	Edmond, OK	363.0	245	Joliet, IL	642.5
341	Boise, ID	431.5	314	El Cajon, CA	484.0	199	Jurupa Valley, CA	749.2
298	Boston, MA	527.2	308	El Monte, CA	495.0	82	Kansas City, KS	1,203.8
321	Boulder, CO	470.8	411	El Paso, TX	270.3	40	Kansas City, MO	1,500.6
383	Brick Twnshp, NJ	349.6	394	Elgin, IL	327.1	271	Kennewick, WA	584.6
145	Bridgeport, CT	943.0	189	Elizabeth, NJ	781.6	217	Kenosha, WI	707.0
165	Brockton, MA	856.5	342	Elk Grove, CA	431.1	120	Kent, WA	1,014.7
369	Broken Arrow, OK	371.4	109	Erie, PA	1,073.8	97	Killeen, TX	1,135.1
248	Brooklyn Park, MN	637.4	300	Escondido, CA	518.4	29	Knoxville, TN	1,581.3
250	Brownsville, TX	632.2	137	Eugene, OR	958.6	108	Lafayette, LA	1,082.6
251	Bryan, TX	632.0	138	Evansville, IN	957.7	406	Lake Forest, CA	286.7
353	Buena Park, CA	414.5	102	Everett, WA	1,106.2	61	Lakeland, FL	1,296.9
38	Buffalo, NY	1,515.0	252	Fairfield, CA	631.1	401	Lakewood Twnshp, NJ	292.3
373	Burbank, CA	364.6	164	Fall River, MA	862.4	328	Lakewood, CA	455.9
322	Cambridge, MA	469.2	354	Fargo, ND	410.7	256	Lakewood, CO	626.3
51	Camden, NJ	1,402.2	404	Farmington Hills, MI	287.6	241	Lancaster, CA	655.3
288	Cape Coral, FL	538.8	236	Fayetteville, AR	668.6	95	Lansing, MI	1,139.6
325	Carlsbad, CA	460.7	10	Fayetteville, NC	1,995.0	224	Laredo, TX	699.6
438	Carmel, IN	138.1	118	Federal Way, WA	1,026.3	208	Largo, FL	728.6
260	Carrollton, TX	619.4	441	Fishers, IN	127.2	125	Las Cruces, NM	992.7
244	Carson, CA	644.6	1	Flint, MI	2,931.2	135	Las Vegas, NV	961.2
417	Cary, NC	262.4	286	Fontana, CA	547.1	231	Lawrence, KS	677.3
197	Cedar Rapids, IA	752.3	360	Fort Collins, CO	401.9	228	Lawrence, MA	690.2
415	Centennial, CO	266.3	21	Fort Lauderdale, FL	1,727.5	30	Lawton, OK	1,579.3
155	Champaign, IL	887.8	75	Fort Smith, AR	1,216.2	385	League City, TX	347.2
318	Chandler, AZ	472.6	185	Fort Wayne, IN	789.1	407	Lee's Summit, MO	286.4
399	Charleston, SC	302.0	104	Fort Worth, TX	1,096.2	142	Lexington, KY	944.0
136	Charlotte, NC	959.9	289	Fremont, CA	537.2	262	Lincoln, NE	611.7
345	Cheektowaga, NY	426.9	89	Fresno, CA	1,166.4	7	Little Rock, AR	2,164.7
331	Chesapeake, VA	454.4	379	Frisco, TX	357.1	368	Livermore, CA	374.4
173	Chicago, IL	839.9	290	Fullerton, CA	535.9	391	Livonia, MI	336.4
154	Chico, CA	893.3				180	Long Beach, CA	808.5

RANK	CITY	RATE	RANK	CITY	RATE	RANK	CITY	RATE
359	Longmont, CO	403.7	247	Pasadena, CA	639.3	344	South Gate, CA	427.2
93	Longview, TX	1,150.8	243	Pasadena, TX	646.3	240	Sparks, NV	659.2
347	Los Angeles, CA	425.1	103	Paterson, NJ	1,100.3	131	Spokane Valley, WA	975.2
114	Louisville, KY	1,051.9	400	Pearland, TX	292.5	16	Spokane, WA	1,803.8
188	Lowell, MA	782.2	296	Pembroke Pines, FL	529.6	46	Springfield, IL	1,425.8
58	Lubbock, TX	1,306.3	269	Peoria, AZ	586.7	41	Springfield, MA	1,499.5
320	Lynchburg, VA	471.9	71	Peoria, IL	1,231.7	55	Springfield, MO	1,376.1
195	Lynn, MA	760.0	190	Philadelphia, PA	780.0	423	Stamford, CT	233.5
11	Macon, GA	1,969.1	80	Phoenix, AZ	1,205.8	410	Sterling Heights, MI	274.7
233	Madison, WI	674.1	179	Pittsburgh, PA	812.8	42	Stockton, CA	1,476.4
191	Manchester, NH	771.5	361	Plano, TX	399.9	358	St. George, UT	405.1
371	McAllen, TX	370.5	182	Plantation, FL	800.4	65	St. Joseph, MO	1,284.1
380	McKinney, TX	356.3	265	Pomona, CA	594.7	31	St. Louis, MO	1,564.6
255	Medford, OR	627.3	69	Pompano Beach, FL	1,245.6	106	St. Paul, MN	1,083.6
172	Melbourne, FL	840.1	313	Port St. Lucie, FL	484.5	86	St. Petersburg, FL	1,181.0
13	Memphis, TN	1,912.7	200	Portland, OR	747.6	384	Sugar Land, TX	348.5
249	Menifee, CA	633.4	66	Portsmouth, VA	1,259.1	372	Sunnyvale, CA	364.9
87	Merced, CA	1,179.4	105	Providence, RI	1,084.4	150	Sunrise, FL	916.6
408	Meridian, ID	284.7	419	Provo, UT	257.5	343	Surprise, AZ	429.7
266	Mesa, AZ	593.9	19	Pueblo, CO	1,737.5	60	Syracuse, NY	1,299.2
107	Mesquite, TX	1,082.8	297	Quincy, MA	528.1	43	Tacoma, WA	1,463.1
93	Miami Beach, FL	1,150.8	53	Racine, WI	1,392.7	47	Tallahassee, FL	1,418.1
91	Miami Gardens, FL	1,160.3	210	Raleigh, NC	721.8	218	Tampa, FL	705.9
117	Miami, FL	1,027.0	436	Ramapo, NY	160.3	274	Temecula, CA	568.6
315	Midland, TX	483.4	163	Rancho Cucamon., CA	862.5	196	Tempe, AZ	752.7
90	Milwaukee, WI	1,164.0	27	Reading, PA	1,634.0	364	Thornton, CO	386.6
72	Minneapolis, MN	1,225.4	84	Redding, CA	1,195.9	429	Thousand Oaks, CA	215.2
230	Miramar, FL	684.1	235	Redwood City, CA	670.4	3	Toledo, OH	2,352.6
425	Mission Viejo, CA	225.9	216	Reno, NV	708.5	226	Toms River Twnshp, NJ	694.7
299	Mission, TX	525.1	139	Renton, WA	957.1	127	Topeka, KS	991.1
101	Mobile, AL	1,111.7	156	Rialto, CA	883.9	377	Torrance, CA	357.8
68	Modesto, CA	1,256.4	232	Richardson, TX	675.9	393	Tracy, CA	333.9
28	Montgomery, AL	1,631.0	45	Richmond, CA	1,445.1	39	Trenton, NJ	1,513.2
122	Moreno Valley, CA	1,010.7	129	Richmond, VA	976.9	427	Troy, MI	221.9
422	Mountain View, CA	234.4	356	Rio Rancho, NM	406.9	141	Tucson, AZ	944.6
176	Murfreesboro, TN	822.3	212	Riverside, CA	716.7	32	Tulsa, OK	1,563.0
367	Murrieta, CA	381.9	134	Roanoke, VA	961.3	64	Tuscaloosa, AL	1,285.2
261	Nampa, ID	612.1	328	Rochester, MN	455.9	398	Tustin, CA	310.1
334	Napa, CA	444.1	49	Rochester, NY	1,404.8	119	Tyler, TX	1,024.6
435	Naperville, IL	178.5	44	Rockford, IL	1,460.3	175	Upland, CA	838.1
340	Nashua, NH	431.7	351	Roseville, CA	422.3	413	Upper Darby Twnshp, PA	268.7
148	Nashville, TN	923.8	339	Roswell, GA	433.0	388	Vacaville, CA	339.5
132	New Bedford, MA	967.4	395	Round Rock, TX	316.3	5	Vallejo, CA	2,279.7
98	New Haven, CT	1,116.7	146	Sacramento, CA	938.8	254	Vancouver, WA	627.5
144	New Orleans, LA	943.3	238	Salem, OR	662.8	211	Ventura, CA	717.0
424	New Rochelle, NY	230.7	186	Salinas, CA	788.8	34	Victorville, CA	1,547.8
426	New York, NY	224.8	140	Salt Lake City, UT	947.7	381	Virginia Beach, VA	351.4
192	Newark, NJ	768.7	96	San Antonio, TX	1,135.3	133	Visalia, CA	961.6
302	Newport Beach, CA	509.8	57	San Bernardino, CA	1,306.6	330	Vista, CA	455.8
278	Newport News, VA	566.7	336	San Diego, CA	440.9	81	Waco, TX	1,205.3
430	Newton, MA	213.4	242	San Francisco, CA	648.1	203	Warren, MI	743.6
149	Norfolk, VA	921.7	293	San Jose, CA	533.2	357	Warwick, RI	405.9
282	Norman, OK	551.9	181	San Leandro, CA	804.7	281	Washington, DC	556.5
166	North Charleston, SC	848.3	346	San Marcos, CA	426.5	263	Waterbury, CT	599.2
223	North Las Vegas, NV	701.7	405	San Mateo, CA	287.0	225	Waukegan, IL	698.6
305	Norwalk, CA	502.4	209	Sandy Springs, GA	724.3	304	West Covina, CA	506.2
403	Norwalk, CT	288.4	306	Sandy, UT	501.1	335	West Jordan, UT	442.6
35	Oakland, CA	1,544.0	397	Santa Ana, CA	310.4	67	West Palm Beach, FL	1,258.5
310	Oceanside, CA	491.4	258	Santa Barbara, CA	620.9	221	West Valley, UT	702.9
204	Odessa, TX	743.0	311	Santa Clara, CA	489.3	227	Westland, MI	690.3
437	O'Fallon, MO	155.0	386	Santa Clarita, CA	343.7	303	Westminster, CA	507.0
162	Ogden, UT	862.7	220	Santa Maria, CA	703.5	375	Westminster, CO	360.9
25	Oklahoma City, OK	1,654.4	246	Santa Monica, CA	642.4	301	Whittier, CA	517.6
420	Olathe, KS	245.0	348	Santa Rosa, CA	424.3	85	Wichita Falls, TX	1,193.5
184	Omaha, NE	792.2	153	Savannah, GA	900.6	121	Wichita, KS	1,014.2
253	Ontario, CA	630.0	280	Scottsdale, AZ	561.7	33	Wilmington, NC	1,548.9
376	Orange, CA	357.9	170	Scranton, PA	842.1	12	Winston-Salem, NC	1,929.8
428	Orem, UT	220.8	116	Seattle, WA	1,040.6	392	Woodbridge Twnshp, NJ	335.9
36	Orlando, FL	1,532.6	83	Shreveport, LA	1,199.5	99	Worcester, MA	1,113.3
402	Overland Park, KS	292.0	396	Simi Valley, CA	314.2	23	Yakima, WA	1,683.8
352	Oxnard, CA	420.2	201	Sioux City, IA	745.6	412	Yonkers, NY	269.6
229	Palm Bay, FL	687.2	275	Sioux Falls, SD	567.7	124	Yuma, AZ	999.3
237	Palmdale, CA	666.5	332	Somerville, MA	450.8			
442	Parma, OH	58.1	22	South Bend, IN	1,720.0			

Source: CQ Press using reported data from the F.B.I. "Crime in the United States 2012"

*Burglary is the unlawful entry of a structure to commit a felony or theft. Attempts are included.

70. Burglary Rate in 2012 (continued)
National Rate = 670.2 Burglaries per 100,000 Population*

RANK	CITY	RATE	RANK	CITY	RATE	RANK	CITY	RATE
1	Flint, MI	2,931.2	75	Fort Smith, AR	1,216.2	149	Norfolk, VA	921.7
2	Cleveland, OH	2,473.5	76	Des Moines, IA	1,212.2	150	Sunrise, FL	916.6
3	Toledo, OH	2,352.6	77	Greensboro, NC	1,211.4	151	Jacksonville, FL	907.9
4	Jackson, MS	2,344.0	78	Decatur, IL	1,209.8	152	Albany, NY	903.4
5	Vallejo, CA	2,279.7	79	Albuquerque, NM	1,205.9	153	Savannah, GA	900.6
6	Birmingham, AL	2,205.7	80	Phoenix, AZ	1,205.8	154	Chico, CA	893.3
7	Little Rock, AR	2,164.7	81	Waco, TX	1,205.3	155	Champaign, IL	887.8
8	Dayton, OH	2,140.9	82	Kansas City, KS	1,203.8	156	Rialto, CA	883.9
9	Gary, IN	2,030.5	83	Shreveport, LA	1,199.5	157	Davenport, IA	879.5
10	Fayetteville, NC	1,995.0	84	Redding, CA	1,195.9	158	Avondale, AZ	874.1
11	Macon, GA	1,969.1	85	Wichita Falls, TX	1,193.5	159	Asheville, NC	869.9
12	Winston-Salem, NC	1,929.8	86	St. Petersburg, FL	1,181.0	160	Austin, TX	869.7
13	Memphis, TN	1,912.7	87	Merced, CA	1,179.4	161	Abilene, TX	865.0
14	Detroit, MI	1,907.5	88	Huntsville, AL	1,178.6	162	Ogden, UT	862.7
15	Cincinnati, OH	1,851.1	89	Fresno, CA	1,166.4	163	Rancho Cucamon., CA	862.5
16	Spokane, WA	1,803.8	90	Milwaukee, WI	1,164.0	164	Fall River, MA	862.4
17	Albany, GA	1,793.4	91	Miami Gardens, FL	1,160.3	165	Brockton, MA	856.5
18	Indianapolis, IN	1,761.6	92	Hammond, IN	1,155.4	166	North Charleston, SC	848.3
19	Pueblo, CO	1,737.5	93	Longview, TX	1,150.8	167	Berkeley, CA	844.6
20	Akron, OH	1,728.4	93	Miami Beach, FL	1,150.8	168	Cicero, IL	843.4
21	Fort Lauderdale, FL	1,727.5	95	Lansing, MI	1,139.6	169	Colorado Springs, CO	842.3
22	South Bend, IN	1,720.0	96	San Antonio, TX	1,135.3	170	Scranton, PA	842.1
23	Yakima, WA	1,683.8	97	Killeen, TX	1,135.1	171	Clearwater, FL	841.2
24	Antioch, CA	1,658.0	98	New Haven, CT	1,116.7	172	Melbourne, FL	840.1
25	Oklahoma City, OK	1,654.4	99	Worcester, MA	1,113.3	173	Chicago, IL	839.9
26	Baton Rouge, LA	1,652.7	100	High Point, NC	1,112.3	174	Hartford, CT	838.6
27	Reading, PA	1,634.0	101	Mobile, AL	1,111.7	175	Upland, CA	838.1
28	Montgomery, AL	1,631.0	102	Everett, WA	1,106.2	176	Murfreesboro, TN	822.3
29	Knoxville, TN	1,581.3	103	Paterson, NJ	1,100.3	177	Gresham, OR	818.8
30	Lawton, OK	1,579.3	104	Fort Worth, TX	1,096.2	178	Denver, CO	816.0
31	St. Louis, MO	1,564.6	105	Providence, RI	1,084.4	179	Pittsburgh, PA	812.8
32	Tulsa, OK	1,563.0	106	St. Paul, MN	1,083.6	180	Long Beach, CA	808.5
33	Wilmington, NC	1,548.9	107	Mesquite, TX	1,082.8	181	San Leandro, CA	804.7
34	Victorville, CA	1,547.8	108	Lafayette, LA	1,082.6	182	Plantation, FL	800.4
35	Oakland, CA	1,544.0	109	Erie, PA	1,073.8	183	Gainesville, FL	794.3
36	Orlando, FL	1,532.6	110	Independence, MO	1,067.0	184	Omaha, NE	792.2
37	Beaumont, TX	1,519.2	111	Edinburg, TX	1,066.8	185	Fort Wayne, IN	789.1
38	Buffalo, NY	1,515.0	112	Indio, CA	1,065.0	186	Salinas, CA	788.8
39	Trenton, NJ	1,513.2	113	Amarillo, TX	1,061.7	187	Corpus Christi, TX	784.5
40	Kansas City, MO	1,500.6	114	Louisville, KY	1,051.9	188	Lowell, MA	782.2
41	Springfield, MA	1,499.5	115	Allentown, PA	1,045.8	189	Elizabeth, NJ	781.6
42	Stockton, CA	1,476.4	116	Seattle, WA	1,040.6	190	Philadelphia, PA	780.0
43	Tacoma, WA	1,463.1	117	Miami, FL	1,027.0	191	Manchester, NH	771.5
44	Rockford, IL	1,460.3	118	Federal Way, WA	1,026.3	192	Newark, NJ	768.7
45	Richmond, CA	1,445.1	119	Tyler, TX	1,024.6	193	Deerfield Beach, FL	767.1
46	Springfield, IL	1,425.8	120	Kent, WA	1,014.7	194	Bloomington, IN	761.9
47	Tallahassee, FL	1,418.1	121	Wichita, KS	1,014.2	195	Lynn, MA	760.0
48	Atlanta, GA	1,416.8	122	Moreno Valley, CA	1,010.7	196	Tempe, AZ	752.7
49	Rochester, NY	1,404.8	123	Grand Rapids, MI	1,009.2	197	Cedar Rapids, IA	752.3
50	Bakersfield, CA	1,404.0	124	Yuma, AZ	999.3	197	Hayward, CA	752.3
51	Camden, NJ	1,402.2	125	Las Cruces, NM	992.7	199	Jurupa Valley, CA	749.2
52	Durham, NC	1,394.1	126	Hesperia, CA	992.6	200	Portland, OR	747.6
53	Racine, WI	1,392.7	127	Topeka, KS	991.1	201	Sioux City, IA	745.6
54	Columbus, GA	1,380.9	128	Athens-Clarke, GA	978.2	202	Billings, MT	745.5
55	Springfield, MO	1,376.1	129	Richmond, VA	976.9	203	Warren, MI	743.6
56	Hollywood, FL	1,347.4	130	Clovis, CA	976.2	204	Odessa, TX	743.0
57	San Bernardino, CA	1,306.6	131	Spokane Valley, WA	975.2	205	Bellingham, WA	742.8
58	Lubbock, TX	1,306.3	132	New Bedford, MA	967.4	206	Duluth, MN	739.4
59	Greenville, NC	1,300.8	133	Visalia, CA	961.6	207	Citrus Heights, CA	734.3
60	Syracuse, NY	1,299.2	134	Roanoke, VA	961.3	208	Largo, FL	728.6
61	Lakeland, FL	1,296.9	135	Las Vegas, NV	961.2	209	Sandy Springs, GA	724.3
62	Dallas, TX	1,296.0	136	Charlotte, NC	959.9	210	Raleigh, NC	721.8
63	Hemet, CA	1,295.4	137	Eugene, OR	958.6	211	Ventura, CA	717.0
64	Tuscaloosa, AL	1,285.2	138	Evansville, IN	957.7	212	Riverside, CA	716.7
65	St. Joseph, MO	1,284.1	139	Renton, WA	957.1	213	Grand Prairie, TX	714.0
66	Portsmouth, VA	1,259.1	140	Salt Lake City, UT	947.7	214	Clarksville, TN	710.6
67	West Palm Beach, FL	1,258.5	141	Tucson, AZ	944.6	215	Columbia, MO	708.6
68	Modesto, CA	1,256.4	142	Lexington, KY	944.0	216	Reno, NV	708.5
69	Pompano Beach, FL	1,245.6	143	Garland, TX	943.9	217	Kenosha, WI	707.0
70	Baltimore, MD	1,242.3	144	New Orleans, LA	943.3	218	Tampa, FL	705.9
71	Peoria, IL	1,231.7	145	Bridgeport, CT	943.0	219	Chino, CA	704.3
72	Minneapolis, MN	1,225.4	146	Sacramento, CA	938.8	220	Santa Maria, CA	703.5
73	Houston, TX	1,223.1	147	Arlington, TX	934.1	221	West Valley, UT	702.9
74	Glendale, AZ	1,221.9	148	Nashville, TN	923.8	222	Davie, FL	702.5

RANK	CITY	RATE	RANK	CITY	RATE	RANK	CITY	RATE
223	North Las Vegas, NV	701.7	297	Quincy, MA	528.1	371	McAllen, TX	370.5
224	Laredo, TX	699.6	298	Boston, MA	527.2	372	Sunnyvale, CA	364.9
225	Waukegan, IL	698.6	299	Mission, TX	525.1	373	Burbank, CA	364.6
226	Toms River Twnshp, NJ	694.7	300	Escondido, CA	518.4	374	Edmond, OK	363.0
227	Westland, MI	690.3	301	Whittier, CA	517.6	375	Westminster, CO	360.9
228	Lawrence, MA	690.2	302	Newport Beach, CA	509.8	376	Orange, CA	357.9
229	Palm Bay, FL	687.2	303	Westminster, CA	507.0	377	Torrance, CA	357.8
230	Miramar, FL	684.1	304	West Covina, CA	506.2	378	Arvada, CO	357.7
231	Lawrence, KS	677.3	305	Norwalk, CA	502.4	379	Frisco, TX	357.1
232	Richardson, TX	675.9	306	Sandy, UT	501.1	380	McKinney, TX	356.3
233	Madison, WI	674.1	307	Bethlehem, PA	500.1	381	Virginia Beach, VA	351.4
234	Hawthorne, CA	671.0	308	El Monte, CA	495.0	382	Danbury, CT	350.5
235	Redwood City, CA	670.4	309	Clinton Twnshp, MI	491.7	383	Brick Twnshp, NJ	349.6
236	Fayetteville, AR	668.6	310	Oceanside, CA	491.4	384	Sugar Land, TX	348.5
237	Palmdale, CA	666.5	311	Santa Clara, CA	489.3	385	League City, TX	347.2
238	Salem, OR	662.8	312	Cranston, RI	488.1	386	Santa Clarita, CA	343.7
239	Concord, CA	662.1	313	Port St. Lucie, FL	484.5	387	Hillsboro, OR	343.2
240	Sparks, NV	659.2	314	El Cajon, CA	484.0	388	Vacaville, CA	339.5
241	Lancaster, CA	655.3	315	Midland, TX	483.4	389	Gilbert, AZ	338.8
242	San Francisco, CA	648.1	316	Hoover, AL	477.3	390	Edison Twnshp, NJ	337.6
243	Pasadena, TX	646.3	317	Dearborn, MI	475.2	391	Livonia, MI	336.4
244	Carson, CA	644.6	318	Aurora, IL	472.6	392	Woodbridge Twnshp, NJ	335.9
245	Joliet, IL	642.5	318	Chandler, AZ	472.6	393	Tracy, CA	333.9
246	Santa Monica, CA	642.4	320	Lynchburg, VA	471.9	394	Elgin, IL	327.1
247	Pasadena, CA	639.3	321	Boulder, CO	470.8	395	Round Rock, TX	316.3
248	Brooklyn Park, MN	637.4	322	Cambridge, MA	469.2	396	Simi Valley, CA	314.2
249	Menifee, CA	633.4	323	Anaheim, CA	465.9	397	Santa Ana, CA	310.4
250	Brownsville, TX	632.2	324	Bloomington, IL	463.0	398	Tustin, CA	310.1
251	Bryan, TX	632.0	325	Carlsbad, CA	460.7	399	Charleston, SC	302.0
252	Fairfield, CA	631.1	326	Coral Springs, FL	457.5	400	Pearland, TX	292.5
253	Ontario, CA	630.0	327	Chino Hills, CA	456.7	401	Lakewood Twnshp, NJ	292.3
254	Vancouver, WA	627.5	328	Lakewood, CA	455.9	402	Overland Park, KS	292.0
255	Medford, OR	627.3	328	Rochester, MN	455.9	403	Norwalk, CT	288.4
256	Lakewood, CO	626.3	330	Vista, CA	455.8	404	Farmington Hills, MI	287.6
257	Green Bay, WI	621.2	331	Chesapeake, VA	454.4	405	San Mateo, CA	287.0
258	Santa Barbara, CA	620.9	332	Somerville, MA	450.8	406	Lake Forest, CA	286.7
259	Ann Arbor, MI	620.8	333	Hialeah, FL	449.6	407	Lee's Summit, MO	286.4
260	Carrollton, TX	619.4	334	Napa, CA	444.1	408	Meridian, ID	284.7
261	Nampa, ID	612.1	335	West Jordan, UT	442.6	409	Colonie, NY	274.9
262	Lincoln, NE	611.7	336	San Diego, CA	440.9	410	Sterling Heights, MI	274.7
263	Waterbury, CT	599.2	337	Baldwin Park, CA	437.1	411	El Paso, TX	270.3
264	College Station, TX	596.5	338	Garden Grove, CA	434.7	412	Yonkers, NY	269.6
265	Pomona, CA	594.7	339	Roswell, GA	433.0	413	Upper Darby Twnshp, PA	268.7
266	Mesa, AZ	593.9	340	Nashua, NH	431.7	414	Bloomington, MN	268.3
267	Costa Mesa, CA	593.1	341	Boise, ID	431.5	415	Centennial, CO	266.3
268	Downey, CA	589.6	342	Elk Grove, CA	431.1	416	Glendale, CA	264.7
269	Peoria, AZ	586.7	343	Surprise, AZ	429.7	417	Cary, NC	262.4
270	Compton, CA	585.4	344	South Gate, CA	427.2	418	Irvine, CA	262.0
271	Kennewick, WA	584.6	345	Cheektowaga, NY	426.9	419	Provo, UT	257.5
272	Inglewood, CA	579.4	346	San Marcos, CA	426.5	420	Olathe, KS	245.0
273	Irving, TX	570.1	347	Los Angeles, CA	425.1	421	Allen, TX	242.2
274	Temecula, CA	568.6	348	Santa Rosa, CA	424.3	422	Mountain View, CA	234.4
275	Boca Raton, FL	567.7	349	Greece, NY	423.8	423	Stamford, CT	233.5
275	Sioux Falls, SD	567.7	350	Clifton, NJ	422.7	424	New Rochelle, NY	230.7
277	Jersey City, NJ	566.9	351	Roseville, CA	422.3	425	Mission Viejo, CA	225.9
278	Newport News, VA	566.7	352	Oxnard, CA	420.2	426	New York, NY	224.8
279	Greeley, CO	563.0	353	Buena Park, CA	414.5	427	Troy, MI	221.9
280	Scottsdale, AZ	561.7	354	Fargo, ND	410.7	428	Orem, UT	220.8
281	Washington, DC	556.5	355	Huntington Beach, CA	409.4	429	Thousand Oaks, CA	215.2
282	Norman, OK	551.9	356	Rio Rancho, NM	406.9	430	Newton, MA	213.4
283	Hampton, VA	549.7	357	Warwick, RI	405.9	431	Beaverton, OR	212.4
284	Hamilton Twnshp, NJ	548.8	358	St. George, UT	405.1	432	Alexandria, VA	192.6
285	Corona, CA	547.2	359	Longmont, CO	403.7	433	Arlington Heights, IL	185.5
286	Fontana, CA	547.1	360	Fort Collins, CO	401.9	434	Amherst, NY	182.0
287	Bellevue, WA	543.6	361	Plano, TX	399.9	435	Naperville, IL	178.5
288	Cape Coral, FL	538.8	362	Alameda, CA	392.2	436	Ramapo, NY	160.3
289	Fremont, CA	537.2	363	Anchorage, AK	387.1	437	O'Fallon, MO	155.0
290	Fullerton, CA	535.9	364	Thornton, CO	386.6	438	Carmel, IN	138.1
291	Bellflower, CA	535.4	365	Alhambra, CA	384.8	439	Clarkstown, NY	133.4
292	Henderson, NV	534.4	366	Daly City, CA	382.3	440	Johns Creek, GA	129.9
293	San Jose, CA	533.2	367	Murrieta, CA	381.9	441	Fishers, IN	127.2
294	Aurora, CO	531.5	368	Livermore, CA	374.4	442	Parma, OH	58.1
295	Denton, TX	531.4	369	Broken Arrow, OK	371.4			
296	Pembroke Pines, FL	529.6	370	Chula Vista, CA	370.7			

Source: CQ Press using reported data from the F.B.I. "Crime in the United States 2012"

*Burglary is the unlawful entry of a structure to commit a felony or theft. Attempts are included.

71. Percent Change in Burglary Rate: 2011 to 2012
National Percent Change = 4.4% Decrease*

RANK	CITY	% CHANGE	RANK	CITY	% CHANGE	RANK	CITY	% CHANGE
256	Abilene, TX	(7.6)	15	Chino Hills, CA	30.9	238	Gainesville, FL	(5.8)
371	Akron, OH	(19.3)	126	Chino, CA	4.9	129	Garden Grove, CA	4.8
251	Alameda, CA	(7.0)	68	Chula Vista, CA	13.4	196	Garland, TX	(2.6)
117	Albany, GA	5.6	112	Cicero, IL	6.2	416	Gary, IN	(37.4)
NA	Albany, NY**	NA	357	Cincinnati, OH	(17.6)	313	Gilbert, AZ	(13.0)
79	Albuquerque, NM	11.2	156	Citrus Heights, CA	2.0	60	Glendale, AZ	15.0
283	Alexandria, VA	(10.0)	NA	Clarkstown, NY**	NA	357	Glendale, CA	(17.6)
140	Alhambra, CA	3.7	406	Clarksville, TN	(28.5)	409	Grand Prairie, TX	(29.3)
NA	Allentown, PA**	NA	18	Clearwater, FL	27.7	200	Grand Rapids, MI	(2.9)
343	Allen, TX	(16.0)	265	Cleveland, OH	(8.3)	NA	Greece, NY**	NA
150	Amarillo, TX	2.5	63	Clifton, NJ	14.7	285	Greeley, CO	(10.3)
NA	Amherst, NY**	NA	311	Clinton Twnshp, MI	(12.7)	7	Green Bay, WI	39.0
74	Anaheim, CA	12.4	143	Clovis, CA	3.3	NA	Greensboro, NC**	NA
111	Anchorage, AK	6.4	305	College Station, TX	(12.2)	NA	Greenville, NC**	NA
12	Ann Arbor, MI	32.4	NA	Colonie, NY**	NA	54	Gresham, OR	16.4
16	Antioch, CA	28.6	105	Colorado Springs, CO	7.4	230	Hamilton Twnshp, NJ	(5.1)
361	Arlington Heights, IL	(17.8)	204	Columbia, MO	(3.3)	273	Hammond, IN	(9.0)
377	Arlington, TX	(20.6)	376	Columbus, GA	(20.5)	249	Hampton, VA	(6.8)
20	Arvada, CO	27.4	408	Compton, CA	(28.6)	355	Hartford, CT	(17.5)
192	Asheville, NC	(2.4)	272	Concord, CA	(8.9)	221	Hawthorne, CA	(4.3)
338	Athens-Clarke, GA	(15.7)	299	Coral Springs, FL	(11.3)	80	Hayward, CA	11.1
372	Atlanta, GA	(19.6)	38	Corona, CA	19.7	304	Hemet, CA	(12.1)
362	Aurora, CO	(18.0)	267	Corpus Christi, TX	(8.4)	98	Henderson, NV	8.5
181	Aurora, IL	(0.9)	23	Costa Mesa, CA	25.9	9	Hesperia, CA	35.6
175	Austin, TX	(0.3)	329	Cranston, RI	(15.0)	220	Hialeah, FL	(4.2)
230	Avondale, AZ	(5.1)	335	Dallas, TX	(15.4)	252	High Point, NC	(7.1)
65	Bakersfield, CA	14.2	32	Daly City, CA	21.5	22	Hillsboro, OR	26.1
115	Baldwin Park, CA	5.8	350	Danbury, CT	(17.2)	245	Hollywood, FL	(6.4)
279	Baltimore, MD	(9.6)	388	Davenport, IA	(22.7)	254	Hoover, AL	(7.2)
275	Baton Rouge, LA	(9.3)	256	Davie, FL	(7.6)	222	Houston, TX	(4.5)
281	Beaumont, TX	(9.8)	199	Dayton, OH	(2.8)	131	Huntington Beach, CA	4.5
331	Beaverton, OR	(15.1)	394	Dearborn, MI	(23.8)	374	Huntsville, AL	(20.3)
77	Bellevue, WA	11.3	364	Decatur, IL	(19.0)	112	Independence, MO	6.2
320	Bellflower, CA	(13.7)	150	Deerfield Beach, FL	2.5	202	Indianapolis, IN	(3.0)
234	Bellingham, WA	(5.5)	92	Denton, TX	8.9	138	Indio, CA	4.0
185	Berkeley, CA	(1.4)	153	Denver, CO	2.4	70	Inglewood, CA	13.2
160	Bethlehem, PA	1.4	179	Des Moines, IA	(0.6)	88	Irvine, CA	9.8
52	Billings, MT	17.1	328	Detroit, MI	(14.9)	382	Irving, TX	(21.5)
364	Birmingham, AL	(19.0)	317	Downey, CA	(13.3)	294	Jacksonville, FL	(11.1)
388	Bloomington, IL	(22.7)	329	Duluth, MN	(15.0)	318	Jackson, MS	(13.5)
153	Bloomington, IN	2.4	348	Durham, NC	(16.8)	169	Jersey City, NJ	0.4
287	Bloomington, MN	(10.7)	83	Edinburg, TX	10.8	390	Johns Creek, GA	(22.9)
190	Boca Raton, FL	(1.9)	184	Edison Twnshp, NJ	(1.3)	161	Joliet, IL	1.2
82	Boise, ID	10.9	217	Edmond, OK	(4.0)	NA	Jurupa Valley, CA**	NA
241	Boston, MA	(5.9)	368	El Cajon, CA	(19.2)	204	Kansas City, KS	(3.3)
173	Boulder, CO	(0.1)	131	El Monte, CA	4.5	162	Kansas City, MO	1.1
375	Brick Twnshp, NJ	(20.4)	209	El Paso, TX	(3.6)	96	Kennewick, WA	8.6
300	Bridgeport, CT	(11.5)	415	Elgin, IL	(36.1)	25	Kenosha, WI	24.5
385	Brockton, MA	(22.0)	338	Elizabeth, NJ	(15.7)	386	Kent, WA	(22.1)
312	Broken Arrow, OK	(12.9)	166	Elk Grove, CA	0.5	402	Killeen, TX	(27.1)
212	Brooklyn Park, MN	(3.8)	294	Erie, PA	(11.1)	75	Knoxville, TN	12.2
76	Brownsville, TX	12.0	10	Escondido, CA	35.5	86	Lafayette, LA	10.4
403	Bryan, TX	(27.8)	124	Eugene, OR	5.1	2	Lake Forest, CA	60.1
92	Buena Park, CA	8.9	119	Evansville, IN	5.3	216	Lakeland, FL	(3.9)
NA	Buffalo, NY**	NA	177	Everett, WA	(0.5)	134	Lakewood Twnshp, NJ	4.3
207	Burbank, CA	(3.5)	47	Fairfield, CA	17.6	101	Lakewood, CA	8.3
261	Cambridge, MA	(7.9)	287	Fall River, MA	(10.7)	196	Lakewood, CO	(2.6)
397	Camden, NJ	(24.2)	136	Fargo, ND	4.2	119	Lancaster, CA	5.3
357	Cape Coral, FL	(17.6)	326	Farmington Hills, MI	(14.2)	379	Lansing, MI	(21.1)
126	Carlsbad, CA	4.9	206	Fayetteville, AR	(3.4)	238	Laredo, TX	(5.8)
4	Carmel, IN	59.3	209	Fayetteville, NC	(3.6)	252	Largo, FL	(7.1)
342	Carrollton, TX	(15.9)	NA	Federal Way, WA**	NA	307	Las Cruces, NM	(12.5)
133	Carson, CA	4.4	1	Fishers, IN	72.4	84	Las Vegas, NV	10.7
200	Cary, NC	(2.9)	352	Flint, MI	(17.3)	41	Lawrence, KS	19.0
315	Cedar Rapids, IA	(13.1)	136	Fontana, CA	4.2	387	Lawrence, MA	(22.2)
345	Centennial, CO	(16.3)	124	Fort Collins, CO	5.1	379	Lawton, OK	(21.1)
26	Champaign, IL	23.2	247	Fort Lauderdale, FL	(6.6)	378	League City, TX	(20.8)
NA	Chandler, AZ**	NA	226	Fort Smith, AR	(4.8)	368	Lee's Summit, MO	(19.2)
411	Charleston, SC	(30.4)	110	Fort Wayne, IN	6.6	NA	Lexington, KY**	NA
298	Charlotte, NC	(11.2)	355	Fort Worth, TX	(17.5)	67	Lincoln, NE	13.8
NA	Cheektowaga, NY**	NA	207	Fremont, CA	(3.5)	275	Little Rock, AR	(9.3)
353	Chesapeake, VA	(17.4)	155	Fresno, CA	2.2	344	Livermore, CA	(16.2)
324	Chicago, IL	(14.1)	302	Frisco, TX	(11.7)	115	Livonia, MI	5.8
3	Chico, CA	59.9	66	Fullerton, CA	14.0	56	Long Beach, CA	15.5

RANK	CITY	% CHANGE	RANK	CITY	% CHANGE	RANK	CITY	% CHANGE
42	Longmont, CO	18.9	306	Pasadena, CA	(12.3)	192	South Gate, CA	(2.4)
58	Longview, TX	15.4	307	Pasadena, TX	(12.5)	269	Sparks, NV	(8.5)
234	Los Angeles, CA	(5.5)	281	Paterson, NJ	(9.8)	203	Spokane Valley, WA	(3.1)
323	Louisville, KY	(13.9)	360	Pearland, TX	(17.7)	21	Spokane, WA	26.3
265	Lowell, MA	(8.3)	383	Pembroke Pines, FL	(21.6)	302	Springfield, IL	(11.7)
284	Lubbock, TX	(10.2)	338	Peoria, AZ	(15.7)	256	Springfield, MA	(7.6)
410	Lynchburg, VA	(29.9)	353	Peoria, IL	(17.4)	107	Springfield, MO	7.3
212	Lynn, MA	(3.8)	182	Philadelphia, PA	(1.0)	158	Stamford, CT	1.7
335	Macon, GA	(15.4)	232	Phoenix, AZ	(5.3)	379	Sterling Heights, MI	(21.1)
89	Madison, WI	9.6	247	Pittsburgh, PA	(6.6)	118	Stockton, CA	5.4
244	Manchester, NH	(6.2)	294	Plano, TX	(11.1)	NA	St. George, UT**	NA
212	McAllen, TX	(3.8)	261	Plantation, FL	(7.9)	90	St. Joseph, MO	9.1
394	McKinney, TX	(23.8)	164	Pomona, CA	0.8	406	St. Louis, MO	(28.5)
17	Medford, OR	28.4	243	Pompano Beach, FL	(6.1)	194	St. Paul, MN	(2.5)
400	Melbourne, FL	(25.8)	405	Port St. Lucie, FL	(28.3)	324	St. Petersburg, FL	(14.1)
238	Memphis, TN	(5.8)	150	Portland, OR	2.5	19	Sugar Land, TX	27.5
86	Menifee, CA	10.4	280	Portsmouth, VA	(9.7)	14	Sunnyvale, CA	31.6
49	Merced, CA	17.5	NA	Providence, RI**	NA	327	Sunrise, FL	(14.6)
8	Meridian, ID	38.5	392	Provo, UT	(23.5)	349	Surprise, AZ	(17.0)
222	Mesa, AZ	(4.5)	43	Pueblo, CO	18.5	NA	Syracuse, NY**	NA
275	Mesquite, TX	(9.3)	290	Quincy, MA	(11.0)	95	Tacoma, WA	8.8
309	Miami Beach, FL	(12.6)	290	Racine, WI	(11.0)	373	Tallahassee, FL	(19.8)
331	Miami Gardens, FL	(15.1)	183	Raleigh, NC	(1.1)	301	Tampa, FL	(11.6)
367	Miami, FL	(19.1)	NA	Ramapo, NY**	NA	119	Temecula, CA	5.3
391	Midland, TX	(23.3)	27	Rancho Cucamon., CA	23.0	384	Tempe, AZ	(21.8)
134	Milwaukee, WI	4.3	130	Reading, PA	4.6	NA	Thornton, CO**	NA
255	Minneapolis, MN	(7.4)	13	Redding, CA	32.1	318	Thousand Oaks, CA	(13.5)
320	Miramar, FL	(13.7)	40	Redwood City, CA	19.5	368	Toledo, OH	(19.2)
85	Mission Viejo, CA	10.5	177	Reno, NV	(0.5)	104	Toms River Twnshp, NJ	8.0
290	Mission, TX	(11.0)	209	Renton, WA	(3.6)	401	Topeka, KS	(26.4)
412	Mobile, AL	(31.0)	228	Rialto, CA	(5.0)	142	Torrance, CA	3.4
35	Modesto, CA	20.6	165	Richardson, TX	0.7	404	Tracy, CA	(28.2)
53	Montgomery, AL	16.9	264	Richmond, CA	(8.2)	69	Trenton, NJ	13.3
237	Moreno Valley, CA	(5.6)	108	Richmond, VA	7.0	396	Troy, MI	(23.9)
123	Mountain View, CA	5.2	43	Rio Rancho, NM	18.5	172	Tucson, AZ	0.1
413	Murfreesboro, TN	(34.8)	114	Riverside, CA	5.9	341	Tulsa, OK	(15.8)
61	Murrieta, CA	14.9	158	Roanoke, VA	1.7	246	Tuscaloosa, AL	(6.5)
188	Nampa, ID	(1.8)	58	Rochester, MN	15.4	194	Tustin, CA	(2.5)
166	Napa, CA	0.5	NA	Rochester, NY**	NA	29	Tyler, TX	21.6
335	Naperville, IL	(15.4)	43	Rockford, IL	18.5	29	Upland, CA	21.6
139	Nashua, NH	3.8	228	Roseville, CA	(5.0)	414	Upper Darby Twnshp, PA	(35.7)
398	Nashville, TN	(24.9)	218	Roswell, GA	(4.1)	29	Vacaville, CA	21.6
222	New Bedford, MA	(4.5)	363	Round Rock, TX	(18.1)	100	Vallejo, CA	8.4
146	New Haven, CT	2.8	108	Sacramento, CA	7.0	98	Vancouver, WA	8.5
331	New Orleans, LA	(15.1)	55	Salem, OR	16.3	49	Ventura, CA	17.5
NA	New Rochelle, NY**	NA	119	Salinas, CA	5.3	11	Victorville, CA	33.6
NA	New York, NY**	NA	96	Salt Lake City, UT	8.6	393	Virginia Beach, VA	(23.6)
289	Newark, NJ	(10.8)	171	San Antonio, TX	0.3	90	Visalia, CA	9.1
176	Newport Beach, CA	(0.4)	47	San Bernardino, CA	17.6	259	Vista, CA	(7.7)
232	Newport News, VA	(5.3)	179	San Diego, CA	(0.6)	263	Waco, TX	(8.0)
322	Newton, MA	(13.8)	36	San Francisco, CA	19.8	250	Warren, MI	(6.9)
169	Norfolk, VA	0.4	33	San Jose, CA	20.9	267	Warwick, RI	(8.4)
270	Norman, OK	(8.6)	145	San Leandro, CA	3.1	286	Washington, DC	(10.6)
345	North Charleston, SC	(16.3)	163	San Marcos, CA	1.0	364	Waterbury, CT	(19.0)
NA	North Las Vegas, NV**	NA	259	San Mateo, CA	(7.7)	NA	Waukegan, IL**	NA
72	Norwalk, CA	12.7	51	Sandy Springs, GA	17.3	143	West Covina, CA	3.3
347	Norwalk, CT	(16.7)	156	Sandy, UT	2.0	56	West Jordan, UT	15.5
46	Oakland, CA	18.1	222	Santa Ana, CA	(4.5)	241	West Palm Beach, FL	(5.9)
126	Oceanside, CA	4.9	147	Santa Barbara, CA	2.7	173	West Valley, UT	(0.1)
28	Odessa, TX	22.9	6	Santa Clara, CA	41.0	227	Westland, MI	(4.9)
270	O'Fallon, MO	(8.6)	103	Santa Clarita, CA	8.1	73	Westminster, CA	12.5
331	Ogden, UT	(15.1)	102	Santa Maria, CA	8.2	188	Westminster, CO	(1.8)
186	Oklahoma City, OK	(1.6)	34	Santa Monica, CA	20.8	147	Whittier, CA	2.7
36	Olathe, KS	19.8	71	Santa Rosa, CA	13.1	147	Wichita Falls, TX	2.7
186	Omaha, NE	(1.6)	273	Savannah, GA	(9.0)	196	Wichita, KS	(2.6)
77	Ontario, CA	11.3	313	Scottsdale, AZ	(13.0)	61	Wilmington, NC	14.9
81	Orange, CA	11.0	140	Scranton, PA	3.7	218	Winston-Salem, NC	(4.1)
38	Orem, UT	19.7	234	Seattle, WA	(5.5)	278	Woodbridge Twnshp, NJ	(9.5)
294	Orlando, FL	(11.1)	315	Shreveport, LA	(13.1)	190	Worcester, MA	(1.9)
92	Overland Park, KS	8.9	24	Simi Valley, CA	25.8	212	Yakima, WA	(3.8)
5	Oxnard, CA	45.8	309	Sioux City, IA	(12.6)	NA	Yonkers, NY**	NA
290	Palm Bay, FL	(11.0)	166	Sioux Falls, SD	0.5	63	Yuma, AZ	14.7
105	Palmdale, CA	7.4	350	Somerville, MA	(17.2)			
NA	Parma, OH**	NA	399	South Bend, IN	(25.1)			

Source: CQ Press using reported data from the F.B.I. "Crime in the United States 2012"

*Burglary is the unlawful entry of a structure to commit a felony or theft. Attempts are included.

**Not available.

71. Percent Change in Burglary Rate: 2011 to 2012 (continued)
National Percent Change = 4.4% Decrease*

RANK	CITY	% CHANGE	RANK	CITY	% CHANGE	RANK	CITY	% CHANGE
1	Fishers, IN	72.4	75	Knoxville, TN	12.2	147	Wichita Falls, TX	2.7
2	Lake Forest, CA	60.1	76	Brownsville, TX	12.0	150	Amarillo, TX	2.5
3	Chico, CA	59.9	77	Bellevue, WA	11.3	150	Deerfield Beach, FL	2.5
4	Carmel, IN	59.3	77	Ontario, CA	11.3	150	Portland, OR	2.5
5	Oxnard, CA	45.8	79	Albuquerque, NM	11.2	153	Bloomington, IN	2.4
6	Santa Clara, CA	41.0	80	Hayward, CA	11.1	153	Denver, CO	2.4
7	Green Bay, WI	39.0	81	Orange, CA	11.0	155	Fresno, CA	2.2
8	Meridian, ID	38.5	82	Boise, ID	10.9	156	Citrus Heights, CA	2.0
9	Hesperia, CA	35.6	83	Edinburg, TX	10.8	156	Sandy, UT	2.0
10	Escondido, CA	35.5	84	Las Vegas, NV	10.7	158	Roanoke, VA	1.7
11	Victorville, CA	33.6	85	Mission Viejo, CA	10.5	158	Stamford, CT	1.7
12	Ann Arbor, MI	32.4	86	Lafayette, LA	10.4	160	Bethlehem, PA	1.4
13	Redding, CA	32.1	86	Menifee, CA	10.4	161	Joliet, IL	1.2
14	Sunnyvale, CA	31.6	88	Irvine, CA	9.8	162	Kansas City, MO	1.1
15	Chino Hills, CA	30.9	89	Madison, WI	9.6	163	San Marcos, CA	1.0
16	Antioch, CA	28.6	90	St. Joseph, MO	9.1	164	Pomona, CA	0.8
17	Medford, OR	28.4	90	Visalia, CA	9.1	165	Richardson, TX	0.7
18	Clearwater, FL	27.7	92	Buena Park, CA	8.9	166	Elk Grove, CA	0.5
19	Sugar Land, TX	27.5	92	Denton, TX	8.9	166	Napa, CA	0.5
20	Arvada, CO	27.4	92	Overland Park, KS	8.9	166	Sioux Falls, SD	0.5
21	Spokane, WA	26.3	95	Tacoma, WA	8.8	169	Jersey City, NJ	0.4
22	Hillsboro, OR	26.1	96	Kennewick, WA	8.6	169	Norfolk, VA	0.4
23	Costa Mesa, CA	25.9	96	Salt Lake City, UT	8.6	171	San Antonio, TX	0.3
24	Simi Valley, CA	25.8	98	Henderson, NV	8.5	172	Tucson, AZ	0.1
25	Kenosha, WI	24.5	98	Vancouver, WA	8.5	173	Boulder, CO	(0.1)
26	Champaign, IL	23.2	100	Vallejo, CA	8.4	173	West Valley, UT	(0.1)
27	Rancho Cucamon., CA	23.0	101	Lakewood, CA	8.3	175	Austin, TX	(0.3)
28	Odessa, TX	22.9	102	Santa Maria, CA	8.2	176	Newport Beach, CA	(0.4)
29	Tyler, TX	21.6	103	Santa Clarita, CA	8.1	177	Everett, WA	(0.5)
29	Upland, CA	21.6	104	Toms River Twnshp, NJ	8.0	177	Reno, NV	(0.5)
29	Vacaville, CA	21.6	105	Colorado Springs, CO	7.4	179	Des Moines, IA	(0.6)
32	Daly City, CA	21.5	105	Palmdale, CA	7.4	179	San Diego, CA	(0.6)
33	San Jose, CA	20.9	107	Springfield, MO	7.3	181	Aurora, IL	(0.9)
34	Santa Monica, CA	20.8	108	Richmond, VA	7.0	182	Philadelphia, PA	(1.0)
35	Modesto, CA	20.6	108	Sacramento, CA	7.0	183	Raleigh, NC	(1.1)
36	Olathe, KS	19.8	110	Fort Wayne, IN	6.6	184	Edison Twnshp, NJ	(1.3)
36	San Francisco, CA	19.8	111	Anchorage, AK	6.4	185	Berkeley, CA	(1.4)
38	Corona, CA	19.7	112	Cicero, IL	6.2	186	Oklahoma City, OK	(1.6)
38	Orem, UT	19.7	112	Independence, MO	6.2	186	Omaha, NE	(1.6)
40	Redwood City, CA	19.5	114	Riverside, CA	5.9	188	Nampa, ID	(1.8)
41	Lawrence, KS	19.0	115	Baldwin Park, CA	5.8	188	Westminster, CO	(1.8)
42	Longmont, CO	18.9	115	Livonia, MI	5.8	190	Boca Raton, FL	(1.9)
43	Pueblo, CO	18.5	117	Albany, GA	5.6	190	Worcester, MA	(1.9)
43	Rio Rancho, NM	18.5	118	Stockton, CA	5.4	192	Asheville, NC	(2.4)
43	Rockford, IL	18.5	119	Evansville, IN	5.3	192	South Gate, CA	(2.4)
46	Oakland, CA	18.1	119	Lancaster, CA	5.3	194	St. Paul, MN	(2.5)
47	Fairfield, CA	17.6	119	Salinas, CA	5.3	194	Tustin, CA	(2.5)
47	San Bernardino, CA	17.6	119	Temecula, CA	5.3	196	Garland, TX	(2.6)
49	Merced, CA	17.5	123	Mountain View, CA	5.2	196	Lakewood, CO	(2.6)
49	Ventura, CA	17.5	124	Eugene, OR	5.1	196	Wichita, KS	(2.6)
51	Sandy Springs, GA	17.3	124	Fort Collins, CO	5.1	199	Dayton, OH	(2.8)
52	Billings, MT	17.1	126	Carlsbad, CA	4.9	200	Cary, NC	(2.9)
53	Montgomery, AL	16.9	126	Chino, CA	4.9	200	Grand Rapids, MI	(2.9)
54	Gresham, OR	16.4	126	Oceanside, CA	4.9	202	Indianapolis, IN	(3.0)
55	Salem, OR	16.3	129	Garden Grove, CA	4.8	203	Spokane Valley, WA	(3.1)
56	Long Beach, CA	15.5	130	Reading, PA	4.6	204	Columbia, MO	(3.3)
56	West Jordan, UT	15.5	131	El Monte, CA	4.5	204	Kansas City, KS	(3.3)
58	Longview, TX	15.4	131	Huntington Beach, CA	4.5	206	Fayetteville, AR	(3.4)
58	Rochester, MN	15.4	133	Carson, CA	4.4	207	Burbank, CA	(3.5)
60	Glendale, AZ	15.0	134	Lakewood Twnshp, NJ	4.3	207	Fremont, CA	(3.5)
61	Murrieta, CA	14.9	134	Milwaukee, WI	4.3	209	El Paso, TX	(3.6)
61	Wilmington, NC	14.9	136	Fargo, ND	4.2	209	Fayetteville, NC	(3.6)
63	Clifton, NJ	14.7	136	Fontana, CA	4.2	209	Renton, WA	(3.6)
63	Yuma, AZ	14.7	138	Indio, CA	4.0	212	Brooklyn Park, MN	(3.8)
65	Bakersfield, CA	14.2	139	Nashua, NH	3.8	212	Lynn, MA	(3.8)
66	Fullerton, CA	14.0	140	Alhambra, CA	3.7	212	McAllen, TX	(3.8)
67	Lincoln, NE	13.8	140	Scranton, PA	3.7	212	Yakima, WA	(3.8)
68	Chula Vista, CA	13.4	142	Torrance, CA	3.4	216	Lakeland, FL	(3.9)
69	Trenton, NJ	13.3	143	Clovis, CA	3.3	217	Edmond, OK	(4.0)
70	Inglewood, CA	13.2	143	West Covina, CA	3.3	218	Roswell, GA	(4.1)
71	Santa Rosa, CA	13.1	145	San Leandro, CA	3.1	218	Winston-Salem, NC	(4.1)
72	Norwalk, CA	12.7	146	New Haven, CT	2.8	220	Hialeah, FL	(4.2)
73	Westminster, CA	12.5	147	Santa Barbara, CA	2.7	221	Hawthorne, CA	(4.3)
74	Anaheim, CA	12.4	147	Whittier, CA	2.7	222	Houston, TX	(4.5)

RANK	CITY	% CHANGE	RANK	CITY	% CHANGE	RANK	CITY	% CHANGE
222	Mesa, AZ	(4.5)	294	Plano, TX	(11.1)	371	Akron, OH	(19.3)
222	New Bedford, MA	(4.5)	298	Charlotte, NC	(11.2)	372	Atlanta, GA	(19.6)
222	Santa Ana, CA	(4.5)	299	Coral Springs, FL	(11.3)	373	Tallahassee, FL	(19.8)
226	Fort Smith, AR	(4.8)	300	Bridgeport, CT	(11.5)	374	Huntsville, AL	(20.3)
227	Westland, MI	(4.9)	301	Tampa, FL	(11.6)	375	Brick Twnshp, NJ	(20.4)
228	Rialto, CA	(5.0)	302	Frisco, TX	(11.7)	376	Columbus, GA	(20.5)
228	Roseville, CA	(5.0)	302	Springfield, IL	(11.7)	377	Arlington, TX	(20.6)
230	Avondale, AZ	(5.1)	304	Hemet, CA	(12.1)	378	League City, TX	(20.8)
230	Hamilton Twnshp, NJ	(5.1)	305	College Station, TX	(12.2)	379	Lansing, MI	(21.1)
232	Newport News, VA	(5.3)	306	Pasadena, CA	(12.3)	379	Lawton, OK	(21.1)
232	Phoenix, AZ	(5.3)	307	Las Cruces, NM	(12.5)	379	Sterling Heights, MI	(21.1)
234	Bellingham, WA	(5.5)	307	Pasadena, TX	(12.5)	382	Irving, TX	(21.5)
234	Los Angeles, CA	(5.5)	309	Miami Beach, FL	(12.6)	383	Pembroke Pines, FL	(21.6)
234	Seattle, WA	(5.5)	309	Sioux City, IA	(12.6)	384	Tempe, AZ	(21.8)
237	Moreno Valley, CA	(5.6)	311	Clinton Twnshp, MI	(12.7)	385	Brockton, MA	(22.0)
238	Gainesville, FL	(5.8)	312	Broken Arrow, OK	(12.9)	386	Kent, WA	(22.1)
238	Laredo, TX	(5.8)	313	Gilbert, AZ	(13.0)	387	Lawrence, MA	(22.2)
238	Memphis, TN	(5.8)	313	Scottsdale, AZ	(13.0)	388	Bloomington, IL	(22.7)
241	Boston, MA	(5.9)	315	Cedar Rapids, IA	(13.1)	388	Davenport, IA	(22.7)
241	West Palm Beach, FL	(5.9)	315	Shreveport, LA	(13.1)	390	Johns Creek, GA	(22.9)
243	Pompano Beach, FL	(6.1)	317	Downey, CA	(13.3)	391	Midland, TX	(23.3)
244	Manchester, NH	(6.2)	318	Jackson, MS	(13.5)	392	Provo, UT	(23.5)
245	Hollywood, FL	(6.4)	318	Thousand Oaks, CA	(13.5)	393	Virginia Beach, VA	(23.6)
246	Tuscaloosa, AL	(6.5)	320	Bellflower, CA	(13.7)	394	Dearborn, MI	(23.8)
247	Fort Lauderdale, FL	(6.6)	320	Miramar, FL	(13.7)	394	McKinney, TX	(23.8)
247	Pittsburgh, PA	(6.6)	322	Newton, MA	(13.8)	396	Troy, MI	(23.9)
249	Hampton, VA	(6.8)	323	Louisville, KY	(13.9)	397	Camden, NJ	(24.2)
250	Warren, MI	(6.9)	324	Chicago, IL	(14.1)	398	Nashville, TN	(24.9)
251	Alameda, CA	(7.0)	324	St. Petersburg, FL	(14.1)	399	South Bend, IN	(25.1)
252	High Point, NC	(7.1)	326	Farmington Hills, MI	(14.2)	400	Melbourne, FL	(25.8)
252	Largo, FL	(7.1)	327	Sunrise, FL	(14.6)	401	Topeka, KS	(26.4)
254	Hoover, AL	(7.2)	328	Detroit, MI	(14.9)	402	Killeen, TX	(27.1)
255	Minneapolis, MN	(7.4)	329	Cranston, RI	(15.0)	403	Bryan, TX	(27.8)
256	Abilene, TX	(7.6)	329	Duluth, MN	(15.0)	404	Tracy, CA	(28.2)
256	Davie, FL	(7.6)	331	Beaverton, OR	(15.1)	405	Port St. Lucie, FL	(28.3)
256	Springfield, MA	(7.6)	331	Miami Gardens, FL	(15.1)	406	Clarksville, TN	(28.5)
259	San Mateo, CA	(7.7)	331	New Orleans, LA	(15.1)	406	St. Louis, MO	(28.5)
259	Vista, CA	(7.7)	331	Ogden, UT	(15.1)	408	Compton, CA	(28.6)
261	Cambridge, MA	(7.9)	335	Dallas, TX	(15.4)	409	Grand Prairie, TX	(29.3)
261	Plantation, FL	(7.9)	335	Macon, GA	(15.4)	410	Lynchburg, VA	(29.9)
263	Waco, TX	(8.0)	335	Naperville, IL	(15.4)	411	Charleston, SC	(30.4)
264	Richmond, CA	(8.2)	338	Athens-Clarke, GA	(15.7)	412	Mobile, AL	(31.0)
265	Cleveland, OH	(8.3)	338	Elizabeth, NJ	(15.7)	413	Murfreesboro, TN	(34.8)
265	Lowell, MA	(8.3)	338	Peoria, AZ	(15.7)	414	Upper Darby Twnshp, PA	(35.7)
267	Corpus Christi, TX	(8.4)	341	Tulsa, OK	(15.8)	415	Elgin, IL	(36.1)
267	Warwick, RI	(8.4)	342	Carrollton, TX	(15.9)	416	Gary, IN	(37.4)
269	Sparks, NV	(8.5)	343	Allen, TX	(16.0)	NA	Albany, NY**	NA
270	Norman, OK	(8.6)	344	Livermore, CA	(16.2)	NA	Allentown, PA**	NA
270	O'Fallon, MO	(8.6)	345	Centennial, CO	(16.3)	NA	Amherst, NY**	NA
272	Concord, CA	(8.9)	345	North Charleston, SC	(16.3)	NA	Buffalo, NY**	NA
273	Hammond, IN	(9.0)	347	Norwalk, CT	(16.7)	NA	Chandler, AZ**	NA
273	Savannah, GA	(9.0)	348	Durham, NC	(16.8)	NA	Cheektowaga, NY**	NA
275	Baton Rouge, LA	(9.3)	349	Surprise, AZ	(17.0)	NA	Clarkstown, NY**	NA
275	Little Rock, AR	(9.3)	350	Danbury, CT	(17.2)	NA	Colonie, NY**	NA
275	Mesquite, TX	(9.3)	350	Somerville, MA	(17.2)	NA	Federal Way, WA**	NA
278	Woodbridge Twnshp, NJ	(9.5)	352	Flint, MI	(17.3)	NA	Greece, NY**	NA
279	Baltimore, MD	(9.6)	353	Chesapeake, VA	(17.4)	NA	Greensboro, NC**	NA
280	Portsmouth, VA	(9.7)	353	Peoria, IL	(17.4)	NA	Greenville, NC**	NA
281	Beaumont, TX	(9.8)	355	Fort Worth, TX	(17.5)	NA	Jurupa Valley, CA**	NA
281	Paterson, NJ	(9.8)	355	Hartford, CT	(17.5)	NA	Lexington, KY**	NA
283	Alexandria, VA	(10.0)	357	Cape Coral, FL	(17.6)	NA	New Rochelle, NY**	NA
284	Lubbock, TX	(10.2)	357	Cincinnati, OH	(17.6)	NA	New York, NY**	NA
285	Greeley, CO	(10.3)	357	Glendale, CA	(17.6)	NA	North Las Vegas, NV**	NA
286	Washington, DC	(10.6)	360	Pearland, TX	(17.7)	NA	Parma, OH**	NA
287	Bloomington, MN	(10.7)	361	Arlington Heights, IL	(17.8)	NA	Providence, RI**	NA
287	Fall River, MA	(10.7)	362	Aurora, CO	(18.0)	NA	Ramapo, NY**	NA
289	Newark, NJ	(10.8)	363	Round Rock, TX	(18.1)	NA	Rochester, NY**	NA
290	Mission, TX	(11.0)	364	Birmingham, AL	(19.0)	NA	St. George, UT**	NA
290	Palm Bay, FL	(11.0)	364	Decatur, IL	(19.0)	NA	Syracuse, NY**	NA
290	Quincy, MA	(11.0)	364	Waterbury, CT	(19.0)	NA	Thornton, CO**	NA
290	Racine, WI	(11.0)	367	Miami, FL	(19.1)	NA	Waukegan, IL**	NA
294	Erie, PA	(11.1)	368	El Cajon, CA	(19.2)	NA	Yonkers, NY**	NA
294	Jacksonville, FL	(11.1)	368	Lee's Summit, MO	(19.2)			
294	Orlando, FL	(11.1)	368	Toledo, OH	(19.2)			

Source: CQ Press using reported data from the F.B.I. "Crime in the United States 2012"

*Burglary is the unlawful entry of a structure to commit a felony or theft. Attempts are included.

**Not available.

72. Percent Change in Burglary Rate: 2008 to 2012
National Percent Change = 8.6% Decrease*

RANK	CITY	% CHANGE	RANK	CITY	% CHANGE	RANK	CITY	% CHANGE
264	Abilene, TX	(16.6)	31	Chino Hills, CA	24.1	376	Gainesville, FL	(34.9)
167	Akron, OH	(5.2)	70	Chino, CA	12.0	231	Garden Grove, CA	(13.0)
255	Alameda, CA	(15.5)	276	Chula Vista, CA	(17.8)	188	Garland, TX	(8.7)
NA	Albany, GA**	NA	NA	Cicero, IL**	NA	15	Gary, IN	38.2
NA	Albany, NY**	NA	146	Cincinnati, OH	(2.7)	367	Gilbert, AZ	(32.9)
106	Albuquerque, NM	2.2	180	Citrus Heights, CA	(7.3)	48	Glendale, AZ	17.7
184	Alexandria, VA	(7.7)	NA	Clarkstown, NY**	NA	335	Glendale, CA	(26.3)
329	Alhambra, CA	(25.6)	384	Clarksville, TN	(37.8)	373	Grand Prairie, TX	(34.6)
NA	Allentown, PA**	NA	101	Clearwater, FL	3.2	249	Grand Rapids, MI	(14.8)
365	Allen, TX	(32.3)	47	Cleveland, OH	17.8	NA	Greece, NY**	NA
274	Amarillo, TX	(17.6)	71	Clifton, NJ	11.3	354	Greeley, CO	(30.8)
NA	Amherst, NY**	NA	297	Clinton Twnshp, MI	(20.9)	157	Green Bay, WI	(4.1)
149	Anaheim, CA	(3.1)	17	Clovis, CA	37.8	388	Greensboro, NC	(38.8)
193	Anchorage, AK	(9.0)	308	College Station, TX	(22.2)	371	Greenville, NC	(34.1)
58	Ann Arbor, MI	14.9	NA	Colonie, NY**	NA	50	Gresham, OR	17.6
2	Antioch, CA	80.9	173	Colorado Springs, CO	(6.3)	86	Hamilton Twnshp, NJ	7.7
NA	Arlington Heights, IL**	NA	246	Columbia, MO	(14.4)	235	Hammond, IN	(13.3)
300	Arlington, TX	(21.3)	301	Columbus, GA	(21.4)	94	Hampton, VA	5.4
186	Arvada, CO	(8.1)	386	Compton, CA	(38.2)	99	Hartford, CT	4.5
346	Asheville, NC	(28.8)	128	Concord, CA	(0.4)	116	Hawthorne, CA	1.0
375	Athens-Clarke, GA	(34.7)	96	Coral Springs, FL	5.2	139	Hayward, CA	(1.8)
323	Atlanta, GA	(24.4)	32	Corona, CA	23.3	44	Hemet, CA	18.3
321	Aurora, CO	(24.1)	378	Corpus Christi, TX	(35.1)	215	Henderson, NV	(11.2)
172	Aurora, IL	(6.2)	29	Costa Mesa, CA	25.2	3	Hesperia, CA	76.4
319	Austin, TX	(23.7)	46	Cranston, RI	18.0	399	Hialeah, FL	(42.4)
337	Avondale, AZ	(26.8)	304	Dallas, TX	(21.8)	395	High Point, NC	(41.7)
74	Bakersfield, CA	9.8	14	Daly City, CA	39.3	73	Hillsboro, OR	10.5
158	Baldwin Park, CA	(4.2)	111	Danbury, CT	1.7	57	Hollywood, FL	15.2
120	Baltimore, MD	0.6	362	Davenport, IA	(32.1)	312	Hoover, AL	(22.6)
132	Baton Rouge, LA	(0.9)	84	Davie, FL	8.2	112	Houston, TX	1.6
241	Beaumont, TX	(13.9)	107	Dayton, OH	2.0	92	Huntington Beach, CA	5.6
370	Beaverton, OR	(33.8)	365	Dearborn, MI	(32.3)	242	Huntsville, AL	(14.0)
149	Bellevue, WA	(3.1)	NA	Decatur, IL**	NA	265	Independence, MO	(16.7)
192	Bellflower, CA	(8.9)	140	Deerfield Beach, FL	(1.9)	125	Indianapolis, IN	(0.2)
188	Bellingham, WA	(8.7)	158	Denton, TX	(4.2)	80	Indio, CA	8.8
306	Berkeley, CA	(22.0)	175	Denver, CO	(6.5)	181	Inglewood, CA	(7.4)
196	Bethlehem, PA	(9.1)	43	Des Moines, IA	19.3	37	Irvine, CA	21.3
30	Billings, MT	24.5	148	Detroit, MI	(3.0)	383	Irving, TX	(37.2)
144	Birmingham, AL	(2.3)	210	Downey, CA	(10.4)	390	Jacksonville, FL	(39.1)
NA	Bloomington, IL**	NA	42	Duluth, MN	19.7	171	Jackson, MS	(5.5)
234	Bloomington, IN	(13.2)	217	Durham, NC	(11.4)	336	Jersey City, NJ	(26.7)
249	Bloomington, MN	(14.8)	199	Edinburg, TX	(9.5)	NA	Johns Creek, GA**	NA
249	Boca Raton, FL	(14.8)	325	Edison Twnshp, NJ	(24.8)	63	Joliet, IL	13.9
294	Boise, ID	(20.4)	262	Edmond, OK	(16.3)	NA	Jurupa Valley, CA**	NA
191	Boston, MA	(8.8)	304	El Cajon, CA	(21.8)	NA	Kansas City, KS**	NA
199	Boulder, CO	(9.5)	153	El Monte, CA	(3.6)	197	Kansas City, MO	(9.3)
142	Brick Twnshp, NJ	(2.0)	294	El Paso, TX	(20.4)	205	Kennewick, WA	(10.0)
114	Bridgeport, CT	1.3	340	Elgin, IL	(27.0)	52	Kenosha, WI	16.2
NA	Brockton, MA**	NA	109	Elizabeth, NJ	1.8	311	Kent, WA	(22.5)
344	Broken Arrow, OK	(28.2)	359	Elk Grove, CA	(31.9)	314	Killeen, TX	(23.1)
323	Brooklyn Park, MN	(24.4)	121	Erie, PA	0.4	75	Knoxville, TN	9.7
350	Brownsville, TX	(29.7)	298	Escondido, CA	(21.2)	235	Lafayette, LA	(13.3)
403	Bryan, TX	(55.3)	255	Eugene, OR	(15.5)	36	Lake Forest, CA	21.8
298	Buena Park, CA	(21.2)	122	Evansville, IN	0.3	51	Lakeland, FL	16.8
NA	Buffalo, NY**	NA	228	Everett, WA	(12.9)	404	Lakewood Twnshp, NJ	(60.6)
380	Burbank, CA	(35.8)	205	Fairfield, CA	(10.0)	58	Lakewood, CA	14.9
40	Cambridge, MA	20.1	177	Fall River, MA	(7.0)	154	Lakewood, CO	(3.7)
221	Camden, NJ	(12.5)	240	Fargo, ND	(13.7)	387	Lancaster, CA	(38.3)
376	Cape Coral, FL	(34.9)	369	Farmington Hills, MI	(33.7)	212	Lansing, MI	(10.8)
216	Carlsbad, CA	(11.3)	228	Fayetteville, AR	(12.9)	328	Laredo, TX	(25.4)
360	Carmel, IN	(32.0)	225	Fayetteville, NC	(12.7)	238	Largo, FL	(13.4)
317	Carrollton, TX	(23.5)	80	Federal Way, WA	8.8	97	Las Cruces, NM	5.1
19	Carson, CA	35.0	118	Fishers, IN	0.9	225	Las Vegas, NV	(12.7)
373	Cary, NC	(34.6)	112	Flint, MI	1.6	313	Lawrence, KS	(23.0)
319	Cedar Rapids, IA	(23.7)	102	Fontana, CA	2.9	302	Lawrence, MA	(21.6)
193	Centennial, CO	(9.0)	352	Fort Collins, CO	(30.4)	124	Lawton, OK	0.0
NA	Champaign, IL**	NA	41	Fort Lauderdale, FL	20.0	384	League City, TX	(37.8)
NA	Chandler, AZ**	NA	152	Fort Smith, AR	(3.4)	400	Lee's Summit, MO	(42.6)
402	Charleston, SC	(53.4)	276	Fort Wayne, IN	(17.8)	NA	Lexington, KY**	NA
389	Charlotte, NC	(39.0)	248	Fort Worth, TX	(14.7)	140	Lincoln, NE	(1.9)
NA	Cheektowaga, NY**	NA	137	Fremont, CA	(1.6)	64	Little Rock, AR	13.8
270	Chesapeake, VA	(17.5)	22	Fresno, CA	33.0	345	Livermore, CA	(28.5)
188	Chicago, IL	(8.7)	349	Frisco, TX	(29.5)	144	Livonia, MI	(2.3)
243	Chico, CA	(14.1)	227	Fullerton, CA	(12.8)	33	Long Beach, CA	22.6

RANK	CITY	% CHANGE	RANK	CITY	% CHANGE	RANK	CITY	% CHANGE
NA	Longmont, CO**	NA	86	Pasadena, CA	7.7	231	South Gate, CA	(13.0)
308	Longview, TX	(22.2)	143	Pasadena, TX	(2.1)	378	Sparks, NV	(35.1)
267	Los Angeles, CA	(17.0)	105	Paterson, NJ	2.5	23	Spokane Valley, WA	31.4
193	Louisville, KY	(9.0)	351	Pearland, TX	(30.1)	5	Spokane, WA	60.2
286	Lowell, MA	(19.7)	257	Pembroke Pines, FL	(15.6)	NA	Springfield, IL**	NA
184	Lubbock, TX	(7.7)	332	Peoria, AZ	(25.7)	66	Springfield, MA	13.3
292	Lynchburg, VA	(20.3)	NA	Peoria, IL**	NA	122	Springfield, MO	0.3
392	Lynn, MA	(39.6)	221	Philadelphia, PA	(12.5)	249	Stamford, CT	(14.8)
179	Macon, GA	(7.1)	109	Phoenix, AZ	1.8	327	Sterling Heights, MI	(24.9)
317	Madison, WI	(23.5)	284	Pittsburgh, PA	(19.0)	131	Stockton, CA	(0.6)
9	Manchester, NH	45.8	356	Plano, TX	(31.4)	358	St. George, UT	(31.7)
394	McAllen, TX	(41.1)	187	Plantation, FL	(8.3)	28	St. Joseph, MO	27.4
209	McKinney, TX	(10.3)	268	Pomona, CA	(17.3)	315	St. Louis, MO	(23.4)
6	Medford, OR	52.7	102	Pompano Beach, FL	2.9	108	St. Paul, MN	1.9
368	Melbourne, FL	(33.5)	353	Port St. Lucie, FL	(30.5)	364	St. Petersburg, FL	(32.2)
284	Memphis, TN	(19.0)	156	Portland, OR	(4.0)	68	Sugar Land, TX	12.6
NA	Menifee, CA**	NA	61	Portsmouth, VA	14.1	18	Sunnyvale, CA	36.6
26	Merced, CA	28.7	135	Providence, RI	(1.1)	90	Sunrise, FL	6.0
329	Meridian, ID	(25.6)	360	Provo, UT	(32.0)	337	Surprise, AZ	(26.8)
169	Mesa, AZ	(5.3)	NA	Pueblo, CO**	NA	NA	Syracuse, NY**	NA
13	Mesquite, TX	39.5	260	Quincy, MA	(16.1)	126	Tacoma, WA	(0.3)
325	Miami Beach, FL	(24.8)	219	Racine, WI	(11.8)	247	Tallahassee, FL	(14.5)
337	Miami Gardens, FL	(26.8)	198	Raleigh, NC	(9.4)	397	Tampa, FL	(42.0)
214	Miami, FL	(11.1)	NA	Ramapo, NY**	NA	292	Temecula, CA	(20.3)
391	Midland, TX	(39.3)	1	Rancho Cucamon., CA	91.8	243	Tempe, AZ	(14.1)
76	Milwaukee, WI	9.4	100	Reading, PA	4.2	NA	Thornton, CO**	NA
269	Minneapolis, MN	(17.4)	7	Redding, CA	46.5	235	Thousand Oaks, CA	(13.3)
329	Miramar, FL	(25.6)	11	Redwood City, CA	43.4	60	Toledo, OH	14.5
98	Mission Viejo, CA	4.9	302	Reno, NV	(21.6)	8	Toms River Twnshp, NJ	46.3
280	Mission, TX	(18.2)	NA	Renton, WA**	NA	308	Topeka, KS	(22.2)
257	Mobile, AL	(15.6)	21	Rialto, CA	33.2	126	Torrance, CA	(0.3)
85	Modesto, CA	8.0	288	Richardson, TX	(20.0)	357	Tracy, CA	(31.6)
166	Montgomery, AL	(5.1)	39	Richmond, CA	20.2	4	Trenton, NJ	71.7
201	Moreno Valley, CA	(9.8)	77	Richmond, VA	9.2	396	Troy, MI	(41.8)
348	Mountain View, CA	(29.2)	270	Rio Rancho, NM	(17.5)	149	Tucson, AZ	(3.1)
279	Murfreesboro, TN	(18.1)	147	Riverside, CA	(2.8)	213	Tulsa, OK	(11.0)
204	Murrieta, CA	(9.9)	205	Roanoke, VA	(10.0)	315	Tuscaloosa, AL	(23.4)
115	Nampa, ID	1.2	243	Rochester, MN	(14.1)	95	Tustin, CA	5.3
208	Napa, CA	(10.2)	NA	Rochester, NY**	NA	24	Tyler, TX	31.0
290	Naperville, IL	(20.1)	287	Rockford, IL	(19.9)	53	Upland, CA	16.0
NA	Nashua, NH**	NA	322	Roseville, CA	(24.3)	382	Upper Darby Twnshp, PA	(36.2)
220	Nashville, TN	(12.1)	343	Roswell, GA	(27.8)	91	Vacaville, CA	5.7
261	New Bedford, MA	(16.2)	280	Round Rock, TX	(18.2)	34	Vallejo, CA	22.0
NA	New Haven, CT**	NA	259	Sacramento, CA	(15.9)	35	Vancouver, WA	21.9
398	New Orleans, LA	(42.2)	176	Salem, OR	(6.8)	72	Ventura, CA	10.9
NA	New Rochelle, NY**	NA	288	Salinas, CA	(20.0)	27	Victorville, CA	27.8
NA	New York, NY**	NA	262	Salt Lake City, UT	(16.3)	296	Virginia Beach, VA	(20.6)
88	Newark, NJ	7.5	283	San Antonio, TX	(18.9)	170	Visalia, CA	(5.4)
210	Newport Beach, CA	(10.4)	44	San Bernardino, CA	18.3	401	Vista, CA	(45.3)
354	Newport News, VA	(30.8)	342	San Diego, CA	(27.6)	347	Waco, TX	(28.9)
163	Newton, MA	(4.6)	158	San Francisco, CA	(4.2)	25	Warren, MI	29.3
53	Norfolk, VA	16.0	9	San Jose, CA	45.8	61	Warwick, RI	14.1
278	Norman, OK	(18.0)	162	San Leandro, CA	(4.4)	228	Washington, DC	(12.9)
372	North Charleston, SC	(34.5)	233	San Marcos, CA	(13.1)	136	Waterbury, CT	(1.4)
341	North Las Vegas, NV	(27.4)	69	San Mateo, CA	12.4	NA	Waukegan, IL**	NA
92	Norwalk, CA	5.6	362	Sandy Springs, GA	(32.1)	137	West Covina, CA	(1.6)
253	Norwalk, CT	(15.2)	270	Sandy, UT	(17.5)	128	West Jordan, UT	(0.4)
15	Oakland, CA	38.2	155	Santa Ana, CA	(3.9)	221	West Palm Beach, FL	(12.5)
128	Oceanside, CA	(0.4)	77	Santa Barbara, CA	9.2	83	West Valley, UT	8.5
282	Odessa, TX	(18.8)	38	Santa Clara, CA	20.4	239	Westland, MI	(13.5)
393	O'Fallon, MO	(39.8)	181	Santa Clarita, CA	(7.4)	218	Westminster, CA	(11.6)
102	Ogden, UT	2.9	56	Santa Maria, CA	15.6	270	Westminster, CO	(17.5)
132	Oklahoma City, OK	(0.9)	116	Santa Monica, CA	1.0	119	Whittier, CA	0.8
NA	Olathe, KS**	NA	266	Santa Rosa, CA	(16.9)	291	Wichita Falls, TX	(20.2)
79	Omaha, NE	9.1	381	Savannah, GA	(36.0)	201	Wichita, KS	(9.8)
82	Ontario, CA	8.7	201	Scottsdale, AZ	(9.8)	89	Wilmington, NC	6.7
66	Orange, CA	13.3	164	Scranton, PA	(4.8)	174	Winston-Salem, NC	(6.4)
254	Orem, UT	(15.4)	161	Seattle, WA	(4.3)	334	Woodbridge Twnshp, NJ	(26.2)
275	Orlando, FL	(17.7)	164	Shreveport, LA	(4.8)	55	Worcester, MA	15.9
134	Overland Park, KS	(1.0)	167	Simi Valley, CA	(5.2)	65	Yakima, WA	13.4
221	Oxnard, CA	(12.5)	48	Sioux City, IA	17.7	NA	Yonkers, NY**	NA
183	Palm Bay, FL	(7.6)	20	Sioux Falls, SD	33.6	12	Yuma, AZ	41.3
177	Palmdale, CA	(7.0)	333	Somerville, MA	(25.9)			
NA	Parma, OH**	NA	306	South Bend, IN	(22.0)			

Source: CQ Press using reported data from the F.B.I. "Crime in the United States 2012"

*Burglary is the unlawful entry of a structure to commit a felony or theft. Attempts are included.

**Not available.

72. Percent Change in Burglary Rate: 2008 to 2012 (continued)
National Percent Change = 8.6% Decrease*

RANK	CITY	% CHANGE	RANK	CITY	% CHANGE	RANK	CITY	% CHANGE
1	Rancho Cucamon., CA	91.8	75	Knoxville, TN	9.7	149	Anaheim, CA	(3.1)
2	Antioch, CA	80.9	76	Milwaukee, WI	9.4	149	Bellevue, WA	(3.1)
3	Hesperia, CA	76.4	77	Richmond, VA	9.2	149	Tucson, AZ	(3.1)
4	Trenton, NJ	71.7	77	Santa Barbara, CA	9.2	152	Fort Smith, AR	(3.4)
5	Spokane, WA	60.2	79	Omaha, NE	9.1	153	El Monte, CA	(3.6)
6	Medford, OR	52.7	80	Federal Way, WA	8.8	154	Lakewood, CO	(3.7)
7	Redding, CA	46.5	80	Indio, CA	8.8	155	Santa Ana, CA	(3.9)
8	Toms River Twnshp, NJ	46.3	82	Ontario, CA	8.7	156	Portland, OR	(4.0)
9	Manchester, NH	45.8	83	West Valley, UT	8.5	157	Green Bay, WI	(4.1)
9	San Jose, CA	45.8	84	Davie, FL	8.2	158	Baldwin Park, CA	(4.2)
11	Redwood City, CA	43.4	85	Modesto, CA	8.0	158	Denton, TX	(4.2)
12	Yuma, AZ	41.3	86	Hamilton Twnshp, NJ	7.7	158	San Francisco, CA	(4.2)
13	Mesquite, TX	39.5	86	Pasadena, CA	7.7	161	Seattle, WA	(4.3)
14	Daly City, CA	39.3	88	Newark, NJ	7.5	162	San Leandro, CA	(4.4)
15	Gary, IN	38.2	89	Wilmington, NC	6.7	163	Newton, MA	(4.6)
15	Oakland, CA	38.2	90	Sunrise, FL	6.0	164	Scranton, PA	(4.8)
17	Clovis, CA	37.8	91	Vacaville, CA	5.7	164	Shreveport, LA	(4.8)
18	Sunnyvale, CA	36.6	92	Huntington Beach, CA	5.6	166	Montgomery, AL	(5.1)
19	Carson, CA	35.0	92	Norwalk, CA	5.6	167	Akron, OH	(5.2)
20	Sioux Falls, SD	33.6	94	Hampton, VA	5.4	167	Simi Valley, CA	(5.2)
21	Rialto, CA	33.2	95	Tustin, CA	5.3	169	Mesa, AZ	(5.3)
22	Fresno, CA	33.0	96	Coral Springs, FL	5.2	170	Visalia, CA	(5.4)
23	Spokane Valley, WA	31.4	97	Las Cruces, NM	5.1	171	Jackson, MS	(5.5)
24	Tyler, TX	31.0	98	Mission Viejo, CA	4.9	172	Aurora, IL	(6.2)
25	Warren, MI	29.3	99	Hartford, CT	4.5	173	Colorado Springs, CO	(6.3)
26	Merced, CA	28.7	100	Reading, PA	4.2	174	Winston-Salem, NC	(6.4)
27	Victorville, CA	27.8	101	Clearwater, FL	3.2	175	Denver, CO	(6.5)
28	St. Joseph, MO	27.4	102	Fontana, CA	2.9	176	Salem, OR	(6.8)
29	Costa Mesa, CA	25.2	102	Ogden, UT	2.9	177	Fall River, MA	(7.0)
30	Billings, MT	24.5	102	Pompano Beach, FL	2.9	177	Palmdale, CA	(7.0)
31	Chino Hills, CA	24.1	105	Paterson, NJ	2.5	179	Macon, GA	(7.1)
32	Corona, CA	23.3	106	Albuquerque, NM	2.2	180	Citrus Heights, CA	(7.3)
33	Long Beach, CA	22.6	107	Dayton, OH	2.0	181	Inglewood, CA	(7.4)
34	Vallejo, CA	22.0	108	St. Paul, MN	1.9	181	Santa Clarita, CA	(7.4)
35	Vancouver, WA	21.9	109	Elizabeth, NJ	1.8	183	Palm Bay, FL	(7.6)
36	Lake Forest, CA	21.8	109	Phoenix, AZ	1.8	184	Alexandria, VA	(7.7)
37	Irvine, CA	21.3	111	Danbury, CT	1.7	184	Lubbock, TX	(7.7)
38	Santa Clara, CA	20.4	112	Flint, MI	1.6	186	Arvada, CO	(8.1)
39	Richmond, CA	20.2	112	Houston, TX	1.6	187	Plantation, FL	(8.3)
40	Cambridge, MA	20.1	114	Bridgeport, CT	1.3	188	Bellingham, WA	(8.7)
41	Fort Lauderdale, FL	20.0	115	Nampa, ID	1.2	188	Chicago, IL	(8.7)
42	Duluth, MN	19.7	116	Hawthorne, CA	1.0	188	Garland, TX	(8.7)
43	Des Moines, IA	19.3	116	Santa Monica, CA	1.0	191	Boston, MA	(8.8)
44	Hemet, CA	18.3	118	Fishers, IN	0.9	192	Bellflower, CA	(8.9)
44	San Bernardino, CA	18.3	119	Whittier, CA	0.8	193	Anchorage, AK	(9.0)
46	Cranston, RI	18.0	120	Baltimore, MD	0.6	193	Centennial, CO	(9.0)
47	Cleveland, OH	17.8	121	Erie, PA	0.4	193	Louisville, KY	(9.0)
48	Glendale, AZ	17.7	122	Evansville, IN	0.3	196	Bethlehem, PA	(9.1)
48	Sioux City, IA	17.7	122	Springfield, MO	0.3	197	Kansas City, MO	(9.3)
50	Gresham, OR	17.6	124	Lawton, OK	0.0	198	Raleigh, NC	(9.4)
51	Lakeland, FL	16.8	125	Indianapolis, IN	(0.2)	199	Boulder, CO	(9.5)
52	Kenosha, WI	16.2	126	Tacoma, WA	(0.3)	199	Edinburg, TX	(9.5)
53	Norfolk, VA	16.0	126	Torrance, CA	(0.3)	201	Moreno Valley, CA	(9.8)
53	Upland, CA	16.0	128	Concord, CA	(0.4)	201	Scottsdale, AZ	(9.8)
55	Worcester, MA	15.9	128	Oceanside, CA	(0.4)	201	Wichita, KS	(9.8)
56	Santa Maria, CA	15.6	128	West Jordan, UT	(0.4)	204	Murrieta, CA	(9.9)
57	Hollywood, FL	15.2	131	Stockton, CA	(0.6)	205	Fairfield, CA	(10.0)
58	Ann Arbor, MI	14.9	132	Baton Rouge, LA	(0.9)	205	Kennewick, WA	(10.0)
58	Lakewood, CA	14.9	132	Oklahoma City, OK	(0.9)	205	Roanoke, VA	(10.0)
60	Toledo, OH	14.5	134	Overland Park, KS	(1.0)	208	Napa, CA	(10.2)
61	Portsmouth, VA	14.1	135	Providence, RI	(1.1)	209	McKinney, TX	(10.3)
61	Warwick, RI	14.1	136	Waterbury, CT	(1.4)	210	Downey, CA	(10.4)
63	Joliet, IL	13.9	137	Fremont, CA	(1.6)	210	Newport Beach, CA	(10.4)
64	Little Rock, AR	13.8	137	West Covina, CA	(1.6)	212	Lansing, MI	(10.8)
65	Yakima, WA	13.4	139	Hayward, CA	(1.8)	213	Tulsa, OK	(11.0)
66	Orange, CA	13.3	140	Deerfield Beach, FL	(1.9)	214	Miami, FL	(11.1)
66	Springfield, MA	13.3	140	Lincoln, NE	(1.9)	215	Henderson, NV	(11.2)
68	Sugar Land, TX	12.6	142	Brick Twnshp, NJ	(2.0)	216	Carlsbad, CA	(11.3)
69	San Mateo, CA	12.4	143	Pasadena, TX	(2.1)	217	Durham, NC	(11.4)
70	Chino, CA	12.0	144	Birmingham, AL	(2.3)	218	Westminster, CA	(11.6)
71	Clifton, NJ	11.3	144	Livonia, MI	(2.3)	219	Racine, WI	(11.8)
72	Ventura, CA	10.9	146	Cincinnati, OH	(2.7)	220	Nashville, TN	(12.1)
73	Hillsboro, OR	10.5	147	Riverside, CA	(2.8)	221	Camden, NJ	(12.5)
74	Bakersfield, CA	9.8	148	Detroit, MI	(3.0)	221	Oxnard, CA	(12.5)

RANK	CITY	% CHANGE	RANK	CITY	% CHANGE	RANK	CITY	% CHANGE
221	Philadelphia, PA	(12.5)	297	Clinton Twnshp, MI	(20.9)	371	Greenville, NC	(34.1)
221	West Palm Beach, FL	(12.5)	298	Buena Park, CA	(21.2)	372	North Charleston, SC	(34.5)
225	Fayetteville, NC	(12.7)	298	Escondido, CA	(21.2)	373	Cary, NC	(34.6)
225	Las Vegas, NV	(12.7)	300	Arlington, TX	(21.3)	373	Grand Prairie, TX	(34.6)
227	Fullerton, CA	(12.8)	301	Columbus, GA	(21.4)	375	Athens-Clarke, GA	(34.7)
228	Everett, WA	(12.9)	302	Lawrence, MA	(21.6)	376	Cape Coral, FL	(34.9)
228	Fayetteville, AR	(12.9)	302	Reno, NV	(21.6)	376	Gainesville, FL	(34.9)
228	Washington, DC	(12.9)	304	Dallas, TX	(21.8)	378	Corpus Christi, TX	(35.1)
231	Garden Grove, CA	(13.0)	304	El Cajon, CA	(21.8)	378	Sparks, NV	(35.1)
231	South Gate, CA	(13.0)	306	Berkeley, CA	(22.0)	380	Burbank, CA	(35.8)
233	San Marcos, CA	(13.1)	306	South Bend, IN	(22.0)	381	Savannah, GA	(36.0)
234	Bloomington, IN	(13.2)	308	College Station, TX	(22.2)	382	Upper Darby Twnshp, PA	(36.2)
235	Hammond, IN	(13.3)	308	Longview, TX	(22.2)	383	Irving, TX	(37.2)
235	Lafayette, LA	(13.3)	308	Topeka, KS	(22.2)	384	Clarksville, TN	(37.8)
235	Thousand Oaks, CA	(13.3)	311	Kent, WA	(22.5)	384	League City, TX	(37.8)
238	Largo, FL	(13.4)	312	Hoover, AL	(22.6)	386	Compton, CA	(38.2)
239	Westland, MI	(13.5)	313	Lawrence, KS	(23.0)	387	Lancaster, CA	(38.3)
240	Fargo, ND	(13.7)	314	Killeen, TX	(23.1)	388	Greensboro, NC	(38.8)
241	Beaumont, TX	(13.9)	315	St. Louis, MO	(23.4)	389	Charlotte, NC	(39.0)
242	Huntsville, AL	(14.0)	315	Tuscaloosa, AL	(23.4)	390	Jacksonville, FL	(39.1)
243	Chico, CA	(14.1)	317	Carrollton, TX	(23.5)	391	Midland, TX	(39.3)
243	Rochester, MN	(14.1)	317	Madison, WI	(23.5)	392	Lynn, MA	(39.6)
243	Tempe, AZ	(14.1)	319	Austin, TX	(23.7)	393	O'Fallon, MO	(39.8)
246	Columbia, MO	(14.4)	319	Cedar Rapids, IA	(23.7)	394	McAllen, TX	(41.1)
247	Tallahassee, FL	(14.5)	321	Aurora, CO	(24.1)	395	High Point, NC	(41.7)
248	Fort Worth, TX	(14.7)	322	Roseville, CA	(24.3)	396	Troy, MI	(41.8)
249	Bloomington, MN	(14.8)	323	Atlanta, GA	(24.4)	397	Tampa, FL	(42.0)
249	Boca Raton, FL	(14.8)	323	Brooklyn Park, MN	(24.4)	398	New Orleans, LA	(42.2)
249	Grand Rapids, MI	(14.8)	325	Edison Twnshp, NJ	(24.8)	399	Hialeah, FL	(42.4)
249	Stamford, CT	(14.8)	325	Miami Beach, FL	(24.8)	400	Lee's Summit, MO	(42.6)
253	Norwalk, CT	(15.2)	327	Sterling Heights, MI	(24.9)	401	Vista, CA	(45.3)
254	Orem, UT	(15.4)	328	Laredo, TX	(25.4)	402	Charleston, SC	(53.4)
255	Alameda, CA	(15.5)	329	Alhambra, CA	(25.6)	403	Bryan, TX	(55.3)
255	Eugene, OR	(15.5)	329	Meridian, ID	(25.6)	404	Lakewood Twnshp, NJ	(60.6)
257	Mobile, AL	(15.6)	329	Miramar, FL	(25.6)	NA	Albany, GA**	NA
257	Pembroke Pines, FL	(15.6)	332	Peoria, AZ	(25.7)	NA	Albany, NY**	NA
259	Sacramento, CA	(15.9)	333	Somerville, MA	(25.9)	NA	Allentown, PA**	NA
260	Quincy, MA	(16.1)	334	Woodbridge Twnshp, NJ	(26.2)	NA	Amherst, NY**	NA
261	New Bedford, MA	(16.2)	335	Glendale, CA	(26.3)	NA	Arlington Heights, IL**	NA
262	Edmond, OK	(16.3)	336	Jersey City, NJ	(26.7)	NA	Bloomington, IL**	NA
262	Salt Lake City, UT	(16.3)	337	Avondale, AZ	(26.8)	NA	Brockton, MA**	NA
264	Abilene, TX	(16.6)	337	Miami Gardens, FL	(26.8)	NA	Buffalo, NY**	NA
265	Independence, MO	(16.7)	337	Surprise, AZ	(26.8)	NA	Champaign, IL**	NA
266	Santa Rosa, CA	(16.9)	340	Elgin, IL	(27.0)	NA	Chandler, AZ**	NA
267	Los Angeles, CA	(17.0)	341	North Las Vegas, NV	(27.4)	NA	Cheektowaga, NY**	NA
268	Pomona, CA	(17.3)	342	San Diego, CA	(27.6)	NA	Cicero, IL**	NA
269	Minneapolis, MN	(17.4)	343	Roswell, GA	(27.8)	NA	Clarkstown, NY**	NA
270	Chesapeake, VA	(17.5)	344	Broken Arrow, OK	(28.2)	NA	Colonie, NY**	NA
270	Rio Rancho, NM	(17.5)	345	Livermore, CA	(28.5)	NA	Decatur, IL**	NA
270	Sandy, UT	(17.5)	346	Asheville, NC	(28.8)	NA	Greece, NY**	NA
270	Westminster, CO	(17.5)	347	Waco, TX	(28.9)	NA	Johns Creek, GA**	NA
274	Amarillo, TX	(17.6)	348	Mountain View, CA	(29.2)	NA	Jurupa Valley, CA**	NA
275	Orlando, FL	(17.7)	349	Frisco, TX	(29.5)	NA	Kansas City, KS**	NA
276	Chula Vista, CA	(17.8)	350	Brownsville, TX	(29.7)	NA	Lexington, KY**	NA
276	Fort Wayne, IN	(17.8)	351	Pearland, TX	(30.1)	NA	Longmont, CO**	NA
278	Norman, OK	(18.0)	352	Fort Collins, CO	(30.4)	NA	Menifee, CA**	NA
279	Murfreesboro, TN	(18.1)	353	Port St. Lucie, FL	(30.5)	NA	Nashua, NH**	NA
280	Mission, TX	(18.2)	354	Greeley, CO	(30.8)	NA	New Haven, CT**	NA
280	Round Rock, TX	(18.2)	354	Newport News, VA	(30.8)	NA	New Rochelle, NY**	NA
282	Odessa, TX	(18.8)	356	Plano, TX	(31.4)	NA	New York, NY**	NA
283	San Antonio, TX	(18.9)	357	Tracy, CA	(31.6)	NA	Olathe, KS**	NA
284	Memphis, TN	(19.0)	358	St. George, UT	(31.7)	NA	Parma, OH**	NA
284	Pittsburgh, PA	(19.0)	359	Elk Grove, CA	(31.9)	NA	Peoria, IL**	NA
286	Lowell, MA	(19.7)	360	Carmel, IN	(32.0)	NA	Pueblo, CO**	NA
287	Rockford, IL	(19.9)	360	Provo, UT	(32.0)	NA	Ramapo, NY**	NA
288	Richardson, TX	(20.0)	362	Davenport, IA	(32.1)	NA	Renton, WA**	NA
288	Salinas, CA	(20.0)	362	Sandy Springs, GA	(32.1)	NA	Rochester, NY**	NA
290	Naperville, IL	(20.1)	364	St. Petersburg, FL	(32.2)	NA	Springfield, IL**	NA
291	Wichita Falls, TX	(20.2)	365	Allen, TX	(32.3)	NA	Syracuse, NY**	NA
292	Lynchburg, VA	(20.3)	365	Dearborn, MI	(32.3)	NA	Thornton, CO**	NA
292	Temecula, CA	(20.3)	367	Gilbert, AZ	(32.9)	NA	Waukegan, IL**	NA
294	Boise, ID	(20.4)	368	Melbourne, FL	(33.5)	NA	Yonkers, NY**	NA
294	El Paso, TX	(20.4)	369	Farmington Hills, MI	(33.7)			
296	Virginia Beach, VA	(20.6)	370	Beaverton, OR	(33.8)			

Source: CQ Press using reported data from the F.B.I. "Crime in the United States 2012"

*Burglary is the unlawful entry of a structure to commit a felony or theft. Attempts are included.

**Not available.

73. Larceny-Thefts in 2012
National Total = 6,150,598 Larceny-Thefts*

RANK	CITY	THEFTS	RANK	CITY	THEFTS	RANK	CITY	THEFTS
189	Abilene, TX	3,185	438	Chino Hills, CA	541	143	Gainesville, FL	3,953
101	Akron, OH	5,884	390	Chino, CA	1,319	225	Garden Grove, CA	2,655
393	Alameda, CA	1,301	192	Chula Vista, CA	3,153	102	Garland, TX	5,866
172	Albany, GA	3,369	398	Cicero, IL	1,225	293	Gary, IN	2,066
179	Albany, NY	3,299	45	Cincinnati, OH	11,590	241	Gilbert, AZ	2,496
21	Albuquerque, NM	20,298	301	Citrus Heights, CA	2,017	49	Glendale, AZ	10,863
255	Alexandria, VA	2,383	381	Clarkstown, NY	1,379	269	Glendale, CA	2,218
387	Alhambra, CA	1,339	232	Clarksville, TN	2,598	178	Grand Prairie, TX	3,316
203	Allentown, PA	2,987	191	Clearwater, FL	3,169	128	Grand Rapids, MI	4,433
404	Allen, TX	1,173	51	Cleveland, OH	10,808	290	Greece, NY	2,069
96	Amarillo, TX	6,184	417	Clifton, NJ	1,080	236	Greeley, CO	2,560
303	Amherst, NY	2,010	358	Clinton Twnshp, MI	1,572	272	Green Bay, WI	2,210
85	Anaheim, CA	7,025	223	Clovis, CA	2,685	72	Greensboro, NC	8,153
63	Anchorage, AK	8,554	333	College Station, TX	1,762	233	Greenville, NC	2,596
318	Ann Arbor, MI	1,898	324	Colonie, NY	1,847	184	Gresham, OR	3,230
313	Antioch, CA	1,920	42	Colorado Springs, CO	12,456	385	Hamilton Twnshp, NJ	1,357
430	Arlington Heights, IL	821	181	Columbia, MO	3,294	282	Hammond, IN	2,143
52	Arlington, TX	10,616	76	Columbus, GA	7,711	157	Hampton, VA	3,637
302	Arvada, CO	2,014	420	Compton, CA	1,006	166	Hartford, CT	3,467
149	Asheville, NC	3,832	222	Concord, CA	2,694	409	Hawthorne, CA	1,138
187	Athens-Clarke, GA	3,210	287	Coral Springs, FL	2,098	267	Hayward, CA	2,227
27	Atlanta, GA	17,212	217	Corona, CA	2,766	310	Hemet, CA	1,955
82	Aurora, CO	7,370	48	Corpus Christi, TX	11,166	169	Henderson, NV	3,386
242	Aurora, IL	2,495	196	Costa Mesa, CA	3,050	402	Hesperia, CA	1,185
8	Austin, TX	33,913	384	Cranston, RI	1,362	105	Hialeah, FL	5,409
219	Avondale, AZ	2,752	9	Dallas, TX	31,148	206	High Point, NC	2,943
58	Bakersfield, CA	9,540	407	Daly City, CA	1,151	337	Hillsboro, OR	1,716
429	Baldwin Park, CA	861	401	Danbury, CT	1,201	110	Hollywood, FL	5,095
26	Baltimore, MD	17,397	207	Davenport, IA	2,912	340	Hoover, AL	1,702
75	Baton Rouge, LA	7,751	234	Davie, FL	2,565	3	Houston, TX	67,978
154	Beaumont, TX	3,717	122	Dayton, OH	4,649	132	Huntington Beach, CA	4,352
406	Beaverton, OR	1,165	246	Dearborn, MI	2,463	93	Huntsville, AL	6,386
226	Bellevue, WA	2,649	373	Decatur, IL	1,445	109	Independence, MO	5,116
428	Bellflower, CA	886	345	Deerfield Beach, FL	1,680	11	Indianapolis, IN	27,525
185	Bellingham, WA	3,223	244	Denton, TX	2,473	370	Indio, CA	1,466
140	Berkeley, CA	4,084	33	Denver, CO	14,544	378	Inglewood, CA	1,389
366	Bethlehem, PA	1,488	89	Des Moines, IA	6,914	231	Irvine, CA	2,599
158	Billings, MT	3,608	28	Detroit, MI	15,968	127	Irving, TX	4,466
59	Birmingham, AL	9,042	315	Downey, CA	1,908	14	Jacksonville, FL	25,403
375	Bloomington, IL	1,396	198	Duluth, MN	3,047	94	Jackson, MS	6,308
245	Bloomington, IN	2,471	95	Durham, NC	6,291	182	Jersey City, NJ	3,291
208	Bloomington, MN	2,908	156	Edinburg, TX	3,666	439	Johns Creek, GA	406
309	Boca Raton, FL	1,965	419	Edison Twnshp, NJ	1,029	220	Joliet, IL	2,723
136	Boise, ID	4,272	388	Edmond, OK	1,330	332	Jurupa Valley, CA	1,779
37	Boston, MA	13,400	363	El Cajon, CA	1,527	124	Kansas City, KS	4,558
258	Boulder, CO	2,337	416	El Monte, CA	1,081	32	Kansas City, MO	15,088
423	Brick Twnshp, NJ	964	36	El Paso, TX	13,425	330	Kennewick, WA	1,795
208	Bridgeport, CT	2,908	360	Elgin, IL	1,546	276	Kenosha, WI	2,194
298	Brockton, MA	2,046	275	Elizabeth, NJ	2,197	173	Kent, WA	3,365
341	Broken Arrow, OK	1,698	251	Elk Grove, CA	2,406	180	Killeen, TX	3,296
304	Brooklyn Park, MN	2,001	260	Erie, PA	2,311	67	Knoxville, TN	8,373
86	Brownsville, TX	6,986	256	Escondido, CA	2,365	106	Lafayette, LA	5,244
320	Bryan, TX	1,889	99	Eugene, OR	6,054	431	Lake Forest, CA	798
374	Buena Park, CA	1,415	126	Evansville, IN	4,531	153	Lakeland, FL	3,735
68	Buffalo, NY	8,371	135	Everett, WA	4,281	432	Lakewood Twnshp, NJ	785
314	Burbank, CA	1,911	281	Fairfield, CA	2,144	380	Lakewood, CA	1,381
243	Cambridge, MA	2,482	346	Fall River, MA	1,659	107	Lakewood, CO	5,180
271	Camden, NJ	2,214	266	Fargo, ND	2,229	295	Lancaster, CA	2,051
238	Cape Coral, FL	2,547	426	Farmington Hills, MI	907	274	Lansing, MI	2,203
371	Carlsbad, CA	1,463	251	Fayetteville, AR	2,406	62	Laredo, TX	8,586
436	Carmel, IN	649	70	Fayetteville, NC	8,298	250	Largo, FL	2,413
257	Carrollton, TX	2,358	174	Federal Way, WA	3,364	186	Las Cruces, NM	3,214
359	Carson, CA	1,558	434	Fishers, IN	693	13	Las Vegas, NV	25,522
367	Cary, NC	1,476	273	Flint, MI	2,207	188	Lawrence, KS	3,190
163	Cedar Rapids, IA	3,503	254	Fontana, CA	2,389	433	Lawrence, MA	743
415	Centennial, CO	1,085	170	Fort Collins, CO	3,379	176	Lawton, OK	3,349
319	Champaign, IL	1,897	92	Fort Lauderdale, FL	6,419	383	League City, TX	1,366
108	Chandler, AZ	5,168	162	Fort Smith, AR	3,524	335	Lee's Summit, MO	1,756
218	Charleston, SC	2,764	84	Fort Wayne, IN	7,073	57	Lexington, KY	9,641
15	Charlotte, NC	22,688	19	Fort Worth, TX	21,648	71	Lincoln, NE	8,244
253	Cheektowaga, NY	2,396	240	Fremont, CA	2,502	54	Little Rock, AR	10,465
115	Chesapeake, VA	4,979	29	Fresno, CA	15,534	390	Livermore, CA	1,319
2	Chicago, IL	72,717	300	Frisco, TX	2,033	354	Livonia, MI	1,601
395	Chico, CA	1,259	211	Fullerton, CA	2,872	77	Long Beach, CA	7,702

RANK	CITY	THEFTS
339	Longmont, CO	1,705
205	Longview, TX	2,946
5	Los Angeles, CA	56,006
22	Louisville, KY	19,411
307	Lowell, MA	1,981
65	Lubbock, TX	8,429
346	Lynchburg, VA	1,659
352	Lynn, MA	1,614
130	Macon, GA	4,371
100	Madison, WI	5,898
212	Manchester, NH	2,848
121	McAllen, TX	4,751
277	McKinney, TX	2,190
152	Medford, OR	3,764
229	Melbourne, FL	2,607
12	Memphis, TN	25,959
413	Menifee, CA	1,109
221	Merced, CA	2,721
421	Meridian, ID	990
53	Mesa, AZ	10,572
141	Mesquite, TX	4,030
81	Miami Beach, FL	7,536
194	Miami Gardens, FL	3,081
31	Miami, FL	15,305
259	Midland, TX	2,313
25	Milwaukee, WI	18,448
40	Minneapolis, MN	12,760
317	Miramar, FL	1,901
425	Mission Viejo, CA	936
331	Mission, TX	1,788
60	Mobile, AL	8,755
90	Modesto, CA	6,906
80	Montgomery, AL	7,548
167	Moreno Valley, CA	3,456
410	Mountain View, CA	1,127
210	Murfreesboro, TN	2,899
403	Murrieta, CA	1,177
356	Nampa, ID	1,590
418	Napa, CA	1,073
336	Naperville, IL	1,748
316	Nashua, NH	1,902
24	Nashville, TN	18,885
311	New Bedford, MA	1,950
133	New Haven, CT	4,351
73	New Orleans, LA	8,051
407	New Rochelle, NY	1,151
1	New York, NY	115,935
138	Newark, NJ	4,093
353	Newport Beach, CA	1,611
129	Newport News, VA	4,431
434	Newton, MA	693
66	Norfolk, VA	8,403
264	Norman, OK	2,252
131	North Charleston, SC	4,363
200	North Las Vegas, NV	3,022
362	Norwalk, CA	1,537
386	Norwalk, CT	1,352
38	Oakland, CA	13,198
202	Oceanside, CA	3,003
234	Odessa, TX	2,565
414	O'Fallon, MO	1,100
195	Ogden, UT	3,051
20	Oklahoma City, OK	21,162
306	Olathe, KS	1,988
39	Omaha, NE	13,120
201	Ontario, CA	3,019
299	Orange, CA	2,044
321	Orem, UT	1,887
47	Orlando, FL	11,222
183	Overland Park, KS	3,238
224	Oxnard, CA	2,677
354	Palm Bay, FL	1,601
291	Palmdale, CA	2,068
440	Parma, OH	398

RANK	CITY	THEFTS
265	Pasadena, CA	2,238
139	Pasadena, TX	4,087
286	Paterson, NJ	2,114
377	Pearland, TX	1,393
190	Pembroke Pines, FL	3,175
165	Peoria, AZ	3,478
171	Peoria, IL	3,370
6	Philadelphia, PA	38,592
7	Phoenix, AZ	35,678
79	Pittsburgh, PA	7,610
111	Plano, TX	5,043
237	Plantation, FL	2,552
199	Pomona, CA	3,044
146	Pompano Beach, FL	3,876
285	Port St. Lucie, FL	2,124
16	Portland, OR	22,398
168	Portsmouth, VA	3,392
119	Providence, RI	4,884
295	Provo, UT	2,051
123	Pueblo, CO	4,642
424	Quincy, MA	943
311	Racine, WI	1,950
55	Raleigh, NC	9,812
437	Ramapo, NY	563
248	Rancho Cucamon., CA	2,427
350	Reading, PA	1,629
215	Redding, CA	2,790
411	Redwood City, CA	1,121
118	Reno, NV	4,909
197	Renton, WA	3,048
328	Rialto, CA	1,798
278	Richardson, TX	2,175
351	Richmond, CA	1,615
97	Richmond, VA	6,138
379	Rio Rancho, NM	1,385
83	Riverside, CA	7,095
159	Roanoke, VA	3,583
283	Rochester, MN	2,137
78	Rochester, NY	7,683
113	Rockford, IL	5,003
239	Roseville, CA	2,536
397	Roswell, GA	1,228
268	Round Rock, TX	2,222
44	Sacramento, CA	12,147
117	Salem, OR	4,958
230	Salinas, CA	2,606
50	Salt Lake City, UT	10,827
4	San Antonio, TX	60,633
114	San Bernardino, CA	4,991
23	San Diego, CA	19,188
10	San Francisco, CA	28,242
34	San Jose, CA	14,498
288	San Leandro, CA	2,094
426	San Marcos, CA	907
372	San Mateo, CA	1,448
322	Sandy Springs, GA	1,871
291	Sandy, UT	2,068
120	Santa Ana, CA	4,779
249	Santa Barbara, CA	2,424
262	Santa Clara, CA	2,273
326	Santa Clarita, CA	1,822
392	Santa Maria, CA	1,318
228	Santa Monica, CA	2,634
216	Santa Rosa, CA	2,777
103	Savannah, GA	5,583
125	Scottsdale, AZ	4,551
329	Scranton, PA	1,796
18	Seattle, WA	21,852
87	Shreveport, LA	6,973
376	Simi Valley, CA	1,394
227	Sioux City, IA	2,645
147	Sioux Falls, SD	3,843
396	Somerville, MA	1,248
214	South Bend, IN	2,798

RANK	CITY	THEFTS
399	South Gate, CA	1,217
338	Sparks, NV	1,710
164	Spokane Valley, WA	3,484
41	Spokane, WA	12,600
112	Springfield, IL	5,033
144	Springfield, MA	3,947
46	Springfield, MO	11,238
368	Stamford, CT	1,472
294	Sterling Heights, MI	2,059
69	Stockton, CA	8,339
405	St. George, UT	1,167
177	St. Joseph, MO	3,344
35	St. Louis, MO	13,520
88	St. Paul, MN	6,938
61	St. Petersburg, FL	8,642
399	Sugar Land, TX	1,217
342	Sunnyvale, CA	1,696
261	Sunrise, FL	2,287
323	Surprise, AZ	1,851
155	Syracuse, NY	3,698
74	Tacoma, WA	7,995
104	Tallahassee, FL	5,463
91	Tampa, FL	6,864
348	Temecula, CA	1,640
98	Tempe, AZ	6,085
247	Thornton, CO	2,431
369	Thousand Oaks, CA	1,470
NA	Toledo, OH**	NA
270	Toms River Twnshp, NJ	2,215
116	Topeka, KS	4,967
325	Torrance, CA	1,823
357	Tracy, CA	1,587
422	Trenton, NJ	986
382	Troy, MI	1,376
NA	Tucson, AZ**	NA
43	Tulsa, OK	12,162
204	Tuscaloosa, AL	2,965
394	Tustin, CA	1,282
175	Tyler, TX	3,350
389	Upland, CA	1,329
349	Upper Darby Twnshp, PA	1,639
361	Vacaville, CA	1,540
344	Vallejo, CA	1,681
134	Vancouver, WA	4,343
213	Ventura, CA	2,825
307	Victorville, CA	1,981
56	Virginia Beach, VA	9,662
151	Visalia, CA	3,778
412	Vista, CA	1,118
137	Waco, TX	4,139
297	Warren, MI	2,049
343	Warwick, RI	1,688
17	Washington, DC	22,196
160	Waterbury, CT	3,538
305	Waukegan, IL	1,999
284	West Covina, CA	2,135
263	West Jordan, UT	2,264
150	West Palm Beach, FL	3,801
142	West Valley, UT	3,972
365	Westland, MI	1,505
289	Westminster, CA	2,086
280	Westminster, CO	2,146
334	Whittier, CA	1,758
161	Wichita Falls, TX	3,532
30	Wichita, KS	15,331
147	Wilmington, NC	3,843
64	Winston-Salem, NC	8,490
364	Woodbridge Twnshp, NJ	1,514
145	Worcester, MA	3,927
193	Yakima, WA	3,106
327	Yonkers, NY	1,799
279	Yuma, AZ	2,162

Source: Reported data from the F.B.I. "Crime in the United States 2012"

*Larceny-theft is the unlawful taking of property. Attempts are included.

**Not available.

73. Larceny-Thefts in 2012 (continued)
National Total = 6,150,598 Larceny-Thefts*

RANK CITY	THEFTS	RANK CITY	THEFTS	RANK CITY	THEFTS
1 New York, NY	115,935	75 Baton Rouge, LA	7,751	149 Asheville, NC	3,832
2 Chicago, IL	72,717	76 Columbus, GA	7,711	150 West Palm Beach, FL	3,801
3 Houston, TX	67,978	77 Long Beach, CA	7,702	151 Visalia, CA	3,778
4 San Antonio, TX	60,633	78 Rochester, NY	7,683	152 Medford, OR	3,764
5 Los Angeles, CA	56,006	79 Pittsburgh, PA	7,610	153 Lakeland, FL	3,735
6 Philadelphia, PA	38,592	80 Montgomery, AL	7,548	154 Beaumont, TX	3,717
7 Phoenix, AZ	35,678	81 Miami Beach, FL	7,536	155 Syracuse, NY	3,698
8 Austin, TX	33,913	82 Aurora, CO	7,370	156 Edinburg, TX	3,666
9 Dallas, TX	31,148	83 Riverside, CA	7,095	157 Hampton, VA	3,637
10 San Francisco, CA	28,242	84 Fort Wayne, IN	7,073	158 Billings, MT	3,608
11 Indianapolis, IN	27,525	85 Anaheim, CA	7,025	159 Roanoke, VA	3,583
12 Memphis, TN	25,959	86 Brownsville, TX	6,986	160 Waterbury, CT	3,538
13 Las Vegas, NV	25,522	87 Shreveport, LA	6,973	161 Wichita Falls, TX	3,532
14 Jacksonville, FL	25,403	88 St. Paul, MN	6,938	162 Fort Smith, AR	3,524
15 Charlotte, NC	22,688	89 Des Moines, IA	6,914	163 Cedar Rapids, IA	3,503
16 Portland, OR	22,398	90 Modesto, CA	6,906	164 Spokane Valley, WA	3,484
17 Washington, DC	22,196	91 Tampa, FL	6,864	165 Peoria, AZ	3,478
18 Seattle, WA	21,852	92 Fort Lauderdale, FL	6,419	166 Hartford, CT	3,467
19 Fort Worth, TX	21,648	93 Huntsville, AL	6,386	167 Moreno Valley, CA	3,456
20 Oklahoma City, OK	21,162	94 Jackson, MS	6,308	168 Portsmouth, VA	3,392
21 Albuquerque, NM	20,298	95 Durham, NC	6,291	169 Henderson, NV	3,386
22 Louisville, KY	19,411	96 Amarillo, TX	6,184	170 Fort Collins, CO	3,379
23 San Diego, CA	19,188	97 Richmond, VA	6,138	171 Peoria, IL	3,370
24 Nashville, TN	18,885	98 Tempe, AZ	6,085	172 Albany, GA	3,369
25 Milwaukee, WI	18,448	99 Eugene, OR	6,054	173 Kent, WA	3,365
26 Baltimore, MD	17,397	100 Madison, WI	5,898	174 Federal Way, WA	3,364
27 Atlanta, GA	17,212	101 Akron, OH	5,884	175 Tyler, TX	3,350
28 Detroit, MI	15,968	102 Garland, TX	5,866	176 Lawton, OK	3,349
29 Fresno, CA	15,534	103 Savannah, GA	5,583	177 St. Joseph, MO	3,344
30 Wichita, KS	15,331	104 Tallahassee, FL	5,463	178 Grand Prairie, TX	3,316
31 Miami, FL	15,305	105 Hialeah, FL	5,409	179 Albany, NY	3,299
32 Kansas City, MO	15,088	106 Lafayette, LA	5,244	180 Killeen, TX	3,296
33 Denver, CO	14,544	107 Lakewood, CO	5,180	181 Columbia, MO	3,294
34 San Jose, CA	14,498	108 Chandler, AZ	5,168	182 Jersey City, NJ	3,291
35 St. Louis, MO	13,520	109 Independence, MO	5,116	183 Overland Park, KS	3,238
36 El Paso, TX	13,425	110 Hollywood, FL	5,095	184 Gresham, OR	3,230
37 Boston, MA	13,400	111 Plano, TX	5,043	185 Bellingham, WA	3,223
38 Oakland, CA	13,198	112 Springfield, IL	5,033	186 Las Cruces, NM	3,214
39 Omaha, NE	13,120	113 Rockford, IL	5,003	187 Athens-Clarke, GA	3,210
40 Minneapolis, MN	12,760	114 San Bernardino, CA	4,991	188 Lawrence, KS	3,190
41 Spokane, WA	12,600	115 Chesapeake, VA	4,979	189 Abilene, TX	3,185
42 Colorado Springs, CO	12,456	116 Topeka, KS	4,967	190 Pembroke Pines, FL	3,175
43 Tulsa, OK	12,162	117 Salem, OR	4,958	191 Clearwater, FL	3,169
44 Sacramento, CA	12,147	118 Reno, NV	4,909	192 Chula Vista, CA	3,153
45 Cincinnati, OH	11,590	119 Providence, RI	4,884	193 Yakima, WA	3,106
46 Springfield, MO	11,238	120 Santa Ana, CA	4,779	194 Miami Gardens, FL	3,081
47 Orlando, FL	11,222	121 McAllen, TX	4,751	195 Ogden, UT	3,051
48 Corpus Christi, TX	11,166	122 Dayton, OH	4,649	196 Costa Mesa, CA	3,050
49 Glendale, AZ	10,863	123 Pueblo, CO	4,642	197 Renton, WA	3,048
50 Salt Lake City, UT	10,827	124 Kansas City, KS	4,558	198 Duluth, MN	3,047
51 Cleveland, OH	10,808	125 Scottsdale, AZ	4,551	199 Pomona, CA	3,044
52 Arlington, TX	10,616	126 Evansville, IN	4,531	200 North Las Vegas, NV	3,022
53 Mesa, AZ	10,572	127 Irving, TX	4,466	201 Ontario, CA	3,019
54 Little Rock, AR	10,465	128 Grand Rapids, MI	4,433	202 Oceanside, CA	3,003
55 Raleigh, NC	9,812	129 Newport News, VA	4,431	203 Allentown, PA	2,987
56 Virginia Beach, VA	9,662	130 Macon, GA	4,371	204 Tuscaloosa, AL	2,965
57 Lexington, KY	9,641	131 North Charleston, SC	4,363	205 Longview, TX	2,946
58 Bakersfield, CA	9,540	132 Huntington Beach, CA	4,352	206 High Point, NC	2,943
59 Birmingham, AL	9,042	133 New Haven, CT	4,351	207 Davenport, IA	2,912
60 Mobile, AL	8,755	134 Vancouver, WA	4,343	208 Bloomington, MN	2,908
61 St. Petersburg, FL	8,642	135 Everett, WA	4,281	208 Bridgeport, CT	2,908
62 Laredo, TX	8,586	136 Boise, ID	4,272	210 Murfreesboro, TN	2,899
63 Anchorage, AK	8,554	137 Waco, TX	4,139	211 Fullerton, CA	2,872
64 Winston-Salem, NC	8,490	138 Newark, NJ	4,093	212 Manchester, NH	2,848
65 Lubbock, TX	8,429	139 Pasadena, TX	4,087	213 Ventura, CA	2,825
66 Norfolk, VA	8,403	140 Berkeley, CA	4,084	214 South Bend, IN	2,798
67 Knoxville, TN	8,373	141 Mesquite, TX	4,030	215 Redding, CA	2,790
68 Buffalo, NY	8,371	142 West Valley, UT	3,972	216 Santa Rosa, CA	2,777
69 Stockton, CA	8,339	143 Gainesville, FL	3,953	217 Corona, CA	2,766
70 Fayetteville, NC	8,298	144 Springfield, MA	3,947	218 Charleston, SC	2,764
71 Lincoln, NE	8,244	145 Worcester, MA	3,927	219 Avondale, AZ	2,752
72 Greensboro, NC	8,153	146 Pompano Beach, FL	3,876	220 Joliet, IL	2,723
73 New Orleans, LA	8,051	147 Sioux Falls, SD	3,843	221 Merced, CA	2,721
74 Tacoma, WA	7,995	147 Wilmington, NC	3,843	222 Concord, CA	2,694

RANK	CITY	THEFTS	RANK	CITY	THEFTS	RANK	CITY	THEFTS
223	Clovis, CA	2,685	297	Warren, MI	2,049	371	Carlsbad, CA	1,463
224	Oxnard, CA	2,677	298	Brockton, MA	2,046	372	San Mateo, CA	1,448
225	Garden Grove, CA	2,655	299	Orange, CA	2,044	373	Decatur, IL	1,445
226	Bellevue, WA	2,649	300	Frisco, TX	2,033	374	Buena Park, CA	1,415
227	Sioux City, IA	2,645	301	Citrus Heights, CA	2,017	375	Bloomington, IL	1,396
228	Santa Monica, CA	2,634	302	Arvada, CO	2,014	376	Simi Valley, CA	1,394
229	Melbourne, FL	2,607	303	Amherst, NY	2,010	377	Pearland, TX	1,393
230	Salinas, CA	2,606	304	Brooklyn Park, MN	2,001	378	Inglewood, CA	1,389
231	Irvine, CA	2,599	305	Waukegan, IL	1,999	379	Rio Rancho, NM	1,385
232	Clarksville, TN	2,598	306	Olathe, KS	1,988	380	Lakewood, CA	1,381
233	Greenville, NC	2,596	307	Lowell, MA	1,981	381	Clarkstown, NY	1,379
234	Davie, FL	2,565	307	Victorville, CA	1,981	382	Troy, MI	1,376
234	Odessa, TX	2,565	309	Boca Raton, FL	1,965	383	League City, TX	1,366
236	Greeley, CO	2,560	310	Hemet, CA	1,955	384	Cranston, RI	1,362
237	Plantation, FL	2,552	311	New Bedford, MA	1,950	385	Hamilton Twnshp, NJ	1,357
238	Cape Coral, FL	2,547	311	Racine, WI	1,950	386	Norwalk, CT	1,352
239	Roseville, CA	2,536	313	Antioch, CA	1,920	387	Alhambra, CA	1,339
240	Fremont, CA	2,502	314	Burbank, CA	1,911	388	Edmond, OK	1,330
241	Gilbert, AZ	2,496	315	Downey, CA	1,908	389	Upland, CA	1,329
242	Aurora, IL	2,495	316	Nashua, NH	1,902	390	Chino, CA	1,319
243	Cambridge, MA	2,482	317	Miramar, FL	1,901	390	Livermore, CA	1,319
244	Denton, TX	2,473	318	Ann Arbor, MI	1,898	392	Santa Maria, CA	1,318
245	Bloomington, IN	2,471	319	Champaign, IL	1,897	393	Alameda, CA	1,301
246	Dearborn, MI	2,463	320	Bryan, TX	1,889	394	Tustin, CA	1,282
247	Thornton, CO	2,431	321	Orem, UT	1,887	395	Chico, CA	1,259
248	Rancho Cucamon., CA	2,427	322	Sandy Springs, GA	1,871	396	Somerville, MA	1,248
249	Santa Barbara, CA	2,424	323	Surprise, AZ	1,851	397	Roswell, GA	1,228
250	Largo, FL	2,413	324	Colonie, NY	1,847	398	Cicero, IL	1,225
251	Elk Grove, CA	2,406	325	Torrance, CA	1,823	399	South Gate, CA	1,217
251	Fayetteville, AR	2,406	326	Santa Clarita, CA	1,822	399	Sugar Land, TX	1,217
253	Cheektowaga, NY	2,396	327	Yonkers, NY	1,799	401	Danbury, CT	1,201
254	Fontana, CA	2,389	328	Rialto, CA	1,798	402	Hesperia, CA	1,185
255	Alexandria, VA	2,383	329	Scranton, PA	1,796	403	Murrieta, CA	1,177
256	Escondido, CA	2,365	330	Kennewick, WA	1,795	404	Allen, TX	1,173
257	Carrollton, TX	2,358	331	Mission, TX	1,788	405	St. George, UT	1,167
258	Boulder, CO	2,337	332	Jurupa Valley, CA	1,779	406	Beaverton, OR	1,165
259	Midland, TX	2,313	333	College Station, TX	1,762	407	Daly City, CA	1,151
260	Erie, PA	2,311	334	Whittier, CA	1,758	407	New Rochelle, NY	1,151
261	Sunrise, FL	2,287	335	Lee's Summit, MO	1,756	409	Hawthorne, CA	1,138
262	Santa Clara, CA	2,273	336	Naperville, IL	1,748	410	Mountain View, CA	1,127
263	West Jordan, UT	2,264	337	Hillsboro, OR	1,716	411	Redwood City, CA	1,121
264	Norman, OK	2,252	338	Sparks, NV	1,710	412	Vista, CA	1,118
265	Pasadena, CA	2,238	339	Longmont, CO	1,705	413	Menifee, CA	1,109
266	Fargo, ND	2,229	340	Hoover, AL	1,702	414	O'Fallon, MO	1,100
267	Hayward, CA	2,227	341	Broken Arrow, OK	1,698	415	Centennial, CO	1,085
268	Round Rock, TX	2,222	342	Sunnyvale, CA	1,696	416	El Monte, CA	1,081
269	Glendale, CA	2,218	343	Warwick, RI	1,688	417	Clifton, NJ	1,080
270	Toms River Twnshp, NJ	2,215	344	Vallejo, CA	1,681	418	Napa, CA	1,073
271	Camden, NJ	2,214	345	Deerfield Beach, FL	1,680	419	Edison Twnshp, NJ	1,029
272	Green Bay, WI	2,210	346	Fall River, MA	1,659	420	Compton, CA	1,006
273	Flint, MI	2,207	346	Lynchburg, VA	1,659	421	Meridian, ID	990
274	Lansing, MI	2,203	348	Temecula, CA	1,640	422	Trenton, NJ	986
275	Elizabeth, NJ	2,197	349	Upper Darby Twnshp, PA	1,639	423	Brick Twnshp, NJ	964
276	Kenosha, WI	2,194	350	Reading, PA	1,629	424	Quincy, MA	943
277	McKinney, TX	2,190	351	Richmond, CA	1,615	425	Mission Viejo, CA	936
278	Richardson, TX	2,175	352	Lynn, MA	1,614	426	Farmington Hills, MI	907
279	Yuma, AZ	2,162	353	Newport Beach, CA	1,611	426	San Marcos, CA	907
280	Westminster, CO	2,146	354	Livonia, MI	1,601	428	Bellflower, CA	886
281	Fairfield, CA	2,144	354	Palm Bay, FL	1,601	429	Baldwin Park, CA	861
282	Hammond, IN	2,143	356	Nampa, ID	1,590	430	Arlington Heights, IL	821
283	Rochester, MN	2,137	357	Tracy, CA	1,587	431	Lake Forest, CA	798
284	West Covina, CA	2,135	358	Clinton Twnshp, MI	1,572	432	Lakewood Twnshp, NJ	785
285	Port St. Lucie, FL	2,124	359	Carson, CA	1,558	433	Lawrence, MA	743
286	Paterson, NJ	2,114	360	Elgin, IL	1,546	434	Fishers, IN	693
287	Coral Springs, FL	2,098	361	Vacaville, CA	1,540	434	Newton, MA	693
288	San Leandro, CA	2,094	362	Norwalk, CA	1,537	436	Carmel, IN	649
289	Westminster, CA	2,086	363	El Cajon, CA	1,527	437	Ramapo, NY	563
290	Greece, NY	2,069	364	Woodbridge Twnshp, NJ	1,514	438	Chino Hills, CA	541
291	Palmdale, CA	2,068	365	Westland, MI	1,505	439	Johns Creek, GA	406
291	Sandy, UT	2,068	366	Bethlehem, PA	1,488	440	Parma, OH	398
293	Gary, IN	2,066	367	Cary, NC	1,476	NA	Toledo, OH**	NA
294	Sterling Heights, MI	2,059	368	Stamford, CT	1,472	NA	Tucson, AZ**	NA
295	Lancaster, CA	2,051	369	Thousand Oaks, CA	1,470			
295	Provo, UT	2,051	370	Indio, CA	1,466			

Source: Reported data from the F.B.I. "Crime in the United States 2012"

*Larceny-theft is the unlawful taking of property. Attempts are included.

**Not available.

74. Larceny-Theft Rate in 2012
National Rate = 1,959.3 Larceny-Thefts per 100,000 Population*

RANK	CITY	RATE	RANK	CITY	RATE	RANK	CITY	RATE
163	Abilene, TX	2,656.7	437	Chino Hills, CA	706.0	109	Gainesville, FL	3,111.7
125	Akron, OH	2,965.9	323	Chino, CA	1,653.0	352	Garden Grove, CA	1,516.5
308	Alameda, CA	1,723.9	398	Chula Vista, CA	1,262.1	182	Garland, TX	2,496.3
18	Albany, GA	4,291.1	366	Cicero, IL	1,453.1	173	Gary, IN	2,567.4
82	Albany, NY	3,359.9	32	Cincinnati, OH	3,912.8	408	Gilbert, AZ	1,164.9
45	Albuquerque, NM	3,666.0	197	Citrus Heights, CA	2,369.8	8	Glendale, AZ	4,662.3
328	Alexandria, VA	1,633.4	309	Clarkstown, NY	1,719.8	412	Glendale, CA	1,138.0
340	Alhambra, CA	1,585.2	278	Clarksville, TN	1,891.4	292	Grand Prairie, TX	1,824.2
180	Allentown, PA	2,503.1	133	Clearwater, FL	2,900.6	200	Grand Rapids, MI	2,333.7
387	Allen, TX	1,321.2	152	Cleveland, OH	2,744.7	234	Greece, NY	2,138.5
105	Amarillo, TX	3,145.9	394	Clifton, NJ	1,275.3	162	Greeley, CO	2,659.0
311	Amherst, NY	1,709.3	330	Clinton Twnshp, MI	1,620.6	242	Green Bay, WI	2,083.3
249	Anaheim, CA	2,039.0	153	Clovis, CA	2,744.6	128	Greensboro, NC	2,952.6
137	Anchorage, AK	2,859.5	291	College Station, TX	1,824.6	121	Greenville, NC	2,988.4
324	Ann Arbor, MI	1,650.3	196	Colonie, NY	2,372.4	122	Gresham, OR	2,985.2
289	Antioch, CA	1,828.4	135	Colorado Springs, CO	2,881.4	350	Hamilton Twnshp, NJ	1,522.8
420	Arlington Heights, IL	1,088.0	123	Columbia, MO	2,977.1	164	Hammond, IN	2,645.4
141	Arlington, TX	2,798.9	31	Columbus, GA	3,930.6	166	Hampton, VA	2,637.3
283	Arvada, CO	1,847.2	424	Compton, CA	1,025.9	146	Hartford, CT	2,769.1
12	Asheville, NC	4,492.6	230	Concord, CA	2,151.7	385	Hawthorne, CA	1,328.0
154	Athens-Clarke, GA	2,732.9	318	Coral Springs, FL	1,678.1	353	Hayward, CA	1,510.6
30	Atlanta, GA	3,938.3	301	Corona, CA	1,758.0	191	Hemet, CA	2,407.3
226	Aurora, CO	2,187.3	55	Corpus Christi, TX	3,572.4	391	Henderson, NV	1,285.2
400	Aurora, IL	1,249.0	156	Costa Mesa, CA	2,707.9	392	Hesperia, CA	1,282.7
23	Austin, TX	4,071.7	313	Cranston, RI	1,695.8	206	Hialeah, FL	2,320.4
62	Avondale, AZ	3,511.8	178	Dallas, TX	2,508.8	150	High Point, NC	2,755.6
160	Bakersfield, CA	2,682.1	417	Daly City, CA	1,114.1	293	Hillsboro, OR	1,823.2
416	Baldwin Park, CA	1,123.4	363	Danbury, CT	1,466.6	66	Hollywood, FL	3,506.2
144	Baltimore, MD	2,781.4	136	Davenport, IA	2,877.7	245	Hoover, AL	2,067.2
85	Baton Rouge, LA	3,348.2	157	Davie, FL	2,701.4	107	Houston, TX	3,122.2
111	Beaumont, TX	3,089.2	92	Dayton, OH	3,270.7	217	Huntington Beach, CA	2,235.5
397	Beaverton, OR	1,262.5	177	Dearborn, MI	2,533.6	72	Huntsville, AL	3,476.5
240	Bellevue, WA	2,102.0	276	Decatur, IL	1,898.0	14	Independence, MO	4,356.5
414	Bellflower, CA	1,137.6	228	Deerfield Beach, FL	2,169.7	91	Indianapolis, IN	3,282.1
33	Bellingham, WA	3,898.9	243	Denton, TX	2,079.2	279	Indio, CA	1,867.5
59	Berkeley, CA	3,552.5	208	Denver, CO	2,313.9	401	Inglewood, CA	1,245.9
266	Bethlehem, PA	1,973.8	87	Des Moines, IA	3,333.7	404	Irvine, CA	1,194.8
77	Billings, MT	3,391.9	216	Detroit, MI	2,258.3	258	Irving, TX	1,993.7
22	Birmingham, AL	4,239.8	317	Downey, CA	1,679.2	120	Jacksonville, FL	3,021.8
296	Bloomington, IL	1,810.5	64	Duluth, MN	3,509.2	53	Jackson, MS	3,585.3
118	Bloomington, IN	3,026.9	161	Durham, NC	2,670.6	388	Jersey City, NJ	1,308.3
75	Bloomington, MN	3,437.5	10	Edinburg, TX	4,563.6	439	Johns Creek, GA	507.3
210	Boca Raton, FL	2,271.9	425	Edison Twnshp, NJ	1,018.7	287	Joliet, IL	1,834.0
254	Boise, ID	2,019.2	335	Edmond, OK	1,593.3	293	Jurupa Valley, CA	1,823.2
237	Boston, MA	2,124.8	356	El Cajon, CA	1,499.1	110	Kansas City, KS	3,096.4
204	Boulder, CO	2,331.0	431	El Monte, CA	937.1	95	Kansas City, MO	3,251.2
395	Brick Twnshp, NJ	1,271.6	261	El Paso, TX	1,987.3	203	Kennewick, WA	2,332.0
259	Bridgeport, CT	1,991.4	376	Elgin, IL	1,416.3	223	Kenosha, WI	2,194.2
231	Brockton, MA	2,150.2	305	Elizabeth, NJ	1,739.8	149	Kent, WA	2,755.9
316	Broken Arrow, OK	1,686.4	346	Elk Grove, CA	1,538.9	181	Killeen, TX	2,497.6
171	Brooklyn Park, MN	2,587.1	213	Erie, PA	2,266.3	9	Knoxville, TN	4,594.1
34	Brownsville, TX	3,857.5	333	Escondido, CA	1,604.6	19	Lafayette, LA	4,268.6
192	Bryan, TX	2,407.0	37	Eugene, OR	3,830.6	427	Lake Forest, CA	1,008.0
310	Buena Park, CA	1,715.0	36	Evansville, IN	3,833.5	42	Lakeland, FL	3,737.5
101	Buffalo, NY	3,189.8	24	Everett, WA	4,064.8	434	Lakewood Twnshp, NJ	837.4
295	Burbank, CA	1,819.0	256	Fairfield, CA	2,001.7	312	Lakewood, CA	1,696.9
207	Cambridge, MA	2,320.0	282	Fall River, MA	1,848.4	60	Lakewood, CO	3,538.2
138	Camden, NJ	2,850.7	252	Fargo, ND	2,029.8	390	Lancaster, CA	1,288.7
334	Cape Coral, FL	1,595.6	415	Farmington Hills, MI	1,129.3	270	Lansing, MI	1,920.9
382	Carlsbad, CA	1,356.1	100	Fayetteville, AR	3,191.5	68	Laredo, TX	3,496.5
436	Carmel, IN	793.2	25	Fayetteville, NC	4,028.8	115	Largo, FL	3,062.8
277	Carrollton, TX	1,894.3	48	Federal Way, WA	3,657.4	97	Las Cruces, NM	3,219.7
319	Carson, CA	1,671.1	433	Fishers, IN	873.1	307	Las Vegas, NV	1,725.2
422	Cary, NC	1,046.7	227	Flint, MI	2,171.6	54	Lawrence, KS	3,577.0
155	Cedar Rapids, IA	2,728.2	405	Fontana, CA	1,189.3	430	Lawrence, MA	956.7
423	Centennial, CO	1,043.0	211	Fort Collins, CO	2,271.0	78	Lawton, OK	3,390.3
202	Champaign, IL	2,332.5	40	Fort Lauderdale, FL	3,757.6	337	League City, TX	1,586.0
236	Chandler, AZ	2,129.2	26	Fort Smith, AR	4,028.2	272	Lee's Summit, MO	1,912.0
219	Charleston, SC	2,231.6	148	Fort Wayne, IN	2,756.2	102	Lexington, KY	3,188.9
140	Charlotte, NC	2,806.2	139	Fort Worth, TX	2,811.1	108	Lincoln, NE	3,120.7
119	Cheektowaga, NY	3,026.1	411	Fremont, CA	1,142.8	5	Little Rock, AR	5,337.8
225	Chesapeake, VA	2,188.3	113	Fresno, CA	3,069.9	336	Livermore, CA	1,593.0
159	Chicago, IL	2,684.9	325	Frisco, TX	1,650.1	321	Livonia, MI	1,667.2
368	Chico, CA	1,445.6	244	Fullerton, CA	2,074.3	327	Long Beach, CA	1,639.1

RANK	CITY	RATE	RANK	CITY	RATE	RANK	CITY	RATE
271	Longmont, CO	1,917.3	332	Pasadena, CA	1,605.7	396	South Gate, CA	1,268.2
56	Longview, TX	3,568.6	165	Pasadena, TX	2,644.2	281	Sparks, NV	1,850.9
367	Los Angeles, CA	1,452.8	370	Paterson, NJ	1,436.6	38	Spokane Valley, WA	3,821.7
131	Louisville, KY	2,913.7	360	Pearland, TX	1,470.9	3	Spokane, WA	5,938.8
290	Lowell, MA	1,825.2	260	Pembroke Pines, FL	1,987.6	17	Springfield, IL	4,296.9
58	Lubbock, TX	3,552.9	222	Peoria, AZ	2,196.4	174	Springfield, MA	2,554.4
232	Lynchburg, VA	2,144.9	130	Peoria, IL	2,923.1	2	Springfield, MO	6,981.8
302	Lynn, MA	1,757.3	179	Philadelphia, PA	2,507.7	406	Stamford, CT	1,185.2
7	Macon, GA	4,708.3	194	Phoenix, AZ	2,401.7	341	Sterling Heights, MI	1,584.2
183	Madison, WI	2,483.3	187	Pittsburgh, PA	2,438.2	142	Stockton, CA	2,788.0
170	Manchester, NH	2,588.1	285	Plano, TX	1,841.7	345	St. George, UT	1,540.0
67	McAllen, TX	3,499.9	132	Plantation, FL	2,909.8	16	St. Joseph, MO	4,324.3
339	McKinney, TX	1,585.7	255	Pomona, CA	2,009.1	21	St. Louis, MO	4,242.7
6	Medford, OR	4,950.2	39	Pompano Beach, FL	3,763.0	195	St. Paul, MN	2,386.7
79	Melbourne, FL	3,379.9	399	Port St. Lucie, FL	1,261.2	71	St. Petersburg, FL	3,479.9
28	Memphis, TN	3,948.5	41	Portland, OR	3,745.3	361	Sugar Land, TX	1,467.6
378	Menifee, CA	1,385.4	65	Portsmouth, VA	3,506.3	407	Sunnyvale, CA	1,181.0
81	Merced, CA	3,360.3	151	Providence, RI	2,745.6	167	Sunrise, FL	2,623.7
393	Meridian, ID	1,281.2	303	Provo, UT	1,754.8	347	Surprise, AZ	1,532.4
199	Mesa, AZ	2,342.1	20	Pueblo, CO	4,256.2	176	Syracuse, NY	2,534.0
143	Mesquite, TX	2,782.9	428	Quincy, MA	1,006.0	29	Tacoma, WA	3,945.3
1	Miami Beach, FL	8,275.3	185	Racine, WI	2,466.6	129	Tallahassee, FL	2,945.6
145	Miami Gardens, FL	2,771.3	201	Raleigh, NC	2,332.9	269	Tampa, FL	1,956.9
44	Miami, FL	3,693.9	438	Ramapo, NY	658.9	338	Temecula, CA	1,585.9
257	Midland, TX	2,000.2	371	Rancho Cucamon., CA	1,433.8	46	Tempe, AZ	3,664.3
112	Milwaukee, WI	3,077.8	286	Reading, PA	1,839.5	265	Thornton, CO	1,974.6
93	Minneapolis, MN	3,269.8	114	Redding, CA	3,066.8	412	Thousand Oaks, CA	1,138.0
354	Miramar, FL	1,508.8	374	Redwood City, CA	1,428.6	NA	Toledo, OH**	NA
429	Mission Viejo, CA	979.1	235	Reno, NV	2,129.8	193	Toms River Twnshp, NJ	2,404.2
220	Mission, TX	2,219.5	94	Renton, WA	3,252.2	35	Topeka, KS	3,855.1
70	Mobile, AL	3,480.9	299	Rialto, CA	1,769.8	402	Torrance, CA	1,233.0
80	Modesto, CA	3,374.9	239	Richardson, TX	2,106.2	280	Tracy, CA	1,866.0
51	Montgomery, AL	3,611.2	351	Richmond, CA	1,518.5	410	Trenton, NJ	1,155.7
306	Moreno Valley, CA	1,730.8	127	Richmond, VA	2,953.8	315	Troy, MI	1,687.0
358	Mountain View, CA	1,484.2	343	Rio Rancho, NM	1,548.1	NA	Tucson, AZ**	NA
172	Murfreesboro, TN	2,582.7	214	Riverside, CA	2,262.9	116	Tulsa, OK	3,048.9
418	Murrieta, CA	1,101.7	46	Roanoke, VA	3,664.3	96	Tuscaloosa, AL	3,223.8
274	Nampa, ID	1,908.4	267	Rochester, MN	1,968.1	322	Tustin, CA	1,656.3
379	Napa, CA	1,365.3	49	Rochester, NY	3,624.2	83	Tyler, TX	3,348.7
403	Naperville, IL	1,223.7	90	Rockford, IL	3,285.1	300	Upland, CA	1,759.5
224	Nashua, NH	2,189.5	246	Roseville, CA	2,063.5	264	Upper Darby Twnshp, PA	1,975.2
117	Nashville, TN	3,041.6	383	Roswell, GA	1,332.7	326	Vacaville, CA	1,639.2
251	New Bedford, MA	2,030.6	241	Round Rock, TX	2,091.6	375	Vallejo, CA	1,425.6
84	New Haven, CT	3,348.6	175	Sacramento, CA	2,548.9	168	Vancouver, WA	2,610.4
221	New Orleans, LA	2,218.7	104	Salem, OR	3,150.9	169	Ventura, CA	2,603.4
359	New Rochelle, NY	1,475.2	314	Salinas, CA	1,687.7	320	Victorville, CA	1,669.1
377	New York, NY	1,398.6	4	Salt Lake City, UT	5,625.4	229	Virginia Beach, VA	2,158.7
362	Newark, NJ	1,467.5	13	San Antonio, TX	4,393.3	126	Visalia, CA	2,960.7
284	Newport Beach, CA	1,845.7	205	San Bernardino, CA	2,321.5	409	Vista, CA	1,163.5
186	Newport News, VA	2,440.1	372	San Diego, CA	1,433.6	98	Waco, TX	3,218.6
435	Newton, MA	799.2	74	San Francisco, CA	3,442.6	349	Warren, MI	1,525.2
76	Norfolk, VA	3,425.6	357	San Jose, CA	1,484.8	248	Warwick, RI	2,051.5
263	Norman, OK	1,976.0	190	San Leandro, CA	2,410.5	63	Washington, DC	3,510.2
15	North Charleston, SC	4,333.7	421	San Marcos, CA	1,057.0	99	Waterbury, CT	3,202.2
381	North Las Vegas, NV	1,362.0	365	San Mateo, CA	1,458.2	218	Waukegan, IL	2,234.3
373	Norwalk, CA	1,432.5	273	Sandy Springs, GA	1,911.3	262	West Covina, CA	1,979.4
342	Norwalk, CT	1,559.5	209	Sandy, UT	2,287.5	238	West Jordan, UT	2,113.9
89	Oakland, CA	3,303.7	369	Santa Ana, CA	1,437.4	43	West Palm Beach, FL	3,711.1
304	Oceanside, CA	1,754.7	158	Santa Barbara, CA	2,697.2	124	West Valley, UT	2,970.3
184	Odessa, TX	2,475.0	275	Santa Clara, CA	1,904.3	297	Westland, MI	1,806.7
380	O'Fallon, MO	1,363.6	426	Santa Clarita, CA	1,016.5	212	Westminster, CA	2,269.7
52	Ogden, UT	3,585.9	389	Santa Maria, CA	1,302.3	268	Westminster, CO	1,960.5
57	Oklahoma City, OK	3,553.0	134	Santa Monica, CA	2,887.7	253	Whittier, CA	2,026.7
344	Olathe, KS	1,546.4	329	Santa Rosa, CA	1,625.3	85	Wichita Falls, TX	3,348.2
106	Omaha, NE	3,139.0	189	Savannah, GA	2,413.9	27	Wichita, KS	3,967.6
298	Ontario, CA	1,797.7	250	Scottsdale, AZ	2,036.9	61	Wilmington, NC	3,513.8
364	Orange, CA	1,463.2	198	Scranton, PA	2,359.5	50	Winston-Salem, NC	3,617.6
247	Orem, UT	2,052.1	69	Seattle, WA	3,485.9	355	Woodbridge Twnshp, NJ	1,504.8
11	Orlando, FL	4,552.3	73	Shreveport, LA	3,449.2	233	Worcester, MA	2,143.0
288	Overland Park, KS	1,828.5	419	Simi Valley, CA	1,100.4	88	Yakima, WA	3,324.8
386	Oxnard, CA	1,326.6	103	Sioux City, IA	3,175.7	432	Yonkers, NY	906.5
348	Palm Bay, FL	1,530.1	188	Sioux Falls, SD	2,426.8	215	Yuma, AZ	2,262.3
384	Palmdale, CA	1,331.7	331	Somerville, MA	1,616.6			
440	Parma, OH	491.6	147	South Bend, IN	2,759.4			

Source: CQ Press using reported data from the F.B.I. "Crime in the United States 2012"

*Larceny-theft is the unlawful taking of property. Attempts are included.

**Not available.

74. Larceny-Theft Rate in 2012 (continued)
National Rate = 1,959.3 Larceny-Thefts per 100,000 Population*

RANK	CITY	RATE	RANK	CITY	RATE	RANK	CITY	RATE
1	Miami Beach, FL	8,275.3	75	Bloomington, MN	3,437.5	149	Kent, WA	2,755.9
2	Springfield, MO	6,981.8	76	Norfolk, VA	3,425.6	150	High Point, NC	2,755.6
3	Spokane, WA	5,938.8	77	Billings, MT	3,391.9	151	Providence, RI	2,745.6
4	Salt Lake City, UT	5,625.4	78	Lawton, OK	3,390.3	152	Cleveland, OH	2,744.7
5	Little Rock, AR	5,337.8	79	Melbourne, FL	3,379.9	153	Clovis, CA	2,744.6
6	Medford, OR	4,950.2	80	Modesto, CA	3,374.9	154	Athens-Clarke, GA	2,732.9
7	Macon, GA	4,708.3	81	Merced, CA	3,360.3	155	Cedar Rapids, IA	2,728.2
8	Glendale, AZ	4,662.3	82	Albany, NY	3,359.9	156	Costa Mesa, CA	2,707.9
9	Knoxville, TN	4,594.1	83	Tyler, TX	3,348.7	157	Davie, FL	2,701.4
10	Edinburg, TX	4,563.6	84	New Haven, CT	3,348.6	158	Santa Barbara, CA	2,697.2
11	Orlando, FL	4,552.3	85	Baton Rouge, LA	3,348.2	159	Chicago, IL	2,684.9
12	Asheville, NC	4,492.6	85	Wichita Falls, TX	3,348.2	160	Bakersfield, CA	2,682.1
13	San Antonio, TX	4,393.3	87	Des Moines, IA	3,333.7	161	Durham, NC	2,670.6
14	Independence, MO	4,356.5	88	Yakima, WA	3,324.8	162	Greeley, CO	2,659.0
15	North Charleston, SC	4,333.7	89	Oakland, CA	3,303.7	163	Abilene, TX	2,656.7
16	St. Joseph, MO	4,324.3	90	Rockford, IL	3,285.1	164	Hammond, IN	2,645.4
17	Springfield, IL	4,296.9	91	Indianapolis, IN	3,282.1	165	Pasadena, TX	2,644.2
18	Albany, GA	4,291.1	92	Dayton, OH	3,270.7	166	Hampton, VA	2,637.3
19	Lafayette, LA	4,268.6	93	Minneapolis, MN	3,269.8	167	Sunrise, FL	2,623.7
20	Pueblo, CO	4,256.2	94	Renton, WA	3,252.2	168	Vancouver, WA	2,610.4
21	St. Louis, MO	4,242.7	95	Kansas City, MO	3,251.2	169	Ventura, CA	2,603.4
22	Birmingham, AL	4,239.8	96	Tuscaloosa, AL	3,223.8	170	Manchester, NH	2,588.1
23	Austin, TX	4,071.7	97	Las Cruces, NM	3,219.7	171	Brooklyn Park, MN	2,587.1
24	Everett, WA	4,064.8	98	Waco, TX	3,218.6	172	Murfreesboro, TN	2,582.7
25	Fayetteville, NC	4,028.8	99	Waterbury, CT	3,202.2	173	Gary, IN	2,567.4
26	Fort Smith, AR	4,028.2	100	Fayetteville, AR	3,191.5	174	Springfield, MA	2,554.4
27	Wichita, KS	3,967.6	101	Buffalo, NY	3,189.8	175	Sacramento, CA	2,548.9
28	Memphis, TN	3,948.5	102	Lexington, KY	3,188.9	176	Syracuse, NY	2,534.0
29	Tacoma, WA	3,945.3	103	Sioux City, IA	3,175.7	177	Dearborn, MI	2,533.6
30	Atlanta, GA	3,938.3	104	Salem, OR	3,150.0	178	Dallas, TX	2,508.8
31	Columbus, GA	3,930.6	105	Amarillo, TX	3,145.9	179	Philadelphia, PA	2,507.7
32	Cincinnati, OH	3,912.8	106	Omaha, NE	3,139.0	180	Allentown, PA	2,503.1
33	Bellingham, WA	3,898.9	107	Houston, TX	3,122.2	181	Killeen, TX	2,497.6
34	Brownsville, TX	3,857.5	108	Lincoln, NE	3,120.7	182	Garland, TX	2,496.3
35	Topeka, KS	3,855.1	109	Gainesville, FL	3,111.7	183	Madison, WI	2,483.3
36	Evansville, IN	3,833.5	110	Kansas City, KS	3,096.4	184	Odessa, TX	2,475.0
37	Eugene, OR	3,830.6	111	Beaumont, TX	3,089.2	185	Racine, WI	2,466.6
38	Spokane Valley, WA	3,821.7	112	Milwaukee, WI	3,077.8	186	Newport News, VA	2,440.1
39	Pompano Beach, FL	3,763.0	113	Fresno, CA	3,069.9	187	Pittsburgh, PA	2,438.2
40	Fort Lauderdale, FL	3,757.6	114	Redding, CA	3,066.8	188	Sioux Falls, SD	2,426.8
41	Portland, OR	3,745.3	115	Largo, FL	3,062.8	189	Savannah, GA	2,413.9
42	Lakeland, FL	3,737.5	116	Tulsa, OK	3,048.9	190	San Leandro, CA	2,410.5
43	West Palm Beach, FL	3,711.1	117	Nashville, TN	3,041.6	191	Hemet, CA	2,407.3
44	Miami, FL	3,693.9	118	Bloomington, IN	3,026.9	192	Bryan, TX	2,407.0
45	Albuquerque, NM	3,666.0	119	Cheektowaga, NY	3,026.1	193	Toms River Twnshp, NJ	2,404.2
46	Roanoke, VA	3,664.3	120	Jacksonville, FL	3,021.8	194	Phoenix, AZ	2,401.7
46	Tempe, AZ	3,664.3	121	Greenville, NC	2,988.4	195	St. Paul, MN	2,386.7
48	Federal Way, WA	3,657.4	122	Gresham, OR	2,985.2	196	Colonie, NY	2,372.4
49	Rochester, NY	3,624.2	123	Columbia, MO	2,977.1	197	Citrus Heights, CA	2,369.8
50	Winston-Salem, NC	3,617.6	124	West Valley, UT	2,970.3	198	Scranton, PA	2,359.5
51	Montgomery, AL	3,611.2	125	Akron, OH	2,965.9	199	Mesa, AZ	2,342.1
52	Ogden, UT	3,585.9	126	Visalia, CA	2,960.7	200	Grand Rapids, MI	2,333.7
53	Jackson, MS	3,585.3	127	Richmond, VA	2,953.8	201	Raleigh, NC	2,332.9
54	Lawrence, KS	3,577.0	128	Greensboro, NC	2,952.6	202	Champaign, IL	2,332.5
55	Corpus Christi, TX	3,572.4	129	Tallahassee, FL	2,945.6	203	Kennewick, WA	2,332.0
56	Longview, TX	3,568.6	130	Peoria, IL	2,923.1	204	Boulder, CO	2,331.0
57	Oklahoma City, OK	3,553.0	131	Louisville, KY	2,913.7	205	San Bernardino, CA	2,321.5
58	Lubbock, TX	3,552.9	132	Plantation, FL	2,909.8	206	Hialeah, FL	2,320.4
59	Berkeley, CA	3,552.5	133	Clearwater, FL	2,900.6	207	Cambridge, MA	2,320.0
60	Lakewood, CO	3,538.2	134	Santa Monica, CA	2,887.7	208	Denver, CO	2,313.9
61	Wilmington, NC	3,513.8	135	Colorado Springs, CO	2,881.4	209	Sandy, UT	2,287.5
62	Avondale, AZ	3,511.8	136	Davenport, IA	2,877.7	210	Boca Raton, FL	2,271.9
63	Washington, DC	3,510.2	137	Anchorage, AK	2,859.5	211	Fort Collins, CO	2,271.0
64	Duluth, MN	3,509.2	138	Camden, NJ	2,850.7	212	Westminster, CA	2,269.7
65	Portsmouth, VA	3,506.3	139	Fort Worth, TX	2,811.1	213	Erie, PA	2,266.3
66	Hollywood, FL	3,506.2	140	Charlotte, NC	2,806.2	214	Riverside, CA	2,262.9
67	McAllen, TX	3,499.9	141	Arlington, TX	2,798.9	215	Yuma, AZ	2,262.3
68	Laredo, TX	3,496.5	142	Stockton, CA	2,788.0	216	Detroit, MI	2,258.3
69	Seattle, WA	3,485.9	143	Mesquite, TX	2,782.9	217	Huntington Beach, CA	2,235.5
70	Mobile, AL	3,480.9	144	Baltimore, MD	2,781.4	218	Waukegan, IL	2,234.3
71	St. Petersburg, FL	3,479.9	145	Miami Gardens, FL	2,771.3	219	Charleston, SC	2,231.6
72	Huntsville, AL	3,476.5	146	Hartford, CT	2,769.1	220	Mission, TX	2,219.5
73	Shreveport, LA	3,449.2	147	South Bend, IN	2,759.4	221	New Orleans, LA	2,218.7
74	San Francisco, CA	3,442.6	148	Fort Wayne, IN	2,756.2	222	Peoria, AZ	2,196.4

RANK	CITY	RATE	RANK	CITY	RATE	RANK	CITY	RATE
223	Kenosha, WI	2,194.2	297	Westland, MI	1,806.7	371	Rancho Cucamon., CA	1,433.8
224	Nashua, NH	2,189.5	298	Ontario, CA	1,797.7	372	San Diego, CA	1,433.6
225	Chesapeake, VA	2,188.3	299	Rialto, CA	1,769.8	373	Norwalk, CA	1,432.5
226	Aurora, CO	2,187.3	300	Upland, CA	1,759.5	374	Redwood City, CA	1,428.6
227	Flint, MI	2,171.6	301	Corona, CA	1,758.0	375	Vallejo, CA	1,425.6
228	Deerfield Beach, FL	2,169.7	302	Lynn, MA	1,757.3	376	Elgin, IL	1,416.3
229	Virginia Beach, VA	2,158.7	303	Provo, UT	1,754.8	377	New York, NY	1,398.6
230	Concord, CA	2,151.7	304	Oceanside, CA	1,754.7	378	Menifee, CA	1,385.4
231	Brockton, MA	2,150.2	305	Elizabeth, NJ	1,739.8	379	Napa, CA	1,365.3
232	Lynchburg, VA	2,144.9	306	Moreno Valley, CA	1,730.8	380	O'Fallon, MO	1,363.6
233	Worcester, MA	2,143.0	307	Las Vegas, NV	1,725.2	381	North Las Vegas, NV	1,362.0
234	Greece, NY	2,138.5	308	Alameda, CA	1,723.9	382	Carlsbad, CA	1,356.1
235	Reno, NV	2,129.8	309	Clarkstown, NY	1,719.8	383	Roswell, GA	1,332.7
236	Chandler, AZ	2,129.2	310	Buena Park, CA	1,715.0	384	Palmdale, CA	1,331.7
237	Boston, MA	2,124.8	311	Amherst, NY	1,709.3	385	Hawthorne, CA	1,328.0
238	West Jordan, UT	2,113.9	312	Lakewood, CA	1,696.9	386	Oxnard, CA	1,326.6
239	Richardson, TX	2,106.2	313	Cranston, RI	1,695.8	387	Allen, TX	1,321.2
240	Bellevue, WA	2,102.0	314	Salinas, CA	1,687.7	388	Jersey City, NJ	1,308.3
241	Round Rock, TX	2,091.6	315	Troy, MI	1,687.0	389	Santa Maria, CA	1,302.3
242	Green Bay, WI	2,083.3	316	Broken Arrow, OK	1,686.4	390	Lancaster, CA	1,288.7
243	Denton, TX	2,079.2	317	Downey, CA	1,679.2	391	Henderson, NV	1,285.2
244	Fullerton, CA	2,074.3	318	Coral Springs, FL	1,678.1	392	Hesperia, CA	1,282.7
245	Hoover, AL	2,067.2	319	Carson, CA	1,671.1	393	Meridian, ID	1,281.2
246	Roseville, CA	2,063.5	320	Victorville, CA	1,669.1	394	Clifton, NJ	1,275.3
247	Orem, UT	2,052.1	321	Livonia, MI	1,667.2	395	Brick Twnshp, NJ	1,271.6
248	Warwick, RI	2,051.5	322	Tustin, CA	1,656.3	396	South Gate, CA	1,268.2
249	Anaheim, CA	2,039.0	323	Chino, CA	1,653.0	397	Beaverton, OR	1,262.5
250	Scottsdale, AZ	2,036.9	324	Ann Arbor, MI	1,650.3	398	Chula Vista, CA	1,262.1
251	New Bedford, MA	2,030.6	325	Frisco, TX	1,650.1	399	Port St. Lucie, FL	1,261.2
252	Fargo, ND	2,029.8	326	Vacaville, CA	1,639.2	400	Aurora, IL	1,249.0
253	Whittier, CA	2,026.7	327	Long Beach, CA	1,639.1	401	Inglewood, CA	1,245.9
254	Boise, ID	2,019.2	328	Alexandria, VA	1,633.4	402	Torrance, CA	1,233.0
255	Pomona, CA	2,009.1	329	Santa Rosa, CA	1,625.3	403	Naperville, IL	1,223.7
256	Fairfield, CA	2,001.7	330	Clinton Twnshp, MI	1,620.6	404	Irvine, CA	1,194.8
257	Midland, TX	2,000.2	331	Somerville, MA	1,616.6	405	Fontana, CA	1,189.3
258	Irving, TX	1,993.7	332	Pasadena, CA	1,605.7	406	Stamford, CT	1,185.2
259	Bridgeport, CT	1,991.4	333	Escondido, CA	1,604.6	407	Sunnyvale, CA	1,181.0
260	Pembroke Pines, FL	1,987.6	334	Cape Coral, FL	1,595.6	408	Gilbert, AZ	1,164.9
261	El Paso, TX	1,987.3	335	Edmond, OK	1,593.3	409	Vista, CA	1,163.5
262	West Covina, CA	1,979.4	336	Livermore, CA	1,593.0	410	Trenton, NJ	1,155.7
263	Norman, OK	1,976.0	337	League City, TX	1,586.0	411	Fremont, CA	1,142.8
264	Upper Darby Twnshp, PA	1,975.2	338	Temecula, CA	1,585.9	412	Glendale, CA	1,138.0
265	Thornton, CO	1,974.6	339	McKinney, TX	1,585.7	412	Thousand Oaks, CA	1,138.0
266	Bethlehem, PA	1,973.8	340	Alhambra, CA	1,585.2	414	Bellflower, CA	1,137.6
267	Rochester, MN	1,968.1	341	Sterling Heights, MI	1,584.2	415	Farmington Hills, MI	1,129.3
268	Westminster, CO	1,960.5	342	Norwalk, CT	1,559.5	416	Baldwin Park, CA	1,123.4
269	Tampa, FL	1,956.9	343	Rio Rancho, NM	1,548.1	417	Daly City, CA	1,114.1
270	Lansing, MI	1,920.9	344	Olathe, KS	1,546.4	418	Murrieta, CA	1,101.7
271	Longmont, CO	1,917.3	345	St. George, UT	1,540.0	419	Simi Valley, CA	1,100.4
272	Lee's Summit, MO	1,912.0	346	Elk Grove, CA	1,538.9	420	Arlington Heights, IL	1,088.0
273	Sandy Springs, GA	1,911.3	347	Surprise, AZ	1,532.4	421	San Marcos, CA	1,057.0
274	Nampa, ID	1,908.4	348	Palm Bay, FL	1,530.1	422	Cary, NC	1,046.7
275	Santa Clara, CA	1,904.3	349	Warren, MI	1,525.2	423	Centennial, CO	1,043.0
276	Decatur, IL	1,898.0	350	Hamilton Twnshp, NJ	1,522.8	424	Compton, CA	1,025.9
277	Carrollton, TX	1,894.3	351	Richmond, CA	1,518.5	425	Edison Twnshp, NJ	1,018.7
278	Clarksville, TN	1,891.4	352	Garden Grove, CA	1,516.5	426	Santa Clarita, CA	1,016.5
279	Indio, CA	1,867.5	353	Hayward, CA	1,510.6	427	Lake Forest, CA	1,008.0
280	Tracy, CA	1,866.0	354	Miramar, FL	1,508.8	428	Quincy, MA	1,006.0
281	Sparks, NV	1,850.9	355	Woodbridge Twnshp, NJ	1,504.8	429	Mission Viejo, CA	979.1
282	Fall River, MA	1,848.4	356	El Cajon, CA	1,499.1	430	Lawrence, MA	956.7
283	Arvada, CO	1,847.2	357	San Jose, CA	1,484.8	431	El Monte, CA	937.1
284	Newport Beach, CA	1,845.7	358	Mountain View, CA	1,484.2	432	Yonkers, NY	906.5
285	Plano, TX	1,841.7	359	New Rochelle, NY	1,475.2	433	Fishers, IN	873.1
286	Reading, PA	1,839.5	360	Pearland, TX	1,470.9	434	Lakewood Twnshp, NJ	837.4
287	Joliet, IL	1,834.0	361	Sugar Land, TX	1,467.6	435	Newton, MA	799.2
288	Overland Park, KS	1,828.5	362	Newark, NJ	1,467.5	436	Carmel, IN	793.2
289	Antioch, CA	1,828.4	363	Danbury, CT	1,466.6	437	Chino Hills, CA	706.0
290	Lowell, MA	1,825.2	364	Orange, CA	1,463.2	438	Ramapo, NY	658.9
291	College Station, TX	1,824.6	365	San Mateo, CA	1,458.2	439	Johns Creek, GA	507.3
292	Grand Prairie, TX	1,824.2	366	Cicero, IL	1,453.1	440	Parma, OH	491.6
293	Hillsboro, OR	1,823.2	367	Los Angeles, CA	1,452.8	NA	Toledo, OH**	NA
293	Jurupa Valley, CA	1,823.2	368	Chico, CA	1,445.6	NA	Tucson, AZ**	NA
295	Burbank, CA	1,819.0	369	Santa Ana, CA	1,437.4			
296	Bloomington, IL	1,810.5	370	Paterson, NJ	1,436.6			

Source: CQ Press using reported data from the F.B.I. "Crime in the United States 2012"

*Larceny-theft is the unlawful taking of property. Attempts are included.

**Not available.

75. Percent Change in Larceny-Theft Rate: 2011 to 2012
National Percent Change = 0.7% Decrease*

RANK	CITY	% CHANGE	RANK	CITY	% CHANGE	RANK	CITY	% CHANGE
151	Abilene, TX	2.7	389	Chino Hills, CA	(14.4)	235	Gainesville, FL	(2.0)
162	Akron, OH	2.1	257	Chino, CA	(2.7)	26	Garden Grove, CA	16.9
257	Alameda, CA	(2.7)	313	Chula Vista, CA	(6.1)	197	Garland, TX	(0.2)
104	Albany, GA	6.1	23	Cicero, IL	17.3	91	Gary, IN	7.6
NA	Albany, NY**	NA	329	Cincinnati, OH	(7.1)	394	Gilbert, AZ	(15.0)
112	Albuquerque, NM	5.6	397	Citrus Heights, CA	(16.3)	215	Glendale, AZ	(1.1)
334	Alexandria, VA	(7.7)	NA	Clarkstown, NY**	NA	369	Glendale, CA	(11.9)
242	Alhambra, CA	(2.2)	286	Clarksville, TN	(4.8)	412	Grand Prairie, TX	(24.6)
NA	Allentown, PA**	NA	254	Clearwater, FL	(2.6)	45	Grand Rapids, MI	12.5
304	Allen, TX	(5.8)	136	Cleveland, OH	3.6	NA	Greece, NY**	NA
352	Amarillo, TX	(9.3)	286	Clifton, NJ	(4.8)	110	Greeley, CO	5.7
NA	Amherst, NY**	NA	205	Clinton Twnshp, MI	(0.5)	20	Green Bay, WI	17.6
29	Anaheim, CA	16.3	170	Clovis, CA	1.8	NA	Greensboro, NC**	NA
67	Anchorage, AK	9.6	411	College Station, TX	(23.6)	NA	Greenville, NC**	NA
235	Ann Arbor, MI	(2.0)	NA	Colonie, NY**	NA	79	Gresham, OR	8.2
16	Antioch, CA	20.5	94	Colorado Springs, CO	7.3	42	Hamilton Twnshp, NJ	12.8
340	Arlington Heights, IL	(8.1)	245	Columbia, MO	(2.4)	325	Hammond, IN	(6.7)
366	Arlington, TX	(11.2)	318	Columbus, GA	(6.2)	373	Hampton, VA	(12.3)
254	Arvada, CO	(2.6)	400	Compton, CA	(16.7)	151	Hartford, CT	2.7
4	Asheville, NC	32.0	24	Concord, CA	17.2	202	Hawthorne, CA	(0.3)
242	Athens-Clarke, GA	(2.2)	338	Coral Springs, FL	(8.0)	6	Hayward, CA	30.2
267	Atlanta, GA	(3.0)	19	Corona, CA	17.9	193	Hemet, CA	0.2
115	Aurora, CO	5.4	294	Corpus Christi, TX	(5.3)	73	Henderson, NV	8.8
353	Aurora, IL	(9.5)	65	Costa Mesa, CA	9.8	214	Hesperia, CA	(0.9)
208	Austin, TX	(0.6)	283	Cranston, RI	(4.3)	272	Hialeah, FL	(3.4)
347	Avondale, AZ	(8.7)	376	Dallas, TX	(12.7)	403	High Point, NC	(18.0)
30	Bakersfield, CA	16.1	377	Daly City, CA	(12.9)	190	Hillsboro, OR	0.3
267	Baldwin Park, CA	(3.0)	185	Danbury, CT	0.5	269	Hollywood, FL	(3.1)
155	Baltimore, MD	2.5	404	Davenport, IA	(18.3)	167	Hoover, AL	1.9
245	Baton Rouge, LA	(2.4)	285	Davie, FL	(4.6)	245	Houston, TX	(2.4)
386	Beaumont, TX	(13.9)	175	Dayton, OH	1.4	17	Huntington Beach, CA	19.9
407	Beaverton, OR	(18.7)	340	Dearborn, MI	(8.1)	197	Huntsville, AL	(0.2)
308	Bellevue, WA	(5.9)	342	Decatur, IL	(8.3)	97	Independence, MO	6.8
261	Bellflower, CA	(2.8)	196	Deerfield Beach, FL	(0.1)	149	Indianapolis, IN	2.8
79	Bellingham, WA	8.2	344	Denton, TX	(8.5)	215	Indio, CA	(1.1)
26	Berkeley, CA	16.9	184	Denver, CO	0.6	291	Inglewood, CA	(5.2)
110	Bethlehem, PA	5.7	336	Des Moines, IA	(7.9)	269	Irvine, CA	(3.1)
272	Billings, MT	(3.4)	240	Detroit, MI	(2.1)	282	Irving, TX	(4.1)
387	Birmingham, AL	(14.1)	333	Downey, CA	(7.5)	235	Jacksonville, FL	(2.0)
41	Bloomington, IL	13.0	362	Duluth, MN	(10.9)	304	Jackson, MS	(5.8)
101	Bloomington, IN	6.4	350	Durham, NC	(8.8)	298	Jersey City, NJ	(5.5)
162	Bloomington, MN	2.1	235	Edinburg, TX	(2.0)	347	Johns Creek, GA	(8.7)
311	Boca Raton, FL	(6.0)	409	Edison Twnshp, NJ	(20.1)	225	Joliet, IL	(1.4)
272	Boise, ID	(3.4)	156	Edmond, OK	2.4	NA	Jurupa Valley, CA**	NA
313	Boston, MA	(6.1)	122	El Cajon, CA	4.6	291	Kansas City, KS	(5.2)
12	Boulder, CO	21.6	294	El Monte, CA	(5.3)	235	Kansas City, MO	(2.0)
197	Brick Twnshp, NJ	(0.2)	176	El Paso, TX	1.3	393	Kennewick, WA	(14.8)
288	Bridgeport, CT	(4.9)	85	Elgin, IL	7.9	313	Kenosha, WI	(6.1)
47	Brockton, MA	12.4	402	Elizabeth, NJ	(17.4)	379	Kent, WA	(13.1)
249	Broken Arrow, OK	(2.5)	127	Elk Grove, CA	4.4	69	Killeen, TX	9.1
356	Brooklyn Park, MN	(10.3)	279	Erie, PA	(3.7)	377	Knoxville, TN	(12.9)
232	Brownsville, TX	(1.7)	76	Escondido, CA	8.4	145	Lafayette, LA	3.1
371	Bryan, TX	(12.1)	145	Eugene, OR	3.1	142	Lake Forest, CA	3.3
36	Buena Park, CA	13.6	71	Evansville, IN	9.0	161	Lakeland, FL	2.2
NA	Buffalo, NY**	NA	410	Everett, WA	(21.5)	210	Lakewood Twnshp, NJ	(0.8)
221	Burbank, CA	(1.3)	133	Fairfield, CA	3.8	104	Lakewood, CA	6.1
203	Cambridge, MA	(0.4)	406	Fall River, MA	(18.5)	85	Lakewood, CO	7.9
208	Camden, NJ	(0.6)	149	Fargo, ND	2.8	59	Lancaster, CA	10.8
375	Cape Coral, FL	(12.6)	185	Farmington Hills, MI	0.5	344	Lansing, MI	(8.5)
119	Carlsbad, CA	5.1	245	Fayetteville, AR	(2.4)	139	Laredo, TX	3.5
382	Carmel, IN	(13.4)	177	Fayetteville, NC	1.2	136	Largo, FL	3.6
96	Carrollton, TX	7.0	NA	Federal Way, WA**	NA	187	Las Cruces, NM	0.4
34	Carson, CA	14.0	90	Fishers, IN	7.7	33	Las Vegas, NV	14.5
383	Cary, NC	(13.5)	195	Flint, MI	0.1	170	Lawrence, KS	1.8
261	Cedar Rapids, IA	(2.8)	240	Fontana, CA	(2.1)	288	Lawrence, MA	(4.9)
54	Centennial, CO	11.3	320	Fort Collins, CO	(6.4)	225	Lawton, OK	(1.4)
18	Champaign, IL	18.6	261	Fort Lauderdale, FL	(2.8)	328	League City, TX	(6.9)
NA	Chandler, AZ**	NA	144	Fort Smith, AR	3.2	122	Lee's Summit, MO	4.6
342	Charleston, SC	(8.3)	133	Fort Wayne, IN	3.8	NA	Lexington, KY**	NA
135	Charlotte, NC	3.7	308	Fort Worth, TX	(5.9)	272	Lincoln, NE	(3.4)
NA	Cheektowaga, NY**	NA	92	Fremont, CA	7.5	98	Little Rock, AR	6.7
371	Chesapeake, VA	(12.1)	148	Fresno, CA	2.9	173	Livermore, CA	1.7
190	Chicago, IL	0.3	121	Frisco, TX	5.0	174	Livonia, MI	1.6
302	Chico, CA	(5.7)	54	Fullerton, CA	11.3	122	Long Beach, CA	4.6

RANK	CITY	% CHANGE
85	Longmont, CO	7.9
76	Longview, TX	8.4
130	Los Angeles, CA	4.3
355	Louisville, KY	(10.1)
182	Lowell, MA	0.8
127	Lubbock, TX	4.4
367	Lynchburg, VA	(11.6)
156	Lynn, MA	2.4
391	Macon, GA	(14.6)
298	Madison, WI	(5.5)
353	Manchester, NH	(9.5)
358	McAllen, TX	(10.5)
170	McKinney, TX	1.8
57	Medford, OR	11.0
384	Melbourne, FL	(13.7)
187	Memphis, TN	0.4
15	Menifee, CA	20.6
5	Merced, CA	31.3
43	Meridian, ID	12.7
346	Mesa, AZ	(8.6)
294	Mesquite, TX	(5.3)
313	Miami Beach, FL	(6.1)
336	Miami Gardens, FL	(7.9)
210	Miami, FL	(0.8)
327	Midland, TX	(6.8)
257	Milwaukee, WI	(2.7)
156	Minneapolis, MN	2.4
291	Miramar, FL	(5.2)
311	Mission Viejo, CA	(6.0)
398	Mission, TX	(16.6)
225	Mobile, AL	(1.4)
7	Modesto, CA	27.0
108	Montgomery, AL	6.0
11	Moreno Valley, CA	22.4
156	Mountain View, CA	2.4
384	Murfreesboro, TN	(13.7)
51	Murrieta, CA	11.9
395	Nampa, ID	(15.6)
313	Napa, CA	(6.1)
230	Naperville, IL	(1.5)
50	Nashua, NH	12.0
325	Nashville, TN	(6.7)
280	New Bedford, MA	(3.8)
112	New Haven, CT	5.6
179	New Orleans, LA	1.1
NA	New Rochelle, NY**	NA
NA	New York, NY**	NA
131	Newark, NJ	4.1
323	Newport Beach, CA	(6.5)
261	Newport News, VA	(2.8)
414	Newton, MA	(27.3)
347	Norfolk, VA	(8.7)
398	Norman, OK	(16.6)
127	North Charleston, SC	4.4
NA	North Las Vegas, NV**	NA
3	Norwalk, CA	32.3
330	Norwalk, CT	(7.3)
1	Oakland, CA	38.5
66	Oceanside, CA	9.7
83	Odessa, TX	8.1
160	O'Fallon, MO	2.3
334	Ogden, UT	(7.7)
145	Oklahoma City, OK	3.1
62	Olathe, KS	10.4
177	Omaha, NE	1.2
249	Ontario, CA	(2.5)
181	Orange, CA	0.9
360	Orem, UT	(10.7)
304	Orlando, FL	(5.8)
225	Overland Park, KS	(1.4)
136	Oxnard, CA	3.6
357	Palm Bay, FL	(10.4)
84	Palmdale, CA	8.0
NA	Parma, OH**	NA

RANK	CITY	% CHANGE
323	Pasadena, CA	(6.5)
85	Pasadena, TX	7.9
53	Paterson, NJ	11.6
103	Pearland, TX	6.3
381	Pembroke Pines, FL	(13.2)
162	Peoria, AZ	2.1
249	Peoria, IL	(2.5)
283	Philadelphia, PA	(4.3)
338	Phoenix, AZ	(8.0)
69	Pittsburgh, PA	9.1
302	Plano, TX	(5.7)
390	Plantation, FL	(14.5)
21	Pomona, CA	17.5
215	Pompano Beach, FL	(1.1)
408	Port St. Lucie, FL	(18.8)
233	Portland, OR	(1.8)
320	Portsmouth, VA	(6.4)
NA	Providence, RI**	NA
396	Provo, UT	(16.2)
2	Pueblo, CO	34.4
387	Quincy, MA	(14.1)
373	Racine, WI	(12.3)
162	Raleigh, NC	2.1
NA	Ramapo, NY**	NA
183	Rancho Cucamon., CA	0.7
78	Reading, PA	8.3
8	Redding, CA	24.6
14	Redwood City, CA	20.9
48	Reno, NV	12.2
68	Renton, WA	9.3
28	Rialto, CA	16.5
63	Richardson, TX	10.3
132	Richmond, CA	3.9
122	Richmond, VA	4.6
40	Rio Rancho, NM	13.4
59	Riverside, CA	10.8
119	Roanoke, VA	5.1
25	Rochester, MN	17.1
NA	Rochester, NY**	NA
104	Rockford, IL	6.1
363	Roseville, CA	(11.0)
298	Roswell, GA	(5.5)
99	Round Rock, TX	6.6
74	Sacramento, CA	8.5
104	Salem, OR	6.1
22	Salinas, CA	17.4
61	Salt Lake City, UT	10.7
197	San Antonio, TX	(0.2)
58	San Bernardino, CA	10.9
95	San Diego, CA	7.2
32	San Francisco, CA	15.4
45	San Jose, CA	12.5
109	San Leandro, CA	5.9
221	San Marcos, CA	(1.3)
54	San Mateo, CA	11.3
117	Sandy Springs, GA	5.2
151	Sandy, UT	2.7
52	Santa Ana, CA	11.8
36	Santa Barbara, CA	13.6
167	Santa Clara, CA	1.9
151	Santa Clarita, CA	2.7
379	Santa Maria, CA	(13.1)
34	Santa Monica, CA	14.0
219	Santa Rosa, CA	(1.2)
401	Savannah, GA	(17.3)
364	Scottsdale, AZ	(11.1)
205	Scranton, PA	(0.5)
197	Seattle, WA	(0.2)
72	Shreveport, LA	8.9
79	Simi Valley, CA	8.2
193	Sioux City, IA	0.2
101	Sioux Falls, SD	6.4
122	Somerville, MA	4.6
405	South Bend, IN	(18.4)

RANK	CITY	% CHANGE
320	South Gate, CA	(6.4)
116	Sparks, NV	5.3
278	Spokane Valley, WA	(3.6)
10	Spokane, WA	23.2
221	Springfield, IL	(1.3)
272	Springfield, MA	(3.4)
234	Springfield, MO	(1.9)
261	Stamford, CT	(2.8)
190	Sterling Heights, MI	0.3
392	Stockton, CA	(14.7)
NA	St. George, UT**	NA
30	St. Joseph, MO	16.1
364	St. Louis, MO	(11.1)
203	St. Paul, MN	(0.4)
179	St. Petersburg, FL	1.1
187	Sugar Land, TX	0.4
9	Sunnyvale, CA	23.9
359	Sunrise, FL	(10.6)
249	Surprise, AZ	(2.5)
NA	Syracuse, NY**	NA
64	Tacoma, WA	10.0
304	Tallahassee, FL	(5.8)
297	Tampa, FL	(5.4)
298	Temecula, CA	(5.5)
368	Tempe, AZ	(11.7)
NA	Thornton, CO**	NA
139	Thousand Oaks, CA	3.5
NA	Toledo, OH**	NA
369	Toms River Twnshp, NJ	(11.9)
290	Topeka, KS	(5.1)
330	Torrance, CA	(7.3)
219	Tracy, CA	(1.2)
210	Trenton, NJ	(0.8)
254	Troy, MI	(2.6)
NA	Tucson, AZ**	NA
205	Tulsa, OK	(0.5)
215	Tuscaloosa, AL	(1.1)
74	Tustin, CA	8.5
271	Tyler, TX	(3.2)
257	Upland, CA	(2.7)
308	Upper Darby Twnshp, PA	(5.9)
13	Vacaville, CA	21.2
249	Vallejo, CA	(2.5)
330	Vancouver, WA	(7.3)
36	Ventura, CA	13.6
318	Victorville, CA	(6.2)
210	Virginia Beach, VA	(0.8)
92	Visalia, CA	7.5
351	Vista, CA	(8.9)
360	Waco, TX	(10.7)
141	Warren, MI	3.4
244	Warwick, RI	(2.3)
89	Washington, DC	7.8
100	Waterbury, CT	6.5
NA	Waukegan, IL**	NA
281	West Covina, CA	(3.9)
272	West Jordan, UT	(3.4)
166	West Palm Beach, FL	2.0
112	West Valley, UT	5.6
142	Westland, MI	3.3
39	Westminster, CA	13.5
167	Westminster, CO	1.9
231	Whittier, CA	(1.6)
117	Wichita Falls, TX	5.2
43	Wichita, KS	12.7
225	Wilmington, NC	(1.4)
221	Winston-Salem, NC	(1.3)
413	Woodbridge Twnshp, NJ	(25.9)
49	Worcester, MA	12.1
79	Yakima, WA	8.2
NA	Yonkers, NY**	NA
261	Yuma, AZ	(2.8)

Source: CQ Press using reported data from the F.B.I. "Crime in the United States 2012"

*Larceny-theft is the unlawful taking of property. Attempts are included.

**Not available.

75. Percent Change in Larceny-Theft Rate: 2011 to 2012 (continued)
National Percent Change = 0.7% Decrease*

RANK	CITY	% CHANGE	RANK	CITY	% CHANGE	RANK	CITY	% CHANGE
1	Oakland, CA	38.5	74	Tustin, CA	8.5	149	Fargo, ND	2.8
2	Pueblo, CO	34.4	76	Escondido, CA	8.4	149	Indianapolis, IN	2.8
3	Norwalk, CA	32.3	76	Longview, TX	8.4	151	Abilene, TX	2.7
4	Asheville, NC	32.0	78	Reading, PA	8.3	151	Hartford, CT	2.7
5	Merced, CA	31.3	79	Bellingham, WA	8.2	151	Sandy, UT	2.7
6	Hayward, CA	30.2	79	Gresham, OR	8.2	151	Santa Clarita, CA	2.7
7	Modesto, CA	27.0	79	Simi Valley, CA	8.2	155	Baltimore, MD	2.5
8	Redding, CA	24.6	79	Yakima, WA	8.2	156	Edmond, OK	2.4
9	Sunnyvale, CA	23.9	83	Odessa, TX	8.1	156	Lynn, MA	2.4
10	Spokane, WA	23.2	84	Palmdale, CA	8.0	156	Minneapolis, MN	2.4
11	Moreno Valley, CA	22.4	85	Elgin, IL	7.9	156	Mountain View, CA	2.4
12	Boulder, CO	21.6	85	Lakewood, CO	7.9	160	O'Fallon, MO	2.3
13	Vacaville, CA	21.2	85	Longmont, CO	7.9	161	Lakeland, FL	2.2
14	Redwood City, CA	20.9	85	Pasadena, TX	7.9	162	Akron, OH	2.1
15	Menifee, CA	20.6	89	Washington, DC	7.8	162	Bloomington, MN	2.1
16	Antioch, CA	20.5	90	Fishers, IN	7.7	162	Peoria, AZ	2.1
17	Huntington Beach, CA	19.9	91	Gary, IN	7.6	162	Raleigh, NC	2.1
18	Champaign, IL	18.6	92	Fremont, CA	7.5	166	West Palm Beach, FL	2.0
19	Corona, CA	17.9	92	Visalia, CA	7.5	167	Hoover, AL	1.9
20	Green Bay, WI	17.6	94	Colorado Springs, CO	7.3	167	Santa Clara, CA	1.9
21	Pomona, CA	17.5	95	San Diego, CA	7.2	167	Westminster, CO	1.9
22	Salinas, CA	17.4	96	Carrollton, TX	7.0	170	Clovis, CA	1.8
23	Cicero, IL	17.3	97	Independence, MO	6.8	170	Lawrence, KS	1.8
24	Concord, CA	17.2	98	Little Rock, AR	6.7	170	McKinney, TX	1.8
25	Rochester, MN	17.1	99	Round Rock, TX	6.6	173	Livermore, CA	1.7
26	Berkeley, CA	16.9	100	Waterbury, CT	6.5	174	Livonia, MI	1.6
26	Garden Grove, CA	16.9	101	Bloomington, IN	6.4	175	Dayton, OH	1.4
28	Rialto, CA	16.5	101	Sioux Falls, SD	6.4	176	El Paso, TX	1.3
29	Anaheim, CA	16.3	103	Pearland, TX	6.3	177	Fayetteville, NC	1.2
30	Bakersfield, CA	16.1	104	Albany, GA	6.1	177	Omaha, NE	1.2
30	St. Joseph, MO	16.1	104	Lakewood, CA	6.1	179	New Orleans, LA	1.1
32	San Francisco, CA	15.4	104	Rockford, IL	6.1	179	St. Petersburg, FL	1.1
33	Las Vegas, NV	14.5	104	Salem, OR	6.1	181	Orange, CA	0.9
34	Carson, CA	14.0	108	Montgomery, AL	6.0	182	Lowell, MA	0.8
34	Santa Monica, CA	14.0	109	San Leandro, CA	5.9	183	Rancho Cucamon., CA	0.7
36	Buena Park, CA	13.6	110	Bethlehem, PA	5.7	184	Denver, CO	0.6
36	Santa Barbara, CA	13.6	110	Greeley, CO	5.7	185	Danbury, CT	0.5
36	Ventura, CA	13.6	112	Albuquerque, NM	5.6	185	Farmington Hills, MI	0.5
39	Westminster, CA	13.5	112	New Haven, CT	5.6	187	Las Cruces, NM	0.4
40	Rio Rancho, NM	13.4	112	West Valley, UT	5.6	187	Memphis, TN	0.4
41	Bloomington, IL	13.0	115	Aurora, CO	5.4	187	Sugar Land, TX	0.4
42	Hamilton Twnshp, NJ	12.8	116	Sparks, NV	5.3	190	Chicago, IL	0.3
43	Meridian, ID	12.7	117	Sandy Springs, GA	5.2	190	Hillsboro, OR	0.3
43	Wichita, KS	12.7	117	Wichita Falls, TX	5.2	190	Sterling Heights, MI	0.3
45	Grand Rapids, MI	12.5	119	Carlsbad, CA	5.1	193	Hemet, CA	0.2
45	San Jose, CA	12.5	119	Roanoke, VA	5.1	193	Sioux City, IA	0.2
47	Brockton, MA	12.4	121	Frisco, TX	5.0	195	Flint, MI	0.1
48	Reno, NV	12.2	122	El Cajon, CA	4.6	196	Deerfield Beach, FL	(0.1)
49	Worcester, MA	12.1	122	Lee's Summit, MO	4.6	197	Brick Twnshp, NJ	(0.2)
50	Nashua, NH	12.0	122	Long Beach, CA	4.6	197	Garland, TX	(0.2)
51	Murrieta, CA	11.9	122	Richmond, VA	4.6	197	Huntsville, AL	(0.2)
52	Santa Ana, CA	11.8	122	Somerville, MA	4.6	197	San Antonio, TX	(0.2)
53	Paterson, NJ	11.6	127	Elk Grove, CA	4.4	197	Seattle, WA	(0.2)
54	Centennial, CO	11.3	127	Lubbock, TX	4.4	202	Hawthorne, CA	(0.3)
54	Fullerton, CA	11.3	127	North Charleston, SC	4.4	203	Cambridge, MA	(0.4)
54	San Mateo, CA	11.3	130	Los Angeles, CA	4.3	203	St. Paul, MN	(0.4)
57	Medford, OR	11.0	131	Newark, NJ	4.1	205	Clinton Twnshp, MI	(0.5)
58	San Bernardino, CA	10.9	132	Richmond, CA	3.9	205	Scranton, PA	(0.5)
59	Lancaster, CA	10.8	133	Fairfield, CA	3.8	205	Tulsa, OK	(0.5)
59	Riverside, CA	10.8	133	Fort Wayne, IN	3.8	208	Austin, TX	(0.6)
61	Salt Lake City, UT	10.7	135	Charlotte, NC	3.7	208	Camden, NJ	(0.6)
62	Olathe, KS	10.4	136	Cleveland, OH	3.6	210	Lakewood Twnshp, NJ	(0.8)
63	Richardson, TX	10.3	136	Largo, FL	3.6	210	Miami, FL	(0.8)
64	Tacoma, WA	10.0	136	Oxnard, CA	3.6	210	Trenton, NJ	(0.8)
65	Costa Mesa, CA	9.8	139	Laredo, TX	3.5	210	Virginia Beach, VA	(0.8)
66	Oceanside, CA	9.7	139	Thousand Oaks, CA	3.5	214	Hesperia, CA	(0.9)
67	Anchorage, AK	9.6	141	Warren, MI	3.4	215	Glendale, AZ	(1.1)
68	Renton, WA	9.3	142	Lake Forest, CA	3.3	215	Indio, CA	(1.1)
69	Killeen, TX	9.1	142	Westland, MI	3.3	215	Pompano Beach, FL	(1.1)
69	Pittsburgh, PA	9.1	144	Fort Smith, AR	3.2	215	Tuscaloosa, AL	(1.1)
71	Evansville, IN	9.0	145	Eugene, OR	3.1	219	Santa Rosa, CA	(1.2)
72	Shreveport, LA	8.9	145	Lafayette, LA	3.1	219	Tracy, CA	(1.2)
73	Henderson, NV	8.8	145	Oklahoma City, OK	3.1	221	Burbank, CA	(1.3)
74	Sacramento, CA	8.5	148	Fresno, CA	2.9	221	San Marcos, CA	(1.3)

RANK	CITY	% CHANGE	RANK	CITY	% CHANGE	RANK	CITY	% CHANGE
221	Springfield, IL	(1.3)	297	Tampa, FL	(5.4)	371	Bryan, TX	(12.1)
221	Winston-Salem, NC	(1.3)	298	Jersey City, NJ	(5.5)	371	Chesapeake, VA	(12.1)
225	Joliet, IL	(1.4)	298	Madison, WI	(5.5)	373	Hampton, VA	(12.3)
225	Lawton, OK	(1.4)	298	Roswell, GA	(5.5)	373	Racine, WI	(12.3)
225	Mobile, AL	(1.4)	298	Temecula, CA	(5.5)	375	Cape Coral, FL	(12.6)
225	Overland Park, KS	(1.4)	302	Chico, CA	(5.7)	376	Dallas, TX	(12.7)
225	Wilmington, NC	(1.4)	302	Plano, TX	(5.7)	377	Daly City, CA	(12.9)
230	Naperville, IL	(1.5)	304	Allen, TX	(5.8)	377	Knoxville, TN	(12.9)
231	Whittier, CA	(1.6)	304	Jackson, MS	(5.8)	379	Kent, WA	(13.1)
232	Brownsville, TX	(1.7)	304	Orlando, FL	(5.8)	379	Santa Maria, CA	(13.1)
233	Portland, OR	(1.8)	304	Tallahassee, FL	(5.8)	381	Pembroke Pines, FL	(13.2)
234	Springfield, MO	(1.9)	308	Bellevue, WA	(5.9)	382	Carmel, IN	(13.4)
235	Ann Arbor, MI	(2.0)	308	Fort Worth, TX	(5.9)	383	Cary, NC	(13.5)
235	Edinburg, TX	(2.0)	308	Upper Darby Twnshp, PA	(5.9)	384	Melbourne, FL	(13.7)
235	Gainesville, FL	(2.0)	311	Boca Raton, FL	(6.0)	384	Murfreesboro, TN	(13.7)
235	Jacksonville, FL	(2.0)	311	Mission Viejo, CA	(6.0)	386	Beaumont, TX	(13.9)
235	Kansas City, MO	(2.0)	313	Boston, MA	(6.1)	387	Birmingham, AL	(14.1)
240	Detroit, MI	(2.1)	313	Chula Vista, CA	(6.1)	387	Quincy, MA	(14.1)
240	Fontana, CA	(2.1)	313	Kenosha, WI	(6.1)	389	Chino Hills, CA	(14.4)
242	Alhambra, CA	(2.2)	313	Miami Beach, FL	(6.1)	390	Plantation, FL	(14.5)
242	Athens-Clarke, GA	(2.2)	313	Napa, CA	(6.1)	391	Macon, GA	(14.6)
244	Warwick, RI	(2.3)	318	Columbus, GA	(6.2)	392	Stockton, CA	(14.7)
245	Baton Rouge, LA	(2.4)	318	Victorville, CA	(6.2)	393	Kennewick, WA	(14.8)
245	Columbia, MO	(2.4)	320	Fort Collins, CO	(6.4)	394	Gilbert, AZ	(15.0)
245	Fayetteville, AR	(2.4)	320	Portsmouth, VA	(6.4)	395	Nampa, ID	(15.6)
245	Houston, TX	(2.4)	320	South Gate, CA	(6.4)	396	Provo, UT	(16.2)
249	Broken Arrow, OK	(2.5)	323	Newport Beach, CA	(6.5)	397	Citrus Heights, CA	(16.3)
249	Ontario, CA	(2.5)	323	Pasadena, CA	(6.5)	398	Mission, TX	(16.6)
249	Peoria, IL	(2.5)	325	Hammond, IN	(6.7)	398	Norman, OK	(16.6)
249	Surprise, AZ	(2.5)	325	Nashville, TN	(6.7)	400	Compton, CA	(16.7)
249	Vallejo, CA	(2.5)	327	Midland, TX	(6.8)	401	Savannah, GA	(17.3)
254	Arvada, CO	(2.6)	328	League City, TX	(6.9)	402	Elizabeth, NJ	(17.4)
254	Clearwater, FL	(2.6)	329	Cincinnati, OH	(7.1)	403	High Point, NC	(18.0)
254	Troy, MI	(2.6)	330	Norwalk, CT	(7.3)	404	Davenport, IA	(18.3)
257	Alameda, CA	(2.7)	330	Torrance, CA	(7.3)	405	South Bend, IN	(18.4)
257	Chino, CA	(2.7)	330	Vancouver, WA	(7.3)	406	Fall River, MA	(18.5)
257	Milwaukee, WI	(2.7)	333	Downey, CA	(7.5)	407	Beaverton, OR	(18.7)
257	Upland, CA	(2.7)	334	Alexandria, VA	(7.7)	408	Port St. Lucie, FL	(18.8)
261	Bellflower, CA	(2.8)	334	Ogden, UT	(7.7)	409	Edison Twnshp, NJ	(20.1)
261	Cedar Rapids, IA	(2.8)	336	Des Moines, IA	(7.9)	410	Everett, WA	(21.5)
261	Fort Lauderdale, FL	(2.8)	336	Miami Gardens, FL	(7.9)	411	College Station, TX	(23.6)
261	Newport News, VA	(2.8)	338	Coral Springs, FL	(8.0)	412	Grand Prairie, TX	(24.6)
261	Stamford, CT	(2.8)	338	Phoenix, AZ	(8.0)	413	Woodbridge Twnshp, NJ	(25.9)
261	Yuma, AZ	(2.8)	340	Arlington Heights, IL	(8.1)	414	Newton, MA	(27.3)
267	Atlanta, GA	(3.0)	340	Dearborn, MI	(8.1)	NA	Albany, NY**	NA
267	Baldwin Park, CA	(3.0)	342	Charleston, SC	(8.3)	NA	Allentown, PA**	NA
269	Hollywood, FL	(3.1)	342	Decatur, IL	(8.3)	NA	Amherst, NY**	NA
269	Irvine, CA	(3.1)	344	Denton, TX	(8.5)	NA	Buffalo, NY**	NA
271	Tyler, TX	(3.2)	344	Lansing, MI	(8.5)	NA	Chandler, AZ**	NA
272	Billings, MT	(3.4)	346	Mesa, AZ	(8.6)	NA	Cheektowaga, NY**	NA
272	Boise, ID	(3.4)	347	Avondale, AZ	(8.7)	NA	Clarkstown, NY**	NA
272	Hialeah, FL	(3.4)	347	Johns Creek, GA	(8.7)	NA	Colonie, NY**	NA
272	Lincoln, NE	(3.4)	347	Norfolk, VA	(8.7)	NA	Federal Way, WA**	NA
272	Springfield, MA	(3.4)	350	Durham, NC	(8.8)	NA	Greece, NY**	NA
272	West Jordan, UT	(3.4)	351	Vista, CA	(8.9)	NA	Greensboro, NC**	NA
278	Spokane Valley, WA	(3.6)	352	Amarillo, TX	(9.3)	NA	Greenville, NC**	NA
279	Erie, PA	(3.7)	353	Aurora, IL	(9.5)	NA	Jurupa Valley, CA**	NA
280	New Bedford, MA	(3.8)	353	Manchester, NH	(9.5)	NA	Lexington, KY**	NA
281	West Covina, CA	(3.9)	355	Louisville, KY	(10.1)	NA	New Rochelle, NY**	NA
282	Irving, TX	(4.1)	356	Brooklyn Park, MN	(10.3)	NA	New York, NY**	NA
283	Cranston, RI	(4.3)	357	Palm Bay, FL	(10.4)	NA	North Las Vegas, NV**	NA
283	Philadelphia, PA	(4.3)	358	McAllen, TX	(10.5)	NA	Parma, OH**	NA
285	Davie, FL	(4.6)	359	Sunrise, FL	(10.6)	NA	Providence, RI**	NA
286	Clarksville, TN	(4.8)	360	Orem, UT	(10.7)	NA	Ramapo, NY**	NA
286	Clifton, NJ	(4.8)	360	Waco, TX	(10.7)	NA	Rochester, NY**	NA
288	Bridgeport, CT	(4.9)	362	Duluth, MN	(10.9)	NA	St. George, UT**	NA
288	Lawrence, MA	(4.9)	363	Roseville, CA	(11.0)	NA	Syracuse, NY**	NA
290	Topeka, KS	(5.1)	364	Scottsdale, AZ	(11.1)	NA	Thornton, CO**	NA
291	Inglewood, CA	(5.2)	364	St. Louis, MO	(11.1)	NA	Toledo, OH**	NA
291	Kansas City, KS	(5.2)	366	Arlington, TX	(11.2)	NA	Tucson, AZ**	NA
291	Miramar, FL	(5.2)	367	Lynchburg, VA	(11.6)	NA	Waukegan, IL**	NA
294	Corpus Christi, TX	(5.3)	368	Tempe, AZ	(11.7)	NA	Yonkers, NY**	NA
294	El Monte, CA	(5.3)	369	Glendale, CA	(11.9)			
294	Mesquite, TX	(5.3)	369	Toms River Twnshp, NJ	(11.9)			

Source: CQ Press using reported data from the F.B.I. "Crime in the United States 2012"

*Larceny-theft is the unlawful taking of property. Attempts are included.

**Not available.

76. Percent Change in Larceny-Theft Rate: 2008 to 2012
National Percent Change = 9.5% Decrease*

RANK	CITY	% CHANGE	RANK	CITY	% CHANGE	RANK	CITY	% CHANGE
87	Abilene, TX	0.9	400	Chino Hills, CA	(35.3)	247	Gainesville, FL	(15.4)
81	Akron, OH	2.2	154	Chino, CA	(6.6)	78	Garden Grove, CA	2.4
144	Alameda, CA	(5.6)	250	Chula Vista, CA	(15.6)	220	Garland, TX	(12.4)
NA	Albany, GA**	NA	NA	Cicero, IL**	NA	7	Gary, IN	39.1
NA	Albany, NY**	NA	63	Cincinnati, OH	5.6	346	Gilbert, AZ	(25.1)
180	Albuquerque, NM	(8.3)	254	Citrus Heights, CA	(15.9)	6	Glendale, AZ	42.6
246	Alexandria, VA	(15.2)	NA	Clarkstown, NY**	NA	318	Glendale, CA	(22.4)
55	Alhambra, CA	7.9	341	Clarksville, TN	(24.6)	395	Grand Prairie, TX	(33.8)
NA	Allentown, PA**	NA	275	Clearwater, FL	(17.2)	381	Grand Rapids, MI	(30.4)
124	Allen, TX	(3.3)	41	Cleveland, OH	11.3	NA	Greece, NY**	NA
278	Amarillo, TX	(17.4)	383	Clifton, NJ	(31.0)	101	Greeley, CO	(0.7)
NA	Amherst, NY**	NA	107	Clinton Twnshp, MI	(1.3)	190	Green Bay, WI	(9.1)
18	Anaheim, CA	20.8	30	Clovis, CA	13.6	337	Greensboro, NC	(24.5)
46	Anchorage, AK	10.4	396	College Station, TX	(34.5)	379	Greenville, NC	(29.5)
294	Ann Arbor, MI	(19.2)	NA	Colonie, NY**	NA	20	Gresham, OR	20.4
4	Antioch, CA	48.4	142	Colorado Springs, CO	(5.5)	47	Hamilton Twnshp, NJ	9.6
NA	Arlington Heights, IL**	NA	84	Columbia, MO	1.3	250	Hammond, IN	(15.6)
351	Arlington, TX	(25.6)	334	Columbus, GA	(24.2)	119	Hampton, VA	(2.9)
121	Arvada, CO	(3.2)	386	Compton, CA	(31.2)	241	Hartford, CT	(14.8)
32	Asheville, NC	13.0	114	Concord, CA	(2.6)	57	Hawthorne, CA	6.8
376	Athens-Clarke, GA	(28.8)	116	Coral Springs, FL	(2.7)	90	Hayward, CA	0.7
156	Atlanta, GA	(6.7)	152	Corona, CA	(6.3)	285	Hemet, CA	(17.9)
121	Aurora, CO	(3.2)	334	Corpus Christi, TX	(24.2)	133	Henderson, NV	(4.4)
392	Aurora, IL	(32.2)	25	Costa Mesa, CA	15.8	177	Hesperia, CA	(8.1)
184	Austin, TX	(8.6)	248	Cranston, RI	(15.5)	337	Hialeah, FL	(24.5)
78	Avondale, AZ	2.4	337	Dallas, TX	(24.5)	343	High Point, NC	(24.9)
172	Bakersfield, CA	(7.7)	309	Daly City, CA	(21.4)	275	Hillsboro, OR	(17.2)
54	Baldwin Park, CA	8.0	140	Danbury, CT	(5.4)	58	Hollywood, FL	6.5
78	Baltimore, MD	2.4	388	Davenport, IA	(31.4)	272	Hoover, AL	(17.0)
108	Baton Rouge, LA	(1.5)	118	Davie, FL	(2.8)	83	Houston, TX	1.9
294	Beaumont, TX	(19.2)	99	Dayton, OH	(0.3)	9	Huntington Beach, CA	32.3
352	Beaverton, OR	(25.7)	330	Dearborn, MI	(23.7)	265	Huntsville, AL	(16.5)
319	Bellevue, WA	(22.6)	NA	Decatur, IL**	NA	291	Independence, MO	(18.6)
322	Bellflower, CA	(22.9)	253	Deerfield Beach, FL	(15.8)	160	Indianapolis, IN	(6.8)
221	Bellingham, WA	(12.6)	98	Denton, TX	(0.2)	22	Indio, CA	16.9
344	Berkeley, CA	(25.0)	10	Denver, CO	30.1	156	Inglewood, CA	(6.7)
332	Bethlehem, PA	(24.0)	194	Des Moines, IA	(9.6)	112	Irvine, CA	(2.2)
67	Billings, MT	4.0	52	Detroit, MI	8.6	391	Irving, TX	(31.9)
333	Birmingham, AL	(24.1)	205	Downey, CA	(10.9)	294	Jacksonville, FL	(19.2)
NA	Bloomington, IL**	NA	258	Duluth, MN	(16.2)	199	Jackson, MS	(10.4)
47	Bloomington, IN	9.6	314	Durham, NC	(21.9)	374	Jersey City, NJ	(28.6)
100	Bloomington, MN	(0.5)	60	Edinburg, TX	6.2	NA	Johns Creek, GA**	NA
326	Boca Raton, FL	(23.2)	399	Edison Twnshp, NJ	(35.1)	177	Joliet, IL	(8.1)
198	Boise, ID	(10.1)	168	Edmond, OK	(7.4)	NA	Jurupa Valley, CA**	NA
316	Boston, MA	(22.3)	363	El Cajon, CA	(27.4)	NA	Kansas City, KS**	NA
142	Boulder, CO	(5.5)	235	El Monte, CA	(13.5)	204	Kansas City, MO	(10.8)
324	Brick Twnshp, NJ	(23.0)	287	El Paso, TX	(18.2)	293	Kennewick, WA	(18.9)
368	Bridgeport, CT	(27.9)	226	Elgin, IL	(12.9)	96	Kenosha, WI	0.2
NA	Brockton, MA**	NA	402	Elizabeth, NJ	(37.8)	232	Kent, WA	(13.3)
77	Broken Arrow, OK	2.5	190	Elk Grove, CA	(9.1)	91	Killeen, TX	0.6
272	Brooklyn Park, MN	(17.0)	70	Erie, PA	3.3	85	Knoxville, TN	1.1
269	Brownsville, TX	(16.8)	187	Escondido, CA	(8.9)	94	Lafayette, LA	0.4
369	Bryan, TX	(28.2)	248	Eugene, OR	(15.5)	40	Lake Forest, CA	12.1
32	Buena Park, CA	13.0	52	Evansville, IN	8.6	202	Lakeland, FL	(10.7)
NA	Buffalo, NY**	NA	312	Everett, WA	(21.6)	359	Lakewood Twnshp, NJ	(26.3)
73	Burbank, CA	2.8	316	Fairfield, CA	(22.3)	125	Lakewood, CA	(3.6)
146	Cambridge, MA	(5.9)	369	Fall River, MA	(28.2)	36	Lakewood, CO	12.7
299	Camden, NJ	(19.4)	260	Fargo, ND	(16.3)	325	Lancaster, CA	(23.1)
347	Cape Coral, FL	(25.2)	306	Farmington Hills, MI	(20.6)	209	Lansing, MI	(11.5)
302	Carlsbad, CA	(20.3)	29	Fayetteville, AR	14.0	355	Laredo, TX	(25.9)
394	Carmel, IN	(33.6)	305	Fayetteville, NC	(20.5)	174	Largo, FL	(7.9)
163	Carrollton, TX	(6.9)	62	Federal Way, WA	5.7	200	Las Cruces, NM	(10.6)
51	Carson, CA	8.7	327	Fishers, IN	(23.3)	230	Las Vegas, NV	(13.1)
350	Cary, NC	(25.5)	189	Flint, MI	(9.0)	205	Lawrence, KS	(10.9)
303	Cedar Rapids, IA	(20.4)	92	Fontana, CA	0.5	397	Lawrence, MA	(34.7)
217	Centennial, CO	(12.3)	236	Fort Collins, CO	(13.9)	19	Lawton, OK	20.5
NA	Champaign, IL**	NA	102	Fort Lauderdale, FL	(0.9)	180	League City, TX	(8.3)
NA	Chandler, AZ**	NA	87	Fort Smith, AR	0.9	156	Lee's Summit, MO	(6.7)
361	Charleston, SC	(26.7)	131	Fort Wayne, IN	(4.3)	NA	Lexington, KY**	NA
372	Charlotte, NC	(28.4)	260	Fort Worth, TX	(16.3)	138	Lincoln, NE	(4.9)
NA	Cheektowaga, NY**	NA	355	Fremont, CA	(25.9)	113	Little Rock, AR	(2.3)
169	Chesapeake, VA	(7.5)	68	Fresno, CA	3.5	147	Livermore, CA	(6.0)
213	Chicago, IL	(11.7)	281	Frisco, TX	(17.6)	87	Livonia, MI	0.9
308	Chico, CA	(21.1)	151	Fullerton, CA	(6.2)	50	Long Beach, CA	8.8

RANK	CITY	% CHANGE	RANK	CITY	% CHANGE	RANK	CITY	% CHANGE
NA	Longmont, CO**	NA	310	Pasadena, CA	(21.5)	16	South Gate, CA	22.8
319	Longview, TX	(22.6)	56	Pasadena, TX	6.9	367	Sparks, NV	(27.8)
131	Los Angeles, CA	(4.3)	68	Paterson, NJ	3.5	8	Spokane Valley, WA	38.3
147	Louisville, KY	(6.0)	193	Pearland, TX	(9.2)	2	Spokane, WA	65.8
197	Lowell, MA	(9.7)	401	Pembroke Pines, FL	(35.6)	NA	Springfield, IL**	NA
187	Lubbock, TX	(8.9)	160	Peoria, AZ	(6.8)	224	Springfield, MA	(12.8)
375	Lynchburg, VA	(28.7)	NA	Peoria, IL**	NA	136	Springfield, MO	(4.6)
38	Lynn, MA	12.4	207	Philadelphia, PA	(11.2)	210	Stamford, CT	(11.6)
217	Macon, GA	(12.3)	313	Phoenix, AZ	(21.8)	154	Sterling Heights, MI	(6.6)
94	Madison, WI	0.4	182	Pittsburgh, PA	(8.5)	360	Stockton, CA	(26.4)
66	Manchester, NH	4.7	307	Plano, TX	(20.7)	358	St. George, UT	(26.0)
383	McAllen, TX	(31.0)	321	Plantation, FL	(22.8)	14	St. Joseph, MO	25.0
147	McKinney, TX	(6.0)	26	Pomona, CA	15.6	224	St. Louis, MO	(12.8)
5	Medford, OR	47.4	111	Pompano Beach, FL	(2.0)	116	St. Paul, MN	(2.7)
223	Melbourne, FL	(12.7)	362	Port St. Lucie, FL	(27.0)	226	St. Petersburg, FL	(12.9)
290	Memphis, TN	(18.5)	128	Portland, OR	(4.1)	230	Sugar Land, TX	(13.1)
NA	Menifee, CA**	NA	240	Portsmouth, VA	(14.7)	289	Sunnyvale, CA	(18.3)
43	Merced, CA	10.9	282	Providence, RI	(17.7)	284	Sunrise, FL	(17.8)
63	Meridian, ID	5.6	226	Provo, UT	(12.9)	210	Surprise, AZ	(11.6)
244	Mesa, AZ	(15.1)	NA	Pueblo, CO**	NA	NA	Syracuse, NY**	NA
257	Mesquite, TX	(16.1)	255	Quincy, MA	(16.0)	285	Tacoma, WA	(17.9)
37	Miami Beach, FL	12.6	267	Racine, WI	(16.6)	216	Tallahassee, FL	(12.1)
347	Miami Gardens, FL	(25.2)	106	Raleigh, NC	(1.2)	390	Tampa, FL	(31.7)
23	Miami, FL	16.3	NA	Ramapo, NY**	NA	63	Temecula, CA	5.6
252	Midland, TX	(15.7)	110	Rancho Cucamon., CA	(1.7)	241	Tempe, AZ	(14.8)
310	Milwaukee, WI	(21.5)	382	Reading, PA	(30.8)	NA	Thornton, CO**	NA
125	Minneapolis, MN	(3.6)	13	Redding, CA	28.1	70	Thousand Oaks, CA	3.3
372	Miramar, FL	(28.4)	364	Redwood City, CA	(27.6)	NA	Toledo, OH**	NA
102	Mission Viejo, CA	(0.9)	385	Reno, NV	(31.1)	31	Toms River Twnshp, NJ	13.1
353	Mission, TX	(25.8)	NA	Renton, WA**	NA	160	Topeka, KS	(6.8)
172	Mobile, AL	(7.7)	1	Rialto, CA	113.7	274	Torrance, CA	(17.1)
104	Modesto, CA	(1.0)	166	Richardson, TX	(7.2)	303	Tracy, CA	(20.4)
190	Montgomery, AL	(9.1)	260	Richmond, CA	(16.3)	393	Trenton, NJ	(32.4)
42	Moreno Valley, CA	11.0	44	Richmond, VA	10.6	109	Troy, MI	(1.6)
364	Mountain View, CA	(27.6)	215	Rio Rancho, NM	(11.9)	NA	Tucson, AZ**	NA
282	Murfreesboro, TN	(17.7)	152	Riverside, CA	(6.3)	244	Tulsa, OK	(15.1)
11	Murrieta, CA	29.8	210	Roanoke, VA	(11.6)	287	Tuscaloosa, AL	(18.2)
170	Nampa, ID	(7.6)	166	Rochester, MN	(7.2)	105	Tustin, CA	(1.1)
349	Napa, CA	(25.3)	NA	Rochester, NY**	NA	145	Tyler, TX	(5.8)
233	Naperville, IL	(13.4)	279	Rockford, IL	(17.5)	376	Upland, CA	(28.8)
NA	Nashua, NH**	NA	341	Roseville, CA	(24.6)	258	Upper Darby Twnshp, PA	(16.2)
322	Nashville, TN	(22.9)	398	Roswell, GA	(35.0)	133	Vacaville, CA	(4.4)
150	New Bedford, MA	(6.1)	121	Round Rock, TX	(3.2)	315	Vallejo, CA	(22.2)
NA	New Haven, CT**	NA	127	Sacramento, CA	(3.8)	92	Vancouver, WA	0.5
214	New Orleans, LA	(11.8)	202	Salem, OR	(10.7)	35	Ventura, CA	12.9
NA	New Rochelle, NY**	NA	182	Salinas, CA	(8.5)	268	Victorville, CA	(16.7)
NA	New York, NY**	NA	277	Salt Lake City, UT	(17.3)	156	Virginia Beach, VA	(6.7)
73	Newark, NJ	2.8	255	San Antonio, TX	(16.0)	133	Visalia, CA	(4.4)
194	Newport Beach, CA	(9.6)	179	San Bernardino, CA	(8.2)	300	Vista, CA	(19.9)
294	Newport News, VA	(19.2)	270	San Diego, CA	(16.9)	298	Waco, TX	(19.3)
353	Newton, MA	(25.8)	49	San Francisco, CA	9.3	28	Warren, MI	14.2
221	Norfolk, VA	(12.6)	72	San Jose, CA	3.1	337	Warwick, RI	(24.5)
217	Norman, OK	(12.3)	260	San Leandro, CA	(16.3)	44	Washington, DC	10.6
243	North Charleston, SC	(14.9)	170	San Marcos, CA	(7.6)	344	Waterbury, CT	(25.0)
233	North Las Vegas, NV	(13.4)	336	San Mateo, CA	(24.3)	NA	Waukegan, IL**	NA
27	Norwalk, CA	14.5	292	Sandy Springs, GA	(18.8)	264	West Covina, CA	(16.4)
186	Norwalk, CT	(8.7)	331	Sandy, UT	(23.8)	194	West Jordan, UT	(9.6)
3	Oakland, CA	48.8	39	Santa Ana, CA	12.3	128	West Palm Beach, FL	(4.1)
60	Oceanside, CA	6.2	17	Santa Barbara, CA	21.1	327	West Valley, UT	(23.3)
237	Odessa, TX	(14.0)	119	Santa Clara, CA	(2.9)	184	Westland, MI	(8.6)
270	O'Fallon, MO	(16.9)	239	Santa Clarita, CA	(14.1)	32	Westminster, CA	13.0
139	Ogden, UT	(5.2)	369	Santa Maria, CA	(28.2)	301	Westminster, CO	(20.1)
86	Oklahoma City, OK	1.0	21	Santa Monica, CA	20.2	24	Whittier, CA	16.0
NA	Olathe, KS**	NA	97	Santa Rosa, CA	(0.1)	387	Wichita Falls, TX	(31.3)
58	Omaha, NE	6.5	366	Savannah, GA	(27.7)	82	Wichita, KS	2.1
140	Ontario, CA	(5.4)	279	Scottsdale, AZ	(17.5)	76	Wilmington, NC	2.7
200	Orange, CA	(10.6)	174	Scranton, PA	(7.9)	208	Winston-Salem, NC	(11.3)
229	Orem, UT	(13.0)	174	Seattle, WA	(7.9)	380	Woodbridge Twnshp, NJ	(29.8)
329	Orlando, FL	(23.6)	130	Shreveport, LA	(4.2)	137	Worcester, MA	(4.7)
114	Overland Park, KS	(2.6)	163	Simi Valley, CA	(6.9)	378	Yakima, WA	(29.3)
237	Oxnard, CA	(14.0)	12	Sioux City, IA	29.3	NA	Yonkers, NY**	NA
73	Palm Bay, FL	2.8	15	Sioux Falls, SD	24.2	165	Yuma, AZ	(7.0)
265	Palmdale, CA	(16.5)	355	Somerville, MA	(25.9)			
NA	Parma, OH**	NA	389	South Bend, IN	(31.6)			

Source: CQ Press using reported data from the F.B.I. "Crime in the United States 2012"

*Larceny-theft is the unlawful taking of property. Attempts are included.

**Not available.

76. Percent Change in Larceny-Theft Rate: 2008 to 2012 (continued)
National Percent Change = 9.5% Decrease*

RANK	CITY	% CHANGE	RANK	CITY	% CHANGE	RANK	CITY	% CHANGE
1	Rialto, CA	113.7	73	Palm Bay, FL	2.8	147	McKinney, TX	(6.0)
2	Spokane, WA	65.8	76	Wilmington, NC	2.7	150	New Bedford, MA	(6.1)
3	Oakland, CA	48.8	77	Broken Arrow, OK	2.5	151	Fullerton, CA	(6.2)
4	Antioch, CA	48.4	78	Avondale, AZ	2.4	152	Corona, CA	(6.3)
5	Medford, OR	47.4	78	Baltimore, MD	2.4	152	Riverside, CA	(6.3)
6	Glendale, AZ	42.6	78	Garden Grove, CA	2.4	154	Chino, CA	(6.6)
7	Gary, IN	39.1	81	Akron, OH	2.2	154	Sterling Heights, MI	(6.6)
8	Spokane Valley, WA	38.3	82	Wichita, KS	2.1	156	Atlanta, GA	(6.7)
9	Huntington Beach, CA	32.3	83	Houston, TX	1.9	156	Inglewood, CA	(6.7)
10	Denver, CO	30.1	84	Columbia, MO	1.3	156	Lee's Summit, MO	(6.7)
11	Murrieta, CA	29.8	85	Knoxville, TN	1.1	156	Virginia Beach, VA	(6.7)
12	Sioux City, IA	29.3	86	Oklahoma City, OK	1.0	160	Indianapolis, IN	(6.8)
13	Redding, CA	28.1	87	Abilene, TX	0.9	160	Peoria, AZ	(6.8)
14	St. Joseph, MO	25.0	87	Fort Smith, AR	0.9	160	Topeka, KS	(6.8)
15	Sioux Falls, SD	24.2	87	Livonia, MI	0.9	163	Carrollton, TX	(6.9)
16	South Gate, CA	22.8	90	Hayward, CA	0.7	163	Simi Valley, CA	(6.9)
17	Santa Barbara, CA	21.1	91	Killeen, TX	0.6	165	Yuma, AZ	(7.0)
18	Anaheim, CA	20.8	92	Fontana, CA	0.5	166	Richardson, TX	(7.2)
19	Lawton, OK	20.5	92	Vancouver, WA	0.5	166	Rochester, MN	(7.2)
20	Gresham, OR	20.4	94	Lafayette, LA	0.4	168	Edmond, OK	(7.4)
21	Santa Monica, CA	20.2	94	Madison, WI	0.4	169	Chesapeake, VA	(7.5)
22	Indio, CA	16.9	96	Kenosha, WI	0.2	170	Nampa, ID	(7.6)
23	Miami, FL	16.3	97	Santa Rosa, CA	(0.1)	170	San Marcos, CA	(7.6)
24	Whittier, CA	16.0	98	Denton, TX	(0.2)	172	Bakersfield, CA	(7.7)
25	Costa Mesa, CA	15.8	99	Dayton, OH	(0.3)	172	Mobile, AL	(7.7)
26	Pomona, CA	15.6	100	Bloomington, MN	(0.5)	174	Largo, FL	(7.9)
27	Norwalk, CA	14.5	101	Greeley, CO	(0.7)	174	Scranton, PA	(7.9)
28	Warren, MI	14.2	102	Fort Lauderdale, FL	(0.9)	174	Seattle, WA	(7.9)
29	Fayetteville, AR	14.0	102	Mission Viejo, CA	(0.9)	177	Hesperia, CA	(8.1)
30	Clovis, CA	13.6	104	Modesto, CA	(1.0)	177	Joliet, IL	(8.1)
31	Toms River Twnshp, NJ	13.1	105	Tustin, CA	(1.1)	179	San Bernardino, CA	(8.2)
32	Asheville, NC	13.0	106	Raleigh, NC	(1.2)	180	Albuquerque, NM	(8.3)
32	Buena Park, CA	13.0	107	Clinton Twnshp, MI	(1.3)	180	League City, TX	(8.3)
32	Westminster, CA	13.0	108	Baton Rouge, LA	(1.5)	182	Pittsburgh, PA	(8.5)
35	Ventura, CA	12.9	109	Troy, MI	(1.6)	182	Salinas, CA	(8.5)
36	Lakewood, CO	12.7	110	Rancho Cucamon., CA	(1.7)	184	Austin, TX	(8.6)
37	Miami Beach, FL	12.6	111	Pompano Beach, FL	(2.0)	184	Westland, MI	(8.6)
38	Lynn, MA	12.4	112	Irvine, CA	(2.2)	186	Norwalk, CT	(8.7)
39	Santa Ana, CA	12.3	113	Little Rock, AR	(2.3)	187	Escondido, CA	(8.9)
40	Lake Forest, CA	12.1	114	Concord, CA	(2.6)	187	Lubbock, TX	(8.9)
41	Cleveland, OH	11.3	114	Overland Park, KS	(2.6)	189	Flint, MI	(9.0)
42	Moreno Valley, CA	11.0	116	Coral Springs, FL	(2.7)	190	Elk Grove, CA	(9.1)
43	Merced, CA	10.9	116	St. Paul, MN	(2.7)	190	Green Bay, WI	(9.1)
44	Richmond, VA	10.6	118	Davie, FL	(2.8)	190	Montgomery, AL	(9.1)
44	Washington, DC	10.6	119	Hampton, VA	(2.9)	193	Pearland, TX	(9.2)
46	Anchorage, AK	10.4	119	Santa Clara, CA	(2.9)	194	Des Moines, IA	(9.6)
47	Bloomington, IN	9.6	121	Arvada, CO	(3.2)	194	Newport Beach, CA	(9.6)
47	Hamilton Twnshp, NJ	9.6	121	Aurora, CO	(3.2)	194	West Jordan, UT	(9.6)
49	San Francisco, CA	9.3	121	Round Rock, TX	(3.2)	197	Lowell, MA	(9.7)
50	Long Beach, CA	8.8	124	Allen, TX	(3.3)	198	Boise, ID	(10.1)
51	Carson, CA	8.7	125	Lakewood, CA	(3.6)	199	Jackson, MS	(10.4)
52	Detroit, MI	8.6	125	Minneapolis, MN	(3.6)	200	Las Cruces, NM	(10.6)
52	Evansville, IN	8.6	127	Sacramento, CA	(3.8)	200	Orange, CA	(10.6)
54	Baldwin Park, CA	8.0	128	Portland, OR	(4.1)	202	Lakeland, FL	(10.7)
55	Alhambra, CA	7.9	128	West Palm Beach, FL	(4.1)	202	Salem, OR	(10.7)
56	Pasadena, TX	6.9	130	Shreveport, LA	(4.2)	204	Kansas City, MO	(10.8)
57	Hawthorne, CA	6.8	131	Fort Wayne, IN	(4.3)	205	Downey, CA	(10.9)
58	Hollywood, FL	6.5	131	Los Angeles, CA	(4.3)	205	Lawrence, KS	(10.9)
58	Omaha, NE	6.5	133	Henderson, NV	(4.4)	207	Philadelphia, PA	(11.2)
60	Edinburg, TX	6.2	133	Vacaville, CA	(4.4)	208	Winston-Salem, NC	(11.3)
60	Oceanside, CA	6.2	133	Visalia, CA	(4.4)	209	Lansing, MI	(11.5)
62	Federal Way, WA	5.7	136	Springfield, MO	(4.6)	210	Roanoke, VA	(11.6)
63	Cincinnati, OH	5.6	137	Worcester, MA	(4.7)	210	Stamford, CT	(11.6)
63	Meridian, ID	5.6	138	Lincoln, NE	(4.9)	210	Surprise, AZ	(11.6)
63	Temecula, CA	5.6	139	Ogden, UT	(5.2)	213	Chicago, IL	(11.7)
66	Manchester, NH	4.7	140	Danbury, CT	(5.4)	214	New Orleans, LA	(11.8)
67	Billings, MT	4.0	140	Ontario, CA	(5.4)	215	Rio Rancho, NM	(11.9)
68	Fresno, CA	3.5	142	Boulder, CO	(5.5)	216	Tallahassee, FL	(12.1)
68	Paterson, NJ	3.5	142	Colorado Springs, CO	(5.5)	217	Centennial, CO	(12.3)
70	Erie, PA	3.3	144	Alameda, CA	(5.6)	217	Macon, GA	(12.3)
70	Thousand Oaks, CA	3.3	145	Tyler, TX	(5.8)	217	Norman, OK	(12.3)
72	San Jose, CA	3.1	146	Cambridge, MA	(5.9)	220	Garland, TX	(12.4)
73	Burbank, CA	2.8	147	Livermore, CA	(6.0)	221	Bellingham, WA	(12.6)
73	Newark, NJ	2.8	147	Louisville, KY	(6.0)	221	Norfolk, VA	(12.6)

RANK	CITY	% CHANGE	RANK	CITY	% CHANGE	RANK	CITY	% CHANGE
223	Melbourne, FL	(12.7)	294	Newport News, VA	(19.2)	369	Santa Maria, CA	(28.2)
224	Springfield, MA	(12.8)	298	Waco, TX	(19.3)	372	Charlotte, NC	(28.4)
224	St. Louis, MO	(12.8)	299	Camden, NJ	(19.4)	372	Miramar, FL	(28.4)
226	Elgin, IL	(12.9)	300	Vista, CA	(19.9)	374	Jersey City, NJ	(28.6)
226	Provo, UT	(12.9)	301	Westminster, CO	(20.1)	375	Lynchburg, VA	(28.7)
226	St. Petersburg, FL	(12.9)	302	Carlsbad, CA	(20.3)	376	Athens-Clarke, GA	(28.8)
229	Orem, UT	(13.0)	303	Cedar Rapids, IA	(20.4)	376	Upland, CA	(28.8)
230	Las Vegas, NV	(13.1)	303	Tracy, CA	(20.4)	378	Yakima, WA	(29.3)
230	Sugar Land, TX	(13.1)	305	Fayetteville, NC	(20.5)	379	Greenville, NC	(29.5)
232	Kent, WA	(13.3)	306	Farmington Hills, MI	(20.6)	380	Woodbridge Twnshp, NJ	(29.8)
233	Naperville, IL	(13.4)	307	Plano, TX	(20.7)	381	Grand Rapids, MI	(30.4)
233	North Las Vegas, NV	(13.4)	308	Chico, CA	(21.1)	382	Reading, PA	(30.8)
235	El Monte, CA	(13.5)	309	Daly City, CA	(21.4)	383	Clifton, NJ	(31.0)
236	Fort Collins, CO	(13.9)	310	Milwaukee, WI	(21.5)	383	McAllen, TX	(31.0)
237	Odessa, TX	(14.0)	310	Pasadena, CA	(21.5)	385	Reno, NV	(31.1)
237	Oxnard, CA	(14.0)	312	Everett, WA	(21.6)	386	Compton, CA	(31.2)
239	Santa Clarita, CA	(14.1)	313	Phoenix, AZ	(21.8)	387	Wichita Falls, TX	(31.3)
240	Portsmouth, VA	(14.7)	314	Durham, NC	(21.9)	388	Davenport, IA	(31.4)
241	Hartford, CT	(14.8)	315	Vallejo, CA	(22.2)	389	South Bend, IN	(31.6)
241	Tempe, AZ	(14.8)	316	Boston, MA	(22.3)	390	Tampa, FL	(31.7)
243	North Charleston, SC	(14.9)	316	Fairfield, CA	(22.3)	391	Irving, TX	(31.9)
244	Mesa, AZ	(15.1)	318	Glendale, CA	(22.4)	392	Aurora, IL	(32.2)
244	Tulsa, OK	(15.1)	319	Bellevue, WA	(22.6)	393	Trenton, NJ	(32.4)
246	Alexandria, VA	(15.2)	319	Longview, TX	(22.6)	394	Carmel, IN	(33.6)
247	Gainesville, FL	(15.4)	321	Plantation, FL	(22.8)	395	Grand Prairie, TX	(33.8)
248	Cranston, RI	(15.5)	322	Bellflower, CA	(22.9)	396	College Station, TX	(34.5)
248	Eugene, OR	(15.5)	322	Nashville, TN	(22.9)	397	Lawrence, MA	(34.7)
250	Chula Vista, CA	(15.6)	324	Brick Twnshp, NJ	(23.0)	398	Roswell, GA	(35.0)
250	Hammond, IN	(15.6)	325	Lancaster, CA	(23.1)	399	Edison Twnshp, NJ	(35.1)
252	Midland, TX	(15.7)	326	Boca Raton, FL	(23.2)	400	Chino Hills, CA	(35.3)
253	Deerfield Beach, FL	(15.8)	327	Fishers, IN	(23.3)	401	Pembroke Pines, FL	(35.6)
254	Citrus Heights, CA	(15.9)	327	West Valley, UT	(23.3)	402	Elizabeth, NJ	(37.8)
255	Quincy, MA	(16.0)	329	Orlando, FL	(23.6)	NA	Albany, GA**	NA
255	San Antonio, TX	(16.0)	330	Dearborn, MI	(23.7)	NA	Albany, NY**	NA
257	Mesquite, TX	(16.1)	331	Sandy, UT	(23.8)	NA	Allentown, PA**	NA
258	Duluth, MN	(16.2)	332	Bethlehem, PA	(24.0)	NA	Amherst, NY**	NA
258	Upper Darby Twnshp, PA	(16.2)	333	Birmingham, AL	(24.1)	NA	Arlington Heights, IL**	NA
260	Fargo, ND	(16.3)	334	Columbus, GA	(24.2)	NA	Bloomington, IL**	NA
260	Fort Worth, TX	(16.3)	334	Corpus Christi, TX	(24.2)	NA	Brockton, MA**	NA
260	Richmond, CA	(16.3)	336	San Mateo, CA	(24.3)	NA	Buffalo, NY**	NA
260	San Leandro, CA	(16.3)	337	Dallas, TX	(24.5)	NA	Champaign, IL**	NA
264	West Covina, CA	(16.4)	337	Greensboro, NC	(24.5)	NA	Chandler, AZ**	NA
265	Huntsville, AL	(16.5)	337	Hialeah, FL	(24.5)	NA	Cheektowaga, NY**	NA
265	Palmdale, CA	(16.5)	337	Warwick, RI	(24.5)	NA	Cicero, IL**	NA
267	Racine, WI	(16.6)	341	Clarksville, TN	(24.6)	NA	Clarkstown, NY**	NA
268	Victorville, CA	(16.7)	341	Roseville, CA	(24.6)	NA	Colonie, NY**	NA
269	Brownsville, TX	(16.8)	343	High Point, NC	(24.9)	NA	Decatur, IL**	NA
270	O'Fallon, MO	(16.9)	344	Berkeley, CA	(25.0)	NA	Greece, NY**	NA
270	San Diego, CA	(16.9)	344	Waterbury, CT	(25.0)	NA	Johns Creek, GA**	NA
272	Brooklyn Park, MN	(17.0)	346	Gilbert, AZ	(25.1)	NA	Jurupa Valley, CA**	NA
272	Hoover, AL	(17.0)	347	Cape Coral, FL	(25.2)	NA	Kansas City, KS**	NA
274	Torrance, CA	(17.1)	347	Miami Gardens, FL	(25.2)	NA	Lexington, KY**	NA
275	Clearwater, FL	(17.2)	349	Napa, CA	(25.3)	NA	Longmont, CO**	NA
275	Hillsboro, OR	(17.2)	350	Cary, NC	(25.5)	NA	Menifee, CA**	NA
277	Salt Lake City, UT	(17.3)	351	Arlington, TX	(25.6)	NA	Nashua, NH**	NA
278	Amarillo, TX	(17.4)	352	Beaverton, OR	(25.7)	NA	New Haven, CT**	NA
279	Rockford, IL	(17.5)	353	Mission, TX	(25.8)	NA	New Rochelle, NY**	NA
279	Scottsdale, AZ	(17.5)	353	Newton, MA	(25.8)	NA	New York, NY**	NA
281	Frisco, TX	(17.6)	355	Fremont, CA	(25.9)	NA	Olathe, KS**	NA
282	Murfreesboro, TN	(17.7)	355	Laredo, TX	(25.9)	NA	Parma, OH**	NA
282	Providence, RI	(17.7)	355	Somerville, MA	(25.9)	NA	Peoria, IL**	NA
284	Sunrise, FL	(17.8)	358	St. George, UT	(26.0)	NA	Pueblo, CO**	NA
285	Hemet, CA	(17.9)	359	Lakewood Twnshp, NJ	(26.3)	NA	Ramapo, NY**	NA
285	Tacoma, WA	(17.9)	360	Stockton, CA	(26.4)	NA	Renton, WA**	NA
287	El Paso, TX	(18.2)	361	Charleston, SC	(26.7)	NA	Rochester, NY**	NA
287	Tuscaloosa, AL	(18.2)	362	Port St. Lucie, FL	(27.0)	NA	Springfield, IL**	NA
289	Sunnyvale, CA	(18.3)	363	El Cajon, CA	(27.4)	NA	Syracuse, NY**	NA
290	Memphis, TN	(18.5)	364	Mountain View, CA	(27.6)	NA	Thornton, CO**	NA
291	Independence, MO	(18.6)	364	Redwood City, CA	(27.6)	NA	Toledo, OH**	NA
292	Sandy Springs, GA	(18.8)	366	Savannah, GA	(27.7)	NA	Tucson, AZ**	NA
293	Kennewick, WA	(18.9)	367	Sparks, NV	(27.8)	NA	Waukegan, IL**	NA
294	Ann Arbor, MI	(19.2)	368	Bridgeport, CT	(27.9)	NA	Yonkers, NY**	NA
294	Beaumont, TX	(19.2)	369	Bryan, TX	(28.2)			
294	Jacksonville, FL	(19.2)	369	Fall River, MA	(28.2)			

Source: CQ Press using reported data from the F.B.I. "Crime in the United States 2012"

*Larceny-theft is the unlawful taking of property. Attempts are included.

**Not available.

77. Motor Vehicle Thefts in 2012
National Total = 721,053 Motor Vehicle Thefts*

RANK	CITY	THEFTS	RANK	CITY	THEFTS	RANK	CITY	THEFTS
316	Abilene, TX	171	415	Chino Hills, CA	65	273	Gainesville, FL	239
121	Akron, OH	721	275	Chino, CA	235	144	Garden Grove, CA	601
236	Alameda, CA	295	82	Chula Vista, CA	1,002	146	Garland, TX	591
283	Albany, GA	224	245	Cicero, IL	285	110	Gary, IN	775
331	Albany, NY	154	73	Cincinnati, OH	1,100	322	Gilbert, AZ	164
33	Albuquerque, NM	2,743	176	Citrus Heights, CA	475	64	Glendale, AZ	1,224
218	Alexandria, VA	326	434	Clarkstown, NY	25	230	Glendale, CA	309
260	Alhambra, CA	255	321	Clarksville, TN	167	138	Grand Prairie, TX	632
208	Allentown, PA	368	312	Clearwater, FL	176	253	Grand Rapids, MI	268
426	Allen, TX	44	22	Cleveland, OH	3,761	409	Greece, NY	77
139	Amarillo, TX	629	343	Clifton, NJ	141	343	Greeley, CO	141
431	Amherst, NY	37	308	Clinton Twnshp, MI	181	381	Green Bay, WI	109
60	Anaheim, CA	1,440	200	Clovis, CA	385	150	Greensboro, NC	566
103	Anchorage, AK	831	420	College Station, TX	60	365	Greenville, NC	119
373	Ann Arbor, MI	114	421	Colonie, NY	56	116	Gresham, OR	742
74	Antioch, CA	1,096	51	Colorado Springs, CO	1,802	352	Hamilton Twnshp, NJ	132
437	Arlington Heights, IL	17	338	Columbia, MO	143	207	Hammond, IN	369
87	Arlington, TX	950	102	Columbus, GA	846	256	Hampton, VA	262
299	Arvada, CO	201	104	Compton, CA	819	105	Hartford, CT	802
214	Asheville, NC	336	132	Concord, CA	659	179	Hawthorne, CA	468
267	Athens-Clarke, GA	242	336	Coral Springs, FL	150	59	Hayward, CA	1,456
15	Atlanta, GA	5,150	163	Corona, CA	516	175	Hemet, CA	479
94	Aurora, CO	898	186	Corpus Christi, TX	443	166	Henderson, NV	501
362	Aurora, IL	126	210	Costa Mesa, CA	361	196	Hesperia, CA	400
41	Austin, TX	2,315	331	Cranston, RI	154	118	Hialeah, FL	737
266	Avondale, AZ	245	8	Dallas, TX	7,062	243	High Point, NC	286
30	Bakersfield, CA	3,220	258	Daly City, CA	257	370	Hillsboro, OR	115
199	Baldwin Park, CA	389	412	Danbury, CT	74	131	Hollywood, FL	660
20	Baltimore, MD	3,982	243	Davenport, IA	286	399	Hoover, AL	85
173	Baton Rouge, LA	482	269	Davie, FL	241	3	Houston, TX	13,070
249	Beaumont, TX	279	126	Dayton, OH	693	223	Huntington Beach, CA	321
380	Beaverton, OR	110	211	Dearborn, MI	357	123	Huntsville, AL	710
319	Bellevue, WA	169	403	Decatur, IL	82	108	Independence, MO	783
168	Bellflower, CA	499	305	Deerfield Beach, FL	184	17	Indianapolis, IN	4,599
345	Bellingham, WA	138	326	Denton, TX	157	171	Indio, CA	489
136	Berkeley, CA	641	23	Denver, CO	3,670	137	Inglewood, CA	638
401	Bethlehem, PA	83	109	Des Moines, IA	782	348	Irvine, CA	135
193	Billings, MT	411	4	Detroit, MI	11,500	151	Irving, TX	564
80	Birmingham, AL	1,042	85	Downey, CA	959	54	Jacksonville, FL	1,639
426	Bloomington, IL	44	314	Duluth, MN	172	69	Jackson, MS	1,136
334	Bloomington, IN	151	124	Durham, NC	704	111	Jersey City, NJ	762
409	Bloomington, MN	77	294	Edinburg, TX	209	439	Johns Creek, GA	16
388	Boca Raton, FL	101	378	Edison Twnshp, NJ	111	325	Joliet, IL	158
326	Boise, ID	157	423	Edmond, OK	47	130	Jurupa Valley, CA	664
55	Boston, MA	1,624	198	El Cajon, CA	394	65	Kansas City, KS	1,208
359	Boulder, CO	128	149	El Monte, CA	578	24	Kansas City, MO	3,590
438	Brick Twnshp, NJ	16	68	El Paso, TX	1,160	361	Kennewick, WA	127
100	Bridgeport, CT	868	406	Elgin, IL	79	389	Kenosha, WI	98
293	Brockton, MA	210	66	Elizabeth, NJ	1,167	101	Kent, WA	864
370	Broken Arrow, OK	115	289	Elk Grove, CA	212	302	Killeen, TX	192
348	Brooklyn Park, MN	135	386	Erie, PA	104	91	Knoxville, TN	914
295	Brownsville, TX	206	113	Escondido, CA	758	269	Lafayette, LA	241
396	Bryan, TX	88	187	Eugene, OR	435	418	Lake Forest, CA	63
230	Buena Park, CA	309	190	Evansville, IN	420	304	Lakeland, FL	185
71	Buffalo, NY	1,107	84	Everett, WA	970	426	Lakewood Twnshp, NJ	44
301	Burbank, CA	199	169	Fairfield, CA	497	229	Lakewood, CA	310
383	Cambridge, MA	107	252	Fall River, MA	273	142	Lakewood, CO	608
124	Camden, NJ	704	328	Fargo, ND	155	194	Lancaster, CA	404
373	Cape Coral, FL	114	362	Farmington Hills, MI	126	255	Lansing, MI	264
337	Carlsbad, CA	149	350	Fayetteville, AR	133	203	Laredo, TX	381
424	Carmel, IN	46	114	Fayetteville, NC	756	356	Largo, FL	130
245	Carrollton, TX	285	106	Federal Way, WA	798	288	Las Cruces, NM	214
153	Carson, CA	550	433	Fishers, IN	27	10	Las Vegas, NV	6,685
418	Cary, NC	63	182	Flint, MI	459	297	Lawrence, KS	203
261	Cedar Rapids, IA	254	81	Fontana, CA	1,006	128	Lawrence, MA	686
409	Centennial, CO	77	341	Fort Collins, CO	142	234	Lawton, OK	299
404	Champaign, IL	81	147	Fort Lauderdale, FL	590	413	League City, TX	69
259	Chandler, AZ	256	307	Fort Smith, AR	183	382	Lee's Summit, MO	108
275	Charleston, SC	235	191	Fort Wayne, IN	417	93	Lexington, KY	904
44	Charlotte, NC	2,138	39	Fort Worth, TX	2,424	228	Lincoln, NE	311
397	Cheektowaga, NY	87	148	Fremont, CA	581	75	Little Rock, AR	1,095
249	Chesapeake, VA	279	19	Fresno, CA	4,301	312	Livermore, CA	176
1	Chicago, IL	17,001	422	Frisco, TX	54	300	Livonia, MI	200
261	Chico, CA	254	221	Fullerton, CA	323	36	Long Beach, CA	2,630

RANK	CITY	THEFTS	RANK	CITY	THEFTS	RANK	CITY	THEFTS
385	Longmont, CO	105	264	Pasadena, CA	250	90	South Gate, CA	918
224	Longview, TX	316	161	Pasadena, TX	524	272	Sparks, NV	240
2	Los Angeles, CA	15,084	92	Paterson, NJ	907	189	Spokane Valley, WA	432
43	Louisville, KY	2,187	401	Pearland, TX	83	45	Spokane, WA	2,095
236	Lowell, MA	295	286	Pembroke Pines, FL	217	267	Springfield, IL	242
115	Lubbock, TX	745	254	Peoria, AZ	266	112	Springfield, MA	760
413	Lynchburg, VA	69	278	Peoria, IL	232	79	Springfield, MO	1,051
251	Lynn, MA	277	12	Philadelphia, PA	6,401	317	Stamford, CT	170
167	Macon, GA	500	7	Phoenix, AZ	7,187	323	Sterling Heights, MI	162
261	Madison, WI	254	155	Pittsburgh, PA	544	206	St. Joseph, MO	371
334	Manchester, NH	151	226	Plano, TX	315	397	St. George, UT	87
291	McAllen, TX	211	303	Plantation, FL	189	28	St. Louis, MO	3,489
386	McKinney, TX	104	70	Pomona, CA	1,110	50	St. Paul, MN	1,805
310	Medford, OR	177	195	Pompano Beach, FL	403	98	St. Petersburg, FL	876
365	Melbourne, FL	119	393	Port St. Lucie, FL	91	432	Sugar Land, TX	35
31	Memphis, TN	2,969	25	Portland, OR	3,585	215	Sunnyvale, CA	335
218	Menifee, CA	326	291	Portsmouth, VA	211	338	Sunrise, FL	143
187	Merced, CA	435	67	Providence, RI	1,164	367	Surprise, AZ	118
436	Meridian, ID	20	376	Provo, UT	113	201	Syracuse, NY	382
96	Mesa, AZ	887	170	Pueblo, CO	493	46	Tacoma, WA	1,906
127	Mesquite, TX	687	368	Quincy, MA	116	161	Tallahassee, FL	524
185	Miami Beach, FL	444	356	Racine, WI	130	143	Tampa, FL	607
192	Miami Gardens, FL	413	89	Raleigh, NC	931	289	Temecula, CA	212
34	Miami, FL	2,711	441	Ramapo, NY	16	171	Tempe, AZ	489
347	Midland, TX	136	176	Rancho Cucamon., CA	475	212	Thornton, CO	350
16	Milwaukee, WI	4,803	158	Reading, PA	536	394	Thousand Oaks, CA	90
49	Minneapolis, MN	1,817	165	Redding, CA	502	62	Toledo, OH	1,334
284	Miramar, FL	221	333	Redwood City, CA	153	430	Toms River Twnshp, NJ	38
425	Mission Viejo, CA	45	97	Reno, NV	881	145	Topeka, KS	597
324	Mission, TX	159	141	Renton, WA	617	213	Torrance, CA	338
152	Mobile, AL	552	99	Rialto, CA	875	242	Tracy, CA	287
52	Modesto, CA	1,799	353	Richardson, TX	131	178	Trenton, NJ	469
72	Montgomery, AL	1,101	47	Richmond, CA	1,866	383	Troy, MI	107
95	Moreno Valley, CA	897	88	Richmond, VA	935	38	Tucson, AZ	2,499
373	Mountain View, CA	114	328	Rio Rancho, NM	155	40	Tulsa, OK	2,410
305	Murfreesboro, TN	184	57	Riverside, CA	1,476	298	Tuscaloosa, AL	202
356	Murrieta, CA	130	265	Roanoke, VA	248	353	Tustin, CA	131
405	Nampa, ID	80	395	Rochester, MN	89	353	Tyler, TX	131
284	Napa, CA	221	140	Rochester, NY	622	209	Upland, CA	366
429	Naperville, IL	41	203	Rockford, IL	381	376	Upper Darby Twnshp, PA	113
400	Nashua, NH	84	277	Roseville, CA	233	314	Vacaville, CA	172
61	Nashville, TN	1,431	392	Roswell, GA	94	58	Vallejo, CA	1,475
233	New Bedford, MA	301	407	Round Rock, TX	78	77	Vancouver, WA	1,091
122	New Haven, CT	714	29	Sacramento, CA	3,346	248	Ventura, CA	282
42	New Orleans, LA	2,215	119	Salem, OR	730	135	Victorville, CA	647
415	New Rochelle, NY	65	78	Salinas, CA	1,082	173	Virginia Beach, VA	482
6	New York, NY	8,190	53	Salt Lake City, UT	1,706	160	Visalia, CA	526
21	Newark, NJ	3,962	13	San Antonio, TX	6,367	217	Vista, CA	329
390	Newport Beach, CA	95	35	San Bernardino, CA	2,710	328	Waco, TX	155
256	Newport News, VA	262	11	San Diego, CA	6,610	117	Warren, MI	739
440	Newton, MA	16	14	San Francisco, CA	5,339	390	Warwick, RI	95
120	Norfolk, VA	727	5	San Jose, CA	8,759	27	Washington, DC	3,549
319	Norman, OK	169	107	San Leandro, CA	792	164	Waterbury, CT	513
157	North Charleston, SC	540	281	San Marcos, CA	229	417	Waukegan, IL	64
86	North Las Vegas, NV	955	338	San Mateo, CA	143	156	West Covina, CA	543
159	Norwalk, CA	533	317	Sandy Springs, GA	170	282	West Jordan, UT	228
378	Norwalk, CT	111	341	Sandy, UT	142	227	West Palm Beach, FL	314
9	Oakland, CA	6,976	56	Santa Ana, CA	1,578	134	West Valley, UT	657
184	Oceanside, CA	445	350	Santa Barbara, CA	133	216	Westland, MI	330
201	Odessa, TX	382	183	Santa Clara, CA	449	221	Westminster, CA	323
435	O'Fallon, MO	21	232	Santa Clarita, CA	304	240	Westminster, CO	289
287	Ogden, UT	216	196	Santa Maria, CA	400	236	Whittier, CA	295
18	Oklahoma City, OK	4,374	309	Santa Monica, CA	178	280	Wichita Falls, TX	230
310	Olathe, KS	177	224	Santa Rosa, CA	316	48	Wichita, KS	1,820
32	Omaha, NE	2,747	132	Savannah, GA	659	205	Wilmington, NC	373
83	Ontario, CA	979	269	Scottsdale, AZ	241	129	Winston-Salem, NC	682
240	Orange, CA	289	368	Scranton, PA	116	370	Woodbridge Twnshp, NJ	115
407	Orem, UT	78	26	Seattle, WA	3,556	180	Worcester, MA	465
63	Orlando, FL	1,304	181	Shreveport, LA	464	75	Yakima, WA	1,095
220	Overland Park, KS	324	364	Simi Valley, CA	124	279	Yonkers, NY	231
154	Oxnard, CA	546	296	Sioux City, IA	204	274	Yuma, AZ	236
346	Palm Bay, FL	137	234	Sioux Falls, SD	299			
239	Palmdale, CA	290	359	Somerville, MA	128			
442	Parma, OH	6	245	South Bend, IN	285			

Source: Reported data from the F.B.I. "Crime in the United States 2012"

*Motor vehicle theft includes the theft or attempted theft of a self-propelled vehicle. Excludes motorboats, construction equipment, airplanes, and farming equipment.

77. Motor Vehicle Thefts in 2012 (continued)
National Total = 721,053 Motor Vehicle Thefts*

RANK	CITY	THEFTS	RANK	CITY	THEFTS	RANK	CITY	THEFTS
1	Chicago, IL	17,001	75	Little Rock, AR	1,095	149	El Monte, CA	578
2	Los Angeles, CA	15,084	75	Yakima, WA	1,095	150	Greensboro, NC	566
3	Houston, TX	13,070	77	Vancouver, WA	1,091	151	Irving, TX	564
4	Detroit, MI	11,500	78	Salinas, CA	1,082	152	Mobile, AL	552
5	San Jose, CA	8,759	79	Springfield, MO	1,051	153	Carson, CA	550
6	New York, NY	8,190	80	Birmingham, AL	1,042	154	Oxnard, CA	546
7	Phoenix, AZ	7,187	81	Fontana, CA	1,006	155	Pittsburgh, PA	544
8	Dallas, TX	7,062	82	Chula Vista, CA	1,002	156	West Covina, CA	543
9	Oakland, CA	6,976	83	Ontario, CA	979	157	North Charleston, SC	540
10	Las Vegas, NV	6,685	84	Everett, WA	970	158	Reading, PA	536
11	San Diego, CA	6,610	85	Downey, CA	959	159	Norwalk, CA	533
12	Philadelphia, PA	6,401	86	North Las Vegas, NV	955	160	Visalia, CA	526
13	San Antonio, TX	6,367	87	Arlington, TX	950	161	Pasadena, TX	524
14	San Francisco, CA	5,339	88	Richmond, VA	935	161	Tallahassee, FL	524
15	Atlanta, GA	5,150	89	Raleigh, NC	931	163	Corona, CA	516
16	Milwaukee, WI	4,803	90	South Gate, CA	918	164	Waterbury, CT	513
17	Indianapolis, IN	4,599	91	Knoxville, TN	914	165	Redding, CA	502
18	Oklahoma City, OK	4,374	92	Paterson, NJ	907	166	Henderson, NV	501
19	Fresno, CA	4,301	93	Lexington, KY	904	167	Macon, GA	500
20	Baltimore, MD	3,982	94	Aurora, CO	898	168	Bellflower, CA	499
21	Newark, NJ	3,962	95	Moreno Valley, CA	897	169	Fairfield, CA	497
22	Cleveland, OH	3,761	96	Mesa, AZ	887	170	Pueblo, CO	493
23	Denver, CO	3,670	97	Reno, NV	881	171	Indio, CA	489
24	Kansas City, MO	3,590	98	St. Petersburg, FL	876	171	Tempe, AZ	489
25	Portland, OR	3,585	99	Rialto, CA	875	173	Baton Rouge, LA	482
26	Seattle, WA	3,556	100	Bridgeport, CT	868	173	Virginia Beach, VA	482
27	Washington, DC	3,549	101	Kent, WA	864	175	Hemet, CA	479
28	St. Louis, MO	3,489	102	Columbus, GA	846	176	Citrus Heights, CA	475
29	Sacramento, CA	3,346	103	Anchorage, AK	831	176	Rancho Cucamon., CA	475
30	Bakersfield, CA	3,220	104	Compton, CA	819	178	Trenton, NJ	469
31	Memphis, TN	2,969	105	Hartford, CT	802	179	Hawthorne, CA	468
32	Omaha, NE	2,747	106	Federal Way, WA	798	180	Worcester, MA	465
33	Albuquerque, NM	2,743	107	San Leandro, CA	792	181	Shreveport, LA	464
34	Miami, FL	2,711	108	Independence, MO	783	182	Flint, MI	459
35	San Bernardino, CA	2,710	109	Des Moines, IA	782	183	Santa Clara, CA	449
36	Long Beach, CA	2,630	110	Gary, IN	775	184	Oceanside, CA	445
37	Stockton, CA	2,503	111	Jersey City, NJ	762	185	Miami Beach, FL	444
38	Tucson, AZ	2,499	112	Springfield, MA	760	186	Corpus Christi, TX	443
39	Fort Worth, TX	2,424	113	Escondido, CA	758	187	Eugene, OR	435
40	Tulsa, OK	2,410	114	Fayetteville, NC	756	187	Merced, CA	435
41	Austin, TX	2,315	115	Lubbock, TX	745	189	Spokane Valley, WA	432
42	New Orleans, LA	2,215	116	Gresham, OR	742	190	Evansville, IN	420
43	Louisville, KY	2,187	117	Warren, MI	739	191	Fort Wayne, IN	417
44	Charlotte, NC	2,138	118	Hialeah, FL	737	192	Miami Gardens, FL	413
45	Spokane, WA	2,095	119	Salem, OR	730	193	Billings, MT	411
46	Tacoma, WA	1,906	120	Norfolk, VA	727	194	Lancaster, CA	404
47	Richmond, CA	1,866	121	Akron, OH	721	195	Pompano Beach, FL	403
48	Wichita, KS	1,820	122	New Haven, CT	714	196	Hesperia, CA	400
49	Minneapolis, MN	1,817	123	Huntsville, AL	710	196	Santa Maria, CA	400
50	St. Paul, MN	1,805	124	Camden, NJ	704	198	El Cajon, CA	394
51	Colorado Springs, CO	1,802	124	Durham, NC	704	199	Baldwin Park, CA	389
52	Modesto, CA	1,799	126	Dayton, OH	693	200	Clovis, CA	385
53	Salt Lake City, UT	1,706	127	Mesquite, TX	687	201	Odessa, TX	382
54	Jacksonville, FL	1,639	128	Lawrence, MA	686	201	Syracuse, NY	382
55	Boston, MA	1,624	129	Winston-Salem, NC	682	203	Laredo, TX	381
56	Santa Ana, CA	1,578	130	Jurupa Valley, CA	664	203	Rockford, IL	381
57	Riverside, CA	1,476	131	Hollywood, FL	660	205	Wilmington, NC	373
58	Vallejo, CA	1,475	132	Concord, CA	659	206	St. Joseph, MO	371
59	Hayward, CA	1,456	132	Savannah, GA	659	207	Hammond, IN	369
60	Anaheim, CA	1,440	134	West Valley, UT	657	208	Allentown, PA	368
61	Nashville, TN	1,431	135	Victorville, CA	647	209	Upland, CA	366
62	Toledo, OH	1,334	136	Berkeley, CA	641	210	Costa Mesa, CA	361
63	Orlando, FL	1,304	137	Inglewood, CA	638	211	Dearborn, MI	357
64	Glendale, AZ	1,224	138	Grand Prairie, TX	632	212	Thornton, CO	350
65	Kansas City, KS	1,208	139	Amarillo, TX	629	213	Torrance, CA	338
66	Elizabeth, NJ	1,167	140	Rochester, NY	622	214	Asheville, NC	336
67	Providence, RI	1,164	141	Renton, WA	617	215	Sunnyvale, CA	335
68	El Paso, TX	1,160	142	Lakewood, CO	608	216	Westland, MI	330
69	Jackson, MS	1,136	143	Tampa, FL	607	217	Vista, CA	329
70	Pomona, CA	1,110	144	Garden Grove, CA	601	218	Alexandria, VA	326
71	Buffalo, NY	1,107	145	Topeka, KS	597	218	Menifee, CA	326
72	Montgomery, AL	1,101	146	Garland, TX	591	220	Overland Park, KS	324
73	Cincinnati, OH	1,100	147	Fort Lauderdale, FL	590	221	Fullerton, CA	323
74	Antioch, CA	1,096	148	Fremont, CA	581	221	Westminster, CA	323

RANK	CITY	THEFTS	RANK	CITY	THEFTS	RANK	CITY	THEFTS
223	Huntington Beach, CA	321	297	Lawrence, KS	203	370	Hillsboro, OR	115
224	Longview, TX	316	298	Tuscaloosa, AL	202	370	Woodbridge Twnshp, NJ	115
224	Santa Rosa, CA	316	299	Arvada, CO	201	373	Ann Arbor, MI	114
226	Plano, TX	315	300	Livonia, MI	200	373	Cape Coral, FL	114
227	West Palm Beach, FL	314	301	Burbank, CA	199	373	Mountain View, CA	114
228	Lincoln, NE	311	302	Killeen, TX	192	376	Provo, UT	113
229	Lakewood, CA	310	303	Plantation, FL	189	376	Upper Darby Twnshp, PA	113
230	Buena Park, CA	309	304	Lakeland, FL	185	378	Edison Twnshp, NJ	111
230	Glendale, CA	309	305	Deerfield Beach, FL	184	378	Norwalk, CT	111
232	Santa Clarita, CA	304	305	Murfreesboro, TN	184	380	Beaverton, OR	110
233	New Bedford, MA	301	307	Fort Smith, AR	183	381	Green Bay, WI	109
234	Lawton, OK	299	308	Clinton Twnshp, MI	181	382	Lee's Summit, MO	108
234	Sioux Falls, SD	299	309	Santa Monica, CA	178	383	Cambridge, MA	107
236	Alameda, CA	295	310	Medford, OR	177	383	Troy, MI	107
236	Lowell, MA	295	310	Olathe, KS	177	385	Longmont, CO	105
236	Whittier, CA	295	312	Clearwater, FL	176	386	Erie, PA	104
239	Palmdale, CA	290	312	Livermore, CA	176	386	McKinney, TX	104
240	Orange, CA	289	314	Duluth, MN	172	388	Boca Raton, FL	101
240	Westminster, CO	289	314	Vacaville, CA	172	389	Kenosha, WI	98
242	Tracy, CA	287	316	Abilene, TX	171	390	Newport Beach, CA	95
243	Davenport, IA	286	317	Sandy Springs, GA	170	390	Warwick, RI	95
243	High Point, NC	286	317	Stamford, CT	170	392	Roswell, GA	94
245	Carrollton, TX	285	319	Bellevue, WA	169	393	Port St. Lucie, FL	91
245	Cicero, IL	285	319	Norman, OK	169	394	Thousand Oaks, CA	90
245	South Bend, IN	285	321	Clarksville, TN	167	395	Rochester, MN	89
248	Ventura, CA	282	322	Gilbert, AZ	164	396	Bryan, TX	88
249	Beaumont, TX	279	323	Sterling Heights, MI	162	397	Cheektowaga, NY	87
249	Chesapeake, VA	279	324	Mission, TX	159	397	St. George, UT	87
251	Lynn, MA	277	325	Joliet, IL	158	399	Hoover, AL	85
252	Fall River, MA	273	326	Boise, ID	157	400	Nashua, NH	84
253	Grand Rapids, MI	268	326	Denton, TX	157	401	Bethlehem, PA	83
254	Peoria, AZ	266	328	Fargo, ND	155	401	Pearland, TX	83
255	Lansing, MI	264	328	Rio Rancho, NM	155	403	Decatur, IL	82
256	Hampton, VA	262	328	Waco, TX	155	404	Champaign, IL	81
256	Newport News, VA	262	331	Albany, NY	154	405	Nampa, ID	80
258	Daly City, CA	257	331	Cranston, RI	154	406	Elgin, IL	79
259	Chandler, AZ	256	333	Redwood City, CA	153	407	Orem, UT	78
260	Alhambra, CA	255	334	Bloomington, IN	151	407	Round Rock, TX	78
261	Cedar Rapids, IA	254	334	Manchester, NH	151	409	Bloomington, MN	77
261	Chico, CA	254	336	Coral Springs, FL	150	409	Centennial, CO	77
261	Madison, WI	254	337	Carlsbad, CA	149	409	Greece, NY	77
264	Pasadena, CA	250	338	Columbia, MO	143	412	Danbury, CT	74
265	Roanoke, VA	248	338	San Mateo, CA	143	413	League City, TX	69
266	Avondale, AZ	245	338	Sunrise, FL	143	413	Lynchburg, VA	69
267	Athens-Clarke, GA	242	341	Fort Collins, CO	142	415	Chino Hills, CA	65
267	Springfield, IL	242	341	Sandy, UT	142	415	New Rochelle, NY	65
269	Davie, FL	241	343	Clifton, NJ	141	417	Waukegan, IL	64
269	Lafayette, LA	241	343	Greeley, CO	141	418	Cary, NC	63
269	Scottsdale, AZ	241	345	Bellingham, WA	138	418	Lake Forest, CA	63
272	Sparks, NV	240	346	Palm Bay, FL	137	420	College Station, TX	60
273	Gainesville, FL	239	347	Midland, TX	136	421	Colonie, NY	56
274	Yuma, AZ	236	348	Brooklyn Park, MN	135	422	Frisco, TX	54
275	Charleston, SC	235	348	Irvine, CA	135	423	Edmond, OK	47
275	Chino, CA	235	350	Fayetteville, AR	133	424	Carmel, IN	46
277	Roseville, CA	233	350	Santa Barbara, CA	133	425	Mission Viejo, CA	45
278	Peoria, IL	232	352	Hamilton Twnshp, NJ	132	426	Allen, TX	44
279	Yonkers, NY	231	353	Richardson, TX	131	426	Bloomington, IL	44
280	Wichita Falls, TX	230	353	Tustin, CA	131	426	Lakewood Twnshp, NJ	44
281	San Marcos, CA	229	353	Tyler, TX	131	429	Naperville, IL	41
282	West Jordan, UT	228	356	Largo, FL	130	430	Toms River Twnshp, NJ	38
283	Albany, GA	224	356	Murrieta, CA	130	431	Amherst, NY	37
284	Miramar, FL	221	356	Racine, WI	130	432	Sugar Land, TX	35
284	Napa, CA	221	359	Boulder, CO	128	433	Fishers, IN	27
286	Pembroke Pines, FL	217	359	Somerville, MA	128	434	Clarkstown, NY	25
287	Ogden, UT	216	361	Kennewick, WA	127	435	O'Fallon, MO	21
288	Las Cruces, NM	214	362	Aurora, IL	126	436	Meridian, ID	20
289	Elk Grove, CA	212	362	Farmington Hills, MI	126	437	Arlington Heights, IL	17
289	Temecula, CA	212	364	Simi Valley, CA	124	438	Brick Twnshp, NJ	16
291	McAllen, TX	211	365	Greenville, NC	119	439	Johns Creek, GA	16
291	Portsmouth, VA	211	365	Melbourne, FL	119	440	Newton, MA	16
293	Brockton, MA	210	367	Surprise, AZ	118	441	Ramapo, NY	16
294	Edinburg, TX	209	368	Quincy, MA	116	442	Parma, OH	6
295	Brownsville, TX	206	368	Scranton, PA	116			
296	Sioux City, IA	204	370	Broken Arrow, OK	115			

Source: Reported data from the F.B.I. "Crime in the United States 2012"

*Motor vehicle theft includes the theft or attempted theft of a self-propelled vehicle. Excludes motorboats, construction equipment, airplanes, and farming equipment.

78. Motor Vehicle Theft Rate in 2012
National Rate = 229.7 Motor Vehicle Thefts per 100,000 Population*

RANK	CITY	RATE	RANK	CITY	RATE	RANK	CITY	RATE
328	Abilene, TX	142.6	400	Chino Hills, CA	84.8	280	Gainesville, FL	188.1
160	Akron, OH	363.4	192	Chino, CA	294.5	166	Garden Grove, CA	343.3
145	Alameda, CA	390.9	138	Chula Vista, CA	401.1	228	Garland, TX	251.5
197	Albany, GA	285.3	171	Cicero, IL	338.1	13	Gary, IN	963.1
315	Albany, NY	156.8	156	Cincinnati, OH	371.4	407	Gilbert, AZ	76.5
97	Albuquerque, NM	495.4	74	Citrus Heights, CA	558.1	89	Glendale, AZ	525.3
245	Alexandria, VA	223.5	433	Clarkstown, NY	31.2	312	Glendale, CA	158.5
187	Alhambra, CA	301.9	354	Clarksville, TN	121.6	164	Grand Prairie, TX	347.7
182	Allentown, PA	308.4	311	Clearwater, FL	161.1	330	Grand Rapids, MI	141.1
424	Allen, TX	49.6	15	Cleveland, OH	955.1	405	Greece, NY	79.6
176	Amarillo, TX	320.0	302	Clifton, NJ	166.5	324	Greeley, CO	146.5
432	Amherst, NY	31.5	282	Clinton Twnshp, MI	186.6	382	Green Bay, WI	102.8
132	Anaheim, CA	418.0	142	Clovis, CA	393.5	262	Greensboro, NC	205.0
206	Anchorage, AK	277.8	418	College Station, TX	62.1	335	Greenville, NC	137.0
387	Ann Arbor, MI	99.1	413	Colonie, NY	71.9	40	Gresham, OR	685.8
10	Antioch, CA	1,043.7	133	Colorado Springs, CO	416.9	322	Hamilton Twnshp, NJ	148.1
437	Arlington Heights, IL	22.5	345	Columbia, MO	129.2	120	Hammond, IN	455.5
229	Arlington, TX	250.5	129	Columbus, GA	431.2	275	Hampton, VA	190.0
286	Arvada, CO	184.4	31	Compton, CA	835.2	52	Hartford, CT	640.6
141	Asheville, NC	393.9	88	Concord, CA	526.3	81	Hawthorne, CA	546.1
261	Athens-Clarke, GA	206.0	356	Coral Springs, FL	120.0	11	Hayward, CA	987.6
7	Atlanta, GA	1,178.4	174	Corona, CA	327.9	65	Hemet, CA	589.8
212	Aurora, CO	266.5	329	Corpus Christi, TX	141.7	274	Henderson, NV	190.2
417	Aurora, IL	63.1	175	Costa Mesa, CA	320.5	128	Hesperia, CA	433.0
205	Austin, TX	277.9	273	Cranston, RI	191.7	177	Hialeah, FL	316.2
181	Avondale, AZ	312.6	69	Dallas, TX	568.8	210	High Point, NC	267.8
21	Bakersfield, CA	905.3	231	Daly City, CA	248.8	352	Hillsboro, OR	122.2
91	Baldwin Park, CA	507.5	397	Danbury, CT	90.4	121	Hollywood, FL	454.2
53	Baltimore, MD	636.6	200	Davenport, IA	282.6	381	Hoover, AL	103.2
258	Baton Rouge, LA	208.2	223	Davie, FL	253.8	61	Houston, TX	600.3
238	Beaumont, TX	231.9	102	Dayton, OH	487.6	306	Huntington Beach, CA	164.9
357	Beaverton, OR	119.2	158	Dearborn, MI	367.2	147	Huntsville, AL	386.5
340	Bellevue, WA	134.1	376	Decatur, IL	107.7	42	Independence, MO	666.8
51	Bellflower, CA	640.7	234	Deerfield Beach, FL	237.6	80	Indianapolis, IN	548.4
301	Bellingham, WA	166.9	341	Denton, TX	132.0	55	Indio, CA	622.9
75	Berkeley, CA	557.6	66	Denver, CO	583.9	68	Inglewood, CA	572.3
371	Bethlehem, PA	110.1	152	Des Moines, IA	377.0	418	Irvine, CA	62.1
148	Billings, MT	386.4	3	Detroit, MI	1,626.4	227	Irving, TX	251.8
101	Birmingham, AL	488.6	29	Downey, CA	844.0	271	Jacksonville, FL	195.0
420	Bloomington, IL	57.1	265	Duluth, MN	198.1	50	Jackson, MS	645.7
284	Bloomington, IN	185.0	190	Durham, NC	298.9	185	Jersey City, NJ	302.9
396	Bloomington, MN	91.0	217	Edinburg, TX	260.2	439	Johns Creek, GA	20.0
362	Boca Raton, FL	116.8	372	Edison Twnshp, NJ	109.9	379	Joliet, IL	106.4
409	Boise, ID	74.2	421	Edmond, OK	56.3	41	Jurupa Valley, CA	680.5
221	Boston, MA	257.5	146	El Cajon, CA	386.8	32	Kansas City, KS	820.6
347	Boulder, CO	127.7	94	El Monte, CA	501.1	34	Kansas City, MO	773.6
438	Brick Twnshp, NJ	21.1	297	El Paso, TX	171.7	304	Kennewick, WA	165.0
63	Bridgeport, CT	594.4	412	Elgin, IL	72.4	389	Kenosha, WI	98.0
247	Brockton, MA	220.7	17	Elizabeth, NJ	924.1	37	Kent, WA	707.6
368	Broken Arrow, OK	114.2	339	Elk Grove, CA	135.6	325	Killeen, TX	145.5
292	Brooklyn Park, MN	174.5	383	Erie, PA	102.0	93	Knoxville, TN	501.5
369	Brownsville, TX	113.7	90	Escondido, CA	514.3	269	Lafayette, LA	196.2
370	Bryan, TX	112.1	207	Eugene, OR	275.2	405	Lake Forest, CA	79.6
154	Buena Park, CA	374.5	161	Evansville, IN	355.3	283	Lakeland, FL	185.1
131	Buffalo, NY	421.8	18	Everett, WA	921.0	426	Lakewood Twnshp, NJ	46.9
278	Burbank, CA	189.4	116	Fairfield, CA	464.0	151	Lakewood, CA	380.9
385	Cambridge, MA	100.0	184	Fall River, MA	304.2	135	Lakewood, CO	415.3
20	Camden, NJ	906.5	330	Fargo, ND	141.1	223	Lancaster, CA	253.8
415	Cape Coral, FL	71.4	314	Farmington Hills, MI	156.9	240	Lansing, MI	230.2
332	Carlsbad, CA	138.1	290	Fayetteville, AR	176.4	317	Laredo, TX	155.2
422	Carmel, IN	56.2	159	Fayetteville, NC	367.1	304	Largo, FL	165.0
242	Carrollton, TX	229.0	26	Federal Way, WA	867.6	253	Las Cruces, NM	214.4
64	Carson, CA	589.9	431	Fishers, IN	34.0	123	Las Vegas, NV	451.9
427	Cary, NC	44.7	124	Flint, MI	451.6	244	Lawrence, KS	227.6
266	Cedar Rapids, IA	197.8	95	Fontana, CA	500.8	24	Lawrence, MA	883.3
410	Centennial, CO	74.0	395	Fort Collins, CO	95.4	186	Lawton, OK	302.7
386	Champaign, IL	99.6	165	Fort Lauderdale, FL	345.4	404	League City, TX	80.1
380	Chandler, AZ	105.5	256	Fort Smith, AR	209.2	360	Lee's Summit, MO	117.6
276	Charleston, SC	189.7	310	Fort Wayne, IN	162.5	189	Lexington, KY	299.0
214	Charlotte, NC	264.4	178	Fort Worth, TX	314.8	359	Lincoln, NE	117.7
372	Cheektowaga, NY	109.9	213	Fremont, CA	265.4	73	Little Rock, AR	558.5
351	Chesapeake, VA	122.6	28	Fresno, CA	850.0	255	Livermore, CA	212.6
54	Chicago, IL	627.7	428	Frisco, TX	43.8	257	Livonia, MI	208.3
195	Chico, CA	291.7	235	Fullerton, CA	233.3	72	Long Beach, CA	559.7

RANK	CITY	RATE
358	Longmont, CO	118.1
149	Longview, TX	382.8
143	Los Angeles, CA	391.3
173	Louisville, KY	328.3
208	Lowell, MA	271.8
179	Lubbock, TX	314.0
398	Lynchburg, VA	89.2
188	Lynn, MA	301.6
83	Macon, GA	538.6
378	Madison, WI	106.9
334	Manchester, NH	137.2
316	McAllen, TX	155.4
408	McKinney, TX	75.3
237	Medford, OR	232.8
318	Melbourne, FL	154.3
124	Memphis, TN	451.6
137	Menifee, CA	407.3
84	Merced, CA	537.2
436	Meridian, ID	25.9
268	Mesa, AZ	196.5
108	Mesquite, TX	474.4
102	Miami Beach, FL	487.6
155	Miami Gardens, FL	371.5
47	Miami, FL	654.3
360	Midland, TX	117.6
33	Milwaukee, WI	801.3
114	Minneapolis, MN	465.6
291	Miramar, FL	175.4
425	Mission Viejo, CA	47.1
267	Mission, TX	197.4
249	Mobile, AL	219.5
25	Modesto, CA	879.1
87	Montgomery, AL	526.7
127	Moreno Valley, CA	449.2
320	Mountain View, CA	150.1
309	Murfreesboro, TN	163.9
353	Murrieta, CA	121.7
394	Nampa, ID	96.0
202	Napa, CA	281.2
434	Naperville, IL	28.7
392	Nashua, NH	96.7
239	Nashville, TN	230.5
180	New Bedford, MA	313.4
79	New Haven, CT	549.5
58	New Orleans, LA	610.4
402	New Rochelle, NY	83.3
388	New York, NY	98.8
4	Newark, NJ	1,420.6
374	Newport Beach, CA	108.8
326	Newport News, VA	144.3
441	Newton, MA	18.5
191	Norfolk, VA	296.4
321	Norman, OK	148.3
85	North Charleston, SC	536.4
130	North Las Vegas, NV	430.4
96	Norwalk, CA	496.8
346	Norwalk, CT	128.0
2	Oakland, CA	1,746.2
218	Oceanside, CA	260.0
157	Odessa, TX	368.6
435	O'Fallon, MO	26.0
222	Ogden, UT	253.9
35	Oklahoma City, OK	734.4
333	Olathe, KS	137.7
44	Omaha, NE	657.2
67	Ontario, CA	583.0
259	Orange, CA	206.9
400	Orem, UT	84.8
86	Orlando, FL	529.0
288	Overland Park, KS	183.0
209	Oxnard, CA	270.6
343	Palm Bay, FL	130.9
281	Palmdale, CA	186.7
442	Parma, OH	7.4

RANK	CITY	RATE
289	Pasadena, CA	179.4
170	Pasadena, TX	339.0
57	Paterson, NJ	616.4
399	Pearland, TX	87.6
338	Pembroke Pines, FL	135.8
300	Peoria, AZ	168.0
264	Peoria, IL	201.2
134	Philadelphia, PA	415.9
105	Phoenix, AZ	483.8
293	Pittsburgh, PA	174.3
365	Plano, TX	115.0
252	Plantation, FL	215.5
36	Pomona, CA	732.6
143	Pompano Beach, FL	391.3
423	Port St. Lucie, FL	54.0
62	Portland, OR	599.5
250	Portsmouth, VA	218.1
46	Providence, RI	654.4
392	Provo, UT	96.7
122	Pueblo, CO	452.0
350	Quincy, MA	123.8
307	Racine, WI	164.4
246	Raleigh, NC	221.4
440	Ramapo, NY	18.7
204	Rancho Cucamon., CA	280.6
59	Reading, PA	605.3
76	Redding, CA	551.8
271	Redwood City, CA	195.0
150	Reno, NV	382.2
43	Renton, WA	658.3
27	Rialto, CA	861.3
348	Richardson, TX	126.9
1	Richmond, CA	1,754.5
126	Richmond, VA	450.0
295	Rio Rancho, NM	173.3
111	Riverside, CA	470.8
226	Roanoke, VA	253.6
403	Rochester, MN	82.0
194	Rochester, NY	293.4
230	Rockford, IL	250.2
277	Roseville, CA	189.6
383	Roswell, GA	102.0
411	Round Rock, TX	73.4
38	Sacramento, CA	702.1
117	Salem, OR	463.9
39	Salinas, CA	700.7
23	Salt Lake City, UT	886.4
119	San Antonio, TX	461.3
5	San Bernardino, CA	1,260.5
98	San Diego, CA	493.8
49	San Francisco, CA	650.8
22	San Jose, CA	897.0
19	San Leandro, CA	911.7
211	San Marcos, CA	266.9
327	San Mateo, CA	144.0
294	Sandy Springs, GA	173.7
313	Sandy, UT	157.1
107	Santa Ana, CA	474.6
323	Santa Barbara, CA	148.0
153	Santa Clara, CA	376.2
298	Santa Clarita, CA	169.6
140	Santa Maria, CA	395.2
270	Santa Monica, CA	195.1
285	Santa Rosa, CA	184.9
198	Savannah, GA	284.9
375	Scottsdale, AZ	107.9
319	Scranton, PA	152.4
70	Seattle, WA	567.3
241	Shreveport, LA	229.5
390	Simi Valley, CA	97.9
233	Sioux City, IA	244.9
279	Sioux Falls, SD	188.8
303	Somerville, MA	165.8
203	South Bend, IN	281.1

RANK	CITY	RATE
14	South Gate, CA	956.6
220	Sparks, NV	259.8
109	Spokane Valley, WA	473.9
12	Spokane, WA	987.4
260	Springfield, IL	206.6
99	Springfield, MA	491.9
48	Springfield, MO	652.9
336	Stamford, CT	136.9
349	Sterling Heights, MI	124.6
30	Stockton, CA	836.8
366	St. George, UT	114.8
106	St. Joseph, MO	479.8
9	St. Louis, MO	1,094.9
56	St. Paul, MN	620.9
162	St. Petersburg, FL	352.7
429	Sugar Land, TX	42.2
235	Sunnyvale, CA	233.3
308	Sunrise, FL	164.1
391	Surprise, AZ	97.7
216	Syracuse, NY	261.8
16	Tacoma, WA	940.6
201	Tallahassee, FL	282.5
296	Tampa, FL	173.1
262	Temecula, CA	205.0
192	Tempe, AZ	294.5
199	Thornton, CO	284.3
416	Thousand Oaks, CA	69.7
113	Toledo, OH	466.4
430	Toms River Twnshp, NJ	41.2
118	Topeka, KS	463.4
243	Torrance, CA	228.6
172	Tracy, CA	337.5
78	Trenton, NJ	549.7
342	Troy, MI	131.2
112	Tucson, AZ	470.1
60	Tulsa, OK	604.2
248	Tuscaloosa, AL	219.6
299	Tustin, CA	169.3
343	Tyler, TX	130.9
104	Upland, CA	484.6
337	Upper Darby Twnshp, PA	136.2
287	Vacaville, CA	183.1
6	Vallejo, CA	1,250.9
45	Vancouver, WA	655.7
219	Ventura, CA	259.9
82	Victorville, CA	545.1
376	Virginia Beach, VA	107.7
136	Visalia, CA	412.2
167	Vista, CA	342.4
355	Waco, TX	120.5
77	Warren, MI	550.1
364	Warwick, RI	115.5
71	Washington, DC	561.3
115	Waterbury, CT	464.3
414	Waukegan, IL	71.5
92	West Covina, CA	503.4
254	West Jordan, UT	212.9
183	West Palm Beach, FL	306.6
100	West Valley, UT	491.3
139	Westland, MI	396.2
163	Westminster, CA	351.4
215	Westminster, CO	264.0
169	Whittier, CA	340.1
251	Wichita Falls, TX	218.0
110	Wichita, KS	471.0
168	Wilmington, NC	341.0
196	Winston-Salem, NC	290.6
367	Woodbridge Twnshp, NJ	114.3
223	Worcester, MA	253.8
8	Yakima, WA	1,172.1
363	Yonkers, NY	116.4
232	Yuma, AZ	246.9

Source: CQ Press using reported data from the F.B.I. "Crime in the United States 2012"

*Motor vehicle theft includes the theft or attempted theft of a self-propelled vehicle. Excludes motorboats, construction equipment, airplanes, and farming equipment.

78. Motor Vehicle Theft Rate in 2012 (continued)
National Rate = 229.7 Motor Vehicle Thefts per 100,000 Population*

RANK	CITY	RATE	RANK	CITY	RATE	RANK	CITY	RATE
1	Richmond, CA	1,754.5	75	Berkeley, CA	557.6	149	Longview, TX	382.8
2	Oakland, CA	1,746.2	76	Redding, CA	551.8	150	Reno, NV	382.2
3	Detroit, MI	1,626.4	77	Warren, MI	550.1	151	Lakewood, CA	380.9
4	Newark, NJ	1,420.6	78	Trenton, NJ	549.7	152	Des Moines, IA	377.0
5	San Bernardino, CA	1,260.5	79	New Haven, CT	549.5	153	Santa Clara, CA	376.2
6	Vallejo, CA	1,250.9	80	Indianapolis, IN	548.4	154	Buena Park, CA	374.5
7	Atlanta, GA	1,178.4	81	Hawthorne, CA	546.1	155	Miami Gardens, FL	371.5
8	Yakima, WA	1,172.1	82	Victorville, CA	545.1	156	Cincinnati, OH	371.4
9	St. Louis, MO	1,094.9	83	Macon, GA	538.6	157	Odessa, TX	368.6
10	Antioch, CA	1,043.7	84	Merced, CA	537.2	158	Dearborn, MI	367.2
11	Hayward, CA	987.6	85	North Charleston, SC	536.4	159	Fayetteville, NC	367.1
12	Spokane, WA	987.4	86	Orlando, FL	529.0	160	Akron, OH	363.4
13	Gary, IN	963.1	87	Montgomery, AL	526.7	161	Evansville, IN	355.3
14	South Gate, CA	956.6	88	Concord, CA	526.3	162	St. Petersburg, FL	352.7
15	Cleveland, OH	955.1	89	Glendale, AZ	525.3	163	Westminster, CA	351.4
16	Tacoma, WA	940.6	90	Escondido, CA	514.3	164	Grand Prairie, TX	347.7
17	Elizabeth, NJ	924.1	91	Baldwin Park, CA	507.5	165	Fort Lauderdale, FL	345.4
18	Everett, WA	921.0	92	West Covina, CA	503.4	166	Garden Grove, CA	343.3
19	San Leandro, CA	911.7	93	Knoxville, TN	501.5	167	Vista, CA	342.4
20	Camden, NJ	906.5	94	El Monte, CA	501.1	168	Wilmington, NC	341.0
21	Bakersfield, CA	905.3	95	Fontana, CA	500.8	169	Whittier, CA	340.1
22	San Jose, CA	897.0	96	Norwalk, CA	496.8	170	Pasadena, TX	339.0
23	Salt Lake City, UT	886.4	97	Albuquerque, NM	495.4	171	Cicero, IL	338.1
24	Lawrence, MA	883.3	98	San Diego, CA	493.8	172	Tracy, CA	337.5
25	Modesto, CA	879.1	99	Springfield, MA	491.9	173	Louisville, KY	328.3
26	Federal Way, WA	867.6	100	West Valley, UT	491.3	174	Corona, CA	327.9
27	Rialto, CA	861.3	101	Birmingham, AL	488.6	175	Costa Mesa, CA	320.5
28	Fresno, CA	850.0	102	Dayton, OH	487.6	176	Amarillo, TX	320.0
29	Downey, CA	844.0	102	Miami Beach, FL	487.6	177	Hialeah, FL	316.2
30	Stockton, CA	836.8	104	Upland, CA	484.6	178	Fort Worth, TX	314.8
31	Compton, CA	835.2	105	Phoenix, AZ	483.8	179	Lubbock, TX	314.0
32	Kansas City, KS	820.6	106	St. Joseph, MO	479.8	180	New Bedford, MA	313.4
33	Milwaukee, WI	801.3	107	Santa Ana, CA	474.6	181	Avondale, AZ	312.6
34	Kansas City, MO	773.6	108	Mesquite, TX	474.4	182	Allentown, PA	308.4
35	Oklahoma City, OK	734.4	109	Spokane Valley, WA	473.9	183	West Palm Beach, FL	306.6
36	Pomona, CA	732.6	110	Wichita, KS	471.0	184	Fall River, MA	304.2
37	Kent, WA	707.6	111	Riverside, CA	470.8	185	Jersey City, NJ	302.9
38	Sacramento, CA	702.1	112	Tucson, AZ	470.1	186	Lawton, OK	302.7
39	Salinas, CA	700.7	113	Toledo, OH	466.4	187	Alhambra, CA	301.9
40	Gresham, OR	685.8	114	Minneapolis, MN	465.6	188	Lynn, MA	301.6
41	Jurupa Valley, CA	680.5	115	Waterbury, CT	464.3	189	Lexington, KY	299.0
42	Independence, MO	666.8	116	Fairfield, CA	464.0	190	Durham, NC	298.9
43	Renton, WA	658.3	117	Salem, OR	463.9	191	Norfolk, VA	296.4
44	Omaha, NE	657.2	118	Topeka, KS	463.4	192	Chino, CA	294.5
45	Vancouver, WA	655.7	119	San Antonio, TX	461.3	192	Tempe, AZ	294.5
46	Providence, RI	654.4	120	Hammond, IN	455.5	194	Rochester, NY	293.4
47	Miami, FL	654.3	121	Hollywood, FL	454.2	195	Chico, CA	291.7
48	Springfield, MO	652.9	122	Pueblo, CO	452.0	196	Winston-Salem, NC	290.6
49	San Francisco, CA	650.8	123	Las Vegas, NV	451.9	197	Albany, GA	285.3
50	Jackson, MS	645.7	124	Flint, MI	451.6	198	Savannah, GA	284.9
51	Bellflower, CA	640.7	124	Memphis, TN	451.6	199	Thornton, CO	284.3
52	Hartford, CT	640.6	126	Richmond, VA	450.0	200	Davenport, IA	282.6
53	Baltimore, MD	636.6	127	Moreno Valley, CA	449.2	201	Tallahassee, FL	282.5
54	Chicago, IL	627.7	128	Hesperia, CA	433.0	202	Napa, CA	281.2
55	Indio, CA	622.9	129	Columbus, GA	431.2	203	South Bend, IN	281.1
56	St. Paul, MN	620.9	130	North Las Vegas, NV	430.4	204	Rancho Cucamon., CA	280.6
57	Paterson, NJ	616.4	131	Buffalo, NY	421.8	205	Austin, TX	277.9
58	New Orleans, LA	610.4	132	Anaheim, CA	418.0	206	Anchorage, AK	277.8
59	Reading, PA	605.3	133	Colorado Springs, CO	416.9	207	Eugene, OR	275.2
60	Tulsa, OK	604.2	134	Philadelphia, PA	415.9	208	Lowell, MA	271.8
61	Houston, TX	600.3	135	Lakewood, CO	415.3	209	Oxnard, CA	270.6
62	Portland, OR	599.5	136	Visalia, CA	412.2	210	High Point, NC	267.8
63	Bridgeport, CT	594.4	137	Menifee, CA	407.3	211	San Marcos, CA	266.9
64	Carson, CA	589.9	138	Chula Vista, CA	401.1	212	Aurora, CO	266.5
65	Hemet, CA	589.8	139	Westland, MI	396.2	213	Fremont, CA	265.4
66	Denver, CO	583.9	140	Santa Maria, CA	395.2	214	Charlotte, NC	264.4
67	Ontario, CA	583.0	141	Asheville, NC	393.9	215	Westminster, CO	264.0
68	Inglewood, CA	572.3	142	Clovis, CA	393.5	216	Syracuse, NY	261.8
69	Dallas, TX	568.8	143	Los Angeles, CA	391.3	217	Edinburg, TX	260.2
70	Seattle, WA	567.3	143	Pompano Beach, FL	391.3	218	Oceanside, CA	260.0
71	Washington, DC	561.3	145	Alameda, CA	390.9	219	Ventura, CA	259.9
72	Long Beach, CA	559.7	146	El Cajon, CA	386.8	220	Sparks, NV	259.8
73	Little Rock, AR	558.5	147	Huntsville, AL	386.5	221	Boston, MA	257.5
74	Citrus Heights, CA	558.1	148	Billings, MT	386.4	222	Ogden, UT	253.9

RANK	CITY	RATE
223	Davie, FL	253.8
223	Lancaster, CA	253.8
223	Worcester, MA	253.8
226	Roanoke, VA	253.6
227	Irving, TX	251.8
228	Garland, TX	251.5
229	Arlington, TX	250.5
230	Rockford, IL	250.2
231	Daly City, CA	248.8
232	Yuma, AZ	246.9
233	Sioux City, IA	244.9
234	Deerfield Beach, FL	237.6
235	Fullerton, CA	233.3
235	Sunnyvale, CA	233.3
237	Medford, OR	232.8
238	Beaumont, TX	231.9
239	Nashville, TN	230.5
240	Lansing, MI	230.2
241	Shreveport, LA	229.5
242	Carrollton, TX	229.0
243	Torrance, CA	228.6
244	Lawrence, KS	227.6
245	Alexandria, VA	223.5
246	Raleigh, NC	221.4
247	Brockton, MA	220.7
248	Tuscaloosa, AL	219.6
249	Mobile, AL	219.5
250	Portsmouth, VA	218.1
251	Wichita Falls, TX	218.0
252	Plantation, FL	215.5
253	Las Cruces, NM	214.4
254	West Jordan, UT	212.9
255	Livermore, CA	212.6
256	Fort Smith, AR	209.2
257	Livonia, MI	208.3
258	Baton Rouge, LA	208.2
259	Orange, CA	206.9
260	Springfield, IL	206.6
261	Athens-Clarke, GA	206.0
262	Greensboro, NC	205.0
262	Temecula, CA	205.0
264	Peoria, IL	201.2
265	Duluth, MN	198.1
266	Cedar Rapids, IA	197.8
267	Mission, TX	197.4
268	Mesa, AZ	196.5
269	Lafayette, LA	196.2
270	Santa Monica, CA	195.1
271	Jacksonville, FL	195.0
271	Redwood City, CA	195.0
273	Cranston, RI	191.7
274	Henderson, NV	190.2
275	Hampton, VA	190.0
276	Charleston, SC	189.7
277	Roseville, CA	189.6
278	Burbank, CA	189.4
279	Sioux Falls, SD	188.8
280	Gainesville, FL	188.1
281	Palmdale, CA	186.7
282	Clinton Twnshp, MI	186.6
283	Lakeland, FL	185.1
284	Bloomington, IN	185.0
285	Santa Rosa, CA	184.9
286	Arvada, CO	184.4
287	Vacaville, CA	183.1
288	Overland Park, KS	183.0
289	Pasadena, CA	179.4
290	Fayetteville, AR	176.4
291	Miramar, FL	175.4
292	Brooklyn Park, MN	174.5
293	Pittsburgh, PA	174.3
294	Sandy Springs, GA	173.7
295	Rio Rancho, NM	173.3
296	Tampa, FL	173.1
297	El Paso, TX	171.7
298	Santa Clarita, CA	169.6
299	Tustin, CA	169.3
300	Peoria, AZ	168.0
301	Bellingham, WA	166.9
302	Clifton, NJ	166.5
303	Somerville, MA	165.8
304	Kennewick, WA	165.0
304	Largo, FL	165.0
306	Huntington Beach, CA	164.9
307	Racine, WI	164.4
308	Sunrise, FL	164.1
309	Murfreesboro, TN	163.9
310	Fort Wayne, IN	162.5
311	Clearwater, FL	161.1
312	Glendale, CA	158.5
313	Sandy, UT	157.1
314	Farmington Hills, MI	156.9
315	Albany, NY	156.8
316	McAllen, TX	155.4
317	Laredo, TX	155.2
318	Melbourne, FL	154.3
319	Scranton, PA	152.4
320	Mountain View, CA	150.1
321	Norman, OK	148.3
322	Hamilton Twnshp, NJ	148.1
323	Santa Barbara, CA	148.0
324	Greeley, CO	146.5
325	Killeen, TX	145.5
326	Newport News, VA	144.3
327	San Mateo, CA	144.0
328	Abilene, TX	142.6
329	Corpus Christi, TX	141.7
330	Fargo, ND	141.1
330	Grand Rapids, MI	141.1
332	Carlsbad, CA	138.1
333	Olathe, KS	137.7
334	Manchester, NH	137.2
335	Greenville, NC	137.0
336	Stamford, CT	136.9
337	Upper Darby Twnshp, PA	136.2
338	Pembroke Pines, FL	135.8
339	Elk Grove, CA	135.6
340	Bellevue, WA	134.1
341	Denton, TX	132.0
342	Troy, MI	131.2
343	Palm Bay, FL	130.9
343	Tyler, TX	130.9
345	Columbia, MO	129.2
346	Norwalk, CT	128.0
347	Boulder, CO	127.7
348	Richardson, TX	126.9
349	Sterling Heights, MI	124.6
350	Quincy, MA	123.8
351	Chesapeake, VA	122.6
352	Hillsboro, OR	122.2
353	Murrieta, CA	121.7
354	Clarksville, TN	121.6
355	Waco, TX	120.5
356	Coral Springs, FL	120.0
357	Beaverton, OR	119.2
358	Longmont, CO	118.1
359	Lincoln, NE	117.7
360	Lee's Summit, MO	117.6
360	Midland, TX	117.6
362	Boca Raton, FL	116.8
363	Yonkers, NY	116.4
364	Warwick, RI	115.5
365	Plano, TX	115.0
366	St. George, UT	114.8
367	Woodbridge Twnshp, NJ	114.3
368	Broken Arrow, OK	114.2
369	Brownsville, TX	113.7
370	Bryan, TX	112.1
371	Bethlehem, PA	110.1
372	Cheektowaga, NY	109.9
372	Edison Twnshp, NJ	109.9
374	Newport Beach, CA	108.8
375	Scottsdale, AZ	107.9
376	Decatur, IL	107.7
376	Virginia Beach, VA	107.7
378	Madison, WI	106.9
379	Joliet, IL	106.4
380	Chandler, AZ	105.5
381	Hoover, AL	103.2
382	Green Bay, WI	102.8
383	Erie, PA	102.0
383	Roswell, GA	102.0
385	Cambridge, MA	100.0
386	Champaign, IL	99.6
387	Ann Arbor, MI	99.1
388	New York, NY	98.8
389	Kenosha, WI	98.0
390	Simi Valley, CA	97.9
391	Surprise, AZ	97.7
392	Nashua, NH	96.7
392	Provo, UT	96.7
394	Nampa, ID	96.0
395	Fort Collins, CO	95.4
396	Bloomington, MN	91.0
397	Danbury, CT	90.4
398	Lynchburg, VA	89.2
399	Pearland, TX	87.6
400	Chino Hills, CA	84.8
400	Orem, UT	84.8
402	New Rochelle, NY	83.3
403	Rochester, MN	82.0
404	League City, TX	80.1
405	Greece, NY	79.6
405	Lake Forest, CA	79.6
407	Gilbert, AZ	76.5
408	McKinney, TX	75.3
409	Boise, ID	74.2
410	Centennial, CO	74.0
411	Round Rock, TX	73.4
412	Elgin, IL	72.4
413	Colonie, NY	71.9
414	Waukegan, IL	71.5
415	Cape Coral, FL	71.4
416	Thousand Oaks, CA	69.7
417	Aurora, IL	63.1
418	College Station, TX	62.1
418	Irvine, CA	62.1
420	Bloomington, IL	57.1
421	Edmond, OK	56.3
422	Carmel, IN	56.2
423	Port St. Lucie, FL	54.0
424	Allen, TX	49.6
425	Mission Viejo, CA	47.1
426	Lakewood Twnshp, NJ	46.9
427	Cary, NC	44.7
428	Frisco, TX	43.8
429	Sugar Land, TX	42.2
430	Toms River Twnshp, NJ	41.2
431	Fishers, IN	34.0
432	Amherst, NY	31.5
433	Clarkstown, NY	31.2
434	Naperville, IL	28.7
435	O'Fallon, MO	26.0
436	Meridian, ID	25.9
437	Arlington Heights, IL	22.5
438	Brick Twnshp, NJ	21.1
439	Johns Creek, GA	20.0
440	Ramapo, NY	18.7
441	Newton, MA	18.5
442	Parma, OH	7.4

Source: CQ Press using reported data from the F.B.I. "Crime in the United States 2012"

*Motor vehicle theft includes the theft or attempted theft of a self-propelled vehicle. Excludes motorboats, construction equipment, airplanes, and farming equipment.

79. Percent Change in Motor Vehicle Theft Rate: 2011 to 2012
National Percent Change = 0.1% Decrease*

RANK	CITY	% CHANGE	RANK	CITY	% CHANGE	RANK	CITY	% CHANGE
211	Abilene, TX	(0.9)	398	Chino Hills, CA	(28.7)	353	Gainesville, FL	(18.3)
291	Akron, OH	(10.2)	98	Chino, CA	15.6	33	Garden Grove, CA	38.7
115	Alameda, CA	12.3	119	Chula Vista, CA	12.0	286	Garland, TX	(9.7)
160	Albany, GA	5.1	162	Cicero, IL	5.0	220	Gary, IN	(2.1)
NA	Albany, NY**	NA	328	Cincinnati, OH	(13.5)	79	Gilbert, AZ	19.7
229	Albuquerque, NM	(3.1)	36	Citrus Heights, CA	38.3	349	Glendale, AZ	(17.2)
335	Alexandria, VA	(14.9)	NA	Clarkstown, NY**	NA	245	Glendale, CA	(4.8)
95	Alhambra, CA	17.0	385	Clarksville, TN	(25.2)	380	Grand Prairie, TX	(23.9)
NA	Allentown, PA**	NA	124	Clearwater, FL	11.3	355	Grand Rapids, MI	(18.4)
411	Allen, TX	(39.9)	267	Cleveland, OH	(7.3)	NA	Greece, NY**	NA
197	Amarillo, TX	1.1	396	Clifton, NJ	(28.3)	259	Greeley, CO	(6.4)
NA	Amherst, NY**	NA	274	Clinton Twnshp, MI	(7.9)	148	Green Bay, WI	6.4
58	Anaheim, CA	27.1	269	Clovis, CA	(7.4)	NA	Greensboro, NC**	NA
47	Anchorage, AK	32.0	115	College Station, TX	12.3	NA	Greenville, NC**	NA
96	Ann Arbor, MI	16.3	NA	Colonie, NY**	NA	81	Gresham, OR	18.6
121	Antioch, CA	11.8	11	Colorado Springs, CO	51.2	69	Hamilton Twnshp, NJ	24.0
359	Arlington Heights, IL	(19.4)	211	Columbia, MO	(0.9)	378	Hammond, IN	(23.5)
308	Arlington, TX	(12.1)	367	Columbus, GA	(20.9)	230	Hampton, VA	(3.2)
155	Arvada, CO	5.7	252	Compton, CA	(5.6)	263	Hartford, CT	(6.8)
174	Asheville, NC	3.6	188	Concord, CA	2.0	80	Hawthorne, CA	19.4
203	Athens-Clarke, GA	0.1	291	Coral Springs, FL	(10.2)	50	Hayward, CA	30.9
261	Atlanta, GA	(6.6)	22	Corona, CA	44.0	75	Hemet, CA	21.0
195	Aurora, CO	1.3	251	Corpus Christi, TX	(5.5)	100	Henderson, NV	15.5
260	Aurora, IL	(6.5)	43	Costa Mesa, CA	33.5	214	Hesperia, CA	(1.2)
163	Austin, TX	4.9	230	Cranston, RI	(3.2)	382	Hialeah, FL	(24.3)
167	Avondale, AZ	4.2	324	Dallas, TX	(12.9)	89	High Point, NC	17.5
45	Bakersfield, CA	32.8	191	Daly City, CA	1.8	325	Hillsboro, OR	(13.0)
241	Baldwin Park, CA	(3.9)	86	Danbury, CT	18.2	109	Hollywood, FL	13.3
248	Baltimore, MD	(5.0)	82	Davenport, IA	18.5	373	Hoover, AL	(22.3)
237	Baton Rouge, LA	(3.6)	335	Davie, FL	(14.9)	164	Houston, TX	4.8
216	Beaumont, TX	(1.7)	135	Dayton, OH	9.1	61	Huntington Beach, CA	25.8
379	Beaverton, OR	(23.8)	352	Dearborn, MI	(18.1)	281	Huntsville, AL	(8.7)
149	Bellevue, WA	6.2	394	Decatur, IL	(27.9)	143	Independence, MO	7.4
120	Bellflower, CA	11.9	267	Deerfield Beach, FL	(7.3)	326	Indianapolis, IN	(13.1)
165	Bellingham, WA	4.6	55	Denton, TX	29.5	53	Indio, CA	29.9
197	Berkeley, CA	1.1	207	Denver, CO	(0.6)	102	Inglewood, CA	14.4
239	Bethlehem, PA	(3.7)	271	Des Moines, IA	(7.6)	111	Irvine, CA	13.1
73	Billings, MT	21.2	188	Detroit, MI	2.0	270	Irving, TX	(7.5)
401	Birmingham, AL	(31.1)	284	Downey, CA	(9.4)	318	Jacksonville, FL	(12.6)
295	Bloomington, IL	(10.5)	173	Duluth, MN	3.7	375	Jackson, MS	(22.8)
318	Bloomington, IN	(12.6)	129	Durham, NC	10.1	317	Jersey City, NJ	(12.5)
321	Bloomington, MN	(12.7)	291	Edinburg, TX	(10.2)	30	Johns Creek, GA	40.8
315	Boca Raton, FL	(12.4)	416	Edison Twnshp, NJ	(47.5)	275	Joliet, IL	(8.0)
294	Boise, ID	(10.3)	340	Edmond, OK	(15.7)	NA	Jurupa Valley, CA**	NA
340	Boston, MA	(15.7)	273	El Cajon, CA	(7.8)	245	Kansas City, KS	(4.8)
196	Boulder, CO	1.2	249	El Monte, CA	(5.1)	159	Kansas City, MO	5.2
393	Brick Twnshp, NJ	(27.7)	372	El Paso, TX	(21.8)	388	Kennewick, WA	(26.3)
351	Bridgeport, CT	(17.6)	298	Elgin, IL	(10.7)	395	Kenosha, WI	(28.2)
414	Brockton, MA	(46.2)	297	Elizabeth, NJ	(10.6)	344	Kent, WA	(15.8)
330	Broken Arrow, OK	(14.2)	407	Elk Grove, CA	(35.2)	192	Killeen, TX	1.6
215	Brooklyn Park, MN	(1.3)	177	Erie, PA	3.1	128	Knoxville, TN	10.4
65	Brownsville, TX	24.7	14	Escondido, CA	50.7	329	Lafayette, LA	(13.8)
276	Bryan, TX	(8.2)	383	Eugene, OR	(24.6)	29	Lake Forest, CA	41.4
290	Buena Park, CA	(10.0)	2	Evansville, IN	81.6	285	Lakeland, FL	(9.5)
NA	Buffalo, NY**	NA	167	Everett, WA	4.2	4	Lakewood Twnshp, NJ	68.1
339	Burbank, CA	(15.4)	28	Fairfield, CA	42.5	92	Lakewood, CA	17.3
403	Cambridge, MA	(31.7)	279	Fall River, MA	(8.4)	70	Lakewood, CO	23.8
308	Camden, NJ	(12.1)	84	Fargo, ND	18.3	171	Lancaster, CA	3.9
205	Cape Coral, FL	(0.3)	77	Farmington Hills, MI	20.2	132	Lansing, MI	9.6
97	Carlsbad, CA	15.9	204	Fayetteville, AR	(0.2)	376	Laredo, TX	(23.0)
41	Carmel, IN	35.4	132	Fayetteville, NC	9.6	63	Largo, FL	24.9
192	Carrollton, TX	1.6	NA	Federal Way, WA**	NA	358	Las Cruces, NM	(19.2)
220	Carson, CA	(2.1)	10	Fishers, IN	54.5	228	Las Vegas, NV	(2.9)
255	Cary, NC	(5.9)	412	Flint, MI	(40.0)	170	Lawrence, KS	4.0
91	Cedar Rapids, IA	17.4	60	Fontana, CA	26.9	405	Lawrence, MA	(33.8)
147	Centennial, CO	6.5	308	Fort Collins, CO	(12.1)	23	Lawton, OK	43.9
340	Champaign, IL	(15.7)	237	Fort Lauderdale, FL	(3.6)	87	League City, TX	17.8
NA	Chandler, AZ**	NA	301	Fort Smith, AR	(10.9)	257	Lee's Summit, MO	(6.2)
334	Charleston, SC	(14.7)	135	Fort Wayne, IN	9.1	NA	Lexington, KY**	NA
207	Charlotte, NC	(0.6)	223	Fort Worth, TX	(2.4)	340	Lincoln, NE	(15.7)
NA	Cheektowaga, NY**	NA	54	Fremont, CA	29.8	206	Little Rock, AR	(0.4)
337	Chesapeake, VA	(15.2)	303	Fresno, CA	(11.0)	38	Livermore, CA	37.2
321	Chicago, IL	(12.7)	415	Frisco, TX	(47.2)	242	Livonia, MI	(4.4)
318	Chico, CA	(12.6)	304	Fullerton, CA	(11.1)	84	Long Beach, CA	18.3

RANK	CITY	% CHANGE	RANK	CITY	% CHANGE	RANK	CITY	% CHANGE
183	Longmont, CO	2.6	299	Pasadena, CA	(10.8)	374	South Gate, CA	(22.6)
111	Longview, TX	13.1	66	Pasadena, TX	24.6	70	Sparks, NV	23.8
239	Los Angeles, CA	(3.7)	330	Paterson, NJ	(14.2)	277	Spokane Valley, WA	(8.3)
235	Louisville, KY	(3.5)	376	Pearland, TX	(23.0)	87	Spokane, WA	17.8
83	Lowell, MA	18.4	392	Pembroke Pines, FL	(27.5)	126	Springfield, IL	11.0
149	Lubbock, TX	6.2	360	Peoria, AZ	(19.5)	243	Springfield, MA	(4.6)
401	Lynchburg, VA	(31.1)	286	Peoria, IL	(9.7)	144	Springfield, MO	7.3
363	Lynn, MA	(20.1)	333	Philadelphia, PA	(14.5)	357	Stamford, CT	(18.8)
283	Macon, GA	(9.2)	256	Phoenix, AZ	(6.1)	262	Sterling Heights, MI	(6.7)
390	Madison, WI	(27.2)	118	Pittsburgh, PA	12.1	18	Stockton, CA	47.1
235	Manchester, NH	(3.5)	371	Plano, TX	(21.6)	NA	St. George, UT**	NA
101	McAllen, TX	14.5	370	Plantation, FL	(21.4)	46	St. Joseph, MO	32.5
314	McKinney, TX	(12.3)	110	Pomona, CA	13.2	169	St. Louis, MO	4.1
89	Medford, OR	17.5	76	Pompano Beach, FL	20.4	230	St. Paul, MN	(3.2)
183	Melbourne, FL	2.6	409	Port St. Lucie, FL	(37.0)	175	St. Petersburg, FL	3.3
330	Memphis, TN	(14.2)	131	Portland, OR	9.7	182	Sugar Land, TX	2.9
72	Menifee, CA	22.9	366	Portsmouth, VA	(20.7)	20	Sunnyvale, CA	46.3
39	Merced, CA	37.1	NA	Providence, RI**	NA	311	Sunrise, FL	(12.2)
406	Meridian, ID	(34.4)	139	Provo, UT	8.7	141	Surprise, AZ	7.8
265	Mesa, AZ	(7.0)	166	Pueblo, CO	4.3	NA	Syracuse, NY**	NA
155	Mesquite, TX	5.7	348	Quincy, MA	(16.7)	299	Tacoma, WA	(10.8)
384	Miami Beach, FL	(24.7)	258	Racine, WI	(6.3)	27	Tallahassee, FL	43.1
410	Miami Gardens, FL	(37.1)	211	Raleigh, NC	(0.9)	264	Tampa, FL	(6.9)
219	Miami, FL	(1.9)	NA	Ramapo, NY**	NA	51	Temecula, CA	30.6
225	Midland, TX	(2.6)	52	Rancho Cucamon., CA	30.0	311	Tempe, AZ	(12.2)
157	Milwaukee, WI	5.5	57	Reading, PA	27.4	NA	Thornton, CO**	NA
197	Minneapolis, MN	1.1	16	Redding, CA	49.3	17	Thousand Oaks, CA	48.9
345	Miramar, FL	(15.9)	104	Redwood City, CA	14.0	280	Toledo, OH	(8.5)
125	Mission Viejo, CA	11.1	31	Reno, NV	39.8	362	Toms River Twnshp, NJ	(19.7)
360	Mission, TX	(19.5)	137	Renton, WA	9.0	200	Topeka, KS	0.9
368	Mobile, AL	(21.1)	6	Rialto, CA	66.2	122	Torrance, CA	11.7
49	Modesto, CA	31.3	404	Richardson, TX	(33.7)	32	Tracy, CA	39.5
44	Montgomery, AL	33.4	42	Richmond, CA	35.2	146	Trenton, NJ	6.7
222	Moreno Valley, CA	(2.3)	202	Richmond, VA	0.2	385	Troy, MI	(25.2)
114	Mountain View, CA	12.5	25	Rio Rancho, NM	43.3	286	Tucson, AZ	(9.7)
227	Murfreesboro, TN	(2.8)	106	Riverside, CA	13.7	216	Tulsa, OK	(1.7)
130	Murrieta, CA	9.8	307	Roanoke, VA	(12.0)	160	Tuscaloosa, AL	5.1
355	Nampa, ID	(18.4)	210	Rochester, MN	(0.8)	62	Tustin, CA	25.6
9	Napa, CA	57.4	NA	Rochester, NY**	NA	400	Tyler, TX	(29.6)
226	Naperville, IL	(2.7)	368	Rockford, IL	(21.1)	180	Upland, CA	3.0
138	Nashua, NH	8.8	177	Roseville, CA	3.1	365	Upper Darby Twnshp, PA	(20.4)
353	Nashville, TN	(18.3)	15	Roswell, GA	49.8	107	Vacaville, CA	13.4
315	New Bedford, MA	(12.4)	19	Round Rock, TX	46.8	35	Vallejo, CA	38.4
381	New Haven, CT	(24.2)	207	Sacramento, CA	(0.6)	68	Vancouver, WA	24.1
346	New Orleans, LA	(16.6)	3	Salem, OR	69.4	24	Ventura, CA	43.5
NA	New Rochelle, NY**	NA	277	Salinas, CA	(8.3)	48	Victorville, CA	31.5
NA	New York, NY**	NA	107	Salt Lake City, UT	13.4	151	Virginia Beach, VA	6.1
145	Newark, NJ	6.8	151	San Antonio, TX	6.1	245	Visalia, CA	(4.8)
93	Newport Beach, CA	17.2	8	San Bernardino, CA	61.7	250	Vista, CA	(5.2)
387	Newport News, VA	(25.7)	171	San Diego, CA	3.9	234	Waco, TX	(3.4)
413	Newton, MA	(41.3)	59	San Francisco, CA	27.0	282	Warren, MI	(8.8)
266	Norfolk, VA	(7.2)	5	San Jose, CA	67.6	194	Warwick, RI	1.5
111	Norman, OK	13.1	40	San Leandro, CA	35.8	363	Washington, DC	(20.1)
140	North Charleston, SC	8.4	26	San Marcos, CA	43.2	77	Waterbury, CT	20.2
NA	North Las Vegas, NV**	NA	183	San Mateo, CA	2.6	NA	Waukegan, IL**	NA
350	Norwalk, CA	(17.4)	176	Sandy Springs, GA	3.2	154	West Covina, CA	5.8
408	Norwalk, CT	(36.9)	391	Sandy, UT	(27.4)	186	West Jordan, UT	2.3
134	Oakland, CA	9.5	73	Santa Ana, CA	21.2	286	West Palm Beach, FL	(9.7)
67	Oceanside, CA	24.5	21	Santa Barbara, CA	45.5	301	West Valley, UT	(10.9)
1	Odessa, TX	107.8	37	Santa Clara, CA	37.7	126	Westland, MI	11.0
397	O'Fallon, MO	(28.6)	56	Santa Clarita, CA	28.8	105	Westminster, CA	13.9
389	Ogden, UT	(26.6)	13	Santa Maria, CA	50.8	327	Westminster, CO	(13.4)
151	Oklahoma City, OK	6.1	254	Santa Monica, CA	(5.8)	98	Whittier, CA	15.6
188	Olathe, KS	2.0	103	Santa Rosa, CA	14.1	218	Wichita Falls, TX	(1.8)
186	Omaha, NE	2.3	305	Savannah, GA	(11.6)	244	Wichita, KS	(4.7)
117	Ontario, CA	12.2	233	Scottsdale, AZ	(3.3)	295	Wilmington, NC	(10.5)
34	Orange, CA	38.6	272	Scranton, PA	(7.7)	201	Winston-Salem, NC	0.6
311	Orem, UT	(12.2)	177	Seattle, WA	3.1	346	Woodbridge Twnshp, NJ	(16.6)
224	Orlando, FL	(2.5)	158	Shreveport, LA	5.4	323	Worcester, MA	(12.8)
180	Overland Park, KS	3.0	93	Simi Valley, CA	17.2	7	Yakima, WA	64.3
12	Oxnard, CA	50.9	63	Sioux City, IA	24.9	NA	Yonkers, NY**	NA
252	Palm Bay, FL	(5.6)	142	Sioux Falls, SD	7.7	123	Yuma, AZ	11.5
399	Palmdale, CA	(29.3)	337	Somerville, MA	(15.2)			
NA	Parma, OH**	NA	306	South Bend, IN	(11.8)			

Source: CQ Press using reported data from the F.B.I. "Crime in the United States 2012"

*Motor vehicle theft includes the theft or attempted theft of a self-propelled vehicle. Excludes motorboats, construction equipment, airplanes, and farming equipment. **Not available.

79. Percent Change in Motor Vehicle Theft Rate: 2011 to 2012 (continued)
National Percent Change = 0.1% Decrease*

RANK	CITY	% CHANGE	RANK	CITY	% CHANGE	RANK	CITY	% CHANGE
1	Odessa, TX	107.8	75	Hemet, CA	21.0	149	Bellevue, WA	6.2
2	Evansville, IN	81.6	76	Pompano Beach, FL	20.4	149	Lubbock, TX	6.2
3	Salem, OR	69.4	77	Farmington Hills, MI	20.2	151	Oklahoma City, OK	6.1
4	Lakewood Twnshp, NJ	68.1	77	Waterbury, CT	20.2	151	San Antonio, TX	6.1
5	San Jose, CA	67.6	79	Gilbert, AZ	19.7	151	Virginia Beach, VA	6.1
6	Rialto, CA	66.2	80	Hawthorne, CA	19.4	154	West Covina, CA	5.8
7	Yakima, WA	64.3	81	Gresham, OR	18.6	155	Arvada, CO	5.7
8	San Bernardino, CA	61.7	82	Davenport, IA	18.5	155	Mesquite, TX	5.7
9	Napa, CA	57.4	83	Lowell, MA	18.4	157	Milwaukee, WI	5.5
10	Fishers, IN	54.5	84	Fargo, ND	18.3	158	Shreveport, LA	5.4
11	Colorado Springs, CO	51.2	84	Long Beach, CA	18.3	159	Kansas City, MO	5.2
12	Oxnard, CA	50.9	86	Danbury, CT	18.2	160	Albany, GA	5.1
13	Santa Maria, CA	50.8	87	League City, TX	17.8	160	Tuscaloosa, AL	5.1
14	Escondido, CA	50.7	87	Spokane, WA	17.8	162	Cicero, IL	5.0
15	Roswell, GA	49.8	89	High Point, NC	17.5	163	Austin, TX	4.9
16	Redding, CA	49.3	89	Medford, OR	17.5	164	Houston, TX	4.8
17	Thousand Oaks, CA	48.9	91	Cedar Rapids, IA	17.4	165	Bellingham, WA	4.6
18	Stockton, CA	47.1	92	Lakewood, CA	17.3	166	Pueblo, CO	4.3
19	Round Rock, TX	46.8	93	Newport Beach, CA	17.2	167	Avondale, AZ	4.2
20	Sunnyvale, CA	46.3	93	Simi Valley, CA	17.2	167	Everett, WA	4.2
21	Santa Barbara, CA	45.5	95	Alhambra, CA	17.0	169	St. Louis, MO	4.1
22	Corona, CA	44.0	96	Ann Arbor, MI	16.3	170	Lawrence, KS	4.0
23	Lawton, OK	43.9	97	Carlsbad, CA	15.9	171	Lancaster, CA	3.9
24	Ventura, CA	43.5	98	Chino, CA	15.6	171	San Diego, CA	3.9
25	Rio Rancho, NM	43.3	98	Whittier, CA	15.6	173	Duluth, MN	3.7
26	San Marcos, CA	43.2	100	Henderson, NV	15.5	174	Asheville, NC	3.6
27	Tallahassee, FL	43.1	101	McAllen, TX	14.5	175	St. Petersburg, FL	3.3
28	Fairfield, CA	42.5	102	Inglewood, CA	14.4	176	Sandy Springs, GA	3.2
29	Lake Forest, CA	41.4	103	Santa Rosa, CA	14.1	177	Erie, PA	3.1
30	Johns Creek, GA	40.8	104	Redwood City, CA	14.0	177	Roseville, CA	3.1
31	Reno, NV	39.8	105	Westminster, CA	13.9	177	Seattle, WA	3.1
32	Tracy, CA	39.5	106	Riverside, CA	13.7	180	Overland Park, KS	3.0
33	Garden Grove, CA	38.7	107	Salt Lake City, UT	13.4	180	Upland, CA	3.0
34	Orange, CA	38.6	107	Vacaville, CA	13.4	182	Sugar Land, TX	2.9
35	Vallejo, CA	38.4	109	Hollywood, FL	13.3	183	Longmont, CO	2.6
36	Citrus Heights, CA	38.3	110	Pomona, CA	13.2	183	Melbourne, FL	2.6
37	Santa Clara, CA	37.7	111	Irvine, CA	13.1	183	San Mateo, CA	2.6
38	Livermore, CA	37.2	111	Longview, TX	13.1	186	Omaha, NE	2.3
39	Merced, CA	37.1	111	Norman, OK	13.1	186	West Jordan, UT	2.3
40	San Leandro, CA	35.8	114	Mountain View, CA	12.5	188	Concord, CA	2.0
41	Carmel, IN	35.4	115	Alameda, CA	12.3	188	Detroit, MI	2.0
42	Richmond, CA	35.2	115	College Station, TX	12.3	188	Olathe, KS	2.0
43	Costa Mesa, CA	33.5	117	Ontario, CA	12.2	191	Daly City, CA	1.8
44	Montgomery, AL	33.4	118	Pittsburgh, PA	12.1	192	Carrollton, TX	1.6
45	Bakersfield, CA	32.8	119	Chula Vista, CA	12.0	192	Killeen, TX	1.6
46	St. Joseph, MO	32.5	120	Bellflower, CA	11.9	194	Warwick, RI	1.5
47	Anchorage, AK	32.0	121	Antioch, CA	11.8	195	Aurora, CO	1.3
48	Victorville, CA	31.5	122	Torrance, CA	11.7	196	Boulder, CO	1.2
49	Modesto, CA	31.3	123	Yuma, AZ	11.5	197	Amarillo, TX	1.1
50	Hayward, CA	30.9	124	Clearwater, FL	11.3	197	Berkeley, CA	1.1
51	Temecula, CA	30.6	125	Mission Viejo, CA	11.1	197	Minneapolis, MN	1.1
52	Rancho Cucamon., CA	30.0	126	Springfield, IL	11.0	200	Topeka, KS	0.9
53	Indio, CA	29.9	126	Westland, MI	11.0	201	Winston-Salem, NC	0.6
54	Fremont, CA	29.8	128	Knoxville, TN	10.4	202	Richmond, VA	0.2
55	Denton, TX	29.5	129	Durham, NC	10.1	203	Athens-Clarke, GA	0.1
56	Santa Clarita, CA	28.8	130	Murrieta, CA	9.8	204	Fayetteville, AR	(0.2)
57	Reading, PA	27.4	131	Portland, OR	9.7	205	Cape Coral, FL	(0.3)
58	Anaheim, CA	27.1	132	Fayetteville, NC	9.6	206	Little Rock, AR	(0.4)
59	San Francisco, CA	27.0	132	Lansing, MI	9.6	207	Charlotte, NC	(0.6)
60	Fontana, CA	26.9	134	Oakland, CA	9.5	207	Denver, CO	(0.6)
61	Huntington Beach, CA	25.8	135	Dayton, OH	9.1	207	Sacramento, CA	(0.6)
62	Tustin, CA	25.6	135	Fort Wayne, IN	9.1	210	Rochester, MN	(0.8)
63	Largo, FL	24.9	137	Renton, WA	9.0	211	Abilene, TX	(0.9)
63	Sioux City, IA	24.9	138	Nashua, NH	8.8	211	Columbia, MO	(0.9)
65	Brownsville, TX	24.7	139	Provo, UT	8.7	211	Raleigh, NC	(0.9)
66	Pasadena, TX	24.6	140	North Charleston, SC	8.4	214	Hesperia, CA	(1.2)
67	Oceanside, CA	24.5	141	Surprise, AZ	7.8	215	Brooklyn Park, MN	(1.3)
68	Vancouver, WA	24.1	142	Sioux Falls, SD	7.7	216	Beaumont, TX	(1.7)
69	Hamilton Twnshp, NJ	24.0	143	Independence, MO	7.4	216	Tulsa, OK	(1.7)
70	Lakewood, CO	23.8	144	Springfield, MO	7.3	218	Wichita Falls, TX	(1.8)
70	Sparks, NV	23.8	145	Newark, NJ	6.8	219	Miami, FL	(1.9)
72	Menifee, CA	22.9	146	Trenton, NJ	6.7	220	Carson, CA	(2.1)
73	Billings, MT	21.2	147	Centennial, CO	6.5	220	Gary, IN	(2.1)
73	Santa Ana, CA	21.2	148	Green Bay, WI	6.4	222	Moreno Valley, CA	(2.3)

RANK	CITY	% CHANGE
223	Fort Worth, TX	(2.4)
224	Orlando, FL	(2.5)
225	Midland, TX	(2.6)
226	Naperville, IL	(2.7)
227	Murfreesboro, TN	(2.8)
228	Las Vegas, NV	(2.9)
229	Albuquerque, NM	(3.1)
230	Cranston, RI	(3.2)
230	Hampton, VA	(3.2)
230	St. Paul, MN	(3.2)
233	Scottsdale, AZ	(3.3)
234	Waco, TX	(3.4)
235	Louisville, KY	(3.5)
235	Manchester, NH	(3.5)
237	Baton Rouge, LA	(3.6)
237	Fort Lauderdale, FL	(3.6)
239	Bethlehem, PA	(3.7)
239	Los Angeles, CA	(3.7)
241	Baldwin Park, CA	(3.9)
242	Livonia, MI	(4.4)
243	Springfield, MA	(4.6)
244	Wichita, KS	(4.7)
245	Glendale, CA	(4.8)
245	Kansas City, KS	(4.8)
245	Visalia, CA	(4.8)
248	Baltimore, MD	(5.0)
249	El Monte, CA	(5.1)
250	Vista, CA	(5.2)
251	Corpus Christi, TX	(5.5)
252	Compton, CA	(5.6)
252	Palm Bay, FL	(5.6)
254	Santa Monica, CA	(5.8)
255	Cary, NC	(5.9)
256	Phoenix, AZ	(6.1)
257	Lee's Summit, MO	(6.2)
258	Racine, WI	(6.3)
259	Greeley, CO	(6.4)
260	Aurora, IL	(6.5)
261	Atlanta, GA	(6.6)
262	Sterling Heights, MI	(6.7)
263	Hartford, CT	(6.8)
264	Tampa, FL	(6.9)
265	Mesa, AZ	(7.0)
266	Norfolk, VA	(7.2)
267	Cleveland, OH	(7.3)
267	Deerfield Beach, FL	(7.3)
269	Clovis, CA	(7.4)
270	Irving, TX	(7.5)
271	Des Moines, IA	(7.6)
272	Scranton, PA	(7.7)
273	El Cajon, CA	(7.8)
274	Clinton Twnshp, MI	(7.9)
275	Joliet, IL	(8.0)
276	Bryan, TX	(8.2)
277	Salinas, CA	(8.3)
277	Spokane Valley, WA	(8.3)
279	Fall River, MA	(8.4)
280	Toledo, OH	(8.5)
281	Huntsville, AL	(8.7)
282	Warren, MI	(8.8)
283	Macon, GA	(9.2)
284	Downey, CA	(9.4)
285	Lakeland, FL	(9.5)
286	Garland, TX	(9.7)
286	Peoria, IL	(9.7)
286	Tucson, AZ	(9.7)
286	West Palm Beach, FL	(9.7)
290	Buena Park, CA	(10.0)
291	Akron, OH	(10.2)
291	Coral Springs, FL	(10.2)
291	Edinburg, TX	(10.2)
294	Boise, ID	(10.3)
295	Bloomington, IL	(10.5)
295	Wilmington, NC	(10.5)

RANK	CITY	% CHANGE
297	Elizabeth, NJ	(10.6)
298	Elgin, IL	(10.7)
299	Pasadena, CA	(10.8)
299	Tacoma, WA	(10.8)
301	Fort Smith, AR	(10.9)
301	West Valley, UT	(10.9)
303	Fresno, CA	(11.0)
304	Fullerton, CA	(11.1)
305	Savannah, GA	(11.6)
306	South Bend, IN	(11.8)
307	Roanoke, VA	(12.0)
308	Arlington, TX	(12.1)
308	Camden, NJ	(12.1)
308	Fort Collins, CO	(12.1)
311	Orem, UT	(12.2)
311	Sunrise, FL	(12.2)
311	Tempe, AZ	(12.2)
314	McKinney, TX	(12.3)
315	Boca Raton, FL	(12.4)
315	New Bedford, MA	(12.4)
317	Jersey City, NJ	(12.5)
318	Bloomington, IN	(12.6)
318	Chico, CA	(12.6)
318	Jacksonville, FL	(12.6)
321	Bloomington, MN	(12.7)
321	Chicago, IL	(12.7)
323	Worcester, MA	(12.8)
324	Dallas, TX	(12.9)
325	Hillsboro, OR	(13.0)
326	Indianapolis, IN	(13.1)
327	Westminster, CO	(13.4)
328	Cincinnati, OH	(13.5)
329	Lafayette, LA	(13.8)
330	Broken Arrow, OK	(14.2)
330	Memphis, TN	(14.2)
330	Paterson, NJ	(14.2)
333	Philadelphia, PA	(14.5)
334	Charleston, SC	(14.7)
335	Alexandria, VA	(14.9)
335	Davie, FL	(14.9)
337	Chesapeake, VA	(15.2)
337	Somerville, MA	(15.2)
339	Burbank, CA	(15.4)
340	Boston, MA	(15.7)
340	Champaign, IL	(15.7)
340	Edmond, OK	(15.7)
340	Lincoln, NE	(15.7)
344	Kent, WA	(15.8)
345	Miramar, FL	(15.9)
346	New Orleans, LA	(16.6)
346	Woodbridge Twnshp, NJ	(16.6)
348	Quincy, MA	(16.7)
349	Glendale, AZ	(17.2)
350	Norwalk, CA	(17.4)
351	Bridgeport, CT	(17.6)
352	Dearborn, MI	(18.1)
353	Gainesville, FL	(18.3)
353	Nashville, TN	(18.3)
355	Grand Rapids, MI	(18.4)
355	Nampa, ID	(18.4)
357	Stamford, CT	(18.8)
358	Las Cruces, NM	(19.2)
359	Arlington Heights, IL	(19.4)
360	Mission, TX	(19.5)
360	Peoria, AZ	(19.5)
362	Toms River Twnshp, NJ	(19.7)
363	Lynn, MA	(20.1)
363	Washington, DC	(20.1)
365	Upper Darby Twnshp, PA	(20.4)
366	Portsmouth, VA	(20.7)
367	Columbus, GA	(20.9)
368	Mobile, AL	(21.1)
368	Rockford, IL	(21.1)
370	Plantation, FL	(21.4)

RANK	CITY	% CHANGE
371	Plano, TX	(21.6)
372	El Paso, TX	(21.8)
373	Hoover, AL	(22.3)
374	South Gate, CA	(22.6)
375	Jackson, MS	(22.8)
376	Laredo, TX	(23.0)
376	Pearland, TX	(23.0)
378	Hammond, IN	(23.5)
379	Beaverton, OR	(23.8)
380	Grand Prairie, TX	(23.9)
381	New Haven, CT	(24.2)
382	Hialeah, FL	(24.3)
383	Eugene, OR	(24.6)
384	Miami Beach, FL	(24.7)
385	Clarksville, TN	(25.2)
385	Troy, MI	(25.2)
387	Newport News, VA	(25.7)
388	Kennewick, WA	(26.3)
389	Ogden, UT	(26.6)
390	Madison, WI	(27.2)
391	Sandy, UT	(27.4)
392	Pembroke Pines, FL	(27.5)
393	Brick Twnshp, NJ	(27.7)
394	Decatur, IL	(27.9)
395	Kenosha, WI	(28.2)
396	Clifton, NJ	(28.3)
397	O'Fallon, MO	(28.6)
398	Chino Hills, CA	(28.7)
399	Palmdale, CA	(29.3)
400	Tyler, TX	(29.6)
401	Birmingham, AL	(31.1)
401	Lynchburg, VA	(31.1)
403	Cambridge, MA	(31.7)
404	Richardson, TX	(33.7)
405	Lawrence, MA	(33.8)
406	Meridian, ID	(34.4)
407	Elk Grove, CA	(35.2)
408	Norwalk, CT	(36.9)
409	Port St. Lucie, FL	(37.0)
410	Miami Gardens, FL	(37.1)
411	Allen, TX	(39.9)
412	Flint, MI	(40.0)
413	Newton, MA	(41.3)
414	Brockton, MA	(46.2)
415	Frisco, TX	(47.2)
416	Edison Twnshp, NJ	(47.5)
NA	Albany, NY**	NA
NA	Allentown, PA**	NA
NA	Amherst, NY**	NA
NA	Buffalo, NY**	NA
NA	Chandler, AZ**	NA
NA	Cheektowaga, NY**	NA
NA	Clarkstown, NY**	NA
NA	Colonie, NY**	NA
NA	Federal Way, WA**	NA
NA	Greece, NY**	NA
NA	Greensboro, NC**	NA
NA	Greenville, NC**	NA
NA	Jurupa Valley, CA**	NA
NA	Lexington, KY**	NA
NA	New Rochelle, NY**	NA
NA	New York, NY**	NA
NA	North Las Vegas, NV**	NA
NA	Parma, OH**	NA
NA	Providence, RI**	NA
NA	Ramapo, NY**	NA
NA	Rochester, NY**	NA
NA	St. George, UT**	NA
NA	Syracuse, NY**	NA
NA	Thornton, CO**	NA
NA	Waukegan, IL**	NA
NA	Yonkers, NY**	NA

Source: CQ Press using reported data from the F.B.I. "Crime in the United States 2012"

*Motor vehicle theft includes the theft or attempted theft of a self-propelled vehicle. Excludes motorboats, construction equipment, airplanes, and farming equipment. **Not available.

80. Percent Change in Motor Vehicle Theft Rate: 2008 to 2012
National Percent Change = 27.2% Decrease*

RANK	CITY	% CHANGE	RANK	CITY	% CHANGE	RANK	CITY	% CHANGE
212	Abilene, TX	(28.8)	285	Chino Hills, CA	(38.6)	341	Gainesville, FL	(48.5)
153	Akron, OH	(20.9)	115	Chino, CA	(13.5)	54	Garden Grove, CA	0.5
53	Alameda, CA	0.6	386	Chula Vista, CA	(58.6)	179	Garland, TX	(24.8)
NA	Albany, GA**	NA	NA	Cicero, IL**	NA	73	Gary, IN	(5.6)
NA	Albany, NY**	NA	169	Cincinnati, OH	(23.1)	378	Gilbert, AZ	(56.9)
324	Albuquerque, NM	(44.1)	200	Citrus Heights, CA	(27.5)	318	Glendale, AZ	(43.4)
130	Alexandria, VA	(17.6)	NA	Clarkstown, NY**	NA	278	Glendale, CA	(38.2)
208	Alhambra, CA	(28.5)	321	Clarksville, TN	(43.7)	377	Grand Prairie, TX	(56.7)
NA	Allentown, PA**	NA	241	Clearwater, FL	(32.6)	296	Grand Rapids, MI	(39.9)
122	Allen, TX	(15.8)	158	Cleveland, OH	(21.6)	NA	Greece, NY**	NA
138	Amarillo, TX	(18.9)	242	Clifton, NJ	(32.9)	254	Greeley, CO	(34.7)
NA	Amherst, NY**	NA	316	Clinton Twnshp, MI	(42.6)	240	Green Bay, WI	(32.5)
15	Anaheim, CA	27.5	11	Clovis, CA	33.3	366	Greensboro, NC	(53.8)
49	Anchorage, AK	1.6	350	College Station, TX	(49.6)	387	Greenville, NC	(59.4)
159	Ann Arbor, MI	(21.8)	NA	Colonie, NY**	NA	51	Gresham, OR	1.2
6	Antioch, CA	53.2	9	Colorado Springs, CO	40.4	135	Hamilton Twnshp, NJ	(18.5)
NA	Arlington Heights, IL**	NA	99	Columbia, MO	(11.2)	227	Hammond, IN	(30.6)
288	Arlington, TX	(39.2)	353	Columbus, GA	(50.1)	232	Hampton, VA	(31.2)
149	Arvada, CO	(20.6)	170	Compton, CA	(23.2)	295	Hartford, CT	(39.8)
210	Asheville, NC	(28.7)	259	Concord, CA	(35.1)	124	Hawthorne, CA	(16.9)
263	Athens-Clarke, GA	(35.7)	237	Coral Springs, FL	(32.1)	47	Hayward, CA	3.7
65	Atlanta, GA	(3.2)	78	Corona, CA	(6.6)	83	Hemet, CA	(8.7)
257	Aurora, CO	(35.0)	301	Corpus Christi, TX	(40.7)	304	Henderson, NV	(41.2)
376	Aurora, IL	(56.3)	30	Costa Mesa, CA	14.8	32	Hesperia, CA	13.5
147	Austin, TX	(20.5)	278	Cranston, RI	(38.2)	394	Hialeah, FL	(62.1)
400	Avondale, AZ	(64.5)	300	Dallas, TX	(40.5)	235	High Point, NC	(31.5)
25	Bakersfield, CA	17.3	198	Daly City, CA	(27.3)	217	Hillsboro, OR	(29.7)
243	Baldwin Park, CA	(33.0)	271	Danbury, CT	(36.7)	125	Hollywood, FL	(17.1)
193	Baltimore, MD	(26.7)	92	Davenport, IA	(10.0)	277	Hoover, AL	(38.1)
361	Baton Rouge, LA	(51.5)	217	Davie, FL	(29.7)	103	Houston, TX	(11.7)
134	Beaumont, TX	(18.1)	262	Dayton, OH	(35.6)	50	Huntington Beach, CA	1.5
336	Beaverton, OR	(47.7)	390	Dearborn, MI	(61.3)	281	Huntsville, AL	(38.3)
299	Bellevue, WA	(40.3)	NA	Decatur, IL**	NA	72	Independence, MO	(5.5)
214	Bellflower, CA	(29.2)	139	Deerfield Beach, FL	(19.0)	232	Indianapolis, IN	(31.2)
256	Bellingham, WA	(34.9)	56	Denton, TX	(0.2)	40	Indio, CA	7.0
301	Berkeley, CA	(40.7)	66	Denver, CO	(3.7)	178	Inglewood, CA	(24.1)
311	Bethlehem, PA	(42.1)	64	Des Moines, IA	(2.9)	265	Irvine, CA	(36.0)
8	Billings, MT	44.4	95	Detroit, MI	(10.4)	312	Irving, TX	(42.2)
338	Birmingham, AL	(47.9)	188	Downey, CA	(25.8)	389	Jacksonville, FL	(61.0)
NA	Bloomington, IL**	NA	56	Duluth, MN	(0.2)	253	Jackson, MS	(34.1)
96	Bloomington, IN	(10.8)	182	Durham, NC	(25.0)	273	Jersey City, NJ	(37.2)
367	Bloomington, MN	(53.9)	357	Edinburg, TX	(50.6)	NA	Johns Creek, GA**	NA
332	Boca Raton, FL	(46.6)	260	Edison Twnshp, NJ	(35.2)	35	Joliet, IL	12.1
217	Boise, ID	(29.7)	244	Edmond, OK	(33.1)	NA	Jurupa Valley, CA**	NA
261	Boston, MA	(35.3)	387	El Cajon, CA	(59.4)	NA	Kansas City, KS**	NA
63	Boulder, CO	(2.2)	104	El Monte, CA	(12.0)	142	Kansas City, MO	(19.7)
398	Brick Twnshp, NJ	(64.1)	392	El Paso, TX	(61.8)	267	Kennewick, WA	(36.3)
210	Bridgeport, CT	(28.7)	364	Elgin, IL	(52.8)	368	Kenosha, WI	(54.1)
NA	Brockton, MA**	NA	97	Elizabeth, NJ	(10.9)	202	Kent, WA	(28.0)
283	Broken Arrow, OK	(38.5)	326	Elk Grove, CA	(45.8)	56	Killeen, TX	(0.2)
303	Brooklyn Park, MN	(40.8)	257	Erie, PA	(35.0)	139	Knoxville, TN	(19.0)
309	Brownsville, TX	(41.5)	145	Escondido, CA	(20.1)	373	Lafayette, LA	(55.9)
382	Bryan, TX	(58.1)	402	Eugene, OR	(68.3)	67	Lake Forest, CA	(4.4)
312	Buena Park, CA	(42.2)	3	Evansville, IN	67.0	352	Lakeland, FL	(49.7)
NA	Buffalo, NY**	NA	171	Everett, WA	(23.3)	399	Lakewood Twnshp, NJ	(64.3)
394	Burbank, CA	(62.1)	125	Fairfield, CA	(17.1)	142	Lakewood, CA	(19.7)
382	Cambridge, MA	(58.1)	153	Fall River, MA	(20.9)	104	Lakewood, CO	(12.0)
228	Camden, NJ	(30.8)	278	Fargo, ND	(38.2)	190	Lancaster, CA	(26.1)
336	Cape Coral, FL	(47.7)	176	Farmington Hills, MI	(23.9)	123	Lansing, MI	(16.4)
209	Carlsbad, CA	(28.6)	36	Fayetteville, AR	11.6	403	Laredo, TX	(80.0)
166	Carmel, IN	(22.7)	217	Fayetteville, NC	(29.7)	314	Largo, FL	(42.4)
147	Carrollton, TX	(20.5)	90	Federal Way, WA	(9.9)	125	Las Cruces, NM	(17.1)
121	Carson, CA	(15.4)	325	Fishers, IN	(44.2)	330	Las Vegas, NV	(46.4)
204	Cary, NC	(28.3)	320	Flint, MI	(43.6)	44	Lawrence, KS	4.2
194	Cedar Rapids, IA	(27.0)	166	Fontana, CA	(22.7)	2	Lawrence, MA	80.8
163	Centennial, CO	(22.3)	327	Fort Collins, CO	(46.3)	20	Lawton, OK	20.9
NA	Champaign, IL**	NA	185	Fort Lauderdale, FL	(25.4)	199	League City, TX	(27.4)
NA	Chandler, AZ**	NA	229	Fort Smith, AR	(30.9)	185	Lee's Summit, MO	(25.4)
346	Charleston, SC	(48.6)	286	Fort Wayne, IN	(38.7)	NA	Lexington, KY**	NA
393	Charlotte, NC	(61.9)	141	Fort Worth, TX	(19.6)	118	Lincoln, NE	(14.9)
NA	Cheektowaga, NY**	NA	173	Fremont, CA	(23.5)	85	Little Rock, AR	(9.1)
269	Chesapeake, VA	(36.6)	39	Fresno, CA	7.1	16	Livermore, CA	26.4
77	Chicago, IL	(6.4)	162	Frisco, TX	(22.2)	187	Livonia, MI	(25.7)
117	Chico, CA	(14.2)	155	Fullerton, CA	(21.0)	84	Long Beach, CA	(9.0)

RANK	CITY	% CHANGE
NA	Longmont, CO**	NA
183	Longview, TX	(25.1)
250	Los Angeles, CA	(33.4)
156	Louisville, KY	(21.1)
251	Lowell, MA	(33.5)
28	Lubbock, TX	15.3
385	Lynchburg, VA	(58.4)
316	Lynn, MA	(42.6)
290	Macon, GA	(39.4)
356	Madison, WI	(50.4)
319	Manchester, NH	(43.5)
373	McAllen, TX	(55.9)
87	McKinney, TX	(9.2)
13	Medford, OR	31.7
348	Melbourne, FL	(49.0)
323	Memphis, TN	(44.0)
NA	Menifee, CA**	NA
21	Merced, CA	20.3
360	Meridian, ID	(51.4)
375	Mesa, AZ	(56.1)
90	Mesquite, TX	(9.9)
341	Miami Beach, FL	(48.5)
363	Miami Gardens, FL	(52.7)
174	Miami, FL	(23.7)
159	Midland, TX	(21.8)
192	Milwaukee, WI	(26.2)
196	Minneapolis, MN	(27.2)
306	Miramar, FL	(41.3)
238	Mission Viejo, CA	(32.4)
396	Mission, TX	(63.2)
341	Mobile, AL	(48.5)
17	Modesto, CA	23.3
23	Montgomery, AL	17.6
116	Moreno Valley, CA	(13.8)
190	Mountain View, CA	(26.1)
110	Murfreesboro, TN	(12.9)
164	Murrieta, CA	(22.5)
359	Nampa, ID	(50.8)
26	Napa, CA	16.9
315	Naperville, IL	(42.5)
NA	Nashua, NH**	NA
283	Nashville, TN	(38.5)
93	New Bedford, MA	(10.1)
NA	New Haven, CT**	NA
331	New Orleans, LA	(46.5)
NA	New Rochelle, NY**	NA
NA	New York, NY**	NA
41	Newark, NJ	5.9
175	Newport Beach, CA	(23.8)
341	Newport News, VA	(48.5)
334	Newton, MA	(47.0)
274	Norfolk, VA	(37.5)
144	Norman, OK	(19.9)
268	North Charleston, SC	(36.4)
288	North Las Vegas, NV	(39.2)
171	Norwalk, CA	(23.3)
338	Norwalk, CT	(47.9)
114	Oakland, CA	(13.3)
131	Oceanside, CA	(17.8)
10	Odessa, TX	34.3
293	O'Fallon, MO	(39.7)
287	Ogden, UT	(39.0)
45	Oklahoma City, OK	4.1
NA	Olathe, KS**	NA
42	Omaha, NE	5.5
120	Ontario, CA	(15.2)
204	Orange, CA	(28.3)
231	Orem, UT	(31.1)
222	Orlando, FL	(29.8)
107	Overland Park, KS	(12.6)
67	Oxnard, CA	(4.4)
106	Palm Bay, FL	(12.4)
370	Palmdale, CA	(55.3)
NA	Parma, OH**	NA

RANK	CITY	% CHANGE
215	Pasadena, CA	(29.3)
7	Pasadena, TX	45.4
81	Paterson, NJ	(8.2)
244	Pearland, TX	(33.1)
348	Pembroke Pines, FL	(49.0)
371	Peoria, AZ	(55.4)
NA	Peoria, IL**	NA
252	Philadelphia, PA	(33.8)
350	Phoenix, AZ	(49.6)
380	Pittsburgh, PA	(57.1)
188	Plano, TX	(25.8)
204	Plantation, FL	(28.3)
69	Pomona, CA	(4.5)
201	Pompano Beach, FL	(27.9)
93	Port St. Lucie, FL	(10.1)
59	Portland, OR	(0.7)
263	Portsmouth, VA	(35.7)
179	Providence, RI	(24.8)
136	Provo, UT	(18.8)
NA	Pueblo, CO**	NA
108	Quincy, MA	(12.8)
238	Racine, WI	(32.4)
87	Raleigh, NC	(9.2)
NA	Ramapo, NY**	NA
34	Rancho Cucamon., CA	12.2
276	Reading, PA	(38.0)
1	Redding, CA	99.8
378	Redwood City, CA	(56.9)
118	Reno, NV	(14.9)
NA	Renton, WA**	NA
31	Rialto, CA	14.4
340	Richardson, TX	(48.3)
75	Richmond, CA	(5.9)
108	Richmond, VA	(12.8)
306	Rio Rancho, NM	(41.3)
111	Riverside, CA	(13.0)
157	Roanoke, VA	(21.2)
372	Rochester, MN	(55.7)
NA	Rochester, NY**	NA
327	Rockford, IL	(46.3)
322	Roseville, CA	(43.9)
275	Roswell, GA	(37.6)
76	Round Rock, TX	(6.0)
247	Sacramento, CA	(33.2)
37	Salem, OR	9.6
136	Salinas, CA	(18.8)
113	Salt Lake City, UT	(13.2)
161	San Antonio, TX	(22.1)
23	San Bernardino, CA	17.6
304	San Diego, CA	(41.2)
89	San Francisco, CA	(9.8)
5	San Jose, CA	62.1
226	San Leandro, CA	(30.1)
146	San Marcos, CA	(20.4)
369	San Mateo, CA	(54.2)
341	Sandy Springs, GA	(48.5)
281	Sandy, UT	(38.3)
43	Santa Ana, CA	5.0
33	Santa Barbara, CA	12.4
48	Santa Clara, CA	3.6
272	Santa Clarita, CA	(36.8)
225	Santa Maria, CA	(30.0)
217	Santa Monica, CA	(29.7)
165	Santa Rosa, CA	(22.6)
355	Savannah, GA	(50.3)
354	Scottsdale, AZ	(50.2)
151	Scranton, PA	(20.8)
79	Seattle, WA	(7.7)
333	Shreveport, LA	(46.7)
133	Simi Valley, CA	(17.9)
12	Sioux City, IA	31.9
22	Sioux Falls, SD	18.1
358	Somerville, MA	(50.7)
310	South Bend, IN	(42.0)

RANK	CITY	% CHANGE
203	South Gate, CA	(28.1)
177	Sparks, NV	(24.0)
70	Spokane Valley, WA	(4.6)
14	Spokane, WA	29.4
NA	Springfield, IL**	NA
128	Springfield, MA	(17.5)
60	Springfield, MO	(1.6)
179	Stamford, CT	(24.8)
151	Sterling Heights, MI	(20.8)
61	Stockton, CA	(1.9)
195	St. George, UT	(27.1)
4	St. Joseph, MO	65.8
247	St. Louis, MO	(33.2)
74	St. Paul, MN	(5.7)
306	St. Petersburg, FL	(41.3)
397	Sugar Land, TX	(63.7)
102	Sunnyvale, CA	(11.6)
347	Sunrise, FL	(48.7)
362	Surprise, AZ	(52.5)
NA	Syracuse, NY**	NA
236	Tacoma, WA	(31.9)
71	Tallahassee, FL	(5.3)
401	Tampa, FL	(66.7)
131	Temecula, CA	(17.8)
365	Tempe, AZ	(53.3)
NA	Thornton, CO**	NA
80	Thousand Oaks, CA	(7.9)
55	Toledo, OH	0.2
222	Toms River Twnshp, NJ	(29.8)
128	Topeka, KS	(17.5)
207	Torrance, CA	(28.4)
62	Tracy, CA	(2.1)
98	Trenton, NJ	(11.1)
265	Troy, MI	(36.0)
381	Tucson, AZ	(57.2)
52	Tulsa, OK	0.7
297	Tuscaloosa, AL	(40.0)
149	Tustin, CA	(20.6)
291	Tyler, TX	(39.5)
38	Upland, CA	8.8
334	Upper Darby Twnshp, PA	(47.0)
232	Vacaville, CA	(31.2)
45	Vallejo, CA	4.1
99	Vancouver, WA	(11.2)
27	Ventura, CA	15.9
19	Victorville, CA	21.2
196	Virginia Beach, VA	(27.2)
213	Visalia, CA	(29.0)
230	Vista, CA	(31.0)
391	Waco, TX	(61.7)
NA	Warren, MI**	NA
249	Warwick, RI	(33.3)
327	Washington, DC	(46.3)
29	Waterbury, CT	15.2
NA	Waukegan, IL**	NA
168	West Covina, CA	(22.8)
112	West Jordan, UT	(13.1)
297	West Palm Beach, FL	(40.0)
216	West Valley, UT	(29.4)
184	Westland, MI	(25.3)
85	Westminster, CA	(9.1)
269	Westminster, CO	(36.6)
99	Whittier, CA	(11.2)
384	Wichita Falls, TX	(58.3)
81	Wichita, KS	(8.2)
255	Wilmington, NC	(34.8)
293	Winston-Salem, NC	(39.7)
224	Woodbridge Twnshp, NJ	(29.9)
244	Worcester, MA	(33.1)
18	Yakima, WA	21.7
NA	Yonkers, NY**	NA
292	Yuma, AZ	(39.6)

Source: CQ Press using reported data from the F.B.I. "Crime in the United States 2012"

*Motor vehicle theft includes the theft or attempted theft of a self-propelled vehicle. Excludes motorboats, construction equipment, airplanes, and farming equipment. **Not available.

80. Percent Change in Motor Vehicle Theft Rate: 2008 to 2012 (continued)
National Percent Change = 27.2% Decrease*

RANK	CITY	% CHANGE	RANK	CITY	% CHANGE	RANK	CITY	% CHANGE
1	Redding, CA	99.8	75	Richmond, CA	(5.9)	149	Arvada, CO	(20.6)
2	Lawrence, MA	80.8	76	Round Rock, TX	(6.0)	149	Tustin, CA	(20.6)
3	Evansville, IN	67.0	77	Chicago, IL	(6.4)	151	Scranton, PA	(20.8)
4	St. Joseph, MO	65.8	78	Corona, CA	(6.6)	151	Sterling Heights, MI	(20.8)
5	San Jose, CA	62.1	79	Seattle, WA	(7.7)	153	Akron, OH	(20.9)
6	Antioch, CA	53.2	80	Thousand Oaks, CA	(7.9)	153	Fall River, MA	(20.9)
7	Pasadena, TX	45.4	81	Paterson, NJ	(8.2)	155	Fullerton, CA	(21.0)
8	Billings, MT	44.4	81	Wichita, KS	(8.2)	156	Louisville, KY	(21.1)
9	Colorado Springs, CO	40.4	83	Hemet, CA	(8.7)	157	Roanoke, VA	(21.2)
10	Odessa, TX	34.3	84	Long Beach, CA	(9.0)	158	Cleveland, OH	(21.6)
11	Clovis, CA	33.3	85	Little Rock, AR	(9.1)	159	Ann Arbor, MI	(21.8)
12	Sioux City, IA	31.9	85	Westminster, CA	(9.1)	159	Midland, TX	(21.8)
13	Medford, OR	31.7	87	McKinney, TX	(9.2)	161	San Antonio, TX	(22.1)
14	Spokane, WA	29.4	87	Raleigh, NC	(9.2)	162	Frisco, TX	(22.2)
15	Anaheim, CA	27.5	89	San Francisco, CA	(9.8)	163	Centennial, CO	(22.3)
16	Livermore, CA	26.4	90	Federal Way, WA	(9.9)	164	Murrieta, CA	(22.5)
17	Modesto, CA	23.3	90	Mesquite, TX	(9.9)	165	Santa Rosa, CA	(22.6)
18	Yakima, WA	21.7	92	Davenport, IA	(10.0)	166	Carmel, IN	(22.7)
19	Victorville, CA	21.2	93	New Bedford, MA	(10.1)	166	Fontana, CA	(22.7)
20	Lawton, OK	20.9	93	Port St. Lucie, FL	(10.1)	168	West Covina, CA	(22.8)
21	Merced, CA	20.3	95	Detroit, MI	(10.4)	169	Cincinnati, OH	(23.1)
22	Sioux Falls, SD	18.1	96	Bloomington, IN	(10.8)	170	Compton, CA	(23.2)
23	Montgomery, AL	17.6	97	Elizabeth, NJ	(10.9)	171	Everett, WA	(23.3)
23	San Bernardino, CA	17.6	98	Trenton, NJ	(11.1)	171	Norwalk, CA	(23.3)
25	Bakersfield, CA	17.3	99	Columbia, MO	(11.2)	173	Fremont, CA	(23.5)
26	Napa, CA	16.9	99	Vancouver, WA	(11.2)	174	Miami, FL	(23.7)
27	Ventura, CA	15.9	99	Whittier, CA	(11.2)	175	Newport Beach, CA	(23.8)
28	Lubbock, TX	15.3	102	Sunnyvale, CA	(11.6)	176	Farmington Hills, MI	(23.9)
29	Waterbury, CT	15.2	103	Houston, TX	(11.7)	177	Sparks, NV	(24.0)
30	Costa Mesa, CA	14.8	104	El Monte, CA	(12.0)	178	Inglewood, CA	(24.1)
31	Rialto, CA	14.4	104	Lakewood, CO	(12.0)	179	Garland, TX	(24.8)
32	Hesperia, CA	13.5	106	Palm Bay, FL	(12.4)	179	Providence, RI	(24.8)
33	Santa Barbara, CA	12.4	107	Overland Park, KS	(12.6)	179	Stamford, CT	(24.8)
34	Rancho Cucamon., CA	12.2	108	Quincy, MA	(12.8)	182	Durham, NC	(25.0)
35	Joliet, IL	12.1	108	Richmond, VA	(12.8)	183	Longview, TX	(25.1)
36	Fayetteville, AR	11.6	110	Murfreesboro, TN	(12.9)	184	Westland, MI	(25.3)
37	Salem, OR	9.6	111	Riverside, CA	(13.0)	185	Fort Lauderdale, FL	(25.4)
38	Upland, CA	8.8	112	West Jordan, UT	(13.1)	185	Lee's Summit, MO	(25.4)
39	Fresno, CA	7.1	113	Salt Lake City, UT	(13.2)	187	Livonia, MI	(25.7)
40	Indio, CA	7.0	114	Oakland, CA	(13.3)	188	Downey, CA	(25.8)
41	Newark, NJ	5.9	115	Chino, CA	(13.5)	188	Plano, TX	(25.8)
42	Omaha, NE	5.5	116	Moreno Valley, CA	(13.8)	190	Lancaster, CA	(26.1)
43	Santa Ana, CA	5.0	117	Chico, CA	(14.2)	190	Mountain View, CA	(26.1)
44	Lawrence, KS	4.2	118	Lincoln, NE	(14.9)	192	Milwaukee, WI	(26.2)
45	Oklahoma City, OK	4.1	118	Reno, NV	(14.9)	193	Baltimore, MD	(26.7)
45	Vallejo, CA	4.1	120	Ontario, CA	(15.2)	194	Cedar Rapids, IA	(27.0)
47	Hayward, CA	3.7	121	Carson, CA	(15.4)	195	St. George, UT	(27.1)
48	Santa Clara, CA	3.6	122	Allen, TX	(15.8)	196	Minneapolis, MN	(27.2)
49	Anchorage, AK	1.6	123	Lansing, MI	(16.4)	196	Virginia Beach, VA	(27.2)
50	Huntington Beach, CA	1.5	124	Hawthorne, CA	(16.9)	198	Daly City, CA	(27.3)
51	Gresham, OR	1.2	125	Fairfield, CA	(17.1)	199	League City, TX	(27.4)
52	Tulsa, OK	0.7	125	Hollywood, FL	(17.1)	200	Citrus Heights, CA	(27.5)
53	Alameda, CA	0.6	125	Las Cruces, NM	(17.1)	201	Pompano Beach, FL	(27.9)
54	Garden Grove, CA	0.5	128	Springfield, MA	(17.5)	202	Kent, WA	(28.0)
55	Toledo, OH	0.2	128	Topeka, KS	(17.5)	203	South Gate, CA	(28.1)
56	Denton, TX	(0.2)	130	Alexandria, VA	(17.6)	204	Cary, NC	(28.3)
56	Duluth, MN	(0.2)	131	Oceanside, CA	(17.8)	204	Orange, CA	(28.3)
56	Killeen, TX	(0.2)	131	Temecula, CA	(17.8)	204	Plantation, FL	(28.3)
59	Portland, OR	(0.7)	133	Simi Valley, CA	(17.9)	207	Torrance, CA	(28.4)
60	Springfield, MO	(1.6)	134	Beaumont, TX	(18.1)	208	Alhambra, CA	(28.5)
61	Stockton, CA	(1.9)	135	Hamilton Twnshp, NJ	(18.5)	209	Carlsbad, CA	(28.6)
62	Tracy, CA	(2.1)	136	Provo, UT	(18.8)	210	Asheville, NC	(28.7)
63	Boulder, CO	(2.2)	136	Salinas, CA	(18.8)	210	Bridgeport, CT	(28.7)
64	Des Moines, IA	(2.9)	138	Amarillo, TX	(18.9)	212	Abilene, TX	(28.8)
65	Atlanta, GA	(3.2)	139	Deerfield Beach, FL	(19.0)	213	Visalia, CA	(29.0)
66	Denver, CO	(3.7)	139	Knoxville, TN	(19.0)	214	Bellflower, CA	(29.2)
67	Lake Forest, CA	(4.4)	141	Fort Worth, TX	(19.6)	215	Pasadena, CA	(29.3)
67	Oxnard, CA	(4.4)	142	Kansas City, MO	(19.7)	216	West Valley, UT	(29.4)
69	Pomona, CA	(4.5)	142	Lakewood, CA	(19.7)	217	Boise, ID	(29.7)
70	Spokane Valley, WA	(4.6)	144	Norman, OK	(19.9)	217	Davie, FL	(29.7)
71	Tallahassee, FL	(5.3)	145	Escondido, CA	(20.1)	217	Fayetteville, NC	(29.7)
72	Independence, MO	(5.5)	146	San Marcos, CA	(20.4)	217	Hillsboro, OR	(29.7)
73	Gary, IN	(5.6)	147	Austin, TX	(20.5)	217	Santa Monica, CA	(29.7)
74	St. Paul, MN	(5.7)	147	Carrollton, TX	(20.5)	222	Orlando, FL	(29.8)

RANK	CITY	% CHANGE	RANK	CITY	% CHANGE	RANK	CITY	% CHANGE
222	Toms River Twnshp, NJ	(29.8)	297	Tuscaloosa, AL	(40.0)	371	Peoria, AZ	(55.4)
224	Woodbridge Twnshp, NJ	(29.9)	297	West Palm Beach, FL	(40.0)	372	Rochester, MN	(55.7)
225	Santa Maria, CA	(30.0)	299	Bellevue, WA	(40.3)	373	Lafayette, LA	(55.9)
226	San Leandro, CA	(30.1)	300	Dallas, TX	(40.5)	373	McAllen, TX	(55.9)
227	Hammond, IN	(30.6)	301	Berkeley, CA	(40.7)	375	Mesa, AZ	(56.1)
228	Camden, NJ	(30.8)	301	Corpus Christi, TX	(40.7)	376	Aurora, IL	(56.3)
229	Fort Smith, AR	(30.9)	303	Brooklyn Park, MN	(40.8)	377	Grand Prairie, TX	(56.7)
230	Vista, CA	(31.0)	304	Henderson, NV	(41.2)	378	Gilbert, AZ	(56.9)
231	Orem, UT	(31.1)	304	San Diego, CA	(41.2)	378	Redwood City, CA	(56.9)
232	Hampton, VA	(31.2)	306	Miramar, FL	(41.3)	380	Pittsburgh, PA	(57.1)
232	Indianapolis, IN	(31.2)	306	Rio Rancho, NM	(41.3)	381	Tucson, AZ	(57.2)
232	Vacaville, CA	(31.2)	306	St. Petersburg, FL	(41.3)	382	Bryan, TX	(58.1)
235	High Point, NC	(31.5)	309	Brownsville, TX	(41.5)	382	Cambridge, MA	(58.1)
236	Tacoma, WA	(31.9)	310	South Bend, IN	(42.0)	384	Wichita Falls, TX	(58.3)
237	Coral Springs, FL	(32.1)	311	Bethlehem, PA	(42.1)	385	Lynchburg, VA	(58.4)
238	Mission Viejo, CA	(32.4)	312	Buena Park, CA	(42.2)	386	Chula Vista, CA	(58.6)
238	Racine, WI	(32.4)	312	Irving, TX	(42.2)	387	El Cajon, CA	(59.4)
240	Green Bay, WI	(32.5)	314	Largo, FL	(42.4)	387	Greenville, NC	(59.4)
241	Clearwater, FL	(32.6)	315	Naperville, IL	(42.5)	389	Jacksonville, FL	(61.0)
242	Clifton, NJ	(32.9)	316	Clinton Twnshp, MI	(42.6)	390	Dearborn, MI	(61.3)
243	Baldwin Park, CA	(33.0)	316	Lynn, MA	(42.6)	391	Waco, TX	(61.7)
244	Edmond, OK	(33.1)	318	Glendale, AZ	(43.4)	392	El Paso, TX	(61.8)
244	Pearland, TX	(33.1)	319	Manchester, NH	(43.5)	393	Charlotte, NC	(61.9)
244	Worcester, MA	(33.1)	320	Flint, MI	(43.6)	394	Burbank, CA	(62.1)
247	Sacramento, CA	(33.2)	321	Clarksville, TN	(43.7)	394	Hialeah, FL	(62.1)
247	St. Louis, MO	(33.2)	322	Roseville, CA	(43.9)	396	Mission, TX	(63.2)
249	Warwick, RI	(33.3)	323	Memphis, TN	(44.0)	397	Sugar Land, TX	(63.7)
250	Los Angeles, CA	(33.4)	324	Albuquerque, NM	(44.1)	398	Brick Twnshp, NJ	(64.1)
251	Lowell, MA	(33.5)	325	Fishers, IN	(44.2)	399	Lakewood Twnshp, NJ	(64.3)
252	Philadelphia, PA	(33.8)	326	Elk Grove, CA	(45.8)	400	Avondale, AZ	(64.5)
253	Jackson, MS	(34.1)	327	Fort Collins, CO	(46.3)	401	Tampa, FL	(66.7)
254	Greeley, CO	(34.7)	327	Rockford, IL	(46.3)	402	Eugene, OR	(68.3)
255	Wilmington, NC	(34.8)	327	Washington, DC	(46.3)	403	Laredo, TX	(80.0)
256	Bellingham, WA	(34.9)	330	Las Vegas, NV	(46.4)	NA	Albany, GA**	NA
257	Aurora, CO	(35.0)	331	New Orleans, LA	(46.5)	NA	Albany, NY**	NA
257	Erie, PA	(35.0)	332	Boca Raton, FL	(46.6)	NA	Allentown, PA**	NA
259	Concord, CA	(35.1)	333	Shreveport, LA	(46.7)	NA	Amherst, NY**	NA
260	Edison Twnshp, NJ	(35.2)	334	Newton, MA	(47.0)	NA	Arlington Heights, IL**	NA
261	Boston, MA	(35.3)	334	Upper Darby Twnshp, PA	(47.0)	NA	Bloomington, IL**	NA
262	Dayton, OH	(35.6)	336	Beaverton, OR	(47.7)	NA	Brockton, MA**	NA
263	Athens-Clarke, GA	(35.7)	336	Cape Coral, FL	(47.7)	NA	Buffalo, NY**	NA
263	Portsmouth, VA	(35.7)	338	Birmingham, AL	(47.9)	NA	Champaign, IL**	NA
265	Irvine, CA	(36.0)	338	Norwalk, CT	(47.9)	NA	Chandler, AZ**	NA
265	Troy, MI	(36.0)	340	Richardson, TX	(48.3)	NA	Cheektowaga, NY**	NA
267	Kennewick, WA	(36.3)	341	Gainesville, FL	(48.5)	NA	Cicero, IL**	NA
268	North Charleston, SC	(36.4)	341	Miami Beach, FL	(48.5)	NA	Clarkstown, NY**	NA
269	Chesapeake, VA	(36.6)	341	Mobile, AL	(48.5)	NA	Colonie, NY**	NA
269	Westminster, CO	(36.6)	341	Newport News, VA	(48.5)	NA	Decatur, IL**	NA
271	Danbury, CT	(36.7)	341	Sandy Springs, GA	(48.5)	NA	Greece, NY**	NA
272	Santa Clarita, CA	(36.8)	346	Charleston, SC	(48.6)	NA	Johns Creek, GA**	NA
273	Jersey City, NJ	(37.2)	347	Sunrise, FL	(48.7)	NA	Jurupa Valley, CA**	NA
274	Norfolk, VA	(37.5)	348	Melbourne, FL	(49.0)	NA	Kansas City, KS**	NA
275	Roswell, GA	(37.6)	348	Pembroke Pines, FL	(49.0)	NA	Lexington, KY**	NA
276	Reading, PA	(38.0)	350	College Station, TX	(49.6)	NA	Longmont, CO**	NA
277	Hoover, AL	(38.1)	350	Phoenix, AZ	(49.6)	NA	Menifee, CA**	NA
278	Cranston, RI	(38.2)	352	Lakeland, FL	(49.7)	NA	Nashua, NH**	NA
278	Fargo, ND	(38.2)	353	Columbus, GA	(50.1)	NA	New Haven, CT**	NA
278	Glendale, CA	(38.2)	354	Scottsdale, AZ	(50.2)	NA	New Rochelle, NY**	NA
281	Huntsville, AL	(38.3)	355	Savannah, GA	(50.3)	NA	New York, NY**	NA
281	Sandy, UT	(38.3)	356	Madison, WI	(50.4)	NA	Olathe, KS**	NA
283	Broken Arrow, OK	(38.5)	357	Edinburg, TX	(50.6)	NA	Parma, OH**	NA
283	Nashville, TN	(38.5)	358	Somerville, MA	(50.7)	NA	Peoria, IL**	NA
285	Chino Hills, CA	(38.6)	359	Nampa, ID	(50.8)	NA	Pueblo, CO**	NA
286	Fort Wayne, IN	(38.7)	360	Meridian, ID	(51.4)	NA	Ramapo, NY**	NA
287	Ogden, UT	(39.0)	361	Baton Rouge, LA	(51.5)	NA	Renton, WA**	NA
288	Arlington, TX	(39.2)	362	Surprise, AZ	(52.5)	NA	Rochester, NY**	NA
288	North Las Vegas, NV	(39.2)	363	Miami Gardens, FL	(52.7)	NA	Springfield, IL**	NA
290	Macon, GA	(39.4)	364	Elgin, IL	(52.8)	NA	Syracuse, NY**	NA
291	Tyler, TX	(39.5)	365	Tempe, AZ	(53.3)	NA	Thornton, CO**	NA
292	Yuma, AZ	(39.6)	366	Greensboro, NC	(53.8)	NA	Warren, MI**	NA
293	O'Fallon, MO	(39.7)	367	Bloomington, MN	(53.9)	NA	Waukegan, IL**	NA
293	Winston-Salem, NC	(39.7)	368	Kenosha, WI	(54.1)	NA	Yonkers, NY**	NA
295	Hartford, CT	(39.8)	369	San Mateo, CA	(54.2)			
296	Grand Rapids, MI	(39.9)	370	Palmdale, CA	(55.3)			

Source: CQ Press using reported data from the F.B.I. "Crime in the United States 2012"

*Motor vehicle theft includes the theft or attempted theft of a self-propelled vehicle. Excludes motorboats, construction equipment, airplanes, and farming equipment. **Not available.

81. Police Officers in 2012
National Total = 670,439 Officers*

RANK	CITY	OFFICERS	RANK	CITY	OFFICERS	RANK	CITY	OFFICERS
NA	Abilene, TX**	NA	NA	Chino Hills, CA**	NA	127	Gainesville, FL	293
88	Akron, OH	418	361	Chino, CA	102	261	Garden Grove, CA	153
394	Alameda, CA	81	181	Chula Vista, CA	210	125	Garland, TX	310
227	Albany, GA	175	265	Cicero, IL	152	163	Gary, IN	235
NA	Albany, NY**	NA	37	Cincinnati, OH	991	172	Gilbert, AZ	222
36	Albuquerque, NM	999	388	Citrus Heights, CA	85	98	Glendale, AZ	397
122	Alexandria, VA	317	251	Clarkstown, NY	159	159	Glendale, CA	240
392	Alhambra, CA	82	142	Clarksville, TN	269	175	Grand Prairie, TX	217
181	Allentown, PA	210	168	Clearwater, FL	228	128	Grand Rapids, MI	292
337	Allen, TX	115	23	Cleveland, OH	1,481	365	Greece, NY	98
118	Amarillo, TX	323	282	Clifton, NJ	144	280	Greeley, CO	145
261	Amherst, NY	153	381	Clinton Twnshp, MI	87	214	Green Bay, WI	183
106	Anaheim, CA	360	374	Clovis, CA	90	64	Greensboro, NC	621
99	Anchorage, AK	372	325	College Station, TX	120	217	Greenville, NC	181
329	Ann Arbor, MI	117	352	Colonie, NY	106	325	Gresham, OR	120
384	Antioch, CA	86	60	Colorado Springs, CO	638	242	Hamilton Twnshp, NJ	166
349	Arlington Heights, IL	107	258	Columbia, MO	156	186	Hammond, IN	207
63	Arlington, TX	623	81	Columbus, GA	467	137	Hampton, VA	277
246	Arvada, CO	163	NA	Compton, CA**	NA	78	Hartford, CT	478
184	Asheville, NC	208	282	Concord, CA	144	368	Hawthorne, CA	96
161	Athens-Clarke, GA	239	194	Coral Springs, FL	197	220	Hayward, CA	179
17	Atlanta, GA	1,775	276	Corona, CA	148	403	Hemet, CA	57
58	Aurora, CO	651	85	Corpus Christi, TX	432	116	Henderson, NV	328
131	Aurora, IL	289	310	Costa Mesa, CA	128	NA	Hesperia, CA**	NA
19	Austin, TX	1,628	292	Cranston, RI	138	NA	Hialeah, FL**	NA
357	Avondale, AZ	103	NA	Dallas, TX**	NA	178	High Point, NC	215
109	Bakersfield, CA	347	352	Daly City, CA	106	305	Hillsboro, OR	131
399	Baldwin Park, CA	68	280	Danbury, CT	145	128	Hollywood, FL	292
8	Baltimore, MD	2,962	246	Davenport, IA	163	NA	Hoover, AL**	NA
57	Baton Rouge, LA	664	245	Davie, FL	164	5	Houston, TX	5,318
NA	Beaumont, TX**	NA	111	Dayton, OH	342	197	Huntington Beach, CA	195
294	Beaverton, OR	137	212	Dearborn, MI	185	95	Huntsville, AL	401
236	Bellevue, WA	170	248	Decatur, IL	160	203	Independence, MO	189
NA	Bellflower, CA**	NA	NA	Deerfield Beach, FL**	NA	20	Indianapolis, IN	1,591
344	Bellingham, WA	110	266	Denton, TX	151	401	Indio, CA	63
233	Berkeley, CA	171	24	Denver, CO	1,388	224	Inglewood, CA	178
270	Bethlehem, PA	150	NA	Des Moines, IA**	NA	191	Irvine, CA	200
288	Billings, MT	141	9	Detroit, MI	2,570	115	Irving, TX	329
42	Birmingham, AL	865	349	Downey, CA	107	21	Jacksonville, FL	1,540
319	Bloomington, IL	122	284	Duluth, MN	143	79	Jackson, MS	468
NA	Bloomington, IN**	NA	73	Durham, NC	537	45	Jersey City, NJ	798
345	Bloomington, MN	109	NA	Edinburg, TX**	NA	402	Johns Creek, GA	61
206	Boca Raton, FL	188	240	Edison Twnshp, NJ	168	156	Joliet, IL	247
134	Boise, ID	283	343	Edmond, OK	111	NA	Jurupa Valley, CA**	NA
14	Boston, MA	2,130	339	El Cajon, CA	112	107	Kansas City, KS	353
231	Boulder, CO	173	329	El Monte, CA	117	28	Kansas City, MO	1,273
306	Brick Twnshp, NJ	130	34	El Paso, TX	1,035	374	Kennewick, WA	90
91	Bridgeport, CT	414	218	Elgin, IL	180	192	Kenosha, WI	199
236	Brockton, MA	170	117	Elizabeth, NJ	326	306	Kent, WA	130
323	Broken Arrow, OK	121	313	Elk Grove, CA	127	165	Killeen, TX	229
356	Brooklyn Park, MN	105	231	Erie, PA	173	92	Knoxville, TN	410
158	Brownsville, TX	242	273	Escondido, CA	149	157	Lafayette, LA	245
292	Bryan, TX	138	203	Eugene, OR	189	NA	Lake Forest, CA**	NA
390	Buena Park, CA	83	132	Evansville, IN	286	175	Lakeland, FL	217
50	Buffalo, NY	759	198	Everett, WA	193	329	Lakewood Twnshp, NJ	117
261	Burbank, CA	153	329	Fairfield, CA	117	NA	Lakewood, CA**	NA
138	Cambridge, MA	276	174	Fall River, MA	218	147	Lakewood, CO	267
145	Camden, NJ	268	288	Fargo, ND	141	NA	Lancaster, CA**	NA
178	Cape Coral, FL	215	357	Farmington Hills, MI	103	201	Lansing, MI	190
339	Carlsbad, CA	112	334	Fayetteville, AR	116	83	Laredo, TX	440
347	Carmel, IN	108	105	Fayetteville, NC	361	298	Largo, FL	134
253	Carrollton, TX	158	319	Federal Way, WA	122	226	Las Cruces, NM	177
NA	Carson, CA**	NA	372	Fishers, IN	91	10	Las Vegas, NV	2,563
218	Cary, NC	180	327	Flint, MI	119	266	Lawrence, KS	151
189	Cedar Rapids, IA	202	220	Fontana, CA	179	329	Lawrence, MA	117
328	Centennial, CO	118	208	Fort Collins, CO	187	233	Lawton, OK	171
339	Champaign, IL	112	77	Fort Lauderdale, FL	501	352	League City, TX	106
123	Chandler, AZ	316	242	Fort Smith, AR	166	306	Lee's Summit, MO	130
94	Charleston, SC	402	84	Fort Wayne, IN	439	76	Lexington, KY	502
18	Charlotte, NC	1,717	22	Fort Worth, TX	1,536	119	Lincoln, NE	320
310	Cheektowaga, NY	128	227	Fremont, CA	175	75	Little Rock, AR	520
104	Chesapeake, VA	365	53	Fresno, CA	736	392	Livermore, CA	82
2	Chicago, IL	11,944	287	Frisco, TX	142	323	Livonia, MI	121
374	Chico, CA	90	290	Fullerton, CA	139	44	Long Beach, CA	801

RANK	CITY	OFFICERS	RANK	CITY	OFFICERS	RANK	CITY	OFFICERS
298	Longmont, CO	134	164	Pasadena, CA	230	397	South Gate, CA	71
256	Longview, TX	157	145	Pasadena, TX	268	347	Sparks, NV	108
3	Los Angeles, CA	9,992	101	Paterson, NJ	371	364	Spokane Valley, WA	99
30	Louisville, KY	1,239	297	Pearland, TX	135	139	Spokane, WA	275
169	Lowell, MA	225	NA	Pembroke Pines, FL**	NA	155	Springfield, IL	249
95	Lubbock, TX	401	210	Peoria, AZ	186	102	Springfield, MA	368
220	Lynchburg, VA	179	183	Peoria, IL	209	121	Springfield, MO	318
220	Lynn, MA	179	4	Philadelphia, PA	6,526	142	Stamford, CT	269
136	Macon, GA	279	7	Phoenix, AZ	2,979	273	Sterling Heights, MI	149
82	Madison, WI	445	41	Pittsburgh, PA	886	114	Stockton, CA	331
180	Manchester, NH	213	112	Plano, TX	339	357	St. George, UT	103
148	McAllen, TX	265	241	Plantation, FL	167	337	St. Joseph, MO	115
256	McKinney, TX	157	266	Pomona, CA	151	25	St. Louis, MO	1,322
361	Medford, OR	102	NA	Pompano Beach, FL**	NA	66	St. Paul, MN	595
NA	Melbourne, FL**	NA	NA	Port St. Lucie, FL**	NA	72	St. Petersburg, FL	541
11	Memphis, TN	2,416	38	Portland, OR	966	273	Sugar Land, TX	149
NA	Menifee, CA**	NA	153	Portsmouth, VA	252	190	Sunnyvale, CA	201
390	Merced, CA	83	86	Providence, RI	427	229	Sunrise, FL	174
384	Meridian, ID	86	363	Provo, UT	100	309	Surprise, AZ	129
49	Mesa, AZ	780	210	Pueblo, CO	186	79	Syracuse, NY	468
173	Mesquite, TX	219	201	Quincy, MA	190	107	Tacoma, WA	353
99	Miami Beach, FL	372	193	Racine, WI	198	110	Tallahassee, FL	346
196	Miami Gardens, FL	196	51	Raleigh, NC	743	39	Tampa, FL	959
33	Miami, FL	1,054	352	Ramapo, NY	106	NA	Temecula, CA**	NA
236	Midland, TX	170	NA	Rancho Cucamon., CA**	NA	113	Tempe, AZ	335
15	Milwaukee, WI	1,906	242	Reading, PA	166	260	Thornton, CO	154
43	Minneapolis, MN	852	365	Redding, CA	98	NA	Thousand Oaks, CA**	NA
198	Miramar, FL	193	381	Redwood City, CA	87	68	Toledo, OH	569
NA	Mission Viejo, CA**	NA	126	Reno, NV	298	270	Toms River Twnshp, NJ	150
284	Mission, TX	143	334	Renton, WA	116	130	Topeka, KS	290
71	Mobile, AL	543	372	Rialto, CA	91	184	Torrance, CA	208
177	Modesto, CA	216	266	Richardson, TX	151	395	Tracy, CA	78
74	Montgomery, AL	529	216	Richmond, CA	182	162	Trenton, NJ	238
NA	Moreno Valley, CA**	NA	56	Richmond, VA	719	374	Troy, MI	90
369	Mountain View, CA	94	314	Rio Rancho, NM	126	40	Tucson, AZ	955
171	Murfreesboro, TN	223	103	Riverside, CA	366	47	Tulsa, OK	783
389	Murrieta, CA	84	150	Roanoke, VA	256	133	Tuscaloosa, AL	285
339	Nampa, ID	112	303	Rochester, MN	132	384	Tustin, CA	86
400	Napa, CA	67	52	Rochester, NY	741	206	Tyler, TX	188
248	Naperville, IL	160	141	Rockford, IL	271	398	Upland, CA	70
229	Nashua, NH	174	334	Roseville, CA	116	314	Upper Darby Twnshp, PA	126
26	Nashville, TN	1,312	278	Roswell, GA	146	380	Vacaville, CA	89
151	New Bedford, MA	253	NA	Round Rock, TX**	NA	371	Vallejo, CA	92
93	New Haven, CT	407	61	Sacramento, CA	627	224	Vancouver, WA	178
29	New Orleans, LA	1,271	208	Salem, OR	187	318	Ventura, CA	123
253	New Rochelle, NY	158	277	Salinas, CA	147	NA	Victorville, CA**	NA
1	New York, NY	34,555	87	Salt Lake City, UT	425	47	Virginia Beach, VA	783
32	Newark, NJ	1,062	12	San Antonio, TX	2,276	298	Visalia, CA	134
303	Newport Beach, CA	132	140	San Bernardino, CA	272	NA	Vista, CA**	NA
88	Newport News, VA	418	16	San Diego, CA	1,866	159	Waco, TX	240
294	Newton, MA	137	13	San Francisco, CA	2,173	194	Warren, MI	197
54	Norfolk, VA	733	31	San Jose, CA	1,094	233	Warwick, RI	171
253	Norman, OK	158	374	San Leandro, CA	90	6	Washington, DC	3,867
123	North Charleston, SC	316	NA	San Marcos, CA**	NA	135	Waterbury, CT	280
142	North Las Vegas, NV	269	357	San Mateo, CA	103	284	Waukegan, IL	143
NA	Norwalk, CA**	NA	310	Sandy Springs, GA	128	374	West Covina, CA	90
239	Norwalk, CT	169	345	Sandy, UT	109	367	West Jordan, UT	97
62	Oakland, CA	626	120	Santa Ana, CA	319	149	West Palm Beach, FL	264
187	Oceanside, CA	203	301	Santa Barbara, CA	133	203	West Valley, UT	189
278	Odessa, TX	146	294	Santa Clara, CA	137	396	Westland, MI	77
349	O'Fallon, MO	107	NA	Santa Clarita, CA**	NA	381	Westminster, CA	87
301	Ogden, UT	133	370	Santa Maria, CA	93	214	Westminster, CO	183
35	Oklahoma City, OK	1,001	187	Santa Monica, CA	203	319	Whittier, CA	122
NA	Olathe, KS**	NA	248	Santa Rosa, CA	160	200	Wichita Falls, TX	191
46	Omaha, NE	795	67	Savannah, GA	588	59	Wichita, KS	642
170	Ontario, CA	224	95	Scottsdale, AZ	401	151	Wilmington, NC	253
259	Orange, CA	155	270	Scranton, PA	150	70	Winston-Salem, NC	547
384	Orem, UT	86	27	Seattle, WA	1,289	212	Woodbridge Twnshp, NJ	185
55	Orlando, FL	721	69	Shreveport, LA	548	90	Worcester, MA	415
NA	Overland Park, KS**	NA	319	Simi Valley, CA	122	290	Yakima, WA	139
165	Oxnard, CA	229	316	Sioux City, IA	125	65	Yonkers, NY	608
261	Palm Bay, FL	153	165	Sioux Falls, SD	229	251	Yuma, AZ	159
NA	Palmdale, CA**	NA	316	Somerville, MA	125			
NA	Parma, OH**	NA	154	South Bend, IN	251			

Source: Reported data from the F.B.I. "Crime in the United States 2012"

*Sworn officers only, does not include civilian employees.

**Not available

81. Police Officers in 2012 (continued)
National Total = 670,439 Officers*

RANK	CITY	OFFICERS	RANK	CITY	OFFICERS	RANK	CITY	OFFICERS
1	New York, NY	34,555	75	Little Rock, AR	520	149	West Palm Beach, FL	264
2	Chicago, IL	11,944	76	Lexington, KY	502	150	Roanoke, VA	256
3	Los Angeles, CA	9,992	77	Fort Lauderdale, FL	501	151	New Bedford, MA	253
4	Philadelphia, PA	6,526	78	Hartford, CT	478	151	Wilmington, NC	253
5	Houston, TX	5,318	79	Jackson, MS	468	153	Portsmouth, VA	252
6	Washington, DC	3,867	79	Syracuse, NY	468	154	South Bend, IN	251
7	Phoenix, AZ	2,979	81	Columbus, GA	467	155	Springfield, IL	249
8	Baltimore, MD	2,962	82	Madison, WI	445	156	Joliet, IL	247
9	Detroit, MI	2,570	83	Laredo, TX	440	157	Lafayette, LA	245
10	Las Vegas, NV	2,563	84	Fort Wayne, IN	439	158	Brownsville, TX	242
11	Memphis, TN	2,416	85	Corpus Christi, TX	432	159	Glendale, CA	240
12	San Antonio, TX	2,276	86	Providence, RI	427	159	Waco, TX	240
13	San Francisco, CA	2,173	87	Salt Lake City, UT	425	161	Athens-Clarke, GA	239
14	Boston, MA	2,130	88	Akron, OH	418	162	Trenton, NJ	238
15	Milwaukee, WI	1,906	88	Newport News, VA	418	163	Gary, IN	235
16	San Diego, CA	1,866	90	Worcester, MA	415	164	Pasadena, CA	230
17	Atlanta, GA	1,775	91	Bridgeport, CT	414	165	Killeen, TX	229
18	Charlotte, NC	1,717	92	Knoxville, TN	410	165	Oxnard, CA	229
19	Austin, TX	1,628	93	New Haven, CT	407	165	Sioux Falls, SD	229
20	Indianapolis, IN	1,591	94	Charleston, SC	402	168	Clearwater, FL	228
21	Jacksonville, FL	1,540	95	Huntsville, AL	401	169	Lowell, MA	225
22	Fort Worth, TX	1,536	95	Lubbock, TX	401	170	Ontario, CA	224
23	Cleveland, OH	1,481	95	Scottsdale, AZ	401	171	Murfreesboro, TN	223
24	Denver, CO	1,388	98	Glendale, AZ	397	172	Gilbert, AZ	222
25	St. Louis, MO	1,322	99	Anchorage, AK	372	173	Mesquite, TX	219
26	Nashville, TN	1,312	99	Miami Beach, FL	372	174	Fall River, MA	218
27	Seattle, WA	1,289	101	Paterson, NJ	371	175	Grand Prairie, TX	217
28	Kansas City, MO	1,273	102	Springfield, MA	368	175	Lakeland, FL	217
29	New Orleans, LA	1,271	103	Riverside, CA	366	177	Modesto, CA	216
30	Louisville, KY	1,239	104	Chesapeake, VA	365	178	Cape Coral, FL	215
31	San Jose, CA	1,094	105	Fayetteville, NC	361	178	High Point, NC	215
32	Newark, NJ	1,062	106	Anaheim, CA	360	180	Manchester, NH	213
33	Miami, FL	1,054	107	Kansas City, KS	353	181	Allentown, PA	210
34	El Paso, TX	1,035	107	Tacoma, WA	353	181	Chula Vista, CA	210
35	Oklahoma City, OK	1,001	109	Bakersfield, CA	347	183	Peoria, IL	209
36	Albuquerque, NM	999	110	Tallahassee, FL	346	184	Asheville, NC	208
37	Cincinnati, OH	991	111	Dayton, OH	342	184	Torrance, CA	208
38	Portland, OR	966	112	Plano, TX	339	186	Hammond, IN	207
39	Tampa, FL	959	113	Tempe, AZ	335	187	Oceanside, CA	203
40	Tucson, AZ	955	114	Stockton, CA	331	187	Santa Monica, CA	203
41	Pittsburgh, PA	886	115	Irving, TX	329	189	Cedar Rapids, IA	202
42	Birmingham, AL	865	116	Henderson, NV	328	190	Sunnyvale, CA	201
43	Minneapolis, MN	852	117	Elizabeth, NJ	326	191	Irvine, CA	200
44	Long Beach, CA	801	118	Amarillo, TX	323	192	Kenosha, WI	199
45	Jersey City, NJ	798	119	Lincoln, NE	320	193	Racine, WI	198
46	Omaha, NE	795	120	Santa Ana, CA	319	194	Coral Springs, FL	197
47	Tulsa, OK	783	121	Springfield, MO	318	194	Warren, MI	197
47	Virginia Beach, VA	783	122	Alexandria, VA	317	196	Miami Gardens, FL	196
49	Mesa, AZ	780	123	Chandler, AZ	316	197	Huntington Beach, CA	195
50	Buffalo, NY	759	123	North Charleston, SC	316	198	Everett, WA	193
51	Raleigh, NC	743	125	Garland, TX	310	198	Miramar, FL	193
52	Rochester, NY	741	126	Reno, NV	298	200	Wichita Falls, TX	191
53	Fresno, CA	736	127	Gainesville, FL	293	201	Lansing, MI	190
54	Norfolk, VA	733	128	Grand Rapids, MI	292	201	Quincy, MA	190
55	Orlando, FL	721	128	Hollywood, FL	292	203	Eugene, OR	189
56	Richmond, VA	719	130	Topeka, KS	290	203	Independence, MO	189
57	Baton Rouge, LA	664	131	Aurora, IL	289	203	West Valley, UT	189
58	Aurora, CO	651	132	Evansville, IN	286	206	Boca Raton, FL	188
59	Wichita, KS	642	133	Tuscaloosa, AL	285	206	Tyler, TX	188
60	Colorado Springs, CO	638	134	Boise, ID	283	208	Fort Collins, CO	187
61	Sacramento, CA	627	135	Waterbury, CT	280	208	Salem, OR	187
62	Oakland, CA	626	136	Macon, GA	279	210	Peoria, AZ	186
63	Arlington, TX	623	137	Hampton, VA	277	210	Pueblo, CO	186
64	Greensboro, NC	621	138	Cambridge, MA	276	212	Dearborn, MI	185
65	Yonkers, NY	608	139	Spokane, WA	275	212	Woodbridge Twnshp, NJ	185
66	St. Paul, MN	595	140	San Bernardino, CA	272	214	Green Bay, WI	183
67	Savannah, GA	588	141	Rockford, IL	271	214	Westminster, CO	183
68	Toledo, OH	569	142	Clarksville, TN	269	216	Richmond, CA	182
69	Shreveport, LA	548	142	North Las Vegas, NV	269	217	Greenville, NC	181
70	Winston-Salem, NC	547	142	Stamford, CT	269	218	Cary, NC	180
71	Mobile, AL	543	145	Camden, NJ	268	218	Elgin, IL	180
72	St. Petersburg, FL	541	145	Pasadena, TX	268	220	Fontana, CA	179
73	Durham, NC	537	147	Lakewood, CO	267	220	Hayward, CA	179
74	Montgomery, AL	529	148	McAllen, TX	265	220	Lynchburg, VA	179

RANK	CITY	OFFICERS	RANK	CITY	OFFICERS	RANK	CITY	OFFICERS
220	Lynn, MA	179	297	Pearland, TX	135	371	Vallejo, CA	92
224	Inglewood, CA	178	298	Largo, FL	134	372	Fishers, IN	91
224	Vancouver, WA	178	298	Longmont, CO	134	372	Rialto, CA	91
226	Las Cruces, NM	177	298	Visalia, CA	134	374	Chico, CA	90
227	Albany, GA	175	301	Ogden, UT	133	374	Clovis, CA	90
227	Fremont, CA	175	301	Santa Barbara, CA	133	374	Kennewick, WA	90
229	Nashua, NH	174	303	Newport Beach, CA	132	374	San Leandro, CA	90
229	Sunrise, FL	174	303	Rochester, MN	132	374	Troy, MI	90
231	Boulder, CO	173	305	Hillsboro, OR	131	374	West Covina, CA	90
231	Erie, PA	173	306	Brick Twnshp, NJ	130	380	Vacaville, CA	89
233	Berkeley, CA	171	306	Kent, WA	130	381	Clinton Twnshp, MI	87
233	Lawton, OK	171	306	Lee's Summit, MO	130	381	Redwood City, CA	87
233	Warwick, RI	171	309	Surprise, AZ	129	381	Westminster, CA	87
236	Bellevue, WA	170	310	Cheektowaga, NY	128	384	Antioch, CA	86
236	Brockton, MA	170	310	Costa Mesa, CA	128	384	Meridian, ID	86
236	Midland, TX	170	310	Sandy Springs, GA	128	384	Orem, UT	86
239	Norwalk, CT	169	313	Elk Grove, CA	127	384	Tustin, CA	86
240	Edison Twnshp, NJ	168	314	Rio Rancho, NM	126	388	Citrus Heights, CA	85
241	Plantation, FL	167	314	Upper Darby Twnshp, PA	126	389	Murrieta, CA	84
242	Fort Smith, AR	166	316	Sioux City, IA	125	390	Buena Park, CA	83
242	Hamilton Twnshp, NJ	166	316	Somerville, MA	125	390	Merced, CA	83
242	Reading, PA	166	318	Ventura, CA	123	392	Alhambra, CA	82
245	Davie, FL	164	319	Bloomington, IL	122	392	Livermore, CA	82
246	Arvada, CO	163	319	Federal Way, WA	122	394	Alameda, CA	81
246	Davenport, IA	163	319	Simi Valley, CA	122	395	Tracy, CA	78
248	Decatur, IL	160	319	Whittier, CA	122	396	Westland, MI	77
248	Naperville, IL	160	323	Broken Arrow, OK	121	397	South Gate, CA	71
248	Santa Rosa, CA	160	323	Livonia, MI	121	398	Upland, CA	70
251	Clarkstown, NY	159	325	College Station, TX	120	399	Baldwin Park, CA	68
251	Yuma, AZ	159	325	Gresham, OR	120	400	Napa, CA	67
253	Carrollton, TX	158	327	Flint, MI	119	401	Indio, CA	63
253	New Rochelle, NY	158	328	Centennial, CO	118	402	Johns Creek, GA	61
253	Norman, OK	158	329	Ann Arbor, MI	117	403	Hemet, CA	57
256	Longview, TX	157	329	El Monte, CA	117	NA	Abilene, TX**	NA
256	McKinney, TX	157	329	Fairfield, CA	117	NA	Albany, NY**	NA
258	Columbia, MO	156	329	Lakewood Twnshp, NJ	117	NA	Beaumont, TX**	NA
259	Orange, CA	155	329	Lawrence, MA	117	NA	Bellflower, CA**	NA
260	Thornton, CO	154	334	Fayetteville, AR	116	NA	Bloomington, IN**	NA
261	Amherst, NY	153	334	Renton, WA	116	NA	Carson, CA**	NA
261	Burbank, CA	153	334	Roseville, CA	116	NA	Chino Hills, CA**	NA
261	Garden Grove, CA	153	337	Allen, TX	115	NA	Compton, CA**	NA
261	Palm Bay, FL	153	337	St. Joseph, MO	115	NA	Dallas, TX**	NA
265	Cicero, IL	152	339	Carlsbad, CA	112	NA	Deerfield Beach, FL**	NA
266	Denton, TX	151	339	Champaign, IL	112	NA	Des Moines, IA**	NA
266	Lawrence, KS	151	339	El Cajon, CA	112	NA	Edinburg, TX**	NA
266	Pomona, CA	151	339	Nampa, ID	112	NA	Hesperia, CA**	NA
266	Richardson, TX	151	343	Edmond, OK	111	NA	Hialeah, FL**	NA
270	Bethlehem, PA	150	344	Bellingham, WA	110	NA	Hoover, AL**	NA
270	Scranton, PA	150	345	Bloomington, MN	109	NA	Jurupa Valley, CA**	NA
270	Toms River Twnshp, NJ	150	345	Sandy, UT	109	NA	Lake Forest, CA**	NA
273	Escondido, CA	149	347	Carmel, IN	108	NA	Lakewood, CA**	NA
273	Sterling Heights, MI	149	347	Sparks, NV	108	NA	Lancaster, CA**	NA
273	Sugar Land, TX	149	349	Arlington Heights, IL	107	NA	Melbourne, FL**	NA
276	Corona, CA	148	349	Downey, CA	107	NA	Menifee, CA**	NA
277	Salinas, CA	147	349	O'Fallon, MO	107	NA	Mission Viejo, CA**	NA
278	Odessa, TX	146	352	Colonie, NY	106	NA	Moreno Valley, CA**	NA
278	Roswell, GA	146	352	Daly City, CA	106	NA	Norwalk, CA**	NA
280	Danbury, CT	145	352	League City, TX	106	NA	Olathe, KS**	NA
280	Greeley, CO	145	352	Ramapo, NY	106	NA	Overland Park, KS**	NA
282	Clifton, NJ	144	356	Brooklyn Park, MN	105	NA	Palmdale, CA**	NA
282	Concord, CA	144	357	Avondale, AZ	103	NA	Parma, OH**	NA
284	Duluth, MN	143	357	Farmington Hills, MI	103	NA	Pembroke Pines, FL**	NA
284	Mission, TX	143	357	San Mateo, CA	103	NA	Pompano Beach, FL**	NA
284	Waukegan, IL	143	357	St. George, UT	103	NA	Port St. Lucie, FL**	NA
287	Frisco, TX	142	361	Chino, CA	102	NA	Rancho Cucamon., CA**	NA
288	Billings, MT	141	361	Medford, OR	102	NA	Round Rock, TX**	NA
288	Fargo, ND	141	363	Provo, UT	100	NA	San Marcos, CA**	NA
290	Fullerton, CA	139	364	Spokane Valley, WA	99	NA	Santa Clarita, CA**	NA
290	Yakima, WA	139	365	Greece, NY	98	NA	Temecula, CA**	NA
292	Bryan, TX	138	365	Redding, CA	98	NA	Thousand Oaks, CA**	NA
292	Cranston, RI	138	367	West Jordan, UT	97	NA	Victorville, CA**	NA
294	Beaverton, OR	137	368	Hawthorne, CA	96	NA	Vista, CA**	NA
294	Newton, MA	137	369	Mountain View, CA	94			
294	Santa Clara, CA	137	370	Santa Maria, CA	93			

Source: Reported data from the F.B.I. "Crime in the United States 2012"

*Sworn officers only, does not include civilian employees.

**Not available

82. Rate of Police Officers in 2012
National Rate = 235 Officers per 100,000 Population*

RANK	CITY	RATE	RANK	CITY	RATE	RANK	CITY	RATE
NA	Abilene, TX**	NA	NA	Chino Hills, CA**	NA	70	Gainesville, FL	231
93	Akron, OH	211	284	Chino, CA	128	390	Garden Grove, CA	87
343	Alameda, CA	107	393	Chula Vista, CA	84	273	Garland, TX	132
79	Albany, GA	223	148	Cicero, IL	180	32	Gary, IN	292
NA	Albany, NY**	NA	20	Cincinnati, OH	335	349	Gilbert, AZ	104
148	Albuquerque, NM	180	362	Citrus Heights, CA	100	179	Glendale, AZ	170
86	Alexandria, VA	217	118	Clarkstown, NY	198	302	Glendale, CA	123
368	Alhambra, CA	97	121	Clarksville, TN	196	311	Grand Prairie, TX	119
160	Allentown, PA	176	96	Clearwater, FL	209	216	Grand Rapids, MI	154
278	Allen, TX	130	12	Cleveland, OH	376	358	Greece, NY	101
198	Amarillo, TX	164	179	Clifton, NJ	170	221	Greeley, CO	151
278	Amherst, NY	130	386	Clinton Twnshp, MI	90	167	Green Bay, WI	173
349	Anaheim, CA	104	380	Clovis, CA	92	76	Greensboro, NC	225
295	Anchorage, AK	124	295	College Station, TX	124	97	Greenville, NC	208
356	Ann Arbor, MI	102	258	Colonie, NY	136	332	Gresham, OR	111
395	Antioch, CA	82	231	Colorado Springs, CO	148	140	Hamilton Twnshp, NJ	186
244	Arlington Heights, IL	142	246	Columbia, MO	141	52	Hammond, IN	256
198	Arlington, TX	164	67	Columbus, GA	238	106	Hampton, VA	201
226	Arvada, CO	150	NA	Compton, CA**	NA	10	Hartford, CT	382
60	Asheville, NC	244	319	Concord, CA	115	329	Hawthorne, CA	112
102	Athens-Clarke, GA	203	209	Coral Springs, FL	158	305	Hayward, CA	121
8	Atlanta, GA	406	374	Corona, CA	94	403	Hemet, CA	70
128	Aurora, CO	193	256	Corpus Christi, TX	138	295	Henderson, NV	124
240	Aurora, IL	145	324	Costa Mesa, CA	114	NA	Hesperia, CA**	NA
123	Austin, TX	195	174	Cranston, RI	172	NA	Hialeah, FL**	NA
276	Avondale, AZ	131	NA	Dallas, TX**	NA	106	High Point, NC	201
367	Bakersfield, CA	98	354	Daly City, CA	103	106	Hollywood, FL	201
388	Baldwin Park, CA	89	157	Danbury, CT	177	NA	Hoover, AL**	NA
2	Baltimore, MD	474	204	Davenport, IA	161	60	Houston, TX	244
35	Baton Rouge, LA	287	167	Davie, FL	173	362	Huntington Beach, CA	100
NA	Beaumont, TX**	NA	64	Dayton, OH	241	83	Huntsville, AL	218
231	Beaverton, OR	148	129	Dearborn, MI	190	204	Independence, MO	161
261	Bellevue, WA	135	95	Decatur, IL	210	129	Indianapolis, IN	190
NA	Bellflower, CA**	NA	NA	Deerfield Beach, FL**	NA	397	Indio, CA	80
267	Bellingham, WA	133	288	Denton, TX	127	206	Inglewood, CA	160
228	Berkeley, CA	149	81	Denver, CO	221	380	Irvine, CA	92
112	Bethlehem, PA	199	NA	Des Moines, IA**	NA	234	Irving, TX	147
267	Billings, MT	133	14	Detroit, MI	363	143	Jacksonville, FL	183
8	Birmingham, AL	406	374	Downey, CA	94	42	Jackson, MS	266
209	Bloomington, IL	158	194	Duluth, MN	165	24	Jersey City, NJ	317
NA	Bloomington, IN**	NA	74	Durham, NC	228	401	Johns Creek, GA	76
282	Bloomington, MN	129	NA	Edinburg, TX**	NA	188	Joliet, IL	166
86	Boca Raton, FL	217	188	Edison Twnshp, NJ	166	NA	Jurupa Valley, CA**	NA
263	Boise, ID	134	267	Edmond, OK	133	65	Kansas City, KS	240
19	Boston, MA	338	338	El Cajon, CA	110	39	Kansas City, MO	274
167	Boulder, CO	173	358	El Monte, CA	101	314	Kennewick, WA	117
175	Brick Twnshp, NJ	171	218	El Paso, TX	153	112	Kenosha, WI	199
36	Bridgeport, CT	284	194	Elgin, IL	165	346	Kent, WA	106
152	Brockton, MA	179	49	Elizabeth, NJ	258	165	Killeen, TX	174
309	Broken Arrow, OK	120	396	Elk Grove, CA	81	76	Knoxville, TN	225
258	Brooklyn Park, MN	136	179	Erie, PA	170	112	Lafayette, LA	199
263	Brownsville, TX	134	358	Escondido, CA	101	NA	Lake Forest, CA**	NA
160	Bryan, TX	176	309	Eugene, OR	120	86	Lakeland, FL	217
358	Buena Park, CA	101	63	Evansville, IN	242	293	Lakewood Twnshp, NJ	125
34	Buffalo, NY	289	143	Everett, WA	183	NA	Lakewood, CA**	NA
237	Burbank, CA	146	340	Fairfield, CA	109	145	Lakewood, CO	182
49	Cambridge, MA	258	62	Fall River, MA	243	NA	Lancaster, CA**	NA
18	Camden, NJ	345	284	Fargo, ND	128	188	Lansing, MI	166
261	Cape Coral, FL	135	284	Farmington Hills, MI	128	152	Laredo, TX	179
349	Carlsbad, CA	104	216	Fayetteville, AR	154	179	Largo, FL	170
273	Carmel, IN	132	163	Fayetteville, NC	175	157	Las Cruces, NM	177
288	Carrollton, TX	127	267	Federal Way, WA	133	167	Las Vegas, NV	173
NA	Carson, CA**	NA	319	Fishers, IN	115	184	Lawrence, KS	169
284	Cary, NC	128	314	Flint, MI	117	221	Lawrence, MA	151
213	Cedar Rapids, IA	157	388	Fontana, CA	89	167	Lawton, OK	173
326	Centennial, CO	113	291	Fort Collins, CO	126	302	League City, TX	123
256	Champaign, IL	138	31	Fort Lauderdale, FL	293	244	Lee's Summit, MO	142
278	Chandler, AZ	130	129	Fort Smith, AR	190	188	Lexington, KY	166
21	Charleston, SC	325	175	Fort Wayne, IN	171	305	Lincoln, NE	121
92	Charlotte, NC	212	112	Fort Worth, TX	199	43	Little Rock, AR	265
201	Cheektowaga, NY	162	397	Fremont, CA	80	366	Livermore, CA	99
206	Chesapeake, VA	160	240	Fresno, CA	145	291	Livonia, MI	126
3	Chicago, IL	441	319	Frisco, TX	115	179	Long Beach, CA	170
354	Chico, CA	103	362	Fullerton, CA	100			

RANK	CITY	RATE	RANK	CITY	RATE	RANK	CITY	RATE
221	Longmont, CO	151	194	Pasadena, CA	165	402	South Gate, CA	74
129	Longview, TX	190	167	Pasadena, TX	173	314	Sparks, NV	117
48	Los Angeles, CA	259	57	Paterson, NJ	252	340	Spokane Valley, WA	109
140	Louisville, KY	186	243	Pearland, TX	143	278	Spokane, WA	130
99	Lowell, MA	207	NA	Pembroke Pines, FL**	NA	91	Springfield, IL	213
184	Lubbock, TX	169	314	Peoria, AZ	117	67	Springfield, MA	238
70	Lynchburg, VA	231	146	Peoria, IL	181	118	Springfield, MO	198
123	Lynn, MA	195	4	Philadelphia, PA	424	86	Stamford, CT	217
29	Macon, GA	301	106	Phoenix, AZ	201	319	Sterling Heights, MI	115
136	Madison, WI	187	36	Pittsburgh, PA	284	332	Stockton, CA	111
127	Manchester, NH	194	295	Plano, TX	124	258	St. George, UT	136
123	McAllen, TX	195	129	Plantation, FL	190	228	St. Joseph, MO	149
324	McKinney, TX	114	362	Pomona, CA	100	6	St. Louis, MO	415
263	Medford, OR	134	NA	Pompano Beach, FL**	NA	101	St. Paul, MN	205
NA	Melbourne, FL**	NA	NA	Port St. Lucie, FL**	NA	83	St. Petersburg, FL	218
13	Memphis, TN	367	201	Portland, OR	162	148	Sugar Land, TX	180
NA	Menifee, CA**	NA	47	Portsmouth, VA	260	252	Sunnyvale, CA	140
356	Merced, CA	102	65	Providence, RI	240	110	Sunrise, FL	200
332	Meridian, ID	111	391	Provo, UT	86	343	Surprise, AZ	107
167	Mesa, AZ	173	175	Pueblo, CO	171	22	Syracuse, NY	321
221	Mesquite, TX	151	102	Quincy, MA	203	165	Tacoma, WA	174
7	Miami Beach, FL	408	58	Racine, WI	250	136	Tallahassee, FL	187
160	Miami Gardens, FL	176	157	Raleigh, NC	177	40	Tampa, FL	273
53	Miami, FL	254	295	Ramapo, NY	124	NA	Temecula, CA**	NA
234	Midland, TX	147	NA	Rancho Cucamon., CA**	NA	104	Tempe, AZ	202
23	Milwaukee, WI	318	136	Reading, PA	187	293	Thornton, CO	125
83	Minneapolis, MN	218	342	Redding, CA	108	NA	Thousand Oaks, CA**	NA
218	Miramar, FL	153	332	Redwood City, CA	111	112	Toledo, OH	199
NA	Mission Viejo, CA**	NA	282	Reno, NV	129	200	Toms River Twnshp, NJ	163
155	Mission, TX	178	295	Renton, WA	124	76	Topeka, KS	225
90	Mobile, AL	216	386	Rialto, CA	90	246	Torrance, CA	141
346	Modesto, CA	106	237	Richardson, TX	146	380	Tracy, CA	92
55	Montgomery, AL	253	175	Richmond, CA	171	38	Trenton, NJ	279
NA	Moreno Valley, CA**	NA	17	Richmond, VA	346	338	Troy, MI	110
295	Mountain View, CA	124	246	Rio Rancho, NM	141	148	Tucson, AZ	180
112	Murfreesboro, TN	199	314	Riverside, CA	117	121	Tulsa, OK	196
399	Murrieta, CA	79	46	Roanoke, VA	262	27	Tuscaloosa, AL	310
263	Nampa, ID	134	304	Rochester, MN	122	332	Tustin, CA	111
392	Napa, CA	85	15	Rochester, NY	350	135	Tyler, TX	188
329	Naperville, IL	112	155	Rockford, IL	178	379	Upland, CA	93
110	Nashua, NH	200	374	Roseville, CA	94	220	Upper Darby Twnshp, PA	152
93	Nashville, TN	211	209	Roswell, GA	158	371	Vacaville, CA	95
45	New Bedford, MA	263	NA	Round Rock, TX**	NA	400	Vallejo, CA	78
26	New Haven, CT	313	273	Sacramento, CA	132	343	Vancouver, WA	107
15	New Orleans, LA	350	311	Salem, OR	119	326	Ventura, CA	113
104	New Rochelle, NY	202	371	Salinas, CA	95	NA	Victorville, CA**	NA
5	New York, NY	417	81	Salt Lake City, UT	221	163	Virginia Beach, VA	175
11	Newark, NJ	381	194	San Antonio, TX	165	348	Visalia, CA	105
221	Newport Beach, CA	151	288	San Bernardino, CA	127	NA	Vista, CA**	NA
73	Newport News, VA	230	253	San Diego, CA	139	136	Waco, TX	187
209	Newton, MA	158	43	San Francisco, CA	265	234	Warren, MI	147
30	Norfolk, VA	299	329	San Jose, CA	112	97	Warwick, RI	208
253	Norman, OK	139	349	San Leandro, CA	104	1	Washington, DC	612
25	North Charleston, SC	314	NA	San Marcos, CA**	NA	55	Waterbury, CT	253
305	North Las Vegas, NV	121	349	San Mateo, CA	104	206	Waukegan, IL	160
NA	Norwalk, CA**	NA	276	Sandy Springs, GA	131	394	West Covina, CA	83
123	Norwalk, CT	195	305	Sandy, UT	121	385	West Jordan, UT	91
213	Oakland, CA	157	369	Santa Ana, CA	96	49	West Palm Beach, FL	258
311	Oceanside, CA	119	231	Santa Barbara, CA	148	246	West Valley, UT	141
246	Odessa, TX	141	319	Santa Clara, CA	115	380	Westland, MI	92
267	O'Fallon, MO	133	NA	Santa Clarita, CA**	NA	371	Westminster, CA	95
215	Ogden, UT	156	380	Santa Maria, CA	92	187	Westminster, CO	167
186	Oklahoma City, OK	168	79	Santa Monica, CA	223	246	Whittier, CA	141
NA	Olathe, KS**	NA	374	Santa Rosa, CA	94	146	Wichita Falls, TX	181
129	Omaha, NE	190	53	Savannah, GA	254	188	Wichita, KS	166
267	Ontario, CA	133	152	Scottsdale, AZ	179	70	Wilmington, NC	231
332	Orange, CA	111	120	Scranton, PA	197	69	Winston-Salem, NC	233
374	Orem, UT	94	100	Seattle, WA	206	142	Woodbridge Twnshp, NJ	184
32	Orlando, FL	292	41	Shreveport, LA	271	75	Worcester, MA	226
NA	Overland Park, KS**	NA	369	Simi Valley, CA	96	228	Yakima, WA	149
326	Oxnard, CA	113	226	Sioux City, IA	150	28	Yonkers, NY	306
237	Palm Bay, FL	146	240	Sioux Falls, SD	145	188	Yuma, AZ	166
NA	Palmdale, CA**	NA	201	Somerville, MA	162			
NA	Parma, OH**	NA	59	South Bend, IN	248			

Source: CQ Press using reported data from the F.B.I. "Crime in the United States 2012"

*Sworn officers only, does not include civilian employees.

**Not available

82. Rate of Police Officers in 2012 (continued)
National Rate = 235 Officers per 100,000 Population*

RANK	CITY	RATE	RANK	CITY	RATE	RANK	CITY	RATE
1	Washington, DC	612	75	Worcester, MA	226	148	Cicero, IL	180
2	Baltimore, MD	474	76	Greensboro, NC	225	148	Sugar Land, TX	180
3	Chicago, IL	441	76	Knoxville, TN	225	148	Tucson, AZ	180
4	Philadelphia, PA	424	76	Topeka, KS	225	152	Brockton, MA	179
5	New York, NY	417	79	Albany, GA	223	152	Laredo, TX	179
6	St. Louis, MO	415	79	Santa Monica, CA	223	152	Scottsdale, AZ	179
7	Miami Beach, FL	408	81	Denver, CO	221	155	Mission, TX	178
8	Atlanta, GA	406	81	Salt Lake City, UT	221	155	Rockford, IL	178
8	Birmingham, AL	406	83	Huntsville, AL	218	157	Danbury, CT	177
10	Hartford, CT	382	83	Minneapolis, MN	218	157	Las Cruces, NM	177
11	Newark, NJ	381	83	St. Petersburg, FL	218	157	Raleigh, NC	177
12	Cleveland, OH	376	86	Alexandria, VA	217	160	Allentown, PA	176
13	Memphis, TN	367	86	Boca Raton, FL	217	160	Bryan, TX	176
14	Detroit, MI	363	86	Lakeland, FL	217	160	Miami Gardens, FL	176
15	New Orleans, LA	350	86	Stamford, CT	217	163	Fayetteville, NC	175
15	Rochester, NY	350	90	Mobile, AL	216	163	Virginia Beach, VA	175
17	Richmond, VA	346	91	Springfield, IL	213	165	Killeen, TX	174
18	Camden, NJ	345	92	Charlotte, NC	212	165	Tacoma, WA	174
19	Boston, MA	338	93	Akron, OH	211	167	Boulder, CO	173
20	Cincinnati, OH	335	93	Nashville, TN	211	167	Davie, FL	173
21	Charleston, SC	325	95	Decatur, IL	210	167	Green Bay, WI	173
22	Syracuse, NY	321	96	Clearwater, FL	209	167	Las Vegas, NV	173
23	Milwaukee, WI	318	97	Greenville, NC	208	167	Lawton, OK	173
24	Jersey City, NJ	317	97	Warwick, RI	208	167	Mesa, AZ	173
25	North Charleston, SC	314	99	Lowell, MA	207	167	Pasadena, TX	173
26	New Haven, CT	313	100	Seattle, WA	206	174	Cranston, RI	172
27	Tuscaloosa, AL	310	101	St. Paul, MN	205	175	Brick Twnshp, NJ	171
28	Yonkers, NY	306	102	Athens-Clarke, GA	203	175	Fort Wayne, IN	171
29	Macon, GA	301	102	Quincy, MA	203	175	Pueblo, CO	171
30	Norfolk, VA	299	104	New Rochelle, NY	202	175	Richmond, CA	171
31	Fort Lauderdale, FL	293	104	Tempe, AZ	202	179	Clifton, NJ	170
32	Gary, IN	292	106	Hampton, VA	201	179	Erie, PA	170
32	Orlando, FL	292	106	High Point, NC	201	179	Glendale, AZ	170
34	Buffalo, NY	289	106	Hollywood, FL	201	179	Largo, FL	170
35	Baton Rouge, LA	287	106	Phoenix, AZ	201	179	Long Beach, CA	170
36	Bridgeport, CT	284	110	Nashua, NH	200	184	Lawrence, KS	169
36	Pittsburgh, PA	284	110	Sunrise, FL	200	184	Lubbock, TX	169
38	Trenton, NJ	279	112	Bethlehem, PA	199	186	Oklahoma City, OK	168
39	Kansas City, MO	274	112	Fort Worth, TX	199	187	Westminster, CO	167
40	Tampa, FL	273	112	Kenosha, WI	199	188	Edison Twnshp, NJ	166
41	Shreveport, LA	271	112	Lafayette, LA	199	188	Joliet, IL	166
42	Jackson, MS	266	112	Murfreesboro, TN	199	188	Lansing, MI	166
43	Little Rock, AR	265	112	Toledo, OH	199	188	Lexington, KY	166
43	San Francisco, CA	265	118	Clarkstown, NY	198	188	Wichita, KS	166
45	New Bedford, MA	263	118	Springfield, MO	198	188	Yuma, AZ	166
46	Roanoke, VA	262	120	Scranton, PA	197	194	Duluth, MN	165
47	Portsmouth, VA	260	121	Clarksville, TN	196	194	Elgin, IL	165
48	Los Angeles, CA	259	121	Tulsa, OK	196	194	Pasadena, CA	165
49	Cambridge, MA	258	123	Austin, TX	195	194	San Antonio, TX	165
49	Elizabeth, NJ	258	123	Lynn, MA	195	198	Amarillo, TX	164
49	West Palm Beach, FL	258	123	McAllen, TX	195	198	Arlington, TX	164
52	Hammond, IN	256	123	Norwalk, CT	195	200	Toms River Twnshp, NJ	163
53	Miami, FL	254	127	Manchester, NH	194	201	Cheektowaga, NY	162
53	Savannah, GA	254	128	Aurora, CO	193	201	Portland, OR	162
55	Montgomery, AL	253	129	Dearborn, MI	190	201	Somerville, MA	162
55	Waterbury, CT	253	129	Fort Smith, AR	190	204	Davenport, IA	161
57	Paterson, NJ	252	129	Indianapolis, IN	190	204	Independence, MO	161
58	Racine, WI	250	129	Longview, TX	190	206	Chesapeake, VA	160
59	South Bend, IN	248	129	Omaha, NE	190	206	Inglewood, CA	160
60	Asheville, NC	244	129	Plantation, FL	190	206	Waukegan, IL	160
60	Houston, TX	244	135	Tyler, TX	188	209	Bloomington, IL	158
62	Fall River, MA	243	136	Madison, WI	187	209	Coral Springs, FL	158
63	Evansville, IN	242	136	Reading, PA	187	209	Newton, MA	158
64	Dayton, OH	241	136	Tallahassee, FL	187	209	Roswell, GA	158
65	Kansas City, KS	240	136	Waco, TX	187	213	Cedar Rapids, IA	157
65	Providence, RI	240	140	Hamilton Twnshp, NJ	186	213	Oakland, CA	157
67	Columbus, GA	238	140	Louisville, KY	186	215	Ogden, UT	156
67	Springfield, MA	238	142	Woodbridge Twnshp, NJ	184	216	Fayetteville, AR	154
69	Winston-Salem, NC	233	143	Everett, WA	183	216	Grand Rapids, MI	154
70	Gainesville, FL	231	143	Jacksonville, FL	183	218	El Paso, TX	153
70	Lynchburg, VA	231	145	Lakewood, CO	182	218	Miramar, FL	153
70	Wilmington, NC	231	146	Peoria, IL	181	220	Upper Darby Twnshp, PA	152
73	Newport News, VA	230	146	Wichita Falls, TX	181	221	Greeley, CO	151
74	Durham, NC	228	148	Albuquerque, NM	180	221	Lawrence, MA	151

RANK	CITY	RATE	RANK	CITY	RATE	RANK	CITY	RATE
221	Longmont, CO	151	295	Henderson, NV	124	371	Salinas, CA	95
221	Mesquite, TX	151	295	Mountain View, CA	124	371	Vacaville, CA	95
221	Newport Beach, CA	151	295	Plano, TX	124	371	Westminster, CA	95
226	Arvada, CO	150	295	Ramapo, NY	124	374	Corona, CA	94
226	Sioux City, IA	150	295	Renton, WA	124	374	Downey, CA	94
228	Berkeley, CA	149	302	Glendale, CA	123	374	Orem, UT	94
228	St. Joseph, MO	149	302	League City, TX	123	374	Roseville, CA	94
228	Yakima, WA	149	304	Rochester, MN	122	374	Santa Rosa, CA	94
231	Beaverton, OR	148	305	Hayward, CA	121	379	Upland, CA	93
231	Colorado Springs, CO	148	305	Lincoln, NE	121	380	Clovis, CA	92
231	Santa Barbara, CA	148	305	North Las Vegas, NV	121	380	Irvine, CA	92
234	Irving, TX	147	305	Sandy, UT	121	380	Santa Maria, CA	92
234	Midland, TX	147	309	Broken Arrow, OK	120	380	Tracy, CA	92
234	Warren, MI	147	309	Eugene, OR	120	380	Westland, MI	92
237	Burbank, CA	146	311	Grand Prairie, TX	119	385	West Jordan, UT	91
237	Palm Bay, FL	146	311	Oceanside, CA	119	386	Clinton Twnshp, MI	90
237	Richardson, TX	146	311	Salem, OR	119	386	Rialto, CA	90
240	Aurora, IL	145	314	Flint, MI	117	388	Baldwin Park, CA	89
240	Fresno, CA	145	314	Kennewick, WA	117	388	Fontana, CA	89
240	Sioux Falls, SD	145	314	Peoria, AZ	117	390	Garden Grove, CA	87
243	Pearland, TX	143	314	Riverside, CA	117	391	Provo, UT	86
244	Arlington Heights, IL	142	314	Sparks, NV	117	392	Napa, CA	85
244	Lee's Summit, MO	142	319	Concord, CA	115	393	Chula Vista, CA	84
246	Columbia, MO	141	319	Fishers, IN	115	394	West Covina, CA	83
246	Odessa, TX	141	319	Frisco, TX	115	395	Antioch, CA	82
246	Rio Rancho, NM	141	319	Santa Clara, CA	115	396	Elk Grove, CA	81
246	Torrance, CA	141	319	Sterling Heights, MI	115	397	Fremont, CA	80
246	West Valley, UT	141	324	Costa Mesa, CA	114	397	Indio, CA	80
246	Whittier, CA	141	324	McKinney, TX	114	399	Murrieta, CA	79
252	Sunnyvale, CA	140	326	Centennial, CO	113	400	Vallejo, CA	78
253	Hillsboro, OR	139	326	Oxnard, CA	113	401	Johns Creek, GA	76
253	Norman, OK	139	326	Ventura, CA	113	402	South Gate, CA	74
253	San Diego, CA	139	329	Hawthorne, CA	112	403	Hemet, CA	70
256	Champaign, IL	138	329	Naperville, IL	112	NA	Abilene, TX**	NA
256	Corpus Christi, TX	138	329	San Jose, CA	112	NA	Albany, NY**	NA
258	Brooklyn Park, MN	136	332	Gresham, OR	111	NA	Beaumont, TX**	NA
258	Colonie, NY	136	332	Meridian, ID	111	NA	Bellflower, CA**	NA
258	St. George, UT	136	332	Orange, CA	111	NA	Bloomington, IN**	NA
261	Bellevue, WA	135	332	Redwood City, CA	111	NA	Carson, CA**	NA
261	Cape Coral, FL	135	332	Stockton, CA	111	NA	Chino Hills, CA**	NA
263	Boise, ID	134	332	Tustin, CA	111	NA	Compton, CA**	NA
263	Brownsville, TX	134	338	El Cajon, CA	110	NA	Dallas, TX**	NA
263	Medford, OR	134	338	Troy, MI	110	NA	Deerfield Beach, FL**	NA
263	Nampa, ID	134	340	Fairfield, CA	109	NA	Des Moines, IA**	NA
267	Bellingham, WA	133	340	Spokane Valley, WA	109	NA	Edinburg, TX**	NA
267	Billings, MT	133	342	Redding, CA	108	NA	Hesperia, CA**	NA
267	Edmond, OK	133	343	Alameda, CA	107	NA	Hialeah, FL**	NA
267	Federal Way, WA	133	343	Surprise, AZ	107	NA	Hoover, AL**	NA
267	O'Fallon, MO	133	343	Vancouver, WA	107	NA	Jurupa Valley, CA**	NA
267	Ontario, CA	133	346	Kent, WA	106	NA	Lake Forest, CA**	NA
273	Carmel, IN	132	346	Modesto, CA	106	NA	Lakewood, CA**	NA
273	Garland, TX	132	348	Visalia, CA	105	NA	Lancaster, CA**	NA
273	Sacramento, CA	132	349	Anaheim, CA	104	NA	Melbourne, FL**	NA
276	Avondale, AZ	131	349	Carlsbad, CA	104	NA	Menifee, CA**	NA
276	Sandy Springs, GA	131	349	Gilbert, AZ	104	NA	Mission Viejo, CA**	NA
278	Allen, TX	130	349	San Leandro, CA	104	NA	Moreno Valley, CA**	NA
278	Amherst, NY	130	349	San Mateo, CA	104	NA	Norwalk, CA**	NA
278	Chandler, AZ	130	354	Chico, CA	103	NA	Olathe, KS**	NA
278	Spokane, WA	130	354	Daly City, CA	103	NA	Overland Park, KS**	NA
282	Bloomington, MN	129	356	Ann Arbor, MI	102	NA	Palmdale, CA**	NA
282	Reno, NV	129	356	Merced, CA	102	NA	Parma, OH**	NA
284	Cary, NC	128	358	Buena Park, CA	101	NA	Pembroke Pines, FL**	NA
284	Chino, CA	128	358	El Monte, CA	101	NA	Pompano Beach, FL**	NA
284	Fargo, ND	128	358	Escondido, CA	101	NA	Port St. Lucie, FL**	NA
284	Farmington Hills, MI	128	358	Greece, NY	101	NA	Rancho Cucamon., CA**	NA
288	Carrollton, TX	127	362	Citrus Heights, CA	100	NA	Round Rock, TX**	NA
288	Denton, TX	127	362	Fullerton, CA	100	NA	San Marcos, CA**	NA
288	San Bernardino, CA	127	362	Huntington Beach, CA	100	NA	Santa Clarita, CA**	NA
291	Fort Collins, CO	126	362	Pomona, CA	100	NA	Temecula, CA**	NA
291	Livonia, MI	126	366	Livermore, CA	99	NA	Thousand Oaks, CA**	NA
293	Lakewood Twnshp, NJ	125	367	Bakersfield, CA	98	NA	Victorville, CA**	NA
293	Thornton, CO	125	368	Alhambra, CA	97	NA	Vista, CA**	NA
295	Anchorage, AK	124	369	Santa Ana, CA	96			
295	College Station, TX	124	369	Simi Valley, CA	96			

Source: CQ Press using reported data from the F.B.I. "Crime in the United States 2012"

*Sworn officers only, does not include civilian employees.

**Not available

83. Percent Change in Rate of Police Officers: 2011 to 2012
National Percent Change = 1.3% Decrease*

RANK	CITY	% CHANGE	RANK	CITY	% CHANGE	RANK	CITY	% CHANGE
NA	Abilene, TX**	NA	NA	Chino Hills, CA**	NA	154	Gainesville, FL	(0.4)
51	Akron, OH	2.4	171	Chino, CA	(0.8)	285	Garden Grove, CA	(3.3)
327	Alameda, CA	(4.5)	356	Chula Vista, CA	(5.6)	337	Garland, TX	(5.0)
27	Albany, GA	3.7	NA	Cicero, IL**	NA	NA	Gary, IN**	NA
NA	Albany, NY**	NA	314	Cincinnati, OH	(4.0)	115	Gilbert, AZ	0.0
281	Albuquerque, NM	(3.2)	178	Citrus Heights, CA	(1.0)	236	Glendale, AZ	(2.3)
51	Alexandria, VA	2.4	311	Clarkstown, NY	(3.9)	95	Glendale, CA	0.8
273	Alhambra, CA	(3.0)	105	Clarksville, TN	0.5	171	Grand Prairie, TX	(0.8)
12	Allentown, PA	6.0	157	Clearwater, FL	(0.5)	336	Grand Rapids, MI	(4.9)
36	Allen, TX	3.2	40	Cleveland, OH	3.0	178	Greece, NY	(1.0)
115	Amarillo, TX	0.0	67	Clifton, NJ	1.8	58	Greeley, CO	2.0
115	Amherst, NY	0.0	228	Clinton Twnshp, MI	(2.2)	268	Green Bay, WI	(2.8)
351	Anaheim, CA	(5.5)	388	Clovis, CA	(9.8)	291	Greensboro, NC	(3.4)
348	Anchorage, AK	(5.3)	71	College Station, TX	1.6	302	Greenville, NC	(3.7)
211	Ann Arbor, MI	(1.9)	163	Colonie, NY	(0.7)	11	Gresham, OR	6.7
392	Antioch, CA	(11.8)	100	Colorado Springs, CO	0.7	275	Hamilton Twnshp, NJ	(3.1)
163	Arlington Heights, IL	(0.7)	291	Columbia, MO	(3.4)	171	Hammond, IN	(0.8)
332	Arlington, TX	(4.7)	191	Columbus, GA	(1.2)	92	Hampton, VA	1.0
19	Arvada, CO	4.9	NA	Compton, CA**	NA	7	Hartford, CT	8.5
21	Asheville, NC	4.3	337	Concord, CA	(5.0)	67	Hawthorne, CA	1.8
40	Athens-Clarke, GA	3.0	249	Coral Springs, FL	(2.5)	351	Hayward, CA	(5.5)
58	Atlanta, GA	2.0	384	Corona, CA	(8.7)	371	Hemet, CA	(6.7)
115	Aurora, CO	0.0	100	Corpus Christi, TX	0.7	311	Henderson, NV	(3.9)
100	Aurora, IL	0.7	337	Costa Mesa, CA	(5.0)	NA	Hesperia, CA**	NA
324	Austin, TX	(4.4)	115	Cranston, RI	0.0	NA	Hialeah, FL**	NA
343	Avondale, AZ	(5.1)	NA	Dallas, TX**	NA	105	High Point, NC	0.5
178	Bakersfield, CA	(1.0)	302	Daly City, CA	(3.7)	10	Hillsboro, OR	6.9
285	Baldwin Park, CA	(3.3)	189	Danbury, CT	(1.1)	366	Hollywood, FL	(6.1)
84	Baltimore, MD	1.3	300	Davenport, IA	(3.6)	NA	Hoover, AL**	NA
43	Baton Rouge, LA	2.9	311	Davie, FL	(3.9)	191	Houston, TX	(1.2)
NA	Beaumont, TX**	NA	115	Dayton, OH	0.0	359	Huntington Beach, CA	(5.7)
218	Beaverton, OR	(2.0)	115	Dearborn, MI	0.0	115	Huntsville, AL	0.0
270	Bellevue, WA	(2.9)	79	Decatur, IL	1.4	300	Independence, MO	(3.6)
NA	Bellflower, CA**	NA	NA	Deerfield Beach, FL**	NA	223	Indianapolis, IN	(2.1)
115	Bellingham, WA	0.0	236	Denton, TX	(2.3)	333	Indio, CA	(4.8)
44	Berkeley, CA	2.8	345	Denver, CO	(5.2)	273	Inglewood, CA	(3.0)
345	Bethlehem, PA	(5.2)	NA	Des Moines, IA**	NA	115	Irvine, CA	0.0
115	Billings, MT	0.0	369	Detroit, MI	(6.2)	285	Irving, TX	(3.3)
191	Birmingham, AL	(1.2)	372	Downey, CA	(6.9)	373	Jacksonville, FL	(7.1)
275	Bloomington, IL	(3.1)	103	Duluth, MN	0.6	13	Jackson, MS	5.6
NA	Bloomington, IN**	NA	4	Durham, NC	10.7	228	Jersey City, NJ	(2.2)
302	Bloomington, MN	(3.7)	NA	Edinburg, TX**	NA	256	Johns Creek, GA	(2.6)
261	Boca Raton, FL	(2.7)	359	Edison Twnshp, NJ	(5.7)	240	Joliet, IL	(2.4)
318	Boise, ID	(4.3)	38	Edmond, OK	3.1	NA	Jurupa Valley, CA**	NA
256	Boston, MA	(2.6)	364	El Cajon, CA	(6.0)	NA	Kansas City, KS**	NA
86	Boulder, CO	1.2	307	El Monte, CA	(3.8)	386	Kansas City, MO	(9.0)
86	Brick Twnshp, NJ	1.2	307	El Paso, TX	(3.8)	94	Kennewick, WA	0.9
240	Bridgeport, CT	(2.4)	115	Elgin, IL	0.0	157	Kenosha, WI	(0.5)
333	Brockton, MA	(4.8)	29	Elizabeth, NJ	3.6	396	Kent, WA	(24.3)
333	Broken Arrow, OK	(4.8)	240	Elk Grove, CA	(2.4)	115	Killeen, TX	0.0
163	Brooklyn Park, MN	(0.7)	86	Erie, PA	1.2	17	Knoxville, TN	5.1
163	Brownsville, TX	(0.7)	370	Escondido, CA	(6.5)	359	Lafayette, LA	(5.7)
31	Bryan, TX	3.5	46	Eugene, OR	2.6	NA	Lake Forest, CA**	NA
178	Buena Park, CA	(1.0)	84	Evansville, IN	1.3	115	Lakeland, FL	0.0
36	Buffalo, NY	3.2	105	Everett, WA	0.5	115	Lakewood Twnshp, NJ	0.0
218	Burbank, CA	(2.0)	64	Fairfield, CA	1.9	NA	Lakewood, CA**	NA
71	Cambridge, MA	1.6	3	Fall River, MA	11.0	228	Lakewood, CO	(2.2)
86	Camden, NJ	1.2	327	Fargo, ND	(4.5)	NA	Lancaster, CA**	NA
201	Cape Coral, FL	(1.5)	71	Farmington Hills, MI	1.6	103	Lansing, MI	0.6
23	Carlsbad, CA	4.0	58	Fayetteville, AR	2.0	70	Laredo, TX	1.7
318	Carmel, IN	(4.3)	268	Fayetteville, NC	(2.8)	205	Largo, FL	(1.7)
95	Carrollton, TX	0.8	163	Federal Way, WA	(0.7)	318	Las Cruces, NM	(4.3)
NA	Carson, CA**	NA	249	Fishers, IN	(2.5)	324	Las Vegas, NV	(4.4)
71	Cary, NC	1.6	115	Flint, MI	0.0	NA	Lawrence, KS**	NA
249	Cedar Rapids, IA	(2.5)	228	Fontana, CA	(2.2)	211	Lawrence, MA	(1.9)
291	Centennial, CO	(3.4)	35	Fort Collins, CO	3.3	205	Lawton, OK	(1.7)
351	Champaign, IL	(5.5)	261	Fort Lauderdale, FL	(2.7)	48	League City, TX	2.5
236	Chandler, AZ	(2.3)	157	Fort Smith, AR	(0.5)	55	Lee's Summit, MO	2.2
153	Charleston, SC	(0.3)	327	Fort Wayne, IN	(4.5)	343	Lexington, KY	(5.1)
281	Charlotte, NC	(3.2)	115	Fort Worth, TX	0.0	281	Lincoln, NE	(3.2)
48	Cheektowaga, NY	2.5	25	Fremont, CA	3.9	53	Little Rock, AR	2.3
64	Chesapeake, VA	1.9	285	Fresno, CA	(3.3)	218	Livermore, CA	(2.0)
197	Chicago, IL	(1.3)	205	Frisco, TX	(1.7)	204	Livonia, MI	(1.6)
351	Chico, CA	(5.5)	307	Fullerton, CA	(3.8)	366	Long Beach, CA	(6.1)

RANK	CITY	% CHANGE	RANK	CITY	% CHANGE	RANK	CITY	% CHANGE
281	Longmont, CO	(3.2)	191	Pasadena, CA	(1.2)	393	South Gate, CA	(11.9)
178	Longview, TX	(1.0)	86	Pasadena, TX	1.2	NA	Sparks, NV**	NA
95	Los Angeles, CA	0.8	27	Paterson, NJ	3.7	44	Spokane Valley, WA	2.8
105	Louisville, KY	0.5	163	Pearland, TX	(0.7)	115	Spokane, WA	0.0
211	Lowell, MA	(1.9)	NA	Pembroke Pines, FL**	NA	34	Springfield, IL	3.4
18	Lubbock, TX	5.0	115	Peoria, AZ	0.0	395	Springfield, MA	(19.6)
5	Lynchburg, VA	10.5	228	Peoria, IL	(2.2)	77	Springfield, MO	1.5
92	Lynn, MA	1.0	223	Philadelphia, PA	(2.1)	261	Stamford, CT	(2.7)
298	Macon, GA	(3.5)	318	Phoenix, AZ	(4.3)	337	Sterling Heights, MI	(5.0)
223	Madison, WI	(2.1)	154	Pittsburgh, PA	(0.4)	67	Stockton, CA	1.8
46	Manchester, NH	2.6	240	Plano, TX	(2.4)	270	St. George, UT	(2.9)
324	McAllen, TX	(4.4)	351	Plantation, FL	(5.5)	115	St. Joseph, MO	0.0
115	McKinney, TX	0.0	58	Pomona, CA	2.0	240	St. Louis, MO	(2.4)
77	Medford, OR	1.5	NA	Pompano Beach, FL**	NA	178	St. Paul, MN	(1.0)
NA	Melbourne, FL**	NA	NA	Port St. Lucie, FL**	NA	79	St. Petersburg, FL	1.4
240	Memphis, TN	(2.4)	115	Portland, OR	0.0	261	Sugar Land, TX	(2.7)
NA	Menifee, CA**	NA	23	Portsmouth, VA	4.0	223	Sunnyvale, CA	(2.1)
307	Merced, CA	(3.8)	387	Providence, RI	(9.4)	105	Sunrise, FL	0.5
115	Meridian, ID	0.0	115	Provo, UT	0.0	25	Surprise, AZ	3.9
40	Mesa, AZ	3.0	390	Pueblo, CO	(11.4)	348	Syracuse, NY	(5.3)
356	Mesquite, TX	(5.6)	48	Quincy, MA	2.5	375	Tacoma, WA	(7.4)
105	Miami Beach, FL	0.5	218	Racine, WI	(2.0)	157	Tallahassee, FL	(0.5)
318	Miami Gardens, FL	(4.3)	261	Raleigh, NC	(2.7)	228	Tampa, FL	(2.2)
275	Miami, FL	(3.1)	275	Ramapo, NY	(3.1)	NA	Temecula, CA**	NA
285	Midland, TX	(3.3)	NA	Rancho Cucamon., CA**	NA	201	Tempe, AZ	(1.5)
64	Milwaukee, WI	1.9	13	Reading, PA	5.6	331	Thornton, CO	(4.6)
199	Minneapolis, MN	(1.4)	115	Redding, CA	0.0	NA	Thousand Oaks, CA**	NA
337	Miramar, FL	(5.0)	175	Redwood City, CA	(0.9)	1	Toledo, OH	38.2
NA	Mission Viejo, CA**	NA	71	Reno, NV	1.6	161	Toms River Twnshp, NJ	(0.6)
115	Mission, TX	0.0	366	Renton, WA	(6.1)	154	Topeka, KS	(0.4)
275	Mobile, AL	(3.1)	380	Rialto, CA	(8.2)	291	Torrance, CA	(3.4)
175	Modesto, CA	(0.9)	261	Richardson, TX	(2.7)	373	Tracy, CA	(7.1)
191	Montgomery, AL	(1.2)	364	Richmond, CA	(6.0)	115	Trenton, NJ	0.0
NA	Moreno Valley, CA**	NA	205	Richmond, VA	(1.7)	394	Troy, MI	(12.7)
115	Mountain View, CA	0.0	79	Rio Rancho, NM	1.4	115	Tucson, AZ	0.0
270	Murfreesboro, TN	(2.9)	205	Riverside, CA	(1.7)	21	Tulsa, OK	4.3
302	Murrieta, CA	(3.7)	112	Roanoke, VA	0.4	161	Tuscaloosa, AL	(0.6)
337	Nampa, ID	(5.0)	95	Rochester, MN	0.8	376	Tustin, CA	(7.5)
356	Napa, CA	(5.6)	113	Rochester, NY	0.3	223	Tyler, TX	(2.1)
256	Naperville, IL	(2.6)	31	Rockford, IL	3.5	379	Upland, CA	(7.9)
38	Nashua, NH	3.1	315	Roseville, CA	(4.1)	115	Upper Darby Twnshp, PA	0.0
211	Nashville, TN	(1.9)	NA	Roswell, GA**	NA	178	Vacaville, CA	(1.0)
86	New Bedford, MA	1.2	NA	Round Rock, TX**	NA	115	Vallejo, CA	0.0
2	New Haven, CT	13.4	382	Sacramento, CA	(8.3)	327	Vancouver, WA	(4.5)
389	New Orleans, LA	(10.0)	249	Salem, OR	(2.5)	115	Ventura, CA	0.0
178	New Rochelle, NY	(1.0)	178	Salinas, CA	(1.0)	NA	Victorville, CA**	NA
178	New York, NY	(1.0)	79	Salt Lake City, UT	1.4	115	Virginia Beach, VA	0.0
285	Newark, NJ	(3.3)	298	San Antonio, TX	(3.5)	211	Visalia, CA	(1.9)
163	Newport Beach, CA	(0.7)	383	San Bernardino, CA	(8.6)	NA	Vista, CA**	NA
15	Newport News, VA	5.5	115	San Diego, CA	0.0	189	Waco, TX	(1.1)
211	Newton, MA	(1.9)	228	San Francisco, CA	(2.2)	31	Warren, MI	3.5
58	Norfolk, VA	2.0	256	San Jose, CA	(2.6)	9	Warwick, RI	7.2
350	Norman, OK	(5.4)	211	San Leandro, CA	(1.9)	178	Washington, DC	(1.0)
380	North Charleston, SC	(8.2)	NA	San Marcos, CA**	NA	291	Waterbury, CT	(3.4)
NA	North Las Vegas, NV**	NA	115	San Mateo, CA	0.0	8	Waukegan, IL	7.4
NA	Norwalk, CA**	NA	71	Sandy Springs, GA	1.6	378	West Covina, CA	(7.8)
57	Norwalk, CT	2.1	95	Sandy, UT	0.8	55	West Jordan, UT	2.2
318	Oakland, CA	(4.3)	362	Santa Ana, CA	(5.9)	302	West Palm Beach, FL	(3.7)
171	Oceanside, CA	(0.8)	197	Santa Barbara, CA	(1.3)	199	West Valley, UT	(1.4)
115	Odessa, TX	0.0	29	Santa Clara, CA	3.6	115	Westland, MI	0.0
163	O'Fallon, MO	(0.7)	NA	Santa Clarita, CA**	NA	362	Westminster, CA	(5.9)
249	Ogden, UT	(2.5)	385	Santa Maria, CA	(8.9)	236	Westminster, CO	(2.3)
291	Oklahoma City, OK	(3.4)	175	Santa Monica, CA	(0.9)	16	Whittier, CA	5.2
NA	Olathe, KS**	NA	275	Santa Rosa, CA	(3.1)	53	Wichita Falls, TX	2.3
105	Omaha, NE	0.5	58	Savannah, GA	2.0	191	Wichita, KS	(1.2)
201	Ontario, CA	(1.5)	261	Scottsdale, AZ	(2.7)	249	Wilmington, NC	(2.5)
256	Orange, CA	(2.6)	115	Scranton, PA	0.0	376	Winston-Salem, NC	(7.5)
315	Orem, UT	(4.1)	240	Seattle, WA	(2.4)	317	Woodbridge Twnshp, NJ	(4.2)
113	Orlando, FL	0.3	390	Shreveport, LA	(11.4)	228	Worcester, MA	(2.2)
NA	Overland Park, KS**	NA	6	Simi Valley, CA	10.3	19	Yakima, WA	4.9
291	Oxnard, CA	(3.4)	79	Sioux City, IA	1.4	249	Yonkers, NY	(2.5)
345	Palm Bay, FL	(5.2)	218	Sioux Falls, SD	(2.0)	240	Yuma, AZ	(2.4)
NA	Palmdale, CA**	NA	210	Somerville, MA	(1.8)			
NA	Parma, OH**	NA	240	South Bend, IN	(2.4)			

Source: CQ Press using reported data from the F.B.I. "Crime in the United States 2012"

*Sworn officers only, does not include civilian employees.

**Not available

83. Percent Change in Rate of Police Officers: 2011 to 2012 (continued)
National Percent Change = 1.3% Decrease*

RANK	CITY	% CHANGE	RANK	CITY	% CHANGE	RANK	CITY	% CHANGE
1	Toledo, OH	38.2	71	Reno, NV	1.6	115	Vallejo, CA	0.0
2	New Haven, CT	13.4	71	Sandy Springs, GA	1.6	115	Ventura, CA	0.0
3	Fall River, MA	11.0	77	Medford, OR	1.5	115	Virginia Beach, VA	0.0
4	Durham, NC	10.7	77	Springfield, MO	1.5	115	Westland, MI	0.0
5	Lynchburg, VA	10.5	79	Decatur, IL	1.4	153	Charleston, SC	(0.3)
6	Simi Valley, CA	10.3	79	Rio Rancho, NM	1.4	154	Gainesville, FL	(0.4)
7	Hartford, CT	8.5	79	Salt Lake City, UT	1.4	154	Pittsburgh, PA	(0.4)
8	Waukegan, IL	7.4	79	Sioux City, IA	1.4	154	Topeka, KS	(0.4)
9	Warwick, RI	7.2	79	St. Petersburg, FL	1.4	157	Clearwater, FL	(0.5)
10	Hillsboro, OR	6.9	84	Baltimore, MD	1.3	157	Fort Smith, AR	(0.5)
11	Gresham, OR	6.7	84	Evansville, IN	1.3	157	Kenosha, WI	(0.5)
12	Allentown, PA	6.0	86	Boulder, CO	1.2	157	Tallahassee, FL	(0.5)
13	Jackson, MS	5.6	86	Brick Twnshp, NJ	1.2	161	Toms River Twnshp, NJ	(0.6)
13	Reading, PA	5.6	86	Camden, NJ	1.2	161	Tuscaloosa, AL	(0.6)
15	Newport News, VA	5.5	86	Erie, PA	1.2	163	Arlington Heights, IL	(0.7)
16	Whittier, CA	5.2	86	New Bedford, MA	1.2	163	Brooklyn Park, MN	(0.7)
17	Knoxville, TN	5.1	86	Pasadena, TX	1.2	163	Brownsville, TX	(0.7)
18	Lubbock, TX	5.0	92	Hampton, VA	1.0	163	Colonie, NY	(0.7)
19	Arvada, CO	4.9	92	Lynn, MA	1.0	163	Federal Way, WA	(0.7)
19	Yakima, WA	4.9	94	Kennewick, WA	0.9	163	Newport Beach, CA	(0.7)
21	Asheville, NC	4.3	95	Carrollton, TX	0.8	163	O'Fallon, MO	(0.7)
21	Tulsa, OK	4.3	95	Glendale, CA	0.8	163	Pearland, TX	(0.7)
23	Carlsbad, CA	4.0	95	Los Angeles, CA	0.8	171	Chino, CA	(0.8)
23	Portsmouth, VA	4.0	95	Rochester, MN	0.8	171	Grand Prairie, TX	(0.8)
25	Fremont, CA	3.9	95	Sandy, UT	0.8	171	Hammond, IN	(0.8)
25	Surprise, AZ	3.9	100	Aurora, IL	0.7	171	Oceanside, CA	(0.8)
27	Albany, GA	3.7	100	Colorado Springs, CO	0.7	175	Modesto, CA	(0.9)
27	Paterson, NJ	3.7	100	Corpus Christi, TX	0.7	175	Redwood City, CA	(0.9)
29	Elizabeth, NJ	3.6	103	Duluth, MN	0.6	175	Santa Monica, CA	(0.9)
29	Santa Clara, CA	3.6	103	Lansing, MI	0.6	178	Bakersfield, CA	(1.0)
31	Bryan, TX	3.5	105	Clarksville, TN	0.5	178	Buena Park, CA	(1.0)
31	Rockford, IL	3.5	105	Everett, WA	0.5	178	Citrus Heights, CA	(1.0)
31	Warren, MI	3.5	105	High Point, NC	0.5	178	Greece, NY	(1.0)
34	Springfield, IL	3.4	105	Louisville, KY	0.5	178	Longview, TX	(1.0)
35	Fort Collins, CO	3.3	105	Miami Beach, FL	0.5	178	New Rochelle, NY	(1.0)
36	Allen, TX	3.2	105	Omaha, NE	0.5	178	New York, NY	(1.0)
36	Buffalo, NY	3.2	105	Sunrise, FL	0.5	178	Salinas, CA	(1.0)
38	Edmond, OK	3.1	112	Roanoke, VA	0.4	178	St. Paul, MN	(1.0)
38	Nashua, NH	3.1	113	Orlando, FL	0.3	178	Vacaville, CA	(1.0)
40	Athens-Clarke, GA	3.0	113	Rochester, NY	0.3	178	Washington, DC	(1.0)
40	Cleveland, OH	3.0	115	Amarillo, TX	0.0	189	Danbury, CT	(1.1)
40	Mesa, AZ	3.0	115	Amherst, NY	0.0	189	Waco, TX	(1.1)
43	Baton Rouge, LA	2.9	115	Aurora, CO	0.0	191	Birmingham, AL	(1.2)
44	Berkeley, CA	2.8	115	Bellingham, WA	0.0	191	Columbus, GA	(1.2)
44	Spokane Valley, WA	2.8	115	Billings, MT	0.0	191	Houston, TX	(1.2)
46	Eugene, OR	2.6	115	Cranston, RI	0.0	191	Montgomery, AL	(1.2)
46	Manchester, NH	2.6	115	Dayton, OH	0.0	191	Pasadena, CA	(1.2)
48	Cheektowaga, NY	2.5	115	Dearborn, MI	0.0	191	Wichita, KS	(1.2)
48	League City, TX	2.5	115	Elgin, IL	0.0	197	Chicago, IL	(1.3)
48	Quincy, MA	2.5	115	Flint, MI	0.0	197	Santa Barbara, CA	(1.3)
51	Akron, OH	2.4	115	Fort Worth, TX	0.0	199	Minneapolis, MN	(1.4)
51	Alexandria, VA	2.4	115	Gilbert, AZ	0.0	199	West Valley, UT	(1.4)
53	Little Rock, AR	2.3	115	Huntsville, AL	0.0	201	Cape Coral, FL	(1.5)
53	Wichita Falls, TX	2.3	115	Irvine, CA	0.0	201	Ontario, CA	(1.5)
55	Lee's Summit, MO	2.2	115	Killeen, TX	0.0	201	Tempe, AZ	(1.5)
55	West Jordan, UT	2.2	115	Lakeland, FL	0.0	204	Livonia, MI	(1.6)
57	Norwalk, CT	2.1	115	Lakewood Twnshp, NJ	0.0	205	Frisco, TX	(1.7)
58	Atlanta, GA	2.0	115	McKinney, TX	0.0	205	Largo, FL	(1.7)
58	Fayetteville, AR	2.0	115	Meridian, ID	0.0	205	Lawton, OK	(1.7)
58	Greeley, CO	2.0	115	Mission, TX	0.0	205	Richmond, VA	(1.7)
58	Norfolk, VA	2.0	115	Mountain View, CA	0.0	205	Riverside, CA	(1.7)
58	Pomona, CA	2.0	115	Odessa, TX	0.0	210	Somerville, MA	(1.8)
58	Savannah, GA	2.0	115	Peoria, AZ	0.0	211	Ann Arbor, MI	(1.9)
64	Chesapeake, VA	1.9	115	Portland, OR	0.0	211	Lawrence, MA	(1.9)
64	Fairfield, CA	1.9	115	Provo, UT	0.0	211	Lowell, MA	(1.9)
64	Milwaukee, WI	1.9	115	Redding, CA	0.0	211	Nashville, TN	(1.9)
67	Clifton, NJ	1.8	115	San Diego, CA	0.0	211	Newton, MA	(1.9)
67	Hawthorne, CA	1.8	115	San Mateo, CA	0.0	211	San Leandro, CA	(1.9)
67	Stockton, CA	1.8	115	Scranton, PA	0.0	211	Visalia, CA	(1.9)
70	Laredo, TX	1.7	115	Spokane, WA	0.0	218	Beaverton, OR	(2.0)
71	Cambridge, MA	1.6	115	St. Joseph, MO	0.0	218	Burbank, CA	(2.0)
71	Cary, NC	1.6	115	Trenton, NJ	0.0	218	Livermore, CA	(2.0)
71	College Station, TX	1.6	115	Tucson, AZ	0.0	218	Racine, WI	(2.0)
71	Farmington Hills, MI	1.6	115	Upper Darby Twnshp, PA	0.0	218	Sioux Falls, SD	(2.0)

RANK	CITY	% CHANGE	RANK	CITY	% CHANGE	RANK	CITY	% CHANGE
223	Indianapolis, IN	(2.1)	291	Waterbury, CT	(3.4)	371	Hemet, CA	(6.7)
223	Madison, WI	(2.1)	298	Macon, GA	(3.5)	372	Downey, CA	(6.9)
223	Philadelphia, PA	(2.1)	298	San Antonio, TX	(3.5)	373	Jacksonville, FL	(7.1)
223	Sunnyvale, CA	(2.1)	300	Davenport, IA	(3.6)	373	Tracy, CA	(7.1)
223	Tyler, TX	(2.1)	300	Independence, MO	(3.6)	375	Tacoma, WA	(7.4)
228	Clinton Twnshp, MI	(2.2)	302	Bloomington, MN	(3.7)	376	Tustin, CA	(7.5)
228	Fontana, CA	(2.2)	302	Daly City, CA	(3.7)	376	Winston-Salem, NC	(7.5)
228	Jersey City, NJ	(2.2)	302	Greenville, NC	(3.7)	378	West Covina, CA	(7.8)
228	Lakewood, CO	(2.2)	302	Murrieta, CA	(3.7)	379	Upland, CA	(7.9)
228	Peoria, IL	(2.2)	302	West Palm Beach, FL	(3.7)	380	North Charleston, SC	(8.2)
228	San Francisco, CA	(2.2)	307	El Monte, CA	(3.8)	380	Rialto, CA	(8.2)
228	Tampa, FL	(2.2)	307	El Paso, TX	(3.8)	382	Sacramento, CA	(8.3)
228	Worcester, MA	(2.2)	307	Fullerton, CA	(3.8)	383	San Bernardino, CA	(8.6)
236	Chandler, AZ	(2.3)	307	Merced, CA	(3.8)	384	Corona, CA	(8.7)
236	Denton, TX	(2.3)	311	Clarkstown, NY	(3.9)	385	Santa Maria, CA	(8.9)
236	Glendale, AZ	(2.3)	311	Davie, FL	(3.9)	386	Kansas City, MO	(9.0)
236	Westminster, CO	(2.3)	311	Henderson, NV	(3.9)	387	Providence, RI	(9.4)
240	Bridgeport, CT	(2.4)	314	Cincinnati, OH	(4.0)	388	Clovis, CA	(9.8)
240	Elk Grove, CA	(2.4)	315	Orem, UT	(4.1)	389	New Orleans, LA	(10.0)
240	Joliet, IL	(2.4)	315	Roseville, CA	(4.1)	390	Pueblo, CO	(11.4)
240	Memphis, TN	(2.4)	317	Woodbridge Twnshp, NJ	(4.2)	390	Shreveport, LA	(11.4)
240	Plano, TX	(2.4)	318	Boise, ID	(4.3)	392	Antioch, CA	(11.8)
240	Seattle, WA	(2.4)	318	Carmel, IN	(4.3)	393	South Gate, CA	(11.9)
240	South Bend, IN	(2.4)	318	Las Cruces, NM	(4.3)	394	Troy, MI	(12.7)
240	St. Louis, MO	(2.4)	318	Miami Gardens, FL	(4.3)	395	Springfield, MA	(19.6)
240	Yuma, AZ	(2.4)	318	Oakland, CA	(4.3)	396	Kent, WA	(24.3)
249	Cedar Rapids, IA	(2.5)	318	Phoenix, AZ	(4.3)	NA	Abilene, TX**	NA
249	Coral Springs, FL	(2.5)	324	Austin, TX	(4.4)	NA	Albany, NY**	NA
249	Fishers, IN	(2.5)	324	Las Vegas, NV	(4.4)	NA	Beaumont, TX**	NA
249	Ogden, UT	(2.5)	324	McAllen, TX	(4.4)	NA	Bellflower, CA**	NA
249	Salem, OR	(2.5)	327	Alameda, CA	(4.5)	NA	Bloomington, IN**	NA
249	Wilmington, NC	(2.5)	327	Fargo, ND	(4.5)	NA	Carson, CA**	NA
249	Yonkers, NY	(2.5)	327	Fort Wayne, IN	(4.5)	NA	Chino Hills, CA**	NA
256	Boston, MA	(2.6)	327	Vancouver, WA	(4.5)	NA	Cicero, IL**	NA
256	Johns Creek, GA	(2.6)	331	Thornton, CO	(4.6)	NA	Compton, CA**	NA
256	Naperville, IL	(2.6)	332	Arlington, TX	(4.7)	NA	Dallas, TX**	NA
256	Orange, CA	(2.6)	333	Brockton, MA	(4.8)	NA	Deerfield Beach, FL**	NA
256	San Jose, CA	(2.6)	333	Broken Arrow, OK	(4.8)	NA	Des Moines, IA**	NA
261	Boca Raton, FL	(2.7)	333	Indio, CA	(4.8)	NA	Edinburg, TX**	NA
261	Fort Lauderdale, FL	(2.7)	336	Grand Rapids, MI	(4.9)	NA	Gary, IN**	NA
261	Raleigh, NC	(2.7)	337	Concord, CA	(5.0)	NA	Hesperia, CA**	NA
261	Richardson, TX	(2.7)	337	Costa Mesa, CA	(5.0)	NA	Hialeah, FL**	NA
261	Scottsdale, AZ	(2.7)	337	Garland, TX	(5.0)	NA	Hoover, AL**	NA
261	Stamford, CT	(2.7)	337	Miramar, FL	(5.0)	NA	Jurupa Valley, CA**	NA
261	Sugar Land, TX	(2.7)	337	Nampa, ID	(5.0)	NA	Kansas City, KS**	NA
268	Fayetteville, NC	(2.8)	337	Sterling Heights, MI	(5.0)	NA	Lake Forest, CA**	NA
268	Green Bay, WI	(2.8)	343	Avondale, AZ	(5.1)	NA	Lakewood, CA**	NA
270	Bellevue, WA	(2.9)	343	Lexington, KY	(5.1)	NA	Lancaster, CA**	NA
270	Murfreesboro, TN	(2.9)	345	Bethlehem, PA	(5.2)	NA	Lawrence, KS**	NA
270	St. George, UT	(2.9)	345	Denver, CO	(5.2)	NA	Melbourne, FL**	NA
273	Alhambra, CA	(3.0)	345	Palm Bay, FL	(5.2)	NA	Menifee, CA**	NA
273	Inglewood, CA	(3.0)	348	Anchorage, AK	(5.3)	NA	Mission Viejo, CA**	NA
275	Bloomington, IL	(3.1)	348	Syracuse, NY	(5.3)	NA	Moreno Valley, CA**	NA
275	Hamilton Twnshp, NJ	(3.1)	350	Norman, OK	(5.4)	NA	North Las Vegas, NV**	NA
275	Miami, FL	(3.1)	351	Anaheim, CA	(5.5)	NA	Norwalk, CA**	NA
275	Mobile, AL	(3.1)	351	Champaign, IL	(5.5)	NA	Olathe, KS**	NA
275	Ramapo, NY	(3.1)	351	Chico, CA	(5.5)	NA	Overland Park, KS**	NA
275	Santa Rosa, CA	(3.1)	351	Hayward, CA	(5.5)	NA	Palmdale, CA**	NA
281	Albuquerque, NM	(3.2)	351	Plantation, FL	(5.5)	NA	Parma, OH**	NA
281	Charlotte, NC	(3.2)	356	Chula Vista, CA	(5.6)	NA	Pembroke Pines, FL**	NA
281	Lincoln, NE	(3.2)	356	Mesquite, TX	(5.6)	NA	Pompano Beach, FL**	NA
281	Longmont, CO	(3.2)	356	Napa, CA	(5.6)	NA	Port St. Lucie, FL**	NA
285	Baldwin Park, CA	(3.3)	359	Edison Twnshp, NJ	(5.7)	NA	Rancho Cucamon., CA**	NA
285	Fresno, CA	(3.3)	359	Huntington Beach, CA	(5.7)	NA	Roswell, GA**	NA
285	Garden Grove, CA	(3.3)	359	Lafayette, LA	(5.7)	NA	Round Rock, TX**	NA
285	Irving, TX	(3.3)	362	Santa Ana, CA	(5.9)	NA	San Marcos, CA**	NA
285	Midland, TX	(3.3)	362	Westminster, CA	(5.9)	NA	Santa Clarita, CA**	NA
285	Newark, NJ	(3.3)	364	El Cajon, CA	(6.0)	NA	Sparks, NV**	NA
291	Centennial, CO	(3.4)	364	Richmond, CA	(6.0)	NA	Temecula, CA**	NA
291	Columbia, MO	(3.4)	366	Hollywood, FL	(6.1)	NA	Thousand Oaks, CA**	NA
291	Greensboro, NC	(3.4)	366	Long Beach, CA	(6.1)	NA	Victorville, CA**	NA
291	Oklahoma City, OK	(3.4)	366	Renton, WA	(6.1)	NA	Vista, CA**	NA
291	Oxnard, CA	(3.4)	369	Detroit, MI	(6.2)			
291	Torrance, CA	(3.4)	370	Escondido, CA	(6.5)			

Source: CQ Press using reported data from the F.B.I. "Crime in the United States 2012"

*Sworn officers only, does not include civilian employees.

**Not available

84. Percent Change in Rate of Police Officers: 2008 to 2012
National Percent Change = 5.2% Decrease*

RANK	CITY	% CHANGE	RANK	CITY	% CHANGE	RANK	CITY	% CHANGE
NA	Abilene, TX**	NA	NA	Chino Hills, CA**	NA	41	Gainesville, FL	4.1
219	Akron, OH	(7.5)	11	Chino, CA	11.3	332	Garden Grove, CA	(15.5)
367	Alameda, CA	(20.1)	382	Chula Vista, CA	(23.6)	261	Garland, TX	(9.6)
158	Albany, GA	(4.7)	162	Cicero, IL	(4.8)	NA	Gary, IN**	NA
NA	Albany, NY**	NA	54	Cincinnati, OH	2.8	59	Gilbert, AZ	2.0
227	Albuquerque, NM	(7.7)	59	Citrus Heights, CA	2.0	5	Glendale, AZ	17.2
162	Alexandria, VA	(4.8)	238	Clarkstown, NY	(8.3)	191	Glendale, CA	(6.1)
81	Alhambra, CA	0.0	112	Clarksville, TN	(1.5)	278	Grand Prairie, TX	(10.5)
165	Allentown, PA	(4.9)	313	Clearwater, FL	(14.0)	230	Grand Rapids, MI	(7.8)
36	Allen, TX	4.8	70	Cleveland, OH	1.1	41	Greece, NY	4.1
81	Amarillo, TX	0.0	333	Clifton, NJ	(15.8)	387	Greeley, CO	(26.7)
200	Amherst, NY	(6.5)	370	Clinton Twnshp, MI	(21.1)	99	Green Bay, WI	(0.6)
358	Anaheim, CA	(18.1)	349	Clovis, CA	(17.1)	179	Greensboro, NC	(5.5)
257	Anchorage, AK	(9.5)	209	College Station, TX	(6.8)	186	Greenville, NC	(5.9)
368	Ann Arbor, MI	(20.9)	110	Colonie, NY	(1.4)	208	Gresham, OR	(6.7)
390	Antioch, CA	(29.9)	341	Colorado Springs, CO	(16.4)	181	Hamilton Twnshp, NJ	(5.6)
261	Arlington Heights, IL	(9.6)	203	Columbia, MO	(6.6)	213	Hammond, IN	(6.9)
77	Arlington, TX	0.6	15	Columbus, GA	10.2	28	Hampton, VA	6.3
55	Arvada, CO	2.7	NA	Compton, CA**	NA	9	Hartford, CT	12.7
216	Asheville, NC	(7.2)	337	Concord, CA	(16.1)	81	Hawthorne, CA	0.0
24	Athens-Clarke, GA	6.8	65	Coral Springs, FL	1.3	277	Hayward, CA	(10.4)
1	Atlanta, GA	33.6	362	Corona, CA	(19.0)	397	Hemet, CA	(35.8)
119	Aurora, CO	(2.0)	286	Corpus Christi, TX	(11.5)	320	Henderson, NV	(14.5)
323	Aurora, IL	(14.7)	381	Costa Mesa, CA	(23.5)	NA	Hesperia, CA**	NA
81	Austin, TX	0.0	154	Cranston, RI	(4.4)	NA	Hialeah, FL**	NA
6	Avondale, AZ	17.0	NA	Dallas, TX**	NA	112	High Point, NC	(1.5)
252	Bakersfield, CA	(9.3)	233	Daly City, CA	(8.0)	7	Hillsboro, OR	13.9
172	Baldwin Park, CA	(5.3)	194	Danbury, CT	(6.3)	267	Hollywood, FL	(9.9)
80	Baltimore, MD	0.4	123	Davenport, IA	(2.4)	NA	Hoover, AL**	NA
46	Baton Rouge, LA	3.6	133	Davie, FL	(2.8)	21	Houston, TX	8.4
NA	Beaumont, TX**	NA	284	Dayton, OH	(11.4)	312	Huntington Beach, CA	(13.8)
26	Beaverton, OR	6.5	334	Dearborn, MI	(15.9)	171	Huntsville, AL	(5.2)
255	Bellevue, WA	(9.4)	145	Decatur, IL	(3.7)	319	Independence, MO	(14.4)
NA	Bellflower, CA**	NA	NA	Deerfield Beach, FL**	NA	144	Indianapolis, IN	(3.6)
182	Bellingham, WA	(5.7)	103	Denton, TX	(0.8)	186	Indio, CA	(5.9)
365	Berkeley, CA	(19.5)	327	Denver, CO	(15.0)	172	Inglewood, CA	(5.3)
153	Bethlehem, PA	(4.3)	NA	Des Moines, IA**	NA	31	Irvine, CA	5.7
81	Billings, MT	0.0	21	Detroit, MI	8.4	313	Irving, TX	(14.0)
4	Birmingham, AL	17.3	169	Downey, CA	(5.1)	300	Jacksonville, FL	(12.9)
200	Bloomington, IL	(6.5)	99	Duluth, MN	(0.6)	32	Jackson, MS	5.6
NA	Bloomington, IN**	NA	10	Durham, NC	12.3	308	Jersey City, NJ	(13.4)
240	Bloomington, MN	(8.5)	NA	Edinburg, TX**	NA	363	Johns Creek, GA	(19.1)
37	Boca Raton, FL	4.3	297	Edison Twnshp, NJ	(12.6)	354	Joliet, IL	(17.8)
257	Boise, ID	(9.5)	248	Edmond, OK	(8.9)	NA	Jurupa Valley, CA**	NA
227	Boston, MA	(7.7)	335	El Cajon, CA	(16.0)	NA	Kansas City, KS**	NA
81	Boulder, CO	0.0	328	El Monte, CA	(15.1)	200	Kansas City, MO	(6.5)
46	Brick Twnshp, NJ	3.6	346	El Paso, TX	(16.8)	359	Kennewick, WA	(18.2)
239	Bridgeport, CT	(8.4)	156	Elgin, IL	(4.6)	94	Kenosha, WI	(0.5)
209	Brockton, MA	(6.8)	219	Elizabeth, NJ	(7.5)	392	Kent, WA	(30.7)
290	Broken Arrow, OK	(11.8)	291	Elk Grove, CA	(12.0)	25	Killeen, TX	6.7
110	Brooklyn Park, MN	(1.4)	16	Erie, PA	9.7	13	Knoxville, TN	10.8
63	Brownsville, TX	1.5	300	Escondido, CA	(12.9)	231	Lafayette, LA	(7.9)
50	Bryan, TX	3.5	61	Eugene, OR	1.7	NA	Lake Forest, CA**	NA
310	Buena Park, CA	(13.7)	73	Evansville, IN	0.8	244	Lakeland, FL	(8.8)
123	Buffalo, NY	(2.4)	249	Everett, WA	(9.0)	NA	Lakewood Twnshp, NJ**	NA
131	Burbank, CA	(2.7)	209	Fairfield, CA	(6.8)	NA	Lakewood, CA**	NA
162	Cambridge, MA	(4.8)	233	Fall River, MA	(8.0)	280	Lakewood, CO	(10.8)
394	Camden, NJ	(33.7)	251	Fargo, ND	(9.2)	NA	Lancaster, CA**	NA
255	Cape Coral, FL	(9.4)	323	Farmington Hills, MI	(14.7)	369	Lansing, MI	(21.0)
297	Carlsbad, CA	(12.6)	137	Fayetteville, AR	(3.1)	172	Laredo, TX	(5.3)
342	Carmel, IN	(16.5)	272	Fayetteville, NC	(10.3)	293	Largo, FL	(12.4)
73	Carrollton, TX	0.8	295	Federal Way, WA	(12.5)	81	Las Cruces, NM	0.0
NA	Carson, CA**	NA	243	Fishers, IN	(8.7)	219	Las Vegas, NV	(7.5)
73	Cary, NC	0.8	395	Flint, MI	(33.9)	18	Lawrence, KS	9.0
65	Cedar Rapids, IA	1.3	329	Fontana, CA	(15.2)	391	Lawrence, MA	(30.1)
115	Centennial, CO	(1.7)	29	Fort Collins, CO	5.9	149	Lawton, OK	(3.9)
305	Champaign, IL	(13.2)	14	Fort Lauderdale, FL	10.6	137	League City, TX	(3.1)
121	Chandler, AZ	(2.3)	94	Fort Smith, AR	(0.5)	81	Lee's Summit, MO	0.0
158	Charleston, SC	(4.7)	149	Fort Wayne, IN	(3.9)	326	Lexington, KY	(14.9)
118	Charlotte, NC	(1.9)	191	Fort Worth, TX	(6.1)	140	Lincoln, NE	(3.2)
116	Cheektowaga, NY	(1.8)	268	Fremont, CA	(10.1)	158	Little Rock, AR	(4.7)
219	Chesapeake, VA	(7.5)	339	Fresno, CA	(16.2)	323	Livermore, CA	(14.7)
203	Chicago, IL	(6.6)	317	Frisco, TX	(14.2)	371	Livonia, MI	(21.3)
145	Chico, CA	(3.7)	335	Fullerton, CA	(16.0)	351	Long Beach, CA	(17.5)

RANK	CITY	% CHANGE	RANK	CITY	% CHANGE	RANK	CITY	% CHANGE
148	Longmont, CO	(3.8)	135	Pasadena, CA	(2.9)	384	South Gate, CA	(24.5)
257	Longview, TX	(9.5)	106	Pasadena, TX	(1.1)	196	Sparks, NV	(6.4)
57	Los Angeles, CA	2.4	379	Paterson, NJ	(23.2)	224	Spokane Valley, WA	(7.6)
137	Louisville, KY	(3.1)	53	Pearland, TX	2.9	288	Spokane, WA	(11.6)
156	Lowell, MA	(4.6)	NA	Pembroke Pines, FL**	NA	203	Springfield, IL	(6.6)
44	Lubbock, TX	3.7	165	Peoria, AZ	(4.9)	378	Springfield, MA	(23.0)
65	Lynchburg, VA	1.3	353	Peoria, IL	(17.7)	79	Springfield, MO	0.5
112	Lynn, MA	(1.5)	261	Philadelphia, PA	(9.6)	261	Stamford, CT	(9.6)
81	Macon, GA	0.0	158	Phoenix, AZ	(4.7)	286	Sterling Heights, MI	(11.5)
106	Madison, WI	(1.1)	46	Pittsburgh, PA	3.6	371	Stockton, CA	(21.3)
142	Manchester, NH	(3.5)	149	Plano, TX	(3.9)	102	St. George, UT	(0.7)
136	McAllen, TX	(3.0)	299	Plantation, FL	(12.8)	81	St. Joseph, MO	0.0
203	McKinney, TX	(6.6)	357	Pomona, CA	(18.0)	34	St. Louis, MO	5.3
58	Medford, OR	2.3	NA	Pompano Beach, FL**	NA	179	St. Paul, MN	(5.5)
NA	Melbourne, FL**	NA	NA	Port St. Lucie, FL**	NA	37	St. Petersburg, FL	4.3
3	Memphis, TN	17.6	257	Portland, OR	(9.5)	17	Sugar Land, TX	9.1
NA	Menifee, CA**	NA	8	Portsmouth, VA	13.5	352	Sunnyvale, CA	(17.6)
374	Merced, CA	(22.7)	329	Providence, RI	(15.2)	56	Sunrise, FL	2.6
20	Meridian, ID	8.8	68	Provo, UT	1.2	361	Surprise, AZ	(18.9)
165	Mesa, AZ	(4.9)	224	Pueblo, CO	(7.6)	268	Syracuse, NY	(10.1)
292	Mesquite, TX	(12.2)	123	Quincy, MA	(2.4)	272	Tacoma, WA	(10.3)
217	Miami Beach, FL	(7.3)	33	Racine, WI	5.5	284	Tallahassee, FL	(11.4)
50	Miami Gardens, FL	3.5	81	Raleigh, NC	0.0	193	Tampa, FL	(6.2)
68	Miami, FL	1.2	NA	Ramapo, NY**	NA	NA	Temecula, CA**	NA
64	Midland, TX	1.4	NA	Rancho Cucamon., CA**	NA	94	Tempe, AZ	(0.5)
169	Milwaukee, WI	(5.1)	383	Reading, PA	(24.0)	244	Thornton, CO	(8.8)
224	Minneapolis, MN	(7.6)	348	Redding, CA	(16.9)	NA	Thousand Oaks, CA**	NA
154	Miramar, FL	(4.4)	307	Redwood City, CA	(13.3)	105	Toledo, OH	(1.0)
NA	Mission Viejo, CA**	NA	375	Reno, NV	(22.8)	116	Toms River Twnshp, NJ	(1.8)
131	Mission, TX	(2.7)	399	Renton, WA	(37.1)	128	Topeka, KS	(2.6)
29	Mobile, AL	5.9	345	Rialto, CA	(16.7)	302	Torrance, CA	(13.0)
342	Modesto, CA	(16.5)	35	Richardson, TX	5.0	293	Tracy, CA	(12.4)
44	Montgomery, AL	3.7	37	Richmond, CA	4.3	398	Trenton, NJ	(36.0)
NA	Moreno Valley, CA**	NA	182	Richmond, VA	(5.7)	396	Troy, MI	(34.5)
268	Mountain View, CA	(10.1)	261	Rio Rancho, NM	(9.6)	237	Tucson, AZ	(8.2)
231	Murfreesboro, TN	(7.9)	252	Riverside, CA	(9.3)	244	Tulsa, OK	(8.8)
189	Murrieta, CA	(6.0)	235	Roanoke, VA	(8.1)	26	Tuscaloosa, AL	6.5
309	Nampa, ID	(13.5)	103	Rochester, MN	(0.8)	354	Tustin, CA	(17.8)
316	Napa, CA	(14.1)	176	Rochester, NY	(5.4)	94	Tyler, TX	(0.5)
305	Naperville, IL	(13.2)	217	Rockford, IL	(7.3)	304	Upland, CA	(13.1)
72	Nashua, NH	1.0	346	Roseville, CA	(16.8)	168	Upper Darby Twnshp, PA	(5.0)
52	Nashville, TN	3.4	18	Roswell, GA	9.0	373	Vacaville, CA	(21.5)
342	New Bedford, MA	(16.5)	NA	Round Rock, TX**	NA	375	Vallejo, CA	(22.8)
81	New Haven, CT	0.0	310	Sacramento, CA	(13.7)	302	Vancouver, WA	(13.0)
393	New Orleans, LA	(31.9)	194	Salem, OR	(6.3)	340	Ventura, CA	(16.3)
366	New Rochelle, NY	(19.8)	375	Salinas, CA	(22.8)	NA	Victorville, CA**	NA
133	New York, NY	(2.8)	209	Salt Lake City, UT	(6.8)	196	Virginia Beach, VA	(6.4)
363	Newark, NJ	(19.1)	43	San Antonio, TX	3.8	176	Visalia, CA	(5.4)
329	Newport Beach, CA	(15.2)	385	San Bernardino, CA	(25.7)	NA	Vista, CA**	NA
109	Newport News, VA	(1.3)	281	San Diego, CA	(10.9)	128	Waco, TX	(2.6)
176	Newton, MA	(5.4)	289	San Francisco, CA	(11.7)	320	Warren, MI	(14.5)
215	Norfolk, VA	(7.1)	380	San Jose, CA	(23.3)	94	Warwick, RI	(0.5)
2	Norman, OK	17.8	313	San Leandro, CA	(14.0)	268	Washington, DC	(10.1)
189	North Charleston, SC	(6.0)	NA	San Marcos, CA**	NA	121	Waterbury, CT	(2.3)
266	North Las Vegas, NV	(9.7)	337	San Mateo, CA	(16.1)	214	Waukegan, IL	(7.0)
NA	Norwalk, CA**	NA	184	Sandy Springs, GA	(5.8)	389	West Covina, CA	(27.8)
126	Norwalk, CT	(2.5)	37	Sandy, UT	4.3	106	West Jordan, UT	(1.1)
354	Oakland, CA	(17.8)	272	Santa Ana, CA	(10.3)	322	West Palm Beach, FL	(14.6)
126	Oceanside, CA	(2.5)	219	Santa Barbara, CA	(7.5)	203	West Valley, UT	(6.6)
141	Odessa, TX	(3.4)	317	Santa Clara, CA	(14.2)	386	Westland, MI	(26.4)
120	O'Fallon, MO	(2.2)	NA	Santa Clarita, CA**	NA	350	Westminster, CA	(17.4)
145	Ogden, UT	(3.7)	388	Santa Maria, CA	(27.6)	99	Westminster, CO	(0.6)
282	Oklahoma City, OK	(11.1)	142	Santa Monica, CA	(3.5)	249	Whittier, CA	(9.0)
NA	Olathe, KS**	NA	360	Santa Rosa, CA	(18.3)	77	Wichita Falls, TX	0.6
12	Omaha, NE	11.1	241	Savannah, GA	(8.6)	152	Wichita, KS	(4.0)
73	Ontario, CA	0.8	61	Scottsdale, AZ	1.7	295	Wilmington, NC	(12.5)
186	Orange, CA	(5.9)	172	Scranton, PA	(5.3)	23	Winston-Salem, NC	6.9
70	Orem, UT	1.1	196	Seattle, WA	(6.4)	282	Woodbridge Twnshp, NJ	(11.1)
252	Orlando, FL	(9.3)	235	Shreveport, LA	(8.1)	279	Worcester, MA	(10.7)
NA	Overland Park, KS**	NA	227	Simi Valley, CA	(7.7)	241	Yakima, WA	(8.6)
272	Oxnard, CA	(10.3)	128	Sioux City, IA	(2.6)	184	Yonkers, NY	(5.8)
244	Palm Bay, FL	(8.8)	46	Sioux Falls, SD	3.6	272	Yuma, AZ	(10.3)
NA	Palmdale, CA**	NA	196	Somerville, MA	(6.4)			
NA	Parma, OH**	NA	81	South Bend, IN	0.0			

Source: CQ Press using reported data from the F.B.I. "Crime in the United States 2012"

*Sworn officers only, does not include civilian employees.

**Not available

84. Percent Change in Rate of Police Officers: 2008 to 2012 (continued)
National Percent Change = 5.2% Decrease*

RANK	CITY	% CHANGE	RANK	CITY	% CHANGE	RANK	CITY	% CHANGE
1	Atlanta, GA	33.6	73	Evansville, IN	0.8	149	Fort Wayne, IN	(3.9)
2	Norman, OK	17.8	73	Ontario, CA	0.8	149	Lawton, OK	(3.9)
3	Memphis, TN	17.6	77	Arlington, TX	0.6	149	Plano, TX	(3.9)
4	Birmingham, AL	17.3	77	Wichita Falls, TX	0.6	152	Wichita, KS	(4.0)
5	Glendale, AZ	17.2	79	Springfield, MO	0.5	153	Bethlehem, PA	(4.3)
6	Avondale, AZ	17.0	80	Baltimore, MD	0.4	154	Cranston, RI	(4.4)
7	Hillsboro, OR	13.9	81	Alhambra, CA	0.0	154	Miramar, FL	(4.4)
8	Portsmouth, VA	13.5	81	Amarillo, TX	0.0	156	Elgin, IL	(4.6)
9	Hartford, CT	12.7	81	Austin, TX	0.0	156	Lowell, MA	(4.6)
10	Durham, NC	12.3	81	Billings, MT	0.0	158	Albany, GA	(4.7)
11	Chino, CA	11.3	81	Boulder, CO	0.0	158	Charleston, SC	(4.7)
12	Omaha, NE	11.1	81	Hawthorne, CA	0.0	158	Little Rock, AR	(4.7)
13	Knoxville, TN	10.8	81	Las Cruces, NM	0.0	158	Phoenix, AZ	(4.7)
14	Fort Lauderdale, FL	10.6	81	Lee's Summit, MO	0.0	162	Alexandria, VA	(4.8)
15	Columbus, GA	10.2	81	Macon, GA	0.0	162	Cambridge, MA	(4.8)
16	Erie, PA	9.7	81	New Haven, CT	0.0	162	Cicero, IL	(4.8)
17	Sugar Land, TX	9.1	81	Raleigh, NC	0.0	165	Allentown, PA	(4.9)
18	Lawrence, KS	9.0	81	South Bend, IN	0.0	165	Mesa, AZ	(4.9)
18	Roswell, GA	9.0	81	St. Joseph, MO	0.0	165	Peoria, AZ	(4.9)
20	Meridian, ID	8.8	94	Fort Smith, AR	(0.5)	168	Upper Darby Twnshp, PA	(5.0)
21	Detroit, MI	8.4	94	Kenosha, WI	(0.5)	169	Downey, CA	(5.1)
21	Houston, TX	8.4	94	Tempe, AZ	(0.5)	169	Milwaukee, WI	(5.1)
23	Winston-Salem, NC	6.9	94	Tyler, TX	(0.5)	171	Huntsville, AL	(5.2)
24	Athens-Clarke, GA	6.8	94	Warwick, RI	(0.5)	172	Baldwin Park, CA	(5.3)
25	Killeen, TX	6.7	99	Duluth, MN	(0.6)	172	Inglewood, CA	(5.3)
26	Beaverton, OR	6.5	99	Green Bay, WI	(0.6)	172	Laredo, TX	(5.3)
26	Tuscaloosa, AL	6.5	99	Westminster, CO	(0.6)	172	Scranton, PA	(5.3)
28	Hampton, VA	6.3	102	St. George, UT	(0.7)	176	Newton, MA	(5.4)
29	Fort Collins, CO	5.9	103	Denton, TX	(0.8)	176	Rochester, NY	(5.4)
29	Mobile, AL	5.9	103	Rochester, MN	(0.8)	176	Visalia, CA	(5.4)
31	Irvine, CA	5.7	105	Toledo, OH	(1.0)	179	Greensboro, NC	(5.5)
32	Jackson, MS	5.6	106	Madison, WI	(1.1)	179	St. Paul, MN	(5.5)
33	Racine, WI	5.5	106	Pasadena, TX	(1.1)	181	Hamilton Twnshp, NJ	(5.6)
34	St. Louis, MO	5.3	106	West Jordan, UT	(1.1)	182	Bellingham, WA	(5.7)
35	Richardson, TX	5.0	109	Newport News, VA	(1.3)	182	Richmond, VA	(5.7)
36	Allen, TX	4.8	110	Brooklyn Park, MN	(1.4)	184	Sandy Springs, GA	(5.8)
37	Boca Raton, FL	4.3	110	Colonie, NY	(1.4)	184	Yonkers, NY	(5.8)
37	Richmond, CA	4.3	112	Clarksville, TN	(1.5)	186	Greenville, NC	(5.9)
37	Sandy, UT	4.3	112	High Point, NC	(1.5)	186	Indio, CA	(5.9)
37	St. Petersburg, FL	4.3	112	Lynn, MA	(1.5)	186	Orange, CA	(5.9)
41	Gainesville, FL	4.1	115	Centennial, CO	(1.7)	189	Murrieta, CA	(6.0)
41	Greece, NY	4.1	116	Cheektowaga, NY	(1.8)	189	North Charleston, SC	(6.0)
43	San Antonio, TX	3.8	116	Toms River Twnshp, NJ	(1.8)	191	Fort Worth, TX	(6.1)
44	Lubbock, TX	3.7	118	Charlotte, NC	(1.9)	191	Glendale, CA	(6.1)
44	Montgomery, AL	3.7	119	Aurora, CO	(2.0)	193	Tampa, FL	(6.2)
46	Baton Rouge, LA	3.6	120	O'Fallon, MO	(2.2)	194	Danbury, CT	(6.3)
46	Brick Twnshp, NJ	3.6	121	Chandler, AZ	(2.3)	194	Salem, OR	(6.3)
46	Pittsburgh, PA	3.6	121	Waterbury, CT	(2.3)	196	Seattle, WA	(6.4)
46	Sioux Falls, SD	3.6	123	Buffalo, NY	(2.4)	196	Somerville, MA	(6.4)
50	Bryan, TX	3.5	123	Davenport, IA	(2.4)	196	Sparks, NV	(6.4)
50	Miami Gardens, FL	3.5	123	Quincy, MA	(2.4)	196	Virginia Beach, VA	(6.4)
52	Nashville, TN	3.4	126	Norwalk, CT	(2.5)	200	Amherst, NY	(6.5)
53	Pearland, TX	2.9	126	Oceanside, CA	(2.5)	200	Bloomington, IL	(6.5)
54	Cincinnati, OH	2.8	128	Sioux City, IA	(2.6)	200	Kansas City, MO	(6.5)
55	Arvada, CO	2.7	128	Topeka, KS	(2.6)	203	Chicago, IL	(6.6)
56	Sunrise, FL	2.6	128	Waco, TX	(2.6)	203	Columbia, MO	(6.6)
57	Los Angeles, CA	2.4	131	Burbank, CA	(2.7)	203	McKinney, TX	(6.6)
58	Medford, OR	2.3	131	Mission, TX	(2.7)	203	Springfield, IL	(6.6)
59	Citrus Heights, CA	2.0	133	Davie, FL	(2.8)	203	West Valley, UT	(6.6)
59	Gilbert, AZ	2.0	133	New York, NY	(2.8)	208	Gresham, OR	(6.7)
61	Eugene, OR	1.7	135	Pasadena, CA	(2.9)	209	Brockton, MA	(6.8)
61	Scottsdale, AZ	1.7	136	McAllen, TX	(3.0)	209	College Station, TX	(6.8)
63	Brownsville, TX	1.5	137	Fayetteville, AR	(3.1)	209	Fairfield, CA	(6.8)
64	Midland, TX	1.4	137	League City, TX	(3.1)	209	Salt Lake City, UT	(6.8)
65	Cedar Rapids, IA	1.3	137	Louisville, KY	(3.1)	213	Hammond, IN	(6.9)
65	Coral Springs, FL	1.3	140	Lincoln, NE	(3.2)	214	Waukegan, IL	(7.0)
65	Lynchburg, VA	1.3	141	Odessa, TX	(3.4)	215	Norfolk, VA	(7.1)
68	Miami, FL	1.2	142	Manchester, NH	(3.5)	216	Asheville, NC	(7.2)
68	Provo, UT	1.2	142	Santa Monica, CA	(3.5)	217	Miami Beach, FL	(7.3)
70	Cleveland, OH	1.1	144	Indianapolis, IN	(3.6)	217	Rockford, IL	(7.3)
70	Orem, UT	1.1	145	Chico, CA	(3.7)	219	Akron, OH	(7.5)
72	Nashua, NH	1.0	145	Decatur, IL	(3.7)	219	Chesapeake, VA	(7.5)
73	Carrollton, TX	0.8	145	Ogden, UT	(3.7)	219	Elizabeth, NJ	(7.5)
73	Cary, NC	0.8	148	Longmont, CO	(3.8)	219	Las Vegas, NV	(7.5)

RANK	CITY	% CHANGE	RANK	CITY	% CHANGE	RANK	CITY	% CHANGE
219	Santa Barbara, CA	(7.5)	297	Carlsbad, CA	(12.6)	371	Livonia, MI	(21.3)
224	Minneapolis, MN	(7.6)	297	Edison Twnshp, NJ	(12.6)	371	Stockton, CA	(21.3)
224	Pueblo, CO	(7.6)	299	Plantation, FL	(12.8)	373	Vacaville, CA	(21.5)
224	Spokane Valley, WA	(7.6)	300	Escondido, CA	(12.9)	374	Merced, CA	(22.7)
227	Albuquerque, NM	(7.7)	300	Jacksonville, FL	(12.9)	375	Reno, NV	(22.8)
227	Boston, MA	(7.7)	302	Torrance, CA	(13.0)	375	Salinas, CA	(22.8)
227	Simi Valley, CA	(7.7)	302	Vancouver, WA	(13.0)	375	Vallejo, CA	(22.8)
230	Grand Rapids, MI	(7.8)	304	Upland, CA	(13.1)	378	Springfield, MA	(23.0)
231	Lafayette, LA	(7.9)	305	Champaign, IL	(13.2)	379	Paterson, NJ	(23.2)
231	Murfreesboro, TN	(7.9)	305	Naperville, IL	(13.2)	380	San Jose, CA	(23.3)
233	Daly City, CA	(8.0)	307	Redwood City, CA	(13.3)	381	Costa Mesa, CA	(23.5)
233	Fall River, MA	(8.0)	308	Jersey City, NJ	(13.4)	382	Chula Vista, CA	(23.6)
235	Roanoke, VA	(8.1)	309	Nampa, ID	(13.5)	383	Reading, PA	(24.0)
235	Shreveport, LA	(8.1)	310	Buena Park, CA	(13.7)	384	South Gate, CA	(24.5)
237	Tucson, AZ	(8.2)	310	Sacramento, CA	(13.7)	385	San Bernardino, CA	(25.7)
238	Clarkstown, NY	(8.3)	312	Huntington Beach, CA	(13.8)	386	Westland, MI	(26.4)
239	Bridgeport, CT	(8.4)	313	Clearwater, FL	(14.0)	387	Greeley, CO	(26.7)
240	Bloomington, MN	(8.5)	313	Irving, TX	(14.0)	388	Santa Maria, CA	(27.6)
241	Savannah, GA	(8.6)	313	San Leandro, CA	(14.0)	389	West Covina, CA	(27.8)
241	Yakima, WA	(8.6)	316	Napa, CA	(14.1)	390	Antioch, CA	(29.9)
243	Fishers, IN	(8.7)	317	Frisco, TX	(14.2)	391	Lawrence, MA	(30.1)
244	Lakeland, FL	(8.8)	317	Santa Clara, CA	(14.2)	392	Kent, WA	(30.7)
244	Palm Bay, FL	(8.8)	319	Independence, MO	(14.4)	393	New Orleans, LA	(31.9)
244	Thornton, CO	(8.8)	320	Henderson, NV	(14.5)	394	Camden, NJ	(33.7)
244	Tulsa, OK	(8.8)	320	Warren, MI	(14.5)	395	Flint, MI	(33.9)
248	Edmond, OK	(8.9)	322	West Palm Beach, FL	(14.6)	396	Troy, MI	(34.5)
249	Everett, WA	(9.0)	323	Aurora, IL	(14.7)	397	Hemet, CA	(35.8)
249	Whittier, CA	(9.0)	323	Farmington Hills, MI	(14.7)	398	Trenton, NJ	(36.0)
251	Fargo, ND	(9.2)	323	Livermore, CA	(14.7)	399	Renton, WA	(37.1)
252	Bakersfield, CA	(9.3)	326	Lexington, KY	(14.9)	NA	Abilene, TX**	NA
252	Orlando, FL	(9.3)	327	Denver, CO	(15.0)	NA	Albany, NY**	NA
252	Riverside, CA	(9.3)	328	El Monte, CA	(15.1)	NA	Beaumont, TX**	NA
255	Bellevue, WA	(9.4)	329	Fontana, CA	(15.2)	NA	Bellflower, CA**	NA
255	Cape Coral, FL	(9.4)	329	Newport Beach, CA	(15.2)	NA	Bloomington, IN**	NA
257	Anchorage, AK	(9.5)	329	Providence, RI	(15.2)	NA	Carson, CA**	NA
257	Boise, ID	(9.5)	332	Garden Grove, CA	(15.5)	NA	Chino Hills, CA**	NA
257	Longview, TX	(9.5)	333	Clifton, NJ	(15.8)	NA	Compton, CA**	NA
257	Portland, OR	(9.5)	334	Dearborn, MI	(15.9)	NA	Dallas, TX**	NA
261	Arlington Heights, IL	(9.6)	335	El Cajon, CA	(16.0)	NA	Deerfield Beach, FL**	NA
261	Garland, TX	(9.6)	335	Fullerton, CA	(16.0)	NA	Des Moines, IA**	NA
261	Philadelphia, PA	(9.6)	337	Concord, CA	(16.1)	NA	Edinburg, TX**	NA
261	Rio Rancho, NM	(9.6)	337	San Mateo, CA	(16.1)	NA	Gary, IN**	NA
261	Stamford, CT	(9.6)	339	Fresno, CA	(16.2)	NA	Hesperia, CA**	NA
266	North Las Vegas, NV	(9.7)	340	Ventura, CA	(16.3)	NA	Hialeah, FL**	NA
267	Hollywood, FL	(9.9)	341	Colorado Springs, CO	(16.4)	NA	Hoover, AL**	NA
268	Fremont, CA	(10.1)	342	Carmel, IN	(16.5)	NA	Jurupa Valley, CA**	NA
268	Mountain View, CA	(10.1)	342	Modesto, CA	(16.5)	NA	Kansas City, KS**	NA
268	Syracuse, NY	(10.1)	342	New Bedford, MA	(16.5)	NA	Lake Forest, CA**	NA
268	Washington, DC	(10.1)	345	Rialto, CA	(16.7)	NA	Lakewood Twnshp, NJ**	NA
272	Fayetteville, NC	(10.3)	346	El Paso, TX	(16.8)	NA	Lakewood, CA**	NA
272	Oxnard, CA	(10.3)	346	Roseville, CA	(16.8)	NA	Lancaster, CA**	NA
272	Santa Ana, CA	(10.3)	348	Redding, CA	(16.9)	NA	Melbourne, FL**	NA
272	Tacoma, WA	(10.3)	349	Clovis, CA	(17.1)	NA	Menifee, CA**	NA
272	Yuma, AZ	(10.3)	350	Westminster, CA	(17.4)	NA	Mission Viejo, CA**	NA
277	Hayward, CA	(10.4)	351	Long Beach, CA	(17.5)	NA	Moreno Valley, CA**	NA
278	Grand Prairie, TX	(10.5)	352	Sunnyvale, CA	(17.6)	NA	Norwalk, CA**	NA
279	Worcester, MA	(10.7)	353	Peoria, IL	(17.7)	NA	Olathe, KS**	NA
280	Lakewood, CO	(10.8)	354	Joliet, IL	(17.8)	NA	Overland Park, KS**	NA
281	San Diego, CA	(10.9)	354	Oakland, CA	(17.8)	NA	Palmdale, CA**	NA
282	Oklahoma City, OK	(11.1)	354	Tustin, CA	(17.8)	NA	Parma, OH**	NA
282	Woodbridge Twnshp, NJ	(11.1)	357	Pomona, CA	(18.0)	NA	Pembroke Pines, FL**	NA
284	Dayton, OH	(11.4)	358	Anaheim, CA	(18.1)	NA	Pompano Beach, FL**	NA
284	Tallahassee, FL	(11.4)	359	Kennewick, WA	(18.2)	NA	Port St. Lucie, FL**	NA
286	Corpus Christi, TX	(11.5)	360	Santa Rosa, CA	(18.3)	NA	Ramapo, NY**	NA
286	Sterling Heights, MI	(11.5)	361	Surprise, AZ	(18.9)	NA	Rancho Cucamon., CA**	NA
288	Spokane, WA	(11.6)	362	Corona, CA	(19.0)	NA	Round Rock, TX**	NA
289	San Francisco, CA	(11.7)	363	Johns Creek, GA	(19.1)	NA	San Marcos, CA**	NA
290	Broken Arrow, OK	(11.8)	363	Newark, NJ	(19.1)	NA	Santa Clarita, CA**	NA
291	Elk Grove, CA	(12.0)	365	Berkeley, CA	(19.5)	NA	Temecula, CA**	NA
292	Mesquite, TX	(12.2)	366	New Rochelle, NY	(19.8)	NA	Thousand Oaks, CA**	NA
293	Largo, FL	(12.4)	367	Alameda, CA	(20.1)	NA	Victorville, CA**	NA
293	Tracy, CA	(12.4)	368	Ann Arbor, MI	(20.9)	NA	Vista, CA**	NA
295	Federal Way, WA	(12.5)	369	Lansing, MI	(21.0)			
295	Wilmington, NC	(12.5)	370	Clinton Twnshp, MI	(21.1)			

Source: CQ Press using reported data from the F.B.I. "Crime in the United States 2012"

*Sworn officers only, does not include civilian employees.

**Not available

III. Metropolitan and City Populations

Please note the following for Tables 1 through 40 and 85 through 87:

- All listings are for Metropolitan Statistical Areas (M.S.A.'s) except for those ending with "M.D."
- Listings with "M.D." are Metropolitan Divisions, which are smaller parts of eleven large M.S.A.'s. These eleven M.S.A.'s divided into M.D.'s are identified using "(greater)" following the metropolitan area name.
- For example, the "Dallas (greater)" M.S.A. includes the two M.D.'s of Dallas-Plano-Irving and Fort Worth-Arlington. The data for the M.D.'s are included in the data for the overall M.S.A. as well.
- The name of a M.S.A. or M.D. is subject to change based on the changing proportional size of the large cities included within it. Percent changes are calculated in this book if the M.S.A. or M.D. has not substantially changed, despite the changes in name. Furthermore, the Office of Management and Budget (OMB) redefined a number of M.S.A.'s in 2013; if the redefined M.S.A. had a population change of 5 percent or greater from the previous definition, its data are treated as not comparable and are not included in the tables showing change over time.
- Some M.S.A. and M.D. names are abbreviated to preserve space within the tables.

Please note the following for Tables 41 through 84 and 88 through 90:
- All listings are for cities of 75,000 or more in population that reported data to the F.B.I. for 2012. The reported populations for crime reporting purposes may vary from Census populations.

85. Metropolitan Population in 2012
National Total = 313,914,040*

RANK	METROPOLITAN AREA	POP	RANK	METROPOLITAN AREA	POP	RANK	METROPOLITAN AREA	POP
253	Abilene, TX	168,908	364	Cheyenne, WY	94,026	96	Gary, IN M.D.	710,891
98	Akron, OH	701,412	5	Chicago (greater), IL-IN-WI	9,511,421	352	Gettysburg, PA	101,598
78	Albany-Schenectady-Troy, NY	876,182	6	Chicago-Joilet-Naperville, IL M.D.	7,300,952	312	Glens Falls, NY	129,692
263	Albany, GA	159,370	215	Chico, CA	222,309	319	Goldsboro, NC	124,923
328	Albany, OR	118,961	42	Cincinnati, OH-KY-IN	2,123,695	354	Grand Forks, ND-MN	99,784
76	Albuquerque, NM	900,072	191	Clarksville, TN-KY	266,196	372	Grand Island, NE	83,197
267	Alexandria, LA	155,419	332	Cleveland, TN	117,799	281	Grand Junction, CO	149,118
86	Allentown, PA-NJ	826,611	295	Coeur d'Alene, ID	142,089	374	Great Falls, MT	82,406
318	Altoona, PA	127,305	209	College Station-Bryan, TX	235,092	193	Greeley, CO	262,216
198	Amarillo, TX	259,729	100	Colorado Springs, CO	669,453	176	Green Bay, WI	310,262
366	Ames, IA	90,011	256	Columbia, MO	165,938	92	Greensboro-High Point, NC	738,208
23	Anaheim-Santa Ana-Irvine, CA M.D.	3,084,081	179	Columbus, GA-AL	304,291	83	Greenville-Anderson, SC	843,836
173	Anchorage, AK	313,529	377	Columbus, IN	78,114	248	Greenville, NC	172,830
167	Ann Arbor, MI	348,215	135	Corpus Christi, TX	437,841	203	Hagerstown-Martinsburg, MD-WV	255,387
330	Anniston-Oxford, AL	118,270	368	Corvallis, OR	86,538	322	Hammond, LA	123,296
213	Appleton, WI	227,986	206	Crestview-Fort Walton Beach, FL	242,539	268	Hanford-Corcoran, CA	155,191
139	Asheville, NC	433,267	349	Cumberland, MD-WV	103,606	118	Harrisburg-Carlisle, PA	553,808
234	Athens-Clarke County, GA	195,380	7	Dallas (greater), TX	6,680,025	316	Harrisonburg, VA	127,957
12	Atlanta, GA	5,434,540	16	Dallas-Plano-Irving, TX M.D.	4,405,585	71	Hartford, CT	1,023,883
186	Atlantic City, NJ	275,689	289	Dalton, GA	144,264	288	Hattiesburg, MS	145,741
290	Auburn, AL	144,044	375	Danville, IL	81,547	163	Hickory, NC	368,179
114	Augusta, GA-SC	575,582	237	Daphne-Fairhope-Foley, AL	187,467	235	Hilton Head Island, SC	191,685
49	Austin-Round Rock, TX	1,810,230	156	Davenport, IA-IL	382,090	376	Hinesville, GA	81,447
80	Bakersfield, CA	859,608	91	Dayton, OH	803,255	296	Homosassa Springs, FL	141,942
27	Baltimore, MD	2,755,459	271	Decatur, AL	154,689	224	Houma, LA	209,817
273	Bangor, ME	153,902	342	Decatur, IL	110,782	8	Houston, TX	6,150,496
217	Barnstable Town, MA	217,689	112	Deltona-Daytona Beach, FL	600,260	141	Huntsville, AL	427,189
88	Baton Rouge, LA	813,022	29	Denver-Aurora, CO	2,635,467	302	Idaho Falls, ID	135,809
346	Bay City, MI	107,188	113	Des Moines-West Des Moines, IA	582,506	46	Indianapolis, IN	1,915,784
151	Beaumont-Port Arthur, TX	411,053	19	Detroit (greater), MI	4,288,943	266	Iowa City, IA	155,494
320	Beckley, WV	124,829	51	Detroit-Dearborn-Livonia, MI M.D.	1,803,403	57	Jacksonville, FL	1,378,810
227	Bellingham, WA	205,660	285	Dothan, AL	147,151	115	Jackson, MS	574,517
259	Billings, MT	162,082	255	Dover, DE	166,643	311	Jackson, TN	131,023
204	Binghamton, NY	251,424	363	Dubuque, IA	95,015	262	Janesville, WI	160,502
68	Birmingham-Hoover, AL	1,136,805	185	Duluth, MN-WI	281,439	280	Jefferson City, MO	150,764
326	Bismarck, ND	119,673	124	Durham-Chapel Hill, NC	518,062	231	Johnson City, TN	201,468
242	Blacksburg, VA	179,827	154	Dutchess-Putnam, NY M.D.	400,079	291	Johnstown, PA	143,961
238	Bloomington, IL	187,221	249	East Stroudsburg, PA	170,157	323	Jonesboro, AR	123,295
260	Bloomington, IN	161,803	245	El Centro, CA	178,699	246	Joplin, MO	177,182
369	Bloomsburg-Berwick, PA	85,911	85	El Paso, TX	836,557	264	Kahului-Wailuku-Lahaina, HI	158,760
105	Boise City, ID	631,917	107	Elgin, IL M.D.	625,305	170	Kalamazoo-Portage, MI	328,443
13	Boston (greater), MA-NH	4,629,025	276	Elizabethtown-Fort Knox, KY	151,716	338	Kankakee, IL	113,751
45	Boston, MA M.D.	1,920,886	367	Elmira, NY	89,320	43	Kansas City, MO-KS	2,033,239
180	Boulder, CO	303,520	184	Erie, PA	281,440	190	Kennewick-Richland, WA	266,723
261	Bowling Green, KY	160,980	165	Eugene, OR	355,926	148	Killeen-Temple, TX	417,760
201	Bremerton-Silverdale, WA	257,130	382	Fairbanks, AK	34,603	174	Kingsport, TN-VA	312,616
75	Bridgeport-Stamford, CT	910,707	219	Fargo, ND-MN	216,055	241	Kingston, NY	183,433
147	Brownsville-Harlingen, TX	420,325	315	Farmington, NM	128,404	82	Knoxville, TN	850,421
337	Brunswick, GA	114,128	128	Fayetteville-Springdale, AR-MO	475,585	373	Kokomo, IN	83,059
67	Buffalo-Niagara Falls, NY	1,140,160	160	Fayetteville, NC	377,864	303	La Crosse, WI-MN	134,905
270	Burlington, NC	154,810	301	Flagstaff, AZ	135,979	229	Lafayette, IN	204,246
343	California-Lexington Park, MD	108,522	143	Flint, MI	422,387	129	Lafayette, LA	473,751
35	Cambridge-Newton, MA M.D.	2,287,271	282	Florence-Muscle Shoals, AL	147,885	79	Lake Co.-Kenosha Co., IL-WI M.D.	874,273
61	Camden, NJ M.D.	1,258,086	225	Florence, SC	208,121	228	Lake Havasu City-Kingman, AZ	204,559
152	Canton, OH	403,843	351	Fond du Lac, WI	102,340	108	Lakeland, FL	617,808
103	Cape Coral-Fort Myers, FL	639,944	177	Fort Collins, CO	309,752	122	Lancaster, PA	524,442
358	Cape Girardeau, MO-IL	97,195	50	Fort Lauderdale, FL M.D.	1,804,461	130	Lansing-East Lansing, MI	465,476
381	Carson City, NV	56,164	183	Fort Smith, AR-OK	283,329	197	Laredo, TX	260,337
378	Casper, WY	77,475	145	Fort Wayne, IN	420,767	221	Las Cruces, NM	213,938
195	Cedar Rapids, IA	261,586	37	Fort Worth-Arlington, TX M.D.	2,274,440	44	Las Vegas-Henderson, NV	1,995,735
279	Chambersburg-Waynesboro, PA	151,055	74	Fresno, CA	951,648	339	Lawrence, KS	112,784
212	Champaign-Urbana, IL	232,445	348	Gadsden, AL	104,722	307	Lawton, OK	132,806
99	Charleston-North Charleston, SC	688,607	188	Gainesville, FL	270,003	306	Lebanon, PA	134,529
214	Charlottesville, VA	223,598	240	Gainesville, GA	185,005	345	Lewiston-Auburn, ME	107,479

Note: All listings are for Metropolitan Statistical Areas (M.S.A.s) except for those ending with "M.D." Listings with "M.D." are Metropolitan Divisions which are smaller parts of eleven large M.S.A.s. See explanatory note at beginning of metropolitan area section.

RANK	METROPOLITAN AREA	POP	RANK	METROPOLITAN AREA	POP	RANK	METROPOLITAN AREA	POP
380	Lewiston, ID-WA	61,959	335	Owensboro, KY	115,625	63	Silver Spring-Frederick, MD M.D.	1,238,384
127	Lexington-Fayette, KY	480,457	84	Oxnard-Thousand Oaks, CA	839,484	250	Sioux City, IA-NE-SD	169,806
347	Lima, OH	106,087	119	Palm Bay-Melbourne, FL	550,983	210	Sioux Falls, SD	235,045
178	Lincoln, NE	308,646	236	Panama City, FL	188,234	171	South Bend-Mishawaka, IN-MI	319,561
95	Little Rock, AR	712,592	365	Parkersburg-Vienna, WV	92,884	172	Spartanburg, SC	318,548
314	Logan, UT-ID	129,186	131	Pensacola, FL	459,402	121	Spokane, WA	535,393
216	Longview, TX	219,910	159	Peoria, IL	379,733	222	Springfield, IL	211,646
350	Longview, WA	103,483	9	Philadelphia (greater) PA-NJ-MD-DE	6,012,363	106	Springfield, MA	627,135
4	Los Angeles County, CA M.D.	9,980,757	41	Philadelphia, PA M.D.	2,144,972	134	Springfield, MO	440,970
3	Los Angeles (greater), CA	13,064,838	18	Phoenix-Mesa-Scottsdale, AZ	4,309,766	300	Springfield, OH	137,682
62	Louisville, KY-IN	1,248,616	355	Pine Bluff, AR	99,299	269	State College, PA	154,973
181	Lubbock, TX	300,321	34	Pittsburgh, PA	2,363,571	325	Staunton-Waynesboro, VA	119,937
202	Lynchburg, VA	256,973	309	Pittsfield, MA	131,619	97	Stockton-Lodi, CA	702,670
208	Macon, GA	235,405	370	Pocatello, ID	84,258	293	St. George, UT	143,580
272	Madera, CA	154,343	138	Port St. Lucie, FL	433,712	317	St. Joseph, MO-KS	127,840
109	Madison, WI	614,928	36	Portland-Vancouver, OR-WA	2,279,873	26	St. Louis, MO-IL	2,798,017
153	Manchester-Nashua, NH	402,466	125	Portland, ME	516,198	344	Sumter, SC	108,482
362	Manhattan, KS	95,402	220	Prescott, AZ	214,201	101	Syracuse, NY	666,129
357	Mankato-North Mankato, MN	97,827	54	Providence-Warwick, RI-MA	1,604,098	87	Tacoma, WA M.D.	815,826
321	Mansfield, OH	123,502	120	Provo-Orem, UT	548,142	161	Tallahassee, FL	374,804
90	McAllen-Edinburg-Mission, TX	809,759	257	Pueblo, CO	162,766	24	Tampa-St Petersburg, FL	2,863,265
226	Medford, OR	206,276	258	Punta Gorda, FL	162,701	247	Terre Haute, IN	173,204
59	Memphis, TN-MS-AR	1,343,608	233	Racine, WI	195,888	278	Texarkana, TX-AR	151,153
192	Merced, CA	262,308	66	Raleigh, NC	1,175,043	356	The Villages, FL	99,090
11	Miami (greater), FL	5,747,489	299	Rapid City, SD	138,237	111	Toledo, OH	608,831
31	Miami-Dade County, FL M.D.	2,589,623	150	Reading, PA	413,447	207	Topeka, KS	235,846
340	Michigan City-La Porte, IN	111,723	243	Redding, CA	179,423	162	Trenton, NJ	368,870
371	Midland, MI	84,124	137	Reno, NV	435,223	72	Tucson, AZ	1,000,369
283	Midland, TX	147,417	64	Richmond, VA	1,232,458	73	Tulsa, OK	952,785
55	Milwaukee, WI	1,566,214	17	Riverside-San Bernardino, CA	4,344,917	211	Tuscaloosa, AL	232,913
21	Minneapolis-St. Paul, MN-WI	3,408,532	175	Roanoke, VA	312,265	218	Tyler, TX	216,577
341	Missoula, MT	110,904	223	Rochester, MN	209,826	182	Utica-Rome, NY	300,058
149	Mobile, AL	414,233	70	Rochester, NY	1,086,565	292	Valdosta, GA	143,826
123	Modesto, CA	523,330	166	Rockford, IL	348,522	146	Vallejo-Fairfield, CA	420,333
244	Monroe, LA	178,701	144	Rockingham County, NH M.D.	420,868	361	Victoria, TX	96,207
277	Monroe, MI	151,670	274	Rocky Mount, NC	153,664	265	Vineland-Bridgeton, NJ	157,869
47	Montgomery County, PA M.D.	1,892,483	360	Rome, GA	97,013	53	Virginia Beach-Norfolk, VA-NC	1,703,542
158	Montgomery, AL	380,129	40	Sacramento, CA	2,196,416	132	Visalia-Porterville, CA	453,419
308	Morgantown, WV	132,255	232	Saginaw, MI	199,233	196	Waco, TX	260,350
334	Morristown, TN	115,676	155	Salem, OR	397,669	379	Walla Walla, WA	64,262
327	Mount Vernon-Anacortes, WA	119,267	142	Salinas, CA	425,810	239	Warner Robins, GA	185,441
331	Muncie, IN	118,029	157	Salisbury, MD-DE	381,281	33	Warren-Troy, MI M.D.	2,485,540
298	Napa, CA	139,368	69	Salt Lake City, UT	1,123,286	10	Washington (greater) DC-VA-MD-WV	5,826,080
169	Naples-Marco Island, FL	332,611	38	San Antonio, TX	2,227,800	14	Washington, DC-VA-MD-WV M.D.	4,587,696
52	Nashville-Davidson, TN	1,712,682	22	San Diego, CA	3,169,187	252	Waterloo-Cedar Falls, IA	168,941
25	Nassau-Suffolk, NY M.D.	2,858,599	15	San Francisco (greater), CA	4,431,755	329	Watertown-Fort Drum, NY	118,546
313	New Bern, NC	129,271	56	San Francisco-Redwood, CA M.D.	1,554,315	304	Wausau, WI	134,744
89	New Haven-Milford, CT	809,772	48	San Jose, CA	1,882,748	58	West Palm Beach, FL M.D.	1,353,405
65	New Orleans, LA	1,220,047	187	San Luis Obispo, CA	274,491	284	Wheeling, WV-OH	147,195
1	New York (greater), NY-NJ-PA	19,791,750	200	San Rafael, CA M.D.	257,396	275	Wichita Falls, TX	152,511
2	New York-Jersey City, NY-NJ M.D.	14,043,153	189	Santa Cruz-Watsonville, CA	266,749	104	Wichita, KS	636,615
32	Newark, NJ-PA M.D.	2,489,919	287	Santa Fe, NM	145,880	333	Williamsport, PA	116,936
93	North Port-Sarasota-Bradenton, FL	719,034	140	Santa Maria-Santa Barbara, CA	430,836	94	Wilmington, DE-MD-NJ M.D.	716,822
286	Norwich-New London, CT	146,391	126	Santa Rosa, CA	492,642	194	Wilmington, NC	262,160
30	Oakland-Hayward, CA M.D.	2,620,044	164	Savannah, GA	359,371	310	Winchester, VA-WV	131,237
168	Ocala, FL	337,066	116	Scranton--Wilkes-Barre, PA	564,136	102	Winston-Salem, NC	651,110
359	Ocean City, NJ	97,077	20	Seattle (greater), WA	3,534,349	81	Worcester, MA-CT	851,171
294	Odessa, TX	142,209	28	Seattle-Bellevue-Everett, WA M.D.	2,718,523	205	Yakima, WA	249,564
110	Ogden-Clearfield, UT	614,396	297	Sebastian-Vero Beach, FL	140,789	136	York-Hanover, PA	437,478
60	Oklahoma City, OK	1,285,907	353	Sebring, FL	99,976	117	Youngstown-Warren, OH-PA	562,899
199	Olympia, WA	259,107	336	Sheboygan, WI	115,444	251	Yuba City, CA	169,050
77	Omaha-Council Bluffs, NE-IA	882,865	324	Sherman-Denison, TX	123,237	230	Yuma, AZ	203,062
39	Orlando, FL	2,200,987	133	Shreveport-Bossier City, LA	447,514			
254	Oshkosh-Neenah, WI	168,129	304	Sierra Vista-Douglas, AZ	134,744			

Source: Reported data from the F.B.I. "Crime in the United States 2012"
*Estimates as of July 2012 based on U.S. Bureau of the Census figures.

85. Metropolitan Population in 2012 (continued)
National Total = 313,914,040*

RANK	METROPOLITAN AREA	POP	RANK	METROPOLITAN AREA	POP	RANK	METROPOLITAN AREA	POP
1	New York (greater), NY-NJ-PA	19,791,750	65	New Orleans, LA	1,220,047	129	Lafayette, LA	473,751
2	New York-Jersey City, NY-NJ M.D.	14,043,153	66	Raleigh, NC	1,175,043	130	Lansing-East Lansing, MI	465,476
3	Los Angeles (greater), CA	13,064,838	67	Buffalo-Niagara Falls, NY	1,140,160	131	Pensacola, FL	459,402
4	Los Angeles County, CA M.D.	9,980,757	68	Birmingham-Hoover, AL	1,136,805	132	Visalia-Porterville, CA	453,419
5	Chicago (greater), IL-IN-WI	9,511,421	69	Salt Lake City, UT	1,123,286	133	Shreveport-Bossier City, LA	447,514
6	Chicago-Joilet-Naperville, IL M.D.	7,300,952	70	Rochester, NY	1,086,565	134	Springfield, MO	440,970
7	Dallas (greater), TX	6,680,025	71	Hartford, CT	1,023,883	135	Corpus Christi, TX	437,841
8	Houston, TX	6,150,496	72	Tucson, AZ	1,000,369	136	York-Hanover, PA	437,478
9	Philadelphia (greater) PA-NJ-MD-DE	6,012,363	73	Tulsa, OK	952,785	137	Reno, NV	435,223
10	Washington (greater) DC-VA-MD-WV	5,826,080	74	Fresno, CA	951,648	138	Port St. Lucie, FL	433,712
11	Miami (greater), FL	5,747,489	75	Bridgeport-Stamford, CT	910,707	139	Asheville, NC	433,267
12	Atlanta, GA	5,434,540	76	Albuquerque, NM	900,072	140	Santa Maria-Santa Barbara, CA	430,836
13	Boston (greater), MA-NH	4,629,025	77	Omaha-Council Bluffs, NE-IA	882,865	141	Huntsville, AL	427,189
14	Washington, DC-VA-MD-WV M.D.	4,587,696	78	Albany-Schenectady-Troy, NY	876,182	142	Salinas, CA	425,810
15	San Francisco (greater), CA	4,431,755	79	Lake Co.-Kenosha Co., IL-WI M.D.	874,273	143	Flint, MI	422,387
16	Dallas-Plano-Irving, TX M.D.	4,405,585	80	Bakersfield, CA	859,608	144	Rockingham County, NH M.D.	420,868
17	Riverside-San Bernardino, CA	4,344,917	81	Worcester, MA-CT	851,171	145	Fort Wayne, IN	420,767
18	Phoenix-Mesa-Scottsdale, AZ	4,309,766	82	Knoxville, TN	850,421	146	Vallejo-Fairfield, CA	420,333
19	Detroit (greater), MI	4,288,943	83	Greenville-Anderson, SC	843,836	147	Brownsville-Harlingen, TX	420,325
20	Seattle (greater), WA	3,534,349	84	Oxnard-Thousand Oaks, CA	839,484	148	Killeen-Temple, TX	417,760
21	Minneapolis-St. Paul, MN-WI	3,408,532	85	El Paso, TX	836,557	149	Mobile, AL	414,233
22	San Diego, CA	3,169,187	86	Allentown, PA-NJ	826,611	150	Reading, PA	413,447
23	Anaheim-Santa Ana-Irvine, CA M.D.	3,084,081	87	Tacoma, WA M.D.	815,826	151	Beaumont-Port Arthur, TX	411,053
24	Tampa-St Petersburg, FL	2,863,265	88	Baton Rouge, LA	813,022	152	Canton, OH	403,843
25	Nassau-Suffolk, NY M.D.	2,858,599	89	New Haven-Milford, CT	809,772	153	Manchester-Nashua, NH	402,466
26	St. Louis, MO-IL	2,798,017	90	McAllen-Edinburg-Mission, TX	809,759	154	Dutchess-Putnam, NY M.D.	400,079
27	Baltimore, MD	2,755,459	91	Dayton, OH	803,255	155	Salem, OR	397,669
28	Seattle-Bellevue-Everett, WA M.D.	2,718,523	92	Greensboro-High Point, NC	738,208	156	Davenport, IA-IL	382,090
29	Denver-Aurora, CO	2,635,467	93	North Port-Sarasota-Bradenton, FL	719,034	157	Salisbury, MD-DE	381,281
30	Oakland-Hayward, CA M.D.	2,620,044	94	Wilmington, DE-MD-NJ M.D.	716,822	158	Montgomery, AL	380,129
31	Miami-Dade County, FL M.D.	2,589,623	95	Little Rock, AR	712,592	159	Peoria, IL	379,733
32	Newark, NJ-PA M.D.	2,489,919	96	Gary, IN M.D.	710,891	160	Fayetteville, NC	377,864
33	Warren-Troy, MI M.D.	2,485,540	97	Stockton-Lodi, CA	702,670	161	Tallahassee, FL	374,804
34	Pittsburgh, PA	2,363,571	98	Akron, OH	701,412	162	Trenton, NJ	368,870
35	Cambridge-Newton, MA M.D.	2,287,271	99	Charleston-North Charleston, SC	688,607	163	Hickory, NC	368,179
36	Portland-Vancouver, OR-WA	2,279,873	100	Colorado Springs, CO	669,453	164	Savannah, GA	359,371
37	Fort Worth-Arlington, TX M.D.	2,274,440	101	Syracuse, NY	666,129	165	Eugene, OR	355,926
38	San Antonio, TX	2,227,800	102	Winston-Salem, NC	651,110	166	Rockford, IL	348,522
39	Orlando, FL	2,200,987	103	Cape Coral-Fort Myers, FL	639,944	167	Ann Arbor, MI	348,215
40	Sacramento, CA	2,196,416	104	Wichita, KS	636,615	168	Ocala, FL	337,066
41	Philadelphia, PA M.D.	2,144,972	105	Boise City, ID	631,917	169	Naples-Marco Island, FL	332,611
42	Cincinnati, OH-KY-IN	2,123,695	106	Springfield, MA	627,135	170	Kalamazoo-Portage, MI	328,443
43	Kansas City, MO-KS	2,033,239	107	Elgin, IL M.D.	625,305	171	South Bend-Mishawaka, IN-MI	319,561
44	Las Vegas-Henderson, NV	1,995,735	108	Lakeland, FL	617,808	172	Spartanburg, SC	318,548
45	Boston, MA M.D.	1,920,886	109	Madison, WI	614,928	173	Anchorage, AK	313,529
46	Indianapolis, IN	1,915,784	110	Ogden-Clearfield, UT	614,396	174	Kingsport, TN-VA	312,616
47	Montgomery County, PA M.D.	1,892,483	111	Toledo, OH	608,831	175	Roanoke, VA	312,265
48	San Jose, CA	1,882,748	112	Deltona-Daytona Beach, FL	600,260	176	Green Bay, WI	310,262
49	Austin-Round Rock, TX	1,810,230	113	Des Moines-West Des Moines, IA	582,506	177	Fort Collins, CO	309,752
50	Fort Lauderdale, FL M.D.	1,804,461	114	Augusta, GA-SC	575,582	178	Lincoln, NE	308,646
51	Detroit-Dearborn-Livonia, MI M.D.	1,803,403	115	Jackson, MS	574,517	179	Columbus, GA-AL	304,291
52	Nashville-Davidson, TN	1,712,682	116	Scranton--Wilkes-Barre, PA	564,136	180	Boulder, CO	303,520
53	Virginia Beach-Norfolk, VA-NC	1,703,542	117	Youngstown-Warren, OH-PA	562,899	181	Lubbock, TX	300,321
54	Providence-Warwick, RI-MA	1,604,098	118	Harrisburg-Carlisle, PA	553,808	182	Utica-Rome, NY	300,058
55	Milwaukee, WI	1,566,214	119	Palm Bay-Melbourne, FL	550,983	183	Fort Smith, AR-OK	283,329
56	San Francisco-Redwood, CA M.D.	1,554,315	120	Provo-Orem, UT	548,142	184	Erie, PA	281,440
57	Jacksonville, FL	1,378,810	121	Spokane, WA	535,393	185	Duluth, MN-WI	281,439
58	West Palm Beach, FL M.D.	1,353,405	122	Lancaster, PA	524,442	186	Atlantic City, NJ	275,689
59	Memphis, TN-MS-AR	1,343,608	123	Modesto, CA	523,330	187	San Luis Obispo, CA	274,491
60	Oklahoma City, OK	1,285,907	124	Durham-Chapel Hill, NC	518,062	188	Gainesville, FL	270,003
61	Camden, NJ M.D.	1,258,086	125	Portland, ME	516,198	189	Santa Cruz-Watsonville, CA	266,749
62	Louisville, KY-IN	1,248,616	126	Santa Rosa, CA	492,642	190	Kennewick-Richland, WA	266,723
63	Silver Spring-Frederick, MD M.D.	1,238,384	127	Lexington-Fayette, KY	480,457	191	Clarksville, TN-KY	266,196
64	Richmond, VA	1,232,458	128	Fayetteville-Springdale, AR-MO	475,585	192	Merced, CA	262,308

Note: All listings are for Metropolitan Statistical Areas (M.S.A.s) except for those ending with "M.D." Listings with "M.D." are Metropolitan Divisions which are smaller parts of eleven large M.S.A.s. See explanatory note at beginning of metropolitan area section.

RANK	METROPOLITAN AREA	POP	RANK	METROPOLITAN AREA	POP	RANK	METROPOLITAN AREA	POP
193	Greeley, CO	262,216	257	Pueblo, CO	162,766	321	Mansfield, OH	123,502
194	Wilmington, NC	262,160	258	Punta Gorda, FL	162,701	322	Hammond, LA	123,296
195	Cedar Rapids, IA	261,586	259	Billings, MT	162,082	323	Jonesboro, AR	123,295
196	Waco, TX	260,350	260	Bloomington, IN	161,803	324	Sherman-Denison, TX	123,237
197	Laredo, TX	260,337	261	Bowling Green, KY	160,980	325	Staunton-Waynesboro, VA	119,937
198	Amarillo, TX	259,729	262	Janesville, WI	160,502	326	Bismarck, ND	119,673
199	Olympia, WA	259,107	263	Albany, GA	159,370	327	Mount Vernon-Anacortes, WA	119,267
200	San Rafael, CA M.D.	257,396	264	Kahului-Wailuku-Lahaina, HI	158,760	328	Albany, OR	118,961
201	Bremerton-Silverdale, WA	257,130	265	Vineland-Bridgeton, NJ	157,869	329	Watertown-Fort Drum, NY	118,546
202	Lynchburg, VA	256,973	266	Iowa City, IA	155,494	330	Anniston-Oxford, AL	118,270
203	Hagerstown-Martinsburg, MD-WV	255,387	267	Alexandria, LA	155,419	331	Muncie, IN	118,029
204	Binghamton, NY	251,424	268	Hanford-Corcoran, CA	155,191	332	Cleveland, TN	117,799
205	Yakima, WA	249,564	269	State College, PA	154,973	333	Williamsport, PA	116,936
206	Crestview-Fort Walton Beach, FL	242,539	270	Burlington, NC	154,810	334	Morristown, TN	115,676
207	Topeka, KS	235,846	271	Decatur, AL	154,689	335	Owensboro, KY	115,625
208	Macon, GA	235,405	272	Madera, CA	154,343	336	Sheboygan, WI	115,444
209	College Station-Bryan, TX	235,092	273	Bangor, ME	153,902	337	Brunswick, GA	114,128
210	Sioux Falls, SD	235,045	274	Rocky Mount, NC	153,664	338	Kankakee, IL	113,751
211	Tuscaloosa, AL	232,913	275	Wichita Falls, TX	152,511	339	Lawrence, KS	112,784
212	Champaign-Urbana, IL	232,445	276	Elizabethtown-Fort Knox, KY	151,716	340	Michigan City-La Porte, IN	111,723
213	Appleton, WI	227,986	277	Monroe, MI	151,670	341	Missoula, MT	110,904
214	Charlottesville, VA	223,598	278	Texarkana, TX-AR	151,153	342	Decatur, IL	110,782
215	Chico, CA	222,309	279	Chambersburg-Waynesboro, PA	151,055	343	California-Lexington Park, MD	108,522
216	Longview, TX	219,910	280	Jefferson City, MO	150,764	344	Sumter, SC	108,482
217	Barnstable Town, MA	217,689	281	Grand Junction, CO	149,118	345	Lewiston-Auburn, ME	107,479
218	Tyler, TX	216,577	282	Florence-Muscle Shoals, AL	147,885	346	Bay City, MI	107,188
219	Fargo, ND-MN	216,055	283	Midland, TX	147,417	347	Lima, OH	106,087
220	Prescott, AZ	214,201	284	Wheeling, WV-OH	147,195	348	Gadsden, AL	104,722
221	Las Cruces, NM	213,938	285	Dothan, AL	147,151	349	Cumberland, MD-WV	103,606
222	Springfield, IL	211,646	286	Norwich-New London, CT	146,391	350	Longview, WA	103,483
223	Rochester, MN	209,826	287	Santa Fe, NM	145,880	351	Fond du Lac, WI	102,340
224	Houma, LA	209,817	288	Hattiesburg, MS	145,741	352	Gettysburg, PA	101,598
225	Florence, SC	208,121	289	Dalton, GA	144,264	353	Sebring, FL	99,976
226	Medford, OR	206,276	290	Auburn, AL	144,044	354	Grand Forks, ND-MN	99,784
227	Bellingham, WA	205,660	291	Johnstown, PA	143,961	355	Pine Bluff, AR	99,299
228	Lake Havasu City-Kingman, AZ	204,559	292	Valdosta, GA	143,826	356	The Villages, FL	99,090
229	Lafayette, IN	204,246	293	St. George, UT	143,580	357	Mankato-North Mankato, MN	97,827
230	Yuma, AZ	203,062	294	Odessa, TX	142,209	358	Cape Girardeau, MO-IL	97,195
231	Johnson City, TN	201,468	295	Coeur d'Alene, ID	142,089	359	Ocean City, NJ	97,077
232	Saginaw, MI	199,233	296	Homosassa Springs, FL	141,942	360	Rome, GA	97,013
233	Racine, WI	195,888	297	Sebastian-Vero Beach, FL	140,789	361	Victoria, TX	96,207
234	Athens-Clarke County, GA	195,380	298	Napa, CA	139,368	362	Manhattan, KS	95,402
235	Hilton Head Island, SC	191,685	299	Rapid City, SD	138,237	363	Dubuque, IA	95,015
236	Panama City, FL	188,234	300	Springfield, OH	137,682	364	Cheyenne, WY	94,026
237	Daphne-Fairhope-Foley, AL	187,467	301	Flagstaff, AZ	135,979	365	Parkersburg-Vienna, WV	92,884
238	Bloomington, IL	187,221	302	Idaho Falls, ID	135,809	366	Ames, IA	90,011
239	Warner Robins, GA	185,441	303	La Crosse, WI-MN	134,905	367	Elmira, NY	89,320
240	Gainesville, GA	185,005	304	Sierra Vista-Douglas, AZ	134,744	368	Corvallis, OR	86,538
241	Kingston, NY	183,433	304	Wausau, WI	134,744	369	Bloomsburg-Berwick, PA	85,911
242	Blacksburg, VA	179,827	306	Lebanon, PA	134,529	370	Pocatello, ID	84,258
243	Redding, CA	179,423	307	Lawton, OK	132,806	371	Midland, MI	84,124
244	Monroe, LA	178,701	308	Morgantown, WV	132,255	372	Grand Island, NE	83,197
245	El Centro, CA	178,699	309	Pittsfield, MA	131,619	373	Kokomo, IN	83,059
246	Joplin, MO	177,182	310	Winchester, VA-WV	131,237	374	Great Falls, MT	82,406
247	Terre Haute, IN	173,204	311	Jackson, TN	131,023	375	Danville, IL	81,547
248	Greenville, NC	172,830	312	Glens Falls, NY	129,692	376	Hinesville, GA	81,447
249	East Stroudsburg, PA	170,157	313	New Bern, NC	129,271	377	Columbus, IN	78,114
250	Sioux City, IA-NE-SD	169,806	314	Logan, UT-ID	129,186	378	Casper, WY	77,475
251	Yuba City, CA	169,050	315	Farmington, NM	128,404	379	Walla Walla, WA	64,262
252	Waterloo-Cedar Falls, IA	168,941	316	Harrisonburg, VA	127,957	380	Lewiston, ID-WA	61,959
253	Abilene, TX	168,908	317	St. Joseph, MO-KS	127,840	381	Carson City, NV	56,164
254	Oshkosh-Neenah, WI	168,129	318	Altoona, PA	127,305	382	Fairbanks, AK	34,603
255	Dover, DE	166,643	319	Goldsboro, NC	124,923			
256	Columbia, MO	165,938	320	Beckley, WV	124,829			

Source: Reported data from the F.B.I. "Crime in the United States 2012"
*Estimates as of July 2012 based on U.S. Bureau of the Census figures.

86. Metropolitan Population in 2011
National Total = 311,587,816*

RANK	METROPOLITAN AREA	POP	RANK	METROPOLITAN AREA	POP	RANK	METROPOLITAN AREA	POP
206	Abilene, TX	168,729	288	Cheyenne, WY	92,473	82	Gary, IN M.D.	711,687
84	Akron, OH	703,715	4	Chicago (greater), IL-IN-WI	9,491,301	NA	Gettysburg, PA**	NA
68	Albany-Schenectady-Troy, NY	874,629	NA	Chicago-Joilet-Naperville, IL M.D.**	NA	249	Glens Falls, NY	129,502
215	Albany, GA	159,379	175	Chico, CA	222,586	256	Goldsboro, NC	124,178
NA	Albany, OR**	NA	37	Cincinnati, OH-KY-IN	2,134,687	282	Grand Forks, ND-MN	99,832
67	Albuquerque, NM	897,005	153	Clarksville, TN-KY	276,234	NA	Grand Island, NE**	NA
216	Alexandria, LA	155,330	262	Cleveland, TN	116,833	228	Grand Junction, CO	149,279
74	Allentown, PA-NJ	823,807	NA	Coeur d'Alene, ID**	NA	292	Great Falls, MT	82,049
252	Altoona, PA	127,494	171	College Station-Bryan, TX	233,472	161	Greeley, CO	257,229
165	Amarillo, TX	255,139	87	Colorado Springs, CO	656,862	144	Green Bay, WI	307,576
289	Ames, IA	90,011	202	Columbia, MO	173,414	NA	Greensboro-High Point, NC**	NA
21	Anaheim-Santa Ana-Irvine, CA M.D.	3,045,620	149	Columbus, GA-AL	298,305	NA	Greenville-Anderson, SC**	NA
143	Anchorage, AK	310,965	295	Columbus, IN	77,186	NA	Greenville, NC**	NA
137	Ann Arbor, MI	344,531	108	Corpus Christi, TX	437,195	NA	Hagerstown-Martinsburg, MD-WV**	NA
259	Anniston-Oxford, AL	119,143	291	Corvallis, OR	86,490	NA	Hammond, LA**	NA
174	Appleton, WI	226,649	196	Crestview-Fort Walton Beach, FL	183,286	217	Hanford-Corcoran, CA	154,780
110	Asheville, NC	430,246	278	Cumberland, MD-WV	104,047	95	Harrisburg-Carlisle, PA	551,228
194	Athens-Clarke County, GA	195,076	5	Dallas (greater), TX	6,505,848	254	Harrisonburg, VA	126,724
10	Atlanta, GA	5,338,234	14	Dallas-Plano-Irving, TX M.D.	4,324,880	62	Hartford, CT	1,022,173
154	Atlantic City, NJ	275,463	234	Dalton, GA	144,100	NA	Hattiesburg, MS**	NA
236	Auburn, AL	140,922	293	Danville, IL	81,871	132	Hickory, NC	370,132
94	Augusta, GA-SC	563,924	NA	Daphne-Fairhope-Foley, AL**	NA	NA	Hilton Head Island, SC**	NA
45	Austin-Round Rock, TX	1,752,404	127	Davenport, IA-IL	381,200	294	Hinesville, GA	78,942
71	Bakersfield, CA	849,502	72	Dayton, OH	842,118	NA	Homosassa Springs, FL**	NA
25	Baltimore, MD	2,736,186	218	Decatur, AL	154,569	183	Houma, LA	210,082
222	Bangor, ME	153,903	270	Decatur, IL	111,101	6	Houston, TX	6,071,933
177	Barnstable Town, MA	217,204	NA	Deltona-Daytona Beach, FL**	NA	115	Huntsville, AL	419,602
77	Baton Rouge, LA	809,822	28	Denver-Aurora, CO	2,587,784	246	Idaho Falls, ID	131,886
274	Bay City, MI	107,690	92	Des Moines-West Des Moines, IA	572,618	NA	Indianapolis, IN**	NA
125	Beaumont-Port Arthur, TX	396,925	15	Detroit (greater), MI	4,293,012	223	Iowa City, IA	153,385
NA	Beckley, WV**	NA	42	Detroit-Dearborn-Livonia, MI M.D.	1,819,213	48	Jacksonville, FL	1,363,935
186	Bellingham, WA	204,296	231	Dothan, AL	146,340	NA	Jackson, MS**	NA
214	Billings, MT	159,454	210	Dover, DE	163,973	NA	Jackson, TN**	NA
167	Binghamton, NY	252,857	287	Dubuque, IA	94,143	213	Janesville, WI	161,030
60	Birmingham-Hoover, AL	1,133,475	151	Duluth, MN-WI	281,781	227	Jefferson City, MO	150,351
271	Bismarck, ND	110,613	101	Durham-Chapel Hill, NC	510,752	190	Johnson City, TN	200,508
209	Blacksburg, VA	164,905	NA	Dutchess-Putnam, NY M.D.**	NA	233	Johnstown, PA	144,137
204	Bloomington, IL	170,082	NA	East Stroudsburg, PA**	NA	258	Jonesboro, AR	121,942
NA	Bloomington, IN**	NA	200	El Centro, CA	176,580	201	Joplin, MO	176,156
NA	Bloomsburg-Berwick, PA**	NA	75	El Paso, TX	817,494	NA	Kahului-Wailuku-Lahaina, HI**	NA
90	Boise City, ID	623,381	NA	Elgin, IL M.D.**	NA	NA	Kalamazoo-Portage, MI**	NA
11	Boston (greater), MA-NH	4,578,146	NA	Elizabethtown-Fort Knox, KY**	NA	267	Kankakee, IL	113,791
40	Boston, MA M.D.	1,899,298	290	Elmira, NY	89,229	38	Kansas City, MO-KS	2,045,034
148	Boulder, CO	299,698	152	Erie, PA	281,461	160	Kennewick-Richland, WA	257,314
253	Bowling Green, KY	126,823	134	Eugene, OR	355,459	121	Killeen-Temple, TX	413,828
166	Bremerton-Silverdale, WA	255,073	298	Fairbanks, AK	34,243	141	Kingsport, TN-VA	312,618
66	Bridgeport-Stamford, CT	901,031	180	Fargo, ND-MN	211,760	195	Kingston, NY	183,313
120	Brownsville-Harlingen, TX	414,768	247	Farmington, NM	131,499	NA	Knoxville, TN**	NA
266	Brunswick, GA	113,849	NA	Fayetteville-Springdale, AR-MO**	NA	NA	Kokomo, IN**	NA
59	Buffalo-Niagara Falls, NY	1,140,613	131	Fayetteville, NC	371,029	243	La Crosse, WI-MN	134,312
224	Burlington, NC	153,047	241	Flagstaff, AZ	136,324	189	Lafayette, IN	202,820
NA	California-Lexington Park, MD**	NA	113	Flint, MI	425,469	NA	Lafayette, LA**	NA
NA	Cambridge-Newton, MA M.D.**	NA	229	Florence-Muscle Shoals, AL	147,845	69	Lake Co.-Kenosha Co., IL-WI M.D.	872,725
54	Camden, NJ M.D.	1,254,841	184	Florence, SC	207,960	188	Lake Havasu City-Kingman, AZ	203,020
123	Canton, OH	404,718	280	Fond du Lac, WI	102,076	91	Lakeland, FL	610,301
88	Cape Coral-Fort Myers, FL	627,187	146	Fort Collins, CO	304,849	98	Lancaster, PA	521,105
286	Cape Girardeau, MO-IL	96,620	44	Fort Lauderdale, FL M.D.	1,771,889	104	Lansing-East Lansing, MI	463,686
297	Carson City, NV	55,740	NA	Fort Smith, AR-OK**	NA	164	Laredo, TX	255,571
296	Casper, WY	76,057	117	Fort Wayne, IN	418,383	181	Las Cruces, NM	211,575
158	Cedar Rapids, IA	259,291	34	Fort Worth-Arlington, TX M.D.	2,180,968	39	Las Vegas-Henderson, NV	1,967,721
NA	Chambersburg-Waynesboro, PA**	NA	65	Fresno, CA	941,388	269	Lawrence, KS	111,530
172	Champaign-Urbana, IL	232,588	277	Gadsden, AL	104,933	NA	Lawton, OK**	NA
NA	Charleston-North Charleston, SC**	NA	156	Gainesville, FL	267,877	244	Lebanon, PA	133,994
187	Charlottesville, VA	203,966	197	Gainesville, GA	182,050	275	Lewiston-Auburn, ME	107,688

Note: All listings are for Metropolitan Statistical Areas (M.S.A.s) except for those ending with "M.D." Listings with "M.D." are Metropolitan Divisions which are smaller parts of eleven large M.S.A.s. See explanatory note at beginning of metropolitan area section.

RANK	METROPOLITAN AREA	POP
NA	Lewiston, ID-WA**	NA
103	Lexington-Fayette, KY	475,361
276	Lima, OH	106,409
145	Lincoln, NE	304,853
83	Little Rock, AR	705,050
251	Logan, UT-ID	127,757
176	Longview, TX	218,879
279	Longview, WA	104,017
3	Los Angeles County, CA M.D.	9,934,033
2	Los Angeles (greater), CA	12,979,653
51	Louisville, KY-IN	1,291,986
150	Lubbock, TX	290,884
163	Lynchburg, VA	255,651
170	Macon, GA	235,351
225	Madera, CA	152,639
NA	Madison, WI**	NA
124	Manchester-Nashua, NH	401,245
NA	Manhattan, KS**	NA
285	Mankato-North Mankato, MN	97,487
255	Mansfield, OH	124,566
79	McAllen-Edinburg-Mission, TX	791,072
185	Medford, OR	205,369
50	Memphis, TN-MS-AR	1,326,648
159	Merced, CA	258,800
9	Miami (greater), FL	5,640,473
29	Miami-Dade County, FL M.D.	2,530,459
268	Michigan City-La Porte, IN	112,036
NA	Midland, MI**	NA
NA	Midland, TX**	NA
47	Milwaukee, WI	1,562,687
19	Minneapolis-St. Paul, MN-WI	3,304,725
272	Missoula, MT	110,269
119	Mobile, AL	414,980
99	Modesto, CA	520,501
199	Monroe, LA	178,055
226	Monroe, MI	151,906
NA	Montgomery County, PA M.D.**	NA
129	Montgomery, AL	376,339
NA	Morgantown, WV**	NA
NA	Morristown, TN**	NA
260	Mount Vernon-Anacortes, WA	118,735
261	Muncie, IN	118,272
240	Napa, CA	138,089
139	Naples-Marco Island, FL	325,902
NA	Nashville-Davidson, TN**	NA
22	Nassau-Suffolk, NY M.D.	2,845,615
NA	New Bern, NC**	NA
76	New Haven-Milford, CT	810,372
56	New Orleans, LA	1,178,445
1	New York (greater), NY-NJ-PA	18,974,419
NA	New York-Jersey City, NY-NJ M.D.**	NA
NA	Newark, NJ-PA M.D.**	NA
81	North Port-Sarasota-Bradenton, FL	711,852
230	Norwich-New London, CT	146,560
27	Oakland-Hayward, CA M.D.	2,589,383
138	Ocala, FL	335,813
283	Ocean City, NJ	97,589
237	Odessa, TX	140,016
NA	Ogden-Clearfield, UT**	NA
53	Oklahoma City, OK	1,266,404
162	Olympia, WA	256,222
70	Omaha-Council Bluffs, NE-IA	872,617
36	Orlando, FL	2,163,500
208	Oshkosh-Neenah, WI	167,722

RANK	METROPOLITAN AREA	POP
265	Owensboro, KY	115,545
73	Oxnard-Thousand Oaks, CA	832,997
96	Palm Bay-Melbourne, FL	550,781
NA	Panama City, FL**	NA
105	Pensacola, FL	455,110
128	Peoria, IL	380,327
7	Philadelphia (greater) PA-NJ-MD-DE	5,988,988
NA	Philadelphia, PA M.D.**	NA
17	Phoenix-Mesa-Scottsdale, AZ	4,252,245
281	Pine Bluff, AR	101,017
31	Pittsburgh, PA	2,363,799
245	Pittsfield, MA	132,019
NA	Pocatello, ID**	NA
111	Port St. Lucie, FL	429,887
32	Portland-Vancouver, OR-WA	2,251,909
100	Portland, ME	514,030
179	Prescott, AZ	214,020
NA	Providence-Warwick, RI-MA**	NA
97	Provo-Orem, UT	536,977
212	Pueblo, CO	161,834
211	Punta Gorda, FL	162,158
193	Racine, WI	196,259
58	Raleigh, NC	1,144,826
NA	Rapid City, SD**	NA
122	Reading, PA	412,754
198	Redding, CA	179,306
112	Reno, NV	429,004
52	Richmond, VA	1,273,282
16	Riverside-San Bernardino, CA	4,274,518
142	Roanoke, VA	312,395
NA	Rochester, MN**	NA
61	Rochester, NY	1,059,061
136	Rockford, IL	350,483
116	Rockingham County, NH M.D.	418,914
221	Rocky Mount, NC	154,324
284	Rome, GA	97,585
35	Sacramento, CA	2,174,392
191	Saginaw, MI	200,018
126	Salem, OR	394,898
114	Salinas, CA	419,936
NA	Salisbury, MD-DE**	NA
57	Salt Lake City, UT	1,145,892
33	San Antonio, TX	2,187,591
20	San Diego, CA	3,131,701
13	San Francisco (greater), CA	4,386,357
43	San Francisco-Redwood, CA M.D.	1,796,974
41	San Jose, CA	1,858,506
155	San Luis Obispo, CA	272,807
NA	San Rafael, CA M.D.**	NA
157	Santa Cruz-Watsonville, CA	265,467
232	Santa Fe, NM	145,783
NA	Santa Maria-Santa Barbara, CA**	NA
102	Santa Rosa, CA	489,566
135	Savannah, GA	352,188
93	Scranton--Wilkes-Barre, PA	565,428
18	Seattle (greater), WA	3,493,774
26	Seattle-Bellevue-Everett, WA M.D.	2,686,073
238	Sebastian-Vero Beach, FL	139,909
NA	Sebring, FL**	NA
264	Sheboygan, WI	116,010
257	Sherman-Denison, TX	123,421
NA	Shreveport-Bossier City, LA**	NA
NA	Sierra Vista-Douglas, AZ**	NA

RANK	METROPOLITAN AREA	POP
55	Silver Spring-Frederick, MD M.D.	1,216,589
NA	Sioux City, IA-NE-SD**	NA
173	Sioux Falls, SD	231,036
140	South Bend-Mishawaka, IN-MI	320,549
NA	Spartanburg, SC**	NA
NA	Spokane, WA**	NA
182	Springfield, IL	210,802
NA	Springfield, MA**	NA
107	Springfield, MO	438,299
239	Springfield, OH	138,434
220	State College, PA	154,481
NA	Staunton-Waynesboro, VA**	NA
85	Stockton-Lodi, CA	693,362
NA	St. George, UT**	NA
250	St. Joseph, MO-KS	127,813
23	St. Louis, MO-IL	2,824,159
273	Sumter, SC	108,707
86	Syracuse, NY	665,555
78	Tacoma, WA M.D.	807,701
130	Tallahassee, FL	372,419
24	Tampa-St Petersburg, FL	2,821,174
203	Terre Haute, IN	173,306
NA	Texarkana, TX-AR**	NA
NA	The Villages, FL**	NA
NA	Toledo, OH**	NA
169	Topeka, KS	235,354
133	Trenton, NJ	367,733
63	Tucson, AZ	994,140
64	Tulsa, OK	947,512
NA	Tuscaloosa, AL**	NA
178	Tyler, TX	214,127
147	Utica-Rome, NY	300,743
235	Valdosta, GA	141,426
118	Vallejo-Fairfield, CA	418,203
NA	Victoria, TX**	NA
NA	Vineland-Bridgeton, NJ**	NA
46	Virginia Beach-Norfolk, VA-NC	1,691,669
106	Visalia-Porterville, CA	447,377
NA	Waco, TX**	NA
NA	Walla Walla, WA**	NA
NA	Warner Robins, GA**	NA
30	Warren-Troy, MI M.D.	2,473,799
8	Washington (greater) DC-VA-MD-WV	5,651,690
12	Washington, DC-VA-MD-WV M.D.	4,435,101
207	Waterloo-Cedar Falls, IA	168,698
NA	Watertown-Fort Drum, NY**	NA
242	Wausau, WI	134,647
49	West Palm Beach, FL M.D.	1,338,125
NA	Wheeling, WV-OH**	NA
219	Wichita Falls, TX	154,490
89	Wichita, KS	627,017
263	Williamsport, PA	116,481
80	Wilmington, DE-MD-NJ M.D.	712,367
NA	Wilmington, NC**	NA
248	Winchester, VA-WV	129,751
NA	Winston-Salem, NC**	NA
NA	Worcester, MA-CT**	NA
168	Yakima, WA	247,047
109	York-Hanover, PA	436,359
NA	Youngstown-Warren, OH-PA**	NA
205	Yuba City, CA	168,854
192	Yuma, AZ	198,522

Source: Reported data from the F.B.I. "Crime in the United States 2011"
*Estimates as of July 2011 based on U.S. Bureau of the Census figures.
**Not available (comparable metro area not included in 2011 crime statistics).

86. Metropolitan Population in 2011 (continued)
National Total = 311,587,816*

RANK	METROPOLITAN AREA	POP	RANK	METROPOLITAN AREA	POP	RANK	METROPOLITAN AREA	POP
1	New York (greater), NY-NJ-PA	18,974,419	65	Fresno, CA	941,388	129	Montgomery, AL	376,339
2	Los Angeles (greater), CA	12,979,653	66	Bridgeport-Stamford, CT	901,031	130	Tallahassee, FL	372,419
3	Los Angeles County, CA M.D.	9,934,033	67	Albuquerque, NM	897,005	131	Fayetteville, NC	371,029
4	Chicago (greater), IL-IN-WI	9,491,301	68	Albany-Schenectady-Troy, NY	874,629	132	Hickory, NC	370,132
5	Dallas (greater), TX	6,505,848	69	Lake Co.-Kenosha Co., IL-WI M.D.	872,725	133	Trenton, NJ	367,733
6	Houston, TX	6,071,933	70	Omaha-Council Bluffs, NE-IA	872,617	134	Eugene, OR	355,459
7	Philadelphia (greater) PA-NJ-MD-DE	5,988,988	71	Bakersfield, CA	849,502	135	Savannah, GA	352,188
8	Washington (greater) DC-VA-MD-WV	5,651,690	72	Dayton, OH	842,118	136	Rockford, IL	350,483
9	Miami (greater), FL	5,640,473	73	Oxnard-Thousand Oaks, CA	832,997	137	Ann Arbor, MI	344,531
10	Atlanta, GA	5,338,234	74	Allentown, PA-NJ	823,807	138	Ocala, FL	335,813
11	Boston (greater), MA-NH	4,578,146	75	El Paso, TX	817,494	139	Naples-Marco Island, FL	325,902
12	Washington, DC-VA-MD-WV M.D.	4,435,101	76	New Haven-Milford, CT	810,372	140	South Bend-Mishawaka, IN-MI	320,549
13	San Francisco (greater), CA	4,386,357	77	Baton Rouge, LA	809,822	141	Kingsport, TN-VA	312,618
14	Dallas-Plano-Irving, TX M.D.	4,324,880	78	Tacoma, WA M.D.	807,701	142	Roanoke, VA	312,395
15	Detroit (greater), MI	4,293,012	79	McAllen-Edinburg-Mission, TX	791,072	143	Anchorage, AK	310,965
16	Riverside-San Bernardino, CA	4,274,518	80	Wilmington, DE-MD-NJ M.D.	712,367	144	Green Bay, WI	307,576
17	Phoenix-Mesa-Scottsdale, AZ	4,252,245	81	North Port-Sarasota-Bradenton, FL	711,852	145	Lincoln, NE	304,853
18	Seattle (greater), WA	3,493,774	82	Gary, IN M.D.	711,687	146	Fort Collins, CO	304,849
19	Minneapolis-St. Paul, MN-WI	3,304,725	83	Little Rock, AR	705,050	147	Utica-Rome, NY	300,743
20	San Diego, CA	3,131,701	84	Akron, OH	703,715	148	Boulder, CO	299,698
21	Anaheim-Santa Ana-Irvine, CA M.D.	3,045,620	85	Stockton-Lodi, CA	693,362	149	Columbus, GA-AL	298,305
22	Nassau-Suffolk, NY M.D.	2,845,615	86	Syracuse, NY	665,555	150	Lubbock, TX	290,884
23	St. Louis, MO-IL	2,824,159	87	Colorado Springs, CO	656,862	151	Duluth, MN-WI	281,781
24	Tampa-St Petersburg, FL	2,821,174	88	Cape Coral-Fort Myers, FL	627,187	152	Erie, PA	281,461
25	Baltimore, MD	2,736,186	89	Wichita, KS	627,017	153	Clarksville, TN-KY	276,234
26	Seattle-Bellevue-Everett, WA M.D.	2,686,073	90	Boise City, ID	623,381	154	Atlantic City, NJ	275,463
27	Oakland-Hayward, CA M.D.	2,589,383	91	Lakeland, FL	610,301	155	San Luis Obispo, CA	272,807
28	Denver-Aurora, CO	2,587,784	92	Des Moines-West Des Moines, IA	572,618	156	Gainesville, FL	267,877
29	Miami-Dade County, FL M.D.	2,530,459	93	Scranton--Wilkes-Barre, PA	565,428	157	Santa Cruz-Watsonville, CA	265,467
30	Warren-Troy, MI M.D.	2,473,799	94	Augusta, GA-SC	563,924	158	Cedar Rapids, IA	259,291
31	Pittsburgh, PA	2,363,799	95	Harrisburg-Carlisle, PA	551,228	159	Merced, CA	258,800
32	Portland-Vancouver, OR-WA	2,251,909	96	Palm Bay-Melbourne, FL	550,781	160	Kennewick-Richland, WA	257,314
33	San Antonio, TX	2,187,591	97	Provo-Orem, UT	536,977	161	Greeley, CO	257,229
34	Fort Worth-Arlington, TX M.D.	2,180,968	98	Lancaster, PA	521,101	162	Olympia, WA	256,222
35	Sacramento, CA	2,174,392	99	Modesto, CA	520,501	163	Lynchburg, VA	255,651
36	Orlando, FL	2,163,500	100	Portland, ME	514,030	164	Laredo, TX	255,571
37	Cincinnati, OH-KY-IN	2,134,687	101	Durham-Chapel Hill, NC	510,752	165	Amarillo, TX	255,139
38	Kansas City, MO-KS	2,045,034	102	Santa Rosa, CA	489,566	166	Bremerton-Silverdale, WA	255,073
39	Las Vegas-Henderson, NV	1,967,721	103	Lexington-Fayette, KY	475,361	167	Binghamton, NY	252,857
40	Boston, MA M.D.	1,899,298	104	Lansing-East Lansing, MI	463,686	168	Yakima, WA	247,047
41	San Jose, CA	1,858,506	105	Pensacola, FL	455,110	169	Topeka, KS	235,354
42	Detroit-Dearborn-Livonia, MI M.D.	1,819,213	106	Visalia-Porterville, CA	447,377	170	Macon, GA	235,351
43	San Francisco-Redwood, CA M.D.	1,796,974	107	Springfield, MO	438,299	171	College Station-Bryan, TX	233,472
44	Fort Lauderdale, FL M.D.	1,771,889	108	Corpus Christi, TX	437,195	172	Champaign-Urbana, IL	232,588
45	Austin-Round Rock, TX	1,752,404	109	York-Hanover, PA	436,359	173	Sioux Falls, SD	231,036
46	Virginia Beach-Norfolk, VA-NC	1,691,669	110	Asheville, NC	430,246	174	Appleton, WI	226,649
47	Milwaukee, WI	1,562,687	111	Port St. Lucie, FL	429,887	175	Chico, CA	222,586
48	Jacksonville, FL	1,363,935	112	Reno, NV	429,004	176	Longview, TX	218,879
49	West Palm Beach, FL M.D.	1,338,125	113	Flint, MI	425,469	177	Barnstable Town, MA	217,204
50	Memphis, TN-MS-AR	1,326,648	114	Salinas, CA	419,936	178	Tyler, TX	214,127
51	Louisville, KY-IN	1,291,986	115	Huntsville, AL	419,602	179	Prescott, AZ	214,020
52	Richmond, VA	1,273,282	116	Rockingham County, NH M.D.	418,914	180	Fargo, ND-MN	211,760
53	Oklahoma City, OK	1,266,404	117	Fort Wayne, IN	418,383	181	Las Cruces, NM	211,575
54	Camden, NJ M.D.	1,254,841	118	Vallejo-Fairfield, CA	418,203	182	Springfield, IL	210,802
55	Silver Spring-Frederick, MD M.D.	1,216,589	119	Mobile, AL	414,980	183	Houma, LA	210,082
56	New Orleans, LA	1,178,445	120	Brownsville-Harlingen, TX	414,768	184	Florence, SC	207,960
57	Salt Lake City, UT	1,145,892	121	Killeen-Temple, TX	413,828	185	Medford, OR	205,369
58	Raleigh, NC	1,144,826	122	Reading, PA	412,754	186	Bellingham, WA	204,296
59	Buffalo-Niagara Falls, NY	1,140,613	123	Canton, OH	404,718	187	Charlottesville, VA	203,966
60	Birmingham-Hoover, AL	1,133,475	124	Manchester-Nashua, NH	401,245	188	Lake Havasu City-Kingman, AZ	203,020
61	Rochester, NY	1,059,061	125	Beaumont-Port Arthur, TX	396,925	189	Lafayette, IN	202,820
62	Hartford, CT	1,022,173	126	Salem, OR	394,898	190	Johnson City, TN	200,508
63	Tucson, AZ	994,140	127	Davenport, IA-IL	381,200	191	Saginaw, MI	200,018
64	Tulsa, OK	947,512	128	Peoria, IL	380,327	192	Yuma, AZ	198,522

Note: All listings are for Metropolitan Statistical Areas (M.S.A.s) except for those ending with "M.D." Listings with "M.D." are Metropolitan Divisions which are smaller parts of eleven large M.S.A.s. See explanatory note at beginning of metropolitan area section.

RANK	METROPOLITAN AREA	POP	RANK	METROPOLITAN AREA	POP	RANK	METROPOLITAN AREA	POP
193	Racine, WI	196,259	257	Sherman-Denison, TX	123,421	NA	Greenville, NC**	NA
194	Athens-Clarke County, GA	195,076	258	Jonesboro, AR	121,942	NA	Hagerstown-Martinsburg, MD-WV**	NA
195	Kingston, NY	183,313	259	Anniston-Oxford, AL	119,143	NA	Hammond, LA**	NA
196	Crestview-Fort Walton Beach, FL	183,286	260	Mount Vernon-Anacortes, WA	118,735	NA	Hattiesburg, MS**	NA
197	Gainesville, GA	182,050	261	Muncie, IN	118,272	NA	Hilton Head Island, SC**	NA
198	Redding, CA	179,306	262	Cleveland, TN	116,833	NA	Homosassa Springs, FL**	NA
199	Monroe, LA	178,055	263	Williamsport, PA	116,481	NA	Indianapolis, IN**	NA
200	El Centro, CA	176,580	264	Sheboygan, WI	116,010	NA	Jackson, MS**	NA
201	Joplin, MO	176,156	265	Owensboro, KY	115,545	NA	Jackson, TN**	NA
202	Columbia, MO	173,414	266	Brunswick, GA	113,849	NA	Kahului-Wailuku-Lahaina, HI**	NA
203	Terre Haute, IN	173,306	267	Kankakee, IL	113,791	NA	Kalamazoo-Portage, MI**	NA
204	Bloomington, IL	170,082	268	Michigan City-La Porte, IN	112,036	NA	Knoxville, TN**	NA
205	Yuba City, CA	168,854	269	Lawrence, KS	111,530	NA	Kokomo, IN**	NA
206	Abilene, TX	168,729	270	Decatur, IL	111,101	NA	Lafayette, LA**	NA
207	Waterloo-Cedar Falls, IA	168,698	271	Bismarck, ND	110,613	NA	Lawton, OK**	NA
208	Oshkosh-Neenah, WI	167,722	272	Missoula, MT	110,269	NA	Lewiston, ID-WA**	NA
209	Blacksburg, VA	164,905	273	Sumter, SC	108,707	NA	Madison, WI**	NA
210	Dover, DE	163,973	274	Bay City, MI	107,690	NA	Manhattan, KS**	NA
211	Punta Gorda, FL	162,158	275	Lewiston-Auburn, ME	107,688	NA	Midland, MI**	NA
212	Pueblo, CO	161,834	276	Lima, OH	106,409	NA	Midland, TX**	NA
213	Janesville, WI	161,030	277	Gadsden, AL	104,933	NA	Montgomery County, PA M.D.**	NA
214	Billings, MT	159,454	278	Cumberland, MD-WV	104,047	NA	Morgantown, WV**	NA
215	Albany, GA	159,379	279	Longview, WA	104,017	NA	Morristown, TN**	NA
216	Alexandria, LA	155,330	280	Fond du Lac, WI	102,076	NA	Nashville-Davidson, TN**	NA
217	Hanford-Corcoran, CA	154,780	281	Pine Bluff, AR	101,017	NA	New Bern, NC**	NA
218	Decatur, AL	154,569	282	Grand Forks, ND-MN	99,832	NA	New York-Jersey City, NY-NJ M.D.**	NA
219	Wichita Falls, TX	154,490	283	Ocean City, NJ	97,589	NA	Newark, NJ-PA M.D.**	NA
220	State College, PA	154,481	284	Rome, GA	97,585	NA	Ogden-Clearfield, UT**	NA
221	Rocky Mount, NC	154,324	285	Mankato-North Mankato, MN	97,487	NA	Panama City, FL**	NA
222	Bangor, ME	153,903	286	Cape Girardeau, MO-IL	96,620	NA	Parkersburg-Vienna, WV**	NA
223	Iowa City, IA	153,385	287	Dubuque, IA	94,143	NA	Philadelphia, PA M.D.**	NA
224	Burlington, NC	153,047	288	Cheyenne, WY	92,473	NA	Pocatello, ID**	NA
225	Madera, CA	152,639	289	Ames, IA	90,011	NA	Providence-Warwick, RI-MA**	NA
226	Monroe, MI	151,906	290	Elmira, NY	89,229	NA	Rapid City, SD**	NA
227	Jefferson City, MO	150,351	291	Corvallis, OR	86,490	NA	Rochester, MN**	NA
228	Grand Junction, CO	149,279	292	Great Falls, MT	82,049	NA	Salisbury, MD-DE**	NA
229	Florence-Muscle Shoals, AL	147,845	293	Danville, IL	81,871	NA	San Rafael, CA M.D.**	NA
230	Norwich-New London, CT	146,560	294	Hinesville, GA	78,942	NA	Santa Maria-Santa Barbara, CA**	NA
231	Dothan, AL	146,340	295	Columbus, IN	77,186	NA	Sebring, FL**	NA
232	Santa Fe, NM	145,783	296	Casper, WY	76,057	NA	Shreveport-Bossier City, LA**	NA
233	Johnstown, PA	144,137	297	Carson City, NV	55,740	NA	Sierra Vista-Douglas, AZ**	NA
234	Dalton, GA	144,100	298	Fairbanks, AK	34,243	NA	Sioux City, IA-NE-SD**	NA
235	Valdosta, GA	141,426	NA	Albany, OR**	NA	NA	Spartanburg, SC**	NA
236	Auburn, AL	140,922	NA	Beckley, WV**	NA	NA	Spokane, WA**	NA
237	Odessa, TX	140,016	NA	Bloomington, IN**	NA	NA	Springfield, MA**	NA
238	Sebastian-Vero Beach, FL	139,909	NA	Bloomsburg-Berwick, PA**	NA	NA	Staunton-Waynesboro, VA**	NA
239	Springfield, OH	138,434	NA	California-Lexington Park, MD**	NA	NA	St. George, UT**	NA
240	Napa, CA	138,089	NA	Cambridge-Newton, MA M.D.**	NA	NA	Texarkana, TX-AR**	NA
241	Flagstaff, AZ	136,324	NA	Chambersburg-Waynesboro, PA**	NA	NA	The Villages, FL**	NA
242	Wausau, WI	134,647	NA	Charleston-North Charleston, SC**	NA	NA	Toledo, OH**	NA
243	La Crosse, WI-MN	134,312	NA	Chicago-Joilet-Naperville, IL M.D.*	NA	NA	Tuscaloosa, AL**	NA
244	Lebanon, PA	133,994	NA	Coeur d'Alene, ID**	NA	NA	Victoria, TX**	NA
245	Pittsfield, MA	132,019	NA	Daphne-Fairhope-Foley, AL**	NA	NA	Vineland-Bridgeton, NJ**	NA
246	Idaho Falls, ID	131,886	NA	Deltona-Daytona Beach, FL**	NA	NA	Waco, TX**	NA
247	Farmington, NM	131,499	NA	Dutchess-Putnam, NY M.D.**	NA	NA	Walla Walla, WA**	NA
248	Winchester, VA-WV	129,751	NA	East Stroudsburg, PA**	NA	NA	Warner Robins, GA**	NA
249	Glens Falls, NY	129,502	NA	Elgin, IL M.D.**	NA	NA	Watertown-Fort Drum, NY**	NA
250	St. Joseph, MO-KS	127,813	NA	Elizabethtown-Fort Knox, KY**	NA	NA	Wheeling, WV-OH**	NA
251	Logan, UT-ID	127,757	NA	Fayetteville-Springdale, AR-MO**	NA	NA	Wilmington, NC**	NA
252	Altoona, PA	127,494	NA	Fort Smith, AR-OK**	NA	NA	Winston-Salem, NC**	NA
253	Bowling Green, KY	126,823	NA	Gettysburg, PA**	NA	NA	Worcester, MA-CT**	NA
254	Harrisonburg, VA	126,724	NA	Grand Island, NE**	NA	NA	Youngstown-Warren, OH-PA**	NA
255	Mansfield, OH	124,566	NA	Greensboro-High Point, NC**	NA			
256	Goldsboro, NC	124,178	NA	Greenville-Anderson, SC**	NA			

Source: Reported data from the F.B.I. "Crime in the United States 2011"
*Estimates as of July 2011 based on U.S. Bureau of the Census figures.
**Not available (comparable metro area not included in 2011 crime statistics).

87. Metropolitan Population in 2008
National Total = 304,059,724*

RANK	METROPOLITAN AREA	POP	RANK	METROPOLITAN AREA	POP	RANK	METROPOLITAN AREA	POP
199	Abilene, TX	159,257	270	Cheyenne, WY	87,931	NA	Gary, IN M.D.**	NA
75	Akron, OH	699,914	NA	Chicago (greater), IL-IN-WI**	NA	NA	Gettysburg, PA**	NA
63	Albany-Schenectady-Troy, NY	856,504	NA	Chicago-Joilet-Naperville, IL M.D.**	NA	232	Glens Falls, NY	129,422
NA	Albany, GA**	NA	168	Chico, CA	219,628	251	Goldsboro, NC	113,923
NA	Albany, OR**	NA	29	Cincinnati, OH-KY-IN	2,150,520	265	Grand Forks, ND-MN	97,825
64	Albuquerque, NM	846,731	148	Clarksville, TN-KY	265,686	NA	Grand Island, NE**	NA
NA	Alexandria, LA**	NA	252	Cleveland, TN	111,956	220	Grand Junction, CO	142,140
67	Allentown, PA-NJ	811,166	NA	Coeur d'Alene, ID**	NA	273	Great Falls, MT	82,142
236	Altoona, PA	125,036	170	College Station-Bryan, TX	205,756	152	Greeley, CO	252,815
157	Amarillo, TX	244,209	81	Colorado Springs, CO	618,723	137	Green Bay, WI	303,250
272	Ames, IA	85,516	194	Columbia, MO	164,226	74	Greensboro-High Point, NC	707,329
18	Anaheim-Santa Ana-Irvine, CA M.D.	3,000,164	143	Columbus, GA-AL	282,227	NA	Greenville-Anderson, SC**	NA
138	Anchorage, AK	301,010	275	Columbus, IN	75,091	190	Greenville, NC	175,515
129	Ann Arbor, MI	350,369	109	Corpus Christi, TX	415,807	NA	Hagerstown-Martinsburg, MD-WV**	NA
NA	Anniston-Oxford, AL**	NA	274	Corvallis, OR	81,844	NA	Hammond, LA**	NA
167	Appleton, WI	219,912	NA	Crestview-Fort Walton Beach, FL**	NA	206	Hanford-Corcoran, CA	150,711
112	Asheville, NC	409,862	264	Cumberland, MD-WV	98,503	91	Harrisburg-Carlisle, PA	531,150
186	Athens-Clarke County, GA	189,226	4	Dallas (greater), TX	6,286,760	243	Harrisonburg, VA	118,335
7	Atlanta, GA	5,396,819	13	Dallas-Plano-Irving, TX M.D.	4,210,336	59	Hartford, CT	1,006,641
146	Atlantic City, NJ	271,795	223	Dalton, GA	135,123	NA	Hattiesburg, MS**	NA
225	Auburn, AL	132,798	NA	Danville, IL**	NA	126	Hickory, NC	363,694
90	Augusta, GA-SC	531,442	NA	Daphne-Fairhope-Foley, AL**	NA	NA	Hilton Head Island, SC**	NA
41	Austin-Round Rock, TX	1,646,660	NA	Davenport, IA-IL**	NA	277	Hinesville, GA	71,471
68	Bakersfield, CA	804,287	66	Dayton, OH	834,203	NA	Homosassa Springs, FL**	NA
23	Baltimore, MD	2,666,452	207	Decatur, AL	150,005	172	Houma, LA	203,144
210	Bangor, ME	148,610	NA	Decatur, IL**	NA	6	Houston, TX	5,752,684
166	Barnstable Town, MA	223,304	96	Deltona-Daytona Beach, FL	501,508	119	Huntsville, AL	393,173
71	Baton Rouge, LA	783,283	24	Denver-Aurora, CO	2,505,132	241	Idaho Falls, ID	121,458
256	Bay City, MI	106,303	87	Des Moines-West Des Moines, IA	556,378	39	Indianapolis, IN	1,717,530
122	Beaumont-Port Arthur, TX	375,242	NA	Detroit (greater), MI**	NA	208	Iowa City, IA	149,310
NA	Beckley, WV**	NA	NA	Detroit-Dearborn-Livonia, MI M.D.**	NA	44	Jacksonville, FL	1,308,904
179	Bellingham, WA	196,614	221	Dothan, AL	140,899	NA	Jackson, MS**	NA
205	Billings, MT	151,343	202	Dover, DE	155,344	NA	Jackson, TN**	NA
155	Binghamton, NY	245,658	268	Dubuque, IA	92,937	198	Janesville, WI	160,438
54	Birmingham-Hoover, AL	1,118,275	145	Duluth, MN-WI	273,527	NA	Jefferson City, MO**	NA
258	Bismarck, ND	104,611	97	Durham-Chapel Hill, NC	488,133	181	Johnson City, TN	194,959
200	Blacksburg, VA	157,811	NA	Dutchess-Putnam, NY M.D.**	NA	216	Johnstown, PA	144,050
NA	Bloomington, IL**	NA	NA	East Stroudsburg, PA**	NA	246	Jonesboro, AR	117,434
187	Bloomington, IN	184,646	195	El Centro, CA	163,673	192	Joplin, MO	172,779
NA	Bloomsburg-Berwick, PA**	NA	72	El Paso, TX	741,662	NA	Kahului-Wailuku-Lahaina, HI**	NA
83	Boise City, ID	603,185	NA	Elgin, IL M.D.**	NA	133	Kalamazoo-Portage, MI	321,552
10	Boston (greater), MA-NH	4,513,046	NA	Elizabethtown-Fort Knox, KY**	NA	NA	Kankakee, IL**	NA
34	Boston, MA M.D.	1,874,072	271	Elmira, NY	87,619	NA	Kansas City, MO-KS**	NA
NA	Boulder, CO**	NA	144	Erie, PA	278,759	162	Kennewick-Richland, WA	234,413
245	Bowling Green, KY	117,583	130	Eugene, OR	346,191	123	Killeen-Temple, TX	375,230
160	Bremerton-Silverdale, WA	237,527	280	Fairbanks, AK	37,407	136	Kingsport, TN-VA	303,904
62	Bridgeport-Stamford, CT	878,111	182	Fargo, ND-MN	194,942	188	Kingston, NY	182,305
118	Brownsville-Harlingen, TX	394,064	239	Farmington, NM	123,156	NA	Knoxville, TN**	NA
NA	Brunswick, GA**	NA	103	Fayetteville-Springdale, AR-MO	447,732	NA	Kokomo, IN**	NA
53	Buffalo-Niagara Falls, NY	1,122,844	128	Fayetteville, NC	351,539	227	La Crosse, WI-MN	131,303
212	Burlington, NC	147,580	234	Flagstaff, AZ	128,071	184	Lafayette, IN	193,802
NA	California-Lexington Park, MD**	NA	104	Flint, MI	430,816	NA	Lafayette, LA**	NA
NA	Cambridge-Newton, MA M.D.**	NA	217	Florence-Muscle Shoals, AL	143,463	NA	Lake Co.-Kenosha Co., IL-WI M.D.**	NA
47	Camden, NJ M.D.	1,248,666	176	Florence, SC	200,297	178	Lake Havasu City-Kingman, AZ	199,207
NA	Canton, OH**	NA	263	Fond du Lac, WI	99,281	85	Lakeland, FL	579,765
82	Cape Coral-Fort Myers, FL	604,488	142	Fort Collins, CO	292,381	95	Lancaster, PA	501,669
267	Cape Girardeau, MO-IL	93,556	37	Fort Lauderdale, FL M.D.	1,754,213	100	Lansing-East Lansing, MI	453,640
279	Carson City, NV	54,316	NA	Fort Smith, AR-OK**	NA	159	Laredo, TX	238,490
276	Casper, WY	73,249	110	Fort Wayne, IN	412,265	175	Las Cruces, NM	201,390
151	Cedar Rapids, IA	255,214	31	Fort Worth-Arlington, TX M.D.	2,076,424	35	Las Vegas-Henderson, NV	1,868,909
NA	Chambersburg-Waynesboro, PA**	NA	61	Fresno, CA	907,820	248	Lawrence, KS	115,531
NA	Champaign-Urbana, IL**	NA	260	Gadsden, AL	103,419	NA	Lawton, OK**	NA
80	Charleston-North Charleston, SC	643,759	150	Gainesville, FL	257,041	233	Lebanon, PA	128,795
183	Charlottesville, VA	194,483	NA	Gainesville, GA**	NA	255	Lewiston-Auburn, ME	106,715

Note: All listings are for Metropolitan Statistical Areas (M.S.A.s) except for those ending with "M.D." Listings with "M.D." are Metropolitan Divisions which are smaller parts of eleven large M.S.A.s. See explanatory note at beginning of metropolitan area section.

RANK	METROPOLITAN AREA	POP
278	Lewiston, ID-WA	60,233
102	Lexington-Fayette, KY	452,390
257	Lima, OH	104,842
140	Lincoln, NE	295,470
78	Little Rock, AR	673,330
237	Logan, UT-ID	124,922
171	Longview, TX	204,851
261	Longview, WA	101,545
3	Los Angeles County, CA M.D.	9,872,263
2	Los Angeles (greater), CA	12,872,427
48	Louisville, KY-IN	1,243,209
147	Lubbock, TX	269,446
156	Lynchburg, VA	244,588
165	Macon, GA	229,719
209	Madera, CA	148,935
NA	Madison, WI**	NA
NA	Manchester-Nashua, NH**	NA
NA	Manhattan, KS**	NA
269	Mankato-North Mankato, MN	91,966
235	Mansfield, OH	125,317
73	McAllen-Edinburg-Mission, TX	729,820
174	Medford, OR	201,601
45	Memphis, TN-MS-AR	1,290,901
154	Merced, CA	248,898
8	Miami (greater), FL	5,395,910
26	Miami-Dade County, FL M.D.	2,373,744
253	Michigan City-La Porte, IN	109,674
NA	Midland, MI**	NA
NA	Midland, TX**	NA
43	Milwaukee, WI	1,548,830
17	Minneapolis-St. Paul, MN-WI	3,231,521
254	Missoula, MT	107,119
116	Mobile, AL	405,797
92	Modesto, CA	516,995
191	Monroe, LA	173,540
203	Monroe, MI	153,241
NA	Montgomery County, PA M.D.**	NA
124	Montgomery, AL	369,292
NA	Morgantown, WV**	NA
NA	Morristown, TN**	NA
244	Mount Vernon-Anacortes, WA	118,241
249	Muncie, IN	114,943
224	Napa, CA	132,946
134	Naples-Marco Island, FL	320,551
NA	Nashville-Davidson, TN**	NA
20	Nassau-Suffolk, NY M.D.	2,877,560
NA	New Bern, NC**	NA
NA	New Haven-Milford, CT**	NA
55	New Orleans, LA	1,114,055
1	New York (greater), NY-NJ-PA	19,004,225
NA	New York-Jersey City, NY-NJ M.D.**	NA
NA	Newark, NJ-PA M.D.**	NA
NA	North Port-Sarasota-Bradenton, FL**	NA
218	Norwich-New London, CT	142,186
25	Oakland-Hayward, CA M.D.	2,481,921
132	Ocala, FL	329,862
266	Ocean City, NJ	95,311
229	Odessa, TX	130,731
NA	Ogden-Clearfield, UT**	NA
50	Oklahoma City, OK	1,206,660
158	Olympia, WA	242,881
65	Omaha-Council Bluffs, NE-IA	838,325
32	Orlando, FL	2,060,706
197	Oshkosh-Neenah, WI	162,698
NA	Owensboro, KY**	NA
69	Oxnard-Thousand Oaks, CA	799,817
89	Palm Bay-Melbourne, FL	537,212
NA	Panama City, FL**	NA
NA	Parkersburg-Vienna, WV**	NA
101	Pensacola, FL	453,297
NA	Peoria, IL**	NA
5	Philadelphia (greater) PA-NJ-MD-DE	5,836,682
16	Philadelphia, PA M.D.	3,891,020
11	Phoenix-Mesa-Scottsdale, AZ	4,283,537
262	Pine Bluff, AR	100,732
27	Pittsburgh, PA	2,345,727
231	Pittsfield, MA	129,918
NA	Pocatello, ID**	NA
114	Port St. Lucie, FL	406,587
28	Portland-Vancouver, OR-WA	2,207,851
94	Portland, ME	513,868
169	Prescott, AZ	217,520
42	Providence-Warwick, RI-MA	1,597,765
93	Provo-Orem, UT	516,198
NA	Pueblo, CO**	NA
204	Punta Gorda, FL	152,292
180	Racine, WI	195,756
56	Raleigh, NC	1,085,760
NA	Rapid City, SD**	NA
117	Reading, PA	405,335
189	Redding, CA	180,598
111	Reno, NV	412,231
49	Richmond, VA	1,223,648
15	Riverside-San Bernardino, CA	4,175,614
139	Roanoke, VA	296,477
NA	Rochester, MN**	NA
57	Rochester, NY	1,029,201
NA	Rockford, IL**	NA
108	Rockingham County, NH M.D.	418,477
NA	Rocky Mount, NC**	NA
NA	Rome, GA**	NA
30	Sacramento, CA	2,119,553
177	Saginaw, MI	199,649
120	Salem, OR	391,860
115	Salinas, CA	406,198
NA	Salisbury, MD-DE**	NA
52	Salt Lake City, UT	1,131,292
33	San Antonio, TX	2,027,812
19	San Diego, CA	2,979,368
12	San Francisco (greater), CA	4,230,321
38	San Francisco-Redwood, CA M.D.	1,748,400
36	San Jose, CA	1,802,847
149	San Luis Obispo, CA	263,017
NA	San Rafael, CA M.D.**	NA
153	Santa Cruz-Watsonville, CA	250,002
215	Santa Fe, NM	144,261
NA	Santa Maria-Santa Barbara, CA**	NA
98	Santa Rosa, CA	462,650
131	Savannah, GA	332,641
88	Scranton--Wilkes-Barre, PA	547,925
NA	Seattle (greater), WA**	NA
NA	Seattle-Bellevue-Everett, WA M.D.**	NA
226	Sebastian-Vero Beach, FL	132,682
NA	Sebring, FL**	NA
250	Sheboygan, WI	114,653
242	Sherman-Denison, TX	119,673
121	Shreveport-Bossier City, LA	391,302
NA	Sierra Vista-Douglas, AZ**	NA
51	Silver Spring-Frederick, MD M.D.	1,169,906
NA	Sioux City, IA-NE-SD**	NA
163	Sioux Falls, SD	233,355
135	South Bend-Mishawaka, IN-MI	316,014
NA	Spartanburg, SC**	NA
99	Spokane, WA	461,536
NA	Springfield, IL**	NA
NA	Springfield, MA**	NA
106	Springfield, MO	426,242
222	Springfield, OH	139,989
213	State College, PA	145,722
NA	Staunton-Waynesboro, VA**	NA
77	Stockton-Lodi, CA	681,786
219	St. George, UT	142,153
240	St. Joseph, MO-KS	123,101
21	St. Louis, MO-IL	2,820,831
259	Sumter, SC	104,311
79	Syracuse, NY	644,461
NA	Tacoma, WA M.D.**	NA
127	Tallahassee, FL	352,043
22	Tampa-St Petersburg, FL	2,734,761
NA	Terre Haute, IN**	NA
NA	Texarkana, TX-AR**	NA
NA	The Villages, FL**	NA
NA	Toledo, OH**	NA
164	Topeka, KS	229,726
125	Trenton, NJ	365,688
58	Tucson, AZ	1,010,650
60	Tulsa, OK	912,415
NA	Tuscaloosa, AL**	NA
173	Tyler, TX	201,817
141	Utica-Rome, NY	294,181
228	Valdosta, GA	130,908
113	Vallejo-Fairfield, CA	408,066
NA	Victoria, TX**	NA
201	Vineland-Bridgeton, NJ	156,078
40	Virginia Beach-Norfolk, VA-NC	1,663,408
105	Visalia-Porterville, CA	426,568
NA	Waco, TX**	NA
NA	Walla Walla, WA**	NA
NA	Warner Robins, GA**	NA
NA	Warren-Troy, MI M.D.**	NA
9	Washington (greater) DC-VA-MD-WV	5,363,413
14	Washington, DC-VA-MD-WV M.D.	4,193,507
196	Waterloo-Cedar Falls, IA	163,606
NA	Watertown-Fort Drum, NY**	NA
230	Wausau, WI	130,393
46	West Palm Beach, FL M.D.	1,267,953
214	Wheeling, WV-OH	144,612
211	Wichita Falls, TX	147,728
84	Wichita, KS	601,018
247	Williamsport, PA	116,368
76	Wilmington, DE-MD-NJ M.D.	696,996
NA	Wilmington, NC**	NA
238	Winchester, VA-WV	123,259
NA	Winston-Salem, NC**	NA
70	Worcester, MA-CT	789,453
161	Yakima, WA	234,618
107	York-Hanover, PA	425,908
86	Youngstown-Warren, OH-PA	566,927
193	Yuba City, CA	166,703
185	Yuma, AZ	193,473

Source: Reported data from the F.B.I. "Crime in the United States 2008"

*Estimates as of July 2008 based on U.S. Bureau of the Census figures.

**Not available (comparable metro area not included in 2008 crime statistics).

87. Metropolitan Population in 2008 (continued)
National Total = 304,059,724*

RANK	METROPOLITAN AREA	POP	RANK	METROPOLITAN AREA	POP	RANK	METROPOLITAN AREA	POP
1	New York (greater), NY-NJ-PA	19,004,225	65	Omaha-Council Bluffs, NE-IA	838,325	129	Ann Arbor, MI	350,369
2	Los Angeles (greater), CA	12,872,427	66	Dayton, OH	834,203	130	Eugene, OR	346,191
3	Los Angeles County, CA M.D.	9,872,263	67	Allentown, PA-NJ	811,166	131	Savannah, GA	332,641
4	Dallas (greater), TX	6,286,760	68	Bakersfield, CA	804,287	132	Ocala, FL	329,862
5	Philadelphia (greater) PA-NJ-MD-DE	5,836,682	69	Oxnard-Thousand Oaks, CA	799,817	133	Kalamazoo-Portage, MI	321,552
6	Houston, TX	5,752,684	70	Worcester, MA-CT	789,453	134	Naples-Marco Island, FL	320,551
7	Atlanta, GA	5,396,819	71	Baton Rouge, LA	783,283	135	South Bend-Mishawaka, IN-MI	316,014
8	Miami (greater), FL	5,395,910	72	El Paso, TX	741,662	136	Kingsport, TN-VA	303,904
9	Washington (greater) DC-VA-MD-WV	5,363,413	73	McAllen-Edinburg-Mission, TX	729,820	137	Green Bay, WI	303,250
10	Boston (greater), MA-NH	4,513,046	74	Greensboro-High Point, NC	707,329	138	Anchorage, AK	301,010
11	Phoenix-Mesa-Scottsdale, AZ	4,283,537	75	Akron, OH	699,914	139	Roanoke, VA	296,477
12	San Francisco (greater), CA	4,230,321	76	Wilmington, DE-MD-NJ M.D.	696,996	140	Lincoln, NE	295,470
13	Dallas-Plano-Irving, TX M.D.	4,210,336	77	Stockton-Lodi, CA	681,786	141	Utica-Rome, NY	294,181
14	Washington, DC-VA-MD-WV M.D.	4,193,507	78	Little Rock, AR	673,330	142	Fort Collins, CO	292,381
15	Riverside-San Bernardino, CA	4,175,614	79	Syracuse, NY	644,461	143	Columbus, GA-AL	282,227
16	Philadelphia, PA M.D.	3,891,020	80	Charleston-North Charleston, SC	643,759	144	Erie, PA	278,759
17	Minneapolis-St. Paul, MN-WI	3,231,521	81	Colorado Springs, CO	618,723	145	Duluth, MN-WI	273,527
18	Anaheim-Santa Ana-Irvine, CA M.D.	3,000,164	82	Cape Coral-Fort Myers, FL	604,488	146	Atlantic City, NJ	271,795
19	San Diego, CA	2,979,368	83	Boise City, ID	603,185	147	Lubbock, TX	269,446
20	Nassau-Suffolk, NY M.D.	2,877,560	84	Wichita, KS	601,018	148	Clarksville, TN-KY	265,686
21	St. Louis, MO-IL	2,820,831	85	Lakeland, FL	579,765	149	San Luis Obispo, CA	263,017
22	Tampa-St Petersburg, FL	2,734,761	86	Youngstown-Warren, OH-PA	566,927	150	Gainesville, FL	257,041
23	Baltimore, MD	2,666,452	87	Des Moines-West Des Moines, IA	556,378	151	Cedar Rapids, IA	255,214
24	Denver-Aurora, CO	2,505,132	88	Scranton--Wilkes-Barre, PA	547,925	152	Greeley, CO	252,815
25	Oakland-Hayward, CA M.D.	2,481,921	89	Palm Bay-Melbourne, FL	537,212	153	Santa Cruz-Watsonville, CA	250,002
26	Miami-Dade County, FL M.D.	2,373,744	90	Augusta, GA-SC	531,442	154	Merced, CA	248,898
27	Pittsburgh, PA	2,345,727	91	Harrisburg-Carlisle, PA	531,150	155	Binghamton, NY	245,658
28	Portland-Vancouver, OR-WA	2,207,851	92	Modesto, CA	516,995	156	Lynchburg, VA	244,588
29	Cincinnati, OH-KY-IN	2,150,520	93	Provo-Orem, UT	516,198	157	Amarillo, TX	244,209
30	Sacramento, CA	2,119,553	94	Portland, ME	513,868	158	Olympia, WA	242,881
31	Fort Worth-Arlington, TX M.D.	2,076,424	95	Lancaster, PA	501,669	159	Laredo, TX	238,490
32	Orlando, FL	2,060,706	96	Deltona-Daytona Beach, FL	501,508	160	Bremerton-Silverdale, WA	237,527
33	San Antonio, TX	2,027,812	97	Durham-Chapel Hill, NC	488,133	161	Yakima, WA	234,618
34	Boston, MA M.D.	1,874,072	98	Santa Rosa, CA	462,650	162	Kennewick-Richland, WA	234,413
35	Las Vegas-Henderson, NV	1,868,909	99	Spokane, WA	461,536	163	Sioux Falls, SD	233,355
36	San Jose, CA	1,802,847	100	Lansing-East Lansing, MI	453,640	164	Topeka, KS	229,726
37	Fort Lauderdale, FL M.D.	1,754,213	101	Pensacola, FL	453,297	165	Macon, GA	229,719
38	San Francisco-Redwood, CA M.D.	1,748,400	102	Lexington-Fayette, KY	452,390	166	Barnstable Town, MA	223,304
39	Indianapolis, IN	1,717,530	103	Fayetteville-Springdale, AR-MO	447,732	167	Appleton, WI	219,912
40	Virginia Beach-Norfolk, VA-NC	1,663,408	104	Flint, MI	430,816	168	Chico, CA	219,628
41	Austin-Round Rock, TX	1,646,660	105	Visalia-Porterville, CA	426,568	169	Prescott, AZ	217,520
42	Providence-Warwick, RI-MA	1,597,765	106	Springfield, MO	426,242	170	College Station-Bryan, TX	205,756
43	Milwaukee, WI	1,548,830	107	York-Hanover, PA	425,908	171	Longview, TX	204,851
44	Jacksonville, FL	1,308,904	108	Rockingham County, NH M.D.	418,477	172	Houma, LA	203,144
45	Memphis, TN-MS-AR	1,290,901	109	Corpus Christi, TX	415,807	173	Tyler, TX	201,817
46	West Palm Beach, FL M.D.	1,267,953	110	Fort Wayne, IN	412,265	174	Medford, OR	201,601
47	Camden, NJ M.D.	1,248,666	111	Reno, NV	412,231	175	Las Cruces, NM	201,390
48	Louisville, KY-IN	1,243,209	112	Asheville, NC	409,862	176	Florence, SC	200,297
49	Richmond, VA	1,223,648	113	Vallejo-Fairfield, CA	408,066	177	Saginaw, MI	199,649
50	Oklahoma City, OK	1,206,660	114	Port St. Lucie, FL	406,587	178	Lake Havasu City-Kingman, AZ	199,207
51	Silver Spring-Frederick, MD M.D.	1,169,906	115	Salinas, CA	406,198	179	Bellingham, WA	196,614
52	Salt Lake City, UT	1,131,292	116	Mobile, AL	405,797	180	Racine, WI	195,756
53	Buffalo-Niagara Falls, NY	1,122,844	117	Reading, PA	405,335	181	Johnson City, TN	194,959
54	Birmingham-Hoover, AL	1,118,275	118	Brownsville-Harlingen, TX	394,064	182	Fargo, ND-MN	194,942
55	New Orleans, LA	1,114,055	119	Huntsville, AL	393,173	183	Charlottesville, VA	194,483
56	Raleigh, NC	1,085,760	120	Salem, OR	391,860	184	Lafayette, IN	193,802
57	Rochester, NY	1,029,201	121	Shreveport-Bossier City, LA	391,302	185	Yuma, AZ	193,473
58	Tucson, AZ	1,010,650	122	Beaumont-Port Arthur, TX	375,242	186	Athens-Clarke County, GA	189,226
59	Hartford, CT	1,006,641	123	Killeen-Temple, TX	375,230	187	Bloomington, IN	184,646
60	Tulsa, OK	912,415	124	Montgomery, AL	369,292	188	Kingston, NY	182,305
61	Fresno, CA	907,820	125	Trenton, NJ	365,688	189	Redding, CA	180,598
62	Bridgeport-Stamford, CT	878,111	126	Hickory, NC	363,694	190	Greenville, NC	175,515
63	Albany-Schenectady-Troy, NY	856,504	127	Tallahassee, FL	352,043	191	Monroe, LA	173,540
64	Albuquerque, NM	846,731	128	Fayetteville, NC	351,539	192	Joplin, MO	172,779

Note: All listings are for Metropolitan Statistical Areas (M.S.A.s) except for those ending with "M.D." Listings with "M.D." are Metropolitan Divisions which are smaller parts of eleven large M.S.A.s. See explanatory note at beginning of metropolitan area section.

RANK	METROPOLITAN AREA	POP	RANK	METROPOLITAN AREA	POP	RANK	METROPOLITAN AREA	POP
193	Yuba City, CA	166,703	257	Lima, OH	104,842	NA	Jackson, TN**	NA
194	Columbia, MO	164,226	258	Bismarck, ND	104,611	NA	Jefferson City, MO**	NA
195	El Centro, CA	163,673	259	Sumter, SC	104,311	NA	Kahului-Wailuku-Lahaina, HI**	NA
196	Waterloo-Cedar Falls, IA	163,606	260	Gadsden, AL	103,419	NA	Kankakee, IL**	NA
197	Oshkosh-Neenah, WI	162,698	261	Longview, WA	101,545	NA	Kansas City, MO-KS**	NA
198	Janesville, WI	160,438	262	Pine Bluff, AR	100,732	NA	Knoxville, TN**	NA
199	Abilene, TX	159,257	263	Fond du Lac, WI	99,281	NA	Kokomo, IN**	NA
200	Blacksburg, VA	157,811	264	Cumberland, MD-WV	98,503	NA	Lafayette, LA**	NA
201	Vineland-Bridgeton, NJ	156,078	265	Grand Forks, ND-MN	97,825	NA	Lake Co.-Kenosha Co., IL-WI M.D.**	NA
202	Dover, DE	155,344	266	Ocean City, NJ	95,311	NA	Lawton, OK**	NA
203	Monroe, MI	153,241	267	Cape Girardeau, MO-IL	93,556	NA	Madison, WI**	NA
204	Punta Gorda, FL	152,292	268	Dubuque, IA	92,937	NA	Manchester-Nashua, NH**	NA
205	Billings, MT	151,343	269	Mankato-North Mankato, MN	91,966	NA	Manhattan, KS**	NA
206	Hanford-Corcoran, CA	150,711	270	Cheyenne, WY	87,931	NA	Midland, MI**	NA
207	Decatur, AL	150,005	271	Elmira, NY	87,619	NA	Midland, TX**	NA
208	Iowa City, IA	149,310	272	Ames, IA	85,516	NA	Montgomery County, PA M.D.**	NA
209	Madera, CA	148,935	273	Great Falls, MT	82,142	NA	Morgantown, WV**	NA
210	Bangor, ME	148,610	274	Corvallis, OR	81,844	NA	Morristown, TN**	NA
211	Wichita Falls, TX	147,728	275	Columbus, IN	75,091	NA	Nashville-Davidson, TN**	NA
212	Burlington, NC	147,580	276	Casper, WY	73,249	NA	New Bern, NC**	NA
213	State College, PA	145,722	277	Hinesville, GA	71,471	NA	New Haven-Milford, CT**	NA
214	Wheeling, WV-OH	144,612	278	Lewiston, ID-WA	60,233	NA	New York-Jersey City, NY-NJ M.D.**	NA
215	Santa Fe, NM	144,261	279	Carson City, NV	54,316	NA	Newark, NJ-PA M.D.**	NA
216	Johnstown, PA	144,050	280	Fairbanks, AK	37,407	NA	North Port-Sarasota-Bradenton, FL**	NA
217	Florence-Muscle Shoals, AL	143,463	NA	Albany, GA**	NA	NA	Ogden-Clearfield, UT**	NA
218	Norwich-New London, CT	142,186	NA	Albany, OR**	NA	NA	Owensboro, KY**	NA
219	St. George, UT	142,153	NA	Alexandria, LA**	NA	NA	Panama City, FL**	NA
220	Grand Junction, CO	142,140	NA	Anniston-Oxford, AL**	NA	NA	Parkersburg-Vienna, WV**	NA
221	Dothan, AL	140,899	NA	Beckley, WV**	NA	NA	Peoria, IL**	NA
222	Springfield, OH	139,989	NA	Bloomington, IL**	NA	NA	Pocatello, ID**	NA
223	Dalton, GA	135,123	NA	Bloomsburg-Berwick, PA**	NA	NA	Pueblo, CO**	NA
224	Napa, CA	132,946	NA	Boulder, CO**	NA	NA	Rapid City, SD**	NA
225	Auburn, AL	132,798	NA	Brunswick, GA**	NA	NA	Rochester, MN**	NA
226	Sebastian-Vero Beach, FL	132,682	NA	California-Lexington Park, MD**	NA	NA	Rockford, IL**	NA
227	La Crosse, WI-MN	131,303	NA	Cambridge-Newton, MA M.D.**	NA	NA	Rocky Mount, NC**	NA
228	Valdosta, GA	130,908	NA	Canton, OH**	NA	NA	Rome, GA**	NA
229	Odessa, TX	130,731	NA	Chambersburg-Waynesboro, PA**	NA	NA	Salisbury, MD-DE**	NA
230	Wausau, WI	130,393	NA	Champaign-Urbana, IL**	NA	NA	San Rafael, CA M.D.**	NA
231	Pittsfield, MA	129,918	NA	Chicago (greater), IL-IN-WI**	NA	NA	Santa Maria-Santa Barbara, CA**	NA
232	Glens Falls, NY	129,422	NA	Chicago-Joilet-Naperville, IL M.D.*	NA	NA	Seattle (greater), WA**	NA
233	Lebanon, PA	128,795	NA	Coeur d'Alene, ID**	NA	NA	Seattle-Bellevue-Everett, WA M.D.**	NA
234	Flagstaff, AZ	128,071	NA	Crestview-Fort Walton Beach, FL*'	NA	NA	Sebring, FL**	NA
235	Mansfield, OH	125,317	NA	Danville, IL**	NA	NA	Sierra Vista-Douglas, AZ**	NA
236	Altoona, PA	125,036	NA	Daphne-Fairhope-Foley, AL**	NA	NA	Sioux City, IA-NE-SD**	NA
237	Logan, UT-ID	124,922	NA	Davenport, IA-IL**	NA	NA	Spartanburg, SC**	NA
238	Winchester, VA-WV	123,259	NA	Decatur, IL**	NA	NA	Springfield, IL**	NA
239	Farmington, NM	123,156	NA	Detroit (greater), MI**	NA	NA	Springfield, MA**	NA
240	St. Joseph, MO-KS	123,101	NA	Detroit-Dearborn-Livonia, MI M.D.*	NA	NA	Staunton-Waynesboro, VA**	NA
241	Idaho Falls, ID	121,458	NA	Dutchess-Putnam, NY M.D.**	NA	NA	Tacoma, WA M.D.**	NA
242	Sherman-Denison, TX	119,673	NA	East Stroudsburg, PA**	NA	NA	Terre Haute, IN**	NA
243	Harrisonburg, VA	118,335	NA	Elgin, IL M.D.**	NA	NA	Texarkana, TX-AR**	NA
244	Mount Vernon-Anacortes, WA	118,241	NA	Elizabethtown-Fort Knox, KY**	NA	NA	The Villages, FL**	NA
245	Bowling Green, KY	117,583	NA	Fort Smith, AR-OK**	NA	NA	Toledo, OH**	NA
246	Jonesboro, AR	117,434	NA	Gainesville, GA**	NA	NA	Tuscaloosa, AL**	NA
247	Williamsport, PA	116,368	NA	Gary, IN M.D.**	NA	NA	Victoria, TX**	NA
248	Lawrence, KS	115,531	NA	Gettysburg, PA**	NA	NA	Waco, TX**	NA
249	Muncie, IN	114,943	NA	Grand Island, NE**	NA	NA	Walla Walla, WA**	NA
250	Sheboygan, WI	114,653	NA	Greenville-Anderson, SC**	NA	NA	Warner Robins, GA**	NA
251	Goldsboro, NC	113,923	NA	Hagerstown-Martinsburg, MD-WV*	NA	NA	Warren-Troy, MI M.D.**	NA
252	Cleveland, TN	111,956	NA	Hammond, LA**	NA	NA	Watertown-Fort Drum, NY**	NA
253	Michigan City-La Porte, IN	109,674	NA	Hattiesburg, MS**	NA	NA	Wilmington, NC**	NA
254	Missoula, MT	107,119	NA	Hilton Head Island, SC**	NA	NA	Winston-Salem, NC**	NA
255	Lewiston-Auburn, ME	106,715	NA	Homosassa Springs, FL**	NA			
256	Bay City, MI	106,303	NA	Jackson, MS**	NA			

Source: Reported data from the F.B.I. "Crime in the United States 2008"

*Estimates as of July 2008 based on U.S. Bureau of the Census figures.

**Not available (comparable metro area not included in 2008 crime statistics).

88. City Population in 2012
National Total = 313,914,040*

RANK	CITY	POP	RANK	CITY	POP	RANK	CITY	POP
212	Abilene, TX	119,886	431	Chino Hills, CA	76,632	194	Gainesville, FL	127,036
115	Akron, OH	198,390	403	Chino, CA	79,792	134	Garden Grove, CA	175,079
439	Alameda, CA	75,467	75	Chula Vista, CA	249,830	84	Garland, TX	234,984
410	Albany, GA	78,512	371	Cicero, IL	84,300	396	Gary, IN	80,472
292	Albany, NY	98,187	63	Cincinnati, OH	296,204	98	Gilbert, AZ	214,264
31	Albuquerque, NM	553,684	365	Citrus Heights, CA	85,112	87	Glendale, AZ	232,997
169	Alexandria, VA	145,892	400	Clarkstown, NY	80,186	119	Glendale, CA	194,902
370	Alhambra, CA	84,469	181	Clarksville, TN	137,356	127	Grand Prairie, TX	181,782
214	Allentown, PA	119,334	242	Clearwater, FL	109,255	122	Grand Rapids, MI	189,953
344	Allen, TX	88,783	46	Cleveland, OH	393,781	300	Greece, NY	96,752
116	Amarillo, TX	196,576	368	Clifton, NJ	84,684	303	Greeley, CO	96,276
219	Amherst, NY	117,591	299	Clinton Twnshp, MI	97,001	261	Green Bay, WI	106,080
53	Anaheim, CA	344,526	295	Clovis, CA	97,828	67	Greensboro, NC	276,134
61	Anchorage, AK	299,143	302	College Station, TX	96,567	352	Greenville, NC	86,869
227	Ann Arbor, MI	115,008	417	Colonie, NY	77,853	249	Gresham, OR	108,202
265	Antioch, CA	105,009	40	Colorado Springs, CO	432,287	342	Hamilton Twnshp, NJ	89,111
440	Arlington Heights, IL	75,463	236	Columbia, MO	110,646	391	Hammond, IN	81,010
49	Arlington, TX	379,295	117	Columbus, GA	196,178	180	Hampton, VA	137,905
245	Arvada, CO	109,029	293	Compton, CA	98,057	200	Hartford, CT	125,203
364	Asheville, NC	85,295	199	Concord, CA	125,205	361	Hawthorne, CA	85,692
220	Athens-Clarke, GA	117,457	201	Coral Springs, FL	125,021	162	Hayward, CA	147,424
39	Atlanta, GA	437,041	151	Corona, CA	157,342	390	Hemet, CA	81,213
54	Aurora, CO	336,952	58	Corpus Christi, TX	312,565	70	Henderson, NV	263,469
112	Aurora, IL	199,765	232	Costa Mesa, CA	112,635	322	Hesperia, CA	92,383
14	Austin, TX	832,901	399	Cranston, RI	80,315	86	Hialeah, FL	233,107
414	Avondale, AZ	78,364	10	Dallas, TX	1,241,549	257	High Point, NC	106,801
51	Bakersfield, CA	355,696	270	Daly City, CA	103,311	313	Hillsboro, OR	94,119
430	Baldwin Park, CA	76,644	384	Danbury, CT	81,891	170	Hollywood, FL	145,313
26	Baltimore, MD	625,474	280	Davenport, IA	101,193	382	Hoover, AL	82,332
88	Baton Rouge, LA	231,500	311	Davie, FL	94,952	4	Houston, TX	2,177,273
211	Beaumont, TX	120,323	174	Dayton, OH	142,139	120	Huntington Beach, CA	194,677
323	Beaverton, OR	92,276	298	Dearborn, MI	97,215	124	Huntsville, AL	183,691
197	Bellevue, WA	126,022	432	Decatur, IL	76,131	221	Independence, MO	117,433
416	Bellflower, CA	77,886	420	Deerfield Beach, FL	77,431	13	Indianapolis, IN	838,650
379	Bellingham, WA	82,665	215	Denton, TX	118,942	411	Indio, CA	78,501
228	Berkeley, CA	114,961	24	Denver, CO	628,545	234	Inglewood, CA	111,488
441	Bethlehem, PA	75,388	105	Des Moines, IA	207,400	96	Irvine, CA	217,528
258	Billings, MT	106,371	18	Detroit, MI	707,096	92	Irving, TX	224,007
99	Birmingham, AL	213,266	231	Downey, CA	113,628	12	Jacksonville, FL	840,660
428	Bloomington, IL	77,107	354	Duluth, MN	86,830	133	Jackson, MS	175,939
386	Bloomington, IN	81,636	83	Durham, NC	235,563	73	Jersey City, NJ	251,554
369	Bloomington, MN	84,596	397	Edinburg, TX	80,332	402	Johns Creek, GA	80,037
358	Boca Raton, FL	86,493	281	Edison Twnshp, NJ	101,007	160	Joliet, IL	148,471
102	Boise, ID	211,569	372	Edmond, OK	83,473	297	Jurupa Valley, CA	97,577
23	Boston, MA	630,648	275	El Cajon, CA	101,864	164	Kansas City, KS	147,201
285	Boulder, CO	100,257	225	El Monte, CA	115,356	36	Kansas City, MO	464,073
436	Brick Twnshp, NJ	75,809	19	El Paso, TX	675,536	429	Kennewick, WA	76,971
167	Bridgeport, CT	146,030	243	Elgin, IL	109,155	287	Kenosha, WI	99,993
310	Brockton, MA	95,156	196	Elizabeth, NJ	126,281	209	Kent, WA	122,102
282	Broken Arrow, OK	100,688	152	Elk Grove, CA	156,344	185	Killeen, TX	131,965
423	Brooklyn Park, MN	77,346	274	Erie, PA	101,972	126	Knoxville, TN	182,254
129	Brownsville, TX	181,102	163	Escondido, CA	147,386	208	Lafayette, LA	122,852
412	Bryan, TX	78,479	149	Eugene, OR	158,043	406	Lake Forest, CA	79,166
381	Buena Park, CA	82,505	217	Evansville, IN	118,194	288	Lakeland, FL	99,934
71	Buffalo, NY	262,434	263	Everett, WA	105,318	315	Lakewood Twnshp, NJ	93,742
264	Burbank, CA	105,057	253	Fairfield, CA	107,110	388	Lakewood, CA	81,382
255	Cambridge, MA	106,981	338	Fall River, MA	89,753	166	Lakewood, CO	146,404
418	Camden, NJ	77,665	239	Fargo, ND	109,813	146	Lancaster, CA	159,155
145	Cape Coral, FL	159,625	398	Farmington Hills, MI	80,316	229	Lansing, MI	114,688
250	Carlsbad, CA	107,879	442	Fayetteville, AR	75,387	78	Laredo, TX	245,558
385	Carmel, IN	81,819	106	Fayetteville, NC	205,966	408	Largo, FL	78,783
202	Carrollton, TX	124,477	326	Federal Way, WA	91,978	289	Las Cruces, NM	99,824
319	Carson, CA	93,233	404	Fishers, IN	79,375	7	Las Vegas, NV	1,479,393
175	Cary, NC	141,016	276	Flint, MI	101,632	341	Lawrence, KS	89,180
192	Cedar Rapids, IA	128,401	111	Fontana, CA	200,874	419	Lawrence, MA	77,661
267	Centennial, CO	104,022	159	Fort Collins, CO	148,792	291	Lawton, OK	98,781
389	Champaign, IL	81,329	137	Fort Lauderdale, FL	170,827	359	League City, TX	86,127
80	Chandler, AZ	242,721	347	Fort Smith, AR	87,483	331	Lee's Summit, MO	91,840
204	Charleston, SC	123,856	72	Fort Wayne, IN	256,625	60	Lexington, KY	302,332
16	Charlotte, NC	808,504	17	Fort Worth, TX	770,101	69	Lincoln, NE	264,175
405	Cheektowaga, NY	79,178	95	Fremont, CA	218,927	118	Little Rock, AR	196,055
91	Chesapeake, VA	227,531	33	Fresno, CA	506,011	378	Livermore, CA	82,800
3	Chicago, IL	2,708,382	205	Frisco, TX	123,205	306	Livonia, MI	96,028
350	Chico, CA	87,090	178	Fullerton, CA	138,455	35	Long Beach, CA	469,893

RANK	CITY	POP	RANK	CITY	POP	RANK	CITY	POP
343	Longmont, CO	88,925	177	Pasadena, CA	139,382	307	South Gate, CA	95,966
380	Longview, TX	82,554	154	Pasadena, TX	154,562	321	Sparks, NV	92,387
2	Los Angeles, CA	3,855,122	165	Paterson, NJ	147,148	333	Spokane Valley, WA	91,164
20	Louisville, KY	666,200	312	Pearland, TX	94,702	100	Spokane, WA	212,163
247	Lowell, MA	108,539	144	Pembroke Pines, FL	159,744	222	Springfield, IL	117,131
82	Lubbock, TX	237,241	148	Peoria, AZ	158,347	155	Springfield, MA	154,518
422	Lynchburg, VA	77,347	226	Peoria, IL	115,288	143	Springfield, MO	160,962
330	Lynn, MA	91,846	5	Philadelphia, PA	1,538,957	203	Stamford, CT	124,201
320	Macon, GA	92,836	6	Phoenix, AZ	1,485,509	186	Sterling Heights, MI	129,974
81	Madison, WI	237,508	59	Pittsburgh, PA	312,112	62	Stockton, CA	299,105
238	Manchester, NH	110,040	68	Plano, TX	273,816	437	St. George, UT	75,780
182	McAllen, TX	135,745	346	Plantation, FL	87,705	424	St. Joseph, MO	77,330
179	McKinney, TX	138,105	158	Pomona, CA	151,511	56	St. Louis, MO	318,667
434	Medford, OR	76,037	272	Pompano Beach, FL	103,003	64	St. Paul, MN	290,700
427	Melbourne, FL	77,133	139	Port St. Lucie, FL	168,416	76	St. Petersburg, FL	248,340
21	Memphis, TN	657,436	29	Portland, OR	598,037	377	Sugar Land, TX	82,924
401	Menifee, CA	80,047	301	Portsmouth, VA	96,739	172	Sunnyvale, CA	143,606
392	Merced, CA	80,976	131	Providence, RI	177,882	349	Sunrise, FL	87,168
425	Meridian, ID	77,270	223	Provo, UT	116,879	210	Surprise, AZ	120,793
37	Mesa, AZ	451,391	244	Pueblo, CO	109,065	168	Syracuse, NY	145,934
171	Mesquite, TX	144,811	316	Quincy, MA	93,736	108	Tacoma, WA	202,646
334	Miami Beach, FL	91,066	407	Racine, WI	79,055	123	Tallahassee, FL	185,461
235	Miami Gardens, FL	111,177	41	Raleigh, NC	420,594	52	Tampa, FL	350,758
43	Miami, FL	414,327	362	Ramapo, NY	85,448	269	Temecula, CA	103,414
224	Midland, TX	115,637	138	Rancho Cucamon., CA	169,276	142	Tempe, AZ	166,061
28	Milwaukee, WI	599,395	345	Reading, PA	88,557	206	Thornton, CO	123,115
47	Minneapolis, MN	390,240	335	Redding, CA	90,974	188	Thousand Oaks, CA	129,171
198	Miramar, FL	125,998	413	Redwood City, CA	78,466	65	Toledo, OH	286,020
308	Mission Viejo, CA	95,599	90	Reno, NV	230,486	325	Toms River Twnshp, NJ	92,131
395	Mission, TX	80,557	317	Renton, WA	93,722	189	Topeka, KS	128,843
74	Mobile, AL	251,516	277	Rialto, CA	101,595	161	Torrance, CA	147,851
107	Modesto, CA	204,631	271	Richardson, TX	103,266	367	Tracy, CA	85,047
103	Montgomery, AL	209,018	259	Richmond, CA	106,357	363	Trenton, NJ	85,317
113	Moreno Valley, CA	199,673	104	Richmond, VA	207,799	387	Troy, MI	81,567
435	Mountain View, CA	75,933	340	Rio Rancho, NM	89,462	32	Tucson, AZ	531,535
233	Murfreesboro, TN	112,247	57	Riverside, CA	313,532	45	Tulsa, OK	398,904
256	Murrieta, CA	106,839	296	Roanoke, VA	97,780	327	Tuscaloosa, AL	91,973
373	Nampa, ID	83,316	246	Rochester, MN	108,582	421	Tustin, CA	77,400
409	Napa, CA	78,589	101	Rochester, NY	211,993	286	Tyler, TX	100,040
173	Naperville, IL	142,840	157	Rockford, IL	152,293	438	Upland, CA	75,531
351	Nashua, NH	86,870	207	Roseville, CA	122,896	376	Upper Darby Twnshp, PA	82,978
27	Nashville, TN	620,886	324	Roswell, GA	92,141	314	Vacaville, CA	93,951
305	New Bedford, MA	96,031	260	Round Rock, TX	106,232	218	Vallejo, CA	117,912
187	New Haven, CT	129,934	34	Sacramento, CA	476,557	141	Vancouver, WA	166,375
50	New Orleans, LA	362,874	150	Salem, OR	157,353	248	Ventura, CA	108,511
415	New Rochelle, NY	78,025	156	Salinas, CA	154,413	216	Victorville, CA	118,687
1	New York, NY	8,289,415	121	Salt Lake City, UT	192,465	38	Virginia Beach, VA	447,588
66	Newark, NJ	278,906	8	San Antonio, TX	1,380,123	193	Visalia, CA	127,604
348	Newport Beach, CA	87,286	97	San Bernardino, CA	214,987	304	Vista, CA	96,087
128	Newport News, VA	181,591	9	San Diego, CA	1,338,477	190	Waco, TX	128,595
356	Newton, MA	86,710	15	San Francisco, CA	820,363	183	Warren, MI	134,340
79	Norfolk, VA	245,303	11	San Jose, CA	976,459	383	Warwick, RI	82,282
230	Norman, OK	113,969	352	San Leandro, CA	86,869	22	Washington, DC	632,323
283	North Charleston, SC	100,675	360	San Marcos, CA	85,810	237	Waterbury, CT	110,486
94	North Las Vegas, NV	221,884	290	San Mateo, CA	99,303	339	Waukegan, IL	89,468
252	Norwalk, CA	107,295	294	Sandy Springs, GA	97,890	251	West Covina, CA	107,861
357	Norwalk, CT	86,693	336	Sandy, UT	90,405	254	West Jordan, UT	107,103
44	Oakland, CA	399,487	55	Santa Ana, CA	332,482	273	West Palm Beach, FL	102,422
135	Oceanside, CA	171,141	337	Santa Barbara, CA	89,871	184	West Valley, UT	133,725
268	Odessa, TX	103,635	213	Santa Clara, CA	119,360	374	Westland, MI	83,299
394	O'Fallon, MO	80,670	130	Santa Clarita, CA	179,248	329	Westminster, CA	91,908
366	Ogden, UT	85,083	279	Santa Maria, CA	101,207	240	Westminster, CO	109,461
30	Oklahoma City, OK	595,607	332	Santa Monica, CA	91,215	355	Whittier, CA	86,740
191	Olathe, KS	128,560	136	Santa Rosa, CA	170,862	262	Wichita Falls, TX	105,488
42	Omaha, NE	417,970	89	Savannah, GA	231,285	48	Wichita, KS	386,409
140	Ontario, CA	167,933	93	Scottsdale, AZ	223,432	241	Wilmington, NC	109,370
176	Orange, CA	139,692	433	Scranton, PA	76,118	85	Winston-Salem, NC	234,687
328	Orem, UT	91,953	25	Seattle, WA	626,865	284	Woodbridge Twnshp, NJ	100,612
77	Orlando, FL	246,513	109	Shreveport, LA	202,164	125	Worcester, MA	183,247
132	Overland Park, KS	177,085	195	Simi Valley, CA	126,686	318	Yakima, WA	93,419
110	Oxnard, CA	201,797	375	Sioux City, IA	83,289	114	Yonkers, NY	198,464
266	Palm Bay, FL	104,635	147	Sioux Falls, SD	158,354	309	Yuma, AZ	95,568
153	Palmdale, CA	155,294	426	Somerville, MA	77,200			
393	Parma, OH	80,963	278	South Bend, IN	101,398			

Source: Reported data from the F.B.I. "Crime in the United States 2012"

*Estimates as of July 2012 based on U.S. Bureau of the Census figures. Charlotte, Indianapolis, Las Vegas, Louisville, Mobile, and Savannah include areas under their police department but outside the city limits. All populations are for area covered by police department.

88. City Population in 2012 (continued)
National Total = 313,914,040*

RANK	CITY	POP
1	New York, NY	8,289,415
2	Los Angeles, CA	3,855,122
3	Chicago, IL	2,708,382
4	Houston, TX	2,177,273
5	Philadelphia, PA	1,538,957
6	Phoenix, AZ	1,485,509
7	Las Vegas, NV	1,479,393
8	San Antonio, TX	1,380,123
9	San Diego, CA	1,338,477
10	Dallas, TX	1,241,549
11	San Jose, CA	976,459
12	Jacksonville, FL	840,660
13	Indianapolis, IN	838,650
14	Austin, TX	832,901
15	San Francisco, CA	820,363
16	Charlotte, NC	808,504
17	Fort Worth, TX	770,101
18	Detroit, MI	707,096
19	El Paso, TX	675,536
20	Louisville, KY	666,200
21	Memphis, TN	657,436
22	Washington, DC	632,323
23	Boston, MA	630,648
24	Denver, CO	628,545
25	Seattle, WA	626,865
26	Baltimore, MD	625,474
27	Nashville, TN	620,886
28	Milwaukee, WI	599,395
29	Portland, OR	598,037
30	Oklahoma City, OK	595,607
31	Albuquerque, NM	553,684
32	Tucson, AZ	531,535
33	Fresno, CA	506,011
34	Sacramento, CA	476,557
35	Long Beach, CA	469,893
36	Kansas City, MO	464,073
37	Mesa, AZ	451,391
38	Virginia Beach, VA	447,588
39	Atlanta, GA	437,041
40	Colorado Springs, CO	432,287
41	Raleigh, NC	420,594
42	Omaha, NE	417,970
43	Miami, FL	414,327
44	Oakland, CA	399,487
45	Tulsa, OK	398,904
46	Cleveland, OH	393,781
47	Minneapolis, MN	390,240
48	Wichita, KS	386,409
49	Arlington, TX	379,295
50	New Orleans, LA	362,874
51	Bakersfield, CA	355,696
52	Tampa, FL	350,758
53	Anaheim, CA	344,526
54	Aurora, CO	336,952
55	Santa Ana, CA	332,482
56	St. Louis, MO	318,667
57	Riverside, CA	313,532
58	Corpus Christi, TX	312,565
59	Pittsburgh, PA	312,112
60	Lexington, KY	302,332
61	Anchorage, AK	299,143
62	Stockton, CA	299,105
63	Cincinnati, OH	296,204
64	St. Paul, MN	290,700
65	Toledo, OH	286,020
66	Newark, NJ	278,906
67	Greensboro, NC	276,134
68	Plano, TX	273,816
69	Lincoln, NE	264,175
70	Henderson, NV	263,469
71	Buffalo, NY	262,434
72	Fort Wayne, IN	256,625
73	Jersey City, NJ	251,554
74	Mobile, AL	251,516
75	Chula Vista, CA	249,830
76	St. Petersburg, FL	248,340
77	Orlando, FL	246,513
78	Laredo, TX	245,558
79	Norfolk, VA	245,303
80	Chandler, AZ	242,721
81	Madison, WI	237,508
82	Lubbock, TX	237,241
83	Durham, NC	235,563
84	Garland, TX	234,984
85	Winston-Salem, NC	234,687
86	Hialeah, FL	233,107
87	Glendale, AZ	232,997
88	Baton Rouge, LA	231,500
89	Savannah, GA	231,285
90	Reno, NV	230,486
91	Chesapeake, VA	227,531
92	Irving, TX	224,007
93	Scottsdale, AZ	223,432
94	North Las Vegas, NV	221,884
95	Fremont, CA	218,927
96	Irvine, CA	217,528
97	San Bernardino, CA	214,987
98	Gilbert, AZ	214,264
99	Birmingham, AL	213,266
100	Spokane, WA	212,163
101	Rochester, NY	211,993
102	Boise, ID	211,569
103	Montgomery, AL	209,018
104	Richmond, VA	207,799
105	Des Moines, IA	207,400
106	Fayetteville, NC	205,966
107	Modesto, CA	204,631
108	Tacoma, WA	202,646
109	Shreveport, LA	202,164
110	Oxnard, CA	201,797
111	Fontana, CA	200,874
112	Aurora, IL	199,765
113	Moreno Valley, CA	199,673
114	Yonkers, NY	198,464
115	Akron, OH	198,390
116	Amarillo, TX	196,576
117	Columbus, GA	196,178
118	Little Rock, AR	196,055
119	Glendale, CA	194,902
120	Huntington Beach, CA	194,677
121	Salt Lake City, UT	192,465
122	Grand Rapids, MI	189,953
123	Tallahassee, FL	185,461
124	Huntsville, AL	183,691
125	Worcester, MA	183,247
126	Knoxville, TN	182,254
127	Grand Prairie, TX	181,782
128	Newport News, VA	181,591
129	Brownsville, TX	181,102
130	Santa Clarita, CA	179,248
131	Providence, RI	177,882
132	Overland Park, KS	177,085
133	Jackson, MS	175,939
134	Garden Grove, CA	175,079
135	Oceanside, CA	171,141
136	Santa Rosa, CA	170,862
137	Fort Lauderdale, FL	170,827
138	Rancho Cucamon., CA	169,276
139	Port St. Lucie, FL	168,416
140	Ontario, CA	167,933
141	Vancouver, WA	166,375
142	Tempe, AZ	166,061
143	Springfield, MO	160,962
144	Pembroke Pines, FL	159,744
145	Cape Coral, FL	159,625
146	Lancaster, CA	159,155
147	Sioux Falls, SD	158,354
148	Peoria, AZ	158,347
149	Eugene, OR	158,043
150	Salem, OR	157,353
151	Corona, CA	157,342
152	Elk Grove, CA	156,344
153	Palmdale, CA	155,294
154	Pasadena, TX	154,562
155	Springfield, MA	154,518
156	Salinas, CA	154,413
157	Rockford, IL	152,293
158	Pomona, CA	151,511
159	Fort Collins, CO	148,792
160	Joliet, IL	148,471
161	Torrance, CA	147,851
162	Hayward, CA	147,424
163	Escondido, CA	147,386
164	Kansas City, KS	147,201
165	Paterson, NJ	147,148
166	Lakewood, CO	146,404
167	Bridgeport, CT	146,030
168	Syracuse, NY	145,934
169	Alexandria, VA	145,892
170	Hollywood, FL	145,313
171	Mesquite, TX	144,811
172	Sunnyvale, CA	143,606
173	Naperville, IL	142,840
174	Dayton, OH	142,139
175	Cary, NC	141,016
176	Orange, CA	139,692
177	Pasadena, CA	139,382
178	Fullerton, CA	138,455
179	McKinney, TX	138,105
180	Hampton, VA	137,905
181	Clarksville, TN	137,356
182	McAllen, TX	135,745
183	Warren, MI	134,340
184	West Valley, UT	133,725
185	Killeen, TX	131,965
186	Sterling Heights, MI	129,974
187	New Haven, CT	129,934
188	Thousand Oaks, CA	129,171
189	Topeka, KS	128,843
190	Waco, TX	128,595
191	Olathe, KS	128,560
192	Cedar Rapids, IA	128,401
193	Visalia, CA	127,604
194	Gainesville, FL	127,036
195	Simi Valley, CA	126,686
196	Elizabeth, NJ	126,281
197	Bellevue, WA	126,022
198	Miramar, FL	125,998
199	Concord, CA	125,205
200	Hartford, CT	125,203
201	Coral Springs, FL	125,021
202	Carrollton, TX	124,477
203	Stamford, CT	124,201
204	Charleston, SC	123,856
205	Frisco, TX	123,205
206	Thornton, CO	123,115
207	Roseville, CA	122,896
208	Lafayette, LA	122,852
209	Kent, WA	122,102
210	Surprise, AZ	120,793
211	Beaumont, TX	120,323
212	Abilene, TX	119,886
213	Santa Clara, CA	119,360
214	Allentown, PA	119,334
215	Denton, TX	118,942
216	Victorville, CA	118,687
217	Evansville, IN	118,194
218	Vallejo, CA	117,912
219	Amherst, NY	117,591
220	Athens-Clarke, GA	117,457
221	Independence, MO	117,433
222	Springfield, IL	117,131

RANK	CITY	POP	RANK	CITY	POP	RANK	CITY	POP
223	Provo, UT	116,879	297	Jurupa Valley, CA	97,577	371	Cicero, IL	84,300
224	Midland, TX	115,637	298	Dearborn, MI	97,215	372	Edmond, OK	83,473
225	El Monte, CA	115,356	299	Clinton Twnshp, MI	97,001	373	Nampa, ID	83,316
226	Peoria, IL	115,288	300	Greece, NY	96,752	374	Westland, MI	83,299
227	Ann Arbor, MI	115,008	301	Portsmouth, VA	96,739	375	Sioux City, IA	83,289
228	Berkeley, CA	114,961	302	College Station, TX	96,567	376	Upper Darby Twnshp, PA	82,978
229	Lansing, MI	114,688	303	Greeley, CO	96,276	377	Sugar Land, TX	82,924
230	Norman, OK	113,969	304	Vista, CA	96,087	378	Livermore, CA	82,800
231	Downey, CA	113,628	305	New Bedford, MA	96,031	379	Bellingham, WA	82,665
232	Costa Mesa, CA	112,635	306	Livonia, MI	96,028	380	Longview, TX	82,554
233	Murfreesboro, TN	112,247	307	South Gate, CA	95,966	381	Buena Park, CA	82,505
234	Inglewood, CA	111,488	308	Mission Viejo, CA	95,599	382	Hoover, AL	82,332
235	Miami Gardens, FL	111,177	309	Yuma, AZ	95,568	383	Warwick, RI	82,282
236	Columbia, MO	110,646	310	Brockton, MA	95,156	384	Danbury, CT	81,891
237	Waterbury, CT	110,486	311	Davie, FL	94,952	385	Carmel, IN	81,819
238	Manchester, NH	110,040	312	Pearland, TX	94,702	386	Bloomington, IN	81,636
239	Fargo, ND	109,813	313	Hillsboro, OR	94,119	387	Troy, MI	81,567
240	Westminster, CO	109,461	314	Vacaville, CA	93,951	388	Lakewood, CA	81,382
241	Wilmington, NC	109,370	315	Lakewood Twnshp, NJ	93,742	389	Champaign, IL	81,329
242	Clearwater, FL	109,255	316	Quincy, MA	93,736	390	Hemet, CA	81,213
243	Elgin, IL	109,155	317	Renton, WA	93,722	391	Hammond, IN	81,010
244	Pueblo, CO	109,065	318	Yakima, WA	93,419	392	Merced, CA	80,976
245	Arvada, CO	109,029	319	Carson, CA	93,233	393	Parma, OH	80,963
246	Rochester, MN	108,582	320	Macon, GA	92,836	394	O'Fallon, MO	80,670
247	Lowell, MA	108,539	321	Sparks, NV	92,387	395	Mission, TX	80,557
248	Ventura, CA	108,511	322	Hesperia, CA	92,383	396	Gary, IN	80,472
249	Gresham, OR	108,202	323	Beaverton, OR	92,276	397	Edinburg, TX	80,332
250	Carlsbad, CA	107,879	324	Roswell, GA	92,141	398	Farmington Hills, MI	80,316
251	West Covina, CA	107,861	325	Toms River Twnshp, NJ	92,131	399	Cranston, RI	80,315
252	Norwalk, CA	107,295	326	Federal Way, WA	91,978	400	Clarkstown, NY	80,186
253	Fairfield, CA	107,110	327	Tuscaloosa, AL	91,973	401	Menifee, CA	80,047
254	West Jordan, UT	107,103	328	Orem, UT	91,953	402	Johns Creek, GA	80,037
255	Cambridge, MA	106,981	329	Westminster, CA	91,908	403	Chino, CA	79,792
256	Murrieta, CA	106,839	330	Lynn, MA	91,846	404	Fishers, IN	79,375
257	High Point, NC	106,801	331	Lee's Summit, MO	91,840	405	Cheektowaga, NY	79,178
258	Billings, MT	106,371	332	Santa Monica, CA	91,215	406	Lake Forest, CA	79,166
259	Richmond, CA	106,357	333	Spokane Valley, WA	91,164	407	Racine, WI	79,055
260	Round Rock, TX	106,232	334	Miami Beach, FL	91,066	408	Largo, FL	78,783
261	Green Bay, WI	106,080	335	Redding, CA	90,974	409	Napa, CA	78,589
262	Wichita Falls, TX	105,488	336	Sandy, UT	90,405	410	Albany, GA	78,512
263	Everett, WA	105,318	337	Santa Barbara, CA	89,871	411	Indio, CA	78,501
264	Burbank, CA	105,057	338	Fall River, MA	89,753	412	Bryan, TX	78,479
265	Antioch, CA	105,009	339	Waukegan, IL	89,468	413	Redwood City, CA	78,466
266	Palm Bay, FL	104,635	340	Rio Rancho, NM	89,462	414	Avondale, AZ	78,364
267	Centennial, CO	104,022	341	Lawrence, KS	89,180	415	New Rochelle, NY	78,025
268	Odessa, TX	103,635	342	Hamilton Twnshp, NJ	89,111	416	Bellflower, CA	77,886
269	Temecula, CA	103,414	343	Longmont, CO	88,925	417	Colonie, NY	77,853
270	Daly City, CA	103,311	344	Allen, TX	88,783	418	Camden, NJ	77,665
271	Richardson, TX	103,266	345	Reading, PA	88,557	419	Lawrence, MA	77,661
272	Pompano Beach, FL	103,003	346	Plantation, FL	87,705	420	Deerfield Beach, FL	77,431
273	West Palm Beach, FL	102,422	347	Fort Smith, AR	87,483	421	Tustin, CA	77,400
274	Erie, PA	101,972	348	Newport Beach, CA	87,286	422	Lynchburg, VA	77,347
275	El Cajon, CA	101,864	349	Sunrise, FL	87,168	423	Brooklyn Park, MN	77,346
276	Flint, MI	101,632	350	Chico, CA	87,090	424	St. Joseph, MO	77,330
277	Rialto, CA	101,595	351	Nashua, NH	86,870	425	Meridian, ID	77,270
278	South Bend, IN	101,398	352	Greenville, NC	86,869	426	Somerville, MA	77,200
279	Santa Maria, CA	101,207	352	San Leandro, CA	86,869	427	Melbourne, FL	77,133
280	Davenport, IA	101,193	354	Duluth, MN	86,830	428	Bloomington, IL	77,107
281	Edison Twnshp, NJ	101,007	355	Whittier, CA	86,740	429	Kennewick, WA	76,971
282	Broken Arrow, OK	100,688	356	Newton, MA	86,710	430	Baldwin Park, CA	76,644
283	North Charleston, SC	100,675	357	Norwalk, CT	86,693	431	Chino Hills, CA	76,632
284	Woodbridge Twnshp, NJ	100,612	358	Boca Raton, FL	86,493	432	Decatur, IL	76,131
285	Boulder, CO	100,257	359	League City, TX	86,127	433	Scranton, PA	76,118
286	Tyler, TX	100,040	360	San Marcos, CA	85,810	434	Medford, OR	76,037
287	Kenosha, WI	99,993	361	Hawthorne, CA	85,692	435	Mountain View, CA	75,933
288	Lakeland, FL	99,934	362	Ramapo, NY	85,448	436	Brick Twnshp, NJ	75,809
289	Las Cruces, NM	99,824	363	Trenton, NJ	85,317	437	St. George, UT	75,780
290	San Mateo, CA	99,303	364	Asheville, NC	85,295	438	Upland, CA	75,531
291	Lawton, OK	98,781	365	Citrus Heights, CA	85,112	439	Alameda, CA	75,467
292	Albany, NY	98,187	366	Ogden, UT	85,083	440	Arlington Heights, IL	75,463
293	Compton, CA	98,057	367	Tracy, CA	85,047	441	Bethlehem, PA	75,388
294	Sandy Springs, GA	97,890	368	Clifton, NJ	84,684	442	Fayetteville, AR	75,387
295	Clovis, CA	97,828	369	Bloomington, MN	84,596			
296	Roanoke, VA	97,780	370	Alhambra, CA	84,469			

Source: Reported data from the F.B.I. "Crime in the United States 2012"

*Estimates as of July 2012 based on U.S. Bureau of the Census figures. Charlotte, Indianapolis, Las Vegas, Louisville, Mobile, and Savannah include areas under their police department but outside the city limits. All populations are for area covered by police department.

89. City Population in 2011
National Total = 311,587,816*

RANK	CITY	POP	RANK	CITY	POP	RANK	CITY	POP
208	Abilene, TX	119,526	431	Chino Hills, CA	75,678	192	Gainesville, FL	126,049
110	Akron, OH	199,256	399	Chino, CA	78,900	133	Garden Grove, CA	172,892
437	Alameda, CA	74,680	76	Chula Vista, CA	246,783	84	Garland, TX	231,650
403	Albany, GA	78,454	366	Cicero, IL	84,144	388	Gary, IN	80,704
289	Albany, NY	98,296	61	Cincinnati, OH	297,160	100	Gilbert, AZ	211,404
31	Albuquerque, NM	551,961	365	Citrus Heights, CA	84,280	87	Glendale, AZ	229,931
172	Alexandria, VA	141,638	396	Clarkstown, NY	79,221	117	Glendale, CA	193,973
367	Alhambra, CA	84,066	179	Clarksville, TN	134,128	127	Grand Prairie, TX	179,087
211	Allentown, PA	118,408	235	Clearwater, FL	109,153	121	Grand Rapids, MI	187,898
350	Allen, TX	86,019	44	Cleveland, OH	397,106	298	Greece, NY	96,527
116	Amarillo, TX	194,708	364	Clifton, NJ	84,416	304	Greeley, CO	94,507
214	Amherst, NY	117,610	296	Clinton Twnshp, MI	96,723	262	Green Bay, WI	104,510
53	Anaheim, CA	340,218	295	Clovis, CA	96,755	67	Greensboro, NC	273,086
62	Anchorage, AK	296,955	299	College Station, TX	95,832	354	Greenville, NC	85,626
226	Ann Arbor, MI	113,848	406	Colonie, NY	77,950	250	Gresham, OR	106,718
263	Antioch, CA	103,575	40	Colorado Springs, CO	423,680	338	Hamilton Twnshp, NJ	88,760
432	Arlington Heights, IL	75,327	236	Columbia, MO	108,894	383	Hammond, IN	81,243
49	Arlington, TX	373,128	118	Columbus, GA	192,385	174	Hampton, VA	139,078
240	Arvada, CO	108,287	293	Compton, CA	97,589	196	Hartford, CT	125,006
361	Asheville, NC	84,450	199	Concord, CA	123,502	358	Hawthorne, CA	85,284
218	Athens-Clarke, GA	117,114	201	Coral Springs, FL	122,746	163	Hayward, CA	145,881
39	Atlanta, GA	425,533	152	Corona, CA	154,165	395	Hemet, CA	79,582
54	Aurora, CO	330,740	57	Corpus Christi, TX	311,637	71	Henderson, NV	259,902
111	Aurora, IL	198,495	230	Costa Mesa, CA	111,253	321	Hesperia, CA	91,233
15	Austin, TX	807,022	390	Cranston, RI	80,290	88	Hialeah, FL	227,731
414	Avondale, AZ	77,317	10	Dallas, TX	1,223,021	255	High Point, NC	105,695
50	Bakersfield, CA	351,568	265	Daly City, CA	102,312	315	Hillsboro, OR	92,586
426	Baldwin Park, CA	76,276	384	Danbury, CT	81,043	169	Hollywood, FL	142,686
22	Baltimore, MD	626,848	279	Davenport, IA	100,207	378	Hoover, AL	82,012
85	Baton Rouge, LA	231,592	310	Davie, FL	93,246	4	Houston, TX	2,143,628
206	Beaumont, TX	120,785	173	Dayton, OH	141,631	119	Huntington Beach, CA	192,226
328	Beaverton, OR	90,759	291	Dearborn, MI	98,079	125	Huntsville, AL	180,972
197	Bellevue, WA	124,283	424	Decatur, IL	76,351	217	Independence, MO	117,255
412	Bellflower, CA	77,517	428	Deerfield Beach, FL	76,040	13	Indianapolis, IN	833,024
376	Bellingham, WA	82,154	220	Denton, TX	115,769	418	Indio, CA	76,930
225	Berkeley, CA	113,903	27	Denver, CO	610,612	231	Inglewood, CA	110,962
434	Bethlehem, PA	75,221	104	Des Moines, IA	204,498	95	Irvine, CA	214,872
256	Billings, MT	105,095	18	Detroit, MI	713,239	92	Irving, TX	220,841
96	Birmingham, AL	213,258	228	Downey, CA	113,086	12	Jacksonville, FL	834,429
420	Bloomington, IL	76,841	344	Duluth, MN	86,931	132	Jackson, MS	174,170
387	Bloomington, IN	80,816	86	Durham, NC	231,225	74	Jersey City, NJ	248,423
370	Bloomington, MN	83,533	400	Edinburg, TX	78,722	409	Johns Creek, GA	77,738
356	Boca Raton, FL	85,542	278	Edison Twnshp, NJ	100,300	158	Joliet, IL	147,877
101	Boise, ID	207,945	375	Edmond, OK	82,276	NA	Jurupa Valley, CA**	NA
23	Boston, MA	621,359	276	El Cajon, CA	100,647	160	Kansas City, KS	146,712
283	Boulder, CO	99,081	222	El Monte, CA	114,809	36	Kansas City, MO	461,458
433	Brick Twnshp, NJ	75,322	20	El Paso, TX	662,780	435	Kennewick, WA	75,077
167	Bridgeport, CT	144,496	238	Elgin, IL	108,514	282	Kenosha, WI	99,650
307	Brockton, MA	94,380	195	Elizabeth, NJ	125,386	308	Kent, WA	93,861
281	Broken Arrow, OK	99,908	150	Elk Grove, CA	154,814	184	Killeen, TX	130,613
423	Brooklyn Park, MN	76,366	267	Erie, PA	102,111	126	Knoxville, TN	180,488
128	Brownsville, TX	178,706	165	Escondido, CA	145,603	202	Lafayette, LA	121,726
408	Bryan, TX	77,804	144	Eugene, OR	157,848	405	Lake Forest, CA	78,172
381	Buena Park, CA	81,477	212	Evansville, IN	118,029	285	Lakeland, FL	98,750
69	Buffalo, NY	262,484	259	Everett, WA	104,635	312	Lakewood Twnshp, NJ	93,152
261	Burbank, CA	104,555	252	Fairfield, CA	106,559	385	Lakewood, CA	80,989
253	Cambridge, MA	105,803	334	Fall River, MA	89,399	166	Lakewood, CO	145,470
411	Camden, NJ	77,604	246	Fargo, ND	107,329	143	Lancaster, CA	158,474
146	Cape Coral, FL	156,408	392	Farmington Hills, MI	79,680	224	Lansing, MI	114,211
251	Carlsbad, CA	106,566	440	Fayetteville, AR	74,137	79	Laredo, TX	241,059
394	Carmel, IN	79,596	106	Fayetteville, NC	203,107	401	Largo, FL	78,706
203	Carrollton, TX	121,603	330	Federal Way, WA	90,707	286	Las Cruces, NM	98,710
314	Carson, CA	92,792	415	Fishers, IN	77,186	7	Las Vegas, NV	1,458,474
177	Cary, NC	136,949	264	Flint, MI	102,357	341	Lawrence, KS	88,200
190	Cedar Rapids, IA	126,988	112	Fontana, CA	198,374	419	Lawrence, MA	76,843
266	Centennial, CO	102,125	162	Fort Collins, CO	146,494	292	Lawton, OK	97,904
382	Champaign, IL	81,299	136	Fort Lauderdale, FL	167,777	357	League City, TX	85,318
80	Chandler, AZ	239,466	345	Fort Smith, AR	86,861	319	Lee's Summit, MO	91,696
204	Charleston, SC	121,481	72	Fort Wayne, IN	254,987	60	Lexington, KY	297,847
16	Charlotte, NC	789,478	17	Fort Worth, TX	756,803	70	Lincoln, NE	260,685
398	Cheektowaga, NY	79,194	94	Fremont, CA	216,606	115	Little Rock, AR	194,988
91	Chesapeake, VA	224,864	33	Fresno, CA	500,480	379	Livermore, CA	81,920
3	Chicago, IL	2,703,713	209	Frisco, TX	119,451	294	Livonia, MI	96,869
343	Chico, CA	87,200	178	Fullerton, CA	136,750	35	Long Beach, CA	467,691

RANK	CITY	POP	RANK	CITY	POP	RANK	CITY	POP
342	Longmont, CO	87,773	175	Pasadena, CA	138,734	301	South Gate, CA	95,506
377	Longview, TX	82,148	156	Pasadena, TX	152,179	323	Sparks, NV	91,025
2	Los Angeles, CA	3,837,207	161	Paterson, NJ	146,685	322	Spokane Valley, WA	91,163
19	Louisville, KY	665,152	311	Pearland, TX	93,172	98	Spokane, WA	212,194
247	Lowell, MA	107,167	145	Pembroke Pines, FL	156,859	219	Springfield, IL	116,600
81	Lubbock, TX	234,404	148	Peoria, AZ	156,246	153	Springfield, MA	153,993
421	Lynchburg, VA	76,471	221	Peoria, IL	115,353	142	Springfield, MO	160,078
326	Lynn, MA	90,880	5	Philadelphia, PA	1,530,873	200	Stamford, CT	122,870
316	Macon, GA	92,554	6	Phoenix, AZ	1,466,097	186	Sterling Heights, MI	129,601
82	Madison, WI	234,225	58	Pittsburgh, PA	308,609	63	Stockton, CA	295,136
234	Manchester, NH	109,708	68	Plano, TX	265,309	439	St. George, UT	74,304
182	McAllen, TX	132,610	349	Plantation, FL	86,113	417	St. Joseph, MO	77,059
181	McKinney, TX	133,876	157	Pomona, CA	150,810	56	St. Louis, MO	320,454
430	Medford, OR	75,704	274	Pompano Beach, FL	101,206	64	St. Paul, MN	287,665
416	Melbourne, FL	77,105	138	Port St. Lucie, FL	166,846	75	St. Petersburg, FL	248,105
21	Memphis, TN	652,725	29	Portland, OR	589,991	389	Sugar Land, TX	80,475
404	Menifee, CA	78,430	297	Portsmouth, VA	96,676	171	Sunnyvale, CA	141,728
391	Merced, CA	79,886	130	Providence, RI	177,830	355	Sunrise, FL	85,590
429	Meridian, ID	75,922	223	Provo, UT	114,659	210	Surprise, AZ	119,181
37	Mesa, AZ	445,256	239	Pueblo, CO	108,452	164	Syracuse, NY	145,822
168	Mesquite, TX	142,766	313	Quincy, MA	92,834	107	Tacoma, WA	201,510
337	Miami Beach, FL	88,975	397	Racine, WI	79,204	122	Tallahassee, FL	183,848
237	Miami Gardens, FL	108,628	42	Raleigh, NC	409,014	52	Tampa, FL	340,284
43	Miami, FL	404,901	362	Ramapo, NY	84,431	273	Temecula, CA	101,274
227	Midland, TX	113,486	137	Rancho Cucamon., CA	167,212	141	Tempe, AZ	164,008
28	Milwaukee, WI	597,426	340	Reading, PA	88,363	205	Thornton, CO	120,841
47	Minneapolis, MN	385,531	324	Redding, CA	90,917	188	Thousand Oaks, CA	128,172
198	Miramar, FL	123,704	410	Redwood City, CA	77,718	65	Toledo, OH	287,418
305	Mission Viejo, CA	94,402	89	Reno, NV	227,120	320	Toms River Twnshp, NJ	91,543
402	Mission, TX	78,679	318	Renton, WA	92,354	187	Topeka, KS	128,283
73	Mobile, AL	251,869	277	Rialto, CA	100,337	159	Torrance, CA	147,148
105	Modesto, CA	203,530	271	Richardson, TX	101,311	369	Tracy, CA	83,897
102	Montgomery, AL	206,754	257	Richmond, CA	104,920	359	Trenton, NJ	85,196
114	Moreno Valley, CA	195,638	103	Richmond, VA	206,654	386	Troy, MI	80,919
436	Mountain View, CA	74,937	339	Rio Rancho, NM	88,500	32	Tucson, AZ	527,479
233	Murfreesboro, TN	109,736	59	Riverside, CA	307,443	45	Tulsa, OK	396,101
258	Murrieta, CA	104,682	290	Roanoke, VA	98,191	325	Tuscaloosa, AL	90,903
374	Nampa, ID	82,459	244	Rochester, MN	107,593	422	Tustin, CA	76,428
407	Napa, CA	77,819	99	Rochester, NY	211,511	284	Tyler, TX	98,939
170	Naperville, IL	142,280	154	Rockford, IL	153,331	438	Upland, CA	74,599
346	Nashua, NH	86,607	207	Roseville, CA	120,184	372	Upper Darby Twnshp, PA	83,059
26	Nashville, TN	612,789	332	Roswell, GA	89,509	309	Vacaville, CA	93,515
300	New Bedford, MA	95,649	269	Round Rock, TX	101,989	215	Vallejo, CA	117,305
185	New Haven, CT	130,019	34	Sacramento, CA	471,972	140	Vancouver, WA	164,329
51	New Orleans, LA	346,974	147	Salem, OR	156,283	243	Ventura, CA	107,684
413	New Rochelle, NY	77,408	155	Salinas, CA	152,210	216	Victorville, CA	117,266
1	New York, NY	8,211,875	120	Salt Lake City, UT	190,038	38	Virginia Beach, VA	443,226
66	Newark, NJ	278,064	8	San Antonio, TX	1,355,339	193	Visalia, CA	125,905
348	Newport Beach, CA	86,187	97	San Bernardino, CA	212,392	303	Vista, CA	94,937
123	Newport News, VA	182,878	9	San Diego, CA	1,316,919	189	Waco, TX	127,431
353	Newton, MA	85,665	14	San Francisco, CA	814,701	180	Warren, MI	133,955
77	Norfolk, VA	245,704	11	San Jose, CA	957,062	373	Warwick, RI	82,572
229	Norman, OK	112,112	351	San Leandro, CA	85,949	25	Washington, DC	617,996
287	North Charleston, SC	98,606	360	San Marcos, CA	84,766	232	Waterbury, CT	110,570
NA	North Las Vegas, NV**	NA	288	San Mateo, CA	98,350	335	Waukegan, IL	89,346
248	Norwalk, CA	106,790	302	Sandy Springs, GA	95,089	245	West Covina, CA	107,345
352	Norwalk, CT	85,761	336	Sandy, UT	89,149	254	West Jordan, UT	105,713
46	Oakland, CA	395,317	55	Santa Ana, CA	328,343	272	West Palm Beach, FL	101,281
135	Oceanside, CA	169,050	333	Santa Barbara, CA	89,449	183	West Valley, UT	131,979
268	Odessa, TX	102,043	213	Santa Clara, CA	117,837	368	Westland, MI	84,031
393	O'Fallon, MO	79,617	129	Santa Clarita, CA	178,393	329	Westminster, CA	90,756
363	Ogden, UT	84,423	275	Santa Maria, CA	100,723	241	Westminster, CO	107,962
30	Oklahoma City, OK	586,208	327	Santa Monica, CA	90,791	347	Whittier, CA	86,334
191	Olathe, KS	126,671	134	Santa Rosa, CA	169,788	249	Wichita Falls, TX	106,753
41	Omaha, NE	412,608	90	Savannah, GA	226,422	48	Wichita, KS	384,796
139	Ontario, CA	165,851	93	Scottsdale, AZ	220,462	242	Wilmington, NC	107,826
176	Orange, CA	138,020	425	Scranton, PA	76,332	83	Winston-Salem, NC	232,529
331	Orem, UT	90,033	24	Seattle, WA	618,209	280	Woodbridge Twnshp, NJ	99,915
78	Orlando, FL	241,548	108	Shreveport, LA	201,134	124	Worcester, MA	182,145
131	Overland Park, KS	174,473	194	Simi Valley, CA	125,698	317	Yakima, WA	92,496
109	Oxnard, CA	200,225	371	Sioux City, IA	83,117	113	Yonkers, NY	196,857
260	Palm Bay, FL	104,596	149	Sioux Falls, SD	155,760	306	Yuma, AZ	94,381
151	Palmdale, CA	154,546	427	Somerville, MA	76,216			
380	Parma, OH	81,661	270	South Bend, IN	101,685			

Source: Reported data from the F.B.I. "Crime in the United States 2011"

*Estimates as of July 2011 based on U.S. Bureau of the Census figures. Charlotte, Indianapolis, Las Vegas, Louisville, Mobile, and Savannah include areas under their police department but outside the city limits. All populations are for area covered by police department.

89. City Population in 2011 (continued)
National Total = 311,587,816*

RANK	CITY	POP	RANK	CITY	POP	RANK	CITY	POP
1	New York, NY	8,211,875	75	St. Petersburg, FL	248,105	149	Sioux Falls, SD	155,760
2	Los Angeles, CA	3,837,207	76	Chula Vista, CA	246,783	150	Elk Grove, CA	154,814
3	Chicago, IL	2,703,713	77	Norfolk, VA	245,704	151	Palmdale, CA	154,546
4	Houston, TX	2,143,628	78	Orlando, FL	241,548	152	Corona, CA	154,165
5	Philadelphia, PA	1,530,873	79	Laredo, TX	241,059	153	Springfield, MA	153,993
6	Phoenix, AZ	1,466,097	80	Chandler, AZ	239,466	154	Rockford, IL	153,331
7	Las Vegas, NV	1,458,474	81	Lubbock, TX	234,404	155	Salinas, CA	152,210
8	San Antonio, TX	1,355,339	82	Madison, WI	234,225	156	Pasadena, TX	152,179
9	San Diego, CA	1,316,919	83	Winston-Salem, NC	232,529	157	Pomona, CA	150,810
10	Dallas, TX	1,223,021	84	Garland, TX	231,650	158	Joliet, IL	147,877
11	San Jose, CA	957,062	85	Baton Rouge, LA	231,592	159	Torrance, CA	147,148
12	Jacksonville, FL	834,429	86	Durham, NC	231,225	160	Kansas City, KS	146,712
13	Indianapolis, IN	833,024	87	Glendale, AZ	229,931	161	Paterson, NJ	146,685
14	San Francisco, CA	814,701	88	Hialeah, FL	227,731	162	Fort Collins, CO	146,494
15	Austin, TX	807,022	89	Reno, NV	227,120	163	Hayward, CA	145,881
16	Charlotte, NC	789,478	90	Savannah, GA	226,422	164	Syracuse, NY	145,822
17	Fort Worth, TX	756,803	91	Chesapeake, VA	224,864	165	Escondido, CA	145,603
18	Detroit, MI	713,239	92	Irving, TX	220,841	166	Lakewood, CO	145,470
19	Louisville, KY	665,152	93	Scottsdale, AZ	220,462	167	Bridgeport, CT	144,496
20	El Paso, TX	662,780	94	Fremont, CA	216,606	168	Mesquite, TX	142,766
21	Memphis, TN	652,725	95	Irvine, CA	214,872	169	Hollywood, FL	142,686
22	Baltimore, MD	626,848	96	Birmingham, AL	213,258	170	Naperville, IL	142,280
23	Boston, MA	621,359	97	San Bernardino, CA	212,392	171	Sunnyvale, CA	141,728
24	Seattle, WA	618,209	98	Spokane, WA	212,194	172	Alexandria, VA	141,638
25	Washington, DC	617,996	99	Rochester, NY	211,511	173	Dayton, OH	141,631
26	Nashville, TN	612,789	100	Gilbert, AZ	211,404	174	Hampton, VA	139,078
27	Denver, CO	610,612	101	Boise, ID	207,945	175	Pasadena, CA	138,734
28	Milwaukee, WI	597,426	102	Montgomery, AL	206,754	176	Orange, CA	138,020
29	Portland, OR	589,991	103	Richmond, VA	206,654	177	Cary, NC	136,949
30	Oklahoma City, OK	586,208	104	Des Moines, IA	204,498	178	Fullerton, CA	136,750
31	Albuquerque, NM	551,961	105	Modesto, CA	203,530	179	Clarksville, TN	134,128
32	Tucson, AZ	527,479	106	Fayetteville, NC	203,107	180	Warren, MI	133,955
33	Fresno, CA	500,480	107	Tacoma, WA	201,510	181	McKinney, TX	133,876
34	Sacramento, CA	471,972	108	Shreveport, LA	201,134	182	McAllen, TX	132,610
35	Long Beach, CA	467,691	109	Oxnard, CA	200,225	183	West Valley, UT	131,979
36	Kansas City, MO	461,458	110	Akron, OH	199,256	184	Killeen, TX	130,613
37	Mesa, AZ	445,256	111	Aurora, IL	198,495	185	New Haven, CT	130,019
38	Virginia Beach, VA	443,226	112	Fontana, CA	198,374	186	Sterling Heights, MI	129,601
39	Atlanta, GA	425,533	113	Yonkers, NY	196,857	187	Topeka, KS	128,283
40	Colorado Springs, CO	423,680	114	Moreno Valley, CA	195,638	188	Thousand Oaks, CA	128,172
41	Omaha, NE	412,608	115	Little Rock, AR	194,988	189	Waco, TX	127,431
42	Raleigh, NC	409,014	116	Amarillo, TX	194,708	190	Cedar Rapids, IA	126,988
43	Miami, FL	404,901	117	Glendale, CA	193,973	191	Olathe, KS	126,671
44	Cleveland, OH	397,106	118	Columbus, GA	192,385	192	Gainesville, FL	126,049
45	Tulsa, OK	396,101	119	Huntington Beach, CA	192,226	193	Visalia, CA	125,905
46	Oakland, CA	395,317	120	Salt Lake City, UT	190,038	194	Simi Valley, CA	125,698
47	Minneapolis, MN	385,531	121	Grand Rapids, MI	187,898	195	Elizabeth, NJ	125,386
48	Wichita, KS	384,796	122	Tallahassee, FL	183,848	196	Hartford, CT	125,006
49	Arlington, TX	373,128	123	Newport News, VA	182,878	197	Bellevue, WA	124,283
50	Bakersfield, CA	351,568	124	Worcester, MA	182,145	198	Miramar, FL	123,704
51	New Orleans, LA	346,974	125	Huntsville, AL	180,972	199	Concord, CA	123,502
52	Tampa, FL	340,284	126	Knoxville, TN	180,488	200	Stamford, CT	122,870
53	Anaheim, CA	340,218	127	Grand Prairie, TX	179,087	201	Coral Springs, FL	122,746
54	Aurora, CO	330,740	128	Brownsville, TX	178,706	202	Lafayette, LA	121,726
55	Santa Ana, CA	328,343	129	Santa Clarita, CA	178,393	203	Carrollton, TX	121,603
56	St. Louis, MO	320,454	130	Providence, RI	177,830	204	Charleston, SC	121,481
57	Corpus Christi, TX	311,637	131	Overland Park, KS	174,473	205	Thornton, CO	120,841
58	Pittsburgh, PA	308,609	132	Jackson, MS	174,170	206	Beaumont, TX	120,785
59	Riverside, CA	307,443	133	Garden Grove, CA	172,892	207	Roseville, CA	120,184
60	Lexington, KY	297,847	134	Santa Rosa, CA	169,788	208	Abilene, TX	119,526
61	Cincinnati, OH	297,160	135	Oceanside, CA	169,050	209	Frisco, TX	119,451
62	Anchorage, AK	296,955	136	Fort Lauderdale, FL	167,777	210	Surprise, AZ	119,181
63	Stockton, CA	295,136	137	Rancho Cucamon., CA	167,212	211	Allentown, PA	118,408
64	St. Paul, MN	287,665	138	Port St. Lucie, FL	166,846	212	Evansville, IN	118,029
65	Toledo, OH	287,418	139	Ontario, CA	165,851	213	Santa Clara, CA	117,837
66	Newark, NJ	278,064	140	Vancouver, WA	164,329	214	Amherst, NY	117,610
67	Greensboro, NC	273,086	141	Tempe, AZ	164,008	215	Vallejo, CA	117,305
68	Plano, TX	265,309	142	Springfield, MO	160,078	216	Victorville, CA	117,266
69	Buffalo, NY	262,484	143	Lancaster, CA	158,474	217	Independence, MO	117,255
70	Lincoln, NE	260,685	144	Eugene, OR	157,848	218	Athens-Clarke, GA	117,114
71	Henderson, NV	259,902	145	Pembroke Pines, FL	156,859	219	Springfield, IL	116,600
72	Fort Wayne, IN	254,987	146	Cape Coral, FL	156,408	220	Denton, TX	115,769
73	Mobile, AL	251,869	147	Salem, OR	156,283	221	Peoria, IL	115,353
74	Jersey City, NJ	248,423	148	Peoria, AZ	156,246	222	El Monte, CA	114,809

RANK	CITY	POP	RANK	CITY	POP	RANK	CITY	POP
223	Provo, UT	114,659	297	Portsmouth, VA	96,676	371	Sioux City, IA	83,117
224	Lansing, MI	114,211	298	Greece, NY	96,527	372	Upper Darby Twnshp, PA	83,059
225	Berkeley, CA	113,903	299	College Station, TX	95,832	373	Warwick, RI	82,572
226	Ann Arbor, MI	113,848	300	New Bedford, MA	95,649	374	Nampa, ID	82,459
227	Midland, TX	113,486	301	South Gate, CA	95,506	375	Edmond, OK	82,276
228	Downey, CA	113,086	302	Sandy Springs, GA	95,089	376	Bellingham, WA	82,154
229	Norman, OK	112,112	303	Vista, CA	94,937	377	Longview, TX	82,148
230	Costa Mesa, CA	111,253	304	Greeley, CO	94,507	378	Hoover, AL	82,012
231	Inglewood, CA	110,962	305	Mission Viejo, CA	94,402	379	Livermore, CA	81,920
232	Waterbury, CT	110,570	306	Yuma, AZ	94,381	380	Parma, OH	81,661
233	Murfreesboro, TN	109,736	307	Brockton, MA	94,380	381	Buena Park, CA	81,477
234	Manchester, NH	109,708	308	Kent, WA	93,861	382	Champaign, IL	81,299
235	Clearwater, FL	109,153	309	Vacaville, CA	93,515	383	Hammond, IN	81,243
236	Columbia, MO	108,894	310	Davie, FL	93,246	384	Danbury, CT	81,043
237	Miami Gardens, FL	108,628	311	Pearland, TX	93,172	385	Lakewood, CA	80,989
238	Elgin, IL	108,514	312	Lakewood Twnshp, NJ	93,152	386	Troy, MI	80,919
239	Pueblo, CO	108,452	313	Quincy, MA	92,834	387	Bloomington, IN	80,816
240	Arvada, CO	108,287	314	Carson, CA	92,792	388	Gary, IN	80,704
241	Westminster, CO	107,962	315	Hillsboro, OR	92,586	389	Sugar Land, TX	80,475
242	Wilmington, NC	107,826	316	Macon, GA	92,554	390	Cranston, RI	80,290
243	Ventura, CA	107,684	317	Yakima, WA	92,496	391	Merced, CA	79,886
244	Rochester, MN	107,593	318	Renton, WA	92,354	392	Farmington Hills, MI	79,680
245	West Covina, CA	107,345	319	Lee's Summit, MO	91,696	393	O'Fallon, MO	79,617
246	Fargo, ND	107,329	320	Toms River Twnshp, NJ	91,543	394	Carmel, IN	79,596
247	Lowell, MA	107,167	321	Hesperia, CA	91,233	395	Hemet, CA	79,582
248	Norwalk, CA	106,790	322	Spokane Valley, WA	91,163	396	Clarkstown, NY	79,221
249	Wichita Falls, TX	106,753	323	Sparks, NV	91,025	397	Racine, WI	79,204
250	Gresham, OR	106,718	324	Redding, CA	90,917	398	Cheektowaga, NY	79,194
251	Carlsbad, CA	106,566	325	Tuscaloosa, AL	90,903	399	Chino, CA	78,900
252	Fairfield, CA	106,559	326	Lynn, MA	90,880	400	Edinburg, TX	78,722
253	Cambridge, MA	105,803	327	Santa Monica, CA	90,791	401	Largo, FL	78,706
254	West Jordan, UT	105,713	328	Beaverton, OR	90,759	402	Mission, TX	78,679
255	High Point, NC	105,695	329	Westminster, CA	90,756	403	Albany, GA	78,454
256	Billings, MT	105,095	330	Federal Way, WA	90,707	404	Menifee, CA	78,430
257	Richmond, CA	104,920	331	Orem, UT	90,033	405	Lake Forest, CA	78,172
258	Murrieta, CA	104,682	332	Roswell, GA	89,509	406	Colonie, NY	77,950
259	Everett, WA	104,635	333	Santa Barbara, CA	89,449	407	Napa, CA	77,819
260	Palm Bay, FL	104,596	334	Fall River, MA	89,399	408	Bryan, TX	77,804
261	Burbank, CA	104,555	335	Waukegan, IL	89,346	409	Johns Creek, GA	77,738
262	Green Bay, WI	104,510	336	Sandy, UT	89,149	410	Redwood City, CA	77,718
263	Antioch, CA	103,575	337	Miami Beach, FL	88,975	411	Camden, NJ	77,604
264	Flint, MI	102,357	338	Hamilton Twnshp, NJ	88,760	412	Bellflower, CA	77,517
265	Daly City, CA	102,312	339	Rio Rancho, NM	88,500	413	New Rochelle, NY	77,408
266	Centennial, CO	102,125	340	Reading, PA	88,363	414	Avondale, AZ	77,317
267	Erie, PA	102,111	341	Lawrence, KS	88,200	415	Fishers, IN	77,186
268	Odessa, TX	102,043	342	Longmont, CO	87,773	416	Melbourne, FL	77,105
269	Round Rock, TX	101,989	343	Chico, CA	87,200	417	St. Joseph, MO	77,059
270	South Bend, IN	101,685	344	Duluth, MN	86,931	418	Indio, CA	76,930
271	Richardson, TX	101,311	345	Fort Smith, AR	86,861	419	Lawrence, MA	76,843
272	West Palm Beach, FL	101,281	346	Nashua, NH	86,607	420	Bloomington, IL	76,841
273	Temecula, CA	101,274	347	Whittier, CA	86,334	421	Lynchburg, VA	76,471
274	Pompano Beach, FL	101,206	348	Newport Beach, CA	86,187	422	Tustin, CA	76,428
275	Santa Maria, CA	100,723	349	Plantation, FL	86,113	423	Brooklyn Park, MN	76,366
276	El Cajon, CA	100,647	350	Allen, TX	86,019	424	Decatur, IL	76,351
277	Rialto, CA	100,337	351	San Leandro, CA	85,949	425	Scranton, PA	76,332
278	Edison Twnshp, NJ	100,300	352	Norwalk, CT	85,761	426	Baldwin Park, CA	76,276
279	Davenport, IA	100,207	353	Newton, MA	85,665	427	Somerville, MA	76,216
280	Woodbridge Twnshp, NJ	99,915	354	Greenville, NC	85,626	428	Deerfield Beach, FL	76,040
281	Broken Arrow, OK	99,908	355	Sunrise, FL	85,590	429	Meridian, ID	75,922
282	Kenosha, WI	99,650	356	Boca Raton, FL	85,542	430	Medford, OR	75,704
283	Boulder, CO	99,081	357	League City, TX	85,318	431	Chino Hills, CA	75,678
284	Tyler, TX	98,939	358	Hawthorne, CA	85,284	432	Arlington Heights, IL	75,327
285	Lakeland, FL	98,750	359	Trenton, NJ	85,196	433	Brick Twnshp, NJ	75,322
286	Las Cruces, NM	98,710	360	San Marcos, CA	84,766	434	Bethlehem, PA	75,221
287	North Charleston, SC	98,606	361	Asheville, NC	84,450	435	Kennewick, WA	75,077
288	San Mateo, CA	98,350	362	Ramapo, NY	84,431	436	Mountain View, CA	74,937
289	Albany, NY	98,296	363	Ogden, UT	84,423	437	Alameda, CA	74,680
290	Roanoke, VA	98,191	364	Clifton, NJ	84,416	438	Upland, CA	74,599
291	Dearborn, MI	98,079	365	Citrus Heights, CA	84,280	439	St. George, UT	74,304
292	Lawton, OK	97,904	366	Cicero, IL	84,144	440	Fayetteville, AR	74,137
293	Compton, CA	97,589	367	Alhambra, CA	84,066	NA	Jurupa Valley, CA**	NA
294	Livonia, MI	96,869	368	Westland, MI	84,031	NA	North Las Vegas, NV**	NA
295	Clovis, CA	96,755	369	Tracy, CA	83,897			
296	Clinton Twnshp, MI	96,723	370	Bloomington, MN	83,533			

Source: Reported data from the F.B.I. "Crime in the United States 2011"

*Estimates as of July 2011 based on U.S. Bureau of the Census figures. Charlotte, Indianapolis, Las Vegas, Louisville, Mobile, and Savannah include areas under their police department but outside the city limits. All populations are for area covered by police department.

90. City Population in 2008
National Total = 304,059,724*

RANK	CITY	POP	RANK	CITY	POP	RANK	CITY	POP
204	Abilene, TX	116,267	403	Chino Hills, CA	75,297	217	Gainesville, FL	113,286
97	Akron, OH	206,845	341	Chino, CA	84,595	138	Garden Grove, CA	165,629
432	Alameda, CA	69,998	86	Chula Vista, CA	223,408	92	Garland, TX	219,135
400	Albany, GA	75,715	369	Cicero, IL	80,428	284	Gary, IN	95,699
292	Albany, NY	94,152	54	Cincinnati, OH	332,608	90	Gilbert, AZ	220,373
33	Albuquerque, NM	527,464	344	Citrus Heights, CA	84,361	69	Glendale, AZ	256,659
167	Alexandria, VA	140,891	379	Clarkstown, NY	78,869	109	Glendale, CA	197,182
333	Alhambra, CA	86,404	198	Clarksville, TN	121,386	141	Grand Prairie, TX	162,706
231	Allentown, PA	107,335	240	Clearwater, FL	104,986	114	Grand Rapids, MI	193,096
352	Allen, TX	83,242	41	Cleveland, OH	433,452	296	Greece, NY	92,932
117	Amarillo, TX	187,674	388	Clifton, NJ	78,180	308	Greeley, CO	91,900
223	Amherst, NY	110,351	283	Clinton Twnshp, MI	96,315	267	Green Bay, WI	100,531
53	Anaheim, CA	333,746	293	Clovis, CA	93,848	75	Greensboro, NC	249,561
64	Anchorage, AK	280,068	363	College Station, TX	81,925	391	Greenville, NC	77,960
208	Ann Arbor, MI	115,148	386	Colonie, NY	78,272	262	Gresham, OR	100,935
263	Antioch, CA	100,702	46	Colorado Springs, CO	378,403	317	Hamilton Twnshp, NJ	90,282
413	Arlington Heights, IL	73,346	260	Columbia, MO	101,033	395	Hammond, IN	76,498
48	Arlington, TX	375,836	119	Columbus, GA	186,217	158	Hampton, VA	145,897
233	Arvada, CO	106,847	289	Compton, CA	94,519	187	Hartford, CT	124,610
406	Asheville, NC	74,215	199	Concord, CA	120,679	342	Hawthorne, CA	84,445
212	Athens-Clarke, GA	113,950	183	Coral Springs, FL	126,222	166	Hayward, CA	140,984
31	Atlanta, GA	533,016	150	Corona, CA	153,193	424	Hemet, CA	71,789
57	Aurora, CO	316,323	61	Corpus Christi, TX	286,558	70	Henderson, NV	256,091
129	Aurora, IL	174,488	227	Costa Mesa, CA	108,898	325	Hesperia, CA	88,853
17	Austin, TX	753,535	371	Cranston, RI	79,987	96	Hialeah, FL	207,908
336	Avondale, AZ	85,376	9	Dallas, TX	1,276,214	251	High Point, NC	102,298
55	Bakersfield, CA	326,046	266	Daly City, CA	100,542	290	Hillsboro, OR	94,373
389	Baldwin Park, CA	78,031	374	Danbury, CT	79,753	165	Hollywood, FL	141,048
20	Baltimore, MD	634,549	272	Davenport, IA	99,070	429	Hoover, AL	70,731
84	Baton Rouge, LA	226,920	318	Davie, FL	90,268	4	Houston, TX	2,238,895
225	Beaumont, TX	109,103	147	Dayton, OH	154,218	113	Huntington Beach, CA	193,241
304	Beaverton, OR	92,198	329	Dearborn, MI	87,482	130	Huntsville, AL	172,794
194	Bellevue, WA	122,459	399	Decatur, IL	76,044	222	Independence, MO	110,376
410	Bellflower, CA	73,488	409	Deerfield Beach, FL	73,665	13	Indianapolis, IN	808,329
381	Bellingham, WA	78,804	200	Denton, TX	120,295	322	Indio, CA	89,486
258	Berkeley, CA	101,170	27	Denver, CO	592,881	216	Inglewood, CA	113,454
418	Bethlehem, PA	72,537	111	Des Moines, IA	196,680	95	Irvine, CA	209,278
248	Billings, MT	103,196	12	Detroit, MI	905,783	105	Irving, TX	200,470
83	Birmingham, AL	228,314	229	Downey, CA	108,184	14	Jacksonville, FL	806,080
414	Bloomington, IL	73,309	346	Duluth, MN	84,171	128	Jackson, MS	174,734
419	Bloomington, IN	72,337	88	Durham, NC	221,785	77	Jersey City, NJ	241,588
366	Bloomington, MN	80,996	425	Edinburg, TX	71,734	439	Johns Creek, GA	59,454
340	Boca Raton, FL	84,630	269	Edison Twnshp, NJ	99,562	154	Joliet, IL	149,617
101	Boise, ID	203,770	376	Edmond, OK	79,529	NA	Jurupa Valley, CA**	NA
23	Boston, MA	604,465	303	El Cajon, CA	92,225	NA	Kansas City, KS**	NA
294	Boulder, CO	93,410	192	El Monte, CA	123,049	38	Kansas City, MO	451,454
387	Brick Twnshp, NJ	78,218	22	El Paso, TX	612,374	437	Kennewick, WA	62,930
172	Bridgeport, CT	136,327	238	Elgin, IL	105,535	282	Kenosha, WI	96,977
285	Brockton, MA	95,650	186	Elizabeth, NJ	124,823	337	Kent, WA	84,966
305	Broken Arrow, OK	92,075	169	Elk Grove, CA	139,395	205	Killeen, TX	115,906
422	Brooklyn Park, MN	71,891	243	Erie, PA	103,881	120	Knoxville, TN	184,559
125	Brownsville, TX	176,893	171	Escondido, CA	136,508	213	Lafayette, LA	113,770
417	Bryan, TX	72,815	153	Eugene, OR	150,297	401	Lake Forest, CA	75,637
377	Buena Park, CA	79,431	206	Evansville, IN	115,639	299	Lakeland, FL	92,669
67	Buffalo, NY	270,289	275	Everett, WA	98,552	428	Lakewood Twnshp, NJ	70,864
244	Burbank, CA	103,640	241	Fairfield, CA	104,927	378	Lakewood, CA	78,894
256	Cambridge, MA	101,362	316	Fall River, MA	90,760	168	Lakewood, CO	139,803
398	Camden, NJ	76,182	297	Fargo, ND	92,883	156	Lancaster, CA	147,017
140	Cape Coral, FL	163,403	382	Farmington Hills, MI	78,602	210	Lansing, MI	114,415
278	Carlsbad, CA	97,670	408	Fayetteville, AR	73,999	87	Laredo, TX	222,870
436	Carmel, IN	65,982	134	Fayetteville, NC	171,457	420	Largo, FL	72,298
184	Carrollton, TX	125,607	339	Federal Way, WA	84,775	307	Las Cruces, NM	91,982
295	Carson, CA	93,170	430	Fishers, IN	70,594	7	Las Vegas, NV	1,353,175
185	Cary, NC	125,277	215	Flint, MI	113,462	313	Lawrence, KS	91,089
181	Cedar Rapids, IA	126,984	115	Fontana, CA	189,253	433	Lawrence, MA	69,812
273	Centennial, CO	98,749	173	Fort Collins, CO	135,785	312	Lawton, OK	91,459
397	Champaign, IL	76,187	121	Fort Lauderdale, FL	182,932	426	League City, TX	71,651
71	Chandler, AZ	253,076	338	Fort Smith, AR	84,847	343	Lee's Summit, MO	84,399
220	Charleston, SC	111,645	73	Fort Wayne, IN	251,194	62	Lexington, KY	281,473
16	Charlotte, NC	758,769	18	Fort Worth, TX	701,345	72	Lincoln, NE	251,550
385	Cheektowaga, NY	78,303	103	Fremont, CA	200,964	116	Little Rock, AR	187,978
89	Chesapeake, VA	220,812	34	Fresno, CA	475,723	370	Livermore, CA	80,258
3	Chicago, IL	2,829,304	271	Frisco, TX	99,472	302	Livonia, MI	92,329
347	Chico, CA	84,086	176	Fullerton, CA	132,776	36	Long Beach, CA	467,055

RANK	CITY	POP	RANK	CITY	POP	RANK	CITY	POP
331	Longmont, CO	86,754	160	Pasadena, CA	144,545	280	South Gate, CA	97,179
394	Longview, TX	77,272	155	Pasadena, TX	147,114	324	Sparks, NV	88,913
2	Los Angeles, CA	3,850,920	159	Paterson, NJ	145,542	335	Spokane Valley, WA	85,551
21	Louisville, KY	629,679	354	Pearland, TX	83,185	102	Spokane, WA	201,491
224	Lowell, MA	110,136	157	Pembroke Pines, FL	146,108	203	Springfield, IL	117,762
91	Lubbock, TX	219,594	151	Peoria, AZ	151,493	152	Springfield, MA	151,249
423	Lynchburg, VA	71,805	214	Peoria, IL	113,616	145	Springfield, MO	155,106
321	Lynn, MA	90,042	6	Philadelphia, PA	1,441,117	202	Stamford, CT	118,597
300	Macon, GA	92,576	5	Phoenix, AZ	1,585,838	180	Sterling Heights, MI	127,697
80	Madison, WI	231,231	58	Pittsburgh, PA	309,757	60	Stockton, CA	293,073
226	Manchester, NH	109,083	68	Plano, TX	265,739	405	St. George, UT	74,356
179	McAllen, TX	130,039	350	Plantation, FL	83,480	396	St. Joseph, MO	76,377
182	McKinney, TX	126,659	149	Pomona, CA	153,201	50	St. Louis, MO	356,204
415	Medford, OR	73,019	253	Pompano Beach, FL	101,769	66	St. Paul, MN	276,083
393	Melbourne, FL	77,286	142	Port St. Lucie, FL	159,735	76	St. Petersburg, FL	243,111
19	Memphis, TN	672,046	29	Portland, OR	553,023	364	Sugar Land, TX	81,763
NA	Menifee, CA**	NA	252	Portsmouth, VA	101,782	178	Sunnyvale, CA	131,052
383	Merced, CA	78,598	135	Providence, RI	170,965	323	Sunrise, FL	89,139
434	Meridian, ID	69,466	201	Provo, UT	119,189	259	Surprise, AZ	101,141
37	Mesa, AZ	456,821	242	Pueblo, CO	104,017	170	Syracuse, NY	138,211
177	Mesquite, TX	132,600	287	Quincy, MA	95,061	110	Tacoma, WA	196,851
348	Miami Beach, FL	83,609	361	Racine, WI	82,226	137	Tallahassee, FL	168,984
228	Miami Gardens, FL	108,657	44	Raleigh, NC	388,661	52	Tampa, FL	336,911
42	Miami, FL	427,740	402	Ramapo, NY	75,433	274	Temecula, CA	98,663
239	Midland, TX	105,049	127	Rancho Cucamon., CA	176,307	126	Tempe, AZ	176,388
25	Milwaukee, WI	602,131	367	Reading, PA	80,860	209	Thornton, CO	114,923
47	Minneapolis, MN	376,753	315	Redding, CA	90,881	189	Thousand Oaks, CA	124,106
219	Miramar, FL	112,055	412	Redwood City, CA	73,369	56	Toledo, OH	317,401
288	Mission Viejo, CA	94,702	93	Reno, NV	218,556	286	Toms River Twnshp, NJ	95,410
435	Mission, TX	68,236	438	Renton, WA	61,536	193	Topeka, KS	122,554
74	Mobile, AL	251,041	270	Rialto, CA	99,485	164	Torrance, CA	141,819
98	Modesto, CA	205,750	264	Richardson, TX	100,597	357	Tracy, CA	82,960
100	Montgomery, AL	204,398	255	Richmond, CA	101,680	362	Trenton, NJ	82,140
112	Moreno Valley, CA	195,649	106	Richmond, VA	199,674	368	Troy, MI	80,491
431	Mountain View, CA	70,401	375	Rio Rancho, NM	79,647	32	Tucson, AZ	528,917
249	Murfreesboro, TN	102,536	59	Riverside, CA	299,384	45	Tulsa, OK	382,954
237	Murrieta, CA	105,666	306	Roanoke, VA	91,983	320	Tuscaloosa, AL	90,157
356	Nampa, ID	83,007	265	Rochester, MN	100,589	427	Tustin, CA	71,272
404	Napa, CA	74,420	99	Rochester, NY	205,341	277	Tyler, TX	98,042
161	Naperville, IL	144,205	143	Rockford, IL	157,262	416	Upland, CA	72,929
330	Nashua, NH	86,845	218	Roseville, CA	112,817	384	Upper Darby Twnshp, PA	78,550
24	Nashville, TN	602,181	327	Roswell, GA	88,069	301	Vacaville, CA	92,424
311	New Bedford, MA	91,473	250	Round Rock, TX	102,411	207	Vallejo, CA	115,330
190	New Haven, CT	123,953	35	Sacramento, CA	467,065	139	Vancouver, WA	163,574
63	New Orleans, LA	281,440	148	Salem, OR	153,831	247	Ventura, CA	103,483
411	New Rochelle, NY	73,376	163	Salinas, CA	143,520	211	Victorville, CA	114,305
1	New York, NY	8,345,075	122	Salt Lake City, UT	180,514	40	Virginia Beach, VA	434,163
65	Newark, NJ	279,788	8	San Antonio, TX	1,351,244	195	Visalia, CA	121,850
373	Newport Beach, CA	79,821	104	San Bernardino, CA	200,617	314	Vista, CA	90,919
123	Newport News, VA	178,308	10	San Diego, CA	1,271,655	191	Waco, TX	123,208
353	Newton, MA	83,191	15	San Francisco, CA	798,144	175	Warren, MI	133,721
79	Norfolk, VA	235,067	11	San Jose, CA	945,197	345	Warwick, RI	84,326
230	Norman, OK	108,016	392	San Leandro, CA	77,474	28	Washington, DC	591,833
298	North Charleston, SC	92,749	365	San Marcos, CA	81,683	232	Waterbury, CT	107,157
82	North Las Vegas, NV	228,363	309	San Mateo, CA	91,650	310	Waukegan, IL	91,487
245	Norwalk, CA	103,612	358	Sandy Springs, GA	82,953	235	West Covina, CA	106,524
349	Norwalk, CT	83,503	281	Sandy, UT	96,998	236	West Jordan, UT	105,772
43	Oakland, CA	401,587	51	Santa Ana, CA	339,674	268	West Palm Beach, FL	100,434
136	Oceanside, CA	169,502	334	Santa Barbara, CA	85,791	188	West Valley, UT	124,128
279	Odessa, TX	97,644	221	Santa Clara, CA	110,712	372	Westland, MI	79,944
380	O'Fallon, MO	78,837	133	Santa Clarita, CA	171,821	326	Westminster, CA	88,730
351	Ogden, UT	83,353	332	Santa Maria, CA	86,744	234	Westminster, CO	106,810
30	Oklahoma City, OK	552,452	328	Santa Monica, CA	87,572	359	Whittier, CA	82,727
197	Olathe, KS	121,472	146	Santa Rosa, CA	154,874	257	Wichita Falls, TX	101,279
39	Omaha, NE	437,238	94	Savannah, GA	211,475	49	Wichita, KS	362,602
131	Ontario, CA	172,543	78	Scottsdale, AZ	238,905	261	Wilmington, NC	100,944
174	Orange, CA	134,852	421	Scranton, PA	72,247	85	Winston-Salem, NC	226,460
291	Orem, UT	94,228	26	Seattle, WA	598,077	276	Woodbridge Twnshp, NJ	98,154
81	Orlando, FL	229,808	108	Shreveport, LA	199,434	124	Worcester, MA	177,151
132	Overland Park, KS	171,909	196	Simi Valley, CA	121,572	355	Yakima, WA	83,027
118	Oxnard, CA	186,434	360	Sioux City, IA	82,404	107	Yonkers, NY	199,615
254	Palm Bay, FL	101,759	144	Sioux Falls, SD	155,110	319	Yuma, AZ	90,245
162	Palmdale, CA	144,109	407	Somerville, MA	74,012			
390	Parma, OH	77,980	246	South Bend, IN	103,561			

Source: Reported data from the F.B.I. "Crime in the United States 2008"

*Estimates as of July 2008 based on U.S. Bureau of the Census figures. Charlotte, Indianapolis, Las Vegas, Louisville, Mobile, and Savannah include areas under their police department but outside the city limits. All populations are for area covered by police department.

90. City Population in 2008 (continued)
National Total = 304,059,724*

RANK	CITY	POP	RANK	CITY	POP	RANK	CITY	POP
1	New York, NY	8,345,075	75	Greensboro, NC	249,561	149	Pomona, CA	153,201
2	Los Angeles, CA	3,850,920	76	St. Petersburg, FL	243,111	150	Corona, CA	153,193
3	Chicago, IL	2,829,304	77	Jersey City, NJ	241,588	151	Peoria, AZ	151,493
4	Houston, TX	2,238,895	78	Scottsdale, AZ	238,905	152	Springfield, MA	151,249
5	Phoenix, AZ	1,585,838	79	Norfolk, VA	235,067	153	Eugene, OR	150,297
6	Philadelphia, PA	1,441,117	80	Madison, WI	231,231	154	Joliet, IL	149,617
7	Las Vegas, NV	1,353,175	81	Orlando, FL	229,808	155	Pasadena, TX	147,114
8	San Antonio, TX	1,351,244	82	North Las Vegas, NV	228,363	156	Lancaster, CA	147,017
9	Dallas, TX	1,276,214	83	Birmingham, AL	228,314	157	Pembroke Pines, FL	146,108
10	San Diego, CA	1,271,655	84	Baton Rouge, LA	226,920	158	Hampton, VA	145,897
11	San Jose, CA	945,197	85	Winston-Salem, NC	226,460	159	Paterson, NJ	145,542
12	Detroit, MI	905,783	86	Chula Vista, CA	223,408	160	Pasadena, CA	144,545
13	Indianapolis, IN	808,329	87	Laredo, TX	222,870	161	Naperville, IL	144,205
14	Jacksonville, FL	806,080	88	Durham, NC	221,785	162	Palmdale, CA	144,109
15	San Francisco, CA	798,144	89	Chesapeake, VA	220,812	163	Salinas, CA	143,520
16	Charlotte, NC	758,769	90	Gilbert, AZ	220,373	164	Torrance, CA	141,819
17	Austin, TX	753,535	91	Lubbock, TX	219,594	165	Hollywood, FL	141,048
18	Fort Worth, TX	701,345	92	Garland, TX	219,135	166	Hayward, CA	140,984
19	Memphis, TN	672,046	93	Reno, NV	218,556	167	Alexandria, VA	140,891
20	Baltimore, MD	634,549	94	Savannah, GA	211,475	168	Lakewood, CO	139,803
21	Louisville, KY	629,679	95	Irvine, CA	209,278	169	Elk Grove, CA	139,395
22	El Paso, TX	612,374	96	Hialeah, FL	207,908	170	Syracuse, NY	138,211
23	Boston, MA	604,465	97	Akron, OH	206,845	171	Escondido, CA	136,508
24	Nashville, TN	602,181	98	Modesto, CA	205,750	172	Bridgeport, CT	136,327
25	Milwaukee, WI	602,131	99	Rochester, NY	205,341	173	Fort Collins, CO	135,785
26	Seattle, WA	598,077	100	Montgomery, AL	204,398	174	Orange, CA	134,852
27	Denver, CO	592,881	101	Boise, ID	203,770	175	Warren, MI	133,721
28	Washington, DC	591,833	102	Spokane, WA	201,491	176	Fullerton, CA	132,776
29	Portland, OR	553,023	103	Fremont, CA	200,964	177	Mesquite, TX	132,600
30	Oklahoma City, OK	552,452	104	San Bernardino, CA	200,617	178	Sunnyvale, CA	131,052
31	Atlanta, GA	533,016	105	Irving, TX	200,470	179	McAllen, TX	130,039
32	Tucson, AZ	528,917	106	Richmond, VA	199,674	180	Sterling Heights, MI	127,697
33	Albuquerque, NM	527,464	107	Yonkers, NY	199,615	181	Cedar Rapids, IA	126,984
34	Fresno, CA	475,723	108	Shreveport, LA	199,434	182	McKinney, TX	126,659
35	Sacramento, CA	467,065	109	Glendale, CA	197,182	183	Coral Springs, FL	126,222
36	Long Beach, CA	467,055	110	Tacoma, WA	196,851	184	Carrollton, TX	125,607
37	Mesa, AZ	456,821	111	Des Moines, IA	196,680	185	Cary, NC	125,277
38	Kansas City, MO	451,454	112	Moreno Valley, CA	195,649	186	Elizabeth, NJ	124,823
39	Omaha, NE	437,238	113	Huntington Beach, CA	193,241	187	Hartford, CT	124,610
40	Virginia Beach, VA	434,163	114	Grand Rapids, MI	193,096	188	West Valley, UT	124,128
41	Cleveland, OH	433,452	115	Fontana, CA	189,253	189	Thousand Oaks, CA	124,106
42	Miami, FL	427,740	116	Little Rock, AR	187,978	190	New Haven, CT	123,953
43	Oakland, CA	401,587	117	Amarillo, TX	187,674	191	Waco, TX	123,208
44	Raleigh, NC	388,661	118	Oxnard, CA	186,434	192	El Monte, CA	123,049
45	Tulsa, OK	382,954	119	Columbus, GA	186,217	193	Topeka, KS	122,554
46	Colorado Springs, CO	378,403	120	Knoxville, TN	184,559	194	Bellevue, WA	122,459
47	Minneapolis, MN	376,753	121	Fort Lauderdale, FL	182,932	195	Visalia, CA	121,850
48	Arlington, TX	375,836	122	Salt Lake City, UT	180,514	196	Simi Valley, CA	121,572
49	Wichita, KS	362,602	123	Newport News, VA	178,308	197	Olathe, KS	121,472
50	St. Louis, MO	356,204	124	Worcester, MA	177,151	198	Clarksville, TN	121,386
51	Santa Ana, CA	339,674	125	Brownsville, TX	176,893	199	Concord, CA	120,679
52	Tampa, FL	336,911	126	Tempe, AZ	176,388	200	Denton, TX	120,295
53	Anaheim, CA	333,746	127	Rancho Cucamon., CA	176,307	201	Provo, UT	119,189
54	Cincinnati, OH	332,608	128	Jackson, MS	174,734	202	Stamford, CT	118,597
55	Bakersfield, CA	326,046	129	Aurora, IL	174,488	203	Springfield, IL	117,762
56	Toledo, OH	317,401	130	Huntsville, AL	172,794	204	Abilene, TX	116,267
57	Aurora, CO	316,323	131	Ontario, CA	172,543	205	Killeen, TX	115,906
58	Pittsburgh, PA	309,757	132	Overland Park, KS	171,909	206	Evansville, IN	115,639
59	Riverside, CA	299,384	133	Santa Clarita, CA	171,821	207	Vallejo, CA	115,330
60	Stockton, CA	293,073	134	Fayetteville, NC	171,457	208	Ann Arbor, MI	115,148
61	Corpus Christi, TX	286,558	135	Providence, RI	170,965	209	Thornton, CO	114,923
62	Lexington, KY	281,473	136	Oceanside, CA	169,502	210	Lansing, MI	114,415
63	New Orleans, LA	281,440	137	Tallahassee, FL	168,984	211	Victorville, CA	114,305
64	Anchorage, AK	280,068	138	Garden Grove, CA	165,629	212	Athens-Clarke, GA	113,950
65	Newark, NJ	279,788	139	Vancouver, WA	163,574	213	Lafayette, LA	113,770
66	St. Paul, MN	276,083	140	Cape Coral, FL	163,403	214	Peoria, IL	113,616
67	Buffalo, NY	270,289	141	Grand Prairie, TX	162,706	215	Flint, MI	113,462
68	Plano, TX	265,739	142	Port St. Lucie, FL	159,735	216	Inglewood, CA	113,454
69	Glendale, AZ	256,659	143	Rockford, IL	157,262	217	Gainesville, FL	113,286
70	Henderson, NV	256,091	144	Sioux Falls, SD	155,110	218	Roseville, CA	112,817
71	Chandler, AZ	253,076	145	Springfield, MO	155,106	219	Miramar, FL	112,055
72	Lincoln, NE	251,550	146	Santa Rosa, CA	154,874	220	Charleston, SC	111,645
73	Fort Wayne, IN	251,194	147	Dayton, OH	154,218	221	Santa Clara, CA	110,712
74	Mobile, AL	251,041	148	Salem, OR	153,831	222	Independence, MO	110,376

RANK	CITY	POP	RANK	CITY	POP	RANK	CITY	POP
223	Amherst, NY	110,351	297	Fargo, ND	92,883	371	Cranston, RI	79,987
224	Lowell, MA	110,136	298	North Charleston, SC	92,749	372	Westland, MI	79,944
225	Beaumont, TX	109,103	299	Lakeland, FL	92,669	373	Newport Beach, CA	79,821
226	Manchester, NH	109,083	300	Macon, GA	92,576	374	Danbury, CT	79,753
227	Costa Mesa, CA	108,898	301	Vacaville, CA	92,424	375	Rio Rancho, NM	79,647
228	Miami Gardens, FL	108,657	302	Livonia, MI	92,329	376	Edmond, OK	79,529
229	Downey, CA	108,184	303	El Cajon, CA	92,225	377	Buena Park, CA	79,431
230	Norman, OK	108,016	304	Beaverton, OR	92,198	378	Lakewood, CA	78,894
231	Allentown, PA	107,335	305	Broken Arrow, OK	92,075	379	Clarkstown, NY	78,869
232	Waterbury, CT	107,157	306	Roanoke, VA	91,983	380	O'Fallon, MO	78,837
233	Arvada, CO	106,847	307	Las Cruces, NM	91,982	381	Bellingham, WA	78,804
234	Westminster, CO	106,810	308	Greeley, CO	91,900	382	Farmington Hills, MI	78,602
235	West Covina, CA	106,524	309	San Mateo, CA	91,650	383	Merced, CA	78,598
236	West Jordan, UT	105,772	310	Waukegan, IL	91,487	384	Upper Darby Twnshp, PA	78,550
237	Murrieta, CA	105,666	311	New Bedford, MA	91,473	385	Cheektowaga, NY	78,303
238	Elgin, IL	105,535	312	Lawton, OK	91,459	386	Colonie, NY	78,272
239	Midland, TX	105,049	313	Lawrence, KS	91,089	387	Brick Twnshp, NJ	78,218
240	Clearwater, FL	104,986	314	Vista, CA	90,919	388	Clifton, NJ	78,180
241	Fairfield, CA	104,927	315	Redding, CA	90,881	389	Baldwin Park, CA	78,031
242	Pueblo, CO	104,017	316	Fall River, MA	90,760	390	Parma, OH	77,980
243	Erie, PA	103,881	317	Hamilton Twnshp, NJ	90,282	391	Greenville, NC	77,960
244	Burbank, CA	103,640	318	Davie, FL	90,268	392	San Leandro, CA	77,474
245	Norwalk, CA	103,612	319	Yuma, AZ	90,245	393	Melbourne, FL	77,286
246	South Bend, IN	103,561	320	Tuscaloosa, AL	90,157	394	Longview, TX	77,272
247	Ventura, CA	103,483	321	Lynn, MA	90,042	395	Hammond, IN	76,498
248	Billings, MT	103,196	322	Indio, CA	89,486	396	St. Joseph, MO	76,377
249	Murfreesboro, TN	102,536	323	Sunrise, FL	89,139	397	Champaign, IL	76,187
250	Round Rock, TX	102,411	324	Sparks, NV	88,913	398	Camden, NJ	76,182
251	High Point, NC	102,298	325	Hesperia, CA	88,853	399	Decatur, IL	76,044
252	Portsmouth, VA	101,782	326	Westminster, CA	88,730	400	Albany, GA	75,715
253	Pompano Beach, FL	101,769	327	Roswell, GA	88,069	401	Lake Forest, CA	75,637
254	Palm Bay, FL	101,759	328	Santa Monica, CA	87,572	402	Ramapo, NY	75,433
255	Richmond, CA	101,680	329	Dearborn, MI	87,482	403	Chino Hills, CA	75,297
256	Cambridge, MA	101,362	330	Nashua, NH	86,845	404	Napa, CA	74,420
257	Wichita Falls, TX	101,279	331	Longmont, CO	86,754	405	St. George, UT	74,356
258	Berkeley, CA	101,170	332	Santa Maria, CA	86,744	406	Asheville, NC	74,215
259	Surprise, AZ	101,141	333	Alhambra, CA	86,404	407	Somerville, MA	74,012
260	Columbia, MO	101,033	334	Santa Barbara, CA	85,791	408	Fayetteville, AR	73,999
261	Wilmington, NC	100,944	335	Spokane Valley, WA	85,551	409	Deerfield Beach, FL	73,665
262	Gresham, OR	100,935	336	Avondale, AZ	85,376	410	Bellflower, CA	73,488
263	Antioch, CA	100,702	337	Kent, WA	84,966	411	New Rochelle, NY	73,376
264	Richardson, TX	100,597	338	Fort Smith, AR	84,847	412	Redwood City, CA	73,369
265	Rochester, MN	100,589	339	Federal Way, WA	84,775	413	Arlington Heights, IL	73,346
266	Daly City, CA	100,542	340	Boca Raton, FL	84,630	414	Bloomington, IL	73,309
267	Green Bay, WI	100,531	341	Chino, CA	84,595	415	Medford, OR	73,019
268	West Palm Beach, FL	100,434	342	Hawthorne, CA	84,445	416	Upland, CA	72,929
269	Edison Twnshp, NJ	99,562	343	Lee's Summit, MO	84,399	417	Bryan, TX	72,815
270	Rialto, CA	99,485	344	Citrus Heights, CA	84,361	418	Bethlehem, PA	72,537
271	Frisco, TX	99,472	345	Warwick, RI	84,326	419	Bloomington, IN	72,337
272	Davenport, IA	99,070	346	Duluth, MN	84,171	420	Largo, FL	72,298
273	Centennial, CO	98,749	347	Chico, CA	84,086	421	Scranton, PA	72,247
274	Temecula, CA	98,663	348	Miami Beach, FL	83,609	422	Brooklyn Park, MN	71,891
275	Everett, WA	98,552	349	Norwalk, CT	83,503	423	Lynchburg, VA	71,805
276	Woodbridge Twnshp, NJ	98,154	350	Plantation, FL	83,480	424	Hemet, CA	71,789
277	Tyler, TX	98,042	351	Ogden, UT	83,353	425	Edinburg, TX	71,734
278	Carlsbad, CA	97,670	352	Allen, TX	83,242	426	League City, TX	71,651
279	Odessa, TX	97,644	353	Newton, MA	83,191	427	Tustin, CA	71,272
280	South Gate, CA	97,179	354	Pearland, TX	83,185	428	Lakewood Twnshp, NJ	70,864
281	Sandy, UT	96,998	355	Yakima, WA	83,027	429	Hoover, AL	70,731
282	Kenosha, WI	96,977	356	Nampa, ID	83,007	430	Fishers, IN	70,594
283	Clinton Twnshp, MI	96,315	357	Tracy, CA	82,960	431	Mountain View, CA	70,401
284	Gary, IN	95,699	358	Sandy Springs, GA	82,953	432	Alameda, CA	69,998
285	Brockton, MA	95,650	359	Whittier, CA	82,727	433	Lawrence, MA	69,812
286	Toms River Twnshp, NJ	95,410	360	Sioux City, IA	82,404	434	Meridian, ID	69,466
287	Quincy, MA	95,061	361	Racine, WI	82,226	435	Mission, TX	68,236
288	Mission Viejo, CA	94,702	362	Trenton, NJ	82,140	436	Carmel, IN	65,982
289	Compton, CA	94,519	363	College Station, TX	81,925	437	Kennewick, WA	62,930
290	Hillsboro, OR	94,373	364	Sugar Land, TX	81,763	438	Renton, WA	61,536
291	Orem, UT	94,228	365	San Marcos, CA	81,683	439	Johns Creek, GA	59,454
292	Albany, NY	94,152	366	Bloomington, MN	80,996	NA	Jurupa Valley, CA**	NA
293	Clovis, CA	93,848	367	Reading, PA	80,860	NA	Kansas City, KS**	NA
294	Boulder, CO	93,410	368	Troy, MI	80,491	NA	Menifee, CA**	NA
295	Carson, CA	93,170	369	Cicero, IL	80,428			
296	Greece, NY	92,932	370	Livermore, CA	80,258			

Source: Reported data from the F.B.I. "Crime in the United States 2008"

*Estimates as of July 2008 based on U.S. Bureau of the Census figures. Charlotte, Indianapolis, Las Vegas, Louisville, Mobile, and Savannah include areas under their police department but outside the city limits. All populations are for area covered by police department.

Appendix

DESCRIPTIONS OF METROPOLITAN AREAS IN 2012

Note: The name of a Metropolitan Statistical Area (MSA) and Metropolitan Division (M.D.) is subject to change based on the changing proportional size of the largest cities included within them. Percent changes are calculated in this book if the MSA or M.D. has not substantially changed, despite the changes in name. In the tables in this book, some MSA and M.D. names are abbreviated to preserve space.

Abilene, TX includes Callahan, Jones, and Taylor Counties

Akron, OH includes Portage and Summit Counties

Albany, GA includes Baker, Dougherty, Lee, Terrell, and Worth Counties

Albany, OR includes Linn County

Albany-Schenectady-Troy, NY includes Albany, Rensselaer, Saratoga, Schenectady, and Schoharie Counties

Albuquerque, NM includes Bernalillo, Sandoval, Torrance, and Valencia Counties

Alexandria, LA includes Grant and Rapides Parishes

Allentown-Bethlehem-Easton, PA-NJ includes Warren County, NJ and Carbon, Lehigh, and Northampton Counties, PA

Altoona, PA includes Blair County

Amarillo, TX includes Armstrong, Carson, Oldham, Potter, and Randall Counties

Ames, IA includes Story County

Anchorage, AK includes Anchorage Municipality and Matanuska-Susitna Borough

Ann Arbor, MI includes Washtenaw County

Anniston-Oxford-Jacksonville, AL includes Calhoun County

Appleton, WI includes Calumet and Outagamie Counties

Asheville, NC includes Buncombe,

Haywood, Henderson, and Madison Counties

Athens-Clarke County, GA includes Clarke, Madison, Oconee, and Oglethorpe Counties

Atlanta-Sandy Springs-Roswell, GA includes Barrow, Bartow, Butts, Carroll, Cherokee, Clayton, Cobb, Coweta, Dawson, DeKalb, Douglas, Fayette, Forsyth, Fulton, Gwinnett, Haralson, Heard, Henry, Jasper, Lamar, Meriwether, Morgan, Newton, Paulding, Pickens, Pike, Rockdale, Spalding, and Walton Counties

Atlantic City-Hammonton, NJ includes Atlantic County

Auburn-Opelika, AL includes Lee County

Augusta-Richmond County, GA-SC includes Burke, Columbia, Lincoln, McDuffie, and Richmond Counties, GA and Aiken and Edgefield Counties, SC

Austin-Round Rock, TX includes Bastrop, Caldwell, Hays, Travis, and Williamson Counties

Bakersfield, CA includes Kern County

Baltimore-Columbia-Towson, MD includes Anne Arundel, Baltimore, Carroll, Harford, Howard, and Queen Anne's Counties and Baltimore City

Bangor, ME includes Penobscot County

Barnstable Town, MA includes Barnstable County

Baton Rouge, LA includes Ascension, East Baton Rouge, East Feliciana, Iberville, Livingston, Pointe Coupee, St. Helena, West Baton Rouge, and West Feliciana Parishes

Bay City, MI includes Bay County

Beaumont-Port Arthur, TX includes Hardin, Jefferson, Newton, and Orange Counties

Beckley, WV includes Fayette and Raleigh Counties

Bellingham, WA includes Whatcom County

Billings, MT includes Carbon, Golden Valley, and Yellowstone Counties

Binghamton, NY includes Broome and Tioga Counties

Birmingham-Hoover, AL includes Bibb, Blount, Chilton, Jefferson, St. Clair, Shelby, and Walker Counties

Bismarck, ND includes Burleigh, Morton, Oliver, and Sioux Counties

Blacksburg-Christiansburg-Radford, VA includes Floyd, Giles, Montgomery, and Pulaski Counties and Radford City

Bloomington, IL includes DeWitt and McLean Counties

Bloomington, IN includes Monroe and Owen Counties

Bloomsburg-Berwick, PA includes Columbia and Montour Counties

Boise City, ID includes Ada, Boise, Canyon, Gem, and Owyhee Counties

Boston-Cambridge-Newton, MA-NH includes the Metropolitan Divisions of Boston, MA; Cambridge-Newton-Framingham, MA; and Rockingham County-Strafford County, NH
- Boston, MA Metropolitan Division includes Norfolk, Plymouth, and Suffolk Counties
- Cambridge-Newton-Framingham, MA Metropolitan Division includes Essex and Middlesex Counties
- Rockingham County-Strafford County, NH Metropolitan Division includes Rockingham and Strafford Counties

Boulder, CO includes Boulder County

Bowling Green, KY includes Allen, Butler, Edmonson, and Warren Counties

Bremerton-Silverdale, WA includes Kitsap County

Bridgeport-Stamford-Norwalk, CT includes Fairfield County

Brownsville-Harlingen, TX includes Cameron County

Brunswick, GA includes Brantley, Glynn,

DESCRIPTIONS OF METROPOLITAN AREAS IN 2012 (continued)

and McIntosh Counties

Buffalo-Cheektowaga-Niagara Falls, NY includes Erie and Niagara Counties

Burlington, NC includes Alamance County

California-Lexington Park, MD includes St. Mary's County

Canton-Massillon, OH includes Carroll and Stark Counties

Cape Coral-Fort Myers, FL includes Lee County

Cape Girardeau, MO-IL includes Alexander County, IL and Bollinger and Cape Girardeau Counties, MO

Carson City, NV includes Carson City

Casper, WY includes Natrona County

Cedar Rapids, IA includes Benton, Jones, and Linn Counties

Chambersburg-Waynesboro, PA includes Franklin County

Champaign-Urbana, IL includes Champaign, Ford, and Piatt Counties

Charleston-North Charleston, SC includes Berkeley, Charleston, and Dorchester Counties

Charlottesville, VA includes Albemarle, Buckingham, Fluvanna, Greene, and Nelson Counties and Charlottesville City

Cheyenne, WY includes Laramie County

Chicago-Naperville-Elgin, IL-IN-WI includes the Metropolitan Divisions of Chicago-Naperville-Arlington Heights, IL; Elgin, IL; Gary, IN; and Lake County-Kenosha County, IL-WI
- Chicago-Naperville-Arlington Heights, IL Metropolitan Division includes Cook, DuPage, Grundy, Kendall, McHenry, and Will Counties
- Elgin, IL Metropolitan Division includes DeKalb and Kane Counties
- Gary, IN Metropolitan Division includes Jasper, Lake, Newton, and Porter Counties
- Lake County-Kenosha County, IL-WI Metropolitan Division includes Lake

County, IL and Kenosha County, WI

Chico, CA includes Butte County

Cincinnati, OH-KY-IN includes Dearborn, Ohio, and Union Counties, IN; Boone, Bracken, Campbell, Gallatin, Grant, Kenton, and Pendleton Counties, KY; and Brown, Butler, Clermont, Hamilton, and Warren Counties, OH

Clarksville, TN-KY includes Christian and Trigg Counties, KY and Montgomery County, TN

Cleveland, TN includes Bradley and Polk Counties

Coeur d'Alene, ID includes Kootenai County

College Station-Bryan, TX includes Brazos, Burleson, and Robertson Counties

Colorado Springs, CO includes El Paso and Teller Counties

Columbia, MO includes Boone County

Columbus, GA-AL includes Russell County, AL and Chattahoochee, Harris, Marion, and Muscogee Counties, GA

Columbus, IN includes Bartholomew County

Corpus Christi, TX includes Aransas, Nueces, and San Patricio Counties

Corvallis, OR includes Benton County

Crestview-Fort Walton Beach-Destin, FL includes Okaloosa and Walton Counties

Cumberland, MD-WV includes Allegany County, MD and Mineral County, WV

Dallas-Fort Worth-Arlington, TX includes the Metropolitan Divisions of Dallas-Plano-Irving and Fort Worth-Arlington
- Dallas-Plano-Irving, TX Metropolitan Division includes Collin, Dallas, Denton, Ellis, Hunt, Kaufman, and Rockwall Counties
- Fort Worth-Arlington, TX Metropolitan Division includes Hood, Johnson, Parker, Somervell, Tarrant, and Wise Counties

Dalton, GA includes Murray and Whitfield Counties

Danville, IL includes Vermilion County

Daphne-Fairhope-Foley, AL includes Baldwin County

Davenport-Moline-Rock Island, IA-IL includes Henry, Mercer, and Rock Island Counties, IL and Scott County, IA

Dayton, OH includes Greene, Miami, and Montgomery Counties

Decatur, AL includes Lawrence and Morgan Counties

Decatur, IL includes Macon County

Deltona-Daytona Beach-Ormond Beach, FL includes Flagler and Volusia Counties

Denver-Aurora-Lakewood, CO includes Adams, Arapahoe, Broomfield, Clear Creek, Denver, Douglas, Elbert, Gilpin, Jefferson, and Park Counties

Des Moines-West Des Moines, IA includes Dallas, Guthrie, Madison, Polk, and Warren Counties

Detroit-Warren-Dearborn, MI includes the Metropolitan Divisions of Detroit-Dearborn-Livonia and Warren-Troy-Farmington Hills
- Detroit-Dearborn-Livonia, MI Metropolitan Division includes Wayne County
- Warren-Troy-Farmington Hills, MI Metropolitan Division includes Lapeer, Livingston, Macomb, Oakland, and St. Clair Counties

Dothan, AL includes Geneva, Henry, and Houston Counties

Dover, DE includes Kent County

Dubuque, IA includes Dubuque County

Duluth, MN-WI includes Carlton and St. Louis Counties, MN and Douglas County, WI

Durham-Chapel Hill, NC includes Chatham, Durham, Orange, and Person Counties

East Stroudsburg, PA includes Monroe County

El Centro, CA includes Imperial County

Elizabethtown-Fort Knox, KY includes Hardin, Larue, and Meade Counties

Elmira, NY includes Chemung County

El Paso, TX includes El Paso and Hudspeth Counties

Erie, PA includes Erie County

Eugene, OR includes Lane County

Fairbanks, AK includes Fairbanks North Star Borough

Fargo, ND-MN includes Clay County, MN and Cass County, ND

Farmington, NM includes San Juan County

Fayetteville, NC includes Cumberland and Hoke Counties

Fayetteville-Springdale-Rogers, AR-MO includes Benton, Madison, and Washington Counties, AR and McDonald County, MO

Flagstaff, AZ includes Coconino County

Flint, MI includes Genesee County

Florence, SC includes Darlington and Florence Counties

Florence-Muscle Shoals, AL includes Colbert and Lauderdale Counties

Fond du Lac, WI includes Fond du Lac County

Fort Collins, CO includes Larimer County

Fort Smith, AR-OK includes Crawford and Sebastian Counties, AR and Le Flore and Sequoyah Counties, OK

Fort Wayne, IN includes Allen, Wells, and Whitley Counties

Fresno, CA includes Fresno County

Gadsden, AL includes Etowah County

Gainesville, FL includes Alachua and Gilchrist Counties

Gainesville, GA includes Hall County

Gettysburg, PA includes Adams County

Glens Falls, NY includes Warren and Washington Counties

Goldsboro, NC includes Wayne County

Grand Forks, ND-MN includes Polk County, MN and Grand Forks County, ND

Grand Island, NE includes Hall, Hamilton, Howard, and Merrick Counties

Grand Junction, CO includes Mesa County

Great Falls, MT includes Cascade County

Greeley, CO includes Weld County

Green Bay, WI includes Brown, Kewaunee, and Oconto Counties

Greensboro-High Point, NC includes Guilford, Randolph, and Rockingham Counties

Greenville, NC includes Pitt County

Greenville-Anderson-Mauldin, SC includes Anderson, Greenville, Laurens, and Pickens Counties

Hagerstown-Martinsburg, MD-WV includes Washington County, MD and Berkeley County, WV

Hammond, LA includes Tangipahoa Parish

Hanford-Corcoran, CA includes Kings County

Harrisburg-Carlisle, PA includes Cumberland, Dauphin, and Perry Counties

Harrisonburg, VA includes Rockingham County and Harrisonburg City

Hartford-West Hartford-East Hartford, CT includes Hartford, Middlesex, and Tolland Counties

Hattiesburg, MS includes Forrest, Lamar, and Perry Counties

Hickory-Lenoir-Morganton, NC includes Alexander, Burke, Caldwell, and Catawba Counties

Hilton Head Island-Bluffton-Beaufort, SC includes Beaufort and Jasper Counties

Hinesville, GA includes Liberty and Long Counties

Homosassa Spring, FL includes Citrus County

Houma-Thibodaux, LA includes Lafourche and Terrebonne Parishes

Houston-The Woodlands-Sugar Land, TX includes Austin, Brazoria, Chambers, Fort Bend, Galveston, Harris, Liberty, Montgomery, and Waller Counties

Huntsville, AL includes Limestone and Madison Counties

Idaho Falls, ID includes Bonneville, Butte, and Jefferson Counties

Indianapolis-Carmel-Anderson, IN includes Boone, Brown, Hamilton, Hancock, Hendricks, Johnson, Madison, Marion, Morgan, Putnam, and Shelby Counties

Iowa City, IA includes Johnson and Washington Counties

Jackson, MS includes Copiah, Hinds, Madison, Rankin, Simpson, and Yazoo Counties

Jackson, TN includes Chester, Crockett, and Madison Counties

Jacksonville, FL includes Baker, Clay, Duval, Nassau, and St. Johns Counties

Janesville-Beloit, WI includes Rock County

Jefferson City, MO includes Callaway, Cole, Moniteau, and Osage Counties

Johnson City, TN includes Carter, Unicoi, and Washington Counties

Johnstown, PA includes Cambria County

Jonesboro, AR includes Craighead and Poinsett Counties

Joplin, MO includes Jasper and Newton Counties

Kahului-Wailuku-Lahaina, HI includes Kalawao and Maui Counties

Kalamazoo-Portage, MI includes Kalamazoo and Van Buren Counties

Kankakee, IL includes Kankakee County

Kansas City, MO-KS includes Johnson, Leavenworth, Linn, Miami, and Wyandotte Counties, KS and Bates, Caldwell, Cass, Clay, Clinton, Jackson, Lafayette, Platte, and Ray Counties, MO

Kennewick-Richland, WA includes Benton and Franklin Counties

Killeen-Temple, TX includes Bell, Coryell, and Lampasas Counties

Kingsport-Bristol-Bristol, TN-VA includes Hawkins and Sullivan Counties, TN and Scott and Washington Counties and Bristol City, VA

Kingston, NY includes Ulster County

Knoxville, TN includes Anderson, Blount, Campbell, Grainger, Knox, Loudon, Morgan, Roane, and Union Counties

Kokomo, IN includes Howard County

La Crosse-Onalaska, WI-MN includes Houston County, MN and La Crosse County, WI

Lafayette, LA includes Acadia, Iberia, Lafayette, St. Martin, and Vermilion Parishes

Lafayette-West Lafayette, IN includes Benton, Carroll, and Tippecanoe Counties

Lake Havasu City-Kingman, AZ includes Mohave County

Lakeland-Winter Haven, FL includes Polk County

Lancaster, PA includes Lancaster County

Lansing-East Lansing, MI includes Clinton, Eaton, and Ingham Counties

Laredo, TX includes Webb County

Las Cruces, NM includes Dona Ana County

Las Vegas-Henderson-Paradise, NV includes Clark County

Lawrence, KS includes Douglas County

Lawton, OK includes Comanche and Cotton Counties

Lebanon, PA includes Lebanon County

Lewiston, ID-WA includes Nez Perce County, ID and Asotin County, WA

Lewiston-Auburn, ME includes Androscoggin County

Lexington-Fayette, KY includes Bourbon, Clark, Fayette, Jessamine, Scott, and Woodford Counties

Lima, OH includes Allen County

Lincoln, NE includes Lancaster and Seward Counties

Little Rock-North Little Rock-Conway, AR includes Faulkner, Grant, Lonoke, Perry, Pulaski, and Saline Counties

Logan, UT-ID includes Franklin County, ID and Cache County, UT

Longview, TX includes Gregg, Rusk, and Upshur Counties

Longview, WA includes Cowlitz County

Los Angeles-Long Beach-Anaheim, CA includes the Metropolitan Divisions of Anaheim-Santa Ana-Irvine and Los Angeles-Long Beach-Glendale
- Anaheim-Santa Ana-Irvine, CA Metropolitan Division includes Orange County
- Los Angeles-Long Beach-Glendale, CA Metropolitan Division includes Los Angeles County

Louisville/Jefferson County, KY-IN includes Clark, Floyd, Harrison, Scott, and Washington Counties, IN and Bullitt, Henry, Jefferson, Oldham, Shelby, Spencer, and Trimble Counties, KY

Lubbock, TX includes Crosby, Lubbock, and Lynn Counties

Lynchburg, VA includes Amherst, Appomattox, Bedford, and Campbell Counties and Bedford and Lynchburg Cities

Macon, GA includes Bibb, Crawford, Jones, Monroe, and Twiggs Counties

Madera, CA includes Madera County

Madison, WI includes Columbia, Dane, Green, and Iowa Counties

Manchester-Nashua, NH includes Hillsborough County

Manhattan, KS includes Pottawatomie and Riley Counties

Mankato-North Mankato, MN includes Blue Earth and Nicollet Counties

Mansfield, OH includes Richland County

McAllen-Edinburg-Mission, TX includes Hidalgo County

Medford, OR includes Jackson County

Memphis, TN-MS-AR includes Crittenden County, AR; Benton, DeSoto, Marshall, Tate, and Tunica Counties, MS; and Fayette, Shelby, and Tipton Counties, TN

Merced, CA includes Merced County

Miami-Fort Lauderdale-West Palm Beach, FL includes the Metropolitan Divisions of Fort Lauderdale-Pompano Beach-Deerfield Beach, Miami-Miami Beach-Kendall, and West Palm Beach-Boca Raton-Delray Beach
- Fort Lauderdale-Pompano Beach-Deerfield Beach, FL Metropolitan Division includes Broward County
- Miami-Miami Beach-Kendall, FL Metropolitan Division includes Miami-Dade County
- West Palm Beach-Boca Raton-Delray Beach, FL Metropolitan Division includes Palm Beach County

Michigan City-La Porte, IN includes La Porte County

Midland, MI includes Midland County

Midland, TX includes Martin and Midland Counties

Milwaukee-Waukesha-West Allis, WI includes Milwaukee, Ozaukee, Washington, and Waukesha Counties

Minneapolis-St. Paul-Bloomington, MN-WI includes Anoka, Carver, Chisago, Dakota, Hennepin, Isanti, Le Sueur, Mille Lacs, Ramsey, Scott, Sherburne, Sibley, Washington, and Wright Counties, MN and Pierce and St. Croix Counties, WI

Missoula, MT includes Missoula County

Mobile, AL includes Mobile County

Modesto, CA includes Stanislaus County

Monroe, LA includes Ouachita and Union Parishes

Monroe, MI includes Monroe County

Montgomery, AL includes Autauga, Elmore, Lowndes, and Montgomery Counties

Morgantown, WV includes Monongalia and Preston Counties

Morristown, TN includes Hamblen and Jefferson Counties

Mount Vernon-Anacortes, WA includes Skagit County

Muncie, IN includes Delaware County

Napa, CA includes Napa County

Naples-Immokalee-Marco Island, FL includes Collier County

Nashville-Davidson--Murfreesboro--Franklin, TN includes Cannon, Cheatham, Davidson, Dickson, Hickman, Macon, Maury, Robertson, Rutherford, Smith, Sumner, Trousdale, Williamson, and Wilson Counties

New Bern, NC includes Craven, Jones, and Pamlico Counties

New Haven-Milford, CT includes New Haven County

New Orleans-Metairie, LA includes Jefferson, Orleans, Plaquemines, St. Bernard, St. Charles, St. James, St. John the Baptist, and St. Tammany Parishes

New York-Newark-Jersey City, NY-NJ-PA includes the Metropolitan Divisions of Dutchess County-Putnam County, NY; Nassau County-Suffolk County, NY; Newark, NJ-PA; and New York-Jersey City-White Plains, NY-NJ
- Dutchess County-Putnam County, NY Metropolitan Division includes Dutchess and Putnam Counties1
- Nassau County-Suffolk County, NY Metropolitan Division includes Nassau and Suffolk Counties1
- Newark, NJ-PA Metropolitan Division includes Essex, Hunterdon, Morris, Somerset, Sussex, and Union Counties, NJ and Pike County, PA
- New York-Jersey City-White Plains, NY-NJ Metropolitan Division includes Bergen, Hudson, Middlesex, Monmouth, Ocean, and Passaic Counties, NJ and Bronx, Kings, New York, Orange, Queens, Richmond, Rockland, and Westchester Counties, NY1

North Port-Sarasota-Bradenton, FL includes Manatee and Sarasota Counties

Norwich-New London, CT includes New London County

Ocala, FL includes Marion County

Ocean City, NJ includes Cape May County

Odessa, TX includes Ector County

Ogden-Clearfield, UT includes Box Elder, Davis, Morgan, and Weber Counties

Oklahoma City, OK includes Canadian, Cleveland, Grady, Lincoln, Logan, McClain, and Oklahoma Counties

Olympia-Tumwater, WA includes Thurston County

Omaha-Council Bluffs, NE-IA includes Harrison, Mills, and Pottawattamie Counties, IA and Cass, Douglas, Sarpy, Saunders, and Washington Counties, NE

Orlando-Kissimmee-Sanford, FL includes Lake, Orange, Osceola, and Seminole Counties

Oshkosh-Neenah, WI includes Winnebago County

Owensboro, KY includes Daviess,

Hancock, and McLean Counties

Oxnard-Thousand Oaks-Ventura, CA includes Ventura County

Palm Bay-Melbourne-Titusville, FL includes Brevard County

Panama City, FL includes Bay and Gulf Counties

Parkersburg-Vienna, WV includes Wirt and Wood Counties

Pensacola-Ferry Pass-Brent, FL includes Escambia and Santa Rosa Counties

Peoria, IL includes Marshall, Peoria, Stark, Tazewell, and Woodford Counties

Philadelphia-Camden-Wilmington, PA-NJ-DE-MD includes the Metropolitan Divisions of Camden, NJ; Montgomery County-Bucks County-Chester County, PA; Philadelphia, PA; and Wilmington, DE-MD-NJ
- Camden, NJ Metropolitan Division includes Burlington, Camden, and Gloucester Counties
- Montgomery County-Bucks County-Chester County, PA Metropolitan Division includes Bucks, Chester, and Montgomery Counties
- Philadelphia, PA Metropolitan Division includes Delaware and Philadelphia Counties
- Wilmington, DE-MD-NJ Metropolitan Division includes New Castle County, DE; Cecil County, MD; and Salem County, NJ
- Phoenix-Mesa-Scottsdale, AZ includes Maricopa and Pinal Counties

Pine Bluff, AR includes Cleveland, Jefferson, and Lincoln Counties

Pittsburgh, PA includes Allegheny, Armstrong, Beaver, Butler, Fayette, Washington, and Westmoreland Counties

Pittsfield, MA includes Berkshire County

Pocatello, ID includes Bannock County

Portland-South Portland, ME includes Cumberland, Sagadahoc, and York Counties

Portland-Vancouver-Hillsboro, OR-WA includes Clackamas, Columbia,

Multnomah, Washington, and Yamhill Counties, OR and Clark and Skamania Counties, WA

Port St. Lucie, FL includes Martin and St. Lucie Counties

Prescott, AZ includes Yavapai County

Providence-Warwick, RI-MA includes Bristol County, MA and Bristol, Kent, Newport, Providence, and Washington Counties RI

Provo-Orem, UT includes Juab and Utah Counties

Pueblo, CO includes Pueblo County

Punta Gorda, FL includes Charlotte County

Racine, WI includes Racine County

Raleigh, NC includes Franklin, Johnston, and Wake Counties

Rapid City, SD includes Custer, Meade, and Pennington Counties

Reading, PA includes Berks County

Redding, CA includes Shasta County

Reno, NV includes Storey and Washoe Counties

Richmond, VA includes Amelia, Caroline, Charles City, Chesterfield, Dinwiddie, Goochland, Hanover, Henrico, King William, New Kent, Powhatan, Prince George, and Sussex Counties and Colonial Heights, Hopewell, Petersburg, and Richmond Cities

Riverside-San Bernardino-Ontario, CA includes Riverside and San Bernardino Counties

Roanoke, VA includes Botetourt, Craig, Franklin, and Roanoke Counties and Roanoke and Salem Cities

Rochester, MN includes Dodge, Fillmore, Olmsted, and Wabasha Counties

Rochester, NY includes Livingston, Monroe, Ontario, Orleans, Wayne, and Yates Counties

Rockford, IL includes Boone and Winnebago Counties

Rocky Mount, NC includes Edgecombe and Nash Counties

Rome, GA includes Floyd County

Sacramento--Roseville--Arden-Arcade, CA includes El Dorado, Placer, Sacramento, and Yolo Counties

Saginaw, MI includes Saginaw County

Salem, OR includes Marion and Polk Counties

Salinas, CA includes Monterey County

Salisbury, MD-DE includes Sussex County, DE and Somerset, Wicomico, and Worcester Counties, MD

Salt Lake City, UT includes Salt Lake and Tooele Counties

San Antonio-New Braunfels, TX includes Atascosa, Bandera, Bexar, Comal, Guadalupe, Kendall, Medina, and Wilson Counties

San Diego-Carlsbad, CA includes San Diego County

San Francisco-Oakland-Hayward, CA includes the Metropolitan Divisions of Oakland-Hayward-Berkeley, San Francisco-Redwood City-South San Francisco, and San Rafael
- Oakland-Hayward-Berkeley, CA Metropolitan Division includes Alameda and Contra Costa Counties
- San Francisco-Redwood City-South San Francisco, CA Metropolitan Division includes San Francisco and San Mateo Counties
- San Rafael, CA Metropolitan Division includes Marin County

San Jose-Sunnyvale-Santa Clara, CA includes San Benito and Santa Clara Counties

San Luis Obispo-Paso Robles-Arroyo Grande, CA includes San Luis Obispo County

Santa Cruz-Watsonville, CA includes Santa Cruz County

Santa Fe, NM includes Santa Fe County

Santa Maria-Santa Barbara, CA includes Santa Barbara County

Santa Rosa, CA includes Sonoma County

Savannah, GA includes Bryan, Chatham, and Effingham Counties

Scranton--Wilkes-Barre--Hazleton, PA includes Lackawanna, Luzerne, and Wyoming Counties

Seattle-Tacoma-Bellevue, WA includes the Metropolitan Divisions of Seattle-Bellevue-Everett and Tacoma-Lakewood
- Seattle-Bellevue-Everett, WA Metropolitan Division includes King and Snohomish Counties
- Tacoma-Lakewood, WA Metropolitan Division includes Pierce County

Sebastian-Vero Beach, FL includes Indian River County

Sebring, FL includes Highlands County

Sheboygan, WI includes Sheboygan County

Sherman-Denison, TX includes Grayson County

Shreveport-Bossier City, LA includes Bossier, Caddo, De Soto, and Webster Parishes

Sierra Vista-Douglas, AZ includes Cochise County

Sioux City, IA-NE-SD includes Plymouth and Woodbury Counties, IA; Dakota and Dixon Counties, NE; and Union County, SD

Sioux Falls, SD includes Lincoln, McCook, Minnehaha, and Turner Counties

South Bend-Mishawaka, IN-MI includes St. Joseph County, IN and Cass County, MI

Spartanburg, SC includes Spartanburg and Union Counties

Spokane-Spokane Valley, WA includes Pend Oreille, Spokane, and Stevens Counties

DESCRIPTIONS OF METROPOLITAN AREAS IN 2012 (continued)

Springfield, IL includes Menard and Sangamon Counties

Springfield, MA includes Hampden and Hampshire Counties

Springfield, MO includes Christian, Dallas, Greene, Polk, and Webster Counties

Springfield, OH includes Clark County

State College, PA includes Centre County

Staunton-Waynesboro, VA includes Augusta County and Staunton and Waynesboro Cities

St. George, UT includes Washington County

St. Joseph, MO-KS includes Doniphan County, KS and Andrew, Buchanan, and De Kalb Counties, MO

St. Louis, MO-IL includes Bond, Calhoun, Clinton, Jersey, Macoupin, Madison, Monroe, and St. Clair Counties, IL and Franklin, Jefferson, Lincoln, St. Charles, St. Louis, and Warren Counties and St. Louis City, MO

Stockton-Lodi, CA includes San Joaquin County

Sumter, SC includes Sumter County

Syracuse, NY includes Madison, Onondaga, and Oswego Counties

Tallahassee, FL includes Gadsden, Jefferson, Leon, and Wakulla Counties

Tampa-St. Petersburg-Clearwater, FL includes Hernando, Hillsborough, Pasco, and Pinellas Counties

Terre Haute, IN includes Clay, Sullivan, Vermillion, and Vigo Counties

Texarkana, TX-AR includes Little River and Miller Counties, AR and Bowie County, TX

The Villages, FL includes Sumter County

Toledo, OH includes Fulton, Lucas, and Wood Counties

Topeka, KS includes Jackson, Jefferson, Osage, Shawnee, and Wabaunsee Counties

Trenton, NJ includes Mercer County

Tucson, AZ includes Pima County

Tulsa, OK includes Creek, Okmulgee, Osage, Pawnee, Rogers, Tulsa, and Wagoner Counties

Tuscaloosa, AL includes Hale, Pickens, and Tuscaloosa Counties

Tyler, TX includes Smith County

Utica-Rome, NY includes Herkimer and Oneida Counties

Valdosta, GA includes Brooks, Echols, Lanier, and Lowndes Counties

Vallejo-Fairfield, CA includes Solano County

Victoria, TX includes Goliad and Victoria Counties

Vineland-Bridgeton, NJ includes Cumberland County

Virginia Beach-Norfolk-Newport News, VA-NC includes Currituck and Gates Counties, NC and Gloucester, Isle of Wight, James City, Mathews, and York Counties and Chesapeake, Hampton, Newport News, Norfolk, Poquoson, Portsmouth, Suffolk, Virginia Beach, and Williamsburg Cities, VA

Visalia-Porterville, CA includes Tulare County

Waco, TX includes Falls and McLennan Counties

Walla Walla, WA includes Columbia and Walla Walla Counties

Warner Robins, GA includes Houston, Peach, and Pulaski Counties

Washington-Arlington-Alexandria, DC-VA-MD-WV includes the Metropolitan Divisions of Silver Spring-Frederick-Rockville, MD and Washington-Arlington-Alexandria, DC-VA-MD-WV
- Silver Spring-Frederick-Rockville, MD Metropolitan Division includes Frederick and Montgomery Counties
- Washington-Arlington-Alexandria, DC-VA-MD-WV Metropolitan Division includes District of Columbia; Calvert,

Charles, and Prince George's Counties, MD; Arlington, Clarke, Culpeper, Fairfax, Fauquier, Loudoun, Prince William, Rapppahannock, Spotsylvania, Stafford, and Warren Counties and Alexandria, Fairfax, Falls Church, Fredericksburg, Manassas, and Manassas Park Cities, VA; and Jefferson County, WV

Waterloo-Cedar Falls, IA includes Black Hawk, Bremer, and Grundy Counties

Watertown-Fort Drum, NY includes Jefferson County

Wausau, WI includes Marathon County

Wheeling, WV-OH includes Belmont County, OH and Marshall and Ohio Counties, WV

Wichita, KS includes Butler, Harvey, Kingman, Sedgewick, and Sumner Counties

Wichita Falls, TX includes Archer, Clay, and Wichita Counties

Williamsport, PA includes Lycoming County

Wilmington, NC includes New Hanover and Pender Counties

Winchester, VA-WV includes Frederick County and Winchester City, VA and Hampshire County, WV

Winston-Salem, NC includes Davidson, Davie, Forsyth, Stokes, and Yadkin Counties

Worcester, MA-CT includes Windham County, CT and Worcester County, MA

Yakima, WA includes Yakima County

York-Hanover, PA includes York County

Youngstown-Warren-Boardman, OH-PA includes Mahoning and Trumbull Counties, OH and Mercer County, PA

Yuba City, CA includes Sutter and Yuba Counties

Yuma, AZ includes Yuma County

COUNTY INDEX: 2012

COUNTY:	IS IN METROPOLITAN:	COUNTY:	IS IN METROPOLITAN:
Acadia, LA	Lafayette, LA	Blue Earth, MN	Mankato-North Mankato, MN
Adams, CO	Denver-Aurora-Lakewood, CO	Boise, ID	Boise City, ID
Adams, PA	Gettysburg, PA	Bollinger, MO	Cape Girardeau, MO-IL
Ada, ID	Boise City, ID	Bond, IL	St. Louis, MO-IL
Aiken, SC	Augusta-Richmond County, GA-SC	Bonneville, ID	Idaho Falls, ID
Alachua, FL	Gainesville, FL	Boone, IL	Rockford, IL
Alamance, NC	Burlington, NC	Boone, IN	Indianapolis-Carmel-Anderson, IN
Alameda, CA	San Francisco-Oakland-Hayward, CA	Boone, KY	Cincinnati, OH-KY-IN
Albany, NY	Albany-Schenectady-Troy, NY	Boone, MO	Columbia, MO
Albemarle, VA	Charlottesville, VA	Boone, WV	Charleston, WV
Alexander, IL	Cape Girardeau, MO-IL	Bossier, LA	Shreveport-Bossier City, LA
Alexander, NC	Hickory-Lenoir-Morganton, NC	Botetourt, VA	Roanoke, VA
Alexandria city, VA	Washington-Arlington-Alexandria, DC-VA-MD-WV	Boulder, CO	Boulder, CO
Allegany, MD	Cumberland, MD-WV	Bourbon, KY	Lexington-Fayette, KY
Allegheny, PA	Pittsburgh, PA	Bowie, TX	Texarkana, TX-AR
Allen, IN	Fort Wayne, IN	Box Elder, UT	Ogden-Clearfield, UT
Allen, KY	Bowling Green, KY	Boyd, KY	Huntington-Ashland, WV-KY-OH
Allen, OH	Lima, OH	Bracken, KY	Cincinnati, OH-KY-IN
Amelia, VA	Richmond, VA	Bradley, TN	Cleveland, TN
Amherst, VA	Lynchburg, VA	Brantley, GA	Brunswick, GA
Anchorage city, AK	Anchorage, AK	Brazoria, TX	Houston-The Woodlands-Sugar Land, TX
Anderson, SC	Greenville-Anderson-Mauldin, SC	Brazos, TX	College Station-Bryan, TX
Anderson, TN	Knoxville, TN	Bremer, IA	Waterloo-Cedar Falls, IA
Andrew, MO	St. Joseph, MO-KS	Brevard, FL	Palm Bay-Melbourne-Titusville, FL
Androscoggin, ME	Lewiston-Auburn, ME	Bristol city, VA	Kingsport-Bristol-Bristol, TN-VA
Anne Arundel, MD	Baltimore-Columbia-Towson, MD	Bristol, MA	Providence-Warwick, RI-MA
Anoka, MN	Minneapolis-St. Paul-Bloomington, MN-WI	Bristol, RI	Providence-Warwick, RI-MA
Appomattox, VA	Lynchburg, VA	Bronx, NY	New York-Newark-Jersey City, NY-NJ-PA
Aransas, TX	Corpus Christi, TX	Brooke, WV	Weirton-Steubenville, WV-OH
Arapahoe, CO	Denver-Aurora-Lakewood, CO	Brooks, GA	Valdosta, GA
Archer, TX	Wichita Falls, TX	Broome, NY	Binghamton, NY
Arlington, VA	Washington-Arlington-Alexandria, DC-VA-MD-WV	Broomfield, CO	Denver-Aurora-Lakewood, CO
Armstrong, PA	Pittsburgh, PA	Broward, FL	Miami-Fort Lauderdale-West Palm Beach, FL
Armstrong, TX	Amarillo, TX	Brown, IN	Indianapolis-Carmel-Anderson, IN
Ascension, LA	Baton Rouge, LA	Brown, OH	Cincinnati, OH-KY-IN
Asotin, WA	Lewiston, ID-WA	Brown, WI	Green Bay, WI
Atascosa, TX	San Antonio-New Braunfels, TX	Brunswick, NC	Myrtle Beach-Conway-North Myrtle Beach, SC-NC
Atlantic, NJ	Atlantic City-Hammonton, NJ	Bryan, GA	Savannah, GA
Augusta, VA	Staunton-Waynesboro, VA	Buchanan, MO	St. Joseph, MO-KS
Austin, TX	Houston-The Woodlands-Sugar Land, TX	Buckingham, VA	Charlottesville, VA
Autauga, AL	Montgomery, AL	Bucks, PA	Philadelphia-Camden-Wilmington, PA-NJ-DE-MD
Baker, FL	Jacksonville, FL	Bullitt, KY	Louisville/Jefferson County, KY-IN
Baker, GA	Albany, GA	Buncombe, NC	Asheville, NC
Baldwin, AL	Daphne-Fairhope-Foley, AL	Burke, GA	Augusta-Richmond County, GA-SC
Baltimore city, MD	Baltimore-Columbia-Towson, MD	Burke, NC	Hickory-Lenoir-Morganton, NC
Baltimore, MD	Baltimore-Columbia-Towson, MD	Burleigh, ND	Bismarck, ND
Bandera, TX	San Antonio-New Braunfels, TX	Burleson, TX	College Station-Bryan, TX
Bannock, ID	Pocatello, ID	Burlington, NJ	Philadelphia-Camden-Wilmington, PA-NJ-DE-MD
Barnstable, MA	Barnstable Town, MA	Butler, KS	Wichita, KS
Barrow, GA	Atlanta-Sandy Springs-Roswell, GA	Butler, KY	Bowling Green, KY
Barry, MI	Grand Rapids-Wyoming, MI	Butler, OH	Cincinnati, OH-KY-IN
Bartholomew, IN	Columbus, IN	Butler, PA	Pittsburgh, PA
Bartow, GA	Atlanta-Sandy Springs-Roswell, GA	Butte, CA	Chico, CA
Bastrop, TX	Austin-Round Rock, TX	Butte, ID	Idaho Falls, ID
Bates, MO	Kansas City, MO-KS	Butts, GA	Atlanta-Sandy Springs-Roswell, GA
Bay, FL	Panama City, FL	Cabarrus, NC	Charlotte-Concord-Gastonia, NC-SC
Bay, MI	Bay City, MI	Cabell, WV	Huntington-Ashland, WV-KY-OH
Beaufort, SC	Hilton Head Island-Bluffton-Beaufort, SC	Cache, UT	Logan, UT-ID
Beaver, PA	Pittsburgh, PA	Caddo, LA	Shreveport-Bossier City, LA
Bedford city, VA	Lynchburg, VA	Calcasieu, LA	Lake Charles, LA
Bedford, VA	Lynchburg, VA	Caldwell, MO	Kansas City, MO-KS
Bell, TX	Killeen-Temple, TX	Caldwell, NC	Hickory-Lenoir-Morganton, NC
Belmont, OH	Wheeling, WV-OH	Caldwell, TX	Austin-Round Rock, TX
Benton, AR	Fayetteville-Springdale-Rogers, AR-MO	Calhoun, AL	Anniston-Oxford-Jacksonville, AL
Benton, IA	Cedar Rapids, IA	Calhoun, IL	St. Louis, MO-IL
Benton, IN	Lafayette-West Lafayette, IN	Calhoun, MI	Battle Creek, MI
Benton, MN	St. Cloud, MN	Calhoun, SC	Columbia, SC
Benton, MS	Memphis, TN-MS-AR	Callahan, TX	Abilene, TX
Benton, OR	Corvallis, OR	Callaway, MO	Jefferson City, MO
Benton, WA	Kennewick-Richland, WA	Calumet, WI	Appleton, WI
Bergen, NJ	New York-Newark-Jersey City, NY-NJ-PA	Calvert, MD	Washington-Arlington-Alexandria DC-VA-MD-WV
Berkeley, SC	Charleston-North Charleston, SC	Cambria, PA	Johnstown, PA
Berkeley, WV	Hagerstown-Martinsburg, MD-WV	Camden, NJ	Philadelphia-Camden-Wilmington, PA-NJ-DE-MD
Berkshire, MA	Pittsfield, MA	Cameron, LA	Lake Charles, LA
Berks, PA	Reading, PA	Cameron, TX	Brownsville-Harlingen, TX
Bernalillo, NM	Albuquerque, NM	Campbell, KY	Cincinnati, OH-KY-IN
Berrien, MI	Niles-Benton Harbor, MI	Campbell, TN	Knoxville, TN
Bexar, TX	San Antonio-New Braunfels, TX	Campbell, VA	Lynchburg, VA
Bibb, AL	Birmingham-Hoover, AL	Canadian, OK	Oklahoma City, OK
Bibb, GA	Macon, GA	Cannon, TN	Nashville-Davidson--Murfreesboro--Franklin, TN
Black Hawk, IA	Waterloo-Cedar Falls, IA	Canyon, ID	Boise City, ID
Blair, PA	Altoona, PA	Cape Girardeau, MO	Cape Girardeau, MO-IL
Blount, AL	Birmingham-Hoover, AL	Cape May, NJ	Ocean City, NJ
Blount, TN	Knoxville, TN	Carbon, MT	Billings, MT

COUNTY INDEX: 2012 (continued)

COUNTY:	IS IN METROPOLITAN:	COUNTY:	IS IN METROPOLITAN:
Carbon, PA	Allentown-Bethlehem-Easton, PA-NJ	Cook, IL	Chicago-Naperville-Elgin, IL-IN-WI
Carlton, MN	Duluth, MN-WI	Copiah, MS	Jackson, MS
Caroline, VA	Richmond, VA	Coryell, TX	Killeen-Temple, TX
Carroll, GA	Atlanta-Sandy Springs-Roswell, GA	Cotton, OK	Lawton, OK
Carroll, IN	Lafayette-West Lafayette, IN	Coweta, GA	Atlanta-Sandy Springs-Roswell, GA
Carroll, MD	Baltimore-Columbia-Towson, MD	Cowlitz, WA	Longview, WA
Carroll, OH	Canton-Massillon, OH	Craighead, AR	Jonesboro, AR
Carson City, NV	Carson City, NV	Craig, VA	Roanoke, VA
Carson, TX	Amarillo, TX	Craven, NC	New Bern, NC
Carter, TN	Johnson City, TN	Crawford, AR	Fort Smith, AR-OK
Carver, MN	Minneapolis-St. Paul-Bloomington, MN-WI	Crawford, GA	Macon, GA
Cascade, MT	Great Falls, MT	Creek, OK	Tulsa, OK
Cass, MI	South Bend-Mishawaka, IN-MI	Crittenden, AR	Memphis, TN-MS-AR
Cass, MO	Kansas City, MO-KS	Crockett, TN	Jackson, TN
Cass, ND	Fargo, ND-MN	Crosby, TX	Lubbock, TX
Cass, NE	Omaha-Council Bluffs, NE-IA	Culpeper, VA	Washington-Arlington-Alexandria, DC-VA-MD-WV
Catawba, NC	Hickory-Lenoir-Morganton, NC	Cumberland, ME	Portland-South Portland, ME
Catoosa, GA	Chattanooga, TN-GA	Cumberland, NC	Fayetteville, NC
Cecil, MD	Philadelphia-Camden-Wilmington, PA-NJ-DE-MD	Cumberland, NJ	Vineland-Bridgeton, NJ
Centre, PA	State College, PA	Cumberland, PA	Harrisburg-Carlisle, PA
Chambers, TX	Houston-The Woodlands-Sugar Land, TX	Currituck, NC	Virginia Beach-Norfolk-Newport News, VA-NC
Champaign, IL	Champaign-Urbana, IL	Custer, SD	Rapid City, SD
Charles City, VA	Richmond, VA	Cuyahoga, OH	Cleveland-Elyria, OH
Charleston, SC	Charleston-North Charleston, SC	Dade, GA	Chattanooga, TN-GA
Charles, MD	Washington-Arlington-Alexandria, DC-VA-MD-WV	Dakota, MN	Minneapolis-St. Paul-Bloomington, MN-WI
Charlottesville city, VA	Charlottesville, VA	Dakota, NE	Sioux City, IA-NE-SD
Charlotte, FL	Punta Gorda, FL	Dallas, IA	Des Moines-West Des Moines, IA
Chatham, GA	Savannah, GA	Dallas, MO	Springfield, MO
Chatham, NC	Durham-Chapel Hill, NC	Dallas, TX	Dallas-Fort Worth-Arlington, TX
Chattahoochee, GA	Columbus, GA-AL	Dane, WI	Madison, WI
Cheatham, TN	Nashville-Davidson--Murfreesboro--Franklin, TN	Darlington, SC	Florence, SC
Chelan, WA	Wenatchee, WA	Dauphin, PA	Harrisburg-Carlisle, PA
Chemung, NY	Elmira, NY	Davidson, NC	Winston-Salem, NC
Cherokee, GA	Atlanta-Sandy Springs-Roswell, GA	Davidson, TN	Nashville-Davidson--Murfreesboro--Franklin, TN
Chesapeake city, VA	Virginia Beach-Norfolk-Newport News, VA-NC	Daviess, KY	Owensboro, KY
Chesterfield, VA	Richmond, VA	Davie, NC	Winston-Salem, NC
Chester, PA	Philadelphia-Camden-Wilmington, PA-NJ-DE-MD	Davis, UT	Ogden-Clearfield, UT
Chester, SC	Charlotte-Concord-Gastonia, NC-SC	Dawson, GA	Atlanta-Sandy Springs-Roswell, GA
Chester, TN	Jackson, TN	De Soto, LA	Shreveport-Bossier City, LA
Chilton, AL	Birmingham-Hoover, AL	De Witt, IL	Bloomington, IL
Chippewa, WI	Eau Claire, WI	Dearborn, IN	Cincinnati, OH-KY-IN
Chisago, MN	Minneapolis-St. Paul-Bloomington, MN-WI	DeKalb, GA	Atlanta-Sandy Springs-Roswell, GA
Chittenden, VT	Burlington-South Burlington, VT	DeKalb, IL	Chicago-Naperville-Elgin, IL-IN-WI
Christian, KY	Clarksville, TN-KY	DeKalb, MO	St. Joseph, MO-KS
Christian, MO	Springfield, MO	Delaware, IN	Muncie, IN
Citrus, FL	Homosassa Springs, FL	Delaware, OH	Columbus, OH
Clackamas, OR	Portland-Vancouver-Hillsboro, OR-WA	Delaware, PA	Philadelphia-Camden-Wilmington, PA-NJ-DE-MD
Clarke, GA	Athens-Clarke County, GA	Denton, TX	Dallas-Fort Worth-Arlington, TX
Clarke, VA	Washington-Arlington-Alexandria, DC-VA-MD-WV	Denver, CO	Denver-Aurora-Lakewood, CO
Clark, IN	Louisville/Jefferson County, KY-IN	Deschutes, OR	Bend-Redmond, OR
Clark, KY	Lexington-Fayette, KY	DeSoto, MS	Memphis, TN-MS-AR
Clark, NV	Las Vegas-Henderson-Paradise, NV	Dickson, TN	Nashville-Davidson--Murfreesboro--Franklin, TN
Clark, OH	Springfield, OH	Dinwiddie, VA	Richmond, VA
Clark, WA	Portland-Vancouver-Hillsboro, OR-WA	District of Columbia, DC	Washington-Arlington-Alexandria, DC-VA-MD-WV
Clayton, GA	Atlanta-Sandy Springs-Roswell, GA	Dixon, NE	Sioux City, IA-NE-SD
Clay, FL	Jacksonville, FL	Dodge, MN	Rochester, MN
Clay, IN	Terre Haute, IN	Doniphan, KS	St. Joseph, MO-KS
Clay, MN	Fargo, ND-MN	Doña Ana, NM	Las Cruces, NM
Clay, MO	Kansas City, MO-KS	Dorchester, SC	Charleston-North Charleston, SC
Clay, TX	Wichita Falls, TX	Dougherty, GA	Albany, GA
Clay, WV	Charleston, WV	Douglas, CO	Denver-Aurora-Lakewood, CO
Clear Creek, CO	Denver-Aurora-Lakewood, CO	Douglas, GA	Atlanta-Sandy Springs-Roswell, GA
Clermont, OH	Cincinnati, OH-KY-IN	Douglas, KS	Lawrence, KS
Cleveland, AR	Pine Bluff, AR	Douglas, NE	Omaha-Council Bluffs, NE-IA
Cleveland, OK	Oklahoma City, OK	Douglas, WA	Wenatchee, WA
Clinton, IL	St. Louis, MO-IL	Douglas, WI	Duluth, MN-WI
Clinton, MI	Lansing-East Lansing, MI	Dubuque, IA	Dubuque, IA
Clinton, MO	Kansas City, MO-KS	DuPage, IL	Chicago-Naperville-Elgin, IL-IN-WI
Cobb, GA	Atlanta-Sandy Springs-Roswell, GA	Durham, NC	Durham-Chapel Hill, NC
Cochise, AZ	Sierra Vista-Douglas, AZ	Dutchess, NY	New York-Newark-Jersey City, NY-NJ-PA
Coconino, AZ	Flagstaff, AZ	Duval, FL	Jacksonville, FL
Colbert, AL	Florence-Muscle Shoals, AL	East Baton Rouge, LA	Baton Rouge, LA
Cole, MO	Jefferson City, MO	East Feliciana, LA	Baton Rouge, LA
Collier, FL	Naples-Immokalee-Marco Island, FL	Eaton, MI	Lansing-East Lansing, MI
Collin, TX	Dallas-Fort Worth-Arlington, TX	Eau Claire, WI	Eau Claire, WI
Colonial Heights city, VA	Richmond, VA	Echols, GA	Valdosta, GA
Columbia, GA	Augusta-Richmond County, GA-SC	Ector, TX	Odessa, TX
Columbia, OR	Portland-Vancouver-Hillsboro, OR-WA	Edgecombe, NC	Rocky Mount, NC
Columbia, PA	Bloomsburg-Berwick, PA	Edgefield, SC	Augusta-Richmond County, GA-SC
Columbia, WA	Walla Walla, WA	Edmonson, KY	Bowling Green, KY
Columbia, WI	Madison, WI	Effingham, GA	Savannah, GA
Comal, TX	San Antonio-New Braunfels, TX	El Dorado, CA	Sacramento--Roseville--Arden-Arcade, CA
Comanche, OK	Lawton, OK	El Paso, CO	Colorado Springs, CO
Contra Costa, CA	San Francisco-Oakland-Hayward, CA	El Paso, TX	El Paso, TX

COUNTY INDEX: 2012 (continued)

COUNTY:	IS IN METROPOLITAN:	COUNTY:	IS IN METROPOLITAN:
Elbert, CO	Denver-Aurora-Lakewood, CO	Green, WI	Madison, WI
Elkhart, IN	Elkhart-Goshen, IN	Gregg, TX	Longview, TX
Ellis, TX	Dallas-Fort Worth-Arlington, TX	Grundy, IA	Waterloo-Cedar Falls, IA
Elmore, AL	Montgomery, AL	Grundy, IL	Chicago-Naperville-Elgin, IL-IN-WI
Erie, NY	Buffalo-Cheektowaga-Niagara Falls, NY	Guadalupe, TX	San Antonio-New Braunfels, TX
Erie, PA	Erie, PA	Guilford, NC	Greensboro-High Point, NC
Escambia, FL	Pensacola-Ferry Pass-Brent, FL	Gulf, FL	Panama City, FL
Essex, MA	Boston-Cambridge-Newton, MA-NH	Guthrie, IA	Des Moines-West Des Moines, IA
Essex, NJ	New York-Newark-Jersey City, NY-NJ-PA	Gwinnett, GA	Atlanta-Sandy Springs-Roswell, GA
Etowah, AL	Gadsden, AL	Hale, AL	Tuscaloosa, AL
Fairbanks North Star, AK	Fairbanks, AK	Hall, GA	Gainesville, GA
Fairfax city, VA	Washington-Arlington-Alexandria, DC-VA-MD-WV	Hall, NE	Grand Island, NE
Fairfax, VA	Washington-Arlington-Alexandria, DC-VA-MD-WV	Hamblen, TN	Morristown, TN
Fairfield, CT	Bridgeport-Stamford-Norwalk, CT	Hamilton, IN	Indianapolis-Carmel-Anderson, IN
Fairfield, OH	Columbus, OH	Hamilton, NE	Grand Island, NE
Fairfield, SC	Columbia, SC	Hamilton, OH	Cincinnati, OH-KY-IN
Falls Church city, VA	Washington-Arlington-Alexandria, DC-VA-MD-WV	Hamilton, TN	Chattanooga, TN-GA
Falls, TX	Waco, TX	Hampden, MA	Springfield, MA
Faulkner, AR	Little Rock-North Little Rock-Conway, AR	Hampshire, MA	Springfield, MA
Fauquier, VA	Washington-Arlington-Alexandria, DC-VA-MD-WV	Hampshire, WV	Winchester, VA-WV
Fayette, GA	Atlanta-Sandy Springs-Roswell, GA	Hampton city, VA	Virginia Beach-Norfolk-Newport News, VA-NC
Fayette, KY	Lexington-Fayette, KY	Hancock, IN	Indianapolis-Carmel-Anderson, IN
Fayette, PA	Pittsburgh, PA	Hancock, KY	Owensboro, KY
Fayette, TN	Memphis, TN-MS-AR	Hancock, MS	Gulfport-Biloxi-Pascagoula, MS
Fayette, WV	Beckley, WV	Hancock, WV	Weirton-Steubenville, WV-OH
Fillmore, MN	Rochester, MN	Hanover, VA	Richmond, VA
Flagler, FL	Deltona-Daytona Beach-Ormond Beach, FL	Haralson, GA	Atlanta-Sandy Springs-Roswell, GA
Florence, SC	Florence, SC	Hardin, KY	Elizabethtown-Fort Knox, KY
Floyd, GA	Rome, GA	Hardin, TX	Beaumont-Port Arthur, TX
Floyd, IN	Louisville/Jefferson County, KY-IN	Harford, MD	Baltimore-Columbia-Towson, MD
Floyd, VA	Blacksburg-Christiansburg-Radford, VA	Harrisonburg city, VA	Harrisonburg, VA
Fluvanna, VA	Charlottesville, VA	Harrison, IA	Omaha-Council Bluffs, NE-IA
Fond du Lac, WI	Fond du Lac, WI	Harrison, IN	Louisville/Jefferson County, KY-IN
Ford, IL	Champaign-Urbana, IL	Harrison, MS	Gulfport-Biloxi-Pascagoula, MS
Forrest, MS	Hattiesburg, MS	Harris, GA	Columbus, GA-AL
Forsyth, GA	Atlanta-Sandy Springs-Roswell, GA	Harris, TX	Houston-The Woodlands-Sugar Land, TX
Forsyth, NC	Winston-Salem, NC	Hartford, CT	Hartford-West Hartford-East Hartford, CT
Fort Bend, TX	Houston-The Woodlands-Sugar Land, TX	Harvey, KS	Wichita, KS
Franklin, ID	Logan, UT-ID	Hawkins, TN	Kingsport-Bristol-Bristol, TN-VA
Franklin, MO	St. Louis, MO-IL	Hays, TX	Austin-Round Rock, TX
Franklin, NC	Raleigh, NC	Haywood, NC	Asheville, NC
Franklin, OH	Columbus, OH	Heard, GA	Atlanta-Sandy Springs-Roswell, GA
Franklin, PA	Chambersburg-Waynesboro, PA	Henderson, KY	Evansville, IN-KY
Franklin, VA	Roanoke, VA	Henderson, NC	Asheville, NC
Franklin, VT	Burlington-South Burlington, VT	Hendricks, IN	Indianapolis-Carmel-Anderson, IN
Franklin, WA	Kennewick-Richland, WA	Hennepin, MN	Minneapolis-St. Paul-Bloomington, MN-WI
Fredericksburg city, VA	Washington-Arlington-Alexandria, DC-VA-MD-WV	Henrico, VA	Richmond, VA
Frederick, MD	Washington-Arlington-Alexandria, DC-VA-MD-WV	Henry, AL	Dothan, AL
Frederick, VA	Winchester, VA-WV	Henry, GA	Atlanta-Sandy Springs-Roswell, GA
Fresno, CA	Fresno, CA	Henry, IL	Davenport-Moline-Rock Island, IA-IL
Fulton, GA	Atlanta-Sandy Springs-Roswell, GA	Henry, KY	Louisville/Jefferson County, KY-IN
Fulton, OH	Toledo, OH	Herkimer, NY	Utica-Rome, NY
Gadsden, FL	Tallahassee, FL	Hernando, FL	Tampa-St. Petersburg-Clearwater, FL
Gallatin, KY	Cincinnati, OH-KY-IN	Hickman, TN	Nashville-Davidson--Murfreesboro--Franklin, TN
Galveston, TX	Houston-The Woodlands-Sugar Land, TX	Hidalgo, TX	McAllen-Edinburg-Mission, TX
Garland, AR	Hot Springs, AR	Highlands, FL	Sebring, FL
Gaston, NC	Charlotte-Concord-Gastonia, NC-SC	Hillsborough, FL	Tampa-St. Petersburg-Clearwater, FL
Gates, NC	Virginia Beach-Norfolk-Newport News, VA-NC	Hillsborough, NH	Manchester-Nashua, NH
Geauga, OH	Cleveland-Elyria, OH	Hinds, MS	Jackson, MS
Gem, ID	Boise City, ID	Hocking, OH	Columbus, OH
Genesee, MI	Flint, MI	Hoke, NC	Fayetteville, NC
Geneva, AL	Dothan, AL	Honolulu, HI	Urban Honolulu, HI
Gilchrist, FL	Gainesville, FL	Hood, TX	Dallas-Fort Worth-Arlington, TX
Giles, VA	Blacksburg-Christiansburg-Radford, VA	Hopewell city, VA	Richmond, VA
Gilpin, CO	Denver-Aurora-Lakewood, CO	Horry, SC	Myrtle Beach-Conway-North Myrtle Beach, SC-NC
Gloucester, NJ	Philadelphia-Camden-Wilmington, PA-NJ-DE-MD	Houston, AL	Dothan, AL
Gloucester, VA	Virginia Beach-Norfolk-Newport News, VA-NC	Houston, GA	Warner Robins, GA
Glynn, GA	Brunswick, GA	Houston, MN	La Crosse-Onalaska, WI-MN
Golden Valley, MT	Billings, MT	Howard, IN	Kokomo, IN
Goliad, TX	Victoria, TX	Howard, MD	Baltimore-Columbia-Towson, MD
Goochland, VA	Richmond, VA	Howard, NE	Grand Island, NE
Grady, OK	Oklahoma City, OK	Hudson, NJ	New York-Newark-Jersey City, NY-NJ-PA
Grainger, TN	Knoxville, TN	Hudspeth, TX	El Paso, TX
Grand Forks, ND	Grand Forks, ND-MN	Hunterdon, NJ	New York-Newark-Jersey City, NY-NJ-PA
Grand Isle, VT	Burlington-South Burlington, VT	Hunt, TX	Dallas-Fort Worth-Arlington, TX
Grant, AR	Little Rock-North Little Rock-Conway, AR	Iberia, LA	Lafayette, LA
Grant, KY	Cincinnati, OH-KY-IN	Iberville, LA	Baton Rouge, LA
Grant, LA	Alexandria, LA	Imperial, CA	El Centro, CA
Grayson, TX	Sherman-Denison, TX	Indian River, FL	Sebastian-Vero Beach, FL
Greene, MO	Springfield, MO	Ingham, MI	Lansing-East Lansing, MI
Greene, OH	Dayton, OH	Iowa, WI	Madison, WI
Greene, VA	Charlottesville, VA	Iredell, NC	Charlotte-Concord-Gastonia, NC-SC
Greenup, KY	Huntington-Ashland, WV-KY-OH	Irion, TX	San Angelo, TX
Greenville, SC	Greenville-Anderson-Mauldin, SC	Isanti, MN	Minneapolis-St. Paul-Bloomington, MN-WI

COUNTY INDEX: 2012 (continued)

COUNTY:	IS IN METROPOLITAN:	COUNTY:	IS IN METROPOLITAN:
Isle of Wight, VA	Virginia Beach-Norfolk-Newport News, VA-NC	Larue, KY	Elizabethtown-Fort Knox, KY
Jackson, IL	Carbondale-Marion, IL	Lauderdale, AL	Florence-Muscle Shoals, AL
Jackson, KS	Topeka, KS	Laurens, SC	Greenville-Anderson-Mauldin, SC
Jackson, MI	Jackson, MI	Lawrence, AL	Decatur, AL
Jackson, MO	Kansas City, MO-KS	Lawrence, OH	Huntington-Ashland, WV-KY-OH
Jackson, MS	Gulfport-Biloxi-Pascagoula, MS	Le Flore, OK	Fort Smith, AR-OK
Jackson, OR	Medford, OR	Le Sueur, MN	Minneapolis-St. Paul-Bloomington, MN-WI
James City, VA	Virginia Beach-Norfolk-Newport News, VA-NC	Leavenworth, KS	Kansas City, MO-KS
Jasper, GA	Atlanta-Sandy Springs-Roswell, GA	Lebanon, PA	Lebanon, PA
Jasper, IN	Chicago-Naperville-Elgin, IL-IN-WI	Lee, AL	Auburn-Opelika, AL
Jasper, MO	Joplin, MO	Lee, FL	Cape Coral-Fort Myers, FL
Jasper, SC	Hilton Head Island-Bluffton-Beaufort, SC	Lee, GA	Albany, GA
Jefferson, AL	Birmingham-Hoover, AL	Lehigh, PA	Allentown-Bethlehem-Easton, PA-NJ
Jefferson, AR	Pine Bluff, AR	Leon, FL	Tallahassee, FL
Jefferson, CO	Denver-Aurora-Lakewood, CO	Lexington, SC	Columbia, SC
Jefferson, FL	Tallahassee, FL	Liberty, GA	Hinesville, GA
Jefferson, ID	Idaho Falls, ID	Liberty, TX	Houston-The Woodlands-Sugar Land, TX
Jefferson, KS	Topeka, KS	Licking, OH	Columbus, OH
Jefferson, KY	Louisville/Jefferson County, KY-IN	Limestone, AL	Huntsville, AL
Jefferson, LA	New Orleans-Metairie, LA	Lincoln, AR	Pine Bluff, AR
Jefferson, MO	St. Louis, MO-IL	Lincoln, GA	Augusta-Richmond County, GA-SC
Jefferson, NY	Watertown-Fort Drum, NY	Lincoln, MO	St. Louis, MO-IL
Jefferson, OH	Weirton-Steubenville, WV-OH	Lincoln, NC	Charlotte-Concord-Gastonia, NC-SC
Jefferson, TN	Morristown, TN	Lincoln, OK	Oklahoma City, OK
Jefferson, TX	Beaumont-Port Arthur, TX	Lincoln, SD	Sioux Falls, SD
Jefferson, WV	Washington-Arlington-Alexandria, DC-VA-MD-WV	Lincoln, WV	Huntington-Ashland, WV-KY-OH
Jersey, IL	St. Louis, MO-IL	Linn, IA	Cedar Rapids, IA
Jessamine, KY	Lexington-Fayette, KY	Linn, KS	Kansas City, MO-KS
Johnson, IA	Iowa City, IA	Linn, OR	Albany, OR
Johnson, IN	Indianapolis-Carmel-Anderson, IN	Little River, AR	Texarkana, TX-AR
Johnson, KS	Kansas City, MO-KS	Livingston, LA	Baton Rouge, LA
Johnson, TX	Dallas-Fort Worth-Arlington, TX	Livingston, MI	Detroit-Warren-Dearborn, MI
Johnston, NC	Raleigh, NC	Livingston, NY	Rochester, NY
Jones, GA	Macon, GA	Logan, OK	Oklahoma City, OK
Jones, IA	Cedar Rapids, IA	Long, GA	Hinesville, GA
Jones, NC	New Bern, NC	Lonoke, AR	Little Rock-North Little Rock-Conway, AR
Jones, TX	Abilene, TX	Lorain, OH	Cleveland-Elyria, OH
Josephine, OR	Grants Pass, OR	Los Angeles, CA	Los Angeles-Long Beach-Anaheim, CA
Juab, UT	Provo-Orem, UT	Loudon, TN	Knoxville, TN
Kalamazoo, MI	Kalamazoo-Portage, MI	Loudoun, VA	Washington-Arlington-Alexandria, DC-VA-MD-WV
Kalawao, HI	Kahului-Wailuku-Lahaina, HI	Lowndes, AL	Montgomery, AL
Kanawha, WV	Charleston, WV	Lowndes, GA	Valdosta, GA
Kane, IL	Chicago-Naperville-Elgin, IL-IN-WI	Lubbock, TX	Lubbock, TX
Kankakee, IL	Kankakee, IL	Lucas, OH	Toledo, OH
Kaufman, TX	Dallas-Fort Worth-Arlington, TX	Luzerne, PA	Scranton--Wilkes-Barre--Hazleton, PA
Kendall, IL	Chicago-Naperville-Elgin, IL-IN-WI	Lycoming, PA	Williamsport, PA
Kendall, TX	San Antonio-New Braunfels, TX	Lynchburg city, VA	Lynchburg, VA
Kenosha, WI	Chicago-Naperville-Elgin, IL-IN-WI	Lynn, TX	Lubbock, TX
Kenton, KY	Cincinnati, OH-KY-IN	Macomb, MI	Detroit-Warren-Dearborn, MI
Kent, DE	Dover, DE	Macon, IL	Decatur, IL
Kent, MI	Grand Rapids-Wyoming, MI	Macon, TN	Nashville-Davidson--Murfreesboro--Franklin, TN
Kent, RI	Providence-Warwick, RI-MA	Macoupin, IL	St. Louis, MO-IL
Kern, CA	Bakersfield, CA	Madera, CA	Madera, CA
Kershaw, SC	Columbia, SC	Madison, AL	Huntsville, AL
Kewaunee, WI	Green Bay, WI	Madison, AR	Fayetteville-Springdale-Rogers, AR-MO
King William, VA	Richmond, VA	Madison, GA	Athens-Clarke County, GA
Kingman, KS	Wichita, KS	Madison, IA	Des Moines-West Des Moines, IA
Kings, CA	Hanford-Corcoran, CA	Madison, IL	St. Louis, MO-IL
Kings, NY	New York-Newark-Jersey City, NY-NJ-PA	Madison, IN	Indianapolis-Carmel-Anderson, IN
King, WA	Seattle-Tacoma-Bellevue, WA	Madison, MS	Jackson, MS
Kitsap, WA	Bremerton-Silverdale, WA	Madison, NC	Asheville, NC
Knox, TN	Knoxville, TN	Madison, NY	Syracuse, NY
Kootenai, ID	Coeur d'Alene, ID	Madison, OH	Columbus, OH
La Crosse, WI	La Crosse-Onalaska, WI-MN	Madison, TN	Jackson, TN
Lackawanna, PA	Scranton--Wilkes-Barre--Hazleton, PA	Mahoning, OH	Youngstown-Warren-Boardman, OH-PA
Lafayette, LA	Lafayette, LA	Manassas city, VA	Washington-Arlington-Alexandria, DC-VA-MD-WV
Lafayette, MO	Kansas City, MO-KS	Manassas Park city, VA	Washington-Arlington-Alexandria, DC-VA-MD-WV
Lafourche, LA	Houma-Thibodaux, LA	Manatee, FL	North Port-Sarasota-Bradenton, FL
Lake, FL	Orlando-Kissimmee-Sanford, FL	Marathon, WI	Wausau, WI
Lake, IL	Chicago-Naperville-Elgin, IL-IN-WI	Maricopa, AZ	Phoenix-Mesa-Scottsdale, AZ
Lake, IN	Chicago-Naperville-Elgin, IL-IN-WI	Marin, CA	San Francisco-Oakland-Hayward, CA
Lake, OH	Cleveland-Elyria, OH	Marion, FL	Ocala, FL
Lamar, GA	Atlanta-Sandy Springs-Roswell, GA	Marion, GA	Columbus, GA-AL
Lamar, MS	Hattiesburg, MS	Marion, IN	Indianapolis-Carmel-Anderson, IN
Lampasas, TX	Killeen-Temple, TX	Marion, OR	Salem, OR
Lancaster, NE	Lincoln, NE	Marion, TN	Chattanooga, TN-GA
Lancaster, PA	Lancaster, PA	Marshall, IL	Peoria, IL
Lancaster, SC	Charlotte-Concord-Gastonia, NC-SC	Marshall, MS	Memphis, TN-MS-AR
Lane, OR	Eugene, OR	Marshall, WV	Wheeling, WV-OH
Lanier, GA	Valdosta, GA	Martin, FL	Port St. Lucie, FL
Lapeer, MI	Detroit-Warren-Dearborn, MI	Martin, TX	Midland, TX
LaPorte, IN	Michigan City-La Porte, IN	Matanuska-Susitna, AK	Anchorage, AK
Laramie, WY	Cheyenne, WY	Mathews, VA	Virginia Beach-Norfolk-Newport News, VA-NC
Larimer, CO	Fort Collins, CO	Maui, HI	Kahului-Wailuku-Lahaina, HI

COUNTY:	IS IN METROPOLITAN:
Maury, TN	Nashville-Davidson--Murfreesboro--Franklin, TN
McClain, OK	Oklahoma City, OK
McCook, SD	Sioux Falls, SD
McDonald, MO	Fayetteville-Springdale-Rogers, AR-MO
McDuffie, GA	Augusta-Richmond County, GA-SC
McHenry, IL	Chicago-Naperville-Elgin, IL-IN-WI
McIntosh, GA	Brunswick, GA
McLean, IL	Bloomington, IL
McLean, KY	Owensboro, KY
McLennan, TX	Waco, TX
Meade, KY	Elizabethtown-Fort Knox, KY
Meade, SD	Rapid City, SD
Mecklenburg, NC	Charlotte-Concord-Gastonia, NC-SC
Medina, OH	Cleveland-Elyria, OH
Medina, TX	San Antonio-New Braunfels, TX
Menard, IL	Springfield, IL
Merced, CA	Merced, CA
Mercer, IL	Davenport-Moline-Rock Island, IA-IL
Mercer, NJ	Trenton, NJ
Mercer, PA	Youngstown-Warren-Boardman, OH-PA
Meriwether, GA	Atlanta-Sandy Springs-Roswell, GA
Merrick, NE	Grand Island, NE
Mesa, CO	Grand Junction, CO
Miami-Dade, FL	Miami-Fort Lauderdale-West Palm Beach, FL
Miami, KS	Kansas City, MO-KS
Miami, OH	Dayton, OH
Middlesex, CT	Hartford-West Hartford-East Hartford, CT
Middlesex, MA	Boston-Cambridge-Newton, MA-NH
Middlesex, NJ	New York-Newark-Jersey City, NY-NJ-PA
Midland, MI	Midland, MI
Midland, TX	Midland, TX
Mille Lacs, MN	Minneapolis-St. Paul-Bloomington, MN-WI
Miller, AR	Texarkana, TX-AR
Mills, IA	Omaha-Council Bluffs, NE-IA
Milwaukee, WI	Milwaukee-Waukesha-West Allis, WI
Mineral, WV	Cumberland, MD-WV
Minnehaha, SD	Sioux Falls, SD
Missoula, MT	Missoula, MT
Mobile, AL	Mobile, AL
Mohave, AZ	Lake Havasu City-Kingman, AZ
Moniteau, MO	Jefferson City, MO
Monmouth, NJ	New York-Newark-Jersey City, NY-NJ-PA
Monongalia, WV	Morgantown, WV
Monroe, GA	Macon, GA
Monroe, IL	St. Louis, MO-IL
Monroe, IN	Bloomington, IN
Monroe, MI	Monroe, MI
Monroe, NY	Rochester, NY
Monroe, PA	East Stroudsburg, PA
Montcalm, MI	Grand Rapids-Wyoming, MI
Monterey, CA	Salinas, CA
Montgomery, AL	Montgomery, AL
Montgomery, MD	Washington-Arlington-Alexandria, DC-VA-MD-WV
Montgomery, OH	Dayton, OH
Montgomery, PA	Philadelphia-Camden-Wilmington, PA-NJ-DE-MD
Montgomery, TN	Clarksville, TN-KY
Montgomery, TX	Houston-The Woodlands-Sugar Land, TX
Montgomery, VA	Blacksburg-Christiansburg-Radford, VA
Montour, PA	Bloomsburg-Berwick, PA
Morgan, AL	Decatur, AL
Morgan, GA	Atlanta-Sandy Springs-Roswell, GA
Morgan, IN	Indianapolis-Carmel-Anderson, IN
Morgan, TN	Knoxville, TN
Morgan, UT	Ogden-Clearfield, UT
Morris, NJ	New York-Newark-Jersey City, NY-NJ-PA
Morrow, OH	Columbus, OH
Morton, ND	Bismarck, ND
Multnomah, OR	Portland-Vancouver-Hillsboro, OR-WA
Murray, GA	Dalton, GA
Muscogee, GA	Columbus, GA-AL
Muskegon, MI	Muskegon, MI
Napa, CA	Napa, CA
Nash, NC	Rocky Mount, NC
Nassau, FL	Jacksonville, FL
Nassau, NY	New York-Newark-Jersey City, NY-NJ-PA
Natrona, WY	Casper, WY
Nelson, VA	Charlottesville, VA
New Castle, DE	Philadelphia-Camden-Wilmington, PA-NJ-DE-MD
New Hanover, NC	Wilmington, NC
New Haven, CT	New Haven-Milford, CT
New Kent, VA	Richmond, VA
New London, CT	Norwich-New London, CT
New York, NY	New York-Newark-Jersey City, NY-NJ-PA
Newport News city, VA	Virginia Beach-Norfolk-Newport News, VA-NC

COUNTY:	IS IN METROPOLITAN:
Newport, RI	Providence-Warwick, RI-MA
Newton, GA	Atlanta-Sandy Springs-Roswell, GA
Newton, IN	Chicago-Naperville-Elgin, IL-IN-WI
Newton, MO	Joplin, MO
Newton, TX	Beaumont-Port Arthur, TX
Nez Perce, ID	Lewiston, ID-WA
Niagara, NY	Buffalo-Cheektowaga-Niagara Falls, NY
Nicollet, MN	Mankato-North Mankato, MN
Norfolk city, VA	Virginia Beach-Norfolk-Newport News, VA-NC
Norfolk, MA	Boston-Cambridge-Newton, MA-NH
Northampton, PA	Allentown-Bethlehem-Easton, PA-NJ
Nueces, TX	Corpus Christi, TX
Oakland, MI	Detroit-Warren-Dearborn, MI
Ocean, NJ	New York-Newark-Jersey City, NY-NJ-PA
Oconee, GA	Athens-Clarke County, GA
Oconto, WI	Green Bay, WI
Oglethorpe, GA	Athens-Clarke County, GA
Ohio, IN	Cincinnati, OH-KY-IN
Ohio, WV	Wheeling, WV-OH
Okaloosa, FL	Crestview-Fort Walton Beach-Destin, FL
Oklahoma, OK	Oklahoma City, OK
Okmulgee, OK	Tulsa, OK
Oldham, KY	Louisville/Jefferson County, KY-IN
Oldham, TX	Amarillo, TX
Oliver, ND	Bismarck, ND
Olmsted, MN	Rochester, MN
Oneida, NY	Utica-Rome, NY
Onondaga, NY	Syracuse, NY
Onslow, NC	Jacksonville, NC
Ontario, NY	Rochester, NY
Orange, CA	Los Angeles-Long Beach-Anaheim, CA
Orange, FL	Orlando-Kissimmee-Sanford, FL
Orange, NC	Durham-Chapel Hill, NC
Orange, NY	New York-Newark-Jersey City, NY-NJ-PA
Orange, TX	Beaumont-Port Arthur, TX
Orleans, LA	New Orleans-Metairie, LA
Orleans, NY	Rochester, NY
Osage, KS	Topeka, KS
Osage, MO	Jefferson City, MO
Osage, OK	Tulsa, OK
Osceola, FL	Orlando-Kissimmee-Sanford, FL
Oswego, NY	Syracuse, NY
Ottawa, MI	Grand Rapids-Wyoming, MI
Ouachita, LA	Monroe, LA
Outagamie, WI	Appleton, WI
Owen, IN	Bloomington, IN
Owyhee, ID	Boise City, ID
Ozaukee, WI	Milwaukee-Waukesha-West Allis, WI
Palm Beach, FL	Miami-Fort Lauderdale-West Palm Beach, FL
Pamlico, NC	New Bern, NC
Parker, TX	Dallas-Fort Worth-Arlington, TX
Park, CO	Denver-Aurora-Lakewood, CO
Pasco, FL	Tampa-St. Petersburg-Clearwater, FL
Passaic, NJ	New York-Newark-Jersey City, NY-NJ-PA
Paulding, GA	Atlanta-Sandy Springs-Roswell, GA
Pawnee, OK	Tulsa, OK
Peach, GA	Warner Robins, GA
Pend Oreille, WA	Spokane-Spokane Valley, WA
Pender, NC	Wilmington, NC
Pendleton, KY	Cincinnati, OH-KY-IN
Pennington, SD	Rapid City, SD
Penobscot, ME	Bangor, ME
Peoria, IL	Peoria, IL
Perry, AR	Little Rock-North Little Rock-Conway, AR
Perry, MS	Hattiesburg, MS
Perry, OH	Columbus, OH
Perry, PA	Harrisburg-Carlisle, PA
Person, NC	Durham-Chapel Hill, NC
Petersburg city, VA	Richmond, VA
Philadelphia, PA	Philadelphia-Camden-Wilmington, PA-NJ-DE-MD
Piatt, IL	Champaign-Urbana, IL
Pickaway, OH	Columbus, OH
Pickens, AL	Tuscaloosa, AL
Pickens, GA	Atlanta-Sandy Springs-Roswell, GA
Pickens, SC	Greenville-Anderson-Mauldin, SC
Pierce, WA	Seattle-Tacoma-Bellevue, WA
Pierce, WI	Minneapolis-St. Paul-Bloomington, MN-WI
Pike, GA	Atlanta-Sandy Springs-Roswell, GA
Pike, PA	New York-Newark-Jersey City, NY-NJ-PA
Pima, AZ	Tucson, AZ
Pinal, AZ	Phoenix-Mesa-Scottsdale, AZ
Pinellas, FL	Tampa-St. Petersburg-Clearwater, FL
Pitt, NC	Greenville, NC
Placer, CA	Sacramento--Roseville--Arden-Arcade, CA

COUNTY:	IS IN METROPOLITAN:	COUNTY:	IS IN METROPOLITAN:
Plaquemines, LA	New Orleans-Metairie, LA	San Juan, NM	Farmington, NM
Platte, MO	Kansas City, MO-KS	San Luis Obispo, CA	San Luis Obispo-Paso Robles-Arroyo Grande, CA
Plymouth, IA	Sioux City, IA-NE-SD	San Mateo, CA	San Francisco-Oakland-Hayward, CA
Plymouth, MA	Boston-Cambridge-Newton, MA-NH	San Patricio, TX	Corpus Christi, TX
Poinsett, AR	Jonesboro, AR	Sandoval, NM	Albuquerque, NM
Pointe Coupee, LA	Baton Rouge, LA	Sangamon, IL	Springfield, IL
Polk, FL	Lakeland-Winter Haven, FL	Santa Barbara, CA	Santa Maria-Santa Barbara, CA
Polk, IA	Des Moines-West Des Moines, IA	Santa Clara, CA	San Jose-Sunnyvale-Santa Clara, CA
Polk, MN	Grand Forks, ND-MN	Santa Cruz, CA	Santa Cruz-Watsonville, CA
Polk, MO	Springfield, MO	Santa Fe, NM	Santa Fe, NM
Polk, OR	Salem, OR	Santa Rosa, FL	Pensacola-Ferry Pass-Brent, FL
Polk, TN	Cleveland, TN	Sarasota, FL	North Port-Sarasota-Bradenton, FL
Poquoson city, VA	Virginia Beach-Norfolk-Newport News, VA-NC	Saratoga, NY	Albany-Schenectady-Troy, NY
Portage, OH	Akron, OH	Sarpy, NE	Omaha-Council Bluffs, NE-IA
Porter, IN	Chicago-Naperville-Elgin, IL-IN-WI	Saunders, NE	Omaha-Council Bluffs, NE-IA
Portsmouth city, VA	Virginia Beach-Norfolk-Newport News, VA-NC	Schenectady, NY	Albany-Schenectady-Troy, NY
Posey, IN	Evansville, IN-KY	Schoharie, NY	Albany-Schenectady-Troy, NY
Pottawatomie, KS	Manhattan, KS	Scott, IA	Davenport-Moline-Rock Island, IA-IL
Pottawattamie, IA	Omaha-Council Bluffs, NE-IA	Scott, IN	Louisville/Jefferson County, KY-IN
Potter, TX	Amarillo, TX	Scott, KY	Lexington-Fayette, KY
Powhatan, VA	Richmond, VA	Scott, MN	Minneapolis-St. Paul-Bloomington, MN-WI
Preston, WV	Morgantown, WV	Scott, VA	Kingsport-Bristol-Bristol, TN-VA
Prince George's, MD	Washington-Arlington-Alexandria, DC-VA-MD-WV	Sebastian, AR	Fort Smith, AR-OK
Prince George, VA	Richmond, VA	Sedgwick, KS	Wichita, KS
Prince William, VA	Washington-Arlington-Alexandria, DC-VA-MD-WV	Seminole, FL	Orlando-Kissimmee-Sanford, FL
Providence, RI	Providence-Warwick, RI-MA	Sequatchie, TN	Chattanooga, TN-GA
Pueblo, CO	Pueblo, CO	Sequoyah, OK	Fort Smith, AR-OK
Pulaski, AR	Little Rock-North Little Rock-Conway, AR	Seward, NE	Lincoln, NE
Pulaski, GA	Warner Robins, GA	Shasta, CA	Redding, CA
Pulaski, VA	Blacksburg-Christiansburg-Radford, VA	Shawnee, KS	Topeka, KS
Putnam, IN	Indianapolis-Carmel-Anderson, IN	Sheboygan, WI	Sheboygan, WI
Putnam, NY	New York-Newark-Jersey City, NY-NJ-PA	Shelby, AL	Birmingham-Hoover, AL
Putnam, WV	Huntington-Ashland, WV-KY-OH	Shelby, IN	Indianapolis-Carmel-Anderson, IN
Queen Anne's, MD	Baltimore-Columbia-Towson, MD	Shelby, KY	Louisville/Jefferson County, KY-IN
Queens, NY	New York-Newark-Jersey City, NY-NJ-PA	Shelby, TN	Memphis, TN-MS-AR
Racine, WI	Racine, WI	Sherburne, MN	Minneapolis-St. Paul-Bloomington, MN-WI
Radford city, VA	Blacksburg-Christiansburg-Radford, VA	Sibley, MN	Minneapolis-St. Paul-Bloomington, MN-WI
Raleigh, WV	Beckley, WV	Simpson, MS	Jackson, MS
Ramsey, MN	Minneapolis-St. Paul-Bloomington, MN-WI	Sioux, ND	Bismarck, ND
Randall, TX	Amarillo, TX	Skagit, WA	Mount Vernon-Anacortes, WA
Randolph, NC	Greensboro-High Point, NC	Skamania, WA	Portland-Vancouver-Hillsboro, OR-WA
Rankin, MS	Jackson, MS	Smith, TN	Nashville-Davidson--Murfreesboro--Franklin, TN
Rapides, LA	Alexandria, LA	Smith, TX	Tyler, TX
Rappahannock, VA	Washington-Arlington-Alexandria, DC-VA-MD-WV	Snohomish, WA	Seattle-Tacoma-Bellevue, WA
Ray, MO	Kansas City, MO-KS	Solano, CA	Vallejo-Fairfield, CA
Rensselaer, NY	Albany-Schenectady-Troy, NY	Somerset, MD	Salisbury, MD-DE
Richland, OH	Mansfield, OH	Somerset, NJ	New York-Newark-Jersey City, NY-NJ-PA
Richland, SC	Columbia, SC	Somervell, TX	Dallas-Fort Worth-Arlington, TX
Richmond city, VA	Richmond, VA	Sonoma, CA	Santa Rosa, CA
Richmond, GA	Augusta-Richmond County, GA-SC	Spalding, GA	Atlanta-Sandy Springs-Roswell, GA
Richmond, NY	New York-Newark-Jersey City, NY-NJ-PA	Spartanburg, SC	Spartanburg, SC
Riley, KS	Manhattan, KS	Spencer, KY	Louisville/Jefferson County, KY-IN
Riverside, CA	Riverside-San Bernardino-Ontario, CA	Spokane, WA	Spokane-Spokane Valley, WA
Roane, TN	Knoxville, TN	Spotsylvania, VA	Washington-Arlington-Alexandria, DC-VA-MD-WV
Roanoke city, VA	Roanoke, VA	Stafford, VA	Washington-Arlington-Alexandria, DC-VA-MD-WV
Roanoke, VA	Roanoke, VA	Stanislaus, CA	Modesto, CA
Robertson, TN	Nashville-Davidson--Murfreesboro--Franklin, TN	Stark, IL	Peoria, IL
Robertson, TX	College Station-Bryan, TX	Stark, OH	Canton-Massillon, OH
Rock Island, IL	Davenport-Moline-Rock Island, IA-IL	Staunton city, VA	Staunton-Waynesboro, VA
Rockdale, GA	Atlanta-Sandy Springs-Roswell, GA	Stearns, MN	St. Cloud, MN
Rockingham, NC	Greensboro-High Point, NC	Stevens, WA	Spokane-Spokane Valley, WA
Rockingham, NH	Boston-Cambridge-Newton, MA-NH	Stokes, NC	Winston-Salem, NC
Rockingham, VA	Harrisonburg, VA	Storey, NV	Reno, NV
Rockland, NY	New York-Newark-Jersey City, NY-NJ-PA	Story, IA	Ames, IA
Rockwall, TX	Dallas-Fort Worth-Arlington, TX	Strafford, NH	Boston-Cambridge-Newton, MA-NH
Rock, WI	Janesville-Beloit, WI	St. Bernard, LA	New Orleans-Metairie, LA
Rogers, OK	Tulsa, OK	St. Charles, LA	New Orleans-Metairie, LA
Rowan, NC	Charlotte-Concord-Gastonia, NC-SC	St. Charles, MO	St. Louis, MO-IL
Rusk, TX	Longview, TX	St. Clair, AL	Birmingham-Hoover, AL
Russell, AL	Columbus, GA-AL	St. Clair, IL	St. Louis, MO-IL
Rutherford, TN	Nashville-Davidson--Murfreesboro--Franklin, TN	St. Clair, MI	Detroit-Warren-Dearborn, MI
Sacramento, CA	Sacramento--Roseville--Arden-Arcade, CA	St. Croix, WI	Minneapolis-St. Paul-Bloomington, MN-WI
Sagadahoc, ME	Portland-South Portland, ME	St. Helena, LA	Baton Rouge, LA
Saginaw, MI	Saginaw, MI	St. James, LA	New Orleans-Metairie, LA
Salem city, VA	Roanoke, VA	St. John the Baptist, LA	New Orleans-Metairie, LA
Salem, NJ	Philadelphia-Camden-Wilmington, PA-NJ-DE-MD	St. Johns, FL	Jacksonville, FL
Saline, AR	Little Rock-North Little Rock-Conway, AR	St. Joseph, IN	South Bend-Mishawaka, IN-MI
Salt Lake, UT	Salt Lake City, UT	St. Louis city, MO	St. Louis, MO-IL
Saluda, SC	Columbia, SC	St. Louis, MN	Duluth, MN-WI
San Benito, CA	San Jose-Sunnyvale-Santa Clara, CA	St. Louis, MO	St. Louis, MO-IL
San Bernardino, CA	Riverside-San Bernardino-Ontario, CA	St. Lucie, FL	Port St. Lucie, FL
San Diego, CA	San Diego-Carlsbad, CA	St. Martin, LA	Lafayette, LA
San Francisco, CA	San Francisco-Oakland-Hayward, CA	St. Mary's, MD	California-Lexington Park, MD
San Joaquin, CA	Stockton-Lodi, CA	St. Tammany, LA	New Orleans-Metairie, LA

COUNTY:	IS IN METROPOLITAN:	COUNTY:	IS IN METROPOLITAN:
Suffolk city, VA	Virginia Beach-Norfolk-Newport News, VA-NC	Washington, AR	Fayetteville-Springdale-Rogers, AR-MO
Suffolk, MA	Boston-Cambridge-Newton, MA-NH	Washington, IA	Iowa City, IA
Suffolk, NY	New York-Newark-Jersey City, NY-NJ-PA	Washington, IN	Louisville/Jefferson County, KY-IN
Sullivan, IN	Terre Haute, IN	Washington, MD	Hagerstown-Martinsburg, MD-WV
Sullivan, TN	Kingsport-Bristol-Bristol, TN-VA	Washington, MN	Minneapolis-St. Paul-Bloomington, MN-WI
Summit, OH	Akron, OH	Washington, NE	Omaha-Council Bluffs, NE-IA
Sumner, KS	Wichita, KS	Washington, NY	Glens Falls, NY
Sumner, TN	Nashville-Davidson--Murfreesboro--Franklin, TN	Washington, OR	Portland-Vancouver-Hillsboro, OR-WA
Sumter, FL	The Villages, FL	Washington, PA	Pittsburgh, PA
Sumter, SC	Sumter, SC	Washington, RI	Providence-Warwick, RI-MA
Sussex, DE	Salisbury, MD-DE	Washington, TN	Johnson City, TN
Sussex, NJ	New York-Newark-Jersey City, NY-NJ-PA	Washington, UT	St. George, UT
Sussex, VA	Richmond, VA	Washington, VA	Kingsport-Bristol-Bristol, TN-VA
Sutter, CA	Yuba City, CA	Washington, WI	Milwaukee-Waukesha-West Allis, WI
Tangipahoa, LA	Hammond, LA	Washoe, NV	Reno, NV
Tarrant, TX	Dallas-Fort Worth-Arlington, TX	Washtenaw, MI	Ann Arbor, MI
Tate, MS	Memphis, TN-MS-AR	Waukesha, WI	Milwaukee-Waukesha-West Allis, WI
Taylor, TX	Abilene, TX	Waynesboro city, VA	Staunton-Waynesboro, VA
Tazewell, IL	Peoria, IL	Wayne, MI	Detroit-Warren-Dearborn, MI
Teller, CO	Colorado Springs, CO	Wayne, NC	Goldsboro, NC
Terrebonne, LA	Houma-Thibodaux, LA	Wayne, NY	Rochester, NY
Terrell, GA	Albany, GA	Wayne, WV	Huntington-Ashland, WV-KY-OH
Thurston, WA	Olympia-Tumwater, WA	Webb, TX	Laredo, TX
Tioga, NY	Binghamton, NY	Weber, UT	Ogden-Clearfield, UT
Tippecanoe, IN	Lafayette-West Lafayette, IN	Webster, LA	Shreveport-Bossier City, LA
Tipton, TN	Memphis, TN-MS-AR	Webster, MO	Springfield, MO
Tolland, CT	Hartford-West Hartford-East Hartford, CT	Weld, CO	Greeley, CO
Tom Green, TX	San Angelo, TX	Wells, IN	Fort Wayne, IN
Tompkins, NY	Ithaca, NY	West Baton Rouge, LA	Baton Rouge, LA
Tooele, UT	Salt Lake City, UT	West Feliciana, LA	Baton Rouge, LA
Torrance, NM	Albuquerque, NM	Westchester, NY	New York-Newark-Jersey City, NY-NJ-PA
Travis, TX	Austin-Round Rock, TX	Westmoreland, PA	Pittsburgh, PA
Trigg, KY	Clarksville, TN-KY	Whatcom, WA	Bellingham, WA
Trimble, KY	Louisville/Jefferson County, KY-IN	Whitfield, GA	Dalton, GA
Trousdale, TN	Nashville-Davidson--Murfreesboro--Franklin, TN	Whitley, IN	Fort Wayne, IN
Trumbull, OH	Youngstown-Warren-Boardman, OH-PA	Wichita, TX	Wichita Falls, TX
Tulare, CA	Visalia-Porterville, CA	Wicomico, MD	Salisbury, MD-DE
Tulsa, OK	Tulsa, OK	Williamsburg city, VA	Virginia Beach-Norfolk-Newport News, VA-NC
Tunica, MS	Memphis, TN-MS-AR	Williamson, IL	Carbondale-Marion, IL
Turner, SD	Sioux Falls, SD	Williamson, TN	Nashville-Davidson--Murfreesboro--Franklin, TN
Tuscaloosa, AL	Tuscaloosa, AL	Williamson, TX	Austin-Round Rock, TX
Twiggs, GA	Macon, GA	Will, IL	Chicago-Naperville-Elgin, IL-IN-WI
Ulster, NY	Kingston, NY	Wilson, TN	Nashville-Davidson--Murfreesboro--Franklin, TN
Unicoi, TN	Johnson City, TN	Wilson, TX	San Antonio-New Braunfels, TX
Union, IN	Cincinnati, OH-KY-IN	Winchester city, VA	Winchester, VA-WV
Union, LA	Monroe, LA	Windham, CT	Worcester, MA-CT
Union, NC	Charlotte-Concord-Gastonia, NC-SC	Winnebago, IL	Rockford, IL
Union, NJ	New York-Newark-Jersey City, NY-NJ-PA	Winnebago, WI	Oshkosh-Neenah, WI
Union, OH	Columbus, OH	Wirt, WV	Parkersburg-Vienna, WV
Union, SC	Spartanburg, SC	Wise, TX	Dallas-Fort Worth-Arlington, TX
Union, SD	Sioux City, IA-NE-SD	Woodbury, IA	Sioux City, IA-NE-SD
Union, TN	Knoxville, TN	Woodford, IL	Peoria, IL
Upshur, TX	Longview, TX	Woodford, KY	Lexington-Fayette, KY
Utah, UT	Provo-Orem, UT	Wood, OH	Toledo, OH
Valencia, NM	Albuquerque, NM	Wood, WV	Parkersburg-Vienna, WV
Van Buren, MI	Kalamazoo-Portage, MI	Worcester, MA	Worcester, MA-CT
Vanderburgh, IN	Evansville, IN-KY	Worcester, MD	Salisbury, MD-DE
Ventura, CA	Oxnard-Thousand Oaks-Ventura, CA	Worth, GA	Albany, GA
Vermilion, IL	Danville, IL	Wright, MN	Minneapolis-St. Paul-Bloomington, MN-WI
Vermilion, LA	Lafayette, LA	Wyandotte, KS	Kansas City, MO-KS
Vermillion, IN	Terre Haute, IN	Wyoming, PA	Scranton--Wilkes-Barre--Hazleton, PA
Victoria, TX	Victoria, TX	Yadkin, NC	Winston-Salem, NC
Vigo, IN	Terre Haute, IN	Yakima, WA	Yakima, WA
Virginia Beach city, VA	Virginia Beach-Norfolk-Newport News, VA-NC	Yamhill, OR	Portland-Vancouver-Hillsboro, OR-WA
Volusia, FL	Deltona-Daytona Beach-Ormond Beach, FL	Yates, NY	Rochester, NY
Wabasha, MN	Rochester, MN	Yavapai, AZ	Prescott, AZ
Wabaunsee, KS	Topeka, KS	Yazoo, MS	Jackson, MS
Wagoner, OK	Tulsa, OK	Yellowstone, MT	Billings, MT
Wake, NC	Raleigh, NC	Yolo, CA	Sacramento--Roseville--Arden-Arcade, CA
Wakulla, FL	Tallahassee, FL	York, ME	Portland-South Portland, ME
Walker, AL	Birmingham-Hoover, AL	York, PA	York-Hanover, PA
Walker, GA	Chattanooga, TN-GA	York, SC	Charlotte-Concord-Gastonia, NC-SC
Walla Walla, WA	Walla Walla, WA	York, VA	Virginia Beach-Norfolk-Newport News, VA-NC
Waller, TX	Houston-The Woodlands-Sugar Land, TX	Yuba, CA	Yuba City, CA
Walton, FL	Crestview-Fort Walton Beach-Destin, FL	Yuma, AZ	Yuma, AZ
Walton, GA	Atlanta-Sandy Springs-Roswell, GA		
Warren, IA	Des Moines-West Des Moines, IA		
Warren, KY	Bowling Green, KY		
Warren, MO	St. Louis, MO-IL		
Warren, NJ	Allentown-Bethlehem-Easton, PA-NJ		
Warren, NY	Glens Falls, NY		
Warren, OH	Cincinnati, OH-KY-IN		
Warren, VA	Washington-Arlington-Alexandria, DC-VA-MD-WV		
Warrick, IN	Evansville, IN-KY		

National Crime Trends: 1993 to 2012

In the 20 years from 1993 to 2012, crime rates in the United States fell significantly. The total crime rate dropped 40.8 percent: from 5,487.1 crimes per 100,000 population in 1993 to a rate of 3,246.1 in 2012. Violent crime rates also decreased, falling 48.2 percent from 1993 to 2012. In addition, property crime rates dropped 39.7 percent.

Among individual crime categories, each recorded declines from 1993 to 2012. The nation's motor vehicle theft rate posted the largest decrease, falling 62.1 percent from 1993 to 2012. The smallest decline was in the rape rate, which dropped 26.9 percent during that same 20-year time frame.

The table below shows rates for each category of crime for every year since 1993. Trends for each individual crime are shown in graphs on the following pages. Violent crimes are murder, rape, robbery, and aggravated assault. Property crimes consist of burglary, larceny-theft, and motor vehicle theft. The total crime rate is simply the sum of the seven specific crimes and was calculated by the editors. All rates are crimes per 100,000 population for the year shown.

Year	Crime	Violent Crime	Property Crime	Murder	Rape	Robbery	Assault	Burglary	Larceny-Theft	Motor Vehicle Theft
1993	5,487.1	747.1	4,740.0	9.5	41.1	256.0	440.5	1,099.7	3,033.9	606.3
1994	5,373.8	713.6	4,660.2	9.0	39.3	237.8	427.6	1,042.1	3,026.9	591.3
1995	5,275.0	684.5	4,590.5	8.2	37.1	220.9	418.3	987.0	3,043.2	560.3
1996	5,087.6	636.6	4,451.0	7.4	36.3	201.9	391.0	945.0	2,980.3	525.7
1997	4,927.3	611.0	4,316.3	6.8	35.9	186.2	382.1	918.8	2,891.8	505.7
1998	4,620.1	567.6	4,052.5	6.3	34.5	165.5	361.4	863.2	2,729.5	459.9
1999	4,266.6	523.0	3,743.6	5.7	32.8	150.1	334.3	770.4	2,550.7	422.5
2000	4,124.8	506.5	3,618.3	5.5	32.0	145.0	324.0	728.8	2,477.3	412.2
2001	4,162.6	504.5	3,658.1	5.6	31.8	148.5	318.6	741.8	2,485.7	430.5
2002	4,125.0	494.4	3,630.6	5.6	33.1	146.1	309.5	747.0	2,450.7	432.9
2003	4,067.0	475.8	3,591.2	5.7	32.3	142.5	295.4	741.0	2,416.5	433.7
2004	3,977.3	463.2	3,514.1	5.5	32.4	136.7	288.6	730.3	2,362.3	421.5
2005	3,900.5	469.0	3,431.5	5.6	31.8	140.8	290.8	726.9	2,287.8	416.8
2006	3,825.9	479.3	3,346.6	5.8	31.6	150.0	292.0	733.1	2,213.2	400.2
2007	3,748.2	471.8	3,276.4	5.7	30.6	148.3	287.2	726.1	2,185.4	364.9
2008	3,673.2	458.6	3,214.6	5.4	29.8	145.9	277.5	733.0	2,166.1	315.4
2009	3,473.2	431.9	3,041.3	5.0	29.1	133.1	264.7	717.7	2,064.5	259.2
2010	3,350.4	404.5	2,945.9	4.8	27.7	119.3	252.8	701.0	2,005.8	239.1
2011	3,292.5	387.1	2,905.4	4.7	27.0	113.9	241.5	701.3	1,974.1	230.0
2012	3,246.1	386.9	2,859.2	4.7	26.9	112.9	242.3	670.2	1,959.3	229.7

Source: Reported data from the F.B.I.
  "Crime in the United States 2012" (Uniform Crime Reports, September 16, 2013)

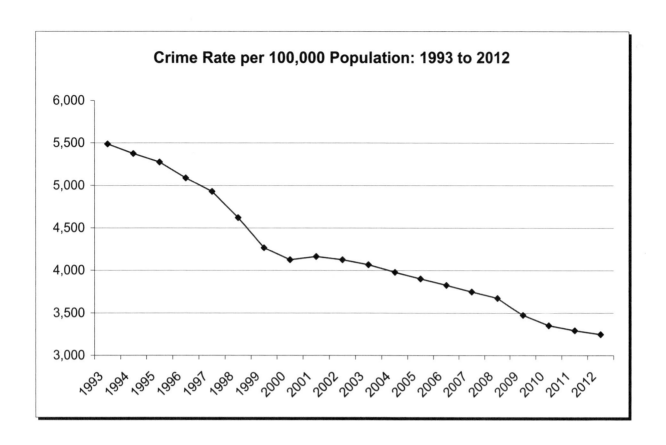

Crime Rate per 100,000 Population: 1993 to 2012

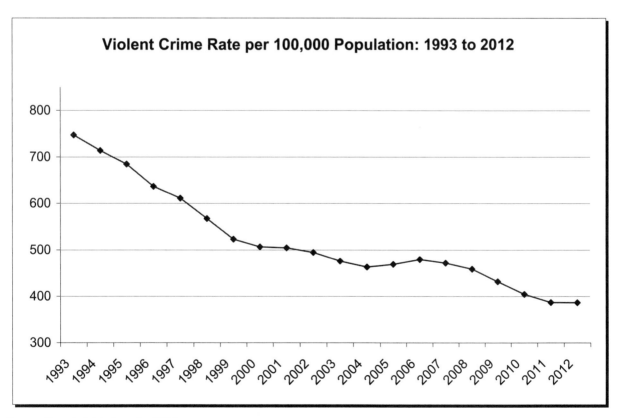

Violent Crime Rate per 100,000 Population: 1993 to 2012

Source: Reported data from the F.B.I.
   "Crime in the United States 2012" (Uniform Crime Reports, September 16, 2013)

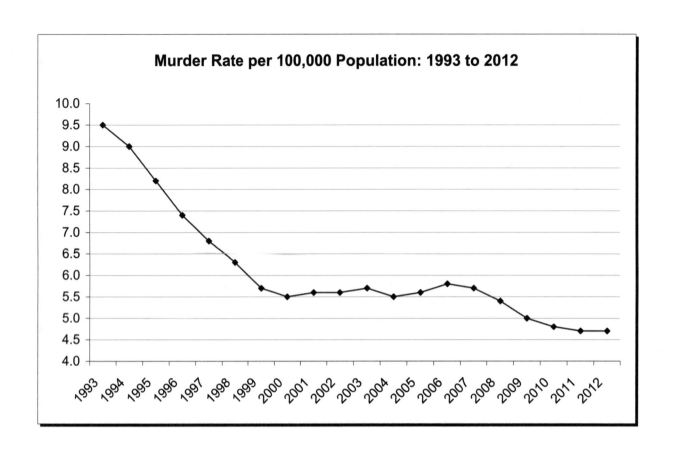

Murder Rate per 100,000 Population: 1993 to 2012

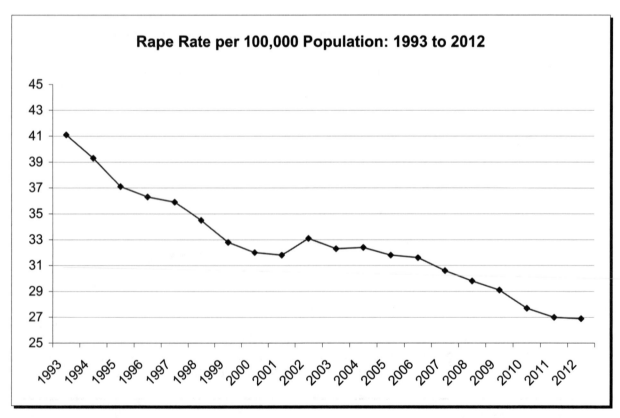

Rape Rate per 100,000 Population: 1993 to 2012

Source: Reported data from the F.B.I.

"Crime in the United States 2012" (Uniform Crime Reports, September 16, 2013)

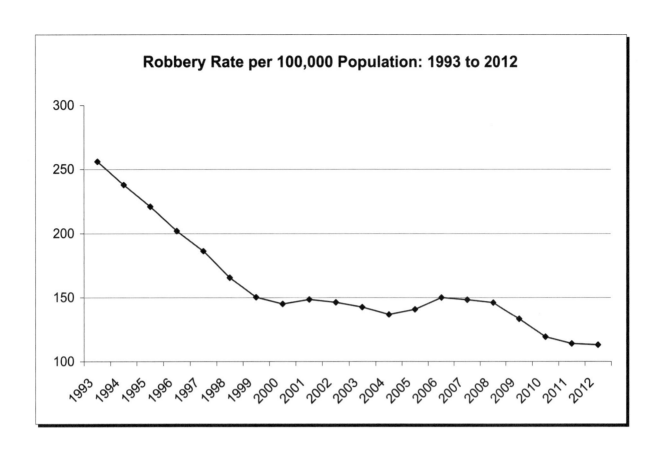

Robbery Rate per 100,000 Population: 1993 to 2012

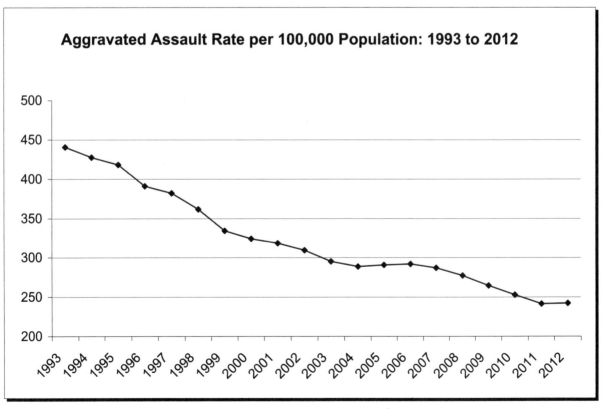

Aggravated Assault Rate per 100,000 Population: 1993 to 2012

Source: Reported data from the F.B.I.
"Crime in the United States 2012" (Uniform Crime Reports, September 16, 2013)

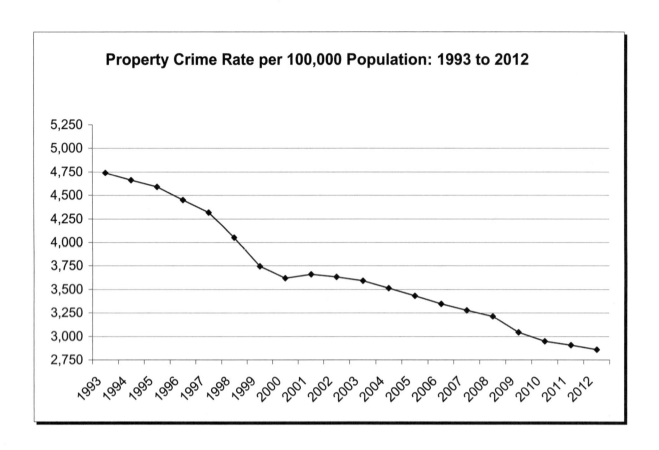

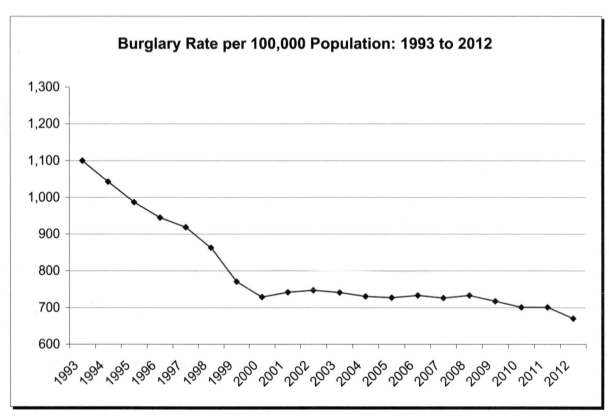

Source: Reported data from the F.B.I.

"Crime in the United States 2012" (Uniform Crime Reports, September 16, 2013)

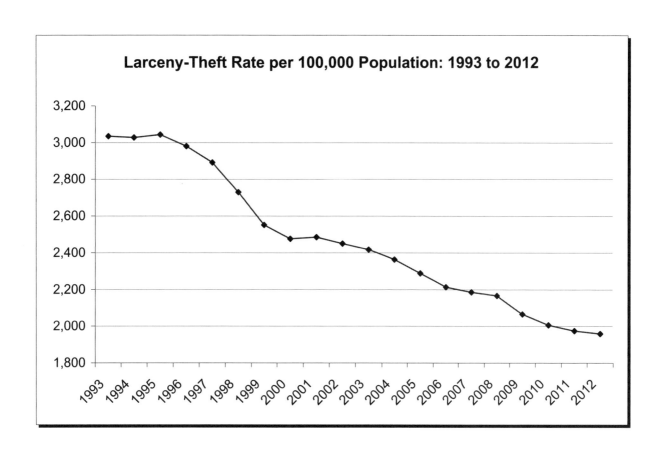

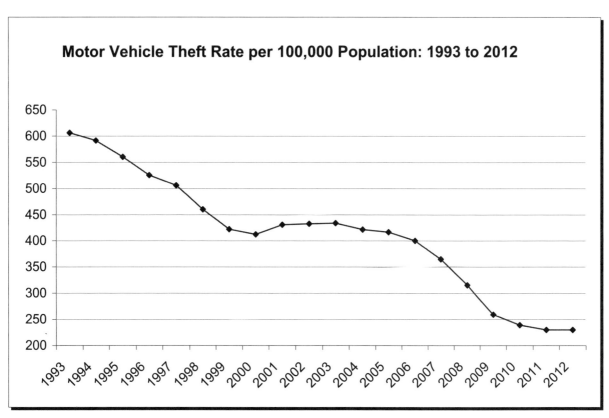

Source: Reported data from the F.B.I.

"Crime in the United States 2012" (Uniform Crime Reports, September 16, 2013)

AAT-6717

NATIONAL, METROPOLITAN, AND CITY CRIME STATISTICS SUMMARY: 2012

	NATIONAL	METRO*	CITY*
Population 2012	313,914,040	266,700,731	88,433,856
Police (Sworn Officers)	670,439		
Rate of Police Officers (per 100,000 Population)	235		
Crimes in 2012	10,189,900	8,959,269	3,872,738
Crime Rate in 2012 (per 100,000 Population)	3,246.1	3,359.2	4,379.2
Percent Change in Crime Rate: 2011 to 2012	(1.4)	(3.3)	(1.5)
Percent Change in Crime Rate: 2008 to 2012	(11.6)	(12.5)	(12.8)
Violent Crimes in 2012	1,214,462	1,092,001	585,176
Violent Crime Rate in 2012 (per 100,000 Population)	386.9	409.4	661.7
Percent Change in Violent Crime Rate: 2011 to 2012	0.0	(4.4)	0.5
Percent Change in Violent Crime Rate: 2008 to 2012	(15.6)	(16.3)	(14.6)
Murders in 2012	14,827	13,175	7,705
Murder Rate in 2012 (per 100,000 Population)	4.7	4.9	8.7
Percent Change in Murder Rate: 2011 to 2012	0.4	(2.0)	1.2
Percent Change in Murder Rate: 2008 to 2012	(12.8)	(14.0)	(13.0)
Rapes in 2012	84,376	70,482	28,468
Rape Rate in 2012 (per 100,000 Population)	26.9	26.4	32.2
Percent Change in Rape Rate: 2011 to 2012	(0.5)	(2.2)	(0.6)
Percent Change in Rape Rate: 2008 to 2012	(9.9)	(9.9)	(6.4)
Robberies in 2012	354,520	341,122	216,061
Robbery Rate in 2012 (per 100,000 Population)	112.9	127.9	244.3
Percent Change in Robbery Rate: 2011 to 2012	(0.8)	(6.0)	(0.9)
Percent Change in Robbery Rate: 2008 to 2012	(22.6)	(23.3)	(21.8)
Aggravated Assaults in 2012	760,739	667,222	332,942
Aggravated Assault Rate in 2012 (per 100,000 Population)	242.3	250.2	376.5
Percent Change in Aggravated Assault Rate: 2011 to 2012	0.4	(3.9)	1.6
Percent Change in Aggravated Assault Rate: 2008 to 2012	(12.7)	(12.9)	(9.9)
Property Crimes in 2012	8,975,438	7,867,268	3,287,562
Property Crime Rate in 2012 (per 100,000 Population)	2,859.2	2,949.8	3,717.5
Percent Change in Property Crime Rate: 2011 to 2012	(1.6)	(3.2)	(1.9)
Percent Change in Property Crime Rate: 2008 to 2012	(11.1)	(12.0)	(12.4)
Burglaries in 2012	2,103,787	1,803,461	754,552
Burglary Rate in 2012 (per 100,000 Population)	670.2	676.2	853.2
Percent Change in Burglary Rate: 2011 to 2012	(4.4)	(4.3)	(6.2)
Percent Change in Burglary Rate: 2008 to 2012	(8.6)	(9.3)	(10.5)
Larceny-Thefts in 2012	6,150,598	5,395,107	2,170,257
Larceny-Theft Rate in 2012 (per 100,000 Population)	1,959.3	2,022.9	2,454.1
Percent Change in Larceny-Theft Rate: 2011 to 2012	(0.7)	(2.6)	(0.6)
Percent Change in Larceny-Theft Rate: 2008 to 2012	(9.5)	(10.4)	(10.1)
Motor Vehicle Thefts in 2012	721,053	668,700	362,753
Motor Vehicle Theft Rate in 2012 (per 100,000 Population)	229.7	250.7	410.2
Percent Change in Motor Vehicle Theft Rate: 2011 to 2012	(0.1)	(4.5)	(0.3)
Percent Change in Motor Vehicle Theft Rate: 2008 to 2012	(27.2)	(28.3)	(27.0)

Source: CQ Press using reported data from the F.B.I.
   "Crime in the United States 2012" (Uniform Crime Reports, September 16, 2013)
*Metro includes population and crime for all metropolitan statistical areas. City statistics are for cities of 100,000 or more in population.